lonely planet

Mexico

John Noble
Susan Forsyth
Ben Greensfelder
Morgan Konn
Monica Lepe
James Lyon
Michele Matter
Alan Murphy
Andrew Dean Nystrom
Vivek Waglé
Allison Wright

D0169936

LONELY PLANET PUBLICATIONS
Melbourne • Oakland • London • Paris

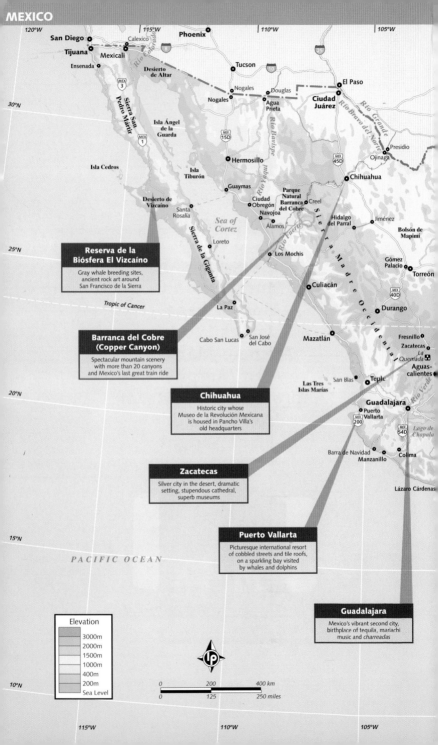

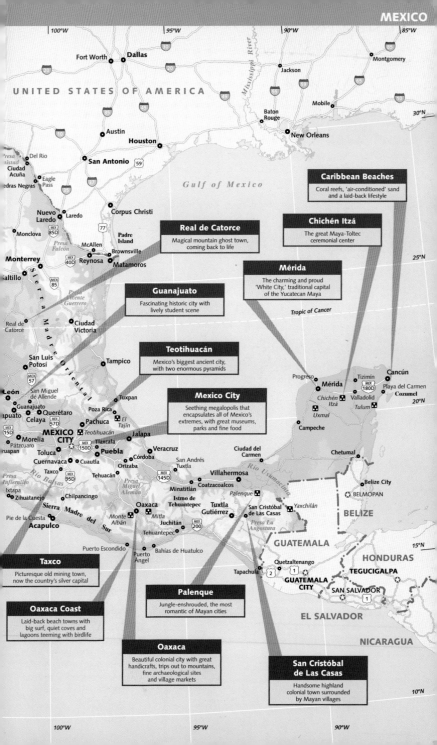

UNITED STATES OF AMERICA

Gulf of Mexico

Caribbean Beaches
Coral reefs, 'air-conditioned' sand and a laid-back lifestyle

Real de Catorce
Magical mountain ghost town, coming back to life

Chichén Itzá
The great Maya-Toltec ceremonial center

Mérida
The charming and proud 'White City,' traditional capital of the Yucatecan Maya

Guanajuato
Fascinating historic city with lively student scene

Teotihuacán
Mexico's biggest ancient city, with two enormous pyramids

Mexico City
Seething megalopolis that encapsulates all of Mexico's extremes, with great museums, parks and fine food

Taxco
Picturesque old mining town, now the country's silver capital

Oaxaca Coast
Laid-back beach towns with big surf, quiet coves and lagoons teeming with birdlife

Palenque
Jungle-enshrouded, the most romantic of Mayan cities

Oaxaca
Beautiful colonial city with great handicrafts, trips out to mountains, fine archaeological sites and village markets

San Cristóbal de Las Casas
Handsome highland colonial town surrounded by Mayan villages

Fort Worth · Dallas
Jackson
Montgomery

Mobile
Austin
Houston
Baton Rouge
New Orleans

Del Rio
Ciudad Acuña
Eagle Pass
Piedras Negras
San Antonio · 59
Corpus Christi

Nuevo Laredo · Laredo
Monclova
77
McAllen
Padre Island
Reynosa · Brownsville
Monterrey
Saltillo · Matamoros

Tropic of Cancer

Ciudad Victoria
Real de Catorce

San Luis Potosí
Tampico
Progreso · Mérida · Tizimin · Cancún
León
San Miguel de Allende
Querétaro
Tuxpan
Chichén Itzá · Valladolid · Playa del Carmen · Cozumel
Guanajuato
Poza Rica
Celaya
Pachuca · El Tajín
Uxmal · Tulum
Irapuato
MEXICO CITY
Teotihuacán
Campeche
Morelia
Pátzcuaro
Tlaxcala
Toluca
Puebla
Chetumal
Uruapan
Cuautla
Veracruz
Jalapa
Córdoba
Ciudad del Carmen
Cuernavaca
Orizaba
Taxco
Tehuacán
San Andrés Tuxtla
Belize City
Chilpancingo
Presa Miguel Alemán
Villahermosa
BELMOPAN
Ixtapa
Minatitlán
Coatzacoalcos
Palenque
Yaxchilán
Zihuatanejo
Oaxaca
Istmo de Tehuantepec
BELIZE
Pie de la Cuesta
Monte Albán
Mitla
Tuxtla Gutiérrez
San Cristóbal de Las Casas
Acapulco
Juchitán
Presa La Angostura
Puerto Escondido
Tehuantepec
GUATEMALA
Puerto Angel
Bahías de Huatulco
HONDURAS
Quetzaltenango
TEGUCIGALPA
Tapachula
GUATEMALA CITY
SAN SALVADOR
EL SALVADOR
NICARAGUA

Mexico
8th edition – September 2002
First published – October 1982

Published by
Lonely Planet Publications Pty Ltd ABN 36 005 607 983
90 Maribyrnong St, Footscray, Victoria 3011, Australia

Lonely Planet Offices
Australia Locked Bag 1, Footscray, Victoria 3011
USA 150 Linden St, Oakland, CA 94607
UK 10a Spring Place, London NW5 3BH
France 1 rue du Dahomey, 75011 Paris

Photographs
Many of the images in this guide are available for licensing from
Lonely Planet Images.
W www.lonelyplanetimages.com

Front cover photograph
Colorful cacti (Bill Bachman)
Mexico City map section photograph
Religious statues for sale (Richard I'Anson)

ISBN 1 74059 028 7

text & maps © Lonely Planet Publications Pty Ltd 2002
photos © photographers as indicated 2002

Printed through Colorcraft Ltd, Hong Kong
Printed in China

Contents

2   Contents

AROUND MEXICO CITY   228

BAJA CALIFORNIA   304

NORTHWEST MEXICO   345

CENTRAL NORTH MEXICO   384

NORTHEAST MEXICO   409

CENTRAL PACIFIC COAST   449

WESTERN CENTRAL HIGHLANDS   541

NORTHERN CENTRAL HIGHLANDS   610

CENTRAL GULF COAST   686

4   Contents

LANGUAGE 996

GLOSSARY 1003

FOOD & DRINK GLOSSARY 1009

THANKS 1013

INDEX 1025

MAP LEGEND 1040

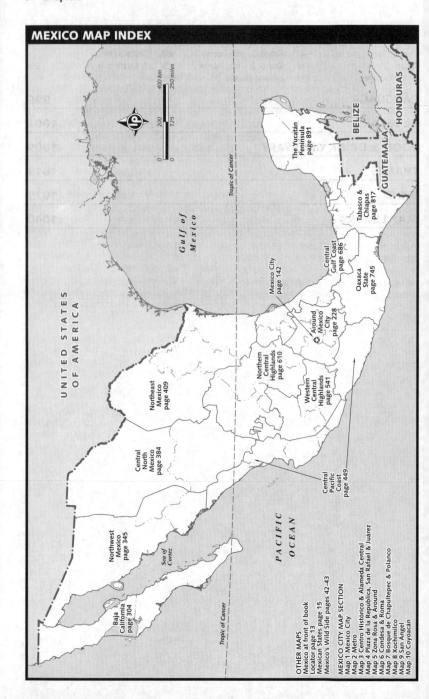

MEXICO MAP INDEX

UNITED STATES OF AMERICA

Gulf of Mexico

PACIFIC OCEAN

Sea of Cortez

BELIZE

GUATEMALA

HONDURAS

Tropic of Cancer

400 km
200
0

250 miles
125
0

The Yucatán Peninsula page 891

Tabasco & Chiapas page 817

Central Gulf Coast page 686

Oaxaca State page 745

Mexico City page 142

Around Mexico City page 228

Northern Central Highlands page 610

Western Central Highlands page 541

Central Pacific Coast page 449

Northeast Mexico page 409

Central North Mexico page 384

Northwest Mexico page 345

Baja California page 304

OTHER MAPS
Mexico at front of book
Locator page 13
Mexican States page 15
Mexico's Wild Side pages 42-43

MEXICO CITY MAP SECTION
Map 1 Mexico City
Map 2 Metro
Map 3 Centro Histórico & Alameda Central
Map 4 Plaza de la República, San Rafael & Juárez
Map 5 Zona Rosa & Around
Map 6 Condesa & Roma
Map 7 Bosque de Chapultepec & Polanco
Map 8 Xochimilco
Map 9 San Ángel
Map 10 Coyoacán

The Authors

John Noble

John comes from the cool, green Ribble valley in northern England. A degree in philosophy led to a career in newspaper journalism, but increasing interruptions for travel eventually saw him abandon Fleet Street for a Lonely Planet trail. At last count, he has covered 19 countries from Indonesia to Lithuania and Uzbekistan to Andorra. He has been coordinating author of many multiauthor titles such as *Brazil*; *Spain*; *Russia, Ukraine & Belarus* and four editions of *Mexico*. John has visited Mexico regularly ever since he took off from the *Sheffield Star* sub-editors' desk for his first long backpacking trip. He's also the author of *Mexico City*. John is based in Spain, together with his wife and coauthor, Susan Forsyth, and their children, Isabella and Jack (also experienced Mexico travelers).

Susan Forsyth

Born and raised in Melbourne, Susan spent a decade teaching in the Victorian state education system. Distracted by her regular visits to Indonesia, she headed off to Sri Lanka for a year's stint as a volunteer lecturer. There she met her husband, writer John Noble, and before long had begun writing for LP, set up home in Europe and had two children. An original author of *Andalucía* and *Spain*, Susan has worked on several editions of *Mexico* as well as *Australia, Indonesia, Sri Lanka* and *Travel With Children* – Mexico remains one of her favorite destinations. Susan and family live in southern Spain, where her children are acquiring a distinct *andaluz* demeanor. Their terrific Spanish makes travel in Mexico very easy but they don't like long bus rides!

Ben Greensfelder

Ben was born and raised in Marin County, California, but left it when the influx of George Bush's 'hot-tubbers' rendered it unaffordable. He attended UC Santa Cruz, skipping terms to travel to Mexico and sail the Pacific coast to Washington State. Under threat of expulsion, he buckled down and got a degree, with honors, in language studies. After college Ben lived in Greece, New York, San Francisco, Monterey, South Korea and elsewhere, pursuing jobs in TESL and publishing. He was the coordinating author of the 4th edition of LP's *Belize, Guatemala & Yucatán,* and he contributed chapters to *Argentina, Uruguay & Paraguay.* Ben and his wife, the renowned author Sandra Bao, make their home in Oakland, California, for the moment.

Morgan Konn & Andrew Dean Nystrom

When not living *la vida aire-condicionada*, Morgan and Andrew dream of sweltering 100% humidity, scabie dogs chasing chickens, hair-raising thunderstorms, naked body surfing, coconut *paletas*, tamales and *telenovelas*, *pozole* on Thursday and co-co-ri-co rooster wakeup calls. When not out *mochilando* (rambling), they garden and perfect their tamale recipes in Berkeley, California, where Morgan makes photos and teaches art. Andrew has contributed other text and images to several other LP publications, including *Out to Eat – San Francisco, Rocky Mountains, San Francisco* and *USA* and the CitySync series of digital city guides. He's currently contemplating a move to Guerrero's Costa Chica, since locals insist that there's no work there. There's more of his writing at www.guidebookwriters.com.

Monica Lepe

Monica first visited Mexico at the age of six. Though she and her family traveled from Mexico City to Tulum, her clearest memories of the trip are of mosquitoes and monkeys. Since then she has returned many times, both to visit family and explore the country. Born and raised in the San Francisco Bay area, she has also traveled through much of Europe, settling for short periods in Madrid and Moscow. Her degree in geography from UC Berkeley helped her land a job as a cartographer at Lonely Planet's Oakland office. After a few fantastic years in Oaktown, restless Monica moved to Brooklyn, New York.

James Lyon

An Australian by birth, a skeptic by nature, and a social scientist by training, James has worked on LP guides to Bali, Mexico, Maldives, South America and the USA. He particularly enjoys Mexico for the depth of its history, the uniqueness of its culture, and the beauty of its colonial towns. For this edition he covered the North Central and Western Highlands and part of the Pacific coast, searching for butterflies, repelling mosquitoes and descending the devil's backbone.

Michele Matter

Michele spent her childhood in Berkeley, California, with breaks spent traveling across the US and to South America with family. After graduating from UC Berkeley, she spent some time traveling, then returned to the Bay Area and began working in Lonely Planet's marketing department. After nearly five years behind the desk promoting travel guides, Michele decided to jump the fence and venture out into the world of travel writing.

Alan Murphy

Born in Perth, Western Australia, Alan had only one aim from the age of 16 when his brother left to wander the globe – try to catch up with him. After four years of tramping through Europe, India and the Middle East, dodgy temp work, a developing fascination for other cultures and a loathing of corporate politics, the realization dawned that travel was to play a major part of life. In 1997 he obtained a journalism degree and, thus armed, approached Lonely Planet. After a brief editing interlude, Alan hit the pavements, researching, updating and writing books, contributing to such guides as *Southern Africa; South Africa; Africa; India; North India* and *Argentina, Uruguay & Paraguay.* Alan lives in Melbourne where tight deadlines, strange working hours and nights at the Retreat Hotel have become life when not researching.

Vivek Waglé

Dragging Vivek kicking and screaming (he was only three) from his native land of India was probably the best way to introduce him to a life of itinerancy. After years of bouncing around the globe from Jakarta, Indonesia, to Washington, DC, with family and friends, he settled down long enough to earn an unbelievably practical degree in philosophy at Harvard University. But the experiential world soon won out over noumenal quandaries, propelling Vivek to enter the travel-writing business. Seeking security and comfort, he headed to Lonely Planet's Oakland office to serve as an editor. After a while, however, LP decided that it was yet again time for him to hit the road – where he remains to this day.

Allison Wright

Allison enjoyed living for almost five years in Mexico City, where she worked as a journalist after her graduation from UC Berkeley in 1995. She returned to the US in 2000 to attend law school at the University of Colorado.

FROM THE AUTHORS

John Noble Extra special thanks to Neil Pyatt, the world's leading authority on Oaxaca nightlife; Tamar Underhill and Tristan Roddis for further priceless Oaxaca tips; Ron Mader for countless pieces of information and advice, great introductions, unflagging dedication to the cause, good coffee, great mezcal and a superb family breakfast; Gina Machorro in Puerto Escondido, undoubtedly the best tourist information officer in *la república;* Dana Burton for a friendly welcome and useful information in San Cristóbal; Adriana Guzmán and all her friendly colleagues for a great *expedición* in Oaxaca's Sierra Norte; SEDETUR in Oaxaca for generous help with information; Jennie Freeman and John Rigdon for writing almost a new book on driving into Mexico; Myra Ingmanson, who now knows more than she ever wanted to about Mexican cell phones; Conner Gorry for info on buses in Guatemala; Izzy and Jack for time-saving help with desk research; Leonie Mugavin and Brett from STA Melbourne for help on airfares from Oz; and last but not least coauthors Alan, Allison, Andrew, Ben, James, Michele, Monica, Susan and Vivek for their patience with my questions, high standards of work and for generally being enjoyable to work with.

Susan Forsyth Susan says thanks to tourist office staff in Oaxaca, Tabasco and Chiapas states, especially Maribel Salazar in Villahermosa, and to the dedicated staff at La Encrucijada and El Triunfo Biosphere Reserve offices in Tuxtla Gutiérrez. Dana Guy Burton was invaluable for tips in San Cristóbal de Las Casas as was the dynamic Ron Mader in Oaxaca. Enthusiastic contributors to the Oaxaca coast research include Gundi in Puerto Ángel, Dan and Carmen in Puerto Escondido, and all at Mexico Lindo y qué Rico in San Agustinillo.

Ben Greensfelder Thanks go again to Raúl Li Causi in Mérida for providing loads of invaluable information, as well as his tireless efforts to improve and expand the hosteling experience in Mexico. Also in Mérida, a big *gracias* to Maritza Fabiola Juárez Galicia for all the bus schedule information. To everyone else in the Yucatán I spoke to, thank you for the generous contributions of time, hospitality and kindness. Sandra, thanks again for all your help and support and the last 11 years. Oakland Lonely Planeteers, Mexico 8 division: the tequila's on me!

Morgan Konn & Andrew Dean Nystrom Mil gracias a Livi in Melaque, Susan in Manzanillo, the brothers who gave us a lift to Tomatlan, Gilberto in Nexpa, Mike at Manzanillo Bay, Pinche Arabe y Jose and Any in Zihua. Finalmente, gracias a Octavio, Reina y Analia para compartir un poquitito del sabor de Guadalajara. Thanks to coordinating author extraordinaire John Noble for his due diligence. Back in the secure homeland, salud to the deceased new media crew. As ever, the continuing adventure would not be possible with out the love and support of our folks – John, Barbara, Joe and Dolores.

Monica Lepe Thanks to John Noble for his support and patience; fellow authors Andrew, Ben, Tracey, Tom, Danny and Myra for helpful advice; the entire cartography department (especially Sean, Patrick and Gina) – I miss you; editors Robert, China, Kevin and Kathryn for helping bring the text up to par; Mariah for letting me do this; Margarita Quintero, Arturo Gutierrez and Gadi Giveon in Creel; Jorge Rodriquez Salazar in Amecameca; Danny, Shirley and Stefan for keeping me company; Jennie Freeman and John Rigdon for making me have fun!

James Lyon Thanks to the staff of the many state and municipal tourist offices who were more than helpful, and especially to Desmond O'Shaughnessy Doyle in Guanajuato and Veronica Selene Ortiz Alvarez in Guadalajara. Thanks also to Mario Raúl in Mazatlán, Luis Miguel López in Morelia, Francisco Castilleja in Erongarícuaro, and as ever, thanks to my family, Pauline, Mike and Ben, for keeping the home fires burning.

Michele Matter Thanks to John Noble and to my fellow authors for their help and advice. Also thanks to Tim for helping me to explore Cabo San Lucas. And thanks to my family, especially to my mother, Ligia, for being a great travel companion.

Alan Murphy Thanks to freelance writer Justine Vaisutis, whose creative linguistic skills and invaluable assistance with research were much appreciated. Tourist offices were a welcoming fountain of information; special thanks to Dulce in Saltillo, Verónica Anchondo and Jossie Aguilar in Chihuahua, and Karime Cámara in Ciudad Victoria. To Martín González Lázcari from the Tamaulipas Secretaría de Desarrollo Urbano y Ecología office in Ciudad Victoria, thanks for your help and advice on the Reserva de la Biósfera El Cielo. Thanks also to LP authors Sandra and Ben for providing a very welcoming pad to crash for a couple days.

Vivek Waglé Thanks to James Lyon for his thorough research, John Noble for his gentle mentorship, Ben Greensfelder and Sandra Bao for showing a novice the ropes, Laura Hernández and Alexandra Larsen for insight into Veracruz's wilder side, and all the hostel owners and tourism officials who helped a li'l lost researcher. Gratefulness to China Williams, Kevin Anglin, Tammy Fortin, Kathryn Ettinger, Michael Johnson and Robert Reid for being some of the best durn editors on this Planet. And, as always, much love to my family and friends.

Allison Wright First off, I would like to thank all of the *chilangos* who help make Mexico City such a wonderful place. I would also like to thank my brother, Jeff, for putting me up and putting up with me all summer. And Sonia, thanks for riding roller coasters, betting on the ponies, drinking tequila and getting caught in the rain with me as I researched the DF. Mostly though, I'd like to thank Nathaniel for being in the right place at the right time.

This Book

This is the eighth edition of *Mexico*. Past authors have included Doug Richmond, Dan Spitzer, Scott Wayne, Mark Balla, Wayne Bernhardson, Tom Brosnahan, Mark Honan, Nancy Keller, Daniel C Schechter, Scott Doggett as well as several authors of this edition. John Noble has been the coordinating author for the past four editions. For this edition he wrote the frontmatter chapters and, along with his wife, Susan Forsyth, Oaxaca State and Tabasco & Chiapas. Allison Wright wrote Mexico City. Monica Lepe wrote Around Mexico City and Northwest Mexico. Alan Murphy wrote Central North Mexico and Northeast Mexcio. James Lyon wrote Western Central Highlands, Northern Central Highlands and the northern part of the Central Pacific Coast. Morgan Konn and Andrew Dean Nystrom wrote the southern part of Central Pacific Coast. Vivek Waglé wrote Central Gulf Coast. Ben Greensfelder wrote the Yucatán Peninsula.

FROM THE PUBLISHER

This is the last time *Mexico* will pass through the hands of an inhouse team (here in the US) who learned to count in Spanish by watching *Sesame Street* as children. Bittersweetly we say goodbye to the Lonely Planet books that helped improve our geography and a spectacular array of people who made it fun to play with others.

China Williams led a great group of editors including Kevin Anglin, Kathryn Ettinger, Michael Johnson, Tammy Fortin, Rebecca Northen, Elaine Merrill, Vivek Waglé, Rachel Bernstein, Don Root, Ann Seward and Sharron Wood. Senior editor Robert Reid smiled upon the work benevolently and smoted villagers who wrought false gods against us. Suki Gear helped out with the layout checks. Ken DellaPenta indexed the book.

Gina Gillich oversaw the mapmaking with help from senior cartographer Sean Brandt, who became a proud father to Ellis Townsend Brandt during the production of this book. Annette Olson filled in for Sean. Narinder Bansal, Buck Cantwell, Justin Colgan, Dion Good, Patrick Huerta, Rachel Jereb, Anneka Imkamp, Sara Nelson, Naoko Ogawa, Carole Nuttall, Don Patterson, Patrick Phelan, Terence Philippe, Kat Smith, Herman So, Ed Turley, Sherry Veverka and Rudie Watzig contributed blood, sweat and a few tears to the masterly maps of this book.

Lora Santiago and Gerilyn Attebery designed the book with oversight from Tracey Croom and Susan Rimerman. Ruth Askevold pitched in for a chapter and a few wry jokes. Justin Marler drew the new illustrations. Other illustrations were drawn by Hugh D'Andrade, Rini Keagy, Beca Lafore, Henia Miedzinski, Hannah Reineck, Lora Santiago and Jim Swanson. Beca Lafore designed the cover and Lora produced it.

The *Mexico* production team would like to dedicate this book to Dr Richard Reid (1939-2002), a man full of humor, warmth and intelligence and the father of Robert Reid, an equally exceptional person.

Foreword

ABOUT LONELY PLANET GUIDEBOOKS

The story begins with a classic travel adventure: Tony and Maureen Wheeler's 1972 journey across Europe and Asia to Australia. There was no useful information about the overland trail then, so Tony and Maureen published the first Lonely Planet guidebook to meet a growing need.

From a kitchen table, Lonely Planet has grown to become the largest independent travel publisher in the world, with offices in Melbourne (Australia), Oakland (USA), London (UK) and Paris (France).

Today Lonely Planet guidebooks cover the globe. There is an ever-growing list of books and information in a variety of media. Some things haven't changed. The main aim is still to make it possible for adventurous travelers to get out there – to explore and better understand the world.

At Lonely Planet we believe travelers can make a positive contribution to the countries they visit – if they respect their host communities and spend their money wisely. Since 1986 a percentage of the income from each book has been donated to aid projects and human rights campaigns, and, more recently, to wildlife conservation.

> Although inclusion in a guidebook usually implies a recommendation, we cannot list every good place. Exclusion does not necessarily imply criticism. In fact, there are a number of reasons why we might exclude a place – sometimes it is simply inappropriate to encourage an influx of travelers.

UPDATES & READER FEEDBACK

Things change – prices go up, schedules change, good places go bad and bad places go bankrupt. Nothing stays the same. So, if you find things better or worse, recently opened or long-since closed, please tell us and help make the next edition even more accurate and useful.

Lonely Planet thoroughly updates each guidebook as often as possible – usually every two years, although for some destinations the gap can be longer. Between editions, up-to-date information is available in our free, quarterly *Planet Talk* newsletter and monthly email bulletin *Comet*. The *Upgrades* section of our Web site (W www.lonelyplanet.com) is also regularly updated by Lonely Planet authors, and the site's *Scoop* section covers news and current affairs relevant to travelers. Lastly, the *Thorn Tree* bulletin board and *Postcards* section carry unverified, but fascinating, reports from travelers.

Tell us about it! We genuinely value your feedback. A well-traveled team at Lonely Planet reads and acknowledges every email and letter we receive and ensures that every morsel of information finds its way to the relevant authors, editors and cartographers.

Everyone who writes to us will find their name listed in the next edition of the appropriate guidebook and will receive the latest issue of *Comet* or *Planet Talk*. The very best contributions will be rewarded with a free guidebook.

We may edit, reproduce and incorporate your comments in Lonely Planet products such as guidebooks, Web sites and digital products, so let us know if you don't want your comments reproduced or your name acknowledged.

How to contact Lonely Planet:
Online: e talk2us@lonelyplanet.com.au, W www.lonelyplanet.com
Australia: Locked Bag 1, Footscray, Victoria 3011
UK: 10a Spring Place, London NW5 3BH
USA: 150 Linden St, Oakland, CA 94607

Introduction

To explore Mexico is to walk through rain forests and along tropical beaches, to traverse vast deserts and to journey around (or up) snow-capped volcanoes; it is to walk the streets of teeming modern conurbations, sleepy villages, chic resorts and the ruined cities of ancient civilizations. Mexico is an experience that offers a multitude of cultures, cuisines, landscapes, activities, music, environments, handicrafts, art and history, and the development of adventure tourism, ecotourism and community tourism in recent years has made a lot more of this variety accessible to visitors. It's easier than ever before to hike remote canyons, watch whales or flamingoes, climb volcanoes, dive waters teeming with tropical fish, bike to remote indigenous villages and kayak to offshore islands.

At the same time, Mexico's long-established virtues as a travel destination have not gone away. Its marvelous Pacific and Caribbean coastlines shelter hundreds of virtually untouched beaches as well as fishing villages and ports and resorts large and small. Cancún, Los Cabos, Mazatlán, Puerto Vallarta, Ixtapa, Zihuatanejo and Acapulco are the names that tumble out of travel agents' brochures. But you'll probably enjoy yourself at least as much in some smaller place you'll never hear of till you get to it, where you can rent a palm-roofed *cabaña,* or just a hammock, and soak up the sun, the surf, good food and some *simpático* company.

If you're in a party mood, there's a *fiesta* – fireworks, parades, music, fun – happening somewhere, every day, and Mexico's cities and hip travel destinations have nightlife to satisfy the most exacting standards.

Scattered around the country – in every type of location from city centers to the middle of impenetrable jungle – is an array of archaeological sites from ancient civilizations that are as fascinating as any in the world: Teotihuacán, El Tajín, Monte Albán, Palenque, Chichén Itzá, Uxmal and Cobá,

to name but a few. From the more recent colonial era Mexico is blessed with many charming, historic towns full of centuries-old stone architecture and plazas with splashing fountains – Zacatecas, Álamos, San Miguel de Allende, Guanajuato, Puebla, Taxco, Cuernavaca, Pátzcuaro, Oaxaca, San Cristóbal de Las Casas, Mérida.

Mexico has world-class museums and galleries – not just the Museo Nacional de Antropología (National Anthropology Museum) in Mexico City and the many other fine archaeological museums, but also the former homes of artists such as Frida Kahlo and Diego Rivera and history-makers such as Hernán Cortés, Leon Trotsky and Pancho Villa, and such establishments as the Museo de las Momias in Guanajuato (a collection of corpses disinterred from a public cemetery) and the Museo Rafael Coronel in Zacatecas (an astonishing display of over 2000 masks used in Mexican dances and rituals).

The country's diversity stems partly from topography. Its Spanish conqueror, Hernán Cortés, when asked to describe Mexico, simply crumpled a piece of paper and set it on a table. The country's endless mountain ranges have always allowed its many peoples to pursue independent destinies. Great cultures and empires, among them the Olmecs, the Maya and the Aztecs, flourished here centuries ago. Their direct descendants – over 50 distinct indigenous peoples, each with their own language – retain their separate identities today amid the country's *mestizo* (mixed-blood) majority and despite the country's ongoing modernization. Tradition and modernity rub shoulders throughout this country where fishing, subsistence agriculture, handwoven textiles and handcrafted ceramics coexist with modern manufacturing, transportation, communications and a big tourism industry. Even as modern highways, television, cell phones and the Internet bring people closer together, being Mexican continues to mean very different things to the distinct peoples of Mexico's many regions. If you're looking for the 'real' Mexico, don't expect just one conclusion.

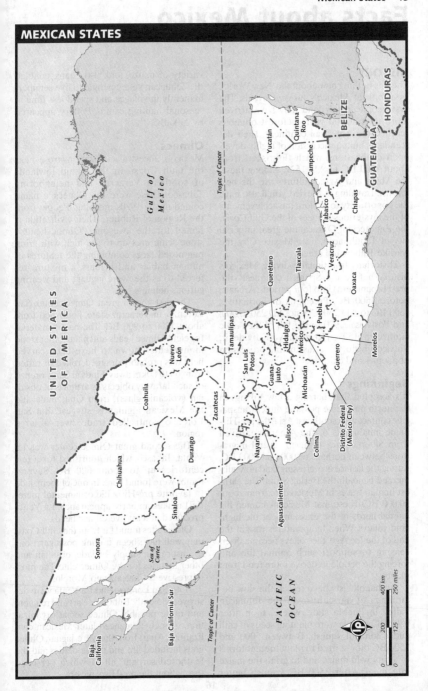

MEXICAN STATES

Facts about Mexico

HISTORY

There is nothing new about the 'New World,' as a look at Mexico's history reveals. The first people in this land may have arrived more than 20,000 years before Columbus reached the American continent. Their descendants built a succession of highly developed civilizations, which flourished from about 1200 BC to AD 1521. Among these, the Maya and Aztec cultures are the best known. Traveling in Mexico, you'll also have the opportunity to explore the achievements of the mysterious Olmecs of the Gulf Coast, the Zapotecs of Oaxaca, the great imperial city of Teotihuacán, near Mexico City, the warlike Toltecs and others.

Historians traditionally divide Mexico's history before the Spanish conquest (the pre-Hispanic era) into four periods: Archaic, before 1500 BC; Preclassic or Formative, 1500 BC to AD 250; Classic, AD 250 to 900; and Postclassic, 900 to the fall of the Aztec empire in 1521. However you divide it, Mexico's history is a fascinating procession of peoples and cultures.

Beginnings

It's accepted that, barring a few Vikings in the north and some possible direct transpacific contact with southeast Asia, the pre-Hispanic inhabitants of the Americas arrived from Siberia. They came in several migrations between perhaps 60,000 and 8000 BC, during the last ice age, crossing land now submerged beneath the Bering Strait. The earliest human traces in Mexico date from about 20,000 BC. These first Mexicans hunted big animal herds in the grasslands of the highland valleys. When temperatures rose at the end of the Ice Age, the valleys became drier, ceasing to support such animal life and forcing the people to derive more food from plants.

Archaeologists have traced the slow beginnings of agriculture in the Tehuacán valley in Puebla state, where, soon after 6500 BC, people were planting seeds of chili and a kind of squash. Between 5000 and 3500 BC they started to plant mutant forms of a tiny wild maize and to grind the maize into meal. After 3500 BC a much better variety of maize, and also beans, enabled the Tehuacán valley people to live semipermanently in villages and spend less time in seasonal hunting camps. Pottery appeared by 2300 BC.

Olmecs

Mexico's ancestral civilization arose near the Gulf Coast, in the humid lowlands of southern Veracruz and neighboring Tabasco. These were the Olmecs, a name coined in the 1920s meaning 'People from the Region of Rubber.' Their civilization is famed for the awesome 'Olmec heads', stone sculptures up to 3m high with grim, pug-nosed faces combining the features of human babies and jaguars, a mixture referred to as the 'were-jaguar', and wearing curious helmets.

The first known great Olmec center, San Lorenzo, in Veracruz state, flourished from about 1200 to 900 BC. The basalt material for eight Olmec heads and many other stone monuments known to have been carved here was probably dragged, rolled or rafted from 60 to 80km away. Finds at San Lorenzo of such faraway objects as artifacts of obsidian (volcanic glass), from Guatemala and the Mexican highlands, suggest that San Lorenzo controlled trade over a large region.

The second great Olmec center was La Venta, Tabasco, which flourished for a few centuries up to about 600 BC. Several tombs were found here. In one of them, jade (a favorite pre-Hispanic ornamental material) makes an early appearance. La Venta produced at least five Olmec heads.

Olmec sites found far from the Gulf Coast may well have been trading posts/garrisons to ensure the supply of jade, obsidian and other luxuries for the Olmec elite. The most impressive is Chalcatzingo, Morelos.

Both San Lorenzo and La Venta were destroyed violently. But Olmec art and religion, and quite possibly Olmec social organization, strongly influenced later Mexican civilizations. Apart from the were-jaguar, Olmec gods included fire and maize deities and the feathered serpent, all of which persisted throughout the pre-Hispanic era.

Teotihuacán

The first great civilization in central Mexico emerged in a valley about 50km northeast of the center of modern Mexico City. Teotihuacán grew into a city of an estimated 125,000 people during its apogee between AD 250 and 600, and it controlled what was probably the biggest pre-Hispanic Mexican empire. Teotihuacán had writing and books, the bar-and-dot number system and the 260-day sacred year (see Calendar under the Classic Maya section, later in this chapter).

The building of a magnificent planned city began about the time of Christ. The greatest of its buildings, the Pirámide del Sol (Pyramid of the Sun; 70m-high, 220m by 220m at its base), was constructed by AD 150. Most of the rest of the city, including the almost-as-big Pirámide de la Luna (Pyramid of the Moon), was built between about AD 250 and 600.

Teotihuacán probably became an imperialistic state sometime after AD 400. It may have controlled the southern two-thirds of Mexico, all of Guatemala and Belize, and bits of Honduras and El Salvador. But it was an empire probably geared toward tribute-gathering rather than full-scale occupation.

Cholula, near Puebla, with a pyramid even bigger than the Pirámide del Sol, was within Teotihuacán's cultural sphere. Teotihuacán may also have had hegemony over the Zapotecs of Oaxaca during the zenith of their capital, Monte Albán, which grew into a city of perhaps 25,000 between about AD 300 and 600. In about AD 400 Teotihuacán invaders reached what's now Guatemala.

In the 7th century Teotihuacán was burned, plundered and abandoned. It is likely that the state had already been weakened by the rise of rival powers in central Mexico or by environmental desiccation caused by the deforestation of the surrounding hillsides.

But Teotihuacán's influence on Mexico's later cultures was huge. Many of its gods, such as the feathered serpent Quetzalcóatl, an all-important symbol of fertility and life (itself inherited from the Olmecs) and Tláloc, the rain and water deity, were still being worshiped by the Aztecs a millennium later.

Classic Maya

By the close of the Preclassic period, in AD 250, the Maya people of the Yucatán Peninsula and the Petén forest of Guatemala were already building stepped temple pyramids. During the Classic period (which ran from about AD 250 to 900), these regions produced pre-Hispanic America's most brilliant civilization.

The Classic Maya region comprised three areas. The northern is the Yucatán Peninsula; the central area is the Petén forest of northern Guatemala and adjacent lowlands in Mexico (to the west) and Belize (to the east); and the southern consists of the highlands of Guatemala and Honduras and the Pacific coast of Guatemala. It was in the northern and central areas that Mayan civilization flowered most brilliantly. Many of the major Mayan ruins sites are outside Mexico, with Tikal in the Petén supreme in splendor.

Scholars used to think the Classic Maya were organized into about 20 independent, often warring city-states. But advances in the understanding of Mayan writing have yielded a new theory that in the first part of the Classic period most of the city-states were grouped into two loose military alliances centered on Tikal and Calakmul, in Mexico's Campeche state. Tikal is believed to have conquered Calakmul in 695, but to have been unable to exert unified control over Calakmul's former subject states.

In the second half of the 8th century, trade between Mayan states started to shrink and conflict began to grow. By the early 10th century the central Mayan area was virtually abandoned, most of its people probably having migrated to the northern area or the highlands of Chiapas. Population pressure and ecological damage have been considered probable reasons for this collapse. Recent research also points to Tikal's inability to control the conquered Calakmul territory after AD 695 as a cause.

Cities A typical Mayan city functioned as the religious, political and market hub for the surrounding farming hamlets. Its ceremonial center focused on plazas surrounded by tall temple pyramids (usually the tombs of probably deified rulers) and lower buildings, so-called palaces, with warrens of small rooms. Stelae and altars were carved with dates, histories and elaborate human and divine figures. Stone causeways called *sacbeob*, probably built for ceremonial use, led out from the plazas.

Classic Maya centers in Mexico fall into four main zones: Chiapas, in the central Mayan area; and Río Bec, Chenes and Puuc, all on the Yucatán Peninsula.

Chiapas – The chief Chiapas sites are Yaxchilán, its tributary Bonampak, Palenque, which to many people is the most beautiful of all Mayan sites, and Toniná. Palenque rose to prominence under the 7th-century ruler Pakal, whose treasure-loaded tomb deep inside the fine Templo de las Inscripciones was discovered in 1952. (See the Tabasco & Chiapas chapter for more information.)

Río Bec & Chenes – These zones, noted for their lavishly carved buildings, are in a wild, little-investigated zone of the southern Yucatán Peninsula. The archaeological sites here, which include Calakmul, draw few visitors (see The Yucatán Peninsula chapter).

Puuc – This zone was another focus of northern Classic Maya culture. Its most important city was Uxmal, south of Mérida. Puuc ornamentation, which reached its peak on the Governor's Palace at Uxmal, featured intricate stone mosaics, part geometric but also incorporating faces of the hook-nosed sky-serpent/rain-god, Chac. The amazing Codz Pop (Palace of Masks) at Kabah, south of Uxmal, is covered with nearly 300 Chac faces. Chichén Itzá, east of Mérida, is another Puuc site, though it also owes much to a later era (see the Toltecs section later in this chapter).

Art Mayan art was elegant, often cluttered, and narrative in content. Fine carved stelae showing historical and mythological events have survived, with those in the central area generally superior to those in the north and south. Mayan potters achieved marvelous multicolored effects on grave vessels that accompanied the dead to the next world. Jade, the most precious substance, was carved into beads or thin plaques.

Calendar The Maya developed a complex, partly pictorial, partly phonetic writing system with 300 to 500 symbols, whose decipherment in the 1980s greatly advanced modern understanding of the culture. They also refined a calendar used by other pre-Hispanic peoples into a tool for the exact recording of earthly and heavenly events. They could predict eclipses of the sun and the movements of the moon and Venus, and they measured time in three ways:

- in *tzolkins* (sacred or almanac years) composed of 13 periods of 20 days
- in *haabs* ('vague' solar years) of 18 20-day 'months,' which were followed by a special five-day 'portentous' period called the *uayeb*; the last day of each 'month' was known as the 'seating' of the next month, in line with the Mayan belief that the future influences the present
- in units of one, 20, 360, 7200 and 144,000 days

All Mexico's pre-Hispanic civilizations used the first two counts, whose interlocking enabled a date to be located precisely within a period of 52 years called a Calendar Round. But the Maya were the preeminent users of the third count, known as the Long Count, which was infinitely extendable. Their inscriptions enumerate the Long Count units elapsed from a starting point (Creation) that corresponds to August 13, 3114 BC. Numbers were written in a system of dots (counted as one) and bars (counted as five).

Religion Religion permeated every facet of Mayan life. The Maya believed in predestination and had a complex astrology. To win the gods' favors they carried out elaborate rituals involving the consumption of the alcoholic drink *balche*; bloodletting from ears, tongues or penises; and dances, feasts and sacrifices. The Classic Maya seem to have practiced human sacrifice on a small scale, the Postclassic on a larger scale. Beheading was probably the most common method. At Chichén Itzá, victims were thrown into a deep *cenote* (well) to bring rain.

The Maya inhabited a universe with a center and four directions (each with a color: east, red; north, white; west, black; south, yellow; the center, green), 13 layers of heavens, and nine layers of underworld to which the dead descended. The earth was the back of a giant reptile floating on a pond. (It's not *too* hard to imagine yourself as a flea on this creature's back as you look across a lowland Mayan landscape!) The current world was just one of a succession of worlds destined to end in cataclysm and be succeeded by another. This cyclical nature of things enabled the future to be predicted by looking at the past.

Mayan gods included Itzamná, the fire deity and creator; Chac, the rain god; Yum

Kaax, the maize and vegetation god; and Ah Puch, the death god. The feathered serpent, known to the Maya as Kukulcán, was introduced from central Mexico in the Postclassic period. Also worshiped were dead ancestors, particularly rulers, who were believed to be descended from the gods.

Classic Veracruz Civilization

Along the Gulf Coast, in what are now central and northern Veracruz, the Classic period saw the rise of a number of statelets with a shared culture, together known as the Classic Veracruz civilization. Their hallmark is a style of abstract carving featuring pairs of curved and interwoven parallel lines. Classic Veracruz appears to have been particularly obsessed with the ball game; its most important center, El Tajín, near Papantla, which was at its height from about AD 600 to 900, contains at least 11 ball courts.

Toltecs

In central Mexico one chief power center after the decline of Teotihuacán was Xochicalco, a hilltop site in Morelos with Mayan influences and impressive evidence of a feathered serpent cult. Cholula may have been another. Tula, 65km north of Mexico City, is thought to have been the capital of a great empire referred to by later Aztec 'histories' as that of the Toltecs (Artificers).

Tula It is particularly hard to disentangle myth and history in the Tula/Toltec story. One version is that the Toltecs were one of a number of semicivilized tribes from the north who moved into central Mexico after the fall of Teotihuacán. Tula became their capital, probably in the 10th century, growing into a city of 30,000 to 40,000. The Tula ceremonial center is dedicated primarily to the feathered serpent god Quetzalcóatl, but annals relate that Quetzalcóatl was displaced by Tezcatlipoca (Smoking Mirror), a newcomer god of warriors and sorcery who demanded a regular diet of the hearts of sacrificed warriors. A king identified with Quetzalcóatl fled to the Gulf Coast and set sail eastward on a raft of snakes, promising one day to return.

Chac, god of rain

Tula seems to have become the capital of a militaristic kingdom that dominated central Mexico, with warriors organized in orders dedicated to different animal-gods: the coyote, jaguar and eagle knights. Mass human sacrifice may have started at Tula.

Tula's influence was great. It is seen at Paquimé in Chihuahua, at Gulf Coast sites such as Castillo de Teayo, and in western Mexico. Pottery from as far south as Costa Rica has been found at Tula, and there's even probable Tula influence in temple mounds and artifacts found in the US states of Tennessee and Illinois.

Tula was abandoned about the start of the 13th century, seemingly destroyed by Chichimecs, as the periodic hordes of barbarian raiders from the north came to be known. Many later Mexican peoples revered the Toltec era as a golden age.

Chichén Itzá Mayan scripts relate that toward the end of the 10th century much of the northern Yucatán Peninsula was conquered by one Kukulcán, who bears many similarities to Quetzalcóatl. The Mayan site of Chichén Itzá, in northern Yucatán, contains many Tula-like features, from flat beam-and-masonry roofs (contrasting with the Mayan corbeled roof) to gruesome chac-mools, reclining human figures holding dishes for human hearts torn out in sacrifices. There's a resemblance that can hardly be coincidental between Tula's Pirámide B (Pyramid B) and Chichén Itzá's Temple of the Warriors. Many writers therefore believe Toltec exiles invaded Yucatán and created a new, even grander version of Tula at Chichén Itzá.

To confuse matters, however, there's a respectable body of opinion that believes the Tula-style features at Chichén Itzá actually *predated* Tula, implying that Chichén Itzá, not Tula, was the epicenter of whatever culture this was.

Aztecs

Aztec legend relates that they were the chosen people of their tribal god Huizilopochtli. Originally nomads from the north or west of Mexico who were led to the Valle

The Ball Game, Then & Now

Probably all pre-Hispanic Mexican cultures played the ball game, which may have varied from place to place and era to era, but had certain lasting features. Special L-shaped ball courts appear at archaeological sites all over Mexico. The game seems to have been played between two teams, and its essence was apparently to keep a rubber ball off the ground by flicking it with hips, thighs and possibly knees or elbows. The vertical or sloping walls alongside the courts were probably part of the playing area, not stands for spectators. The game had, at least sometimes, deep religious significance. It perhaps served as an oracle, with the result indicating which of two courses of action should be taken. Games could be followed by the sacrifice of one or more of the players – whether winners or losers, no one is sure.

The ancient ball game survives, somewhat modified and without human sacrifice, in the form of *la pelota mixteca* (Mixtec ball game), a five-a-side team sport played regularly in some towns and villages in Oaxaca state. Participants wear a thick heavy glove with which to hit the ball. Some 25 Oaxacan teams play championship competitions lasting three months, twice a year. One place you can see the game played is Bajos de Chila near Puerto Escondido. Oaxacan migrants have even exported the game to Fresno, California.

de México (site of present-day Mexico City) by their priests, the Aztecs settled on islands in the lakes that then filled much of the valley.

The Aztec capital, Tenochtitlán, was founded on one of those islands in the first half of the 14th century. Around 1427 the Aztecs rebelled against Azcapotzalco, then the strongest statelet in the valley, and themselves became the most powerful people in the valley.

In the mid-15th century the Aztecs formed the Triple Alliance with two other valley states, Texcoco and Tlacopan, to wage war against Tlaxcala and Huejotzingo, east of the valley. The prisoners they took would form the diet of sacrificed warriors that

their god Huizilopochtli demanded to keep the sun rising every day. For the dedication of Tenochtitlán's Templo Mayor (Great Temple) in 1487, the Aztec king Ahuizotl had 20,000 captives sacrificed.

The Triple Alliance brought most of central Mexico from the Gulf Coast to the Pacific (though not Tlaxcala) under its control. The total population of the empire's 38 provinces may have been about 5 million. The empire's purpose was to exact tribute of resources absent from the heartland. Jade, turquoise, cotton, paper, tobacco, rubber, lowland fruits and vegetables, cacao and precious feathers were needed for the glorification of the Aztec elite and to support the many nonproductive servants of its war-oriented state.

Ahuizotl's successor was Moctezuma II Xocoyotzin, a reflective character who believed, perhaps fatally, that the Spaniard Hernán Cortés, who arrived on the Gulf Coast in 1519, might be Quetzalcóatl, returned from the east to reclaim his throne (see the Spanish Conquest, later in this chapter).

Economy & Society By 1519 Tenochtitlán and the adjoining Aztec city of Tlatelolco probably had more than 200,000 inhabitants, and the Valle de México, as a whole, over a million. They were supported by a variety of intensive farming methods using only stone and wooden tools, including irrigation, terracing and swamp reclamation.

The basic unit of Aztec society was the *calpulli*, consisting of a few dozen to a few hundred extended families, owning land communally. The king held absolute power but delegated important roles such as priest or tax collector to members of the *pilli* (nobility). Military leaders were usually *tecuhtli*, elite professional soldiers. Another special group was the *pochteca*, militarized merchants who helped extend the empire, brought goods to the capital and organized large markets, which were held daily in big towns. At the bottom of society were pawns (paupers who could sell themselves for a specified period), serfs and slaves.

Culture & Religion Tenochtitlán-Tlatelolco had hundreds of temple complexes. The greatest, located on and around modern Mexico City's Zócalo, marked the center of the universe. Its main temple pyramid was dedicated to Huizilopochtli and the rain god, Tláloc.

Much of Aztec culture was drawn from earlier Mexican civilizations. They had writing, bark-paper books and the Calendar Round. They observed the heavens for astrological purposes. Celibate priests performed cycles of great ceremonies, typically including sacrifices and masked dances or processions enacting myths.

The Aztecs believed they lived in the 'fifth world,' whose four predecessors had each been destroyed by the death of the sun and of humanity. Aztec human sacrifices were designed to keep the sun alive. Like the Maya, the Aztecs saw the world as having four directions, 13 heavens and nine hells. Those who died by drowning, leprosy, lightning, gout, dropsy or lung disease went to the paradisiac gardens of Tláloc, the god who had killed them; warriors who were sacrificed or died in battle, merchants killed while traveling far away, and women who died giving birth to their first child all went to heaven as companions of the sun; everyone else traveled for four years under the northern deserts, in the abode of the death god named Mictlantecuhtli, before reaching the ninth hell, where they vanished altogether.

Other Postclassic Civilizations

On the eve of the Spanish conquest most Mexican civilizations shared deep similarities. Each was politically centralized and divided into classes, with many people occupied in specialist tasks, including professional priests. Agriculture was productive despite the lack of draft animals, metal tools and the wheel. Maize tortillas and *pozol* (maize gruel) were staple foods. Beans provided important protein, and a great variety of other crops were grown in different regions: squash, tomatoes, chilies, avocados, peanuts, papayas and pineapples. Luxury foods for the elite included turkey, domesticated hairless dog, game and chocolate drinks. War was widespread, often in connection with the need to take prisoners for sacrifice to a variety of gods.

Yucatán The 'Toltec' phase at Chichén Itzá lasted until about 1200. After that, the city of Mayapán dominated most of the Yucatán Peninsula until the 15th century, when rebellions broke out and the peninsula became a quarreling-ground of numerous city-states, with a culture much decayed from Classic Mayan glories.

Oaxaca After about 1200 the remaining Zapotec settlements, such as Mitla and Yagul, were increasingly dominated by the Mixtecs, who were famed metalsmiths and potters from the uplands around the Oaxaca-Puebla border. Mixtec and Zapotec cultures became entangled before much of their territory fell to the Aztecs in the 15th and 16th centuries.

Gulf Coast The Totonacs, a people who may have occupied El Tajín in its later years, established themselves in much of Veracruz state. To their north, the Huastecs, who inhabited another web of probably independent statelets, flourished from 800 to 1200. In the 15th century the Aztecs subdued most of these areas.

The West One group who avoided conquest by the Aztecs were the Tarascos, who ruled modern Michoacán from their capital, Tzintzuntzan, about 200km west of Mexico City. They were skilled artisans and jewelers.

Spanish Conquest

Ancient Mexican civilization, nearly 3000 years old, was shattered in the two short years from 1519-21 by a tiny group of invaders. These conquerors destroyed the Aztec empire, brought a new religion and reduced the native people to second-class citizens and slaves. So alien to each other were the newcomers and the indigenous people that each doubted whether the other was human (the Pope gave the Mexicans the benefit of the doubt in 1537).

From this traumatic encounter arose modern Mexico. Most Mexicans are *mestizo*, of mixed indigenous and European blood, and thus descendants of both cultures. But while Cuauhtémoc, the last Aztec emperor, is now an official hero, Cortés, the leader of the Spanish conquerors, is seen as a villain, and his indigenous allies as traitors.

Early Expeditions The Spaniards had been in the Caribbean since Columbus

A Historical Who's Who

Ahuizotl (d 1502) This Aztec emperor from 1486-1502 expanded the empire.

Allende, Ignacio (1779-1811) He was an instigator of the independence struggle in 1810.

Alvarado, Pedro de (1486-1541) One of the leading conquistadors, Alvarado accompanied Cortés and later conquered Guatemala and El Salvador.

Axayácatl This Aztec emperor from 1469-81 was the father of Moctezuma II Xocoyotzin.

Calles, Plutarco Elías (1877-1945) This Mexican Revolution leader was president from 1924-28.

Cárdenas, Cuauhtémoc (b 1933) Son of Lázaro Cárdenas, he ran for president as a left-of-center opposition candidate in 1988 and is thought by many to have been cheated of victory through PRI fraud; he was elected to be the mayor of Mexico City in 1997 and stood for presidency again in 1994 and 2000.

Cárdenas, Lázaro (1895-1970) A general and a statesman, he was considered a true president of the people, serving from 1934-40. Cárdenas carried out major land reforms and expropriated foreign oil company operations.

Carlota, Marie Charlotte Amélie (1840-1927) Daughter of King Leopold I of Belgium, she married Archduke Maximilian of Hapsburg and accompanied him to Mexico in 1864 to become empress. After her husband's execution in 1867 she lived on for 60 years, mentally unstable, a ward of the Vatican.

Carranza, Venustiano (1859-1920) This leader of the Constitutionalist side in the Mexican revolution, which opposed to Pancho Villa and Emiliano Zapata, was president from 1917-20; he was overthrown by an alliance led by Álvaro Obregón and later assassinated, which effectively ended the revolution.

Cortés, Hernán (1485-1547) This Spanish conquistador, sometimes known as Hernando or Fernando, invaded Mexico and conquered the Aztecs. Today much maligned in Mexico, Cortés was the person chiefly responsible for introducing Hispanic civilization into Mexico.

Cuauhtémoc (c 1495-1525) The last Aztec emperor, he was defeated and later executed by Cortés.

Cuitláhuac (d 1520) This Aztec emperor succeeded Moctezuma II Xocoyotzin in 1520, but died the same year.

Díaz, Porfirio (1830-1915) Elected president in 1877 and reelected on numerous occasions on a slogan of 'order and progress,' he became a dictator who pursued public-works projects and foreign investment at the expense of the poor and of civil liberties. His policies precipitated the Mexican Revolution in 1910.

Díaz del Castillo, Bernal (1492-1581) Captain in Cortés' army, he wrote *History of the Conquest of New Spain*, his eyewitness account of the Spanish conquest of Mexico and Guatemala.

Echeverría, Luis (b 1922) A left-leaning president from 1970-76, he aided agriculture and expanded rural social services, but his term was blighted by violent unrest and the beginnings of severe corruption.

Guerrero, Vicente (1782-1831) A leader in the later stages of the struggle for independence from Spain, he subsequently became a liberal president but was deposed by conservatives in 1829 and executed in 1831.

Hidalgo y Costilla, Miguel (1753-1811) This parish priest of Dolores sparked the independence struggle in 1810 with his famous *grito*, or call for independence.

Huerta, Victoriano (1854-1916) Leader of Madero's forces against a 1913 counterrevolution, he switched sides to become president himself. One of Mexico's most disliked and ineffective leaders, he was forced to resign in 1914.

A Historical Who's Who

Iturbide, Agustín de (1783-1824) An officer in the royalist army against Guerrero, he switched sides to negotiate with the rebels and achieve Mexico's independence from Spain (1821). Iturbide set himself up as Emperor Agustín I of Mexico, but his reign lasted less than a year (1822-23).

Juárez, Benito (1806-72) A Zapotec lawyer from Oaxaca, Juárez was prominent in the group of liberals who deposed Santa Anna and then passed laws against the church, precipitating the three-year War of the Reform. Elected president in 1861, he was forced to flee because of the French takeover by Napoleon III and Emperor Maximilian. After the French left, Juárez resumed the presidency until his death.

Las Casas, Bartolomé de (1474-1566) This bishop of Chiapas in the 1540s was a leading campaigner for indigenous peoples' rights.

Madero, Francisco (1873-1913) A liberal politician, Madero began the Mexican Revolution, leading the first major opposition to Porfirio Díaz and forcing him to resign. But he proved unable to quell factional fighting, and his presidential term (1911-13) ended in front of a firing squad.

Malinche, La (Doña Marina; c 1501-50) Cortés' indigenous mistress and interpreter, she is considered to have had a major influence on Cortés' strategy in subduing the Aztecs.

Ferdinand Maximilian (1832-67) Hapsburg archduke sent by Napoleon III of France in 1864 to rule as emperor of Mexico. His rule was short-lived and he was forced to surrender to Juárez's forces, who executed him by firing squad in 1867.

Moctezuma I Ilhuicamina He was the Aztec emperor from 1440-69.

Moctezuma II Xocoyotzin (1466-1520) Aztec emperor from 1502-20, he was an indecisive leader and failed to fend off the Spanish invasion led by Cortés.

Morelos y Pavón, José María (1765-1815) A liberal priest like Hidalgo, he assumed leadership of the independence movement after Hidalgo's execution and proved a brilliant leader and strategist, but was captured and executed in 1815. His home city Valladolid was renamed Morelia in his honor.

Obregón, Álvaro (1880-1928) This revolutionary leader supported Madero, then Carranza, but rebelled when Carranza tried to keep power illegally. Obregón's presidency (1920-24) saw revolutionary reforms, especially in education. He was assassinated in 1928.

Salinas de Gortari, Carlos (b 1948) President from 1988-94, Salinas revived the economy, but his term was clouded by the Zapatista uprising in Chiapas and the assassination of his chosen successor, Luis Donaldo Colosio. Salinas' reputation disintegrated after he left power when he was blamed for the 1994-95 peso crash and suspected of links with drug mobs. He took up residence in Ireland.

Santa Anna, Antonio López de (1794-1876) Santa Anna unseated Iturbide in 1823 and headed 11 of the 50 governments in Mexico's first 35 years of independence, a period of chronic economic decline and corruption. He was a leading player in conflicts with the USA in which Mexico lost huge tracts of territory.

Villa, Francisco 'Pancho' (1878-1923) Bandit in Chihuahua and Durango, he became a charismatic fighting leader in the revolution but fell out with Carranza. He was assassinated in 1923.

Zapata, Emiliano (1879-1919) A peasant leader from Morelos state, Zapata was the most radical of the revolution's leaders, fighting for the return of land to the peasants. He was at odds both with the conservative supporters of the old regime and their liberal opponents. After winning numerous battles (some in association with Pancho Villa), he was ambushed and killed in 1919 on Carranza's orders.

Zedillo Ponce de León, Ernesto (b 1951) PRI president from 1994-2000, Zedillo steered Mexico out of economic crisis and effected a peaceful transition to democratic rule, handing over power to the first non-PRI president in 70 years, Vicente Fox.

arrived in 1492, with their main bases on the islands of Hispaniola and Cuba. Realizing that they had not reached the East Indies, they began looking for a passage through the land mass to their west, but were distracted by tales of gold, silver and a rich empire there.

Early expeditions from Cuba, led by Francisco Hernández de Córdoba in 1517 and Juan de Grijalva in 1518, were driven back from Mexico's Gulf Coast by hostile locals. In 1518 the governor of Cuba, Diego Velázquez, asked Hernán Cortés, a Spanish colonist on the island, to lead a new expedition westward. As Cortés gathered ships and men, Velázquez became uneasy about the costs and Cortés' loyalty. He tried to cancel the expedition, but Cortés ignored him and set sail on February 15, 1519, with 11 ships, 550 men and 16 horses.

The confrontation between the Machiavellian Cortés and the Aztecs, no shabby players of military politics themselves, would be one of the most bizarre in history.

Cortés & the Aztecs The Spaniards landed first at Cozumel, off the Yucatán Peninsula, then sailed around the coast to Tabasco, where they defeated local resisters and Cortés delivered the first of many lectures to Mexicans on the importance of Christianity and the greatness of King Carlos I of Spain. The locals gave him 20 maidens, among them Doña Marina (La Malinche), who became his interpreter, aide and lover.

The expedition next put in near the present city of Veracruz. In the Aztec capital of Tenochtitlán, tales of 'towers floating on water,' bearing fair-skinned beings, reached Moctezuma II, the Aztec god-king. Lightning struck a temple, a comet sailed through the night skies and a bird 'with a mirror in its head' was brought to Moctezuma, who saw warriors in it. According to the Aztec calendar, 1519 would see the legendary god-king Quetzalcóatl return from the east. Unsure if Cortés really was the god returning, Moctezuma sent messengers to attempt to discourage Cortés from traveling to Tenochtitlán.

The Spaniards were well received at the Gulf Coast communities of Zempoala and Quiahuiztlán, which resented Aztec dominion. Cortés thus gained his first indigenous

allies. He set up a coastal settlement called Villa Rica de la Vera Cruz and then apparently scuttled his ships to stop his men from retreating. Leaving about 150 men at Villa Rica, Cortés set off for Tenochtitlán. On the way he won over the Tlaxcalan people, who became valuable allies.

After considerable vacillation, Moctezuma finally invited Cortés to meet him, denying responsibility for an ambush at Cholula that had resulted in the Spanish massacring many of that town's inhabitants. The Spaniards and 6000 indigenous allies thus approached the Aztecs' lake-island capital, a city bigger than any in Spain. Entering Tenochtitlán on November 8, 1519, along one of the causeways that linked it to the lakeshore, Cortés was met by Moctezuma, who was carried by nobles in a litter with a canopy of feathers and gold. The Spaniards were lodged, as befitted gods, in the palace of Axayácatl, Moctezuma's father.

Though entertained in luxury, the Spaniards were trapped. But Moctezuma continued to behave hesitantly, and the Spaniards took him hostage. Believing Cortés a god, Moctezuma told his people he went willingly, but hostility rose in the city, aggravated by the Spaniards' destruction of Aztec idols.

Fall of Tenochtitlán When the Spaniards had been in Tenochtitlán about six months, Moctezuma informed Cortés that another fleet had arrived on the Veracruz coast. It was led by Pánfilo de Narváez, sent by Diego Velázquez to arrest Cortés. Cortés left 140 Spaniards under Pedro de Alvarado in Tenochtitlán and sped to the coast with the others. They routed Narváez's much bigger force, and most of the defeated men joined Cortés.

Meanwhile, things boiled over in Tenochtitlán. Apparently fearing an attack, the Spaniards struck first and killed about 200 Aztec nobles trapped in a square during a festival. Cortés and his enlarged force returned to the Aztec capital and were allowed to rejoin their comrades – only then to come under fierce attack. Trapped in Axayácatl's palace, Cortés persuaded Moctezuma to try to pacify his people. According to one version of the events, the king went up to the roof to address the crowds but was wounded by missiles and died soon afterward;

other versions of the story have it that the Spaniards killed him.

The Spaniards fled on the night of June 30, 1520, but several hundred of them, and thousands of their indigenous allies, were killed on this Noche Triste (Sad Night). The survivors retreated to Tlaxcala, where they prepared for another campaign by building boats in sections, which could be carried across the mountains for a waterborne assault on Tenochtitlán. When the 900 Spaniards reentered the Valle de México they were accompanied by some 100,000 native allies. For the first time, the odds were in their favor.

Moctezuma had been succeeded by his nephew, Cuitláhuac, who then died of smallpox, brought to Mexico by one of Narváez's soldiers. He was succeeded by another nephew, the 18-year-old Cuauhtémoc. The attack started in May 1521. Cortés had to resort to razing Tenochtitlán building by building. By August 13, 1521, the resistance had ended. The captured Cuauhtémoc asked Cortés to kill him, but was kept alive until 1525 as a hostage, undergoing occasional foot-burning as the Spanish tried to make him reveal the whereabouts of treasure.

Colonial Era

Encomienda System The Spaniards renamed Tenochtitlán 'México' and rebuilt it as the capital of Nueva España (New Spain), as they named their new colony.

Cortés granted his soldiers *encomiendas*, which gave rights to the labor or tribute of groups of indigenous people. The settlers were also supposed to convert, protect and 'civilize' these people, but in reality the system often produced little more than slavery. In 1528, on a visit to Spain, Cortés himself received 22 towns as encomiendas and was given the title Marqués del Valle de Oaxaca by the Spanish crown, but he was denied the role of governor. He finally returned to Spain in 1540 and died there in 1547. The rest of the 16th century saw a long, eventually successful struggle by the Spanish crown to restrict the power of the conquistadors in the colony. By the 17th century the number of encomiendas had fallen drastically, and the system was abolished in the 18th century.

Nueva España By 1524 virtually all the Aztec empire, plus other Mexican regions

such as Colima, the Huasteca area and the Isthmus of Tehuantepec, had been brought under at least loose control of the colony. In 1527 Spain set up Nueva España's first *audiencia*, a high court with government functions. Its leader, Nuño de Guzmán, was among the worst of Mexican history's long list of corrupt, violent leaders. After leading a bloody expedition to western Mexico, from Michoacán up to Sonora, he was eventually recalled to Spain.

The second audiencia (1530-35) brought some order to the colony. The king subsequently appointed Antonio de Mendoza as Nueva España's first viceroy – his personal representative to administer the colony. Mendoza, who ruled for 15 years, brought stability, limited the worst exploitation of the indigenous people, encouraged missionary efforts and ensured steady revenue to the Spanish crown.

Central America had been conquered in the 1520s by Spanish forces from Mexico and Panama, and in the 1540s the subjection of the Yucatán Peninsula, by two men both named Francisco de Montejo, was accomplished. In the north, Nueva España's territory ended at the 'Chichimec frontier,' a line running roughly between modern Tampico and Guadalajara, beyond which dwelt fierce seminomads.

Big finds of silver in Zacatecas in the mid-1540s, followed by further finds at Guanajuato, San Luis Potosí and Pachuca, spurred Spanish attempts to subdue the north. They did not succeed until the 1590s, when the Spanish offered the Chichimecs food and clothing in return for peace. By 1700 the viceroyalty of Nueva España, still ruled from Mexico City, also officially included Spain's Caribbean islands and the Philippines. In practice, Central America, the Caribbean and the Philippines were governed separately.

The northern borders were slowly extended by missionaries and a few settlers, and by the early 19th century Nueva España included most of the modern US states of Texas, New Mexico, Arizona, California, Utah and Colorado, though control there was tenuous.

Indigenous People & Missionaries

Despite the efforts of Viceroy Mendoza and Mexico City's first bishop, Juan de

A Different Sort of Liberator

The Spanish invaders of the Americas acquired a reputation for brutality toward the indigenous peoples: the notorious 'Black Legend' of the Spaniards' deliberate sadism. Accounts by the subjugated Aztecs and the conquering Spanish themselves are full of descriptions of beheadings, amputations, burnings, brandings and various other tortures and punishments inflicted on the populace by the newcomers.

In the invaders' footsteps followed representatives of the Catholic Church, enforcing 'Christian principles' among peoples they regarded as pagans. Since those early days, the official church has often been identified with brutal authority, but a strong counter-current of thought began in early colonial times and has survived to the present.

The outstanding figure was Bartolomé de Las Casas. Born in Seville in 1474, Las Casas joined a 1502 expedition against the indigenous people of Higuey, on the island of Hispaniola; he soon held encomiendas there and in Cuba. However, he experienced a conversion that convinced him of the evils of the system and devoted the rest of his life to the cause of justice for the indigenous peoples of Spanish America.

Renouncing his encomiendas, Las Casas returned to Spain to argue passionately for reform of the abuses he had observed in the Indies. His polemical *Very Brief Account of the Destruction of the Indies* persuaded King Carlos I to enact the New Laws of 1542, which included a major reform of the encomienda system. Though the New Laws went largely unenforced because they nearly caused a rebellion among encomienda holders, Las Casas continued to speak out against corrupt officials and encomenderos from his position as bishop of Chiapas, and then as Protector of the Indians at the Spanish court in Madrid, until his death in 1566.

Before the royal court, the audacious Dominican reported one cacique's statement that if Spaniards went to heaven, the native people would prefer hell. Las Casas went so far as to defend the practice of cannibalism, to advocate restitution for all the wealth that Spain had plundered from the Americas, and even to imply that the lands themselves should be returned to the indigenous people in the interests of good government:

'When we entered there… would we have found such great unions of peoples in their towns and cities if they had lacked the order of a good way of life, peace, concord and justice?'

Las Casas' advocacy undoubtedly mitigated some of the worst abuses against the indigenous Americans. In this sense, he was a role model for the Latin American activist clergy of recent decades, which, inspired by liberation theology, has worked to alleviate poverty and human-rights abuses despite great personal risk. Las Casas was the original liberation theologist.

Las Casas also left valuable observations of indigenous customs and history. His is a broad legacy with great modern relevance. One who has followed in his footsteps in modern times is Samuel Ruiz García, the long-time bishop of San Cristóbal de Las Casas, the Chiapas town named after Bartolomé de Las Casas. As bishop, Ruiz stood up to the political and religious establishments with his outspoken support for oppressed indigenous people in Chiapas, who came to regard him almost as a guardian angel. Since retiring in 1999 Ruiz has continued to speak out, both as a Bishop Emeritus of San Cristóbal and as a leader of the activist human rights organization he founded and named for his illustrious predecessor – the Centro de Derechos Humanos Fray Bartolomé de Las Casas.

Zumárraga, the populations of the conquered peoples declined disastrously, mainly from epidemics, many of them new diseases brought by the Spaniards. The population of Nueva España fell from an estimated 25 million at the conquest to little over a million by 1605.

The indigenous peoples' only real allies were some of the monks who started arriving in Nueva España in 1523 to convert them. Many of these monks were compassionate, brave men; the Franciscan and Dominican orders distinguished themselves by protecting the local people from the colonists' worst excesses (see 'A Different Sort of Liberator').

The monks' missionary work helped extend Spanish control over Mexico. By 1560 they had built more than 100 monasteries, some fortified, and had carried out millions of conversions. Under the second viceroy, Luis de Velasco, indigenous slavery was abolished in the 1550s, to be partly replaced by black slavery. Forced labor on encomiendas was also stopped, but a new system of about 45 days' forced labor a year (the *cuatequil*) was introduced for all indigenous people. That system too was widely abused by the Spaniards until abolished about half a century later.

Criollos A person's place in Mexican colonial society was determined by skin color, parentage and birthplace. Spanish-born colonists – known as *peninsulares* or, derisively, *gachupines* – were a minuscule part of the population but were at the top of the tree and considered nobility in Nueva España, however humble their origins in Spain.

Next on the ladder were *criollos*, people born of Spanish parents in Nueva España. By the 18th century some criollos had acquired fortunes in mining, commerce, ranching or agriculture. *Haciendas*, large estates, had begun to grow up as early as the 16th century. Not surprisingly, criollos sought political power commensurate with their wealth.

Below the criollos were the mestizos, and at the bottom of the pile were the indigenous people and African slaves. Though the poor were, by the 18th century, paid for their labor, they were paid very little. Many were *peones*, bonded laborers tied by debt to their employers. Indigenous people still had to pay tribute to the crown.

Aware of the threat to Nueva España from British and French expansion in North America, Spain's King Carlos III (1759-88) sought to bring the colony under firmer control and improve the flow of funds to the crown. He reformed the colonial administration and expelled the Jesuits, whom he suspected of disloyalty, from the entire Spanish empire. The Jesuits in Nueva España had played major roles in missionary work, education and administration, and two-thirds of them were criollos.

Continuing its attack on the powerful Catholic Church in Nueva España, the Spanish crown in 1804 decreed the transfer of many church assets to the royal coffers. The church had to call in many debts, which hit criollos hard and created widespread discontent.

The catalyst for rebellion came in 1808, when France's Napoleon Bonaparte occupied most of Spain and put his brother Joseph on the Spanish throne. Direct Spanish control over Nueva España evaporated. Rivalry between peninsulares and criollos in the colony intensified.

Independence

War of Independence In 1810 a criollo coterie based in Querétaro began planning a rebellion. News of the plans leaked to the colonial authorities, so the group acted immediately. On September 16 one of its members, Miguel Hidalgo y Costilla, priest of the town of Dolores, summoned his parishioners and issued his now-famous call to rebellion, the Grito de Dolores, whose exact words have been lost to history but whose gist was:

My children, a new dispensation comes to us this day. Are you ready to receive it? Will you be free? Will you make the effort to recover from the hated Spaniards the lands stolen from your forefathers 300 years ago? We must act at once...Long live Our Lady of Guadalupe! Death to bad government!

A mob formed and marched on San Miguel, Celaya and Guanajuato, massacring peninsulares in Guanajuato. Over the next month and a half the rebels captured Zacatecas, San Luis Potosí and Morelia. On October 30 their army, numbering about 80,000, defeated loyalist forces at Las Cruces outside Mexico City, but Hidalgo hesitated to attack the capital. The rebels occupied Guadalajara but then were pushed northward by their opponents, their numbers shrank, and in 1811 their leaders, including Hidalgo, were captured and executed.

José María Morelos y Pavón, a former student of Hidalgo and also a parish priest, assumed the rebel leadership, blockading Mexico City for several months. He convened a congress at Chilpancingo, which adopted guiding principles for the independence movement including universal male suffrage, popular sovereignty and abolition of slavery. Morelos was captured and executed in 1815, and his forces split into several guerrilla bands, the most successful of which was led by Vicente Guerrero in the state of Oaxaca.

Emperor Agustín I In 1821 the royalist general Agustín de Iturbide defected during an offensive against Guerrero and conspired with the rebels to declare independence from Spain. Iturbide and Guerrero worked out the Plan de Iguala, which established three guarantees – religious dominance by the Catholic Church, a constitutional monarchy and equal rights for criollos and peninsulares. The plan won over all influential sections of society, and the incoming Spanish viceroy in 1821 agreed to Mexican independence. Iturbide, who had command of the army, soon arranged his own nomination to the throne, which he ascended as Emperor Agustín I in 1822.

Mexican Republic

Iturbide was deposed in 1823 by a rebel army led by another opportunistic soldier, Antonio López de Santa Anna. A new constitution in 1824 established a federal Mexican republic of 19 states and four territories. Guadalupe Victoria, a former independence fighter, became its first president. Mexico's southern boundary was the same as it is today (Central America had set up a separate federation in 1823). In the north, Mexico included much of what's now the southwestern USA.

Vicente Guerrero stood as a liberal candidate in the 1828 presidential elections and was defeated, but was eventually awarded the presidency after another Santa Anna-led revolt. Guerrero abolished slavery but was deposed and executed by his conservative vice president, Anastasio Bustamante. The struggle between liberals, who favored social reform, and conservatives, who opposed it, would be a constant theme in 19th-century Mexican politics.

Santa Anna Intervention in politics by ambitious military men was also becoming a habit. Santa Anna, a national hero after defeating a small Spanish invasion force at Tampico in 1829, overthrew Bustamante and was elected president in 1833. Thus

began 22 years of chronic instability in which the presidency changed hands 36 times; 11 of those terms went to Santa Anna. Economic decline and corruption became entrenched, and Santa Anna quickly turned into a conservative. His main contributions to Mexico were manifestations of his megalomaniacal personality. Most memorably, he had his amputated, mummified leg (lost in an 1838 battle with the French) disinterred in 1842 and paraded through Mexico City.

Santa Anna is also remembered for helping to lose large chunks of Mexican territory to the USA. North American settlers in Texas, initially welcomed by the Mexican authorities, grew restless and declared Texas independent in 1836. Santa Anna led an army north and wiped out the defenders of an old mission called the Alamo in San Antonio, but he was routed on the San Jacinto River a few weeks later.

In 1845 the US Congress voted to annex Texas, and US president Polk demanded further Mexican territory. That led, in 1846, to the Mexican-American War, in which US troops captured Mexico City. At the end of the war, by the Treaty of Guadalupe Hidalgo (1848), Mexico ceded Texas, California, Utah, Colorado, and most of New Mexico and Arizona to the USA. The Santa Anna government sold the remainder of New Mexico and Arizona to the USA in 1853 for US$10 million, in the Gadsden Purchase. This loss precipitated the liberal-led Revolution of Ayutla, which ousted Santa Anna for good in 1855.

Mexico almost lost the Yucatán Peninsula, too, in the so-called War of the Castes in the late 1840s, when the Maya people rose up against their criollo overlords and narrowly failed to drive them off the peninsula.

Juárez & the French Intervention The new liberal government ushered in the era known as the Reform, in which it set about dismantling the conservative state that had developed in Mexico. The key figure was Benito Juárez, a Zapotec from Oaxaca and a leading lawyer and politician. Laws requiring the church to sell much of its property helped precipitate the internal War of the Reform (1858-61) between the liberals, with their 'capital' at Veracruz, and conservatives, based in Mexico City. The liberals eventually won, and Juárez became president in 1861. But Mexico was in disarray and heavily in debt to Britain, France and Spain. These three countries sent a joint force to collect their debts, but France's Napoleon III decided to go further and take over Mexico, leading to yet another war.

Though the French were defeated at Puebla by General Ignacio Zaragoza on May 5, 1862, they took Puebla a year later and went on to capture Mexico City. In 1864 Napoleon invited the Austrian archduke, Maximilian of Hapsburg, to become emperor of Mexico. The French army drove Juárez and his government into the provinces.

Maximilian and Empress Carlota entered Mexico City on June 12, 1864, and moved into the Castillo de Chapultepec. But their reign was brief. In 1866, under pressure from the USA, Napoleon began to withdraw his troops. Maximilian refused to abandon his task but was defeated at Querétaro in 1867 by forces loyal to Juárez, and executed there by firing squad.

Juárez immediately set an agenda of economic and educational reform. For the first time, schooling was made mandatory. A railway was built between Mexico City and Veracruz. A rural police force, the *rurales*, was organized to secure the transport of cargo through Mexico.

The Porfiriato Juárez died in 1872. When his successor, Sebastián Lerdo de Tejada, stood for reelection in 1876, Porfirio Díaz, an ambitious liberal, launched a rebellion on the pretext that presidents should not serve more than one term of office. The following year Díaz, the sole candidate, won the presidential elections, and for the next 33 years he ran Mexico, brushing aside any 'no reelection' principles to serve six successive presidential terms from 1884. Díaz brought Mexico into the industrial age, launching public-works projects throughout the country, particularly in Mexico City. Telephone and telegraph lines were strung and the railway network spread.

Díaz kept Mexico free of the civil wars that had plagued it for over 60 years, but at a cost. Political opposition, free elections and a free press were banned. Many of Mexico's resources went into foreign ownership, peasants were cheated out of their land by new laws, workers suffered appalling conditions,

and the country was kept quiet by a ruthless army and the now-feared rurales. Land and wealth became concentrated in the hands of a small minority. Some hacienda owners amassed truly vast landholdings (in Chihuahua, Don Luis Terrazas had at least 14,000 sq km) and commensurate political power. Many rural workers were tied by debt to their bosses, just like their colonial forebears.

In the early 1900s a liberal opposition formed, but it was forced into exile in the USA. In 1906 the most important group of exiles issued a new liberal plan for Mexico from St Louis, Missouri. Their actions precipitated strikes throughout Mexico, some of which were violently suppressed. All this led, in late 1910, to the Mexican Revolution.

Mexican Revolution

The revolution was a 10-year period of shifting allegiances between a spectrum of leaders, in which successive attempts to create stable governments were wrecked by new outbreaks of devastating fighting.

Madero & Zapata Francisco Madero, a wealthy liberal from Coahuila, campaigned for the presidency in 1910 and would probably have won if Díaz hadn't jailed him. On his release Madero drafted the Plan de San Luis Potosí, which called for the nation to rise in revolution on November 20. The call was heard, and the revolution spread quickly across the country. When revolutionaries under the leadership of Francisco 'Pancho' Villa took Ciudad Juárez in May 1911, Díaz resigned. Madero was elected president in November 1911.

But Madero was unable to contain the factions fighting for power throughout the country. The basic divide was between liberal reformers like Madero and more radical leaders such as Emiliano Zapata from the state of Morelos, who was fighting for the transfer of hacienda land to the peasants with the cry '*¡Tierra y Libertad!*' ('Land and Freedom!'). Madero sent federal troops to disband Zapata's forces, and the Zapatista movement was born.

In November 1911 Zapata promulgated the Plan de Ayala, calling for restoration of all land to the peasants. Zapatistas won several battles against government troops in central Mexico. Other forces of varied political complexion took up local causes elsewhere. Soon all Mexico was plunged into military chaos.

Huerta In February 1913 two conservative leaders – Félix Díaz, nephew of Porfirio, and Bernardo Reyes – commenced a counter-revolution that brought 10 days of fierce fighting, the 'Decena Trágica,' to Mexico City. The fighting ended only after the US ambassador to Mexico, Henry Lane Wilson, persuaded Madero's general, Victoriano Huerta, to switch to the rebel side and help depose Madero's government. Huerta himself became president; Madero and his vice president, José María Pino Suárez, were executed.

Huerta only fomented greater strife. In March 1913 three revolutionary leaders in the north united against him under the Plan de Guadalupe: Venustiano Carranza, a Madero supporter, in Coahuila; Pancho Villa in Chihuahua; and Álvaro Obregón in Sonora. Zapata too was fighting against Huerta. Terror reigned in the countryside as Huerta's troops fought, pillaged and plundered. Finally he was defeated and forced to resign in July 1914.

Constitutionalists versus Radicals Carranza called the victorious factions to a conference in Aguascalientes but failed to unify them, and war broke out again. This time Obregón and Carranza (known as the 'Constitutionalists,' with their capital at Veracruz) were pitted against the 'Radicals,' including populist Villa and the real radical Zapata. But Villa and Zapata, despite a famous meeting in Mexico City, never formed a serious alliance, and the fighting became increasingly anarchic. Villa never recovered from a defeat by Obregón in the battle of Celaya (1915). Carranza eventually emerged the victor, to form a government that was recognized by the USA. A new reformist constitution, still largely in force today, was enacted in 1917.

In Morelos the Zapatistas continued to demand reforms. Carranza had Zapata assassinated in 1919, but the following year Obregón turned against Carranza and, together with fellow Sonorans Adolfo de la Huerta and Plutarco Elías Calles, raised an army, chased Carranza out of office and had him assassinated.

The 10 years of violent civil war cost an estimated 1.5 to 2 million lives (roughly one in eight Mexicans) and shattered the economy.

From Revolution to WWII

Obregón & Calles As president from 1920-24, Obregón turned to national reconstruction. More than a thousand rural schools were built, and some land was redistributed from big landowners to the peasants. Education minister José Vasconcelos commissioned top artists, such as Diego Rivera, David Alfaro Siqueiros and José Clemente Orozco, to decorate important public buildings with large, vivid murals on social and historical themes.

Plutarco Elías Calles, president from 1924-28, built more schools and distributed more land. He also closed monasteries, convents and church schools, and prohibited religious processions. These measures precipitated the bloody Cristero Rebellion by Catholics, which lasted until 1929.

At the end of Calles' term, in 1928, Obregón was elected president again but was assassinated by a Cristero. Calles reorganized his supporters to found the Partido Nacional Revolucionario (PNR, National Revolutionary Party), a precursor of today's PRI and the initiator of a long tradition of official acronyms.

Cárdenas Lázaro Cárdenas, former governor of Michoacán, won the presidency in 1934 with the PNR's support and stepped up the reform program. Cárdenas redistributed almost 200,000 sq km of land – nearly double the amount distributed before him – mostly through the establishment of *ejidos* (peasant landholding cooperatives). Thus, most of Mexico's arable land had been redistributed, and nearly one-third of the population had received land. Cárdenas also set up the million-member Confederación de Trabajadores Mexicanos (CTM, Confederation of Mexican Workers, a labor union) and boldly expropriated foreign oil-company operations in Mexico in 1938, forming Petróleos Mexicanos (Pemex, the Mexican Petroleum Company). After the oil expropriation, foreign investors avoided Mexico, which slowed the economy.

Cárdenas reorganized the PNR into the Partido de la Revolución Mexicana (PRM), a coalition of representatives from agriculture, the military, labor and the people at large.

Following Cárdenas, the presidency of Manuel Ávila Camacho (1940-46) marked a transition toward more conservative government at the end of the first two postrevolutionary decades. Camacho sent Mexican troops to help the WWII Allies in the Pacific and supplied raw materials and labor to the USA. The war's curtailment of manufactured imports boosted Mexican industry and exports.

Modern Mexico

As the Mexican economy expanded, new economic and political groups demanded influence in the ruling PRM. To recognize their inclusion, the party was renamed the Partido Revolucionario Institucional (PRI, or 'El Pree'). President Miguel Alemán (1946-52) continued development by building hydroelectric stations, irrigation projects and UNAM, the National Autonomous University of Mexico, and by extending the road system. Pemex grew dramatically and, with the rise of other industries, spawned some of Mexico's worst corruption.

Alemán's successor, Adolfo Ruiz Cortines (1952-58), began to confront a new problem: explosive population growth. In two decades Mexico's population had doubled, and many people began migrating to urban areas to search for work. Adolfo López Mateos (1958-64), one of Mexico's most popular post-WWII presidents, redistributed 120,000 sq km of land to small farmers, nationalized foreign utility concessions, implemented social welfare and rural education programs, and launched health campaigns. These programs were helped by strong economic growth, particularly in tourism and exports.

Unrest, Boom & Bust President Gustavo Díaz Ordaz (1964-70) was a conservative with an agenda that emphasized business. Though he fostered education and tourism, and the economy grew by 6% a year during his term, he is better remembered for his repression of civil liberties. He sacked the president of the PRI, Carlos Madrazo, who had tried to democratize the party. University students in Mexico City were the first to express their outrage with the Díaz Ordaz administration. Discontent came to a head

in the months preceding the 1968 Olympic Games in Mexico City, the first ever held in a developing nation. Single-party rule and restricted freedom of speech were among the objects of protest. More than half a million people rallied in Mexico City's Zócalo on August 27. On October 2, with the Olympics only a few days away, a rally was organized in Tlatelolco, Mexico City. The government sent in heavily armed troops and police. Several hundred people died in the ensuing massacre.

The following president, Luis Echeverría (1970-76), sought to distribute wealth more equitably than in the past. He instituted government credit for the troubled agricultural sector, launched family-planning programs, and expanded rural clinics and the social security system. But unrest increased, and there was a guerrilla insurrection in Guerrero state, all fueled partly by the corruption that was now rife among government officials.

José López Portillo (1976-82) presided during the jump in world oil prices caused by the OPEC embargo of the early 1970s. He announced that Mexico's main problem now was how to manage its enormous prosperity: on the strength of the country's vast oil reserves, international institutions began lending Mexico billions of dollars. Then, just as suddenly, a world oil glut sent prices plunging. Mexico's worst recession for decades began.

Miguel de la Madrid (1982-88) was largely unsuccessful in coping with the problems he inherited. The population continued to grow at Malthusian rates; the economy made only weak progress, crushed by the huge debt from the oil boom years; and the social pot continued to simmer. Things were not helped by the 1985 Mexico City earthquake, which killed at least 10,000 people, destroyed hundreds of buildings and caused more than US$4 billion in damage.

In a climate of economic helplessness and rampant corruption, dissent grew, even inside the PRI. There were sometimes violent protests over the PRI's now-routine electoral fraud and strong-arm tactics.

Salinas Cuauhtémoc Cárdenas, son of the 1930s president Lázaro Cárdenas, walked out of the PRI to stand as a presidential candidate for the new center-left Frente

Democrático Nacional (FDN, National Democratic Front) in 1988. It's widely believed that Cárdenas received more votes than the PRI candidate, Carlos Salinas de Gortari, but vote counting was interrupted by a mysterious computer failure. In the end Salinas was awarded 50.7% of the vote – less than any PRI candidate before him.

Harvard-educated Salinas (1988-94) transformed Mexico's state-dominated economy into one of private enterprise and free trade. The apex of this program was NAFTA, the North American Free Trade Agreement (see Economy, later in this chapter), which came into effect on January 1, 1994. Salinas' term did not end in a blaze of glory, however. Far from it. Firstly, January 1, 1994 also saw the start of the Zapatista uprising in Mexico's southernmost state, Chiapas (see the Zapatista Movement, later). Then in March 1994 Luis Donaldo Colosio, Salinas' chosen successor as PRI presidential candidate, was assassinated in Tijuana. Conspiracy theories abound about the killing (by the time of the murder relations between Salinas and Colosio had deteriorated markedly), but by 2002 the only person who had been convicted was the one who pulled the trigger and was captured on the spot.

After the Zapatista uprising Salinas pushed through electoral reforms against ballot-stuffing and double voting, and the 1994 presidential election was regarded as the cleanest yet, though on polling day at least a million voters still found they were mysteriously not on the electoral roll. Colosio's replacement as PRI candidate, 43-year-old Ernesto Zedillo, won the election with 50% of the vote. Before he took office in December, another top-level PRI leader, José Francisco Ruiz Massieu, the party's secretary-general (and ex-husband of President Salinas' sister), was assassinated in Mexico City.

During Salinas' term, drug trafficking grew into a huge business in Mexico (see the Drug Trade section, later) and many Mexicans believe President Salinas and his brother Raúl and other PRI high-ups were deeply involved in drug business. Raúl was arrested in 1995, after Carlos left office, and soon afterwards Carlos himself departed Mexico for the USA, then Canada, then the Caribbean. Eventually he resurfaced in Ireland, which doesn't have an extradition treaty with Mexico. Vilified also for the economic crisis into which Mexico plunged after he left office, Carlos Salinas ended up as the ex-president that Mexicans most love to hate.

Zedillo Ernesto Zedillo (1994-2000) was a quiet, uncharismatic economist president, but he brought the Mexican economy back from a nasty slump engendered by his predecessor. He also made real history by reforming the country's politics so that power was peacefully transferred to a non-PRI successor – the first ever peaceful change of regime in Mexican history.

Within days of President Zedillo's taking office in late 1994, Mexico's currency, the peso, suddenly collapsed, bringing on a rapid and deep economic recession that hit everyone hard, and the poor hardest. It led to, among other things, a big increase in crime, intensified discontent with the PRI, and large-scale Mexican emigration to the USA. It was estimated that by 1997 more than 2.5 million Mexicans a year were entering the USA illegally. Zedillo's policies pulled Mexico gradually out of recession and by the end of his term in 2000, Mexicans' purchasing power was again approaching what it had been in 1994.

Zedillo was perceived as more honest than his predecessors. He replaced en masse the notoriously partial supreme court, and it was under his administration that Raúl Salinas was arrested and convicted of masterminding the 1994 murder of Ruiz Massieu. That an ex-president's brother would be arrested for anything was a surprise, for him to receive such a conviction was unheard of. Zedillo was unable to make many inroads into the burgeoning power of Mexico's drug mobs, however (see the Drug Trade section, later).

Zedillo set up a new, independent electoral apparatus that, first, oversaw free and fair elections for the federal Chamber of Deputies in 1997 (the PRI lost control of the chamber for the first time ever), then saw a non-PRI national president elected to succeed Zedillo, when Vicente Fox of the right-of-center Partido de Acción Nacional (PAN, National Action Party) defeated the PRI's Francisco Labastida in 2000. The PRI also refrained from its traditional strong-arm, corrupt methods in most local elections.

By 2000, 11 of Mexico's 31 states had elected non-PRI governors and half the population (including Mexico City) had non-PRI mayors.

The PRI remained at its most repressive and antediluvian in southern states such as Guerrero and Chiapas, both, hardly surprisingly, scenes of armed left-wing insurgency (see the Zapatista Movement, later). When Guerrero's famed Pacific resort Acapulco elected a mayor from the left-wing Partido de la Revolución Democrática (PRD, Party of the Democratic Revolution) in 1999, several prominent PRD figures and members of their families suddenly found themselves arrested, kidnapped, tortured and in one case killed.

The Drug Trade Mexico has long been a marijuana and heroin producer, but a huge impetus to its drug gangs was given by a mid-1980s US crackdown on drug shipments from Colombia through the Caribbean to Florida. As a result, drugs being transported from South America to the USA went through Mexico instead. Three main Mexican cartels emerged: the Pacific or Tijuana cartel, headed by the Arellano Félix brothers; the (Ciudad) Juárez cartel, run by Amado Carrillo Fuentes; and the Matamoros-based Gulf cartel of Juan García Ábrego. These cartels bought up politicians, top antidrug officials and whole police forces.

Many Mexicans believe organized crime in the early 1990s was actually controlled by the PRI, with President Carlos Salinas and his brother Raúl deeply involved. Many believe the 1994 murders of PRI secretary general José Francisco Ruiz Massieu and of presidential candidate Luis Donaldo Colosio (see the Salinas section, earlier) were both related to the drug trade. In 1999 Raúl Salinas was sentenced to 50 years in prison (reduced on appeal to 27½ years) for plotting the Ruiz Massieu murder. In 2001 he was indicted on drug trafficking charges by authorities from Switzerland, where he had been suspected of depositing millions of dollars in drug trade pay-offs.

By 1997 most illegal drugs entering the USA were going through Mexico – an annual flow of about 770 tons of cocaine, 7700 tons of marijuana, and 6 tons of heroin, plus growing quantities of metham-

phetamine (speed). The Mexican cartels were taking up to half the Colombian cocaine shipments themselves and rapidly developing their own production of heroin and speed. Drug gang profits amounted to US$15 billion or more a year.

President Zedillo brought the armed forces into the fight against the drug mobs, but in 1997 his trusted top drug fighter, General Jesús Gutiérrez Rebollo, was himself arrested on charges of being in the pay of the Juárez mob. Zedillo scored some successes. In 1996 Juan García Ábrego, of the Gulf cartel, was captured, deported to the USA and jailed for life in Houston. It was rumored that he had lost a crucial protector when Raúl Salinas was arrested in 1995. Amado Carrillo Fuentes, of the Juárez mob, was reportedly killed in 1997 in Mexico City by surgeons performing plastic surgery on him. But despite his death (if indeed he really did die, which many Mexicans doubt) the Juárez mob and the Pacific (Tijuana) cartel emerged as Mexico's two big drug gangs.

Tijuana was the scene of literally hundreds of drug-related murders, including those of judges, witnesses, honest police and journalists, in the late 1990s. The mobs were just too powerful and had too many highly placed friends to be easily defeated. In 1999 Mario Villanueva, the PRI state governor of Quintana Roo, on Mexico's Caribbean coast, disappeared eight days before his term of office (and immunity from prosecution) expired. Quintana Roo is reportedly the Mexican arrival point of a lot of the cocaine smuggled to USA by the Juárez mob, and Villanueva was finally arrested in 2001 for conspiring with drug traffickers.

The Fox Presidency Rancher, former chief of Coca-Cola's Mexican operation and former state governor of Guanajuato, Vicente Fox stands at almost 2m tall and has a penchant for wearing jeans and cowboy boots. He is Mexico's first non-PRI president since the PRI (or, strictly speaking, its predecessor the PNR) was invented in 1929. Although Fox represents the right-of-center PAN, he is more of a centrist social democrat himself, and he entered office with the goodwill of a wide range of Mexicans who hoped a change of ruling party would betoken real change in the country. Fox picked a broad-based ministerial team ranging from ex-PRI officials to left-wing academics, and did not, as incoming Mexican administrations traditionally do, replace the entire governing apparatus with his own mates and hangers-on.

He made an early, though unsuccessful, attempt to resolve the Zapatista conflict in Chiapas (see the Zapatista movement section, following). Another early Fox initiative was to try to resolve some of the problems of the Mexico/US border and Mexican immigration to the USA. The 8 million undocumented workers in the USA include some 4 million Mexicans (2 million of them in California). The number of people apprehended while trying to cross illegally from Mexico to the USA was approaching 1.8 million a year in 2000. About 400 die each year in the attempt to cross, mostly from drowning, thirst (in the deserts straddling the border) or being hit by vehicles on US highways. Those who make it across, some paying as much as US$3000 to a *'coyote'* (person-smuggler), are vulnerable to ill treatment and exploitation in the USA. (Ironically, sectors of the US economy, such as fruit farming and construction, rely very heavily on Mexican labor). From talks between Fox and US President George W Bush, the possibility emerged of legalization for at least some undocumented Mexicans in the US, in return for greater Mexican vigilance of the border.

One year into Fox's term he was being criticized for having achieved little and his popularity ratings were poor. The assassination of a prominent human rights lawyer, Digna Ochoa, and the lack of official protection she had been given after receiving death threats, made people ask how committed Fox really was to human rights and to rooting out corruption.

He had been bequeathed a booming economy by President Zedillo, only to have things seriously complicated by the recession of 2001. Fox wanted to raise taxes to pay for better education and social welfare programs, increase the time an average Mexican spends in school from seven to 10 years, and reduce the number of Mexicans living in poverty by one-third. He was not being helped by tensions with the orthodox establishment of his own party nor by the PAN's lack of overall majority in Congress, which made it harder for him to push through reforms.

The Zapatista Movement On January 1, 1994, around two thousand indigenous peasant rebels calling themselves the Ejército Zapatista de Liberación Nacional (EZLN, Zapatista National Liberation Army) shocked Mexico by taking over San Cristóbal de Las Casas and three other towns in the country's southernmost state, Chiapas. They wanted to end decades of evictions, discrimination and disappearances in their impoverished state, over which a wealthy minority had maintained a near-feudal grip since before the Mexican Revolution.

Though the EZLN was driven out of the towns within a few days (about 150 people were killed in the uprising), these events struck a chord among all Mexicans who felt that NAFTA and President Salinas' other economic policies were merely widening the gap between rich and poor. To many, the Mexican system prevented real social or political change. The rebels retreated under a truce to a base in the Chiapas jungle, and their leader, Subcomandante Marcos, became a folk hero.

In February 1995 Salinas' successor as president, Ernesto Zedillo, sent in the army to 'arrest' Marcos and other leaders. The rebels escaped deeper into the jungle. On-and-off negotiations eventually brought an agreement on indigenous rights in 1996 (the San Andrés accords; see 'The Zapatistas' in the Tabasco & Chiapas chapter), but Zedillo balked at turning the agreement into law. Chiapas remained tense, with the army and armed paramilitary groups (often supported or organized by the state authorities) harassing Zapatista supporters. In

Vicente Fox

1997 pro-PRI paramilitaries massacred 45 people, mostly women and children, in a chapel in the village of Acteal, in the worst single incident of the conflict.

A smaller left-wing rebel movement, the Ejército Popular Revolucionario (EPR, People's Revolutionary Army), emerged in 1996 in two other impoverished southern states, Guerrero (where 17 peasant political activists had been killed by police in the 1995 Aguas Blancas massacre) and Oaxaca.

The installation in 2000 of Vicente Fox as Mexico's first non-PRI president for over half a century spawned hopes of a peace settlement in Chiapas. The Zapatistas soon staged the 'Zapatour' – a much-publicized two-week journey from Chiapas to Mexico City – and in April 2001 the national Congress approved constitutional changes granting some special rights to Mexico's indigenous peoples. The trouble was, Congress approved only a watered-down version of the original draft endorsed by Fox (which had been based closely on the 1996 San Andrés accords). The new law still denied indigenous communities recognition as legal entities, and instead of 'collective use and enjoyment' of the lands they live on, indigenous peoples were awarded 'preferential use.' The Zapatistas rejected the congressional version, so it was back to the drawing board. Meanwhile, the Mexican army adopted a lower profile in Chiapas, but didn't actually pull many troops out.

GEOGRAPHY

Covering almost 2 million sq km, Mexico is big: it's nearly 3500km as the crow flies from Tijuana, in the northwest, to Cancún in the southeast (or about 4600km by road). To get from the US border at Ciudad Juárez to Mexico City, you must travel 1850km (about 24 hours by bus). From Mexico City to the Guatemalan border at Ciudad Cuauhtémoc is over 1200km.

Mexico curves from northwest to southeast, narrowing to the Isthmus of Tehuantepec in the south and then continuing northeast to the Yucatán Peninsula. To the west and south it's bordered by the Pacific Ocean. The Sea of Cortez (Golfo de California) lies between the mainland and Baja California, the world's longest peninsula – 1300km of mountains, deserts, plains and beaches. Mexico's east coast is bordered by the Gulf of Mexico all the way from the US border to the northeastern tip of the Yucatán Peninsula. The eastern Yucatán Peninsula faces the Caribbean Sea.

The country has a 3326km northern border with the US, the eastern half of which is formed by the Río Bravo del Norte (or Rio Grande, as it's called by the folk from north of that border). In the south and southeast are a 962km border with Guatemala and a 250km border with Belize.

Topography
Sierra Madre & Altiplano Central
Northern and central Mexico – as far south as the latitude of Mexico City – have coastal plains on the east and west and two north-south mountain ranges, the Sierra Madre Oriental and Sierra Madre Occidental, framing a group of broad central plateaus known as the Altiplano Central.

On the west coast a relatively dry coastal plain stretches south from Mexicali, on the US border, almost to Tepic, in Nayarit state. Inland from this plain is the rugged Sierra Madre Occidental, crossed by only two main transport routes: the Barranca del Cobre (Copper Canyon) railway from Chihuahua to Los Mochis, and the dramatic highway 40 from Durango to Mazatlán.

The Altiplano Central is divided into northern and central parts, themselves split by minor ranges, and varies in altitude from about 1000m in the north to more than 2000m in the center of the country. The northern plateau extends northward into Texas and New Mexico. The central plateau is mostly a series of rolling hills and broad valleys and includes some of the best farm and ranch land in Mexico.

The altiplano is delimited on the east by the Sierra Madre Oriental, which runs as far south as the state of Puebla and includes peaks as high as 3700m. The Gulf Coast plain, crossed by many rivers flowing down from the Sierra Madre, is an extension of a similar coastal plain in Texas. In northeastern Mexico the plain is wide and semi-marshy near the coast, but as it nears the port of Veracruz it narrows.

Cordillera Neovolcánica The Altiplano Central and the two Sierra Madres end where they meet the Cordillera Neovolcánica. This volcanic range, running east-west across the middle of Mexico, includes the active volcanoes Popocatépetl (5452m) and Volcán de Fuego de Colima (3960m), as well as the nation's other highest peaks – Pico de Orizaba (5611m) and Iztaccíhuatl (5286m) – and its youngest volcano, Paricutín (2800m), which appeared only in 1943. Mexico City lies in the heart of the volcanic country, 70km northwest of Popocatépetl.

The South South of Cabo Corrientes (west of Guadalajara), the Pacific lowlands narrow to a thin strip. The main mountain range in the south of Mexico is the Sierra Madre del Sur, which stretches across the states of Guerrero and Oaxaca to the low Isthmus of Tehuantepec, the narrowest part of Mexico at just 220km wide. The north side of the isthmus is part of a wide, marshy plain, strewn with meandering rivers, that stretches from Veracruz to the Yucatán Peninsula.

In the southernmost state, Chiapas, the Pacific lowlands are backed by the Sierra Madre de Chiapas, behind which is the Río Grijalva basin and then the Chiapas highlands. East of these highlands is a tropical rain-forest area stretching into northern Guatemala. The jungle melts into a region of tropical savanna on the flat, low Yucatán Peninsula. The tip of the peninsula is arid, almost desertlike.

CLIMATE

The tropic of Cancer cuts across Mexico north of Mazatlán and Tampico. South of the tropic it's hot and humid along the coastal plains on either side of the country and on the Yucatán Peninsula. Inland, at higher elevations, such as in Guadalajara or Mexico City, the climate is much more dry and temperate, and the mountain peaks are often capped with snow.

The hottest months, May to October, are also the wettest. The hottest and wettest periods of all fall between June and September for most of the country. Low-lying coastal areas are wetter and hotter than elevated inland ones, but there's considerable local variation: among coastal resorts, Acapulco receives twice as much rain as Mazatlán (nearly all of it between May and October); Acapulco and Cancún share similar temperatures, but Mazatlán and Cozumel are a few degrees cooler.

Mexico City's rainfall and temperatures are on the low side for an inland Mexican city: Taxco and Pátzcuaro get about twice as much rain as the capital and are a few degrees warmer; Oaxaca is also a few degrees warmer but similarly dry.

Northwestern Mexico and inland northern areas are drier than the rest of the country. In the east rainfall is particularly high on the eastern slopes of the Sierra Madre Oriental and on the northern side of the Isthmus of Tehuantepec. North winds can make inland northern Mexico decidedly chilly in winter, with temperatures sometimes down to freezing.

ECOLOGY & ENVIRONMENT

Bridging temperate and tropical regions and lying in the latitudes that contain most of the world's deserts, Mexico has an enormous range of natural environments. Its rugged, mountainous topography creates countless microclimates, which support one of the most diverse arrays of plant and animal species on the planet. But many of Mexico's species are endangered. The human impact on the environment has been enormous, and the country has a list of environmental problems as long as a rain-forest liana; these problems threaten not only the fauna and flora but the people too.

Problems

Mexico's environmental crises are typical of a developing country with an exploding population. From early in the 20th century, urban industrial growth, intensive chemical-based agriculture, and the destruction of forests for logging, grazing and development were seen as paths toward prosperity, and scant attention was paid to the environmental effects of these actions. A growth in environmental awareness since the 1970s has achieved only limited changes.

The country's most infamous environmental problem is the pollution from traffic and industry, which chokes the air of Mexico's ever-growing cities, above all the capital, where it brings residents a host of health problems (see 'Mexico City's Air' in the Mexico City chapter).

Forest Depletion Before the Spanish conquest, about two-thirds of Mexico was forested, from cool pine-clad highlands to

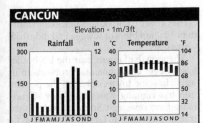

CANCÚN
Elevation - 1m/3ft

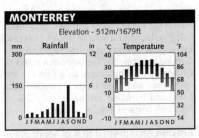

MONTERREY
Elevation - 512m/1679ft

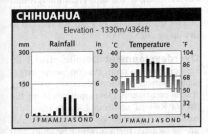

CHIHUAHUA
Elevation - 1330m/4364ft

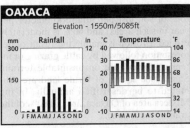

OAXACA
Elevation - 1550m/5085ft

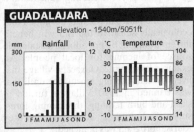

GUADALAJARA
Elevation - 1540m/5051ft

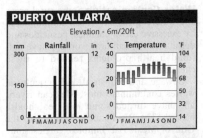

PUERTO VALLARTA
Elevation - 6m/20ft

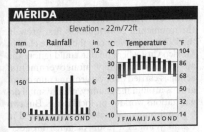

MÉRIDA
Elevation - 22m/72ft

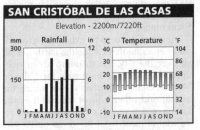

SAN CRISTÓBAL DE LAS CASAS
Elevation - 2200m/7220ft

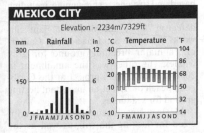

MEXICO CITY
Elevation - 2234m/7329ft

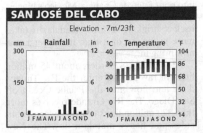

SAN JOSÉ DEL CABO
Elevation - 7m/23ft

tropical jungle. Today only around 15% (or 300,000 sq km) remains forested, and this is being reduced at a rate of about 11,000 sq km a year for grazing, logging and new farming settlements. The southern states of Chiapas and Tabasco are said to have lost more than half their tropical jungles since 1980, and by some estimates only 2% of Mexico's tropical jungles remain.

Erosion An estimated 13% of Mexican soil is severely eroded (with more than 1000 tons of soil lost per square kilometer per year in such areas) and 66% is moderately eroded. Erosion is mainly the result of deforestation followed by cattle grazing or intensive agriculture on unsuitable terrain. Some 2000 sq km of fertile land are estimated to be desertified annually. In the Mixteca area of Oaxaca, around 80% of the arable land is gone.

Water Contamination Some rural areas and watercourses have been contaminated by excessive use of chemical pesticides and defoliants. Agricultural workers have suffered health problems related to these chemicals.

Sewage and industrial and agricultural wastes contaminate most Mexican rivers, and have turned some into real health hazards. The Río Pánuco, flowing into the Gulf of Mexico at Tampico, carries some 2000 tons of untreated sewage a day, mainly from Mexico City, which expels it via a 50km tunnel.

Mexico City, despite extracting groundwater at a rate that causes the earth to sink all over the city, has to pump about one-third of its water from outside the Valle de México. One of the rivers from which the capital and other cities take water is the Lerma, which receives raw sewage and industrial effluent from 95 towns on its way into poor Lago de Chapala, Mexico's biggest natural lake, near Guadalajara. Chapala itself is shrinking because Guadalajara takes more water out of it than its feeder rivers now bring in.

Along the US border, about 45 million liters of raw sewage enter the Río Tijuana daily and flow into the Pacific Ocean off San Diego. The Rio Grande receives more than 370 million liters of raw sewage, pesticides and heavy metals a day. The New River, entering California from Mexicali, carries about 100 toxic substances and more than 1 billion liters of sewage and industrial waste daily.

The growth of towns near the US border has brought environmental problems in its wake. In some towns, only half the population has running water and only slightly more have sewerage. So much water is extracted from the Rio Grande that it dries up before reaching the sea. The underground aquifer supplying water to Ciudad Juárez and its US neighbor, El Paso, is expected to dry up by 2025.

Overdevelopment Despite official lip service paid to conservation, some large-scale tourism developments are wrecking fragile ecosystems. Developments along the 'Maya Riviera' south of Cancún may very well kill off large sections of coral reef, mangrove swamp, turtle-nesting beaches and everything in between.

In some places in Mexico, it's hoped that ecologically sensitive tourism will benefit the environment by providing a sustainable source of income for local people. An example is Mazunte, Oaxaca, a village that lived by slaughtering sea turtles until that was banned in 1990. Villagers turned to slash-and-burn farming, threatening forest survival, before a successful low-key tourism program was launched.

Environmental Movement

Environmental consciousness first grew in the 1970s, initially among the middle class in Mexico City, where no one could ignore the air pollution. Today nongovernmental action is carried out by a growing number of groups around the country, mainly small organizations working on local issues. But two big environmental victories were scored in recent years as a result of much broader-based and sustained campaigning, including support from outside Mexico. One was the defeat in 2000 of the plan for a giant saltworks at Laguna San Ignacio, Baja California, a major breeding ground for gray whales. The other was the annulment in 2001 of a large hotel project at the Caribbean beach of Xcacel, an important nesting ground for sea turtles.

Mexican governments are routinely criticized for lacking the will, as well as the money, to tackle environmental problems really seriously. Since the mid-1980s the federal government has, in public at least, recognized the need for economic development to be environmentally sustainable. President Salinas tried to tackle Mexico City's air pollution problem, banned the hunting of sea turtles and set up an important conservation and research agency, CONABIO (National Commission for the Knowledge and Use of Biodiversity). President Zedillo in 1994 placed most government environmental agencies under one secretariat, currently called SEMARNAT (Secretaría de Medio Ambiente y Recursos Naturales, Department of Environment & Natural Resources).

FLORA & FAUNA

Mexico is one of the most biologically diverse countries on earth. It's home to 1041 bird species, 439 mammals, 989 amphibians and reptiles, and about 26,000 plants – in each case, about 10% of the total number of species on the planet, on just 1.4% of the earth's land. Just a dozen or so tropical countries harbor two-thirds of the earth's plant and animal species, and Mexico is among them. Many Mexican species are endemic, including more than half of its reptiles and amphibians, and 139 of its mammals. Over one-third of all the world's marine mammals have been found in the Sea of Cortez. The southern state of Chiapas alone has some 10,000 plant species, more than 600 birds (twice as many as the USA) and 1200 butterflies (more than twice as many as the USA and Canada combined).

Flora

Northern Deserts Northern Mexico is dominated by two deserts: the Desierto Sonorense (Sonoran Desert) west of the Sierra Madre Occidental, and the Desierto Chihuahuense (Chihuahuan Desert) occupying much of the Altiplano Central. The deserts are sparsely vegetated with cacti, agaves, yucca, scrub and short grasses. West of Monclova in Coahuila state, the Cuatrociénegas valley is an oasis in the desert, renowned for its varied wildlife with dozens of endemic species including several each of turtle and fish. Between the Desierto Chihuahuense and the Sierra Madre Occidental and Oriental, as well as in the northeast

of Mexico, a lot of land has been turned over to irrigation or grazing, or has become wasteland, but there are still natural grasslands dotted with mesquite, a hardy bush of the bean family. Both deserts stretch north into the USA; the Desierto Sonorense also extends down into Baja California (although Baja has a surprising range of other habitats too, and because of its isolation, rather specialized flora and fauna). Most of the world's 1000 or so cactus species are found in Mexico.

Mountain Forests The Sierra Madre Occidental and Oriental, the Cordillera Neovolcánica (which runs east-west across the middle of the country), and the Sierra Madre del Sur still have some big stretches of pine forest and (at lower elevations) oak forest, though human occupation has stripped away much of the forest around the valleys.

In the southern half of the country, high-altitude pine forests are often covered in clouds, turning them into cloud forests, an unusual environment with lush, damp vegetation and epiphytes growing on tree branches. The Sierra Norte of Oaxaca and El Triunfo Biosphere Reserve in Chiapas preserve outstanding cloud forests.

Tropical Forests The natural vegetation of much of low-lying southeast Mexico, from southern Veracruz to eastern Chiapas and on to Quintana Roo, is evergreen tropical forest (rain forest in parts). The forest is dense and diverse, with ferns, epiphytes, palms, tropical hardwoods such as mahogany, and fruit trees such as the mamey and the chicozapote (sapodilla), which yields chicle (natural chewing gum). Perhaps Mexico's biggest ecological tragedy of all is the destruction of the Selva Lacandona (Lacandón Jungle) in eastern Chiapas; it is the largest remaining tropical forest area in the country. The Yucatán Peninsula changes from rain forest in the south to dry thorny forest in the north.

On the drier, western side of mainland Mexico – the western slopes of the Sierra Madre Occidental, the western and southern portions of the Cordillera Neovolcánica, and much of the southern states of Oaxaca and Chiapas – there's deciduous and semi-deciduous tropical forest, which is less varied than the eastern tropical forests. Much of this plant community has in fact been turned into ranches and cropland.

Thorn Forests Along the dry Pacific coastal plain, from the southern end of the Desierto Sonorense to the state of Guerrero, as well as on the northern Gulf Coast plain and in the northern Yucatán Peninsula, the predominant vegetation is thorn forest, composed of thorny bushes and small trees, including many acacias. Some of this flora occurs naturally, some occurs on overgrazed grassland or abandoned slash-and-burn farmland.

Fauna
Land Mammals & Reptiles In the north, domesticated grazing animals have pushed the larger wild beasts, such as the puma (mountain lion), wolf, deer and coyote, into isolated, often mountainous, pockets. Raccoons, armadillos, skunks, rabbits and snakes are still fairly common, however. The last four are found in much of the rest of Mexico too. Vampire bats live in deep sinkholes, known as *sótanos*, in the northeast and emerge at night to drink the blood of cattle and horses. In large numbers they can weaken animals, but otherwise they're harmless except when they carry diseases such as rabies.

The surviving tropical forests of the south and east still harbor (in places) howler and spider monkeys, jaguars, ocelots, tapirs, anteaters, peccaries (a type of wild pig), deer and some mean tropical reptiles, including boa constrictors. The big cats are reduced to isolated pockets mainly in eastern Chiapas, though they also exist around Celestún in Yucatán. You may well see howler monkeys, or at least hear their eerie growls, near the Mayan ruins at Palenque and Yaxchilán.

In all warm parts of Mexico you'll come across two harmless, though sometimes alarming, reptiles: the iguana, a lizard that can grow a meter or so long and comes in many different colors, and the gecko, a tiny, usually green lizard that may shoot out from behind a curtain or cupboard when disturbed. Geckos might make you jump, but they're good news because they eat mosquitoes. Less welcome are scorpions, also common in warmer parts of the country.

Marine Life Mexico's coasts, from Baja California to Chiapas and from the northeast to the Yucatán Peninsula, are among the world's chief breeding grounds for sea turtles (see 'Mexico's Turtles' in the Oaxaca State chapter).

Dolphins can be seen off much of the Pacific coast, while some wetlands, mainly in the south of the country, harbor crocodiles or caimans.

Baja California is a famous site for whale-watching in the early months of the year, but it's also a breeding ground for other big sea creatures such as sea lions and elephant seals.

Underwater life is richest along the Yucatán Peninsula's Caribbean coast, where there are coral reefs.

Birds & Butterflies Coastal Mexico is a major bird habitat, especially on the estuaries, lagoons, islands, mangroves and wetlands of Tamaulipas state, northern Veracruz state, the Yucatán Peninsula and the Pacific coast. Inland Mexico abounds with eagles, hawks and buzzards, and innumerable ducks and geese winter in the northern Sierra Madre Occidental.

Tropical species such as trogons, parrots, parakeets, tanagers and many others start to appear south of Tampico in the east of the country and from around Mazatlán in the west. The forests of the southeast are still home to colorful macaws, toucans, parrots and even a few quetzals. Yucatán has spectacular flamingo colonies at Celestún and Río Lagartos.

Another unforgettable marvel is the Santurio Mariposa Monarca in Michoacán, where the trees and earth are turned orange by the arrival of millions of monarch butterflies every winter.

Protected Areas
Sadly, many protected areas in Mexico are protected in name only. Governments have never had the money to properly police protected areas against unlawful hunting, logging, farming, grazing or animal and plant collection.

About 8% of Mexico (144,000 sq km) is under federal, state or municipal protection in a large number of different categories. The two most important protective categories are Parque Nacional (National Park) and Reserva de la Biósfera (Biosphere Reserve).

National Parks Mexico has 64 national parks, totaling around 14,000 sq km. Many are tiny (smaller than 10 sq km) and most were created between 1934 and 1940, often for their archaeological, historical, scenic or recreational value rather than for biological or ecological reasons. Some have no visitor infrastructure and draw few people, others are alive with weekend picnickers.

Mexico's national parks officially restrict many forms of human exploitation, but little attempt has ever been made to find alternative sources of income for the local people. Consequently, destructive activities such as tree-cutting, hunting and grazing have continued illegally. Nevertheless, national parks have succeeded in giving some protection to big tracts of forest, especially the high coniferous forests of central Mexico.

Among the better-known and most interesting national parks are the mountainous, coniferous-forested Constitución de 1857 and Sierra San Pedro Mártir, both in Baja California; Pico de Orizaba, La Malinche, Iztaccíhuatl-Popocatépetl, Nevado de Toluca and Nevado de Colima, all in the central volcanic belt; the coastal Lagunas de Chacahua, in Oaxaca; Palenque, Cañón del Sumidero and Lagos de Montebello, diverse environments in Chiapas; and Dzibilchaltún and Tulum, archaeological parks on the Yucatán Peninsula. Marine national parks, created in the 1990s to protect aquatic ecosystems, cover the Cozumel reefs and the west coast of Isla Mujeres, both off the Yucatán Peninsula, and the Bahía de Loreto in Baja California Sur.

Biosphere Reserves Biosphere reserves came into being as a result of a 1970s initiative by UNESCO, which recognized that it was impractical for developing countries to take ecologically important areas out of economic use. Biosphere reserves encourage local people to take part in planning and developing sustainable economic activities outside the reserves' strictly protected *zonas núcleo* (core areas). Today Mexico has 23 biosphere reserves, covering 87,610 sq km. Twelve of these are included in the UNESCO biosphere reserves network; the others are recognized only at a national

level. All focus on whole ecosystems with genuine biodiversity, ranging from deserts through dry and temperate forests to tropical forests and coastal areas. Sian Ka'an Biosphere Reserve on the Yucatán Peninsula is a UNESCO World Heritage Site. El Vizcaíno Biosphere Reserve in Baja California Sur includes whale sanctuaries that constitute another World Heritage Site.

Mexican biosphere reserves have had varied success. Sian Ka'an is one of the most successful: some villagers have turned from slash-and-burn farming and cattle grazing to drip irrigation and multiple crops, thus conserving the forest and increasing food yields; lobster fishers have seen lobster numbers cease to fall after they accepted a two-month off-season for egg-laying and began returning pregnant females to the sea.

Biosphere reserves tend to be harder to access than national parks, but controlled tourism is seen as an important source of income in several of them. Among the most visited or most interesting reserves are El Vizcaíno and Sierra de la Laguna, in Baja California Sur; El Pinacate y Gran Desierto de Altar, in Sonora; El Cielo (Tamaulipas) and Sierra Gorda (Querétaro), both in the Sierra Madre Oriental; Montes Azules, La Encrucijada and El Triunfo, all in Chiapas; and Calakmul, Ría Lagartos and Sian Ka'an, on the Yucatán Peninsula, and Banco Chinchorro, a coral atoll 40km off it.

Mexico's Wild Side

You're not likely to bump into very much of Mexico's wildlife unless you go looking for it, and sometimes you need to head for some pretty remote areas. But as interest in Mexican nature increases, the possibilities for doing just this are growing. Fascinating, beautiful areas that were once impossible for the nonspecialist to reach are opening up, and a growing number of operators offer their services to help you visit them.

Ecotourism has been a buzz word in Mexico for a while. Some cynical opportunists use it to describe mass-tourism activities that could not be much less ecological. (Some of the overpriced 'eco-parks' along the overdeveloped 'Maya Riviera' south of Cancún leap to mind.) Visitors who want to experience Mexico's natural wonders in a more harmonious and sensitive manner will however find enthusiastic help available

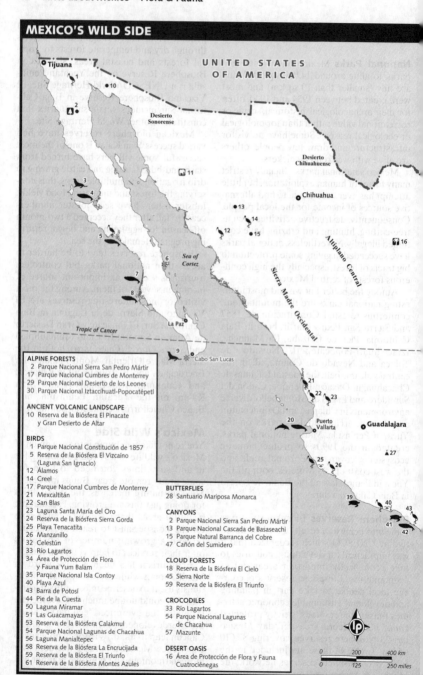

MEXICO'S WILD SIDE

UNITED STATES OF AMERICA

Tijuana

Desierto Sonorense

Desierto Chihuahuense

Chihuahua

Sea of Cortez

La Paz

Tropic of Cancer

Cabo San Lucas

Sierra Madre Occidental

Altiplano Central

Puerto Vallarta

Guadalajara

ALPINE FORESTS
2 Parque Nacional Sierra San Pedro Mártir
17 Parque Nacional Cumbres de Monterrey
29 Parque Nacional Desierto de los Leones
30 Parque Nacional Iztaccíhuatl-Popocatépetl

ANCIENT VOLCANIC LANDSCAPE
10 Reserva de la Biósfera El Pinacate
y Gran Desierto de Altar

BIRDS
1 Parque Nacional Constitución de 1857
5 Reserva de la Biósfera El Vizcaíno
(Laguna San Ignacio)
12 Álamos
14 Creel
17 Parque Nacional Cumbres de Monterrey
21 Mexcaltitán
22 San Blas
23 Laguna Santa María del Oro
24 Reserva de la Biósfera Sierra Gorda
25 Playa Tenacatita
26 Manzanillo
32 Celestún
33 Río Lagartos
34 Área de Protección de Flora
y Fauna Yum Balam
35 Parque Nacional Isla Contoy
40 Playa Azul
43 Barra de Potosí
44 Pie de la Cuesta
50 Laguna Miramar
51 Las Guacamayas
53 Reserva de la Biósfera Calakmul
54 Parque Nacional Lagunas de Chacahua
56 Laguna Manialtepec
58 Reserva de la Biósfera La Encrucijada
59 Reserva de la Biósfera El Triunfo
61 Reserva de la Biósfera Montes Azules

BUTTERFLIES
28 Santuario Mariposa Monarca

CANYONS
2 Parque Nacional Sierra San Pedro Mártir
13 Parque Nacional Cascada de Basaseachi
15 Parque Natural Barranca del Cobre
47 Cañón del Sumidero

CLOUD FORESTS
18 Reserva de la Biósfera El Cielo
45 Sierra Norte
59 Reserva de la Biósfera El Triunfo

CROCODILES
33 Río Lagartos
54 Parque Nacional Lagunas
de Chacahua
57 Mazunte

DESERT OASIS
16 Área de Protección de Flora y Fauna
Cuatrociénegas

0   200   400 km
0   125   250 miles

MEXICO'S WILD SIDE

DOLPHINS
20 Bahía de Banderas
55 Puerto Escondido
57 Mazunte

ELEPHANT SEALS & SEA LIONS
3 Isla Cedros
9 Cabo San Lucas

MANGROVES
25 Playa Tenacatita
40 Playa Azul
58 Reserva de la Biósfera
    La Encrucijada

MONKEYS & TROPICAL FOREST FAUNA
36 Reserva de la Biósfera Sian Ka'an
49 Palenque
50 Laguna Miramar
52 Yaxchilán
53 Reserva de la Biósfera Calakmul
58 Reserva de la Biósfera La Encrucijada

REEFS
6 Parque Marino Nacional Bahía de Loreto
10 Cabo San Lucas
37 Reserva de la Biósfera Banco Chinchorro
38 Cozumel

SEA TURTLES
19 La Pesca
33 Río Lagartos
39 Playa Maruata
41 Playa Troncones
54 Parque Nacional Lagunas de Chacahua
55 Puerto Escondido
57 Mazunte
58 Reserva de la Biósfera La Encrucijada

TROPICAL RAINFORESTS
36 Reserva de la Biósfera Sian Ka'an
50 Laguna Miramar
53 Reserva de la Biósfera Calakmul
61 Reserva de la Biósfera Montes Azules

VOLCANOES
27 Volcán Paricutín
30 Parque Nacional Iztaccíhuatl-Popocatépetl
31 Parque Nacional Pico de Orizaba
60 Tacaná

WHALES
4 Reserva de la Biósfera El Vizcaíno
   (Laguna Ojo de Liebre)
5 Reserva de la Biósfera El Vizcaíno
   (Laguna San Ignacio)
7 Puerto López Mateos
8 Puerto San Carlos
20 Bahía de Banderas
42 Zihuatanejo

ZOOS
11 Centro Ecológico de Sonora, Hermosillo
46 Zoológico Miguel Álvarez del Toro (ZOOMAT),
    Tuxtla Gutiérrez
48 Parque-Museo La Venta, Villahermosa

Alpine Forests	Dolphins	Sea Turtles
Birds	Elephant Seals & Sea Lions	Tropical Rainforests
Butterflies	Mangroves	Volcanoes
Crocodiles	Monkeys & Tropical Forest Fauna	Whales
Desert Oasis	Reefs	Zoos

Monterrey
17

Sierra Madre Oriental

18

24

Tropic of Cancer

33   34   35

Cancún

Gulf of Mexico

32   Mérida

38

Yucatán
Peninsula

36

MEXICO CITY
28
29   30   31

48   49

37

Sierra Madre del Sur

45

52

BELIZE

44   Acapulco   Oaxaca

46   47

50

51

54   56

59

53

55   57   58

60   61

GUATEMALA

HONDURAS

EL SALVADOR

PACIFIC OCEAN

from many smaller-scale operators and organizations (see Organized Tours in the Getting Around chapter), some of them run by local communities themselves If you use such local services, the money you spend may well help to conserve ecosystems that would otherwise be threatened by less sustainable modes of extracting a livelihood.

The corresponding map shows the best places for observing Mexican fauna and flora – from the whales of Baja California to the howler monkeys and toucans of the southeastern jungles – plus a few outstanding geological features. Refer to the destination chapters of this book for details of how and when to visit these places. The Web site Eco Travels in Latin America (ⓦ www.planeta.com) brims with information and links for those wanting to experience Mexican flora and fauna firsthand. For readers of Spanish, the site of CONABIO, Mexico's national biodiversity commission (ⓦ www.conabio.gob.mx), is another excellent resource. Some useful and fascinating books on Mexico's environment and plant and animal life – including practical ecotourism guidebooks – are mentioned under Books in the Facts for the Visitor chapter.

GOVERNMENT & POLITICS

Mexico is a federal republic of 31 states and one federal district, with the states further divided into 2394 *municipios* (municipalities). A two-chamber federal congress, with a 128-member upper chamber, the Cámara de Senadores (Senate), and a 500-member lower chamber, the Cámara de Diputados (Chamber of Deputies), makes the laws. A directly elected president carries out the laws, and an independent judiciary decides disputes according to Napoleonic law. Women gained the vote in 1954, and an Equal Rights Amendment was added to the constitution in 1974. The legislatures and governors of Mexico's states are elected by their citizens, as are the *ayuntamientos* (town councils), which run the municipios, and their mayors *(alcaldes)*.

Such is the theory. In practice, Mexican political life was dominated for most of the 20th century by one party, the Partido Revolucionario Institucional (PRI, Institutional Revolutionary Party), and its predecessors, with the national president ruling in the tradition of strong, centralized leadership going back to Moctezuma. Accusations of fraud, corruption, bribery, intimidation and violence has long accompanied the all-conquering PRI's election tactics and style of governing at every level.

Mexican politics celebrated its equivalent of the dismantling of the Berlin wall in 2000, when Vicente Fox Quesada of the Partido de Acción Nacional (PAN, National Action Party) was elected president; he was the first non-PRI president since the PRI was invented (under a different name, PNR) in 1929. This sea change was the fruit of growing discontent with the PRI's one-party rule since the mid-1980s, fostered by events such as the 1985 Mexico City earthquake, when the authorities left the people to do most of the rescue and clean-up work themselves; unusually obvious fraud at the 1988 presidential elections; particularly sordid behavior among the circle of the president 'elected' then, Carlos Salinas de Gortari; and the economic crash of the mid-1990s.

In a Gorbachev-like attempt to hang on to power by relaxing its grip, the PRI under Salinas allowed the center-right PAN to win the state governorships of Baja California, Chihuahua and Guanajuato (the first occasion the PRI had ever not won a state governor election), and they introduced limited anticorruption measures for the elections for Salinas' successor in 1994. The winner, President Ernesto Zedillo of the PRI, responding to mounting Mexican dissatisfaction and to pressure from other countries that came with NAFTA, turned Mexico towards being a genuine pluralist democracy, despite opposition from the PRI old guard, which benefited from absence of change. Zedillo allowed the newly independent election-organizing body, the Instituto Federal Electoral (IFE), to spend hundreds of millions of dollars to build an electoral apparatus transparent enough to overcome fraud.

The first elections under this new setup, in 1997, were for all 500 seats in the Chamber of Deputies and a quarter of the Senate. At the same time a popular election was held for the new Mexico City mayor, after decades of the capital's being run directly by the federal government. The PRI, unprecedentedly, lost overall control of the Chamber of Deputies, and the Mexico City mayoralty went to Cuauhtémoc Cárdenas, of the Partido de la Revolución Democrática (PRD, Party of the

Democratic Revolution), who had lost the 1988 presidential election to Salinas. The elections were hailed as the freest and fairest in Mexico since 1911.

For 2000 all three main parties broke new ground by using a primary-election system to choose their presidential candidates. This was particularly historic in the case of the PRI, whose candidates had previously been picked by the *'dedazo'* (fingering) method in which the outgoing president, who is forbidden by law from serving more than one *sexenio* (six-year term), chose a candidate to succeed him from within PRI ranks. That candidate had invariably become president.

In the presidential elections in July 2000, Vicente Fox (PAN) won 43% of the votes, Francisco Labastida (PRI) gained 36% and Cuauhtémoc Cárdenas (PRD) took 16%. Fox took office in December 2000.

However successful Fox's sexenio turns out, his election as president was the biggest event in Mexican politics since the forming of the PRI in the chaotic aftermath of the revolution in the early 20th century. Democratization, meanwhile, continued at other levels of Mexican politics too; by 2002 there were 15 state governorships in non-PRI hands (eight PAN, five PRD and two PAN-PRD alliance).

Defeat did not cause the PRI to split asunder between 'modern' free-marketeers and 'old-guard' statists, as some had predicted, but it did leave it with a serious identity crisis. Without power, its *raison-d'être* for 70 years, it also lacked a convenient niche from which to operate as opposition, now that the PRD represented the left of the political spectrum, the PAN the right, and President Fox (never orthodox even within his own party) the social democratic center.

ECONOMY
Resources & Products

The 20th century saw Mexico transform from a backward agricultural economy to one of Latin America's most industrialized nations. Manufacturing employs about 18% of the workforce and produces about a quarter of the gross national product and most of the country's exports. Motor vehicles, processed food, steel, chemicals, paper and textiles have joined more traditional products such as sugar, coffee, silver, lead, copper and zinc. Among Mexico's biggest national assets are its oil reserves (the eighth largest in the world) and its gas reserves. Concentrated mainly along the Gulf Coast and belonging to a government-owned monopoly (Pemex), these reserves yield about one-tenth of Mexico's export

Slim in Name, Plump in Wallet

Heard of Carlos Slim? Chances are you haven't, but Slim is easily Mexico's richest person. And chances are that while in Mexico you'll add to his personal wealth. This self-made multi-billionaire was worth US$10.8 billion according to *Forbes* magazine in 2001. This made him the 25th wealthiest person in the world and easily the richest in Latin America. Slim was born in 1940 into a family of Lebanese Christian immigrants who had a haberdasher's shop in Mexico City. As a child he sold candies to his brothers and cousins from a shop under the stairs, and by the age of 15 he already had 44 shares in Banamex (Banco Nacional de México).

Today Slim's fortune is based on telecommunications, retailing and financial services. He controls Telmex, Mexico's biggest phone company, plus the Telcel cellular phone company and the Internet provider Prodigy. He also has a big stake in another telecom company, América Móvil, is a director of Philip Morris, and has further investments from Brazil to the USA as well as owning the Sanborns store and restaurant chain and the Mixup music store chain. Slim is an art lover too: the Museo Soumaya in Mexico City, inaugurated in 1994 and named for his wife (who died in 2000), opened his superb collection, especially of sculptor Auguste Rodin, to public view.

In the ranks of wealthy Mexicans, Slim is followed at some distance by Emilio Azcárraga Jean, head of the country's biggest TV network Televisa, and Ricardo Salinas Pliego, head of the second biggest TV network, TV Azteca, and the Elektra retail chain. The pair were ranked 151st equal in *Forbes'* 2001 list, with a worth of US$3 billion each.

earnings and one-third of the government's revenues.

Half of Mexico's output is produced within 150km of Mexico City, though northern states such as Nuevo León, Chihuahua and Baja California are increasingly important, aided by their proximity to that major export market, the USA, and by their many *maquiladoras*. Maquiladoras are factories (usually foreign-owned) that import materials, parts and equipment for processing or assembly by inexpensive Mexican laborers, then export the products, usually to the USA. Maquiladoras employ more than 1 million Mexicans and produce nearly half of Mexico's exports. The border cities of Tijuana and Ciudad Juárez are the capitals of maquiladora industry.

Mining, Mexico's main income source in colonial times, now accounts for only 1% of the national product.

About 30% of the workforce is in service industries. Tourism is one of the most important of these. Some 20 million foreign visitors a year, more than half of them cross-border day-trippers, bring in around US$8 billion of foreign exchange (petrochemical exports are of a similar order), and the domestic tourism business is three times as big.

Agriculture occupies 23% of Mexico's workers but produces only 4% of the national product. Around 10% of Mexico is planted with maize, wheat, rice and beans, but the country still imports more grain than it exports. Small farming plots became prevalent after the redistribution of hacienda land to ejidos following the revolution. These plots are often farmed at subsistence level, their owners lacking the technology and capital to render them more productive. Larger-scale farming goes on primarily along the Gulf Coast (coffee and sugarcane), in the north and northwest (livestock, wheat, fruit and cotton), and in the Bajío area, north of Mexico City (wheat and vegetables).

NAFTA

The oil boom of the 1970s encouraged Mexico to spend wildly, piling up a big national debt that could not be paid when revenues slumped in the 1980s oil bust. In response, particularly from 1988-94 under President Salinas, debt was rescheduled, austerity measures were introduced, and

government enterprises from banks and utilities to steel mills were sold off. By 2000, the number of state-owned enterprises had fallen from over 1000 in 1982 to less than 200 and the formerly state-dominated, protectionist Mexican economy had become one of the most open in Latin America. Inflation was cut from well over 100% to less than 10% under Salinas. By the early 1990s Mexico was showing steady growth, and the peso had been stabilized.

The key to Salinas' plans was the North American Free Trade Agreement (NAFTA), which took effect in 1994. NAFTA (known to Mexicans as the TLC, Tratado de Libre Comercio) is steadily (over a 15-year period) eliminating restrictions on trade and investment between the US, Mexico and Canada. The hope was that NAFTA would bring Mexico increased employment, growing exports and cheaper imports. International trade certainly soared; Mexico's combined exports and imports jumped from US$117 billion in 1993 to US$341 billion in 2000. Critics of NAFTA argue that it makes Mexico's economic welfare more dependent on that of the US, and that the wide gap between Mexico's rich and poor is being made even wider as new imports damage uncompetitive sectors of the Mexican economy. Much of Mexican agriculture, consisting of small one-family plots on ejidos (communal landholdings), is just unable to compete with the cheaper products of larger-scale farming.

Peso Crisis & Recovery

NAFTA had not long been in existence before the Mexican economy was devastated by the peso collapse of 1994-95, which took years to get over. When, for a range of temporary reasons, foreign investment in Mexico slowed to a trickle in 1994, the Salinas government spent nearly all of its foreign reserves in a futile attempt to support the peso. Salinas' successor Ernesto Zedillo had no option but to let the peso float. It fell far and fast, and Mexico had to be bailed out by a multibillion-dollar package of emergency credit from the US, Canada and international financial bodies. The government raised taxes and interest rates, cut spending and announced new privatizations. More than 1.5 million people lost their jobs, prices and crime soared, production and standards of living fell, borrowers went broke. Inflation in 1995 was more than 50%. One 1997 study concluded that more than one-fifth of the people in the Distrito Federal (which encompasses about half of Mexico City) were living on 'marginal levels of basic subsistence.' Yet the majority of Mexico's 20 to 25 million poorest people live in rural areas, which receive far less welfare spending than cities. More Mexicans looked to (usually illegal) migration to the USA as the only way out of poverty.

Zedillo's austerity measures, coupled with big help for exports from NAFTA and the cheap peso, began to pull Mexico out of the slump surprisingly quickly. Mexico repaid most of its emergency debt ahead of schedule, and national production grew by an average 5% a year from 1996-2000. By 2000, growth was 7% and inflation was well below 10%. Close economic links, through NAFTA, to a booming USA were key to this success. Almost 90% of Mexican exports were now going to the US, which had only one larger trading partner (Canada).

By 2000 even Mexico's many poor citizens were beginning to feel the benefits of the recovery. People's purchasing power was again approaching 1994 levels.

Recession & Challenge

The global recession of 2001 changed things again. Even before the September 11 attacks on the USA, Mexico's national production had suddenly ceased to grow. The maquiladoras and northern Mexico, in general, were particularly badly hit because of their dependence on exports to the USA. Maquiladoras had shed 100,000 jobs even before September 11.

For many Mexicans, there will never be a way out of poverty. Few Mexican workers earn more than US$10 a day. Then there are the millions (an estimated one-quarter of Mexico's workforce) in the 'informal economy'; these include street hawkers, traffic signal fire-eaters, buskers, home workers, criminals and anybody who is unregistered and doesn't pay taxes. Few of these people scrape together much more than US$5 a day.

The Fox government aimed to raise the government's tax revenue from 11% of the national product to 17% in order to pay for better education and social welfare. Another challenge is Mexico's own north-south divide: average incomes in many of the country's northern states are around three times what they are in the poor southern states of Oaxaca and Chiapas. The Fox government proposed the so-called Puebla-Panama Plan, which is a series of joint development schemes with Central American countries involving new roads, electrical and telecommunications links, investment promotion and so on, as a means of boosting southern Mexico's prospects.

POPULATION & PEOPLE

In 2000 Mexico's population was counted at 97.5 million. In 1940 it was counted at 20 million, in 1960 at 35 million, in 1970 at 49 million, in 1980 at 67 million and in 1990 at 81 million. In addition, an estimated 4 million Mexicans are living illegally in the USA at any given moment.

About 60% of Mexicans live in towns or cities of more than 15,000 people, and one-third are aged under 15. The biggest cities are Mexico City (with perhaps 20 million people), Guadalajara (with a conurbation estimated at 5 million) and Monterrey (conurbation estimated at 3.4 million). Tijuana, Puebla, Ciudad Juárez and the conurbations of León and Torreón all have populations above 1 million. The most populous state is the state of México, which includes the rapidly growing outer areas of Mexico City and has more than 13 million people.

By official figures, the population grew by an average of 1.85% a year in the 1990s, which is down from rates of more than 3% between 1950 and 1980 but still means an extra 1.8 million mouths to feed every year. Of even more concern is the growth of the cities, which attract thousands of newcomers from the poorer countryside every day.

Ethnic Groups

The major ethnic division is between mestizos and *indígenas* or *indios* (indigenous people). Mestizos are people of mixed ancestry of usually Spanish and indigenous, although African slaves and other Europeans were also significant elements. Indigenous people are descendants of Mexico's pre-Hispanic inhabitants who have retained their sense of a distinct identity. Mestizos are the overwhelming majority, and together with the few people of supposed pure Spanish descent they hold most positions of power in Mexican society. (If you were to judge from Mexican TV soap operas, all Mexicans are of pure Spanish descent, but let's not worry about that for now.)

Researchers have listed at least 139 vanished indigenous languages. The 50 or so indigenous cultures that have survived, some now with only a few hundred people, have done so largely because of their rural isolation. Indigenous people in general remain second-class citizens, often restricted to the worst land or forced to migrate to city slums or the USA in search of work. Their main wealth is traditional and spiritual, their way of life imbued with communal customs and rituals bound up with nature. Indigenous traditions, religion, arts, crafts and costumes are fascinating; you will find more information on them in the various regional chapters, in this chapter under Arts and Religion, and in the Artesanías special section.

Official figures count as indigenous only those who list themselves in censuses as speakers of indigenous languages. They number about 7 million, though people of predominantly indigenous ancestry may total as many as 25 million. The biggest indigenous group is the Nahua, descendants of the Aztecs. At least 1.7 million Nahuatl speakers are spread around central Mexico, chiefly in Puebla, Veracruz, Hidalgo, Guerrero and San Luis Potosí states. There are approximately 1 million Maya speakers on the Yucatán Peninsula; 500,000 Zapotecs, mainly in Oaxaca; 500,000 Mixtecs, mainly in Oaxaca, Guerrero and Puebla; 260,000 Totonacs, in Veracruz and Puebla; and 130,000 Purépecha in Michoacán – each group directly descended from a well-known pre-Hispanic people. (Purépecha is the most common name for the descendants of the pre-Hispanic Tarascos).

Descendants of lesser-known pre-Hispanic peoples include the approximately 330,000 Otomí, mainly in Hidalgo and México states; 150,000 Mazahua, in México state; and 150,000 Huastecs in San Luis Potosí and northern Veracruz. The Tzotzils and Tzeltals of Chiapas are probably descendants of the Maya who migrated to the highlands at the time of the Classic Maya downfall. Among less numerous indigenous peoples, the Huichol of Jalisco and Nayarit are renowned for the importance of the hallucinogenic drug peyote in their spiritual life, and the Mazatecs of northern Oaxaca for their use of hallucinogenic mushrooms.

ARTS
Painting & Sculpture
Mexicans have had a talent for painting since pre-Hispanic times. Today the many murals decorating Mexican walls and the wealth of modern and historic art in Mexico's many galleries are among the highlights of the country for many visitors. Mexican creativity is also expressed in myriad folk arts, which are very much a living tradition. (See the Artesanías special section for more information.)

Pre-Hispanic Art Mexico's first civilization, the Olmecs of the Gulf Coast, produced remarkable stone sculptures, depicting deities, animals, and wonderfully lifelike human forms. Most awesome are the huge Olmec heads, which combine the features of human babies and jaguars. The earliest outstanding Mexican murals are found at Teotihuacán, where the colorful *Paradise of Tláloc* depicts in detail the delights awaiting those who died at the hands of the water god, Tláloc. The Teotihuacán mural style spread to other places in Mexico, such as Monte Albán in Oaxaca.

The Classic Maya of southeast Mexico, at their cultural height from about AD 250 to 800, were perhaps ancient Mexico's most artistic people. They left countless beautiful stone sculptures, of complicated design and meaning but possessing an easily appreciable delicacy of touch – a talent also expressed in their unique architecture. Subjects are typically rulers, deities and ceremonies. The art of the Aztecs (whose civilization lasted from about 1350-1521) reflects their harsh worldview, with many carvings of skulls and complicated symbolic representations of gods.

Other pre-Hispanic peoples with major artistic legacies include the Toltecs of central Mexico (10th-13th centuries), who had a fearsome, militaristic style of carving; the Mixtecs of Oaxaca and Puebla (13th to 16th centuries), who were excellent goldsmiths and jewelers; and the Classic Veracruz civilization (about AD 400-900), which left a wealth of pottery and stone sculpture.

Pre-Hispanic art can be found at archaeological sites and museums throughout

Mexico. The Museo Nacional de Antropología, in Mexico City, provides an excellent overview.

Colonial Period Mexican art during Spanish rule was heavily Spanish-influenced and chiefly religious in subject, though later in the period portraits grew in popularity under wealthy patrons. The influence of indigenous artisans is seen in the elaborate altarpieces and sculpted walls and ceilings, overflowing with tiny detail, in churches and monasteries, as well as in fine frescoes such as those at Actopan monastery in Hidalgo state. Miguel Cabrera (1695-1768), from Oaxaca, was probably the leading painter of the era; his scenes and figures have a sureness of touch lacking in others' more labored efforts. They can be seen in churches and museums scattered all over Mexico.

Independent Mexico The landscapes of José María Velasco (1840-1912) capture the magical qualities of the country around Mexico City and areas farther afield, such as Oaxaca.

The years before the 1910 revolution saw a real break from European traditions and the beginnings of socially conscious art. Slums, brothels and indigenous poverty began to appear on canvases. The cartoons and engravings of José Guadalupe Posada (1852-1913), with their characteristic *calavera* (skull) motif, satirized the injustices of the Porfiriato period and were aimed at a wider audience than most previous Mexican art. Gerardo Murillo (1875-1964), who took the name Doctor Atl (from a Náhuatl word meaning 'water'), displayed some scandalously orgiastic paintings at a 1910 show marking the centenary of the independence movement.

The Muralists In the 1920s, immediately following the Mexican Revolution, education minister José Vasconcelos commissioned leading young artists to paint a series of murals on public buildings to spread a sense of Mexican history and culture and the need for social and technological change. The trio of great muralists were Diego Rivera (1885-1957), José Clemente Orozco

(1883-1949) and David Alfaro Siqueiros (1896-1974).

Rivera's work carried a clear left-wing message, emphasizing past oppression of indigenous people and peasants. His art pulled the country's indigenous and Spanish roots together into one national identity through colorful, crowded tableaus depicting historical people and events or symbolic scenes of Mexican life, with a simple moral message. They're realistic, if not always lifelike. To appreciate them you need a little knowledge of Mexican history and, preferably, an explanation of the details. Many of Rivera's greatest works are in and around Mexico City (see 'Diego & Frida' in the Mexico City chapter).

Siqueiros, who fought on the Constitutionalist side in the revolution (while Rivera was in Europe), remained a political activist afterward, spending time in jail as a result and leading an attempt to kill Leon Trotsky in Mexico City in 1940. His murals lack Rivera's realism but convey a more clearly Marxist message through dramatic, symbolic depictions of the oppressed and grotesque caricatures of the oppressors. Some of his best works are at the Palacio de Bellas Artes, Castillo de Chapultepec and Ciudad Universitaria, all in Mexico City.

Orozco was less of a propagandist; he conveyed emotion, character and atmosphere and focused more on the universal human condition than on historical specifics. By the 1930s Orozco grew disillusioned with the revolution. His work is reckoned to have reached its peak in Guadalajara from 1936-39, particularly in the 50-odd frescoes in the Instituto Cultural

David Alfaro Siqueiros, Diego Rivera and José Clemente Orozco

Cabañas. Other powerful works, such as those in the Palacio de Bellas Artes in Mexico City, depict oppressive scenes of degradation, violence and injustice.

Rivera, Siqueiros and Orozco were also great artists on a smaller scale. Some of their portraits, drawings and other works can be seen in places like the Museo de Arte Moderno and Museo de Arte Carrillo Gil in Mexico City and in the Casa de Diego Rivera in Guanajuato.

Among later muralists Rufino Tamayo (1899-1991) from Oaxaca, also represented in the Palacio de Bellas Artes, was relatively unconcerned with politics and history, but was absorbed by abstract and mythological scenes and effects of color. Juan O'Gorman (1905-81), a Mexican of Irish ancestry, was even more realistic and detailed than Rivera. His mosaic on the Biblioteca Central at Mexico City's Ciudad Universitaria is probably his best-known work.

Other 20th-Century Artists Frida Kahlo (1907-54), physically crippled by a road accident and mentally tormented in her tempestuous marriage to Diego Rivera, painted anguished, penetrating self-portraits and grotesque, surreal images that expressed her left-wing views and externalized her inner tumult. Kahlo's work suddenly seemed to strike an international chord in the 1980s, almost overnight becoming hugely popular and as renowned as Rivera's.

After WWII, young Mexican artists reacted against the muralist movement, which they saw as too didactic and too obsessed with *Mexicanidad* (Mexicanness). They opened Mexico up to world trends such as abstract expressionism and op art. The Museo José Luis Cuevas, in Mexico City, was founded by and named after one of the leaders of this trend. Other interesting artists to look for include Zacatecans Francisco Goitia (1882-1960) and Pedro Coronel (1923-85) and Oaxacans Francisco Toledo (b 1940) and Rodolfo Morales (1925-2001). Along with Mexico City, Oaxaca currently has one of the liveliest art scenes in the country. A good place to catch up on the contemporary art scene is W www.arte-mexico.com.

Architecture

Pre-Hispanic The ancient civilizations of Mexico produced some of the most spectac-ular, eye-pleasing architecture ever built. At sites such as Teotihuacán near Mexico City, Monte Albán in Oaxaca, and Chichén Itzá and Uxmal in Yucatán, you can still see fairly intact pre-Hispanic cities. Their spectacular ceremonial centers, used by the religious and political elite, were designed to impress, with great stone pyramids, palaces and ball courts. Pyramids usually functioned as the bases for small shrines on their summits. Mexico's three biggest pyramids are the Pirámide del Sol and Pirámide de la Luna, both at Teotihuacán, and the Great Pyramid of Cholula, near Puebla.

There are many differences in style between pre-Hispanic civilizations: while Teotihuacán, Monte Albán and Aztec buildings were relatively simple, designed to awe by their grand scale, Mayan architecture paid more attention to aesthetics, with intricately patterned façades, delicate 'combs' on temple roofs, and sinuous carvings. Buildings at Mayan sites such as Uxmal, Chichén Itzá and Palenque are some of the most beautiful human creations in Mexico. Some speculate that Mayan roof combs, formed by gridlike arrangements of stone with multiple gaps through which the breeze could pass, may have functioned as sacred wind instruments. Most roof combs would originally have been taller than what remains of them today. Maya buildings are also characterized by the corbeled vault, their version of the arch: two stone walls leaning toward one another, nearly meeting at the top and surmounted by a capstone.

Colonial One of the first preoccupations of the Spanish was to replace pagan temples with Christian churches. A classic case is the Great Pyramid of Cholula, now topped by a small colonial church. Many of the fine mansions, churches, monasteries and plazas that today contribute so much to Mexico's beauty were created during the 300 years of Spanish rule. Most were in basically Spanish styles, but with unique local variations.

Gothic & Renaissance These styles dominated colonial building in Mexico in the 16th and early 17th centuries. Gothic, which originated in medieval Europe, is typified by soaring buttresses, pointed arches, clusters of round columns and ribbed ceiling vaults. The Renaissance style saw a return to the disciplined ancient Greek and Roman ideals of harmony and proportion: columns and shapes such as the square and circle predominated. The usual Renaissance style in Mexico was plateresque, which is from *platero* (silversmith), because its decoration resembled the elaborate ornamentation that went into silverwork. Plateresque was commonly used on the façades of buildings, particularly church doorways, which had round arches bordered by classical columns and stone sculpture. A later, more austere Renaissance style was called Herreresque, after the Spanish architect Juan de Herrera. Two of Mexico's outstanding Renaissance buildings are Mérida's cathedral and Casa de Montejo. Mexico City and Puebla cathedrals mingle Renaissance and baroque styles.

Gothic and Renaissance influences were combined in many of the fortified monasteries that were built as Spanish monks carried their missionary work to all corners of the country. Monasteries usually had a large church, a cloister, a big atrium (churchyard) and often a *capilla abierta* (open chapel), from which priests could address large crowds of local people. Notable monasteries include Actopan and Acolman in central Mexico, and Yanhuitlán, Coixtlahuaca and Teposcolula, in Oaxaca.

The influence of the Muslims, who had ruled much of Spain until the 15th century, was also carried to Mexico. Examples of Mudéjar, a Muslim-influenced Spanish Christian style, can be seen in some beautifully carved wooden ceilings and in the *alfiz*, a rectangle framing a round arch. The 49 domes of the Capilla Real in Cholula almost resemble a mosque.

Baroque Baroque style, which reached Mexico in the early 17th century, was a reaction against strict Renaissance styles, combining classical influences with other elements and aiming at dramatic effect rather than pure proportion. Curves, color, contrasts of light and dark, and increasingly elaborate decoration were among its hallmarks. Painting and sculpture were integrated with architecture, most notably in ornate, often enormous altar pieces *(retablos)*.

Early, more restrained baroque buildings include the churches of Santiago Tlatelolco in Mexico City, San Felipe Neri in Oaxaca and San Francisco in San Luis Potosí.

Among later baroque works are the marvelous façade of Zacatecas' cathedral and the churches of San Cristóbal in Puebla and La Soledad in Oaxaca.

Mexican baroque reached its final form, Churrigueresque, between 1730 and 1780. Named after a Barcelona architect, José Benito Churriguera, this style was characterized by riotous surface ornamentation. Its hallmark is the *estípite*, a pilaster (a vertical pillar projecting only partly from a wall) in the form of a very narrow upside-down pyramid. The estípite helped give Churrigueresque its typical 'top-heavy' effect.

Outstanding Churrigueresque churches include the Sagrario Metropolitano in Mexico City; San Martín, Tepotzotlán; San Francisco, La Compañía and La Valenciana in Guanajuato; Santa Prisca and San Sebastián in Taxco; and the Ocotlán sanctuary at Tlaxcala.

Mexican indigenous artisans added profuse, detailed sculpture in stone and colored stucco to many baroque buildings. Among the most exuberant examples are the Capilla del Rosario in Santo Domingo church, Puebla, and the nearby village church of Tonantzintla. Arabic influence continued with the popularity of *azulejos* (colored tiles) on the outside of buildings, particularly in and around Puebla.

Neoclassical Neoclassical style was another return to Greek and Roman ideals. In Mexico it lasted from about 1780 to 1830. Outstanding examples include the Colegio de Minería in Mexico City, the Alhóndiga de Granaditas in Guanajuato and the second tiers of the Mexico City cathedral's towers. Eduardo Tresguerras and Spanish-born Manuel Tolsá were the most prominent neoclassical architects.

19th & 20th Centuries Independent Mexico in the 19th century saw revivals of Gothic and colonial styles typically copying French or Italian styles. The Palacio de Bellas Artes in Mexico City is one of the finest buildings from this era.

After the revolution of 1910-21, art deco appeared in some buildings such as the Frontón México in Mexico City, but more important was an attempt to return to pre-Hispanic roots in the search for a national identity. This trend was known as Toltecism, and many public buildings exhibit the heaviness of Aztec or Toltec monuments. It culminated in the 1950s with the UNAM campus in Mexico City, where many buildings are covered with colorful murals.

More modern architects have provided Mexico, especially Mexico City and Monterrey, with some eye-catching and adventurous buildings. Among these are the 1960s Museo Nacional de Antropología (Mexico City), with a large umbrella-like stone fountain in its central courtyard; the early 1990s Centro Bursátil, a skyward-pointing arrowhead of reflecting glass beside the capital's main boulevard, Paseo de la Reforma; Monterrey's Faro del Comercio, a tall orange concrete slab erected in the 1980s in the city's main plaza; and the Centro de Tecnología Avanzada para la Producción at Monterrey's Instituto Tecnológico, a building that appears to have been sliced in two, leaving the halves toppling away from each other.

Music

In Mexico live music may start up at any time on streets, plazas or even buses. The musicians play for a living and range from marimba (wooden xylophone) teams and mariachi bands (trumpeters, violinists, guitarists and a singer, all dressed in smart cowboy-like costumes) to ragged lone buskers with out-of-tune guitars and sandpaper voices. Mariachi music (perhaps the most 'typical' Mexican music of all) originated in the Guadalajara area but is played nationwide (see 'Mariachis' in the Western Central Highlands chapter). Marimbas are particularly popular in the southeast and on the Gulf Coast.

On a more organized level, Mexico has a thriving popular music business. Its outpourings can be heard live at fiestas, nightspots and concerts or bought from music shops or cheap bootleg-tape vendors. (Ask tape vendors to play cassettes before you buy them, as there are many defective or blank copies.)

Rock & Pop Mexican rock was pretty raw and basic until the late 1980s, when a more sophisticated music began to emerge. El Tri, still together after more than 30 years, head up the earlier generation with their still-energetic rock & roll. The changes of the '80s were spearheaded by mystical Def Leppard-type rockers Caifanes, a middle-class Mexico City group typical of the sort of Mexicans exposed earliest to North American and European music. (Caifanes are still together under the name Jaguares, whose 1999 double album *Bajo el Azul de tu Misterio* was a big success in both Mexico and the USA.)

Foreign rock acts were not allowed to play live in Mexico until the late '80s. Their arrival greatly broadened rock's appeal and today Mexico, so close to the big US Spanish-speaking market, is arguably the most important hub of Spanish-language rock. Talented and versatile Mexico City bands such as Café Tacuba and Maldita Vecindad took *rock en español* to new heights and new audiences (well beyond Mexico) in the '90s, mixing a huge range of influences – from rock & roll, ska and punk to traditional Mexican *son*, bolero or mariachi. Four-piece Café Tacuba's exciting handling of so many styles, yet with their own very strong musical identity, led the *New York Times* to compare their 1994 album *Re* with the Beatles' *White Album*. *Re*, *Avalancha de Éxitos* (1996) and *Tiempo Transcurrido* (2001) are all full of great songs. The 1999 double album *Revés/YoSoy* is more instrumental. Maná from Guadalajara are an unashamedly commercial band with British and Caribbean influences sounding strongly reminiscent of the Police. They have been around since the '80s and get ever stronger. Important late '90s arrivals were mostly from Monterrey, notably the politically minded hip-hop trio Control Machete; crude, rude rappers Molotov; and the twosome Plastilina Mosh (programmer Alejandro Rosso and vocalist/guitarist Jonas), a kind of Mexican Beastie Boys whose 1998 debut album *Aquamosh* was a huge success, selling over 1 million copies. *Juan Manuel* followed in 2000.

Meanwhile, balladeer Luis Miguel (born in Veracruz in 1970) is probably the most widely known Mexican pop act. If you don't know his voice you will probably have read about his love life. You probably also heard about Gloria Trevi, dubbed the 'Mexican Madonna' until she vanished in 1998 after Chihuahua authorities ordered the arrest of her and her manager Sergio Andrade

Sánchez for alleged sexual abuse and kidnapping of minors. The story went that the school for young female talent run by Trevi was actually a harem for Andrade. In a saga that gripped Mexico and produced hundreds of false 'sightings' all over the world, the pair were on the run for over a year before being arrested in Rio de Janeiro in 2000.

Mexican Regional Music The deepest-rooted Mexican folk music is *son* (literally, 'sound'), a broad term covering a range of country styles that grew out of the fusion of indigenous, Spanish and African musical cultures. Son is essentially guitars plus harp or violin, often played for a foot-stamping dance audience, with witty, often improvised lyrics. The independent label Discos Corasón has done much to promote these most traditional of Mexican musical forms.

Celebrated brands of Mexican son come from Jalisco *(sones jaliscenses* originally formed the repertoire of many mariachi bands); Veracruz, whose *son jarocho*, performed preeminently by harpist La Negra Graciana, is particularly African-influenced; and the hot Río Balsas basin southwest of Mexico City with the elaborate violin passages of its *sones calentanos*. This last region produced perhaps the greatest son musician of recent decades, violinist Juan Reynoso. Another area renowned for its son is the Huasteca, whose *son huasteco* trios feature a solo violinist and two guitarists singing falsetto between soaring violin passages. Keep an eye open for son festivals or performances by such groups as Camperos de Valles or Trio Tamazunchale if you're traveling in the Huasteca or Hidalgo state or northern Puebla.

More modern regional music is rooted in a strong rhythm from several guitars, with voice, accordion, violin or brass providing the melody. *Ranchera* is Mexico's urban 'country music.' Developed in the expanding towns and cities of the 20th century, it's mostly melodramatic stuff with a nostalgia for rural roots: vocalist-and-combo music, maybe with a mariachi backing. The hugely popular Vicente Fernández, Juan Gabriel and Alejandro Fernández are leading ranchera artists now that past generations of female stars such as Lola Beltrán, Lucha Reyes and Amalia Mendoza are gone.

Norteño is country ballad and dance music, originating in northern Mexico, but nationwide in popularity. Its roots are in *corridos* – heroic narrative ballads with the rhythms of European dances such as the polka or waltz, which were brought to southern Texas by 19th-century German and Czech immigrants. Originally the songs were tales of latino/anglo strife in the borderlands or themes from the Mexican Revolution. Today's ballads tend to deal with small-time crooks, such as drug-runners or *coyotes*, trying to survive amid big-time corruption and crime, and with the injustices and problems faced by Mexican immigrants in the USA. There's even a sub-genre called *narco-corridos*, sung by such groups as Los Tucanes de Tijuana, Los Huracanes del Norte and Raza Obrera. Norteño *conjuntos* (groups) go for 10-gallon hats, and backing for the singer is centered on the accordion and the bajo sexto (a 12-string guitar), along with bass and drums. Los Tigres del Norte, the superstars of the genre, added saxophone and absorbed popular *cumbia* rhythms from Colombia. Other big names are vocalist Marco Antonio Solis and the group he used to front, Los Bukis. Accordionist Flaco Jiménez gained international recognition after working with Ry Cooder, the American rock star whose ventures into world music have also yielded *Buena Vista Social Club*, *Talking Timbuktu* and other hit collaborations.

Banda is a 1990s development of norteño, substituting large brass sections for guitars and accordion, playing a combination of Latin and more traditional Mexican rhythms. Banda del Recodo from Mazatlán are the biggest name in banda. This music also gave birth to an energetic new dance, *la quebradita*.

Grupera, a feebler blend of ranchera, norteño and cumbia, is also popular, especially at fiestas deep in rural Mexico. Límite and Banda Machos are grupera stars.

Música Tropical Though its origins lie in the Caribbean and South America, several brands of *música tropical* or *música afroantillana* have become integral parts of the Mexican musical scene. Two types of dance music – *danzón*, originally from Cuba, and cumbia, from Colombia – both took deeper root in Mexico than in their original homelands (see the Dance section, following). Some banda and norteño groups play a lot of cumbia. The leading Mexican exponents were probably Los Bukis (who split in 1995).

Trova Also called *canto nuevo, nueva canción* or *nueva trova*, this is the genre of troubadour-type folk songs, often with a protest theme and poetic lyrics, typically performed by singer-songwriters *(cantautores)* with a solitary guitar. Fernando Delgadillo and Alberto Escobar are leading Mexican artists, while others such as Betsy Pecanins and the versatile Eugenia León have moved on to other styles such as norteño, ranchera and, in Pecanins' case, blues.

Dance
Indigenous Dance Colorful traditional indigenous dances are an important part of Mexican fiestas. Many bear traces of pre-Hispanic ritual. There are hundreds of them, some popular in several parts of the country, others danced only in a single town or village. Nearly all require special costumes, sometimes including masks. Among the most superb costumes are those of the Zapotec Danza de las Plumas (Feather Dance), from Oaxaca state, and the Nahua Danza de los Quetzales (Quetzal Dance), from Puebla state, which feature enormous feathered headdresses or shields.

Some dances have evolved from old fertility rites. Others tell stories of Spanish or colonial origin (the Danza de las Plumas represents the Spanish conquest of Mexico). *Moros y Cristianos* is a fairly widespread type of dance that reenacts the victory of Christians over Muslims in 15th-century Spain. The costumes of Los Viejitos (The Old Men), to be seen in Pátzcuaro, Michoacán, originated in mockery of the Spanish, whom the local Tarasco people thought aged very fast.

Some dances are these days performed outside their religious context as simple spectacles. The Ballet Folklórico in Mexico City brings together traditional dances from all over the country. Other folkloric dance performances can be seen in several cities and at festivals such as the Guelaguetza, in Oaxaca on the last two Mondays of July, and the Atlixcáyotl, in Atlixco, Puebla, on the last Sunday in September.

Latin Dance Caribbean and South American dance and dance music, which is broadly described as *música afroantillana* or *música tropical*, have become highly popular in Mexico. This is tropical ballroom dancing, to percussion-heavy, infectiously rhythmic music that often includes electric guitars or brass. Mexico City has a dozen or more clubs and large dance halls devoted to this scene; *aficionados* can go to a different hall each night of the week, often with big-name bands from the Caribbean and South America. One of the more formal, old-fashioned varieties of Latin dance is danzón, originally from Cuba and associated particularly with the port city of Veracruz. For danzón, high heels and a dress are de rigueur for women, a Panama hat for men. Steps are small, movement is from the hips down, and danzón can be danced only to danzón music. Cumbia, originally from Colombia but now with its adopted home in Mexico City, has set steps too but is livelier, more flirtatious and less structured than danzón: you move the top half of your body too. Musically it rests on thumping bass lines with an addition of brass, guitars, mandolins and sometimes marimbas.

Salsa developed in New York in the 1950s when jazz met the son, cha-cha and rumba brought by immigrants from Cuba and Puerto Rico. Musically it boils down to brass (with trumpet solos), piano, percussion, singer and chorus – the dance is a hot one with a lot of exciting turns. *Merengue*, mainly from Colombia and Venezuela, is a cumbia/salsa blend with a hopping step; the rhythm catches the shoulders, and the arms go up and down. The music is strong on maracas, and its musicians go for puffed-up sleeves.

Literature
Mexico's best-known novelist internationally is probably Carlos Fuentes (b 1928), and his most highly regarded novel is *Where the Air is Clear*, written in the 1950s. Like his *Death of Artemio Cruz*, it's an attack on the failure of the Mexican Revolution. Fuentes' *Aura* is a magical book with one of the most stunning endings of any novel. *The Old Gringo* is a novel-form version of the mysterious disappearance of San Francisco journalist Ambrose Bierce while covering Pancho Villa during the Mexican Revolution.

In Mexico, Juan Rulfo is generally regarded as the country's supreme novelist.

His *Pedro Páramo* (1955), set before and during the revolution, is a work of desolate magical realism that has been described as '*Wuthering Heights* set in Mexico and written by Kafka.' Among younger writers, Laura Esquivel achieved a big success with *Like Water for Chocolate* (1989), a passionate love story interwoven with both fantasy and cooking recipes set in rural Mexico at the time of the revolution.

Octavio Paz (1914-98), poet, essayist and winner of the 1990 Nobel Prize in Literature, wrote perhaps the most probing examination of Mexico's myths and the Mexican character in *The Labyrinth of Solitude* (1950).

The brightest star among younger contemporary fiction writers is Carmen Boullosa (b 1954), who has had two of her novels published in English: *Leaving Tabasco*, a powerful, imaginative tale of a childhood in an all-female southern Mexican household, and *They're Cows, We're Pigs*, which vividly evokes the world of 17th-century Caribbean pirates.

SOCIETY & CONDUCT

Mexicans are in general friendly, humorous and helpful to visitors – the more so if you address them in Spanish, however rudimentary.

Traditional Culture

Roman Catholicism is one deep fount of traditional culture. Its calendar is filled with saints' days and major festivals including Semana Santa (Holy Week), Día de Muertos (Day of the Dead, November 2), Día de la Virgen de Guadalupe (December 12) and Christmas. These events lead people to gather for the same processions and rituals, dance the same dances in the same costumes and create the same special handicrafts year after year in traditions that evolve only slowly and in some cases go back hundreds of years.

Another vital thread of tradition predates the arrival of Catholicism with the Spanish. The ways of life of many of Mexico's surviving indigenous peoples are still governed, in varying degrees, by pre-Hispanic traditions, ranging from colorful costumes and traditional crafts to the agricultural calendar and communalist social organization.

Mexican traditions often interweave indigenous and Hispanic influences. Día de Muertos, for instance, is in Catholic terms All Souls' Day, yet the manner in which it's celebrated in Mexico has strong overtones of ancestor worship.

The faith that so many Mexicans have in their traditional form of medicine (a mixture of charms, chants, herbs, candles, incense) is further evidence of the strength of pre-Hispanic tradition.

You'll find more information on Mexican traditional culture in sections of this book such as Music, Dance and Religion (this chapter), Public Holidays & Special Events (Facts for the Visitor), and the Artesanías special section, as well as in regional chapters where local traditions are covered.

The Family & Machismo Traditional family ties remain very strong in Mexico. Some have even observed that Mexicans only truly reveal themselves to their families.

An invitation to a Mexican home is quite an honor for an outsider; as a guest you will probably be treated royally and will enter a part of real Mexico to which few outsiders are admitted.

Connected with Mexican family dynamics is the phenomenon of machismo, an exaggerated masculinity aimed at impressing other males as well as women. Its manifestations range from aggressive driving and the carrying of weapons to heavy drinking. The macho image may have roots in Mexico's often-violent past and seems to hinge on a curious network of family relationships. Since it's common for Mexican husbands to have mistresses, wives in response tend to lavish affection on their sons, who end up idolizing their mothers and, unable to find similar perfection in a wife, take a mistress....The strong mother-son bond also means that it's crucial for a Mexican wife to get along with her mother-in-law. And while the virtue of daughters and sisters has to be protected at all costs, other women – including foreign tourists without male companions – may be seen as fair game by Mexican men. The other side of the machismo coin is women who emphasize their femininity.

Such stereotyping, however, is not universal and is under pressure from more modern influences. Machismo is much less overt among many younger Mexicans today.

Dos & Don'ts

In many parts of Mexico, most tourists and travelers are assumed to be citizens of the USA. Away from tourist destinations, your presence may bring any reaction from curiosity to fear or, very occasionally, brusqueness. But any negative response will usually evaporate as soon as you show that you're friendly.

Language difficulties may be the biggest barrier to friendly contact. Some people just don't imagine a conversation is possible, and just a few words of Spanish will often bring smiles and warmth, probably followed by questions. Then someone who speaks a few words of English will pluck up the courage to try them out.

Some indigenous peoples adopt a cool attitude toward visitors: they have learned to mistrust outsiders after five centuries of exploitation. They don't like being gawked at by tourists and can be very sensitive about cameras: if in doubt about whether it's OK to take a photo, always ask first.

In general, it's recommended that women dress conservatively in towns and in off-the-beaten-track places; avoid shorts, sleeveless tops, etc. Everyone should lean toward the more respectful end of the dress spectrum when visiting churches.

Nationalism

Most Mexicans are fiercely proud of their own country at the same time as they despair of it ever being governed well. Their independent-mindedness has roots in Mexico's 11-year war for independence from Spain in the 19th century and subsequent struggles against US and French invaders. Any threat or suspicion of foreign economic domination, as many Mexicans fear is resulting from recent governments' leaning to competitive capitalist economics, is deeply resented. The classic Mexican attitude toward the USA is a combination of the envy and resentment that a poor neighbor feels for a rich one. The word *gringo*, incidentally, isn't exactly a compliment, but it's not necessarily an insult either: the term can simply be, and often is, a neutral synonym for 'American' or 'citizen of the USA.'

Time

The fabled Mexican attitude toward time – '*mañana, mañana…*' – has probably become legendary simply from comparison with the USA. But it's still true, especially outside the big cities, that the urgency Europeans and North Americans are used to is often lacking. Most Mexicans value *simpatía* (congeniality) over promptness. If something is really worth doing, it gets done. If not, it can wait. Life should not be a succession of pressures and deadlines. According to many Mexicans, life in the 'businesslike' cultures has been de-sympathized. You may come away from Mexico convinced that the Mexicans are right!

Treatment of Animals

As in most countries where humans may not have enough to eat, animals in Mexico are rarely mollycoddled as they can be in wealthier societies. In general Mexicans view animals in terms of their direct practical use as food, protection, beasts of burden and, in the case of some wild animals (despite some protective legislation) sources of money for their hides, shells, feathers or eggs. Mexicans may not be as sensitive to animal welfare as some other cultures but they don't in general wantonly mistreat animals. Bullfighting and cockfighting, it may be argued, are evidence to the contrary; but such is the weight of tradition and ritual around these activities, especially bullfighting, that Mexicans could hardly be expected to regard them as anything other than sport or art.

RELIGION
Roman Catholicism

Nearly 90% of Mexicans profess Catholicism. Though its grip over emerging generations today is perhaps marginally less strong than over their predecessors, Catholicism's dominance is remarkable considering the rocky history that the Catholic Church has had in Mexico, particularly in the last two centuries.

The church was present in Mexico from the very first days of the Spanish conquest. Until independence it remained the second most important institution after the crown's representatives and was really the only unifying force in Mexican society. Almost everyone belonged to the church because, spirituality aside, it was the principal provider of social services and education.

The Jesuits were among the foremost providers and administrators, establishing missions and settlements throughout Mexico. Their expulsion from the Spanish empire in the 18th century marked the beginning of stormy church-state relations in Mexico. In the 19th and 20th centuries (up to 1940), Mexico passed numerous measures restricting the church's power and influence. The bottom line was money and property, both of which the church tended to amass faster than the generals and political bosses. The 1917 Mexican constitution prevented the church from owning property or running schools or newspapers, and banned clergy from voting, from wearing clerical garb and from speaking out on government policies and decisions. Church-state relations reached their nadir in the 1920s, when the Cristeros (Catholic rebels) burned government schools, murdered teachers and assassinated a president, while government troops killed priests and looted churches. Most of the anti-church provisions in the constitution ceased to be enforced during the second half of the 20th century, and in the early 1990s President Salinas had them removed from the constitution. In 1992 Mexico finally established diplomatic relations with the Vatican.

The Mexican Catholic Church is one of Latin America's more conservative. Only in the south of the country have its leaders gotten involved in political issues such as human rights and poverty. The most notable figure in this regard is Samuel Ruiz, long-time bishop of San Cristóbal de Las Casas, who retired in 1999.

The Mexican church's most binding symbol is *Nuestra Señora de Guadalupe*, the dark-skinned Virgin of Guadalupe, a manifestation of the Virgin Mary who appeared to an indigenous Mexican in 1531 on a hill near Mexico City. The Guadalupe Virgin became a crucial link between Catholic and indigenous spirituality, and as Mexico grew into a mestizo society she became the most potent symbol of Mexican Catholicism. Today she is the country's patron, her blue-cloaked image is ubiquitous, and her name is invoked in religious ceremonies, political speeches and literature.

Other Christian Faiths

Around 7% of Mexicans profess other varieties of Christianity. Some are members of the Methodist, Baptist, Presbyterian or Anglican churches set up by US missionaries in the 19th century. Others were converted by a wave of American Pentecostal, evangelical, Mormon, Seventh-Day Adventist and Jehovah's Witness missionaries in the last few decades of the 20th century. These churches have gained millions of converts, particularly among the rural and indigenous peoples of southeast Mexico, sometimes leading to serious strife with Catholics, notably in and around San Juan Chamula in Chiapas.

Indigenous Religions

The missionaries of the 16th and 17th centuries won the indigenous people over to Catholicism by grafting it onto pre-Hispanic religions. Often old gods were simply identified with Christian saints, and the old festivals continued to be celebrated, much as they had been in pre-Hispanic times, on the nearest saint's day. Acceptance of the new religion was greatly helped by the appearance of the Virgin of Guadalupe in 1531.

Today, despite modern inroads into indigenous life, indigenous Christianity is still fused with more ancient beliefs. In some remote regions Christianity is only a veneer at most. The Huichol people of Jalisco have two Christs, but neither is a major deity. Much more important is Nakawé, the fertility goddess. The hallucinogenic drug peyote is a crucial source of wisdom in the Huichol world. Elsewhere, among peoples such as the Tarahumara and many Tzotzil people in highland Chiapas, drunkenness is an almost sacred element at festival times.

Even among the more orthodox Christian indigenous peoples, it's not uncommon for spring saints' festivals, or the pre-Lent carnival, to be accompanied by remnants of fertility rites. The famous Totonac voladores (see 'Outdoing the Dervishes' in the Central Gulf Coast chapter) enact one such ritual. The Guelaguetza dance festival, which draws thousands of visitors to Oaxaca every summer, has roots in pre-Hispanic maize-god rituals.

In the traditional indigenous world almost everything has a spiritual dimension – trees, rivers, plants, wind, rain, sun, animals and hills have their own gods or spirits. Even Coca-Cola is believed to have supernatural powers by the Tzotzil people of San Juan Chamula, Chiapas.

Witchcraft, magic and traditional medicine survive. Illness may be seen as a 'loss of soul' resulting from the sufferer's wrongdoing or from the malign influence of someone with magical powers. A soul can be 'regained' if the appropriate ritual is performed by a *brujo* (witch doctor) or *curandero* (curer).

LANGUAGE

The predominant language of Mexico is Spanish. Mexican Spanish is unlike Castilian Spanish, the language of much of Spain, in two main respects: in Mexico the Castilian lisp has more or less disappeared and numerous indigenous words have been adopted.

Travelers in cities, towns and larger villages can almost always find someone who speaks at least some English. All the same, it is advantageous and courteous to know at least a few words and phrases of Spanish. Mexicans will generally respond much more positively if you attempt to speak to them in their own language.

About 50 indigenous languages are spoken as their mother tongue by 7 million or more people in Mexico, of whom about 15% do not speak Spanish.

For a guide to Spanish pronunciation and vocabulary, see the Language chapter.

ARTESANÍAS

Mexico is so richly endowed with appealing *artesanías* (handicrafts) that even the most hardened nonhunter of souvenirs might find it hard to get home without at least one pair of earrings or a little model animal. Such a huge and colorful range of arts and crafts can be found, at mostly reasonable prices, that virtually everyone is irresistibly attracted to something, somewhere along the way.

Selling folk art to tourists and collectors has been a growing business for Mexican artisans since before WWII, but bringing in tourist dollars is only one of the roles handicrafts play in Mexican life. For one thing, Mexicans themselves are eager buyers and collectors of such handicrafts. The colorful, highly decorative crafts that catch the eye in shops and markets today are, in a way, counterparts to the splendid costumes, beautiful ceramics and elaborate jewelry used by the nobility of Aztec, Mayan and other pre-Hispanic cultures.

On a more mundane level, contemporary artisans still turn out countless handmade objects – pots, hats, baskets, toys, clothes, sandals – for everyday use, just as they did centuries before the Spanish came. Many modern crafts are easily traced to their pre-Hispanic origins, and some techniques, designs and materials have remained unchanged.

The Spanish brought their own artistic methods, styles and products, and, although these mingled to some extent with older traditions, indigenous crafts were generally regarded as inferior during the colonial period. But with the search for a national identity after the Mexican Revolution in the early 20th century, a new interest – inspired partly by artists such as Frida Kahlo and Diego Rivera – arose in older, specifically Mexican,

Below: Huichol man working on beaded animal sculpture

DAVID PEEVERS

craft traditions. A lot of handicrafts today show a clear fusion of pre-Hispanic and Spanish inspirations, and sometimes eclectic modern influences, too. Because many of Mexico's indigenous peoples maintain age-old skills and traditions, it's no surprise that the areas producing the most exciting artesanías are often those with prominent indigenous populations, in states such as Chiapas, Guerrero, México, Michoacán, Nayarit, Oaxaca, Puebla and Sonora.

Buying Handicrafts

You can buy artesanías in the villages where they are produced, or in shops and markets in urban centers. In towns and cities you'll generally find a wider range of wares, usually of good quality. But traveling to the villages gives you more of a chance to observe artisans at work, and if you buy there you'll have the satisfaction of knowing that more of your money is likely to go to the artisans themselves, and less to entrepreneurs.

Prices are not necessarily lower in the villages. For example, in Oaxaca city, which is the major clearinghouse for handicrafts from all over the state of Oaxaca, the number of stores and markets selling crafts helps keep prices competitive. Prices also are lower in Oaxaca than they would be after shipping to Mexico City or elsewhere.

City shops devoted to artesanías will give you a good overview of what's available. Some towns and cities with large numbers of resident foreigners or tourists interested in crafts – Mexico City, Guadalajara, San Miguel de Allende, Puerto Vallarta, Oaxaca – have stores offering handicrafts from all over the country. In other cities, you'll find shops with wares from around the local region. Even if you don't buy in these stores, they'll show you good-quality crafts and give you a basis for price comparisons.

Museums can also be good sources of information and examples of handicrafts. Many towns have artesanías museums showing local crafts and techniques, sometimes with items for sale. The upper floor of the Museo Nacional de Antropología, in Mexico City, is devoted to the modern lifestyles of many of Mexico's indigenous peoples, and it's interesting to compare these displays with the artifacts of their pre-Hispanic ancestors in the ground-floor archaeological sections of the museum.

Markets, of course, are a major source of handicrafts. A few cities have special markets devoted to crafts, but ordinary daily or weekly markets always sell some handicrafts – often regional specialties that attract buyers from farther afield, as well as everyday objects, such as pots and baskets, used by local people. The quality of market goods may not be as high as in stores, but you'll usually pay less; bargaining is expected in markets, whereas shops generally have fixed prices.

Specific shops, markets, villages and museums with notable handicrafts are listed in this book's regional sections.

Textiles

Traditional Costume

Although traditional indigenous clothing is rarely worn in towns nowadays, if you get out to some of Mexico's villages you'll be intrigued by the variety of colorful everyday attire, differing from area to area and often from village to village. In general, the more remote an area is, the more intact its costume traditions tend to be. One town where you will come across indigenous people in traditional dress is San Cristóbal de

Las Casas, in Chiapas, which is visited every day by numerous people from nearby villages. Traditional costume – more widely worn by women than men – serves as a mark of the community to which a person belongs and may also have meanings related to a person's status in the community or to religious or spiritual beliefs.

Much laborious, highly skilled work goes into creating such clothing. Many of the garments and the methods by which they are made – and even some of the designs worked into them – are little changed since before the Spanish reached Mexico.

The following four types of women's garment have been in use since long before the Spanish conquest:

Huipil – a sleeveless tunic, often reaching as low as the thighs or ankles, though some are shorter and may be tucked into a skirt. The huipil is found mainly in the southern half of the country.

Quechquémitl – a shoulder cape with an opening for the head, now worn mainly in the center and north of the country.

Enredo – a wraparound skirt, almost invisible if worn beneath a long huipil.

Faja – a waist sash that holds the enredo in place.

Blouses, introduced by Spanish missionaries who thought the quechquémitl immodest when worn without a huipil, are now often embroidered with just as much care and detail as the more traditional garments. They have caused quechquémitls to shrink in size and have replaced huipiles in some places.

The *rebozo*, which probably appeared in the Spanish era, is a long shawl that may cover the shoulders or head or be used for carrying.

Indigenous men's garments are less traditional than women's. In Spanish times the church encouraged modesty, so loose shirts and *calzones* (long baggy shorts) were introduced. Indigenous men may carry shoulder bags because their clothes lack pockets, though many of them have adopted ordinary modern clothing. The male equivalent of the rebozo, also dating from the Spanish era, is the sarape, a blanket with an opening for the head.

Most eye-catching about Mexican indigenous garments – especially those of women – are the intensely colorful, intricate designs that are woven or embroidered into them. Some garments are covered with a web of stylized animal,

Embroidered Chiapas blouse

human, plant and mythical shapes that can take months to complete.

The basic materials of indigenous weaving are cotton and wool, which were once home-produced and homespun. Today, the use of factory yarn, including synthetic fibers, is common.

Colors, too, are often synthetic – Mexicans use bright modern shades in some highly original combinations – but some natural dyes are still in use or are being revived. Among the colors produced by natural dyes are deep blues from the indigo plant; reds and browns from various woods; reds, pinks and purples from the cochineal insect (chiefly used in Oaxaca state); and purples and mauves from a secretion of the *caracol púrpura* (purple sea snail), found on rocks along the south-western coast of Oaxaca. Cloth with natural dyes is highly valued, but it's tough for the untrained eye to tell the difference between natural and artificial colors. Thread dyed from the caracol púrpura, however, is said to always retain the smell of the sea.

The basic indigenous weaver's tool – now, as in the old days, used only by women – is the *telar de cintura* (back-strap loom). In simple terms, the warp (long) threads are stretched between two horizontal bars, one of which is fixed to a post or tree, while the other is attached to a strap that goes around the weaver's lower back; the weft (cross) threads are then woven in. The length of a cloth woven on a back-strap loom is almost unlimited, but the width is restricted to the weaver's arm span.

A variety of sophisticated weaving techniques, including tapestry and brocading, is used to create amazing patterns in the cloth. Embroidery is another widespread decorative technique. The intricacy of some products has to be seen to be believed. Huipiles, skirts, blouses, sashes, quechquémitls and other garments and cloth are decorated in these ways.

The huipiles of indigenous women in the south and southeast of the country are among Mexico's most intricate and eye-catching garments. In the state of Oaxaca some of the finest, most colorful designs are created by the Mazatecs, Chinantecs, Triquis, coastal Mixtecs, and some Zapotecs in villages such as Yalalag. The Amuzgos, whose communities straddle the southern part of the Oaxaca-Guerrero border, also are superb textile artisans. In Chiapas, the most skilled weavers are the high-land Tzotzils, and the Maya of the Yucatán Peninsula also create some attractive huipiles.

There are immense differences of color and pattern in the clothing of different indigenous peoples. In some areas there are even big differ-ences between the styles of neighboring villages. This is especially no-ticeable around San Cristóbal de Las Casas, in Chiapas, where each of the dozen or so indigenous villages within about 30km of the town has a distinct clothing design. Differences also can be seen between every-day huipiles and special ceremonial huipiles, and each individual huipil is likely to have its own unique features.

Some especially beautiful embroidered blouses and quechquémitls are created by Nahua women in Puebla state, by the Mazahua in the western part of México state, and by the Huichol people, who live in a remote region on the borders of Nayarit, Jalisco and Durango states.

An exception to the generally less elaborate design of indigenous men's clothing occurs in southwestern Oaxaca; the garb of the Tacuate people is embroidered with hundreds of tiny, colorful birds, animals and insects – an idea now widely copied on clothing commercially produced elsewhere.

Indigenous clothing is not embellished simply for the joy of decora-tion. Costume and its patterning may have a magical or religious role, usually of pre-Hispanic origin. In some cases, the exact significance has been forgotten, but among the Huichol, for instance, waist sashes are identified with snakes, which are themselves symbols of rain and fertil-ity, so the wearing of a waist sash is a symbolic prayer for rain. Diamond shapes on some huipiles from San Andrés Larrainzar, in Chiapas, repre-sent the universe of the villagers' Mayan ancestors, who believed that the earth was a cube and the sky had four corners. Wearing a garment with a saint's figure on it is also a form of prayer, and the sacred nature of traditional costume in general is shown by the widespread practice of dressing saints' images in old, revered garments at festival times.

Indigenous costume is not something you're likely to buy for practical use, but collectors purchase many items as works of art, which the finest examples certainly are. Outstanding work doesn't come cheap: the finest huipiles in shops in Oaxaca and San Cristóbal de Las Casas might cost hundreds of dollars. A less expensive representation of Mexican costume comes in the form of the cloth dolls found in several parts of the country. Some are quite detailed in their reproduction of indigenous dress.

Other Textiles

One textile art that's practiced by men is weaving on a treadle loom, a machine introduced to Mexico by the Spanish, which is operated by foot pedals. The treadle loom can weave wider cloth than the back-strap loom and tends to be used for blankets, rugs and wall hangings, as well as rebozos, sarapes and skirt material. It allows for great intricacy in design. Mexico's most famous blanket- and rug-weaving village is Teotitlán del Valle, Oaxaca, which produces, among other things, fine textile copies of pre-Hispanic and modern art, including versions of works by Picasso, Escher, Rivera and Miró, as well as pre-Hispanic geometric patterns.

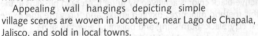

Appealing wall hangings depicting simple village scenes are woven in Jocotepec, near Lago de Chapala, Jalisco, and sold in local towns.

Also suitable as a wall hanging is the cloth embroidered with multitudes of highly colorful birds, animals and insects by the Otomí people of San Pablito, a remote, traditional village in northern Puebla state. This cloth is found in many shops and markets around central Mexico.

The 'yarn paintings' of the Huichol people – created by pressing strands of wool or acrylic yarn onto a wax-covered board – make for colorful and unique decorations. The scenes resemble visions experienced under the influence of the hallucinatory drug peyote, which is central to Huichol culture and believed to put people in contact with the gods. Huichol crafts are found mainly in the states of Nayarit and Jalisco, on whose remote borders the Huichol live. There's a museum in Zapopan, Guadalajara, where you can buy Huichol crafts, and some galleries in Puerto Vallarta sell Huichol work, also. Huichol artisans can be found at work most of the year at the Centro Huichol, in Santiago Ixcuintla, Nayarit.

Not to be forgotten beside the more authentic textile products is the wide range of commercially produced clothing based to varying degrees on traditional designs and widely available in shops and markets throughout Mexico. Some of these clothes are very attractive and of obvious practical use.

Also useful and decorative are the many tablecloths and shoulder bags found around the country. Commercially woven tablecloths can be a good buy, as they're often reasonably priced and can serve a variety of purposes. Lovely ones are found in Oaxaca and Michoacán. Bags come in all shapes and sizes, many incorporating pre-Hispanic indigenous designs. Those produced and used by the Huichol are among the most authentic and original.

Ceramics

Mexicans have been making ceramics of both simple and sophisticated design for several millennia. Because of its durability, pottery has told us much of what we know about Mexico's ancient cultures. Wonderful human, animal and mythical ceramic figures can be seen in almost any archaeological museum.

Today the country has many small-scale potters' workshops, turning out everything from the plain cooking or storage pots that you'll see in markets to elaborate decorative pieces that are true works of art.

A number of village potters work without a wheel: molds are employed by some, while others use a board resting on a stone or two upturned dishes, one on top of the other, as devices for turning their pots. Two villages producing attractive, inexpensive and unique unglazed pottery by these methods are Amatenango del Valle, Chiapas, and San Bartolo Coyotepec, Oaxaca. Amatenango women make jars and plates turned on boards, but the village is best known for its *animalitos* (tiny animal figures), many of which are made by children. Amatenango pottery is fired by the pre-Hispanic method of burning a mound of wood around a pile of pots, and painted with colors made from local earth.

San Bartolo is the source of all the shiny, black, surprisingly lightweight pottery you'll see in Oaxaca and farther afield. It comes in hundreds of shapes and forms: candlesticks, jugs and vases, decorative animal and bird figures, you name it. Turning is by the two-dish method. The distinctive black color is achieved by firing pottery in pit-kilns in the ground; this method minimizes oxygen intake and turns the iron oxide in the local clay black. Burnishing and polishing give the shine.

A more sophisticated and highly attractive type of Mexican pottery is Talavera, named after a town in Spain whose pottery it resembles. Talavera has been made in the city of Puebla since colonial times; Dolores Hidalgo is another Talavera production center. Talavera comes in two main forms: tableware and tiles. Bright colors (blue and yellow are often prominent) and floral designs are typical, but tiles may bear any kind of design. In Puebla, Talavera tiles, some painted with people or animals, adorn the exteriors of many colonial-era buildings. The basic Talavera method involves two firings, with a tin and lead glaze and the painted design applied between the two.

Another of Mexico's distinctive ceramic forms is the *árbol de la vida* (tree of life). These highly elaborate candelabra-like objects, often a meter or more high, are molded by hand and decorated with numerous tiny figures of people, animals, plants and so on. Trees of life may be brightly or soberly colored. The most common themes are Christian, with the Garden of Eden a frequent subject, but trees of life may be devoted to any theme the potter wishes. Some of the best are made in Acatlán de Osorio and Izúcar de Matamoros, Puebla, and Metepec, in the state of México. Artesanías shops in several major centers sell trees of life, as well as striking clay suns from Metepec.

The Guadalajara suburbs of Tonalá and Tlaquepaque are also renowned pottery centers. Tonalá is the source of most of the better

Woven dolls at the Mercado Municipal, San Cristóbal de Las Casas

Oaxacan rug with geometric designs, Tlacolula

Mayan patterns in Tzotzil clothing, San Cristóbal

Handmade woven goods being sold on the streets of Palenque

JOHN NEUBAUER

Pottery for sale in Morelia

JAMES LYON

Ceramic tea set

RICHARD I'ANSON

Centro de Artesanías La Ciudadela, Mexico City

RICHARD I'ANSON

Famous Talavera pottery

Alebrijes, brightly painted copal animals and imaginary beasts, San Martín Tilcajete

Calla lilies carved from wood

Ironwood carvings by the Seri, Hermosillo

Toy skeletons in honor of Día de Muertos, San Miguel de Allende

Woven fruit bowl

Sombreros, Mexico City

Painted tabletop, San Martín Tilcajete

Bark painter, Taxco

Retablo, a small painting giving thanks for answered prayers or miracles, Zacatecas

work, and its products are sold in both places, as well as farther afield. The towns produce a wide variety of ceramics; among the most outstanding work is Jorge Wilmot's heavy 'stoneware' – mostly tableware in delicate blue colors, fired at very high temperatures.

One truly eye-catching method of decoration, employed by the Huicholes (practitioners of so many unusual techniques), is to cover the ceramics in dramatic, bright patterns of glass beads pressed into a wax coating. The Huicholes also use this technique on masks and gourds and even to create pictures.

A walk around almost any Mexican market or craft shop will reveal interesting ceramics. All kinds of decorative animal and human figurines, often with strong pre-Hispanic influence, are sold around the country. Copies of pre-Hispanic pottery can be attractive as well, one notable example being figures of the pudgy, playful, hairless Tepezcuintle dogs that formed part of the diet of ancient western Mexicans. Many pottery Tepezcuintles have been unearthed around the city of Colima, and skillful reproductions of them are sold in several places in the city.

Before you go overboard buying pottery, remember that it needs very careful packing to get it home unbroken.

Masks & Headdresses

Like so many other Mexican crafts, mask-making dates back to pre-Hispanic times. In authentic use, masks were and are worn for magical and religious purposes in dances, ceremonies and shamanistic rites: the wearer temporarily becomes the creature, person or deity depicted by the mask. The exact meanings of some masked dances performed in indigenous festivals today may be forgotten, but often the dances enact a mythical story intended to bring fertility or scare away enemies or other evil forces. These dances often have a curious mixture of pre-Hispanic and Christian or Spanish themes. In some cities, traditional dances, some with masks, are regularly performed in *folklórico* shows.

A huge range of masks is employed, differing from region to region and dance to dance. Though masks obviously have much more life when in use, you can still admire their variety and artistry at museums in cities such as San Luis Potosí, Zacatecas, Morelia and Colima, and at artesanías shops and markets around the country. The southern state of Guerrero has produced probably the broadest range of fine masks.

Wood is the basic material of most masks, but papier-mâché, clay, wax and leather are also used. A mask will often be painted or embellished with real teeth, hair, feathers or other adornments. 'Tigers' – often looking more like leopards or jaguars – are fairly common, as are other animals and birds, actual and mythical. Also numerous are masks depicting Christ, devils and Europeans, whose pale, wide-eyed, mustachioed features obviously looked pretty comical to the native Mexicans.

Today, masks are also made for hanging on walls. While these may not have the mystique that surrounds genuine ceremonial masks, some of which are of considerable age, they're often brighter and in better condition. Even miniature masks can be attractive. Distinguishing genuine dance masks from imitations can be nearly impossible for the uninitiated. Some new masks are even treated so that they will appear old.

Unless you know something about masks or have expert guidance, the best policy when buying them is simply to go for what you like – if the price seems right.

Another spectacular element of some dance costumes is the brilliant feathered headdress, recalling the famous ones that adorned the Aztec emperor Moctezuma and other ancient Mexican nobles. Unless you're lucky enough to be present at a festival in Puebla state where the Danza de los Quetzales, (Quetzal Dance) is being performed, or in Oaxaca state for the Zapotecs' stately Danza de las Plumas (Feather Dance), the best chance you'll have of seeing these magnificent creations is at folklórico dance shows. The conchero dance, frequently staged by informal groups in the Mexico City Zócalo to the accompaniment of loud, upbeat drumming, features feathered headdresses that are almost as superb. Huicholes also adorn some of their hats with impressive feather arrays.

Lacquerware & Woodwork

Gourds, the hard shells of certain squash-type fruits, have been used in Mexico since antiquity as bowls, cups and small storage vessels. Today they serve many other uses, including children's rattles, maracas and even hats. Since pre-Hispanic times, too, gourds have been decorated. The most eye-catching technique is the lacquer process, in which the outside of the gourd is coated with layers of paste or paint, each left to harden before the next is applied. The final layer is painted with the artisan's chosen design, then coated with oil varnish to seal the lacquer. All this makes the gourd nonporous and, to some extent, heat resistant. The painted designs often show birds, plants or animals, but the possibilities are infinite.

Wood, too, can be lacquered, and today the majority of lacquerware you'll see in Mexico – sold all over the central and southern portions of the country – is pine or a sweetly scented wood from the remote village of Olinalá, in the northeastern part of Guerrero state. Characteristic of Olinalá crafts are boxes, trays, chests and furniture lacquered by the *rayado* method, in which designs are created by scraping off part of the top coat of paint to expose a different-colored layer below. Other lacquering centers are Chiapa de Corzo, in Chiapas, and Uruapan and Pátzcuaro, in Michoacán. Some lacquer artists in Uruapan practice the *embutido* method, in which they scrape a design in the top layer of lacquer and fill in the resulting depressions with different colors.

Among the finest wooden crafts made in Mexico are the polished *palo fierro* (ironwood) carvings done by the Seri people of the northwestern state of Sonora. The hard wood is worked into dramatic human, animal and sea-creature shapes. Seris sell their work in Hermosillo, Kino Viejo and Kino Nuevo.

Other attractive woodcrafts are the brightly painted copal animals and dragons and other imaginary beasts produced by villagers in San Martín Tilcajete, Arrazola and La Unión Tejalapan, near Oaxaca city. Multitudes of these creatures, called *alebrijes,* are arrayed in shops and markets in Oaxaca. The craft emerged as a form of souvenir only in the late 1980s, from toys the local people had been carving for their children for generations. It has brought relative wealth to many families in the villages involved.

The Tarahumara people of the Barranca del Cobre (Copper Canyon) area in northwest Mexico produce dolls, toys and animals. Quiroga, near Pátzcuaro in Michoacán, is well known for its brightly painted wooden furniture.

San Miguel de Allende and Cuernavaca are other wooden furniture centers.

Musical Instruments

Mexico's finest guitars are produced in Paracho, near Uruapan in Michoacán, which also turns out violins, cellos and other instruments. There are many shops and workshops in the town, which holds a guitar festival every August. The Tarahumara also make violins.

Elsewhere you'll come across maracas, tambourines, whistles, scrape boards and a variety of drums in markets and shops. Interesting to look out for, though not particularly common, are 'tongue drums' – hollowed-out pieces of wood, often cylindrical in shape and attractively carved or decorated, with two central tongues of wood, each giving a different note when struck.

Bark Paintings

Colorful paintings on *amate*, paper made from tree bark, are sold in countless souvenir shops. While many are cheap, humdrum productions for an undiscriminating tourist market, others certainly qualify as art, showing village life in skillful detail.

Bark paper has been made in Mexico since pre-Hispanic times, when some codices – pictorial manuscripts – were painted on it. It has always been held sacred. The skills for making amate survive only in one small, remote area of central Mexico where the states of Hidalgo, Puebla and Veracruz converge. A chief source of the paper is the Otomí village of San Pablito. The paper is made by women, who boil the bark, then lay out the fibers and beat them until they blend together. The resulting paper is dried in the sun. Most of it is then bought by Nahua villagers from the state of Guerrero, who have been creating bark paintings since the 1960s. More recently, San Pablito villagers have taken up bark painting, some producing unorthodox designs representing San Pablito's traditional deities.

Shamans in San Pablito still use bark paper cutouts portraying the deities for fertility and medicinal rites, and some of these highly unusual works are also sold.

Leather

Leather belts, bags, *huaraches* (sandals), shoes, boots and clothes are often of good quality in Mexico and usually much cheaper than at home. They're widely available in shops and markets all over the country, but you'll find especially well crafted gear in northern and central ranching towns such as Zacatecas, Jerez, Hermosillo, Monterrey, Saltillo, León and Guadalajara. These towns are also the places to look for a Mexican saddle or pair of spurs.

León is renowned as Mexico's shoe capital and has dozens of shoe stores, but every other sizable city has plenty of good ones, too. Check quality and fit carefully before you buy. Mexicans use metric footwear sizes.

Jewelry & Metalwork

Some ancient Mexicans were expert metal smiths and jewelers, as museum exhibits show. The Spanish fever for Mexico's gold and silver led to indigenous people being banned from working those metals for a time during the colonial period, during which European styles of jewelry predominated. Indigenous artisanship was revived in the 20th century, however – most famously in central Mexico by the American William Spratling, who initiated a silver-craft industry that now supplies more than 300 shops in Taxco. Silver is much more widely available than gold in Mexico, and is fashioned in all manner of styles and designs, with artistry ranging from the dully imitative to the superb. Earrings are particularly popular. It's quite possible to buy good pieces at sensible prices. (See Shopping, in the Taxco section of the Around Mexico City chapter, for hints on buying silver jewelry.) For gold, including some delicate filigree work, Guanajuato and Oaxaca cities are two good places to look.

Necklaces are a wide variety of materials, including glass or stone beads, wood, seeds and coral, are worn by many Mexican women and are quite easy to come by. Many original jewelry creations, mostly from inexpensive materials, are also sold at the weekend market in the Mexico City suburb of Coyoacán and by vendors in travelers' haunts such as Oaxaca and San Cristóbal de Las Casas.

Precious stones are much less common than precious metals. True jade, beloved of ancient Mexicans, is a rarity; most 'jade' jewelry is actually jadeite, serpentine or calcite. One abundant stone is the opal, which is mined in Querétaro state. The town of San Juan del Río, near Tequisquiapan, has become quite a gem and jewelry center.

Santa Clara del Cobre, Michoacán, is a center for copperware, with dozens of workshops turning out shining plates, pots, candlesticks, lamps and more. Oaxaca city is the center of a thriving craft of tin plates, stamped into low relief and painted with hundreds of attractive, colorful, small shapes.

Retablos

An engaging Mexican custom is to adorn the sanctuaries of specially revered saints or holy images with retablos, small paintings giving thanks to the saint in question for answered prayers. Typically done on small sheets of tin, but sometimes on glass, wood, cardboard or other materials, the retablos depict these miracles in touchingly literal images painted by their beneficiaries. They may show a cyclist's hair's-breadth escape from a hurtling bus, a sailor's survival of a shipwreck or an invalid rising from a sickbed, beside a representation of the saint and a brief message along the lines of 'Thanks to San Milagro for curing my rheumatism – María Suárez González, 6 June 1999.' The Basílica de Guadalupe in Mexico City, the Santuario de Plateros near Fresnillo in Zacatecas and the church at Real de Catorce in San Luis Potosí state all have fascinating collections of retablos. Diego Rivera was among the first to treat these works as real folk art, and the Museo Frida Kahlo in Coyoacán, Mexico City, the former home of his artist wife, displays some of his collection.

Baskets, Hats & Hammocks

Handmade baskets of multifarious shapes and sizes are common in Mexican markets. If you take a fancy to one, at least you can use it to carry other souvenirs home. Materials used to make baskets include cane, bamboo, and rush or palm-leaf strips. The latter may be wound around a filling of grasses. The more pliable materials enable a coiled construction, but weaving is most common. Many baskets are attractively patterned or colored.

The classic wide-brimmed, high-crowned Mexican sombrero is now largely a thing of the past, except on a few mariachi musicians and in a few souvenir shops. Contemporary everyday men's hats are smaller but still often woven from palm strips, either in factories or by hand. The best are considered to be the *jipijapas* (Panama hats) made in caves at Becal, Campeche, where the humidity prevents the fibers from becoming too brittle during the production process. Mérida is a good place to buy a jipijapa.

Another product of practical use to many travelers is the hammock. A hammock is the most comfortable and economical place to sleep in many hot, southern areas. Generally made of cotton or nylon, hammocks come in a variety of widths and an infinite number of color patterns. Notable places where they're made or sold include Mérida, in Yucatán state; Palenque, in Chiapas; and Mitla and Juchitán, in Oaxaca. You can watch them being made in Tixcocob, near Mérida. (Also see 'Yucatecan Hammocks: The Only Way to Sleep' in the Yucatán Peninsula chapter).

Festival Crafts

Some Mexican crafts are produced for specific events. The national obsession with skull and skeleton motifs, by which Mexicans continually remind themselves of their own mortality, reaches a crescendo in the weeks before Día de Muertos (Day of the Dead, November 2), when the souls of the dead are believed to revisit the earth and people gather in graveyards with gifts for them. As the Day of the Dead approaches, families build altars in their homes, and shops and markets fill with countless toy coffins and skeletons made of paper, cardboard or clay, many of them engaged in very un-skeletonlike activities such as riding a bicycle, playing music or getting married. Most amazing are the rows of chocolate and candy skulls, skeletons and coffins that appear in market stalls – proof of the almost joyful nature of the festival, which reunites the living with their dead.

Most Mexican children's birthdays would be incomplete without a piñata, a large, brightly decorated star, animal, fruit or other figure, constructed around a clay pot or papier-mâché mold. At party time, the piñata is stuffed with small toys, sweets and fruit and suspended on a rope. Blindfolded children take turns bashing it with a stick until it breaks open and showers everyone with the gifts inside. Piñatas also are broken after the traditional pre-Christmas processions called posadas, which are still held in some towns.

Another Christmas craft is the creation of *nacimientos*, nativity scenes, in homes or town plazas. Clay or wood figures of the personages in these scenes may be reused year after year. Some larger-scale nacimientos even feature live sheep and goats.

Facts for the Visitor

HIGHLIGHTS

Reducing the marvels of Mexico to a finite 'best of' list is a tough task and any result is bound to be very subjective. Travel highlights are personal and much depends on the company you're in, the food you just ate and so on. And Mexico has so many marvels…but here goes:

Coasts

Baja California – There are fine beaches around the resorts of La Paz, San José del Cabo and Cabo San Lucas as well diving, surfing and other watersports opportunities in several places on the peninsula.

Pacific Coast – Mazatlán, still-picturesque Puerto Vallarta and Acapulco are classic larger resorts with lots of fine beaches; smaller resorts and towns, such as San Blas, Cuyutlán, Puerto Escondido, Zipolite and Puerto Arista, have untouched beaches and more local character; there's great surfing to be found at San Blas and Puerto Escondido.

Gulf Coast – Revel in the tropical port atmosphere of Veracruz.

Yucatán Peninsula – Cancún has beautiful white sand and azure Caribbean waters but unsympathetic mega-resort development; nearby Isla Mujeres is a lot more laid back and has good snorkeling and diving; Playa del Carmen offers good beaches, outdoor activities, food and nightlife; at

Top 10 Beaches

Where along Mexico's varied and lengthy coastline should you plant your beach blanket? The 10 authors who worked on this edition threw down their towels for the following:

Bahía Manzanillo, near Troncones, Guerrero
Chacahua, Oaxaca
Playa del Carmen (two votes)
Playa El Burro, near Mulegé
Playa Norte, Isla Mujeres
Playa Zicatela, Puerto Escondido
Tulum
Unnamed beach one hour's walk south of Todos Santos, Baja California
Zipolite, Oaxaca

Cozumel island there's legendary diving; Tulum sports ancient Mayan ruins and palm-fringed white sand; Xcalak area is little developed, with pretty beaches and access to the large but little-explored coral atoll Banco Chinchorro.

Archaeological Sites

Northern Mexico – Head for Paquimé at Casas Grandes, Chihuahua, an adobe-built trading center of 900-1340 AD.

Central Mexico – Don't miss Teotihuacán, with its giant Pyramids of the Sun and Moon. Elsewhere in central Mexico, the hilltop ruins at Xochicalco, Tula with its fearsome warrior statues, and Cacaxtla with its colorful battle frescoes are all well worth journeying to. El Tajín, near the Gulf Coast, was a classic Veracruz capital and has the very unusual Pyramid of the Niches.

Southern Mexico – In the state of Oaxaca, the large ancient Zapotec capital Monte Albán has a superb hilltop setting. Farther east, in Chiapas, you enter the Mayan region: Palenque has a site of exquisite architecture surrounded by emerald rain forest, while the more remote Yaxchilán and Bonampak (the latter with famous murals) are in the midst of the Lacandón Jungle.

On the Yucatán Peninsula, don't miss the great, well-restored city of Chichén Itzá, which fuses Mayan and central Mexican styles, or Uxmal with its elaborate temples dedicated to the Mayan rain god Chac. With time at your disposal, you can travel the Puuc Route of four separate Mayan sites near Uxmal, and seek out other important, but more remote, Mayan sites in the Xpujil vicinity or deep in the jungle at Cobá.

Colonial Cities

Mexico is blessed with many charming, historic, Spanish-built towns full of centuries-old carved-stone architecture, plazas with splashing fountains and often lively modern cultural and entertainment scenes. Many of their fine old courtyarded mansions are now charming hotels. Outstanding colonial cities include Zacatecas, with its stupendous cathedral; San Miguel de Allende, home to many artists and expatriates; Guanajuato, a city in a ravine with a great student life; Puebla, with perhaps the greatest concentration of colonial buildings in the country; Taxco, the hillside 'silver town' of winding, cobbled streets; Cuernavaca, famed for its language schools; Oaxaca, remote yet cosmopolitan with beautifully clear southern light; San Cristóbal de Las Casas, a big travelers' center in the cool highlands of Chiapas; and Mérida, the proud capital of Yucatán state with its narrow streets and shady parks.

Small Towns

South of Monterrey, don't miss Real de Catorce, a mountain silver-mining town that went 'ghost' but is now coming back to life. In northwest Mexico are Creel, surrounded by pine forests in the midst of the awesome Barranca del Cobre (Copper Canyon), and Álamos, with cobbled streets lined by Moorish-influenced buildings created by 16th-century Andalusian architects (a good spot for nature-lovers, too).

East of Mexico City, Cuetzalan sits in a mountainous but lush coffee-growing region and is famed for its Sunday market attended by indigenous Nahua people in traditional dress. North of the capital is Tequisquiapan, a charming little spa of clean, colonial streets and brilliant purple bougainvillea. Westward lies Pátzcuaro, a highland town with stately colonial architecture at the heart of indigenous Purépecha country, famous for its Day of the Dead celebrations; and south of the capital there's Tepoztlán, legendary birthplace of the ancient plumed serpent god Quetzalcóatl, in a valley beneath jagged cliffs and now an international new-age energy center.

Nature

Watch whales at Laguna Ojo de Liebre, Laguna San Ignacio or Puerto López Mateos in Baja California, or off Puerto Vallarta. Observe sea turtles near Puerto Vallarta, Zihuatanejo, Mazunte or La Pesca in Tamaulipas.

Climb or just gaze at the dormant and not-so-dormant peaks of central Mexico's volcanic belt: Pico de Orizaba, La Malinche, Iztaccíhuatl, Popocatépetl, Nevado de Toluca and Paricutín.

See teeming birdlife on lagoons and estuaries near the Pacific coast, as at Mexcaltitán, San Blas, Playa Tenacatita, Manialtepec and the Reserva de la Biósfera La Encrucijada. On the Yucatán Peninsula, bird-lovers should head for Celestún and Río Lagartos (both famous for flamingoes), Isla Contoy and San Felipe. Inland biosphere reserves famous for their birds include El Cielo in Tamaulipas (northeast Mexico) and the rare cloud forests of El Triunfo, Chiapas.

Swim amid the majesty of Mexico's northern deserts at the spring-fed pools of Cuatrociénegas. Visit pristine Laguna Miramar in the rain forests of Chiapas' Lacandón Jungle and seek out howler and spider monkeys, toucans, macaws and even jaguars.

Marvel at trees and earth turned orange by millions of monarch butterflies at the Reserva de la Biósfera Mariposa Monarca in Michoacán.

Explore the spectacular Barranca del Cobre (Copper Canyon) area in the Sierra Madre Occidental in Mexico's northwest – actually 20 canyons, some over 2000m deep.

Also see the the Flora & Fauna section in the Facts about Mexico chapter.

Museums

Mexico has some world-class museums. Museo Nacional de Antropología, in Mexico City, is the monarch of Mexican museums and is full of stupendous relics of the country's pre-Hispanic culture. Also in Mexico City, Museo Frida Kahlo is the former home of the haunted artist. Museo Dolores Olmedo Patiño displays a magnificent collection of Diego Rivera and Frida Kahlo art, amid beautiful gardens in Mexico City.

Museo de la Revolución Mexicana, Chihuahua, is Pancho Villa's old headquarters and now a museum of the Mexican Revolution. A creative, interactive survey of the whole of Mexican history – and rain forest ecology – can be found at the Museo de Historia Mexicana in Monterrey.

Instituto Cultural de Cabañas, Guadalajara, has a chapel with 50-odd masterpiece frescoes by 20th-century muralist José Clemente Orozco. Museo de las Mómias, Guanajuato, displays corpses disinterred from a public cemetery, a quintessential example of Mexico's obsession with death.

Museo de Antropología de la Universidad Veracruzana, Jalapa, is the world's best display of ancient Olmec artifacts. Museo de las Culturas de Oaxaca has an extensive and beautifully conceived telling of Oaxaca's history, in a well-restored monastery.

Miscellaneous Favorites

What shouldn't you miss in Mexico? Here's an unscientific survey of the 10 authors' top picks.

Bosque de Chapultepec, Mexico City, on Sunday

Cenote Ik-Kil, near Pisté

El Espinazo del Diablo, between Durango and Mazatlán

Laguna San Ignacio

Las Pozas, Xilitla, San Luis Potosí (two votes)

Palenque ruins

San Cristóbal de Las Casas

Villa del Oeste, near Durango

Yaxchilán ruins and howler monkeys, Chiapas

Parque-Museo La Venta, Villahermosa is an excellent open-air combination of an Olmec archaeological museum and a zoo of Tabasco wildlife.

Grab Bag

Perhaps Mexico's most unforgettable journey is the Ferrocarril Chihuahua al Pacífico, otherwise known as the Copper Canyon Railway, which traverses the awesome Barranca del Cobre (see Nature, above).

When it comes to big cities, you can't beat the Really Big Three – Mexico City, Guadalajara and Monterrey – for, well, big-city atmosphere...bustle, nightlife, the sense of things happening. Guadalajara, the 'most Mexican' city, is a center of music, art and, at heart, a colonial city. Monterrey, by contrast, is the most *norteamericano* city, with the raw energy of a brash industrial capital.

And Mexico City? It's ancient, modern, beautiful, ugly, it's rich, poor, enormous. With nearly a quarter of the nation's people, it's the center of Mexico's culture, economy, politics. It's got everything – except clean air.

Finally, four highlights you'll encounter throughout Mexico:

Music – Mexico is rarely without music: marimbas on the plaza in Veracruz, buskers on the Mexico City metro, brass bands on bandstands everywhere, mariachis tootling on the street in Saltillo, international megastars at vast Mexico City au-

ditoriums, a *son* trio in a Cuetzalan doorway, Plastilina Mosh. Tune in and turn on. And make sure you hear Café Tacuba.

Handicrafts – Mexicans love color and are endlessly inventive with their hands – see the Artesanías special section.

Fiestas – fireworks, parades, music, fun – there's something happening, somewhere, every day (see Public Holidays & Special Events, later in this chapter)

Mexicans – *¡simpáticos, hombre!*

SUGGESTED ITINERARIES

Where you should go in Mexico depends, for one thing, on where you enter the country and where you're going to exit it from. Please take the following suggestions of routes from two major gateways, Mexico City and Cancún, as mere starting points for developing your own itinerary, using other chapters of this book to point you along some of the roads less traveled.

A classic travelers' route through the south of the country runs from Mexico City to Oaxaca to the Oaxaca coast to San Cristóbal de Las Casas to Palenque to Campeche to Mérida to Chichén Itzá to the Caribbean coast (Playa del Carmen, Tulum, Cozumel, Cancún). You need at least three weeks to enjoy all that, before you even start talking about side trips or heading on to Guatemala or Belize.

Travelers coming overland from the USA have a host of further options; they could travel along the Gulf coast (the quickest route to southeast Mexico), or south through Chihuahua and the center of the country with its deserts and beautiful colonial silver cities, or through Baja California, the world's longest peninsula with endless opportunities for outdoor pursuits, or along the mainland Pacific coast with its small and big resorts and countless bays and beaches. The Ferrocarril Chihuahua al Pacífico (Copper Canyon Railway), between Chihuahua and Los Mochis via the Barranca del Cobre (Copper Canyon), provides a spectacular route linking central north Mexico and the Pacific coast.

One Week

If one week is all you've got, pick one good base and make a couple of day-trips out from it. Good bases include Loreto (Baja California), Guanajuato, San Miguel de

Allende, Mexico City, Oaxaca, Mérida, Playa del Carmen and Pacific resorts such as Manzanillo, Puerto Vallarta, Zihuatanejo or Acapulco. The Barranca del Cobre (Copper Canyon) in northwest Mexico, with its spectacular train ride and great hiking, is a unique area worth a week's exploration. Or maybe you've just got your own favorite spot to go back to....

Two Weeks

Two weeks make it worth moving around a bit. Starting in Mexico City (and not missing a side trip to Teotihuacán), you could explore south to Tepoztlán, Cuernavaca, Taxco and maybe on to the Pacific coast at Acapulco; or west to Morelia, Pátzcuaro, Volcán Paricutín, Guadalajara and the Pacific coast at Puerto Vallarta; or northwest to fascinating and beautiful colonial cities such as Querétaro, San Miguel de Allende, Guanajuato or Zacatecas; or east/southeast to Puebla, Jalapa, Veracruz and Oaxaca.

From Cancún, another major gateway city, a two-week Yucatán Peninsula circuit neatly combining ancient Mayan ruins, colonial cities and the Caribbean coast might take in Valladolid, Chichén Itzá, Mérida, Uxmal and Cobá, winding up with beach and snorkeling/diving time at Playa del Carmen, Tulum, Cozumel or the quieter 'Costa Maya' to the south.

One Month

With one month you can explore a bit more of Mexico simply by expanding on or combining a couple of the basic routes already mentioned. Also consider fitting in the Barranca del Cobre – a true highlight of northern Mexico. Starting from Cancún you could add Chiapas (San Cristóbal de Las Casas, Palenque and a side-trip to Yaxchilán), and maybe even the great Mayan ruins at Tikal (Guatemala) and on to the Yucatán Peninsula.

Two Months

Now you're talking! Starting in Mexico City, take one or two of the routes described in Two Weeks (see earlier) and again consider fitting in the Barranca del Cobre, then head to Oaxaca and its coast and on to Chiapas and the Yucatán Peninsula. Returning to Mexico City you might take in Villahermosa, Veracruz and Jalapa.

Starting from Cancún, you could do a more in-depth Yucatán Peninsula trip *and* have time for Chiapas, Oaxaca, highlights of Guatemala and/or Belize and maybe even some of central Mexico.

PLANNING
When to Go

Any time is a good time to visit Mexico, though the coastal and lowland regions, particularly in the southern half of the country, are fairly hot and humid from May to September. The interior of the country has a more temperate climate than the coasts. In fact it's sometimes decidedly chilly in the north and the central highlands in winter (November to February).

July and August are peak holiday months for both Mexicans and foreigners. Other big holiday seasons are mid-December to early January (for both foreigners and Mexicans), and a week either side of Easter (for Mexicans). At these times the coastal resorts attract big tourist crowds, room prices go up in popular places and rooms and public transportation are heavily booked, so advance reservations are often advisable.

Maps

The GeoCenter, Nelles Verlag, ITMB and the AAA (American Automobile Association) all produce good country maps of Mexico suitable for travel planning, available internationally for under US$10. The map scales vary between 1:2,500,000 (1cm:25km)

0 out of 10

Not surprisingly, border towns and bathrooms rank high on the authors' worst of Mexico list.

Acapulco
Any pool hall bathroom in *la provincia*
Any toilet with a basket full of used paper
Ciudad Juárez
Escárcega, Campeche
La Revo, Tijuana
Long lines for free museums on Sunday, Mexico City
Mexico City traffic and pollution
Poza Rica
Tapachula, Chiapas

and 1:3,675,000 (1cm:36.75km). The GeoCenter map is recommendable for its combination of relief (terrain) shading, archaeological sites, national parks, roads graded by quality and settlements graded by size. For information on road atlases, see the Car & Motorcycle section in the Getting Around chapter.

City, town and regional maps of varying quality are available free from local tourist offices in Mexico, and you can often find commercially published ones at bookstores or newsstands. INEGI (Instituto Nacional de Estadística, Geografía e Informática) publishes large-scale series of 1:50,000 (1cm:500m) and 1:250,000 (1cm:2.5km) maps covering all of Mexico. INEGI has an office in every Mexican state capital, and at least three shops in Mexico City (see the Maps section in the Mexico City chapter), where you can buy these maps for US$4 to US$6 each.

What to Bring

The clothing you should bring depends on how, when and where you want to travel, and how you would like to be perceived by Mexicans.

Mexicans tend to dress informally but conservatively. Even in the hot regions, men wear long trousers. A *guayabera,* a fancy shirt decorated with tucks and worn outside the belt, may substitute for a jacket and tie on more formal occasions. Many women wear stylish dresses, blouses or skirts.

The local people do not expect you to dress as they do, but you'll soon realize that, except in beach resorts, shorts and T-shirts are the marks of the tourist. In the hotter regions, these plus light cotton trousers or skirts, light blouses or shirts, trainers or light boots, and a pair of sandals, should see you through most of the time. But also bring a light sweater or jacket; you'll need it on air-conditioned buses or even for some boat rides on the coasts. Jeans are often uncomfortably heavy in warm, humid areas but are good for upland areas in the cooler months. A light rain jacket, preferably loose-fitting, is good to have from October to May and is a necessity from May to October. If you plan to party in the nightspots in cities or resorts, don't forget a couple of suitable garments for that purpose.

In lowland areas such as the Pacific and Gulf Coasts, Yucatán and Tabasco, everyone should have a hat and sunblock. These are usually obtainable on the spot if you don't bring them. If your complexion is particularly fair or you burn easily, consider wearing long sleeves and long pants.

Basic toiletries such as shampoo, shaving cream, razors, soap and toothpaste are readily available throughout Mexico except in small or remote villages. You should bring your own contact lens solution, tampons, contraceptives and insect repellent; they are available in Mexico, but not always readily so.

Other recommended items are sunglasses, a flashlight (torch), a pocketknife, a traveler's alarm clock, a couple meters of cord, a small sewing kit, a money belt or pouch that you can wear under your clothes, a small padlock and a small Spanish dictionary.

For carrying it all, a backpack is the most convenient if you'll be doing much traveling. You can make it reasonably theft-proof with small padlocks. A light daypack, too, is useful.

RESPONSIBLE TOURISM

A responsible tourist is, perhaps, one who treats the visited place as if it were home. Would you wander into your hometown church and start taking flash photos during a service? If the drains at your home were blocked, would you put paper down to block them further?

Most places you're likely to go in Mexico welcome tourism as a money earner, but be sensitive with indigenous peoples, who have some delicate traditions and unusual beliefs. Respect their ceremonies. Many have a deep dislike of being photographed; only snap them if you've been granted permission.

As for Mexico's environment, well, some of it's a mess, but there's still a lot of glorious nature out there. You can do your bit by, for instance, not buying turtle, iguana or black coral products, and patronizing projects that promote sustainable development. If the human inhabitants of forests and wetlands can earn a living from hosting low-impact ecotourism, instead of cutting down their forests, fishing their lagoons dry or abandoning their villages to work illegally in the US, it's win-win. As the saying goes, take only photos, leave only footprints – but don't leave footprints on the coral.

Many of the most ecologically conscious enterprises in Mexico are community-run, and community initiatives ensure that any profit made from your visit goes to the people you have visited (who are usually poor), and not to entrepreneurs from elsewhere. Another way you can do this is to buy crafts and commodities direct from producer cooperatives, villages or from the artisans themselves.

TOURIST OFFICES
Local Tourist Offices
Just about every place of interest to tourists has a national, state or city/town tourist office. They can be helpful with maps and brochures, and often some staff members speak English.

You can call the Mexico City office of the national tourism ministry SECTUR (☎ 55-5250-0123, 800-903-92-00) at any time – 24 hours a day, seven days a week – for information or help in English or Spanish.

Tourist Offices Abroad
In the USA and Canada you can call ☎ 800-446-3942 for Mexican tourist information. You can also contact a Mexican Government Tourism Office at the following locations:

Chicago (☎ 312-606-9252), 300 North Michigan Ave, 4th Floor, IL 60601

Houston (☎ 713-772-2581), 4507 San Jacinto, Suite 308, TX 77004

Los Angeles (☎ 213-351-2075), 2401 W 6th St, 5th Floor, CA 90057

Miami (☎ 305-718-4095), 1200 NW 78th Avenue, No 203, FL 33126

Montreal (☎ 514-871-1052), 1 Place Ville Marie, Suite 1931, H3B 2C3

New York (☎ 212-821-0314), 21 East 63rd St, NY 10021

Toronto (☎ 416-925-0704 ext 22 or 23), 2 Bloor St West, Suite 1502, M4W 3E2

Vancouver (☎ 604-669-2845), 999 West Hastings St, Suite 1110 V6C 2W2

Look for the following Mexican Government Tourism Offices in Europe:

France (☎ 01 42 86 96 12), 4 rue Notre Dame des Victoires, 75002 Paris

Germany (☎ 069-253-509), Taunusanlage 21, 60325 Frankfurt-am-Main

Italy (☎ 06-487-4698), Via Barberini 3, 00187 Rome

Spain (☎ 91-561-18-27), Calle Velázquez 126, Madrid 28006

UK (☎ 020-7488-9392), 41 Trinity Square, Wakefield House, London EC3N 4DJ

VISAS & DOCUMENTS
Visitors to Mexico should have a valid passport. Visitors of some nationalities have to obtain visas, but others (when visiting as tourists) require only the easily obtained Mexican government tourist card. Because the regulations sometimes change, it's wise to confirm them at a Mexican Government Tourism Office or Mexican embassy or consulate before you go. Several Mexican embassies and consulates, and foreign embassies in Mexico, have Web sites with useful information on tourist permits, visas and so on (see Embassies & Consulates, later), but they don't all agree with each other, so you should back up any Internet findings with some phone calls. The Lonely Planet Web site (Ⓦ www.lonelyplanet.com) has links to updated visa information.

Travelers under 18 who are not accompanied by *both* parents need special documentation (see Under-18 Travelers, later).

Passport
Though it's not recommended, US tourists can enter Mexico without a passport if they have official photo identification, such as a driver's license, plus some proof of their citizenship, such as a birth certificate certified by the issuing agency or a naturalization certificate (not a copy). Citizens of other countries who are permanent residents in the USA have to take their passports and Permanent Resident Alien Cards.

Canadian tourists may enter Mexico with official photo identification plus proof of citizenship, such as a birth certificate or notarized affidavit of it. Naturalized Canadian citizens, however, require a valid passport.

It is much better to have a passport, because officials are used to passports and may delay people who have other documents. This also applies to officials at reentry points to the USA or Canada as well as to Mexico. In Mexico you will often need your passport when you change money, as well.

Citizens of other countries should have a passport valid for at least six months after they arrive in Mexico.

Dual Nationals Mexicans with dual nationality must carry proof of both their citizenships and must identify themselves as Mexican when entering or leaving Mexico. They are considered Mexican by the Mexican authorities but are not subject to compulsory military service.

Visas

Citizens of the USA, Canada, the EU countries, Australia, New Zealand, Argentina, Brazil, Chile, the Czech Republic, Hungary, Iceland, Israel, Japan, Norway, Poland, Singapore, Slovenia, Switzerland and Uruguay are among those who do not require visas to enter Mexico as tourists. The list changes from time to time; check well ahead of travel with your local Mexican embassy or consulate. Visa procedures, for those who need them, can sometimes take several weeks.

All tourists must obtain a Mexican government tourist card (see Travel Permits).

Non-US citizens passing through the USA on the way to or from Mexico, or visiting Mexico from the USA, should check their US visa requirements.

Travel Permits

The Mexican tourist card – officially the Forma Migratoria para Turista (FMT) – is a brief card document that you must fill out and get stamped by Mexican immigration when you enter Mexico and must keep till you leave. It's available free of charge at official border crossings, international airports and ports, and often from airlines, travel agencies, Mexican consulates and Mexican government tourism offices. At the US-Mexico border you won't usually be given one automatically; you have to ask for it.

At many US-Mexico border crossings you don't *have* to get the card stamped at the border itself, as the Instituto Nacional de Migración (INM, National Immigration Institute) has control points on the highways into the interior where it's also possible to do it; but it's preferable to get it done at the border itself, in case there are difficulties elsewhere.

One section of the card deals with the length of your stay in Mexico, and this section is filled out by the immigration officer. The maximum is 180 days but immigration officers will often put a much lower number (as little as 15 or 30 days in some cases) unless you tell them specifically that you need, say, 90 or 180 days. It's always advisable to ask for more days than you think you'll need, in case you are delayed or change your plans. Ultimately it's down to the whim of the individual immigration officer: while researching this book, some of authors were given 180 days without even asking for it, while another asked for 60 but was given 30 and told to get an extension later!

People entering Mexico in Chiapas (from Guatemala) are never given more than 30 days initially. This can be extended by a further 30 days at INM offices in Chiapas, and up to a total 180 days at INM offices outside Chiapas (see Extensions & Lost Cards, later).

Look after your tourist card, as it will probably be checked when you leave the country.

Tourist cards are not needed for visits shorter than 72 hours within the frontier zones along Mexico's northern and southern borders. The frontier zone is the territory between the border itself and the INM's control points on the highways leading into the Mexican interior (usually 20 to 30km from the border). A few extra zones are also exempt from the tourist card requirement for visits of less than 72 hours, including the Tijuana-Ensenada corridor in Baja California; San Felipe, Baja California; and the Sonoita-Puerto Peñasco corridor in Sonora.

A tourist card only permits you to engage in what are considered to be tourist activities (including sports, health, artistic and cultural activities). In recent years Mexico has expelled, especially from Chiapas, dozens of foreigners it considered to be pursuing activities not permitted by a tourist card. If the purpose of your visit is to work (even voluntarily), to report or to study, or to participate in humanitarian aid or human rights observation, you may well need a visa. Check with a Mexican embassy or consulate.

Tourist Fee Foreign tourists and business travelers visiting Mexico are all charged a fee of about US$20 called the Derecho para

No Inmigrante (DNI, Nonimmigrant Fee). The exact amount changes each year.

If you enter Mexico by air, the fee is included in the price of your air ticket. If you enter by land you must pay it at a branch of any of the Mexican banks listed on the back of your tourist card, at any time before you reenter the frontier zone on your way out of Mexico (or before you check in at an airport to fly out of Mexico). It makes sense to get the job done as soon as possible, and at least some Mexican border posts have on-the-spot bank offices where you can do so.

When you pay at a bank, your tourist card or business visitor card will be stamped to prove that you have paid.

Tourists only have to pay the fee once in any 180-day period. You are entitled to leave and reenter Mexico as many times as you like within 180 days without paying again. A similar multi-entry rule applies to business travelers, but their limit is 30 days. If you are going to return within the stipulated period, retain your card when you leave Mexico.

The fee does not have to be paid by people visiting Mexico for less than 72 hours and who remain in seaports or within the frontier zone or certain nearby exempted areas: Tijuana-Ensenada, Mexicali-San Felipe, Sonoita-Puerto Peñasco, Ciudad Juárez-Paquimé, Piedras Negras-Santa Rosa, and Reynosa-China-Presa El Cuchillo.

Extensions & Lost Cards If the number of days given on your tourist card is for some reason less than the 180-day maximum, its validity may be extended one or more times, at no cost, up to the maximum. To get a card extended you have to apply to the INM, which has offices in many towns and cities. The procedure costs around US$20 and should take between half an hour and three hours, depending on the cooperation of each particular immigration office. (One reader reported spending 10 hours, spread over two days, extending a card at Playa del Carmen on the Caribbean coast.) You'll need your passport, tourist card, photocopies of the important pages of these documents, and, at some offices, evidence of 'sufficient funds.' A major credit card is usually OK for the latter, or an amount in traveler's checks anywhere from US$100 to US$1000 depending on the office.

Most INM offices will not extend a card until a few days before it is due to expire; don't bother trying earlier.

If you lose your card or need further information, contact the SECTUR tourist office in Mexico City (☎ 55-5250-0123, ☎ 800-903-92-00) or your embassy or consulate. Your embassy or consulate may be able to give you a letter enabling you to leave Mexico without your card, or at least an official note to take to your local INM office, which will have to issue a duplicate.

Travel Insurance

A travel insurance policy to cover theft, loss and medical problems is a good idea. It's also a good idea to buy insurance as early as possible. If you buy it the week before you fly, you may find, for example, that you're not covered for delays to your flight caused by strikes.

Mexican medical treatment is generally inexpensive for common diseases and minor treatment, but if you suffer some serious medical problem, you may want to find a private hospital or fly out for treatment. Travel insurance can typically cover the costs. Some US health insurance policies stay in effect (at least for a limited time) if you travel abroad, but it's worth checking exactly what you'll be covered for in Mexico. For people whose medical insurance or national health systems don't extend to Mexico – which includes most non-Americans – a travel policy is advisable.

You may prefer a policy that pays doctors or hospitals directly rather than requiring you to pay on the spot and claim later. If you have to claim later, keep all documentation. Some policies ask you to call collect to a center in your home country, where an immediate assessment of your problem is made. Check that the policy covers ambulances or an emergency flight home.

Some policies offer lower and higher medical-expense options; the higher ones are chiefly for countries such as the USA, which have extremely high medical costs. There is a wide variety of policies available, so check the small print.

Some policies specifically exclude 'dangerous activities,' which can include scuba diving, motorcycling and even trekking. A locally acquired motorcycle license is not valid under some policies.

Driver's License & Permits

If you're thinking of driving in Mexico, take your driver's license and a major credit card with you. For more information on car rentals, see the Getting Around chapter. For the paperwork involved in taking your own vehicle into Mexico, see the Getting There & Away chapter.

Hostel, Student & Teacher Cards

The ISIC student card, the GO25 card for any traveler aged 12 to 25, and the ITIC card for teachers can help you obtain reduced-price air tickets to or from Mexico at student- and youth-oriented travel agencies. In Mexico, reduced prices for students at museums, archaeological sites and so on are usually only for those with Mexican education credentials, but in practice the ISIC card will sometimes get you a reduction. It may also get you discounts on some bus tickets and in a few hostel-type accommodations. The GO25 and ITIC are less recognized, but worth taking along.

All three cards can be obtained in Mexico. One outlet is the youth/student travel agency Mundo Joven (W www.mundojoven.com), with offices in Mexico City and several other cities. You need proof of your student/teacher status to obtain the ISIC/ITIC.

An HI (Hostelling International) card will save you US$1 or so in some hostels in Mexico. Take this card along if you have one, but it's not worth getting one specially.

Documents for Under-18 Travelers

To prevent international child abduction, minors (people under 18) entering Mexico without one or both of their parents may be, and often are, required to show a notarized consent form, signed by the absent parent or parents, giving permission for the young traveler to enter Mexico. A form for this purpose is available from Mexican consulates. In the case of divorced parents, a custody document may be acceptable instead. If one or both parents are dead, or the traveler has only one legal parent, a notarized statement saying so may be required.

These rules are aimed primarily at visitors from the USA and Canada but may also apply to people from elsewhere. Procedures vary from country to country; contact a Mexican consulate to find out exactly what you need to do.

Copies

All important documents (passport data pages and visa pages, birth certificate, vehicle papers, credit or bank cards, travel insurance papers, air tickets, driver's license, traveler's check receipts or serial numbers, etc) should be copied before you leave home. Leave one copy with someone at home and keep another with you, separate from the originals. When you get to Mexico, add a photocopy of your tourist permit and, if you're driving, vehicle import papers.

EMBASSIES & CONSULATES
Mexican Embassies & Consulates

Unless otherwise noted, details are for embassies or their consular sections. Updated details can be found at W www.sre.gob.mx, which also has links to the embassies' and consulates' own Web sites. Some of these sites, such as the Mexican consulates in New York, San Diego and Los Angeles and the Mexican embassy in London, are useful sources on visas and related matters.

Australia (☎ 02-6273-3963), 14 Perth Ave, Yarralumla, Canberra, ACT 2600

Belize (☎ 02-30-193, W www.embamexbelize .gob.mx), 18 North Park St, Fort George Area, Belize City

Canada (☎ 613-233-9917/9272, W www.embamex can.com), 45 O'Connor St, Suite 1500, Ottawa, ON K1P 1A4
Consulates: (☎ 514-288-2502), 2000 rue Mansfield, Suite 1015, Montreal, PQ H3A 2Z7
(☎ 416-368-8490), Commerce Court West, 199 Bay St, Suite 4440, Toronto, ON M5L 1E9
(☎ 604-684-3547), 710-1177 West Hastings St, Vancouver, BC V6E 2K3

France (☎ 01 53 70 27 70, W www.sre.gob.mx/ francia), 9 rue de Longchamps, 75116 Paris
Consulate: (☎ 01 42 86 56 20), 4 rue Notre Dame des Victoires, 75002 Paris

Germany (☎ 030-269-3230, W www.embamex.de), Klingelhöferstrasse 3, 10785 Berlin
Consulate: (☎ 069-299-8750), Taunusanlage 21, 60325 Frankfurt-am-Main
Consulate: (☎ 040-450-1580), Hallerst 76, 20146 Hamburg

Guatemala (☎ 333-7254), Edificio Centro Ejecutivo, 15a Calle No 3-20, Nivel 7, Zona 10, Guatemala City
Consulates: (☎ 339-1009), Avenida Reforma 6-

64, Edificio Plaza Corporativa Reforma, Zona 9, Torre Jardín 3rd Floor, Oficinas J-300 y J-2, Guatemala City (☎ 767-5542), 21a Avenida 8-64, Zona 3, Quetzaltenango (☎ 776-8181), 1a Avenida 4-01, Zona 1, Ciudad Tecún Umán

Ireland (☎ 01-260-0699), 43 Ailesbury Rd, Ballsbridge, Dublin 4

Italy (☎ 06-441151, W www.target.it/messico), Via Lazzaro Spallanzani 16, 00161 Rome
Consulate: (☎ 02-7602-0541), Via Cappuccini 4, 20122 Milan

Netherlands (☎ 070-345-2569), Nassauplein 17, 2585 EB The Hague

New Zealand (☎ 04-472-5555), 8th Floor, 111-115 Customhouse Quay, Wellington

Spain (☎ 91-369-2814, W www.embamex.es), Carrera de San Jerónimo 46, 28014 Madrid
Consulate: (☎ 93-201-1822), Avinguda Diagonal 626, 08021 Barcelona

UK (☎ 020-7235-6393, W www.embamex.co.uk), 8 Halkin St, London SW1X 7DW

USA (☎ 202-728-1600, W www.sre.gob.mx/eua), 1911 Pennsylvania Ave NW, Washington, DC 20006
Consulate: (☎ 202-736-1000), 2827 16th St NW, Washington, DC 20009

Other Mexican Consulates in the USA

There are consulates in many other US cities besides Washington, DC, particularly in the border states.

Arizona

Douglas	☎ 520-364-3107
Nogales	☎ 520-287-2521
Phoenix	☎ 602-242-7398
Tucson	☎ 520-882-5595

California

Calexico	☎ 760-357-3863
Fresno	☎ 559-233-9770
Los Angeles	☎ 213-351-6800
	W www.consulmex-la.com
Sacramento	☎ 916-441-3287
San Bernardino	☎ 909-889-9837
San Diego	☎ 619-231-8414,
	W www.sre.gob.mx/sandiego
San Francisco	☎ 415-392-6576
San Jose	☎ 408-294-3414 ext 120

Colorado

Denver	☎ 303-331-1110

Florida

Miami	☎ 305-716-4977
Orlando	☎ 407-422-0514

Georgia

Atlanta	☎ 404-266-2233

Illinois

Chicago	☎ 312-855-1380

Louisiana

New Orleans	☎ 504-522-3596

Massachusetts

Boston	☎ 617-426-4181

Michigan

Detroit	☎ 313-964-4515

Missouri

St Louis	☎ 314-436-3233

New Mexico

Albuquerque	☎ 505-247-2139

New York

New York	☎ 212-217-6400
	W www.consulmexny.org

Oregon

Portland	☎ 503-274-1450

Pennsylvania

Philadelphia	☎ 215-922-3834

Texas

Austin	☎ 512-478-2866
Brownsville	☎ 956-542-4431
Corpus Christi	☎ 361-882-3375
Dallas	☎ 214-252-9250
Del Rio	☎ 830-775-2352
Eagle Pass	☎ 830-773-9255
El Paso	☎ 915-533-3644
Houston	☎ 713-271-6800
Laredo	☎ 956-723-6369
McAllen	☎ 956-686-0243
Midland	☎ 915-687-2334
San Antonio	☎ 210-271-9728

Utah

Salt Lake City	☎ 801-521-8502

Washington state

Seattle	☎ 206-448-3526

Embassies & Consulates in Mexico

All embassies are in Mexico City. Many countries also have consulates in other cities around Mexico. Embassies and consulates often keep limited business hours (typically from around 9am or 10am to 1pm or 2pm Monday to Friday) and usually close on both Mexican and their own national holidays. But many embassies provide 24-hour emergency telephone contact. Embassy addresses in the selective list that follows include the *colonias* (neighborhoods) of Mexico City in which they are located and any metro stations convenient to them. All telephone numbers given include area codes.

It's important to realize what your embassy can and can't do to help you if you get into trouble. Generally speaking, it won't be much help in emergencies if the trouble you're in is remotely your own fault. You are bound by the laws of the country you are in. Your embassy will not be sympathetic if you end up in jail after committing a crime locally, even if such actions are legal in your own country. In genuine emergencies you might get some assistance, but only if other channels have been exhausted. For example, if you need to get home urgently, a free ticket home is exceedingly unlikely – the embassy would expect you to have insurance. If you have all your money and documents stolen, it might assist with getting a new passport, but a loan for onward travel is out of the question.

Australia (☎ 55-5531-5225, W www.mexico .embassy.gov.au), Rubén Darío 55, Polanco; ⓜ Polanco or Auditorio
Consulates: Guadalajara (☎ 33-3615-7418), Privada Vista Alegre 945, Colonia Lomas Valle
Monterrey (☎ 81-8158-0791), Avenida Munich 195, Colonia Cuauhtémoc, San Nicolás de los Garza

Belize (☎ 55-5520-1274), Bernardo de Gálvez 215, Lomas de Chapultepec
Consulates: Cancún (☎ 998-887-86-31), Avenida Náder 34, 1st floor (enter via Lima)
Chetumal (☎ 983-832-18-03), Armadas de México 91

Canada (☎ 55-5724-7900, ☎ 800-706-29-00, W www .canada.org.mx), Schiller 529, Polanco; 400m north of the Museo Nacional de Antropología; ⓜ Polanco
Consulates: Acapulco (☎ 744-484-13-05), Centro Comercial Marbella, Local 23
Cancún (☎ 998-883-32-32), Plaza Caracol 330
Guadalajara (☎ 33-3616-5642), Hotel Fiesta Americana, Local 31, Aceves 225, Colonia Vallarta Poniente
Mazatlán (☎ 669-913-73-20), Hotel Playa Mazatlán, Loaiza 202, Zona Dorada
Monterrey (☎ 81-8344-3200), Edificio Kalos, C1 floor, Local 108A, Zaragoza 1300 Sur
Oaxaca (☎ 951-513-37-77), Pino Suárez 700, Local 11B
Puerto Vallarta (☎ 322-222-53-98), Zaragoza 160, Interior 10, Colonia Centro
San José del Cabo (☎ 624-142-43-33), Plaza José Green, Local 9, Boulevard Mijares s/n
Tijuana (☎ 664-684-04-61), Gedovius 5-202, Zona Río

France (☎ 55-5280-9700, W www.francia.org.mx), Campos Elíseos 339, Polanco; ⓜ Auditorio
Consulate-General: (☎ 55-5282-9840) Lafontaine 32, Polanco; open 9 am to 1 pm Monday to Friday; ⓜ Auditorio
Consulates: Acapulco (☎ 744-469-12-08), Hyatt Regency Hotel, La Costera 1
Cancún (☎ 998-884-88-48), Avenida Náder 34

Guadalajara (☎ 33-3616-5516), López Mateos Nte 484
Mazatlán (☎ 669-985-12-28), Belisario Domínguez 1008 Sur, Colonia Centro
Mérida (☎ 999-925-28-86), Calle 33B No 528
Monterrey (☎ 81-8336-4498), 2 de Abril No 789 Ote, San Pedro Garza

Germany (☎ 55-5283-2200, W www.embajada alemana.org.mx), Lord Byron 737, Polanco; open 9am to noon Monday to Friday; ⓜ Polanco
Consulates: Acapulco (☎ 744-484-18-60), Alaminos 26, Casa Tres Fuentes, Colonia Costa Azul
Cancún (☎ 998-884-18-98), Punta Conoco No 36
Guadalajara (☎ 33-3613-9623, ☎ 800-021-11-70), Corona 202
Mazatlán (☎ 669-982-28-09), Jacarandas 10, Colonia Loma Linda
Mérida (☎ 999-981-29-76), Calle 7 No 217, Colonia Chuburna de Hidalgo
Monterrey (☎ 81-8355-1784), Calzada del Valle 400, Local 77, Colonia del Valle

Guatemala (☎ 55-5540-7520), Avenida Explanada 1025, Lomas de Chapultepec
Consulates: Cancún (☎ 998-884-82-96), Avenida Náder 34, 1st floor (enter via Lima)
Chetumal (☎ 983-832-30-45), Avenida Independencia 326
Comitán (☎ 963-632-04-91), 1a Calle Sur Pte 26
Tapachula (☎ 962-626-12-52), 2a Calle Pte 3

Italy (☎ 55-5596-3655, W www.embitalia.org.mx), Paseo de las Palmas 1994, Lomas de Chapultepec
Consulates: Cancún (☎ 998-884-12-61), Alcatraces 39
Guadalajara (☎ 33-3616-1700), Avenida López Mateos Nte 790, 1st floor, Fraccionamiento Ladrón de Guevara
Monterrey (☎ 81-8378-2444), Prolongación Moralillo 109, Colonia Lomas del Valle

Netherlands (☎ 55-5258-9921), Avenida Vasco de Quiroga 3000, 7th floor, Santa Fe
Consulates: Acapulco (☎ 744-486-82-10), Hotel Qualton Club Acapulco, La Costera 159
Cancún (☎ 998-886-01-34), Martinair office, Cancún International Airport
Guadalajara (☎ 33-3673-2211), Avenida Vallarta 5500, Lomas Universidad
Mérida (☎ 999-924-31-22), Calle 64 No 418

New Zealand (☎ 55-5283-9460), Lagrange 103, 10th floor, Los Morales

Spain (☎ 55-5282-2974), Galileo 114, Polanco; ⓜ Auditorio
Consulates: Acapulco (☎ 744-485-72-05), Llantera del Pacífico, Avenida Universidad 2, Fraccionamiento Magallanes
Cancún (☎ 998-885-24-37), Edificio Oásis, Boulevard Kukulcán Km 6.5
Guadalajara (☎ 33-3630-0450), Torre Sterling, mezzanine izquierdo, Francisco de Quevedo 117, Sector Juárez

Mérida (☎ 999-927-15-20), Calle 3 No 237, Fraccionamiento Campestre
Oaxaca (☎ 951-518-00-31), Calzada Porfirio Díaz 340, Colonia Reforma

UK (☎ 55-5207-85-00; **w** www.embajadabritanica.com.mx), Río Lerma 71, Colonia Cuauhtémoc; north of the Monumento a la Independencia; open 8.30 am to 3.30 pm Monday to Friday; consular section at rear (☎ 55-5242-8500), Río Usumacinta 30; open 9am to 2pm Monday to Friday; **M** Insurgentes
Consulates: Acapulco (☎ 744-481-17-70), Casa Consular, Centro Internacional Acapulco, La Costera
Cancún (☎ 998-881-01-00), Hotel Royal Sand, Boulevard Kukulcán Km 16.5
Guadalajara (☎ 33-3343-2296), Paseo del Eden 2449-4, Prolongación Colinas de San Javier
Mérida (☎ 999-928-6152, fax 999-928-3962), Calle 53 No 489
Monterrey (☎ 81-8356-5359), Avenida Ricardo Margain Zozaya 240, 2nd floor, Colonia Valle del Campestre, San Pedro Garza García
Tijuana (☎ 664-686-53-20) Boulevard Salinas 1500, Fraccionamiento Aviación Tijuana

USA (☎ 55-5080-2000, **w** www.usembassy-mexico.gov), Paseo de la Reforma 305 at Río Danubio, Colonia Cuauhtémoc; open 8.30am to 5.30pm Monday to Friday; **M** Insurgentes
Consulates: Acapulco (☎ 744-469-05-56), Hotel Acapulco Continental, La Costera 121, Local 14
Cabo San Lucas (☎ 624-143-3566), Plaza Náutica, Office No C4
Cancún (☎ 998-883-02-72), Plaza Caracol II, 3rd floor, Local 320-323, Boulevard Kukulcán Km 8.5
Ciudad Juárez (☎ 656-611-30-00), López Mateos 924 Nte
Guadalajara (☎ 33-3825-2700), Progreso 175
Ixtapa (☎ 755-553-21-00), Plaza Ambiente, Office 9
Matamoros (☎ 868-812-44-02), Calle 1 No 2002
Mazatlán (☎ 669-916-58-89), Hotel Playa Mazatlán, Loaiza 202, Zona Dorada
Mérida (☎ 999-925-50-11, after-hours emergency ☎ 999-947-22-85), Paseo de Montejo 453
Monterrey (☎ 81-8345-2120), Avenida Constitución 411 Pte
Nogales (☎ 631-313-48-20), San José s/n, Fraccionamiento Los Álamos
Nuevo Laredo (☎ 867-714-05-12), Allende 3330, Colonia Jardín (US citizens can call the Laredo, Texas number ☎ 210-727-9661 for after-hours emergency assistance)
Oaxaca (☎ 951-514-30-54), Alcalá 407 (Plaza Santo Domingo), Interior 20
Puerto Vallarta (☎ 322-223-00-69), Zaragoza 160, Colonia Centro
San Miguel de Allende (☎ 415-152-23-57), Hernández Macías 72
Tijuana (☎ 664-681-74-00), Tapachula 96, Colonia Hipódromo

CUSTOMS

Things that visitors are allowed to bring into Mexico duty-free include items for personal use such as clothing; a camera and video camera; up to 12 rolls of film or videocassettes; a cellular phone; a laptop computer; a portable cassette player; medicine for personal use, with prescription in the case of psychotropic drugs; 3L of wine, beer or liquor; 400 cigarettes; and US$300 worth of other goods.

The normal routine when you enter Mexico is to complete a customs declaration form (which lists duty-free allowances), then place it in a machine. If the machine shows a green light, you pass without inspection. If a red light shows, your baggage will be searched.

MONEY
Currency

Mexico's currency is the peso. The peso is divided into 100 centavos. Coins come in denominations of five, 10, 20 and 50 centavos and one, two, five, 10, 20 and 50 pesos, and there are notes of 10, 20, 50, 100, 200 and 500 pesos.

The '$' sign is used to refer to pesos in Mexico. Any prices quoted in US dollars will normally be written 'US$5,' '$5 Dlls' or '5 USD' to avoid misunderstanding.

Coins and notes minted between 1993 and 1995 bear the wording 'nuevos pesos' (new pesos), or the abbreviation 'N$.' They are worth exactly the same as more recent coins and notes which simply say 'pesos' or '$.'

Since the peso's exchange value is sometimes unstable, prices in this book are given in US dollar equivalents.

Exchange Rates

Exchange rates as this book went to press were:

country	unit		N$
Australia	A$1	=	4.77 pesos
Belize	BZ$1	=	4.58 pesos
Canada	C$1	=	5.67 pesos
European Union	€1	=	7.92 pesos
Guatemala	Q1	=	1.15 pesos
Japan	¥10	=	6.80 pesos
New Zealand	NZ$1	=	3.94 pesos
UK	£1	=	12.89 pesos
USA	US$1	=	9.03 pesos

Exchanging Money

The most convenient form of money in Mexico is a major international credit card or debit card. Cards such as Visa, American Express and MasterCard can be used to obtain cash easily from ATMs and are accepted for payment by virtually all airlines, car rental companies and travel agents in Mexico, and by many hotels, restaurants and shops. As a backup it's best also to take some traveler's checks and a little cash.

Traveler's Checks & Cash If you have a credit card or bank card, as a backup you should still take along some major-brand traveler's checks (best denominated in US dollars), and a few cash US dollars. If you don't have a credit or bank card, use US-dollar traveler's checks. American Express is a good brand to have because it's recognized everywhere, which can prevent delays. In Mexico, you can call American Express toll-free at ☎ 800-504-04-00.

You should be able to change Canadian dollars, British pounds and euros, in cash or as checks, in main cities, but it might be time-consuming.

Banks & Casas de Cambio You can exchange money in banks or at *casas de cambio* ('exchange houses,' often single-window kiosks). Banks go through a more time-consuming procedure than casas de cambio and usually have shorter exchange hours (typically 9am to 3pm or 4pm Monday to Friday). Casas de cambio can easily be found in just about every large or medium-size town and in many smaller ones. They're quick and often open evenings or weekends, but some don't accept traveler's checks, which rarely happens in banks.

Exchange rates vary a little from one bank or casa de cambio to another. Different rates are also often posted for *efectivo* (cash) and *documento* (traveler's checks).

If you have trouble finding a place to change money, particularly on a weekend, you can always try a hotel; though the exchange rate won't be the best.

ATMs You can use major credit cards and some bank cards, such as those on the Cirrus and Plus systems, to withdraw cash pesos from ATMs (bank cash machines, which are very common in Mexico) and

over the counter at banks. ATMs are generally the easiest source of cash. Despite the handling fee that may be charged to your account, you win by using ATMs because you get a good exchange rate and avoid the commission you would pay when changing cash or traveler's checks.

Mexican banks call their ATMs by a variety of names – usually something like *caja permanente* or *cajero automático*. Each ATM displays the cards it will accept. If an ATM refuses to give you money, try another one nearby.

If you're worried about an ATM swallowing your card, look for Banorte machines, in which you generally just swipe your card through a slot.

International Transfers Should you need money wired to you in Mexico, an easy and quick, though not cheap, method is the Western Union 'Dinero en Minutos' (Money in Minutes) service. It's offered by the approximately 300 Elektra electronics and domestic goods stores around Mexico (most are open 9am to 9pm daily), by the *telégrafos* (telegraph) offices in many cities, and by some other shops – all are identified by black-and-yellow signs bearing the words 'Western Union' and 'Dinero en Minutos.' Your sender pays the money over at a Western Union branch, along with a fee, and gives the details on who is to receive it and where. When you pick it up, take along photo identification. You can expect the exchange rate used to be well in Western Union's favor. Western Union has offices worldwide; information can be obtained at ☎ 800-12-13-13 in Mexico, ☎ 800-325-6000 in the USA, or ⓦ www.westernunion.com.

Security

Ideally, when you're out and about, carry only what you'll need that day. Leave the rest in the hotel's *caja fuerte* (safe), preferably after counting it in front of the clerk when you hand it in. If there isn't a safe, you have to decide whether it's better to carry your funds with you or try to secretly hide them in your room. Baggage that you can lock up is an advantage here. It's also a good idea to divide your funds into several stashes kept in different places.

To guard against robbery when using ATMs, try to use them during working hours and choose ones that are securely inside a bank building, rather than ones open to the street or enclosed only by glass.

Be wary of attempts at credit card fraud. One method is the cashier swipes your card twice (once for the transaction and once for nefarious purposes). Keep your card in sight at all times; do not let waiters or others take it away. If you sign an older-style receipt with carbon-paper inserts, ask for the inserts and destroy them after use.

Costs

In most of Mexico a single budget traveler can expect to pay US$12 to US$25 a day for the basics of staying in budget accommodations and eating two meals a day in restaurants. (Exception areas include Baja California, the city of Monterrey and the Yucatán Peninsula's Caribbean coast, in all of which rooms can cost up to double what they do elsewhere.) Add in other costs (snacks, drinks, entry to archaeological sites, buses, etc) and you'll spend more like US$20 to US$35 a day. If there are two or more of you sharing rooms, costs per person drop considerably. Double rooms often cost only a few dollars more than singles, and triples or quadruples only a few dollars more than doubles.

In the middle range you can live well in most of Mexico for US$40 to US$70 per person per day. Two people can usually find a clean, modern room with private bath and TV for US$30 to US$45 and have the rest to pay for food, admission fees, transport and incidentals.

At the top of the scale are a few hotels and resorts that charge upwards of US$200 for a room, and restaurants where you can pay US$50 per person, but you can also stay at classy smaller hotels for US$60 to US$90 a double and eat extremely well for US$25 to US$40 per person per day.

These figures do not take account of extra expenses like internal airfares or car rentals, or of any shopping you do in Mexico – which you should certainly budget for!

Tipping & Bargaining

In general, workers in small, cheap restaurants don't expect much in the way of tips, while those in expensive resorts expect you to be lavish in your largesse. Tipping in the resorts frequented by foreigners (such as Acapulco, Cancún, Cozumel) is up to US levels of 15%; elsewhere 10% is usually plenty. If you stay a few days in one place, you should leave up to 10% of your room costs for the people who have kept your room clean (assuming they have). A porter in a mid-range hotel would be happy with US$1 for carrying two bags. Taxi drivers don't generally expect tips unless they provide some special service, but gas station attendants do (US$0.25 to US$0.50).

Hotel room rates are pretty firm, though you can attempt to bargain some prices down, especially in cheaper places and in the off-season, if you are going to stay more than a couple of nights. In markets bargaining is the rule, and you may pay much more than the going rate if you accept the first price quoted. You should also bargain with drivers of unmetered taxis.

Taxes

Mexico's Impuesto de Valor Agregado (Value-Added Tax), abbreviated IVA ('EE-bah'), is levied at 15%. By law the tax must be included in virtually any price quoted to you and should not be added afterward. Signs in shops and notices on restaurant menus often state *'IVA incluido.'* Occasionally they state instead that IVA must be added to the quoted prices.

Impuesto Sobre Hospedaje (ISH, 'ee-ESS-e-AH-che,' the Lodging Tax) is levied on the price of hotel rooms. Each Mexican state sets its own rate, but in most it's 2%.

Some accommodations, especially in the budget range, will not charge you the taxes unless you want a receipt. Generally, though, IVA and ISH are included in quoted prices. In top-end hotels a price may often be given as, say, 'US$100 *más impuestos*' (plus taxes), in which case you must add about 17% to the figure. When in doubt, ask, *'¿Están incluidos los impuestos?'* ('Are taxes included?')

Prices in this book all, to the best of our knowledge, include IVA and ISH, where payable.

Domestic and international airline tickets are subject to departure taxes, see the Getting There & Away and Getting Around chapters. For details of the tourist fee of around US$20, payable by all tourists, see Visas & Documents earlier in this chapter.

POST & COMMUNICATIONS
Postal Rates

An airmail letter or postcard weighing up to 20g costs US$0.50 to the US or Canada, US$0.60 to Europe and US$0.70 to Australasia. Items weighing between 20g and 50g cost US$0.80, US$1 and US$1.25 respectively.

Sending Mail

Almost every town in Mexico has an *oficina de correos* (post office) where you can buy stamps and send or receive mail. They're usually open Saturday mornings as well as long hours Monday to Friday.

Delivery times are elastic, and packages in particular sometimes go missing. If you're sending something by airmail, clearly mark it 'Vía Aérea.' Registered *(registrado)* service helps ensure delivery and costs just US$0.90 extra for international mail. An airmail letter from Mexico to the USA or Canada can take four to 14 days to arrive (but don't be surprised if it takes longer). Mail to Europe may take between one and three weeks, to Australasia a month or more.

If you're sending a package internationally from Mexico, be prepared to open it for customs inspection at the post office; take packing materials with you, or don't seal it until you get there.

The Mexpost express mail service, available at some post offices, supposedly takes four to five working days to anywhere in the world; it costs US$15.50 to send up to 500g to the US or Canada, or US$23 to Europe.

For assured and speedy delivery, you can use one of the more expensive international courier services, such as UPS (☎ 800-902-92-00, Ⓦ www.ups.com), Federal Express (☎ 800-900-11-00, Ⓦ www.fedex.com), DHL (☎ 55-5345-7000, Ⓦ www.dhl.com) or Mexico's Estafeta (☎ 55-5249-9100, Ⓦ www.estafeta.com.mx). Packages up to 500g cost about US$23 to the US or Canada or US$33 to Europe.

Receiving Mail

You can receive letters and packages care of a post office if they're addressed as follows: Have lista de correos mail addressed this way:

Albert JONES (last name in capitals)
Lista de Correos
Oficina Central de Correos
México 06002 DF
MEXICO

When the letter reaches the post office, the name of the addressee is placed on an alphabetical list, which is updated daily. If you can, check the list yourself – it's often pinned on the wall – because the item may be listed under your first name instead of your last. To claim your mail, present your passport or other identification. There's no charge, but many post offices only hold 'Lista' mail for 10 days before returning it to the sender. If you think you're going to pick mail up more than 10 days after it has arrived, have it sent to:

Jane SMITH (last name in capitals)
Poste Restante
Correo Central
Acapulco
Guerrero 00000 (post code)
MEXICO

Poste restante may hold mail for up to a month, but there is no posted list of what has been received. Again, there's no charge for collection.

If you have an American Express card or American Express traveler's checks, you can have mail sent to you c/o any of the 50-plus American Express offices in Mexico (the Mexico City office holds mail for about a month before returning it to the sender).

Inbound mail usually takes as long to arrive as outbound mail does, and may go missing, just like outbound mail.

Telephone

Local calls are cheap. International calls can be expensive, but needn't be if you call from the right place at the right time.

Internet telephony (calls carried through an Internet server line instead of a phone line) has appeared at Internet cafés in Mexico City and will very likely spread around the country. It's a lot cheaper than regular phone calls, at around US$0.35 per minute to the USA or US$0.50 per minute to Canada or Europe.

Internet telephony aside, there are three main types of places where you can make a call from. Generally, the cheapest are public pay phones. Following in affordability are call stations, *casetas de teléfono* or *casetas telefónicas*, in a shop or restaurant, where an on-the-spot operator connects the call for you. The third option is to call from your hotel, but hotels can, and do, charge what they like for this service. It's nearly always cheaper to go elsewhere.

Public Pay Phones These are common in towns and cities: you'll usually find some at airports, bus stations and around the main square. Easily the most common, and most reliable on costs, are those marked with the name of the country's biggest phone company, Telmex. To use a Telmex pay phone you need a *tarjeta telefónica* or *tarjeta Ladatel* (phone card). These come in denominations of 30, 50 or 100 pesos (about US$3.50, US$5.50 and US$11) and they are sold at many kiosks and shops – look for the blue-and-yellow signs reading *'De venta aquí Ladatel.'*

Beware the misleadingly named 'Savings' service advertised on many Telmex phones. Available for collect calls, credit-card calls and calls with some US calling cards, this service is actually a lot more expensive than a normal call; for example costs can be US$3.50 a minute to the USA, Canada or Europe.

Especially in parts of Mexico frequented by US tourists, you may notice a variety of other pay phones that advertise that they accept credit cards or that you can make easy collect calls to the USA on them. While some of these phones may be fair value, there are others on which very high rates (for example US$30 for three minutes) are charged. We suggest being very sure about what you'll pay before making a call on a non-Telmex phone.

Casetas de Teléfono Casetas cost almost the same as Telmex pay phones, and you don't need a phone card to use them, and they eliminate street noise. Many offer the same off-peak discounts as pay phones and private phones. Casetas usually have a telephone symbol outside, or signs saying *'teléfono,'* 'Lada' or 'Larga Distancia.' In Baja California they are known as *cabinas*.

Prefixes & Codes When dialing a call in Mexico, you need to know what *prefijo* (prefix) and *claves* (country or area codes) to dial before the number.

If you're calling a number in the town or city you're in, simply dial the local number (eight digits in Mexico City, Guadalajara and Monterrey, seven digits everywhere else). So if you're in Mexico City and you want to call the Mexico City number ☎ 5876-5432, just dial ☎ 5876-5432.

To call another town or city in Mexico, dial the long-distance prefix ☎ 01, followed by the area code (two digits for Mexico City, Guadalajara and Monterrey; three digits for everywhere else) and then the local number. For example, to call from Mexico City to the Oaxaca number ☎ 517-65-43, dial ☎ 01, then the Oaxaca area code ☎ 951, then ☎ 517-65-43. You'll find area codes listed immediately underneath city and town headings in this book. If calling from one town to another that has the same area code, you still have to dial 01 and the area code.

For international calls, dial the international prefix ☎ 00, followed by the country code, area code and local number. For example, to call the New York City number ☎ 987-6543 from Mexico, dial ☎ 00, then the US country code ☎ 1, then the New York City area code ☎ 212, then ☎ 987-6543.

Mexicans may present their phone numbers and area codes in all sorts of bizarre arrangements of digits (a consequence of having all their numbers changed once, and all their area codes twice, in the three years from 1999-2001); but if you just remember that the area code and the local number always total 10 digits, you shouldn't go far wrong.

To call a number in Mexico from another country, dial your international access code, then the Mexico country code (☎ 52), then the area code and number.

Toll-Free & Operator Numbers Mexican toll-free numbers – all ☎ 800 followed by seven digits – always require the ☎ 01 prefix. You can call them from Telmex pay phones without inserting a telephone card.

International Country Codes

Australia ☎ 61	Ireland ☎ 353
Belize ☎ 501	Italy ☎ 39
Canada ☎ 1	Mexico ☎ 52
Cuba ☎ 53	New Zealand ☎ 64
France ☎ 33	Spain ☎ 34
Germany ☎ 49	UK ☎ 44
Guatemala ☎ 502	USA ☎ 1

Most US and Canadian toll-free numbers are ☎ 800 or 888 followed by seven digits. Some of these can be reached from Mexico (dial ☎ 00-1 before the 800), but you may have to pay a charge for the call.

For a Mexican domestic operator, call ☎ 020; for an international operator, call ☎ 090. For Mexican directory information, call ☎ 040.

Costs Costs per minute from a Telmex pay phone or typical telephone caseta are approximately US$0.05 for local calls, US$0.50 for calls to other places in Mexico or to cellular (mobile) phones, US$1 to the USA, Canada or Central America, and US$2.25 to the rest of the world. Caseta charges are similar except that you'll more likely pay US$0.25 a minute for local calls.

Telmex off-peak discounts include 50% off domestic long-distance calls from 8pm to 8am Monday to Saturday, and all day Sunday; 33% off calls to the USA or Canada from 7pm to 7am Monday to Friday, all day Saturday, and midnight to 5pm Sunday; and 33% off calls to Europe from 6pm to 6am Monday to Friday and all day Saturday and Sunday.

Collect Calls A *llamada por cobrar* (collect call) can cost the receiving party much more than if *they* call *you*, so you may prefer to pay for a quick call to the other party to ask them to call you back.

If you do need to make a collect call, you can do so from pay phones without a card. Call an operator on ☎ 020 for domestic calls, or ☎ 090 for international calls, or use a Home Country Direct service (see later). Mexican international operators can usually speak English.

Some telephone casetas and hotels will make collect calls for you, but they usually charge for the service. We've also come across casetas and shops that proudly announce that you can place collect calls for free, but then charge exorbitant rates to the receiving party. So take care.

Home Country Direct service, by which you make an international collect call via an operator in the country you're calling, is available to many countries. You can make these calls from pay phones without any card. Mexican international operators may know access numbers for some countries,

but it's best to get information from your phone company before you leave for Mexico. The Mexican term for Home Country Direct is *País Directo*.

Telephone Cards Lonely Planet's eKno global communication service provides low-cost international calls; for local calls you're usually better off with a local phone card. The eKno service also offers free messaging services, email, travel information and an online travel vault, where you can securely store all your important documents. You can join online at www.ekno.lonelyplanet .com, where you will find the local-access numbers for the 24-hour customer-service center. Once you have joined, always check the eKno Web site for the latest access numbers for each country and updates on new features.

Many North American calling cards can be used for calls from Mexico to the USA or Canada by dialing special access numbers (ask the phone company about these before you leave for Mexico).

Warning: If you get an operator who asks for your Visa or MasterCard number instead of your calling card number, or says the service is unavailable, hang up. There have been scams in which calls are rerouted to super-expensive credit-card phone services.

Cellular Phones When calling to Mexican cellular (mobile) phones whose numbers start with 044, you must always dial the area code after the 044, even if it is a local call.

Few cellular phones from the US, Canada, Europe or Australasia will work in Mexico; and if they do, they're likely to be expensive (contact your service provider for coverage information, or visit Ⓦ www.gsm coverage.co.uk). But you can rent Mexican cell phones in the international area at Mexico City airport and at some other large airports.

At the time of writing, Telcel Digital (Ⓦ www.telcel.com) provided spotty TDMA (Time Division Multiple Access) in Mexico, but no GSM (Global System for Mobile Communications) coverage. Development of more standard GSM coverage was on the horizon, however.

Coverage by the very expensive Globalstar satellite-based telephony (Ⓦ www.buy phone.com/satellite) includes the USA,

Canada and Mexico. At the time of writing Globalstar USA customers could make outbound calls from Mexico, but receiving incoming calls was not yet possible.

Sanborns and some other department stores in Mexico sell a range of cell phones. At the time of writing a Samsung N275, with good national and international coverage and clear connections, cost US$243 including US$34 of air time, while a Telcel Amigo Kit P8190 cost US$276 including US$56 of air time. Ericsson phones were cheaper but you would need to get a new number if you took one to the US. Before buying a phone, ascertain which parts of Mexico it will have coverage in. Cards for additional air time in some local areas are sold at newsstands and mini-marts in denominations of 100, 200 and 400 pesos (approximately US$11, US$22 and US$44, respectively).

Most Mexican cell phones work on an *'el que llama paga'* (caller pays) basis. Nextel is one of the few companies where you pay for calls received; but the charge on all calls is lower, so it's a better deal for those who mostly make calls rather than receiving.

Fax

Public fax service is offered in many Mexican towns by the public *telégrafos* (telegraph) office or offices of the companies Telecomm and Computel. Also look for *'Fax'* or *'Fax Público'* signs on shops, businesses and telephone casetas, and in bus stations and airports. Typically you will pay around US$1 to US$2 a page to the US or Canada.

Email & Internet Access

An easy way of accessing the Internet and email while you're on the road is through cybercafes and other public access points. You'll find these in just about every town and city in Mexico, and many are listed in this book. Costs are usually US$1 to US$2 an hour. The more travelers and students in a city, the cheaper the Internet access. If you have a web-based email account, you can access it anywhere in the world from any Internet-connected computer. Several such accounts are available free through eKno (see Telephone Cards earlier), Yahoo! (W www.yahoo.com) or Hotmail (W www.hotmail.com).

Traveling with a portable computer is also a great way to stay in touch with the rest of the world, but it has potential problems. The power supply voltage abroad may vary from that at home (see Electricity, later in this chapter), risking damage to your equipment. The best investment is a universal AC adaptor for your appliance, which will enable you to plug it in anywhere without frying the innards. You'll also need a plug adapter for each country you visit – often it's easiest to buy these before you leave home.

Your PC-card modem may or may not work outside your home country, and you won't know for sure until you try. The safest option is to buy a reputable 'global' modem before leaving home, or buy a local PC-card modem if you're spending an extended time in one country. Telephone sockets in Mexico may differ from those at home, so ensure that you have at least a US RJ-11 telephone adapter that works with your modem. You can almost always find an adapter that will convert from RJ-11 to the local variety. For more information on traveling with a portable computer, see W www.teleadapt.com or W www.warrior.com.

Some Mexican hotel rooms have direct-dial phones and phone sockets that allow you to unplug the phone and insert a phone jack that runs directly to your computer. In others you're confronted with switchboard phone systems and/or room phones with a cord running directly into the wall, both of which make it impossible to go online from your room. In such cases reception will often let you borrow a line for a couple of minutes.

It's also possible to plug in your computer at some telephone casetas.

Major global Internet service providers (ISP) such as AOL (W www.aol.com) and CompuServe (W www.compuserve.com) have dial-in nodes throughout Mexico. It's best to download a list of the dial-in numbers before you leave home. If you access an email account through a smaller ISP or your office or school network, and you want to use it on the road, your best option is to rely on cybercafes or other public Internet access points; and you'll need three pieces of information, your incoming (POP or IMAP) mail server name, your account name and your password. Your ISP or network supervisor will be able to give you these.

INTERNET RESOURCES

The World Wide Web is a rich resource for travelers. You can research your trip, hunt down bargain airfares, book hotels, check weather conditions or chat with locals and other travelers about the best places to visit (or avoid!).

Lonely Planet

There are few better places to start your Web explorations than the Lonely Planet Web site (W www.lonelyplanet.com). Here you'll find succinct summaries on traveling to most places on earth, postcards from other travelers, and the Thorn Tree bulletin board where you can ask questions before you go or dispense advice when you get back. You can also find travel news, updates of our most popular guidebooks, and the subway section, which links you to the most useful travel resources elsewhere on the Web.

Mexico-Specific Sites

Mexico Connect (W www.mexconnect.com) and Mexico Online (W www.mexonline .com) both combine news, message/chat centers and a huge variety of other content and links. The friendly and colorful W www.mexicanwave.com is 'Europe's gateway to Mexico,' with a growing fund of travel, culture, food and business-related material. A quirky mix of ecology, community projects, travel, volunteer work opportunities and more can be found at W www.ecoturismolatino.com.

Eco Travels in Latin America (W www .planeta.com) is a marvelous resource for anyone interested in Mexican travel or the Mexican environment. You'll find articles, lists and links covering birds, butterflies, books, language schools, protected areas, rugby and a whole lot more on this constantly growing site, hosted by a dedicated Mexico-based American, Ron Mader.

The Mexico site at the University of Texas, W http://lanic.utexas.edu/la/mexico, has the best broad collection of Mexico links we know.

Web sites focusing on specific areas or aspects of Mexico are covered in specific sections of this book.

BOOKS

The Mexican-published titles mentioned here are widely available, but it's wise to obtain other books before going to Mexico. You can buy books in English in most major centers in Mexico, but only Mexico City, Oaxaca and Guadalajara have an extensive choice. A few libraries in places such as Mexico City, San Miguel de Allende, Oaxaca and San Cristóbal de Las Casas have good collections of English-language books on Mexico.

Most books are published in different editions by different publishers in different countries. As a result, a book might be a hardcover rarity in one country while it's readily available in paperback in another. Fortunately, bookshops and libraries search by title or author, so your local bookshop or library is the best place to advise you on the availability of the following recommendations.

Lonely Planet

Lonely Planet has several guides covering specific parts of Mexico in detail: *Mexico City, Yucatán, Baja California* and *San Diego & Tijuana. Belize, Guatemala & Yucatán* combines coverage of southeast Mexico and the two neighboring countries – the whole Mayan cultural area – in one volume.

Handy companions for anyone traveling in Mexico are Lonely Planet's *Healthy Travel Central & South America* and *Latin American Spanish phrasebook*. The latter contains practical, up-to-date words and expressions in Latin American Spanish.

Lonely Planet's *Read This First: Central & South America* offers more tips on preparing for a trip to Mexico.

Lonely Planet's *World Food Mexico* is an intimate, full-color guide to exploring Mexico and its cuisine. This book covers every food or drink situation the traveler could encounter and plots the evolution of Mexican cuisine. Its language section includes a definitive culinary dictionary and useful phrases.

Diving & Snorkeling Baja California and *Diving & Snorkeling Cozumel* are good guides for divers.

Green Dreams: Travels in Central America by Stephen Benz, in the Lonely Planet Journeys series, is a wry tale of 'green' tourism in southern Mexico and Central America.

Guidebooks

The People's Guide to Mexico by Carl Franz (motto: 'Wherever you go…there you are') has for a quarter of a century been an invaluable, amusing resource for anyone on an extended trip. It's a great all-round introduction to Mexico, written from plenty of personal experience.

A good resource if you're keen to experience Mexico's natural wonders is Ron Mader's *Mexico – Adventures in Nature*, with practical information on visiting some 60 sites of natural interest all around Mexico. *Backpacking in Mexico* by Tim Burford gives detailed hiking directions for about a dozen walks in diverse regions and points the reader to many more areas of archaeological interest. *Mexico's Volcanoes* by RJ Secor covers routes up the main peaks of Mexico's central volcanic belt.

Blue Guide Mexico by John Collis and David M Jones is a comprehensive, authoritative guide to the country's archaeology, architecture and art.

Several series of straightforward guides to single sites or regions are fairly widely available in Mexico. The INAH-SALVAT *Official Guide* booklets on museums and archaeological sites cost around US$5 to US$6. Also useful, and a little cheaper, is the *Easy Guide* series by Richard Bloomgarden.

Travel & Living in Mexico

Incidents of Travel in Central America, Chiapas & Yucatan and *Incidents of Travel in Yucatan* by John L Stephens are fascinating accounts of adventure and discovery by a 19th-century American, which provided the outside world's first serious look at many Mayan archaeological sites.

Graham Greene's *Lawless Roads* traces his wanderings down eastern Mexico to Chiapas in the 1930s, a time of conflict between Catholics and the atheistic state. Greene found Mexican food to be 'all a hideous red and yellow, green and brown.'

Time Among the Maya by Ronald Wright is a search for the Mayan concept of time, yielding an insightful understanding of the peoples and cultures, ancient and modern, of southeast Mexico, Belize and Guatemala. The book also confronts the subject of violence against the Mayan peoples.

Christopher Shaw's *Sacred Monkey River* (2000) explores, by means of a series of canoe trips, the basin of the remote Río Usumacinta, which divides Mexico from Guatemala; the river is a cradle both of

ancient Mayan civilization and modern Zapatista revolution, and home to much of the remaining tropical jungles of Mexico and Guatemala. The book is a great read.

In *Sliced Iguana: Travels in Unknown Mexico* (2001), young travel writer Isabella Tree takes peyote with the Huicholes and meets the matriarchs of Juchitán. It's a warm and perceptive account of Mexico and its indigenous cultures, old and new. Another recently successful book, *On Mexican Time* by Tony Cohan, is a gringo's account of making a new life in San Miguel de Allende, among a cast of assorted Mexicans and other expats.

Anthropologist Pierre L Van Den Berghe takes an interesting look at travelers looking at Mexicans in *The Quest for the Other: Ethnic Tourism in San Cristobal, Mexico* – food for thought.

History & Society

General Lesley Byrd Simpson's *Many Mexicos* is a classic collection of short essays ranging from pre-Hispanic times to the present. *Sons of the Shaking Earth* by Eric Wolf is a classic, very readable 1960s introduction to Mexican history and Mesoamerican ethnology. Michael C Meyer & William L Sherman's *The Course of Mexican History* is one of the best general accounts of Mexican history and society.

Ancient Mexico Two books by Michael D Coe – *The Maya* and *Mexico* – give a learned but concise and well-illustrated picture of all ancient Mexico's great cultures. Both have gone through several editions. Coe's *Breaking the Maya Code* tells the fascinating story of the decipherment of Mayan writing, and his *Reading the Maya Glyphs* will help you actually to read ancient inscriptions.

Nigel Davies' *Ancient Kingdoms of Mexico* is a succinct but scholarly study of the Olmec, Teotihuacán, Toltec and Aztec civilizations. Diagrams, illustrations, plans and maps complement the text.

Jacques Soustelle's *Daily Life of the Aztecs* (1962) is a classic on its subject. Also good is *The Aztecs* by Richard F Townsend. *The Cities of Ancient Mexico* by Jeremy A Sabloff has fascinating descriptions of Mexico's ancient cities and what it was like to live in them.

Maya World Archaeology by Victor Vera Castillo is an attractive little introduction to the Maya and to 75 sites in five countries; it is well illustrated but not too big to carry with you.

Spanish Conquest William Henry Prescott's mammoth *History of the Conquest of Mexico* (1843) remains well regarded, even though its author never went to Mexico. Not until 1993 did the 20th century produce an equivalent tome: Hugh Thomas' *Conquest: Montezuma, Cortes & The Fall of Old Mexico* (called *The Conquest of Mexico* in Britain). *History of the Conquest of New Spain*, by Bernal Díaz del Castillo, is an eye-witness account of the Spanish arrival by one of Cortés' lieutenants.

Modern Mexico Alan Riding's *Distant Neighbors*, published in the 1980s, remains a good introduction to Mexico and its love-hate relationship with the US. (In Britain it's called *Mexico, Inside the Volcano*.) *The Mexicans* by Patrick Oster is a sort of microcosmic counterpart to Riding's book, focusing on the lives of 20 individual Mexicans.

Living Maya by Walter F Morris Jr and Jeffrey J Foxx captures in words and pictures the lives of the modern Maya of southeast Mexico and Guatemala.

Art, Architecture & Crafts
The Art of Mesoamerica by Mary Ellen Miller, in the Thames & Hudson World of Art series, is a good survey of pre-Hispanic art and architecture. On colonial architecture, the most important book is George Kubler's *Mexican Architecture of the Sixteenth Century* (1948).

Good books on Mexico's 20th-century artists include Diego Rivera's autobiography *My Art, My Life*; Patrick Marnham's 1998 biography of Rivera, *Dreaming with his Eyes Open*; *The Fabulous Life of Diego Rivera* by BD Wolfe; *Frida: A Biography of Frida Kahlo* by Hayden Herrera; *Frida Kahlo* by Malka Drucker; and *The Mexican Muralists* by Alma M Reed.

Mexico City bookstores are full of beautifully illustrated coffee-table books on Mexican arts, crafts, archaeology and anthropology. One such is *Mask Arts of Mexico* by Ruth D Lechuga and Chloe Sayer a finely illustrated work by two

experts in the field. Sayer has also written the fascinating *Arts & Crafts of Mexico*, tracing the evolution of crafts from pre-Hispanic times to the present, with dozens of beautiful photos.

Flora, Fauna & Environment
Joel Simon's *Endangered Mexico: An Environment on the Edge* examines Mexico's varied environmental crises, from dumping on the northern border to the destruction of the Lacandón Jungle, with the benefit of a lot of excellent first-hand journalistic research; it is a compelling and frightening read. *Defending the Land of the Jaguar* by Lane Simonian is the absorbing story of Mexico's long, if weak, tradition of conservation.

Dedicated birders should seek out the Spanish-language *Aves de México* by Roger Tory Peterson and Edward L Chalif. The English-language version of this book, *A Field Guide to Mexican Birds*, omits illustrations of birds that also appear in Peterson's guides to US birds (but still has over 700 color paintings). Alternatives are *A Field Guide to the Birds of Mexico & Adjacent Areas* by Ernest Preston Edwards, with color drawings of 850 species, and *A Guide to the Birds of Mexico & Northern Central America* by Steve NG Howell and Sophie Webb. Howell's *A Bird-Finding Guide to Mexico* is a guide to where the birds are and covers over 100 sites.

Roland H Wauer's *Naturalist's Mexico* (1992) describes visits to dozens of areas of natural interest all around Mexico based on three decades of annual trips. Wauer has also penned *Birder's Mexico*.

Tropical Mexico: The Ecotravellers' Wildlife Guide by Les Beletsky is a field guide to wildlife from Oaxaca to the Yucatán Peninsula, with color illustrations of more than 500 creatures. See Guidebooks, earlier, for further books likely to appeal to nature lovers.

Fiction
Many foreign novelists have been inspired by Mexico. *The Power and the Glory* by Graham Greene dramatizes the state-church conflict that followed the Mexican Revolution. *Under the Volcano* (1938) by British dipsomaniac Malcolm Lowry follows a British diplomat who drinks himself to death on the Day of the Dead in a fictionalized

Cuernavaca. It delves into the Mexican psyche, as well as Lowry's own, at a time of deep conflict. DH Lawrence's *Mornings in Mexico* is a readable collection of short stories set in both Mexico and New Mexico.

B Traven is best known as the author of that classic 1935 adventure story of gold and greed in northwest Mexico, *The Treasure of the Sierra Madre* (made into an equally classic John Huston/Humphrey Bogart film in 1948). Traven wrote many other novels set in Mexico, chiefly the six of the Jungle series – among them *The Rebellion of the Hanged*, *General from the Jungle* and *Trozas* – focusing on oppression in Chiapas in the years before the Mexican Revolution. The identity of Traven himself is one of literature's big mysteries.

Carlos Castaneda's *Don Juan* series, which reached serious cult status in the 1970s, tells of a North American's experiences with a peyote guru somewhere in northwestern Mexico.

The 1990s brought some fine new English-language novels set in Mexico. Cormac McCarthy's marvelous *All the Pretty Horses* is the laconic, tense, poetic tale of three young latter-day cowboys riding south of the border. *The Crossing* and *Cities of the Plain* completed his Border Trilogy. James Maw's exciting *Year of the Jaguar* catches the feel of Mexican travel superbly taking its youthful English protagonist from the US border to Chiapas, in search of the father he has never met.

Travel Advisory: Stories of Mexico by David Lida (2000) is a fine debut short-story collection that disturbingly, at times humorously, evokes the dark underside of Mexican life – and its odd interactions with Americans.

For information on Mexican literature, see the Arts section in the Facts about Mexico chapter.

Books Published in Mexico

Mexican publisher Minutiae Mexicana produces a range of interesting booklets, including *A Guide to Mexican Witchcraft, A Guide to Mexican Mammals & Reptiles, The Maya World, A Guide to Mexican Ceramics* and even *A Guide to Tequila, Mezcal & Pulque*. They're widely available at around US$5 each. A similar Mexican-produced paperback series with many titles in English is Panorama.

NEWSPAPERS & MAGAZINES

English Language

The long-established English-language daily paper *The News* is published in Mexico City and distributed throughout Mexico. It covers main items of Mexican and foreign news, has long stock exchange listings and occasional interesting Mexico features, and will keep you in touch with Mexican as well as foreign sports. Find it online at **W** www.thenewsmexico.com.

Most cities that attract long-stay English-speakers – San Miguel de Allende, Guadalajara, Oaxaca, Puerto Vallarta and Puerto Escondido, for example – have small English-language newspapers, magazines or newsletters.

You can find US papers and magazines, and sometimes Canadian and European ones, a day or more old, on sale in the major cities and tourist towns.

Spanish Language

Mexico has a thriving local press, as well as national newspapers such as *Crónica*, *Reforma*, *Excelsior*, *El Universal* and *Uno más Uno*. In theory the press is free. In practice it's subject to pressure from businesses, politicians and drug barons. *La Jornada* is an outstanding national daily with a non-establishment viewpoint; it covers a lot of stories other papers don't.

Arqueología Mexicana (Mexican Archaeology) magazine is beautifully illustrated and full of fascinating features. *México Desconocido* (Unknown Mexico) is another colorful monthly magazine, with intelligent coverage of many interesting, little known places to visit. Both magazines are sold at newsstands and you can often find back numbers or special issues of both magazines relating to sites or areas you are visiting.

You can access about 300 Mexican newspapers and magazines on the Internet at the excellent **W** www.zonalatina.com.

RADIO & TV

Mexico has around 1000 AM and FM radio stations, most of them privately run (many by Televisa). They offer a variety of music, often that of the region. In the evening you may be able to pick up US stations on the AM (medium wave) band. Visit **W** www.zonalatina.com if you want to learn heaps more about Mexican TV and radio.

Mexican TV is dominated by Televisa, the biggest TV company in the Spanish-speaking world, which runs four of the six main national channels: channels 2 ('El Canal de las Estrellas'), 4, 5 and 9. Its rival, TV Azteca, has two main channels: Azteca Siete (7) and Azteca Trece (13). Mexican airtime is devoted mainly to ads, low-budget *telenovelas* (soaps), soccer, game/chat/variety shows, movies and comedy. Nudity, graphic violence and offensive language are pretty much kept off the screen. Better than the commercial channels, but not available everywhere, are two cultural channels: Once TV (Eleven TV), run by Mexico City's Instituto Politécnico Nacional, and Canal 22, run by Conaculta, the National Culture & Arts Council.

Cable and satellite TV are widespread, and you'll find at least a few channels in many mid-range and top-end hotel rooms, often including MTV, CNN in English, and Fox or ESPN sports channels.

VIDEO SYSTEMS

Videotapes on sale in Mexico (like the rest of the Americas and Japan) nearly all use the NTSC image registration system. This is incompatible with the PAL system common to most of Western Europe and Australia and the SECAM system used in France.

PHOTOGRAPHY & VIDEO
Film & Equipment

Camera and film processing shops, pharmacies and hotels all sell film. Most types of film (with the general exception of Kodachrome slide film) are available in larger cities and resorts. A 36-exposure 100-ASA print film generally costs US$6 to US$7 to buy and about the same to process. Film on sale at lower prices may be outdated. If the date on the box is obscured by a price sticker, look under the sticker. Avoid film from sun-exposed shop windows.

If your camera breaks down, you'll be able to find a repair shop in most sizable towns, and prices will be agreeably low.

Technical Tips

Mexico is a photographer's paradise. You'll get better results if you take pictures in the morning or afternoon rather than at midday, when the bright sun bleaches out colors and contrast. Wide-angle and zoom lenses are useful, and it helps to have a polarizing filter to cut down the glare from reflections of sunlight on the ocean.

Photographing People

Be sensitive about photographing people; if in doubt, ask first. Indigenous people in particular can be reluctant to be photographed. It also isn't a good idea to photograph soldiers.

TIME

If you think time doesn't exist in Mexico, you're wrong. The politicians are in a tangle about it, and the odds are it'll catch *you* napping before your trip's over.

Daylight Saving

Daylight saving was introduced by President Zedillo in 1996, on the theory that it would cut energy costs and help Mexican companies coordinate with businesses in the USA. Initially it ran from the first Sunday in April to the last Sunday in October. Many Mexicans however grew very upset about disruption to their time-honored seasonal routines and their biological clocks, and in 2001 President Fox tried to appease them by shortening the daylight saving period. Daylight saving was thenceforth to run from the first Sunday in May to the last Sunday in September. But Mexico City mayor Andrés Manuel López Obrador, sensing a chance to score votes, challenged Fox's decree as unconstitutional. His arcane argument was that the annual switchovers to and from daylight saving would produce days that were not 24 hours long – contravening Congress' right to determine Mexico's system of weights and measures. In September 2001 Mexico's Supreme Court ruled in López Obrador's favor, meaning that Fox would have to get Congress to legislate the new timetable into existence. If it didn't, Mexico City would have the right to ignore daylight saving. At press time the outcome was still being awaited; when you get to Mexico City you'll have to ask half a dozen people to get an estimation of what time it is.

Meanwhile the northwestern Mexican state of Sonora had been quietly ignoring daylight saving for a few years already (just like its US neighbor Arizona), and Baja California (Norte) still maintained daylight saving from the first Sunday in April to the last Sunday in October. Furthermore, a few remote rural zones, such as the Sierra Norte of Oaxaca and the Marqués de Comillas area of eastern Chiapas, have ignored daylight saving all along (to the perdition of bus schedules from nearby towns such as Oaxaca and Palenque).

Mexicans refer to daylight saving variously as *horario de verano* (summer time), *horario de Zedillo* or *horario de Fox.*

Time Zones
Most of Mexico is on Hora del Centro, the same as US Central Time (that's GMT minus six hours in winter, and GMT minus five hours during daylight saving). Five northern and western states, Chihuahua, Nayarit, Sinaloa, Sonora and Baja California Sur, are on Hora de las Montañas, the same as US Mountain Time or GMT minus seven hours in winter, GMT minus six hours during daylight saving (except of course that Sonora ignores daylight saving, so is GMT minus seven hours all year).

Another state, Durango, has been talking about switching from Central to Mountain Time as from the start of daylight saving in 2002. Baja California (Norte) observes Hora del Pacífico, the same as US Pacific Time or GMT minus eight hours in winter, GMT minus seven hours during daylight saving.

ELECTRICITY
Electrical current in Mexico is the same as in the USA and Canada: 110V, 60 Hz. Though most plugs and sockets are the same as in the USA, Mexico actually has three different types of electrical sockets: older ones with two equally sized flat slots, newer ones with two flat slots of differing sizes, and a few with a round hole for a grounding (earth) pin. If your plug doesn't fit the Mexican socket, the best thing to do is get an adapter or change the plug. Mexican electronics stores have a variety of adapters and extensions that should solve the problem.

WEIGHTS & MEASURES
Mexico uses the metric system. For conversion between metric and US or Imperial measures, see the table at the back of this book.

LAUNDRY
Sizable Mexican towns have *lavanderías* (laundries) where you can take in a load of washing and have it done for you the same or next day. A 3kg load costs around US$5. Only at a few laundries can you do your own washing to reduce the cost.

TOILETS
Public toilets are rare, so take advantage of facilities in places such as hotels, restaurants, bus stations and museums. If there's a bin beside the toilet, put paper, etc, in it because the drains can't cope otherwise.

HEALTH
Travel health depends on your predeparture preparations, your daily health care while traveling and how you handle medical problems that develop. While the potential dangers can seem quite frightening, in reality few travelers experience anything more than upset stomachs.

Predeparture Planning
Immunizations Plan ahead for vaccinations: some of them require more than one injection, while some should not be given together. You should seek medical advice at least six weeks before travel.

Discuss your requirements with your doctor (there is often a greater risk of disease with children and with women during pregnancy), but vaccinations you should consider for this trip include the following (for more details about the diseases themselves, see the individual disease entries later in this section). Carry proof of your vaccinations, especially yellow fever, as this is needed for travelers arriving in Mexico from infected countries.

Diphtheria & Tetanus Vaccinations for these two diseases are usually combined and are recommended for everyone. After an initial course of three injections (usually given in childhood), boosters are necessary every 10 years.

Polio Everyone should keep up to date with this vaccination, which is given in childhood. A booster every 10 years maintains immunity.

Hepatitis A Hepatitis A vaccine (eg Avaxim, Havrix 1440 or VAQTA) provides long-term immunity (possibly more than 10 years) after an initial injection and a booster at six to 12 months.

Alternatively, an injection of gamma globulin can provide short-term protection against hepatitis A (two to six months, depending on the dose given). It is not a vaccine, but it is a ready-made antibody collected from blood donations. It is

Medical Kit Check List

Here is a list of items you should consider including in your medical kit – consult your pharmacist for brands available in your country.

❑ **Aspirin or paracetamol** (acetaminophen in the USA) – for pain or fever

❑ **Antihistamine** – for allergies, (hay fever); to ease the itch from insect bites or stings; and to prevent motion sickness

❑ **Cold and flu tablets, throat lozenges and nasal decongestant**

❑ **Multivitamins** – consider for long trips, when dietary vitamin intake may be somewhat inadequate

❑ **Antibiotics** – consider including these if you're traveling well off the beaten track; see your doctor, as they must be prescribed, and carry the prescription with you

❑ **Loperamide or diphenoxylate** –'blockers' for diarrhea

❑ **Prochlorperazine or metaclopramide** – for nausea and vomiting

❑ **Rehydration mixture** – to prevent dehydration, which may occur, for example, during bouts of diarrhea; particularly important when traveling with children

❑ **Insect repellent, sunscreen, lip balm and eye drops**

❑ **Calamine lotion, sting relief spray or aloe vera** – to ease irritation from sunburn and insect bites or stings

❑ **Antifungal cream or powder** – for fungal skin infections and thrush

❑ **Antiseptic (such as povidone-iodine)** – for cuts and grazes

❑ **Bandages, Band-Aids (plasters) and other wound dressings**

❑ **Water purification tablets or iodine**

❑ **Scissors, tweezers and a thermometer** – note that mercury thermometers are prohibited by airlines

❑ **Sterile kit (sealed medical kit containing syringes and needles** – in case you need injections in an area with medical hygiene problems (most likely in remote, rural areas); discuss with your doctor

reasonably effective and, unlike the vaccine, it is protective immediately, but because it is a blood product, there are current concerns about its long-term safety.

Hepatitis A vaccine is also available in a combined form, Twinrix, with hepatitis B vaccine. Three injections over a six-month period are required, the first two providing substantial protection against hepatitis A.

Hepatitis B Travelers who should consider vaccination against hepatitis B include those on a long trip and those visiting developing countries (like Mexico) where there are high levels of hepatitis B infection, where blood transfusions may not be adequately screened or where sexual contact or needle sharing is a possibility. Vaccination involves three injections, with a booster at 12 months. More rapid courses are available if necessary.

Typhoid Vaccination against typhoid may be advised if you are traveling for more than a couple of weeks in Central or South America. It is available as an injection or oral capsules.

Yellow Fever Yellow fever is not present in Mexico, but the country requires travelers arriving from areas infected with the disease (which are all in tropical South America or Africa) to have had yellow fever vaccination and to carry a yellow fever certificate. Discuss this with your doctor if necessary.

Malaria Medication Antimalarial drugs do not prevent you from being infected but kill the malaria parasites during a stage in their development and significantly reduce the risk of becoming very ill or dying. Expert advice on medication should be sought, as there are many factors to consider, including the area to be visited, the risk of exposure to malaria-carrying mosquitoes, the side effects of medication, your medical history and whether you are a child or an adult or pregnant. In Mexico at the time of writing there was malaria risk in rural areas of Campeche, Chiapas, Guerrero, Michoacán, Nayarit, Oaxaca, Quintana Roo, Sinaloa and Tabasco states, in the mountainous northern area of Jalisco, and in the area between latitudes 24° and 28° north and longitudes 106° and 110° west (this last represents an approximate triangle with its corners at Chihuahua, Ciudad Obregón and Mazatlán).

Health Insurance Make sure that you have adequate health insurance. See Travel Insurance under Visas & Documents earlier in this chapter for details.

Travel Health Guides Lonely Planet's *Healthy Travel Central & South America* is a handy pocket-size book packed with useful information including pretrip planning, emergency first aid, immunization and disease information, and what to do if you get sick on the road. *Travel with Children* from Lonely Planet includes advice on travel health for younger children.

There are a number of excellent travel health sites on the Internet. There are links to the World Health Organization and the US Centers for Disease Control & Prevention from the Lonely Planet Web site (W www.lonelyplanet.com/weblinks/wlheal.htm).

Other Preparations Make sure you're healthy before you start traveling. If you are going on a long trip, make sure your teeth are OK. If you wear glasses, take a spare pair and your prescription.

If you require a particular medication, take an adequate supply, as it may not be available locally. Take part of the packaging showing the generic name rather than the brand, which will make getting replacements easier. It's a good idea to have a legible prescription or letter from your doctor to show that you use the medication legally.

Basic Rules

Food A colonial adage goes: 'If you can cook it, boil it or peel it you can eat it…otherwise forget it.' Vegetables and fruit should be washed with purified water or peeled where possible. Beware of ice cream that might have melted and refrozen; if there's any doubt (eg a power outage in the last day or two), steer well clear. Shellfish such as mussels, oysters and clams should be avoided, as should undercooked meat, particularly in the form of mince. Steaming does not make shellfish safe for eating.

If a place looks clean and well run and the vendor looks clean and healthy, then the food is probably safe. The food in busy restaurants is cooked and eaten quite quickly and is probably not reheated.

Water The number one rule is *be careful* of the water, especially of ice. If you don't know for certain that the water is safe, assume the worst. Reputable brands of bottled water or soft drinks are generally fine. Only use water from containers with a serrated seal – not tops or corks. Many Mexican hotels have large bottles of purified water from which you can fill a water bottle or canteen. Take care with fruit juice, particularly if water may have been added. Milk should be treated with suspicion, as it might be unpasteurized, though boiled milk is fine if it is kept hygienically. Coffee and tea should also be OK, since the water should have been boiled.

The simplest way of purifying water is to boil it thoroughly. At high altitude it should be boiled for longer because it boils at a lower temperature, meaning that germs are less likely to be killed.

For a long trip, consider purchasing a water filter. There are two main kinds of filter. Total filters remove all parasites, bacteria and viruses and make water safe to

---

Nutrition

If your diet is poor or limited in variety, if you're traveling hard and fast and therefore missing meals or if you simply lose your appetite, you can soon start to lose weight and place your health at risk.

Make sure your diet is well balanced. Cooked eggs, tofu, beans, lentils (dhal in India) and nuts are all safe ways to get protein. Fruit you can peel (bananas, oranges or mandarins, for example) is usually safe and a good source of vitamins. Melons can harbor bacteria in their flesh and are best avoided. Try to eat plenty of grains (including rice) and bread. Remember that although food is generally safer if it is cooked well, overcooked food loses much of its nutritional value. If your diet isn't well balanced or if your food intake is insufficient, it's a good idea to take vitamin and iron pills.

In hot climates, make sure you drink enough – don't rely on feeling thirsty to indicate when you should drink. Not needing to urinate or voiding small amounts of very dark-yellow urine is a danger sign. Always carry a water bottle on long trips. Excessive sweating can lead to loss of salt and therefore muscle cramping. Salt tablets are not a good idea as a preventative, but in places where salt is not used much, adding salt to food can help.

drink. They are often expensive, but they can be more cost-effective than buying bottled water. Simple filters (even such as a nylon mesh bag) remove dirt and larger foreign bodies from the water so that chemical solutions work much more effectively; if water is dirty, chemical solutions may not work at all.

When buying a filter it's very important to read the specifications, so that you know exactly what it removes from the water and what it doesn't. Use of a simple filter will not remove all dangerous organisms, so if you cannot boil water it should be treated chemically. Chlorine tablets will kill many pathogens, but not some parasites like giardia and amoebic cysts. Iodine is more effective in purifying water and is available in tablet form. Follow the directions carefully and remember that too much iodine can be harmful. The Spanish for 'water purification tablets/drops' is *'pastillas/gotas para purificar agua.'*

Medical Problems & Treatment
We know from experience that it is possible to take dozens of journeys in every region of Mexico, climbing volcanoes, trekking to pyramids in remote jungle, camping out, staying in cheap hotels and eating in all sorts of markets and restaurants without getting anything worse than occasional traveler's diarrhea. But some of us *have* experienced hepatitis, dysentery and giardiasis, and we have known people who caught

Everyday Health

Normal body temperature is up to 37°C (98.6°F); more than 2°C (4°F) higher indicates a high fever. The normal adult pulse rate is 60 to 100 per minute (children 80 to 100, babies 100 to 140). As a general rule, pulse increases about 20 beats per minute for each 1°C (2°F) rise in fever.

Respiration (breathing) rate is also an indicator of illness. Count the number of breaths per minute: Between 12 and 20 is normal for adults and older children (up to 30 for younger children, 40 for babies). People with a high fever or serious respiratory illness breathe more quickly than normal. More than 40 shallow breaths a minute may indicate pneumonia.

dengue fever and typhoid, so we know that these things can happen.

Self-diagnosis and treatment can be risky, so you should always seek medical help. An embassy, consulate or good hotel can usually recommend a local doctor or clinic. Almost every Mexican town and city has a hospital and/or a clinic, as well as Cruz Roja (Red Cross) emergency facilities. In big cities and major tourist resorts you should be able to find an adequate hospital. Care in more remote areas is limited. In some serious cases it may be best to fly elsewhere for treatment.

Hospitals are generally inexpensive for common ailments (diarrhea, dysentery) and minor treatments (stitches, sprains). Most have to be paid at the time of service, and doctors usually require immediate cash payment. Some facilities may accept credit cards.

Note that drug dosages given in this section are for emergency use only. Correct diagnosis is vital. The generic names for medications have been given here; check with a pharmacist for brands available locally.

Antibiotics should ideally be administered only under medical supervision. Take only the recommended dose at the prescribed intervals and use the whole course, even if the illness seems to be cured earlier. Stop immediately if there are any serious reactions and don't use the antibiotic at all if you are unsure that you have the correct one. Some people are allergic to commonly prescribed antibiotics such as penicillin; carry this information (eg on a bracelet) when traveling.

Environmental Hazards
Altitude Sickness Lack of oxygen at high altitudes (over 2500m) affects most people to some extent. The effect may be mild or severe and occurs because less oxygen reaches the muscles and brain, requiring the heart and lungs to work harder. Symptoms of Acute Mountain Sickness (AMS) usually develop during the first 24 hours at high altitude, but may be delayed up to three weeks. Mild symptoms include headache, lethargy, dizziness, difficulty sleeping and loss of appetite. AMS may become more severe without warning and can be fatal. Severe symptoms include breathlessness, a

dry, irritative cough (which may progress to the production of pink, frothy sputum), severe headache, lack of coordination and balance, confusion, irrational behavior, vomiting, drowsiness and unconsciousness. There is no hard-and-fast rule as to what is too high: AMS has been fatal at 3000m, although 3500m to 4500m is the usual range.

Treat mild symptoms by resting at the same altitude until recovery, usually a day or two. Paracetamol or aspirin can be taken for headaches. If symptoms persist or become worse, however, *descend immediately*; even 500m can help. Drug treatments should never be used to avoid descent or to enable further ascent.

The drugs acetazolamide and dexamethasone are recommended by some doctors for the prevention of AMS, but their use is controversial. They can reduce the symptoms, but they may also mask warning signs; severe and fatal AMS has occurred to people taking these drugs. In general, we do not recommend them for travelers.

To prevent acute mountain sickness:

- Ascend slowly – have frequent rest days, spending two to three nights at each rise of 1000m. It is always wise to sleep at a lower altitude than the greatest height reached during the day. Above 3000m, care should be taken not to increase the sleeping altitude by more than 300m per day.
- Drink extra fluids. Mountain air is dry and cold and moisture is lost as you breathe. Evaporation of sweat may occur unnoticed and result in dehydration.
- Eat light, high-carbohydrate meals for more energy.
- Avoid alcohol as it may increase the risk of dehydration.
- Avoid sedatives.

Heat Exhaustion Dehydration and salt deficiency can cause heat exhaustion. Take time to acclimatize to high temperatures, drink sufficient liquids and do not do anything too physically demanding.

Salt deficiency is characterized by fatigue, lethargy, headaches, giddiness and muscle cramps; salt tablets may help, but adding extra salt to your food is better.

Anhydrotic heat exhaustion, which is caused by an inability to sweat, is rare. It tends to affect people who have been in a hot climate for some time, rather than newcomers.

It can progress to heatstroke. Treatment involves removal to a cooler climate.

Heatstroke This serious, occasionally fatal, condition can occur if the body's heat-regulating mechanism breaks down and body temperature rises to dangerous levels. Long, continuous periods of exposure to high temperatures and insufficient fluids can leave you vulnerable to heatstroke.

Symptoms are feeling unwell, not sweating very much (or at all) and a high body temperature (39°C to 41°C, 102°F to 106°F). Where sweating has ceased, the skin becomes flushed and red. Severe, throbbing headaches and lack of coordination also occur, and the sufferer may be confused or aggressive. Eventually the victim becomes delirious or convulses. Hospitalization is essential, but in the interim get victims out of the sun, remove their clothing, cover them with a wet sheet or towel and then fan continually. Give fluids if they are conscious.

Hypothermia Too much cold can be just as dangerous as too much heat. If you are outdoors at high altitudes, particularly at night, be prepared.

Hypothermia occurs when the body loses heat faster than it can produce it and the core temperature of the body falls. It is surprisingly easy to progress from very cold to dangerously cold due to a combination of wind, wet clothing, fatigue and hunger, even if the air temperature is above freezing. It's best to dress in layers; silk, wool and some of the new artificial fibers are all good insulating materials. A hat is important, as a lot of heat is lost through the head. A strong, waterproof outer layer (and a 'space' blanket for emergencies) are essential. Carry basic supplies, including food containing simple sugars to generate heat quickly and fluid to drink.

Symptoms of hypothermia are exhaustion, numb skin (particularly toes and fingers), shivering, slurred speech, irrational or violent behavior, lethargy, stumbling, dizzy spells, muscle cramps and violent bursts of energy. Irrationality may take the form of sufferers claiming they are warm and trying to take off their clothes.

To treat mild hypothermia, first get victims out of the wind and/or rain and replace wet clothing with dry, warm clothing.

Give them hot liquids (not alcohol) and some high-calorie, easily digestible food. Do not rub victims; instead, allow them slowly to warm themselves. This should be enough to treat the early stages of hypothermia. Early recognition and treatment of mild hypothermia are the only ways to prevent severe hypothermia, which is a critical condition.

Jet Lag This is experienced when you travel by air across more than three time zones. You may experience fatigue, disorientation, insomnia, anxiety, impaired concentration and loss of appetite. These effects will usually be gone within three days, but to minimize the impact of jet lag:

• Try to rest for a couple of days prior to departure.
• Select flight schedules that minimize your sleep deprivation.
• During the flight, avoid excessive eating (which bloats the stomach) and alcohol (which causes dehydration). Drink plenty of noncarbonated, nonalcoholic drinks such as fruit juice or water.
• Avoid smoking.
• Wear loose-fitting clothes and perhaps bring an eye mask and earplugs to help you sleep.
• Try to sleep at the appropriate time for the time zone you are traveling to.

Motion Sickness Eating lightly before and during a journey will reduce the chances of motion sickness. Try to find a place that minimizes movement – near the wing on aircraft, close to midships on boats, near the center on buses. Fresh air usually helps; reading and cigarette smoke don't. Commercial motion-sickness preparations, which can cause drowsiness, have to be taken before the trip commences. Ginger (available in capsule form) and peppermint (including mint-flavored sweets) are natural preventatives.

Prickly Heat This is an itchy rash caused by excessive perspiration trapped under the skin. It usually strikes people who have just arrived in a hot climate. Keeping cool, bathing often, drying the skin and using a mild talcum or prickly-heat powder, or resorting to air-conditioning may help.

Sunburn In the tropics or deserts or at high altitude, you can get sunburned surprisingly quickly, even through cloud cover. Use a sunscreen, a hat, and barrier cream for your nose and lips. Calamine lotion or a commercial after-sun preparation are good for mild sunburn. Protect your eyes with good-quality sunglasses, particularly if you will be near water, sand or snow.

Infectious Diseases
Diarrhea Simple things such as a change of water, food or climate can cause a mild bout of diarrhea, but a few rushed toilet trips with no other symptoms are not indicative of a major problem.

Dehydration is the main danger with any diarrhea, particularly in children or the elderly. Under all circumstances, *fluid replacement* (at least equal to the volume lost) is the most important thing to remember. Weak black tea with a little sugar, soda water, or soft drinks allowed to go flat and diluted 50% with clean water are all good. With severe diarrhea, a rehydrating solution is preferable to replace minerals and salts lost. Commercially available oral rehydration salts (ORS) are very useful; add them to boiled or bottled water. In an emergency, you can make a solution of six teaspoons of sugar and a half teaspoon of salt to a liter of boiled or bottled water. You need to drink at least the same volume of fluid that you are losing in bowel movements and vomiting. Urine is the best guide to the adequacy of replacement – if you have small amounts of concentrated urine, you need to drink more. Keep drinking small amounts often. Stick to a bland diet as you recover.

Gut-paralyzing drugs such as loperamide or diphenoxylate can be used to bring relief from the symptoms, although they do not actually cure the problem. Only use these drugs if you do not have access to toilets, eg if you *must* travel. Note that these drugs are not recommended for children under 12 years.

In certain situations antibiotics may be required: diarrhea with blood or mucus (dysentery), any diarrhea with fever, profuse watery diarrhea, persistent diarrhea not improving after 48 hours, and severe diarrhea. These suggest a more serious cause of diarrhea and gut-paralyzing drugs should be avoided.

In these situations, a stool test may be necessary to diagnose what bug is causing your diarrhea, so you should seek medical help urgently. Where this is not possible the recommended drugs for bacterial diarrhea (the most likely cause of severe diarrhea in travelers) are norfloxacin (400mg twice daily for three days) or ciprofloxacin (500mg twice daily for five days). These are not recommended for children or pregnant women. The drug of choice for children would be co-trimoxazole with dosage dependent on weight. A five-day course is given. Ampicillin or amoxycillin may be given in pregnancy, but medical care is necessary.

Two other causes of persistent diarrhea in travelers are giardiasis and amoebic dysentery.

Giardiasis is caused by a common parasite, *Giardia lamblia*. Symptoms include stomach cramps, nausea, a bloated stomach, watery, foul-smelling diarrhea and frequent gas. Giardiasis can appear several weeks after you have been exposed to the parasite. The symptoms may disappear for a few days and then return; this can go on for several weeks.

Amoebic dysentery, caused by the protozoan *Entamoeba histolytica*, is characterized by a gradual onset of low-grade diarrhea, often with blood and mucus. Cramping abdominal pain and vomiting are less likely than in other types of diarrhea, and fever may not be present. It will persist until treated and can recur and cause other health problems.

You should seek medical advice if you think you have giardiasis or amoebic dysentery, but where this is not possible, tinidazole or metronidazole are the recommended drugs. Treatment is a 2g single dose of tinidazole or 250mg of metronidazole three times daily for five to 10 days.

See also Cholera, under Less Common Diseases later.

Fungal Infections These occur more commonly in hot weather and are usually found on the scalp, between the toes (athlete's foot) or fingers, in the groin and on the body (ringworm). You can get ringworm (which is not a worm) from infected animals or other people. Moisture encourages these infections.

To prevent fungal infections, wear loose, comfortable clothes, avoid artificial fibers, wash frequently and dry carefully. If you get an infection, wash the infected area at least daily with a disinfectant or medicated soap and water, and rinse and dry well. Apply an antifungal cream or powder like tolnaftate. Try to expose the infected area to air or sunlight as much as possible, and wash towels and underwear in hot water, change them often and let them dry in the sun.

Hepatitis Hepatitis is a general term for inflammation of the liver. It is common worldwide. Several different viruses can cause hepatitis, and they differ in the ways they are transmitted. The symptoms are similar in all forms of the illness, and include fever, chills, headache, fatigue, feelings of weakness and aches and pains, followed by loss of appetite, nausea, vomiting, abdominal pain, dark urine, light-colored feces, jaundiced (yellow) skin and yellowing of the whites of the eyes. People who have had hepatitis should avoid alcohol for some time after the illness, as the liver needs time to recover.

Hepatitis A is transmitted by contaminated food and drinking water. You should seek medical advice, but there is not much you can do apart from rest, drink lots of fluids, eat lightly and avoid fatty foods. Hepatitis E is transmitted in the same way as hepatitis A; it can be particularly serious in pregnant women.

Incidence of Hepatitis B is low in Mexico, although it's classed as intermediate in neighboring Guatemala. Hepatitis B is spread through contact with infected blood, blood products or body fluids – for example through sexual contact, unsterilized needles, blood transfusions or contact with blood via small breaks in the skin. Other risk situations include getting a shave, tattoo or body piercing with contaminated equipment. The symptoms of hepatitis B may be more severe than type A and the disease can lead to long term problems such as chronic liver damage, liver cancer or a long term carrier state. Hepatitis C and D are spread in the same ways as hepatitis B and can also lead to long term complications.

There are vaccines against hepatitis A and B, but there are currently no vaccines against the other types of hepatitis. Following the basic rules about food and water (hepatitis A and E) and avoiding risk situations (hepatitis B, C and D) are important preventative measures.

HIV & AIDS Infection with the human immunodeficiency virus (HIV) may lead to acquired immune deficiency syndrome (AIDS), which is a fatal disease. By the end of 2000 an estimated 64,000 people had contracted AIDS in Mexico (a much lower percentage of the population than in any of its three neighbors: the USA, Guatemala and Belize) and there were around 150,000 people with HIV. Any exposure to blood, blood products or body fluids may put the individual at risk. The disease is often transmitted through sexual contact or dirty needles – vaccinations, acupuncture, tattooing and body piercing can be potentially as dangerous as intravenous drug use. HIV/AIDS can also be spread through infected blood transfusions; in developing countries such as Mexico it is possible that blood for a transfusion will not have been screened for HIV. If you do need an injection, ask to see the syringe unwrapped in front of you, or take a needle and syringe pack with you.

Fear of HIV infection should never preclude treatment for serious medical conditions.

Intestinal Worms These parasites are most common in rural, tropical areas. Different worms have different ways of infecting people. Some may be ingested on food such as undercooked meat (eg tapeworms) and some enter through your skin (eg hookworms). Infestations may not show up for some time, and although they are generally not serious, if left untreated some can cause severe health problems later. Consider having a stool test when you return home to check for these and determine the appropriate treatment.

Schistosomiasis Also known as bilharzia, this disease is transmitted by minute worms. They infect certain varieties of freshwater snails found in rivers, streams, lakes and particularly behind dams. The worms multiply and are eventually discharged into the water. The worm enters through the skin and attaches itself to the intestines or bladder. The first symptom may be a general feeling of being unwell, or a tingling and sometimes a light rash around the area where it entered. Weeks later, a high fever may develop. Once the disease is established, abdominal pain and blood in the urine are other signs. The infection often causes no symptoms until the disease is well established (several months to years after exposure) and damage to internal organs irreversible.

The main method of prevention is to avoid swimming or bathing in fresh water where bilharzia is present. Even deep water can be infected. If you do get wet, dry off quickly and dry your clothes as well.

A blood test is the most reliable test, but it will not show positive until a number of weeks after exposure.

Sexually Transmitted Diseases (STDs) HIV/AIDS and hepatitis B can be transmitted through sexual contact; see the relevant sections earlier for more details. Other STDs include gonorrhea, herpes and syphilis; sores, blisters or rashes around the genitals, and discharges or pain when urinating, are common symptoms. In some STDs, such as wart virus or chlamydia, symptoms may be less marked or not observed at all, especially in women. Chlamydia infection can cause infertility in men and women before any symptoms have been noticed. Syphilis symptoms eventually disappear completely but the disease continues and can cause severe problems in later years. While abstinence from sexual contact is the only 100% effective way of preventing STDs, using condoms is also effective. The treatment of gonorrhea and syphilis is with antibiotics. Each STD requires specific antibiotics.

Typhoid Typhoid fever is a dangerous gut infection caused by contaminated water and food. Medical help must be sought.

In its early stages, sufferers may feel they have a bad cold or flu on the way, as early symptoms are headache, body aches and a fever that rises a little each day until it is around 40°C (104°F) or more. The victim's pulse is often slow relative to the degree of fever present – unlike a normal fever, where the pulse increases. There may also be vomiting, abdominal pain, diarrhea or constipation.

In the second week, the high fever and slow pulse continue and a few pink spots may appear on the body; trembling, delirium, weakness, weight loss and dehydration may occur. Complications such as pneumonia, perforated bowel or meningitis may occur.

Insect-Borne Diseases

Chagas' disease and leishmaniasis are insect-borne diseases, but they do not pose a great risk to travelers. For information on them see Less Common Diseases later.

Malaria This serious, potentially fatal disease is spread by mosquito bites. When in endemic areas, it is extremely important to avoid mosquito bites and to take tablets to prevent malaria. Symptoms range from fever, chills and sweating, headache, diarrhea and abdominal pains to a vague feeling of ill health. Seek medical help immediately if malaria is suspected. Without treatment, malaria can rapidly become more serious and can be fatal.

If medical care is unavailable, malaria tablets can be used for treatment. You need to use a different malaria tablet than the one you were taking when you contracted malaria. The standard treatment dose of mefloquine is two 250mg tablets and another two six hours later. For Fansidar, it's a single dose of three tablets. If you were previously taking mefloquine and cannot obtain Fansidar, other alternatives are Malarone (atovaquone-proguanil; four tablets once daily for three days), halofantrine (three doses of two 250mg tablets every six hours) or quinine sulphate (600mg every six hours). There is a greater risk of side effects with these dosages than in normal use if used with mefloquine, so medical advice is preferable. Halo-fantrine is no longer recommended by the WHO as emergency standby treatment, because of side effects, and should only be used if no other drugs are available.

Travelers are advised to prevent mosquito bites at all times. In general mosquitoes in Mexico are most bothersome from dusk to dawn and during the rainy season (May to October in most places). To avoid being bitten by a mosquito, follow these precautions:

- Wear light-colored clothing.
- Wear long trousers and long-sleeved shirts.
- Use mosquito repellents containing the compound DEET on exposed areas (prolonged overuse of DEET may be harmful, especially to children, but its use is considered preferable to being bitten by disease-transmitting mosquitoes).
- Avoid perfumes or aftershave.

- Impregnate clothes and mosquito nets with repellent (permethrin); it may be worth taking your own net.

Dengue Fever This viral disease is transmitted by mosquitoes and is fast becoming one of the top public health problems in the tropical world. Unlike the malaria mosquito, the *Aedes aegypti* mosquito, which transmits the dengue virus, is most active during the day, and is found mainly in urban areas, in and around human dwellings.

Signs and symptoms of dengue fever include a sudden onset of high fever, headache, joint and muscle pains (hence its old name, 'breakbone fever') and nausea and vomiting. A rash of small red spots sometimes appears three to four days after the onset of fever. In the early phase of illness, dengue may be mistaken for other infectious diseases, including malaria and influenza. Minor bleeding such as nose bleeds may occur in the course of the illness, but this does not necessarily mean that you have progressed to the potentially fatal dengue haemorrhagic fever (DHF), which is characterized by heavy bleeding. Recovery even from simple dengue fever may be prolonged, with tiredness lasting several weeks.

Seek medical attention as soon as possible if you think you may be infected. A blood test can exclude malaria and indicate the possibility of dengue fever. There is no specific treatment for dengue. Aspirin should be avoided, as it increases the risk of hemorrhaging. Nor is there a vaccine against dengue fever. The best prevention is to avoid mosquito bites at all times by covering up, using insect repellents containing the compound DEET and mosquito nets (see Malaria, earlier, for advice on avoiding mosquito bites).

Cuts, Bites & Stings

See Less Common Diseases for details of rabies, which is passed through animal bites.

Cuts & Scratches Wash any cut well and treat it with an antiseptic, such as povidone-iodine. When possible, avoid bandages and Band-Aids, which can keep wounds wet. Coral cuts are notoriously slow to heal, and if they are not adequately cleaned, small pieces of coral can become embedded in the wound.

Bedbugs & Lice Bedbugs live in various places, but particularly in dirty mattresses and bedding, evidenced by spots of blood on bedclothes or on the wall. Bedbugs leave itchy bites in neat rows. Calamine lotion or a sting relief spray may help.

All lice cause itching and discomfort. They make themselves at home in your hair (head lice), your clothing (body lice) or in your pubic hair (crabs). You catch lice through direct contact with infected people or by sharing combs, clothing and the like. Powder or shampoo treatment will kill the lice and infected clothing should then be washed in very hot, soapy water and left in the sun to dry.

Bites & Stings Bee and wasp stings are usually painful rather than dangerous. However, in people who are allergic to them severe breathing difficulties may occur and require urgent medical care. Calamine lotion or a sting relief spray will give relief, and ice packs will reduce the pain and swelling. Some spiders have dangerous bites, but antivenins are usually available. Scorpion stings are notoriously painful and in some parts of Central America can be fatal. Scorpions often shelter in shoes or clothing.

Various sea creatures can sting or bite dangerously or are dangerous to eat; seek local advice.

Jellyfish Avoid contact with these sea creatures, which have stinging tentacles. Stings from most jellyfish are simply rather painful. Dousing in vinegar will deactivate any stingers that have not 'fired.' Calamine lotion, antihistamines and analgesics may reduce the reaction and relieve the pain.

Leeches & Ticks Leeches may be present in damp rainforest conditions; they attach themselves to your skin to suck your blood. An insect repellent may keep them away. Salt or a lighted cigarette end will make them fall off. Do not pull them off, as the bite is then more likely to become infected. Clean and apply pressure if the point of attachment is bleeding.

You should always check all over your body if you have been walking through a potentially tick-infested area, as ticks can cause skin infections and other more serious diseases. If a tick is found attached, press down around the tick's head with tweezers, grab the head and gently pull upwards.

Snakes To minimize your chances of being bitten, wear boots, socks and long trousers when walking through undergrowth where snakes may be lurking. Don't put your hands into holes and crevices, and be careful when collecting firewood.

Snake bites do not cause instantaneous death, and antivenins are usually available. Immediately wrap the bitten limb tightly, as you would for a sprained ankle, and then attach a splint to immobilize it. Keep the victim still and seek medical help, and take the dead snake along for identification if possible. Don't attempt to catch the snake if there is a possibility of being bitten again. Tourniquets and sucking out the poison are now comprehensively discredited.

Women's Health
Gynecological Problems Antibiotic use, synthetic underwear, sweating and contraceptive pills can contribute to fungal vaginal infections in hot climates. Good personal hygiene, loose-fitting clothes and cotton underwear will help prevent these infections.

Fungal infections are characterized by a rash, itch and discharge, and can be treated with a vinegar or lemon-juice douche or with yogurt. Nystatin, miconazole or clotrimazole pessaries or vaginal cream are the usual treatments.

Sexually transmitted diseases are a major cause of vaginal problems. Symptoms include a smelly discharge, painful intercourse and sometimes a burning sensation when urinating. Medical attention should be sought and male sexual partners must also be treated. For more details see Sexually Transmitted Diseases earlier. Besides abstinence, the best thing is to practice safe sex by using condoms.

Pregnancy Some vaccinations normally used to prevent serious diseases are not advisable during pregnancy, making travel to some places inadvisable. In addition, some diseases, such as malaria, are much more serious for pregnant women, and may increase the risk of a stillborn child.

Most miscarriages occur during the first three months of pregnancy. Miscarriage is not uncommon and can occasionally lead to severe bleeding. The last three months should also be spent within reasonable distance of good medical care. A baby born as early as 24 weeks stands a chance of survival, but only in a good modern hospital. Pregnant women should avoid all unnecessary medication, although vaccinations and malarial prophylactics should still be taken where needed. Additional care should be taken to prevent illness and particular attention should be paid to diet and nutrition. Alcohol and nicotine, for example, should be avoided.

Less Common Diseases

The following diseases pose a small risk to travelers, and so are only mentioned in passing. Seek medical advice if you think you may have any of them.

Chagas' Disease In remote rural areas of Latin America this parasitic disease is transmitted by a bug that hides in the wall crevices and thatched roofs of mud huts and on palm fronds. It bites at night and a hard, violet-coloured swelling appears in about a week. Chagas' disease can be treated in its early stages, but untreated infections can lead to death some years later.

Cholera This is the worst of the watery diarrheas and medical help should be sought. Outbreaks of cholera are generally widely reported, so you can avoid such problem areas. Fluid replacement is the most vital treatment; the risk of dehydration is severe as you may lose up to 20L a day. If there is a delay in getting to the hospital, then begin taking tetracycline. The adult dose is 250mg four times daily. It is not recommended for children under nine years nor for pregnant women. Tetracycline may help shorten the illness, but adequate fluids are required to save lives.

Leishmaniasis This is a group of parasitic diseases transmitted by sandflies. Cutaneous leishmaniasis, types of which occur in the Yucatán Peninsula, Belize and Guatemala, affects the skin tissue causing ulceration and disfigurement. Visceral leishmaniasis, which is rare, affects the internal organs. Seek medical advice, as laboratory testing is required for diagnosis and correct treatment. The best precaution is to avoid sandfly bites by covering up and applying repellent.

Rabies This fatal viral infection occurs throughout Latin America. Many animals can be infected (such as dogs, cats, bats and monkeys). The disease is transmitted through the infected animals saliva and any bite, scratch or even lick from an animal should be cleaned immediately and thoroughly. Scrub with soap and running water, and then apply alcohol or iodine solution. Medical help should be sought promptly to receive a course of injections to prevent the onset of symptoms and death.

Tetanus This disease is caused by a germ that lives in the soil and in the feces of horses and other animals. It enters the body via breaks in the skin. The first symptom may be discomfort in swallowing, or stiffening of the jaw and neck; this is followed by painful convulsions of the jaw and whole body. The disease can be fatal, but it can be prevented by vaccination.

Tuberculosis TB is a bacterial infection usually transmitted from person to person by coughing, but which may also be transmitted through consumption of unpasteurized milk. Milk that has been boiled is safe to drink, and the souring of milk to make yoghurt or cheese also kills the bacilli. Travelers are usually not at great risk as close household contact with the infected person is usually required before the disease is passed on.

WOMEN TRAVELERS

In this land that invented machismo, women have to make some concessions to local custom – but don't let that put you off. In general, Mexicans are great believers in the difference (rather than the equality) between the sexes. Lone women must expect some catcalls and attempts to chat them up. Normally these men only want to talk to you, but it can get tiresome. The best way to discourage unwanted attention is to avoid eye contact (sunglasses help here) and, if possible, ignore the attention altogether. Otherwise, use a cool but polite initial response and a consistent, firm 'No.' It is possible to turn uninvited attention into a worthwhile conversation by making clear that you *are* willing to talk, but no more.

Don't put yourself in peril by doing things Mexican women would not do, such as challenging a man's masculinity, drinking in a cantina, hitchhiking, or going alone to isolated places.

Wearing a bra will spare you a lot of unwanted attention. A wedding ring and talk of your husband may help, too. Except in beach resorts, it's advisable to wear shorts only when at a swimming pool. You might even consider swimming in shorts and a T-shirt, as some Mexican women do.

GAY & LESBIAN TRAVELERS

Though its reputation might suggest otherwise, Mexico is more broad-minded than visitors might expect. Gays and lesbians tend to keep a low profile but in general rarely attract open discrimination or violence. Gay and lesbian travelers will find active scenes in cities such as Mexico City, Cancún, Puerto Vallarta, Acapulco, Guadalajara and Ciudad Juárez.

A good source of information on the Internet is the Gay Mexico Network (W www.gaymexico.net). It includes information on gay-friendly hotels and tours in Mexico. *Sergay* is a Spanish-language magazine, focused on Mexico City, but with bar, disco and cruising-spot listings for the whole country. You can find it on the Internet at W www.sergay.com.mx.

The *Man's Guide to Mexico and Central America* by Señor Cordova, published in 1997, has sections on where to eat, stay and go in about 10 Mexican cities. *Damron Women's Traveller*, with listings for lesbians, and *Damron Men's Travel Guide* are both published annually by Damron Company of San Francisco. *Men's Travel in Your Pocket*, *Women's Travel in Your Pocket* and *Gay Travel A to Z* (for men and women), all published by Ferrari Guides, and *Gay Mexico: The Men of Mexico,* by Eduardo David, are also useful. They can be obtained at any good bookstore or on the Internet.

DISABLED TRAVELERS

Mexico is not yet very disabled-friendly, though some hotels and restaurants (mostly towards the top end of the market) and some public buildings now provide wheelchair access. Mobility is easiest in the major tourist resorts and the more expensive hotels. Bus transportation can be difficult; flying or taking a taxi are easier.

Mobility International USA (☎ 541-343-1284, W www.miusa.org), PO Box 10767, Eugene, OR 97440, USA, advises disabled travelers on mobility issues, runs exchange programs (including in Mexico), and publishes *A World of Options: A Guide to International Educational Exchange, Community Service, and Travel for People with Disabilities*.

Twin Peaks Press (☎ 360-694-2462, W www.pacifier.com/~twinpeak), PO Box 129, Vancouver, WA 98666-0129 USA, publishes useful material including the *Disability News You Can Use* newsletter, with a travel section in each issue. Cost is $US49 annually in the USA, US$55 in Canada, US$65 elsewhere.

In the UK, RADAR (☎ 020-7250-3222, W www.radar.org.uk), 250 City Rd, London EC1V 8AF, is run by and for disabled people. Its excellent Web site has links to good travel-specific sites, as does the Australian site W www.acrod.org.au.

Another excellent information source for disabled travelers is Access-able Travel Source (W www.access-able.com).

SENIOR TRAVELERS

The well-known American Association of Retired Persons (AARP, ☎ 800-424-3410, W www.aarp.org), 601 E St NW, Washington, DC 20049, USA, is an advocacy and service group for Americans 50 years and older and a good resource for travel bargains. Membership costs US$10 a year.

Elderhostel (☎ 877-426-8056, W www.elderhostel.org), 11 Avenue de Lafayette, Boston, MA 02111, USA, is a nonprofit organization providing educational travel programs to people over age 55. It has many fascinating cultural and historical programs in Mexico, typically costing around US$1000 to US$1200 a week including airfares from the USA.

Grand Circle Travel (☎ 800-955-1034, W www.gct.com) specializes in escorted tours for the over-50s and has itineraries in Mexico.

TRAVEL WITH CHILDREN

Mexicans as a rule like children. Any child whose hair is less than jet black will get called *güeróa* (blond). Children are welcome at all kinds of hotels and in virtually every café and restaurant.

Children are excited and stimulated by the colors, sights and sounds of Mexico, but most don't like traveling all the time; they're happier if they can settle into places for a while and make friends. Try to give them time to get on with some of what they like doing back home.

Children are likely to be more affected than adults by heat or disrupted sleeping patterns. They need time to acclimatize and extra care to avoid sunburn. Take care to replace fluids if a child gets diarrhea (see the Health section).

Apart from the obvious attractions of beaches and swimming pools, in some places you'll find excellent special attractions such as amusement parks, zoos, aquariums, wildlife and boat rides. Kids don't have to be very old to enjoy snorkeling, riding bicycles or riding horses.

Archaeological sites are fun if the kids are into climbing pyramids and exploring tunnels (who isn't?). In Mexico City don't miss the hands-on children's museum, Papalote Museo del Niño.

Diapers (nappies) are widely available, but you may not easily find creams, lotions, baby foods or familiar medicines outside larger cities and tourist towns. Bring what you need.

It's usually not hard to find an inexpensive baby-sitter if the grown-ups want to go out on their own; just ask at your hotel.

On flights to and within Mexico, children under two generally travel for 10% of the adult fare, as long as they do not occupy a seat, and those aged two to 11 normally pay 67%. Children under 13 pay half-price on many Mexican long-distance buses and if they're under three, and small enough to sit on your lap, they will usually go free.

Lonely Planet's *Travel with Children* has lots of practical advice on the subject, as well as firsthand stories from many Lonely Planet authors, and others, who have done it.

DANGERS & ANNOYANCES

Mexico – especially its big cities and above all Mexico City – experienced a big increase in crime after the economic crisis of the mid-1990s. Generally, with a few precautions, you can minimize danger to your physical safety. But lone women, and even pairs of women, should always be very cautious about going to remote beach spots, and everyone should be extremely careful with taxis in Mexico City. On the whole, though, it's your possessions that are more at risk, particularly possessions that you carry around with you.

Official information can make Mexico sound more alarming than it really is, but for a variety of useful information on travel

---

Mexico According to Miss Noble

What I Liked in Mexico
I liked the sea and the beaches. The sea was really warm compared to Europe, where I live, and the sand was great for making sandcastles. Another thing I liked in Mexico were the markets in San Cristóbal and Oaxaca. There were really nice handmade clothes, tablecloths, hammocks and mats, which were selling at reasonable prices. At Rancho Esmeralda (Chiapas) there are loads of animals that I really liked looking after. And make sure you try the Oaxacan hot chocolate.

What I Didn't Like in Mexico
I didn't like the 14-hour bus trip from Puerto Escondido to San Cristóbal. The flight from Mexico City to Huatulco was terrible too. There was a big storm and I kept thinking the plane was going to crash. And then riding a bike through Frontera Corozal was not very nice either, because everyone was laughing at me.

– Isabella M Noble (authors' daughter, age 11)

to Mexico, including potential risks, you can consult your country's foreign affairs department, by telephone or on the Internet: Australia (☎ 1300 555 135, ⓦ www.dfat .gov.au); Canada (☎ 613-944-6788, ☎ 800-267-6788, ⓦ www.dfait-maeci.gc.ca); UK (☎ 020-7008-0233, ⓦ www.fco.gov.uk); USA (☎ 202- 647-5225, ⓦ http://travel.state.gov). If you're already in Mexico, you can contact your embassy.

Theft & Robbery

Tourists are vulnerable as they are generally presumed to be wealthy (by Mexican standards) and to be carrying valuables. Pocket-picking and purse- or bag-snatching are risks in large Mexican cities, particularly Mexico City. Crowded buses, bus stops, bus stations, airports, the Mexico City metro, markets, thronged streets and plazas, and anywhere frequented by large numbers of tourists are all possible haunts of these thieves. Robbery or mugging is more likely in less crowded places such as empty pedestrian underpasses, remote beach spots and quiet streets after dark.

Violent crimes are rare in major coastal resorts, which tend to have a large and visible police presence.

Pickpockets often work in teams: one or two of them may grab your bag or camera (or your arm and leg), and while you're trying to get it free another will pick your pocket. Or one may 'drop' something as a crowd jostles onto a bus and as he or she 'looks for it,' a pocket will be picked or a bag slashed. The objective is to distract you. If your valuables are *underneath* your clothing, the chances of losing them are greatly reduced.

Robberies and muggings are less common than pocket-picking and purse-snatching, but they are more alarming and more serious, as resistance may be met with violence (do NOT resist). Robbers may force you to remove your money belt or neck-strap pouch, watch, rings, etc. They may be armed. Usually they will not harm you: what they want is your money, fast. But there have been cases of robbers beating victims, or forcing them to drink large amounts of alcohol, to extract credit or bank card personal numbers. Sometimes the police themselves have been the criminals. Mexico City taxis, which have become notorious for (sometimes violent) robberies, are especially dangerous if you take the wrong kind of cab (see 'Taxi Crime' in the Mexico City chapter).

Precautions To avoid being robbed in cities, do not go where there are few other people. This includes empty streets or empty metro cars at night, little-used pedestrian underpasses and similarly lonely places.

On beaches and in the countryside, do not camp overnight in lonely places unless you are absolutely sure they're safe.

As you travel in Mexico, you will develop a sense of which situations and places are more threatening than others. But you must always protect yourself, or you may lose a considerable amount.

In Mexican cities adhere to the following precautions:

- Unless you have immediate need of them, leave most of your cash, traveler's checks, passport, jewelry, air tickets, credit cards, watch, and perhaps your camera in a sealed, signed envelope in your hotel's safe. Virtually all hotels except the very cheapest provide safekeeping for guests' valuables.
- Leaving valuables in a locked suitcase in your hotel room is often safer than carrying them on the streets of most Mexican cities.
- Carry a small amount of ready money – just enough for the outing you're on – in a pocket. If you have to carry valuables, keep them in a money belt, shoulder wallet, or a pouch on a string around your neck, *underneath your clothing*. Visible round-the-waist money belts are an invitation to thieves.
- Walk with purpose and be alert to people around you.
- Don't keep money (cash or plastic), purses, bags or cameras in open view any longer than you have to. At ticket counters in bus stations and airports, keep your bag between your feet.
- Use ATMs only in secure locations, not those open to the street.
- Do not leave anything valuable-looking visible in a parked vehicle.

Highway Robbery Bandits occasionally hold up buses, cars and other vehicles on intercity routes, especially at night, taking luggage or valuables. Sometimes buses are robbed by people who board as passengers. The best ways to avoid highway robbery are not to travel at night and to travel on toll highways as much as possible. Deluxe and 1st-class buses use toll highways, where they exist; 2nd-class buses do not and are therefore more vulnerable. Roads with particularly bad reputations include highway 200 along the Pacific coast, especially in the states of Guerrero and Oaxaca, highways 15 and 15D in Sinaloa state, highway 134 between Ixtapa/Zihuatanejo and Ciudad Altamirano, roads linking the Yucatán Peninsula with Tabasco and Chiapas states, and highway 147 from Tuxtepec to Palomares (Oaxaca state).

LEGAL MATTERS
Mexican Law

Mexican law is based on the Napoleonic code, presuming an accused person is guilty until proven innocent.

The minimum jail sentence for possession of more than a token amount of any narcotic, including marijuana and amphetamines, is 10 years. As in most other countries, the purchase of controlled medication requires a doctor's prescription.

It's against Mexican law to take any weapon or ammunition into the country (even unintentionally) without a permit from a Mexican embassy or consulate.

Road travelers should expect occasional police or military checkpoints. They are normally looking for drugs, weapons or illegal migrants. Drivers found with drugs or weapons on board may have their vehicle confiscated and may be detained for months while their cases are investigated. See the Getting Around chapter for information on legal aspects of road accidents.

Useful warnings on Mexican law are found in the US State Department's *Tips for Travelers to Mexico* and in State Department consular information sheets, public announcements or travel warnings on Mexico. All are available on the Internet at **w** http://travel.state.gov.

Help

If arrested, you have the right to notify your embassy or consulate. Consular officials can tell you your rights and provide lists of local lawyers. They can also monitor your case, make sure you are treated humanely, and notify your relatives or friends; but they can't get you out of jail. More Americans are in jail in Mexico than in any other country except the USA – about 450 at any one time. By Mexican law the longest a person can be detained by police without a specific accusation is 72 hours.

Most of Mexico's 31 states have a Protección al Turista (Tourist Protection) department, often found in the same building as the state tourist office (and contactable through tourist offices). Protección al Turista exists to help you with legal problems such as complaints or reporting crimes or lost articles. The national tourism ministry, SECTUR (☎ 55-5250-0123, ☎ 800-903-92-00), offers 24-hour telephone advice on tourist protection laws and where tourists can obtain help.

If you wish to lodge a complaint about bad service or defective merchandise in Mexico, you can do so to the Procuraduría Federal del Consumidor (PROFECO, Federal Consumer Protection Office). PROFECO has the power to investigate consumer complaints, mediate disputes and order hearings. You can talk with PROFECO in English at ☎ 55-5211-1723 (in Mexico City), 9am to 3pm Monday to Friday. They also have a toll-free line, ☎ 800-903-13-00, open daily. PROFECO's Web site (**w** www.profeco.gob.mx) has an 'Attention to Foreigners' section where you can print a complaint form to fill out.

If you are the victim of a crime, your embassy or consulate, or SECTUR, can give advice. In some cases, you may feel there is little to gain by going to the police, unless you need a statement to present to your insurance company. If you go to the police and your Spanish is poor, take a more fluent speaker. Also take your passport and tourist card, if you still have them. If you just want to report a theft for purposes of an insurance claim, say you want to '*poner una acta de un robo*' (make a record of a robbery). This should make it clear that you merely want a piece of paper and you should get it without too much trouble.

If Mexican police wrongfully accuse you of an infraction (as they have often been known to do in the hope of obtaining a bribe), you can ask for the officer's identification or to speak to a superior or to be shown documentation about the law you have supposedly broken. You can also note the officer's name, badge number, vehicle number and department (federal, state or municipal). Pay any traffic fines at a police station and get a receipt. Then make your complaint to Protección al Turista or to SECTUR.

BUSINESS HOURS

Shops are generally open from 9am or 10am to 7pm or 8pm Monday to Saturday. In hot regions and small towns some businesses may close for siesta from around 2pm to 4pm, then stay open till 9pm. Some shops don't open Saturday afternoon. Shops in malls and tourist resorts are often open Sunday.

Offices have similar Monday to Friday hours, with greater likelihood of the 2pm to 4pm lunch break. Those with tourist-related business might open for a few hours on Saturday.

Some Mexican churches – particularly those that contain valuable works of art – are locked when not in use by the congregation. Most churches are in frequent use so be careful not to disturb services when you visit them.

Archaeological sites are usually open daily from 8am or 9am to about 5pm. This is unfortunate, because in many hot regions the hours before 8am and after 5pm, especially in summer, are cooler and much more pleasant than daytime hours, and there's plenty of golden light. If they have a closing day, it's usually Monday. Museums often close Monday, too. On Sunday nearly all archaeological sites and museums are free, and the major ones can get very crowded on this day.

PUBLIC HOLIDAYS & SPECIAL EVENTS

Mexico's many fiestas are full-blooded, highly colorful affairs that often go on for several days and add much spice to everyday life. There's a major national holiday or celebration just about every month, to which each town adds nearly as many local saints' days, regional fairs, arts festivals and so on.

The chief Mexican holiday periods are Christmas-New Year, Semana Santa (the week leading up to Easter and a couple of days afterwards), and mid-July to mid-August. Transportation and tourist accommodations get heavily booked at these times.

National Holidays

Banks, post offices, government offices and many shops throughout Mexico are closed on the following days:

January 1 – *Año Nuevo* (New Year's Day)

February 5 – *Día de la Constitución* (Constitution Day)

February 24 – *Día de la Bandera* (Day of the National Flag)

March 21 – *Día de Nacimiento de Benito Juárez* (Anniversary of Benito Juárez's birth)

May 1 – *Día del Trabajo* (Labor Day)

May 5 – *Cinco de Mayo* is the anniversary of Mexico's 1862 victory over the French at Puebla, where it is grandly celebrated.

September 16 – *Día de la Independencia* commemorates the start of Mexico's war for independence from Spain; the biggest celebrations are in Mexico City, the evening before.

October 12 – *Día de la Raza* commemorates Columbus' discovery of the New World and the founding of the *mestizo* (mixed-ancestry) Mexican people.

November 20 – *Día de la Revolución* is the anniversary of the 1910 Mexican Revolution.

December 25 – *Día de Navidad* (Christmas Day) is traditionally celebrated with a feast in the early hours of December 25 after midnight mass.

Other National Celebrations

Though not official holidays, some of these are among the most important festivals on the Mexican calendar. Many offices and businesses close.

January 6 – *Día de los Reyes Magos* (Three Kings' Day or Epiphany) is the day that Mexican children traditionally receive gifts, rather than at Christmas (but some get two loads of presents!).

February 2 – *Día de la Candelaría* (Candlemas) commemorates the presentation of Jesus in the temple 40 days after his birth; it is celebrated in Mexico with processions, bullfights and dancing in many towns.

Late February or early March – *Carnaval* takes place the week or so before Ash Wednesday (which falls 46 days before Easter Sunday) and is a big bash preceding the 40-day penance of Lent; it's celebrated most festively in Mazatlán, Veracruz and La Paz, with huge parades and masses of music, food, drink, dancing, fireworks and fun.

March or April – *Semana Santa* (Holy Week) starts on Palm Sunday (*Domingo de Ramos*); businesses close usually from Good Friday (*Viernes Santo*) to Easter Sunday (*Domingo de*

Resurrección); particularly colorful celebrations are held in San Miguel de Allende, Taxco and Pátzcuaro; most of Mexico seems to be on the move at this time.

September 1 – *Informe Presidencial* is the president's state of the nation address to the Mexican legislature.

November 1 – *Día de Todos los Santos* (All Saints' Day)

November 2 – *Día de Muertos* (Day of the Dead) is Mexico's most characteristic fiesta (see 'Día de Muertos').

December 12 – *Día de Nuestra Señora de Guadalupe* (Day of Our Lady of Guadalupe) honors Mexico's national patron, the manifestation of the Virgin Mary who appeared to an indigenous Mexican, Juan Diego, in 1531; a week or more of celebrations throughout Mexico leads up to the big day, with children taken to church dressed as little Juan Diegos or indigenous girls; the biggest festivities are at the Basílica de Guadalupe in Mexico City.

December 16-24 – Candlelit parades of children and adults, reenact the journey of Mary and Joseph to Bethlehem; it is held for nine nights and is more important in small towns than big cities.

Local Fiestas

Every city, town, *barrio* (neighborhood) and village has its own fiestas, often in honor of its patron saint(s). Street parades of holy images, special costumes, fireworks, dancing, lots of music, plenty of drinking – even bull-running through the streets in some places – are all part of the scene. There are festivals of arts, dance, music and handicrafts, and celebrations for harvests of avocados, grapes and even radishes. Trade and business fairs often serve as a focus for wider festivities.

ACTIVITIES

Active tourism in Mexico is growing fast, thanks to the desire of more and more Mexicans and foreigners to do more with their free time than just lie on beaches, sightsee, shop, eat and drink. To help you plan your travels, this section is a very brief introduction to where you can *do* things in Mexico. Refer to this book's destination sections for the details on equipment rentals and availability and advisability of guides. This chapter's Books section mentions some useful guidebooks for hikers, divers and nature lovers.

Good Internet sources on active tourism agencies in Mexico are ⓦ www.planeta.com

(Eco Travels in Latin America), ⓦ www.mexonline.com (Mexico Online) and ⓦ www.amtave.com. This last is the site of AMTAVE, a grouping of over 80 Mexican adventure travel and ecotourism operators.

Hiking

Hiking trails in the Barranca del Cobre (Copper Canyon), Baja California (Sierra de la Laguna, Parque Nacional San Pedro Mártir, Sierra de la Giganta) and Oaxaca (Pueblos Mancomunados, Santiago Apoala) are among the most popular and developed. Parque Nacional El Chico, the Reserva de la Biósfera El Cielo, Álamos, San Miguel de Allende, Nevado de Toluca, Volcán Paricutín, Volcán Nevado de Colima, La Malinche, Iztaccíhuatl and Volcán Tacaná are other places where you can stretch your legs without any technical climbing skills (though the summit of Iztaccíhuatl is a different matter). A guide is a very good idea for many routes, as route marking is incipient. Walking alone across remote territory is not advised for safety reasons.

Mountain Biking

In a growing number of places around Mexico you'll find mountain bikes available for excursions or guided trips of up to several days. These include Mexico City, Creel, Baja California's Sierra de la Giganta, Oaxaca (Oaxaca City, Pueblos Mancomunados, Santiago Apoala), Parque Nacional El Chico, Reserva de la Biósfera El Cielo, San Miguel de Allende and San Cristóbal de Las Casas. There's limitless magnificent country to ride across. On the Internet, Eco Travels in Latin America (ⓦ www.planeta.com) has a 'Mexico Biking Guide.'

Horse Riding

This is another increasingly popular activity. Locations include the Sierra de la Giganta (Baja California), Álamos, Creel and the Barranca del Cobre, Real de Catorce, San Miguel de Allende, San Cristóbal de Las Casas and Toniná in Chiapas, Volcán Paricutín and Pacific coastal spots such as Puerto Vallarta, Zihuatanejo, Pie de la Cuesta and Bahías de Huatulco.

Mountain & Rock Climbing

Mexico's mecca for technical climbers is the limestone of Potrero Chico, north of

Día de Muertos

The Day of the Dead has its origins in the pre-Hispanic Tarasco people's belief that the dead could return to their homes on one day each year to visit their loved ones. The underlying philosophy is that death does not represent the end of a life, but the continuation of the same life in a parallel world, the Cumiehchúcuaro (translated as 'Inframundo' in Spanish, or 'Underworld' in English).

This day when the dead could return was set in the ancient calendar, a month after the autumn equinox. The occasion required preparations to help the spirits find their way home, and to make them welcome. An arch made of bright yellow marigold flowers was put up in each home, as a symbolic door or gateway to and from the underworld. Tamales, fruits, corn and salt were placed in front of the arch on an altar, along with containers of water because spirits always arrived thirsty after their journey. A path of marigold petals and resin lamps marked the way to the altar. Traditionally, the spirits of departed children visited on the first night (when toys and sweets were added to the altar), and the spirits of dead adults came on the following night, when they joined their living relatives to eat, drink, talk and sing.

The Spanish conquest, and the evangelical mission of the Catholic Church, suppressed some pre-Hispanic beliefs but allowed others to continue in new manifestations. The Catholic celebrations of All Saints' Day (November 1) and All Souls' Day (November 2) were easily superimposed on the old Tarasco 'day of the dead' traditions, which shared a similar date and much of the same symbolism – flowers for the dead, offerings of food and drink, and the burning of candles. All Souls' Day is the Catholic day of prayers for those in purgatory, which the Tarasco were able to reconcile with their own concept of a day when the dead come back for a celebration. All Saints' Day was understood as a visit by the spirits of children who immediately became *angelitos* (little angels) when they died. A cross was added to the design of the symbolic archway above the altar and the offerings. Indigenous people had always buried their dead near their homes so the Catholic practice of burying the dead in community graveyards added a new gateway for spirits to pass between the earth and the underworld, and a new venue for Day of the Dead observances. The growing mestizo community, of mixed European and indigenous ancestry, evolved a new tradition of visiting graveyards and decorating graves where family members were buried.

Archaeological evidence suggests that all the indigenous cultures of Mexico believed in places where people went after death, and in deities who ruled over the worlds of the dead. The Aztecs, for example, believed the dead went to one of several after-worlds, depending on the cause of death (see the History section of the Facts about Mexico chapter), much as Catholics believed in heaven, purgatory and hell. The idea that the dead could return to visit on a specific day of the year seems to have been unique to the Tarasco people, but as the Catholic Church endorsed an annual day of prayer for the dead, other indigenous beliefs, symbols and rituals about death were also adapted and attached to the occasion. (The tendency to combine the beliefs and practices of different religions is known as 'syncretism', and is evident throughout Latin America.) Thus the Aztec death god Mictlantecutli, who was often depicted with a skull-like face in pre-Hispanic artefacts, reappeared symbolically as a skull on the Day of the Dead, alongside Christian images like the cross. Catholic Church authorities may have actively encouraged syncretism because they knew they could not eliminate traditional beliefs, so deliberately helped to transform them into Catholic rituals.

Día de Muertos persisted in the guise of Catholic celebration throughout the colonial period, when the idea of death as a great leveller and as a release from earthly suffering must have

Monterrey, with over 600 routes developed. Popocatépetl, the famous volcano east of Mexico City, was off-limits at the time of writing because of a spell of volcanic activity that began in 1994. However two other peaks in Mexico's central volcanic belt – Iztaccíhuatl and Pico de Orizaba (Mexico's highest) – offer a good challenge. Go with a guide. Oaxaca is a nascent climbing center.

Día de Muertos

provided comfort for the overwhelmingly poor mestizo and indigenous people. After independence it remained a popular event in the Mexican year, and poets used the occasion to publish verses ridiculing members of the social elite by portraying them as dead, with all their wealth and pretensions rendered futile. The great Mexican engraver José Guadalupe Posada (1852-1913) expressed this in his famous depictions of *calaveras* – skeletal figures of death cheerfully engaging in the business of everyday life, working, dancing, courting, drinking and riding horses into battle. One of his best known and most enduring characters is *La Calavera Catrina*, a female skeleton in an elaborate low-cut dress and flamboyant flower-covered hat, suggestively revealing a bony leg and an ample bust that is all ribs and no cleavage.

The occasion is still observed throughout the country, but there are some important differences in the practices and the underlying beliefs. In predominantly indigenous communities, most notably the Purépecha of Michoacán, it is still very much a religious and spiritual event. For these people, the observance is more appropriately called Noche de Muertos (the Night of the Dead) because families will spend a whole night at the graveyard – the night of October 31 and November 1 with the sprits of dead children, the following night with the spirits of dead adults.

For the mestizo and European people, who comprise about 80% of Mexico's population, Día de Muertos is more of a popular folk festival and family occasion. The mestizos may visit a graveyard to clean and decorate family graves, but they do not usually maintain an all-night vigil. And though they may pray for the souls of the departed, the Catholic belief is that those souls are in heaven or in purgatory, not actually in the graveyard on a visit from the underworld. Sugar skulls, chocolate coffins and toy skeletons are sold in markets everywhere as gifts for children as well as graveyard decorations, though they derive as much from Posada's work as from the icons of the ancient death cults. And though these sweets and toys make fun of death, they have as much spiritual significance as a chocolate Easter egg.

A more recent influence is the North American Halloween tradition, now widely seen in pumpkin heads, friendly ghosts and kid's costume parties, and inadvertently promoted by tourists who give candy to children for 'trick or treat.' There is concern amongst Mexicans about *norteamericano* impacts on Mexican culture, and about commercialization of the event, but Día de Muertos expresses a uniquely Mexican attitude to life and death that is deeply rooted, profoundly fatalistic yet eternally optimistic. It will probably absorb the pagan festival of Halloween just as it adapted to Catholicism over 400 years ago.

Water Sports

Most imaginable activities in, on and under water are practiced along Mexico's coasts. Most resorts offer snorkel gear rentals and can arrange boat and fishing trips. Water-skiing, parasailing, jet skis and 'banana' riding are widespread resort activities too. Cast an eye over the equipment before taking off.

Inland are many *balnearios*, bathing places with swimming pools, often centered on hot springs in picturesque natural surroundings.

Sea Kayaking This is rapidly advancing in popularity. You can do it around La Paz, Cabo San Lucas and Loreto (center of the Parque Marino Nacional Bahía de Loreto) in Baja California; and at places like Puerto Vallarta, Barra de Navidad, Playa Troncones, Pie de la Cuesta, Acapulco and Bahías de Huatulco on the Pacific coast.

Snorkeling & Diving There are wonderful waters along both the Caribbean and Pacific coasts, with diving available in many places. Good visibility is more predictable on the Caribbean and great diving spots include Isla Mujeres, Playa del Carmen, Cozumel, Akumal, Paamul, Punta Allen and the Banco Chinchorro coral atoll. The inland site of Nohoch Nah Chich is the world's largest underwater cavern system.

On the Pacific coast, strap on your tanks at Mazatlán, Puerto Vallarta, Barra de Navidad, Manzanillo, Zihuatanejo, Acapulco, Puerto Escondido, Puerto Ángel, or Bahías de Huatulco. Mulegé, Isla del Carmen (off Loreto), La Paz and Cabo San Lucas are the chief diving spots in Baja California. On the Gulf coast, Veracruz and Tuxpan have possibilities.

Top snorkeling spots include most of the sites mentioned above as well as Playa Tenacatita, Playa Troncones, Faro de Bucerías, Zihuatanejo, Acapulco on the Pacific coast; and Isla Contoy, Punta Allen and Xcalak on the Caribbean. Mexico's most unusual snorkeling site has got to be the lagoons of Cuatrociénegas – in the middle of the Chihuahuan Desert!

When renting diving equipment, try to make sure that it's up to standard. And beware of dive shops that promise certification after just a few hours' tuition.

Surfing & Windsurfing The Pacific coast has some superb waves. Among the very best are the summer breaks at spots between San José del Cabo and Cabo San Lucas (Baja California); the 'world's longest wave,' on Bahía de Matanchén (near San Blas); and the 'Mexican Pipeline,' at Puerto Escondido. Other fine spots include Ensenada, Mazatlán, Sayulita, Barra de Navidad, Manzanillo, Boca de Pascuales (near El Paraíso), Playa La Ticla, Barra de Nexpa, Playa Azul, Playa Troncones, Saladita, Ixtapa, Playa Revolcadero (near Acapulco), Chacahua and Barra de la Cruz (east of Bahías de Huatulco). As always, many surf beaches are easiest reached with your own vehicle.

Los Barriles is Baja California's windsurfing capital. Farther south, Puerto Vallarta and Manzanillo can be good.

Rafting & Canoeing Veracruz state, where rivers fall dramatically from the Sierra Madre to the coastal plain, is the epicenter of this newly popular activity, called *descenso de ríos* in Mexico. The Río Filo-Bobos, with class 2 rapids, is often used for beginners' trips, as is the class 2-3 Río Actopan.

Río Antigua and its tributary Río Pescados are more challenging, especially the upper reaches where the class 4 Barranca Grande rapids are navigable in winter. Jalapa, a base for several rafting operators, is a convenient starting point.

In Chiapas, it's now possible to make raft or canoe trips along some of the rivers of the Lacandón Jungle.

Always use a reliable company with good equipment and experienced guides.

Fishing
There's lake and reservoir fishing inland, and lagoon, river and sea fishing along the Gulf and Caribbean coasts, but it's sport fishing off the Pacific coast that Mexico is justly famous for. See destination sections in the Baja California and Central Pacific Coast chapters for more detail on fishing for marlin, swordfish, sailfish and tuna. Locations include Ensenada, San Felipe, La Paz, San José del Cabo, Cabo San Lucas, Mazatlán, Puerto Vallarta, Barra de Navidad, Manzanillo, Zihuatanejo, Acapulco, Puerto Escondido, Puerto Ángel and Bahías de Huatulco. Fishing permits are required; contact a Mexican Government Tourism Office or a Mexican consulate for information.

Wildlife & Bird-Watching
Observing Mexico's varied and exotic fauna is an increasingly popular and increasingly practicable pastime: see Flora & Fauna in the Facts about Mexico chapter for an introduction to what you can see and where.

COURSES

Taking classes in Mexico can be a great way to meet people and get an inside angle on local life as well as study the language or culture. Mexican universities and colleges often offer tuition to complement courses you may be taking back home. For long-term study in Mexico you'll need a student visa; contact a Mexican consulate.

The Web site Study Mexico (W http://edumexico.org) has a comprehensive directory of higher education opportunities in the country.

Two good US sources on study possibilities in Mexico are the University of Minnesota's International Service and Travel Center (ISTC, ☎ 612-626-4782, W www.istc.umn.edu) and The Council on International Educational Exchange (CIEE, ☎ 888-268-6245, W www.ciee.org). There are also helpful links on the Lonely Planet site (W www.lonelyplanet.com).

Language

Many of Mexico's most attractive cities are home to Spanish language schools, among them Cuernavaca, Guadalajara, Guanajuato, Mérida, Mexico City, Morelia, Oaxaca, Puerto Vallarta, San Cristóbal de Las Casas, San Miguel de Allende and Taxco. Some schools are private, some affiliated to universities.

Course lengths range from a few days to a year. In some places you can enroll on the spot and start any Monday. You may be offered accommodations with a local family as part of the deal. This will help your language skills as much as any formal tuition. In some schools, courses in art, crafts or in-depth study of Mexico are also available.

Costs per week, with accommodations and meals included, can range from around US$150 to over US$400, depending on the city, the school and how intensively you study.

Useful information is available from the National Registration Center for Study Abroad (☎ 414-278-0631, W www.nrcsa.com), 823 N 2nd St, PO Box 1393, Milwaukee, WI 53201, USA. There are also language-school listings on the Web sites Eco Travels in Latin America (W www.planeta.com), Mexico Online (W www.mexonline.com) and Mexican Wave (W www.mexicanwave.com).

The Latin America office of the Institute of International Education (W www.iie.org/latinamerica) publishes *Spanish Study in Mexico*, profiling 43 Spanish-language schools in Mexico.

AmeriSpan (☎ 215-751-1100, W www.amerispan.com), PO Box 40007, Philadelphia, PA 19106-0007, USA, is a 'language travel company' with partner schools in many Mexican and other Latin American cities; it is worth looking at if finding the best program is a problem.

Cooking

Fans of Mexican food can learn from experts how to prepare the whole enchilada at several cookery schools around the country; Tlaxcala and Oaxaca City have several good ones.

WORK

Mexicans themselves need jobs, and people who enter Mexico as tourists are not legally allowed to take employment. The many expats working in Mexico have usually been posted there by their companies with all the necessary papers.

English-speakers (and, though much less likely, German or French speakers) may find teaching jobs in language schools, *preparatorias* (high schools) or universities, or can offer personal tutoring. Mexico City is the best place to get English-teaching work; Guadalajara is also good. It's possible in other major cities. The pay is low, but you can live on it.

The News and cities' telephone yellow pages are sources of job opportunities. Ads in *The News* – mostly for work in Mexico City – quote pay rates up to US$12 an hour. Positions in high schools or universities are more likely to become available with the beginning of each new term; contact institutions that offer bilingual programs or classes in English; for universities, arrange an appointment with the director of the language department. Language schools tend to offer short courses, so teaching opportunities with them come up more often and your commitment is for a shorter time, but they may pay less than high schools and universities.

A foreigner working in Mexico normally needs a permit or government license, but a school will often pay a foreign teacher in the form of a *beca* (scholarship), and thus circumvent the law, or the school's administration will procure the appropriate papers.

It's helpful to know at least a little Spanish, even though some institutes insist that only English be spoken in class.

Teaching apart, you might find a little bar or restaurant work in tourist areas. It's likely to be part-time and short-term.

Volunteer Work

Many opportunities exist for unpaid work in Mexico, short-term or longer. Projects range from sea turtle conservation to human-rights observation to work with abused children. The Web site of the International Service and Travel Center has a database listing many volunteer possibilities and the Council on International Educational Exchange also has information on volunteer programs in Mexico (see Courses, earlier). Check out the Alliance of European Voluntary Service Organisations (W www.alliance-network.org) or UNESCO's Coordinating Committee on International Voluntary Service (W www.unesco.org/ccivs) for information on opportunities for non-US residents. *Volunteer Vacations* by Bill McMillon and *International Directory of Voluntary Work* by Louise Whetter and Victoria Pybus list lots of volunteer organizations and information sources.

Amigos de las Americas (☎ 800-231-7796, W www.amigoslink.org), 5618 Star Lane, Houston, TX 77057, USA, sends paying volunteers to work on summer public-health projects in Latin America. Volunteers receive prior training. AmeriSpan (see Courses, earlier) offers a range of volunteer opportunities in Mexico.

Global Exchange (☎ 415-255-7296, W www.globalexchange.org), 2017 Mission St No 303, San Francisco, CA 94110, USA, wants Spanish-speaking volunteer human-rights observers to live for six to eight weeks in peace camps in Chiapas villages threatened by violence. This program is run in collaboration with the Centro de Derechos Humanos Fray Bartolomé de Las Casas, a human-rights center in San Cristóbal de Las Casas. SIPAZ (W www.sipaz.org), another peace group, needs Spanish-speaking volunteers to work for a year or more in Chiapas.

One World Workforce (☎ 800-451-9564, W www.1ww.org), PO Box 20006, Boulder, CO 80308, USA, sends paying volunteers to work on sea turtle protection projects in Mexico. Cost is around US$700 for a week (plus roundtrip transportation). Earthwatch (☎ 800-776-0188, W www.earthwatch.org), with offices in the USA, Britain, Australia and Japan, also runs environmental projects in Mexico that you pay to take part in (usually around US$1000 per week).

The Casa de los Amigos (see Places to Stay in the Mexico City chapter) has files on volunteer opportunities in Latin America and can place Spanish-speaking volunteers with projects in Mexico City, focusing on issues such as education, street children, AIDS, refugees, and women's rights. Contact Convive at the Casa de los Amigos for more information on volunteer placement and the application process. Further volunteer projects in Mexico are featured at W www.ecoturismolatino.com.

ACCOMMODATIONS

Accommodations in Mexico range from hammocks, palm-thatched huts and campgrounds through hostels and *casas de huéspedes* (guesthouses) to hotels of every imaginable category and world-class luxury resorts.

Almost any tourism-related Internet site can connect you to plenty of Mexican hotel Web sites and provide hotel information.

Seasons & Reservations

The tourism high seasons in most places are Semana Santa (the week before Easter and a couple of days after it), most of July and August, and the Christmas-New Year holiday period of about two weeks. In popular destinations at these times it's best to go early in the day to the place of your choice to try to secure a room. You can try to reserve in advance, by telephone, email or fax, asking whether a deposit is required and how to send it, and requesting confirmation. Some places now take bookings on their Web sites or by email. Others are reluctant to take bookings at all: if you telephone they might say they're full or that they can't hold a room after 7pm. Don't worry: you'll always end up with a room somewhere.

During these peak seasons, many mid-range and top-end establishments in tourist destinations raise their room prices, by anything from 10% to 50% over low-season rates. Budget places to stay are more likely to keep the same rates all year. Annual price hikes usually happen in December or January.

You can often avoid paying the IVA and ISH taxes (totaling 17%) on your room price if you don't require a receipt. The room rates that most establishments quote are those that they expect most of their customers will want to pay – which will be without taxes in many budget and some mid-range places.

Camping

Most organized campgrounds are actually trailer parks, set up for RVs (camper vans) and trailers (caravans), but they accept tent campers at lower rates. Some are very basic, others quite luxurious. Expect to pay about US$3 to US$5 to pitch a tent for two, and US$10 to US$20 for two people with a vehicle, using the full facilities of a good trailer park. Some restaurants or guesthouses in small beach spots will let you pitch a tent on their patch for a couple of dollars per person.

Campgrounds are most common on the Yucatán Peninsula, in Baja California and along the Pacific coast. Recommendable are *The People's Guide to RV Camping in Mexico* by Carl Franz and *Traveler's Guide to Mexican Camping* by Mike & Terri Church.

All Mexican beaches are considered public property. You can camp for nothing on most of them, but security is nonexistent.

Hammocks & Cabañas

These are mainly found in low-key beach spots in the south of the country.

You can rent a hammock and a place to hang it – usually under a palm roof outside a small casa de huéspedes or beach restaurant – for US$2 in some places, though it might reach US$10 on the more expensive Caribbean coast. If you have your own hammock the cost comes down a bit. It's easy enough to buy hammocks in Mexico; Mérida specializes in them, and you'll find them on sale in many places in Oaxaca, Chiapas and the Yucatán Peninsula. Mosquito repellent is handy if you're sleeping in a hammock.

Cabañas are, basically, huts with a palm-thatched roof. Some have dirt floors and

Top 10 Places to Stay

Lonely Planet authors stay in a lot of hotels; sometimes a different one each night. On top of that, they nose around even more. This list of best places to take a snooze was crafted from the expert opinions of the 10 authors who worked on this edition.

Caesar Park Beach & Golf Resort, Cancún
El Castillo, Xilitla
El Moro Hotel, La Paz
Hotel Los Arcos, Taxco
Hotel Posada San Javier, Taxco
Hotel Quinta Real, Zacatecas
Hotel Tierra Maya, Xcalak
Hotel Urdiñola, Saltillo
México Lindo y que Rico!, San Agustinillo, Oaxaca
Rancho Esmeralda, Toniná, Chiapas

nothing inside but a bed; others are deluxe, with electric light, mosquito nets, fans, fridge, bar and decor. Prices for simple cabañas range from around US$10 to US$35, and the most expensive ones of course are on the Caribbean where you'll also find luxury cabañas costing over US$100!

Hostels

Hostels for international budget travelers are a recent phenomenon in Mexico. Since the mid-1990s Mexico City, the central highlands and the southeast of the country (from Oaxaca to the Yucatán Peninsula) have sprouted a few dozen such places, providing dormitory accommodation for US$5 to US$10 per person, plus communal kitchens, bathrooms and living space. Aside from being cheap, they're generally relaxed, and good places to meet other travelers.

All these hostels are independent, but some are loosely grouped in small chains affiliated to Hostelling International (HI, the former International Youth Hostel Federation). The more prominent chain is AMAJ (Asociación Mexicana de Albergues Juveniles, Mexican Youth Hostels Association; w www.hostels.com.mx). The other is REMAJ (Red Mexicana de Alojamiento para Jóvenes, Mexican Youth Lodging Network; w www.hostellingmexico.com).

Hostel cards are not generally required in hostels, though they will get you a small discount in some.

For a long time the only hostels in Mexico were *villas deportivas* or *albergues de juventud* attached to youth sports centers in university and resort cities. These still exist but tend to be inconveniently located and full of Mexican youth groups. They usually have single-sex dormitories. Prepared meals are often available, but there's no guest kitchen. A bunk can cost anywhere between US$3 and US$10.

Casas de Huéspedes & Posadas

Other cheap and often congenial accommodations are often to be found at a casa de huéspedes, a home converted into simple guest lodgings. Good casas de huéspedes are usually family-run, with a relaxed, friendly atmosphere. Rooms may or may not have a private bathroom. A double typically costs US$10 to US$20, though a few places are more comfy and more expensive. Many *posadas* (inns) are like casas de huéspedes; others are small hotels.

Hotels

Cheap hotels exist in every Mexican town. There are clean, friendly ones and dark, dirty, smelly ones. You can get a decent double room with private shower and hot water for under US$20 in most of the country (prices are higher in Baja California and on the Caribbean coast). Fortunately for small groups of travelers, many hotels have rooms for three, four or five people that cost not much more than a double.

Mexico specializes in good mid-range hotels where two people can get a room with private bath, TV and perhaps air-con for US$25 to US$50. Often there's an elevator and a restaurant and bar. You can expect these places to be pleasant, respectable, safe and comfortable.

Among the most charming lodgings are the many old mansions, inns, even convents, turned into hotels. Some date from colonial times, others from the 19th century. Most are wonderfully atmospheric, with fountains gurgling in old stone courtyards. Some are a bit spartan (but relatively low in price), others have been modernized and can be posh and expensive. These are often the lodgings you will remember most fondly after your trip.

Mexico also has plenty of large, modern hotels, particularly in the largest cities and resorts. They offer the expected levels of luxury at expectedly lofty prices. If you like to stay in luxury but also enjoy saving some money, choose a Mexican hotel that's not part of an international chain.

Note that *cuarto sencillo* (literally, single room) usually means a room with one bed, which is often a *cama matrimonial* (double bed). Sometimes one person can occupy such a room for a lower price than two people, sometimes the price is the same. A *cuarto doble* is usually a room with two beds, often both 'matrimonial.'

Apartments

In some places there are *apartamentos* with fully equipped kitchens designed for tourists. Some are very comfortable, and they can be a good value for three or four people. Tourist offices and ads in local papers (especially English-language papers) are good sources of information on apartments.

FOOD

Mexican cuisine is enormously varied, full of regional differences and subtle surprises. You'll eat well in Mexico, and the choice is wide in all sizable towns. In addition to the Mexican fare, there's all sorts of international food, even some good vegetarian restaurants. For inexpensive fresh fruit, vegetables, tortillas, cheese and bread, pop into the local market. Seafood is good along the coasts and in the major cities. But be suspicious of it in out-of-the-way mountain towns, and take care with uncooked seafood.

You'll find a Food & Drink Glossary of Spanish terms at the back of the book.

Meals & Staples

Mexicans eat three meals a day: *desayuno* (breakfast), *comida* (lunch) and *cena* (supper). Each includes one or more of three national staples: *tortillas, frijoles* and *chiles*.

Tortillas are thin round patties of pressed corn *(maíz)* dough or wheat-flour *(harina)* dough, cooked on griddles. Both can be wrapped around or served under any type of food. Frijoles are beans, eaten boiled, fried or refried in soups, on tortillas, or with just about anything.

Chiles refer to the spicy chili peppers, which come in dozens of varieties and can be consumed in hundreds of ways. Some types, such as the *habanero* and *serrano*, are always very hot, while others, such as the *poblano*, vary in spiciness according to when they were picked. If you're unsure about your tolerance for hot chilies, ask if they are *dulce* (sweet), *picante* (hot) or *muy picante* (very hot).

Breakfast The simplest breakfast is coffee or tea and *pan dulce* (sweet rolls), a basket of which is set on the table; you pay for the number consumed. Many restaurants offer combination breakfasts for about US$2 to US$4.50, typically composed of *jugo o fruta* (fruit juice or fruit), *café* (coffee), *bolillo* (bread roll) or *pan tostado* (toasted sliced bread) with *mantequilla* (butter) and *mermelada* (jam), *huevos* (eggs, which can be served in a variety of ways) and probably frijoles and tortillas.

Mexicans often eat meat for breakfast, but in many places frequented by travelers, items such as granola, fruit salad *(ensalada de frutas)*, Corn Flakes and even porridge *(avena)* are equally available.

Lunch *La comida* or *el almuerzo*, the main meal of the day, is usually served between 1 and 3 or 4pm. Most restaurants offer not only á la carte fare but also special fixed-price menus called *comida corrida*, *cubierto* or *menú del día*. These menus are Mexico's best food bargains, because you get several courses (often with some choice) for much less than such a meal would cost á la carte. Prices may range from US$1.75 at a market stall for a simple meal of soup, a meat dish, rice and coffee to US$12 or more for elaborate meals beginning with oyster stew and finishing with *profiteroles* (chocolate mousse). Typically you'll get soup, maybe a plate of rice served as a separate course, a meat or fish main dish, a dessert *(postre*, typically a small afterthought to the meal), and a fruit drink and/or coffee, for US$3 to US$5.

Dinner/Supper *La cena*, the evening meal, is usually lighter than lunch. Fixed-price meals are rarely offered.

Snacks

Antojitos, or 'little whims' – nowadays called *especialidades mexicanas* or *platillos*

mexicanos on some menus – are traditional Mexican snacks or light dishes. Burritos, tacos, enchiladas, quesadillas, tamales and tortas are all antojitos. Some are small meals in themselves. They can be eaten at any time, on their own or as part of a larger meal. There are many, many varieties, some of which are peculiar to local areas.

Street & Market Meals

The cheapest food in Mexico is served up by the thousands of street stands selling all manner of hot and cold food and drinks. At these places you can often get a taco or a glass of orange juice for less than US$0.40. Many are very popular and well patronized, but hygiene can be a risk. Deciding whether to use them is a matter of judgment; those with a lot of customers are likely to be the best and safest.

A grade up from street fare are the *comedores* which are found in many markets. They offer Mexico's cheapest sit-down meals – you sit on benches at long tables and the food is prepared in front of you. Usually comedores serve typical local fare, and at the best ones you are likely to get a meal that's close to home cooking. It's best to go at lunchtime, when ingredients are fresher, and pick a comedor that's busy – which usually means it's good.

DRINKS

In a country with a climate as warm as Mexico's, quenching your thirst is an important activity, and Mexicans have invented some delicious ways of doing it. A huge variety of *bebidas* (drinks) are imbibed in Mexico. Don't drink any water, ice or drinks made with water unless you're sure the water has been purified or boiled (see the Health section, earlier in this chapter). You can buy bottles of inexpensive purified or mineral water everywhere. You will find a Food & Drink Glossary of Spanish terms at the back of the book.

Nonalcoholic Drinks

Tea & Coffee Ordinary Mexican *café*, grown mostly near Córdoba and Orizaba and in Chiapas and Oaxaca, is flavorful but often served weak. Fortunately for caffeine addicts more and more real cafés are now appearing around the country; these places serve a decent-strength shot of the dark brown stuff, native or imported. A few places serve Mexican organic coffee, from Oaxaca or Chiapas. In other places it's often better to ask for 'Nescafé,' which can mean any brand of instant coffee. Tea, invariably in bags, is a profound disappointment to any real tea drinker.

Fruit & Vegetable Drinks Pure fresh juices *jugos* are popular, and readily available from street-side stalls and juice bars. If you see the fruit being squeezed in front of you, as is often the case, it will almost certainly be safe to drink. Every fruit, including some succulent tropical ones, and a few of the squeezable vegetables are used.

Licuados are blends of fruit or juice with water and sugar. *Licuados con leche* use milk instead of water. The delicious combinations are practically limitless. In juice bars you can expect that purified water is used, but don't assume the same for street-side juice stalls.

Aguas de fruta (also called *aguas frescas* or *aguas preparadas*) are made by adding sugar and water to fruit juice or a syrup made from mashed grains or seeds. You'll often see them in big glass jars on the counters of juice stands. A jug of agua de fruta is a great thirst-quencher with a meal.

Atole is a sweet, hot drink thickened with *masa* (corn dough) and flavored with chocolate, cinnamon or various fruits. It's often consumed at breakfast with tamales.

Chocolate (hot chocolate, often flavored with cinnamon) is a favorite warming drink in the south. It's traditionally drunk from a bowl, with sweet bread to dip into it.

Soft Drinks *Refrescos* are bottled or canned soft drinks, and there are some interesting and tasty local varieties.

Many brands of *agua mineral* (mineral water) are derived from Mexican springs – Tehuacán and Garci Crespo are two of the best and are sometimes available with refreshing flavors, as well as plain.

Alcoholic Drinks

Mexico produces a fascinating variety of alcoholic drinks made from grapes, grains

---

How to Drink Tequila Like a Pro

There's almost as much mystique about drinking tequila or mezcal as there is about the Japanese tea ceremony. Some insist that if you don't want to look silly you must:

    1) lick the back of your hand and sprinkle salt on it
    2) lick the salt
    3) down the shot *(trago)* in one gulp
    4) suck on a wedge of lime
    5) lick more salt
    6) if you're drinking mezcal, eat the worm when the bottle is finished

In fact, Mexicans may equally well suck a lime before downing the shot instead of after it. Nor is there any law whatsoever against savoring tequila or mezcal in a much more measured manner like, say, a glass of brandy. In fact, some real tequila aficionados argue that a quality tequila or mezcal is wasted if thrown back in one.

and cacti. Foreign liquors are widely available, too.

Those for whom alcohol is a problem, not a pleasure, will find Alcoholics Anonymous schedules for Mexico (many meetings are in English), and other tips about staying off the bottle, on the Mexico Mike Internet site (**W** www.mexicomike.com).

Drinking Places Everyone knows about Mexican cantinas, those pits of wild drinking and wilder displays of machismo. A friend was once in a cantina in Mexico City where it was hardly noticed when a man drew his pistol and fired several rounds into the ceiling. Cantinas are generally loud but not quite that loud.

Cantinas are usually for men only. They don't typically have 'Cantina' signs outside, but can be identified by Wild West-type swinging half-doors, signs prohibiting minors, and a generally raucous atmosphere. Those who enter must be prepared to drink hard. They might be challenged by a local to go one-for-one at a bottle of tequila, mezcal or brandy. If you're not up to that, excuse yourself and beat a retreat.

Some of the nicer cantinas don't get upset about the presence of a woman if she is accompanied by a man, preferably a regular patron. It's best to leave judgment of the situation up to a local, though.

In fact, most Mexican drinking establishments are far less daunting than cantinas. Most travelers and a great number of Mexicans do any drinking they do in cafés, bars, lounges or 'pubs' where anyone will feel at home. Plenty of bars are geared to a young, sociable crowd, with recorded music and themed decor.

Mezcal, Tequila & Pulque Mezcal can be made from the sap of several species of the maguey plant, a spray of long, thick spikes sticking out of the ground. Tequila is made only from the maguey *Agave tequilana weber*, grown in Jalisco and a few other states. The production method for both is similar (see 'Tequila' in the Western Central Highlands chapter), except that for mezcal the chopped up *piña* (core) of the plant is baked, whereas for tequila it's steamed. The final product is a clear liquid (sometimes artificially tinted) which is at its most potent as tequila. The longer the aging process, the

---

Top 10 Places to Drink

Raise a glass to Mexico's best drinking ponds! After countless, seemingly bottomless pitchers, the 10 authors on this edition came to these staggering conclusions.

   Cafe El Infinito, Monterrey
   El Alquimista, Zipolite
   El Chile Willie, Loreto
   Ixchel, Colonia Roma, Mexico City
   La Casa de la Condesa, Veracruz
   La Parrilla, Cancún (for the piña coladas)
   On the beach, at night, with friends
   On the street in Guanajuato during the
      Cervantino festival
   Plazuela Machado, old Mazatlán
   Zócalo, Oaxaca

---

smoother the drink and the higher the price. A repugnant *gusano* (worm) is added to some bottles of mezcal.

For foreigners not used to the potency of straight tequila, Mexican bartenders invented the margarita, a concoction of tequila, lime juice and liquor served in a salt-rimmed glass. Sangrita is a sweet, nonalcoholic, tomato, citrus, chile and spice drink often downed as a tequila chaser.

Pulque is fermented maguey juice, a cheap drink much less potent than tequila or mezcal. The foamy, milky, slightly sour liquid spoils quickly and cannot easily be bottled and shipped. Most pulque is produced around Mexico City and served in male-dominated, working-class *pulquerías*.

Beer Breweries were established in Mexico by German immigrants in the late 19th century. Mexico's several large brewing companies produce more than 25 brands of *cerveza* (beer), many of which are excellent. Each major company has a premium beer, such as Bohemia and Corona de Barril (usually served in bottles); several standard beers, such as Carta Blanca, Superior and Dos Equis (Two Xs); and 'popular' brands, such as Corona, Tecate and Modelo. All are blond lagers meant to be served chilled. Each of the large companies also produces an *oscura* (dark) beer, such as Negra Modelo or Dos Equis Oscura. There are some regional beers, too, brewed to similar tastes.

Wine Wine is far less popular than beer and tequila, and homegrown wines are usually the cheapest on any Mexican restaurant's wine list, but the country's few large wine growers, all around Ensenada in Baja California, produce some quite drinkable vintages.

Pedro Domecq has the highest profile. Its Cabernet Sauvignon XA, costing around US$20 in restaurants, is probably the most popular Mexican red. Its Zinfandel XA is of similar quality. Domecq's Calafia and Los Reyes reds and whites cost little over half that.

Three of the top wineries in quality are Chateau Camou, Bodegas de Santo Tomás and Monte Xanic. The very best wines fetch US$75 a bottle in upmarket restaurants.

Other northern centers, such as Zacatecas and Parras (home of the Americas' oldest winery), produce less polished but still very drinkable wines.

Wine mixed with fruit juice is the basis of the tasty *sangría*.

ENTERTAINMENT

Little beats a Mexican fiesta for entertainment, but if none happens to be in progress where you happen to be, you have plenty of alternatives. People-watching from a café on a plaza is up on the list. Larger cities and resorts have thriving bar, club and music scenes. In the big cities you'll also find opera, classical concerts, and Spanish-language theater. Cinemas screen many foreign movies, always in their original language with Spanish subtitles, unless they are children's films.

One thing specially worth making an effort to see is a performance of Mexican folk dance, always colorful and interesting (see Arts in the Facts about Mexico chapter). If you can't catch dance in its natural setting (at a fiesta) some good regular shows are put on in theaters and hotels. The most dazzlingly elaborate is Mexico City's Ballet Folklórico.

SPECTATOR SPORTS

Events such as soccer games, bullfights and *charreadas* (rodeos) can be fascinating; if the action doesn't enthrall you, the crowd probably will.

Soccer (Football)

Fútbol is Mexico's favorite sport. The country has a 19-team national Primera División (one team takes a rest each week) and some impressive stadiums. Mexico City's Estadio Azteca (Aztec Stadium) hosted the 1970 and 1986 World Cup finals.

The two most popular teams in the country are América, of Mexico City, nicknamed Las Águilas (the Eagles), and Guadalajara (Las Chivas, the Goats). They attract large followings wherever they play. Other leading clubs are UNAM (Universidad Autónoma de Mexico, nicknamed Las Pumas), Cruz Azul, Atlante, Toros Neza and Necaxa, all from Mexico City; Universidad de Guadalajara, Universidad Autónoma de Guadalajara (Los Tecos), and Atlas, all from Guadalajara; Monterrey and Universidad Autónoma de Nuevo León (Los Tigres), also from Monterrey; Toluca, Pachuca, Puebla, Celaya and Santos (of Torreón).

The biggest games of the year are those between América and Guadalajara, known as 'Los Clásicos.' These teams attract crowds of 100,000 when they meet at the Estadio Azteca. Crowds at other games range from a few thousand to around 70,000. Games are spaced over the weekend from Friday to Sunday; details are printed in *The News* and the Spanish-language press.

Attending a game is fun; rivalry between opposing fans is generally good-humored. Tickets can be bought at the gate and can cost from less than US$1 to US$10, depending on the quality of your seat.

Mexico's soccer calendar is divided into a *torneo de invierno* (winter season, August to December) and a *torneo de verano* (summer season, January to May), each ending in eight-team playoffs (La Liguilla) and eventually a two-leg final to decide the champion.

The Spanish-language Web site **w** www .futbolmundial.com.mx has scores, standings and other things fans need to know.

Baseball

Professional *béisbol* is fairly popular. The winner of the October to January Liga Mexicana del Pacífico (**w** www.ligadel pacifico.com.mx), with teams from the northwest, represents Mexico in the February Serie del Caribe (the biggest event in Latin American baseball) against the champions of Venezuela, Puerto Rico and the Dominican Republic. Younger American players on the way up often play in the Pacific league. The Liga Mexicana de

The Fiesta Brava

To many gringo eyes the *corrida de toros* (bullfight) hardly seems to be sport or, for that matter, entertainment. Mexicans see it as both and more. It's as much a ritualistic dance as a fight, and it's said that Mexicans arrive on time for only two events – funerals and bullfights.

The corrida de toros (literally, running of the bulls) or *fiesta brava* (wild festival) begins promptly at an appointed time on Sunday afternoon. To the sound of music, usually a Spanish *paso doble*, the *matador* (literally, killer), in his *traje de luces* (suit of lights), and the *toreros* (his assistants) give the traditional *paseíllo* (salute) to the fight authorities and the crowd. Then the first of the day's bulls (there are usually six in an afternoon) is released from its pen for the first of the ritual's three *suertes* (acts) or *tercios* (thirds).

The cape-waving toreros tire the bull by luring him around the ring. After a few minutes two *picadores*, on heavily padded horses, enter and jab long lances *(picas)* into the bull's shoulders to weaken him. Somehow this is often the most gruesome part of the whole process.

After the picadores leave the ring the *suerte de banderillas* begins, as the toreros attempt to stab three pairs of elongated darts into the bull's shoulders without getting impaled on his horns. After that comes the *suerte de muleta*, the climax in which the matador has exactly 16 minutes to kill the bull. Starting with fancy cape work to tire the animal, the matador then exchanges his large cape for the smaller *muleta* and takes sword in hand, baiting the bull to charge before delivering the fatal *estocada* (lunge) with his sword. The matador must deliver the estocada into the neck from a position directly in front of the animal.

If the matador succeeds, and he usually does, the bull collapses and an assistant dashes into the ring to slice its jugular. If the applause from the crowd warrants, he will also cut off an ear or two and sometimes the tail for the matador. The dead bull is dragged from the ring to be butchered for sale.

A 'good' bullfight depends not only on the skill and courage of the matador but also the spirit of the bulls. Animals lacking heart for the fight bring shame on the ranch that bred them. Very occasionally, a bull that has fought outstandingly is *indultado* (spared) – an occasion for great celebration – and will then retire to stud.

In northern Mexico the bullfighting season runs from March or April to August or September. In Mexico City's Monumental Plaza México, one of the world's biggest bullrings, and other southerly rings the main season is from October or November to March.

The veteran Eloy Cavasos, from Monterrey, is often acclaimed as Mexico's top matador. Eulalio 'Zotoluco' López is another big name. Paco González, Ignacio Garibay, Fernando Ochoa and Jerónimo are younger stars. Bullfights also featuring star matadors from Spain, such as Enrique Ponce, El Juli, José Tomás or El Cordobés, have added spice. *The News* runs an informative weekly bullfighting column called Blood on the Sand.

Béisbol (W www.lmb.com.mx), with 16 teams spread down the center and east of the country from Monclova to Cancún, plays from March to September. *Afición* newspaper has good baseball coverage.

Other Sports

A **charreada** is a rodeo, held particularly in the northern half of the country during fiestas and at regular venues often called *lienzos charros*. **Horse racing** takes place

Friday to Sunday at Mexico City's Hipódromo de las Américas.

The fast, exciting Basque game *pelota,*
brought to Mexico by the Spanish, is played
in Mexico as **jai alai** ('HIGH-lie'). It's a bit
like squash played on a long court with a
hard ball and with curved baskets attached
to the arm. Sadly, the game has been in a
decline recently and at the time of writing
you could no longer see semiprofessionals
in action in Mexico City or Tijuana. **Pelota
mixteca** is something entirely different – a
modern version of the pre-Hispanic ball
game, still played in parts of Oaxaca state
(see 'The Ball Game, Then & Now' in the
Facts about Mexico chapter).

More showbiz than sport is **lucha libre**,
wrestling. Participants give themselves names
like Shocker, Los Karate Boy and Heavy
Metal, then clown around in fancy dress.

SHOPPING

See the Artesanías special section for words
and pictures on the wonderful range of
(handicrafts), which are Mexico's outstanding buys. If you buy crafts in the villages
where they are made or at local markets –
and not from shops or large centralized
crafts markets – then a lot more of your
money will go to the (usually poor) people
who make them, instead of to entrepreneurs.

For everyday purchases and consumer
goods, wealthier urban Mexicans like to shop
in glitzy modern malls, big super/hypermar-
kets and department stores. These are usually
in residential districts where travelers have
little reason to go (unless you're actually
looking for a back-home-type shopping experience). In city centers you're more likely
to find smaller, older shops and markets, with
a lot more character!

Getting There & Away

AIR

Most visitors to Mexico arrive by air.

Airports & Airlines

About 30 Mexican cities receive direct flights from the USA or Canada, and you can fly to Mexico without changing planes from at least 25 US and Canadian cities. There are one-stop connecting flights to and from many other cities in all three countries. Mexico City receives more flights from the north than any other Mexican city, followed by Guadalajara, Cancún, Monterrey and Acapulco.

Airlines with the most service from the USA or Canada to Mexico include Air Canada, Alaska, America West, American, Continental, Delta, Northwest, United and the two main Mexican airlines, Aeroméxico and Mexicana. Another Mexican airline, Aero California, operates flights between California, USA, and northwest Mexico.

From Europe there are flights to Mexico City and Cancún. Only a few airlines fly nonstop, among them Aeroméxico, Air France, British Airways, Iberia, KLM and Lufthansa. An alternative is to fly with a US airline or alliance partner, changing planes in the USA.

From Havana, Cuba, you can fly into Mexico City by Mexicana and to Cancún and six other southeast Mexican cities by Aerocaribe, a Mexicana subsidiary. Mexicana and Guatemala's Aviateca fly Guatemala-Mexico routes including Guatemala City-Flores-Cancún and Guatemala City-Mexico City.

From other Central American countries, you generally have to fly into Mexico City unless you change planes in Guatemala. Airlines include Mexicana, Aviateca, TACA of El Salvador, LACSA of Costa Rica, Nica of Nicaragua and Panama's Copa.

Flights from South America go to Mexico City and Cancún. Carriers between South America and Mexico include Mexicana, Aeroméxico, American Airlines, Continental, Avianca, Copa, LACSA, Lloyd Aéreo Boliviano, Varig and Aerolíneas Argentinas.

See the Getting There & Away sections under individual cities for more on who flies where.

Buying Tickets

The cost of flying to Mexico depends on what time of year and day of the week you fly (you pay more around Christmas and New Year's, during the summer holidays and at weekends), how long you're traveling (you'll usually pay less on a roundtrip ticket if you come back within 90 days) and whether you can find a discount or advance-purchase fare or promotional offer. If you are going to take flights within Mexico, it is often cheaper to book them before you go, in conjunction with an international roundtrip ticket, than to buy them individually in Mexico.

Start shopping for airfares as soon as you can; the cheapest tickets often have to be bought months in advance, and popular flights sell out early. Generally, there is nothing to be gained by buying a ticket direct from the airline. Discounted tickets are released to selected travel agents and specialist discount agencies, and these are usually the cheapest deals going. From time

Warning

The information in this chapter is particularly vulnerable to change: prices for international travel are volatile, routes are introduced and canceled, schedules change, special deals come and go, and rules and visa requirements are amended. Airlines and governments seem to take a perverse pleasure in making price structures and regulations as complicated as possible. You should check directly with the airline or a travel agent to make sure you understand how a fare (and any ticket you may buy) works. In addition, the travel industry is highly competitive, and there are many lurks and perks.

The upshot of this is that you should get opinions, quotes and advice from as many airlines and travel agents as possible before you part with your hard-earned cash. The details given in this chapter should be regarded as pointers and are not a substitute for your own careful, up-to-date research.

Airline Contact Details

Many airlines have toll-free 800 telephone numbers that you can call from anywhere in Mexico:

Airline	Web Site	Telephone
Aero California		☎ 55-5207-1392
Aerocaribe	w www.aerocaribe.com	☎ 800-502-20-00
Aerocozumel	w www.aerocaribe.com	☎ 800-502-20-00
Aerolíneas Internacionales		☎ 800-004-17-00
Aerolitoral	w www.aeromexico.com	☎ 800-021-40-00
Aeromar	w www.aeromar-air.com	☎ 800-704-29-00
Aeroméxico	w www.aeromexico.com	☎ 800-021-40-00
Air Canada	w www.aircanada.ca	☎ 55-5207-6611
Alaska Airlines	w www.alaska-air.com	☎ 55-5533-1747
America West	w www.americawest.com	☎ 800-533-68-62
American Airlines	w www.aa.com	☎ 800-904-60-00
Aviacsa		☎ 800-006-22-00
AVIATECA	w www.grupotaca.com	☎ 55-5553-3366
British Airways	w www.britishairways.com	☎ 800-006-57-00
Continental Airlines	w www.continental.com	☎ 800-900-50-00
Delta Airlines	w www.delta-air.com	☎ 55-5279-0909
Iberia	w www.iberia.com	☎ 55-5130-3030
KLM	w www.klm.com	☎ 800-900-08-00
Mexicana	w www.mexicana.com	☎ 800-502-20-00
Northwest Airlines	w www.nwa.com	☎ 800-225-25-25
United Airlines	w www.ual.com	☎ 800-003-07-70

to time, airlines do have promotional fares and special offers, but generally they only sell fares at the official listed price. An exception to this is booking on the Internet. Some airlines offer excellent fares to Web surfers. They may sell seats by auction or simply cut prices to reflect the reduced cost of electronic selling.

Many travel agents have Web sites too, which can make the Internet an easy way to compare prices. There is also an increasing number of online agents who operate only on the Internet. Online ticket sales work well for a simple one-way or return trip on specified dates. But there's no substitute for a travel agent who knows about special deals and can offer advice on many other aspects of your flight and trip.

You may find the cheapest flights are advertised by obscure agencies. Most such firms are honest and solvent, but there are some rogue outfits around. Paying by credit card generally offers protection, as most card issuers provide refunds if you can prove you didn't get what you paid for.

Similar protection can be obtained by buying a ticket from a bonded agent, such as one covered by the Air Travel Organiser's Licence (ATOL) scheme in the UK (more details available at w www.atol .org.uk). Agents who accept only cash should hand over the tickets straight away. After you've made a booking or paid your deposit, call the airline and confirm that the booking was made. It's generally not advisable to send money (even checks) through the post unless the agent is very well established. Some travelers have reported being ripped off by fly-by-night mail-order ticket agents.

If you purchase a ticket and later want to make changes to your route or get a refund, you need to contact the original travel agent. Airlines only issue refunds to the purchaser of a ticket, usually the travel agent who bought the ticket on your behalf. Many travelers change their routes halfway through their trips, so think carefully before buying a ticket which is not easily refunded.

Student & Youth Fares Full-time students and people under 26 have access to better deals than other travelers (cheaper fares and/or more flexibility to change flights or routes). You have to show a document proving your date of birth or a valid International Student Identity Card (ISIC) when buying your ticket and boarding the plane.

Travelers with Special Needs
If they're warned early enough, airlines can often make special arrangements such as wheelchair assistance at airports, vegetarian meals on the flight, or 'Skycots' or baby food for infants. The disability-friendly Web site W www.allgohere.com has an airline directory that provides information on the facilities offered by various airlines.

Departure Tax
A departure tax equivalent to about US$25 is levied on international flights from Mexico. It's usually included in your ticket cost, but if it isn't, you must pay with cash during airport check-in. Ask your travel agent in advance.

The USA & Canada
Discount travel agents in the USA and Canada are known as consolidators (although you won't see a sign on the door saying 'Consolidator'). You can locate them through the yellow pages and they also advertise in newspapers and magazines, listing tables of destinations and fares and toll-free numbers to call. San Francisco is the ticket consolidator capital of the USA, although good deals can also be found in Los Angeles, New York and other big cities.

The *New York Times, Los Angeles Times, Chicago Tribune* and *San Francisco Chronicle* all produce weekly travel sections in which you'll find a number of travel agency ads. In Canada, the *Globe & Mail, Toronto Star, Montreal Gazette* and *Vancouver Sun* are good places to look for cheap fares.

Council Travel, America's largest student travel organization, has around 60 offices in the USA. Call it for the office nearest you (☎ 800-226-8624) or visit its Web site at W www.counciltravel.com. STA Travel (☎ 800-777-0112) has offices in Boston, Chicago, Miami, New York, Philadelphia,

San Francisco and other major cities. Call the toll-free 800 number for office locations or visit its Web site at W www.statravel.com.

Travel CUTS (☎ 800-667-2887) is Canada's national student travel agency and has offices in all major cities. Its Web address is W www.travelcuts.com.

Other Internet sites well worth looking at include W www.expedia.com, W http://air.one travel.com and W www.smarterliving.com.

Here are some typical examples of discounted roundtrip fares at one week's notice in the low season:

from	to Mexico City	to Cancún	to Acapulco
Chicago	US$390	US$570	US$540
Dallas/ Fort Worth	US$455	US$530	US$480
Los Angeles	US$350	US$540	US$460
Miami	US$420	US$450	US$470
New York	US$400	US$470	US$565
Toronto	C$840	C$975	C$1120

Another possibility for a shortish trip, say, three weeks or less, is a package-tour flight. Check newspaper travel ads and call a package-tour agent, asking if you can buy 'air only' (just the roundtrip air transportation, not the hotel or other features). This is often cheaper than a discounted roundtrip ticket.

Europe
Typically, a discounted or advance-purchase roundtrip fare from anywhere in western Europe to Mexico City or Cancún costs between UK£350 and UK£600 (€560 to €960). You get prices towards the lower end of that range by flying outside the peak seasons of July, August and mid-December to mid-January, and booking well ahead.

With a normal roundtrip ticket, you can often change the date of the return leg, subject to seat availability, at little or no cost. It's worth checking before you buy the ticket. Open-jaw tickets can be useful if you want to hop from one part of Mexico to another, or between Mexico and elsewhere in the Americas, without backtracking. With an open-jaw, you usually depart from, and return to, the same city in Europe.

Most ticket types are available at discount rates from cheap ticket agencies in

Air Travel Glossary

Alliances Many of the world's leading airlines are now intimately involved with each other, sharing everything from reservations systems and check-in to aircraft and frequent-flier schemes. Opponents say that alliances restrict competition. Whatever the arguments, there is no doubt that big alliances are the way of the future.

Courier flights These are a great bargain if you're lucky enough to find one. They are occasionally advertised in the newspapers, or you could contact air-freight companies listed in the phone book. You may even have to go to the air-freight company to get an answer – the companies aren't always keen to give out information over the phone. For more information, contact International Association of Air Travel Couriers (IAATC; in the USA ☎ 561-582-8320) or visit its Web site at Ⓦ www.courier.org. Joining this organization does not guarantee that you'll get a courier flight.

Fares Airlines traditionally offer 1st-class (coded F), business-class (coded J) and economy-class (coded Y) tickets. These days, there are so many promotional and discounted fares available that few passengers pay full fare.

Lost Tickets If you lose your airline ticket, an airline will usually treat it as a traveler's check and, after inquiries, issue you with another one. Legally, however, an airline is entitled to treat it as cash, so if you lose it, then it could be gone forever. Take very good care of your tickets.

Open-Jaw Tickets These are return tickets used to fly out to one place but return from another. If available, this can save you from having to backtrack to your arrival point.

Overbooking Since every flight has some passengers who fail to show up, airlines often book more passengers than they have seats. Usually excess passengers make up for the no-shows, but occasionally somebody gets bumped onto the next available flight. Who is it most likely to be? The passengers who check in late. If you do get bumped, you are normally offered some form of compensation.

Reconfirmation Some airlines require you to reconfirm your flight at least 72 hours prior to departure. Check your travel documents to see if this is the case.

Restrictions Discounted tickets often have various restrictions on them – such as mandatory advance payment and penalties for alterations or cancellations. Others have restrictions on the minimum and maximum period you must be away.

Round-the-World Tickets RTW tickets give you a limited period (usually a year) in which to circumnavigate the globe. You can go anywhere the carrying airlines go, as long as you don't backtrack. The number of stopovers or the total number of separate flights is decided before you set off, and these tickets usually cost a bit more than a basic return flight.

Transferred Tickets Airline tickets cannot be transferred from one person to another. Travelers sometimes try to sell the return half of their tickets, but officials can ask you to prove that you are the person named on the ticket. On an international flight, the name on the ticket is compared with the name on the passport.

Europe's bargain flight centers, such as London, Amsterdam and Paris.

If you're planning on traveling via the USA, be sure that you remember to check US visa requirements.

Ticket Agents in the UK Discount air travel is big business in London. Advertisements for many travel agencies appear in the travel pages of the weekend broadsheet newspapers (such as the *Sunday Times, The Independent* and the *Daily Telegraph)*, in *Time Out,* the *Evening Standard* and in the free magazine *TNT.*

An excellent place to start your fare inquiries for Mexico is Journey Latin America (☎ 020-8747-3108), 12 & 13 Heathfield Terrace, Chiswick, London W4 4JE. Its Web site is Ⓦ www.journeylatinamerica.co.uk.

For students or travelers under 26 years, a popular travel agency is STA Travel (☎ 020-7361 6262, Ⓦ www.statravel.co.uk), which has an office at 86 Old Brompton Rd, London SW7, and branches across the country. It sells tickets to all travelers but caters especially to young people and students.

One Internet site well worth investigating for good fares is Ⓦ www.ebookers.com.

Ticket Agents Elsewhere in Europe

Agencies specializing in cheap tickets and student/youth travel include the following:

France – Nouvelles Frontières (☎ 08 25 00 08 25, W www.nouvelles-frontieres.fr), 87 blvd de Grenelle, 75015 Paris, with dozens of offices around the country

OTU Voyages (☎ 01 40 29 12 12, W www.otu.fr), 39 ave Georges Bernanos, 75005 Paris: youth/student agency with branches across the country

Germany – STA Travel (☎ 030-311 0950), Goethesttrasse 73, 10625 Berlin: youth/student agency with branches in major cities across the country

Italy – CTS Viaggi (☎ 06-462 0431, W www.cts.it), Via Genova 16, Rome: youth/student agency with branches all over Italy

Passagi (☎ 06-474 0923), Stazione Termini FS, Galleria Di Tesla, Rome

Netherlands – Holland International (☎ 070-307 6307), with offices in most cities

Scandinavia – Kilroy Travels (W www.kilroy travels.com): youth/student agency with branches in many cities

Spain – Halcón Viajes (☎ 902-300 600), with over 500 branches

Viajes Zeppelin (☎ 902-384 253, W www .v-zeppelin.es), Plaza Santo Domingo 2, 28013 Madrid

An interesting Web site to check for fares from France, Switzerland or Belgium is W www.degriftour.com.

Australia & New Zealand

There are no direct flights from Australia or New Zealand to Mexico. The cheapest way to get there is usually via the USA (normally Los Angeles).

At the time of writing some bargain fares were available via Japan on Japan Airlines. Tickets with stopovers in South America were hard to obtain. From Sydney, Melbourne or Auckland to Mexico City via Los Angeles, typical roundtrip fares are around A$2500 or NZ$2600; add a couple of hundred dollars between mid-December and the end of February. Check US visa requirements if you're traveling via the USA.

It often works out cheaper to keep going right round the world on a Round-the-World (RTW) ticket rather than do a U-turn on a return ticket. RTW fares from Sydney or Melbourne, including Mexico, can be had for little over A$2000.

Two well-known agents for cheap fares are STA Travel and Flight Centre. STA Travel (☎ 03-9349 2411) has its main office at 224 Faraday St, Carlton, Melbourne, with offices in all major Australian cities and on many university campuses. Call ☎ 131 776 Australiawide for the location of your nearest branch or visit its Web site at W www.statravel.com.au. In New Zealand STA Travel's main office is at 10 High St, Auckland (☎ 09-309 0458). Other offices in Auckland include Hamilton, Palmerston North, Wellington, Christchurch and Dunedin. The Web address is www.sta travel.co.nz. Flight Centre (☎ 131 600 Australiawide) has a central office at 82 Elizabeth St, Sydney, and a large central office (☎ 09-309 6171) in Auckland at National Bank Towers (corner Queen and Darby Sts), plus many branches throughout Australia and New Zealand. Its Web address is W www.flightcentre.com.au.

Some discount ticket agencies, particularly smaller ones, advertise cheap airfares in the weekend newspapers, such as the *Age* in Melbourne and the *Sydney Morning Herald*. The *New Zealand Herald* has a travel section in which travel agents advertise fares.

Good Web sites for fares are W www.travel .com.au and W www.travel.co.nz.

South America

Roundtrip flights to Mexico City start at around US$500 from Caracas, US$750 from Lima, US$850 from Buenos Aires or US$950 from São Paulo. Fares to Cancún are usually US$100 to US$300 lower. Student/youth fares are available from agencies such as IVI Tours (☎ 02-993 6082, W www.ividiomas.com), Residencia La Hacienda, Piso Bajo, Local 1-4-T, Final Avenida Principal de las Mercedes, Caracas, Venezuela; ASATEJ (☎ 011-4511 8700, W www.asatej.org), Florida 835, 3rd floor, oficina 320 (1005), Buenos Aires, and 15 other offices in Argentina; and the Student Travel Bureau (☎ 55-21-2512 8577, W www .stb.com.br), Rua Visconde de Pirajá 550, Ipanema, Rio de Janeiro, with 28 other branches around Brazil.

For online airfares from Argentina, Brazil, Chile, Uruguay or Venezuela, try W www.viajo.com.

LAND
Border Crossings

There are about 40 official road crossing points on the US-Mexico border, including the following:

Arizona – Douglas/Agua Prieta, Nogales/Nogales, San Luis/San Luis Río Colorado and Naco/Naco (all open 24 hours); Sasabe/El Sásabe (open 8am to 10pm); Lukeville/Sonoita (open 8am to midnight)

California – Calexico/Mexicali (two crossings, one open 24 hours); San Ysidro/Tijuana (open 24 hours); Otay Mesa/Mesa de Otay (near Tijuana airport; open 6am to 10pm); Tecate/Tecate (open 6am to midnight)

New Mexico – Columbus/General Rodrigo M Quevedo (also called Palomas; open 24 hours)

Texas – Brownsville/Matamoros, McAllen/Reynosa, Laredo/Nuevo Laredo, Del Rio/Ciudad Acuña, El Paso/Ciudad Juárez, Presidio/Ojinaga and Eagle Pass/Piedras Negras (all open 24 hours)

There are 10 official road border crossings between Guatemala and Mexico, and two between Belize and Mexico. The following are the most frequently used:

Ciudad Cuauhtémoc/La Mesilla on the Pan-American Highway (between San Cristóbal de Las Casas, Mexico and Huehuetenango, Guatemala), open 24 hours daily

Ciudad Hidalgo/Ciudad Tecún Umán and Talismán/El Carmen (both between Tapachula, Mexico and Quetzaltenango, Guatemala), both open 24 hours daily

Subteniente López/Santa Elena (between Chetumal, Mexico and Corozal, Belize)

More information on many of these crossings can be found in the regional chapters.

The USA

Bus Since 1997 buses have been permitted to travel between cities in the US and Mexican interiors (previously, they had to terminate at frontier towns). But cross-border buses can suffer delays at the border, and it's usually no great inconvenience or greater expense to make your way to the border on one bus, cross it on foot, and then catch an onward bus on the other side. Greyhound (☎ 800-846-0754 in the USA, ⓦ www.greyhound.com) serves many US border cities; to reach others, transfer to a smaller bus line.

Bus companies providing cross-border service include Greyhound and its Mexican partners Autobuses Crucero (serving Mexico's Pacific coast down to Los Mochis), Autobuses Amigos (Gulf coast down to Tampico) and Autobuses Americanos (central Mexico as far south as Querétaro). The greatest number of cross-border buses run to and from Texas, but many farther-flung US cities (such as Denver, Chicago and Los Angeles) have direct bus links by these and other companies to cities inside Mexico. The daily Denver-Chihuahua run on Americanos, for instance, costs US$62. Greyhound itself goes mostly to/from Mexican border cities such as Tijuana (US$15 from Los Angeles), Nuevo Laredo (US$29 from Houston), Matamoros (US$49 from Austin, Texas) and Mexicali and Reynosa – though it also does a Los Angeles-Hermosillo run (US$72, 16 hours).

ADO Trailways runs daily service from McAllen, Texas to Oaxaca for US$84. You'll find further detail on international bus services in this book's city sections.

Train Taking a train to the Mexican border may not be much cheaper than flying when you add the cost of meals and other expenses. Trains tend to be a little more expensive and less frequent than buses. Amtrak (☎ 800-872-7245, ⓦ www.amtrak.com) serves four US cities from which access to Mexico is easy: cross from San Diego, California, to Tijuana; from El Paso, Texas, to Ciudad Juárez; from Del Rio, Texas, to Ciudad Acuña; and from San Antonio, Texas, take a bus to the border at Eagle Pass or Laredo.

South of the border, you have to resort to road transportation. None of the very few Mexican passenger trains that still exist come anywhere near the border.

Car & Motorcycle Driving into Mexico is not for everyone. You should know some Spanish and have basic mechanical aptitude, reserves of patience and access to some extra cash for emergencies. You should also note warnings about risk areas for highway robbery (see Dangers & Annoyances in the Facts for the Visitor chapter) and avoid intercity driving at night.

Cars are most useful for travelers who:

• have plenty of time
• plan to go to remote places

- will be camping a lot
- have surfboards, diving equipment or other cumbersome luggage
- will be traveling with a group of four or more

Don't take a car if you are on a tight schedule, have a small budget, plan to spend most of your time in urban areas or will be traveling alone.

Cars are fairly expensive to rent or buy in Mexico, so your best option is to take one in from the USA. If that means buying it first, you may need a few weeks to find a good vehicle at a reasonable price. It may also take time at the end of your trip to sell the thing.

Good makes of car to take to Mexico are Volkswagen, Nissan, General Motors and Ford, which have manufacturing or assembly plants in Mexico and dealers in most big Mexican towns. Big cars are unwieldy on narrow roads and use a lot of gasoline. A sedan with a trunk (boot) provides safer storage than a station wagon or hatchback. Volkswagen camper vans are economical, and parts and service are easy to find.

Mexican mechanics are resourceful, and most repairs can be done quickly and inexpensively, but it still pays to take as many spare parts as you can manage and know what to do with (spare fuel filters are very useful). Tires (including spare), shock absorbers and suspension should be in good condition. For security, have something to immobilize the steering wheel, such as 'the Club'; you should also consider getting a kill switch installed.

Motorcycling in Mexico is not for the faint-hearted. Roads and traffic can be rough, and parts and mechanics hard to come by. The only parts you'll find will be for Kawasaki, Honda and Suzuki bikes.

The rules for taking a vehicle into Mexico, described in the next sections, change from time to time. You can check with the American Automobile Association (AAA, W www.aaa.com), a Mexican consulate or a Mexican Government Tourist Office, or call the Mexican tourist information number (☎ 800-446-3942 in the USA). For more on driving and motorcycling in Mexico, see the Getting Around chapter.

Buying a Car in the USA The border states (particularly California and Texas) have many car lots, and every town has magazines and newspapers with ads from private sellers. Cars there are also likely to have aircon – very desirable in Mexico. To get an idea of used-car prices and trade-in values, consult the *Kelley Blue Book,* on the Internet (W www.kbb.com) and at most libraries. About US$2000 to US$3000 should buy a car that will take you around Mexico and still be worth something at journey's end.

You have to take with you to Mexico either the vehicle's registration document or your certificate of title for it (see Vehicle Permit, later). The registration document can usually be obtained in one day, while the certificate of title can take a week, even if you ask for rush service. If a lienholder's name (for example, a bank that has lent money for the vehicle) is shown on the certificate of title, you'll need a notarized letter giving their permission for you to take the vehicle into Mexico.

Motor Insurance It is very foolish to drive in Mexico without Mexican liability insurance. If you are involved in an accident, you can be jailed and have your vehicle impounded while responsibility is assessed, or, if you are to blame for an accident causing injury or death, until you guarantee restitution to the victims and payment of any fines. This could take weeks or months. A valid Mexican insurance policy is regarded as a guarantee that restitution will be paid, and it will also expedite release of the driver. Mexican law recognizes only Mexican motor *seguro* (insurance), so a US or Canadian policy is of no use.

Mexican insurance is sold in US border towns; as you approach the border from the USA you will see billboards advertising offices selling Mexican policies. At the busiest border crossings (to Tijuana, Mexicali, Nogales, Agua Prieta, Ciudad Juárez, Nuevo Laredo, Reynosa and Matamoros), there are insurance offices open 24 hours a day. Some deals are better than others.

Check the yellow pages in US border towns. Two organizations worth looking into, both of which also offer lots of useful travel information, are Sanborn's (☎ 800-222-0158, W www.sanbornsinsurance.com) and American Automobile Association (AAA, W www.aaa.com). Short-term insurance is about US$15 a day for full coverage on a car worth under US$10,000; for periods of more than two weeks it's often cheaper to get an annual policy. Liability-only insurance costs around half what full coverage costs. The AAA can provide its members with Mexican insurance and the forms needed for taking a vehicle into Mexico.

Driver's License To drive a motor vehicle in Mexico, you need a valid driver's license from your home country. Mexican police are familiar with US and Canadian licenses. Those from other countries may be scrutinized more closely, but they are still legal.

Vehicle Permit You will need a *permiso de importación temporal de vehículos* (temporary vehicle import permit) if you want to take a vehicle beyond Baja California, beyond Puerto Peñasco in Sonora state or beyond the border zone that extends 20 to 30km into Mexico along the rest of the US frontier and up to 70km from the Guatemalan and Belize frontiers.

Customs officials at Instituto Nacional de Migración (INM; National Immigration Institute) posts in the border zones along the US, Guatemalan and Belizean borders, and at the Baja California ports for ferries to mainland Mexico, will want to see the permit for your vehicle. You must get this at the *aduana* (customs) office at a border crossing or, in Baja, at the Pichilingue (La Paz) ferry terminal. (Permits are not available at Santa Rosalía, the other Baja ferry port.)

The person importing the vehicle will need originals and at least one photocopy of each of the following documents, which must all be in his/her own name (people at the office may make photocopies for a small fee):

- tourist card (FMT): go to *migración* before you go to the aduana
- certificate of title or registration certificate for the vehicle
- a valid Visa, MasterCard or American Express credit card, issued by a non-Mexican institution; if you don't have one you must pay a very large cash bond (see below)
- proof of citizenship or residency such as passport, birth certificate, voter's registration card or residency card
- driver's license

If the vehicle is financed or leased or is a rental car or company car, you need a notarized letter of permission from the lender,

lienholder or rental company, and in the case of leased or rented vehicles, the original contract (plus a copy), which must be in the name of the person importing the car. In practise few US rental firms allow their vehicles to be taken into Mexico.

One person cannot bring in two vehicles. If you have a motorcycle attached to your car, you'll need another adult traveling with you to obtain a permit for the motorcycle and he/she will need to have all the right papers for it. If the motorcycle is registered in your name, you'll need a notarized affidavit authorizing the other person to take it into Mexico. A special type of import permit is needed for vehicles weighing more than 3000kg (about 3.3 US tons).

At the border there will be a building with a parking area for vehicles awaiting permits. Go inside and find the right counter to present your papers. After some signing and stamping of papers, you sign a promise to take the car out of the country, the Banco del Ejército (also called Banjército; it's the army bank) charges a fee of about US$15 to your credit card, and you go and wait with your vehicle. Make sure you get back the originals of all documents. Eventually someone will come out and give you your vehicle permit and a sticker to be displayed on your windshield.

If you don't have an international credit card, you will have to pay a large refundable cash deposit or bond to the Banco del Ejército or an authorized Mexican *afianzadora* (bonding company) at the border. The required amounts are determined by official tables of vehicle values and range from US$500 to US$20,000 depending on the age and type of the vehicle. The bond (minus administrative charges) or the deposit should be refunded when the vehicle finally leaves Mexico and the temporary import permit is canceled. If you plan to leave Mexico at a different border crossing, make sure you will be able to obtain a refund there. There are offices for Banco del Ejército and authorized Mexican bonding companies at or near all the major border points.

Your vehicle permit entitles you to take the vehicle in and out of Mexico for the period shown on your tourist card. If the car is still in Mexico after that time, the aduana may start charging fines to your credit card and the car can be confiscated. The permit allows the vehicle to be driven by other people if the owner is in the vehicle.

When you leave Mexico for the last time, you must have the permit canceled by the Mexican authorities. An official may do this as you enter the border zone, usually 20 to 30km before the border itself. If not, you'll have to find the right official at the border crossing. If you leave Mexico without having the permit canceled, once the permit expires the authorities may assume you've left the vehicle in the country illegally and start charging fines to your credit card.

Only the owner may take the vehicle out of Mexico. If the vehicle is wrecked completely, you must contact your embassy or consulate or a Mexican customs office to make arrangements to leave without it.

If you are visiting the state of Sonora only, and are entering Mexico at Nogales and going to leave by the same route after not more than six days, you do not have to pay the US$15 fee or a bond. You just need to show – at the Km 21 checkpoint on highway 15 south of Nogales – your valid driver's license and proof of ownership or legal possession of the vehicle (such as registration, title, lease contract or notarized permission from leasing company or bank).

Guatemala & Belize

Bus The Mexico/Guatemala borders on the Pacific slope at Ciudad Hidalgo/Ciudad Tecún Umán and Talismán/El Carmen are both easily accessible by frequent local transportation from the nearest Mexican city, Tapachula. From Ciudad Tecún Umán frequent buses, and from El Carmen less frequent buses, head east into Guatemala along the Carretera al Pacífico (Coatepeque, Retalhuleu, Mazatenango, Escuintla and Guatemala City). Daily direct international bus services also run between Tapachula and Guatemala City (around US$20, 6 hours). For more details, see the Tapachula and Around Tapachula sections in the Tabasco & Chiapas chapter.

Inland, the Pan-American Highway crosses from Mexico into Guatemala at Ciudad Cuauhtémoc/La Mesilla. Frequent buses or *combis* link this crossing with the Mexican towns of Comitán and San Cristóbal de Las Casas and with the Guatemalan towns

of Huehuetenango, Quetzaltenango and Guatemala City. Lago de Atitlán and Chichicastenango (244km, 5 hours) both lie a few kilometers off the Guatemala City road. A couple of agencies in San Cristóbal de Las Casas run shuttle services all the way through to Quetzaltenango, Panajachel and Antigua (9½ hours, US$60). For more information see the San Cristóbal and Ciudad Cuauhtémoc sections in the Tabasco & Chiapas chapter.

Several daily 1st-class buses run between Flores, Guatemala and Chetumal, Mexico (US$36, 8 hours).

See the River section, following, for other routes between Mexico and Guatemala.

Frequent buses run between Chetumal, Mexico, and Belize City (3 to 4 hours, US$5 to US$6.75) via Orange Walk and Corozal in northern Belize. There's more information in the Yucatán Peninsula chapter.

Car & Motorcycle Drivers entering Mexico from the south must go through the same procedures as those entering from the USA (see earlier section). Some 'borderzone' checkpoints of the INM are a lot farther from the border than they are in the north – up to 70km.

Note that when crossing from Mexico into Belize or Guatemala you must carry both the vehicle's certificate of title *and* the registration document.

RIVER

River routes across the jungle-straddled Mexico-Guatemala border are fun for the mildly adventurously inclined. There are three main routes, all of which can be used to travel between the great Mayan ruins at Palenque, Mexico and the great Mayan ruins at Tikal, Guatemala.

The busiest and easiest route – which also enables you to visit the Mayan ruins at Yaxchilán and Bonampak, Mexico – is via a short boat ride on the Río Usumacinta between Frontera Corozal, Mexico and Bethel, Guatemala. The others (each with a river ride of four hours or so) are between Benemérito de las Américas, Chiapas and Sayaxché, Guatemala; and between La Palma, Tabasco, Mexico and El Naranjo, Guatemala. In each case, bus services reach the start and end of the river sections. You'll find details on all three of these river routes in the Tabasco & Chiapas chapter.

ORGANIZED TOURS

If you want just a short, easy holiday in Mexico, consider signing up for one of the many package deals offered by travel agents and in newspaper travel sections. Mexican government tourist offices can give you armfuls of brochures about these trips. Costs depend on where and when you go (peak time is usually December to February), but some packages give you flights and accommodations for little more than the cost of an individually bought airfare. For example, a seven-night off-season package trip from New York to Cancún or Acapulco can cost as little as US$500. Some packages even include a rental car and airport transfers in the price.

If on the other hand you are looking for an adventure- or activity-focused group trip to Mexico, you'll find a wide selection, mainly from North America but also from Europe. Great Web sites to check are Eco Travels in Latin America (W www.planeta .com), GORP (Great Outdoor Recreation Pages, W www.gorp.com) and Mexico Online (W www.mexonline.com). Following is a selection of tour operators with offerings to Mexico.

Adventure Center (☎ 800-228-8747, W www .adventurecenter.com), 1311 63rd St, Suite 200, Emeryville, CA 94608 USA – ecologically-minded, community-focused small group camping and hotel trips in Mexico and Central and South America

Adventure Specialists (☎ 719-783-2519, W www .gorp.com/adventur), Bear Basin Ranch, West-cliffe, CO 81252 USA – Barranca del Cobre (Copper Canyon) expeditions

Columbus Travel (☎ 800-843-1060, W www .canyontravel.com), 900 Ridge Creek Lane, Bul-verde, TX 78163 USA – Barranca del Cobre ex-plorations for individuals and small groups (using local naturalist guides and private ecolodges)

Dragoman (☎ 01728-861133, W www.dragoman .co.uk), Camp Green, Debenham, Stowmarket, Suffolk IP14 6LA, UK – longish (four to 27 weeks) camping or hotel overland trips, includ-ing Mexico among other countries in North, Central or South America

Explore Worldwide (☎ 800-227-8747 in the USA, ☎ 01252-760000 in the UK, ☎ 02-8913-0755 in Australia, W www.explore.co.uk) – small-group land trips with interesting itineraries

Field Guides (☎ 800-728-4953, W www.field guides.com), 9433 Bee Cave Rd, Building 1, Suite 150, Austin, TX 78733 USA – bird-watching trips to southern Mexico

GAP Adventures (☎ 800-465-5600, W www.gap .ca), 19 Duncan St, Suite 401, Toronto, Ontario M5H 3H1, Canada; (☎ 800-692-5495), 760 N Bedford Rd No 246, Bedford Hills, New York 10507 USA – small-group tours in southern Mexico and neighboring Maya lands, mainly using local transportation and simple accommo-dations; also overland expeditions combining Mexico with other parts of the Americas

Global Exchange (☎ 415-255-7296, 800-497-1994 W www.globalexchange.org), 2017 Mission St Nc 303, San Francisco, CA 94110 USA – 'Reality Tours' to Chiapas and the US/Mexico border in which you get an in-depth look at the problems and conditions of people in problem regions meeting community leaders, peace and social justice workers and other folk; a one-week trip typically costs around US$750

Green Tortoise (☎ 800-867-8647, W www.green tortoise.com), 494 Broadway, San Francisco, CA 94133 USA – long-running 'alternative' bus company operating casual, inexpensive 'self-service adventure travel vacations'; you spend lots of nights on the bus (the seats convert to beds) and some camping. Trips might be Baja loops from California, Yucatán loops, one-way rides from San Francisco to Mexico City or vice-versa. Read a sort-of description at W www.magic-bus.com/buslinks.shtml

Journey Latin America (☎ 020-8747-3108 W www.journeylatinamerica.co.uk), 12 & 13 Heathfield Terrace, Chiswick, London W4 4JE UK – two- or three-week tours on a budget or more comfy basis, also Baja sea-kayaking trips

Mayatours (☎ 800-392-6292, W www.mayatour .com), 2608 N Ocean Blvd Suite 108, Pompano Beach, FL 33062 USA – tours and travel services to Mexico and Central America with emphasis on Maya archaeology, ecology and diving

Suntrek (☎ 800-786-8735, W www.suntrek.com) Sun Plaza, 77 W Third St, Santa Rosa, CA 95401 USA; (☎ 08024-474490), Marktplatz 17, 83607 Holzkirchen, Germany – small international-group camping tours

TrekAmerica (☎ 800-221-0596 in the USA, ☎ 01295-256777 in the UK, W www.trek america.com), PO Box 189, Rockaway, NJ 07866 USA – small-group camping expeditions; most participants are in their early 20s

Getting Around

The Mexican holiday periods of Semana Santa (the week before Easter and a couple of days after it), mid-July to mid-August, and the Christmas-New Year holiday period of about two weeks are hectic and heavily booked throughout the country. Try to book transportation in advance for those periods.

For some useful words and phrases when traveling, see the Language chapter at the back of this book.

AIR

All large and many smaller cities in Mexico have passenger airports. Aeroméxico and Mexicana are easily the country's two largest airlines. There are also numerous smaller ones, often flying routes between provincial cities that the big two don't bother with. The larger of these smaller airlines include Aero California (serving Mexico City and a variety of other cities, chiefly in northern and western Mexico, including Baja California); Aerocaribe and Aerocozumel (Mexico City, the Gulf Coast, the south and southeast); Aerolíneas Internacionales (Mexico City, central and northern Mexico); Aerolitoral (central highlands, western and northern Mexico, Baja California); Aeromar (Mexico City and scattered cities around the country); Aviacsa (Mexico City, Guadalajara, Monterrey, Hermosillo, Tijuana, Acapulco, Oaxaca, southeast Mexico); Azteca (Mexico City, Cancún, Manzanillo, Guadalajara, Chihuahua, Tijuana); and Magnicharters (Mexico City, Guadalajara, Monterrey, Bajío, Puerto Vallarta, Ixtapa, Cancún, Mérida, Huatulco). Most of the aforementioned will be included in travel agents' computerized reservation systems in Mexico and abroad, but you may find it impossible to get information on other, even smaller airlines until you reach a city served by them.

Aerolitoral and Aeromar are feeder airlines for Aeroméxico and normally share its ticket offices and booking networks. A similar arrangement exists between Aerocaribe, Aerocozumel and Mexicana.

Fares

Depending on the fare you get, flying can be a good value for the money, especially considering the long bus trip that is probably the alternative. Fares can vary considerably between airlines and also depend on whether you fly at a busy or quiet time of day, week or year, and how far ahead you book and pay. Domestic flights within Mexico are often cheaper if you book them before you go, in conjunction with an international roundtrip ticket, than if you buy them individually in Mexico.

High season generally corresponds to the Mexican holiday seasons (see this chapter's opening paragraph). You'll normally save money if you pay for the ticket a few days ahead or if you fly late in the evening. Independent airlines such as Aviacsa, Aero California and Magnicharters are worth looking into as they often offer fares significantly lower than the government-controlled (though due to be sold off) Aeroméxico and Mexicana. Roundtrip fares are usually simply twice the price of one-way tickets, though some advance-payment cheaper deals do exist.

Here are some examples of one-way, low-season, Aeroméxico/Mexicana fares from Mexico City, including taxes:

destination	fare
Acapulco	US$166
Cancún	US$265
Guadalajara	US$155
Mérida	US$168
Monterrey	US$200
Oaxaca	US$165
Puerto Vallarta	US$275
Tijuana	US$200

Information on specific flights is given in the Getting There & Away sections under individual cities in this book. See 'Airline Contact Details' in the Getting There & Away chapter for a list of airlines' Internet addresses and toll-free telephone numbers.

Domestic Departure Tax

There are two taxes on domestic flight fares: IVA, the consumer tax (15% of the fare), and TUA, an airport tax of about US$16.

Taxes are normally included in quoted fares and paid when you buy the ticket.

BUS

Mexico has a good intercity road and bus network. Intercity buses are frequent and go almost everywhere, typically for between US$4 and US$6 an hour (70 to 80km) on 1st-class buses. For trips of up to three or four hours on busy routes, you can usually just go to the bus terminal, buy a ticket and head out without too much delay. For longer trips, or routes with infrequent service, book a ticket at least a day in advance, preferably two or three.

Seats on any service of the UNO, ADO, Maya de Oro, Cristóbal Colón, Altos and Rápidos del Sur lines (serving Mexico City, Puebla, the Gulf coast, Yucatán Peninsula, Oaxaca and Chiapas) can be booked through Ticket Bus, a reservations service with offices in city centers (and more than 20 branches in Mexico city), which saves you having to trek out to the bus station to buy an advance ticket. You can also make reservations on Ticket Bus's toll-free national reservations line, ☎ 800-702-80-00. Ticket Bus also has an erratic Web site, ⓦ www.ticketbus.com.mx.

Immediate cash refunds of 80% to 100% are available from many bus companies if you cancel your ticket more than a couple of hours before the listed departure time. The Cristóbal Colón, ADO and UNO lines, for instance, serving eastern and southeast Mexico, give 100% refunds up to 30 minutes before departure on tickets paid for in cash, if you show some identification (such as your passport). To check whether refunds apply, ask '¿Hay cancelaciones?'

All deluxe and most 1st-class buses, and some 2nd-class buses, are air-conditioned, so bring a sweater or jacket. Most have computerized ticket systems that allow you to select your seat from an on-screen diagram when you buy your ticket. Try to avoid the back of the bus, which is where the toilets are and also tends to give a bumpier ride. On non-air-conditioned 2nd-class buses, it's a good idea to get a window seat so that you have some control over the window (other travelers may have different ideas about what's too warm or too cool). See Classes of Service, below, for more on the differences between classes.

Baggage is safe if stowed in the bus's baggage hold, but always get a receipt for it when you hand it over. This is usually a numbered ticket matching a receipt that an attendant attaches to the bag. Keep your most valuable documents (passport, money, etc) in the cabin with you – and keep them closely protected.

Food and drinks in bus stations are overpriced; bringing your own is cheaper. Drinks and snacks are provided on some deluxe services. The better buses have toilets, but it's a good idea to carry some toilet paper.

Highway robbery happens very occasionally. The risk is higher at night, on isolated stretches of highway far from cities, and in 2nd-class buses. See Classes of Service, later, and Dangers & Annoyances in Facts for the Visitor for more information.

Terminals & Schedules

Most cities and towns have a single, modern, main bus station where all long-distance buses arrive and depart. It's usually called the Terminal de Autobuses, Central Camionera, Central de Autobuses, Central de Camiones or simply El Central. Note the crucial difference between the Central (the bus station) and the Centro (the city center), which are usually a long way apart! (It helps reduce heavy traffic in downtown areas.) Frequent local buses link bus stations with city centers.

If there is no single main terminal, bus companies will have their own terminals scattered around town.

Most bus lines have schedules posted at their ticket desks in the bus station, but the schedules aren't always comprehensive. If your destination isn't listed, ask – it may be en route to one that is. From bigger cities, many different bus companies may run on the same routes, so compare fares and classes of service.

Classes of Service

Long-distance buses range enormously in quality, from comfortable, nonstop, air-conditioned super-deluxe services to decaying, suspensionless ex-city buses grinding out their dying years on dirt roads to remote settlements. The differences between the classes are not completely clear-cut, and terms such as *de lujo* (deluxe) and *primera clase* (1st-class) can cover quite a wide range of standards.

How Many Stops?

It is important to know the types of service offered:

Sin escalas Nonstop
Directo Very few stops
Semi-directo A few more stops than directo
Ordinario Stops wherever passengers want to get on or off; deluxe and 1st-class buses are never ordinario
Express Nonstop on short to medium-length trips; very few stops on long trips
Local Bus that starts its journey at the bus station you're in and usually leaves on time; preferable to *de paso*
De paso Bus that started its journey somewhere else but is stopping to let off and take on passengers. A de paso bus may be late and may or may not have seats available; unless the bus company has a computer booking system, you also may have to wait until it arrives before any tickets are sold. If the bus is full, you may have to wait for the next one
Viaje redondo Roundtrip

Generally, deluxe or 1st-class will give you a perfectly comfortable and rapid ride. Unless your budget is very tight, the money you save by traveling 2nd-class is hardly worth the discomfort or extra journey time entailed. Second-class buses tend to take slow, non-toll roads in and out of big cities and will stop anywhere to pick up passengers. They may also be more vulnerable to being boarded by bandits in some areas, such as around Mexico City. Out in the remoter areas, however, you'll often find that only 2nd-class buses will be available.

The one definite advantage of 2nd-class buses is that they do not subject their passengers to the movies that 1st-class and deluxe bus travelers are obliged to watch. These are all third-grade US-made films obsessed with hitting, kicking, shooting and killing. Unless you close your eyes, you cannot avoid watching them as all seats in the bus face a video screen. So much for sitting back and enjoying the scenery.

Broadly, buses fall into three categories:

De lujo Deluxe services run mainly on the busy routes. They are swift, modern and comfortable. Most bus lines with 'Plus' in their name are deluxe. They may cost just 10% or 20% more than 1st class, or double for the most luxurious lines, such as ETN, UNO and Turistar Ejecutivo, which offer reclining seats, plenty of legroom, few or no stops, snacks, drinks and toilets on board. Some people regard the super-deluxe buses as a class of their own – *ejecutivo* (executive). For simplicity, this book groups them with other deluxe services.

Primera (1ª) clase First-class buses have a comfortable *numerado* (numbered) seat for each passenger. Their standards of comfort are perfectly adequate. They usually have a toilet, and they stop infrequently. All sizable towns have 1st-class bus service. As with deluxe buses, you buy your ticket in the bus station before boarding.

Segunda (2ª) clase Second-class buses serve small towns and villages and provide cheaper, slower travel on some intercity routes. A few are almost as quick and comfortable as 1st-class buses; others are old and shabby. They're also liable to break down, and will stop anywhere for someone to get on or off, which can add hours to the duration of a long journey. Second-class buses may be less safe than 1st-class or better ones, for reasons of maintenance, driver standards and vulnerability to robbery. Except on some major routes, there's no apparent limit on capacity, which means that if you board mid-route you might make some of the trip standing. If you board mid-route, you pay your fare to the conductor. Fares are about 10% or 20% lower than for 1st-class. *Microbuses* or *'micros'* are small, usually fairly new, 2nd-class buses with around 25 seats, usually running short routes between nearby towns.

Mexbus

Mexbus (**W** www.mexbus.net) is a backpackers' bus service that had just started up as this edition went to press. Launched by the enterprising folk from Hostal Moneda in Mexico City, the service initially ran just between Mexico City and Oaxaca (daily) but the plan was to extend it to San Cristóbal de Las Casas, Palenque, Campeche, Mérida, Cancún and possibly Panajachel (Guatemala). The service runs comfortable vans door-to-door between popular hostels and budget hotels used by travelers in these cities, at prices below those of 1st-class buses. You can book or get updated information at all the accommodations served by Mexbus and (in English or Spanish) at the toll-free telephone number ☎ 800-523-94-12.

Vans, Combis, Pickups & Trucks

In some areas (mainly rural), a variety of other vehicles performs the service of moving people from A to B. Volkswagen combis and more comfortable passenger-carrying vans, such as Chevrolet Suburbans, operate shuttle services between some towns, usually leaving whenever they have a full load of passengers. Fares are typically a little less than 1st-class buses. More primitive are passenger-carrying *camiones* (trucks) and *camionetas* (pickups). Standing in the back of a lurching truck with a couple of dozen *campesinos* (farm workers) and their machetes and animals is at least an experience to remember. Fares are similar to a 2nd-class bus fare.

TRAIN

The spectacular Ferrocarril Chihuahua al Pacífico between Los Mochis and Chihuahua, known in English as the Copper Canyon Railway, is one of the highlights of Mexico travel: see the Northwest Mexico chapter for details. But the rest of Mexico's passenger train system, after being in decline for decades, has in effect ceased to exist. The private firms that bought the country's railroads from the government in the 1990s simply stopped running passenger trains because they were so unprofitable. The very few services remaining are either on routes of no interest to travelers or are tourist excursion/entertainment services of equally little use for actually getting from one place to another.

CAR & MOTORCYCLE

Driving in Mexico is not as easy as it is north of the border, but it is often easier and more convenient than the bus, and it's sometimes the only way to get to some of the most beautiful places or isolated towns and villages.

See Dangers & Annoyances in Facts for the Visitor for a warning about risks of highway robbery in some areas, and the Getting There & Away chapter for information about the requirements for bringing a vehicle into Mexico.

The Language chapter in the back of the book includes lists of some useful Spanish words and phrases for drivers. Two useful Web sites for drivers in Mexico are ⓦ www.mexicomike.com and ⓦ www.sanbornsinsurance.com.

Maps

Town and country roads are often poorly or idiosyncratically signposted. It pays to get the best road maps you can. The Mexican *Guía Roji Por Las Carreteras de México* road atlas is an excellent investment. In Mexico it costs US$11 from decent bookstores and some city newsstands. It's available in the US, or from Internet booksellers, for around US$18 to US$20 (sometimes in an English-language version). This atlas is updated annually and includes new highways, though minor roads may be overlooked or imperfect. Sanborn's Insurance supplies free and highly detailed 'Travelogs' (mile-by-mile companions for the driver) to their customers.

Road Rules

Drive on the right-hand side of the road.

Traffic laws and speed limits rarely seem to be enforced on the highways. Obey the rules in the cities so you don't give the police an excuse to demand a 'fine' payable on the spot. (The standard bribe for minor traffic infringements is US$5.) Speed limits are usually 100km per hour on highways and 40km per hour or 30km per hour in towns and cities.

Antipollution rules in Mexico City prohibit every vehicle from driving there on one day each week. (See 'Driving Restrictions' in the Mexico City chapter.)

Accidents

Under Mexico's legal system, all drivers involved in a road accident are detained and their vehicles impounded while responsibility is assessed. For minor accidents, drivers will probably be released if they have insurance to cover any damage they may have caused. But the culpable driver's vehicle may remain impounded until damages are paid. If the accident causes injury or death, the responsible driver will be jailed until he or she guarantees restitution to the victims and payment of any fines. Determining responsibility *could* take weeks or even months. (Mexican drivers often *don't* stop after accidents.)

Your embassy can give you only limited help (see Legal Matters in the Facts for the Visitor chapter). Adequate Mexican insurance coverage is the only real protection: the policy will be treated as a guarantee of payment for damages, and can speed up your release. Insurance is considered invalid if the driver is under the influence of alcohol or drugs.

Fuel & Service

All *gasolina* (gasoline) and diesel fuel in Mexico is sold by the government's monopoly, Pemex (Petróleos Mexicanos), for cash only (no credit cards). Most towns, even small ones, have a Pemex station, and the stations are pretty common on most major roads. Nevertheless, in remote areas it's better to fill up when you can.

The gasoline on sale is all *sin plomo* (unleaded). There are two varieties: Magna Sin, equivalent to US regular unleaded, and Premium, equivalent to US super unleaded. At the time of research, Magna Sin cost about US$0.60 a liter (US$2.40 a US gallon), and Premium about US$0.70. Diesel fuel is widely available at around US$0.50 a liter. Regular Mexican diesel has a higher sulfur content than US diesel, but there is a 'Diesel Sin' with less sulfur than before. If diesel drivers change their oil and filter about every 3500km, they should have no problems.

Gas stations have pump attendants (who expect a small tip).

Road Conditions

Mexican highways, even some toll highways, are not up to the standards of European or North American ones. Still, the main roads are serviceable and fairly fast when traffic is not heavy. A common problem is steep shoulders, so if your wheels go off the road surface the car tilts alarmingly. Sometimes there's a deep gutter, and if you go into it you may roll the car.

Driving at night is best avoided since unlit vehicles, rocks, pedestrians and animals on the roads are common. Hijacks and robberies do occur. Generally, it's unsafe to pull over and sleep in your parked vehicle. Plan to reach accommodations well before nightfall.

On some roads, especially those heading south from the US border, the army and police conduct fairly frequent drug and weapon searches.

In towns and cities, be especially wary of *Alto* (Stop) signs, *topes* (speed bumps) and holes in the road. They are often not where you'd expect, and missing one can cost you in traffic fines or car damage. Speed bumps are also used to slow traffic on highways that pass through built-up areas: they are usually signed, but not always, and some of them are severe.

One-way streets are the rule in towns. Priority at street intersections is indicated by thin black and red rectangles containing white arrows. A black rectangle means you have priority and a red one means you don't. Arrows indicate the direction of traffic on the cross street.

Mexicans on the whole drive as cautiously and sensibly as people anywhere. The density of traffic, poor surfaces and frequent hazards (potholes, topes, dogs, livestock, bicycles and children) all help keep speeds down.

Toll Roads Mexico has more than 6000km of *autopistas* (toll roads), usually four-lane. They are generally in much better condition and a lot quicker than the alternative free roads. They also have a reputation for being safer from highway robbery. Some are operated by the federal government, others by private concessions. *Cuotas* (tolls) vary from highway to highway: on average you pay about US$1 for every 10km to 20km.

Motorcycle Hazards Certain aspects of Mexican roads make them particularly hazardous for bikers:

- poor signage of road and lane closures (there may be nothing more than a rock placed 20m before where the work is being done)
- lack of hotels/motels on some stretches of highway
- lots of dogs on the roads
- debris and deep potholes
- vehicles without taillights and lack of highway lighting

Breakdown Assistance

The Mexican tourism ministry, SECTUR, maintains a network of *Ángeles Verdes* (Green Angels). These are bilingual mechanics in green uniforms and green trucks, who patrol major stretches of highway throughout the country daily during daylight hours looking for motorists in trouble. They make minor repairs, change tires, provide fuel and oil, and arrange towing and other assistance if necessary. Service is free; parts, gasoline and oil are provided at cost. If you are near a telephone when your car has problems, you can call their 24-hour hot line in Mexico City (☎ 55-5250-8221) or contact them through the national 24-hour tourist assistance numbers in Mexico City (☎ 55-5250-0123, 800-903-92-00).

Most serious mechanical problems can be fixed efficiently and inexpensively by mechanics in towns and cities as long as the parts are available. Volkswagen, Ford, Nissan and General Motors parts are among the easiest to obtain; others may have to be ordered from the USA. For parts suppliers, consult the telephone directory's yellow pages under *Refacciones y Acesorios para Automóviles y Camiones*. For authorized dealer service, look under *Automóviles – Agencias*.

City Parking

It's not a good idea to park on the street overnight, and most cheap city hotels don't provide parking. Sometimes you can leave a car out front and the night porter will keep an eye on it. Usually, you have to use a commercial *estacionamiento* (parking lot) that might cost US$5 to US$7 overnight and US$1 per hour during the day. Hotels with parking tend to be the more expensive ones.

If you're just overnighting and moving on in the morning, often you can find decent motels with easy parking on highways just outside cities.

Rental

Auto rental in Mexico is expensive by US or European standards, but it can be worthwhile if you want to visit several places in a short time and have three or four people to share the cost. It can also be useful for getting off the beaten track, where public transport is slow or scarce.

Cars can be rented in most of Mexico's cities and resorts, at airports and sometimes at bus and train stations. Most big hotels can arrange a car. Sometimes it's recommendable to book a couple of days ahead.

Renters must provide a valid driver's license (your home license is OK), passport and major credit card, and are usually required to be at least 21 (sometimes as much as 25). You should get a signed rental agreement and read the small print.

In addition to the basic daily or weekly rental rate, you pay for insurance, tax and fuel. Ask exactly what the insurance covers. Sometimes it covers only 90% of the car's value in case of theft and doesn't cover 'partial theft,' such as wiper blades or tires. And since Mexican law permits the jailing of drivers after an accident until they have met their obligations to third parties (see Accidents, earlier), you should make sure you have plenty of liability coverage.

Most agencies offer a choice between a per-kilometer deal or unlimited kilometers. The latter is usually preferable if you intend to do some hard driving. (If you don't, why are you renting a car?) Local firms are often cheaper than the big international ones. The cheapest car available (often a Volkswagen Beetle) can cost anywhere between US$45 and US$75 a day (depending on where you are) including unlimited kilometers, insurance and tax. The extra charge for drop-off in another city, when available, is usually about US$0.40 per kilometer.

You can book cars in Mexico through the large international agencies in other countries. Doing this may get you lower rates. Here's contact information for some major firms operating in Mexico. See city sections in regional chapters for more information on car rental agencies.

Alamo
☎ 800-462-5266 in the USA
☎ 800-849-80-01 toll-free in Mexico
W www.goalamo.com

Avis
☎ 800-230-4898 in the USA
☎ 55-5588-8888 in Mexico City
W www.avis.com

Budget
☎ 800-472-3325 in the USA
☎ 55-5271-4322 in Mexico City
W www.drivebudget.com

Dollar
☎ 800-300-3665 in the USA
☎ 33-3825-5080 in Guadalajara
W www.dollar.com

Europcar
☎ 877-940-6900 in the USA
☎ 55-2801-1111 in Mexico City
W www.europcar.com

Hertz
- ☎ 800-654-3001 in the USA
- ☎ 800-709-50-00 toll-free in Mexico
- Ⓦ www.hertz.com

Thrifty
- ☎ 800-847-4389 in the USA
- ☎ 55-5207-1100 in Mexico City
- Ⓦ www.thrifty.com

Motorbikes or scooters are available to rent in a few tourist centers. You're usually required to have a driver's license and credit card.

BICYCLE

With the exception of Baja California, bicycling is not a common way to tour Mexico. The size of the country, reports of highway robbery, poor road surfaces and road hazards (see Road Conditions under Car & Motorcycle, earlier) are all deterrents. However, this method of getting around Mexico is certainly not impossible if you're prepared for the challenges. You should be very fit, use the best equipment you can muster and be fully able to handle your own repairs. Take the mountainous topography and hot climate into account when planning your route.

A valuable help to anyone cycling in Mexico is *Bicycling Mexico* by Erica Weisbroth and Eric Ellman, published in 1990 but still applicable.

You can rent bikes in some Mexican towns and cities for local rides, and a growing number of mountain bike tours are offered in places such as Baja California, Oaxaca and San Cristóbal de Las Casas (see city and town sections).

If you're interested in more than just a local ride, consider the two- and three-week Pacific coast, Yucatán Peninsula and Chiapas cycling tours offered by El Tour (Ⓦ http://eltour.itgo.com), based at Los Pingüinos in San Cristóbal de Las Casas, Chiapas (see the Around San Cristóbal section of the Tabasco & Chiapas chapter). These small-group trips, with English-speaking guides, usually last two or three weeks, for US$625 to US$925 per person.

HITCHHIKING

Hitchhiking is never entirely safe in any country in the world, and is not recommend it. Travelers who decide to hitch should understand that they are taking a small but potentially serious risk. People who do choose to hitch will be safer if they travel in pairs and let someone know where they are planning to go. A woman traveling alone certainly should not hitchhike in Mexico, and even two women alone is not advisable.

However, some people do choose to hitchhike, and it's not an uncommon way of getting to some of the off-the-beaten-track archaeological sites and other places that tend to be poorly served by bus. Always be alert to possible dangers wherever you are.

If the driver is another tourist or a private motorist, you may get the ride for free. If it is a work or commercial vehicle, you should offer to pay.

BOAT

Vehicle and passenger ferries between Santa Rosalía and Guaymas, La Paz and Mazatlán and La Paz and Topolobampo connect Baja California with the Mexican mainland. There are also ferries running to Isla Mujeres, Cozumel and Isla Holbox, off the Yucatán Peninsula. For details, see the relevant city and island sections. Information regarding the Baja ferries is also available on the Web site of the ferry company Sematur (Ⓦ www.ferrysematur.com.mx).

LOCAL TRANSPORTATION

Mexican street naming and numbering can be confusing. When asking directions, it's better to ask for a specific place, such as the Hotel Central or the Museo Regional, rather than the street it's on. To achieve a degree of certainty, ask three people.

Bus

Generally known as *camiones,* local buses are the cheapest way to get around cities and to nearby villages. They run everywhere frequently and are cheap. Fares in cities are rarely more than US$0.50. Older buses are often noisy, dirty and crowded, but in some cities there are fleets of small, modern microbuses that tend to be more pleasant.

City buses halt only at specific *paradas* (bus stops), that may or may not be marked.

Colectivos, Combis & Peseros

Colectivos are minibuses or microbuses that function as something between a taxi and a bus. (A *combi* is a VW minibus; *pesero* is a

Mexico City word for colectivo.) They're cheaper than taxis and quicker and less crowded than buses. They run along set routes – sometimes displayed on the windshield – and will pick you up or drop you off on any corner along that route.

If you're not at the start of a colectivo's route, go to the curb and wave your hand when you see one. Tell the driver where you want to go. Usually, payment is made at the end of the trip and the fare depends on how far you go.

Metro

Mexico City, Guadalajara and Monterrey have metro (subway, underground railway) systems. Mexico City's, in particular, is a quick, cheap and useful way of getting around.

Taxi

Taxis are common in towns and cities. They're often surprisingly economical, and they're useful if you have a lot of baggage or need to get from point A to point B quickly. (But see the Mexico City Information section for a warning on that city's taxi crime epidemic.) Many Mexican taxis are Volkswagen Beetles. If a taxi has a meter, ask the driver if it's working ('¿Funciona el taxímetro?'). If it's not, or if the taxi doesn't have a meter, establish the price of the ride *before* getting in. (This usually involves a bit of haggling.)

Some airports and big bus stations have taxi *taquillas* (kiosks), where you buy a fixed-price ticket to your destination and then hand it to the driver instead of paying cash. This can save haggling and major rip-offs, but fares are usually higher than you could get on the street.

In some (usually rural) areas, some taxis operate on a colectivo basis, following set routes, often from one town or village to another, and picking up or dropping off passengers anywhere along that route. Fares per person are around one-fifth of the normal cab fare.

Boat

Here and there you may find yourself traveling by boat to an outlying beach or along a river or across a lake or lagoon. The craft are usually fast fiberglass outboard *lanchas* (launches). You may have to haggle a bit, but fares for such excursions are often fixed.

ORGANIZED TOURS

Taking a guided tour can be an easy way of getting a quick introduction to big cities, or of visiting nearby major archaeological sites and other tourist attractions. More interestingly, group trips can also be the most practical way of getting out to remote natural attractions and other areas where public transportation isn't the greatest – places such as the canyons, cascades and rivers of the Barranca del Cobre (Copper Canyon) area; the Cuatrociénegas desert lagoons, in the north; the Sierra Norte, the Mixteca or the Lagunas de Chacahua, in Oaxaca; the Reserva de la Biósfera Sian Ka'an and some archaeological sites on the Yucatán Peninsula; and, in Chiapas, places like Laguna Miramar, the waterfalls near Palenque, or the Bonampak and Yaxchilán ruins. A knowledgeable and enthusiastic guide can add much to your understanding and enjoyment of a place. A guide is also a necessity in some protected areas where visitors are not allowed unaccompanied, such as the Sierra de San Francisco rock art sites in Baja California, the Grutas de Loltún caverns in Yucatán, or the El Triunfo cloud forest in Chiapas.

A new generation of adventure/activity tourism is emerging in some parts of Mexico, with enthusiastic guides offering the chance to hike, bike, climb, raft and meet local people (in areas you'd probably never even know about without them). Trips run by, or in cooperation with, local community tourism organizations have the additional attraction that they channel funds directly to local people.

You'll find details on all these tours, and others, in the regional chapters. Most are best arranged locally (with some advance notice, in a few cases). See the Activities section in the Facts for the Visitor chapter for an introduction to the more active ways of spending your time in Mexico.

Good Web sites to look at are Earthfoot (W www.earthfoot.org), which provides links to small-scale, low-impact, local eco-tourism providers (in Mexico and around the world); Eco Travels in Latin America (W www.planeta.com); and AMTAVE (W www.amtave.com). AMTAVE is a grouping of over 80 'alternative tourism' operators around Mexico; its office (☎ 998-884-95-80, 800-509-76-78) is located at Camarón 32, sm 27, Cancún, Quintana Roo.

Before signing up for any tour, be sure to find out whether the price includes tariffs, taxes *(tarifas y impuestos)*, or refunds. If problems should happen to arise you can call the Office of Consumer Protection (PROFECO; see the Legal Matters section in the Facts for the Visitor chapter for details).

Mexico City

• pop 20 million (approx) • elev 2240m ☎ 55
Mexico City is a place to love and loathe.
Spread across more than 2000 sq km of a
single valley high in Mexico's central
uplands, it encapsulates the best and worst
of Mexico the country. The result is a
seething, cosmopolitan megalopolis that is

Highlights

• Museo Nacional de Antropología – a
treasure-house of Mexican archaeological
marvels

• Bosque de Chapultepec – a large inner-
city woodland expanse with several good
museums

• Coyoacán and San Ángel – old suburbs
vibrant with weekend markets and
memories of Diego Rivera and Frida Kahlo

• Zócalo – one of the world's biggest
plazas, surrounded by the presidential
palace, the cathedral and the remains of
the most important Aztec temple

• Murals – marvelous works by 20th-
century Mexican masters in the Palacio
Nacional, Palacio de Bellas Artes, Museo
Mural Diego Rivera and elsewhere

• Xochimilco – the ancient Aztec waterways and the Museo Dolores Olmedo
Patiño, with its superb Rivera collection

• Colonia Condesa – delightful dining at
relaxed sidewalk bistros

• Ballet Folklórico de México – spectacular
dance show in the beautiful Palacio de
Bellas Artes

by turns exhilarating and overpowering.
One moment Mexico City is music, glamour
and excitement; the next it's drabness,
poverty, overcrowding and foul smells. This
is a city of colonial palaces and sprawling
slums; of ear-splitting traffic and peaceful
plazas; of huge wealth and miserable
poverty; of green parks and brown air.

Despite its problems, Mexico City is a
magnet for Mexicans and visitors alike,
because with nearly a quarter of the
country's population, it far outstrips anywhere else in the country in economic, cultural and political importance. One resident
summarized the city's dominance with this
saying: *'Lo que ocurre en México, ocurre en
el DF'* ('What happens in Mexico, happens
in Mexico City').

The city is known to Mexicans simply as
México ('MEH-hee-ko'). If they want to dis-
tinguish it from Mexico the country, they call
it either *la ciudad de México* or *el DF* ('el de
EFF-eh'). The DF is the Distrito Federal
(Federal District), in which in fact only half
the city lies. The outlying parts of Mexico
City lie in the state of México, which surrounds the Distrito Federal on three sides,
and the state of Morelos is on the fourth.

HISTORY

As early as 10,000 BC, humans were attracted to the Lago de Texcoco, the lake that
then covered much of the floor of the Valle
de México. After 7500 BC the lake began to
shrink, hunting became more difficult, and
the inhabitants turned to agriculture. A
loose federation of farming villages had
evolved around Lago de Texcoco by approximately 200 BC. The biggest, Cuicuilco,
was destroyed by a volcanic eruption about
AD 100.

After that the big influence in the
area was Teotihuacán, 25km northeast of
the lake. For centuries Teotihuacán was the
capital of an empire stretching to Guatemala
and beyond, but it fell in the 7th century.
Among several city-states in the region in
the following centuries, the Toltec empire,
based at Tula, 65km north of modern Mexico
City, was the most important. By the 13th
century the Tula empire had collapsed,

leaving a number of small statelets around the lake to compete for control of the Valle de México. It was the Aztecs who emerged supreme.

Aztec Mexico City

The Aztecs, or Mexica ('meh-SHEE-kah'), a wandering Chichimec tribe from northern or western Mexico, settled first on the western shore of Lago de Texcoco, but other Valle de México inhabitants objected to Aztec habits such as wife-stealing and human sacrifice (to appease the Aztecs' guardian god, Huizilopochtli). In the early 14th century, fighting as mercenaries for Coxcox, ruler of Culhuacán, on the southern shore of the lake, the Aztecs defeated nearby Xochimilco and sent Coxcox 8000 human ears as proof of their victory. Coxcox granted them land and rashly allowed them to make his daughter an Aztec goddess. As described in *The Course of Mexican History,* by Michael Meyer and William Sherman:

The princess was sacrificed and flayed. When her father attended the banquet in his honor, he was horrified to find that the entertainment included a dancer dressed in the skin of his daughter…Coxcox raised an army which scattered the barbarians.

Some time between 1325 and 1345 the Aztecs, wandering around the swampy fringes of the lake, finally founded their own city, Tenochtitlán, on an island near the lake's western shore. (Today the island site is the downtown area around the main square, the Zócalo.) The island was chosen, legend says, because there the Aztecs saw an eagle standing on a cactus eating a snake; they interpreted this as a sign to stop their wanderings and build a city.

About 1370 the Aztecs began to serve as mercenaries for Azcapotzalco, on the western shore of the lake. When they rebelled against Azcapotzalco (about 1427), they became the greatest power in the Valle de México. Tenochtitlán rapidly became a sophisticated city-state whose empire would, by the early 16th century, stretch across most of central (modern-day) Mexico from the Pacific to the gulf and down into far southern Mexico. The Aztecs' sense of their own importance as the chosen people of the voracious Huizilopochtli grew too. In the mid-15th century they formed the Triple Alliance

The legendary symbol of Mexico

with the lakeshore states Texcoco and Tlacopan to conduct wars against Tlaxcala and Huejotzingo, which lay east of the valley. The purpose was to gain a steady supply of the prisoners needed to sate Huizilopochtli's vast hunger for sacrificial victims, so that the sun would continue to rise each day and floods and famines could be avoided. In four days in 1487, no less than 20,000 prisoners were sacrificed to dedicate Tenochtitlán's newly rebuilt main temple.

The Aztecs built a large city on a grid plan, with canals as thoroughfares. In the marshier parts they created raised gardens by piling up vegetation and mud and planting willows. These chinampas (versions of which can still be seen at Xochimilco in southern Mexico City) gave three or four harvests a year but were still not enough to feed the growing population. The Aztecs also needed to extract tribute from conquered tribes to supplement their resources, leading to more imperial expansion in the 15th century. At the city's heart stood the main teocalli (sacred precinct), with its temple dedicated to Huizilopochtli and the water god, Tláloc. The remains of this temple, the Templo Mayor, can be seen today just off the Zócalo. Causeways linked the city to the lakeshore. This was the city that amazed the Spanish when they arrived in 1519, by which time its population was an estimated 200,000. That of the whole Valle de México was perhaps 1.5 million, making it already one of the world's biggest and densest urban areas.

So assiduously did the Spanish raze Tenochtitlán that only a handful of Aztec structures remain in Mexico City today. The Templo Mayor is easily the most interesting of these, followed by the small pyramids of Tlatelolco, north of the center. Dedicated ruin-hunters must venture to the pyramids at Tenayuca and Santa Cecilia Acatitlán, respectively 11km and 13km northwest of the Zócalo, to see more. It's a similar story throughout central Mexico. The most impressive remaining Aztec structures (at Tepoztlán, Cuernavaca, Calixtlahuaca and Malinalco) pale by comparison with the monuments left by earlier civilizations at places like Teotihuacán, Tula and Cholula. A more enduring legacy is represented by the Nahua indigenous people, who are spread all over central Mexico; numbering around 2 million, they make up the country's largest indigenous group. The Nahua are direct descendants of the people of the Aztec empire, and their language, Náhuatl, is the language the Aztecs spoke. For more information on Aztec culture, society and religion see History in the Facts about Mexico chapter.

Capital of Nueva España
Wrecked during and after the Spanish conquest, the Aztec capital Tenochtitlán was rebuilt as a Spanish city. The native population of the Valle de México shrank drastically – from more than 1.5 million to fewer than 100,000 within a century of the conquest, by some estimates. But the city itself emerged by 1550 as the prosperous and elegant, if unsanitary, capital of Nueva España. Broad, straight streets were laid out, and buildings were constructed to Spanish designs with local materials such as *tezontle*, a light-red volcanic rock that the Aztecs had used for their temples. Hospitals, schools, churches, palaces, parks and a university were built. But right up to the late 19th century the city suffered floods caused by the partial destruction in the 1520s of the Aztecs' canals. Lago de Texcoco often overflowed into the city, damaging streets and buildings, bringing disease and forcing the relocation of thousands of people.

Independence
On October 30, 1810, some 80,000 independence rebels had Mexico City at their mercy after defeating Spanish loyalist forces at Las Cruces, just west of the capital. But their leader Miguel Hidalgo decided against advancing on the city – a mistake that cost Mexico 11 more years of fighting before independence was achieved. By 1821 the city had a population of 160,000, which made it the biggest in the Americas.

Mexico City entered the modern age under the despotic Porfirio Díaz, who ruled Mexico for most of the period from 1877 to 1911 and attracted much foreign investment. Díaz ushered in a construction boom in the city and had railways built to the provinces and the USA. Some 150km of electric tramways threaded the streets, industry grew, and by 1910 the city had 471,000 inhabitants. A drainage canal and tunnel finally succeeded in drying up much of the Lago de Texcoco, allowing the city to expand farther.

Modern Megalopolis
After Díaz fell in 1911, the Mexican Revolution brought war and hunger to the city's streets. In the 1920s the post-revolution minister of education, José Vasconcelos, commissioned talented young artists – among them Diego Rivera, David Alfaro Siqueiros and José Clemente Orozco – to decorate numerous public buildings with dramatic, large-scale murals conveying a new sense of Mexico's past and future.

Shantytowns

Mexico City's notorious shantytowns are on its fringes, where most of the city's expansion is taking place. You may glimpse some of them as you enter or leave the city by road, though most of the main routes are lined by more established communities. Many of the oldest shantytowns – such as the vast Ciudad Nezahualcóyotl, east of the airport and home to well over a million people – are no longer really shantytowns, as they have succeeded in gaining services such as running water and electricity. Now these areas are sprawling gritty industrial slums with pockets of middle-class areas where some inhabitants have earned enough money to build themselves relatively comfortable homes.

After the Great Depression, a drive to industrialize attracted more and more money and people to the city. By 1940 the population reached 1.7 million. In the 1940s and '50s factories and skyscrapers rose almost as quickly as the population, which was increasing by 7% a year. The supply of housing, jobs and services could not keep pace with the influx of people; shantytowns appeared on the city's fringes, and Mexico City began growing into the urban monster we know today.

Despite continued economic growth into the 1960s, political and social reform lagged behind. Student-led discontent came to a head as Mexico City prepared for the 1968 Olympic Games. On October 2, just 10 days before the games started, about 5000 to 10,000 student marchers gathered in Tlatelolco, north of the city center, to demonstrate against alleged official repression, including police brutality, torture and 'disappearances' of left-wing social activists. The demonstrators were encircled by troops and police, and to this day, no one is certain how many people died in the ensuing massacre; the official count was just 24 dead, but estimates have been put at several hundred. In early 2002 Mexico's attorney general, responding to an order issued by the Supreme Court, finally began an official investigation into the event.

Mexico City continued to grow at a frightening rate in the 1970s, spreading beyond the Distrito Federal into the state of México and developing some of the world's worst traffic and pollution problems, only partly alleviated by the metro system (opened in 1969) and by attempts in the 1990s to limit traffic.

People continued to pour into Mexico City despite the earthquake of September 19, 1985, which registered more than eight on the Richter scale, killed at least 10,000 (possibly 20,000) people, displaced thousands more and caused more than US$4 billion in damage.

Today the city's population is estimated at 20 million, and an estimated 1100 newcomers arrive daily. Since 1940 Mexico City has multiplied in area more than 10 times, yet it's still one of the world's most crowded metropolitan areas. It is the industrial, retail, financial, communications and cultural center of the country; its industries generate more than one-third of Mexico's wealth, and its people consume two-thirds of Mexico's energy. Its cost of living is the highest in the nation.

Heavy subsidies are needed to keep the place from seizing up, and more than half the country's spending on social welfare is used here. Water extraction from the subsoil makes the city sink steadily – as much as 45cm a year in some fringe areas. Parts of the city center sank 10m in the 20th century. Even so, one-third of the city's water has to be pumped in at great cost from outside the Valle de México. The challenges of supplying water to the city's growing population and disposing of waste water threaten to exceed even those of combating air pollution.

The poverty and overcrowding that always existed alongside the city's wealth were exacerbated by the recession of the mid-1990s. In 1996 it was estimated that more than one-fifth of the people in the Distrito Federal were living on marginal levels of basic subsistence, and another two-thirds were barely able to cover the expense of material necessities. And those figures did not include the outer parts of the city, where most of the newer shantytowns lie. One effect of the crisis was a big rise in crime. During the economic boom of the late 1990s crime levels went down; but when the economic hard times returned in 2001, it was feared the trends might re-reverse themselves.

From 1928 to 1997 the Distrito Federal was ruled directly by the federal government, with federally appointed 'regents' heading notoriously corrupt administrations. Since 1997 the DF has had political autonomy, electing its own mayor for the first time that year. The winner, Cuauhtémoc Cárdenas of the left-of-center PRD party, headed an administration widely seen as honest and well intentioned, and made the first serious efforts to combat police corruption, a major factor in the high crime levels. Cárdenas resigned in 1999 to campaign instead for the national presidency, and although he lost his presidential bid, his party held onto the mayoralty. Under democratically elected governments, Mexico City has visibly improved its infrastructure, landscaping and public services.

ORIENTATION

Mexico City's 350 *colonias* (neighborhoods) sprawl across the ancient bed of Lago de Texcoco and beyond. Though this vast urban expanse is daunting at first, the main areas of interest to visitors are fairly well defined and easy to traverse.

Centro Histórico & Alameda Central

The historic heart of the city is the wide plaza known as the Zócalo, surrounded by the presidential palace, the city's cathedral and the excavated site of the Templo Mayor, the main temple of Aztec Tenochtitlán. The Zócalo and its surrounding neighborhoods are known as the Centro Histórico (Historic Center) and are full of notable old buildings and interesting museums. North, west and south of the Zócalo are many good, economical hotels and restaurants.

Avenida Madero and Avenida 5 de Mayo (or Cinco de Mayo) link the Zócalo with the Alameda Central park, eight blocks to the west. On the east side of the Alameda stands the magnificent Palacio de Bellas Artes. The landmark Torre Latinoamericana (Latin American Tower) pierces the sky a block south of the Bellas Artes, beside one of the city's main north-south arterial roads, the Eje Central Lázaro Cárdenas.

Plaza de la República

Some 750m west of the Alameda, across Paseo de la Reforma, is the Plaza de la República, marked by the somber, domed art deco-style Monumento a la Revolución. This is a fairly quiet, mostly residential area with many budget and mid-range hotels. The districts called San Rafael and Juárez are respectively west and south of here.

Paseo de la Reforma

Mexico City's grandest boulevard, flanked by major hotels, embassies and banks, runs for many kilometers across the city's heart, connecting the Alameda to the Zona Rosa and the Bosque de Chapultepec.

Zona Rosa

The Zona Rosa (Pink Zone) is a glitzy shopping, eating, hotel and nightlife district bound by Paseo de la Reforma to the north, Avenida Insurgentes to the east, and Avenida Chapultepec to the south.

Bosque de Chapultepec

The woods of Chapultepec, known to gringos as Chapultepec Park, is to the west

of the aforementioned districts. It's Mexico City's 'lungs,' a large expanse of greenery and lakes, and holds many major museums, including the renowned Museo Nacional de Antropología. Northwest of the park is the swanky Polanco district, filled with embassies and upscale shopping and dining establishments.

North of the Centro

Five kilometers north of the center is the Terminal Norte, the largest of the city's four major bus terminals. Six kilometers north of the center is the Basílica de Guadalupe, Mexico's most revered shrine.

South of the Centro

Avenida Insurgentes Sur connects Paseo de la Reforma to most points of interest in the south. Just south of the Zona Rosa and stretching southeast and a bit southwest of Insurgentes is the Roma, a quaint middle-class area. Just west of Roma, 1 to 2km south of the Zona Rosa, is Colonia Condesa, a trendy but relaxed neighborhood with pleasant parks, quiet streets, and plentiful restaurants and coffee bars. Five to 10km farther south are the atmospheric former villages of San Ángel and Coyoacán and the vast campus of UNAM, the National Autonomous University of Mexico. In the area to the southeast are the canals and gardens of Xochimilco.

The Eje System

Besides their regular names, many major streets in Mexico City are termed Eje (axis). The Eje system superimposes a grid of priority roads on this sprawling city's maze of smaller streets, making transport easier and quicker. The key north-south Eje Central Lázaro Cárdenas, running all the way from Coyoacán in the south to Tenayuca in the north, passes just east of the Alameda Central. Major north-south roads west of the Eje Central are termed Eje 1 Poniente (also called Guerrero, Rosales and Bucareli as it passes through the central area), Eje 2 Poniente (Avenida Florencia, Monterrey) etc. Major north-south roads to the east of the Eje Central are called Eje 1 Oriente (Alcocer, Anillo de Circunvalación), Eje 2 Oriente (Avenida Congreso de la Unión) and so on. The same goes for major east-west roads to the north and south of the Alameda

Central and Zócalo – Rayón is Eje 1 Norte, Fray Servando Teresa de Mier is Eje 1 Sur.

Maps

Maps handed out by tourist offices in Mexico City are currently pretty basic. You can buy better maps of the city and country in many bookstores (including those in the Sanborns chain stores and at top-end hotels) and at the shops of INEGI, Mexico's national geographical institute. One convenient INEGI outlet is at Local (Office) CC23, Glorieta Insurgentes, just outside Insurgentes metro station. This shop stocks INEGI's own maps plus a variety of other maps of Mexico City, Mexico, Mexican states and other Mexican cities. It's open 8am to 8pm Monday to Friday, 8.30am to 4pm Saturday. There are other INEGI map shops at Local 61 in the airport and in the Roma at Baja California 272 (Map 6) at Culiacán, near Chilpancingo metro station.

The *Guía Roji Ciudad de México* street atlas, costing US$11.50, has a comprehensive index and is updated annually.

Finding an Address

Some major streets, such as Avenida Insurgentes, keep the same name for many kilometers, but the names (and numbering) of many lesser streets switch every few blocks. Full addresses normally include the name of a colonia (neighborhood). Except for well-known center districts, you may need help. Often the easiest way to find an address is by asking where it is in relation to the nearest metro station.

INFORMATION
Tourist Offices

The Mexico City Ministry of Tourism has 11 tourist information offices in central areas and two others at the airport and the Terminal Norte bus station (see Getting There & Away). Offices provide information on Mexico City only, but they have some good maps. Often at least one member of staff in each office can speak English.

The offices are all open from 9am to 6pm daily, and a few of the offices stay open until 7pm. The offices include the following:

Alameda Central (☎ 5518-1003), Juárez 66

Monte de Piedad (no ☎; Ⓜ Zócalo; Map 3), next to the Catedral Metropolitana

Zona Rosa (☎ 5208-1030; Ⓜ Insurgentes; Map 5), Amberes 54 at Londres

Bosque de Chapultepec (☎ 5286-3867; Ⓜ Chapultepec; Map 7), Kiosk 30, just across Paseo de la Reforma from the Tláloc monument in front of the Museo Nacional de Antropología, on Reforma and Gandhi

Xochimilco (☎ 5653-5209; Map 8), at the Embarcadero Nuevo Nativitas on Mercado and Galeana

San Ángel (☎ 5616-4252; Ⓜ MA de Quevedo; Map 9), at Avenida Revolución and Madero in the Casa de la Cultura

Coyoacán (☎ 5659-6009; Ⓜ Coyoacán; Map 10), Jardín Hidalgo 1, in the former town hall, also called the Casa de Cortés

Plaza de las Américas (no ☎; Ⓜ Basílica-La Villa), by the Basílica de Guadalupe

The tourist office of SECTUR (☎ 5250-0123, 800-903-92-00; Ⓜ Polanco; Map 7), the national tourism ministry, is located, inconveniently for most tourists to Mexico City, at Avenida Presidente Masaryk 172, on the corner of Hegel in Polanco about 700m north of the Bosque de Chapultepec. The ministry has multilingual staff who willingly answer visitors' queries on the whole country and can provide computer printouts on some specific historical or cultural subjects.

SECTUR's two phone lines are staffed 24 hours, seven days a week, to provide tourist information and help with problems and emergencies. The office itself is open 8am to 6pm Monday to Friday and 10am to 3pm Saturday.

The Cámara Nacional de Comercio de la Ciudad de México (Mexico City National Chamber of Commerce, ☎ 5592-2677 ext 1015; Ⓜ Juárez; Map 4), Paseo de la Reforma 42, 4th floor, is open 9am to 2pm and 3pm to 6pm Monday to Friday and has a tourist office providing information on the city only.

Tourist Card Extensions

The Instituto Nacional de Migración (☎ 5387-2400) has an office at Homero 1832, Polanco. The office is open 9am to 1pm Monday to Friday. It's advisable to phone the office first to ask what documents are needed.

Money

Exchange rates vary a bit among Mexico City's numerous money-changing outlets, so

Mexico City's Air

Mexico City has some of the world's worst air. Severe pollution from traffic and industry is intensified by the mountains that ring the Valle de México, preventing air from dispersing, and by the city's altitude and consequent lack of oxygen.

Pollution is at its worst in the cooler months, especially November to February, when an unpleasant phenomenon called thermal inversion is most likely to occur: warm air passing over the Valle de México stops cool, polluted air near ground level from rising and dispersing. But at any time the pollution and altitude may make a visitor feel breathless and tired or may cause a sore throat, headache, runny nose or insomnia. People with serious lung, heart, asthmatic or respiratory problems are advised to consult a doctor before visiting Mexico City.

The major culprit is ozone, too much of which causes respiratory and eye problems in humans and corrodes rubber, paint and plastics. Leaks of unburned LPG (liquefied petroleum gas), used for cooking and heating, are a factor in ozone levels. But the primary problem is reckoned to be low-lead gasoline, introduced in 1986 to counter lead pollution, which until then was the city's worst atmospheric contaminant. The reaction between sunlight and combustion residues from low-lead gasoline produces a great deal of ozone. Mexico City's average ozone level is almost twice the maximum permitted in the USA and Japan.

In an attempt to reduce traffic pollution, since 1989 many cars in the city have been banned from the streets on one day each week by a program called Hoy No Circula (Don't Drive Today), and catalytic converters have been compulsory in all new cars in Mexico since the early 1990s. But ozone levels have remained high. Hoy No Circula unwittingly encouraged people to buy or rent

---

it's worth checking two or three before you part with your money. Most banks and *casas de cambio* (exchange offices) will change both cash and traveler's checks; some give a better rate for cash, others for traveler's checks. Some will change only US or Canadian dollars.

The greatest concentration of banks, ATMs and casas de cambio is on Paseo de la Reforma between the Monumento a Cristóbal Colón and the Monumento a la Independencia, but there are others all over the city, including at the airport, where some casas de cambio are open 24 hours.

Banks & ATMs Mexico City is chock-full of banks, most open 9am to 5pm Monday to Friday. Many have ATMs. In addition some newer supermarkets have branches that are open until around 2pm Saturday. To see Mexico City's most beautiful bank, step into the Banamex, Isabel la Católica 44 at Venustiano Carranza, in the old palace of the Counts of San Mateo Valparaiso.

Casas de Cambio The city's dozens of casas de cambio have longer hours and quicker procedures than banks. One downtown place with good rates is Cambios Exchange at Avenida Madero 15 between Mata and Condesa (open 10am to 7.30pm daily).

The area around the Monumento a la Independencia on Paseo de la Reforma, near the Zona Rosa, is a fertile hunting ground for exchange houses. Casa de Cambio Tíber, Río Tíber 112 at Río Lerma, gives good rates and is open 8.30am to 5pm Monday to Friday, 8.30am to 2pm Saturday. Money Exchange, Paseo de la Reforma at Sevilla, gives good rates for cash and American Express traveler's checks and is open 9am to 5.30pm Monday to Friday, 9am to 2.30pm Saturday.

extra cars to get around the once-a-week prohibition. There are expected to be 5 million cars in the city by 2005; the number has more than doubled since 1980.

The News publishes daily air quality reports and forecasts. Hourly reports (from 7am to 8pm) are usually posted on the Mexico City Air Quality Report Internet site (**w** www.sima.com.mx); this excellent site also explains in detail, in English and Spanish, how the pollution is measured. Ozone concentrations are worst around midday on sunny days.

Mexico City's air contamination is measured by the Índice Metropolitana de Calidad de Aire (IMECA, Metropolitan Air Quality Index). IMECA assesses five pollutants: ozone, sulfur dioxide, nitrogen dioxide, carbon monoxide and suspended particles. Readings below 100 are classed as 'satisfactory,' 101 to 200 is 'unsatisfactory,' 201 to 300 is 'bad,' and over 300 is 'very bad.' Ozone readings of more than 240, which may occur several times a year, or suspended particle levels of over 175 trigger phase one of the city's environmental contingency plan, which includes the Doble Hoy No Circula (Double Don't Drive Today) rule, which takes more vehicles off the streets. Three successive days of phase one trigger phase two, which immobilizes further vehicles, reduces industrial activity by 30% to 40%, and stops outdoor activities at schools. Phase three (rare) stops all industry and permits only emergency traffic.

The more exotic remedies suggested for the pollution crisis have included fleets of helicopters to sweep the smog away, and exploding a hole in the ring of mountains around the city, then using giant fans to blow the smog through it. More feasible, conceivably, is the idea of ionizing the air to create winds that would disperse pollution. Large ionizing antennae would alter the rate at which water vapor condenses, releasing heat and thus creating winds which would, it's hoped, blow pollution away. Tests of this proposal began in 1998 and 1999 in the Parque Ecológico de Xochimilco in the southeast section of the city; the scientists responsible claimed that it significantly lowered levels of ozone and other pollutants.

Meanwhile Bicitekas, a group of cyclists with their feet somewhat closer to the ground, is campaigning for people to use bicycles instead of cars in Mexico City; see the Cycling section, later in this chapter, for how to participate in their weekly *paseorecorridomanifestación* ('ridetourprotest').

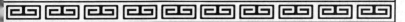

In the Zona Rosa, Money Exchange, Liverpool 162, is open 9am to 8pm Monday to Friday, 9am to 5pm Saturday and has reasonable rates for cash, but poor rates for traveler's checks. Londres, between Génova and Florencia, has many more casas de cambio.

American Express In a new building facing the Monumento a la Independencia, American Express (☎ 5207-7282; **◎** Insurgentes; Map 5) is at Paseo de la Reforma 350 on the corner of Florencia. It's open 9am to 6pm Monday to Friday, 9am to 1pm Saturday. You can change American Express traveler's checks here at good rates. The office also has other financial and card services, a travel bureau and a mail pick-up desk.

Wire Transfers The money wiring service Western Union 'Dinero en Minutos' is available at Telecomm (**◎** Revolución; Map 4), Insurgentes 114, 1½ blocks north of Reforma; it is open 8am to 9pm Monday to Friday, 9am to 1pm Saturday.

Elektra Electronics Stores, with three locations open 9am to 9pm daily, also offers this service. Its branches are at Pino Suárez at El Salvador, three blocks south of the Zócalo (**◎** Pino Suárez; Map 3); Balderas 62, two blocks south of the Alameda Central (**◎** Juárez; Map 3); and on the east side of Insurgentes Sur at Durango (**◎** Insurgentes; Map 6).

Post
The Correo Mayor, Mexico City's central post office, is a lovely early-20th-century building in Italian Renaissance style on Eje Central Lázaro Cárdenas at Tacuba, across from the Palacio de Bellas Artes (**◎** Bellas Artes; Map 3). The building is open 8am to 8pm Monday to Saturday, 8am to 4pm

Sunday. The stamp windows are marked '*estampillas.*' The *lista de correos* window is not marked, as the building is undergoing some remodeling, so ask at the front stamp window. For other information ask at the third window on the right from the front corner, 9am to 3pm Monday to Saturday, or call the postal services information line at ☎ 5709-9600, or check out their Web site at Ⓦ www.sepomex.gob.mx.

Other post offices in the city are generally open 9am to 3pm Monday to Friday, 9am to 1pm Saturday, and a few offices have extended hours until 5pm Monday to Friday. Here are a few:

Zócalo (Map 3), inside Plaza de la Constitución 7, on the west side of the Zócalo

Plaza de la República (Ⓜ Revolución; Map 4), on the corner of Mariscal and Arriaga

Plaza Colón (Map 4), Reforma at Ramírez

Zona Rosa (Ⓜ Insurgentes or Sevilla; Map 5), corner of Varsovia and Londres; closes at 5pm

If you carry an American Express card or American Express traveler's checks, you can use the American Express office (see Money) as your mailing address in Mexico City. The office holds mail for about one month before returning it to the sender. Have mail addressed this way:

Lucy CHANG (last name in capitals)
Client Mail
American Express
Paseo de la Reforma 350
México 06600 DF
MEXICO

Telephone & Fax

There are thousands of pay phones on the streets of Mexico City. Shops selling phone cards are also plentiful, including at the airport – look for blue-and-yellow 'De Venta Aqui Ladatel' signs.

Internet telephony – a call carried through an Internet server line instead of a phone line – is increasingly being provided at Internet cafés. One good place is Mac Coffee, a sleek new Internet café in the Zona Rosa (see Email & Internet Access, later). One minute to the USA costs US$0.35, and a minute to Canada or Europe costs US$0.50.

Java Chat (see Email & Internet Access) offers the same services US$0.05 per minute cheaper, but it may be much more crowded.

You can send and receive faxes at Mac Coffee. Sending one page to the USA or Canada costs about US$1 to US$2 depending on the time of day; receiving a fax costs US$0.30. Many telephone *casetas*, shops and businesses, including at the airport and bus stations, offer fax service; look for 'fax' or '*fax público*' signs.

Email & Internet Access

Mexico City has many public Internet and email services. Prices in the following listings are for an hour online.

Centro Histórico (Map 3):

Esperanto (☎ 5512-4123), Independencia 66; US$2.75; open 9am to 8pm Monday to Saturday, noon to 6pm Sunday

Zona Rosa (Map 5):

Café Internet (no ☎), Hamburgo 165, just east of Florencia; rates US$2.75; open 10am to 10pm Monday to Friday, 11am to 10pm Saturday and 1pm to 8pm Sunday

Java Chat, Génova 44K; US$4.25; open 9am to 11.30pm Monday to Friday, 10am to 11pm Saturday and Sunday; Internet phone service and free coffee

Mac Coffee (☎ 5525-4385; Ⓜ Insurgentes), Londres 152, just west of Amberes; rates US$1.75; open 10am to 10pm Monday to Saturday; ring the buzzer to be let in, then walk up one flight

Other Areas:

Café Punto Com (☎ 5281-3516; Map 7), Virgilio 25, Polanco; US$4.25; open 10am to 8pm Monday to Thursday, 10am to 7pm Friday, 11.30am to 5pm Saturday

Coffee Net (☎ 5286-7104; Map 6), Nuevo León 104B, Condesa; rates US$2.75; open 10am to 10pm Monday to Saturday, noon to 6pm Sunday; pleasant environment, drinks available

Escape (☎ 5550-7684; Map 9), Avenida de la Paz 23, San Ángel; rates US$2.15; open 8am to 11pm Monday to Saturday, 11am to 7pm Sunday

Internet Resources

One of the better introductions to the city on the Internet is Mexico City Virtual Guide (Ⓦ www.mexicocity.com.mx/mexcity.html, in English, or Ⓦ www.mexicocity.com.mx/index.html, in Spanish). It has a broad range of materials on sights, hotels and restaurants (mainly top-end), books and interesting links. The Spanish-language version has more information than the English one. The

Distrito Federal tourism department's site (W www.mexicocity.gob.mx) has exhaustive listings of museums and galleries and what's on in them, and contact details for countless hotels, restaurants, travel agencies and transportation companies (in English and Spanish).

Tiempo Libre magazine's helpful Web site (W www.tiempolibre.com.mx) has heaps of useful information, including listings of clubs, restaurants and shows (the magazine itself covers the current week's entertainment in Mexico City). Another good site, in Spanish, is W www.chilangolandia.com.

Some other sites are mentioned in relevant sections of this chapter.

Travel Agencies

A number of mid-range and top-end hotels have an *agencia de viajes* (travel agent's desk) on-site or can recommend travel agencies nearby.

Mundo Joven (W www.mundojoven.com) specializes in cheap travel tickets for youths, students and teachers, and has worthwhile fares on domestic and one-way international flights from Mexico City. Mundo Joven can issue ISIC, ITIC and GO25 cards for US$12; for the first two you need a card or letter from your college showing that you are a full-time student or teacher. For a GO25 you need your passport (and you have to be under 26). The company has three locations: (☎ 5661-3233), Insurgentes Sur 1510, Local D; at the Casa de Francia (☎ 5525-0407), Havre 15, Zona Rosa; and (☎ 5518-1755), Guatemala 4, Centro. You can reach the Insurgentes office on a 'San Ángel' minibus south from Metro Insurgentes; it's just south of Avenida Río Mixcoac.

Two other youth/student travel agencies are notable. Viajes Educativos (☎ 5661-4235; Ⓜ Barranca del Muerto), Insurgentes Sur 1690 at Francia, can issue ISIC cards (US$12) and HI cards (US$22), and for US$25 can change dates on student and youth air tickets. Cosmo Educación (☎ 5550-3373; Map 9), Avenida de la Paz 58, Local 9, San Ángel, and (☎ 5282-1021; Map 7), France 17A, Polanco, can issue all of the aforementioned cards and can also help find cheap student and teacher tickets.

The following travel agencies are also worth looking into for reasonably priced air tickets: Tony Pérez (☎ 5533-1148,

W www.tonyperez.com.mx; Map 5), Río Volga 1 at Río Danubio, Zona Rosa; and Viajes Universales (☎/fax 5512-7120; Map 4), Bucareli 12, 3rd floor.

Bookstores

Books in English and other non-Spanish languages can be found in bookstalls in top-end hotels, Sanborns stores and major museums, as well as most of the following recommended bookstores.

In the Centro Histórico, American Bookstore (☎ 5512-0306; Map 3), Bolívar 23, has novels and books on Mexico in English as well as Mexico City's best selection of Lonely Planet guides. (They have other branches in the city as well; see the Web site W www.americanbookstore.org, then click on *sucursales*.)

Gandhi (☎ 5510-4231; Map 3), Avenida Juárez 4, is a good source of books about Mexico and Mexico City and novels in English. Opening hours are 10am to 9pm Monday to Saturday, 11am to 8pm Sunday. A Gandhi's in San Ángel (☎ 5661-0911; Map 9), Avenida MA de Quevedo 121 to 134, is a Mexico City hangout spot with a worthwhile music section and a popular upstairs café.

The Palacio de Bellas Artes (☎ 5521-9251; Map 3), Avenida Juárez 1, has an excellent arts bookstore with some English-language titles on Mexico. It is open 10am to 9pm Tuesday to Sunday, 11am to 6pm Monday.

In the Zona Rosa, three stores are especially worth seeking out. La Bouquinerie (☎ 5511-3151; Map 5), in the Casa de Francia, Havre 15, is a small French bookstore with French-language magazines. It is open 10am to 8pm Monday to Friday, 1pm to 6pm Saturday. There is a larger branch in San Ángel (☎ 5616-6066; Map 9), Camino al Desierto de los Leones 40. Tower Records (☎ 5525-4829; Map 5), Niza 19, has a good selection of books and magazines in English and Spanish and is open 10am to 9pm Sunday to Thursday, 10am to 10pm Friday and Saturday.

In the Roma look for Nueva Librería Italiana (☎ 5511-6180; Map 6), Plaza Río de Janeiro 53 at Durango, which mostly stocks Italian-language books and magazines, as well as some titles in French and English; it is open 10am to 7pm Monday to Friday, 10am to 2pm Saturday.

Librería Pegaso (☎ 5208-0174; Map 6), Obregón 99, in the Centro Cultural Casa Lamm, deals mostly with Spanish-language books but also stocks titles in French and English, and you can help yourself to coffee and sit on a couch while browsing. It is open 11am to 8pm daily.

In Polanco CENCA (☎ 5280-1666; Map 7), Temistocles 73-B at Avenida Presidente Masaryk, has a huge variety of magazines in Spanish and English, and also sells best-sellers in English. It is open 8am to 10pm Monday to Friday, 9am to 9pm Saturday and Sunday.

Las Sirenas (☎ 5550-3112; Map 9), Avenida de la Paz 57, is in San Ángel and is open 11am to 8pm Tuesday to Saturday, 12.30pm to 7pm Sunday. Another good bookstore is Nalandra Libros (☎ 5554-7522; Map 10), Centenario 16, Coyoacán; it is open 10am to 8pm Monday to Saturday, 10am to 7pm Sunday.

Media

Mexico's English-language newspaper, *The News,* and the weekly *Tiempo Libre,* the city's Spanish-language what's-on magazine, are sold at many downtown and Zona Rosa newsstands, as well as by several of the bookstores mentioned earlier.

Mexico City's best Spanish-language newspaper is *Reforma,* sold in convenience stores, grocery stores and bookstores. It's also sold on the street by authorized salespeople, although it's not available at outdoor newsstands.

North American and European newspapers and magazines are sold at hotel newsstands and some of the above bookstores. *La Casa de la Prensa* (Ⓜ Insurgentes; Map 5), Avenida Florencia 57 and Hamburgo 141, Zona Rosa, sells major British and American newspapers and magazines, plus a few French, Spanish and German ones. The Florencia branch is open 8am to 10pm Monday to Friday, 9am to 6pm Saturday to Sunday; the Hamburgo branch is open 9am to 10pm Monday to Friday, 11am to 7.30pm Saturday to Sunday.

Libraries

There are several useful foreign-run libraries in Mexico City:

Biblioteca Benjamín Franklin (☎ 5080-2000 ext 2801; Ⓜ Cuauhtémoc; Map 4), Londres 16, west of Berlín, is open 9am to 5pm Monday to Friday and is run by the US embassy. It has a wide range of books about Mexico, plus English language periodicals. Users must be 20 or older

Canadian Embassy Library (☎ 5724-7960; Ⓜ Cuauhtémoc; Map 7), Schiller 529, Polanco, is open 9am to 1pm Monday to Friday and contains many Canadian books and periodicals in English and French.

Casa de Francia (☎ 5511-3151; Ⓜ Insurgentes Map 5), Havre 15, Zona Rosa, is open 10am to 8pm Monday to Saturday and is a good French library equipped with computers.

Consejo Británico (British Council, ☎ 5566-4500 ext 2527; Ⓜ San Cosme; Map 4), Antonio Caso 127, San Rafael, is open 8am to 3pm Monday to Friday and has lots of books and magazines in English, plus aging British newspapers.

Instituto Goethe (☎ 5533-0441; Ⓜ Insurgentes Map 6), Tonalá 43, Roma, is open 9am to 1pm and 4pm to 7.30pm Tuesday to Thursday and has collections in German.

Cultural Centers

The Consejo Británico and Instituto Goethe (see Libraries) and the Institut Français d'Amérique Latine (☎ 5566-0777 Ⓜ San Cosme or Insurgentes; Map 4), Río Nazas 43, all put on films, exhibitions, concerts and other events from their home countries. The Casa de Francia (see Libraries) has a French bookstore and café and an exhibition hall.

Laundry

The following three laundries all charge around US$4 for you to wash and dry 3kg or US$5.25 for a 3kg service wash:

Lavandería Automática Édison (Ⓜ Revolución Map 4), Édison 91, near Plaza de la República, open 10am to 7pm Monday to Friday, 10am to 6pm Saturday

Lavandería Las Artes (☎ 5535-7474; Map 4) Antonio Caso 82, near the Jardín del Arte; open 9am to 7.30pm Monday to Friday, 9am to 8pm Saturday

Lavandería Automática (Map 5), Río Danubio 119B, north of Zona Rosa; open 8.15am to 5.30pm Monday to Friday, 8.30am to 4pm Saturday

Medical Services

For recommendation of a doctor, dentist or hospital, you can call your embassy or the

[continued on page 172]

MAP 1 MEXICO CITY

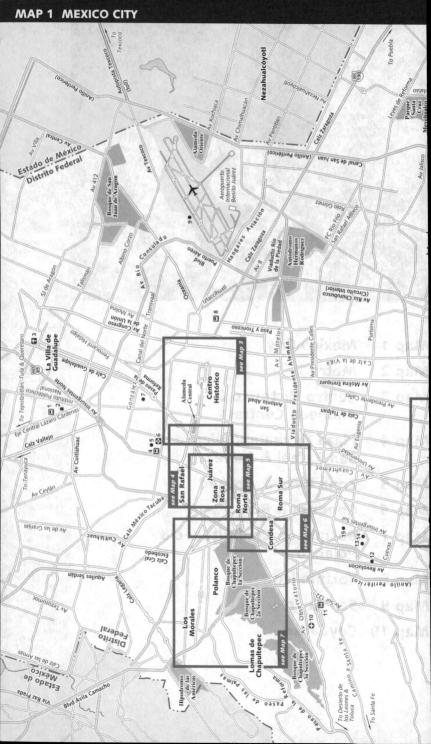

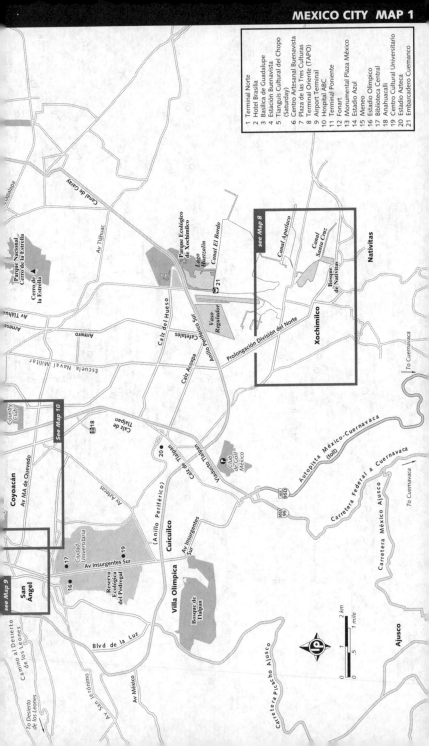

1 Terminal Norte
2 Hotel Brasilia
3 Basílica de Guadalupe
4 Estación Buenavista
5 Tianguis Cultural del Chopo (Saturday)
6 Centro Artesanal Buenavista
7 Plaza de las Tres Culturas
8 Terminal Oriente (TAPO)
9 Airport Terminal
10 Hospital ABC
11 Terminal Poniente
12 Fonart
13 Monumental Plaza México
14 Estadio Azul
15 Meneo
16 Estadio Olímpico
17 Biblioteca Central
18 Anahuacalli
19 Centro Cultural Universitario
20 Estadio Azteca
21 Embarcadero Cuemanco

MAP 2 METRO

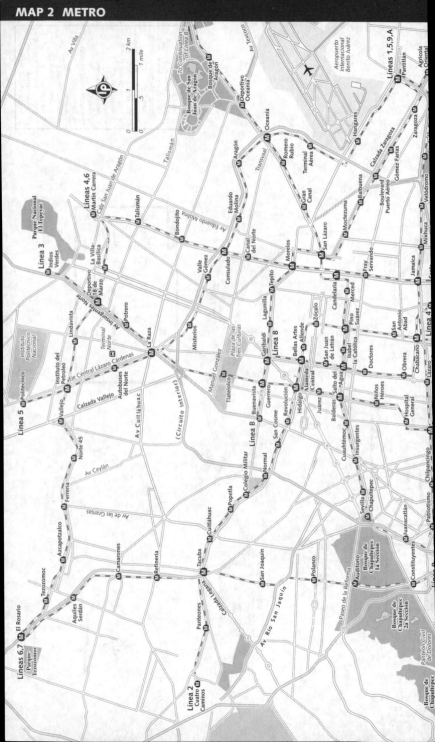

Continuation of Linea A

0 1 2 km
0 .5 1 mile

Linea A

La Paz
Los Reyes
Santa Marta
Acatitla
Peñón Viejo
Guelatao
Tepalcates
Canal de San Juan
Calz. Ignacio Zaragoza
Av. Juárez

Parque
Santa
Cruz
Meyehualco

Canal de San Juan

Linea 8

Constitución
de 1917
Purísima
Iztapalapa
Cerro de
la Estrella
Atlalilco
Escuadrón 201
Aculco
Apatlaco
Iztacalco
Coyuya

Ave Río Churubusco (Circuito Interior)

Av Jalisco
Leyes de Reforma
Rojo Gómez
Oriente 253

Calz Ermita Iztapalapa

Parque
Nacional de
Cerro de
la Estrella

Calzada de la Viga

Av Molina Enríquez

Xola
Villa de Cortes
Portales
Ermita
Nativitas
Xola

Calzada de Tlalpan

Av Presidente Calles

General Anaya
Tasqueña
Terminal
Sur
Ciudad Jardín
La Virgen
Xotepingo
Nezahualpilli
Registro Federal
Textitlan
El Vergel

Linea 2

Country
Club

Las Torres

Av Azteca

Etiopía
Eugenia
División
del Norte
Zapata
Coyoacán
Viveros
MA de
Quevedo

Av Cuauhtémoc
Av División del Norte
Av Coyoacán
Av Universidad
Av Río Churubusco (Circuito Interior)
Av MA de Quevedo

Viveros de
Coyoacán

Henríquez Ureña

Copilco
Universidad

Linea 3

Ciudad
Universitaria

Av Insurgentes Sur

Reserva
Ecológica
del Pedregal

Paseo del Pedregal

Blvd López Mateos (Anillo Periférico)

Observatorio

Linea 1

Terminal
Poniente

San Pedro
de los Pinos
San Antonio
Mixcoac

Barranca
del Muerto

Linea 7

Viaducto Presidente
Av Insurgentes Sur

Rodríguez

A   Metro Line Terminus
M Metro Transfer Station
M Metro Station
T   Tren Ligero Station

MAP 3 CENTRO HISTÓRICO & ALAMEDA CENTRAL

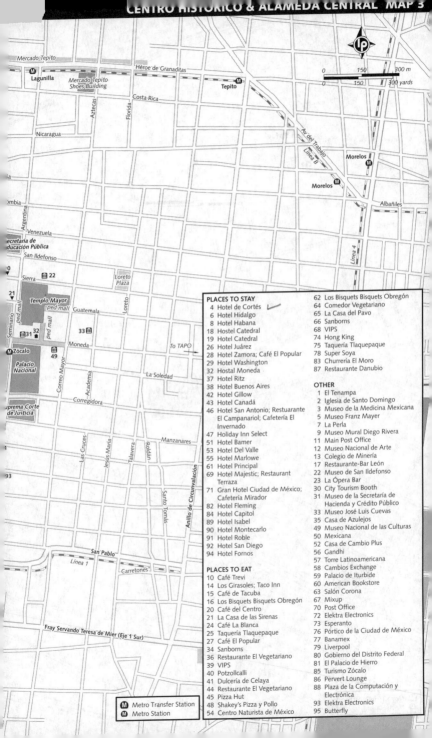

PLACES TO STAY
- 4 Hotel de Cortés
- 6 Hotel Hidalgo
- 8 Hotel Habana
- 18 Hostel Catedral
- 19 Hotel Catedral
- 26 Hotel Juárez
- 28 Hotel Zamora; Café El Popular
- 29 Hotel Washington
- 32 Hostal Moneda
- 37 Hotel Ritz
- 38 Hotel Buenos Aires
- 42 Hotel Gillow
- 43 Hotel Canadá
- 46 Hotel San Antonio; Restuarante El Campanario!; Cafetería El Invernado
- 47 Holiday Inn Select
- 51 Hotel Bamer
- 53 Hotel Del Valle
- 55 Hotel Marlowe
- 61 Hotel Principal
- 69 Hotel Majestic; Restaurant Terraza
- 71 Gran Hotel Ciudad de México; Cafetería Mirador
- 82 Hotel Fleming
- 84 Hotel Capitol
- 89 Hotel Isabel
- 90 Hotel Montecarlo
- 91 Hotel Roble
- 92 Hotel San Diego
- 94 Hotel Fornos

PLACES TO EAT
- 10 Café Trevi
- 14 Los Girasoles; Taco Inn
- 15 Café de Tacuba
- 16 Los Bisquets Bisquets Obregón
- 20 Café del Centro
- 21 La Casa de las Sirenas
- 24 Café La Blanca
- 25 Taquería Tlaquepaque
- 27 Café El Popular
- 34 Sanborns
- 36 Restaurante El Vegetariano
- 39 VIPS
- 40 Potzollcalli
- 41 Dulcería de Celaya
- 44 Restaurante El Vegetariano
- 45 Pizza Hut
- 48 Shakey's Pizza y Pollo
- 54 Centro Naturista de México

- 62 Los Bisquets Bisquets Obregón
- 64 Comedor Vegetariano
- 65 La Casa del Pavo
- 66 Sanborns
- 68 VIPS
- 74 Hong King
- 75 Taquería Tlaquepaque
- 78 Super Soya
- 83 Churrería El Moro
- 87 Restaurante Danubio

OTHER
- 1 El Tenampa
- 2 Iglesia de Santo Domingo
- 3 Museo de la Medicina Mexicana
- 5 Museo Franz Mayer
- 7 La Perla
- 9 Museo Mural Diego Rivera
- 11 Main Post Office
- 12 Museo Nacional de Arte
- 13 Colegio de Minería
- 17 Restaurante-Bar León
- 22 Museo de San Ildefonso
- 23 La Ópera Bar
- 30 City Tourism Booth
- 31 Museo de la Secretaría de Hacienda y Crédito Público
- 33 Museo José Luis Cuevas
- 35 Casa de Azulejos
- 49 Museo Nacional de las Culturas
- 50 Mexicana
- 52 Casa de Cambio Plus
- 56 Gandhi
- 57 Torre Latinoamericana
- 58 Cambios Exchange
- 59 Palacio de Iturbide
- 60 American Bookstore
- 63 Salón Corona
- 67 Mixup
- 70 Post Office
- 72 Elektra Electronics
- 73 Esperanto
- 76 Pórtico de la Ciudad de México
- 77 Banamex
- 79 Liverpool
- 80 Gobierno del Distrito Federal
- 81 El Palacio de Hierro
- 85 Turismo Zócalo
- 86 Pervert Lounge
- 88 Plaza de la Computación y Electrónica
- 93 Elektra Electronics
- 95 Butterfly

M Metro Transfer Station
M Metro Station

0   150   300 m
0   150   300 yards

MAP 4 PLAZA DE LA REPÚBLICA, SAN RAFAEL & JUÁREZ

San Rafael

Juárez

Jardín del Arte

Plaza

María Isabel Sheraton Hotel

Metro Transfer Station
Metro Station

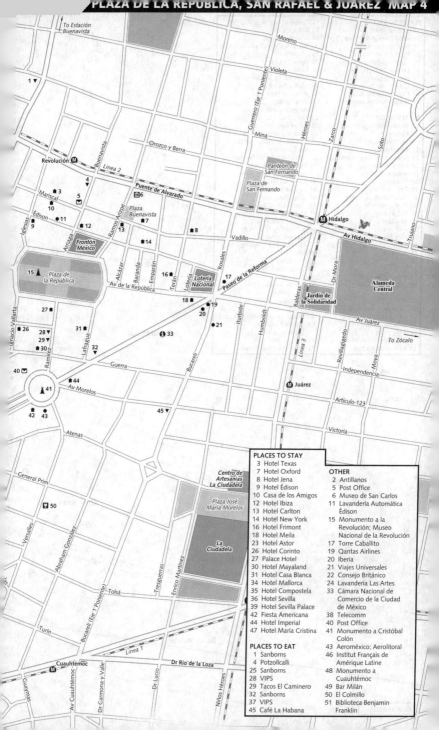

PLACES TO STAY
3 Hotel Texas
7 Hotel Oxford
8 Hotel Jena
9 Hotel Édison
10 Casa de los Amigos
12 Hotel Ibiza
13 Hotel Carlton
14 Hotel New York
16 Hotel Frimont
18 Hotel Meila
23 Hotel Astor
26 Hotel Corinto
27 Palace Hotel
30 Hotel Mayaland
31 Hotel Casa Blanca
34 Hotel Mallorca
35 Hotel Compostela
36 Hotel Sevilla
39 Hotel Sevilla Palace
42 Fiesta Americana
44 Hotel Imperial
47 Hotel María Cristina

PLACES TO EAT
1 Sanborns
4 Potzollcalli
25 Sanborns
28 VIPS
29 Tacos El Caminero
32 Sanborns
37 VIPS
45 Café La Habana

OTHER
2 Antillanos
5 Post Office
6 Museo de San Carlos
11 Lavandería Automática
   Édison
15 Monumento a la
   Revolución; Museo
   Nacional de la Revolución
17 Torre Caballito
19 Qantas Airlines
20 Iberia
21 Viajes Universales
22 Consejo Británico
24 Lavandería Las Artes
33 Cámara Nacional de
   Comercio de la Ciudad
   de México
38 Telecomm
40 Post Office
41 Monumento a Cristóbal
   Colón
43 Aeroméxico; Aerolitoral
46 Institut Français de
   Amérique Latine
48 Monumento a
   Cuauhtémoc
49 Bar Milán
50 El Colmillo
51 Biblioteca Benjamin
   Franklin

MAP 5 ZONA ROSA & AROUND

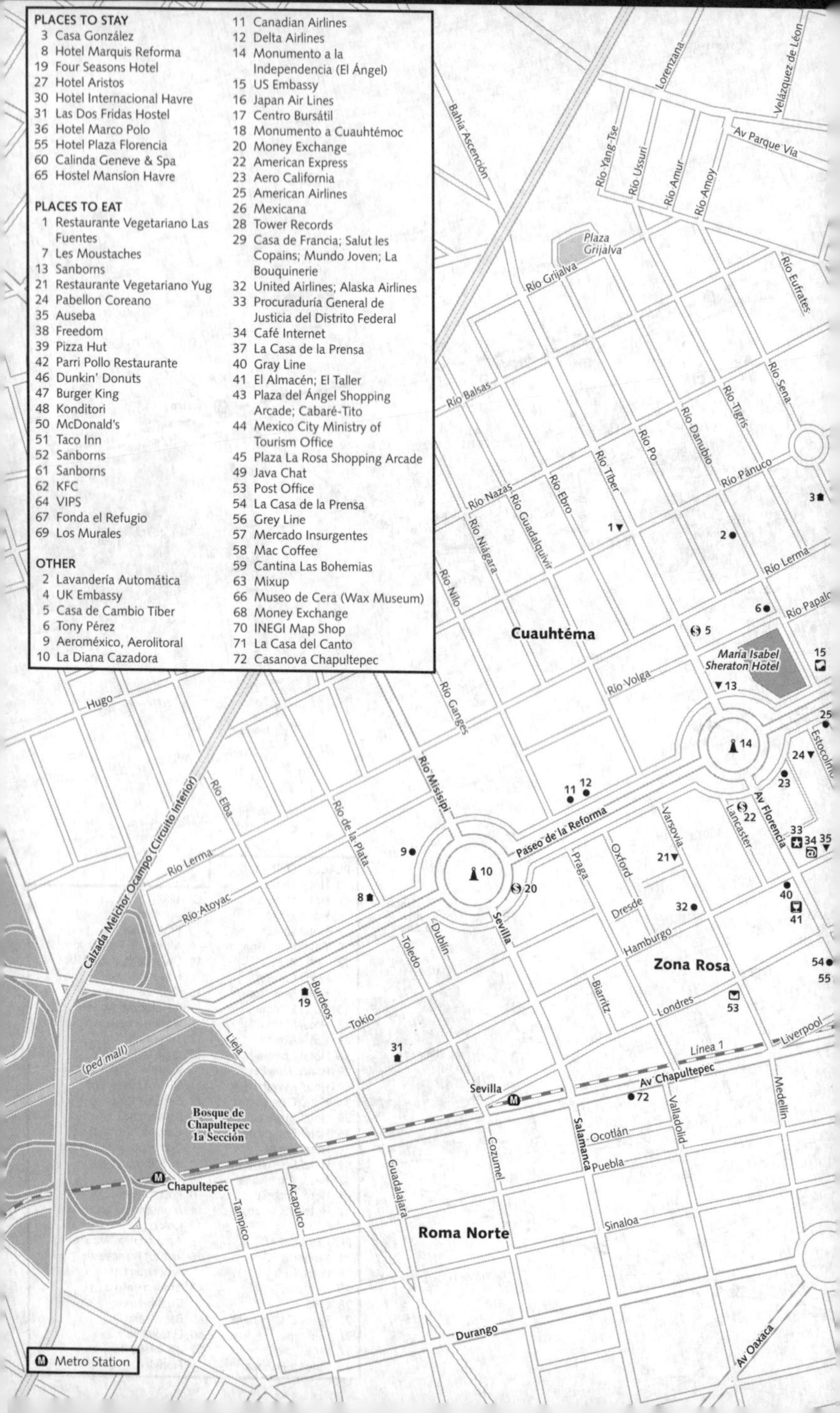

Velázquez de León

Lorenzana

Av Parque Vía

Bahía Ascención

Río Yang-Tse

Río Ussuri

Río Amur

Río Amoy

Plaza Grijalva

Río Grijalva

Río Eufrates

Río Balsas

Río Po

Río Danubio

Río Tigris

Río Sena

Río Nazas

Río Ebro

Río Tiber

Río Pánuco

Río Guadalquivir

1 ▼

2 ●

3 ●

Río Lerma

Río Níagara

Río Nilo

6 ●

Río Papalo

Cuauhtéma

(●) 5

María Isabel Sheraton Hotel

15

Río Volga

▼ 13

Hugo

Río Ganges

Calzada Melchor Ocampo (Circuito Interior)

Río Elba

Río Mississpi

25

â 14

Estocolmo

24 ▼

23

Río Lerma

Paseo de la Reforma

11 12

Varsovia

Lancaster

(●) 22

Av Florencia

33

34 35

Río Atoyac

9 ●

Toledo

Dublín

Sevilla

â 10

(●) 20

Praga

Oxford

21 ▼

Dresde

32 ●

40

41

Hamburgo

Zona Rosa

54 ●

55

Burdeos

8 ■

Río de la Plata

19

Biarritz

Londres

53

Tokio

31

Lieja

Linea 1

Liverpool

Medellín

Sevilla Ⓜ

Av Chapultepec

● 72

Valladolid

(ped mall)

Bosque de Chapultepec la Sección

Cozumel

Salamanca

Ocotlán

Puebla

Ⓜ Chapultepec

Tampico

Acapulco

Guadalajara

Sinaloa

Roma Norte

Durango

Av Oaxaca

Ⓜ Metro Station

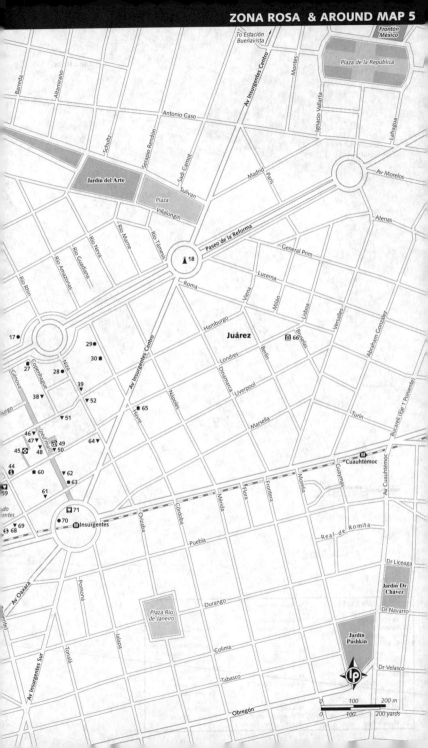

MAP 6 CONDESA & ROMA

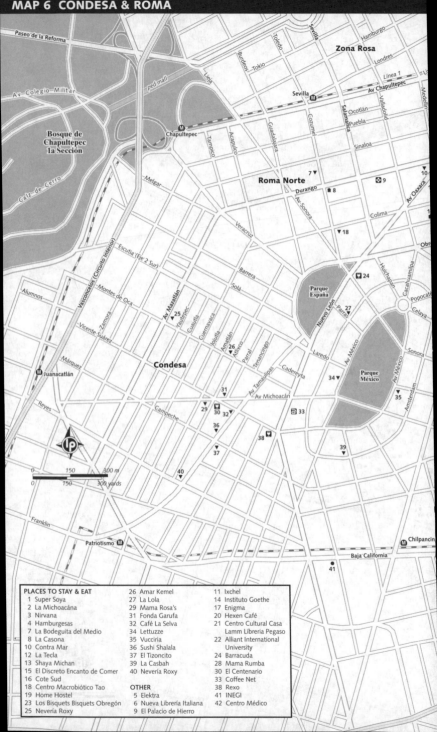

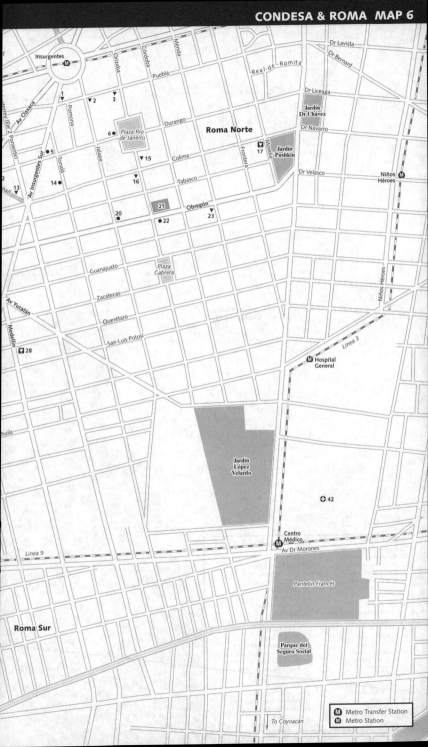

Insurgentes

Dr Lavista
Dr Bernard

Córdoba
Orizaba
Mérida

Puebla

Real-de-Romita

Dr Liceaga

Pomona

Durango

Dr Navarro

Jardín
Dr Chávez

Roma Norte

1
2
3

Plaza Río
de Janeiro

6

Jalapa

15

Colima

Morelia

Frontera

17

Jardín
Pushkin

Dr Velasco

Niños
Héroes

5
Tonalá

14

16

Tabasco

Dr Velasco

13
Av Insurgentes Sur
Av Oaxaca

20

21

Obregón

22

23

Guanajuato

Plaza
Cabrera

Av Yucatán

Zacatecas

Querétaro

Niños Héroes

Medellín

San Luis Potosí

Línea 3

28

Hospital
General

Jardín
López
Velardo

42

Centro
Médico

Línea 9

Av Dr Morones

Panteón Francés

Roma Sur

Parque del
Seguro Social

To Coyoacán

Ⓜ	Metro Transfer Station
Ⓜ	Metro Station

MAP 7 BOSQUE DE CHAPULTEPEC & POLANCO

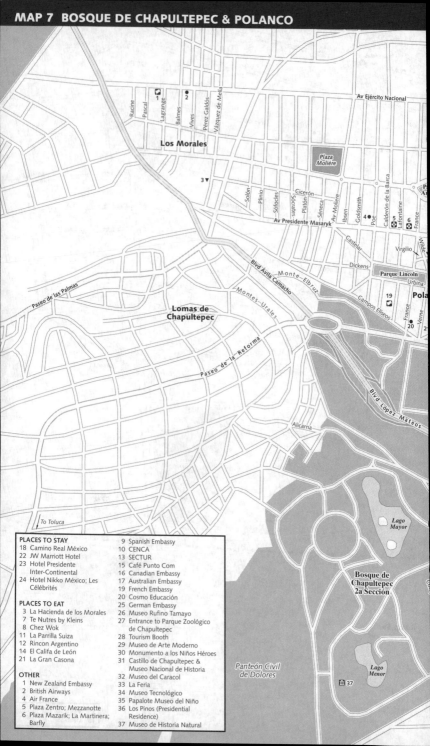

Los Morales

Plaza Molière

Av Ejército Nacional

Av Presidente Masaryk

Blvd Ávila Camacho

Monte-Elbruz

Montes-Urales

Lomas de Chapultepec

Paseo de las Palmas

Paseo de la Reforma

Parque Lincoln

Pola...

Blvd López Mateos

Alicarna

Castelar

Virgilio

Dickens

To Toluca

Lago Mayor

Bosque de Chapultepec 2a Sección

Lago Menor

Panteón Civil de Dolores

PLACES TO STAY
18 Camino Real México
22 JW Marriott Hotel
23 Hotel Presidente Inter-Continental
24 Hotel Nikko México; Les Célébrités

PLACES TO EAT
3 La Hacienda de los Morales
7 Te Nutres by Kleins
8 Chez Wok
11 La Parrilla Suiza
12 Rincon Argentino
14 El Califa de León
21 La Gran Casona

OTHER
1 New Zealand Embassy
2 British Airways
4 Air France
5 Plaza Zentro; Mezzanotte
6 Plaza Mazarik; La Martinera; Barfly

9 Spanish Embassy
10 CENCA
13 SECTUR
15 Café Punto Com
16 Canadian Embassy
17 Australian Embassy
19 French Embassy
20 Cosmo Educación
25 German Embassy
26 Museo Rufino Tamayo
27 Entrance to Parque Zoológico de Chapultepec
28 Tourism Booth
29 Museo de Arte Moderno
30 Monumento a los Niños Héroes
31 Castillo de Chapultepec & Museo Nacional de Historia
32 Museo del Caracol
33 La Feria
34 Museo Tecnológico
35 Papalote Museo del Niño
36 Los Pinos (Presidential Residence)
37 Museo de Historia Natural

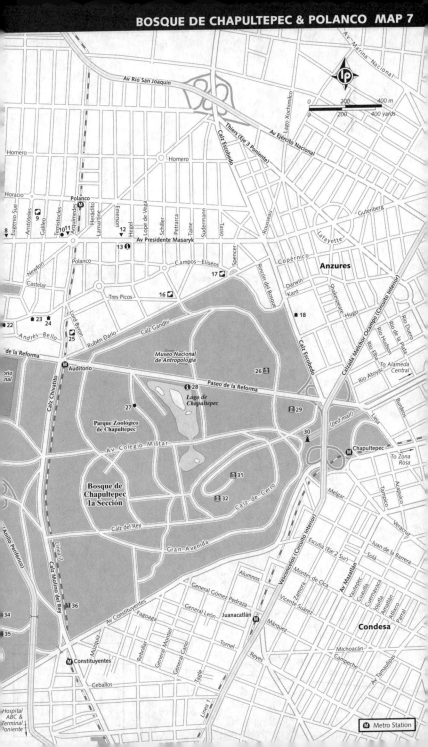

Av Marina Nacional

Av Río San Joaquín

Lago Xochimilco

Thiers (Eje 3 Poniente)

Av Ejército Nacional

Calz Escobedo

0   200   400 m
0   200   400 yards

Homero

Homero

Horacio

Eugenio Sue

Aristóteles

Galileo

Temístocles

Arquímedes

Polanco

9
10 11

8

Heráclito

Lamartine

Emerson

Lope de Vega

Schiller

Petrarca

Taine

Sudermann

Tasso

Hegel

12

Av Presidente Masaryk

13

Polanco

Newton

Castelar

Tres Picos

Campos-Elíseos

17

16

Spencer

Rincón del Bosque

Copérnico

Anzures

Darwin

Kant

Rousseau

Gutenberg

Lafayette

Shakespeare

Hugo

Calzada Melchor Ocampo (Circuito Interior)

23
24

22

Andrés Bello

Lord Byron

25

Rubén Darío

Calz Gandhi

Museo Nacional
de Antropología

26

18

Río Duero

Río de la Plata

Río Hudson

Río Elba

Río Atoyac

To Alameda
Central

de la Reforma

Calz Chivatito

Auditorio

28

Paseo de la Reforma

27

Lago de
Chapultepec

29

Parque Zoológico
de Chapultepec

Av Colegio-Militar

30

(ped mall)

Lieja

Burdeos

Chapultepec

To Zona
Rosa

Bosque de
Chapultepec
1a Sección

31

32

Calz de Cerro

Melgar

Tampico

Acapulco

Veracruz

Calz del Rey

Calz Molino del Rey

Linea 7

Gran-Avenida

Alumnos

General Gómez Pedraza

General León

Juanacatlán

General Morelos

Anillo Periférico

36

34

35

Av Constituyentes

Fagoaga

Múzquiz

Rebollar

General Cano

Tornel

Reyes

Vicente Suárez

Vasconcelos (Circuito Interior)

Montes de Oca

Escuta (Eje 2 Sur)

Márquez

Av Mazatlán

Yautepec

Cuautla

Guernavaca

Joquila

Amatlán

Atlixco

Parral

Condesa

Michoacán

Campeche

Av Tamaulipas

Juan de la Barrera

Solá

Constituyentes

Ceballos

Tagle

Hospital
ABC &
Terminal
Poniente

M Metro Station

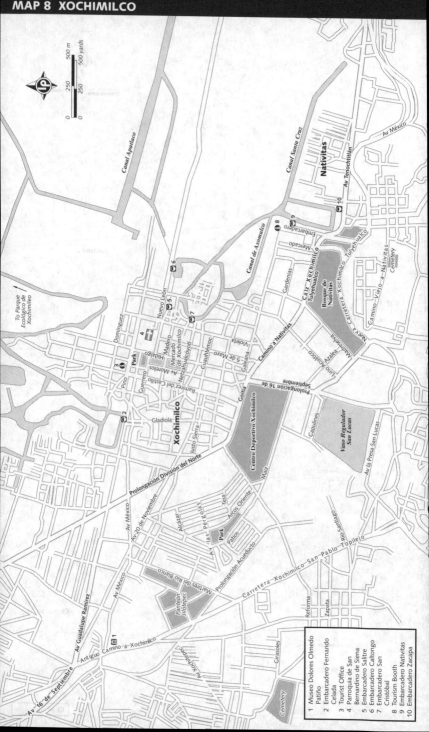

MAP 8 XOCHIMILCO

To Parque Ecológico de Xochimilco

Canal Apatlaco

Canal Santa Cruz

Nativitas

Av México

Av Tenochtitlán

Canal de Axomulco

Bosque de Nativitas

Cementery

Camino Viejo a Nativitas

Caltz Xochimilco Tulyehualco

Mercado

Embarcadero

Gardenias

Nueva Carretera Xochimilco Tulyehualco

Madreselva

Nuevo León

Madero

Mercado de Xochimilco Nezahualcóyotl

Hidalgo

Pino

Guerrero

Av Morelos

Ramírez del Castillo

Cuauhtémoc

5 de Mayo

Galeana

Violeta

Lirio Acuático

Lino Azules

Camino a Nativitas

Prolongación 16 de septiembre

Park

Gladiola

Justo Sierra

Goitia

Capulines

Vaso Regulador San Lucas

Av la Presa San Lucas

Dominguez

Xochimilco

Prolongación División del Norte

Centro Deportivo Xochimilco

Malix

Av 20 de Noviembre

Av México

Alcázar

Arcos Oriente

Tejar

Av las Peñolas

Park

Patio

Prolongación Acueducto

Mártires del Río Blanco

Carretera Xochimilco–San Pablo–Topilejo Río Santiago

Reforma

Zapata

Panteón Ilicotepec

Av Guadalupe Ramírez

Antiguo Camino a Xochimilco

Girasoles

Cristóbal

Av Xochimilco

Cementery

Av 16 de Septiembre

1 Museo Dolores Olmedo Patiño
2 Embarcadero Fernando Celada
3 Tourist Office
4 Parroquia de San Bernardino de Siena
5 Embarcadero Salitre
6 Embarcadero Caltongo
7 Embarcadero San Cristóbal
8 Tourism Booth
9 Embarcadero Nativitas
10 Embarcadero Zacapa

500 m
500 yards
0 250

MAP 9 SAN ÁNGEL

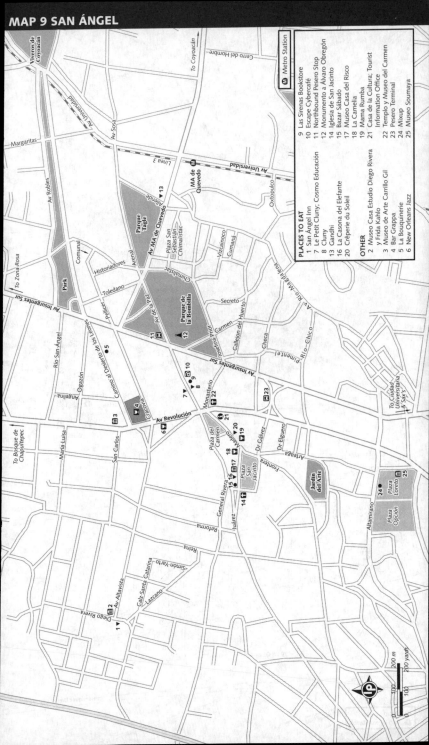

PLACES TO EAT
1 San Angel Inn
7 Le Petit Cluny; Cosmo Educación
8 Cluny
13 Gandhi
16 La Casona del Elefante
20 Crêperie du Soleil

OTHER
2 Museo Casa Estudio Diego Rivera
   y Frida Kahlo
3 Museo de Arte Carrillo Gil
4 Bar Grappa
5 La Bouquinerie
6 New Orleans Jazz

9 Las Sirenas Bookstore
10 Escape Cybercafé
11 Northbound Pesero Stop
12 Monumento a Alvaro Obregón
14 Iglesia de San Jacinto
15 Bazar Sábado
17 Museo Casa del Risco
18 La Camelia
19 Mama Rumba
21 Casa de la Cultura; Tourist
   Information Office
22 Templo y Museo del Carmen
23 Pesero Terminal
24 Mixup
25 Museo Soumaya

Ⓜ Metro Station

MAP 10 COYOACÁN

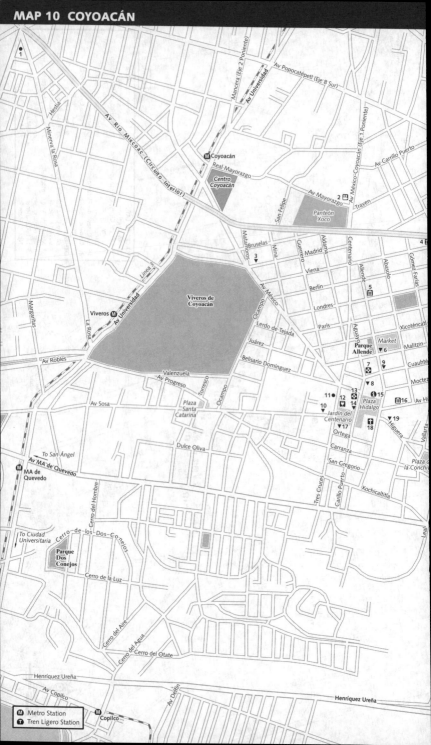

Mancera (Eje 2 Poniente)
Av Universidad
Av Popocatépetl (Eje 8 Sur)
Hesta
Minerva la Rosa
Av Río Mixcoac (Circuito Interior)
M Coyoacán
Real Mayorazgo
Av Carrillo Puerto
Av Mayorazgo (Eje 1 Poniente)
Centro Coyoacán
San Felipe
2
Traven
Panteón Xoco
4
Matamoros
Bruselas
Mina
Guerrero
Madrid
Aldama
Centenario
Allende
Abasolo
Gómez Farías
3
Viena
Linea 3
Berlin
5
Viveros M Viveros
Av Universidad
La Rosa
Viveros de Coyoacán
Ocampo
Av México
Londres
Paris
Xicoténcatl
Margaritas
Lerdo de Tejada
Aguayo
Parque Allende
Market 6
Malitzin
Av Robles
Juárez
Belisario Domínguez
7
9
Cuauhté
Moctez
Valenzuela
Torresco
Av Progreso
Ocampo
8
Av Sosa
Plaza Santa Catarina
11
12
13
14
Plaza Hidalgo
15
16 Av H
10
Jardín del Centenario
17
19
To San Ángel
Av MA de Quevedo
Dulce Oliva
18
Ortega
Higuera
Vallarta
M MA de Quevedo
Carranza
San Gregorio
Plaza la Conchi
Cerro del Hombre
Xochicaltitla
Tres Cruces
Carrillo Puerto
To Ciudad Universitaria
Cerro-de-los-Dos-Conejos
Parque Dos Conejos
Leal
Cerro de la Luz
Cerro del Aire
Cerro del Agua
Cerro del Otate
Henríquez Ureña
Av Copilco
Av Delfín
Henríquez Ureña

M Metro Station
T Tren Ligero Station
M Copilco

PLACES TO EAT
3 El Shiek
6 El Jardín del Pulpo
8 El Tizoncito
9 Café Jarocho
10 Moheli
14 Sanborns
17 Entre Vero
19 Quesadilla Stands

OTHER
1 Mundo Joven
2 Cineteca Nacional
4 Museo Léon Trotsky
5 Museo Frida Kahlo
7 Pasaje Coyoacán
11 Nalandra Libros
12 El Hijo del Cuervo
13 Bazar Artesanal de
   Coyoacán
15 Casa de Cortés,
   Tourist Information
16 Museo Nacional de
   Culturas Populares
18 Parroquia de San
   Juan Bautista
20 Terminal Sur

To Alameda
Central & Zócalo

Av División del Norte

Av General Emiliano Zapata

Panamá (Eje Central Lázaro Cárdenas)

Calz de Tlalpan

Oriente 172

Línea 2

Av Popocatépetl

Ⓜ Ermita

Calz Ermita Iztapalapa

Privada Corina

Corina

Ausco

Av Río Churubusco (Circuito Interior)

Ex-Convento de
Churubusco
(Museo Nacional
de las Intervenciones)

Centro Nacional
de las Artes

20 de Agosto

Av del Convento

Calz de Tlalpan

Ciclistas
Ⓜ General
Anaya

Calz General-Anaya

García-Torres

Country Club

Mártires Irlandeses

Irlanda

Canadá

Pallares y Portillo

Tepalcatitla

América

Inglaterra

Cerro de Jesús

Av MA de Quevedo

Pacífico

Av División del Norte

Av Tasqueña

20 🏠

Ⓜ Tasqueña
ⓣ

Terminal Sur
Bus Station

ⓣ Las Torres

Calz de Tlalpan

Monserrat

Av Canal de Miramontes

ⓣ Ciudad
Jardín

0   200   400 m
0   200   400 yards

To Anahuacalli

To Estadio
Azteca

[continued from page 152]

24-hour help line of the tourism ministry SECTUR (☎ 5250-0123). A private doctor's consultation generally costs between US$25 and US$40.

One of the best hospitals in all Mexico is the Hospital ABC (American British Cowdray Hospital, ☎ 5230-8000; Map 1), Calle Sur 136 No 116, just south of Avenida Observatorio in Colonia Las Américas, south of the Bosque de Chapultepec. There's an outpatient section and many of the staff speak English, but fees can be steep so adequate medical insurance is a big help. The nearest metro station is Observatorio, about 1km southeast.

For an ambulance, you can call the Cruz Roja (Red Cross, ☎ 5395-1111) or the general emergency numbers for ambulance, fire and police (☎ 061 and ☎ 080).

You can buy many medicines at pharmacies, such as the well-respected pharmacies of the Sanborns chain.

Emergency

SECTUR (see Tourist Offices) is available by phone 24 hours a day (☎ 5250-0123, 800-903-92-00) to help tourists with problems and emergencies.

The Procuraduría General de Justicia del Distrito Federal (Federal District Attorney General) maintains mobile tourist-assistance police units to go to the aid of visitors who are victims or witnesses of crime. Call ☎ 061 for help on the spot from these units.

The Procuraduría General de Justicia also has police offices to aid tourists with legal questions and problems. You can report crimes at these offices. One office (☎ 5242-6328, 5346-8730; Ⓜ Insurgentes; Map 5), Avenida Florencia 20, Zona Rosa, is always open and has English-speaking staff available.

Dangers & Annoyances

The recession of the mid-1990s brought a big increase in crime in Mexico City, with foreigners among the juicier and often easier

Taxi Crime

In 1999 the US State Department warned: 'Robbery assaults on passengers in taxis are frequent and violent, with passengers subjected to beating, shootings and sexual assault.' The warning was still current at press time. (For more updates visit Ⓦ http://travel.state.gov/travel_warnings.html.) Ask any foreigner living in Mexico City: if it hasn't happened to them, it has happened to someone they know. Many victims had hailed a cab on the street and were attacked or robbed by armed accomplices of the driver.

At the airport, use only the official yellow 'Transportación Terrestre' airport cabs (see Getting Around). Elsewhere in the city, you can telephone a radio taxi or a *sitio* (taxi stand) and ask the dispatcher for the driver's name and the cab's license plate number. These cabs are more expensive than ordinary cruising street cabs, but the extra money buys you security. Radio taxi firms include Super Sitio 160 (☎ 5271-9146, 5271-9058), Taxi-Mex (☎ 5538-1440, 5519-7690), Taxi Radio Mex (☎ 5584-0571, 5574-4596), Sitio 101 (☎ 5566-0077, 5566-7266) and Servitaxis (☎ 5516-6020). Cab firms are listed under 'Sitios de Automóviles' or simply 'Taxis' in the telephone yellow pages. Hotels and restaurants will nearly always be able to call a reliable cab for you. The State Department specifically warns against taking taxis parked outside the Palacio de Bellas Artes, in front of nightclubs or restaurants, or cruising anywhere in the city.

If you *have* to hail a cab on the street – and it's much better never to do so – check that the cab has license plates and that the number on them matches the number painted on the bodywork. Additionally make sure the plates are actual taxi plates. Sitio cabs have the letter S at the start of their license plate and an orange stripe along the bottom of the plate. *Libre* (cruising) taxis have the letter L and a green stripe. Also check the *carta de identificación* (also called the *tarjetón*), a postcard-sized ID card which should be displayed visibly inside the cab, to see that the driver matches the photo. If a cab does not pass these tests, get another one.

For more safety tips see Dangers & Annoyances in this chapter and in the Facts about Mexico chapter; for information on taxis, see this chapter's Getting Around section.

targets for pickpockets, purse snatchers, thieves and armed robbers. Despite a reported decline in crime beginning in 1999, levels remain high and foreigners have been the victims of far too many violent incidents (including assaults *by* the police) for anyone to deny the risks. But there's no need to walk in fear whenever you step outside your hotel: a few precautions greatly reduce any dangers. (Please read Dangers & Annoyances in the Facts for the Visitor chapter for general hints applicable throughout Mexico.)

Do not travel alone after dark, and do not carry ATM cards, credit cards or large amounts of cash. A fairly common practice among robbers is to force hijack victims to tour the city and withdraw cash from ATMs. Robbers will also hold people past the stroke of midnight in order to withdraw the daily limit imposed by the victim's bank – twice.

Mexico City's metro, buses and *peseros* (minibuses) are favorite haunts of pickpockets and thieves, particularly when they're crowded. Second-class buses can be dangerous also, but taxis are perhaps the most notorious for robberies (see 'Taxi Crime').

Using the metro only at less busy times enables you to find a less crowded car (at one end of the train), where thieves will find it harder to get close to you without being noticed (but avoid near-empty cars). During peak hours (roughly 7.30am to 10am and 5pm to 7pm) all trains and buses in the central area are packed tight, which suits pickpockets. Hold on to any belongings tightly. Also avoid getting on or off trains at Hidalgo station, where pickpockets and bag snatchers wait for foreigners and follow them onto crowded trains. If you're on a train that's going through Hidalgo, use only the last cars, so that thieves waiting in the station are less likely to spot you.

Robberies or assaults are also most likely to happen in areas where foreigners most often go. These include central metro stations, the Bosque de Chapultepec, around the Museo Nacional de Antropología, the Zona Rosa and the area around the US embassy. Steer clear of empty streets after dark.

Do not walk into a pedestrian underpass that is empty or nearly so; robbers may intercept you in the middle.

If you participate in any Mexican festivities (such as rallies or celebrations in the Zócalo) be aware that half the pickpockets in the city will be there too.

Be aware of your surroundings and on your guard at the airport and bus stations, and be sure to keep your bag or pack between your feet when checking in.

Drivers should not drive alone at night. Thieves have stopped lone drivers at night and robbed them of ATM and credit cards. Police have also been known to assault and rob people after pulling them over at night.

If you become a robbery victim, don't resist. Give the perpetrator your valuables, which are not worth risking injury or death. In February 2001, a US tourist was murdered in a bungled robbery in daylight near Mexico City's upscale San Ángel handicraft market.

CENTRO HISTÓRICO (MAP 3)

A good place to start your explorations of Mexico City is where the city began. The area known as the Centro Histórico focuses on the city's large main plaza, the Zócalo, and stretches for several blocks in each direction from there.

The Centro Histórico is full of historic sites from the Aztec and colonial eras, and it contains some of the city's finest art and architecture and is home to a number of absorbing museums. It also bustles with modern-day street life. Sunday is a particularly good day to explore this innermost part of the inner city; traffic and street crowds are thinner, a relaxed atmosphere prevails, and museums are free.

A few years ago the Centro Histórico had become rather rundown, but since then it has been spruced up to better fit the image of the hub of a proud nation. Some streets have been pedestrianized, buildings have been refurbished, new museums have opened, and many glossy eateries, shops and fashionable bars have appeared. The city authorities fight an ongoing battle with the operators of the many small sidewalk stalls in the Centro Histórico. Attempts to expel them – which would please shopkeepers by making it easier to walk around – generally bring protests and riots and succeed only temporarily.

Zócalo

The heart of Mexico City is the Plaza de la Constitución, more commonly known as the

Zócalo. The Spanish word *zócalo,* which means plinth or stone base, was adopted in 1843 when a tall monument to independence was constructed only as far as the base. The plinth is long gone, but the name remains – and has been adopted informally by a lot of other Mexican cities for their main plazas.

The center of Aztec Tenochtitlán, the ceremonial precinct known as the Teocalli, lay immediately north and northeast of the Zócalo. Today *conchero* dancers remind everyone of this heritage with daily get-togethers in the Zócalo to carry out a sort of pre-Hispanic aerobics, in feathered headdresses and *concha* (shell) anklets and bracelets, to the rhythm of booming drums.

In the 1520s Cortés paved the plaza with stones from the ruins of the Teocalli and other Aztec buildings. Until the early 20th century, the Zócalo was more often a maze of market stalls than an open plaza. With each side measuring more than 200m, it's one of the world's largest city squares.

The Zócalo is the home of the powers-that-be in Mexico City. On its east side is the Palacio Nacional (the presidential palace), on the north the Catedral Metropolitana, on the south the offices of the Distrito Federal government. The plaza is also a place for political protesters to make their points, and it's often dotted with makeshift camps of strikers or campaigners.

Each day at 6pm the huge Mexican flag flying in the middle of the Zócalo is ceremonially lowered by the Mexican army and carried into the Palacio Nacional.

Palacio Nacional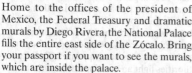

Home to the offices of the president of Mexico, the Federal Treasury and dramatic murals by Diego Rivera, the National Palace fills the entire east side of the Zócalo. Bring your passport if you want to see the murals, which are inside the palace.

The first palace on this spot was built of tezontle by Aztec emperor Moctezuma II in the early 16th century. Cortés destroyed the palace in 1521 and rebuilt it with a large courtyard so he could entertain visitors with Nueva España's first recorded bullfights. In 1562 the crown bought the palace from Cortés' family to house the Spanish viceroys of Nueva España. Destroyed during riots in 1692, it was rebuilt again and remained in

use as the viceregal residence until Mexican independence in the 1820s.

As you face the palace you will see three portals. On the right (south) is the guarded entrance for the president and other officials. High above the center door hangs the **Campaña de Dolores** (Bell of Dolores), rung in the town of Dolores Hidalgo by Padre Miguel Hidalgo in 1810 at the start of the Mexican War of Independence and later moved to this place of honor.

Enter the palace through the center door. The colorful **Diego Rivera murals** around the courtyard present Rivera's view of Mexican civilization from the arrival of Quetzalcóatl (the Aztec plumed serpent god whom some believed to be personified in Hernán Cortés) to the 1910 revolution. Painted between 1929 and 1935, the murals are open for public viewing 9am to 5pm daily (free). Detailed English-language guide booklets to the murals are sold (together with a set of 10 postcards) for US$4.25 at the foot of the stairs inside the entrance.

Catedral Metropolitana

Construction of the Metropolitan Cathedral, on the north side of the Zócalo, began in 1573. In Aztec times part of the cathedral site was occupied by a large *tzompantli* (rack for the skulls of sacrifice victims). Cortés reportedly found more than 136,000 skulls here and nearby.

The cathedral offers three regular **tours** *(11am-2pm & 4pm-6pm Mon-Sat)* – one visits the bell tower, another offers a glimpse at the sacristy, and the third goes inside the choir room, which houses the wooden choir stalls (see Interior). Visitors can buy tours individually for US$1, or get all three for US$2.75; buy tickets at the information booth just inside the church entrance.

Another tour, the *voces de catedral* tour *(voices of the cathedral, tickets US$27; 8.30pm-10pm Mon & Wed),* includes a light and choir show and a guided tour (in Spanish) around the installations. Space is limited to 80 people, so book at least a week in advance. To obtain tickets, contact Ticketmaster (see Entertainment, later) or visit the church ticket booth *(open 9.30am-7.30pm Tues-Sat, 9.30am-2.30pm Sun- Mon).*

General admission to the cathedral is still free and the building is open daily, but tourists are asked not to visit during mass (unless they plan on attending). Since the hours the guided tours are offered do not coincide with mass, they are a good time to visit even if you do not plan on taking a formal tour.

Exterior With a three-nave basilica design of vaults on semicircular arches, the cathedral was built to resemble those of Toledo and Granada in Spain. Several parts have been added or replaced over the years. The grand portals facing the Zócalo, built in the 17th century in baroque style, have two levels of columns and marble panels with bas-reliefs. The central panel shows the Assumption of the Virgin Mary, to whom the cathedral is dedicated. The tall north portals facing Calle Guatemala, dating from 1615, are in pure Renaissance style.

The upper levels of the towers, with their unique bell-shaped tops, were added in the late 18th century. The exterior was completed in 1813, when architect Manuel Tolsá added the clock tower – topped by statues of Faith, Hope and Charity – and a great central dome, all in neoclassical style, to create some unity and balance.

Interior The cathedral's chief artistic treasure is the gilded 18th-century Altar de los Reyes (Altar of the Three Kings), behind the main altar. It's a masterly exercise in controlled elaboration and a high point of the Churrigueresque style. The two side naves are lined by 14 richly decorated chapels. At the cathedral's southwest corner, the Capilla de los Santos Ángeles y Arcángeles (Chapel of the Holy Angels and Archangels) is another exquisite example of baroque sculpture and painting, with a huge main altarpiece and two smaller ones decorated by the 18th-century painter Juan Correa.

A lot of other art in the cathedral was damaged or destroyed in a 1967 fire. The intricately carved late-17th-century wooden choir stalls by Juan de Rojas and the huge, gilded Altar de Perdón (Altar of Pardon), all in the central nave, have been restored.

Sagrario Metropolitano Adjoining the east side of the cathedral is the 18th-century sacristy (open to visitors 7.30am-7.30pm daily), built to house the archives and vestments of the archbishop. Its exterior is a superb example of the ultradecorative Churrigueresque style and has recently undergone a 10-year restoration project.

Templo Mayor
The Teocalli of Aztec Tenochtitlán, demolished by the Spaniards in the 1520s, stood on the site of the cathedral and the blocks to its north and east. It wasn't until 1978, after electricity workers by chance dug up an 8-ton stone-disc carving of the Aztec goddess Coyolxauhqui, that the decision was taken to demolish colonial buildings and excavate the Teocalli's Templo Mayor (Main Temple, ☎ 5542-0606, Seminario 8; admission US$3.75, free Sun; open 9am-5pm Tues-Sun). The temple is thought to be on the exact spot where the Aztecs saw their symbolic eagle with a snake in its beak perching on a cactus – still the symbol of Mexico today. In Aztec belief this was, literally, the center of the universe.

The entrance to the temple site is just east of the cathedral. The admission fee includes entrance to the Museo del Templo Mayor.

A walkway around the site reveals the temple's multiple layers of construction. Explanatory material is all in Spanish. Like many other sacred buildings in Tenochtitlán, the temple, first begun in 1375, was enlarged several times, with each rebuilding accompanied by the sacrifice of captured warriors. In 1487 these rituals were performed at a frenzied pace to rededicate the temple after one major reconstruction. Michael Meyer and William Sherman write in The Course of Mexican History:

In a ceremony lasting four days sacrificial victims taken during campaigns were formed in four columns, each stretching three miles. At least twenty thousand human hearts were torn out to please the god.... In the frenzy of this ghastly pageant, the priests were finally overcome by exhaustion.

What we see today are sections of several of the temple's different phases. Unfortunately hardly anything is left of the seventh and last version, built about 1502, which was seen by the Spanish conquistadors. A replica of the Coyolxauhqui stone lies near the west side of the site. At the center is a platform dating from about 1400; on its southern half, a sacrificial stone stands in front of a shrine to Huizilopochtli, the Aztec tribal god. On the northern half is a chac-mool figure before a shrine to the water god, Tláloc. By the time the Spanish arrived, a 40m-high double pyramid towered above this spot, with steep twin stairways climbing to shrines of the same two gods.

Other features of the site include a late-15th-century stone replica of a tzompantli, carved with 240 stone skulls, and the mid-15th-century Recinto de los Guerreros Águila (Sanctuary of the Eagle Warriors, an elite band of Aztec fighters), decorated with colored bas-reliefs of military processions.

Museo del Templo Mayor This excellent museum within the Templo Mayor site houses artifacts from the site and gives a good overview (in Spanish) of Aztec civilization, including their *chinampa* agriculture, their systems of government and trade, and their beliefs, wars and sacrifices. Pride of place is given to the great wheel-like stone of Coyolxauhqui (She of Bells on her Cheek). She is shown decapitated – the result of her murder by Huizilopochtli, her brother, who also killed his 400 brothers en route to becoming top god. Other outstanding exhibits include full-size terra-cotta eagle warriors.

Calle Moneda

As you walk back down Seminario toward the Zócalo from the Templo Mayor, Moneda is the first street on your left. Many of its buildings are made of tezontle. This east side of the Zócalo is a commercial area lacking the glitz of the west side.

Museo de la Secretaría de Hacienda y Crédito Público (*Museum of the Secretariat of Finance, ☎ 5228-1245, Moneda 4; admission US$0.80, free Sun; open 10am-5.30pm Tues-Sun*) houses a good collection of Mexican art. Pieces range from works by the 18th-century master Juan Correa to 20th-century giants Diego Rivera and Rufino Tamayo and interesting contemporary artists. The setting, a colonial archbishop's palace with two lovely courtyards, adds to the attraction.

Museo Nacional de las Culturas (*National Museum of Cultures, ☎ 5512-7452, Moneda 13; admission free; open 9.30am-5.45pm Tues-Sun*), in a fine courtyard building constructed in 1567 as the colonial mint, has exhibits showing the art, dress and handicrafts of several world cultures.

A block farther east, then a few steps north, is a former convent housing the **Museo José Luis Cuevas** (*☎ 5542-8959, Academia 13; admission US$0.80, free Sun; open 10am-6pm Tues-Sun*), founded by Cuevas, a leading modern Mexican artist. There are engravings by Picasso, drawings by Rembrandt, and work by Cuevas himself and other moderns.

Nacional Monte de Piedad

Facing the west side of the cathedral is Mexico's national pawnshop (*☎ 5278-1800, cnr Avenida 5 de Mayo & Monte de Piedad; open 8.30am-6pm Mon-Fri, 8.30am-3pm Sat*). Founded in 1775, it's now one of the world's largest secondhand shops.

Plaza Santo Domingo

This plaza, two blocks north of the cathedral, is a less formal affair than the Zócalo. Modern-day scribes, with typewriters and antique printing machines, work beneath the **Portal de Evangelistas**, along its west side. Those condemned to die during the Inquisition passed through this plaza on the way to their executions.

The pink stone **Iglesia de Santo Domingo**, dating from 1736, is a beautiful baroque church, decorated on its east side with carved stone figures of Santo Domingo (St Dominic) and San Francisco (St Francis). Below the figures, the arms of both saints are symbolically entwined as if to convey a unity of purpose in their lives. The church's front, or southern, façade is equally beautiful, with 12 columns around the main entrance. Between the columns are statues of San Francisco and San Agustín (St Augustine), and in the center at the top is a bas-relief of the Assumption of the Virgin Mary.

Opposite the big church is the 18th-century Escuela Nacional de Medicina (formerly the Palacio de la Inquisición), built as the headquarters of the Inquisition in Mexico. It now houses the interesting **Museo de la Medicina Mexicana** (*Museum of Mexican Medicine, ☎ 5526-7827, Brasil 33 at Venezuela; admission free; open 10am-6pm daily*). This museum has displays that range from a model of a *baño de temazcal* – a kind of indigenous sauna, used for spiritual purification – to a reconstruction of a 19th-century pharmacy.

Café Tacuba – Calle de Opera
Calle Tacuba

Murals

Outstanding murals on diverse subjects connected with the people of Mexico adorn the **Secretaría de Educación Pública** (*Secretariat of Education, no ☎, Argentina 28; admission free; open 9am-5pm Mon-Fri*), 3½ blocks north of the Zócalo. Sometimes the attendants ask for ID, so it's best to take your passport. The two front courtyards are lined with 120 fresco panels done by Diego Rivera and assistants in the 1920s. On the ground floor you'll find themes of industry, agriculture and class struggle, as well as artisan and festival scenes. The middle floor features murals covering science, work and coats of arms of the Mexican states. On the top floor, the first courtyard holds portraits of Mexican heroes, such as Emiliano Zapata and the Aztec king Cuauhtémoc, and panels on themes such as brotherhood, women and the arts; the second courtyard offers scenes of capitalist decadence and proletarian and agrarian revolution. The likeness of Frida Kahlo can be spotted in one called *En El Arsenal*. The building's rear courtyard has a staircase adorned with *Patricios y Patricidas* by Siqueiros and others.

A block back toward the Zócalo, then half a block east, is the **Museo de San Ildefonso** (*☎ 5789-2505, Justo Sierra 16; admission US$3.25, free Tues; open 10am-5.30pm Tues-Sun*). Built in the 16th century as the Jesuit college of San Ildefonso, it served from 1867 to 1878 as the Escuela Nacional Preparatoría, a prestigious teacher training college. From 1923 to 1933, Rivera, Orozco, Siqueiros and others were brought in to adorn it with murals. Most of the work in the main patio and on the grand staircase is by Orozco, inspired by the recently ended Mexican Revolution. Some interesting temporary exhibitions are held in the building. The amphitheater, off the lobby, holds a gigantic Creation mural by Rivera.

Museo Nacional de Arte

Several blocks west of the Zócalo is the National Museum of Art (*☎ 5530-3400, Tacuba 8; admission US$3.25, free Sun; open 10am-5.30pm Tues-Sun*). This museum contains exclusively Mexican work. In front stands a distinctive bronze equestrian statue of the Spanish king Carlos IV (who reigned from 1788 to 1808) by the sculptor and architect Manuel Tolsá. The statue, called *El Caballito*

(the Little Horse), originally stood in the Zócalo but was moved here in 1852. A sign points out that the work is preserved as an art piece (not, it's implied, out of respect for the Spanish king).

The museum, once the Secretariat of Communications, was built around 1900 in the style of an Italian Renaissance palace, with a grand marble staircase. The collections represent every style and school of Mexican art up to the early 20th century. The work of José María Velasco, depicting Mexico City and the countryside in the late 19th and early 20th centuries, is a highlight. Velasco's landscapes show the Lago de Texcoco still filling half the Valle de México, and Guadalupe and Chapultepec far outside the city in the 1870s.

Colegio de Minería

Opposite the Museo Nacional de Arte is the Colegio de Minería (*College of Mining, ☎ 5521-4022, Tacuba 5; admission free; open 9am-8pm Mon-Fri*). This neoclassical building was designed by Manuel Tolsá and built between 1797 and 1813. Four meteorites found in Mexico are displayed in its entrance.

Send buses.   – bark

Casa de Azulejos   machine.

A block south of the Museo Nacional de Arte, between Avenida 5 de Mayo and Avenida Madero, stands one of the city's gems. The Casa de Azulejos (House of Tiles) dates from 1596, when it was built for the Condes (Counts) del Valle de Orizaba. Although the superb tile work that has adorned the outside walls since the 18th century is Spanish and Moorish in style, most of the tiles were actually produced in China and shipped to Mexico on the Manila *naos* (Spanish galleons used up to the early 19th century).

The building now houses a Sanborns store and restaurant and is a good place to buy a newspaper or have a snack. The main restaurant is in a covered courtyard around a Moorish fountain, with odd murals of mythical landscapes. The staircase climbing from the main restaurant to the upper floor has a 1925 mural by Orozco.

Torre Latinoamericana

The Latin American Tower (*cnr Avenida Madero & Eje Central Lázaro Cárdenas; admission US$3.75; open 9.30am-10.30pm daily*) is a landmark 1950s skyscraper with an observation deck and café on its 43rd and 44th floors. The views are spectacular, smog permitting. Tickets are sold at the street entrance on the Eje Central side of the building.

Palacio de Iturbide

A block east of the Casa de Azulejos rises the beautiful baroque façade of the Iturbide Palace (☎ 5225-0109, Avenida Madero 17; admission free; open 10am-7pm daily). Built between 1779 and 1785 for colonial nobility, it was claimed in 1821 by General Agustín Iturbide, a hero of the Mexican struggle for independence from Spain. Responding favorably to a rent-a-crowd that gathered before the palace in 1822 and beseeched him to be their emperor, Iturbide proclaimed himself Emperor Agustín I. But he abdicated less than a year later, after General Santa Anna announced the birth of a republic.

Acquired and restored by Banamex bank in 1965, the palace now houses the Fomento Cultural Banamex (the cultural promotion section of Banamex). Some excellent art and crafts exhibitions are shown in the fine courtyard.

ALAMEDA CENTRAL & AROUND (MAP 3)

A little less than 1km west of the Zócalo is the pretty Alameda Central, Mexico City's only sizable downtown park. In the blocks around the Alameda are some of the city's most interesting buildings and museums.

Bellas Artes metro station is at the northeast corner of the Alameda, and the Hidalgo metro station is on the northwest corner. You can also reach the Alameda from the Zócalo area on a 'M(etro) Chapultepec,' 'M(etro) Hidalgo' or 'M(etro) Auditorio' pesero heading west on Avenida 5 de Mayo.

Alameda Central

This verdant park was once an Aztec marketplace. In early colonial times it became the site of autos-da-fé, in which heretics were sentenced and often burned or hanged. In 1592 Viceroy Luis de Velasco decided the growing city needed a pleasant area of pathways, fountains and trees. He created the Alameda, which took its name from the álamos (poplars) with which it was planted. By the late 19th century the park was dotted

with European-style statuary, lit by gas lamps, and had a bandstand for free concerts. Today the Alameda is a popular, easily accessible refuge from the city streets. It's particularly busy on Sunday, when you may catch a rock or salsa band playing open-air.

Palacio de Bellas Artes

Dominating the east end of the Alameda is the splendid white-marble Palace of Fine Arts (☎ 5521-9251, Avenida Juárez 1; admission US$2.75, free Sun; open 10am-5.30pm Tues-Sun; box office open 11am-7pm Mon-Sat, 9am-7pm Sun), a concert hall and arts center that was commissioned by President Porfirio Díaz. Construction of the building began in 1904 under Italian architect Adamo Boari, who favored neoclassical and art nouveau styles. But the building's heavy marble shell began to sink into the spongy subsoil, and work was halted. Architect Federico Mariscal eventually finished the interior in the 1930s, with new designs reflecting the more modern art deco style.

Some of Mexico's finest murals dominate immense wall spaces on the 2nd and 3rd floors. On the 2nd floor are two large, striking, early 1950s works by Rufino Tamayo: México de Hoy (Mexico Today) and Nacimiento de la Nacionalidad (Birth of Nationality), a symbolic depiction of the creation of the Mexican mestizo identity.

At the west end of the 3rd floor is Diego Rivera's famous El Hombre, Contralor del Universo (Man, Controller of the Universe), which was first commissioned for Rockefeller Center in New York. The Rockefeller family had the original destroyed because of its anticapitalist themes, but Rivera recreated it even more dramatically here in 1934. Capitalism, with accompanying death and war, is shown on the left; socialism, with health and peace, is on the right.

On the north side of the 3rd floor are David Alfaro Siqueiros' three-part La Nueva Democracía (New Democracy), painted in 1944-45, and Rivera's four-part Carnaval de la Vida Mexicana (Carnival of Mexican Life), from 1936. At the east end is José Clemente Orozco's eye-catching La Katharsis (Catharsis), from 1934 to 1935, in which violence and degradation result from the conflict between 'natural' and 'social' poles of human nature, symbolized by naked and clothed figures, but a giant bonfire threatens to consume all in a spiritual rebirth.

On the 4th floor is the interesting *Museo de Arquitectura* (National Architecture Museum).

The palace's theater has a beautiful stained-glass stage curtain depicting the Valle de México, based on a design by Mexican painter Gerardo Murillo (also called Dr Atl). Tiffany Studios of New York assembled the curtain from almost a million pieces of colored glass. It's normally lit up for public viewing on Sunday mornings and just before performances.

The palace also stages some top-class temporary art exhibitions and is home to the famous Ballet Folklórico (see Entertainment). A good bookstore and elegant café are on the premises too.

Museo Franz Mayer

On little Plaza de Santa Veracruz, opposite the north side of the Alameda, the Franz Mayer Museum (☎ 5518-2265, *Avenida Hidalgo 45; admission US$2.15, free Tues; open 10am-5pm Tues-Sun*) displays a sumptuous collection of mainly Mexican art and crafts in the lovely 16th-century Hospital de San Juan de Dios. This oasis of calm and beauty is the fruit of the efforts of Franz Mayer, who was born in Mannheim, Germany, in 1882. He later moved to Mexico, became a citizen, earned the name Don Pancho and amassed a collection of Mexican silver, textiles, ceramics and furniture masterpieces.

The way into the main part of the museum is to the right as you enter. To the left is a gorgeous colonial garden courtyard. The suite of rooms on the courtyard's west side is done in antique furnishings and is very fine, especially the lovely chapel. On the north side is the delightful Cafetería del Claustro (see Places to Eat).

Museo Mural Diego Rivera

Among Diego Rivera's most famous murals is *Sueño de una Tarde Dominical en la Alameda* (Dream of a Sunday Afternoon in the Alameda), 15m long by 4m high, painted in 1947. The artist imagines many of the figures who walked in the city from colonial times onward, among them Cortés, Juárez, Santa Anna, Emperor Maximilian, Porfirio Díaz, and Francisco Madero and his nemesis, General Victoriano Huerta. All are grouped around a skeleton dressed in prerevolutionary women's garb. Rivera himself (as a pug-faced child) and his artist wife, Frida Kahlo, are depicted next to the skeleton.

The museum (☎ 5510-2329, *cnr Balderas & Colon; admission US$1, free Sun; open 10am-6pm Tues-Sun*) housing this work is just west of the Alameda, fronting the Jardín de la Solidaridad. It was built in 1986 specifically for this mural, which had stood in the Hotel del Prado, nearby on Avenida Juárez, until the hotel was wrecked in the 1985 earthquake.

Charts in English and Spanish identify all the characters. There are also photos and other material on Rivera's life and work.

PLAZA DE LA REPÚBLICA & AROUND (MAP 4)

This plaza, 600m west of the Alameda Central, is dominated by the huge, domed Monumento a la Revolución. Revolución metro station is nearby.

Monumento a la Revolución

The Revolution Monument, begun in the 1900s under Porfirio Díaz, was originally meant to be not a monument at all, but a meeting chamber for senators and deputies. But construction (not to mention Díaz's presidency) was interrupted by the revolution. The structure was modified and given a new role in the 1930s: the tombs of the revolutionary and postrevolutionary heroes Pancho Villa, Francisco Madero, Venustiano Carranza, Plutarco Elías Calles and Lázaro Cárdenas are inside its wide pillars (not open to the public).

The interesting but small **Museo Nacional de la Revolución** (*National Museum of the Revolution,* ☎ 5546-2115, *Plaza de la República; admission US$0.65, free Sun; open 9am-5pm Tues-Sat, 9am-5pm Sun*) houses exhibits on the revolution and preceding decades. Enter from the northeast quarter of the garden around the monument.

Frontón México

On the north side of Plaza de la República is the Frontón México, a now defunct grand art deco arena for the sport of jai alai.

Museo de San Carlos

Occupying the former mansion of the Conde (Count) de Buenavista, the Museum of San Carlos (☎ 5566-8522, Puente de Alvarado 50 at Ramos Arizpe; admission US$2.75, free Mon; open 10am-6pm Wed-Mon) exhibits a nice collection of European art. The mansion was designed by Manuel Tolsá in the late 18th century and later became home to Alamo victor Santa Anna. It subsequently served as a cigar factory, lottery headquarters and school before being reborn as an art museum in 1968.

The museum's permanent collection includes works by Goya, Rubens, Van Dyck, Zurbarán and Ingres. Good temporary exhibitions are also staged.

PASEO DE LA REFORMA (MAPS 4 & 5)

Paseo de la Reforma, Mexico City's main boulevard and one of its status addresses, runs southwest across the city from the Alameda Central and through the Bosque de Chapultepec. It's said that Emperor Maximilian of Hapsburg laid out the boulevard to connect his castle on Chapultepec Hill with the older section of the city. He could look along it from his bedroom and ride along it to work in the Palacio Nacional, on the Zócalo.

You'll almost certainly pass along Reforma at some time, or call at one of the nearby banks, shops, hotels, restaurants or embassies. Reforma is dotted with striking architecture and sculpture.

A couple of blocks west of the Alameda Central on Reforma, in front of the Torre Caballito office building, is **El Caballito**, a huge golden-yellow creation by the sculptor Sebastián. It represents a horse's head, in memory of the other El Caballito sculpture which once stood here and today is in front of the Museo Nacional de Arte. A few blocks southwest on Reforma is the **Glorieta Cristóbal Colón**, a traffic circle with a statue of Christopher Columbus at its center. The statue was created by French sculptor Charles Cordier in 1877.

Reforma's busy intersection with Avenida Insurgentes is marked by the **Monumento a Cuauhtémoc**, memorializing the last Aztec emperor. Two blocks northwest of this intersection is the **Jardín del Arte**, a sliver of shady park that becomes an interesting open-air artists' bazaar from 9am to 6pm on Sunday.

The most striking modern building on Reforma is the **Centro Bursátil**, an arrow of reflecting glass housing Mexico City's stock exchange. It's at Reforma 255, about 600m southwest of Insurgentes in Zona Rosa.

On Reforma, on the northwest flank of the Zona Rosa, stands the symbol of Mexico City, the **Monumento a la Independencia** (cnr Paseo de la Reforma & Florencia; admission free; open 9am-6pm daily). This gilded statue of Victory on a tall pedestal, called by locals simply 'El Ángel' (the Angel), was created by sculptor Antonio Rivas Mercado and inaugurated in 1910. The female figures around the base portray Law, Justice, War and Peace; the male ones are Mexican independence heroes such as Miguel Hidalgo, Vicente Guerrero and José María Morelos. Inside the monument are the skulls of Hidalgo, Ignacio Allende, Juan Aldama and Mariano Jiménez (retrieved from an 1811-21 stint hanging outside the Alhóndiga de Granaditas in Guanajuato) and caskets containing the ashes or remains of Morelos, Guerrero and others.

A few blocks farther west, at Reforma's intersection with Sevilla, is **La Diana Cazadora** (Diana the Huntress), a 1942 bronze statue of a female archer by Juan Fernando Olaguíbel. Southwest from here, Reforma crosses the Bosque de Chapultepec and then becomes the main road to Toluca.

Getting There & Away

Hidalgo metro station (see Dangers & Annoyances) is on Reforma at the Alameda Central; Insurgentes station is at the southern tip of the Zona Rosa, 500m south of Reforma; Chapultepec station is just south of Reforma at the east end of the Bosque de Chapultepec.

From the Zócalo area, westbound 'M(etro) Chapultepec' and 'M(etro) Auditorio' peseros on Avenida 5 de Mayo go along Reforma to the Bosque de Chapultepec. If you get fed up with waiting for them, you can take the metro or walk to Reforma and catch another pesero there. Any 'M(etro) Auditorio,' 'Reforma Km 13' or 'Km 15.5 por Reforma' pesero or bus heading southwest on Reforma will continue along Reforma through the Bosque de Chapultepec.

In the opposite direction, the 'Zócalo' peseros heading east on Reforma will transport you to the Zócalo. 'M(etro) Hidalgo,' 'M(etro) La Villa' and 'M(etro) Indios Verdes' buses and peseros all head northeast up Reforma to the Alameda Central or beyond.

ZONA ROSA (MAP 5)

The Zona Rosa, a restaurant, hotel, shopping and entertainment district, lies on the south side of Reforma roughly 2km from the Alameda Central. This neighborhood, both glossy and sleazy, is an integral piece of the Mexico City jigsaw, and people-watching from its sidewalk cafés reveals plenty of variety among the passing parade of pedestrians. For details of how to spend money here, see Places to Stay, Places to Eat, Entertainment and Shopping.

Museo de Cera de la Ciudad de México *(Wax Museum, ☎ 5546-3784, Londres 6; admission US$5/2.75 adults/children; open 11am-7pm Mon-Fri, 10am-7pm Sat-Sun)* is worth a trip. While famous figures from all over the globe have their likenesses displayed in wax here, the museum also memorializes a number of famous Mexican figures such as film stars Jorge Negrete and María Félix.

CONDESA & ROMA (MAP 6)

Condesa is a trendy but relaxed neighborhood south of the Zona Rosa. It has a couple of pleasant parks, some attractive 1930s and '40s neocolonial architecture and a huge number of good, informal restaurants and coffee bars.

A focus is the peaceful, beautifully kept **Parque México**, full of trees, well-maintained paths, benches with cute little roofs, and signs exhorting everyone to demonstrate their eco-consciousness and treat their park nicely. **Parque España**, two blocks northwest, has a children's fun fair. Parque México is a 500m walk north from Chilpancingo metro station (or a 1km walk south from Sevilla station); or you can get a pesero south on Avenida Insurgentes from Insurgentes metro station to the intersection with Avenida Michoacán (there's a Woolworth store on the corner), and walk two blocks west.

The main cluster of Condesa bistro-type eateries (see Places to Eat) is about 500m west of Parque México, near the intersection of Michoacán and Tamaulipas. Patriotismo and Juanacatlán metro stations are also within walking distance.

Roma, a mostly residential neighborhood, is one of Mexico City's oldest and was once home to members of Mexico's ruling elite and movie stars. Although its heyday is over, it's filled with interesting architecture and funky cafés. This was also the neighborhood favored by the beatniks, and the site where William S Burroughs fatally shot his wife Joan during a William Tell exercise in which he aimed for a martini glass on her head.

Centro Cultural Casa Lamm

The highlight of Casa Lamm *(☎ 5525-3938, Obregón 99; admission free; open 10am-5pm Tues-Sun)* is the Manuel Álvarez Bravo photo collection. This new permanent photo exhibit includes more than 2,000 original photos by masters such as Álvarez Bravo himself, as well as Ansel Adams, Man Ray, Dorothea Lange and Walker Evans.

BOSQUE DE CHAPULTEPEC (MAP 7)

According to legend, one of the last kings of the Toltecs took refuge in the Chapultepec woods after fleeing from Tula. Later, the hill in the park served as a refuge for the wandering Aztecs before eventually becoming a summer residence for Aztec nobles. Chapultepec means 'Hill of Grasshoppers' in the Aztec language, Náhuatl. In the 15th century – when Chapultepec was still separated from Tenochtitlán, the site of modern central Mexico City, by the waters of Lago de Texcoco – Nezahualcóyotl, ruler of nearby Texcoco, gave permission for the area to be made a forest reserve.

The Bosque de Chapultepec has remained Mexico City's largest park to this day. It now covers more than 4 sq km and has lakes, a zoo and several excellent museums. It has also remained an abode of Mexico's high and mighty. It contains both the current presidential residence, Los Pinos, and a former imperial and presidential palace, the Castillo de Chapultepec.

The Bosque de Chapultepec attracts thousands of visitors daily, particularly on Sunday, when vendors line its main paths and throngs of families come to picnic, relax and crowd into the museums. The park is divided into two main sections by two big roads: Calzada Molino del Rey/Calzada Chivatito and Boulevard López Mateos/Anillo Periférico, which run north-south across the middle. Most of the major attractions are in or near the eastern *1ª Sección*

(First Section), which is open 5am to 4.30pm daily except Monday. Most of the museums in the park offer free admission on Sunday and holidays.

Monumento a los Niños Héroes

The six columns of the Monument to the Boy Heroes, near Chapultepec metro, mark the main entrance to the park. They commemorate six brave cadets at the national military academy, which used to be housed in the Castillo de Chapultepec. Legend has it that on September 13, 1847, when invading American troops reached Mexico City, the six cadets, having defended their school as long as they could, wrapped themselves in Mexican flags and leapt to their deaths rather than surrender.

Castillo de Chapultepec

Part of the castle on Chapultepec Hill was built in 1785 as a residence for the viceroys of Nueva España. The building was converted into a military academy in 1843. When Emperor Maximilian and Empress Carlota arrived in 1864, they refurbished it as their main residence. After their fall, the castle became home to Mexico's presidents, until 1940 when President Lázaro Cárdenas converted it into the **Museo Nacional de Historia** (National History Museum, ☎ 5286-0700, Bosque de Chapultepec, 1ª Sección; admission US$3.25, free Sun; open 9am-4.30pm Tues-Sun).

Two floors of exhibits chronicle the rise and fall of colonial Nueva España, the establishment of independent Mexico, the dictatorship of Porfirio Díaz and the Mexican Revolution. Several of the 1st-floor rooms are decorated with impressive murals on historical themes by famous Mexican artists. These include Juan O'Gorman's *Retablo de la Independencia* (Thanksgiving Panel for Independence), room 5; José Clemente Orozco's *La Reforma y la Caída del Imperio* (The Reform and Fall of the Empire), room 7; and David Alfaro Siqueiros' *Del Porfirismo a la Revolución* (From Porfirism to the Revolution), room 13. The rooms where Maximilian and Carlota lived, at the east end of the castle, are furnished in period style, including Carlota's marble bath. Above them are Porfirio Díaz's sumptuous rooms, flanking a patio with expansive views.

Last tickets at the museum are sold at 4pm. To reach the castle, walk up the road that curves up the right-hand side of the hill behind the Monumento a los Niños Héroes. Alternatively, a little road-train (US$0.50 roundtrip) runs up this road every 10 minutes or so while the castle is open.

Museo del Caracol

From the Castillo de Chapultepec, the Museo del Caracol (☎ 5553-6285, Bosque de Chapultepec, 1ª Sección; admission US$3.25, free Sun; open 9am-5.30pm Tues-Sun) is just a short distance back down the approach road. Shaped somewhat like a *caracol* (snail shell), this is officially a 'Galería de Historia' on the subject of the Mexican people's struggle for liberty. Displays cover social and political life from colonial days, the divisions of Nueva España in the 18th century, Miguel Hidalgo's leadership in the struggle for independence, and Francisco Madero's leadership in the revolution. The self-guided tour ends in a circular hall that contains only one item – a replica of the 1917 Constitution of Mexico. This museum is closed for remodeling until the middle of 2002.

Museo de Arte Moderno

The two rounded buildings of the Museum of Modern Art (☎ 5553-6233, southeast corner of Paseo de la Reforma & Gandhi; admission US$1.50, free Sat-Sun; open 10am-6pm Tues-Sun) stand in their own sculpture garden just northwest of the Monumento a los Niños Héroes. The entrance faces Paseo de la Reforma. The museum's permanent collection includes work by Mexico's most famous 20th-century artists, including Dr Atl, Rivera, Siqueiros, Orozco, Kahlo, Tamayo and O'Gorman. Some of these artists' more intimate works, such as portraits, are shown here. Rotating temporary exhibitions feature prominent Mexican and foreign artists.

Parque Zoológico de Chapultepec

The first zoo in Chapultepec – and the Americas – is said to have been established by King Nezahualcóyotl well before the Spanish arrived. Cortés added a bird sanctuary. In 1975 a gift from China brought pandas, which are thriving. Rebuilt in the mid-1990s for US$30 million, the Chapultepec Zoo (☎ 5553-6229, *Bosque de Chapultepec, 1ª Sección; admission free, venomous reptile exhibit US$2.25; open 9am-4.30pm Tues-Sun*) is a mainly open-air place with a wide range of the world's creatures in relatively large enclosures. Something went badly wrong in 1998, when almost 400 of the 1800 animals here died in nine months, but today the zoo is back to normal.

There's an inexpensive snack area inside.

Museo Nacional de Antropología

The National Museum of Anthropology (☎ 5553-6381, *cnr Paseo de la Reforma & Gandhi; admission US$4, free Sun; open 9am-7pm Tues-Sat, 10am-6pm Sun*), one of the finest museums of its kind in the world, stands in an extension of the Bosque de Chapultepec.

The museum is fascinating and very large, offering more than most people can absorb (without brain strain) in a single visit. A good plan is to concentrate on the regions of Mexico that you plan to visit or have visited, with a quick look at some of the other eye-catching exhibits. Labeling is in Spanish, but some of the spectacular exhibits need little explanation.

In a clearing about 100m in front of the museum's entrance, indigenous Totonac people perform their spectacular *voladores* rite – 'flying' from a 20m-high pole – several times a day, collecting money from onlookers afterward (see 'Outdoing the Dervishes' in the Central Gulf Coast chapter).

The spacious museum building, constructed in the 1960s, is the work of Mexican architect Pedro Ramírez Vásquez. Its long, rectangular courtyard is surrounded on three sides by the museum's two-story display halls. An immense umbrella-like stone fountain rises up from the center of the courtyard.

The ground-floor *salas* (halls) are dedicated to pre-Hispanic Mexico. The upper level covers how modern Mexico's indigenous peoples, the descendants of those pre-Hispanic civilizations, live today. With a few exceptions, each ethnological section upstairs covers the same territory as the archaeological exhibit below it; for example, you can see the great Mayan city of Palenque as it was in the 7th century, then go upstairs and see how Mayan people live

today. Here's a brief guide to the ground-floor halls, proceeding counterclockwise around the courtyard:

Introducción a la Antropología does just that – introduces the visitor to anthropology, ethnology and pre-Hispanic culture in general.

Sala Origenes, the Origins Room, shows evidence of the first people in the Americas, explaining their arrival from Asia and the beginnings of agriculture.

Sala Preclásica shows exhibits from the Preclassic period, which lasted from about 1500 BC to AD 250. These exhibits highlight the indigenous peoples' transition from a nomadic hunting life to a more settled farming life.

Sala Teotihuacana displays models and objects from the wondrous city of Teotihuacán, near Mexico City – the Americas' first great and powerful state. The exhibit includes a full-size color model of part of the Templo de Quetzalcóatl.

Sala Tolteca covers cultures of central Mexico between about AD 650 and AD 1250 and is named for one of the most important of these, the Toltecs. Exhibits include a huge stone statue of Quetzalcóatl from Tula.

Sala Mexica, at the west end of the courtyard, is devoted to the Mexica, or Aztecs. Come here to see the famous sun (or calendar) stone, which bears the face of the sun god, Tonatiuh, at the center of a web of symbols representing the five worlds, the four directions, the 20 days and more; and the statue of Coatlicue (She of the Skirt of Snakes), the mother of the Aztec gods, found (like the sun stone) beneath the Zócalo in 1790. Other exhibits include a replica of a carved stone tzompantli, an 'aerial view' painting of Tenochtitlán, and other graphic evidence of this awesome culture.

Sala Oaxaca is devoted to Oaxaca state's cultural heights, scaled by the Zapotec and Mixtec peoples. Two tombs from the hilltop site of Monte Albán are reproduced full-size.

Sala Golfo de México spotlights the important ancient civilizations along the Gulf of Mexico including the Olmec, Classic Veracruz, Totonac and Huastec. There are very fine stone carvings here, including two magnificent Olmec heads.

Sala Maya has wonderful exhibits not only from southeast Mexico but from Guatemala, Belize and Honduras too. The full-scale model of the tomb of King Pakal, discovered deep in the Templo de las Inscripciones at Palenque, is breathtaking. On the outside patio are replicas of the famous wall paintings of Bonampak and of Edificio II at Hochob, in Campeche, constructed as a giant mask of the rain god, Chac.

Sala Norte covers the Casas Grandes (Paquimé) site and other cultures from dry northern

Mexico. Similarities can be seen with indigenous cultures of the US Southwest.

Sala Occidente profiles cultures of western Mexico from Nayarit, Jalisco, Michoacán, Colima and Guerrero states.

Museo Rufino Tamayo

This museum (☎ 5286-6519, northwest cnr of Paseo de la Reforma & Calzada Gandhi; admission US$1.75, free Sun; open 10am-6pm Tues-Sun) is a multilevel concrete and glass structure about 250m east of the Museo Nacional de Antropología. It was built to house the fine collection of international modern art donated by Rufino Tamayo and his wife, Olga, to the people of Mexico. More than 150 artists, including Picasso, Warhol and Tamayo himself, are represented in the permanent collection, but you may find that their works have all been put away to make room for temporary exhibitions.

Segunda (2ª) Sección

The second section of the Bosque de Chapultepec lies west of Boulevard López Mateos. The nearest metro station is Constituyentes, near the park's southern perimeter.

One highlight is **La Feria** (☎ 5230-2112, Circuito Bosque de Chapultepec; admission US$6.50/1 adults/children; open 9am-8pm Mon-Fri, 9am-9pm Sat-Sun Jul-Aug, 10am-6pm Mon-Fri, 10am-9pm Sat-Sun rest of year), a large amusement park with some hair-raising rides. A children's ticket includes 23 children's rides and 6 adult rides; an adult ticket includes all the rides except the Bumper Cars, the House of Horror and the Go-Carts.

Another highlight is **Papalote Museo del Niño** (☎ 5224-1260, ⓦ www.papalote.org.mx; Circuito Bosque de Chapultepec; admission US$6/4.25 adults/seniors & children 2-11; open 9am-1pm & 2pm-6pm Fri-Wed & 7pm-11pm Thur, 10am-2pm and 3pm-7pm Sat-Sun; call for summer hours). This hands-on children's museum is a surefire hit if you have children in tow. Attractions range from a tunnel slide and a conventional playground to a giant-soap-bubble maker and all manner of technical/scientific gadget-games. The museum also has an IMAX movie theater (separate admission US$4.25/3.75). Everything is attended by young, child-friendly supervisors, and you can be

sure that your kids will not want to leave. During school vacations the weekend hours apply daily. Tickets can also be purchased from Ticketmaster; advance purchase is recommended and prices are for one four-hour session.

Also in Chapultepec's Segunda Sección are two lakes (Lago Mayor and Lago Menor) and two more museums: the **Museo Tecnológico** (Museum of Technology, ☎ 5516-0964, Circuito Bosque de Chapultepec between La Feria & Children's Museum; admission free; open 9am-5pm daily), which showcases Mexico's technological development and is surrounded by pretty and interesting grounds dotted with railcars, oil-drilling machines and other examples of industrial equipment; and the interesting **Museo de Historia Natural** (Natural History Museum, ☎ 5515-2222, Circuito Bosque de Chapultepec; admission US$1.75, free Tues; open 10am-5pm Tues-Sun).

Getting There & Away

Chapultepec metro station is at the east end of the Bosque de Chapultepec, near the Monumento a los Niños Héroes and Castillo de Chapultepec. Auditorio metro station is on the north side of the park, 500m west of the Museo Nacional de Antropología.

You can also reach the park from the Zócalo area on a 'M(etro) Chapultepec' or 'M(etro) Auditorio' pesero westbound on Avenida 5 de Mayo. From anywhere on Paseo de la Reforma west of the Alameda Central, peseros and buses saying 'M(etro) Chapultepec,' 'M(etro) Auditorio,' 'Km 15.5 por Reforma' or 'Reforma Km 13' will reach Chapultepec metro station, and all except 'M(etro) Chapultepec' vehicles will cross the first section of the park on Paseo de la Reforma; you can get off right outside the Museo Nacional de Antropología (watch out for pickpockets in the area around the museum).

Returning downtown, 'Zócalo' peseros heading east on Paseo de la Reforma will take you to the Zócalo. Any 'M(etro) Hidalgo,' 'M(etro) Garibaldi,' 'M(etro) Villa,' 'M(etro) La Villa' or 'M(etro) Indios Verdes' pesero or bus, from Chapultepec metro station or heading east on Reforma, will go along Reforma at least as far as Hidalgo metro station.

POLANCO (MAP 7)

In this affluent residential quarter north of the Bosque de Chapultepec, the streets are named after writers and scientists, and the spring blossoms are even more of a treat than elsewhere in the city. Polanco contains lots of restaurants, several art galleries and embassies, some expensive hotels and shops, and the SECTUR tourist office (see Information). Much of the architecture is in the appealing neocolonial style of the 1930s and '40s, with prettily carved stone doorways and window surrounds. You could visit this part of the city before or after the nearby Museo Nacional de Antropología (see the Bosque de Chapultepec section).

XOCHIMILCO & AROUND (MAP 8)

About 20km south of downtown Mexico City, the urban sprawl is strung with a network of canals lined by gardens and houses with patches of waterside lawn. These are the 'floating gardens' of Xochimilco ('so-chi-MEEL-co'), remnants of the chinampas where the Aztecs grew much of their food. A gondola trip along the canals is a tranquil experience. Nearby are the enjoyable Parque Ecológico de Xochimilco and one of the city's best art museums, the Museo Dolores Olmedo Patiño.

Museo Dolores Olmedo Patiño

The Olmedo Patiño museum (☎ 5555-1016, Avenida México 5843; admission US$2.75, free Tues; open 10am-6pm Tues-Sun), a little over 2km west of Xochimilco, has perhaps the biggest and most important Diego Rivera collection of all. It's a fascinating place, set in a peaceful 16th-century hacienda with large gardens.

Dolores Olmedo Patiño, who still lives in part of the mansion, was a rich socialite and a patron of Diego Rivera, amassing a large collection of his art. The museum's 137 Rivera works – oils, watercolors, drawings and lithographs from many periods of his life – are displayed with a fine collection of memorabilia and pre-Hispanic pottery figures and metalwork. There's also a room of Frida Kahlo paintings. Elsewhere in the museum you'll find Emperor Maximilian's 365-piece silverware set and a colorful collection of Mexican folk art.

To get there take the metro to Tasqueña, then the Tren Ligero (streetcar) from Tasqueña metro station to La Noria. Leaving La Noria station, turn left at the top of the steps, walk down to the street and continue ahead to an intersection with a footbridge over it. Here turn a sharp left, almost doubling back on your path, onto Antiguo Camino Xochimilco. The museum is 300m down this street. Altogether the trip is about one hour from the city center.

Xochimilco

Xochimilco means 'Place where Flowers Grow' in Náhuatl. Pre-Hispanic inhabitants piled up vegetation and lake mud in the shallow waters of Lago de Xochimilco, a southern offshoot of Lago de Texcoco, to make fertile gardens called chinampas, which became an economic base of the Aztec empire. As the chinampas proliferated, much of the lake was transformed into a series of canals. About 180km of these canals remain today. Partly thanks to a recent environmental-recovery program, Xochimilco's canals remain one of city residents' favorite destinations for a bit of fun and relaxation.

In addition to the city-sponsored tourist office, Xochimilco also boasts its own tourist information office (☎ 5676-0810), Pino 36 just off the central plaza, open 9am to 9pm Monday to Friday, 8am to 8pm Saturday and Sunday. Plaza-area highlights include the Mercado de Xochimilco, a bustling daily market occupying the two blocks south of the plaza; and the Parroquia de San Bernardino de Siena (☎ 5676-0148, east side of plaza; open 7am-1pm & 4.30pm-8pm daily), a 16th-century church with pretty gardens and an elaborate, gold-painted retablo.

Most people board their trajinera (gondola) at one of the embarcaderos (boat landings) near the center of Xochimilco such as Salitre or San Cristóbal, both 400m east of the plaza, or Fernando Celada, 400m west on Guadalupe Ramírez. Hundreds of colorful trajineras, each punted by one man with a pole, wait to cruise the canals with parties of merrymakers or tourists.

On weekends, especially Sunday, a fiesta atmosphere takes over as the town and waterways of Xochimilco become jammed with people arranging boats, cruising the canals or trying to talk you into buying something. For a more relaxed atmosphere, come on a weekday.

Official prices for the boats are posted at the embarcaderos and you needn't pay more. At all of the embarcaderos a four-person boat (yellow roof) is US$7.50 an hour; six-person boat (red), US$9.75; 12-person boat (blue), US$12; and 20-person boat (green), US$14. On Saturday, Sunday and holidays, 60-person *lanchas colectivas* (motor boats) charging US$7 (one-way) or US$14 (roundtrip) a person depart from the Salitre and Caltongo embarcaderos.

Fixed prices for food, drink and even mariachi and marimba music on the boats are also posted at the embarcaderos. You can get a taste of Xochimilco in one hour, but it's worth going for longer; you can see more and get a proper chance to relax.

To reach Xochimilco, you can take the metro to Tasqueña station, then take the Tren Ligero (streetcar, US$0.15), which starts there, to its last stop, Embarcadero. From Embarcadero station, walk to the left (north) along Avenida Morelos to the market, plaza and church. Five of the eight embarcaderos are within 500m of the plaza.

Alternatively, 'Xochimilco' buses and peseros run from outside Tasqueña metro station. It's about 45 minutes from Tasqueña to Xochimilco either way. The last Tren Ligero back to Tasqueña leaves Embarcadero station about 11pm.

A sitio cab will cost between US$12 and US$18 from downtown Mexico City to Xochimilco.

Parque Ecológico de Xochimilco (Map 1)

About 3km north of downtown Xochimilco, this 2-sq-km park (☎ 5673-8061, *Periférico Oriente 1; admission US$1.75; open 9am-6pm daily*) contains lakes, an incipient botanical garden and a truly surprising number and variety of water birds. It's enjoyable to walk around the pathways – despite the lack of shade – but you can also move around by bicycle, pedal boat or tra-jinera. There's a visitor center with displays on the plants and birds.

Just 2km west of the park is the Embarcadero Cuemanco, the best place to take a trajinera if you want to see the genuine chi-nampas of northern Xochimilco.

To reach Parque Ecológico de Xochimilco, take a 'Tlahuac' pesero northbound on Calzada de Tlalpan outside General Anaya metro station. You reach the park entrance – beside a blue footbridge with blue-and-red spiral towers near each end – after 20 to 30 minutes.

SAN ÁNGEL (MAP 9)

Sixty years ago San Ángel, 8.5km south of the Bosque de Chapultepec, was a village separated from Mexico City by open fields. Today it's one of the city's most charming suburbs, with many quiet cobbled streets lined by both old colonial houses and expensive modern ones, and a variety of other things to see and do. The museums are closed on Monday.

Avenida Insurgentes Sur runs north-south through eastern San Ángel.

Plaza San Jacinto & Bazar Sábado

Every Saturday the Bazar Sábado (see Markets in the Shopping section) brings a festive atmosphere, masses of color and crowds of people to San Ángel's pretty little Plaza San Jacinto.

The 16th-century **Iglesia de San Jacinto** and its peaceful gardens, where you can take refuge from the crowded market area, are entered by walking 50m west up Benito Juárez from the northwest corner of the plaza. The **Museo Casa del Risco** (☎ *5616-2711, Plaza San Jacinto 15; admission free; open 10am-5pm Tues-Sun*) occupies an 18th-century mansion with two pretty courtyards and a spectacular tile mosaic fountain. Inside you'll find a permanent exhibition of 14th- to 19th-century European art and 17th- to 19th-century Mexican art, as well as rotating temporary exhibitions.

Museo Casa Estudio Diego Rivera y Frida Kahlo

One kilometer northwest of Plaza San Jacinto is the Diego Rivera & Frida Kahlo Studio Museum (☎ *5550-1189, Rivera 2 at Altavista; admission US$1, free Sun; open 10am-6pm Tues-Sun*). The famous artist couple (see 'Diego & Frida') lived in this 1930s avant-garde abode – with a separate house for each of them – from 1934 to 1940, when they divorced. Rivera stayed on until his death in 1957.

The museum has only a few examples of Rivera's art and none of Kahlo's, but it holds a lot of memorabilia. Rivera's house (the pink one) has an upstairs studio. Across the street is the San Ángel Inn restaurant (see Places to Eat), in the 18th-century Ex-Hacienda de Goicoechea, once the home of the marquises of Selva Nevada and the counts of Pinillos. If your budget won't run to a meal here, you can still have a stroll in the gardens and perhaps a drink in the cocktail bar. (The margaritas here are the best in the city!)

Museo de Arte Carrillo Gil

The Carrillo Gil Art Museum (☎ 5550-6289, Avenida Revolución 1608; admission US$1.75, free Sun; open 10am-6pm Tues-Sun) has a permanent collection by first-rank Mexican artists, with numerous works by Rivera, Siqueiros and Orozco (including some of Orozco's grotesque, satirical early drawings and watercolors). Temporary exhibits are excellent too. There's a pleasant bookstore-café in the basement.

Templo y Museo del Carmen

The cool, peaceful Templo del Carmen, a tile-domed church dating from the 17th century, houses its museum (☎ 5616-2816, Avenida Revolución 4; admission US$3.50, free Sun; open 10am-5pm Tues-Sun) in the former monastic quarters. The museum is mainly devoted to colonial-era furniture and religious art, but its big tourist attraction is the mummified bodies in the crypt, which are thought to be 18th-century monks, nuns and gentry. You can also walk out into the pretty garden, which was once much bigger (when cuttings and seeds from the garden were sent all over colonial Mexico).

Parque de la Bombilla

This pleasant park lies just east of Avenida Insurgentes. The **Monumento a Álvaro Obregón** marks the spot where the Mexican president was assassinated during a banquet in 1928. Obregón's killer was a young Christian fanatic, José de León Toral, who was involved in the Cristero rebellion against the government's anti-Church policies.

Plaza Loreto

Plaza Loreto, a 600m walk south of Plaza San Jacinto, is Mexico City's most attractive mall, converted from an old paper factory. Several patios and courtyards are set between the brick buildings, and it's more than just a place to shop. Visitors to the mall will find a mini-amphitheater for performances, two multi-screen cinemas (one of them, Cinemanía, endowed with nice little lobby bar), a variety of eateries and the excellent **Museo Soumaya** (☎ 5616-3731; admission US$1, free Sun-Mon; open 10.30am-6.30pm Thur-Mon, 10.30am-7.30pm Wed). The museum houses one of the world's three major collections (70 pieces) of the sculpture of Auguste Rodin (1840-1917), plus work by Degas, Matisse, Renoir, Tamayo and other renowned artists.

Getting There & Away

'San Ángel' peseros and buses run south on Insurgentes from at least as far north as Buenavista train station. Most terminate on Dr Gálvez between Insurgentes and Avenida Revolución.

Alternatively, take the metro to Viveros or MA de Quevedo station, then walk (20 to 30 minutes) or board a 'San Ángel' pesero or bus at either place.

Returning north to the city center, 'M(etro) Indios Verdes' and 'M(etro) La Raza' buses and peseros run all the way up Insurgentes to the northern part of the city; 'M(etro) Insurgentes' vehicles go to Insurgentes metro station. A good place to catch any of these is the corner of Insurgentes and Avenida La Paz.

Returning from central San Ángel to the metro stations, 'M(etro) Viveros' peseros head east on Avenida Robles, and 'M(etro) Tasqueña' peseros and buses east on Avenida MA de Quevedo go to MA de Quevedo metro station.

To Coyoacán, a 'M(etro) Tasqueña' pesero or bus will take you to the corner of Carrillo Puerto (2.5km), from which you can walk the five blocks north to the Jardín del Centenario.

CIUDAD UNIVERSITARIA (MAP 1)

The University City, on the east side of Avenida Insurgentes 2km south of San Ángel, is the main campus of Latin America's biggest university, the Universidad Nacional Autónoma de México (UNAM), and one of the nation's modern architectural showpieces. To see a map check out **w** www.mapa.unam.mx.

The university was founded in the 1550s but was suppressed from 1833 to 1910. Most of the Ciudad Universitaria was built between 1950 and 1953 by a team of 150 young architects and technicians headed by José García Villagrán, Mario Pani and Enrique del Moral. It's a monument both to national pride, with its buildings covered in optimistic murals linking Mexican and global themes, and to an idealistic education system in which almost anyone is entitled to university tuition. In recent years, however, UNAM has struggled to compete academically with increasingly prestigious private universities.

UNAM has some 270,000 students and 30,000 teachers. It has often been a center of political dissent, most notably in the lead-up to the 1968 Mexico City Olympics.

In 1999-2000 the university was closed by a student strike for 9½ months. Initially protesting a proposed rise in tuition fees (from a token US$0.02 a semester to an average US$65), the strikers quickly developed wider demands such as a far-reaching reorganization of the university. The strike also became a broader protest against the Zedillo government's international free-market economic policies. But leadership of the strike passed increasingly into the hands of radicals, and support for it waned. Eventually police retook the occupied UNAM campus. It was a testament to the scars left on Mexico's psyche by the 1968 Tlatelolco massacre that they carried no firearms and no one was injured.

Anyone is free to wander around the campus. Most of the faculty buildings are scattered over an area about 1km square at the north end. As you enter from Insurgentes, it's easy to spot the **Biblioteca Central** (Central Library), which is 10 stories high, almost windowless, and covered on every side with mosaics by Juan O'Gorman. The south wall, with two prominent circles toward the top, covers colonial times. The theme of the north wall is Aztec culture. The east wall shows the creation of modern Mexico. The west wall is harder to interpret but may be dedicated to Latin American culture as a whole.

La Rectoría, the Rectorate administration building, southwest of the library, at the top (west) end of the wide, grassy Jardín Central, has a vivid 3-D Siqueiros mosaic on its south wall, showing students urged on by the people.

The building south of the Rectorate contains the university's modern art museum, the **Museo Universitario Contemporaneo de Arte** (☎ 5622-0298; admission free; open 10am-7pm Mon-Fri, 10am-6pm Sat-Sun).

The **Auditorio Alfonso Caso**, at the bottom (east) end of the Jardín Central, bears a mural by José Chávez Morado showing the conquest of energy, with humanity progressing from the shadow of a primitive jaguar god into an ethereal future. A little farther east, on the west wall of the **Facultad de Medicina**, a mosaic by Francisco Eppens interprets the theme of life and death. The central mask has a Spanish profile on the left and a Mexican indigenous one on the right, together making up a mestizo face in the middle. A maize cob and symbols of Aztec and Mayan gods represent forces of life and death.

The **Estadio Olímpico** (Olympic Stadium), on the west side of Insurgentes opposite this northern part of the campus, is designed to resemble a volcano cone and holds up to 80,000 people. A Rivera mosaic adorns the main entrance.

A second main section of the campus, about 2km farther south, contains the **Centro Cultural Universitario** (University Cultural Center), hosting the performing arts in its concert halls and theaters as well as the visual arts in its cinemas (see Entertainment, later), and the **Museo Universitario de Ciencias** (Universum, ☎ 5622-8238, 5622-7336, W www.universum.unam.mx; admission US$3.25; open 9am-5pm Mon-Fri, 10am-5pm Sat-Sun), the university's science museum. Other attractions on this section of campus include the university's botanical gardens; the Unidad Bibliográfica, housing part of Mexico's National Library; and the Espacio Escultórico (Sculptural Space), focused on a striking work by Mathias Goeritz consisting of triangular concrete blocks encircling a crater-shaped lava bed.

There are student cafés, open to everyone when school is in session, in the Facultad de Economía and the Unidad Posgrado, both off the east end of the Jardín Central, and in the Centro Cultural Universitario.

Getting There & Away

Any pesero or bus marked 'Villa Olímpica,' 'Perisur' or 'Cuicuilco' traveling south on

Insurgentes from Paseo de la Reforma or San Ángel will take you to the Ciudad Universitaria. You can also take one marked 'San Ángel' and change at San Ángel.

For the northern part of the campus, get off at the first yellow footbridge crossing Insurgentes, a little more than 1km from San Ángel, just before the Estadio Olímpico. For the southern part of the campus, get off at the second yellow footbridge *after* the Estadio Olímpico.

Returning to the north, the 'San Ángel,' 'M(etro) Insurgentes,' 'M(etro) La Raza' and 'M(etro) Indios Verdes' buses or peseros go along Insurgentes as far as their respective destinations.

Copilco metro station is near the northeast edge of the campus, 1km east of the Biblioteca Central; the Universidad metro station is at the eastern edge of campus.

COYOACÁN (MAP 10)

About 10km south of downtown Mexico City, Coyoacán ('Place of Coyotes' in the Aztec language, Náhuatl) was Cortés' base after the fall of Tenochtitlán. It remained a small town outside Mexico City until urban sprawl reached it 50 years ago. Close to the university and once home to Leon Trotsky and Frida Kahlo (whose houses are now fascinating museums), Coyoacán still has its own identity, with narrow colonial-era streets, plazas, cafés and a lively atmosphere. Especially on Saturday and Sunday, assorted musicians, mimes and crafts markets (see Shopping, later) draw large but relaxed crowds from all walks of life to Coyoacán's central plazas.

Viveros de Coyoacán

A pleasant way of approaching Coyoacán is via the Viveros de Coyoacán (Coyoacán Nurseries), a swath of greenery, popular with joggers, about 1km west of Coyoacán's central plazas. You can stroll here any day between 6am and 6pm. From Viveros metro station, walk south along Avenida Universidad, then take the first street on the left, Valenzuela, to enter the Viveros.

A block south of the Viveros, along Ocampo, is the pretty little **Plaza Santa Catarina**. The 700m walk east from here along Avenida Sosa to Coyoacán's central plazas takes you past some fine 16th- and 17th-century houses.

Plaza Hidalgo & Jardín del Centenario

The focuses of Coyoacán life, and scenes of most of the weekend fun, are its twin central plazas – the eastern Plaza Hidalgo, with a statue of Miguel Hidalgo, and the western Jardín del Centenario, with a coyote fountain.

The Coyoacán tourist office is housed in the former Coyoacán town hall, also called the **Casa de Cortés**, on the north side of Plaza Hidalgo. It's said that on this spot the Spanish tortured the defeated Aztec emperor Cuauhtémoc to try to make him reveal the whereabouts of treasure. The building was the headquarters of the Marquesado del Valle de Oaxaca, the Cortés family's lands in Mexico, which included Coyoacán.

The 16th-century **Parroquia de San Juan Bautista**, Coyoacán's church, and its adjacent ex-monastery stand by the southern part of Plaza Hidalgo. Half a block east of Plaza Hidalgo is the **Museo Nacional de Culturas Populares** *(National Museum of Popular Culture,* ☎ *5658-1265, Avenida Hidalgo 289; admission free; open 10am-6pm Tues-Thur, 10am-8pm Fri-Sun),* which has exhibitions on popular cultural forms such as *lucha libre* (wrestling), *nacimientos* (nativity models) and circuses.

Museo Frida Kahlo

The 'Blue House' *(*☎ *5554-5999, Londres 247; admission US$2.75; open 10am-6pm Tues-Sun),* six blocks north of Plaza Hidalgo, was the longtime home of artist Frida Kahlo (see 'Diego & Frida').

Kahlo and her husband, Diego Rivera, were part of a glamorous but far from harmonious leftist intellectual circle (which included, in the 1930s, Leon Trotsky), and the house is littered with mementos of the couple. As well as some of their own and other artists' work, it contains pre-Hispanic objects and Mexican crafts collected by the couple.

The Kahlo art on display consists mostly of lesser works, but it still expresses the anguish of her existence; one painting, *El Marxismo Dará la Salud* (Marxism Will Give Health), shows her casting away her crutches. In the upstairs studio an unfinished portrait of Stalin, who became Kahlo's hero when she and Rivera fell out with Trotsky (after she'd had an affair with Trotsky),

MEXICO CITY

Diego & Frida

Diego Rivera, born in Guanajuato in 1886, first met Frida Kahlo, 21 years his junior, when he was working on a mural at Mexico City's prestigious Escuela Nacional Preparatoria (National Preparatory School), where she was a student in the early 1920s. Rivera was already at the forefront of Mexican art and a socialist; his commission at the school was the first of many semi-propagandistic murals on public buildings that he was to execute over three decades. He was also already an inveterate womanizer; he had fathered children by two Russian women in Europe and in 1922 married Lupe Marín in Mexico. She bore him two more children before their marriage broke up in 1928.

Kahlo, born in Coyoacán in 1907, had contracted polio at the age of six, which left her right leg permanently thinner than her left. At school she was a tomboyish character. In 1925 she was horribly injured in a bus accident that broke her back, right leg, collarbone, pelvis and ribs. She made a mirac-ulous recovery but suffered much pain thereafter and underwent many operations to try to alleviate it. It was during convalescence from her accident that she began painting. Pain – physical and emotional – was to be a dominating theme of her art.

Kahlo and Rivera both moved in left-wing artistic circles and met again in 1928. They married the following year. The liaison, which has been described as a union between an elephant and a dove (he was big and fat, she short and thin), was always a passionate love-hate affair. Rivera wrote: 'If I ever loved a woman, the more I loved her, the more I wanted to hurt her. Frida was only the most obvious victim of this disgusting trait.' Both had many extramarital affairs.

Kahlo's beauty, bisexuality and unconventional behavior – she drank tequila, told dirty jokes and held wild parties – fascinated many people. In 1934 the pair, after a spell in the USA, moved into a new home built by Juan O'Gorman in San Ángel; the place had separate houses for each of them, linked by an aerial walkway. In 1937 exiled Russian revolutionary Leon Trotsky arrived in Mexico with his wife, Natalia. The Trotskys moved into the 'Blue House' in Coyoacán, where Kahlo had been born, a few kilometers from San Ángel. Kahlo and Trotsky wound up having an affair. In 1939 Rivera quarreled with Trotsky, and the Trotskys moved to a different house in Coyoacán.

stands before a poignantly positioned wheelchair. The folk art collection includes Mexican regional costumes worn by Kahlo, and Rivera's collection of retablo paintings.

Museo Léon Trotsky

Having come second to Stalin in the power struggle in the Soviet Union, Trotsky was expelled from that country in 1929 and con-demned to death *in absentia*. In 1937 Trotsky found refuge in Mexico, thanks to the support of Diego Rivera and Frida Kahlo. At first Trotsky and his wife, Natalia, lived in Frida Kahlo's Blue House, but after falling out with Kahlo and Rivera in 1939 they moved a few streets away, to this house

(☎ 5554-0687, *Viena 45; admission US$2.25; open 10am-5pm Tues-Sun*).

The house has been left much as it was on the day in 1940 when a Stalin agent finally caught up with Trotsky and killed him here. High walls and watchtowers (once occupied by armed guards) surround the house and its small garden. These defenses were built after a first attempt on Trotsky's life, on May 24, 1940, when attackers led by the Mexican artist Siqueiros (a Stalinist) pumped bullets into the house. Trotsky and Natalia survived by hiding under their bedroom furniture. The bullet holes remain.

The final, fatal attack took place in Trotsky's study. The assassin had several iden-

Diego & Frida

The following year Rivera and Kahlo divorced, and Rivera went to San Francisco. Soon afterward, Trotsky was assassinated at his Coyoacán home. Kahlo and Rivera remarried but she moved into the Blue House and he stayed at San Ángel – a state of affairs that endured for the rest of their lives, though their relationship endured too. Kahlo remained Rivera's most trusted critic, and Rivera was Kahlo's biggest fan.

Kahlo had only one exhibition in Mexico in her lifetime, in 1953. She arrived at the opening on a stretcher. Rivera said of the exhibition, 'Anyone who attended it could not but marvel at her great talent.' She died, at the Blue House, in 1954. The final words in her diary were, 'I hope the leaving is joyful and I hope never to return.' Rivera called the day of her death 'the most tragic day of my life… Too late I realized that the most wonderful part of my life had been my love for Frida.'

In 1955 Rivera married Emma Hurtado, his dealer. He died in 1957.

Kahlo & Rivera Sites in Mexico City

There's much more of his work than hers on view – partly because he was a more prolific, public and versatile artist, partly because some of her best work is in private collections or other countries.

Anahuacalli – fortresslike museum designed by Rivera to house his pre-Hispanic art collection (see the Coyoacán section)

Museo Casa Estudio Diego Rivera y Frida Kahlo – their double house (San Ángel)

Museo de Arte Moderno – includes works by Kahlo and Rivera (Bosque de Chapultepec)

Museo de San Ildefonso – the former Escuela Nacional Preparatoria (Centro Histórico)

Museo Dolores Olmedo Patiño – 137 Rivera works and a room of Kahlos in the excellent collection of a Rivera associate (see Xochimilco & Around)

Museo Frida Kahlo – the 'Blue House' (Coyoacán)

Museo Mural Diego Rivera – holds Rivera's mural *Sueño de una Tarde Dominical en la Alameda* (Alameda Central & Around)

Palacio de Bellas Artes – 1930s Rivera murals (Alameda Central & Around)

Palacio Nacional – Rivera's mural history of Mexican civilization (Centro Histórico)

Secretaría de Educación Pública – 120 fresco panels painted by Rivera and helpers in the 1920s (Centro Histórico)

tities but is usually known as Ramón Mercader, a Catalan. He had become the lover of Trotsky's secretary and gained the confidence of the household. On August 20, 1940, Mercader went to Trotsky at his desk and asked him to look at a document. Mercader then pulled an ice ax from under his coat and smashed the pick end of it into Trotsky's skull. Trotsky died the next day; Mercader was arrested and spent 20 years in prison. Books and magazines on Trotsky's desk and in bookcases give an intriguing glimpse of the revolutionary's preoccupations.

Other memorabilia and biographical notes are displayed in outbuildings. The garden contains a tomb holding the Trotskys' ashes.

To enter the house, go to its northern entrance, at Avenida Río Churubusco 410, near the corner of Morelos.

Ex-Convento de Churubusco

The 17th-century former Monastery of Churubusco, scene of one of Mexico's heroic military defeats, stands less than 1.5km east of the Trotsky Museum, east of Avenida División del Norte.

On August 20, 1847, an American army was advancing on Mexico City from Veracruz. Mexicans who defended this old monastery fought until they ran out of ammunition and were finally beaten only after hand-to-hand fighting. General Pedro Anaya, when asked by US general David Twiggs to surrender his ammunition, is said to have answered, 'If there was any, you wouldn't be here.' Cannons and memorials outside the monastery recall these events.

Most of the monastery is now occupied by the interesting **Museo Nacional de las Intervenciones** *(National Interventions Museum,* ☎ *5604-0699, cnr 20 de Agosto & General Anaya; admission US$3.25, free Sun; open 9am-6pm Tues-Sun).* Displays include an American map showing operations in 1847 (note how far outside the city Churubusco was then) and material on the French occupation in the 1860s and the plot by US ambassador Henry Lane Wilson to bring down the Madero government in 1913. Parts of the peaceful old monastery gardens are also open.

You can reach Churubusco on an eastbound 'M(etro) Gral Anaya' pesero or bus; catch it on Xicoténcatl at Allende, a few blocks north of Coyoacán's Plaza Hidalgo. Alternatively, it's a 500m walk from the General Anaya metro station.

Anahuacalli

This dramatic museum *(* ☎ *5617-3797, Calle del Museo 150; admission US$2.25; open 10am-6pm Tues-Sun),* 3.5km south of central Coyoacán, was designed by Diego Rivera to house his own collection of pre-Hispanic art. It also contains one of his studios and some of his work.

The fortresslike building is made of dark volcanic stone and incorporates many pre-Hispanic stylistic features. Its name means 'House of Anáhuac' (Anáhuac was the Aztec name for the Valle de México). If the air is clear, there's a great view over the city from the roof.

The archaeological exhibits are mostly of pottery and stone figures, chosen primarily for their artistic qualities. Among Rivera's own art, the most interesting pieces are studies for major murals such as *El Hombre, Contralor del Universo,* which is in the Palacio de Bellas Artes.

From Coyoacán, catch a 'Villa Coapa' pesero south on Tres Cruces. This will eventually travel south on Avenida División del Norte. Three kilometers from Coyoacán, get off at Calle del Museo (there are traffic lights and a church at the intersection) and walk 600m southwest along Calle del

Museo, curving to the left at first, then going slightly uphill. Returning northward, take a 'M(etro) División del Norte' pesero or bus along Avenida División del Norte.

Getting There & Away

The nearest metro stations (1.5 to 2km) to the center of Coyoacán are Viveros, Coyoacán and General Anaya. If you don't fancy a walk, from Viveros station walk south to Valenzuela and catch an eastbound 'M(etro) Gral Anaya' pesero to Allende; or from Coyoacán station take a 'Coyoacán' pesero southeast on Avenida México. From General Anaya station too, many peseros and buses go to central Coyoacán.

To return to these metro stations from central Coyoacán, there are 'M(etro) Viveros' peseros going west on Malitzin from Allende, 'M(etro) Coyoacán' peseros north on Aguayo, and 'M(etro) Gral Anaya' peseros east on Xicoténcatl from Allende.

To reach San Ángel from Coyoacán, there are 'San Ángel' peseros and buses heading west on Malitzin from Allende, or west on Avenida MA de Quevedo, five blocks south of Plaza Hidalgo. To reach the Ciudad Universitaria, take a 'M(etro) Copilco' pesero west on Malitzin, from Allende.

PARQUE NACIONAL DESIERTO DE LOS LEONES

This 20-sq-km national park *(open 6am-5pm daily),* full of cool and fragrant pine, fir and oak forests echoing to the sound of birdsong, lies some 23km southwest of downtown Mexico City, east of the town of La Venta on highway. It's 800m higher than the city center, in the hills on the rim of the Valle de México, and a fine place to head when the city's carbon monoxide and concrete get to be too much.

The park's name comes from the **Ex-Convento del Desierto de Santa Fe** *(open 10am-5pm Tues-Sun),* the 17th-century former Carmelite monastery in the park. The Carmelites called their isolated monasteries 'deserts' to commemorate Elijah, who lived as a recluse in the desert near Mt Carmel. 'Leones' probably stems from José Manuel de León who at one stage administered the monastery's finances.

The monastery was built in 1606-11, wrecked by an earthquake in 1711 and rebuilt in 1722-23. In 1801 the monks left in order to escape the too wet, too cool climate and their too frequent visitors.

Today the Ex-Convento has been restored with exhibition halls and a medium-to-expensive restaurant. There are pretty patios within, and lovely gardens around the buildings. The rest of the park has extensive walking trails and is very popular with weekend picnickers. Sometimes robberies are reported in the park, so take care of your things and don't wander off the main paths.

One good walk is from the spot known as **Cruz Blanca** at 3130m up to the chapel-crowned Cerro San Miguel at about 3800m. The route (1½ to two hours one-way) follows part of the Barda de la Ex-Comunión, the perimeter wall of the old monastery's property. To reach Cruz Blanca, turn right up a side road, immediately before a barrier where a US$1 charge on vehicles is levied, halfway from highway 15 to the Ex-Convento. It's about 4km from here up to Cruz Blanca, where you should find a *vigilante* (forest warden) who can direct you to Cerro San Miguel.

Getting There & Away

On Saturday and Sunday there are peseros to the Ex-Convento from near Tacubaya metro station. Take the 'Av Jalisco Calle Manuel Dublan' exit from the station's line 9 platforms, cross the street outside and walk through to the far end of the market.

Any day, you can take one of Flecha Roja's frequent 'Toluca Intermedio' buses from the Terminal Poniente bus station to La Venta, which is on the Toluca-bound highway 15. The ride takes about 20 minutes (US$1). Tell the driver you are going to the Desierto de los Leones and you should be dropped at a yellow footbridge over a tangle of merging highways just short of a *caseta de cobro* (toll station). Cross the footbridge, and toward its far end you'll see, on your right, the Desierto de los Leones signpost on a side road to the south. On Saturday and Sunday, peseros or taxis may wait here to take people up the 4km paved road to the Ex-Convento. Other days you'll probably have to walk, but traffic will be light and it's a pleasant stroll, gently rising nearly all the way.

TLATELOLCO & GUADALUPE (MAP 1)
Plaza de las Tres Culturas

About 2km north of the Alameda Central up the Eje Central is the Plaza de las Tres Culturas (Plaza of the Three Cultures), so called because it symbolizes the fusion of pre-Hispanic and Spanish roots into the Mexican mestizo identity. The Aztec pyramids of Tlatelolco, the 17th-century Spanish Templo de Santiago, and the modern Secretaría de Relaciones Exteriores (Foreign Ministry) building, on the plaza's south side, represent the three cultures.

Tlatelolco was founded by Aztecs in the 14th century as a separate dynasty from Tenochtitlán, on a separate island in Lago de Texcoco. In pre-Hispanic times it was the scene of the largest market in the Valle de México. Cortés defeated Tlatelolco's Aztec defenders, led by Cuauhtémoc, here in 1521. An inscription about that battle in the plaza today translates: 'This was neither victory nor defeat. It was the sad birth of the mestizo people that is Mexico today.'

Tlatelolco is also a symbol of more modern troubles. On October 2, 1968, 300 to 400 student protesters were massacred by government troops on the eve of the Mexico City Olympic Games. And in 1985, the area suffered some of the worst damage and casualties in the Mexico City earthquake when apartment blocks collapsed, killing hundreds of people.

Though it's a calm oasis amid the city, the plaza is haunted by echoes of its somber history. You can view the remains of Tlatelolco's main pyramid-temple and other Aztec buildings from a walkway around them. Recognizing the religious significance of the place, the Spanish built a monastery here before erecting the Templo de Santiago in 1609. Just inside the main (west) doors of this church is the baptismal font of Juan Diego (see Basílica de Guadalupe, following). Outside the north wall of the church, a monument erected in 1993 honors the victims of the 1968 massacre. The full truth about the massacre has never come out: the traces were hastily cleaned away, and Mexican schoolbooks still do not refer to it. (See Modern Megalopolis in the History section, earlier, for more on the massacre.)

Northbound 'Eje Central, Central Camionera, Tenayuca' peseros and buses pass right by the Plaza de las Tres Culturas. You can catch them on the Eje Central at Donceles, one block north of the Palacio de Bellas Artes. Alternatively, take the metro to Tlatelolco station, exit on to the busy Manuel González, and turn right. Walk to the first major intersection (Eje Central Lázaro Cárdenas), turn right, and you'll soon see the plaza on the far (east) side of the road, 900m from the metro station.

Basílica de Guadalupe

On December 9, 1531, the story goes, a Mexican indigenous Christian convert named Juan Diego, standing on the Cerro del Tepeyac (Tepeyac Hill), site of an old Aztec shrine, saw a vision of a beautiful lady in a blue mantle trimmed with gold. He told the local priest that he had seen the Virgin Mary, but the priest didn't believe him. Juan returned to the hill, saw the vision again, and an image of the lady was miraculously emblazoned on his cloak. Eventually the church accepted his story, and a cult grew up around the place.

Over the following centuries Nuestra Señora de Guadalupe (Our Lady of Guadalupe), as this Virgin became known – after a Spanish manifestation of the Virgin whose cult was particularly popular in early colonial times – came to receive credit for all manner of miracles, hugely aiding the acceptance of Catholicism by Mexicans. In 1737, after she had extinguished a typhoid outbreak in Mexico City, she was officially declared the Patrona Principal (Principal Patron) of Nueva España. Today her image is seen throughout the country, and her shrines around the Cerro del Tepeyac are the most revered in Mexico, attracting thousands of pilgrims daily from all over the country and hundreds of thousands on the days leading up to her feast day, December 12. See Special Events for more on these festivities.

Some pilgrims travel the last meters to the modern **Basílica de Nuestra Señora de Guadalupe**, at the foot of the Cerro del Tepeyac, on their knees. By the 1970s the old yellow-domed basilica here, built around 1700, was swamped by worshipers and began to sink slowly into the soft earth beneath it. So the new basilica was built next door. Designed by Pedro Ramírez Vásquez, architect of the Museo Nacional de Antropología, it's a vast, rounded, open-plan structure with the capacity to hold thousands of worshipers. The sound of so many people singing together is quite thrilling. The image of the Virgin hangs above the main altar, with moving walkways beneath it to bring visitors as close as possible.

The rear of the Antigua Basílica (Old Basilica) is now the **Museo de la Basílica de Guadalupe** (☎ 5577-6022, *Plaza de las Américas 1; admission US$0.50; open 10am-6pm Tues-Sun*), with a fine collection of *retablos* (small paintings done by the devout to give thanks for miracles) and colonial religious art.

Stairs behind the Antigua Basílica climb about 100m to the hilltop **Capilla del Cerrito** (Hill Chapel), on the spot where Juan Diego saw his vision. From here, stairs lead down the east side of the hill to the **Jardín del Tepeyac** (Tepeyac Garden), from which a path leads back to the main plaza, reentering it beside the 17th-century **Capilla de Indios** (Chapel of Indians). This is next to the spot where, according to tradition, Juan Diego lived from 1531 until his death in 1548.

An easy way to reach the Basílica de Guadalupe is to take the metro to La Villa-Basílica station, then follow the crowds two blocks north along Calzada de Guadalupe. You can reach the same metro station on any 'M(etro) La Villa' pesero or bus heading northeast on Paseo de la Reforma. A 'M(etro) Hidalgo' or 'M(etro) Chapultepec' pesero or bus south down Calzada de los Misterios, a block west of Calzada de Guadalupe, will return you to downtown.

CYCLING

Bicitekas (*no ☎, W www.bicitekas.org*) is an urban cycling organization that organizes weekly rides (known as Critical Mass) starting from the Monumento a la Independencia (El Ángel) at 9pm every Wednesday. Trips consist of a group of about 50 riders in tight formation, protected by rotating lights. Helmets are obligatory, and bikes can be borrowed by contacting Bicitekas at least one week in advance (English spoken). For organized bike tours, see Organized Tours later.

COURSES

Centro de Enseñanza Para Extranjeros (*Foreigners' Teaching Center, ☎ 5622-2470, fax 5616-2672, e marta@servidor.unam.mx, W www.cepe.unam.mx, Avenida Universidad*

3002, Ciudad Universitaria) US$375 for 6-week intensive Spanish-language and Latin American-culture courses. Beginners and others will find courses that cater to them. Though classes can be quite large (up to 18 students), the courses have received good reports.

Alliant International University (☎ 5264-2187, fax 5264-2188, e *info@usiumexico .edu*, w *www.usiumexico.edu*, *Álvaro Obregón 110, Roma; Map 6*) US$150 beginner, US$165 intermediate, US$180 advanced, plus US$14 placement exam. Formerly US International University, this small, private university has well-qualified staff and offers a total of 12 languages. The school also puts on a variety of other events and activities, such as guided cultural tours and open lectures and seminars, many of which can be joined on a one-time basis. If you're in the city for more than a few days, it's worth popping by to see what's coming up.

ORGANIZED TOURS

Many travel agencies, including those in most top-end and mid-range hotels, can book you on bus tours within and outside the city, with English-language guides. A half-day whirl around the Zócalo area and the Museo Nacional de Antropología costs around US$30. Full-day tours to Teotihuacán cost US$33.

Gray Line (☎ 5514-3080, *Hamburgo 182B, Zona Rosa*) Map 5. This international tour company is one well-established agency offering such tours.

Beware: Readers have warned of negative experiences when dealing with a negative alternative (no relation to Gray Line) called **Grey Line** (☎ 5208-1163, *Londres 166, Zona Rosa*) Map 5.

Mountain Bike Mexico (☎ 5846-0793, e *mtbmexico@prodigy.net.mx*, w *www.mtb mexico.com*) This company specializes in mountain bike trips outside the city, from one to five days' duration. Guides are bilingual.

Río y Montaña Expediciones (☎ 5520-2041, w *www.rioymontana.com*, *Prado Norte 450, Lomas de Chapultepec*) If you're looking for a guided adventure or ecotourism trip elsewhere in Mexico, check out this group, which receives good reports. Rafting, climbing, mountain-biking and hiking are their stocks in trade.

SPECIAL EVENTS

Every major Mexican festival described in the Facts for the Visitor chapter is celebrated in Mexico City. Some unique local events (and countrywide celebrations having a special flavor in the capital) are listed below. Visit w www.cultura.df.gob.mx for information (in Spanish only) about festivals and museum events.

Semana Santa – The most evocative events of Holy Week (in late March or early April) are in the humble Iztapalapa district, about 9km southeast of the Zócalo (M Iztapalapa), where more than 150 locals act out realistic scenes from the Passion and death of Christ. Palm Sunday sees Christ's triumphal entry into Jerusalem. On Holy Thursday the betrayal by Judas and the Last Supper are played out in Iztapalapa's plaza, and Christ's address in Gethsemane is enacted on Cerro de la Estrella, the hill rising to the south. The most emotive scenes begin at noon on Good Friday, in the plaza. Christ is sentenced, beaten, and crowned with real thorns, then carries his 90kg cross 4km up Cerro de la Estrella, where he is tied to the cross and 'crucified.' Afterward he is carried down the hill and taken to the hospital.

Día de la Independencia – On the evening of September 15 thousands gather in the Zócalo to hear the president of Mexico recite a version of the Grito de Dolores (Cry of Dolores), Miguel Hidalgo's famous rallying call to rebellion against the Spanish in 1810, from the central balcony of the National Palace at 11pm. The president then rings the ceremonial Campaña de Dolores (Bell of Dolores), and there's lots of cheering, fireworks and throwing of confetti, usually in the faces of other merrymakers.

Día de Nuestra Señora de Guadalupe – At the Basílica de Guadalupe in the northern part of the city, December 12, the Day of Our Lady of Guadalupe, caps 10 days of festivities honoring Mexico's religious patron. From December 3, ever-growing crowds flood toward the basilica and its broad plaza. On December 11 and 12 groups of indigenous dancers and musicians from all over Mexico perform on the plaza in uninterrupted succession for two days. The numbers of pilgrims reach the millions by December 12, when religious services go on in the basilica almost round the clock.

Christmas & Día de los Reyes Magos – For the couple of weeks before Christmas (December 25) the Alameda Central is ringed with brightly lit fairy-tale castles and polar grottoes, where families flock in and children pose for photos with Santa Clauses and their reindeer. Between Christmas and January 6 (Day of the Three Kings or Reyes Magos), Santa Claus is replaced by the Three Kings, who are equally popular and look, if anything, even more ill at ease than the Santas.

PLACES TO STAY

Mexico City has a full range of accommodations, from basic to classy. Accommodations are described here first by neighborhood and then by price range. Remember that many hotels have rooms for three or four people, costing not much more than a double.

Budget places typically charge anywhere up to US$30 for a double room. Several hostels geared to international budget travelers have opened in the last few years, to provide a welcome alternative to cheap hotels. Hotel rooms in the budget range have private baths unless otherwise mentioned. Many also have TV and carafes or bottles of purified water. Hot water supplies are erratic in some.

In general, the best cheap and moderately priced rooms are in the areas west of the Zócalo, near the Alameda Central and near the Plaza de la República.

Mid-range hotels charge US$30 to US$100 a double. Hotels in this range provide comfortable and attractive, if sometimes small, rooms in modern or colonial buildings. All rooms have private bath (usually with shower, sometimes with tub) and color TV. For the hotels in the Best Western group you can call ☎ 800-528-1234 in the USA or Canada for reservations.

Top-end hotel rooms run from US$100 up to the sky and range from comfortable medium-sized, tourist-oriented hotels to modern luxury high-rises for business travelers. The concentration of top-end places can be found in the Zona Rosa, along Paseo de la Reforma and in the Polanco district.

Please note that when two prices are listed for a double room, the first price is for one large bed and the second price is for two small beds.

Centro Histórico (Map 3)

Most of the suitable places in the Centro Histórico are on Avenida 5 de Mayo and the streets to its north and south.

Budget *Hostal Moneda* (☎ 5552-5821, ☎/fax 5522-5803, ☎ 800-221-72-65, Ⓦ www.hostal moneda.com.mx, Moneda 8) Ⓜ Zócalo. Dorm beds US$10, doubles US$12, triples

US$11. Just a stone's throw from the Zócalo, this hostel is a member of the HI-affiliated group AMAJ and opened in 2000. It has 98 beds in double and triple rooms and six-person dormitories. A kitchen, roof garden, café, TV areas, Internet and laundry facilities, and recycling and energy-conserving technologies are all part of the project. The hostel also offers daily tours to the Basílica de Guadalupe and Teotihuacán for US$14.50 (excluding admission fees), and an airport pick-up service at lower rates than the Transportación Terrestre cabs; call ☎ 800-221-72-65 (preceded by the long-distance access code, ☎ 01) and they'll pick you up at the airport in about 20 minutes.

Hostel Catedral (☎ 5518-1726, fax 5510-3442, Ⓦ www.hostelcatedral.com, Guatemala 4) Ⓜ Zócalo. Dorm beds US$10/11 members/nonmembers, private rooms US$25 per person, all including breakfast. Almost as close to the Zócalo as the Hostal Moneda is this 209-bunk hostel, which also opened in early 2000. Rooms hold from four to six people, and each bed includes a locker that can accommodate a large backpack. The hostel, open 24 hours, is the flagship of the HI-affiliated hostel group REMAJ, and it incorporates a restaurant, guest kitchen, Internet center, laundry, pool table and travel agency.

Hotel Isabel (☎ 5518-1213, Isabel la Católica 63 at El Salvador) Ⓜ Isabel la Católica. Singles/doubles US$16/20 with private bath, US$10/12 with shared bath. This hotel is popular with budget travelers because of its convenient location, comfy if old-fashioned rooms, and decent, moderately priced restaurant. All rooms have TV and some are very large; those overlooking the street are noisy but brighter, and some have good views.

Hotel Juárez (☎ 5512-6929, 1ª Cerrada de 5 de Mayo 17) Ⓜ Zócalo or Allende. Singles US$13, doubles US$14/15. This 39-room hotel is on a quiet side street off Avenida 5 de Mayo, only 1½ blocks from the Zócalo. It's simple but clean and presentable, with 24-hour hot water and low prices. All rooms have TV, but only a few have windows. Those fronting the street can be noisy. If you're there by 2pm you should be able to get a room without prior reservations.

Hotel Habana (☎ 5518-1589, Cuba 77) Ⓜ Allende. Singles/doubles US$20/27. This place is an excellent value. It has 40 clean, decent-sized rooms, painted a variety of pastel shades; rooms have TV and good tiled bathrooms.

Hotel San Antonio (☎ *5512-9906, 2ª Cerrada de 5 de Mayo 29*) ⓜ Zócalo or Allende. Singles & doubles US$18. This hotel is just south of the Hotel Juárez, across Avenida 5 de Mayo on the corresponding side street. All the 43 small, clean rooms have TV, and the hotel is quiet and convenient. Rooms on the street side are brighter.

Hotel Zamora (☎ *5512-8245, Avenida 5 de Mayo 50*) ⓜ Zócalo or Allende. Singles & 1-bed doubles with shared/private bath US$8/10, 2-bed doubles US$12/16. Between La Palma and Isabel la Católica, the Zamora has absolutely no frills, but it's clean, friendly and cheap, with hot showers and a safe.

Hotel Principal (☎ *5521-1333, Bolívar 29*) ⓜ Zócalo or Allende. Singles/doubles with shared bath US$7.50/10, with private bath US$18/20. Between Avenidas Madero and 16 de Septiembre, this is a friendly place with most rooms opening on to a plant-draped central hall. Rooms also have TVs and safes.

Hotel Washington (☎ *5512-3502, Avenida 5 de Mayo 54 at La Palma*) ⓜ Zócalo or Allende. Singles US$17, doubles US$18.50-21.50. Near Hotel Juárez, this hotel has small but adequate rooms with TV.

Hotel Roble (☎ *5522-7830, Uruguay 109*) ⓜ Zócalo or Pino Suárez. Singles US$21.50, doubles US$25-28. This hotel is two blocks south of the Zócalo. It's at the top end of the budget range with good rooms. A bright, busy restaurant adjoins.

Hotel Buenos Aires (☎ *5518-2104, Motolinía 21*) ⓜ Allende. Singles with shared/private bath US$7.50/10.25, doubles with private bath US$12.50/14. This hotel has good prices. Rooms are plain but clean, and management is friendly. Rooms with private bath also have TV.

Hotel Montecarlo (☎ *5518-1418, Uruguay 69*) ⓜ Zócalo. Singles/doubles with shared bath US$12/14, with private bath US$15/16. DH Lawrence once stayed here. Though renovated and clean, it's rather cavernous. But its closeness to the Zócalo and its prices make it worth considering.

Mid-Range *Hotel Canadá* (☎ *5518-2106, Avenida 5 de Mayo 47*) ⓜ Allende. Singles US$30, doubles US$33/36. East of Isabel la Católica is this bright, modern and tidy hotel. The location is excellent, though the 100 rooms are modestly sized; exterior ones get some street noise. They all have safes and bottled drinking water.

Hotel Catedral (☎ *5518-5232, Donceles 95*) ⓜ Zócalo. Singles US$31, doubles US$42/48. Just a block north of the Catedral Metropolitana, the Hotel Catedral is shiny and bright, with a reasonable restaurant off the lobby. The 120 rooms are well kept and pleasant. There's a roof terrace with good views.

Hotel Gillow (☎ *5518-1440, Isabel la Católica 17 at Avenida 5 de Mayo*) ⓜ Allende. Singles US$36, doubles US$38/49. This hotel has a pleasant leafy lobby and cheerful rooms. There's a moderately priced restaurant too.

Hotel Capitol (☎ *5512-0460, Uruguay 12*) ⓜ San Juan de Letrán. Singles/doubles US$35/42. This hotel is close to the Torre Latinoamericana. Rooms, mostly around a central hall with a fountain, are modern and pleasant.

Hotel Ritz (☎ *5518-1340*, ⓔ *hotelritzdf@ hotelritzdf.com.mx, Avenida Madero 30*) ⓜ Allende. Singles/doubles US$60/65, breakfast included. The Ritz, 3½ blocks west of the Zócalo, caters to business travelers and north-of-the-border tour groups. It offers 120 comfortable rooms with mini-bars. There's a restaurant and a good little bar with live piano music. It's a Best Western hotel.

Top End *Holiday Inn Select* (☎ *5521-2121, ☎ 800-990-99-99, Avenida 5 de Mayo 61*) ⓜ Zócalo. Singles & doubles US$111. This is a 110-room recent addition, with a prime site just across the street from the Catedral Metropolitana. The rooms are modern, pleasant and comfortable without being huge. The rooftop restaurant has marvelous views.

Gran Hotel Ciudad de México (☎ *5510-4040*, ⓦ *www.granhotel.com.mx, Avenida 16 de Septiembre 82*) ⓜ Zócalo. Singles & doubles US$111. Just off the Zócalo, this 124-room hotel is a feast of century-old Mexican art nouveau. Sit on one of the plush settees in the spacious lobby, listen to the songbirds in the large cages, and watch the open ironwork elevator glide toward the brilliant canopy of art nouveau stained glass high above you. The standard rooms are large and comfortable. Buffet breakfasts are a specialty of the hotel's restaurants.

Hotel Majestic (☎ 5521-8600, e majestic@ supernet.com.mx, w www.majestic.com.mx, Avenida Madero 73) ❶ Zócalo. Singles & doubles US$130. The long-established Majestic, on the west side of the Zócalo, has lots of colorful tiles in the lobby and a few rooms (the more expensive ones) overlooking the vast plaza. Avoid the rooms facing Madero (too noisy) and around the inner glass-floored courtyard (unless you don't mind people looking through your windows). The 7th-floor café-restaurant has a good Zócalo view. This is yet another Best Western hotel.

Alameda Central & Around (Map 3)

This is a convenient, if drab, area.

Budget *Hotel Del Valle* (☎ 5521-8067, Independencia 35) ❶ San Juan de Letrán or Juárez. Singles US$12, doubles US$13-16. Just a block from the Alameda, this is a friendly place with reasonably priced, medium-sized, slightly worn rooms with TVs.

Hotel San Diego (☎ 5521-6010, Moya 98) ❶ Salto del Agua. Singles US$14-16, doubles US$27. This hotel, 5½ blocks from the Alameda, is a bit far from the action but offers a good value. The 87 spacious, modern rooms boast satellite TV and tiled bathrooms. There's a good restaurant, a bar and a garage.

Hotel Hidalgo (☎ 5521-8771, Santa Veracruz 37) ❶ Bellas Artes. Singles/ doubles US$23/29. One block north of the Alameda, this hotel is on a fairly grungy street, but the 100 rooms are modern and excellent. It has a restaurant and garage.

Mid-Range *Hotel Bamer* (☎ 5521-9060, Avenida Juárez 52) ❶ Bellas Artes or Juárez. Singles/doubles US$49/54, smaller singles/doubles US$24/30. The Hotel Bamer faces the Alameda, and many of the 111 large, comfortable, air-conditioned rooms have fantastic views of the park. The smaller rooms at the sides are without Alameda

views or bathtub but do come with a shower. The ground-floor cafeteria serves good, reasonably priced breakfasts and lunches.

Hotel Fleming (☎ 5510-4530, Revillagigedo 35) ❶ Juárez. Singles US$33, doubles US$39-42. The Fleming, 2½ blocks south of the Alameda, has 100 comfortable rooms with large tiled bathrooms; some on the higher floors have great views. There's a nice restaurant and parking.

Hotel Marlowe (☎ 5521-9540, Independencia 17) ❶ San Juan de Letrán. Singles US$37, doubles US$43-47. This hotel is one short block south of the Alameda. It's bright and comfortable, and the 120 rooms are pleasant, tasteful and quite big.

Hotel Fornos (☎ 5521-9594, Revillagigedo 92) ❶ Balderas. Singles/doubles US$18/35. This place is 700m from the Alameda and has pleasant, smallish rooms. The hotel has a parking lot and restaurant.

Hotel de Cortés (☎ 5518-2181, e reservaciones@hoteldecortez.com.mx, Avenida Hidalgo 85) ❶ Hidalgo. Singles & doubles US$91. Facing the north side of the Alameda, this place has a somewhat forbidding façade of dark tezontle stone, but inside is a charming small colonial hotel. Originally built in 1780 as a monks' hospice, it now has modern, comfortable rooms with small windows that look out on the courtyard. Noise can be a problem, though. There's a nightly marimba and traditional dance show in the courtyard restaurant. It's another Best Western hotel.

Plaza de la República & Around (Map 4)

This area, about 1km west of the Alameda and near the Monumento a la Revolución, is slightly less convenient, but prices are good and the neighborhood is mainly quiet and residential. The closest metro station is Revolución.

Budget *Hotel Ibiza* (☎ 5566-8155, Arriaga 22 at Édison) Singles/doubles US$13/17. This small hotel is a good value. The little rooms are nice and clean, with brightly colored bedspreads and TV.

Hotel Édison (☎ 5566-0933, Édison 106) Singles US$20, doubles US$22/24. For a bit more comfort try the Édison, which has 45 pleasant, clean rooms around a small, plant-filled courtyard. There's a garage, and a bakery is just across the street.

Hotel Frimont (☎ 5705-4169, Terán 35) Singles US$17, doubles US$19/22. This hotel is a good value with 100 clean, carpeted, decent-sized rooms and an inexpensive restaurant.

Hotel Texas (☎ 5705-5782, Mariscal 129) Singles US$20, doubles US$21/23. The Texas has helpful staff and 60 cozy, clean rooms with free bottled water. There's also a garage.

Hotel Carlton (☎ 5566-2911, Mariscal 32B at Ramos Arizpe) Singles/doubles US$13/16. This old budget favorite is almost done with a remodeling project. The rooms are carpeted, have TV and are vaguely cozy. A few prostitutes look for work in Plaza Buenavista, the quiet little square in front of the hotel.

Hotel Oxford (☎ 5566-0500, Mariscal 67) Singles/doubles US$13/15. This hotel, also on Plaza Buenavista, is still waiting for refurbishment; the carpets don't appear to have been washed for a decade. But the hotel has large rooms with TVs. Upper rooms overlook the plaza.

Casa de los Amigos (☎ 5705-0521, ⓔ friends@avantel.net, Mariscal 132) Dorm beds US$10, singles/doubles with shared bath US$11/19, doubles with private bath US$20, studio apartments US$28; all prices are suggested donations. This Quaker center offers lodging to people interested in participating in its community or in becoming involved with other social concerns, such as doing research or community service in Mexico (see Work in the Facts for the Visitor chapter). There's a two-night minimum stay, and the Casa requires the completion of a brief questionnaire before accepting bookings, which can be done by email. It's a good place for meeting people with an informed interest in Mexico and Central America. The 45-bed guesthouse has both single-sex dormitories and private rooms. There's a guest kitchen, security boxes and a US$1.75 breakfast served Monday to Friday. Alcohol and smoking are not permitted in the building.

Mid-Range Hotel Mayaland (☎ 5566-6066, Antonio Caso 23) Singles US$34, doubles US$37/45. This hotel is a good value. The 100 rooms are small but clean and pleasing, with air-con, drinking water and about 100 channels on TV. There's a decent little restaurant and parking.

Palace Hotel (☎ 5566-2400, Ramírez 7) Singles US$37, doubles US$39/52. This 200-room hotel has a bustling lobby and comfortable rooms, some recently remodeled. Some rooms hold up to six people. The hotel also has a restaurant, bar and garage.

Hotel Corinto (☎ 5566-6555, Ignacio Vallarta 24) Singles US$34, doubles US$37/44. This place is sleek and polished, with a good restaurant, a bar, helpful staff and even a small rooftop pool. The 155 rooms, though small, are comfortable, quiet and air-conditioned.

Hotel New York (☎ 5566-9700, Édison 45) Singles US$28, doubles US$34/47. Northeast of Plaza de la República, this 45-room, recently upgraded hotel has bright, comfy rooms of a reasonable size, and a nice little restaurant.

Hotel Jena (☎ 5566-0277, Terán 12 at Mariscal) Singles US$49, doubles US$51/57. This modern, gleaming building has a posh feel. Its 120-plus rooms are ultraclean and among the most luxurious in the middle range. There's a piano bar and a slightly pricey restaurant.

Hotel María Cristina (☎ 5703-1212, fax 5592-3447, Río Lerma 31) Singles/doubles US$61/67. This colonial-style gem is 600m north of the Zona Rosa center near the Jardín del Arte. It has 150 comfy rooms, small manicured lawns, baronial public rooms and a patio with a fountain. There's a fine medium-priced restaurant, a bar and parking.

The Jardín del Arte is a small park about 1km north of the Zona Rosa, close to the Reforma and Insurgentes intersection. The following four decent midsize hotels, all with parking, are on Serapio Rendón within a block of the park. Buses and peseros pass nearby on Insurgentes and Reforma.

Hotel Mallorca (☎ 5566-4833, Serapio Rendón 119) Singles/doubles US$26/28, larger doubles US$30-33. This hotel has clean, pleasant, carpeted rooms. It's popular with Mexican couples and families. The 'doble chico' and 'doble grande' are large.

Hotel Sevilla (☎ 5566-1866, Serapio Rendón 124) Singles & doubles US$27-31, new singles & doubles US$47-60. The

Sevilla has a *sección tradicional* with decent enough rooms, and a nicer *sección nueva* with some rooms overlooking the park. Rooms are moderately sized. The hotel also has a shop, travel agency and restaurant.

Hotel Compostela (☎ 5566-0733, *Sullivan 35 at Serapio Rendón*) Singles US$24, doubles US$30/33. The Compostela has smallish but pleasant rooms.

Hotel Astor (☎ 5148-2644, *Antonio Caso 83 at Serapio Rendón*) Singles US$39, doubles US$47/50. This clean and modern 96-room hotel has a restaurant and parking; the rooms in the back are quieter.

Top End Several mainly business-oriented hotels on and near Paseo de la Reforma provide a convenient location between the Centro Histórico and Zona Rosa.

Fiesta Americana (☎ 5705-1515, **w** *www .fiestaamericana.com.mx, Reforma 80*) Singles & doubles US$157. This is a 26-story, 610-unit slab with stylish rooms.

Hotel Casa Blanca (☎ 5705-1300, **e** *hotel@hotel_casablanca.com.mx, Lafragua 7*) Singles/doubles US$86/105. Just north of Reforma, the Casa Blanca has 300 comfy rooms.

Hotel Meliá (☎ 5128-5000, **e** *melia .mexico@solmelia.es*, **w** *www.solmelia.com, Reforma 1*) Rooms US$307. This is a 490-room luxury hotel.

Hotel Sevilla Palace (☎ 5566-8877, **w** *www.sevillapalace.com.mx, Reforma 105*) Singles & doubles US$130. This hotel has helpful service and good, modern rooms.

Hotel Imperial (☎ 5705-4911, **e** *imperial@ internet.com.mx*, **w** *www.hotelimperial.com .mx, Reforma 64*) Singles & doubles US$143. This cozy 64-room hotel is beautifully kept and a national historic monument. It was built in 1902 as then-dictator Porfirio Díaz's private residence and later served as the US embassy during the 1940s. It was also the Hotel Francis for a time, named after the wife of famous Mexican comedian Mario Moreno 'Cantinflas.' The hotel has an upscale restaurant, a bar and a moderately priced cafeteria in the basement.

Zona Rosa & Around (Map 5)

Accommodations right in the posh Zona Rosa are expensive, but a couple of excellent and popular mid-range places are nearby (book these ahead if you can). The nearest metro station is Insurgentes.

Budget *Las Dos Fridas Hostel* (☎ 5286-3849, **e** *info@mail.2fridashostel.com*, **w** *www .2fridashostel.com, Hamburgo 301*) **❻** Sevilla. Dorm beds US$12, singles/doubles US$16/23. This cozy new hostel has four- and five-bed dorms and private rooms. It offers discounts for ISIC members and long stays. Amenities include a guest kitchen, 24-hour hot water, laundry facilities, TV room, Internet, telephone and fax access and tourist information. It is open 24 hours.

Hostel Mansión Havre (☎ 5533-1271, **e** *mansionhavre@hotmail.com, Havre 40*) Dorm beds US$9. This hostel, part of the HI-affiliated AMAJ hostel group, has 84 spaces in 12 rooms with two, four, six or eight beds. It also has showers, lockers, an Internet café, guest kitchen and a TV lounge. It is open 24 hours.

Mid-Range *Casa González* (☎ 5514-3302, fax 5511-0702, **e** *J_Ortiz_Moore@hotmail .com, Río Sena 69*) Singles US$28-38, doubles US$32-63, family rooms US$109. This guesthouse, with two beautiful houses set in small plots, is a 500m walk north from the heart of the Zona Rosa, in a quieter neighborhood. It's an exceptional place run by a charming family, perfect for those staying more than one or two nights, and a good value. Good home-cooked meals are available in the pretty dining room. They may have parking. No sign marks the houses: ring the bell to enter. French and English are spoken.

Hotel Aristos (☎ 5211-0112, *Reforma 276*) Singles & doubles US$79. This 326-room hotel is on the corner of the popular restaurant street Copenhague. Rooms are not huge but are comfortable and pleasant enough. The hotel sports a bar with mariachis and two nightclubs. Promotions often cut the room prices by more than half.

Hotel Internacional Havre (☎ 5211-0082, *Havre 21*) Singles & doubles US$106, including breakfast; discounts available for longer stays, breakfast not included. This hotel has 48 big, comfy rooms with nice furniture and TV; there are fine views from the top floors. Management is helpful, and there's free guarded parking and an on-site restaurant.

Top End *Hotel Plaza Florencia* (☎ 5242-4700, ⓦ *www.plazaflorencia.com.mx, Avenida Florencia 61*) ⓜ Insurgentes. Rooms US$113. This hotel is pleasant and modern, with 142 tasteful, though not huge, rooms all with one or two double beds, air-con, mini-bar and cable TV. There's also a restaurant.

Calinda Geneve & Spa (☎ 5211-0071, ☎ 877-657-5799 in the USA, ☎ 877-609-6940 in Canada, ⓔ *reservas@prodigy.net.mx,* ⓦ *www.hotelescalinda.com.mx, Londres 130)* Singles & doubles US$200. West of Génova, this place is older than most Zona Rosa hotels. It is well kept, with a formal colonial lobby from which you can walk into a glass-canopied Sanborns restaurant or, at the other end, the popular Café Jardín. The 320 rooms, with a bit of period style, have air-con, mini-bar and cable TV. As the name advertises, there's also a spa.

Hotel Marquis Reforma (☎ 5229-1200, *Paseo de la Reforma 465 at Río de la Plata)* ⓜ Sevilla. Deluxe rooms US$174-204. This hotel opened in 1991 with design and decor that draw from the city's rich art deco heritage and updated for the 21st century. It has lots of colored marble, well-trained multilingual staff, and facilities such as an outdoor spa with whirlpool baths. There are 98 deluxe rooms and 110 lavish suites.

María Isabel-Sheraton Hotel (☎ 5242-5555, 800-325-3535 in the USA, ⓦ *www.sheraton.com, Paseo de la Reforma 325)* Singles & doubles weekdays/weekends US$320/164. This hotel is older (1962) than the other top-end hotels, but it's as attractive and solidly comfortable as ever. It has spacious public rooms, excellent food and drink, nightly mariachi entertainment and all the services of a classy hotel, including pool, fitness and medical centers and two lighted tennis courts. The 755 reasonably sized rooms and suites offer all the comforts.

Hotel Marco Polo (☎ 5511-1839, 800-310-96-93, ⓔ *marcopolo@data.net.mx,* ⓦ *www.marcopolo.com.mx, Amberes 27)* Singles/doubles US$170/189. This trendy lodging attracts foreign customers from the art and business worlds. It has 60 stylishly modern rooms.

Four Seasons Hotel (☎ 5230-1818, ⓦ *www.fourseasons.com, Reforma 500)* ⓜ Sevilla. Singles weekdays/weekends around US$292/234; add US$30 for each additional person. This is Mexico City's top hotel; it is

refined, modern and business-oriented. Most of its 240 spacious rooms overlook a handsome garden-courtyard.

Condesa & Roma (Map 6)
Home Hostel (☎ 5511-1683, ⓔ *wmaster@hostelhome.com.mx,* ⓦ *www.hostelhome.com.mx, Tabasco 303)* ⓜ Insurgentes. Dorm beds US$7/8 members/nonmembers. This pleasant, small hostel sits on a quiet, leafy street between the groovy Roma and Condesa districts, south of the Zona Rosa. It accommodates 20 people, each in four separate-sex bunk rooms. There's a kitchen and TV/sitting room and Internet access. Home Hostel is in the HI-affiliated AMAJ and REMAJ hostel groups.

La Casona (☎ 5286-3001, ⓔ *casona@data.net.mx,* ⓦ *www.hotellacasona.com.mx, Durango 280)* ⓜ Sevilla. Singles & doubles US$178, including breakfast. This elegant small hotel in a modernized early-20th-century mansion has tasteful rooms. There's also a reasonably priced little restaurant on site. Book ahead.

Polanco (Map 7)
The Polanco area, just north of Bosque de Chapultepec, has some of the city's best business hotels, including three high-rises in a row along Campos Elíseos. The closest metro station is Auditorio, unless otherwise stated.

Camino Real México (☎ 5263-8888, ⓦ *www.caminoreal.com, Calzada General Escobedo 700)* ⓜ Chapultepec. Singles & doubles weekdays/weekends US$242/171. This hotel has bold, modern architecture and 713 rooms.

Hotel Nikko México (☎ 5280-1111, 800-908-88-00, ⓦ *www.nikkohotel.com, Campos Elíseos 204)* Singles & doubles US$328. The Nikko México is a 745-room high-rise blending modern luxury with excellent service in a dramatically designed building. Discounts may be available Friday to Sunday.

Hotel Presidente Inter-Continental (☎ 5327-7700, 800-904-44-00, *Campos Elíseos 218)* Singles & doubles weekdays/weekends US$234/169. The Presidente Inter-Continental has six quality restaurants and 659 spacious, modern rooms.

JW Marriott Hotel (☎ 5282-8888, ⓦ *www.marriott.com, Andrés Bello 29)*

MEXICO CITY

Singles & doubles weekdays/weekends US$304/215. The Marriott has 312 rooms and suites and is very classy and comfortable.

Terminal Norte

Hotel Brasilia (☎ 5587-8577, e mhbrasilia@ wm.com.mx, Avenida de los Cien Metros 4823) ⓜ Autobuses del Norte. Singles/ doubles US$23/35. This hotel is a five- to eight-minute walk south of the northern bus terminal. It has 200 decent rooms, a restaurant and bar.

PLACES TO EAT

This cosmopolitan capital has eateries for all tastes and budgets, with plenty of European, Middle Eastern, Asian and Argentine restaurants as well as Mexican ones. Some of the best places are cheap; some of the more expensive ones are well worth the extra money. In the formal restaurants, men should wear a jacket and tie, and women something commensurate. Phone numbers are given for places where it's worth reserving a table.

The city's cheapest food is at its thousands of street stands.

The city is also liberally laced with modern chain restaurants whose predictable menus make for a sound fallback if you fancy somewhere easy and reliable, if not often inspired. Numerous branches of *VIPS* and *Sanborns*, with Mexican and international food, are found in affluent and touristy parts of the city such as the Zona Rosa, the Alameda area and Paseo de la Reforma. At both places salads, *antojitos* and toasted sandwiches cost around US$2.50 to US$4.50, with most main dishes from US$4 to US$7. You'll find several branches of these major chains shown on this chapter's maps. Less widespread chains include the cheery *Taco Inn* (tacos), *Potzoll-calli* (Mexican food) and the wide-ranging *Los Bisquets Bisquets Obregón* and *El Portón*. International chains such as *Pizza Hut*, *McDonald's* and *KFC* are here too.

Centro Histórico (Map 3)

For places to eat overlooking the Zócalo, see 'Square Meals: Eating Around the Zócalo.'

Budget *Café El Popular* (☎ 5518-6081, Avenida 5 de Mayo 52) Breakfast, set lunches US$2-3. Open 24 hrs. This good, cheap neighborhood place with tightly packed tables is 1½ blocks west of the Zócalo. In addition to good combination

---

Square Meals: Eating Around the Zócalo

Shakey's Pizza y Pollo US$5.75-12 At the northwest corner of the Zócalo (Map 3), this restaurant has sidewalk tables that are good for watching the city in action. It does pizzas, chicken nuggets and so on.

Restaurante El Campanario/Cafetería El Invernadero (☎ 5521-2121, 5 de Mayo 61) Breakfast buffet US$9.50 Mon-Fri, US$10 Sat-Sun; mains US$3-5.50. Open 7am-11pm daily. For a truly marvelous view, head to the restaurant on the roof of the Holiday Inn Select hotel. This dining area is almost within touching distance of the Catedral Metropolitana's bells and has a magnificent panorama over the Zócalo and much of the rest of the city.

Restaurante Terraza (☎ 5521-8600, Avenida Madero 73) Daily breakfast buffet US$9.50, buffet lunch 1pm-6pm US$10 Mon-Fri, US$17 Sat-Sun. Open 7am-midnight daily. Restaurante Terraza overlooks the Zócalo from the 7th floor of the Hotel Majestic. In addition to the buffets, à la carte items are available, and if it's not too busy you can enjoy the view for the price of a drink.

Cafetería Mirador (☎ 5510-4040, Avenida 16 de Septiembre 82) Buffet breakfast US$8.75. Open 7am-10.30pm daily. On the top floor of the Gran Hotel Ciudad de México, Cafetería Mirador has a small terrace with a great view over the Zócalo.

La Casa de las Sirenas (☎ 5704-3225, Guatemala 32) Mains US$12-15, desserts US$3.75. Open 8am-11pm Mon-Sat, 8am-6pm Sun. In a 17th-century house just behind the cathedral, this lovely restaurant serves excellent *alta cocina Mexicana* on its terrace, which has views of the Zócalo, Palacio Nacional and Templo Mayor. Enjoy a meat, seafood or poultry main dish and finish off with a crêpe. And to drink? Well, the Sirenas offers some 50 varieties of tequila, costing from US$3.75 to US$20 a shot, in the restaurant or in the Salones Tequila on the lower floors.

breakfasts (fruit, eggs, frijoles, roll and coffee), they serve all sorts of other food, such as a quarter chicken with mole, or *carne asada a la tampiqueña*. Good, strong *café con leche* is US$1. A second branch (☎ 5510-9176, *Avenida 5 de Mayo 10*) has the same menu, more space and bright yellow plastic furnishings.

Café La Blanca (☎ 5510-0399, *Avenida 5 de Mayo 40*) 3-course lunch US$4.75. This café, west of Isabel la Católica, is big, always busy and good for people-watching over a café con leche (US$1.50).

Los Bisquets Bisquets Obregón (no ☎, *Madero 29 and Tacuba 85*) À la carte dishes US$2.25-4.25. Open 7.30am-10.30pm daily. This chain is a good place to start the day. It serves combination breakfasts (US$4.50 to US$7) that include coffee, juice, a roll, *pan dulce*, and a main egg or meat dish. At lunchtime a two-course *comida* with a drink costs the same.

La Casa del Pavo (☎ 5518-4282, *Motolinía 40A*) 4-course meal US$3.25. Open 8am-10pm daily. The chefs here wear white aprons and slice roast turkeys all day long, serving them up at low prices. The four-course *comida corrida* offers a good value, and there are turkey tacos and turkey *tortas* too.

Taco Inn (no ☎, *Plaza Tolsá*) Prices from US$1.75. This taco chain is outside the Museo Nacional de Arte and offers more than 30 taco choices, but the Hawaiiano Inn (four tacos with beef, pineapple, cheese and ham) is especially good. There's also a three-taco *vegetariano* option.

Taquería Tlaquepaque (no ☎, *Isabel la Católica 16*) 3 tacos US$0.25-1. Open 7am-2am Mon-Thur, 7am-4am Fri-Sat, 8am-1am Sun. This is a good answer to late-night hunger. You can get three tasty tacos for a varying price depending on what's in them.

Potzollcalli (☎ 5521-4253, *Avenida 5 de Mayo 39 at Motolinía*) Prices from US$3.50. Open 7.30am-11.30pm Mon-Fri, 7.30am-1am Sat-Sun. This is one in a chain of clean, bright and good Mexican restaurants, with specialties like *taquiza mixta* (five types of taco with rice) and chicken or meat grills. It also has tasty vegetarian options like squash blossoms or potato quesadillas.

A number of popular *lunch places* along 1ª Cerrada de 5 de Mayo serve up set meals (US$2.25) from 1pm to 5pm Monday to Saturday.

Restaurante El Vegetariano (☎ 5521-6880, *Avenida Madero 56*) 3- to 4-course lunch US$4.50-5. Open 8.30am-6.30pm Mon-Sat. Don't be put off by the unimpressive stairway entrance to this restaurant. Upstairs are three busy, high-ceilinged rooms where a pianist plunks out old favorites as you dine. The food is tasty, filling and an excellent value. Nearby is a more modern, street-level branch (☎ 5510-0113, *Mata 13*).

Comedor Vegetariano (no ☎, *Motolinía 31-5*) Prices US$3.75. Open 1pm-6pm daily. This place serves up a good comida.

Super Soya (no ☎, *Avenida 16 de Septiembre 79*) Prices from US$0.75. Open 9am-9pm Mon-Sat, 10am-7pm Sun. Opposite the Gran Hotel Ciudad de México is this juice bar veggie joint. It has an array of gaudy signs listing all the juices, *licuados*, fruit salads, tortas and tacos it can manage. You could wash down a couple of vegetarian tacos with a Dracula (beetroot, pineapple, celery and orange juice). There are other branches at Brasil 11 and Bolívar 31.

Dulcería de Celaya (☎ 5521-1787, *Avenida 5 de Mayo 39*) Prices from US$2.25. Open 10.30am-7.30pm daily. Set in a beautifully ornate old building west of Isabel la Católica, this traditional Mexican candy store has been around since 1874 selling delicate Mexican sweets such as candied fruits, sugared almonds and crystallized strawberries, as well as honey and fruit jams.

Café del Centro (no ☎, *opposite Hotel Catedral on Donceles*) Prices from US$1. This place has good coffee, cakes, muffins and burritos too.

Mid-Range & Top End *Café de Tacuba* (☎ 5518-4950, *Tacuba 28*) 5-course lunch US$11.75, mains US$5-11. Open 8am-11.30pm daily. Just west of Allende metro station is this gem of old-time Mexico City; it opened in 1912. Colored tiles, stained glass, brass lamps and oil paintings set the mood. The cuisine is traditional Mexican and delicious.

Restaurante Danubio (☎ 5512-0976, *Uruguay 3*) Set lunch US$11.25, mains US$7.50-15. Open 1pm-10pm daily. This place has been here, specializing in seafood, since the 1930s, and still does it well. It serves a huge and excellent six-course set-price lunch including fish *and* meat courses.

There are also à la carte options. *Langosta* (lobster) and *langostinos* (Dublin Bay prawns) are the specialties, but prices for them are stratospheric. You'll be lucky to get a table here for Sunday lunch.

Los Girasoles (☎ 5510-0630, Tacuba 1 at Plaza Tolsá) Starters from US$3.25, mains US$6.25-10. Open 1pm-1am Mon-Sat, 1.30pm-8pm Sun. Beside the Museo Nacional de Arte, this is one of the best of a recent wave of restaurants specializing in *alta cocina mexicana*. Recipes are either traditional or innovative, but all have a very Mexican flavor. You might start with *crema de tres quesos* (three-cheese soup) and follow up with Sonoran ranch-style beef medallions with *chipotle*. There are pleasant outside tables as well as indoor seating.

Alameda Central & Around (Map 3)
Budget *Cafetería del Claustro* (Cloister Café, ☎ 5518-2265, Avenida Hidalgo 45) Prices US$1.25-3.25. Open 10am-5pm Tues-Sun. In the Museo Franz Mayer, opposite the north side of the Alameda, this café is one of the prettiest, most peaceful restaurants in the city. Entrance fee of US$0.50 gives you access to both the café and the cloister. On Tuesday entrance is free. Marble-top tables are set in the lovely courtyard, with taped baroque music setting the mood. The good, self-service food includes sandwiches, salads, quiche and excellent cakes.

Café Trevi (☎ 5512-3020, Colon 1 at Dr Mora) Breakfast US$2-3, set meals US$3, mains US$4-6. Open 8am-11.30pm daily. Facing the west side of the Alameda is this good Italian and Mexican restaurant. It serves breakfasts till noon and has a six-course set-price daily meal, pasta dishes and one-person pizzas.

Taquería Tlaquepaque (☎ 5521-3082, Independencia 4) 3 tacos US$1-4. Open 8am-3am Sun-Thur, 8am-4am Fri-Sat. One block south of the southeast corner of the Alameda, there's a cluster of bright, inexpensive eateries around the intersection of Independencia and López. The pick of the bunch is the Taquería Tlaquepaque, a clean, bustling place where bow-tied waiters serve up dozens of types of tacos. The *chuletas, nopales y queso* (chopped pork, cactus tips and cheese) taco, at the top of the range, is delicious.

Centro Naturista de México (☎ 5512-5377, Dolores 10B) Set lunch US$2-3.50. Open 1pm-6pm daily. Half a block south of the Alameda, this health food shop with a vegetarian restaurant serves lunches of soup, veggie mains, salad, bread, fruit *aguas frescas*, tortillas and dessert. There is also Mexican à la carte fare.

For a taste of lingering Spain, you can't beat a helping of *churros y chocolate*. Churros are long, thin, deep-fried doughnuts, just made to be dipped in a cup of thick hot chocolate.

Churrería El Moro (no ☎, San Juan de Letrán 42) Hot chocolate with 4 churros US$2.25, café con leche with 4 churros US$1.75. Open 24 hrs daily. A fine spot for the churros experience is Churrería El Moro, 2½ blocks south of the Torre Latinoamericana. It's often busy in the wee hours with people winding down after a night on the town.

Mid-Range *Café del Palacio* (☎ 5512-0807, inside Palacio de Bellas Artes) Prices US$3.50-7. Open 11am-7pm Tues-Sun, 1pm-5pm Mon. This elegant café serves salads and tempting *emparedados* (sandwiches), including smoked salmon, smoked turkey and cream cheese varieties.

Hong King (☎ 5512-6703, Dolores 25-A) Set meals US$6-13. Dishes US$4-7. Open 12.30pm-11pm daily. This is one of the best restaurants in Mexico City's small Chinatown. It has set meals (minimum two people) and menus in Chinese, Spanish and English. It also serves à la carte dishes with some vegetarian offerings; try the tofu with veggie stir-fry.

Plaza de la República & Around (Map 4)
This is not a great area to eat in, but there are a couple of good chain restaurants here.

Potzollcalli (☎ 5546-3261, Arriaga 5) This restaurant, just south of Puente de Alvarado, has the same menu and prices as the Avenida 5 de Mayo branch (see Centro Histórico, earlier in this Places to Eat section).

Tacos El Caminero (☎ 5566-4913, Ramírez 17) Prices US$3 and up. Open 10am-midnight Mon-Thur, 10am-1am Fri-Sat, 11am-11pm Sun. This is a busy, slightly upscale taquería doling out good tacos. You will find it about 100m south of Plaza de la República next to a branch of VIPS.

Café La Habana (☎ 5546-0255, *Morelos 62 at Bucareli*) Coffee from US$1, breakfasts from US$2.25, daily set meals US$5.25. Open 7.30am-11pm Mon-Sat, 8am-10pm Sun. This is Mexico City's best coffee place. Rumor has it that Che and Castro were known to stop here for java while plotting the Cuban revolution.

Zona Rosa & Around (Map 5)

The Zona Rosa is packed with places to eat and drink. Some streets are closed to traffic, making the sidewalk cafés more pleasant.

Budget Some of the cheapest meals are at the *Mercado Insurgentes* on Londres. One corner of this crafts market is given over to typical Mexican market *comedores*, serving hot lunches daily to customers who sit on benches in front of the cooks and their stoves. You'll find the same typical Mexican dishes here as you would in restaurants but at much lower prices (around US$2.75 for a comida corrida). Pick one that's busy. A bit farther west from Mercado Insurgentes along Londres on both sides of Florencia are some of the area's most economical restaurants, the best of them packed at lunchtime.

Taco Inn (☎ 5511-2103, *Hamburgo 96*) Prices US$1-3. Near the hub of the Zona Rosa, this place is part of the same chain as the Taco Inn on Plaza Tolsá (see Centro Histórico, earlier in this Places to Eat section).

Auseba (☎ 5511-3769, *Hamburgo 159B*) Prices US$1.50-3. The Auseba has glass cases filled with enticing cakes and other sweet offerings and large windows for watching the traffic on Hamburgo. You can get cakes and pastries including *pan danés* (Danish pastry), as well as good tea and coffee, and good cheap breakfasts.

Super Soya (☎ 5511-7426, *Insurgentes Sur 168*) Open 9am-9pm Mon-Sat, 10am-7pm Sun. This is part of the same chain as the Super Soya in the Centro.

Junk-food junkies will be in heaven on Génova between Hamburgo and Liverpool, where **Dunkin' Donuts**, **Burger King**, **Mc-Donald's** and **KFC** all congregate.

Mid-Range *Konditori* (☎ 5511-2300, *Génova 61*) Prices US$5.25-10. Open 7am-11.30pm daily. This perennially popular restaurant serves a mixture of Italian, Scandinavian and Mexican fare in its elegant small dining rooms and spacious sidewalk café, and there are good cakes and pastries too. It is also a good spot for people-watching on the Zona Rosa's busiest pedestrian street.

Parri Pollo Restaurante (☎ 5525-5353, *Hamburgo 154*) Tacos US$2.50, mains from US$5.75. Open 8am or 9am until midnight or later daily. This is a busy, barnlike place serving grilled beef, pork and chicken in various ways, from tacos to steaks or whole birds.

One of the Zona Rosa's busiest restaurant streets is Copenhague, a single block lined with bustling mid-range and upscale eateries.

Freedom (☎ 5525-7346, *Copenhague 25*) Prices US$6-8. This good Tex-Mex restaurant does barbecued ribs, nachos, pasta, burgers, salads and the like; it also has a lively bar.

Fonda el Refugio (☎ 5525-8128, *Liverpool 166*) Mains US$8-10. Open 1pm-midnight Mon-Sat, 1pm-10pm Sun. In a charming old house, this spot offers Mexican fine-dining, including regional specialties such as *escamole* (fried ant larva).

Pabellon Coreano (☎ 5525-2509, *Estocolmo 16*) Prices US$5-9. Open 1pm-11pm Mon-Fri, 1pm-10pm Sat-Sun. This is one of the hottest Korean places in town.

Salut les Copains (no ☎, *Havre 15*) Prices US$7-10. Open 10am-6pm Mon-Sat. Cash only. Inside the Casa de Francia compound, this excellent French spot has daily and weekly menus, reliable service and a great atmosphere.

Restaurante Vegetariano Yug (☎ 5333-3296, *Varsovia 3*) Prices from US$3. Open 7am-10pm Mon-Fri, 8am-8pm Sat, 1pm-8pm Sun. This good restaurant, just south of Reforma, does a US$5.50 lunch buffet from 1pm-5pm daily, and daily four-course comidas corridas with good whole-wheat bread. There's à la carte fare too. The clientele is mostly local office workers. A scaled-down cafeteria version of this chain is in the Roma district (☎ 5553-3872, *Puebla 326-6*); open 10am-8pm Mon-Sat.

Restaurante Vegetariano Las Fuentes (☎ 5514-8187, *Río Pánuco 127*) Breakfast US$4.50, meals US$8. Open 8am-6pm daily.

A couple of blocks north of the Zona Rosa is this attractive place, which serves tasty food in large portions. It offers full meals of soup, salad bar, home-style mains and a drink. Breakfasts here are big.

Los Murales (☎ 5726-9911, Liverpool 152) Mains US$6. Open 1.30pm-5pm Mon-Fri. This veggie restaurant in the bottom floor of the Century Hotel serves a decent vegetarian buffet lunch.

Top End Les Moustaches (☎ 5533-3390, Río Sena 88) Prices US$8-18. Open 1pm-11.30pm Mon-Sat. This is one of the city's best sophisticated and formal French restaurants. It lies 1½ blocks from the Zona Rosa, just north of Reforma. Try the pâté de foie gras starter and choose a main course of chicken, duck, beef or fish. For dessert, there are tempting crêpes and soufflés. Many tables are in an elegant greenery-filled patio.

Condesa (Map 6)

This relaxed, fashionable and agreeable neighborhood 1 to 2km south of the Zona Rosa has, since the mid-1990s, become the hub of the Mexico City eating-out scene. Its leafy streets have sprouted dozens of informal, mid-range, bistro-style restaurants and good cafés, many with sidewalk tables. Cuisines from all over the globe are represented here.

Condesa's culinary heart is the intersection of Avenida Michoacán, Vicente Suárez and Atlixco, 500m west of Parque México, as well as along Tamaulipas on either side of Michoacán. In addition, several good restaurants and cafés can be found along Amsterdam and Avenida México, two roads that encircle the park.

Fonda Garufa (☎ 5286-8295, Avenida Michoacán 91) Prices from US$4. Open 1pm-midnight Mon-Wed, 1pm-1am Thur-Sat, 1pm-11pm Sun. This long-established restaurant serves a big range of good pasta, vegetarian brochettes and salads, plus seafood and other grills, including ostrich.

Mama Rosa's (☎ 5211-1640, Atlixco 105) Prices from US$8. Open 8am-1am Mon-Sat, 8am-12pm Sun. On the same intersection as Fonda Garufa, the hugely popular Mama Rosa's is in a similar vein, serving almost everything, including gourmet wood-oven pizzas and good breakfasts. Go by about 8pm to ensure a table for dinner.

Amar Kemel (☎ 5211-2649, Montes de Oca 43) Prices from US$3.50. Open 10am-12pm daily. Amar Kemel serves generous quantities of excellent Middle Eastern food: falafel, kebabs, tabbouleh and hummus. There are also soups, salads and dishes based on kepe (ground beef), rice, fish and chicken.

La Casbah (☎ 5564-6826, Amsterdam 194) Prices US$7-10. Open 2pm-10.30pm Tues-Sat, 1.30pm-7.30pm Sun. This excellent spot on tree-lined Amsterdam is the place to go for couscous, which is served up with vegetables, lamb or chicken.

Vucciria (☎ 5264-0993, Avenida México 157) Prices US$4.50-12. Open 11am-midnight daily. This Italian restaurant, right on the park, serves excellent food and has an extensive wine list.

La Lola (☎ 5211-3705, Amsterdam 71) Prices US$3.50-10. Open 2pm-midnight Mon-Wed, 2pm-1am Thur-Sat, 2pm-7pm Sun. This French-style bistro has tasty food and pleasant outdoor tables; try the tuna in sun-dried-tomato sauce.

Sushi Shalala (☎ 5286-5406, Avenida Tamaulipas 73) Sushi rolls from US$3.25. Open 1pm-11pm Sat-Thur, 1pm-midnight Fri, 1pm-8pm Sun. If you want sushi this Japanese deli is the place to go; try the uramaki special. The restaurant also serves good soups and noodle and rice dishes.

El Tizoncito (☎ 5286-7321, Avenida Tamaulipas 122 at Campeche) Prices from US$0.75. Open till 3.30am Sun-Thur, till 4.30am Fri-Sat. This hugely popular place serves up excellent tacos al pastor, with fillings such as fish, shrimp, nopales y queso (cactus tips and cheese) and chicken. If there are no seats, try the bigger location two blocks east on Campeche.

Lettuzze (no ☎, Avenida México 67) Salad bar US$3.25, set lunch US$4.50. Open 2pm-5pm Mon-Sat. This decent vegetarian place has a lovely garden patio and a fantastic salad bar. It also has a set lunch (which includes the salad bar) and à la carte items.

Café La Selva (☎ 5211-5170, Vicente Suárez 38) Prices from US$1. Open 8am-11pm daily. This café serves good organic coffee from Chiapas, produced by a group of small-scale indigenous coffee growers.

Nevería Roxy (no ☎, Fernando Montes 89 at Mazatlán) Scoops from US$0.75, banana splits US$3. Open 11am-9pm daily July-Aug, 11am-8pm daily Sept-June. This old-fashioned ice cream counter is a Condesa classic, and it makes fresh ice cream on site. You can watch them do it when it gets slow. Another branch is open for business at Tamaulipas 161 at Alfonso Reyes.

Roma (Map 6)
While Roma is not Mexico City's famous eating zone, there are still plenty of gems worth trying here, as well as several vegetarian restaurants.

Budget On weekends, Calle de Oro between the Plaza de Cíbeles and Insurgentes hosts the crowded Mercado del Oro, which offers lots of *food stands* in its southernmost aisle. Among these is *Parrilladas Bariloche*, an Argentine steak house that sets up here at noon and 6pm Saturday and Sunday and sells delicious steaks (from US$3) and good salads.

Hamburguesas (no ☎, Medellín 34 at Sinaloa) Prices US$1.50. This popular hamburger stand cooks up delicious burgers that can be made with cheese or pineapple.

La Michoacana (no ☎, Puebla 160) Prices US$0.50-2. Open 10am-10pm daily. This Mexican popsicle chain that began in Tocumbo, Michoacán, opened its doors in the DF in 1943 and now has over 1000 branches in Mexico City alone. It makes its own delicious ice cream and Popsicles on site; try the *mango con chile paleta de agua* (spicy mango).

La Bodeguita del Medio (☎ 5553-0411, Cozumel 37) Prices from US$3. Open 1.30pm-2am Thur-Sat, 1.30pm-midnight Sun-Wed. Mexico's Bodeguita del Medio opened in the Roma in 1998 and is a branch of the famous Havana (Cuba) Bodeguita. Try the *mojitos*, a Cuban concoction of rum and mint leaves (US$3.25).

Shaya Michan (☎ 5514-5510, Calle de Oro 11) Set lunches US$3 from 1pm-5pm. Open 10.30am-5pm Mon-Fri, 10.30am-3.30pm Sat. On the 7th floor of the Shaya Michan building, this vegetarian restaurant has cheap food and a nice view of the Roma.

Nirvana (☎ 5525-1326, Puebla 120) Buffet US$5. Open 1pm-5.30pm daily. Enjoy an all-you-can-eat vegetarian buffet amid chirping birds, fountains and indoor gardens in this Roma establishment.

Centro Macrobiótico Tao (☎ 5211-4641, Cozumel 76) Set menu US$6. Open 1.30pm-5pm Mon-Sat. This restaurant serves typical macrobiotic fare such as seaweed, pickled vegetables and whole grains.

Mid-Range & Top End *Contra Mar (☎ 5514-3169, Durango 200)* Prices US$4-13. Open 1.30pm-6.30pm daily. This is one of the hottest seafood restaurants in town; try the tuna Contra Mar.

La Tecla (☎ 5525-4920, Durango 186A) Prices US$3-10. Open 1.30pm-midnight Mon-Sat, 1.30pm-6pm Sun. Some of the best alta cocina mexicana in Mexico City is served here, at reasonable prices in an intimate atmosphere. Try the shrimp in tamarind sauce or the fish stuffed with squash blossoms in a *huitlacoche* (corn fungus) sauce.

Cote Sud (☎ 5219-2981, Orizaba 87) Starters US$3.50-6, mains US$7-10. Open 8am-5pm Mon-Tues, 8am-11pm Wed-Sat. This charming French place has cute red-checkered tablecloths, excellent service and good food.

El Discreto Encanto de Comer (☎ 5525-5756, Orizaba 70) Main courses US$15-25. Open 1.30pm-6pm Sun-Tues, 1.30pm-11pm Wed-Sat. At this ritzy French-Mexican restaurant the food is expensive but excellent.

Polanco (Map 7)
Budget & Mid-Range *La Parrilla Suiza (☎ 5538-8015, cnr Avenida Presidente Masaryk & Arquímedes)* Prices US$1.50-6. Open noon-midnight or later daily. For hungry meat eaters, a good economical choice in Polanco is La Parilla Suiza on the traffic circle 600m northwest of the Museo Nacional de Antropología. It gets packed at lunchtime when it serves a comida. They also have mixed grills and tacos.

El Califa de León (☎ 5280-6443, Virgilio 9) Prices US$2-5. Open 1.30pm-3.30am daily. This taco joint serves good tacos and spicy salsa. Try the nopales, a uniquely simple but delicious dish of whole grilled cactus leaves.

For other moderately priced fare in Polanco, head for the section of Avenida Presidente Masaryk between Dumas and France, where a string of sidewalk cafés lines the south side of the street. One of these is:

Te Nutres by Klein's (☎ 5281-3749, *Avenida Presidente Masaryk 360B*) Prices from US$3.50. Open 7.30am-midnight daily. This place serves breakfasts, antojitos, hot and cold tortas, veggie burgers and meat, fish and chicken dishes.

Top End *Rincón Argentino* (☎ 5254-8775, *Avenida Presidente Masaryk 177*) Prices US$28-55. Open 12.30pm-11pm. This Argentine eatery serves the best steaks in town.

Chez Wok (☎ 5281-3410, *Tennyson 117*) Prices around US$14-66. Open 1.30pm-5pm & 7.30pm-11.45pm Mon-Sat, 1.30pm-5pm Sun. Chez Wok makes Mexico's best Chinese food. The menu changes, but everything is excellent. This restaurant is formal and reservations are recommended.

La Gran Casona (☎ 5280-5150, *Dumas 4*) Prices US$5-15. Open 1pm-12.30am Mon-Sat, till 11.30pm Sun. This formal restaurant offers tip-top Mexican cuisine in an elegant setting.

La Hacienda de los Morales (☎ 5281-4554, *Vázquez de Mella 525*) Prices US$25-40. Open 1pm-1am daily. This place is south of Avenida Ejército Nacional. It's easiest to go by taxi. Once a colonial country hacienda, it's now surrounded by the city, which makes the spacious rooms and pretty gardens all the more appealing. Excellent Mexican and international dishes, with some particularly good fish choices, are served in numerous dining rooms by the experienced staff. Reservations are advisable, and dress is formal for dinner (though not for lunch).

Les Célébrités (☎ 5280-1111, *Hotel Nikko México, Campos Elíseos 204*) Full dinner US$30-50. Open 7am-11am, 1.30pm-4.30pm & 7.30pm-11pm Mon-Fri. Polanco's luxury hotels contain some of the city's best restaurants, including this French highlight. Les Célébrités is formal and reservations are recommended.

San Ángel (Map 9)
Budget & Mid-Range *La Casona del Elefante* (☎ 5616-2208, *Plaza San Jacinto 9*) Prices from US$5. Open 1pm-1am Mon-Sat, 1pm-11pm Sun. This Indian restaurant has a few pleasant outdoor tables and is not

a bad value. Try any of the excellent curries or a seafood kabob. Vegetarian *thali* plates are available too.

Crêperie du Soleil (☎ 5616-2682, *Madero 4*) Prices from US$2.50. Open 9am-7pm Tues-Sun. Near Plaza del Carmen, this café does tempting crêpes (sweet and savory), tortas and coffee.

Gandhi (☎ 5292-1394, *Avenida MA de Quevedo 128-132*) Prices from US$2.25. Open 9am-11pm Mon-Fri, 10am-10pm Sat-Sun. This famous bookstore, 400m east of Parque de la Bombilla, has a friendly café where customers linger over coffee, snacks, books, newspapers and chess.

Avenida de la Paz between Revolución and Insurgentes is thick with places to eat.

Cluny (☎ 5550-7350, *Avenida de la Paz 57*) Prices US$4-8. Open 1pm-midnight Mon-Sat, 1pm-10pm Sun. Cluny serves up a scrumptious variety of crêpes both savory and sweet. You'll often have to wait for a table in the evening.

Saxs (☎ 5615-1500, *Insurgentes Sur 1641*) Prices US$3-7. Open 7.30am-midnight Tues-Sat, 7.30am-11pm Sun-Mon. For elegant upscale and delicious vegetarian dining head to Saxs.

Top End *Le Petit Cluny* (☎ 5616-2288, *Avenida de la Paz 58*) Prices from US$9, US$1.50 table charge. Open 8am-midnight Tues-Sat, 8am-10.30pm Sun. Across the street from Cluny's, this is probably San Ángel's best and most popular Italian restaurant. It serves quality pizza and pasta.

San Ángel Inn (☎ 5616-1402, *Diego Rivera 50*) Prices US$5-15, US$2 table charge. Open 1pm-1am daily. To dine in style, head for the San Ángel Inn, a 15-minute walk northwest of Plaza San Jacinto. This is an ex-hacienda with a lovely flowery courtyard and gardens, transformed into a restaurant serving delicious Mexican and European cuisine. Ordering carefully, you can eat two courses cheaply, but you could easily spend a lot on a full meal. If the food prices are too steep, consider just having a drink in the bar; the town's best margaritas (from US$7) are served here.

Coyoacán (Map 10)
For inexpensive Mexican fare, leave Plaza Hidalgo along Higuera. The municipal building on the left is filled with *quesadilla stands*.

El Tizoncito (☎ 5554-7712, Aguayo 3) Prices from US$0.75. If you go half a block north from the plaza, you will find this cheerful place, which is part of the same chain featured in Condesa.

Moheli (☎ 5554-6221, Sosa 1) Prices from US$2.75. Open 9am-10pm daily. This is a good spot for breakfast, snacks or coffee. It is a café-cum-gallery, a few steps from the Jardín del Centenario. You can have yogurt, fruit, granola and honey, a Greek salad, or a bagel with salami.

Entre Vero (☎ 5659-0066, Jardín del Centenario 14-C) Prices US$7-15. Open 11am-11pm daily. This excellent Uruguayan restaurant serves up a variety of meat, seafood, chicken and pasta dishes. The Punta Estena, a fresh seafood salad, is a very good choice.

El Jardín del Pulpo (The Octopus's Garden, ☎ 5658-6152, cnr Allende & Malitzin) Prices US$1-7. Open 10am-6pm daily. On the corner of Coyoacán's main market, 2½ blocks north of Plaza Hidalgo, this excellent restaurant serves fish platters and seafood cocktails or *caldos* (broths). Everyone sits on benches at long tables.

El Sheik (☎ 5659-3311, Madrid 129) Prices from US$2.75. Open 8am-6pm daily. Across the street from the Viveros de Coyoacán, this good Mediterranean place serves up tasty salads, falafel, hummus and meat dishes.

Café El Jarocho (☎ 5658-5029, Cuauhtémoc 134 at Allende) Open 8am-8pm daily. This immensely popular Cuban coffee joint churns out US$0.65 coffees.

ENTERTAINMENT

There's a vast choice of entertainment in Mexico City, as a glance through *Tiempo Libre,* the city's fairly comprehensive what's-on magazine, will show. *Tiempo Libre,* published every Thursday, is sold at newsstands (US$0.70) and appears on the Internet at Ⓦ www.tiempolibre.com.mx. Even with limited Spanish, it's not too hard to decipher what's going on, from music and movies to exhibitions and lots of entertainment for children. *The News* and Mexican newspapers also carry some what's-on information. For art-related events check Ⓦ www.arte-mexico.com.

Auditorio Nacional (☎ 5280-9250, Paseo de la Reforma 50, Bosque de Chapultepec) Major gigs by Mexican and visiting rock and pop performers often take place here.

The ticket agency Ticketmaster (☎ 5325-9000) sells tickets for many of these and other big events, listing them in its free monthly leaflet, *La Guía de Entretenimiento.* Ticketmaster sales outlets can be found at Auditorio Nacional, Paseo de la Reforma 50, Bosque de Chapultepec; and El Palacio de Hierro, Durango 230, Colonia Roma (Map 6). They're also at several locations of Mixup music store, including Avenida Madero 51, Centro Histórico (Map 3); Génova 76, Zona Rosa (Map 5); and Plaza Loreto, San Ángel (Map 9).

'Primera Fila,' a Friday supplement in *Reforma,* also has a lot of good information on all sorts of entertainment.

Dance, Classical Music & Theater

Palacio de Bellas Artes Box office open 11am-7pm Mon-Sat, 9am-7pm Sun. Beside the Alameda Central, the Palacio is home to the Orquesta Sinfónica Nacional (National Symphony Orchestra). It is a big venue for classical music in general, but it's most famous for the Ballet Folklórico de México, a two-hour festive blur of costumes, music and dance from all over Mexico. This famous company has been performing such shows since the 1950s, and they are as spectacular and professional as ever. Tickets are not cheap, however, at US$20 to US$35.50. Performances are normally at 8.30pm Wednesday and 9.30am and 8.30pm Sunday. Tickets are usually available on the day of the show or the day before at the *taquillas* (ticket windows) in the Palacio de Bellas Artes lobby. You can also get them from Ticketmaster (see earlier this Entertainment section for outlets).

On the UNAM campus, *Centro Cultural Universitario* hosts many interesting cultural events; information is available at ☎ 5665-0709 or on the Web at Ⓦ http://difusion.cultural.unam.mx.

The city also offers a big choice of other classical concerts, ballet and contemporary dance, as well as Spanish-language theater; check *Tiempo Libre* for current events.

Cinemas

Foreign movies (except for children's and educational films) are always shown in their original language, with Spanish subtitles.

Cinema tickets are usually around US$3.75, though they're half price in most cinemas on Wednesday. Classic and art-house films are shown at the *Cineteca Nacional* (☎ 5422-1100, Avenida México-Coyoacán 389; Map 10), 700m east of the Coyoacán metro station; the *Centro Cultural Universitario* (☎ 5622-7003, Avenida Insurgentes Sur 3000), in the Ciudad Universitaria; and elsewhere.

The News has partial cinema listings on Friday and Sunday. *Reforma* has daily listings of movies by their original names and their Spanish titles; it also lists addresses of the cinemas covered and includes movie reviews.

Mariachis

Plaza Garibaldi, five blocks north of the Palacio de Bellas Artes (Ⓜ Bellas Artes or Garibaldi), is where the city's mariachi bands gather in the evenings. Outfitted in their fancy costumes, they tootle their trumpets, tune their guitars and stand around with a drink until approached by someone who'll pay for a song (about US$5) or whisk them away to entertain at a party. You can wander and listen to the mariachis in the plaza for free, then stay on in one of the bars or clubs around the plaza, some of which have live Latin dance music as a change from the mariachis. The bars usually have no entry fee and typically charge around US$3 for a shot of tequila or US$50 for a bottle; ask prices *before* you order drinks in these places.

El Tenampa (☎ 5526-6176, Plaza Garibaldi 12) This bar, on the north side of the plaza, has in-house mariachis and is daubed with murals of Mexican film stars.

Plaza Garibaldi gets going by about 8pm and stays busy till around midnight. For food, try the taquerías in the northeast corner of the plaza.

Nightlife

The 'Espectáculos Nocturnos,' 'Espectáculos Populares' and 'Bares y Cantinas' sections in *Tiempo Libre* have fairly good information on live music events, bars/clubs, dance halls, cabaret, jazz and more. Prices for drinks vary quite a bit, but generally beers can always be had for US$1.50 to US$3, and mixed drinks range from US$2 to US$10, depending upon what you order;

rum is cheaper, whiskey and tequilas are usually more expensive.

Centro Histórico & Alameda Central (Map 3)

The downtown area offers a mix of venerable bars and youthful clubs. Thursday, Friday and Saturday nights, from about 10pm, are the happening times. Places veer rapidly in and out of style, but those listed below have been staples of the club and bar scene for years. Hip new places can also be found by looking in the various entertainment guides published in the city.

Pervert Lounge (☎ 5518-0976, Uruguay 70) Ⓜ Isabel la Católica. Admission US$8.50. Open 11pm-6am Thur-Sat. There is a hip and offbeat crowd here, and the music is house, trip-hop and acid jazz.

Restaurante-Bar León (☎ 5510-3093, Brasil 5) Ⓜ Allende and Zócalo. Admission US$5.50, free for women Thur. Open 9.30pm-3am Thur-Sat. This is a very different type of little club, neither flashy nor trendy but a lot of fun. Live salsa, merengue and rumba rhythms drive customers to the tightly packed dance floor.

La Ópera Bar (☎ 5512-8959, Avenida 5 de Mayo 14) Ⓜ Allende or Bellas Artes. Open 1pm-11pm Mon-Sat, 1pm-6pm Sun. Two blocks east of the Palacio de Bellas Artes is this ornate early-20th-century watering hole that opened its doors to women in the 1970s. Booths of dark wood and a massive bar are all original, and there's a hole in the ceiling said to have been made by a bullet from Pancho Villa. There are also lots of midpriced food choices, and musicians serenade. It's a fun place to spend a couple of hours.

Salón Corona (no ☎, Bolívar 24) Ⓜ Bellas Artes. Open 8am-11.30pm daily. Beer lovers should make for this no-frills place. Amiable staff serve up *tarros* (mugs) of light or dark *cerveza de barril* (draft beer) and bottles of almost every known Mexican beer for US$1.50 each. The bar has been going since 1928.

La Perla (no ☎, Cuba 44 at Allende) Ⓜ Bellas Artes. Admission US$4.25. Open at 11pm Thur-Sat. This place has great techno music on Thursday and drag shows at 11.30pm and 1.30am Friday and Saturday.

Zona Rosa (Map 5)

The glitzy Zona Rosa (Ⓜ Insurgentes) peaks from about 11pm to

2am or 3am on Friday and Saturday. At times the Zona can seem pretty sleazy with so many dark-suited bouncers and touts trying to lure business into strip joints and brothels. For the fans of fully clothed entertainment, there are plenty of fun places too. These clubs change by the year and the hot spots tend to be around Hamburgo, Londres, Niza, Avenida Florencia and Génova, as well as on Copenhague.

Cantina Las Bohemias (☎ *5207-4384, Londres 142 at Amberes*) Open 1.30pm-1.30am Mon-Sat. This bright, jolly place is popular with women as well as men.

La Casa del Canto (*no* ☎, *Glorieta Insurgentes CC-04*) Admission US$2. Open 6pm-midnight daily. Live, very raw heavy rock can be experienced at this place near the exit of Insurgentes metro station. It's a small, very basic place, which unleashes the decibels' full effect.

Juárez (Map 4) There are two popular spots a few blocks east of the Zona Rosa in the Juárez area:

El Colmillo (☎ *5592-6114, Versalles 52*) Admission US$13/5.50 men/women. Open 10pm-2am Wed-Sat. This is a groovy hangout owned by a pair of British clubbers. Downstairs there's loud dance music, a dance floor and a bar-lounge area; upstairs there's jazz Thursday to Saturday. The line at the door doesn't keep people waiting long.

Bar Milán (☎ *5592-0031, Milán 18*) Open 9pm-2am Tues-Sun. This is really a fairly straightforward music bar. It plays great, varied music and gets packed by about midnight Thursday through Saturday.

Condesa & Roma (Map 6) The Roma and Condesa areas have recently become dotted with fun and hip bars and dance spots with a mix of young Mexican and foreign patrons.

Mama Rumba (☎ *5564-6920, Querétaro 230*) Admission US$5.50, free for women Tues. Open 9pm-5am Tues-Sat. *The* spot for live Cuban music is this place in Roma, 1km south of the Zona Rosa. The music starts around 11pm and it's funkiest from Thursday to Saturday. The bar is small and tightly packed, but you can't miss its bright neon lights as you approach.

Barracuda (☎ *5211-9346, Nuevo León 4A at Sonora*) Open 7pm-2am daily. This groovy place has a long bar and comfy booths, and while you can't sit at the booths unless you eat, fortunately the food is great. They have live Latin music from 11pm Thursday and a DJ spinning from 11pm Sunday.

Ixchel (☎ *5208-4055, Medellín 65*) Open 1.30pm-midnight Mon-Tues, 1.30pm-2am Wed-Sat. You can enjoy a martini in Ixchel's room draped in blue velvet, or sit outside on the patio. It also has a good restaurant.

Rexo (☎ *5553-5337, Saltillo 1 at Nuevo León*) Open 1pm-2am Tues-Sat, 1pm-1am Sun-Mon. Superhip and supercrowded Rexo also offers a dining area where you can escape the crowds and enjoy the excellent, but expensive, food.

El Centenario (☎ *5553-4454, Vicente Suárez 42*) Open 10am-midnight Mon-Sat. This traditional-style cantina is classy and fun, attracting a young crowd of both men and women.

Hexen Café (☎ *5514-5969, Jalapa 104*) Admission US$3-7. Open 4pm-11pm Mon-Sat. This café and German cultural center has good music ranging from jazz to Brazilian bossa nova to opera Thursday to Saturday nights. It also hosts a German chat night on Tuesday.

Polanco (Map 7) This well-heeled neighborhood north of the Bosque de Chapultepec gets quite lively after dark.

La Martinera (☎ *5281-7235, Avenida France 120*) Open 6pm-midnight Mon-Fri, 11am-midnight Sat, 4pm-midnight Sun. In Plaza Mazarik, between France and Lafontaine, is this hip spot to sip martinis.

Barfly (☎ *5282-2906*) Admission US$5.50. Open 11.30pm-3am Tues-Sat. In the same complex as La Martinera, this place jumps to live Cuban sounds.

Mezzanotte (☎ *5282-0130, cnr Lafontaine & Avenida Presidente Masaryk*) Open 1.30pm-2am daily. In neighboring Plaza Zentro, between Lafontaine and Calderón, is this thriving Italian restaurant that transforms itself into a New York-style dance club after midnight Thursday to Saturday.

San Ángel (Map 9) & Insurgentes Sur *Rockotitlán* (☎ *5687-7893, Insurgentes Sur 953*) Once a time-honored live stage for homegrown Mexican rock music, Rockotitlán, on Plaza Baja California, had been closed for almost a year at the time of writing. It's expected to reopen, however. It formerly opened nightly except Monday, usually at 10pm, and entry price depended on who was on, but ranged from US$1 to US$10. You can drop by to pick up a schedule when (and if) it reopens. About the easiest way to get there is by a 'San Ángel' pesero southbound on Insurgentes from Insurgentes metro station for 4.5km.

La Casona del Elefante (☎ 5616-2208, *Plaza San Jacinto 9)* Admission free with mandatory appetizer order. In San Ángel, this Indian restaurant puts on live jazz from 9.30pm to 1am Friday and Saturday.

Just east toward Revolución is *La Camelia*, a seafood restaurant that becomes a lively music bar for an 18-35 crowd until midnight daily. Across the street from La Camelia is another *Mama Rumba*, with hours and prices the same as the Roma branch.

New Orleans Jazz (☎ 5550-1908, *Avenida Revolución 1655)* Admission US$5.25. Open 8pm-1am Tues-Sun. This place serves up good, varied jazz and is a restaurant too.

Bar Grappa (☎ 5616-4504, *Avenida Revolución & Camino al Desierto de los Leones)* Admission US$10.75. Open 10pm until the crowd dies down, usually around 4am Thur-Sat. Upstairs in Pabellón Altavista mall is this fun place with a youngish, chic crowd. The space is long and dark with a large video screen and loud mixed music.

Coyoacán (Map 10) For free entertainment, you can't beat the musicians, comedians and mimes who turn Coyoacán's central plazas into a big open-air party most evenings and all day Saturday and Sunday. There are also good cafés and bars around the plaza, where you can take in the atmosphere.

El Hijo del Cuervo (☎ 5658-7824, *Jardín del Centenario 17)* Open 5pm-midnight Mon-Wed, 1pm-midnight Thur-Sun. This place, with a youngish crowd of Mexicans and foreigners, plays a mixture of recorded Mexican and gringo rock. It also stages occasional live music or theater and gets busy most evenings.

Dance Halls The city's many Latin dance aficionados have a whole circuit of large *salones de baile*, some capable of holding thousands of people. You need to dress smart and know how to dance salsa, merengue, cumbia or danzón to really enjoy

these places, and it's best to go in a group, or at least with someone to dance with.

Antillanos (☎ 5592-0439, *Pimentel 78, San Rafael)* ⓜ San Cosme. Map 4. Admission US$8.50. Open 8pm-3.30am Thur-Sat. Just north of Jardín del Arte, this is a good place to dance. Top bands from Mexico, Cuba, Puerto Rico or Colombia grind out infectious rhythms.

Meneo (☎ 5523-9448, *Nueva York 315)* Map 1. Admission US$8.50. Open 9pm-3am Thur-Sat. Just west of Insurgentes Sur, the Meneo has salsa and merengue bands. Men must wear a jacket here. To reach this club, take a 'San Ángel' pesero 5km south from Insurgentes metro station.

Salon México (☎ 5518-0931, *2ª Callejón San Juan de Dios 25, Colonia Guerrero)* Open 9pm-3am Thur-Sat. This traditional dance hall attracts fabulous dancers who come strictly to cut a rug; alcohol is not served.

There are several other good dance halls around town, such as the festive *Maraka* (☎ 5682-0636, *cnr Eugenia & Mitla, Colonia Narvarte)*, which is open 9pm-4am Thur-Sat.

Gay & Lesbian Venues *Sergay* magazine, available free in some clubs and bars, has useful information on the Mexico City gay scene. It's on the Internet at ⓦ www.sergay.com.mx. *Tiempo Libre* also has long gay listings on its Web site. The Zona Rosa is the focus of the gay scene.

El Almacén (☎ 5207-0727, *Avenida Florencia 37A)* Map 5. Open 4pm-3am daily. One of the longest-established spots is this relaxed bar, welcoming lesbians as well as gay men.

El Taller (☎ 5533-4984) Map 5. Admission US$5.25. Open 4pm-3am daily. Downstairs from El Almacén is this pounding disco-bar; it is men-only except on Thursday, Friday and Saturday, when women are allowed in.

Cabaré-Tito (☎ 5514-9455, *Londres 161, Plaza del Ángel, Local 20A Interior)* Map 5. Admission US$5.25. Open 4pm-4am daily. This is an innovative gay bar-disco-theater often featuring cabaret, drama or discussion sessions. The venue attracts a wide range of people including some heterosexuals.

Butterfly (☎ 5761-1351, *Izazaga 5, Centro Histórico)* ⓜ Salto del Agua. Map 3. Admission US$5.25. Open 9pm-4am daily, drag shows 11.30pm and 1.30am Fri-Sat. Just a few steps east of Eje Central Lázaro Cárdenas, the Butterfly is a big, hi-tech dance club with great music. The cover charge includes two drinks.

Enigma (☎ 5207-7367, Morelia 111, Roma) Map 6. Admission US$5.25. Open 9pm-4.30am Wed-Sun. About 700m south of Cuauhtémoc metro station, this mainly lesbian disco-bar has regular transvestite shows.

SPECTATOR SPORTS
Soccer
The capital stages two or three *fútbol* (soccer) matches in the national Primera División almost every weekend from August to May. *The News* carries details on upcoming games. Mexico City has five teams: América, nicknamed Las Águilas (the Eagles); Las Pumas, of UNAM; Cruz Azul (known as Los Cementeros); Atlante; and Necaxa, which is due to move to the city of Aguascalientes in 2003.

The biggest match of all is El Clásico, between América and Guadalajara; this game fills the awesome Estadio Azteca with 100,000 flag-waving fans – an occasion surprising for the friendliness of the rivalry between the two bands of fans. This is about the only game of the year in the capital where you should get a ticket in advance.

Match days and times vary somewhat to suit the TV companies, but usually América and Necaxa kick off their home games at 7pm Saturday at the *Estadio Azteca* (☎ 5617-8080, ⓦ *www.esmas.com/estadio azteca, Calzada de Tlalpan 3465; Map 1)*. When games are on, peseros run to the stadium from Tasqueña metro station; you can also get there by the Tren Ligero (streetcar) from Tasqueña metro station to Estadio Azteca station.

The Pumas play home games usually at noon on Sunday in the *Estadio Olímpico* (☎ 5616-2045, Insurgentes Sur, Ciudad Universitaria)*.

Cruz Azul and Atlante play home games usually at 5pm Saturday in the *Estadio Azul* (☎ 5563-9525, Indiana 255, door 1)*, which is next door to the Monumental Plaza México bullring.

Tickets are usually available at the gate right up to game time; prices range from US$2 to US$11.

Baseball
Mexico City has one team in the Liga Mexicana de Béisbol. The Diablos Rojos (officially Club México) play at least three games a week, and games usually start at 6.30pm. Games are staged at the *Foro Sol (☎ 5764-8646, Avenida Río Churubusco, in front of the Palacio de Deportes; ⓜ Cuidad Deportiva)*. The season runs from March to August. Ticketmaster (see Entertainment) sells tickets for games and lists dates in its *La Guía de Entretenimiento. Afición* sports paper also details upcoming games.

Bullfights
One of the largest bullrings in the world, *Monumental Plaza México (☎ 5563-3961, Rodin 241)* is a deep concrete bowl holding 48,000 spectators. It's a few blocks west of Avenida Insurgentes Sur, 5.5km south of Paseo de la Reforma and a 10-minute walk from San Antonio metro station. 'Plaza México' peseros run along Insurgentes Sur on bullfight afternoons.

If you're not put off by its very concept, a *corrida de toros* (bullfight) is quite a spectacle, from the milling throngs and hawkers outside the arena to the pageantry and drama in the ring itself and the response it provokes. Six bulls are usually fought in an afternoon, two each by three matadors.

From October or November to March, professional fights are held at the Monumental most Sundays starting at 4pm. From June to October, junior matadors fight young bulls. *The News* runs a weekly bullfighting column, 'Blood on the Sand,' which will tell you what's in store.

The taquillas (ticket windows) by the main entrance on Rodin have printed lists of ticket prices. The cheapest seats, less than US$2, are in the *Sol General* section, the top tiers of seating on the sunny side of the arena. These are OK if the weather's not too hot – and many of them fall into shade as the afternoon goes on, in any case. Seats in the *Sombra General* section, the top tiers on the shady side, cost slightly more. The best seats are in the *Barreras,* the seven rows nearest the arena, and normally cost US$43. Between the Barreras and the General sections are first the *Primer (1er) Tendido,* then the *Segundo (2°) Tendido.*

Except for the biggest corridas, tickets are available right up to the time the third bull is killed, though the best seats may sell out early. You can buy advance tickets from 9.30am to 1pm and 3.30pm to 7pm Thursday to Saturday, and from 9.30am onward Sunday. Most travel agencies also sell tickets, at a mark-up.

For more on bullfights, see 'The Fiesta Brava' in the Facts for the Visitor chapter.

Horse Races

If you have a hankering to bet, head over to the beautifully renovated *Hipódromo de las Américas* (☎ 5387-0600, **w** *www .hipodromo.com.mx, Avenida Industria Militar, Colonia Residencial Militar*) to watch the ponies run. The races start at 3pm, Friday to Sunday, and last until 8.30pm. General admission is US$1.50, and a seat in the boxes costs an additional US$4.50 per person up to eight people (minimum purchase four people). If it's sunny or rainy, be advised the second level is more sheltered from the elements. Tickets can be purchased in advance through Ticketmaster. There is also a sport book here. The installations are a 20-minute walk from the Cuatro Caminos metro; just turn left upon leaving the station and walk along Avenida Casa de la Moneda, turn right onto Avenida Río San Joaquín, cross the Anillo Periférico, turn right onto Avenida Río San Joaquín, which will become Avenida del Conscripto, then turn left onto Puente Tecamachalco, where an entrance is located.

SHOPPING
Shops

The well-heeled residents of Mexico City do a lot of their shopping in department stores and modern malls. The malls are full of designer clothing and shoe stores, toy shops, jewelers, cosmeticians, sometimes a music store. Among the more interesting of them, for their design or for the shops themselves, are *Plaza Loreto*, between Altamirano and Río de la Magdalena in San Ángel; *Pabellón Altavista*, Avenida Revolución and Camino al Desierto de los Leones, San Ángel; *Perisur*, Periférico Sur 4690, near the intersection with Avenida Insurgentes Sur, with several large department stores; and *Plaza Molière*, at Molière and Horacio in Polanco.

Fonart (☎ 5563-0306, *Patriotismo 691*) Map 1. Open 9am-8pm daily. One of the biggest and best handicrafts stores in the city is this government-run place between the Bosque de Chapultepec and San Ángel (600m north of Mixcoac metro station). The store holds beautiful wares from around the country, ranging from Olinalá lacquered boxes and Oaxacan *alebrijes* (whimsical

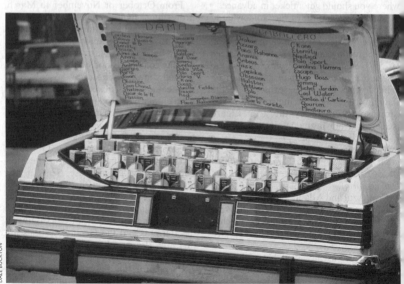

A trunkbed of good smells

representations of animals in wood or papier-mâché) to blankets from Teotitlán del Valle, all sorts of attractive pottery and a big variety of glassware. Prices are fixed and fair.

Centro Histórico (Map 3) The streets south, west and north of the Zócalo are full of shops specializing in everyday goods, from shoes or screws to fireworks or cakes. You'll find clusters of shops selling similar items all together on the same street or block – photography supplies and camera repair around the intersection of Brasil and Donceles, sports gear and backpacks on Carranza west of Bolívar, bridal gowns on Chile north of Tacuba, shoes on Avenida 16 de Septiembre, Pino Suárez and 20 de Noviembre, stationery on El Salvador between Cinco de Febrero and Bolívar. About 50 computer stores huddle in the Plaza de la Computación y Electrónica on Eje Central Lázaro Cárdenas, south of Uruguay.

There are also two large department stores, both open daily, within a block south of the Zócalo: *El Palacio de Hierro* (☎ 5728-9905, 20 de Noviembre 3) and *Liverpool* (☎ 5133-2800, Venustiano Carranza 92).

Zona Rosa (Map 5) This is a good area for boutiques and art and antique shops. Plaza La Rosa, an arcade between Hamburgo and Londres just west of Génova, is a good place to start if you're after clothes. Plaza del Ángel, another arcade between Hamburgo and Londres, this time just west of Amberes, has many classy antique and art shops; more are strung along Hamburgo between Amberes and Florencia and up Estocolmo.

Two of the biggest music stores in the city are *Tower Records* (☎ 5525-4829, Niza 19) and *Mixup* (☎ 5225-3011, Génova 76).

Polanco (Map 7) Designer clothing houses are strung along Avenida Presidente Masaryk in the blocks west of France. The futuristic-looking Plaza Molière mall at Molière and Horacio includes a branch of *El Palacio de Hierro* department store, dealing mainly in clothes, toys and cosmetics.

Markets

There are numerous interesting markets around the city where you can buy all sorts of Mexican handicrafts, souvenirs and everyday goods. For a primer on Mexican handicrafts see the Artesanías special section.

Mercado Insurgentes (Londres between Avenida Florencia & Amberes) Map 5. ⓜ Insurgentes. Open 9.30am-7.30pm Mon-Sat, 10am-4pm Sun. This market in the Zona Rosa is packed with Mexican crafts – silver, textiles, pottery, leather and carved wood figures. You need to bargain a bit to get sensible prices.

Centro de Artesanías La Ciudadela (Balderas at Dondé) Map 3. ⓜ Balderas. Open 10am-6pm daily. About 600m south of Alameda, this market is full of crafts at prices that are fair even before you try to bargain. You'll find brightly dyed sarapes, pretty lacquerware boxes and trays, silver jewelry, pottery, Huichol bead masks, guitars, maracas and baskets of every shape and size, some large enough to hide in.

Mercado de Artesanías San Juan (Dolores & Ayuntamiento) ⓜ San Juan de Letrán. Open 9am-7pm Mon-Sat, 9am-4pm Sun. Four blocks east of Centro de Artesanías La Ciudadela, this market has a similar range of goods and prices that are, if anything, a little cheaper.

Two of the city's biggest markets, both open daily, merge into each other along Rayón and Héroe de Granaditas, 1km north of the Zócalo. Both deal mainly in everyday wares, and they're lively, crowded places. Garibaldi metro station is just west of La Lagunilla, and Lagunilla metro station serves both markets.

La Lagunilla (Map 3) is centered on three large buildings. Building No 1 is full of clothes and fabrics, No 2 is for furniture, and No 3 is devoted to *comestibles* (food). On Sunday the Lagunilla market spreads out from the corner of Allende and Rayon in a sprawl of street stands that hawk everything under the sun, including great antiques.

Tepito (Map 3) takes over where La Lagunilla ends and stretches several hundred meters east along Rayón and Héroe de Granaditas and deep into most of the side streets. Much of what's sold here is said to be *fayuca* (contraband), and the market has a reputation for pickpockets and thieves – so take care. The market is composed mainly of street-side stalls and focuses on clothes (new and secondhand), antiques and leisure goods such as videotapes, CD players, TVs, Rollerblades and toys. The only large building, at Héroe de Granaditas and Aztecas, is packed with every kind of shoe and boot you could imagine.

Centro Artesanal Buenavista (☎ 5526-0315, Aldama 187) Map 1. Open 9am-6pm daily. Just east of the Buenavista train station, this large handicrafts 'market' is actually a huge fixed-price store. Much advertised and often visited by tour groups, it has a vast assortment of stuff. Some of it is quality, but bargains can be scarce.

Tianguis Cultural del Chopo Map 1. Open 10am-4pm Sat. This unusual little market, just north of the Centro Artesanal Buenavista on Hidalgo, is devoted mainly to punk and death-metal music and fashions, but some stalls specialize in other musical genres such as rock, Cuban music and Mexican regional sounds.

Mercado La Merced (1km southeast of the Zócalo) occupies four whole blocks dedicated to the buying and selling of Mexicans' daily needs, which makes for an interesting wander. A couple of blocks south, on the south side of Fray Servando Teresa de Mier, is *Mercado Sonora*, which has four diverse specialties: toys, caged birds, herbs and folk medicine. Merced metro station is in the middle of La Merced market.

Bazar Sábado (Plaza San Jacinto 11) Map 9. Open 10am-7pm Sat. In the southern suburb of San Ángel, this is a showcase for some of Mexico's very best handcrafted jewelry, woodwork, ceramics and textiles. Prices are high but so is quality. At the same time, artists and artisans display work in Plaza San Jacinto itself, in surrounding streets and in nearby Plaza del Carmen. There are some interesting *boutiques* and *antique shops* between the two plazas too.

On Saturday and Sunday a colorful jewelry and crafts market spreads over much of Coyoacán's central Jardín del Centenario (Map 10). Hippie jewelry, Mexican indigenous crafts, leather work and tie-dye clothes are among the stocks-in-trade. Other markets in the neighborhood include *Bazar Artesanal de Coyoacán*, on the west side of the adjoining Plaza Hidalgo, open 10.30am to 8.30pm Saturday and Sunday only; and *Pasaje Coyoacán*, 1½ blocks farther north at Aguayo and Cuauhtémoc, open 11am to 8pm Tuesday to Sunday.

GETTING THERE & AWAY
Air
Airport Aeropuerto Internacional Benito Juárez (☎ 5571-3600; Map 1; ⓜ Terminal Aérea), 6km east of the Zócalo, is Mexico City's only passenger airport.

The single terminal is divided into six salas (halls):

Sala A – domestic arrivals

Sala B – check-in for Aeroméxico, Mexicana and Aero California, Aeromar and some other domestic flights; Hotel Marriott

Sala C – check-in for Aviacsa and Aerolíneas Internacionales

Sala D – check-in for other domestic flights

Sala E – international arrivals

Sala F – check-in for international flights; Hilton Hotel

The terminal has hosts of shops and facilities, including some good bookstores. You can change money at many bank branches and casas de cambio; Tamize in Sala E is one casa de cambio that stays open 24 hours. You can also obtain pesos from numerous ATMs.

There are plenty of pay phones and telephone casetas, plus shops selling cards for the pay phones. In Salas A and E are car rental agencies and luggage lockers (open 24 hours; US$5 for up to 24 hours). Sala A has a tourist information office (☎ 5782-9002), which is open 9am to 7pm daily (it will book hotel rooms for you), and post and telegraph offices. The airport is a bad place to buy film; you'll almost certainly find a better selection and lower prices at your destination.

Direct buses to Cuernavaca, Querétaro, Celaya, Pachuca, Toluca and Puebla depart from outside Sala D. Most go roughly hourly from about 7am to 9pm.

Airlines If you already have an onward air ticket from Mexico City, you're all set. If not, a visit to a couple of the city's many travel agencies (see Information, earlier) is a good way of finding a suitable ticket. Here's where to find the offices of major domestic and international airlines:

Aero California (☎ 5207-1392; Map 5), Paseo de la Reforma 332, Zona Rosa

Aerocaribe (☎ 5536-9046), Xola 535, 28th floor, Colonia del Valle, or through Mexicana

Aerolíneas Argentinas (☎ 5523-7097), Xola 535, 4th floor, Colonia del Valle

Aerolíneas Internacionales (☎ 5543-1223), Beistegui 815, Colonia del Valle

Aerolitoral (see Aeroméxico)

Aeromar (☎ 5784-1139), airport

Aeroméxico (☎ 5133-4000), 14 offices around the city, including Paseo de la Reforma 80 (Map 4) and Paseo de la Reforma 445 (Map 5)

Air France (☎ 5627-6060; Map 7), Poe 90, Polanco

Alaska Airlines (☎ 5533-1747; Map 5), Hamburgo 213, 10th floor, Zona Rosa

Alitalia (☎ 5533-5590), Río Tiber 103, 6th floor, Colonia Cuauhtémoc

Allegro (☎ 5265-0034, 5584-2527), Orizaba 154, Roma Sur

America West (☎ 5511-9779, 800-533-68-62), Río Tiber 103, 6th floor, Colonia Cuauhtémoc

American Airlines (☎ 5209-1400; Map 5), Paseo de la Reforma 300, Zona Rosa

Aviacsa (☎ 5716-9004), airport

Avianca (☎ 5566-8550), Paseo de la Reforma 195

British Airways (☎ 5387-0300), Balmes 8, Colonia Los Morales

Canadian Airlines (☎ 5208-1883; Map 5), Paseo de la Reforma 389, 14th floor

Continental Airlines (☎ 800-706-68-00), Andrés Bello 45, Polanco

Delta Airlines (☎ 5279-0909; Map 5), Paseo de la Reforma 381

Iberia (☎ 5130-3030; Map 4), Paseo de la Reforma 24

Japan Air Lines (☎ 5242-0140; Map 5), Paseo de la Reforma 295

KLM (☎ 5279-5390), Paseo de las Palmas 735, 7th floor, Lomas de Chapultepec

Lufthansa (☎ 5230-0000), Paseo de las Palmas 239, Lomas de Chapultepec

Mexicana (☎ 5448-3000), 19 offices around the city, including Avenida Juárez 82 at Balderas (Map 3) and Paseo de la Reforma 312 at Amberes (Map 5)

Northwest Airlines (☎ 5279-5390), Paseo de las Palmas 735, 7th floor, Lomas de Chapultepec

Qantas (☎ 5628-0547; Map 4), Paseo de la Reforma 10

United Airlines (☎ 5627-0222; Map 5), Hamburgo 213, Zona Rosa

Bus

Mexico City has four main long-distance bus terminals, basically serving the four points of the compass: Terminal Norte (north), Terminal Oriente (called TAPO, east), Terminal Poniente (west) and Terminal Sur (south).

All terminals have baggage checkrooms or lockers charging US$2.25 to US$6.75 per item per 24 hours depending on size. (Beware: Always ask how long luggage can be left before it is considered abandoned and disposed of, and never leave valuables in your luggage!) There are also toilets, newsstands, pay phones or casetas where you can make long-distance calls, post and fax offices, cash machines and cafeterias.

There are also a few buses to nearby cities from Mexico City airport (see Airport under Air, earlier).

For trips up to five hours, it usually suffices to just go to the bus station, buy your ticket and go. For longer trips, many buses leave in the evening or at night, and service may well sell out, so buy your ticket in advance. One helpful resource that could save you an extra trip out to one of the bus stations is Ticket Bus (☎ 5133-2424; W www.ticketbus.com.mx), an agency that sells and reserves tickets for 17 bus lines leaving out of the eastern, northern and southern stations. They have 25 outlets to pick up tickets across Mexico City and a Web site, which provides information about routes as well as the amenities offered by the bus lines.

Turismo Zócalo (☎ 5510-9219; Map 3), Carranza 67, Centro Histórico, sells tickets for the deluxe ETN, UNO and ADO GL services (see the introductory Getting Around chapter).

If you speak some Spanish, you can call the bus companies to ask about schedules; they're listed in the phone directory's yellow pages under 'Camiones y Automóviles Foráneos para Pasajeros.'

Most destinations are served by just one of the four terminals, but for a few major destinations you have a choice of terminals. Some companies require you to check in luggage at their counter at least 30 minutes prior to departure.

The backpackers' van service Mexbus (W www.mexbus.net) began operations in 2001 with daily service between Mexico City and Oaxaca for US$28, running door-to-door between hostels and budget hotels in Oaxaca and downtown Mexico City. It was planned to extend to destinations in Chiapas and the Yucatán Peninsula in 2002. You can book Mexbus at any of the accommodations where it stops, or call ☎ 800-523-94-12.

Second-class buses are more vulnerable to highway robbery on some routes in and out of Mexico City.

Destinations See the 'Buses from Mexico City' table for a list of daily services from Mexico City to a selection of destinations. More information can be found in other town and city sections of this book. It's all subject to change, of course.

Terminal Norte (CN) Terminal Central de Autobuses del Norte (☎ 5587-5200; Map 1; Ⓜ Autobuses del Norte), Avenida de los Cien Metros 4907, is about 5km north of the Zócalo. It is the largest of the four terminals. It serves places north of Mexico City (including cities on the US border), plus some places to the west, including Guadalajara and Puerto Vallarta. Over 30 different bus companies have services from the terminal. Deluxe and 1st-class counters are mostly in the southern half of the terminal, 2nd-class counters are in the northern half. There are luggage-storage areas at the far south end (open 24 hours) and in the central passageway. Near the middle of the main concourse is a tourist information module (☎ 5719-1201), open 9am-7pm daily. There is also a Banorte ATM and a casa de cambio giving poor rates.

Terminal Oriente (TAPO) The Terminal de Autobuses de Pasajeros de Oriente, usually known by its acronym TAPO (☎ 5762-5977; Map 1; Ⓜ San Lázaro), Calzada Ignacio Zaragoza 200 at Avenida Eduardo Molina, is about 2km east of the Zócalo. This is the terminal for buses serving places east and southeast of Mexico City, including Puebla, central and southern Veracruz, Yucatán, Oaxaca and Chiapas.

There's a Banamex ATM in the passage between the metro and the terminal's circular main hall. Luggage lockers are located across from the Banamex ATM.

Terminal Sur Terminal Central de Autobuses del Sur (☎ 5689-9795; Map 10; Ⓜ Tasqueña), Avenida Tasqueña 1320, 10km south of the Zócalo, serves Tepoztlán, Cuernavaca, Taxco, Acapulco and other towns. There are no money-changing facilities here.

Terminal Poniente The Terminal Poniente de Autobuses (☎ 5271-4519; Map 1; Ⓜ Ob-

servatorio), Avenida Sur 122 at Avenida Río de Tacubaya, is south of the Bosque de Chapultepec, 8km southwest of the Zócalo. This is the place for frequent shuttle services to nearby Toluca and for most buses to the state of Michoacán.

Train
All passenger train services from Mexico City have been closed.

Car & Motorcycle
Touring Mexico City by car is strongly discouraged, unless you are familiar with the streets and have a healthy reserve of stamina and patience. You may, however, want to rent a car here for travel outside the city. If you're traveling through Mexico by car, find a hotel that has off-street parking (many do). For safety reasons, avoid driving alone at night in the city.

Another constant hazard is the bogus traffic fine or bribe, extracted by traffic cops as a routine means of increasing their miserly salaries. The airport area is especially rife with corrupt cops.

Rental Many car rental companies have offices at the airport and in or near the Zona Rosa; ask at any of the large hotels there. Most hotels can refer you to a rental agent (who may be the hotel owner's brother-in-law). Prices vary quite a lot. The seemingly better deals offered by some small ones should be compared with a larger chain before you take the plunge. One local firm offering good rates is Casanova Chapultepec (☎ 5514-0449; Map 5), Avenida Chapultepec 442 near the Zona Rosa, with economy-sized Chevys for US$45 a day, including tax, insurance and unlimited kilometers (minimum two days, book one day ahead).

Roadside Assistance The Green Angels (Ángeles Verdes, see the Getting Around chapter) can be contacted in Mexico City at ☎ 5250-8221. Apoyo Vial (☎ 5532-3800), another road-assistance program, can be contacted 7am to 9pm Monday to Friday, 9am to 9pm Saturday to Sunday. These roving mechanics, suited up in yellow jumpsuits and mounted on motorcycles, buzz through the city providing on-the-spot help to motorists in need, with the aim of keeping traffic flowing smoothly.

Buses from Mexico City

Destination	Distance (km)	Journey (hours)	Terminal in Mexico City	Class	Bus Company	No of Daily Departures	Price (US$)
Acapulco	400	5-6	Sur	deluxe	Estrella de Oro	6	38
				deluxe	Turistar Ejecutivo	3	38
				1st	Futura	5	25
				1st	Estrella de Oro	25	25
				2nd	Futura	21	21
Bahías de Huatulco	850	15-17	Oriente (TAPO)	deluxe	Cristóbal Colón Plus	1	50
			Oriente (TAPO)	1st	Cristóbal Colón	2	43
Campeche	1155	16-17	Oriente (TAPO)	deluxe	ADO-GL	1	82
				1st	ADO	3	72
			Norte	1st	ADO	1	72
Cancún	1649	23	Oriente (TAPO)	deluxe	ADO-GL	1	112
				1st	ADO	3	95
Chetumal	1345	24	Oriente (TAPO)	1st	ADO	2	65
Chihuahua	1487	20	Norte	1st	Transportes Chihuahuenses	19	97
				1st	Ómnibus de México	9	85
Ciudad Juárez	1863	26	Norte	1st	Futura/Elite	18	122
				1st	Ómnibus de México	1	122
Cuernavaca	90	1¼	Sur	1st	Pullman de Morelos	frequent	5
			Airport	1st	Pullman de Morelos	16	9.50
Guadalajara	535	7-8	Norte	deluxe	ETN	23	53
				1st	Primera Plus	27	38
				1st	Futura/Elite	19	38
				2nd	Flecha Amarilla	22	30
			Poniente	deluxe	ETN	7	53
Guanajuato	365	4½	Norte	deluxe	ETN	9	31
				1st	Primera Plus	10	25
				2nd	Flecha Amarilla	4	17.50
Jalapa	315	5	Oriente (TAPO)	deluxe	ADO-Gl	6	20
				1st	ADO	21	17
				2nd	AU	19	11
Matamoros	975	15	Norte	1st	Futura/Elite	5	70

MEXICO CITY

Buses from Mexico City

Destination	Distance (km)	Journey (hours)	Terminal in Mexico City	Class	Bus Company	No of Daily Departures	Price (US$)
Mazatlán	1041	15	Norte	1st	Futura/Elite	18	67
				2nd	Transportes del Norte de Sonora	frequent	60
Mérida	1332	19	Oriente (TAPO)	deluxe	ADO-GL	1	93
				1st	ADO	3	81
			Norte	1st	ADO	1	81
Mexicali	2667	40	Norte	1st	Futura/Elite	16	128
				1st	Transportes del Pacífico	12	128
				2nd	Transportes Norte de Sonora	9	110
Monterrey	934	11–12	Norte	deluxe	Turistar	10	83
				1st	Futura/Elite	18	64
Morelia	304	4	Poniente	deluxe	ETN	28	26
				1st	Pegasso Plus	35	20
				2nd	Herradura de Plata	11	16
				2nd	Vía Plus/2000	13	17
			Norte	1st	Primera Plus	19	20
				2nd	Flecha Amarilla	59	16
Nogales	2227	33	Norte	1st	Futura/Elite	5	130
				1st	Transportes del Pacífico	4	131
Nuevo Laredo	1158	15	Norte	deluxe	Turistar	6	107
				1st	Estrella Blanca	18	79
Oaxaca	470	6½	Oriente (TAPO)	deluxe	UNO	6	41
					ADO-GL	6	31
				1st	Cristóbal Colón	3	27
					ADO	16	27
				2nd	AU	12	21
			Sur			4	20
			Sur	deluxe	Cristóbal Colón-Plus	3	31
				1st	ADO	6	26
				1st	Cristóbal Colón	4	27
				2nd	AU	13	20
Palenque	1010	12	Oriente (TAPO)	1st	ADO	2	57
Papantla	290	5	Norte	1st	ADO	5	15
Pátzcuaro	370	5	Poniente	1st	Pegasso Plus	10	22
				2nd	Flecha Amarilla	2	18
			Norte	1st	Primera Plus	2	22
				2nd	Herradura de Plata	6	18

Buses from Mexico City

Destination	Distance (km)	Journey (hours)	Terminal in Mexico City	Class	Bus Company	No of Daily Departures	Price (US$)
Puebla	123	2	Oriente (TAPO)	deluxe	Estrella Roja	24	9
				deluxe	ADO-GI	23	9
				1st	Primera Más	53	8
				1st	ADO	frequent	8
				2nd	Estrella Roja	84	7
				2nd	AU	102	7
			Norte	1st	ADO	55	8
			Sur	1st	Cristóbal Colón	16	8
			Airport	2nd	Estrella Roja	42	12.50
Puerto Escondido	750	18	Sur	1st	Cristóbal Colón	1	44
Puerto Vallarta	880	12-13	Norte	1st	Futura/Elite	4	70
Querétaro	215	2½-3	Norte	deluxe	ETN	37	20
				1st	Primera Plus	48	16
				1st	Futura/Elite	48	16
				1st	Ómnibus de México	38	15
				2nd	Flecha Amarilla	82	12
			Airport	1st	Aero Plus	14	20
San Cristóbal de Las Casas	1065	16	Oriente (TAPO)	deluxe	UNO	1	102
				deluxe	Maya de Oro	1	71
				1st	Cristóbal Colón	3	59
				1st	Altos	1	55
San Luis Potosí	417	5-6	Norte	deluxe	ETN	16	36
				1st	Primera Plus	6	30
				1st	Futura/Elite	24	28
				1st	Ómnibus de México	15	28
				2nd	Flecha Amarilla	19	25
San Miguel de Allende	280	3½-4	Norte	deluxe	ETN	4	23
				1st	Primera Plus	3	20
				1st	Pegasso Plus	2	20
				2nd	Flecha Amarilla	30	16
				2nd	Herradura de Plata	29	16
Tapachula	1157	19	Oriente (TAPO)	deluxe	UNO	1	100
				1st	Cristóbal Colón	6	65
			Norte	1st	Cristóbal Colón	2	65
			Sur	1st	Cristóbal Colón	1	65
Taxco	170	2	Sur	1st	Futura	1	10
				1st	Estrella de Oro	6	9

MEXICO CITY

Buses from Mexico City

Destination	Distance (km)	Journey (hours)	Terminal in Mexico City	Class	Bus Company	No of Daily Departures	Price (US$)
Teotihuacán	50	1	Norte	2nd	Autobuses México-San Juan Teotihuacan	33**	2
Tepoztlán	80	1	Sur	1st	Cristóbal Colón	frequent	5
					Pullman de Morelos	hourly till 8pm	5
Tijuana	2848	42	Norte	1st	Futura/Elite	18	139
				2nd	Transportes del Norte de Sonora	frequent	121
Toluca	64	1	Poniente	deluxe	ETN	40	4.75
				1st	TMT	frequent	3.50
				2nd	Flecha Roja	frequent	3.25
			Airport	1st	TMT	19	5
Tula	65	1¼	Norte	1st	Ovnibus	21	4.25
				2nd	AVM	72	3
Tuxtla Gutiérrez	1015	14	Oriente (TAPO)	deluxe	UNO	1	95
				deluxe	Maya	2	68
				1st	Cristóbal Colón	4	57
				1st	ADO	2	59
Uruapan	402	6	Poniente	deluxe	ETN	10	35
				1st	Vía Plus/2000	11	28
				1st	Flecha Amarilla	5	28
			Norte	1st	Primera Plus	6	29
				2nd	Flecha Amarilla	3	20
Veracruz	402	5	Oriente (TAPO)	deluxe	UNO	1	39
				deluxe	ADO-GL	4 per week	28
				1st	ADO	17	24
				2nd	AU	18	20
			Norte	1st	ADO	7	27
Villahermosa	768	11	Oriente (TAPO)	deluxe	UNO	3	78
				deluxe	ADO-GL	1	57
				1st	ADO	5	50
				2nd	AU	3	45
			Norte	deluxe	ADO-GL	1	57
				1st	ADO	5	50
Zacatecas	600	6-8	Norte	1st	Ómnibus de México	1	42
Zihuatanejo	640	9	Sur	deluxe	Estrella de Oro	1	52
				1st	Estrella de Oro	3	37
				1st	Futura	6	38

**7 am to 3 pm; make sure your bus is heading for 'Los Pirámides'

GETTING AROUND

Crime levels make some precautions advisable on all transport – please read the Dangers & Annoyances section earlier in this chapter.

Mexico City has a good, cheap, easy-to-use metro (underground railway). Peseros (minibuses), buses and/or trolley buses ply all main routes and are also cheap and useful. Taxis are plentiful but some are potentially hazardous (see Dangers & Annoyances in the Information section, earlier this chapter).

Obvious though it may sound, always look both ways when you cross a street. Some one-way streets have bus lanes running counter to the flow of the rest of the traffic, and traffic on some divided streets runs in the same direction on both sides.

To/From the Airport

Unless you are renting a car, use a taxi or the metro to travel to and from the airport. No bus or pesero runs directly between the airport and city center.

Metro Officially, you're not supposed to travel on the metro with anything larger than a shoulder bag – and at busy times the crowds make it inadvisable in any case. However, this rule is often not enforced at quieter times, especially before 7am, after 9pm and on Sunday.

The airport metro station is Terminal Aérea, on *Línea* (Line) 5. It's 200m from the airport terminal building: leave the terminal by the exit at the end of Sala A (the domestic-flight arrivals area) and continue walking in the same direction until you see the metro logo, a stylized 'M,' and the steps down to the station. One ticket costs US$0.15. To get to hotels in the city center, follow signs for 'Dirección Pantitlán'; at Pantitlán station you have to change trains: follow signs for 'Dirección Tacubaya' (Línea 9). Change trains again at Chabacano, where you follow signs for 'Dirección Cuatro Caminos' (Línea 2), which takes you to the Zócalo, Allende, Bellas Artes, Hidalgo and Revolución stations (but note the warning about Hidalgo in Dangers & Annoyances). To get to the Zona Rosa take 'Dirección Observatorio' (Línea 1) at the

Pantitlán station and get off at Metro Insurgentes.

Line A and the lines from Tasqueña to Embarcadero (to Xochimilco) are served by the *tren ligero* (above-ground streetcar) system. There are ambitious plans for light-rail commuter lines, but currently the two spur extensions of the metro are the only additional lines available.

Taxi Do not take green street cabs from the airport. Safe and comfortable 'Transportación Terrestre' taxis to/from the airport are reliable and controlled by a fixed-price ticket system.

To reserve a Transportación Terrestre taxi *to* the airport call ☎ 5571-9344. At the airport, three kiosks in the terminal sell Transportación Terrestre tickets: one is in the international baggage-collection area, one is in Sala E (the international arrivals area), and the other is in Sala A (domestic arrivals). Maps on display near the kiosks divide the city into *zonas* (zones) that determine the fare from the airport. You can choose between *ordinario* (sedans) and more expensive *ejecutivo* (vans). The Zócalo is in zona 2 (US$8.50 ordinario), the Alameda Central is in zona 3 (US$10.75) and the Zona Rosa is in zona 4 (US$12). One ticket is valid for up to four people and luggage that will fit in the trunk of the cab. If you simply mention a landmark such as 'Zócalo' or 'Plaza de la República' to the ticket clerk, you should receive a ticket for the correct zone. But it's advisable to check the map, and count your change, as rip-offs are not unknown.

Walk to the taxi stand (taxi rank) and hand the ticket to the driver after getting into the car. (Porters may want to take your ticket and your luggage the few steps to the taxi and will then importune you for a tip.) The driver is not supposed to expect a tip for the ride, but may expect one for helping with your bags.

To/From the Bus Terminals

The metro is the fastest and cheapest way to any bus terminal, but the prohibition against luggage bigger than a shoulder bag may keep you from using it. Each terminal is also reachable by bus, pesero and/or trolley bus. Do not take street taxis away from the bus stations. All the stations operate ticket-taxi systems; these *taxis autorizados* are cheaper than those from the airport.

Terminal Norte (CN) From Terminal Norte you can reach the Centro by trolley bus, pesero or bus. Trolley buses marked 'Eje Central,' 'Tasqueña,' 'Terminal Sur' or 'Central Camionera del Sur' waiting in front of the terminal head south along Eje Central Lázaro Cárdenas, going within one block of the Alameda Central and six blocks from the Zócalo, and terminate at the Terminal Sur at Tasqueña, some 15km from the Terminal Norte. Fare is US$0.15. For peseros or buses going from Terminal Norte to downtown, cross under the road through the underpass. Vehicles heading for central areas include those marked 'M(etro) Insurgentes,' 'M(etro) Revolución,' 'M(etro) Hidalgo' and 'M(etro) Bellas Artes.'

To reach the Terminal Norte from central areas, you can take peseros, trolley buses or buses heading north on Eje Central at Donceles, one block north of the Palacio de Bellas Artes. They're marked with some variation of the terminal's name such as 'Central Camionera Norte,' 'Central Norte,' 'Terminal Norte' or 'Central Camionera.' On Avenida Insurgentes, anywhere north of Insurgentes metro station, take a northbound 'Central Camionera' or 'Central Norte' bus or pesero.

The metro station (on Línea 5) serving Terminal Norte goes by several different names; outside the front door of the station it is named Autobuses del Norte, but on some maps it's marked 'Central Autobuses del Norte,' or 'Autobuses Norte,' or just 'TAN' (for Terminal de Autobuses del Norte). Traveling from the Terminal Norte to the Centro, follow signs for 'Dirección Pantitlán,' then change at La Raza, or at Consulado then Candelaria. At La Raza you must walk for seven or eight minutes.

The terminal's *taxi autorizado* kiosk is in the central passageway; a cab for one to four people to the Plaza de la República, Alameda, Zócalo or Terminal Oriente (TAPO), all in zone 3, costs US$4.50 (add US$1.50 to fares between 10pm and 6am).

Terminal Oriente (TAPO) For peseros or city buses from TAPO, follow the signs

to Calle Eduardo Molina; the bus stop is on the road outside. Peseros marked 'Zócalo' or 'Alameda' run to the city center, passing a few blocks north of the Zócalo.

This bus terminal is next door to San Lázaro metro station.

The taxi autorizado fare to the Zócalo (zona 1) is US$2.25; to the Zona Rosa (zona 3), US$3.75. Add US$1.50 between 9pm and 6am.

To get to TAPO from central parts of the city, you can take a 'M(etro) San Lázaro' pesero on Arriaga at Mariscal near Plaza de la República, or heading east on Donceles north of the Zócalo.

Terminal Sur 'Eje Central' and 'Central Camionera Norte' trolley buses run north from Terminal Sur along Eje Central Lázaro Cárdenas to the Palacio de Bellas Artes in the city center then on to the Terminal Norte. Walk to the left from Terminal Sur's main exit, and you'll find the trolley buses waiting on the far side of the main road.

Heading south from the city center to Terminal Sur, trolley buses are marked with some combination of 'Eje Central,' 'Tasqueña/Taxqueña,' 'Autobuses Sur,' 'Terminal Sur' or 'Central Camionera del Sur.' You can pick them up one block north of the Palacio de Bellas Artes, on the Eje Central at Santa Veracruz. From San Ángel or Coyoacán, you can take a 'M(etro) Tasqueña' pesero or bus east on Avenida Miguel Ángel de Quevedo.

Tasqueña metro station is a two-minute walk from Terminal Sur through a crowded hawkers' market.

A taxi autorizado from Terminal Sur costs US$5.50 to the Zona Rosa, Alameda or Zócalo (zona 4), and US$6.25 to the streets north of Plaza de la República (zona 5). Add US$1.50 between 10pm and 6am.

Terminal Poniente Observatorio metro station is a couple of minutes' walk from the terminal. A taxi ticket to the Zona Rosa costs US$5.50, to the Zócalo US$6.50. Add US$1.50 between 9pm and 6am.

Bus, Pesero & Trolley Bus

About 2.5 million people use Mexico City's thousands of peseros (also called

RICHARD I'ANSON

ural detail from Casa de Cortés, Mexico City

RICHARD I'ANSON

Palacio de Bellas Artes, Mexico City

RICHARD I'ANSON

ztec performer, Mexico City's Zócalo

RICHARD NEBESKY

Wall of skulls, Templo Mayor, Mexico City

GREG ELMS

ood stalls at a Mexico City market

Off to work, Mexico City

Palacio de Iturbide, Mexico City

Mexico City's mega-skyline

'One more bite and I'll buy that flying elephant

micros or *minibuses)* and buses daily. The peseros and buses operate from about 5am to midnight and are most crowded during the rush hours, which are roughly 7.30am to 10am and 5pm to 7pm. During other hours, the routes of most use to travelers are not too crowded.

Peseros are usually gray and green minibuses, but occasionally, in the outer suburbs, they're Volkswagen *combi* vehicles. They run along fixed routes, often starting or ending at metro stations, and will stop to pick up or drop off at virtually any street corner. Route information is displayed on the front of vehicles, often painted in random order on the windshield. Fares are US$0.20 for trips of up to 5km, US$0.25 for 5 to 12km, and US$0.35 for more than 12km. Add 20% between 10pm and 6am.

Municipally operated full-size buses are gradually replacing peseros, which are privately owned, on many routes. Buses, and the few trolley bus services, are more limited in their stops than peseros; fares are US$0.20 or so. There are a few express buses, which stop only every kilometer or so.

Information on services to specific places around the city is given in the relevant sections of this chapter.

Metro

The metro system offers the quickest and most crowded way to get around Mexico City. The fare is US$0.20 a ride, including transfers.

About 4.7 million people ride the metro on an average weekday, making it the world's third-busiest underground railway, after Moscow's and Tokyo's. At last count it had 167 stations and 191km of track on 11 *líneas* (lines).

The stations are generally clean and well organized but are often crowded, sometimes fearfully so. Cars at the ends of trains are usually the least crowded. The platforms can become dangerously packed with passengers during the morning and evening rush hours (roughly 7.30am to 10am and 5pm to 7pm). At these times some trains have cars reserved for women and children, boarded through special *'Solo Mujeres y Niños'* lanes. Generally speaking, the best times to ride the metro are late morning, in the evening and Sunday.

All lines operate 5am to 11.30pm Monday to Friday, 6am to 12.30am Saturday (into Sunday) and 7am to 11.30pm Sunday.

With such crowded conditions, it's not surprising that pickpocketing is popular and that luggage bigger than a shoulder bag is not allowed. Be careful with belongings. Hidalgo station is particularly notorious for thefts.

The metro is easy to use. Signs in stations reading 'Dirección Pantitlán,' 'Dirección Universidad' and so on name the stations at the ends of the metro lines. Check a map for the *dirección* you want. Buy a *boleto* (ticket), or several at once, at the booth, feed it into the turnstile, and you're on your way.

When changing trains, look for 'Correspondencia' (Transfer) signs.

Taxi

Please see 'Taxi Crime,' earlier in this chapter.

Mexico City has several classes of taxi. The cheapest are the regular cruising street cabs, mostly Volkswagen Beetles but also small Nissans and other Japanese models. They have license plate numbers beginning with the letter L (for *libre*, or free) and a green stripe along the bottom of the license plate. Larger and more expensive, but safer, are radio taxis, Transportación Terrestre cabs from the airport, and *sitio* (taxi stand) cabs, which have license plates beginning with S and bearing an orange stripe.

Driving Restrictions

To help combat pollution, Mexico City operates its Hoy No Circula (Don't Drive Today) program banning many vehicles, wherever they are registered, from being driven in the city between 5am and 10pm on one day each week. The major exceptions are cars of 1993 model or newer (supposedly less polluting), which have a *calcomanía de verificación* (verification hologram sticker) numbered 0. This sticker is obtained under the city's notoriously corrupt (and in the process of being reformed) vehicle pollution assessment system.

For other vehicles (including foreign-registered ones), the last digit of the license plate number determines the day when they cannot circulate. Any car may operate on Saturday and Sunday:

day	prohibited last digits
Monday	5, 6
Tuesday	7, 8
Wednesday	3, 4
Thursday	1, 2
Friday	9, 0

Several times a year, when ozone readings in the city top 240 IMECA points (see 'Mexico City's Air'), the city's environmental contingency plan comes into action, with a Doble Hoy No Circula (Double Don't Drive Today) rule. This rule affects foreign-registered vehicles and vehicles with verification hologram No 2 (older, more polluting vehicles). Those with plates ending in an even digit are banned on the first day, and those ending in an odd digit are banned the next. If the contingency lasts into a third day, all hologram No 2 vehicles are banned. Doble Hoy No Circula remains in effect even during weekends.

Cars with hologram No 1 (intermediate polluters) follow the simple Hoy No Circula restrictions all the time, even during contingency phases one and two. Further information on the driving restriction program is available at **w** www.sima.com.mx.

In cruising cabs, fares are computed by *taxímetro* (digital meter). At this writing, they should start with 4.80 pesos on the meter. The total cost of a 3 or 4km ride in moderate traffic – from the Zócalo to the Zona Rosa – should be about US$1.50 to US$2. Between 11pm and 6am, 20% is added to fares.

A radio or sitio cab costs three or four times as much, but it can't be emphasized enough that the extra cost brings a degree of security you could never have in a cruising cab.

You need not tip taxi drivers unless they have provided some special service.

Around Mexico City

Some of the best things to see and do in Mexico are within a day's travel of the capital. Many of them, such as the ancient city of Teotihuacán or the picturesque town of Tepoztlán, can easily be visited as day trips. Other destinations, such as the colonial cities of Puebla and Taxco, are a bit farther away and have so many attractions that you should plan to spend at least one night.

Alternatively, you can stop at most of the places covered in this chapter on your way between the capital and other parts of Mexico. This chapter is divided into four sections – north, east, south and west of Mexico City – and each covers at least one major route to/from the capital. Another option is a circular tour around the capital, which would make a fascinating trip. The roads going around the Distrito Federal generally are not quite as good as those going to and from it, but it is still quite feasible to take this option, either in your own vehicle or on local buses.

Geographically, the whole area is elevated. South of Mexico City, the Cordillera Neovolcánica, with Mexico's highest volcanoes, runs from Pico de Orizaba in the east to Nevado de Toluca in the west (and continues as far west as Colima). North of this range is the Altiplano Central (Central Plateau). The altitude makes for a very pleasant climate, cooler and less humid than the lowlands, with rain falling in brief summer downpours. It also makes for a variety of landscapes, from dramatic gorges to fertile plains, fragrant pine forests and snow-capped peaks. Geologically, it remains an active area, with some still-smoking volcanoes and natural hot springs.

Historically, the area was home to a succession of important indigenous civilizations (notably Teotihuacán, Toltec and Aztec) and a crossroads of trade and cultural exchange. By the late 15th century, all but one of the small states of central Mexico were under the domination of the Aztec empire. Remnants of pre-Hispanic history can be seen at many archaeological sites and in museums rich with artifacts; the Museo Amparo in Puebla gives an excellent overview of the area's history and culture.

After the conquest, the Spanish transformed central Mexico, establishing ceramic industries at Puebla, mines at Taxco and Pachuca, and haciendas producing wheat, sugar and cattle. Most towns still have a

Highlights

- Teotihuacán – Mexico's biggest ancient city and the site of two enormous, spectacular pyramids

- Volcanoes – the towering volcanoes of Popocatépetl, a smoking behemoth ringed by tranquil villages, and Iztaccíhuatl, a snowcapped challenge for mountaineers

- Cacaxtla ruins – with their vividly colored frescoes of warriors in battle

- Puebla – a charming city which faithfully preserves the Spanish imprint

- Taxco – Mexico's picturesque silver capital, a gorgeous colonial antique

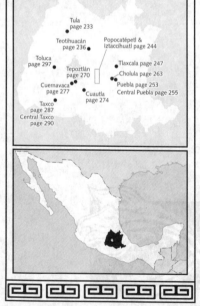

central plaza surrounded by Spanish colonial buildings. The Catholic church used the area as a base for its missionary activities in Mexico and left a series of fortified monasteries and imposing churches.

Despite the rich historical heritage, this is a modern part of Mexico, with large industrial plants and up-to-date transport and urban infrastructure. On weekends, many places near Mexico City typically attract crowds of visitors from the capital. Generally, this means that there are ample facilities available during the week, and if a place is crowded it likely won't be with foreigners.

North of Mexico City

Two main routes go to the north of Mexico City. Highway 57D goes past the colonial town of Tepotzotlán, swings northwest past the turnoff for Tula with its Toltec ruins, and continues to Querétaro (see the Northern Central Highlands chapter). Highway 130D goes northeast from the capital to Pachuca, a mining town since colonial times. Highway 132D branches east off 130D past the old monastery at Acolman and the vast archaeological zone of Teotihuacán, then cuts across a starkly beautiful plateau before reaching Tulancingo, the state of Hidalgo's second largest city. From Pachuca, routes go north into the Huasteca region or east to the Gulf Coast (see the Central Gulf Coast chapter), traversing some spectacular landscapes as the fringes of the Sierra Madre descend to the coastal plain.

TEPOTZOTLÁN
• pop 39,000 • elev 2300m ☎ 55
About 41km north of central Mexico City, just beyond its urban sprawl, the town of Tepotzotlán has a pleasant central plaza, an extreme example of Churrigueresque architecture and the Museo Nacional del Virreinato (National Museum of the Viceregal Period).

The Jesuit Iglesia de San Francisco Javier, beside the *zócalo,* was originally built from 1670 to 1682; elaborations carried out in the 18th century made it one of Mexico's most lavish churches. The façade, with its single tower, is a phantasmagoric array of carved saints, angels, people, plants and more, while the interior walls, and the Camarín del Virgen adjacent to the altar, are covered with a circus of gilded and multicolored ornamentation.

Access to the Iglesia de San Francisco Javier is through the adjacent monastery. In the 1960s both the church and monastery were restored and transformed into the **Museo Nacional del Virreinato** *(admission US$3.50, free Sun; open 10am-5pm Tues, 9am-6pm Wed-Sun).* Among the fine art and folk art gathered here are silver chalices, pictures created from inlaid wood, porcelain, furniture and some of the finest religious paintings and statues from the epoch. Don't miss the Capilla Doméstica, whose Churrigueresque main altarpiece is thick with mirrors. To get to the church, turn to the right after you enter, go down the hall and then downstairs.

Tepotzotlán's highly regarded Christmas *pastorelas,* or Nativity plays, are performed inside the former monastery. Tickets for the event, which includes Christmas dinner and piñata smashing, can be purchased at La Hostería de Tepotzotlán (see Places to Stay & Eat).

Places to Stay & Eat
Tepotzotlán is primarily geared to daytrippers, but several good hotels make an overnight stay possible.

Hotel Posada San José (☎ 5876-0835, *Plaza Virreinal 3)* Interior rooms US$17, rooms with view of the church US$23-34. On the south side of the zócalo, this colonial-style hotel has lovely rooms with TV and private bath.

Posada del Cid (☎ 5876-0064, *Insurgentes 12)* Singles/doubles US$13.50/20. This hotel is about 500m from the zócalo on the way to the *autopista.* The rooms have no frills, but they're clean and cheap and they don't smell bad.

Hotel Posada del Virrey (☎/fax 5876-1864, *Insurgentes 13)* Singles/doubles with TV US$23/34. Across the street from the Posada del Cid, this hotel is a brighter, more comfortable option. It has clean, colorful rooms on two arcaded levels around a dirt courtyard/parking lot. Some rooms are equipped with Jacuzzi. The entrance is on Colón.

La Hostería de Tepotzotlán (☎ 5876-0243, *Plaza Virreinal 1)* Prices US$2.50-7.

AROUND MEXICO CITY

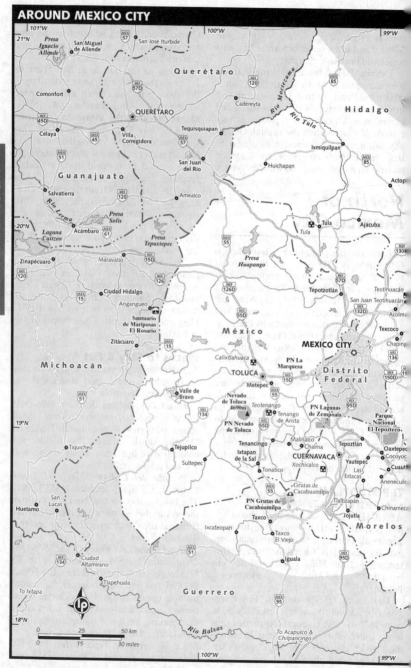

AROUND MEXICO CITY

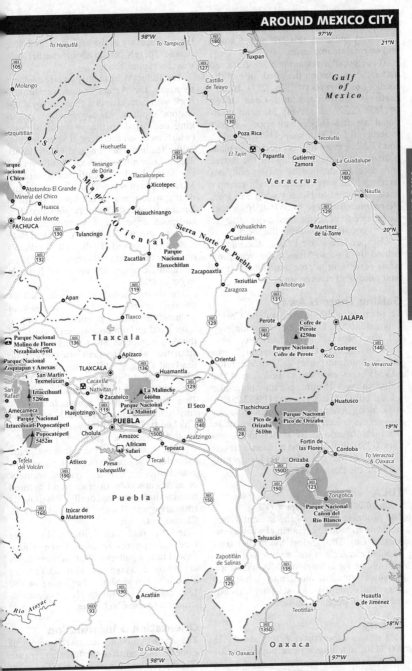

AROUND MEXICO CITY

To Huejutla
98°W
To Tampico
MEX 180
97°W
21°N

Tuxpan

MEX 105

Molango

Castillo de Teayo

Gulf of Mexico

etzquitlán

MEX 127

MEX 130

Sierra

Huehuetla

Poza Rica

Tecolutla

MEX 130

El Tajín

Papantla

Gutiérrez Zamora

La Guadalupe

arque acional l Chico

Tenango de Doria

Tlacuilotepec

Madre

Xicotepec

MEX 180

Veracruz

Nautla

Atotonilco El Grande

Mineral del Chico

Huasca

Huauchinango

Oriental

Yohualichán

Cuetzalan

Martinez de la Torre

MEX 129

20°N

Real del Monte

PACHUCA

MEX 130

Tulancingo

Sierra Norte de Puebla

Zacatlán

Parque Nacional Eloxochitlan

Zacapoaxtla

Teziutlán

Altotonga

MEX 132

Zaragoza

MEX 131

Apan

MEX 119

Perote

Cofre de Perote 4250m

JALAPA

Tlaxco

MEX 129

MEX 140

Parque Nacional Molino de Flores Nezahualcóyotl

Tlaxcala

Parque Nacional Cofre de Perote

Coatepec

MEX 140

Xico

To Veracruz

Parque Nacional Zoquiapan y Anexas

Apizaco

MEX 136

TLAXCALA

MEX 136

Huamantla

Oriental

San Martín Texmelucan

Cacaxtla

Nativitas

Huatusco

San Rafael

Iztaccíhuatl 5286m

Zacatelco

La Malinche 4460m

MEX 129

El Seco

Tlachichuca

Parque Nacional Pico de Orizaba

Amecameca

Huejotzingo

MEX 119

Parque Nacional La Malintzi

Parque Nacional Iztaccíhuatl-Popocatépetl

PUEBLA

MEX 150D

MEX 140

Pico de Orizaba 5610m

MEX 28

Popocatépetl 5452m

Cholula

Amozoc

Acatzingo

Fortín de las Flores

Córdoba

Tetela del Volcán

Atlixco

Africam Safari

Tepeaca

Tecali

Orizaba

To Veracruz & Oaxaca

MEX 190

Presa Valsequillo

MEX 150D

Puebla

MEX 150

MEX 150

MEX 123

Zongolica

MEX 160

Izúcar de Matamoros

Parque Nacional Cañón del Río Blanco

Tehuacán

Zapotitlán de Salinas

MEX 135

MEX 190

Acatlán

MEX 125

MEX 93

Huautla de Jiménez

Río Atoyac

Teotitlán

MEX 135D

18°N

To Oaxaca

To Oaxaca

Oaxaca

98°W

97°W

Open 10am-5pm Tues, 9am-6pm Wed-Sun. Occupying a pretty courtyard within the monastery museum, this café serves soups and original main courses.

Three popular restaurants are clustered under the arcades on the north side of the zócalo: *Los Virreyes* (☎ 5876-0235), *Montecarlo* (☎ 5876-0586) and *Casa Mago* (☎ 5876-0229), all serving Mexican traditional favorites. They're a bit pricey – expect to shell out US$3 for soup, US$4 for salad, and US$8 or more for beef or chicken main courses – but you're paying for the festive ambiance, heightened by roving *ranchero* bands, which play Mexican-style country music. Adjacent to Hotel Posada San José, *Restaurant-Bar Pepe* (☎ 5876-0520) is similarly priced but smaller and more intimate than its counterparts across the zócalo.

Cheaper fare is available at the market behind the Palacio Municipal, where *food stalls* serve fine *pozole, quesadillas,* fresh fruit juices and chicken soup.

Getting There & Away

Tepotzotlán is 1.5km west of the Caseta Tepotzotlán, the first tollbooth on highway 57D from Mexico City to Querétaro.

From Mexico City's Terminal Norte station, Autotransportes Valle de Mezquital (AVM) buses en route to Tula stop at the tollbooth every 15 minutes. From there, take a local bus (US$0.30) or taxi (US$2.25), or walk along Avenida Insurgentes. You can also take a colectivo or bus to Tepotzotlán from the Rosario metro station in Mexico City (US$0.90). Returning buses, marked 'Rosario,' depart from Avenida Insurgentes opposite the Posada San José.

TULA

• pop 26,000 • elev 2060m ☎ 773

The probable capital of the ancient Toltec civilization stood 65km north of what is now Mexico City. Though less spectacular than Teotihuacán, Tula is still an absorbing site, best known for its fearsome 4.5m-high stone warrior figures. The modern town has a refinery and cement works on its outskirts, but the center is pleasant enough.

History

Tula was an important city from about AD 900-1150, reaching a peak population of about 35,000. The Aztec annals tell of a king called Topiltzin – fair-skinned, long-haired and black-bearded – who founded a city in the 10th century as the capital of his Toltec people. There's debate about whether Tula was this capital, though.

The Toltecs were mighty empire-builders to whom the Aztecs themselves looked back with awe, claiming them as royal ancestors. Topiltzin was supposedly a priest-king dedicated to the peaceful worship (which included sacrifices of animals only) of the feathered serpent god Quetzalcóatl. Tula is known to have housed followers of the less likable Tezcatlipoca (Smoking Mirror), god of warriors, witchcraft, life and death; worshiping Tezcatlipoca required human sacrifices. The story goes that Tezcatlipoca appeared in various guises in order to provoke Topiltzin. As a naked chili-seller, he aroused the lust of Topiltzin's daughter and eventually married her; as an old man, he persuaded the sober Topiltzin to get drunk.

Eventually, the humiliated leader left for the Gulf Coast, where he set sail eastward on a raft of snakes, promising one day to return and reclaim his throne. (This caused the Aztec emperor Moctezuma much consternation when Hernán Cortés arrived on the Gulf Coast in 1519.) The conventional wisdom is that Topiltzin set up a new Toltec state at Chichén Itzá in Yucatán, while the Tula Toltecs built a brutal, militaristic empire that dominated central Mexico. (See Chichén Itzá in the History section of Facts about Mexico for a rival theory.)

Tula was evidently a place of some splendor – legends speak of palaces of gold, turquoise, jade and quetzal feathers, of enormous cobs of maize and colored cotton that grew naturally. Possibly its treasures were looted by the Aztecs or Chichimecs.

In the mid-12th century, the ruler Huémac apparently moved the Toltec capital to Chapultepec after factional fighting at Tula, then committed suicide. Tula was abandoned around the beginning of the 13th century, seemingly after violent destruction by the Chichimecs.

Orientation & Information

The Zona Arqueológica (Archaeological Zone) is 2km north of the town center (see Getting Around for directions). The main

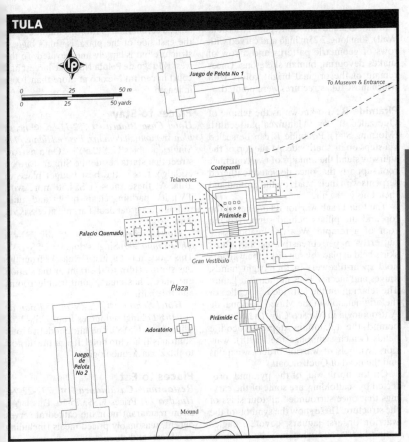

TULA

Juego de Pelota No 1

To Museum & Entrance

0   25   50 m
0   25   50 yards

Coatepantli

Telamones

Pirámide B

Palacio Quemado

Gran Vestíbulo

Plaza

Adoratorio

Pirámide C

Juego de Pelota No 2

Mound

street is Zaragoza, which runs from the outskirts of town to the zócalo. There are a couple of banks on Juárez, a block-long pedestrian street off the zócalo. Pay phones abound.

Town Center

The fortress-like church on Zaragoza was part of the 16th-century fortified monastery of San José. Inside, its vault ribs are picked out in gold. On the library wall in the zócalo is a mural of Tula's history.

Zona Arqueológica

The old settlement of Tula covered nearly 16 sq km and stretched to the far side of the modern town, but the present focus is the **ruins** (*admission US$3.50, video camera US$3.50 extra, free Sun; open 9am-5pm daily*) of the main ceremonial center, perched on a hilltop with good views over rolling countryside.

Half a kilometer from the entrance, there's a **museum** displaying pottery and several large sculptures taken from the site (signs in Spanish only). After another 700m, you will reach the center of the ancient city. At the site, there are explanatory signs in English, Spanish and Náhuatl.

Juego de Pelota No 1 This I-shaped ball court, a copy of an earlier one at Xochicalco, is the first large structure you'll reach from the museum. Researchers believe its walls were once decorated with sculpted panels that were removed under Aztec rule.

Coatepantli Near the north side of Pirámide B stands the Coatepantli (Serpent Wall), 40m long, 2.25m high and carved with rows of geometric patterns and a row of snakes devouring human skeletons. Traces remain of the original bright colors with which most Tula structures were painted.

Pirámide B Also known as the temple of Quetzalcóatl or Tlahuizcalpantecuhtli (Morning Star), Pirámide B can be scaled via steps on its south side. At the top of the stairway stand the remains of two columnar roof supports that once depicted feathered serpents with their heads on the ground and their tails in the air.

The four basalt warrior-telamones at the top and the pillars behind supported the roof of a temple. Wearing headdresses, butterfly-shaped breastplates and short skirts held in place by sun disks, the warriors hold spear-throwers in their right hands, knives and incense bags in their left hands. The telamon on the left side is a replica of the original, now in the Museo Nacional de Antropología in Mexico City. The columns behind the telamones depict crocodile heads (which symbolize the Earth), warriors, symbols of warrior orders, weapons and the head of Quetzalcóatl.

On the north wall of the pyramid, protected by scaffolding, are some of the carvings that once surrounded all four sides of the structure. These show the symbols of the warrior orders: jaguars, coyotes, eagles eating hearts, and what may be a human head in the mouth of Quetzalcóatl.

Gran Vestíbulo Now roofless, the Great Vestibule extends along the front of the pyramid, facing the plaza. The stone bench carved with warriors originally ran the length of the hall, possibly to seat priests and nobles observing ceremonies in the plaza.

Palacio Quemado The Burnt Palace, immediately to the west of Pirámide B, is really a series of halls and courtyards with more low benches and relief carvings, one showing a procession of nobles. It was probably used for meetings or ceremonies.

Plaza The plaza in front of Pirámide B would have been the scene of religious and military displays. At its center is the *adoratorio*, a ceremonial platform. **Pirámide C**, on the east side of the plaza, is Tula's biggest structure but is largely unexcavated. To the west is **Juego de Pelota No 2**, the largest ball court in central Mexico at more than 100m in length.

Places to Stay

Hotel Casa Blanca (☎ 732-11-86, e hcasablanca@hotmail.com.mx, Pasaje Hidalgo 11) Singles/doubles US$13.50/18. On a narrow street that starts beside the Singer store on Hidalgo, this is the best budget place in Tula. At these rates (US$4.50 more with TV), its sparkling clean, bright and quiet rooms are a great deal. Parking access is via Zaragoza.

Hotel Lizbeth (☎ 732-00-45, fax 732-48-34, Ocampo 200) Singles/doubles US$32/37. This modern hotel, just 1½ blocks from the bus station (turn to the right at the station entrance), has clean, comfortable rooms and free parking.

Hotel Sharon (☎ 732-09-76, Callejón de la Cruz 1) Singles/doubles from US$42/52, suites from US$80. The ultramodern Hotel Sharon is Tula's top hotel. It is at the turnoff to the Zona Arqueológica.

Places to Eat

Restaurant Casablanca (☎ 732-22-74, Hidalgo 14) Prices US$3.75-10. This large, clean restaurant near the cathedral serves decent, reasonably priced meals (including breakfast) and *antojitos*.

Fonda Naturística Maná Prices from US$1. Next door to Hotel Casa Blanca is this vegetarian restaurant where at least half a dozen family members busily prepare veggie burgers, quesadillas, fruit salads, vegetable juices, *licuados* and other meatless fare, both liquid and solid.

Getting There & Away

Tula's bus depot is on Xicoténcatl, three blocks from the cathedral. First-class Ovnibus buses go to/from Mexico City's Terminal Norte every 40 minutes (1¼ hours, US$4.25) and to/from Pachuca every hour (1¾ hours, US$4). AVM has second-class buses that travel to the same two destinations every 15 minutes (US$3.50). Flecha Amarilla has daily service to Querétaro, Guanajuato, León and Morelia.

Getting Around

If you arrive in Tula by bus, the easiest way to get to the Zona Arqueológica is to catch a taxi (US$2.25) from outside the depot. From the center, microbuses (US$0.40) labeled 'Actopan' depart from 5 de Mayo and Zaragoza and drop you off 100m from the site entrance.

ACOLMAN
• pop 3800 • elev 2250m

Thirty-two kilometers north of Mexico City, just beside highway 132D (the toll road to Teotihuacán), you'll see what look like battlements surrounding the **Ex-Convento de San Agustín Acolman**. The historic building, with its massive thick walls, colonnaded courtyards and carved stonework, contains many frescoes. The adjacent church of San Agustín, built between 1539 and 1560, has a spacious Gothic interior and one of the earliest examples of a plateresque façade. The old monastery now houses a **museum** (☎ 957-16-44, admission US$3, free Sun; open 9am-6pm daily) with artifacts and paintings from the early Christian missionary period. This is a very pleasant stop on the way to or from Teotihuacán. Buses go to Acolman from Indios Verdes metro station in Mexico City for US$1.75. It's not far from Teotihuacán; if there's no convenient bus you can get a taxi for about US$5. Frequent colectivos also make the journey from Avenida Guerrero in San Juan Teotihuacán (US$0.50).

TEOTIHUACÁN
• pop 18,000 • elev 2300m ☎ 594

If there is any must-see attraction near Mexico City, it is the archaeological zone Teotihuacán ('teh-oh-tih-wah-KAN'), 50km northeast of downtown Mexico City in a mountain-ringed offshoot of the Valle de México. Site of the huge Pirámides del Sol y de la Luna (Pyramids of the Sun and Moon), Teotihuacán was Mexico's biggest ancient city and the capital of what was probably Mexico's largest pre-Hispanic empire (see Teotihuacán under History in the Facts about Mexico chapter for an outline of its importance). If you don't let the hawkers get you down, a day here can be an awesome experience.

A grid plan for the city was developed around the early part of the 1st century AD,

and the Pyrámide del Sol was built – over an earlier cave shrine – by AD 150. Most of the rest of the city was built between about AD 250 and 600. Social, environmental and economic factors hastened its decline and eventual collapse in the 7th century AD.

The city was divided into quarters by two great avenues that met near La Ciudadela (the Citadel). One, running roughly north-south, is the famous Calzada de los Muertos (Avenue of the Dead) – so called because the later Aztecs believed the great buildings lining it were vast tombs, built by giants for Teotihuacán's first rulers. The major buildings are typified by a *talud-tablero* style, in which the rising portions of stepped, pyramid-like buildings consist of both sloping (talud) and upright (tablero) sections. They were often covered in lime and colorfully painted. Most of the city was made up of residential compounds, some of which contain elegant and refined frescoes.

Centuries after its fall, Teotihuacán was still a pilgrimage site for Aztec royalty, who believed that all of the gods had sacrificed themselves here to start the sun moving at the beginning of the 'fifth world,' inhabited by the Aztecs. To this day it is still an important pilgrimage site, as thousands of Mexicans flock to the pyramids every year to celebrate the vernal equinox and soak up the mystical energies they believe to converge there on that day.

Orientation

Though ancient Teotihuacán covered more than 20 sq km, most of what there is to see now lies along nearly 2km of the Calzada de los Muertos. Buses arrive at a traffic circle by the southwest entrance (Gate 1); four other entrances are reached by a road that circles the site. There are ticket booths and parking lots at all five entrances. If you wish to exit, your ticket allows you to go back in at any of them on the same day. The museum is just inside the main east entrance (Gate 5).

Information

An information booth inside the old museum building, near the southwest entrance (Gate 1), is staffed from 9am to 4pm. Free site tours by authorized guides, in Spanish only, may be available from this point if a sizable group forms.

TEOTIHUACÁN

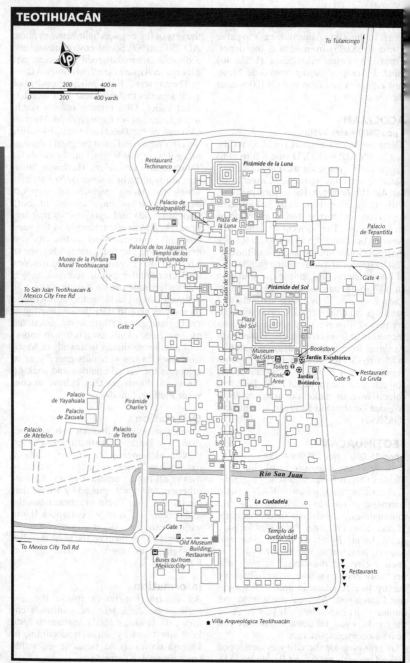

To Tulancingo

0   200   400 m
0   200   400 yards

Restaurant Techinanco

Palacio de Quetzalpapálotl

Pirámide de la Luna

Plaza de la Luna

Palacio de los Jaguares, Templo de los Caracoles Emplumados

Palacio de Tepantitla

Museo de la Pintura Mural Teotihuacana

Gate 4

To San Juan Teotihuacan & Mexico City Free Rd

Calzada de los Muertos

Pirámide del Sol

Gate 2

Plaza del Sol

Museum del Sitio

Bookstore

Jardín Escultórica

Toilets

Restaurant La Gruta

Picnic Area

Jardín Botánico

Gate 5

Palacio de Yayahuala

Pirámide Charlie's

Palacio de Zacuala

Palacio de Atetelco

Palacio de Tetitla

Río San Juan

La Ciudadela

Templo de Quetzalcóatl

Gate 1

To Mexico City Toll Rd

Old Museum Building, Restaurant

Buses to/from Mexico City

Restaurants

Villa Arqueológica Teotihuacán

Crowds at the ruins *(admission US$4, video camera US$3.50 extra, free Sun & holidays; open 7am-6pm daily)* are thickest from 10am to 2pm, and the site is busiest on Sunday, holidays and on the vernal equinox (March 21). Numerous tours from Mexico City go to the ruins. *Bestours (☎ 5514-3080 in Mexico City, Hamburgo 18210, Colonia Juárez)* runs several Teotihuacán excursions daily. Excursions are led by English-speaking guides for US$34 including transportation and admission to the site.

Most of the year, you should bring a hat and water; you may walk several kilometers, and the midday sun can be brutal. Because of the heat and the altitude, take your time exploring the expansive ruins and climbing the steep pyramids. Afternoon rain showers are common from June to September.

Calzada de los Muertos

Centuries ago the Avenue of the Dead, the axis of the site, must have seemed incomparable to its inhabitants, who saw its buildings at their best. Gate 1 brings you to the avenue in front of La Ciudadela. For 2km to the north, the avenue is flanked by former palaces of Teotihuacán's elite and other major structures such as the Pirámide del Sol. At the northern end stands the Pirámide de la Luna.

La Ciudadela

The large, square complex called the Citadel is believed to have been the residence of the city's supreme ruler. Four wide walls, 390m long, topped by 15 pyramids, enclose a huge open space of which the main feature, toward the east side, is a pyramid called the **Templo de Quetzalcóatl**. The temple is flanked by two large, ruined complexes of rooms and patios, which may have been the city's administrative center.

The fascinating feature of the Templo de Quetzalcóatl is the façade of an earlier structure (from around AD 250-300), which was revealed by excavating the more recent pyramid that had been superimposed on it. The four surviving steps of this façade (there were originally seven) are encrusted with striking carvings. In the tablero panels the sharp-fanged feathered serpent deity, its head emerging from a necklace of 11 petals, alternates with a four-eyed, two-fanged creature often identified as the rain god

Tláloc but perhaps more authoritatively reckoned to be the fire serpent, bearer of the sun on its daily journey across the sky. On the sloping panels are side views of the plumed serpent.

Museum

Continuing along the Calzada de los Muertos toward the pyramids, a path to the right on the other side of the river leads to the museum at a point just south of the Pirámide del Sol. The museum makes a refreshing stop midway through the site. Around the building, there's a lovely sculpture garden with Teotihuacán artifacts, a botanical garden, public toilets, a snack bar, picnic tables and a bookstore.

The museum is thematically divided with explanations in Spanish and English. There are excellent displays of artifacts, fresco panels and an impressive large-scale model of the city set under a Plexiglas walkway, from which the real Pirámide del Sol can be viewed through a wall-size window.

Pirámide del Sol

The world's third-largest pyramid (surpassed in size only by the pyramid of Cholula and Egypt's Cheops) stands on the east side of the Calzada de los Muertos. The base is base of 222m long on each side, and it is now just over 70m high. The pyramid was built around AD 100, from 3 million tons of stone, brick and rubble without the use of metal tools, pack animals or the wheel.

The Aztec belief that the structure was dedicated to the sun god was validated in 1971, when archaeologists uncovered a 100m-long underground tunnel leading from near the pyramid's west side to a cave directly beneath its center, where they found religious artifacts. It is thought that the sun was worshiped here before the pyramid was built and that the city's ancient inhabitants traced the very origins of life to this grotto.

At Teotihuacán's height, the pyramid's plaster was painted bright red, which must have been a radiant sight at sunset. You can climb the pyramid's 248 steps for an overview of the entire ancient city.

Pirámide de la Luna

The Pyramid of the Moon, at the north end of Calzada de los Muertos, is not as big as the Pirámide del Sol, but it is more grace-fully proportioned. Its summit is nearly the same height, because it is built on higher ground. It was completed around AD 300.

The Plaza de la Luna, in front of the pyramid, is a handsome arrangement of 12 temple platforms. Some experts attribute as-tronomical symbolism to the total 13 (made by the 12 platforms plus the pyramid), a key number in the day-counting system of the Mesoamerican ritual calendar. The altar in the plaza's center is thought to have been the site of religious dancing.

Palacio de Quetzalpapálotl

Off the southwest corner of the Plaza de la Luna is the Palace of the Quetzal Butterfly, where it is thought a high priest lived. A flight of steps leads up to a roofed portico with an abstract mural and, just off that, a well-restored patio whose thick columns are carved with images of the quetzal bird or a hybrid quetzal butterfly.

The **Palacio de los Jaguares** (Jaguar Palace) and **Templo de los Caracoles Em-plumados** (Temple of the Plumed Conch Shells) lie behind and below the Palacio de Quetzalpapálotl. On the lower walls of several of the chambers off the patio of the Palacio de los Jaguares are parts of murals showing the jaguar god in feathered head-dresses, blowing conch shells and appar-ently praying to the rain god Tláloc.

The Templo de los Caracoles Empluma-dos, entered from the Palacio de los Jaguares patio, is a now-subterranean structure of the 2nd or 3rd century AD. Carvings on what was its façade show large shells – possibly used as musical instruments – decorated with feathers and four-petal flowers. The base on which the façade stands has a green, blue, red and yellow mural of birds with water streaming from their beaks.

Palacio de Tepantitla

Teotihuacán's most famous fresco, the worn **Paradise of Tláloc**, is in the Tepantitla Palace, a priest's residence about 500m northeast of the Pirámide del Sol. The mural flanks a doorway in a covered patio in the northeast corner of the building. The rain god Tláloc, attended by priests, is shown on both sides. Below, on the right of the door, appears his paradise, a gardenlike place with people, animals and fish swim-

ming in a mountain-fed river. Left of the door, tiny human figures are engaged in a unique ball game. Frescoes in other rooms show priests with feather headdresses.

Palacio de Tetitla & Palacio de Atetelco

Another group of palaces lies west of the site's main area, several hundred meters from Gate 1. Their many murals, discovered in the 1940s, are often well-preserved or re-stored and perfectly intelligible. Inside the sprawling Tetitla Palace, no fewer than 120 walls have murals, with Tláloc, jaguars, serpents and eagles among the easiest figures to make out. Some 400m west is the Atetelco Palace, whose vivid jaguar or coyote murals – a mixture of originals and restorations – are in the so-called Patio Blanco in the northwest corner. Processions of these creatures in shades of red perhaps symbolize warrior orders.

About 100m farther north lie Zacuala and Yayahuala, a pair of enormous walled compounds that probably served as living quarters for large groups of families. Sepa-rated by the original alleyways, the two structures are made up of numerous rooms and patios but few entranceways, perhaps to discourage unwanted guests.

Museo de la Pintura Mural Teotihuacana

On the ring road between Gates 2 and 3, this impressive new museum (☎ 958-20-81; admission free with site ticket; open 10am-6pm daily) showcases murals from Teoti-huacán as well as reconstructions of murals you'll see in the ruins. Explanations of the modern exhibits are in Spanish only, but the museum is definitely worth a stop.

Places to Stay

Villa Arqueológica Teotihuacán (☎ 956-09-09, e oper@df1.prodigy.net.mx) Singles/doubles US$67/76. This Club Med-run hotel, on the south end of the road that en-circles the ancient city, has small yet charm-ing rooms. It also has a heated pool, tennis court, billiards table and restaurant.

The town of San Juan Teotihuacán, 3km west of the Pirámide del Sol, features several less costly options for spending the night.

Trailer Park Teotihuacán (☎ 956-03-13, López Mateos 17) Tent sites US$4.50 per person, trailer sites US$7. You can camp here on a peaceful street behind a 16th-century Jesuit church. The park has baths with hot showers.

Hotel Posada Teotihuacán (☎ 956-04-60, Canteroco 7) Singles/doubles US$20/27. Two blocks east of the central plaza on Canteroco, the Posada Teotihuacán offers clean rooms with TVs and friendly service.

Hotel Posada Sol y Luna (☎ 956-23-68, fax 956-23-74, Jiménez Cantú 13) Doubles/triples US$26/40, suites with Jacuzzi from US$39. At the east end of town, closer to the pyramids, is this superior-value hotel with luxurious rooms.

Hotel Quinto Sol (☎ 956-18-81, fax 956-19-04, Avenida Hidalgo 26) Singles/doubles US$55/65 This new hotel has luxurious rooms with every service you'd need, including hairdryers, coffeemakers, cable TV and phones.

Motel Quinto Sol (behind the Hotel Quinto Sol) Room with one king-size bed US$34, with Jacuzzi US$45. The motel offers clean, modern rooms, each comes with one king-size bed, above private garages.

Places to Eat

Except for some dusty eateries along the ring road on the southeast side of the archaeological site, meals are pricey in the vicinity of the ruins. The most convenient place is on the 3rd floor of the old museum building, where there's a **restaurant** with views of La Ciudadela.

Restaurant Techinanco (☎ 958-22-94, ring road behind Pirámide de la Luna) Prices US$1.75-7.25. This modest, friendly restaurant serves delicious moles and other tasty Mexican dishes at very reasonable prices. The mole de huitlacoche is divine.

Pirámide Charlie's (ring road south of Gate 2) Prices US$4.50-20. Undeniably a tourist trap, this place serves savory but costly soup, chicken, beef and seafood dishes.

Restaurant La Gruta (the Cave, ☎ 956-01-04, 75m east of Gate 5) Prices US$5-15.50. Meals have been served in this cool, wide-mouthed natural cave for a century; Porfirio Díaz (Mexican president for 33 years prior to the Mexican Revolution) ate here in 1906. The food's quite good and fairly priced.

Getting There & Away

Autobuses México-San Juan Teotihuacán runs 2nd-class buses from Mexico City's Terminal Norte to the ruins every 15 minutes during the day (one hour, US$2). The ticket office is at the north end of the terminal. Make sure your bus is going to 'Los Pirámides' as opposed to the nearby town of San Juan Teotihuacán.

Buses arrive and depart from the traffic circle near Gate 1, also making stops at Gates 2 and 3. Return buses are more frequent after 1pm. The last bus back to the capital from the traffic circle leaves about 6.30pm. Some terminate at the Indios Verdes metro station in the north of Mexico City, but most continue to Terminal Norte.

Getting Around

To get to the pyramids from San Juan Teotihuacán, take any combi labeled 'San Martín' departing from Avenida Hidalgo beside the central plaza (US$0.30). Combis returning to San Juan make stops at Gates 1, 2 and 3.

PACHUCA

• pop 226,000 • elev 2426m ☎ 771

Pachuca, capital of the state of Hidalgo, lies 90km northeast of Mexico City. It has grown rapidly in the last few years, and brightly painted houses climb the dry hillsides around the town. Pachuca has a few interesting sights, and is a good departure point for trips north and east into the dramatic Sierra Madre Oriental.

Silver was found in the area as early as 1534, and the mines of Real del Monte, 9km northeast, still produce substantial amounts of the metal. Pachuca was also the gateway through which soccer entered Mexico, brought by miners from Cornwall, England, in the 19th century. Further evidence of the Cornish influence, the meat pies known as pasties (pastes) are sold in bakeries and restaurants around town.

Orientation

The rectangular **Reloj Monumental** (Clock Tower), built between 1904 and 1910 to commemorate the independence centennial, stands at the north end of Pachuca's Plaza de la Independencia (zócalo) which is flanked by Avenida Matamoros on the east and Avenida Allende on the west. Guerrero runs parallel to Allende, about 100m to the west. To the south, by about 700m, both Guerrero and Matamoros reach the modern Plaza Juárez.

Information

There's a tourist module (☎ 715-14-11) in the base of the clock tower, theoretically open 10am to 6pm daily, but in reality the desk is often unoccupied. Small maps are available.

There are banks (with ATMs) on Plaza de la Independencia. The post office is three blocks south of Plaza Juárez on the corner of Juárez and Iglesias. Internet access is available at Café Internet, one block east of the zócalo on the corner of Hidalgo and Leandro Valle, for US$1.75 per hour.

Lookout Points

For a jaw-dropping view of the city, catch a 'Mirador' bus (US$0.30) from Plaza de la Constitución a few blocks northeast of the zócalo to an observation point on the road to Real del Monte. Even more extraordinary views can be had from the Cristo Rey monument on the Cerro de Santa Apolonia north of town.

Centro Cultural de Hidalgo

The Ex-Convento de San Francisco has become the Centro Cultural de Hidalgo (cnr Hidalgo & Arista; admission free; open 10am-6pm Tues-Sun), which embodies two museums and a gallery, theater, library and several lovely plazas. It is four blocks east of Plaza Juárez.

The **Museo Nacional de la Fotografía** (admission free; open 10am-6pm Tues-Sun) displays early photographic technology and selections from the 1.5 million photos in the archives of the Instituto Nacional de Antropología e Historia (INAH). The photos – some by Europeans and Americans, many more by pioneer Mexican photojournalist Agustín Victor Casasola – provide fascinating glimpses of Mexico from 1873 to the present.

Museo de Minería

Just two blocks southeast of the zócalo, this museum (Mina 110; admission US$1.10; open 10am-2pm & 3pm-6pm Wed-Sun) provides an interesting overview of the mining industry that has shaped the region. Well-

displayed photos show conditions in the mines from early years to the present. Also on display are helmets and headlamps, old mining maps and shrines taken from mines. Half a block east of Avenida Matamoros, it has guided tours (in Spanish) with a video program.

Places to Stay

Hotel de los Baños (☎ 713-07-00, fax 715-14-41, Avenida Matamoros 205) Singles/doubles US$19.50/23. This hotel, half a block southeast of the zócalo, has a skylight over a handsomely enclosed courtyard. Rooms vary in price and quality, but all have TVs, phones and clean baths.

Hotel Noriega (☎ 715-15-55, Avenida Matamoros 305) Singles/doubles US$19.50/23. This colonial-style hotel, one block south of Hotel de los Baños, is another good choice. There's a leaf-covered courtyard, stately staircase and decent restaurant. Have a look at a few rooms, though, before checking in – some are tiny and claustrophobic, while others are large and airy. You pay US$2 more for TV. Parking is available behind the hotel for US$1.70.

Hotel Emily (☎ 715-08-68, Plaza Independencia) Singles/doubles US$35/40. The modern Hotel Emily, on the south side of the zócalo, has large comfortable rooms, some facing a back patio, others with balconies on the plaza. There's a parking garage underneath the hotel.

Hotel Ciro's (☎ 715-40-83, e hotelciros@hotmail.com.mx, Plaza Independencia 110) Singles/doubles US$32/36. This hotel, owned by members of the same family, stands on the opposite side of the plaza from the Emily. The building is very different, but the style and quality of the rooms are similar.

Gran Hotel Independencia (☎ 715-05-15, Avenida Independencia 116) Singles/doubles US$28/37 Sun-Thur, US$34/43 Fri & Sat. This hotel occupies an imposing building on the west side of the zócalo but is much less impressive inside. The rooms are sizable but bare. Parking is available in the courtyard.

Places to Eat

Pasties are available all over town, including at the bus station. Baked in pizza ovens, they contain a variety of fillings probably never imagined by those Cornish miners, such as *mole verde,* beans, pineapple and rice pudding. *Pastes Kiko's* in the arcade opposite the Juárez monument on Plaza Juárez and *Pastes San Juan,* nearby on Fernando Soto, are especially popular.

Restaurant-Bar Cabales (Avenida Matamoros 205) Prices from US$0.50. Next door to the Hotel de los Baños is this attractive restaurant which features a bar ringed with swiveling stools and good, reasonably priced food (the five-course meal of the day runs US$4).

Mina La Blanca Restaurant Bar (☎ 715-19-64, Avenida Matamoros 201) Prices US$3.75-9. On the southwest corner of the zócalo, this place serves 'authentic' pasties, filled with potatoes, leeks, parsley, ground beef and black pepper. Decorated with stained-glass panels of mining scenes, the cavernous dining hall also offers set breakfasts, salads and antojitos.

Mi Antiguo Café (Matomoros 15) Set breakfast US$4-5.50. This charming café on the southeast side of Plaza Independencia serves crêpes, tasty Mexican breakfasts and espresso.

Getting There & Away

First-class buses leave Mexico City's Terminal Norte for Pachuca every 15 minutes (US$5). From Pachuca, there is 1st-class service daily to the following: Mexico City, every 15 minutes (1¼ hours, US$5); Poza Rica, seven buses (5 hours, US$9.50); and Tampico, two buses (8 hours, US$25). Buses serving destinations closer to Pachuca are nearly all 2nd-class; these frequently go to/ from Tula, Tulancingo and Tamazunchale, while several go daily to/from Huejutla and Querétaro.

Getting Around

The bus station is several kilometers southwest of downtown, beside the road to Mexico City. Green-striped colectivos marked 'Centro' take you to Plaza Constitución (US$0.30), a short walk from the zócalo; in the reverse direction, you can hop on along Avenida Allende. The trip by taxi costs US$2.75.

AROUND PACHUCA

Three scenic roads ascend into the forested, sometimes foggy Sierra Madre. Highway 105 goes north to Huejutla and Tampico.

Highway 85 – the Pan-American Highway – goes via Actopan and Ixmiquilpan to Tamazunchale and Ciudad Valles in the Huasteca (see the Central Gulf Coast chapter). Highway 130 goes east to Tulancingo and Poza Rica.

Parque Nacional El Chico
☎ 771

Nine kilometers north of Pachuca, a road branches northwest (left) off highway 105 and winds 20km or so to the picturesque old mining town of **Mineral del Chico**, located in Parque Nacional El Chico. The park has spectacular rock formations popular with climbers, pine forests with lovely walks, and rivers and dams for fishing.

Río y Montaña Expediciones (☎ 55-5292-5032, ⊠ www.rioymontana.com) in Mexico City organizes three-day expeditions to El Chico for groups of eight or more persons. The company supplies all climbing and camping equipment, but you must arrange your own transportation to the park. For further information, consult their Web site.

Places to Stay & Eat *La Cabaña del Lobo (☎ 55-5776-2222 in Mexico City)* Singles/ doubles with bath US$29/40. Five kilometers from highway 105 (on the road toward Mineral del Chico) is a right turn that leads 1.2km by bumpy dirt road to La Cabaña. It is in a remote valley ringed by pine-covered mountains. The hotel features a row of cozy rooms with clean baths and hot water overlooking a campfire/playground area and a restaurant. Some of the rooms have fireplaces – it can be chilly up here.

There are several **campgrounds** with rudimentary facilities between Km 7 and Km 10 of the road to Mineral del Chico, all charging about US$2 per tent plus US$0.30 per person.

In Mineral del Chico, there are a couple of nice hotels. These places fill up fast on weekends, but are empty during the week.

Hospedaje El Chico (☎ 715-47-41, Avenida Corona del Rosal 1) Singles/doubles US$22/28. On the plaza, this place is sparkling clean and comfortable. The entrance is at the door to the right of a shop called Casa Brisa; there's no sign.

La Posada del Amanacer (☎ 715-01-90, ⊠ www.hotelesecoturisticos.com.mx,

Morelos 3) Rooms US$54 Sun-Thur, US$67 Fri & Sat. Rooms with fireplaces cost US$11 extra. Just up the street from Hospedaje El Chico is this adobe structure with 11 rooms on two levels beside a lovely patio. Rooms come with one or two double beds. The hotel also offers hiking or bike tours into the park.

Getting There & Away From Pachuca, colectivos depart frequently from Calle Galeana (west of the market, through an arch labeled 'Barrio el Arbolito') for US$0.80. Flecha Roja runs three 2nd-class buses daily to Mineral del Chico (1 hour, US$1) from Pachuca's bus station.

Highway 105

Two kilometers past the park turnoff for Parque Nacional El Chico, **Real del Monte** (also known as Mineral del Monte) was the scene of a miners' strike in 1776 – commemorated as the first strike in the Americas. Most of the town was settled in the 19th century, after a British company took over the mines. The field opposite the Dolores mine was the first place in the country where soccer was played. Cornish-style cottages line many of the steep cobbled streets, and there is an English cemetery nearby. Flecha Roja buses leave from the Pachuca bus station every half hour for Real del Monte (1/2 hour, US$0.50).

Eleven kilometers north of Real del Monte is a turnoff east to **Huasca** (or Huasca de Ocampo), which has a 17th-century church, *balnearios* and a variety of local crafts. Some old haciendas have been converted into attractive hotels. Nearby is a canyon with imposing basalt columns and a waterfall.

At **Atotonilco el Grande**, 34km from Pachuca, there's a 16th-century fortress-monastery and a balneario beside some hot springs. Market day is Thursday. The highway then descends to Metzquititlán, in the fertile Río Tulancingo valley (see Tampico & the Huasteca in the Central Gulf Coast chapter for information about other places along this route).

Actopan

• **pop 24,000** • **elev 2400m** ☎ **772**

Actopan, 37km northwest of Pachuca on highway 85, has one of the finest of Hidalgo's many 16th-century fortress-monasteries.

Founded in 1548, **Convento de San Nicolás de Tolentino** is in an excellent state of preservation. Its church has a lovely plateresque façade and a single tower showing Moorish influence. Mexico's best 16th-century frescoes are in the cloister: hermits are depicted in the Sala De Profundis, and saints, Augustinian monks and a meeting between Fray Martín de Acevedo (an important early monk at Actopan) and two indigenous nobles (Juan Inica Actopa and Pedro Ixcuincuitlapilco) are shown on the stairs. To the left of the church, a vaulted *capilla abierta* is also adorned with frescoes.

Wednesday is market day in Actopan, and has been for at least 400 years. Local handicrafts are sold, along with regional dishes such as barbecued lamb.

PAI (Pachuca-Actopan-Ixmiquilpan) runs 1st-class buses every 12 minutes from Pachuca to Actopan (20 minutes, US$2.25). There is frequent 2nd-class service from Mexico City's Terminal Norte.

Ixmiquilpan

• **pop 31,000** • **elev 1700m** ☎ **759**

Ixmiquilpan, 75km from Pachuca on highway 85 (1½ hours by frequent buses), is a former capital of the Otomí people, ancient inhabitants of Hidalgo. The arid Mezquital Valley in which the town stands remains an Otomí enclave; about half of Mexico's 350,000 Otomí live in Hidalgo. Traditional Otomí women's dress is a *quechquémitl,* an embroidered shoulder cape worn over an embroidered cloth blouse. The Mezquital Valley Otomí make Mexico's finest *ayates,* cloths woven from *ixtle,* the fiber of the maguey cactus.

The busy Monday *market* is the best place to find Otomí crafts such as miniature musical instruments made of juniper wood with pearl or shell inlay, colorful drawstring bags or embroidered textiles. During the rest of the week, you can go to the nearby community of El Nith (east of Ixmiquilpan) to find such items. Combis depart from Jesús del Rosal near the market; taxis make the trip for US$3.50.

Ixmiquilpan's **monastery** was founded by Augustinians in the mid-1500s. The nave of its church, crowned by a huge Gothic vault, is unusual for a band of frescoes depicting indigenous warriors in combat. The murals show a clash between soldiers in Aztec military garb and scantily clad warriors using obsidian swords. Experts speculate the murals were painted by Mexica artists as propaganda against Chichimec invaders.

PAI runs 1st-class buses every 12 minutes from Pachuca to Ixmiquilpan (1½ hours, US$4).

Highway 130

Just 46km east of Pachuca is **Tulancingo** (population 94,000, altitude 2140m), which was briefly the Toltec capital before Tula. There's a Toltec pyramid at the foot of a cliff at **Huapalcalco**, 3km north. Market day is Thursday.

The Otomí village of **Tenango de Doria** is a rugged 40k north of Tulancingo by sometimes impassable roads. The residents make cotton fabric colorfully embroidered with animals and plants. In **Huehuetla**, 50km north of Tulancingo, there is one of the few communities of the tiny Tepehua indigenous group, who embroider floral and geometric patterns on their quechquémitls and *enredos* (wraparound skirts).

Beyond Tulancingo, highway 130 descends toward Huauchinango in the state of Puebla (see the Northern Veracruz section in the Central Gulf Coast chapter).

East of Mexico City

Toll highway 150D goes east to Puebla across a high, dry region studded with volcanic peaks, including Popocatépetl, Iztaccíhuatl and La Malinche. The mountains offer scope for anything from pleasant alpine strolls to demanding technical climbs – though Popocatépetl is off-limits because of recent volcanic activity. Just north of the highway, the tiny state of Tlaxcala (population 912,000) features a charming capital and relics from a rich pre-Hispanic and colonial history.

Puebla itself is one of Mexico's best preserved colonial cities, a pivot of its history and a lively modern metropolis with a lot to see and do. Nevertheless, the state of Puebla is predominantly rural, with about half a million indigenous people. The indigenous presence helps give Puebla a rich handicraft output, including pottery, carved onyx and fine handwoven and embroidered textiles.

You can continue east from Puebla on highway 150D, past Pico de Orizaba (Mexico's highest mountain), and descend from the highlands to the coast of Veracruz state (see the Central Gulf Coast chapter). Alternatives are to swing north on highway 140 toward the remote Sierra Norte de Puebla, or descend to the Gulf Coast via Jalapa. South and east of Puebla, there's a choice of scenic routes through the mountains to the state and city of Oaxaca.

POPOCATÉPETL & IZTACCÍHUATL

Mexico's second and third highest mountains, Popocatépetl ('po-po-ka-TEH-pet-l') and Iztaccíhuatl ('iss-ta-SEE-wat-l'), form the eastern rim of the Valle de México, 72km southeast of Mexico City and 43km west of Puebla. While the craterless Iztaccíhuatl remains dormant, Popocatépetl in recent years has spouted plumes of gas and ash, forced the evacuation of 25,000 people, and spurred experts to issue warnings to the 30 million people who live within striking distance of the volcano. At the time of writing, leading vulcanologists were continuing to watch Popocatépetl with concern.

After explosions under the 5452m volcano Popocatépetl – which is Náhuatl for 'Smoking Mountain' – sent 5000 tons of hot ash into the sky, soldiers evacuated 16 nearby villages on December 22, 1994. Popo, as the volcano is called locally, has been occasionally spewing ash since then. In first few months of 2001, several eruptions sent ash up to 8km into the atmosphere.

The federal agency Cenapred (National Disaster Prevention Center) keeps an eye on volcanic activity via variations in gas emissions and seismic intensity, and provides information to the public through its Web site (W www.cenapred.unam.mx).

Historically, Popo has been relatively kind. It has had 14 eruptive periods since the Spanish arrived in 1519, but none have caused a major loss of life or property. It has been over a thousand years since Popo delivered a really big blast, but experts don't discount the possibility of one now, and it is for this reason that Mexican authorities are not allowing anyone on the mountain except scientists monitoring its activity.

Iztaccíhuatl (White Woman), 20km from Popo summit to summit, remains open to climbers and is perhaps all the more fetching because of her neighbor's unpredictable outbursts. Legend has it that Popo was a

AROUND MEXICO CITY

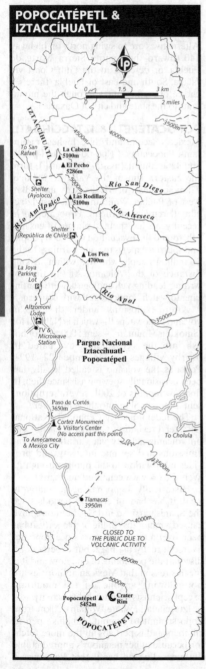

POPOCATÉPETL &
IZTACCÍHUATL

warrior who was in love with Izta, the emperor's daughter. As the story goes, Izta died of grief while Popo was away at war. Upon his return, he created the two mountains, laid her body on one and stood holding her funeral torch on the other. With some imagination, Izta does resemble a woman lying on her back. From the Mexico City side, you can, if the sky's clear, make out four peaks from left to right known as La Cabeza (the Head), El Pecho (the Breast), Las Rodillas (the Knees) and Los Pies (the Feet).

Amecameca
• pop 32,000 • elev 2480m ☎ 597

From the Mexico City side, the town of Amecameca, 60km by road from the city, is the key staging post for an Izta climb. But with a pair of volcanoes as a backdrop for the town's everyday activities and a few 16th-century churches, it makes an interesting destination in itself. There are ATMs around the plaza and a post office in the city hall on the southwest corner of the plaza. The best way to get around town is by bicycle-taxi (US$0.40). There is a lively *market* next to the church.

The **Santuario del Sacromonte**, 90m above Amecameca to the west, is an important pilgrimage site built over a cave that was the retreat of the Dominican friar Martín de Valencia in the early 16th century. It makes a delightful walk with awesome views of the town spread out beneath the volcanoes. Go through the arch on the southwest side of the plaza and walk down Avenida Fray Martín about two blocks, until you see the stairs ascending the hill on the right. From there, follow the stations of the cross uphill to the sanctuary.

Hotel San Carlos (☎ 978-07-46, Plaza de la Constitucion 10), on the southeast corner of the plaza, has 33 clean, comfortable rooms (singles/doubles US$9/18, US$5.50 more with TV).

From Mexico City's TAPO, the 2nd-class Volcanes bus line runs every 15 minutes to/from Amecameca (1¼ hours, US$2) and Cuautla. From the Amecameca bus station, turn right and walk two blocks to the plaza.

Hiking

Izta's highest peak is El Pecho at 5286m, and all routes to it require a night on the mountain. Between the starting point at La Joya parking lot and Las Rodillas, there is a shelter hut that could be used during an ascent of El Pecho. On average, it takes five hours to reach the hut from La Joya, another six hours from the hut to El Pecho, and six hours back to the base. Before making the ascent, climbers need to call ahead and arrange permission from the Parque National Iztaccíhuatl-Popocatépetl office (☎ 597-978-38-29), at Plaza de la Constitución 1, on the southeast side of Amecameca's zócalo. The office is open 9am to 6pm Monday to Friday. Technically, you do not need permission to climb Izta, but if you're starting from Amecameca, you'll need the permit to pass the military checkpoint near Paso de Cortés. Alternately, you can depart from the village of San Rafael, 8km north of Amecameca, a longer and more rigorous climb.

If you'd rather not climb Izta but would still like to spend a day enjoying the mountain scenery, Paso de Cortés has plenty of lower-altitude trails through pine forests and grassy meadows; some offer breathtaking glimpses of the nearby peaks. Trails begin at La Joya. Again, you need to arrange for a permit, otherwise the guards will only allow you to stay at Paso de Cortés for 10 minutes. Taxis departing from in front of the national park office will take you to La Joya (40 minutes) and back for US$34.

Shelter is available at Paso de Cortés' visitors center and at *Altzomoni Lodge* nearby. The lodge is by a TV and microwave station roughly halfway between the visitors center at the Paso and La Joya. Bring bedding and drinking water.

Climate & Conditions It can be windy and well below freezing on the upper slopes of Izta any time of year, and it is nearly always below freezing near the summit at night. Ice and snow are fixtures here; the average snow line is 4200m. The best months for ascents are October to February, when there is hard snow for crampons. The rainy season, April to September, brings with it the threat of whiteouts, thunderstorms and avalanches.

Anyone can be affected by altitude problems, including life-threatening altitude sickness. Even the Paso de Cortés (3650m), the turnoff for Izta, is at a level where you should know the symptoms (see Altitude Sickness in the Health section of the Facts for the Visitor chapter).

Guides Iztaccíhuatl should be attempted by experienced climbers *only,* and because of hidden crevices on the ice-covered upper slopes, a guide is highly recommended.

Mexico City-based guide Mario Andrade has led many Izta ascents. His fee for leading climbers up Izta is US$350 for one person; the price goes down for groups. The cost includes transportation from Mexico City to Izta and back, lodging and the use of rope. Contact Andrade, who speaks Spanish and English, by email (e mountainup@ hotmail.com) or at his Mexico City home (☎ 55-5875-0105). His mailing address is PO Box M-10380, México DF, Mexico. In Amecameca, José Luis Ariza (☎ 978-13-35), a member of the rescue squad Búsqueda y Salvamento who has scaled peaks throughout Latin America, leads climbers up Izta's peak year-round. He charges US$100 for one person and US$50 for each additional person (transportation and equipment rental cost extra).

TEXCOCO
• **pop 102,000** • **elev 2778m** ☎ **595**

Some of Diego Rivera's finest mural work can be found at the agriculture school of the **Universidad Autónoma de Chapingo** just outside Texcoco, 67km from Mexico City via highway 136. In the **Capilla Riveriana** *(admission US$3.50; open 10am-3pm Mon-Fri, 10am-5pm Sat & Sun)* of the former hacienda, now part of the university's administration building, sensual murals intertwine images of the Mexican struggle for agrarian reform and the Earth's fertility cycles. One of the 24 panels covering the chapel's walls and ceiling depicts buried martyrs of reform symbolically fertilizing the land and thus the future. From Mexico City take a local bus from metro Zaragoza, or a direct bus from TAPO, to downtown Texcoco where there are 'Chapingo' combis. From the main entrance, the hacienda is at the end of the tree-lined path.

Also worth visiting in this area are the **Parque Nacional Molino de Flores Nezahualcóyotl**, 3km east of Texcoco, and the archaeological site **Baños de Nezahualcóyotl**, 5km farther. Established in 1585 as the first wheat mill in the region, the Molino later served as a *pulque* hacienda before being expropriated by the government in 1937. Today many of the original buildings are in ruins, but some have been partly restored and opened to the public. Works of local artists are exhibited in the *tinacal* where pulque was processed. A walk past the main buildings will take you to an unusual little church built into the side of a gorge, accessible on one side by a hanging bridge. To get to the park, take a 'Molino de Flores' combi from downtown Texcoco.

The little known, but interesting, Baños de Nezahualcóyotl contain the remains of temples, a palace, fountains, spring-fed aqueducts and baths built by the Texcocan poet-king, Nezahualcóyotl. He was perhaps the only Mesoamerican ruler to observe a type of monotheistic religion, worshiping an abstract god with feminine and masculine qualities. The site is on a hilltop with a view as far as Xochimilco (when the pollution isn't bad). To get there, take a 'Tlamincas' combi from downtown Texcoco, or from the right fork just outside the national park's entrance, and get off at the sign pointing to the site. From there, it's a kilometer walk to the summit.

TLAXCALA
• pop 69,000 • elev 2252m ☎ 246
About 120km east of Mexico City and 30km north of Puebla, this quiet colonial town is the capital of Tlaxcala state, Mexico's smallest. Stopping here makes a pleasant day trip from either city.

History
In the last centuries before the Spanish conquest, numerous small warrior kingdoms *(señoríos)* arose in the Tlaxcala area. Some of them formed a loose federation that managed to stay independent of the Aztec empire as it spread from the Valle de México in the 15th century. The most important kingdom seems to have been Tizatlán, now on the edge of Tlaxcala city.

When the Spanish arrived in 1519 the Tlaxcalans fought fiercely at first, but then became Cortés' staunchest allies against the Aztecs (with the exception of one chief, Xicoténcatl the Younger, who tried at least twice to rouse his people against the Spanish

and is now a Mexican hero). The Spanish rewarded the Tlaxcalans with privileges and used them to help pacify and settle Chichimec areas to the north. In 1527 Tlaxcala became the seat of the first bishopric in Nueva España, but a plague in the 1540s decimated the population and the town never played an important role again.

Orientation
Two central plazas meet on the corner of Independencia and Muñoz. The northern one, surrounded by colonial buildings, is the zócalo, called Plaza de la Constitución. The other, Plaza Xicohténcatl, has a crafts market on weekends. Tlaxcala's bus station is 1km west of the plazas.

Information
The Tlaxcala state tourist office (☎ 800-509-75-57, ⓦ www.tlaxcala.gob.mx/turismo), on the corner of Juárez and Lardizabal, is open 9am to 6pm Monday to Friday and 10am to 6pm Saturday and Sunday. Its accommodating staff speak some English. The office runs tours of the city and most of the outlying areas on Saturday, with departures scheduled from the Hotel Posada San Francisco at 10.15am (US$1.75, including transport).

The post office is on the west side of the zócalo; Bancrecer has a branch (with ATM) on the southeast corner. There is an Internet café on Independencia just south of Guerrero, open 9am to 8pm daily.

Zócalo
The spacious, shady zócalo is one of the best looking in Mexico. Most of its north side is taken up by the 16th-century **Palacio Municipal**, a former grain storehouse, and the **Palacio de Gobierno**; inside the latter there are more than 450 sq m of vivid murals of Tlaxcala's history by Desiderio Hernández Xochitiotzin. The 16th-century building on the northwest side of the zócalo, adjacent to the post office, is the **Palacio de Justicia**, the former Capilla Real de Indios, constructed for the use of indigenous nobles. The handsome mortar bas-reliefs around its doorway depict the seal of Castilla y León and a two-headed eagle, symbol of the Hapsburg monarchs who ruled Spain in the 16th and 17th centuries. Just off the zócalo's northwest

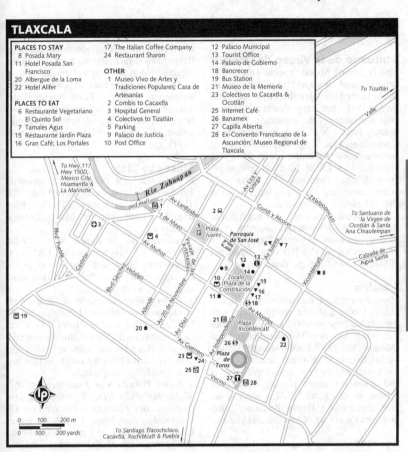

TLAXCALA

PLACES TO STAY
8 Posada Mary
11 Hotel Posada San Francisco
20 Albergue de la Loma
22 Hotel Alifer

PLACES TO EAT
6 Restaurante Vegetariano El Quinto Sol
7 Tamales Agus
15 Restaurante Jardín Plaza
16 Gran Café; Los Portales

17 The Italian Coffee Company
24 Restaurant Sharon

OTHER
1 Museo Vivo de Artes y Tradiciones Populares; Casa de Artesanías
2 Combis to Cacaxtla
3 Hospital General
4 Colectivos to Tizatlán
5 Parking
9 Palacio de Justicia
10 Post Office

12 Palacio Municipal
13 Tourist Office
14 Palacio de Gobierno
18 Bancrecer
19 Bus Station
21 Museo de la Memoria
23 Colectivos to Cacaxtla & Ocotlán
25 Internet Café
26 Banamex
27 Capilla Abierta
28 Ex-Convento Franciscano de la Asunción; Museo Regional de Tlaxcala

To Tizatlán

To Hwy 117; Hwy 150D, Mexico City, Huamantla & La Malinche

Río Zahuapan

ped mall

Av Lardizabal

1 de Mayo

Blvd - Puebla

Castelar

Blvd Sánchez - Hidalgo

Av Muñoz

Pasaje de las Artesanías

Allende

Av 20 de Noviembre

Av Díaz

Av Guerrero

Av Lira y Ortega

Zitelpopocatl

Gundi y Alcocer

Av Juárez

Xicohténcatl

Plaza Juárez

Parroquia de San José

Zócalo (Plaza de la Constitución)

Av Morelos

Plaza Xicohténcatl

Av Independencia

Plaza de Toros

Vecino

To Santuario de la Virgen de Ocotlán & Santa Ana Chiautempan

Calzada de Agua Santa

To Santiago Tlacochcalco, Cacaxtla, Xochitécatl & Puebla

0   100   200 m
0   100   200 yards

AROUND MEXICO CITY

corner is the pretty brick, tile and stucco **Parroquia de San José**.

Ex-Convento Franciscano de la Asunción

This former monastery is up a steep, shaded path from the southeast corner of Plaza Xicohténcatl. It was one of Mexico's earliest monasteries built between 1537 and 1540, and its church – the city's cathedral – has a beautiful Moorish-style wooden ceiling. Next to the church is the **Museo Regional de Tlaxcala** *(admission US$3.50, free Sun & holidays; open 10am-5pm Tues-Sun)*.

Just below the monastery, beside the 19th-century bullring, is a **capilla abierta**, unique for the Moorish style of its three arches.

Museo Vivo de Artes y Tradiciones Populares

This museum *(Blvd Sánchez 1; admission US$0.70; open 10am-6pm Tues-Sun)*, at the end of 1 de Mayo, has displays on Tlaxcalan village life, bell-making, weaving and pulque-making, sometimes with demonstrations. Next door, the Casa de Artesanías has handicrafts that are worth a look if you're in the market.

Museo de la Memoria

This museum *(☎ 466-07-91, Plaza Xicohténcatl 3; admission US$1.25; open 10am-5pm Tues-Sun)* takes a multimedia approach to Tlaxcala's history. Exhibits on indigenous government, agriculture and contemporary festivals are well presented, though explanations are in Spanish only.

Santuario de la Virgen de Ocotlán

This is one of Mexico's most spectacular churches, and an important pilgrimage site owing to the belief that the Virgin appeared here in 1541 – her image stands on the main altar in memory of the apparition. The 18th-century façade is a classic example of the Churrigueresque style, with white stucco 'wedding cake' decorations contrasting with plain red tiles. In the 18th century, indigenous Mexican Francisco Miguel spent 25 years decorating the altarpieces and the chapel beside the main altar.

The church is on a hill 1km northeast of the zócalo. Walk north on Juárez for three blocks, then turn right onto Zitlalpopocatl, or take an 'Ocotlán' colectivo at the corner of Guerrero and Independencia.

Tizatlán

These are the scant remains of Xicoténcatl's palace. Under a shelter are two altars with some faded frescoes of the gods Tezcatlipoca (Smoking Mirror), Tlahuizcalpantecuhtli (Morning Star) and Mictlantecuhtli (Underworld). Templo San Esteban, next to the ruins, has a 16th-century Franciscan capilla abierta and frescoes of angels playing instruments. The site is on a small hill 4km north of the town center; take a 'Tizatlán Parroquia' colectivo from the corner of Sánchez and Muñoz.

Courses

Estela Silva's Mexican Home Cooking program (☎ 468-09-78, fax 462-49-98, ⓦ www.mexicanhomecooking.com; postal address Apdo 64, Tlaxcala, Tlax, Mexico 90000) Program fee US$1000. This course offers visitors hands-on instruction in the preparation of classic Mexican dishes. A basic five-day course that focuses on Puebla cuisine is set in the Talavera-tiled kitchen of Silva's hacienda-style home, which is in the small village of Santiago Tlacochcalco, a few kilometers south of Tlaxcala. The cost of the program includes lodging (she has three double rooms with private baths and fireplaces) and three meals daily for a week.

Special Events

On the third Monday in May, the figure of the Virgin of Ocotlán is carried from its hilltop residence to other churches, attracting crowds of believers and onlookers. Throughout the month, processions commemorating the miracle attract pilgrims from around the republic and as far away as Canada.

The neighboring town of Santa Ana Chiautempan hosts the Feria Nacional del Sarape (National Sarape Fair) for two weeks on either side of July 26 to correspond with the celebration of its patron saint's day.

Places to Stay

Posada Mary (☎ 462-96-55, *Xicohténcatl 19*) Singles/doubles with bath US$11/13. This is the cheapest option in Tlaxcala. It's a friendly if basic concrete shell enclosing a parking lot.

Albergue de la Loma (☎ 462-04-24, *Guerrero 58*) Singles/doubles US$18/24. This modern hotel, at the top of 61 steps, has big, clean rooms with tiled bathrooms, some offering views of the city.

Hotel Alifer (☎ 462-56-78, ⓔ halifer@ prodigy.net.mx, *Morelos 11*) Singles/doubles US$28/39. The central Hotel Alifer has clean rooms, with TVs and phones, around a paved parking lot. The hillside hotel is less than two blocks from the zócalo, but the last 50m stretch is a steep climb.

Hotel Posada San Francisco (☎ 462-60-22, fax 462-68-18, ⓔ info@posadasn francisco.com, *Plaza de la Constitución 17*) Singles/doubles from US$71/87, suites US$120. This hotel, on the south side of the zócalo in a restored 19th-century mansion, has a couple of restaurants, tennis courts, billiards and an inviting pool.

Places to Eat

Restaurant Vegetariano El Quinto Sol (☎ 466-18-57, *Juárez 12*) Prices from US$3.50. For healthy snacks and meals, try this popular place. It features fresh salads, veggie burgers, hearty breakfasts and a large variety of juices. The fixed-price meals here are good values.

Tamales Agus (*Juárez 25*) Prices US$0.30. Across the street from Vegetariano El Quinto Sol, this tiny place serves delicious mole and salsa verde *tamales* along with assorted *atole* drinks.

There's a row of places under the arcades on the east side of the zócalo. *Restaurante Jardín Plaza* is the best of the bunch, with regional food served in a pleasant indoor/ outdoor setting. *Gran Café* and *Los Portales* serve very popular dinner buffets featuring a wide variety of traditional dishes for US$8. *The Italian Coffee Company* a Mexican franchise, offers top-notch espresso, cappuccino and other coffee drinks, as well as a variety of gourmet teas.

Restaurant Sharon (*Guerrero 14*) 3 tacos US$3. Open 1pm-7pm Sun-Fri. For scrumptious tacos, try this clean, unpretentious place near Independencia.

Shopping
Embroidered capes and *huipiles* from Santa Ana Chiautempan, carved canes from Tizatlán, amaranth candies from San Miguel del Milagro and other local handicrafts are sold Monday to Friday along the Pasaje de las Artesanías, which forms an arc northeast of the Muñoz-Allende intersection.

Getting There & Away
The bus station is west of the zócalo. Second-class Flecha Azul buses travel to and from Puebla every ten minutes for US$1.25. To and from Mexico City's TAPO, Autobuses Tlaxcala-Apizaco-Huamantla (ATAH) operates its 1st-class 'expresso' buses every 20 minutes (2 hours, US$7.50) and 'ordinario' buses every half hour (2½ hours, US$4.75).

Getting Around
Buses and colectivos in Tlaxcala cost US$0.30. Most colectivos at the bus station go to the town center. From the center to the bus station, catch a blue-and-white colectivo along the east side of Boulevard Sánchez. There is a 24-hour parking lot underneath Plaza Juárez.

CACAXTLA & XOCHITÉCATL
The hilltop ruins at Cacaxtla ('ca-CASHT-la') feature vividly colored and well-preserved frescoes showing, among many other scenes, nearly life-size jaguar and eagle warriors engaged in battle. The ruins were discovered in September 1975 when a group of men from the nearby village of San Miguel del Milagro, in search of a reputedly valuable cache of relics, dug a tunnel and came across a mural.

The much older ruins at Xochitécatl ('so-chi-TEH-catl'), 2km away, include an exceptionally wide pyramid as well as a circular pyramid. A German archaeologist led the first systematic exploration of the site in 1969, but it wasn't until 1994 that the pyramids were uncovered and opened to the public. The two archaeological sites, 32km northwest of Puebla and 20km southwest of Tlaxcala, are among Mexico's most interesting.

Though both sites can be toured on one's own, explanatory signs tend to be either sketchy or overly technical. One alternative is to join a Sunday tour (US$1.75) conducted by the *Tlaxcala tourist office* (☎ 800-509-7557, cnr Juárez & Lardizabal, Tlaxcala) departing from the Hotel Posada de San Francisco in Tlaxcala at 10.15am and returning at 2.30pm. The fee includes transport and entry to both sites and explanations by authorized guides. It is also possible to hire a guide at the site between Thursday and Sunday.

History
Cacaxtla was the capital of a group of Olmeca-Xicallanca or Putún Maya, who first came to central Mexico as early as AD 400. After the decline of Cholula (which they may have helped bring about) around AD 600, they became the chief power in southern Tlaxcala and the Puebla valley. Cacaxtla peaked from AD 650-900 before being abandoned by AD 1000 in the face of possibly Chichimec newcomers.

Two kilometers west of Cacaxtla, atop a higher hill, the ruins of Xochitécatl predate Christ by a millennium. Just who first occupied the area is a matter of dispute, but experts agree that whereas Cacaxtla primarily served as living quarters for the ruling class, Xochitécatl was chiefly used for gory ceremonies to honor Quecholli, the fertility god. That isn't to say Cacaxtla didn't hold similar ceremonies; the skeletal remains of more than 200 mutilated children found there attest to Cacaxtla's bloody past.

Cacaxtla
From the parking lot, which is opposite the entrance to the site (*admission US$4, free Sun & holidays; open 10am-5pm daily*), it's a 200m walk to the ticket office, museum, shop and restaurant.

From the ticket office, it's another 300m to the main attraction – a natural platform 200m long and 25m high called the Gran

Basamento (Great Base), which is now under a huge metal roof. Here stood Cacaxtla's main religious and civil buildings and the residences of its ruling priestly classes. At the top of the entry stairs is an open space called the Plaza Norte. From here, you will follow a clockwise path around the ruins until you reach the **murals**.

Archaeologists have yet to determine the identity of the muralists; many of the symbols found in the murals are clearly from the Mexican highlands, yet a Mayan influence, from Yucatán, appears in all of them. The combined appearance of Mayan style and Mexican-highlands symbols in a mural is unique to Cacaxtla and the subject of much speculation.

Before reaching the first mural you come to a small patio whose main feature is an altar fronted by a small square pit in which numerous human remains were discovered. Just beyond the altar, along the west edge of the complex, you come upon the Templo de Venus, which contains two anthropomorphic figures in blue – a man and a woman – wearing short jaguar skins. The name of the temple is attributed to the appearance of numerous half-stars around the female figure, which are associated with the planet Venus.

On the opposite side of the path toward the Plaza Norte, the Templo Rojo (named for the amount of red paint used) contains four murals, only one of which is currently visible. Its weird imagery is dominated by a row of maize crops whose husks contain human heads.

Facing the north side of the Plaza Norte is the long Mural de la Batalla (Battle Mural), dating from before AD 700. It shows two groups of warriors, one wearing jaguar skins and the other bird feathers, engaged in ferocious battle. The Olmeca-Xicallanca (the jaguar-warriors with round shields) are clearly repelling invading Huastecs (the bird-warriors adorned with jade ornaments and deformed skulls).

At the end of the Mural de la Batalla, turn left and climb some steps to see the second main group of murals, to your right behind a fence. The two major murals, from about AD 750, show a figure in jaguar costume and a black-painted figure in bird costume (who is believed to be the Olmeca-Xicallanca priest-governor) standing upon a plumed serpent.

Xochitécatl

From the parking lot at the Xochitécatl site *(admission US$3, free Sun & holidays; open 10am-5.30pm Tues-Sun),* follow a path around to the circular Pirámide de la Espiral, atop which there's a cross put there by people from a neighboring village long before they knew the hill contained a pyramid. The path then leads to three other pyramids – the lowest in stature is Basamento de los Volcanes, the next is the mid-size Pirámide de la Serpiente, and the last is the quite large Pirámide de las Flores.

Pirámide de la Espiral Because of its outline and the materials used, archaeologists believe this circular pyramid was built between 1000 and 800 BC. Its form and location atop a high hill suggest it may have been used as an astronomical observation post or as a temple to Ehecatl, the wind god.

Basamento de los Volcanes Only the base of this pyramid remains, and it is made of materials from two periods. Cut square stones were placed over the original stones, visible in some areas, and then stuccoed over. The colored stones used to build Tlaxcala's municipal palace appear to have come from this site.

Pirámide de la Serpiente This structure gets its name from a large piece of carved stone with the head of a snake at one end. Its most interesting feature is the huge pot found at its center, carved from a single boulder that was hauled from another region. Scientists surmise it was used to hold water.

Pirámide de las Flores Experts speculate that rituals honoring the fertility god were held at this pyramid, within which were found several sculptures and the remains of 30 sacrificed infants. Near the pyramid's base – the fourth widest in Latin America – is a pool carved from a massive rock, where the infants were believed to have been washed before being killed.

Getting There & Away

The Cacaxtla site is 1.5km uphill from a back road between San Martín Texmelucan (near highway 150) and highway 119, which is the secondary road between Puebla and Tlaxcala. By car, turn west off highway 119 just south of Tlaxcala. A sign 1.5km west of the village of Nativitas points to Cacaxtla and to the nearby village of San Miguel del Milagro.

By public transport from Tlaxcala, take a 'San Miguel del Milagro' colectivo from the corner of 20 de Noviembre and Lardizabal; it will drop you off about 500m from Cacaxtla. Alternatively, a 'Nativitas-Texoloc-Tlaxcala' colectivo, which departs from the same corner, goes to the town of Nativitas, 3km from Cacaxtla; from there, catch a 'Zona Arqueológica' colectivo directly to the site. From Cacaxtla to Xochitécatl, take a taxi (US$3), or hike the 2km.

LA MALINCHE

This dormant 4460m volcano, named after Cortés' indigenous interpreter and lover, is 43km southeast of Tlaxcala and 73km northeast of Puebla. Its long, sweeping slopes dominate the skyline north of Puebla.

The main route to the summit is from highway 136; turn south at the sign 'Centro Vacacional Malintzi.' Before you reach the center, you must register at the entrance to Parque Nacional La Malintzi, which is open 24 hours daily.

Centro Vacacional Malintzi (☎ 246-462-40-98, 55-5238-2701 in Mexico City, fax 246-461-07-00) has campsites (US$3.50 per person) and cabins (US$50 up to six people, or US$80 up to nine people). Rates are lower during the week. This resort, run by the Mexican Social Security Institute (IMSS), has woodsy grounds and fine views of the peak. Cabins come with fireplaces, kitchens and basic accommodations. The center charges US$0.70 per person for day visits. Those not staying at the center may be able to leave their car in its parking lot for a small fee.

Above the center, the road becomes impassable by car. Then it's 1km by footpath, through trees initially, on to a ridge from which it is an arduous hike of about five hours to the top. Hikers should take precautions against altitude sickness (see Health in Facts for the Visitor). La Malinche is snow-capped only a few weeks each year.

There are three buses a day (8am, noon and 4pm) that go to the Centro Vacacional Malintzi (US$1.75) from downtown Apizaco, at Avenida Hidalgo and Aquiles Serdán, in front of the Comex store. Apizaco can be

reached via frequent buses from Tlaxcala, Huamantla or Puebla.

HUAMANTLA

• **pop 39,000** • **elev 2500m** ☎ **247**
This town dates from 1534 and is a national historic monument. Two of the most notable buildings are the 16th-century **Ex-Convento de San Francisco** and the 17th-century baroque **Parroquia de San Luis Obispo de Tolosa**.

During the first three weeks of August, Huamantla celebrates its feria. A day before the feast of the Assumption (August 15), inhabitants cover the town's streets with beautiful carpets made of flowers and colored sawdust. The Saturday following this event, there is a 'running of the bulls,' similar to that in Pamplona, Spain – but much more dangerous, because there is nothing to hide behind and the bulls charge from two directions.

Worthy hotels in the area include the following two. Rates nearly double during Huamantla's feria, for which rooms are booked well in advance.

Hotel Mesón del Portal (☎ 472-26-26, Parque Juárez 9) Singles/doubles US$16/21. This hotel has basic but cheery rooms with TV and bath.

Hotel Cuamanco (☎ 472-22-09, Highway 136 Km 146.5) Singles/doubles US$18/25. East of town, this surprisingly tasteful motel has clean, sizable rooms, some of which have balconies overlooking the surrounding fields.

Suriano runs frequent buses from Puebla and ATAH runs frequent buses from Tlaxcala.

PUEBLA

• **pop 1.3 million** • **elev 2162m** ☎ **222**
Few Mexican cities preserve the Spanish imprint as faithfully as Puebla. There are more than 70 churches and, in the central area alone, a thousand other colonial buildings – many adorned with the hand-painted tiles for which the city is famous. Located on the Veracruz-Mexico City road, and set in a broad valley with Popocatépetl and Iztaccíhuatl rising to the west, Puebla has always played a main role in national affairs.

Strongly Catholic, *criollo* and conservative, its people *(poblanos)* maintained Spanish affinities longer than most in Mexico. In the

The Quake of '99

On June 15 1999, an earthquake centered in Huajuapan de León, Oaxaca, sent tremors through the states of Oaxaca, Puebla and México. The city of Puebla was one of the worst hit, with at least 20 people killed and many buildings in the colonial center suffering serious damage. During the 40-second quake, which measured 6.9 on the Richter scale, the roof of the Palacio del Ayuntamiento on the north side of the zócalo caved in, while façade damage and cracks in naves and vaults occurred in varying degrees in almost all of the city's churches. Many of the historic buildings and museums mentioned here were still closed for repairs at the time of writing.

19th century, their patriotism was regarded as suspect, and today Puebla's Spanish-descended families have a reputation among other Mexicans for snobbishness. Nevertheless, it's a lively city with much to see and do. The historic center, where a great deal of conservation and restoration has taken place, has a prosperous modern dimension too, with its share of fancy boutiques. Cerro de Guadalupe is a peaceful retreat from city noises, as well as the site of a celebrated Mexican military victory and a clutch of museums. On the negative side, some areas of Puebla are squalid, polluted and unsafe to walk at night.

History
Founded by Spanish settlers in 1531 as Ciudad de los Ángeles with the aim of surpassing the nearby pre-Hispanic religious center of Cholula, the city became known as Puebla de los Ángeles eight years later and quickly grew into an important Catholic center. Fine pottery had always been made from the local clay, and after the colonists introduced new materials and techniques, Puebla pottery became both an art and an industry. By the late 18th century, the city was also an important textile and glass producer. With 50,000 people living in Puebla by 1811, it remained Mexico's second-biggest city until Guadalajara overtook it in the late 1800s.

The French invaders of 1862 expected a welcome in Puebla, but General Ignacio de Zaragoza fortified Cerro de Guadalupe, and on May 5 his 2000 men defeated a frontal attack by 6000 French, many of whom were handicapped by diarrhea. This rare Mexican military success is the excuse for annual national celebrations and hundreds of streets named in honor of Cinco de Mayo (May 5). No one seems to remember that the following year the reinforced French took Puebla and occupied the city until 1867.

Architecture
In the 17th century, local tiles – some in Arabic designs – began to be used to fine effect on Puebla church domes and, with red brick, on Puebla façades. In the 18th century, alfeñique – elaborate white stucco ornamentation named after a candy made from egg whites and sugar – became popular. Throughout the colonial period, the local gray stone was carved into a variety of forms to embellish many buildings. Also notable is the local indigenous influence, best seen in the prolific stucco decoration of buildings such as the Capilla del Rosario in the Templo de Santo Domingo and Tonantzintla village church (see Around Cholula later in this chapter).

Pottery
Puebla's colorful hand-painted ceramics, known as Talavera (after a town in Spain), take many forms – plates, cups, vases, fountains and azulejos (tiles). Designs show Asian, Spanish-Arabic and Mexican indigenous influences. Before the conquest, Cholula was the most important town in the area, and it had artistic influence from the Mixtecs to the south. The colorful glazed Mixteca-Cholula-Puebla pottery was the finest in the land when the Spanish arrived; Moctezuma, it was said, would eat off no other. The finest Puebla pottery of all is the white ware called majolica.

Orientation
The center of the city is the spacious, shady zócalo, with the cathedral on its south side. The majority of places to stay, eat and visit are within a few blocks of here. Farther away are dirtier, poorer streets. The area of smart, modern restaurants and shops along

Avenida Juárez, about 2km west of the zócalo, is known as Zona Esmeralda.

Buses arrive at a modern bus station, the Central de Autobuses de Puebla (CAPU), on the northern edge of the city.

The crucial intersection for the complicated naming system of Puebla's grid plan of streets is the northwest corner of the zócalo. From here, Avenida 5 de Mayo goes north, Avenida 16 de Septiembre heads south, Avenida Reforma goes west and Avenida Palafox y Mendoza goes east. Other north-south streets are suffixed Norte (Nte) or Sur, and west-east streets Poniente (Pte) or Oriente (Ote). These are designated with rising sequences of either odd or even numbers as you move away from the center.

Information

Tourist Offices The helpful state tourist office (☎ 246-12-85, e securep@infosel .net.mx) is at Calle 5 Ote 3, facing the cathedral yard. Open 9am to 8.30pm Monday to Saturday, and 9am to 2pm on Sunday, the office is staffed by English speakers. The office operates a tour of downtown Puebla by trolley car. The tour leaves every half hour from the south side of the zócalo (US$3.50).

The municipal tourist office (☎ 232-03-57) is on the zócalo, near the corner of Avenida Palafox y Mendoza and Calle 2 Nte, and is open 9am to 8pm Monday to Friday.

Money Several city-center banks change money and travelers checks, including

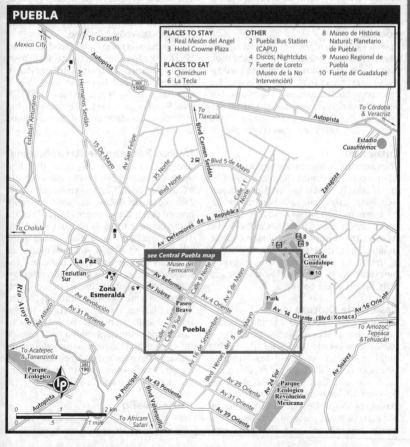

PUEBLA

PLACES TO STAY
1 Real Mesón del Angel
3 Hotel Crowne Plaza

PLACES TO EAT
5 Chimichurri
6 La Tecla

OTHER
2 Puebla Bus Station (CAPU)
4 Discos; Nightclubs
7 Fuerte de Loreto (Museo de la No Intervención)

8 Museo de Historia Natural; Planetario de Puebla
9 Museo Regional de Puebla
10 Fuerte de Guadalupe

Banamex, Bancomer and Bital, all on Avenida Reforma within two blocks west of the zócalo. All have ATMs.

Post & Communications The main post office is on Avenida 16 de Septiembre, south of the cathedral. The Telecomm office next door to the post office has telegram, fax, Internet, money transfer and telex services. There are a pair of good Internet cafés half a block north and south of the Museo Amparo: Cybercafé, at Calle 2 Sur 907, charges US$1.75 per hour; and Cyberbyte, at Calle 2 Sur 505B, charges US$2 per hour but is closed on Sunday.

Medical Services The Hospital Universidad Popular Autónomo del Estado de Puebla (UPAEP, ☎ 246-60-99) is at Calle 5 Pte 715, between Calles 7 Sur and 9 Sur.

Zócalo

Puebla's central plaza was a marketplace where hangings, bullfights and theater took place before it acquired its current garden-like appearance in 1854. The nearby arcades date from the 16th century. The zócalo fills with entertainers (mostly clowns) on Sunday evening, when the streetside tables at the Restaurant Royalty are especially popular.

Cathedral

The cathedral, whose image appears on the 500 peso bill, occupies the block south of the zócalo. It blends severe Herreresque-Renaissance style and early baroque. Building began in 1550 but most of it took place under bishop Juan de Palafox in the 1640s. At 69m, the towers are the highest in the country. The cathedral's bells are celebrated in the traditional rhyme *Para mujeres y campanas, las poblanas* – 'For women and bells, Puebla's (are best).'

Casa de la Cultura

Occupying the whole block facing the south side of the cathedral, the former bishop's palace is a classic brick-and-tile Puebla building that now houses government offices, including the state tourist office, and the Casa de la Cultura *(open 10am-8pm)*, devoted to local cultural activities. The posting boards in Casa de la Cultura's hallways are a great place to find announcements for musical and theater events

throughout the city. Upstairs is the **Biblioteca Palafoxiana**, with thousands of valuable books, including the 1493 Nuremberg Chronicle with more than 2000 engravings. The library was closed for earthquake repairs at the time of research.

Museo Amparo

This excellent modern museum *(☎ 246-42-10, Calle 2 Sur 708; admission US$1.75, video camera US$5.50 extra, free Mon; open 10am-6pm Wed-Mon)* at Calles 2 Sur and 9 Ote, is a must-see. It is housed in two linked colonial buildings. The first has eight rooms with superb pre-Hispanic artifacts, which are well displayed with explanations (in English and Spanish) of their production techniques, regional and historical context and anthropological significance. Crossing to the second building, you enter a series of rooms rich with the finest art and furnishings from the colonial period.

An audiovisual system (headset rental US$1.10) offers information in Spanish, English, French, German, Portuguese and Japanese. Guided tours are available in English (US$15.50) and Spanish (US$7.75, free Sunday at noon). The museum has a library, a cafeteria and a very good bookstore.

Museo Poblano de Arte Virreinal

Inaugurated in 1999, this is another top-notch museum *(☎ 246-58-58, Calle 4 Nte 203; admission US$1.75, includes admission to the Museo Casa del Alfeñique; open 10am-5pm)*, housed in the 17th-century Hospital de San Pedro between Calle 4 Ote and Calle 2 Ote. The galleries were once wings of the hospital. On the walls, it is still possible to see numbers that at one time indicated the spaces of patients' beds. One gallery displays temporary exhibits on the art of the viceregal period (16th to 19th century) in Mexico, another has temporary exhibits of contemporary Mexican art, and the last houses a fascinating permanent exhibit on the hospital's history, including a fine model of the building. The museum features a library and an excellent bookstore, with many art and architecture books in English.

Museo Bello

This house *(Calle 3 Pte 302; admission US$1.25, free Tues; open 10am-5pm)* is filled

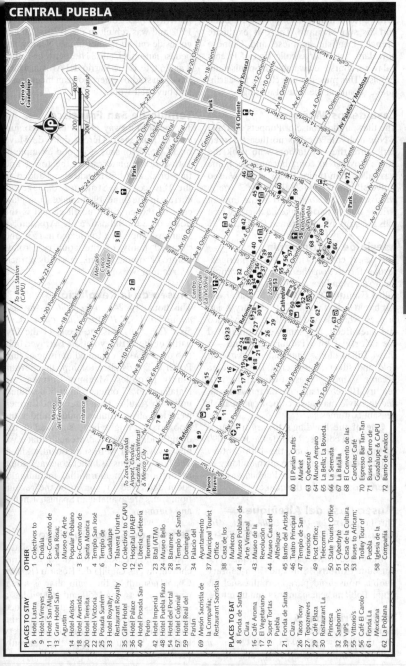

CENTRAL PUEBLA

PLACES TO STAY
5   Hotel Lastra
9   Hotel Virreyes
11 Hotel San Miguel
13 Gran Hotel San
    Agustín
14 Hotel Aristos
18 Hotel Avenida
20 Hotel Teresita
22 Hotel Victoria
25 Posada Suném
33 Hotel Royalty;
    Restaurant Royalty
35 Gilfer Hotel
36 Hotel Palace
40 Hotel Posada San
    Pedro
42 Hotel Imperial
48 Hotel Puebla Plaza
54 Hotel del Portal
57 Hotel Colonial
59 Hotel Real del
    Parián
69 Mesón Sacristía de
    la Compañía;
    Restaurant Sacristía

PLACES TO EAT
8   Fonda de Santa
    Clara
16 Café Aroma
17 El Vegetariano
19 Super Tortas
    Puebla
21 Fonda de Santa
    Clara
26 Tacos Tony
27 Tepozníeves
29 Café Plaza
30 Restaurant La
    Princesa
32 Sanbom's
39 VIPS
55 Vittorio's
56 Café El Carolo
61 Fonda La
    Mexicana
62 La Poblana

OTHER
1   Colectivos to
    Cholula
2   Ex-Convento de
    Santa Rosa;
    Museo de Arte
    Popular Poblano
3   Ex-Convento de
    Santa Monica
4   Templo San José
6   Templo de
    Guadalupe
7   Talavera Uriarte
10 Colectivos to CAPU
12 Hospital UPAEP
15 Librería Cafetería
    Teorema
23 Bital (ATM)
24 Museo Bello
28 Banamex
31 Templo de Santo
    Domingo
34 Palacio del
    Ayuntamiento
37 Municipal Tourist
    Office
38 Casa de los
    Muñecos
41 Museo Poblano de
    Arte Virreinal
43 Museo de la
    Revolución
44 Museo Casa del
    Alfeñique
45 Barrio del Artista
46 Teatro Principal
47 Templo de San
    Francisco
49 Post Office;
    Telecomm
50 State Tourist Office
51 Cyberbyte
52 Casa de la Cultura
53 Buses to African;
    Trolley Tour of
    Puebla
58 Iglesia de la
    Compañía
60 El Parián Crafts
    Market
63 Cybercafé
64 Museo Amparo
65 La Bella; La Boveda
66 La Serenata
67 La Batalla
68 El Convento de las
    Carolinas Café
70 Espresso Bar Tan-Tan
71 Buses to Cerro de
    Guadalupe & CAPU
72 Barrio de Analco

with the diverse art and crafts collection of 19th-century industrialist José Luis Bello and his son Mariano. There is exquisite French, English, Japanese and Chinese porcelain, and a large collection of Puebla Talavera. Tours are available in Spanish and English. This museum was closed for earthquake repairs at the time of writing.

Casa de los Muñecos

The tiles on the House of Puppets on Calle 2 Nte, near the zócalo's northeast corner, caricature the city fathers who took the house's owner to court because his home was taller than theirs. Inside is the **Museo Universitario** (☎ 246-28-99, Calle 2 Nte 2; admission US$0.60) (closed at the time of writing due to earthquake damage), which tells the story of education in Puebla.

Iglesia de la Compañía

This Jesuit church with a 1767 Churrigueresque façade, on the corner of Avenida Palafox y Mendoza and Calle 4 Sur, is also called Espíritu Santo. Beneath the altar is a tomb said to be that of a 17th-century Asian princess who was sold into slavery in Mexico and later freed. She supposedly originated the colorful China Poblana costume – a shawl, frilled blouse, embroidered skirt and gold and silver adornments. This costume became a kind of 'peasant chic' in the 19th century. But china also meant maidservant, and the style may have come from Spanish peasant costumes.

One of the building's towers fractured and a cupola collapsed during the June 1999 earthquake. Next door, the 16th-century Edificio Carolino, now the main building of Universidad Autonoma de Puebla, was also severely damaged by the quake.

Museo Casa del Alfeñique

This house (☎ 246-04-58, Calle 4 Ote 416; admission US$1.75; open 10am-5pm Tues-Sun) is an outstanding example of the 18th-century decorative style alfeñique. The museum exhibits 18th- and 19th-century Puebla household paraphernalia such as China Poblana gear, paintings and furniture.

Teatro Principal & Barrio del Artista

The theater (☎ 232-60-85, Calle 8 Ote at Calle 6 Nte; open 10am-5pm) dates from 1759, making it one of the oldest in the Americas – sort of. It went up in flames in 1902 and was rebuilt in the 1930s. You can go inside only if it's not in use. Nearby, the pedestrian-only Calle 8 Nte, between Calles 4 and 6 Ote, is the Barrio del Artista, which has open studios where you can meet artists and buy their work.

Templo de San Francisco

The north doorway of San Francisco, just east of Boulevard Héroes del 5 de Mayo on 14 Ote (Xonaca), is a good example of 16th-century plateresque; the tower and fine brick-and-tile façade were added in the 18th century. Structural damage occurred in the June 1999 quake. In a glass case in the church's north chapel is the body of San Sebastián de Aparicio, a Spaniard who came to Mexico in 1533 and planned many of the country's roads before becoming a monk. His body attracts a stream of worshipers.

Museo de la Revolución

This house (☎ 242-10-76, Calle 6 Ote 206; admission US$1.10, free Tues; open 10am-5pm Tues-Sun) was the scene of the first battle of the 1910 revolution. Betrayed only two days before a planned uprising against Porfirio Díaz's dictatorship, the Serdán family (Aquiles, Máximo, Carmen and Natalia) and 17 others fought 500 soldiers until only Aquiles, their leader, and Carmen were left alive. Aquiles, hidden under the floorboards, might have survived if the damp hadn't provoked a cough that gave him away. Both were subsequently killed. The house retains its bullet holes and some revolutionary memorabilia, including a room dedicated to women of the revolution. Tours are available in Spanish, English and German.

Templo de Santo Domingo

Santo Domingo, 2½ blocks north of the zócalo on Avenida 5 de Mayo, is a fine church, and its Capilla del Rosario (Rosary Chapel), south of the main altar, is a real gem. Built between 1650 and 1690, it has a sumptuous baroque proliferation of gilded plaster and carved stone with angels and cherubim popping out from behind every leaf. See if you can spot the heavenly orchestra.

ying tortillas, Mexico City

GREG ELMS

Mercado La Merced, Mexico City

GREG ELMS

ast food: chips and limes, Mexico City

GREG ELMS

La Bandera Mexicana, a potent trio of drinks

GREG ELMS

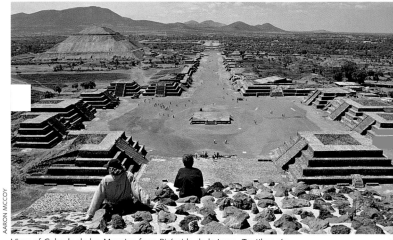
AARON MCCOY

View of Calzada de los Muertos from Pirámide de la Luna, Teotihuacán

JOHN NEUBAUER

Carnaval folk dancer, Tlaxcala

GREG ELMS

Sopes and other treats, Tepoztlán

ROSS BARNETT

Sunset over Valle de México

STUART WASSERMAN

Aztec performance, Teotihuacán

Ex-Convento de Santa Rosa & Museo de Arte Popular Poblano

This 17th-century ex-nunnery (☎ 232-92-40, enter at Calle 14 Pte between Calles 3 & 5 Nte; admission US$1.10, free Tues; open 10am-5pm Tues-Sun) houses an extensive collection of Puebla state handicrafts. You must take one of the hourly tours with a guide, who may try to rush you through the fine displays of traditional indigenous costumes, pottery, onyx, glass and metal work. Tours are in Spanish, but there are occasionally English-speaking guides available. Mole poblano is said to have been created in the kitchen of the ex-convent (see 'Puebla Originals,' later in this section).

Museo del Ferrocarril

A dozen vintage locomotives from the majestic to the quaint repose outside the old station (Calle 11 Nte 1005; admission free; open 10am-6pm daily).

Cerro de Guadalupe

The hilltop park, 2km northeast of the zócalo, contains the historic forts of Loreto and Guadalupe and the Centro Cívico 5 de Mayo, a group of museums and exhibitions. Good views, relatively fresh air and eucalyptus woods add to the appeal. Take a 'Plaza de Loreto' bus (US$0.30) north on Boulevard Héroes del 5 de Mayo.

Fuerte de Loreto, at the west end of the hilltop, was one of the Mexican defense points on May 5, 1862, during the victory over the invading French. Today, it houses **Museo de la No Intervención** (admission US$3; open 10am-4.30pm), which has displays of uniforms and documents relating to the French occupation of Mexico.

A short walk east of the fort, beyond the domed auditorium, are the **Museo Regional de Puebla** (☎ 235-97-20; admission US$3.50; open 10am-5pm Tues-Sun), which traces human history in the state, **Museo de Historia Natural** (☎ 235-34-19; admission US$2.25; open 10am-5pm Tues-Sun) and the pyramid-shaped **Planetario de Puebla** (☎ 235-20-99; admission US$2.75), which shows IMAX movies as well as light shows. At the east end of the hilltop you will find the **Fuerte de Guadalupe** (admission US$3; open 9am-6pm daily), which also played a part in the battle of May 5, 1862.

Places to Stay

Despite Puebla's abundance of hotels, which are easily recognizable by the big red 'H' signs over their doors, decent budget options tend to fill up fast, with most places catering toward a higher-end market. Reasonably priced hotels are most densely clustered along the streets west of the cathedral.

Budget Hotel Avenida (☎ 232-21-04, Calle 5 Pte 336) Singles/doubles without bath US$8/13.50, with bath US$11/17. Near the center, this lively hotel is very popular with young foreigners. It offers very basic rooms facing a central courtyard. It's about as clean as a hotel with flaking plaster and missing tiles can be.

Hotel Victoria (☎ 232-89-92, Calle 3 Pte 306) Singles/doubles US$11/17. Around the block from the Avenida is this gloomy and faded, but friendly enough and clean, hotel.

Hotel Virreyes (☎ 242-48-68, Calle 3 Pte 912) Singles/doubles without bath US$9/11, with bath US$14.50/19. A few blocks west of Hotel Victoria, the Virreyes has large, clean, wood-beamed rooms along two wide balconies above a courtyard parking lot. It's a bit run-down and not entirely bug-free, but not bad.

Hotel Real del Parián (☎ 246-19-68, Calle 2 Ote 601) Singles/doubles US$14.50/24. Just south of El Parián crafts market is this friendly place. Its brightly painted rooms are large and clean. If possible, choose a room with a balcony; interior rooms are stuffier.

Posada Suném (☎ 296-82-70, e posada sunem@hotmail.com, Calle 3 Pte 301) Rooms US$22. This tiny place, next to Fonda de Santa Clara, has large sunny rooms with high ceilings and tiled floors around a tiled courtyard.

Mid-Range Hotel Teresita (☎ 232-70-72, Calle 3 Pte 309) Singles/doubles US$19/29. Located 1½ blocks west of the zócalo, this hotel offers carpeted rooms with good beds and cable TV. You pay slightly more for those with windows facing the street.

Gran Hotel San Agustín (☎ 232-50-89, Calle 3 Pte 531) Singles/doubles with breakfast US$20/26. One block west of the Hotel Teresita, the San Agustín has small, rather stuffy rooms, each named after a town in the Puebla state, with TVs and unreliable

AROUND MEXICO CITY

fluorescent lighting. The price includes a space in the Hotel Virreyes parking lot.

Hotel San Miguel (☎ 242-48-60, Calle 3 Pte 721) Singles/doubles with bath US$23/29. Just up the street from the San Agustín, the San Miguel has clean, respectably sized rooms with TVs. Parking is unavailable, but you're entitled to a discount at a garage on the next block.

Hotel Puebla Plaza (☎ 246-31-75, fax 242-57-92, w www.hotelpueblaplaza.com, Calle 5 Pte 111) Singles/doubles with bath US$31/43. This attractively remodeled hotel, just west of the cathedral, offers rooms with wood-beamed ceilings, colonial-style furniture, tiled baths and TVs.

Hotel Imperial (☎ 242-49-80, Calle 4 Ote 212) Singles/doubles US$30/43, executive singles/doubles US$36/50. The Imperial caters to its guests' every need, offering free breakfast and dinner, laundry service, parking, some exercise equipment, a pool table and golfito – a two-hole miniature golf course in the back patio. With 64 comfortable rooms, the Imperial charges more for the stylish rooms in the new 'executive' wing.

Hotel Palace (☎ 232-24-30, fax 242-55-99, e hotpalas@prodigy.net.mx, Calle 2 Ote 13) Singles/doubles US$37/49. This is yet another pleasant and centrally located mid-range place. Rooms have cable TV. Parking costs US$5 extra.

Gilfer Hotel (☎ 246-06-11, fax 242-34-85, Calle 2 Ote 11) Singles/doubles US$45/55. Next door to the Hotel Palace, the more modern but similarly priced Gilfer has 92 comfortable rooms with TVs, phones and a safe.

Hotel Colonial (☎ 246-41-99, e colonial@giga.com, Calle 4 Sur 105) Singles/doubles US$44/54. On the corner of 3 Ote facing the university, this hotel has 70 lovely rooms. Most rooms are big and tiled, and have TVs and phones. Upstairs exterior rooms are best. Once part of a Jesuit monastery, the hotel maintains a hearty colonial atmosphere despite modernization. The Colonial may be the best value in Puebla. It's often full, so reserve ahead.

Hotel Royalty (☎ 242-47-40, fax 242-47-43, e royalty@prodigy.net.mx, Portal Hidalgo 8) Singles/doubles US$46/58. This 45-room hotel is another friendly, well-kept colonial-style place, on the zócalo. The

rooms are comfortable and colorful, with carpet and TVs.

Hotel del Portal (☎ 246-02-11, fax 232 31-94, Avenida Palafox y Mendoza 205 Singles/doubles US$46/61, with balcony US$54/67. This outwardly colonial hotel half a block from the zócalo, has a modern interior. Rooms are modest but comfortable, with phones and TVs.

Top End **Hotel Posada San Pedro** (☎ 246-50-77, e/mail hotel@posadasanpedro.com.mx Calle 2 Ote 202) Rooms US$78, suites from US$130. Just a block away from the zócalo this tastefully decorated hotel has a pool restaurant, bar and quiet courtyard. The large rooms are comfortable if not elegant.

Hotel Aristos (☎ 232-05-65, e avz01@ prodigy.net.mx, Avenida Reforma 533 Singles & doubles with air-con US$84. This big, fancy place has 120 rooms that aren' particularly spacious, but the rate drops to a more reasonable US$50 Friday to Sunday.

Mesón Sacristía de la Compañía (☎ 242 35-54, e sacristia@mail.g-networks.net Calle 6 Sur 304) Singles & doubles US$134 suites US$167. Honeymooners, or those ready for a splurge, may consider a stay at this hotel. The 18th-century building is in the heart of the Barrio de los Sapos and combines modern comfort with colonial splendor – at a price. The suites are fabulous with fine, dramatic furniture (most of which is for sale).

Hotel Lastra (☎ 235-97-55, Calzada de los Fuertes 2633) Rooms US$89. The 51-room Lastra, 2km northeast of the zócalo on the Cerro de Guadalupe, offers a peaceful location, good views, easy parking and a pleasant garden. Rooms come in various shapes and sizes.

There are a few top hotels outside the city center, but you miss out on the charm of central Puebla.

Real Mesón del Angel (☎ 223-83-00, e reservaciones@gruporeal.com.mx, Avenida Hermanos Serdán 807) Rooms from US$150 suites from US$206. Located 6km northwest of the center, just off the Mexico City highway, this is the best of the hotels here. Its 192 rooms have every amenity, and the grounds are quite attractive and peaceful.

Hotel Crowne Plaza (☎ 248-60-55, fax 213-70-00, e reservas@crowneplaza puebla.com.mx, Avenida Hermanos Serdán

141) Rooms from US$189. This hotel, geared toward business travelers, is 3km nearer the center. Its clean and well-appointed rooms surround a courtyard pool.

Places to Eat

Near the Zócalo *Restaurant La Princesa* *(Portal Juárez 101)* Prices US$2-7. This large dining hall on the zócalo's west side is packed at lunchtime for its five-course *cubiertos* (set meals) (US$3.25) and fresh fruit drinks (melon, papaya, mango).

Vittorio's (☎ *232-79-00, Portal Morelos 106)* Prices US$3-15. This Italian-run restaurant is one of the zócalo's culinary highlights. It bills itself as 'La Casa de la Pizza Increíble' in memory of a 20 sq m monster pizza baked back in 1981. The pizzas are good, but not cheap.

Restaurant Royalty (☎ *242-47-40, Portal Hidalgo 8)* Prices US$3.50-9. On the north side, this smart place has outdoor tables where you can watch the world go by for the price of a cappuccino. It also has tasty fish and meat dishes.

Café El Carolo *(Avenida Palafox y Mendoza 231)* Prices from US$2. Half a block east of the zócalo, this café serves fruit salad, yogurt and other less healthy stuff. It also has a *comida corrida*.

Sanborns *(Calle 2 Ote 6)* and *VIPS* *(Calle 2 Nte 8)* have branches just north of the zócalo.

Zona Esmeralda The upscale stretch of Juárez between Paseo Bravo and the La Paz area has lots of slick, international-style restaurants.

La Tecla (☎ *246-60-66, Juárez 1909)* Prices from US$5.50. Open 1.30pm-2am daily. Near Calle 21 Sur, La Tecla offers an enticing array of *alta cocina Mexicana* in a stylish setting. Try the *filete tecla*, a tender steak served over a *huitlacoche*/white sauce and graced with Roquefort cheese.

Chimichurri *(cnr Calle 27 Sur & Juárez)* Prices US$4.25-20. This is a popular Argentinian restaurant that serves steaks and pastas.

Poblano Specialties *Fonda de Santa Clara* (☎ *242-26-59, Calle 3 Pte 307)* Prices US$5-9.50. This is a super place to try poblano food. Santa Clara has delicious chicken mole and enchiladas. Also quite

tasty is the *mixiote* – a stew of sliced mutton tied in a maguey-leaf bundle – served with guacamole. The restaurant has a second branch (☎ *246-19-52, Calle 3 Pte 920)* a bit farther from the center. The food here is equally as good and the atmosphere is more festive.

Restaurant Sacristía (☎ *242-35-54, Calle 6 Sur 304)* Prices from US$7. Another good option for traditional poblano cuisine is here in the delightful patio of a colonial

AROUND MEXICO CITY

Puebla Originals

Mole poblano, which is found on almost every menu in Puebla and imitated throughout Mexico, is a spicy chocolate sauce usually served over turkey *(pavo* or *guajolote)* or chicken – a real taste sensation if well prepared. Supposedly invented by Sor (Sister) Andrea de la Asunción of the Convento de Santa Rosa for a visit by the viceroy, it traditionally contains fresh chile, chipotle (smoked jalapeño), pepper, peanuts, almonds, cinnamon, aniseed, tomato, onion, garlic and, of course, chocolate.

A seasonal Puebla dish, available in July, August and September, is *chiles en nogada*, said to have been created in 1821 to honor Agustín de Iturbide, the first ruler of independent Mexico. Its colors are those of the national flag: large green chilies stuffed with dried fruit and meat are covered with a creamy white walnut sauce and sprinkled with red pomegranate seeds.

In April and May you can try *gusanos de maguey*, and in March *escamoles* – respectively maguey worms and ant larvae.

A substantial poblano snack is the *cemita*, a sesame roll filled with *chiles rellenos*, white cheese or ham and seasoned with the essential herb *pápalo*...sort of a super torta.

Camotes are sticks of sweetened sweet potato paste flavored with various fruits. You can also buy sweet potatoes in a different form from Puebla's distinctive camote vendors. They wheel around a wood-burning stove with an ear-shattering whistle not unlike a steam engine. Inside are roasted sweet potatoes and plantains that you can eat plain or garnished with sugar and *lechera* (sweetened condensed milk).

mansion. Try the *mole Sacristía,* made from roasted *chipotle* chilies.

***Fonda La Mexicana** (Avenida 16 de Septiembre 708)* Prices from US$3.50. This unassuming restaurant, three blocks south of the zócalo, serves a great mole poblano plus other Puebla specialties at low prices.

***La Poblana** (Calle 7 Ote 17)* Prices US$1.50-2. This place, around the corner from the Museo Amparo, fixes authentic Puebla *cemitas* (see 'Puebla Originals').

The ***food court*** on the upper level of the Centro Comercial Victoria is an inexpensive place to sample Puebla specialties like mole and *chalupas.*

Vegetarian *El Vegetariano (☎ 246-54-62, Calle 3 Pte 525)* Prices from US$2.50. El Vegetariano has a long menu of meatless dishes such as *chiles rellenos, nopales rellenos* (stuffed cactus paddles) and *enchiladas suizas,* all of which come with salad, soup and a drink.

Cheap Eats & Snacks *Tacos Tony (Calle 3 Pte 147)* Prices from US$0.75. You can get a *pan árabe* taco (with pita bread instead of tortillas) here, a block west of the zócalo, where a trio of enormous cones of seasoned pork are kept grilling until 9pm.

***Super Tortas Puebla** (Calle 3 Pte 311)* Prices US$1.50-4. The tabletops at this place are set with dishes of marinated chilies, carrots and onions to spice up your sandwich.

***Tepoznieves** (Calle 3 Pte at Calle 3 Sur)* Prices US$1.50-2.75. This is Puebla's top traditional Mexican ice cream shop – fig with mezcal and mango with chile are among its long list of exotic flavors.

***Café Aroma** (Calle 3 Pte 520)* Prices from US$1. Open 8am-9pm. Across the street from El Vegetariano, this is the place to go for good coffee. It has only six tables and they're usually occupied.

***Café Plaza** (Calle 3 Pte 145)* Prices from US$1. Just off the zócalo, this café also brews a mean cup of java from a fresh-ground blend of Coatepec, Sierra de Puebla and Chiapas beans; the same blend is sold by the sack.

Entertainment

***Librería Cafetería Teorema** (cnr Avenida Reforma & Calle 7 Nte)* Admission US$2. This bookstore-cum-café fills up in the evenings with an arty/student crowd. There's live music most nights from 9.30pm to 1am.

***El Convento de las Carolinas Café** (Calle 3 Ote 403)* Popular with students from the nearby university, this café near the Callejón de los Sapos serves up live jazz, folk and blues.

***Espresso Bar Tan-Tan** (☎ 246-42-37, Calle 3 Ote 615A)* This dimly lit, cellar-like café, a block north of Plazuela de los Sapos, serves beer and wine as well as espresso. It hosts live jazz and rock Wednesday to Saturday at 8pm.

At night, mariachis lurk around the Callejón de los Sapos, Calle 6 Sur between Avenidas 3 and 7 Ote, but they are being crowded out by the bars on the nearby Plazuela de los Sapos. The tables at these bars, especially ***La Bella,*** are crowded every night of the week. Many of these become live music venues after dark. ***La Batalla*** favors folk music, while ***La Boveda*** and ***La Serenata,*** a large hall with a good sound system, feature rock 'n' roll bands.

In the Zona Esmeralda, there are a number of trendy discos and *antros* (music bars) on Juárez near Boulevard Norte just east of the La Paz neighborhood. Among the current hot spots are the disco ***Tasaja,*** ***Portos Tropical*** for salsa and merengue and the cutting-edge ***Bar y Tono***; an average US$2 to US$3 cover is charged at these places.

Check with the tourist offices and Casa de la Cultura for the word on cultural events.

Shopping

Quite a few shops along Calle 18 Pte, west of the Ex-Convento de Santa Mónica, display and sell the pretty Puebla ceramics. The big pieces are expensive and difficult for a traveler to carry, but you could buy a small hand-painted Talavera tile for US$3 to US$5, or a plate for around US$12.

***Talavera Uriarte** (☎ 232-15-98, Calle 4 Pte 911)* Hardly any Talavera shops make pottery on site anymore, but Talavera Uriarte still does, and has a factory and showroom. Factory tours are given at 11am, noon and 1pm Monday to Friday.

Indigenous textiles and pottery can be found at the state-run handicraft shop ***Patio del los Geranios*** on the 7 Ote side of the Casa de la Cultura.

El Parián crafts market (*between Calles 6 nd 8 Nte & Avenidas 2 and 4 Ote*) has local alavera, onyx and trees of life, as well as the orts of leather, jewelry and textiles that you nd in other cities. Much of the work is hoddy, but there is some good stuff and rices are reasonable. *Antique shops* domi- ate the Callejón de los Sapos, and on Sunday he Plazuela de los Sapos is the site of a lively *outdoor antiques market*. It's great for brows- ng, with a wonderful variety of old books, urniture, bric-a-brac and junk. Also on unday, there is a major *market* in the Barrio le Analco on the east side of Boulevard Héroes del 5 de Mayo, where flowers, sweets, aintings and other items are sold.

Along Calle 6 Ote east of Avenida 5 de Mayo, a number of *shops* sell traditional Puebla sweets such as *camotes* (candied weet potato sticks) and *jamoncillos* (bars of pumpkin seed paste). Stay away if you're afraid of bees!

Getting There & Away

Air Aeropuerto Hermanos Serdán, 22km west of Puebla on the Cholula-Huejotzingo road, has flights to/from Guadalajara and Tijuana by Aero California, and to/from León and Mexico City by Aeromar.

Bus Puebla's bus station, Central de Auto- buses de Puebla (CAPU), is 4km north of the zócalo and 1.5km off the autopista, by the corner of Boulevards Norte and Carmen Serdán. It has a left-luggage facility, phone office, Banca Serfin branch (with ATM), restaurant and various shops.

Buses to/from Puebla use Mexico City's TAPO. The 130km trip takes about two hours. Three bus lines have frequent serv- ices: ADO, a 1st-class service, has direct buses leaving every 20 minutes (US$8); AU, a 2nd-class service, has direct buses leaving every 14 minutes (US$7); Estrella Roja has 1st-class buses leaving every 20 minutes (US$8) and 2nd-class buses every 10 minutes (US$7). Estrella Roja also runs buses to Mexico City airport hourly from 3am to 8pm, for US$12.50.

There is daily bus service from Puebla to just about everywhere in the south and east of Mexico, including:

Cuernavaca – 175km, 3 hours; 4 deluxe (US$13), 8 1st-class (US$9), hourly 2nd-class (US$9)

Jalapa – 185km, 3 hours; 8 1st-class (US$9.50), hourly 2nd-class (US$8.50)

Oaxaca – 320km, 4½ hours; 1 deluxe UNO (US$58), 2 deluxe ADO GL (US$24), 7 1st-class (US$21), 3 2nd-class directos (US$16)

Tampico – 730km, 11 hours; 1 deluxe (US$27), 7 1st-class (US$21)

Tuxtla Gutiérrez – 870km, 13 hours; 1 deluxe UNO (US$80), 3 1st-class (US$53)

Veracruz – 300km, 3½ hours; 7 deluxe ADO GL (US$20), 10 1st-class (US$17), hourly 2nd-class (US$15) taking 4½ hours

Villahermosa – 690km, 8 hours; 1 deluxe UNO (US$64), 1 deluxe ADO GL (US$47), 2 1st-class (US$40)

Frequent colectivos to Cholula leave from the corner of Calles 6 Pte and 13 Nte in Puebla (30 minutes, US$0.50).

Car & Motorcycle Puebla is 123km from Mexico City by a fast autopista, highway 150D (tolls total about US$11). East of Puebla, 150D continues to Córdoba (nego- tiating a cloudy, winding 22km descent from the 2385m Cumbres de Maltrata en route) and Veracruz.

Getting Around

Most hotels and places of interest are within walking distance of the zócalo. From the bus station, you can take a taxi to the city center (US$3.50 ticket from the kiosk, US$4.50 after 10pm); or exit the station at the 'Auto- buses Urbanos' sign, and go up a ramp leading to the bridge over Boulevard Norte. On the other side of the bridge over Boule- vard Norte, walk west (toward VIPS) and stop in front of the Chedraui supermarket. From there, you can catch a No 40 combi to Avenida 16 de Septiembre, four blocks south of the zócalo. The ride takes 15 to 20 minutes.

From the city center to the bus station, climb aboard any northbound 'CAPU' co- lectivo from Boulevard Héroes del 5 de Mayo at Avenida Palafox y Mendoza, three blocks east of the zócalo. All city buses and colectivos cost US$0.30.

AROUND PUEBLA
Africam Safari

One of the best places in Mexico to see wildlife is this safari park (*☎ 281-70-00, Km 16.5 on road to Presa Valsequillo; adult/child US$8.50/7.75; open 10am-5pm daily*). The

over 3000 animals – among them rhinoc-
eros, bears and tigers – are in spacious
'natural' settings, and you can view them up
close from within your car, a taxi or an
Africam bus. It's best to arrive at the park in
the morning, when the animals are most
active. Estrella Roja runs daily buses from
CAPU to Africam and back, including admission and a four-hour tour of the park, for
US$12.50, US$11 for children. Tours also
depart from the zócalo Tuesday to Sunday
at 11am and 2pm for the same price.

CHOLULA
• pop 69,000 • elev 2170m ☎ 222

Ten kilometers west of Puebla stands the
widest pyramid ever built, Pirámide
Tepanapa – the Great Pyramid of Cholula.
By the 4th century AD, it measured 450m
along each side of the base and 65m high,
making it larger in volume than Egypt's
Pyramid of Cheops. But overgrown and
topped by a church, it's difficult even to recognize the huge grassy mound as a pyramid.
The town of Cholula is fairly unimpressive,
but the University of the Americas, with
many foreign students, adds a cosmopolitan
touch, and there's a hearty nightlife. The
nearby villages of Tonantzintla and Acatepec have splendid churches.

A 1999 earthquake measuring 6.9 took
its toll on some of Cholula's historic buildings, including the pyramid-top Santuario
de Nuestra Señora de los Remedios.

History
Between around AD 1 and AD 600,
Cholula grew into one of central Mexico's
largest cities and an important religious
center, while powerful Teotihuacán flourished 100km to the northwest. The Great
Pyramid was built over several times.
Around AD 600, Cholula fell to the
Olmeca-Xicallanca, who built nearby Cacaxtla. Sometime between AD 900 and
1300, Toltecs and/or Chichimecs took over.
Later it fell under Aztec dominance. There
was also artistic influence from the Mixtecs
to the south.

By 1519, Cholula's population had
reached 100,000, and the Great Pyramid
was already overgrown. Cortés, having
made friends with the nearby Tlaxcalans,
traveled here at Moctezuma's request.
Aztec warriors set an ambush, but unfortunately for them, the Tlaxcalans tipped of
Cortés about the plot and the Spanis
struck first. Within one day, they killed 600
Cholulans before the city was looted by th
Tlaxcalans. Cortés vowed to build a churc
here for each day of the year, or one on to
of every pagan temple, depending on whic
legend you prefer. Today there are 39 – fa
from 365 but still a lot for a small town.

The Spanish developed nearby Puebla t
overshadow the old pagan center, and
Cholula never regained its importance, es
pecially after a severe plague in the 1540
decimated the indigenous population.

Orientation & Information
Arriving buses and colectivos drop you of
two or three blocks north of the zócalo. Two
long blocks to the east, the pyramid with it
domed church on top is a clear landmark
The helpful tourist office (☎ 247-31-16)
open 10am to 5pm Monday to Friday and
10am to 3pm Saturday and Sunday, is a
Calle 4 Pte 103A, half a block northwest of
the zócalo. No English is spoken here, bu
maps are available. Bancomer, Bital and
Banamex, on the south side of the zócalo
change money and have ATMs. Casa de
Cambio de Puebla is on the same block; the
post office is three blocks west at Calle 7 Su
505. The IMSS (Social Security Institute)
Hospital is on Calle 4 Nte between Calles
10 and 12 Ote. El Globo Lavandería a
Calle 5 Ote 9 charges US$1 per kilogram
(minimum 3kg) to wash your clothes.

Zona Arqueológica
Pirámide Tepanapa Probably originally
dedicated to Quetzalcóatl, Cholula's
pyramid is topped by the church of **Nuestra
Señora de los Remedios**. It's a classic
symbol of conquest, but possibly an inad-
vertent one as the church may have been
built before the Spanish knew the mound
contained a pagan temple. The June 1999
earthquake sent deep fractures through the
church structure, but the pyramid suffered
no damage. You can climb to the church,
which was being reconstructed at the time
of writing, by a path from the pyramid's
northwest corner (no charge).

The Zona Arqueológica (*admission
US$3.50, video camera US$3.50 extra, free
Sun & holidays; open 9am-6pm Tues-Sun*)
comprises the excavated areas around the

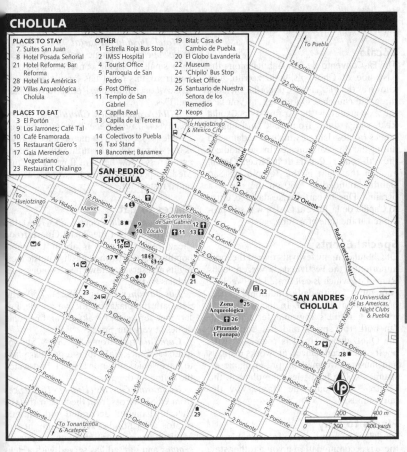

CHOLULA

PLACES TO STAY	OTHER	19 Bital; Casa de Cambio de Puebla
7 Suites San Juan	1 Estrella Roja Bus Stop	20 El Globo Lavandería
8 Hotel Posada Señorial	2 IMSS Hospital	22 Museum
21 Hotel Reforma; Bar Reforma	4 Tourist Office	24 'Chipilo' Bus Stop
28 Hotel Las Américas	5 Parroquia de San Pedro	25 Ticket Office
29 Villas Arqueológica Cholula	6 Post Office	26 Santuario de Nuestra Señora de los Remedios
	11 Templo de San Gabriel	27 Keops
PLACES TO EAT	12 Capilla Real	
3 El Portón	13 Capilla de la Tercera Orden	
9 Los Jarrones; Café Tal	14 Colectivos to Puebla	
10 Café Enamorada	16 Taxi Stand	
15 Restaurant Güero's	18 Bancomer; Banamex	
17 Gaia Merendero Vegetariano		
23 Restaurant Chialingo		

pyramid and the tunnels underneath. Enter via the tunnel on the north side. The small **museum** *(admission free with site ticket)*, across the road from the ticket office and down some steps, has the best introduction to the site – a large cutaway model of the pyramid mound showing the various superimposed structures.

Several pyramids were built on top of each other in various reconstructions. Over 8km of tunnels have been dug beneath the pyramid by archaeologists to penetrate each stage. From the tourist access tunnel, a few hundred meters long, you can see earlier layers of the building. Guides at the tunnel entrance charge US$7 for a one-hour tour or US$3.50 for a 15-minute tour of just the tunnels; a few speak English. You don't

need a guide to follow the tunnel through to the structures on the south and west sides of the pyramid, but they can be useful in pointing out and explaining various features as nothing is labeled.

The access tunnel emerges on the east side of the pyramid, from where you can take a path around to the **Patio de los Altares**, or Great Plaza, on the south side. This was the main approach to the pyramid, and it is ringed by platforms and unique diagonal stairways. Three large stone slabs on its east, north and west sides are carved in the Veracruz interlocking-scroll design. At its south end is an Aztec-style altar in a pit dating from shortly before the Spanish conquest. On the west side of the mound is a reconstructed section of the latest pyramid, with two earlier layers exposed to view.

Zócalo

The **Ex-Convento de San Gabriel**, along the east side of Cholula's wide zócalo, also known as the Plaza de la Concordia, includes three fine churches. On the left, as you face the ex-convent, is the Arabic-style **Capilla Real**, which dates from 1540 and has 49 domes (almost half of which were damaged during the 1999 earthquake). In the middle is the 19th-century **Capilla de la Tercera Orden**, and on the right is the **Templo de San Gabriel**, founded in 1530 on the site of a pyramid. Due to earthquake damage, entry to Capilla de la Tercera Orden was still prohibited at the time of writing.

Special Events

Of Cholula's many festivals, one of the most important is the Festival de la Virgen de los Remedios, which is celebrated the week of September 1 with daily traditional dances on the Great Pyramid. In the weeks that follow, Cholula's regional feria is held. On both the spring and fall equinoxes, the Quetzalcóatl ritual is reenacted with poetry, sacrificial dances, fireworks displays and music performed on pre-Hispanic instruments. The festivities take place in the Centro Ceremonial de Danzas by the fairgrounds.

Places to Stay

Cholula is an easy day trip from Puebla, but there is accommodation if you'd rather stay.

Hotel Reforma (☎ 247-01-49, Calle 4 Sur 101) Singles/doubles with bath US$18/27. The Reforma, located midway between the zócalo and the pyramid, is the oldest hotel in Cholula. All 13 rooms are nice and have hot water, but size and features vary.

Hotel Las Américas (☎ 247-09-91, Calle 14 Ote 6) Singles/doubles with TV & bath US$13/23. This hotel, three blocks east of the pyramid, is a little farther from the action, but offers clean and comfortable rooms for a very reasonable price. There's a restaurant, a pleasant courtyard garden and a pool.

Suites San Juan (☎ 247-02-78, Calle 5 Sur 103) Singles/doubles US$28/39. Half a block from the market, the San Juan has large, clean rooms with enormous beds and TVs;

windows face a noisy street. The parking lo is open to the public during the day.

Hotel Posada Señorial (☎ 247-03-41 Portal Guerrero 5) Singles/doubles US$43/50 In a small shopping center inside Porta Guerrero, this hotel has large rooms with rustic wooden furniture. Rooms have phones and TVs.

Villa Arqueológica Cholula (☎ 247-19-66, fax 247-15-08, Calle 2 Pte 601) Singles doubles US$84/95. The nicest place in town is this 44-room hotel, south of the pyramid and across a few fields of flowers. A Club-Med property, it has lush gardens, a pool and a restaurant.

Places to Eat

Café Enamorada Prices US$3-7. At the southern corner of the Portal Guerrero on the zócalo, this café is about the most popular place in town. It has live music most nights and serves sandwiches, tostadas, quesadillas and tacos.

Los Jarrones Prices US$2.50-7.50. Underneath the plaza's attractive arcade, Los Jarrones serves set breakfasts and regional dishes at very fair prices.

Café Tal Prices from US$0.80. Next door to Los Jarrones, Café Tal is a popular place to have some coffee or a snack and watch the action on the plaza.

Restaurant Güero's (Hidalgo 101) Prices from US$2. Across from the zócalo, this is a cheerful hangout, decorated with antique photos of Cholula. Among the hearty Mexican favorites on the menu are pozole, cemitas and quesadillas served with a delicious salsa roja.

Gaia Merendero Vegetariano (Calle 3 Pte 102) Prices US$2.75-4.50. This small, cheery restaurant serves up wholesome breakfasts, meatless versions of popular Mexican dishes and fresh fruit and vegetable juices.

El Portón (Hidalgo at Calle 3 Sur) Set menu US$4. One block west of the zócalo, this place is popular for its daily set menu, which typically includes a choice of three soups, a main course (chicken, beef or vegetables), dessert and coffee.

Restaurant Chialingo (☎ 247-28-31, Calle 7 Pte 113) Prices US$3.50-7.50. A few short blocks away, this is a much finer place, overlooking a lovely courtyard. It offers salads, chicken and seafood.

Entertainment

Bar Reforma Next to the Hotel Reforma, southeast of the zócalo, this is Cholula's oldest drinking spot and serves freshly prepared sangrias and snacks.

Discos and antros, including **Rocka**, **El Alebrije** and **La Adelita**, are clustered near the university exit of the 'Recta,' as the highway to Puebla is known.

Closer to the center on Calle 14 Pte east of the pyramid, there are several bars and discos, including Keops *(cnr Calles 14 Pte & 16 de Septiembre)*. This quiet area comes alive after about 10pm Thursday to Saturday.

Getting There & Away

Frequent colectivos to Puebla leave from the corner of Calles 5 Pte and 3 Sur. They cost US$0.50 and take 20 minutes. Estrella Roja has frequent buses between Mexico City's TAPO and Puebla that stop in Cholula on Calle 12 Pte (US$4).

AROUND CHOLULA
Tonantzintla & Acatepec

The interior of the small **Templo de Santa María** *(open 9am-6pm daily)* in Tonantzintla is among the most exuberant in Mexico. Under the dome, the surface is covered with colorful stucco saints, devils, flowers, fruit, birds and more – a great example of indigenous artisanship applied to Christian themes. Tonantzintla celebrates the Festival of the Assumption on August 15 with a procession and traditional dances.

The **Templo de San Francisco** *(open 10am-1pm & 3pm-5pm daily)* in Acatepec, 1.5km southeast of Tonantzintla, dates from about 1730. The brilliant exterior is beautifully decorated with blue, green and yellow Talavera tiles set in red brick on an ornate Churrigueresque façade.

Getting There & Away

Autobuses Puebla-Cholula runs 'Chipilo' buses from the Puebla bus station to Tonantzintla and Acatepec. In Cholula, you can pick them up on the corner of Calle 7 Pte and Miguel Alemán. Between the two villages you can wait for the next bus or walk.

Huejotzingo

• pop 19,000 • elev 2280m ☎ 227

Huejotzingo ('weh-hot-SIN-goh'), 14km northwest of Cholula on highway 190, is known for its cider and sarapes. The fine 16th-century plateresque-style monastery has been restored as a **museum** *(Plazuela Fray Juan de Alameda; admission US$3, free Sun; open 10am-4.30pm Tues-Sun)* with exhibits on the Spanish missions and monastic life. The fortified church is stark but imposing, with Gothic ribbing on its ceiling. There are old frescoes and excellent carved stonework. On Shrove Tuesday, masked Carnaval dancers re-enact a battle between French and Mexican forces. Estrella Roja buses service Huejotzingo from Puebla, Cholula and Mexico City.

SIERRA NORTE DE PUEBLA

The mountains covering much of remote northern Puebla state rise to over 2500m before falling away to the Gulf coastal plain. Despite deforestation, it's beautiful territory, with pine forests and, at lower altitudes, semitropical vegetation. Sierra Norte handicrafts – among them *rebozos*, quechquémitls and baskets – are sold in markets at Cuetzalan, Zacapoaxtla, Teziutlán, Tlatlauquitepec and elsewhere.

The area has a large indigenous population, mostly Nahua and Totonac (see 'The Nahua,' later, and 'The Totonacs' in the Central Gulf Coast chapter).

Cuetzalan

• pop 5000 • elev 1000m ☎ 233

The colonial town of Cuetzalan, in the center of a lush coffee-growing region, is famed for a Sunday market that fills its zócalo and attracts scores of indigenous people in traditional dress.

Orientation & Information The main road into town from the south passes a tiny bus depot before ending 100m later at the zócalo. The center is on a hillside; from the zócalo most hotels and restaurants are uphill. Children will offer to guide you around for a small fee; most are friendly and helpful. There's a tourist office (☎ 331-00-04) on Hidalgo west of the zócalo (two doors down from a door with the large blue letters 'SEP' above it). It's open 9am to 4pm Wednesday to Sunday. No English is spoken, but maps of the town are available. Banamex on Alvarado has an ATM.

Things to See & Do Two towers rise above Cuetzalan: the tall gothic spire of the zócalo's **Parroquia de San Francisco** and the tower of **Santuario de Guadalupe** to the west, with unusual decorative rows of clay vases. There's a regional **museum** opposite Posada Jackeline.

Two lovely waterfalls called **Las Brisas** are 4km and 5km northeast of town. To reach them, catch one of the colectivos behind the Parroquia de San Francisco heading for the village of San Andrés, or simply walk along the dirt road that begins just west of the bus depot, keeping to the right when it forks, until you come to San Andrés and its church with a striking green-tile dome. There, at least one child will offer to take you to the falls for US$3. You should accept the offer, as there are many trails in the forest and no signs to the falls. Bring bathing gear as the natural pools under the falls are enticing. Some of the area's 32km network of caves can be explored at **Atepolihui**, accessible from the village of San Miguel a half hour walk from the end of Hidalgo.

Special Events For several lively days around October 4, Cuetzalan celebrates both the festival of San Francisco de Assisi and the Feria del Café y del Huipil. A traditional dance festival in mid-July attracts groups from all over the area.

The Nahua

Puebla state has about 400,000 of Mexico's most numerous indigenous people, the Nahua – more than any other state. Another 200,000 Nahua live in western parts of Veracruz state adjoining Puebla. The Nahua language (Náhuatl) was spoken by the Aztecs and, like the Aztecs, the Nahua were probably of Chichimec origin. Traditional Nahua women's dress consists of a black wool *enredo* (waist sash) and embroidered blouse and *quechquémitl* (shoulder cape). The Nahua are Christian but often also believe in a pantheon of supernatural beings, including *tonos* (people's animal 'doubles') and witches who can become blood-sucking birds and cause illness.

Places to Stay *Posada Jackeline* (☎ 331 03-54, 2 de Abril 2) Singles/doubles US$11/17. On the uphill side of the zócalo this hotel's basic but large and clean rooms are good values.

Hotel Posada Cuetzalan (☎ 331-01-54 Zaragoza 10) Singles/doubles US$34/45 Located 100m from the zócalo, this hotel has 40 rooms with blue walls, lots of lightly stained wood and TVs. It has a swimming pool, a restaurant, and two lovely interior courtyards.

Hotel La Casa de la Piedra (☎ 331-00-30, García 11) Singles/doubles US$35/44 This is the best place in town, two blocks below the zócalo. The old stone house has been superbly renovated in *rústico* style with fine wood floors and large picture windows. Two-level suites accommodate up to four people and offer views of the valley. downstairs rooms have double beds. Secure parking is available.

Several places near Cuetzalan are designed for maximum appreciation of the area's beautiful landscapes.

Taselotzin (☎ 331-04-80, e maseualsina@ laneta.apc.org, Barrio Zacatipan) Dorm beds US$8.50, singles/doubles US$18/32. Just outside Cuetzalan on the Puebla road, the Taselotzin is run by local Nahua craftswomen. It has five cozy cabins, as well as dormitory-style lodging amid peaceful gardens. The restaurant serves traditional dishes of the region.

Cabañas Metzintli (☎ 249-04-72, e luna06@correoweb.com) Rooms from US$34, cabins from US$61. About 1km from the town center on the road to Yohualichán, Metzintli has lovely rustic rooms and cabins for rent. The grounds include a soccer field and a small basketball court. Horses and four-wheel all-terrain vehicles are available for rent.

Places to Eat *Restaurant Yoloxochitl* (☎ 331-03-35, across the street from Posada Jackeline) Prices US$1.50-3. This restaurant has lots of charm, a lovely view and OK food. It offers salads, antojitos and meat dishes. In season, mushrooms are served pickled, in chipotle sauce, and in a cocktail.

La Terraza (☎ 331-06-62, Hidalgo 33) Prices US$2-7. This is one of several good restaurants along Hidalgo. It offers an assortment of seafood, salads and pastas.

Bar El Calate (☎ 331-05-66, *Morelos 9B*) Prices from US$0.30. On the west side of the zócalo, this is a great place to try home-made alcoholic drinks made from coffee, limes and berries, as well as *yolixpán*, a medicinal liqueur made from local herbs.

Restaurant Peña Los Jarritos (☎ 331-05-58, *Plazuela López Mateos 7*) Prices from US$3. This restaurant is under the same ownership as Casa de la Piedra. It hosts Saturday night *peñas*, featuring regional dishes and drinks, folk music, quetzal dancers, local *uapango* bands and *voladores* (literally 'fliers,' the Totonac ritual in which men, suspended by their ankles, whirl around a tall pole). Book early.

Getting There & Away First-class ADO buses (3¾ hours, US$10) leave Puebla for Cuetzalan at 4.15pm daily, and Cuetzalan for Puebla at 5.30am daily. Second-class Vía buses (US$9) make the same run hourly. On weekends, ADO runs an additional 8.30am bus from Puebla and a 6.30pm departure from Cuetzalan. Get your return tickets early. Autotransportes Mexico-Texcoco runs six 1st-class buses daily (5½ hours, US$14) to/from Mexico City's TAPO.

Yohualichán

About 8km from Cuetzalan by cobblestone road, this pre-Hispanic site *(admission US$2.50, free Sun; open 8am-5pm daily)* has niche pyramids similar to El Tajín. The site is adjacent to the Yohualichán town plaza. To get there, catch any colectivo taking the road out of Cuetzalan from the end of Hidalgo (US$0.30), and get off when it stops beside the blue sign with a pyramid image on it. It's a half-hour walk from this turnoff.

SOUTHERN PUEBLA

The main route from Puebla to Oaxaca is a modern toll highway that turns south off highway 150D, 83km east of Puebla. Two older roads, highways 150 and 190, go through southern Puebla state toward Oaxaca.

Highway 150

Heading east from Puebla, this road parallels the 150D autopista, but it's a lot slower and more congested. Second-class buses stop at the towns en route. **Amozoc**, 17km

from Puebla, produces pottery and many of the fancy silver decorations worn by *charros* (Mexican cowboys). **Tepeaca**, 38km from Puebla, has a big Friday market, mainly for everyday goods, and a 16th-century Franciscan monastery. The village of **Tecali**, 11km southwest of Tepeaca, is a center for the carving of onyx from the nearby quarries.

Tehuacán

- **pop 192,000** • **elev 1640m** ☎ 238

Modern Tehuacán, on highway 150, 122km southeast of Puebla, is a pretty town with a fine zócalo. It's famed for its mineral water (the town's name is the generic term for the water), which is sold in bottles all over Mexico; tours of the impressive **Peñafiel** plant, 100m north of the Casas Cantarranas hotel (see Places to Stay, later in this section), are offered from 9am to 12pm and 4pm to 6pm daily except Friday. Just up the road, competitor Garci-Crespo offers informative tours of its facilities 10am to 4pm daily, including a visit to its underground springs.

The high, dry Tehuacán Valley was the site of some of the earliest agriculture in Mexico. By 7000-5000 BC, people were planting avocados, chilies, cotton and maize. Pottery, the sign of a truly settled existence, appeared about 2000 BC. The **Museo del Valle de Tehuacán** *(admission US$1.25; open 10am-6pm Tues-Sun),* inside the Ex-Convento del Carmen three blocks northwest of the zócalo, explains some of the archaeological discoveries and exhibits tiny preserved cobs of maize that were among the first to be cultivated. The museum was closed for earthquake repairs at the time of writing.

Orientation & Information The main road into town coming from Puebla, Avenida Independencia, passes the ADO bus station before reaching the north side of Parque Juárez – the zócalo. The main north-south road is Avenida Reforma. The city's most popular restaurants are located around the zócalo. There's a tourist information kiosk in the zócalo open from 10am to 2pm and 4 to 7pm daily.

Special Events October 15 starts the two-week festival La Matanza, in which goats are slaughtered en masse. *Mole de cadera* is the regional specialty resulting from the carnage (available year-round at Restaurant Danny Richard, across the street from the Ex-Convento del Carmen).

Places to Stay *Hotel Monroy* (☎ 382-04-91, *Reforma Nte 217)* Singles/doubles US$20/26. The Monroy offers no frills, but the rooms are clean and spacious.

Bogh Suites Hotel (☎ 382-34-74, fax 382-33-73, *Calle 1 Nte 102)* Singles/doubles US$29/34. Rooms on the fourth floor are discounted (no elevator). On the northwest side of the zócalo, Bogh Suites has small but attractive rooms with TVs, phones and fans. Parking, at a lot across the street, is included in the price.

Hotel México (☎ 382-24-19, **w** *hotel mexico.hypermart.net, cnr Reforma Nte & Independencia Pte)* Singles/doubles US$46/53. This hotel is central but quite tranquil with large, comfortable rooms, several courtyards, a restaurant and a swimming pool.

Casas Cantarranas (☎ 383-49-22, **e** *hotelcc@acnet.net, Avenida José Garci-Crespo 2215)* Singles/doubles US$67/77. This resort features a large, blue-tile pool, spacious gardens and 45 fine rooms with every amenity.

Getting There & Away ADO, at Independencia 119, has 1st-class buses running every half hour to/from Puebla (2 hours, US$6.50), an hourly service to/from Mexico City (4 hours, US$13), two buses a day to Veracruz (4½ hours, US$12) and five buses a day to Oaxaca (3 hours, US$16).

Around Tehuacán

Twenty-five kilometers southwest of Tehuacán, **Jardín Botánico** (☎ 383-68-45; admission US$1; open 8am-6pm daily) displays some 250 species of local plants, mainly cactus, along well-maintained trails. It's 3km before Zapotitlán de Salinas, on highway 125 to Huajuapan de León. To get there, catch a green-and-white bus along Calle 1 Sur, south of the cathedral. On weekends, you may be better off hiring a taxi roundtrip as bus service is infrequent.

Highway 190

Highway 190 swings southwest from Puebla to **Atlixco**, 31km away, a town known for its mineral springs, avocados, near-perfect climate – and the weeklong Atlixcáyotl festival of traditional indigenous culture in September, which culminates in a spectacular dance display by groups from all parts of Puebla state on the last Sunday of the month. Another 36km brings you to **Izúcar de Matamoros**, which also has therapeutic balnearios but is best known for ceramic handicrafts.

South of Mexico City

Heading south from Mexico City, highway 95 and highway 95D (the toll road) climb to more than 3000m from the Valle de México into refreshing pine forests, then descend to Cuernavaca, capital of Morelos state and longtime popular retreat from Mexico City. On the way, highway 115D branches southeast to Tepoztlán, nestled beneath high cliffs, and to balnearios at Oaxtepec and Cuautla.

Morelos is one of Mexico's smallest and most densely populated states. Valleys at different elevations have a variety of microclimates, and many fruits, vegetables and grains have been cultivated since pre-Hispanic times. Archaeological sites at Cuernavaca, Tepoztlán and Xochicalco show signs of the agricultural Tlahuica civilization and the Aztecs who subjugated them. In the colonial era, most of the state was controlled by a few families, including descendants of Cortés. Their palaces and haciendas can still be seen, along with churches and monasteries from as early as the 16th century. Unsurprisingly, the *campesinos* of Morelos became fervent supporters of the Mexican Revolution, and local lad Emiliano Zapata is the state's hero.

South of Cuernavaca, spurs of highway 95D go to the remarkable silver town of Taxco and to the industrial city of Iguala, both in mountainous Guerrero state. The Iguala branch continues south as highway 95 (no autopista pretensions) to Chilpancingo and Acapulco (see the Central Pacific Coast chapter). The main highway 95D takes a more direct route to Chilpancingo and Acapulco. On this expensive superhighway, you can drive the 400km between Mexico City and Acapulco in three hours – the frequent tolls can total more than US$44. The alternative sections of free road are consequently heavily used, slow and dangerous. Driving at night in Guerrero is inadvisable because cars are sometimes stopped and robbed. The route from Iguala to Ixtapa via highways 51 and 134 is said to be particularly risky.

TEPOZTLÁN
• pop 14,000 • elev 1701m ☎ 739

Eighty kilometers from Mexico City, Tepoztlán (Place of Copper) sits in a valley surrounded by high, jagged cliffs. It was the legendary birthplace, more than 1200 years ago, of Quetzalcóatl, the omnipotent serpent god of the Aztecs. The town retains indigenous traditions, with many older people still speaking Náhuatl, and younger people now learning it in secondary school. Now something of an international hippie venue, Tepoztlán attracts writers, artists and astrologers, who claim the place has a creative energy, as well as many more conventional weekend visitors from Mexico City. Developers hoping to profit from the destination's popularity planned an enormous golf club complex a few years ago, but locals who feared their water supplies would be threatened organized against it successfully.

Orientation & Information
Everything here is easily accessible by walking, except the Pirámide de Tepozteco on the clifftop to the north. Street names change in the center of town; for example, Avenida 5 de Mayo becomes Avenida Tepozteco north of the plaza.

The Telecomm office on the north side of the main plaza has fax and telegram service. The post office is in an interior courtyard accessible through a black door marked 'Municipio del Tepoztlán' on Avenida Tepozteco near Zaragoza. Long-distance and local telephone calls can be made from pay phones around town. There's a Bancomer on the west side of the plaza. Café El Navegante, opposite Museo Arqueológico Carlos Pellicer on Pablo González, is an Internet café that actually serves coffee! They charge US$1.75 per hour for Internet access.

Ex-Convento Domínico de la Natividad
This monastery (admission free; open 10am-5pm Tues-Sun) and the attached church were built by Dominican priests between 1560 and 1588 and are the chief feature of the town. The plateresque church façade has Dominican seals interspersed with indigenous symbols, floral designs and various figures including the sun, moon and stars, animals, angels and the Virgin Mary.

The arched entryway to the monastery is an elaborate mural of pre-Hispanic history and symbolism composed of 60 varieties of seeds. Every year, during the first week of September, local artists create a new mural.

The 400-year-old monastery section has been undergoing a major restoration since 1993. Some 4500 sq m of murals from the 16th and 17th centuries have been meticulously restored. Upstairs, the cells of the west wing house a museum covering the region's natural history, economy, social organization and religion.

Museo Arqueológico Carlos Pellicer
This museum (☎ 395-10-98, Pablo González 2; admission US$0.60; open 10am-6pm Tues-Sun) behind the Dominican church has a small but interesting collection of pieces from many parts of Mexico, donated to the people of Tepoztlán by the Tabascan poet Carlos Pellicer Cámara. The objects on display here are lively and vibrant, with an emphasis on human figures, but also include some animals. The stone fragments depicting a pair of rabbits – the symbol for Ometochtli, one of the 400 gods of pulque – were discovered at the Tepozteco pyramid site.

Though there is no tourist office in Tepoztlán, the museum's knowledgeable staff can answer most of your questions.

Pirámide de Tepozteco
The 10m-high Pyramid of Tepozteco (admission US$3, free Sun; open 9am-5.30pm daily) was built on a cliff 400m above Tepoztlán in honor of Tepoztécatl, the Aztec god of the harvest, fertility and pulque. It's accessible by a steep path beginning at the end of Avenida Tepozteco; the 1.3km walk can take up to 1½ hours and may be too strenuous for some. At the top, you may be rewarded with a panorama of Tepoztlán and the valley, depending on haze levels. Hiking boots or at least good tennis shoes are recommended.

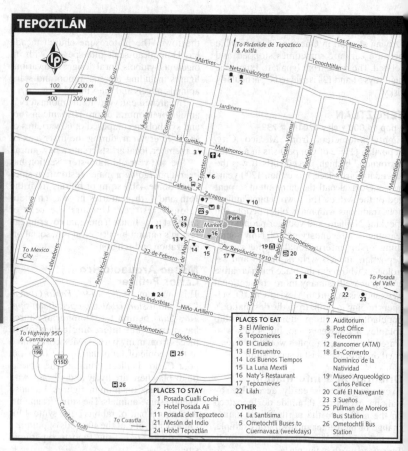

TEPOZTLÁN

PLACES TO EAT
3 El Milenio
6 Tepoznieves
10 El Ciruelo
13 El Encuentro
14 Los Buenos Tiempos
15 La Luna Mextli
16 Naty's Restaurant
17 Tepoznieves
22 Lilah

7 Auditorium
8 Post Office
9 Telecomm
12 Bancomer (ATM)
18 Ex-Convento
   Dominico de la
   Natividad
19 Museo Arqueológico
   Carlos Pellicer
20 Café El Navegante
23 3 Sueños
25 Pullman de Morelos
   Bus Station
26 Ometochtli Bus
   Station

PLACES TO STAY
1 Posada Cualli Cochi
2 Hotel Posada Ali
11 Posada del Tepozteco
21 Mesón del Indio
24 Hotel Tepoztlán

OTHER
4 La Santisima
5 Ometochtli Buses to
   Cuernavaca (weekdays)

Special Events

Tepoztlán is a festive place, with many Christian feasts superimposed on pagan celebrations. On the five days preceding Ash Wednesday, Carnaval features the colorful dances of the Huehuenches and Chinelos with feather headdresses and beautifully embroidered costumes. On September 7, an all-night celebration takes place on Tepozteco hill near the pyramid, with copious consumption of *ponche* and pulque in honor of Tepoztécatl. The following day is the Fiesta del Templo, a Catholic celebration featuring theater performances in the Náhuatl language and the re-creation of the seed mural upon the monastery's entrance arch (see Ex-Convento Domínico de la Natividad earlier in this section). The holiday was first in-

tended to coincide with, and perhaps supplant, the pagan Tepoztécatl festival, but the pulque drinkers get a jump on it by starting the night before.

Places to Stay

It can be difficult to find decent inexpensive accommodations here on weekends.

Mesón del Indio (☎ 395-02-38, Revolución 44) Rooms with bath US$18. This hotel is about the cheapest place in town; its sign is barely larger than a loaf of bread. It is a friendly place with eight small moldy rooms beside a garden, each with hot water.

Hotel Posada Ali (☎ 395-19-71, Netzahualcóyotl 2C) Rooms from US$56, suites from US$78. The Posada Ali, north of the center, is a very homey place, with a sitting room and a small swimming pool. No two of its attractive, spacious rooms are alike.

Posada Cualli Cochi (☎ 395-03-93, *Netzahualcóyotl 2)* Rooms with shared bath US$23, singles/doubles with bath US$28/45. This new hotel, just west of Posada Ali, has sparsely furnished, clean rooms with TVs. Parking is available.

The better hotels cater to the weekend crowd from Mexico City, and are expensive.

Hotel Tepoztlán (☎ 395-05-22, *fax 395-05-03, Las Industrias 6)* Singles/doubles US$74/85. This is a health resort-style hotel with 36 rooms, a pool, vegetarian restaurant and bar. Spa services are also available.

Posada del Tepozteco (☎ 395-00-10, w *posadadeltepozteco.com.mx,* e *tepozhot@ prodigy.net.mx, Paraíso 3)* Rooms from US$139, suites US$179. Rates are discounted Sunday to Thursday. This gorgeous hotel was built as a hillside hacienda in the 1930s and has two pools, a *temazcal* (pre-Hispanic steam bath), a restaurant-bar and terraces with spectacular views of the town and valley. It has 18 rooms, and the suites come with private spa baths.

Posada del Valle (☎ 395-05-21, *fax 395-19-47, Camino a Mextitla 5)* Rooms US$87 Mon-Thur only, weekend spa packages for two US$329. Posada del Valle has quiet, romantic rooms and a pool. Spa services are available Friday to Sunday. The weekend package includes two nights at the hotel, breakfast, massages and a visit to the *temazcal.* It's 2km from town (take Revolución east, follow signs the remaining 100m to the hotel).

Places to Eat

If fine dining is your goal, try to arrive on the weekend. During the week most of the nicer restaurants are closed. Avenida Revolución has a varied string of restaurants.

Naty's Restaurant (*Avenida Revolución 7)* Prices from US$3. This is an inexpensive place to have breakfast and watch the action in the market.

La Luna Mextli (*Avenida Revolución 16)* Prices from US$4.50. This is a combination restaurant, bar and art gallery. Tables surround a pleasant interior courtyard.

El Milenio (*cnr Avenida Tepozteco & La Cumbre)* Prices from US$1.50. This vegetarian café is a nice place to stop for a healthy snack before climbing up to the pyramid. They serve veggie burgers, tacos and juices.

El Encuentro (*cnr Buena Vista & Avenida 5 de Mayo)* Prices from US$4. This friendly restaurant serves an odd mix of Italian and Asian dishes, including fantastic pizzas, pastas, and curries.

Lilah (☎ 395-03-87, *Avenida Revolución 60)* Prices from US$4.50. Open Fri & Sat 1pm-10pm, Sun 1pm-7pm. You will find this place at the bottom of the street where the asphalt begins. It offers delicious originals fusing elements from various cuisines. Wonderful salads consist of organic ingredients from the restaurant's garden. There are many veggie options and cappuccino and herbal teas.

El Ciruelo (☎ 395-12-03, *Zaragoza 17)* Prices US$4-14. Open 1pm-6pm Mon-Thur, 1pm-10pm Fri & Sat. This is an elegant restaurant-bar serving pizzas, salads and international dishes. Try the steak in tequila sauce.

Axitla (☎ 395-05-19) Prices US$4-13. Open 10am-7pm Wed-Sun. At the beginning of the trail to the archaeological site, Axitla has a jungly setting. It offers abundant portions of fine Mexican and international food.

Tepoznieves (*Avenida Revolución across from the convent)* Prices US$0.70-1.50. This ice cream emporium scooping up 70 heavenly flavors, including exotics like cactus and pineapple/chili is an obligatory stop in Tepoztlán. It has a second branch at Tepozteco 8.

Los Buenos Tiempos (☎ 395-05-19, *Avenida Revolución 10)* Prices from US$1. This cozy café serves perhaps Tepoztlán's finest coffee and espresso. Their homemade strudels are delicious.

Shopping

On Saturday and Sunday, Tepoztlán's **market stalls** sell a mélange of handicrafts, including sarapes, embroidery, weavings, carvings, baskets and pottery. Shops in the adjacent streets also have interesting wares (some from Bali and India) at upscale prices. A popular local craft product is miniature houses and villages carved from the corklike spines of the local *pochote* tree.

3 Sueños (*Revolución 64)* This shop, just down the street from Lilah, sells work by local artists and craftspeople, as well as secondhand clothing, jewelry and books in English, French, German and Spanish.

AROUND MEXICO CITY

Getting There & Away

Pullman de Morelos has an hourly 1st-class service to/from Mexico City (Terminal Sur) until 8pm (1 hour, US$5), with buses departing from, and arriving at, Avenida 5 de Mayo 35, at the southern entrance to town. Frequent buses to Oaxtepec (15 minutes, US$1) and Cuautla (14 minutes, US$1.50) depart from the *caseta* (tollbooth) on the autopista outside town. Pullman de Morelos runs free combis between the 5 de Mayo terminal and the gas station near the autopista entrance; from there, walk down the left (exit) ramp to the caseta.

Ometochtli buses leave for Cuernavaca, 23 km away, every 10 minutes from 5am to 9pm (30 minutes, US$1.50). The terminal is on the road south of town on the way to the autopista. Monday to Friday you can catch the bus on the corner of Galeana and Avenida Tepozteco downtown.

If you're driving north from Cuernavaca on highway 95D, don't get off at the 'Tepoztlán' exit, which will put you on the slow federal highway. Take the exit marked 'Cuautla/Oaxtepec.'

OAXTEPEC & COCOYOC

In Oaxtepec ('wahs-teh-PEC'; pop 6000, elev 1400m, ☎ 735) the 200,000-sq-m **Centro Vacacional Oaxtepec** is a balneario with numerous pools and sulfur springs. The giant park was divided into two areas in 1999: a privately run **aquatic amusement park** *(☎ 356-01-01; adult/ child US$9/4; open 10am-6pm daily)* with a wave pool and giant slides; and a **recreational center** *(☎ 356-01-01, adult/child US$4.50/2.25; open 8am-6pm daily)*- operated by the Mexican Social Security Institute (IMSS) though open to the general public – with pools, a stadium, restaurants and a cable car. Cocoyoc (pop 8600, elev 1300m, ☎ 735) is about 4km southwest of Oaxtepec.

Places to Stay

IMSS facility (☎ 356-01-01, 5639-4173 in Mexico City) Camping adult/child US$7/3.50 per person, rooms from US$45. For overnight stays, this facility has campgrounds, five-person cabins and a hotel. With reservations, there's a 50% discount on admission to the aquatic amusement park . If you don't have a reservation, stop by the *hospedaje* office near the entrance to the complex to arrange lodging.

Hacienda Cocoyoc (☎ 356-22-11, w www.cocoyoc.com, highway 113 Km 32.5) Rooms from US$129, suites from US$196. This hacienda was built in the 17th century, later becoming an important sugar refinery until Zapata declared war on all sugar plantations during the revolution. Today it is a refreshing resort hotel and spa with pools, restaurants, horseback riding and a nine-hole golf course. You can get a suite here with a private pool.

Getting There & Away

Oaxtepec is just north of highway 115D, 100km south of Mexico City. Cocoyoc is about 3km south of the Oaxtepec turnoff. Frequent 1st-class buses go from the capital's Terminal Sur to the Oaxtepec bus station beside the entrance to the springs complex (1½ hours, US$7). There are also buses to/ from Tepoztlán, Cuernavaca, Cuautla and Puebla. Taxis and combis to Cocoyoc also depart from the entrance to the complex.

CUAUTLA

• pop 143,000 • elev 1290m ☎ 735

The balnearios at Cuautla ('KWOUT-la') and its pleasant year-round climate have been attractions since the time of Moctezuma, who reputedly enjoyed soaking in the sun and sulfur springs. These days, however, the city is uninspiring and spread out, though the center is pleasant enough.

José María Morelos y Pavón, one of Mexico's first leaders in the independence struggle, used Cuautla as a base, but the royalist army besieged the city from February 19 to May 2 1812. Morelos and his army were forced to evacuate when their food gave out. A century later, Cuautla was a center of support for the revolutionary army of Emiliano Zapata. Now, every April 10, the Agrarian Reform Minister lays a wreath at Zapata's monument in Cuautla, quoting the revolutionary's principles of land reform.

Orientation

Cuautla spreads north to south roughly parallel to the Río Cuautla. The two main plazas – Plaza Fuerte de Galeana, more commonly known as the Alameda, and the zócalo – lie along the main avenue, whose name changes from Avenida Insurgentes to Batalla 19 de Febrero, then to

Galeana, Los Bravos, Guerrero and Ordiera, on its way through town.

The zócalo has arcades with restaurants on the northern side, a church on the east, the Palacio Municipal on the west and the Hotel Colón on the south. Bus lines have separate terminals in the blocks east of the plaza.

Information

The tourist office (☎ 352-52-21) is three blocks north of the zócalo, on the platform of the old train station, housed in the 16th-century Ex-Convento de San Diego. Open 9am to 8pm daily, the office is a font of information, well stocked with literature on convents, balnearios, handicrafts and history, as well as a good map of Cuautla – very necessary since streets change names each block. The staff speak Spanish only.

Several banks can be found throughout the town (see Cuautla map for locations). A block north of the tourist office on Batalla 19 de Febrero, Computación de Cuautla provides Internet access for US$1.50 per hour. The Hospital General (☎ 353-61-93) is on Avenida Reforma in the north of town near the Autopista México.

Things to See & Do

Mexico's only steam-powered train departs from the old railroad station (in the Ex-Convento de San Diego), where in August 1911 presidential candidate Francisco Madero embraced Emiliano Zapata. The train does a circuit of Cuautla (US$0.70) on Saturday and Sunday after 5pm.

The former residence of José María Morelos, on the southwest side of the plaza, houses the **Museo Histórico del Oriente**

Emiliano Zapato

(☎ 352-83-31, Callejón del Castigo 3; admission US$3, free Sun; open 9am-6pm Tues-Sun). Each room covers a different historical period with well-lit displays of pre-Hispanic pottery, good maps and early photos of Cuautla and Zapata.

Plazuela Revolución del Sur is one of Cuautla's loveliest plazas. In its center stands an imposing **Zapata** monument, underneath which lie the rebel's remains.

Balnearios

The best-known balneario in Cuautla is **Agua Hedionda** (Stinky Water) on the east side of the river at the end of Avenida Progreso. Waterfalls replenish two lake-sized pools with the spring's cool sulfur-scented waters. To get to the complex (adult/child US$3.50/1.75; open 6.30am-5.30pm daily), take an 'Agua Hedionda' combi (US$0.50) from Plazuela Revolución del Sur.

Other balnearios you might find worth a visit in town include **El Almeal** (adult/child US$3/1.75; open 9am-6pm) and **Los Limones** (Centinela 14; adult/child US$3/2.25; open 8.30am-6.30pm). Both of these balnearios are served by the same spring (no sulfur) and have pleasant wooded grounds.

Places to Stay

Cheap hotels include:

Hotel Colón (☎ 352-29-90, Portal Guerrero) Singles/doubles US$11/16. Hotel Colón is on the main plaza. The rooms here are basic but nice enough for the price.

Hotel Jardines de Cuautla (☎ 352-00-88, 2 de Mayo 94) Singles/doubles US$15/19. Opposite the Cristóbal Colón bus terminal, this hotel has clean, modern rooms, parking, a garden and two tiny swimming pools. Unfortunately, quite a bit of noise intrudes from the busy streets below.

Hotel España (☎ 352-21-86, 2 de Mayo 22) Singles/doubles US$20/23. Half a block east of the Hotel Colón, the España has parking and 27 spacious rooms with hot water.

Hotel Defensa del Agua (☎ 352-16-79, Defensa del Agua 34) Singles/doubles US$19/27. Two blocks east of the Alameda, the Defensa del Agua surrounds a small garden/parking area with two small pools. Its pleasant colonial-style rooms, named after Cuautla war heroes, have cable TV, phones and ceiling fans. Avoid rooms with windows on the street.

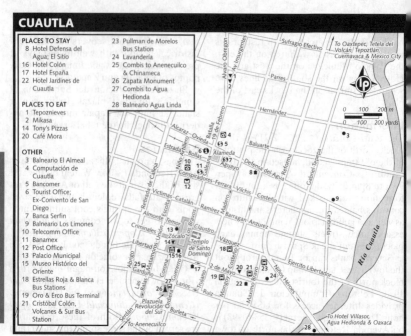

CUAUTLA

PLACES TO STAY
8   Hotel Defensa del
    Agua; El Sitio
16 Hotel Colón
17 Hotel España
22 Hotel Jardines de
    Cuautla

PLACES TO EAT
1   Tepoznieves
2   Mikasa
19 Tony's Pizzas
20 Café Mora

OTHER
3   Balneario El Almeal
4   Computación de
    Cuautla
5   Bancomer
6   Tourist Office;
    Ex-Convento de San
    Diego
7   Banca Serfin
9   Balneario Los Limones
10 Telecomm Office
11 Banamex
12 Post Office
13 Palacio Municipal
15 Museo Histórico del
    Oriente
18 Estrellas Roja & Blanca
    Bus Stations
19 Oro & Erco Bus Terminal
21 Cristóbal Colón,
    Volcanes & Sur Bus
    Station

23 Pullman de Morelos
    Bus Station
24 Lavandería
25 Combis to Anenecuilco
    & Chinameca
26 Zapata Monument
27 Combis to Agua
    Hedionda
28 Balneario Agua Linda

Hotel Villasor (☎ 352-65-21, fax 352-65-62, e villasor@mail.cem-sa.com.mx, *Avenida Progreso across from Agua Hedionda*) Singles/doubles US$39/50. If you're only visiting Cuautla for the Agua Hedionda park, Hotel Villasor, a stone's throw from the balneario, is the place to stay. Comfortable rooms come with TVs, fans and phones.

Places to Eat

The Alameda has several popular *cafés* with outdoor seating; they serve sandwiches, cappuccino, ice cream and milkshakes.

Tony's Pizzas (☎ 352-04-02, *Portal Matamoros 6*) Prices US$3.75-12. On the zócalo, Tony's serves a variety of pizzas plus hamburgers, sandwiches, pasta and cocktails.

El Sitio (*Hotel Defensa del Agua, Defensa del Agua 34*) Prices US$4.50-11, set lunch US$6. This is an elegant alternative to the cafés, with salads, meat and seafood dishes. Its set lunch features exotic local options.

Café Mora (*2 de Mayo 91*) Prices from US$0.80. Across the street from the Hotel Jardines de Cuautla is this café which serves Cuautla's finest espresso.

Mikasa (☎ 352-51-02, *Obregón 112*) This place serves a wide variety of Japanese dishes including sushi, udon and teriyaki. It's not fine Japanese cuisine, but it's among the best you'll find in Mexico.

Tepoznieves (*Obregón 9E*) Next door to Mikasa, you'll find a branch of this heavenly ice cream shop. They have dozens and dozens of flavors, including some with chile or alcohol. Every one of them is delicious.

Getting There & Away

Cristóbal Colón, a 1st-class line, and Sur and Volcanes, both 2nd-class, share a bus station at the eastern end of 2 de Mayo. Pullman de Morelos is across the street at Maximo Bravo 53D, with 1st-class service to Tepoztlán and Oaxtepec every 15 minutes until 9.15pm. A block west is the Estrella Roja (2nd-class) and Estrella Blanca bus station; an elevated restaurant separates the two lines. A block south at the corner of 2 de Mayo and Mongoy is the Oro and Erco station. Useful services include:

Cuernavaca – 42km, 1¼ hours; Estrella Roja every 15 minutes, 5am to 7.30pm (US$3)

Mexico City (TAPO) – 70km, 2½ hours via Amecameca; Volcanes every 20 minutes (US$3.50)

Mexico City (Terminal Sur) – 70km, 1¾ hours; frequent Colón, Estrella Roja and Pullman de Morelos (US$6)

Oaxaca – 410km, 7 hours; 3 Sur (US$16.50)

Puebla – 125km, 2½ hours; Estrella Roja and Oro hourly (US$6.50)

AROUND CUAUTLA

The road south of Cuautla leads through some significant territory of the revolutionary period, where General Emiliano Zapata was born, fought and met his death at the hands of treacherous federalists. North of Cuautla, off highway 115 to Amecameca, a road heads east along the southern slopes of the active volcano Popocatépetl (see Popocatépetl & Iztaccíhuatl in the East of Mexico City section, earlier in this chapter), passing an extraordinary series of small towns with magnificent monasteries. Here you will get a good glimpse of how traditional ways of life go on, apparently undisturbed by their proximity to the smoking behemoth.

Ruta de Zapata

In Anenecuilco, about 5km south of Cuautla, what's left of the adobe cottage where Zapata was born on August 8 1879, is now a **museum** (Avenida Zapata s/n; admission free, donation requested; open 8am-8pm Tues-Sun) featuring photographs of the rebel leader. Outside is a mural by Roberto Rodríguez Navarro which depicts Zapata exploding with the force of a volcano into the center of Mexican history, sundering the chains that bound his countrymen.

About 20km directly south you will find the **Ex-Hacienda de San Juan Chinameca**, where in 1919 Zapata was lured into a fatal trap by Colonel Jesús Guajardo following orders of President Venustiano Carranza, who was eager to get rid of the rebel leader and consolidate the post-revolutionary government. Pretending to defect to the revolutionary forces, Guajardo set up a meeting with Zapata, who arrived at Chinameca accompanied by a guerrilla escort. Guajardo's men gunned down the general before he crossed the threshold of the abandoned hacienda.

The hacienda, with a small **museum** (Cárdenas s/n; donation requested; open 9.30am-5pm daily), is on the left at the end of the town's main street, where there's a statue of Zapata astride a rearing horse. The museum exhibits are pretty meager (photos and newspaper reproductions), but you can still see the bullet holes in the walls.

From Chinameca, highway 9 heads northwest 20km to Tlaltizapán, site of the **Cuartel General de Zapata** (Guerrero 2; donation requested; open 10am-6pm Tues-Sun), the revolutionary forces' main barracks. It contains relics of General Zapata, including the bed where he slept, his rifle (the trigger retains his fingerprints) and the hat and clothing he was wearing at the time of his death (they are riddled with bullet holes and stained with blood).

From Cuautla, the yellow 'Chinameca' combis traveling to Anenecuilco and Chinameca (US$0.50) leave from Garduño and Matamoros every 10 minutes.

Tetela del Volcán
• **pop 7900 • elev 2220 ☎ 731**

This village 22km east of highway 115 is one of several built around Augustinian monasteries on Popo's southern slopes. From the outside of Tetela's 16th-century **Ex-Convento de San Juan Bautista**, there are majestic views of the monastery crowned by the volcano. Like other villages in Popo's vicinity, Tetela has a notable military presence standing by should an evacuation be necessary. There's a civil protection headquarters off the plaza, keeping residents posted on the latest volcanic activity.

A fine place to stay is the **Albergue Suizo** (☎ 357-00-56, cnr Avenida Morelos & Allende). This tall brick hotel is approached by the first left after you go through Tetela's entryway arches. The hotel's interior is austere and unadorned, but the friendly staff makes it seem cozy. The large rooms have a view (though not of Popo) and spacious baths with copious hot water for US$11/17 singles/doubles. Popo can be glimpsed through a wall of windows around the top-level dining room.

About a 15-minute drive east of Tetela, on the way to Hueyapan, is the pristine **Río Amatzinac**. You can hike along an old cobblestone road and over stone bridges spanning the river.

From Cuautla, microbuses to Tetela depart from near the Estrella Roja station (40 minutes).

CUERNAVACA

• pop 346,000 • elev 1480m ☎ 777

With a mild climate, once described as 'eternal spring,' Cuernavaca ('kwehr-nah-VAH-kah') has been a retreat from Mexico City since colonial times. It attracts the wealthy and fashionable from Mexico and abroad, many of whom have stayed on to become temporary or semipermanent residents. A number of their residences have become attractions in themselves, now housing museums, galleries, expensive restaurants and hotels. As the local population grows and more and more visitors come, especially on weekends, Cuernavaca is unfortunately losing some of its charm and acquiring the problems that people from the capital try to escape – crowds, traffic, smog and crime.

Much of the city's elegance is hidden behind high walls and in colonial courtyards, and is largely inaccessible to the casual visitor on a tight budget. A stroll through the lively zócalo costs nothing, but try to allow a few extra pesos to enjoy the food and ambiance at some of the better restaurants. Cuernavaca is also worth visiting to see the famed Palacio de Cortés, and the nearby pre-Hispanic sites and balnearios. A lot of visitors stay longer to enroll in one of the many Spanish-language schools.

History

The people settling in the valleys of modern Morelos around AD 1220 developed a highly productive agricultural society based at Cuauhnáhuac (Place at the Edge of the Forest). The Mexica (Aztecs), who dominated the Valle de México, called them 'Tlahuica,' which means 'people who work the land.' In 1379, a Mexica warlord conquered Cuauhnáhuac, subdued the Tlahuica and required them to pay an annual tribute that included 8000 sets of clothing, 16,000 pieces of amate bark paper and 20,000 bushels of maize. The tributes payable by the subject states were set out in a register the Spanish later called Códice Mendocino in which Cuauhnáhuac was represented by a three-branched tree; this symbol now appears on the city's coat of arms.

The successor to the Mexican lord married the daughter of the Cuauhnáhuac leader, and from this marriage was born Moctezuma I Ilhuicamina, the great 15th-century Aztec king who was a predecessor of the Moctezuma II Xocoyotzin encountered by Cortés. The Tlahuica prospered under the Aztec empire, themselves dominating small states to the south and trading extensively with other regions. Their city was also a center for religious ceremonies and learning, and archaeological remains show they had a considerable knowledge of astronomy.

When the Spanish arrived, the Tlahuica were fiercely loyal to the Aztec empire, savagely resisting the advance of the conquistadors. In April 1521, they were finally overcome, and Cortés torched the city. Destroying the city pyramid, Cortés used the stones to build a fortress-palace on the pyramid's base. He also had built from the rubble the Catedral de la Asunción, another fortress-like structure in a walled compound; in the 1520s, there was not much reason to trust in the benign favor of the new Catholic 'converts.' Soon the city became known as Cuernavaca, a more pronounceable (to the Spanish) version of its original name.

In 1529, Cortés received his somewhat belated reward from the Spanish crown when he was named Marqués del Valle de Oaxaca, with an estate that covered 22 towns, including Cuernavaca, and a charge of 23,000 indigenous Mexicans. He introduced sugar cane and other crops, and new farming methods, which resulted in Cuernavaca becoming an agricultural center for the Spanish, as it had been for the Aztecs. Cortés made Cuernavaca his home for the rest of his stay in Mexico, and his descendants dominated the area for nearly 300 years.

With its pleasant climate, rural surroundings and colonial elite, Cuernavaca became a refuge and a retreat for the rich and powerful. One of these was José de la Borda, the 18th-century Taxco silver magnate. His lavish home and garden were later a retreat for Emperor Maximilian and Empress Carlota. Cuernavaca also attracted artists and writers, and achieved literary fame as the setting for Malcolm Lowry's 1947 novel Under the Volcano. The very rich of Mexico City are now just as likely to go to Acapulco or Dallas for the weekend, but many still have magnificent properties in the suburbs of Cuernavaca.

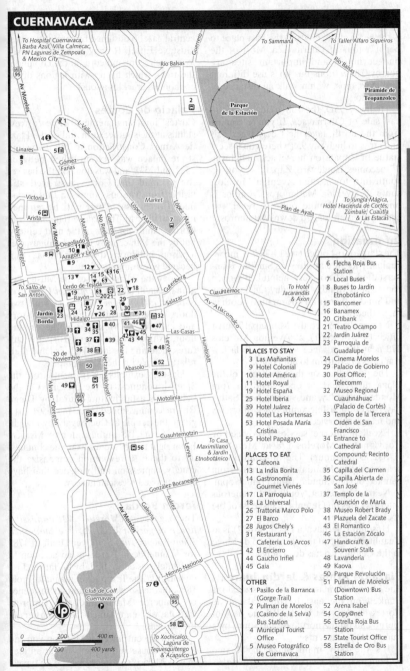

CUERNAVACA

PLACES TO STAY
3 Las Mañanitas
9 Hotel Colonial
10 Hotel América
11 Hotel Royal
19 Hotel España
25 Hotel Iberia
39 Hotel Juárez
40 Hotel Las Hortensas
53 Hotel Posada María Cristina
55 Hotel Papagayo

PLACES TO EAT
12 Cafeona
13 La India Bonita
14 Gastronomía Gourmet Vienés
17 La Parroquia
18 La Universal
26 Trattoria Marco Polo
27 El Barco
28 Jugos Chely's
31 Restaurant y Cafetería Los Arcos
42 El Encierro
44 Gaucho Infiel
45 Gaia

OTHER
1 Pasillo de la Barranca (Gorge Trail)
2 Pullman de Morelos (Casino de la Selva) Bus Station
4 Municipal Tourist Office
5 Museo Fotográfico de Cuernavaca
6 Flecha Roja Bus Station
7 Local Buses
8 Buses to Jardín Etnobotánico
15 Bancomer
16 Banamex
20 Citibank
21 Teatro Ocampo
22 Jardín Juárez
23 Parroquia de Guadalupe
24 Cinema Morelos
29 Palacio de Gobierno
30 Post Office; Telecomm
32 Museo Regional Cuauhnáhuac (Palacio de Cortés)
33 Templo de la Tercera Orden de San Francisco
34 Entrance to Cathedral Compound; Recinto Catedral
35 Capilla del Carmen
36 Capilla Abierta de San José
37 Templo de la Asunción de María
38 Museo Robert Brady
41 Plazuela del Zacate
43 El Romantico
46 La Estación Zócalo
47 Handicraft & Souvenir Stalls
48 Lavandería
49 Kaova
50 Parque Revolución
51 Pullman de Morelos (Downtown) Bus Station
52 Arena Isabel
54 Copy@net
56 Estrella Roja Bus Station
57 State Tourist Office
58 Estrella de Oro Bus Station

Orientation

The zócalo, also called the Plaza de Armas, is the heart of the city and the best place to begin a tour of Cuernavaca. Most of the budget hotels and important sites are nearby. The various bus lines use different terminals, most within walking distance of the zócalo.

Highway 95D, the toll road, skirts the east side of Cuernavaca. If you're coming from the north, take the Cuernavaca exit and cross to highway 95 (where you'll see a statue of Zapata on horseback). Highway 95 becomes Boulevard Zapata as you go south into town, then Avenida Morelos; south of Avenida Matamoros, Morelos is one-way, northbound only. To reach the center, veer left and go down Matamoros.

Information

The state tourist office (☎ 314-38-72), inconveniently located at Morelos Sur 187, is understaffed and not very helpful. It's open 8am to 5pm Monday to Friday. On Saturday and Sunday there's an information booth in the cathedral.

Nearer the center, the Municipal Tourist office (☎ 318-75-61), at Avenida Morelos 278 near the entrance to Pasilla de la Barranca, is open 10am to 8pm daily.

The post office, on the south side of the Plaza de Armas, is open 8am to 7pm Monday to Friday, and 9am to 1pm Saturday. Next door a Telecomm office offers fax and telegram services.

Excellent Internet service is provided by Copy@net at Morelos 178 at Motolinía (US$2.75 per hour). The air-conditioned space is open Monday to Saturday from 8am to 9pm and Sunday from 11am to 5pm.

Nearer the center, you'll find numerous Internet cafés on Gutenberg just east of the zócalo.

Hospital Cuernavaca (☎ 311-24-82) is at Cuauhtémoc 305 at the corner of 5 de Mayo in the Colonia Lomas de la Selva.

Plaza de Armas & Jardín Juárez

The Plaza de Armas, Cuernavaca's zócalo, is flanked on the east by the Palacio de Cortés, on the west by the Palacio de Gobierno and on the northeast and south by a number of restaurants.

It's the only main plaza in Mexico *without* a church, chapel, convent or cathedral overlooking it. Adjoining the northwest corner is the smaller Jardín Juárez, with a central gazebo designed by tower specialist Gustave Eiffel. Roving vendors sell balloons, ice cream and corn on the cob under the trees, which fill up with legions of cacophonous grackles at dusk.

Palacio de Cortés

Cortés' imposing medieval-style fortress stands at the southeastern end of the Plaza de Armas. Construction of this two-story stone palace was accomplished between 1522 and 1532, and was done on the base of the pyramid that Cortés destroyed, still visible from various points on the ground floor. Cortés resided here until he returned to Spain in 1540. The palace remained with Cortés' family for most of the next century, but by the 18th century it was being used as a prison, and during the Porfirio Díaz era it became government offices.

Today the palace houses the **Museo Regional Cuauhnáhuac** (*admission US$2, free Sun; open 9am-6pm Tues-Sun*), with two floors of exhibits highlighting the history and cultures of Mexico. On the ground floor, exhibits focus on pre-Hispanic cultures, including the local Tlahuica and their relationship with the Aztec empire.

Upstairs, exhibits cover events from the Spanish conquest to the present. On the balcony is a fascinating mural by Diego Rivera, commissioned in the mid-1920s as a gift to the people of Cuernavaca by Dwight Morrow, the US ambassador to Mexico. From right to left, scenes from the conquest up to the 1910 revolution emphasize the cruelty, oppression and violence that have characterized Mexican history.

Jardín Borda

These gardens (*Morelos 271; admission house & garden US$1.25, free Sun; open 10am-5.30pm Tues-Sun*) were built in 1783 for Manuel de la Borda, as an addition to the stately residence built by his father, José de la Borda, the Taxco silver magnate. From 1866, the house was the summer residence of Emperor Maximilian and Empress Carlota, who entertained their courtiers in the gardens.

From the entrance on Morelos, you can tour the house and gardens to get an idea of how Mexico's aristocracy lived. In typical colonial style, the buildings are arranged around courtyards. In one wing, the **Museo de Sitio** has exhibits on daily life during the empire period, and original documents with the signatures of Morelos, Juárez and Maximilian.

Several romantic paintings on the walls of the Sala Manuel M Ponce, a recital hall near the entrance, show scenes of the garden in Maximilian's time. One of the most famous paintings of the collection depicts Maximilian in the garden with La India Bonita, the 'pretty Indian' who was to become his lover.

The gardens are formally laid out on a series of terraces, with paths, steps and fountains, and they originally featured a botanical collection with hundreds of varieties of fruit trees and ornamental plants. The vegetation is still exuberant, with large trees and semitropical shrubs, though there is no longer a wide range of species, and the pretty pond you see in the painting now looks more like a dirty concrete swimming pool. Also, because of a water shortage in the city, the fountains have been turned off, which greatly diminishes the aesthetic appeal of the gardens. You can hire a little boat and go rowing for US$2.25 an hour. A café near the entrance serves cake and *empanadas*.

Beside the house is the Parroquia de Guadalupe, also built by José de la Borda, and dedicated in December 1784.

Recinto de la Catedral

Cuernavaca's cathedral stands in a large high-walled compound *(recinto)* on the corner of Morelos and Hidalgo (the entrance gate is on Hidalgo). Like the Palacio de Cortés, the cathedral was built on a grand scale and in a fortress-like style, as a defense against the natives and to impress and intimidate them. Franciscans started work under Cortés in 1526, using indigenous labor and stones from the rubble of Cuauhnáhuac; it was one of the earliest Christian missions in Mexico. The first part to be built was **Capilla Abierta de San José**, the open chapel on the west side of the cathedral.

The cathedral itself, **Templo de la Asunción de María**, is plain and solid, with an unembellished façade. The side door, which faces north to the compound's entrance, shows a mixture of indigenous and European features – the skull and crossbones above it is a symbol of the Franciscan order. Inside are frescoes discovered early in the 20th century. They are said to show the persecution of Christian missionaries in Japan, though it's difficult to decipher them. Cuernavaca *was* a center for Franciscan missionary activities in Asia, and the frescoes were supposedly painted in the 17th century by a Japanese convert to Christianity.

The cathedral compound also holds two smaller churches, one on either side of the Hidalgo entrance. On the right as you enter is the **Templo de la Tercera Orden de San Francisco**, which was commenced in 1723; its exterior was carved in 18th-century baroque style by indigenous artisans, and its interior has ornate, gilded decorations. Left as you enter is the 19th-century **Capilla del Carmen**, where believers seek cures for illness. Mass in English is given here at 9.30am on Sunday.

Museo Robert Brady

Robert Brady (1928-86), an American artist and collector, lived in Cuernavaca for 24 years. His home, the Casa de la Torre, was originally part of the monastery within the Recinto de la Catedral. Brady had it extensively renovated and decorated with paintings, carvings, textiles, antiques and decorative and folk arts he'd acquired in his travels around the world. There are several paintings by well-known Mexican artists, including Tamayo, Kahlo and Covarrubias, but the main attraction is the sheer size and diversity of the collection and the way it is arranged with delightful combinations and contrasts of styles, periods and places.

The museum *(☎ 316-85-54, Netzahualcóyotl 4; admission US$2.25; open 10am-6pm Tues-Sun)* is a short walk from the zócalo.

Salto de San Antón

This 36m waterfall *(admission free; open 10am-6pm Tues-Sun)*, surrounded by lush vegetation, is less than 1km west of the Jardín Borda. A walkway is built into the cliff face so you can go right behind the falls, where there are a few picnic tables. The village of San Antón, above the falls, is a traditional center for pottery. The Ruta 4 bus, marked 'Salto,' goes from the corner of Abasolo and Morelos directly to the entrance.

Language Courses in Cuernavaca

Many foreigners come to Cuernavaca to study Spanish. The best schools offer small-group or individual instruction, at all levels, with four to five hours per day of intensive instruction plus a couple of hours' conversation practice. Classes begin each Monday, and most schools recommend a minimum enrollment of four weeks, though you can study for as many weeks as you want.

Tuition fees vary from US$140 to US$250 per week, usually payable in advance. You may get a discount outside the peak months of January, February, July and August; some schools offer discounts if you stay more than four weeks. Most schools also charge a nonrefundable one-time enrollment fee of US$75 to US$100.

The schools can arrange for students to live with a Mexican family to experience 'total immersion' in the language. The host families charge about US$18 per day with shared room and bath, or about US$25 per day with private room and bath; the price includes three meals daily. The schools can often help with hotels too. For free brochures, write or call:

CALE – Center of Art and Languages
(☎/fax 313-06-03, **w** www.gl.com.mx/cale) Nueva Tabachin 22B, Colonia Tlaltenango, CP 62170 Cuernavaca, Morelos, Mexico; former students cite CALE's personalized approach to learning as its best asset.

Cemanahuac Educational Community
(☎ 318-64-07, fax 312-54-18, **w** www.cemanahuac.com) Apdo Postal 5-21, CP 62051 Cuernavaca, Morelos, Mexico; emphasis is placed on language acquisition and cultural awareness.

Center for Bilingual Multicultural Studies
(☎ 317-10-87, 800-932-2068 in the USA, fax 317-05-33, **w** www.bilingual-center.com) Apdo Postal 1520, CP 62179 Cuernavaca, Morelos, Mexico; the center is accredited by the Universidad Autónoma del Estado de Morelos and affiliated with more than 100 foreign universities.

Centro International
(☎ 312-32-33, fax 312-32-55, **w** www.internationalcenter.edu.mx) Leyva 96, CP 62000 Cuernavaca, Morelos, Mexico; close to the center, Centro International offers classes for students at various levels of proficiency as well as excursions to nearby cultural sites.

Cetlalic Alternative Language School
(☎/fax 313-26-37, **w** www.cetlalic.org.mx) Apdo Postal 1-201, CP 62000 Cuernavaca, Morelos, Mexico; emphasis is placed on language learning, cultural awareness and social responsibility.

Cuauhnáhuac Spanish Language School
(☎ 312-36-73, fax 318-26-93, **w** www.cuauhnahuac.edu.mx) Apdo Postal 5-26, CP 62051 Cuernavaca, Morelos, Mexico; the school helps students earn university language credits and members of the business and medical communities develop language interests.

Encuentros Comunicación y Cultura
(☎/fax 312-50-88, http://cuernavaca.infosel.com.mx/encuentros/spanish.htm) Morelos 36,

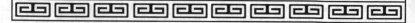

Casa Maximiliano

In Cuernavaca's suburbs, 1.5km southeast of the center, this 1866 house was once a rural retreat for the Emperor Maximilian, where he would meet his Mexican lover. It was called La Casa del Olvido (the House of Forgetfulness), because Maximilian 'forgot' to include a room for his wife there. He did remember to include a small house in the back for his lover; it is now the **Museo de**

Language Courses in Cuernavaca

Colonia Acapantizingo, CP 62440 Cuernavaca, Morelos, Mexico; the program focuses on professionals and travelers needing to learn Spanish.

Experiencia – Centro de Intercambio Bilingüe y Cultural
(☎ 312-65-79, 888-397-8363 in the USA, fax 318-52-09, **w** www.experiencia.com/cuernavaca.html) Leyva 200, Colonia Las Palmas, CP 62050 Cuernavaca, Morelos, Mexico; the Intercambio program offers two-hour, twice-weekly conversational exchanges between Mexican and international students.

IDEAL Latinoamerica
(☎ 311-75-51, fax 311-59-10, **w** www.giga.com/~ideal) Apdo Postal 2-65, CP 62158 Cuernavaca, Morelos, Mexico; the program immerses the student in the Spanish language and Mexican culture, while respecting the individual's pace and style of learning.

IDEL – Instituto de Idiomas y Culturas Latinoamericanas
(☎/fax 313-01-57, **w** http://idel-site.tripod.com/main.html) Apdo Postal 1271-1, CP 62001 Cuernavaca, Morelos, Mexico; IDEL complements language study with excursions to places of historical interest in and around Cuernavaca, video presentations, cultural events and parties.

Instituto de Idiomas y Cultura en Cuernavaca
(☎/fax 317-04-55, **w** www.idiomaycultura.com) Apdo Postal 2-42, CP 62158 Cuernavaca, Morelos, Mexico; a different teacher each week gives students exposure to different voices and personalities.

Prolingua Instituto Español Xochicalco
(☎/fax 318-42-86, **w** www.prolingua.edu.mx) Calle Hidalgo 24, Colonia Acapantzingo, CP 62400 Cuernavaca, Morelos, Mexico; the program helps develop conversational fluency while building awareness of Mexican culture, history and traditions through lectures.

Spanish Language Institute
(☎ 311-00-63, fax 317-52-94, **w** www.sli-spanish.com.mx) Apdo Postal 2-3, CP 62191 Cuernavaca, Morelos, Mexico; cultural courses include Mexican customs and Latin American literature.

Universal Centro de Lengua y Comunicación
(☎ 318-29-04, fax 318-29-10, **w** www.universal-spanish.com) Apdo Postal 1-1826, CP 62000 Cuernavaca, Morelos, Mexico; Universal mixes language study with visits to local communities and visits from local politicians, community leaders and scholars.

Universidad Autónoma del Estado de Morelos
(☎ 316-16-26, fax 322-35-13, **w** www2.uaem.mx/clahpe) Rio Pánuco 20, Colonia Lomas del Mirador, CP 62350 Cuernavaca, Morelos, Mexico; the university's Centro de Lengua, Arte e Historia para Extranjeros uses a communicative approach augmented by authentic audio, video and print source materials.

Medicina Tradicional y Herbolaria (*admission free; open 9am-4.30pm daily*), a museum of traditional herbal medicine. Around the museum, the **Jardín Etnobotánico** has a collection of 455 herbs and medicinal plants from around the world, all labeled with their botanical names. Catch a Ruta 6 'Jardines' bus from the corner of Morelos and Degollado. Catch the return bus on 16 de Septiembre behind the garden.

Pirámide de Teopanzolco

This small archaeological site *(cnr Río Balsas & Ixcateopan; admission US$3, free Sun; open 9am-5.30pm daily)* is in the Colonia Vista Hermosa. There are actually two pyramids, one inside the other. You can climb upon the outer base and see the older pyramid within, with a double staircase leading up to the remains of a pair of temples. The older pyramid was built over 800 years ago by the Tlahuicas; the outside one was under construction by the Aztecs when Cortés arrived and was never completed. The name Teopanzolco means 'Place of the Old Temple,' and may relate to an ancient construction to the west of the current pyramid, where artifacts dating from around 7000 BC have been found as well as others with an Olmec influence.

Several other smaller platform structures surround the double pyramid. Near the rectangular platform to the west a tomb was discovered, containing the remains of 92 men, women and children mixed with ceramic pieces. They are believed to be victims of human sacrifice in which decapitation and dismemberment were practiced.

No buses go directly to the entrance. Catch a Ruta 4 'Barona' bus at Degollado and Guerrero, get off at Río Balsas, turn right and walk four blocks; or take a taxi to the site.

Other Things to See & Do

The great Mexican muralist David Alfaro Siqueiros had his workshop *(taller)* and home in Cuernavaca from 1964 until his death in 1974. The **Taller Alfaro Siqueiros** *(☎ 315-11-15, Venus 52; admission free; open 10am-5pm Tues-Sun)* is in Fraccionamiento Jardines de Cuernavaca. On display are four murals left unfinished at the artist's death and some mementos of his life.

If you are interested in history, the **Museo Fotográfico de Cuernavaca** *(Güemes 1; admission free; open 10am-6pm Tues-Sun)* has a few early photographs and maps of the city. It's in a cute little 1897 building called the Castillito, 1km north of the zócalo. By the fountain at the base of Güemes is the entrance to the **Pasillo de la Barranca**, a walkway that follows a deep gorge bursting with flowers and butterflies, well below the roar of traffic. There are a few waterfalls along the half-kilometer trail,

which emerges by the arches at Guerrero and Gómez Farías.

Jungla Mágica *(☎ 315-87-76, Bajada de Chapultepec 27; adult/child US$2.25/1.50; open 10.30am-6pm Thur-Sun)* is a children's park with a jungle theme and a popular bird show, as well as boating and picnicking facilities where you can swim with dolphins. To get there, take a Ruta 17 bus and tell the driver you're going to 'La Luna,' which is a roundabout; walk two blocks along Bajada de Chapultepec and you'll come to the entrance of the park.

Special Events

These are among the festivals and special events you can see in Cuernavaca:

Carnaval – In the five days before Ash Wednesday (late February or early March), this colorful celebration features street performances by the Chinelo dancers of Tepoztlán, parades, art exhibits and more.

Feria de la Primavera – The Spring Fair (late March to early April) includes cultural and artistic events, concerts and a beautiful exhibit of the city's spring flowers.

Places to Stay

Accommodations in Cuernavaca don't offer great value for the money. The cheap places tend to be depressingly basic, the mid-range ones are lacking in charm, and the top-end hotels are wonderful but very expensive. On weekends and holidays, the town fills up with visitors from the capital, so phone ahead or try to secure your room early in the day.

Budget The cheapest places are on Aragón y León between Morelos and Matamoros – a section of street worked by a handful of hookers.

Hotel América *(☎ 318-61-27, Aragón y León 14)* Singles/doubles US$14.50/23. This is the best of the cheap places – basic but very clean. Rooms come with hot water; TVs cost extra.

Hotel Colonial *(☎ 318-14-64, Aragón y León 19)* Singles/doubles with bath US$17/28. Up the street from the Hotel América, the rooms here are pleasant with some facing a cute garden.

Hotel Iberia *(☎ 312-60-40, fax 312-30-61, Rayón 7)* Singles/doubles US$18/22. This place has long been patronized by travelers and foreign students. It has small, basic rooms set around a tiled parking lot and is only a short walk to the zócalo. Rooms have cable TV.

Hotel Las Hortensas (☎ *318-52-65, Hidalgo 13*) Singles/doubles US$18/24. One block from the zócalo, Las Hortensas has tiny, dark rooms with baths. The rooms are clean enough, but location and price are the only reasons to stay here.

Villa Calmecac (☎ *310-21-03,* e *info@ turismoalternativo.org, Zacatecas 114, Colonia Buenavista*) Dorm beds with breakfast US$21, 10% less with HI card. This hostel, affiliated with Hostelling International (HI), is very pleasant though quite a distance from the center. Made of adobe and wood, the building is equipped with rainwater-collection and sewage-recycling devices and surrounded by organic gardens of local plants. Breakfast is an all-natural buffet and the bunk beds are in rustic-style rooms. There are two sparkling clean baths, each with three shower stalls and toilets. Villa Calmecac is 800m west of the Mexico City autopista. From the town center, it's a 20-minute ride on a Ruta 1, 2 or 3 bus from Morelos and Degollado. Zacatecas is two blocks past the Zapata monument on the left. Visitors must check in before 9pm.

Mid-Range *Hotel España* (☎ *318-67-44, fax 310-19-34, Morelos 190*) Singles/doubles US$22/27. This colonial hotel may boast shower curtains and decent ventilation, but in other cities its fairly worn rooms (US$3 extra for color TV) would cost less. The downstairs restaurant specializes in Spanish cuisine.

Hotel Royal (☎ *318-64-80, fax 314-40-18, Matamoros 11*) Singles/doubles US$23/26. Around the corner from the Hotel América, the Royal features clean rooms with hot water. It also has a central parking lot.

Hotel Juárez (☎ *314-02-19, Netzahualcóyotl 19*) Singles/doubles US$25/28. Centrally located next to the cathedral, the Juárez offers 12 simple but spacious and airy rooms with 24-hour hot water, as well as a swimming pool encircled by a lawn.

Hotel Papagayo (☎ *314-17-11, fax 314-19-24,* e *hotelpapagayo@prodigy.net.mx, Motolinía 13*) Singles/doubles with breakfast US$40/57. This attractive place has 77

modern rooms, two swimming pools, a playground (bordered by poinsettias and mango trees) and plenty of parking. The rate includes breakfast at the central restaurant served with complimentary lounge music on weekends.

Top End *Las Mañanitas* (☎ *314-14-66,* w *www.lasmananitas.com.mx, Linares 107*) Rooms from US$132, suites from US$180. Renowned for its large private garden where peacocks stroll around while guests enjoy the pool, this is one of the finest hotels in Mexico and has been included in several listings of the world's best hotels. There are both standard rooms and gorgeous garden suites. Its restaurant is also justly famous.

Hotel Posada María Cristina (☎ *318-57-67,* w *www.maria-cristina.com, Juárez 300*) Doubles US$167, suites US$205-255. This hotel is one of Cuernavaca's longtime favorites, with 20 tastefully appointed rooms in a nicely restored colonial building, two restaurants, lovely hillside gardens and an inviting pool.

Hotel Jacarandas (☎ *315-77-77,* w *www .jacarandas.com.mx, Cuauhtémoc 133*) Rooms US$156, suites US$362. Rooms at the Jacarandas are not very large or fancy, but the rambling grounds are graced with lots of trees, gardens and three pools at varying temperatures. Suites here have terraces. It's east of the center in the Colonia Chapultepec. There are buses along Cuauhtémoc to the center.

Hotel Hacienda de Cortés (☎ *316-08-67, fax 315-00-35,* w *www.haciendadecortes.com, Plaza Kennedy 90*) Suites from US$167. Built in the 17th century by Martín Cortés, who succeeded Hernán Cortés as Marqués del Valle de Oaxaca, the Hacienda de San Antonio Atlacomulco was renovated in 1980 to become this hotel. It has 23 luxurious suites, each with its own terrace and garden. There's a swimming pool built around old stone columns. About 4km southeast of the center, in Atlacomulco, it's worth visiting even if you're not staying at the hotel, just to stroll the lovely grounds and have lunch underneath the magnificent colonial arches of the restaurant.

Places to Eat
Budget For a simple, healthy snack of yogurt with fruit, *escamochas* (a kind of

fruit salad), corn on the cob or ice cream, you could patronize one of the booths at the Jardín Juárez gazebo, then eat your treat on one of the park's many benches.

Jugos Chely's Prices from US$1.50. Heading south down Galeana from Jardín Juárez, Jugos Chely's has fresh fruit juice combos such as *zanayogui* (carrot and orange), *toronjil* (grapefruit, pineapple and parsley) and *mexicano* (nopal, orange and lime), as well as burgers and quesadillas. Along this noisy street are several small greasy joints that all hang out numerous signs shouting their offerings – these places are best avoided.

El Barco (☎ 314-10-20, *Rayón 5F*) Prices from US$2-4.50. This popular place serves Guerrero-style *pozole* from a clean, tiled kitchen with plenty of clay pottery. Small or large bowls of pozole verde or rojo (shredded pork and hominy in delicious broth) are served with oregano, chili, chopped onions and limes. Specify '*maciza*' unless you want your pozole to include bits of fat. El Barco also serves pitchers of ice-cold *agua de jamaica* and various tequilas.

Cafeona (☎ 318-27-57, *Morrow 6*) Prices from US$1.75. This café, just west of Matamoros, is a little corner of Chiapas in Cuernavaca. It's a cool hangout, decorated with Chiapan crafts and serving organic coffee from the southern state, as well as pies, tamales and fruit salads with granola.

Mid-Range *La Parroquia* (☎ 318-58-20, *Guerrero 102*) Prices from US$4. Open 7.30am-midnight. On the east side of Jardín Juárez, this is one of Cuernavaca's favorite restaurants. Come here for the location – the food is nothing special.

La Universal (☎ 318-59-76, *cnr Gutenberg & Guerrero*) Prices from US$4.50. Open 9am-midnight. La Universal occupies a strategic position on the corner of the two central plazas, with tables under an awning facing the Plaza de Armas. Like La Parroquia, this popular place is all about location. The food is just average and a bit overpriced.

Restaurant y Cafeteria Los Arcos (☎ 312-15-10, *Jardín de los Héroes 4*) Prices from US$2.50. Open 10am-midnight. On the south side of the Plaza de Armas, this is a popular meeting place among the international student crowd. Have a seat under the umbrellas of its outdoor tables, sip a coffee

or a soda and watch the action on the plaza. The varied bilingual menu has something for everyone and is not too expensive.

El Encierro Prices US$1.75-3.75. This place on the Plazuela del Zacate at Galeana and Hidalgo serves tasty sandwiches and hot dogs.

Gaucho Infiel (*Las Casas 2*) Prices from US$5. East of El Encierro, the plazuela funnels into Las Casas, which is where you'll find this good Argentine steak place with a charcoal grill. It has steaks and *parrilladas* (various assortments of meats and sausages that typically feed two).

La India Bonita (☎ 318-69-67, *Morrow 106*) Prices from US$5. Open 8.30am-7.30pm Tues-Sat, 8.30am-6.30pm Sun. Northwest of Jardín Juárez, this is a lovely courtyard restaurant with tasty, traditional Mexican food. The house specialties are chicken in mole sauce, chicken breast stuffed with squash flowers and huitlacoche sauce, and a special platter with seven different tacos.

Gastronomía Gourmet Vienés (☎ 318-40-44, *Lerdo de Tejada 4*) Prices from US$6, set lunch US$10. Vienés offers middle-European dishes, such as knackwurst with sauerkraut and German fried potatoes. They also serve the best cakes, cookies, cream puffs and chocolate-rum truffles you've tasted since the last time you were in Vienna. Their superb coffee comes with free refills.

Trattoria Marco Polo (☎ 318-40-32, *Hidalgo 30*) Prices US$5-23. The Marco Polo makes excellent pizzas, with single-serving and large pies. There's a lovely view of the cathedral compound from the balcony tables.

Top End *Restaurant Las Mañanitas* (☎ 314-14-66, *Linares 107*) Prices from US$13-34. Open 1pm-5pm & 7pm-11pm daily. If you can afford an indulgence, try this restaurant at the hotel of the same name. One of Mexico's best and most famous restaurants, it has tables inside the mansion or on the garden terrace where you can see peacocks and flamingos strolling through an emerald-green garden. The menu, which waiters will show you on a large blackboard, features meals from around the world. You should bring at least US$20 in cash per person, unless you have an American Express card. If you'd rather not spend all that cash, you may have a drink in the garden. Reservations are recommended.

Gaia (☎ 312-36-56, Boulevard Juárez 102) Prices US$9-17. In a converted mansion that once belonged to actor Mario Moreno (Cantinflas), this creative restaurant blends Mediterranean and Mexican ingredients resulting in some fabulous dishes. The walls have been torn down to provide diners with a view of the pool, the bottom of which is adorned with a mosaic designed by Diego Rivera.

Entertainment

Hanging around the central plazas is always a popular activity in Cuernavaca, especially on Sunday and Thursday from 6pm on, when open-air concerts are often held.

Cinema Morelos (☎ 318-10-62 ext 243, Avenida Morelos 188) This is the state theater of Morelos, hosting a variety of cultural offerings, including quality film series, plays and dance performances.

Teatro Ocampo (☎ 318-63-85, Jardín Juárez 2) On the west side of Jardín Juárez, this theater stages contemporary plays; a calendar of cultural events is posted at its entrance.

Arena Isabel (☎ 318-59-16, cnr Juárez & Abasolo) Less highbrow entertainment is available here in the form of *lucha libre* (wrestling). Look for posters around town for lineups.

Plazuela del Zacate and adjacent Las Casas come alive in the evening with many bars featuring live music. *Bar Eclipse* has performers on two levels, folk on the bottom and rock on top. As the name implies, *El Romántico* is a venue for ballad singers.

La Estación Zócalo (☎ 315-04-77, cnr Juárez & Hidalgo) Across the street from Palacio de Cortés, this popular bar blares loud rock music from two brightly colored, but dimly lit floors.

The better discos charge a cover of at least US$7; women are usually admitted free Friday and Saturday nights. Some discos enforce dress codes, and the trendier places post style police at the door. *Barba Azul* (Prado 10) in Colonia San Jeronimo, and *Kaova* (Avenida Morelos 241), near the corner of Abasolo, are two of the most popular places. Glitzy *Sammaná* (☎ 313-47-27, Domingo Diéz 1522), across the street from Carlos & Charlie's, is another local favorite. It's open Wednesday to Saturday. For live salsa dance music, *Zúmbale* (Bajada de Chapultepec 13), near Glorieta La Luna, is the place to go.

Since public transport is sparse during these hours, taxi is the best way to get to the clubs. The fare to Zúmbale or Sammaná from the center should be about US$4.

Shopping

Cuernavaca has no distinctive handicrafts, but if you want an onyx ashtray, a leather belt or some second-rate silver, try the stalls just south of the Palacio de Cortés. Assorted ceramic figurines of *campesina* women, animals and miniature buildings are sold on 3 de Mayo, south of the center, at prices far lower than you'd find elsewhere.

Getting There & Away

Bus Quite a few bus companies serve Cuernavaca. The main lines operate five separate long-distance terminals:

Pullman de Morelos (PDM) – There are two stations; one on the corner of Abasolo and Netzahualcóyotl, and the other at Casino de la Selva, northeast of the center.

Estrella de Oro (EDO) – Avenida Morelos Sur 900

Estrella Roja (ER) – Corner of Galeana and Cuauhtemotzin

Flecha Roja (FR) – Avenida Morelos 503, between Arista and Victoria

To get to the Estrella de Oro terminal, which is 1.5km south of the center, take a Ruta 20 bus down Galeana; in the other direction, catch any bus up Morelos. Ruta 17 buses up Morelos stop within one block of the Pullman de Morelos terminal at Casino de la Selva. The rest of the terminals are within walking distance of the zócalo. Many local buses and those to nearby towns go from the southern corner of the city market.

Daily 1st-class buses from Cuernavaca include:

Acapulco – 315km, 4 hours; frequent EDO (US$20, deluxe US$22), 7 FR (US$22)

Chilpancingo – 180km, 2 hours; 5 EDO (US$11), 7 FR (US$11)

Cuautla – 42km, 1¼ hours; ER every 15 minutes (US$3)

Grutas de Cacahuamilpa – 80km, 2 hours; 6 FR (US$3)

Mexico City (Terminal Sur) – 89km, 1¼ hours; deluxe PDM from downtown terminal every 15

AROUND MEXICO CITY

minutes (US$5.25), 'ejecutivo' PDM from Casino de la Selva every 25 minutes (US$6.25), frequent FR (US$5.25)

Mexico City Airport – 100km, 1¾ hours; PDM hourly from Casino de la Selva (US$9.50, tickets may be purchased at PDM downtown terminal)

Oaxtepec – 25km, 1 hour; ER every 15 minutes (US$2.75)

Puebla – 175km, 3¾ hours; 15 ER (US$8.75)

Taxco – 80km, 1½ hours; 14 FR (US$4.50), 3 EDO (US$4.50)

Tepoztlán – 23km, 30 minutes; every 15 minutes till 10pm from the local bus terminal at the city market (US$1.50)

Toluca – 153km, 2½ hours; FR every half hour (US$4.50)

Zihuatanejo – 450km, 7 hours; 2 EDO (US$28)

Car & Motorcycle Cuernavaca is 89km south of Mexico City, a 1½ hour drive on highway 95 and a one-hour trip on the toll highway 95D (US$7). Both roads continue south to Acapulco; highway 95 goes through Taxco, and highway 95D is more direct and much faster (US$37).

Getting Around

You can walk to most places of interest in central Cuernavaca. The local buses (US$0.40) have their destinations marked on their windshields. Taxis will go to most places in town for under US$4. Radio taxi services include Citlalli (☎ 317-75-26) and Independéncia (☎ 313-14-14).

AROUND CUERNAVACA

Many places can be visited on day trips from Cuernavaca, on the way north to Mexico City or south to Taxco.

Xochicalco

Atop a desolate plateau 15km southwest of Cuernavaca as the crow flies but about 38km by road is the ancient ceremonial center of Xochicalco *('so-chee-CAL-co'; admission US$4, free Sun; open 9am-5pm daily)*, one of the most important archaeological sites in central Mexico. In Náhuatl, the language of the Aztecs, Xochicalco means 'Place of the House of Flowers.'

Today it is a collection of white stone ruins covering approximately 10 sq km, many yet to be excavated. They represent the various cultures – Toltec, Olmec, Zapotec, Mixtec and Aztec – for which

Xochicalco was a commercial, cultural or religious center. When Teotihuacán began to weaken around AD 650-700, Xochicalco began to rise in importance, achieving its maximum splendor between AD 650 and 850 with far-reaching commercial and cultural relations. Around the year 650, a congress of spiritual leaders met in Xochicalco, representing the Zapotec, Mayan and Gulf Coast peoples, to correlate their respective calendars.

The most famous monument here is the Pirámide de Quetzalcóatl (Pyramid of the Plumed Serpent). Archaeologists have surmised from its well-preserved bas-reliefs that astronomer-priests met here at the beginning and end of each 52-year cycle of the pre-Hispanic calendar. Xochicalco remained an important center until around 1200, when its excessive growth caused a fall similar to that of Teotihuacán. Signs at the site are in English and Spanish, but information appearing beside displays at an impressive museum 200m from the ruins is in Spanish only.

Getting There & Away Take a 'Cuautepec' bus from the local bus station near the Cuernavaca market (US$0.75). It will drop you off at the entrance to the site. The buses run every half hour. The last bus back to town leaves around 6pm. Alternatively, Pullman de Morelos runs buses every 40 minutes that will drop you off within 4km of the site. Flecha Roja runs buses by the same intersection every two hours. From there, you can walk (uphill) or catch a taxi (if you're lucky enough to find one).

Laguna de Tequesquitengo

This lake, 37km south of Cuernavaca, is a popular location for water sports, particularly water-skiing. There are hotels, restaurants and other facilities around the lakeshore.

In the area are several of the state of Morelos' famous balnearios – often natural springs that have been used as bathing and therapeutic places for hundreds of years.

Hotel Hacienda Vista Hermosa (☎ 734-345-53-61, 55-5662-4912 in Mexico City, **e** tourbymexico@infosel.net.mx), 2km north of the lake, was a cane-alcohol refinery in the 16th century. Accommodations are in 105 rooms (without/with meals US$142/198) and suites, some retaining their original colonial-era furniture, amid 80,000 sq m of lush gardens and palm-lined pathways. You may visit the grounds and use the pool and sports facilities without staying at the hotel for US$4.50 per day.

Pullman de Morelos runs five or more buses daily from Cuernavaca to the town of Tequesquitengo, on the southeast edge of the lake (1½ hours, US$2.50).

Las Estacas

Set amid botanical gardens with plenty of flowers, Las Estacas *(adult/child under 1.25m tall US$10/7; open 8am-6pm daily)* is designed for relaxation in nature. At this balneario near the town of Tlaltizapán, you can swim in numerous pools or in a cool, clear river, replenished by underground springs at the rate of 7500 liters per second. There's scuba diving equipment for rent and diving classes are offered. Try to arrive Monday to Friday if you're seeking tranquility.

Fuerte Bambú (☎ 734-345-00-77, 55-5563-2428 in Mexico City, ℮ informes@ lasestacas.com) is Las Estacas' HI-affiliated hostel and resembles a jungle village. It features a row of cool, well-ventilated adobe/reed houses, referred to as *villas ecológicas*. There are three bunk beds in each of the houses (dorm beds adult/child US$24/19). Spacious bathhouses are adjacent to the villas. Other accommodations include a 14-room hotel (singles/doubles US$54/63) and a cluster of four-person, palm-thatched huts (US$19), or you can camp. The fee for any of these options includes park admission. Reservations for the hostel, hotel, huts or camping are encouraged.

Getting There & Away Combis from Jojutla (50 minutes south of Cuernavaca by frequent Pullman de Morelos buses) go directly to the park entrance (US$0.75). By car, take the Cuautla exit off the Mexico City-Acapulco autopista, then take highway 138 east to Yautepec. From there head south on highway 2 toward Tlaltizapán and follow signs to Las Estacas.

Parque Nacional Lagunas de Zempoala

Only 25km northwest of Cuernavaca, by winding roads, is a group of seven lakes

high in the hills. Some of them are stocked with fish for anglers, and the surrounding forest offers pleasant walks and camping. Departing every half hour from Cuernavaca, Flecha Roja buses to Toluca make a stop at the park. The journey takes an hour.

TAXCO
* pop 52,000 • elev 1800m ☎ 762

The old silver-mining town of Taxco ('TASS-co'), 160km southwest of Mexico City, is a gorgeous colonial antique, and one of the most picturesque and pleasant places in Mexico. Clinging to a steep hillside, its narrow, cobblestone streets twist and turn between well-worn buildings, open unexpectedly onto pretty plazas and reveal delightful vistas at every corner. Unlike many

TAXCO

To Las Grutas de Cacahuamilpa, Cuernavaca & Mexico City

PLACES TO STAY
7 Hotel de la Borda
9 Posada de la Misión
10 Hotel Loma Linda

OTHER
1 Teleférico to Hotel Monte Taxco
2 Instituto de Artes Plásticos; UNAM Campus
3 Los Arcos
4 State Tourism Office
5 Tourist Information Office
6 Pemex
8 Templo de Chavarrieta

see Central Taxco map

AROUND MEXICO CITY

Reversals of Fortune

Taxco was called Tlachco (literally, 'place where ball is played') by the Aztecs, who dominated the region from 1440 until the Spanish arrived. In 1529, the colonial city was founded by Captain Rodrigo de Castañeda, acting under a mandate from Hernán Cortés. Among the town's first Spanish residents were three miners – Juan de Cabra, Juan Salcedo and Diego de Nava – and the carpenter Pedro Muriel. In 1531, they established the first Spanish mine on the North American continent.

The Spaniards came searching for tin, which they found in small quantities, but by 1534 they had discovered tremendous lodes of silver. That year the Hacienda El Chorrillo was built, complete with water wheel, smelter and aqueduct – the remains of which form the old arches (Los Arcos) over the highway at the northern end of present-day Taxco. The hacienda has gone through several metamorphoses and now houses the Instituto de Artes Plásticos and a branch of the Universidad Nacional Autónoma de México's Spanish-language institute. The prospectors quickly emptied the first veins of silver from the hacienda and left Taxco. Further quantities of silver were not discovered until two centuries later, in 1743. Don José de la Borda, who had arrived in 1716 from France at the age of 16 to work with his miner brother, accidentally uncovered one of the area's richest veins. According to a Taxco legend, Borda was riding near where the Templo de Santa Prisca now stands when his horse stumbled, dislodged a stone and exposed the silver.

Borda went on to make three fortunes and lose two. He introduced new techniques of draining and repairing mines, and he reportedly treated his indigenous workers much better than those working in other colonial mines. The Templo de Santa Prisca was the devout Borda's gift to Taxco. He is remembered for the saying 'Dios da a Borda, Borda da a Dios' ('God gives to Borda, Borda gives to God').

His success attracted many more prospectors and miners, and new veins of silver were found and emptied. With most of the silver gone, Taxco became a quiet town with a dwindling population and economy. In 1929, an American professor and architect named William (Guillermo) Spratling arrived and, at the suggestion of then US ambassador Dwight Morrow, set up a small silver workshop as a way to rejuvenate the town. (Another version has it that Spratling was writing a book in Taxco and resorted to the silver business because his publisher went broke. A third has it that Spratling had a notion – and acted on it – to design and create jewelry that synthesized pre-Hispanic motifs with art deco modernism.) The workshop became a factory, and Spratling's apprentices began establishing their own shops. Today there are more than 300 silver shops in Taxco.

Mexican towns from the colonial era, it has not surrounded itself with industrial suburbs. A fleet of VW taxis and combis scurries through the labyrinth like ants on an anthill. And few streetscapes are defaced with rows of parked cars, because there's simply no room for them.

The federal government has declared the city a national historical monument, and local laws preserve Taxco's colonial-style architecture and heritage. Old buildings are preserved and restored wherever possible, and any new buildings must conform to the old in scale, style and materials – have a look at the colonial Pemex station.

Though Taxco's silver mines are almost exhausted, handmade silver jewelry is one of the town's main industries. There are hundreds of silver shops, and visiting them is an excellent reason to wander the streets. Taxco's hotels and restaurants tend to be priced higher than elsewhere in Mexico, but they are generally so appealing that they are a good value anyway.

Orientation

Taxco's twisting streets may make you feel like a mouse in a maze, and even maps of the town look confusing at first, but you'll learn your way around – in any case it's a nice place to get lost. Plaza Borda, also called the zócalo, is the heart of the town, and its church, the Parroquia de Santa Prisca, is a good landmark.

Highway 95 becomes Avenida de los Plateros beyond the remains of the old aqueduct (Los Arcos) at the north end of town, hen winds its way around the eastern side of central Taxco. Both bus stations are on Avenida de los Plateros. La Garita branches west from Avenida de los Plateros opposite the Pemex station, and becomes the main horoughfare through the middle of town. It follows a convoluted route, more or less southwest (one-way only), to the Plaza Borda, changing its name to Juárez on the way. Past the plaza, this main artery becomes Cuauhtémoc, and goes down to the Plazuela de San Juan. Most of the essentials are along this La Garita-Juárez-Cuauhtémoc route, or pretty close to it. Several side roads go east back to Avenida de los Plateros, which is two-way and therefore the only way a vehicle can get back to the north end of town. The basic combi route is a counterclockwise loop going north on Avenida de los Plateros and south through the center of town.

Information

The Secretaría de Fomento Turístico (☎ 622-66-16) has an office in the Centro de Convenciones de Taxco, on Avenida de los Plateros at the north end of town, where the old aqueduct crosses the highway. Helpful English-speaking staff arrange guided tours of Taxco (US$32 for groups up to ten). The office is open 9am to 8pm daily. A non-government Tourist Information Office (☎ 622-07-98), 1km farther south along Avenida de los Plateros, functions primarily to arrange city tours, but its knowledgeable English (and French and German) speaking staff can answer most questions. The Flecha Roja bus station also has a tourist information booth.

There are several banks with ATMs around the town's main plazas.

The post office, which is open 8am to 4pm Monday to Friday and 9am to 1pm Saturday, is at Avenida de los Plateros 382, at the south end of town. There are card phones near Plaza Borda and in hotel lobbies; cards are sold at hotels, banks and stores.

Ciber Café (Hidalgo 9), open from 9am to 10pm, offers Internet access for US$2.25 per hour. Bora Bora Pizza and Freddie's Café (see Places to Eat) are also convenient places to get on the net.

Parroquia de Santa Prisca

On Plaza Borda, this church of rose-colored stone is a treasure of baroque architecture; its façade is decorated in the Churrigueresque style with elaborately sculpted figures. Over the doorway, the oval bas-relief depicts Christ's baptism. Inside, the intricately sculpted altarpieces covered with gold are equally fine examples of Churrigueresque art.

The local Catholic hierarchy allowed Don José de la Borda to donate this church to Taxco on the condition that he mortgage his personal mansion and other assets to guarantee its completion. It was designed by Spanish architects Diego Durán and Juan Caballero and constructed between 1751 and 1758, and it almost bankrupted Borda.

Museo Guillermo Spratling

This three-story museum of archaeology and history (☎ 622-16-70, Delgado 1; admission US$3.50; open 9am-6pm Tues-Sat, 9am-3pm Sun) is directly behind the Templo de Santa Prisca. Pre-Hispanic art exhibits on the two upper floors include jade statuettes, Olmec ceramics and other interesting pieces, mostly from the private collection of William Spratling.

Museo de Arte Virreinal

On Ruiz de Alarcón, a couple of blocks down the hill from the Plazuela de Bernal, is one of the oldest colonial homes in Taxco. It is commonly known as **Casa Humboldt**, though the German explorer and naturalist Friedrich Heinrich Alexander von Humboldt stayed here for only one night in 1803. The restored building now houses a museum of colonial religious art (☎ 622-55-01, Ruiz de Alarcón 12; admission US$1.75; open 10am-5pm Tues-Sat), with a small but well-displayed collection, labeled in English and Spanish. An interesting exhibit describes some of the restoration work on the Templo de Santa Prisca, during which some fabulous material was found in the basement.

Casa Borda (Museo de Arte Popular de Guerrero)

Built by José de la Borda in 1759, the Casa Borda (off Plaza Borda; admission free; open 10am-5pm Tues-Sun) now serves as a cultural center exhibiting sculpture, painting and photos by artists from Taxco and elsewhere. The building, though, is the main

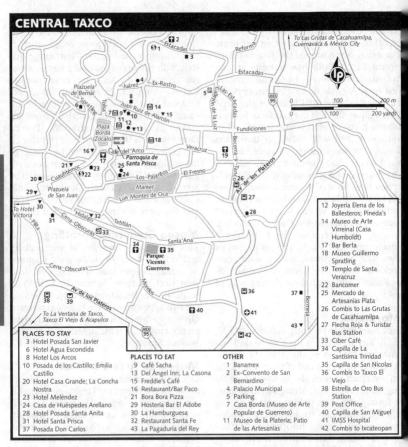

CENTRAL TAXCO

To Las Grutas de Cacahuamilpa,
Cuernavaca & México City

PLACES TO STAY
3 Hotel Posada San Javier
6 Hotel Agua Escondida
8 Hotel Los Arcos
10 Posada de los Castillo; Emilia
    Castillo
20 Hotel Casa Grande; La Concha
    Nostra
23 Hotel Meléndez
28 Hotel Posada Santa Anita
31 Hotel Santa Prisca
37 Posada Don Carlos

PLACES TO EAT
9 Café Sacha
13 Del Ángel Inn; La Casona
15 Freddie's Café
16 Restaurant/Bar Paco
21 Bora Bora Pizza
29 Hostería Bar El Adobe
30 La Hamburguesa
32 Restaurant Santa Fe
43 La Pagaduría del Rey

OTHER
1 Banamex
2 Ex-Convento de San
   Bernardino
4 Palacio Municipal
5 Parking
7 Casa Borda (Museo de Arte
   Popular de Guerrero)
11 Museo de la Platería; Patio
    de las Artesanías
12 Joyería Elena de los
    Ballesteros; Pineda's
14 Museo de Arte
    Virreinal (Casa
    Humboldt)
17 Bar Berta
18 Museo Guillermo
    Spratling
19 Templo de Santa
    Veracruz
22 Bancomer
25 Mercado de
    Artesanías Plata
26 Combis to Las Grutas
    de Cacahuamilpa
27 Flecha Roja & Turistar
    Bus Station
33 Ciber Café
34 Capilla de La
    Santísima Trinidad
35 Capilla de San Nicolas
36 Combis to Taxco El
    Viejo
38 Estrella de Oro Bus
    Station
39 Post Office
40 Capilla de San Miguel
41 IMSS Hospital
42 Combis to Ixcateopan

attraction. Due to the unevenness of the terrain, the rear window looks out on a precipitous four-story drop, even though the entrance off Plaza Borda is on the ground floor.

Museo de la Platería

The small museum of silverwork (*Patio de las Artesanías; admission US$1; open 10am-6pm Tues-Sun*) exhibits some superb examples of the silversmith's art and outlines (in Spanish) its development in Taxco. Included are some classic designs by William Spratling and prize-winning pieces from national and international competitions. Notice the very colorful, sculptural combinations of silver with semiprecious minerals such as jade, lapis lazuli, turquoise, malachite, agate and obsid-

ian – a feature of much of the silverwork for sale in the town and a link with pre-Hispanic stone-carving traditions.

To get to the museum, enter the Patio de las Artesanías building on the corner of Plaza Borda, on your left as you face Santa Prisca, turn left and go to the end of the hall and down the stairs.

Teleférico & Monte Taxco

From the northern end of Taxco, near Los Arcos, a Swiss-made cable car (*roundtrip adult/child US$3.50/2.25; open 8am-7pm daily*) ascends 173m to the luxurious Hotel Monte Taxco (see Places to Stay), affording fantastic views of Taxco and the surrounding mountains. To find it, walk uphill from the south side of Los Arcos and turn right through

he gate of the Instituto de Artes Plásticos;
'ou can see the terminal from the gate.

Courses

The ***Centro de Enseñanza Para Extranjeros***
(*CEPE, ☎ 622-01-24, e espino@servidor
unam.mx; postal address: Apdo Postal No 70,
40220 Taxco, Gro, Mexico; courses from
US$275*), a branch of the Universidad Nacio-
nal Autónoma de México (UNAM), offers
six-week Spanish language courses in the Ex-
Hacienda El Chorrillo, just south of Los
Arcos. Advanced students may take additional courses in Mexican art history, geography, literature and Chicano Studies. The basic
cost covers one language course and two
culture/history courses. CEPE arranges
lodging with families in Taxco.

Special Events

Try to time your visit to Taxco during one of
its annual festivals, but be sure to reserve a
hotel room in advance. During Semana
Santa, in particular, visitors pour into the
city to see the processions and events.

Fiestas de Santa Prisca & San Sebastián – The festivals of Taxco's two patron saints are celebrated
on January 18 (Santa Prisca) and January 20 (San
Sebastián), when people parade by the entrance
of the Templo de Santa Prisca with their pets and
farm animals in tow for an annual blessing.

Jueves Santo – On the Thursday before Easter, the
institution of the Eucharist is commemorated
with beautiful presentations and street processions of hooded penitents, some of whom flagel-
late themselves with thorns as the procession
winds through town.

Jornadas Alarconianas – In memory of Taxco-
born playwright Juan Ruiz de Alarcón, a cultural festival takes place in the summertime
(check with the tourist office for exact dates).
Taxco's convention center, plazas and churches
all host concerts and dance performances by internationally renowned performing artists.
Other concerts take place inside the Grutas de
Cacahuamilpa.

El Día del Jumil – This unusual festival is cele-
brated on the first Monday after the Day of the
Dead at the start of November (see 'El Día del
Jumil').

Feria de la Plata – The weeklong national silver
fair is held during the last week in November or
the first week in December (check with the
tourist office for exact dates). Silverwork competitions are held in various categories (such as
statuary and jewelry), and some of Mexico's best
silverwork is on display. Other festivities include

El Día del Jumil

Jumiles are small beetles (about 1cm long),
which migrate annually to the Cerro de
Huixteco (the hill behind Taxco) to reproduce. They begin to arrive around September; the last ones are gone by about January
or February. During this time, the jumiles are
a great delicacy for the people of Taxco, who
eat them alone or mixed in salsa with tomatoes, garlic, onion and chilies, or even alive,
rolled into tortillas. (You can buy live jumiles
in the market during this time; the Restaurant Santa Fe serves salsa de jumil prepared
in the traditional way.)

Traditionally, the entire population of the
town climbs the Cerro de Huixteco on Día
del Jumil (the first Monday after the Day of
the Dead, usually the first week of November) to collect jumiles, bring picnic baskets
and share food and fellowship. Many families come early and camp on the hill over the
preceding weekend. The celebration is said
to represent the jumiles giving energy and
life to the people of Taxco for another year.

organ recitals in Santa Prisca, rodeos, burro
races, concerts and dances.

Las Posadas – From December 16 to 24, nightly
candlelit processions pass through the streets of
Taxco singing from door to door. Children are
dressed up to resemble various Biblical characters, and at the end of the processions, they
attack piñatas.

Places to Stay

Budget *Hotel Casa Grande* (*☎ 622-09-69,
fax 622-11-08, Plazuela de San Juan 7*)
Singles/doubles with shared bath US$12/20,
with private bath US$14/23. Occupying the
upper level of the former mining court
building, the Casa Grande has 26 clean,
basic rooms around an inner courtyard. The
shared bathroom is both tiny and dirty. It
can be noisy; adjacent La Concha Nostra
(see Places to Eat) hosts very loud live
music on Saturday. Laundry facilities are
available.

Casa de Huéspedes Arellano (*☎ 622-02-
15, Los Pajaritos 23*) Dorm bed US$11,
singles/doubles with shared bath US$14/20,
with private bath US$28/39. Next to the
silver market, this hotel offers 10 simple but

clean rooms. It's a family-run place with terraces for sitting and a place on the roof for washing clothes. To find it, walk down the alley on the south side of Santa Prisca until you reach a staircase going down to your right. Follow it past the stalls to a flight of stairs to your left; the Casa de Huéspedes is 30 steps down, on the left.

Mid-Range *Hotel Posada Santa Anita* (☎ 622-07-52, *Avenida de los Plateros 302*) Singles/doubles US$20/28. Near the Flecha Roja bus station, this hotel has small, quiet rooms.

Hotel Posada San Javier (☎ 622-31-77, fax 622-23-51, ℮ posadasanjavier@ hotmail.com, *Estacadas 32*) Singles/doubles US$30/33, junior suites from US$33. One of the most attractive places to stay in Taxco at any price is this one, a block down the hill from the Palacio Municipal. Though centrally located, it's peaceful, with a private parking area and a lovely, large enclosed garden around a big swimming pool. Many of its comfortable, high-ceilinged rooms come with private terraces.

Hotel Los Arcos (☎ 622-18-36, *Ruiz de Alarcón 4*) Singles/doubles US$29/39. This hotel has 26 clean, spacious rooms. The former 17th-century monastery retains a wonderful courtyard, lounging areas, a spectacular rooftop terrace and lots of character.

Posada de los Castillo (☎/fax 622-13-96, *Juan Ruiz de Alarcón 7*) Singles/doubles US$23/33. Across the road from the Hotel Los Arcos, owned by a renowned family of silver workers, this place has colonial charm and reasonable prices. The hotel's patio contains a shop displaying Emilia Castillo's unique silver designs.

Hotel Meléndez (☎ 622-00-06, *Cuauhtémoc 6*) Singles/doubles US$33/40. This is an older place with pleasant terrace sitting areas and a good location between the Plazuela de San Juan and Plaza Borda. Because of its location, quite a bit of street noise penetrates into the rooms.

Hotel Santa Prisca (☎ 622-09-80, fax 622-29-38, ℮ htl_staprisca@yahoo.com, *Cena Obscuras 1*) Singles/doubles US$30/46, suites US$64. On the south side of the Plazuela de San Juan, the elegant Santa Prisca features a quiet interior patio and a pleasant restaurant. Most rooms have private terraces. The parking lot is reached through a tunnel at the hotel's uphill end.

Top End *Hotel Loma Linda* (☎ 622-02-06, ꓪ hotellomalinda.com, *Avenida de los Plateros 52*) Singles/doubles US$56/63. A kilometer north of the Santa Anita at a bend in the highway, the Loma Linda is perched on the edge of a vast chasm. The back rooms have vertigo-inducing views of a lush green valley. There's a restaurant, swimming pool and motel-style parking.

Posada Don Carlos (☎ 622-00-75, *Calle del Consuelo 8*) Rooms from US$56. This hotel has eight tastefully appointed rooms, six with balconies offering superb views of Taxco. There's a small swimming pool on a terrace facing town. The hill to the Don Carlos is a tough climb – take a taxi for US$1.50.

Hotel Victoria (☎ 622-00-04, fax 622-00-10, *Carlos J Nibbi 14*) Singles/doubles US$62/73, deluxe rooms US$89. This sprawling place, on a street named after the American who ran the place in the 1950s, dominates Taxco's southern hills. It feels like a colonial village wrapped around a bend in the mountainside complete with cobblestone streets and little overgrown nooks.

Hotel Agua Escondida (☎ 622-07-26, ꓪ www.aguaescondida.com, *Plaza Borda 4*) Singles/doubles US$62/76. Right on the zócalo, the Agua Escondida has large and small swimming pools on a high terrace and a basement garage. Its 65 comfy rooms have TVs and phones.

Hotel de la Borda (☎ 622-00-25, *Cerro del Pedregal 2*) Rooms US$91, suites US$167. This four-star hotel is a sprawling, mission-style complex perched on a hill, with a pool and a large dining room. The hotel's spacious rooms, some with panoramic city views, are less elegant than you'd expect for the price.

Posada de la Misión (☎ 622-00-63, ꓪ www.posadamision.com, *Cerro de la Misión 32*) Singles/doubles with breakfast & dinner US$162/185. A more expensive but far superior option to the other top-end hotels is this luxurious place. Most of its large rooms feature private terraces with fine views of Taxco. Overlooking the large pool is a mosaic mural of the Aztec emperor Cuauhtémoc designed by Juan O'Gorman.

Hotel Monte Taxco (☎ 622-13-00) Rooms US$110, suites US$200. Way up on top of the mountain that it's named after, this five-star hotel is considered the most fabulous place to stay in Taxco, but magnificent views and nicer rooms can be had elsewhere for far less. It can be reached by car, taxi or cable car. Rates, which are more on weekends, include use of the swimming pool but not of the hotel's tennis courts, underequipped gym or steam baths. There are also restaurants, bars, a disco and a state-run handicrafts shop.

Places to Eat

Bora Bora Pizza (☎ 622-17-21, Delicias 4) Prices US$4-10. Open 1.30pm-11.30pm. Just off Cuauhtémoc near the Plaza Borda, this restaurant serves the best pizza in Taxco. It also has Internet access for US$2.25 per hour.

La Hamburguesa (☎ 622-09-41, Plazuela de San Juan 5) Prices from US$1.50. Open 8am-midnight. For late-night snacks, try this place on the west side of Plazuela San Juan. It has burger/fries combinations and excellent enchiladas.

La Concha Nostra (☎ 622-79-44, Plazuela de San Juan 5) Prices US$2.25-7. This is a laid-back bar-restaurant within the Casa Grande Hotel. It serves pizza, salads and various snacks until well after midnight. From the balcony, you can watch the action on Plazuela San Juan.

Freddie's Café (☎ 622-48-18, inside Plaza Taxco) Prices from US$1.25. Coffee aficionados will appreciate this place in the Plaza Taxco shopping center next door to Casa Humboldt. In addition to the cappuccino and espresso, Freddie's serves good grilled cheese sandwiches. Seating is on a long balcony with a view of Monte Taxco. There is also Internet access for US$3.25 per hour.

Café Sacha (☎ 628-51-50; Ruiz de Alarcón 1A) Prices US$1.75-7. Just up the street from Posada de los Castillo, this little bohemian café serves a variety of international snacks and vegetarian dishes. This is a great place to have breakfast or to just hang out and have some good coffee.

Restaurant Santa Fe (☎ 622-11-70, Hidalgo 2) Prices from US$3. A few doors downhill from the Plazuela de San Juan, this place is often recommended by locals, and it does indeed serve good food at fair prices,

though service can be brusque. It offers set breakfasts, and the comida corrida includes four courses.

Restaurant/Bar Paco (☎ 622-00-64, Plaza Borda 12) Prices US$5-14. Overlooking Plaza Borda through large picture windows, this restaurant is great for people-watching. The food is good too, but you pay for the view. Try the delicious enchiladas with mole. The Paco hosts live music Friday and Saturday evenings.

Del Ángel Inn (☎ 622-55-25, Muñoz 4) Prices US$4.50-14.50, set lunch US$8.50. On the left side of the Santa Prisca, the Del Ángel Inn has a spectacular roof terrace with a bar. It's definitely tourist-oriented but the food isn't bad. The set lunch includes fresh bread with herbed butter, soup, a main course and dessert. There are also salads, pastas and Mexican dishes.

La Casona (☎ 622-10-71, Muñoz 4) Prices US$3.50-9.50. Next door to the Del Ángel Inn, La Casona has similar fare for a little cheaper, as well as an excellent balcony with a view down the hillside of Taxco.

Hostería Bar El Adobe (Plazuela de San Juan 13) Prices US$3.75-11. This place has a less captivating view but a lovely interior. Regional specialties include garlic soup with shrimp and Taxco-style *cecina* (salted strip steak) served with diced chicken and sliced *chiles poblanos*.

The top two restaurants in Taxco are on hills facing the city center and are best reached by taxi.

La Ventana de Taxco (☎ 622-05-87, Paraje del Solar s/n) Prices US$8-14. South of town, this restaurant specializes in Italian food. Its *piccata lombarda* (veal sautéed in a lemon, butter and parsley sauce) is superb.

La Pagaduría del Rey (Colegio Militar 8) Prices US$6-20. In the Barrio Bermeja outside of the center of town is this equally fancy place. It offers salads, pastas and Mexican dishes. It's a great place simply to sip a drink and admire the view.

Bar Berta Prices from US$3. Just off the Plaza Borda at the beginning of Cuauhtémoc, this is a fine place for a drink. With simple green tables on two levels and bullfight posters on the walls, it's the sort of place Hemingway would have felt at home in. Try the house specialty, a Berta, which is tequila, honey, lime and mineral water.

Shopping

Silver With more than 300 shops selling silverwork, the selection is mind-boggling. Look at some of the best places first, to see what's available, then try to focus on the things you're really interested in, and shop around for those. If you are careful and willing to bargain a bit, you can buy wonderful pieces at reasonable prices.

Most shops are both *menudeo* and *mayoreo* (retail and wholesale); to get the wholesale price you will have to buy about 1kg of silver.

The price of a piece is principally determined by its weight; the creative work serves mainly to make it salable, though items with exceptional artisanship can command a premium. If you're serious about buying silver, find out the current peso-per-gram rate and weigh any piece before you agree on a price. All the silver shops have scales, mostly electronic devices that should be accurate. If a piece costs less than the going price per gram, it's not real silver. Don't buy anything that doesn't have the Mexican government '.925' stamp, which certifies that the piece is 92.5% sterling silver (most pieces also bear a set of initials identifying the workshop where they were made). If a piece is too small or delicate to stamp, a reputable shop will supply a certificate as to its purity. Anyone who is discovered selling forged .925 pieces is sent to prison.

The shops in and around Plaza Borda tend to have higher prices than those farther from the center, but they also tend to have more interesting work. The shops on Avenida de los Plateros are often branches of downtown businesses, set up for the tourist buses that can't make it through the narrow streets.

Several shops are in the Patio de las Artesanías building on the Plaza Borda. *Pineda's* on the corner of Muñoz and the plaza is a famous shop; a couple of doors down Muñoz, the *Joyería Elena de los Ballesteros* (☎ 622-37-67) is another. The tableware on display in the showroom of *Emilia Castillo* (☎ 622-34-74), inside Posada de los Castillo, is a unique blend of porcelain and silver.

For quantity rather than quality, see the stalls in the *Mercado de Artesanías Plata* which have vast quantities of rings, chains and pendants. The work is not as well-displayed here, but you can often spot something special.

Other Crafts It's easy to overlook them among the silver, but there are other things to buy in Taxco. Finely painted wood and papier-mâché trays, platters and boxes are sold along the Calle del Arco, on the south side of Santa Prisca, as well as bark paintings and wood carvings. Quite a few shops sell semiprecious stones, fossils and mineral crystals, and some have a good selection of masks, puppets and semi-antique carvings.

Getting There & Away

Taxco has two long-distance bus terminals, both on Avenida de los Plateros. First-class Flecha Roja and Futura buses and deluxe Turistar buses, as well as several 2nd-class lines, use the terminal at Avenida de los Plateros 104. The Estrella de Oro (1st-class) terminal is at the south end of town. Combis pass both terminals every few minutes and will take you up the hill to the Plaza Borda for US$0.30 (see Getting Around). Book early for buses out of Taxco as it can be hard to get a seat.

Daily long-distance departures (directos unless otherwise stated) include:

Acapulco – 266km, 4½ hours; 5 Estrella de Oro, 4 Turistar (US$13.50)

Chilpancingo – 130km, 2 hours; 5 Estrella de Oro (US$6.50), 4 Turistar (US$7.50)

Cuernavaca – 80km, 1½ hours; 3 Estrella de Oro, hourly Flecha Roja until 7pm (US$4.25)

Iguala – 35km, 45 minutes; various 2nd-class operators every 15 minutes (US$1.25)

Ixtapan de la Sal – 68km, 1½ hours; 3 Turistar (US$2.75), 18 Tres Estrellas departing from Flecha Roja terminal (US$3)

Mexico City (Terminal Sur) – 170km, 3 hours; 6 Estrella de Oro (US$7.75), Futura hourly (1st-class US$7.75, deluxe US$8.50)

Toluca – 145km, 3 hours; 3 Turistar, 18 Tres Estrellas departing from Flecha Roja terminal (US$7)

Getting Around

Apart from walking, combis and taxis are the most popular ways of getting around the steep, winding streets of Taxco. Combis (white Volkswagen minibuses) are frequent and cheap (US$0.30) and operate from 7am to 8pm. The 'Zócalo' combi departs from Plaza Borda, goes down Cuauhtémoc to the

Plazuela de San Juan, then heads down the hill on Hidalgo. It turns right at Morelos, left at Avenida de los Plateros and goes north until La Garita, where it turns left and goes back to the zócalo. The 'Arcos/Zócalo' combi follows basically the same route except that it continues past La Garita to Los Arcos, where it does a U-turn and heads back to La Garita. Combis marked 'PM' for 'Pedro Martín' go to the south end of town, past the Estrella de Oro bus station. Taxis cost US$1 to US$1.50 for trips around town.

A large parking garage is at the Plaza Taxco shopping center, charging US$1 an hour. Access is off Avenida de los Plateros via Estacadas. An elevator takes you up to the shopping center, on Ruiz de Alarcón next door to the Casa Humboldt.

AROUND TAXCO
Taxco El Viejo
The original site of Taxco was 11km south at Taxco El Viejo, where the indigenous Tlahuica mined tin and silver deposits, which were later heavily exploited by the Spaniards. The principal attraction of the area today is a pair of ranches north and south of Taxco El Viejo where silver is crafted in peaceful settings.

Ex-Hacienda San Juan Bautista Just south of Taxco El Viejo, the Ex-Hacienda San Juan Bautista is one of seven silver refining facilities established around Taxco and Taxco El Viejo during the region's first silver boom. The old hacienda, which today houses the School of Earth Sciences of the Universidad Autónoma de Guerrero, is worth exploring for its lovely, poinsettia-lined patios and remnants of its former use.

Enter through an archway on the left side of the highway, then turn left and downhill past some new school buildings. An architectural innovation of the facility was the intra-wall conduits for transporting water from the main aqueduct to the tanks in the patios, where mercury was added to extract silver (a process that polluted extensive groundwater sources). The building also contains the university's mineralogy museum.

Rancho Spratling Although William Spratling died in 1967, his former workshop (☎ 762-622-60-50; open 9am-1pm & 2pm-5pm Mon-Sat) continues to produce some of the finest silver in Mexico and employs the same handcrafted methods and classic designs that have made Spratling pieces collectibles. The former Spratling ranch, just south of the Ex-Hacienda San Juan Bautista, has been pridefully maintained, and a new generation of artisans adhere to Spratling's standards under the guidance of maestro Don Tomás, one of Spratling's principal workers for many years.

Visitors are encouraged to enter the workshop and see how fine silver is crafted. Also on the premises is a showroom displaying work designed by Spratling; a second room features new designs by Don Tomás' apprentices. Prices are in US dollars.

Rancho Cascada Los Castillo The metal workshops of the Castillo family (open 9am-6pm Mon-Fri, 9am-1pm Sat) are on the lovely grounds of the Rancho Cascada Los Castillo, off the highway north of Taxco El Viejo. On the way to the workshops, through rambling gardens, is a museum in a circular hut displaying the antiquities collection of Antonio Castillo, a master craftsman and contemporary of Spratling's. Inside the workshops, which are housed in a series of low buildings, craftspeople create silver, copper, tin and *alpaca* (nickel silver) objects. There is no shop on the premises, but those interested can buy their products online (W www.silverzeal.com).

Getting There & Away Taxco El Viejo is 25 minutes south of Taxco on highway 95. From Taxco, catch any of the frequent 2nd-class buses heading for Iguala at the Flecha Roja terminal. Combis to Taxco El Viejo leave Taxco just north of the IMSS hospital. Ask the driver to let you off at either of the *ranchos* or the ex-hacienda, as all have entrances along the highway. To visit all three destinations, you could get off at the Rancho Spratling, walk back up the highway to the Ex-Hacienda San Juan Bautista (half a kilometer), then catch a bus back toward Taxco and get off at the Rancho Cascada Los Castillo. From there, take any bus or combi heading north to return to Taxco.

Ixcateopan
The village of Ixcateopan, southwest of Taxco, was the birthplace of Cuauhtémoc,

the final Aztec emperor, who was defeated and later executed by Cortés. The emperor's remains were returned to his native village and entombed in the church on the town plaza, also the site of the historical **Museo de la Mexicanidad**. Marble is quarried nearby and, being the most common stone in the area, was often used in construction – Ixcateopan is one of the few towns in the world with marble streets.

Getting There & Away A combi marked 'Ixcateopan' departs Taxco, from about 100m south of the Seguro Social building, approximately every half hour from 7am to 5pm (1½ hours, US$2).

Grutas de Cacahuamilpa

The caverns of Cacahuamilpa (*cave tours adult/child US$3.50/2.25; open 10am-7pm, last ticket sold at 5pm*) are a beautiful natural wonder of stalactites, stalagmites and twisted rock formations, with huge chambers up to 82m high. Thirty kilometers northeast of Taxco, they are protected as a national park and well worth visiting.

You must tour the caves with a group and a guide, through 2km of an illuminated walkway. Many of the formations are named for some fanciful resemblance – 'the elephant,' 'the champagne bottle,' 'Dante's head,' 'the tortillas' and so on – and the lighting is used to enhance these resemblances. Much of the guide's commentary focuses on these, but the geological information is minimal. After the tour, you can return to the entrance at your own pace. The entire tour takes two hours.

From the cave entrance, a path goes down the steep valley to Río Dos Bocas, where two rivers emerge from the caves. The pretty walk down and back takes 30 minutes.

Cave tours, in Spanish, depart from the visitor's center every hour on the hour from 10am to 5pm. An English-speaking guide *might* be available for large groups of foreigners. There are restaurants, snacks and souvenir shops at the visitor's center.

Getting There & Away From Taxco, bluestriped combis depart every two hours in front of the Flecha Roja bus terminal and go right to the visitor's center at the caves (one hour, US$2.25). Alternatively, you can take any bus heading for Toluca or Ixtapan de la

Sal, get off at the 'Grutas' crossroads and walk 1km down the road to the entrance, on your right. The last combis leave the site at 5pm on Monday to Friday and 6pm on Saturday to Sunday; after this you might be able to catch a bus to Taxco at the crossroads.

West of Mexico City

The main road west from the capital, highway 15D, goes to Toluca, which has a pleasant center, an interesting museum and several art galleries. There are ruins nearby and some of the surrounding villages are known for their handicrafts. The countryside to the east, south and west of Toluca is scenic, with pine forests, rivers and a huge volcano. Valle de Bravo is a lakeside resort and colonial gem 70km west of Toluca. Two highways head south from Toluca: highway 55 passes handicraft centers, impressive pyramids and spas at Ixtapan de la Sal and Tonatico, then continues on to Taxco; toll highway 55D is the fast route to Ixtapan de la Sal.

TOLUCA
• pop 418,000 • elev 2660m ☎ 722

Toluca, 64km west of Mexico City, is 400m higher than the capital, and the extra altitude is noticeable. The eastern outskirts are an industrial area, but the colonial-era city center has attractive plazas and lively arcades. Its cultural sites include a good number of museums and art galleries.

Toluca was an indigenous settlement from at least the 13th century; the Spanish founded the city in the 16th century after defeating the Aztecs and Matlazincas who lived in the valley. It became part of the Marquesado del Valle de Oaxaca, Hernán Cortés' personal estates in Mexico. Since 1830, it has been capital of the state of México, which surrounds the Distrito Federal on three sides like an upside-down U.

Orientation

The main road from Mexico City becomes Paseo Tollocan, a dual carriageway, as it approaches Toluca. On reaching the east side of the city proper, Paseo Tollocan bears southwest and becomes a ring road around

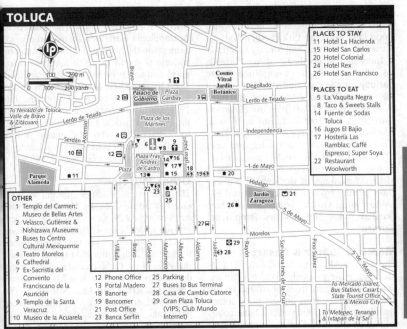

TOLUCA

PLACES TO STAY
11 Hotel La Hacienda
15 Hotel San Carlos
20 Hotel Colonial
24 Hotel Rex
26 Hotel San Francisco

PLACES TO EAT
5 La Vaquita Negra
8 Taco & Sweets Stalls
14 Fuente de Sodas Toluca
16 Jugos El Bajío
17 Hostería Las Ramblas; Caffé Espresso; Super Soya
22 Restaurant Woolworth

OTHER
1 Templo del Carmen; Museo de Bellas Artes
2 Velasco, Gutiérrez & Nishizawa Museums
3 Buses to Centro Cultural Mexiquense
4 Teatro Morelos
6 Cathedral
7 Ex-Sacrística del Convento Franciscano de la Asunción
9 Templo de la Santa Veracruz
10 Museo de la Acuarela
12 Phone Office
13 Portal Madero
18 Banorte
19 Bancomer
21 Post Office
23 Banca Serfín
25 Parking
27 Buses to Bus Terminal
28 Casa de Cambio Catorce
29 Gran Plaza Toluca (VIPS; Club Mundo Internet)

the south side of the city center. The bus station and the large Mercado Juárez are 2km southeast of the city center, just off Paseo Tollocan.

The vast Plaza de los Mártires, with the Palacio de Gobierno and the cathedral, is the center of town, but most of the life is in the block to the south, a pedestrian precinct that is surrounded by arched colonnades on its east, south and west sides. These arcades are lined with shops and restaurants and thronged with people most of the day. The pleasant Parque Alameda is three blocks to the west along Hidalgo.

Information

The state tourist office (☎ 212-60-48) is 2km from the center in the Edificio de Servicios Administrativos, office 110-A, at the corner of Urawa and Paseo Tollocan. Good maps of Toluca and the state of México are available, and English is spoken.

There are many banks with ATMs near the Portal Madero; Banca Serfín at Matamoros will change money or travelers checks. Casa de Cambio Catorce is next to the VIPS restaurant on Juárez.

The main post office is on the corner of Hidalgo and Sor Juana Inés de la Cruz, 500m east of Portal Madero. There are pay phones all around the arcade, and a phone office, near the north end of the underground parking lot west of the cathedral, open 7am to 8.30pm daily for long-distance phone calls and faxes.

Club Mundo Internet, in the Gran Plaza Toluca shopping mall, provides Internet access 9am to 9.30pm daily and charges US$2.25 an hour.

The hospital, Sanatorio Toluca (☎ 217-78-00), is at Peñaloza 233, a little west of the center southwest along Paseo Tollocan.

City Center

The 19th-century **Portal Madero**, running 250m along Avenida Hidalgo, is lively and bustling, as is the arcade along the pedestrian street to the east. A block north, the big, open expanse of the **Plaza de los Mártires** is surrounded by fine old government buildings; the 19th-century **cathedral** and the 18th-century **Templo de la Santa Veracruz** are on its south side. The octagonal-shaped building in the plaza beside the cathedral was once the sacristy of the Convento Franciscano de la Asunción, which stood here until the 19th century. Today it is used as a meeting hall for city functions.

Immediately northeast of the Plaza de los Mártires is the fountained **Plaza Garibay**, at the east end of which stands the unique **Cosmo Vitral Jardín Botánico** (*Cosmic Stained-Glass Window Botanical Garden; cnr Juárez & Lerdo de Tejada; admission US$1.25; open 10am-6pm Tues-Sun*). Built in 1909 as a market, and until 1975 the site of the weekly *tianguis* (regional market), this now houses 3500 sq m of lovely gardens, lit through 48 stained-glass panels by the Tolucan artist Leopoldo Flores. On the north side of Plaza Garibay is the 18th century **Templo del Carmen**.

Mercado Juárez & Casart

The Juárez Market (*cnr Fabela & 5 de Mayo; open daily*) is behind the bus station. On Friday, villagers from all around swarm in to buy and sell fruit, flowers, pots, clothes and plastic goods. The market is huge, colorful and chaotic, but it's not a great place to buy local handicrafts.

You can see quality arts and crafts of the region in more peaceful surroundings here at the state crafts store, **Casart** (*Casa de Artesanía; open 10am-6.45pm daily*). There's a big range, and the crafts sold at the store are often the top-end pieces from the villages where the crafts are made. Prices are fixed and higher than you can get with some haggling in the markets, but you can gauge prices and quality here before going elsewhere to buy. You can watch craftspeople, such as basket weavers from San Pedro Actopan, at work in the store. Honey cookies from Sultepec and Tejupilco are baked on the premises.

Centro Cultural Mexiquense

The impressive **State of México Cultural Center** (*Boulevard Reyes Herdes 302; admission US$2, free Sun; all museums open 10am-6pm daily*), 4.5km west of the city center, comprises three very good museums and a library. The **Museo de Culturas Populares** has superb examples of the traditional arts and crafts of México state, with some astounding trees of life, whimsical Day of the Dead figures and a fine display of charro

equipment – saddles, sombreros, swords, pistols, ropes and spurs. The **Museo de Antropología e História** features top-notch exhibits on the history of the state from prehistoric times to the 20th century, with a good collection of pre-Hispanic artifacts. The **Museo de Arte Moderno** traces the development of Mexican art from the late 19th century Academia de San Carlos to the Nueva Plástica, and includes paintings by Tamayo, Orozco and many others. 'Centro Cultural' buses go along Lerdo de Tejada, passing Plaza Garibay (US$0.50).

Other Museums

The ex-convent buildings adjacent to Plaza Garibay house Toluca's **Museo de Bellas Artes** (*☎ 215-53-29, Santos Degollado 102; admission US$0.25; open 10am-6pm Tues-Sun*), which has paintings from the colonial period to the early 20th century. On Bravo, opposite the Palacio de Gobierno, are art museums devoted to the work of José María Velasco, Felipe Gutiérrez and Luis Nishizawa. The latter was an artist of Mexican-Japanese parentage whose work shows influences from both cultures. The **Museo de la Acuarela** (*☎ 214-73-04, Pedro Ascencio 13; admission free; open 10am-6pm Tues-Sat, 10am-3pm Sun*) displays a fine collection of watercolors by Mexican and American artists, including a wonderful series of cathedral façades by Vicente Mendiola.

Places to Stay

Hotel Rex (*☎ 215-93-00, Matamoros Sur 101*) Singles/doubles US$20/24. The rooms here, some facing the arcade, have TVs and hot water. They're basic but acceptable.

Hotel San Carlos (*☎ 214-43-36, Portal Madero 210*) Singles/doubles US$20/30. Across the street from the Rex, this friendly place is a bit shabby but is clean and has large bathrooms. Neither hotel has parking but a lot on Matamoros charges US$5 for the night.

Hotel La Hacienda (*☎ 214-36-34, Hidalgo Poniente 508*) Singles/doubles US$23/39. Half a block east of the Alameda, the rooms here are overpriced, but most are decent with colonial touches like wood-beam ceilings. There's also a garage.

Hotel Colonial (*☎ 215-97-00, fax 214-70-66, Hidalgo Oriente 103*) Singles/doubles US$28/34. For true colonial ambiance, try this hotel just east of Juárez. It has well-maintained, stylish rooms around an interior courtyard. Guests can use a parking lot on Juárez, the next left turn off of Hidalgo.

Hotel San Francisco (☎/fax 213-44-15, W *www.hotelsanfrancisco.com.mx, Rayón Sur 104*) Singles/doubles US$56/67. Around the corner from the Gran Plaza Toluca, this hotel has pretensions to luxury, including a glass-walled elevator shaft for viewing the slick skylit atrium restaurant. The rooms are modern and there's plenty of parking.

Places to Eat
Toluqueños like to snack, and you can join them in the arcades around the Plaza Fray Andrés de Castro, beside the cathedral. Stalls selling authentic *tacos de obispo,* a sausage from Tenancingo, are easily found because there are crowds of people flocking around them. The contents of these arm-width sausages – barbecued chopped beef spiced with epazote, nuts, raisins, almonds and marrow – are stuffed into tortillas and sold in large quantities. Other stalls sell *jamoncillos* and *mostachones* (sweets made of burned milk) and candied fruit accompanied by lots of bees.

Jugos El Bajío Prices from US$1.50. This place, in the arcade opposite the Templo de la Santa Veracruz, offers *tortas,* fresh fruit juices and fruit cocktails.

Fuente de Sodas Toluca Prices from US$1.50. Around the corner from Jugos El Bajío, this café is exactly the same in design and menu.

La Vaquita Negra Prices US$1.50-2. On the northwest corner of the arcades, this place with green and red sausages hanging over the counter serves first-rate tortas. You can garnish the tortas with pickled peppers and onions, which are also sold in jars.

Hostería Las Ramblas Prices from US$5. On the pedestrian mall, this is one of Toluca's best and most atmospheric places. It serves a variety of tasty antojitos, including *sopes,* mole verde and *sesos* (brains) *a la mexicana.*

Caffé Espresso Prices from US$1. Two doors down from Hostería Las Ramblas is this relaxing hangout serving espresso and hot and cold cappuccinos.

Restaurant Woolworth Set breakfast from US$3.50. Opposite the Hotel San Carlos, the Woolworth offers large set breakfasts with unlimited free coffee refills.

VIPS (inside Grand Plaza Toluca shopping mall) Prices US$4-10. This is a terribly popular place serving bland fare at inflated prices. It serves burgers and Mexican specialties.

Super Soya Prices US$1.75 Next to Café Espresso, this ultrapopular spot serves semi-healthy ice cream and fruit concoctions.

Getting There & Away
Toluca's bus station is at Berriozábal 101, 2km southeast of the center. Ticket offices for many destinations are at the gate entrances, or right on the platforms. There are frequent departures to Querétaro (gate 2), Morelia (gate 5), Valle de Bravo (gate 6), Chalma and Malinalco (gate 9), Metepec (platform 10) and Cuernavaca, Taxco and Ixtapan de la Sal (platform 12).

In Mexico City, Toluca buses use the Terminal Poniente. The 1st-class TMT line runs buses between the two cities every five minutes from 5.30am to 10pm; the trip takes an hour (US$3.50).

Getting Around
'Centro' buses go from outside the bus station to the town center along Lerdo de Tejada; 'Terminal' buses go from Juárez (south of Lerdo de Tejada) in the center to the bus station (US$0.50). Taxis from the bus station to the city center cost about US$4.50. Taxis around town are considerably cheaper.

AROUND TOLUCA
Calixtlahuaca
This Aztec site *(admission US$3, free Sun; open 10am-5pm daily)* is 2km west of highway 55, 8km north of Toluca. It's partly excavated and restored. The site has some unusual features, such as a circular pyramid that supported a temple to Quetzalcóatl and Calmecac, believed to have been a school for the children of priests and nobles. You can catch a bus in front of Suburbia (near Mercado Juárez) in Toluca that goes to within a short walk of the site.

Metepec
• pop 167,000 • elev 2610m ☎ 722
Basically a suburb of Toluca, 7km to the south on highway 55, Metepec is the center

for producing elaborate and symbolic pottery *árboles de la vida* (trees of life) and Metepec suns (earthenware discs brightly painted with sun and moon faces). A number of shops along the so-called Corredor Artesanal, on Comonfort south of Paseo San Isidro, sell árboles de la vida. Prices range from US$6 for a miniature árbol de la vida up to US$130 for a meter-high tree. Just north of Paseo San Isidro is the Corral Artesanal, a series of small shops along an arcade selling local crafts, and a restaurant.

The *potters' workshops (alfarerías)* are spread out all over town; there's a map painted on the wall of the triangular tourism module in front of the Cerro del Calvario that shows their locations. The workshop of Beto Hernández *(Altamirano 58),* between Allende and Ascencio, is itself a work of art with fountains, altars, and designs embedded in the cobblestone walkway, and a sort of chapel built around the lavishly decorated kiln. Within the various display rooms are some pretty amazing trees, many unpainted, at reasonable prices. The most elaborate and expensive trees are in the front gallery. A few doors down, the workshop of Adrián Luis González *(Altamirano 212)* is equally remarkable; the floor of the upstairs gallery is adorned with butterflies and suns made by González. A fascinating genealogical tree shows members of the González family (Adrián himself is near the top) with their accoutrements. The tree demonstrates the process of its own creation, with subsequent levels at different stages of production – from unbaked clay at the bottom to a bright paint finish at the top.

A pleasant hike with great views can be made to the top of Cerro del Calvario, a hill decorated with a huge pottery mural.

Frequent 2nd-class buses reach Metepec from the Toluca bus station.

NEVADO DE TOLUCA

The extinct volcano Nevado de Toluca (or Xinantécatl), 4690m high, lies across the horizon south of Toluca. A road runs 48km up to its crater, which contains two lakes, El Sol and La Luna. The earlier you reach the summit, the better the chance of clear views. The summit area is snowy *(nevado)* from November to March, and sometimes OK for cross-country skiing, but the park is closed during the heaviest snows.

Buses on highway 134, the Toluca-Tejupilco road, will stop at the turnoff for highway 10 to Sultepec, which passes the park entrance 8km to the south. On weekends, it should be possible to hitch a ride the 27km from the junction of highways 134 and 10 to the crater. Taxis from Toluca will take you to the top for US$30, or there and back (including some time for you to look around) for US$50. Be sure to pick a newer taxi; the road up is very rough.

From the park entrance, a road winds 3.5km up to the main gate at an area called **Parque de los Venados** *(admission US$1).* From there, it's a 17km drive along an unsurfaced road up to the crater. Six kilometers from the crater, there's a boom gate, a shelter and a café. From that point, the crater can also be reached by a 2km hike via the Paso del Quetzal, a very scenic walking track *(admission US$0.25).* Dress warmly; it can be very cold at the top.

Places to Stay & Eat

You can stay at any of the following places. Camping is permitted by the first two.

Posada Familiar Rooms with shared bath US$9. Posada Familiar has 11 rooms with hot showers. There's a kitchen without utensils, and a common area with a fireplace. Bring extra blankets. It's closed on Monday and Tuesday. It's in the Parque de los Venados.

Albergue Ejidal Dorm beds US$4. Albergue Ejidal has 64 bunk beds (sleeping bag required), hot water and a large dining area with a huge fireplace. Before you go up, ask the attendant in the Parque de los Venados or someone at Posada Familiar to open it up for you. It is 2km farther up.

The *state-run shelter* near the summit (at 4050m) has foam mattresses but no bathrooms for US$1.75.

On weekends, food is served at stalls in the Parque de los Venados and at the gate near the summit. During the week, bring your own food and water.

VALLE DE BRAVO
• pop 22,000 • elev 1800m ☎ 726

About 70km west of Toluca, Valle de Bravo was a quiet colonial-era village in the hills until the 1940s, when it became a base for construction of a dam and hydroelectric station. The new lake gave the town a waterside location and it was soon a popular weekend and holiday spot for the wealthy. Nevertheless, this vibrant country community still retains its colonial charm.

Sailing on the lake is the main activity in Valle de Bravo – there are hour-long cruises by colectiva boat *(US$7 per person)*. You can rent a private boat for about US$25 per hour. Water-skiing, horse riding and hang gliding are also popular.

You can walk and camp in the hills around town, which attract monarch butterflies from December to March. A climb up the rock promontory La Peña, northwest of the center, will give you a view of the whole lake.

Places to Stay & Eat

The town's budget hotels are a cut above those found elsewhere.

Hotel Los Girasoles *(☎ 262-29-67, Plaza Independencia 1)* Singles/doubles US$17/27. The simple, clean rooms have small bathrooms and TVs.

Hotel Blanquita *(☎ 262-17-66,* e *hotel blanquita@hotmail.com, Villagran 100)* Rooms from US$28 Mon-Thur, from US$39 Fri-Sun. This hotel is in the same building on the plaza and has cheerfully painted rooms with a rustic, cowboy look.

Posada Casa Vieja *(☎ 262-03-18, Juárez 101)* Singles/doubles US$34/46. This hotel offers very good values. Pleasant rooms face an idyllic patio with a fountain and lots of chirping birds. There's parking in the courtyard, but the entranceway is a tight squeeze.

Centro Vacacional ISSEMYM *(☎ 262-00-04, Independencia 404)* Singles/doubles US$37/65, or US$43 per person with three meals. Just above the market, this is a holiday center for state workers but it accepts other guests. Featuring several pools and other recreational facilities, it's a good deal.

There are scores of restaurants and cafés around the zócalo and near the pier, but the fancier places only open Friday to Sunday.

Los Veleros *(☎ 262-32-79, Salitre 104)* Prices US$7-14. This restaurant is in an elegant adobe brick building with tables on a balcony overlooking a large garden. The restaurant offers seafood main courses.

For ambiance, have a drink and/or a light meal at the floating lakefront restaurant-bars ***La Balsa Avándaro*** *(☎ 262-25-53)* and ***Los Pericos*** *(☎ 262-05-58)* (open 10am to 6pm Wednesday to Monday).

Getting There & Away

The bus terminal is on 16 de Septiembre. Autobuses Zinacantepec runs hourly 2nd-class directos until 5.30pm to Mexico City's Terminal Poniente, all of which make a stop near Toluca's terminal (3 hours, US$8). There is also frequent service to Zitácuaro (US$4). If you're driving between Toluca and Valle de Bravo, the southern route via highway 134 is quicker and more scenic.

TEOTENANGO

Tenango de Arista, 25km south of Toluca on highway 55, is overlooked from the west by the large, well-restored hilltop ruins of Teotenango *(admission ruins & museum US$1.25, free Wed; open 9am-5pm Tues-Sun)*, a Matlazinca ceremonial center dating from the 9th century. The site is quite extensive – several pyramids, plazas and a ball court – and has great views. **Museo Arqueológico del Estado de México**, near the entrance, has Teotenango pottery and sculpture, as well as a section devoted to the prehistory of the region.

From Toluca bus station, buses run every 10 minutes to the center of Tenango, from which you can walk to the site in 20 to 30 minutes or take a taxi (US$1.25).

Driving from Toluca on highway 55, pass the toll highway and turn right into Teotenango; signs show you where to make a right turn on to a road that passes north of the hill.

MALINALCO

• pop 6500 • elev 1740m ☎ 714

One of the few reasonably well-preserved Aztec temples stands above beautiful but little-visited Malinalco, 20km east of Tenancingo. The site *(admission US$3.50, free Sun; open 9am-5.30pm Tues-Sun)* is 1km west of the town center, approached by a well-maintained footpath with signs about the area in Spanish, English and Náhuatl. The views over the valley from the summit have inspired legions of painters.

The Aztecs conquered this area in 1476 and were still building a ritual center here when they were themselves conquered by the Spanish. El Cuauhcalli, thought to be the Temple of Eagle and Jaguar Warriors, where sons of Aztec nobles were initiated into warrior orders, survived because it is hewn from the mountainside itself. Its entrance is carved in the form of a fanged serpent.

Malinalco also has a fine 16th-century Augustinian convent, fronted by a tranquil tree-lined yard. Floral and herbal frescoes adorn its cloister. The tourist office (☎ 147-01-11, ext 21) open 9am to 3pm Monday to Saturday, is next door to the Palacio Municipal. There's an ATM on Hidalgo, on the north side of the convent.

Places to Stay

Like other destinations near Mexico City, Malinalco is geared toward weekend visitors, which means you'll have no trouble finding a room Sunday to Thursday nights but your dining options may be limited. Conversely, weekend hotel reservations are recommended.

Villa Hotel (☎ 147-00-01, *Guerrero 101*) Rooms with shared bath US$13.50, other rooms US$34. This hotel is on the south side of the plaza. It is a friendly place with 12 rooms, six basic ones with cliff views sharing a single bath and six elegant ones facing the plaza.

Hotel Marmil (☎ 147-09-16, fax 147-09-16, *Progreso 606*) Singles/doubles US$20/29. The Marmil, in the ocher building near the northern entrance into town, is Malinalco's best place to stay. Standard rooms have large comfy beds.

Hotel Las Cabañas (☎ 147-01-01, *Progreso 1*) Cabins US$17 per person. Just north of the Marmil in a woodsy area, Las Cabañas has a swimming pool and 20 country cabins, each with two bedrooms, a fireplace and a kitchen with refrigerator and gas stove.

Places to Eat

Malinalco has many good restaurants serving a wide variety of cuisines, but only a few are open during the week.

Las Palomas (☎ 147-01-22, *Guerrero 104*) Prices US$3.50-8. This elegant place has a tiled country kitchen at the front, citrus and mango trees on the patio and a *palapa* bar. Its reasonably priced menu consists of all-natural Mexican originals, with healthy, creative salads, meat dishes and trout dishes.

Los Placeres (☎ 147-08-55) Prices from US$4. Open Fri-Sun. On the plaza, this is an excellent choice, with a laid-back atmosphere, good music and great views of the cliffs in back. Its varied menu features hearty breakfasts with good coffee and tea, bagels with cheese or salmon, original salads, crêpes and exotic specials.

Restaurant Huehuetl Prices US$2.25-7. Under the arcade on the south side of the plaza is this other weekend place; an Italian-run restaurant that serves good pastas and salads.

Les Chefs (☎ 147-04-01, *Morelos 107*) Prices from US$2.50-8.50. Behind the convent, this is a double restaurant: one serves pizzas, the other serves French cuisine with a strong Mexican flavor. The French chef has at least seven delicious ways of making trout.

Beto's (☎ 147-03-11, *Morelos 8*) Prices from US$2. Open noon-8pm daily. Across the street from Les Chefs, this bar serves seafood, including shark *empanadas* and terrific shrimp cocktails.

Getting There & Away

You can reach Malinalco by bus from Tenancingo or from the Toluca bus station. From Mexico City's Terminal Poniente, there are two direct buses at 5.10pm and 5.50pm; alternatively, take one of many buses to Jajalpa (en route to Tenancingo), then get a local bus. By car from Mexico City, turn south at La Marquesa and follow the signs to Malinalco.

Direct buses back to Mexico City depart at 5.10pm daily. There is frequent colectivo service to Tenango, from where you can catch a Toluca or Mexico City bus.

CHALMA

One of Mexico's most important shrines is in the village of Chalma, 12km east of Malinalco. In 1533, an image of Christ, El Señor de Chalma, miraculously appeared in a cave to replace one of the local gods, Oxtéotl, and proceeded to stamp out dangerous beasts and do other wondrous things. The Señor now resides in Chalma's 17th-century church. The biggest of many annual pilgrimages here is for Pentecost (the seventh Sunday after Easter) when thousands of people camp, hold a market and perform traditional dances.

Tres Estrellas del Centro runs hourly 2nd-class buses from Toluca to Chalma (US$3). A number of companies run

2nd-class buses from Mexico City's Terminal Poniente. There is also frequent bus service from Malinalco.

IXTAPAN DE LA SAL
• pop 14,000 • elev 1880m ☎ 721

The spa town of Ixtapan features a kind of giant curative water park, the **Balneario, Spa y Parque Acuático Ixtapan** (☎ 143-30-00; *adult/child US$12/6; spa section open 8am-7pm, aquatic park open 10am-6pm daily*), combining thermal water pools with waterfalls, lakes, water slides, a wave pool and a miniature railway. It's unashamedly a tourist town, but it's worth a stop if you want to take the waters or give your kids a fun day.

Hotels are clustered along Juárez south of the aquatic park, with a good range of lodging. About 5km farther on highway 55 is **Tonatico** with its own water park **Balneario Municpal Tonatico** (*adult/child US$3.50/2.25*). It's about a tenth of the size of Ixtapan de la Sal's and consequently more relaxed. There is an economical hotel on the grounds. At the south end of town is a spectacular waterfall (El Salto).

From the new bus terminal on highway 55 between Ixtapan and Tonatico, Tres Estrellas del Centro runs frequent buses to Toluca (US$3.50), Taxco (US$3.75) and Cuernavaca (US$4.25). There is also an hourly service to Mexico City via autopista until 6pm daily (US$7.25). Buses to/from the terminal go up and down Juárez in Ixtapan (US$0.30); taxis charge US$1.25.

Going north to Toluca, toll highway 55D parallels part of highway 55, bypassing Tenango and Tenancingo. Going south to Taxco, you could pass on the Grutas de la Estrella, but the Grutas de Cacahuamilpa are a must (see Around Taxco in the South of Mexico City section, earlier in this chapter).

Baja California

Highlights

- Tijuana – world's most-visited border town; historically notorious for lowlife partying but now an impressive locus of commerce, education and cultural activities

- Reserva de la Biósfera El Vizcaíno – an extensive biosphere reserve that includes major gray whale breeding sites at Laguna Ojo de Liebre and Laguna San Ignacio

- Loreto – historic first capital of the Californias, notable for two restored missions: its own and nearby San Francisco Javier; also known for kayaking on the Sea of Cortez and mountain-biking in the Sierra de la Giganta

- La Paz – capital of Baja California Sur, providing beautiful beaches, a palm-lined *malecón*, a handful of colonial buildings and spectacular sunsets over the bay

- Los Cabos – an uneasy mixture of nightclubs and time-shares (Cabo San Lucas), unpretentious tropical retreats (San José del Cabo), artists' colonies (Todos Santos) and biological and natural wonders (Sierra de la Laguna, probably the best hiking area on the entire peninsula)

Tijuana
pages 308-309
Mexicali
page 317
Central Mexicali
page 319
U S A
Ensenada
page 313
P A C I F I C   O C E A N
Loreto
page 328
Sea of Cortez
La Paz
pages 332-333
Cabo San Lucas
page 341
San José del Cabo
page 338
OTHER MAPS
Baja California page 305

Baja California attracts more than 50 million visitors a year. The draws are duty-free shopping, sumptuous seafood and myriad activities, such as horseback riding, diving, snorkeling, windsurfing, clamming, whale-watching, fishing, sailing, kayaking, cycling, surfing and hiking.

Baja's pre-Hispanic native peoples left memorable murals in caves and on canyon walls, and permanent European settlement failed to reach the world's longest peninsula until the Jesuit missions of the 17th and 18th centuries. The missions collapsed as indigenous people fell prey to European diseases, but ranchers from the mainland, miners and fisherfolk settled when foreigners built port facilities and acquired huge land grants in the 19th century. During US prohibition, Baja became a popular south-of-the-border destination for gamblers, drinkers and other 'sinners.'

Travelers to Baja California will find that prices are generally a bit higher than elsewhere in Mexico. The cost of food can range from US$1 for a taco at a stand to US$28 for a lobster at a restaurant, but a good, moderately priced meal tends to cost around US$8.

Hurricane Juliette in 2001 did a lot of damage to Baja's roads (in particular the roads from Loreto southward, and along the tip of the peninsula), but repairs were undertaken swiftly and the roads should be more or less back to normal by the time you get there.

Northern Baja

The northernmost part of the state of Baja California is referred to as La Frontera. The region includes the border towns of Tijuana and Tecate and extends down south to San Quintín. La Frontera corresponds roughly to the area colonized by the Dominicans, who established nine missions north of El Rosario from 1773 to 1821. Many view its cities and beaches as hedonistic enclaves, but Tijuana and Mexicali are major manufacturing centers, and Mexicali's Río Colorado hinterland is a key agricultural zone.

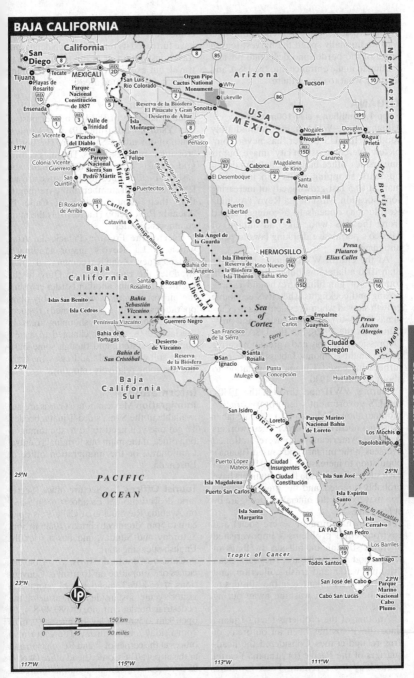

BAJA CALIFORNIA

The region attracts many undocumented border crossers, both experienced migrants who traditionally spend the harvest season north of the border and desperate novices waiting to make entrance into the USA and learning what to expect there.

TIJUANA
• pop 1.15 million • elev 100m ☎ 664

Tijuana ('tee-WHA-nah'), immediately south of the US border, has never completely overcome its 'sin city' image, but its universities, office buildings, housing developments, shopping malls and industries mark it as a fast-growing city of increasing sophistication. Most of 'La Revo' (Avenida Revolución) appeals to a younger crowd from the US who take advantage of Mexico's permissive drinking laws to party until dawn.

At the end of WWI Tijuana had fewer than 1000 inhabitants, but it soon drew US tourists for gambling, greyhound racing, boxing and cockfights. The city's economic growth slowed when President Lázaro Cárdenas (1934-40) outlawed casinos and prostitution in the 1930s, but the USA's Great Depression probably had a greater negative impact on the economy. Jobless Mexican returnees increased Tijuana's population to about 16,500 by 1940.

During WWII and through the 1950s, the US government's temporary *bracero* program allowed Mexicans to alleviate labor shortages north of the border. These workers replaced Americans who were stationed overseas in the military and caused Tijuana's population to increase to 180,000 by 1960. In each succeeding decade those numbers have probably doubled, and the present population may exceed the official census figure by at least half.

Growth has brought severe social and environmental problems – impoverished migrants still inhabit hillside dwellings of scrap wood and cardboard. They lack clean drinking water and trash collection, and worn tires are implanted in the hillsides to keep the soil from washing away during storms.

Another of the problems facing Tijuana since the 1990s has been an outbreak of drug-related crimes. Considered the headquarters of the Pacific (or 'Tijuana') cartel headed by the Arellano Félix brothers,

Tijuana has had its share of well-publicized crimes that have put it in the spotlight and have furthered its reputation as a dangerous travel destination. It is still a safe place to travel, but exercise caution when traveling at night or in isolated areas.

Orientation
Tijuana is south of the US border post of San Ysidro, California, 19km (12 miles) south of downtown San Diego. The border crossing is open 24 hours. Tijuana's central grid consists of north-south *avenidas* and east-west *calles* (most of the latter are referred to by their numbers more frequently than their names). South of Calle 1ª, Avenida Revolución (La Revo) is the main commercial center.

East of the Frontón Palacio Jai Alai, which is La Revo's major landmark, Tijuana's 'new' Zona Río commercial center straddles the river. Mesa de Otay, to the northeast, contains another border crossing, the airport, *maquiladoras* (assembly-plant operations, usually foreign-owned), residential neighborhoods and shopping areas. In the late 1990s, the city changed to a new numbering system, and though some businesses still use their old addresses, the transition is going relatively smoothly.

Information
Immigration Mexican tourist cards are not available at the San Ysidro-Tijuana border. To get one you need to go to the immigration office at the main bus terminal (Central Camionera) or the immigration office at Ensenada.

Tourist Offices The Secture office (Secretaría de Turismo del Estado, ☎ 688-05-55), on Avenida Revolución at Calle 1ª, is open 8am to 5pm Monday to Friday, 10am to 5pm Saturday and Sunday, and has a friendly, English-speaking staff.

Cotuco (Comité de Turismo y Convenciones or Committee on Tourism & Conventions, ☎ 684-05-37 head office) operates a visitor's center just inside the turnstiles at the pedestrian border entrance (☎ 683-49-87); it's open 9am to 5pm Sunday to Thursday, 9am to 7pm Friday and Saturday. There are also offices at the corner of 4ª and Revolución and at the airport. The Cotuco head office (☎ 684-05-37, e convistj@omnitec.com) is located at

Paseo de los Héroes 9365, Suite 201, in the Zona Río, and is open 9am to 6pm Monday to Friday.

Money Everyone accepts US dollars, but countless *casas de cambio* keep long hours. There are banks all along Paseo de los Héroes, all with ATMs. Travelers heading south or east by bus can use the casa de cambio at the Central Camionera.

Post & Communications Tijuana's central post office, at Avenida Negrete and Calle 11ª, is open 8am to 4pm Monday to Friday, 9am to 1pm Saturday.

Public telephones and long-distance offices are common.

The Internet Café (☎ 688-02-38), Calle 8ª No 8187, charges US$1.50 per half hour.

Travel Agencies There are numerous travel agencies in town, but Viajes Honold's (☎ 688-11-11), on Avenida Revolución near Calle 2ª, is one of the longest established.

Bookstores The book department in San-borns department store (☎ 688-14-62), Revolución 1102 at Calle 8ª, has a large selection of US and Mexican newspapers and magazines.

Medical Services Tijuana's Hospital General (☎ 684-00-78) is north of the river on Avenida Padre Kino, northwest of the junction with Avenida Rodríguez, but Tijuana has many other medical facilities catering to visitors from north of the border.

Dangers & Annoyances *Coyotes* and *polleros* – smugglers of humans – and their clients congregate along the river west of the San Ysidro crossing. After dark, avoid this area and Colonia Libertad, east of the crossing.

Things to See & Do
South of Calle 1ª, **La Revo** (Avenida Revolución) is the heart of Tijuana's tourist area. Every visitor braves at least a brief stroll up this raucous avenue of crowded discos, fine restaurants, seedy bars with bellowing hawkers, brash taxi drivers, tacky souvenir shops and street photographers with zebra-striped *burros*.

Jai alai tournaments used to be held at the **Frontón Palacio Jai Alai** (☎ 685-78-33, *Revolución & Calle 8ª*), but have been discontinued. The Frontón, however, remains a landmark and centerpiece for La Revo.

Vinícola LA Cetto (*LA Cetto winery*, ☎ 685-30-31, *Cañón Johnson 2108; open 10am-6pm Mon-Fri, 10am-5pm Sat*), southwest of Avenida Constitución, offers tours and tasting for a modest charge.

A modern landmark, Mexico's federal government built the **Centro Cultural Tijuana** (*Cecut,* ☎ 687-96-00, *cnr Paseo de los Héroes & Avenida Independencia*), in the Zona Río, to reinforce the Mexican identity of its border populations. The cultural center is a facility of which any comparably sized city north of the border would be proud. It houses an art gallery, the **Museo de las Identidades Mexicanas** (*Museum of Mexican Identities; admission to museum & art gallery US$2; open 9am-6pm Tues-Sun*), a theater and the globular **Cine Planetario** (*colloquially known as La Bola – 'the Ball'; programs from US$4.50; open 2pm-9pm Mon-Fri, 11am-9pm Sat & Sun*).

Places to Stay
Hotel Lafayette (☎ 685-39-40, *Revolución 926*) Singles/doubles US$22/29. Perhaps downtown's best budget hotel is the Lafayette, above Café La Especial, but it's often full, especially on weekends.

Motel Plaza Hermosa (☎ 685-33-53, *Constitución 1821*) Singles/doubles US$28/34. This hotel is a good value and has secure parking.

Hotel Catalina (☎ 685-97-48, *Calle 5ª No 2039*) Singles/doubles US$18/26. This hotel is clean and feels secure.

Hotel Nelson (☎ 685-43-03, fax 685-43-02, w *www.bajavisual.com/hotelnelson, Revolución 721*) Doubles US$53. The Nelson is a longtime favorite for its central location and tidy, carpeted rooms. Rooms come with color TV, a view and the less-than-soothing sounds of La Revo.

Hotel Caesar (☎ 685-16-06, fax 685-34-92, *Revolución 827*) Singles/doubles US$39/50. Bullfight posters and photographs adorn the walls here; its restaurant claims to have created the Caesar salad.

Hotel La Villa de Zaragoza (☎ 685-18-32, fax 685-18-37, e *rey@telnor.net, Avenida Madero 1120*) Singles/doubles US$39/48.

BAJA CALIFORNIA

TIJUANA

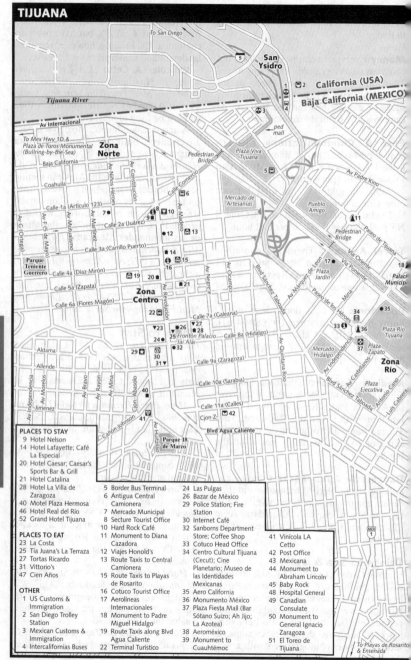

PLACES TO STAY
9 Hotel Nelson
14 Hotel Lafayette; Café
    La Especial
20 Hotel Caesar; Caesar's
    Sports Bar & Grill
21 Hotel Catalina
28 Hotel La Villa de
    Zaragoza
40 Motel Plaza Hermosa
46 Hotel Real del Río
52 Grand Hotel Tijuana

PLACES TO EAT
23 La Costa
25 Tía Juana's La Terraza
27 Tortas Ricardo
31 Vittorio's
47 Cien Años

OTHER
1 US Customs &
   Immigration
2 San Diego Trolley
   Station
3 Mexican Customs &
   Immigration
4 Intercalifornias Buses

5 Border Bus Terminal
6 Antigua Central
   Camionera
7 Mercado Municipal
8 Secture Tourist Office
10 Hard Rock Café
11 Monument to Diana
    Cazadora
12 Viajes Honold's
13 Route Taxis to Central
    Camionera
15 Route Taxis to Playas
    de Rosarito
16 Cotuco Tourist Office
17 Aerolíneas
    Internacionales
18 Monument to Padre
    Miguel Hidalgo
19 Route Taxis along Blvd
    Agua Caliente
22 Terminal Turístico

24 Las Pulgas
26 Bazar de México
29 Police Station; Fire
    Station
30 Internet Café
32 Sanborns Department
    Store; Coffee Shop
33 Cotuco Head Office
34 Centro Cultural Tijuana
    (Cecut); Cine
    Planetario; Museo de
    las Identidades
    Mexicanas
35 Aero California
36 Monumento México
37 Plaza Fiesta Mall (Bar
    Sótano Suizo; Ah Jijo;
    La Azotea)
38 Aeroméxico
39 Monument to
    Cuauhtémoc

41 Vinícola LA
    Cetto
42 Post Office
43 Mexicana
44 Monument to
    Abraham Lincoln
45 Baby Rock
48 Hospital General
49 Canadian
    Consulate
50 Monument to
    General Ignacio
    Zaragoza
51 El Toreo de
    Tijuana

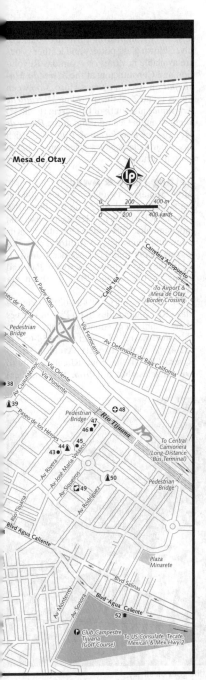

Mesa de Otay

Rooms at this newer and excellent hotel, directly behind the Frontón, include TV, telephone, heat and air-con. This is a nice place to stay, especially if you want to get a little bit away from the noise of La Revo. There's a nice restaurant and off-street parking.

Hotel Real del Río (☎ 634-31-00, fax 634-30-53, Velasco 1409A) Singles/doubles US$83/90. Modern and efficient, the Real del Río is located in the Zona Río.

Grand Hotel Tijuana (☎ 681-70-00, fax 681-70-16, W www.grandhoteltijuana.com, Agua Caliente 4500) Rooms from US$163. This 23-story structure houses a shopping mall, offices, restaurants, a pool and convention facilities, and it has golf-course access.

Places to Eat

Café La Especial (☎ 685-66-54, Revolución 718) Mains US$3-6. A mainstay since 1952, this restaurant is on the east side of Avenida Revolución, at the foot of the stairs near the corner of Calle 3ª. It offers decent Mexican food at reasonable prices and is far quieter than the average eatery on La Revo.

Tortas Ricardo (☎ 685-40-31, Avenida Madero 1410) Breakfast US$3-5, tortas US$2-4. Open 24 hours. One of Tijuana's best values is this bright and cheerful diner-style place. The breakfasts are excellent and the tortas are among the best in town.

Tía Juana's La Terraza (☎ 685-60-24, Revolución 1420) Mains US$6-12. This popular gringo hangout is next to the Frontón Palacio Jai Alai. It serves standard Mexican entrees, steak and seafood.

Vittorio's (☎ 685-17-29, Revolución 1687) Pizzas US$6-8. For generous portions of reasonably priced pizza and pasta, try Vittorio's.

Bar Sótano Suizo (☎ 684-88-34, Plaza Fiesta mall, Paseo de los Héroes & Independencia) Mains US$9-14. This place has a nice atmosphere and moderate prices.

La Costa (☎ 685-31-24, Calle 7ª No 8131) Dinner US$10-20. La Costa is where you should head for seafood. For US$30, the combination plate provides a sample of crab, shrimp, lobster, octopus and fish fillet.

Cien Años (☎ 634-30-39, Velasco 1407) Dinner US$10-15. With a menu of traditional Mexican dishes, this formal restaurant in Zona Río is the place to go for a culinary treat.

BAJA CALIFORNIA

Entertainment

Rowdy Avenida Revolución is the place for 'upside-down margaritas' and ear-splitting live and recorded music at places such as **Hard Rock Café** (☎ 685-02-06, Revolución 520). Always crowded, this popular spot is open until 2am.

For a sense of the nightlife away from the craziness of La Revo, try the bars **Ah Jijo** or **La Azotea**, which are frequented by the young crowd of Tijuana; both are in the Plaza Fiesta mall in the Zona Río.

Equally or more interesting are *banda/norteña* venues like **Las Pulgas** (☎ 685-95-94, Revolución 1127).

Most fancier discos are in the Zona Río, such as the kitschy **Baby Rock** (☎ 634-24-04, Avenida Diego Rivera 1482), which charges a cover of US$10 on Saturday night.

Spectator Sports

From May to September, Sunday bullfights take place at two bullrings: **El Toreo de Tijuana**, on Boulevard Agua Caliente northwest of Club Campestre Tijuana, and the oceanfront **Plaza de Toros Monumental**. Call ☎ 686-15-10 for reservations at either bullring (☎ 619-232-5049 in San Diego). Tickets cost US$19 to US$45.

Shopping

Jewelry, wrought-iron furniture, baskets, silver, blown glass, pottery and leather goods are available in stores on Avenidas Revolución and Constitución; at the **Mercado Municipal** on Avenida Niños Héroes between Calles 1ª and 2ª; at the sprawling **Mercado de Artesanías** just south of Comercio (Calle 1ª) along Avenida Ocampo; and at the **Bazar de México** (cnr Revolución & Calle 7ª), which has a particularly good selection of hand-crafted furniture.

Getting There & Away

Air Aeroméxico (☎ 686-55-88, 683-10-63 at the airport), Local A 12-1 in the Plaza Río Tijuana, at Paseo de los Héroes and Avenida Independencia, also houses the office for its commuter subsidiary Aerolitoral. Besides serving many mainland Mexican destinations, they have nonstops to La Paz and flights to Tucson and Phoenix, both via Hermosillo.

Aero California (☎ 684-21-00), also in the Plaza Río Tijuana, flies to La Paz and serves many mainland destinations from Mexico City northward. Mexicana (☎ 634-65-66, 682-41-83 at the airport), Avenida Diego Rivera 1511, in the Zona Río, flies daily to Los Angeles (but not *from* Los Angeles)

In Tijuana the nightlife goes on all day.

and also serves many mainland Mexican cities.

Aerolíneas Internacionales (☎ 684-07-27), Vía Poniente 4246, in the Plaza Jardín in the Zona Río, flies to mainland destinations from Hermosillo to Mexico City.

Bus Only Suburbaja (a subsidiary of ABC, ☎ 688-00-45) and the US-based Greyhound (☎ 688-19-79) use the handy downtown bus terminal, Antigua Central Camionera, at Madero and Comercio (Calle 1ª). Suburbaja buses leave for Ensenada every hour (2 hours, US$8), Playas de Rosarito every three hours (1 hour, US$1) and Tecate every 20 minutes (1½ hours, US$3.50); these are all local buses that make many stops.

From Plaza Viva Tijuana near the border, ABC (☎ 683-56-81) and Estrella de Baja California (☎ 683-56-22) offer inexpensive Ensenada buses. Buses leave every 30 minutes between 6am and 9.30pm for US$8 one-way, US$15 roundtrip.

The main bus terminal is the Central Camionera (☎ 621-29-82), about 5km southeast of downtown, where Elite and Crucero offer 1st-class buses with air-con and toilets to mainland Mexico. Autotransportes del Pacífico, Norte de Sonora and ABC operate mostly 2nd-class buses to mainland Mexico's Pacific coast and around Baja California. ABC's Servicio Plus resembles Elite and Crucero. ABC has buses to Ensenada (US$9.50 1st-class, US$8 2nd-class), Tecate (US$4), Mexicali (2½ hours, US$14 1st-class, US$12 2nd-class), San Felipe (6 hours, US$25), Guerrero Negro (13 hours, US$43), Loreto (17 hours, US$69) and La Paz (22 hours, US$89).

Elite and Crucero have express buses to Guadalajara (35 hours, US$74) and Mexico City (42 hours, US$105). Autotransportes del Pacífico and Norte de Sonora are comparable to Elite and Crucero. All lines stop at major mainland destinations.

Mexicoach runs frequent buses (US$1) from its San Ysidro terminal (☎ 619-428-9517), 4570 Camino de la Plaza, to Terminal Turístico (☎ 685-14-70) at Revolución 1025, between Calle 6ª and Calle 7ª. Between 5.45am and 10.35pm, Greyhound (☎ 686-06-95, 800-231-2222 in the USA), 120 West Broadway in San Diego, stops at San Ysidro (☎ 619-428-1194), 799 East San Ysidro Boulevard, en route to Tijuana's downtown

terminal (☎ 686-06-95) or the Central Camionera. Fares to both locations are US$6.50 one-way, US$9.50 roundtrip Monday to Friday, an extra dollar Saturday and Sunday. Intercalifornias (☎ 683-62-81), on the east side of the road just south of the San Ysidro border crossing, goes to Los Angeles (US$15) and US California's Central Valley.

Trolley San Diego's popular light-rail trolley (☎ 619-233-3004) runs from downtown San Diego to San Ysidro every 15 minutes from about 5am to midnight (US$2). From San Diego's Lindbergh Field airport, city bus No 992 goes directly to the Plaza America trolley stop in downtown San Diego, across from the Amtrak depot.

Car & Motorcycle The San Ysidro border crossing, a 10-minute walk from downtown Tijuana, is open 24 hours, but motorists may find the Otay Mesa crossing (open 6am to 10pm) much less congested.

For rentals, agencies in San Diego are the cheapest option, but most of them allow rentals only as far as Ensenada. California Baja Rent-A-Car (☎ 619-470-7368), in Spring Valley, California, 32km (20 miles) from downtown San Diego and 24km (15 miles) from San Ysidro, is a good option if you plan to continue driving beyond Ensenada.

Getting Around
To/From the Airport Sharing can reduce the cost of a taxi (about US$12 if hailed on the street) to busy Aeropuerto Internacional Abelardo L Rodríguez (☎ 683-24-18) in Mesa de Otay, east of downtown. Alternatively, take any 'Aeropuerto' bus from the street just south of the San Ysidro border taxi stand (about US$0.30); from downtown, catch it on Calle 5ª between Avenidas Constitución and Niños Héroes.

Bus & Taxi For about US$0.30, local buses go everywhere, but slightly pricier route taxis are much quicker. To get to the Central Camionera take any 'Buena Vista,' 'Centro' or 'Central Camionera' bus from Calle 2ª, east of Constitución. For a quicker and more convenient option, take a gold-and-white 'Mesa de Otay' route taxi from Avenida Madero between Calles 2ª and 3ª (US$0.60).

BAJA CALIFORNIA

Tijuana taxis lack meters, but most rides cost about US$5 or less. However, beware of the occasional unscrupulous taxi driver.

AROUND TIJUANA
Playas de Rosarito
• pop 100,000

South of Tijuana, the valley of Rosarito marks the original boundary between mainland California and Baja California. The town of Playas de Rosarito dates from 1885, but the Hotel Rosarito (now the landmark Rosarito Beach Hotel) and its long, sandy beach pioneered local tourism in the late 1920s. The town's main street – the noisy commercial strip of Boulevard Juárez (part of the Carretera Transpeninsular, highway 1) – has many good restaurants and affordable accommodations.

The amphitheater at the beachfront **Parque Municipal Abelardo L Rodríguez** contains Juan Zuñiga Padilla's impressive 1987 mural *Tierra y Libertad* (Land and Liberty).

From downtown Tijuana, route taxis for Playas de Rosarito leave from Avenida Madero between Calles 3ª and 4ª (US$1).

Tecate
• pop 40,200

About 55km east of Tijuana by highway 2, the east-west route linking Tijuana and Mexicali, Tecate resembles more of a mainland Mexican village than a border town, but hosts several popular tourist events, such as bicycle races. Its landmark **brewery** (☎ 654-11-11, Hidalgo & Obregón; open for tours by reservation only) produces two of Mexico's best-known beers, Tecate and Carta Blanca, but maquiladoras drive the local economy. The border crossing, open 6am to midnight daily, is less congested than either Tijuana or Mesa de Otay.

ENSENADA
• pop 229,000 ☎ 646

In the late 1990s, Ensenada went through a major renovation. Both the waterfront *malecón* (promenade) and sidewalks along Avenida López Mateos (Calle 1ª) from Avenida Castillo to Avenida Macheros have been widened to accommodate outside patios for restaurants and shops. And even though you still have a smattering of Americans strolling the streets with shopping lists of pharmaceuticals (which are generally

much cheaper in Ensenada than in the US), the town has a very quaint feel to it. Outdoor activities such as fishing and surfing are popular, and Ensenada is the locus of Baja's wine industry. US visitors sometimes make the city a reluctant host for spontaneous Fourth of July celebrations.

History
In colonial times, Ensenada de Todos los Santos occasionally sheltered Acapulco-bound galleons returning from Manila, but the first permanent settlement was established in 1804. The discovery of gold in 1870 at Real del Castillo, 35km inland, brought a short-lived boom. Ensenada was capital of Baja territory from 1882 to 1915, but the capital shifted to Mexicali during the revolution. After the revolution the city catered to 'sin' industries until the federal government outlawed gambling in the 1930s.

Orientation
Near the water, hotels and restaurants line Boulevard Costero, also known as Boulevard Cárdenas. Avenida López Mateos (Calle 1ª) parallels Boulevard Costero for a short distance inland (north). The tourist district is between Avenidas Ryerson and Castillo.

North of town, highway 3 heads northeast to Tecate: at the southeast edge of town it leads east toward Ojos Negros and Parque Nacional Constitución de 1857 (Laguna Hanson) before continuing south to the Valle de Trinidad and San Felipe.

Information
The immigration office (Delegación del Instituto Nacional de Migración, ☎ 174-01-64), Azueta 101, is open 8am to 3pm daily.

Ensenada's Cotuco tourist office (☎ 178-24-11), Azueta 540, at the corner of Boulevard Costero, carries maps, brochures and current hotel information. It's open 9am to 7pm Monday to Friday, 10am to 6pm Saturday, 11am to 3pm Sunday. The Secture tourist office (☎ 172-30-22), Boulevard Costero 1477, near Riviera, is open 9am to 7pm Monday to Friday, 9am to 3pm Saturday and Sunday. During June and July, the hours change to 8am to 5pm Monday to Friday, 10am to 3pm Saturday and Sunday.

Most banks and casas de cambio are near the intersection of Avenidas Ruiz and

ENSENADA

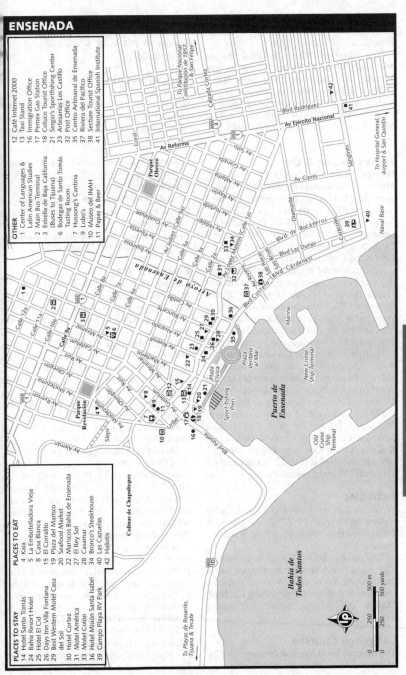

PLACES TO STAY
14 Hotel Santo Tomás
24 Bahia Resort Hotel
25 Hotel El Cid
26 Days Inn Villa Fontana
29 Best Western Motel Casa del Sol
30 Hotel Cortez
31 Motel América
33 Motel Colón
36 Hotel Misión Santa Isabel
39 Campo Playa RV Park

PLACES TO EAT
4 Kaia
5 La Embotelladora Vieja
8 Casa Blanca
15 El Corralito
19 Plaza del Marisco
Seafood Market
22 Mariscos Bahia de Ensenada
27 El Rey Sol
28 Casamar
34 Bronco's Steakhouse
40 Las Cazuelas
42 Haliotis

OTHER
1 Center of Languages & Latin American Studies
2 Main Bus Terminal
3 Estrella de Baja California (Buses to Tijuana)
6 Bodegas de Santo Tomás Tasting Room
7 Hussong's Cantina
9 Lobo's
10 Museo del INAH
11 Papas & Beer
12 Café Internet 2000
13 Taxi Stand
16 Immigration Office
17 Pemex Gas Station
18 Cotuco Tourist Office
21 Sergio's Sportfishing Center
23 Artesanías Los Castillo
32 Post Office
35 Centro Artesanal de Ensenada
37 Riviera del Pacífico
38 Secture Tourist Office
41 International Spanish Institute

Juárez. Only banks provide cash advances, but there are numerous ATMs throughout Ensenada.

The main post office is at López Mateos and Club Rotario; it's open 8am to 7pm Monday to Friday, 9am to 1pm Saturday.

There are pay phones throughout town.

The best option for getting online is at Café Internet 2000 (☎ 175-70-11), López Mateos 582, which charges US$2 per half hour.

Things to See & Do

Bodegas de Santo Tomás (☎ 178-33-33, *Miramar 666; tour admission US$2-5; open 8am-5pm)* holds tours of its cellars and wine tastings at 10am, noon and 3pm daily.

Opened in the early 1930s as Hotel Playa Ensenada, the extravagant **Riviera del Pacífico**, a Spanish-style former casino on Boulevard Costero, features an impressive three-dimensional mural of the Californias that emphasizes mission sites. Now a cultural center *(Centro Social, Cívico y Cultural Riviera, ☎ 177-05-95; admission US$0.50; open 9am-2pm & 3pm-5pm)*, it houses a renovated museum and the Bar Andaluz, and offers retrospective film showings and art exhibitions.

Built in 1886 by the US-owned International Company of Mexico, Ensenada's oldest public building houses the **Museo del INAH** *(Instituto Nacional de Antropología e Historia, ex-Aduana Marítima de Ensenada, ☎ 178-25-31, Avenida Ryerson 1; admission free; open 10am-5pm Mon-Fri)*. It had passed to the British-owned Mexican Land & Colonization Company before Mexican customs acquired it in 1922. It's currently a historical/cultural museum.

Activities

From December to March, the **Caracol Museo de Ciencias** *(☎ 178-71-92, Obregón 1463)* arranges offshore whale-watching cruises.

Ensenada is known for its sport fishing. There are many charter companies to be found along the newly renovated malecón. One option is **Sergio's Sportfishing Center & Marina** *(☎ 178-21-85, on the sport-fishing pier)*.

Language Courses

The *International Spanish Institute* *(☎ 176-01-09, Boulevard Rodríguez 377)* offers in-tensive Spanish instruction, as does the *Center of Languages and Latin American Studies* *(☎ 174-56-88, W www.bajacal.com, Riveroll 1287)*.

Special Events

The events listed below constitute a tiny sample of the 70-plus sporting, tourist and cultural happenings that take place each year. Dates change, so contact tourist offices for details.

Carnaval – Mardi Gras; sometime between mid-February and early March

Baja 500 – off-road car race; June

Fiesta de la Vendimia – wine harvest; mid-August

Fiestas Patrias – Mexican independence days; mid-September

Desfile Navideño Club Amigos de Ensenada – Christmas parade; mid-December

Places to Stay

Campo Playa RV Park (☎ 176-29-18, e camplaya@telnor.net, Las Dunas & Sanginés) Tent sites US$13, RV sites US$16-20. Close to downtown, this place offers shady sites.

Motel América (☎ 176-13-33, López Mateos 1309) Singles/doubles US$22/28. The rooms here are simple and have kitchenettes.

Motel Colón (☎ 176-19-10, Guadalupe 174) Rooms from US$22-45. The Motel Colón offers off-street parking. All the rooms are comfortable and have TV and fans. The older rooms are a good deal and include kitchenettes.

Days Inn Villa Fontana (☎ 178-34-34, fax 178-38-37, W www.villafontana.com.mx, López Mateos 1050) Rooms with air-con Mon-Thur/Fri & Sat US$46/60. Located between Avenidas Blancarte and Alvarado, this renovated hotel has comfortable rooms with views, cable TV and Jacuzzis; plus, there's a swimming pool.

Hotel Cortez (☎ 178-23-07, fax 178-39-04, e hcz@bajainn.com, López Mateos 1089) Singles & doubles with air-con Mon-Fri/Sat & Sun US$60/70. Rooms at Hotel Cortez come with TV, pool access and gym; it often fills up early.

Bahía Resort Hotel (☎ 178-21-03, fax 178-14-55, e htlbahia@telnor.net, López Mateos 850) Singles/doubles US$55/85. This popular hotel covers a block between Riveroll and Alvarado and offers similar amenities to Hotel Cortez (see above). The rooms are carpeted and have balconies.

Hotel Misión Santa Isabel (☎ *178-33-45, fax 178-36-16,* e *hmision@telnor.net, Boulevard Costero 1119)* Singles/doubles from US$40/65. This is one of the most striking buildings in Ensenada, and offers clean, comfortable rooms.

Hotel Santo Tomás (☎ *178-15-03, 800-303-2684 in the USA, fax 178-15-04,* e *bajainn@telnor.net, Boulevard Costero 609)* Rooms US$60. Between Miramar and Macheros, this hotel is conveniently central. Rates here go up on Friday and Saturday.

Best Western Motel Casa del Sol (☎ *178-15-70, fax 178-20-25,* e *casa@telnor.net, López Mateos 1001)* Singles/doubles with air-con US$78/94. The rooms here have TV and pool access.

Hotel El Cid (☎ *178-24-01, fax 178-36-71,* w *www.hotelcid.com, López Mateos 993)* Singles/doubles from US$65/90. Situated across from the Villa Fontana, the El Cid has a swimming pool, an outstanding restaurant and a disco.

Places to Eat

At the **seafood market** near the sport-fishing piers on the malecón running parallel to Boulevard Costero, try the deep-fried fish or shrimp tacos. **Plaza del Marisco**, on Boulevard Costero across from the Pemex station, is a similar cluster of seafood-taco stands of good quality.

El Corralito (☎ *178-23-70, López Mateos 627)* Dinner US$7. This modest café offers decent tacos and seafood.

Casa Blanca (☎ *174-03-16, Ruiz 254)* Prices US$6. The Casa Blanca offers decent fixed-price lunches.

Las Cazuelas (☎ *176-10-44, Sanginés & Boulevard Costero)* Seafood meals around US$12. Near the corner of Boulevard Costero, Las Cazuelas has a pricey seafood menu, but *antojitos* are more reasonable.

Haliotis (☎ *176-37-20, Delante 179)* Dinner US$12-20. Situated east of Avenida Ejercito, this is a good option for seafood – the restaurant's name means 'abalone' (not 'bad breath').

Casamar (☎ *174-04-17, Cárdenas 197)* Standard dinner US$15, lobster US$26. A popular spot, the specialty is seafood.

El Rey Sol (☎ *178-17-33, López Mateos 1000)* Mains US$30. Most meals are expensive at this venerable Franco-Mexican institution, but selective diners can find good-value options.

La Embotelladora Vieja (☎ *174-08-07, Miramar & Calle 7ª)* Dinner US$20. Closed Tues. This cavernous place has been modernized for upscale dining, with huge wine casks and other features intact. It has good food, particularly lobster.

Bronco's Steakhouse (☎ *176-48-92, López Mateos 1525)* Dinner US$15. If you crave steak, try this place.

Kaia (☎ *178-22-38, Moctezuma 479)* Dinner US$15-20. This cozy, romantic Basque restaurant is tucked away from the street.

Mariscos Bahía de Ensenada (☎ *178-10-15, Riveroll 109)* Standard dinner US$10, lobster US$25. Seafood lovers will love this place, where portions are generous and prices are reasonable.

Entertainment

Historic **Hussong's Cantina** (☎ *178-32-10, Ruiz 113)* is the oldest cantina in the Californias (unlike some cantinas, it's an OK place for all). **Papas & Beer** (☎ *174-01-45, López Mateos & Ruiz)* is a popular restaurant and nightclub. **Lobo's** (☎ *178-23-85, Ruiz 447)* is also a hot nightspot that stays open until 3am.

Shopping

Galería de Pérez Meillon (☎ *174-03-94, Local 39, Centro Artesanal de Ensenada, Boulevard Costero 1094)* sells pottery and other crafts from Baja California's Paipai, Kumiai and Cucapah peoples, as well as from Chihuahua state's Tarahumara peoples.

Taxco's famous silver is available at **Artesanías Los Castillo** (☎ *178-29-62, López Mateos 815).*

Getting There & Around

Air Aerocedros (☎ *177-35-34),* at Aeropuerto El Ciprés, south of town, flies to Guerrero Negro and Isla Cedros (see the Southern Baja section, later in this chapter).

Bus Ensenada's main bus terminal (☎ *178-66-80)* is at Riveroll 1075. Elite (☎ *178-67-70)* and Norte de Sonora (☎ *178-66-77)* serve mainland Mexican destinations as far as Guadalajara (35 hours, US$126) and

Mexico City (45 hours, US$95). Norte de Sonora's 2nd-class fares are about 15% cheaper.

ABC (☎ 178-66-80) serves Tecate (1½ hours, US$10), Tijuana (1½ hours, US$9.50 1st-class, US$8 2nd-class), Mexicali (3½ hours, US$21 1st-class, US$18 2nd-class), San Felipe (3 hours, US$18), Guerrero Negro (10 hours, US$35) and La Paz (18 hours, US$85). If you are going to Tijuana, make sure to specify whether you want to go to the main terminal, or to the border ('La Línea').

Estrella de Baja California (☎ 178-85-21), Riveroll 861, goes to Tijuana (US$8) hourly from 5am to 6pm.

Taxi Taxis are available 24 hours a day. The main stand is at the corner of López Mateos and Miramar.

AROUND ENSENADA

About 32km northeast of Ensenada at Km 78 on highway 3, some Dominican mission ruins remain at the village of **Guadalupe** (pop 1220). Early 20th-century Russian immigrants settled here; their history is now documented by the **Museo Comunitario de Guadalupe** (admission US$0.50; open 10am-6pm Tues-Sun). The Fiesta de la Vendimia (Wine Harvest Festival) takes place in August; the Domecq and Cetto wineries are open for tours.

PN CONSTITUCIÓN DE 1857

From Ojos Negros, east of Ensenada at Km 39 on highway 3, a 43km dirt road climbs to the Sierra de Juárez and Parque Nacional Constitución de 1857, the highlight of which is the marshy, pine-sheltered **Laguna Hanson** (also known as Laguna Juárez). At 1200m, the lake abounds with migratory birds from August to November.

Camping is pleasant, but livestock have contaminated the water, so bring your own. Firewood is scarce along the lake but abundant in the hills. Only pit toilets are available. Nearby granite outcrops offer stupendous views but tiring ascents through dense brush and massive rock falls – beware of ticks and rattlesnakes. Technical climbers will find short but challenging routes.

The park is also accessible by a steeper road east of Km 55.2, 16km southeast of the Ojos Negros junction.

PN SIERRA SAN PEDRO MÁRTIR

In the Sierra San Pedro Mártir, east of San Telmo and west of San Felipe, Baja's most notable national park comprises 630 sq km of coniferous forests, granite peaks exceeding 3000m and deep canyons cutting into its steep eastern scarp. The elusive desert bighorn sheep inhabits some remote areas of the park. Snow falls in winter, and the area gets summer thunderstorms.

Camping areas and hiking trails are numerous, but maintenance is limited; carry a compass and a topographic map, along with cold- and wet-weather supplies, canteens and water purification tablets. Below 1800m, beware of rattlesnakes.

Observatorio Astronómico Nacional (☎ 554-54-70; open 11am-1pm Sat only, call for reservations) is Mexico's national observatory. It's 2km from the parking area at the end of the San Telmo road.

Few climbers who attempt **Picacho del Diablo** (Devil's Peak), the peninsula's highest point, reach the 3095m summit, because finding routes is so difficult. The Baja Adventure Book, by Walt Peterson, includes a good map and describes possible routes.

From San Telmo de Abajo, south of Km 140 on the Transpeninsular (highway 1), and about 52km south of San Vicente, a graded dirt road climbs through San Telmo to the park entrance, about 80km east. The road is passable to most passenger vehicles, but you do have to cross a river along the way, and snowmelt can raise it to hazardous levels.

MEXICALI
• pop 601,000 ☎ 686

Many visitors pass through Mexicali en route to San Felipe or mainland Mexico; the state capital does not pander to tourists, but the Centro Cívico-Comercial (Civic and Commercial Center), on Calzada Independencia, features government offices, a medical school, the Plaza de Toros Calafia bullring, cinemas, a bus station, hospitals and restaurants.

European settlement came late to the Río Colorado lowlands, but the Mexicali area grew rapidly – in more than one sense: irrigation allowed early-20th-century farmers to take advantage of rich alluvial lowlands and a long, productive agricultural season.

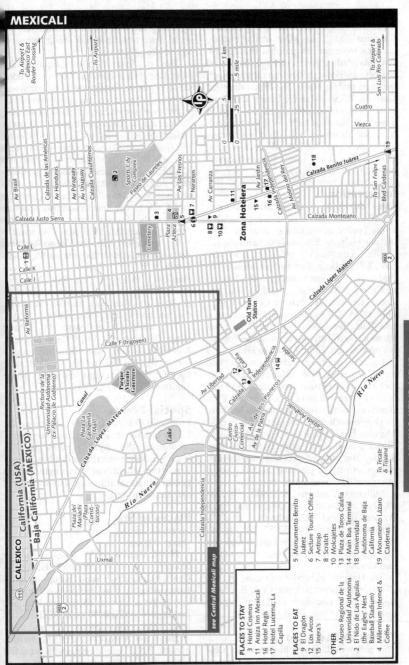

MEXICALI

PLACES TO STAY
3 Hotel Cosmos
11 Araiza Inn Mexicali
16 Hotel Regis
17 Hotel Lucerna; La
    Capilla

PLACES TO EAT
9 El Dragón
12 Los Arcos
15 Jinera's

OTHER
1 Museo Regional de la
   Universidad Autónoma
2 El Nido de Las Águilas
   (the Eagles' Nest
   Baseball Stadium)
4 Millennium Internet &
   Coffee

5 Monumento Benito
   Juárez
6 Secure Tourist Office
7 Antrojo
8 Scratch
10 Molcajetes
13 Plaza de Toros Calafia
14 Main Bus Terminal
18 Universidad
    Autónoma de Baja
    California
19 Monumento Lázaro
    Cárdenas

Orientation

Mexicali straddles the Río Nuevo, south of Calexico, California. Most of the historic center's main streets parallel the border. Avenida Madero passes through the central business district of modest restaurants, shops, bars and budget hotels. The broad diagonal Calzada López Mateos heads southeast through newer industrial and commercial areas and becomes highway 2 (to Sonora). Many of Mexicali's hotels and restaurants are in the Zona Hotelera, which runs along Calzadas Sierra and Juárez (which becomes highway 5 to San Felipe).

Information

The Calexico-Mexicali border crossing is open 24 hours. Vehicle permits are available at the border, as are tourist cards for those traveling beyond Ensenada or San Felipe.

The Secture tourist office (☎ 566-11-16, 566-12-77) is open 8am to 5pm Monday to Friday, 10am to 3pm Saturday, and is located at Calzadas Montejano and Juárez in the Zona Hotelera. The private Cotuco tourist office (☎ 557-23-76), at Calzada López Mateos and Camelias, is opposite the Teatro del Estado, about 3km southeast of the border. It's open 8am to 5pm Monday to Friday.

Casas de cambio are abundant and keep long hours, while banks offer exchange services Monday to Friday mornings only. Most banks in Mexicali and Calexico have ATMs. Bancomer is on Azueta at Avenida Madero.

The post office, on Avenida Madero near Morelos, is open 8am to 6.30pm Monday to Friday, 8am to 3pm Saturday, 9am to 1pm Sunday. Both pay phones and *cabinas* (call offices; mostly in pharmacies, but also in other small businesses) are common.

Millennium Internet & Coffee (☎ 568-43-47), Calzada Sierra 1700-6, in the Plaza Azteca, charges US$2 per hour.

Librería Alethia (☎ 552-57-76), Altamirano 420A, has a good selection of books on Mexican history, archaeology, anthropology and literature.

The Hospital México-Americano (☎ 552-27-49), at Reforma 1000 and Calle B, is close to the border. Locally trained dentists offer quality work at very good prices.

Things to See & Do

The country's largest Chinatown, **La Chinesca**, is south of Calzada López Mateos,centered around Avenida Juárez and Altamirano; the nearby Plaza del Mariachi is a good place to hear banda groups rehearse in the late afternoon.

Most of Mexicali's historic buildings are northeast of Calzada López Mateos. **Catedral de la Virgen de Guadalupe**, at Reforma and Morelos, is the city's major religious landmark. Now the rectory of the Universidad Autónoma de Baja California, the former **Palacio de Gobierno** (built between 1919 and 1922) interrupts Avenida Obregón just east of Calle E. To the north, at Reforma and Calle F, the former headquarters of the **Colorado River Land Company** dates from 1924 and is now used as office space. At Zaragoza and Calle E, two blocks southwest of the rectory, the former brewery **Cervecería Mexicali** (opened in 1923) now sits vacant.

The modest eight-room **Museo Regional de la Universidad Autónoma de Baja California** *(☎ 552-57-15, Reforma & Calle L; admission US$1; open 9am-6pm Mon-Fri, 10am-4pm Sat & Sun)* features exhibits on geology, paleontology, human evolution, colonial history and photography.

The ultramodern **Teatro del Estado** *(State Theater, ☎ 554-64-18, Calzada López Mateos & Milton)*, just north of Compresora, seats 1100. The Instituto de Cultura de Baja California presents film cycles at the Teatro del Estado's Café Literario.

Special Events

From mid-October to early November, the Fiesta del Sol (Festival of the Sun) commemorates the city's founding in 1903. Events include concerts, art exhibits, a crafts exposition, theatrical performances and parades. It also features local industrial and agricultural products.

Places to Stay

Mexicali doesn't really have any decent cheap lodgings.

Hotel México (☎ 554-06-69, Lerdo de Tejada 476) Singles/doubles US$30/34. Central Mexicali's best budget option is this family-oriented hotel between Altamirano and Morelos; air-con, TV, private bath and parking are available. Keep in mind that this hotel is not in the safest part of town.

Hotel del Norte (☎ 552-81-01, Avenida Madero 205) Singles/doubles with breakfast US$48/57. Convenient to the border, the

CENTRAL MEXICALI

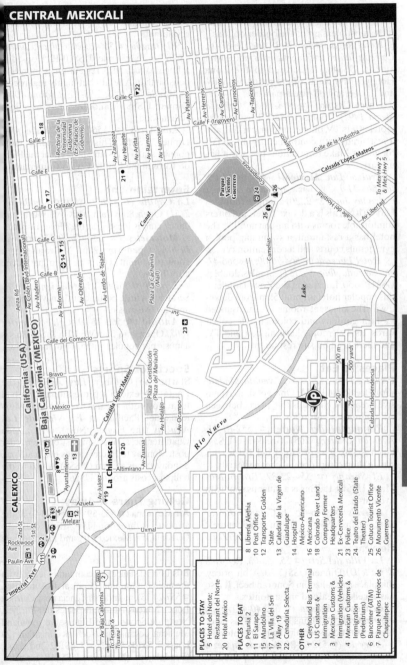

PLACES TO STAY
5 Hotel del Norte;
  Restaurant del Norte
20 Hotel México

PLACES TO EAT
9 Petunia 2
11 El Sarape
15 Mandolino
17 La Villa del Seri
19 Alley 19
22 Cenaduría Selecta

OTHER
1 Greyhound Bus Terminal
2 US Customs &
  Immigration
3 Mexican Customs &
  Immigration (Vehicles)
4 Mexican Customs &
  Immigration
  (Pedestrians)
6 Bancomer (ATM)
7 Parque Niños Héroes de
  Chapultepec

8 Librería Alethia
10 Post Office
12 Transportes Golden
   State
13 Catedral de la Virgen de
   Guadalupe
14 Hospital
16 México-Americano
   Mexicana
18 Colorado River Land
   Company Former
   Headquarters
21 Ex-Cervecería Mexicali
23 Police
24 Teatro del Estado (State
   Theater)
25 Cotuco Tourist Office
26 Monumento Vicente
   Guerrero

landmark Hotel del Norte has 52 rooms, some with color TV and air-con. This hotel is the most pleasant of the border options.

Hotel Regis (☎ 566-34-35, fax 566-88-02, Calzada Juárez 2150) Singles/doubles with air-con US$40/52. Located in the Zona Hotelera, the Regis offers rooms with TV and phone, and off-street parking.

Hotel Cosmos (☎ 568-11-55, Calzada Sierra 1493) Rooms US$50. This popular motel offers TV, phone, air-con, parking and a restaurant with complimentary breakfast for guests. Make reservations because it fills up early.

Araiza Inn Mexicali (☎ 564-11-00, fax 564-11-13, W www.araizainn.com.mx, Calzada Juárez 2220) Singles/doubles US$92/108. This is a deluxe hotel, and offers comfortable rooms with air-con and TV. The hotel has a restaurant, a swimming pool, a gym, tennis courts and a convention center.

Hotel Lucerna (☎ 564-70-00, fax 566-47-06, Calzada Juárez 2151) Singles/doubles US$139/150. Located in the Zona Hotelera, this popular hotel is about 5km from downtown. The pleasant rooms are surrounded by lush gardens and colonial-style courtyards. Its 192 rooms have air-con and TV, and there is an on-site restaurant.

Places to Eat

Petunia 2 (☎ 552-69-51, Avenida Madero 436) Breakfast US$4. One good, inexpensive breakfast choice is this place, between Altamirano and Morelos.

Restaurant del Norte (☎ 552-81-01, Avenida Madero 205) Breakfast US$4, lunch US$6. Part of Hotel del Norte, this coffee shop offers decent, cheap specials.

El Sarape (☎ 554-22-87, Bravo 140) Mains US$10-15. This is a raucous spot with live music.

Jinera's (☎ 566-01-11, Calzada Juárez 1342) Mains US$5-10. For an excellent meal of Mexican food, try Jinera's in the Zona Hotelera.

La Villa del Seri (☎ 553-55-03, Reforma & Calle D) Dinner US$15-20. A bit pricey, this place specializes in Sonoran beef. It also has excellent seafood and antojitos.

Cenaduría Selecta (☎ 552-40-47, Arista 1510 at Calle G) Mains US$6-10. This place is an institution, specializing in antojitos.

Alley 19 (☎ 552-95-20, Avenida Juárez 8 near Azueta) Mains US$5-8. Opened in 1928, the inexpensive Alley 19 is Mexicali's oldest continuously operating Chinese restaurant.

El Dragón (☎ 566-20-20, Calzada Juárez 1830) Lunch & dinner US$10-12. Housed in a huge pagoda, this restaurant is more expensive than Alley 19 but highly regarded.

Mandolino (☎ 552-95-45, Reforma 1070) Dinner US$8. Mandolino has excellent Italian food.

Los Arcos (☎ 556-08-86, Calafia 454) Dinner US$10. This is Mexicali's most popular seafood restaurant; it's near the Plaza de Toros in the Centro Cívico-Comercial.

Entertainment

La Capilla (☎ 564-70-00, Calzada Juárez 2151) Open 8pm-2am. This live music and dance club is located at the Hotel Lucerna.

Molcajetes (☎ 556-07-00, Montejano 1100A) Open 1pm-2am. Molcajetes is a good restaurant with a popular bar scene after 10pm.

Scratch (☎ 557-03-95, Montejano 1100B) Scratch is a little bit fancier than Molcajetes and has live music.

Antrojo (☎ 568-21-29, Calzada Juárez 1807) Open 9pm-2am Wed, Fri & Sat. This is a music bar popular with the younger crowd.

Spectator Sports

Starting in October, **Las Águilas** (the Eagles), Mexicali's professional baseball team, hosts other teams from the Liga Mexicana del Pacífico at **El Nido de Las Águilas** (the Eagles' Nest), on Calzada Cuauhtémoc, about 5km east of the border post. Monday to Friday games begin at 7pm, Sunday games at 1pm (US$8). A taxi to the ballpark costs around US$6.

Getting There & Away

Air Mexicana (☎ 553-59-20, 552-93-91 at the airport), Obregón 1170, flies daily to Guadalajara, Mexico City and intermediate points.

Bus Long-distance bus companies leave from the main bus terminal (Central de Autobuses, ☎ 557-24-15), on Independencia near Calzada López Mateos. Autotransportes del Pacífico, Norte de Sonora and Elite serve mainland Mexican destinations such as Mazatlán (24 hours, US$104 1st-class, US$102 2nd-class), Guadalajara (33 hours, US$118 1st-class,

FIREWORKS

reworks and plastic flamingoes – together at last, Tijuana

RAY LASKOWITZ

Arco, Baja California Sur

ROSS BARNETT

'Wait, my moustache comb!'

COREY RICH

unset on a building's façade in La Paz, Baja California Sur

STUART WASSERMAN

Discover gold upon the Sea of Cortez, Sonora

Pancho Villa met his death here in Hidalgo del Parral.

Barranca del Cobre (Copper Canyon)

Chihuahua state's vast emptiness

US$60 2nd-class) and Mexico City (40 hours, US$134 1st-class, US$88 2nd-class). When you cross the state line into Sonora, some 70km east of Mexicali, you enter a new time zone, so put your watch forward one hour – except during daylight saving (first Sunday in May to last Sunday in September), because Sonora does not observe daylight saving.

ABC destinations from the Central de Autobuses include Tijuana (2 hours, US$14 1st-class; 2½ hours, US$12 2nd-class), Ensenada (3½ hours, US$21 1st-class, US$18 2nd-class), Guerrero Negro (10 hours, US$57), Loreto (19 hours, US$83) and La Paz (24 hours, US$103). ABC buses to San Felipe (2 hours, US$13) depart at 8am, noon, 4pm, 6pm and 8pm.

From a stop on the south side of Calzada López Mateos, near Melgar and the border, Transportes Golden State (☎ 553-61-69) goes to Los Angeles (5 hours, US$35) and intermediate points at 8am, 11.30am, 2.30pm, 6pm and 10.30pm. The Calexico, California, stop is at Church's Fried Chicken, 344 Imperial Ave.

In Calexico, Greyhound (☎ 760-357-1895), 121 1st St, is directly across from the border. There are five departures daily from the Los Angeles terminal (☎ 213-629-8400) to Calexico and back (US$29/53 one-way/roundtrip).

Car & Motorcycle The main border crossing is open 24 hours, but US and Mexican authorities have opened a second border complex east of downtown to ease congestion. It's open 6am to 10pm.

Getting Around

Cabs to Aeropuerto Internacional General Rodolfo Sánchez Taboada (☎ 553-67-42), 12km east of town, cost US$15 but may be shared.

Most city buses start from Avenida Reforma, just west of López Mateos; check the placard for the destination. Local fares are about US$1.

A taxi to the Centro Cívico-Comercial or Zona Hotelera from the border averages about US$5; agree on the fare first.

SAN FELIPE
• pop 20,000 ☎ 686
This once-tranquil fishing community on the Sea of Cortez (Golfo de California),

200km south of Mexicali, suffers blistering summer temperatures, roaring motorcycles, firecrackers, real-estate speculators and aggressive restaurateurs who almost yank patrons off the sidewalk. Sport fishing and warm winters have attracted many retirees from the US to sprawling trailer parks, while younger Americans flock here to party. Farther south, **Puertecitos** is the starting point for a rugged southbound alternative to the Transpeninsular highway; the road is due to be paved in the near future, so check its status first.

Buses to Mexicali (2 hours, US$13) leave at 6am, 7.30am, noon, 4pm and 8pm; Ensenada-bound buses (3 hours, US$18) leave at 8am and 6pm daily.

Southern Baja

Cochimís once foraged the vast Desierto Central (Central Desert), which extends from El Rosario to Loreto, and its coastline along the Sea of Cortez. Baja's colonial and later historical heritage is more palpable here than it is farther north – well-preserved or restored mission churches and modest plazas reveal close links to mainland Mexico.

The sinuous 125km stretch of highway between El Rosario and the desert pit stop of Cataviña traverses a surrealistic desert landscape of granite boulders among *cardón* cacti and the contorted *cirio,* or 'boojum tree.' South of the 28th parallel, the border between the states of Baja California and Baja California Sur, the hour changes; Mountain time (to the south) is an hour ahead of Pacific time (to the north). Here you also enter the 25,000-sq-km Reserva de la Biósfera El Vizcaíno, Latin America's largest protected area, not including those linked to others. It sprawls from the Península Vizcaíno across to the Sea of Cortez and includes the major gray-whale calving areas of Laguna San Ignacio and Laguna Ojo de Liebre and the Sierra de San Francisco, with its pre-Hispanic rock art.

Beyond Guerrero Negro and the desolate Desierto de Vizcaíno, the oasis of San Ignacio augurs the semitropical gulf coast between Mulegé and Cabo San Lucas. Paralleling the gulf, the Sierra de la Giganta divides the region into an eastern

BAJA CALIFORNIA

subtropical zone and a western zone of elevated plateaus and dry lowlands.

South of Loreto, the Transpeninsular highway turns west to the Llano de Magdalena (Magdalena Plain), a rich farming zone, which also offers fishing, whale-watching, surfing and windsurfing.

The southernmost part of the peninsula contains the city of La Paz and areas to its south including the popular resorts of Los Cabos. Los Cabos refers to the towns of San José del Cabo and Cabo San Lucas, as well as to the Los Cabos Corridor (the strip of beaches and luxury resorts that lines the coastline between the two towns). This is the costliest and most tourist-oriented part of the peninsula.

GUERRERO NEGRO
• pop 10,200 ☎ 615

The town of Guerrero Negro is renowned for nearby Laguna Ojo de Liebre (known in English as Scammon's Lagoon), which annually becomes the mating and breeding ground of California gray whales. Each year, the whales migrate 9660km (6000 miles) from the Bering Sea to the lagoon, where they stay from early January through March. About 24km from the junction of highway 1, the lagoon is south of the town's evaporative saltworks (the largest of its kind in the world).

Orientation & Information
The town comprises two distinct sectors: a disorderly strip along Boulevard Zapata, west of the Transpeninsular, and an orderly company town farther west, run by Exportadora de Sal (ESSA). Nearly all accommodations, restaurants and other services are along Boulevard Zapata.

There's a Banamex with an ATM at the far end of the commercial district on Boulevard Zapata, just at the start of the company town.

Whale-Watching
Guerrero Negro travel agencies arrange whale-watching trips on Laguna Ojo de Liebre's shallow waters for about US$40. A bit farther south, *pangueros* (boatmen) from Ejido Benito Juárez take visitors for whale-watching excursions for about US$15 (US$10 for children).

Whales are not usually present until after January 1.

Places to Stay & Eat
About 8km south of Guerrero Negro, an excellent graded road leads 25km west to Ojo de Liebre, where the US$3 parking fee includes the right to camp; the *ejido* (communal landholding) runs a simple but very good restaurant.

The whale-watching season can strain local accommodations; reservations are advisable from January to March.

Malarrimo Trailer Park (☎/fax 157-01-00, ⓦ www.malarrimo.com, cnr Zapata & Guerrero) Tent/RV sites US$5/12. This camping site is located at the eastern entrance to town. Hot water is plentiful and toilets are clean, but check electrical outlets.

Cabañas Don Miguelito (☎ 157-01-00, ⓦ www.malarrimo.com, cnr Zapata & Guerrero) Singles/doubles US$30/35. This is part of the Malarrimo complex and offers pleasant rooms.

Motel Las Ballenas (☎/fax 157-01-16, cnr Victoria Sánchez & Casillas) Singles/doubles US$18/22. Las Ballenas offers hot water and color TV in every room.

Hotel El Morro (☎ 157-04-14, Boulevard Zapata) Singles/doubles US$25/31. Located on the north side of Boulevard Zapata, this hotel has comfortable but basic rooms.

Guerrero Negro's many *taco stands* keep erratic hours.

Malarrimo (☎ 157-01-00) Mains US$10-15. Specializing in seafood, both as antojitos and as sophisticated international dishes, the Malarrimo (part of the Malarrimo complex) is not cheap, but portions are generous.

Getting There & Away
The Aeroméxico subsidiary Aerolitoral (☎ 157-17-33), on the north side of Boulevard Zapata near the Pemex station, flies Monday, Wednesday and Friday to Hermosillo (US$216), connecting to mainland Mexican cities and Phoenix, Arizona. It leaves from the airfield 2km north of the state border, west of the Transpeninsular highway.

Aerocedros (☎ 157-16-26), on the south side of Boulevard Zapata, flies to Isla Cedros (US$51) and Ensenada (US$103) Tuesday and Friday.

The bus station (☎ 157-06-11) is on the south side of Boulevard Zapata. Northbound services include Ensenada (10 hours, US$35) and Tijuana (13 hours, US$44 1st-class,

California Gray Whales

Each year, gray whales migrate 9700km from the Bering Sea to the warmer waters of Baja California. You can view gray whales almost anywhere on the peninsula: all waterfront towns offer some type of whale-watching expe- 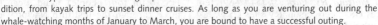 dition, from kayak trips to sunset dinner cruises. As long as you are venturing out during the whale-watching months of January to March, you are bound to have a successful outing.

If you want an up-close-and-personal whale experience, go to one of the lagoons of Ojo de Liebre, San Ignacio or Bahía Magdalena. These lagoons offer an ideal, protected place for whales to mate, give birth and nurture their offspring. The whale-watching tours in these lagoons gener- ally entail hiring a small boat for a two- to six-hour outing.

Just south of Guerrero Negro, Laguna Ojo de Liebre (Scammon's Lagoon) has a reputation as the location with the greatest number of whales of any of Baja's main whale-watching sites.

Laguna San Ignacio is probably the best spot for contact with friendly whales, who seem com- pletely receptive to contact with human visitors (petting the whales is permitted).

In the south, the two main whale-watching areas are in Bahía Magdalena. Puerto López Mateos and Puerto San Carlos are both gray whale breeding grounds. Of the two locations, Puerto López Mateos is reputed to be the slightly more accessible site. The lagoon is smaller and narrower than at Puerto San Carlos, so it takes less time to get to the whales.

Whale-watching season for all sites officially begins December 15 and lasts until April 15. See this chapter's sections on Guerrero Negro, Laguna San Ignacio (in the Around San Ignacio section) and Around Ciudad Constitución for more details on watching whales.

US$43 2nd-class); southbound services include Mulegé (4 hours, US$21 1st-class, US$18 2nd-class), Loreto (6 hours, US$29 1st-class, US$26 2nd-class) and La Paz (11 hours, US$50 1st-class, US$47 2nd-class).

ISLA CEDROS
• pop 1470 ☎ 615

Isla Cedros is not a touristy destination – it has few services, and you can't even get a margarita – but this mountainous north- ward extension of Península Vizcaíno sup- ports unusual flora, marine mammals such as elephant seals and sea lions, and the en- dangered Cedros mule deer. The hiking is good here, but water is scarce.

Most of the island's inhabitants live in the port of Cedros on the eastern shore, but a fair number live at Punta Morro Redondo, the transshipment point for salt barged over from Guerrero Negro.

Manuel Aguilar maintains a basic *guest house*, with rooms for US$12. *La Paceñita* has good, reasonably priced antojitos, fish and shrimp.

Aerocedros (☎ 615-157-16-26 in Gue- rrero Negro) flies Tuesday and Friday to and from Guerrero Negro (US$51) and Ense- nada (US$103). Flights leave Ensenada at 9.30am and stop at Isla Cedros before going on to Guerrero Negro at noon. Return flights to Ensenada originate in Guerrero Negro, stop briefly on the island and con- tinue on to Ensenada around 4pm.

Taxis charge about US$5 per person from Cedros port to the airfield at Punta Morro Redondo, 8km south of town.

SAN IGNACIO
• pop 760 • elev 200m ☎ 615

Jesuits located Misión San Ignacio de Kadakaamán in this soothing oasis in 1728, planting dense groves of date palms and citrus trees, but it was Dominicans who supervised construction of the striking church (finished in 1786) that still domi- nates the cool, laurel-shaded plaza. With lava-block walls nearly 1.2m thick and sur- rounded by bougainvillea, this is one of Baja's most beautiful churches.

The lush village of San Ignacio proper is about 1.6km south of the Transpeninsular and is a welcome sight after the scrub brush and dense cacti of the Desierto de Vizcaíno. Most services are around the plaza, including public telephones, but there is no bank.

Places to Stay & Eat

El Padrino RV Park (☎ 154-00-89) Tent sites US$4 per person, RV sites US$9. Just south of Hotel La Pinta, on the west side of the road into town, this palm-shaded park has around 50 sites, 16 with full hookups.

Rice & Beans RV Park (☎ 154-02-83) RV sites US$17. This park is on the way to San Lino, just off the Transpeninsular west of town. Although the site is a little barren, the owners are very friendly, and the on-site *restaurant* is worth the stop for the shrimp burritos. Antojitos are US$5 to US$10.

Motel La Posada (☎ 154-03-13, *Carranza 22*) Doubles US$20. Southeast of the plaza, La Posada has spartan rooms with hot showers. It's a bit difficult to find: take Avenida Hidalgo east from the plaza, turn right at Callejón Ciprés, then turn left onto Venustiano Carranza.

Hotel La Pinta (☎ 154-03-00) Singles & doubles US$69. This pseudo-colonial hotel, on the main road just before entering San Ignacio, appeals to more affluent travelers.

Hotel La Pinta has a decent *restaurant*. Mains are US$7 to US$15. Specializing in local beef, it also offers the typical antojitos.

Rene's (☎ 154-01-53) Mains US$5-10, lobster US$18. A block west of Motel La Posada, Rene's serves good, reasonably priced antojitos and seafood dishes.

Flojos (☎ 154-00-89, *El Padrino RV Park*) Mains around US$5-10. Flojos prepares good, fresh seafood at reasonable prices.

Getting There & Away

San Ignacio now has an official bus station, and buses will no longer pick up passengers at the old stop at the San Lino junction outside of town. The new bus station (☎ 154-02-04) is located at the La Muralla restaurant on the road into town.

AROUND SAN IGNACIO
San Francisco de la Sierra

From Km 118 on the Transpeninsular, 43km northwest of San Ignacio, a graded but poorly consolidated road climbs east to San Francisco de la Sierra, the gateway to the Desierto Central's most spectacular pre-Hispanic rock art. **Cueva del Ratón**, about 2.5km before San Francisco, is the most accessible site. Excursions to Cueva del Ratón, which has representations of *monos* (human figures), *borregos* (bighorn sheep) and deer, requires hiring a guide (US$6 to US$10 for four people). Guides can be hired through the **Instituto Nacional de Antropología e Historia** (*INAH*, ☎ 154-02-22; open 8am-3pm Mon-Sat). The INAH office is in San Ignacio adjacent to the Misión San Ignacio on the plaza.

In the dramatic Cañón San Pablo, **Cueva Pintada**, **Cueva de las Flechas** and other sites are better preserved. Cueva Pintada's rock overhang is the most impressive. The awesome mule-back descent of Cañón San Pablo requires at least two days, preferably three. Visitors must refrain from touching the paintings, smoking at sites or employing flash photography (400 ASA film suffices even in dim light). Excursions to Cañón San Pablo involve hiring a guide with a mule through INAH for US$13 per day, plus a mule for each individual in the party for US$10 per day, and additional pack animals to carry supplies. Visitors must also provide food for the guide.

The best season for visiting is early spring, when the days are fairly long but temperatures are not yet unpleasantly hot. Backpacking is permitted, but you must still hire a guide and mule.

Laguna San Ignacio

Along with Laguna Ojo de Liebre and Bahía Magdalena, Laguna San Ignacio is one of the Pacific coast's major winter whale-watching sites, with three-hour excursions costing around US$30 per person. **Kuyima** (☎ 154-00-70, ☒ www.kuyima.com, 23 Morelos), a cooperative based at the east end of the plaza in San Ignacio, can arrange transport and accommodations. The 65km drive to the campsite La Fridera takes about two hours, but the road can be pretty rough.

A plan for a giant saltworks at the lagoon by the Mexican-Japanese company Exportadora de Sal (ESSA) – which already has the world's largest evaporative saltworks at Guerrero Negro – was killed off by President Zedillo in 2000. This represented a major victory for environmentalists, who had campaigned hard against the proposal for several years, chiefly on the grounds of the threat to the whales.

In other seasons the area offers outstanding bird-watching in the stunted mangroves and at **Islas El Pelícano**, where ospreys and cormorants nest (landing of airplanes on the island is prohibited).

SANTA ROSALÍA
* pop 10,500 ☎ 615

Imported timber frames the clapboard houses lining the main streets of Santa Rosalía, a copper town built on the Sea of Cortez coast by the French-owned Compañía del Boleo in the 1880s. The French also assembled a prefabricated church here that was designed by Alexandre Gustave Eiffel (the same!) for Paris' 1889 World's Fair. And they bequeathed a bakery that sells Baja's best baguettes.

Orientation & Information
Central Santa Rosalía nestles in the canyon of its namesake *arroyo* (stream), west of the Transpeninsular, but French administrators built their houses on the northern Mesa Francia, now home to municipal authorities and the historic Hotel Francés. Santa Rosalía's narrow avenidas run east-west, while its short calles run north-south; one-way traffic is the rule. Plaza Benito Juárez, four blocks west of the highway, is the town center.

Travelers bound for Mulegé, which has no banks, should change US cash or traveler's checks here, where Banamex also has an ATM. The post office is at Avenida Constitución at Calle 2. Hotel del Real, on the exit road from town, has long-distance cabinas.

Iglesia Santa Bárbara
Designed and erected in Paris, disassembled and stored in Brussels, intended for West

---

The Rock Art of the Desierto Central

When Jesuit missionaries inquired as to who created the giant rock paintings of the Sierra de San Francisco and about the meaning of those paintings, the Cochimís responded with a bewilderment that was, in all likelihood, utterly feigned. The Cochimís claimed ignorance of both symbols and techniques, but it was not unusual, when missionaries came calling, to deny knowledge of the profound religious beliefs which those missionaries wanted to eradicate.

At sites such as Cueva Pintada, Cochimí painters and their predecessors decorated high rock overhangs with vivid red and black representations of human figures, bighorn sheep, pumas and deer, as well as with more abstract designs. It is speculated that the painters built scaffolds of palm logs to reach the ceilings. Post-contact motifs do include Christian crosses, but these are few and small in contrast to the dazzling pre-Hispanic figures surrounding them.

Cueva de las Flechas, across Cañón San Pablo, has similar paintings, but the uncommon feature of arrows through some of the figures is the subject of serious speculation. One interpretation is that these paintings depict a period of warfare. Similar opinions suggest that they record a raid or an instance of trespass on tribal territory or perhaps constitute a warning against such trespass. One researcher, however, has hypothesized that the arrows represent a shaman's metaphor for death in the course of a vision quest.

Such speculation is impossible to prove since the Cochimís no longer exist, but in the mid-1990s the Instituto Nacional de Antropología e Historia (INAH) undertook the largest systematic archaeological survey of a hunter-gatherer people yet attempted in Mexico. Results revealed that, besides well-known features such as rock art sites and grinding stones, the Cochimís left evidence of permanent dwellings. In recognition of its cultural importance, the Sierra de San Francisco has been declared a UNESCO World Heritage Site. It is also part of the Reserva de la Biósfera El Vizcaíno.

The sierra is an INAH-protected archaeological zone, which means that foreigners need entry permits to conduct research – not everyone has been scrupulous in that regard. INAH has instituted regulations for tourists. Visitors must contact INAH to obtain permission and to hire a guide in order to visit the sites.

BAJA CALIFORNIA

Africa, Gustave Eiffel's prefab church was finally shipped here when a Compañía del Boleo director chanced upon it in 1895. It was reassembled by 1897. It has attractive stained-glass windows.

Places to Stay & Eat

Las Palmas RV Park (☎ 152-01-09, Km 192 *on Transpeninsular)* Tent sites US$6 per person, RV sites US$13. Located just south of town, Las Palmas has grassy sites with hot showers, clean toilets and laundry.

Motel San Victor (☎ 152-01-16, Avenida *Progreso 32)* Singles & doubles US$10. This family-run motel has a dozen tidy rooms with ceiling fans, air-con and tiled baths.

Hotel Francés (☎/fax 152-20-52, Calle Jean Michel Cousteau 15) Rooms US$46. This historic hotel offers an atmospheric bar, views of the rusting copper works, air-con and a small swimming pool.

Hotel El Morro (☎ 152-04-14, on the *Transpeninsular about 1.5km south of town)* Singles/doubles with air-con US$30/38. With a small pool and balconies overlooking the water, this is Santa Rosalía's most upscale accommodations.

Taco stands are numerous along Avenida Obregón.

Cenaduría Gaby (☎ 152-01-55, Calle 5 No 3) Antojitos US$3-4.50. This restaurant, just north of Obregón, serves good fish tacos.

Restaurant Selene (☎ 152-06-85, on the *malecón)* Mains US$8-10. South of downtown, this waterfront restaurant serves sumptuous though pricey seafood.

Panadería El Boleo (☎ 152-03-10, *Obregón 30 between Calles 3 & 4)* This is an obligatory stop for Mexican and French-style baked goods. A loaf of bread costs about US$0.50. Baguettes usually sell out early.

Getting There & Away

Bus At least six buses daily in each direction stop at the terminal (☎ 152-01-50), which is south of town on the west side of the Transpeninsular, about 250m south of the ferry terminal. Northbound destinations include San Ignacio (1½ hours, US$5.50), Guerrero Negro (3 hours, US$15), Ensenada (12 hours, US$50) and Tijuana (14 hours, US$59); southbound fares include Mulegé (1½ hours, US$5.50), Loreto (3 hours, US$13), Ciudad Constitución (5 hours, US$22) and La Paz (8 hours, US$34).

Boat Sematur passenger/auto ferries sail to Guaymas at 10pm Monday and Thursday, arriving at 9am; the return ferry to Santa Rosalía sails at 9.30am Monday and Thursday, arriving at 8pm. Strong winter winds may cause delays.

Ticket windows at the terminal (☎ 152-00-13), on the highway, are open 8am to 3.30pm Monday, Wednesday and Thursday; 8am to 11am and 7pm to 9.30pm Tuesday and Friday; 9am to 12.45pm Saturday; and are closed Sunday. See the accompanying chart for vehicle fares. Make reservations at least three days in advance and, even if you have reservations, arrive early at the ticket office. Passenger fares are US$51 for *salón* class, US$115 for *turista*, US$141 for *cabina*, and US$166 for *especial*. Vehicle rates vary with vehicle length:

vehicle	length	rate
car	up to 5m	US$244
	5.01 to 6.5m	US$314
car with trailer	up to 9m	US$432
	9.01 to 17m	US$811
motorcycle		US$80

Before shipping any vehicle to the mainland, officials require a vehicle permit (see the Car & Motorcycle section of the Getting There & Away chapter for details on bringing a car into Mexico). Vehicle permits are not obtainable in Santa Rosalía, so get them in Tijuana, Ensenada, Mexicali or La Paz.

MULEGÉ
• pop 3170 ☎ 615

Beyond Santa Rosalía, the Transpeninsular hugs the eastern scarp of the Sierra de la Giganta before winding through the Sierra Azteca and dropping into the subtropical oasis of Mulegé, a popular divers' destination. The village of Mulegé straddles the palm-lined Arroyo de Santa Rosalía (Río Mulegé), 3km inland from the gulf.

Information

Most services, including the post office, are on or near Jardín Corona, the town plaza. Mulegé has no bank, but merchants change cash dollars or accept them for payment. There are a number of pay phones on the plaza.

Things to See & Do

Across the highway, near the south bank of the arroyo, the hilltop **Misión Santa Rosalía de Mulegé** was founded in 1705, completed in 1766, and abandoned in 1828. A short path climbs to a scenic overlook of the palm-lined arroyo.

Desperately needing major restoration, the former territorial prison is now the **Museo Mulegé** *(Barrio Canenea; admission free; open 9am-3pm)*, overlooking the town. Its eclectic artifacts include cotton gins, antique diving equipment and firearms.

Diving

Cortez Explorers *(☎ 153-05-00, Moctezuma 75A; open 10am-1pm & 4pm-7pm Mon-Sat, Sunday excursions available by reservation)* offers diving instruction and excursions, snorkel equipment rental and bike rental. Book trips one day in advance. Prices for scuba-diving excursions range from US$50 to US$80 per person, depending on the package. Snorkeling packages cost about US$30 per person. There's a US$100 minimum for the scuba charters and a US$70 minimum for the snorkeling charters.

Places to Stay

Huerta Saucedo RV Park *(☎ 153-03-00)* Tent sites US$5, RV sites US$15-18, cabins US$65-110. This friendly place, south of town on the gulf side of the highway, rents 35 RV spaces. Cabins are situated on the river and there are canoe and paddleboat rentals available.

Canett Casa de Huéspedes *(☎ 153-02-72, Madero)* Rooms US$11-14. East of Jardín Corona, this hotel isn't bad, but don't plan on sleeping in; the church bells next door start ringing at 6am.

Casa de Huéspedes Manuelita *(☎ 153-01-75, Moctezuma)* Singles/doubles around US$13/16 or US$19 with air-con. This hotel is basic but decent.

Hotel Las Casitas *(☎ 153-00-19, Madero 50)* Singles/doubles with bath & air-con US$28/33. Poet Alán Gorosave once inhabited this shady hotel near Martínez.

Hotel Hacienda *(☎ 153-00-21, e hotel hacienda_mulege@hotmail.com, Madero 3)* Rooms US$33. Rooms come with twin beds, fridge, air-con and hot shower, plus there's a small pool.

Places to Eat

Asadero Ramón *(formerly Dany's, Madero & Romerio Rubio)* Tacos US$2. This place offers the closest the humble taco will ever get to haute cuisine, with various fillings and a cornucopia of tasty condiments at reasonable prices.

Las Casitas *(☎ 153-01-19, Madero 50)* Antojitos US$6, seafood US$10-14. Located in its namesake hotel, try this place for antojitos and a few seafood dishes.

Los Equipales *(☎ 153-03-30, Moctezuma)* Lunch & dinner US$4-7. Just west of Zaragoza, this restaurant has outstanding meals (ranging from hamburgers to a Mexican combination platter) that are a good value for the money.

El Candil *(Zaragoza)* Mains US$5-10. Located near the plaza, El Candil has filling meat and seafood dishes at moderate prices; its bar is a popular meeting place.

Getting There & Away

Half a dozen buses pass daily in each direction at the Y-junction ('La Y Griega') on the Transpeninsular at the western edge of town.

LORETO

• pop 8300 ☎ 613

In 1697 Jesuit Juan María Salvatierra established the Californias' first permanent European settlement at this modest port of cobbled streets some 135km south of Mulegé, between the Transpeninsular and the gulf. Loreto is home to Baja's marine national park, Parque Marino Nacional Bahía de Loreto, with 2065 sq km of shoreline, ocean and offshore islands protected from pollution and uncontrolled fishing.

Orientation

Loreto has an irregular street plan. Most hotels and services are near the landmark mission church on Salvatierra, while the attractive malecón (waterfront boulevard) is ideal for evening strolls. The Plaza Cívica is just north of Salvatierra, between Madero and Davis.

Information

Loreto's Municipal Department of Tourism *(☎ 135-04-11)*, on the west side of the Plaza Cívica, is open 8am to 3pm Monday to Friday. A helpful English-speaking staff is

BAJA CALIFORNIA

LORETO

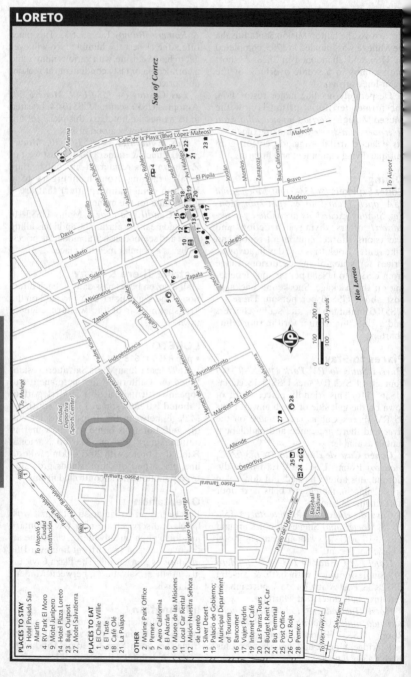

PLACES TO STAY
3   Hotel Posada San Martin
4   RV Park El Moro
9   Motel Junipero
14 Hotel Plaza Loreto
23 Baja Outpost
27 Motel Salvatierra

PLACES TO EAT
1   El Chile Willie
6   El Taste
18 Café Olé
21 La Palapa

OTHER
2   Marine Park Office
5   Pemex
7   Aero California
8   El Alacrán
10 Museo de las Misiones
11 Local Car Rental
12 Misión Nuestra Señora de Loreto
13 Silver Desert
15 Palacio de Gobierno; Municipal Department of Tourism
16 Bancomer
17 Viajes Pedrin
19 Internet Café
20 Las Parras Tours
22 Budget Rent A Car
24 Bus Terminal
25 Post Office
26 Cruz Roja
28 Pemex

BAJA CALIFORNIA

usually on duty, and it has a good selection of brochures and flyers. The marine park office (☎ 135-04-77), alongside the marina, is where you pay the US$6 entrance fee to the park. The staff at the marine park office is also a good source of information for all water activities in the area. The office is open 9am to 3pm Monday to Saturday.

Bancomer, at Salvatierra and Madero, has an ATM and changes US cash and traveler's checks Monday to Friday.

The post office is on Deportiva, north of Salvatierra; it's open 8am to 3pm Monday to Saturday. Several businesses along Salvatierra have long-distance cabinas, but they charge for international collect calls.

The Internet Café (☎ 135-08-02), on Madero next to Café Olé, is open 9am to 2pm and 4pm to 7pm Monday to Friday, and 9am to 2.30pm Saturday. Computers are available at US$3 per half hour.

Things to See & Do

Above the entrance to **Misión Nuestra Señora de Loreto**, the inscription 'Cabeza y Madre de Las Misiones de Baja y Alta California' (Head and Mother of the Missions of Lower and Upper California) aptly describes the mission's role in the history of the Californias.

Alongside the church, INAH's revamped **Museo de las Misiones** (☎ 135-04-41, Salvatierra & Misioneros; admission US$3; open 9am-1pm & 1.45pm-6pm Tues-Fri) chronicles the settlement of Baja California, paying more attention to the indigenous heritage than it once did.

Activities

Loreto is an ideal location for all types of outdoor activities, and a number of outfitters cover the range from kayaking and diving along the reefs around Isla del Carmen to horseback riding, hiking and mountain biking in the Sierra de la Giganta.

Las Parras Tours (☎ 135-10-10, Madero 16) offers diving, as well as kayaking, biking and hiking trips to Misión San Francisco Javier. **Baja Outpost** (☎ 135-12-29, e outpost@ bajaoutpost.com, w www.bajaoutpost.com, Boulevard López Mateos), between Jordán and Hidalgo, a well-run outfitter, offers diving, snorkeling, whale-watching and kayaking expeditions.

Places to Stay

RV Park El Moro (☎/fax 135-05-42, Rosendo Robles 8) RV sites US$12, singles/doubles US$30/40. Half a block from the beach, the friendly Park El Moro has 12 sites with full hookups. It has clean baths and hot showers and the rooms here are clean and comfortable.

Hotel Posada San Martín (☎ 135-07-92, Juárez & Davis) Rooms US$12-40. The rooms here are basic, but it's often full.

Motel Salvatierra (☎ 135-00-21, Salvatierra 123) Singles/doubles US$24/27. The Salvatierra has clean but worn rooms with air-con and hot showers.

Hotel Plaza Loreto (☎ 135-02-80, fax 135-08-55, e hotelplazaloreto@prodigy.net.mx, w www.hotelplazaloreto.com, Hidalgo 2) Singles/doubles US$51/62. This hotel is central and very attractive.

Motel Junípero (☎ 135-01-22, Hidalgo) Singles/doubles US$30/40. Across the street from the Plaza Loreto, this family-run hotel has pleasant rooms.

Baja Outpost (☎ 135-11-34) Rooms US$56. Located on the waterfront between Jordán and Hidalgo, Baja Outpost specializes in activities such as scuba diving and kayaking, but also offers beautiful rooms and pleasant bungalows.

Places to Eat

Café Olé (☎ 135-04-96, Madero 14) Mains US$1.50-5. This inexpensive café is the place to stop for breakfast.

El Taste (☎ 135-14-89, Juárez & Zapata) Dinners US$13-20. This restaurant serves the best steak in Loreto: be prepared to eat well, because the plates are giant.

La Palapa (☎ 135-11-01, Hidalgo between Boulevard López Mateos & El Pipila) Dinner US$6-12. This popular seafood restaurant is a direct descendant of the now defunct Caesar's.

El Chile Willie (☎ 135-06-77, Boulevard López Mateos) Mains US$6-11. This waterfront restaurant is becoming something of a Loreto institution. The food is good and the margaritas are strong.

Shopping

Try **El Alacrán** (☎ 135-00-29, Salvatierra 47) for varied handicrafts. For silver artwork and jewelry, visit **Silver Desert** (☎ 135-06-84, Salvatierra 36).

BAJA CALIFORNIA

Getting There & Away

Aero California (☎ 135-05-00), on Juárez between Misioneros and Zapata, flies daily to Los Angeles. Aerolitoral, represented by Viajes Pedrín (☎ 135-02-04), on the south side of Hidalgo at Madero, flies daily to and from La Paz and to Los Angeles.

Loreto's bus station (☎ 135-07-67) is near the convergence of Salvatierra, Paseo de Ugarte and Paseo Tamaral. Northbound buses head to Santa Rosalía (3 hours, US$13), Guerrero Negro (6 hours, US$29), Tijuana (17 hours, US$69) and Mexicali (19 hours, US$83). Southbound buses for La Paz (5 hours, US$20) and intermediate stops leave five times daily, from 8am to midnight.

Both Local and Budget car-rental agencies are located on Hidalgo.

Getting Around

Taxis to Aeropuerto Internacional de Loreto (☎ 135-04-99), reached by a lateral road off the highway south of the Río Loreto, cost US$12.

AROUND LORETO

About 2km south of Loreto on the Transpeninsular is the junction for the spectacular 35km mountain road to beautifully preserved **Misión San Francisco Javier de Viggé-Biaundó**. Every December 3, pilgrims celebrate the saint's fiesta at this mission founded in 1699.

Restaurant Palapa San Javier Prices US$2-5. This restaurant, located just at the entrance to the village, serves simple meals, cold sodas and beer and offers simple accommodations.

CIUDAD CONSTITUCIÓN
• pop 35,500 • elev 50m ☎ 613

Conveniently close to whale-watching sites, inland Ciudad Constitución, 215km northwest of La Paz, has grown dramatically with the development of commercial agriculture. Most services are within a block or two of the north-south Transpeninsular, commonly known as Boulevard Olachea.

The post office is on Galeana, west of Olachea; for phone service, try the cabinas on the east side of Olachea between Matamoros and Mina. For information on whale-watching, see the Around Ciudad Constitución section, later.

The Internet Café, across from the Banamex on Olachea, is open 10am to 2pm and 4.30pm to 8.30pm Monday to Friday, and 9am to 2.30pm Saturday. Computers are available for US$3 per hour.

Places to Stay

Manfred's RV Trailer Park (☎ 132-11-03) Tent/RV sites US$7/9. At the north end of town, near the junction of the highway to Puerto López Mateos, this Austrian-run trailer park has spacious, shady sites. It gives a break to cyclists, motorcyclists and car campers.

Hotel Casino (☎ 132-14-15, Guadalupe Victoria) Singles/doubles US$21/23. This hotel is situated east of the Hotel Maribel. Rooms are simple but decent.

Hotel Conchita (☎ 132-02-66, Olachea 180) Singles/doubles US$18/21. The Conchita has basic rooms with TV; a few rooms have air-con.

Hotel Maribel (☎ 132-01-55, Guadalupe Victoria 156) Singles/doubles US$30/35. Located near Olachea, the Maribel is more expensive, but the rooms are just as spartan.

Places to Eat

Constitución's many taco stands and the **Mercado Central**, on Olachea at Morelos, have the cheapest eats with tacos costing around US$2. *Estrella del Mar* (☎ 132-09-55) and *Rincón Jarocho* (☎ 132-25-25), on the east side of Olachea, are seafood restaurants. Meals cost US$5 to US$10. Another seafood choice is *Mariscos El Delfín* (Olachea & Zapata).

Getting There & Away

Long-distance buses stop at the terminal (☎ 132-03-76), at Zapata and Juárez. You can also catch buses to nearby Puerto San Carlos (US$5) at 10.45am and 5.15pm and Puerto López Mateos (US$5) at 12.45pm and 7.45pm from this terminal.

AROUND CIUDAD CONSTITUCIÓN
Puerto López Mateos
• pop 2390 ☎ 613

Shielded from the open Pacific by the offshore barrier of Isla Magdalena, Puerto Adolfo López Mateos is one of Baja's best whale-watching sites. Whales are visible from the shore near Playa El Faro. Three-hour *panga* (skiff) excursions cost about US$55 per hour for up to six people and are easy to arrange.

Free *camping*, with pit toilets only (bring water), is possible at tidy Playa Soledad, which is near Playa El Faro.

The only other accommodations in Puerto López Mateos are at the small but tidy *Posada Ballena López*. Singles/doubles cost US$10/15.

Besides a couple of so-so taco stands, López Mateos has several decent restaurants. *Restaurant California* (☎ 131-52-08) Prices US$5-8. You will find this good restaurant across from the church.

La Ballena Gris Meals US$5-8. At the entrance to town, this place offers good seafood.

Puerto López Mateos is 34km west of Ciudad Insurgentes by a good paved road. Autotransportes Águila has buses from Ciudad Constitución (US$5) at 12.45pm and 7.45pm daily; return service to Constitución leaves at 6.30am and 12.30pm.

Puerto San Carlos
• pop 3640 ☎ 613

On Bahía Magdalena, 56km west of Ciudad Constitución, Puerto San Carlos is a deep-water port from which Llano de Magdalena produce is shipped. From January through March, pangueros take up to five or six passengers for whale-watching excursions for US$55 per hour.

Accommodations can be tougher to find during whale-watching season, but free *camping* is possible north of town on the public beach. There are no toilets at the beach.

Motel Las Brisas (☎ 136-01-52, Madero) Singles/doubles US$15/18. The rooms here are basic but clean.

Hotel Palmar (☎ 136-00-35, Puerto Morelos) Singles/doubles US$22/26. The Palmar offers pleasant rooms.

Hotel Alcatraz (☎ 136-00-17, Puerto La Paz) Singles/doubles US$50/70. The Hotel Alcatraz offers rooms with TV.

Restaurant Bar El Patio (☎ 136-00-17) Lunch & dinner US$5-10. At the Hotel Alcatraz, this is the town's best eatery.

Mariscos Los Arcos (Puerto La Paz) Tacos US$2. This place has tremendous shrimp tacos and seafood soup.

From a small house on Calle Puerto Morelos, Autotransportes Águilar runs buses

at 7.30am daily to Ciudad Constitución (US$5) and La Paz (US$15). This is the only public transportation from Puerto San Carlos.

LA PAZ
• pop 169,000 ☎ 612

Hernán Cortés established Baja's first European outpost near La Paz, but permanent settlement waited until 1811. US troops occupied the city during the Mexican-American War (1846-48). In 1853 the quixotic American adventurer William Walker proclaimed a 'Republic of Lower California,' but he soon left under Mexican pressure.

After Walker's fiasco La Paz settled down. It had a rich pearl industry but that pretty nearly disappeared during the revolution of 1910-20. Today the capital of Baja California Sur is a peaceful place with beautiful beaches, a palm-lined malecón, a handful of colonial buildings and spectacular sunsets over the bay. It is also a popular winter resort, and its port of Pichilingue receives ferries from the mainland ports of Topolobampo and Mazatlán.

Orientation

Approaching La Paz from the southwest, the Transpeninsular becomes Abasolo as it runs parallel to the bay. Four blocks east of 5 de Febrero, Abasolo becomes Paseo Obregón, leading along the palm-lined malecón toward Península Pichilingue.

La Paz's grid makes basic orientation easy, but the center's crooked streets and alleys change names almost every block. The city's heart is Jardín Velasco (Plaza Constitución), three blocks southeast of the tourist pier.

Information

Immigration There's an immigration office (☎ 125-34-93) at Paseo Obregón 2140 in the Edificio Milhe, between Allende and Juárez; it's open 9am to 5pm Monday to Friday.

Tourist Offices The well-organized staff at the Coordinación Estatal de Turismo tourist office (☎ 124-01-99, w www.gbcs.gob.mx), on the waterfront at Paseo Obregón and 16 de Septiembre, distribute a variety of leaflets and keep a current list of hotel rates. It's open 8am to 11pm Monday to Friday, 12am to 12pm Saturday and Sunday.

BAJA CALIFORNIA

Money Most banks (many with ATMs) and casas de cambio are located on or around 16 de Septiembre.

Post & Communications The post office is at Constitución and Revolución. Pay phones are numerous throughout the city. Internet cafés have opened up throughout the city. One location is at Servicios Turisticos (☎ 122-68-37), at Obregón and Muelle; it's open 8am to 8pm. The cost is about US$3 per half hour.

Travel Agencies Turismo Express (☎ 125-63-10, W www.turismoexpress.com), at Paseo Obregón and 16 de Septiembre, is alongside the tourist office on the Muelle Turístico.

Bookstores The Museo Regional de Antropología e Historia (see below) has a good selection of Spanish-language books on Baja California and mainland Mexico; it's open 8am to 3pm Monday to Friday. Libros Libros Books Books (☎ 122-14-10), Constitución 195, stocks books in English and Spanish.

Things to See & Do
The **Museo Regional de Antropología e Historia** *(☎ 122-01-62, 5 de Mayo & Altamirano; admission free; open 8am-6pm Mon-Fri, 9am-2pm Sat)* chronicles the peninsula from prehistory to the revolution of 1910 and its aftermath. It also has an attractive cactus garden.

Across from the Jardín Velasco, La Paz's former Casa de Gobierno is now the **Biblioteca de la Historia de las Californias** *(Madero & Independencia; open 8am-8pm Mon-Fri),* a history library.

A sprawling concrete edifice, the **Teatro de la Ciudad** *(☎ 125-02-07)* is the most conspicuous element of the **Unidad Cultural Profesor Jesús Castro Agúndez** *(☎ 125-90-40; open 8am-8pm Mon-Fri),* a cultural center that takes up most of the area bounded by Altamirano, Navarro, Héroes de la Independencia and Legaspi. At the entrance to the theater, on Legaspi, the *Rotonda de los Hombres Ilustres* (Rotunda of Distinguished Men) is a sculptural tribute to figures who fought against William Walker's invasion of La Paz in 1853 and the French mainland intervention of

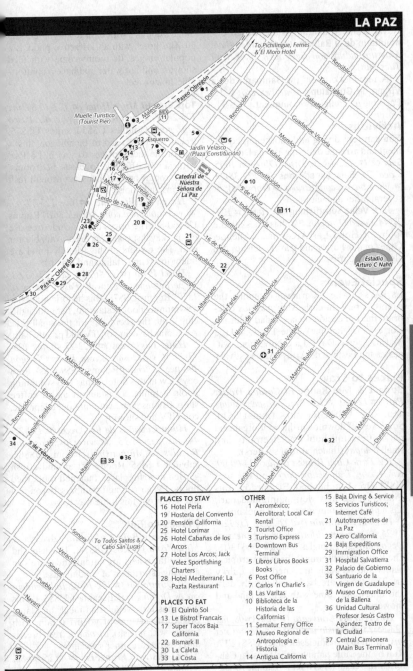

LA PAZ

To Pichilingue, Ferries & El Moro Hotel

Muelle Turístico (Tourist Pier)

Jardín Velasco (Plaza Constitución)

Catedral de Nuestra Señora de La Paz

Estadio Arturo C Nahtl

To Todos Santos & Cabo San Lucas

BAJA CALIFORNIA

PLACES TO STAY
16 Hotel Perla
19 Hostería del Convento
20 Pensión California
25 Hotel Lorimar
26 Hotel Cabañas de los Arcos
27 Hotel Los Arcos; Jack Velez Sportfishing Charters
28 Hotel Mediterrané; La Pazta Restaurant

PLACES TO EAT
9 El Quinto Sol
13 Le Bistrot Francais
17 Super Tacos Baja California
22 Bismark II
30 La Caleta
33 La Costa

OTHER
1 Aeroméxico; Aerolitoral; Local Car Rental
2 Tourist Office
3 Turismo Express
4 Downtown Bus Terminal
5 Libros Libros Books Books
6 Post Office
7 Carlos 'n Charlie's
8 Las Varitas
10 Biblioteca de la Historia de las Californias
11 Sematur Ferry Office
12 Museo Regional de Antropología e Historia
14 Antigua California

15 Baja Diving & Service
18 Servicios Turísticos; Internet Café
21 Autotransportes de La Paz
23 Aero California
24 Baja Expeditions
29 Immigration Office
31 Hospital Salvatierra
32 Palacio de Gobierno
34 Santuario de la Virgen de Guadalupe
35 Museo Comunitario de la Ballena
36 Unidad Cultural Profesor Jesús Castro Agúndez; Teatro de la Ciudad
37 Central Camionera (Main Bus Terminal)

1862. At the periphery of the grounds at Navarro and Altamirano is the **Museo Comunitario de la Ballena** (*Community Whale Museum; admission free; open 10am-1pm Tues-Sun*).

A few blocks west, the **Santuario de la Virgen de Guadalupe** (*5 de Febrero*) is La Paz's biggest religious monument.

Activities

You can rent diving and snorkeling equipment and arrange day trips at **Baja Diving & Service** (☎ 122-18-26, *Paseo Obregón 1665, Local 2*); **Baja Expeditions** (☎ 125-38-28, **w** *www.bajaex.com, Bravo & Obregón*); or several other agencies.

Jack Velez Sportfishing Charters (☎ 122-27-44, *Paseo Obregón 498*) has a desk in the lobby of Hotel Los Arcos, near Allende. Other major hotels and travel agencies can also arrange trips.

Special Events

La Paz's pre-Lent Carnaval is among the country's best. In early May, *paceños* celebrate the Fundación de la Ciudad (Hernán Cortés' 1535 landing). June 1 is Día de la Marina (Navy Day). Late November witnesses the Festival de Artes (Arts Festival).

Places to Stay

Budget & Mid-Range *El Cardón Trailer Park* (☎ 124-00-78, *Km 4 on Transpeninsular*) Tent sites US$8, RV sites from US$14. Southwest of downtown, this well-organized park offers full hookups, electricity and small *palapas* (thatched-roof shelters).

RV Park Casa Blanca (☎/fax 124-00-09, *Km 4.5 on Transpeninsular*) Tent/RV sites US$12/15. Just beyond El Cardón, this shady, secure and well-maintained park has a pool, a restaurant and full hookups.

Pensión California (☎ 122-28-96, fax 123-35-25, **e** *pensioncalifornia@prodigy.net.mx, Degollado 209*) Singles/doubles US$13/18. The Pensión California is shaded by tropical plants and its walls are lined with quirky art. The rooms are basic and slightly dark and dingy, but come with ceiling fans and showers.

Hostería del Convento (☎ 122-35-08, fax 123-35-25, **e** *pensioncalifornia@prodigy.net .mx, Madero 85*) Singles/doubles US$12/17. Run by the same family as the Pensión California, this clean hotel offers 30 simple rooms.

Hotel Lorimar (☎ 125-38-22, *Bravo 110*) Singles/doubles with bath & air-con US$22/30. This hotel, with an attractive patio, is a popular choice. Its rooms come with tiled showers and hot water and have a comfortable, homey feel.

Top End *El Moro Hotel* (☎ 122-40-84, fax 125-28-28, **e** *elmoro@prodigy.net.mx, Paseo Obregón*) Doubles US$50, suites US$75. Located on the road to Pichilingue, this is one of the nicest places to stay in La Paz, with suites offering spacious bedrooms, living rooms and kitchens, set around lush gardens and pools.

Hotel Mediterrané (☎/fax 125-11-95, **w** *www.hotelmed.com, Allende 36B*) Rooms US$60-80. The prices here include free use of the kayaks; bikes are also available for rent. The owners of this friendly hotel are fluent in French, Italian and English.

Hotel Perla (☎ 122-07-77, fax 125-53-63, **e** *perla@lapaz.cromwell, Paseo Obregón 1570*) Rooms US$78. This historic hotel has a swimming pool, restaurant, bar and nightclub – but the rooms are on the small side. All rooms have air-con, TV and private bath.

Hotel Los Arcos (☎ 122-27-44, fax 125-43-13, **w** *www.losarcos.com, Paseo Obregón 498 near Allende*) Rooms US$90. Ask for a bay view at this hotel. It has two swimming pools, a sauna, a restaurant and a coffee shop. Rooms come with air-con, telephone, color TV and shower.

Hotel Cabañas de los Arcos (☎ 122-27-44, fax 125-43-13, **w** *www.losarcos.com, Rosales & Mutualismo*) Rooms US$65, cabañas US$85. Rooms set around a lush garden have fireplaces, thatched roofs, tiled floors, TV, air-con and minibars. If you feel like splurging, this is the way to go.

Places to Eat

Super Tacos Baja California (*Arreola & Mutualismo*) Tacos US$1-2. The fish and shrimp tacos here are a treat, and there's an amazing assortment of condiments.

El Quinto Sol (☎ 122-16-92, *Independencia & Domínguez*) Breakfast US$3-4. This place has tasty vegetarian meals and large breakfast servings of yogurt (plain, with fruit or with muesli). *Licuados*, fresh breads and pastries are other specialties.

Le Bistrot Francais (☎ 125-60-80, **e** *bistrot@prodiby.net.mx, Esquerro 10*)

Breakfast US$3-4. The crêpes here are especially good, and the French owners are very friendly.

La Caleta (☎ 112-02-87, on the malecón at Pineda) Mains US$6-12, margaritas US$5. This popular restaurant serves reasonably priced meals and is an ideal spot to drink a margarita on a deck overlooking the bay.

La Pazta Restaurant (☎ 125-11-95, Allende 36B) Dinner US$8-12. Located in the Hotel Mediterrané, La Pazta has moderately priced Italian specials.

Bismark II (☎ 122-48-54, Degollado & Altamirano) Antojitos US$7, lobster US$28. The Bismark II offers generous seafood platters.

La Costa (☎ 122-88-08, Topete & Navarro) Mains US$10, lobster US$22. La Costa offers some of the best seafood in Baja: it's the place to go for lobster.

Entertainment

Las Varitas (☎ 125-20-25, W www.lasvaritas .com, Independencia 111) Admission US$4. Open 9pm-3am. Located near Domínguez, Las Varitas has live music and dancing.

Carlos 'n Charlie's (☎ 122-92-90, Paseo Obregón & 16 de Septiembre) Admission US$4. This is another popular nightspot – lines are always long.

Keep in mind that women walking alone at night are bound to get heckled – cabs are sometimes the best way to get from hotel to bar.

Shopping

Antigua California (☎ 125-52-30, Paseo Obregón 220) This place features a wide selection of crafts from throughout the country.

Getting There & Away

Air Aeroméxico (☎ 122-00-91), on Paseo Obregón between Hidalgo and Morelos, has flights every day but Sunday between La Paz and Los Angeles, Tijuana, Tucson and mainland Mexican cities. Its subsidiary Aerolitoral, at the same address and phone number, flies daily to Loreto.

Aero California (☎ 125-10-23) has offices at the airport and at Paseo Obregón 550, near the corner of Bravo; it operates daily nonstops between La Paz and Los Angeles, one daily nonstop to Tijuana, and daily flights to Tucson via Hermosillo. Aero

California also flies to mainland Mexican destinations, including Los Mochis (for the Copper Canyon Railway), Mazatlán and Mexico City.

Bus ABC (☎ 122-30-63) and Autotransportes Águila (☎ 122-42-70) use the Central Camionera (main bus terminal) at Jalisco and Héroes de la Independencia. Northbound ABC buses go to Ciudad Constitución at 11am (2 hours, US$11), Loreto at 1.30pm and 6pm (5 hours, US$20), Mulegé at 9am and noon (6 hours, US$28), San Ignacio at 9am and noon (9 hours, US$38), Guerrero Negro at 9pm (11 hours, US$50), Ensenada at 8pm (18 hours, US$85) and Tijuana at 8pm (22 hours, US$89).

Frequent southbound ABC buses serve San José del Cabo (3 hours, US$11) and intermediate points via the Transpeninsular. Autotransportes Águila takes highway 19 to Todos Santos (US$5.50) and Cabo San Lucas (US$11) at least five times daily.

Buses by Autotransportes de La Paz (☎ 122-7-51) leave from Prieto and Degollado for Todos Santos (1 hour, US$5), Cabo San Lucas (2 hours, US$9.50) and San José del Cabo (3 hours, US$10) eight times daily, from 6.45am to 7.45pm.

Car Rental rates start around US$55 per day with 300km free; taxes and insurance are extra. Local (☎ 122-51-40) is on Paseo Obregón between Morelos and Hidalgo. There are a number of other agencies along Paseo Obregón.

Boat Ferries to Mazatlán and Topolobampo leave from Pichilingue, 23km north of La Paz, but the Sematur office (☎ 125-23-46, W www.ferrysematur.com.mx) is at Prieto and 5 de Mayo in La Paz. There is an on-site tourist agency that can help you with travel arrangements.

Before shipping any vehicle to the mainland, officials require a vehicle permit (see the Car & Motorcycle section of the Getting There & Away chapter for more information). Vehicle permits are obtainable at the Pichilingue ferry terminal 8am to 3pm Monday to Friday, 9am to 1pm Saturday and Sunday, but it's probably safer to get one in Tijuana, Mexicali or Ensenada. Confirm tickets by 2pm the day before departure; at 3pm that day, unconfirmed

BAJA CALIFORNIA

cabins are sold on a first-come, first-served basis.

Weather permitting (high winds often delay winter sailings), the ferry to Mazatlán departs at 3pm daily, arriving at 9am the following day; the return schedule is identical. Occasionally, the ferry carries cargo only and doesn't take passengers. Approximate passenger fares are US$51 in *salón* (numbered seats), US$115 in *turista* (two- to four-bunk cabins with shared bath), US$141 in *cabina* (two bunks with private bath), and US$167 in *especial* (suite).

The Topolobampo ferry sails at 9pm Wednesday and Friday, arriving at 10am the next day, and also at 11am Sunday, arriving at 7pm; the return ferries leave at 10pm Tuesday and Saturday, arriving at 8am. Passenger fares are US$40 in *salón,* US$90 in *turista,* US$115 in *cabina,* US$131 in *especial.* Vehicle rates vary with vehicle length:

vehicle	length	Mazatlán	Topolobampo
car	up to 5m	US$394	US$244
	5.01 to 6.5m	US$511	US$314
car & trailer	up to 9m	US$716	US$432
	9.01 to 17m	US$1328	US$811
motorcycle		US$94	US$80

Between November and March, the Marina de La Paz, southwest of central La Paz, can be a good place to hitch a lift on a yacht to mainland Mexico.

Getting Around
The government-regulated Transporte Terrestre minivan service (☎ 125-11-56) charges US$14 per person to or from the airport. Private taxis cost approximately US$16.50, but they may be shared.

From the downtown bus terminal (☎ 122-78-98), at Paseo Obregón and Independencia, Autotransportes Águila goes to the Pichilingue ferry terminal (US$2) hourly between 7.30am and 7.30pm.

AROUND LA PAZ
Beaches
On Península Pichilingue, the beaches nearest to La Paz are **Playa Palmira** (with the Hotel Palmira and a marina), and **Playa Coromuel** and **Playa Caimancito** (both with restaurant-bars, toilets and palapas). **Playa Tesoro**, the next beach north, also has a restaurant.

Camping is possible at **Playa Pichilingue**, 100m north of the ferry terminal, and it has a restaurant and bar, toilets and shade. The road is paved to **Playa Balandra** and **Playa Tecolote** (where kayak and windsurfer rentals are available). Tecolote also has a restaurant. Balandra is problematic for camping because of insects in the mangroves, but it's one of the more beautiful beaches, with an enclosed cove. **Playa Coyote**, on the gulf, is more isolated. Particularly stealthy thieves break into campers' vehicles in all these areas, especially the more remote ones.

LOS BARRILES
• pop 590 ☎ 624

South of La Paz, the Transpeninsular brushes the gulf at Los Barriles, Baja's windsurfing capital. Brisk westerlies, averaging 20 to 25 knots, descend the 1800m cordillera. Keep in mind that from April to August the winds really die down, and windsurfing is pretty much impossible.

Several fairly good dirt roads follow the coast south. Beyond Cabo Pulmo and Bahía Los Frailes, they are rough but passable for vehicles with good clearance and a short wheelbase. However, south of the junction with the road going to the village of Palo Escopeta and Los Cabos international airport, the road is impassable for RVs and difficult for most other vehicles, rendered so by the rains of November 1993. Pedestrians, mountain bikers, burros and mules will do just fine.

Places to Stay & Eat
Martín Verdugo's Beach Resort (☎ 141-00-54, e mverdugo@bajaquest.com, 20 de Noviembre) Tent/RV sites US$11/13, rooms US$46-56. This crowded beach resort offers hot showers, full hookups, laundry and a sizable paperback book exchange. There is camping available as well as a range of rooms, some with kitchenettes.

Hotel Los Barriles (☎ 141-00-24, e hotel losbarriles@cabonet.net.mx) Singles/doubles US$45/55. This place offers clean, comfortable rooms.

Tío Pablo has a good pizza menu and massive portions of Mexican specialties like chicken fajitas. Despite the raucous decor and satellite TV, it's fairly sedate.

RESERVA DE LA BIÓSFERA SIERRA DE LA LAGUNA

Even travelers who deplore the ugly coastal development around Los Cabos will enjoy the Sierra de la Laguna, an ecological treasure between La Paz and Los Cabos. Several foothill villages provide access to these unique interior mountains.

Tranquil **Santiago**, 10km south of the junction for La Rivera and 2.5km west of the Transpeninsular, once witnessed a bloody Pericú indigenous revolt against the Jesuits.

Cañón San Dionisio, about 25km west of Santiago, is the northernmost of three major east-west walking routes across the sierra; the others are **Cañón San Bernardo**, west of Miraflores, and **Cañón San Pedro**, west of Caduaño, which is about 10km south of Santiago. San Dionisio offers scenic hiking in an ecologically unique area where cacti, palms, oaks, aspens and pines grow side by side. The trail requires scrambling over large granite boulders; if rainfall has been sufficient, there are pools suitable for swimming.

The best guide for hiking these routes is Walt Peterson's *Baja Adventure Book*.

Hotel Palomar (☎ 122-21-90, Santiago) Tent sites US$5, rooms US$20. This modest hotel has basic rooms amid pleasant grounds. There is a bar and restaurant as well, but the seafood is a little pricey.

SAN JOSÉ DEL CABO
• pop 21,700 ☎ 624
San José del Cabo is still a quaint town of narrow streets, Spanish-style buildings and shady plazas, despite its growth as a major tourist resort. Grandiose plans for a yacht marina at the outlet of the ecologically sensitive Arroyo San José fizzled because of local opposition, and, having maintained its open space, San José remains one of the most pleasant destinations in Baja.

Orientation
San José del Cabo consists of San José proper, about 1.5km inland, and a *zona hotelera* of tacky beachfront hotels, condos and time-shares. Linking the two areas, just south of shady Plaza Mijares, Boulevard Mijares is a *gringolandia* of restaurants and souvenir shops.

Information
As of October 2001, the Plaza Mijares was undergoing a total reconstruction, and the building that housed the tourist office had been torn down. The tourist office will probably be reopened once the project has been completed.

The casa de cambio at Aeropuerto Internacional Los Cabos offers very poor rates, so avoid changing money until you get to town, where several casas de cambio keep long hours. Banks pay better rates but keep shorter hours. Bancomer, at the corner of Zaragoza and Morelos, and Banca Serfin, at Zaragoza and Degollado, both cash traveler's checks and have ATMs.

The post office is on Boulevard Mijares, north of González Conseco. Pay phones are numerous throughout the town.

The Internet café WebLand (☎ 142-52-82), at Boulevard Mijares 29, charges US$3 per half hour.

Libros Libros Books Books (☎ 142-44-33), at Boulevard Mijares 41, stocks books in English and Spanish.

Things to See & Do
The colonial-style **Iglesia San José** faces the shady Plaza Mijares.

Between raids on Spanish galleons, 18th-century pirates took refuge at the freshwater **Arroyo San José**, now a protected wildlife area replenished by a subterranean spring. Among the common bird species to be found are coots, pelicans, herons, egrets and plovers.

The beaches at the south end of Boulevard Mijares (known as Playa de California) have a dangerous current so are not good for swimming. The best beaches for swimming are along the road to Cabo San Lucas. **Playa Santa Maria** at Km 13 is one of the nicest beaches in Los Cabos.

The Fiesta de San José, on March 19, celebrates the town's patron saint.

Fishing & Surfing
Victor's Sportfishing (☎ 142-10-92, in the Hotel Posada Real) arranges fishing excursions and sells and rents tackle. Fisherfolk at **Pueblo La Playa**, a small fishing community about 2.5km east of the junction of Juárez and Boulevard Mijares, arrange similar trips; ask them in the late afternoon as they cut up the day's catch on the beach.

BAJA CALIFORNIA

SAN JOSÉ DEL CABO

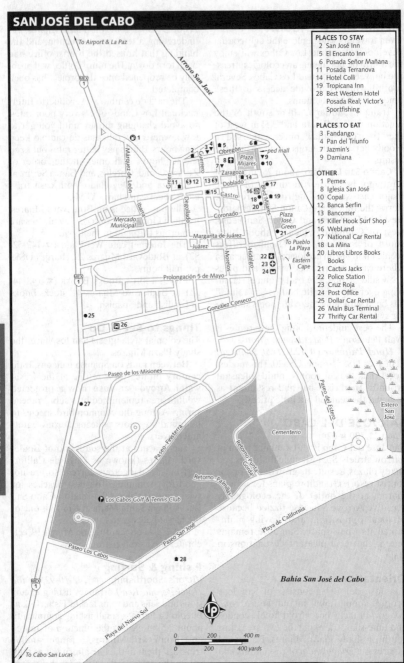

PLACES TO STAY
2 San José Inn
5 El Encanto Inn
6 Posada Señor Mañana
11 Posada Terranova
14 Hotel Colli
19 Tropicana Inn
28 Best Western Hotel
   Posada Real; Victor's
   Sportfishing

PLACES TO EAT
3 Fandango
4 Pan del Triunfo
7 Jazmin's
9 Damiana

OTHER
1 Pemex
8 Iglesia San José
10 Copal
12 Banca Serfin
13 Bancomer
15 Killer Hook Surf Shop
16 WebLand
17 National Car Rental
18 La Mina
20 Libros Libros Books
   Books
21 Cactus Jacks
22 Police Station
23 Cruz Roja
24 Post Office
25 Dollar Car Rental
26 Main Bus Terminal
27 Thrifty Car Rental

BAJA CALIFORNIA

The best source of surfing information is **Killer Hook Surf Shop** (☎ 142-24-30, *Guerrero & Doblado*).

Places to Stay

Budget & Mid-Range Free *camping* is possible at Pueblo La Playa, east of the center.

San José Inn (☎/fax 142-24-64, *Obregón & Guerrero*) Singles/doubles with bath US$13/22. Though urgently in need of a plasterer and painter, the friendly San José, between Degollado and Guerrero, has spacious rooms with ceiling fans and hot water.

Hotel Colli (☎/fax 142-07-25, *Hidalgo*) Rooms US$39. The rooms are small but clean.

Posada Señor Mañana (☎ 142-04-62, *Obregón 1*) Rooms US$33-44. This woodsy, casual hotel, just north of Plaza Mijares, has a small pool and access to a shared kitchen.

Posada Terranova (☎ 142-05-34, fax 142-09-02, ℮ terranova@1cabonet.com.mx, De-gollado & Doblado*) Rooms US$55. This inviting hotel also has a good restaurant.

Top End *Tropicana Inn* (☎ 142-23-11, fax 142-15-90, ⩊ http://tropicanacabo.com, *Boulevard Mijares 30*) Rooms in June/Dec US$69/89. Probably the best hotel in San José proper, the inconspicuous Tropicana has doubles with satellite TV, a patio and pool. Prices vary with the season.

El Encanto Inn (☎ 142-03-88, fax 142-46-20, ⩊ www.elencantoinn.com, *Morelos 133*) Rooms US$65-75. One of the nicest places in town is this charming inn, with a beautifully landscaped garden and thoughtfully decorated rooms.

Best Western Hotel Posada Real (☎ 142-01-55, fax 142-04-60, ℮ pr2cabos@prodigy.net.mx, *Paseo San José*) Rooms from US$99. Ocean-view rooms are in a three-floor structure wrapped around a beautiful cactus garden.

Places to Eat

The very clean *Mercado Municipal* (*Ibarra between Coronado & Castro*) has numerous stalls offering simple and inexpensive but good and filling meals.

Pan del Triunfo (☎ 142-57-20, *Morelos & Obregón*) This place has delicious pastries for around US$0.50 each.

Jazmín's (☎ 142-17-60, *Morelos & Zaragoza*) Breakfast US$4, dinner US$10-12. Jazmín's offers a wide variety of tasty breakfasts, plus lunches and dinners at mid-range prices, with excellent but unobtrusive service and, incongruously, a paperback book exchange.

Damiana (☎ 142-04-99, *Plaza Mijares 8*) Standard meal US$15. This romantic seafood restaurant is in a restored 18th-century house.

Fandango (☎ 142-22-26, *Obregón 19*) Mains US$15. This place offers Pacific Rim cuisine in a relaxed setting.

Entertainment

Noisy nightlife doesn't dominate San José the way it does Cabo San Lucas. *Cactus Jacks* (☎ 142-56-01, *Boulevard Mijares & Juárez*) hosts the occasional live band.

Shopping

Copal (☎ 142-30-70, *Plaza Mijares 10*) Located on the east side of Plaza Mijares, Copal has an interesting assortment of crafts, especially masks.

La Mina (☎ 142-37-47, *Boulevard Mijares 33-C*) This shop sells gold and silver jewelry in an imaginative setting.

Getting There & Away

Air All airlines have their offices at Los Cabos airport, which serves both San José and Cabo San Lucas.

Mexicana (☎ 142-65-02) flies daily to Los Angeles and Mexico City, less frequently to Denver, Colorado.

Alaska Airlines (☎ 142-10-15) flies to/from Los Angeles, Phoenix, San Diego, San Francisco and San Jose, California (USA).

Aero California (☎ 146-52-52, fax 146-52-22) flies daily to/from Denver, Los Angeles and Phoenix.

Continental Airlines (☎ 142-38-40, 800-900-5000 in the USA) flies between Houston and Los Cabos.

Aeroméxico (☎ 142-03-41) flies daily to/from San Diego and many mainland Mexican destinations, with international connections via Mexico City.

Bus & Car Frequent buses leave for Cabo San Lucas (30 minutes, US$2) and La Paz (3 hours, US$11) from the main bus terminal (☎ 142-11-00), on González Conseco, east of the Transpeninsular.

Offering car rental, Dollar (☎ 142-01-00, 142-50-60 at the airport) is on the Transpeninsular just north of the intersection with González Conseco, and Thrifty (☎ 146-50-30) is a block south on the Transpeninsular.

Getting Around

The official, government-run company Aeroterrestre (☎ 142-05-55) runs bright yellow taxis and minibuses to Aeropuerto Internacional Los Cabos, 10km north of San José, for about US$12. Local buses from the terminal on González Conseco to the airport junction cost less than US$2, but taking one means a half-hour walk to the air terminal. A taxi to the airport will cost around US$9.

LOS CABOS CORRIDOR

West of San José, all the way to Cabo San Lucas, a string of luxury resorts lines the once-scenic coastline. Along this stretch of the Transpeninsular, commonly referred to as 'the Corridor,' there are choice **surfing beaches** at Km 27, at Punta Mirador near Hotel Palmilla, and at Km 28. The reefs off Playa Chileno are excellent for diving, and experienced surfers claim that summer reef and point breaks at Km 28 (popularly known as Zipper's) match Hawaii's best.

CABO SAN LUCAS

• pop 28,500 ☎ 624

Cabo San Lucas has become a mecca for both the fishing and golfing crowd and for younger Americans who treat Cabo as the quintessential party town, ideal for a weekend getaway or bachelor party. On many levels the town seems to have the feel of an endless playground. It has an amazing array of activities to offer, from beautiful beaches and water sports such as diving and kayaking to an endless string of bars and nightclubs that provide a continuous party.

Many residents seem a bit perplexed by the explosion of development in the last decade, and partially resent the time-share sellers who have metamorphosed a placid fishing village into a jumble of exorbitantly priced hotels and rowdy bars. But overall, Cabo has the feel of a place that will provide a good time, in a very laid-back atmosphere.

Orientation

Northwest of Cárdenas, central Cabo has a fairly regular grid, while southeast of Cárdenas, Boulevard Marina curves along the Harbor Cabo San Lucas toward Land's End (or 'Finisterra'), the tip of the peninsula where the Pacific Ocean and the Sea of Cortez meet. Few places have street addresses, so you will need to refer to the map to locate them.

Information

There's an immigration office (☎ 143-01-35) at Cárdenas and Gómez Farías northeast of downtown; it's open 9am to 2pm.

Several downtown banks cash traveler's checks and have ATMs, including Banca Serfin, at Cárdenas and Zaragoza.

The post office is on the east side of Cárdenas, near 16 de Noviembre, north of downtown. Long-distance cabinas have sprung up in many shops and pharmacies, and pay phones are abundant.

You'll find Internet service at Café Cabo Mail (☎ 143-77-97), in the Plaza Arámburo at the corner of Cárdenas and Zaragoza.

You'll encounter aggressive time-share sellers on Boulevard Marina; they distribute town maps and happily provide information (along with their sales pitch). Pedestrians should also be wary of the traffic: drivers seem to speed along with no regard for pedestrians.

Things to See & Do

The **Casa de Cultura** houses a theater, and has a small park and a *mirador*. Built into the one hill in downtown Cabo, the mirador is surrounded by landscaped gardens and offers a view of all of Cabo. It is a peaceful retreat from the craziness of Cabo. The entrance is on Niños Héroes.

For sunbathing and calm waters **Playa Médano**, in front of the Hacienda Beach Resort, on the Bahía de Cabo San Lucas, is ideal. **Playa Solmar**, on the Pacific, has a reputation for unpredictable, dangerous breakers. Nearly unspoiled **Playa del Amor**, near Land's End, is accessible by boat.

Diving

Among the best diving areas are Roca Pelícano, the sea lion colony off Land's End, and the reef off Playa Chileno, at Bahía Chileno east of town.

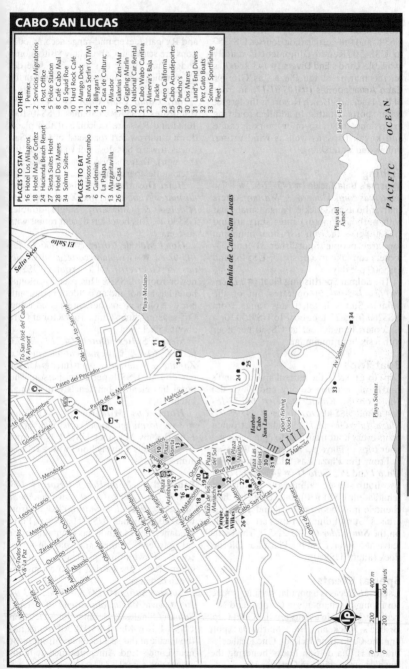

CABO SAN LUCAS

PLACES TO STAY
16 Hotel Los Milagros
18 Hotel Mar de Cortez
24 Hacienda Beach Resort
27 Siesta Suites Hotel
28 Hotel Dos Mares
34 Solmar Suites

PLACES TO EAT
3 Mariscos Mocambo
6 Gardenias
7 La Palapa
13 Margaritaville
26 Mi Casa

OTHER
1 Pemex
2 Servicios Migratorios
4 Post Office
5 Police Station
8 Café Cabo Mall
9 El Squid Roe
10 Hard Rock Café
11 Mango Deck
12 Banca Serfin (ATM)
14 Billygan's
15 Casa de Cultura;
   Mirador
17 Galerías Zen–Mar
19 Giggling Marlin
20 National Car Rental
21 Cabo Wabo Cantina
22 Minerva's Baja
   Tackle
23 Aero California
25 Cabo Acuadeportes
29 Pancho's
30 Dos Mares
31 Land's End Divers
32 Pez Gato Boats
33 Solmar Sportfishing
   Fleet

BAJA CALIFORNIA

At most shops, two-tank dives cost around US$70, introductory courses around US$90 and full-certification courses US$350 to US$450. Rental equipment is readily available. **Land's End Divers** (☎ 143-22-00) is on the marina at the Plaza Las Glorias. **Cabo Acuadeportes** (☎ 143-01-17), in front of the Hacienda Beach Resort, is the largest water-sports outfitter. In addition to diving excursions, they also offer snorkel, canoe and kayak trips, as well as windsurfing, sailing and waterskiing.

Fishing

Minerva's Baja Tackle (☎ 143-12-82, W *www .minervas.com, Madero & Marina*) offers charter boats and tackle. Panga (small boat with outboard motor) rates start around US$30 per hour, with a six-hour minimum for three people; Sportfisher 31- and 33-footers can take five or six for US$465 and US$500 per day.

The **Solmar Sportfishing Fleet** (☎ 143-06-46, fax 143-04-10) operates out of the Solmar Suites hotel. Rates range from US$260 for a 26-foot boat to US$650 for a 42-footer; Pangas rent at US$30 per hour with a six-hour minimum.

Boat Trips

Trips to El Arco (the natural arch at Land's End), the sea lion colony and Playa del Amor on the **Kaleidoscope** (☎ 148-73-18) cost about US$40. **Dos Mares** (☎ 143-89-71, *Plaza Las Glorias*) sails glass-bottomed boats every hour from 9am to 3pm for three-hour trips to Playa del Amor (US$10).

From the Plaza Las Glorias dock, **Pez Gato I** and **Pez Gato II** (☎ 143-37-97) offer two-hour sunset sailings on catamarans (child/adult US$15/30), and segregate their clientele into 'booze cruises' and 'romantic cruises.' Sunset dinner cruises are available on the **Sun Rider** (☎ 143-22-52). The boats leave at 5.30pm from the Plaza Las Glorias dock (adults US$40).

Special Events

Cabo San Lucas is a popular staging ground for fishing tournaments in October and November. The main events are the Gold Cup, Bisbee's Black and Blue Marlin Jackpot, and the Cabo Tuna Jackpot. One local celebration is Día de San Lucas, honoring the town's patron saint, on October 18.

Places to Stay

Budget & Mid-Range Except for camping and RV parks, even mid-range accommodations are scarce in Cabo. Many visitors on a budget may prefer to stay in San José del Cabo, which is cheaper and close enough for day trips.

Surf Camp Club Cabo (☎ 143-33-48) Campsites US$7.50, cabañas US$40-100. Tents and RVs are welcome at this place, down a narrow dirt road east of Cabo San Lucas, toward San José del Cabo (look for the sign). There is also a cabaña and two kitchenette apartments.

Hotel Dos Mares (☎ 143-03-30, e *hotel dosmares@cabonet.net.mx, Zapata between Hidalgo & Guerrero*) Singles/doubles US$36/47. This hotel has decent rooms with air-con.

Hotel Mar de Cortez (☎ 143-00-32, fax 143-02-32, W *www.mardecortez.com, Cárdenas & Guerrero*) Older rooms US$46, newer rooms US$56. This pseudo-colonial hotel has a pool and an outdoor restaurant-bar. The older rooms here are a good value. Off-season rates (June to October) are about 15% lower.

Siesta Suites Hotel (☎ 143-27-73, fax 143-64-94, e *siesta@cabonet.net.mx, Zapata & Guerrero*) Apartments US$50 per double, US$10 per extra person. This hotel has clean rooms each with a small kitchen.

Hotel Los Milagros (☎ 143-45-66, W *www.losmilagroshotel.com, Matamoros 116*) Rooms May-Oct US$50, Nov-April US$72. This is a lovely hotel with a relaxed atmosphere.

Top End Hacienda Beach Resort (☎ 143-06-63, fax 143-06-66, W *www.hacienda cabo.com, Paseo de la Marina*) Rooms from US$140, cabañas US$250. Near Playa Médano, the Hacienda has fountains, tropical gardens, tennis and paddle-tennis courts, a swimming pool and a putting green. There are garden patio rooms and beach cabañas.

Solmar Suites (☎ 143-35-35, fax 143-04-10, W *www.solmar.com, at end of Avenida Solmar*) Singles & doubles June-Oct from US$164, Nov-May US$180. All rooms face the Pacific at this secluded beachfront resort near Land's End. Amenities include tennis courts and a pool.

Places to Eat

Gardenias (☎ *143-24-65, Paseo de la Marina*) Tacos US$1. Open for lunch only. Consistently delicious tacos (fish, beef, pork, shrimp) are served here.

Mariscos Mocambo (☎ *143-21-22, Vicario & 20 de Noviembre*) Mains US$15. The impressive seafood platter is the ideal way to sample the various dishes at this lively restaurant.

La Palapa (*143-08-88, Zaragoza & Niños Héroes*) Mains US$12. This popular restaurant serves good seafood.

Margaritaville (☎ *143-00-10, Plaza Bonita, Boulevard Marina*) Dinner US$10-15, margaritas US$7.50. This lively restaurant serves gigantic margaritas to go along with great seafood.

Mi Casa (☎ *143-19-33, Cabo San Lucas*) Dinner US$21-31. The upscale Mi Casa, across from Parque Amelia Wilkes, has a pleasant environment and excellent seafood.

Entertainment

One of the quintessential activities for the young Cabo tourist is drinking a margarita on the beach. Two popular destinations for beach party-goers and people-watchers are *Mango Deck* (☎ *143-09-01*) and *Billygan's* (☎ *143-04-02*), both at Playa Médano. Both offer two-for-one margaritas for around US$6. Another seemingly required stop on the Cabo drinking tour is the *Giggling Marlin* (☎ *143-11-82, Matamoros & Boulevard Marina*), in the center.

Cabo Wabo Cantina (☎ *143-11-88, Guerrero & Madero*) Gold records and rock photos line the walls at this spot, which features live music from late at night to early in the morning.

Pancho's (☎ *143-09-73, Hidalgo & Marina*) Barhoppers will reportedly find Mexico's largest selection of tequilas at this place.

The *Hard Rock Café* (☎ *143-37-79, Cárdenas & Boulevard Marina*) is a popular nightspot. It's not as rowdy as some of the other bars.

For a late-night dance club, try *El Squid Roe* (☎ *143-12-69, cnr Cárdenas & Zaragoza*), which stays open till 4am. Friday and Saturday there's a two-drink minimum.

Shopping

Cabo's most comprehensive shopping area is the sprawling *Mercado Mexicano*, at Madero and Hidalgo, containing dozens of stalls with crafts from all around the country.

Galerías Zen-Mar (☎ *143-06-61, Cárdenas between Matamoros & Ocampo*) This shop offers Zapotec weavings, bracelets and masks, as well as traditional crafts from other mainland indigenous peoples.

Getting There & Away

The closest airport is Los Cabos, north of San José del Cabo; for flight information, see the San José del Cabo Getting There & Away section, earlier. Aero California's main office (☎ 143-37-00, fax 143-39-27) is in the Plaza Náutica mall, on Boulevard Marina near Madero.

From the main bus terminal (☎ 143-78-80), at Zaragoza and 16 de Septiembre, buses leave for San José del Cabo (30 minutes, US$2) and La Paz (express 2 hours, US$12; regular 3½ hours, US$11). Autotransportes de La Paz has a separate terminal at the junction of highway 19 and the Cabo bypass, north of downtown, as does Enlaces Terrestres. These buses go to La Paz only.

Numerous rental agencies have booths along Boulevard Marina and elsewhere in town. National (☎ 143-14-14), at Boulevard Marina and Matamoros, offers rentals for around US$60.

Getting Around

The government-regulated airport minibus (☎ 146-53-54), costing US$13 per person, leaves Plaza Las Glorias at 10am, noon, 2.30pm and 4.30pm. For US$45, shared taxis (☎ 143-01-04) are another option.

Cabs are plentiful but not cheap; fares within town average about US$3 to US$5.

TODOS SANTOS

• pop 3770 ☎ 612

Founded in 1723 but nearly destroyed by the Pericú rebellion in 1734, Misión Santa Rosa de Todos los Santos limped along until its abandonment in 1840. In the late 19th century Todos Santos became a prosperous sugar town with several brick *trapiches* (mills), but depleted aquifers have nearly eliminated this thirsty industry. In the last 10 years, Todos Santos has seen a North American invasion, including artists from Santa Fe and Taos, New Mexico, and organic farmers whose produce gets premium prices north of the border.

Orientation & Information

Todos Santos has a regular grid, but residents rely more on landmarks than street names for directions. The plaza is surrounded by Márquez de León, Legaspi, Avenida Hidalgo and Centenario.

Todos Santos' de facto tourist office is El Tecolote (☎ 145-02-95), at the corner of Juárez and Avenida Hidalgo among a cluster of shops. This English-language bookstore distributes a very detailed town map and a sketch map of nearby beach areas.

You can change cash Monday through Friday mornings at BanCrecer, at the corner of Juárez and Obregón, which has an ATM.

The post office is on Heroico Colegio Militar between Hidalgo and Márquez de León. The Message Center (☎ 145-00-33, fax 145-02-88), adjacent to El Tecolote at Juárez and Hidalgo, provides phone, fax and Internet services. It's open 8am to 3pm Monday to Friday, 8am to 2pm Saturday. Use of the computers costs US$2 per half hour.

Things to See & Do

Scattered around town are several former trapiches, including **Molino El Progreso**, at what was formerly El Molino restaurant, and **Molino de los Santana**, on Juárez opposite the hospital. The restored **Teatro Cine General Manuel Márquez de León** is on Legaspi, facing the plaza.

Nationalist and revolutionary murals at the **Centro Cultural Todosanteño**, a former schoolhouse on Juárez near Topete, date from 1933. The subjects range from indigenous people, Spanish conquistadors and Emiliano Zapata to athletics and 'emancipation of the rural spirit.'

Special Events

Todos Santos' two-day Festival de Artes (Arts Festival) is held in late January. At other times it's possible to visit local artists in their home studios.

Places to Stay

Motel Guluarte (☎ 145-00-06, Juárez & Morelos) Singles/doubles US$19/28. The rooms are small but clean, and there's a swimming pool.

Hostería Las Casitas (☎ 145-02-55, W www.mexonline.com/laspalmas, Rangel between Obregón & Hidalgo) Doubles US$45-65 including breakfast. This Canadian-run B&B has a superb breakfast and also offers inexpensive tent sites.

The Todos Santos Inn (☎/fax 145-00-40, e todossantosinn@yahoo.com, Legaspi 33) Rooms US$90-130. This B&B, in a converted 19th-century building, provides the most genteel accommodations in town.

Places to Eat

Taco stands, along Heroico Colegio Militar between Márquez de León and Degollado, offer fish, chicken, shrimp or beef at bargain prices.

Caffé Todos Santos (☎ 145-03-00, Centenario 33) Breakfast US$4-7. The coffee-conscious can consume cappuccinos with savory pastries or enticing fruit salads here, between Topete and Obregón.

Las Fuentes (☎ 145-02-57, Degollado at Heroico Colegio Militar) Antojitos US$5-10, seafood US$15. This moderately priced restaurant, in a bougainvillea-shaded patio with three refreshing fountains, has delicious antojitos (try the chicken with *mole* sauce) and seafood specialties.

Café Santa Fe (☎ 145-03-40, Centenario 4) Mains US$15-25. The Santa Fe attracts patrons from La Paz and Cabo San Lucas to its plaza location for Italian dining. Prices are high here but it's worth the splurge.

Shopping

Galería de Todos Santos (☎ 145-05-00, Legaspi 33) This gallery features imaginative artwork by Mexican and North American artists.

Galería Santa Fe (☎ 145-03-40, Centenario 4), alongside its namesake restaurant on the south side of the plaza, is well worth a visit, as is the *Stewart Gallery* (☎ 145-02-65, Obregón between Legaspí & Centenario).

Getting There & Away

At least six buses daily go to La Paz (1½ hours, US$5.50) and to Cabo San Lucas (1½ hours, US$5.50) from the bus station at Heroico Colegio Militar and Zaragoza.

Northwest Mexico

This chapter covers the northwestern state of Sonora, as well as portions of Chihuahua and Sinaloa, including the spectacular Barranca del Cobre (Copper Canyon) in the Sierra Madre Occidental and the Ferrocarril Chihuahua al Pacífico, the railway that runs through it.

Not to be missed, Copper Canyon is actually a system of more than 20 canyons, nine of which are deeper than the Grand Canyon in Arizona. Many travelers begin their journey through the canyons at Los Mochis, which can be reached by a ferry from La Paz in Baja California.

Alternatively, travelers coming from the USA work their way south through Sonora, a large state known for its beef and agriculture (principally wheat and cotton). Much of the state is part of the great Desierto Sonorense (Sonoran Desert).

Highway 15, Mexico's principal Pacific coast highway, begins at the border town of Nogales, Sonora, opposite Nogales, Arizona, about 1½ hours south of Tucson. This is one of the most convenient border crossings between western Mexico and the USA. From Nogales, highway 15/15D heads south through the Desierto Sonorense for about four hours to Hermosillo and then cuts over to the coast at Guaymas, about 1½ hours south of Hermosillo. From Guaymas the highway parallels the beautiful Pacific coast for about a thousand kilometers, finally turning inland at Tepic (see the Central Pacific Coast chapter) and heading on to Guadalajara and Mexico City. There are regular toll booths along highway 15 (including two between Nogales and Hermosillo, each charging US$11 per car).

It can be dangerous to travel on Sinaloense highways after dark. (For more information see the Dangers & Annoyances section of the Facts for the Visitor chapter.)

NOGALES
• pop 160,000 • elev 1170m ☎ 631

Like its border-city cousins Tijuana, Ciudad Juárez, Nuevo Laredo and Matamoros, Nogales is a major transit point for goods and people traveling between the USA and Mexico. On the northern side of the border

in Arizona, its smaller US counterpart is also named Nogales. (The name means 'walnuts,' which is a reference to the many walnut trees that once flourished in the general area.)

Nogales presents an easier introduction to Mexico than do the larger border cities. Nogales has everything they have – curio shops overflowing with Mexican handicrafts, trinkets and souvenirs, Mexican restaurants, cheap bars and plenty of liquor stores and pharmacies – but all on a much smaller scale.

Highlights

• Hermosillo's Centro Ecológico de Sonora – displaying the diversity of the Sonoran Desert's flora and fauna with cacti galore and more than 300 plant species

• Álamos – a tranquil town in the foothills of Sierra Madre, with well-restored colonial mansions, cobblestone streets, and Mexican jumping beans

• Barranca del Cobre (Copper Canyon) – a breathtaking network of more than 20 canyons covered with cool pine forests

• Ferrocarril Chihuahua al Pacífico (Copper Canyon Railway) – traveling through deep gorges and at dizzying heights on one of the world's most scenic train trips

• Batopilas – a tropical village deep in the heart of the canyon country

OTHER MAPS
Northwest Mexico page 346

Sea of Cortez

USA

Nogales page 347

Hermosillo page 351

Guaymas page 356

Creel page 377

Navojoa Bus Stations page 360

Barranca del Cobre page 371

Álamos page 361

Los Mochis page 366

PACIFIC OCEAN

NORTHWEST MEXICO

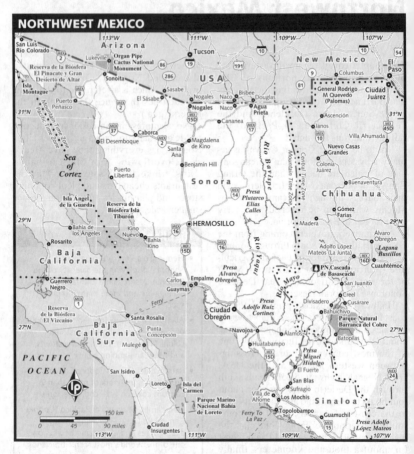

NORTHWEST MEXICO

On the Arizona side, the small **Pimería Alta Historical Society Museum** (☎ 520-287-4621, 136 N Grand Ave; admission free; open 10am-4pm Thur-Sat), one block from the border crossing at the intersection of Grand Ave and Crawford St, has interesting exhibits on the history of Nogales.

Orientation

The commercial section of Nogales is only a few blocks wide, being hemmed in on either side by hills. The main commercial street is Obregón, two blocks west of the border crossing, which eventually runs south into Mexico's highway 15. Almost everything you'll need is within walking distance of the border crossing.

Information

Immigration If you are heading farther south into Mexico, pick up a Mexican tourist permit at the immigration office in the large, modern white building at the border crossing, on the west side of the big white arches. The office is open 24 hours a day. No one will tell you to get this tourist permit, and if you're staying within 21km of the border you don't need it. If you're heading farther south, however, you must have it.

The tourist permit is also available at the vehicle checkpoint, 21km south of the border, and if you're driving, it is more convenient to get it there. Buses don't stop there, so if you're traveling by bus, be sure to pick up your permit at the immigration office. See the Facts for the Visitor chapter for more information on crossing the border between Mexico and the USA.

Tourist Offices The tourist office (☎ 312-06-66) occupies a tiny stone building beside the large white building on the west side of the big white arches at the border crossing. It is open 8.30am to 6pm daily.

Money There are plenty of *casas de cambio,* where you can change US dollars to pesos or vice versa, on both sides of the border crossing (no commission is charged). On the Mexican side, dollars and pesos are used interchangeably.

Bancomer on Campillo between Juárez and Obregón has an ATM. On the US side there's a Wells Fargo Bank with ATM at the corner of Grand Ave and Crawford St.

Post & Communications On the Mexican side, the post office is on the corner of Juárez and Campillo, and is open 9am to 3pm Monday to Friday. The Telecomm office, with telegram, telex and fax, is next door. Telephone *casetas* and pay phones for long-distance calls are everywhere in the small Nogales shopping district. On the US side, the post office is at 300 N Morley Ave, three blocks north of the border crossing.

Places to Stay

Hotel San Carlos (☎ 312-13-46, *Juárez 22*) Singles/doubles US$28/43. The San Carlos is very clean and has a helpful staff, parking, and rooms with air-con, TV and phone.

Hotel Regis (☎ 312-51-81, *Juárez 34*) Rooms US$36. Similar to the San Carlos in quality, the Regis is another good choice.

Hotel Granada (☎ 312-29-11, *cnr López Mateos & González*) Singles/doubles US$38/40. Seven blocks south of the border crossing, the Granada is further from the action and a bit more peaceful. Rooms have TV, phone and air-con.

Hotel Fray Marcos de Niza (☎ 312-16-51, *Campillo 91*) Singles/doubles US$45/50. This is the fancy hotel on the Mexican side. The rooms are well appointed if not elegant. The hotel has a restaurant and bar.

Sometimes when all the hotels on the Mexican side of Nogales are full, you can find rooms on the US side of the border.

NOGALES

PLACES TO STAY & EAT
6 Elvira's Restaurant
8 Hotel San Carlos; Hotel Regis
12 Cafeteria Leo's
13 Hotel Fray Marcos de Niza
15 El Cid Restaurant
16 El Greco Restaurant

OTHER
1 Wells Fargo
2 Pimería Alta Historical Society Museum
3 Greyhound & Crucero Bus Station
4 Unión Transportes de Nogales
5 US Border Crossing; Immigration
7 Bancomer
9 Post Office; Telecomm
10 Mexican Border Crossing; Immigration
11 Tourist Office
14 Local Buses to Long-Distance Bus Stations

Mi Casa RV Travel Park (☎ 520-281-1150, *2901 N Grand Ave*) RV sites US$16. Located 5km north of town at exit 8, this park offers spaces with weekly and monthly discounts.

Motel 6 (☎ 520-281-2951, *141 W Mariposa Rd*) Singles/doubles US$36/49. Predictable and inexpensive, Motel 6 has comfortable rooms with air-con and cable TV.

Best Western Siesta Motel (☎ 520-287-4671, *673 N Grand Ave*) Singles/doubles US$56/67. Price includes a continental breakfast. Rooms have cable TV, microwaves and refrigerators.

Places to Eat

Cafeteria Leo's (*cnr Obregón & Campillo*) Prices US$3-6. Bright, clean and cute, this is a good place for economical meals. The food is tasty and fast.

Parador Restaurant (*in Hotel Granada*) Prices US$3.50-9. Open 7am-midnight daily. This little restaurant has a good selection of Mexican-style breakfasts, beef dishes and *antojitos*.

Elvira's Restaurant (☎ 312-47-73, *Obregón 1*) Prices US$6-15. Just two blocks from the border crossing, at the corner of Internacional, Elvira's serves Mexican and international dishes in a cheerful setting.

El Greco Restaurant (☎ 312-43-58, *Obregón 152*) Prices US$7-29. For something fancier, this is an enjoyable spot with air-con, attractive décor and good food. Menu items range from chiles rellenos to lobster thermidor. Enter via the stairs at the rear of the shop on the corner of Pierson.

El Cid Restaurant (☎ 312-15-00, *Obregón 124*) Prices US$6-25. El Cid is similar to El Greco in menu and price, but not as elegant. But they have something El Greco doesn't – frogs' legs! Enter via the stairs at the rear of a shopping arcade.

Getting There & Away

Air The nearest airport is in Tucson, Arizona, about 100km (1½ hours) north of Nogales.

Bus

Mexico The main bus station is on highway 15, about 8km south of the city center. Elite, Transportes Norte de Sonora and TAP (Transportes y Autobuses del Pacífico) have 1st-class air-conditioned buses that head south along highway 15 to Guadalajara and on to Mexico City. Crucero buses travel across the border from here to the Greyhound station on the Arizona side and to Tucson, Phoenix and Los Angeles (USA).

Tufesa has its own station, two blocks north of the main bus station, and has hourly 1st-class buses 24 hours a day that go south as far as Culiacán. Next door, Transportes Baldomero Corral serves the major cities along highway 15, with a 1st-class bus departing every two hours, 10.30am to 12.30am; stops include Hermosillo (3½ hours, US$14) and Álamos (9 hours, US$32). They also have three daily buses to Phoenix (3½ hours, US$27).

Buses departing from the main bus station include:

Chihuahua – 962km, 12 hours; 5 daily (US$35-55)

Guadalajara – 1694km, 26 hours; 12 daily (US$71-82)

Guaymas – 416km, 5 hours; 16 daily (US$10-23)

Hermosillo – 277km, 3½ hours; every half hour (US$7.50-14.50)

Los Mochis – 765km, 10 hours; every half hour (US$24-40)

Mazatlán – 1194km, 16 hours; hourly buses (US$54-88)

Mexico City (Terminal Norte) – 2236km, 33 hours; 12 daily (US$105-154)

Tepic – 1480km, 24 hours; 12 daily (US$66-103)

The USA From Tucson's Greyhound station (2 S 4th Ave), the Golden State bus arrives at the Nogales, Arizona, Greyhound station (35 N Terrace Ave), a block from the border crossing. The 1-hour ride costs US$4. The Greyhound station in Nogales also has three daily direct buses to Phoenix (3½ hours, US$22) and Los Angeles (9 hours, US$50), and four to Hermosillo (3 hours, US$18) and Ciudad Obregón (6 hours, US$31).

Opposite the Greyhound station, Unión Transportes de Nogales, 42 N Terrace Ave, has shuttle vans that take you to your door if you live in Tucson (1 hour, US$6) or Phoenix (3 hours, US$30). Buses operate from 6am to 8pm and depart whenever five people are on hand for the trip.

Car & Motorcycle Approaching Nogales from Tucson, the left lanes go to central Nogales. The right lanes, which go to a vehicular border crossing outside the city (favored by trucks), are the quickest way to enter Mexico, but the crossing is only open from 6am to 10pm. Outside these hours, you'll have to come through the city, where the border crossing is open 24 hours a day. As you approach Nogales, you'll see plenty of signs for Mexican auto insurance, which you'll need if you're bringing a vehicle into Mexico.

Temporary vehicle import procedures are dealt with at the Aguazarca inspection site at the 21km point on the highway south of Nogales. See the Car & Motorcycle section in the Getting There & Away chapter for more on bringing a vehicle into Mexico and on simplified procedures for those who are only visiting Sonora.

On the Arizona side of Nogales, Enterprise Rent-A-Car (☎ 520-281-0425, 800-325-8007, 1831 N Grand Ave) allows you to take its rental vehicles to Mexico. You can pick up the vehicle in either Nogales or Tucson (including the Tucson airport), and must return it where you got it. Hertz (☎ 520-287-2012, 800-654-3131, 1012 N Grand Ave) also rents vehicles for trips into Mexico from either Tucson or Nogales.

On the Arizona side of Nogales, several attended lots near the border crossing offer parking for US$5.50 per day.

Getting Around

For the bus station, city buses marked 'Central' or 'Central Camionera' depart frequently from a corner on López Mateos, two blocks south of the border crossing (US$0.30). Everything else you'll need in Nogales is within easy walking distance of the border crossing. Taxis wait on either side of the border crossing, but are not allowed to cross it.

OTHER BORDER CROSSINGS

The Nogales border crossing is the quickest and easiest route in this region. Other 24-hour border crossings between Sonora and Arizona include **San Luis Río Colorado**, west of Nogales on the banks of the Río Colorado (Colorado River), 42km southwest of Yuma, Arizona, and **Agua Prieta**, about 130km east of Nogales opposite Douglas, Arizona. **Sonoita**, opposite Lukeville, Arizona, and immediately south of the picturesque Organ Pipe Cactus National Monument, has a border crossing open 8am to midnight daily. All these crossings are on Mexican highway 2, with frequent bus services from the Mexican side to places deeper into Mexico (though possibly not on the US side between San Luis Río Colorado and Yuma).

El Sásabe, opposite Sasabe, Arizona, about 60km west of Nogales, is in the middle of nowhere, with no bus connections on either side of the border and nowhere to get your Mexican car insurance if you're driving south. The border crossing is open 8am to 10pm daily, but you're probably better off crossing somewhere else with a little more life. About 90km east of Nogales, **Naco**, opposite Naco, Arizona, has a 24-hour crossing.

AROUND NORTHERN SONORA

On the northeast coast of the Sea of Cortez (Golfo de California), **Puerto Peñasco** (population 30,000) is a popular destination for travelers with trailers and RVs, making tourism an even more profitable industry than the shrimping and fishing for which this small town is also known. About a 1½-hour drive south of the Sonoita border crossing, this is southern Arizona's nearest beach.

Growing rapidly, Puerto Peñasco has many good hotels, motels, trailer parks and restaurants and a marina. Fishing, surfing, scuba diving, kayaking and yacht cruises are popular activities. English is widely spoken and local businesses are as keen to take US dollars as pesos.

Puerto Peñasco's tourist office (☎ 638-383-61-22), Boulevard Juárez 320B, open 9am to 5pm Monday to Friday and 9am to 2pm Saturday, can help with activities and accommodations. In the USA, Rocky Point Reservations (☎ 602-439-9004, 800-427-6259) also arranges stays in Puerto Peñasco.

Northwest of Puerto Peñasco is the **Reserva de la Biósfera El Pinacate y Gran Desierto de Altar**, a reserve containing several extinct volcanic craters, a large lava flow, cinder cones, a cinder mine and vast sand dunes. Visitors must register at the entrance, reached by going down a 10km gravel road heading south from a turnoff about 10km east of Los Vidrios, which is on highway 2 west of Sonoita. Until 1993, part of the reserve formed the Parque Nacional El Pinacate, a title still sometimes used.

The small town of **Cananea**, on highway 2 about halfway between Santa Ana and Agua Prieta, is a mining town that is not of much note today, but it is significant in Mexican history because the miners' revolt that broke out here on June 1, 1906, near the end of the rule of Porfirio Díaz, helped to precipitate the Mexican Revolution. Displays in the small town **museum** tell the story of the strike.

HERMOSILLO

• pop 610,000 • elev 238m ☎ 662

On highway 15 about 280km south of Nogales, Hermosillo ('ehrr-mo-SEE-yo') was founded in 1700 by Juan Bautista Escalante for the resettlement of indigenous Pima and is now the large, bustling, multi-industry capital of the Sonora state. Like many cities in Mexico, Hermosillo industrialized quickly. In the early 1980s, it was little more than an agricultural and administrative center of 45,000 people. Many travelers pass through Hermosillo heading north or south. Smack in the middle of the great Desierto Sonorense, Hermosillo gets unbearably hot in summer; the rest of the year it's quite pleasant.

Orientation

Highway 15 enters Hermosillo from the northeast and becomes Boulevard Francisco Eusebio Kino, a wide street lined with orange and laurel trees. Boulevard Kino continues west through the city, curves southwest and becomes Rodríguez, then Rosales as it passes through the city center, then Vildosola before becoming highway 15 again south of the city. The major business and administrative sections of Hermosillo lie on either side of Boulevard Rosales and along Boulevard Encinas, which transects the city center from northwest to southeast. The Periférico, once a beltway around Hermosillo, has become practically an inner loop due to the city's rapid expansion.

Both tourist offices (see Information) offer a good free city map. Many of the nicer hotels and restaurants also hand out copies of the map.

Information

Tourist Offices The tourist office (☎ 217-00-76, 217-00-44, 800-716-25-55 in Mexico, ☎ 800-476-6672 in the USA, ⓦ www.sonora.gob.mx/turismo) is on the 3rd floor of the south wing of the giant Centro de Gobierno building, which straddles Comonfort just south of Paseo Río Sonora Sur, on the south side of the city center. It's open 8am to 5pm Monday to Friday.

Another tourist information office, on highway 15 at the checkpoint about 15km north of Hermosillo, is open 8am to 8pm daily. Both have information on all Sonora and links with the Arizona tourist office in Phoenix.

Money Banks and casas de cambio are scattered along Hermosillo's Boulevards Rosales and Encinas. The American Express agent, Hermex Travel (☎ 213-44-15), is on the corner of Boulevard Rosales and Monterrey.

Post & Communications The main post office, on the corner of Boulevard Rosales and Serdán, is open 8am to 7pm Monday to Friday, 8am to noon Saturday. The Telecom office, with telegram, telex, fax and Internet, is in the same building. Pay phones and telephone casetas are everywhere in central Hermosillo. Copynet, on the corner of Pino Suárez and Monterrey, has Internet access.

Travel Agencies Hermex Travel (see Money) and Turismo Palo Verde (☎ 213-47-01), at Hotel San Alberto, are helpful travel agencies.

Laundry Lavandería Automática de Hermosillo, on the corner of Yañez and Sonora, is open 8am to 8pm Monday to Saturday, 8am to 2pm Sunday.

Things to See & Do

Hermosillo has two principal plazas: **Plaza Zaragoza** and **Jardín Juárez**. Plaza Zaragoza is especially pleasant at sundown when thousands of yellow-headed blackbirds roost in the trees for the night. On the west side of the plaza is the lovely **Catedral de la Ascensión**, also called the Catedral Metropolitana. On the east side, the gray-and-white **Palacio de Gobierno** has a courtyard with colorful, dramatic murals depicting episodes in the history of Sonora.

The **Capilla del Carmen**, on Jesús García facing No Reelección, is not as impressive as the cathedral but it's a fine little 19th-century chapel, built from 1837 to 1842.

The **Cerro de la Campana** (Hill of the Bell) is the most prominent landmark in the area and an easy point of reference night or day. The panoramic view from the top is beautiful and well worth the walk or drive to get up there. Hugging the east side of the hill, the **Museo de Sonora** (☎ 217-27-14, Jesús García s/n; admission US$3, free Sun & holidays; open 10am-5pm Tues-Sat, 9am-4pm Sun) has fine exhibits on the history and anthropology of Sonora. The building itself is also interesting. It served as the Sonora state penitentiary from 1907 to 1979 before reopening as a museum in 1985; the dungeon is downstairs, under the courtyard. It's an easy walk, or take local bus No 8 ('La Matanza') from the corner of Elías Calles and Garmendia to the museum entrance.

HERMOSILLO

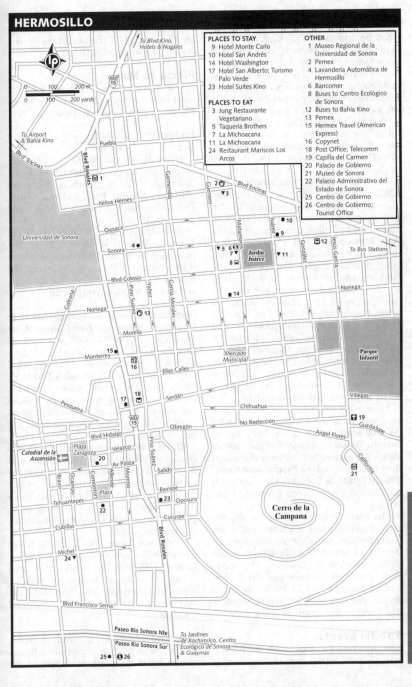

PLACES TO STAY
9 Hotel Monte Carlo
10 Hotel San Andrés
14 Hotel Washington
17 Hotel San Alberto; Turismo Palo Verde
23 Hotel Suites Kino

PLACES TO EAT
3 Jung Restaurante Vegetariano
5 Taquería Brothers
7 La Michoacana
11 La Michoacana
24 Restaurant Mariscos Los Arcos

OTHER
1 Museo Regional de la Universidad de Sonora
2 Pemex
4 Lavandería Automática de Hermosillo
6 Bancomer
8 Buses to Centro Ecológico de Sonora
12 Buses to Bahía Kino
13 Pemex
15 Hermex Travel (American Express)
16 Copynet
18 Post Office; Telecomm
19 Capilla del Carmen
20 Palacio de Gobierno
21 Museo de Sonora
22 Palacio Administrativo del Estado de Sonora
25 Centro de Gobierno
26 Centro de Gobierno; Tourist Office

The University of Sonora has a museum complex, the **Museo Regional de la Universidad de Sonora** (☎ *212-06-09, cnr Boulevards Rosales & Encinas; admission free; open 9am-5pm Mon-Sat*), which has a history section on the ground floor and an archaeology section upstairs. Downstairs on the corner of the building is the **university art gallery** (☎ *213-42-67, admission free; open 9am-7pm Mon-Fri*). Events and exhibits are presented at the university throughout the year; check with the university's Difusión Cultural office (☎ 213-52-08) or the tourist office for details.

The **Centro Ecológico de Sonora** (☎ *250-12-25; admission US$2.25; open 8am-6pm Tues-Sun*) is a zoo and botanical garden with plants and animals of the Desierto Sonorense and other ecosystems of northwest Mexico. It's well worth visiting – there's more variety of desert life than you'd probably expect. The zoo also contains animals from around the world. There is also an **observatory** (*admission US$2.50; open 7.30pm-10.30pm Thur-Sat*) there, with telescope viewing sessions. The center is about 5km south of central Hermosillo, past the Periférico Sur and just off highway 15. The 'Luis Orcí' local bus, departing from the west side of Jardín Juárez and heading south on Boulevard Rosales, stops at a gate about 500m from the entrance – ask the driver where to get off, as there are no signs.

Hermosillo has some impressively large government buildings, including the **Centro de Gobierno**, which is the huge brown complex straddling Comonfort just south of Paseo Río Sonora Sur on the south side of the city center; and the **Palacio Administrativo del Estado de Sonora** (see its courtyard) on Tehuantepec between Comonfort and Allende.

Hermosillo boasts a couple of enjoyable recreation parks with miniature golf, boats, bathing pools and other activities for children and adults: **Mundo Divertido** (☎ *260-35-05, Boulevard Colosio 653; open 1pm-8pm Mon-Fri, noon-9pm Sat & Sun*) and **La Sauceda** (☎ *212-05-09, Boulevard Serna; admission US$0.80; open 9am-6pm Tues-Sun*), east of Cerro de la Campana.

Special Events

The city's major annual event, the Exposición Ganadera (the Sonora state fair) is held in the Unión Gándara each year for 10 days near the end of April. La Vendimia, or the Fiesta de la Uva (Festival of the Grape), is held on a weekend in late June.

Places to Stay

If you spend a night here in summer, you must have a room with air-con that works. Check the room before you accept it.

Budget Price is not the only indicator of quality.

Hotel Washington (☎ *213-11-83, Noriega 68 Pte*) Singles/doubles US$16/18. Hotel Washington has a cheerfully decorated lobby, vending machines and free coffee. The rooms are basic but large, clean and comfortable.

Hotel Monte Carlo (☎/*fax 212-33-54, cnr Juárez & Sonora*) Rooms US$20-37. The only thing the Monte Carlo has going for it is its location – right on Jardín Juárez. The hotel is in disrepair, is not particularly clean, and its staff is rather disorganized.

Mid-Range On a convenient site near Boulevard Rosales is *Hotel Suites Kino* (☎ *213-31-31, 800-711-54-60, w www.hotelsuiteskino.com, Pino Suárez 151 Sur*) Standard singles/doubles US$29/40, 'Plus' singles/doubles US$42/46, suites US$48-55. Hotel Kino has a small indoor swimming pool, secure parking, travel agency, a pleasant restaurant, and cool air-con throughout. 'Plus' rooms are larger and have desks and bigger TVs.

Hotel San Alberto (☎ *213-18-40, cnr Boulevard Rosales & Serdán*) Singles/doubles US$36/39. The San Alberto has the feeling of a hotel whose time has past. It's no longer in great shape, though it's still a decent value. It has a swimming pool, parking, travel agency, bookstore and 80 air-conditioned rooms.

Hotel San Andrés (☎ *217-30-99, e san andres@infosel.net.mx, Oaxaca 14*) Singles/doubles US$38/40. The Hotel San Andrés, a block from Jardín Juárez, has parking, a restaurant, a bar and 80 modern air-conditioned rooms around a pleasant courtyard.

Top End Many of Hermosillo's better hotels and motels are strung along Boulevard Kino in the northeast corner of the

Carnaval dancers in Mazatlán, just south of the tropic of Cancer

One of Acapulco's *clavadistas* (cliff divers)

Gearing up in San Blas

Puerto Vallarta's tropical charm

Aquatic childhood, Acapulco

Real de Catorce, an abandoned mining town

Mask, Museo Rafael Coronel, Zacatecas

Historic aqueduct of Zacatecas

Balcony in San Miguel de Allende

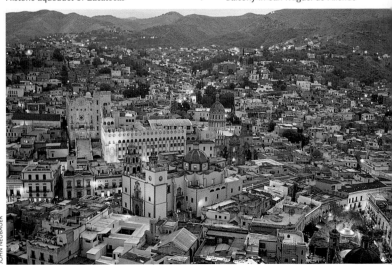
Guanajuato is prettily packed into serpentine ravines.

city. Among these are **Araiza Inn** (☎ 210-27-17, Boulevard Kino 353), **Fiesta Americana** (☎ 259-60-00, Boulevard Kino 369) and **Holiday Inn** (☎ 214-45-70, cnr Boulevard Kino & Corral).

Places to Eat

Some of the cheapest food in Hermosillo can be bought from the hot-dog carts on many street corners. The hot dogs are surprisingly good, especially when piled high with guacamole, refried beans, chilies, relish and/or mustard. Another street-cart treat is the *pico de gallo* – chunks of orange, apple, pineapple, cucumber, jicama, watermelon and coconut – refreshing on a hot day.

For a cool fruit salad, yogurt with fruit, ice cream, fruit or vegetable juice or other cold drinks, check out the many branches of **La Michoacana**. The two bordering Jardín Juárez, open till 9pm, are convenient for getting snacks to take out on the plaza.

There are cheap food stalls in **Mercado Municipal**, on Matamoros between Elías Calles and Monterrey.

Taquería Brothers (cnr Sonora & Guerrero) Tacos from US$1. This is a simple stall serving great tacos and quesadillas.

Jung Restaurante Vegetariano (☎ 213-28-81, Niños Héroes 75D) Buffets from US$5.50-8. Located near Boulevard Encinas, this is a clean, cheerful, air-conditioned vegetarian restaurant and health food store with a vast, reasonably priced menu as well as buffets at breakfast, lunch and dinner.

The air-conditioned restaurant at **Hotel Suites Kino** (see Places to Stay) has reasonable meals, with breakfast and dinner for US$4.50 and a *comida corrida* for US$5.50. **Hotel San Andrés** also has a restaurant.

Restaurant Mariscos Los Arcos (☎ 213-22-20, Michel 43) Prices US$6-12. This pleasant restaurant, on the corner of Ocampo, is famous for its seafood.

Jardines de Xochimilco (☎ 250-40-89, Obregón 51) Dinner special US$20. Open 11am-9pm daily. Hermosillo's best-known restaurant, it serves the beef for which Sonora is famous and has mariachi bands. The dinner special for two is a memorable feast. It's in Villa de los Seris, an old part of town just south of the center. Come in a taxi at night, as the neighborhood is not the best. Reservations are advised in the evening.

Shopping

If you always wanted to buy a pair of cowboy boots and a 10-gallon hat, you'll probably find what you want in Hermosillo. The city has one of the best selections of cowboy gear in Mexico. Ironwood carvings made by the Seri people are another distinctive product of the region and are sold in front of the post office and at other places around town.

Getting There & Away

Air The airport, about 10km from central Hermosillo on the road to Bahía Kino, is served by Aero California, Aerolitoral, Aeroméxico, America West, and Mexicana. Daily direct flights, all with connections to other centers, go to Chihuahua, Ciudad Juárez, Ciudad Obregón, Culiacán, Guadalajara, Guaymas/San Carlos, Guerrero Negro, La Paz, Los Angeles, Los Mochis, Mexicali, Mexico City, Monterrey, Phoenix, Tijuana and Tucson.

Bus The main bus terminal on Boulevard Encinas is about 2km southeast of the city center. First-class service is offered by Crucero, Elite, Estrella Blanca (EB), Transportes del Pacífico (TP), Transportes Norte de Sonora (TNS) and others. Other companies have separate terminals nearby – Transportes Baldomero Corral (TBC) is next door. Across the street is Tufesa, and about a block west of Boulevard Encinas is Estrellas del Pacífico (EP). Services to many destinations depart around the clock. Daily 1st-class departures include:

Guadalajara – 1417km, 23 hours; frequent buses (US$70) from the main bus terminal via Los Mochis, Mazatlán and Tepic

Guaymas – 134km, 1¾ hours; frequent buses by most companies (US$4-6.75)

Los Angeles (California) – 1167km, 15 hours; 3 Crucero (US$72)

Mexico City (Terminal Norte) – 1959km, 30 to 33 hours; frequent buses from the main bus terminal (US$108-120)

Nogales – 277km, 4 hours; frequent buses by most companies (US$7.50-19)

Phoenix (Arizona) – 565km, 8 hours; 5 Crucero, 4 TBC (US$35-42)

Tijuana – 889km, 13 hours; frequent buses by most companies (US$44)

Tucson (Arizona) – 385km, 5½ hours; 5 Crucero, 5 TBC (US$22-29)

NORTHWEST MEXICO

Second-class buses to Bahía Kino depart from the AMH & TCH bus terminal in central Hermosillo, on Sonora between González and Jesús García, 1½ blocks east of Jardín Juárez. They depart hourly between 5.30am and 11.30am and at 1.30pm, 3.30pm, 5pm and 7pm; the two-hour trip costs US$5.

Getting Around

Local buses operate 5.30am to 10pm daily (US$0.30). To get to the main bus terminal, take any 'Central,' 'Central Camionera' or 'Ruta 1' bus from Juárez on the east side of Jardín Juárez.

BAHÍA KINO

• pop 4040 ☎ 662

Named for Father Eusebio Kino, a Jesuit missionary who established a small mission here for the indigenous Seri people in the late 17th century, the bayfront town of Kino, 110km west of Hermosillo, is divided into old and new parts that are as different as night and day.

Kino Viejo, the old quarter on your left as you drive into Kino, is a dusty, run-down fishing village. Kino Nuevo, on your right, is basically a single beachfront road stretching about 8km north along the beach, lined with the holiday homes and retreats of wealthy gringos and Mexicans. It's a fine beach with soft sand and safe swimming. From around November to March the 'snowbirds' drift down in their trailers from colder climes. The rest of the time it's not crowded – but it's always a popular day outing for families from Hermosillo escaping the city. The beach has many *palapas* providing welcome shade.

In winter, the snowbirds migrate south.

The **Museo de los Seris** *(admission US$0.60; open 8am-3pm Tues-Fri)*, about halfway along the beachfront road in Kino Nuevo, has fascinating exhibits about the Seri, the traditionally nomadic indigenous people of this area. There's a Seri *artesanías* shop next door. Seri ironwood carvings are sold in both Kino Nuevo and Viejo.

Places to Stay & Eat

Kino Nuevo Most people come to Kino for the day from Hermosillo, but there are several places to stay. Prices tend to be considerably higher than in Hermosillo. There are plenty of palapas all along the beach – you could easily string up a hammock and camp out under one of these for free.

Kino Bay RV Park (☎ 242-02-16) Tent/trailer sites US$12/18. At the far north end of Kino Nuevo, opposite the beach at the end of the bus line, this clean, attractive and well-equipped park has 200 tent or trailer spaces with full hookups.

Parador Bellavista (☎ 242-01-39) Tent/trailer sites US$13/18, rooms US$50. The beachfront Bellavista has trailer and camping spaces and two air-conditioned rooms with kitchenette.

Posada Santa Gemma (☎ 242-00-26) Tent & trailer sites US$18, bungalows US$160. Also located on the beach, the Santa Gemma offers tent and trailer spaces without hookups as well as bungalows; prices seem to be negotiable.

Hotel Saro (☎/fax 242-00-07) Singles/doubles US$34/45. This beachfront place has air-conditioned rooms with fridge as well as TV.

Hotel Posada del Mar (☎/fax 242-01-55) Singles/doubles from US$38/45. This hotel is located across the road from the beach on tree-covered grounds. It has a pool.

Most of these places offer both weekly and monthly discounts.

Various places to eat – all specializing in fresh seafood, of course – lie along the beachfront road and in some of the hotels. *Restaurant La Palapa* (☎ 242-02-10), *Pargo Rojo* (☎ 242-02-05) and *Taco Bar* (☎ 242-02-10) are all recommended.

Kino Viejo On the beach is *Islandia Marina* (☎/fax 242-00-81) Tent sites US$10, trailer sites US$15, bungalows US$39-45. This is a trailer park with tent and trailer

The Seris

The Seris are the least numerous indigenous people in Sonora, but one of the most recognized due to their distinctive handicrafts. Traditionally a nomadic people living by hunting, gathering and fishing – not agriculture, as was prevalent among many other indigenous groups in Mexico – the Seris roamed along the Sea of Cortez from roughly El Desemboque in the north to Bahía Kino in the south, and inland to Hermosillo.

The Seris are one of the few indigenous peoples who do not work for outsiders, preferring to live by fishing, hunting and handicrafts. Their most famous handicrafts are their ironwood carvings of animals, humans and other figures. Other important traditional handicrafts, including pottery and basketry, are no longer as important. The Seris were once one of the very few peoples in the world who were nomadic and also made pottery.

Though the Seris are no longer strictly nomadic, they still often move from place to place in groups; sometimes you can see them camped at Bahía Kino, or traveling up and down the coast. You will also see Seris in Hermosillo, where some sell ironwood carvings outside the post office. Many, though, live far from modern civilization on the large, protected Isla Tiburón (which belongs to the Seri) or in other inconspicuous places along the Sonora coast, and they still maintain many of their old traditions reflecting the rhythms of living between the desert and the sea.

A visit to the Museo de los Seris in Kino Nuevo is rewarding. The exhibits encompass the Seri's distinctive clothing, their traditional houses with frames of ocotillo cactus, their musical instruments and handicrafts, and their nomadic social structure and nature-based religion.

spaces, plus eight free-standing self-contained bungalows. Beachfront bungalows cost more; bring your own bed linen and dishes.

A block away, the pricey, air-conditioned **Restaurant Marlin** and **Roberto's** are popular restaurants. Other small open-air *eateries*, serving fresh barbecued fish or tacos, are dotted around Kino Viejo.

Getting There & Away

Buses to Hermosillo leave from Kino Nuevo roughly every hour on the half hour, with the last bus departing from Kino Nuevo at 5.30pm and Kino Viejo at 6pm. If you come at a busy time (on a Sunday, for example, when lots of families are there) and you want to get the last bus of the day, catch it at the first stop, on the north end of Kino Nuevo, while there is still space. Be aware that this is the only public transportation in Kino; there are no local buses or taxis.

If you're driving, you can make the trip from Hermosillo to Bahía Kino in about an hour. From central Hermosillo, head northwest out of town on Boulevard Encinas and just keep going.

GUAYMAS
• pop 130,000 ☎ 622

Founded in 1769 by the Spaniards at the site of Yaqui and Guaymenas indigenous villages on the shores of a sparkling blue bay, Guaymas is Sonora's main port. Fishing and commerce are its main economic activities. A ferry connects Guaymas with Santa Rosalía, Baja California. The tourist resort town of San Carlos is 20km northwest of Guaymas.

You can enjoy the view of the fishing boats, town and surrounding hills from the statue of 'El Pescador' (the fisherman) in the Plaza del Pescador. The town's other notable features include the Plaza de los Tres Presidentes, which commemorates the three Mexican presidents hailing from Guaymas, the 19th-century Iglesia de San Fernando and its Plaza 13 de Julio, the Palacio Municipal (built in 1899) and the old jail (1900).

Orientation & Information

Highway 15 becomes Boulevard García López as it passes along the northern edge of Guaymas. Central Guaymas and the port area are along Avenida Serdán, the town's main drag, running parallel to and just south of García López; everything you'll need is on or near Avenida Serdán. García López and Serdán intersect a few blocks west of the Guaymas map's extents.

The tourist office (☎/fax 224-41-14), at the corner of Avenida 6 and Calle 19, is

GUAYMAS

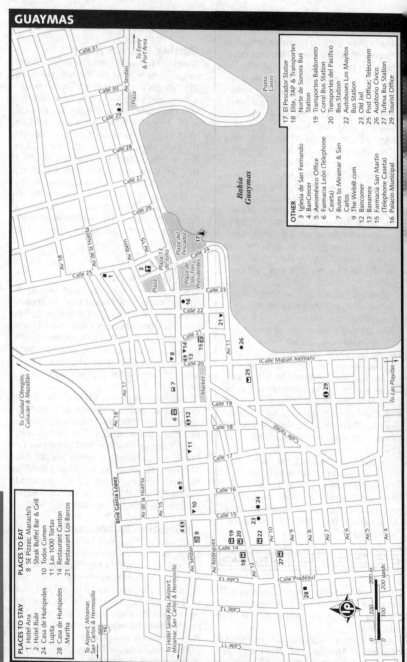

PLACES TO STAY
1 Hotel Ana
2 Hotel Rubí
24 Casa de Huéspedes Lupita
28 Casa de Huéspedes Martha

PLACES TO EAT
8 SE Pizzas; Mariachi's Steak Buffet Bar & Grill
10 Todos Comen
11 Las 1000 Tortas
14 Restaurant Canton
21 Restaurant Los Barcos

OTHER
3 Iglesia de San Fernando
4 BanCrecer
5 Aeroméxico Office
6 Farmacia León (Telephone Caseta)
7 Buses to Miramar & San Carlos
9 The Web@.com
12 Bancomer
13 Banamex
15 Farmacia San Martín (Telephone Caseta)
16 Palacio Municipal
17 El Pescador Statue
18 Elite, TAP & Transportes Norte de Sonora Bus Station
19 Transportes Baldomero Corral Bus Station
20 Transportes del Pacífico Bus Station
22 Autobuses Los Mayitos Bus Station
23 Old Jail
25 Post Office, Telecomm
26 Auditorio Cívico
27 Tufesa Bus Station
29 Tourist Office

NORTHWEST MEXICO

open 9am to 3pm Monday to Friday. They're planning to build a new office in the seafront park near the Pescador statue.

The post office, Avenida 10 between Calles 19 and 20, is open 9am to 3pm Monday to Friday and 9am to 1pm Saturday. Telecomm, with telegram, telex and fax, is next door. Two pharmacies downtown have telephone/fax casetas: Farmacia San Martín, on the corner of Calle 21 and Avenida Rodríguez (open 8am to midnight daily), and Farmacia León, on Avenida Serdán at Calle 19. For Internet access, The Web@.com on Avenida Serdán at Calle 14 is open 9am to 9pm Monday to Saturday.

Several banks on Avenida Serdán have ATMs, including BanCrecer at Calle 15, Bancomer at Calle 18, and Banamex at Calle 20.

Special Events

Carnaval is celebrated in a big way in Guaymas. Festivities occur on the Thursday to Tuesday preceding Ash Wednesday. Día de la Marina is on June 1, and the Fiestas de San Juan Bautista on June 24.

Places to Stay

Casa de Huéspedes Lupita (☎ 222-84-09, Calle 15 No 125) Singles/doubles with shared bath US$6.75/9, with private bath US$9/13.50. For budget accommodations you can't beat this hotel located between Avenidas 10 and 12, 1½ blocks from the bus stations. It's not fancy, but it's clean and popular with foreign travelers.

Casa de Huéspedes Martha (☎ 222-83-32, Avenida 9 near Calle 13) Singles/doubles with bath US$9/13.50. This smaller hotel has a friendly atmosphere, off-street parking and 15 rooms with fan or air-con. In the summer, the rooms with air-con cost more.

Hotel Ana (☎ 222-30-48, Calle 25 No 135) Rooms US$19. The Hotel Ana has parking and air-conditioned rooms with TV around a courtyard.

Hotel Rubí (☎ 224-01-69, Avenida Serdán s/n) Singles/doubles US$19/21. Located between Calles 29 and 30, this hotel has quiet, air-conditioned rooms opening onto a courtyard.

On Avenida Serdán at the west end of town are a couple of US-style motels with not much personality, but they're clean, with air-con, TV and parking.

Hotel Santa Rita (☎ 224-14-64, cnr Avenida Serdán & Calle 9) Singles/doubles US$23/28. This hotel has small tiled rooms and a patio that is several degrees cooler than the street outside.

Motel Santa Rita (☎ 224-19-19, Avenida Serdán 590 Pte) Singles/doubles US$34/39. Situated in the next block from the Santa Rita, this motel has an air-conditioned restaurant and two computers available for Internet access.

Places to Eat

As in most Mexican towns, Guaymas supports a *market*, which has stalls where you can sit down to eat for cheap; it's a block south of Avenida Serdán, on Avenida Rodríguez between Calles 19 and 20, and opens at around 5am.

Avenida Serdán has many restaurants.

Todos Comen (between Calles 15 & 16) Prices from US$2.75. Open 7am-midnight daily. This small air-conditioned place has economical meals, with a comida corrida for US$3.25.

SE Pizzas (near Calle 20) Prices from US$2.75. This place has an all-you-can-eat pizza and salad buffet and the beer's cheap too. Watching the mad rush for pizza is also a good form of entertainment (unless you're very hungry).

Mariachi's Steak Buffet Bar & Grill (cnr Calle 20) Prices US$3.50. Next door to SE Pizzas, Mariachi's serves an ample buffet.

Restaurant Canton (between Calles 20 & 21) Prices from US$2.50. The Canton offers inexpensive Chinese fare as well as some Mexican dishes.

Las 1000 Tortas (between Calles 17 & 18) Prices from US$2. This is a good snack shop that serves tortas and hamburgers.

Motel Santa Rita (cnr Calle 9) Prices US$3.75-10. Resembling an American diner with its vinyl-clad booths, the Santa Rita serves a variety of seafood dishes and antojitos. The menu is in English and Spanish.

Restaurant Los Barcos (cnr Avenida 11 & Calle 22) Prices US$4-11. You can sample the seafood for which Guaymas is famous at this popular seafront restaurant. It offers seafood, steak, seafood cocktails and salads.

Getting There & Away

Air The airport is about 10km northwest of Guaymas on the highway to San Carlos. Aeroméxico (☎ 222-01-23) offers direct flights to Phoenix and La Paz. Its office is on the corner of Avenida Serdán and Calle 16. America West (☎ 221-22-66) offers direct flights to Phoenix.

Bus Guaymas has five small bus stations, all on Calle 14, about two blocks south of Avenida Serdán. Elite, TAP (Transportes y Autobuses del Pacífico) and Transportes Norte de Sonora share a terminal at the corner of Calle 14 and Avenida 12; Transportes del Pacífico is opposite. All these have far-ranging northbound and southbound routes departing hourly, 24 hours. Transportes Baldomero Corral (TBC), beside Transportes del Pacífico, goes hourly to Hermosillo, Nogales, Ciudad Obregón and Navojoa, and also has two buses daily (3.45pm and 8.45pm) direct to Álamos. Autobuses Los Mayitos, between Avenidas 10 and 12, operates hourly buses north to Hermosillo and south to Navojoa, 7am to 9pm. Tufesa, at the corner of Avenida 10, has hourly buses heading south to Culiacán, and heading north to Hermosillo and Nogales, 24 hours a day. All run 1st-class buses, though Transportes del Pacífico also has 2nd-class buses. Distances, trip times and 1st-class fares include:

Álamos – 247km, 4 hours; TBC only, US$7.75
Guadalajara – 1276km, 20 hours; US$53-82
Hermosillo – 134km, 1¾ hours; US$3.50-7.25
Los Mochis – 349km, 5 hours; US$10-17.50
Mazatlán – 770km, 11 hours; US$43-49
Mexico City (Terminal Norte) – 1811km, 28 hours; US$87-122
Navojoa – 194km, 3 hours; US$5-9
Nogales – 416km, 5 hours; US$11-21
Tepic – 1060km, 16 hours; US$49-65
Tijuana – 1026km, 15 hours; US$39-45

Boat Ferries connect Guaymas with Santa Rosalía, Baja California. The ferry *(transbordador)* terminal (☎ 222-23-24) is on Avenida Serdán at the east end of town. Ferries depart at 9.30am on Monday and Thursday and arrive in Santa Rosalía at 8pm. Ferries depart Santa Rosalía at 10pm on Monday and Thursday and arrive in Guaymas at 9am.

Vehicle reservations are accepted by telephone a week in advance. Passenger tickets are sold at the ferry office on the morning of departure, or a few days before. Make reservations at least three days in advance and, even if you have reservations, arrive early at the ticket office. The office is open 8am to 3pm Monday to Friday and 9am to noon Saturday. Passenger fares are US$51 for seats and US$116 to US$166 for cabins. See the Santa Rosalía section in the Baja California chapter for vehicle fares.

Getting Around

To get to the airport, catch a bus from Avenida Serdán heading to Itson or San José, or take a taxi (US$9). Local buses run along Avenida Serdán frequently between 6am and 9pm daily (US$0.40). Several eastbound buses stop at the ferry terminal; ask for 'transbordador.'

AROUND GUAYMAS

The closest beach is **Miramar**, on the Bahía de Bacochibampo about 5km west of Guaymas. It's not a big tourist destination like San Carlos, but it does have an interesting industry – pearl farming.

Hotel Playa de Cortés (☎ 622-221-01-35, Bahía de Bacochibampo) Trailer sites US$23, rooms US$90-129. This sprawling beachfront hotel has 150 rooms, plus a 90-space trailer park with full hookups and access to all hotel facilities. 'Miramar' buses head west on Avenida Serdán (starting from between Calles 19 and 20) every 30 minutes between 7am and 8pm (US$0.50).

San Carlos

• pop 1440 ☎ 622

On Bahía San Carlos, about 20km northwest of Guaymas, San Carlos is a beautiful desert-and-bay landscape. Twin-peaked Cerro Tetakawi is the symbol of the town. From around October to April, the town is full of *norteamericanos* and their trailers; the rest of the year it's quiet, except for a flurry of Mexican tourists in July and August.

San Carlos has two marinas: Marina San Carlos, which is in the heart of town, and the newer Marina Real at Algodones, which is in the northernmost sector of town. San Carlos is bursting with outdoor activities such as snorkeling, diving, sailing, fishing, kayaking, mountain biking, motorcycling, horseback riding and golfing. There are also local tours, bay cruises, gyms and an Internet café. The view from the *mirador* (lookout) is spectacular, especially at sunset. Cañon de Nacapule, with lush green vegetation, is good for a 2½-hour circuit hike.

San Carlos has a helpful bilingual tourist office (☎ 226-02-02, e hdtours@prodigy .net.mx), in the Edificio Hacienda Plaza on Boulevard Manlio Beltrones, the main road into San Carlos. It's open 9am to 5pm Monday to Friday, 9am to 2pm Saturday.

Special Events Annual events include Carnavalito, which is held the week following the Carnaval celebration in Guaymas; a skydiving exhibition in March; a women's fishing tournament in May; an international fishing tournament in July; the Labor Day fishing tournament in September; a sailboat competition in October; and golf tournaments throughout the year.

Places to Stay & Eat Find a room or bring your own at *Best Western Hacienda Teta Kawi – Hotel & RV Park* (☎ 226-02-20, e bwtetakawi@hotmail.com, *Boulevard Manlio Beltrones s/n)* Tent/RV sites US$10/15, rooms US$64, suites US$74-85. Campers at the adjacent trailer park can use all the hotel's facilities.

El Mirador RV Park (☎ 227-02-13, w www.elmiradorrv.com) Sites US$22. This park, overlooking Marina Real, has great views, many amenities, and 90 spaces.

Posada del Desierto (☎ 226-04-67) Apartments US$34-38 for up to 4 people. The Posada del Desierto, San Carlos' most economical hotel, overlooks Marina San Carlos. It has seven basic air-conditioned studio apartments with kitchen; cheaper weekly and monthly rates are available.

Motel Creston (☎ 226-00-20, *Boulevard Manlio Beltrones Km 10)* Rooms US$39. The Creston has a swimming pool, air-conditioned rooms and parking.

Hotel Fiesta San Carlos (☎ 226-02-29, *Boulevard Manlio Beltrones Km 8.5)* Rooms US$61-95, including breakfast. This is a popular hotel with a swimming pool, restaurant, bar, and beachfront rooms with balconies.

Loma Bonita Condohotel & Vacation Club (☎ 226-14-13, *Carretera San Carlos Km 11)* Condos Sun-Thur/Fri & Sat US$73/89

for up to 6 people. Operated by Los Jitos Hotel & Spa next door, this hotel has two-story condos with two bedrooms, two baths, a kitchen and TV.

San Carlos Plaza Hotel, Resort & Convention Center (☎ 227-00-77, fax 227-00-98, *Mar Bermejo Norte No 4, Algodones)* Rooms US$182-217, suites US$220-945. This luxurious beachfront hotel has a pool, Jacuzzi, two restaurants, a bar and an incredibly expensive presidential suite.

Good restaurants in San Carlos include the *San Carlos Grill* (☎ 226-05-09, *Plaza Comercial San Carlos)*, which serves a variety of seafood and Mexican dishes; *Piccolo's* (☎ 226-05-03, *Creston 305)*, an Italian restaurant; and *El Bronco* (☎ 226-11-30, *Creston 178)*, a steakhouse serving Sonoran beef.

Getting There & Around Buses to San Carlos from Guaymas run west along Avenida Serdán (starting from between Calles 19 and 20) every 10 minutes between 5.30am and 11pm (US$0.90). San Carlos also has a local bus, serving all its various sectors, 7am to 8pm (US$0.30).

CIUDAD OBREGÓN
• pop 251,000 ☎ 644

Heading southeast 125km from Guaymas, highway 15D passes through Ciudad Obregón, a large, modern agricultural center. There is little of interest to the tourist in Ciudad Obregón. However, if you do stop here, be sure to visit the **Museo de los Yaquis** (cnr Allende & 5 de Febrero, inside *the Biblioteca Pública; admission US$1; open 8am-6pm Mon-Fri)*. This small museum has interesting exhibits on the history, traditions and art of the local Yaqui tribe.

NAVOJOA
• pop 98,000

Navojoa, 194km from Guaymas, is a similarly mundane place. However, it is a significant hub for those heading to the picturesque town of Álamos, 53km east on highway 13.

Navojoa has five bus stations within 6 blocks. Transportes del Pacífico, Transportes Norte de Sonora and Elite each have hourly 1st-class buses, 24 hours a day, going north and south on highway 15D. Second-class buses to Álamos depart from the Transportes

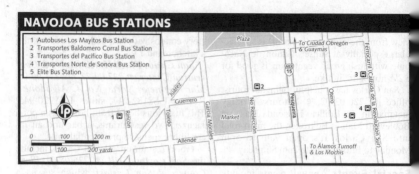

NAVOJOA BUS STATIONS

1 Autobuses Los Mayitos Bus Station
2 Transportes Baldomero Corral Bus Station
3 Transportes del Pacifico Bus Station
4 Transportes Norte de Sonora Bus Station
5 Elite Bus Station

Baldomero Corral (TBC) station on the corner of Guerrero and No Reelección every half hour, between 7.30am and 7pm, and at 8pm, 10pm and midnight (1 hour, US$2). TBC also has 1st-class service, including 12 daily buses north to Hermosillo (5 hours, US$10), eight daily buses to Nogales (8 hours, US$20) and three daily buses to Tucson (11 hours, US$37) and Phoenix (13 hours, US$50). From the Autobuses Los Mayitos station on the corner of Guerrero and Rincón, 2nd-class buses to Álamos depart every half hour from 6.30am to 6pm and 1st-class buses north to Hermosillo depart hourly between 6am and 6pm.

ÁLAMOS

• pop 8000 • elev 432m ☎ 647

This small, quiet town in the foothills of the Sierra Madre Occidental, 53km east of Navojoa, has been declared a national historic monument. Its beautifully restored Spanish colonial architecture has a Moorish influence, brought by 17th-century architects from Andalucía in southern Spain. The façades of colonial mansions line narrow cobblestone streets, concealing courtyards lush with bougainvillea. Several of the old mansions have been converted to hotels and restaurants. The whole town has a distinctly peaceful, timeless feel. Sunday evenings are often spent strolling and people-watching on the Plaza de Armas – a lovely old tradition, enjoyed by locals and visitors alike.

Álamos is on the border of two large ecosystems: the great Desierto Sonorense to the north and the lush tropical jungles of Sinaloa to the south. Nature-lovers are attracted by the area's 450 species of birds and animals (including some endangered and endemic species) and over 1000 species of plants. Horseback riding, hunting, fishing, hiking and swimming are popular activities.

From mid-October to mid-April, when the air is cool and fresh, norteamericanos arrive to take up residence in their winter homes and the town begins to hum with foreign visitors. Quail and dove hunting season, from November to February, also attracts many visitors. Mexican tourists come in the scorching hot summer months of July and August, when school is out. At other times you may find scarcely another visitor.

History

In 1540, this was the campsite of Francisco Vázquez de Coronado, future governor of Nueva Galicia (the colonial name for much of western Mexico), during his wars against the indigenous Mayo and Yaqui (the Yaqui resisted all invaders until 1928). If he had known about the vast amounts of gold and silver that prospectors would later find, he would have stayed.

In 1683, silver was discovered at Promontorios, near Álamos, and the Europa mine was opened. Other mines soon followed and Álamos became a boom town of more than 30,000, one of Mexico's principal 18th-century mining centers. Mansions, haciendas, a cathedral, tanneries, metalworks, blacksmiths' shops and later a mint were built. El Camino Real (the King's Highway), a well-trodden Spanish mule trail through the foothills, connected Álamos with Culiacán and El Fuerte to the south.

After Mexican independence, Álamos became the capital of the newly formed province of Occidente, a vast area including all of the present states of Sonora and Sinaloa. Don José María Almada, owner of

ÁLAMOS

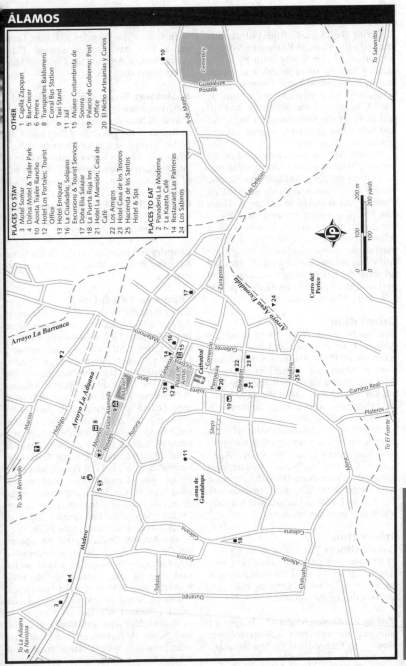

PLACES TO STAY
3 Motel Somar
4 Dolisa Motel & Trailer Park
10 Acosta Trailer Rancho
12 Hotel Los Portales; Tourist Office
13 Hotel Enriquez
16 La Ciudadela; Solipaso Excursions & Tourist Services
17 Doña Elia Salazar
18 La Puerta Roja Inn
21 Hotel La Mansión; Casa de Café
22 Los Amigos
23 Hotel Casa de los Tesoros
25 Hacienda de los Santos Hotel & Spa

PLACES TO EAT
2 Panadería La Moderna
7 La Kazeta Café
14 Restaurant Las Palmeras
24 Los Sabinos

OTHER
1 Capilla Zapopan
5 BanCrecer
6 Pemex
8 Transportes Baldomero Corral Bus Station
9 Taxi Stand
11 Jail
15 Museo Costumbrista de Sonora
19 Palacio de Gobierno; Post Office
20 El Nicho Artesanías y Curíos

the richest silver mine in Álamos, was appointed as governor.

During the turmoil of the 19th century and up to the Mexican Revolution, Álamos was attacked repeatedly, both by rebels seeking its vast silver wealth and by the fiercely independent Yaqui. The years of the revolution took a great toll on the town. By the 1920s, most of the population had left and many of the once-beautiful haciendas had fallen into disrepair. Álamos became practically a ghost town.

In 1948, Álamos was reawakened by the arrival of William Levant Alcorn, a Pennsylvania dairy farmer who moved to Álamos, bought the 15-room Almada mansion on Plaza de Armas and restored it as the Hotel Los Portales. Alcorn brought publicity to the town and made a fortune selling Álamos real estate. A number of norteamericanos crossed the border, bought the crumbling old mansions for good prices and set about the task of lovingly restoring them to their former glory. Many of these people still live in Álamos today.

Orientation

The paved road from Navojoa enters Álamos from the west and leads to the green, shady Plaza Alameda, with outdoor cafés at either end where you can get a drink and sit and watch the world go by. The market is at the east end of Plaza Alameda; the other main square, Plaza de Armas, is two blocks south of the market.

The Arroyo La Aduana (Customs House Stream, which is usually dry) runs along the town's northern edge; the Arroyo Agua Escondida (Hidden Waters Stream, also usually dry) runs along the southern edge. Both converge at the east end of town with the Arroyo La Barranca (Ravine Stream), which runs from the northwest.

Information

Tourist Offices The tourist office (☎ 428-04-50, Juárez 6), under the Hotel Los Portales on the west side of Plaza de Armas, is open 9am to 7pm daily. Opening hours are cut back during the summer.

Money BanCrecer, Madero 37, is open for changing money from 8.30am to 3pm Monday to Friday, 10am to 2pm Saturday. This bank also has an ATM.

Post & Communications The post office, inside the Palacio de Gobierno on Juárez, is open 9am to 3pm Monday to Friday. There are a few pay phones around Plaza Alameda. Los Amigos (see Places to Stay) offers Internet access.

Bookstores Books about Álamos, and a variety of other books in English, are available at El Nicho artesanías shop behind the cathedral, at the gift shop of the Hotel Casa de los Tesoros, and at Los Amigos. *A Brief History of Álamos* is an excellent source of information on the town. *The Stately Homes of Álamos* by Leila Gillette tells stories of many of the town's old homes. *The Álamos Guide* by BK Hamma and Donna McGee has tons of practical information for visitors as well as potential residents.

Laundry The laundry is at the Dolisa Motel & Trailer Park, on Madero at the entrance to town.

Things to See & Do

The **cathedral** is the tallest building in Álamos and also one of its oldest – construction lasted from 1786 to 1804 on the site of an early 17th-century adobe Jesuit mission. Legend relates that every family in Álamos contributed to the construction of the church. The high-ranking Spanish ladies of the town contributed plates from their finest sets of china to be placed at the base of the pilasters in the church tower. Inside, the altar rail, lamps, censers and candelabra were fashioned from silver, but were all ordered to be melted down in 1866 by General Ángel Martínez after he booted out French imperialist troops from Álamos. Subterranean passageways between the church and several of the mansions – probably built as escape routes for the safety of the rich families in time of attack – were blocked off in the 1950s.

The **Museo Costumbrista de Sonora** (☎ 428-00-53, Plaza de Armas; admission US$1.25; open 9am-6pm Wed-Sun), on the east side of the plaza, is a fine little museum with exhibits on the history and traditions of the people of Sonora. Occupying a former silk factory behind the cathedral, **El Nicho Artesanías y Curios** (cnr Juárez & Parroquia) is a fascinating shop brimming with antiques, curios, folk art and handicrafts from all over Mexico.

Mexican Jumping Beans

Mexican jumping beans, or *brincadores,* are not really beans, and it's not really the 'beans' themselves that jump – it's the larvae of a small moth, the *Carpocapsa saltitans.* The moth lays its eggs on the flower of a shrub called the *Sebastiana palmieri* or *Sebastiana pavoniana,* of the spurge family. When the egg hatches, the caterpillar burrows into the plant's developing seed pod, which continues to grow and closes up leaving no sign that a caterpillar is inside. The larva eats the seed in the pod and builds itself a tiny web. By yanking the web, the caterpillar makes the pod 'jump.'

The brincadores only jump at certain times of the year, and they can only be found in one small part of the world – an area of about 650 sq km in southern Sonora and northern Sinaloa. Álamos is known as the 'jumping bean capital,' and the beans play a significant role in the economy of the town.

Twenty days after the first rain of the season, sometime in June, the seed pods with the caterpillars inside start jumping. People from Álamos and other small towns in the region take to the hills to gather the beans, locating them by the sound of rustling leaves. The hotter the weather, the more the jumping beans jump. They keep on jumping for about three to six months; the larva then spins a cocoon inside the seed, mutates and eventually emerges as a moth.

If you're in Álamos at the right time of year, you can go into the hills and find some brincadores yourself, or simply buy them from vendors in front of the cathedral. José Trinidad, a popular tour guide, has been dubbed the 'jumping bean king.' He sells brincadores (about 40) in a small bag for US$2, or by the liter (about 1200) for US$40. He can send them internationally; write (in English or Spanish) to José Trinidad Hurtado S, Apartado Postal 9, Álamos, Sonora 85760, Mexico, or fax him at 647-428-00-22. The brincadores are sent out around July to September (minimum order 1L). If you get some jumping beans and they don't jump very much, close your hand around them to warm them up.

Interestingly, though Mexican jumping beans are sold as a curiosity in other parts of the world including the USA, Europe and Asia, they are almost never sold in other parts of Mexico.

A couple of good **vantage points** offer views of the town. One is the scenic overlook atop a small hill on the south side of town. The other is on a small hill just west of the cathedral. This one is closer to the center, but the view is better from the overlook.

A **tianguis** (flea market) is held from about 6am to 2pm Sunday beside the Arroyo La Aduana on the north side of town.

Organized Tours

The *Home & Garden Tour*, sponsored by Los Amigos de Educación, starts at 10am Saturday in front of the museum. The tour costs US$8 and is given from around mid-October to mid-May.

At other times, Álamos' tour guides can take you to some of the homes. Álamos has six professional tour guides. Ask at the tourist office; a two-hour tour costs around US$9 per person. The superb *Hacienda de los Santos* (see Places to Stay) offers one-hour tours at 2pm daily for US$3.50.

Solipaso Excursions & Tourist Services (☎/fax 428-04-66, Ⓦ www.solipaso.com, *Cárdenas 15; mountain-bike rental day/week US$15/70*), run by Jennifer and David MacKay, offers nature tours including trips on the Río Mayo and Sea of Cortez and of the former silver mining town of La Aduana. They also lead bird-watching, hiking and mountain bike tours from October through May. They have a guesthouse (see Places to Stay) and rent mountain bikes.

Craig Leonard (☎ 428-01-42) offers Río Mayo rafting trips from December to March. *Felipe Acosta* (☎ 428-01-82), who runs a hunting lodge, offers bird-watching or bird-hunting trips and horseback riding. Expert biologist **Stephanie Meyer** (☎/fax 428-03-88, e hotelrio@cybernet.com.mx) leads a variety of natural history tours around Álamos and southern Sonora.

Special Events
Festival Dr Alfonso Ortíz Tirado, a high-quality cultural festival held the last 10 days of January, attracts thousands of visitors each year. The fiesta of the Virgen de Concepción, the town's patron saint, is December 8. Singing competitions are held December 4 to 14. Traditional *posadas* (processions) begin on December 16 and continue to Christmas Eve.

Places to Stay
Budget Near the entrance to town is **Dolisa Motel & Trailer Park** (☎ 428-01-31, Madero 72) Tent/trailer sites US$9/17, rooms US$34-45. This property has 40 spaces with full hookups, and pleasant, air-conditioned rooms.

Acosta Trailer Rancho (☎ 428-02-46, fax 428-02-79, cnr 5 de Mayo & Guadalupe Posada) Tent sites US$5.50, trailer sites US$9-15, rooms US$50. Located about 1km east of the town center, the Acosta has 20 sites with full hookups, barbecue areas, shady trees and two swimming pools. They also have eight rooms (for up to three people) with chimneys, air-con and bath.

Hotel Enríquez (☎ 428-03-10, Juárez 4) Singles/doubles with shared bath US$11.25/17, with private bath US$17/23. This 250-year-old building with a central courtyard stands on the west side of Plaza de Armas. This is the cheapest hotel in Álamos, but it's not a great value. It's dirty, noisy and a little creepy. But, hey, cheap is good.

Mid-Range At the entrance to town is **Motel Somar** (☎ 428-01-95, Madero 110) Singles/doubles with bath US$23/27, with air-con US$34/38. The Somar has parking and decent, reasonably sized rooms.

Hotel Los Portales (☎ 428-02-11, Juárez 6) Singles/doubles US$29/50. The restored mansion of the Almada family, on the west side of Plaza de Armas, is the least impressive of Álamos' Spanish colonial buildings – but still a fine place.

Doña Elia Salazar (☎ 428-01-44, Rosales 67) rents rooms in her home for US$28. The tourist office keeps a list of other *casas particulares* (private homes) that rent rooms.

Dolisa Motel & Trailer Park and **Acosta Trailer Rancho** also rent rooms in this price range (see Budget).

Top End Breakfast is only one of the attractions at **La Puerta Roja Inn** (☎ 428-01-42, w www.lapuertarojainn.com, Galeana 46) Rooms US$50-67. Teri Arnold's hotel is not central but has a small swimming pool. She rents three charming rooms, plus a *casita* (small house) with kitchen out back; ask about weekly rates for the casita.

Los Amigos (☎ 428-10-14, w www.alamosmexico.com/losamigos, Obregón 3) Singles/doubles US$72/84 including continental breakfast. Prices are considerably lower from April through October. Los Amigos is a B&B, café, gallery and bookstore all in one small building. They rent three large rooms and allow those on a budget to camp on their roof (US$11 plus US$5.50 for bedding if needed).

La Ciudadela (☎ 428-04-66, w www.solipaso.com, Cárdenas 15) Rooms US$70-100, 'dungeon' room US$40. Jennifer and David MacKay of Solipaso (see Organized Tours, above) run this guesthouse just off Plaza de Armas. It was the first jail in Álamos and is one of its oldest buildings. One of the four rooms is expandable to a two-room suite. They also have a secluded casita in the back.

Hotel La Mansión (☎ 428-02-21, Obregón 2) Rooms US$106 including breakfast. Recently reopened, La Mansión has rooms with king-size beds and chimneys around a sunny courtyard.

Hotel Casa de los Tesoros (☎ 428-00-10, Obregón 10) Rooms US$94-119 including breakfast. Rates are lower June through October. Formerly an 18th-century convent, this is now a handsome hotel with a swimming pool, cozy bar and courtyard restaurant with entertainment. Rooms come with air-con and a fireplace.

Hacienda de los Santos Hotel & Spa (☎ 428-02-17, w www.haciendadelossantos.com, Molina 8) Rooms US$165-1100. The most luxurious hotel in Álamos, the Hacienda de los Santos has three swimming pools, a gym, spa treatments, restaurant, bar and beautiful courtyards (also see Organized Tours, earlier).

Places to Eat

Some of the cheapest food can be had at the food stalls in and around the **market**.

La Kazeta Café, a simple snack bar on the west end of Plaza Alameda, is a nice place to watch the people.

Restaurant Las Palmeras (☎ 428-00-65, *Cárdenas 9*) Prices US$3-9. This place on the north side of Plaza de Armas is a town favorite. The food is tasty and the prices are good too.

Los Sabinos Prices US$3-8. This place, located across Arroyo Agua Escondida, consists of a few tables on a family's front porch. They offer a variety of *antojitos* (light dishes such as quesadillas or tostadas) and seafood or meat dishes.

Casa de Café (inside Hotel La Mansión) Prices from US$1.25. Open 7.30am-noon daily Oct-Apr. Sally Hoff, whose café has hopped around several hotels in the last few years, is now back at her original location and still serving great coffee and pastries.

The restaurant/bar at the *Hacienda de los Santos* (see Places to Stay) serves breakfast, lunch, dinner and Sunday brunch, and a trio provides music every evening. Reservations are required. At *Hotel Casa de los Tesoros* (see Places to Stay), you can dine in the air-conditioned restaurant, on the courtyard, or in the cozy bar. Indigenous dances are performed Saturday nights in winter; there's live dinner music all other evenings in winter, but only on Saturday in summer.

Panadería La Moderna (Macías s/n) Bread & pastries US$0.50. Located across the Arroyo La Aduana on the north edge of town, this is Álamos' favorite bakery. The best time to come is around 1pm, when the baked goods emerge from the outdoor oven.

Getting There & Away

Access to Álamos is via highway 13 from Navojoa. Transportes Baldomero Corral and other bus companies have frequent service to Álamos (see the Navojoa section, earlier, for information).

Álamos' Transportes Baldomero Corral bus station is on the north side of Plaza Alameda. Buses depart for Navojoa at 4am, half-hourly from 6am to 12.30pm, hourly from 12.30pm to 6.30pm and at 9.15pm (1 hour, US$2). A bus to Phoenix departs nightly at 9.15pm (14 hours, US$53).

There's a taxi stand on the east end of Plaza Alameda, opposite the market.

AROUND ÁLAMOS

El Chalatón, a park about 2km southwest of town, is popular for swimming in summer. About 10km east of town, **Arroyo de Cuchujaqui** has a delightful swimming hole and is enjoyable for fishing, camping and bird-watching. **Presa El Mocuzari** is also good for swimming, camping and fishing, with abundant largemouth bass, bluegill and catfish. Take the turnoff on the Navojoa-Álamos road, about 20km west of Álamos; the reservoir is about 12km from the turnoff.

Several small historic villages near Álamos make interesting day excursions. Check out **Minas Nuevas**, about 9km from Álamos on the Navojoa-Álamos road; the bus to Navojoa will drop you off there for US$0.70. Other historic villages near Álamos include **La Aduana** and **Promontorios**. You can visit all these places on your own, or the tourist office can arrange a guide to take you.

Casa La Aduana Gourmet Restaurant & Inn (☎ 642-482-25-25) Guest rooms US$50, suites US$80; meals US$15-20. Restaurant open noon-8pm daily. In La Aduana, on the plaza in front of the church, Samuel and Donna Beardsley operate this restaurant specializing in international gourmet meals; allow about two hours for a four-course meal.

LOS MOCHIS
• pop 201,000 ☎ 668

Los Mochis (Place of Turtles) is a modern city without much history. It was founded in 1903 by American Benjamin Johnston, who established sugarcane plantations and a sugar factory here.

Many travelers pass through Los Mochis, as it's the western terminus of the famous Ferrocarril Chihuahua al Pacífico (Chihuahua-Pacific Railway), which runs through the Barranca del Cobre (Copper Canyon) region. Topolobampo, 24km southwest of Los Mochis, is the mainland terminus of a ferry serving La Paz, Baja California. Los Mochis is unremarkable otherwise, but it does have everything travelers may need.

Plazuela 27 de Septiembre, a pleasant plaza with flowers and a gazebo, is in front of the Parroquia del Sagrado Corazón de Jesús, on the corner of Obregón and Mina. With its white tower the church looks old on the outside, but inside it looks quite new. Parque Sinaloa y Jardín Botánico, a large park and botanical garden, is behind and to the left of the big Plaza Las Palmas shopping center at the intersection of Boulevards Castro and Rosales. There is also a small museum, the **Museo Regional del Valle del Fuerte** *(Rosales & Obregón; admission US$0.60; open 10am-1pm & 4pm-7pm Tues-Sat, 10am-1pm Sun)*, which has somewhat static exhibits (in Spanish only) on the history and culture of northwest Mexico.

Orientation

The streets are laid out on a grid. The main street through the city, running southwest from highway 15D directly into the center of town, changes names from Calzada López Mateos to Leyva as it enters the center. Boulevard Castro is another major artery.

Some blocks in the center are split by smaller streets (not shown on the Los Mochis map) running parallel to the main streets.

Information

Tourist Offices The very helpful tourist office (☎/fax 815-10-90, ⓔ tursina@ prodigy.net.mx), on the ground floor of the large government building on Allende at Ordóñez, is open 9am to 4pm Monday to Friday.

Money Banks are dotted around the city center. Many have ATMs, including Bancomer, at Leyva and Juárez. Casas de cambio, which have longer opening hours, include two branches of Servicio de Cambio. The American Express agent is Viajes Araceli (☎ 812-20-84, ⓦ www.viaje saracely.com, Obregón 471A Pte), between Leyva and Flores.

Post & Communications The post office, on Ordóñez between Zaragoza and Prieto, is open 8am to 6pm Monday to Friday and 9am to 1pm Saturday.

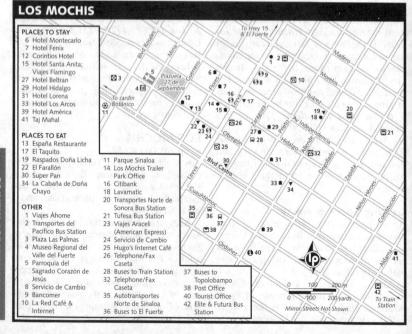

LOS MOCHIS

PLACES TO STAY
6 Hotel Montecarlo
7 Hotel Fenix
12 Corintios Hotel
15 Hotel Santa Anita;
    Viajes Flamingo
27 Hotel Beltran
29 Hotel Hidalgo
31 Hotel Lorena
33 Hotel Los Arcos
39 Hotel América
41 Taj Mahal

PLACES TO EAT
13 España Restaurante
17 El Taquito
19 Raspados Doña Licha
22 El Farallón
30 Super Pan
34 La Cabaña de Doña
    Chayo

OTHER
1 Viajes Áhome
2 Transportes del
   Pacífico Bus Station
3 Plaza Las Palmas
4 Museo Regional del
   Valle del Fuerte
5 Parroquia del
   Sagrado Corazón de
   Jesús
8 Servicio de Cambio
9 Bancomer
10 La Red Café &
    Internet

11 Parque Sinaloa
14 Los Mochis Trailer
    Park Office
16 Citibank
18 Lavamatic
20 Transportes Norte de
    Sonora Bus Station
21 Tufesa Bus Station
23 Viajes Araceli
    (American Express)
24 Servicio de Cambio
25 Hugo's Internet Café
26 Telephone/Fax
    Caseta
28 Buses to Train Station
32 Telephone/Fax
    Caseta
35 Autotransportes
    Norte de Sinaloa
36 Buses to El Fuerte

37 Buses to
    Topolobampo
38 Post Office
40 Tourist Office
42 Elite & Futura Bus
    Station

There's a telephone/fax caseta on Leyva between Obregón and Hidalgo; another is on Allende near Hidalgo. Both offer discounts after 8pm. Pay phones are plentiful around the city center.

La Red Café & Internet, Juárez 272 Pte, offers Internet access 9am to 9pm Monday to Saturday. Hugo's Internet Café, Leyva 537 Sur, has similar opening hours.

Laundry Lavamatic, Allende 228 Sur between Juárez and Independencia, is open 7.30am to 7pm Monday to Saturday and 8am to 1pm Sunday.

Places to Stay

Budget Pitch a tent or park an RV at *Los Mochis Trailer Park* (☎ 812-68-17, Calzada López Mateos) Tent/RV sites US$13.50/20. The park, 1km west of highway 15D, has 140 spaces with full hookups. You can reserve and pay at the *Trailer Park office* (☎ 812-00-21, Hidalgo 419C Pte), on the ground floor of the Hotel Santa Anita; the entrance is around the corner from the hotel entrance.

Hotel Los Arcos (☎ 812-32-53, Allende 524 Sur) Singles/doubles with shared bath US$9/15.50. This is the cheapest hotel in Los Mochis. It's not particularly clean and by staying here you may risk exposure to rats, prostitutes and loud music late into the night. You have been warned.

Hotel Hidalgo (☎ 818-34-53, e hhidalgo@ lmm.megared.net.mx, Hidalgo 260 Pte, 2nd floor) Rooms with bath & fan US$17; rooms with bath, air-con & TV US$20-25. Located between Zaragoza and Prieto, the Hidalgo has small, basic rooms.

Mid-Range The following are all clean, with private bath, air-con and cable TV in the rooms.

Hotel Fenix (☎ 812-26-23, Flores 365 Sur) Singles/doubles/triples US$25/30/33. Recently remodeled, the Fenix is the most attractive and comfortable hotel in its price range. It has a small restaurant.

Hotel Beltran (☎ 812-07-10, fax 815-71-00, Hidalgo 281 Pte) Singles/doubles/triples US$29/33/36. Hotel Beltran, on the corner of Zaragoza, has 55 clean, well-kept rooms that don't smell as strongly of industrial cleanser as the rest of the hotels in Los Mochis do.

The following three hotels have enclosed parking where you can leave a vehicle while you visit the Copper Canyon.

Hotel Lorena (☎ 812-02-39, Obregón 186 Pte) Singles/doubles/triples US$22/26/30. This hotel, on the corner of Prieto, has an inexpensive upstairs restaurant.

Hotel Montecarlo (☎/fax 812-18-18, Flores 322 Sur) Singles/doubles/triples US$24/29/31. Situated at the corner of Independencia, the Montecarlo has rooms around a sunny courtyard with a bar at one end and a little restaurant at the other.

Hotel América (☎ 812-13-55, fax 812-59-83, Allende 655 Sur) Singles/doubles/triples US$30/34/39. Located between Boulevard Castro and Cuauhtémoc, the Hotel América has a little restaurant. Rooms facing the rear are quieter.

Top End Near the new bus terminal but far from the city center is *Taj Mahal* (☎ 818-70-95, Obregón 400 Ote) Rooms US$50, suites US$64. The rooms in this brand-new hotel have air-con, phone and cable TV.

Corintios Hotel (☎ 818-22-24, 800-690-30-00, Obregón 580 Pte) Singles/doubles US$57/65, suites US$72-99. With its airy, pale green rooms, the Corintios is easily the most charming of Los Mochis' hotels.

Hotel Santa Anita (☎ 818-70-46, fax 812-00-46, e santaanita@mexicoscoppercanyon .com, cnr Leyva & Hidalgo) Singles/doubles US$100/111, suites US$122. The overpriced Santa Anita has an English-speaking staff, air-con, restaurant, bar, travel agent and parking. A bus for hotel guests only (US$4.50 per person) departs daily at 5.15am for the Ferrocarril Chihuahua al Pacífico; you can park a vehicle here while you visit the canyon.

Places to Eat

La Cabaña de Doña Chayo (Obregón 99 Pte) Prices from US$1.25. Open 8am-1am daily. This air-conditioned place, on the corner of Allende, has been serving tasty quesadillas and handmade corn and flour tortillas filled with *carne asada* (grilled beef) and *machaca* (spiced shredded dried beef) since 1963.

El Taquito (Leyva 333 Sur) Prices US$2.75-6. Open 24 hr. The economical El Taquito, located between Hidalgo and Independencia, has air-con, plastic booths and a varied bilingual menu.

España Restaurante (☎ 812-22-21, *Obregón 525 Pte*) Prices from US$7.25-18. This elegant restaurant serves Spanish cuisine. Try the house specialty, *paella especial de la casa*.

El Farallón (☎ 812-12-73, cnr *Flores & Obregón*) Prices US$7.75-12.50. This is a good seafood restaurant that serves creative sushi in addition to Mexican favorites.

Super Pan (cnr *Blvd Castro & Zaragoza*) This is an especially good Mexican bakery.

Raspados Doña Licha (cnr *Allende & Juárez*) Prices US$1. This place serves *raspados* (shaved ice covered with sweet fruit syrup).

Getting There & Away

Air The airport is about 12km southwest of the city, on the road to Topolobampo.

Daily direct flights (all with connections to other cities) are offered by Aeroméxico/Aerolitoral (☎ 815-25-70) to Chihuahua, Hermosillo, La Paz, Los Cabos and Mazatlán. Aero California (☎ 818-16-16) flies to Ciudad Obregón, Culiacán, Guadalajara, Hermosillo, La Paz, Mexico City and Tijuana.

Bus Los Mochis is on highway 15D; several major bus lines offer hourly buses heading north and south, 24 hours a day. Elite, Futura, Turistar, TAP (Transportes y Autobuses del Pacífico) and Transportes Chihuahuenses (all 1st class) share a large new terminal on Boulevard Castro, just a few blocks east of the center. Other 1st-class bus lines have their own terminals. Transportes Norte de Sonora is on Degollado between Juárez and Morelos. Transportes del Pacífico is on Morelos between Zaragoza and Leyva. All serve the same places.

Tufesa is on Zapata between Juárez and Morelos. It only goes north (except to Culiacán in the south) and has fewer buses. Autotransportes Norte de Sinaloa, on the corner of Zaragoza and Ordóñez, has expensive 2nd-class buses going south to Culiacán and Mazatlán.

Distances, times and 1st-class fares include:

Guadalajara – 927km, 13 hours; US$34-35
Guaymas – 349km, 5 hours; US$14.50-16
Hermosillo – 483km, 7 hours; US$14.50-24
Mazatlán – 421km, 6 hours; US$16-25

Mexico City (Terminal Norte) – 1462km, 24 hours; US$73-83
Navojoa – 155km, 2 hours; US$5-7
Nogales – 765km, 12 hours; US$23-38
Tepic – 711km, 12 hours; US$28-39
Tijuana – 1375km, 20 hours; US$45-68

Second-class buses to Topolobampo (24km, 45 minutes, US$1.25) leave from Cuauhtémoc at the corner of Prieto. Departures are every 15 minutes between 5.45am and 8pm. Second-class buses to El Fuerte (78km, 2 hours, US$4.75) leave from the corner of Zaragoza on the same block of Cuauhtémoc. Departures are at 7.30am, 9am, 10.30am, 11.30am, 12.30pm, 2.30pm, 3.25pm, 3.45pm, 4.30pm, 4.45pm, 5.30pm, 6pm, 7.30pm and 8pm.

Train The train station in Los Mochis (☎ 824-11-51, fax 824-11-61) is east of the center on Serrano. The ticket window is open 5am to 7am daily for the morning's departures. Tickets are also sold inside the office, which is open 9am to 6pm Monday to Friday, 9am to noon Saturday and 9am to 11am Sunday.

You can buy *primera express* (1st class) tickets up to one week in advance of travel. Tickets for *clase económica* (economy class) trains are sold an hour before the train departs, or the day before. You can also purchase tickets for either class one day in advance through Viajes Flamingo travel agency (☎ 812-16-13, e hotelsbal@tsi.com.mx) at Hotel Santa Anita. They charge an additional 8% for tickets for clase económica and a 5% service charge for credit cards.

The primera express train leaves Los Mochis at 6am, clase económica at 7am. See the Ferrocarril Chihuahua al Pacífico section, later in this chapter, for fares and detailed schedules.

Boat Ferries go from nearby Topolobampo to La Paz, Baja California. Tickets are sold at the ferry terminal in Topolobampo (see the Topolobampo section, later in this chapter, for more information).

Getting Around

Nearly everything in Los Mochis is within walking distance of the city center.

A taxi to the airport costs US$17.

'Estación' buses to the train station (20 minutes, US$0.40) depart every five minutes between 5am and 8pm from Zaragoza between Hidalgo and Obregón. You can take the bus to get to the station for the clase económica train, which departs at 7am, but for the 6am primera express departure it is probably safer to fork out US$9 for a taxi to get to the station in plenty of time. If arriving in Los Mochis by train, you can catch a group taxi to the city center for US$3.

TOPOLOBAMPO
• pop 7300 ☎ 668

Topolobampo, 24km southwest of Los Mochis, is the terminus for a ferry route to/from La Paz, Baja California.

Topolobampo has no hotels, but Mexicans love to come here to eat fresh seafood (both in town and at Playa El Maviri), go to the beach and enjoy the town's natural surroundings. A five-minute bus ride from Topolobampo is Playa El Maviri, a popular beach with plenty of seafood restaurants. Everyone recommends the *pescado zarandeado* (charcoal-grilled fish wrapped in foil). On the way to Playa El Maviri, you pass Cueva de los Murciélagos (Cave of Bats); you cannot enter this protected area, but it's beautiful to see the bats emerging at sunset and returning at sunrise.

Inexpensive *lanchas* (small motorized boats) will take you from either Topolobampo or Playa El Maviri to some beautiful natural spots that attract large populations of the animals they are named for. **Isla de Pájaros** (Island of Birds) is home to hundreds of birds, and **Santuario de Delfines** is a dolphin sanctuary. Other spots include **Playa Las Copas**, **Isla Santa María** with dunes where you can camp and **Isla El Farallón** with seals and sea lions, or you can also visit **El Delfín 'El Pechocho,'** a friendly dolphin who likes to swim with people.

Ferry tickets are sold the day of departure in the Sematur office (☎/fax 862-01-41), Cerro de las Gallinas s/n, at the Topolobampo ferry terminal; it's open 8am to 10pm when there's a ferry, 8am to 3pm on off days. Seats are US$40 and cabins are US$90 to US$140. Viajes Ahomé in Los Mochis (☎ 815-61-20), Leyva 121 Sur, sells tickets up to a month in advance. Passenger ferries usually leave every Tuesday and Saturday at 10pm arriving in La Paz at 8am; returning ferries leave La Paz Wednesday and Friday at 9pm, arriving in Topolobampo at 10am the next day. Days of passenger service may vary, so call to confirm before making the trek to Topolobampo. See Getting There & Away in the La Paz section of the Baja California chapter for vehicle fares.

CULIACÁN
• pop 540,000 ☎ 667

Capital of the state of Sinaloa, Culiacán is equidistant from Los Mochis and Mazatlán – about 210km (a three-hour drive) from either place. Primarily a commercial, administrative and agricultural center, the city has little to attract tourists but is a good point to break up the journey. If you spend some time here, you could check out the 17th-century cathedral, Palacio Municipal at Obregón & Escobedo and the *malecón* walkway along the Río Tamazula and Río Humaya.

Barranca del Cobre (Copper Canyon)

The name Barranca del Cobre (Copper Canyon) refers specifically to the awe-inspiring canyon of the Río Urique, southeast of the village of Divisadero, and generally to this and more than 20 nearby canyons carved out of the Sierra Tarahumara by at least six different rivers. Together, these canyons are four times larger than Arizona's Grand Canyon. Nine of them are deeper than it is. At an altitude of only 500m, the canyons' deepest point (Barranca de Urique, depth 1879m) has a subtropical climate, while the peaks high above are 2300m above sea level and home to conifers and evergreens. One of Mexico's most numerous indigenous peoples, the Tarahumara, still retains a traditional lifestyle here (see 'The Tarahumara').

The most popular way to see the canyons is by riding the Ferrocarril Chihuahua al Pacífico (Chihuahua-Pacific Railway, also known as the Copper Canyon Railway), which travels between Los Mochis near the Sea of Cortez and Chihuahua in the interior of northern Mexico. There are several stops in the Barranca del Cobre area.

NORTHWEST MEXICO

The Tarahumara

More than 50,000 indigenous Tarahumara live in the Sierra Tarahumara's numerous canyons, including the famous Barranca del Cobre (Copper Canyon). Isolated within this formidable topography, the Tarahumara retain many of their traditions; many still live in caves and log cabins (some of these dwellings can be seen near Creel) and they subsist on very basic agriculture of maize and beans.

The Tarahumara are well known for their eye-catching traditional apparel, especially the women, who wear full, pleated skirts and blouses made of brightly colored, patterned fabric. The men wear loincloths and ample, long-sleeved shirts also made from bright fabric. Both men and women wear the traditional sandals – now made from tire tread and leather straps.

They are also famous for running long distances. Running is so significant to the Tarahumara's culture that in their own language they call themselves Rarámuri – 'those who run fast.' Traditionally, the Tarahumara hunted by chasing down and exhausting deer, then driving the animals over cliffs to be impaled on wooden sticks strategically placed at the bottom of the canyon. Today, they run grueling footraces of 160km (or more), without stopping, through rough canyons, kicking a small wooden ball ahead of them.

A tradition of quite a different sort is the *tesquinada*, a raucous gathering in which they consume copious amounts of *tesquino*, a potent maize beer.

Catholic missionaries have made some progress improving living conditions for the Tarahumara, but they haven't been entirely successful in converting them to Catholicism. Many of the Tarahumara attend church services, but continue to worship their ancestral gods, particularly Raiénari, the sun god and protector of men, and Mechá, the moon god and protector of women. Sorcerers are as important as Catholic priests and are the only members of the Tarahumara permitted to consume peyote, a hallucinogen derived from a small cactus. They often take peyote in order to perform a bizarre dance to cure the sick.

Creel, approximately eight hours from Los Mochis, is probably the best place in the Barranca del Cobre region to break the journey and explore the canyon. It's only a small town but it has several economical places to stay and plenty of tours and things to do (see the Creel section, later in this chapter, for more information).

In between Los Mochis and Creel, the charming town of El Fuerte is a good alternative starting point for your journey. Once in the canyons, overnight stays are possible at Cerocahui, Urique, Posada Barrancas and Divisadero, allowing you 24 hours before the train passes by again – time enough to get a closer look and explore into the canyons.

Many travelers prefer to visit the area in spring or autumn, when the temperatures are not too hot at the bottom of the canyon (as in summer), or too cold at the top (as in winter).

A particularly good time to visit is late September and October (after the summer rains), when the vegetation is still green. Things dry up February to June, but you can still see some wildflowers.

FERROCARRIL CHIHUAHUA AL PACÍFICO (COPPER CANYON RAILWAY)

The Ferrocarril Chihuahua al Pacífico is among Mexico's most scenic rail journeys. A considerable feat of engineering, it has 39 bridges and 86 tunnels along 655km of railway line, connecting the mountainous, arid interior of northern Mexico with the Pacific coast. It was opened in 1961 after taking many decades to build. The major link between Chihuahua and the coast, the line is used heavily by passengers and for shipping freight. The beauty of the landscape it traverses has made it one of the country's prime tourist excursions as well.

The Ferrocarril Chihuahua al Pacífico (CHP, which is pronounced 'CHE-pe') operates two trains: the first-class primera express, which makes fewer stops and has a restaurant, bar and reclining seats; and the cheaper and slower clase económica, which has food provided by vendors and a snack bar. Cars on both trains have air-con and heating. It takes about 14 hours to make the trip on the primera express, and at least two hours longer on the clase económica, which stops frequently along the way.

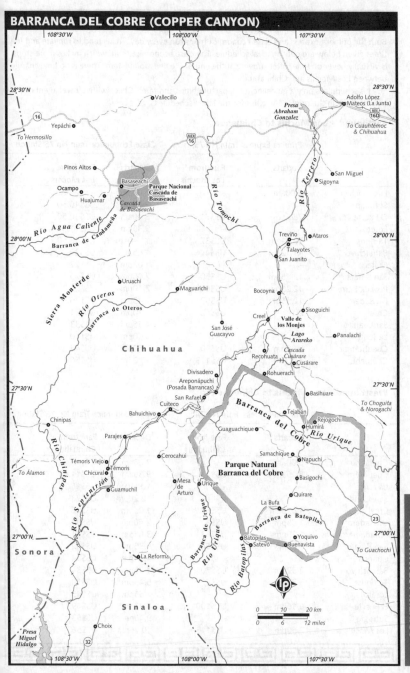

BARRANCA DEL COBRE (COPPER CANYON)

108°30'W · 108°00'W · 107°30'W

28°30'N · 28°00'N · 27°30'N · 27°00'N

Vallecillo · Yepáchi · To Hermosillo · Pinos Altos · Ocampo · Huajúmar · Basaseachi · Cascada de Basaseachi · Parque Nacional Cascada de Basaseachi · Río Agua Caliente · Barranca de Candameña · Sierra Monterde · Uruachi · Maguarichi · Río Oteros · Barranca de Oteros · Chihuahua · San José Guacayvo · Creel · Valle de los Monjes · Lago Arareko · Sisoguichi · Panalachi · Cascada Cusárare · Recohuata · Cusárare · Rohuerachi · Divisadero · Areponápuchi (Posada Barrancas) · San Rafael · Cuiteco · Bahuichivo · Barranca del Cobre · Tejabán · Basihuare · To Choguita & Norogachi · Chinipas · Parajes · Guaguachique · Humirá · Rejogochi · Río Urique · Cerocahui · Témoris Viejo · Chicural · Témoris · Guamuchil · Río Septentrión · Mesa de Arturo · Urique · Parque Natural Barranca del Cobre · Samachique · Napuchi · Basigochi · Quirare · La Bufa · Barranca de Batopilas · Batopilas · Satevó · Yoquivo · Buenavista · To Guachochi · La Reforma · Río Chinipas · To Álamos · Sonora · Barranca de Urique · Río Urique · Río Batopilas · Sinaloa · Choix · Presa Miguel Hidalgo

Presa Abraham Gonzalez · Adolfo López Mateos (La Junta) · To Cuauhtémoc & Chihuahua · San Miguel · Sigoyna · Río Tomochi · Río Terrero · Treviño · Ataros · Talayotes · San Juanito · Bocoyna

0   10   20 km
0   6   12 miles

Railway Schedule – Ferrocarril Chihuahua al Pacífico

Both the primera express and clase económica trains run every day. Trains tend to run late and the times given below are only an ideal schedule. The clase económica train, which makes more stops, is virtually never on time, often arriving at the end of the line around 1am. There is no time change between Los Mochis and Chihuahua.

This schedule is only a guideline for departure times and fares. Check with a travel agent or the train stations in the originating cities for the latest schedules.

Eastbound – Los Mochis to Chihuahua

	Primera Express Train No 73		Clase Económica Train No 75 Station	
	Departs	Fare from Los Mochis	Departs	Fare from Los Mochis
Los Mochis	6.00am	–	7.00am	–
Sufragio	–	–	7.55am	US$10.50
El Fuerte	7.26am	US$21	8.40am	US$10.50
Loreto	–	–	9.35am	US$11.50
Témoris	10.11am	US$37	11.40am	US$18.50
Bahuichivo	11.12am	US$44	12.50pm	US$22
Cuiteco	–	–	1.02pm	US$22
San Rafael	12.15pm	US$50	2.00pm	US$25
Posada Barrancas	12.25pm	US$51	2.10pm	US$25
Divisadero	12.55pm	US$52	2.45pm	US$26
Creel	2.14pm	US$62	4.10pm	US$31
San Juanito	–	–	4.55pm	US$33
La Junta	–	–	6.50pm	US$40
Cuauhtémoc	5.25pm	US$90	7.50pm	US$45
Chihuahua	7.50pm	US$113	10.25pm	US$56

Westbound – Los Mochis to Chihuahua

	Primera Express Train No 74		Clase Económica Train No 76 Station	
	Departs	Fare from Chihuahua	Departs	Fare from Chihuahua
Chihuahua	6.00am	–	7.00am	–
Cuauhtémoc	8.15am	US$23	9.35am	US$11.50
La Junta	–	–	10.40am	US$16
San Juanito	–	–	12.20pm	US$23
Creel	11.26am	US$52	1.05pm	US$26
Divisadero	1.05pm	US$62	2.50pm	US$31
Posada Barrancas	1.20pm	US$63	3.05pm	US$31
San Rafael	1.40pm	US$64	3.35pm	US$32
Cuiteco	–	–	4.14pm	US$34
Bahuichivo	2.32pm	US$70	4.35pm	US$34
Témoris	3.30pm	US$77	5.45pm	US$38
Loreto	–	–	7.55pm	US$45
El Fuerte	6.16pm	US$100	8.42pm	US$49
Sufragio	–	–	9.40pm	US$53
Los Mochis	7.50pm	US$113	10.25pm	US$56

ELEVATION OF FERROCARRIL CHIHUAHUA AL PACÍFICO

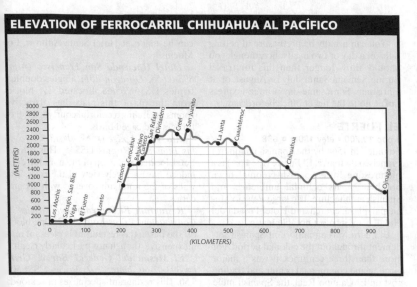

If you're heading toward Los Mochis from Chihuahua, take the primera express, as the clase económica, which runs later and is often late, passes the best scenery (between Creel and Loreto) after dark, especially in winter when the sun sets earlier. Heading in the other direction, you should be able to see the best views on either train, unless the clase económica is excessively delayed.

The majority of the good views are on the right side of the carriage heading inland (east), while the left side is best for trips going to the coast (west). Passengers often congregate in the vestibules between cars (where the windows open) to take photos.

Between Los Mochis and El Fuerte, the train passes through flat, gray farmland. Shortly after El Fuerte, it begins to climb through fog-shrouded hills speckled with dark pillars of cacti. It passes over the long Río Fuerte bridge and through the first of 86 tunnels about three hours after leaving Los Mochis. It cuts through small canyons and hugs the sides of cliffs as it climbs higher and higher through the mountains of the Sierra Tarahumara. The trip becomes an exciting sequence of dramatic geological images – craggy cliffs, sheer canyon walls and the riverbed far below. The highlight of the ride is when the train stops at Divisadero and you get your first and only glimpse of the actual Barranca del Cobre.

If you're traveling only between Creel and Chihuahua, you may prefer to take the bus, as it's quicker and the schedule is more convenient.

Tickets
Primera express tickets can be purchased up to one week in advance, while tickets for clase económica trains can only be purchased one day in advance.

At the train station in Chihuahua (☎ 614-439-72-12), tickets are sold 5am to 7am and 9am to 6pm Monday, Wednesday and Friday; 5am to 6am and 9am to 6pm Tuesday and Thursday, 5am to 6am and 9am to noon Saturday and Sunday.

At the train station in Los Mochis (☎ 668-824-11-51, fax 668-824-11-61), the ticket window is open 5am to 7am daily for the morning's departures. Tickets are also sold inside the office, which is open 9am to 6pm Monday to Friday, 9am to noon Saturday and 9am to 11am Sunday.

The Viajes Flamingo travel agency (☎ 668-812-16-13, e hotelsbal@tsi.com.mx, w www.tsi.com.mx/coppercanyon/index2.htm) at the Hotel Santa Anita in Los Mochis sells tickets one day in advance. They sell primera express tickets for the same price as that at train stations, but apply an 8% charge for clase económica and a 5% charge for credit cards.

You can usually be pretty sure of getting a ticket a day or two in advance, though you should allow longer than this for travel during Semana Santa, July or August, or at Christmas. For a same-day primera express ticket, go to the ticket office before 5am.

EL FUERTE
• pop 10,700 • elev 180m ☎ 698

Founded in 1564 by the Spanish conqueror Francisco de Ibarra, El Fuerte (the Fort) is a picturesque little Spanish colonial town notable for its colonial ambience and Spanish architecture. The large Palacio Municipal, plaza, church and Hotel Posada del Hidalgo are its most notable features.

El Fuerte was an important Spanish settlement throughout the colonial period. For more than three centuries, it was a major farming and commercial center and trading post on El Camino Real, the Spanish mule trail between Guadalajara to the southeast, the mines of Álamos to the north and the Sierra Madre Occidental to the northeast. In 1824, El Fuerte became the capital of the state of Sinaloa, a title it retained for several years.

You can get a great view of the town, the Río Fuerte and surrounding area by walking up the small mirador hill behind the Posada del Hidalgo, just off the plaza. At the top, there's a replica of the original fort for which El Fuerte was named. Excursions around El Fuerte include a three-hour round-trip (on your own or with a guide) to a set of petroglyphs. El Fuerte's two reservoirs (Domínguez and Hidalgo) are excellent for fishing.

Bancomer, at the corner of Constitución and Juárez, one block off the plaza, is open 8.30am to 2.30pm Monday to Friday and has an ATM.

Places to Stay & Eat
Hotel Posada del Hidalgo (☎ 893-11-92, W www.mexicoscoppercanyon.com/posada hidalgo.htm, cnr Hidalgo & 5 de Mayo) Singles/doubles/triples US$100/111/123. The rich silver-mining Almada family of Álamos had strong connections in El Fuerte. In 1890, Rafael Almada built an opulent mansion that is now this hotel, in the center of El Fuerte behind the church. It has beautiful interior gardens, swimming pool, restaurant/bar and 50 rooms. Reservations can be made at Hotel Santa Anita in Los Mochis.

Hotel Hacienda San Francisco (☎/fax 893-00-55, Obregón 201) Singles/doubles/triples US$56/65/68. Located 2½ blocks from the plaza, this place has attractive rooms encircling a colorful courtyard full of flowers and caged birds.

Río Vista Lodge (☎ 893-04-13, Cerro de las Pilas s/n) Rooms US$45. This quirky hotel, located at the top of the mirador, does indeed have a lovely view of the river. The walls of the hotel are covered with art and curios.

Restaurant El Supremo (cnr Rosales & Constitución) Prices from US$2. One block off the plaza, this restaurant is pleasant and inexpensive, though not particularly clean.

El Mesón del General Bar & Grill (☎ 893-02-60, Juárez 202) Prices US$1.50-5.50. This restaurant specializes in seafood; its tables are set around a shaded courtyard.

There's also a restaurant at *Hotel Posada del Hidalgo*. And for less expensive fare, you can try one of the many taco stands on 16 de Septiembre at Juárez near the bus stop.

Langostino (crayfish) and *filete de lobina* (fillet of bass) are El Fuerte specialties.

Getting There & Around
In El Fuerte, buses to Los Mochis (78km, 2 hours, US$4.75) depart hourly between 5.30am and 6.30pm, from the corner of Juárez and 16 de Septiembre.

El Fuerte makes a good alternative to Los Mochis as a starting or ending point for a trip on the Ferrocarril Chihuahua al Pacífico. The train station is a few kilometers east of town. The eastbound primera express train departs El Fuerte at 7.26am; clase económica leaves at 8.40am. The westbound primera express leaves at 6.16pm and clase económica at 8.42pm. Tickets are sold on board. You can take a taxi to the station for about US$5.50.

CEROCAHUI
• elev 1600m ☎ 635

Cerocahui, about 16km from the Bahuichivo train stop, is a picturesque village in a valley with apple and peach orchards and pine and madrone trees. Its church, San Francisco Javier de Cerocahui, was founded in 1680 by the Jesuit Padre Juan María de Salvatierra. Cerocahui is an excellent place for bird-watching; over 168 species of birds have been spotted here. Any of the hotels here can arrange trips into the canyon. There is a restaurant in town on the plaza.

Places to Stay

Hotel Paraíso del Oso (☎ 614-421-33-72 in Chihuahua, ☎ 800-844-3107 in the USA, **W** www.mexicohorse.com) Camp sites US$5.50, dorm beds US$11, singles/doubles US$105/155 including all meals. Named after the rock formation resembling a cartoon bear that looms over it, Paraíso del Oso occupies a peaceful and picturesque spot 5km north of Cerocahui village. Camping sites are next to the river. Campers may shower and arrange meals at the hotel. There is one dorm room with eight beds. The management can arrange horseback or hiking trips as far as Batopilas.

Hotel Raramuri Singles/doubles around US$11/17. Enrique Mancinas and his wife operate this small hotel on the far side of the church. It is clean and popular with backpackers. They don't have a phone, but you can contact them through the town caseta (☎ 456-06-19).

Hotel Misión Singles/doubles US$170/249 including all meals. This former hacienda, with bar, restaurant, gardens and a small vineyard, is the oldest and best-known hotel in Cerocahui. The rooms here are certainly adequate and comfortable, but not really worth the price. Reservations are made at the Hotel Santa Anita (☎ 668-818-70-46) in Los Mochis.

Margarita's Cerocahui Wilderness Lodge Singles & doubles US$160 including all meals. This luxurious hotel, on a cliff about a 25-minute drive from Cerocahui, offers spectacular views. The brightly painted rooms have electricity but are lit with kerosene lamps for ambience. Reservations must be made in advance through Hotel Margarita's Plaza Mexicana (☎ 635-456-02-45) in Creel.

Getting There & Away

All the hotels except Raramuri will pick you up at the Bahuichivo train station. If you're going to Raramuri you can hitch or catch a ride with one of the other hotels' buses. The daily bus from Bahuichivo to Urique may drop you off in Cerocahui if it's not too full (see the Urique section). See the Ferrocarril Chihuahua al Pacífico section for information on getting to Bahuichivo by train.

URIQUE
• elev 550m ☎ 635

This village, at the bottom of the impressive Barranca de Urique, is also accessed from the Bahuichivo train stop and is a good base for all kinds of canyon hikes lasting anywhere from one to several days. The two- to three-day hike between Batopilas and Urique is a popular trek.

Urique has a surprising number of accommodations for its size.

Hotel Figueroa Rooms US$5.50. This hotel has eight rooms that share one bathroom. The rooms don't lock while you're inside of them and there are plenty of roaches. Inquire at Calle Principal 170, across from the plaza.

Hotel Cañón de Urique (☎ 456-60-24, Calle Principal s/n) Singles/doubles US$11/17. This hotel is often recommended by travelers. Rooms are nothing fancy, but they're a good value.

Hotel Estrella del Río (☎ 456-60-03) Singles/doubles US$34/61 including breakfast & dinner. This brand-new hotel has huge, bright rooms overlooking Río Urique. The rooms have electric fans and plenty of hot water. When in Urique, inquire about rooms at Restaurant Plaza, across from the plaza.

Keith, an American, also rents **rooms** and has a camping area at his ranch (on the road to Guadalupe). You can camp at **La Playita** beside the Río Urique; ask permission at the Presidencia Municipal.

A bus (actually a Suburban) heads down to Urique from Bahuichivo train station once a day after the last train passes the station (around 5pm). The jarring ride takes four hours and costs US$8. It departs for the return trip at 7am, so plan on staying for two nights. Alternately, you may be able to arrange transportation with your hotel in Urique.

AREPONÁPUCHI (POSADA BARRANCAS)
• elev 2220m ☎ 635

About 5km southwest of Divisadero, Posada Barrancas station is next to Areponápuchi, the only village on the train line that is right on the rim of the canyon. Often referred to as Arepo, this village has magnificent views of the canyon, several places to stay and is a good point for going into the canyon by foot, car or horseback.

Places to Stay

Lucy González (☎ 578-30-07) rents rooms in Arepo, with TV, carpet and private hot bath, for US$28 per day. *Loly Mancinas* rents rooms for US$34. Both women sell food at the Divisadero train station; if you get off there, they'll make sure you get a ride to Arepo.

Cabañas Díaz (☎ 578-30-08) 1-3-person cabañas with shared bath US$23, 1-3-person cabañas with private bath & fireplace US$45, 3-5-person cabañas with private bath & heater US$56, large room with 10 bunk beds US$110; meals US$5.50. This place is known for its hospitality, delicious meals and tranquil, relaxing atmosphere. They'll organize any kind of canyon trip you would like, be it a hike to the rim of the canyon, halfway down or all the way down to the Río Urique. Van, horse and burro tours are all available. If no one from the family comes to meet the train, just walk down the main road into the village until you see their sign on the right (about 10 minutes).

Hotel Rancho Posada (Ⓦ *www.mexico scoppercanyon.com*) Singles/doubles US$98/124. This hotel is located right at the train stop and just a five-minute walk from the viewpoint. Meals are not included, but can be purchased at Hotel Posada Mirador's spectacular dining room. Reservations are made at the Hotel Santa Anita (☎ 668-818-70-46) in Los Mochis.

Hotel Mansión Tarahumara (☎ 614-415-47-21 in Chihuahua, Ⓔ *mansion@ buzon.online.com.mx*) Singles/doubles US$135/191 including all meals & a walking tour. Located near the train station, this place is also known as El Castillo because it looks like a medieval stone castle. It has a variety of cozy, rustic cabins. The hotel has a Jacuzzi, bar and restaurant.

Hotel Posada Mirador (Ⓦ *www .mexicoscoppercanyon.com*) Singles/doubles US$170/249 including all meals. Perched on the rim of the canyon, the Posada Mirador has 48 luxury rooms and suites – all with private terraces and magnificent views.

Reservations are made at the Hotel Santa Anita (☎ 668-818-70-46) in Los Mochis.

Getting There & Away

See the Ferrocarril Chihuahua al Pacífico section for information on getting to Posada Barrancas by train. Buses between San Rafael and Creel will drop you off in Areponápuchi at the highway entrance (see Getting There & Around in the Creel section for more information). The bus is much faster and cheaper than the train, but it's a couple of kilometers from the highway to the hotels and there are no taxis in town.

DIVISADERO

• elev 2240m

About seven hours out of Los Mochis, the train stops for 20 minutes at **Divisadero** for an excellent view of the Barranca del Cobre. For the rest of the trip, the train runs through pine forests skirting the edge of canyons, but not close enough to see down into them. The viewpoint at Divisadero is the first and only chance you'll get to see into the 1760m-deep canyon from the train. This will also probably be the first time you will see some of the Tarahumara people who inhabit the canyon. The Tarahumara come to the train station to display and sell their handicrafts to visitors. Hotels in Divisadero organize short trips into the canyon, but you can arrange a far better deal yourself with one of the Tarahumara who meet the train to sell handicrafts and food. If you hire a guide, you must have your own food for the trip; there are two restaurants and some snack stalls, but no stores in Divisadero. Your guide will lead you 1000m down to the Río Urique. Carry enough water for the descent and be prepared for a change in climate from cool – Divisadero is 2240m high – to warm and humid near the river. Autumn is the best time to come; flash floods and suffocatingly high temperatures are a problem in summer. You could spend more time here if you switch from a primera express to clase económica train, which is roughly two hours behind. Be aware that you will need two separate tickets to do this.

Next to the viewpoint, *Hotel Divisadero Barrancas* (☎ 614-415-11-99 in Chihuahua) has 48 luxurious rooms, all with views of the canyon. Singles/doubles here cost US$180/210; the price includes three meals daily and a walking tour. Rates are lower in the summer. The restaurant/bar, with a spectacular view, is open to the public. The hotel will arrange guided tours into the canyon.

Buses between San Rafael and Creel will drop you off at Divisadero (see Getting There & Around in the Creel section for more information). For information on getting to Divisadero by train, see the Ferrocarril Chihuahua al Pacífico section.

CREEL
• pop 4600 • elev 2338m ☎ 635

Creel, a pleasant small town surrounded by pine forests and interesting rock formations, is many travelers' favorite stop on the Ferrocarril Chihuahua al Pacífico. You can stock up on maps and staples and catch a bus to Batopilas, a village 140km away deep in the heart of the Tarahumara canyon country. Creel is also a regional center for the Tarahumara people. You will see many Tarahumara in traditional dress and numerous shops selling Tarahumara handicrafts.

Its high elevation means Creel can be very cold, even snowy, especially in winter. In summer, the cool air and piney aroma from the town's lumber mill are a welcome relief from the heat of the tropical coastal lowlands or the deserts of northern Mexico.

Orientation

Creel is a very small town. Most things you need, including many hotels and restaurants, are on Avenida López Mateos, the town's main street, which leads south from the town plaza, where there are two churches, the post office, the bank and the Artesanías Misión shop. The train station is one block north of the plaza. Across the tracks are a couple more hotels and restaurants and the bus station.

Avenida Gran Visión is the highway through town; it heads northeast to Chihuahua and southeast to Guachochi, passing Lago Arareko and Cusárare. There is a paved road that runs southwest from Creel through Divisadero and on to San Rafael. Avenida López Mateos and Avenida Gran Visión intersect a couple of kilometers south of the center of town.

Maps A large map of Creel is posted on the outside wall of Banca Serfin, on the north side of the plaza. Maps of the surrounding

CREEL

PLACES TO STAY
1 Hotel Nuevo
3 Hotel Korachi
10 Casa Margarita
18 Casa de Huéspedes Pérez
20 La Posada de Creel
23 Cabañas Berti's
26 Hotel Margarita's Plaza Mexicana
28 Hotel Los Pinos; Buses to Batopilas
29 Hotel Parador de la Montaña
30 Motel Cascada Inn
32 Casa Valenzuela
33 Best Western - The Lodge at Creel; Sierra Madre Pub Steakhouse

PLACES TO EAT
5 Hospital Para Crudos
17 Cafetería Mí Café
24 Restaurant Verónica
25 Restaurant La Cabaña
27 Restaurant Lupita
31 El Caballo Bayo
34 Restaurant Estela

OTHER
2 Autotransportes Noroeste Bus Station
4 Estrella Blanca Bus Station
6 Artesanías Misión Shop
7 Banca Serfin
8 Tarahumara Tours
9 Church
11 Church
12 Laundry (Familia Mendoza González)
13 Casa de las Artesanías del Estado de Chihuahua y Museo
14 Post Office
15 Museo de Paleontología; Casa del Artesano Indígena
16 Divisas La Sierra
19 Umarike Expediciones
21 Papelería de Todo
22 Complejo Ecoturístico Arareko Office

To Chihuahua

Av Gran Visión
Av Rarajipa
Cristo Rey
Villa
Av Ferrocarril
Villa
Arroyo del Creel
Av Tarahumara
Train Station
Plaza
Plaza
Flores
Av López Mateos
Elfido Batista
Cuesta
Batopilas
Ferrocarril Chihuahua al Pacífico

0   50   100 m
0   50   100 yards

To Complejo Ecoturístico Arareko, Lago Arareko, Divisadero & San Rafael

To Villa Mexicana, Hotel Pueblo Viejo, Complejo Ecoturístico Arareko, Lago Arareko, Divisadero & San Rafael

NORTHWEST MEXICO

area, including a series of topographical maps of the canyons, are sold next door at the Artesanías Misión shop. This shop also sells a number of fine books about the Barranca del Cobre and the Tarahumara, in Spanish and English.

Umarike Expediciones, on Villa at Cristo Rey, sells probably the best map for hiking or biking in the area (it's to scale!), as well as some topographical maps of the area.

Information

Creel has no formal tourist office, but information about local attractions is available from the tour operators, most of the places to stay, and the Artesanías Misión shop.

Banca Serfin on the plaza changes money; it's open 9am to 4pm Monday to Friday and has an ATM. Divisas La Sierra, just southeast of the plaza, changes US dollars and traveler's checks.

The post office on the plaza is open 9am to 3pm Monday to Friday. Pay phones are plentiful on López Mateos. The Papelería de Todo shop on López Mateos has a telephone caseta and Internet access.

The public laundry at the Best Western – The Lodge at Creel is open 9am to 6pm Monday to Saturday. Laundry service is available in the large two-story yellow house on Villa, across the tracks from the plaza; there's no sign except for the family name, Familia Mendoza González. It's open 9am to 7pm Monday to Saturday. Another public laundry is at the Villa Mexicana campground, south of town.

Museums

The **Casa de las Artesanías del Estado de Chihuahua y Museo** (admission US$0.60; open 9am-2pm & 4pm-7pm Tues-Sun), overlooking the plaza, contains excellent exhibits on Tarahumara culture and crafts. Don't miss it.

The **Museo de Paleontología** (admission US$1.25; open 9am-1pm & 3pm-6pm daily), on the smaller plaza, is less impressive. It has a hodgepodge of exhibits on Chihuahuan history, ranging from fossils and rocks to antiques and Mennonite artifacts.

Organized Tours

Most of Creel's hotels offer tours of the surrounding area, with trips to canyons, rivers, hot springs, waterfalls and other places.

Trips range from a seven-hour tour to Río Urique, at the bottom of the Barranca de Urique, passing several indigenous villages to an eight-hour excursion to Mennonite settlements in Cuauhtémoc, including a visit to a Mennonite cheese factory and lunch at a Mennonite home (see the Cuauhtémoc section in the Central North Mexico chapter for more on the Mennonites). See the Around Creel, Cascada de Basaseachi and Batopilas sections for information on other tour destinations.

Tarahumara Tours (☎ 456-00-65, W www.umarike.com.mx/coppercanyon/taratours.htm), with an office on the plaza, offers all the same tours as the hotels, often at better prices. There's also **Umarike Expediciones** (☎ 456-02-48, W www.umarike.com.mx, Villa at Cristo Rey), which offers guided hiking and mountain bike tours, rock climbing excursions and instruction; rents mountain bikes and camping gear; and offers maps and information for do-it-yourself trips.

Tara Adventures (☎/fax 614-417-38-04 in Chihuahua, W www.umarike.com.mx/coppercanyon/tara_adventures.htm, Privada de José Martí No 5716, Colonia Granjas, Chihuahua, Chihuahua CP 31160), operated by popular bilingual naturalist and guide Pedro Palma Gutiérrez, has an excellent reputation for Copper Canyon adventures. (Tours can originate in Chihuahua, Creel or any place you like.)

All tours require a minimum number of people. The easiest place to get a group together is often at Casa Margarita, but any hotel will organize a tour if there are enough people wanting to go, usually four or five. Most hotels don't require that you be a guest in order to go on a tour. Expect to pay about US$11/25 per person for a half/full-day tour, but shop around – the pricier hotels tend to have more expensive tours. If you have your own transport you can do many of these excursions on your own. If you take any tour from Casa Margarita, they include a box lunch. One or more destinations may be combined on the same tour.

You could also hire your own guide. Expect to pay around US$25 per person, per day. Inquire at the office of the Complejo Ecoturístico Arareko on López Mateos, the Tarahumara Tours office on the plaza, Umarike Expediciones, or ask around at the hotels.

Places to Stay

Camping & Cabins About 7km south of Creel, *Complejo Ecoturístico Arareko* offers camping and lodging near Lago Arareko (see Around Creel, later in this chapter).

Villa Mexicana (☎ 456-06-65, **w** *www .koacoppercanyon.com, Prolongacion López Mateos s/n)* Dorm beds US$9, with breakfast US$12, tent sites US$5.50 per person, RV sites with no/partial/full hookups US$12/18/20, 4/6-person cabins US$109/124. This new, well-equipped campground is on the south side of Creel, about a 15-minute walk from the center of town; head south on López Mateos and just keep going. Cheaper weekly and monthly rates are available. Facilities include a communal kitchen, baths, restaurant, bar, small shop, laundry and tours.

Hotel Pueblo Viejo (☎ 456-02-95) Singles/doubles with breakfast US$67/78, with all meals US$90/115. Nestled in at the base of the hills behind Villa Mexicana, the whimsical Pueblo Viejo features several cabins in various sizes and styles, from log cabin to fortress, which together resemble a small town. All cabins have a heater, water cooler, coffee maker and bath. They'll pick up guests at the train station.

Guesthouses & Hotels The most popular local accommodations is *Casa Margarita* (☎ 456-00-45, López Mateos 11) Mattress on floor US$5.50, dorm beds US$8, rooms with bath from US$23. It's situated on the northeast corner of the plaza between the two churches, with a variety of accommodations and prices. There are beds in cramped dorms and nicer private rooms. All prices include both breakfast and dinner. Casa Margarita is a great place to meet other travelers, as everyone gathers at the table to eat together – often in shifts, since the place is so popular. They run a variety of tours daily, which there is some pressure to join. They also rent bicycles and have laundry machines. At the time of writing, two new floors were being added to the house, with plans to include Internet access, a juice bar and lounge.

Casa de Huéspedes Pérez (☎ 456-00-47, Flores 257) 1-6-person rooms US$9 per person. This hotel has a communal kitchen, friendly family atmosphere and simple rooms. Only the first-floor rooms have heaters.

Casa Valenzuela (☎ 456-01-04, López Mateos 68) Singles/doubles US$9/17. This place is a bit stark and quiet, but the rooms are adequate. Some rooms share a bath.

Cabañas Berti's (López Mateos 31) Singles/doubles US$17/23. The cozy rooms here come with either a heater or fireplace. They don't currently have a phone, but you can call the caseta across the street (☎ 456-01-22) to contact them; ask for Paola.

La Posada de Creel (☎ 456-01-42, Avenida Ferrocarril s/n) Rooms with shared bath US$8 per person, singles/doubles with private bath US$17/20. The rooms at Posada de Creel are attractive in a small, dark kind of way.

Hotel Los Pinos (☎ 456-00-44, López Mateos 39) Singles/doubles US$26/34. The Hotel Los Pinos has aging but tidy rooms with heaters, plus off-street parking.

Hotel Korachi (☎ 456-00-64, Villa 16) Singles/doubles/triples/quads with bath US$14.50/20/25/34, cabaña-style singles/ doubles/triples/quads US$24/34/39/45. Across the tracks from the plaza, the rooms here are simple. The cabañas are dated in style – lacquered log walls – but are comfy enough and have woodstoves. There is private parking. They also have seven rustic *country houses* in the countryside, 2km from Creel. Each can hold up to eight people.

Hotel Nuevo (☎ 456-00-22, fax 456-00-43, Villa 121) Singles/doubles US$28/50, cabaña-style rooms US$73. Located across from the train station, the Nuevo offers both standard rooms as well as large, log-and-stone cabaña-style rooms.

Hotel Margarita's Plaza Mexicana (☎ 456-02-45, Elfido Batista s/n) Singles/ doubles US$39/50. The family that runs the Casa Margarita also runs this comfortable hotel, a block from López Mateos. It has a restaurant, bar and 26 spacious rooms around a courtyard. Prices here include breakfast and a three-course dinner.

Motel Cascada Inn (☎ 456-02-53, López Mateos 49) Rooms from US$53. The Cascada Inn has a covered swimming pool, parking, restaurant and bar. Its 32 rooms each have TV and two double beds.

Hotel Parador de la Montaña (☎ 456-00-75, López Mateos 44) Rooms from US$71. This hotel is larger than the Cascada Inn and similarly priced. Rooms have tile floors, high ceilings, TV and heaters.

NORTHWEST MEXICO

Best Western – The Lodge at Creel (☎ 456-00-71, ⚏ *www.thelodgeatcreel.com, López Mateos 61*) Cabins for 2 US$111, honeymoon suite US$167, including breakfast. This attractive hotel offers spacious, comfortable, self-contained wooden cabins, each with gas woodstove, two double beds and TV. The honeymoon suite comes with a private Jacuzzi and kitchenette.

Places to Eat
Plenty of restaurants are on López Mateos, in the few blocks south of the plaza. Most are open from around 7.30am to 10pm daily. *Restaurant Verónica* and *Restaurant La Cabaña* are both popular. They serve steak, seafood and Mexican dishes. The casual *Restaurant Lupita* is less expensive and popular with locals. Homey *Restaurant Estela* serves good, economical meals for US$3.50 each. *Cafetería Mí Café*, on the east side of the plaza, has good coffee.

Hospital Para Crudos Prices US$2.25-5.50. Next to the tracks just south of the train station, Hospital Para Crudos specializes in hangover remedies like *menudo,* hence the name. They also have a variety of burritos and other snack food.

El Caballo Bayo Prices US$3.50-9. This restaurant, across the street from the Best Western, caters to tourists with a bilingual menu that features both Mexican and American dishes.

Sierra Madre Pub Steakhouse (in Best Western – The Lodge at Creel) Prices US$3.50-15. For more upscale dining, try this attractive place, with good food and a bar. It offers breakfasts, pizza, and a full-on dinner including soup, salad, main course and dessert. Bottles of wine here range from US$3 to US$38.

Shopping
Many shops in Creel sell Tarahumara handicrafts, including baskets, colorful dolls, wood carvings, violins, flutes, archery sets, pottery, clothing and more. Prices are very reasonable.

The *Artesanías Misión* shop, on the north side of the plaza, is the best place to buy handicrafts. All of the store's earnings go to support the Catholic mission hospital, which provides free medical care for the Tarahumara.

Getting There & Around
Bus Travel between Creel and Chihuahua may be more convenient via bus rather than train, as the trip is shorter and the schedule more flexible. The Estrella Blanca bus station, across the tracks from the plaza, has nine daily buses to Chihuahua (256km, 4½ hours, US$17), passing through San Juanito (30km, 45 minutes, US$2.50), La Junta (102km, 2 hours, US$8) and Cuauhtémoc (170km, 3 hours, US$11) on the way. A bus to Ciudad Juárez (10 hours, US$40) departs at 8.30am daily.

Estrella Blanca also has three daily buses to San Rafael (55km, 1½ hours, US$4) via Divisadero (45km, 1 hour, US$3) and Posada Barrancas (Areponápuchi; 49km, 1 hour, US$3.25). They depart Creel daily at 11am, 3pm and 6pm. Autotransportes Noroeste, just north of Estrella Blanca, has two departures for San Rafael (US$4) at 10.30am and 6.30pm and three departures for Chihuahua (US$17) at 9.15am, 11am and 3pm.

A bus to Batopilas (140km, 5 hours, US$18) leaves from outside the Hotel Los Pinos on López Mateos, two blocks south of the plaza. The bus leaves Creel at 7.30am Tuesday, Thursday and Saturday, and at 9.30am Monday, Wednesday and Friday. The road between Creel and Batopilas is paved initially, but the rest of the ride is very bumpy and rough.

Train Creel's train station is half a block from the main plaza. Per the train schedule, the westbound primera express train departs Creel 11.26am and clase económica at 1.05pm; the eastbound trains depart at 2.14pm and 4.10pm. However, they are usually late. Check the board inside the train station for the estimated times of arrival that day. See the Ferrocarril Chihuahua al Pacífico section, earlier, for schedule and ticket information.

Car & Motorcycle Now there's a paved road all the way from Creel to Divisadero and on to San Rafael. From San Rafael, if you have a sturdy 4WD vehicle, you could go to El Fuerte in the dry season (March to May is the best time) via Bahuichivo, Mesa de Arturo, La Reforma and Choix, crossing the Colosio reservoir in a two-vehicle ferry. Or you could go from San Rafael to Álamos via Bahuichivo, Témoris and Chinipas, crossing he Río Chinipas. Both of these roads are very rough; assaults have also occurred on these roads, making them dangerous.

Bicycle Umarike Expediciones, on Villa, rents mountain bikes for US$11.50/17 a half/full day; prices include map, helmet and tool kit. The Complejo Ecoturístico Arareko office on López Mateos also rents mountain bikes for US$2.25/22 per hour/day.

AROUND CREEL

The area around Creel is rich in natural wonders, with everything from waterfalls to hot springs to rocks shaped like frogs only a day's hike, bike ride or drive from town. Local guides offer a variety of tours, some of which you can do on your own with a bicycle or even on foot. However, do not walk into the countryside by yourself: at least one woman has been assaulted while walking to Lago Arareko alone.

As for the Ferrocarril Chihuahua al Pacífico, east of Creel it goes through **Cuauhtémoc**, the center of northern Mexico's Mennonite population, and ends at **Chihuahua**, the capital of the state of Chihuahua. See the Central North Mexico chapter for information on these places.

Complejo Ecoturístico Arareko

An excellent local hike (or drive) is to the Complejo Ecoturístico Arareko *(admission US$1.75)*, a Tarahumara *ejido* (landholding cooperative) with over 200 sq km of pine forest with waterfalls, hot springs, caves (inhabited by the Tarahumara) and other rock formations. There are also deep canyons, farmlands, villages and **Lago Arareko**.

About 7km from Creel, the lake is an easy hike or drive south along the road to Cusárare; hitchhiking is also relatively easy. A few caves inhabited by Tarahumara can be seen along the way. The lake is surrounded by boulders and pine forests; there's also an old log cabin which was used as a set for the filming of the Mexican movie *El Refugio del Lobo* (Refuge of the Wolf).

There's a *campground* on the northeast shore of Lago Arareko. It has sites with barbecue pits, picnic areas, water and bathrooms for US$1.75 per person.

It also operates two lodges:

Albergue de Batosárachi Beds US$17 per person. This lodge, 1km south of Lago Arareko, has three rustic cabins with bunk beds or individual rooms, and hot showers; you can cook in the communal kitchen or arrange to have meals prepared. It can accommodate 70 people.

Cabaña de Segórachi Beds US$39 per person. This place, on the south shore of Lago Arareko, is more luxurious than Albergue de Batosárachi, with the use of a rowboat and other amenities included; it holds 15 people.

You can make reservations for both of the lodges and arrange to rent bikes or boats for excursions on the lake at Complejo Ecoturístico Arareko's *office* (☎ 635-456-01-26), which can be found on López Mateos in Creel. They'll pick up lodge guests at the train or bus station.

To get to the ejido from Creel, head south on López Mateos and veer left off López Mateos, passing the town cemetery on your left. About 1.5km south of town there's a gate where the US$1.75 entrance fee is charged and you're given a map and printed information about the ejido. Continue straight ahead; caves and farmlands will appear on both sides of the road before you eventually arrive at the small Tarahumara village of San Ignacio, where there's a 400-year-old mission church.

Visitors often get lost trying to reach the lake from this point (the map isn't the best). Here's how to do it: from San Ignacio, continue straight ahead past the church, taking the trail up the hill. At the top of the hill, take the trail straight ahead through the next valley, and you'll come to the lake. If you do get lost, just remember that the highway is running parallel to you, on your right (west); it's an easy hitch back to Creel.

Valle de los Monjes

The vertical rock formations found in this valley gave rise to its traditional Tarahumara name of Bisabírachi, meaning the Valley of the Erect Penises. The valley, also sometimes called the Valley of the Gods, is 9km from Creel and is considered a day trip by horse. Along the way you'll pass a couple other valleys named after the rock formations found there: Valley of the Toads and Valley of the Mushrooms. Tour operators can either rent horses or tell you where to get them.

Cascada Cusárare

The 30m-high Cusárare waterfall is 22km south of Creel, near the Tarahumara village of Cusárare. Tour operators in Creel offer a four- to five-hour tour that involves going 22km by car, stopping at Lago Arareko on the way and then hiking 2.5km to the waterfall. To do it yourself, if you're coming from Creel, don't take the first turnoff you see on your right where large signs point to the waterfall – this entrance leaves you with a longer, less inter-esting hike to reach the falls. Continue on for about another 5km, passing the sign to Cusárare village pointing off to your left, until you reach a small, inconspicuous sign point-ing to your right saying 'Cascada Cusárare – Cusárare Waterfall.' Turn here, follow the road until you reach the small shop and a hotel, *Copper Canyon Sierra Lodge* (☎ 800-776-3942 in the USA, W *www.sierratrail.com*), and park there. You could camp here too, beside the river. The waterfall (*entrance US$1.75*) is about a 40-minute walk along the river, on an easy-to-follow trail.

Recohuata Hot Springs

These small natural hot springs are about 35km southwest of Creel at the bottom of Barranca Tararecua. A popular seven-hour tour from Creel begins with a 1½-hour truck ride and then a scenic hike down 607m into the canyon to the hot springs (*en-trance US$1.75*).

CASCADA DE BASASEACHI

Basaseachi Falls, 140km northwest of Creel, is a dramatic 246m-high waterfall (the highest in Mexico), especially spectacular in the rainy season. It takes all day to visit the falls – a bumpy three-hour drive, then about two hours walking down, half an hour at the waterfall, three hours walking up again, and a bumpy three-hour return ride. If you're up for it, it's worth it. If you're not up for the walk down into the canyon, you can still enjoy views of the falls and the canyon, from up on the rim. *Rancho San Lorenzo* (☎ 614-421-26-56) has several large cabins and an attractive camping area a five-minute walk from the falls.

BATOPILAS

• pop 1175 • elev 495m ☎ 649

Batopilas, a serene 19th-century silver-mining village 140km south of Creel, is deep in the heart of the canyon country. The journey from Creel to Batopilas is a thrilling ride from an altitude of 2338m at Creel to 495m at Batopilas, with dramatic descents and ascents through several canyons, cli-mates and vegetative zones. Batopilas' climate is distinctly warmer and more trop-ical than Creel's. You are now surrounded by stands of tropical fruit trees rather than Creel's cool-loving pine forests.

Batopilas is a great starting point for many short and long treks; any hotel can help arrange canyon trips. An interesting 8km walk is to the Catedral Perdida (Lost Cathedral) at **Satevó**. It's a mystery why such an elaborate cathedral was built in a hauntingly beautiful but uninhabited canyon where there has never been a size-able settlement. It was built so long ago that its origins are lost in the distant past. The two- to three-day hike to the town of Urique is also very popular.

There is a map of the town painted inside El Zaguán Bar, showing the locations of some interesting sites such as the ruins of Hacienda San Miguel and some abandoned mines. If you decide to explore the mines, do not go in without a flashlight as there are some deep holes you'll want to avoid.

Most tour operators offer a two-day ex-cursion from Creel to Batopilas. But if you don't have two days to spare to visit Batopi-las, a tour to **La Bufa** lets you experience some of that spectacular scenery in one day, with plenty of stops along the way. The nine-hour tour takes you 105km from Creel through five spectacular canyons to the viewpoint at La Bufa, overlooking the town of the same name in a canyon 1750m deep with a cool river at the bottom.

Places to Stay & Eat

Hotel Mary Singles/doubles US$11.50/17. Opposite the church, this place is a favorite with travelers. It has simple rooms and a good little restaurant. It can be a little noisy due to the bar next door.

La Casa Monse (☎ 456-90-27, *on Main Plaza*) Rooms US$11.25 per person. Casa Monse has a communal kitchen and patio. The price goes down to US$8.50 if you stay more than one night.

Hotel Juanita's (☎ 456-90-43, *Nigromante 7*) Singles/doubles US$23/34. The clean, comfortable rooms here are a good value.

Real de Minas *(☎ 456-90-45, cnr Guerra & Ochoa)* Rooms US$39. Real de Minas has brightly decorated rooms around a lovely courtyard.

Hacienda del Río Rooms US$160 including all meals. This beautiful new hotel has 10 luxurious rooms decorated with tile and stained glass windows. The rooms are lit with oil lamps for atmosphere. It's located on the road from Creel, about a 10-minute walk from Batopilas. Reservations must be made in advance through Hotel Margarita's Plaza Mexicana *(☎ 635-456-02-45)* in Creel.

El Quinto Patio *(in Hotel Mary)* Prices US$1-4.50. This unassuming restaurant serves inexpensive, flavorful meals.

Restaurant Clarita *(on main street)* Prices US$3.50 per meal. The Clarita serves good basic meals. They also offer the cheapest accommodations in town (US$3.50 per person).

Doña Mica's Prices US$5.50 per meal. This restaurant, located near the plaza, is a good place to eat; let her know an hour ahead of time if you want to eat here.

A recently opened *café*, which is just half a block from the plaza, serves palatable cups of coffee for US$0.80.

Getting There & Away

The bus to Creel (140km, 5 hours, US$18) departs from the plaza in Batopilas at 5am Monday to Saturday. On Tuesday, Thursday and Saturday the bus goes all the way from Batopilas to Chihuahua (396km, 8 hours, US$34).

Central North Mexico

This chapter covers much of the state of Chihuahua, the entire state of Durango and a tiny part of the state of Coahuila. The roads through this area follow a long-used travel route between central Mexico and what is now the USA, along the high plains parallel to the Sierra Madre Occidental. The countryside is flat or undulating, with occasional rocky ranges jutting from the plains. Remote desert landscapes are the rule, but the arid, sparsely populated region is intersected by muddy rivers flowing intermittently from the mountains. The irrigated areas are verdant oases where fruit, cotton as well as other crops are grown, and where most of the towns and villages have been established.

Highlights

- Paquimé ruins – a restored complex of adobe structures that once were part of a major indigenous trading settlement

- Chihuahua's Museo de la Revolución Mexicana – history buffs will love this place, housed in Pancho Villa's former headquarters

- Durango – lively Plaza de Armas, and the movie locations for many classic Westerns

- Around Madera – a forested region with pre-Hispanic cliffside dwellings

Most travelers hurry through the Central North area on their way to better-known attractions, but the region holds plenty of interest. History and archaeology buffs in particular will enjoy exploring the ruins at Paquimé and Cuarenta Casas – remnants of once-flourishing settlements of northern Mexico's indigenous peoples. And though most of the region's towns, with the notable exception of Durango, tend to be rough and run-down, some colonial gems are hidden amid the modern urban detritus.

Chihuahua state is in the Hora de las Montañas (Mountain Time) time zone, one hour behind Durango and Coahuila. The time in Chihuahua is the same as in the neighboring US state of New Mexico (and far west Texas around El Paso) and in the neighboring Mexican states of Sinaloa and Sonora – except for the daylight-saving period (first Sunday in May to last Sunday in September), in Sonora's case, because Sonora does not observe daylight saving.

CIUDAD JUÁREZ
• pop 1,107,400 • elev 1145m ☎ 656

Ciudad Juárez is a grimy, noisy, booming border town, inextricably linked with El Paso, its American neighbor just across the Rio Grande. Most travelers do not linger here, using the city's excellent bus and road connections as a springboard for exploration farther south, or as a gateway to the US. Fortunately Ciudad Juárez is not representative of the rest of the Central North.

This river crossing lies on a travel route used long before the conquistador Cabeza de Vaca found El Paso del Norte in the 16th century. Modern travelers use this same crossing in droves, making El Paso/Juárez the second-busiest port of entry on the US-Mexico border.

The two cities are a study in the economic disparity 'across the line,' and for many short-term visitors, the main attractions of Juárez are cheap dental work and bargain shopping – along with under-21 drinking. But Juárez and El Paso also have much in common. Bustling nightclubs in both cities, including a number of gay bars, draw revelers from miles around. And both

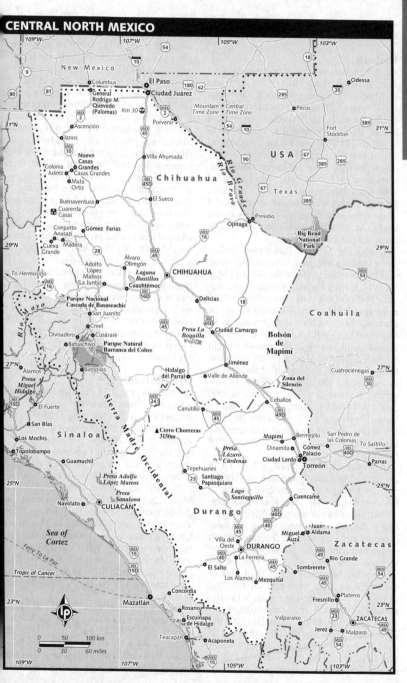

sides of the border share a relatively benevolent climate.

History

In 1848, following the Mexican-American War, the Rio Grande (Río Bravo del Norte to Mexicans) became the border between the US state of Texas and the Mexican state of Chihuahua. In the 1860s, the river changed course, shifting southward so that an additional couple of square kilometers came to be on the US side. The resulting border dispute was the subject of international arbitration in 1911, but wasn't resolved until 1963, when a treaty was signed that provided for engineering works to move the channel of the Rio Grande and transfer some of the land to Mexico. This land is now the Parque Chamizal in Ciudad Juárez.

During the Mexican Revolution, Juárez had a strategic importance beyond its small size. Pancho Villa stormed the town on May 10, 1911, forcing the resignation of the dictator Porfirio Díaz. After the February 1913 coup against legitimately elected President Francisco Madero, Villa sought refuge in El Paso. In March 1913, he recrossed the Rio Grande with just eight followers to begin the reconquest of Mexico. Within months, he had recruited and equipped an army of thousands, La División del Norte. In November he conquered Juárez for a second time – this time by loading his troops onto a train, deceiving the defenders into thinking it was one of their own, and steaming into the middle of town in a modern version of the Trojan-horse tactic.

After the implementation of NAFTA in the mid-1990s industry mushroomed in the city, as US manufacturers took advantage of low-cost labor in Mexico and markets grew on both sides of the border. With 13 industrial parks and more than 360 *maquiladoras* (assembly plants, usually foreign-owned) pumping out electronic goods and automotive parts, the area became a magnet for job-seeking Mexicans, more than half of them women. The beginning of the 21st century saw a different story, with the slowing of the US economy bringing increased hardship to Juárez. In late 2001 the city had an additional 40,000 people out of work with the expectation that this would lead to increased levels of crime and more people attempting to slip across the border.

There were job losses of around 13% in maquiladoras; many of the women who had come to work in the factories were struggling to find even a cleaning job. For the first time since NAFTA was introduced, exports to the US were expected to drop in 2002.

This border city suffers from an image problem due to its association with the notorious drug cartel that bears its name. Juárez is considered a key transit point for illicit drugs entering the US. Much of the city's crime is drug related and the justice system is hopelessly swamped. In 2000 there were 183 murders. Fewer than half the cases even reached the courts. In response to demands by Juárez's exasperated mayor, who insisted his city was being unfairly slandered, the Mexican attorney general's office ordered that in legal proceedings the Juárez cartel be referred to instead as the Cartel of Vicente Carrillo, after its leader.

In 2001 President Fox vowed a new campaign to curb drug trafficking, labeling it 'a war without mercy.' However, with juveniles increasingly being favored as drug couriers – from January to June 2001, 100 juveniles crossing into El Paso were arrested on smuggling charges – the president has his work cut out.

Orientation

Ciudad Juárez and El Paso sprawl on both sides of the Rio Grande, but most places of interest to travelers are concentrated in the central areas of the two cities, along the streets connected by the international bridges: El Paso's Santa Fe St, which becomes Avenida Juárez on the Mexican side, and Stanton St, which becomes Avenida Lerdo.

You can walk across either bridge into Mexico, but to return on foot you must use the Avenida Juárez/Santa Fe St bridge. If for some reason you have been in Mexico so long that you needed a tourist card (see the Information section below), you must first go to the immigration office at the end of the Avenida Lerdo/Stanton St bridge, then cross into the US via the Avenida Juárez/Santa Fe St bridge.

By car, you must take Stanton St going south and Avenida Juárez going north – the vehicle toll is US$2 each way. Avenida Juárez, lined with shops, restaurants, bars and seedy hotels, is the main tourist street in Ciudad Juárez and leads to the center of

CIUDAD JUÁREZ

PLACES TO STAY
1 Gardner Hotel
16 Hotel del Río
17 Hotel Impala
24 Plaza Continental Hotel;
   Cafetería El Coyote
30 Hotel Imperial
36 Hotel Lucerna
37 Hotel Chula Vista
38 Villa del Sol

PLACES TO EAT
7 The Tap
19 Burritos El Padrino
23 Villa del Mar
34 Los Arcos
35 Ajua!!

OTHER
2 Post Office
3 El Paso Tourist
   Information Center
4 Amtrak
5 Greyhound Station
6 Valuta
8 The New Old Plantation
9 Mexican Consulate
10 Tourist Information Center
11 Immigration Office
12 US Consulate
13 Mexican Immigration
14 Juárez Turf Club
15 Kentucky Club
20 Cathedral; Misión de
   Guadalupe
21 Bancomer; Comisiones
   San Luis
22 Museo Histórico
25 Banamex
26 Mercado Juárez
27 Post Office
28 Local Buses to El Paso
29 Gay Bars
31 Buses to Bus Station
32 Tourist Information
   Module
33 Local Buses to El Paso

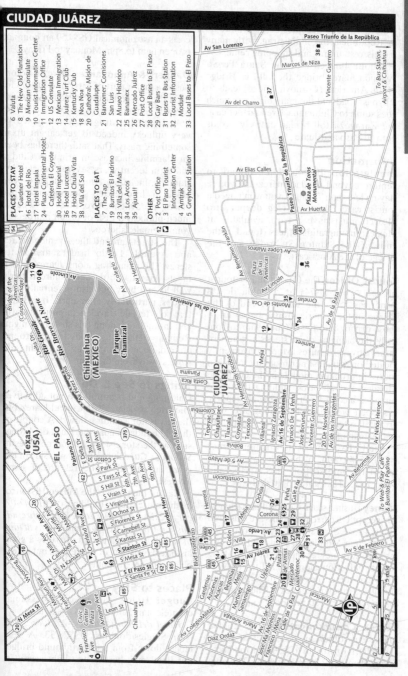

town. Avenida 16 de Septiembre heads east from Lerdo and becomes Paseo Triunfo de la República, the main drag, with many motels, restaurants and shopping centers.

About 4km east of the Santa Fe St/ Avenida Juárez bridge, the toll-free Bridge of the Americas (Cordova Bridge) leads to a bypass road and the main highway, which goes south to Chihuahua. Even farther east, the Zaragoza toll bridge entirely avoids both El Paso and Juárez.

Information

Immigration If you don't intend to venture beyond Ciudad Juárez and you're staying less than 72 hours, you won't need a tourist card. Those moving deeper into Mexico must have a card, available at Mexican immigration offices (found at the ends of the Stanton St bridge and the Bridge of the Americas).

Tourist Offices The Ciudad Juárez tourist office (☎ 611-31-74) at Avenida de las Américas 2551 (the southern end of the Bridge of the Americas) may be useful to those driving into town. Open 9am to 9pm daily, the bilingual office stocks a variety of informative brochures. More conveniently located on Villa just north of Guerrero is a tourist information module in the Garita de Metales, a small brick building that once served as a control point for metals exports. It's open weekdays but hours are very erratic; it offers many of the same materials as the main office.

The El Paso Tourist Information Center (☎ 915-544-0061), in the little round pavilion at the intersection of Santa Fe and Main, is open 8.30am to 5pm daily.

Money Businesses in Ciudad Juárez generally accept US currency. Banks are clustered along 16 de Septiembre, with most open 9am to 5pm Monday to Friday. Of the numerous currency exchange booths along Juárez, only Comisiones San Luis (☎ 614-20-33), at the corner of 16 de Septiembre, changes traveler's checks. The *casa de cambio* at the bus station does too.

Post & Communications The Ciudad Juárez post office, at the corner of Lerdo and Peña, is open 8am to 5.30pm Monday to Friday, 9am to 12.30pm Saturday. The only Internet café is a fair way out of the city: Web & Play Cafe, at Ejército Nacional 7624, costs an astronomical US$4.50 an hour and is open 6am to 8pm Monday to Friday.

Dangers & Annoyances Juárez is notorious as a major port of entry into the US for illicit drugs (see History earlier). Most visitors will remain oblivious to mob activities linked with the drug trade and you'd be very unlucky indeed to get caught up in something nasty. That said, there has been an alarming increase in crime in Ciudad Juárez in recent years; several innocent bystanders, including Americans, have been killed in drug-related shootings in public places in daylight. Also, there has been a much-publicized rash of brutal murders of young female laborers.

The streets around the Avenida Juárez and Avenida Lerdo bridges are pretty sleazy. The main drag along Juárez until it meets Avenida 16 de Septiembre is fairly well lit and busy but also potentially dangerous, particularly after dark. It is likely that solo female travelers in particular will feel intimidated along this stretch at night. Remain vigilant, use taxis to get around after dark and don't stray into unlit side streets away from the main drag.

Things to See & Do

Charming and beautiful are not adjectives one often associates with Ciudad Juárez, but the city is not a cultural desert. A couple of the old buildings near the Plaza de Armas, such as the stone-sided **Misión de Nuestra Señora de Guadalupe** on the west side of the plaza next to the cathedral, are of some interest.

East of the plaza is the **Museo Histórico**, in the old customs building (☎ 612-47-07, *cnr Avenidas Juárez & 16 de Septiembre; admission US$1; closed for renovations at time of research*). The museum provides a good historical overview of the region, but all explanations are in Spanish.

Places to Stay

Budget Hotels without a professional clientele start at about US$28 single.

Hotel del Río (☎ 615-55-25, *Juárez 488 Nte*) Singles/doubles US$28/33. A few blocks down from the northbound bridge, this hotel may be the best-kept secret in own. It's easy to miss the staircase leading up to the establishment's 18 neat, cozy rooms.

Hotel Impala (☎ *615-04-91, Lerdo 670 Nte*) Singles/doubles US$36/38 including breakfast. Near the Stanton St bridge on a rather seedy section of Lerdo is this old standby, with pleasing rooms and firm beds. It has a restaurant and a parking lot, which is entered from Tlaxcala.

Hotel Imperial (☎ *615-03-23, Guerrero 206*) Singles/doubles US$28/31. This cordial hotel, a block east of the Plaza de Armas, is another good deal; it has cheery rooms with TVs. Room size can vary so have a look before deciding.

Gardner Hotel (☎ *915-532-3661,* e *epi hostl@whc.net, 311 E Franklin*) Dorm beds US$17 for HI members, plus US$2 for sheets; doubles US$45. Across the border in El Paso is this top budget/mid-range choice for those who don't want to stay overnight in Juárez. The Gardner, between Stanton and Kansas, has a hostel section with lodging in a four-bed dorm with air-con and shared bath (HI memberships are available at the hotel). Clean, comfortable hotel rooms with cable TV are also available.

Mid-Range *Plaza Continental Hotel* (☎ *615-00-84,* e *hotelcon@prodigy.net.mx, Lerdo 112 Sur*) Singles & doubles US$45. Located between 16 de Septiembre and Peña, the Plaza Continental offers affordable luxury in the center of town. Some travelers will be charmed by the hotel's ornate chandeliered lobby and pleasant lounge areas; others will appreciate the beer-dispensing machine in the corridor. The large carpeted rooms come with cable TV. There's parking in an adjacent lot.

Hotel Chula Vista (☎ *617-12-07, Paseo Triunfo de la República 3555*) Singles/doubles US$32/42. Among the scores of roadside inns east of the center, this place is one of the better deals. The sprawling hotel includes a small pool, a restaurant, a bar/disco and a guarded parking area. They have spacious comfortable rooms with two double beds and color TVs and smaller single rooms in an older wing by the highway.

Villa del Sol (☎ *617-24-24, Triunfo de la República 339*) Singles & doubles US$52. At the east end of Triunfo de la República is this classy hotel. Amenities include a large pool, satellite TV and a good restaurant; rooms are slightly cheaper on weekends.

Top End *Hotel Lucerna* (☎ *629-99-00, Paseo Triunfo de la República 3976*) Singles & doubles US$227. Catering to Juárez's business class, this hotel, at López Mateos, offers the city's finest accommodations. Little expense was spared on its poolside restaurant, palm-studded gardens or lounge areas. Rates here are 10% less Friday to Sunday.

Places to Eat
Inexpensive, filling fare can be found at the *Mercado Cuauhtémoc* beside the Plaza de Armas. A number of stalls on the lower level serve tacos, *tortas*, soups, *antojitos* and seafood.

Cafeteria El Coyote (☎ *614-25-71, Lerdo 118 Sur*) Breakfast or lunch US$4. Open 24 hours. Located next to Plaza Continental Hotel (there's also a branch on Juárez near the bridge), this diner-style, central café is very convenient for breakfast, lunch or a late-night snack after the clubs have closed.

Juárez is famous for its burritos, and some of the most authentic can be found at *Burritos El Padrino*, which has branches on Mejía at Américas (☎ *616-65-19*) and at Ejército Nacional 5125 (☎ *611-58-55*). At US$1.25 apiece, these mega-burritos are filled with beans, *mole,* shredded beef in *salsa verde* and so on.

Ciudad Juárez also boasts some excellent seafood restaurants.

Los Arcos (☎ *616-86-08, Paseo Triunfo de la República 2220*) Starters US$3, mains US$5.50-12. At the corner with Américas, you'll receive a fine catch of smoked marlin tacos and fresh fish fillets here.

Villa del Mar (☎ *612-58-90, Villa 130*) Mains US$5.50-9, house specialties US$7. Just off 16 de Septiembre, this place is clean, cheap and busy; try the *pescado entero normandi* if black bass stuffed with shrimp and oysters and smothered in white salsa sounds good to you (US$9.50).

Ajuua!! (☎ *616-69-35, Ornelas 162 Nte*) Mains US$6.75-13.50. Open 8am-1am Sun-Thur, 8am-2am Fri & Sat. A large restaurant-bar popular with Texans, Ajuua!! offers the full Mexican experience. Decorated to resemble a *pueblito mexicano*, complete with mariachis, the restaurant serves all the classics, including *chiles en nogada* (chilies stuffed with ground meat and fruit mixture) and *enmoladas* (tortillas drenched in mole sauce).

The Tap *(408 E San Antonio)* Main dishes US$4.50-6. Open until 2am daily. Most of downtown El Paso shuts down by 6pm; an exception is this buzzing place. Though it looks more like a bar than a restaurant, the Tap prepares tasty Mexican dishes.

Entertainment

Kentucky Club *(Juárez 643)* Open until late. The bars and discos extending from the bridge down Juárez tend to be grimy and depressing, this venerable one being the greatest exception. The Kentucky's polished wood bar is a fine place to sip a margarita – legend has it that this cocktail made its first appearance here.

Noa Noa *(Juárez 240)* Admission US$2.50. This bar, named after a hit song by bar owner Juan Gabriel, features a pool table and good *norteño* bands.

The city's gay bars are concentrated near the corner of Peña and Lerdo with the *Ritz* (on *Peña*) and *Club Olímpico* *(Lerdo 210)* among the more popular spots; they open around 1am nightly.

The New Old Plantation *(☎ 915-533-6055, 301 S Ochoa)* Admission free Fri & Sat before 10pm. Open 9pm-2am Thur & Sun, 9pm-4am Fri & Sat. Across the border in El Paso, this is the most popular watering hole. Although predominantly gay, the multilevel bar/disco is a hit with straights too.

Spectator Sports

Plaza de Toros Monumental *(☎ 613-16-56, Paseo Triunfo de la República)* Juárez's bullfighting season is April through August. Events at the Plaza Monumental typically begin at 6pm Sunday. Off-track betting is available at the Juárez Turf Club, a block from the Juárez bridge.

Getting There & Away

Air The Juárez airport (Aeropuerto Internacional Abraham González) is just east of highway 45D, about 18km south of the center of town. Direct flights are available to/from Mexico City, Chihuahua, Guadalajara, Mazatlán and Tijuana. Flights to most other major cities go via Chihuahua or Mexico City. The main Mexican carriers are Aeroméxico (☎ 800-021-40-00) and Aero California (☎ 618-33-99).

Bus The Juárez bus station (Central de Autobuses) is on Teófilo Borunda, a long way from town. For information on getting there, see Getting Around. Main destinations, with daily departures, are:

Chihuahua – 373km, 5 hours; 3 deluxe (US$32), frequent 1st-class (US$23)

Mexico City (Terminal Norte) – 1840km, 24 hours; frequent 1st-class (US$116)

Nuevo Casas Grandes – 315km, 4 hours; hourly 1st-class (US$14)

Frequent 1st-class buses also go to Durango, Monterrey, San Luis Potosí and Zacatecas. Autobuses Americanos buses going direct to US cities (for example, Albuquerque, Dallas and Denver) are generally cheaper than Greyhound from El Paso.

The El Paso Greyhound station (☎ 915-532-2365) has its main entrance on Santa Fe between Overland and San Antonio. Several buses a day travel to Los Angeles (16 hours, US$45), Chicago (34 hours, US$99), Miami (35 hours, US$99), New York (48 hours, US$99) and other major US cities.

Train El Paso's Amtrak station (☎ 915-545-2247) is at 700 San Francisco, three blocks west of the Civic Center Plaza. Trains run three times a week to Los Angeles (15 hours, US$128), Chicago (48 hours, US$153), Miami (48 hours, US$172) and New York (60 hours, US$259).

Car & Motorcycle If you're driving into the Mexican interior, you must obtain a vehicle permit (see the Getting There & Away chapter). The only place to do so in the Ciudad Juárez area (even if you're heading in another direction) is at the major customs checkpoint at Km 30 on highway 45D south.

Beyond the checkpoint, the highway to Chihuahua is in good condition but it comes with a US$10 toll. Highway 2 to Nuevo Casas Grandes branches west at a traffic circle 25km south of town.

For liability and vehicle insurance coverage while in Mexico, compare the policies of these companies in El Paso: Sanborn's

☎ 915-779-3538), 2401 E Missouri Ave, or AAA (☎ 915-778-9521), 1201 Airway Blvd.

Getting Around
Local buses to the Juárez bus station leave from Guerrero just west of Villa (in front of the Hotel Aremar). Catch a blue-striped 'C Camionera' bus or a green-top 'Permision- arios Unidos' bus (US$0.40); it's a 25-minute trip. From the bus station to the town center, turn left and go out to the highway; any bus labeled 'Centro' will drop you near the cathedral. Inside the bus station, a booth sells tickets for authorized taxis into town (US$7.75).

You can bypass central Juárez altogether if you take one of the hourly direct buses between the El Paso and Juárez bus stations (1 hour, US$5).

Autobuses Twin Cities runs a shuttle service between the Juárez and El Paso downtown areas. Blue vans depart from the corner of Villa and Galeana every 10 minutes (US$0.30).

OTHER BORDER CROSSINGS
Though El Paso-Juárez is the most impor- tant and frequently used port of entry between central north Mexico and the USA, there are some alternative crossing points.

Columbus (New Mexico)- General Rodrigo M Quevedo
The small border town of General Rodrigo M Quevedo (also called Palomas) is about 150km west of Juárez. The crossing is open 24 hours a day. Motorists can obtain a vehicle permit in one of the trailers beside the border checkpoint. There's a motel and an inexpensive hotel, as well as 2nd-class bus connections to Ciudad Juárez.

Columbus has a campground and a motel, but no public transport connections into the USA. Pancho Villa sacked the town in 1916 (see 'Pancho Villa: Bandit-Turned-Revolu- tionary' in this chapter). A museum in Columbus has some exhibits about the attack.

Presidio (Texas)-Ojinaga
This little-used border crossing is 209km northeast of Chihuahua. A few buses run between Chihuahua and Ojinaga daily. From Presidio, Greyhound offers daily service to San Antonio, Houston and Dallas; there's no depot, just a bus stop on the corner of O'Riley and Anderson. Both Presidio and Ojinaga have some cheap places to stay and eat.

NUEVO CASAS GRANDES & CASAS GRANDES
Nuevo Casas Grandes (pop 55,300, elev 1463m, ☎ 636) is a four-hour bus trip south- west of Ciudad Juárez. You could make it here for a quiet first night in Mexico. It's a peaceful, prosperous country town with wide streets, serving the surrounding farmlands. The substantial brick houses around town, which look like they should be in the US Midwest, were built by Mormon settlers in the late 19th century. The main reason to visit is to see the ruins of Paquimé, adjacent to the nearby village of Casas Grandes (pop 3430).

Orientation & Information
Most of the facilities useful to visitors are within a few blocks of 5 de Mayo and Con- stitución (the street with railway tracks down the middle). Available services include banks (ATMs at Banamex and Ban- comer), a casa de cambio next to the Hotel California, and a post office. For Internet and email, try Verssus Internet Cafe at Juárez 1408, 1km north of town; it's open daily and charges US$3.25 per hour.

Paquimé Ruins
The name 'Casas Grandes' (Big Houses) comes from the Paquimé Ruins – the crum- bling adobe remnants of what was the major trading settlement in northern Mexico between AD 900 and 1340. Par- tially excavated and restored, the networks of eroded walls now resemble roofless mazes.

The Paquimé people had a flourishing civilization with significant ties to the pre- Hispanic cultures of Arizona and New Mexico. The structures here are similar to Pueblo houses of the US Southwest, with distinctive T-shaped door openings. (Ar- chaeologists speculate that the design allowed doors to be closed against the cold, while smoke from cooking fires still escaped.) Timber beams set into the walls supported roofs and upper floors, some of which have been reconstructed. The largest dwellings had up to three levels.

The Paquimé irrigated the land to grow maize crops, and they built adobe cages to breed *guacamayas* (macaws), whose feathers were valued for ceremonial uses. As the city grew, it was influenced through trade with southern civilizations, particularly the Toltecs. Paquimé acquired some Toltec features, such as a ball court, of which there are remnants. At its peak, the local population is estimated to have been around 10,000.

Despite fortifications, Paquimé was invaded, perhaps by Apaches, in 1340. The city was sacked, burned and abandoned, and its great structures were left alone for more than 600 years. The site was partially excavated in the late 1950s, and subsequent exposure to the elements led to erosion of the walls. Today the walls have been dutifully restored, and some of the unique interior water systems and hidden cisterns have been rebuilt.

The Paquimé were great potters and produced earthenware with striking red, brown or black geometric designs over a cream background. Other pieces were made from black clay. Fine examples can be seen in the impressive **Museo de las Culturas del Norte** (☎ 692-41-40, near the ruins; admission to museum & ruins US$4, video US$3.25; museum & ruins open 10am-5pm Tues-Sun), which also displays large-scale models of the Paquimé complex and other key northern trade centers. The museum gift shop sells locally made pottery in the Paquimé style, but better-quality items are sold at lower prices in a shop near the site entrance.

To reach the ruins, take a 'Casas Grandes/Col Juárez' bus from Constitución in the center of Nuevo Casas Grandes; they run every half hour during the day. The 8km journey takes about 15 minutes (US$0.50). You will be let off at the picturesque main plaza of Casas Grandes, and from there signs direct you to the ruins, a 15-minute walk.

Places to Stay

A range of places to stay can be found in Nuevo Casas Grandes.

Hotel Juárez (☎ 694-02-33, Obregón 110) Singles/doubles US$10/11. Most budget travelers stay at this dingy place, just south of 5 de Mayo and close to the bus station. There's no heating or air-con (although some rooms have a fan), but for one or two nights it's tolerable.

Hotel California (☎ 694-11-10, fax 694-08-34, Constitución 209) Singles/doubles with bath US$31/37. This hospitable hotel in the heart of town is an excellent choice, offering sparkling clean, air-conditioned rooms.

Motel Piñón (☎ 694-06-55, Juárez 605) Singles/doubles US$40/49. On Juárez as you enter town from the north, the Piñón features well-designed air-conditioned rooms, cleverly incorporating Paquimé motifs into the decor. It also has a swimming pool (summer only).

Hotel Hacienda (☎ 694-10-46, e hotel hacienda@paquinet.com.mx, Juárez 2603) Singles/doubles US$57/67. Top honors go to the Hacienda, 1.5km north of town on highway 10, with a garden courtyard, swimming pool, restaurant and comfortable air-conditioned rooms. The hotel also organizes guide services to the ruins.

Places to Eat

Nuevo Casas Grandes has several good, reasonably priced restaurants.

Constantino (☎ 694-10-05, cnr Juárez & Minerva) Breakfast US$3.50. Other meals US$4.50-7.75. Open 7am-midnight daily. Located just north of the main plaza, the Constantino is popular with locals all day and serves fresh, tasty meals.

Dinno's Pizza (☎ 694-33-54, cnr 5 de Mayo & Obregón) Pizzas US$3.25-10, Chinese dishes US$6.75-10. In addition to its pizzas, this clean and popular place offers Chinese food including Szechuan-style dishes.

Restaurant Malmedy (cnr Juárez & Calle 5a) Mains US$6.75-9. Nuevo Casas Grandes' classiest choice – though not a terribly expensive one – is here in a grand old house in the old Mormon community of Colonia Dublán at the north end of town. The chef prepares dishes from his native Belgium, such as shrimp *beignets*, in addition to original versions of Mexican favorites; portions are huge.

Getting There & Away

Daily buses run to/from Ciudad Juárez (315km, 4 hours, US$14), to/from Chihuahua (352km, 4½ hours, US$18) and to/from Madera (242km, 4 hours, US$17). Other buses go daily to Cuauhtémoc, Monterrey and Zacatecas.

Driving south to Madera, turn right onto highway 28 at Buenaventura. This road climbs through scenic mountains dotted with oaks and short stubby cacti on its way to Zaragoza and Gómez Farías. It's best driven in daylight.

AROUND NUEVO CASAS GRANDES

Trips in the areas west and south of Nuevo Casas Grandes take in some interesting little towns, cool forests and several archaeological sites. Most can be reached by bus, but to see the ancient rock carvings in the rugged **Arroyo de los Monos**, 35km to the south, you will need a vehicle with good clearance.

A good day trip could include the Mormon village of **Colonia Juárez** and the **Hacienda de San Diego** (a 1902 mansion owned by the Terrazas family, who controlled most of prerevolutionary Chihuahua state). The mountain-flanked community of **Mata Ortiz** is 30km south of Nuevo Casas Grandes via unpaved roads. Mata Ortiz is a center for the production of pottery using materials, techniques and decorative styles like those of the ancient Paquimé culture. Juan Quezada, credited with reviving the Paquimé pottery tradition, is the most famous of the village's 300 potters, the best of whom can command US$1000 per piece.

There are two hotels in Mata Ortiz, both offering full board: the **Posada de las Ollas** (☎ 636-698-64-10) has singles/doubles for US$39/59; and the more expensive and luxurious **Hotel del Adobe** (☎ 636-694-62-83) has rooms for US$45/75. It may be possible to find cheaper accommodations in **private homes**.

One bus a day makes the journey from Nuevo Casas Grandes to Mata Ortiz (1½ hours, US$3.75), departing at 4pm from the market and returning the following morning at 8am.

MADERA & AROUND
• pop 14,000 • elev 2092m ☎ 652

In the sierra south of Nuevo Casas Grandes, the Madera area retains some forest despite a hearty timber industry. There are several archaeological sites too, as well as natural attractions.

About 66km west of Madera, **Cueva Grande** sits behind a waterfall during the rainy season; inside the cave are some ancient adobe buildings in the architectural style of the Mogollon culture, closely associated with Paquimé. More of these cliff dwellings can be seen at **Conjunto Anasazi**, about 35km west of Madera; a strenuous 4km ascent is required. In the same area are the **Puente Colgante** (Suspension Bridge) over the Río Huápoca, and some **thermal springs**.

The unpaved road to Cueva Grande should be attempted with a 4WD vehicle only. *Motel Real del Bosque (see Places to Stay)* offers guided van excursions that take in the Conjunto Anasazi, Cueva Grande and other points west for US$22 per person (minimum of eight participants). English-speaking taxi driver **Salvador Chacón** (☎ 572-09-38) will drive you to the Conjunto Anasazi and act as a guide for US$50. You can find him at the taxi stand opposite the bus station.

Cuarenta Casas

The existence of cliff dwellings at Cuarenta Casas *(Forty Houses; admission US$1; open 9am-3pm daily)* was known to the Spaniards as early as the 16th century, when explorer Álvar Núñez Cabeza de Vaca wrote in his chronicles, '…and here by the side of the mountain we forged our way inland more than 50 leagues and found 40 houses.' The number may have been exaggerated: about a dozen adobe apartments are carved into the west cliffside of a dramatic canyon at La Cueva de las Ventanas (Cave of the Windows). Last occupied in the 13th century, Cuarenta Casas is believed to have been an outlying settlement of Paquimé, perhaps a garrison for defense of commercial routes to the Pacific coast. Though the site is not as well preserved as the dwellings at Casas Grandes, its extraordinary natural setting makes it well worth a visit.

Cuarenta Casas is 43km north of Madera via a good paved road through pine forest. From the turnoff, a dirt road leads 1.5km to the entrance, where a trail descends into the Arroyo del Garabato and climbs the western slopes to the cave. Signs in English, Spanish and Tarahumara provide historical background along the way. The 1.5km hike isn't easy and takes about 80 minutes roundtrip. Expect freezing temperatures in winter and be off the premises by 4pm.

From Madera, an 11.30am bus (US$4.50) goes by Cuarenta Casas en route to the town of Largo. In the reverse direction, it stops at the site at around 4pm, allowing just enough time to make a day trip from Madera.

Places to Stay & Eat

Motel Mara's (cnr Calle 5 & Juárez) Singles/doubles US$11/17. For budget lodging, try this simple place with its battered but clean rooms and running hot water.

Hotel María (☎ 572-03-23, cnr Calle 5 & 5 de Mayo) Singles/doubles US$21/27. The rooms here are cramped but comfortable; second-floor rooms are the best.

Parador de la Sierra (☎ 572-02-77, cnr Calle 3 & Independencia) Singles/doubles US$24/27. Large wood-paneled rooms here come with heaters and face a secluded courtyard. The next-door disco can make sleep difficult.

Motel Real del Bosque (☎ 572-05-38) Singles & doubles US$39. The nicest place in town is this one on the highway coming in from Chihuahua, with spacious rooms. The cable TV setup is peculiar – every room has to watch the same station, which is controlled by the reception office! The motel also conducts tours of the ruins and natural attractions in the area.

Madera's lumberjacks support a number of cheap, simple *restaurants* in town, especially along Calle 5 around the bus station.

El Mexicano Restaurant (cnr Calle 3 & Guerrero) Mains US$3.25-6.75. This friendly place gets our vote for its cheap, filling meals of seafood, steak and Mexican food. The refreshing *limonadas* (lemonades) here are huge!

Getting There & Away

The bus station is on Calle 5. Second-class buses run hourly to/from Cuauhtémoc (US$11) and Chihuahua (US$17); twice a day to/from Nuevo Casas Grandes (US$18); and three times a day to/from Ciudad Juárez (US$33). The winding yet scenic cliff road linking Madera and Nuevo Casas Grandes should not be driven at night.

CHIHUAHUA

• pop 682,500 • elev 1455m ☎ 614

Chihuahua is the prosperous capital city of the state of Chihuahua (Mexico's largest state). Some fine colonial buildings dot the city's center, while newer suburbs and industries sprawl around the edges. Most travelers stay here as an overnight stop on a journey to the north or south, or at the start or finish of a Copper Canyon Railway trip.

Chihuahua's main attractions are Pancho Villa's old house, Quinta Luz, and the museum of the Mexican Revolution that now occupies it. Among the city's other sights of interest is the market, visited early morning by Mennonites and colorfully attired Tarahumaras. Around town you'll see lots of men wearing cowboy hats and boots – a reminder that this is cattle country, as it has been since the days of the great haciendas.

History

Chihuahua, in the indigenous Nahua language, means 'dry and sandy zone.' The city of Chihuahua grew in size from the first few Spanish settlers to become both an administration center for the surrounding territory and a commercial center for cattle and mining interests. In the War of Independence, rebel leader Miguel Hidalgo fled here, only to be betrayed, imprisoned by the Spaniards and shot. President Benito Juárez made Chihuahua his headquarters for a while when forced to flee northward by the French troops of Emperor Maximilian. The city also served as a major garrison for cavalry guarding vulnerable settlements from the incessant raids of the Apaches, until the tribe was subdued by the legendary 'Indian fighter,' Colonel Joaquín Terrazas.

The Porfirio Díaz regime brought railways to Chihuahua and helped consolidate the wealth of the huge cattle fiefdoms – one family held lands the size of Belgium.

After Pancho Villa's forces took Chihuahua in 1913 during the Mexican Revolution, Villa established his headquarters here. He had schools built and arranged other civic works, contributing to his status as a local hero. A statue of Villa graces the intersection of Universidad and División del Norte.

Orientation

Most areas of interest in Chihuahua are within a dozen blocks of the central Plaza de Armas – sometimes meaning a long walk or a taxi ride. Independencia, running approximately northwest-southeast, divides

CHIHUAHUA

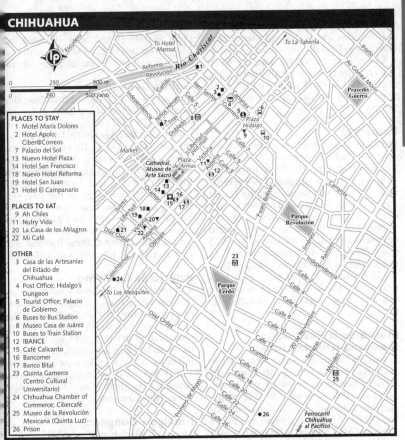

PLACES TO STAY
1 Motel María Dolores
2 Hotel Apolo;
    Ciber@Correos
7 Palacio del Sol
13 Nuevo Hotel Plaza
14 Hotel San Francisco
18 Nuevo Hotel Reforma
19 Hotel San Juan
21 Hotel El Campanario

PLACES TO EAT
9 Ah Chiles
11 Nutry Vida
20 La Casa de los Milagros
22 Mi Café

OTHER
3 Casa de las Artesanías
    del Estado de
    Chihuahua
4 Post Office; Hidalgo's
    Dungeon
5 Tourist Office; Palacio
    de Gobierno
6 Buses to Bus Station
8 Museo Casa de Juárez
10 Buses to Train Station
12 IBANCE
15 Café Calicanto
16 Bancomer
17 Banco Bital
23 Quinta Gameros
    (Centro Cultural
    Universitario)
24 Chihuahua Chamber of
    Commerce; Cibercafé
25 Museo de la Revolución
    Mexicana (Quinta Luz)
26 Prison

the downtown and serves as a sort of 'zero' point for addresses. Streets parallel to it ascend by odd numbers (Calle 3, 5, 7 etc) as one goes northeast, and by even numbers as one goes southwest.

Information

Tourist Offices On the ground floor of the Palacio de Gobierno, near the entrance on Aldama, the state tourist office (☎ 410-10-77, 800-849-52-00, e cturismo@buzon. chihuahua.gob.mx) has an extraordinarily helpful, English-speaking staff. It's open 8.30am to 6pm Monday to Friday and 10am to 5pm Saturday and Sunday.

Money Most of the larger banks are around the Plaza de Armas and most are

open 9am to 5pm Monday to Friday. You'll find casas de cambio on Aldama southwest of the cathedral; IBANCE, at Aldama 8, is open 8am to 8pm Monday to Saturday and changes traveler's checks. Banco Bital, a block east from Bancomer, also has a foreign exchange service.

Post & Communications The main post office is in the Palacio Federal on Juárez between Guerrero and Carranza. It's open 8am to 6pm Monday to Friday, 9am to 1pm Saturday.

The Chihuahua Chamber of Commerce (Canaco), the stone-and-glass structure at Cuauhtémoc 1800, houses the Cibercafé, offering Internet access from 8.30am to 7.30pm Monday to Friday, 9am to 1pm Saturday

(US$3.25 per hour). Director Alfredo Sosa hands out maps and brochures on the state of Chihuahua and can answer your tourism questions, in English.

Ciber@Correos, next to Hotel Apolo on Juárez, is more conveniently located and charges US$2.25 an hour. It's open 9am to 9pm Monday to Saturday, 10am to 6pm Sunday.

Cathedral

Chihuahua's *catedral* towers majestically over the Plaza de Armas. Although construction began in 1726, frequent raids by indigenous tribes postponed completion until 1789. Its marvelous baroque façade contrasts with the simpler Doric-style interior, with 16 Corinthian columns. On the southeast side is the entrance to the **Museo de Arte Sacro** (☎ 413-63-04; admission US$1; open 10am-2pm & 4pm-6pm Mon-Fri), which displays 38 religious paintings from the 18th century. The painters represented were among the founders of Mexico City's first art schools, notably the Academia de San Carlos.

Museo de la Revolución Mexicana (Quinta Luz)

Housed in the mansion and former headquarters of Pancho Villa, the Museum of the Mexican Revolution (☎ 416-29-58, Calle 10; admission US$1; open 9am-1pm & 3pm-7pm Tues-Sat, 9am-5pm Sun) is a must-see for history buffs. After his assassination in 1923, a number of Villa's 'wives' (a list of whom is at the ticket counter) filed claim for his estate. Government investigations determined that Luz Corral de Villa was the generalísimo's legal spouse; the mansion was awarded to her and became known as Quinta Luz (quinta means villa or country house).

When Luz died in 1981, the government acquired the estate and made it a museum. Inside are rooms with their original furnishings, a veritable arsenal of weaponry, historical documents and some exceptional photographs of the revolution and its principals. The accompanying explanations are in Spanish. Parked in a courtyard is the black Dodge that Villa was driving when he was murdered. It's been restored, except for the bullet holes.

You can walk to the museum from the city center or take any bus designated 'Avaloz' or 'Juárez' running southeast on Ocampo. Get off at the corner of Méndez, cross the street and walk downhill on Méndez for two blocks. Quinta Luz will be on your right, with the entrance on Calle 10.

Quinta Gameros

Manuel Gameros started building this mansion (☎ 416-66-84, cnr Bolívar & Calle 4; adult/child US$2.50/1.25; open 11am-2pm & 4pm-7pm Tues-Sun) in 1907 as a wedding present for his fiancée. By the time it was finished four years later, she had fallen in love with the architect, the Colombian Julio Corredor Latorre, and decided to marry him instead. It's a gorgeous building with striking art nouveau decoration – the wood carvings in the dining room are particularly exuberant. The upstairs rooms serve as galleries for the **Centro Cultural Universitario**, Universidad de Chihuahua's art collection.

Palacio de Gobierno

This handsome, 19th-century building is on Aldama facing Plaza Hidalgo. Colonnades of arches surround the classic courtyard, and murals showing the history of Chihuahua cover the walls; the tourist office, in the same building, has a leaflet to help you follow them. On one side of the courtyard is a small room with an eternal flame – actually a red lightbulb – marking the place where Hidalgo was shot.

Hidalgo's Dungeon

The cell in which Hidalgo was held prior to his execution is beneath the post office in the Palacio Federal (a later construction). The entrance is on Juárez – look for the cracked eagle's head inscribed 'Libertad' (admission US$0.50; open 9am-6.30pm Tues-Sun). The cell contains Hidalgo's crucifix, pistol and other personal effects, and a plaque recalls the verses the revolutionary priest dedicated to his captors in his final hours. Despite modern lighting, a real dungeon ambiance remains.

Museo Casa de Juárez

The home and office of Benito Juárez during the period of French occupation now holds this museum (☎ 410-42-58, Juárez 321; admission US$0.50; open 9am-7pm Tues-Sun), which exhibits documents and artifacts related to the great reformer.

Places to Stay

Budget Calle Victoria, southwest of Ocampo, is a budget traveler's haven with a pair of low-priced favorites:

Hotel San Juan (☎ 410-00-35, *Victoria 823*) Singles/doubles US$11/12. This basic place is an excellent value for the price. It has character, its patio entrance is attractively tiled, and it offers parking.

Nuevo Hotel Reforma (☎ 410-03-47, *Victoria 809*) 1 or 2 people US$13.50, 3 or 4 people US$17.50. The Reforma is definitely a superior option to the San Juan, with fairly clean, spacious rooms and overhead fans. Choose a rear rooftop room for a peaceful night's sleep.

Nuevo Hotel Plaza (☎ 415-58-34, *Calle 4 No 206*) Singles/doubles US$9/10. Chihuahua's least expensive option is this hotel, directly behind the cathedral. Rooms are quite decent for the price, with central air-con, ample hot water and lots of what once was polished wood.

Motel María Dolores (☎ 410-47-70, *Niños Héroes 917*) Singles/doubles US$19/22. At the corner of Calle 9, the rooms here are a very good deal – modern and air-conditioned. It's also a hospitable place leaving little doubt as to why it fills up so fast.

Mid-Range *Hotel Apolo* (☎ 416-11-00, e *hapolo@chih1.telmex.net.mx, Juárez 907*) Singles/doubles US$42/47. Opposite the post office, this is Chihuahua's oldest inn, with a Greco-Roman lobby and good rooms with old-fashioned furniture. The singles face noisy Avenida Carranza.

Hotel El Campanario (☎ 415-45-45, *Díaz Ordaz*) Singles/doubles with bath US$47/50. A fine choice with large comfortable rooms, El Campanario is situated between Libertad and Victoria.

Hotel Marrod (☎ 419-03-23, *Tecnológico 10111*) Singles/doubles US$50/53 including breakfast. Visitors driving to Chihuahua will find a number of motels on the main roads into town. The Marrod, located along the approach from Ciudad Juárez, offers air-conditioned rooms.

Top End *Hotel San Francisco* (☎ 416-75-50, e *hsanfco@chihuahua.podernet.com.mx, Victoria 409*) Singles/doubles US$125/134. Sitting behind the cathedral, this hotel has luxurious rooms with satellite TV and voice-mail service. A fine restaurant and cocktail lounge are on the premises.

Palacio del Sol (☎ 416-60-00, e *palacio@ infosel.net.mx, Independencia 116*) Singles & doubles US$125. You'll probably be offered rates of 30% less Friday to Sunday at this high-rise, deluxe hotel on the corner of Niños Héroes.

Places to Eat

Mi Café (☎ 410-12-38, *Victoria 1000*) Large breakfast from US$4.50, mains US$4.50-9. Just up the street from the Nuevo Hotel Reforma, this is a popular breakfast place, serving fresh juices and fruit salads besides the usual egg platters, in comfy booths with friendly service.

La Casa de los Milagros (☎ 437-06-93, *Victoria 812*) Mains US$3.50-5.50. Open from 5pm daily. Stellar service and stylish presentation make this restaurant a fine choice for lunch or dinner. Housed in a beautiful old mansion, it takes on a special candlelit ambiance in the evenings, when you can dine under the stars in the open-roofed courtyard. The menu features original salads, hearty sandwiches and wonderful *quesadillas.*

Ah Chiles (☎ 437-09-77, *Aldama 712*) Tacos from US$2.50. Near Guerrero, Ah Chiles offers a variety of tacos, which are sold by the eighth- and quarter-kilo, and *montados,* which are similar to burritos but folded instead of rolled.

Los Mezquites (☎ 411-66-99, *Cuauhtémoc 2009*) Beef dishes from US$10. In a region famed for its beef, Los Mezquites, a few blocks southwest of Díaz Ordaz, takes pride in its quality cuts, which are broiled over mesquite charcoal. Prices are reasonable for a 125g *arrachera* (skirt steak) or a 250g T-bone.

Nutry Vida (*Aldama 117*) Prices US$1-7. Near Calle 3, and *the* place to stock up for the train journey, this natural-foods market sells a variety of whole wheat breads and pastries, veggie sandwiches and homemade yogurts.

Entertainment

Hotel San Juan (*see Places to Stay*) The bar inside this hotel has lots of character and entertainment in the form of *norteño* troubadours.

Pancho Villa: Bandit-Turned-Revolutionary

Although best known as a hero of the Mexican Revolution, for much of his adult life Francisco 'Pancho' Villa was a murderous thief more given to robbing and womanizing than to any noble cause. Born Doroteo Arango on June 5, 1878, in the village of La Coyotada in rural Durango, the future revolutionary legend lived the rather unremarkable childhood of a typical peasant boy who later found work on a farm. That peaceful life took an abrupt turn on September 22, 1894, when 16-year-old Doroteo took the law into his own hands.

Accounts of what happened that day vary, but the popular version involves an alleged affront to the honor of his 12-year-old sister, Martina. According to this account, Doroteo was returning from work in the fields when he came upon the landowner attempting to abduct Martina. Doroteo ran to a cousin's house, took a pistol down from a wall, then ran down the landowner and shot him. Fearing reprisal, Doroteo took to the hills and abandoned his baptismal name, calling himself Francisco Villa. 'Pancho,' as his associates called him, spent the next 16 years as a bandit and cattle thief, variously riding with three vicious gangs.

Although the life of Pancho Villa the Revolutionary is well documented, his years as a bandit are obscured by contradictory claims, half-truths and outright lies. According to one story, Villa was once captured by three bounty hunters and would have been executed had he not killed a guard and escaped from prison. Another tale has Villa taking his new name from a bandito who was slain in a shoot-out – an action Villa supposedly took to demonstrate his authority over the dead man's gang. The tales abound, but one thing is certain: although an outlaw and ever the bully, Villa detested alcohol, and the sight of excessive drinking made his blood boil. In his *Memorias*, Villa gleefully recalled how he once stole a magnificent horse from a man who was preoccupied with getting drunk in a cantina.

Long after his outlaw years, Pancho Villa became uncharacteristically mum whenever the subject of his criminal past came up. When he did admit to banditry, he described his deeds in the loftiest terms, often referring to himself as the Mexican Robin Hood. But unlike the legendary English outlaw famed for robbing the rich and giving to the poor, Villa and the gangs he rode with killed many innocent people. For instance, José Solís, who rode with Villa as part of the Ignacio Parra gang, once killed an old man because he wouldn't sell him some bread.

By 1909, at age 31, Villa had bought a house in Chihuahua and was running a peaceful, if not entirely legitimate, business trading in horses and meat from dubious sources. That spring, Chihuahua's revolutionary governor Abraham González began recruiting men to break dictator Porfirio Díaz's grip on Mexico, and among the people he lobbied was Villa. González knew about Villa's past, but he also knew that he needed men like Villa – natural leaders who knew how to fight – if he ever hoped to depose Díaz. Thus, González encouraged Villa to return to marauding, but this time for a noble cause: agrarian reform. The idea appealed to Villa, and a year later he joined the revolution.

Villa had no trouble finding men to fight beside him against federal troops. There was much poverty, and rich Mexicans and Americans seemed to own all the land in Mexico. Villa's knowledge of the sierra and bandit tactics greatly aided him in battle; federal troops, who had been taught

---

Café Calicanto (☎ 410-44-52, *Aldama 411*) Open 4pm-1am Sun-Thur, 4pm-2am Fri & Sat. A block away from the San Juan, Café Calicanto provides pleasant outdoor seating in a tree-lined patio and live folk music and jazz nightly, accompanied by tasty regional snacks.

Chihuahua's nightlife percolates in the section of Juárez just above Colón.

La Taberna (☎ 416-83-32, *Juárez*) Open till late. This place, which is located just behind Restaurant La Olla, is a lot of fun for wasting a few hours away. A multilevel bar/restaurant/game room complex, linked by giant brewery vats, La Taberna features a neon-lit rooftop terrace with live rock music and cold draft beer available for the thirsty masses by the pitcher.

Pancho Villa: Bandit-Turned-Revolutionary

only to march in perfect step and fire in volleys, knew nothing about how to deal with these mobs of men who, armed with hand bombs and rifles, attacked one minute then disappeared the next. Villa's guerrilla tactics – lightning strikes, ambushes and night attacks – confounded them. When rebels under Villa's leadership took Ciudad Juárez in May 1911, Díaz resigned. Francisco Madero, a wealthy liberal from the state of Coahuila, was elected president in November 1911.

But Madero was unable to contain the various factions fighting for control throughout the country, and in early 1913 he was toppled from power by one of his own commanders, General Victoriano Huerta, and executed. Pancho Villa fled across the US border to El Paso, but within a couple of months he was back in Mexico, one of four revolutionary leaders opposed to Huerta. Villa quickly raised an army of thousands, the División del Norte, and by the end of 1913 he had taken Ciudad Juárez (again) and Chihuahua. His victory at Zacatecas the following year is reckoned to be one of his most brilliant. Huerta was finally defeated and forced to resign in July 1914. With his defeat, the four revolutionary forces split into two camps, with the liberal Venustiano Carranza and Álvaro Obregón on one side and the more radical Villa and Emiliano Zapata on the other, though the latter pair never formed a serious aloned to be one of his most brilliant. Huerta was finally defeated and forced to resign in July 1914. With his defeat, the four revolutionary forces split into two camps, with the liberal Venustiano Carranza and Álvaro Obregón on one side and the more radical Pancho Villa and Emiliano Zapata on the other, though the latter pair never really formed a serious alliance. Villa was defeated by Obregón in the big battle of Celaya (1915) and never recovered militarily.

But before their fighting days were over, Villa's soldiers would go down in history for, among other things, being one of the few forces ever to invade the United States. Angered by troop support provided to Obregón by the US government in the battle of Celaya, and by the refusal of American merchants to sell them contraband despite cash advances for goods, in 1916 the Villistas ravaged the town of Columbus, New Mexico, and killed 18 Americans. The attack resulted in the US sending 12,000 soldiers into Mexico to pursue the invaders, but the slow-moving columns never did catch Villa's men.

In July 1920, after 10 years of revolutionary fighting, Villa signed a peace treaty with Adolfo de la Huerta, who had been chosen provisional president two months earlier. Villa pledged to lay down his arms and retire to a hacienda called Canutillo, 80km south of Hidalgo del Parral, for which the Huerta government paid 636,000 pesos. In addition, Villa was given 35,926 pesos to cover wages owed to his troops. He also received money to buy farm tools, pay a security guard and help the widows and orphans of the División del Norte.

For the next three years, Villa led a relatively quiet life. He bought a hotel in Parral and regularly attended cockfights. He installed one of his many 'wives,' Soledad Seañez, in a Parral apartment, and kept another at Canutillo. Then, one day while he was leaving Parral in his big Dodge touring car, a volley of shots rang out from a two-story house. Five of the seven passengers in the car were killed, including the legendary revolutionary. An eight-man assassin team fired the fatal shots, but just who ordered the killings remains a mystery.

Shopping

Casa de las Artesanías del Estado de Chihuahua (☎ 437-12-92, Juárez 705) Open 9am-7pm Mon-Fri, 9am-5pm Sat & Sun. Paquimé pottery, Urique baskets and Tarahumara clothing are reasonably priced here, across from the post office. The state-run store purchases its crafts directly from the producers.

Getting There & Away

Air Chihuahua's airport has five flights a day to Mexico City and daily flights to Los Angeles and to major cities in northern Mexico.

Bus The bus station contains restaurants, a luggage storage facility and a telephone *caseta*. Chihuahua is a major center for buses in every direction. The ones most likely to interest travelers are:

Ciudad Juárez – 373km, 5 hours; hourly 1st-class (US$23)

Creel – 256km, 5 hours; hourly 2nd-class (US$17)

Cuauhtémoc – 103km, 1½ hours; 1st-class every half hour (US$6)

Durango – 667km, 9 hours; frequent 1st-class (US$37)

Hidalgo del Parral – 220km, 3 hours; frequent 1st-class (US$13), 5 2nd-class (US$9)

Madera – 276km, 3 hrs; hourly 2nd-class (US$17)

Mexico City (Terminal Norte) – 1468km, 18-22 hours; frequent 1st-class (US$92)

Nuevo Casas Grandes – 352km, 4½ hours; 6 1st-class (US$18.50), 7 2nd-class (US$16)

Zacatecas – 849km, 12 hours; frequent 1st-class (US$52)

Other buses go to Mazatlán, Ojinaga, Monterrey, Saltillo, San Luis Potosí, Torreón and Tijuana. Omnibus Americanos departs daily for Phoenix, Los Angeles, Albuquerque and Denver.

Train Chihuahua is the northeastern terminus of the Chihuahua al Pacífico line for Barranca del Cobre (Copper Canyon) trains. The station is near the intersection of Méndez and Calle 24. Tickets are sold 5am to 7am and 9am to 6pm Monday, Wednesday and Friday; 5am to 6am and 9am to 6pm Tuesday and Thursday; 5am to 6am and 9am to noon Saturday and Sunday.

The air-conditioned *primera express,* No 74, departs daily at 6am for the 14-hour run through the canyon country to Los Mochis. Train No 73 from the coast arrives in Chihuahua at 7.50pm. Fare is US$113 each way. The *clase económica* train, No 76, leaves Chihuahua daily at 7am and takes at least two hours longer. Though not as luxurious as the 1st-class train, it's quite comfortable and air-conditioned. This train in turn has two fare categories: *turista* for US$56 and *subsidio* for much less but available only to locals with identification. For more information on the trains and stops along the way, see the Barranca del Cobre (Copper Canyon) section in the Northwest Mexico chapter.

Getting Around

The bus station is a half-hour ride east of town along Avenida Pacheco. To get there,

catch a 'Circunvalación 2 Sur' bus on Carranza across the street from Plaza Hidalgo (US$0.40). From the bus stop in front of the station, the 'Circunvalación Maquilas' bus goes back to the center.

For the Chihuahua al Pacífico station, take a 'Cerro de la Cruz' bus on Carranza at Plaza Hidalgo, get off at the prison (it looks like a medieval castle), then walk behind the prison to the station.

A taxi stand on Victoria near the cathedral charges standard rates to the train station (US$3.25), bus station (US$5.50) and airport (US$10).

CUAUHTÉMOC
• pop 89,400 • elev 2010m ☎ 625

West of Chihuahua, Cuauhtémoc is a center for the Mennonite population of northern Mexico. From the town's west end, highway 65 runs north through the principal Mennonite zone, with entrances to the numbered *campos* (villages) along the way (see 'The Mennonites' in this chapter).

Logi-Q Computación on the plaza provides Internet connections for US$3.25 an hour and is open 9am to 2pm and 3.30pm to 7pm Monday to Friday, 9am to 3pm Saturday.

The travel agency **Cumbres Friessen** (☎ 582-54-57, ⓔ info@divitur.com.mx, Calle 3 No 466; 4½-hour tours US$28 per person) conducts tours in English that include visits to a local cheese-maker and to traditional Mennonite homes and schools.

Loewen's RV Park (☎ 582-65-23, highway 65 Km 14) RV sites US$13. This park outside of town is a Mennonite-run establishment, on the east side of highway 65. It has 40 hookups, along with bathrooms and laundry facilities.

Hotel San Francisco (☎ 582-31-52, Calle 3 No 132) Singles/doubles US$10.50/11.50 including breakfast. Near Morelos, the Hotel San Francisco has spotless, modern rooms – it's a real bargain. Rooms with TV are about US$3 extra.

Motel Tarahumara Inn (☎ 581-19-19, cnr Calle 5 & Allende) Singles & doubles US$58. This is a very comfortable hotel with clean rooms and parking outside your front door.

Restaurant El Duff (☎ 582-44-61, highway 65 Km 11) Meals US$4. You can sample home-cooked Mennonite dishes such as *kilge* (noodles with lots of cream and smoked ham) at this restaurant outside town.

Cuauhtémoc is 1½ hours by bus (US$6) or 3½ hours by train from Chihuahua. By car, one can head west via La Junta to the spectacular Cascada de Basaseachi waterfalls; see the Barranca del Cobre (Copper Canyon) section in the Northwest Mexico chapter.

HIDALGO DEL PARRAL
• pop 109,400 • elev 1652m ☎ 627

Parral is a pleasant if scruffy town, as well as the most interesting place to break a journey between Chihuahua and Durango. You'll be surprised by the remarkable courtesy of its drivers, who customarily halt for pedestrians! Parral is most famous as the place where Pancho Villa was murdered on July 20, 1923 (see 'Pancho Villa: Bandit-Turned-Revolutionary' in this chapter). A hero to the *campesinos* of the state of Chihuahua, Villa was buried in Parral, with 30,000 attending his funeral. (The story has a sordid postscript: shortly after the general's burial, his corpse was beheaded by unknown raiders.) In 1976, Villa's body was moved to Mexico City. The building from which Villa was shot, on Avenida Juárez at the west end of town, is now a library with a small collection of photos, guns and memorabilia upstairs. Outside to the right of the entrance, a star marks the spot where Villa hit the ground.

Founded as a mining settlement in 1631, the town took the 'Hidalgo' tag later but is still commonly called just 'Parral.' Throughout the 17th century, enslaved natives mined the rich veins of silver, copper and lead from La Negrita mine, whose installations still loom above town but are no longer in use.

Orientation & Information
With its narrow, winding one-way streets, Parral can be confusing at first. Two main squares, Plaza Principal and Plaza Guillermo Baca, are roughly in a line along the north side of the river, linked by busy Avenida Herrera (also called Mercaderes). The bus station at the east end of town is connected to the center of town by Avenida Independencia, which ends at the Hidalgo monument. From there, turn left and go over the bridge to Plaza Principal.

The Mennonites

Founded by the Dutchman Menno Simonis in the 16th century, the Mennonite sect maintains a code of beliefs that, from the start, put it at odds with several governments of the world: members take no oaths of loyalty other than to God and they eschew military service. Persecuted for their beliefs, the Mennonites moved from Germany to Russia to Canada, and thousands settled in the tolerant, post-revolutionary Mexico of the 1920s.

In villages around Cuauhtémoc you might encounter Mennonite men in baggy overalls and straw hats and women in American Gothic dresses and black bonnets speaking their own dialect of old German. As much as their clothing, their northern European physical features set them apart – they seem to tower over their Mexican neighbors. Traditionally, they lead a spartan existence, speak little Spanish, and marry only among themselves, though their refusal to use machinery has been long forgotten; horse-and-buggy transport has been replaced by tractors and pickup trucks.

The Mennonite villages, called *campos* and numbered instead of named, are clustered along route 65, a four-lane highway heading straight north from Cuauhtémoc's western approach. Wide unpaved roads crisscross the campos through vast cornfields interrupted by the occasional farm building and suburban-type dwellings. It feels more like Iowa than Mexico. The Mennonites' best-known product is their cheese *(queso menonito)*, which is sold in many Cuauhtémoc shops.

The Cámara Nacional de Comercio (☎ 522-00-18), at Colegio 28 across from Hotel Acosta, functions as a tourist office, distributing maps and brochures. It's open 9am to 1pm and 3pm to 7pm Monday to Friday, 9am to 1pm Saturday.

There are banks and cambios around Plaza Principal, including Bancomer, which has an ATM.

Infosel at Herrera 26 (enter through the Iris sewing shop) provides fast Internet connections from 9.30am to 1pm and 4pm to

7.30pm Monday to Friday, 10am to 1pm Saturday (US$2.25 per hour).

Special Events

Pancho Villa is honored during the Jornadas Villistas in the latter half of July, featuring a series of cultural events plus parades and fireworks. The general's 1923 assassination is reenacted on July 20 with guns blazing from the Avenida Juárez library, and the following day a cavalcade of some 300 riders descends on Parral on horseback after a six-day journey from the north, recalling Villa's famous marathons.

Places to Stay & Eat

Hotel Acosta (☎ 522-02-21, *Barbachano 3*) Singles/doubles US$18/24. Near Plaza Principal, this is the best-value hotel in town and very friendly; ask for a 3rd-floor room and be sure to check out the view from the roof.

Hotel Fuentes (☎ 522-00-16, e *coadriana@ infosel.net.mx, Mercaderes (Herrera) 79*) Small/large rooms US$13/15. The cheapest decent place is the Fuentes, recognizable by its pink stone façade, opposite the cathedral. Rooms at this cheerful establishment vary in size, but all are clean. English is spoken.

Hotel Los Arcos (☎ 523-05-97, *Pedro de Lille 5*) Singles/doubles US$40/46. A stone's throw from the bus station, this hotel is a good mid-range option, featuring nifty rooms around an elegant courtyard or along an outer terrace. It has almost doubled in price in recent times, however, making it less of a bargain than it used to be.

Motel El Camino Real (☎ 523-02-02, cnr *Avenida Independencia & Pedro de Lille*) Singles/doubles US$49/57. Comfortable, spacious, more upscale rooms and a covered swimming pool can be found here, around the corner from the Hotel Los Arcos.

Parral isn't exactly a culinary capital, but you won't go hungry.

Restaurant Turista (☎ 523-41-00, *Hotel Turista, Plaza Independencia 12*) Breakfast under US$3.50. This restaurant whips up a fine traditional Mexican breakfast.

Restaurant La Fuente (cnr *Coronado & Benítez*) Breakfast US$2.25-5, mains US$3-7. Meat dishes including steak, chicken, tongue and fish are the order of the day here. It's a relaxed, open restaurant with large windows fronting the street, 1970s furniture and no-nonsense dining.

J Quissime Bar & Grill (☎ 523-34-44, *Independencia*) Steaks under US$8, other dishes US$4.50-9. Perhaps Parral's most atmospheric restaurant, J Quissime is also one of the few places open after 10pm. It is decorated with Tarahumara paraphernalia and is located opposite Motel El Camino Real. The food, including Mexican dishes, steaks or black bass, is nothing to get excited about, but it isn't expensive either.

Getting There & Around

The bus station, on the southeast outskirts of town, is most easily reached by taxi (US$3). Regular 1st-class buses run to Chihuahua (3 hours, US$13) and Durango (6 hours, US$23). Frequent 2nd-class buses head to Valle de Allende (30 minutes, US$1.25) from Independencia, near the bus station, opposite the hospital.

AROUND HIDALGO DEL PARRAL

The road east to Jiménez goes through dry, undulating country, but just south of this road, the village of **Valle de Allende** is lush with trees and surrounded by green farmland. The stream through the valley is fed by mineral springs that start near **Ojo de Talamantes**, a few kilometers west, where there's a small bathing area.

Canutillo, 80km south of Parral on the road to Durango, is where Pancho Villa spent the last three years of his life (see 'Pancho Villa: Bandit-Turned-Revolutionary' in this chapter). His former hacienda, attached to a 200-year-old church, is now a museum. The two front rooms contain photographs of Villa, along with displays of his guns and other personal artifacts. Unfortunately, the roofs of the remaining rooms long ago collapsed, and the floors have given way to weeds.

TORREÓN

• pop 517,200 • elev 1150m ☎ 871

Torreón, in the state of Coahuila, is part of a large metropolitan area that includes the contiguous cities of Gómez Palacio and Ciudad Lerdo, both in Durango. The city boasts an attractive central plaza and it makes a good base for exploring the surrounding desert region. Nevertheless, few tourists make it to Torreón – in summer it feels like a steaming concrete jungle. For a panoramic view, take a taxi up to the **Cerro del Cristo de las Noas** lookout. The Christ statue, flanked by TV antennas, is the second-tallest in the Americas.

The 1910 battle for Torreón was Pancho Villa's first big victory in the Mexican Revolution, giving him control of the railways that radiate from the city. Villa waged three more battles for Torreón over the next few years, during which his troops in their revolutionary zeal slaughtered some 200 Chinese immigrants.

Orientation & Information

The whole district around Torreón is known as La Laguna. Torreón fans out east of the Río Nazas, with the central grid lying at the west end of town and the Plaza de Armas at the west end of the grid. Avenidas Juárez and Morelos extend east from the plaza, past the main government plaza and, east of Colón, several large shaded parks. The Torreón bus station is 6km east of the center on Juárez.

The modern Protursa tourist office (☎ 732-22-44, e promotos@prodigy.net.mx), 5km east of the center at Paseo de la Rosita 308D, hands out maps and guides of Torreón and the region. Some staff members speak English. It's open 9am to 2pm and 4pm to 7pm Monday to Friday, 9am to 2pm Saturday. There are Internet cafés around the Alameda park; most are open daily and charge US$2.50 per hour.

Be aware that the city center can be fairly seedy after dark, particularly along Morelos, so be careful if walking around after about 9pm.

Museo de la Revolución

Pancho Villa's Torreón escapades are documented in this tiny museum *(cnr Múzquiz & Constitución; admission by donation; open 10am-2pm Tues-Sun)*, beside the bridge to Gómez Palacio. Built in the 19th century to regulate the irrigation canal for a cotton plantation, the building now houses an unruly collection of photos, cannonballs, swords, posters and other memorabilia pertaining to the revolution.

Special Events

Starting in late August, the month-long Feria del Algodón (cotton fair) has a little of everything: *charro* singers, games, rides, a circus, regional food specialties, prize livestock and – the best reason to attend – an enormous beer garden with room for thousands.

Places to Stay & Eat

Hotel Galicia (☎ 716-18-19, Cepeda 273) Singles & doubles US$13. This is the cheapest place to stay and very basic. It's a study in faded elegance, with tiled halls, stained glass and battered furniture. The Galicia is on the east side of Torreón's main plaza.

Hotel del Paseo (☎ 716-03-03, fax 716-08-81, Morelos 574) Singles/doubles US$26/31. The Paseo, offering pleasant rooms with firm beds, is a major step up in price and quality from the Galicia. The air-con works in some rooms only.

Hotel Calvete (☎ 716-15-30, fax 712-03-78, w www.hotelcalvete.com.mx, cnr Juárez & Corona) Singles/doubles from US$40/45. This hotel is a big white block, featuring spacious air-conditioned rooms with large balconies. It has a restaurant downstairs and parking across the street.

Restaurant Del Granero (☎ 712-91-44, Morelos 444 Pte) Gorditas US$0.50, mains US$3. Open 8am-9pm daily. Vegetarians and others will enjoy this little gem, located between Corona and Vicario. It serves excellent whole-wheat *gorditas* (round corn cakes) and burritos with tasty meatless fillings. There is also a huge selection of fresh juices. Next door is a bakery doing whole-wheat versions of standard Mexican pastries.

Casa Alameda (☎ 712-68-88, Guerra 205) Snacks US$4, mains US$6.75-9.50. For Spanish and Mexican cuisine in a relaxed pub-style setting, try this roomy, bright place across the street from the Alameda park. It offers snacks as well as main courses.

Getting There & Around

There are bus stations in both Torreón and Gómez Palacio, and long-distance buses will stop at both or transfer you from one to the other without charge. Buses depart regularly for Chihuahua (6 hours, US$28), Durango (3½ hours, US$16), Mexico City (14 hours, US$64), Saltillo (3 hours, US$19) and Zacatecas (6 hours, US$21). Taxis are the best way to get from the Torreón bus station to downtown (about US$2.50).

The tolls on the highway to Durango total US$25. To Saltillo, highway 40D costs

US$16; most vehicles take the slightly slower free road.

AROUND TORREÓN

The deserts north of La Laguna are starkly beautiful, with strange geological formations around **Dinamita** and many semiprecious stones for gem hunters. Farther north, the village of **Mapimí** was once the center of an incredibly productive mining area and served the nearby Ojuela mine between periodic raids by Cocoyomes and Tobosos. Benito Juárez passed through Mapimí in the mid-19th century during his flight from French forces. The house where he stayed, near the northwest corner of the Mapimí plaza, is now a small history museum (closed Wednesday) displaying some very good sepia photos of Ojuela in its heyday.

At the end of the 19th century, the Ojuela mine supported an adjacent town of the same name with a population of over 3000. Today a cluster of abandoned buildings clings to a hillside as a silent reminder of Ojuela town's bonanza years. A spectacular 300m-long suspension bridge, the **Puente de Ojuela**, was built over a 100m-deep gorge to carry ore trains from the mine. You can walk across the bridge, fortified with 5cm steel cables, to the mine entrance. A site guide *(suggested fee US$5)* will accompany you through the 800m tunnel, and you'll emerge at a point that affords good views of the Bermejillo area.

To reach Mapimí from Torreón, go 40km north on highway 49 to Bermejillo, then 35km west on highway 30. It's easiest to get there with your own transport, but Agencia Contraste (☎ 871-715-20-51), at Miguel Alemán 128 in Torreón, arranges tours. From Torreón's bus station, Autobuses de la Laguna 2nd-class buses depart every half hour for Mapimí (US$3.25). To visit Puente de Ojuela, get off 3km before Mapimí, at a shop selling rocks and minerals. From there, a narrow road winds 7km up to the bridge. It's an hour walk, but you may be able to hitch a ride. Four kilometers from the turnoff, the road narrows further as the surface becomes cobblestoned and more suitable for hiking than driving.

At Ceballos, 130km north of Torreón, a rough road goes east 40km to the **Zona del Silencio**, so called because conditions in the area are said to prevent propagation of radio waves. Peppered with meteorites, the Zona is also believed to be a UFO landing site. The mysterious overtones associated with the region amplified after a NASA test rocket crashed there during the 1970s. The ensuing search for the craft by US teams was of course veiled in secrecy, giving rise to all manner of suspicions.

The Zona del Silencio is in the **Reserva de la Biósfera Bolsón de Mapimí**, a desert biosphere reserve dedicated to the study of arid-region plants and animals, including a very rare tortoise. This is a remote area with rough roads.

DURANGO

• **pop 411,800** • **elev 1912m** ☎ **618**

Don't be too put off by the modernization on the outskirts of this city – proceed directly to Durango's delightful Plaza de Armas, where you'll discover fine colonial architecture.

The city was founded in 1563 by conquistador Don Francisco de Ibarra and named after the Spanish city of his birth. Just north of town, Cerro del Mercado is one of the world's richest iron ore deposits and was the basis of Durango's early importance along with gold and silver from the Sierra Madre.

Other industries of the area include farming, grazing, timber and paper. Durango is also in the movie business, with several locations outside the city, especially for Westerns. Many of the restaurants have movie or cowboy decor, and lots of shops sell cowboy boots, belts and hats. It's a fun town, and very friendly.

Orientation

Durango is a good town to walk around in, and most of the interesting places to see and stay are within a few blocks of the two main squares, the Plaza de Armas and the Plaza IV Centenario. For some greenery, go to the extensive Parque Guadiana on the west side of town.

Information

Tourist Offices The state tourist office (☎ 811-11-07, e turismor@prodigy.net.mx), which doubles as the state film board, is at Florida 1006. The staff, some of whom speak English, are helpful and have a variety of printed materials. The office is open 8am to 8pm Monday to Friday.

Money Several banks (with ATMs) are on the west side of the Plaza de Armas. For currency exchange, try Bancomer, which is open 8.30am to 4pm Monday to Friday, 10am to 2pm Saturday. A casa de cambio located next to the Hotel Roma has quicker service but lower exchange rates. American Express (☎ 817-00-23) has an office at 20 de Noviembre 810 Ote, which is open 9am to 7pm Monday to Friday, 10am to 5pm Saturday.

Post & Communications The post office is on 20 de Noviembre at Roncal, about 1.5km east of the Plaza de Armas. Hours are 8am to 6pm Monday to Friday, 9am to noon Saturday.

Email services include Internet Calvario, on Florida next to the tourist information office, and Virus Internet Cafe, which can be found at Constitución 101, opposite Hotel Posada San Jorge. Both of these establishments charge US$1.25 per hour and are open Monday to Saturday.

Walking Tour

The Plaza de Armas is attractive, especially on Sunday when musicians perform on the bandstand and locals promenade. Below the bandstand is the university-sponsored handicrafts shop. Facing the plaza's north side is the **Catedral Basílica Menor**, with its imposing baroque façade, constructed from 1695 to 1750. Walk west on 20 de Noviembre and on your right you will see the elegant **Teatro Ricardo Castro**, which has served as a cinema and boxing arena in its century of existence.

Turn south on Martínez, past the **Teatro Victoria**, to the Plaza IV Centenario. On its north side is the **Palacio de Gobierno**, built on the estate of a Spanish mine owner and expropriated by the government after the War of Independence. Inside are colorful murals depicting the history of the state. On the plaza's east side is the **Universidad Juárez**, originally a Jesuit monastery. From there, walk east on 5 de Febrero to the **Casa del Conde de Suchil**, the 18th-century home of the Spanish governor of Durango, now the Banamex building. Two blocks farther east is the **Mercado Gómez**

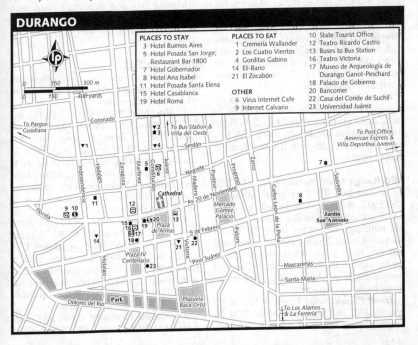

DURANGO

PLACES TO STAY	PLACES TO EAT	
3 Hotel Buenos Aires	1 Cremería Wallander	10 State Tourist Office
5 Hotel Posada San Jorge;	2 Los Cuatro Vientos	12 Teatro Ricardo Castro
Restaurant Bar 1800	4 Gorditas Gabino	13 Buses to Bus Station
7 Hotel Gobernador	14 Eli-Bano	16 Teatro Victoria
8 Hotel Ana Isabel	21 El Zocabón	17 Museo de Arqueología de
11 Hotel Posada Santa Elena		Durango Ganot-Peschard
15 Hotel Casablanca	**OTHER**	18 Palacio de Gobierno
19 Hotel Roma	6 Virus Internet Cafe	20 Bancomer
	9 Internet Calvario	22 Casa del Conde de Suchil
		23 Universidad Juárez

CENTRAL NORTH MEXICO

Palacio, which is a good place for a snack and a rest.

Museo de Arqueología de Durango Ganot-Peschard

Opened in 1998, the museum *(Zaragoza 315 Sur; admission US$0.50, free Tues; open 10am-6pm Tues-Fri, 11am-7pm Sat & Sun)* is a visual feast innovatively presenting the archaeological record of the region's indigenous cultures, from prehistoric times to the Spanish conquest. Highlights include a photographic exhibit on rock paintings and an interesting section demonstrating the archaeological method. All descriptions are in Spanish. The museum is located between 5 de Febrero and 20 de Noviembre.

Places to Stay

Budget *Villa Deportiva Juvenil (☎ 818-70-71, Colegio Militar)* Dorm beds US$4, plus US$2.25 deposit. Durango's cheapest digs can be found at this youth hostel, 400m south of the bus station. It offers clean dorm beds.

Hotel Buenos Aires (☎ 812-31-28, Constitución 126 Nte) Singles US$8, doubles with bath US$14.50. In the center of town, the Buenos Aires has tidy little rooms, some with bathrooms and hot water, and a rather complicated pricing system. Singles come with black-and-white TV; doubles come with color TV. Other configurations are available; the chart by the reception desk sets it all down for you.

Hotel Ana Isabel (☎ 813-45-00, 5 de Febrero 219 Ote) Singles/doubles US$19/25. Just a stone's throw east of León de la Peña, the rooms here are lovely, some with balconies over a courtyard. It's an excellent budget option.

Mid-Range *Hotel Roma (☎ 812-01-22, 20 de Noviembre 705 Pte)* Singles/doubles US$25/32, suites US$35, including breakfast. The friendly Roma is in a large century-old building catercorner from the Teatro Ricardo Castro. The rooms here are small but in pretty good shape. Room 218, a *media suite,* is the best deal, including two double beds, two balconies and an enormous bathroom with tub.

Hotel Posada Santa Elena (☎ 812-78-18, Negrete 1007 Pte) Singles/doubles US$34/41. Friendly, small and quiet, this hotel is a find.

It features 10 tastefully furnished rooms, some with their own little courtyard.

Hotel Casablanca (☎ 811-35-99, fax 811-47-04, e casabca@infosel.net.mx, 20 de Noviembre 811 Pte) Singles/doubles US$53/59. Located a block west of the Roma is this place with large well-appointed rooms. If you're going to stay here it's worth shelling out an additional US$5.50 for an *habitación panorámica,* featuring king-size bed, marble tub and jaw-dropping views.

Hotel Posada San Jorge (☎ 813-32-57, fax 811-60-40, Constitución 102 Sur) Singles/doubles US$57/63, suites US$80. Posada San Jorge, in a handsome 19th-century building, is one of Durango's finest hotels. Its colonial-style rooms and junior suites, the latter with sofas and walk-in closets, are well worth the price tag. Little luxuries, such as being able to make a fresh cup of coffee in the morning, make a stay very memorable.

Top End *Hotel Gobernador (☎ 813-19-19, fax 811-14-22, 20 de Noviembre 257 Ote)* Singles & doubles US$118. The Gobernador is the best hotel in town, featuring a swimming pool and an elegant restaurant. The rooms here include air-con, phone, TV and the works. It's 1km east of the Plaza de Armas.

Places to Eat

Durango boasts plenty of good restaurants, and those craving variety will find a range of ethnic establishments.

El Zocabón (☎ 811-80-83, 5 de Febrero 513) Breakfast US$2.25-3.25. Open 7.30am-11pm daily. A large, pleasant café that makes a good spot for breakfast, El Zocabón serves big mugs of fresh steaming coffee with your *desayuno* (breakfast). Next door *Fuente de Sodas* serves ice creams, flavored coffees and other tasty treats to satisfy your sweet tooth.

Gorditas Gabino (☎ 812-11-92, Constitución 100A Nte) Gorditas US$0.75, other meals under US$5.50. A good snacking option is here at the corner of Serdán, serving up huge, delicious gorditas stuffed with avocados, shredded beef in *salsa verde* and other tasty things. Fresh-squeezed juices and *licuados* are available too.

Los Cuatro Vientos (☎ 813-53-10, Constitución 154 Nte) Mains US$3.25-5.50. Open for breakfast & lunch. Just up the street from Gorditas Gabino, this very popular place offers quality seafood in an unpretentious setting. Choose from a hearty bowl of shrimp soup, octopus salad and fresh fish fillets. Service is rapid and portions are plentiful.

Eli-Bano (☎ 813-40-04, Hidalgo 310 Sur) Mains US$4.50-10. Fans of Middle Eastern cuisine should head for this place, where you will find appetizers like hummus, tabbouleh and stuffed grape leaves.

Restaurant Bar 1800 (☎ 811-03-25) Mains US$8-13. In an elegant courtyard of the Hotel Posada San Jorge (see Places to Stay), this restaurant serves outstanding Mexican food, steaks, seafood and chicken dishes. The succulent steaks (US$10) are simply delicious – very tender and served with a variety of fillings.

Cremería Wallander (☎ 813-86-33, Independencia 128 Nte) Prices from US$2.50. This is a good place to stock up for a picnic or bus journey, offering locally made yogurt, honey and granola. The bakery/gourmet deli prepares extraordinary tortas with special German cold cuts and Mennonite cheese on fresh-baked seeded rolls.

Getting There & Away

Good bus connections are available from Durango to many of the places that travelers want to go. Daily departures include:

Chihuahua – 667km, 9 hours; 6 1st-class (US$37)

Hidalgo del Parral – 396km, 6 hours; 9 1st-class (US$23)

Mazatlán – 322km, 7 hours; 3 deluxe (US$36), 10 1st-class (US$27), 6 2nd-class (US$24)

Mexico City (Terminal Norte) – 920km, 12 hours; 1 deluxe (US$77), 7 1st-class (US$57)

Torreón – 247km, 3½ hours; frequent 1st-class (US$16), 8 2nd-class (US$14.50)

Zacatecas – 290km, 4 hours; frequent 1st-class (US$18), 5 2nd-class (US$14.50)

Getting Around

The bus station is on the east side of town; white Ruta 2 buses departing from the far side of the parking lot will get you to the Plaza de Armas for US$0.30. Taxis, which are metered, charge about US$2.25 to the center.

To reach the bus station from downtown, catch a blue-striped 'Camionera' bus from 20 de Noviembre beside the plaza. Get off at the intersection of Colegio Militar (a major thoroughfare), then go left toward the Villa monument and take the overpass across Pescador.

AROUND DURANGO
Movie Locations

The clear light and stark countryside have made Durango a popular location for Hollywood movies. Around 120 films have been shot in the area – mostly Westerns, including John Wayne vehicles and films by directors John Huston and Sam Peckinpah. Movie fans will enjoy visiting the sets, which appear to be undergoing a renaissance; a number of Mexican TV series and US productions are planned. Be sure to check with the tourist office before going out to the sets, as they may be off limits during production.

Villa del Oeste (off highway 45; admission US$0.50; open noon-6pm Sat & Sun) is 12km north of Durango. After its use in a number of Westerns, the 'main street,' known locally as Calle Howard, was left undisturbed. When not in production, it's open to visitors. To get there, take a 2nd-class bus for Chupaderos from the bus station (every half hour; US$1) and tell the driver to drop you at Villa del Oeste. To get back to Durango, just flag down any passing bus headed toward the city. Note that opening hours are changeable so it's best to check with the tourist office in Durango before heading out there.

Southwest of Durango is **Los Álamos** (open daily), a '1940s town' where Fat Man and Little Boy was filmed in 1989; the movie, about the making of the first A-bomb, starred Paul Newman. To get there, take Boulevard Arrieta south of town and stay on it for about 30km, past dramatic mesas and a steep river gorge. Watch for a rusty sign on the right announcing the turnoff for the set. From there it's another 1.5km over a rough road. Buses are not an option.

Museo de Arte Guillermo Ceniceros

Originally the site of a British-built ironworks, the Ferrería de los Flores in 1998 was converted into a museum (☎ 618-826-03-64, La Ferrería; admission US$0.50; open 10am-6pm Tues-Sun) to display the art of Durango native Guillermo Ceniceros. Profoundly influenced by his teacher, the formidable muralist David Alfaro Siqueiros,

Ceniceros developed his own method of visual expression. Mysterious landscapes and feminine figures are his preferred subjects. La Ferrería is 4km southwest of Durango on the way to Los Álamos. Regular 'Ferrería' buses depart from the Plazuela Baca Ortiz in the center of town.

En Route to Mazatlán

The road west from Durango to the coastal city of Mazatlán (see the Central Pacific

Coast chapter) is particularly scenic, with a number of worthwhile natural attractions. In the vicinity around **El Salto**, you can trek to waterfalls, canyons and forests. About 160km from Durango is a spectacular stretch of road called **El Espinazo del Diablo** (which means the Devil's Backbone).

You enter a new time zone when you cross the Durango-Sinaloa state border; Sinaloa is one hour behind Durango.

Northeast Mexico

This chapter covers the state of Nuevo León and most of the states of Tamaulipas and Coahuila – together, a huge area stretching nearly 1000km from north to south and 500km from east to west. Many travelers enter Mexico at one of the region's five main border crossings from the USA, and take one of the several routes heading south to the Bajío region, central Mexico or the Gulf Coast. Most of them pass through this area as quickly as possible to get to what is seen as the 'real' Mexico. This is not surprising, as northeast Mexico does not have impressive pre-Hispanic ruins, charming colonial towns, or pretty palm-fringed beaches. What it does have is a geography unlike anywhere else in Mexico, and a unique emerging culture.

Geographically, the deserts of northeast Mexico are the southern extension of the Great Plains of the USA and Canada, impressive for their stark, rugged beauty and sheer expanse. The Rio Grande (Río Bravo del Norte to Mexicans) is vital for irrigation in this arid region, and has been developed as a resource by joint Mexican-US projects. In fact, it might have been overdeveloped, and attention is now being paid to environmental quality along the river. The coastal areas have remote beaches, lagoons and wetlands, home to diverse marine life and a winter stopover for many migratory birds. Inland, numerous winding roads climb to the eastern and northern edges of the Sierra Madre Oriental, offering spectacular scenery and a refreshing highland climate.

Culturally, northeast Mexico and the south-central USA comprise a frontier of epic proportions. It was here that the two great colonizing movements, Spanish from the south and Anglo-Saxon from the north, confronted each other and displaced the indigenous peoples. The war between Mexico and the USA (1846-48) was probably inevitable, and though it established the Rio Grande as the political border between the two countries, the cultural and economic boundaries remain much less distinct. There is so much Mexican influence in southern Texas that Spanish seems to be more widely spoken there than English, while cities such

Highlights

- Monterrey – a vibrant state capital, home to some of Mexico's finest modern architecture and to the hottest nightlife scene in the northeast

- Area de Protección de Flora y Fauna Cuatrociénegas – an isolated protected area in the Desierto Chihuahuense (Chihuahuan Desert), with hundreds of crystalline pools, amazing white gypsum sand dunes and numerous endemic species

- Saltillo – the high-sierra capital of Coahuila, with its pleasant climate and lovely colonial buildings

- Parras – a tranquil town and desert oasis in Coahuila that is home to the Americas' oldest winery, Casa Madero

USA

Nuevo Laredo
page 412

Monterrey
page 427
Central Monterrey
page 430-431

Reynosa
page 415

Matamoros
page 418

Saltillo
page 444

Gulf
of
Mexico

Ciudad Victoria
page 423

OTHER MAPS
Northeast Mexico page 410

as Monterrey, the capital of Nuevo León, represent the most Americanized parts of Mexico. Economically, the two sides of the river seem worlds apart, but money and resources surge back and forth across the line. The Texas economy is largely dependent on Mexican labor while American investment is integral for the *maquiladoras* (assembly-plant operations, usually foreign-owned), which are so key to the economy of northern

NORTHEAST MEXICO

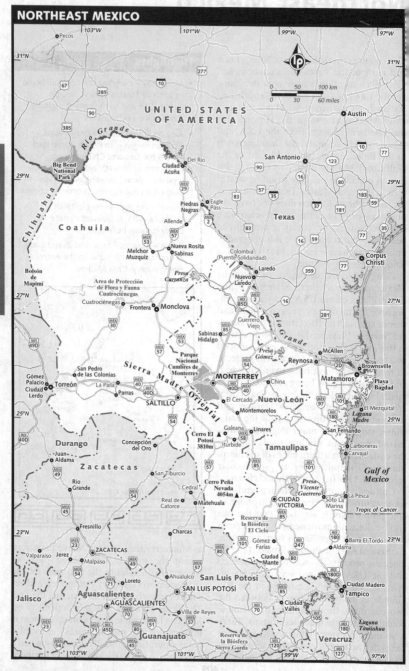

Mexico. Mexico sends about 90% of its exports to its northern neighbor and the slowdown in the US economy in 2001, with consequent sluggish investment in maquiladoras, augured a couple of tough years here.

If you're just looking for tourist attractions you might be disappointed in northeast Mexico, but if you want to see a fascinating, evolving region you should spend at least a few days here. It might be a window to the future of Mexico in the age of NAFTA – a place where Tex-Mex is more than a burrito.

Tamaulipas

NUEVO LAREDO
• pop 307,600 • elev 438m ☎ 867

More foreign tourists enter Mexico through Nuevo Laredo than any other town on the northeast border. As border towns go, the Laredo/Nuevo Laredo pairing is almost a classic example, and not unpleasant, though the heat can be unbearable. Nuevo Laredo has many restaurants, bars and souvenir shops catering to day-trippers from the USA. Most accept US currency and quote prices in dollars. 'Across the water,' in Laredo, there are supermarkets, motels and fast-food joints, all staffed with Spanish-speaking workers.

History
In 1836 Texas seceded from Mexico and became an independent republic. From 1839 to 1841 the Rio Grande valley, and much of what is now northeastern Mexico, also declared itself a separate republic, the Republic of the Rio Grande, with its capital at Laredo.

The US annexation of Texas in 1845 precipitated the Mexican-American War, with the Rio Grande subsequently becoming the border between the USA and Mexico. Mexicans established a new town, Nuevo Laredo, south of the river. Nuevo Laredo now collects more in tariffs and customs revenue than any other Mexican port of entry. It also has more than 60 maquiladoras producing goods for the US market.

Orientation
Two international bridges link the two Laredos. Puente Internacional No 1 is the one to use if you're walking into Mexico – there's a US$0.40 pedestrian toll. It leaves you at the north end of Avenida Guerrero, Nuevo Laredo's main thoroughfare, which stretches for 2km (one way going south). Northbound traffic heading for Puente Internacional No 1 is directed via Avenida López de Lara on the western side of the city.

Puente Internacional No 2 is for vehicles only. It is preferred by drivers bypassing Nuevo Laredo's center, as it feeds directly into Boulevard Luis Colosio, skirting the city to the east. On the US side, Interstate 35 goes north to San Antonio.

A third international bridge, the Puente Solidaridad, crosses the border 38km to the northwest, enabling motorists in a hurry to bypass Laredo and Nuevo Laredo altogether.

The Plaza Hidalgo is seven blocks from Puente Internacional No 1, with a kiosk in the middle, the Palacio de Gobierno on the east side, and a few hotels and restaurants around it.

Information
Immigration Both international bridges have Mexican immigration offices at the southern end where you can get your tourist card, if you plan to go further south into Mexico. You have to go to the *aduana* (customs) office in town to get a vehicle permit (see Getting There & Away).

Tourist Offices A tourist office (☎ 712-73-97, ⓔ turismolider@hotmail.com) at the corner of Herrera and Juárez is open 8am to 8pm Monday to Friday (sometimes staffed on weekends). The friendly staffers, one of whom speaks English, distribute maps and brochures.

Money Most *casas de cambio* will not change traveler's checks but most businesses will accept them with a purchase, and the main Mexican banks should change them. Businesses also accept US currency, but the exchange rate can be low. Banca Serfin and Banamex on Avenida Guerrero have ATMs.

Post & Communications The post office is on Camargo, behind the government offices on the east side of the plaza. It's open 8am to 6pm Monday to Friday,

NORTHEAST MEXICO

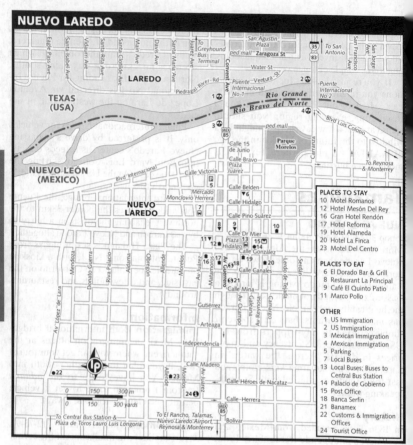

NUEVO LAREDO

LAREDO

TEXAS (USA)

Rio Grande
Rio Bravo del Norte

NUEVO LEÓN (MEXICO)

NUEVO LAREDO

Parque Morelos

PLACES TO STAY
10 Motel Romanos
12 Hotel Mesón Del Rey
16 Gran Hotel Rendón
17 Hotel Reforma
19 Hotel Alameda
20 Hotel La Finca
23 Motel Del Centro

PLACES TO EAT
6 El Dorado Bar & Grill
8 Restaurant La Principal
9 Café El Quinto Patio
11 Marco Pollo

OTHER
1 US Immigration
2 US Immigration
3 Mexican Immigration
4 Mexican Immigration
5 Parking
7 Local Buses
13 Local Buses; Buses to Central Bus Station
14 Palacio de Gobierno
15 Post Office
18 Banca Serfin
21 Banamex
22 Customs & Immigration Offices
24 Tourist Office

0   150   300 m
0   150   300 yards

To Central Bus Station & Plaza de Toros Lauro Luis Longoria

To El Rancho, Talamas, Nuevo Laredo Airport, Reynosa & Monterrey

8am to 2pm Saturday. Two kinds of pay phones stand around the plaza and the center: Ladatel card-operated phones, and special coin-operated phones for calls across the border.

Talamas, a music store on Guerrero, offers Internet access on its upper level for US$3.25 per hour. It's open 9am to 11pm Monday to Saturday, 11am to 10pm Sunday.

Special Events

Nuevo Laredo holds an agricultural, livestock, industrial and cultural fair the second and third weeks of September. The founding of Nuevo Laredo in 1848 is celebrated June 13-15 with music, baseball games and bullfights.

Places to Stay

All the hotels listed here have air-con, a necessity during Nuevo Laredo's blistering summers. There are more upmarket places on highway 85 heading south.

Hotel La Finca (☎ 712-88-83, *Avenida Reynosa 811*) Singles/doubles US$25/28. South of González, this hotel is the least expensive decent place in town, with clean, comfortable rooms that have cable TV.

Motel Romanos (☎ 712-23-91, *Dr Mier 2420*) Singles & doubles US$31. Three blocks east of the plaza, Motel Romanos, with its Romanesque façade, is almost as good as La Finca, although a bit snooty.

Gran Hotel Rendón (☎ 712-00-66, *cnr González & Avenida Juárez*) Singles/doubles US$33/39. This hotel is built around an attractive open courtyard. It has simple, tidy rooms with small bathrooms. Parking is available.

Hotel Alameda (☎ 712-50-50, González 2715) Singles/doubles US$23/38. On the south side of the plaza, the Alameda has clean, airy rooms that are much better than the hotel facade and foyer would suggest.

Hotel Reforma (☎ 712-62-50, Avenida Guerrero 822) Singles/doubles US$40/47. A half block north of Canales, the Reforma has bright, clean rooms with color TV, phone and firm mattresses. Some of the doorways are small, so mind your head! There is also a restaurant and bar here.

Hotel Mesón Del Rey (☎ 712-63-60, Avenida Guerrero 718) Singles/doubles US$34/42. The friendly Mesón Del Rey, on the west side of the plaza, features spacious, quiet rooms and chilly central air-con. The entrance to the hotel's parking lot is on González.

Motel Del Centro (☎ 712-13-10, Héroes de Nacataz 3330) Singles & doubles US$42. This little oasis near the tourist office has palm trees that adorn the parking lot, and one wing wraps around a swimming pool. It has large, comfortable rooms (some with king-size beds), although they're looking a little faded these days.

Places to Eat
There are numerous eating possibilities, though the places on Avenida Guerrero, just south of the bridge, can be overpriced tourist joints.

El Dorado Bar & Grill (☎ 712-00-15, cnr Belden & Ocampo) Starters US$3-7, mains US$16-20. Five blocks south of the bridge, this place has been a haunt for South Texans since opening in 1922 as the casino-restaurant 'El Caballo Blanco.' It still harbors a significant number of gringos, attracted by its 'Old West' atmosphere, Cajun cuisine and special cocktails – notably the New Orleans 'gin fizz' (US$4.50). In addition to soft-shell crabs and frog's legs, the El Dorado offers a variety of border favorites such as *cabrito* (roasted young goat); all at about US$16.

Restaurant La Principal (☎ 712-13-01, Avenida Guerrero 624) Mains US$7.75-11, parrillada for 2 US$33. For authentic *norteño* fare, check out La Principal, half a block north of the plaza; look for goats

roasting over coals in the window. The popular restaurant offers all the cabrito variations – a substantial order of *pierna* comes with salsa, salad, tortillas and beans.

Marco Pollo (☎ 712-87-00, cnr Dr Mier & Matamoros) Mains US$4-10. Charcoal-grilled chicken is the main attraction at this pleasant restaurant, which has overhead fans and tiled tables. A whole chicken (US$8) is served with salsa and tortillas. Large pizzas (US$10) are also offered.

Café El Quinto Patio (cnr Ocampo & Dr Mier) Mains US$3.50. This is a popular hangout for cowboys and other local characters. The air-conditioned café serves pretty good enchiladas and *lonches* (rolls stuffed with avocado, ground beef or eggs).

El Rancho (☎ 714-80-18, Avenida Guerrero 2134) Mains US$5-9. Between Venezuela and Lincoln, a kilometer or so down Avenida Guerrero from the international bridge, is this taco-and-beer hall frequented by families. Aside from the wide variety of tacos (US$1.25) and regional dishes, meat lovers can buy slabs by the kilo here.

Spectator Sports
Plaza de Toros Lauro Luis Longoria (☎ 712-71-92, Avenida Monterrey 4101) Admission US$6-8. Two or three bullfights each month are held here, near Anáhuac.

Shopping
It's worth browsing around some of the shops and markets for the odd souvenir. There's a **crafts market** on the east side of Avenida Guerrero half a block north of the main plaza, and the **Mercado Monclovio Herrera** on the west side of Avenida Guerrero, between Hidalgo and Belden, where you'll find an assortment of T-shirts, silver, rugs, liquor, hats, leather and pottery.

Getting There & Away
Air Nuevo Laredo airport is off the Monterrey road, 14km south of town. Mexicana (☎ 718-14-92), with an office at the corner of Paseo Colón and Obregón, has direct flights to/from Mexico City and Guadalajara.

Bus Nuevo Laredo's central bus station is 3km south of Puente Internacional No 1 on Anáhuac. There's a left-luggage service opposite the bus ticket counters (US$0.30 per hour). First- and 2nd-class buses serve every city in northern Mexico. Daily service from Nuevo Laredo includes:

Ciudad Victoria – 510km, 7 hours; 6 1st-class (US$34)

Mexico City (Terminal Norte) – 1158km, 14 hours; 3 deluxe (US$97), 8 1st-class (US$75), 1 2nd-class (US$66)

Monclova – 248km, 4 hrs; 5 1st-class (US$19)

Monterrey – 224km, 3 hours; 1st-class every half hour (US$17), frequent 2nd-class (US$13)

Reynosa – 251km, 4 hours; 8 1st-class (US$16)

Saltillo – 310km, 4½ hours; hourly 1st-class (US$22), 2 2nd-class (US$19)

San Luis Potosí – 740km, 10 hours; hourly 1st-class (US$48), 4 2nd-class (US$40)

Zacatecas – 683km, 8 hours; 6 1st-class (US$44)

Buses also go to Aguascalientes, Durango, Guadalajara and Querétaro, and to major cities in Texas.

There are also direct buses to cities in Mexico from the Greyhound terminal across the border in Laredo, Texas (610 Salinas Ave, ☎ 956 723-4324), but these are more expensive than services from Nuevo Laredo. You can sometimes use these buses to go between Laredo and Nuevo Laredo bus stations, but you have to ask the driver (it's less hassle and often quicker just to walk over the international bridge).

Car & Motorcycle For a vehicle permit you must go to the customs office (open 24 hours) at Avenida López de Lara and Héroes de Nacataz. From Puente Internacional No 1, turn right onto Boulevard Internacional and follow the 'vehicle permit' signs. After about 10 blocks, bear left onto Avenida López de Lara, moving into the left lane. Just past the train station on your left is a low white wall labeled 'Importación Temporal de Vehículos Extranjeros'; swing around to the other side of the boulevard at the traffic circle, pull in at the entrance and park. The low building left of the parking lot entrance houses an immigration office and customs bureau. The office is always open and should issue a permit without hassle if your papers are in order (see the Getting There & Away chapter). To avoid a fine, don't forget to cancel the permit when you leave the country.

The route south via Monterrey is the most direct to central Mexico, the Pacific Coast and the Gulf Coast. An excellent toll road, highway 85D is fast but expensive (tolls total US$18 to Monterrey). The alternative free road (highway 85) is longer, rougher and slower. Highway 2 is a rural road following the Rio Grande to Reynosa and Matamoros.

Getting Around

Frequent city buses (US$0.40) make getting around Nuevo Laredo simple enough. Many buses go down Avenida Guerrero from the plaza; 'Carretera – Central' buses with an aquamarine stripe, go to the central bus station. To get from Puente Internacional No 1 to the nearest bus stop, go two blocks on Boulevard Internacional to Avenida Juárez, then left five blocks to Pino Suárez. From the bus station, local buses go back into town.

A taxi to the bridge from the bus station will cost about US$6, and about a dollar more in the reverse direction.

There's a secure parking garage four blocks south of the bridge on Victoria, west of Avenida Guerrero (US$1.50 per hour).

REYNOSA
● **pop 360,100** ● **elev 90m** ☎ **899**

Reynosa is one of northeast Mexico's most important industrial towns, with oil refineries, petrochemical plants, cotton mills, distilleries and maquiladoras. Pipelines from here carry natural gas to Monterrey and into the USA.

As a commercial border crossing, Reynosa is busier than Matamoros, but less important than Nuevo Laredo. It has good road connections into Mexico and Texas, but most travelers will probably find one of the other crossings more direct and convenient. Across the Rio Grande is the town of McAllen.

The tourist trade is geared to short-term Texan visitors, with restaurants, nightclubs, bars and bawdier diversions.

Reynosa was founded in 1749 as Villa de Nuestra Señora de Guadalupe de Reynosa, 20km from its present location: flooding forced the move in 1802. Reynosa was one of the first towns to rise up in the independence movement of 1810, but little of historical interest remains.

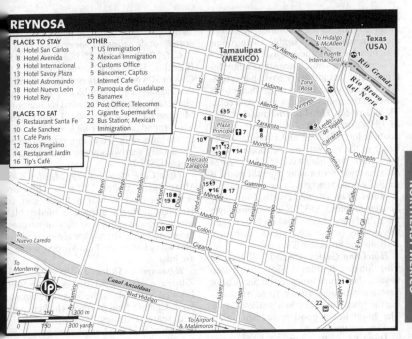

REYNOSA

PLACES TO STAY
4 Hotel San Carlos
8 Hotel Avenida
9 Hotel Internacional
13 Hotel Savoy Plaza
17 Hotel Astromundo
18 Hotel Nuevo León
19 Hotel Rey

PLACES TO EAT
6 Restaurant Santa Fe
10 Cafe Sanchez
11 Café Paris
12 Tacos Pingüino
14 Restaurant Jardín
16 Tip's Café

OTHER
1 US Immigration
2 Mexican Immigration
3 Customs Office
5 Bancomer; Captus
Internet Cafe
7 Parroquia de Guadalupe
15 Banamex
20 Post Office; Telecomm
21 Gigante Supermarket
22 Bus Station; Mexican
Immigration

NORTHEAST MEXICO

Orientation

Reynosa's central streets are laid out on a grid pattern, between the Rio Grande and the Canal Anzalduas. The main plaza, on a rise a few blocks southwest of the Puente Internacional, is the site of the town hall, banks, hotels and a modern church, the Parroquia de Guadalupe.

South of the plaza, on Hidalgo, is a pedestrian mall lined with shops and cafés, extending to Gigante at the southern edge of the grid. Between the bridge and the center lies the Zona Rosa, with its restaurants, bars and nightclubs.

If you're driving in from Mexico, follow the signs to the Puente Internacional. Avoid the maze of streets in the industrial zone south of the canal.

Information

US and Mexican immigration bureaus are at their respective ends of the bridge, and there's another Mexican post in the Reynosa bus station. Get a tourist card stamped at either Mexican post if you're proceeding beyond Reynosa deeper into Mexico.

You can change traveler's checks at Banamex, on Guerrero between Hidalgo and Juárez. The main banks have ATMs, some dispensing US dollars as well as pesos, and there are several casas de cambio along Zaragoza near the bridge.

The post office, adjacent to a Telecomm office on the corner of Díaz and Colón, is open 9am to 4pm Monday to Friday, 9am to 1pm Saturday.

Captus Internet Cafe, on the north side of the plaza at Zaragoza, is open 8.30am to 9pm Monday to Saturday, 9am to 7pm on Sunday. Internet connections are US$2.25 an hour.

Special Events

The festival of Nuestra Señora de Guadalupe, on December 12, is the town's major event. Pilgrims start processions a week before and there are afternoon dance performances in front of the church. Reynosa's *feria* is held from late July to early August.

Places to Stay

Hotel Nuevo León (☎ 922-13-10, Díaz 580) Singles & doubles US$17 (more for air-con).

This is probably the best budget option in the area (and only a few minutes' walk from the main square) with sizable, clean rooms with fans. Be quick though, as it fills early.

There are two hotels near the Puente Internacional that are fairly basic, but probably of better value in this range than hotels closer to the center. Rooms come with cable TV and air-con. *Hotel Internacional* (☎ 922-23-18, Zaragoza 1050 Ote) has singles/doubles for US$27/33 and is probably the better of the two with no-frills accommodations. *Hotel Avenida* (☎ 922-05-92, Zaragoza 885), just two blocks away from the plaza, is similarly priced and runs a close second.

Hotel Rey (☎ 922-29-80, Díaz 556) Singles/doubles US$32/38. Two doors down from the Nuevo León, this hotel has bright, tidy rooms (some have views) with firm beds, air-con and cable TV.

Hotel San Carlos (☎ 922-12-80, Hidalgo 970) Singles/doubles US$50/55. A step toward the luxury bracket, the San Carlos has air-conditioned rooms, some overlooking the plaza, furnished in a medieval style. The hotel has a good restaurant and a parking garage.

Hotel Savoy Plaza (☎ 922-00-67, Juárez 860 Nte) Singles & doubles US$55. Half a block south of the Parroquia de Guadalupe, this pleasant hotel has modern, air-conditioned rooms.

Hotel Astromundo (☎ 922-56-25, e astromundo@infosel.net.mx, Juárez 675 Nte) Singles/doubles US$72/83. The top downtown place is the Astromundo, between Guerrero and Méndez. It features large, clean rooms with spotless bathrooms, cable TV, email access, parking and a restaurant.

Places to Eat
Reynosa boasts quite a few centrally located places to eat, many offering hearty, inexpensive fare.

Tacos Pingüino (☎ 922-66-65, Morelos 665) Mains US$4. Open until 9pm daily. Tasty Mexican snacks can be found here, on the south side of the plaza.

Cafe Sanchez (☎ 924-35-08, Morelos 575) Breakfast US$1.75-4, lunch US$3.25. A popular spot with locals, Sanchez has lots of egg dishes, some English-speaking waiters and a cool interior.

Restaurant Jardín (☎ 961-74-94, Juárez) Meat dishes, including cabrito US$11. Open

7am-11pm Mon-Thur, 7am-12pm Fri & Sat, 7am-10pm Sun. This is *the* place for norteño-style *cabrito al pastor*.

Café Paris (☎ 922-55-35, Hidalgo 815, Breakfast US$2.25-3.25, mains US$3.25-8) One of Reynosa's most popular options is this elegant cafe, half a block south of the plaza, featuring breakfasts and scrumptious Mexican dishes. Waiters wheel carts of pastries around and serve *café lechero*, pouring coffee and milk from separate pitchers. Their tasty sandwiches are an inexpensive lunch (US$1.75).

Tip's Café (☎ 922-60-19, Méndez 640) Most meals under US$3.25. This air-conditioned café, half a block east of Hidalgo, features attractive tiled tables where you can enjoy a variety of burritos, tacos and *tortas*. The nachos are some of the best we've had in northern Mexico; servings are huge.

Restaurant Santa Fe (☎ 922-85-16, Zaragoza 690) Most dishes US$5.50-9. Located on the plaza, the Santa Fe claims to serve Chinese food. It offers chicken, pork and seafood dishes. Portions are large enough to feed two hungry people.

Entertainment
The Zona Rosa has a slew of restaurants, bars and nightclubs, but comes to life only on the nights when the young Texas crowd comes in. Much sleazier entertainment (exotic dancing and prostitution) is the rule at 'boys' town, a few kilometers west, just beyond where Aldama becomes a dirt road.

Getting There & Away
Air Reynosa airport is 8km out of town, off the Matamoros road. There are daily Aeroméxico flights direct to Mexico City, and to/from Guadalajara. Several other small airlines operate here, such as Aerolíneas Internacionales (☎ 926-73-00) which flies to and from Aguascalientes and Tijuana.

Bus The bus station is on the southeastern corner of the central grid, opposite the parking lot of the Gigante supermarket. Buses run to almost anywhere you'd want to go in Mexico. Daily service from Reynosa includes:

Aguascalientes – 808km, 12 hours; hourly 1st-class (US$48)

Ciudad Victoria – 330km, 4½ hours; frequent 1st-class (US$18.50)

Guadalajara – 990km, 15 hours; 8 1st-class (US$64)

Matamoros – 104km, 2 hours; frequent 1st-class (US$6), 5 2nd-class (US$5.75)

Mexico City (Terminal Norte) – 970km, 14 hours; 4 1st-class (US$65)

Monterrey – 220km, 3 hours; frequent 1st-class (US$15.50)

Saltillo – 305km, 5 hours; frequent 1st-class (US$19)

San Luis Potosí – 737km, 10 hours; frequent 1st-class (US$38)

Tampico – 580km, 7 hours; frequent 1st-class (US$27)

Torreón – 536km, 9 hours; 9 1st-class (US$34)

Zacatecas – 678km, 10 hours; frequent 1st-class (US$45)

First-class buses also serve Chihuahua, Ciudad Juárez, Durango, Puebla, Querétaro, Veracruz and Villahermosa. Second-class buses serving mainly local destinations are also available. There are also direct buses to Houston daily (US$26) and to Chicago twice a week (US$105).

McAllen, Texas The nearest Texas transport center, McAllen, is 9km from the border. Valley Transit Company (☎ 956-686-5479 in McAllen) runs buses between the McAllen and Reynosa bus stations every 30 minutes between 6am and 10pm (US$1.75). In Reynosa, tickets can be purchased at the Noreste Senda counter in the left-hand corner of the bus station as you enter.

Coming from McAllen, if you don't want to go all the way to the Reynosa bus station, get off on the US side and walk over the bridge into Reynosa.

Car & Motorcycle East of the bridge, there's an aduana office that can issue car permits. To get there, turn left up Avenida Alemán after clearing immigration, and follow the yellow arrows. Take the first left after the Matamoros turnoff; the entrance is at the end of the street.

Going west to Monterrey (220km), the toll highway 40D is excellent and patrolled by Green Angels; the tolls total US$18. (The less direct, toll-free highway 40 follows roughly the same route.) Highways 97 and 180 south to Tampico are two-lane, surfaced

roads, but not too busy. Highway 101 branches off highway 180 to Ciudad Victoria and the scenic climb to San Luis Potosí. If you want to follow the Rio Grande upstream to Nuevo Laredo, highway 2 is not in bad shape, but it's quicker to travel on the US side. Side roads off highway 2 reach a number of obscure border crossings and the Presa Falcón (Falcon Reservoir), as well as Guerrero Viejo, a town that was submerged after the dam's construction in 1953, and moved to its current site at Nuevo Ciudad Guerrero, 33km to the southeast. It's a smooth 40-minute drive east to Matamoros via the toll highway 2D, which begins just past Reynosa airport (US$4.50).

Getting Around

Battered yellow microbuses rattle around Reynosa, providing cheap but jarring transport. From the international bridge to the bus station, catch one of the Valley Transit Company coaches coming from McAllen with 'Reynosa' on the front (US$1.75).

To get from the bus station to the town center, turn left after exiting the station and go half a block, then cross the Gigante parking lot to the bus stop on Colón. Take one of the buses labeled 'Olmo' (US$0.40).

Taxis between the bus station and the bridge should not cost more than US$5.50. Expect to pay around US$15 for a taxi ride to/from the airport.

MATAMOROS
• pop 363,800 • elev 14m ☎ 868

Matamoros is an energetic place, with many shops and restaurants targeting day-trippers from the other side of the border. Enthusiastic shop owners around Mercado Juárez try to bundle passers-by through their doors.

The city is no historical monument, but there is more evidence of the past here than in most border towns, and the town center, with its church and plaza, looks typically Mexican. South of the central area is a broad circle of newer industrial zones. Matamoros also is a commercial center for a large agricultural hinterland.

First settled during the Spanish colonization of Tamaulipas in 1686 as Los Esteros Hermosas (The Beautiful Estuaries), this city was renamed in 1793 after Padre Mariano Matamoros. In 1846, Matamoros was the first Mexican city to be taken by US

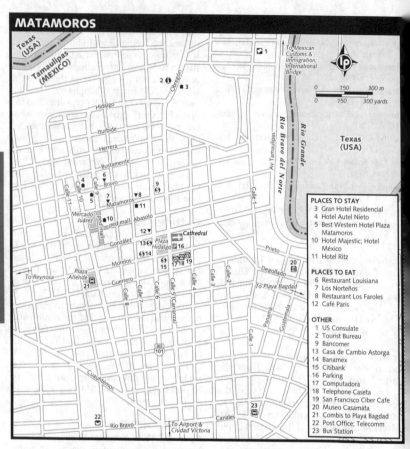

MATAMOROS

PLACES TO STAY
3 Gran Hotel Residencial
4 Hotel Autel Nieto
5 Best Western Hotel Plaza
   Matamoros
10 Hotel Majestic; Hotel
   México
11 Hotel Ritz

PLACES TO EAT
6 Restaurant Louisiana
7 Los Norteños
8 Restaurant Los Faroles
12 Café Paris

OTHER
1 US Consulate
2 Tourist Bureau
9 Bancomer
13 Casa de Cambio Astorga
14 Banamex
15 Citibank
16 Parking
17 Computadora
18 Telephone Caseta
19 San Francisco Ciber Cafe
20 Museo Casamata
21 Combis to Playa Bagdad
22 Post Office; Telecomm
23 Bus Station

forces in the Mexican-American War;
Zachary Taylor then used it as a base for his
attack on Monterrey. During the US Civil
War, when sea routes to the Confederacy
were blockaded, Matamoros transshipped
cotton out of Confederate Texas, and supplies and war material into it.

Orientation

Matamoros lies across the Rio Grande from
Brownsville, Texas. The river is spanned by a
bridge with border controls at each end. The
Rio Grande is a disappointing trickle in this
area, as most of its water has been siphoned
off upstream for irrigation.

From the southern end of the bridge,
Obregón winds around toward the town's
central grid, 1.5km to the southwest.

Information

Immigration The Mexican border post
waves most pedestrians through on the assumption that they are there just for a day's
shopping or eating, but some cars will get
the red light to be checked. If you're planning to proceed farther south into Mexico,
go to the immigration office and ask for a
tourist card and have it stamped before you
leave Matamoros.

Tourist Offices An informal 'tourist
bureau' can be found in the green and white
shack on Obregón across from the Gran
Hotel Residencial. Someone's usually there
9am to 1pm and 3pm to 7pm daily. English
is spoken but information other than directions to Mercado Juárez might be hard to

obtain. If you need maps, brochures or printed giveaways try the Brownsville Chamber of Commerce (☎ 956-542-4341, e info@brownsvillechamber.com), at 1600 E Elizabeth St, about 300m east of the bridge, open 8am to 5pm Monday to Friday.

Money Several banks on Plaza Hidalgo have ATMs; Citibank's machine dispenses dollars and pesos. Banamex on Calle 7 will change cash or traveler's checks. Often you get a better rate for cash in the exchange houses around the central area, but few change traveler's checks; Casa de Cambio Astorga, on González just west of the plaza, is an exception.

In Brownsville, there are exchange houses on International Boulevard, which is the road running straight north from the international bridge. Some are open 24 hours a day.

Post & Communications A post office and a Telecomm office with fax service are situated 1km south of the center at Calle 11 and Río Bravo. Both are open 8am to 6pm Monday to Friday, 9am to 1pm Saturday. A telephone caseta, open 7am to 10pm daily, is on Morelos between Calle 4 and Calle 5.

Computadora and San Francisco Ciber Café (open 8am to 9pm) are two Internet cafés on Morelos, near the south east corner of Plaza Hidalgo. They charge about US$2.25 an hour.

Museo Casamata
This fort dates from 1845 (cnr Guatemala & Degollado; admission free; open 8am-4pm Tues-Fri, 9am-2pm Sat & Sun). One of a series of walls and fortifications built in the 19th century to defend the city, it was the scene of fighting in the Mexican-American War. It now contains memorabilia of the Mexican Revolution, early photos of Matamoros and some ill-assorted miscellany. Explanations are in Spanish only.

Playa Bagdad
Matamoros' beach, formerly known as Playa Lauro Villar, adopted the name of Bagdad from a town at the mouth of the Rio Grande that prospered during the US Civil War, but later succumbed to floods, hurricanes and military attacks. It's 37km east of Matamoros on highway 2, with a wide stretch of clean sand and a few beach-

side seafood restaurants. Some mid-range motels are along the road approaching the beach. Blue combis (vans) to Playa Bagdad leave hourly from Calle 10 on the east side of Plaza Allende (1½ hours, US$2.20).

Special Events
From late June to early July, Expo Fiesta Matamoros features an amusement park, handicrafts displays and popular entertainers. In October the International Autumn Festival is the occasion for a variety of cultural events, from chamber music concerts to traditional dance displays.

Places to Stay
There are a couple of basic options near the center of town for less than US$20 a double. Mid-range lodging, with air-con and parking, starts at around US$40, and there's not much in between.

Hotel Majestic (☎ 813-36-80, Abasolo 131) Singles/doubles with bath US$14.50/17. This family-run place has excellent, spacious rooms with firm beds and clean, good-sized bathrooms. There's no air-con but it's the best budget option in the center of town.

Hotel México (☎ 812-08-56, Abasolo) Singles & doubles with bath US$15.50, larger rooms US$22. A few doors up from Hotel Majestic, this place is an option if Majestic is full. The basic rooms have ceiling fans and hot water in the mornings and evenings. Top-level rooms are cooler with a pretty good view of the Hotel Ritz from the balcony.

Hotel Autel Nieto (☎ 813-08-57, Calle 10 No 1508) Singles/doubles US$34/41. Autel Nieto, between Bustamante and Bravo, has large, old-fashioned rooms, with cable TV, phone and laundry services. It's an old place that doesn't look like much from the outside, but it's a very good deal at this price.

Hotel Ritz (☎ 812-11-90, e ritz1@infosel.net.mx, Matamoros 612) Singles/doubles including breakfast US$64/81. More expensive and luxurious than the Autel Nieto, the Ritz offers a gym, fax and laundry services, a sports bar and a car rental agency. The rooms are small but lovely, with Talavera-tiled furniture.

Best Western Hotel Plaza Matamoros (☎ 816-16-98, fax 816-16-96, e salcas46@hotmail.com, cnr Calle 9 & Bravo) Singles/doubles US$79/90. Pricier than the Hotel Ritz, the Hotel Plaza Matamoros has a

NORTHEAST MEXICO

handsome restaurant/atrium and fine spacious rooms with plush carpeting. Rooms on weekends are a mere US$75.

Gran Hotel Residencial (☎ *813-94-40, fax 813-27-77, Obregón 249*) Singles/doubles US$85/98. Matamoros' top hotel, 1.2km south of the international bridge, has 120 air-conditioned rooms, with terraces surrounding pleasant gardens and a few swimming pools.

Places to Eat

Café Paris (☎ *816-03-10, González 125*) Breakfast US$2.50, mains US$2.25-5.50. This large operation with many booths is usually packed in the morning. Assorted pastries are brought around on carts; coffee and hot milk are poured from separate pitchers for *café lechero*. There are breakfast specials and Mexican *antojitos* (snacks, such as tacos and enchiladas).

Restaurant Los Faroles (☎ *812-11-90, cnr Calle 7 & Matamoros*) Mains US$5.50-10. Open 7am-11pm daily. The food is very good at this cozy place with big booths and an American-style menu. Main dishes include grilled chicken, prawns and filet mignon, and there's a breakfast buffet.

Restaurant Louisiana (☎ *812-10-96, Bravo 807*) Sandwiches US$4.50, mains US$8-11. This elegant restaurant offers entrées including rib-eye steak with mushrooms (US$10), quail and shish kebab. Except for the frog's legs, however, there's no Cajun food on the menu.

Los Norteños (☎ *813-00-37, Matamoros 109*) Mains US$4.50, cabrito US$11. For authentic northern-Mexican cuisine, head for Los Norteños. A cantina-style restaurant with a bar, simple tables and attentive waiters, it offers cabrito al pastor, served with salad, tortillas and *frijoles charros* (cowboy beans).

Shopping

The 'new market,' or *Mercado Juárez*, occupies the blocks bordered by Calles 9 and 10, and Abasolo and Matamoros. A lot of the stuff is second-rate but there's plenty of variety. Prices are 20% to 30% higher than the cheapest markets farther south, but you can bargain them down a bit.

Getting There & Away

Air Matamoros has an airport 17km out of town on the road to Ciudad Victoria.

Aeromexico (☎ 812-24-60) has daily flights to/from Mexico City, while Aero California (☎ 812-22-00) flies to Mexico City and Ciudad Victoria.

Bus Both 1st- and 2nd-class buses run from the bus station on Canales, near the corner of Guatemala. The station has a 24-hour restaurant, a post office, left-luggage service and a telephone caseta (which also sells city maps).

Daily service from Matamoros includes

Ciudad Victoria – 320km, 4 hours; frequent 1st class (US$18)

Mexico City (Terminal Norte) – 975 km 15 hours 1 deluxe (US$86), 7 1st-class (US$65), 2 2nd class (US$57)

Monterrey – 324km, 5 hours; frequent 1st-class (US$22)

Reynosa – 102km, 2 hours; hourly 1st-class (US$6.75), 5 2nd-class (US$5.75)

Saltillo – 410km, 7 hours; frequent 1st-class (US$25)

Tampico – 500km, 7 hours; frequent 1st-class (US$27)

Torreón – 640km, 9 hours; 8 1st-class (US$39)

Buses go to many other destinations including Chihuahua, Durango, Guadalajara, San Luis Potosí, Tijuana, Veracruz and Zacatecas. Greyhound (☎ 816-66-15, 800-550-6210 in USA) runs daily buses to Houston and Atlanta, and El Expreso Bus Company (☎ 813-79-72) has daily departures to points throughout the southeast US.

Brownsville, Texas You can get buses from the Brownsville bus station direct to several cities inside Mexico, but they cost more than from Matamoros, and they might take up to two hours to get over the international bridge and through customs and immigration. It's quicker to walk across the bridge and take local transport to the Matamoros bus station.

The Brownsville bus station (☎ 956-546-7171) is at 1134 East Saint Charles on the corner of 12th St. Facing the USA from the north end of the international bridge, go left (west) on Elizabeth, then two blocks south on 12th. There are buses to all the major cities in Texas, and connections to other US cities.

Car & Motorcycle Driving across the bridge to/from Brownsville costs US$1.60. At the Mexican end there is a turnoff immediately before the aduana building; pull in there to obtain your temporary vehicle permit. To cancel your permit on the way out, turn left through the opening in the median before you reach the toll booth, then park in the lane beside the aduana building.

The main routes on into Mexico are highway 180 south to Tampico and highway 101 southwest to Ciudad Victoria and into the Bajío region (see South of Matamoros, below, for more information on highways 180 and 101). These unfrequented two-lane roads are both in fair condition and free of tolls. Officials at various checkpoints will want to see your tourist card and vehicle permit, and might check your vehicle for drugs or firearms. You can also go west to Monterrey via Reynosa.

Getting Around

Matamoros is served by small buses called maxi-taxis, which charge US$0.50 to anywhere in town. You can stop them on any street corner. Ruta 2 maxi-taxis pass by the bus station and go to the center of town. From the international bridge, regular taxis are on the right side of Obregón, maxi-taxis on the left beyond the taco stalls. Ruta 3 maxi-taxis go to the bus station. Alternatively, you could catch a free city tour bus in front of the García crafts shop on Obregón near the bridge. Every half hour between 9am and 6pm, the service shuttles visitors from the bridge to Mercado Juárez and back.

Taxis from the bus station to the bridge or center of town cost about US$6.

SOUTH OF MATAMOROS

For its first 183km, the 500km highway 180 to Tampico is the same road as highway 101 to Ciudad Victoria. Most of the highway runs 30 to 40km inland, crossing unspectacular lowlands where sugarcane is the chief crop, though there are some more scenic stretches where the outliers of the Sierra Madre Oriental come close to the coast. Budget and mid-range hotels are found in San Fernando (137km from Matamoros), Soto La Marina (267km) and Aldama (379km). Side roads go east to the coast, most of which consists of lagoons separated

from the gulf by narrow sand spits. The longest is the Laguna Madre, extending some 230km along the northern Tamaulipas coast. (The lagoon dried up in the mid-20th century, forcing many to leave the area. When a 1967 hurricane replenished it, the area was resettled by *veracruzanos*.) The lagoons, sand dunes and coastal wetlands support a unique ecosystem, with many bird species and excellent fishing.

About 20km south of Matamoros, just past the airport, a side road crosses marshland for 60km before reaching **El Mezquital**, a small fishing village with a lighthouse and beach on the long thin spit of land that divides the Laguna Madre from the Gulf. From San Fernando, 120km farther south, a road leads to **Carboneras**, another small fishing village facing the lagoon. There's not much here, but you might be able to get a boat out to the lagoon barrier island, where porpoises can sometimes be seen. Food and gas are available, but there are no rooms for rent in either village.

From Soto La Marina, about 130km south of San Fernando, highway 70 heads east for 50km, paralleling the Río Soto La Marina, to La Pesca (see below). Farther south, a 45km road runs east from Aldama, through the eastern fringes of the Sierra de Tamaulipas, to **Barra del Tordo**, another fishing village with a beach and good sport fishing. Facilities include budget and mid-range hotels, restaurants and a campground.

La Pesca
• pop 1226 ☎ 835

Despite resort development plans, La Pesca still has the ramshackle feel of an ordinary fishing village. There's a long, wide beach 6km east of town – Playa La Pesca – with shady *palapas* and seaside restaurants. The Río Soto La Marina and the Laguna Morales have abundant rainbow trout, kingfish, sea bass, porgy and sole. Most of the hotels can arrange boat rentals with fishing guides for around US$65 a day. A fishing tournament for sea bass takes place in November. Other activities include surfing on the beaches that face the Gulf of Mexico.

There are about half a dozen riverside *hotels* along the approach to La Pesca all featuring piers with lights for night-fishing and grills for cooking your catch. Designed for family weekends, most places charge around US$45 for a two- or three-bed room, but will reduce rates for solo travelers during the week.

In the village there are also hotels with varying standards, including the friendly **Rivera del Rio** (☎ 327-06-58), which has large, plain rooms with TV and air-con for US$33 (double this when it's busy). Fishing and self-catering facilities are also available here. There is a good **restaurant** attached serving trout and sea bass dishes (US$8).

The nondescript village also has a few **grocery stores** and several **taco stalls**.

Transportes Tamaulipecos De La Costa runs nine buses a day between Ciudad Victoria's bus terminal and Playa La Pesca (3½ hours, US$9). You also can catch one of these buses from Soto La Marina's central plaza, an hour from La Pesca (US$3).

Turtle Reserves

The Kemp's ridley, currently classified as the world's most endangered sea turtle, digs its nests on the beaches from Tampico north to La Pesca from March to July (see 'Mexico's Turtles' in the Oaxaca State chapter). Working in tandem with the US Fish and Wildlife Service, government-administered turtle protection centers along this stretch of coast have had considerable success in reversing the decline of the Kemp's ridley. The centers collect the turtles' eggs and store them in corrals, keeping them out of reach of poachers. Researchers estimate that 75 percent of the eggs collected hatch successfully. Hatchlings are then released into the Gulf from June until September.

The Tamaulipas state environmental authority has one such **center** (☎ 834-312-60-18 in Ciudad Victoria for information, 800m north of the main beach; open daily) at La Pesca, the northern limit of the turtles' nesting grounds. Visitors are educated about protection efforts and offered a first-hand glimpse of the process during the months of peak activity. They might even have a chance to help crews release the hatchlings.

CIUDAD VICTORIA
• pop 258,800 • elev 333m ☎ 834
About 40km north of the Tropic of Cancer, the capital of Tamaulipas state is a clean

and pleasant city. It's around 310km south of Matamoros and Reynosa, well served by buses in every direction, and a good spot to break a journey between central Mexico and the Texas border. A late-afternoon stroll around Plaza Hidalgo is a great way to stretch the legs and tap into the lethargy of this laid-back place. With the Sierra Madre forming an impressive backdrop to the city, there's just enough altitude to moderate the steamy heat of the coastal plains or the Rio Grande valley.

Orientation

Three highways converge at Ciudad Victoria, and a ring road allows through traffic to move between them without entering the city itself. The center is laid out in a grid pattern. The north-south streets have both numbers (Calle 7, Calle 8, etc) and names (Díaz, Tijerina, respectively, etc).

Information

The tourist office (☎ 314-11-12, e fidetam@ prodigy.net.mx) is twelve blocks north of Plaza Hidalgo at Tijerina (Calle 8) 1287. It's open 9am to 6pm daily; on weekends call ☎ 800-710-6532. Some of the friendly staff here speak English. Pick up a free copy of Victoria magazine, a city guide with maps.

The main post office is on Morelos, north east of the plaza in the Palacio Federal building. There is also a post office and a telecommunications center at the bus station (see Getting There & Away). There are plenty of Internet cafes around town charging about US$1.50 an hour for Internet access. If you need to get wired a handy outlet is Chat (☎ 315-35-55), next to Hotel Sierra Gorda on Hidalgo, open 10am to 11pm daily.

Things to See & Do

Ciudad Victoria has no compelling tourist attractions, but there is the **Museo de Antropología e Historia**, one block north of Plaza Hidalgo, run by the University of Tamaulipas (☎ 318-18-31, Matamoros; admission free; open 9.30am-7pm Mon-Fri). It's a grab bag of mammoth bones, indigenous artifacts, colonial memorabilia, revolutionary photos and one vintage carriage.

Ciudad Victoria also has some interesting public buildings, such as the **Palacio de Gobierno del Estado**, on Juárez between Calles 15 and 16, and the **Teatro Juárez**, facing the

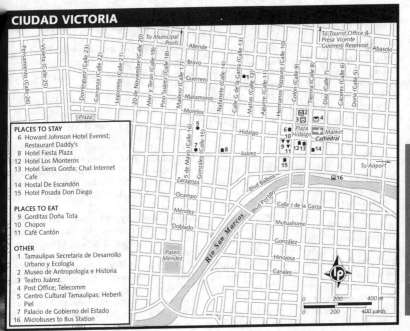

CIUDAD VICTORIA

PLACES TO STAY
6 Howard Johnson Hotel Everest;
   Restaurant Daddy's
8 Hotel Fiesta Plaza
12 Hotel Los Monteros
13 Hotel Sierra Gorda; Chat Internet
   Cafe
14 Hostal De Escandón
15 Hotel Posada Don Diego

PLACES TO EAT
9 Gorditas Doña Tota
10 Chopos
11 Café Cantón

OTHER
1 Tamaulipas Secretaría de Desarrollo
   Urbano y Ecología
2 Museo de Antropología e Historia
3 Teatro Juárez
4 Post Office; Telecomm
5 Centro Cultural Tamaulipas; Heberli
   Piel
7 Palacio de Gobierno del Estado
16 Microbuses to Bus Station

north side of the Plaza Hidalgo, both with large murals. The Paseo Méndez on the corner of Rosales and 5 de Mayo has plenty of greenery, and a couple of **public pools** (admission US$1; open 7pm-10pm daily). There is an entrance to Paseo Méndez on Calle 19 (Mier y Terán) between Berriozabal and Carrera Torres.

About 40km northeast of Ciudad Victoria, **Presa Vicente Guerrero** is a huge reservoir that attracts Mexicans and US citizens for bass fishing.

Places to Stay

Hostal De Escandón (☎ 312-90-04, Tijerina 143) Singles/doubles US$14/17.50, 3/4-person rooms US$20/23. This is the best budget deal in town, with dormitory-style lodging on three levels around an inexpensive dining hall. Rooms are very clean and secure, with color TV, phones and fans. Air-con is extra.

Hotel Los Monteros (☎ 312-03-00, Plaza Hidalgo 962) 1 or 2 person rooms without/with air-con US$22/28. A classic budget hotel, the Los Monteros is a busy place with a fine colonnaded courtyard and garden.

Rooms are simply furnished, spacious, clean and some boast fine views over the plaza.

Hotel Posada Don Diego (☎ 312-12-79, Juárez 814 Ote) Singles/doubles US$21/22. Another decent inexpensive option is the Posada Don Diego, located between Hermanos Vázquez and Colón. The small rooms come with TVs; add US$4 for air-con.

Hotel Fiesta Plaza (☎ 312-78-77, Juárez 401) Singles/doubles US$33/37. A block east of the Palacio de Gobierno, Fiesta Plaza is a welcoming place with spacious, comfortable air-conditioned rooms with phones and cable TV.

Hotel Sierra Gorda (☎ 312-20-10, Hidalgo 990) Singles/doubles US$40/45. This elegant hotel on the south side of Plaza Hidalgo has a lot of style; there's a barber shop, a tobacco shop and a bar. Rooms are spacious and have TV, air-con and phones.

Howard Johnson Hotel Everest (☎ 318-70-70, e hotelera@prodigy.net.mx, Colón 126) Rooms US$109. This tall structure on the west side of the plaza has luxurious, modern rooms (those in front have balconies with excellent plaza views). Ask about discount specials, as there are often promotions. The hotel features an indoor pool and a parking garage.

Places to Eat

Café Cantón (☎ *312-16-43, Colón 114)* Breakfast US$3, other meals US$3-5.50. This humble café has very good coffee and stick-to-your-ribs breakfasts – perhaps that's why it's packed in the morning. Try the excellent *huevos machacados*, a norteño classic. There are several members of this chain around town.

Gorditas Doña Tota *(Hidalgo)* Gorditas from US$0.50. Near the corner of Vazquez, Doña Tota serves cheap, tasty gorditas; seating and munching is at the counter.

Restaurant Daddy's (☎ *312-67-84)* Mains US$5.50-11. This restaurant, under the Howard Johnson Hotel Everest, offers a sophisticated dining ambience and a relaxed, cool interior with a clientele to match the Howard Johnson's. Dishes include tasty steaks, seafood, antojitos and pastas. The desserts are simply excellent and there are menus in English.

Chopos *(Hidalgo)* Ice creams from US$0.70. Just up from Gorditas Doña Tota, this paletería and nevería is just what the doctor ordered on a hot day. Delicious ice creams come in many different flavors.

Shopping

Ciudad Victoria is a good place to find garments made of Tamaulipas leather, distinctive for their hand-embroidered patterns.

Heberli Piel (☎ *312-19-54, Centro Cultural Tamaulipas, Pino Suárez 402 Sur)* Try this place, opposite the Palacio de Gobierno del Estado, for leather goods, particularly clothing.

For an assortment of handicrafts and local sweets have a browse through the informal *market stalls* in front of the Centro Cultural Tamaulipas building.

Getting There & Away

Air Aeropuerto Nacional General Pedro J Méndez is east of town off the Soto La Marina road. There are flights to Matamoros and Mexico City with Aero California (☎ 315-18-50) and to Mexico City with Aeromar (☎ 316-96-96).

Bus The bus station, on the east side of town near the ring road, has a left-luggage

service. There is frequent 1st-class service to the following destinations, unless indicated:

Ciudad Mante – 141 km, 2½ hrs; (US$7.75)
Matamoros – 306km, 4¼ hours; (US$18)
Mexico City (Terminal Norte) – 702km, 10 hours; 2 1st-class (US$47)
Monterrey – 285km, 3¾ hours; (US$18)
San Luis Potosí – 350km, 5½ hours; (US$18)
Tampico – 245km, 4 hours; (US$14)

Five buses a day serve La Pesca from Ciudad Victoria (3½ hours, US$9) and there are frequent services south to Gómez Farías (1½ hours, US$5.75), for those wanting to visit Reserva de la Biósfera El Cielo.

Car & Motorcycle From Ciudad Victoria, you can go southeast to Tampico for the Huasteca region or the Gulf Coast, or take one of the steep roads heading west ascending the Sierra Madre Oriental. For San Luis Potosí, take highway 101 southwest – an incredibly scenic route. For Mexico City, highway 85 south, via Ciudad Mante and Ciudad Valles, is the most direct.

Getting Around

From the bus station to the center of town, take a Ruta 25 bus, which goes down Bravo, three blocks north of Plaza Hidalgo (US$0.35). In the other direction, microbuses labeled 'Palmas' depart from Boulevard Balboa at the bridge over the Río San Marcos. Taxis charge around US$3 for the same trip, or from Plaza Hidalgo to the tourist office.

SOUTH OF CIUDAD VICTORIA
Reserva de la Biósfera El Cielo
☎ 832

A reserve of 1440 sq km, El Cielo covers a range of altitudes on the slopes of the Sierra, and is a transition zone between tropical, semi-desert and temperate ecosystems. Declared an international biosphere reserve by the UN in 1987, it marks the northern limit for a number of tropical species of plants and animals. Forty varieties of orchids can be found here, mostly within the cloud forest zone between 800 and 1400m. The reserve is also habitat to half the bird species in Mexico and 40 kinds of bats.

Though currently you don't need a permit to enter the reserve, the **Tamaulipas Secretaría** de Desarrollo Urbano y Ecología (☎ 834-315-55-80, @ direcc_nat@terra.com.mx, Garza 475; open 9am-6pm Mon-Fri) in Ciudad Victoria recommends you register with them beforehand as a safety measure. (You can also register in the village of Gómez Farías in El Cielo; look for the brown cabin in front of Restaurant La Cabaña, near the plaza.) Martín González Lázcari works in the Secretaría office in Ciudad Victoria and is very helpful. He speaks English and can tell you about conditions in the reserve as well as providing contact details for local guides. The Casa de Piedra (see Places to Stay) can also arrange guides and transport to the reserve and has a shop with food and hiking supplies.

Several trails take off from the village of Gómez Farías, which is within the reserve, 11km up a side road off highway 85, about 100km south of Ciudad Victoria and 40km north of Ciudad Mante. One strenuous trail climbs 5km to the village of Alta Cima, the starting point for hikes into the cloud forest. Guides can be hired in Gómez Farías and Alta Cima.

Places to Stay There are two lodging options in Gómez Farías. *Hotel Posada Campestre* (☎ 232-66-71, @ hotelposada campestre@correoweb.com, Hidalgo) has seven basic rooms for US$27 per person. *Casa de Piedra* (☎ 834-316-69-41 in Ciudad Victoria, @ famenco@prodigy.net.mx, Hidalgo) has four rooms with two to four beds and fan. Singles/doubles with bath and breakfast at Casa de Piedra are US$33/44 and the price might include a ride from the highway turnoff.

Canindo Research Station (☎ 232-08-88, 304-20-58, within cloud forest) Cabins US$12 per person. The basic cabins here can accommodate 36 people, call beforehand to book and get directions.

Rancho el Huasteco (☎ 312-22-01, 317-27-70) 8-10 person cabin US$111, camping US$5.50. In a lovely forest setting in El Cielo, this ranch has a single cabin (more on the way) and the owner can organize plenty of activities in the reserve such as three-hour kayaking trips (US$39), fishing (US$11 for three fish), abseiling (rappelling) and mountain biking. It's a 15-minute drive from Gómez Farías; call ahead for directions.

Getting There & Away From Ciudad Mante, buses go directly to Gómez Farías. Frequent buses also go directly from Ciudad Victoria (1½ hours US$5.75). You might be able to find someone in Gómez Farías to take you into the cloud forest by 4WD vehicle; it costs about US$165 for up to 15 passengers.

Ciudad Mante
• pop 91,200 • elev 190m ☎ 831

Ciudad Mante is a center for processing sugarcane and cotton grown in the area. It's a quiet, clean place to stop for a night, with some cheap to mid-range hotels, motels and restaurants. You can cool off at the *balnearios* (spas), La Aguja and El Nacimiento, outside of town.

Nuevo León

It was the crown's search for silver and slaves, and the church's desire to proselytize, that brought the Spanish to this sparsely inhabited region. In 1579, Luis de Carvajal was commissioned to found Nuevo León. He set up abortive settlements in Monterrey and Monclova. It was not until 1596 and 1644, respectively, however, that the Spanish established themselves at those sites, with help from native Mexicans from Tlaxcala and other areas to the south. In the late 17th century, Nuevo León and Coahuila were the starting points for Spanish expansion into Texas.

Silver was never found, but ranching slowly became viable around the small new towns, despite raids by hostile Chichimecs from the north that continued into the 18th century. Nuevo León had an estimated 1.5 million sheep by 1710.

As the 19th century progressed and the railways arrived, ranching continued to expand and industry developed, especially in Monterrey. By 1900, Nuevo León had 328,000 inhabitants.

MONTERREY
• pop 1,214,800 • elev 538m ☎ 81

Monterrey, capital of Nuevo León, is Mexico's second-biggest industrial center and third-biggest city (its metropolitan area is home to to 3½ million residents). It's perhaps the most Americanized city in

Mexico, and parts of it, with leafy suburbs, 7-Eleven convenience stores and giant air-conditioned malls, look just like suburbs in Texas or California. Industry and commerce drive Monterrey, and its pursuit of profit also seems more American than Mexican.

The city's historic center was ambitiously made over in the mid-1980s, with a series of linked plazas and gardens, a pedestrian precinct on the west side and a historical zone on the east. Jagged mountains, including the distinctive saddle-shaped Cerro de la Silla (1288m), make a dramatic backdrop for the city, and provide opportunities for some worthwhile side trips; the surrounding countryside offers caves, canyons, lakes and waterfalls.

Most travelers bypass Monterrey in their haste to get to other parts of Mexico, but the city truly is a fascinating mixture of old and new, industry and style, tradition and efficiency. There's a lot to see here, particularly if you like modern art and architecture. The city is also a good place to party with a buzzing nightlife scene in the Barrio Antiguo, the old part of town. For budget travelers, Monterrey's disadvantage is that lodging is expensive and the cheaper places are mainly in a seedy area outside the city center. The smog and the weather can be bad, too, but you are just as likely to find fresh breezes, blue skies and clear, dry desert air.

History

After several unsuccessful attempts to found a city here, in 1596 Diego de Montemayor christened his 34-person settlement Ciudad Metropolitana de Nuestra Señora de Monterrey, after the Conde de Monterrey, then the viceroy of Mexico. Monterrey struggled as an outpost, but it slowly became the core of a sheep-ranching area. Its importance grew with the colonization of Tamaulipas in the mid-18th century, since it was on the trade route to the new settlements. In 1777, when Monterrey had about 4000 inhabitants, it became the seat of the new bishopric of Linares.

In 1824, Monterrey became the capital of the state of Nuevo León in newly independent Mexico. In the Mexican-American War, Monterrey was occupied by US troops led by Zachary Taylor after three days of fierce fighting. The city was occupied again in the 1860s by French troops, who were driven out by Benito Juárez's forces in 1866.

Monterrey's proximity to the USA gave it advantages in trade and smuggling: In the US Civil War it was a staging post for cotton exports by the blockaded Confederates. Monterrey began to emerge as an industrial center in the 1860s. During the Porfiriato (the rule of Porfirio Díaz, from 1876 to 1910), the city's railway lines and industrial tax exemptions attracted Mexican, US, British and French investment. By the early 20th century Monterrey was one of Mexico's biggest cities; its population grew from 27,000 in 1853 to about 80,000 in 1910.

The city was the site of the first heavy industry in Latin America – the iron and steel works of the Compañía Fundidora de Fierro y Acero de Monterrey. Two inter-married families, the Garzas and the Sadas, came to dominate business and built a huge empire (the Monterrey Group) that owned many of the city's biggest companies. After the 1940s, scores of new industries developed but little planning went into the city's growth, and the environment was generally ignored. Education was promoted by the Garza and Sada families, however, and today Monterrey has four universities and a prestigious technological institute.

Economic success and distance from the national power center have given Monterrey's citizens, called *regiomontanos*, an independent point of view. Monterrey resents any 'meddling' in its affairs by the central government, which in turn often accuses the city of being too capitalist or, worse, too friendly with the USA. In the early 1970s the Garzas and Sadas broke the Monterrey Group into two parts: the Alfa Group and the VISA Group (now known as Femsa). The economic crisis of the 1980s struck Monterrey hard and the Alfa Group almost went broke.

Today Monterrey is profiting from NAFTA, the 1994 free-trade agreement, with more than 450 US and Canadian firms basing their regional operations in Nuevo León's capital. It remains the pillar of a state economy that produces over 9% of Mexico's manufactured goods and close to 6% of the country's exports.

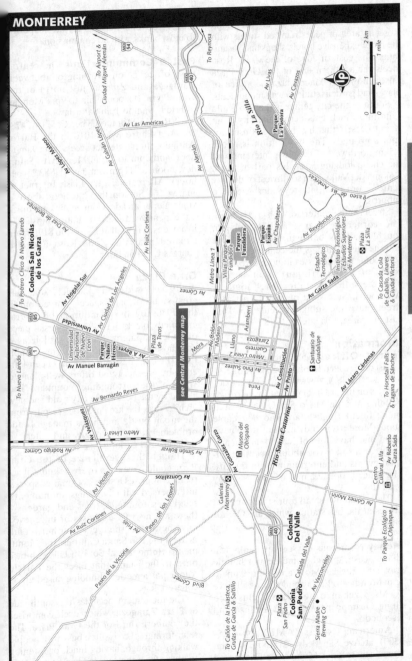

NORTHEAST MEXICO

Orientation

Central Monterrey focuses on the Zona Rosa, an area of pedestrianized streets with the more expensive hotels, shops and restaurants. The eastern edge of the Zona Rosa meets the southern end of the Gran Plaza (also known as Macroplaza), a series of plazas and gardens studded with monuments.

South of the city center is the Río Santa Catarina, which cuts across the city from west to east – the dry riverbed is used for sports grounds. The bus station is about 2.5km northwest of the city center; most of the cheap lodging is in this part of town. Colonia del Valle, 6km southwest of the city center, is one of Monterrey's most exclusive suburbs.

Streets in the center are on a grid pattern. The corner of Juárez and Aramberri, roughly halfway between the Zona Rosa and the bus station, is the center of town – zero point for addresses in both directions. North of Aramberri, north-south streets have the suffix 'Norte' or 'Nte'; south of Aramberri, 'Sur.' West of Juárez, east-west streets have the suffix 'Poniente' or 'Pte'; east of Juárez, 'Oriente' or 'Ote.'

Information

Tourist Offices Monterrey's modern tourist office called Infotur (☎ 8345-7010, 800-832-22-00 in USA, ⓦ www.monterrey-mexico .com) is on the 3rd floor of the Elizondo Paez building at 5 de Mayo 525 Ote. The staff speak fluent English, are knowledgeable about Monterrey and the state of Nuevo León and have lots of leaflets and maps. They can also tell you about upcoming cultural events and entertainment in the city. The office is open 9am to 6.30pm Monday to Friday.

There also two small tourist information offices at the bus station which are OK for basic stuff.

Money Numerous city-center banks will change cash, though some do not handle traveler's checks. Most are open 9am to 5pm Monday to Friday and almost all have ATMs. Exchange houses are clustered along Ocampo between E Carranza and Escobedo.

American Express (AMEX; ☎ 8318-3300), at Ave San Pedro 215 Nte, is open from 9am to 6pm Monday to Friday and 9am to 1pm on Saturday. They change AMEX traveler's checks at rates superior to most banks, with no commission.

Post & Communications The central post office is on Washington between Zaragoza and Zuazua, just north of the Gran Plaza. It's open 9am to 7pm Monday to Friday, 9am to 1pm Saturday.

El Rincón Morado Cyber Café (☎ 8478-0891) at Padre Mier 1010 in the Barrio Antiguo, offers Internet access from 9am to noon and 2pm to 11pm Monday to Saturday, noon to 11pm Sunday (US$2.25 per hour). Alternatively, try Flash Internet at Juárez 164 Sur on the 2nd floor above a video games arcade. Connections are quick but expensive at US$4 an hour. Ships 2000, in a pedestrian mall at Escobedo 819, is well situated near the Zona Rosa and also charges US$4 an hour.

Gran Plaza

A city block wide and a kilometer long, this great swath of open space – carved out in the 1980s by the demolition of several entire city blocks – is a controversial piece of redevelopment. Many regard it as a grandiose monument to Monterrey's ambition. The once desolate space has been softened by greenery and offers well-planned vistas of the surrounding mountains. Enclosed by the best of the city's old and new architecture, the area provides respite from the urban bustle and helps manage traffic problems with underpasses and extensive underground parking lots.

Though the overall size of the Gran Plaza could have been overwhelming, it actually comprises a series of smaller spaces, interspersed with buildings, monuments, sculptures, fountains, trees and gardens – there are no vast expanses of unrelieved pavement. At the very southern end, nearest the Río Santa Catarina, the **Monumento Homenaje al Sol** is a tall sculpture on a traffic island that faces the **Palacio Municipal**, a modern building raised up on concrete legs.

The monument occupies the south side of **Plaza Zaragoza**, which itself comprises the southern third of the Gran Plaza. The semi-formal space is often busy with people walking through, having lunch or listening to music from the covered bandstand.

Facing the southeast corner of Plaza Zaragoza is the **Museo de Arte Contemporáneo** *(MARCO;* ☎ *8342-4820, cnr Zuazua & Jardón; admission US$3.25, free Wed; open 10am-6pm Tues & Thur-Sun, 10am-8pm Wed)* with its gigantic black dove sculpture by Juan Soriano. MARCO has major exhibitions of work by Mexican and international artists. Just north of MARCO is the baroque façade of the **cathedral**, built between 1635 and 1770. The south bell tower was not completed until 1899. Facing the cathedral across the plaza is the 19th-century Palacio Municipal, which now houses the **Museo Metropolitano de Monterrey** *(*☎ *8344-1971, Zaragoza; admission free; open 8am-6pm daily).* This museum has several upstairs galleries featuring the work of contemporary painters and sculptors. North of the museum, new and old buildings flank the east end of **Calle Morelos**, a bustling pedestrian mall.

The centerpiece of Plaza Zaragoza is the stunning **Faro del Comercio** (Beacon of Commerce), a tall, flat, orange concrete slab designed by the architect Luis Barragán in the love-it-or-hate-it-but-you-can't-ignore-it style. If you're lucky you'll see green laser beams from the top sweep over the city at night.

Across Padre Mier is the **Fuente de la Vida** (Fountain of Life) with Neptune riding a chariot. North of this, the modern **Teatro de la Ciudad** and **Congreso del Estado** buildings face each other from the east and west sides of the plaza. Farther north again, the **Biblioteca Central** (State Library) and **Palacio de Justicia** (Courthouse) stand on either side of the **Parque Hundido** (Sunken Garden), a favorite spot for couples.

North again and down some steps, you come to the **Explanada de los Héroes** (Esplanade of the Heroes), also called the Plaza Cinco de Mayo, with statues of national heroes in each corner. It's the most formal and traditional of the spaces in the Gran Plaza and looks like a standard Plaza de Armas with the 1908 neoclassical **Palacio de Gobierno** on its north side. From the steps of the building you can look back down the length of the Gran Plaza to the south side of the river and toward the hills beyond. Behind the Palacio de Gobierno, a small park faces the 1930s **post office** and

federal government building, providing yet another architectural contrast.

Just east of the Explanada de los Héroes is yet another wide open space, the **Plaza 400 Años**. Graced with fountains and pools, it serves as a grand entryway to the **Museo de Historia Mexicana** *(*☎ *8345-9898, Plaza 400 Años; admission Wed-Sat US$1.25, Sun US$0.75, Tues free; open 11am-8pm Tues-Sun),* a 1994 addition to the Gran Plaza. The museum presents an exhaustive chronological survey of Mexican history, dividing its vast subject matter into four periods: Ancient Mexico, the Colonial Era, the 19th Century and Modern Mexico. There's also an area on rainforest ecology. Creatively designed and displayed, the museum appeals to kids and adults, with interactive exhibits on the Maya calendar and pre-Hispanic math, a number of touch-screen computer terminals, and excellent models of all the major pre-Conquest cities. There are superb examples of sacred art of the colonial period. All explanations are in Spanish only but English **tours** can be arranged by phoning in advance.

Bordering the Plaza 400 Años to the southeast is the Paseo Santa Lucia, a canal-side promenade with restaurants that is popular with weekend strollers.

Zona Rosa

This is the area of top hotels, restaurants and shops just west of Plaza Zaragoza. It's bounded roughly by Morelos to the north, Zaragoza to the east, Hidalgo to the south, and E Carranza to the west. Two of the streets are pedestrian-only and it's usually a bustling place where it's a pleasure to walk around, window-shop or find a place to eat or drink.

Barrio Antiguo

This is the old neighborhood, east of the Gran Plaza, and it's one of the few parts of Monterrey where you can admire traditional architecture. In recent years it has become a rather trendy area of art galleries, antique shops and cafés. Friday and Saturday nights, streets are closed to traffic and it becomes a major party zone with an excellent assortment of bars and clubs.

Alameda

Occupying eight city blocks a kilometer northwest of the city center, this lovely park

CENTRAL MONTERREY

PLACES TO STAY
6 Fastos Hotel; Fastory Restaurant
7 Hotel Posada
8 Hotel Amado Nervo
11 Hotel Mundo
12 Hotel Nuevo León
13 Days Inn Hotel Patricia
14 Hotel 5a Avenida
15 Hotel Calinda Plaza
16 Gran Hotel Yamallel
22 Hotel Fiesta Versalles
28 Fundador Hotel
38 Sheraton Ambassador; Hertz
41 Hotel Colonial
42 Hotel Ancira; Bar 1900
45 Howard Johnson Gran Plaza Monterrey
Radisson Plaza Gran

PLACES TO EAT
3 Cafetería Coliseo
10 Las 4 Milpas
17 Los Cabritos
19 Taqueria Juárez
24 Restaurante Vegetariano Superbom
32 Café El Paraiso
34 Restaurant La Puntada
35 Las Monjitas
36 Mi Tierra
44 Las Monjitas
49 Casa de Maíz; Akbal Lounge
53 El Rey de Cabrito

OTHER
1 Salón de la Fama; Cervecería Cuauhtémoc
2 Museo del Vidrio
4 Bus Station
5 Parking
9 Kumbala
18 Flash Internet
20 Infotur
21 Post Office
23 Museo de Historia Mexicana
25 Ships 2000
26 Fuente de la Vida
27 La Tumba
29 Café Iguana
30 Café La Galería
31 Fonda San Miguel
33 El Rincón Morado Cyber Café
37 Tienda Carapan
39 Excell RentaCar
40 Budget
43 Sultana Internacional
46 Museo Metropolitano de Monterrey
47 Faro del Comercio
48 Museo de Arte Contemporáneo
50 Café El Infinito
51 US Consulate
52 Monumento Homenaje al Sol

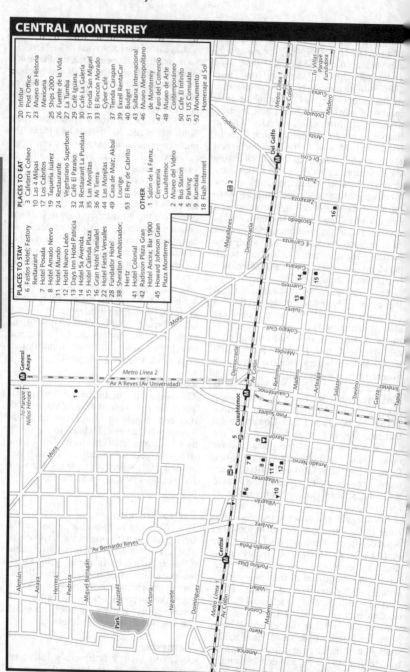

CENTRAL MONTERREY

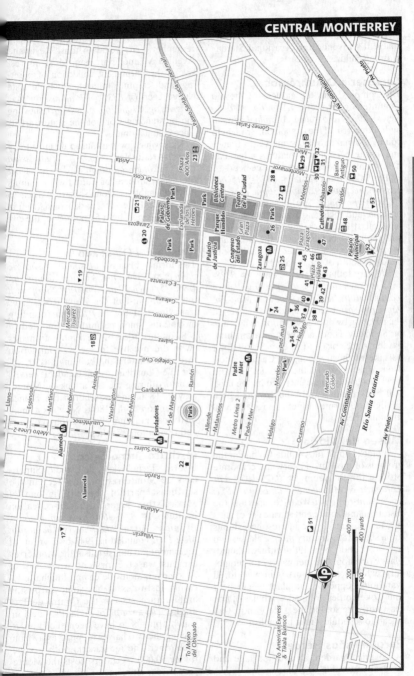

offers fountains, paths and tall shade trees in pleasant contrast to the surrounding chaos. It's a venue for occasional Sunday morning children's concerts.

Cervecería Cuauhtémoc

This complex is in the gardens of the old Cuauhtémoc brewery (*Avenida Alfonso Reyes 2202 – also called Avenida Universidad*), 1km north of the bus station. Brought to you by the maker of Bohemia, Carta Blanca and Tecate beer, it now features a baseball hall of fame, brewery tours and free beer!

The **Salón de la Fama** (☎ *8328-5815; admission free; open 9.30am-5.30pm Tues-Fri, 10.30am-6pm Sat & Sun*) has photos, memorabilia, and facts and figures on Mexican baseball. It features many Mexican players who made the big leagues in the USA, and some Americans whose careers made more headway south of the border.

Brewery tours are given hourly (☎ *8328-5355 for reservation,* e *jlarrher@ccm.femsa.com.mx; tours free; open 9am-5pm Mon-Fri, 9am-2pm Sat*). Tours in English are given in the morning by prior reservation or anytime on Saturday. There is a very pleasant little garden, a nice place to sit even if you don't partake of the free mug of Carta Blanca. There's also a café on the museum's ground level in a lovely space enclosed by the original brick factory walls and crowned by a skylight. Gourmet lunches are US$5.50 including beer.

Museo del Vidrio

Two blocks north of Avenida Colón, on the grounds of the Vitro factory and corporate offices, this museum (☎ *8329-1052, cnr Zaragoza & Magallanes; admission US$1; open 9am-6pm Fri-Wed*) focuses on the history, manufacture and artistic use of glass in Mexico. Among the interesting exhibits are a set of 18th-century *pulque* glasses and a reproduction of a 19th-century stained-glass workshop. Another gallery for temporary exhibits of glass art is in a restored warehouse opposite the plant where beer and Coke bottles are made; samples of fine glasswork are sold in the gallery shop. Call ahead to schedule a tour in English.

Parque Niños Héroes

A botanical garden, an aviary, a lake and several museums are among the recreational and cultural facilities in this large park (*admission US$1*), north of the city center between Avenida Alfonso Reyes and Avenida Manuel Barragán. Most impressive is the permanent collection of paintings and sculpture found at **Pinacoteca de Nuevo León** (☎ *8331-5462; admission free; galleries open 10am-6pm Tues-Sun*), showing the outstanding work of the state's artists since colonial times.

Kids will enjoy the **Museo de la Fauna y Ciencias Naturales** (☎ *8351-7077; admission US$0.50; open 9am-6pm daily*), featuring life-sized dioramas of stuffed wildlife in its 'natural' habitats, from Saharan Africa to the Arctic. Enter the park from Avenida Alfonso Reyes, about 5km north of the city center.

Museo del Obispado

The former bishop's *obispado (bishopric palace;* ☎ *8346-0404, Verguer; admission US$3.25; open 10am-5pm Tues-Sun*), on a hill 2.5km west of the Zona Rosa, gives fine views of the city and surrounding mountains, smog permitting. Initiated in 1787 on the orders of the bishop of Linares (who did not live to see its completion three years later), the building has an admirable Churrigueresque façade. It served as a fort during the US attack on Monterrey in 1846, and weathered the French intervention of the 1860s. Now it's a small historical museum with various colonial and revolutionary relics.

Instituto Tecnológico

Instituto Tecnológico y de Estudios Superiores de Monterrey, or the 'Tec,' in the southeast part of the city, is one of Mexico's best-regarded higher-education institutes (☎ *8328-4080 for campus tours, Avenida Garza Sada; tours 10am-4pm Mon-Fri*). Founded in 1943 by a group of regiomontano industrialists, the Monterrey campus was the first of what was to become a nationwide chain of higher education institutes. It has some surprising architecture, such as the Centro de Tecnología Avanzada para la Producción, which appears to have been sliced apart, leaving the two halves toppling away from each other. The Tec stadium, with a capacity for 30,000 spectators, hosts the Monterrey soccer club, one of the city's two top teams (see Spectator Sports). Campus tours are given, departing from the Rectoría building (the one with the mural) near the entrance. English tours can be arranged with at least three days notice.

Centro Cultural Alfa

This cultural complex (☎ 8303-0002, Roberto Garza Sada 1000; admission US$6.75; open 3pm-8.30pm Tues-Fri, 2pm-8.30pm Sat, 12pm-8.30pm Sun) off Gómez Morín in Colonia del Valle is sponsored by the Alfa industrial group. It's well worth the trip. The main building, which looks like a water tank tipping over, has floors devoted to computers, astronomy, physics, Mexican antiquities and temporary exhibitions. The scientific displays have lots of educational hands-on exhibits, and everything is well lit and carefully labeled (in Spanish only). In the center of the building is the planetarium and an Omnimax cinema.

Outside is the Jardín Prehispánico, with replicas of some of the great Mexican archaeological finds. El Universo, a superb glass mural, was created by Rufino Tamayo for the headquarters of the Alfa group, but was considered so beautiful that a special building was constructed to display it to a wider audience. It's in the Pabellón building, which resembles a covered wagon.

Special buses go every hour from the Alameda, at the intersection of Washington and Villagrán (every half hour on Sunday); the last bus departs from the planetarium at 9pm.

Parque Ecológico Chipinque

Several kilometers up the hill and south of Colonia del Valle, this park (☎ 8303-0000; admission pedestrians/cyclists US$1/1.50; open 6am-10pm daily) is the most accessible section of the Parque Nacional Cumbres de Monterrey, offering city dwellers ample opportunities for hiking, mountain biking and bird watching. Trails are well maintained, and it doesn't take long to get into some pretty dense pine and oak forest, though much of the area was destroyed in an April 1998 blaze. From the entrance, a 7km drive brings you to the Meseta de Chipinque where there's a luxury hotel and access to the park's highest peak, Copete de las Águilas (2200m). Trail maps and snacks are available at the visitor's center, near the park entrance.

Cyclists are required to display an identification badge, which can be purchased at the entrance. Parking at the visitor's center is US$2.25; to drive up to the meseta, there's a charge of US$5.50 per car.

To get to Chipinque, take Avenida Constitución west (keep right), and turn south at Avenida Morín. By public transport, take a ruta 130 bus (from Ramón and Juárez) to 'Los Tubos,' and catch a taxi from there.

Organized Tours

Troley Tours (tours US$0.50; tour times 4pm-9pm Tues-Sun) operates several pseudo trolley cars that make a loop around downtown every half hour with commentary in Spanish. You can hop on at Howard Johnson Gran Plaza Monterrey (see Places to Stay, below) or the Museo de Historia Mexicana at the Gran Plaza.

Special Events

Aniversario de Independencia – Monterrey's biggest celebrations are held on September 16, Mexico's independence day, with fireworks, free tequila and a big parade.

Expo Monterrey – The annual trade and cultural fair happens in September, in the Parque Niños Héroes.

Festival Cultural del Barrio Antiguo – In late November, this series of concerts, art expositions and literary conferences takes place in clubs and museums throughout Monterrey's old quarter.

Nuestra Señora de Guadalupe – Celebrations of the December 12 event begin as early as the last week of November. In the days leading up to the 12th, thousands of pilgrims head for the Santuario de Guadalupe, the pyramid-shaped structure south of the river. The festival is also celebrated in a big way in Abasolo, a village off the Monclova road.

Places to Stay

If you're willing to spend upward of US$50 a double, you'll find a wide range of decent hotels in Monterrey. Below that, quality is less consistent. Nearly all of the cheaper hotels, and some of the mid-range ones, are within a few blocks of the bus station, while the top-end places are in the Zona Rosa.

Budget Budget hotels in Monterrey fill up fast, especially on weekends. There is often a significant price increase for air-con. A room

NORTHEAST MEXICO

away from the noisy street is a plus. Some of the best budget accommodations can be found on Amado Nervo, in the two blocks running south of the enormous bus station.

Hotel Posada (☎ 8372-3908, *Amado Nervo 1138*) Singles/doubles US$23/27, with air-con US$27/32. The first place you come to from the bus station is this one, which has small, neat rooms with fans, TV and plenty of hot water. Several rooms on the upper floors have sweeping views, but front rooms can be terribly noisy.

Hotel Amado Nervo (☎ 8375-4632, *fax 8372-5488, Amado Nervo 1110*) Singles/doubles US$21/24. This hotel, around the corner from the Posada, has some good though small rooms with TV and other re-modeled units. Only double rooms have air-con. It's a bit ramshackle inside but is one of the best budget options in the area.

Hotel Mundo (☎ 8374-6850, *Reforma 736 Pte*) 1 or 2 person rooms without/with air-con US$28/36. Around the corner from the Amado Nervo, the Mundo is the best value around if you can stand the area. It might not be much to look at from the outside but its rooms are spacious, well maintained and quite comfortable. The only drawback is there's no hotel parking lot.

Hotel Nuevo León (☎ 8374-1900, *Amado Nervo 1007*) Singles/doubles US$18/28, with air-con & TV US$28/44. The rooms here are large enough to include lounge furniture but are in need of a facelift. The hotel features an elevator and a parking garage. It's not as nice as the Mundo but would do at a pinch.

Villas Parque Fundidora (☎ 8355-7370, *Madero 3500 Ote*) Dorm beds with breakfast US$8. Monterrey's cheapest accommodations are at this youth hostel designed for large student groups but open to individual travelers. East of the center beside the rusting smokestacks of the old foundry (closed in 1986), the squat, white building features several air-conditioned dormitory rooms, the largest of which has 36 bunk beds (and one TV). You must call ahead during office hours to reserve: 8am to 1.30pm and 3pm to 11pm Monday to Friday. To get there, take a Ruta 2 bus up Madero, and tell the driver to let you off at 'Parque Acero.'

Mid-Range Never judge books by their covers. These hotels are comfortable and reasonable.

Hotel 5a Avenida – called *quinta Avenida* – (☎ 8375-6565, *fax 8374-2639, Madero 243 Ote*) Singles/doubles US$38/39. This place has good, clean rooms on the smallish side with TV and phone – some with fine views. The rooms look a lot better than the foyer. Downstairs is Restaurant York, offering a buffet breakfast.

Days Inn Hotel Patricia (☎ 8375-0750, e *daysinnzaragoza@hotelesexpressmty.com, Madero 123 Ote*) Singles/doubles US$57/61. The Patricia is a quantum leap in comfort and price from the 5a Avenida. It has a lobby-restaurant and is modern and air-conditioned, although the rooms are characterless.

Hotel Calinda Plaza (☎ 8375-7700, e *calindaplaza@hotelesexpressmty.com, Madero 250 Ote*) Singles & doubles US$68. This place is similar in style to the Patricia – it also has a lobby-restaurant, as well as fax and laundry services. The elegant rooms have plush carpeting, polished wood, big comfortable beds and variable air-con. The parking lot entrance is on Galeana.

Gran Hotel Yamallel (☎ 8375-3500, *fax 8374-1185*, e *hyamallel@unet.com.mx, Zaragoza 912 Nte*) Singles & doubles on weekends/weekdays US$53/59. This tower-ing hotel is nine blocks east of Cuauhtémoc Metro station. Modern in style, it offers a parking garage, a restaurant, satellite TV and majestic views over the city from the upper floors. Some of the rooms are quite small so you should ask to see a few.

Fastos Hotel (☎ 8372-3250, w *www.fastoshotel.com.mx, Avenida Colón 956 Pte*) Rooms US$78. In contrast to the sur-rounding area (it's located opposite the bus station), the Fastos is a classy and comfort-able hotel. Elegant, air-conditioned rooms each feature a pair of large, firm beds.

Hotel Fiesta Versalles (☎/fax 8340-2281, e *hfv@nl1.telmex.net.mx, Ramón 360 Pte*) Single/doubles US$55/61. Nine blocks west of the Gran Plaza and just south of the Alameda, this friendly place is a good value. Its air-conditioned rooms are spacious and attractively furnished. There's a café and a travel agency downstairs, and a parking lot across the street. Weekend specials might be available.

Hotel Colonial (☎ 8380-6800, *fax 8380-6801*, w *www.hotelcolonialmty.com, Hidalgo 475 Ote*) Twins/doubles including breakfast

US$74/82. In the Zona Rosa, the Colonial is even more central than the Fiesta Versalles and is a tempting splurge as it's the cheapest option in this hotel zone. Unfortunately the rooms are not as large or fancy as you'd expect. Local telephone calls are included in the tariff. Weekend specials are available.

Fundador Hotel (☎ 8343-6464, **e** *hotel fundador@mail.sedein.com, Montemayor 802*) Singles & doubles without/with air-con US$39/45. Undoubtedly the bargain of Monterrey, this huge old-style place has a great central courtyard and is very well-located on the edge of the late-night action around Barrio Antiguo. Rooms are spotless, spacious and have TV. The entrance to the hotel is located on the corner of Montemayor and Matamoros.

Top End At all of these downtown places you can expect restaurants and bars, and carpeted rooms with air-con, heater, TV and phone. Prices listed in this section are the same for singles or doubles. Note that most places have weekend specials.

Sheraton Ambassador (☎ 8380-7000, fax 8345-1984, Hidalgo 310 Ote) Rooms US$162. Across the street from Hotel Royalty, this is the one of Monterrey's premier luxury hotels, with 239 rooms and suites.

Howard Johnson Gran Plaza Monterrey (☎ 8380-6000, 800-832-40-00, fax 8380-6090, Morelos 574 Ote) Rooms US$127. Fronting the Plaza Zaragoza, this hotel is one of the more popular top-end places. Formerly the Hotel Monterrey, it's been remodeled as a business hotel with an office center and non-smoking floors. Its 198 rooms, many with views of the Gran Plaza, have all the modern conveniences, including a direct line to Domino's Pizza and a microwave oven for heating up your order.

Radisson Plaza Gran Hotel Ancira (☎ 8150-7000, 800-830-60-00, fax 8345-1121, **w** www.hotel-ancira.com, cnr Hidalgo & Escobedo) Rooms including breakfast US$255. For atmosphere, nothing rivals the Radisson on the corner of Escobedo and Plaza Hidalgo. It's been around since 1912, and it's said that Pancho Villa once rode into the lobby, which now has shops, a piano player, a restaurant and hovering waiters. It has big rooms and plenty of old-fashioned elegance.

Places to Eat
Bus Station Area Both of these eateries are open at all times.

Fastory Restaurant (☎ 8372-3250, Avenida Colón 956) Breakfast US$3.25-5.50, mains US$5-8. This all-night restaurant in the Fastos Hotel offers Mexican food and coffee shop standards in a bland but reassuring setting with prompt service. Dishes on offer include spaghetti bolognese (no trimmings) and enchiladas. Breakfast is also available.

Cafetería Coliseo (Avenida Colón, next to bus station) Breakfast US$1.75-3.25, mains US$3-5.50. Across from the Fastory Restaurant is this more reasonably priced and personable café with fresh juices and *licuados* (fruit drinks), sandwiches and a variety of homemade *guisados* (stews).

Zona Rosa Almost every block of the Zona Rosa seems to have at least one restaurant or café.

Restaurant La Puntada (Hidalgo 123 Ote) Mains US$3. Closed Sunday. This ever-popular restaurant has a long list of Mexican items, as well as T-bone steak. Everything is done with exemplary style and attention to quality, and portions are ample.

Mi Tierra (Morelos) Mains US$3.25. West of E Carranza, Mi Tierra serves up tasty tacos and quesadillas.

Las Monjitas (☎ 8344-6713, Escobedo 903) Mains US$3.25-6.75, specials US$5.50-6.75. For good international fare in a bizarre setting, try this restaurant just above Plaza Hidalgo, where the waitresses are dressed as nuns. There's another *branch* at the corner of Morelos and Galeana.

Restaurante Vegetariano Superbom (☎ 8345-2663, upstairs at Padre Mier 300) Buffet US$6.75, meals of the day US$5. Open 8am-5pm Sun-Fri. Vegetarians will find a haven here – the buffet lunch is excellent.

Taquería Juárez (☎ 8340-1956, Galeana 123 Nte) Mains US$2.50. Open 10.30am-11pm Thur-Tues. Watch your *flautas*, tacos and enchiladas being prepared by at least 10 white-capped women behind a long window at this veritable *antojito* factory. An order of five items, combined according to your preference, is served with guacamole and salad.

Sierra Madre Brewing Co (☎ 8378-6001, Ave Vasconcelos 564 Ote, Colonia del Valle) Mains US$11-17, pizzas US$5-9, burgers

US$6-9.50. Open noon-1am daily. Serving similar food to TGI Fridays, this place about 3km southwest of the city center was brought to our attention by a reader. It has good quality food with prices to match. It is also a microbrewery and has fine quality beers on offer. Try the sampler (US$4.50), which comes with five different beers. The restaurant is in a huge brick brewery and features 'Alice in Wonderland' armchairs; after a couple of their samplers you might begin to feel like the 'Mad Hatter'!

Barrio Antiguo A stroll around the Antiguo is the best way to find a place to eat to your liking. Prices can be expensive and there might be a wait on weekend nights as the cafes and restaurants here are very popular.

Café El Paraíso (☎ *8344-6616, Morelos 958)* Mains US$3.25-5.50. Open 9am-midnight Mon-Wed, 9am-2am Thur-Sat, 4.30pm-midnight Sunday. A great spot to stop for a meal before hitting the bars and clubs in the Antiguo, this café has filling meals of nachos, salads and crepes, but

fajitas are the specialty of the house. Come here for the food and drinks not the décor. On Saturday nights beers are two for the price of one.

La Casa de Maíz (☎ *8340-4332, Abasolo 870)* Mains US$5. The Casa prepares a variety of corn-based snacks from southern Mexico, including *memelas, tlacoyos* and *molotes*. All are creatively presented and served in healthy portions. Be sure to order a pitcher of refreshing *agua de fruta*.

Entertainment

Monterrey has numerous cinemas and an active cultural life including concerts, theater and art exhibitions. The tourist office can tell you what's happening, and posters listing events are placed in strategic spots around town.

Monterrey's affluent younger set supports an active nightlife. On weekend nights, the Barrio Antiguo is very much the center of action – join the club-hopping crowds along Padre Mier east of Dr Coss. The establishments named here are but a few of the nightspots.

Norteño Cuisine

Goat dishes rule in Monterrey and throughout northeast Mexico, owing to the animal's ability to thrive in this arid desert area. Restaurants throughout northeast Mexico use their windows to display *cabrito* – whole young goats split open, flattened on racks and roasted over coals for several hours.

Every part of the animal is eaten. You can order *pierna* (leg), *pecho* (breast), *paleta* (shoulder) or *riñonada* (a section of the lower back that is considered the best – crisp on the outside, tender and juicy as spring lamb on the inside). Even the *cabeza* (head) is relished, particularly for the tongue, though some may be unnerved by the sight of a baby goat's head sitting on a plate next to a pile of salad. Other goat variations include *machitos* (goat liver wrapped in tripe), and *fritada* (a sort of goat's blood broth – thick like gravy and not for everyone).

Steak, too, is good and very reasonable in Monterrey – a big, tender T-bone can cost as little as US$6. Beef is also eaten as *fajitas*, grilled strips of marinated skirt steak served with flour tortillas and salsas and often sold by the kilo.

Vegetarians shouldn't completely lose hope in Monterrey, however, as thick corn cakes known as *gorditas* may be stuffed with a variety of meatless fillings, such as *nopales* (chopped cactus paddles), beans and white cheese.

Perhaps the premier place in Monterrey to sample cabrito is *El Rey de Cabrito* (☎ *8345-3352, Avenida Constitución 817 Ote)*, a vast dining hall at the southern edge of the Barrio Antiguo near MARCO (Museo de Arte Contemporaneo). Your cabrito (US$10) arrives at the table still sizzling on a bed of onions, with a large salad and tortillas. Similar but less expensive restaurants specializing in cabrito include *Las 4 Milpas* (☎ *8374-5454, Madero 911)*, near the bus station, and *Los Cabritos* (☎ *8342-8376, Aramberri 1010 Pte)* near the Alameda.

Café La Galería (☎ 8342-5071, Morelos 902) A popular cafe/bar, Galería has a funky tribal vibe. The young and beautiful quaff cocktails from a huge menu, with delights such as Ticket to Fly and Astronaut (US$5)…you get the picture.

La Tumba (☎ 8345-6860, Padre Mier 827 Ote) Admission US$5.50. This excellent coffeehouse has continuous live folk music and there's a quiet area for chilling where you don't have to pay the admission.

Cafe el Infinito (☎ 8340-3634, Jardón 904 Ote) Coffee US$1.50-3.25, frappes US$4. Trendy in a bohemian way, laid-back and almost sleepy, Infinito gets our vote as the coolest, friendliest spot in the Antiguo for a quiet drink. The exposed sandstone walls here are adorned with sketches of naked bodies and rows of books. Delicious fruit frappes are the specialty – try the Jamaican Limon.

Akbal Lounge (☎ 8340-4332, Abasolo 870 Ote) Upstairs from La Casa de Maíz, Akbal is a dim, cozy bar with an industrial decor setting, where the town's style-cats plant themselves on sofas, chairs and cushions. After a few drinks it isn't difficult to lose yourself to the sexy, soulful beats in the background.

Fonda San Miguel (☎ 8342-6848, Morelos 924 Ote) Admission US$5.50. Open 10pm-late Thur & Fri, 9pm-late Sat. This is a throbbing club with a big stage, a good sound system and rock by popular bands.

Café Iguana (☎ 8343-0822, Montemayor 927 Sur) Admission US$5.50. More a space than a room, the Iguana features comfortable lounging areas inside and out, modern/ ancient art and cutting-edge DJs.

Bar 1900 (☎ 8150-7000, Gran Hotel Ancira, Ocampo 443 Ote) The Zona Rosa has this elegant after-hours cabaret/bar inside the Ancira hotel. Sedate in comparison to venues in the Barrio Antiguo, it's good for a quiet drink.

Barroco (☎ 8378-1277, Tamazunchale 306) In the club district known as Centrito Valle in Colonia del Valle you'll find Barroco, where you should be elegantly dressed, bring plenty of cash for drinks and taxis, and not arrive before 10 or 11pm.

Kumbala (cnr Reforma & Rayón) Much less formal entertainment can be found at this 'ladies' bar' (for men and women) near the bus station, featuring hot norteño music

nightly. It's not the trendiest place, but Monday and Tuesday night beers are two for US$1.75.

The *Sierra Madre Brewing Co* (see Places to Eat earlier) is definitely worth checking out if fine beer is your idea of a good night out.

Spectator Sports

Plaza de Toros Lorenzo Garza (☎ 8374-0450, Alfonso Reyes 2401 Nte, Colonia del Prado) During bullfight season, March to August, *corridas* are held here at 5pm on Sunday.

The professional soccer season is from August to May. Games are played over the weekend at either the *Estadio Tecnológico* (☎ 8358-2000) at the Instituto Tecnológico de Monterrey, home of the Monterrey club (nicknamed the Pandilla Rayada, 'Striped Gang'), or the *Estadio Universitario* (☎ 8376-0524), home of the Tigres (Universidad de Nuevo León).

Estadio de Béisbol Monterrey (☎ 8351-0209, Parque Niños Héroes) Monterrey's Sultanes baseball team plays from March to August near the university. Check the newspaper *El Norte* for further details.

There are occasional *charreadas* in which *charros* (cowboys) appear in all their finery to demonstrate their skills. Contact Infotur (see Tourist Offices, earlier in this section) for the current venues.

Shopping

Interesting shops with quality handicrafts from different parts of Mexico include:

Tienda Carápan (☎ 8345-4422, Hidalgo 305 Ote) Open 9am-7pm Mon-Sat. Across the street from the Sheraton Ambassador is Tienda Carápan where, despite the extensive array of goodies, it is unfortunately difficult to browse in peace as staff constantly try to engage potential buyers in pleasant conversation.

Tikal (☎ 8335-1740, Río Missouri 316 Pte, Colonia del Valle) Open 9am-7pm Mon-Fri, 9am-6pm Sat. There are no bargains here, but some items are reasonably priced given their quality.

The two main downtown markets, *Mercado Colón* and *Mercado Juárez*, are big, bustling places selling everyday items. The wealthier regiomontanos prefer to shop at one of the big air-conditioned malls, such

NORTHEAST MEXICO

Mexico's Home of Baseball

Ever since Monterrey's first baseball team, Carta Blanca, played an exhibition match in 1939, the city has enjoyed an increasing love affair with the US imported game. Now called Los Sultanes, the team has been labeled 'the decade's champion' after winning three tournaments during the 1990s.

The people of Monterrey have embraced their team and indeed the sport as a whole; no short order considering their existing devotion to all things soccer. Monterrey now boasts 50 little league networks and the Salón de la Fama (Mexican Baseball Hall of Fame), not to mention Mexico's largest and most spectacular baseball park. This depth of support was enough to catch the attention of the US Major League, which consequently opened its 1999 season at Monterrey's Estadio de Béisbol. Tickets to the event – which featured an emotional tribute to famous Mexican baseball stars and chili peanuts rather than the typical US staple of hotdogs – sold out in 3 hours.

If you are in the city during the season, which runs from March to August, taking in a game will not only reward sports fans, but also anyone who is interested in experiencing a slice of Monterrey community and culture.

— Justine Vaisutis

as *Plaza la Silla* (☎ 8369-1777, *Avenida Garza Sada*), south of the city center; *Plaza San Pedro* (*Humberto Lobo 520*), southwest in the suburb of San Pedro; or *Galerías Monterrey* (☎ 8348-4989, *Avenida Insurgentes 2500*), west of town.

Getting There & Away

Air There are direct flights, usually at least daily, to all major cities in Mexico and connections to just about anywhere else. Connections to most international destinations are best made through Houston. Airlines serving Monterrey are listed below, along with their nonstop destinations.

Aero California (☎ 8345-9700), Ocampo 145 Ote – Los Angeles, Guadalajara, Hermosillo, Mexico City

Aeromexico (☎ 8343-5560), Cuauhtémoc 818 Sur – Guadalajara, Houston, Mazatlán, Mexico City, Monclova, Puebla, Puerto Vallarta, Querétaro, San Antonio, Tijuana, Torreón and others

Aviacsa (☎ 8153-4300), Humberto Lobo 660, Colonia Del Valle – Cancún, Guadalajara, Houston, Las Vegas, Mexico City, Tijuana

Mexicana (☎ 8340-5311), Hidalgo 922 Pte – Cancún, Guadalajara, Mérida, Mexico City, Puebla, Tijuana, Veracruz, Villahermosa and others

Bus Monterrey's huge bus station (Central de Autobuses) occupies three blocks along Avenida Colón, between Villagrán and Rayón. It's a small city unto itself, with restaurants, pay phones, an exchange house, a 24-hour left-luggage service (US$0.40 an hour) and ticket desks strung out along its whole length. The platform for local bus lines is accessed via a tunnel from Gate 5. First-class lines include Sendor (☎ 8375-0014), Ómnibus de México (☎ 8375-7063), and Futura (☎ 8318-3737); deluxe service is provided by Turistar (☎ 8318-3737). Autobuses Americanos (☎ 8375-0358) is the line for Texas destinations. Daily service from Monterrey includes:

Aguascalientes – 588km, 8 hours; 1 deluxe (US$46), frequent 1st-class (US$35)

Chihuahua – 783km, 12 hours; 2 deluxe (US$62), frequent 1st-class (US$50)

Ciudad Victoria – 285km, 4 hours; hourly 1st-class (US$18), frequent 2nd-class (US$16)

Durango – 573km, 9 hours; 4 deluxe (US$52), 9 1st-class (US$39)

Guadalajara – 778km, 12 hours; 3 deluxe (US$67), 7 1st-class (US$50)

Matamoros – 324km, 4½ hours; frequent 1st-class (US$22)

Mexico City (Terminal Norte) – 934km, 11 hours; 8 deluxe (US$79), 9 1st-class (US$59)

Nuevo Laredo – 224km, 2½ hours; 4 deluxe (US$25), frequent 1st-class (US$17) and 2nd-class (US$13)

Reynosa – 220km, 3 hours; frequent 1st-class (US$15.50), 2 2nd-class (US$13)

Saltillo – 85km, 1¾ hours; 1 deluxe (US$6.75), frequent 1st- and 2nd-class (US$5)

San Luis Potosí – 517km, 7 hours; 3 deluxe (US$43), frequent 1st-class (US$31) and 2nd-class (US$24)

Tampico – 530km, 7¼ hours; 2 deluxe (US$48), frequent 1st-class (US$33)

Torreón – 316km, 4 hours; 5 deluxe (US$30), frequent 1st-class (US$23)

Zacatecas – 458km, 6 hours; frequent 1st-class (US$27), 7 2nd-class (US$22)

First-class buses also serve Acapulco, Ciudad Juárez, Mazatlán, Puebla and Querétaro, and there are six trips a day to the remote border towns of Piedras Negras (US$33) and Ciudad Acuña (US$36). Buses also serve US destinations including Laredo, San Antonio, Dallas and Houston.

Car There is enough to see within a day's drive of Monterrey that renting a car is worth considering. (See the Around Monterrey section later in this chapter.) Big companies such as Avis (☎ 8190-6673), Hertz (☎ 8369-0822) and Budget (☎ 8369-0819) have branches at the airport and in town as well. You might get a cheaper deal at one of the smaller local outfits: Alal (☎ 8340-7611) at Hidalgo 426 Ote; Excell RentaCar (☎ 8340-8684) at Hidalgo 400 Sur; or Sultana Internacional (☎ 8344-6363) at Escobedo 1011 Sur. Be careful when using a credit card at one of the smaller companies. Check that the correct amount has been debited, and only sign for the agreed rate. You are better off using cash.

Getting Around

To/From the Airport Monterrey airport is off highway 54 to Ciudad Alemán, about 15km northeast of the city center. A taxi costs around US$14 from one of the downtown hotels, or via radio taxi service (☎ 8372-4370, 8372-4371). From the airport you can purchase a ticket for an authorized taxi at a booth in the arrivals area.

Metro Monterrey's Metro is a sensible alternative for getting around town. Its very simple plan consists of two lines: the elevated Línea 1 runs east to west in the north of the city, primarily going to outlying residential areas; and the underground Línea 2 runs north to south from near the Cuauhtémoc brewery (General Anaya station), past the bus station (Cuauhtémoc), and down to the Zona Rosa (Padre Mier) and the Gran Plaza (Zaragoza). The Metro's two lines cross at the intersection of Avenida Colón and Cuauhtémoc, where the giant overhead Cuauhtémoc Metro station is located.

The fare is US$0.50/0.90 for a one-way/return journey anywhere on the network; tickets are dispensed from machines at the station entrances and can be purchased for multiple trips. The Metro runs from 5am to midnight daily. There are ATMs at many station entrances.

Bus Frequent buses (US$0.35) go almost everywhere in Monterrey, but often by circuitous routes. The following routes might be useful:

Bus station to center – No 18, from the corner of Amado Nervo and Reforma, goes down Juárez to the edge of the Zona Rosa – get off at Padre Mier, Hidalgo or Ocampo.

Center to bus station – No 1 (blue) can be picked up on Juárez at Padre Mier. It takes you to Avenida Colón, within two blocks of the bus station.

Center to Museo del Obispado – No 4 (red & black) goes west along Padre Mier. For the Obispado, get off when the bus turns left at Degollado, walk up the hill and turn left, then take the first right (a 10-minute walk).

Center to Del Valle/San Pedro – Ruta 131 (orange) from the corner of Juárez and Hidalgo goes to the big traffic circle in Colonia Del Valle, then heads west along Avenida Vasconcelos.

Center to Instituto Tecnológico – Take No 1 ('San Nicolás-Tecnológico') from the corner of Hidalgo and Pino Suárez.

Car There are large parking lots underneath the Gran Plaza, charging only US$2 for the whole night. Another lot, just east of the bus station off Avenida Colón, is US$7 for 24 hours.

AROUND MONTERREY

A number of sights near Monterrey are easily accessible in your own vehicle, and somewhat less accessible by bus.

Grutas de García

An illuminated, 2.5km route leads through 16 chambers in this **cave system** (☎ 81-8347-1533, admission US$5.50 – including funicular ride; open 9am-5pm daily) high in the

NORTHEAST MEXICO

Sierra El Fraile. The caves, reached by a 700m funicular railway, are 50 million years old, with lots of stalactites and stalagmites, as well as petrified seashells. A parish priest found the caves in 1843.

This is a popular weekend outing. On Saturday and Sunday mornings, Transportes Villa de García runs buses directly to the caves from local platforms 17-19 in the Monterrey bus station, returning in the afternoon. On other days the same line runs frequent buses to Villa de García, 9km from the caves (US$0.60); taxis go the rest of the way. Driving from Monterrey, take highway 40 toward Saltillo. After 22km a sign points the way to the caves; turn right and go another 18km to the base of the funicular.

Cañón de la Huasteca

About 16km west of Monterrey's city center, this canyon (☎ 81-8331-6785, admission US$0.50 per person, US$1 per vehicle; open 9am-6pm daily) is 300m deep and has some dramatic rock formations, as well as cliffside drawings (evidence of its prehistoric inhabitants). There is a town at one end of it and a playground in the middle, somewhat reducing its attraction as a wilderness area. Reach the mouth of the canyon by taking a Ruta 206 bus, labeled 'Aurora,' from the corner of Ramón and Cuauhtémoc in Monterrey. If driving, take Avenida Constitucion west out of the city center.

Cascada Cola de Caballo

Horsetail Falls (admission US$2.75; open 9am-7pm daily) is 6km up a rough road from El Cercado, a village 35km south of Monterrey on highway 85. The site has its share of hawkers and food stalls, but it's quite pretty and attracts a lot of picnickers. Horses and donkeys can be hired for the last kilometer to the falls (US$4.50). Farther up the valley, vegetation flourishes on the slopes of the sierra. Autobuses Amarillos runs frequent buses to El Cercado from the Monterrey bus station (US$2); you'll have to catch a local bus from there to the falls.

If you have your own vehicle, you can drive 33km up a rough road from El Cercado to the **Laguna de Sánchez**, a mountain lake surrounded by pine forests.

SOUTH OF MONTERREY

The excellent highway 40 (the main route toward Mexico City) goes southwest from Monterrey to Saltillo (85km), alongside the towering cliffs of the Sierra San José de los Nuncios.

Going southeast on highway 85 toward Ciudad Victoria, you follow the edge of the Sierra Madre Oriental through Mexico's most important citrus-growing area, centered on the towns of Allende, Montemorelos and Linares.

South of Montemorelos, the **Bioparque Estrella** (☎ 8190-3100, admission US$7.75; open 9am-7pm Fri-Sun; Tues-Sun July & Aug) has a variety of large animals from

Scaling the Potrero Chico

Interested in rock climbing? Potrero Chico is arguably among the 10 best places in the world for learning the sport and it's only 1½ hours north of Monterrey, near the town of Hidalgo. Climbs range from 30m to 300m, with a range of features that will challenge both beginners and experienced climbers. Expert tuition is available on site for all levels.

The limestone crags of the canyon currently support about 600 different routes (some requiring an overnight stay) with more being added all the time. Although routes have been established in the Potrero for over 30 years, it owes its current status to a group of American climbers who have been developing the area for the last 13 years, opening many of the new routes and setting up accommodation and a Web site.

Near the canyon is *Rancho Cerro Gordo*, where you can camp for US$5 a night. There are also two casitas, which have modern facilities and are very comfortable. They are priced at US$40 (sleeps up to four people) and US$60 (sleeps up to eight people).

From Monterrey a taxi will cost about US$40, or you can catch a bus to Hidalgo. For more information about climbing the Potrero Chico see the excellent Web site **w** www.potrerochico.com.

Africa, Asia and the Americas, easily observed from the park's palapa-mobiles. To get there, take the turnoff for Rayones to the park entrance; turn left just past the 9km sign.

Sierra Madre Oriental

From Linares, scenic highway 58 heads west up into the Sierra Madre Oriental to the town of Iturbide (64km). Cut into the cliff beside the road is Los Altares, a giant bas-relief by Nuevo León sculptor Federico Cantú; it's dedicated to road builders. Beyond Iturbide, an 8km northward detour climbs another 1000m to **Galeana**, high on a wheat-producing plateau. The birthplace of the 1860s Republican general Mariano Escobedo, Galeana has a few hotels. It also has one of the few *cenotes* (pools in collapsed caverns) outside of Yucatán, the Pozo del Gavilán. Nine kilometers north (turn right at the Río San Lucas junction) is a 15m-high natural bridge, the **Puente de Dios**, over which a local road passes. The best view is from the flat area to the left just before the bridge. The 3700m **Cerro El Potosí**, one of the state's highest peaks, is 35km west of Galeana. It's superb up on the sierra, with clear air, sparkling streams and unspoiled landscapes.

Highway 58 continues west down to the Altiplano Central, where it meets highway 57 between Saltillo and Matehuala.

Coahuila

The state of Coahuila is large, mostly desert and sparsely populated. The border crossings into Coahuila from Texas are less frequently used than those farther southeast in Tamaulipas, because the road connections into Mexico and the USA are not as convenient for most travelers. Yet the remoteness and the harsh, arid landscape will appeal to some, and the state capital, Saltillo, is definitely worth a visit. For information about the west of the state, including the city of Torreón and the Zona del Silencio, see the Central North Mexico chapter.

History

The Spanish came to Coahuila in search of silver, slaves and souls. The region was explored by the Spanish as early as 1535 and the state capital, Saltillo, was founded 42 years after, but incessant attacks by indigenous Chichimecs and, later, Apaches discouraged widespread settlement until the early 19th century. In 1800, Coahuila still had fewer than 7000 people. A few big landowners came to dominate the area. In southeast Coahuila, one holding of 890 sq km was bought from the crown for US$33 in 1731, and grew to 58,700 sq km by 1771, becoming the Marquesado de Aguayo, protected by a private cavalry.

After 1821, in the early years of independence, Coahuila and Texas were one state of the new Mexican republic, but Texas was lost after the Mexican-American War. As the 19th century progressed, ranching grew in importance, helped by the arrival of railways. By 1900, Coahuila had 297,000 inhabitants. In the 20th century, a steel foundry was established in Monclova, giving Coahuila a major industrial center.

BORDER CROSSINGS
Ciudad Acuña
• pop 79,200 • elev 1250m ☎ 877

Ciudad Acuña, across from the US town of Del Rio, is a fairly busy border crossing, open 24 hours a day. About 20km upriver, the **Presa de la Amistad** (Friendship Reservoir) is a joint Mexican-US water management project, offering good fishing and boating facilities. In October, the Fiesta de la Amistad is celebrated by both towns in a cross-border display of friendship. From Ciudad Acuña to Saltillo it's an eight-hour bus ride (US$29) on good two-lane roads.

Piedras Negras
• pop 122,900 • elev 1450m ☎ 878

The border crossing between Piedras Negras and the US town of Eagle Pass is a major commercial route. Piedras Negras attracts quite a few short-term visitors from Texas. There's a crafts shop in the old San Bernardino mission that features work from all over Mexico, and the *casa de cultura* has occasional displays of Mexican art, music and dance.

Legend has it that Piedras Negras is the birthplace of the nacho – said to have been invented by Don Ignacio (Nacho) Anaya, a bar owner, to satisfy the snacking needs of his patrons from both sides of the border – and the town holds its International Nacho Festival in early October.

Highway 57 goes southeast to Allende, Sabinas and Monclova and continues to Saltillo, about seven hours away by bus (US$26).

MONCLOVA
• pop 202,800 • elev 1200m ☎ 866

Not an attractive city, Monclova nevertheless offers a convenient stopover for those on their way to the Cuatrociénegas protected area. The city's Altos Hornos iron and steel works (AHMSA), founded in 1942, is one of the largest in Mexico.

The Monclova tourist office (☎ 634-42-22, e promotorac@prodigy.net.mx), in the Canaco building on Boulevard Harold Pape, is open 9am to 12pm and 4pm to 7pm Monday to Friday and 9am to 1pm on Saturday. Its helpful, English-speaking staff can give you excellent maps of Monclova and Coahuila's main destinations.

Monclova has a few fine 18th-century buildings, notably the **Parroquia de Santiago** on the Plaza Principal. The **Museo Harold R Pape** (☎ 631-16-56, Boulevard Harold Pape; admission free; open 8am-8pm Tues-Sun) is an incongruous cylindrical structure functioning primarily as a monument to the American industrialist who built up AHMSA. It also houses a small collection of pre-Hispanic objects, exhibits on the steel industry and works of modern art.

There are several decent, inexpensive **hotels** on Privada Cuauhtémoc, beside the bus station. If you prefer your creature comforts you could try **Hotel Flores Hill** (☎ 632-10-10, Miguel Blanco 107), which has comfortable singles/doubles for US$44/51; less if you don't require a receipt. **Hotel Las Misiones** (☎ 634-36-36, Boulevard Suárez 2105) is a step up the luxury scale with well-appointed singles/doubles for US$72/83. Ask about weekend specials.

The main bus terminal is on Carranza, two blocks west of the plaza, with 1st- and 2nd-class service to/from Ciudad Acuña, Piedras Negras, Saltillo, Monterrey, Torreón and Mexico City. Second-class buses to Cuatrociénegas depart every two hours (1½ hours, US$4).

Highway 57 runs south to Saltillo, about 190km away, three hours by bus. About 25km south of Monclova, highway 53 branches southeast to Monterrey (there are no fuel stations on this highway). Highway 30 heads west for 82km to Cuatrociénegas, then southwest to Torreón.

CUATROCIÉNEGAS
• pop 9190 • elev 750m ☎ 869

In this valley in the middle of the Desierto Chihuahuense (Chihuahuan Desert), a network of underground springs forms rivers and numerous crystalline pools, creating the conditions for a desert habitat of extraordinary biological diversity. The Galapagos-like isolation of the area also contributes to the existence of dozens of endemic species, including several kinds of turtles and eight kinds of fish. Because of the fragility of the ecosystem, in 1994 federal authorities created the **Área de Protección de Flora y Fauna Cuatrociénegas**, an 843 sq km protected area, but some of the pools have been set aside as recreational spots, ideal for swimming and snorkeling. Within the clear blue waters of these desert aquariums, you can observe a wide variety of small fish, as well as organisms called *estromatolitos*, formed by calcified algae colonies, which biologists believe are akin to the planet's first oxygen-producing forms of life.

Equally impressive is the area called Las Arenales, where glistening white sand dunes, formed by the crystallization of gypsum in the nearby Laguna Churince, create an eerily beautiful effect against a backdrop of six mountain ranges ringing the valley. The nearby town of Cuatrociénegas has several points of historical interest as well as a few hotels and restaurants, making it a good base for exploration of the reserve.

Visiting the Reserve
Access to the reserve is south of town along highway 30. Though it's possible to explore on your own, the desert tracks are minimally labeled. Authorized guides will escort you through the reserve (US$22), but you'll need your own vehicle. A good alternative is to arrange a **tour** through the Cuatrociénegas tourist office (☎ 696-05-74, e pturismo@yahoo.com, Zaragoza 101; day tour US$50, up to 15 people).

A **visitor's center** (Poza Las Tortugas; open 9am-5pm Tues-Sun) 7km south of town has maps and illustrated explanations, in Spanish, of the relevant natural phenomena. In the reserve area there are over 170 cerulean pools, or *pozas*, some up to 13m deep. **Poza La**

Becerra (☎ *696-05-74 for information; admission adult/child US$4/2)*, about 16km from the visitor's center, is set up as a recreational facility with a diving pier, bathrooms and showers. Swimming amid the desert landscape is a marvelous experience. Though the water temperature can get as high as 32°C (90°F) in summer, cooler water spouts up from spring sources. Wearing suntan lotion is prohibited when swimming in the pozas. You can get a bus here from town.

You can also swim at the peaceful **Río Los Mezquites**, cooler than the pozas, with some shady palapas and picnic areas along the banks. Access to the river is 6.5km south of town: Turn left at the blue swimmer sign and go another 1.5km on an unpaved track.

The entrance to Las Arenales is left of the Poza La Becerra; it's about a 4.5km drive out. Reaching heights of 13m, the white dunes are spotted with low desert brush, and you'll come across evidence of coyotes, rabbits, roadrunners and scorpions. Summer temperatures can be extreme, so bring plenty of water and avoid midday excursions.

The scorpion is one ornery bugger.

Places to Stay & Eat
You may set up a tent within the protected area at **Río Los Mezquites** or **Poza La Becerra**. There are two decent hotels in the town of Cuatrociénegas.

Motel Santa Fe (☎ *696-04-25, Boulevard Juárez)* Singles/doubles US$28/36. Along the approach from Monclova, about 4km out of town, this motel is a good deal for large, comfortable rooms if you don't mind the racket made by the air-con unit.

Hotel Plaza (☎ *696-00-66, Hidalgo 202)* Singles/doubles US$37/47. A central hotel, just east of the plaza, this place has beautiful colonial-style rooms.

El Doc (*Zaragoza 103)* Mains US$3-8. For breakfast, lunch and dinner stop in here,

on the east side of the plaza – it's about the only game in town.

Getting There & Away
The bus terminal occupies the south side of the plaza. There's frequent 2nd-class service to/from both Monclova (one hour, US$4) and Torreón (3½ hours, US$12). Several buses a day journey to each of the nearest border crossings at Ciudad Acuña and Piedras Negras.

SALTILLO
• pop 547,900 • elev 1599m ☎ 844

Set high in the arid Sierra Madre Oriental, Saltillo was founded in 1577, making it the oldest city in the northeast. It has a quiet central area with a small-town feel, making it a popular destination, though there are extensive new suburbs and major industries on the city's outskirts. The city, with its lovely colonial buildings, temperate climate, great restaurants and dignified hotels, embodies what most travelers are seeking from a small town – a relaxing place to observe and experience northern Mexican life. It's on the main routes between the northeast border and central Mexico, making it an ideal spot to break a journey.

In the late 17th century, Saltillo was capital of an area that included Coahuila, Nuevo León, Tamaulipas, Texas and 'all the land to the north which reaches toward the pole.'

History
The first mission was established here in 1591 as a center for the education and religious conversion of the local indigenous populations. Native Tlaxcalans were brought to help the Spanish stabilize the area, and they set up a colony beside the Spanish one at Saltillo. The Tlaxcalans' skill on the treadle-loom and the abundance of wool in the area led to the development of a unique type of sarape, for which Saltillo became famous in the 18th and 19th centuries.

Capital of the state of Coahuila (and Texas after Mexican independence), the city was occupied by US troops under Zachary Taylor during the Mexican-American War in 1846. At Buenavista, south of Saltillo, the 20,000-strong army of General Santa Anna was repulsed by Taylor's force, a quarter the size, in the decisive battle for control of the northeast during that war.

NORTHEAST MEXICO

NORTHEAST MEXICO

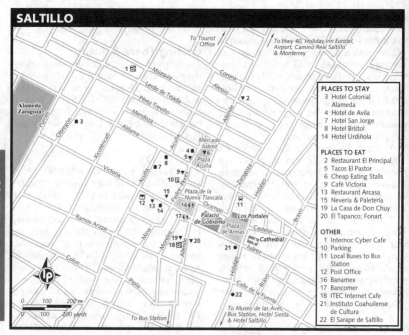

SALTILLO

PLACES TO STAY
3 Hotel Colonial
   Alameda
4 Hotel de Avila
7 Hotel San Jorge
8 Hotel Bristol
14 Hotel Urdiñola

PLACES TO EAT
2 Restaurant El Principal
5 Tacos El Pastor
6 Cheap Eating Stalls
9 Café Victoria
13 Restaurant Arcasa
15 Nevería & Paletería
19 La Casa de Don Chuy
20 El Tapanco; Fonart

OTHER
1 Internoc Cyber Cafe
10 Parking
11 Local Buses to Bus
   Station
12 Post Office
16 Banamex
17 Bancomer
18 ITEC Internet Cafe
21 Instituto Coahuilense
   de Cultura
22 El Sarape de Saltillo

President Benito Juárez came to Saltillo during his flight from the invading French forces in 1864, and the city was occupied again by foreign troops before being freed in 1866. During the Porfiriato, agriculture and ranching prospered in the area, and the coming of the railway helped trade and the first industries in the city, but Monterrey was by this time quickly overtaking Saltillo in size and importance.

These days Saltillo is still a center for a large livestock and agricultural area, and in recent decades it has expanded to include automobile and petrochemical plants.

Orientation

Saltillo spreads over a large area, but most places of interest are located in the blocks around the two central plazas. Periférico Echeverría, a ring road, enables traffic to bypass the inner-city area.

The junction of Hidalgo and Juárez, at the southeast corner of the plaza, serves as a dividing point for Saltillo's street addresses, with those located to the south suffixed 'Sur,' those to the east 'Ote' (Oriente), and so on.

The bus station is on the south side of town, on Periférico Echeverría Sur – a 10-minute bus ride from the center.

Information

In the old train station on the corner of Boulevard Coss and Acuña, about 1.5km north of downtown, the state tourist office (☎ 412-51-22, e protursa@prodigy.net.mx) has a friendly English-speaking staff and abundant handouts including multiple-map guides to every region in the state. It's open 9am to 7pm Monday to Friday, 9am to 12pm Saturday and 10am to 6pm Sunday.

You can change cash and traveler's checks at the banks near the Plaza de Armas (all have ATMs). There are casas de cambio on Victoria, open until 6pm Monday to Friday, until 1pm on Saturday.

The post office is centrally located at Victoria 223 Pte, a few doors from the Hotel Urdiñola. It's open 9am to 3pm Monday to Friday, 9am to 1pm Saturday.

There are a couple of Internet cafes around town: Internoc Cyber Cafe on Múzquiz, near the corner of Xicoténcatl, charges US$1.75 per hour and is open from

8am to 12pm Monday to Saturday and 12pm to 10pm Sunday. ITEC Internet Cafe at Allende 238 is shabby but does the job at US$2.25 an hour.

Catedral de Santiago

Built between 1745 and 1800, Saltillo's cathedral dominates the plaza and has one of Mexico's finest Churrigueresque façades, with columns of elaborately carved pale gray stone. It's particularly splendid when lit up at night. Inside, the transepts are full of gilt ornamentation – look for the human figure perched on a ledge at the top of the dome.

Palacio de Gobierno

Facing the plaza are the state government headquarters. You are free to wander into this elegant 19th-century building. A mural in its second-floor passageway traces Coahuila's history and depicts its historical figures, most prominently Venustiano Carranza, who, as governor of the state during the Revolution, launched a revolt against the provisional president Victoriano Huerta.

Plaza de la Nueva Tlaxcala

Behind the Palacio is this plaza, built in 1991 to commemorate the fourth centennial of Saltillo's foundation. A sculpted scene on its southern end alludes to the colonization of Coahuila. Allende, the plaza's east side, once divided the two sections of the old town – to the east was the section occupied by the Spaniards, to the west the area where the Tlaxcalans lived.

Instituto Coahuilense de Cultura

This gallery (☎ 410-20-33, cnr Juárez & Hidalgo; admission free; open 9am-6pm Tues-Sun), on the south side of the plaza, exhibits paintings, sculpture and crafts by artists from Coahuila and elsewhere.

Alameda Zaragoza

Full of shady trees and pathways, this park has a playground and is a favorite spot for young couples. A pond at the southern end has an island shaped like Mexico. It is reached by going west down Victoria from behind the Palacio de Gobierno.

Museo de las Aves

A few blocks south of the plaza you'll find this museum (☎ 414-01-67, cnr Hidalgo & Bolívar; admission US$1, free Sat; open 10am-6pm Tues-Sat, 11am-6pm Sun) devoted to the birds of Mexico. It's definitely worth a visit. Mexico ranks sixth in the world in avian diversity. Most of the exhibits are birds stuffed and mounted in convincing dioramas of their natural habitat. There are special sections on nesting, territoriality, birdsongs, navigation and endangered species. Over 670 bird species are displayed, along with bird skeletons, fossils and eggs.

Special Events

The Aniversario de Saltillo commemorates the city's foundation and is celebrated with a nine-day cultural festival in late July, followed by the annual fair.

For the Día del Santo Cristo de la Capilla celebration, in the week leading up to August 6, dance groups from around Coahuila perform on the esplanade in front of the cathedral, in honor of Saltillo's patron saint. The date commemorates the arrival of a statue of the crucified Christ brought over from Spain in 1608 and now housed in the Capilla del Santo Cristo within the cathedral.

Places to Stay

Budget *Hotel De Avila* (☎ 412-59-16, Padre Flores 211) Singles/doubles US$14/18. This hotel is in a good location at the northwest corner of Plaza Acuña (another sign calls it Hotel Jardín). Rooms are basic (with TV) and the price is right.

Hotel Bristol (☎ 410-43-37, Aldama 405 Pte) Singles/doubles US$15/19. A good budget deal and somewhat better than the De Avila is the Bristol, entered through a clothing store between Acuña and Padre Flores. Rooms are a little shabby but clean, and there's a pleasant sunlit courtyard with sofas.

Hotel Siesta (☎ 417-07-24, Echeverría) Singles & doubles US$24, larger rooms US$33. Another decent budget option, this place is across the road from the bus station. Airy, upstairs rooms have good light and come with fan and TV.

Mid-Range *Hotel Saltillo* (☎ 417-22-00, Echeverría 249) Singles & doubles US$33. Beside the Siesta stands the Saltillo, beckoning visitors with its neon lights. It's a friendly place featuring modern, clean rooms with color TV, phone and ceiling fan. The hotel's 24-hour restaurant specializes in seafood.

Hotel Urdiñola (☎ 414-09-40, Victoria 251 Pte) Singles/doubles US$35/38. A place that offers heaps of character and great value is the excellent Urdiñola. There's a sparkling white lobby with a wide stairway sweeping up to a stained-glass window. Large, airy rooms face a long courtyard with pleasant gardens. The hotel also has a decent inexpensive restaurant, helpful staff and parking just up the street.

Hotel Colonial Alameda (☎ 410-00-88, Obregón 222) Rooms US$69. This hotel is an excellent choice. The Spanish colonial-style building features 21 large, elegant, rooms each containing a pair of huge beds.

Hotel San Jorge (☎ 412-22-22, Acuña 240 Nte) Singles/doubles US$65/69. Not as impressive as the Colonial Alameda, but still good, is this modern well-maintained establishment with a restaurant, a small rooftop swimming pool and comfortable rooms (some with terrific views).

Top End There are several four- and five-star hotels, aimed at business-class travelers, along the highways heading north and east from Saltillo.

Holiday Inn Eurotel (☎ 415-10-00, W www.holidayinneurotel.com, V Carranza 4100) Rooms on weekdays/weekends US$145/77. The Holiday Inn is located on highway 40 to Monterrey just south of the Carranza monument and has all the modern luxuries; weekend deals are a bargain.

Camino Real Saltillo (☎ 438-00-00, W www.caminoreal.com, Los Fundadores 2000) Rooms US$232 Mon-Fri, US$118 Sat & Sun. This classy establishment is as good as it gets in Saltillo, with two restaurants and a lovely outdoor grassed area. The weekend deals bring room prices within reach of most mortals.

Places to Eat

There are cheap *eating stalls* with outdoor seating in front of Mercado Juárez, overlooking Plaza Acuña.

For cooling down on a hot day, check out the ice creams at **Nevería & Paletería**, across the street from the Hotel Urdiñola; a bucket with two scoops is US$1.50.

Tacos El Pastor (cnr Padre Flores & Aldama) 4 tacos US$2.50. On the southwest corner of Plaza Acuña, this busy place prepares tasty tacos *al pastor* (grilled spiced pork carved off a meter-high cone) and tacos *de lengua* (beef tongue).

Restaurant Arcasa (☎ 412-64-24, Victoria 251) Set breakfast US$3.25, sandwiches US$2.25, Mexican dishes US$3.25. Next to the Hotel Urdiñola, Arcasa is a big, bright place with an extensive, cheap menu.

Café Victoria (☎ 412-91-31, Padre Flores 221) Breakfast US$2.50, set 3-course lunches US$4.50. This is a popular hangout with a lunch counter, serving *café con leche*, sandwiches, tacos, hamburgers and enchiladas.

Restaurant El Principal (☎ 412-71-31, Allende 702 Nte) Cabrito dishes US$7-12, steak dishes US$13. Norteño-style cabrito is the specialty at this restaurant, four blocks down the hill from Plaza Acuña. It offers assorted goat parts, steaks and attentive service.

El Tapanco (☎ 414-43-39, Allende 225 Sur) Mains from US$11. If you're looking for fine cuisine in splendid surroundings try Tapanco. You can dine alfresco on the back patio. The menu features a tempting array of salads, seafoods, pastas and crepes – the *huitlacoche* crepes are superb.

La Casa de Don Chuy (☎ 414-97-62, Allende 160) Steak dishes from US$13, seafood dishes US$9.50. Similar to El Tapanco, this elegant restaurant offers courtyard dining in style – it's a favorite with tourists and a bit cheaper than its neighbor.

Shopping

Saltillo used to be so famous for its sarapes that a certain type was known as a 'Saltillo' even if it was made elsewhere in Mexico. The technique involves leaving out color fixatives in the dyeing process so that the different bands of color 'weep' or blend into each other. The finest sarapes have silk or gold and silver threads woven into them. These days the local workshops have stopped making classic all-wool sarapes and seem to be obsessed with jarring combinations of bright colors. But you can still get ponchos and blankets in more 'natural' colors, some of which are pure wool.

El Sarape de Saltillo (☎ 412-48-89, Hidalgo 305) Open 9am-1pm & 3pm-7pm Mon-Sat. You can see sarapes and other handicrafts at this shop, a couple of blocks up the hill from the cathedral. Wool is dyed and woven on treadle looms inside the shop.

Other places worth a look include the **Mercado Juárez**, next to Plaza Acuña, which also has a selection of sarapes, as well as hats, saddles and souvenirs; and *Fonart* on Allende, just south of Juárez, a branch of the government-run crafts shop with a variety of pottery, textiles and jewelry from around Mexico.

Getting There & Away

Air Mexicana (☎ 415-03-43), with an office at the airport, has flights between Mexico City and Saltillo. Continental Airlines (☎ 488-31-14) flies to/from Houston.

Bus Saltillo's modern bus station is on the ring road at Libertad. First-class lines have ticket desks to the right end of the hall as you enter; 2nd-class is to the left.

Lots of buses serve Saltillo but few start their journeys here. This means that on some buses, 2nd-class ones in particular, you often can't buy a ticket until the bus has arrived and they know how much room there is for new passengers. You'd be better off taking a 1st-class bus. The 1st-class lines include Transportes del Norte and Ómnibus de México, while Transportes Frontera and Línea Verde are 2nd-class; Turistar is the deluxe bus line. Daily departures include the following:

Aguascalientes – 503km, 7 hours; 14 1st-class (US$30)

Durango – 488km, 8 hours; 4 1st-class (US$34)

Guadalajara – 693km, 10 hours; 15 1st-class (US$44)

Matamoros – 410km, 7 hours; 13 1st-class (US$25)

Mexico City (Terminal Norte) – 870km, 10 hours; 2 deluxe (US$72), 9 1st-class (US$53), 2 2nd-class (US$46)

Monterrey – 85km, 1½ hours; 3 deluxe (US$7), frequent 1st-class (US$5)

Nuevo Laredo – 310km, 4 hours; 8 1st-class (US$22), 4 2nd-class (US$19)

Parras – 160km, 2½ hours; 7 2nd-class (US$6.75)

San Luis Potosí – 455km, 6 hours; frequent 1st-class (US$26), 2 2nd-class (US$24)

Torreón – 231km, 3½ hours; frequent 1st-class (US$19) and 2nd-class (US$17.50)

Zacatecas – 373km, 5 hours; 10 1st-class (US$22), 7 2nd-class (US$19)

Buses also go to Chihuahua, Ciudad Acuña, Ciudad Juárez, Mazatlán, Monclova, Morelia, Piedras Negras, Reynosa, Querétaro and Tijuana. Autobuses Americanos serves Chicago, Dallas, Houston and San Antonio.

Car & Motorcycle Saltillo is a junction of major roads. Highway 40 going northeast to Monterrey is a good four-lane road, with no tolls until you reach the Monterrey bypass. Going west to Torreón (277km), highway 40D splits off highway 40 after 30km, becoming an overpriced toll road (US$16). Highway 40 is free and perfectly all right.

Highway 57 goes north to Monclova (192km), penetrating the dramatic Sierra San Marcos y Pinos at Cima de la Muralla (a butterfly migration zone in the summer months), and onward to Piedras Negras (441km). Going south to Mexico City (852km), highway 57 climbs to over 2000m, then descends gradually along the Altiplano Central to Matehuala (260km) and San Luis Potosí (455km), through barren but often scenic country. To the southwest, highway 54 crosses high, dry plains toward Zacatecas (363km) and Guadalajara (680km).

Getting Around

The airport is 15km northeast of town on highway 40; catch a 'Ramos Arizpe' bus along Xicoténcatl (US$0.40) or a taxi. To reach the city center from the bus station, take minibus No 9 (US$0.30), which departs from Libertad, the first street on the right as you leave the station. To reach the bus station from the center, catch a No 9 on Aldama between Zaragoza and Hidalgo. Taxis between the center and the bus station cost US$3.50.

PARRAS

• pop 32,200 • elev 1580m ☎ 842

Parras, 160km west of Saltillo off the Torreón road, is an oasis in the Coahuilan Desert. Underground streams from the sierra come to the surface here as springs, used to irrigate the grapevines (*parras*) for which the area is famous and giving the town its full name – Parras de la Fuente.

Parras was the birthplace of Francisco Madero, an important leader in the Mexican Revolution. An obelisk on Calle Arizpe honors him.

Orientation & Information

Treat street numbers in Parras with some skepticism as, at times, they don't appear to follow any numerical order.

The Parras tourist office (☎ 422-02-59) is on the roadside 3km north of town. Open 10am to 1pm and 3.30pm to 7pm daily, it has a helpful staff and plenty of useful maps and brochures.

The Interworld Ciber Cafe on Madero opposite the parish church charges US$2.25 for Internet connections.

Things to See & Do

The first winery in the Americas was established at Parras in 1597, a year before the town itself was founded. The winery, now called **Casa Madero** *(☎ 422-01-11; admission free; tours 9am to 4pm daily)*, is about 4km north of town in San Lorenzo on the road going to the main highway. Tours are conducted in Spanish and last about an hour; you can buy quality wine and brandy on site.

The town has an old aqueduct, some colonial buildings, and three *estanques* (large pools where water from the springs is stored) that are great for swimming. The **Iglesia del Santo Madero**, on the southern edge of town, sits on the plug of an extinct volcano. Expansive views reward those who make the steep climb.

An important manufacturer of *mezclilla* (denim), Parras is a good place to buy jeans. Its fig, date and nut orchards provide the basis for delectable fudgy sweets, on sale around town.

Special Events

The grape fair, the Feria de la Uva, goes on for most of the month of August, featuring parades, fireworks, horse races, religious celebrations on the Día de la Asunción (August 15), and traditional dances by descendants of early Tlaxcalan settlers.

Places to Stay

Hotel Parras *(☎ 422-06-44, Arizpe 105)* Singles & doubles US$8. Parras' cheapest option, the Hotel Parras at Reforma, might also be the friendliest. Its clean, very basic rooms face an unruly interior garden – room No 6 is the airiest.

Hotel La Siesta *(☎ 422-03-74, Acuña 9,* Singles/doubles US$20/24. This is another reasonably priced place, around the corner from the bus station, with small homey rooms. The trees give it a cool feel in summer.

Hotel Posada Santa Isabel *(☎ 422-05-72, Madero 514)* Singles/doubles US$31/33. The best value for the money by far is this hotel with a swimming pool, restaurant and spacious air-conditioned rooms around a pretty courtyard. Look for the 'Restaurant Posada' sign on Madero.

Rincón del Montero *(☎ 422-05-40, fax 422-08-72, 3km north of town)* Rooms & cabins US$107. A few kilometers north of town is this resort with golf, tennis, swimming and horseback riding. Approaching from the north, turn left off the main road just below the tourist information module.

Places to Eat

Restaurant Posada *(☎ 422-05-72, Madero 514)* Breakfast US$3.25, dinner US$4.50. With its pleasant courtyard dining amid lots of greenery, this restaurant is at Hotel Posada Santa Isabel and serves excellent food at affordable prices.

The restaurants **El Tiburón** *(Reforma 17)* and **Chávez** *(☎ 422-00-52, Reforma 19)*, just north of Madero, serve decent, inexpensive seafood (US$4) and pizza (US$9), respectively.

Getting There & Away

Only 2nd-class buses serve Parras; there are seven daily to/from Saltillo (2½ hours, US$6.75) and five to/from Torreón (2½ hours, US$9). A 1st-class bus from Saltillo or elsewhere might drop you at La Paila, from where you can find local transport. Parras is easy to reach by car; at La Paila, about halfway between Saltillo and Torreón, turn off the highway and go 27km south.

Central Pacific Coast

Stretching from Mazatlán south to the Oaxacan border, the central Pacific coast is home to some of Mexico's principal beach resorts – Mazatlán, Puerto Vallarta, Manzanillo, Ixtapa, Zihuatanejo and Acapulco – and many lesser-known but equally enchanting hideaways.

Frequent bus services and an improving coastal highway 200 make travel up and down the coast easy, while several scenic highways connect the coast to the western highlands. There are regular domestic and international air services to all the main tourist resorts.

MAZATLÁN
• pop 324,700 ☎ 669

Just 13km south of the tropic of Cancer, Mazatlán is Mexico's principal Pacific coast port for fishing and trade, as well as a prime Pacific resort area. It's famous for sport fishing, with thousands of sailfish and marlin tagged and released each year, and is home to Latin America's largest fleet of commercial shrimp vessels.

In pre-Hispanic times Mazatlán (which means 'place of deer' in Náhuatl) was populated by Totorames, who lived by hunting, gathering, fishing and agriculture. A group of 25 Spaniards led by Nuño de Guzmán officially founded a settlement here on Easter Sunday in 1531, but almost three centuries elapsed before a permanent colony was established in the early 1820s. The port was blockaded by US forces in 1847, and by the French in 1864, but Mazatlán was little more than a fishing village for the next 80 years. 'Old' Mazatlán, the traditional town center, dates from the 19th century. Tourists started coming in the 1930s, mainly for fishing and hunting, and some hotels appeared along Playa Olas Altas, Mazatlán's first tourist beach, in the 1950s. From the 1970s onward, a long strip of modern hotels and tourist facilities has spread north along the coast.

Today's visitors have a choice between a luxury package-tour resort, some old-style Mexican ambiance, or the very basic beach-bum option. One big attraction is free for all – the daily spectacle of rocky islands sil-

Highlights

- Luxury, international resorts – Acapulco, Ixtapa and Puerto Vallarta
- Charming seaside towns – Playa Azul, San Blas, Cuyutlán and El Paraíso
- Superb coastal scenery – blue sea, white sand, verdant jungle backdrop
- Succulent seafood – lobster, shrimp, shellfish and sizzling *mahi mahi*
- Tropical daze – sun, sea, sand and snoozing
- Tropical nights – fiery sunsets, cool breezes, long drinks and hot dance clubs
- Tropical action – surfing, fishing, diving, boat trips, treks and bungee jumps

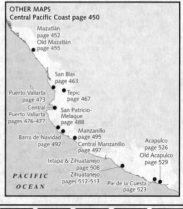

OTHER MAPS
Central Pacific Coast page 450

Mazatlán page 452
Old Mazatlán page 455
San Blas page 463
Puerto Vallarta page 473
Tepic page 467
Central Puerto Vallarta pages 476-477
San Patricio-Melaque page 488
Barra de Navidad page 492
Manzanillo page 495
Central Manzanillo page 497
Ixtapa & Zihuatanejo page 508
Zihuatanejo pages 512-513
Acapulco page 526
Old Acapulco page 529
Pie de la Cuesta page 523

PACIFIC OCEAN

houetted against the tropical sunset, as the fiery red sun fades into the sea, and another starry night begins.

Orientation

Old Mazatlán, the city center, is concentrated near the southern end of a peninsula, bounded by the Pacific Ocean on the west and the Bahía Dársena on the east. The center of the old city is the cathedral, on Plaza Principal, surrounded by the standard rectangular street grid. At the southern tip of the peninsula El Faro (the lighthouse)

CENTRAL PACIFIC COAST

stands on a rocky prominence, over looking Mazatlán's sport fishing fleet and the La Paz ferry terminal.

A beachside boulevard (which changes names frequently) runs along the Pacific side of the peninsula from Playa Olas Altas, around some rocky outcrops, and north around the wide arc of Playa Norte to the Zona Dorada (Golden Zone), a concentration of hotels, bars, and businesses catering mainly to package tourists. Farther north are more hotels, a marina and some time-share condominium developments.

East of the Mazatlán peninsula (and comprising a separate municipality), Isla de la Piedra is a short boat ride from town, though it's not really an island any more – landfill from the airport construction has joined it to the mainland. The wide, sandy beach here is lined with open-sided, palm-thatched *palapas* restaurants.

Information

Tourist Offices The Coordinación General de Turismo (☎ 916-51-60/65, e tursina@prodigy.net.mx, w www.sinaloa.gob.mx/turismo/index2.htm) is on the fourth floor of the Banrural building, Avenida Camarón-Sábalo s/n, north of the Zona Dorada (open 8am to 3pm Monday to Saturday).

The El Cid Mega Resort information booth, at the northern end of the Zona Dorada, is mainly there to sell boat trips, water sports and timeshare presentations, but the staff are helpful and well informed about all sorts of things to see and do.

Free bilingual tourist newspapers – *Pacific Pearl* and *Mazatlán Interactivo* – are available at the tourist office and at many hotels and tourist-oriented businesses.

Money Banks, most with ATMs, and casas de cambio are plentiful in both old and new Mazatlán. A visitor to the city will find Bancomer and Banamex branches near Plaza Principal, and a Banamex on Avenida Camarón-Sábalo in the Zona Dorada. American Express (☎ 913-06-00) is in the Centro Comercial Balboa shopping center on Avenida Camarón-Sábalo, in the Zona Dorada; it's open 9am to 6pm Monday to Friday, 9am to 1pm Saturday.

Post & Communications The main post office, on Juárez on the eastern side of Plaza Principal, is open 8am to 7pm Monday to Friday and 9am to 1pm Saturday. Next door, Telecomm has telegraph, telex, fax and Internet services and pay phones and opens similar hours. Miscelanea Hermes, at Serdán 1510, a block east of the cathedral, offers telephone, fax and Internet services, as does Computel next door. Internet access is also available (US$1.75 per hour) at Telefonía Automática, Flores 810, and Ahorra-Net, Flores 508. In the Zona Dorada, there's Netscape Café Internet on Avenida Camarón-Sábalo. Pay phones are plentiful around the city.

Old Mazatlán

The heart of Old Mazatlán is the large 19th-century **cathedral** at Juárez and 21 de Marzo, with its high, yellow twin towers and beautiful statues inside. Built from 1875 to 1890, it faces **Plaza Principal**, which has lush trees and a bandstand. The **Palacio Municipal** is on the western side of the Plaza Principal.

A couple of blocks southwest of Plaza Principal, the attractive **Plazuela Machado**, at Avenida Carnaval and Constitución, is the center of a large historic area of Mazatlán that has been undergoing a massive renewal program. It's surrounded by historic buildings and attractive sidewalk cafés, restaurants and bars. Half a block south of the Plazuela Machado, **Teatro Ángela Peralta** (*Carnaval 47*) was built in 1860, and reopened in 1992 after a five-year restoration project. Cultural events of all kinds are presented here (see Entertainment), and the opulent interior is open for viewing most days.

Four blocks toward Playa Olas Altas, the **Museo Arqueológico** (☎ 981-14-55, *Sixto Osuna 76; admission free; open 9.30am-4pm Mon-Fri*) is an interesting little archaeological museum with some labels in English. Opposite, the **Museo de Arte** (☎ 985-35-02, *cnr Sixto Osuna & Carranza; admission US$0.60; open 10am-2pm & 5pm-8pm Tues-Sun*) has permanent and changing exhibits of work by Mexican artists.

West of the center, **Playa Olas Altas** is a small beach in a small cove where Mazatlán's tourism began in the 1950s. The seafront road, Paseo Olas Altas, has a few faded '50s hotels facing the water, though erosion and construction have reduced the beach to a small crescent at the northern

MAZATLÁN

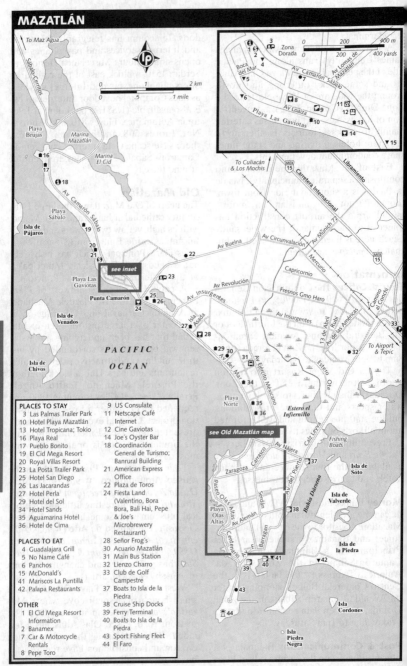

PLACES TO STAY
3   Las Palmas Trailer Park
10 Hotel Playa Mazatlán
13 Hotel Tropicana; Tokio
16 Playa Real
17 Pueblo Bonito
19 El Cid Mega Resort
20 Royal Villas Resort
23 La Posta Trailer Park
25 Hotel San Diego
26 Las Jacarandas
27 Hotel Perla
29 Hotel del Sol
34 Hotel Sands
35 Aguamarina Hotel
36 Hotel de Cima

PLACES TO EAT
4   Guadalajara Grill
5   No Name Café
9   Panchos
15 McDonald's
41 Mariscos La Puntilla
42 Palapa Restaurants

OTHER
1   El Cid Mega Resort Information
2   Banamex
7   Car & Motorcycle Rentals
8   Pepe Toro

9   US Consulate
11 Netscape Café Internet
12 Cine Gaviotas
14 Joe's Oyster Bar
18 Coordinación General de Turismo; Banrural Building
21 American Express Office
22 Plaza de Toros
24 Fiesta Land (Valentino, Bora Bora, Bali Hai, Pepe & Joe's Microbrewery Restaurant)
28 Señor Frog's
30 Acuario Mazatlán
31 Main Bus Station
32 Lienzo Charro
33 Club de Golf Campestre
37 Boats to Isla de la Piedra
38 Cruise Ship Docks
39 Ferry Terminal
40 Boats to Isla de la Piedra
43 Sport Fishing Fleet
44 El Faro

nd of the cove. Look for two of the town's
many seafront monuments: the **Escudo de
Sinaloa y Mazatlán** (Sinaloa and Mazatlán
shield) at the southern end of the cove and
the **Monumento al Venado** (Monument to
the Deer) at the northern end (a tribute to
the city's Náhuatl name).

Farther north, around the rocky outcrop
called **Cerro de la Nevería** (Icebox Hill) is
the **Monumento a la Continuidad de la Vida**
(Monument to the Continuity of Life), featuring two naked humans and a group of
dolphins. Also along here is the platform
from which the **cliff divers** *(clavadistas)*
plunge into the ocean swells below. There's
no fixed schedule, but you're mostly likely
to see the divers perform around lunch time
on weekends and holidays.

Paseo Olas Altas continues around
another rocky promontory, where the
cannons of the old fort point out to sea past
one of Mazatlán's best surf breaks. Changing
its name to Avenida del Mar, the seafront
road passes **Playa Norte**, a sunset fishing spot
for pelicans and other birds, and the **Monumento al Pescador** (Monument to the Fisherman), another of Mazatlán's nude statues.

At the southern end of the peninsula, a
particularly prominent rocky outcrop provides the base for **El Faro**, 157m above sea
level and supposedly the second-highest
lighthouse in the world (after Gibraltar).
You can climb up there for a spectacular
view of the city and coast. The hill, called
Cerro del Crestón, was once an island, but a
causeway built in the 1930s now joins it to
the mainland. Mazatlán's sport fishing fleet,
the ferry to La Paz and some of the tourist
boats (see Organized Tours, later in this
section) dock in the marina on the eastern
side of the causeway.

Beaches & Zona Dorada
Mazatlán has 16km of sandy beaches stretching north from Old Mazatlán to beyond the
Zona Dorada. Playa Norte begins just north
of Old Mazatlán and arcs toward Punta
Camarón, a rocky point dominated by the
conspicuous white walls and turrets of the
Fiesta Land nightclub complex. The traffic
circle here marks the southern end of the
Zona Dorada, an unashamed tourist precinct
of hotels, restaurants, bars and souvenir
shops. The fanciest hotels face the fine
beaches of **Playa Las Gaviotas** and **Playa**

Sábalo, which extends north of the Zona
Dorada. The 'Sábalo-Centro' buses pass
along all of these beaches.

North of Playa Sábalo, large-scale work
continues on the extensive Marina Mazatlán. Other resort hotels and new condominium developments line the beaches
north of the marina – **Playa Brujas** (Witches'
Beach) and, farther north, **Playa Cerritos**.

Children's Attractions
Between the center and the Zona Dorada,
Acuario Mazatlán *(☎ 981-78-15, Avenida de
los Deportes s/n; adult/child US$5.50/3; open
9.30am-5.30pm daily)*, a block inland from
Playa Norte, has 52 tanks with 250 species of
fresh and saltwater fish and other creatures.
Sea lion and bird shows are presented four
times daily.

North of the marina, **Mazagua** *(☎ 988-00-
41, Entronque Habal-Cerritos s/n; admission
US$8.75; open 10am-6pm daily Mar-Dec)* is
a family aquatic park with water toboggans,
a wave pool and other entertainment. The
'Cerritos-Juárez' bus takes you there.

Islands
Three rocky islands are clearly seen from
Mazatlán's beaches – **Isla de Chivos** (Island
of Goats) is on the left, and **Isla de Pájaros**
(Island of Birds) is on the right.

In the middle, **Isla de Venados** (Deer
Island) has been designated a natural reserve
for protection of native flora and fauna; petroglyphs have also been found on the island.
Secluded beaches on the island are wonderful for a day trip, and the clear waters offer
great snorkelling. Boats depart from the
Aqua Sport Centre at El Cid Mega Resort
(☎ 916-34-68), on Avenida Camarón-Sábalo
s/n. A round-trip costs US$10. Boats leave at
10am, noon and 2pm daily, with the last boat
returning at 4pm.

Isla de la Piedra
Isla de la Piedra (Stone Island) is actually a
long, thin peninsula whose tip is opposite
the southern end of the city. Its beautiful,
long, sandy beach is bordered by coconut
groves, and a row of palapa restaurants,
some of which have music and dancing on
Sunday afternoons and holidays, when the
beach is popular with locals. Good surf
breaks offshore, and some very cheap accommodations make it popular with surfers.

CENTRAL PACIFIC COAST

To get to Isla de la Piedra, take a small boat from one of two docks. One is near the ferry terminal (boats leave 9.30am to 6pm), and boats from there will drop you at a jetty just a short walk from the Isla de la Piedra beach. The other dock is farther north, near the end of Avenida Nájera (boats leave 6am to midnight), and boats from there will take you to the village on Isla de la Piedra, slightly farther from the beach (a *pulmonía* taxi will take you right to the beach for US$2). Boats depart from this northerly departure point every 10 minutes for the five-minute ride to the island (US$1 round-trip).

Water Sports

The **Aqua Sport Centre** (*El Cid Mega Resort, ☎ 916-24-68 ext 6598*), is the place to go for water sports, including scuba diving, water-skiing, catamaran sailing, parasailing, boogie boarding and riding the 'big banana.' Water-sports equipment can also be hired on the beaches in front of most of the other large beachfront hotels.

The best surf breaks are the right hander at Punta Camarón, and 'Cannons,' the left off the point near the old fort on Paseo Olas Altas, as well as the breaks off Isla de la Piedra.

Sport Fishing

Mazatlán is world famous for its sport fishing – especially for marlin, swordfish, sailfish, tuna and *dorado* (dolphinfish). It's an expensive activity (around US$360 for a day in a boat with three people fishing), though small-game fishing is less expensive, especially with a group of five or six. Established big-game fishing operators include **El Cid Mega Resort** (*☎ 916-24-68 ext 6598*), **Star Fleet** (*☎ 982-26-65*) and **Flota Bibi** (*☎ 981-36-40*). Some of these are based at Marina El Cid and Marina Mazatlán, while others are at the dock near the foot of El Faro, along with quite a few less-expensive operators such as **Viking** (*☎ 986-34-84) and* **Flota Saballo** (*☎ 981-27-61*). For the winter high season, make fishing reservations as far in advance as you can. All operators should offer tag-and-release options.

Golf & Tennis

There's golf at the **Club de Golf Campestre** (*☎ 980-15-70, highway 15*), east of town; the **Estrella del Mar Golf Club** (*☎ 982-33-00, Isla*

de la Piedra), south of the airport by th coast; and El Cid Mega Resort (*☎ 913-3: 33, Avenida Camarón-Sábalo s/n*), north the Zona Dorada. Play tennis at th **Racquet Club Gaviotas** (*☎ 913-59-39, cr Iris & Bravo*) in the Zona Dorada, at El Ci resort and at almost any of the large hote north of the center.

Language Courses

Centro de Idiomas (*☎ 985-56-06, Domíngue 1908,* **w** *www.go2mazatlan.com/spanish*) hour/5-hour classes US$120/150. The cente offers Spanish courses daily Monday t Friday with a maximum of six students pe class. You can begin any Monday and stud for as many weeks as you like; registration every Saturday morning, 9am to noor There are discounts if you sign up for fou weeks. Homestays (shared/private roor US$130/150 per week) can be arranged wit a Mexican family and include three meals day (30-day advance notice required).

Organized Tours

Marlin Tours (*☎ 913-53-01,* **w** *www .go2mazatlan.com/marlin*) Tours US$15-32 Marlin offers a three-hour city tou (US$15); a colonial tour to the foothil towns of Concordia and Copala (US$28) an ecological tour to Teacapan, Rosario an Agua Caliente (US$32); and a ranch tour tc La Noria and Las Moras (US$17).

Vista Tours (*☎ 986-83-83*) Tours US$20 87. Vista has an even bigger range of possi bilities including Cosalá and the Sar Ignacio Missions.

There's also *Mazatleco* (*☎ 916-59-33*) which does kayak tours, bird-watching trips and sailboat rentals.

Call tour companies directly (they wil pick you up from your hotel), or have a travel agent book a tour.

As well as trips to Isla de Venados (see Islands, earlier), several boats do three-hour sightseeing trips, mostly leaving from the marina near El Faro at 11am (around US$12 including hotel transfers). Two-hour sunset cruises, sometimes called 'booze cruises,' include hors d'oeuvres and an open bar (US$16). To find out what's going on, look for flyers around town, talk to a tour agent, or call the operators of boats like *Costalegre* (*☎ 914-24-77*), *Kolonahe* (*☎ 916-34-68*) or *Yate Fiesta* (*☎ 913-06-24*).

OLD MAZATLÁN

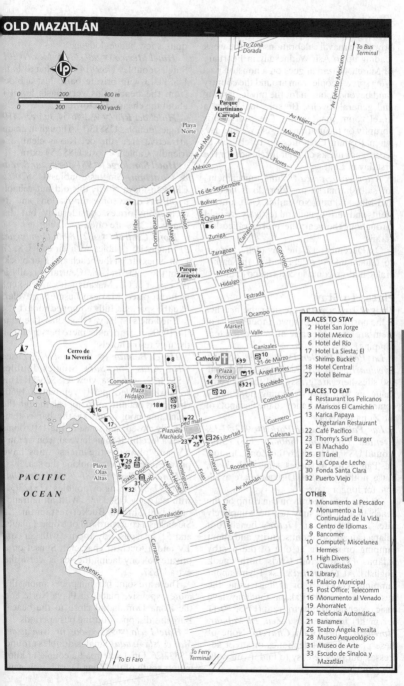

PLACES TO STAY
2 Hotel San Jorge
3 Hotel México
6 Hotel del Río
17 Hotel La Siesta; El
   Shrimp Bucket
18 Hotel Central
27 Hotel Belmar

PLACES TO EAT
4 Restaurant los Pelícanos
5 Mariscos El Camichín
13 Karica Papaya
   Vegetarian Restaurant
22 Café Pacífico
23 Thorny's Surf Burger
24 El Machado
25 El Túnel
29 La Copa de Leche
30 Fonda Santa Clara
32 Puerto Viejo

OTHER
1 Monumento al Pescador
7 Monumento a la
   Continuidad de la Vida
8 Centro de Idiomas
9 Bancomer
10 Computel; Miscelanea
   Hermes
11 High Divers
   (Clavadistas)
12 Library
14 Palacio Municipal
15 Post Office; Telecomm
16 Monumento al Venado
19 AhorraNet
20 Telefonía Automática
21 Banamex
26 Teatro Ángela Peralta
28 Museo Arqueológico
31 Museo de Arte
33 Escudo de Sinaloa y
   Mazatlán

CENTRAL PACIFIC COAST

Special Events

Mazatlán has one of Mexico's most flamboyant Carnaval celebrations. For the week leading up to Ash Wednesday in February or March, Mazatlán goes on a nonstop partying spree. People from around the country (and beyond) pour in for the music, dancing and general revelry. Be sure to reserve a hotel room in advance. The party ends abruptly on the morning of Ash Wednesday, when Roman Catholics go to church to receive ash marks on their foreheads for the first day of Lent.

A *torneo de pesca* (fishing tournament) for sailfish, marlin and dorado is held in mid-May and mid-November. Golf tournaments and various cultural festivals are held throughout the year; the tourist office has details.

On December 12, the day of the Virgen de Guadalupe is celebrated at the cathedral. Children come in colorful costumes.

Places to Stay

Budget Trailer parks are near the beaches at the northern end of town, though most of them are not especially attractive for tent camping.

La Posta Trailer Park (☎ 983-53-10, *Avenida Buelna 7*) Sites from US$11. The 180 sites here are grassy and there's some shade, as well as a swimming pool and a common room. It's handy to the fleshpots of the Zona Dorada.

Las Palmas Trailer Park (☎ 913-53-11, *Avenida Camarón- Sábalo 333*) Sites around US$16. Handy to the Zona Dorada, Las Palmas has 68 spaces, some with shade, but is nothing special. Discounts are available for longer stays.

On Isla de la Piedra you can camp on the beach though this may not be completely safe. The people at *Victor's* beachfront palapa can advise about security, and about camping or staying at one of the nearby palapas (Victor and Chris both speak English). At *Carmelita's*, ask Elvira about camping (US$3.50), or at least using the fresh-water showers. Palapas that may have basic beachside rooms for rent (US$5.50-11 per night) include *Casa Zen*, *El Palmar*, *Florencio's* and *Doña Chavela*. None of these places have telephones or street addresses, but they're easy to find if you walk along the beach.

Old Mazatlán may not have great beaches, but it's an interesting area with quite a few budget lodgings.

Hotel México (☎ 981-38-06, *México 201*) Singles/doubles US$9/14 with shared bath, US$11/13 with private bath. Just a block from the beach, this very basic hotel is about the cheapest in town.

Hotel del Río (☎ 982-46-54, *Juárez 2410*) Singles/doubles US$13/19. Though in an unattractive area, the del Río is clean and friendly. Cable TV costs US$2.50 extra.

Hotel San Jorge (☎ 981-36-95, *cnr Serdán & Gastelum*) Singles/doubles US$20/25. Close to Playa Norte, this old but reliable hotel has done some renovations and increased its prices considerably, but discounts of 25% are often available.

Hotel Central (☎ 982-18-66, *Domínguez 2*) Singles & doubles with air-con US$27. Four blocks from the beach and four blocks from the cathedral, the Central is really in the center of Old Mazatlán. It's a well-kept well-run place; Mexican business travelers like the spacious, fully equipped rooms.

The hotels on Playa Olas Altas date from the 1960s, and are much more personal than the new resort hotels.

Hotel Belmar (☎ 985-11-11/12, *Paseo Olas Altas 166 Sur*) Singles/doubles US$23/27, with sea view US$26/31. This somewhat faded, partly renovated 1960s classic has definite retro appeal, though the swimming pool is murky, the bar is temporarily closed, and some of the 150 rooms need a facelift. Rooms have air-con or fans, TV and phone – the nicest ones have private balconies overlooking the sea.

Hotel La Siesta (☎ 981-26-40, *Paseo Olas Altas 11 Sur*) Singles/doubles US$27/31, with sea view US$33/38. With an entrance beside El Shrimp Bucket restaurant, La Siesta has a courtyard full of tropical plants, and 51 spacious, tidy rooms, with air-con, TV and a touch of character. Sunset on a private balcony facing the sea is worth the extra US$7.

There are some bargain prices among the more expensive places in Playa Norte and the Zona Dorada, all close to the beach. Bargains disappear during busy periods.

Hotel Perla (☎ 985-33-66, *cnr Avenida del Mar & Isla Asada*) Singles/doubles around US$22/26. On a side road a couple of kilometers south of the Zona Dorada, this new,

:mon-yellow hotel is cheaply built and heaply priced.

Las Jacarandas (☎ 984-11-77, Avenida del Mar 2500) Rooms US$20, with TV US$22, with air-con and TV is US$25. This good, modern, motel-style place is just a few hundred meters from the main nightlife area.

Hotel San Diego (☎ 983-57-03, W www hotelsandiego.tripod.com, cnr Avenidas del Mar & Buelna) Rooms US$22-26. At the southern end of the Zona Dorada, very close to the after-dark action, the San Diego offers clean, pleasant, economical rooms with air-con and TV.

Mid-Range There are some good mid-range hotels on Avenida del Mar, opposite Playa Norte, with frequent buses heading north and south. All have swimming pools, car parking and air-conditioned rooms with TV and phone.

Hotel del Sol (☎ 985-11-03, Avenida del Mar 800) Rooms US$42, with kitchen US$53. The bigger rooms with kitchens are good for families.

Hotel Sands (☎ 982-00-00, W www.sands arenas.com, Avenida del Mar 1910) Singles/doubles US$38/49, with sea view US$49/60. Also good for kids, the Sands has a restaurant-bar, and rooms with balcony, fan, satellite TV and refrigerator.

Hotel de Cima (☎ 985-18-55, 800-696-06-00, Avenida del Mar 48) Rooms from US$32. Another enjoyable place to stay, this one features a tunnel to the beach so you don't risk your life crossing Avenida del Mar.

Hotel Tropicana (☎ 983-80-00, W www .torretropicana.com.mx, Avenida Loaiza 27) Rooms from US$45, special rates US$32. The Tropicana doesn't face the beach, and it's not much different from other resort hotels, but its special rates are a great value.

Top End Rooms at top-end hotels can be booked most economically as part of a holiday package – see your travel agent at home.

Aguamarina Hotel (☎ 981-70-80, W www .aguamarina.com, Avenida del Mar 110) Rooms US$90, discount rates from US$55. One of the few top-end places at the southern end of Playa Norte, the Aguamarina has a pool, restaurant-bar, parking, travel agency and rooms with cable TV and phone.

The most luxurious top-end hotels are on the beaches north of the Zona Dorada:

El Cid Mega Resort (☎ 913-33-33, W www.elcid.com.mx, Avenida Camarón-Sábalo s/n) Rooms from US$190. This 1230-room resort is the most imposing of the luxury hotels – it actually has facilities at several locations.

Pueblo Bonito (☎ 914-37-00, W www .pueblobonito.com, Avenida Camarón-Sábalo 2121) Rooms US$105-140. Facing a fine stretch of uncrowded beach, this classy-looking place has all the facilities you'd expect.

Playa Real (☎ 913-11-11, Punta del Sábalo s/n) Rooms US$100-130, with ocean view US$130-150. The former Camino Real sits on a prominent peninsula, and features beautifully landscaped gardens.

Royal Villas Resort (☎ 916-61-61, 800-696-70-00, W www.royalvillas.com.mx, Avenida Camarón-Sábalo 500) Rooms US$205-445. All rooms here have kitchens and dining rooms, and accommodate up to six people.

Places to Eat

Mazatlán is famous for fresh seafood – the shrimp especially is fantastic. Also try *pescado zarandeado*, a delicious charcoal-broiled fish stuffed with onion, celery and spices. A whole kilo, feeding two people well, usually costs around US$10, while shrimp is around US$6 to US$12 per dish. The standard Mexican meat and chicken dishes are available at most places too, and generally cost much less than seafood.

Old Mazatlán In the heart of Old Mazatlán, Plazuela Machado is a delightful space with real Mexican tropical ambiance. It's sublime in the evening when the plaza is softly lit, music plays, kids frolic, and outdoor tables offer cool drinks, snacks and meals in a very romantic atmosphere.

Café Pacífico (☎ 981-39-72, Constitución 501) Mains US$6-9. Open 9am-2am daily. A bar, café or restaurant, depending on your needs, the Pacífico has been a mainstay on Plazuela Machado for years, offering solid food, stiff drinks and friendly service.

El Machado (☎ 981-13-75, Sixto Osuna 34) Mains around US$4. Open 9am-midnight. The outdoor tables here are the perfect place for a cold beer and a tasty fish taco or three.

Thorny's Surf Burger *(Sixto Osuna 510B)* Mains US$4. Another pleasant place with tables on the plaza, Thorny's specializes in substantial US-style burgers for the very hungry and/or homesick.

El Túnel *(Avenida Carnaval 1205)* Mains around US$4. Open 6pm-10pm Thur-Tues. Opposite Teatro Ángela Peralta, El Tunel is a *cenaduría* – a modest eatery serving traditional Mexican dishes like *gorditas*, *pozole* or the special local *tamales*.

Other streets in Old Mazatlán have eateries catering to local workers.

Karica Papaya Vegetarian Restaurant *(☎ 981-79-52, Ángel Flores 509)* Mains US$4. Open 8.30am-5pm daily. This place is great for vegetarians, serving fresh fruit juices and wholemeal breads for breakfast and lunch.

Around the seafront, along Paseo Claussen and Paseo Olas Altas, assorted restaurants-cum-bars specialize in seafood and cold drinks. Most have outdoor tables, or open-sided areas.

Mariscos El Camichín *(☎ 985-01-97, Paseo Claussen 97)* Mains US$5-11. Open 11am-10pm daily. Facing Playa Norte, this popular open-air patio restaurant serves delicious seafood under a cool palapa roof.

Restaurant Los Pelícanos *(cnr Paseo Claussen & Uribe)* Mains US$4-7. Open 10am-6pm Tues-Sun. This small open-air thatched-roof place does some of the cheapest and tastiest seafood in Mazatlán. It has a great view of the entire arc of Playa Norte, and catches any sea breezes coming by.

El Shrimp Bucket *(☎ 981-63-50, Paseo Olas Altas 11)* Mains US$6-20. Open 6am-11pm daily. Opened in 1963, the Bucket was the first of the international chain of Carlos Anderson restaurants. It has a large and varied menu, tables outside on the street and a very air-conditioned interior. Live music adds to the lively atmosphere.

La Copa de Leche *(☎ 982-57-53, Paseo Olas Altas 122)* Mains US$5-8. Open 7.30am-11pm. This sidewalk restaurant-bar is popular with the local gentry, for breakfast, a filling and economical *comida corrida*, a snack, a drink or an evening coffee. Nearby ***Fonda Santa Clara*** is almost identical.

Pueto Viejo *(☎ 928-82-26, Paseo Olas Altas 25)* Mains US$3-5. Open 11am-11pm Mon-Fri, 11am-1am Sat & Sun. This very casual, inexpensive, seafood restaurant and watering hole is popular with locals and expats, especially at sunset and in the evening, when the sea breeze comes through the open sides. A large shrimp cocktail is about the most expensive thing on the menu (US$5). Local bands play here some nights.

Mariscos La Puntilla *(☎ 982-88-77, Flote Playa Sur s/n)* Mains US$5-15. Open 10am-6pm daily. This open-air seafood specialist is popular with Mexican families, especially on weekends – it's very relaxed and the food is good. It's near the Isla de la Piedra ferries on a small point with a view across the water.

Zona Dorada & Around

Zona Dorada restaurants cater to the tourist trade.

No Name Café *(☎ 913-20-31, Avenida Loaiza 417)* Mains US$5-15. Open 8am-1am daily. A US-style sports bar boasting 'the best damn ribs you'll ever eat' has to be worth a try. No Name delivers with a huge norteamericano-mexicano menu, a mile-long drink list, big screens and a tropical patio.

Guadalajara Grill *(☎ 913-50-65, Avenida Camarón-Sábalo 335)* Mains US$5-15. Another Carlos Anderson outlet, this cheerful, barn-sized restaurant serves up safe, substantial Mexican meals at full tourist prices, for breakfast, lunch, dinner or snacks.

Señor Frog's *(☎ 985-11-10, Avenida del Mar s/n)* Mains US$6-12. Open noon-1am daily (food served until midnight). Halfway between the Zona Dorada and the center is a Mazatlán landmark, and another link in the Carlos Anderson chain. The food is OK (perhaps overpriced), but Frog's is mainly a party place (and merchandizing gimmick).

Tokio *(☎ 986-16-33, Avenida Loaiza 27)* Meals US$4-10. Mazatlán seafood makes pretty good sushi. Try it here, in air-conditioned comfort in front of Hotel Tropicana.

Panchos *(☎ 914-09-11, Avenida Loaiza 408/1B)* Mains US$5-15. Right next to Playa Las Gaviotas, Panchos is perfect for a tasty Mexican or American breakfast, light lunch, sunset snack or big dinner. It's super-clean, slightly pricey, but well worth it.

sla de la Piedra Stroll along the beach ere and enjoy choosing where to eat. Check what's on offer at the open kitchens nder the *palapas*. It's hard to beat a fresh barbecued fish and a cold beer as you wiggle your toes in the sand.

Entertainment

Cultural Events *Teatro Ángela Peralta* (☎ 982-44-47, *Carnaval 47 near Plazuela Machado*) Events of all kinds – movies, concerts, opera (Mazatlán has its own opera company), theater and more – are presented at this historic theatre; a kiosk on the walkway in front of the theater announces current and upcoming cultural events here and at other venues around the city.

If you get a chance, try to hear a rousing traditional *banda sinaloense* – a boisterous brass band unique to the state of Sinaloa and especially associated with Mazatlán.

Bars & Discos The incongruous white castle on Punta Camarón, at the southern end of the Zona Dorada, is *Fiesta Land* (☎ 984-16-66, *Avenida del Mar s/n*), a nightlife fun zone where several of Mazatlán's major venues are concentrated. There's a central ticket office, with information about what's on at each venue.

Valentino (☎ 984-16-66) Admission US$6. Well-dressed Mexican and foreign tourists, mostly 20- and 30-somethings, flock to this well-known disco-club.

Bora Bora (☎ 984-16-66) Cover US$6. This very popular beachfront bar has a sand volleyball court, swimming pool and beachside dance floor, but people still dance on the bar.

The *Bali Hai* bar, *Pepe & Joe's Microbrewery Restaurant* and *Mikonos* are also in the Fiesta Land complex.

Joe's Oyster Bar (☎ 983-53-33, *Avenida Loaiza 100*) Cover US$5.50. Open 11am-2am. About 500m north of Fiesta Land, behind Hotel Los Sábalos, this beachfront bar is fine for a quiet drink until early evening, but it goes ballistic after about 11pm, when it's packed with college kids dancing on tables, chairs and each other.

Several hotels have nightclubs, music and dancing, though most are pretty sedate.

El Caracol (☎ 913-33-33, *in El Cid Mega Resort, Avenida Camarón-Sábalo s/n*) Cover US$4-14 (depending on how many drinks are included). Open 9pm-4am. An upmarket crowd comes to El Caracol for loud techno music and fantastic lighting.

Hotel Playa Mazatlán (☎ 913-44-44, *Avenida Loaiza 202*) Open 7pm-midnight. The beachside restaurant-bar at this posh hotel attracts the 30s-and-up age group for dancing under the stars.

Señor Frog's (☎ 985-11-10, *Avenida del Mar s/n*) Open noon-1am daily. Wild party place for teens and 20s, Frog's plays loud dance music to a packed dance floor almost every night.

Pepe Toro (☎ 914-41-76, W www.pepetoro .com.mx, *Avenida de las Garza 18*) Open 9pm-4am Thur-Sun. This gay bar and disco is usually fun, with a good music mix, party nights and occasional drag acts.

On Sunday afternoon there's live music and dancing at a couple of *palapas* on the beach at Isla de la Piedra, patronized mostly by hard-drinking, hot-dancing locals.

Fiesta Mexicana Mazatlán offers a few places where package tourists can get a dose of packaged Mexican culture. *Hotel Playa Mazatlán* (☎ 913-44-44, *Avenida Loaiza 202*) Admission US$27. Open 7pm-10.30pm Tues, Thur & Sat. Fiesta Mexicana ('Mexican Party') features a Mexican buffet dinner, open bar, folkloric floor show and live Latin dance music. Call the hotel for reservations or reserve at a travel agency.

Cinemas Check the local daily newspapers *El Sol del Pacífico* and *El Noroeste* for movie listings.

Cine Gaviotas (*Avenida Camarón-Sábalo s/n*) Admission US$3.50. This modern, six-screen movie house shows recent-release movies, some dubbed into Spanish and some with original English soundtrack and Spanish subtitles.

Spectator Sports

The Plaza de Toros, on Avenida Buelna, inland from the Zona Dorada traffic circle, hosts *bullfights* 4pm Sunday from Christmas to Easter; the 'Sábalo-Cocos' bus will drop you there. Tickets are sold at travel agencies, at major hotels, at the Bora Bora shop beside Valentino disco and at the Salón Bacanora (☎ 986-91-55) beside the Plaza de Toros.

Charreadas (rodeos) are held at the **Lienzo Charro** (☎ 986-35-10) in Colonia Juárez.

Getting There & Away

Air The Mazatlán international airport (☎ 928-04-38) is 20km southeast of the city. Airlines serving the airport include Aero California (☎ 913-20-42), Aeroméxico (☎ 982-34-44), America West (☎ 981-11-84) and Mexicana (☎ 982-77-22).

Bus The main bus station (Central de Autobuses) is just off Avenida Ejército Méxicano on Avenida de los Deportes, about three blocks inland from the beach, and ringed by inexpensive hotels. First- and 2nd-class bus lines operate from separate halls in the main terminal; buses to small towns nearby (such as Concordia, Copala and Rosario) operate from a smaller terminal, behind the main terminal. Daily services include:

Durango – 321km, 7 hours; 3 Estrella Blanca 1st-
   class (US$27), 7 2nd-class (US$23)
Guadalajara – 506km, 8 hours; 3 Estrella Blanca
   1st-class (US$29), hourly 2nd-class (US$25)
Mexico City (Terminal Norte) – 1041km, 17 hours;
   3 1st-class (US$66), hourly 2nd-class de paso
   (US$58)
Puerto Vallarta – 459km, 8 hours; 1 Elite 1st-class
   (US$32), or take a bus to Tepic, where buses
   depart frequently for Puerto Vallarta
Tepic – 290km, 5 hours; Estrella Blanca 1st-class
   (US$14), 2nd-class (US$12) hourly, or even
   more frequently than that

To get to San Blas (290km), go first to Tepic then get a bus from there. This involves some backtracking, but the alternative (getting off the bus at Crucero San Blas, and waiting there for a local bus to San Blas) is not safe. Travelers have been accosted at Crucero San Blas.

Car Mazatlán's car rental agencies include Aga (☎ 981-35-80), Budget (☎ 913-20-00), Hertz (☎ 913-60-60), National (☎ 913-60-00), and Quality (☎ 916-53-77). Shop around for the best rates, but don't expect to find much under US$50 per day.

Boat Sematur (☎ 981-70-20/21, **W** www .ferrysematur.com.mx) operates ferries between Mazatlán and La Paz, Baja California Sur (actually to the port of Pichilingue,

23km from La Paz). The ferry terminal is a the southern end of town; the office is ope 8am to 2pm daily. The ferry to Pichilingu usually departs at 3pm daily except som Saturdays and the day before some holi days. Occasionally, the ferry carries carg only, and doesn't take passengers. Ticket are sold from two days in advance until th morning of departure. See the La Pa: section in the Baja California chapter fo schedule and fare details.

Getting Around

To/From the Airport *Colectivo* vans and a bus operate from the airport to town, bu not from town to the airport. Taxis are about US$20.

Bus Local buses operate every day from around 5.30am to 10.30pm. Regular white buses cost US$0.40; Urban Pluss air-cor green buses cost US$0.80. Useful routes for visitors include:

Sábalo-Centro travels from the market in the
   center to the beach via Juárez, then north on
   Avenida del Mar to the Zona Dorada and
   farther north on Avenida Camarón-Sábalo.
Playa Sur travels south along Avenida Ejército
   Méxicano near the bus station and through the
   city center, passing the market, then to the ferry
   terminal and El Faro.

To get into the center of Mazatlán from the bus terminal, go to Avenida Ejército Mexicano and catch any bus going south (to your right if the bus terminal is behind you). Alternatively, you can walk 500m from the bus station to the beach and take a 'Sábalo-Centro' bus heading south (left) to the center.

Motorcycle Various companies on Avenida Camarón-Sábalo in the Zona Dorada rent motor scooters for getting around town – you'll see the bikes lined up beside the road. Prices are somewhat negotiable, around US$25 per day. You need a driver's license to hire one; a car license from any country will do.

Pulmonías & Taxis Mazatlán has a special type of taxi called a pulmonía (pneumonia), a small open-air vehicle similar to a golf cart – usually a modified VW. There are also regular red-and-white taxis and green-and-white taxis called 'eco-taxis' that have rates from US$2.25 to US$4.50 for trips around town. Pulmonías can be slightly cheaper, depending on your bargaining skills and the time of day.

AROUND MAZATLÁN

Several small, picturesque colonial towns in the Sierra Madre foothills make pleasant day trips from Mazatlán. **Concordia**, founded in 1565, has an 18th-century church with a baroque façade and elaborately decorated columns. Hot mineral springs are nearby. The village is known for its manufacture of high-quality pottery and hand-carved furniture. It's about a 45-minute drive east of Mazatlán; head southeast on highway 15 for 20km to Villa Unión, turn inland on highway 40 (the highway to Durango) and go another 20km.

Also founded in 1565, **Copala**, 40km past Concordia on highway 40, was one of Mexico's first mining towns. It still has its colonial church (1748), colonial houses and cobblestone streets.

Rosario, 76km southeast of Mazatlán on highway 15, founded in 1655, is another colonial mining town. Its most famous feature is the gold-leaf altar in its church, Nuestra Señora del Rosario.

In the mountains north of Mazatlán, **Cosalá** is a beautiful colonial mining village dating from 1550. It has a 17th-century church, a historical and mining museum in a colonial mansion on the plaza, and two simple but clean hotels. Attractions nearby include **Vado Hondo**, a *balneario* (bathing resort) with a large natural swimming pool and three waterfalls, 15km from town; **La Gruta México**, a large cave 18km from town; and the **Presa El Comedero** reservoir, 20km from town, with rowboats for hire for fishing. To get to Cosalá, go north on highway 15 for 113km to the turnoff (opposite the turnoff for La Cruz de Alota on the coast) and then go about 45km up into the mountains.

Buses to all these places depart from the small bus terminal at the rear of the main bus station in Mazatlán. Alternatively, there are tours (see Organized Tours in the Mazatlán section). Vista, among others, does Cosalá.

SANTIAGO IXCUINTLA
• pop 18,000 ☎ 323

Santiago Ixcuintla is mainly of interest as the jumping-off point for Mexcaltitán. It's

not a tourist town, but it does have the **Centro Huichol** (☎ 235-11-71, *Calle 20 de Noviembre 452 Pte; open 10am-7pm Mon-Sat),* a handicrafts center where indigenous Huicholes make their distinctive arts and crafts; it's on the outskirts of town toward Mexcaltitán.

A couple of hotels are near the market. *Hotel Casino* (☎ 235-08-50, *Ocampo 40)* is a pleasant hotel with ample parking, a restaurant-bar and air-conditioned rooms (singles/doubles US$19/22).

Getting There & Away
Turn off highway 15 63km northwest of Tepic; Santiago Ixcuintla is about 7km west of the turnoff. Buses to Santiago leave frequently from Tepic and Mazatlán. Combis from Santiago Ixcuintla to La Batanga (the departure point for boats to Mexcaltitán) depart from the market. Transportes del Pacífico runs 2nd-class buses to La Batanga four times a day (37km, 1 hour, US$2).

MEXCALTITÁN
• pop 1100 ☎ 323

A small, ancient island village, Mexcaltitán is a fascinating place to visit. Tourism has scarcely touched the island, though it does have a few facilities and a small museum. To get there you must take a *lancha* (motor boat) through a large mangrove lagoon full of fish and birds (and mosquitoes – bring insect repellent!).

The island was originally called Aztlán (Place of Egrets), and some believe it was the original homeland of the Aztec people. Around 1116, it's believed, they left here and began the generations-long migration that eventually led them to Tenochtitlán (modern Mexico City) around 1325.

Mexcaltitán is sometimes called the 'Venice of Mexico.' It's completely surrounded by water, and sometimes actually covered with water. The lagoon rises after heavy rains near the end of the rainy season. Around September to November, at the end of the rainy season, the lagoon rises and water flows through the streets between high cement sidewalks, and all travel is done in canoes.

Orientation & Information
The island is a small oval, about 350m from east to west, 400m from north to south. The

central plaza has a church on its eastern side, and the museum on its northern side. The hotel is a block behind the museum.

All the telephones on the island go through one operator, who has a switchboard in the sitting room of her house. From outside the island, phone the switchboard (☎ 232-02-11) and ask for the extension you want.

Things to See & Do

The **Museo Aztlán del Origen** *(admission US$0.50; open 9am-2pm & 4pm-7pm daily)*, on the northern side of the plaza, is small but enchanting. Among the exhibits are many interesting ancient objects and a fascinating long scroll, the Códice Ruturini, telling the story of the peregrinations of the Aztec people, with notes in Spanish.

You can arrange for **boat trips** on the lagoon for bird-watching, fishing and sightseeing – every family has one or more boats.

Special Events

Semana Santa is celebrated in a big way here. On Good Friday a statue of Christ is put on a cross in the church, then taken down and carried through the streets. The Fiesta de San Pedro Apóstol, the patron saint of fishing, is celebrated on June 29. Statues of St Peter and St Paul are taken out into the lagoon in decorated lanchas for the blessing of the waters. Festivities start around June 20, leading up to the big day.

Places to Stay & Eat

Hotel Ruta Azteca (☎ 232-02-11 ext 128, Venecia 5) Singles/doubles US$11/17. This simple hotel is not the best in town – it's the only one in town.

Restaurant Alberca (☎ 232-02-11 ext 128) Mains US$5. Open 9am-8pm daily. This attractive restaurant is on the eastern shore, accessible by a rickety wooden walkway, and has a great view of the lagoon. It specializes in shrimp dishes. Several other restaurants on the island also offer fresh seafood.

Getting There & Away

From Santiago Ixcuintla, take a bus, taxi or *colectivo* to La Batanga, a small wharf where lanchas depart for Mexcaltitán. Colectivo lanchas' arrival and departure times are coordinated with the bus schedule. The boat journey takes 15 minutes and costs US$1 per person. If you miss the colectivo lancha you can hire a private lancha for US$5, between 8am and 6pm.

SAN BLAS
• **pop 8700 ☎ 323**

The small fishing village of San Blas, 70km northwest of Tepic, was an important Spanish port from the late 16th to the 19th century. The Spanish built a fortress here to protect their *naos* (trading galleons) from marauding British and French pirates. Today's visitors come to enjoy isolated beaches, abundant bird life and tropical jungle reached by riverboats.

San Blas has the amenities of a small beach resort, but retains the character of a Mexican village. One suspects that the real reason the village hasn't been developed as a major resort is the proliferation of *jejenes* (sandflies), tiny gnatlike insects with huge appetites for human flesh; their bites will leave you with an indomitable itch. Abundant mosquitoes compete with the jejenes for your blood. During daylight hours they're not too active, but around sunset they appear from nowhere to attack. Use insect repellent, and get a hotel room with good window screens. (Certain times seem to be relatively free of insects – if you find these warnings exaggerated, count yourself lucky.)

Orientation

San Blas sits on a tongue of land situated between Estuario El Pozo and Estuario San Cristóbal, with Playa El Borrego on the Pacific Ocean on the southern side. A 36km paved road connects San Blas with highway 15, the Tepic-Mazatlán road. This road goes through town as Avenida Juárez, the town's main east-west street. At the small *zócalo* it crosses Batallón de San Blas (Batallón for short), the main north-south street, which heads south to the beach. Everything in town is within walking distance.

Information

The small Secretaría de Turismo (☎ 285-00-05, 285-03-81), is in the Casa de Gobierno, on the eastern side of the Zócalo. It's open 9am to 1pm and 5pm to 8pm Monday to Saturday (plus Sunday in high season). The office has a few maps and brochures about the area and the state of Nayarit and can

SAN BLAS

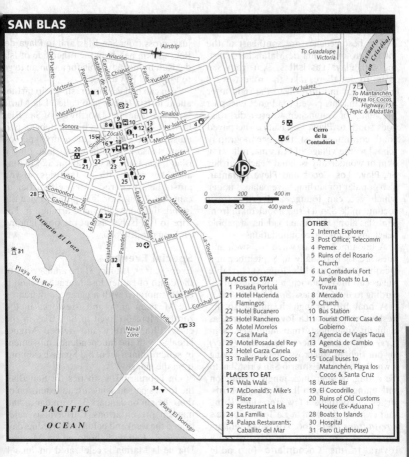

OTHER
2 Internet Explorer
3 Post Office; Telecomm
4 Pemex
5 Ruins of del Rosario Church
6 La Contaduría Fort
7 Jungle Boats to La Tovara
8 Mercado
9 Church
10 Bus Station
11 Tourist Office; Casa de Gobierno
12 Agencia de Viajes Tacua
13 Agencia de Cambio
14 Banamex
15 Local buses to Matanchén, Playa los Cocos & Santa Cruz
18 Aussie Bar
19 El Cocodrillo
20 Ruins of Old Customs House (Ex-Aduana)
28 Boats to Islands
30 Hospital
31 Faro (Lighthouse)

PLACES TO STAY
1 Posada Portolá
21 Hotel Hacienda Flamingos
22 Hotel Bucanero
25 Hotel Ranchero
26 Motel Morelos
27 Casa María
29 Motel Posada del Rey
32 Hotel Garza Canela
33 Trailer Park Los Cocos

PLACES TO EAT
16 Wala Wala
17 McDonald's; Mike's Place
23 Restaurant La Isla
24 La Familia
34 Palapa Restaurants; Caballito del Mar

recommend a guide or boat operator for specialized tours and boat trips.

Banamex, on Avenida Juárez a block east of the zócalo, open 8am to 2pm Monday to Friday, has an ATM. Nearby, Agencia de Cambio is open 8am to 2pm, Monday to Saturday.

The post office is on Sonora at Echeverría, with Telecomm next door. Several public telephones are on the zócalo. Internet Explorer, Canalizo 4, will connect you for US$2.25 per hour.

Agencia de Viajes Tacua is a travel agency at Sinaloa 20, just off the zócalo.

Cerro de la Contadurá
Just west of the bridge over Estuario San Cristóbal, the road passes the Cerro de la Contaduría. Climb up and see the ruins of the 18th-century Spanish fortress and church (admission US$0.70); there's a fine view from the top.

Ex-Aduana
The handsome but crumbling ruins of the old Aduana (customs house), on Avenida Juárez three blocks west of the zócalo, are a reminder of the days when San Blas was an important port on Mexico's Pacific coast.

Beaches
The nearest beach is **Playa El Borrego**, at the end of Azueta. It's a wide, sandy surf beach with a few palapa restaurants at the towns end. The surf here can be treacherous in

CENTRAL PACIFIC COAST

some conditions – beware of rip currents and heed locals' warnings.

The best beaches are southeast of the village around Bahía de Matanchén, starting with **Playa Las Islitas**, 7km from San Blas. To get there, take the road toward highway 15, and turn off to the right after about 4km. This paved road goes east past the village of Matanchén, where a dirt road goes south to Playa Las Islitas. The paved road continues past the oceanography school to the village of Aticama, following 8km of wonderfully isolated beach. Farther on, **Playa Los Cocos** and **Playa Miramar**, also popular for surfing, have palapas under which you can lounge and drink fresh coconut milk. Santa Cruz, about 16km from San Blas along the same road, has a pebble beach and simple accommodations.

A few times a year, when the swell and tides are right (usually in September and October), the world's longest surfable waves curl into Matanchén bay – 1.7km according to the *Guinness Book of Records*.

A **boat trip** through the jungle to the freshwater spring of **La Tovara** is a San Blas highlight. Small boats (maximum 13 passengers) depart from the *embarcadero* (jetty) to your right as you cross the bridge leaving town. Boats go up Estuario San Cristóbal to the spring, passing thick jungle vegetation and mangroves; you'll see exotic birds, turtles and perhaps a few crocodiles. Bring your swimsuit to swim at La Tovara; there's a *restaurant* there too. For a few dollars more, you can extend the trip from La Tovara to the **Cocodrilario** (crocodile nursery), where reptiles are reared in captivity for later release in the wild. The extra few miles of river are especially interesting, even if the nursery doesn't appeal. For a group of up to four people, it costs US$27 to go to La Tovara (3½ hours), US$36 to the Cocodrilario (4 hours). Each extra person costs US$7/9 to La Tovara/Cocodrilario. Shorter boat trips to La Tovara can be made from near Matanchén village, farther up the river; they take an hour less and are a few dollars cheaper.

A five-hour bird-watching trip up the Estuario San Cristóbal to the **Santuario de Aves** (Bird Sanctuary), can be arranged at the same embarcadero by the bridge. Other boat trips depart from a landing on Estuario El Pozo. They include a trip to **Piedra Blanca** to visit the statue of the Virgin; to **Estero Casa Blanca** to gather clams; to **Isla del Rey** just across from San Blas; and to **Playa del Rey**, a 20km beach on the other side of Isla del Rey. It's not advisable for a woman to go to Playa del Rey alone.

You can make an interesting trip farther afield to **Isla Isabel**, also called Isla María Isabelita, four hours northwest of San Blas by boat. The island is a bird-watcher's paradise, with colonies of many species. There's also a volcanic crater lake on the island. Isla Isabel is only about 1.5km long and 1km wide, with no facilities, so you must be prepared for self-sufficient camping. Permission is required to visit the island; the boat pilots can arrange it. For trips to Isla Isabel, ask at the boat landing on Estuario El Pozo.

Special Events

Every year on January 31 the anniversary of the death of Father José María Mercado is commemorated with a parade, a march by the Mexican navy and fireworks in the zócalo. Mercado lived in San Blas in the early 19th century and helped Miguel Hidalgo with the independence movement by sending him a set of old Spanish cannons from the village.

On February 3, festivities for San Blas, the town's patron saint, are an extension of those begun on January 31, with dance and musical presentations. Carnaval is celebrated the weekend before Ash Wednesday. Virgen de Fátima is honored on May 13. Día de la Marina is celebrated on June 1 with burro races on the beach, sporting events, dances and partying.

Places to Stay

Budget Travelers watching their wallets can camp, or choose from a number of hotels. Campers should be prepared for the swarms of insects, especially at sunset.

Trailer Park Los Cocos (☎ 285-00-55, *Azueta s/n*) Tent sites US$13, trailer sites with hookup US$15. Near Playa El Borrego, about 1km from the town center, this park is a grassy area with lots of trees.

Playa Amor (*Playa Los Cocos*) Tent sites US$8, trailer sites with hookup US$15. About a 15-minute drive from town, this attractive beachfront trailer park has a fine view of the sunset and coast, no mosquitoes, and some palapa restaurants nearby.

Hotel Ranchero (☎ *285-08-92, Batallón de San Blas 102*) Rooms with shared/private bath US$13/17. At the corner of Michoacán, this clean, friendly place has eight rooms and is popular with travelers. It has kitchen and laundry facilities for guests.

Motel Morelos (*no* ☎, *Batallón de San Blas 108*) Singles & doubles US$17. Opposite the Ranchero, and run by the same family, this is another clean, simple guesthouse with a homey atmosphere. Rooms are around a central courtyard.

Casa María (☎ *285-08-92, Canalizo 67*) Singles & doubles US$22. One block east of the Morelos, and also run by the same extended family, Casa María has comfortable rooms facing a pretty courtyard garden.

Posada Portolá (☎ *285-03-86, Paredes 118*) Bungalows US$17-20. Three blocks north of the Zócolo, this place has eight spacious, family-sized bungalows with simple kitchens.

Hotel Bucanero (☎ *285-01-01, Avenida Juárez 75*) Singles/doubles US$16/22. Two blocks west of the zócalo, the Bucanero is old, but full of character. A large stuffed crocodile greets you at the door, and the rooms (with one to six beds) are set around a wide, palm-filled courtyard. There's off-street parking, and a big swimming pool that's useable sometimes.

Mid-Range Several hotels offer more comfort, but only one has real charm.

Hotel Posada del Rey (☎ *285-01-23, Campeche 10*) Singles/doubles with fan & air-con US$27/33. This attractive, clean, modern place has pleasant rooms, a small swimming pool and a third-floor bar and grill with ocean views.

Hotel Hacienda Flamingos (☎/*fax 285-04-85, Avenida Juárez 105*) Singles/doubles US$53/73; more in Dec-Jan. The classiest place in town offers luxurious rooms set around a lovely courtyard in a superbly restored old building. A large garden and swimming pool are off to one side.

Hotel Garza Canela (☎/*fax 285-01-12,* Ⓦ *www.garzacanela.com, Paredes 106 Sur*) Singles/doubles/triples from US$65/76/87. The Garza Canela has a large garden, an outdoor swimming pool, an air-conditioned restaurant-bar, and 42 large rooms with air-

con and satellite TV. Suites with kitchens are also available.

Places to Eat
McDonald's (☎ *285-04-32, Avenida Juárez 36*) Mains US$3-8. Open 7am-10pm daily. Just west of the zócalo, this old travelers' hangout serves filling food at reasonable prices (it's no relation to the burger chain).

Wala Wala (☎ *285-08-63, Avenida Juárez 94*) Mains US$5-10. Open 8am-10pm daily. Another popular travelers' place, this cheerfully decorated restaurant has inexpensive breakfasts and lunches, and some very good main dishes – try the *pollo con naranja*.

Restaurant La Isla (☎ *285-04-07, cnr Paredes & Mercado*) Mains US$5-8. Open 2pm-9pm Tues-Sun. Fresh seafood is perfectly done at this family-run restaurant, also notable for its almost overdone nautical decor.

La Familia (☎ *285-02-58, Batallón de San Blas 16*) Mains US$6-10. Open 8am-10pm daily. This pleasantly decorated family restaurant asks moderate prices for tasty seafood and Mexican dishes.

There's a good selection of places to eat on the beaches, too, with seafood the specialty (of course), served under shady palapas, right on the sand. They all have the same languid, tropical ambiance, and they all charge about US$1.50 for a nice cold beer.

Caballito del Mar (*Playa El Borrego*) Mains US$5-7. Caballito del Mar (Seahorse) is the first palapa you'll see as you come from town. It does remarkably sophisticated seafood dishes – try the sensational *pescado con queso* or the super fresh oyster cocktails.

Entertainment
El Cocodrilo (*Avenida Juárez 6*) Open 5.30pm-10.30pm daily. This pleasant bar-restaurant on the zócalo attracts gringos in the evening.

Mike's Place (*Avenida Juárez 36*), upstairs over McDonald's restaurant, Mike's is a relaxed lounge with occasional live music.

Aussie Bar (*Avenida Juárez 34*) is an upstairs pool room and bar, frequented by surfers, travelers and local youth.

Getting There & Around
The little bus station is on the corner of Sinaloa and Canalizo, at the northeast

corner of the zócalo. Most buses are Estrella Blanca 2nd-class. For many destinations to the south and east, it may be quicker to go to Tepic first.

Guadalajara – 242km, 5 hours; 7am daily (US$19)

Mazatlán – 290km, 4½ hours; 12.30 pm daily (US$19), or go via Tepic (Don't go to the highway and wait at Crucero San Blas for a Mazatlán bus – it's not a safe place to wait.)

Puerto Vallarta – 175km, 3½ hours; 2 daily (US$11)

Santa Cruz – 16km, 20 minutes; hourly (US$0.60)

Santiago Ixcuintla – 70km, 1 hour; hourly (US$4.50)

Tepic – 62km, 1 hour; frequently (US$4.25)

There are also small buses departing from the corner of Sinaloa and Paredes several times a day, serving all the villages and beaches on Bahía de Matanchén, including Matanchén, Playa Las Islitas, Aticama, Playa Los Cocos, Playa Miramar and Santa Cruz, at the far end of the bay.

Taxis will take you around town and to nearby beaches – a good option with two or more people. Rent bicycles from Wala Wala restaurant for about US$1 per hour.

TEPIC
• pop 261,000 • elev 900m ☎ 311

Tepic is the bustling capital of the small state of Nayarit. It's where highway 15/15D meets the start of highway 200; from here highway 15/15D turns inland toward Guadalajara and Mexico City, while highway 200 runs southwest to the coast. Local time is one hour behind Puerto Vallarta and Guadalajara in the neighboring state of Jalisco.

Many travelers pass through the outskirts of Tepic without stopping off. But it doesn't take long to visit the city, and there are a few things of interest, including a large neo-Gothic cathedral and several museums. Indigenous Huicholes are often seen here, wearing their colorful traditional clothing, and Huichol artwork is sold on the street and in several shops. Tepic's climate is noticeably cooler than on the coast.

Orientation
Plaza Principal, with the large cathedral at the eastern end, is the heart of the city. Avenida México, the city's main street, runs south from the cathedral to Plaza Consti-

tuyentes, past banks, restaurants, the state museum and other places of interest. The bus station is on the southeastern side of the city. Peripheral roads allow traffic to pass through Tepic without entering the city center.

Information
The state tourist office (☎ 216-56-61, 212-08-84, W www.turismonayarit.gob.mx), just off Plaza Principal at the corner of Puebla Nte and Nervo Pte, is open 9am to 8pm daily, with free maps and information on Tepic and the state of Nayarit. The Secretaría de Turismo (☎ 214-80-71), at the Ex-Convento de la Cruz de Zacate at the foot of Avenida México, is open 8am to 8pm Monday to Saturday, 9am to 3pm Sunday.

Banks and casas de cambio line Avenida México Nte between the two plazas.

The post office, on Durango Sur between Allende Pte and Morelos Pte, is open 8am to 5pm Monday to Friday and 8.30am to noon Saturday. Telecomm, with telegram, telex and fax, Avenida México 50 Nte on the corner of Morelos, is open 8am to 7.30pm Monday to Friday, 8am to 4pm Saturday. Post and Telecomm offices, and pay phones, are also found in the bus station.

You can access the Internet at Cafetería La Parroquia, Nervo 18 (see Places to Eat) – it's inexpensive and open long hours. Publicaciones Azteca (☎ 216-08-11, Avenida México 29 Nte) has books in Spanish and a good selection of magazines in English.

Things to See & Do
The large **cathedral** on Plaza Principal was dedicated in 1750; the towers were completed in 1885. Opposite the cathedral is the **palacio municipal** (city hall), where colorfully dressed Huicholes sell handicrafts under the arches at very reasonable prices. On Avenida México, south of the plaza, look inside the Palacio de Gobierno and the Cámara de Diputados to see some impressive and colorful **murals**.

The 18th-century **Templo y Ex-Convento de la Cruz de Zacate** is at the end of Avenida México on the corner of Calzada del Ejército, about 2km south of the cathedral. It was here in 1767 that Father Junípero Serra organized his expedition that established the chain of Spanish missions in the Californias; you can visit the room where he stayed, but there's not

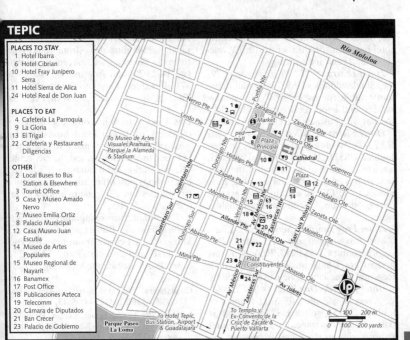

TEPIC

PLACES TO STAY
1 Hotel Ibarra
6 Hotel Cibrian
10 Hotel Fray Junípero
    Serra
11 Hotel Sierra de Alica
24 Hotel Real de Don Juan

PLACES TO EAT
4 Cafetería La Parroquia
9 La Gloria
13 El Trigal
22 Cafetería y Restaurant
    Diligencias

OTHER
2 Local Buses to Bus
   Station & Elsewhere
3 Tourist Office
5 Casa y Museo Amado
   Nervo
7 Museo Emilia Ortiz
8 Palacio Municipal
12 Casa Museo Juan
    Escutia
14 Museo de Artes
    Populares
15 Museo Regional de
    Nayarit
16 Banamex
17 Post Office
18 Publicaciones Azteca
19 Telecomm
20 Cámara de Diputados
21 Ban Crecer
23 Palacio de Gobierno

much else to see. In the southwest section of the city is the large **Parque Paseo de la Loma**.

Museo Regional de Nayarit (☎ 212-19-00, Avenida México 91 Nte; admission US$3.50; open 9am-7pm Mon-Fri, 9am-3pm Sat), displays a variety of exhibits on pre-Hispanic times, ancient tomb artifacts, colonial painting and Huichol culture. The **Casa y Museo Amado Nervo** (☎ 212-29-16, Zacatecas 284 Nte; admission free; open 10am-2pm & 4pm-7pm Mon-Fri, 10am-2pm Sat) celebrates the life of the poet Amado Nervo, who was born in this house in 1870. The **Casa Museo Juan Escutia** (no ☎, Hidalgo 71 Ote; admission free; open 9am-2pm & 4pm-7pm Mon-Fri, 10am-2pm Sat) was the home of Juan Escutia, one of Mexico's illustrious Niños Héroes, who died in 1847 at age 17 defending Mexico City's Castillo de Chapultepec from US forces. Opposite, the **Museo de Artes Populares Casa de los Cuatro Pueblos** (☎ 212-17-05, Hidalgo 60 Ote; admission free; open 9am-2pm & 4pm-7pm Mon-Fri, 9am-2pm Sat & Sun) has contemporary popular arts of the Nayarit's Huichol, Cora, Nahua and Tepehuano peoples, including clothing, yarn art, weaving, musical instruments, ceramics and beadwork.

Aramara (☎ 216-42-46, Allende 329 Pte; admission free; open 9am-2pm & 4pm-7pm Mon-Sat, 10am-3pm Sun) is another museum of visual arts. The **Museo Emilia Ortiz** (☎ 212-26-52, Lerdo 192 Pte; admission free; open 9am-7pm Mon-Sat) honors the painter Emilia Ortiz and her work.

Places to Stay

Trailer Park Los Pinos (☎ 213-12-32, Boulevard Tepic-Xalisco 150) Trailer sites US$11, bungalows US$16. About 5km south of town, this park offers 18 bungalows, all with kitchens, and 27 trailer spaces with full hookups.

The cheapest hotels are near the bus station, but are accessible to the center by local buses.

Hotel Tepic (☎ 213-13-77, fax 214-76-15, Dr Martinez 438 Ote) Singles/doubles with bath US$9/11. This hotel has 85 small, clean rooms; add US$1.75 for TV.

There's a good selection of mid-range and better hotels in the center.

Hotel Cibrian (☎ 212-86-98, *Nervo 163 Pte*) Singles/doubles US$16/19. This central hotel has clean, bright rooms with TV, telephone and enclosed parking.

Hotel Ibarra (☎ 212-38-70, *Durango 297 Nte*) Singles/doubles US$21/23. Smallish but comfortable rooms, cable TV, telephone, parking and good service make this place popular with business travelers on a budget.

Hotel Sierra de Alica (☎ 212-03-24, fax 212-13-09, *Avenida México 180 Nte*) Singles/doubles US$21/26, with air-con US$33/42. Just a block south of the cathedral, the standard rooms at this hotel have ceiling fans, phones, cable TV and exterior windows and are a good value. Air-con rooms are slightly bigger.

Hotel Fray Junípero Serra (☎ 212-25-25, W *www.frayjunipero.com.mx, Lerdo 23 Pte*) Singles/doubles US$48/53. Rooms in this modern hotel have all the facilities you'll need, and some have a view over the plaza.

Hotel Real de Don Juan (☎/fax 216-18-88, *Avenida México 105 Sur*) Singles & doubles US$57, suites US$77. Though it looks old, and has some character, this hotel is thoroughly modern and is possibly the best place to stay in downtown Tepic.

Places to Eat

Cafetería La Parroquia (*Nervo 18*) Snacks US$2-4. Open 8am-9.30pm Mon-Sat, 2pm-9.30pm Sun. On the northern side of the Plaza, upstairs under the arches, this place is very pleasant for breakfasts, drinks and inexpensive light meals, and it does good coffee.

Cafetería y Restaurant Diligencias (☎ 212-15-35, *Avenida México 29 Sur*) Mains around US$3. Open 7am-10pm Mon-Sat, 5pm-10pm Sun. Popular with locals for its comida corrida, Diligencias serves up quality coffee, snacks and full meals all day long.

El Trigal (☎ 216-40-04, *Veracruz 112 Nte*) Mains US$3. Open 8.30am-9pm daily. This inexpensive vegetarian restaurant has tables in an attractive courtyard. Offerings include wholemeal quesadillas, veggie burgers and an excellent *menú del día*.

La Gloria (☎ 217-04-22, *cnr Lerdo & Avenida México*) Mains US$6-10. With live music and tables on a balcony overlooking the plaza, La Gloria is an especially enjoyable place for an evening meal. The menu is a little more adventurous than the average, and includes a selection of fresh seafood.

Getting There & Away

Air Tepic's airport (☎ 214-18-50) is in Pantanal, a 25-minute drive from Tepic, going toward Guadalajara. Aero California (☎ 214-23-20) and Aeroméxico (☎ 213-90-47) offer direct flights to Mexico City and Tijuana, with connections to other centers.

Bus The bus station is on the southeastern outskirts of town; local buses marked 'Central' and 'Centro' make frequent trips between the bus station and the city center. The bus station has a cafeteria, left-luggage office, shops, post office, tourist information, pay phones and a Telecomm office with fax, telegram and telex.

The main bus companies are Elite, Futura, Estrella Blanca and Ómnibus de México (all 1st-class), Transportes del Pacífico (1st- and 2nd-class) and TNS (2nd-class). Buses include the following:

Guadalajara – 216km, 3 hours; frequent 1st-class (US$17.50) and 2nd-class (US$15)

Ixtlán del Río – 88km, 1 hour; take an Ómnibus de México bus toward Guadalajara that is not *por autopista* (US$5)

Mazatlán – 290km, 4½-5 hours; hourly 1st-class (US$14) and 2nd-class (US$12)

Mexico City (Terminal Norte) – 751km, 10-11 hours; hourly 1st-class (US$51) and 2nd-class (US$48)

Puerto Vallarta – 169km, 3½ hours; Elite 1st-class 9pm (US$13), hourly Transportes del Pacífico 2nd-class 3am to 10pm (US$12)

San Blas – 62km, 1¼ hours; hourly TNS 6am to 7pm (US$4)

Santiago Ixcuintla – 70km, 1½ hours; half-hourly TNS 5.30am to 8pm (US$3.75)

Getting Around

Local buses operate from around 6am to 9pm (US$0.30). Combis operate along Avenida México from 6am to midnight (US$0.30). There are also plenty of taxis.

AROUND TEPIC
Laguna Santa María del Oro

Idyllic Laguna Santa María del Oro (elevation 730m), surrounded by steep, forested mountains, is in a volcanic crater 2km around and thought to be over 100m deep. The clear, clean water takes on colors ranging from turquoise to slate. You can take some very pleasant walks around the lake and in the surrounding mountains, seeing numerous birds (some 250 species) and butterflies along the way. You can also climb to an abandoned gold mine, cycle, swim, row on the lake, kayak, or fish for black bass and perch. A few small restaurants serve fresh lake fish.

Koala Bungalows & RV Park (☎ 327-214-05-09, e *koala45@latinmail.com*) Tent sites US$3 per person, trailer sites with hookup US$9, bungalows from US$40. This attractive, peaceful park has a restaurant, campsites and well-maintained bungalows in several sizes (with cheaper monthly rates). It's owned and operated by a friendly Englishman, who's an excellent source of information about the lake.

To get there, take the Santa María del Oro turnoff about 40km from Tepic along the Guadalajara road; from the turnoff it's about 10km to Santa María del Oro, then another 8km from the village to the lake. Buses to the lake depart from in front of the bus station in Tepic at 10.30am, 2pm and 8pm (1½ hours, US$2.50). Alternatively, buses to the village of Santa María del Oro depart from the bus station in Tepic every half-hour; from there you can take another bus (or a taxi) to the lake.

Volcán Ceboruco

This extinct volcano, with a number of old craters, interesting plants and volcanic forms, has several short, interesting walks at the top. The 15km cobblestone road up the volcano passes lava fields and fumaroles (steam vents), with plenty of vegetation growing on the slopes. The road begins at the village of Jala, 7km off the highway from Tepic to Guadalajara; the turnoff is 76km from Tepic, 12km before you reach Ixtlán del Río.

Ixtlán del Río

The small town of Ixtlán del Río, one hour (88km) from Tepic on the road to Guadalajara, is unremarkable in itself, but Carlos Castaneda fans will remember that this is where Don Juan took Carlos in the book *Journey to Ixtlán*. Outside Ixtlán, **Los Toriles** archaeological site has an impressive round stone temple, the Templo a Quetzalcóatl, open 9am-5pm daily. Buses that take highway 15 between Tepic and Guadalajara will drop you at Ixtlán, but

those that go *por autopisa* (highway 15D) will fly straight past.

Mirador del Águila

This lookout on highway 15, about 11km north of Tepic, offers a wide view over a lush jungle canyon; bird-watching is best in the early morning and late afternoon.

CHACALA

The tiny coastal fishing village of Chacala is about 30km north of Rincón de Guayabitos and about 10km west of Las Varas, the turnoff on highway 200. Chacala occupies an amazingly beautiful little cove, with a lovely 1km beach bordered by lush green slopes. Camping and some very basic accommodations are available on and near the palm-fringed beach. Ask at one of the palapa seafood restaurants – there are about 15 of them on the beach.

On the beach at the southern end of the cove, you'll find *Mar de Jade* (☎ 327-294-11-63, w *www.mardejade.com, Playa Chacala s/n)*, an ecological resort and retreat center. Accommodations range from dorm beds (US$60), to single/double rooms (US$100/150), suites (US$120/170) and spacious apartments (from US$330). These rates include three healthy buffet-style meals per day and various exercise and activity programs. Discounts are available off-season, for three-week programs, and for doing several hours of volunteer work a day. Activities include yoga, spa and arts retreats, medical conferences, immersion Spanish courses and a teenage summer camp. See the Web site for details.

For Chacala, get off a Puerto Vallarta-Tepic bus at Las Varas and take a taxi from there (15 minutes, US$4.50).

RINCÓN DE GUAYABITOS
• pop 3000 ☎ 327

On the coast about 60km north of Puerto Vallarta, Rincón de Guayabitos ('Guayabitos' for short) is a tailor-made beach resort town that caters to Mexican holiday makers and winter visitors from Canada and other cold places; it's extremely busy during the Mexican vacation times of Semana Santa, Christmas and the July and August school holidays. If you come at these times, reserve rooms in advance and be prepared for crowds and higher hotel prices. At other times, you can have the beautiful beach practically all to yourself, and relax, relax, relax. More energetic activities include swimming, fishing, horseback riding, and hiking up to the cross on the hill for the fine view. You can also take a boat out to Isla Islote, where you can rent snorkelling gear and eat in the restaurant. Boats do whale-watching trips November to March.

Orientation & Information

Rincón de Guayabitos is on the beach, just west of highway 200. At the northern entrance to town, a high water tower is a distinctive landmark; turn into town here, follow the curve around, and you'll be on Guayabitos' main street, Avenida Sol Nuevo, lined with shops, restaurants and hotels. More restaurants and hotels are along the beach, two blocks over – they're reached by side streets as there's no road along the waterfront.

Near the water tower, the Delegación de Turismo (☎/fax 274-06-93) provides information on the local area and the state of Nayarit. It's open 9am to 2pm and 4pm to 6pm Monday to Saturday, 9am to 2pm Sunday.

Guayabitos has basic services including shops and a post office. For more extensive shopping and an Internet café, locals go to La Peñita de Jaltemba, a larger and less touristy town a couple of kilometers north on highway 200.

Places to Stay & Eat

Guayabitos has plenty of places to stay. Many of them are mid-range places pitched at families, offering bungalows with kitchen facilities and accommodation for two, four or more people.

Bungalows San Miguel (☎ 274-01-33, *Retorno Laureles s/n*) Low-season/high-season singles & doubles US$27/43, 4-person/8-person bungalows US$32/54 in low season, US$51/86 in high season. Only half a block from the beach, San Miguel has a small swimming pool and a good choice of comfortable accommodation.

Posada Jaltemba (☎ 274-01-65, *cnr Avenida Sol Nuevo & Retorno Laureles*) Singles & doubles US$30-65, bungalows US$38-85. Also half a block from the beach, Jaltemba has a variety of accommodations to choose from.

Villas Buena Vida (☎ 274-02-31, W *www.villasbuenavida.com, Retorno Laureles s/n*) Low-season/high-season villas US$66/88, suites US$112-146. This luxurious beachfront hotel is a great place to splash out, with its beachfront swimming pool and balconies overlooking the ocean. Villas sleep one to four people; suites sleep five to six people.

Many eateries along Avenida del Sol Nuevo serve ice cream, coffee, pizza and barbecued chicken.

Beto's (☎ 274-05-75, *Avenida del Sol Nuevo s/n*) Mains US$8-12. In a block with several other restaurants, Beto's stands out for its fine seafood.

Rincón Mexicano (☎ 274-06-63, *cnr Cedro & Retorno Laureles*) Mains US$7-12. Open 8am-9pm Thur-Tues. Attached to the beachfront Hotel Estancia San Carlos, this restaurant has a lunch and dinner menu with BBQ ribs, interesting beef dishes and imaginative dishes such as shrimp in mango and red-wine sauce.

Getting There & Away

Second-class buses coming from Puerto Vallarta (1½ hours, US$6) or Tepic (2 hours, US$7) may drop you on the highway at Rincón de Guayabitos, but sometimes they don't stop here. A couple of kilometers toward Tepic, La Peñita is a sure stop. Colectivo vans operate frequently between La Peñita and Guayabitos (10 minutes, US$0.50), or you can take a taxi (US$3).

AROUND RINCÓN DE GUAYABITOS

Other pleasant little beach towns south of Rincón de Guayabitos make good day trips from either Guayabitos or Puerto Vallarta; they all have places to stay and eat, if you want to stay over. Check places like **Playa Los Ayala**, about 2km south of Guayabitos, **Lo del Marco**, 13km south, and **San Francisco**, 22km south.

SAYULITA
● pop 1000 ☎ 322

Tiny Sayulita is a low-key fishing village on a beautiful sandy beach, shaded by a backdrop of coconut trees. Many surfers and beachgoers come here from Puerto Vallarta, an hour away by bus, and some like it enough to stay. You can rent surfboards on the beach and arrange bicycles, boat trips, horseback riding, trekking and kayaking from operators in the main street.

Sayulita Trailer Park & Bungalows (☎ 275-02-02, e *sayupark@prodigy.net.mx, Miramar s/n*) Tent & trailer sites with hookup US$13, 2-bed garden bungalows US$28-54. Coconut palms shade the well-tended lawn at this attractive beachfront park. Prices are lower for longer stays.

Diamante International Hotel *(no ☎, Miramar 40)* Singles & doubles US$11, in high season US$22. A short walk from the beach, and a little farther to town, this hotel offers basic standards, but it's cheap.

Bungalows Las Gaviotas (☎ 275-02-26, *Gaviotas 12)* Singles/doubles US$19/24, bungalows with kitchen June-Oct US$35, Nov-May US$48. This friendly place is half a block from the plaza and half a block from the beach.

Several cheap and cheerful *cafés* are near the plaza, but the most pleasant places are the *palapas* on the beach, where a seafood meal and a beer will cost about US$7.

Don Pedro's (☎ 275-02-29, *Marlin 02)* Mains US$8-12. Open 11am-11pm. This up-market version of the beachfront palapa offers fine seafood with Greek and Italian influences.

To reach Sayulita, turn off highway 200 about 35km north of Puerto Vallarta and 25km south of Rincón de Guayabitos. Sayulita is 3km from the turnoff. Ten buses per day operate between Sayulita and the Puerto Vallarta bus terminal (1 hour, US$2); otherwise, any 2nd-class bus will drop you at the turnoff. (Note the time difference between Sayulita, which is in Nayarit state, and Puerto Vallarta, one hour ahead, in Jalisco.)

PUERTO VALLARTA
• pop 132,000 ☎ 322

Puerto Vallarta stretches around the sparkling blue Bahía de Banderas (Bay of Flags), backed by green, palm-covered mountains. It's in Jalisco state, one hour ahead of neighboring Nayarit.

Formerly a quaint seaside village, Puerto Vallarta (or PV) has been transformed into a world-famous resort city hosting millions of visitors every year, nearly half of them from other countries. Some of the most beautiful beaches, secluded and romantic just a few years ago, are now dominated by giant luxury mega-resorts. Tourism – Vallarta's only industry – has made it a bilingual city, with English almost as commonly spoken as Spanish. But the cobblestone streets, old-fashioned white adobe buildings and red-tile roofs still make Vallarta one of Mexico's most picturesque coastal cities. If the pretty town and white-sand beaches aren't enough, you can venture out on cruises, horseback rides, dive trips and day tours, explore shops and art galleries; and enjoy numerous restaurants and a vibrant nightlife.

History

Indigenous peoples probably lived in this area, and elsewhere along the coast, for centuries before European settlement. In 1851, the Sánchez family came and made their home by the mouth of the Río Cuale. Farmers and fisherfolk followed, and farmers began shipping their harvests from a small port north of the Río Cuale. In 1918 the settlement was named 'Vallarta,' in honor of Ignacio Luis Vallarta, a former governor of the state of Jalisco.

Tourists began to visit Vallarta in 1954 when Mexicana airlines started a promotional campaign and initiated the first flights here, landing on a dirt airstrip in Emiliano Zapata, an area that is now the center of Vallarta. A decade later, John Huston chose the nearby deserted cove of Mismaloya as a location for the film of Tennessee Williams' *The Night of the Iguana*. Hollywood paparazzi descended on the town to report on the tempestuous romance between Richard Burton and Elizabeth Taylor. Burton's co-star Ava Gardner also raised more than a few eyebrows. Puerto Vallarta suddenly became world-famous, with an aura of steamy tropical romance. Tour groups began arriving not long after the film crew left, and they've been coming ever since.

Orientation

The 'old' town center, called El Centro, is the area north and south of Río Cuale, with the small Isla Cuale in the middle of the river. Two road bridges and a pedestrian bridge allow easy passage between the two sides of town. Many fine houses, quite a few owned by foreigners, are found farther up the Río Cuale valley, also known as Gringo Gulch.

Bahía de Banderas

Bahía de Banderas (Bay of Flags) was supposedly formed by an extinct volcano slowly sinking into the ocean. It now has a depth of some 1800m and is home to an impressive variety of marine life – almost every large marine animal is found here, except for sharks. Apparently dolphins mount an anti-shark patrol at the entrance to the bay, to protect the young dolphins that are born here all year round.

The bay is something of a mating center and marine nursery for several species. For example, giant manta rays mate here in April. During that month they jump above the water's surface, flashing their 4m wingspan in acrobatic displays that you can sometimes see from boats or even from the shore.

Humpbacks are the bay's most numerous and oft-sighted whales – they hang out here from around November to the end of March to mate, and to bear the calves that were conceived the year before. Bride whales are much less numerous, but unlike humpbacks they are not a migratory whale – they remain in tropical waters all year round, so there's a chance of seeing one at any time of year. Even gray whales, which migrate between Alaska and Baja California every year, are very occasionally seen this far south.

North of the city are a strip of giant luxury hotels called the Zona Hotelera; Marina Vallarta, a large yachting marina (9km from the center); the airport (10km); the bus station (12km); and Nuevo Vallarta, a new resort area of hotel and condominium development (25km). To the south of the city are a few more large resorts and some of the most beautiful beaches in the area.

The heart of El Centro is **Plaza Principal**, also called Plaza de Armas, beside the sea between Morelos and Juárez, the city's two principal thoroughfares. On the sea side of the plaza is an amphitheater backed by **Los Arcos**, a row of arches that have become a symbol of the city. The Malecón, a wide seaside walkway, stretches about 10 blocks north from the amphitheater, dotted with bars, restaurants, nightclubs and boutiques. Uphill from the plaza, the crown-topped steeple of the **Templo de Guadalupe** is another PV icon.

South of the river, the **Zona Romántica** is another tourist district with smaller hotels, restaurants and bars. It has the only two beaches in the city center: **Playa Olas Altas** (which doesn't actually have 'high waves,' despite the name) and **Playa de los Muertos** (Beach of the Dead), which takes its strange name from a fierce fight there sometime in the distant past.

City traffic has been reduced dramatically by the opening of a bypass road *(libramiento)* on the inland side of the city center, diverting traffic away from the center.

Information

Tourist Offices Vallarta's municipal tourist office (☎ 223-25-00 ext 230/231/232), in the municipal building on the northeast corner of Plaza Principal, has free maps, multilingual tourist literature and friendly bilingual staff; it's open 8am to 4pm Monday to Friday. A good Web site is ⓦ www.puertovallarta.net, sponsored by the visitors bureau and tourist board.

Club Paco Paco (☎ 222-18-99, ⓔ info@pacopaco.com, ⓦ www.pacopaco.com), Vallarta 278, acts as an informal center for Vallarta's gay community (see Entertainment); open noon to 6am daily. Pick up its free *Paco Paco Tourist Info & Map*, with information on gay hotels, cruises, tours and entertainment. Another useful resource is ⓦ www.gaypuertovallarta.info.

Money Most businesses in Vallarta accept US dollars as readily as they accept pesos, though the rate of exchange they give is usually less favorable than at banks. Several banks are found around Plaza Principal, but they sometimes have long queues. Banamex, on the southern side of the plaza, is open 9am to 5pm Monday to Friday, 9am to 2pm Saturday. Most banks have ATMs.

Vallarta has many casas de cambio; it may pay to shop around, since rates differ.

PUERTO VALLARTA

PLACES TO STAY
2 KOA
6 Westin Regina Resort;
   Garibaldi's
9 Tacho's Trailer Park
10 Hotel Krystal Vallarta;
   Bogart's; Christine
11 Fiesta Americana
14 Sheraton Buganvilas
15 Camino Real
16 Presidente
   Inter-Continental
18 La Jolla de Mismaloya

PLACES TO EAT
19 Le Kliff
20 Chino's Paraíso
21 Chico's Paradise
22 El Edén

OTHER
1 Los Flamingos Golf Club
3 Splash Parque Acuático
4 Bus Station
5 Marriot Hotel Tennis
   Courts
7 Marina Vallarta
   Country Club
8 Plaza de Toros
12 Tennis Club at
   Continental Plaza Hotel
13 Mario's Moto Rent
17 Bungee Jump; Raptor
   Tours

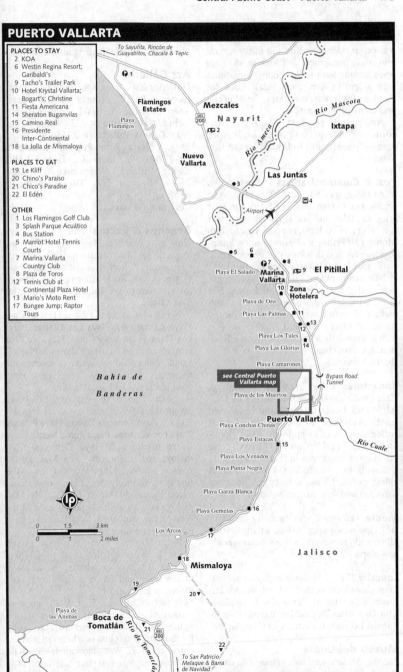

To Sayulita, Rincón de
Guayabitos, Chacala & Tepic

Flamingos
Estates

Playa
Flamingos

Mezcales

Nayarit

Nuevo
Vallarta

Río Ameca

Río Mascota

Ixtapa

Las Juntas

Airport

Playa El Salado

Marina
Vallarta

El Pitillal

Zona
Hotelera

Playa de Oro

Playa Las Palmas

Playa Los Tules

Playa Las Glorias

Playa Camarones

see Central Puerto
Vallarta map

Playa de los Muertos

Bahía de
Banderas

Bypass Road
Tunnel

Puerto Vallarta

Playa Conchas Chinas

Playa Estacas

Playa Los Venados

Playa Punta Negra

Playa Garza Blanca

Playa Gemelas

Los Arcos

Río Cuale

Jalisco

0   1.5   3 km
0   1   2 miles

Playa de
las Ánimas

Boca de
Tomatlán

Mismaloya

Río de Tomatlán

To San Patricio-
Melaque & Barra
de Navidad

CENTRAL PACIFIC COAST

Though their rates are less favorable than the banks', the difference may be slight, and the longer opening hours and faster service may make using them worthwhile. Most are open around 9am to 7pm daily, sometimes with a 2pm to 4pm lunch break. Look for them on Insurgentes, Vallarta, the Malecón and many other streets.

American Express (☎ 223-29-55), at the corner of Morelos and Abasolo, is open 9am to 5pm Monday to Friday, 9am to 1pm Saturday.

Post & Communications The post office, Mina 188, is open 8am to 4.30pm Monday to Friday, 9am to 1pm Saturday. Telecomm, with telegram, telex and fax, at Hidalgo 582 near the corner of Aldama, is open 8am to 7pm Monday to Friday and 9am to noon Saturday, Sunday and holidays. Pay phones (card only) are plentiful everywhere in town.

Numerous places offer Internet access, especially in the Zona Romántica. Net House, Vallarta 232, is open 7am to midnight. Cafe.com Internet Café & Bar, at the corner of Olas Altas and Badillo, is open 8am to 1am daily. Virtual Reality, on F Rodríguez, offers cheap phone calls as well as Internet access.

Bookstores A Page in the Sun Bookshop-Café (☎ 222-36-08), on the corner of Olas Altas and Diéguez, buys and sells used English-language books, and serves great coffee; open 8am to midnight daily. Book-Store (☎ 223-11-77), Corona 172, has a good selection of magazines in English, and quite a few books (including Lonely Planet guides); open 9.30am to 8.30pm Monday to Saturday and 4pm to 8pm Sunday.

Media *Vallarta Today*, a daily English-language newspaper, is free at the tourist office and elsewhere, as is a similar weekly newspaper, *PV Tribune*.

Laundry There are many laundries around town. Those south of the Río Cuale include Lavandería Quinter, Madero 407A; Lavandería Elsa, Olas Altas 385; and Lavandería Púlpito, Púlpito 141 near the corner of Olas Altas.

Museo del Cuale

The tiny Museo del Cuale *(Paseo Isla Cuale s/n; admission free; open 10am-2pm & 4pm-*

7pm Tues-Sat), near the western end of Isla Cuale, has a small collection of ancient objects, as well as changing art exhibitions.

Art Galleries

Galleries have been sprouting like mushrooms in Puerto Vallarta for many years. Some of the better-known galleries include **Galería Uno** *(☎ 222-09-08, Morelos 561),* **Galería Vallarta** *(☎ 222-02-90, Juárez 263),* **Galería Arte Popular Mexicana** *(☎ 222-69-60, Libertad 285)* and Judith Ewing Morlan Contemporary Art *(☎ 223-21-79, Miramar 237).* There are plenty more in El Centro – look on Juárez and Corona for a start.

Beaches & Excursions

Only two beaches, Playa Olas Altas and Playa de los Muertos, are handy to the city center; they're both south of the Río Cuale. Gay guys go to the southern end of Playa de los Muertos, to the stretch of beach called **Blue Chairs**.

North of town, in the Zona Hotelera, are **Playa Camarones**, **Playa Las Glorias**, **Playa Los Tules**, **Playa Las Palmas**, **Playa de Oro**. Farther north, at Marina Vallarta, is **Playa El Salado**. Nuevo Vallarta also has beaches and there are others, less developed, right around the bay to Punta de Mita.

South of town, accessible by minibuses plying the superbly scenic coastal highway 200, are **Playa Conchas Chinas**, **Playa Estacas**, **Playa Los Venados**, **Playa Punta Negra**, **Playa Garza Blanca** and **Playa Gemelas**. **Mismaloya**, the location for *The Night of the Iguana*, is about 12km south of town. The tiny cove, formerly deserted, is now dominated by the 303-room La Jolla de Mismaloya hotel, and the buildings used in the film, on the southern side of the cove, have now been transformed into restaurants.

From Mismaloya you can head inland along a riverside dirt road to Chino's Paraíso, 2km upriver, where you can swim in the river and enjoy a full lunch (see Places to Eat, later in this section). About 5km farther upriver, El Edén is another restaurant and swimming place, promoted as the set of the movie *Predator*, accounting for the burned-out hull of a helicopter at the entrance. Here you also can take jungle walks and explore two waterfalls just a little upriver. To get to these places you can drive, or take a bus to Mismaloya and taxi from there. The walk back is downhill all the way and makes a pleasant stroll.

Farther southwest along the coast, about 4km past Mismaloya, **Boca de Tomatlán** is a peaceful, less commercialized seaside village in a small cove where the Río de Tomatlán meets the sea – a jungly place with quiet water, a beach and several small restaurants. The road swings inland here, and you can follow it up to Chico's Paradise, another place offering good meals, cool drinks and swimming in a refreshing river.

Farther around the southern side of the bay are the more isolated beaches of Las Ánimas, Quimixto and Yelapa, accessible only by boat. **Playa de las Ánimas** (Beach of the Spirits), a lovely beach with a small fishing village and some *palapa* restaurants offering fresh seafood, is said to be the most beautiful beach on the bay. **Quimixto**, not far from Las Ánimas, has a waterfall accessible by a half-hour hike, or you can hire a pony on the beach to take you up.

Yelapa, farthest from town, is probably Vallarta's most popular cruise destination. This picturesque cove is crowded with tourists, restaurants and parasailing operators during the day, but empties out when the tourist boats leave in late afternoon. The charming village at Yelapa has a sizable colony of foreign residents; you can easily find a place to stay if you ask around. Take a hike upriver to see the waterfalls.

Come aboard the Chrysler of cruises.

Water Sports

Snorkeling, scuba diving, deep-sea fishing, water-skiing, windsurfing, sailing, parasailing, riding the 'banana' and just plain swimming are all popular in Vallarta. Most activities can be arranged on the beaches in front of any of the large hotels. The tourist offices can help connect you with operators.

The most spectacular spots for diving and snorkeling are **Los Arcos**, the rocky islands in the bay just south of town (now a protected ecological zone), and **Islas Marietas** at the entrance to the bay, which are surrounded by impressive reefs, underwater caves, tunnels and walls. Dolphins, whales and giant manta rays are often sighted between December and April.

Vallarta has several diving and snorkeling operators. **Chico's Dive Shop** (☎ 222-18-95, ⓦ www.chicos-diveshop.com, Paseo Díaz Ordaz 772; open 8am-10pm daily; 2-dive trips US$83-113; PADI open-water diver certification course US$316), on the Malecón, is the biggest outfit, offering several good diving and snorkeling trips. The cost of a two-tank diving trip varies, depending on where you go. The PADI open-water course takes three days; advanced courses are also available.

Deep-sea fishing is popular all year, with a major international sailfish tournament held every November. Prime catches are sailfish, marlin, tuna, red snapper and sea bass. The tourist office can recommend fishing operators for the type of trip you have in mind.

See the Getting Around section for information on hiring private yachts and lanchas for snorkeling and fishing trips.

Kids will enjoy **Splash Parque Acuático** (☎ 297-07-08, Carratera Tepic Km 155; entry US$9; open 10am-7pm daily), which has 12 water slides, a lazy river swimming pool and a daily dolphin show.

Dolphin- & Whale-Watching

Always wanted to swim with dolphins? You can do it in Vallarta at the dolphin center operated by Vallarta Adventure (see Organized Tours, later in this section) for US$141. Dolphins are present in the bay all year round; you're likely to see some if you go out on a boat. Whale-watching trips operate from December to March, when humpback whales are in the bay mating,

CENTRAL PACIFIC COAST

CENTRAL PUERTO VALLARTA

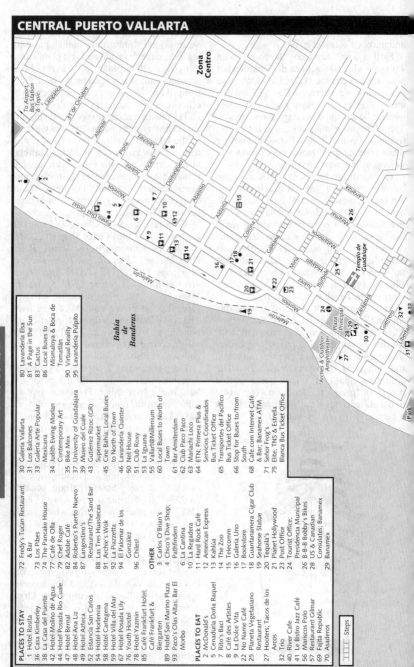

PLACES TO STAY
1 Hotel Rosita
36 Casa Kimberley
38 La Casa del Puente
44 Hotel Molino de Agua
47 Hotel Posada Río Cuale
47 Hotel Bernal
48 Hotel Ana Liz
49 Hotel Azteca
52 Estancia San Carlos
54 Hotel Hortencia
58 Hotel Cartegena
59 Hotel Villa del Mar
67 Hotel Posada Lily
76 Youth Hostel
78 Hotel Yazmin
85 Café Frankfurt Hotel;
   Café Frankfurt &
   Biergarten
89 Hotel San Marino Plaza
93 Paco's Olas Altas; Bar El
   Morbo

PLACES TO EAT
2 McDonald's
5 Cenaduría Doña Raquel
7 Rito's Baci
8 Café des Artistes
9 La Dolce Vita
22 No Name Café
25 Planeta Vegetariano
   Restaurant
27 Hooters; Tacos de los
   Arcos
32 Trio
40 River Cafe
41 Le Bistro Jazz Café
56 Mariscos Polo
57 Restaurant Gilmar
69 Fajita Republic
70 Asaderos

72 Fredy's Tucan Restaurant
   & Bar
73 Los Pibes
74 The Pancake House
77 Café de Olla
79 Chef Roger
82 Adobe Café
84 Roberto's Puerto Nuevo
87 Langostino's
   Restaurant/The Sand Bar
88 Las Tres Huastecas
91 Archie's Wok
92 La Piazzetta
94 El Palomar de los
   González
96 Chiles!

OTHER
3 Carlos O'Brian's
4 Chico's Dive Shop;
   Pathfinders
6 La Cantina
10 La Regadera
11 Hard Rock Café
12 American Express
13 Kahlúa
14 The Zoo
15 Telecomm
16 Galería Uno
17 Bookstore
18 Guantanamera Cigar Club
19 Seahorse Statue
20 Tequila's
21 Planet Hollywood
23 Post Office
24 Tourist Office;
   Presidencia Municipal
26 B-B-B Bobby's Bikes
28 US & Canadian
   Consulates; Banamex
29 Banamex

30 Galería Vallarta
31 Los Balcones
33 Galería Arte Popular
   Mexicana
34 Judith Ewing Morían
   Contemporary Art
35 Bike Mex
37 University of Guadalajara
39 Museo del Cuale
43 Gutiérrez Rizoc (GR)
   Supermarket
45 Cine Bahía; Local Buses
   to North of Town
46 Lavandería Quinter
50 Net House
51 Club Roxy
53 La Iguana
55 Vallart@Millenium
60 Local Buses to North of
   Town
61 Bar Amsterdam
62 Club Paco Paco
63 Mariachi Loco
64 ETN; Primera Plus &
   Servicios Coordinados
   Bus Ticket Office
65 Transportes del Pacífico
   Bus Ticket Office
66 Stop for Buses to/from
   South
68 Cafe.com Internet Café
   & Bar; Banamex ATM
71 Señor Frog's
75 Elite; TNS & Estrella
   Blanca Bus Ticket Office

80 Lavandería Elsa
81 A Page in the Sun
83 Cactus
86 Local Buses to
   Mismaloya & Boca de
   Tomatlán
90 Virtual Reality
95 Lavandería Púlpito

IIII Steps

CENTRAL PUERTO VALLARTA

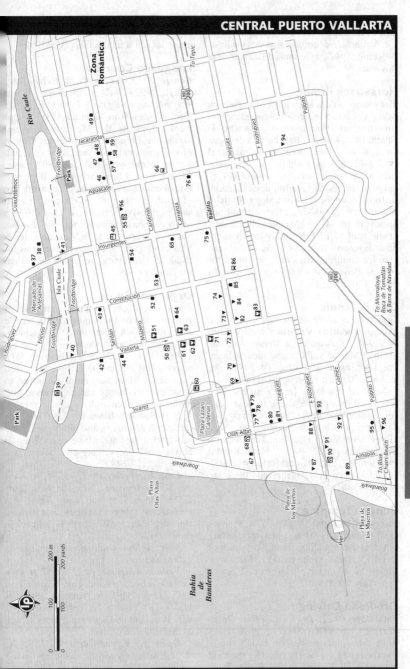

bearing young and caring for new calves. Open Air Expeditions is a popular operator; Vallarta Adventure also does whale-watching trips (see Organized Tours, later in this section).

Horseback Riding

The tourist offices keep a list of horseback riding operators. Some established operators, not far from town, are **Rancho El Charro** (☎ 224-01-14), **Rancho Ojo de Agua** (☎ 224-06-07) and **Rancho Palma Real** (☎ 221-12-36) – they will provide transport from your hotel. Costs are around US$11 per hour, or US$85 for a full-day excursion, including lunch. At Mismaloya, **Rancho Manolo** (☎ 228-00-18) offers three-hour horseback trips from Mismaloya beach up a jungle trail to El Edén, plus longer nine-hour mountain trips. For a short ride, suitable for children, there may be horses for rent on Playa Olas Altas, near the western end of Carranza.

Golf & Tennis

Golf courses north of the city include the exclusive **Marina Vallarta Country Club** (☎ 221-01-71, Paseo de la Marina s/n), just north of Marina Vallarta, and the less fancy **Los Flamingos Golf Club** (☎ 298-06-06, highway 200 s/n), 13km north of town.

Most of the large luxury hotels have tennis courts; phone them to reserve a court. **John Newcombe Tennis Club** (☎ 224-43-60 ext 500) is at the Continental Plaza Hotel in the Zona Hotelera. The **Sheraton Buganvilias** (☎ 223-04-04), **Hotel Krystal** (☎ 224-02-02) and **Marriott Hotel** (☎ 221-00-04) all have courts available, and there are plenty of others.

Bungee Jumping

The **bungee jump** (☎ 228-0670, W www .vallarta-action.com) is a platform jutting out over the sea cliffs, about 9km south of Puerto Vallarta on the road to Mismaloya. Make the 40-meter plunge from 10am to 6pm daily (US$55).

Off-Road Driving

Pathfinders (☎ 222-18-75, Paseo Díaz Ordaz 772), at Chico's Dive Shop, arranges three-hour dune buggy trips on rough roads, riverbeds and the nearby hills, 'for the road warrior in all of us' (US$125). **Raptor Tours**

(☎ 228-0670, W www.vallarta-action.com) based at the bungee jump, does seven-hour excursions in similar terrain (US$196).

Language Courses

Centro de Estudios Para Extranjeros (CEPE, ☎ 223-20-82, e cipv@cepe.edu.mx W www.cepe.udg.mx, Libertad 105-1, Tuition fees from around US$100 per week. Opposite the Mercado de Artesanías, the Foreign Student Study Center of the University of Guadalajara specializes in teaching Spanish and can arrange lodging with a Mexican family. Beginner intermediate and advanced courses are offered year-round, plus intensive and super-intensive sessions. It also offers a one-week 'basic skills for tourists' session. Summer courses include Mexican culture, Mexican history, and language sessions for children. University credit can be earned for most courses.

Organized Tours

The tourist offices and travel agents can set you up with city tours, jungle tours, bicycle tours, horseback riding tours and archaeological tours, among others.

Bike Mex (☎ 223-16-80, Guerrero 361), offers hiking and mountain bike tours with experienced bilingual guides, tailored to your level of fitness and experience, plus mountain bike rentals for self-guided tours.

B-B-Bobby's Bikes (☎ 223-00-08, cnr Iturbide & Miramar), also offers guided and self-guided mountain bike tours. Rentals cost around US$6/28 per hour/day; guided tours start at US$45.

Casa Kimberley (☎ 222-13-36, W www .casakimberley.com, Zaragoza 445) Tours US$8. Open 9am-6pm daily. There are guided daily tours of the house that Richard Burton bought for Elizabeth Taylor back in the 1960s.

Several tour companies specialize in nature and outdoor tours.

Vallarta Adventure (☎ 221-06-57, W www .vallarta-adventures.com, Calle Mastil Local 13C, Marina Vallarta) Tours & activities US$60-130. Vallarta Adventure operates a variety of land and sea nature tours, as well as their dolphin center.

Open Air Expeditions (☎ 222-33-10, e openair@vivamexico.com, W www .vallartawhales.com, Guerrero 339) Open

Timeshares

If you can endure a 90-minute sales pitch for a timeshare condominium, and do a tour of the project, you can be rewarded (or compensated) with a free or discounted dinner, tour, horseback ride, jeep rental or boat cruise. Touts in tour company offices and in Puerto Vallarta's most touristy areas are eager to offer you freebies, if you'll only attend the presentation. The touts won't tell you any details about the timeshare deal – their job is just to get you to the hard-sell session.

Generally you must be over 25 years old, a US or Canadian resident, and have a major credit card and a job. Some deals require that you be married, and that both husband and wife attend the presentation. The promoter will pay the taxi fare from your hotel to the project. You are under no obligation to buy or sign anything – pressure, yes, obligation, no.

People have mixed reactions to a timeshare presentation. Some say it's a relatively painless way to get a cheap jeep, a good meal, a tour or a cruise. Others are still angry days later, after fending off the 'hard sell.' A few are still paying for it years later, after failing to fend off the 'hard sell.'

Air offers whale-watching, sea kayaking, snorkeling, bird-watching, hiking and customized tours.

A host of daytime, sunset and evening cruises are available in Vallarta, some emphasizing beach visits and snorkeling stops, some in sail boats, and others that are accurately described as 'booze cruises.' The most popular are probably the cruises to Yelapa and Las Ánimas beaches (around US$25 to US$40); other cruises go to the Islas Marietas, farther out. The tourist office or any travel agency can tell you which cruises are operating, details of where they go, what they offer (many include meals, open bar, live music and dancing) and what they cost.

For something different, try the **Marigalante** (☎ 223-08-75, **w** *www.marigalante .com.mx*), a reproduction Spanish galleon that does daytime cruises (9am to 5pm, US$49) and an evening cruise (6pm to 11pm, US$65) that culminates in a mock pirate attack on the Malecón. The **Rainbow Dancer** (☎ 223-19-33) does a gay cruise, with lots of food, drink and Donna Summer music.

If you just want to visit the beaches, a cheaper way to get there is by water taxi (see Getting Around).

Special Events

Semana Santa (Easter week) is the busiest holiday of the year in Puerto Vallarta. Hotels fill up and hundreds (or thousands) of excess visitors camp out on the beaches and party. It's a wild time.

Fiestas de Mayo, a citywide fair with cultural and sporting events, music concerts, carnival rides and art exhibits, is held throughout May.

A big, international torneo de pesca is held each year in mid-November; dates vary according to the phase of the moon, which must be right for fishing.

Día de Santa Cecilia (November 22) honors the patron saint of mariachis, with all the city's mariachis forming a musical procession to the Templo de Guadalupe in the early evening. They come playing and singing, enter the church and sing homage to their saint, then go out into the plaza and continue to play. During the entire day one or another group of mariachis stays in the church making music.

All Mexico celebrates December 12 as the day of honor for the country's religious patron, the Virgen de Guadalupe. In Puerto Vallarta the celebrations are more drawn out, with pilgrimages and processions to the cathedral both day and night from November 30 until the big bash on December 12.

Places to Stay

Vallarta has a good selection of accommodations in every price range. Most hotel prices are higher during Vallarta's high season, roughly from December to April. For accommodations at the very busiest times – Semana Santa or between Christmas and New Year's – be sure to reserve in advance.

Places to Stay

Budget Camping is possible at a couple of trailer parks, but they're a ways north of town.

Tacho's Trailer Park (☎ 224-21-63, *Camino Nuevo al Pitillal s/n)* Tent & trailer sites US$16. Opposite Colonia Aramara, this place has a swimming pool and 125 tent/trailer spaces with full hookups.

KOA (☎ 298-08-53, *highway 200 at Km 149)* Tent/trailer sites US$13/20, cabins US$27. About 10km north of town, the KOA has tent sites, trailer spaces with full hookups and 'kamping kabins.'

Vallarta's cheapest lodgings are south of the Río Cuale, particularly along Madero. All rooms are basic but clean, with fan and private bath.

Youth Hostel (☎ 222-21-08, *Aguacate 302A)* Dorm beds US$8. This clean and pleasant hostel offers even cheaper rates for longer stays. It's closed from noon to 6pm daily.

Hotel Villa del Mar (☎ 222-07-85, *Madero 440)* Singles US$16-19, doubles $19-27. This hotel has tasteful, clean, good-sized rooms; the pricier ones feature private balconies with chairs and flowering plants. Rooftop sitting areas offer a view over town.

Hotel Azteca (☎ 222-27-50, *Madero 473)* Singles/doubles US$16/21, rooms with kitchenette & cable TV US$30. Though it's a few blocks east of the action, this clean, pleasant place still offers good value.

Hotel Bernal (☎ 222-36-05, *Madero 423)* Singles/doubles US$15/18. A longtime budget travelers' standby, the Bernal has basic, cleanish, fan-cooled rooms around a courtyard.

Hotel Cartagena (☎ 222-69-14, *Madero 428)* and *Hotel Ana Liz* (☎ 222-17-57, *Madero 429)* are other acceptable, inexpensive choices.

Mid-Range The following places are a considerable step up in price, comfort and ambience.

Hotel Hortencia (☎ 222-24-84, *Madero 336)* Singles/doubles US$27/33. A little better than most budget hotels on Madero, but considerably more expensive, the Hortencia offers telephone, refrigerator and air-con for an extra US$2 to $5.

Café Frankfurt Hotel (☎ 222-34-03, Ⓦ *www.hotelfrankfurt.com, Badillo 300)*

Rooms US$28, cabañas US$38, 1-/2-bedroom apartments with kitchen US$38/55. This is an older hotel with a friendly family atmosphere, a garden café and enclosed parking. All prices include accommodations for two children; rates are cheaper monthly.

Hotel Posada Lily (☎/fax 222-00-32, *Badillo 109)* Singles/doubles Apr-Nov US$22/33, Dec-Mar US$27/44. At the corner of Badillo and Olas Altas, with its entrance inconspicuously located half a block from a great beach, this hotel is a great value in a great location. Rooms have refrigerators, TV and, for an extra few dollars, air-con – some have balconies with fine views.

Hotel Yazmín (☎ 222-00-87, *Badillo 168)* Singles/doubles US$29/34, air-con US$5 extra. This oft-recommended hotel is clean and friendly, with courtyard gardens. There are lots of restaurants nearby, and it's just a block from Playa de los Muertos, the most popular beach in Vallarta.

Estancia San Carlos (☎/fax 222-54-84, *Constitución 210)* 2-person/4-person apartments US$38/65. These mid-range apartments have fully-equipped kitchens, air-con, TV and private balconies. Other amenities include a courtyard swimming pool and covered parking. Monthly rates are an even better deal.

Hotel Posada Río Cuale (☎/fax 222-04-50, *Serdán 242)* Air-conditioned singles/doubles May-Nov US$27/33, Dec-Apr US$48/54. Well located on the corner of Vallarta, this pleasant hotel has a swimming pool with a poolside restaurant and bar.

Hotel Rosita (☎ 222-10-33, Ⓔ reserva@hotelrosita.com, Paseo Díaz Ordaz 901) Singles & doubles US$49-$85. Beside the beach at the northern end of the Malecón, this popular older hotel has a beachside swimming pool, restaurant and bar. Interior rooms with fans are the cheapest; suites with sea view and air-con cost the most.

La Casa del Puente (☎ 222-07-49, Ⓔ casadelpuente@yahoo.com, Libertad s/n) Apartments June-Oct US$41, Nov-May US$81. This tiny guesthouse is tucked in behind the Restaurant La Fuente del Puente, overlooking the Río Cuale. It has just two apartments, but they're very spacious, stylish and comfortable, and Mollie Muir, the owner, is an entertaining hostess full of fascinating local information.

Paco's Olas Altas (☎ 223-43-47, e *pacos olasaltas@hotmail.com, Olas Altas 465)* Singles/doubles with breakfast US$30/40. Located above the Bar El Morbo, this gay men's hotel has clean but smallish rooms and a rooftop spa. It's the least expensive of the three hotels run by Club Paco Paco, the gay bar-disco (see Entertainment). See the Web site w www.pacopaco.com for information about the other two, *Descanso del Sol* (☎ 223-02-77, *Suárez 583)* and *Paco's Hidden Paradise*, on a private beach near Boca de Tomatlán, accessible only by boat.

Top End At the top end of the market, Puerto Vallarta has a few small, stylish places, and lots of large luxury hotels for package tourists. From mid-April to mid-December, low-season discounts bring some of the finest places down to a more affordable level.

Hotel Molino de Agua (☎ 222-19-07, *Vallarta 130)* Singles & doubles May-Nov from US$85, mid-Dec–mid-Apr from US$121. The 59 comfortable cabins, rooms and suites here are set among tropical gardens covering two city blocks, extending down to the beach on the southern side of Río Cuale. It's remarkably quiet and peaceful, but an easy walk to nearby restaurants and nightspots.

Casa Kimberley (☎/fax 222-13-36, w www.casakimberley.com, *Zaragoza 445)* Singles & doubles Apr-Oct US$60, Nov-May US$90. The villas used by Elizabeth Taylor and Richard Burton (see Organized Tours) are now a super-stylish but friendly B&B, with swimming pool, great views and movie-themed decor.

Top-end hotels line the beach at Playa de los Muertos. Typically they are high-rises with air-con, beachfront swimming pools and restaurants.

Hotel San Marino Plaza (☎ 222-30-50, w www.hotelsanmarino.com, *Rodolfo Gómez 111)* All-inclusive doubles from US$108 in low season, US$160 in high season. Right on the beach, this large hotel has a big swimming pool and well-equipped rooms. Prices include three meals a day, and all recreational activities.

Many five-star and Grand Tourism category hotels, often with hundreds of rooms, line the beaches north and south of town. They all do big business in package tours, which can be arranged by good travel agents everywhere, probably for rates considerably lower than the 'walk-in' rates quoted here. Note that rates can vary widely with the time of year and the type of room.

In the Zona Hotelera, *Sheraton Buganvilias* (☎ 223-04-04, w *www.buganvilias.com, Carretera Aeropuerto 999)* has singles/doubles from US$145/154 to US$296/338; *Hotel Krystal Vallarta* (☎ 224-02-02, w *www.krystal.com.mx, Avenida Las Garzas s/n)* has singles/doubles from US$136/148 to US$292/325; and *Fiesta Americana* (☎ 224-20-10, w *www.fiesta mexico.com, Paseo de las Palmas s/n)* has singles/doubles from US$125/134 to US$286/318.

Farther north, in Marina Vallarta, you'll find *Westin Regina Resort* (☎ 226-11-00, w *www.westinpv.com, Paseo de la Marina Sur 105)* has singles/doubles from US$144/170 to US$185/215.

South of Puerto Vallarta, many top-end places have fantastic views from cliff-top positions. *Camino Real* (☎ 221-50-00, w *www.pvr-caminoreal.com, highway 200 Km 3.5)* has singles/doubles from US$121/135 to US$247/400; *Presidente Inter-Continental* (☎ 228-05-07, w *puertovallarta.interconti .com, highway 200 Km 8.5)* has singles/doubles from US$189/210 to US$270/330; and *La Jolla de Mismaloya* (☎ 226-06-60, w *www.lajollamismaloya.com, Bahía de Mismaloya)* has singles/doubles from US$216/245 to US$301/359.

Places to Eat

South of Río Cuale Madero sprouts some *taco stands* early in the evening, with some of the best and cheapest food in town. There are also several small, economical, family-run restaurants along Madero.

Restaurant Gilmar (☎ 222-39-23, *Madero 418)* Mains US$4-7. Gilmar provides good tasty Mexican dishes and seafood at reasonable prices; the comida corrida (US$3.50) includes three courses and a drink.

Mariscos Polo (*Madero 362)* Mains US$4-7. This little local seafood specialist serves incredibly tasty stuff – try the seafood burrito (US$4).

Other restaurants south of the river are a step up in class, catering to Mexican and foreign tourists. Badillo in particular has emerged as Puerto Vallarta's 'restaurant row,' and offers an excellent choice.

Two restaurants on Badillo claim to serve the best breakfast in town, both offering Mexican standards like *huevos Mexicanos*, and American treats like eggs Benedict, cheese blintzes, omelettes with hash browns and 20 varieties of pancake.

Fredy's Tucan Restaurant & Bar (☎ 222-08-36, cnr Badillo & Vallarta) Mains US$3-6, breakfast US$5. Open 8am to 2.30am. Fredy's Tucan serves breakfast, lunch, dinner, snacks and drinks. The food is fine, though the coffee could be better.

The Pancake House (☎ 222-62-72, Badillo 289) Mains US$3-6, breakfast US$5. Open 8am-2pm daily. The 'Casa de Hotcakes' does very well-prepared breakfasts and light meals, as well as US-style pancakes and a mean waffle.

There are a number of other interesting eateries on Badillo.

Los Pibes (☎ 223-20-44, Badillo 261) Mains US$10-28. Open 2pm-midnight Wed-Mon. A vegetarian-free zone, this old favourite Argentine restaurant does large and juicy steaks.

Asaderos Mains US$8. A great value for hungry meat eaters, Asaderos offers all the barbecued chicken, steak, ribs and Mexican sausage you can eat for US$8. Salad and bread is included, but drinks are a considerable extra.

Fajita Republic (☎ 222-31-31, cnr Badillo & Suárez) Mains US$6-12. Open 1pm-11pm. Enjoy substantial Mexican, American and seafood dishes in a delighful courtyard setting.

Chef Roger (☎ 222-59-00, Badillo 180) Mains US$13-22. Open 6.30pm-11pm Mon-Sat. Recently re-located to this street, Chef Roger has an excellent and longstanding reputation. The fabulous Swiss-style menu is not for the faint of wallet, but it's really very good value for cuisine of this quality.

Café de Olla (☎ 223-16-26, Badillo 168A) Mains US$4-7. Open 10am-11pm Wed-Mon. This small, busy, very pleasant tourist-oriented restaurant serves good traditional Mexican food.

Adobe Café (☎ 222-67-20, Badillo 252) Mains US$10-20. Open 6pm-11pm Wed-Mon. This stylish, air-conditioned café has a varied menu of well-prepared, slightly pricey international dishes.

Roberto's Puerto Nuevo (☎ 222-62-10, Badillo 284) Mains US$7-15. Open noon-11.30pm daily. The popular Roberto's serves fine Italian cuisine and super-fresh seafood.

Café Frankfurt & Biergarten (☎ 222-34-03, cnr Badillo & Constitución) Mains US$6-10. In the pleasant garden courtyard of the Café Frankfurt Hotel, this is the place for German food and cool beers.

Plenty more interesting eateries are found close to the beaches.

Langostino's Restaurant/The Sand Bar (☎ 222-08-94, Playa de los Muertos) Mains US$5-15. Open 7am-11pm. These two places sit under a shady palapa, side by side facing the sea. The menu 'aims to please everyone' with seafood, ribs, burgers, salads and tacos.

Las Tres Huastecas (cnr Olas Altas & F Rodríguez) Mains US$3-7. Open 7am to 6pm. This simple restaurant serves beautiful, bargain-priced Mexican favorites.

La Piazzetta (☎ 222-06-50, cnr Olas Altas & Gómez) Mains US$5-7. Open 1pm-midnight Mon-Sat. This Italian restaurant-bar-pizza place is recommended for a pasta-pizza fix.

Chiles! (Púlpito 122) Mains US$4-6. Open 11am-6pm Mon-Sat Nov-May. Chiles! is a high-end hamburger joint, turning out huge beef burgers, veggie burgers, roast chicken, salad and vegetarian chili-with-beans, to eat in or take out.

Archie's Wok (☎ 222-04-11, F Rodríguez 130) Mains US$7-12. Open 2pm-11pm Mon-Sat. Half a block from Playa de los Muertos pier, this very well-known restaurant was created by the former personal chef of film director John Huston. Archie's features Asian fusion cuisine, with dishes like Hoi Sin ribs, Thai noodles, Indian chicken-cashew curry and Philippine egg rolls.

El Palomar de los González (☎ 222-07-95, Aguacate 425) Mains US$10-20. Open 6pm-11pm. The superb view over the city and bay is a big draw at this hillside restaurant, especially at sunset. Jumbo shrimp and fillet steak are specialties. It's a steep climb up here, so get a taxi or work up an appetite.

Gutiérrez Rizoc (GR; cnr Constitución & Serdán) Open 6.30am-11pm daily. For self-catering or a small indulgence, visit this well-stocked air-conditioned supermarket on the southern side of the Río Cuale.

Isla Cuale The island located in the middle of the Río Cuale has several atmospheric restaurants.

Le Bistro Jazz Café (☎ 222-002-83, Isla Río Cuale 16A) Mains US$8-14. The enjoyable Jazz Café has good (but pricey) food, great jazz recordings and exceptionally beautiful tropical scenery.

River Cafe (☎ 223-07-88, Isla Río Cuale 4) Mains US$10-20. Imaginative seafood dishes are a highlight of this well-regarded and delightfully situated restaurant. Try shrimp with pecans and orange sauce, or the yummy shellfish salad.

North of Río Cuale Just north of the river, the *Mercado de Artesanías* has simple stalls upstairs serving typical Mexican market foods. The blocks farther north have numerous upmarket shops, nightclubs and restaurants, and a few surprises.

Planeta Vegetariano Restaurant (☎ 222-30-73, Iturbide 270) Meals US$6. Open 11.30am-10pm Mon-Sat. Readers have raved about the all-you-can-eat vegetarian buffet (US$6) at this small restaurant, up the steps from Hidalgo.

Cenaduría Doña Raquel (Vicario 131) Mains US$3-5. Open 6pm-11.30pm Tues-Sun. Half a block off the Malecón, Doña Raquel serves traditional Mexican food at very non-tourist prices.

Rito's Baci (☎ 222-64-48, Domínguez 181) Mains US$7-20. Open 1pm-11.30pm daily. This tiny Italian restaurant with delicious food serves pastas, pizzas, salads and seafood. Reservations suggested. Phone for free delivery within the city.

Trio (☎ 222-21-96, Guerrero 264) Mains US$10-18. Open 6pm-midnight Jan-Dec, also noon-4pm Nov-Apr. The extremely classy Trio is a European-style restaurant-bar-bistro created and operated by two German chefs who combine Mediterranean and Mexican styles.

Café des Artistes (☎ 222-32-28, Sánchez 740) Mains US$10-22. Open 6pm-11.30pm. With fine views over the town, this distinguished restaurant has a romantic ambiance to match its exquisite French cuisine. Local seafood is featured in many of the dishes, such as grilled swordfish in green tomato sauce, or tuna in sesame seeds with wasabe mousse. Reservations are recommended.

Paseo Díaz Ordaz, the street fronting the Malecón, is thick with restaurants and bars. Many have upstairs terraces offering fine views of the bay. Prices are considerably

higher than in other p... a few places that ar... venues are not reall... their meals.

La Dolce Vita (☎ ... Ordaz 674) Mains US$6-12. Open noon ... The wood-fired pizza ovens run hot at this popular, often crowded Italian restaurant.

No Name Café (☎ 223-25-08, cnr Morelos & Mina) Mains US$5-20. Open 8am-1am. Facing the Malecón near the seahorse statue, this fun restaurant and sports bar serves All-American favorites like BBQ pork spareribs and deep-dish Chicago-style pizzas; phone for free delivery.

Tacos de los Arcos (Zaragoza 120) Tacos from US$1. This clean, slightly upmarket taquería faces the amphitheater and Los Arcos (downstairs from the heavily promoted Hooters). It serves simple, economical and quite authentic Mexican fare.

Elsewhere North of town, the top-end hotels in the Zona Hotelera and Marina Vallarta all have top-end restaurants, at appropriately top-end prices. Good examples are *Bogart's* (☎ 224-02-02 ext 2077), at Hotel Krystal Vallarta, for gourmet international cuisine; and *Garibaldi's* (☎ 226-11-50 ext 4419), at Westin Regina Resort, for fine seafood in a beachfront setting.

South of town, apart from the fancy hotel restaurants, there are several places notable for lush tropical locations.

Chino's Paraíso Mains US$8-16. Open 11am-6pm. On rocky ledges overlooking a perfect swimming hole, 2km from Mismaloya up a small river, Chino's is an elegantly rustic seafood restaurant. You can choose your fish before it's cooked.

El Edén Mains US$5-13. Open 11am-6pm. About 5km farther upriver, Edén is not quite so appealing to look at, but the food is good, and considerably cheaper, and there are more activities on offer in the area.

Chico's Paradise (☎ 222-07-47, Carretera Colima/highway 200 Km 20) Mains US$6-16. Open 10am-6pm daily. Though farther from town, Chico's is beside a main road, and is quite accessible by car or public bus. The dining areas are in rustic palapas on stilts beside a rushing river. Sunbathe and relax on the large rocks and enjoy the lush jungle backdrop. The food is pretty good too.

and Mismaloya, several restaurant-are perched on clifftops with stunning a views and sunsets.

Le Kliff (☎ *224-09-75, Carretera Colima Km 17.5)* Mains US$10-25. Open noon-11pm. The dramatic position of Le Kliff is matched by its super seafood menu – try the tequila jumbo shrimp, or go all the way with the seafood carousel, a lobster-shrimp-fish combination.

Entertainment

Dancing and drinking are Vallarta's main forms of nighttime entertainment. At night many people stroll down the Malecón, where they can choose from romantic open-air restaurant-bars and discos with riotous reveling. Entertainment is often presented in the amphitheater by the sea, opposite Plaza Principal. Softly lit Isla Cuale is a quiet haven for a romantic promenade in the early evening.

Bars, Clubs & Discos Along the Malecón are a bunch of places where teen and twenty-something tourists get trashed and dance on tables. On a good night, they all stay open to about 5am. You can see from the street which one has the most action. Usually there's no cover charge, but drinks are on the expensive side, except during the 'happy hours,' which can be any time from 8pm to 11pm. Vallarta mainstays include *Carlos O'Brian's* (☎ *222-14-44, Paseo Díaz Ordaz 786)*, *Kahlúa* (☎ *222-24-86, cnr Paseo Díaz Ordaz & Abasolo)* and *The Zoo* (☎ *222-49-45, Paseo Díaz Ordaz 638)*.

Hard Rock Café (☎ *222-55-32, Paseo Díaz Ordaz 652)* is in the same area, but gets an older, more sedate crowd, as does *Planet Hollywood* (☎ *223-27-10, cnr Morelos & Galeana)*, a few blocks farther south.

Young locals drink and dance to loud Latin music at the rambling *La Cantina* *(Morelos 700)*, or drink and do karaoke at *La Regadera (Morelos 664)*. Both these places are busy on Thursday, Friday and Saturday nights.

South of the Río Cuale, a wider variety of nightspots caters to a more diverse clientele, and drink prices are generally lower than on the Malecón scene.

Club Roxy (Vallarta 217) Live music at the Roxy covers rock, blues and reggae clas-sics and attracts a good mix of locals and visitors, young and not-so-young.

Bar Amsterdam (Vallarta 264) A very popular hangout for Europeans and assorted travelers, the Amsterdam does drink promotions most nights.

Señor Frog's (☎ *222-51-71, cnr Vallarta & Carranza)* Another PV party scene, Señor Frog's blasts out live rock and disco music. Youthful patrons dance on top of the bar while under the influence.

Cactus (☎ *222-03-91, Vallarta 399)* This popular disco-dance club does different promotions throughout the week. Some nights it's a wet T-shirt contest; other nights there's an open bar (US$22 for men, free for women), which does nothing to promote responsible drinking.

North of the city, some of the large resort hotels have bars and nightclubs, but they're usually low-energy, high-priced affairs. They might get busier at holiday times, when very well dressed Mexicans strut their stuff. To cut the cost of the cover charge, look for discount coupons offered by time share touts.

Christine (☎ *224-69-90)* Cover US$6-15. At Hotel Krystal Vallarta in the Zona Hotelera, this flashy disco is livelier than most places in the area, but you'll need good clothes and good moves to cut it on the dance floor here.

Gay Venues The gay scene is huge in PV, with accommodations, tours, cruises and nightspots all catering to the gay market.

Club Paco Paco (☎ *222-18-99, Vallarta 278)* Open noon-6am daily. This popular bar-disco is the place for contacts and information on Puerto Vallarta's thriving gay scene. It's also a lot of fun, with regular floor shows, strippers and drag acts. Paco runs a couple of other gay nightspots around town, including *Bar El Morbo* (☎ *223-43-47, Olas Altas 465)*, in the same building as Paco's Olas Altas hotel.

Los Balcones (☎ *222-46-71, Juárez 182)* Cover US$2-4. Upstairs near the corner of Libertad you'll see the little balconies where the trendy clientele of this bar-disco-dance club like to be seen.

Blue Chairs, a beach bar at the southern end of Playa de los Muertos, is a popular gay meeting place in the afternoon and evening.

Mariachis Two places present regular mariachi music. One attracts mostly tourists; the other is mainly for Mexicans.

Tequila's (☎ 222-57-25, Galeana 104) On the Malecón near the seahorse statue, this upstairs restaurant-bar features live mariachi music every night except Monday, starting around 7.30pm or 8pm.

Mariachi Loco (☎ 223-22-05, cnr Cárdenas & Vallarta) Cover US$3.50. Usually attracting an enthusiastic, all-Mexican crowd, this restaurant-bar presents an entertaining (if slightly amateur) show of music, comedy and mariachi every night, and some afternoons as well. It's a great bit of local color, but you'll need good Spanish to enjoy it.

Fiestas Mexicanas These folkloric shows give tourists a crash course in not-very-contemporary Mexican culture.

La Iguana (☎ 222-01-05, Cárdenas 311) Open 7pm-11pm Thur & Sun. Admission US$30. Said to be the original of this much-copied tourist entertainment, the deal here includes a Mexican buffet, open bar, live music, folkloric dances, mariachis, cowboy rope tricks, bloodless cockfights and a piñata.

Some of the big resort hotels also do Fiesta Mexicana nights, including the *Sheraton Buganvilias* (☎ 226-04-04) and *Hotel Krystal Vallarta* (☎ 224-02-02).

Cinemas For less frenetic evening entertainment, catch a movie in air-con comfort.

Cine Bahía (cnr Insurgentes & Madero) Admission US$4. This cinema shows recent release movies, often in English with Spanish subtitles.

Cigar Clubs For PV's classiest cancer enhancer, try what Uncle Sam won't let you buy.

Guantanamera Cigar Club (☎ 223-25-07, Corona 186B) Open 10am-10pm Mon-Sat. Have your cigars rolled to order, or buy Cubanos, and enjoy them with a drink in the comfortable lounge bar.

Spectator Sports

Bullfights are held at 4pm Wednesday, November to May, in the Plaza de Toros opposite the marina.

Shopping

Shops and boutiques in Puerto Vallarta sell fashion clothing, beachwear and just about every type of handicraft made in Mexico, but prices tend to be high.

Mercado de Artesanías (☎ 223-09-25, A Rodríguez 260) Open 9am-8pm Mon-Sat, 9am-2pm Sun. The municipal craft market is the place for anything from Taxco silver, *sarapes* and *huaraches* to wool wall-hangings and blown glass. The market has more than 150 shops and stalls. Many other shops line A Rodríguez, facing the market.

Getting There & Away

Air Puerto Vallarta's international airport (PVR), on highway 200 about 10km north of the city, is served by several national and international airlines:

Aeroméxico (☎ 224-27-77, 800-021-40-10) flies to Guadalajara, León, Los Angeles, Mexico City and Tijuana.

Alaska Airlines (☎ 221-13-50, 800-252-75-22) flies to Los Angeles, San Francisco, Seattle and Phoenix.

America West (☎ 221-13-33) flies to Phoenix.

American Airlines (☎ 221-17-99) flies to Dallas.

Continental (☎ 221-10-25, 800-900-50-00) flies to Houston and Newark.

Mexicana (☎ 224-89-00, 800-366-5400) flies to Chicago, Guadalajara and Mexico City.

Bus Vallarta's long-distance bus station is just off highway 200, about 12km north of the city center and a kilometer or two north of the airport.

Most intercity bus lines also have offices south of the Río Cuale, where you can buy tickets without having to make a trip to the bus station. They include Elite, TNS and Estrella Blanca, on the corner of Badillo and Insurgentes; ETN, Primera Plus and Servicios Coordinados, at Cárdenas 268; and Transportes del Pacífico, at Insurgentes 282.

Buses depart from the main bus station. Some buses make an additional stop in town – for example, Transportes Cihuatlán's southbound buses make a stop on Carranza at the corner of Aguacate after leaving the main terminal, and will drop off passengers there by request when arriving from the south.

Daily departures from the main terminal include the following:

Barra de Navidad – 225km, 3½-4 hours, 6 1st-class (US$12), and same buses as to Manzanillo

CENTRAL PACIFIC COAST

Guadalajara – 344km, 5 hours; 11 ETN deluxe (US$39), frequent Futura, Transportes del Pacífico and Primera Plus 1st-class (US$29)

Manzanillo – 285km, 5 hours; 7 Primera Plus, Elite and Autocamiones Cihuatlán 1st-class (US$17-18), Servicios Coordinados 2nd-class (US$15)

Mazatlán – 459km, 8 hours; 4 Transportes del Pacífico (US$27), or take a bus to Tepic, where buses depart frequently for Mazatlán

Mexico City (Terminal Norte) – 880km, 12-13 hours; 1 ETN deluxe (US$89), regular Elite, Futura, Transportes del Pacífico and Primera Plus 1st-class (US$65)

Rincón de Guayabitos – 60km, 1½ hours; same buses as to Tepic (US$6)

San Blas – 175km, 3½ hours; TNS 2nd-class 10am and 12.15pm (US$11)

San Patricio-Melaque (Melaque) – 225km, 3½-4 hours; 7 1st-class (US$14), regular 2nd-class (US$12), and same buses as to Manzanillo

Sayulita – 38km, 1 hour; 10 Transportes del Pacífico 2nd-class (US$3.50)

Tepic – 169km, 3½ hours; frequent Transportes del Pacífico 2nd-class (US$12)

Car & Motorcycle Car rental agencies in Puerto Vallarta include the following:

Avis	☎ 221-11-12
Budget	☎ 222-29-80
De Alba	☎ 222-29-59
Dollar	☎ 222-42-56
Hertz	☎ 221-14-73
MagnoCar	☎ 222-65-45
National	☎ 221-12-26
Quick	☎ 222-00-06

To rent a vehicle you must be at least 25 years old and hold a valid driver's license (a foreign one will do). If you don't have a credit card you'll have to pay a large cash deposit. Rates vary, so it pays to shop around, but you won't get much cheaper than US$44 per day.

Mario's Moto Rent (☎ 044-322-229-81-42, Avenida Ascencio 998), opposite the Sheraton Buganvilias hotel, rents trail bikes and motor scooters at US$38 for 12 hours, US$48 for 24 hours.

Getting Around
To/From the Airport Colectivo vans operate from the airport to town, but not from town to the airport. The cheapest way to get to/from the airport is on a local bus for US$0.30. 'Aeropuerto,' 'Juntas' and 'Ixtapa' buses from town all stop right at the airport entrance; 'Centro' or 'Olas Altas' buses go into town from beside the airport entrance. A taxi from the city center costs around US$6. From the airport to the city, taxis ask as much as US$13, but shouldn't be more than US$8 for most parts of the city.

Bus Local buses marked 'Ixtapa' and 'Juntas' go from the center of town to the bus station; 'Centro' or 'Olas Altas' buses run into town from beside the bus-station parking lot. A taxi between the center and the bus station costs US$6 to US$8.

Local buses operate every five minutes, 5am to 11pm, on most routes and cost US$0.40. Plaza Lázaro Cárdenas at Playa Olas Altas is a major departure hub. Northbound local bus routes also stop in front of the Cine Bahía, on Insurgentes near the corner of Madero.

Northbound buses marked 'Hoteles,' 'Aeropuerto,' 'Ixtapa,' 'Pitillal' and 'Juntas' pass through the city heading north to the airport, the Zona Hotelera and Marina Vallarta; the 'Hoteles,' 'Pitillal' and 'Ixtapa' routes can take you to any of the large hotels north of the city.

Southbound 'Boca de Tomatlán' buses pass along the southern coastal highway through Mismaloya (20 minutes, US$0.50) to Boca de Tomatlán (30 minutes, US$0.75). They depart from Constitución near the corner of Badillo every 10 minutes, from 6am to 10pm.

Taxi Cab prices are regulated by zones; the cost for a ride is determined by how many zones you cross. Always determine the price of the ride before you get in.

Bicycle See Organized Tours for companies that hire bicycles and give guided cycle tours.

Boat In addition to taxis on land, Vallarta also has water taxis to beautiful beaches on the southern side of the bay that are accessible only by boat.

Water taxis departing from the pier at Playa de los Muertos head south around the bay, making stops at Playa Las Ánimas (25 minutes), Quimixto (30 minutes) and Yelapa (45 minutes); the roundtrip fare is

US$31 for any destination. Boats depart at 10am, 11am and 4pm, and return in mid-afternoon (the 4pm boat returns in the morning).

A water taxi also goes to Yelapa from the beach just south of Hotel Rosita, on the northern end of the Malecón, departing at 11.30am, Monday to Saturday (30 minutes, US$14.50 one-way).

Cheaper water taxis to the same places depart from Boca de Tomatlán, south of town, which is easily reachable by local bus. Water taxis to Playa Las Ánimas (15 minutes), Quimixto (20 minutes) and Yelapa (30 minutes) depart here daily at 10.30am and 11.30am, 1pm, 2pm, 4pm and 5.30pm, or more frequently if enough people want to make the trip; one-way fare is US$8 to any destination (double for roundtrip).

Private yachts and lanchas can be hired from the southern side of the Playa de los Muertos pier. They'll take you to any secluded beach around the bay; most have gear aboard for snorkeling and fishing. Lanchas can also be hired privately at Mismaloya and Boca de Tomatlán, but they are expensive.

LA CRUZ DE LORETO

This small village, west of highway 200, 90km south of Puerto Vallarta, is adjacent to a wetland estuary and nature reserve. It's also the closest village to one of Mexico's most attractive and eco-friendly luxury hotels.

Hotelito Desconocido (☎ *322-222-25-26, fax 322-223-02-93,* Ⓦ *www.hotelito.com)* Singles/doubles June-Sep from US$437/546, Oct-May from US$560/737. On a spit of land between the Pacific Ocean and El Ermitaño estuary, this rusticated yet luxurious resort offers serenity, scenery and superb cuisine. The rates include all meals and activities including horseback riding, canoeing, yoga classes, and wildlife-watching excursions. Bird-watching is excellent here, and a sea turtle protection project operates June to February.

COSTALEGRE BEACHES & RESORTS

Just south of Puerto Vallarta, the stretch of Mexico's Pacific coast from Chamela to Barra de Navidad is blessed with many fine beaches. Tourism promoters refer to this shoreline as the 'Costalegre' (Happy Coast), while more gung-ho developers prefer the term 'Mexican Riviera.'

Due to increased development, several pristine hideaways along here (such as Los Ángeles Locos) have effectively been commandeered by private interests, notwithstanding federal laws prohibiting privatization of the shoreline. Thankfully, several noteworthy beaches remain publicly accessible.

From north to south they include (with kilometer numbers as measured from the highway 80/200 junction just outside San Patricio-Melaque): the broad and sheltered **Playa Pérula** (Km 76), at the north end of tranquil 11km-long Bahía de Chamela; the once-untouched **Playa Chamela** (Km 72), where tourism is slowly creeping in; pristine **Playa Negrito** (Km 64), at the south end of Bahía de Chamela; **Playa Careyes** and **Playa Careyitos** (Km 52), where endangered hawksbill sea turtles are making a comeback with the help of local activists; deserted white-sand **Playa Tecuán** (Km 33), 10km off the highway near an abandoned resort; **Playa Tenacatita** (Km 30), with crystal clear snorkeling waters and a large mangrove lagoon with good bird-watching; the wide-open 10km-long **Playa Boca de Iguanas** (Km 19), on Bahía Tenacatita (where RVs rule); sheltered **Playa La Manzanilla** (Km 13), marking the south end of public access to Bahía Tenacatita; and pleasant **Playa Cuastecomates**, 3km west of San Patricio-Melaque.

SAN PATRICIO-MELAQUE
• pop 8000 ☎ 315

Known by easygoing locals simply as Melaque ('may-LAH-kay'), the peaceful beach resort of San Patricio-Melaque is 60km southeast of Chamela on lovely Bahía de Navidad. Melaque is a bit larger than its twin, Barra de Navidad, but Barra sees more gringo tourists.

Two foreign-owned haciendas – San Patricio (on the east side) and Melaque (on the west) – once stood side by side here, with the dividing line between them running where Calle López Mateos is today. Settlements gradually grew around the haciendas and eventually merged into today's sleepy town.

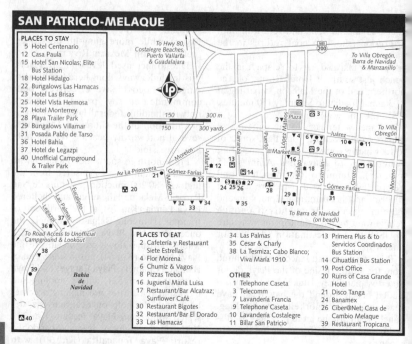

SAN PATRICIO-MELAQUE

PLACES TO STAY
5 Hotel Centenario
12 Casa Paula
15 Hotel San Nicolas; Elite Bus Station
18 Hotel Hidalgo
22 Bungalows Las Hamacas
23 Hotel Las Brisas
25 Hotel Vista Hermosa
27 Hotel Monterrey
28 Playa Trailer Park
29 Bungalows Villamar
31 Posada Pablo de Tarso
36 Hotel Bahía
37 Hotel de Legazpi
40 Unofficial Campground & Trailer Park

PLACES TO EAT
2 Cafetería y Restaurant Siete Estrellas
4 Flor Morena
6 Chumiz & Vagos
8 Pizzas Trebol
16 Juguería María Luisa
17 Restaurant/Bar Alcatraz; Sunflower Café
30 Restaurant Bigotes
32 Restaurant/Bar El Dorado
33 Las Hamacas
34 Las Palmas
35 Cesar & Charly
38 La Tesmiza; Cabo Blanco; Viva María 1910

OTHER
1 Telephone Caseta
3 Telecomm
7 Lavandería Francia
9 Telephone Caseta
10 Lavandería Costalegre
11 Billar San Patricio
13 Primera Plus & to Servicios Coordinados Bus Station
14 Cihuatlán Bus Station
19 Post Office
20 Ruins of Casa Grande Hotel
21 Disco Tanga
24 Banamex
26 Ciber@Net; Casa de Cambio Melaque
39 Restaurant Tropicana

Besides being a popular vacation destination for Mexican families and a low-key winter hangout for snowbirds (principally Canadians), the town is famous for its week-long Fiesta de San Patricio (St Patrick's Day Festival) in March.

The crumbling ruins of the Casa Grande Hotel, now home to squatter families, are an imposing reminder of the 1995 earthquake and subsequent *maremotos* (tidal waves) that severely damaged the region.

Orientation & Information

Everything in Melaque is within walking distance. Most of the hotels, restaurants and public services are concentrated on or near east-west Gómez Farías, which parallels the beach, and north-south López Mateos, the main highway 200 exit. Building numbers on Gómez Farías and some other streets are not consecutive – refer to the map for locations. Barra de Navidad is 5km southeast of Melaque via highway 200 or 2.5km by walking 30 to 45 minutes along the beach. Barra's tourist office has some basic information on Melaque.

Banamex, near the bus terminal on Gómez Farías, is open 9am to 3pm Monday to Friday. US and Canadian cash is changed during these hours; traveler's checks are changed 9am to noon only. Casa de Cambio Melaque (No 11 in rear of the Pasaje Comercial, opposite the bus station off Gómez Farías) changes cash and traveler's checks 9am to 2pm and 4pm to 7pm Monday to Saturday, 9am to 2pm Sunday.

The post office is on Orozco near Corona; open 8am to 3pm Monday to Friday, 8am to noon Saturday. Telecomm, at Morelos 53 near the plaza, offers telegram, telex and fax service 9am to 2.30pm Monday to Friday. Several telephone *casetas* have fax service, among them one near the northeast corner of the plaza at Morelos and Hidalgo, another at Corona 60 between Hidalgo and Guzmán, and one on Gómez Farías beside the bus station. Ciber@Net, Gómez Farías 27A (in the Pasaje Comercial Melaque, opposite the bus station), offers Internet access (US$4 per hour) 9.30am to 2.30pm and 4pm to 8pm Monday to Saturday.

Lavandería Costalegre, Juárez 63, is open 8am to 8pm Monday to Saturday. Lavandería Francia, a block west on Juárez between Hidalgo and Guzmán, is open 9am to 10pm daily. Both charge around US$1.25 per kilo.

Things to See & Do
Melaque is the perfect place to simply relax and take it easy. The main activities are swimming, lazing on the beach (or beachcombing), watching pelicans fish at sunrise and sunset, climbing to the *mirador* (lookout) at the bay's west end, prowling the plaza and public market, or walking to Barra de Navidad. A *tianguis* (flea market) is held every Wednesday starting around 8am; it's on Orozco two blocks east of the plaza.

Special Events
Melaque's biggest annual celebration is the **Fiesta de San Patricio** honoring the town's patron saint. A week of festivities – including all-day parties, rodeos, a carnival, music, dances and nightly fireworks – leads up to St Patrick's Day (March 17), which is marked with a mass and the blessing of the fishing fleet. Take care when the *borrachos* (drunks) take over after dark.

Places to Stay
Rates vary greatly depending on the season; the town fills up with families during Mexican school holidays in July and August, in December and at Semana Santa, so accommodation prices are higher then and it's best to reserve ahead. The rest of the year it's pretty quiet, and many hotels will give discounts. Bungalows – apartments with kitchens where kids stay for no extra charge – are common here, and it never hurts to ask for cheaper weekly rates. Prices generally get cheaper as you go inland.

Budget The unofficial beachfront *campground* at the far west end of Avenida La Primavera doesn't have any facilities (you can buy water and beer from trucks that make the rounds), but the price is right; someone may come by to collect US$1 per night in the high season. Most of the nearby *enramadas* (palapa restaurants) charge a nominal fee for showers and bathroom usage.

Playa Trailer Park (☎ 355-50-65, *Gómez Farías 250)* Tent camping US$5 per person, full RV hookups US$11 for two, US$1.50 per extra person. Friendly *fútbol*-playing, English-speaking manager Amador welcomes long-term visitors to his crowded beachfront RV park, which offers 45 shadeless spaces under the radio tower.

Hotel San Nicolás (☎ 355-50-66, *Gómez Farías 54)* Rooms US$8 per person. Upstairs, the street-facing rooms have private balconies with ocean views, but rooms downstairs are dark.

Casa Paula (☎ 355-50-93, *Vallarta 6)* Singles/doubles US$11/16. This simple, family-run place has four courtyard rooms with bath.

Hotel Centenario (☎ 355-63-08, *Corona 38)* Singles/doubles/triples US$10/18/24. Above the market, the Centenario has nine mostly bright rooms with bath – look at a few before settling in.

Bungalows Villamar (☎/fax 355-50-05, *Hidalgo 1)* Singles/doubles US$16.50/18, 2-bed bungalows US$25 per couple, US$10 per extra person. The *'estilo Californiano'* Villamar has five spacious but worn garden bungalows, a pool and a beachfront terrace. It's popular with norteamericanos since owner Roberto speaks English.

Hotel Hidalgo (☎ 355-50-45, *Hidalgo 7)* Singles/doubles US$16/19, US$3 per extra person. The Hidalgo has a courtyard, communal kitchen and simple rooms. The upstairs rooms are brighter.

Hotel Bahía (☎ 355-56-81, *Legazpi 5)* Singles/doubles with bath US$22/27. This pleasant little family-run hotel, also known as Casa Rafa, is half a block from the beach at the west end of town. One of Melaque's best deals, it's a clean, well-maintained place with a communal open-air kitchen. Two of the 20 rooms have a private kitchen and are slightly more expensive.

Mid-Range *Hotel de Legazpi* (☎ 355-53-97, e *hlegazpi@prodigy.net.mx, Las Palmas 3)* Doubles May-Sept US$33, Oct-Apr US$40, US$4 extra with kitchenette. On the beach near Hotel Bahía, the Legazpi has a swimming pool and 16 large, bright rooms, some with a balcony and sea view.

Bungalows Las Hamacas (☎/fax 355-51-13, *Gómez Farías 13)* Singles/doubles US$25/33, bungalows from US$60. Stylish beachfront Las Hamacas has a small swimming pool, secure parking, an inexpensive restaurant and large bungalows (with up to six beds) with full kitchens.

Hotel Monterrey (☎ 355-50-04, *Gómez Farías 27*) Singles/doubles US$25/35, bungalows US$44 per double (two kids under 7 stay free). This hotel has beachfront terraces and a lovely sea view, plus a large swimming pool, restaurant/bar and parking.

Hotel Vista Hermosa (☎ 355-50-02, *Gómez Farías 23*) Singles/doubles US$32/38, bungalow singles/doubles from US$40/50. The beachfront Vista Hermosa has a pool, standard rooms and a variety of one-, two- and three-bedroom bungalows.

Posada Pablo de Tarso (☎ 355-51-17, *Gómez Farías 408*) Singles/doubles with air-con US$25/40, bungalows from US$50. This budget posada has a large beachfront pool, worn rooms and bungalows for one to three folks.

Hotel Las Brisas (☎/fax 355-51-08, *Gómez Farías 9*) Singles/doubles US$33/46, bungalows US$65 per double. Las Brisas has a pool, outdoor communal cooking facilities and rooms with fridge, air-con and TV. Bungalows with private kitchens are also available.

Places to Eat

From 6pm to midnight, *food carts* serve inexpensive Mexican fare a block east of the plaza along Juárez; a tummyful of *carne asada* (grilled beef) costs around US$3. Lots of little eateries await along Corona in the two market alleys on either side of López Mateos, and several good, cheap places surround the plaza.

Flor Morena (*Juárez s/n*) Dinner US$1-3. Open 6pm-11pm Tues-Sun. On the south side of the plaza, this flower is an inexpensive and immensely popular typical Mexican eatery. The shrimp *pozole* (hearty hominy stew), the most expensive thing on the menu at US$3, is worth every centavo. Or try an order of four tamales or crispy tacos with salad. Everything is made fresh daily and most items are available vegetarian.

Cafetería y Restaurant Siete Estrellas (☎ 355-64-21, *López Mateos 49*) Mains US$2-7. Open 7am-midnight daily. On the west side of the plaza, this is another simple family place serving good, inexpensive Mexican dishes; phone for free delivery.

Pizzas Trebol (☎ 355-63-84, *cnr Juárez & Guzmán*) Pizzas US$3-10. Open 10am-10.30pm daily. Trebol, a block east of the plaza, also offers free delivery.

Juguería María Luisa (*cnr López Mateos & Corona*) Mains US$1-2.50. Open 7am-11pm daily. María Luisa whips up fresh fruit and vegetable juices, *licuados*, yogurt and granola, *tortas* and good burgers.

Restaurant/Bar Alcatraz (*cnr López Mateos & Gómez Farías*) Mains US$3-15. Open 2pm-10.30pm Fri-Wed. This small, cheerful upstairs restaurant serves lunch and dinner under a lofty palapa. The chateaubriand (US$15) serves two. Downstairs, the *Sunflower Café*, open 8am-noon and 6pm-9pm daily, serves good coffee and superb baked goods.

Chumiz & Vagos (*Juárez 43*) Mains US$2-5. Open 6pm-11pm daily. Chumiz has a pool table and is fun and casual. It has separate bar and restaurant sections, so you can sit upstairs under the palapa or under the stars and enjoy some decent pub grub.

Several more upmarket restaurant/bars are right on the beach.

Cesar & Charly (*south end of Carranza*) Dinner US$4-10. Open 7am-10pm daily. Behind Hotel Monterrey and Hotel Vista Hermosa, this pleasant beachfront place serves a variety of inexpensive dishes, including healthy 'light-hearted fare.' Try a steamed or grilled vegetable plate with chicken, shrimp or fish, a huge Mexican plate or the house specialty Hawaiian-style shrimp.

Restaurant Bigotes (*south end of López Mateos*) Seafood US$5-10. Open 8am-9pm daily. Seafood is the specialty at this pleasant beachfront palapa; try the *huachinango a la naranja* (red snapper à l'orange) or *camarones al cilantro* (cilantro shrimp). The two-for-one happy hour (2pm-8pm) is popular.

A row of pleasant palapa restaurants stretches along the beach at the west end of town. *Cabo Blanco* is a favorite with locals and visitors alike; nearby *Restaurant La Tesmiza* and *Viva María 1910* are also good. A bit closer to town, the fancier *Restaurant/ Bar El Dorado* has live music on Friday and Saturday nights. Nearby, *Las Palmas* and *Las Hamacas* are a bit cheaper.

Entertainment

On the beach at the west end of town, *Restaurant Tropicana* showcases a Sunday afternoon dance that's popular with young locals. Sunday night, locals gather in the plaza to snack, socialize and enjoy the balmy evening air. *Chumiz & Vagos* and *El Dorado* (see Places to Eat) are both popular nighttime hangouts. In summer, keep an eye out for the arrival of the *circus*.

Billar San Patricio (cnr Juárez & Orozco) Open until 11pm daily. Billiard tables US$1.50 an hour. This poolroom has large tables with smooth felt.

Disco Tanga (cnr Gómez Farías & Madero) Open 10pm-3am daily in high season, 10pm-3am Fri-Sun rest of year. Disco Tanga is Melaque's only dedicated disco.

Spectator Sports

During the winter and spring, *corridas de toros* (bullfights) occasionally liven up the bullring off highway 200 near the Barra turnoff. Watch for flyers promoting *charreadas* (Mexican-style rodeos), and keep an ear out for cruising, megaphone-equipped cars scratchily announcing *béisbol* games and *fútbol* (soccer) matches.

Getting There & Away

Air See the Barra de Navidad Getting There & Away section.

Bus Melaque has three bus stations. Transportes Cihuatlán and Primera Plus/Servicios Coordinados are on opposite sides of Carranza at the corner of Gómez Farías. Both have 1st- and 2nd-class buses and ply similar routes for similar fares. Buses trundling out of these stations serve the following destinations:

Barra de Navidad – 5km, 10 minutes; every 15 minutes 6am-9pm (US$0.30), or take any southbound long-distance bus

Guadalajara – 294km, 5-7½ hours; 17 1st-class (US$21), 14 2nd-class (US$17.50)

Manzanillo – 65km, 1-1½ hours; 11 1st-class (US$4), 2nd-class at least hourly 3am-11.30pm (US$3.50)

Puerto Vallarta – 220km, 3½-5 hours; 4 1st-class (US$14), 17 2nd-class (US$12)

The 1st-class Elite bus station is a block east on Gómez Farías. Two buses daily go to Puerto Vallarta (3½ hours, US$13) then continue up the coast and on to Tijuana.

Elite's southbound buses depart from Manzanillo.

Local buses for Villa Obregón and Barra de Navidad (15-20 minutes, US$0.40) stop near the plaza by the Paletería Michoacán every 15 minutes.

Taxi A taxi between Melaque and Barra should cost no more than US$4.50, or as little as US$3.25, depending on how well *tu hablas espanglish*.

BARRA DE NAVIDAD
• pop 4000 ☎ 315

The beach resort of Barra de Navidad (usually simply called 'Barra') is squeezed onto a sandbar between Bahía de Navidad and Laguna de Navidad, around the bay from San Patricio-Melaque. Local surfers prefer Barra to Melaque since Barra's waves are bigger, especially in January. The Grand Bay Hotel's marina is a popular yachtie port November to May.

Orientation

Legazpi, the main drag, parallels the beach. Veracruz, the town's other major artery and the highway feeder, parallels Legazpi before merging with it at the south end of town, which terminates in a fingerlike sandbar.

Information

The regional tourist office (☎/fax 355-51-00), Jalisco 67, is open 9am to 5pm Monday to Friday, 9am to 2pm Saturday. It has free maps and also runs an information kiosk on the jetty during the high tourist season.

Barra is now blessed with an air-conditioned Banamex ATM, at the southeast corner of the plaza. Change money at Vinos y Licores Barra de Navidad, on Legazpi near the southwest corner of the plaza (open 8.30am to 11pm daily), or at the casa de cambio at Veracruz 212.

The post office is on Nueva España, six blocks north and four blocks east of the bus stations. It's open 8am to 3pm Monday to Friday, 9am to 1pm Saturday.

Telecomm, near the northeast corner of the plaza on Veracruz, is open 9am to 3pm Monday to Friday and offers fax and telex service. Mini-Market Hawaii, on Legazpi at Sonora, has telephone and fax services

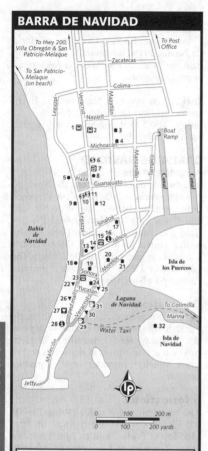

BARRA DE NAVIDAD

To Hwy 200,
Villa Obregón & San
Patricio-Melaque

To San Patricio-
Melaque
(on beach)

To Post
Office

Zacatecas

Colima

Nayarit

Michoacan

Boat
Ramp

Plaza

Guanajuato

Bahia
de
Navidad

Sinaloa

Jalisco

Isla de
los Puercos

Sonora

Yucatán

Laguna
de Navidad

To Colimilla

Marina

Water Taxi

Isla de
Navidad

Jetty

0   100   200 m
0   100   200 yards

PLACES TO STAY
3 Bungalows Mar Vida
4 Hotel Posada Pacífico
9 Hotel Barra de Navidad
12 Polo's Bungalows
17 Hotel San Lorenzo
19 Hotel Caribe
20 Hotel Delfin
21 Hotel Sands; El Galeón
   Disco
24 Casa de Huéspedes
   Mama Laya
32 Grand Bay Hotel Isla
   Navidad

PLACES TO EAT
14 Restaurant Ambar
22 Sea Master Café
25 Veleros; Restaurant Eloy
26 Mariscos Nacho
30 El Manglito

OTHER
1 Primera Plus Bus Station
2 Transportes Cihuatlán
   Bus Station

5 Biblioteca Publica
   (Library)
6 Casa de Cambio;
   Telephone Caseta
7 Ciber@Money
8 Nauti-Mar Dive Shop;
   Telecomm
10 Vinos y Licores Barra de
   Navidad
11 Banamex ATM
13 Crazy Cactus, Z Pesca
15 Telephone Caseta
16 Delegación Regional de
   Turismo; Lavandería
   Jardín
18 Fantasía Pesca Deportiva
23 Mini-Market Hawaii;
   Telephone Caseta
27 Piper Lovers Bar
28 Tourist Information Kiosk
   (high season only)
29 Water Taxi to Marina,
   Grand Bay Hotel
31 Sociedad Cooperativa de
   Servicios Turísticos Office

and is open noon to 10pm daily. Another caseta, at Veracruz 102, has narrowband, sometimes-on Internet access and is open 9am to 10.30pm daily.

Ciber@Money, adjacent to the casa de cambio on the 200 block of Veracruz, is open 9am to 2pm and 4pm to 7pm Monday to Friday, 9am to 6.30pm Saturday and charges US$4 an hour. Other Internet access nodes are sprouting up faster than annoying pop-up ads.

Lavandería Jardín, Jalisco 71, claims to be open 9am to 2pm and 4pm to 7pm Monday to Friday, 9am to noon Saturday, but may take longer siestas in the *temporada baja* (low season). If nobody's home, try Mak y Mar at Hotel Caribe (see Places to Stay).

Activities
The beach is Barra's prime attraction. The lagoon may also look tempting for a swim, but before diving in, consider the possibility of bilharzia contamination.

Surfboards, body boards, snorkeling gear, kayaks, bicycles, cars and apartments can be rented from **Crazy Cactus** (☎ 355-60-99, *Jalisco 8; open 9.30am-6pm Mon-Sat)*. **Nauti-Mar** (☎ 355-57-91, *Veracruz 204)* dive shop rents outfits for all manner of aquatic sports.

Organized Tours
Sociedad Cooperativa de Servicios Turísticos (Veracruz 40) Tours US$15-160. Dock open 7am-8pm daily. The local *lancha* cooperative offers a variety of boat excursions ranging from half-hour trips around the lagoon to all-day jungle trips to Tenacatita. One popular tour heads across the lagoon to the village of Colimilla (US$11). Prices (good for up to eight people) are posted at the open-air lagoon-side office. The coop also offers fishing, snorkeling and diving trips.

For a short jaunt out on the water, you could also catch a water taxi from a nearby dock and head over to the Grand Bay Hotel on Isla de Navidad (US$1 roundtrip; see Getting There & Away later in this section).

If a serious **deep-sea fishing** expedition is what you have in mind, pass on the lanchas and check out **Z Pesca** (☎ 355-60-99, *Jalisco 8, at Crazy Cactus)* or **Fantasía Pesca Deportiva** (☎ 355-68-24, *Legazpi 213)*, both of which have better boats and equipment. A six-hour all-inclusive (except beer) trip costs US$100 to US$200 depending on the size of the boat and number of fisherfolk.

Special Events
Big-money international fishing tournaments are held annually for marlin, sailfish, tuna and dorado. The most important, the three-day Torneo Internacional de Pesca, is held around the third week in January. The second most important is the two-day Torneo Internacional de Marlin, held during late May or early June, with another two-day tournament in mid-August. The final tournament of the year is held around Independence Day on September 15 and 16.

Places to Stay
Budget *Casa de Huéspedes Mama Laya* *(no ☎, Veracruz 69)* Singles/doubles with shared bath US$10/16.50. Cheapest in town, this very basic place has a quiet rooftop terrace with good views. You can also pitch a tent on the roof.

Hotel Caribe (☎ 355-59-52, Sonora 15) Singles/doubles with private bath US$14.50/20. The popular Caribe is one of Barra's best budget deals. It has a rooftop terrace, hot water, laundry service and clean rooms, some of which are larger than others.

Hotel Posada Pacífico (☎ 355-53-59, fax 355-53-49, Mazatlán 136 at Michoacán) Singles/doubles US$14/20, bungalows with kitchen from US$35. Friendly Posada Pacífico has 25 large, clean rooms, plus a few bungalows sleeping up to four people. Some English is spoken.

Hotel San Lorenzo (☎/fax 355-51-39, Sinaloa 7, near Mazatlán) Singles/doubles US$15/17, doubles with two beds US$18.50. Try the less drab upstairs rooms at bright orange San Lorenzo if all the other budget hotels in town are full.

Mid-Range & Top End *Hotel Delfín* *(☎ 355-50-68, fax 355-60-20, e hoteldelfin@ barradenavidad.zzn.com, Morelos 23)* Singles/doubles May-Nov US$23/27, Dec-Apr US$35. The four-story Delfín is one of Barra's best hotels. Its large, clean, pleasant rooms open onto wide shared balconies; most rooms have views of the lagoon. A good-value breakfast buffet is served poolside year-round. Repeat customers often fill the place in winter. Note

Christ of the Cyclone

The Christ figure hanging on the cross of Barra de Navidad's San Antonio church is unlike any other in Mexico; its arms hang at its sides, rather than being outstretched on the cross. The figure originally had its arms outstretched, but at dawn on September 1, 1971, when Hurricane Lily hit Barra with full force, the statue's arms fell from the cross. Locals believe that when the figure's arms fell, it calmed the hurricane and saved the town. Ever since, they have believed that the 'Cristo del Ciclón' has miraculous powers.

that the thumping bass from Hotel Sands' disco across the street can be a nuisance after dark.

Hotel Sands (☎/fax 355-50-18, reservations ☎ 33-3616-2859 in Guadalajara, Morelos 24) Singles/doubles with breakfast US$35/49, bungalows with kitchen from US$80 (bargain for up to 50% off in low season). The party-oriented Sands has a lagoonside swimming pool and a poolside restaurant/bar. Some rooms are a bit rough around the edges, but few folks seem to mind after the popular high-season happy hour (4pm to 6pm daily). Request a room away from the adjacent El Galeón disco if you've forgotten your earplugs.

Polo's Bungalows (☎ 355-64-10, Veracruz 174) 1-bed/2-bed double-occupancy bungalows US$33/55. This modern, luxurious complex has secure parking and deluxe rooms with kitchen, air-con, hot water and cable TV. Inquire about monthly rates.

Bungalows Mar Vida (☎ 355-59-11, Mazatlán 168) Apartments US$55. The fine little Mar Vida has a swimming pool and five studio apartments, all with air-con and cable TV. English is spoken.

Hotel Barra de Navidad (☎ 355-51-22, fax 355-53-03, w www.hotelbarradenavidad .com, Legazpi 250) Singles US$60, US$7 per extra person. This modern hotel has a beachside swimming pool and 60 attractive rooms with air-con and cable TV.

Grand Bay Hotel Isla Navidad (☎ 355-50-50, fax 355-60-71) Suites US$322-2925. On a peninsula in the lagoon, this superluxury resort is spendy but magnificent. Golf,

CENTRAL PACIFIC COAST

tennis and other packages are available (three-night minimum stay).

Places to Eat

Of Barra's many good restaurants, several are on beachfront terraces with beautiful sunset views, and several more overlook the lagoon. Simple, inexpensive little indoor-outdoor places line Calle Veracruz in the center of town.

Restaurant Ambar (cnr Veracruz & Jalisco) Dinner US$6-15. Open 8am-noon & 5pm-11pm daily, Nov-Apr & July-Aug. This treasure, hidden upstairs under a high palapa roof, is good for evening meals. Verónica, the French owner/cook, offers high-quality food and a good wine list. Imaginatively prepared crêpes are the house specialty.

At several other good beachfront places near the corner of Legazpi and Yucatán, full dinners run US$8 to US$15. *Mariscos Nacho* features a wide selection of breakfasts and seafood, and it proudly proclaims itself *'el rey del pescado asado'* ('king of grilled fish'). The *Sea Master Café (cnr Legazpi & Yucatán)* is another decent bar and grill. Nearby, also with fine views overlooking the lagoon on Veracruz, are *Restaurant Eloy*, *Veleros* and *El Manglito*.

Entertainment

Adjacent to Hotel Sands, *El Galeón* (open November to Easter) is a disco with a popular poolside bar. The daily happy hour (4pm to 6pm) includes use of the pool. Happy hour at *Piper Lovers Bar (Legazpi near Yucatán)* runs 5pm to 6pm and 9pm to 10pm daily year-round; loud live music often follows in high season.

Getting There & Around

Air Barra de Navidad and Melaque are served by Playa de Oro International Airport (ZLO), 25km southeast on highway 200, which also serves Manzanillo. To get to town from the airport, take a taxi (30 minutes, US$24), or take a bus 15km to Cihuatlán and a cheaper taxi from there. See the Manzanillo section for flight details.

Bus See San Patricio-Melaque earlier in this chapter; long-distance buses stopping there also stop here (15 minutes before or after). Transportes Cihuatlán's station is at Veracruz 228; Primera Plus is almost opposite (look right).

In addition to the long-distance buses, colorful local buses connect Barra and Melaque (every 15 minutes 6am to 9pm, US$0.40), stopping in Barra at the long-distance bus stations (buses stopping on the southbound side of the road loop round Legazpi and back to Melaque).

Taxis between Barra and San Patricio-Melaque run US$3.25 to US$4.

Boat Water taxis operate on demand 24 hours a day from the dock at the south end of Veracruz, offering service to the Grand Bay Hotel (US$1), the marina, the golf course and Colimilla. Also see Activities, earlier in this section, for information on boat tours.

MANZANILLO

• pop 95,000 ☎ 314

The 'little apple' is an industrial city and major port of call dominated by shipping piers, train tracks and a bustling central district. Away from the center, fine beaches ring nearby Bahía de Santiago and Bahía de Manzanillo, and the lagoons surrounding town offer good bird-watching. Deep-sea fishing is also popular here. In fact, boosters call Manzanillo the 'World Capital of Sailfish' – more than 300 *pez vela* were caught here during a three-day fishing tournament in 1957.

Orientation

Manzanillo extends 16km, northwest to southeast. The resort hotels and finest beaches begin at Playa Azul, across the bay from Playa San Pedrito, the closest beach to the center. Farther around the bay is Peninsula de Santiago, a rocky outcrop holding Las Hadas Resort and Playa La Audiencia. Just west of the peninsula, Bahía de Santiago is lined with three excellent stretches of sand: Playas Santiago, Olas Altas and Miramar. Just west of Playa Miramar are Laguna de Juluapan and Playa La Boquita.

Central Manzanillo is bound by Bahía de Manzanillo to the north, the Pacific Ocean to the west and Laguna de Cuyutlán to the south. Avenida Morelos, the main drag, runs along the north edge of town center, beside the sea. On its east end it meets Avenida Niños Héroes, which leads to highway 200.

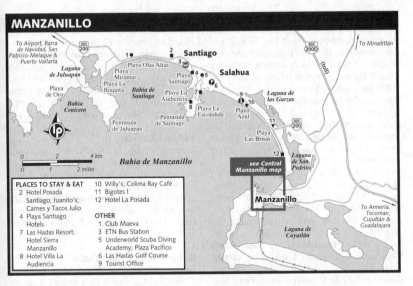

MANZANILLO

To Airport, Barra
de Navidad, San
Patricio-Melaque &
Puerto Vallarta

To Minatitlán

Laguna
de Juluapan

Playa Olas Altas

Santiago

Playa
Miramar
Playa La
Boquita

Bahía de
Santiago

Playa
Santiago

Salahua

Playa
de Oro

Bahía
Cenicero

Playa La
Audiencia

Laguna de
las Garzas

Playa La
Escondida

Playa
Azul

Península
de Juluapan

Península
de Santiago

Playa
Las Brisas

Bahía de Manzanillo

see Central
Manzanillo map

Laguna
de San
Pedrito

Manzanillo

0   2   4 km
0   1   2 miles

To Armería,
Tecoman,
Cujutlán &
Guadalajara

Laguna de
Cuyutlán

PLACES TO STAY & EAT
2 Hotel Posada
   Santiago; Juanito's;
   Carnes y Tacos Julio
4 Playa Santiago
   Hotels
7 Las Hadas Resort;
   Hotel Sierra
   Manzanillo
8 Hotel Villa La
   Audiencia

10 Willy's; Colima Bay Café
11 Bigotes I
12 Hotel La Posada

OTHER
1 Club Maeva
3 ETN Bus Station
5 Underworld Scuba Diving
   Academy; Plaza Pacifico
6 Las Hadas Golf Course
9 Tourist Office

The city center begins at the *zócalo* (also known as the *jardín central*) and continues south along Avenida México, a major artery. The east-west streets crossing Avenida México change names on either side of it.

Information

The municipal Departamento de Turismo (☎ 332-10-02 ext 247) operates a sidewalk tourist information desk in front of the Presidencia Municipal; open 9am to 7pm daily. The tourist police are stationed behind the Presidencia Municipal. The helpful state-run Secretaría de Turismo (☎ 333-22-77/64) is at Boulevard Miguel de la Madrid 1033, around the bay in Playa Azul (between the Fiesta Mexicana and Marbella hotels). It's open 9am to 2pm and 5pm to 7.30pm Monday to Friday, 10am to 2pm Saturday.

Several banks with ATMs are scattered around the city center. Bital, on Avenida México a block south of the zócalo, is open 8am to 7pm Monday to Friday, 9am to 2.30pm Saturday.

The post office, south of the zócalo at Galindo 30, is open 9am to 5.30pm Monday to Friday, 9am to 1pm Saturday. Telecomm, with telegram and fax service, is in the Presidencia Municipal, on the southeast corner of the zócalo; open 8am to 7.30pm Monday to Friday, 9am to 12.30pm Saturday, Sunday and holidays.

Public telephones are plentiful around the center. Computel, with long-distance telephone and fax service, has offices at Avenida Morelos 144 and Avenida México 302, both open 7am to 10pm daily.

The most central Internet café is in La Luna silver shop, Avenida México 69, half a block south of the zócalo. A few blocks farther south, redundant Internet Online, Carrillo Puerto 223, is open until 8pm and charges US$2 an hour.

The air-conditioned public library is on Avenida Morelos opposite the zócalo; open 10am to 2pm and 4pm to 8pm Monday to Saturday.

Lavandería Lavimatic, on Madero near Serdán, is within walking distance of the center.

Museo Universitario de Arqueología

University of Colima's archaeological museum (☎ 332-22-56, Niños Héroes at Glorieta San Pedrito; admission US$1.25; open 10am-2pm & 5pm-8pm Tues-Sat, 10am-1pm Sun) presents interesting objects from ancient Colima and some other parts of Mexico. The university art gallery is opposite.

Beaches

Playa San Pedrito, 1km northeast of the zócalo, is the closest beach to town. The next closest stretch of sand, spacious **Playa Las Brisas**, caters to a few hotels. **Playa Azul** stretches northwest from Las Brisas and curves around to Las Hadas and the best beaches in the area: **La Audiencia, Santiago, Olas Altas** and **Miramar**. Miramar and Olas Altas have the best surfing and bodysurfing waves in the area; surfboards can be rented at Miramar. Playa La Audiencia, lining a quiet cove on the west side of Peninsula de Santiago, has more tranquil water and is thus popular for water-skiing and other noisy motorized water sports.

Getting to these beaches from the town center is easy: local buses marked 'Santiago,' 'Las Brisas' and 'Miramar' head around the bay to San Pedrito, Salahua, Santiago, Miramar and beaches along the way and take 40 minutes. 'Las Hadas' buses take a more circuitous, scenic route down Peninsula de Santiago. These buses depart from Avenida México, from the corner of Juárez and 21 de Marzo near the zócalo and from the main bus station, every 10 minutes from 6am to 11pm. Fares (pay driver as you board) are US$0.30 to US$0.60, depending on how far down the line you're going.

Activities

Water sports rule here. Snorkeling, scuba diving, windsurfing, sailing, water-skiing and deep-sea fishing are all popular around the bay. Susan and Carlos at **Underworld Scuba Diving Academy** (☎ 333-06-42, cellular ☎ 044-314-358-50-42, fax 333-36-78, e scuba@gomanzanillo.com, w www .gomanzanillo.com, Plaza Pacífico), on Peninsula de Santiago, offer CMAS, PADI and YMCA certification courses and charge around US$100 (with low-season discounts) for two boat dives, including equipment. Highlights include feeding eels by hand at Playa La Audiencia, or exploring a sunken cargo ship that lies 9m down off Playa Miramar.

Special Events

In early February a sailing regatta, which comes from San Diego, Alta California, in even-numbered years and from Puerto Vallarta in odd-numbered years, ends with celebrations at Las Hadas.

The Fiestas de Mayo celebrate Manzanillo's anniversary with sporting competitions and other events over the first 10 days

in May. Here, as elsewhere in Mexico, the Fiesta de Nuestra Señora de Guadalupe is held December 1-12 in honor of Mexico's revered manifestation of the Virgin Mary.

Sailfish season runs November to March, with marlin, red snapper, sea bass and tuna also plentiful. The biggest international tournament is held in November, with a smaller national tournament in February.

Places to Stay

Central Manzanillo is safe and clean, and the best places to stay are within a block or two of the zócalo. More places to stay lie a few blocks south of the city center, but that area is comparatively squalid. Around the bay, where the better beaches are, hotels tend to be more expensive; Playa Santiago, half an hour away by bus, is the exception.

Budget *Hotel Emperador* (☎ 332-23-74, Dávalos 69) Singles/1-bed doubles US$9/11, 2-bed doubles US$13. Half a block from the zócalo, this simple but clean refuge has some top-floor rooms that are brighter than the rest. The hotel's restaurant is good and is one of the cheapest in town.

Hotel Flamingos (☎ 332-10-37, Madero 72) Singles/doubles US$9/11.50. This nicely furnished, low-budget place is half a block south of the zócalo.

Casa de Huéspedes Petrita (☎ 332-01-87, Allende 24) Singles/1-bed doubles with shared bath US$6.50/8, doubles with private bath US$16.50. Last-ditch Petrita's is very basic, but it's clean and economical.

Mid-Range *Hotel Colonial* (☎/fax 332-10-80, 332-06-68, Bocanegra 100) Singles/doubles with air-con & TV US$18.50/22. A block south of the zócalo, this pleasant older place has parking and a popular restaurant/bar.

Hotel San Pedrito (☎/fax 332-05-35, Teniente Azueta 3) Singles/doubles US$22-29. The only option close to both the beach and downtown, this beachfront hotel has a swimming pool fronting Playa San Pedrito. Generous exterior and second-story rooms are less dank than interior ones. From the zócalo, walk 15 leisurely minutes east along the Malecón, or catch a local bus and get off at the archaeology museum.

The following four fine hotels are a winding 10- or 15-minute walk (or five-minute

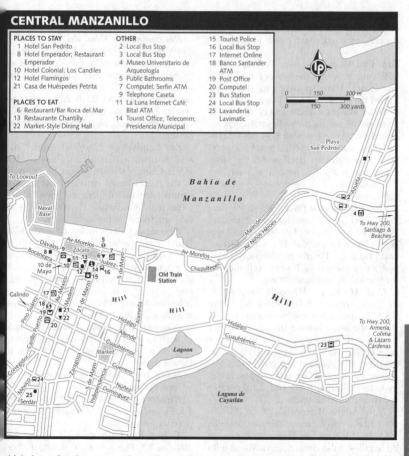

CENTRAL MANZANILLO

PLACES TO STAY
1 Hotel San Pedrito
8 Hotel Emperador; Restaurant Emperador
10 Hotel Colonial; Los Candiles
12 Hotel Flamingos
21 Casa de Huéspedes Petrita

PLACES TO EAT
6 Restaurant/Bar Roca del Mar
13 Restaurante Chantilly
22 Market-Style Dining Hall

OTHER
2 Local Bus Stop
3 Local Bus Stop
4 Museo Universitario de Arqueología
5 Public Bathrooms
7 Computel; Serfin ATM
9 Telephone Caseta
11 La Luna Internet Café; Bital ATM
14 Tourist Office; Telecomm; Presidencia Municipal

15 Tourist Police
16 Local Bus Stop
17 Internet Online
18 Banco Santander ATM
19 Post Office
20 Computel
23 Bus Station
24 Local Bus Stop
25 Lavandería Lavimatic

ride) from Santiago town down the road leading off highway 200 past the ETN bus station and several well-placed coconut and *coctel de frutas* vendors. The hotels perch on a bluff overlooking Playa Santiago, and all except the Anita have beachfront swimming pools; the Marlyn and Playa de Santiago also have restaurant/bars:

Hotel Anita (☎ 333-01-61) Singles/doubles US$11/22. Bare-bulb Anita is the cheapest of the four, with 36 large if fading-fast rooms.

Hotel Marlyn (☎ 333-01-07, reservations ☎ 33-3613-8411 in Guadalajara) Singles & doubles US$43-60, suites US$109-130. Next door to the Anita, Hotel Marlyn has rates that vary depending on views and amenities. All rooms have private balconies, and some

have air-con. Larger six-person kitchen suites are available.

Hotel Brillamar (☎ 334-11-88) Singles & doubles US$20-35, bungalows sleeping up to six US$60-90. Just past the Marlyn, the attractive Brillamar has breezy rooms with air-con and TV, plus a variety of kitchen bungalows.

Hotel Playa de Santiago (☎ 333-02-70, fax 333-03-44, e hoplasan@bay.net.mx) Singles & doubles US$55/65 low/high season. Two children under 10 stay for no extra charge. At the end of the road, this hotel has rooms with private sea-view balconies.

Another option in this price range is: **Hotel Posada Santiago** (☎ 333-00-14, Blvd Miguel de la Madrid Km 13.5) Low/high season US$16.50/27 for two. Two blocks west of Santiago's sleepy plaza, this simple, bright yellow posada lacks a sign but is surrounded by good, cheap places to eat.

Top End Most of Manzanillo's upmarket hotels are on or near the beaches outside the city center. Many sprawl along the beach side of the main road near Playa Azul.

Hotel Villas La Audiencia (☎ 333-08-61, *Santiago Peninsula near Playa Audiencia*) Doubles US$55, villas with 1-3-beds US$70-140. This moderately priced hotel is a good value, especially for families. All the villas come with a kitchen, air-con and satellite TV, and there's a swimming pool and restaurant/bar.

Hotel La Posada (☎/fax 333-18-99, *Cárdenas 201*) Singles/doubles with breakfast US$65/70 low season, US$80/90 mid-Dec-Apr. Closer to town at Playa Las Brisas, beachfront La Posada is a friendly lodge with a swimming pool. It's also well-situated for snorkeling and windsurfing.

Club Maeva (☎ 331-08-75 or 800-523-84-54 in Mexico, ☎ 800-466-2382 in the USA & Canada, ⓦ www.maevaresorts.com, *Playa Miramar*) Rooms from US$105 per person off-season, up to US$179 per person in winter. Santiago Bay's all-inclusive Club Maeva has more than 500 rooms and is great for active types. Rates include unlimited food and drink, water sports and entertainment.

Hotel Sierra Manzanillo (☎/fax 333-20-00, *Playa Audiencia*) Singles/doubles US$176/212. Near Las Hadas on Peninsula de Santiago, all-inclusive Sierra Manzanillo offers a similar deal to Club Maeva.

Las Hadas Resort (☎ 334-00-00, *Playa Audiencia*) Doubles May-Nov US$240, mid-Dec-Apr US$305. The best known of the Santiago Peninsula's expensive hotels is this 220-room Arabian-style complex where the film *10,* featuring Bo Derek, was made. It's worth a visit for a meal or a drink.

Places to Eat

A number of good places to eat surround the zócalo.

Restaurante Chantilly (☎ 332-01-94, *Juárez 44*) Mains US$3-10. Open 7.30am-10.30pm Sun-Fri. On the south side of the zócalo, this crowded *cafetería* and *nievería* has lots of reasonably priced meals and snacks, plus a generous *comida corrida*

(US$4.50), genuine espresso and good ice cream.

Restaurant/Bar Roca del Mar (☎ 332-03-02, *Morelos 225*) Mains US$4-12. On the east side of the zócalo, this slightly more spacious and formal eatery, featuring a full bar and sidewalk seating, is good for people-watching and meals. Among its specialties is a seafood comida corrida (US$8) with seafood soup, rice, fish or shrimp and dessert.

Los Candiles (☎ 332-10-80, *Hotel Colonial, Bocanegra 100*) Mains US$4-10. The Hotel Colonial's restaurant, a block south of the zócalo, opens onto a pleasant patio, features surf-and-turf fare and has a full bar. Other highlights include the comida corrida ($5) and sports on the satellite TV.

Restaurant Emperador (☎ 332-23-74, *Hotel Emperador, Dávalos 69*) Mains US$2-4.50. Open 8am-11.30pm daily. Half a block west of the zócalo, this small ground-floor restaurant is simple, but has good, cheap food. Highlights include set breakfasts and the meat-and-seafood comida corrida (US$3).

A *market-style dining hall* at the corner of Madero and Cuauhtémoc is open 7am to 9pm daily and has a number of stalls to choose from.

Many more restaurants are spread out around the bay.

Bigotes I (☎ 334-08-31, *highway 200 Km 1.5, Playa Las Brisas*) Mid-range Bigotes is popular for seafood.

Colima Bay Café (☎ 333-11-50, *highway 200 Km 6.5, Playa Azul*) This fun, if overpriced, chain place tries hard to put on a good time for tourists. It features music, good food and lots to drink.

Willy's (☎ 333-17-92, *1 Lotee Manza s/n, Playa Azul*) Dinner US$10-25. Arguably Playa Azul's best restaurant, Willy's offers fine French and international cuisine.

In Santiago, west of the plaza, are a few other noteworthy places:

Carnes y Tacos Julio Open noon-1am daily. This place offers excellent inexpensive meat dishes. A few doors down, *Julio's* is also cheap (everything less than US$3) and good.

Juanito's (☎ 333-13-88, *highway 200 Km 14.3*) Open 8am-11pm daily. Across the road from the Julio twins and 100m west, Juanito's is a popular mid-range gringo hangout.

Entertainment

If you're in town on a Sunday evening, stop by the zócalo, where multiple generations come out to enjoy an ice cream and the warm evening air. This tradition, which is fast disappearing in many parts of post-NAFTA Mexico, still thrives here. On the most atmospheric of nights, a band belts out traditional music from the gazebo. It's also worth stopping by the zócalo at sunset to hear the cacophony of the exuberant *zanates* (blackbirds) as they settle into their roosts. Tourist nightlife is spread out around the bay.

At Playa Azul, *Vog* is a popular disco. Next door, *Bar de Felix* has no cover charge, and many people like it better for dancing. Near the Hotel Fiesta Mexicana, *Teto's Bar* offers live music and dancing. *Kitzias Discotheque* (highway 200 Km 10.5) is another popular disco, and *Ole Ole* (highway 200 Km 7.5) is the place to dance to live salsa music.

Near Las Hadas in Santiago, *Cantina del Vaquero* (☎ 334-19-69, Blvd Miguel de la Madrid 5010) features carne asada and dance music. On Playa Miramar, *Club Maeva* (☎ 335-05-96) houses *Disco Boom Boom* and *Tropical Hut*, which present theme entertainment several nights weekly; phone for reservations.

Getting There & Away

Air Playa de Oro International Airport (ZLO) is 35km northwest of Manzanillo's Zona Hotelera on highway 200. Aero California, Aeromar and Mexicana fly direct to/from Mexico City. Aerolitoral (under Aeroméxico) flies to/from Guadalajara, Ixtapa, Monterrey and Puerto Vallarta. Aero California and Alaska both fly to/from Los Angeles. America West flies to/from Phoenix during the high season.

Bus ETN (☎ 334-10-50) offers deluxe and 1st-class service from its own terminal near Santiago at highway 200 Km 13.5. The other companies use Manzanillo's bus terminal, 1.5km east of the center; ticket offices, luggage storage, a telephone caseta and restaurants huddle in a dusty row where a terminal once stood prior to the 1995 earthquake.

Destinations include:

Armería – 45km, 45 minutes; 2nd-class Autobuses Nuevo Horizonte every 15 minutes 4am-10pm (US$2.50), 2nd-class Autotransportes del Sur de Jalisco hourly 2am-10pm (US$2.50)

Barra de Navidad – 60km, 1-1½ hours; 1st-class/2nd-class Transportes Cihuatlán at least hourly 4.30am-midnight (US$4.50/3.50)

Colima – 101km, 1½-2 hours; eight daily, deluxe ETN (US$6), 1st-class La Línea Plus (US$5), 2nd-class Autobuses Nuevo Horizonte and Autotransportes del Sur de Jalisco every half hour 2am-10pm (US$4)

Guadalajara – 325km, 4½-8 hours; frequent 1st-class La Línea Plus, Transportes Cihuatlán and ETN (US$15-22); 19 2nd-class Transportes Cihuatlán and Autotransportes del Sur de Jalisco (US$14-18)

Lázaro Cárdenas – 313km, 6 hours; 1st-class Elite at 2am & 6am (US$21); 6 2nd-class Autotransportes del Sur de Jalisco and Galeana (US$15)

Mexico City (Terminal Norte) – 843km, 12 hours; *via corta* (short route) or via Morelia; deluxe Elite at 7.30pm & 9pm (US$53), 1st-class ETN at 7.30pm (US$35)

Puerto Vallarta – 285km, 5-6½ hours; 1st-class Elite at 4pm, 7.30pm & 9.30pm (US$18.50), 1st-class Transportes Cihuatlán at 8am & noon (US$19), 9 2nd-class Transportes Cihuatlán (US$16)

San Patricio-Melaque – 65km, 1-1½ hours; same as to Barra de Navidad

Getting Around

Transportes Turísticos Benito Juárez (☎ 334-15-55) shuttles door-to-door to/from Playa de Oro airport. Fare is US$22 for private *particular* service (one or two people) or US$8 per person *colectivo* when three or more people share the ride. A taxi from the airport to Manzanillo's center or most resort hotels runs US$18 to US$22.

Local buses heading around the bay to San Pedrito, Salahua, Santiago, Miramar and beaches along the way depart every 10 minutes 6am to 11pm from all along Avenida México, as well as from the corner of Juárez and 21 de Marzo near the zócalo and from the main bus station. Fares (pay driver as you board) are US$0.30 to US$0.60, depending on how far you're going.

Taxis are plentiful in Manzanillo. From the zócalo, cab fare is around US$1.50 to the bus station, US$3 to Playa Azul, US$4.50 to Playa Santiago and US$6 to Playa Miramar. Agree with the driver on the price *before* you get into the cab.

CUYUTLÁN & EL PARAÍSO

The small, black-sand-beach resort towns of Cuyutlán (population 1000, ☎ 313) and Cuyutlán & El Paraíso (population 300, ☎ 313) are seldom visited by norteamericanos, but are popular with Mexican families. Cuyutlán is at the southeastern end of Laguna de Cuyutlán, 40km southeast of Manzanillo and 12km west of Armería. As the crow flies, sleepy El Paraíso is 6km southeast of Cuyutlán along the coast, but by road it's more like 12km. The choice of hotels is better in more developed Cuyutlán, but the beach is less crowded and more tranquil in the much smaller fishing village of El Paraíso.

Orientation & Information

Most of Cuyutlán's tourist facilities are clustered near the beach. If you arrive in town by bus you'll be dumped off on Hidalgo, on the east side of the zócalo. Walk four blocks toward the ocean on Hidalgo and you'll land right in the middle of the beachfront hotel and restaurant area.

Cuyutlán has a post office (El Paraíso does not), but neither town has a bank; for this you'll have to visit Armería. Both towns have public telephones and long-distance casetas near their zócalos.

Things to See & Do

Aside from its long stretch of relatively isolated beach, Cuyutlán is known for its *ola verde* (green wave), appearing just offshore in April and May. This phenomenon is supposedly caused by little green phosphorescent critters, but it's the subject of much local debate. Bigger green critters can be seen at the **Centro Tortuguero** *(admission US$1; open 10am-5.30pm Tues-Sun)*, a beachfront turtle sanctuary and environmental-education center 4km toward Paraíso.

Cuyutlán lies near the *salinas* (salt ponds) at the southeast end of Laguna de Cuyutlán. In an old wooden warehouse a block north of the plaza, the free **Museo de Sal** depicts the process of salt production in miniature (all signs are in Spanish) and has historic photos of life around the lagoon; the retired salt workers who act as caretakers appreciate donations.

Good **surfing** can be found 3km south of El Paraíso near Boca de Pascuale.

Places to Stay & Eat

Beachfront accommodation here costs less than in most other electrified Pacific-coast locales. Reserve in advance for Christmas and Semana Santa, when Cuyutlán's hotels are booked solid by Mexican families. During these holidays, many hotels require you to take three meals a day; cost for room and board will be at least US$25 per person. Rates quoted here are for the off-season unless otherwise noted.

Cuyutlán You can camp on the empty sands on either side of the hotels – when in doubt, ask the closest palapa owner for permission. Several of the beachfront enramadas rent showers. Tent camping and RV parking is also welcomed at the Centro Tortuguero (see Things to See & Do).

As you approach the beach on Hidalgo, you'll cross Veracruz one block before the pedestrian-only beachfront Malecón. Hotel Morelos and Hotel Fénix, Cuyutlán's best budget hotels (both with good open-air restaurants), anchor this corner, and several other hotels and beachfront seafood restaurant/bars lie a block or two to either side.

Hotel Morelos (☎ 326-40-13, *Hidalgo 185 at Veracruz)* Rooms with bath and hot water US$10/25 per person without/with three meals, high season. The old-school Morelos has 35 clean, spacious rooms (some remodeled, check a few), hot water, a swimming pool and a good, if greasy, restaurant (open daily 7.30am-10pm; comida corrida US$4.50).

Hotel Fénix (☎/fax *326-40-82, Hidalgo 201 at Veracruz)* Rooms US$8 per person downstairs, US$10 upstairs. Opposite Hotel Morelos and a block off the beach, the Fénix has 14 rooms with private bath. The breezier and brighter 2nd-floor rooms are worth the extra pesos. Look for the friendly English-speaking management behind the bar in the open-air restaurant.

Hotel El Bucanero (☎ *326-40-05, cnr Hidalgo & Malecón)* Interior/sea-view rooms US$8/11 per person. Fronting the beach behind Hotel Fénix, the salt-encrusted Buccaneer may appear rough around the edges, but it has some nice rooms with new mattresses and a decent cheap restaurant, El Galeón Viejo.

Hotel María Victoria (☎ *326-40-04, Veracruz 10)* Rooms US$23 per person. Opposite El Bucanero, also right on the beach, this large *Miami Vice*-inspired hotel is Cuyutlán's most luxurious. The sea-view restaurant serves fresh typical Mexican fare at high-roller prices.

Hotel San Rafael (☎ 326-40-15, Veracruz 46) Interior/exterior rooms US$13/16 per person. Next to the María Victoria, the re-modeled San Rafael has a swimming pool and beachfront restaurant/bar. Sea-view rooms, which share a large breezy balcony, are the most inviting.

El Paraíso Once you roll into dusty one-lane El Paraíso, it's either left or right at the T intersection. *Hotel Valencia (☎ 322-00-25)* Singles/doubles US$11/15. *A la derecha* (to the right), the simple eight-room Valencia is one of several ad-hoc places charging similar (seasonally negotiable) rates for spartan accommodation.

Hotel Paraíso (☎ 322-10-32) Rooms US$25 for up to two adults and two children. *A la izquerda* (left), the Paraíso is the fanciest hotel in town, but that's not saying much. It has 60 rooms, a swimming pool, pleasant terraces and the town's most expensive seafood restaurant.

Otherwise you can *camp* on the beach or string up a hammock at one of El Paraíso's beachfront *enramadas*. All the enramadas serve basically the same food at similar prices; expect to spend US$5 to US$10 per person for a full, fresh meal.

Getting There & Away

Cuyutlán and Paraíso are connected to the rest of the world through Armería, a friendly little service center on highway 200, 46km southeast of Manzanillo and 55km southwest of Colima. From Armería to Cuyutlán it's 12km down a paved road past orchards and coconut plantations; a similar road runs 8km south-west from Armería to El Paraíso.

To reach either place by bus involves a transfer in Armería. Two bus lines – Sociedad Cooperativo de Autotransportes Colima Manzanillo and Auto-

transportes Nuevo Horizonte – have offices and stops a couple of doors down on Armería's main street. They both operate 2nd-class buses to Manzanillo every half hour, 5am to 12.30am (45 minutes, US$2.50) and to Colima every half hour, 5.45am to 10.30pm (45 minutes, US$2.50). Buses go every 20 minutes to Tecomán (25 minutes, US$0.70), where you can connect with Elite, Galeana and other buses heading southeast on highway 200 to Lázaro Cárdenas and elsewhere. Flecha Amarilla runs 2nd-class buses to Mexico City and Guadalajara. Across the street, Autotransportes del Sur de Jalisco serves Colima and Manzanillo.

Buses to Cuyutlán and El Paraíso depart from Armería's market, one block north and one block east of the long-distance bus depots. To Cuyutlán, they depart every half hour, 6am to 7.30pm (20 minutes, US$0.80). To El Paraíso, they go every 45 minutes, 6am to 7.30pm (15 minutes, US$0.70).

No buses shuttle directly between Cuyutlán and El Paraíso. To go by bus, you must return to Armería and change buses again. It's not as difficult as it sounds, but taxis are also available to link any of the towns directly. Approximate cab fares are: Cuyutlán to Armería, US$5.50; El Paraíso to Armería, US$4; and Cuyutlán to El Paraíso, US$5.

MICHOACÁN COAST

Much improved highway 200 traces the shoreline most of the way along the beautiful 250km coast of Michoacán, one of Mexico's most beautiful states. The route passes dozens of untouched beaches – some with wide expanses of golden sand, some tucked into tiny rocky coves, some at river mouths where quiet estuaries harbor multitudes of birds. Several have gentle lapping waves good for swimming, while others have big breakers suitable for surfing. Many of the beaches are uninhabited, but some have small communities. Mango, coconut, papaya and banana plantations line the highway, while the green peaks

Carefree accommodations

of the Sierra Madre del Sur form a lush backdrop inland.

At the Michoacán-Colima border, **Boca de Apiza**, deposited at the mouth of the Río Coahuayana, is a mangrove-lined beach with many competing seafood enramadas; turn off highway 200 at the town of Coahuayana. Kilometer markers begin counting down from Km 231 at the state border.

Twenty kilometers south, after the highway meets the coast, **San Juan de Alima** (Km 211) is an attractive community with beachfront restaurants and several modern hotels.

A short distance down the coast, **Las Brisas** (Km 207) is another beachside community with places to stay. Still farther along, **Playa La Ticla** (Km 183) is a popular surfing beach, with beachfront *cabañas* for rent.

The next stop is **Faro de Bucerías** (Km 173), known for its clear, pale-blue waters, yellow sand and rocky islands. It's a good spot for camping, swimming and snorkeling, and the local Nahua community prepares fresh seafood.

Farther along, white-sand **Playa Maruata** (Km 150) is one of Michoacán's most beautiful beaches, with clear turquoise waters. This is the principal Mexican beach where black sea turtles lay their eggs; these and other species of sea turtles are set free here each year by conservation programs. Camping and discreet nude bathing are possible, and services include rustic cabañas and some palapas serving fresh seafood.

Farther south, **Pichilinguillo** (Km 95) is in a small bay, good for swimming. Farther still are beautiful unsigned **Barra de Nexpa** (Km 56), popular with surfers; **Caleta de Campos** (Km 50), on a lovely little bay (see the next section); **La Soledad** (the Lonely Place), a very beautiful, tranquil little beach; and **Las Peñas**, another good surfing beach. Playa Azul, 24km northwest of Lázaro Cárdenas, is another laid-back beach community that is easy to visit and has surfable waves (see the Playa Azul section).

CALETA DE CAMPOS
• pop 2000 ☎ 753

A friendly little town on a bluff overlooking a lovely azure bay, 'Caleta' (Km 50) is a quiet place, but since it's a regional service center it has a pair of good, clean hotels and several friendly, satisfying places to eat.

Caleta's paved main drag has all the essentials, including a telephone caseta, late-night *taquerías* and torta shops, a pharmacy and several grocery stores. The beach, however, is more accessible at nearby surfing mecca Barra de Nexpa.

Hotel Los Arcos (☎ 531-50-38) Singles/doubles US$16.25/21.75 with fan and cold water, seaview rooms with fan and cold water US$25, seaview rooms with air-con and hot water US$35. Towards the ocean off the main drag, Los Arcos is Caleta's best choice, with friendly owners and a bird's eye view of the Bahía de Bufadero's blowhole. TV is available in any room for US$6 extra.

Hotel Yuritzi (☎ 531-50-10, Calle Corregidora 10) Singles/doubles with fan US$17.50/22, with air-con & TV US$32/38. Business travelers prefer the Yuritzi for its secure parking, and families like it for its swimming pool and homemade ice cream, but the rooms lack hot water.

First-class Ruta Paraíso and 2nd-class Galeana buses depart Caleta for Lázaro Cárdenas every 25 minutes, 5am to 7pm (1½ hours, US$3). In Lázaro Cárdenas, these buses depart from the Galeana terminal on Avenida Lázaro Cárdenas. A taxi between Caleta de Campos and Nexpa runs US$4; it's a bit less to the Nexpa turnoff on highway 200.

PLAYA AZUL
• pop 3500 ☎ 753

Playa Azul is a small beach resort backed by lagoons that are fed by tributaries of the Río Balsas. The town attracts Mexican families during Semana Santa and the Christmas holidays, when all the hotels fill up, prices rise and reservations are necessary. The rest of the time it's pretty quiet here, with a trickle of foreign travelers enjoying the long beach and surfable waves. A strong undertow, however, makes swimming touch-and-go; also beware of stray stingrays on the sand. Swimming is better at Laguna Pichi, a couple of kilometers east along the beach, where boat trips take visitors to view the plants, birds and other animals that inhabit the surrounding mangrove forest.

Orientation & Information
Playa Azul is so small and everything is so close that there's little need for street names. Basically, five main streets parallel

the beach. The beachside street, usually referred to as the Malecón, is officially named Zapata. Heading inland, the next four streets are Carranza, Madero, Independencia and Justo Sierra, in that order.

A Pemex station *(la gasolinera)* on the corner of Independencia represents the beginning of town as you enter from the highway. This station used to be the last opportunity to fill up on *magna sin* (unleaded) until Tecomán, 270km north, but new stations were being built on either side of Caleta de Campos in late 2001. The gasolinera is a major landmark where buses and combis congregate. The beach is three blocks straight ahead. A few blocks east (left as you face the sea) is a large plaza. Almost everything you need is somewhere between the plaza and the gasolinera. A long row of seafood enramadas stretches along the coast.

The post office, on Madero at the northwest corner of the plaza, is open 9am to 3pm Monday to Friday. Telecomm, with fax and telex service, is in the same building (different entrance). There are several telephone casetas, including one on Carranza and another near the gasolinera.

Activities

For swimming, pools provide a safer alternative to the turbulent ocean. Behind Hotel Playa Azul, **Balneario Playa Azul** *(Malecón; admission US$1.50, free to Hotel Playa Azul guests; open 10am-6pm Sat & Sun)* has a large swimming pool, a water slide and a restaurant/bar. Hotel Playa Azul and Hotel María Teresa also have courtyard pools with poolside restaurants (see Places to Stay & Eat).

A few kilometers southeast down the beach, **Laguna de Pichi** makes for a good excursion; lanchas can be hired for lagoon tours, and the estuary is good for swimming and bird-watching. You can walk there in half an hour or take a taxi (US$3).

Places to Stay & Eat

You can string up a hammock at most of the beachfront enramadas; ask permission from the family running the restaurant, who probably won't mind, especially if you eat there once or twice. If you don't have your own hammock they may loan you one. A couple of enramadas provide public toilets and showers.

Among the dozen or so hotels in town, a few stand out:

Hotel Costa de Oro *(☎ 536-02-51, Madero s/n)* Singles/doubles US$16.50/22. Near the plaza, this friendly family-run hotel has clean, spacious rooms with warm water.

Hotel María Isabel *(☎ 536-00-16, Madero s/n)* Singles/doubles US$21/25, 6-bed rooms US$45. On the far (east) side of the plaza, Hotel María has a swimming pool and 30 clean, spacious rooms with fans and hot water. Air-con is US$6.50 extra.

Hotel Playa Azul *(☎ 536-00-24/91, Carranza s/n) Económica* doubles US$30, singles/doubles with fan/air-con US$35/55, RV sites with full hookups US$20. The upmarket, 73-room Playa Azul has a small trailer park and nice rooms around the pool. The poolside Las Gaviotas restaurant/bar (open 7.30am to 10.30pm daily) is a travelers' favorite; if you eat or drink here, you can use both the hotel's pool and the adjacent Balneario Playa Azul.

Hotel María Teresa *(☎ 536-00-05, Independencia 626)* Singles/doubles US$33/38. This attractive place on the inland side of the plaza is a better value than Hotel Playa Azul. It has a swimming pool and poolside restaurant/bar, parking and 42 clean, comfortable rooms, all with air-con and TV. Note that the disco across the street can be loud on Friday and Saturday nights.

Playa Azul's beachfront enramadas prepare a similar selection of fresh seafood at competitive prices – the fanciest are to the right as you face the beach. Try the regional-specialty *pescado relleno*, a fried fillet of fish stuffed with shrimp, octopus and sundry seafood.

Two small family restaurants, *Restaurant Galdy* and *Restaurant Familiar Martita*, both on the market street near Madero, around the corner from Hotel Playa Azul, are recommended by locals. Both serve fresh-squeezed juices and good cheap grub (comida corrida US$3) and are open 7am to 11pm daily.

Getting There & Away

Combis run every 10 minutes, 5am to 9pm, between Playa Azul and Lázaro Cárdenas (24km, 30 minutes, US$1.25). They enter Playa Azul and follow Carranza, dropping you off anywhere along the way. In Playa

Azul, catch combis on Carranza or as they loop back on Independencia.

Intercity buses don't pass through Playa Azul; they will drop you off 7km to the north at the highway 200 junction in La Mira. To skip Lázaro Cárdenas and go from Playa Azul to Caleta de Campos or beyond, catch the northbound bus at La Mira.

Taxis between Playa Azul and Lázaro Cárdenas cost around US$11.

LÁZARO CÁRDENAS
• pop 65,000 ☎ 753

The significant port of Lázaro Cárdenas is Michoacán's largest coastal city. Originally named Melchor Ocampo, its name was changed in 1970 to honor Lázaro Cárdenas, Michoacán's reform-minded governor (1928-32) and Mexico's president (1934-40), who is most famous for nationalizing foreign (mostly US) oil assets during his tenure.

An industrial city, Lázaro has nothing of real interest to travelers – but since it's the terminus of several bus routes, travelers do pass through. Reasons to stop here include changing buses, stocking up on provisions, and heading 24km west to Playa Azul (see the Playa Azul section). If you must spend the night here, you'll find several adequate hotels near the bus stations.

Orientation & Information
The eponymous main drag, Avenida Lázaro Cárdenas, caters to travelers' needs. Near the bus terminals along Lázaro Cárdenas, the town center is a busy commercial area with travel agencies and banks, including Banamex, open 9am to 1pm Monday to Friday for money exchange, and Bancomer, open 8.30am to 5.30pm Monday to Friday, 10am to 2pm Saturday.

The state-run Delegación Regional de Turismo (☎ 532-15-47), Nicolás Bravo 475, is in front of Hotel Casablanca, four blocks northwest of the Galeana bus station and a block east of Avenida Lázaro Cárdenas. It offers free city and regional maps and is open 9am to 7pm Monday to Friday, 10am to 1pm Saturday.

Places to Stay & Eat
Hotel Reyna Pio (☎ 532-06-20, Corregidora 78) Singles/doubles with air-con & TV US$11/14. This good budget hotel is at the corner of 8 de Mayo, a block west o Avenida Lázaro Cárdenas.

Hotel Viña del Mar (☎ 532-04-15, Javie Mina 352) Singles/doubles US$18/21. Half a block west of Avenida Lázaro Cárdenas, the Viña del Mar has a small courtyard swimming pool and rooms with air-con, TV and phone.

Hotel Casablanca (☎ 537-34-80, Nicolás Bravo 475) Singles/doubles US$27/39. This business-minded luxury hotel is a block east of Avenida Lázaro Cárdenas.

Many restaurants cluster around the bus terminals. Locals recommend *Restaurant El Tejado* (*Lázaro Cárdenas, between Corregidora & Javier Mina*) for an ample, economical meal.

Getting There & Away
Air The Lázaro Cárdenas airport (LZC) is 6km from the center – 5 minutes by taxi (US$4) or colectivo (US$0.50). Aeromar flies to/from Mexico City; Aero Cuahonte flies to/from Uruapan, Morelia and Guadalajara; and Aeroméxico flies to/from Mexico City, Monterrey, Tijuana and Veracruz.

Bus Lázaro has four bus terminals, all within a few blocks of each other. Galeana (☎ 532-02-62) and Parhikuni (☎ 532-30-06), with services northwest to Manzanillo and inland to Uruapan and Morelia, share a terminal at Lázaro Cárdenas 1810, on the corner of Constitución de 1814. Opposite, at Lázaro Cárdenas 1791, Autobuses de Jalisco, La Línea, Vía 2000 and Sur de Jalisco (☎ 537-18-50) share a terminal and serve the same destinations, plus Colima, Guadalajara and Mexico City.

Estrella Blanca's big terminal (☎ 532-11-71), Francisco Villa 65, two blocks west behind the Galeana terminal, is also home base for Cuauhtémoc and Elite. From here buses head southeast to Zihuatanejo and Acapulco; up the coast to Manzanillo, Mazatlán and Tijuana; and inland to Uruapan, Morelia and Mexico City. Estrella de Oro (☎ 532-02-75), Corregidora 318, two blocks southwest of Estrella Blanca, serves Acapulco, Cuernavaca, Mexico City and Zihuatanejo.

Buses from Lázaro Cárdenas include:

Acapulco – 340km, 6-7 hours; 12 1st-class Estrella Blanca (US$17.50), 1st-class Estrella de Oro at

Highway 200: Road Conditions & Warnings

At the time of writing, highway 200 between Lázaro Cárdenas and Zihuatanejo was not very good, making for slow driving. Authorities claim the road was slowly being improved, but no one could guess when (or if) it would become a good road. Several readers have written to warn other travelers that driving between Lázaro Cárdenas and Zihuatanejo took them much longer than they would have expected from looking at the map; they ended up driving late at night, which they wanted to avoid.

A new *autopista* (superhighway) connecting Lázaro Cárdenas with Mexico City via Pátzcuaro and Morelia is scheduled to be built, but no one knows when this highway will be started, let alone finished.

Locals all along the coast repeatedly warned us not to travel the entire stretch of highway 200 from Tecomán to Acapulco at night – not only because of poor road conditions, but also because of rapacious *bandidos*. Due to several missed bus connections, we ended up traveling on this highway at night and arrived none the worse for the experience. Nevertheless, we received so many warnings about this that it seems like a good idea to pass the warning along.

6.30am (US$14), hourly 2nd-class Estrella Blanca (US$15), hourly 2nd-class Estrella de Oro (US$11.50).

Caleta de Campos – 65km, 1½ hours; 2nd-class Galeana every 25 minutes 5am-8pm (US$3.25)

Colima – 320km, 6-6½ hours; same buses as to Guadalajara by Autobuses de Jalisco/La Línea (US$19.50) and Sur de Jalisco (US$16.50)

Guadalajara – 540km, 9-11 hours; Autobuses de Jalisco/La Línea 'Plus' service at 10.30am, direct service at 8.15pm & 9.15pm (US$34), 1st-class at 11.15pm (US$31); 2nd-class Sur de Jalisco at 2am, 7am & 1pm (US$24)

Manzanillo – 313km, 6-7 hours; 1st-class Estrella Blanca at noon, 2.30pm & 1am (US$22), 4 2nd-class Galeana (US$14.50), 2nd-class Sur de Jalisco at 2.30pm & 5.30pm (US$14.50); or take Sur de Jalisco's Tecomán bus; 5½ hours (US$13) and then a frequent local bus from there

Mexico City (Terminal Poniente) – 711km, 12 hours; 2 1st-class Vía 2000 (US$42)

Mexico City (Terminal Sur) – 711km, 10-11 hours; 1st-class Estrella Blanca at 8am & 8.05pm (US$41-43), 1st-class Estrella de Oro at 5.50am, 9.50am, 7pm, 8pm & 9pm (US$38)

Morelia – 406km, 8 hours; 14 'Plus' Galeana/Parhikuni (US$25), 3 1st-class Vía 2000 (US$25), 1st-class Estrella Blanca at 11pm (US$21), 14 2nd-class Galeana/Parhikuni (US$20)

Uruapan – 280km, 6 hours; same buses as to Morelia (US$17.50-18.50)

Zihuatanejo – 120km, 2-3 hours; same buses as to Acapulco (US$3.50-7)

Combis to Playa Azul via La Mira trawl Avenida Lázaro Cárdenas every 10 minutes, 5am to 9pm (24km, 30 minutes, US$1.25),

stopping to rebait outside the Autobuses de Jalisco terminal, opposite Galeana. A taxi between Lázaro Cárdenas and Playa Azul fetches US$10 to US$12.

TRONCONES, BAHÍA MANZANILLO & MAJAHUA
• pop around 500 ☎ 755

A 25-minute drive or one-hour bus ride northwest of Zihuatanejo, Playa Troncones is a beach on the open sea with several beachfront seafood restaurants. It's a popular outing for Zihuatanejo families and home to a growing number of gringo expats. Just to the north is Playa Manzanillo, which lines Bahía Manzanillo – a lovely little bay. And just north of the bay is the quiet little fishing village of Majahua.

Orientation

The one-burro village of Troncones, 100m inland from the beach, has just two roads: the 3km paved road coming in from highway 200, and another dirt track stretching along the beach for 5km. The village surrounds the end of the paved road, but most of what you'll probably be looking for is along the unpaved beachfront road. Where the road coming in from the highway meets the sea, the Burro Borracho is 1km to the left, the Casa de la Tortuga 1.5km to the right (north), Playa Manzanillo is 2km north of that, and Majahua is a 10-minute walk past Playa Manzanillo. From Majahua, another dirt road (rough in wet season) leads to highway 200 near Km 32.

Activities

Playa Troncones has several world-class **surfing** breaks; it's best to get out in the morning, before 11am when the breeze picks up, or around sunset when the surf gets glassy. Troncones Point is a popular spot, and there are at least 20 other surfing spots, good for beginning to advanced surfers, along the coast within 20km. Saladita, 7km from Troncones, has an awesome half-mile left-hand break.

There's good **snorkeling** at Manzanillo Point, at the north end of Troncones. Other **water activities** in the area include fishing, sea kayaking, body-boarding, horseback riding, hiking, bird-watching and turtle-watching – you can observe sea turtles lay their eggs here in the sand on moonlit nights. Relaxing on the beach is another major 'activity.'

Places to Stay

While still a sleepy hideaway, Troncones has been experiencing a gringo-backed building boom since the ejidos went up for public sale in December 1995. Troncones' pristine 5km shoreline now boasts more than 80 beachfront rooms, and Playa Manzanillo and Majahua appear poised to follow a similar development trajectory.

Aside from hanging a hammock or pitching a tent, the cheapest sleeps are the basic rooms over *Miscelanea Jasmín*, an in-town *abarrotes* shop asking around US$15. Inquire at other Troncones shops for similarly priced off-beach deals.

Walking from town along the beach road south (left, facing the ocean), you'll come to:

La Puesta del Sol (☎ 553-28-18, reservations ☎ 323-913-0423 in the USA, fax 323-913-1246 in the USA, e troncones@yahoo.com, W www.mexonline.com/troncones) Basic double May-Oct/Nov-Apr US$25/35, mountain-view room US$45/70, ocean-view minisuite with kitchen US$70/90, penthouse US$150/190. This attractive four-room, three-story *palapa* offers a variety of rooms – from a simple 'surfers' room' to a superluxurious penthouse apartment.

Burro Borracho (cellular ☎ 044-755-553-28-34, e tortuga@cdnet.com.mx) Tent sites US$5, RV hookups US$10 including shower

and toilets, singles/doubles with breakfas May-July US$25/35, Nov-Apr US$50/60 This popular beachfront restaurant/bar ha six basic stone bungalows, all with ho water, big beds, hammocks on beachfron terraces and use of a communal outdoo kitchen.

Down the northern side of the unpavec beachfront road (right, facing the ocean) from nearest to farthest, are:

Casa Ki (☎ 553-28-15, e casaki@ yahoo.com, W www.casa-ki.com) Nov-Ap single/double bungalows US$75/85 with breakfast, 2-bedroom house sleeping ₄ US$165 (3-day minimum); 30% discoun May-Oct. Ed and Ellen Weston's charming B&B retreat includes a variety of ocean view rooms and a thoughtfully furnishec main house with a full kitchen. Reservations recommended.

Casa de la Tortuga (cellular ☎ 044-755 557-07-32, fax 553-24-17, e casadetortuga@ troncones.net, W www.casadelatortuga.net, Doubles with breakfast US$50-80. Oper ated by a friendly American couple, this pleasant guesthouse has two types of doubles: two beds and shared bath, or one big bed and private bath. Rooms are half-price May to November, but it may close June to August if business is slow.

Casa Delfín Sonriente (☎ 553-328-03, ☎/ fax 831-688-6578 in the USA, e enovey@ sasq.net, W www.casadelfinsonriente.com) Bungalows for two with shared bath US$65, air-conditioned rooms with private bath from US$85, suites US$120, complete villa rental (sleeps 8-12) from US$360/2500 day/ week; 40% discount May-Oct. This Spanish Mediterranean seaside B&B villa offers a variety of well-furnished accommodations. All units have access to the swimming pool, artists' workshop and communal master kitchen.

Inn at Manzanillo Bay (☎ 553-28-84, fax 553-28-83, e manzanillobay@aol.com, W www.manzanillobay.com) Single/double bungalows US$98/108 mid-Nov-April, US$58/65 May-mid-Nov. Troncones' nicest newcomer is really an old Mexico hand. El Burro Borracho's former owner, Mike Bensal, has thoughtfully refurbished the former Las Chozas resort and created a peaceful poolside paradise that caters to surfers. The well-appointed thatched-roof bungalows lie within earshot of a classic point break. Amenities include free Internet access, a surf shop and a gourmet restaurant and beachfront bar with satellite TV.

Hacienda Edén (☎ 553-28-02, fax 801-340-9883 in the USA, e evaandjim@ aol.com, w www.edenmex.com) Double rooms with breakfast US$65-75, bungalows US$80, US$15 extra per person. Open Nov-Apr. North of Troncones on tranquil Playa Manzanillo, this beachfront guesthouse has 10 beautifully decorated rooms, a gourmet restaurant and a full bar. The friendly proprietors, Eva and Jim, are gracious hosts. They may allow camping – just one tent – for free, if you eat a few meals here.

If you need a cheaper place to stay, ask around. You can also camp free on Playa Manzanillo or on the beach at Majahua.

Places to Eat

The cheapest dining options are in Troncones and Majahua. Both towns have several taco stands where you can eat well for under US$3, as well as a few enramadas where US$10 goes a long way. Good Mexican-owned beachfront restaurants include **Costa Brava**, north of the T intersection just across the bridge, and nearby **Doña Nica's Enramada**, just south of the T intersection.

A few shuffles farther south, the **Tropic of Cancer** restaurant/bar, run by Quebecois expat Anita LaPointe, is another popular spot with rooms for rent, Internet access and ice for sale; open 10am to 6pm most days.

A few paces farther along, locals and expats mingle with travelers at the popular beachfront **Burro Borracho** restaurant/bar. The Burro is also Troncones' main information center, with a bulletin board and an English-language lending library. The friendly proprietors will lend you body boards and sea kayaks for no charge.

At the south end of Bahía Manzanillo, you'll find **Restaurant Playa Manzanillo** (also known as María's), a traditional Mexican seafood enramada, and the **Inn at Manzanillo Bay** (see Places to Stay), where the California Culinary Academy-trained owner/chef offers his own innovative recipes – don't miss his signature Thai-style fried shrimp tacos – as well as gringo-inspired gourmet takes on traditional Mexican dishes.

Farther north around Bahía Manzanillo at Hacienda Edén, **La Cosina del Sol** is open for all meals (one dinner seating only, at 7pm, reservations recommended). Sundays there's breakfast and a barbecue. If you eat here, you can use their body boards and sea kayaks for free.

In Majahua, **Las Brisas Mexicanas** is a good Mexican seafood restaurant with fresh lobster and oysters.

Getting There & Away

If you're driving to Troncones from Ixtapa or Zihuatanejo, head northwest on highway 200 toward Lázaro Cárdenas. Just north of Km 30 you'll see the marked turnoff for Troncones; follow this winding paved road 3km west to the beach.

There are no direct buses from Ixtapa or Zihuatanejo, but 2nd-class buses heading northwest toward Lázaro Cárdenas or La Unión will let you off at the turnoff for Troncones. In Zihua, buses heading for Lázaro Cárdenas depart from the long-distance bus terminals; in La Unión, buses depart from the lot a couple of blocks east of the market. Ask to be let off at the Troncones turnoff (30-60 minutes, US$1.25).

A microbus shuttles between highway 200 and Troncones every half hour or so in the morning and evening, and every hour or so around siesta time (US$0.70). We found it safe and easy to hitch from the turnoff into Troncones, and also vice versa, but locals note: you'll probably have better luck and more success flagging down a bus on highway 200 for the return trip to Zihua during daylight hours. If someone offers, ride to Pantla, halfway to Zihua, then catch a micro or 2nd-class bus (both US$1.25) from there.

A taxi from Ixtapa or the Zihua airport costs around US$35/50 one-way/roundtrip. Taxis from Zihua to Troncones can be bargained down to around US$20/35 one-way/roundtrip, and taxis from Troncones back to Zihua can be even cheaper.

IXTAPA

● pop 1500 ☎ 755

Not so long ago, Ixtapa ('eeks-TAH-pah') was a coconut plantation and nearby Zihuatanejo was a sleepy fishing village. Then in 1970, Fonatur, the Mexican government tourism-development organization that conceived Cancún, decided that the Pacific coast needed a Cancún-like resort. After many

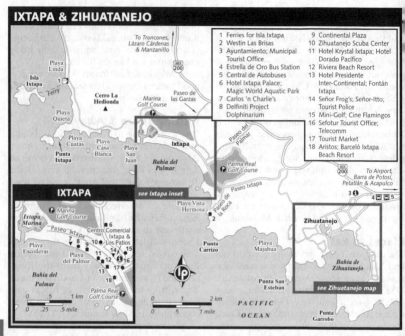

IXTAPA & ZIHUATANEJO

1 Ferries for Isla Ixtapa
2 Westin Las Brisas
3 Ayuntamiento; Municipal Tourist Office
4 Estrella de Oro Bus Station
5 Central de Autobuses
6 Hotel Ixtapa Palace; Magic World Aquatic Park
7 Carlos 'n Charlie's
8 Delfiniti Project Dolphinarium
9 Continental Plaza
10 Zihuatanejo Scuba Center
11 Hotel Krystal Ixtapa; Hotel Dorado Pacifico
12 Riviera Beach Resort
13 Hotel Presidente Inter-Continental; Fontán Ixtapa
14 Señor Frog's; Señor-Itto; Tourist Police
15 Mini-Golf; Cine Flamingos
16 Sefotur Tourist Office; Telecomm
17 Tourist Market
18 Aristos; Barceló Ixtapa Beach Resort

focus groups, Fonatur sagely selected Ixtapa, 210km northwest of Acapulco, for its resort complex. Proximity to the USA, an average temperature of 27°C, tropical vegetation and fine beaches were its criteria. Fonatur bought the coconut plantation, platted streets, dug reservoirs, strung electrical lines and rolled out the red carpet for hotel chains.

Today, Ixtapa boasts a string of luxurious resort hotels spread out along Bahía del Palmar; Club Med and some fine beaches are farther west beyond Punta Ixtapa. It's a beautiful spot, but many travelers cringe at the purpose-built glitz targeted primarily at gringos and a growing Mexican middle class.

Information

The state-run Sefotur office (☎/fax 553-19-67) is in Plaza Los Patios, opposite the Hotel Presidente Inter-Continental. It's open 8am to 8.30pm Monday to Friday, 8am to 3pm Saturday. The state-run Sefotur office (☎/fax 553-19-67) is in Plaza Los Patios, opposite the Hotel Presidente Inter-Continental. It's open 8am to 8.30pm Monday to Friday, 8am to 3pm Saturday. The tourist police station (☎ 553-10-67) is

nearby. Note: Ixtapa has several offices and sidewalk kiosks offering tourist information. They may provide free maps and answer queries, but their ultimate purpose is to promote time-share schemes.

Ixtapa has banks and casas de cambio where you can change US dollars and traveler's checks. American Express (☎ 553-08-53), at Hotel Krystal Ixtapa, is open 9am to 6pm Monday to Friday, 9am to 2pm Saturday.

The town doesn't have a post office, but you can drop mail at big hotels. The Telecomm office is behind Sefotur and is open 9am to 3pm Monday to Friday.

Beaches

Ixtapa's big hotels line **Playa del Palmar**, a long, broad stretch of white sand that's often overrun by parasail and jet-ski outfits. Be very careful if you swim here: the large waves crash straight down and there's a powerful undertow. The west end of this beach, just before the entrance to the lagoon, is locally called **Playa Escolleras** and is a favorite spot for surfing.

Farther west, past the marina, are **Playa San Juan, Playa Casa Blanca** and **Playa**

Cuatas. These small, beautiful beaches are among the best in the area. Unfortunately, they've all been effectively privatized by new developments; unless you can gain access by skiff or helicopter, you're probably out of luck, since the Mexican public-access law appears to have been overlooked.

To the west, past Punta Ixtapa, are **Playa Quieta** and **Playa Linda**, both popular with locals. From Playa Linda's pier, boats run every half hour (if there are enough passengers) to **Isla Ixtapa**, which is just offshore and has four beaches good for **snorkeling**; you can rent gear there for about US$5 a day. The roundtrip boat ride (five minutes each way) costs US$3.50; boats operate 8am to 5pm daily.

Activities

Bicycling is a breeze along a new 15km *ci-clopista* (bicycle path) that stretches from Playa Linda north of Ixtapa practically into Zihuatanejo. Bicycles can be rented at several places in Ixtapa (see Getting There & Around).

Scuba-diving is a popular pastime in the area's warm clear waters. NAUI-affiliated **Zihuatanejo Scuba Center** (☎/fax 554-21-47, e divemexico@email.com, w www.dive mexico.com) offers daily morning and afternoon dives at more than 30 dive sites. The company's Ixtapa office is in the Centro Comercial Ixtapa.

The **Ixtapa Club de Golf Palma Real** (☎ 553-10-62) and the **Marina Ixtapa Golf Club** (☎ 553-14-10) both have 18-hole courses, tennis courts and swimming pools. Children will enjoy the mini-golf near Ixtapa's Cine Flamingos. There's a **yacht club** (☎ 553-11-31, Porto Ixtapa) beside the Ixtapa Marina. **Horseback riding** is available on Playa Linda (see Beaches).

Kid-stuff is the specialty of the Hotel Krystal Ixtapa's **Krystalitos Children's Club** (☎ 553-03-33; admission ages 4-12 yrs US$13; open 10am-5pm daily). Drop your children off at 10am to enroll; they'll be fed breakfast and lunch, enjoy fun activities all day long and receive a club T-shirt and hat. The club is open to everyone, not just guests of the hotel.

Magic World (☎ 553-13-59; admission US$4.50; open 10.30am-5.30pm Tues-Sun), an aquatic park beside the Hotel Ixtapa Palace, has rides, water slides, toboggans and other amusements.

Next to Carlos 'n Charlie's, the new **Delfiniti Project Dolphinarium** (☎ 553-27-07, w www.delfiniti.com; US$65 for 20 min or US$110 for 45 min) offers visitors the chance to swim with and learn about dolphins. Daily sessions start at 10am, noon and 4pm.

If your idea of a fun activity is shopping, head to Ixtapa's **Tourist Market**, opposite the Barceló Ixtapa Beach Resort.

Places to Stay

Ixtapa's resorts are all top-end, costing upward of US$200 a night in the winter high season (mid-December to Easter) and just a bit less the rest of the year. Zihuatanejo's lodgings are more reasonable. If you want to stay in Ixtapa, try arranging a package deal through a travel agent, including airfare from your home country.

Among the hotels in Ixtapa – all with top-notch amenities – are the ***Barceló Ixtapa Beach Resort*** (☎ 553-18-58), ***Continental Plaza*** (☎ 553-11-75), ***Pacifica Resort*** (☎ 553-30-33), ***Pacifica Resort*** (☎ 553-10-27), ***Riviera Beach Resort*** (☎ 553-10-66) and ***Westin Las Brisas*** (☎ 553-21-21).

Ixtapa resorts with all-inclusive rates include ***Aristos*** (☎ 553-00-11), ***Club Med*** (☎ 553-00-40), ***Fontán Ixtapa*** (☎ 553-16-66), ***Hotel Presidente Inter-Continental*** (☎ 553-00-18), ***Melía Azul*** (☎ 550-00-00) and ***Qualton Club*** (☎ 552-00-80).

Travel agents can arrange packages at any of these places.

Places to Eat

Ixtapa has plenty of restaurants in addition to those in the big hotels.

Sitting like three ducks in a row, ***Carlos 'n Charlie's*** (☎ 553-00-85, Paseo del Palmar s/n), ***Señor Frog's*** (☎ 553-02-72, Blvd Ixtapa s/n) and ***Señor-Itto*** (☎ 553-02-72, Blvd Ixtapa s/n) deliver decent meals and good times. The latter two are side by side in the Centro Comercial, opposite the Presidente Inter-Continental; Carlos 'n Charlie's is farther west, by Hotel Posada Real.

Beccofino (☎ 553-17-70, Veleros Lote 6, Ixtapa Marina Plaza) Dinner US$15-30. Open 9am-11pm daily. Indoor-outdoor Beccofino enjoys a good reputation for delicious Italian cuisine, especially seafood. Several other good restaurants ring the marina.

Villa de la Selva (☎ 553-03-62, *Paseo de la Roca Lote D)* Dinner US$15-30. Open 6pm-11.30pm daily; reservations recommended. For a special night out with a great sunset view, try this elegant Mexican-Mediterranean restaurant in the former home of Mexican president Luis Echeverría. The cliffside villa overlooks the ocean, near the Westin.

Entertainment

All the big hotels have bars and nightclubs, and most also have discos. The best disco is Hotel Krystal Ixtapa's *Christine* (☎ 553-04-56 *for reservations),* with no cover on Monday. The Barceló Ixtapa Beach Resort's *Sanca Bar* is popular for dancing to Latin music. The best lobby bar is at the *Westin. Liquid* is in Ixtapa's Centro Comercial. Also popular in Ixtapa are *Carlos 'n Charlie's* and *Señor Frog's,* lively chain restaurant/bars with dancing.

Behind Señor Frog's in the Centro Comercial Ixtapa, *Los Mandiles* (☎ 553-03-79) restaurant/bar has popular Bongo's disco upstairs. Inside the Magic World aquatic park, the newer *Millenium* disco (☎ 553-27-10, *Paseo de las Garzas s/n)* is open Wednesday to Saturday. At the top of a 25m-high lighthouse, *El Faro* (☎ 553-10-27, *Paseo Ixtapa)* is a great bar for watching the sunset and also has music and dancing.

Several of Ixtapa's big hotels hold evening 'Fiestas Mexicanas,' which typically include a Mexican buffet and open bar, entertainment (traditional Mexican dancing, mariachis and cockfighting demonstrations), door prizes and dancing; total price is usually US$35 to US$40. The *Barceló Ixtapa Beach Resort* holds fiestas year round; in the high season several other hotels, including the *Dorado Pacífico* (☎ 553-04-76), also present fiestas. The *Riviera Beach Resort* (☎ 553-10-66) holds a weekly show with a pre-Hispanic theme; *Club Med* and the *Melía Azul Ixtapa* present a variety of international theme shows. Reservations can be made directly or through travel agents.

Ixtapa's relatively new and plush *Cine Flamingos* (☎ 553-24-90; *admission US$4),* behind the tourist office and opposite the Plaza Ixpamar and mini-golf, screens two films nightly, usually in English with Spanish subtitles.

Getting There & Around

For information on getting to Ixtapa, see Getting There & Away in the Zihuatanejo section. Private colectivo vans provide transport from the airport to Ixtapa for US$6 per person, but not in the other direction. A taxi to the airport costs US$10 to US$12 from Ixtapa.

Local 'Directo' and 'B Viejo' buses run frequently between Ixtapa and Zihua, a 15 minute ride. They depart every 15 minutes 6am to 11pm (US$0.50). In Ixtapa, buses stop all along the main street, in front of all the hotels. In Zihua, buses depart from the corner of Juárez and Morelos. Buses marked 'Zihua-Ixtapa-Playa Linda' continue through Ixtapa to Playa Linda (US$0.70), stopping near Playa Quieta on the way, and operate 7am to 7pm.

Cabs are plentiful in Ixtapa. You should always agree on the fare before climbing into the cab. Prices between Zihua and Ixtapa are around US$3.50. If you can't hail a taxi on the street, call Radio Taxi UTAAZ (☎ 554-33-11).

Ixtapa has several places renting motorbikes (around US$40 per hour), including Rent-A-Car (☎ 553-16-30, 553-16-30), in the Centro Comercial Los Patios (open 7am to 10pm daily). Most motorcycle rental places also rent mountain bikes for around US$3.50/20 per hour/day. You'll probably need a driver's license and credit card to rent.

ZIHUATANEJO

• pop 59,000 ☎ 755

Like its sister city Ixtapa, cacophonous Zihuatanejo ('see-wah-tahn-NAY-ho') is quite touristy. Nevertheless, it retains an easygoing, coastal ambiance, and its setting on a beautiful bay with several fine beaches makes it a gratifying place to visit. Small-scale fishing is still an economic mainstay; if you stroll down by the pier early in the morning, you can join the pelicans in greeting successful fisherfolk and inspecting the morning's catch. Needless to say, seafood is superb here.

Orientation

Though Zihua's suburbs are growing considerably, spreading around Bahía de Zihuatanejo and climbing the hills behind town, in the city's center everything is compressed within a few square blocks. It's difficult to get lost; there are only a few streets

..nd their names are clearly marked. Ixtapa, ..km northwest, is easily reached by fre- ..uent local buses or by taxi. At press time, ..ihua's street-numbering scheme was ..hanging: new blue metal number plates ..vere posted around town but hadn't offi- ..ially been adopted yet. New numbers are ..iven here wherever they were available.

..nformation

..ourist Offices Zihua's municipal Direc- ..ión de Turismo (☎/fax 553-19-68, **w** www ..ixtapa-zihuatanejo.com) is upstairs in the ..yuntamiento (City Hall), Zihuatanejo Pte ..s/n, Colonia La Deportiva, 2km northeast ..of the town center (local buses between ..Ixtapa and Zihuatanejo stop out front); ..open 8am to 4pm Monday to Friday. ..During the high season the office operates ..a helpful kiosk in the heart of town, on ..Álvarez immediately east of the basketball ..court. It offers free information, maps and ..brochures from 9am to 8pm daily.

..Money Zihuatanejo has many banks and ..casas de cambio where you can change US ..dollars and traveler's checks. Bancomer and ..Banca Serfin are on Juárez at Bravo, Ban- ..Crecer is on Juárez at Ejido, and Banamex ..is on Ejido at Guerrero. All have 24-hour ..air-conditioned ATMs and are open 9am to ..4pm or 5pm Monday to Friday, 10am to ..2pm Saturday. A less-busy Banamex ATM, ..inside Farmapronto at Juárez 12, is open ..until 10pm daily.

Casas de cambio offer slightly less favor- able rates but are open longer. Casa de Cambio Guiball, Galeana 4, is open 8am to 9pm daily.

Post & Communications Zihua's post office, a few blocks northeast of the town center, is open 8am to 3pm weekdays. Several other places in town also sell stamps; among them is Byblos bookstore (see Book- stores later in this section), at Galeana 2.

The Telecomm office, with telegram, Mexpost and fax service, is beside the post office; open 8am to 7.30pm Monday to Friday, 9am to noon Saturday and Sunday. Long-distance telephone and fax services are available at several Zihuatanejo tele- phone casetas, including two on the corner of Galeana and Ascencio. Public Lada tele- phones are all around town.

Zihuatanejo is crawling with Internet cafés, and competition is fierce. Four- terminal Zihua@.com, Ejido 32 at Cuauhté- moc, is open late depending on demand and · charges as little as US$1 per hour (one-hour minimum) for a 56k dial-up connection. ServiNet (☎ 554-87-23), Cuauhtémoc 46 at González, also has telephone and fax serv- ices; open 9am to 8pm Monday to Saturday. Several others stay open as late as midnight.

Travel Agencies Various agencies provide general travel services and arrange local tours. Two of Zihua's biggest agencies are Turismo Internacional del Pacífico (TIP, ☎ 554-75-10, 554-75-11), Juárez at Álvarez, open 9am to 2pm and 4pm to 7pm daily, and América-Ixtamar Viajes (☎ 554-35-90), at Cuauhtémoc and Bravo.

Bookstores Byblos (☎/fax 554-38-11), Galeana 2 near Bravo, stocks a small selec- tion of English-language newspapers, mag- azines and books (including a few Lonely Planet guides) and a wider Spanish- language selection. It also sells cappuccino, desserts and stamps, and has a mailbox outside. Hours are 9am to 9pm Monday to Saturday.

Laundry Lavandería Super Clean (☎ 554- 23-47), González 11 at Galeana, offers free pickup/delivery within Zihuatanejo; a 3kg (minimum) wash costs US$4. Lavandería Express (☎ 554-43-93), Cuauhtémoc 44, offers pickup/delivery for US$1.75. Both are open 8am to 8pm Monday to Saturday. Lavandería y Tintorería Premium, Cuauhté- moc 34, does laundry and dry cleaning; open 9am to 8pm Monday to Saturday.

Museo Arqueológico de la Costa Grande

At the east end of Zihua's Paseo del Pescador, this small museum (☎ 554-75-52; admission US$0.50; open 10am-6pm Tues- Sun) houses exhibits on the history, archae- ology and culture of the Guerrero coast, with Spanish captions; a free English- language brochure has translations.

Beaches

Waves are gentle at all Bahía de Zihuata- nejo's beaches. If you want big ocean waves, head west toward Ixtapa.

Playa Municipal, in front of town, is the least appealing swimming beach on Bahía de Zihuatanejo. From it you can see several other beaches spread around the bay, starting with Playa Madera just past the rocky point on your left, then the long, white stretch of Playa La Ropa past that, and finally, directly across the bay, Playa Las Gatas.

Playa Madera was formerly isolated from Playa Municipal by a couple of rocky points, but now an unlit concrete walkway around the rocky sections makes it an easy five-minute walk from town.

Walk over the hill along the steep Carretera Escénica for another 15-20 minutes from Playa Madera, past the mirador, and you'll reach the broad, 2km expanse of **Playa La Ropa**, bordered by palm trees and seafood restaurants. It's a pleasant walk, with the road rising up onto cliffs offering a fine view over the water. One of Zihua's most beautiful beaches, La Ropa is great for swimming, parasailing, water-skiing and sand-soccer. You can also rent sailboards and sailboats.

Opposite Zihuatanejo, **Playa Las Gatas** is a protected beach, crowded with sunbeds and restaurants. It's good for snorkeling (there's some coral) and as a swimming spot for children, but beware of sea urchins. According to legend, Calzontzin, a Tarascan chief, built a stone barrier here in pre-Hispanic times to keep the waves down and prevent sea creatures from entering, making it a sort of private swimming pool. Beach shacks and restaurants rent snorkeling gear for around US$5 per day.

Boats to Playa Las Gatas depart frequently from the Zihuatanejo pier, 8am to 5pm daily. Tickets (US$3.50 roundtrip) are sold at the ticket booth at the foot of the pier; one-way tickets can be bought on board. Or you can reach Playa Las Gatas by walking around the bay from Playa La Ropa; a road takes you half the way, then scramble up and down slippery rocks 15 to 20 minutes before reaching the Las Gatas pier.

Between Zihuatanejo and Ixtapa, **Playa Majahua** is accessible via a road serving a new hotel zone there, similar to Ixtapa. The beach, facing the open sea, has large waves and similar conditions to Ixtapa.

A boat goes to **Isla Ixtapa** (see Beaches in the Ixtapa section, earlier in this chapter)

PLACES TO STAY
4 Hotel Lari's
7 Hotel Posada Coral
12 Bungalows Pacíficos
13 Bungalows Sotelo
14 Bungalows Allec; Bungalows Ley
15 Hotel Palacios
17 Hotel Raúl Tres Marías
20 La Casa Que Canta
22 Las Gatas Beach Club
24 Villa Mexicana
25 Trailer Park Los Cabañas
26 Trailer Park La Ropa
28 Villa del Sol
30 Hotel Paraíso Real; Zihuatanejo Scuba Center
33 Owen's Beach Club Bungalows
35 Casa de Huéspedes Miriam
37 Hotel Imelda
47 Hotel Casa Aurora
49 Hotel Amueblados Valle
53 Hotel Casa Bravo
69 Hotel Ulises
70 Hotel Raúl Tres Marías Centro; Garrobo's
75 Hotel Amueblados Isabel
78 Posada Citlali
80 Hotel Susy
89 Hotel Avila; Restaurant/Bar Tata's; Casa de Huéspedes La Playa

PLACES TO EAT
11 La Reina Panadería y Pastelería
16 Casa Puntarenas
18 Restaurant Kau-Kan
19 Puesta del Sol
29 La Perla
31 Rossy's
32 La Gaviota
34 Restaurante Oliverio; Chez Arnoldo's
41 Los Braceros
42 Tamales y Atoles Any
44 Cafe Costa del Sol
45 Cafetería Nueva Zelanda
48 Il Paccolo
51 Fonda Económica Susy
52 Pollos Locos
66 Cenaduría Antelia
67 Paul's
76 JJ's Grill; Panificadora El Buen Gusto
77 Pizzas Locas
82 La Sirena Gorda
84 Casa Elvira; Sport Fishing Operators
85 Café Marina; El Jumil
88 Mariscos Los Paisanos

OTHER
1 Post Office; Telecomm; Mexpost
2 Local Buses to Ixtapa
3 Sanborns
5 Public Library
6 'La Correa' Route Bus Stop (To Long-Distance Bus Stations)
8 Buses to Petatlán, La Unión
9 Café Internet
10 Church
21 Mirador
23 Pemex Marine Gas Station
27 Tourist Police
36 Lavandería Super Clean
38 Mercado Municipal de las Artesanías
39 Lavandería Express; ServiNet
40 Lavandería y Tintorería Premium
43 'Coacoyul' Route Bus Stop (To Playa Larga & Airport)
46 Plata de Taxco
50 Banamex
54 Bancrecer
55 Bancomer
56 Banamex ATM; Late-Night Pharmacy
57 Banca Serfín
58 Cine Paraíso; América-Ixtamar Viajes
59 Byblos
60 Casa de Cambio Guiball
61 Telephone Casetas
62 D'Latino
63 Ventaneando
64 Mexicana
65 Hertz
68 Turismo Internacional del Pacífico (TIP)
71 Aero Cuahonte
72 Aeroméxico
73 Church
74 Bital Air-Con ATM
79 Coco's Cabaña
81 Public Bathrooms & Showers
83 Sport Fishing Operators
86 Basketball Court
87 Tourist Office (high season only)
90 Museo Arqueológico de la Costa Grande
91 Ticket Office for Boats to Playa Las Gatas, Isla Ixtapa
92 Harbor Master

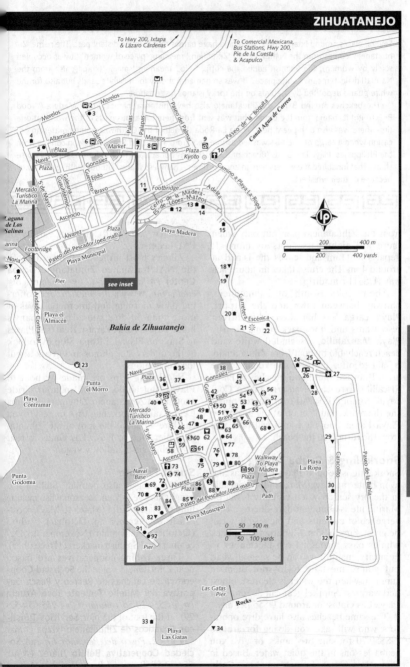

ZIHUATANEJO

To Hwy 200, Ixtapa
& Lázaro Cárdenas

To Comercial Mexicana,
Bus Stations, Hwy 200,
Pie de la Cuesta
& Acapulco

Canal Agua de Correa

Paseo del Palmar

Paseo de la Bonita

Morelos

Morelos

Altamirano

Palmas

Juárez

Palapas

Mangos

Cocos

Plaza

Market

Plaza
Kyoto

Nava
Plaza

Galeana

Cuauhtémoc

Guerrero

Ejido

Bravo

González

Camino a Playa La Ropa

Footbridge

Adelita

Cerro de la Madera

Mercado
Turístico
La Marina

5 de Mayo

5 de López Mateos

Laguna
de Las
Salinas

arina

Ascencio

Álvarez

Plaza

Footbridge

Playa Madera

Noria

Paseo del Pescador (ped mall)

Playa Municipal

Pier

see inset

Playa el
Almacén

Bahía de Zihuatanejo

Carretera Escénica

Punta
el Morro

Playa
Contramar

Andador Contramar

Punta
Godoma

Nava
Plaza

Mercado
Turístico
La Marina

5 de Mayo

Galeana

Cuauhtémoc

Guerrero

Ejido

Bravo

González

Ascencio

Naval
Base

Álvarez

Plaza

Paseo del Pescador (ped mall)

Playa Municipal

Pier

Walkway
To Playa
Madera

Plaza

Path

Playa
La Ropa

Caracolito

Paseo de la Bahía

Las Gatas
Pier

Rocks

Playa
Las Gatas

CENTRAL PACIFIC COAST

0   200   400 m
0   200   400 yards

0   50   100 m
0   50   100 yards

'Las Gatas' Were Not Cats...& Other Twisted Zihua Tales

Several places around Ixtapa and Zihuatanejo have names rooted in the distant past. The name 'Zihuatanejo' comes from the Náhuatl word 'Zihuatlán,' meaning 'place of women' (it was occupied solely by women); the Spanish added the suffix '-ejo,' meaning 'small.' 'Ixtapa,' also from the Náhuatl dialect, means 'white place.' It was so named not only for its white sands but also for the white guano deposited by seabirds on the rocky islands just offshore.

The beaches around Bahía de Zihuatanejo also have historical names. Playa Madera (Wood Beach) got its name from the timber that was sent from here to various parts of the world; at one time there was also a shipyard here. Playa La Ropa (Beach of the Clothes) commemorates an occasion when a cargo of fine silks washed ashore here from a wrecked Spanish galleon coming from the Philippines. Playa Las Gatas (Beach of the Cats) was not actually named for cats, but for nurse sharks that inhabited the waters here in ancient times – harmless sharks without teeth, called 'cats' because of their whiskers.

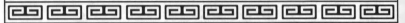

from the Zihuatanejo pier, but only when there are eight passengers or more. It departs at 11am and leaves the island at around 4pm. The cruise takes an hour each way (US$11 roundtrip).

About 10km south of Zihuatanejo, halfway between town and the airport, **Playa Larga** has big waves, beachfront restaurants and horseback riding. Nearby **Playa Manzanillo**, a secluded white-sand beach reachable by boat from Zihuatanejo, is said to offer the best snorkeling in the area. Between these two beaches is **Playa Riscalillo**. To reach Playa Larga, take a 'Coacoyul' combi (US$0.70) from Juárez opposite the market and get off at the turnoff to Playa Larga; another combi will take you from the turnoff to the beach.

Snorkeling & Scuba Diving

Snorkeling is good at Playa Las Gatas and even better at Playa Manzanillo, especially in the dry season when visibility is better. Marine life is abundant here due to a convergence of currents, and the visibility can be great – up to 35m. Migrating humpback whales pass through from December to February; manta rays can be seen all year, but you're most likely to spot them in summer, when the water is clearest, bluest and warmest. Snorkel gear can be rented at Playa Las Gatas for around US$5 per day.

The same beaches also have dive operators, who will take you diving for around US$50/70 for one/two tanks, or give you scuba lessons in the quiet water. Based in Playa Las Gatas, French-speaking **Carlo**

Scuba (☎ 554-35-70) offers a variety of PADI courses.

Zihua's most professional dive outfit is the NAUI-affiliated **Zihuatanejo Scuba Center** (☎/fax 554-21-47, e divemexico@email.com, w www.divemexico.com), offering daily morning and afternoon dives at more than 30 dive sites. The company's home base is Hotel Paraíso Real (see Places to Stay) on Playa La Ropa. Stop by to look at the underwater photos and to ask about local conditions.

Snorkeling trips are made by boat to Playa Manzanillo, about an hour's ride south from Zihuatanejo. Zihuatanejo Scuba Center takes snorkeling trips there. Or you can hire a boat at the foot of the Zihuatanejo pier, stop at Playa Las Gatas to rent snorkeling gear, and off you go.

Sport Fishing

Sport fishing is also popular. Sailfish are caught here year-round; seasonal fish include blue or black marlin (March to May), roosterfish (September to October), wahoo (October), mahi mahi (November to December) and Spanish mackerel (December).

Three fishing cooperatives are based near Zihuatanejo's pier: the **Sociedad Cooperativa de Lanchas de Recreo y Pesca Deportiva del Muelle Teniente José Azueta** (☎/fax 554-20-56, cellular ☎ 044-755-559-52-79), at the foot of the pier; **Servicios Turísticos Acuáticos de Zihuatanejo Ixtapa** (☎/fax 554-41-62, Paseo del Pescador 6); and **Sociedad Cooperativa Benito Juárez** (☎/fax 554-37-58, Paseo del Pescador 20-2). Any of these can arrange deep-sea fishing trips, from around US$150 for up to four people including equipment. Alternatively, you can walk along the pier and negotiate, as chatting it up in a friendly lazy style will certainly yield the best deal here. French and English (and aquavit) are spoken next door at Whisky Water World (☎ 554-01-47, e whisky@prodigy.net.mx).

Organized Tours

Most travel agencies offer a wide array of tours (see Travel Agencies). Interesting possibilities include: pre-Columbian La Soledad de Maciel archaeological zone, also called La Chole, 20km southeast of Zihua; Pantla, a brick-making center on highway 200 a half hour northwest of Zihuatanejo; and Petatlán, a colonial town on highway 200 a half hour southeast of Zihuatanejo (see South of Ixtapa & Zihuatanejo).

A couple of sailboat cruises tour local waters and can include snorkeling as part of the package.

Tristar (☎ 554-26-94, 554-82-70) This 67-foot trimaran based in Bahía de Zihuatanejo offers a couple of different excursions. The 'Sail & Snorkel' trip (10am to 2.30pm, US$55) goes outside the bay for brief snorkeling (gear-rental US$5) at Playa Manzanillo, about an hour's cruise away. The trip includes lunch, an open bar, flying from the spinnaker and a great party. The 2½-hour sunset cruise (6pm to 8.30pm, US$45) heads around the bay and out along the coast of Ixtapa. Add US$3 for transport to/from any hotel in Ixtapa. Reservations are required; private charters are also available.

Nirvana (☎/fax 554-59-15) The *Nirvana*, a 65-foot Australian-built wooden cutter, offers day-sailing trips (US$70) including snorkeling, swimming, sailing and lunch, as well as sunset cruises (US$50 with snacks and open bar) and private charters. Ring ahead for reservations.

Places to Stay

Unlike Ixtapa, Zihuatanejo does have some reasonably priced places to stay. But during the high season many hotels here fill up, so phone ahead to reserve a room; if you don't like what you get, you can always look for another room early the next day. The busiest times of year are Semana Santa and the week between Christmas and New Year;

at these times you must reserve a room and be prepared to pony up extra pesos. Tourism is much slower and rates are often negotiable from mid-April to mid-December. Most places in Zihua will offer 10% to 20% (negotiable) off rack rates for longer stays, if asked.

Budget Camping is available in Playa La Ropa at two small, basic trailer parks – actually just the backyards of a couple of friendly families. Both offer spaces for tents (US$4) and trailers (from US$10, depending on size). Compare the two to see which will best meet your needs.

Trailer Park La Ropa (☎ 554-60-30) Beside the Mercado de Artesanías, behind Marisquería Mary's, this place has no sign, but it does have tent spaces and six trailer spaces with full hookups.

Trailer Park Los Cabañas (☎ 554-47-18) Near the north end of the beach, the Cabaña family's backyard has four spaces with electric hookups (for everything but air-con); no water hookups. Tents and camping gear are available for rent.

The town's budget hotels are all in central Zihuatanejo. These include:

Casa de Huéspedes La Playa (☎ 554-22-47, Álvarez 6-7) Rates (negotiable) under US$10 per person. Fronting Playa Municipal, this humble hotel beside the larger Hotel Ávila is a basic guesthouse with six simple rooms with private bath (no hot water). From December to March it's always filled with satisfied snowbirds who no doubt reserve for the following year as they check out. English is spoken.

Hotel Ulises (☎ 554-37-51, Armada de México 9) Singles/doubles US$11/16.50. Across from the sleepy Club Naval, this family-run hotel is a good deal, with 16 simple rooms with hot water bath. Upstairs rooms are brighter.

Casa de Huéspedes Miriam (☎ 554-39-86, Nava 17) Rooms US$6.50 per person. This simple but clean and quiet guesthouse offers fan-only rooms with cold-water private bath.

Hotel Lari's (☎/fax 554-37-67, Altamirano 28) Singles/doubles US$15/19. Lari's is similar to Casa de Huéspedes Miriam, with off-street parking.

Hotel Posada Coral (☎ 554-54-77, cnr Los Mangos & Las Palmas) Singles/doubles

US$13/16.50. Near the main market, the Coral has clean rooms with tiled bathrooms.

Hotel Casa Aurora (☎ *554-36-92, Bravo 27*) Singles/doubles US$22/28, air-con US$5.50 extra. Casa Aurora has a nice 2nd-floor terrace, and the upstairs rooms are better.

Hotel Casa Bravo (☎ *554-25-48, Bravo 12*) Singles/doubles US$22/27, air-con US$5.50 extra. This remodeled hotel has clean, pleasant rooms with cable TV; some have air-con. Traffic outside can make the exterior rooms noisy, but the interior rooms are darker.

Posada Citlali (☎/*fax 554-20-43, Guerrero 3*) Singles/doubles May-Nov US$27/33, Dec-Apr US$38/43. This pleasant older posada features terrace sitting areas around a leafy courtyard. The rooms have hot water and are clean and comfortable. Credit cards are accepted.

Hotel Susy (☎ *554-23-39, Guerrero 2 at Álvarez*) Singles/doubles US$22/27. Next door to Posada Citlali, this older place is also clean and well located, but rooms can feel cramped.

Hotel Raúl Tres Marías (☎ *554-21-91, 554-25-91*, ✉ *r3mariasnoria@yahoo.com, La Noria 4*) Singles/doubles May-Nov US$17/22, Dec-Apr US$22/25. Across the lagoon from town, over the footbridge, this clean place in Colonia Lázaro Cárdenas is many a frequent visitor's home away from home. Many of its rooms (with cold-water showers and portable fans) open onto large shared flowery terraces with nice views over town and the bay, but the wooden shuttered windows let in lots of noise. French and some English are spoken.

Mid-Range Downtown holds several mid-range places, but other options are available just east of downtown in the Playa Madera area. Another interesting choice is across the bay in Playa Las Gatas.

Central Zihuatanejo Lodgings in the heart of town provide easy access to banks, restaurants and other services.

Hotel Imelda (☎ *554-76-62, González 70*) Rooms with 1-3 beds May-Nov US$43-65, Dec-Apr US$70-100. The popular Imelda has two swimming pools, enclosed parking and a high-season restaurant/bar. The rooms are clean and have cable TV and air-con.

Hotel Raúl Tres Marías Centro (☎ *554-67-06, 554-57-29, Álvarez 214*) Singles/doubles with air-con US$33/45. Upstairs from Garrobo's restaurant, this hotel has simple but clean rooms that are cheaper by the week. French and English are spoken.

Hotel Ávila (☎ *554-20-10, fax 554-85-92, Álvarez 8*) Singles/doubles without sea view May-Nov US$49/55, with sea view May-Nov US$55/65, doubles without/with sea view Dec-Apr US$65/82. Fronting Playa Municipal, the Ávila has terraces overlooking the bay, private parking and large, well-equipped rooms with air-con, fan and cable TV.

Hotel Amueblados Valle (☎/*fax 544-32-20, Guerrero 33*) 1-bed/2-bed apartments May-Nov US$30/45, Dec-Apr US$40/60. This apartment-style hotel is a good deal, with five large, airy units equipped with everything you need, including full kitchens. Three-bedroom apartments are also available, but everything is often taken during the high-season, so reserve ahead if possible. Ask owner Luis about other Playa La Ropa apartments, which may be cheaper, especially for longer stays.

Hotel Amueblados Isabel (☎ *554-36-61, Ascencio 11*) 2-bed/3-bed apartments May-Nov US$71/82, Dec-Apr US$76/87. This apartment-style place also has fully equipped rooms with air-con, telephone and TV.

Playa Madera A five-minute walk east from the center on quiet Eva S de López Mateos, the Playa Madera area has several good places to stay. Most are bungalows with full kitchens, and all have large terraces offering fine views of the bay.

Bungalows Pacíficos (☎/*fax 554-21-12*, ✉ *bungalowspacificos@zihua.net, López Mateos s/n*) Double-occupancy bungalows US$50-70. This place, the closest to town on Cerro de la Madera, has six attractive bungalows with ample sea-view terraces and fully equipped kitchens. Anita Hahner, the Swiss owner, is a gracious hostess who speaks English, Spanish and German. She'll help you find anything from good restaurants to the best bird-watching spots.

Bungalows Sotelo (☎ *554-63-07*, ✉ *betty_sotelo@cdnet.com.mx, López Mateos 13*) Bungalows with 1-3 double beds US$65-200, half-price May-June & Sept-Nov. Air conditioning is available for an extra charge at these funky 1970s stucco bungalows.

Bungalows Allec (☎/*fax 554-20-02*, e *josesauro@hotmail.com, López Mateos s/n*) 1-bed/2-bed bungalows with sea view US$40/85 high season, US$27/33 low season, studios US$27/33 low/high season. Next door to Bungalows Sotelo, Allec rents bright green fan-only bungalows and smaller studios for couples. English is spoken by friendly assistant manager José.

Bungalows Ley (☎ *554-45-63, 554-40-87*, e *bungalowsley@prodigy.net.mx, López Mateos s/n*) 1-bed/2-bed bungalows with air-con from US$33/75 low season, US$55/100 high season (June-Aug & Nov-Apr). Next door to Bungalows Allec, the nicer and newer Ley has clean well-appointed suites with cable TV, hot water and overhead fans.

Hotel Palacios (☎/*fax 554-20-55, Adelita s/n*) Singles/doubles with fan & breakfast Dec-Apr US$45/55, with air-con & breakfast US$45/60. Overlooking the east end of Playa Madera, pleasant Hotel Palacios is a family place with a swimming pool and beachfront terrace. Low-season rates are cheaper (around US$30 to US$50) but don't include breakfast.

Playa Las Gatas Way out at Playa Las Gatas, far from the maddening crowd, hermit types will find one more mid-range option.

Owen's Las Gatas Beach Club (☎/*fax 554-83-07, fax 554-47-62*, w *www.lasgatas beachclub.com*) 3-person bungalows May-Nov US$60, Dec-Apr US$80, US$20 per extra person. The Beach Club's seven large freestanding bungalows sit on peaceful grounds where you'll hear only the rhythmic sound of the surf and the sea breezes rustling through the palms. The unique bungalows are made of natural building materials, and some sleep up to eight people. This tranquil tropical hideaway is operated by Owen Lee, an ex-New Yorker who has been living in Playa Las Gatas since 1969 and 'loving every minute of it.' One of the first American divers to work with Jacques-Yves Cousteau, and author of a large book about diving and snorkeling, Owen also wrote a useful guidebook to Zihuatanejo and Ixtapa. The restaurant/bar is open only seasonally, but plenty of good seafood palapas are just a coconut-toss away.

Top End Ixtapa has most of the top-end resorts, but Playa La Ropa has a few good luxury hotels.

Hotel Paraíso Real (☎ *554-38-73, fax 554-21-47*, e *divemexico@email.com*, w *www .divemexico.com, southern end of Playa La Ropa*) Doubles May-14 Nov US$65, 15 Nov-Apr US$105. This ecologically conscious hideaway offers both garden and beachfront rooms. Operated by Zihuatanejo Scuba Center, the hotel also offers lodging-and-dive packages and some good low-season student deals.

Villa del Sol (☎ *554-22-39, 888-389-2645 in the USA & Canada, northern end of Playa La Ropa*) Doubles Apr-Dec from US$189, Jan-Mar US$200-270. A breakfast-and-dinner plan (US$60 per person) is mandatory in winter, but optional the rest of the year at this luxury resort. Children under 14 are not allowed in winter.

Villa Mexicana (☎ *554-36-36, fax 554-37-76, northern end of Playa La Ropa*) Doubles Mar-Nov US$85-110, Dec-Feb US$100-150. This recently revamped hotel complex has many nicely furnished (if sterile) rooms and package deals that attract a loyal return snowbird crowd.

Hotel Sotavento-Catalina (☎ *554-20-32, fax 554-68-70*, w *www.giga.com/~sotavent, northern end of Playa La Ropa*) Doubles Dec-Apr US$90-150, May-Nov US$45-90. On a hill overlooking Playa La Ropa, this place features one of Zihuatanejo's most beautiful settings. It's an old favorite, and its white terraces are visible from around the bay. Rates vary, depending on room size, view and amenities. Children under 12 stay for free.

La Casa Que Canta (☎ *554-70-30, 800-710-93-45 in Mexico*, ☎ *888-523-5050 in the USA, fax 554-70-40*, w *www.lacasaquecanta .com, Carretera Escénica s/n*) Doubles May-Dec US$285-295, Jan-Apr from US$330. Perched on the cliffs between Playa Madera and Playa La Ropa, this small luxury hotel, whose reddish adobe-style walls and thatched awnings are also visible all around the bay, is where part of *When a Man Loves a Woman* with Meg Ryan and Al Pacino was filmed.

Places to Eat
You won't find them on many menus, but *tiretas* (slivers of raw fish marinated with

onion, green chile and vinegar and served with soda crackers and chile picante) are Zihua's specialty – look for them at carts near the bus stations, or request them at any good beachfront enramada. A hearty inexpensive breakfast or lunch is also available in the street market, on Juárez between Nava and Gonzáles, from 8am to 6pm daily. *Comercial Mexicana supermarket* (open 8am to 10pm daily) is behind the Estrella Blanca bus station. *La Reina Panadería y Pastelería (Paseo de la Boquita 15A)* is Zihua's reigning queen of baked goods.

Paseo del Pescador Seafood here is fresh and delicious; many popular (if touristy) fish central Zihuatanejo paralleling Playa Municipal. The best options, from west to east, are:

La Sirena Gorda (☎ 554-26-87, Paseo del Pescador 90) Dinner US$5-10, house specialties US$10-17.50. Open 9am-11pm Thur-Tues. Closest to the pier, the Fat Mermaid is a casual open-air place famous for its seafood tacos, plus delicious burgers, shrimp and traditional Mexican dishes.

Casa Elvira (☎ 554-84-25, Paseo del Pescador 8) Dinner US$10-20. Open 8am-10pm daily. This longtime favorite serves some of the best seafood in town.

Garrobo's (☎ 554-67-06, Álvarez 214) Dinner US$8-18. Behind Casa Elvira in Hotel Raúl Tres Marías Centro, Garrobo's is a popular post-fishing hangout. Try the house specialty paella (US$17).

Café Marina (Paseo Pescador, west side of plaza) Pizzas US$5-10. Closed Sun and June-Sept. Tiny Café Marina tosses good pizzas, bakes fabulous chocolate cake (US$3.50) and has an English-language book exchange.

Just east of the basketball court on Paseo del Pescador, insistent touts will no doubt invite you into *Mariscos Los Paisanos* and *Tata's*. Both are good-value seafood specialists with popular happy hours, and both are open from 8am until late in the evening. At either one you can sit inside or at shaded beachfront tables with fine views of the bay.

Central Zihuatanejo – Inland Many good inexpensive options lie a couple of blocks from the beach.

Cafe Costa del Sol (☎ 554-47-16, Juárez 114) Open 8am-9pm daily. This storefront café has fresh-brewed locally grown

organic coffee, sugary sweets and whole beans by the kilo.

Fonda Económica Susy (Bravo 18) Comida corrida US$2.50. Open 8am-8pm daily. Susy serves some of the cheapest food in town, including a dependable comida corrida. *Telenovela* (soap opera) devotees gather outside on the sidewalk at the late-night *taquería* next door.

Cafetería Nueva Zelanda (☎ 554-23-40, Cuauhtémoc 23-30) Entrees US$2.50-4.50. Open 7am-10pm daily. English is spoken at this popular dineresque café with entrances on Cuauhtémoc and Galeana. It's best for breakfast, everything is available *para llevar* (to go) and they steam a decent cappuccino. Nearby *Byblos* (see Bookstores, under Information earlier this section) makes even better espresso and offers dessert on its sidewalk patio.

Los Braceros (☎ 554-48-58, Ejido 21) Combination plates US$5. Open 8am-1am daily. Los Braceros specializes in grilled and skewered meat and veggie combinations, and you can watch your selection being prepared at the sidewalk grill. There are 30 combinations to choose from and many other tasty meat dishes, with more than 100 items on the menu. Thirty-five cent mini, double-tortilla pork tacos attract many late-night diners.

Pollos Locos (☎ 554-40-44, Bravo 15) Whole chicken US$4. Open 1pm-10.30pm daily. This simple open-air place serves inexpensive wood-grilled chicken and other meats.

Cenaduría Antelia (☎ 554-50-11, Bravo 14 at Andador Pellicer) Everything less than US$2. Open 6am-4pm & 7pm-midnight daily. This simple, family-style open-air eatery has been dishing out superb *antojitos Mexicanos* (traditional Mexican snacks) and desserts since 1975. The beer is always cold, the TV is always on, and the social atmosphere spills out into the alley on balmy evenings. Tuck into a chile-verde tamal (US$0.50) or a bursting bowl of the *muy rico* pozole (typical *guerrerense* pork stew, US$1.50).

Tamales y Atoles Any (☎ 554-73-73, Ejido 15 at Guerrero) Everything less than US$6. Open 8am-midnight Mon-Sat. Friendly owners Any and José deserve a big post-meal *'buen provecho'* for their excellent offerings. The faux-rustic ambiance, with a high palapa roof, is colorful and inviting, and the menu features an amazing variety of reasonably priced dishes, including huge piping-hot tamales (US$1 to US$2), sweet atoles and traditional regional Mexican antojitos. Phone for free delivery. Every Thursday is a pozole fiesta, featuring all the locally produced mezcal you can drink for only US$6.

Il Paccolo (*Pacco's, Bravo 22 near Guerrero*) Pizzas US$6-9. Open 4pm-midnight daily. Pacco's supercheesy lasagna (US$6.50), the most authentic this side of the Sierra Madre, is delicious. Other options include pizza, pasta, meats and seafood. The ambiance is low-key and the bar is friendly.

A couple more pizzerias are on Guerrero between Álvarez and Bravo; try *Pizzas Locas*, which will deliver its brick-oven baked pies (US$5 to US$14).

JJ's Grill (☎ 554-83-80, *Guerrero 6*) Mains US$3-12. Open 11am-2am daily. JJ's is a gringo haven with a popular restaurant, sports bar and pool tables. The food is classic American, including giant burgers, filet mignon sandwiches, grilled tuna steak and clam chowder. Happy hour runs 10pm to midnight daily.

Panificadora El Buen Gusto (*Guerrero 8A*) Open 7.30am-10pm daily. On the same block as JJ's, this delightful little bakery makes mouthwatering chicken mole empanadas (US$1.25). The open-air café next door has an espresso machine.

Paul's (☎ 554-65-28, *Juárez near Bravo*) Mains US$10-20. Open 3pm-late Mon-Sat. This gourmet restaurant is named after its Swiss owner/chef, who consistently creates some of Zihua's best fancy food, with good vegetarian options. The adjacent *El Mascarero* piano bar is a mellow after-hours hangout.

Casa Puntarenas (*La Noria, near Hotel Raúl Tres Marías*) Open 8.30am-11am & 6pm-9pm daily Dec-Mar. Across the lagoon from town, this simple, family-run eatery has a relaxed atmosphere and attracts a steady crowd with its hearty portions of good, cheap Mexican food.

Around the Bay *Puesta del Sol* (☎ 554-83-42, *Carretera Escénica s/n*) Dinner US$10-20. Open 2pm-midnight daily; reservations recommended in high season. Hanging on the cliffs between Playa Madera and Playa La Ropa, Puesta del Sol (Spanish for 'sunset') offers moderately priced full dinners, spectacular bay views and stunning sunset vistas.

Restaurant Kau-Kan (☎ 554-84-46, *Carretera Escénica 7*) Dinner US$10-20. Open 1pm-midnight daily (6pm-midnight low season). On the cliffs near Puesta del Sol, pricier gourmet Kau-Kan enjoys the same great views.

La Casa Que Canta (☎ 554-70-30, *Carretera Escénica s/n*) Full dinner US$40-65. Open 6.30pm-10.30pm. The gourmet restaurant at this luxurious resort is the most expensive in Zihuatanejo. Reservations required.

On Playa La Ropa, *Rossy's*, *La Perla* and *La Gaviota* are all good seafood restaurants. On Playa Las Gatas, *Restaurante Oliverio* and *Chez Arnoldo's* also feature fresh seafood, or try:

Owen's Las Gatas Beach Club (☎ 554-83-07, *Playa Las Gatas*) Open 8am-5.30pm high season, with dinner by arrangement. The Las Gatas Beach Club (see Places to Stay) has a sublimely situated restaurant, and its water taxi provides evening transport from town.

Entertainment

For big-time nightlife, head to Ixtapa. Zihuatanejo has a more mellow vibe.

Many beachfront bars have a happy hour. *Restaurant/Bar Tata's* and *Mariscos Los Paisanos*, side by side on Zihuatanejo's Playa Municipal, attract jolly sunset crowds.

Hotel Sotavento-Catalina (☎ 554-20-32, *Playa La Ropa*) Open 3pm-11pm. Perched on the cliffs over Playa La Ropa, the Sotavento-Catalina (see Places to Stay) is a great spot to watch the sunset. Its lobby bar affords a magnificent view over the whole bay. Happy hour runs 6pm to 8pm. Nearby, the bar/restaurant *Puesta del Sol* (see Places to Eat) has a similar beautiful view.

Club D'Latino (*cnr Bravo & Guerrero*) Zihuatanejo's only real discothèque, Club D'Latino is an open-air street-corner bar serving cheap draft Corona.

Ventaneando (*Guerrero 24*) Across the street from Club D'Latino, Ventaneando is a popular '*canta baile bar*' that attracts a steady crowd of karaoke-loving local teens.

Psst, Hey, My Friend – Don't Buy the Coral

In Zihuatanejo, don't buy things like dried sea horses, coral and shells. These species are being wiped out, and the tourist industry causes this devastation. Resources are not infinite here, and this commercial trade contributes to the destruction of Mexico's beautiful marine ecology. The purchase of coral, in particular, should be avoided, as coral is the basis of an endangered habitat that sustains much other sea life.

Zihua's only cinema is *Cine Paraíso* (*Cuauhtémoc near Bravo, admission US$2-3*). It shows two films nightly, usually in English with Spanish subtitles.

Shopping

Mexican handicrafts, including ceramics, *típica* clothing, leatherwork, Taxco silver, wood carvings and masks from around the state of Guerrero are all in abundance.

Zihuatanejo's *Mercado Turístico La Marina* on Cinco de Mayo has the most stalls. A few more are in the *Mercado Municipal de las Artesanías* on González near Juárez. A new Sanborns department store (*cnr Juárez & Morelos*) should be open by the time you read this.

El Jumil (☎ 554-61-91, *Paseo del Pescador 9*) This friendly artesanía shop (in the block west of the basketball court) specializes in authentic guerrerense masks. Guerrero is known for its variety of interesting masks, and El Jumil stocks some museum-quality examples, many starting around US$15. English is spoken and the owners are a good source of local information.

Coco's Cabaña (☎ 554-25-18, *cnr Guerrero & Álvarez*) Next door to Coconuts restaurant, Coco's Cabaña stocks an impressive selection of handicrafts from all over Mexico.

Several shops along Cuauhtémoc, including *Plata de Taxco* (*cnr Cuauhtémoc & Bravo*) sell good selections of quality Taxco silver.

Getting There & Away

Air The Ixtapa/Zihuatanejo international airport (ZIH) is 19km southeast of Zihuatanejo, a couple of kilometers off highway 200 heading toward Acapulco. Airlines serving this airport, and their direct flights, are listed below; all have connections to other hubs.

Aero Cuahonte (☎ 554-39-88, 554-70-61), Álvarez 34; flies to Lázaro Cárdenas, Morelia, Uruapan

Aeroméxico (☎ 554-20-18/19, airport ☎ 554-22-37, 554-26-34), Álvarez 34; flies to Guadalajara, Los Angeles, Mexico City, Oaxaca

Alaska (☎ 554-84-57); flies to Los Angeles, San Francisco

America West (☎ 800-235-92-92); flies to Phoenix

Continental (☎ 554-42-19, 800-900-50-00); flies daily to Houston

Mexicana (☎ 554-22-08/9, 800-502-20-00, airport ☎ 554-22-27), Guerrero 22; also (☎ 553-22-08/9) Hotel Dorado Pacífico, Ixtapa; flies to Guadalajara, Mexico City

Bus The large Estrella Blanca bus terminal (Central de Autobuses, ☎ 554-34-77) is on highway 200, about 2km out of Zihuatanejo heading toward Acapulco; 1st-class Cuauhtémoc, Elite, Futura and Plus buses operate from here. Estrella de Oro (☎ 554-21-75) has its own smaller terminal, across a side road from the Estrella Blanca terminal, heading toward town. Buses include:

Acapulco – 239km, 4 hours; 1st-class Estrella Blanca hourly 5am-9.30pm (US$10-14.50), 3 1st-class Estrella de Oro (US$10), 2nd-class Estrella de Oro hourly 5.30am-5pm (US$7.75), 2nd-class Estrella Blanca (US$7.50)

Lázaro Cárdenas – 120km, 2 hours; 11 1st-class Estrella Blanca 1am-9.30pm (US$5.50-7.75), 2nd-class Estrella Blanca hourly 9am-10pm (US$3.50), 2nd-class Estrella de Oro every 1-2 hours 5.40am-6pm (US$3.50)

Manzanillo – 433km, 8 hours; 1st-class Estrella Blanca at 10am, noon & 9pm (US$28)

Mexico City (Terminal Norte) – 640km, 10 hours; 1st-class Estrella Blanca at 6.30pm (US$50)

Mexico City (Terminal Sur) – 640km, 8-9 hours; deluxe Estrella Blanca 'Ejecutivo' at 10.30pm (US$50), deluxe Estrella de Oro 'Diamante' at 9.15pm (US$50), 10 1st-class Estrella de Oro (US$33), 5 1st-class Futura (US$35)

Petatlán – 32km, 30 minutes; 1st-class. Estrella Blanca every half hour 3.45am-11.20pm

(US$1.50), 2nd-class. Estrella de Oro hourly 5.30am-6pm (US$1.50); most buses to Acapulco also stop in Petatlán – or take a local bus (30 minutes, US$1.25) from the bus lot a couple of blocks east of the market in Zihuatanejo

Manzanillo-bound buses continue to Puerto Vallarta (718km, 14 hours, US$46) and Mazatlán (1177km, 24 hours, US$75); the noon bus goes all the way to Tijuana (US$156).

Car & Motorcycle Car rental companies in Ixtapa and Zihuatanejo include:

Alamo	☎ 553-02-06, 800-849-80-01, airport ☎ 558-84-29
Avis	☎ 554-22-48, 554-22-75
Budget	☎ 553-03-97, airport ☎ 554-48-37
Econo Car Rental	☎ 554-78-07
Galgo	☎ 554-53-66, airport ☎ 554-23-14
Hertz	☎ 554-22-55, airport ☎ 554-25-90
Quick	☎ 553-18-30, 553-03-33
Rent-A-Car	☎ 553-16-30

Getting Around
To/From the Airport The cheapest way to get to the airport is via a public 'Coacoyul' colectivo (US$0.70) with a plane on the windshield, departing from Juárez near González. Private colectivo vans provide transport from the airport to Ixtapa or Zihua (US$6 per person), but they don't offer service *to* the airport. A taxi to the airport costs US$8 from Zihua.

Bus Local 'Directo' and 'B Viejo' buses run between Ixtapa and Zihua every 15 minutes, 6am to 11pm (15 minutes, US$0.50). In Zihua, buses depart from the corner of Juárez and Morelos. In Ixtapa, buses stop all along the main street, in front of all the hotels. Buses marked 'Zihua-Ixtapa-Playa Linda' continue through Ixtapa to Playa Linda (US$0.70), stopping near Playa Quieta on the way; they operate 7am to 7pm.

The 'Correa' route goes to the Central de Autobuses, 6am to 9.30pm (US$0.40). Catch it on Juárez at the corner of Nava.

'Playa La Ropa' buses head south on Juárez and out to Playa La Ropa every half hour, 7am to 8pm (US$0.70).

'Coacoyul' colectivos heading toward Playa Larga depart from Juárez near the corner of González, every five minutes 6am to 10pm (US$0.70).

Taxi Cabs are plentiful in Zihuatanejo. Always agree on the fare before getting in. Approximate sample fares (from central Zihua) include: US$3.50 to Ixtapa, US$2.50 to Playa La Ropa, US$5 to Playa Larga and US$1.50 to the Central de Autobuses. If you can't hail a taxi streetside, ring Radio Taxi UTAAZ (☎ 554-33-11).

SOUTH OF IXTAPA & ZIHUATANEJO
Barra de Potosí
A 40-minute drive southeast of Zihuatanejo, Barra de Potosí is a popular day-trip area with a long, sandy, open-sea beach (beautiful, but dangerous for swimming) and another beach on a large lagoon with good swimming. You can take boat trips, rent a canoe and paddle around the estuary (good bird-watching) or go horseback riding or hiking on local trails.

Seafood restaurants line the beach – try the *pescado a la talla* (broiled fish fillets) or *tiretas* (sashimi slivers smothered in salsa), both local specialties.

Hotel Barra de Potosí (☎ 554-82-90/91, fax 554-34-45, e lbaker@sd70.bc.ca) Singles & doubles US$40-60. Right on the beach, this Canadian-owned hotel has a swimming pool, parking and a variety of comfy rooms.

To get here, head southeast on highway 200 toward Acapulco; turn off at the town of Los Achotes, 25km from Zihua, and head for the sea, another 10km. Any bus heading to Petatlán (see Getting There & Away in the Zihuatanejo section) will drop you at the turnoff. Tell the driver you're going to Barra de Potosí; you'll be let off where you can meet a minibus going the rest of the way. The total cost is about US$2.50 if you go by bus; a taxi from Zihua costs US$35/45 one-way/roundtrip (negotiable).

Petatlán
A colonial town half an hour southeast of Zihua, Petatlán is best known for its Santuario Nacional del Padre Jesús de Petatlán, a large, modern church attracting pilgrims from near and far. Gold is sold cheaply from many shops beside the church. Petroglyphs

CENTRAL PACIFIC COAST

and other pre-Hispanic artifacts are displayed in the town center. During Semana Santa there's a traditional fair with food, music and handicrafts exhibitions. Petatlán's religious festival is held on August 6.

Petatlán is on highway 200, 32km southeast of Zihua heading toward Acapulco. See Getting There & Away under Zihuatanejo, earlier, for bus information.

La Barrita

An hour southeast of Zihua off highway 200, La Barrita is a small town on an attractive beach. Not many tourists stop here; there's one no-name *hotel* with double rooms for around US$8. Second-class buses heading south from Zihua or north from Acapulco will drop you at La Barrita.

PIE DE LA CUESTA
☎ 744

Ten kilometers northwest of Acapulco, Pie de la Cuesta is a narrow 2km strip of land bordered by a wide beach and the ocean on one side and by the large, freshwater Laguna de Coyuca on the other. Known for its relaxed beach scene, Pie de la Cuesta is quieter, cleaner, closer to nature and much more peaceful than neighboring Acapulco. Swimming in the surf can be dangerous, however, due to a riptide and the shape of the waves; each year a number of people drown here. Laguna de Coyuca, three times as large as Bahía de Acapulco, is better for swimming; in the lagoon are the islands of Montosa, Presido and Pájaros, which is a bird sanctuary.

Pie de la Cuesta has many oceanfront restaurants specializing in seafood, and it's a great place for watching the sunset. The only nightlife is the billiards parlor, so if you're looking for excitement you're better off in Acapulco. Water-skiing is popular on Laguna de Coyuca; several water-skiing clubs provide the equipment (US$30 to US$40 per hour). Boat trips on the lagoon, where Sylvester Stallone filmed *Rambo,* are also an option. Negotiate for your own launch any time, or take one of the regularly scheduled colectivos (US$5 per person). You can also go horseback riding on the beach for around US$11 an hour.

Places to Stay

For accommodation, Pie de la Cuesta is a good alternative to Acapulco. You can

easily check out the 15 or so hotels that line the single, 2km road. Every hotel provides safe parking.

Budget Camping is available, and you'll find plenty of small, friendly, family-run lodgings near the beach.

Camping Pie de la Cuesta proper has two pleasant trailer parks at the far end of the road near the military base: larger *Acapulco Trailer Park & Mini-Super* (☎ 460-00-10) and less-secure *Trailer Park Quinta Dora* (☎ 460-11-38). Quinta Dora has a bar and restaurant. Both have full hookups and are good for tents (US$10) and trailers (US$15). Take a look at both and ask for prices (negotiable) before you choose your spot; they're only a two-minute walk from each other, but most campers have a distinct preference for one or the other. Each place has camping areas on both the beach and lagoon sides of the road.

KOA (☎ 444-40-62, fax 483-22-81, ⓦ www .koa.com, Playa Luces) Tent/trailer sites US$14/22, double-size 'premier' beachfront spaces US$27, simple rooms US$33, US$90 weekly, US$300 monthly. Four kilometers north of Pie de la Cuesta, this large, 110-space landscaped campground has trailer spaces with full hookups. Amenities include a large beachfront swimming pool, a restaurant/bar, children's playgrounds and Internet service (US$3.25 per hour). The 'Pie de la Cuesta – Playa Luces' bus stops at the gate upon request.

Hotels & Guesthouses Places are listed below in order from east to west.

Casa de Huéspedes & Restaurant Rocío (☎ 460-10-08, Calzada Pie de la Cuesta s/n) Rooms with 1-3-beds US$25-44. Félix López, the resident bartender, chef and guitarist, provides music and good times at this beachfront hotel/restaurant/bar. Newer oceanside rooms with large balconies cost the same as other doubles.

Villa Nirvana (☎ 460-16-31, fax 460-35-73, ⓔ nirvana@acabtu.com.mx, ⓦ www .lavillanirvana.com, rear of Calzada Pie de la Cuesta 302) Doubles US$22, beach cottage US$44, 6-person apartment US$87; rates 25% more in high season. Villa Nirvana's friendly new American owners have thoughtfully revamped this cheerful

PIE DE LA CUESTA

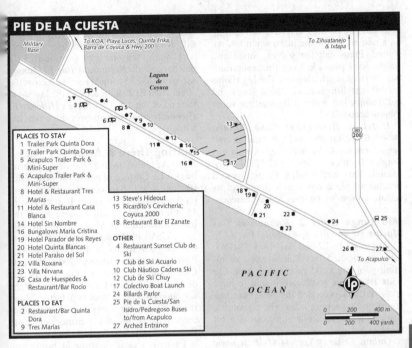

PLACES TO STAY
1 Trailer Park Quinta Dora
3 Trailer Park Quinta Dora
5 Acapulco Trailer Park & Mini-Super
6 Acapulco Trailer Park & Mini-Super
8 Hotel & Restaurant Tres Marías
11 Hotel & Restaurant Casa Blanca
14 Hotel Sin Nombre
16 Bungalows María Cristina
19 Hotel Parador de los Reyes
20 Hotel Quinta Blancas
21 Hotel Paraíso del Sol
22 Villa Roxana
23 Villa Nirvana
26 Casa de Huespedes & Restaurant/Bar Rocío

PLACES TO EAT
2 Restaurant/Bar Quinta Dora
9 Tres Marías

13 Steve's Hideout
15 Ricardito's Cevichería; Coyuca 2000
18 Restaurant Bar El Zanate

OTHER
4 Restaurant Sunset Club de Ski
7 Club de Ski Acuario
10 Club Náutico Cadena Ski
12 Club de Ski Chuy
17 Colectivo Boat Launch
24 Billards Parlor
25 Pie de la Cuesta/San Isidro/Pedregoso Buses to/from Acapulco
27 Arched Entrance

eight-room beachfront property. Pamela lovingly tends to the rare palms and blossoming butterfly garden, while her partner Daniel designed the new rooms in the airy elevated annex. A beachside swimming pool, pleasant open-air restaurant (breakfast only) and bar, and complimentary (but limited, please) Internet access round out the good-value offering.

Villa Roxana (☎ *460-32-52, front of Calzada Pie de la Cuesta 302*) Singles/doubles/triples US$18/22/27 low season. To get to Villa Nirvana, you must go straight through the Villa Roxana, which inevitably means meeting Roxana. Her villa is a similarly attractive and spotlessly clean place, with nice gardens with plenty of shaded hammocks, a small swimming pool, a restaurant and bar, and attractively furnished rooms. Guests should note that Villa Nirvana's facilities are off-limits to Roxana's guests. Check out both places before deciding which one suits your needs.

Hotel Quinta Blancas (☎ *460-03-12/13, Calzada Pie de la Cuesta 307*) Singles/doubles US$16.50/22. Under new ownership, this sprawling, spiffed-up place has a

big swimming pool and 24 large rooms, with air-con promised soon.

Hotel Paraíso del Sol (☎ *460-04-12, Calzada Pie de la Cuesta s/n*) Rooms US$27, 4-bed rooms US$44 low season. About 50m off the main road down a narrow lane, this excellent beachfront choice, formerly known as Hotel Puesta del Sol, has a lovely shaded garden, a swimming pool and a restaurant/bar.

Hotel Parador de los Reyes (☎ *460-01-31, Calzada Pie de la Cuesta 305*) Rooms US$6.50 per person low season. This clean, economical choice is right beside the road and has a small courtyard swimming pool.

Bungalows María Cristina (☎ *460-02-62, Calzada Pie de la Cuesta s/n*) Doubles US$33, beachfront bungalows US$70. Run by English-speaking Enrique and his friendly family, this is a clean, well-tended, relaxing place with a barbecue and hammocks overlooking the beach. The large bungalows have kitchens and sleep five or six people.

Hotel Sin Nombre (☎ *460-31-51, Calzada Pie de la Cuesta s/n*) Doubles US$33 low season, air-con US$12 extra. Formerly

CENTRAL PACIFIC COAST

Hotel Lago Mar & Club de Ski, this lovely hotel has new owners who were still settling on a new name for the place when last we visited. Plans call for serving sushi and Italian food poolside from the restaurant/bar overlooking the lagoon. The big rooms exhibit a stylish flair, with tiled floors and bathrooms, but were still awaiting some long-overdue TLC.

Hotel & Restaurant Casa Blanca (☎ 460-03-24, fax 460-40-27, **e** casablanca@acanet.com.mx, Calzada Pie de la Cuesta s/n) Singles/doubles/triples US$27/33/44 low season. This well-tended French-owned beachfront place has a new pool, and its restaurant retains a homey atmosphere.

Mid-Range *Hotel & Restaurant Tres Marías* (☎ 460-01-78, Calzada Pie de la Cuesta s/n) 1-bed/2-bed doubles US$49/65. Long-established Tres Marías has a swimming pool and good rooms with king-size beds. Its seaside restaurant is said to have some of the best food in the area, but some complain that service is lax. The lagoonside restaurant serves similar fare but is a bit more expensive.

Quinta Erika (☎/fax 444-41-31, **w** www.quintaerika.de.vu, Playa Luces) Singles/Doubles with breakfast US$45/50 year-round, bungalow US$120. Six kilometers northeast of Pie de la Cuesta at Playa Luces this small, quality lagoonside lodging has five large rooms and one family-size bungalow on two well-tended hectares. The price includes boat tours and use of the hotel's kayaks and small *lancha*. Quinta Erika takes pride in being quiet, restful and attentive. Reservations are strongly suggested, but walk-ins with their Lonely Planet in hand are welcome. English, German and Spanish are spoken.

Places to Eat

Restaurants here are known for fresh seafood. Plenty of open-air places front the beach, though some close early in the evening. Most of the hotels and guesthouses have restaurants, as do many of the water-skiing clubs. Food prices tend to be higher here than in Acapulco, so it may be worth bringing some groceries and getting a room with kitchen access, as many local families do on Saturday and Sunday.

About halfway down to the military base, locally owned *Coyuca 2000* serves good traditional Mexican fare and exhibits a special flair with seafood. Nearby, lagoon-side *Ricardito's Cevichería* does wonders with marinated *mariscos* (seafood). In a pinch, roadside *Restaurant Bar El Zanate* serves a US$2.25 comida corrida. Across the street from El Zanate, around the lagoon at the end of the dirt road, *Steve's Hideout/El Escondite*, built on stilts over the water, has a fine view.

Getting There & Away

From Acapulco, take a 'Pie de la Cuesta' bus on La Costera opposite the post office (the one next to Sanborns, near the zócalo), on the bay side of the street. Buses go every 15 minutes, 6am until around 8pm; the bumpy, roundabout 35- to 50-minute ride costs US$0.40. Buses marked 'Pie de la Cuesta – San Isidro' or 'Pie de la Cuesta – Pedregoso' stop on highway 200 at Pie de la Cuesta's arched entrance; those marked 'Pie de la Cuesta – Playa Luces' continue all the way along to Playa Luces, 6km farther along toward Barra de Coyuca. VW microbus colectivos (US$0.40) continue on from Barra de Coyuca back out to highway 200.

Colectivo taxis operate 24 hours and charge US$1.25 one-way. A taxi from Acapulco costs anywhere from US$6 to US$9 one-way (more after dark), but typically you'll pay only US$4.50 to US$6 to return to Acapulco, since the cabbies hate to go home empty-handed.

ACAPULCO
• pop 800,000 ☎ 744

Acapulco is the granddaddy of Mexican coastal resorts. Commerce and tourism are the city's primary industries and have been since the Spanish conquistadors pioneered trade routes between Europe and Asia in the early 16th century. Today, the name Acapulco evokes images of golden beaches, towering resort hotels, glitzy nightlife and La Quebrada's daredevil, swan-diving *clavadistas* (cliff divers).

Acapulco is a fast-growing city of dual personalities. Around the curve of Bahía de Acapulco stretches an arc of beautiful beaches, luxury hotels, jet-set discos, air-conditioned shopping plazas and restaurants with trilingual menus (many French Canadians come here). Just inland is a none-too-glamorous commercial center with crowded sidewalks, congested traffic and ranks of constantly honking taxis and colorful customized buses menacing pedestrians.

Throughout the year you can expect average daytime temperatures of 27° to 33°C and nighttime temperatures of 21° to 27°C. Refreshing afternoon showers are common from June to September but are rare the rest of the year.

Orientation

Acapulco occupies a narrow coastal sliver along the 11km shore of Bahía de Acapulco (aka Bahía de Santa Lucía). Accessible via highway 200 from the east and west and by highways 95 and 95D from the north, it's 400km south of Mexico City and 240km southeast of Ixtapa and Zihuatanejo. Street signs are as scarce as safe crosswalks, and building numbers are erratic and often obscured or unused, but inquiring on the street eventually will lead you to your destination. As in most Spanish colonial cities, the cathedral and adjacent zócalo dominate the heart of the old central commercial district.

Acapulco can be divided into three parts: Old Acapulco (which tourism promoters once called 'Acapulco Tradicionál' and now call 'Acapulco Naútico') is the western (old) part of the city; Acapulco Dorado heads around the bay east from Playa Hornos; and Acapulco Diamante is a newer luxury resort area 18km southeast of Acapulco proper, between Bahía de Acapulco and the airport. Tourism is more low-key in Pie de la Cuesta (see that section, earlier), 10km northwest of Acapulco off highway 200.

At Bahía de Acapulco's west end, Península de las Playas juts south from Old Acapulco. South of the peninsula is Isla de la Roqueta. From Playa Caleta on the south edge of the peninsula, Avenida López Mateos climbs west and then north to Playa La Angosta and La Quebrada before curling east back toward the city center.

Playa Caleta also marks the beginning of Acapulco's principal bayside avenue, Avenida Costera Miguel Alemán – often called 'La Costera' or 'Miguel Alemán'. From Playa Caleta, La Costera traverses Península de las Playas and then hugs the shoreline all the way around the bay to Playa Icacos and the naval base at the eastern end of Bahía de Acapulco. Most of Acapulco's major hotels, restaurants, discos and other points of interest are along or near La Costera. Just after the naval base, La Costera becomes La Carretera Escénica (Scenic Highway), which rejoins the main route of highway 200 after 9km. Highway 200 then leads south toward Puerto Marqués and the airport.

Information

Immigration You can extend visas free at Migración (☎ 484-90-14/21), corner of La Costera and Elcano, open 8am to 2pm Monday to Friday.

Tourist Offices Procuduría de la Turista (☎/fax 484-44-16), La Costera 4455, in the yellow building in front of the Centro de Convenciones, provides visitor information and assistance 9am to 11pm daily; services include free medical care, money exchange and a handicrafts store. The office also sells tickets for local attractions and for bus and air travel – tickets are cheaper here than at travel agencies, since it's a government service and no commissions are charged. The state tourist office (Sefotur, ☎ 484-24-23, fax 481-11-60, e sefotur@yahoo.com), inside the Centro de Convenciones, has information on Acapulco and Guerrero; open 9am to 3pm and 6pm to 8pm Monday to Friday, 9am to 3pm Saturday.

The Casa Consular (☎/fax 481-25-33), in the Centro de Convenciones, provides consular assistance to visitors of all nationalities; it is open 9am to 2pm and 5pm to 7pm Monday to Friday.

Money Many places in Acapulco are eager to change your money. Omnipresent banks give the best rates. Conspicuous casas de cambio pay a slightly lower rate, but are open longer hours and are less busy than banks; shop around, as rates vary. Banks and casas de cambio cluster around the zócalo and line La Costera. Hotels will also change money, but their rates are usually extortionate.

In La Gran Plaza, American Express (☎ 485-99-08), La Costera 1628, changes the company's traveler's checks at bank rates, sans crowds, 10am to 7pm Monday to Friday, 10am to 3pm Saturday.

Post & Communications The main post office (☎ 483-53-63), La Costera 125, is in

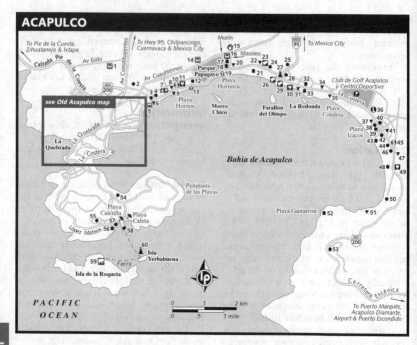

ACAPULCO

the Palacio Federal beside Sanborns, a couple of blocks east of the zócalo; open 8am to 5.30pm Monday to Friday, 8am to 1pm Saturday. In the same building, Telecomm (☎ 484-69-76), with fax and telex service, is open 8am to 7pm Monday to Friday, 9am to noon Saturday and Sunday.

Another post office (open 8am to 4pm Monday to Friday, 9am to 1pm Saturday) and Telecomm office (open 8am to 7.30pm Monday to Friday, 9am to noon Saturday, Sunday and holidays) are at the Estrella de Oro bus station, Cuauhtémoc at Massieu, upstairs on the outside right corner of the building. You can also post mail from the Centro de Convenciones.

Long-distance calls can be made from Telmex pay phones – plentiful throughout the city – or from private telephone casetas (with signs saying 'larga distancia'). Telephone and fax services are available on the west side of the zócalo at Caseta Alameda, on La Paz. Many other casetas are near the zócalo and along La Costera.

It's impossible to walk more than a few blocks without passing a cybercafé in Acapulco's major hotel districts – Internet places now possibly outnumber discos. Most places with online access are run by friendly younger folks and stay open late. Air-conditioned Tequila@.com, La Costera 326, a few blocks east of the zócalo, is open 9am to midnight Monday to Saturday and noon to 10pm Sunday. It charges US$1.75 an hour and also offers telephone, fax and copy services. A few blocks west of the zócalo, C@afe Internet, La Quebrada 21, charges US$1.25 an hour and is open until around 8pm. Several other non-air-conditioned places charging around US$1 an hour (some as little as US$0.50 per hour during low season) are near the Mercado de Artesanías, by the corner of Mina and Galeana. Fly-by-night cybercafés sprout like mushrooms in moist duff along the east half of La Costera.

Bookstores For its size, Acapulco is woefully lacking good bookstores. All Sanborns locations have English-language books and magazines; the outlet a couple of blocks east of CICI (☎ 484-20-44), La Costera 3111, stocks a larger selection than the other location near the zócalo.

ACAPULCO

PLACES TO STAY
7 Playa Suave Trailer Park
17 Auto Hotel Ritz
18 Hotel Jacqueline; Hotel del Valle
21 Hotel Costa Club Acapulco; Centro Comercio Plaza Bahía; Museo Histórico Naval de Acapulco; Aerolíneas Internacionales
32 Romano Palace Hotel
33 AJ Hackett Bungee; Delfines Paradise; Fiesta Americana Condesa
43 Hotel Quinta Mica; Suites Selene
48 Hyatt Regency Acapulco; Mexicana Airlines
52 Radisson Resort
53 Las Brisas
56 Hotel Boca Chica

PLACES TO EAT
6 100% Natural
8 100% Natural; Banamex ATM
9 El Amigo Miguel
20 VIPS; La Gran Plaza; American Express; ATM
22 Hotel Club del Sol; American Airlines
31 Pancho's
34 Carlos 'n Charlie's
35 Sanborns; VIPS

37 Mariscos Pipo's
41 Fersato's; Immigration Office (Migración); German Consulate; El Fogón; Baby 'O disco
47 24-hour VIPS; Wal-Mart; Swedish Consulate
51 Señor Frog's

OTHER
1 Estrella Blanca 1st-Class Bus Station (Central Ejido)
2 Unidad Deportiva Acapulco
3 Comercial Mexicana; Aeroméxico; Mercado de Artesanías Papagayo; Pemex Gas Station; Bital ATM; Banamex ATM
4 Mercado de Artesanías Noa Noa
5 Local Bus Stops
10 Banamex
11 Tequila's Le Club; Bodega Gigante
12 Bodega Aurrera
13 Public Bathrooms
14 Estrella Blanca 1st-Class Bus Station (Central Papagayo)
15 Pemex Gas Station
16 Estrella de Oro Bus Station; Post Office; Telecomm; ATM
19 Public Bathrooms
23 Netherlands Consulate

24 Mercado de Artesanías Dalia
25 Sam's Club; Comercial Mexicana
26 US Consulate
27 Diana Statue (La Diana)
28 Mercado de Artesanías La Diana; Pemex Gas Station
29 Canadian Consulate
30 Disco Beach
36 Centro de Convenciones; Procuduría de la Turista; Sefotur; Casa Consular; French Consulate
38 Hard Rock Café; Planet Hollywood; Nina's
39 CICI & Acapulco Mágico
40 Comercial Mexicana
42 Casa de la Cultura
44 Sanborns; Alamo Rent-A-Car; Salon Q
45 Bancomer ATM; Saad Rent-A-Car
46 Andromedas
49 El Alebrije
50 Icacos Naval Base
54 Yacht Club
55 Plaza de Toros
57 Mercado de Artesanías La Caletilla
58 Mágico Mundo Marino
59 Zoo
60 La Capilla Submarina (Underwater Chapel)

Comercial Mexicana, on La Costera opposite CICI, has a few magazines in English. Wal-Mart, farther east on La Costera, has a limited English-language selection. La Tienda, at the Fuerte de San Diego museum, has the city's best Spanish-language academic section plus a limited selection of paperbacks and periodicals in English.

Laundry Lavandería Lavadín (☎ 482-28-90), corner of La Paz and Iglesias a couple of blocks west of the zócalo, is open 8am to 10pm Monday to Saturday; pickup and delivery service costs US$2.75. Lavandería y Tintorería Coral (☎ 480-07-35), Juárez 12, next door to Hotel Mama Hélène, charges US$1.25 per kilo and also does dry cleaning; open 9am to 2pm and 4pm to 7pm Monday to Friday, 9am to 2pm Saturday. Several other laundries line La Costera, including one at the Hotel Club del Sol (☎ 485-66-00), La Costera at Ascencio.

Emergency Locatel (☎ 481-11-00), operated by Sefotur, is a 24-hour hot line for all types of emergencies. Rouse the tourist police at ☎ 485-04-90. The Cruz Roja (Red Cross, ☎ 485-59-12) provides ambulance service.

Fuerte de San Diego

This impressively restored pentagonal fort was built in 1616 atop a hill just east of the zócalo. Its mission was to protect from marauding Dutch and English buccaneers the Spanish *naos* (galleons) conducting trade between the Philippines and Mexico. It must have been effective because this trade route lasted until the early 19th century. Apparently the fort was also strong enough to forestall for four months the takeover of the city by independence leader José María Morelos y Pavón in 1812.

After a 1776 earthquake damaged most of Acapulco, the fort had to be rebuilt. It remains basically unchanged today, having been recently restored to top condition by

Acapulco's Long & Illustrious History

The name 'Acapulco' is derived from ancient Náhuatl words meaning 'where the reeds stood' or 'place of giant reeds.' Archaeological finds show that when the Spaniards arrived, people had been living around Bahía de Acapulco and the nearby bay of Puerto Marqués for around 2000 years, developing from a hunting and gathering society to an agricultural one.

Spanish sailors discovered the Bay of Acapulco in 1512. Port and shipbuilding facilities were subsequently established here because of the substantial natural harbor.

In 1523 Hernán Cortés, Juan Rodríguez Villafuerte and merchant Juan de Sala joined forces to finance an overland trade route between Mexico City and Acapulco. This route, known as the 'Camino de Asia,' was the principal trade route between Mexico City and the Pacific; the 'Camino de Europa,' from Mexico City to Veracruz on the Gulf Coast, completed the overland link between Asia and Spain.

Acapulco became the only port in the New World authorized to receive *naos* (Spanish trading galleons) from China and the Philippines. During the annual springtime Acapulco Fair, lasting up to two months after the galleons arrived from Manila, traders converged on Acapulco from Mexico City, Manila and Peru.

By the 17th century, trade with Asia was flourishing, and English and Dutch pirate ships were thriving in the Pacific and along the coastlines of mainland Mexico and Baja California. To fend off freebooters, the Fuerte de San Diego was built atop a low hill overlooking Bahía de Acapulco. It was not until the end of the 18th century that Spain permitted its American colonies to engage in free trade, ending the monopoly of the naos and the Manila-Acapulco trade route. The naos continued trading until the early 19th century.

Upon gaining independence, Mexico severed most of its trade links with Spain and Spanish colonies, and Acapulco declined as a port city. It became relatively isolated from the rest of the world until a paved road linked it with Mexico City in 1927 (look for the older green signs along La Costera). As Mexico City flourished, its citizens began vacationing on the Pacific coast. A new international airport was built, Hollywood filmed a few flicks here, and by the 1950s Acapulco was on its way to becoming a glitzy jet-set resort.

the Instituto Nacional de Antropología e Historia (INAH). The panorama of Acapulco you'll get from the fort is free and alone worth the trip.

The fort is now home to the **Museo Histórico de Acapulco** (☎ 482-38-28; *admission US$3.50, free Sun & holidays and always free for students with ID; open 9.30am-6.30pm Tues-Sun*), which offers interesting exhibits detailing the city's history, with Spanish and English captions.

The new **Casa de las Máscaras** mask museum is nearby on the pedestrian portion of Morelos, just downhill past the parking lot through the fort's front entrance gate; open 10am to 6pm Monday to Saturday.

Museo Histórico Naval de Acapulco

This insightful museum (☎ 463-29-84, *Centro Comercial Plaza Bahía, La Costera*

125, 1st floor, Local 48; admission US$1.25; open 10am-2pm & 5pm-10pm daily) preserves maps, photos and intricate wooden models of historic ships, a couple of which are on display in Fuerte de San Diego. The intricate, navigable 1:250 scale models are crafted here by museum director Marcelo Adano; stop by for a guided tour and a peek inside his workshop.

La Quebrada Cliff Divers

The famous *clavadistas* (cliff divers) of La Quebrada (☎ 483-14-00; *admission US$1.75, children under 8 yrs free; shows at 12.45pm, 7.30pm, 8.30pm, 9.30pm & 10.30pm daily*) have been dazzling audiences ever since 1934, swan diving with graceful finesse from heights of 25 to 35m into the narrow ocean cove below. Understandably, the divers pray at a small shrine before leaping over the edge, as did Elvis

OLD ACAPULCO

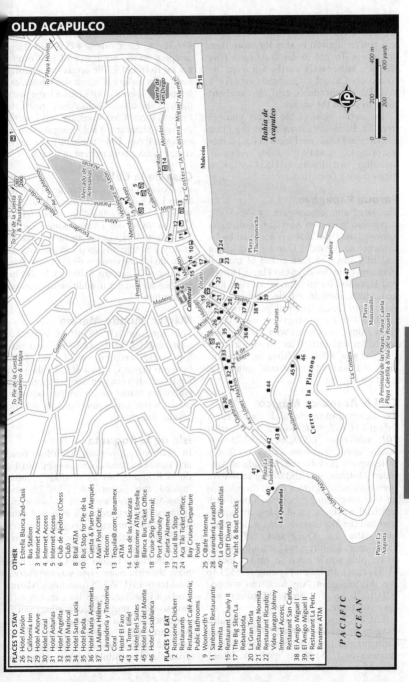

PLACES TO STAY
26 Hotel Misión
27 California Inn
29 Hotel Anorve
30 Hotel Coral
31 Hotel Asturias
32 Hotel Angelita
33 Hotel Mariscal
34 Hotel Santa Lucía
35 Hotel Paola
36 Hotel María Antonieta
37 La Mama Hélène; Lavandería y Tintorería Coral
42 Hotel El Faro
43 La Torre Eiffel
44 Hotel Etel Suites
45 Hotel Real del Monte
46 Hotel Casablanca

PLACES TO EAT
2   Rotisserie Chicken Restaurants
7   Restaurant Café Astoria; Public Bathrooms
9   Woolworth's
11 Sanborns; Restaurante Normita
15 Restaurant Charly II
17 The Big Slice/La Rebanadota
20 La Gran Torta
21 Restaurante Normita
22 Restaurant Ricardo; Video Juegos Johnny Internet Access; Restaurant San Carlos
38 El Amigo Miguel I
39 El Amigo Miguel II
41 Restaurant La Perla; Banamex ATM

OTHER
1   Estrella Blanca 2nd-Class Bus Station
3   Internet Access
4   Internet Access
5   Internet Access
6   Club de Ajedrez (Chess Club)
8   Bital ATM
10 Bus Stop for Pie de la Cuesta & Puerto Marqués
12 Main Post Office; Telecom
13 Tequila@.com; Banamex ATM
14 Casa de las Máscaras
16 Bancomer ATM; Estrella Blanca Bus Ticket Office
18 Cruise Ship Terminal; Port Authority
19 Caseta Alameda
23 Local Bus Stop
24 Aca Tiki Ticket Office; Bay Cruises Departure Point
25 C@afe Internet
28 Lavandería Lavadín
40 La Quebrada Clavadistas (Cliff Divers)
47 Yacht & Boat Docks

CENTRAL PACIFIC COAST

Presley in the 1963 flick *Fun in Acapulco*. At least three divers perform each time, and you're allowed to stay for more than one show. To get to La Quebrada (the Ravine), either walk up the hill from the zócalo on Calle La Quebrada or take a taxi. La Quebrada is also an excellent place to watch the sunset.

The aerial view of the divers you get from La Perla restaurant/bar at the Plaza Las Glorias Hotel (see Places to Eat) comes at a price. Cover while the diving's going on, including two drinks, is US$17.50, with meals costing twice that.

Parque Papagayo

This large amusement park (☎ 485-71-77; *admission free; open 8am-8pm daily, rides operate 3pm-10pm daily*) is bounded by La Costera and Avenidas Cuauhtémoc, Morín and El Cano. The park is full of tropical trees and provides access to Playas Hornos and Hornitos. Its attractions, for both kids and adults, include a roller-skating rink, skateboard area, a lake with paddleboats, a children's train, quadricycles, mechanical rides, animal enclosures with deer, rabbits, crocodiles and turtles, an aviary, a restaurant/bar and a hill affording an excellent view. A 1.2km 'interior circuit' pathway is good for jogging.

CICI & Acapulco Mágico

The Centro Internacional de Convivencia Infantil (CICI, ☎ 484-82-10, *La Costera 101; admission US$5.50, US$2.75 low season; open 10am-6pm daily*) is a family water-sports park on the east side of Acapulco. Dolphin, seal and diving shows are presented several times daily; there's also an 80m-long water toboggan, a pool with artificial waves, a small tide-pool aquarium and the Sky Coaster ride, which simulates the La Quebrada cliff-diving experience. Children two and up pay full price, plus you'll need to rent a locker (US$1) and an inflatable ring (US$2) to use the toboggan. Any local bus marked 'CICI,' 'Base' or 'Puerto Marqués' will take you there.

CICI's new attraction is **Acapulco Mágico** (☎ 481-02-94, 484-19-70), featuring swimming with dolphins; US$55 for 20 minutes or US$100 for an hour. Phone ahead for reservations.

Centro de Convenciones

Acapulco's convention center (☎ 484-71-52, 484-70-98, *La Costera 4455*) is a large complex on the north side of La Costera not far from CICI. The center has a permanent crafts gallery (Galería de Artesanías), temporary special exhibitions, a large plaza, theaters and concert halls. Also here are the tourist offices, Casa Consular and Locatel. A Fiesta Mexicana is held several evenings each week (see Entertainment). Phone the center to ask about current offerings.

Casa de la Cultura

Set around a garden just southeast of CICI down La Costera, this complex of buildings (☎ 484-23-90, 484-38-14 for schedules, La Costera 4834; open 10am-6pm Mon-Fri, 10am-3pm Sat) houses an innovative art gallery, a handicrafts shop and the Salon de Fama de los Deportistas de Guerrero (Hall of Fame of Guerrero Athletes). It also has an open-air theater in addition to an indoor auditorium.

Mágico Mundo Marino

This aquarium (☎ 483-93-44; *admission adult/child 3-12 yrs US$3.25/1.75; open 9am-6pm daily*) stands on a small point of land between Playas Caleta and Caletilla. Highlights include a sea lion show; the feeding of crocodiles, turtles and piranhas; swimming pools; water toboggans; and an oceanographic museum.

Isla de la Roqueta

In addition to a popular (crowded) beach and snorkeling and diving possibilities, Isla de la Roqueta has an obviously underfunded **zoo** (*admission US$0.70; open 10am-5pm daily*) with lots of exotic cats (pumas, jaguars, leopards etc) and other jungle critters in small cages. You can rent snorkeling gear, kayaks and other watersports equipment on the beach.

From Playas Caleta and Caletilla, boats make the eight-minute one-way trip every 20 minutes or so (US$3.25 roundtrip). Alternatively, a glass-bottomed boat makes a circuitous trip to the island, departing from the same beaches but traveling via La Capilla Submarina (the Underwater Chapel), a submerged bronze statue of the Virgen de Guadalupe – visibility varies with water conditions. Roundtrip fare is US$5.50; the rip takes about an hour, depending on how many times floating vendors accost your boat. You can alight on the island and take a later boat back, but find out when the last boat leaves, usually around 5.30pm.

Beaches

Visiting Acapulco's beaches tops most visitors' lists of must-dos here. The beaches heading east around the bay from the zócalo – Playas **Hornos**, **Hornitos**, **Condesa** and **Icacos** – are the most popular. The high-rise hotel district begins on Playa Hornitos, on the east side of Parque Papagayo, and heads east from there. City buses constantly ply La Costera, making it easy to get up and down this long arc of beaches.

Playas **Caleta** and **Caletilla** are two small, protected beaches beside one another in a cove on the south side of Peninsula de las Playas. They're especially popular among families with small children, as the water is very calm. All buses marked 'Caleta' heading down La Costera go there. The Mágico Mundo Marino aquarium sits on a tiny point of land separating the two beaches; boats go regularly from there to Isla de la Roqueta.

Playa La Angosta is in a tiny, protected cove on the west side of the peninsula. From the zócalo it takes about 20 minutes to walk there. Or you can take any 'Caleta' bus and get off near the Hotel Avenida, on La Costera, just one short block from the beach.

Farther afield are other good beaches, including **Puerto Marqués** and **Playa Revolcadero** (see Around Acapulco, later this chapter) and **Pie de la Cuesta** (see Pie de la Cuesta, earlier this chapter).

Water Sports

Just about everything that can be done on, under or above the water is done in Acapulco. On Bahía de Acapulco, water-skiing, boating, 'banana-boating' and parasailing are all popular activities. The smaller Playas Caleta and Caletilla have all of these, plus sailboats, fishing boats, motorboats, pedal boats, canoes, snorkel gear, inner tubes and water bicycles for rent.

Scuba-diving trips and instruction can be arranged through several diving operators, including **Arnold Brothers** (☎ 482-18-77, La Costera 205), **Divers de México** (☎ 482-13-98, 483-60-20, La Costera 100), **Mantarraya**

(☎/fax 482-41-76, Gran Vía Tropical 23) and the **Swiss Divers Association** (☎ 482-13-57, Centro Comercial Las Palmas, Local 25).

Deep-sea fishing is another possibility. Divers de México and Mantarraya both offer fishing trips, as does **Fish 'R' Us** (☎ 482-22-22, 482-82-82, La Costera 100). The cost for a six-hour fishing trip starts around US$200 per boat, depending on the size of the boat; Fish 'R' Us offers half-day trips from US$75 per person.

Other Activities

The **Unidad Deportiva Acapulco** (☎ 486-10-33, Calle Chiapas s/n, Colonia Progreso; admission stadium track US$0.30, children's pool US$0.50, pool US$1; open noon-6pm Tues, 9am-6pm Wed-Sun) has an Olympic-size pool, children's pool, gymnasium, stadium, sports courts and grass fields.

For tennis, try **Club de Golf Acapulco** (☎ 484-65-83), **Club de Tenis Hyatt** (☎ 469-12-34), **Villa Vera Racquet Club** (☎ 484-03-34), **Hotel Panoramic** (☎ 481-01-32) or **Fairmont Acapulco Princess Hotel** (☎ 469-10-00).

Acapulco also has gyms, squash courts and other recreation facilities. The tourist office has information on sports in Acapulco.

Organized Tours

Various boats and yachts offer cruises, which depart from the Malecón near the zócalo. Cruises (from US$20 low season) are available day and night; they range from multilevel boats with blaring salsa music and open bars to yachts offering quiet sunset cruises around the bay. All take basically the same route – they leave from the Malecón, go around Peninsula de las Playas to Isla de la Roqueta, pass by to see the cliff divers at La Quebrada, cross over to Puerto Marqués and then come back around Bahía de Acapulco.

The *Hawaiano* (☎ 482-21-99, 482-07-85), the *Fiesta* and *Bonanza* (☎ 482-20-55), and the large *Aca Tiki* catamaran (☎ 484-61-40) are all popular; you can make reservations directly or through travel agencies and most hotels.

Special Events

Probably the busiest time of year for tourism in Acapulco is Semana Santa, when there's lots of action in the discos, on the beaches and all over town.

Tianguis Turístico, Mexico's major annual tourism trade fair, is held the second or third week in April. The **Festivales de Acapulco**, held for one week in May, feature Mexican and international music at venues around town.

International film festivals include the Festival de Cine Negro (Black Film Festival), held in early June, and the weeklong Festival de Cine Francés (French Film Festival) in late November. The festival for Mexico's favorite figure, the Virgen de Guadalupe, is celebrated all night on December 11 and all the following day; it's marked by fireworks, folk dances and street processions accompanied by small marching bands. The processions converge at the cathedral in the zócalo, where children dressed in costumes congregate.

Places to Stay

Acapulco has more than 30,000 hotel rooms in all categories. Rates vary widely by season; high season is from the middle of December until the end of Easter, with another flurry of activity during the July and August school holidays. Most hotels raise their rates during these times, to as much as double the low-season price, though some do this for only part of the season. At other times of year you can often bargain for a better rate, especially if you plan to stay a while. During Semana Santa or between Christmas and New Year's Day, it's essential to book ahead.

Budget *Playa Suave Trailer Park* (☎ 485-18-85, La Costera 276) Tent & trailer sites US$15. Closest park to town, Playa Suave has 38 tent and trailer spaces with full hookups. The entrance is on Vasco Núñez de Balboa, between Mendoza and Malaespina, a block behind La Costera.

Trailer Park Diamante (☎ 466-02-00, Copacabana 8, Fraccionamiento Playa Diamante) Tent & trailer sites with full hookups US$15. Southeast of town in the Diamante area, this place is 3km from the beach but has two swimming pools.

Trailer Park El Coloso is at Carretera Pinotepa Nacional Km 2.5 in Colonia La Sábana.

Other trailer parks are in Pie de la Cuesta, half an hour northwest of town (see Pie de la Cuesta, earlier in this chapter).

Most of Acapulco's budget hotels are concentrated around the zócalo and on Calle La Quebrada, the street heading up the hill from behind the cathedral to La Quebrada, where the divers take the plunge.

Hotel Maria Antonieta (☎ 482-50-24, Azueta 17) Rooms US$10 per person. Maria Antonieta is a good but cavernous place near the zócalo with reasonably quiet rooms and a communal kitchen.

California Inn (☎ 482-28-93, La Paz 12) Singles/doubles US$13/22. The California is another good choice. Its clean, pleasant rooms are set around a leafy courtyard, and English is spoken.

Hotel Añorve (☎ 482-32-62, Juárez 17) Singles/doubles US$9/16.50. One block from the zócalo, this humble hotel has simple, clean rooms with hot water and ceiling fans.

Hotel Paola (☎ 482-62-43, Azueta 16) Rooms US$10 per person. The positively pink Paola is yet another clean place. The outside rooms have small private balconies, the interior rooms are quieter, and all are outfitted in pastels.

Hotel Santa Lucía (☎ 482-04-41, López Mateos 33) Rooms US$8 per person. The family-run Santa Lucía also has clean rooms.

La Mama Hélène (Casa Héléne, ☎ 482-23-96, Juárez 12) Singles/doubles US$9/13. Less desirable Casa Hélène has rooms set around a covered interior courtyard.

Hotel Angelita (☎ 483-57-34, La Quebrada 37) Singles/doubles US$11/16.50. Angelita is clean and popular, with a guests' sitting room out front.

Hotel Mariscal (☎ 482-00-15, La Quebrada 35) Rooms US$14.50 per person high season; cheaper by the week. Next door to the Angelita, the homey Mariscal has clean rooms with hot water. Some rooms have private balconies.

Hotel Asturias (☎/fax 483-65-48, La Quebrada 45) Doubles US$16/32 low/high season, one room with air-con an extra US$5.50. This friendly family-run hotel is popular, very clean and well tended, with pleasant rooms on a courtyard, cable TV in the lobby and a small swimming pool.

Hotel Coral (☎ 482-07-56, La Quebrada 56) Rooms US$6.50 per person. The clean Coral also has a small swimming pool.

Up the hill at the top of Calle La Quebrada is Plaza La Quebrada, overlooking the sea. The large attended parking lot here is a safe place to park, but it can get very loud in the evening when the cliff divers perform. Hotels here are somewhat cooler than places down in town, since they catch the sea breezes.

La Torre Eiffel (☎ 482-16-83, Inalámbrica 110) Singles/doubles US$11/16 low season. Perched on a hill above Plaza La Quebrada, the 30-year-old Torre Eiffel has a small swimming pool and huge balconies with sitting areas facing the sea. The rooms have non-cable color TV and are bright and airy, and the sunset views are great, but the place shows its age in malfunctioning details.

Hotel El Faro (☎ 482-13-65, La Quebrada 83) Singles/doubles May-Nov US$9/16.50, Dec-Apr US$11/22. On Plaza La Quebrada, El Faro has large rooms with private balconies and a shared balcony overlooking the noisy plaza. Last time we checked in late 2001, it was for sale and looking a bit neglected.

Mid-Range *Hotel Misión* (☎ 482-36-43, Valle 12) Doubles from US$25/35 low/high season. Near the zócalo, this relaxing colonial-style place has stylish rooms with tiles and heavy Spanish furniture. Rooms are set around a shady courtyard where your choice of continental breakfast (US$3) or complete breakfast (US$6) is served.

Hotel Jacqueline (☎ 485-93-38, Morín 205 at La Costera) Doubles with air-con low/high season US$39/50. On the east side of Parque Papagayo, near La Costera and popular Playa Hornitos, the Jacqueline has 10 rooms around a pleasant little garden.

Hotel del Valle (☎ 485-83-36/88, Espinosa 8) Doubles with fan/air-con US$32/39 low season. Just inland from La Costera near Parque Papagayo, this place has a small swimming pool and kitchens (US$6.50 surcharge per day). The nearest street sign indicates Morín (which actually starts a block north).

Auto Hotel Ritz (☎ 482-52-42, 800-715-40-54, Massieu s/n) Doubles US$55/65 low/high season. Half a block from Playa Hornitos is this six-story hotel with indoor parking. Rooms come with air-con, cable TV, dank carpet and private terraces overlooking the swimming pool.

There are a number of hotels near CICI and Playa Icacos, including two with large apartments, swimming pools, parking, air-con and fully equipped kitchens:

Suites Selene (☎/fax 484-36-43, e suites selene@hotmail.com, Colón 175) Singles/doubles US$40/45, 1-bed/2-bed apartments with kitchen US$55/110 Dec-Apr; rates 20% less May-Nov. One door from the beach, Selene is the best option. It has basic rooms and attractive air-conditioned apartments. Ask for a sea-view room; they have spacious balconies and cost the same.

Hotel Quinta Mica (☎ 484-01-21, fax 484-25-99, Colón 115) Double-occupancy apartments Mon-Thur US$45, Fri-Sun US$55. These air-conditioned apartments are simpler and more worn than Selene's. The Comercial Mexicana supermarket nearby is convenient to both for groceries.

High-rise hotels along La Costera tend to be expensive.

Romano Palace Hotel (☎ 484-77-30, 800-090-15-00, w www.romanopalace.com.mx, La Costera 130) 1-4 person rooms US$65/80 low/high season. One of the more economical hotels is the 22-story Romano Palace, whose luxurious rooms have private balconies and floor-to-ceiling windows with great bayfront views; ask for an upper-story room.

Hotel Boca Chica (☎ 483-63-88, fax 483-95-13, e bocach@acabtu.com.mx, w http://acapulco-bocachica.com, Playa Caletilla) Singles/doubles with breakfast Dec-Apr US$75/89, from US$60 low-season. This lovely waterside hotel has a natural seaside swimming pool, gardens with a view of Isla de la Roqueta, an open-air restaurant/bar and air-conditioned rooms with fine vistas.

Three classy hotels perched on a hill on Peninsula de las Playas offer magnificent views.

Hotel Real del Monte/Hotel Casablanca (☎ 482-12-12/13, Cerro de la Pinzona 80) 1-4 person rooms with fan/air-con from US$38/45. This connected pair of neocolonial hotels has a swimming pool and panoramic views.

Hotel Etel Suites (☎ 482-22-40/41, Cerro de la Pinzona 92) Doubles US$30/40 low/high season, furnished suites US$40/50. High atop the hill overlooking Old Acapulco, this friendly hotel's good-value, spotless suites have expansive terraces with views of La Quebrada and the bay. Amenities include full kitchens, two swimming pools and well-manicured gardens. Recommended, especially for larger groups.

Top End If you're on a junket or have wads of cash burning a hole in your disco trousers, there's plenty of opportunity to splash out at Acapulco's numerous deluxe 'grand tourism' and ultraluxe 'special category' hotels. Many of the luxury hotels are in the newer Acapulco Diamante zone, east of Puerto Marqués, and beachfront along La Costera; the original high-rise zone begins at the eastern end of Parque Papagayo and curves east around the bay. Off-season package rates and special promotions, which can be less than half standard holiday rack rates, dip as low as US$129 per night for double occupancy – ask reservation agents for special deals. During the high season, the sky is truly the limit.

Impressive special category hotels include:

Camino Real Acapulco Diamante (☎/fax 435-10-10/20, ☎ 800-722-6466 in the USA, **w** www.caminoreal.com, Carretera Escénica Km 14)

Fairmont Acapulco Princess (☎ 484-21-24, 800-441-1414 in the USA, **w** www.fairmont.com, Playa Revolcadero s/n)

Fairmont Pierre Marqués (☎ 466-05-66, 800-441-1414 in the USA, **w** www.fairmont.com, Villa 741, Playa Revolcadero s/n)

Hyatt Regency Acapulco (☎ 469-1234, 800-005-00-00 in Mexico, ☎ 800-233-1234 in the USA, **w** www.acapulco.hyatt.com, La Costera 1)

Las Brisas (☎ 469-69-00, 800-227-47-27 in Mexico, ☎ 888-559-4329 in the USA, fax 446-53-28, **w** www.brisas.com.mx, Carretera Escénica s/n)

Noteworthy grand tourism hotels include:

Costa Club Acapulco (☎ 485-90-50, 800-903-49-00, La Costera 123)

Fiesta Americana Condesa (☎ 484-28-28, **w** www.fiestaamericana.com, La Costera 97)

Radisson Resort (☎ 446-65-65, **w** www.radisson.com, Costera Guitarrón 110)

Vidafel Mayan Palace (☎ 466-23-93, fax 466-00-38, Costera de las Palmas 1121)

Villa Vera Hotel Spa (☎ 484-03-34, fax 484-74-79, Lomas del Mar 35)

Places to Eat
Old Acapulco On the northeast side of the zócalo, the **Big Slice/La Rebanadota**, open 10am to 3am Wednesday to Monday during the high season, is a popular place with tasty, economical food and attractive tables both out on the plaza (great for people-watching) and inside where it's air-conditioned. Specialties include pizza, pasta and salads, and their 'big slices' (US$1.50) are gigantic.

La Gran Torta (☎ 483-84-76, La Paz 6) US$4. Open 8am-midnight daily. Popular with local families, the Big Torta serves hearty breakfasts, good espresso, a US$3 comida corrida and tasty tortas.

Restaurant Café Astoria (Plaza Álvarez, Edificio Pintos 4-C) Everything less than US$4. Open 8am-11pm daily. Hidden away at the back of the plaza, this café has outdoor tables in a shady, quietish spot just east of the cathedral. Prices are reasonable and the comida corrida, served 1pm to 4pm, is good.

Restaurant Charly II (Carranza s/n) Tacos US$2-3, comida corrida US$2.50. Open 7.30am-11pm daily. Around the corner from Café Astoria, on the pedestrian callejón Carranza, economical Charly II has shady sidewalk tables.

Woolworth's (☎ 482-23-45, Escudero 250) Set breakfasts and lunches US$4-6.50, set dinners US$5.50-7. Open 7am-10pm. This department store's air-conditioned restaurant is popular with locals for its good-value meal deals.

Sanborns (☎ 482-61-67, cnr Escudero & La Costera) Near Woolworth's, Sanborns also has an air-conditioned restaurant serving similar, but more spendy, Mexi-American fare and a couple more locations along La Costera.

Emerging from the zócalo's west side, Calle Juárez has at least a dozen restaurants.

Restaurant San Carlos (Juárez 5) Comida corrida US$3. Open 8am-10pm daily. The San Carlos has an open-air patio, good traditional Mexican fare and ample ambiance.

Restaurant Ricardo (Juárez 9) Comida corrida US$3. Open 8am-midnight daily. A couple of doors farther from the zócalo, Ricardo's is popular with locals for its cheap set meals and robust café con leche.

Restaurante Normita (La Paz 7-13) Breakfast US$2.75, comida corrida US$3. Open 8am-8pm daily. Just one block west of the zócalo, friendly Restaurante Normita's dishes out no-nonsense *comida casera* (home-style cooking) and free fruit salad with set breakfasts. Dinner features a succinct selection of antojitos and mariscos.

El Amigo Miguel (☎ 485-77-64, 483-69-81, Juárez 31 at Azueta) Everything less than US$7. Open 10am-9pm daily. This cheery open-air restaurant is one of the busiest, featuring cheap and delicious seafood. Miguel has two restaurants opposite one another, on the same corner, with other branches around town. Several other good seafood places are nearby.

For eat-in or takeout rotisserie roasted chicken, head for 5 de Mayo, where there are four places side by side, plus a *Mr Taco* joint across the street.

La Costera Dozens of restaurants line La Costera heading east toward the high-rise hotels.

Fersato's (☎ 484-39-49, La Costera 44) Comida corrida US$4. Open 8am-midnight daily. Opposite the Casa de la Cultura, this long-standing family establishment features delicious Mexican food.

Mariscos Pipo's (☎ 484-01-65, cnr La Costera & Nao Victoria) Dinner US$10-20. Open 1pm to 9.30pm daily. Near Plaza Canadá, Pipo's used to be known as one of Acapulco's best *marisquerías*, but it's far from the best value on the beach; the combination seafood cocktail (US$14/17 small/large) might feed two.

Hotel Club del Sol (☎ 485-66-00, La Costera at Ascencio) Breakfast/dinner buffets US$8/15, including drinks. This restaurant serves a popular breakfast buffet 9am to noon Monday to Thursday and a dinner buffet 6pm to 10pm Monday to Saturday.

VIPS (☎ 486-85-74, Gran Plaza, cnr La Costera & Massieu) Mains US$5-10. Open 7am-midnight Sun-Thur, 7am-2am Fri & Sat. The Mexican version of Denny's is a big, bright, air-conditioned place, more popular with locals than tourists. There are a couple more locations along La Costera, including one at Playa icacos that's open 24 hours.

Carlos 'n Charlie's (☎ 484-00-39, La Costera 112) Mains US$5-15. Open 1pm-midnight daily. Carlos Anderson's chain place isn't cheap, but it sends the tourists home happy with rowdy music and a quirky bilingual menu.

Señor Frog's (☎ 446-57-34, Carretera Escénica 28, Centro Comercial La Vista) Mains US$5-15. Open 1pm-1am daily. On the east side of Bahía de Acapulco, this famously boisterous place has great views and less great food.

Pancho's (☎ 484-10-96, La Costera 109) Dinner US$6-15. Open 6pm-midnight daily. This open-air restaurant is reasonably priced and serves tasty Mexican and international meals, especially grilled and barbecued meats.

Many other open-air beachfront restaurant/bars are opposite the Romano Palace Hotel. Stroll along, browse the posted menus, and take your pick.

Health-conscious *100% Natural* chain outlets, serving mid-range, mostly vegetarian fare, are found throughout Acapulco; there are five along La Costera, including a 24-hour branch (☎ 485-39-82) at La Costera 200. Another chain, *El Fogón*, serves its traditional Mexican dishes at several La Costera branches, including one (☎ 484-50-79) at La Costera 10 that's open daily until midnight. Many fast food chains also litter La Costera, especially near the east end.

Playa Caletilla Many open-air seafood restaurants are under the big trees lining the rear of Playa Caletilla. All have similar inexpensive menus.

Hotel Boca Chica (☎ 483-63-88, Playa Caletilla) Buffets US$10-15. Lunch 12.30pm-2.30pm daily, dinner 7.30pm-10pm daily. This attractive open-air restaurant at the west end of the beach, under a high palapa roof with a view across to Isla de la Roqueta, serves buffet lunch and dinner.

La Quebrada *Restaurant La Perla* (☎ 483-11-55, Plaza Las Glorias Hotel, Plazoleta La Quebrada 74) Dinner US$15-30, served 7pm-11pm daily. This scenic restaurant is a nice splurge. The nightly à la carte meal on candlelit terraces under the stars is overpriced (US$30 per person), but the great view of the clavadistas (see La Quebrada Cliff Divers, earlier in the Acapulco section) makes for a special evening.

Grocery Stores The huge air-conditioned *Comercial Mexicana*, *Bodega Aurrera* and *Bodega Gigante* combination supermarkets and big-box discount department stores (open 8am to 10pm daily) are along La Costera between the zócalo and Parque Papagayo. Another Comercial Mexicana is opposite CICI. **Sam's Club** and yet another **Comercial Mexicana** are on highway 95, just inland from the La Diana traffic circle. **Wal-Mart**, on the east end of the city, has a pharmacy and is open 24 hours. **Costco** is farther east.

Entertainment

Discos, Clubs & Bars Acapulco's active nightlife rivals its beaches as the main attraction. Much of it revolves around discos and nightclubs, with new ones continually opening up to challenge the old. Most of the discos open around 10pm and have a cover charge of at least US$10, which sometimes includes an open bar. You can identify the most popular of-the-moment places by comparing the length of the VIP lines.

Enigma (☎ 446-57-11, Carretera Escénica s/n) and **Palladium** (☎ 446-54-90, Carretera Escénica s/n) are popular places in the Las Brisas area in the southeast part of Acapulco; Palladium attracts the younger crowd. Some locals say these two are Acapulco's best.

Andromedas (☎ 484-88-15/16, cnr La Costera & La Fragata Yucatán) Another popular disco with a techno-pop feel and a nautical theme.

Salon Q (☎ 484-32-52, 481-01-14, La Costera 23) Open 10pm-4am, impersonator shows begin at 12.45am. Cover at this 'catedral de la salsa' includes an open bar. Nightly entertainment includes Latin rhythms, impersonators and live music; reservations recommended.

Baby'O (☎ 484-74-74, La Costera 22) Baby'O has a laser light show and is reputedly one of the best discos in Acapulco, attracting a younger crowd.

El Alebrije (☎ 484-59-04, La Costera 12) Located 400m south of Baby'O, this disco/concert hall bills itself as 'one of the largest and most spectacular discos in the world.'

Disco Beach (☎ 484-8230, La Costera s/n, Playa Condesa) This popular disco is in the line of beachfront restaurant/bars opposite the Romano Palace Hotel, right on Playa Condesa.

Hard Rock Cafe (☎ 484-66-80, La Costera 37) Restaurant and bar open noon-2am daily. It's hard to miss the Hard Rock.

Just west of CICI, the chain's Acapulco branch has live music 11pm to 1.30am.

Planet Hollywood (☎ 484-42-84, La Costera 2917) Restaurant and bar open noon-2am daily. Planet Hollywood has dancing from around 11pm.

Nina's (☎ 484-24-00, La Costera 41) On the other side of the Hard Rock, Nina's specializes in live Latin music.

Gay Venues Acapulco has an active gay scene and several predominantly gay bars and clubs. Drag shows are only one feature of the multifaceted scene:

Tequila's Le Club (☎ 485-86-23, 483-82-36, Urdaneta 29) Cover usually US$10-12; reservations recommended. Three blocks behind the Gigante supermarket, this club presents a famous transvesti (transvestite) show 11.30pm to 1am Monday to Saturday during the high season (Thursday to Saturday during low season), with an international show at 11.15pm and a Latin show at 1.30am. Chippendale, a ladies-only male stripper show, is presented 8.45pm to 11pm Thursday and Saturday.

Dance, Music & Theater As an alternative to the discos, most of the big hotels along La Costera have bars with entertainment, be it quiet piano music or live bands.

Centro de Convenciones (reservations ☎ 484-71-52, La Costera s/n) Admission US$45-50 for buffet, open bar and show, US$25 for show & bar only. Buffet starting at 7pm, show from 8pm-10pm, Mon, Wed & Fri. The convention center presents a Fiesta Mexicana three nights a week, featuring regional dances from many parts of Mexico, mariachis, the famous Papantla voladores and a rope performer.

Other theaters at the Centro de Convenciones present plays, concerts, dance and other cultural performances, as does the **Casa de la Cultura** (☎ 484-23-90, 484-38-14); phone or stop by for current schedules. **Parque Papagayo** (☎ 485-71-77, 485-96-23) also sometimes hosts alfresco events.

Cinemas Acapulco has several cinemas – at least three front La Costera, and several more are scattered around town. Show times are listed in the Acapulco Novedades and Sol de Acapulco newspapers.

Spectator Sports

Plaza de Toros (☎ 482-11-82, 483-95-61, *up the hill from Playa Caletilla*) 'Caleta' buses from Old Acapulco from US$35. Bullfights at 5.30pm every Sun, Dec-Mar. Bullfights are held at the bullring, southeast of La Quebrada and northwest of Playa Caleta. Buy tickets at the ring (from 4.30pm on fight day) or at travel agencies.

Shopping

Acapulco's huge *Mercado Central* is a 20-minute walk northeast of the zócalo on Constituyentes. The main crafts market, the 400-stall *Mercado de Artesanías*, is a few blocks east of the zócalo between Cuauhtémoc and Vicente de León. Paved and pleasant, it's a good place to get better deals on everything you see in the hotel shops – sarapes, hammocks, jewelry, huaraches, clothing and T-shirts, but don't expect to find any artisans at work here. Bargaining is definitely the rule; open 9am to 8pm daily.

Other artesanías markets include the *Mercados de Artesanías Papagayo*, *Noa Noa*, *El Pueblito*, *Dalia* and *La Diana*, all on La Costera, and another at Playa Caletilla. Many artisans now come down from the mountains with their wares every Monday after the famous Sunday market in Chilapa (see Around Chilpancingo later in this chapter), saving a potentially time-consuming trip for crafts-hounds who are short on time and longer on *dinero*.

Getting There & Away

Air Acapulco's busy airport (ACA, ☎ 466-94-34) has many international flights, most connecting through Mexico City or Guadalajara – both short hops from Acapulco. Airlines serving Acapulco and their direct flights (all with connections to other cities) include:

Aerolíneas Internacionales (☎ 486-56-30, 486-00-02) La Costera 127, Local 9; flies to Cuernavaca

Aeroméxico/Aerolitoral (☎ 485-16-25, 485-16-00, airport ☎ 466-92-04, 800-021-26-22) La Costera 286; flies to Guadalajara, Mexico City

America West (☎ 466-92-75, 800-235-92-92); flies to Phoenix

American Airlines (☎ 481-01-61, 800-904-60-00) La Costera 116, Plaza Condesa, Local 109; flies to Dallas

Continental Airlines (☎ 466-90-46, 800-900-50-00); flies to Houston

Mexicana (☎ 486-75-85, 800-502-20-00) La Costera 1632, La Gran Plaza; flies to Mexico City

Northwest (☎ 800-900-08-00); flies to Minneapolis (one Saturday flight, Dec-Apr)

Bus Acapulco has two major 1st-class long-distance bus companies: Estrella de Oro and Estrella Blanca. The tony, air-conditioned Estrella de Oro terminal (☎ 485-93-60), with free toilets and a Banamex ATM, is on the corner of Cuauhtémoc and Massieu. Estrella Blanca has two 1st-class terminals: Central Papagayo (☎ 469-20-80), Cuauhtémoc 1605, just north of Parque Papagayo, and Central Ejido (☎ 469-20-28/30), Ejido 47. Estrella Blanca also has a 2nd-class terminal (☎ 482-21-84), Cuauhtémoc 97, which sells tickets for all buses, but only has departures to nearby towns. Estrella Blanca tickets are also sold at several agencies around town, including Agencia de Viajes Zócalo (☎ 482-49-76), La Costera 207, Local 2, a couple of blocks east of the zócalo.

Both companies offer frequent services to Mexico City, with various levels of luxury; journey durations depend on whether they use the faster autopista (highway 95D) or the old federal highway 95. Destinations include:

Chilpancingo – 132km, 1½-3 hours; 1st-class or Plus every 1-2 hours 6.40am-11.30pm by Estrella de Oro (US$5.50), semidirect at least hourly by Estrella de Oro (US$5.50), 6 Futura (US$5.50), 1 Ejecutivo by Estrella Blanca (US$6.50, from Central Papagayo), 2nd-class every half hour 5am-7pm by Estrella Blanca (US$4.50, from 2nd-class terminal)

Cuernavaca – 315km, 4-5 hours; 3 Primera (US$19), 3 Plus (US$21) and frequent 2nd-class (US$16) by Estrella de Oro; 7 Primera (US$18.50), 1 Plus (US$20) and 1 Futura by Estrella Blanca (US$22, from Central Ejido); 3 Futura by Estrella Blanca (US$22, from Central Papagayo)

Iguala – 231km, 3 hours; 10 Primera by Estrella de Oro (US$11); Ordinario (2nd-class) hourly 6am-8.30pm by Estrella de Oro (3½ hours, US$9), 17 Primera by Estrella Blanca (US$11, from Central Ejido)

Mexico City (Terminal Norte) – 400km, 6 hours; 1 Plus by Estrella de Oro (US$25), 9 Futura (US$24), 1 Ejecutivo by Estrella Blanca (US$38,

Central Papagayo), 2 Económico (US$23) and 2 Futura by Estrella Blanca (US$24, Central Ejido)

Mexico City (Terminal Sur) – 400km, 5 hours; 20 Plus (US$25), 5 Crucero (US$26) and 6 Diamante (US$38) by Estrella de Oro, Futura at least hourly 7am to midnight (US$24), 4 Ejecutivo by Estrella Blanca (US$38, from Central Papagayo), 5 Primera and 8 Futura by Estrella Blanca (US$23-24, from Central Ejido)

Puerto Escondido – 400km, 7 hours; 3 Primera by Estrella Blanca (US$17.50, from Central Ejido)

Taxco – 266km, 4 hours; 5 Primera by Estrella de Oro (US$16); 4 Primera by Estrella Blanca (US$13, from Central Ejido)

Zihuatanejo – 239km, 4-5 hours; 3 Primera (US$10), 15 Primera (US$10.50), 2 Futura by Estrella Blanca (US$15, from Central Ejido), 2nd-class hourly 4.50am-5.30pm by Estrella de Oro (US$7.50)

Car Many car rental companies rent Jeeps as well as cars; several have offices at the airport as well as in town, and some offer free delivery to you. As always, it's a good idea to shop around to compare prices. Rental companies include:

Alamo	☎ 484-33-05, 466-94-44, 800-700-17-00
Avis	☎ 466-91-90, 462-00-75
Budget	☎ 481-24-33, 466-90-03
Europcar	☎ 466-02-46, 466-07-00
Galgo	☎ 484-30-66, 484-35-47
Hertz	☎ 485-89-47, 466-91-72
Saad	local rentals only, ☎ 484-34-45, 466-91-79

Getting Around

To/From the Airport Acapulco's airport is 25km southeast of the zócalo, beyond the junction for Puerto Marqués, about 30 minutes by car. Arriving by air, buy a ticket for transport into town from the colectivo desk before you leave the terminal; it's around US$8.50 per person for a ride directly to your hotel.

Leaving Acapulco, phone Móvil ACA (☎ 462-10-95/99, 462-03-09) 24 hours in advance to reserve a shuttle to the airport (US$9 per person). They'll pick you up 90 minutes before your domestic flights, two hours prior to your international flights. The US$15 to US$20 range is a good place to start bargaining for taxis from the center to the airport if hailed in the street; 'hotel rates' are higher.

Bus Acapulco has a good city bus system with buses going every few minutes to most places you'd want to go. They operate 5am to 11pm daily and cost US$0.40; fancier, air-conditioned buses cost a bit more, around US$0.50. Near the zócalo, the bus stop opposite Sanborns department store on La Costera, two blocks east of the zócalo, is a good place to catch buses – it's the beginning of several bus routes so you can usually get a seat. The most useful city routes are:

Base-Caleta – from the Icacos Naval Base at the southeast end of Acapulco, along La Costera past the zócalo to Playa Caleta

Base-Cine Río-Caleta – from the Icacos Naval Base, cuts inland from La Costera on Avenida Wilfrido Massieu to Avenida Cuauhtémoc, heads down Cuauhtémoc through the business district, turning back to La Costera just before reaching the zócalo, continuing west to Caleta

Puerto Marqués-Centro – from opposite Sanborns, along La Costera to Puerto Marqués

Zócalo-Playa Pie de la Cuesta – from opposite Sanborns to Pie de la Cuesta; buses marked 'Playa' or 'Luces' go all the way down the Pie de la Cuesta beach road; those marked 'San Isidro' or 'Pedregoso' stop at the entrance to Pie de la Cuesta

Taxi Cabs are plentiful in Acapulco and taxi drivers are happy to take gringos for a ride, especially for fares higher than the official rates. Always agree on the fare before you climb into the cab; it never hurts to bargain with taxi drivers. Ask locals how much you can expect to pay for a particular ride, and don't hesitate to flag down another ride should a driver try to shake you down.

AROUND ACAPULCO

The cove at **Puerto Marqués**, 18km southeast of Acapulco, is much smaller than Bahía de Acapulco. You get a magnificent view of Bahía de Acapulco as the Carretera Escénica climbs south out of the city. Puerto Marqués' calm surf is good for water-skiing and sailing. Frequent 'Puerto Marqués' buses run along Acapulco's La Costera every 10 minutes, 5am to 9pm (US$0.30).

Heading out toward the airport past Puerto Marqués, **Playa Revolcadero** is the long, straight beach of the new Acapulco Diamante luxury tourism developments. Waves are large and surfing is popular here, especially in summer, but a strong undertow makes swimming dangerous. Horseback riding along the beach is also popular.

During Semana Santa, the Passion of Christ is acted out in the town of **Treinta**, 30km northeast of Acapulco; the Acapulco tourist office has details.

COSTA CHICA

The coast of Guerrero is known as the **Costa Grande** (Large Coast) from Acapulco northwest to the border of Michoacán, and as the **Costa Chica** (Small Coast) from Acapulco southeast to the less-traveled Oaxacan border.

On highway 200, 60km (about an hour) east of Acapulco, **San Marcos** is an unremarkable town, but it provides essential services. Similarly small **Cruz Grande** is on highway 200 about 40km farther east.

Almost three hours southeast of Acapulco, **Playa Ventura** is a pristine beach with soft white and gold sand, clear water, a number of simple beachfront seafood restaurants and simple places to stay. From Playa Ventura you can walk about 1km to another good beach, **Playa La Piedra**. Horseback riding is available. You won't find Playa Ventura on any map – it's labeled **Juan Álvarez**. To get there from Acapulco, first take a bus heading southeast on highway 200 from Acapulco to **Copala** (120km, 2 hours, US$4.50). Buses depart from Estrella Blanca's 2nd-class terminal on Avenida Cuauhtémoc every half hour, 3.30am to 7pm. In Copala, *camionetas* and microbuses depart for Playa Ventura every half hour (13km, 30 minutes, US$1.25).

Marquelia, 20km east of Copala on highway 200, is another town providing essential services, including several inexpensive hotels. From Marquelia you can take a combi (US$0.40) to the nearby **Playa La Bocana**, where the Río Marquelia meets the sea and forms a lagoon. Another beach, **Playa Las Peñitas**, is 5km from La Bocana. There's no public transport from Marquelia to Playa Ventura; this operates from Copala. The same buses that depart Acapulco for Copala also continue to Marquelia (140km, 2½ hours, US$1.75).

Punta Maldonado, also sometimes referred to as **El Faro**, is a more remote Costa Chica beach. On a small bay fine for swimming, the tiny hamlet of Punta Maldonado has some seafood restaurants on the beach and one small hotel, which unfortunately is none too beautiful. To reach Punta Maldonado, take a camioneta from **Cuajinicuilapa** (aka 'Cuaji'), a small town on highway 200, some 200km southeast of Acapulco. Camionetas depart hourly from Cuaji (45 minutes, US$1.75), or you can take a taxi. Coming from Acapulco, 2nd-class buses to Cuaji depart hourly, 3.30am to 6.30pm (200km, 5 hours, US$10) from Estrella Blanca's Central Ejido terminal.

CHILPANCINGO
- pop 135,000 • elev 1360m ☎ 747

Chilpancingo, capital of the state of Guerrero, is a university city and agricultural center. It lies on highways 95 and 95D, 130km north of Acapulco and 270km south of Mexico City. As an administrative center, it's a rather nondescript place between the much more compelling destinations of Taxco and Acapulco.

Murals in the former **Palacio Municipal** showing the 1813 Congress of Chilpancingo are the only remaining signs of the city's important place in Mexico's history. In the spring of 1813, rebel leader José María Morelos y Pavón encircled Mexico City with his guerrilla army and demanded a congress in Chilpancingo. The congress issued a Declaration of Independence and began to lay down the principles of a new constitution. Their achievements, however, were short-lived – Spanish troops breached the circle around Mexico City and recaptured most of the city of Guerrero, including Chilpancingo. Morelos was tried for treason and executed by firing squad.

The state-operated tourist office (☎ 472-95-66) in Chilpancingo is at Moisés Guevara 8, Colonia Cuauhtémoc Norte. It's open 9am to 3pm and 6pm to 9pm Monday to Friday, providing information on the town, the region and the state of Guerrero.

Places to Stay & Eat
Hotel El Presidente (☎ 472-97-31, Calle 30 de Agosto 1) Singles/doubles US$22/26, suites US$37. The tidy Presidente is only a block from the bus station and is visible from the highway and the bus terminal.

Hotel Laura Elena (☎ 472-48-80, Madero 1 at Abasolo) Singles/doubles US$18/20. Closer to the university and the downtown plaza, this is another safe choice.

Hotel El Presidente has a popular mid-range restaurant/bar, and several other cheaper places are visible from the bus station. The lively public market's upstairs *fondas* are cheap places to fuel up if you're waylaid here – don't miss the pork specialties and *pozole* with *chicharrones* (pork rinds) on Thursday.

Getting There & Away

Chilpancingo is served by two bus companies: Estrella Blanca (☎ 472-06-34) and Estrella de Oro (☎ 472-21-30). Buses operate to/from Acapulco (1½ hours), Chilapa (45 minutes), Iguala (1½ hours), Mexico City (3½ hours) and Taxco (2 hours).

AROUND CHILPANCINGO
Chilapa
The tiny town of Chilapa, 45 minutes east of Chilpancingo by 2nd-class bus, holds a traditional market every Sunday, starting very early in the morning. Market day has almost a pre-Hispanic feel; indigenous people pour out of the hills, and all types of foodstuffs, handicrafts and animals are on display. Many vendors from this market cart their leftover wares to Acapulco on Monday. Virgen de Guadalupe devotees shouldn't miss the church clock; at noon daily Juan Diego emerges from the Virgen and showers the plaza below with flowers.

Grutas de Juxtlahuaca
Southeast of Chilpancingo, near the tiny settlement of Juxtlahuaca, the Grutas de Juxtlahuaca are an impressive 1.5km-long cave system with a subterranean river and 19 caverns. **Cave tours** are available from Profesor Andrés Ortega Jiménez', known as 'El Chivo,' and from his brother Enrique Ortega Jiménez (☎ 756-7474-7006).

Olinalá
The small, remote town of Olinalá is famous throughout Mexico for its beautiful lacquered boxes and other locally produced lacquered woodcraft. Linaloe, the fragrant wood used to make the boxes, grows in this area. Olinalá is waaaay up in the mountains (altitude 1350m) and not often visited. If you do make it here, you'll find simple hotels around the plaza and a few places to eat. Second-class buses from Chilpancingo to Tlapa will drop you at the crossroads for Olinalá (4½ hours); then catch another bus (3rd-class, one more hour) to Olinalá.

Western Central Highlands

West of Mexico City, the highland region comprising the inland parts of Jalisco, Michoacán and Colima states is off the major tourist routes but rewards travelers with much to see. Here you'll find Guadalajara, capital of Jalisco and Mexico's second-largest city; Morelia, the fine capital of Michoacán; Pátzcuaro, a lovely colonial town and center of Michoacán's indigenous Purépecha culture; Volcán Paricutín, the volcano that rose in 1943 from the lush Michoacán countryside; and, in eastern Michoacán, a special biosphere reserve protecting prime wintering grounds for the monarch butterfly. In addition, the region's little-visited backcountry beckons explorers with its rugged landscapes, fertile valleys and timeless villages.

(See the Central Pacific Coast chapter for information on the narrow coastal plains of Jalisco, Michoacán and Colima.)

History

The western central highlands were remote from the country's pre-Hispanic empires, though a fairly advanced agricultural village society flourished in parts of the region as early as 200 BC. In the 14th to 16th centuries AD, the Tarascos of northern Michoacán developed a major pre-Hispanic civilization with its capital at Tzintzuntzan, near Pátzcuaro. The zenith of the Tarascan empire coincided with the Aztec empire, but the Tarascos always managed to fend off Aztec attacks. West of the Tarascos – and occasionally at war with them – was the Chimalhuacán confederation of four indigenous kingdoms, in parts of what are now Jalisco, Colima and Nayarit states. To the north were Chichimecs, whom the Aztecs regarded as barbarians.

Colima, the leading Chimalhuacán kingdom, was conquered by the Spanish in 1523, but the region as a whole was not brought under Spanish control until the 1529-36 campaigns of Nuño de Guzmán, who tortured, killed and enslaved indigenous people from Michoacán to Sinaloa in his pursuit of riches, territory and glory. Guzmán was appointed governor of most of what he had conquered, but eventually his

Highlights

- Guadalajara – the country's most Mexican city, birthplace of mariachi music, tequila and *charreadas* (Mexican rodeos)
- Morelia – distinguished colonial architecture, fine food, Spanish courses and a lively student population
- Santuario Mariposa Monarca (Monarch Butterfly Reserve) – winter resort for millions of migratory butterflies
- Pátzcuaro – handsome little highland town in the homeland of the Purépecha people
- Volcano Treks – unforgettable trekking up the extinct Nevado de Colima or the still-steaming Volcán Paricutín

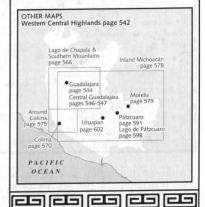

OTHER MAPS
Western Central Highlands page 542

Lago de Chapala & Southern Mountains page 566
Inland Michoacán page 578
Guadalajara page 544
Central Guadalajara pages 546-547
Morelia page 579
Around Colima page 575
Uruapan page 602
Pátzcuaro page 591
Lago de Pátzcuaro page 598
Colima page 570

PACIFIC OCEAN

misdeeds caught up with him and in 1538 he was sent back to Spain. These territories came to be called Nueva Galicia and retained some autonomy from the rest of Nueva España until 1786.

A rebellion in Jalisco in 1540 set that area aflame in what is known as the Mixtón War; it was ended the next year by an army led by the Spanish viceroy. Guadalajara was established in its present location in 1542, after three earlier settlements were abandoned in the face of attacks by hostile indigenous groups.

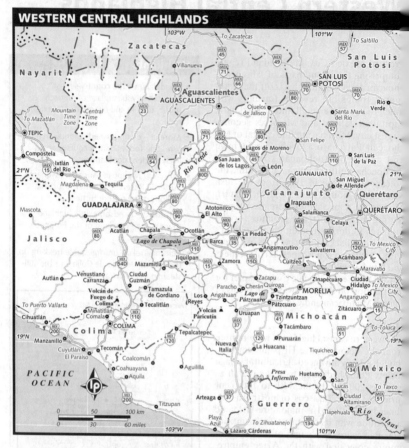

WESTERN CENTRAL HIGHLANDS

Although the region was slower to develop than mineral-rich areas such as Zacatecas or Guanajuato, it did develop. Ranching and agriculture grew, and Guadalajara, always one of Mexico's biggest cities, became the 'capital of the west.' The church helped by fostering small industries and handicraft traditions in its effort to ease the poverty of the indigenous people.

In the 1920s Michoacán and Jalisco were hotbeds of the Cristero rebellion by Catholics against government antichurch policies. Lázaro Cárdenas of Michoacán, as state governor (1928-32) and then as Mexican president (1934-40), instituted reforms that did much to allay antigovernment sentiments.

Geography

The western central highlands reach from the southern outliers of the Sierra Madre Occidental, in the north of Jalisco, to the western extremities of the Sierra Madre del Sur, which rise behind the Pacific coast. In between, part of the Cordillera Neovolcánica sweeps east-west across the region, strewn with extinct and active volcanoes. One of these, Volcán de Fuego de Colima, is among the country's most active. The main ranges are interspersed with lesser hills, valleys and basins that make up some of Mexico's richest agricultural land.

The region is drained by major rivers. Río Lerma flows down from the east along the border of Michoacán and Jalisco and into Lago de Chapala, Mexico's largest natural ke. Río Balsas carries almost all the runoff from the southern side of the Cordillera Neovolcánica.

Climate

Warm and dry most of the year, the region has a distinct rainy season from June to September, when some 200mm of rain per month falls in most areas. At lower altitudes, like the areas near Uruapan and Colima, temperature and humidity rise, and tropical plants abound. In higher-altitude places, such as Pátzcuaro, winter nights can get chilly.

Population & People

The region is home to about 10% of the nation's people. Well over half of Jalisco's six million inhabitants live in the extended Guadalajara urban area. Michoacán has about four million people and Colima about half a million. The population is predominantly mestizo, with the 130,000 Purépecha of Michoacán and 60,000 Huichol in northern Jalisco forming the only large indigenous groups.

Guadalajara & Around

The city of Guadalajara is the major attraction of inland Jalisco, but travelers mustn't ignore worthwhile day trips. Head northwest to Tequila for central highlands scenery and a taste of Mexico's best-known beverage. Or travel 40km south of Guadalajara to Lago de Chapala, where the idyllic climate has attracted many US and Canadian expatriates. Farther south and west, Jalisco's mountain region – the Zona Montaña – is home to several small towns that are ideal for exploration.

GUADALAJARA

• pop 1,646,000 • elev 1540m ☎ 33

Guadalajara's contributions to Mexican life include mariachi music, tequila, the broad-rimmed sombrero hat, *charreadas* (rodeos) and the Mexican Hat Dance. The second-largest city in Mexico, it also is western Mexico's biggest industrial center and has its share of museums, galleries, festivals, historic buildings, nightlife, culture and good places to stay and eat.

Nonetheless, many visitors are disappointed with Guadalajara. The renovated downtown area is on a grand scale and quite elegant, but it doesn't have the quaint charm of Mexico's nicest colonial cities. The traffic and pollution aren't nearly as bad as in Mexico City, but central Guadalajara can still be congested, noisy and stifling, while the vast, sprawling urban area is not easy to negotiate. The most appealing places are suburbs like Zapopan, Tlaquepaque and Tonalá, formerly separate communities that have retained their small-town charm.

History

Guadalajara was established on its present site only after three settlements elsewhere had failed. In 1532, Nuño de Guzmán and 63 Spanish families founded the first Guadalajara near Nochistlán (now in Zacatecas state), naming it after Guzmán's home city in Spain. Water was scarce, the land was hard to farm and the indigenous people were hostile, so in 1533 Captain Juan de Oñate ordered the settlement moved to the pre-Hispanic village of Tonalá, today a suburb of Guadalajara. Guzmán, however, disliked Tonalá and in 1535 had the settlement moved to Tlacotán, northeast of the modern city. In 1541 this was destroyed by a confederation of indigenous tribes led by the chief Tenamaxtli. The surviving colonists picked a new site in the valley of Atemajac beside San Juan de Dios Creek, which ran where Calzada Independencia is today. The new Guadalajara was founded by Oñate on February 14, 1542, near where the Teatro Degollado now stands.

This Guadalajara prospered, and in 1560 it was declared the capital of Nueva Galicia province. The city quickly grew into one of colonial Mexico's most important population centers and the heart of a rich agricultural region. It also was the starting point for Spanish expeditions and missions to western and northern Nueva España – and as far away as the Philippines. Miguel Hidalgo, a leader in the struggle for Mexican independence, set up a revolutionary government in Guadalajara in 1810 but was defeated near the city in 1811, not long before his capture and execution in Chihuahua. The city was also the object of heavy fighting during the War of the Reform (1858-61) and between Constitutionalist and Villista armies in 1915.

WESTERN CENTRAL

GUADALAJARA

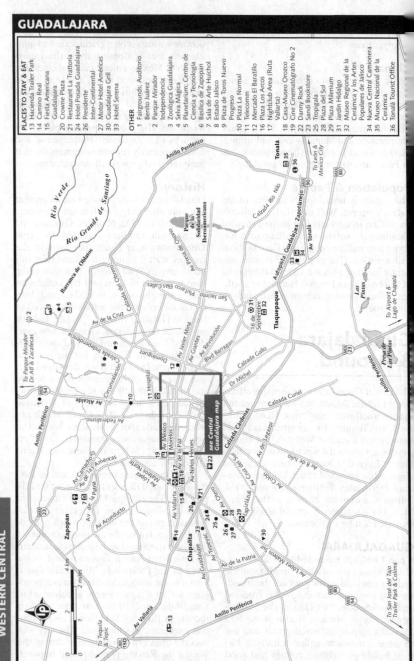

PLACES TO STAY & EAT
13 Hacienda Trailer Park
14 Camino Real
15 Fiesta Americana
   Guadalajara
20 Crowne Plaza
21 Restaurant La Trattoria
24 Hotel Posada Guadalajara
26 Presidente
27 Inter-Continental
30 Motor Hotel Américas
33 Guadalajara Grill
   Hotel Serena

OTHER
1 Fairgrounds; Auditorio
   Benito Juárez
2 Parque Mirador
   Independencia
3 Zoológica Guadalajara
4 Selva Mágica
5 Planetarium; Centro de
   Ciencia y Tecnología
6 Basílica de Zapopan
7 Sala de Arte Huichol
8 Estadio Jalisco
9 Plaza de Toros Nuevo
   Progreso
10 Plaza La Normal
11 Telecomm
12 Mercado El Baratillo
16 Plaza Los Arcos
17 Nightclub Area (Ruta
   Vallarta)
18 Casa-Museo Orozco
19 Cine Cinematógrafo No 2
22 Danny Rock
23 Sandi Bookstore
25 Plaza del Sol
28 Plaza Milenium
29 Jardín Hidalgo
31 Jardín Regional de la
   Cerámica y los Artes
   Populares de Jalisco
34 Nueva Central Camionera
35 Museo Nacional de la
   Cerámica
36 Tonalá Tourist Office

By the late 19th century Guadalajara had overtaken Puebla as Mexico's second-biggest city. Its population has mushroomed since WWII, and now the city is a huge commercial, industrial and cultural center and the communications hub for a large region.

Orientation

Guadalajara's giant twin-towered cathedral at the heart of the city is surrounded by four lovely plazas. The plaza east of the cathedral, Plaza de la Liberación, extends two blocks to the Teatro Degollado, also a city landmark. The area from the cathedral to the theater, and the surrounding blocks, is known as the Centro Histórico.

East of Teatro Degollado, the Plaza Tapatía pedestrian precinct extends half a kilometer to the Instituto Cultural de Cabañas, another historically significant building. Just south of Plaza Tapatía is Mercado Libertad, a three-story market covering four city blocks.

Calzada Independencia is a major north-south central artery. From Mercado Libertad, it runs south to Parque Agua Azul and the Antigua Central Camionera (Old Bus Station), still used by short-distance regional buses. Northward, it runs to the zoo, the Plaza de Toros (Bullring) and Barranca de Oblatos (Oblates Canyon). Don't confuse Calzada Independencia with Avenida Independencia, the east-west street one block north of the cathedral. In the city center, north-south streets change names at Hidalgo, the street running along the north side of the cathedral.

About 21 blocks west of the cathedral, the north-south Avenida Chapultepec is Guadalajara's Zona Rosa, a smart area with modern office blocks, shops and a few fine restaurants. In the southwest of the city, Plaza del Sol, on Avenida López Mateos Sur, is a huge modern shopping mall with restaurants, entertainment and a number of brand-name hotels.

The long-distance bus station is the Nueva Central Camionera (New Bus Station), 9km southeast of the city center past the suburb of Tlaquepaque.

Information

Tourist Offices The state tourist office (☎ 3668-1600, 800-362-22-00, ⓦ http://vive.guadalajara.gob.mx), Morelos 102, is in Plaza Tapatía behind the Teatro Degollado. It's open 9am to 8pm Monday to Friday, 9am to 1pm Saturday and Sunday. This is the place to come for free maps and information on Guadalajara and the state of Jalisco. English is spoken, and information is available on anything you could want to know, from local bus routes to retirement in Mexico. The information desk in the Palacio de Gobierno, facing the Plaza de Armas just south of the cathedral, is open 9am to 3pm and (generally) 4pm to 8pm Monday to Friday, 9am to 1pm Saturday. Information kiosks are provided around the central area too, especially during cultural events and festivals.

Money Banks are plentiful in Guadalajara and are generally open for currency exchange and other services from about 9am to 5pm Monday through Friday and 9am to 1pm Saturday. Most have ATMs. *Casas de cambio* on López Cotilla, in the three blocks between 16 de Septiembre and Molina, offer competitive exchange rates, quicker service and sometimes longer hours.

The American Express office (☎ 3818-2319), Avenida Vallarta 2440, is in the small Plaza Los Arcos shopping center. It's open 9am to 6pm Monday to Friday and 9am to 1pm Saturday, but it issues traveler's checks only Monday to Friday 9am to 2pm and 4pm to 4.30pm. Banamex will change Canadian-dollar traveler's checks.

Post & Communications The main post office is on Carranza, between Juan Manuel and Independencia. It's open 8am to 6pm Monday through Friday, 9am to 1pm Saturday.

The Telecomm office, with telegram, telex and fax services, is nine blocks north of the city center, in the Palacio Federal on the corner of Avenida Alcalde and Álvarez, opposite the Santuario church. It's open 9am to 7pm Monday to Friday, 9am to noon Saturday. There's a post office branch there too.

Computel, with long-distance telephone and fax services, has several offices around the city. There's one on Corona, in a shopping center opposite the Hotel Fénix. Another is at 16 de Septiembre 599.

Several places around the central area offer Internet access for US$2 to US$3 per hour. CCCP Internet, upstairs on Avenida Alcalde at Juan Manuel, is open

CENTRAL GUADALAJARA

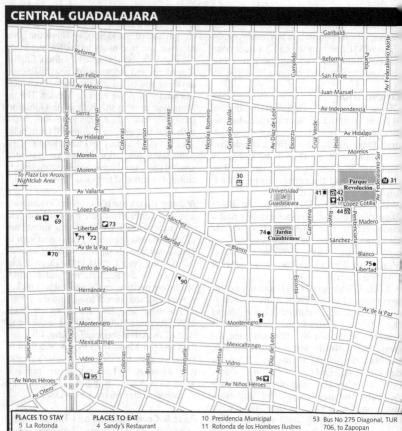

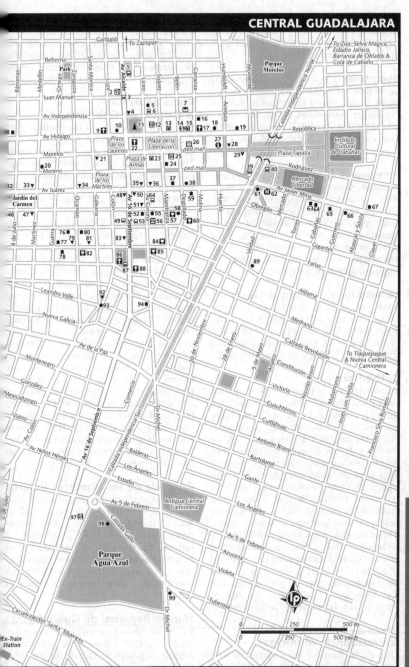

CENTRAL GUADALAJARA

approximately 9am to 9pm daily; Cyber-cafe and CMC, both on Parque Revolución, 10 blocks west of the city center, are open about 10am to 10pm daily.

Bookstores A fair selection of books and magazines in English is available in the gift shops of most major hotels and at many of the larger bookstores. Sandi Bookstore (☎ 3121-4210), Avenida Tepeyac 718, about 1km west of Avenida López Mateos, has a good travel section.

Newspapers & Magazines The Spanish-language *Público*, the city's most prominent daily newspaper, offers exhaustive entertainment listings on Friday (see Entertainment). *Guadalajara Weekly* is a free but not very informative visitor newsletter, available at the tourist office and some hotels. Many of the newsstands in central Guadalajara sell English-language periodicals.

Laundry There's a laundry at Aldama 125, open 9am to 8pm Monday to Saturday. Drop your stuff off and return for it two hours later; it'll be waiting, clean and folded, in the same sack you brought it in. They charge about US$3.50 for a machine load.

Cathedral

Guadalajara's twin-towered cathedral is the city's most famous symbol and most conspicuous landmark. Begun in 1558 and consecrated in 1618, the cathedral is almost as old as the city itself. Up close you can see that it's a stylistic hodgepodge. The exterior decorations, some of which were completed long after the consecration, are in Churrigueresque, baroque, neoclassical and other styles. The towers date from 1848; they're much higher than the originals, which were destroyed in an earthquake 30 years before. The interior includes Gothic vaults, Tuscany-style pillars and 11 richly decorated altars given to Guadalajara by King Fernando VII of Spain (1784-1833). In the sacristy, which an attendant can open for you on request, is *La Asunción de la Virgen,* painted by Spanish artist Bartolomé Murillo in 1650.

Plaza de los Laureles & Presidencia Municipal

Directly in front of the cathedral's west façade, Plaza de los Laureles is planted with laurel trees, hence the name. On its north side is the Presidencia Municipal (City Hall), which was built between 1949 and 1952 but looks much older. Above its interior stairway is a mural by Gabriel Flores depicting the founding of Guadalajara.

Plaza de Armas & Palacio de Gobierno

The Plaza de Armas, on the south side of the cathedral, is a nice place to sit and imagine how the city was in colonial times. The fine central kiosk is attractively supported by bronze art nouveau ladies. Free concerts of Jaliscan music are often held here on Thursday and Sunday evening, starting at about 6pm.

On the east side of Plaza de Armas is the Palacio de Gobierno (Palace of Government), finished in 1774, which houses state offices. Like the cathedral, it was built in a combination of styles: a mix of simple, neo-classical features and riotous Churrigueresque decorations. Its most interesting artistic feature is the huge 1937 portrait of Miguel Hidalgo painted by José Clemente Orozco in a mural over the interior stairway. In it, an angry Hidalgo, father of Mexico's movement for independence from Spain, brandishes a torch high in one fist while the masses struggle at his feet. In this mural Orozco also comments on the pressing issues of his time: communism, fascism and religion. Another Orozco mural in the upstairs Congreso (Congress Hall) depicts Hidalgo, Benito Juárez and other figures important in Mexican history. The murals can be viewed from 9am to 9pm daily.

Rotonda de los Hombres Ilustres

The plaza on the north side of the cathedral is ringed by bronze sculptures of 12 of Jalisco's favorite characters: a poet, a composer, a writer, an architect, a university reformer and others. Six of them are buried beneath the Rotonda de los Hombres Ilustres (Rotunda of Illustrious Men), the round pillared monument in the center of the plaza.

Museo Regional de Guadalajara

Facing the Rotonda de los Hombres Ilustres on the east, this museum is also called Museo Regional de Occidente (☎ 3614-2227, Liceo 60; admission US$3.50, free for hildren 12 and under, free for all ages Sun & ues; open 9am-4pm Tues-Sun). This must-ee museum has an eclectic collection covring the history and prehistory of western Mexico. Displays in the ground-floor arhaeological section include the skeleton of woolly mammoth. Upstairs are galleries of olonial paintings, a history gallery covering he area since the Spanish conquest and an thnography section with displays about inigenous life in Jalisco, and about *charros*, r Mexican cowboys. The museum building s the former seminary of San José, a late-7th-century baroque structure with two tories of arcades and an inner court.

Plaza de la Liberación

East of the cathedral, Plaza de la Liberación s a lively and impressive space that was reated by a 1980s urban renovation project nvolving the demolition of two whole plocks of colonial buildings. The redevelopment is still controversial.

On the north side of the Plaza de la Libración is the **Palacio Legislativo**, where he state congress meets, distinguished by nassive stone columns in its interior courtyard.

On the south side of the plaza, the **Museo de Cera** (☎ 3614-8487, Morelos 217; admision adult/child US$3/2; open 11am-8pm daily) is a good place to meet the heroes, eaders and popular figures of Mexico's past and present. They're all here in wax effigy form, along with some international celebriies and the usual chamber of horrors. In the same location, the new **Ripley's Aunque Usted No Lo Crea** has the same hours and the same admission prices. It includes the usual Ripley's Believe it or Not-type exhibits, but it lacks any particularly Mexican feel. Combined admission to both attractions costs US$4.50/3.

Teatro Degollado

At the east end of Plaza de la Liberación, the imposing neoclassical-style Teatro Degollado (☎ 3614-4773; admission free; open for viewing 10am-1pm Tues-Sat) was begun in 1856, inaugurated 30 years later and has been reconstructed several times since. Over the columns on its front is a frieze depicting Apollo and the Nine Muses. The five-tiered theater's interior is decorated with red velvet and gold and is crowned by a Gerardo Suárez mural based on the fourth canto of Dante's *Divine Comedy*. The theater hosts frequent performances of music, dance and drama.

Palacio de Justicia & Templo de Santa María de Gracia

Across Hidalgo from the Teatro Degollado, the Palacio de Justicia (State Courthouse) was built in 1588 as part of the Convento de Santa María, Guadalajara's first nunnery. A 1965 mural by Guillermo Chávez, depicting Benito Juárez and other legendary Mexican lawmakers, graces the interior stairway.

Also near the theater, at the corner of Hidalgo and Carranza, is the Templo de Santa María de Gracia, which served as the city's first cathedral (1549-1618).

Plaza Tapatía

Just behind Teatro Degollado, Plaza Tapatía is a modern pedestrian mall, comprising shops, restaurants, street performers, fountains and the tourist office. It stretches half a kilometer east to the Instituto Cultural de Cabañas. Calzada Independencia passes underneath it at about its midpoint.

Instituto Cultural de Cabañas

The huge neoclassical gem at the east end of Plaza Tapatía was built between 1805 and 1810 as the Hospicio Cabañas, an orphanage and home for invalids founded by Bishop Don Juan Cruz Ruiz de Cabañas. Designed by Spanish architect Manuel Tolsá and featuring 23 separate courtyards, the building continued to serve mainly as an orphanage for over 150 years, often housing up to 3000 children at a time. At one time or another it has also served as an insane asylum, military barracks and jail.

Between 1936 and 1939 José Clemente Orozco painted murals in the building's main chapel. They are widely regarded as his finest works. Most notable is *El Hombre de Fuego* (Man of Fire) in the dome; it's been the subject of widely varying interpretations. Fifty-three other frescoes cover the walls and ceiling of the chapel, which is furnished with benches on which you can lie back and look straight up. A small book in English and Spanish, *The Murals of Orozco in the Cabañas Cultural Institute,* on sale at the main entrance, gives information on the artist and the murals.

Today the building houses the Instituto Cultural de Cabañas (☎ 3617-4248, Cabañas 8; admission US$1.25, free Sun; open 10am-6pm Tues-Sat, 10am-3pm Sun), a cultural institute with a museum, theater and school. Tours in English and Spanish are available. The museum features a permanent exhibition of more than 100 Orozco drawings and paintings, plus temporary exhibitions of painting, sculpture and engraving. The institute also hosts dance festivals, drama performances and concerts.

Plaza de los Mariachis

The Plaza de los Mariachis, near the intersection of Avenida Javier Mina and Calzada Independencia Sur, is arguably the birthplace of mariachi music. It's more like a short pedestrian street than a plaza, but you can't miss the outdoor tables, where people sit, eat and drink while wandering mariachis offer their musical services – for about US$5 per song. Unfortunately the plaza attracts some unpleasant types after dark, so it's probably unwise to linger after 9pm.

Colonial Churches

In addition to the cathedral and the Templo de Santa María de Gracia, central Guadalajara holds 13 other churches, some quite impressive. The baroque **Templo de La Merced**, near the cathedral on the corner of Hidalgo and Loza, was built in 1650; inside are several fine large paintings, crystal chandeliers and lots of gold decoration.

The **Santuario de Nuestra Señora del Carmen**, facing the small plaza on the corner of Juárez and 8 de Julio, is another lovely church, with lots of gold decoration, old paintings and murals in the dome.

On the corner of 16 de Septiembre and Blanco, the **Templo de Aranzazú**, built 1749-52, has three ornate Churrigueresque golden altars. Beside it is the less showy **Templo de San Francisco**, built two centuries earlier.

Parque Agua Azul

About 20 blocks south of the city center, Parque Agua Azul (Calzada Independencia Sur; admission adult/child US$0.40/0.20; open 10am-6pm Tues-Sun) is a large verdant park offering pleasant relief from the city hubbub. It features an orchid house, butterfly house, aviary and children's playground.

The orchids are at their best in October, November, April and May. Bus No 60 or 6 heading south on Calzada Independencia will take you there from the city center.

The **Museo de Arqueología del Occidente de México** (☎ 3619-0101, Calzada Independencia Sur; admission US$0.40; open 10am-2pm & 5pm-7pm daily), opposite the entrance to the park, houses a small collection including some pre-Hispanic figurines and artifacts from Jalisco and the states of Nayarit and Colima.

The **Casa de las Artesanías de Jalisco** (☎ 3619-4664, Calzada Gallo s/n; admission free; open 10am-6pm Mon-Fri, 11am-3pm Sat, 11am-2pm Sun) is on the north side of the park but has its own separate entrance on Calzada Gallo. It displays handicrafts and arts from all over Jalisco, and everything is for sale. Prices are reasonable, and there are some excellent quality artesanías to choose from.

Universidad de Guadalajara

West of the city center, where Juárez meets Federalismo, is another shady park, **Parque Revolución**. Three blocks farther west at Juárez 975 is the **Paraninfo** (Theater Hall), one of the main buildings of the University of Guadalajara. Inside, the stage backdrop and dome feature large, powerful murals by Orozco.

Casa Museo José Clemente Orozco

During the 1940s, the great tapatío painter and muralist José Clemente Orozco (1883-1949) lived and worked in this house (☎ 3616-8329, Aurelio Aceves 29; admission free; open 9am-5pm Mon-Fri). Personal effects, documents, photographs, a mural and a few paintings are on display.

Zoológico Guadalajara, Selva Mágica & Planetario

The zoo, Selva Mágica amusement park and the planetarium are near one another on the northern outskirts of the city. Buses No 60 and 62 (marked 'Zoológico'), heading north on Calzada Independencia, will drop you at the entrance monument. From there, it's a 10-minute walk to the actual entrances to the three sites.

The Zoológico Guadalajara (☎ 3674-4230, off Calzada Independencia Nte; admission dult/child US$3/1.50; open 10am-7pm Wed-un) is a large, older zoo with two pyramid-haped aviaries, a snake house, a children's etting zoo and a train that will take you round if you don't feel like walking. The orth end of the site provides a view of Barranca de Oblatos. The zoo opens on Monday and Tuesday during the holidays.

Located beside the zoo is Selva Mágica (☎ 3674-0138, off Calzada Independencia Nte; admission US$3-6 depending on he attractions package; open 10am-8pm daily), a children's amusement park with a dolphin-and-seal show, a trained-bird how and mechanical rides.

About a five-minute walk from the zoo is he planetarium at the Centro de Ciencia y Tecnología (☎ 3674-4106, off Calzada Independencia Nte; admission US$1; open 9am-pm Tues-Sun). It has exhibits on astronomy, space, airplanes, the body and other science-related topics. Planetarium shows are held hourly from 10.30am to about 4.30pm.

Barranca de Oblatos & Cascada Cola de Caballo

You can see 670m-deep Oblates Canyon from the zoo. Otherwise, take bus No 60 north on Calzada Independencia to Parque Mirador Independencia, a little past the entrance to the zoo. The park is always open and overlooks the canyon.

In the canyon, the Cola de Caballo (Horse Tail) waterfall flows all year but is most impressive during the summer rainy season. For a view of the falls, take a local bus from the city center north on Alcalde about 10 blocks to Plaza La Normal. From there get an Ixcatan bus and ask to be let off at Parque Mirador Dr Atl.

Zapopan

About 8km from downtown, on the north-western edge of Guadalajara, the suburb of Zapopan (population 911,000) was a village before the Spanish arrived and an important maize-producing center in colonial times.

The Zapopan tourist office (☎ 3818-2200), Guerrero 233, is upstairs in the Casa de la Cultura, a block west of the Zapopan basilica. It's open 9am to 8pm Monday to Friday, 9am to 1pm Saturday. Staff give out maps of Zapopan and leaflets, in Spanish, detailing places of interest in and around the suburb.

The large **Basílica de Zapopan**, built in 1730, is home to Nuestra Señora de Zapopan (Virgin of Zapopan), a tiny statue visited by pilgrims from near and far. On October 12, during Guadalajara's Fiestas de Octubre, the statue, which has been visiting other churches in Jalisco before reaching Guadalajara, is taken from Guadalajara's cathedral and returned to its home in Zapopan amid throngs of people and much merrymaking. The statue receives a new car each year for the procession, but the engine is never turned on; instead, the car is hauled along by ropes.

To the right of the basilica entrance, the small **Sala de Arte Huichol** (☎ 3636-4430, Plaza de las Américas; admission US$0.60; open 10am-2pm & 4pm-7pm Mon-Sat, 10am-2pm Sun) exhibits many colorful yarn paintings and other fine examples of Huichol arts and crafts. Many Huichol handicrafts are available for purchase.

Bus No 275 Diagonal and TUR bus 706, heading north on 16 de Septiembre or Alcalde, stop beside the basilica; the trip takes 20 minutes.

Tlaquepaque

About 7km southeast of downtown Guadalajara, Tlaquepaque ('tlah-keh-PAH-keh'; population 459,000) was also a village before the Spanish arrived and is a center for ceramics production. In colonial times it was one of the first stops on the long road to Mexico City, and the Guadalajara gentry built substantial mansions here in the 19th century. Tlaquepaque's most historically important moment was June 13, 1821, when the Plan de Iguala, which established the paradigms of an independent Mexican state, was signed in a house on the corner of Independencia and Medellín.

More recently, Tlaquepaque has capitalized on its creative talents and colonial heritage by renovating several blocks around the central Jardín Hidalgo, converting old country homes into stylish restaurants and galleries. Flowers, small benches, monuments and a fountain grace the plaza, and a few new B&Bs have been established in charming old buildings. The city center in general is now a very appealing precinct of pedestrian streets, popular with local people for a long lunch (especially on Saturday and Sunday) and with Mexican and international tourists who come to browse and buy. The numerous upscale shops are full of ceramics, papier-mâché animals, bronze figures, hand-made glassware, embroidered clothing and other items from all over Mexico. Many shops are closed on Sunday, but the restaurants are especially busy for Sunday lunch. See Places to Eat for suggestions.

The Tlaquepaque tourist office (☎ 3635-5756), Prieto 80, is next to the post office and open 9am to 9pm Monday to Friday. There's also an information booth on the plaza.

The **Museo Regional de la Cerámica** (☎ 3635-5404, Independencia 237; admission free; open 10am-6pm Tues-Sat, 10am-3pm Sun) has many exhibits showing the different types and styles of ceramic work made in Tlaquepaque.

To get to Tlaquepaque, take local bus No 647 or TUR bus 706 heading south on 16 de Septiembre. The trip takes about 30 minutes. After turning off Avenida Revolución, watch for a brick pedestrian bridge then a small traffic circle. Get off here. On the left is Calle Independencia, which will take you to the heart of Tlaquepaque.

Tonalá

The suburb of Tonalá (population 315,000), beyond Tlaquepaque, about 13km southeast of the center of Guadalajara, is a less developed and less touristic relative of Tlaquepaque. The shops here call themselves factories, not galleries – an accurate description considering that many of them manufacture the glassware and ceramics found in Tlaquepaque and in other parts of Guadalajara. On Thursday and Sunday most of the town becomes a street market that takes hours to explore. The best crafts are found in the factories, but you can pick up some bargains at the market (check the bargain pieces carefully because many of them are seconds). Other attractions in Tonalá are several old churches of interest, and a charreada, starting between 4pm and 5pm Saturday.

The Tonalá tourist office (☎ 3683-0047, 3683-6047), Tonaltecas 140 in the Casa de Artesanos, is open 9am to 8pm Monday to Friday, 9am to 1pm Saturday. The office gives out maps and information in Spanish.

The **Museo Nacional de la Cerámica** (☎ 3635-5404, Constitución 110; admission free; open 10am-5pm Tues-Sun) houses an eclectic array of pots from all over Mexico.

Local bus No 275 Diagonal or TUR bus 706, heading south on 16 de Septiembre, will take you to Tonalá. The trip takes 4. minutes to an hour. As you enter Tonalá, get off on the corner of Avenidas Tonalá and Tonaltecas, then walk three blocks north on Tonaltecas to the tourist office and Casa de Artesanos. From the Casa de Artesanos, it's three blocks east and two blocks north to the Plaza Principal.

Courses

A number of schools in Guadalajara teach language and cultural courses.

CEPE (☎ 3616-4399, fax 3616-4013, ⓦ www.cepe.udg.mx, Universidad de Guadalajara, Apartado Postal 1-2130, Guadalajara, Jalisco 44100) Registration US$95; tuition fees US$607 per 5-week session (4 hours of instruction per day Mon-Fri). With over 180,000 students, the Universidad de Guadalajara is the second-largest university in Mexico and the most established of Guadalajara's language schools. Its Centro de Estudios para Extranjeros (Foreign Student Studies Center), or CEPE, offers 10 levels of intensive five-week Spanish-language courses, as well as classes in Mexican history, culture, politics, economics, literature in addition to other subjects, all taught in Spanish. Workshops in topics such as folkloric dance, guitar and singing are also offered, as are special cultural events and excursions to other parts of Mexico. The workshops and excursions are an optional extra expense.

Lodging and three meals daily can be arranged with local Mexican families at a cost of about US$743 per session. Singles/doubles in the university's guesthouse cost US$417/534 per session.

Organized Tours

During holiday periods (Easter, mid-July to late August, and the second half of December), the tourist office runs **free guided walking tours** (mostly in Spanish) of the Centro Histórico. They start at 9.30am at the Plaza de Armas and take about three hours; book at the tourist office the day before.

Panoramex (☎ 3810-5057, Federalismo Sur 944) This company offers numerous tours with English-, French- and Spanish-speaking guides. The tours can be booked at he tourist office, and they start at Jardín San Francisco, on Corona, at 9.30am. Standard offerings include:

Tour No 1 (Monday to Saturday) – visits some of the main sights of Guadalajara and Tlaquepaque (5 hours, US$11)

Tour No 2 (Wednesday, Thursday, Saturday and Sunday) – visits Chapala and Ajijic (6 hours, US$14)

Tour No 3 (Monday, Wednesday, Friday) – visits the town of Tequila, including the agave fields and a tequila distillery (5 hours, US$14)

Special Events

Several major festivals are celebrated in Guadalajara and its suburbs. They include:

Feria de Tonalá – Annual handicrafts fair in Tonalá, specializing in ceramics, is held the week before and the week after Semana Santa.

Fiestas de Tlaquepaque – Tlaquepaque's annual fiesta and handicrafts fair takes place mid-June to the first week of July.

Fiesta Internacional del Mariachi – In late August and early September, mariachis come from everywhere to hear, play and celebrate the latest sounds.

Fiestas de Octubre – Beginning with a parade on the first Sunday in October, the October Fiestas, lasting all month, are Guadalajara's principal annual fair. Free entertainment takes place from noon to 10pm daily in Benito Juárez auditorium at the fairgrounds, while elsewhere around the city are livestock shows, art and other exhibitions and sporting and cultural events. On October 12 a religious element enters the festivities with a procession from the cathedral to Zapopan carrying the miniature statue of the Virgin of Zapopan (see Zapopan, earlier).

Feria Internacional del Libro – This is one of the biggest book promotions in Latin America; last week of November and first week of December.

Places to Stay

Budget Guadalajara has two trailer parks, both offering full hookups and spaces for tents, trailers and motor homes.

San José del Tajo Trailer Park (☎ 3686-1738, highway 54/80 Km 15.5) Trailer sites US$22, tent sites US$18. This 150-site park is southwest of the city center on the main road to Colima. Facilities include a pool, tennis court and laundry.

Hacienda Trailer Park (☎ 3627-1724, Circunvalación Pte 66, Ciudad Granja) Tent & trailer sites US$18. The Hacienda is 10km

west of the city center, between Avenida Vallarta and the Periférico. Call for directions. Amenities include a pool, laundry and plenty of trees. The communal clubhouse has a barbecue and tables for billiards and ping-pong.

The city center has some budget-priced accommodation, though all places fill up during the numerous special events and whenever there's a big football game. It's always wise to secure your room early in the day. These places are handy to the central attractions, though not necessarily on attractive streets.

Hotel Hamilton (☎ 3614-6726, Madero 381) Singles/doubles US$9/11, TV US$2.50 extra. The popular Hamilton offers simple, small rooms that are clean and generally quiet. All rooms have 24-hour hot water. If you stay five or more nights and pay in advance, the rate is slightly lower.

Posada San Pablo (☎ 3614-2811, Madero 429) Singles/doubles with shared bath US$13/19, with private bath US$16/21. A block west from the Hamilton, this quiet, friendly, family-run hotel doesn't look like a hotel and there's no sign. Just ring the bell at the front door. Its 10 rooms surround an open courtyard. Hot water is usually available.

Hotel Sevilla (☎ 3614-9172, Sánchez 413) Singles/doubles US$15/22. The slightly shabby-looking Sevilla has good little rooms with carpet, phone and TV (no cable). It's well located and has plenty of off-street parking.

Hotel Hidalgo (☎ 3613-5067, Hidalgo 14) Singles & doubles with private bath US$5.50. On a street with all the charm of a freeway off-ramp, this almost-clean dive has warm water and austere rooms with no mod-cons. But it's just a couple of blocks from Plaza Tapatía, the very center of town, and it's dirt cheap.

Hotel Las Américas (☎ 3613-9622, Hidalgo 76) Singles/doubles US$16/22. In the same central but unattractive location, this hotel offers good facilities for the price. The 49 rooms are clean and fairly modern, with TV, phone, carpeting, 24-hour hot water and large windows. Rooms on the street side are noisy.

Hotel Posada San Rafael Inn (☎ 3614-9146, e posadasanrafael@usa.net, López Cotilla 619) Singles/doubles US$13/18. This small, family-run place is more guesthouse than hotel, and it's popular with budget travelers for its cheerful decor and friendly atmosphere. The 12 rooms have high ceilings and large bathrooms, and they face a covered courtyard with lots of plants.

Hotel Jorge Alejandro (☎ *3658-1051, Hidalgo 656*) Singles/doubles US$26/33. Seven blocks west of the cathedral, the Jorge Alejandro is a former convent with 28 clean, quiet, slightly stuffy rooms, all facing into the courtyard. There's plenty of hot water, and every room has a TV and fan.

Posada Regis (☎ *3614-8633, e posada regis@usa.net, Corona 171*) Singles/doubles/triples US$22/27/36. The pleasant, friendly Posada Regis is upstairs in a converted 19th-century French-style mansion with high ceilings and ornate details. The 19 original rooms open onto a covered patio and are great value. Rooms overlooking the street can be noisy.

Hotel Continental (☎ *3614-1117, Corona 450*) Singles/doubles US$23/30. About seven blocks south of the cathedral, the Continental has parking and 124 fairly clean, comfortable, 1960s-style rooms with phone and cable TV. It's in need of a facelift, but OK for the price.

Avenida Javier Mina, east of Mercado Libertad and the Plaza de los Mariachis, has a good selection of budget hotels. This part of town is not especially pleasant and possibly not as safe as the city center, but you can find a cheap room here when every other place is full.

Hotel Ana Isabel (☎ *3617-7920, Javier Mina 164*) Singles/doubles with bath US$17/20. The best of the cheap hotels in this area is this one opposite the Mercado Libertad. It has 50 clean rooms lined up along three floors of walkways draped with plants. Rooms come with TV and ceiling fan. Hot water is always available, and there's off-street parking.

Hotel México 70 (☎ *3617-9978, Javier Mina 230*) Singles/doubles US$13/15. This hotel has 80 clean rooms. The bigger rooms have two or more beds, 24-hour hot water, TV and decent mattresses.

Hotel Imperio (☎ *3617-5042, Javier Mina 180*) Singles/doubles US$16/18. Nothing special to look at, but this hotel is basic but respectable and comfortable enough.

Hotel San Jorge (☎ *3617-9779, Javier Mina 284*) Singles/doubles US$13/15. The San Jorge is another ordinary but inexpensive place.

Hotel Azteca (☎ *3617-7465, Javier Mina 311*) Rooms with one/two beds US$27/44. The five-story Azteca is better and more modern than the other neighborhood hotels, though also pricier. It has 70 clean rooms, all with good plumbing, phone, TV and ceiling fan. There's a restaurant and parking too. If you don't mind the roughish neighborhood, it's a great value.

Mid-Range *Hotel del Parque* (☎ *3825-2800, Juárez 845*) Singles & doubles US$56. About 10 blocks west of the city center and easily reached by bus or trolley, this attractive hotel is near Parque Revolución. It has a pleasant restaurant, a lobby bar and sidewalk café tables. The 81 rooms are all well equipped and are a good value if you can get a discount on the asking price.

Hotel Internacional (☎ *3613-0330, Moreno 570*) Singles & doubles US$63. More central than the Hotel del Parque but with less style, the Internacional has 120 carpeted rooms with TV, air-con and phone.

La Rotonda (☎ *3614-1017, Liceo 130*) Singles/doubles US$48/58. In an old but completely renovated building, this small hotel is well run by a helpful and friendly staff.

Hotel Francés (☎ *3613-1190, 800-853-09-00, w www.hotelfrances.com, Maestranza 35*) Singles & doubles US$60, suites from US$66. This historic hotel, the oldest in Guadalajara, was founded in 1610 as an inn. Horses were kept in the arched stone courtyard, which is now a comfortable lobby bar. The 52 rooms have tiled floors, satellite TV, phone and fan, but they vary considerably in size, and some are not nearly as genteel as the handsome exterior and entrance might suggest. If you want something elegant, check the more expensive rooms.

Hotel Cervantes (☎ *3613-6846, Sánchez 442*) Singles/doubles US$59/71. A swank modern alternative is this hotel with five floors, 100 elegant rooms and all the amenities, including underground parking, a 2nd-floor pool, and a phone beside every bathtub.

If you come into town late, consider spending the night near the Nueva Central Camionera and finding a more central place in the morning.

Hotel Serena (☎ 3600-0910, Antigua Carretera Zapotlanejo 1500) Singles & Doubles US$39. Across the road from Módulo 1 of the Nueva Central Camionera, the Serena has 377 clean, functional rooms with color TV, and it often gives discounts that make it a very good value. There are two reception areas (head for the one on the right under the 'hotel' sign) and two swimming pools (at least one might be usable).

Avenida López Mateos is Guadalajara's 'motel row.'

Motor Hotel Américas (☎ 3631-4415, López Mateos Sur 2400) Singles/doubles US$52/60. Opposite the Plaza del Sol mall, this four-star place is designed unashamedly in US motel style and has a swimming pool, air-con and other amenities. Some of the 101 rooms have kitchens and cost a few dollars more.

Plenty of other motels are near the Plaza del Sol. Bus No 258 heading west on San Felipe will bring you here from the city center.

Motel Isabel (☎ 3826-2630, Montenegro 1572) Singles/doubles US$55/60. This fine motel is southwest of the city center, about six blocks south of Vallarta. Its 50 rooms have TV, phones and firm beds, and amenities include a pool, restaurant and parking.

Top End *Hotel de Mendoza* (☎ 3613-4646, 800-361-26-00, fax 3613-7310, W www.demendoza.com.mx, Carranza 16) Singles/doubles US$80/96, suites US$98/116. On the north side of the Teatro Degollado, this place was built as the convent to the church of Santa María de Gracia, which is still standing at one side. The convent has been beautifully refurbished and today is a fashionable four-star hotel with 104 modern rooms and all the amenities: satellite TV, air-con, restaurant, bar, pool and parking. Some rooms have bathtubs and private balconies.

Hotel Calinda Roma (☎ 3614-8650, 800-368-26-00, fax 3614-2629, W www.hoteles calinda.com.mx, Juárez 170) Singles & doubles from US$64. The central and modern Calinda Roma has a rooftop pool and 172 rooms.

Best Western Hotel Plaza Génova (☎ 3613-7500, fax 3614-8253, W www.hplaza genova.com, Juárez 123) Singles & doubles US$120. This hotel offers rooms with air-con, phone, cable TV and minibar, and rates include an American breakfast. Facilities include parking, a gym and a travel agency in the lobby.

Hotel Fénix (☎ 3614-5714, 800-361-11-00, Corona 160) Singles & doubles US$78. The Fénix has big, bright, pleasant rooms. Exterior rooms have balconies. It's well set up for business travelers and gives discounts at quiet times.

Hotel Lafayette (☎ 3615-0252, 800-362-22-00, fax 3630-1112, e lafayete@mpsnet .com.mx, Avenida de la Paz 2055) Singles/doubles US$101/108. This lovely hotel, in the Zona Rosa just west of Avenida Chapultepec, has a pool, an attractive café and 181 rooms with wall-to-wall carpeting, color TV and air-con.

Hotel Posada Guadalajara (☎ 3121-2022, fax 3122-1834, López Mateos Sur 1280) Singles/doubles US$74/76. This place has a popular bar and restaurant and 170 modern rooms on six floors. In cute Mexican style, all rooms flank an open courtyard, which has a swimming pool in the center.

Guadalajara has its quota of upscale chain hotels catering mainly to corporate travelers. Most are on the west side of town, on or near Avenida López Mateos. Among these are:

Fiesta Americana Guadalajara (☎ 3825-3434, 800-504-50-00, W www.fiestamericana .com, Aceves 225) Singles & doubles US$164.

Crowne Plaza (☎ 3634-1034, 800-365-55-00, fax 3631-9393, W www.crowneplaza.com .mx, López Mateos Sur 2500) Singles & doubles from US$198.

Presidente Inter-Continental (☎ 3678-1234, fax 3678-1222, W www.interconti.com/ mexico/guadalajara/hotel_guaic.html, López Mateos Sur at Moctezuma) Singles & doubles US$328.

Camino Real (☎ 3134-2424, 800-901-23-00, W www.caminoreal.com, Vallarta 5005) Singles/doubles US$178. A little farther from the city center, the Camino Real has the most luxurious ambience of the city's chain hotels.

The attractive old precinct of Tlaquepaque, southeast of the busy city center, now has several upscale B&Bs in renovated old buildings. The Tlaquepaque tourist office has a full list.

Casa de las Flores *(☎ 3659-3186,* W *www.casadelasflores.com, Santos Degollado 175)* Singles/doubles US$59/76. Three blocks from Tlaquepaque's main plaza, this old adobe building was once a country house. It now has spacious rooms surrounding a delightful, flower-filled courtyard. The management is especially helpful in arranging sightseeing, shopping and dining out.

La Villa del Ensueño *(☎ 3635-8792,* e *ensueno1@prodigy.net.mx, Florida 305)* Singles & doubles US$76-100. A few blocks northwest of Tlaquepaque's tourist zone, the 'Villa of Dreams' has a variety of accommodation, including some units with two bedrooms. The pool, gardens, shaded patios and bar make it an ideal place to relax.

Places to Eat

Most eateries in the center of town serve up standard Mexican fare, with higher prices buying better atmosphere rather than more creative cuisine. Guadalajara's best restaurants are scattered around the suburbs, along with a surfeit of fast-food franchises.

Centro Histórico & Around The Mercado Libertad, just east of the city center, has scores of *food stalls* serving maybe the cheapest eats you'll find in town. Sensitive stomachs beware: the hygiene here is not ideal.

The pedestrian zone around the tourist office has several good eateries, enjoyed by locals as well as visitors.

La Rinconada *(☎ 3613-9914, Morelos 86)* Mains US$8-10. Open 8am-9pm. Enjoy well-prepared Mexican and US-style meals in this fashionable restaurant with its covered courtyard. It's very clean, and the service is good.

El Mexicano *(☎ 3658-0345, Morelos 79)* Mains US$4-10. The walls of this festive, gym-size eatery are lined with photos of revolutionary figures and murals depicting village life. The *comida corrida* is a good value, and there's a choice of big barbecued meat dishes. It's not low-fat cooking, but the food is tasty, the prices are right, and live music plays most nights from 6pm to 10pm.

The streets around the central plazas harbor places catering to shoppers and office workers.

Sandy's Restaurant *(☎ 3614-4236, cnr Alcalde & Independencia, upstairs)* Mains US$4-8. Open 8am-9pm. Beside the Rotonda de los Hombres Ilustres is one of the city's several Sandy's establishments. This one is noted for its set-price buffet breakfasts and great-value lunches.

Sanborns Restaurant *(☎ 3613-6680, cn. 16 de Septiembre & Juárez)* Mains US$4-8 Like other Sanborns restaurants, this place is popular with well-dressed locals who presumably come for the squeaky-clean surroundings or to see waitresses wearing ersatz traditional dress. The menu is ordinary, the food is nothing special, and the service can be slow.

Sanborns Café *(☎ 3613-6496, Juárez 305)* Mains US$4-8. On the other side of 16 de Septiembre is another Sanborns, this one specializing in cakes, coffee, ice cream and snacks. Though a little pricey, it's popular with locals, and super-clean. For a more substantial meal, go upstairs to **La Esquina**, yet another Sanborns eatery, with a larger selection of dishes and balcony tables that are delightful for people-watching.

Café Madrid *(☎ 3614-9604, Juárez 264)* Mains about US$5. Open 8am-10pm daily. A Guadalajara favorite, the Madrid serves good, moderately priced food and excellent coffee. Smiling waiters in white coats and black bow ties offer brisk, efficient service. The '50s-style decor is reminiscent of a US diner, with a huge window opening onto the street.

Restaurant La Terraza Oasis *(☎ 3613-8285, cnr Morelos & Galeana, upstairs)* Mains US$3-5. Just off the Plaza de los Laureles, this big, popular, no-frills place serves economical meals, including hamburgers, steaks and chicken dishes.

La Terraza *(☎ 3658-3690, Juárez 442)* Snacks and light fare US$2-4. This second La Terraza near Ocampo serves only *antojitos* (snacks) and cheap beer. It's often crowded, mostly with young people, and seldom quiet.

Chong Wa *(☎ 3613-9950, Juárez 558)* Mains about US$5. Open noon-11pm daily. This big, bustling budget place has a pretty standard Westernized Chinese menu, but the food is tasty, the servings are huge, and the service is efficient.

La Playita *(cnr Juárez & Corona)* Antojitos US$2-4. Open 8am-11.30pm. About the best bargain eats in the city center are the tacos, tortas and quesadillas at this reasonably hygienic hole-in-the-wall taco joint, hugely popular with students and unpretentious locals.

Restaurant La Chata (☎ 3613-0588, Corona 126) Mains about US$5. Open 8am-midnight daily. La Chata has been cooking quality Mexican food for over 50 years. Their specialty is a *platillo jalisciense*: a quarter chicken, potatoes, soup, an enchilada and a flauta. They also have *pozole* (hominy soup) and chiles rellenos.

Café/Restaurant Málaga (☎ 3614-3815, 16 de Septiembre 210) Mains US$4-8. Open 7am-10pm daily. This spacious restaurant is a reasonably priced place with main dishes, various salads, enchiladas and breakfasts. Sometimes it's packed; sometimes empty.

All the fancy hotels have fashionable restaurants. The ones at Hotel Francés and Hotel de Mendoza are magnificent old dining rooms, beautifully done up.

The blocks south and west of the city center have a few inexpensive eateries offering healthy, natural fare.

Villa Madrid (☎ 3613-4250, López Cotilla 223) Mains US$3-4. Open noon-9pm Mon-Sat. This is not an exclusively vegetarian restaurant, but its tasty light meals include vegetarian options like soya burgers, veggie burritos and salads. The chicken burritos with mole, and the yogurt with fruit, are superb.

Alta Fibra (☎ 3613-6980, Sánchez 370B) Mains US$3. 'High Fiber' features a fine range of vegetarian dishes, especially the soya ceviche, soya burgers, *choco de soya* (drinking chocolate) and assorted salads.

Egipto Al Natural (☎ 3613-6277, Sánchez 416) Mains about US$3. Open 9.30am-6pm Mon-Sat. This friendly restaurant is a combined vegetarian restaurant and health-food store, popular for its filling comida corrida. It also serves soy-based meals, fresh vegetable juices and yogurt with fruit.

Plaza de las Nueve Esquinas About 10 blocks southwest of the city center, the 'Plaza of the Nine Corners' is a small, untouristy, triangular space where several small streets intersect. It's a cute little neighborhood with a number of eateries, many specializing in *birria*, a thick stew of mutton and onions.

Birrería las Nueve Esquinas (☎ 3613-6260, Colón 384) Mains US$2-4. Open 9am-

10pm. This place serves some of the best birria around, in a charming little dining area with windows on three sides. Open for all to see, the spotlessly clean, classic Mexican kitchen has tiled work surfaces, suspended utensils and delicious aromas.

Near Avenida Chapultepec Guadalajara's Zona Rosa is basically the few blocks of Avenida Chapultepec north and south of Avenida Vallarta. It's hardly a full-on nightlife and entertainment district, but it does have some pleasant restaurants on quiet streets nearby. From the city center, catch the 'Par Vial' bus heading west on Independencia and get off at Chapultepec and Vallarta (about 10 minutes).

Sandy's Restaurant (☎ 3616-1841, Chapultepec 152 at López Cotilla) Mains US$5-8. Open 8am-10pm daily. A block south of Avenida Vallarta, this is a reliable place where shoppers and office workers get breakfast and lunch.

Cafetería Azteca (☎ 3825-5599, Chapultepec 201 at Libertad) Mains about US$4. Open 8am-11.30pm daily. This café serves up sandwiches, burgers, tacos and meat dishes, indoors and outdoors. It's a breezy place with open sides and outdoor tables, and you can linger over the fine coffee.

Restaurant/Bar Recco (☎ 3825-0724, Libertad 1981) Mains US$8-11. Open 1pm-11.45pm Mon-Sat, 1pm-10pm Sun. Just east of Chapultepec and two blocks south of Vallarta, this classy European-style restaurant serves classic Italian dishes (the lasagna is excellent), seafood (try the sea bass in beer batter) and salads.

Suehiro (☎ 3826-0094, La Paz 1701) Mains US$9-15. Open 1.30pm-5.30pm & 7.30pm-11.30pm daily. About 500m east of Avenida Chapultepec, Suehiro is arguably the best of the 30-odd Japanese restaurants in town.

Near Avenida López Mateos About 15 blocks west of Avenida Chapultepec, Avenida López Mateos is the avenue of up-market hotels, shopping centers and restaurants. Bus No 258 from San Felipe in the city center runs along López Mateos to, or near, all these restaurants (a 30-minute trip).

Restaurant La Trattoria (☎ 3122-4425, Niños Héroes 3051) Mains US$6-10. Open 1pm-midnight daily. A block east of López

Mateos Sur, this is one of the top Italian restaurants in Guadalajara, but not overly pricey. Superbly prepared main courses include scaloppini, saltimbocca and a selection of homemade pastas.

Guadalajara Grill (☎ 3631-5622, *López Mateos Sur 3711*) Mains US$5-15. Open 1.30pm-1am Mon-Sat, 1.30pm-6pm Sun. One of several US-style steak bars in the area, the Guadalajara Grill, about 1km south of Plaza del Sol, is part of the Carlos Anderson chain. It's a large, fun place with a lively atmosphere, good music and dancing in the bar. Steak, chicken, shrimp, red snapper and big salads are on the menu.

Tlaquepaque Southeast of Tlaquepaque's main plaza, Jardín Hidalgo, *El Parián* is a block of little restaurant-bars around an enclosed courtyard full of chairs and tables. It's best on Saturday and Sunday, when it's crowded with people eating inexpensive antojitos, drinking moderately expensive beer and enjoying mariachi music. More expensive restaurants dot the pedestrian streets around Tlaquepaque's main plaza; most offer outdoor dining as well as fine food.

El Patio (☎ 3635-1108, *Independencia 186*) Mains about US$8. Open 1pm-11pm daily. With tables set in a pretty patio, this long-popular restaurant serves fine versions of classic Mexican favorites.

Restaurant Sin Nombre (☎ 3635-9677, *Madero 80*) Mains US$7-16. Open noon-11.30pm. The 'Restaurant with No Name' is a local favorite for its innovative Spanish and nouvelle-Mexican dishes. The garden setting, with parrots, peacocks and live music, is especially attractive.

Entertainment

Guadalajara is in love with music of all kinds, and live performers can be heard any night of the week. Theaters, cinemas and bars are also plentiful, but there aren't many dance venues accessible from the city center or affordable to the budget traveler.

For entertainment information, you can stop by the tourist office and view its weekly schedule of events; the bilingual staff will help you find something to suit your fancy. Or check out the Friday edition of the daily newspaper *Público*; its entertainment insert, *Ocio*, includes a cultural-events calendar for the upcoming week and is *the* place to look

for information on restaurants, movies, exhibits and the club scene. *Occidental* and *Informador,* also Spanish-language dailies, have entertainment listings, as does the weekly booklet *Ciento Uno*.

Popular cultural-arts venues hosting a range of drama, dance and music performances include **Teatro Degollado** (☎ 3658-3812) and the **Instituto Cultural de Cabañas** (☎ 3617-4248), both downtown cultural centers (see their respective sections, earlier), as well as the **Ex-Convento del Carmen** (☎ 3614-7184, *Juárez 638*).

Ballet Folklórico *Ballet Folklórico de la Universidad de Guadalajara* (☎ 3614-4773) US$3 in the gallery to US$16 in the best seats. The university's folkloric dance troupe stages grand performances at the Teatro Degollado at 8.30pm Thursday and 10am Sunday.

Ballet Folklórico del Instituto Cultural de Cabañas (☎ 3668-1640 ext 1004) US$4.50. This company performs at the Cabañas Cultural Institute at 8.30pm every Wednesday.

Mariachis Pay your respects to the mariachi tradition in its home city. The Plaza de los Mariachis, just east of the historic center, is a good place to get a taste of it, but it's unwise to linger here after about 9pm. Most tourists now get their mariachi experience in one of the sanitized (but safe) venues provided for the purpose.

La Feria (☎ 3613-7150, *Corona 291*) Mains US$6-10. Shows at 3.30pm and 10pm. You can eat and drink in this lofty former mansion, then listen to traditional and modern mariachi music and enjoy whatever other Mexican-style entertainment is offered. It's pretty touristy but a lot of fun, and many Mexicans come along for the ride.

Casa Bariachi (☎ 3616-9180, *Vallarta 2221*) Open 6pm-3am daily. This brightly decorated, barnlike space features a bar, restaurant, big margaritas and lots of mariachis. It's popular with groups of locals who like to party.

Near Tlaquepaque's main plaza, the *El Parián* quadrangle is another mariachi magnet.

Other Live Music The state band presents *free concerts* of typical *música tapatía* in the

Mariachis

In many minds, no image captures the spirit of Mexico better than that of proud-faced mariachis, in matching garb and broad-rimmed sombreros, belting out traditional Mexican ballads before a festive crowd. But the origin of the word 'mariachi' is something of a mystery.

Some historians contend that 'mariachi' is a corruption of the French word *mariage* (marriage) and that the name stems from the time of the French intervention in 1861-67. Mariachi bands were said to have played at wedding ceremonies during that period, hence the name.

Others say that the word was in use before the French arrived and that it arose from festivals honoring the Virgin Mary at which musicians performed. They note that the mariachi is indigenous to the region south of Guadalajara, probably derived from the name María with the Náhuatl diminutive '-chi' tacked on.

Still others point out that in the 1870s a Mexican poet designated as *mariache* the stage upon which dancers and musicians performed *jarabes*. A jarabe consisted of an ensemble that played and sang while a couple – a man attired as a Mexican cowboy in chaps and a wide-rimmed hat and a woman in a hand-woven shawl and full, brightly colored skirt – danced beside them.

Today's mariachi bands are of two types. The original version consists of musicians who play only stringed instruments and who limit their repertoire to traditional tapatío melodies. The lead instrument of modern, more commercial mariachi bands is the trumpet, and these bands have quite a broad repertoire. Both types can be heard in Guadalajara's Plaza de los Mariachis and at indoor venues devoted to mariachi music.

Plaza de Armas at 6.30pm on most Thursdays and Sundays, and on other days as well during holiday seasons.

Instituto Cultural Mexicano Norteamericano de Jalisco (☎ 3825-5838, *Díaz de León 300*) often hosts classical music concerts and recitals.

Peña Cuicacalli (☎ 3825-4690, *Niños Héroes 1988*) Admission US$4-11. This popular *peña* (folk-music club) presents a varied program of contemporary Mexican and Latino folk ballads, called *trova*, and other Latin sounds, jazz, comedy and more.

Bars The historic center has a few bars serving snacks, drinks and sometimes live music. If you stroll south of Plaza de la Liberación, down streets like Maestranza and Degollado, you'll find quite a few places that are lively at night.

La Maestranza (☎ 3613-5878, *Maestranza 179*) Open 1pm-2am. Decorated with a vast array of bullfighting memorabilia, this hip cantina attracts lots of 20- and 30-somethings with its cheap beer, salty snacks and lively music.

Hotel Francés (☎ 3613-1190, *Maestranza 35*) The lobby piano bar at this hotel near the Plaza de la Liberación is a sedate but stylish option. It's popular with gringos and worth a look for the architecture alone.

Copenhagen (☎ 3587-6596, *cnr López Costilla & Castellanos*) Facing the west side of Parque Revolución, about 800m west of the city center, this upstairs restaurant serves good paella and (after 9pm) 'gourmet jazz' to an older audience.

¡Qué Pues! (☎ 3826-9114, *Niños Héroes 1554*) For most of the week this is a standard restaurant/bar showing rock videos from the US, but it's worth checking out on Tuesday night when it hosts live rock music with local bands.

Discos & Dance Clubs West of the city center, Avenida Juárez becomes Avenida Vallarta, which has a concentration of nightspots. Discos and clubs on the 'Ruta Vallarta' attract young, affluent locals who dress to impress. No track shoes or jeans, please.

La Marcha (☎ 3615-8999, *Vallarta 2648*) Admission US$15/9 for men/women. If you're young, rich and gorgeous, you'll feel right at home at La Marcha, bopping to the techno beat and sipping expensive drinks.

El Mito (☎ 3615-2855, *Avenida Vallarta 2425*) Open 10.30pm-3am Wed-Sat. Admission US$0-5.50. Mainly for people 25 years and over, El Mito is in the Centro Magno shopping center and has music from the '60s, '70s, '80s and '90s, as well as special shows on Friday and Saturday.

Hard Rock Café (☎ 3616-4564, *Vallarta 2425*) Admission varies from nothing to about US$8, depending on time, day, and what's happening. As well as the usual slick decor and clientele, this Hard Rock Café, also in the Centro Magno, regularly features local bands doing polished covers of rock classics.

More nightlife venues cluster around Plaza del Sol, on López Mateos Sur south of Vallarta.

Tropigala (☎ 3122-5903, *López Mateos Sur 2011*) Admission US$5. Open 9pm-4am Tues-Sat. This is a large, very hip, multilevel club with live salsa, meringue and popular Mexican music.

Danny Rock (☎ 3121-1363, *Otero 1989*) Admission US$7. Open 9pm-3am. A disco and video bar, Danny Rock draws a mixed crowd with music dating from the '60s to the '90s.

Gay & Lesbian Venues Central venues include:

Maskara (☎ 3614-8103, *Maestranza 238*) This is a colorful bar with discount drink specials.

Los Caudillos (☎ 3613-5445, *cnr Sánchez & Ocampo*) Open 3pm-3am. This bar has cheap drinks, dancing, loud music and late hours.

Flama Latina (*no* ☎, *Degollado 187*) A typical looking salsa bar, the 'Latin Flame' is a gay-friendly place attracting a diverse crowd.

Angels (☎ 3615-2525, *López Cotilla 1495*) A glittery gay disco/bar, Angels features

techno and Latin sounds and a well-dressed clientele.

Cinemas Several cinemas show international films and classics. Check *Ocio* or the local newspapers. Some of the best places to catch them are:

Alianza Francesa (☎ 3825-5595, *López Cotilla 1199*)
Cine Cinematógrafo No 1 (☎ 3825-0514, *Vallarta 1102*), No 2 (☎ 3630-1208, *México 2222*) & No 3 (☎ 3629-4780, *Patria 600, Plaza de la Amistad shopping center, Zapopan*)
Cine-Teatro Cabañas (☎ 3617-4322, *Instituto Cultural de Cabañas*)

The big shopping centers like Plaza del Sol and Plaza Milenium have multiscreen facilities showing recent movie releases. *Cinepolis* (☎ 3630-1076, *Vallarta 2425*), in the Centro Magno, shows new releases in its state-of-the-art, 14-screen facility.

Spectator Sports
Bullfights & Charreadas *Plaza de Toros Nuevo Progreso* (☎ 3637-9982, *north end of Calzada Independencia*) Admission US$3-25. The bullfighting season is October to March, and the fights are held on select Sundays starting at 4.30pm. A couple of fights will almost certainly take place during the October fiestas; the rest of the schedule is sporadic. Check at the bullring or tourist office.

Lienzo Charros de Jalisco (*Agua Azul*, ☎ 3619-0315, *Dr Michel 577*). Admission from US$3. Charreadas are held at noon most Sundays in this ring behind Parque Agua Azul. Charros come from all over Jalisco and Mexico to show off their skills. *Escaramuzas* (cowgirls) also compete in daring displays of their sidesaddle riding.

Soccer (Football) *Fútbol* is Guadalajara's favorite sport. The city usually has at least three teams playing in the national top-level *primera división*: Guadalajara (Las Chivas), the second most popular team in the country after América of Mexico City; Atlas (Los Zorros); and Universidad Autónoma de Guadalajara (Los Tecos).

Estadio Jalisco (☎ 3637-0563, *Siete Colinas 1772*) Admission US$2-12 (more for a really big game). The summer soccer season is January to May; winter season

August to December. The teams play at stadiums around the city, but this main venue has hosted several World Cup matches. Contact the stadium or tourist office for schedule information.

Shopping

Handicrafts from Jalisco, Michoacán and other Mexican states are available in Guadalajara. (See the Tlaquepaque and Tonalá sections, earlier in this chapter, for information on these two craft-making suburbs.) The *Casa de las Artesanías de Jalisco*, 20 blocks south of the city center, has a good selection. See Parque Agua Azul, earlier.

Mercado Libertad (☎ 3658-1514, cnr Javier Mina & Calzada Independencia) Open daily. Just east of the Centro Histórico, this general market has three floors of stalls spread over an area of several city blocks.

Mercado El Baratillo Vast and popular, this Sunday flea market stretches blocks in every direction on and around Javier Mina. To get there, take a 'Par Vial' bus east along Hidalgo.

El Charro (☎ 3614-7599, cnr Juárez & Degollado) This is the place to buy the cowboy boots, Mexican hat and mariachi suit you've always wanted. Several similar (and cheaper) shops are on Juárez east of El Charro.

Guadalajara's most prosperous citizens prefer to shop at one of the several big shopping centers around town.

Plaza del Sol (López Mateos Sur, about 7km southwest of the city center) This shopping mall has a huge variety of shops, eateries and entertainment.

Plaza Milenium (López Mateos Sur at Otero) A little south of Plaza del Sol, the newer Plaza Milenium also holds a wide range of hot shopping opportunities. Take bus Nos 258 or 258A west on San Felipe to get to these.

Getting There & Away

Air Guadalajara's Aeropuerto Internacional Miguel Hidalgo (code GDL, ☎ 3688-5248) is 17km south of downtown, just off the highway to Chapala. The many airlines serving the airport offer direct flights to more than 20 cities in Mexico and about 10 cities in the US and Canada, as well as one-stop connections to many other places. You'll find a tourist office in the terminal.

Book flights with one of the many travel agencies in Guadalajara. Look in the phone-directory yellow pages under 'Agencias de Viajes.' A number of airlines and travel agents, as well as American Express, have offices in Plaza Los Arcos, Vallarta 2440. Airline offices in Guadalajara include:

Aero California	☎ 3616-2525
Aeroméxico	☎ 3122-0200
Aerolitoral	☎ 3688-5341
Aeromar	☎ 3615-8511
Air France	☎ 3630-3707
American Airlines	☎ 3616-4402
Continental	☎ 3647-0107
Delta	☎ 3630-3130
Mexicana	☎ 3112-0011
United Airlines	☎ 3616-9393

Bus Guadalajara has two bus stations. The long-distance bus station is the Nueva Central Camionera, a huge modern terminal with seven separate buildings, called *módulos* (modules) or *salas* (waiting rooms), in a V shape on two sides of a large triangular parking lot. It's 9km southeast of the Guadalajara city center, past Tlaquepaque.

Each *módulo* has ticket desks for a number of bus lines, plus places to eat and pay phones. Most *módulos* have a place to leave luggage.

Buses, often frequent, travel to and from just about everywhere in western, central and northern Mexico. The same destination can be served by several companies in several different *módulos*; the companies suggested below have the most frequent departures to the cities indicated. Distances, travel times, frequencies, typical 1st-class prices and departure modules are as follows:

Barra de Navidad – 291km, 5 hours; 11 Autocamiones de Cihuatlán (US$21, Módulo 3), 3 Primera Plus (US$21, Módulo 1)

Colima – 202km, 2½-3 hours; frequent Primera Plus (US$14, Módulo 1)

Guanajuato – 296km, 4 hours; 7 Primera Plus (US$21, Módulo 1)

Mazatlán – 506km, 8 hours; regular Elite, Pacífico (US$29, Módulo 3)

Mexico City (Terminal Norte) – 535km, 7-8 hours; regular Primera Plus (US$37-40, Módulo 1), regular Omnibus de México (US$37-40, Módulo 6)

Morelia – 278km, 3½ hours; regular Primera Plus (US$20, Módulo 1), regular La Línea (US$20, Módulo 2)

Puerto Vallarta – 344km, 5 hours; frequent Pacífico, Futura, Elite (US$26-29, Módulos 3 and 4)

Querétaro – 350km, 4½ hours; twice-hourly Primera Plus (US$22, Módulo 1)

San Miguel de Allende – 380km, 6 hours; 1 Primera Plus direct at 1pm (US$29, Módulo 1), 1 Omnibus de México direct at 5.30pm (US$29, Módulo 2)

Tepic – 216km, 3 hours; regular Elite and Futura (US$19, Módulo 3), regular Omnibus de México (US$19, Módulo 6)

Uruapan – 305km, 3½ hours; regular Primera Plus (US$17, Módulo 1)

Zacatecas – 320km, 5 hours; frequent Omnibus de México (US$22, Módulo 6)

For deluxe buses to many of these destinations (at considerably higher fares), try ETN, Módulo 2.

Bus tickets can be bought in the city center at Turismo MaCull, López Cotilla 163, near the corner of Degollado. It's open 9am to 7pm Monday to Friday, 9am to 1pm Saturday.

Guadalajara's other bus station is the Antigua Central Camionera (Old Bus Station), about 1.5km south of the cathedral, near Parque Agua Azul. It occupies the block bounded by Avenida 5 de Febrero, Los Ángeles and Dr Michel (which is the southward continuation of Avenida Corona). The Antigua Central Camionera has 2nd-class buses to and from destinations nearer Guadalajara. There are two sides and two sets of ticket booths: Sala A is for destinations to the east and northeast; Sala B is for destinations northwest, southwest and south.

Transportes Guadalajara-Chapala buses depart Sala B every half hour from 6am to 9pm for Chapala (40km, 45 minutes, US$3), Ajijic (47km, 55 minutes, US$3) and Jocotepec (68km, 1 hour, US$3.25).

Rojo de Los Altos buses depart from Sala B every 15 or 20 minutes from 6am to 9pm for Tequila (62km, 1¾ hours, US$2.75) via Amatitán (49km, 1¼ hours, US$2.25).

Train The only train serving Guadalajara is the Tequila Express – a tourist excursion to the nearby town of Tequila (see the Tequila section).

Car & Motorcycle Guadalajara is 535km northwest of Mexico City and 344km east of Puerto Vallarta. Highways 15, 15D, 23, 54, 54D, 80, 80D and 90 all converge here, combining temporarily to form the Periférico, a ring road around the city.

Guadalajara has many car rental agencies, listed in the telephone yellow pages under 'Automóviles – Renta de.' Several of the large US companies are represented, but you may get a cheaper deal from a local company. Agencies include:

Auto Rent de Guadalajara	☎ 3826-2013, 800-800-40-00
Budget	☎ 3613-0027, 800-700-17-00
Dollar	☎ 3826-7959, 3688-5659
Hertz	☎ 3688-5633, 800-654-30-30
National	☎ 3614-7994, 800-227-73-68
Quick Rent A Car	☎ 3614-6006, 3614-2247

Getting Around

To/From the Airport The airport (☎ 3688-5248) is 17km south of downtown, just off the highway to Chapala. Bus No 176, going north on Corona about every 20 minutes, will eventually wind its way to the airport. Tell the driver you're going to the *aeropuerto,* and you'll be dropped two blocks from the airport. You should allow a good hour for the trip (US$0.60). Buses to Chapala from the Antigua Central Camionera also pass the airport (US$0.80).

The company Autotransportaciónes Aeropuerto (☎ 3612-4278) provides shuttle service between the airport and many downtown hotels (40 minutes, US$10-16). Taxis between the airport and the city center cost about US$13 on the meter.

To/From the Bus Stations To reach the city center from the Nueva Central Camionera, you can take any 'Centro' or No 644 city bus, or the more comfortable TUR 707 bus, from the loop road within the station (immediately outside your módulo). These are not very frequent so it's often quicker to walk out of the station between Módulo 1 and the Hotel Serena and take an orange bus No 275, going to the right (north) along the road outside. These run every 15 minutes from 5.30am to 10.30pm and bring you into the city center along Avenida 16 de Septiembre.

All the city's taxis now have meters, but most taxi drivers at the bus station prefer not to use them and will quote a flat fee to the city center. US$6.50 is reasonable, but the asking price varies from about US$6 to US$9. Don't be afraid to haggle.

From the city to the Nueva Central Camionera, catch bus No 275 Diagonal southward on 16 de Septiembre, anywhere between the cathedral and Calzada Revolución. They run frequently but tend to be crowded and can take 40 to 50 minutes to get there. A taxi should cost about US$6.50.

Bus Nos 60 and 60D south on Calzada Independencia will take you from the city center to the Antigua Central Camionera.

Bus Nos 616 and 000 run between the two bus stations.

Bus Guadalajara has a comprehensive city bus system, but the buses are pretty basic: they can be crowded, and they sometimes give passengers a rough ride as they accelerate, swerve and brake suddenly in the heavy traffic. On the major routes, buses run every five minutes or so from 6am to 10pm daily; they cost US$0.40. Many buses pass through the center of town, so for an inner suburban destination you'll have a few stops to choose from. The routes diverge as they get farther from the city center, and you need to know the bus number for the

suburb you want. Some bus route numbers are followed by an additional letter indicating which circuitous route they will follow in the outer suburbs.

The TUR buses, painted a distinctive turquoise color, are a more comfortable alternative on some routes. They have air-con and everyone gets a seat. The fare is US$0.70. If they roar past without stopping, they're probably full.

The tourist office has a list of the many bus routes in Guadalajara and can help you figure out how to get anywhere you want to go. The table below lists some of the most common suburban destinations, the buses that go to those destinations, and suggestions on where to catch the buses in the Centro Histórico.

Metro The subway system (☎ 3827-0000) has two lines that cross the city. Stops are marked around town by a 'T' symbol. The subway is quick and comfortable enough, but doesn't serve many points of visitor interest. Línea 1 stretches north-south for 15km all the way from the Periférico Nte to the Periférico Sur. It runs more or less below Federalismo (seven blocks west of the city center) and Avenida Colón. You can catch it at Parque Revolución, on the corner of Avenida Juárez.

Línea 2 runs east-west for 10km below Avenidas Juárez and Mina.

Guadalajara Bus Routes

Destination	Bus Number(s)	Route in Centro
Antigua Central Camionera	No 60, 62 or 174	south on Calzada Independencia
Nueva Central Camionera	No 275 Diagonal or TUR 706	south on 16 de Septiembre
Parque Agua Azul	No 60, 62 or 62A	south on Calzada Independencia
Plaza de Toros, Zoo, Selva Mágica	No 60, 62 or 62D, or Par Vial 600	north on Calzada Independencia
Plaza del Sol	No 258 TUR 707	west on San Felipe west on Juárez
Tlaquepaque	No 275 Diagonal, No 647 or TUR 706	south on 16 de Septiembre
Tonalá	No 275 Diagonal or TUR 706	south on 16 de Septiembre
Zapopan	any No 275 or TUR 706	north on 16 de Septiembre
Zona Rosa	Par Vial 400	west on Avenida Independencia

Taxi Cabs are plentiful in the city center. All Guadalajara taxis now have meters, but many taxi drivers prefer not to use them and will quote a flat fee for a trip. Generally, it's cheaper to go by the meter, though the driver may take a circuitous route to increase the fare anyway. For a flat fee, try to negotiate a discount. Typical fares from the city center are: US$3 to the Antigua Central Camionera or Parque Agua Azul; US$4 to Plaza del Sol; US$4.50 to Tlaquepaque or the zoo; US$5 to Zapopan; US$6.50 to the Nueva Central Camionera; US$7.50 to Tonalá; and US$13 to the airport. Settle the fare before you get into the taxi.

TEQUILA
• pop 22,000 • elev 1219m ☎ 374

The town of Tequila, 50km northwest of Guadalajara, has been home to the liquor of the same name since the 17th century. Fields of blue agave, the cactuslike plant from which tequila is distilled, surround the town. You can almost get drunk just breathing the heavily scented air that drifts from the town's distilleries. The tourist office, on Plaza Principal, organizes distillery tours (US$3.50) throughout the day.

The **Museo del Tequila** (☎ 742-24-10, Coran 34; admission US$0.60; open 10am-5pm Tues-Sat), near the plaza, gives a history of the industry. The two largest distilleries are also near the plaza. Ask at the tourist office for details. Sauza tequila runs the Perseverencia distillery (☎ 742-02-43, Francisco Javier Sauza Mora 80; tours US$2.50; open 9am-2pm Mon-Fri), noted for its tequila-inspired mural. Cuervo tequila is made in the La Rojena distillery (☎ 742-13-82, José Cuervo 73; tours US$1.50; open 9am-6pm), the biggest in town. Tours of these and other distilleries include samples of the product.

The **Tequila Express** (☎ 33-3122-9020 in Guadalajara; US$60) starts at Guadalajara train station at 10am. Tours include a train ride through the agave fields, a distillery visit, music, a mariachi show, snacks, lunch and an open bar with *mucho* tequila.

The **Tequila Bus** (☎ 33-3813-3594 in Guadalajara; US$44) picks up tour groups from a couple of locations in Guadalajara at about 10am daily. The trip includes a walk in the agave fields, visits to distilleries

and the tequila museum, a dinner with mariachi music and a folkloric show, and plentiful tastings of tequila.

If you want to do it yourself, just get one of the frequent Rojo de los Altos public buses to Tequila from the Antigua Central Camionera in Guadalajara (62km, 1¾ hours, US$2.75).

Another option for tequila tourism is **Amatitán**, 49km from Guadalajara on the road to Tequila. This old-fashioned town is the home of Herradura brand tequila, produced at the old San José del Refugio hacienda using traditional methods. Tours of the hacienda can be arranged (☎ 33-3613-9585 in Guadalajara; tours 9am-noon).

LAGO DE CHAPALA
Mexico's largest natural lake, Lago de Chapala, lies 40km south of Guadalajara. Though picturesque, the lake suffers from a significantly declining water level; towns that were once by the shore now overlook a swath of sand and grass several hundred meters wide. Guadalajara's water needs exceed the flow of water into the lake, and the main river feeding the lake, Río Lerma, is diminished because water is pumped out to supply Mexico City. The Lerma water that does reach the lake is often polluted with fertilizers that nourish water hyacinth, a fast-growing plant that clogs the water surface almost as fast as mechanical cutters can remove it.

Still, the near-perfect climate and lovely countryside around the small lakeside towns of Chapala, Ajijic and Jocotepec have attracted some 5000 full-time residents from the USA and Canada; many are retirees who enjoy lower living costs and higher temperatures than at home.

Getting There & Around
Chapala is easy to reach by bus from Guadalajara's Antigua Central Camionera (see Getting There & Away in the Guadalajara section), while Ajijic, Jocotepec and other lakeside towns can be reached from the small bus station in Chapala. Large buses ply the main road between Chapala and Jocotepec every half hour from 7am to 10pm (50 minutes, US$0.50), stopping on the roadside in each village. Smaller buses, running every 15 minutes or so, follow the same road but

Tequila

In ancient times, the plant we call *Agave tequilana weber* (blue agave) was used by indigenous Mexicans as a source of food, cloth and paper. The plant even was used in torture. The needlelike tips of its long leaves were customarily thrust into human flesh as penance to the gods. Today, the blue agave is known more widely as the source of Mexico's national drink: tequila.

To ensure quality control, the Mexican government allows blue agave to be grown only in the state of Jalisco and in parts of Nayarit, Michoacán, Guanajuato and Tamaulipas states. It is here, and nowhere else in Mexico, distillers say, that conditions are right for the blue agave to produce a good-tasting tequila. At any given moment more than 100 million tequila agaves are in cultivation within this designated territory.

In some ways the production of tequila has changed little since the drink was invented near Guadalajara hundreds of years ago. The blue agaves are still planted and harvested by hand, and the heavy pineapple-like hearts, from which the alcohol is derived, are still removed from the fields on the backs of mules.

When planted, the agave heart is no bigger than an onion. Its blue-gray, swordlike leaves give the plant the appearance of a cactus, although it is more closely related to the lily. By the time the agave is ready for harvesting, eight to 12 years after planting, its heart is the size of a beach ball and can weigh 50kg.

The harvested agave heart, called a *piña,* is chopped to bits, fed into ovens and cooked for up to three days. After cooking, the softened plants are shredded and juiced. The juice, called *aguamiel* (honey water) for its golden, syrupy appearance, is then pumped into vats, where it typically is mixed with sugarcane and yeast before being allowed to ferment. By law, the mixture can contain no less than 51% agave. A bottle of tequila made from 100% agave will bear a label stating so.

There are four varieties of tequila. Which is best is a matter of personal opinion. White or silver *(blanco)* tequila is not aged, and no colors or flavors are added. The gold variety *(dorado)* also is not aged, but color and flavor, usually caramel, are added. Tequila *reposado* (rested) has been aged at least two months in oak barrels, and coloring and flavoring agents usually have been added. Tequila *añejo* (aged) has spent at least one year in oak barrels, also with added coloring and flavoring.

frequently make detours through the side streets of San Antonio, Ajijic in addition to San Juan Cosalá.

There's also a *ciclopista* (bike path) between Chapala and Ajijic, for cycling, jogging or walking.

A scenic road around the south shore of the lake makes an attractive alternative route to Michoacán if you're driving. You can also catch the scenery and some local color by taking a 2nd-class bus from Chapala to Zamora.

Chapala
• pop 18,000 • elev 1560m ☎ 376

The largest of the settlements toward the western end of the lake, Chapala took off as a resort when president Porfirio Díaz vacationed here every year from 1904 to 1909. DH Lawrence wrote most of *The Plumed Serpent* in the house at Zaragoza 307. Templo de San Francisco, at the lake end of Avenida Madero (the main street), figures in the book's final pages. Today Chapala might get busy some Saturdays, Sundays and holidays, but mostly it's a quiet place catering to older expatriates.

Orientation & Information From the bus station it's a 10-minute walk down Avenida Madero to the lakeside (or what was the lakeside before the water level fell). Hidalgo heads to the west off Madero 200m before the lake to become the road leading to Ajijic. All services can be found on and around Madero or Hidalgo.

The tourist office (☎ 765-31-41, 800-363-22-00), upstairs at Madero 407, is open 9am to 7pm Monday to Friday, 9am to 1pm Saturday and Sunday.

Libros de Chapala (☎ 765-25-34, Madero 230A), opposite the plaza, has many US magazines, plus some newspapers and books in English.

A small produce market is situated on the east side of the plaza.

Things to See & Do At the foot of Avenida Madero, where the waterfront used to be, are a small park and a row of souvenir stalls, some selling attractive weavings from Jocotepec, most selling schlock.

There's also a covered crafts market, the **Mercado de Artesanías**, about 400m east along Paseo Corona. Farther east, the expansive **Parque La Cristiania** has a big swimming pool, a playground and nice picnic lawns. It's entered from Avenida Cristiania, off Ramón Corona, the road east around the lake.

On the embarcadero at the foot of Madero, an office sells tickets for the passenger boats that cruise the lake. From the ticket office, it's a longish walk down to the water and the boats (most companies now have a vehicle to drive passengers there).

Two islands in the lake are popular destinations. **Isla de los Alacranes** (Scorpion Island), 6km south, has some restaurants and more souvenir stalls, but it's mainly just an excuse for an opportunity to get out on the lake. A round trip, with 30 minutes on the island, costs US$22 per boat, for one to eight people. **Isla de Mezcala**, also called Isla El Presidio, about 15km east, has ruins of a fort and other buildings. Mexican independence fighters heroically held out there from 1812 to 1816, repulsing several Spanish attempts to dislodge them and finally

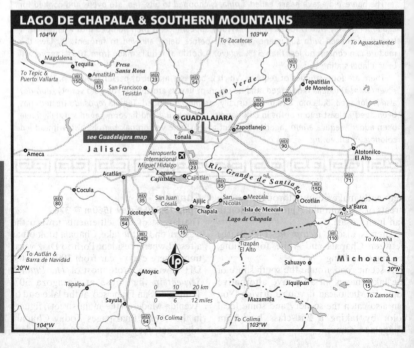

LAGO DE CHAPALA & SOUTHERN MOUNTAINS

winning a full pardon from their enemies. A boat there and back, with an hour to look around, will cost about US$41 for up to eight people.

Places to Stay The least-expensive accommodation option is *Casa de Huéspedes Las Palmitas* (☎ 765-30-70, *Juárez 531*) Singles/doubles with bath US$16/20. This place just south of the east side of the market has 15 clean rooms with cable TV and 24-hour hot water.

Villa Montecarlo (☎ 765-22-16, *Hidalgo 296*) Singles & doubles from US$74. This luxurious mansionlike place, 1km west of town center, is surrounded by lush gardens extending down to the lakeshore. A thermal swimming pool and strutting peacocks add to the atmosphere. Each room has a private balcony.

Places to Eat Chapala's specialty is fish of various sorts, but very little now comes from Lago de Chapala, which suffers from overfishing and pollution. The small *pescado blanco* (whitefish) is sold in many places, but it's expensive and probably comes from a fish farm. Another specialty, *charales,* are tiny fish, deep-fried and sold at many stalls near the embarcadero. They're fatty and salty, but not bad with lemon and a beer.

Several places on the east side of Madero offer a good range of decent food at reasonable prices. The sidewalk tables and high standards of cleanliness appeal to expatriates.

Café Paris (☎ 765-23-43, *Madero 411*) Light meals US$4. Good for breakfast and snacks, the Paris also makes an economical comida corrida.

Restaurant Superior (☎ 765-21-80, *Madero 415*) Mains US$3.50. Serving Mexican and American standards, this place is also popular for a quiet beer or three.

El Arbol de Café (☎ 765-39-08, *Hidalgo 236*) Snacks US$3. This café keeps sporadic hours but is recommended for its coffee and cakes.

East of the souvenir stalls along Ramón Corona, a whole slew of fishy restaurants compete for customers to sit at tables overlooking what used to be the lake. The water view is now somewhat distant, and the seafood is all imported, but these places are still pleasant and reasonably priced.

Ajijic
• pop 8500 • elev 1555m ☎ 376

Ajijic ('ah-hee-HEEK'), about 7km west of Chapala along the lakeside, is a pretty, friendly little town of cobbled streets and brightly painted houses. It's home to a sizeable colony of Mexican, US and Canadian artists. Usually Ajijic is fairly sleepy, except during the nine-day Fiesta de San Andrés, at the end of November, and over Easter, when a reenactment of Christ's trial and crucifixion is staged over three days.

The bigger buses will drop you on the highway at the top of Colón, the main street, which leads two blocks down to the main plaza and four more blocks down to the lake. A small information office (☎ 766-31-31, *Guadalupe Victoria 8*), a block east of the plaza, doubles as a bookstore. The chapel on the north side of the plaza, two blocks down, dates from the 18th century and possibly even earlier. A handful of galleries (look for Colección Moon) and some upmarket crafts shops lie on and off Colón.

The Lake Chapala Society, a club for expat residents, provides a library and does other good works for local kids. Its attractive premises are a block or so southeast of the plaza.

Places to Stay & Eat Tents are not encouraged at *PAL Trailer Park* (☎ 766-00-40, *Allen W Lloyd 149, San Antonio*) RV sites US$16 for one or two people. Two kilometers east of central Ajijic, just off the highway from Chapala, this park has a pool, laundry and 105 grassy sites with full hookups.

Hotel Italo (☎ 766-22-21, *Guadalupe Victoria 10*) Singles/doubles with breakfast US$25/33. A couple of blocks east of the plaza, the Italo has a bar, restaurant and 30 clean, spacious rooms with cable TV. Visit the rooftop terrace for a nice view of the nearby lake.

Hotel Ajijic Plaza Suites (☎ 766-03-83, **w** *www.ajijichotel.com, Colón 33*) Singles/doubles US$49/54. On the west side of the plaza, this friendly, well-run place has sizeable, modern two-room suites.

La Nueva Posada (☎ 766-14-44, **e** *nueva posada@laguna.com.mx, Donato Guerra 9*) Singles/doubles without lake view US$57/61, with lake view US$59/65. Down by the lakeshore, this lovely hotel is run by a friendly Canadian family. It has 17 large, tastefully decorated rooms, an inviting pool and an excellent restaurant that spills out into a fine lakeside garden. Most meat or fish dishes are US$8 to US$10, but there are cheaper daily specials.

Trattoria di Giovanni (☎ 766-17-33, *Carretera Ote 28*) Mains US$4-10. On the Chapala road, 1½ blocks east of Colón, this popular restaurant serves some of the best food in town, including chicken, seafood, pasta and pizzas.

The main cluster of cheap cafés and restaurants is around the plaza on Colón and a block or so to the south.

San Juan Cosalá

At San Juan Cosalá, 10km west of Ajijic toward Jocotepec, there's a thermal spa (admission US$5) in an attractive lakeside setting. The spa has its own natural geyser and several swimming pools.

Motel Balneario San Juan Cosalá (☎ 387-761-02-22, *La Paz 420*) Singles/doubles US$40/46. This comfortable motel is right beside the spa, and guests get free use of the pools.

Jocotepec

• pop 15,000

Jocotepec ('ho-co-teh-PEC'), 21km west of Chapala and a kilometer from the lake, is far less gringo-influenced than Chapala or Ajijic. It's a pleasant town, but there's nothing special to see or do except look for the handsome blankets, sarapes and wall hangings that are woven here and sold along Hidalgo. The main festival is the two-week Fiesta del Señor del Monte in early January.

SOUTHERN MOUNTAINS

South and west of Lago de Chapala, the mountainous region of Jalisco known as the Zona Montaña is an increasingly popular weekend getaway for Guadalajarans, who seem to enjoy the rural landscapes and cute colonial villages rather than wilderness experiences.

On the slopes of the Sierra Tapalpa about 130km south of Guadalajara, **Tapalpa** was once a mining town, and it retains its impressive church and quaint old buildings with balconies and red tiled roofs. There's wonderful walking in the surrounding area, which features some impressive rock formations, pine forests, fishing streams and a fine waterfall. Accommodation is available at a dozen hotels and guesthouses, though they can all be full on Saturday, Sunday and holidays (and still overpriced at other times). The basic *Hotel Tapalpa* (☎ 343-432-06-07, *Matamoros 35)* is the cheapest, while the rustic *Casa de Maty* (☎ 343-432-01-09, *Matamoros 69)* is the most charming and about the most expensive. Hourly buses run to Tapalpa from Guadalajara's Antigua Central Camionera, Sala B (3½ hours, US$9).

Another good base for visiting the mountains is **Mazamitla**, in the Sierra del Tigre, south of Lago de Chapala and 132km by road from Guadalajara. It's a tidy town of cobbled streets, tiled roofs and whitewashed buildings. About 4km west of town, the forest called Monteverde is noted for its lush flowers and plush holiday homes. *Cabañas Monteverde* (☎ 382-538-01-50, [W] *www.monteverde.com.mx, cnr Chavarria & Constitucion)* offers comfortable accommodation in a woodsy setting for high prices. *Fiesta Mazamitla* (☎ 382-538-00-50, *Reforma 14)* and *Posada Alpina* (☎ 382-538-01-04, *Reforma 8)* provide adequate and much more affordable alternatives. Most buses between Colima and Zamora will stop at Mazamitla, and you also might be able to get a 2nd-class bus from Chapala.

East of Mazamitla, on the road toward Zamora, the pleasant little town of **Jiquilpan** (properly called Jiquilpan de Juárez) is actually in the state of Michoacán, but it's a short detour from the Lago de Chapala circuit. It was the birthplace of Lázaro Cárdenas (1895-1970), Michoacán governor and reformist Mexican president (1934-40), and it's worth a stop to see the Orozco mural in the public library. Another choice for charm and mountainous surroundings is **Ciudad Guzmán**, also called Zapotlán el Grande.

Inland Colima

The tiny (5191 sq km) state of Colima enjoys a widely varied landscape, from tall volcanoes on its northern fringes to shallow lagoons near the Pacific coast. The climate is similarly diverse: cool in the highlands and hot along the coast. This section deals with the upland area of the state; the narrow coastal plain, including the beach resorts of Manzanillo, Cuyutlán and Paraíso, is covered in the Central Pacific Coast chapter.

Colima, the semitropical state capital, is a small, little-visited but pleasant city. Overlooking it from the north are two spectacular volcanoes: the active, constantly steaming Volcán de Fuego de Colima (3820m), and the extinct, snowcapped Volcán Nevado de Colima (4240m). Both can be reached relatively easily if you have a taste for adventure and a not-too-tight budget, though access to the Volcán de Fuego is usually barred for safety reasons.

The state's main agricultural products are coconuts, limes, bananas and mangoes. Its biggest industry is mining – one of Mexico's richest iron deposits is near Minatitlán.

History

Pre-Hispanic Colima was remote from the major ancient cultures of Mexico. Sea-borne contacts with more distant places might have been more important: there's a legend that one king of Colima, Ix, had regular treasure-bearing visitors from China.

Colima produced some remarkable pottery, which has been found in over 250 sites, mainly tombs, dating from about 200 BC to AD 800. The pottery includes a variety of figures, often quite comical and expressive of emotion and movement. Best known are the rotund figures of hairless dogs, known as Tepezcuintles. In some ancient Mexican cultures, dogs were buried with their owners. It was believed that they were able to carry the dead to paradise. Dogs also were part of the indigenous diet.

Archaeologists believe the makers of the pottery lived in villages spread around the state. The type of grave in which much of the pottery was found, the shaft tomb, occurs not only in the western Mexican states of Colima, Michoacán, Jalisco and Nayarit, but in Panama and South America as well, which suggests seaborne contacts with places much farther south.

When the Spanish reached Mexico, Colima was the leading force in the Chimalhuacán indigenous confederation that dominated Colima and parts of Jalisco and Nayarit. Two Spanish expeditions were defeated by the Colimans before Gonzalo de Sandoval, one of Cortés' lieutenants, conquered them in 1523. That same year he founded the town of Colima, the third Spanish settlement in Nueva España, after Veracruz and Mexico City. The town was moved to its present site, from its unhealthy original lowland location near Tecomán, in 1527.

COLIMA

- pop 134,000 • elev 550m ☎ 312

Colima lives at the mercy of the forces of nature. Volcán de Fuego de Colima, clearly visible 30km to the north, has had nine major eruptions in the past four centuries. Of even greater concern are earthquakes; the city has been hit by a series of them over the centuries, the most recent major one occurring in 1941. Because of these devastating natural events, Colima has few colonial buildings, despite having been the first Spanish city in western Mexico.

Today Colima is a small, pleasant place, graced by palm trees and ringed by mountains. Few tourists come here, but there are a number of interesting things to see and do in town and in the surrounding countryside. Though only 45km from the coast, Colima is at a higher elevation and, consequently, is cooler and less humid. The rainy months are July through September.

Orientation

Central Colima spreads around three plazas, with Plaza Principal (also known as Jardín Libertad) at the center of things. Portal Medellín is the row of arches on the north side of the plaza; Portal Morelos is on the south side. Jardín Quintero lies directly behind the cathedral, and three blocks farther east is Jardín Núñez. Street names change at Plaza Principal. Some of the sights are eight or 10 blocks from the city center, so be prepared for some walking.

The shiny modern main bus terminal is about 2km east of the city center, on the Guadalajara-Manzanillo road.

Information

Tourist Offices The state tourist office (☎ 312-43-60, e turiscol@palmera.colimanet .com.mx, w www.visitacolima.com.mx) is in a domed white building at Hidalgo and Ocampo. It's open 8.30am to 8pm Monday to Friday, 10am to 2pm Saturday. The

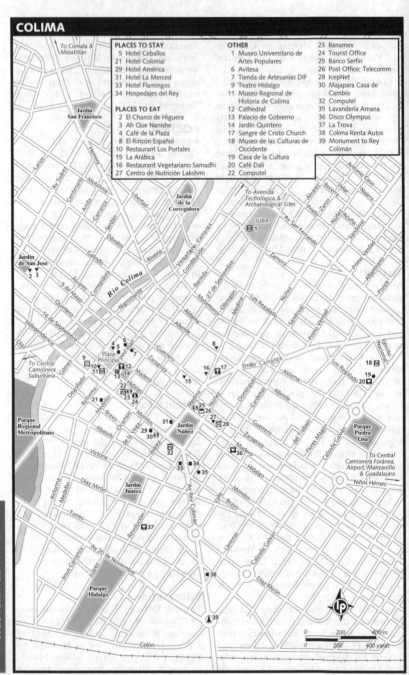

COLIMA

PLACES TO STAY
5   Hotel Ceballos
21 Hotel Colonial
29 Hotel América
31 Hotel La Merced
33 Hotel Flamingos
34 Hospedajes del Rey

PLACES TO EAT
2   El Charco de Higuera
3   Ah Que Nanishe
4   Café de la Plaza
8   El Rincón Español
10 Restaurant Los Portales
15 La Arábica
16 Restaurant Vegetariano Samadhi
27 Centro de Nutrición Lakshmi

OTHER
1   Museo Universitario de Artes Populares
6   Avitesa
7   Tienda de Artesanías DIF
9   Teatro Hidalgo
11 Museo Regional de Historia de Colima
12 Cathedral
13 Palacio de Gobierno
14 Jardín Quintero
17 Sangre de Cristo Church
18 Museo de las Culturas de Occidente
19 Casa de la Cultura
20 Café Dali
22 Computel

23 Banamex
24 Tourist Office
25 Banco Serfin
26 Post Office; Telecomm
28 IcepNet
30 Majapara Casa de Cambio
32 Computel
35 Lavandería Amana
36 Disco Olympus
37 La Trova
38 Colima Renta Autos
39 Monument to Rey Colimán

friendly, helpful staff (some speak English) gives out maps, brochures and information on the city and state of Colima.

Money You can change money at numerous banks around the city center. Banamex, on Hidalgo a block east of the cathedral, has an ATM and is open 9am to 5pm Monday to Friday, 10am to 2pm Saturday. Banco Serfin, on Jardín Núñez, has similar hours.

Majapara Casa de Cambio, at the southwest corner of Jardín Núñez, is open 9am to 2pm and 4.30pm to 7pm Monday to Saturday. Other money changers are nearby.

Post & Communications The post office, at Madero 247, is at the northeast corner of Jardín Núñez. It's open from 8am to 7pm Monday to Friday, 8am to noon Saturday. The Telecomm office, offering telegram, telex and fax services, is one door to the left of the post office. It's open 9am to 8pm Monday to Friday, 9am to 1pm Saturday.

Several pay phones can be found beside Plaza Principal and Jardín Núñez. Computel offices with telephone and fax service are at Morelos 236, facing Jardín Núñez, and Medellín 55, near the corner of Hidalgo (open 7am to 10pm daily).

IcepNet, Madero 295, is a computer school offering public Internet access for US$1.75 per hour. It's open 7am to 9pm daily.

Laundry Lavandería Amana, on Domínguez at Morelos, charges US$3.50 to wash and dry a 3kg load of clothes.

Around Plaza Principal

The **cathedral**, or Santa Iglesia, on the east side of Plaza Principal has been rebuilt several times since the Spanish first erected a cathedral here in 1527. The most recent reconstruction dates from just after the 1941 earthquake.

Next to the cathedral is the **Palacio de Gobierno**, built between 1884 and 1904. Local artist Jorge Chávez Carrillo painted the murals on the stairway to celebrate the 200th anniversary of the birth of independence hero Miguel Hidalgo, who was once parish priest of Colima. The murals depict Mexican history from the Spanish conquest to independence.

On the south side of the plaza, **Portal Morelos** is a handsome colonnade shading

outdoor tables. The **Museo Regional de Historia de Colima** (☎ 312-92-28, Portal Morelos 1; admission US$3; open 9am-6pm Tues-Sat, 5pm-8pm Sun) is well worth a visit to see ceramic vessels and figurines (mostly people and cute Tepezcuintle dogs) unearthed in Colima state. Other permanent displays include masks, textiles, costumes, basketry and shellwork from the Colima coast and exhibits on the 19th- and 20th-century history of the state.

Teatro Hidalgo, on the corner of Degollado and Independencia, one block south of Plaza Principal, was built in neoclassical style between 1871 and 1883 on a site originally donated to the city by Miguel Hidalgo. The theater was destroyed by the earthquakes of 1932 and 1941, and reconstruction was undertaken in 1942.

Museo de las Culturas de Occidente & Casa de la Cultura

The chief attraction of Colima state's large, modern cultural complex is the Museum of Western Cultures (☎ 313-06-08, cnr Calzada Galván & Ejército Nacional; admission US$1.75; open 9am-7pm Tues-Sun), a little over 1km east of the city center. The well-lit museum exhibits hundreds of pre-Hispanic ceramic vessels, figurines and musical instruments from Colima state, with explanations in Spanish. Most impressive are the human figures and Tepezcuintle dogs, but the wide variety of other figures includes mammals, reptiles, fish and birds, depicted with a cartoonlike expressiveness that would make Disney proud.

South of the museum, the Casa de la Cultura is a complex of several architecturally interesting modern buildings. Its art gallery hosts temporary exhibitions and displays a permanent collection of works by renowned Colima modernist painter Alfonso Michel (1897-1957). The Complex also holds a theater and the Edificio de Talleres, a building housing a workshop with a bar/café on the ground floor.

Museo Universitario de Artes Populares

The University Museum of Popular Arts (☎ 312-68-69, cnr 27 de Septiembre & Gallardo; admission US$1, free Sun; open 10am-2pm & 5pm-8pm Tues-Sat, 10am-1pm Sun) is about 900m north of Plaza Principal in the Instituto Universitario de Bellas Artes (IUBA). It displays folk art from Colima and other states, with a particularly good section of costumes and masks used in traditional Colima dances. Other fascinating exhibits include textiles, ceramics, models and furniture.

Adjacent to the museum, the interesting **Taller de Reproducciones** is a workshop making reproductions of ancient Coliman ceramic figures. Some of these figures may be on sale at the museum shop, which stocks an assortment of inexpensive folk-art souvenirs.

Parks

The **Parque Regional Metropolitano**, on Degollado a few blocks southwest of the city center, has a small zoo, a swimming pool, a café and a forest with an artificial lake. You can rent bikes to explore the forest paths, or rowboats to cruise the lake.

East of the city center on Calzada Galván, **Parque Piedra Lisa** is named after its famous Sliding Stone, which is visible from the park entrance (close to the traffic circle where Galván and Aldama meet). Legend says that visitors who slide on this stone will some day return to Colima, either to marry or to die.

Archaeological Sites

On the north side of town are two archaeological sites dating from as early as 1500 BC. Both are still being excavated. **La Campana** (*Avenida Tecnológico s/n; admission US$2.50, free Sun; open 9am-5pm Tues-Sun*) is easily accessible by a No 7 or No 22 bus from the city center. It's next to the Plaza Diamante shopping center. Several low, pyramid-like structures have been excavated and restored, along with a small tomb you can look into and a space that appears to be a ball court (very unusual in western Mexico). The structures seem to be oriented due north toward Volcán de Fuego, which makes an impressive backdrop to the site. The other site, **El Chanal**, is in the countryside about 4km north of Avenida Tecnológico. It's much more difficult to reach and not as interesting.

Special Events

Many masked dances are performed at fiestas in Colima state. The Museo Universitario de Artes Populares has a good display of the masks and costumes worn by the dancers, and plenty of information on the subject. The following festivals take place in or very near Colima city:

Ferias Charro-Taurinas San Felipe de Jesús – For 10 days in late January and early February, this celebration honors the Virgen de la Candelaria (February 2) and takes place in Villa de Álvarez, about 5km north of the city center. Each day of the festival except Tuesday and Friday, a large crowd parades through the streets accompanied by giant *mojigangos* (caricature figures of the village's mayor and wife) and groups of musicians. They start at Colima's cathedral and go to Villa de Álvarez where the celebrations continue with food, music, rodeos and bullfights.

Feria de Todos los Santos – Also called the Feria de Colima, the Colima state fair (late October and early November) includes agricultural and handicraft exhibitions, cultural events and carnival rides.

Día de la Virgen de Guadalupe – From about December 1 to the actual feast day, on December 12, women and children dress in costume to pay homage at the Virgin's altar in the cathedral. In the evenings the Jardín Quintero behind the cathedral fills with busy food stalls.

Places to Stay

Budget Rooms in budget hotels can vary in size, quality and features, so ask to see a couple before registering. *Hotel Colonial* (☎ *313-08-77, Medellín 142*) Singles/doubles with private bath US$17/18, with shared bath US$9/10. This central, old-style hotel is friendly and quite appealing for the price, with 46 clean, cool, well-maintained rooms.

Hotel La Merced (☎ *312-69-69, Juárez 82*) Singles/doubles US$16/19, twins US$20. Another old-style budget place, La Merced is a small tidy hotel with adequate off-street parking. Every room has a private bath and fan, and the twin rooms are generously sized. The best rooms are in the older section well back from the street.

Hotel Flamingos (☎ *312-25-25, Avenida Rey Colimán 18*) Singles/doubles US$14/20. This 1960s-style hotel has 56 clean, modern rooms with private bath and fan. All rooms have balconies and big windows. Rooms on the upper floors offer a view out over the town. The cheapest rooms are small, with a single bed. There's a restaurant on the ground floor.

Hospedajes del Rey (☎ *313-36-83, Rey Colimán 125*) Singles & doubles US$24, twins US$28. The small, friendly Hospeda-jes del Rey has spotless rooms, all with cable TV and fan.

Mid-Range & Top End On the north side of Plaza Principal is *Hotel Ceballos* (☎ 312-44-44, e *hotelceballos@ucol.mx, Portal Medellín 12)* Singles & doubles US$63. This stately building, dating from 1880, has been the home of three state governors. The 63 clean, pleasant rooms have high ceilings, air-con, TV and phone, and some have French windows opening onto small balconies.

Hotel América (☎ 312-74-88, fax 314-44-25, e *hamerica@prodigy.com.mx, Morelos 162)* Singles & doubles about US$65. A modern hotel catering to business travelers and the local wedding and convention trade, the América's 75 spacious rooms have high ceilings, air-con, satellite TV and more.

Places to Eat

The food is good in Colima, thanks to an abundance of fresh fruit and vegetables, savory seafood and choice coffee. Many small restaurants around Plaza Principal offer good simple fare. Some just sell cold drinks, ice cream and frozen juices; others offer meals, snacks and drinks at outdoor tables.

Restaurant Los Portales (☎ 312-85-20, *Portal Morelos 25)* Mains US$3-8. Open 7am-10pm daily. In the *portales* (arched verandas) on the south side of Plaza Principal, this reasonable all-purpose eatery serves Mexican food and *mariscos* (shellfish). The four-course comida corrida is only US$3.

Café de la Plaza (Portal Medellín 20) Mains US$4. Open 8am-10pm Mon-Sat, 8am-5pm Sun. Beside the Hotel Ceballos, this café is particularly pleasant, with high ceilings and a jukebox full of Mexican and US music. Nothing is high priced, and the menu includes a large traditional US- or Mexican-style breakfast.

Ah Que Nanishe (☎ 314-21-97, Calle 5 de Mayo 267) Mains US$5-10. Open 1pm-10pm Wed-Mon. The name of this restaurant means 'How delicious!' – an apt moniker considering the fine Oaxacan specialties served here. Mole fans will have to choose between *mole negro* (a black mole with chocolate, spices and peppers), *mole verde* (made with a variety of vegetables) and *mole colorado* (sweet red mole made with only one solitary chili. Six blocks west of the city center, it's well worth the walk.

El Charco de Higuera (☎ 313-01-92, *Jardín de San José s/n)* Mains US$4-7. This place is also about six blocks west of the city center, beside the little Jardín de San José. The menu is pretty standard, with the usual Mexican soups, antojitos and grills, but the outdoor tables and the lively atmosphere make it an enjoyable place to eat.

El Rincón Español (cellular ☎ 044-312-311-65-18, Medina 167) Mains US$7-12. Tapas, paella and other Spanish dishes are well prepared (if a trifle too salty) and beautifully presented at El Rincón Español, a Spanish restaurant with an elegant courtyard and relaxed indoor spaces.

Restaurant Vegetariano Samadhi (☎ 313-24-98, Medina 125) Mains US$2-3. Open 8.30am-10pm Fri-Wed, 8.30am-6pm Thur. Vegetarians shouldn't miss this restaurant, three blocks north of Jardín Núñez. It occupies an arched courtyard with a large palm tree and other tropical plants. The extensive menu includes soy burgers with salad, mushroom crêpes and fresh fruit and yogurt drinks. The buffet breakfast and the comida corrida are both great value.

Centro de Nutrición Lakshmi (☎ 312-64-33, Madero 265) Healthy snacks and light meals US$2. Near Jardín Núñez, this wholegrain bakery and health-products store also has a café serving light breakfasts, soy burgers, yogurts and more.

La Arábica (☎ 314-70-01, Guerrero 162 near Obregón) Coffee from US$1.25. Open 8am-3pm & 4pm-8.30pm Mon-Sat. La Arábica is a small coffeehouse where people come to chat at the tables in front or on the shady patio out back.

Entertainment

Colima is basically a quiet city, but there are a few things you can do in the evening: hanging around the plaza, lingering over coffee or beer, is a well-practiced pastime here. To help with the relaxed mood, the state band plays in Plaza Principal every Thursday and Sunday from 6pm to 8pm.

Café Dalí (Calzada Galván s/n) Open 6pm-midnight daily. An older clientele comes to this sedate spot for quiet music and romantic atmosphere. Most nights there's a crooner after 9pm.

La Trova (☎ 314-11-59, *Revolución 363*) Open 8pm-2am. This *'bar bohemio'* is another relaxed place with live music, attracting affluent older couples rather than ragged bohemians.

Disco Olympus (☎ 313-42-81, *Madero s/n*) Open 9pm-3am Wed-Sat. About the liveliest place within walking distance of the city is this flashy disco, which is newly popular with local students.

Argenta (☎ 313-80-12, *Sevilla del Río 574*) Open 10pm-3am Wed-Sat. Admission US$0-3. A fashionable hot spot for dance and Latin sounds, the Argenta attracts a mostly well-dressed 20- to 30-something crowd with some very smooth movers. It's a couple of kilometers northeast of the city center. Take a taxi.

Shopping

Tienda de Artesanías DIF (*cnr Zaragoza & Constitución*) This government handicrafts shop, a block north of Plaza Principal, has a good range of Colima artesanías, including attractive reproduction Tepezcuintle dogs.

Getting There & Away

Air Aeromar (☎ 313-55-88) and Aero California (☎ 314-48-50) both serve Mexico City daily (with onward connections) and Tijuana several times a week. Avitesa travel agency (☎ 312-19-84), on the corner of Constitución and Zaragoza, a block north of Plaza Principal, can make flight arrangements.

Bus Colima has two bus stations. The main long-distance terminal is Central Camionera Foránea (also called Terminal Nuevo), 2km east of the city center at the junction of Avenida Niños Héroes and the city's eastern bypass. The terminal has pay phones, a telephone caseta, a pharmacy and some places to eat. Daily departures from here include:

Guadalajara – 220km, 2½ hours; 6 deluxe ETN (US$20); frequent 1st-class Primera Plus, Ómnibus de México, Servicios Coordinados (US$12-14)

Manzanillo – 101km, 1½ hours; 7 deluxe ETN (US$7); many 1st-class La Línea, Primera Plus, Servicios Coordinados (US$4.50); frequent Autobuses Nuevo Horizonte, Autotransportes del Sur de Jalisco 2nd-class (via Tecomán and Armería 2 hours, US$4)

Mexico City (Terminal Norte) – 740km, 10 hours; 1 deluxe ETN (US$66); several 1st-class Primera Plus, Servicios Coordinados and Ómnibus de México (US$47-51); 6 2nd-class Autobuses de Occidente (US$41)

Autobuses de Occidente also runs many buses daily to Ciudad Guzmán, Morelia and Uruapan.

The second bus station is Central Camionera Suburbana, also known as the Terminal Suburbana, about 1.5km west of Plaza Principal on the Carretera a Coquimatlán. This is the station for buses to Comala and nearby places, and for 2nd-class Autobuses Colima-Manzanillo buses, which go frequently to Manzanillo (1½ hours, US$3.50), Tecomán (45 minutes, US$2.50) and Armería (45 minutes, US$2.50).

Getting Around

To/From the Airport Colima's airport is near Cuauhtémoc, 12km northeast of the city center off the highway to Guadalajara. A taxi to or from the city center is about US$14.

Bus & Taxi Local buses (US$0.40) run 6am to 9pm daily. Ruta 4 buses from the Central Camionera Foránea will take you to the city center; to return to the bus station you can catch Ruta 4 on 5 de Mayo or Zaragoza. To reach Central Camionera Suburbana, take a Ruta 2 or Ruta 4 bus west along Morelos. Taxi fares within town are US$1.25 to US$1.75.

Car Colima's not a bad place to rent a car, and you might want one to explore the volcanoes and the nearby villages. Try Colima Renta Autos (☎ 312-95-84), at the junction of Llerenas and Rey Colimán, which has VW beetles at US$44 for one day with 400 free kilometers; less per day for longer periods.

AROUND COLIMA
Comala
• pop 7700 • elev 600m ☎ 312

A picturesque town 9km north of Colima, Comala is known for its fine handicrafts, especially wood furniture. It is also a popular weekend outing from Colima; on Sunday there are markets for browsing.

The plaza has a fine white gazebo, pretty flowering trees and a cute little church. Under the arches along one side of the plaza are some inviting *centros botaneros,* which are bars where minors are allowed (but not served alcohol) and where each beverage is accompanied by a free snack. They're open from about noon to 6pm. Many people come to Comala just to enjoy these restaurants.

Sociedad Cooperativa Artesanías Pueblo Blanco *(☎ 315-56-00, Carretera Colima-Comala Km 6)* Open 9am-6pm Mon-Fri, 9am-2pm Sat. A good place to buy local crafts is this place, which is famous for colonial-style hand-carved furniture, wood paintings and ironwork. It's 1km south of town just beside the road from Colima.

Comala buses leave Colima's Central Camionera Suburbana approximately every 10 minutes; the fare is US$0.80 for the 15-minute ride. In Comala, the buses back to Colima depart from the plaza.

Zona Mágica

Approximately 6km north of Comala there's a stretch of road that seems to slope downhill, but if you let your car roll…hey! It stops, then goes backward. This convincing optical illusion works in both directions: if you're heading south, you can put your car in neutral and it will roll 'uphill.'

Suchitlán

• pop 3200 • elev 1200m ☎ 318

The village of Suchitlán, 8km northeast of Comala and 1km east of the main road, is famous for its animal masks and its witches. The masks are carved in the village and worn by the dancers in the traditional Danza de los Morenos, which takes place here during Semana Santa. The dance commemorates the legend that dancing animals enabled the Marys to rescue Christ's body by distracting the Roman guards. You'll have to ask around for the homes of the mask makers, who often have masks for sale.

Restaurant Portales de Suchitlán *(☎ 395-44-52, Galeana 10)* Mains US$4-9. At the southwest corner of the plaza, this place is popular for a leisurely lunch on Saturday and Sunday. Delicious and inexpensive local cuisine is served at a host of indoor-outdoor tables. The walls are decorated with dozens of animal masks.

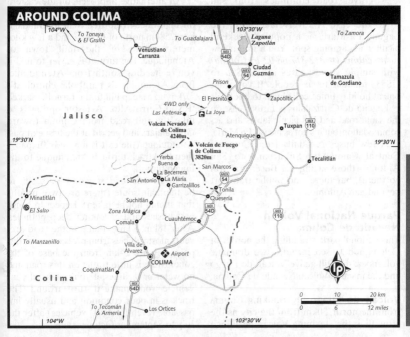

AROUND COLIMA

Buses to Suchitlán leave from Central Camionera Suburbana in Colima.

San Antonio, La María & Carrizalillos

From Suchitlán the road winds about 10km north to the almost invisibly small village of San Antonio. Just before you get there, on the east side of the road, look for signs marking the driveway to *El Jacal de San Antonio*, an unusual restaurant where tables under big *palapas* have an unsurpassed view of Volcán de Fuego de Colima. It's definitely worth a stop, but it's open only on Saturday and Sunday.

Mahakua – Hacienda de San Antonio (☎ *312-313-44-11, fax 312-314-37-27,* ⓦ *www.mahakua.com)* Singles/doubles around US$1030/1158, including all meals, house beverages and activities. The paved road ends here at this superb, superluxurious resort hotel (one of the Aman group) is a beautifully restored and renovated 19th-century *casa grande,* set on a former coffee farm. The suites are fabulously furnished with tapestries, antiques and original artworks.

A gravel road continues from San Antonio to La María, about a kilometer or so to the east. A lovely lake here, the Laguna La María, is a popular weekend picnic and camping spot. You'll find a few rustic *cabins* (☎ *312-317-68-02 in Colima)* with simple stoves; rates are US$25 to US$30 for four to six people. If you want one at holiday times, call ahead to book.

Laguna de Carrizalillos is farther east on the same road and has picnic tables and accommodation, but it's not as nice as La María.

A few buses run daily from Colima's Central Camionera Suburbana to San Antonio (those saying 'La Becerrera' will go there), but there's no public transport beyond San Antonio.

Parque Nacional Volcán Nevado de Colima

This national park, straddling the border of Colima and Jalisco, includes two dramatic volcanoes: the still-active Volcán de Fuego and the inactive Volcán Nevado de Colima.

Volcán de Fuego Overlooking Colima from the north, 30km from the city as the crow flies, the steaming Volcán de Fuego de Colima (3820m) is also called Volcán de Fuego (Volcano of Fire) or Fuego de Colima. It has erupted 30 times in the past four centuries, with a big eruption about every 70 years. A major eruption in 1913 spelled the end of one cycle of activity. Another began in the 1960s and is ongoing. Some 3km of new lava emerged in 1998, and intermittent fireworks persisted in 1999.

No major activity occurred during 2000 and 2001, but the crater continues to emit steam, and ongoing geological monitoring indicates that the volcano is far from dormant. The authorities are maintaining an 'exclusion zone' within a 6.5km radius of the summit, as well as an emergency alert system for all communities within an 11.5km radius. Information on the current condition of the volcano is posted (in Spanish) on the University of Colima's Web site: ⓦ www.ucol.mx/volcan.

The closest accessible settlement to the volcano is the village of Yerba Buena, on the southern slopes, northeast of San Antonio. You'll need your own transport to get there.

An alternative approach, on the eastern slopes, is via the 32km track that turns west off highway 54 (the free road to Guadalajara), 58km north of Colima and a few kilometers south of the mill town of Atenquique. The turnoff is easier to find if you're heading south from Atenquique: from Atenquique's parabolic church it's 2.7km up a steep hill to the turnoff, marked 'RMO Cerro Alto.' A faster option is to take the toll road from Colima toward Guadalajara and get off at the first exit past Atenquique (the exit is marked 'Tuxpan'), then backtrack through Atenquique to the Fuego turnoff.

On the side road, stay on what seems to be the main route (there are two turnoffs that should not be taken). Expect to brush past bushes and encounter deep potholes. After 18km, a large bump in the road prevents most vehicles from proceeding; at this point you are 14km from the base of the cone. There is little traffic on this road and no water or facilities; if you're fearful your vehicle won't make it, turn around. The track is in poor condition and usually impassable (even for 4WD vehicles) after the July to September/October rains.

Volcán Nevado de Colima The higher and more northerly peak of Nevado de Colima (4240m) is accessible for most of the year, but the best months for climbing it are September through February. Remnants of a pine forest cover most of Nevado, and alpine desert appears at the highest altitudes. Snow is possible on the upper slopes between December and March – *nevado* means 'snowy' or 'snow-covered.'

For help with transport and organization, contact the family of Agustín Ibarra (☎ 313-414-70-03), at Montes 85 in the town of El Fresnito. Sr Ibarra no longer does guided treks up the mountain, but his son is sometimes available to provide 4WD transport up the rough road to Las Antenas (the radio masts; also referred to as *micro-ondas,* the microwave station). It's wise to camp here for a night to acclimatize to the altitude, though there are no facilities. Bring all the supplies you'll need, including water. From Las Antenas it's about a 90-minute walk to the top on a reasonably well-marked trail.

If you can't get help with 4WD transport, a car with reasonably good ground clearance should get you as far as La Joya, a *refugio* (mountain hut) at 3500m. A Volkswagen beetle should make it in reasonable road conditions. You can camp here and get drinking water, but don't count on sleeping in the refugio, because it's often locked. From La Joya it's about a 90-minute walk (all uphill) to Las Antenas.

Without a car, it's possible to walk up from El Fresnito to Las Antenas in six to eight hours. It's about 22km, uphill. The Ibarra family has a couple of basic rooms at their house in El Fresnito to rent to climbers.

To get to El Fresnito by car, take the free highway 54 almost to Ciudad Guzmán, some 83km from Colima. Or take the toll route 54D as far as the Tuxpan junction, but at the traffic circle take the free road toward Guadalajara ('Guadalajara Libre'). Shortly before Ciudad Guzmán, turn left (west) at the road to 'El Grullo.' Follow this road west past the conspicuous prison, and continue 3.4km to near the village of El Fresnito. On the way you'll pass a small side road to the left with a sign 'Viajes al Nevado....' This directs you to the Ibarras' house. At El Fresnito, the road turns sharply right. Continue 1km to a side road climbing steeply on your left. On this rough road, by

4WD it will take almost two hours to cover the 20km to the *refugio* of La Joya and another 20 minutes to reach Las Antenas.

By bus, take one of the frequent Autotransportes del Sur de Jalisco 2nd-class buses from Colima's main bus station to Ciudad Guzmán (1½ hours, US$3.75). From there, take another bus to El Fresnito. They are much more frequent in the morning.

Tampumacchay
Some interesting shaft tombs from about AD 200 perch on the edge of a ravine at Tampumacchay, near the town of Los Ortices about 15km south of Colima. For a small fee you can enter the tombs and someone will guide you around. Buses go from Colima's Central Camionera Suburbana to Los Ortices, but you'll have to walk the last 5km unless you happen upon a taxi.

Minatitlán
* pop 4000 * elev 740m
Minatitlán is an iron-ore mining town 55km west of Colima. It's on a scenic route through the mountains from Colima to the coast that drivers might consider as a long alternative to the main toll road or the main free road. About 7km south of Minatitlán, in the direction of Manzanillo, is a lovely waterfall with a natural swimming pool. The last half kilometer to the waterfall is on a steep section of road better traveled on foot.

Inland Michoacán

Michoacán is a beautiful state pierced by the Cordillera Neovolcánica, the volcanic range that gives the region both fertile soils and a striking mountainous landscape. Along a 200km stretch of the cordillera across the northern part of Michoacán are found a number of fascinating destinations, including the spectacular Monarch Butterfly Reserve; the handsome state capital, Morelia; the beautiful colonial town of Pátzcuaro, set near scenic Lago de Pátzcuaro; the town of Uruapan, with its miniature tropical national park; and the famous Volcán Paricutín, a short distance beyond Uruapan.

The name Michoacán is an Aztec word meaning 'Place of the Masters of Fish.' Northern Michoacán was once an extensive

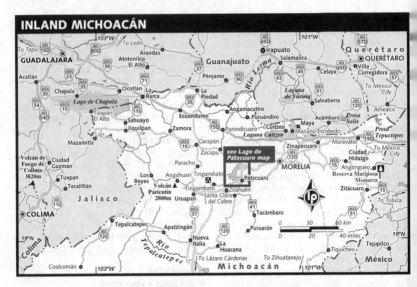

region of lakes, but most were drained to create farmland during the colonial period. Traditional 'butterfly' nets are still used on Lago de Pátzcuaro, although nowadays the catch is more tourists' pesos than fish.

The more tropical coastal areas of Michoacán, reached by spectacular highway 37 down through the hills from Uruapan, are covered in the Central Pacific Coast chapter.

MORELIA

• pop 537,000 • elev 1920m ☎ 443

Morelia, the capital of Michoacán, lies in the northeastern part of the state, 315km west of Mexico City and 278km southeast of Guadalajara. It's a well-preserved colonial city with a university, an active cultural scene and a number of language schools offering Spanish courses. It's a good place for an extended visit, as many foreigners have discovered.

Morelia was one of the first Spanish cities in Nueva España, officially founded in 1541, although a Franciscan monastery had been in the area since 1537. The first viceroy, Antonio de Mendoza, named it Valladolid after the Spanish city of that name, and he encouraged families of Spanish nobility to move here. The families remained and maintained Valladolid as a very Spanish city, at least architecturally, until 1828.

By that time, Nueva España had become the independent republic of Mexico, and the city had been renamed Morelia in honor of local hero José María Morelos y Pavón, a key figure in Mexico's independence movement.

Morelia's downtown streets are lined with colonial buildings, and it still looks nearly as Spanish as it did before independence. City ordinances require that all new construction in the city center be done in colonial style with arches, baroque façades and walls of pink stone.

Orientation

The imposing, twin-towered cathedral is the center of town and a major landmark. It's flanked on its east side by the Plaza Ocampo and on its west side by the handsome Plaza de Armas (also called the zócalo). Almost everything of interest is within walking distance of here.

Avenida Madero, along the north side of the zócalo, is the major downtown avenue; to the west of the cathedral it's Madero Pte, to the east it's Madero Ote. Other east-west streets change names at the cathedral while north-south streets change names at Madero. On Madero, the elegant row of arched verandas facing the zócalo is commonly called Portal Hidalgo; the arches on Abasolo facing the west side of the plaza are called Portal Matamoros. Ten blocks

MORELIA

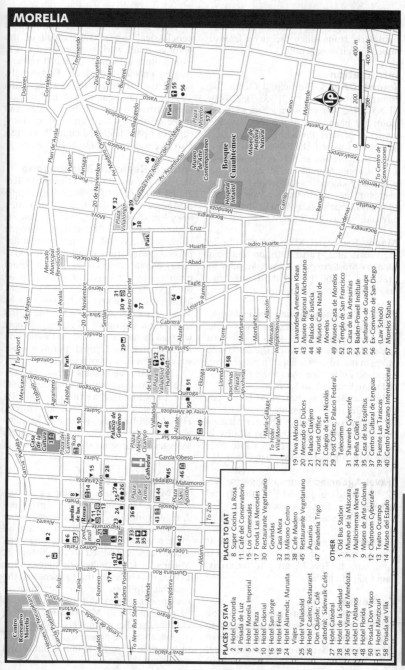

PLACES TO STAY
2 Hotel Concordia
4 Posada de Luz
5 Hotel Morelia Imperial
6 Hotel Plaza
10 Hotel Colonial
16 Hotel San Jorge
18 Hotel Fénix
24 Hotel Alameda; Maruata Viajes
25 Hotel Valladolid
26 Hotel Casino; Restaurant Don Quijote; Café Catedral; Sidewalk Cafés
27 Hotel Catedral
28 Hotel de la Soledad
32 Hotel Virrey de Mendoza
42 Hotel D'Atilanos
48 Hotel Florida
50 Posada Don Vasco
51 Hotel Mintzicuri
58 Posada de Villa

PLACES TO EAT
8 Super Cocina La Rosa
11 Café del Conservatorio
15 Los Comensales
17 Fonda Las Mercedes
30 Restaurante Vegetariano Govindas
32 Casa Mora
33 Mikono Centro
38 Cafe Madero
45 Restaurante Vegetariano Acuarius
47 Panadería Trigo

OTHER
1 Old Bus Station
3 Museo de la Máscara
7 Multicinemas Morelia
9 Museo de Arte Colonial
12 Chatroom Cybercafe
13 Teatro Ocampo
14 Museo del Estado
19 Viva México
20 Mercado de Dulces
21 Palacio Clavijero
22 Tourist Office
23 Colegio de San Nicolás
29 Post Office; Palacio Federal; Telecomm
31 Shareweb Cybercafe
34 Peña Colibrí
35 Casa de los Espíritus
37 Centro Cultural de Lenguas
39 Fuente Las Tarascas
40 Centro Mexicano Internacional
41 Lavandería American Klean
43 Museo Regional Michoacano
44 Palacio de Justicia
46 Museo Casa Natal de Morelos
49 Museo Casa de Morelos
52 Templo de San Francisco
53 Casa de las Artesanías
54 Baden-Powell Institute
55 Santuario de Guadalupe
56 Ex-Convento de San Diego (Law School)
57 Morelos Statue

WESTERN CENTRAL

east of the cathedral on Madero, the Fuente Las Tarascas (Tarascan Fountain) is another landmark, from which the city's famous aqueduct runs southeast.

Information

Tourist Offices The helpful Oficina de Información Turística (☎ 317-23-71, 312-80-81, 800-450-23-00, W www.michoacan-travel .com) is a block west of the zócalo on the corner of Madero Pte and Nigromante, on an outside corner of the Palacio Clavijero. It has free maps and leaflets in Spanish and English about Morelia and Michoacán, plus a monthly calendar of films and cultural events in the city. Hours are 9am to 8pm Monday through Friday, 9am to 7pm Saturday and 9am to 3pm Sunday.

Money Banks and ATMs are plentiful in the zócalo area, particularly on and near Madero. Most are open all day Monday to Friday and until 2pm Saturday, but some may change currency only until about 1pm.

Post & Communications The main post office is in the Palacio Federal, Madero Ote 369, and open 8am to 4pm Monday to Friday, 8am to 1pm Saturday. The Telecomm office, in the same building, offers telegram, telex and fax services 9am to 8pm Monday to Friday, 9am to 1pm Saturday.

Internet access is available at Chatroom Cybercafe, on Nigromante, just north of Ocampo. It's open to about 10pm most days ($1.75 per hour). Another possibility is Shareweb Cybercafe, Madero Ote 573, open daily till 10pm (US$1.50 per hour).

Travel Agencies Maruata Viajes (☎ 317-12-10), Madero Pte 313 in the Hotel Alameda building, is a central agency for air and ETN bus tickets.

Laundry Lavandería American Klean, at Corregidora 787 on the corner of Bravo, is open 9am to 7pm Monday to Saturday, 9am to 2pm Sunday.

Cathedral

The cathedral dominating the zócalo took more than a century to build, from 1640 to 1744. Architecturally, it is a combination of Herreresque, baroque and neoclassical styles. Its twin 70m-high towers, for instance, have classical Herreresque bases, baroque midsections and multicolumned neoclassical tops. Inside, much of the baroque relief work was replaced in the 19th century with more balanced and calculated neoclassical pieces. Fortunately, one of the cathedral's interior highlights was preserved: a sculpture of the Señor de la Sacristía made from dried maize and topped with a gold crown from the 16th-century Spanish king, Felipe II. There's also a very large organ with 4600 pipes.

Museo Regional Michoacano

Just off the zócalo, the Michoacán Regional Museum (☎ 312-04-07, Allende 305 & Abasolo; admission US$3.50, free Sun; open 9am-7pm Tues-Sat, 9am-2pm Sun) is housed in the late-18th-century baroque palace of Isidro Huarte. The museum displays a great variety of pre-Hispanic artifacts, colonial art and relics, contemporary paintings by local artists and exhibits on the geology and fauna of the region. A highlight is the mural on the stairway by Mexican painter Alfredo Alce. The mural is in halves: the right half portrays people who have had a positive influence on Mexico, while the left half portrays those who have had a negative influence.

The **Palacio de Justicia**, across Abasolo from the museum, was built between 1682 and 1695 to serve as the city hall. Its façade is an eclectic but well-done mix of French and baroque styles, and the stairway in the courtyard has a dramatic mural by Agustín Cárdenas showing Morelos in action.

Museo del Estado

The Michoacán State Museum (☎ 313-06-29, Prieto 176; admission free; open 9am-2pm & 4pm-8pm Mon-Fri, 9am-2pm & 4pm-7pm Sat, Sun & holidays) is a good place to learn about this interesting state. Downstairs is devoted to the history of Michoacán from prehistoric times to the first contact between the Tarascos and the Spanish. Upstairs, the story continues to the present, with exhibits on many aspects of modern life in Michoacán including clothing, handicrafts and agriculture.

Ask about the program of free cultural events such as regional music, dance and *artesanías*.

Morelos Sites

José María Morelos y Pavón, one of the most important figures in Mexico's struggle for independence from Spain, was born in the house on the corner of Corregidora and García Obeso on September 30, 1765. Two centuries later, the house was declared a national monument and made into the **Museo Casa Natal de Morelos** (*Morelos Birthplace Museum,* ☎ *312-27-93, Corregidora 113; admission free; open 9am-7pm Mon-Fri*). Morelos memorabilia fill two rooms; a public library, auditorium and projection room occupy the rest of the house. An eternal torch burns next to the projection room. Free international films and cultural events are held at the museum (see Entertainment).

In 1801 Morelos bought the Spanish-style house on the corner of Avenida Morelos and Soto y Saldaña. He added a second story in 1806. This house is now the **Museo Casa de Morelos** (*Morelos House Museum,* ☎ *313-85-06, Morelos Sur 323; admission US$2.50, free Sun; open 9am-7pm daily*), with exhibits on Morelos' life and his role in the independence movement.

Morelos studied at the **Colegio de San Nicolás** (*cnr Madero Pte & Nigromante*), one block west of the zócalo. The Colegio later became the foundation for the Universidad Michoacana and is still in use as a part of the university. Upstairs, the Sala de Melchor Ocampo is a memorial room to another Mexican hero, a reformer and governor of Michoacán. Here are preserved Ocampo's library and a copy of the document he signed to donate his library to the college, just before being shot by firing squad on June 3, 1861. Visitors can enter the university buildings Monday to Friday during term time.

Palacio Clavijero & Mercado de Dulces

From 1660 to 1767, the Clavijero Palace was home to the Jesuit school of St Francis Xavier. After the Jesuits were expelled from Spanish dominions, the building served variously as a warehouse, prison and seat of the state legislature. In 1970 it was completely restored and renovated for use as state government offices. The majestic main patio has imposing colonnades and stonework so pink it almost glows. Look for the elaborate carvings over the main entrance on Nigromante.

Be sure to visit the arcade on the western side of the palace to taste some of the goodies on sale in the **Mercado de Dulces** (*Market of Sweets, open 9am-10pm daily*). Some folksy Michoacán handicrafts and souvenirs are also sold in the arcade, but for high-quality handicrafts you'll do better at the Casa de las Artesanías.

Casa de la Cultura & Around

Three blocks north of the cathedral, facing Plaza del Carmen in baroque buildings that were once a church and convent, the Casa de la Cultura hosts dance and music performances, films and art exhibitions. Stop by for a free monthly brochure describing cultural events in the city. Inside the Casa de la Cultura, the **Museo de la Máscara** (☎ *313-13-20, Avenida Morelos Nte 485; admission free; open 10am-2pm & 4pm-8pm Mon-Fri, 10am-6pm Sat & Sun*) has masks from around Mexico, each labeled with the ethnic group and the particular dance it's associated with.

South of Plaza del Carmen, the **Museo de Arte Colonial** (☎ *313-92-60, Juárez 240; admission free; open 10am-2pm & 5pm-8pm daily*) contains 18th-century religious paintings, crucifixes and some models of galleons.

Casa de las Artesanías

The House of Handicrafts (☎ *312-12-48, Plaza Valladolid; open 10am-3pm & 5pm-8pm daily*) occupies the Ex-Convento de San Francisco, attached to the Templo de San Francisco, three blocks east of the zócalo. Arts and handicrafts from all over Michoacán are displayed and sold; they're expensive but some of the best you'll see anywhere in the state. There's also a small selection of cassettes of regional music. Upstairs, small shops represent many of Michoacán's towns, with craftspeople demonstrating how the specialties of their area are made. You'll find guitars from Paracho, copperware from Santa Clara del Cobre, lacquerware, weaving and much more. The shops keep individual hours, which may vary somewhat from those listed above.

Fuente Las Tarascas & El Acueducto

At the east end of Madero Ote, nine blocks from the cathedral, the *fuente* (fountain) spouts from a tray of fruit

José María Morelos

One of Mexico's greatest heroes, the priest and revolutionary José María Morelos y Pavón (1765-1815) gives his name to streets and plazas all over the country. His home city of Valladolid was renamed Morelia in his honor. Noted for his determination, Morelos came from a humble mestizo family and was well educated at the city's Colegio de San Nicolás, where Miguel Hidalgo was rector. Hidalgo, even then, had fallen out of favor because of his unorthodox views, and he was later transferred to become a parish priest in rural Dolores, where the church authorities hoped he would be less influential.

Morelos was ordained in 1797, at a time when the Catholic Church was a hotbed of anti-Spanish sentiment. Priests saw firsthand the effects of Spanish policies on the poor of Mexico, and the Spanish crown greatly alienated the church by an 1804 decree confiscating church assets. Along with other priests, Morelos was active in a secret society working toward independence. The group included Hidalgo, who launched the independence war with his famous Grito (Cry for Independence) in September 1810.

Valladolid was among the first towns to fall to the independence movement, and from here Hidalgo's ragtag army began its ill-fated march toward Mexico City. After two major defeats and the capture and beheading of Hidalgo and three other insurgent leaders in 1811, Morelos became commander of the insurgent forces. For a man trained as a Catholic priest, Morelos had an amazing talent for military leadership, reorganizing and equipping his small army and leading it to a string of victories over well-trained royalist forces. From February to May 1812, Morelos and his troops held the town of Cuautla against great odds, then escaped the siege and went on to defeat the royalist forces at Orizaba and Oaxaca. In his most brilliant tactical encounter, Morelos led the capture of Fuerte de San Diego, and hence the port of Acapulco, in 1812. In all these towns, Morelos established a well-organized administration to protect and assist the people.

By spring 1813 Morelos' forces had encircled Mexico City. He then attempted to impose a unity of purpose on the various factions within the independence movement. Convening a congress in Chilpancingo, Morelos proclaimed his Sentimientos de la Nación, a statement of his goals for the new nation. They included independence from Spain, the abolition of slavery, equality before the law, free trade and the protection of private property. After months of debate, the Congress of Chilpancingo incorporated his principles in its Declaration of Independence, and Morelos emerged as a social and political visionary as well as a military genius.

Unfortunately, this time-out for independence politics enabled the royalists to regroup, and led by General Félix Calleja they broke the circle around Mexico City and inflicted a major defeat on Morelos at his home town of Valladolid in late 1813. Forced to fight a running, defensive campaign, and weakened by disputes within the independence movement, Morelos was defeated again and taken prisoner. He was first disgraced and defrocked by the Inquisition, then handed over to the Spanish authorities, who executed him by firing squad on December 22, 1815.

Now the stern face of Morelos frowns from murals, monuments and banknotes all over the country, and the question many ask is – why does he always have that handkerchief tied around his head? None of the other independence heroes has one, so it couldn't be a military uniform or an early 19th-century fashion statement. Contemporaries of Morelos noted that he suffered badly from headaches, and he apparently tied a cloth (called a *paleacatte*) tightly around his head to relieve the pain. Looking at portraits of Morelos, it's easy to imagine he was a man under pressure, and one wonders whether his biggest headache was fighting a guerrilla war, trying to forge Mexico's races and classes into a nation, or contemplating the fate of Hidalgo and the other leaders who had lost their heads for the independence cause.

supported by three bare-breasted Tarascan women. The original fountain here vanished mysteriously in 1940, and this replacement was installed in the 1960s. Adjacent Plaza Villalongin has another fine fountain.

El Acueducto (the Aqueduct) runs for several kilometers along Avenida Acueducto and makes a couple of bends around Plaza Villalongin. The aqueduct was built between 1785 and 1788 to meet the city's growing water needs. Its 253 arches make an impressive sight, especially at night when they are illuminated by floodlights.

Plaza Morelos & Around

Running roughly east from the Fuente Las Tarascas, the cobbled Calzada Fray Antonio de San Miguel is a broad and elegant pedestrian promenade lined by fine old buildings. It leads about 500m to Plaza Morelos, an irregular but finely proportioned space surrounding the landmark **Estatua Ecuestre al Patriota Morelos**, a statue of Morelos on horseback trotting to battle. Sculpted by the Italian artist Giuseppe Ingillieri between 1910 and 1913, it makes a fine focal point in this very attractive area.

On the northeast edge of the plaza, the **Santuario de Guadalupe** is a lavishly overdone baroque church built 1708-16; the ornate mauve-and-gold interior, the icing on the cake, dates from 1915. Beside the church, the **Ex-Convento de San Diego** was built in 1761 as a monastery and now houses the law school of the Universidad Michoacana. Check the elaborate façade, and look inside to see the bronze fountain.

The aqueduct delineates the south side of the plaza, and on the other side of that is **Bosque Cuauhtémoc**, a large park with lots of trees, children's amusements and a couple of museums. The **Museo de Arte Contemporáneo** (☎ 312-54-04, Acueducto 18; admission free; open 10am-2pm & 4pm-8pm Tues-Sat, 10am-5pm Sun) is a French-style 19th-century building housing a permanent collection of works by modern Mexican artists, as well as changing exhibitions of contemporary art. The small **Museo de Historia Natural** (☎ 312-00-44, Calzada Puente s/n), on the east side of the park, has displays of stuffed, dissected and skeletal animals.

Centro de Convenciones

The Convention Center complex, about 1.5km south of Bosque Cuauhtémoc on Calzada Ventura Puente, holds several places of interest on its extensive parklike grounds. You can reach it on the Ruta Roja (red) combi heading east on Tapia or 20 de Noviembre.

Inside the complex are the **Planetario de Morelia** (☎ 314-24-65; shows US$2.25, 7pm Fri & Sat, 5pm & 6.30pm Sun), a planetarium with 164 projectors simulating stars on a dome 20m in diameter; and the **Orquidario** (Orchid House, ☎ 314-62-02; admission US$0.50; open 9am-6pm Mon-Fri, 10.30am-3pm & 4pm-6pm Sat & Sun), which exhibits nearly 3000 species of wild and hybrid orchids.

Parque Zoológico Benito Juárez

The zoo (☎ 314-04-88, Calzada Juárez s/n; admission US$1.50; open 10am-5pm daily) is 3km south of the zócalo. It's a pleasant place with many animals in naturalistic settings, a lake with rowboats for hire, a small train, picnic areas and a playground.

The Ruta Guinda (pink) combi, heading south on Nigromante from the stop on the east side of the Palacio Clavijero, will drop you at the zoo entrance.

Markets

Mercado Independencia is on Ruiz de Alarcón, about 10 blocks southeast of the zócalo; and **Mercado Municipal Revolución** is on the corner of Revolución and Plan de Ayala, about 10 blocks northeast of the zócalo.

Courses

Several schools in Morelia offer Spanish-language and Mexican-culture courses.

Centro Cultural de Lenguas (☎/fax 312-05-89, Ⓦ www.ccl.com.mx, Madero Ote 560) Group lessons US$220 per week, private lessons US$260 per week. This centrally located school offers Spanish-language courses running from two to four weeks, four hours daily (three hours of classroom work and an hour spent on workshops related to Mexican history, literature and culture). Living with Mexican families is encouraged (US$18 to US$20 per day, including all meals) and organized by the school.

Baden-Powell Institute (☎/fax 312-40-70, [W] *www.baden-powell.com, Alzate 565)* Private lessons US$12 per hour. Three blocks south of Madero Ote on Alzate, this small school offers courses in Spanish language, as well as Mexican politics, cooking, culture, guitar playing and folk dancing. This is done mostly on a one-to-one basis, although group classes can be arranged. Most students take four hours of instruction per day. Lodging with a Mexican family is US$20 per day, including three meals.

Centro Mexicano Internacional (☎ 312-45-96, fax 313-98-98, [W] *www.spanish-language.com, Calzada Fray Antonio de San Miguel 173)* Intensive courses US$358/485/700/915 for 1/2/3/4 weeks. In a large colonial building, this school offers courses in Spanish language and Mexican culture. Classes run four hours daily in groups of five or fewer students. Family living costs about US$17 a day.

Organized Tours

Tranvía Kuanari (cellular ☎ 044-443-027-74-09, cnr Jardín de las Rosas & Nigromante) Tours US$3. This company offers two different loop tours of the city in imitation antique trolley cars.

For organized tours to places outside the city, ask the tourist office to recommend an authorized guide or tour company. One good one is *Mex Mich Guías (☎ 320-11-57,* [e] *mexmich@prodigy.net.mx,* [W] *www.mmg.com.mx),* which provides personalized tours and transport to many area destinations, including the monarch butterfly reserve.

Special Events

As well as the usual Mexican celebrations, Morelia's many annual festivals include:

Feria de Morelia – Morelia's major fair sports exhibits of handicrafts, agriculture and livestock from around Michoacán, plus regional dances, bullfights and fiestas. The anniversary of the founding of Morelia in 1541 is celebrated on May 18 with fireworks, displays of historical photos and more; three weeks in mid-May.

Feria de Órgano – This international organ festival is held during the first two weeks of the Feria de Morelia.

Festival Internacional de Música – International music festival occurs the last week of July and first week of August.

Cumpleaños de Morelos – Morelos' birthday is celebrated with a parade, fireworks and more; September 30.

Día de la Virgen de Guadalupe – The Day of the Virgin of Guadalupe is celebrated on December 12 at the Templo de San Diego; in the preceding weeks, typical Mexican foods are sold on the pedestrian street Calzada Fray Antonio de San Miguel.

Feria Navideña – Christmas Fair, with traditional Christmas items, foods and handicrafts from Michoacán, is celebrated approximately December 1 to January 6.

Places to Stay

Budget *Las Villas (☎ 313-31-77, cnr Oaxaca & Chiapas)* Dorm beds US$9. Open 7am-11pm. The cheapest place to stay in Morelia is this hostel in the Imjude sports complex, a 20-minute walk southwest of the zócalo. The hostel is clean and has separate men's and women's areas, with four beds and a locker in each room. HI members get a discount. The complex houses a pool, gym and several athletic fields.

Hotel Colonial (☎ 312-18-97, 20 de Noviembre 15) Singles/doubles US$12/16, US$18/20 with TV. This 25-room colonial-style hotel is two blocks northeast of the cathedral. Street-facing rooms are large, with high beamed ceilings and small balconies, but they catch a lot of traffic noise. The interior rooms are quieter.

Posada de Luz (☎ 317-48-78, Calle del Trabajo 23) Singles/doubles US$13/16, US$20 with two beds. Opposite the Casa de la Cultura, Posada de Luz offers small, clean, colorful, cheerful rooms with private bath and TV.

Hotel Fénix (☎ 312-05-12, Madero Pte 537) Singles/doubles US$10/13 with private bath, US$7/9 with shared bath. A few blocks west of the city center, Fénix offers basic, clean, well-maintained rooms with firm mattresses. There's no shortage of hot water, and it's a good value for its central location. The hotel even has a couple of parking spaces available.

Hotel San Jorge (☎ 312-46-10, Victoria 26) Singles/doubles from US$11/14. Four blocks west of the city center, the San Jorge has a variety of rooms, some much bigger, brighter and better furnished than others. Ask to see the room before registering.

Posada Don Vasco (☎ 312-14-84, Vasco de Quiroga 232) Singles/doubles US$17/21.

Southeast of the city center, this colonial-style hotel has rooms around a courtyard with sitting areas and plants. The rooms are varied, but all have carpet, phone and private bath. The price is a real bargain if you get one of the better rooms.

Hotel Mintzicuri (☎ 312-05-90, *Vasco de Quiroga 227*) Singles/doubles US$17/21. Just opposite the Don Vasco, the Mintzicuri has 37 small, clean rooms around a courtyard. All have carpet and a phone, and some parking is available. A few larger rooms are available at higher prices.

Posada de Villa (☎ 312-72-90, *Padre Lloreda 176*) Singles/doubles US$15/19. About 10 blocks southeast of the city center, this comfortable motel-style place is not elegant, but it has spacious, comfortable rooms and plenty of parking.

Mid-Range Several relatively modern hotels around the old bus station offer reasonable standards and are not far from the city center, but the area is unappealing and possibly unsafe at night.

Hotel Plaza (☎ 312-30-95, *Gómez Farías 278*) Singles/doubles US$22/27. Nowhere near a plaza, this modern hotel offers clean and comfortable rooms. The rooms facing the street have little balconies and big windows, but interior rooms are quieter.

Hotel Concordia (☎ 312-30-53, *Gómez Farías 328*) Singles/doubles US$27/30. Very similar to the Hotel Plaza, the Concordia has slightly less character and slightly better rooms.

Hotel Morelia Imperial (☎ 313-23-00, 800-711-16-62, *Guadalupe Victoria 245*) Singles & doubles from US$35. About eight blocks from the heart of town, but miles away in character, this modern, business travelers' hotel has a bar, conference rooms and 110 clean, pleasant rooms, all with TV, phone and carpet. Other amenities include plenty of enclosed parking and a popular restaurant at the center of a covered courtyard.

The center of town is a delightful area to be, and the lodgings have a lot more character.

Hotel Casino (☎ 313-13-28, 800-450-21-00, ⓦ *www.hotelcasino.com.mx, Portal Hidalgo 229*) Singles/doubles US$49/65. On the north side of the zócalo, this Best Western hotel has 48 cozy rooms, all with carpet, phone and color TV. Those facing

the street have balconies overlooking the zócalo; the interior rooms open onto a covered courtyard with a popular restaurant on the ground floor. Special discount prices are sometimes available.

Hotel Valladolid (☎ 312-46-63, *Portal Hidalgo 241 cnr Prieto*) Singles & doubles from US$38. In the historic block facing the north side of the Plaza de Armas, this hotel has a great location, an elegant lobby and OK rooms.

Hotel D'Atilanos (☎ 312-01-21, *Corregidora 465*) Singles/doubles US$25/28. About four blocks southwest of the city center, this well-kept colonial-style hotel has 27 large, comfy rooms, all with color TV and phone, arranged around a covered courtyard. It's nice, but customer relations could be better.

Hotel Florida (☎ 312-18-19, *Morelos Sur 161*) Singles/doubles US$25/36. Just a block southeast of the cathedral, this hotel is well located, clean and comfortable enough, but doesn't offer much charm.

Top End A range of prices exists even among these top properties. *Hotel Catedral* (☎ 313-04-67, ⓔ *hotel_catedral@infosel .net.mx, Zaragoza 37*) Singles & doubles US$89. This hotel has a great location opposite the cathedral, though the entrance is around the corner on the side street. It's a very attractive colonial-style hotel with cushy rooms around a covered courtyard. The price is OK if you get one of the lovely rooms with a view of the cathedral; if you take one of the other rooms, try for a discount.

Hotel de la Soledad (☎ 312-18-88, *Zaragoza 90*) Singles/doubles US$73/82. This gorgeous colonial building was built in about 1700. It has been a carriage house, a convent and a private mansion. Just a block north of the cathedral, it has 49 standard rooms plus nine suites.

Hotel Alameda (☎ 312-20-23, ⓦ *www .hotel-alameda.com.mx, Madero Pte 313*) Singles & doubles US$81. Thoroughly modernized, but with old-fashioned charm, the Alameda is ideally situated on the corner of the zócalo. It offers business facilities, a popular restaurant and bar, and great views from its rooftop.

Hotel Virrey de Mendoza (☎ 312-49-40, ⓦ *www.hotelmex.com/hotelvirrey, Madero Pte 310*) Singles & doubles from US$81, suites US$119-263. Undoubtedly the classiest accommodations in Morelia, the former mansion of Antonio de Mendoza, the first viceroy of Mexico, has been converted to a hotel with magnificent public areas. The 55 rooms and suites are all different and all elegantly furnished with antiques and crystal chandeliers. It's wonderful.

Hotel Villa Montaña (☎ 314-02-31, *Patzimba 201*) Singles & doubles US$130-255, presidential suite US$330. About 3km south of the city center, in one of Morelia's best suburbs, the Villa Montaña offers sweeping views over the city. The 40 spacious rooms are like cottages in a lush garden and have all the modern conveniences. The heated swimming pool is especially attractive.

Places to Eat

Dulces morelianos – delicious sweets made mainly of milk and sugar – are a local specialty. Try them at street stalls, markets and *dulcerías*.

Plaza San Agustín (*cnr Abasolo & Corregidora*) One block south of the zócalo, this plaza has food stalls and tables under the covered arches running around three of its sides. The vendors serve all manner of Mexican meals, snacks and taste treats from approximately 3pm until 1am daily. It's an entertaining and economical place to eat.

Super Cocina La Rosa (☎ 313-08-52, *cnr Tapia & Prieto*) Mains about US$2.25. Open 8.30am-4.30pm. For an inexpensive breakfast or lunch in a friendly family setting, stop by this unpretentious place, two blocks north of the plaza. Try a filling comida corrida (US$3.50), or select a typical Mexican main course.

On the north side of the zócalo, under the arches of Portal Hidalgo, is a row of restaurants and sidewalk cafés open from about 8am to 10pm daily.

Café Catedral (☎ 312-32-89, *Portal Hidalgo 211*) Light meals from US$3. Some local people seem to spend the whole day at the sidewalk tables here, lingering over coffee, snacks, or a light meal in the evening. You could do worse.

Restaurant Don Quijote (☎ 313-13-28, *Portal Hidalgo 229*) Light meals US$2-5. This popular restaurant at the Hotel Casino has tables both inside and out on the sidewalk. The *menú del día* makes a substantial lunch, and you get great people-watching in the early evening for the price of a beer.

Other inexpensive eateries within a few blocks of the cathedral cater to shoppers, students and others not in a hurry.

Café del Conservatorio (☎ 312-86-01, *Tapia 363*) Mains US$5-8. Open 8am-10pm Mon-Fri, noon-10pm Sat & Sun. A peaceful place to have coffee is this often-busy café facing the shady Jardín de las Rosas. Classical music plays as you nibble on a pastry or bite into a baguette while sipping wine, coffee or juice.

Panadería Trigo (☎ 313-42-32, *Valladolid 8*) Light meals about US$3. Open 7am-9pm. A popular stop for shoppers is this bakery and deli off the southeast corner of Plaza Melchor Ocampo. The café upstairs serves delicious breakfasts, light lunches and substantial sandwiches for moderate prices.

Mikono Centro (☎ 312-40-44, *Madero Pte 410*) Meals US$6-10. Open noon-11pm. For something different, get your sushi or sashimi fix here.

If you're visiting the aqueduct and Fuente Las Tarascas, you can find refreshment and a place to sit down at any of several places around Plaza Villalongin. On the south side of the plaza, *Cafe Madero* does a good line in coffee and ice cream, while on the northeast side, duck under the aqueduct to *Casa Mora*, a pleasant place that doubles as a crafts shop.

For more formal dining, Morelia has some truly excellent restaurants combining fine food and superb settings.

Fonda Las Mercedes (☎ 312-61-13, *Guzmán 47*) Mains US$9-15. Open 1.30pm-midnight. You can choose a table in a classic covered courtyard with stately potted palms, or in a vast stone hall with atmospheric lighting and an open fire. The imaginative, international menu offers a fine choice of pasta dishes and main courses using chicken, beef or seafood. The house specialty is *sábana Mercedes*: grilled, thinly sliced fillet of beef lightly covered with fresh parsley, garlic and olive oil. One delicious serving covers an entire dinner plate (veggies and a baked potato arrive separately). The fruit crêpe is a divine dessert. Budget on US$20 or so per person, and it will be a highlight of your trip.

Los Comensales (☎ 312-93-61, *Zaragoza 148*) Mains US$5-12. Open 8am-10pm daily. This is another restaurant with great atmosphere, 1½ blocks north of the zócalo. The restaurant has tables in several rooms of a lovely colonial building and under the arches around its central courtyard. The menu is mainly Mexican, with antojitos, lots of seafood choices, chicken mole, steak or sizzling paella.

Vegetarian *Restaurante Vegetariano Acuarius* (☎ 368-95-96, Hidalgo 75) Light meals US$3-4. Open 9am-5pm daily. South of the zócalo in an informal covered courtyard, this restaurant makes healthy breakfasts combining fruit, yogurt and granola. For lunch there's a good comida corrida featuring salad, soup and veggie burgers.

Restaurante Vegetariano Govindas (Madero Ote 549) Mains about US$3. Open 1pm-7pm. This upstairs café serves soy burgers, salads, soups and vegetarian versions of Mexican standards.

Entertainment

Being a university town as well as the capital of one of Mexico's most interesting states, Morelia has a lively cultural life. Stop by the tourist office or the Casa de la Cultura for *Cartelera Cultural,* a free weekly listing of films and cultural events around Morelia, published every Monday. Daily newspapers *El Sol de Morelia, La Voz de Michoacán* and *El Cambio de Michoacán* have cultural sections with events notices and theater and cinema ads.

International film series are presented by various cinema clubs, with admission often free. Venues are the **Museo Regional Michoacano**, the **Casa Natal de Morelos** (both screening films several times a week) and the **Casa de la Cultura**. For recent-release movies, check *Multicinemas Morelia* (☎ 312-12-88, cnr Tapia & Farías).

The Casa Natal de Morelos also presents free talks and other cultural events at its Viernes Culturales, at 7pm Friday. At the **Museo del Estado**, regional dances, music, stories and exhibitions from the state of Michoacán are presented at 7.30pm most Wednesdays.

For theater, check what's on at *Teatro Ocampo* (☎ 312-37-34, cnr Ocampo & Prieto), notable for its lavish interior, or *Teatro Morelos* (☎ 314-62-02, cnr Camelinas & Ventura Puente), part of the Centro de Convenciones complex.

One of the many traditional regional dances, the Danza de los Viejitos (Dance of the Old Men) is performed in the bar of the Hotel Alameda at 9pm most Fridays and Saturdays. The costumed dancers, wearing comical masks of grinning *viejitos* with long gray hair, hooked noses, rosy cheeks and no teeth, enter hobbling on skinny canes. Their dance gets more and more animated, with wooden sandals clacking on the floor, until finally they hobble off again, looking as if they barely can make it to the door. It's a little contrived but great fun for the price of a drink or two.

Two peña places near the zócalo host live music and other performances.

Peña Colibrí (☎ 312-22-61, Galeana 36) Open 11am-1am. This longstanding venue presents various styles of Latin music, including trova, samba, folk and Cuban, and even performances of the Viejitos dance.

La Casa de los Espíritus (☎ 334-31-18, Galeana 70) This blues/rock/folk venue hosts local live acts on Thursday, Friday and Saturday nights.

Billed as a restaurant/bar/galería, *Viva México* (☎ 317-20-31, Madero Pte 525) is another unassuming place with drinks, students, rock and contemporary Mexican music.

Quite a few dance clubs rock the posh suburbs. For the current hot spot, ask at the tourist office, dress up, and take a taxi.

Getting There & Away

Air The Francisco J Múgica airport (☎ 312-65-14) is 27km north of Morelia, on the Morelia-Zinapécuaro highway. Plenty of flights are available to cities in Mexico, and limited flights serve cities elsewhere in North America. Some flights are with new small airlines, so it's worth checking with a travel agent for current options.

Mexicana (☎ 324-38-08), in the lobby of the Hotel Fiesta Inn at the Centro de Convenciones, offers daily flights to and from San Francisco, Chicago and Los Angeles. Aeromar (☎ 324-67-77), also at Hotel Fiesta Inn, has daily flights to and from Mexico City and Tijuana. Aeroméxico (☎ 324-24-24) offers daily direct flights to and from Tijuana. AeroCuahonte (☎ 315-39-69) flies daily to Lázaro Cárdenas and thrice weekly to Zihuatanejo.

Bus In late 2001, Morelia's new bus station opened up on the northwest side of town, at Periférico República 5555, opposite the football stadium. The old (but more conveniently located) bus station, a few blocks northwest of the zócalo, may still be used for buses to nearby towns, so check at the tourist office before you go all the way out to the new one. Daily departures include:

Guadalajara – 278km, 3½-5 hours; 8 ETN deluxe (US$26), regular Primera Plus and Servicios Coordinados 1st-class (US$17-20); frequent 2nd-class (US$15)

Guanajuato – 176km, 4 hours; 4 Servicios Coordinados 2nd-class (US$11)

Lázaro Cárdenas – 406km, 7 hours; regular Parhikuni 1st-class (US$37), regular 2nd-class (US$25)

León – 197km, 3½-4 hours; 17 deluxe Primera Plus (US$13), 7 1st-class Servicios Coordinados (US$12), 2nd-class Flecha Amarilla every 20 minutes (US$10.50)

Mexico City (Terminal Poniente or Terminal Norte) – 304km, 4 hours; 24 ETN deluxe (US$26), frequent Primera Plus and Herradura de Plata 1st-class (US$20), and Autobuses de Occidente 2nd-class (US$17)

Pátzcuaro – 62km, 1 hour; 4 Parhikuni 1st-class (US$3), frequent Galeana and Flecha Amarilla 2nd-class (US$3)

Querétaro – 259km, 3-4 hours; 3 ETN deluxe (US$15), frequent Primera Plus, Elite and Servicios Coordinados 1st-class (US$10-11)

Toluca – 211km, 3¾ hours; regular Herradura de Plata 1st-class (US$13)

Uruapan – 124km, 2 hours; 5 ETN deluxe (US$11), frequent Parhikuni and Primera Plus 1st-class (US$8), 5 Flecha Amarilla 2nd-class (US$7)

Zitácuaro – 150km, 2½-3 hours; 8 Servicios Coordinados 1st-class (US$8), frequent Autobuses de Occidente, Transportes Frontera 2nd-class (US$7)

Car To rent a car, call both Hertz (☎ 313-53-28) and Budget (☎ 314-70-07), discuss the price, and expect to pay over US$60 per day.

Getting Around

The several airport taxi services (☎ 315-63-53, 315-06-46, 313-10-43, 312-22-21 or 316-37-78) all charge about US$16.50 for the trip between the airport and the city center. To the new long-distance bus station, take a Ruta Cafe (brown) combi going west on Corregidora.

Around town, local combis (white VW vans) and small buses operate from 6am to 10pm daily and cost US$0.40. Their routes are designated by the color of their stripe: Ruta Roja (red), Ruta Amarilla (yellow), Ruta Guinda (pink), Ruta Azul (blue), Ruta Verde (green), Ruta Cafe (brown) and so on. In the middle of town they mostly follow pretty straight routes. If you need to cross the central area, just hop on a combi that's going your way.

Taxis are plentiful in the city center; the average taxi ride costs about US$2.25, or a little more to outer areas like the Centro de Convenciones.

SANTUARIO MARIPOSA MONARCA

In the easternmost part of Michoacán, straddling the border of México state, is the 160-sq-km monarch butterfly reserve (ⓔ mmonarca@conanp.gob.mx; admission US$2.25; open 9am-6pm daily), which has been decreed a Reserva Especial de la Biosfera. Many millions of monarch butterflies come to these forested highlands every autumn, after flying more than 4000km from the Great Lakes region of the US and Canada. At night and in the early morning the butterflies cluster together, covering whole trees and weighing down the branches. As the day warms up, they begin to flutter around like gold and orange snowflakes, descending to the humid forest floor for the hottest part of the day. By midafternoon they might cover the ground completely and you can't avoid crushing many of them, so it's best to make your visit in the morning.

The reserve comprises five separate sanctuaries, of which only two, Sierra Chincua and El Campanario, are open to visitors. Sierra Chincua is about a half-hour's slow drive north of Angangueo, a once-substantial mining town. El Campanario, commonly called El Rosario, is much more frequently visited. It lies above the small village of El Rosario, almost an hour's drive up a very rough road from the larger village of Ocampo.

The butterflies arrive from late October to early November; visitors are usually excluded until about mid-November, to allow the butterflies time to consolidate their colonies and begin their hibernation, which lasts through the winter. In the warm spring weather of late March, after hibernation, the butterflies reach their sexual maturity and mate – abdomen to abdomen, with the males flying around carrying the females underneath. The exhausted males die shortly afterward, and the pregnant females fly north to sites in the southeastern US where they lay their eggs in milkweed bushes, then die themselves. The eggs hatch into caterpillars that feed on the milkweed, then make cocoons and emerge in late May as a new generation of monarch butterflies. These monarchs fly north to forests in the Great Lakes region, where they mate, and by mid-August yet another generation of monarch butterflies is ready to make the long trip south to central Mexico. No single generation makes the entire circle.

In January 2002 an unusually severe storm struck central Mexico, dumping more than 100mm of rain on the butterfly sanctuaries, followed by freezing temperatures. A vast number of butterflies perished in the fatal combination of wet and cold conditions, especially in areas where the forest cover has been depleted by logging and the level of natural protection reduced. The death toll is estimated at well over 200 million insects. Though this amounts to some 70% or 80% of the total population it's unlikely to lead to the extinction of the species, because many non-migratory monarchs remain in parts of the USA during the winter. What is in danger is the migratory behavior itself, with the smaller number of migratory monarchs now increasingly vulnerable to predation, disease and uncertain weather in the course of what was always a long and hazardous journey. The monarch population wintering in Mexico has always been highly variable, and whether it will recover to pre-2002 levels, only time will tell.

Visiting the Reserve

Angangueo is the most popular base for visits to the reserve, but it's also possible to do a day trip from Zitácuaro, a bigger town on highway 52. To do a day visit from Morelia, you'd need your own transport and an early start. It's easiest with an organized tour (see the tourist office in Morelia to contact a tour operator). From Zitácuaro, public buses run frequently to Ocampo (23km), and from there two buses a day ascend the rough road to the village of El Rosario (12km, 1½ hours). From El Rosario, it's a little farther to the entrance (marked by a double row of souvenir stalls) of El Campanario sanctuary, then a steep uphill walk of 3 or 4km to where the butterflies will be. Just head for where the swarms of butterflies (or sightseers) are the most concentrated.

Pickup trucks and small, basic vans can be chartered to take groups of visitors to the El Campanario (El Rosario) sanctuary. It's a *very* bumpy, uncomfortable ride. Most of them operate from Angangueo (2 hours), but you might also get one from Ocampo (ask around) or from Zitácuaro (ask at your hotel or the tourist office, ☎ 715-153-06-75). The vehicle will cost about US$33 roundtrip from Angangueo, with two hours' waiting time, so it's more economical if you get a group together (10-12 people). Negotiate for enough waiting time, and make it clear that you want to go to the sanctuary entrance, not just to the village of El Rosario.

The entrance to the Sierra Chincua sanctuary is about a half-hour drive north from Angangueo on a sealed road, but the truck drivers are not as keen to take people there. It's also a long walk from the entrance to the butterfly colonies, which can be difficult to find. The entrance charge is supposed to include a guide, but he probably won't speak English or do any more than point you up the hill. If you want to visit this sanctuary, you might do best taking an organized tour.

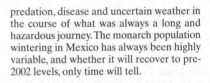

WESTERN CENTRAL

Angangueo
• pop 5000 • elev 2980m ☎ 715

Angangueo is an old mining town that still extracts some lead and silver from the rugged hillsides. It's spread out along a single main street (variously called Nacional and Morelos) with the Plaza de la Constitución and two churches at the uphill end. The town is enjoyable to stroll around, and a miner monument offers good views. A tourism office, open in the butterfly season, is just downhill from the plaza.

Places to Stay & Eat Angangueo has several places to stay along its main drag.

Casa de Huéspedes El Paso de la Monarca (☎ 156-01-87, Morelos 20) Singles/doubles with bath US$16/18. A few blocks down from the plaza, this place has simple rooms set round a tiered garden with views of the hills.

Casa de Huéspedes Juárez (no ☎, Morelos 15) Singles & doubles US$16. A rose-filled courtyard here is surrounded by clean, basic rooms.

Albergue Don Bruno (☎ 156-00-26, Morelos 92) Singles/doubles US$54/67. The first accommodation you'll encounter as you come into town is this appealing hotel, where the better rooms have open fireplaces and some have fine views. Packages with a buffet breakfast and dinner are available.

Outside the butterfly season, when the town is practically devoid of visitors, all these places might charge a little less (if they're open at all).

Restaurant Los Geranios (Morelos 92) Mains US$5-6. This restaurant, at Albergue Don Bruno, has great views and does a fine comida corrida and other meals.

Restaurant Los Arcos (☎ 716-01-20, Plaza de la Constitución 5A) Mains US$3-5. With a pleasing outlook over the plaza, Los Arcos is an enjoyable, economical place for a meal or a snack.

Getting There & Away Autobuses de Occidente has infrequent 2nd-class buses direct to Angangueo from Mexico City's Terminal Poniente (about 4 hours, US$9), but it's probably better to go first to Zitácuaro, then take one of the local buses from there to Angangueo. They leave every 15 minutes (1 hour, US$1.75).

PÁTZCUARO
• pop 49,000 • elev 2175m ☎ 434

Pátzcuaro is a lovely highland town in the heart of Purépecha country. The center of town, with some stately colonial architecture, lies 3.5km from the southeast shore of Lago de Pátzcuaro, almost equidistant between Morelia and Uruapan (both are about 60km away on the good highway 14). Mexican tourists come in large numbers over Christmas and New Year, for Semana Santa and for the area's famous Day of the Dead celebrations on November 1 and 2. It can get chilly in this mountainous area in winter. Bring at least a warm sweater.

History
Pátzcuaro was the capital of the Tarasco people from about AD 1325 to 1400. Then, on the death of King Tariácuri, the Tarascan state became a three-part league comprising Pátzcuaro and, on the east side of the lake, Tzintzuntzan and Ihuatzio. First Pátzcuaro dominated, then Ihuatzio, then Tzintzuntzan. The league repulsed Aztec attacks. The Spanish first came to the area in 1522, when they received a friendly reception. Then they returned in 1529 under Nuño de Guzmán, a conquistador of legendary cruelty.

Guzmán's inhumanity to the indigenous people was so severe that the Catholic Church and the colonial government sent Bishop Vasco de Quiroga, a respected judge and cleric from Mexico City, to clean up the mess Guzmán left. Quiroga, who arrived in 1536, established a bishopric (based initially at Tzintzuntzan, then, from 1540, at Pátzcuaro) and pioneered village cooperatives based on the humanitarian ideas of Sir Thomas More's *Utopia*.

To avoid dependence on Spanish mining lords and landowners, Quiroga successfully encouraged education and agricultural self-sufficiency in the villages around Lago de Pátzcuaro, with all villagers contributing equally to the community. He also helped each village develop its own craft specialty. The Utopian communities declined after his death in 1565, but the crafts traditions continue to this day. Not surprisingly, Tata Vascu, as the Tarascos called him, is much venerated for his work. Streets, plazas, restaurants and hotels all over Michoacán are named after him.

PÁTZCUARO

PLACES TO STAY
5 Hotel Fiesta Plaza
10 Hotel Valmen
11 Posada de la Basílica
14 Hotel Posada de la Salud
16 Hotel San Agustín
17 Hotel Posada de la Rosa
18 Hotel de la Concordia
20 Gran Hotel
26 Hotel Mansión Iturbe
29 Hotel Los Escudos
37 Hotel Misión San Manuel
38 Hotel Posada de San Rafael
43 Posada Mandala
45 Hotel Mesón del Gallo

PLACES TO EAT
3 Food Stalls
19 Restaurante Don Rafa
27 Restaurant Doña Paca
39 El Patio
40 El Primer Piso
41 Casa de las Once Pizzas

OTHER
1 Telecomm
2 Post Office
4 Buses & Colectivos to Lake
6 Teatro Emperador Caltzontzin; Computel
7 Colectivos to Bus Station
8 Mercado de Artesanías
9 Biblioteca Gertrudis Bocanegra
12 State Tourist Office
13 Basílica de Nuestra Señora de la Salud
15 Templo El Santuario
21 Numismática del Lago
22 Meganet
23 Bancomer
24 Banco Bital
25 Icser
28 Museo de Artes Populares
30 Municipal Tourist Office
31 Ex-Colegio Jesuita
32 Templo de la Compañía
33 Lavandería San Francisco
34 Bicipartes Chávez
35 Templo San Francisco
36 Templo San Juan de Dios
42 Templo del Sagrario
44 CELEP Language School
46 Casa de los Once Patios

Orientation

Pátzcuaro has a handsome core of lovely colonial buildings and some less attractive outlying areas stretching as far as the lake. Central Pátzcuaro focuses on the fine Plaza Vasco de Quiroga and the smaller but busier Plaza Gertrudis Bocanegra one block farther north, with the town market on its west side. The city center is fairly flat, but some streets climb steeply to the basilica east of the plazas.

Ahumada heads north from Plaza Vasco de Quiroga toward the old Morelia-Uruapan highway, 2km away, veering west and changing its name first to Avenida Cárdenas then to Avenida de las Américas along the way (these last two names are sometimes used interchangeably). Lago de Pátzcuaro is half a kilometer north of the highway.

The bus station is on a ring road on the southwest side of town, a kilometer from the city center.

Information

Tourist Offices The municipal tourist office (☎ 342-02-15), at Portal Hidalgo 1 on the west side of Plaza Vasco de Quiroga, is open 10am to 3pm and 4.30pm to 7pm Monday to Saturday, 10am to 3pm Sunday.

The state tourist office, Delegación Regional de Turismo (☎ 342-12-14), Calle Buena Vista 7, is in a new location, up the hill near Basílica de Nuestra Señora de la Salud. It's open 9am to 3pm and 4pm to 7pm daily. The staff are charming and helpful, though not all of them speak English.

Money You can change dollars or traveler's checks at several banks on and around the two main plazas, all of which have ATMs. Some will change money only between 10am and noon, but Bancomer, at Mendoza 23, and Banco Bital on Iturbe will do so during regular business hours. Numismática del Lago, at Iturbe 30, changes cash and checks 9am to 7pm Monday to Friday, 9am to 2pm Saturday and Sunday, with slightly lower rates and considerably less paperwork.

Post & Communications The post office, at Obregón 13 half a block north of Plaza Gertrudis Bocanegra, is open 8am to 4pm Monday to Friday, 9am to 1pm Saturday. The Telecomm office, at Títere 15, offers telegram and fax services. Computel, on the north side of Plaza Gertrudis Bocanegra, has long-distance and fax services. It's open 6am to midnight daily.

Meganet, Mendoza 8, offers Internet access for US$2 per hour (open 9am to 9pm daily). Around the corner on Plaza Vasco de Quiroga, Icser charges US$1.50 per hour and stays open a little later.

Laundry Lavandería San Francisco, Terán 6, near Templo San Francisco, will wash and dry 3kg for US$4. It's open 9am to 8pm Monday to Saturday.

Plaza Vasco de Quiroga

Pátzcuaro's wide and well-proportioned main plaza is one of the loveliest in Mexico. A tall statue of Vasco de Quiroga gazes benignly down from the central fountain. The plaza is ringed by trees and flanked by portales that form part of the façades of 17th-century buildings. Originally grand mansions, these buildings are now mostly used as hotels, restaurants and shops. The sides of the plaza are named (independently of the street names) Portal Hidalgo (west side), Portal Aldama (south side) and Portal Matamoros (east side). The north side is Portal Allende east of Iturbe and Portal Morelos west of Iturbe.

Plaza Gertrudis Bocanegra

Pátzcuaro's second main plaza is named after a local heroine who was shot by firing squad in 1818 for her support of the independence movement. Her statue adorns the center of the plaza, and she looks like a tough woman.

The town's **market** bustles away on the west side of the plaza, especially on Sunday, Monday and Friday. You can find everything from fruit, vegetables and fresh lake fish to herbal medicines, crafts, and clothing, including the region's distinctive striped shawls, sarapes and *peruanas* (a kind of sarape-shawl worn by women).

The **Biblioteca Gertrudis Bocanegra** (*Gertrudis Bocanegra Library,* ☎ 342-54-41, cnr Lloreda & Títere; open 9am-8pm Mon-Sat) occupies the 16th-century former San Agustín church on the north side of the plaza. A large, colorful Juan O'Gorman mural covering the rear wall depicts the history of Michoacán from pre-Hispanic times to the 1910 revolution.

A small **Mercado de Artesanías** operates in the side street next to the library. Crafts sold here include grotesque Tocuaro masks, carved wooden forks and knives from Zirahuén, and pottery. The quality is variable but the prices are about the lowest you'll find.

On the west side of the library, the **Teatro Emperador Caltzontzin** was a convent until it was converted to a theater in 1936. Movies and occasional cultural events are presented here.

Basílica de Nuestra Señora de la Salud

On a hilltop three blocks east of the south end of Plaza Gertrudis Bocanegra, the Basílica de Nuestra Señora de la Salud was built atop a pre-Hispanic ceremonial site. Vasco de Quiroga intended the church to be the centerpiece of his Michoacán community and big enough for 30,000 worshipers. The building you see today wasn't completed until the 19th century and is only the central nave of the original design. Quiroga's tomb, the Mausoleo de Don Vasco, is just to the left inside the main west doors.

Behind the altar at the east end stands a much revered figure of the Virgin, Nuestra Señora de la Salud (Our Lady of Health). The image was made by Tarascos in the 16th century, on Quiroga's request, from a corncob-and-honey paste called *tatzingue.* Soon people began to experience miraculous healings, and Quiroga had the words

'Salus Infirmorum' (Healer of the Sick) inscribed at the figure's feet. Ever since, pilgrims have come from all over Mexico to ask this Virgin for a miracle. Many make their way on their knees across the plaza, into the church and along its nave. You can walk up the stairs behind the image to see the many small tin representations of hands, feet, legs and so on that pilgrims have offered to the Virgin.

Museo de Artes Populares

One block south of the basilica, this museum of folk arts (☎ 342-10-29, cnr Enseñanza & Alcantarillas; admission US$3.50, free Sun; open 9am-7pm Tues-Sat, 9am-3pm Sun) is housed in a spacious old colonial building. On this site in 1540, Quiroga founded the original Colegio de San Nicolás, arguably the first university in the Americas. The institution was later moved to Valladolid (as Morelia was then called), and much of the present structure dates from the early 18th century. In fact, the whole lot is superimposed on pre-Hispanic stone structures, some of which can be seen behind the museum courtyards.

Exhibits of Michoacán arts and crafts include delicate white lace *rebozos* (shawls) from Aranza, hand-painted ceramics from Santa Fe de la Laguna and copperware from Santa Clara del Cobre. One room is set up as a typical Michoacán kitchen with a tremendous brick oven and a full set of ceramic and copper utensils. Also note the tasteful use of cows' knuckle bones as decorations between the flagstones on the floor.

Templo de la Compañía & Ex-Colegio Jesuita

Built in the 16th century, the Templo de la Compañía (cnr Lerín & Alcantarillas) and the adjacent plain white building became a Jesuit training college in the 17th century. The church is still in use and houses some relics from Vasco de Quiroga. The college building fell into ruin after the expulsion of the Jesuits. Restored in the early 1990s, it is now used for cultural and community activities.

Other Churches

Pátzcuaro has several other old churches of interest, including del Sagrario, San Juan de Dios, San Francisco and El Santuario. All are shown on the map.

Casa de los Once Patios

House of the 11 Courtyards, a block southeast of Plaza Vasco de Quiroga on the cobbled Calle de la Madrigal de las Altas Torres, is a fine rambling building built as a Dominican convent in the 1740s. (Before that, the site held one of Mexico's first hospitals, founded by Vasco de Quiroga.) Today the house is a warren of small artesanías shops, each specializing in a particular regional craft. Browsers will discover copperware from Santa Clara del Cobre, straw goods from Tzintzuntzan and musical instruments from Paracho, as well as goldleaf-decorated lacquerware, hand-painted ceramics and attractive textiles. In some shops you can see the artisans at work. Most of the shops are open 10am to 7pm daily.

El Estribo

El Estribo, a lookout point on a hill 4km west of the town center, offers a magnificent view of the entire Lago de Pátzcuaro area. It takes up to an hour to get there on foot but only a few minutes in a vehicle. Either way, you take Ponce de León from the southwest corner of Plaza Vasco de Quiroga and follow the signs. It's best to do this on a Saturday or Sunday, when lots of people are walking the trails. People walking here at other times have been threatened and robbed. It would be wise to check with the tourist office before you go.

Courses

Centro de Lenguas y Ecoturismo de Pátzcuaro (CELEP, ☎ 342-47-64, e celep@rds2000.crefal.edu.mx, w www.celep.com, Navarrete 47A) Two-week language course US$250; language and culture programs US$390. CELEP offers courses in two-week blocks, starting with an evaluation every Monday. Courses involve four hours of classes every morning, and the cultural programs include activities every afternoon. Accommodation and meals with local families can be arranged for US$18 per day.

Organized Tours

See the Around Pátzcuaro section for local tour operators.

Special Events

Aside from the famous local events for Day of the Dead (see 'The Tarascos, the

Purépecha & Day of the Dead'), Pátzcuaro stages some interesting events at other times as well.

Pastorelas – These dramatizations of the journey of the shepherds to see the infant Jesus are staged in Plaza Vasco de Quiroga on several evenings around Christmas. *Pastorelas indígenas,* on the same theme but including mask dances, enact the struggle of angels against the devils that are trying to hinder the shepherds. Pastorelas are held in eight villages around Lago de Pátzcuaro on different days between December 26 and February 2. Rodeos and other events accompany them.

Semana Santa – The week leading up to Easter is full of events in Pátzcuaro and the lakeside villages: Palm Sunday processions in several places; Viacrucis processions on Good Friday morning, enacting Christ's journey to Calvary and the crucifixion itself; candlelit processions in silence on Good Friday evening; and, on Easter Sunday evening, a ceremonial burning of Judas in Plaza Vasco de Quiroga. There are many local variations.

Nuestra Señora de la Salud – A colorful procession to the basilica honors the Virgin of Health. Traditional dances are performed, including Los Reboceros, Los Moros, Los Viejitos and Los Panaderos.

Places to Stay

Budget Camping options include: *Hotel Villa Pátzcuaro (☎ 342-07-67, Avenida de las Américas 506)* Tent sites US$5.50 per person, trailer sites US$12-15. On the road to the lake, 2km north of the town center, this hotel has a small camping area, a helpful manager, clean showers, a small kitchen, very pleasant grounds and a swimming pool.

Trailer Park El Pozo (☎ 342-09-37, highway 190 s/n) Tent & trailer sites US$5.50 per person. This park is on the lakeside, just off the highway to Morelia 1km east of its junction with Avenida de las Américas. Watch for the sign pointing across the train tracks to the grassy field which has 20 sites (most shaded) with full hookups.

Budget hotels are also available. Note that during special events and festivals, especially around Day of the Dead, every hotel room fills up and prices will be higher than those quoted here.

Hotel Posada de la Rosa (☎ 342-08-11, Portal Juárez 29) Singles & doubles with shared bath US$9, with private bath US$16.

The Tarascos, the Purépecha & Day of the Dead

The territory inhabited by Michoacán's 130,000 Purépecha people extends from around Lago de Pátzcuaro to west of Uruapan. The Purépecha are direct descendants of the Tarascos, who emerged around Lago de Pátzcuaro in about the 14th century and developed western Mexico's most advanced pre-Hispanic civilization. Their origins are obscure. They might have originated as semibarbaric Chichimecs from farther north, but neither the modern Purépecha language nor the old Tarasco language has any established links to any other tongue (though connections with languages such as Zuni, from the US Southwest, and Quechua, from Peru, have been suggested). The Spanish supposedly began calling them Tarascos because they often used a word that sounded like that.

The old Tarascos were noted potters and metalsmiths, and many Purépecha villages still specialize in these crafts. The modern Purépecha also maintain some of the country's most vital and ancient religious traditions. Día de Muertos (Day of the Dead) observances around Lago de Pátzcuaro are particularly famous.

Best known – and attracting an overwhelming number of sightseers – are the events at Isla Janitzio, culminating in a parade of decorated canoes late in the evening on November 1. Many events, including crafts markets, dancing, exhibitions and concerts, are held in Pátzcuaro and nearby villages in the days before and after the Día de Muertos. In Jarácuaro, dance groups and musicians stage a traditional contest of their skills in the village square on the evening of November 1. Parades, dances and ceremonies take place in other villages around the lake, including Tzintzuntzan, Ihuatzio, Jarácuaro and Tzurumútaro. The state tourist office in Pátzcuaro can provide details.

On the west side of Plaza Gertrudis Bocanegra, this is the cheapest decent place in town. Its rooms, along an upstairs patio, all have two beds, and there's lots of hot water.

Hotel San Agustín (☎ 342-04-42, Portal Juárez 27) Singles/doubles with bath US$7.75/13. Go upstairs from the portales to reach the small but clean rooms of this basic hotel. Rooms on one side of the hall have windows overlooking the market; those on the other side are stuffy, dark and depressing.

Hotel de la Concordia (☎ 342-00-03, Portal Juárez 31) Singles/doubles with shared bath US$10/21, with TV & private bath US$20/35. A few doors down from the San Agustín, this atmospheric hotel has big, old, dark rooms with high ceilings.

Hotel Valmen (☎ 342-11-61, Padre Lloreda 34) Singles & doubles at about US$8 per person. One block east of Plaza Gertrudis Bocanegra, the Valmen is pretty worn but it's OK for the price and has nice atmosphere. The 16 rooms are around covered patios with lurid green tiles. They're of various sizes and shapes – most have large windows and plenty of light, but look before registering.

Hotel Posada de la Salud (☎ 342-00-58, Serrato 9) Singles/doubles US$21/27. Half a block east of the basilica, this well-kept little place has 15 clean, pleasant rooms. It's a bit away from the town center, very quiet (except for noisy plumbing) and more suited to pilgrims than partyers, but it's a pretty good value budget place to stay.

Mid-Range Several of the 17th-century mansions around Plaza Vasco de Quiroga have been turned into elegant colonial-style hotels, all with restaurants.

Hotel Los Escudos (☎ 342-01-38, fax 342-06-49, Portal Hidalgo 73) Singles/doubles US$31/41, twins US$58. An attractive colonial building on the west side of Plaza Quiroga, this hotel has 30 nicely decorated rooms set around two traditional-style patios. All rooms have carpet, private bath, phone, and satellite TV; some have fireplaces.

Hotel Misión San Manuel (☎ 342-13-13, Portal Aldama 12) Singles & doubles US$43, twins US$60. A fantastic old-world feel permeates the original part of this former monastery on the south side of the plaza. The 42 rooms have carpeting, tiled

bathrooms and high, beamed ceilings. Some have fireplaces.

Hotel Posada de San Rafael (☎ 342-07-70, Portal Aldama 18) Singles/doubles US$27/31. This hotel occupies another handsome old colonial building. The 105 rooms are modestly sized but quite OK, and all have carpet and TV. It's a good value.

Hotel Mesón del Gallo (☎ 342-14-74, e hmeson@ml.com.mx, Dr Coss 20) Singles/doubles with breakfast US$35/42. One block south of Plaza Vasco de Quiroga, this 20-room place is less historic than the hotels on the plaza, but it has a swimming pool, lawn and a pleasant restaurant and bar. Special discounts are sometimes offered.

Posada Mandala (☎ 342-41-76, e matias@ hotmail.com, Lerín 14) Singles/doubles with breakfast US$18/31 to US$25/38. As well as an excellent vegetarian restaurant, the Mandala, just east of Casa de los Once Patios, has four very comfortable and attractive rooms. The downstairs rooms share a modern bathroom. The upstairs rooms – two of the nicest rooms in town – have a fine view, private bath and a higher price tag.

Gran Hotel (☎ 342-04-43, W www.galeon .com/granhotel, Plaza Bocanegra 6) Singles & doubles US$28. This hotel is nothing special, but the rooms are small, clean, nicely furnished and quite a good value.

Hotel Villa Pátzcuaro (☎ 342-07-67, Avenida de las Américas 506) Singles & doubles US$33. This pleasant hotel is set back from the road to the lake, about 2km from the center of town. The 12 cozy rooms all have fireplaces, and there's a swimming pool. It's most convenient if you have a vehicle, but local buses to the lake or town pass by every few minutes. The manager here is helpful, knows the area well and speaks good English.

Top End Splurges in Pátzcuaro include: **Hotel Mansión Iturbe** (☎ 342-03-68, W www.mexonline.com/iturbe.htm, Portal Morelos 59) Singles & doubles with breakfast US$76-98. On the north side of Plaza Vasco de Quiroga, this hotel retains all of its colonial elegance, with high ceilings, wood beams and antique furnishings. Each room is different (some have deep bathtubs, others private balconies and so on), so have a look before checking in. Prices include a newspaper, two hours' bicycle use and coffee at any time. The hotel also has an art gallery and a good restaurant and bar.

Posada de la Basílica (☎ 342-11-08, 🖃 hotelpb@hotmail.com, Arciga 6) Singles/ doubles US$54/76. On a hill opposite the basilica, this hotel has cheerful, sizeable rooms around an open courtyard overlooking the town's red-tile roofs. Most rooms have fireplaces, and firewood is provided. Try for a room with a balcony and a view. The restaurant here is an enjoyable place for breakfast.

Hotel Fiesta Plaza (☎ 342-25-15, Plaza Bocanegra 24) Singles & doubles US$71. The Fiesta Plaza is a modern, well-run place in colonial style. It has 60 pleasant, amply sized rooms on three floors around two courtyards.

Posada de Don Vasco (☎ 342-24-90, Avenida de las Américas 450) Singles/ doubles US$67/105. This Best Western hotel is about 1.5km north of the town center on the way to the lake. It was established as a resort hotel in 1938, in a vague semi-art-deco neocolonial style. Considerably renovated and enlarged, it now has 101 comfortable rooms, plus a tennis court, swimming pool, game room, restaurant and bar. Older rooms have a little character; those in the newer blocks are bigger and brighter and come with all the modern amenities. Special rates of about US$50 sometimes are available.

Places to Eat

The best-known Pátzcuaro specialty is the small pescado blanco (white fish), traditionally caught on Lago de Pátzcuaro using canoes and 'butterfly' nets. Now the pescado blanco is as likely to come from a fish farm, and the taste is OK but nothing special. Until the new sewer system is finished, most of Pátzcuaro's wastewater pours untreated into the lake, so you might think twice about local fish. By contrast, another specialty, *sopa Tarasca*, is a true taste sensation: a rich tomato-based soup with cream, dried chili and bits of crisp tortilla. Another specialty worth trying is *corundas* – tamales with a pork, bean and cream filling. Eating in Pátzcuaro can be exceptionally good.

The market on the northwest corner of Plaza Gertrudis Bocanegra has a great choice of **food stalls** serving everything from homemade yogurt and fruit salad for breakfast, to filling *tortas* for lunch, to a chicken dinner with vegetables and tortillas for less than US$3.

El Patio (☎ 342-04-84, Plaza Vasco de Quiroga 19) Mains US$4-8. Open 8am-10pm. El Patio specializes in regional food at reasonable prices. Its sopa Tarasca is delicious, and the rich reddish-brown sauce on the *pollo en mole* will make you drool.

El Primer Piso (☎ 342-01-22, Plaza Vasco de Quiroga 29) Mains US$8-10. Open 1pm-10pm. This place is on the 2nd floor of a very old building, and its four balconies are a favorite of romantics and people-watchers. Its menu is eclectic contemporary Mexican, with French, Spanish and Middle Eastern influences, resulting in imaginative dishes like birria-stuffed chiles, along with soups, salads and pastas. The coffee and desserts are excellent, and you can come in late and sit on the balcony.

All the mansions-turned-hotels on Plaza Vasco de Quiroga have restaurants.

Restaurant Doña Paca (☎ 342-03-68, Portal Morelos 59) Mains US$7-10. One of the best hotel restaurants, the Doña Paca, at the Hotel Mansión Iturbe (see Places to Stay), makes excellent, upmarket versions of traditional street-market fare like tacos, *gorditas* and enchiladas, all beautifully presented.

Casa de las Once Pizzas (☎ 342-00-62, Plaza de Quiroga 33) Mains US$5. On the east side of the main plaza, this unassuming colonial courtyard pizzeria will fill most people with one very tasty medium-size pizza. The house wine is drinkable and affordable.

Restaurante Don Rafa (☎ 342-03-68, Mendoza 30) Mains US$4-8. Between the main plazas, this place is clinically clean and does a popular comida corrida and a divine sopa Tarasca.

Posada de la Basílica (☎ 342-11-008, Arciga 6) Mains US$5-8. For a meal with a view, try this restaurant which is open only for breakfast and lunch. Thick tablecloths and heavy Michoacán ceramic plates might inspire some shopping.

Mandala (☎ 342-41-76, Lerín 14) Mains about US$4. Vegetarians and others will enjoy the atmosphere at this place, a short walk east of Plaza Vasco de Quiroga. It's bright, friendly and charmingly decorated,

nd it uses fresh, flavorful vegetables for sat-
sfying salads, soups and pastas.

A cheap place to try local fish is beside
he main jetty on the lake, where the boats
lepart for Isla Janitzio. Several *fish stands*
ere all charge about US$6 for pescado
)lanco and US$3 for a cupful of charales
tiny fish that are eaten whole) or a *caldo
)escado* (fish soup). You can choose your
ish, and they'll fry it up on the spot.

Entertainment
Pátzcuaro is a quiet town. The main evening
iction is lingering over coffee in one of the
'estaurants, most of which close at 10pm.
Hotel Fiesta Plaza (see Places to Stay) has
ive music some Friday and Saturday
evenings. *Teatro Emperador Caltzontzin*
iosts occasional performances of theater,
nusic and dance in addition to the usual
are of cinema in small-town Mexico.

Shopping
The *Casa de los Once Patios* is the first
place to look for Michoacán crafts, but you
can also try the main market and the
Mercado de Artesanías, both next to Plaza
Gertrudis Bocanegra (see the earlier entries
or Casa de los Once Patios and Plaza
Gertrudis Bocanegra). On Friday morning a
ceramics market, with pottery from different villages, is held in Plaza San Francisco,
one block west of Plaza Vasco de Quiroga.

Getting There & Away
Pátzcuaro's bus station is on the southwest
edge of town, on the ring road variously
called Avenida Circunvalación or El Libramiento. It has a cafetería, pay phones
and a *guarda equipaje* where you can store
your luggage. Buses from Pátzcuaro (2nd-
class unless otherwise stated) include:

Erongarícuaro – 18km, 25 minutes; Autobuses de
Occidente every 5 minutes, 7am to 8pm (US$0.90)

Guadalajara – 347km, 5½ hours; 1 Servicios Coordinados 1st-class at 11.30pm (US$14), 1 Piedad
2nd-class at 11.50pm (US$12)

Lázaro Cárdenas – 342km, 6 hours; Galeana
hourly, 6am to 6.30pm (US$17)

Mexico City – 366km, 5 hours; 10 Herradura de
Plata 1st-class to Terminal Poniente, 7 to Terminal Norte (US$20), 5 Flecha Amarilla 2nd-class
to Terminal Poniente (US$16)

Morelia – 62km, 1 hour; 5 Herradura de Plata 1st-
class (US$3.50), hourly Galeana and Flecha
Amarilla 2nd-class (US$3)

Quiroga – 22km, 30 minutes; Galeana every 15
minutes, 5.50am to 8.45pm (US$0.90)

Santa Clara del Cobre – 20km, 30 minutes;
Galeana hourly, 5.45am to 8.25pm (US$0.60)

Tzintzuntzan – 15km, 20 minutes; same buses as to
Quiroga (US$0.60)

Uruapan – 62km, 1 hour; Galeana every 15
minutes (US$3.50)

Zirahuén – 20km, 40 minutes; 6 Occidente
(US$0.70)

Minibuses to some nearby towns depart
from Plaza Gertrudis Bocanegra (see
Getting Around below).

Getting Around
'Centro' buses and *colectivos,* from the yard
to your right when you walk out of the bus
station, will take you to Plaza Gertrudis Bocanegra. Returning to the bus station, catch
a 'Central' vehicle from Plaza Gertrudis Bocanegra – colectivos stop on the north side
of the plaza, buses on the west side. For the
jetty where boats leave for Isla Janitzio, take
a 'Lago' bus or colectivo from the northwest
corner of Plaza Gertrudis Bocanegra. Buses
cost US$0.40, colectivos slightly more. They
run from about 6am to 10pm.

Bicipartes Chávez *(Terán 14)* usually has
a few bikes available for rent at a very reasonable US$11 per day.

AROUND PÁTZCUARO
The most interesting day trips from
Pátzcuaro are to the surrounding villages –
all of which can be reached, or nearly
reached, by local buses (see Getting There
& Away in the Pátzcuaro section). From
Pátzcuaro it's possible to circle the lake by
bus, stopping at villages along the way.
You'll need to change buses at Quiroga and
Erongarícuaro in order to get around.

Organized Tours
Francisco Castilleja (☎ 434-344-01-67)
Typical day trip about US$25, some of which
goes to Purépecha villagers. Based at Erongarícuaro on the west side of the lake, Francisco offers guided tours with an emphasis on
local ecology and indigenous communities.
Typical tours visit Purépecha villages, check

the local crafts industry, learn about the local environment and include a traditional lunch. Mostly it's done on public buses or by walking, but arrangements are flexible. Tours meet at 10am in Pátzcuaro at the Hotel Mansión Iturbe or at the tables outside.

Jorge Guzmán Orozco (☎ *434-342-25-79*) Day tours US$27-38 per person. Jorge is another well-recommended local guide who can be contacted through the municipal tourist office. He leads tours to Isla Janitzio, Isla Pacanda and Tzintzuntzan, and he can also arrange trips to Santa Clara del Cobre or Lago de Zirahuén.

Lago de Pátzcuaro

The lake has one very touristy island and a couple of others that are much less visited.

Streams and aquifers feeding the lake are being depleted or diverted, and at the current rate of shrinkage the lake won't exist at all in 50 years. You may find the lake to be prettier from a distance than up close. Swimming in the lake is not recommended.

Isla Janitzio Janitzio (population 2000) the largest island in Lago de Pátzcuaro, is heavily devoted to tourism, and on Saturday, Sunday and holidays it is overrun with day-trippers. It has all the hallmarks of a tourist trap, so don't feel bad if you miss it. The 20-minute launch trip to the island offers distant views of villages along the shore. Local people will come alongside to demonstrate the use of their famous butterfly-shaped fishing nets and solicit tips

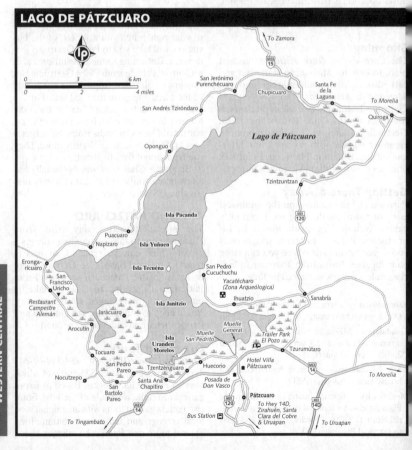

LAGO DE PÁTZCUARO

To Zamora

MEX 15

San Jerónimo Purenchécuaro
Chupicuaro
Santa Fe de la Laguna
To Morelia
San Andrés Tziróndaro
Quiroga

Lago de Pátzcuaro

Oponguo

Tzintzuntzan

MEX 120

Isla Pacanda

Puacuaro
Napizaro
Isla Yuñuen

Eronga-rícuaro
San Francisco Uricho
Isla Tecuéna
San Pedro Cucuchucho
Yacatécharo (Zona Arqueológica)
Ihuatzio
Sanabría

Restaurant Campestre Alemán
Jarácuaro
Isla Janitzio
Arocutin

Muelle General
Trailer Park El Pozo

Tocuaro
Isla Uranden Morelos
Muelle San Pedrito
Tzurumútaro

San Pedro Pareo
Tzentzénguaro
Huecorio
Hotel Villa Pátzcuaro
MEX 14
To Morelia

Nocutzepo
Santa Ana Chapitiro
Posada de Don Vaso

San Bartolo Pareo
MEX 14
Pátzcuaro
MEX 120
To Hwy 14D, Zirahuén, Santa Clara del Cobre & Uruapan
MEX 14D
To Uruapan

To Tingambato
Bus Station
To Uruapan

0   3   6 km
0   2   4 miles

The island itself has plenty of fish restaurants and cheap souvenir shops. You can see everything in an hour. An unattractive 40m-high **statue** (admission US$0.60) of independence hero José María Morelos y Pavón stands on its highest point. Inside the statue is a set of murals depicting Morelos' life. The pictures are hard to appreciate from the walkways, however, and the captions are impossible. You can climb all the way up to its wrist and poke your head through narrow gaps to see the panoramic view.

Isla Yuñuen This smaller island (population 100) has a strong Purépecha community and is developing some small-scale tourism.

Cabañas de Yuñuen (☎ 434-342-44-73) Cabins about US$38. Rates for the six comfortable cabins here vary, depending on the season and the number of people. Call ahead to arrange a stay.

Getting There & Away For boat trips on the lake, head to the *muelles* (docks), 3km north of central Pátzcuaro. The Muelle General is well served by local buses and combis marked 'Lago' from Plaza Gertrudis Bocanegra in Pátzcuaro. It has a slew of cheap fish restaurants and souvenir shops, and a ticket office for boat trips. The roundtrip fare is US$3 to Isla Janitzio, US$3.25 to Isla Yuñuen and Isla Pacanda. Launches leave when they're full, which is about every 30 minutes for Isla Janitzio, less frequently for the other two islands. Keep your ticket for the return trip.

Muelle San Pedrito, a short distance around the lake to the west, is smaller and not as well served by public transport, but the launches are slightly cheaper from here, and it might be a better place to charter a boat if you have a group of people.

Ihuatzio
• pop 3200 • elev 2035m

Ihuatzio, 14km from Pátzcuaro near the eastern shore of the lake, was capital of the Tarascan league after Pátzcuaro but before Tzintzuntzan. Buses run to this village from Plaza Gertrudis Bocanegra. Yacatécharo, a large partially excavated **archaeological site** holding Tarasco ruins (admission US$0.60; open 10am-3pm daily), is a short walk northwest from the village. The main

feature is an open ceremonial space 200m long with two pyramids at its west end. The unexcavated areas include walled causeways and a round-based building thought to have been an observatory. The ruins are more memorable than those at Tzintzuntzan, especially at sunset, mainly because they appear in a more natural setting.

Tzintzuntzan
• pop 3200 • elev 2050m

The interesting little town of Tzintzuntzan ('tseen-TSOON-tsahn') is about 15km from Pátzcuaro near the northeastern corner of Lago de Pátzcuaro. It has impressive buildings from both the pre-Hispanic Tarasco empire and the early Spanish missionary period, and there are modern handicrafts on sale.

Tzintzuntzan is a Purépecha name meaning Place of Hummingbirds. It was the capital of the Tarascan league at the time of invasions by the Aztecs in the late 15th century (which were repulsed) and by the Spanish in the 1520s. The Purépecha chief came to peaceable terms with Cristóbal de Olid, leader of the first Spanish expedition in 1522, but this did not satisfy Nuño de Guzmán, who arrived in 1529 in his quest for gold and had the chief burned alive.

Vasco de Quiroga established his first base here when he reached Michoacán in the mid-1530s, and Tzintzuntzan became the headquarters of the Franciscan monks who followed him. But the town declined in importance after Quiroga shifted his base to Pátzcuaro in 1540.

Just along the main street from the Ex-Convento de San Francisco, craftspeople sell a variety of straw goods (a local specialty), ceramics and other Michoacán artesanías. You can reach the lakeshore by continuing straight down this street for about 1km.

Las Yácatas The centerpiece of pre-Hispanic Tzintzuntzan is an impressive group of five round-based temples, known as *yácatas*, on a large terrace of carefully fitted stone blocks. They stand on the hillside just above the town, on the east side of the road from Pátzcuaro. The site entrance is a 700m walk from the center of the town. You can climb to the higher levels for good views, then nose around a few other structures and a small **museum** (admission US$3; open 9am-6pm daily).

Ex-Convento de San Francisco On the west side of Avenida Lázaro Cárdenas (the main street) is a complex of religious buildings constructed partly with stones from Las Yácatas, which the Spanish wrecked. Here Franciscan monks began the Spanish missionary effort in Michoacán in the 16th century. The olive trees in the churchyard are said to have been brought from Spain and planted by Vasco de Quiroga; they're believed to be the oldest olive trees in the Americas.

Straight ahead as you walk into the churchyard is the still-functioning Templo de San Francisco, built for the monks' own use. Inside, halfway along its north side, is the Capilla del Señor del Rescate (Chapel of the Savior), with a much-revered painting of Christ. This painting is the focus of a week-long festival in February. The cloister of the old monastery adjoining the church contains the parish offices and some old, weathered murals. On the north side of the churchyard stands the church built for the Tarascos, the Templo de Nuestra Señora de la Salud, with a holy image of El Cristo de Goznes (the Christ of Hinges). In the old enclosed yard beside this church is an old open chapel, the Capilla Abierta de la Concepción.

Quiroga
• pop 13,000 • elev 2074m

The town of Quiroga lies 7km northeast of Tzintzuntzan, at the junction of highway 120 and highway 15 between Morelia and Zamora. In existence since pre-Hispanic times, the town is named after Vasco de Quiroga, who was responsible for many of its buildings and handicrafts. These days Quiroga has few original old buildings and is not very pretty, but it's a great place to shop for artesanías, especially brightly painted wooden products, leatherwork, wool sweaters and sarapes.

On the first Sunday in July, the Fiesta de la Preciosa Sangre de Cristo (Festival of the Precious Blood of Christ) is celebrated with a long torchlight procession. The procession is led by a group carrying an image of Christ crafted from a paste made of corncobs and honey.

Buses run west out of Quiroga to Erongarícuaro every 90 minutes.

Erongarícuaro
• pop 2500 • elev 2080m

On the southwest edge of Lago de Pátzcuaro, a pretty 18km trip from Pátzcuaro, Erongarícuaro (often just called 'Eronga') is one of the oldest settlements on the lake. It's a peaceful little town where you can enjoy strolling along streets still lined with old Spanish-style houses. French artist André Breton (1896-1966) lived here for a time in the 1950s, visited occasionally by Diego Rivera and Frida Kahlo. Breton made the unusual wrought-iron cross in the forecourt of the church – see if you can spot the various Christian and pre-Hispanic symbols. The fine old seminary attached to the church is being restored. Downhill from the plaza, toward the lake, the Muebles Finos factory specializes in decorating furniture with beautiful hand-painted flowers, landscapes and other images.

On January 6, the Fiesta de los Reyes Magos (Festival of the Magic Kings) is celebrated with music and dance.

Restaurant Campestre Alemán (☎ 434 344-00-06, *Carretera Pátzcuaro-Erongarícuaro Km14*) Mains about US$10. Just south of Erongarícuaro, near the friendly village of San Francisco Uricho, this restaurant specializes in German-style smoked trout. It's slightly upmarket, with a lovely outlook, and it's popular with locals for long lunches on Saturday and Sunday (don't count on fast service).

Tocuaro
• pop 600 • elev 2035m

Some of Mexico's finest mask makers live in this sleepy, one-bus-stop town 10km from Pátzcuaro, although you wouldn't know it. Many families in Tocuaro are involved in mask making, but none have shops. A few now have small signs on their gates, but locating the town's mask makers is still a bit of a hit-or-miss affair.

To find Tocuaro's most famous mask maker, Juan Orta Castillo, you should walk up the street that runs from the bus stop to the church; when you're about halfway to the church, knock on a door on the left side of the street and politely repeat his name. If you're at his home, you'll be invited in and

hown masks for sale; if not, you'll be
ointed the right way. If you're lucky, you
ill see Orta at work. He has won Mexico's
National Mask Maker competition several
times. Tocuaro's other highly regarded mask
makers include Gustavo Horta, Felipe Terra
and Felipe Anciola.

One thing you won't find is a bargain –
uality mask making is a recognized art, and
fine mask takes many hours to make. The
best ones are wonderfully expressive, realis-
ic and surrealistic, but they'll cost hundreds
of dollars.

Santa Clara del Cobre
• pop 12,000 • elev 2180m

Santa Clara del Cobre (also called Villa Es-
alante), 20km south of Pátzcuaro, was a
copper-mining center from 1553 onward.
Though the mines are closed, this nice little
own still specializes in copperware, with
over 50 workshops making things from
cobre (copper). The small **Museo del Cobre**
*(cnr Morelos & Pino Suárez; open 10am-
3pm and 5pm-7pm Tues-Sat, 10am-4pm
Sun)* exhibits some interesting pieces and
shows how copper is beaten into shape and
decorated.

A weeklong Feria del Cobre (Copper
Fair) is held each August; exact dates vary.

Lago de Zirahuén
• pop 2250 • elev 2240m

Smaller than Lago de Pátzcuaro, but much
deeper and cleaner, the blue lake beside the
colonial town of Zirahuén, about 20km
from Pátzcuaro off the road to Uruapan,
makes a peaceful spot for a day trip or for
camping. At the lake are some *cabañas*
(☎ 434-342-07-58 in Pátzcuaro), a few
casual lakeside eateries, and launches offering excursions. Six buses a day go from the
Pátzcuaro bus station to Zirahuén; the last
bus back is at 5.30pm.

URUAPAN
• pop 215,000 • elev 1620m ☎ 452

When the Spanish monk Fray Juan de San
Miguel arrived here in 1533, he was so im-
pressed with the Río Cupatitzio and the
lush vegetation surrounding it that he gave
the area the Purépecha name Uruapan
('oo-roo-AH-pahn'), which means 'a time
when a plant bears flowers and fruit simul-
taneously.' We tend to translate it as

'Eternal Spring.' Uruapan is 500m lower in
altitude than Pátzcuaro and is much
warmer.

Fray Juan had a large market square, hospital and chapel built, and he arranged
streets in an orderly checkerboard pattern.
Under Spanish rule, Uruapan quickly grew
into a productive agricultural center, and
today it's renowned for high-quality *agua-
cates* (avocados) and fruit. It bills itself as
the Capital Mundial del Aguacate and has
an avocado fair in November. The town's
craftspeople are famed for their hand-
painted cedar lacquerware, particularly
trays and boxes.

Uruapan is a larger, less tidy place than
Pátzcuaro, with far less colonial ambience.
But it's still attractive with its red-tile roofs
and lush hillside setting. A splendid little
national park, Parque Nacional Eduardo
Ruiz, is just 15 minutes' walk from the town
center. Uruapan is also the best base for visiting the remarkable volcano Paricutín,
35km west.

Orientation
The city slopes down from north to south,
with the Río Cupatitzio running down its
west side. Most of the streets are still
arranged in the grid pattern laid down in
the 1530s. Apart from the bus station in the
northeast of town, everything of interest to
travelers is within walking distance of the
300m-long main plaza. This is actually three
joined plazas named, from east to west, El
Jardín Morelos, La Pérgola Municipal and
El Jardín de los Mártires de Uruapan. A
colonial church stands at each end of the
north side of the plaza. The portales facing
the plaza are named independently of the
streets; Portal Degollado is the east side of
the plaza, while Portal Carrillo and Portal
Matamoros run along the south side.

Street names change at the plaza and at
other points. The busy street along the south
side of the plaza is called Emilio Carranza
to the west and Obregón to the east. Farther
east, it changes again to Sarabia, which in-
tersects Paseo Lázaro Cárdenas, the main
road south to the coast.

Information
Tourist Offices The state Delegación de
Turismo (☎ 524-71-99), Juan Ayala 16, is a
couple of blocks northwest of the plaza. It

URUAPAN

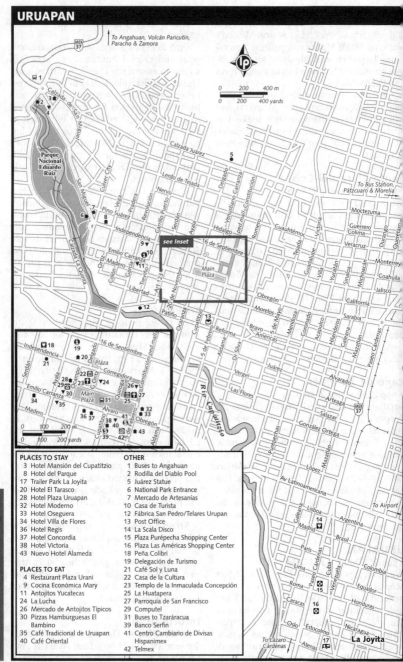

To Angahuan, Volcán Paricutín,
Paracho & Zamora

Parque
Nacional
Eduardo
Ruiz

see Inset

Main
Plaza

To Bus Station,
Pátzcuaro & Morelia

To Airport

To Lázaro
Cárdenas

La Joyita

PLACES TO STAY
3 Hotel Mansión del Cupatitzio
8 Hotel del Parque
17 Trailer Park La Joyita
20 Hotel El Tarasco
28 Hotel Plaza Uruapan
32 Hotel Moderno
33 Hotel Oseguera
34 Hotel Villa de Flores
36 Hotel Regis
37 Hotel Concordia
38 Hotel Victoria
43 Nuevo Hotel Alameda

PLACES TO EAT
4 Restaurant Plaza Urani
9 Cocina Económica Mary
11 Antojitos Yucatecas
24 La Lucha
26 Mercado de Antojitos Típicos
30 Pizzas Hamburguesas El
    Bambino
35 Café Tradicional de Uruapan
40 Café Oriental

OTHER
1 Buses to Angahuan
2 Rodilla del Diablo Pool
5 Juárez Statue
6 National Park Entrance
7 Mercado de Artesanías
10 Casa de Turista
12 Fábrica San Pedro/Telares Urupan
13 Post Office
14 La Scala Disco
15 Plaza Purépecha Shopping Center
16 Plaza Las Américas Shopping Center
18 Peña Colibrí
19 Delegación de Turismo
21 Café Sol y Luna
22 Casa de la Cultura
23 Templo de la Inmaculada Concepción
25 La Huatapera
27 Parroquia de San Francisco
29 Computel
31 Buses to Tzaráracua
39 Banco Serfin
41 Centro Cambiario de Divisas
    Hispanimex
42 Telmex

tocks brochures (some in English) and a simple map of Uruapan. The office is open 'am to 2.30pm and 4pm to 7pm Monday to Saturday.

The municipal Casa del Turista (☎ 524-50-91), in the courtyard at Emilio Carranza 44, often has material on local writers, history and cultural traditions, and the staff are keen to talk about these things. It stocks few brochures, but it does have some crafts for sale and a limited Web site: w www.uruapan.gob.mx. The office is open 9am to 7pm daily.

Money Several banks and ATMs are near the central plaza, especially on Cupatitzio in the first two blocks south of the plaza. Most banks are open 9am to 5.30pm Monday to Friday and 9am to 1pm Saturday, but some have shorter hours for foreign exchange. Centro Cambiario de Divisas Hispanimex, at Portal Matamoros 19 near the east end of the plaza, will change cash or traveler's checks until 7pm Monday to Friday and until 2pm Saturday.

Post & Communications The main post office, at Reforma 13, is just west of 5 de Febrero, three blocks south of the central plaza. It's open 8am to 7pm Monday to Friday, 9am to 1pm Saturday.

There's a Computel caseta on Ocampo opposite the west end of the plaza. The Telecomm office, a block north on Ocampo, offers fax and money-transfer service.

The small Telmex office on 5 de Febrero, just south of the plaza, has public phones as well as Internet connections (US$1.50 per hour). Café Sol y Luna, at Independencia 15A, also has inexpensive Internet access.

Travel Agencies A helpful travel agency for booking flights is Viajes Tzitzi (☎ 523-34-19), beside the entrance to Hotel Plaza Uruapan. The office also sells ETN and Primera Plus bus tickets.

La Huatapera

Near the northeast corner of the central plaza, La Huatapera is a low, colonnaded, colonial building around two sides of a timeworn stone patio. One of the institutions established in the 1530s under the auspices of Vasco de Quiroga, it was reputedly the first hospital in the Americas. The deco-

rations around the doors and windows were carved by Purépecha artisans in a Mudéjar (Moorish) style. The building houses the Museo Regional de Arte Popular, but it's currently closed to the public for major restoration work.

Parque Nacional Eduardo Ruiz

This lovely tropical park (main entrance: Calzada La Quinta at end of Independencia; admission adult/child US$0.90/0.50; open 8am-6pm daily) is only 1km west of the central plaza. It follows the lushly vegetated banks of the Río Cupatitzio from its source at the Rodilla del Diablo pool, at the park's north end. Legend has it that the devil knelt here and left the mark of his knee. Many paths guide a shady stroll down the gorge, over bridges and past waterfalls and fountains – the park is famous for its water features. Boys dive into the river's deepest pools and ask for coins.

Walk, or take a 'Parque' bus up Independencia from Ocampo. Maps and leaflets on the park's history are on sale at the ticket kiosk.

Special Events

Uruapan's festivals include the following:

Semana Santa – Palm Sunday is marked by a procession through the city streets. Figures and crosses woven from palm fronds are sold after the procession. A ceramics contest takes place, and a weeklong exhibition/market of Michoacán handicrafts fills up the central plaza; prices get lower as the week goes on.

Día de San Francisco – St Francis, the patron saint of Uruapan, is honored with colorful festivities on October 4.

Festival de Coros y Danzas – Around October 17-18, the Choir & Dance Festival is a contest of Purépecha dance and musical groups.

Feria del Aguacate – For two weeks in November, the Avocado Fair is a big event, with bullfights, cockfights, concerts and agricultural, industrial and handicraft exhibitions.

Places to Stay

Budget Camping and cheap hotels are available.

Trailer Park La Joyita (☎ 523-03-64, Estocolmo 22) Tent & trailer sites US$4.50 per person. This park is 1½ blocks east of Paseo Lázaro Cárdenas at the southern end of town. It has full hookups for 10 trailers, a

WESTERN CENTRAL

lawn area for tents, a barbecue and 24-hour hot water in the showers.

Hotel del Parque (☎ 524-38-45, Independencia 124) Singles/doubles US$13/15.50, twins US$16. Very handy to the national park, but 6½ blocks west of the central plaza, this place is still the most pleasant of Uruapan's cheap lodgings. The rooms are clean with tile floors, private bath and 24-hour hot water. Other amenities include a rear patio area and enclosed parking.

A row of uninspiring but inexpensive hotels lines up along Portal Santos Degollado at the east end of the plaza.

Hotel Moderno (☎ 524-02-12, Degollado 4) Singles/doubles US$9/15. Not exactly modern, this hotel offers habitable rooms, minimal comforts and reasonably reliable 24-hour hot water.

Hotel Oseguera (☎ 523-98-56, Degollado 2) Singles/doubles US$11/22. The well-worn Oseguera has mostly smaller, darker rooms, though you might get a nicer one overlooking the plaza.

Mid-Range **Hotel Villa de Flores** (☎ 524-28-00, Emilio Carranza 15) Singles/doubles US$30/37. This well-kept colonial-style hotel is just 1½ blocks west of the central plaza. Its colorful pink courtyard is surrounded by 27 smallish but comfortable rooms, all with cable TV and fan. The two-bed rooms on the rear courtyard are newer and brighter.

Hotel Regis (☎ 523-58-44, Portal Carrillo 12) Singles/doubles US$24/30. On the south side of the plaza, the Regis has 40 brightly decorated, mostly well-lit rooms with fans, phones and TV, plus its own restaurant and parking.

Hotel Concordia (☎ 523-04-00, W www .hotelconcordia.com.mx, Portal Carrillo 8) Singles/doubles US$31/38. Next door to the Regis is this comfortable, modern hotel with 58 large, spotless rooms and four suites, all with TV, phone and carpeting. It also has parking, a restaurant and laundry service.

Nuevo Hotel Alameda (☎ 523-41-00, 5 de Febrero 11) Singles/doubles US$24/31. Half a block south of the central plaza, this is another good, modern, mid-range hotel. Rooms are clean and comfortable, with air-con, heating, TV and phone. It advertises private parking, plus hygiene and morality.

Hotel El Tarasco (☎ 524-15-00, Independencia 2) Singles/doubles US$50/62. Half a block north of the plaza, the El Tarasco is a step up in quality, with 65 large and bright rooms, plus a restaurant and a swimming pool. There are good views from some of the upper floors.

Hotel Victoria (☎ 524-25-00, 800-420-3900, Cupatitzio 11) Singles/doubles US$52/60. The four-story, 80-room Victoria has nice rooms that offer all the modern conveniences but no views.

Top End **Hotel Plaza Uruapan** (☎ 523-37-00, fax 523-39-80, W www.hotelplaza uruapan.com.mx, Ocampo 64) Singles/doubles US$59/74, suites US$95. Catering mainly to business travelers, this place is at the west end of the main plaza and has a business center, meeting rooms and a gym. The exterior rooms have great views through floor-to-ceiling windows.

Hotel Mansión del Cupatitzio (☎ 523-21-00, fax 524-67-72, Calzada Fray Juan de San Miguel s/n) Singles/doubles US$77/97. This hacienda-style place at the north end of Parque Nacional Eduardo Ruiz is the most pleasant hotel in Uruapan. It's right next to the park, and its restaurant overlooks the Rodilla del Diablo pool where the Río Cupatitzio begins. The hotel has a swimming pool, lovely grounds, a gift shop, laundry service and so forth. Rates are more for a view of the park.

Places to Eat

Uruapan is a great place for low-budget taste treats.

Mercado de Antojitos Típicos (Constitución s/n) Open 6am-midnight daily. For those with tight budgets and adventurous eating habits, this market is a wonderful place to sample local food. Just one short block north of the plaza, under a big, barn-like roof, some 40 stalls serve authentic, typical Michoacán dishes – the real deal at a bargain price. It looks like one of the most hygienic markets in Mexico, but pick a stall that seems popular, to be on the safe side.

Several places on the south side of the plaza serve good breakfasts, economical comidas corridas and adequate à la carte meals for dinner. **Café La Pérgola** (Portal Carrillo 4) and **Café Oriental** (Portal Matamoros 16) are two examples of such stablishments, very similar in their quality and in their menus.

Cafetería La Placita (☎ 523-34-88,)campo 64) Light meals US$4. Open 7am-1pm daily. Beneath the Hotel Plaza Uruapan at the west end of the plaza, La *lacita does a good breakfast with fruit alad, yogurt and granola, and egg dishes. ater in the day come antojitos, snacks and a more expensive dinner menu.

Pizzas Hamburguesas El Bambino ☎ 524-38-82, Emilio Carranza 8) Basic student food US$3. Open 8am-10.30pm daily. For a slice of junk-food heaven, visit this place a few steps west of the central plaza. The burgers and burritos are particularly good, and the tasty pizzas have generous toppings – the *chica* size is plenty for one person.

Cocina Económica Mary (no ☎, Independencia 57) Mains US$3.50. Open 8.30am-5.30pm Mon-Sat. About 3½ blocks west of the central plaza, this well-patronized, family-run place serves a delicious homestyle meal of soup followed by a choice of several main courses from *bístek ranchero* to *pollo con mole*, plus a soda or glass of fresh juice.

Antojitos Yucatecas (☎ 524-61-52, Emilio Carranza 37) Mains under US$5. Also about 3½ blocks west of the town center, this tidy little place specializes in delicious dishes from Yucatán – *tacos cochinita pibil* is one of the most typical. It's highly recommended.

Restaurant Plaza Urani (☎ 524-86-98, Calzada Fray Juan de San Miguel s/n) Mains US$5-8. This restaurant opposite Hotel Mansión del Cupatitzio has beautifully situated open-air tables looking over the north end of the national park. The specialty is fresh *trucha arco iris* (rainbow trout), from the little trout farm in the park.

Cafés Locally grown coffee is a specialty in Uruapan.

La Lucha (☎ 524-03-75, García Ortiz 20) Coffee US$3. Sit back in the solid wooden furniture and enjoy a good, strong cup at this café, half a block north of the central plaza.

Café Tradicional de Uruapan (☎ 523-56-80, Emilio Carranza 5B) Coffee and cake US$3.50. Open 8.30am-10pm. Half a block west of the plaza, this is another good spot offering breakfasts, snacks, cakes and a large selection of coffees.

Entertainment

You might find one or two things to do after dark besides lingering over coffee or going to church.

Casa de la Cultura (García Ortiz 1) Half a block north of the plaza, this place hosts exhibitions, occasional concerts and other events. Check with the tourist office (☎ 524-71-99) to see what's cooking during your stay in Uruapan.

Café Sol y Luna (☎ 524-06-29, Independencia 15A) Open 10am-11pm. This place bills itself as an art café and is popular with a student crowd. It has a full bar, as well as good coffee, Internet connections and live jazz, blues or rock on some nights.

Peña Colibri (☎ 524-52-57, Independencia 18) This peña offers food and drink as well as a variety of live music – *canto nuevo, trova Cubana,* Mexican and other Latin American music.

La Scala Disco (☎ 524-26-09, Madrid 12) Admission US$2.50-5. Open 6pm-3am Tues-Sun. La Scala is a favorite dance venue for well-dressed, well-heeled young locals. The cover charge depends on the night and your gender.

Shopping

Telares Uruapan (☎ 524-06-77, Miguel Treviño s/n) The old Fábrica San Pedro – a late-19th-century factory now operated by Telares Uruapan – still turns out traditional Míchoacan costumes (*ropa típica*), as well as bedspreads, tablecloths, curtains etc, from pure wool and cotton. Products can be bought directly from the factory, beside the river a few blocks southwest of the town center.

Local crafts such as lacquered trays and boxes can be bought at the **Mercado de Artesanías**, opposite the entrance to Parque Nacional Eduardo Ruiz. A few **shops** nearby on Independencia sell the same sort of thing. The town **market**, which stretches more than half a kilometer up Constitución from the central plaza to Calzada Juárez, is worth a browse too.

Getting There & Away

Air Aeromar (☎ 523-50-50 at the airport) flies daily to and from Mexico City via Morelia.

Bus The bus station is 3km northeast of central Uruapan on the highway to

Pátzcuaro and Morelia. It has a post office, telegraph and fax office, telephone caseta, cafetería and a *guardería* for leaving luggage.

Buses run daily to cities all over central and northern Mexico, including:

Colima – 400km, 6-8 hours; 1 La Línea 1st-class at 9.45pm (US$18), 1 Autobuses de Occidente 2nd-class at 11.15am (US$15); it may be more convenient to go first to Zamora or even to Guadalajara

Guadalajara – 305km, 3½-5 hours, via La Barca; 5 deluxe by ETN (US$21), Primera Plus and La Línea Plus (US$17); regular Servicios Coordinados 1st-class (US$15); for the more scenic route around the south side of Lake Chapala, you need to change to a local bus at Zamora

Lázaro Cárdenas – 280km, 6 hours or less; 15 Parhikuni, La Línea Plus and Vía 2000 1st-class (US$16-17), hourly Galeana 2nd-class (US$14)

Mexico City (Terminal Poniente or Terminal Norte) – 430km, 6 hours; 6 ETN deluxe (US$35), frequent Primera Plus, Vía 2000 Plus and Vía 2000 1st-class (US$25-27), 4 Servicios Coordinados 2nd-class (US$21)

Morelia – 124km, 2 hours; 2 ETN deluxe (US$11), frequent Primera Plus and Parhikuni 1st-class (US$8), Galeana Ruta Paraíso 2nd-class every 15 minutes (US$5)

Pátzcuaro – 62km, 1 hour; Galeana or Ruta Paraíso 2nd-class every 15 minutes (US$3.50)

Zamora – 115km, 2-2½ hours; 3 ETN deluxe (US$9), 5 Primera Plus 1st-class (US$6.50), frequent Flecha Amarilla 2nd-class (US$5)

Getting Around

To/From the Airport The airport is on Avenida Latinoamericana about 8km southeast of the city center, a 15-minute drive. A taxi costs about US$4.

Bus Local buses marked 'Centro' run from the door of the bus station to the central plaza. If you want a taxi, buy a ticket from the *taquilla* in the station (US$1.75). On the return trip catch a 'Central Camionera' or 'Central' bus on the south side of the central plaza.

The local buses run from about 6am to 9pm daily. They cost US$0.40.

Car If you need wheels, try the local car rental agency Del Cupatitzio (☎ 523-11-81, cellular ☎ 044-452-500-69-19, @ autorent@prodigy.net.mx).

AROUND URUAPAN
Cascada de Tzaráracua

Ten kilometers south of Uruapan just off highway 37, the Río Cupatitzio falls 30m into two pools flanked by lush vegetation. Two kilometers upstream is another lovely waterfall, the smaller Tzararacuita, which is better and safer for swimming – local kids will show you the way for a tip. Tzaráracua buses depart from the middle of the south side of Uruapan's main plaza. They go every half hour on Saturday, Sunday and holidays, when the falls attract crowds. Other days these buses go only every couple of hours, so it's better to take an Autotransportes Galeana bus heading for Nueva Italia from the Uruapan bus station; these depart every 20 minutes and will drop you off at Tzaráracua. The buses stop at a car park. From there, it's a steep descent of about 1km to the main falls.

Tingambato
• **pop 6100** • **elev 1980m**

At Tingambato, a village about 30km from Uruapan on the road to Pátzcuaro, are ruins of a ceremonial site that existed from about AD 450 to 900. They show Teotihuacán influence and date from well before the Tarascan empire. The ruins include a ball court (rare in western Mexico), temple pyramids and an underground tomb where a skeleton and 32 skulls were found. A blue sign with a white pyramid points to the site from the highway, about 1km away.

Paracho
• **pop 16,000** • **elev 2220m**

Paracho, 40km north of Uruapan on highway 37, is a small Purépecha town famous for its handmade guitars. It's worth visiting if you want to buy an instrument or watch some of the country's best guitar makers at work. The local artisans are also known for their high-quality violins, cellos and other woodcrafts, including furniture. The liveliest time to come is during the annual Feria Nacional de la Guitarra (National Guitar Fair), a big weeklong splurge of music, dance, exhibitions, markets and cockfights in early August.

Many buses from Uruapan to Zamora will stop in Paracho. Autotransportes Galeana 2nd-class buses leave Uruapan every 15 minutes (1 hour, US$2.50).

VOLCÁN PARICUTÍN

On the afternoon of February 20, 1943, a Purépecha farmer, Dionisio Pulido, was plowing his cornfield some 35km west of Uruapan when the ground began to shake and swell and to spurt steam, sparks and hot ash. The farmer tried at first to cover the moving earth, but when that proved impossible, he fled. A volcano started to rise from the spot. Within a year it had risen 410m above the surrounding land and its lava had engulfed the Purépecha villages of San Salvador Paricutín and San Juan Parangaricutiro. No one was hurt: the lava flow was gradual, giving the villagers plenty of time to flee.

The volcano continued to spit lava and fire and to increase in size until 1952. Today its large black cone stands mute, emitting gentle wisps of steam. Near the edge of the 20-sq-km lava field, the top of San Juan's church protrudes eerily from the sea of solidified, black lava. It's the only visible trace of the two buried villages.

An excursion to Paricutín from Uruapan makes a fine day trip, to see San Juan's church engulfed in a jumble of black boulders and to climb the volcanic cone. At 2800m, the volcano is not particularly high – the much bigger Tancítaro towers to the south – but it's certainly memorable and fairly easy to access. If you want to do it in one day from Uruapan, as most people do, start early.

Angahuan & Around

Angahuan is the jumping-off point for treks and sightseeing around the volcano. It's a typical Purépecha village with wooden houses, dusty streets, little electricity and loudspeakers booming out announcements in the Purépecha language. On the main plaza is the 16th-century **Iglesia de Santiago Apóstol**, with some fine carving around its door done by a Moorish stonemason who accompanied the early Spanish missionaries here.

The ruined church of **Templo San Juan Parangaricutiro** is a 45-minute walk down a path that begins near the entrance to Las Cabañas (see Centro Turístico de Angahuan, below). The path is wide, gray with volcanic ash, and at times flanked by barbed-wire fences. It's an easy, enjoyable walk, and it costs nothing to visit the church. Getting around the site is surprisingly difficult, as the walls are filled with, and surrounded by, huge boulders of black volcanic rock. The missing tower was not a casualty of the volcano – it was never completed.

Centro Turístico de Angahuan (☎ 525-83-83, Camino al Paricutín s/n) Cabins US$44, dorm beds US$8. This sprawling, low-key tourist complex, commonly called 'Las Cabañas,' offers food, accommodation and some information about the volcano. There's supposedly an entry charge to the complex, though the fee isn't always collected. The restaurant has a minimal menu and sometimes shows an interesting video about the eruption, which helps fill in the long wait for your order. There's also a small exhibition of photos and press clippings on the volcano and its history. A lookout point provides good views of the lava field, the protruding San Juan church tower and the volcano itself.

Apart from staying at Las Cabañas, *camping* may be possible in the Angahuan area (ask at the municipal tourist office in Uruapan), or a guide may offer you *homestay* lodging at about US$7 per person.

Getting There & Away Angahuan is 32km from Uruapan on the road to Los Reyes, which branches west off highway 37 about 15km north of Uruapan. Galeana 2nd-class buses leave the Uruapan bus station for Angahuan every 30 minutes from 5am to 7pm. Alternatively, flag down a 'Los Reyes' bus near the Calzada de San Miguel traffic circle, just north of Parque Nacional Eduardo Ruiz in Uruapan. This will save some time getting out to the bus station east of town, then doubling back to the west side, but it won't guarantee you a seat on the bus. The one-hour bus ride to Angahuan (US$1) passes the now-forested stumps of a dozen or so older volcanoes.

To reach Las Cabañas on foot from the Angahuan bus stop, walk west into the village center, turn right at the main plaza, then left at the fork after 200m, where there's a building with a TV satellite dish. From the fork, the track leads straight to Las Cabañas, about 20 minutes away.

Buses back to Uruapan will pick up at the Angahuan turnoff (about 1km from the village) until at least 7pm nightly.

Climbing Paricutín

Bring some water and food from Uruapan as there's none on the route and precious little available in Angahuan.

At the Angahuan bus stop, guides with horses will offer to take you 1km to the Centro Turístico de Angahuan ('Las Cabañas'), the starting point for trips onto the lava field. The guides are mainly interested in taking you on a longer trip, to the church or to the volcano. If you want to go by horse, you can start negotiating at the bus stop. You probably won't get any better choice of guides or horses in town or at the tourist center, and the prices won't be any lower. To the ruined San Juan church you'll pay about US$8 for a horse and a guide, but it's an easy walk and you don't really need either.

To go up the volcano you can ride a horse to the base and climb up the last few hundred meters, or you can walk all the way, but either way you should hire a guide to show you the way. To ride to the base of the volcano and be guided up to the top will cost about US$30 (including the guide, the guide's horse and your horse). With a guide plus two tourists, it's about US$43. Most of the horses are pretty sedate and the guide should be able to lead them if necessary, but if you're not accustomed to riding, you might find four or five hours on a hard Mexican saddle is pretty wearing. If you'd rather walk to the volcano, you'll still need a guide (about US$18 per day), but walking guides are harder to find.

Some guides are young boys, with very little experience, poor equipment, little Spanish and zero English. Make sure you deal with the actual person who will be guiding you, and don't agree to go with someone who isn't able to look after himself. Make sure your guide brings something to eat and drink.

Trails to the Volcano Two routes lead to the crater. The more **direct route** begins behind the restaurant at Las Cabañas, to the left of the viewing area. The path is narrow and winds for 500m through a pine forest that can be disorienting. There are a lot of small tracks created by wood gatherers and tree planters, and it's easy to get lost.

A little beyond the pine forest you'll cross a dirt road and pick up the trail on the other side. Within 30m you should pass through a gate, and soon afterward the path begins to slope upward considerably. The trail weaves through thickets where wild flowers bloom much of the year. About here, you'll have to leave your horse and continue on foot. (It's not really worth having a horse on this route, but it may be difficult to find a guide willing to walk the whole way.) After about 30 minutes of hiking, there's a campsite (sadly, it may be covered with litter) and then the woods give way to a barren lava field. The path to the crater, over jagged black rock, is marked occasionally with splashes of paint.

About 150m from the summit, the rock gives way to a sandy ash and you'll see steam rising from fumaroles on knolls to the left of the trail. A narrow 40m trail links the main trail to the knolls, which are worth visiting. They are covered with bright yellow, sulfurous rock that is quite striking amid the surrounding black lava. You can feel steam rising from the crevices around you.

The lip of the crater has two high points. Beneath the northern lip, on the outside of the cone, is a dust slide that is fun to bound down at a fast, high-stepping walk. This brings you down near the flat, dusty horse trail (see below) that returns via the San Juan church. To return across the lava field and through the forest to Las Cabañas, pass on the dust slide and go back the way you came. Using this route most people need 3½ or four hours to reach the summit from Las Cabañas, and another three hours for the return trip.

The **horse trail** to the base of the cone is longer, but not as steep or rugged. This trail starts beside the entrance to Las Cabañas and skirts the southeastern edge of the lava field to San Juan church. From the church, the trail follows a road past some farms, then narrows and passes through brush before reaching an open, sandy area 15 minutes' walk from the foot of the volcano. There the horses are tied up under a shade tree while their riders make the final, 20-minute ascent on foot. The ride takes about two hours each way.

ZAMORA

● pop 121,000 ● elev 1560m ☎ 351

Zamora de Hidalgo (to give it its full name), about 115km northwest of Uruapan and

190km southeast of Guadalajara, is a pleasant town in the center of a rich agricultural region known for its strawberries and potatoes. Zamora's delicious *dulces* (sweets) are also famous, and on sale at numerous stalls in the market.

Founded in 1574, Zamora has an inordinate number of churches, including the so-called **Catedral Inconclusa**, started in 1898 and still not quite finished.

Fifteen kilometers southeast of Zamora, a short distance off highway 15 at Tangancícuaro, is the clear, spring-fed, tree-shaded **Laguna de Camécuaro**, a lovely spot for drivers to stop and picnic.

If you need to spend the night, Zamora has half a dozen hotels.

Hotel Nacional (☎ 512-42-24, Corregidora Ote 106) Single/doubles US$15/17. Rooms are small but clean at this inexpensive, respectable hotel, handy to the market and the center of town.

Zamora is something of a regional transport hub, and its bus station has regular connections to Guadalajara, Colima, Uruapan, Pátzcuaro and Morelia.

Northern Central Highlands

Northwest from Mexico City stretches a fairly dry, temperate upland region comprising the southern part of the Altiplano Central. This was where the Spanish found most of the silver and other precious metals central to their colonial ambitions in Mexico – and where they built some of the country's most magnificent cities from the silver's great fortunes. The most spectacular of these cities are Guanajuato and Zacatecas, which along with Potosí in Bolivia were the major silver-producing centers of the Americas. San Miguel de Allende, Querétaro and San Luis Potosí also have a wealth of colonial architecture, as well as lively arts and entertainment scenes. It's a highly rewarding region to visit, the distances are not huge and the landscape between the cities is always impressive.

The flatter, more fertile land, in an arc from Querétaro through Celaya and León to Aguascalientes, is known as the Bajío ('ba-HEE-o'), and has long been one of Mexico's major agricultural zones. From colonial times, the Bajío supplied food and other goods to the mining towns, and it formed an important transport corridor to Mexico City. Bajío cities have developed as industrial centers, though many of them retain a core of colonial architecture and have an important place in Mexico's history. It was here that the movement for independence from Spain began in 1810, and thus the region is known to Mexicans as La Cuna de la Independencia (the Cradle of Independence). The town of Dolores Hidalgo, where the uprising started, and nearby places like San Miguel de Allende, Querétaro and Guanajuato are full of key sites from this historic movement.

Before the Spanish reached Mexico, the northern central highlands were inhabited by fierce seminomadic tribes known to the Aztecs as Chichimecs. They resisted Spanish conquest longer than any other Mexican peoples and were finally pacified in the late 16th century by an offer of food and clothing in return for peace. The wealth subsequently amassed in the region by the Spanish was at the cost of the lives of many of these people, who were used as virtual slave labor in the mines.

Highlights

- Zacatecas – stylish silver city with a sublime cathedral, museums, mountains and a nightclub in a mine tunnel
- Real de Catorce – ghost town of miracles, magic, stark mountains and fine Italian food
- Guanajuato – student city with colonial mansions, crooked cobbled alleyways and a very quixotic festival
- San Miguel de Allende – traditional city merges with expat chic for exuberant fiestas, top-notch food and super shopping
- Highway 120 through Sierra Gorda – remote region of archaeological sites

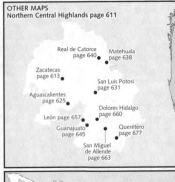

OTHER MAPS
Northern Central Highlands page 611

This chapter encompasses the states of Zacatecas, Aguascalientes, Guanajuato and Querétaro, and most of San Luis Potosí state. Eastern San Luis Potosí state is covered in the Central Gulf Coast chapter.

NORTHERN CENTRAL HIGHLANDS

Zacatecas State

The state of Zacatecas ('zak-a-TEK-as') is one of Mexico's largest in area (73,252 sq km) but smallest in population (1.35 million). It's a dry, rugged, cactus-strewn expanse on the fringe of Mexico's northern semideserts, with large tracts almost blank on the map. The fact that it has any significant population is largely due to the mineral wealth the Spanish discovered here, mainly around the capital city Zacatecas. The climate is generally delightful – dry, clear and sunny, but not too hot.

ZACATECAS
- pop 108,200 • elev 2445m ☎ 492

If you've come down from the north, welcome to the first of Mexico's justly fabled silver cities. If you've been visiting more southerly silver cities like Guanajuato, it's worth coming a few hours farther north, because Zacatecas is a particularly beautiful and fascinating city.

Some of Mexico's finest colonial buildings, including perhaps its most stunning cathedral, cluster along narrow, winding streets at the foot of a spectacular rock-topped hill called Cerro de la Bufa. Set amid dry, arid country, this historic city has much to detain you, from trips into an old silver mine to some excellent museums and the ascent of la Bufa itself by *teleférico* (cable car). A state capital and university city, Zacatecas is sophisticated for its size, and though it's popular with Mexican and European visitors, its off-center location insulates it from hordes of tourists.

History

Before the Spanish arrived, the area was inhabited by the Zacatecos – one of the Chichimec tribes. Indigenous people had mined local mineral deposits for centuries before the Spanish arrived; it's said that the silver rush here was started by a Chichimec giving a piece of the fabled metal to a conquistador. The Spaniards founded a settlement and, in 1548, started mining operations, virtually enslaving many indigenous people in the process. Caravan after caravan of silver was sent off to Mexico City. While some treasure-laden wagons were raided by hostile tribes, enough silver reached its destination to create fabulously wealthy silver barons. Agriculture and ranching developed to serve the rapidly growing town.

In the first quarter of the 18th century, Zacatecas' mines were producing 20% of Nueva España's silver. At this time the city became an important base for missionaries spreading Catholicism as far north as what are now the US states of Arizona and New Mexico.

In the 19th century political events diminished the flow of silver as various forces fought to control the city. Although silver production later improved under Porfirio Díaz, the revolution disrupted it. And it was here in 1914 that Pancho Villa, through brilliant tactics, defeated a stronghold of 12,000 soldiers loyal to the unpopular President Victoriano Huerta.

After the revolution, Zacatecas continued to thrive on silver. It remains a mining center to this day, with the 200-year-old El Bote mine still productive.

Orientation

The city center lies in a valley between Cerro de la Bufa, with its strange rocky cap, to the northeast, and the smaller Cerro del Grillo to the northwest. Most facilities and attractions are within walking distance of the center, and this is a wonderful city in which to walk. The two key streets are Avenida Hidalgo, running roughly north-south, with the cathedral toward its north end; and Avenida Juárez, running roughly east-west across the south end of Avenida Hidalgo. If you get lost, just ask the way back to one of these two streets. Avenida Hidalgo becomes Avenida González Ortega south of its intersection with Avenida Juárez.

Information

The state tourist office (☎ 924-40-47, 800-712-4078, w www.turismozacatecas.gob.mx) is upstairs in an old colonial building at Avenida Hidalgo 403, open 9am to 8pm Monday to Saturday, 10am to 7pm Sunday. They're very helpful and have plenty of brochures, in Spanish, on Zacatecas city and state. Some staff members speak English.

Plenty of banks around the central area change traveler's checks and cash, from about 9am to 5pm Monday to Friday, 10am to 1pm Saturday. Nearly all have ATMs.

The post office is at Allende 111, just east of Avenida Hidalgo, open 8am to 7pm Monday to Friday, 9am to 1pm Saturday.

Telephone casetas are in the bus station and on Callejón de las Cuevas, off Avenida Hidalgo beside Café Zas. The Telecomm office, on Hidalgo at Juárez, offers public fax service.

Internet access is inexpensive here. Two good places, both charging about US$1.75 per hour, are CyberNovus, upstairs on Lancaster near Villalpando (9am to 9pm daily), and Juegos en Red, on Dr Hierro at the corner of Callejón de la Caja (9am to 10pm daily).

Lavandería El Indio Triste, Tolusa 826 does a wash, dry and fold for US$1.50 per kg. It's open 9am to 9pm Monday to Friday, 9am to 3pm Saturday.

Plaza de Armas

Plaza de Armas is the open space on the north side of the pink-stone **cathedral** which is perhaps the ultimate expression of Mexican baroque. The cathedral was built chiefly between 1729 and 1752, just before baroque edged into its final Churrigueresque phase. And in this city of affluent silver barons, no expense was spared.

The highlight is the stupendous main façade, which faces Avenida Hidalgo. This wall of amazingly detailed yet harmonious carvings has been interpreted as a giant symbol of the tabernacle, which is the receptacle for the wafer and the wine that confer communion with God, the heart of Catholic worship. A tiny figure of an angel holding a tabernacle can be seen at the middle of the design, the keystone at the top of the round central window. Above this, at

ZACATECAS

PLACES TO STAY
12 Hotel Continental Plaza
13 Casa Santa Lucia
21 Posada de la Moneda
30 Hostal Villa Colonial
33 Hotel Mesón de Jobito
41 Hostel del Río
43 Hotel Condesa
47 Posada de los Condes
50 Hotel Zamora
51 Hotel del Parque
52 Hotel Quinta Real
55 Hotel María Conchita
56 Hotel Gami
58 Hotel Colón

PLACES TO EAT
2 Cafetería Rancho Grande
23 Restaurant Cazadores
25 Nueva Galicia; Zacatecas 450
26 La Cantera Musical
28 Café y Nevería Acropolis
35 Café Zas
42 Restaurant Condesa
44 Mercado El Laberinto

46 Restaurant Fonda El Jacalito
48 El Pastor
49 Mercado Arroyo de la Plata

OTHER
1 Museo Rafael Coronel
3 Fuente de los Conquistadores
4 Mina El Edén (East Entrance)
5 Museo Manuel Felguérez
6 Lavandería El Indio Triste
7 Mina El Edén (West Entrance); Disco El Malacate
8 Museo Pedro Coronel

9 Plazuela de Santo Domingo
10 Templo de Santo Domingo
11 Palacio de la Mala Noche
14 Salzacatecas
15 Palacio de Gobierno
16 IMSS Hospital
17 CyberNovus
18 Museo Zacatecano
19 IMSS Casa de Moneda
20 Tourist Office; El Pueblito
22 Juegos en Red
24 Teatro Calderón
27 El Paraíso
29 El Claustro

31 Ex-Templo de San Agustín
32 Rectoria
34 Jardín Juárez
36 Post Office
37 Málaga
38 Cactus
39 Telecomm
40 Banamex; ATM
45 Museo Francisco Goitia
53 Centro Comercial Zacatecas (Old Bus Station)
54 Local buses to Guadalupe
57 Budget Rent-a-Car

the center of the third tier, is Christ, and above Christ is God. The other main statues are the 12 apostles, while a smaller figure of the Virgin stands immediately above the center of the doorway. The whole façade is now shrouded in a fine mesh, which is scarcely visible and a lot less intrusive than a crust of pigeon poop.

The south and north façades, though simpler, are also very fine. The central sculpture on the southern façade is of La Virgen de los Zacatecas, the city's patroness. The north façade shows Christ crucified, attended by the Virgin Mary and St John.

The interior of the cathedral is disarmingly plain, though it was once adorned with elaborate gold and silver ornaments and festooned with tapestries and paintings. This wealth was plundered in the course of Zacatecas' turbulent history.

The **Palacio de Gobierno** on the plaza's east side was built in the 18th century for a family of colonial gentry. It was acquired by the state in the 19th century. In the turret of its main staircase is a mural of the history of Zacatecas state, painted in 1970 by Antonio Rodríguez.

The lovely white **Palacio de la Mala Noche** on the west side of the plaza was built in the late 18th century for the owner of the Mala Noche mine near Zacatecas. It houses state government offices.

Plazuela Francisco Goitia

A block south of the cathedral a broad flight of stairs descends from Avenida Hidalgo to Tacuba, forming a charming and beautifully proportioned open space overlooked by terraces on either side. The plazuela is a popular meeting place and is often used as an informal amphitheater for buskers, clowns and street musicians.

North of the plazuela, **Mercado González Ortega** is an impressive iron-columned building from the 1880s that used to hold Zacatecas' main market. In the 1980s the upper level, entered from Avenida Hidalgo, was renovated into an upscale shopping center. The lower level, facing Tacuba, was once used for *bodegas* (storage rooms) and now houses several restaurants.

Opposite the plazuela on Hidalgo, the 1890s **Teatro Calderón** (☎ 922-81-20) dates from the Porfiriato period. This lovely theater is as busy as ever staging plays, concerts, films and art exhibitions; check out the architectural model in the foyer.

Plazuela de Santo Domingo

A block west of the cathedral, the Plazuela de Santo Domingo is dominated by the **Templo de Santo Domingo** and reached from the Plaza de Armas by a narrow lane, Callejón de Veyna. Although the church is done in a more sober baroque style than the cathedral, it has some fine gilded altars and paintings and a graceful horseshoe staircase. Built by the Jesuits in the 1740s, the church was taken over by Dominican monks when the Jesuits were expelled in 1767.

Museo Pedro Coronel (☎ 922-80-21, *Plaza de Santo Domingo s/n; admission US$2.25; open 10am-5pm Fri-Wed*) is housed in a 17th-century former Jesuit college beside Santo Domingo. Pedro Coronel (1923-85) was an affluent Zacatecan artist who bequeathed to his hometown his great collection of art and artifacts from all over the world, as well as much of his own work. The collection includes 20th-century prints; drawings and paintings by Picasso, Rouault, Chagall, Kandinsky and Miró; some entertaining Hogarth lithographs; and many fine ink drawings by Francisco de Goya (1746-1828). The pre-Hispanic Mexican artifacts seem to have been chosen as much for their artistic appeal as their archaeological importance, and there's an amazing collection of masks and other pieces from ancient Egypt, Greece, Rome, Asia, Africa, and even New Guinea. It all adds up to one of provincial Mexico's best art museums.

Calles Dr Hierro & Auza

Dr Hierro, leading south from Plazuela de Santo Domingo, and its continuation Auza, are quiet, narrow streets. About 100m from Plazuela de Santo Domingo is the **Casa de Moneda**, which housed the Zacatecas mint (Mexico's second biggest) during the 19th century. A little farther down is the **Museo Zacatecano** (☎ 922-65-80, *Dr Hierro 301; admission US$1.50; open 10am-5pm Wed-Mon*), largely devoted to Huichol art.

Another 100m south is the **Ex-Templo de San Agustín**, built as a church for Augustinian monks in the 17th century. During the anticlerical movement of the 19th century, the church was turned into a casino. Then, in 1882, it was purchased by American Presbyterian missionaries who destroyed its 'too Catholic' main façade, replacing it with a blank white wall. In the 20th century the church returned to Catholic use, and its adjoining former monastery is now the seat of the Zacatecas bishopric. The church's finest feature is the plateresque carving of the conversion of St Augustine over the north doorway.

The street ends at **Jardín Juárez**, a tiny rectangle of a park. The Rectoría, or administrative headquarters, of the Universidad Autónoma de Zacatecas is housed in a neoclassical building on its west side.

Mina El Edén

El Edén Mine *(☎ 922-30-02; tours US$2.25, every 15 minutes 10am to 6pm daily)*, once one of Mexico's richest, is a 'must' for visitors to Zacatecas because of the dramatic insight it gives into the source of wealth in this region and the terrible price paid for it. Digging for fabulous hoards of silver, gold, iron, copper and zinc, the enslaved indigenous people, including many children, worked under horrific conditions. At one time up to five people a day died from accidents or diseases like silicosis and tuberculosis.

El Edén was worked from 1586 until the 1950s. Today the fourth of its seven levels is kept open for visitors. The lower levels are flooded. A miniature train or an elevator takes you deep inside the Cerro del Grillo, the hill in which the mine is located. Then guides – who may or may not speak a little English – lead you along floodlit walkways past deep shafts and over subterranean pools.

The mine has two entrances. To reach the higher one (the east entrance), walk about 100m to the southwest from the Cerro de Grillo teleférico station; from this entrance, tours start with an elevator descent. To reach the west entrance from the town center, walk west along Parque Avenida Juárez and stay on it after its name changes to Torreón at the Alameda. Turn right immediately after the big IMSS hospital above the park (a Ruta 7 bus from the corner of Avenida Hidalgo will go up Avenida Juárez and past the hospital) and a short walk will bring you to the mine entrance where tours begin with a descent on the narrow-gauge railway. For information about Disco El Malacate, the mine's nighttime alter ego, see the Entertainment section.

Teleférico

The most exhilarating ride in Zacatecas, and the easiest way to reach Cerro de la Bufa, is the teleférico *(☎ 922-01-70; admission US$2.25, open 10am-6pm daily)* that crosses high above the city from Cerro del Grillo. Just walk to the east from Mina El Edén (east entrance) and you'll reach the teleférico's Cerro del Grillo station after a couple of minutes. Alternatively, walk up the steep steps of Callejón de García Rojas, which lead straight up to the teleférico from Genaro Codina; you can see the teleférico cables, so it's easy to find the terminal.

The Swiss-built teleférico operates every 15 minutes (except when it's raining or when winds exceed 60km/h), and the trip takes seven minutes.

Cerro de la Bufa

Cerro de la Bufa is the rock-topped hill that dominates Zacatecas from the northeast. The most appealing of the many explanations for its name is that *bufa* is an old Spanish word for wineskin, which is certainly what the rocky formation atop the hill looks like. The views from the top are superb, and there's an interesting group of monuments, a chapel and a museum up there.

The small **Museo de la Toma de Zacatecas** *(☎ 922-80-66; admission US$1.50; open 10am-5pm Tues-Sun)* commemorates the 1914 battle fought on the slopes of la Bufa in which the revolutionary División del Norte, led by Pancho Villa and Felipe Ángeles, defeated the forces of President Victoriano Huerta. This gave the revolutionaries control of Zacatecas, which was the gateway to Mexico City. The museum features descriptions of the battle and contemporary newspaper cuttings, all in Spanish.

La Capilla de la Virgen del Patrocinio, adjacent to the museum, is named after the patron saint of miners. Above the altar of this 18th-century chapel is an image of the Virgin that is said to be capable of healing the sick. Thousands of pilgrims make their way here each year during the weeks either side of September 8, when the image is carried to the cathedral.

Just east of the museum and chapel stand three imposing equestrian **statues** of the victors of the battle of Zacatecas – Villa, Ángeles, and Pánfilo Natera. A path behind the Villa and Natera statues leads to the rocky **summit** of La Bufa, where there are marvelous views on all sides, stretching over the city and away to mountain ranges far in the distance. The hill is topped by a metal cross that is illuminated at night.

A path along the foot of the rocky hilltop, starting to the right of the statues, leads to the **Mausoleo de los Hombres Ilustres de Zacatecas**, with the tombs of Zacatecan heroes from 1841 to the present day.

An exciting and convenient way to ascend la Bufa is by the teleférico (see earlier section). More strenuously, you can walk up it (start by going up Calle del Ángel from the east end of the cathedral). To reach it by car, take Carretera a la Bufa, which begins at Avenida López Velarde beside the university library. A taxi will cost about US$4.50. All three routes bring you to the monuments, chapel and museum. Just above the teleférico station, the quaint round building is a meteorological observatory.

You can return to the city by the teleférico or by a footpath leading downhill from the statues.

Museo Manuel Felguérez

This newly opened museum (☎ 924-37-05, cnr Colón & Seminario; admission US$2.25; open 10am-5pm Wed-Mon) is a couple of blocks west of Tolusa, up some steep callejones (alleys). It specializes in abstract art, particularly the work of Zacatecan artist Manuel Felguérez, but also includes paintings, sculptures and installations by other artists on temporary or permanent exhibition; it's a varied, exciting and stunning collection. The building itself, originally a seminary, was later used as a prison, and has now been renovated to create some remarkable exhibition spaces.

Museo Rafael Coronel

The Rafael Coronel Museum (☎ 922-81-16, cnr Abasolo & Matamoros; admission US$2.25; open 10am-5pm Thur-Tues), imaginatively housed in the ruins of the lovely 16th-century ex-Convento de San Francisco in the north of the city, contains Mexican folk art collected by the Zacatecan artist Rafael Coronel, brother of Pedro Coronel and son-in-law of Diego Rivera. The highlight is the astonishing, colorful display of over 2000 masks used in traditional dances

and rituals. This is probably the biggest collection of Mexican masks in the country. Also to be seen are pottery, puppets, pre-Hispanic objects and drawings and sketches by Rivera.

Museo Francisco Goitia

The Francisco Goitia Museum (☎ 922-80-66, Estrada 102; admission US$2.25; open 10am-5pm Tues-Sun) displays work by several major Zacatecan artists of the 20th century. Set in a fine former governor's mansion, above the pleasant Parque Enrique Estrada south of the city's central area, it's well worth the short walk from the center. Francisco Goitia (1882-1960) himself did some particularly good paintings of indigenous people. There's also a very striking Goitia self-portrait in the museum. Other artists represented include Pedro Coronel, Rafael Coronel and Manuel Felguérez.

Organized Tours

A couple of companies run tours of city sights and places of interest out of town. Typical offerings are a four-hour city tour including the mine and the teleférico (US$17); four-hour tours to Guadalupe (US$17); and a six-hour trip to the archaeological site of La Quemada and the town of Jerez (US$21). The tourist office can recommend tour companies, including **Viajes Mazzocco** (☎ 922-899-54, Fátima 115) or **De La O Tours** (☎ 922-234-64, Matamoros 153-C).

Special Events

La Morisma Usually held on the last Friday, Saturday and Sunday in August, this festival features the most spectacular of the many mock battles staged at Mexican fiestas commemorating the triumph of the Christians over the Muslims (Moors) in old Spain. Rival 'armies' parade through the city streets in the mornings, then, accompanied by bands of musicians, enact two battle sequences, one around midday and one in the afternoon, between Lomas de Bracho in the northeast of the city and Cerro de la Bufa. One sequence portrays a conflict between Emperor Charlemagne and Almirante Balam, king of Alexandria. The other deals with a 16th-century Muslim rebellion led by Argel Osmán. The enactments develop over the festival's three days, both culminating in Christian victory on Sunday.

Church services and other ceremonies also form part of the celebrations.

Feria de Zacatecas Zacatecas stages its annual fair from about September 5 to 21. Renowned matadors come to fight the famous local bulls; *charreadas* (rodeos), concerts, plays and agricultural and craft shows are staged; and on September 8 the image of La Virgen del Patrocinio is carried to the cathedral from its chapel on the Cerro de la Bufa.

Rodeo rider at the Fería de Zacatecas

Places to Stay

Budget Zacatecas' cheap lodgings tend to be in extreme contrast to the stately beauty of its colonial architecture. The cheaper places don't have parking, but public lots in the center are only US$1 or so per night.

Hostal Villa Colonial (☎/fax 922-19-80, e hostalvillacolonial@hotmail.com, cnr 1 de Mayo & Callejón Mono Prieto) Dorm beds US$9, private rooms US$20. Centrally located near the cathedral, this new HI-affiliated hostel is a great place for budget travelers. Facilities include kitchen, laundry, a TV lounge and Internet access.

Hotel Zamora (☎ 922-12-00, Plazuela Zamora 303) Singles/doubles US$12/16. The least expensive hotel in the center of town, the Zamora is two blocks south of Jardín Independencia, and some of the better rooms overlook pretty Plazuela Zamora. All rooms have minimal facilities.

The cheaper ones can be small and gloomy, so check first.

Hostal del Río (☎ 924-00-35, fax 922-78-33, Avenida Hidalgo 116) Singles/doubles US$18/22. Often full, this small hotel has a great location, a bit of character and an assortment of clean, comfortable rooms of various sizes and prices.

Hotel del Parque (☎ 922-04-79, Avenida González Ortega 202) Singles/doubles US$11/14. About 1.5km southwest of the cathedral and up the hill behind Parque Enrique Estrada, this hotel is popular choice. Rooms are a good size and clean enough, but a bit short on natural light.

Other cheapies are farther out, on and around Boulevard López Mateos.

Hotel María Conchita (☎ 922-14-94, Boulevard López Mateos 401) Singles/doubles US$14/16. This modern hotel has clean rooms with TV and phone and is a good option at this price. Traffic noise may be a problem in the front rooms.

Hotel Gami (☎ 922-80-05, Boulevard López Mateos 309) Singles/doubles US$16/22. Down the hill from the María Conchita, the Gami's small rooms are quite pleasant and recently repainted, and all have TV.

Hotel Colón (☎ 922-89-25, fax 922-04-64, Boulevard López Mateos 106) Singles/doubles US$22/28. The Colón is between two busy streets (its second address is Avenida López Velarde 508), and a pleasant walk from the center of town. Rooms are reasonably sized and well kept, and include TV and phone.

Mid-Range Mid-range and top-end hotels hike their prices in high season (Christmas, August and Semana Santa). At other times you may be able to get a discount on the prices given here. All these places have TV and phone in the rooms.

Hotel Condesa (☎ 922-11-60, Avenida Juárez 12) Singles/doubles US$26/30 to US$38/43. Centrally located near the corner of Avenida Hidalgo, the Condesa has 60 rooms around a covered courtyard. Nearly all have exterior windows; those facing northeast have fine views of La Bufa and a few have balconies. Some rooms are renovated and more expensive, but the less expensive, unrenovated rooms are quite OK and a better value.

Posada de los Condes (☎ 922-10-93, Avenida Juárez 18) Singles/doubles US$26/30. Across the street from the Condesa, this colonial building is over three centuries old, but a recent modernization has removed most evidence of its age from the interior. The carpeted rooms are pleasant, modern and well kept, though most are lacking an exterior window.

Posada de la Moneda (☎ 922-08-81, Avenida Hidalgo 413) Singles/doubles US$37/53. An imposing old building and a perfect location, a block south of the cathedral, make this one of the most attractive-looking hotels in town. The spacious rooms are very comfortable and nicely decorated, though not with as much old-fashioned charm as you might expect.

Motel del Bosque (☎ 922-07-45, Paseo Díaz Ordaz s/n) Singles/doubles US$40/50. This motel is on the Periférico (ring road) on the northwest side of town, uphill from the cable car terminal. It's ideal if you have a vehicle but don't want to drive in the congested central area; you can easily walk to the center, but the climb back will be harder! Quiet, comfortable rooms come with all modern conveniences, and some have great views over the city.

Top End Hotel Continental Plaza (☎ 922-61-83, fax 922-62-45, w http://hotel.sidek .com.mx, Avenida Hidalgo 703) Singles & doubles US$130. This hotel is superbly located in a renovated colonial building facing the Plaza de Armas. The 115 air-conditioned rooms and suites have comfortable, modern furnishings, minibars and cable TV, but not much colonial charm. The upstairs restaurant has a great view of the cathedral.

Casa Santa Lucia (☎ 924-49-00, 800-711-00-59, e mazzocco@zac1.telmex.net.mx, Avenida Hidalgo 717) Singles/doubles US$54/70. Once the bishop's residence, this old building is just a short walk from the cathedral. It's now a small and very appealing hotel with a comfortable, rustic character.

Hotel Mesón de Jobito (☎ 924-17-22, fax 924-35-00, e hmjobito@logicnet .com.mx, Jardín Juárez 143) Singles & doubles & suites from US$140. Several restored buildings and a small colonial street have all been incorporated into a superb luxury hotel. The finely decorated rooms,

excellent restaurant, bar and lobby are all rich with charm and historic character.

Hotel Quinta Real (☎ 922-91-04, fax 922-84-40, w www.quintareal.com, Rayón 434) Suites US$225. The best hotel in town, the Quinta Real is spectacularly constructed around Zacatecas' former main bullring, with the arches of the fine old El Cubo aqueduct running across the front of the hotel. The least expensive rooms are large and very comfortable 'master suites.'

Places to Eat

Many restaurants have local specialties using such ingredients as nopal, pumpkin, and pumpkin seeds. Locally produced wine is good. You might also like to try *aguamiel* (honey water), a nutritional drink made from a type of cactus. Early in the day, look on and around Avenida Hidalgo for burros carrying pottery jugs of the beverage.

There are two produce markets in the center. **Mercado El Laberinto** has its main entrance on Avenida Juárez. Budget eateries abound in the small streets around this market. A little to the southeast, **Mercado Arroyo de la Plata** can be entered from the curved street Arroyo de la Plata.

There are lots of mid-range possibilities on Avenida Hidalgo and Avenida Juárez, serving well-prepared Mexican standards, as well as items from the ice cream/hamburger/french fries food group.

Avenida Hidalgo Area It's a pleasure to walk this lively street, trying to choose between the many excellent eateries. Most are open daily from around 8am to 10pm or even later.

Café y Nevería Acrópolis (☎ 922-12-84, cnr Hidalgo & Plazuela Candelario Huizar) Prices US$3-6. Just south of the cathedral, this café is popular with locals and visitors for excellent coffee, delicious cakes and light meals.

La Cantera Musical (☎ 922-88-28, Tacuba 2) Prices US$4-8. Open 8am-11pm. In the old storerooms underneath Mercado González Ortega, this restaurant has classic and truly delicious Mexican food. It's a fun place with the kitchen in full view and live music some nights. Set breakfasts cost about US$5, and full meals, snacks and drinks are dispensed all day long.

Nueva Galicia (☎ 922-80-46, *Plazuela Goitia 102*) Prices US$5-9. This smart restaurant-bar is on the corner of Hidalgo, beside a lively little plaza. It offers a good choice of breakfasts, and well-prepared, slightly pricey meals for lunch and dinner.

Zacatecas 450 (no ☎, *Plazuela Goitia 104*) Prices US$3-7. This hole-in-the-wall beside Plazuela Goitia does grills, *mariscos,* enchiladas etc, from morning until late at night.

Restaurant Cazadores (☎ 924-22-04, *Callejón de la Caja 104*) Prices US$8. 'Cazadores' means 'hunters,' and this restaurant is suitably decorated with animal heads and has a very meaty menu. The main attraction, though, is the location, upstairs and opposite the lively Plazuela Goitia – try to get a window seat.

El Pueblito (☎ 924-38-18, *Hidalgo 403*) Prices US$4-8. In the same building as the tourist office, El Pueblito offers tasty renditions of most standard Mexican dishes and local Zacatecan specialties. It has bright decor, light entertainment and an enjoyable atmosphere.

Café Zas (☎ 922-70-89, *Hidalgo 201*) Prices US$4-7. Popular, clean and friendly, Café Zas, near the south end of Hidalgo, serves decent breakfasts, *antojitos* (appetizers), and substantial chicken or meat meals.

Cafetería Rancho Grande (no ☎, *Plazuela de García s/n*) Prices around US$3. From the cathedral, continue north on Hidalgo for about six blocks to this small, family-style café, a few blocks north of the cathedral. It's a good stop before or after Museo Rafael Coronel, for typical dishes like red enchiladas and cheese or a filling comida corrida.

Jardín Independencia Area *Restaurant Fonda El Jacalito* (☎ 922-07-71, *Avenida Juárez 18*) Prices US$3-8. This bright, airy place is the best on the street, offering set breakfasts from US$4, an economical comida corrida, and tasty versions of traditional favorites.

Restaurant Condesa (☎ 922-11-60, *Avenida Juárez 12*) Prices US$4-8. Attached to the Hotel Condesa, this is another standard eatery, but OK for an inexpensive breakfast or lunch.

El Pastor (☎ 922-16-35, *Independencia 24*) Prices US$3. Open 8am-9pm. This friendly, family-run restaurant is on the south side of Jardín Independencia, just off the east end of Avenida Juárez. It's busy serving up charcoal-roasted chicken, tortilla chips and salad. Pay a little more for chicken *mole* and rice.

Hotel Quinta Real (☎ 922-91-04, *on Rayón*) Prices US$10-20. About six blocks south of Jardín Independencia, the restaurant at Hotel Quinta Real is especially memorable for its outlook to the bullring and aqueduct, as well as for its elegant ambiance and excellent Mexican-international cuisine.

Entertainment

Disco El Malacate (☎ 922-30-02, *Dovali s/n*) Admission US$5.50. Open 9.30pm-2.30am Thur-Sat. Get down in a gallery of the Mina El Edén to a mix of US and Latin music with a big crowd of locals and domestic and international tourists. The essential Zacatecas nightlife experience, it really gets going around 11.30pm. Drinks are reasonably priced. Space is limited, so it's a good idea to reserve a table.

In the center of the city several other dance clubs jump on Thursday, Friday and Saturday nights.

El Claustro (☎ 044-492-927-05-55, *Aguascalientes 10*) Admission US$5.50. Open 9pm-3am Fri-Sat. Loud music and crowds outside make it easy to find this disco-nightclub-party place, on a small street east off Tacuba. It's been popular for years.

Cactus (☎ 922-05-09, *Avenida Hidalgo 111*) Admission US$3.50 Fri & Sat. Open 9pm-3am Mon-Sat. Cactus is an enjoyable video-and-billiards bar open until late every night, with music and dancing (and a cover charge) on Friday and Saturday.

El Paraíso (☎ 922-61-64, *cnr Avenida Hidalgo & Plazuela Goitia*) A smart bar in the southwest corner of the Mercado González Ortega, El Paraíso has a friendly, varied, mostly 30s clientele and is open nightly; it's busy on Friday and Saturday.

Salzacatecas (☎ 924-39-90, *Avenida Hidalgo 634*) Open Thur-Sat. As the name suggests, this is Zacatecas' salsa centro, with live music and a lively, mixed crowd schmoozing, smooching and sashaying in a series of upstairs rooms.

Teatro Calderón (☎ 922-81-20) is the top central venue for cultural events.

For Whom the Horn Toots

Zacatecas has a tradition of *callejoneadas* – a custom from Spain in which a group of professional musicians in costume leads a crowd of revelers through the city, drinking wine, singing and telling stories along the way. In Zacatecas it's usually horn players leading the parade. There doesn't seem to be a regular schedule but during fiestas and on some weekends callejoneadas set off around 8pm from Teatro Calderón. You can join in for free; ask for details at the tourist office.

Shopping

Zacatecas is known for fine leather, silver and colorful sarapes. Try along Arroyo de la Plata and in the indoor market off this street. *Mercado González Ortega* is somewhat upmarket with silver jewelry; another shop specializes in local wines; and yet another in *charrería* gear – boots, saddles, chaps, belts, sarapes and more.

The Zacatecas silversmithing industry is being revived in a number of workshops at the *Centro Platero*, east of town, between Zacatecas and Guadalupe. Tour companies can arrange visits to these workshops, or you can take a taxi.

Getting There & Away

Air Mexicana (☎ 922-74-29) flies direct daily to/from Mexico City, Acapulco, Cancún, Monterrey and Tijuana. They also have several direct flights weekly to/from Chicago and Los Angeles, and one to/from Denver. Aero California (☎ 925-24-00) connects to Mexico City and Tijuana.

Bus The Zacatecas bus station is on the southwest edge of town, about 3km from the center. Many buses are *de paso* (stopping here en route between other cities). The station has a checkroom for baggage (open 7am to 10pm), telephone casetas and a fax office. The old bus station (Centro Comercial Zacatecas) is on Boulevard López Mateos and handles only a few destinations.

Aguascalientes – 130km, 2 hours; regular 1st-class Futura, Chihuahuenses, Ómnibus de México

(US$7.50), half-hourly 2nd-class Estrella Blanca (US$6.50)

Durango – 290km, 4½ hours; 13 1st-class Ómnibus de México (US$18.50), 6 2nd-class Estrella Blanca (US$17)

Fresnillo – 60km, 1-1½ hours; hourly 1st-class Futura (US$3), hourly 2nd-class Estrella Blanca and Camiones de los Altos (US$2.50), every 10 minutes, 6am to 9.30pm, 2nd-class buses (US$2.25)

Guadalajara – 318km, 4 hours; frequent 1st-class Ómnibus de México and Chihuahuenses (US$22.50), hourly 2nd-class Estrella Blanca/Rojo de los Altos (US$19.50)

Guanajuato – 310km; take a León bus and change there for Guanajuato

León – 257km, 3 hours; 10 1st-class Ómnibus de México and Chihuahuenses (US$14)

Mexico City (Terminal Norte) – 600km, 6-8 hours; 1 deluxe (US$53), 16 1st-class Futura, Chihuahuenses and Ómnibus de México (US$42)

Monterrey – 450km, 5 hours; 5 1st-class Transportes del Norte (US$26), 10 2nd-class Estrella Blanca and Rojo de los Altos (US$22)

San Luis Potosí – 188km, 3 hours; 12 1st-class Futura and Ómnibus de México (US$10), 15 2nd-class Estrella Blanca (US$9.50)

There are also frequent buses to Torreón and several a day to Chihuahua, Ciudad Juárez, Saltillo and Nuevo Laredo.

Car Budget (☎ 922-94-58) has a rental office next to the Hotel Colón on Boulevard López Mateos. Lloguer (☎ 922-34-07), Héroes de Chapultepec 119, offers discounts for guests of several hotels, including Hotel Condesa and Posada de los Condes.

Getting Around

Zacatecas' airport is about 20km north of the city. The cheapest way to/from the center is a combi (☎ 922-59-46, US$5.50). Taxis are about US$16.

Ruta 8 buses from the bus station run directly to the cathedral (US$0.30). Heading back out from the center, they go south on Villalpando. Ruta 7 buses from the bus station run to the intersection of Avenida González Ortega and Avenida Juárez. Taxis from the bus station to the center cost US$3.

GUADALUPE
● pop 65,200 ☎ 492

About 10km east of the Zacatecas city center, Guadalupe has an historic former monastery and an impressive church that still attracts pilgrims. It also has one of Mexico's best collections of colonial art, and it's worth the side trip from Zacatecas if you have any interest in colonial history, art or architecture.

The Convento de Guadalupe was established by Franciscan monks in the early 18th century as a Colegio Apostólica de Propaganda Fide (Apostolic College for the Propagation of the Faith). It developed a strong academic tradition and a renowned library and was a base for missionary work in northern Nueva España until it closed in the 1850s. The convento now houses the **Museo Virreinal de Guadalupe** (☎ 923-23-86, Jardín Juárez s/n; admission US$3, free Sun; open 10am-4.30pm daily), with many paintings by Miguel Cabrera, Juan Correa, Antonio Torres and Cristóbal Villalpando. The art is almost entirely religious – lots of saints, angels and bloody crucifixions. The building itself has a wonderful medieval feeling, and visitors can see part of the library and step into the choir on the upper floor of the monastery church (templo), with its fine carved and painted chairs. From the choir you can look down into the beautifully decorated 19th-century Capilla de Nápoles on the church's north side.

Beside the Museo Virreinal, the newer **Museo Regional de Historia** (☎ 923-23-86; admission free; open 10am-4pm daily) has a limited number of exhibits on Zacatecas' history, including a small collection of old carriages and cars.

The town holds its annual fair December 3-13, focused on the Día de la Virgen de Guadalupe (December 12).

Getting There & Away
From Zacatecas, Transportes de Guadalupe buses run to Guadalupe every few minutes (20 minutes, US$0.30); catch one at the bus stop on Boulevard López Mateos opposite the old bus station. Get off at a small plaza in the middle of Guadalupe where a 'Museo Convento' sign points to the right, along Madero. Walk about 250m along Madero to Jardín Juárez, a sizable plaza. The museums are on the left side of the plaza. To return to Zacatecas, you can pick up the bus where you disembarked.

FRESNILLO & PLATEROS
☎ 493
Fresnillo (population 88,600) is an unexciting town 60km north of Zacatecas, beside the road to Torreón and Durango. The village of Plateros, 5km northeast of Fresnillo, is the site of the Santuario de Plateros, one of Mexico's most visited shrines. If you're particularly interested in Mexican Catholicism, you might find the shrine worth visiting. Otherwise, give both Fresnillo and Plateros a miss.

Orientation
Fresnillo's bus station is on Ébano, about 1km northeast of the center of town on local bus Ruta 3. You can get a bus direct to Plateros from the Fresnillo bus station. If you need to go into Fresnillo for a meal or a room, you'll find it's a higgledy-piggledy place with three main plazas. The most pleasant of the three is Jardín Madero with the colonial church of Nuestra Señora de la Purificación on its north side.

Santuario de Plateros
Pilgrims flock to Plateros every day of the year to see El Santo Niño de Atocha, a quaint image of the infant Jesus holding a staff and basket and wearing a colonial pilgrim's feathered hat. The figure is on the altar of Santuario de Plateros church. The courtyard in front of the 18th-century church is regularly packed with pilgrims, and the surrounding streets are lined with stalls selling a vast array of gaudy religious artifacts – Santo Niño souvenirs especially.

A series of rooms to the right of the church entrance is lined with thousands of retablos, new and old, giving thanks to the Santo Niño for all manner of miracles. Some older ones go back to WWII, while others recall traffic accidents, muggings and medical operations. More recent ones include copies of school reports and academic records.

Places to Stay
There are a few hotels in Plateros for pilgrims planning a 6am mass, but they aren't a very restful option. If you want to stay the night, Fresnillo has several satisfactory places.

Hotel Lirmar (☎ 932-45-98, cnr Durango & Ébano) Singles/doubles US$16/22. Right by the Fresnillo bus station, this fairly modern hotel has clean, comfortable rooms.

Hotel Maya (☎ 932-03-51, Ensaye 9) Singles/doubles US$14/17. If you want to stay in central Fresnillo, the Hotel Maya, one block south of Avenida Juárez and one block west of Avenida Hidalgo, has bright, fairly clean rooms with TV.

Hotel Casa Blanca (☎ 932-12-88, García Salinas 503) Singles/doubles US$38/47. Mainly for business travelers, this mid-range option, three blocks east of Jardín Hidalgo, offers clean, quiet, well-furnished rooms.

Getting There & Away

Fresnillo is well served by long-distance buses, though many are de paso. The bus station has a telephone caseta, luggage storage and an impressive mural. Frequent 1st-class buses go to Durango (230km, 3¼ hours, US$13), Torreón (330km, 5 hours, US$20) and Zacatecas (60km, 1 hour, US$2.25); 2nd-class buses are even more frequent.

To Plateros, buy a ticket at the Parques Industriales counter for one of the frequent 2nd-class buses (US$0.70). Ruta 6 local buses also run to Plateros, from Calle Emiliano Zapata, 2½ blocks east of the Jardín Madero (US$0.60).

JEREZ
• pop 36,600 ☎ 494

A small country town 30km southwest of Zacatecas, Jerez de García Salinas (to use its full name) has some surprisingly fine 18th- and 19th-century buildings that testify to the wealth that silver brought to even the lesser towns of the Zacatecas region. Jerez holds a lively Easter fair with charreadas, cockfights and other activities, starting on Good Friday and continuing for about 10 days.

Orientation & Information

Jardín Páez, the town's main plaza, has an old-fashioned gazebo and plenty of trees, birds and seats. Streets on the south and east sides are closed to traffic. The local tourist office (☎ 945-68-24) is two blocks north, at Guanajuato 28. A booth in the plaza may also have information. The efficient Cafe Cybernet, one block north at Salinas 2A, charges US$2 per hour (open 10am-10pm). You'll find pay phones and

several banks (with ATMs) on the plaza and the nearby streets.

Things to See & Do

The 18th-century **Parroquia de la Inmaculada Concepción** and the 19th-century **Santuario de la Soledad** have fine stone carvings. To find them go one block south from the southeast corner of Jardín Páez, then one block east for the church, or one block west for the shrine. Just past the shrine, on the north side of Jardín Hidalgo, is a beautiful little 19th-century theater, **Teatro Hinojosa**.

Places to Stay & Eat

Hotel Plaza (☎ 945-20-63, Plaza Principal Sur 8) Singles/doubles US$11/12. Like several other cheapies on the plaza, this hotel offers small, bare, clean rooms with bathroom and TV.

Posada Santa Cecilia (945-24-12, Constitución 4) Singles/doubles US$18/21. This old building has been completely renovated, and offers modern comforts and very appealing rooms. It's a half block north of the plaza.

Leo Hotel (☎ 945-20-01, e hotelleo@ jereznet.com.mx, Calzada La Suave Patria s/n) Singles & doubles US$51. On the east side of town, this modern, multistory hotel is the fanciest place around, with its own swimming pool and cinema next door.

Several places around the plaza serve up the standard chicken, *bistec* (steak) and beans at very nontouristic prices.

Azul Cafe (☎ 044-4942-6461, Constitución 2) Prices US$4. A restaurant and bar set in an attractive old courtyard, the 'Blue Cafe' is just north of the plaza, and a cut above the basic eateries there. The fajitas are especially tasty.

Getting There & Away

The turnoff to Jerez is near Malpaso, on the Zacatecas-Guadalajara road 29km south of Zacatecas. The Zacatecas-Jerez line runs 2nd-class buses from Zacatecas bus station to Jerez every 30 minutes from 5am to 9pm (US$3). There are also services by Ómnibus de México and Estrella Blanca/Rojo de los Altos. Jerez's bus station is on the east side of town, about 1km from the center along Calzada La Suave Patria. 'Centro-Central' buses, from inside the bus station, run to/from the center (US$0.30). There are also several buses a day to/from Fresnillo (US$2.25).

LA QUEMADA

The impressive ruins of La Quemada *(admission US$3; open 10am-5pm daily)* stand on a hill overlooking a broad valley about 45km south of Zacatecas, 2km east of the Zacatecas-Guadalajara road. They're also known as Chicomostoc, because they were once thought to be the place of that name where the Aztecs halted during their legendary wanderings toward the Valle de México. The ruins' remote and scenic setting makes them well worth the trip from Zacatecas. The site museum *(admission US$0.80; open 10am-4pm daily)* has fascinating exhibits on the archaeology of the area and is an interesting piece of architecture in itself. Both the museum and the site have explanatory labels in English as well as Spanish.

La Quemada was inhabited between about AD 300 and AD 1200 and probably peaked between AD 500 and AD 900 with as many as 15,000 people. From around AD 400 it was part of a regional trade network linked to Teotihuacán, but fortifications at the site suggest that La Quemada later tried to dominate trade in this part of Mexico. Traces of a big fire indicate that its final downfall was violent.

Some of the ruins can be seen up on the hill to the left as you approach from the Zacatecas-Guadalajara road. Of the main structures, the nearest to the site entrance is the Salón de las Columnas (Hall of the Columns), which was probably a ceremonial hall. A bit farther up the hill are a ball court, a steep offerings pyramid and an equally steep staircase leading toward the upper levels of the site. From the upper levels of the main hill, a path leads westward to a spur hilltop with the remains of a cluster of buildings called La Ciudadela (the Citadel). A stone wall, thought to have been built for defensive purposes late in La Quemada's history, stretches across the slopes to the north.

Getting There & Away

From the old bus station (Centro Comercial Zacatecas) in Zacatecas, take a 2nd-class bus (US$3) heading to Villanueva and ask to be let off at *'las ruinas'*; you'll be deposited at the Restaurant Las Siete Cuevas, where you can walk 2km along the paved road going east to the site. When returning to Zacatecas, you may have to wait a while before a bus shows up, and don't leave the ruins too late. Ómnibus de México and Rojo de los Altos have regular service from Zacatecas' 1st-class bus station to Villanueva and Guadalajara, and these may also stop at the La Quemada turnoff. You can also do an organized tour from Zacatecas for about US$21. See Organized Tours in Zacatecas, earlier, for company recommendations.

SOMBRERETE

• pop 30,000 ☎ 433

Looking like something from a Western movie, Sombrerete is an archetypical old Mexican town, its traditional streets and timeworn buildings almost totally intact. The first settlements here were in the 1550s, and mines began extracting silver and other minerals that financed a rich legacy of churches, mansions and public buildings.

The municipal tourist office (☎ 935-00-88), Avenida Hidalgo s/n, doesn't see many tourists, but they can answer questions (in Spanish) about the town and the surrounding area. The small **Museo de la Ciudad** *(no ☎, Hidalgo 207; admission US$0.75; open 10am-4pm Mon-Sat)* has folksy but well-displayed exhibits on Sombrerete's history.

Hotel Hidalgo (☎ 935-00-98, Hidalgo 145) Singles/doubles US$9/11. Bathrooms have been added on and electricity installed, but everything else about this place seems straight out of the 19th century, from the tiled courtyard to the high ceilings.

Sombrerete's bus station is not far from the center of town, and numerous buses stop here between Zacatecas and Durango. If you're driving yourself, the main street is just south of highway 48.

SIERRA DE ÓRGANOS

High on the western edge of Zacatecas state, the Sierra de Órganos is named for its distinctive rock formations, some of which resemble organ pipes. The clear sky and striking high desert scenery make an ideal setting for western movies: the original *Cisco Kid, The Guns of San Sebastian* and *The Sons of Katie Elder* have all filmed scenes here. The area has recently been declared a **national park** *(admission US$1.25),* and a visitors center is under construction. There are a few campsites and picnic areas, but no other facilities, and no year-round water source. Most people come on a day trip, and some good day hikes are possible (carry water and wear a hat).

To get there, turn north off highway 45 about 15km west of Sombrerete, follow the dirt roads for about 10km until you see rocky formations on your left, then take the next left to the park entrance. You really need your own transport.

ALTAVISTA

The unusual archaeological site of Altavista was used for astronomical observations and ceremonial purposes from about AD 200 to AD 1000. Numerous short, round columns, arranged in rows and clusters, act as a calendar, star chart and sundial; the structure called El Laberinto reaches a perfect alignment on the spring equinox.

The site is near the village of Chalchihuites, about 55km southwest of Sombrerete, and has almost no visitor facilities. You'll need your own transport to get there; the tourist office in Sombrerete may be able to arrange a tour.

Aguascalientes State

The state of Aguascalientes, bordered on the south by Jalisco and surrounded on its other sides by Zacatecas, is one of Mexico's smallest. It was originally part of Zacatecas; according to tradition, a kiss planted on the lips of dictator Santa Anna by the attractive wife of a prominent local politician brought about the creation of a separate Aguascalientes state.

Industry is concentrated in and around the capital city, also called Aguascalientes, but the rest of the state is primarily agricultural, producing maize, beans, chilies, fruit, grapes and grain grown on its fertile lands. Livestock is also important, and the state's ranches produce beef cattle as well as bulls, which are slaughtered at bullfights all over Mexico.

AGUASCALIENTES

• pop 586,200 • elev 1800m ☎ 449

Named for its hot springs, this is a prosperous industrial city, with a few handsome colonial buildings in the well-planned central area. Aguascalientes also has several modern shopping malls and a very modern bullring. If you're interested in Mexican art, the museums devoted to José Guadalupe Posada and Saturnino Herrán will justify a visit. Even by Mexican standards, Aguascalientes is a very friendly town.

History

Some time before the Spanish invasion, a labyrinth of catacombs was built here, so the first Spaniards called it La Ciudad Perforada – the perforated city. Archaeologists have little understanding of the tunnels, which are off-limits to visitors.

Pedro de Alvarado came to subdue this region in 1522 but was driven back by the Chichimecs. A small garrison was founded here in 1575 to protect silver convoys from Zacatecas to Mexico City. Eventually, as the Chichimecs were pacified, the region's hot springs at Ojo Caliente served as the basis for the growth of a town; a large tank beside the springs helped irrigate local farms where fruits, vegetables and grains were cultivated for sale to the hungry mining districts.

The city's industries began with processing agricultural products into textiles, wine, brandy, leather and preserved fruits, but now include a huge Nissan plant just south of town. Today, more than half of the state's population lives in the city.

Orientation

Aguascalientes is flat and easy to get around. The center of town is Plaza de la Patria, surrounded by some pleasant pedestrian streets. Shops, hotels, restaurants and some fine buildings are within a few blocks. Avenida Chávez/5 de Mayo is the main north-south artery; it passes through a tunnel beneath Plaza de la Patria. Avenida López Mateos, the main east-west artery across the central part of the city, is a couple of blocks south of the plaza. The bus station is on the south side of town.

Information

The state tourist office (☎ 915-95-04, 800-949-49-49) is in the Palacio de Gobierno on Plaza de la Patria. Open 9am to 8pm daily (except holidays), it gives out free city maps and information on the city and state of Aguascalientes, mostly in Spanish.

AGUASCALIENTES

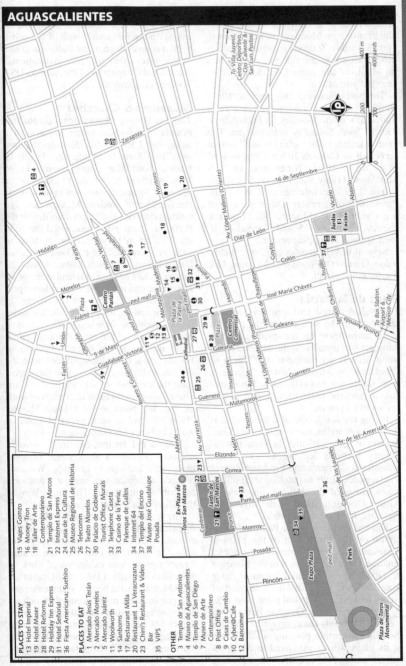

There are plenty of banks with ATMs around Plaza de la Patria. Hours are generally 9am to 5pm Monday to Friday, 9am to 1pm Saturday. Casas de cambio include Money Tron, half a block east of the plaza on Montoro, and several on Hospitalidad, near the post office.

The post office is at Hospitalidad 108, a couple of blocks northeast of Plaza de la Patria. It's open Monday to Friday from 8am to 5pm, Saturday 9am to 1pm. The main Telecomm office, with fax and Internet service, is at Galeana 102, a block west of Plaza de la Patria (open 8am to 6pm Monday to Friday, 9am to noon Saturday).

You'll find an Internet café in Centro Parián shopping center. Other good ones are Cyber@Cafe, Madero 402, Internet Express, Carranza 415, and Internet 64, in the Expoplaza shopping center.

Several travel agencies can book flights. Viajes Gomzo (☎ 916-61-92), Montoro 114, is especially helpful.

Plaza de la Patria

The well-restored 18th-century baroque **cathedral**, on the west side of the plaza, is more magnificent on the inside than the outside. Over the altar at the east end of the south aisle is a painting of the Virgin of Guadalupe by Miguel Cabrera. There are more Cabrera works in the cathedral's *pinacoteca* (picture gallery); ask one of the priests to let you in.

Facing the south side of the cathedral is the **Teatro Morelos**, scene of the 1914 Convention of Aguascalientes, in which revolutionary factions led by Pancho Villa, Venustiano Carranza and Emiliano Zapata tried unsuccessfully to patch up their differences. Busts of these three, plus one of Álvaro Obregón, stand in the foyer, and there are a few exhibits upstairs.

The red and pink stone **Palacio de Gobierno** on the south side of the plaza is Aguascalientes' most noteworthy colonial building. Once the mansion of the Marqués de Guadalupe, a colonial baron, it dates from 1665 and has a striking courtyard of arches and pillars. A mural painted in 1992 by the Chilean artist Osvaldo Barra is on the wall just inside the courtyard. It depicts the 1914 convention, pointing out that some of its ideas were crystallized in Mexico's still-governing 1917 constitution – including

the eight-hour workday. Barra, whose mentor was Diego Rivera, also painted the mural on the far (south) wall of the courtyard, a compendium of the historic and economic forces that forged Aguascalientes (look for the depiction of the Mexico-USA border being drawn).

Museums & Churches

The fascinating **Museo José Guadalupe Posada** (☎ 915-45-56, *Jardín El Encino s/n; admission US$0.50, free Sun; open 11am-6pm Tues-Sun*) is beside the Jardín El Encino, about 450m south of Avenida López Mateos Oriente. Posada (1852-1913), a native of Aguascalientes, was in many ways the founder of modern Mexican art. His satirical cartoons and engravings during the Porfiriato dictatorship broadened the audience for art in Mexico, drew attention to social problems and inspired later artists like Diego Rivera. Posada's hallmark was the *calavera* (skull or skeleton), and many of his calavera engravings have been widely reproduced. Less well known are the engravings of current events for periodicals; the series on executions by firing squad conveys some of the violence of the revolutionary period. The museum has a large collection of Posada prints, each displayed alongside the original etched zinc plate so you can appreciate the demands of the printmaker's art. There's also a permanent exhibition of work by Posada's predecessor Manuel Manilla (1830-90), and temporary exhibitions of works by other Mexican artists.

Templo del Encino, beside the Posada museum, contains a black statue of Jesus that some believe is growing. When it reaches an adjacent column, a worldwide calamity is anticipated. The huge 'Way of the Cross' murals are also noteworthy.

The handsome neoclassical **Museo de Aguascalientes** (☎ 915-90-43, *Zaragoza 507; admission US$1.25, free Sun; open 11am-6pm Tues-Sun*), northeast of the center, houses a permanent exhibition of work by Saturnino Herrán (1887-1918), another great Mexican artist born in Aguascalientes. In a graphic style reminiscent of French art nouveau, his portraits and illustrative work depict Mexican people and places with great technical skill and sensitivity. The museum also hosts temporary exhibitions of work by other artists. The very sensual sculpture *Malgretout* on the patio is a fiberglass copy of the marble original by Jesús Contreras.

Opposite the museum, the **Templo de San Antonio** is a crazy quilt of architectural styles built around 1900 by local self-taught architect Refugio Reyes. The interior is highly ornate, with huge round paintings and intricate decoration highlighted in gold.

Museo Regional de Historia (*☎ 916-52-28, Carranza 118; admission US$1.25, free Sun; open 10am-3pm & 4pm-7pm Tues-Sun*), two blocks west of the cathedral, was designed by Refugio Reyes as a family home. It has several rooms of exhibits on Aguascalientes' history from the big bang to the *revolución*.

Museo de Arte Contemporáneo (*☎ 918-69-01, cnr Morelos & Primo Verdad; admission US$1.25, free Sun; open 10am-6pm Tues-Sun*) is a modern museum displaying recent products of Aguascaliente's artists – it's well worth a look. **Taller de Arte Contemporáneo** (*☎ 994-00-74, Montoro 222; admission free; open 10am-8pm Tues-Sun*) is a workshop-studio-gallery for printmakers and graphic designers; there are frequently fine prints for sale here.

Expoplaza & Around

About a kilometer west of Plaza de la Patria, via Avenida López Mateos or Nieto, Expoplaza is a modern US-style shopping center with lots of shops, a few cafés, and a multiscreen cinema. On the south side of the mall, the wide and somewhat soulless pedestrian boulevard comes alive during the annual Feria de San Marcos. At its west end, the mammoth **Plaza de Toros Monumental** is notable for its modern-colonial treatment of traditional bullring architecture.

On the east side of Expoplaza, Calle Pani, also called Paseo de la Feria, runs two blocks north to the 18th-century Templo de San Marcos and the shady Jardín de San Marcos. The Palenque de Gallos, in the Casino de la Feria building on Pani, is the city's cockfighting arena. Near the northeast corner of Jardín de San Marcos, the Ex-Plaza de Toros de San Marcos, the old bullring, is now a school for aspiring practitioners of the bullfighters' art.

Thermal Springs

It's no surprise that a town called Aguascalientes has hot springs. The best known are at the **Centro Deportivo Ojo Caliente** (*☎ 970-06-98, Carretera San Luis Potosí Km 1; admission US$3; open 7am-7pm Wed-Fri, 7am-8pm Sat, Sun & holidays*), on the east edge of the city. Bus No 12, along Avenida López Mateos, will get you there. The large pool and some other smaller pools have warmish water; the hot water is in private pools (from US$5). The large parklike grounds have tennis, volleyball and squash courts and a restaurant.

The **Baños Termales de Ojocaliente** (*☎ 970-07-21, Tecnológico 102; admission US$3; open 8am-7pm daily*) are less sporty and more elegant, and worth seeing for the restored 1808 architecture.

Organized Tours

El Tranvía, an imitation trolley car, does two different tour routes through the city, including a guided visit to the Palacio de Gobierno, departing six times per day. Get information and buy tickets at the state tourist office (*☎ 915-95-04; US$3*).

Special Events

Feria de San Marcos This is the biggest annual fair in Mexico, attracting around a million visitors each year for exhibitions, bullfights, cockfights, rodeos, free concerts and an extravaganza of cultural events, including an international film festival. The fair starts in mid-April and lasts 22 days. The big parade takes place on the saint's day, April 25. Programs of cultural events can be picked up at theaters and museums. Expoplaza is the hub of things.

Festival de las Calaveras From October 25 to November 4, Aguascalientes celebrates the Día de los Muertos with an emphasis on the symbolism of skeletons (calaveras), as depicted by local artist Posada from the 19th century.

Places to Stay

Prices skyrocket during the Feria de San Marcos and places to stay are completely booked for the fair's final weekend; local residents run a lucrative homestay service at this time. Ask around at the fair if you're stuck.

Budget *Villa Juvenil* (*☎ 970-06-78, cnr Avenida Circunvalación Ote & Jaime Nunó*) Dorm beds US$4.50. This youth hostel, about 3km east of the center on the ring road, is mainly for visiting sports teams, but it does accommodate travelers too. The sign out front says 'Instituto Aguascalentense del Deporte.' The hostel has 72 beds in clean separate-sex dormitories. In the park-like grounds are a cafeteria, swimming pool, gym and various ball courts. Bus No 20 from the bus station or the red bus east along Avenida López Mateos will take you to Avenida Circunvalación; walk north about 200m to the hostel.

Hotel Señorial (☎ 915-16-30, 915-14-73, *Colón 1040*) Singles/doubles US$16/22. This friendly, family-run hotel, just off the south-east corner of Plaza de la Patria, has 32 reasonable rooms with TV and phone. There's a variety of rooms, some with balconies, and some larger ones with several beds.

Hotel Reforma (☎ 915-11-07, *Nieto 118 at Galeana*) Singles/doubles US$10/13. A block west of the plaza is this wonderful old building where rooms with high ceilings are set around a covered courtyard. It's aging, the rooms are dark, and the service is not too sharp, but it's decent and it has character.

Hotel Maser (☎ 915-35-62, *Montoro 303*) Singles/doubles US$14/18, US$20 with TV. A few blocks east of the center, this hotel has helpful management and 47 simple, very clean rooms around a covered inner courtyard. There's enclosed parking behind the hotel.

Mid-Range & Top End *Hotel Imperial* (☎ 915-16-64, *5 de Mayo 106*) Singles & doubles US$25-31. Well located on the north side of the Plaza de la Patria, the Imperial is a fine-looking building outside, though the lobby is unimpressive. Rooms are spacious, modern and clean, with fan, TV and phone. Interior rooms are darker, quieter and cheaper than the exterior ones.

Holiday Inn Express (☎ 916-16-66, ✉ hiexp@ags.podernet.com.mx, *Nieto 102*) Singles & doubles US$105. On the south-west corner of Plaza de la Patria, this is the center's most comfortable option. It has 92 rooms with all modern conveniences, and full facilities for business travelers. Discounts of 25% are available some weekends.

Fiesta Americana (☎ 918-60-10, fax 918-51-18, ⊠ www.fiestaamericana.com, *Laureles s/n*) Singles & doubles US$140. This luxury 192-room hotel has all the amenities

you'd expect, including a very attractive swimming pool.

Other luxurious resort-style hotels are on the outskirts of the city, including *Hotel Quinta Real* (☎ 978-58-18, fax 978-56-16, *Avenida Aguascalientes Sur 601*) and *Hotel Las Trojes* (☎ 973-00-66, fax 973-04-34, cnr *Zacatecas & Campestre*).

Places to Eat

Fresh produce is available in three markets a few blocks north of Plaza de la Patria: *Mercado Juárez, Mercado Jesús Terán* and *Mercado Morelos*. Quite a few places around and north of the plaza cater to local workers and shoppers.

Sanborns (☎ 915-87-74, *Madero 101*) Prices US$4-7. On the east side of the plaza above the Sanborns store, in the restored Hotel Francia building, this restaurant is a delightful place for a meal or a snack. They serve fixed price breakfasts and lunches, as well as a choice of à la carte Mexican dishes. It's popular with well-to-do locals.

Woolworth (☎ 918-41-98, *5 de Mayo 122*) Prices US$4-7. Very near the center just short of Allende, Woolworth has good-value breakfasts, lunches and snacks, plus decent coffee.

Restaurant Mitla (☎ 916-61-57, *Madero 220*) Prices US$5-10. Open 8am-10pm daily. A block east of Plaza de la Patria, this large, clean and pleasant restaurant has been going since 1938. It's popular with local people and welcomes *extranjeros* (foreigners). There's a choice of good-value set breakfasts, four-course comida corrida and a variety of well-prepared Mexican and local specialties. You can linger here over coffee or a drink.

Restaurant La Veracruzana (☎ 915-44-38, *Hornedo 402*) Prices US$2. Open 8.30am-5pm Mon-Sat. Two blocks east and a block south of Plaza de la Patria, this small, simple, family-run restaurant does solid home-style cooking at rock bottom prices: the four-course comida corrida is a bargain and the frijoles are some of the best in Mexico!

There's a good selection of mid-price eateries on Avenida Carranza and on the pedestrian street Pani going south to Expoplaza.

Chirri's Restaurant & Video Bar (☎ 953-23-31, *Avenida Carranza 301*) Prices

US$3-7. This is a smart place where you can get a big salad and well-prepared meat, poultry and fish dishes. It's also good for a drink, and sometimes has live music or big sports events on TV.

VIPS (☎ 918-42-61, Centro Comercial Expoplaza) Prices US$5-9. Inside the Expoplaza shopping center is another link in the reliable chain of VIPs restaurants.

Aguascalientes also has some true top-end restaurants.

Suehiro (☎ 915-51-17, Laureles s/n) Prices US$5-20. Probably the best of several Japanese restaurants catering to visiting Nissan executives, the Suehiro is in the Fiesta Americana hotel. The food is very good, and the kimono-clad señoritas provide excellent service.

Villa Andrea (☎ 970-31-86, cnr Alameda & Tecnológico) Prices US$10-16. In the Hotel Andrea Alameda, east of the center, this fine French-Continental restaurant is regarded as one of the best in Mexico.

Entertainment

Casa de la Cultura, in a fine 17th-century building on Carranza just west of Galeana, hosts art exhibitions, concerts, theater, dance and other cultural events. Stop in to look at their schedule.

Teatro Morelos, on Plaza de la Patria, and *Teatro de Aguascalientes*, on Chávez at Avenida Aguascalientes in the south of the city, both stage a variety of cultural events. Free concerts, dance and theater are presented some Sunday lunchtimes in the courtyard of the *Museo José Guadalupe Posada*.

Pani, the pedestrian street between the Expoplaza and Jardín de San Marcos, is lively in the evenings, with a good selection of restaurants and bars, for eating, drinking and dancing. The trendy, classy nightspots are out in the suburbs; *Centro Comercial Galerias (☎ 912-66-12, Avenida Independencia 2351)* is a shopping mall with several bars and discos, including the popular *El Reloj*.

Getting There & Away

Air Jesús Terán airport (☎ 915-81-32) is 22km south from Aguascalientes on the road to Mexico City. Aeroméxico (☎ 916-13-62), Madero 474, flies direct daily to/from Mexico City and Tijuana, and three times a week to/from Los Angeles. Aerolitoral (same office as Aeroméxico) flies daily to/from Monterrey,

San Luis Potosí and San Antonio (Texas). Aero California (☎ 915-24-00), Madero 319, and Aerolíneas Internacionales (☎ 915-85-05), Avenida Las Américas 110, fly to Mexico City and Tijuana.

Bus The bus station (Central Camionera) is about 2km south of the center on Avenida Circunvalación Sur, also called Avenida Convención, at the corner of Quinta Avenida. It has post and fax offices, pay phones, a cafeteria and luggage storage. Daily departures include:

Guadalajara – 250km, 2½-4 hours; 4 deluxe ETN (US$22), frequent 1st-class Elite, Futura, Ómnibus de México, Primera Plus (US$17) and Estrella Blanca (US$16)

Guanajuato – 180km, 3 hours; 1 1st-class de paso Primera Plus (US$16), 3 2nd-class Flecha Amarilla (US$10); more frequent buses from León

León – 128km, 2 hours; frequent 1st-class Primera Plus (US$9)

Mexico City (Terminal Norte) – 513km, 6 hours; 8 deluxe ETN (US$45), frequent 1st-class Futura or Ómnibus de México (US$33), 5 2nd-class Flecha Amarilla (US$29)

San Luis Potosí – 171km, 3 hours; 14 1st-class Futura (US$12), hourly 2nd-class Estrella Blanca (US$9.50)

Zacatecas – 130km, 2 hours; 13 1st-class Ómnibus de México and Futura (US$8), 2nd-class half-hourly Rojo de los Altos (US$6.50)

There's also frequent service to Ciudad Juárez, Monterrey, Morelia and Torreón, and two buses daily to San Miguel de Allende.

Getting Around

Most places of interest are within easy walking distance of the center. Regular city buses run from 6am to 10pm and cost US$0.30; the red buses are slightly more comfortable, cost US$0.40, and follow the same routes.

Bus Nos 3, 4 and 9 run from the bus station to the city center. Get off at the first stop after the tunnel under Plaza de la Patria; this will be on 5 de Mayo or Rivero y Gutiérrez. To go from the city center to the bus station, take any 'Central' bus on Moctezuma opposite the north side of the cathedral, or around the corner on Galeana.

Within town and to the bus station, the standard taxi fare is US$2.75; to the airport it's about US$8.50.

San Luis Potosí State

The state of San Luis Potosí ('poh-toh-SEE') has two of the most interesting destinations between Mexico City and the US border: the mountain ghost town of Real de Catorce and the city of San Luis Potosí itself, a major colonial town steeped in history.

Most of the state is high (average altitude around 2000m) and dry, with little rainfall. The exception is its eastern corner, which drops steeply to the tropical valleys near the Gulf coast (see Tampico & the Huasteca in the Central Gulf Coast chapter for information about this area).

Before the Spanish conquest in 1521, western San Luis Potosí was inhabited by warlike hunters and collectors known as Guachichiles, the Aztec word for 'sparrows,' after their widespread custom of wearing only loincloths and, sometimes, pointed headdresses resembling sparrows' heads.

A couple of Christian missionaries entered the southwest of the state in the 1570s and 1580s, but it was the discovery of silver in the Cerro de San Pedro hills that really awakened Spanish interest in that region. San Luis Potosí city was founded near these deposits in 1592, and Tlaxcalans, Tarascans and Otomíes were brought in to work the mines and cattle ranches.

In the 18th century the area had a reputation for maltreatment of indigenous people. This was partly because a number of parishes were transferred from the Franciscans, who had done their best to protect indigenous people, to other clergy. Appalling conditions in the mines, and discontent over the expulsion of the Jesuits (who ran the best schools in Mexico and managed their estates relatively well), culminated in an uprising in 1767.

Under Spanish reforms in 1786, the city of San Luis Potosí became capital of a huge area covering the modern states of San Luis Potosí, Tamaulipas, Nuevo León, Coahuila and Texas. This lasted only until Mexican independence, and in 1824 the state of San Luis Potosí was formed with its present area.

Today it's a fairly prosperous state. The northern silver mines are some of the richest in the country, and gold, copper, lead and zinc are also extracted. Agriculture (maize, beans, wheat and cotton) and livestock are other major sources of wealth, as is industry which is mainly concentrated in the capital city. Tourism is a growing industry.

SAN LUIS POTOSÍ

• pop 623,500 • elev 1860m ☎ 444

The state capital was a major colonial city and has been a mining center, a seat of governments-in-exile and a hotbed of revolutionaries. Today its main importance is as a regional capital and center of industries, including brewing, textiles and metal foundries. Flat and laid out in an orderly grid, San Luis is less spectacular than colonial cities like Zacatecas or Guanajuato, but its historic heart has fine buildings, congenial pedestrian areas, expansive plazas, museums, markets, cafés and a general air of elegance. It's also a university town, with cultural attractions and an active nightlife. Don't be put off by the industrial outskirts – San Luis is lovely in the middle.

History

Founded in 1592, 20km west of the silver deposits in the Cerro de San Pedro hills, San Luis is named Potosí after the immensely rich Bolivian silver town of that name, which the Spanish hoped it would rival.

Yields from the mines started to decline in the 1620s, but the city was well enough established as a ranching center to remain the major city of northeastern Mexico until overtaken by Monterrey at the start of the 20th century.

It was known in the 19th century for its lavish houses and luxury goods imported from the USA and Europe. San Luis was twice the seat of President Benito Juárez's government during the French intervention of the 1860s. In 1910 the dictatorial president Porfirio Díaz jailed Francisco Madero, his liberal opponent, in that year's presidential election in San Luis. Bailed out after the election, Madero hatched his Plan de San Luis Potosí (a strategy to depose Díaz), announcing it in San Antonio, Texas, in October 1910. The plan declared the recent election illegal, named Madero provisional president and designated November 20 as the day for Mexico to rise in revolt.

Orientation

Central San Luis Potosí stretches about 500m from the Alameda park in the east to

SAN LUIS POTOSÍ

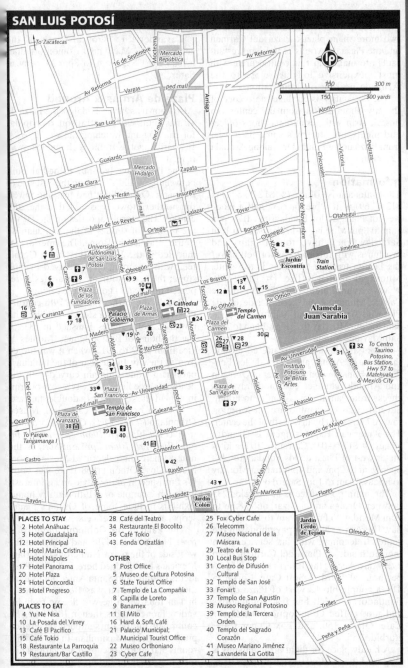

PLACES TO STAY
2 Hotel Anáhuac
3 Hotel Guadalajara
12 Hotel Principal
14 Hotel María Cristina;
    Hotel Nápoles
17 Hotel Panorama
20 Hotel Plaza
24 Hotel Concordia
35 Hotel Progreso

PLACES TO EAT
4 Yu Ne Nisa
10 La Posada del Virrey
13 Café El Pacífico
15 Café Tokio
18 Restaurante La Parroquia
19 Restaurant/Bar Castillo
28 Café del Teatro
34 Restaurante El Bocolito
36 Café Tokio
43 Fonda Orizatlán

OTHER
1 Post Office
5 Museo de Cultura Potosina
7 State Tourist Office
7 Templo de La Compañía
8 Capilla de Loreto
9 Banamex
11 El Mito
16 Hard & Soft Café
21 Palacio Municipal;
    Municipal Tourist Office
22 Museo Orthoniano
23 Cyber Cafe
25 Fox Cyber Cafe
26 Telecomm
27 Museo Nacional de la
    Máscara
29 Teatro de la Paz
30 Local Bus Stop
31 Centro de Difusión
    Cultural
32 Templo de San José
33 Fonart
37 Templo de San Agustín
38 Museo Regional Potosino
39 Templo de la Tercera
    Orden
40 Templo del Sagrado
    Corazón
41 Museo Mariano Jiménez
42 Lavandería La Gotita

Plaza de los Fundadores and Plaza San Francisco in the west. Within this triangle lie two more main plazas, Plaza del Carmen and the Plaza de Armas. Hotels and restaurants are mainly in this central area, with most inexpensive lodgings close to the Alameda, near the old train station.

The bus station is on the eastern edge of the city, about 2.5km from the center. An upscale strip, with restaurants, shops, offices and nightspots, stretches some 3km west from Plaza de los Fundadores along Avenida Carranza.

Information

The state tourist office (☎ 812-23-57, fax 812-67-69) is at Obregón 520, half a block west of Plaza de los Fundadores. It's open 8am to 8pm Monday to Friday, 9am to 1pm Saturday. They have tourist maps and brochures with lots of ideas for getting off the beaten track in San Luis Potosí state. Municipal tourist office (☎ 812-27-70, w www.ayuntamientoslp.gob.mx), in the Palacio Municipal on the east side of the Plaza de Armas, is also helpful. It's open 8am to 7pm Monday to Friday, 10am to 2pm Saturday and Sunday.

Banks and ATMs are scattered around the Plaza de Armas and Plaza de los Fundadores. Banamex, on the corner of Obregón and Allende, changes cash and traveler's checks from 9am to 2pm Monday to Friday. Several casas de cambio are on Morelos, toward Mercado Hidalgo north of the center. The American Express agent is Grandes Viajes (☎ 817-60-04), Carranza 1077, a kilometer west of Plaza de los Fundadores. It's open 9am to 2pm and 4pm to 6pm Monday to Friday, 10am to 1pm Saturday.

The main post office is at Morelos 235 between Ortega and Salazar, open 8am to 7pm Monday to Friday, 9am to 1pm Saturday. There are plenty of pay phones in the center. Telecomm, with fax service, is on the south side of Plaza del Carmen, open every day. Access the Internet for US$1.75 per hour at Hard & Soft Café, Carranza 416, a couple blocks west of Plaza de los Fundadores, which has fast connections and good coffee. Other options are Cyber Cafe, Othón 150, and Fox Cyber Cafe, Iturbide 355.

A handy place for flight arrangements is Wagons Lits (☎ 813-04-18), Carranza 1026.

Grandes Viajes (see above) is another big travel agency.

Lavandería La Gotita, south of the center on 5 de Mayo near Comonfort, does a load for US$3, 9am to 8pm Monday to Saturday.

Plaza de Armas & Around

Also known as Jardín Hidalgo, the Plaza de Armas is the city's central square, popular for chatting and watching the world go by. It's fairly quiet as traffic is channeled away from it.

The three-nave baroque **cathedral**, built between 1660 and 1730, is on the east side of the plaza. Originally it had just one tower; the northern tower was added in the 20th century. The marble apostles on the façade are replicas of statues in the San Juan de Letrán Basilica in Rome. The interior, remodeled in the 19th century, has a Gothic feel, with sweeping arches carved in pink stone; the leaf motif on the arches is repeated in blue and gold on the ceiling.

Beside the cathedral, the 19th-century **Palacio Municipal** is a stocky building with powerful stone arches. Finished in 1838, it was the home of Bishop Ignacio Montes de Oca from 1892 to 1915, when it was turned over to the city. In the rear of the building's patio is a stone fountain carved with the heads of three lions. The city's coat of arms in stained glass overlooks a double staircase.

Located behind the cathedral, **Museo Othoniano** (☎ 812-74-12, Othón 225; admission US$0.30; open 10am-2pm and 4pm-6pm Tues-Fri, 10am-2pm Sat-Sun) is the house where the celebrated Mexican poet Manuel José Othón (1858-1906) was born. It's furnished in period style and is interesting as an example of a 19th-century home. Exhibits include some of Othón's manuscripts and personal effects.

The **Palacio de Gobierno** (admission free), built between 1798 and 1816, lines the west side of the plaza. Numerous important Mexicans have lodged here, including Presidents Iturbide and Santa Anna, but its most illustrious occupant was Benito Juárez – first in 1863 when he was fleeing from invading French forces, then in 1867 when he confirmed the death sentence on French puppet emperor Maximilian. In the upstairs rooms that Juárez occupied are various historical artifacts, including a life-size model of Juárez with Princess Inés de Salm-Salm kneeling before him. An American who had married into Maximilian's family, Salm-Salm came to San Luis in June 1867 to make one last plea for his life. The Palacio de Gobierno is open during business hours; go left at the top of the stairs and ask a custodian to open the Salón de Juárez.

Plaza de los Fundadores & Around

The busy Founders' Plaza, also called Plaza Juárez, is where the city started. On the north side is a large building housing offices of the **Universidad Autónoma de San Luis Potosí**. It was probably on this site that Diego de la Magdalena, a Franciscan friar, started a small settlement of Guachichiles around 1585. The building, which has a lovely courtyard, was constructed in 1653 as a Jesuit college.

To the west of these offices is **Templo de la Compañía**, also called del Sagrario, built by the Jesuits in 1675 with a baroque façade. A little farther west is the **Capilla de Loreto**, a Jesuit chapel from 1700 with unusual twisted pillars.

One and a half blocks northwest of the plaza, the **Museo de Cultura Potosina** (☎ 812-18-33, *Arista 340; admission US$0.30; open 10am-2pm and 4-6pm Tues-Fri, 10am-2pm Sat-Sun*) has models and dioramas explaining the city's history, mainly for children.

Plaza San Francisco & Around

Dominated by the red bulk of the Templo de San Francisco, this quiet square is one of the most beautiful in the city.

The interior of the 17th- and 18th-century **Templo de San Francisco** was remodeled in the 20th century but the sacristy (priest's dressing room), reached by a door to the right of the altar, is original and has a fine dome and carved pink stone. The Sala De Profundis, through the arch at the south end of the sacristy, has more paintings and a stone fountain carved by indigenous artisans. A beautiful crystal ship hangs from the main dome.

Museo Regional Potosino (☎ 814-35-72, *Galeana 450; admission US$2.50; open 10am-5pm Tues-Sun*) along the street to the west of the Templo de San Francisco, was originally part of a Franciscan monastery founded in 1590. The ground floor has ex-

hibits on pre-Hispanic Mexico, especially the indigenous people of the Huasteca. Upstairs is the lavish Capilla de Aranzazú, an elaborate private chapel for the monks constructed in the mid-18th century. It is dedicated to the cult of the Virgin of Aranzazú: according to legend, a Spanish shepherd found a statue of the Virgin in a thornbush and named it Aranzazú, a Basque word meaning 'Among thorns, you.'

The small **Templo de la Tercera Orden** and **Templo del Sagrado Corazón**, both formerly part of the Franciscan monastery, stand together at the south end of the plaza. Tercera Orden, on the west, was finished in 1694 and restored in 1959 and 1960. Sagrado Corazón dates from 1728-31.

A couple of blocks south and west of the plaza, **Museo Mariano Jiménez** (☎ 814-73-93, *5 de Mayo 610; admission free; open 10am-2pm & 4pm-6pm Tues-Fri, 9am-3pm Sat, 10am-2pm Sun*), also called the Museo de las Revoluciones, covers some of the most dramatic events in Mexican history, with a good account of indigenous resistance to the Spanish conquest.

Plaza del Carmen

Plaza del Carmen is dominated by the **Templo del Carmen**, a Churrigueresque church built between 1749 and 1764 and the most spectacular building in San Luis. On the vividly carved stone façade, perching and hovering angels show the touch of indigenous artisans. The Camarín de la Virgen, with a splendid golden altar, is to the left of the main altar inside. The entrance and roof of this chapel are a riot of small plaster figures.

Teatro de la Paz, built between 1889 and 1894, is near the church. It contains a concert hall and exhibition gallery as well as a theater. Posters announce upcoming events; there's usually something on (see Entertainment).

Museo Nacional de la Máscara (*National Mask Museum,* ☎ 812-22-47, *Carranza 1815; admission US$0.50; open 10am-2pm & 5pm-7pm Tues-Sat, 10am-2pm Sun*) is a distinguished 19th-century neoclassical building on the south side of the plaza. Inside, ceremonial masks from many parts of Mexico are displayed with explanations of the dances and rituals in which they are used. Look for the *gigantes* (papier-mâché giants).

Alameda & Around

The Alameda Juan Sarabia marks the eastern boundary of the downtown area. It used to be the vegetable garden of the monastery attached to the Templo del Carmen. Today it's a large, attractive park with shady paths.

Inside the **Templo de San José**, facing the south side of the Alameda, is the image of El Señor de los Trabajos, a Christ figure attracting pilgrims from near and far. Numerous retablos around the statue testify to prayers answered in finding jobs, regaining health and passing exams.

Instituto Potosino de Bellas Artes (☎ 822-12-06, cnr Universidad & Constitución), a modern building in 'neo-indigenous' architectural style, hosts art exhibitions and performances. Two blocks to the east, **Centro de Difusión Cultural** (☎ 812-43-33, cnr Universidad & Negrete; admission free; galleries open 10am-2pm & 5pm-8pm Tues-Sun) is another interesting example of modern Mexican architecture, with a shape inspired by a spiral sea shell. Inside, art galleries show changing exhibitions.

Just over the railway bridge east of the Alameda is the **Centro Taurino Potosino**, comprising the Plaza de Toros (Bullring) and the **Museo Taurino** (☎ 822-15-01, cnr Universidad & Triana; open 11am-2pm & 5.30pm-8pm Tues-Sat), a bullfighting museum displaying intricately decorated matador suits and capes, historical posters and photos, stuffed bulls' heads and more. The museum is only open when there's a bullfight.

Parque Tangamanga I

This large 3.3-sq-km park (Boulevard Diagonal Sur), about 2km southwest of the center, has a planetarium, outdoor theater, amusement park, two lakes, sports fields and acres of green open spaces. **Museo de las Culturas Populares** (☎ 817-29-76; admission US$0.30; open 9am-4pm Tues-Sun) exhibits typical crafts and clothing from all over the state, with some quite good pieces for sale. To get to the park, take a southbound 'Perimetral' bus, or Bus No 25 or 26, from the west end of the Alameda.

Organized Tours

Tranvía (☎ 814-22-26) does a two-hour loop (US$3) around the historic center in an imitation antique trolley car, starting from the Hotel Panorama. A few of the driver/conductors speak English; ask when you book.

Special Events

Among San Luis' many festivals are the following:

Semana Santa – Holy Week is celebrated with concerts, exhibitions and other activities; on Good Friday morning Christ's passion is reenacted in the barrio of San Juan de Guadalupe, followed by a silent procession through the city.

Festival Internacional de Danza – This national festival of contemporary dance is held in the last two weeks of July.

Feria Nacional Potosina – The San Luis Potosí National Fair, normally in the last two weeks of August, includes concerts, bullfights, rodeos, cockfights, sports events and livestock and agriculture shows.

Día de San Luis Rey de Francia – On August 25 the city's patron saint, St Louis, King of France, is honored as the highlight of the Feria Nacional. Events include a large parade with floats and gigantes (papier-mâché giants).

Places to Stay

Budget You'll enjoy San Luis Potosí more if you choose a hotel room in the pedestrianized center, away from the traffic and in the midst of the attractive architecture.

Hotel Plaza (☎ 812-46-31, Jardín Hidalgo 22) Singles & doubles US$21-24. In an 18th-century building on the south side of the Plaza de Armas, this hotel has loads of character and a perfect location. The rooms at the front, overlooking the plaza, are the best and cost a little more. The others open onto two upstairs patios and tend to be darker, stuffier and a little more worn.

Hotel Progreso (☎/fax 812-03-66, Aldama 415) Singles/doubles US$20/21. The Progreso is another older hotel, with art nouveau statues of ladies overlooking the staircase and lobby. In its day it was probably an elegant place. The 51 rooms have been modernized, but retain their high ceilings and spacious feel.

Hotel Principal (☎ 812-07-84, Sarabia 145) Singles/doubles US$16/22. Just three blocks east of the central plazas, the Principal has 18 reasonable rooms and a convenient location.

Near the old train station, about six blocks east of the center, a couple of places provide inexpensive accommodations and off-street parking.

Hotel Anáhuac (☎ 812-65-05, fax 814-49-94, *Xóchitl 140*) Singles/doubles US$17/23 o US$20/25. The Anáhuac has 78 clean, modern rooms that vary in size, outlook, and the presence of a TV.

Hotel Guadalajara (☎ 812-46-12, *Jiménez 253*) Singles/doubles US$25/31. On the small plaza west of the old station, this hotel has enclosed parking and 33 clean, comfortable, well ventilated rooms with color TV and fan.

Mid-Range *Hotel María Cristina* (☎ 812-94-08, fax 812-88-23, ⓦ www.mariacristina .com.mx, *Sarabia 110*) Singles/doubles US$45/52. A short block northwest of the Alameda, the María Cristina has parking, a restaurant and modern, comfortable, bright rooms with cable TV, carpet, fan and phone.

Hotel Nápoles (☎ 812-84-18, fax 812-22-60, *Sarabia 120*) Singles/doubles US$42/48. Next door to the María Cristina, this hotel has similar facilities and slightly lower prices.

Hotel Concordia (☎ 812-06-66, fax 812-69-79, ⓔ concrdia@prodigy.net.mx, cnr Othón & Morelos) Singles/doubles US$39/43. Slightly more central, this is a modernized hotel in an old building; its 94 rooms all have TV, carpeting and other amenities. Exterior rooms are nicer than the interior ones. There's parking and an inexpensive restaurant.

Hotel Panorama (☎ 812-17-77, fax 812-45-91, ⓔ hpanoram@compaq.net.mx, Carranza 315) Singles & doubles US$63. Near the southwest corner of Plaza de los Fundadores is this very smart 10-story hotel. All 126 comfortable rooms have floor-to-ceiling windows, and most on the south side have private balconies overlooking the swimming pool.

Top End *Hotel María Dolores* (☎ 822-18-82, fax 822-06-02, highway 57 s/n) Singles & doubles US$73. This is one of several upscale motel-style places east of the city on highway 57. Just opposite the bus station, it has a nightclub, bar, restaurant, pool and 213 fully equipped rooms.

Hotel Real de Minas (☎ 818-26-16, fax 818-69-15, ⓦ www.realdeminasdesanluis.com, highway 57 s/n) Singles & doubles US$97. The very nice-looking Real de Minas has landscaped grounds, a big pool, restaurant, bar and 178 rooms. The hotel offers heavily discounted promotional rates when it needs to fill its rooms.

Places to Eat
One local specialty is tacos *potosinos* – tacos stuffed with chopped potato, carrots, lettuce and loads of *queso blanco* (white cheese), then smothered in salsa roja. Lots of places do their own version, and it's usually yummy. For the lowdown on SLP's upscale eateries, ask the tourist office for the booklet *Guía de Restaurantes,* which includes many interesting options outside the city center.

Center *La Posada del Virrey* (☎ 812-70-55, *Jardín Hidalgo 3*) Prices US$6-8. Open 7am-11.30pm daily. On the north side of Plaza de Armas, the former home of Spanish viceroys dates from 1736 and has been a popular restaurant with the local gentry for the last few decades. Some lunchtimes, live music plays in the attractive covered courtyard. Breakfast specials are available as well as the comida corrida and generous meat and seafood meals, though most of the menu is unadventurous Mexican fare.

Restaurant/Bar Castillo (Madero 145) Prices US$2-6. Open 8am-11pm daily. Side by side café, bakery and bar, Castillo is a small, cozy, inexpensive spot half a block west of the Plaza de Armas. You can get a big breakfast, with eggs, beans and salad, set lunches and main courses for dinner.

Café Tokio (☎ 814-61-89, cnr Zaragoza & Guerrero) Prices US$4-6. Open 7am-11pm daily. This slick and sizable café, two blocks south of the Plaza de Armas has no trace of Japanese influence. It serves up the usual Mexican and fast-food standards, and is popular for an economical comida corrida or a late night snack.

Restaurante La Parroquia (☎ 812-66-81, Carranza 303) Prices US$5-8. Open 7am-midnight daily. A popular place with *potosinos,* this restaurant has big windows looking over the southwest corner of Plaza de los Fundadores. It offers a four-course comida corrida and many à la carte dishes, including *cabrito* (kid) and enchiladas potosinas. A huge buffet spread appears at breakfast on Saturday and Sunday.

Yu Ne Nisa (☎ 814-36-31, Arista 360) Prices US$3-5. Open 9.30am-8.30pm Mon-Sat. Northwest of Plaza de los Fundadores, this small vegetarian restaurant and health food shop offers healthy snacks – sandwiches, quesadillas, gorditas and soyburgers – plus mouth-watering juices and smoothies. It also does a full comida corrida for US$4.50.

Restaurante El Bocolito (☎ 812-76-94, Guerrero 2) Prices US$3-7. Open 7.30am-10.30pm daily. An interesting option is this restaurant with friendly atmosphere and a great location at the northeast corner of charming Plaza San Francisco. It serves up huge platters of Huasteca-style food, with dishes like *gringa, sarape* and *mula india,* which are combinations of meats fried up with herbs, onion, chili, tomato and green pepper, often with melted cheese on top. It also offers tasty tacos and cheap breakfasts. It's a cooperative venture of the Casas José Martí, benefiting young indigenous students, and often features live music in the evening.

Café Tokio (☎ 812-58-99, Othón 415) Prices US$4-6. Open 7am-11pm daily. This large, air-conditioned café facing the northwest corner of the Alameda, is the original of which the central Café Tokio is a branch, with the same food, prices and hours. It's popular for ice cream or coffee after a stroll in the park.

Café El Pacífico (☎ 812-79-89, cnr Los Bravos & Constitución) Prices US$3-6. Open 24 hr. This café is not so slick, but it's locally popular for an inexpensive meal, coffee or a snack. The menu has the usual antojitos, chicken and meat.

Café del Teatro (☎ 814-07-33, Villaries 205) Prices US$5-7. Open 11am-midnight daily. Beside the Teatro de la Paz, this quirky, inexpensive place is good for a coffee, a meal, a drink or all three. It's also a regular live music venue.

Fonda Orizatlán (☎ 814-67-86, Hernández 240) Prices US$6-9. Open 8am-11pm daily. About eight blocks south of the center, Fonda Orizatlán is locally renowned for its first-class Huasteca-style cuisine. Friday and Saturday nights feature folkloric dances.

Avenida Carranza There's a selection of upscale restaurants along Avenida Carranza ('La Avenida'), west of the center.

La Corriente (☎ 812-93-04, Avenida Carranza 700) Prices US$6-11. Open 8am-midnight Mon-Sat, 8am-6pm Sun. One of the most attractive restaurants in town, La Corriente is just 400m west of Plaza de los Fundadores, at the start of the La Avenida strip. It specializes in regional and ranch-style food, served in an elegant dining room or delightful plant-filled courtyard. A good four-course comida corrida is served Monday to Saturday, and in the evenings the à la carte dinner has antojitos and main dishes. Sometimes there's music in the evenings.

La Virreina (☎ 812-37-50, Carranza 830) Prices US$7-12. Open 1pm-midnight. A long-established gourmet restaurant, the Virreina has a menu of classic international and Mexican dishes, award-winning desserts and an excellent reputation.

Entertainment

San Luis has quite an active entertainment scene. Ask in the tourist office for what's going on and keep your eye out for posters. The free monthly booklet *Guiarte* lists cultural attractions; *Guiarte* schedules also appear as posters.

Teatro de la Paz (☎ 812-52-09) has something most nights and Sunday around noon. Concerts, theater, exhibitions and other events are also presented at places like the *Teatro de la Ciudad*, an open-air theater in Parque Tangamanga I, and the *Casa de la Cultura* (☎ 813-22-47, Carranza 1815), about 2.5km west of Plaza de los Fundadores.

El Mito (☎ 814-41-57, cnr Jardín Hidalgo & Hidalgo) Admission US$5.50. Open 9pm-2am Fri-Sat. The hottest nightspot in the center of town, El Mito attracts the young and the beautiful with full blast pop, Latin and dance sounds. It's periodically closed by the authorities, which could be a recommendation in itself.

Other nightclubs are along Avenida Carranza or in the hotels and malls on the outskirts of town.

Staff (☎ 814-30-74, Avenida Carranza 423) Admission US$3.50. Open Fri-Sat nights. This is one of the most convenient clubs on Carranza, where a mixed crowd gets off on rock and *norteño* music.

El Ozz (Centro Comercial Mexicano, Avenida Muñoz) In a shopping mall northwest of the center, this is another popular disco, bar and music venue.

Shopping

The main area of shops is between the Plaza de Armas and the Mercado Hidalgo, four blocks north. Just a few blocks farther northeast is the larger, more interesting *Mercado República*.

Fonart (☎ 812-39-98, Plaza San Francisco) Like other Fonart stores, this place has a selection of quality handicrafts from all parts of Mexico.

La Casa del Artesano (☎ 814-89-90, Carranza 540) For more local products, try this shop, a couple of blocks west of Independencia. It stocks potosino pottery, masks, woodwork and canework.

Milky, sugary sweets are a local specialty and can be found in the markets and at shops along Avenida Carranza.

Getting There & Away

Air The airport is 23km north of the city on highway 57. Aeromar (☎ 817-79-36), Carranza 1030, flies to/from Mexico City several times daily and to San Antonio, Texas. Aerolitoral (☎ 822-22-29), at the airport, flies direct to/from Guadalajara and Monterrey. Aero California (☎ 811-80-50) goes to Mexico City, Tijuana and Bajío international airport (León).

Bus San Luis Potosí is a major bus hub. Its bus station, the Terminal Terrestre Potosina (TTP), on highway 57, 2.5km east of the center, has deluxe, 1st-class and some 2nd-class services. Facilities include pay phones, a telephone caseta, luggage storage (open 24 hours) and two cafés. Daily departures include:

Guadalajara – 340km, 5-6 hours; 9 deluxe ETN (US$36), 8 1st-class Transportes del Norte (US$22), hourly 2nd-class Estrella Blanca (US$19)

Guanajuato – 215km, 4 hours; 5 1st-class Flecha Amarilla (US$13)

Matehuala – 192km, 2½ hours; hourly 1st-class Sendor (US$11), hourly 2nd-class Estrella Blanca (US$10)

Mexico City (Terminal Norte) – 417km, 5-6 hours; 16 deluxe ETN (US$36), frequent 1st-class Primera Plus and Ómnibus de México (US$28), 8 2nd-class Flecha Amarilla (US$23)

Monterrey – 517km, 6 hours; hourly 1st-class Futura (US$30), 12 2nd-class Estrella Blanca (US$27)

Querétaro – 202km, 2½-3½ hours; 2 deluxe ETN (US$18.50), frequent 1st-class Futura, Ómnibus

de México (US$13), frequent 2nd-class Flecha Amarilla (US$11)

San Miguel de Allende – 180km, 4 hours; 7 1st-class Flecha Amarilla (US$10.50)

Tampico – 401km, 7-8 hours; 4 1st-class Oriente, Ómnibus de México and Futura (US$27), 16 2nd-class Vencedor and Oriente (US$25)

Zacatecas – 190km, 3 hours; 6 1st-class Ómnibus de México (US$10), regular 2nd-class Estrella Blanca (US$9)

There are also many buses to Aguascalientes, Ciudad Juárez, Ciudad Valles, Ciudad Victoria, Chihuahua, Dolores Hidalgo, León, Morelia, Nuevo Laredo, Saltillo, and Torreón, and daily direct Americanos buses to US cities including Laredo, Austin, Houston, Memphis and Chicago.

Car Car rental agencies include Budget (☎ 811-47-25) and Hertz (☎ 812-95-00).

Getting Around

A taxi to/from the airport will cost around US$12 for the half-hour trip.

To reach the center from the bus station, walk out, turn left, take the foot bridge over the busy road, and take any 'Centro' bus; No 5, 'Central TTP,' is the most direct. A convenient place to get off is on the Alameda, outside the train station. A booth in the bus station sells taxi tickets to the center for US$3.

From the center to the bus station, take a 'Central TTP' bus southbound on Constitución on the west side of the Alameda.

City buses run from 6.30am to 10.30pm. The basic *blanco* (white) buses cost US$0.35; the better ones, in various colors, cost US$0.40. For places along Avenida Carranza, catch a 'Morales' or 'Carranza' bus in front of the train station or anywhere on Carranza west of Reforma, 400m west of Plaza de los Fundadores.

SANTA MARÍA DEL RÍO
• pop 11,000 ☎ 485

Forty-seven kilometers south of San Luis Potosí, just off the highway to Mexico City, this small town is known for its excellent handmade *rebozos* and inlaid woodwork. The rebozos are usually made of synthetic 'silk' thread called *artisela*, in less garish colors than in many Mexican textile centers. You can see and buy them at the Escuela del Rebozo (Rebozo School) on the central

Plaza Hidalgo, and in a few private workshops. A Rebozo Fair is held each year in the first half of August.

MATEHUALA
• pop 64,500 • elev 1600m ☎ 488

The only town of any size on highway 57 between Saltillo and San Luis Potosí, Matehuala ('ma-te-WAL-a') is an unremarkable but quite pleasant and prosperous place high on the Altiplano Central. It was founded in the 17th century but has little left in the way of colonial charm. Most travelers just use it to get to Real de Catorce.

Highway 57 bypasses the town to the east. There is a large parabolic 'arch of welcome' at each end of town – the arches are something of a Matehuala trademark, though they look like they've been recycled from a McDonald's restaurant.

Orientation & Information

Central Matehuala lies between two plazas about 300m apart: the shady Plaza de Armas with a kiosk in the middle, and the bustling Placita del Rey to the north, with its big new concrete cathedral. Cheaper hotels and the town's restaurants are in this area. Between the center and highway 57 is the shady Parque Vicente Guerrero.

The bus station is just west of the highway and about 2km south of the center. To walk to the center, turn left out of the bus station and go straight along Avenida 5 de Mayo for about 1.5km, then turn left on Insurgentes for a few blocks to reach the Plaza de Armas.

The tourist office (☎ 882-50-05), at the Motel El Dorado on the west side of the highway just north of town, has information about attractions in the state of San Luis Potosí.

On Hidalgo, Banco Serfin and other banks have ATMs and will change cash or traveler's checks, but you'll get quicker service at casas de cambio, like Cambio Internacional, in the same area. There are pay phones around the plazas, and a Telecomm office, with fax service, on the corner of Bocanegro and Juárez. To access the Internet, try @isn, Betancort 422, which charges US$1.50 per hour (open 9am to 10pm).

Places to Stay

In Town *Hotel Matehuala* (☎ 882-06-80, cnr Bustamante & Hidalgo) Singles/doubles US$22/24. This is the most atmospheric place, with high ceilings and dark rooms, set around a large, covered courtyard. It has become somewhat overpriced, but they may give a discount. It's convenient for buses to Real de Catorce.

Hotel Álamo (☎ 882-00-17, Guerrero 116A) Singles/doubles US$11/22. This hotel is slightly brighter than the Matehuala and much more modern. It's also convenient for buses to Real de Catorce.

Hotel María Esther (☎ 882-07-14, Madero 111) Singles/doubles US$17.50/19.50. Perhaps the best budget place is the family-run María Esther. There is hot water, TV, parking and a restaurant; the best rooms are next to a plant-filled patio out back.

MATEHUALA

1 Telecomm
2 Hotel María Esther
3 @isn
4 Cambio Internacional
5 Banca Serfin
6 Hotel Matehuala
7 Restaurant Fontella
8 Hotel Álamo
9 Stop for Buses to Real de Catorce
10 Restaurant Santa Fe

0   100   200 m
0   100   200 yards

To Motel Las Palmas,
Motel El Dorado & Saltillo

Parque Vicente Guerrero

To Bus Station,
San Luis Potosí
& Mexico City

Parque Obregón

On the Highway Several very '60s-style motels dot highway 57 as it passes Matehuala.

Las Palmas (☎ 882-00-02, highway 57 Km 617) Trailer sites US$23, singles/doubles US$63/77. On the east side of the highway, Las Palmas has very nice rooms around landscaped gardens with a pool and also a camping area/trailer park with full hookups.

El Dorado (☎ 882-01-74, highway 57 Km 614) Singles/doubles US$35/43. On the other side of the highway, the El Dorado's rooms all have air-conditioning and cable TV.

Places to Eat

Restaurant Santa Fe (☎ 882-07-53, Morelos 709) Prices US$3-6. Beside the shady Plaza de Armas, the long-standing Santa Fe is big, clean and reasonably priced, with generous portions of good plain food. The comida corrida is US$4, and the big breakfasts are inexpensive.

Restaurant Fontella (☎ 882-02-43, Morelos 618) Prices US$4. Just north of the plaza, the relaxed Fontella does a solid, four-course comida corrida (US$3.50) and has interesting regional dishes. Their fresh fruit salad makes a healthy breakfast.

Getting There & Away

Fairly frequent 1st- and 2nd-class buses head north and south, but Matehuala is mid-route so they may not have seats available. Daily departures include:

Mexico City (Terminal Norte) – 609km, 8 hours; 8 1st-class directo (US$37), frequent 2nd-class de paso (US$31)

Monterrey – 325km, 5 hours; 16 1st-class (US$19) and frequent 2nd-class (US$17)

Saltillo – 261km, 3 hours; 3 1st-class (US$16) and frequent 2nd-class (US$13)

San Luis Potosí – 192km, 2 hours; hourly 1st-class (US$11) and frequent 2nd-class (US$10)

Sendor runs 1st-class buses from the Matehuala bus station to Real de Catorce at 6am, 8am, 10am, noon, 2pm and 5.45pm (1½ hours, US$4); the bus can be caught in town about 15 minutes later on Guerrero, a little to the east of and across the street from the Hotel Álamo. During festivals and holidays, buses to Real may be full. When you arrive at the bus station in Matuehuala, ask if you need to buy a ticket to Real in advance, and whether you can catch the bus in town the next day. If you buy a roundtrip ticket, note the time stated for the return journey; you may have difficulty getting on a bus at a different time!

Getting Around

Beige buses marked 'Centro' run from the bus station to the town center but aren't very frequent; buses marked 'Central' go the other way. It can be quicker to walk. A taxi costs about US$2.

REAL DE CATORCE
• pop 920 • elev 2756m ☎ 488

This reborn ghost town has a touch of magic. High on the fringes of the Sierra Madre Oriental, Real de Catorce was a wealthy and important silver-mining town of 40,000 people until early in the 20th century. A few years ago it was almost deserted, its paved streets lined with crumbling stone buildings, its mint a ruin and a few hundred people eking out an existence from old mine workings and the annual influx of pilgrims.

Recently, Real has begun to attract trendier residents – wealthy Mexicans and gringos looking for an unusual retreat. Foreigners have been restoring old buildings and setting them up as hotels, while a few Europeans have established shops and restaurants. Artists have settled here, and filmmakers use the town and the surrounding hills. The cast and crew of *The Mexican,* including Julia Roberts and Brad Pitt, virtually took over the town in July and August 2000. One day Real may become another Taxco or San Miguel de Allende, but it has a long way to go.

The Huichol people, who live 400km away on the Durango-Nayarit-Jalisco-Zacatecas borders, believe that the deserts around Real are a spiritual homeland called Wirikuta, where their peyote and maize gods live. In May or June every year the Huichol make a pilgrimage here for rituals involving peyote (see 'Huichol Visions'). This hallucinogenic cactus has great cultural and spiritual significance, and its indiscriminate use by foreigners is regarded as offensive, even sacrilegious. There is also a concern that if too many peyote plants are taken from accessible areas to meet tourist demands, the Huichol will have increasing difficulty obtaining what they need for religious and ceremonial purposes.

NORTHERN CENTRAL

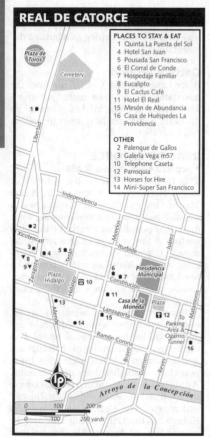

REAL DE CATORCE

PLACES TO STAY & EAT
1   Quinta La Puesta del Sol
4   Hotel San Juan
5   Pousada San Francisco
6   El Corral de Conde
7   Hospedaje Familiar
8   Eucalipto
9   El Cactus Café
11 Hotel El Real
15 Mesón de Abundancia
16 Casa de Huéspedes La
    Providencia

OTHER
2   Palenque de Gallos
3   Galería Vega m57
10 Telephone Caseta
12 Parroquia
13 Horses for Hire
14 Mini-Super San Francisco

You can take a day trip to Real de
Catorce from Matehuala, but it's worth
staying a few days to explore the surrounding hills and soak up the atmosphere.

History

The name Real de Catorce literally means
'Royal of 14': the '14' probably comes from
14 Spanish soldiers killed here by indigenous resisters in about 1700, though this is
uncertain. The town was founded in the mid-
18th century, and the church built between
1783 and 1817. The original name, Villa Real
de Minas de Nuestra Señora de la Limpia
Concepción de Guadalupe de los Álamos de
Catorce, was shortened for some reason.

The mines had their ups and downs.
During the independence war years (1810-

21) some of the shafts were flooded, and in
1821 and 1822 an Englishman, Robert
Phillips, made a yearlong journey from
London to Catorce bringing a 'steam
machine' for pumping the water out of the
mines.

Real de Catorce reached its peak in the
late 19th century when it was producing an
estimated US$3 million in silver a year. It
had a bullring, and shops selling luxury
goods from Europe. Caruso once performed in the town's theater. A number of
large houses from this period of opulence
are still standing. The dictator Porfirio Díaz
journeyed here from Mexico City in 1895 to
inaugurate two mine pumps purchased
from California. Díaz had to travel by train,
then by mule-carriage and then on horseback to reach Catorce.

Just why Catorce was transformed into a
ghost town within three decades is a bit of a
mystery. Locals in the town will tell you
that during the revolution years (1910-20)
bandidos took refuge here and scared away
the other inhabitants. The official state
tourist guidebook explains, perhaps more
plausibly, that the price of silver slumped
after 1900.

Orientation & Information

The bus from Matehuala drops you off after
passing through the 2.3km Ogarrio tunnel.
If you drive yourself, leave your car in the
dusty open space here – local kids will
hassle you to watch it all day for a few
pesos. Or they'll pester you to hire them as
guides or to take you to a place to stay.

Walk a few steps up from the parking area
to Lanzagorta, a stony street heading west
through a row of shops, past the church at the
center of town. The town's new telephone
caseta is on the east side of Plaza Hidalgo.
Mini-Super San Francisco, one block south
of Plaza Hidalgo, may change cash dollars if
they have plenty of pesos, but don't count on
it – bring enough pesos with you.

Parroquia

The charmingly timeworn parish church is
an impressive neoclassical building, the
Templo de la Purísima Limpia, always
called simply la Parroquia. The attraction
for thousands of Mexican pilgrims is the reputedly miraculous image of St Francis of
Assisi on one of the side altars. A cult has

grown up around the statue, whose help is sought in solving problems. Some believe it can cleanse their sins.

Walk through the door to the left of the altar to find a roomful of retablos. These small pictures usually show some life-threatening situation from which St Francis has rescued the victim, and include a brief description of the incident and some words of prayer and gratitude. Car accidents and medical operations are common themes. Retablos have become much sought after by collectors and are sometimes seen in antique or souvenir shops. Many of those on sale have been stolen from old churches; stealing and purchasing such sacred items must be very bad karma.

Underneath the church, behind an old door on Lanzagorta, is the small Museo Parroquial (cnr Lanzagorta & Reyes; admission US$0.30; open very occasionally), containing photos, documents and other miscellanea rescued from the crumbling town, including an ancient, rusting car, said to have been the second to reach Catorce. The museum may have closed, but the hours were so irregular anyway that it's hard to say.

Casa de la Moneda
Opposite the façade of the church, the old mint made coins for a few years in the 1860s, but is now used only for occasional art exhibitions and community classes. It is in bad repair, though a few rooms have been made usable – a total restoration is needed.

Plaza Hidalgo
Farther west along Lanzagorta, past the church and mint, this small plaza is terraced into the hillside. The plaza dates from 1888 and originally had a fountain in the middle, where the small rotunda now stands. It's a beautiful little space, with a sleepy bar-poolroom on the north side that's straight out of a Western movie.

Galeria Vega m57
Real's new art gallery (Zaragoza 3), in a restored colonial building, shows temporary exhibitions of work in a variety of media, by local artists and others. You might see a giant mobile in the courtyard, an installation in one of the spaces and displays of modern jewelery in another.

Palenque de Gallos & Plaza de Toros
A block or so northwest of the plaza lies a monument to the town's heyday – a cock-fighting ring built like a little Roman amphitheater. It was restored in the 1970s and sometimes hosts theater or dance performances. Follow Zaragoza north to the edge of the town where the restored Plaza de Toros is used for football (soccer) practice; the panteón (cemetery) across the street is also worth a look.

Horseback Riding & Walking
Numerous trails lead out into the stark and stunning countryside around Real. Guided trail rides include a three-hour trip to Montaña Sagrada (Sacred Mountain), a big hill, and offers wonderful views. Another good trip is to Pueblo Fantasmo (Ghost Town). Guides and people with horses congregate every morning on the south side of Plaza Hidalgo. Rates are around US$85 for two people for a day, including horses and a guide. Jeep trips and guided walking trips can also be arranged. Ask your hotel to suggest a guide, or try *Ted Douglas* (Morelos 20), who has been recommended by readers.

If you want to trek by yourself, you can simply walk out from Real in almost any direction. But be prepared with water, a hat and strong footwear; it's unforgiving country.

Special Events
Real is usually very quiet, but Semana Santa and Christmas are big events, and Fiesta San Francisco is huge. Between September 25 and October 12, over 150,000 pilgrims come to pay homage to the figure of St Francis of Assisi in the town's church. Many of them just come for the day, by the busload to the Ogarrio tunnel, and from there on rickety horse-drawn carts. Thousands stay in the town too, filling every hotel and every let-table room, and also sleeping rough in the plazas. The streets are temporarily lined with stalls selling religious souvenirs and food, while the town's trendy Italian restaurants close for a month. Tourists who want to get the ghost town experience should keep well away until later in October.

Places to Stay
Real de Catorce has assorted cheap *casas de huéspedes* that cater mainly to pilgrims; kids

in the parking area of town will take you to the more obscure ones. Some excellent mid-range accommodations are in old buildings, newly restored. During Semana Santa, July/August, festival of St Francis and Christmas-New Year, all the accommodations can fill up. At these times, it's wise to find a room early.

Casa de Huéspedes La Providencia *(no ☎, Lanzagorta 19)* Singles/doubles with bath US$16/22. The closest place to the tunnel is this place with very ordinary rooms that are not a great value. If there aren't many visitors in town, ask for a discount. A few superior rooms have bathrooms and fine views down the valley. The attached restaurant does an inexpensive comida corrida (US$3).

Hospedaje Familiar *(☎ 887-50-09, Constitución 21)* Singles & doubles with shared bath US$13, twins US$16. As the name suggests, this place provides 'family lodgings,' for budget travelers and poor pilgrims. The

rooms are small and plain, but clean, and they may have discount rates at quiet times.

Pousada San Francisco *(no ☎, Terán s/n)* Singles/doubles US$11/16, with shared bath US$8. Just uphill from Plaza Hidalgo, the friendly San Francisco has a few small, basic rooms, some with private bath and balcony.

Hotel San Juan *(no ☎, cnr Constitución & Zaragoza)* Singles/doubles US$16/22. A 'new' hotel in an old building, the San Juan has small, rustic rooms, some with a nice outlook over Plaza Hidalgo.

Quinta La Puesta del Sol *(☎ 887-50-10, fax 887-50-11, Libertad s/n)* Singles/doubles US$33/44, suites US$49, including breakfast. On the far side of town, on the road to the bullring, this rambling hotel has little old-world charm but a superb view down the valley to the west. Amenities include satellite TV, restaurant and car parking.

Hotel El Real *(☎ 887-50-58, Morelos 20)* Singles & doubles US$33. Another re

---

Huichol Visions

The remote Sierra Madre Occidental, in and around the far north of Jalisco, is the home of the Huichol, one of Mexico's most distinctive and enduring indigenous groups. Even in pre-Hispanic times the Huichol were an independent people, one of the few groups that were not subjugated by the Aztecs, Toltecs or any of the other dominant kingdoms. Traditionally, they lived by cultivating small, scattered fields of corn in the high valleys and by hunting deer.

The arrival of the Spanish had little immediate effect on the Huichol, and it wasn't until the 17th century that the first Catholic missionaries reached the Huichol homelands. Rather than convert to Christianity, the Huichol incorporated various elements of Christian teachings into their traditional animist belief systems. In Huichol mythology, the elements of nature take a personal form as well as a supernatural form. The gods become personalized as plants, animals and natural objects, while their supernatural form is revealed in religious rituals. For example, rain is personified as a snake, and visions of snakes can indicate when rain might be expected.

Every year the Huichol leave their isolated homeland and make a pilgrimage of about 400km across Mexico's central plateau to what is now northern San Luis Potosí state. In this harsh desert region, they seek out the mescal cactus *(Lophophora williamsii;* often called peyote cactus), a small, well-camouflaged plant that scarcely grows above ground level. The rounded 'buttons' on the top of the cactus contain peyote, a powerful hallucinogenic drug (whose chief element is mescaline) central to the Huichol's rituals and complex spiritual life. Most of the buttons are collected, dried and carried back to the tribal homelands, but a small piece is eaten on the spot, as a gesture to the plant. Small amounts of peyote help to ward off hunger, cold and fatigue, while larger amounts are taken by the Huichol on ritual occasions, such as the return from the annual pilgrimage. In particular, peyote is used by shamans whose visions inform them about when to plant and harvest corn, where to hunt deer or how to treat illnesses.

stored building houses the El Real where the comfortable, well-decorated bedrooms are on three floors around an open courtyard. Some have views over the town and the hills. The restaurant is open all day, every day, and serves good Italian, vegetarian and Mexican food, but it's quite pricey, with pasta dishes from US$5 to US$8.

El Corral del Conde (☎ 887-50-48, *cnr Morelos & Constitución*) Doubles with breakfast US$38, rooms with 4 beds & breakfast US$58. Perhaps the most stylish of all the hotels, this one features spacious stone-walled rooms that could be from a medieval castle, though they're tastefully furnished and very comfortable.

Mesón de Abundancia (☎ 882-37-33, *Lanzagorta 11*) Singles & doubles US$27, US$49 and US$70. A block west of the church, this 19th-century bank building has been renovated and is now run as a hotel and restaurant by a Swiss-Mexican couple.

There are several different rooms and all are large, quaint and decorated with local crafts. Three have great views.

Hotel Ruinas del Real (☎ 887-50-65, *Lerdo s/n*) Singles/doubles US$44/54, suite US$81. Real's latest boutique hotel, in a rebuilt stone building, is on the west side of town, about two blocks from Plaza Hidalgo. The rooms are colorful, spacious and nicely decorated. The suite is wonderful and it's where Julia Roberts stayed.

Places to Eat
A few *food stalls* along Lanzagorta serve standard Mexican snacks, while several restaurants compete (with each other and with the better hotels) to do the best Italian cuisine in town.

El Cactus Café (*Plaza Hidalgo*) Prices US$6-10. On the west side of the plaza, this is the original Italian restaurant in Real, and it's still the real deal, for fine Italian dishes in a rustic ambiance.

Huichol Visions

The Huichol resisted absorption into the mine and ranch economy of colonial Mexico, and only a few migrated to the growing urban areas in the 19th century. They have not generally intermarried with other indigenous groups or with the mestizo population, most retain the Huichol language, and many still take part in the annual pilgrimages and peyote rituals. Some Huichol do seasonal work on the coastal plantations, and many speak Spanish as well as their own language, but mostly they are on the margins of the modern market economy and materially poor. Development of a unique artistic style has brought new recognition to Huichol culture and provided many Huichol people with a source of income.

Traditionally, the main Huichol art forms were stories of the supernatural (as revealed by peyote hallucinations) and the making of masks, ritual items and colorful, detailed geometric embroidery. In the last few decades, the Huichol have been depicting their myths and visions graphically, using brightly colored beads or yarn pressed into a beeswax-covered substrate. Beadwork generally uses abstract patterns and is often done on wooden bowls, animal skulls or masks. The 'yarn pictures' are notable for their wealth of symbolism and surreal imagery. The mouth of a deer might be linked by wavy lines to a crescent moon, combining with other shapes to form an eagle, all surrounded by a circular design representing the sun. Weird shapes and brilliant colors interweave in psychedelic style. Snakes, birds and rabbits often appear, along with ritual items like feathers, candles, drums and, of course, peyote cactus.

Huichol artwork is sold in craft markets, shops and galleries in many big cities and tourist resorts. If you buy from a market stall, there's a good chance that the artist, or the artist's family, will be there to explain the various elements of a picture; sometimes the story is written on the back. Prices are usually fixed, and the Huichol don't like to haggle. Huichol art is expensive compared with some souvenirs, but it takes a long time to produce, and each piece is unique. To see the best work, visit one of the specialist museums in Zapopan (near Guadalajara), Tepic, Puerto Vallarta or Zacatecas.

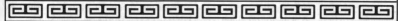

Eucalipto *(Constitución s/n)* Prices US$7-11. Eucalipto is up the small street northwest of the plaza, and it also does excellent Italian and international dishes. Try to visit both of these Italian restaurants!

The restaurant part of ***Mesón de Abundancia*** (see Places to Stay) has a wonderful atmosphere, and the Italian-Mexican meals are very good and moderately priced (US$2-7).

Getting There & Away

See Getting There & Away in the Matehuala section for bus information.

From highway 57 north of Matehuala turn off to Cedral, 20km west on a mostly paved road. After Cedral, you turn south to reach Catorce on what must be one of the world's longest cobblestone streets. It's a slow but spectacular drive, up a steep mountainside, past various abandoned buildings. The Ogarrio tunnel, part of the old mine, is only wide enough for one vehicle; workers stationed at each end with telephones control traffic. You may have to wait up to 20 minutes for traffic in the opposite direction to pass. If it's really busy, you'll have to leave your car at the tunnel entrance and continue to Catorce by pick-up, cart or whatever.

Guanajuato State

The state of Guanajuato has historically been one of Mexico's richest. After silver was found in Zacatecas, Spanish prospectors combed the rugged lands north of Mexico City and were rewarded by discoveries of silver, gold, iron, lead, zinc and tin. For two centuries 30% to 40% of the world's silver was mined in Guanajuato. Silver barons in Guanajuato city lived opulent lives at the expense of indigenous people who worked the mines, first as slave labor and then as wage slaves.

Eventually the well-heeled criollo class of Guanajuato and Querétaro states began to resent the dominance and arrogance of the Spanish-born in the colony. After the occupation of much of Spain by Napoleon Bonaparte's troops in 1808 and subsequent political confusion in Mexico, some provincial criollos began – while meeting as 'literary societies' – to draw up plans for rebellion.

The house of a member of one such group in Querétaro city was raided on September 13, 1810. Three days later a colleague, parish priest Miguel Hidalgo declared independence in the town of Dolores, Guanajuato (later called Dolores Hidalgo). After Dolores, San Miguel de Allende was the next town to fall to the rebels, Celaya the third, and Guanajuato the fourth. Guanajuato state is proud to have given birth to Mexico's most glorious moment and is visited almost as a place of pilgrimage by people from far and wide.

In addition to the quaint colonial towns of Guanajuato and San Miguel de Allende, which are major tourist attractions, the state of Guanajuato has important industrial centers like León (famous for its shoes and leather goods), Salamanca (with a big oil refinery), Celaya and Irapuato. It's also a fertile agricultural state, producing grains, vegetables and fruit – the strawberries grown around Irapuato are famous. And it's still an important source of silver, gold and fluorspar. In the late 1990s the state thrived under its PAN governor, Vicente Fox Quesada, with the lowest unemployment rate in Mexico and an export rate three times the national average, though critics claimed that the poorest people did not benefit from the improved economy. Fox was chosen as the PAN candidate for the 2000 presidential election, and his record as Guanajuato state governor was one of the key elements in his victory (see Facts about Mexico for more on the watershed election result of 2000).

The state government Web site, **W** www .guanajuato.gob.mx, has information for potential visitors, investors and voters.

GUANAJUATO
• **pop 73,400** • **elev 2017m** ☎ **473**
Gorgeous Guanajuato is a city crammed onto the steep slopes of a ravine, with narrow streets that twist around the hillsides and dive underground into a series of tunnels. This impossible topography was settled in 1559 because the silver and gold deposits found here were among the richest in the world. Much of the fine architecture built from this wealth remains intact, making Guanajuato a living monument to a prosperous, turbulent past; it is listed by UNESCO as a World Heritage Site.

GUANAJUATO

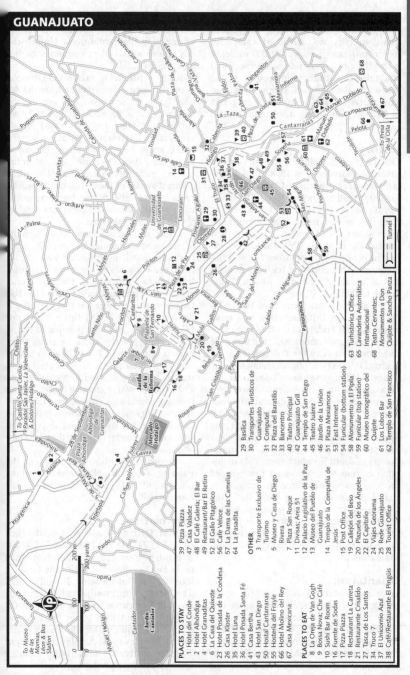

PLACES TO STAY
1 Hotel del Conde
2 Hotel Alhóndiga
4 Hotel Granaditas
6 La Casa del Quixote
23 Hotel Posada de la Condesa
26 Casa Kloster
35 Hotel Luna
36 Hotel Posada Santa Fé
41 Casa Bertha
43 Hotel San Diego
50 Hostal Cantarranas
55 Hostería del Frayle
66 Hotel Molino del Rey
67 Casa Mexicana

PLACES TO EAT
8 La Oreja de Van Gogh
9 Bossa Nova; Che Café
10 Sushi Bar Room
16 Fuente de Sodas
17 Pizza Piazza
18 Restaurant La Carreta
21 Restaurante Crisálido
27 Tasca de los Santos
34 Truco 7
37 El Unicornio Azul
38 Café/Restaurante El Pingüis

39 Pizza Piazza
47 Casa Valadez
48 El Café Galería; El Bar
49 Restaurant/Bar El Retiro
52 El Gallo Pitagórico
56 Cafe Veloce
57 La Dama de las Camelias
64 La Pasadita

OTHER
3 Transporte Exclusivo de
  Turismo
5 Museo y Casa de Diego
  Rivera
7 Plaza San Roque
11 Divisas; Area 51
12 Palacio Legislativo de la Paz
13 Museo del Pueblo de
  Guanajuato
14 Templo de la Compañía de
  Jesús
15 Post Office
19 Callejón del Beso
20 Plazuela de los Ángeles
22 El Capitolio
24 Viajes Georama
25 Rede Guanajuato
28 Tourist Office

29 Basílica
30 Transportes Turísticos de
  Guanajuato
31 Computel
32 Plaza del Baratillo
33 Bancentro
40 Teatro Principal
42 Guanajuato Grill
44 Templo de San Diego
45 Teatro Juárez
46 Jardín de la Unión
51 Plaza Mexiamora
53 Fast Internet
54 Funicular (bottom station)
58 Monumento a El Pípila
59 Funicular (top station)
60 Museo Iconográfico del
  Quijote
61 Los Lobos Bar
62 Templo de San Francisco

63 Turhística Office
65 Lavandería Automática
  Internacional
68 Teatro Cervantes;
  Monumentos a Don
  Quijote & Sancho Panza

But it's not only the past that resounds from Guanajuato's narrow cobbled streets. The University of Guanajuato, known for its arts programs, has over 21,000 students, giving the city a youthfulness, vibrancy and cultural life that are as interesting to the visitor as the colonial architecture and exotic setting. The city's cultural year peaks in October with the Festival Internacional Cervantino.

History

One of the hemisphere's richest veins of silver was uncovered in 1558 at La Valenciana mine, 5km north of Guanajuato, and for 250 years the mine produced 20% of the world's silver. Colonial barons benefiting from this mineral treasure were infuriated when King Carlos III of Spain slashed their share of the wealth in 1765. The king's 1767 decree banishing Jesuits from Spanish dominions further alienated both the wealthy barons and the poor miners, who held allegiance to the Jesuits.

This anger found a focus in the War of Independence. In 1810 the priest and rebel leader Miguel Hidalgo set off Mexico's independence movement with his Grito de Independencia (Cry for Independence) in nearby Dolores (see 'Miguel Hidalgo' in the Dolores Hidalgo section). The citizens of Guanajuato joined the independence fighters and defeated Spanish and loyalists, seizing the city in the first military victory of the independence rebellion. When the Spaniards eventually retook the city they retaliated by conducting the infamous 'lottery of death,' in which names of Guanajuato citizens were drawn at random and the 'winners' were tortured and hanged.

Independence was eventually won, freeing the silver barons to amass further wealth. From this wealth arose many of the mansions, churches and theaters that make Guanajuato one of Mexico's most handsome cities.

Orientation

Guanajuato's central area is quite compact, with a few major streets and lots of tiny back alleys (callejones). It's ideal for walking, but tricky to drive around. The main street, running roughly west-east, is called Juárez from the Mercado Hidalgo to the basilica on Plaza de la Paz. East of the basilica, this street is now closed to vehicles but it continues as a pedestrian street called Obregón to the Jardín de la Unión (the city's main plaza), then continues farther east as Sopeña.

Roughly parallel to Juárez and Obregón is another long street, running from the Alhóndiga to the university, and bearing the names 28 de Septiembre, Pocitos and Lascuraín de Retana along the way. Hidalgo, also called Cantarranas, parallels Sopeña and is another important street. Once you know these streets you can't get lost in the center – just walk downhill until you find yourself on one of them. You can, however, have a great time getting lost among the maze of narrow, crooked callejones winding up the hills from the center.

Traffic on these main arteries through the center is one-way, going east to west. Vehicles (including public buses) going west to east must use the main underground roadway, Subterránea Padre Miguel Hidalgo, a one-way route along the dried-up bed of the Río Guanajuato. (The river was diverted after it flooded the city in 1905.) This is mainly for vehicular traffic, but it is possible to access some underground sections by stairs (look around just south of Plaza Baratillo to find one good access point). At least eight other tunnels were constructed in the 1980s and 1990s to cope with increasing traffic without damaging the historic streetscapes. The Tunel Noreste Ingeniero Ponciano Aguilar and Tunel Santa Fe, running one-way east to west, enable vehicles to bypass the city center altogether.

Surrounding central Guanajuato is the winding Carretera Panorámica, which offers wonderful views of the town and surrounding hills.

Information

Tourist Offices The state tourist office (☎ 732-15-74, 800-714-10-86, fax 732-42-51, e turismo@guanajuato.gob.mx) is at Plaza de la Paz 14, almost opposite the basilica; look for the 'Información Turística' sign. The friendly staff, mostly English-speaking, give out free city maps and brochures (in Spanish and English) about the city and state of Guanajuato. The office is open 9am to 7pm Monday to Wednesday, 9am to 8pm Thursday and Friday, 10am to 4pm Saturday and 10am to 2pm Sunday.

Money Banks along Avenida Juárez change cash and traveler's checks (some only until 2pm), and have ATMs. Bancentro, opposite the state tourist office, is convenient and relatively quick. Divisas, at Juárez 33A, is a casa de cambio with reasonable rates, open 9am to 8pm Monday to Saturday, 10am to 5pm Sunday. The American Express agent is at Viajes Georama (☎ 732-51-01), Plaza de la Paz 34.

Post & Communications The main post office is at the eastern end of Lascuraín de Retana, opposite the Templo de la Compañía, and there's a post office agency in the bus station.

Pasaje de los Arcos, an alley off the south side of Obregón near the tourist office, has pay phones in reasonably quiet surroundings. Computel, opposite the post office, has a telephone caseta and fax service; it's open daily.

Quite a few places offer Internet access, including Fast Internet, on Plaza Constancia behind the Teatro Principal; Rede Guanajuato, Alonso 70B; and Area 51, lower level, Juárez 33.

Laundry Lavandería Automática Internacional, Doblado 28, on the corner of Hidalgo, will do a 3kg load for about US$4.

Walking Tour

A slow walk around the main plazas is a good introduction to Guanajuato's historic center. Starting from the east, pretty **Jardín de la Unión**, surrounded by restaurants and shaded by trees, is the social heart of the city. The elegant Teatro Juárez is on its southeastern corner. Walk west on Obregón to **Plaza de la Paz**, the small triangle beside the basilica, surrounded by the former homes of wealthy silver lords.

Wander west and south along the curving Avenida Juárez to **Plazuela de los Ángeles**, where the steps and ice-cream stands are popular gathering spots for students. The Callejón del Beso is just a few meters from here.

Continue on Juárez to the handsome **Jardín de la Reforma**, behind the row of classical columns. This leads on to **Plaza San Roque**, where *entremeses* (theatrical sketches) are performed during the Cervantino festival (see Special Events). Nearby is the pleasant, shady **Plazuela San**

Fernando. These three linked spaces form a superbly picturesque detour northwest of Avenida Juárez.

Farther west on Juárez is the bustling area in front of Mercado Hidalgo, busy with shoppers and souvenir sellers. A block north, **Plaza Alhóndiga** is a usually bare and empty space with wide steps leading up to the Alhóndiga. From there, head back east along 28 de Septiembre (which changes names several times), past museums and the university, and a few twists and turns, to **Plaza del Baratillo** with its Florentine fountain. A right turn and a short block south from there should bring you back to Jardín de la Unión, where tourists and the local well-to-do congregate in the late afternoon, along with street musicians, shoe shiners and snack vendors.

Teatro Juárez & Other Theaters

The magnificent Teatro Juárez (☎ 732-01-83, *Sopeña s/n; admission US$1; open 9am-1.45pm & 5pm-7.45pm Tues-Sun when no performances are scheduled*) was built between 1873 and 1903 and inaugurated by the dictator Porfirio Díaz, whose lavish tastes are reflected in the plush red and gold interior. The outside is festooned with columns, lampposts and statues; inside the impression is Moorish, with the bar and lobby gleaming with carved wood, stained glass and precious metals. The steps outside are a popular place to watch the scene on the plaza.

Teatro Principal (☎ 732-15-23, *Hidalgo s/n*) and **Teatro Cervantes** (☎ 732-11-69, *Plaza Allende s/n*) are not as spectacular as Teatro Juárez, but they all host a full schedule of performances during the Cervantino festival, and less regular shows at other times. Statues of Don Quixote and Sancho Panza grace the small Plaza Allende, in front of Teatro Cervantes.

Basilica & Other Churches

The Basílica de Nuestra Señora de Guanajuato, on Plaza de la Paz, one block west of the Jardín de la Unión, contains a jewel-covered image of the Virgin, patron of Guanajuato. The wooden statue was supposedly hidden from the Moors in a cave in Spain for 800 years. Felipe II of Spain gave it to Guanajuato in thanks for the wealth it provided to the crown.

Other fine colonial churches include **Templo de San Diego**, opposite the Jardín de la Unión; **Templo de San Francisco**, on Doblado; and the large **Templo de la Compañía de Jesús**, on Navarro, which was completed in 1747 for the Jesuit seminary whose buildings are now occupied by the University of Guanajuato.

Universidad de Guanajuato
The University of Guanajuato, whose ramparts are visible above much of the city, is on Lascuraín de Retana one block up the hill from the basilica. It is considered one of Mexico's finest schools for music, theater, mine engineering, industrial relations and law. Some of the buildings originally housed a large Jesuit seminary, but the distinctive multistory white and blue building with the crenellated pediment dates from the 1950s. The design was controversial at the time, but it's now recognized as a very successful integration of a modern building into an historic cityscape.

On the ground floor of the main building, **Museo de Historia Natural Alfredo Dugés** (☎ 732-00-66, Lascuraín de Retana 5; admission US$0.80; open 10am-6pm Mon-Fri) honors one of the university's pioneering naturalists with a collection of preserved and stuffed animals, birds, reptiles and insects; look for the two-headed goat and a so-called Australian kiwi.

Museo del Pueblo de Guanajuato
Located beside the university, this art museum (☎ 732-29-90, Pocitos 7; admission US$1.75; open 10am-6.30pm Tues-Sat, 10am-2pm Sun) has a collection ranging from colonial to modern times. The museum occupies the former mansion of the Marqueses de San Juan de Rayas, who owned the San Juan de Rayas mine. The private church upstairs in the courtyard contains a powerful mural by José Chávez Morado.

Museo y Casa de Diego Rivera
The birthplace of Diego Rivera is now a museum (☎ 732-11-97, Pocitos 47; admission US$1.75; open 10am-6.30pm Tues-Sat, 10am-2.30pm Sun) honoring the painter. Rivera and a twin brother were born in this house in 1886 (his twin died at the age of two), and lived here until the family moved to Mexico City six years later.

In conservative Guanajuato, where Catholic influence prevails, the Marxist Rivera was *persona non grata* for years. The city now honors its once blacklisted son with a small collection of his work in this house. The 1st floor contains the Rivera family's 19th-century antiques and fine furniture. On the 2nd and 3rd floors are some 70 to 80 paintings and sketches by the master, including portraits of peasants and indigenous people, a nude of Frida Kahlo and sketches for some of Rivera's memorable murals. The upper floors also have temporary exhibitions of work by Mexican and international artists.

Alhóndiga de Granaditas
The Alhóndiga de Granaditas, site of the first major rebel victory in Mexico's War of Independence, is now a history and art museum (☎ 732-11-12, 28 de Septiembre; admission US$3.50, free Sun, video camera US$3.50 extra; open 10am-1.30pm & 4pm-5.30pm Tues-Sat, 10am-2.30pm Sun).

The Alhóndiga was a massive grain and seed storehouse built between 1798 and 1808. In 1810 it became a fortress for Spanish troops and loyalist leaders. They barricaded themselves inside when 20,000 rebels led by Miguel Hidalgo attempted to take Guanajuato. It looked as if the outnumbered Spaniards would be able to hold out. Then, on September 28, 1810, a young miner named Juan José de los Reyes Martínez (better known as El Pípila), under orders from Hidalgo, tied a stone slab to his back and, thus protected from Spanish bullets, was able to set the gates ablaze. While the Spaniards choked on smoke, the rebels moved in and took the Alhóndiga, killing most of those inside. (El Pípila probably perished in the battle, but some versions of the story have it that he survived and lived to a ripe old age.)

The Spaniards later took their revenge: the heads of four leaders of the rebellion – Aldama, Allende, Jiménez and Hidalgo himself, who was executed in Chihuahua – were displayed on the four outside corners of the Alhóndiga from 1811 to 1821. The metal cages in which the heads hung are now exhibited inside, and the hooks can still be seen outside. The Alhóndiga was used as a prison for a century, beginning in 1864, then became a museum in 1967. Historical sections of the museum cover Guanajuato's pre-Hispanic past, its great flood of 1905 and modern times. There's also a fine art gallery that houses a permanent collection as well as temporary exhibits. Don't miss Chávez Morado's dramatic murals of Guanajuato's history on the staircases.

Callejón del Beso
The narrowest of the many narrow alleys that climb the hills from Guanajuato's main streets is Callejón del Beso, where the balconies of the houses on either side of the alley practically touch. In a Guanajuato legend, a fine family once lived on this street, and their daughter fell in love with a common miner. They were forbidden to see each other, but the miner rented a room opposite, and the lovers exchanged furtive kisses (besos) from these balconies. Of course the romance was discovered and the couple met a tragic end. From the Plazuela de los Ángeles on Juárez, walk about 40m up Callejón del Patrocinio and you'll see tiny Callejón del Beso to your left.

Monumento a El Pípila
The monument to El Pípila honors the hero who torched the Alhóndiga gates on September 28, 1810, enabling Hidalgo's forces to win the first victory of the independence movement. The statue shows El Pípila holding his torch high over the city. On the base is the inscription 'Aún hay otras Alhóndigas por incendiar' ('There are still other Alhóndigas to burn').

It's worth going up to the statue for the magnificent view over the city; you can climb up inside the statue (one peso) to about shoulder level but the view is just as good from the terraces at its feet. Two routes from the center of town go up steep, picturesque lanes. One goes east on Sopeña from Jardín de la Unión, then turns right on Callejón del Calvario (you'll see the 'Al Pípila' sign). Another ascent, unmarked, goes uphill from the small plaza on Alonso. If the climb is too much for you, the 'Pípila-ISSSTE' bus heading west on Juárez will let you off right by the statue, or you can ride up in the new funicular.

Funicular
This new incline railway (Plaza Constancia s/n; admission US$1.25/2.25 one-way/roundtrip; open 9am-10pm Mon-Sat, 10am-9pm Sun) inches up the slope behind the Teatro Juárez to a terminal just south of the El Pípila monument. The modern track and the terminals both seem a little incongruous in this ancient town, but it's a scenic trip for tourists, and a great boon for those who live in steep hillside suburbs south and west of the center.

Museo Iconográfico del Quijote
This excellent and surprisingly interesting museum (☎ 732-67-21, Doblado 1; admission free; open 10am-6.30pm Tues-Sat, 10am-3pm Sun) is on the tiny plaza in front of the Templo de San Francisco. Every exhibit relates to Don Quixote de la Mancha, the famous hero of Spanish literature, and it's fascinating to see the same subject depicted in so many different media by different artists in different styles. There's everything from room-size murals to a tiny picture on an eggshell. Paintings, statues, tapestries, even chess sets, clocks and postage stamps all feature Don Quixote and his companion Sancho Panza.

Museo de las Momias
The famous Museum of the Mummies (☎ 732-12-45, Camino a las Momias s/n; admission child/adult US$1.75/2.25, cameras/videos US$0.70/1.75; open 9am-6pm daily) at the panteón (cemetery) on the western side of town, is a quintessential example of Mexico's obsession with death. Visitors from far and wide come to see scores of corpses disinterred from the public cemetery, and there can be a long queue to enter.

The first remains were dug up in 1865, when it was necessary to remove some bodies from the cemetery to make room for more. What the authorities uncovered were not skeletons but flesh mummified with grotesque forms and facial expressions. The mineral content of the soil and extremely dry atmosphere had combined to preserve the bodies in this unique way.

Today 119 mummies are on display in the museum, including the first mummy to be discovered, the 'smallest mummy in the world,' a pregnant mummy and plenty more. Since space is still tight in the cemetery, bodies continue to be exhumed if the relatives don't keep paying the fees to keep them there. It takes only five or six years for a body to become mummified here, though only 1% or 2% of the bodies exhumed have turned into 'display quality' mummies. The others are cremated.

In the same building as the Museo de las Momias, the **Salón de Culto a la Muerte** is a series of hokey horror-show exhibits that you can see for an extra US$0.90.

Museo de Mineralogía

The Mineralogy Museum (☎ 732-38-64, *Panorámica Tramo s/n; admission free; open 9am-3pm Mon-Fri*), at the university's Escuela de Minas campus, has over 20,000 specimens from around the world, including some extremely rare minerals. The school of mines is a little more than 1km directly northwest of the center of town, but the trip there on the winding La Valenciana road is more than twice that distance. Take a 'Presa-San Javier' bus heading west on Juárez and ask to get off at the Escuela de Minas.

Casa de las Leyendas

East of the town center, the 'House of Legends' (☎ 731-01-92, *cnr Panorámica & Subida del Molino; admission US$3; open 10am-2pm & 4pm-7pm Thur-Tue*) is corny, but kind of fun. Dioramas and models depict various legends from Guanajuato's colorful past, from monsters in the mines to treachery in high-ranking families, but you'll need good Spanish to enjoy it.

Galeras de la Inquisición

On the road to Valenciana, the old Hacienda del Cochero (☎ 733-03-44, *Calle de la Cochera 11; admission US$2.25; open 10am-6pm daily*) has a new tourist trap in its cellars. Allegedly used as torture chambers during the Inquisition, the cellars now contain scarecrowlike dummies being tormented on reproduction racks, wheels and iron maidens. The rote commentary is in Spanish.

Mina & Templo La Valenciana

For 250 years **La Valenciana mine** (☎ 732-05-07; *admission US$0.50; open 8am-7pm daily*), on a hill overlooking Guanajuato about 5km north of the center, produced 20% of the world's silver, in addition to quantities of gold and other minerals. Shut down after the Mexican Revolution, the mine reopened in 1968 and is now run by a cooperative. It still yields silver, gold, nickel and lead, and you can see the ore being lifted out and miners descending the immense main shaft, 9m wide and 500m deep. Guides in the mine compound will show you around (they expect a tip), though you can't go inside the mine.

On the main road near the mine is the magnificent **Templo La Valenciana**, also called the Iglesia de San Cayetano. One legend says that the Spaniard who started the mine promised San Cayetano that if it made him rich, he would build a church to honor the saint. Another says that the silver baron of La Valenciana, Conde de Rul, tried to atone for exploiting the miners by building the ultimate in Churrigueresque churches. Whatever the motive, ground was broken in 1765, and the church was completed in 1788. La Valenciana's façade is spectacular, and its interior is dazzling with ornate golden altars, filigree carvings and giant paintings.

Just downhill behind the church **Bocamina Valenciana** (☎ 732-05-70) is a section of mine shaft you can actually enter for a small fee, if it's open.

To get to La Valenciana, take a 'Cristo Rey' or 'Valenciana' bus (every 15 minutes) from the bus stop on Alhóndiga just north of 28 de Septiembre. Get off at Templo La Valenciana (be sure to look at the interior), then cross the road to the entrance to the mine area and follow the dirt track, veering left, about 400m to the mine itself.

Ex-Hacienda San Gabriel de Barrera

Built at the end of the 17th century, this was the grand hacienda of Captain Gabriel de Barrera, whose family was descended from the first Conde de Rul of the famous La Valenciana mine. Opened as a museum in 1979, the hacienda (☎ 732-06-19, *Camino Antiguo a Marfil Km 2.5; admission US$1.75, camera US$1.50, video US$2.25; open 9am-6pm daily*) has been magnificently restored with period European furniture and art; inside the chapel is an ornate gold-covered altar.

The large grounds, originally devoted to processing ore from La Valenciana, were converted in 1945 to beautiful terraced gardens with pavilions, pools, fountains and footpaths – a lovely and tranquil retreat from the city.

The house and garden are about 2.5km west of the city center. Take one of the frequent 'Marfil' buses heading west on Juárez and tell the driver you want to get off at Hotel Misión Guanajuato. From where they drop you, just walk downhill past the hotel; the ex-hacienda is almost opposite the hotel.

Presa de la Olla
In the hills at the east end of the city are two small reservoirs, Presa de la Olla and Presa de San Renovato, with a green park between them and a lighthouse on the hill above. It's a popular family park on Sunday, when you can bring a picnic and hire small rowboats. The rest of the week it's quiet and peaceful, though not especially scenic. Any eastbound 'Presa' bus, from the underground stop down the steps at the southwest corner of the Jardín de la Unión, will take you there.

Language Courses
Guanajuato is a university town and has an excellent atmosphere for studying Spanish.

Academia Falcón (☎/fax 731-07-45, e infalcon@redes.int.com.mx, ⓦ www.instituto falcon.com, Paseo de la Presa 80; postal address Instituto Falcón, Callejón de la Mora 158, 36000 Guanajuato, Gto, Mexico) Registration US$75, weekly fees for 3 55-minute classes a day US$85, 5 classes a day US$110, 1 private class a day US$70, 3 private classes a day US$210. This well-established institute has language courses with two to five students per class, from beginners to advanced level. It offers cultural courses and weekend recreational trips too. Registration is every Saturday morning. The institute can arrange accommodations with Mexican families, with three meals a day, for about US$19 or US$16 with shared facilities.

Universidad de Guanajuato (☎ 732-00-06 ext 8001, fax 732-72-53, e idioma@ quijote.ugto.mx; postal address Centro de Idiomas, Universidad de Guanajuato, Lascuraín de Retana 5, 36000 Guanajuato, Gto, Mexico) Placement test US$5.50, 4 weeks of classes US$590. This school offers summer courses in basic, intermediate and advanced Spanish, plus classes in Mexican and Latin American culture; sessions begin in early June and early July with registration in February and May. The university also offers a range of semester-long courses in language and culture, beginning in January and July. Students must register in person and take a placement test the week before the courses begin. Staying with Mexican families costs from US$16 per day.

Escuela Mexicana (☎ 732-50-05, ⓦ www .escuelamexicana.int.com.mx, Sóstenes Rocha 28) 55-minute class US$5/9 for group/private. This small school conducts classes in Spanish (grammar, conversation, literature) and other topics from pre-Hispanic art to business culture. Accommodation with a Mexican family costs US$13 to US$21.

Instituto Tonali (☎ 732-73-52, ⓦ www .az-net.com/azteca/tonali, Juárez 4) Classes US$4.50-6.60 per hour; individual lessons US$10 per hour. Tonali (formerly Instituto Calmecac) offers Spanish classes at all levels, dance and craft programs, and arranges homestays (US$16).

Organized Tours
A few different companies offer very similar tours of Guanajuato's major sights (usually in Spanish). You can reach all the same places on local buses, but if your time is limited a tour may be useful.

Transporte Exclusivo de Turismo (☎ 732-59-68), in a kiosk on the corner of Juárez & 5 de Mayo, and *Transportes Turísticos de Guanajuato* (☎ 732-21-34), below the front courtyard of the basilica, both offer 'Guanajuato Colonial' tours, which include the mummies, La Valenciana mine and church, the Pípila monument and the Carretera Panorámica with a view over the town. Trips depart up to three times daily, last 3 to 3½ hours, and cost US$7.50. Longer tours go to Cristo Rey (US$9) or make an 8-hour circuit through Dolores Hidalgo and San Miguel de Allende (US$16). Night tours (5 hours, US$12) take in Guanajuato's views and nightspots and the walking street parties called callejoneadas (see Entertainment).

Turhistorica (☎ 732-89-56, e turhis@ int.com.mx, Hidalgo 68) arranges in-depth cultural and architectural tours for individuals and groups. Professional guides can arrange customized itineraries.

Special Events
Baile de las Flores The Flower Dance takes place on the Thursday before Semana

Santa. The next day, many mines are open to the public for sightseeing and celebrations. Miners decorate altars to La Virgen de los Dolores, a manifestation of the Virgin Mary who looks out for miners.

Fiestas de San Juan y Presa de la Olla The Fiestas de San Juan are celebrated at the Presa de la Olla park in late June. The 24th is the big bash for the saint's day itself, with dances, music, fireworks and picnics. On the first Monday in July, everyone comes back to the park for another big party celebrating the opening of the dam's floodgates.

Dia de la Cueva Cave Day is a country fair held on July 31, when locals walk to a cave in the nearby hills, to honor San Ignacio de Loyola, and enjoy a picnic and party.

Fiesta de la Virgen de Guanajuato This festival, on August 9, commemorates the date when Felipe II gave the people of Guanajuato the jeweled wooden Virgin that now adorns the basilica.

Festival Internacional Cervantino Guanajuato's arts festival (W www.festival cervantino.gob.mx) is dedicated to the Spanish writer Miguel Cervantes, author of *Don Quixote*. In the 1950s the festival was merely entremeses (sketches) from Cervantes' work performed by students. It has grown to become one of the foremost arts extravaganzas in Latin America. Music, dance and theater groups converge on Guanajuato from around the world, performing work that nowadays may have nothing whatsoever to do with Cervantes. (A recent festival included Argentine orchestras, Australian writers, Nigerian dancers, Polish drama and new Japanese cinema.) The festival lasts two to three weeks starting around October 10. If your visit to Mexico coincides with it, don't miss it.

While some events are held in the Teatro Juárez and other theaters, the most spectacular entremeses, with galloping horses and medieval costumes, are performed in the historic settings of Plaza San Roque and Plaza Alhóndiga.

Many events, in fact some of the biggest, are free. The festival opens at Plaza Alhóndiga, and you should arrive a couple hours early if you want to find a seat. On Saturday and Sunday, when Guanajuato's population swells to many times its normal size, there's music – from children's ensembles to rock/hip-hop bands – on practically every corner.

Cervantino events are organized into morning, afternoon and evening sessions, for which tickets range from around US$7.50 to US$25. Tickets and hotels should be booked in advance. Travelers wanting to buy tickets to Cervantino events can do so through Ticketmaster (☎ 5325-9000 in Mexico City, W www.ticketmaster .com.mx). In Guanajuato, buy tickets from the ticket office (Sopeña s/n) on the southeast side of Teatro Juárez (not in the theater ticket office).

Places to Stay
Prices given here are for the summer season. They may be lower in other months, but may be even higher at Christmas, Semana Santa and during the Festival Internacional Cervantino.

Budget *Casa Kloster* (☎ 732-00-88, *Alonso 32*) Dorm beds US$10, singles/doubles US$13/20. This budget backpackers' choice is near the center of town, a short block down an alley from the basilica. Birds and flowers grace the sunny courtyard, and the well-tended rooms with shared bath are clean and comfortable. Those facing the street can be noisy. The cost is slightly more in the larger rooms. It's a relaxed, friendly place, but don't leave valuables lying around in your room. Arrive early because the Casa is often booked.

Casa Bertha (☎ 732-13-16, fax 732-06-00, e casaberthagto@hotmail.com, *Tamboras 9*) Singles/doubles US$11/22. The friendly, family-run Casa Bertha, a few minutes east of the Jardín de la Unión, is a casa de huéspedes offering nine doubles and three apartments suitable for families. It's homey, well kept and centrally located, with modern bathrooms and a rooftop terrace with views over the town. Walk up the street beside the Teatro Principal to Plaza Mexiamora. Head straight uphill, take the first right, then turn left and follow the path to the door directly ahead.

Casa Mexicana (☎ 732-50-05, e escuela mexicana@hotmail.com, *Sostenes Rocha 28*)

Singles & doubles with shared bath US$9 per person, with private bath US$12 per person. This is another cheapie, about 300m south east of the Jardín de la Unión. Smallish rooms are centred around a central courtyard. It's a clean, friendly, family-run place, connected to the Escuela Mexicana language school.

Hotel Posada de la Condesa (☎ 732-14-62, *Plaza de la Paz 60*) Singles & doubles from US$14. Cheap, central lodgings are available here, just northwest of the basilica. Rooms have private baths with 24-hour hot water and are passably clean, but they're pretty worn and can be noisy. Some are large and have balconies; others are dark, without windows or ventilation. The price is OK for the better rooms but too much for the bad ones.

Hotel Granaditas (☎ 732-10-39, *Juárez 109*) Singles/doubles US$16/22. The best of the cheap hotels in the area around Mercado Hidalgo, the Granaditas has clean rooms with hot water and TV.

Mid-Range There are several medium-priced hotels just off Alhóndiga, the street heading north from Plaza Alhóndiga.

Hotel Alhóndiga (☎ 732-05-25, *Insurgencia 49*) Singles/doubles US$18/26. Visible from the plaza, Hotel Alhóndiga has clean, comfortable 'colonial' rooms with color TV; some have small private balconies. Covered parking is included.

Hotel del Conde (☎ 732-14-65, *Rangel de Alba 1*) Singles/doubles US$22/27. This hotel is OK, and the rooms are spacious and well furnished, though the interior ones can be gloomy.

At the east end of town are some more mid-range options.

Hostal Cantarranas (☎ 732-51-44, *Hidalgo 50*) Singles/doubles US$31/42. A short hop southeast of the Jardín, the Cantarranas is an old building with eight pleasant, bright apartments. They have two to six beds, a kitchen, sitting room, TV and phone.

Hotel Molino del Rey (☎ 732-22-23, *cnr Campanero & Belaunzaran*) Singles/doubles US$30/43. An easy stroll southeast from the Cantarranas, the Molino del Rey is a good choice for its convenient but quiet location. Its 35 rooms are set around a pretty patio, though some are nicer than others. The small restaurant on the ground floor serves tasty, inexpensive meals.

Motel de las Embajadoras (☎ 731-01-05, *cnr Embajadoras & Paseo Madero*) Singles/doubles US$50/70. If you have a car but wish to avoid driving in the congested center, this motel beside Parque Embajadoras has plenty of parking and is only five minutes east of the center on an 'Embajadoras' or 'Presa' bus (you can catch one on Sostenes Rocha). The restaurant/bar is elegant but inexpensive, and the lovely courtyard is full of plants, trees and birds. Clean, comfortable rooms have color TV and phone.

Top End The classiest address is Jardín de la Unión, where several venerable hotels charge extra for exterior rooms overlooking the lively but traffic-free plaza.

Hotel San Diego (☎ 732-13-00, *fax 732-56-26*, e *sandiego@redes.int.com.mx, Jardín de la Unión 1*) Rooms US$85, with balcony US$103. The San Diego has 55 comfortable rooms and suites, a large roof terrace and a subterranean bar.

Hotel Posada Santa Fé (☎ 732-00-84, *fax 732-46-53*, e *santafe@redes.int.com.mx, Jardín de la Unión 12*) Singles/doubles US$80/95, with plaza view US$123. Overlooking the north end of the Jardín, this 19th-century mansion has a great location and very comfortable rooms, though they're not as classy as the elegant lobby might suggest.

Hotel Luna (☎ 732-97-20, w *www.nafta connect.com/hotelluna, Jardín de la Unión 6*) Singles & doubles US$89, with plaza view US$104. Another handsome building on the plaza, this 100-year old hotel has been completely restored and modernized. The rooms combine contemporary facilities with old-style charm.

Hostería del Frayle (☎/fax 732-11-79, *Sopeña 3*) Singles/doubles US$64/89. A block southeast of the Jardín, this very attractive hotel has rooms with high wood-beamed ceilings, color TV and other comforts. It's right in the center of town, but thick adobe walls keep things quiet.

Some quaint old buildings in various parts of town are being restored ·as small boutique hotels.

La Casa del Quixote (☎/fax 732-39-23, *Pocitos 37*) Singles & doubles US$60. This small hotel is built right into a steep hillside overlooking the north side of town. The colorful, comfortable rooms are a real delight, and some have brilliant views.

The road to La Valenciana has several posh places with elevated locations.

Castillo Santa Cecilia (☎ *732-04-85, fax 732-01-53,* e *castillo@guanajuato-turistico .com, Camino a La Valenciana Km 1*) Singles & doubles US$82. This large stone building really looks like a castle, and the lobby, dining room and bars all aim for a medieval ambiance. In fact it's a modern hotel, and the rooms have all the modern facilities, and there's a swimming pool, tennis courts and an excellent restaurant.

Parador San Javier (☎ *732-06-26, fax 732-31-14,* e *hpsjgto@redes.int.com.mx, Plaza Aldama 92*) Singles & doubles US$100. Farther out on the same road as the Castillo Santa Cecilia, the San Javier offers luxurious accommodations and service in a superbly restored colonial setting.

Other upmarket places are in Marfil, west of town.

Hotel Misión Guanajuato (☎ *732-39-80, fax 732-74-60,* e *misiongt@prodigy .net.mx, Camino Antiguo a Marfil Km 2.5*) Singles & doubles from US$126. The Misión Guanajuato has a restaurant, bar, swimming pool, tennis courts and 160 luxury rooms. It is west of the city beside the ex-Hacienda San Gabriel de Barrera.

La Casa de Espíritus Alegres (☎/fax *753-10-13,* w *www.casaspirit.com, Real de Marfil s/n*) Singles & doubles from US$111. For something different, go farther west to the suburb of Marfil, where this attractive B&B has enough artifacts to fill a museum of Mexican folk arts. It has individually decorated rooms in a restored hacienda. The sign out front says 'ex-Hacienda La Trinidad,' and buses to/from the center pass every 10 minutes.

Places to Eat

Jardín de la Unión & Around The hotels on the west side of the Jardín de la Unión have good but quite expensive restaurants where you can enjoy the atmosphere of the plaza. At the tables outside *Posada Santa Fé*, well-prepared antojitos will cost US$4 to US$8, and steak dishes around US$10, and you might allow extra for wandering musicians. The adjoining *Hotel Luna* restaurant also has outdoor tables and a good, if uninspired, selection.

On the southwest corner of the Jardín, *Hotel San Diego* has an elegant upstairs restaurant with several balcony tables overlooking the plaza; the breakfast specials and the comida corrida are the best values here.

On the southeast side of the Jardín, several simple places offer cheap eats like pizza slices, hamburgers and ice cream.

Café/Restaurante El Pingüis (☎ *732-14-14, Jardín de la Unión 21*) Prices US$2-4. Open 8.30am-9.30pm daily. This unpretentious café at the northeast end of the Jardín is one of the most consistently popular places in town. The menu mixes Mexican and fast-food standards, with good coffee, egg dishes, enchiladas, big sandwiches and a solid comida corrida, all at very reasonable prices.

Casa Valadez (☎ *732-11-57, Jardín de la Unión 3, cnr Sopeña*) Prices US$6-9. Open 8.30am-11pm daily. The cavernous but classy Valadez, opposite Teatro Juárez, is pretty upmarket, but serves economical breakfasts and a good value comida corrida – it's never empty.

El Café Galería (☎ *732-25-66, Sopeña 10*) Prices from $4. A lively, popular, mid-priced place, El Café has more tables under umbrellas across the street, next to the Teatro Juárez.

Restaurant/Bar El Retiro (☎ *732-06-22, Sopeña 12*) Prices US$4-7. El Retiro has a good *menú del día* for about US$4, and live music in the evenings.

Cafe Veloce (☎ *736-67-26, Sopeña 3*) Prices US$5. The menu is mostly mid-priced Italian dishes and includes an excellent pasta selection. The name is a reference to the 1950s motorcycle racing theme.

El Gallo Pitagórico (☎ *732-94-89, Constancia 10*) Prices US$4-11. South of the Jardín, up the steep path behind Templo San Diego, this restaurant is in a bright blue building with a wonderful view over the city. The fine Italian cuisine includes assorted antipasti, rich minestrone and a range of pastas. It's well worth the walk.

Truco 7 (☎ *732-83-74, Truco 7*) Prices US$4-6. Open 8.30am-11.30pm daily. This small, intimate, artsy café-restaurant-gallery is in the short street beside the basilica. It has great atmosphere, delicious food and a mixed crowd of students, teachers and travelers. The comida corrida lunches are inexpensive and the choices for breakfast and dinner are more imaginative than in most places. Background music includes jazz, blues and classical.

La Pasadita (Cantarranas 70) Prices US\$2-3. Open 10pm-6am daily. A basic, cheap Mexican eatery, La Pasadita is open later than just about anywhere else in town.

El Unicornio Azul (☎ 732-07-00, Plaza Baratillo 2) Prices US\$2. Mainly a health food store, this little place has a few tables where you can enjoy a yogurt and fruit breakfast or a soyburger, or get wholemeal cookies to go.

Avenida Juárez & Around *Tasca de Los Santos (☎ 732-19-98, Plaza de la Paz 23)* Prices US\$9. This place has outdoor tables on picturesque Plaza de la Paz for tapas, paella and other Spanish specialties. It's a little pricey, but worth it for the great flavors and European ambiance.

Sushi Bar Room (☎ 732-05-79, Juárez 25A) Prices US\$3-7. Not the best sushi and teppanyaki you'll ever taste, but quite OK and a good change from the usual Mexican fare.

Pizza Piazza (☎ 732-59-17, Juárez 69A) Prices US\$4-5. One of several branches of a popular local pizza provider, this one offers a wide choice of toppings on suitably gooey pizzas at reasonable prices.

Restaurant La Carreta (☎ 732-43-58, Juárez 96) Prices US\$3-4. La Carreta does a good version of the standard Mexican grilled chicken with large portions of rice and salad.

Fuente de Sodas (no ☎, Juárez 120) Prices US\$2. This standard sandwich and juice bar is good for a quick inexpensive *licuado,* fruit salad or torta.

For fresh produce and local sweets, the *Mercado Hidalgo* is just a little farther west on Juárez.

Restaurante Crisalido (no ☎, Callejón de Calixto 20) Prices US\$4. Open 2-4pm Tues-Sun. Just uphill from Plazuela de los Ángeles, this peaceful place serves a tasty lunch of comida Hindu.

Plazuela San Fernando This little plaza is delightful in the evening, for a drink, a snack or a meal.

La Oreja de Van Gogh (☎ 732-69-03, Plazuela San Fernando) Prices US\$6. The Ear of Van Gogh has Vincentish murals

inside, congenial tables outside, cheap beer at the 5pm happy hour and a menu of your favorite Mexican dishes.

Other pleasant places include *Bossa Nova Cafe* and *Che Cafe.*

Entertainment

Every evening, the Jardín de la Unión comes alive with tourists and others crowding the outdoor tables, strolling, people-watching and listening to the street musicians. The *state band* and other groups give free concerts in the gazebo some evenings from around 7pm.

On Friday, Saturday and Sunday evenings around 8pm or 8.30pm, callejoneadas (or *estudiantinas)* depart form in front of San Diego church on the Jardín de la Unión. The callejoneada tradition is said to have come from Spain. A group of professional songsters and musicians, dressed in traditional costumes, starts up in front of the church, a crowd gathers, then the whole mob winds through the ancient alleyways of the city, playing and singing heartily. On special occasions they take along a burro laden with wine; at other times wine is stashed midpoint on the route. Stories and jokes are told between songs, though these are unintelligible unless you understand Spanish well. It's good fun and one of Guanajuato's most enjoyable traditions. There's no cost except a small amount for the wine you drink. Tour companies and others try to sell you tickets for the callejoneadas, but you don't need them!

Bars & Clubs *El Bar (☎ 732-25-66, Sopeña 10)* Open about 10pm until late, Tues-Sat. Upstairs above Café Galería, this popular, friendly place swings to salsa music, attracting a mixed but mostly young crowd. Good dancers will feel right at home. Others can ask about the Thursday evening salsa classes.

Guanajuato Grill (☎ 732-02-85, Alonso 20) This casual disco and drink spot is frequented by affluent, energetic students who like loud dance music. It's really packed after midnight on Friday and Saturday. On quieter nights they try to pull in the patrons with drink specials from 9pm to 10pm.

El Capitolio (☎ 732-08-10, Plaza de la Paz 62) Open 9pm-3am Tues-Sat. Another discotheque blasting techno and dance music to big weekend crowds, but Capitolio has slightly more stylish ambiance and clientele than the Grill.

La Dama de las Camelias *(Sopeña 34)* For Latin sounds in an artsy, gay-friendly atmosphere, check out La Dama de las Camelias, playing live and recorded salsa, flamenco and Andean music.

Los Lobos Bar *(Doblado s/n)* This basic, often busy rock music joint sometimes features good bands doing classic rock covers for an appreciative golden oldies crowd.

Performing Arts Guanajuato has three fine theaters, *Teatro Juárez* (☎ 732-01-83), *Teatro Principal* (☎ 732-15-23, *Hidalgo s/n*) and *Teatro Cervantes* (☎ 732-11-69, *Plaza Allende s/n)*, none far from the Jardín de la Unión. Check their posters to see what's on. International films are shown in several locations, including the Teatro Principal, Teatro Cervantes and Museo y Casa de Diego Rivera.

The Viva la Magia program runs every weekend from March to September, with Guanajuato's theaters hosting a variety of music, dance and literary events on Thursday, Friday and Saturday evenings. The tourist office has details of what's on each week.

Getting There & Away

Air Guanajuato is served by Bajío international airport (BJX), which is about 35km from Guanajuato, halfway between Léon and Silao. See the León section for specific flight information.

Bus Guanajuato's Central de Autobuses is way out on the southwest outskirts of town. It has a post office, telephone caseta, restaurant and luggage checkroom. Deluxe and 1st-class bus tickets can be bought in town at Viajes Frausto (☎ 732-35-80, *Obregón 10)*. Daily departures include:

Dolores Hidalgo – 54km, 1 hour; frequent 2nd-class Flecha Amarilla (US$3.50)

Guadalajara – 302km, 4 hours; 6 deluxe ETN (US$28), 8 1st-class Primera Plus (US$21), 8 2nd-class Flecha Amarilla (US$18)

León – 54km, 1 hour; 6 deluxe ETN (US$4.50), 7 1st-class Primera Plus (US$3.50), frequent 2nd-class Flecha Amarilla and Flecha de Oro (US$3)

Mexico City (Terminal Norte) – 365km, 4½ hours; 9 deluxe ETN (US$31), 10 1st-class Primera Plus (US$25), 2 1st-class Futura and Ómnibus de México (US$23)

San Luis Potosí – 215km, 4 hours; 5 1st-class Flecha Amarilla (US$13)

San Miguel de Allende – 94km, 1½ hours; 2 deluxe ETN (US$9), 3 1st-class Primera Plus (US$7), 9 2nd-class Flecha Amarilla (US$5)

There are also frequent 2nd-class Flecha Amarilla buses to Celaya and Morelia, plus five to Querétaro and six to Aguascalientes. For Morelia, take a bus to Irapuato and change there.

Getting Around

A taxi to Bajío international airport will cost about US$33. A cheaper option is a bus to Silao, and a taxi from there (US$9).

'Central de Autobuses' buses run frequently between the bus station and city center up to midnight. From the center, you can catch them heading west on Juárez, or on the north side of the basilica. A taxi costs US$3.

You won't want a car in town, but if you want one to explore the surrounding area, try Lloguer (☎ 733-36-90).

City buses (US$0.30) run from around 5am to 10pm. The tourist office is very helpful with bus information. Taxis are plentiful in the center and charge about US$2 for short trips around town.

CRISTO REY

Cristo Rey (Christ the King) is a 20m bronze statue of Jesus erected in 1950 on the summit of the Cerro de Cubilete about 15km west of Guanajuato and is said to be the exact geographical center of Mexico. For religious Mexicans there is a special significance in having Jesus at the heart of their country, and the statue is a popular attraction for Mexicans visiting Guanajuato.

Tour companies offer 3½-hour trips to the statue (see Organized Tours in the Guanajuato section, earlier), but you can go on your own for only US$1.75 each way by an Autobuses Vasallo de Cristo bus from the Guanajuato bus station. They depart daily at 6am, 7am, 9am, 10am, 11am, 12.30pm, 2pm, 4pm and 6pm, with additional buses on Saturday, Sunday and holidays. From the bus station it is possible to see the statue up on the hill in the distance.

LEÓN

• pop 987,300 • elev 1854m ☎ 477

The industrial city of León, 56km west of Guanajuato, is a big bus interchange point and a likable enough place if you need to stay a few hours or overnight. From the 16th century it became the center of the cattle-raising district, providing meat for the mining towns and processing hides into bags, belts, boots, saddles and harnesses that were essential for mine work in the early days. León is still famous for its leather goods, though fashion footwear now outsells fancy saddles. The city's other products include steel, textiles and soap.

In January/February, the Guanajuato State Fair attracts over 5 million visitors with agricultural displays, food and craft stalls, music, dancing, carnival rides, bull-fights and cockfights. Some 300 or so shoe-makers display their wares in the **Centro de Exposiciones** *(Conexpo, ☎ 771-25-00, cnr Boulevard López Mateos & Francisco Villa)* during the state fair. Like Guanajuato, León also celebrates a Cervantino cultural festi-val, starting mid-October.

Orientation & Information

The heart of the city is the wide main Plaza de los Mártires del 2 de Enero (also called Plaza Principal), a pleasant pedestrian space with the Palacio Municipal on its west side. The adjoining Plaza de los Fundadores, to the north, and several nearby streets are also traffic-free. A board in the Plaza de los Mártires del 2 de Enero shows a big map of

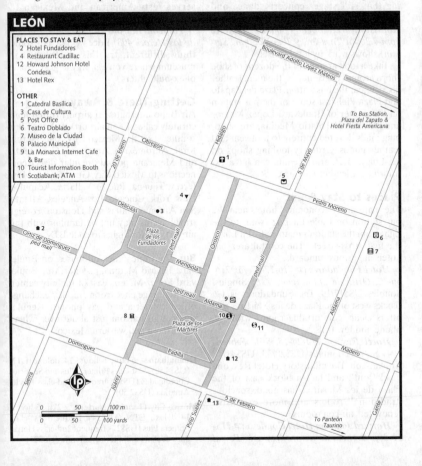

LEÓN

PLACES TO STAY & EAT
2 Hotel Fundadores
4 Restaurant Cadillac
12 Howard Johnson Hotel
   Condesa
13 Hotel Rex

OTHER
1 Catedral Basílica
3 Casa de Cultura
5 Post Office
6 Teatro Doblado
7 Museo de la Ciudad
8 Palacio Municipal
9 La Monarca Internet Cafe
   & Bar
10 Tourist Information Booth
11 Scotiabank; ATM

To Bus Station,
Plaza del Zapato &
Hotel Fiesta Americana

To Panteón
Taurino

the city center, and an information booth nearby is staffed sporadically. You could also try calling the regional tourism office (☎ 763-19-92), Vasco de Quiroga 101. La Monarca Internet Cafe & Bar, upstairs at 5 de Mayo 103, has Internet connections at US$2.25 per hour.

Things to See & Do

Walking around the historic heart of the city is the main attraction; look out for fine buildings like the **Casa de Cultura**, on the smaller, northern plaza. The big, twin-towered, baroque **Catedral Basílica** is a block northeast of the Casa de Cultura on the corner of Obregón and Hidalgo. On Aldama, a block east of the main plaza, the **Teatro Doblado** is a neoclassical 1869 building that still stages concerts, dance and drama. **Museo de la Ciudad** (*Aldama 134; admission free; open 9.30am-2.30pm & 5pm-7.30pm Tues-Fri, 9.30am-2.30pm Sat-Sun*) shows work by local artists.

Take a look at some of the dozens of shoe shops around the center, or the main leather district near the bus station. **Plaza del Zapato** and **Plaza Piel**, just south of the bus station on the corner of Boulevard López Mateos and Boulevard Hilario Medina, are shopping malls devoted entirely to footwear and leather goods. Ordinary-looking shops on La Luz and Hilario Medina can have extraordinary leather bargains.

Places to Stay & Eat

There are many economical hotels near the bus station on Calle La Luz (walk to the right from the station's main exit – La Luz is the first cross-street). The central area has hotels at various standards.

Hotel Fundadores (☎ 716-17-27, fax 716-66-12, Ortiz de Domínguez 218) Singles/doubles US$17/19. The Fundadores is 1½ blocks west of the Plaza de los Mártires and offers clean, comfortable rooms with TV, phone and few frills.

Hotel Rex (☎ 714-24-15, 5 de Febrero 104) Singles/doubles US$28/33, US$41/48 with air-con. The multistory Hotel Rex, one block south and half a block east of the Plaza de los Mártires, has good, spacious 'traditional' rooms, and more expensive renovated, air-con rooms.

Howard Johnson Hotel Condesa (☎ 713-11-20, e hcondesa@prodigy.net, Portal Bravo 14) Singles & doubles US$76. On the east side of Plaza de los Mártires, Hotel Condesa has very comfortable rooms, and a busy restaurant with outdoor tables; the buffet lunch costs US$6.50.

Fiesta Americana (☎ 713-60-40, e resfale@fiestaamericana.com.mx, Boulevard López Mateos 1102) Singles & doubles from US$154. This is the most expensive and luxurious of the several top-end hotels on López Mateos, the boulevard that runs east of the center and becomes highway 45 to the airport.

Restaurant Cadillac (☎ 716-84-07, Hidalgo 107) Prices US$4-7. On a pedestrian street north of the plazas, the Cadillac is decorated with Hollywood posters. The set lunch menu is an excellent value, and it serves tasty American and Mexican favorites until late at night.

Panteón Taurino (☎ 713-49-69, Calzada de los Héroes 408) Prices US$8. For something different, try this restaurant-bar-museum where you eat off the gravestones of ex-bullfighters.

Getting There & Away

Air Bajío international airport (often inaccurately called León airport) is about 12km southeast on the Mexico City road. Aerolitoral, Aeroméxico, American, Continental and Mexicana provide regular direct connections to Mexico City, Guadalajara, Monterrey, Tijuana, Puerto Vallarta, Acapulco, New York, Chicago, Los Angeles, Atlanta, San Antonio, Dallas and Houston. Foreign travel agents may not be familiar with this airport; ask for flights to code BJX.

Bus The Central de Autobuses, on Boulevard Hilario Medina, just north of Boulevard López Mateos east of the city center, has a luggage checkroom, money exchange office, cafeteria and pay phones. Regular services go to/from just about everywhere in northern and western Mexico.

Guanajuato – 54km, 1 hour; 14 deluxe ETN (US$4.50), 7 1st-class Primera Plus and Servicios Coordinados (US$3), frequent 2nd-class Flecha Amarilla (US$2.50)

Mexico City (Terminal Norte) – 392km, 5 hours; 14 deluxe ETN (US$34), frequent 1st-class Primera Plus (US$27), frequent 2nd-class Herradura de Plata and Flecha Amarilla (US$21)

San Miguel de Allende – 138km, 2¼ hours; 2 deluxe ETN (US$15), 3 1st-class Primera Plus and Servicios Coordinados (US$11), 2 2nd-class Flecha Amarilla (US$9)

Getting Around

There are no bus services from BJX airport to central León – a taxi will cost about US$13. The closest long-distance bus station to the airport is at Silao. A taxi from the airport will cost about US$9.

From the bus station, turn left (south) and walk 150m to López Mateos, where 'Centro' buses go west to the city center (US$0.40). To return to the bus station, catch a 'Central' bus east along López Mateos, two blocks north of the Plaza Principal. A taxi between the center and the bus station costs around US$3.50.

DOLORES HIDALGO

• **pop 46,000** • **elev 1955m** ☎ **418**

This is where the Mexican independence movement began in earnest. At 5am on September 16, 1810, Miguel Hidalgo, the parish priest, rang the bells to summon people to church earlier than usual and issued the Grito de Dolores, whose precise words have been lost to history but which boiled down to 'Long live Our Lady of Guadalupe! Death to bad government and the *gachupines!*' ('Gachupines' was a derisive term for the Spanish-born overlords who ruled Mexico.)

Hidalgo, Ignacio Allende and other conspirators had been alerted to the discovery of their plans for an uprising in Querétaro, so they decided to launch their rebellion immediately from Dolores. After the Grito they went to the lavish Spanish house on the plaza, today the Casa de Visitas, and captured the local representative of the Spanish viceroy and the Spanish tax collector. They freed the prisoners from the town jail and set off for San Miguel at the head of a growing band of criollos, *mestizos* and *indígenas*.

Today Hidalgo is Mexico's most revered hero, rivaled only by Benito Juárez in the number of streets, plazas and statues dedicated to him throughout the country. Dolores was renamed in his honor in 1824. Visiting Dolores Hidalgo has acquired pilgrimage status for Mexicans, though it's not a very attractive town. If you're interested in the country's history, it's worth a day trip

from Guanajuato or San Miguel de Allende, or a stop between them.

Orientation & Information

Everything of interest is within a couple of blocks of the Plaza Principal, which is two or three blocks north of the bus station.

The tourist office (☎ 182-11-64) is on the north side of the Plaza Principal in the Presidencia Municipal building. The staff can answer, in Spanish, any questions about the town. The office is open 10am to 3pm and 5pm to 7pm Monday to Friday, 10am to 6pm weekends, but these hours are not totally reliable.

Cash and traveler's checks can be changed at several banks around the Plaza Principal, 9am to 5pm Monday to Friday, 10am to 1pm Saturday – they all have ATMs. There are some casas de cambio too.

The post office and Telecomm (with fax service) are in the same building at Puebla 22, on the corner of Veracruz. Pay phones are in the post office, outside the tourist office and at the Flecha Amarilla bus stations.

Plaza Principal & Around

The **Parroquia de Nuestra Señora de Dolores**, the church where Hidalgo issued the Grito, is on the north side of the plaza. It has a fine 18th-century Churrigueresque façade; inside, it's fairly plain. Some say that Hidalgo uttered his famous words from the pulpit, others that he spoke at the church door to the people gathered outside.

To the west of the church is **Presidencia Municipal**, which has two colorful murals on the theme of independence. The plaza contains a **statue of Hidalgo** (in Roman garb, on top of a tall column) and a tree that, according to a plaque beneath it, was a sapling of the tree of the Noche Triste (Sad Night), under which Cortés is said to have wept when his men were driven out of Tenochtitlán in 1520.

Casa de Visitas (*cnr San Luis Potosí & Michoacán*), on the west side of the plaza, was the residence of Don Nicolás Fernández del Rincón and Don Ignacio Díaz de la Cortina, the two representatives of Spanish rule in Dolores. On September 16, 1810, they became the first two prisoners of the independence movement. Today, this is where Mexican presidents and other dignitaries stay when they come to Dolores for ceremonies.

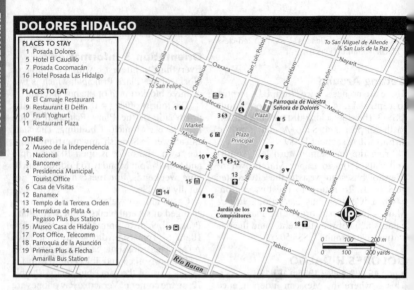

DOLORES HIDALGO

PLACES TO STAY
1   Posada Dolores
5   Hotel El Caudillo
9   Posada Cocomacán
16 Hotel Posada Las Hidalgo

PLACES TO EAT
8   El Carruaje Restaurant
9   Restaurant El Delfin
10 Fruti Yoghurt
11 Restaurant Plaza

OTHER
2   Museo de la Independencia
    Nacional
3   Bancomer
4   Presidencia Municipal,
    Tourist Office
6   Casa de Visitas
12 Banamex
13 Templo de la Tercera Orden
14 Herradura de Plata &
    Pegasso Plus Bus Station
15 Museo Casa de Hidalgo
17 Post Office, Telecomm
18 Parroquia de la Asunción
19 Primera Plus & Flecha
    Amarilla Bus Station

Museo de la Independencia Nacional

Half a block west of the Plaza Principal, this museum (no ☎, Zacatecas 6; admission US$1, free Sun; open 9am-5pm daily) has few relics but plenty of information on the independence movement and its background. It charts the appalling decline in Nueva España's indigenous population between 1519 (an estimated 25 million) and 1605 (1 million), and identifies 23 indigenous rebellions before 1800 as well as several criollo conspiracies in the years leading up to 1810. There are vivid paintings, quotations and some details on the heroic last 10 months of Hidalgo's life.

Museo Casa de Hidalgo

Miguel Hidalgo lived in this house (☎ 182-01-71, cnr Hidalgo & Morelos; admission US$2.25, free Sun; open 10am-5.45pm Tues-Sat, 10am-4.45pm Sun), one block south of the Plaza Principal, when he was parish priest to the town. It was here in the early hours of September 16, 1810, Hidalgo, Ignacio Allende and Juan de Aldama decided to launch the uprising against colonial rule. It is now something of a national shrine. One large room is devoted to a big collection of memorials, wreaths and homages to Hidalgo. Other rooms contain replicas of Hidalgo's furni-

ture and documents of the movement for independence, including the order for Hidalgo's excommunication.

The house is one block south of the Plaza Principal.

Special Events

Dolores is the scene of major celebrations on the Día de la Independencia, September 16, when the Mexican president often officiates. Festivities start September 6.

Places to Stay

Most visitors stay here just long enough to see the church and museums and eat an ice cream on the plaza. Accommodations can fill up during special events and holiday weekends; at other times you may get a discount on these prices.

Posada Dolores (☎ 182-06-42, Yucatán 8) Singles/doubles with shared bath US$7/13, with private bath US$13/16, with TV US$22. This basic, friendly casa de huéspedes, one block west of the Plaza Principal, has the cheapest rooms in town, though they're pretty small. The bigger rooms are worth the extra pesos.

Hotel El Caudillo (☎ 182-01-98, Querétaro 8) Singles/doubles US$17.50/25. Opposite the east side of the church, El Caudillo has 32 carpeted rooms that are clean enough, but a little cramped.

Miguel Hidalgo

The balding head of the visionary priest Father Miguel Hidalgo y Costilla is familiar to anyone who's looked at Mexican murals or statues. He was, it seems, a genuine rebel idealist, who had already sacrificed his own career at least once before that fateful day in 1810. And he launched the independence movement clearly aware of the risks to his own life.

Born on May 8, 1753, son of a criollo hacienda manager in Guanajuato, he studied at the Colegio de San Nicolás in Valladolid (now Morelia), earned a bachelor's degree and, in 1778, was ordained a priest. He returned to teach at his old college and eventually became rector. But he was no orthodox cleric: Hidalgo questioned the virgin birth and the infallibility of the pope, read banned books, gambled, danced and had a mistress.

In 1800 he was brought before the Inquisition. Nothing was proven, but a few years later, in 1804, he found himself transferred as priest to the hick town of Dolores.

Hidalgo's years in Dolores show that he was interested not only in the religious welfare of the local people but also in their economic and cultural welfare. Somewhat in the tradition of Don Vasco de Quiroga of Michoacán, founder of the Colegio de San Nicolás where Hidalgo had studied, he started new industries in the town. Silk was cultivated, olive groves planted and vineyards established, all in defiance of the Spanish colonial authorities. Earthenware building products such as bricks and roof tiles were the foundation of the ceramics industry that today produces fine glazed tiles and pots.

When Hidalgo met Ignacio Allende from San Miguel, they shared a criollo discontent with the Spanish stranglehold on Mexico. But Hidalgo's standing among the mestizos and indigenous people of his parish was vital in broadening the base of the rebellion that followed.

On October 13, 1810, shortly after his Grito de Independencia, Hidalgo was formally excommunicated for 'heresy, apostasy and sedition.' He answered by proclaiming that he never would have been excommunicated had it not been for his call for the independence of Mexico and furthermore stated that the Spanish were not truly Catholic in any religious sense of the word, but only for political purposes, specifically to rape, pillage and exploit Mexico. A few days later, on October 19, Hidalgo dictated his first edict calling for the abolition of slavery in Mexico.

Hidalgo led his growing forces from Dolores to San Miguel, Celaya and Guanajuato, north to Zacatecas, south almost to Mexico City, and west to Guadalajara. But then, pushed northward, their numbers dwindled and on July 30, 1811, having been captured by the Spanish, Hidalgo was shot by a firing squad in Chihuahua. His head was returned to the city of Guanajuato, where his army had won its first major victory. It hung in a cage for 10 years on an outer corner of the Alhóndiga de Granaditas, along with the heads of independence leaders Allende, Aldama and Jiménez. Rather than intimidating the people, this lurid display kept the memory, the goal and the example of the heroic martyrs fresh in everyone's mind. After independence the cages were removed, and the skulls of the heroes are now in the Monumento a la Independencia in Mexico City.

Posada Cocomacán (☎ *182-61-49, Plaza Principal 4)* Singles/doubles US$38/49. This hotel on the east side of the plaza has 50 rooms, all with private bath, good ventilation and parquet floors.

Hotel Posada Las Hidalgo (☎/*fax 182-04-77, Hidalgo 15)* Singles/doubles US$29/33. This comfortable, modern hotel is conveniently located between the bus stations and the Plaza Principal. It's very well managed and super clean, though somewhat sterile.

Places to Eat

Dolores is famous not only for its historical attractions but also for its ice cream. On the southwest corner of the Plaza Principal you can get cones in a variety of unusual flavors including *mole, chicharrón,* avocado, corn, cheese, honey, shrimp, whiskey, tequila and about 20 tropical fruit flavors. The *Fruti Yoghurt* fruit stand, just down Hidalgo, is a fresh and healthful alternative. Also look for the delicious locally made *dulces* at street stalls and in the markets.

Restaurant Plaza (☎ *182-02-59, Plaza Principal 17B*) Prices US$5. Open 8am-10pm. On the south side of the plaza, this good family restaurant does filling Mexican breakfasts, enchiladas and other antojitos, and a four-course comida corrida for US$5.50.

In the same price range as the Restaurant Plaza, the restaurant/bar at the *Hotel El Caudillo* is cool and pleasant. À la carte breakfasts are inexpensive and there's a good range of antojitos and main dishes. It stays open after 11pm, when most other eateries have closed, and it makes good coffee.

El Carruaje Restaurant (☎ *182-04-74, Plaza Principal 8*) Prices US$7. This cavernous restaurant on the east side of the plaza caters well to day-tripping families with its US$6.50 comida corrida.

Restaurant El Delfín (☎ *182-22-99, Veracruz 2*) Prices US$5-8. Open 9am-7pm daily. For surprisingly good seafood, try this pleasant place one block east of the Plaza Principal. Fare includes fish dishes, seafood soup and large shrimp servings.

Shopping

Ceramics, especially Talavera ware (including tiles), have been the special handicraft of Dolores ever since Padre Hidalgo founded the town's first ceramics workshop in the early 19th century. A number of shops sell these and other craft items. If you've got wheels, stop by the *ceramics workshops* along the approach roads to Dolores. An increasing number of workshops make 'antique,' colonial-style furniture.

Getting There & Away

Nearly all buses to/from Dolores are 2nd class. The station for Flecha Amarilla and Primera Plus is on Hidalgo, 2½ blocks south of the Plaza Principal. Herradura de Plata and Pegasso Plus are in a small station on Chiapas at Yucatán. Daily departures include:

Guanajuato – 54km, 1 hour; frequent 2nd-class Flecha Amarilla (US$3.50)

Mexico City (Terminal Norte) – 325km, 5 hours; 1 (at noon) 1st-class Pegasso Plus (US$19), frequent 2nd-class Herradura de Plata and Flecha Amarilla (US$16)

San Miguel de Allende – 43 km, 45 minutes; half-hourly 2nd-class Flecha Amarilla and Herradura de Plata (US$2.25)

There are also regular 2nd-class connections to Querétaro (US$5), León (US$6) and San Luis Potosí (US$8).

SAN MIGUEL DE ALLENDE
• pop 55,500 • elev 1840m ☎ 415

A charming colonial town in a beautiful setting, San Miguel is well known for its large expatriate community. The influx started in the 1940s, when artists, writers and other creative types came to San Miguel's Escuela de Bellas Artes. US citizens in particular came to study at the Instituto Allende. Now several thousand foreigners have retired here permanently, many others come for the winter months, and hundreds more come for crash courses in Spanish. Inevitably, the town has lost much of its bohemian character, real estate offices outnumber art galleries, and English is widely spoken.

For all the foreign influence (and partly because of it), San Miguel has preserved its lovely old buildings and quaint cobbled streets, often with unexpected vistas over the plains and distant hills. To protect its charm, the Mexican government has declared the entire town a national monument. The San Miguel locals seem especially fond of festivals, fireworks and parades, making the place even more colorful. It's easy for visitors to feel at home here, the restaurants and bars are many and varied, and every other facility is available, though low-budget lodging can be in short supply.

San Miguel has two peak periods for visitors. The main one is from mid-December to the end of March, when many *norteamericanos* come to escape the northern winter, and there's another influx from June to August. San Miguel has a very agreeable climate and superbly sharp light, which is another reason it attracts artists. It's cool and clear in winter, and warm and clear in summer, with occasional thunderstorms and heavy rain.

History

The town, so the story goes, owes its founding to a few hot dogs. These hounds were dearly loved by a courageous barefooted Franciscan friar, Juan de San Miguel, who started a mission in 1542 near an often-dry river 5km from the present town. One day the dogs wandered off from the mission, to

SAN MIGUEL DE ALLENDE

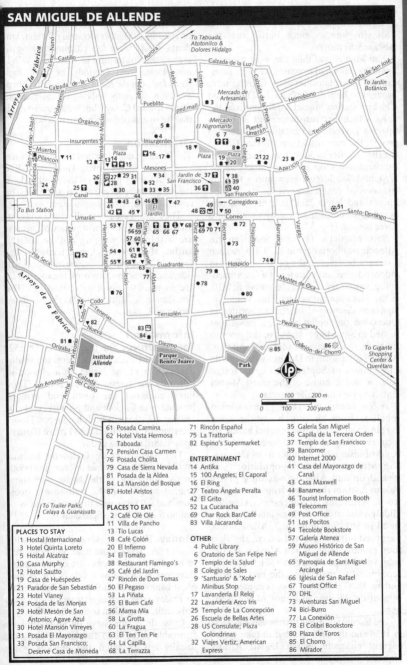

61 Posada Carmina
62 Hotel Vista Hermosa Taboada
72 Pensión Casa Carmen
76 Posada Cholita
79 Casa de Sierra Nevada
81 Posada de la Aldea
84 La Mansión del Bosque
87 Hotel Aristos

PLACES TO EAT
2 Café Olé Olé
13 Tío Lucas
18 Café Colón
20 El Infierno
34 El Tomato
38 Restaurant Flamingo's
45 Café del Jardín
47 Rincón de Don Tomas
50 El Pegaso
53 La Piñata
55 El Buen Café
56 Mama Mía
58 La Grotta
60 La Fragua
63 El Ten Ten Pie
64 La Capilla
68 La Terrazza

71 Rincón Español
75 La Trattoria
82 Espino's Supermarket

ENTERTAINMENT
14 Antika
15 100 Ángeles; El Caporal
16 El Ring
27 Teatro Ángela Peralta
42 El Grito
52 La Cucaracha
69 Char Rock Bar/Café
83 Villa Jacaranda

OTHER
4 Public Library
6 Oratorio de San Felipe Neri
7 Templo de la Salud
8 Colegio de Sales
9 'Santuario' & 'Xote' Minibus Stop
17 Lavandería El Reloj
22 Lavandería Arco Iris
25 Templo de La Concepción
26 Escuela de Bellas Artes
28 US Consulate; Plaza Golondrinas
32 Viajes Vertiz; American Express

35 Galería San Miguel
36 Capilla de la Tercera Orden
37 Templo de San Francisco
39 Bancomer
40 Internet 2000
41 Casa del Mayorazgo de Canal
43 Casa Maxwell
44 Banamex
46 Tourist Information Booth
48 Telecomm
49 Post Office
51 Los Pocitos
54 Tecolote Bookstore
57 Galería Atenea
59 Museo Histórico de San Miguel de Allende
65 Parroquia de San Miguel Arcángel
66 Iglesia de San Rafael
67 Tourist Office
70 DHL
73 Aventuras San Miguel
74 Bici-Burro
77 La Conexión
78 El Colibrí Bookstore
80 Plaza de Toros
85 El Chorro
86 Mirador

PLACES TO STAY
1 Hostal Internacional
3 Hotel Quinta Loreto
5 Hostal Alcatraz
10 Casa Murphy
12 Hotel Sautto
19 Casa de Huéspedes
21 Parador de San Sebastián
23 Hotel Vianey
24 Posada de las Monjas
29 Hotel Mesón de San Antonio; Agave Azul
30 Hotel Mansión Virreyes
31 Posada El Mayorazgo
33 Posada San Francisco; Deserve Casa de Moneda

be found later reclining at the spring called El Chorro in the south of the present town. This site was so much better that the mission was moved.

San Miguel was then the most northern Spanish settlement in central Mexico. Tarascan and Tlaxcalan allies of the Spanish were brought to help pacify the local Otomí and Chichimecs. San Miguel barely survived the fierce Chichimec resistance, and in 1555 a Spanish garrison was established there to protect the new road from Mexico City to the silver center of Zacatecas. Then Spanish ranchers and crop growers settled in the area, and San Miguel grew into a thriving commercial center known for its textiles, knives and horse tackle. It also became home to some of the wealthy Guanajuato silver barons.

San Miguel's favorite son, Ignacio Allende, was born here in 1779. He became a fervent believer in the need for Mexican independence and a leader of a Querétaro-based conspiracy that set December 8, 1810, as the date for an armed uprising. When the plan was discovered by the authorities in Querétaro on September 13, a messenger rushed to San Miguel and gave the news to Juan de Aldama, another conspirator. Aldama sped north to Dolores where, in the early hours of September 16, he found Allende at the house of the priest Miguel Hidalgo, also one of the coterie.

A few hours later Hidalgo proclaimed rebellion from his church. By the same evening, San Miguel was in rebel hands. Its local regiment had joined forces with the band of insurgents arriving from Dolores. San Miguel's Spanish population was locked up and Allende was only partly able to restrain the rebels from looting the town. After initial successes, Allende, Hidalgo and other rebel leaders were captured in 1811 in Chihuahua. Allende was executed almost immediately, Hidalgo four months later. When Mexico finally achieved independence in 1821 they were recognized as martyrs to the new nation, and in 1826 the town was renamed San Miguel de Allende in honor of the local hero.

The Escuela de Bellas Artes was founded in 1938 and the town started to take on its current character when David Alfaro Siqueiros began mural-painting courses that attracted artists of every persuasion from Mexico and the USA. The Instituto Allende opened in 1951, also attracting foreign students. Many were US citizens seeking to escape the conformity of their post-WWII homeland. Neal Cassady, hero of Jack Kerouac's *On the Road,* died here in February 1968, allegedly walking on the railroad tracks toward Celaya, but another version is that he overdosed at a house in town.

Orientation

The Plaza Principal, called the Jardín, is the focal point of the town. The Gothic-like spires of the parroquia on the south side of the plaza can be seen from far and wide. The town slopes up from west to east.

The central area is small with a straightforward layout, and most places of interest are within easy walking distance of the Jardín. Most streets change names at the Jardín. Canal/San Francisco, on its north side, and Umarán/Correo, on the south side, are the main streets of the central area. The bus station is a little over 1km west of the Jardín on Canal.

Information

Tourist Offices The tourist office (☎ 152-65-65), Plaza Principal s/n, is on the southeast corner of the Jardín, in a glassed-in office by the Iglesia de San Rafael. They have maps of the town and printed brochures in English and Spanish, and can answer questions in both languages. Hours are 10am to 5pm Monday to Friday, 10am to 2pm Saturday and Sunday.

The Asociación de Guías de Turistas (☎ 154-51-31) has a tourist information booth on the north side of the Jardín, with some printed information; the staff answer questions and sell tours with the local guide association (open 10am to 5pm daily).

Money There are several banks with *cajeros* (ATMs) on and near San Francisco in the couple of blocks east of the Jardín. Banamex is on the west side of the Jardín. Most banks are open 9am to 5pm Monday to Friday (some change traveler's checks only until 2pm), 10am to 2pm Saturday.

Casas de cambio have only slightly less favorable rates than the banks, and are usually less crowded and quicker, with longer hours. Deserve Casa de Moneda, in the Posada San Francisco on the Jardín, is open 9am to 7pm Monday to Friday, 9am to 5pm Saturday.

American Express (☎ 152-18-56) is at Viajes Vertiz, Hidalgo 1A, half a block north of the Jardín. It's open 9am to 2pm and 4pm to 6.30pm Monday to Friday, 10am to 2pm Saturday.

Post & Communications The post office is two blocks east of the Jardín, on the corner of Correo and Corregidora, open 8am to 6pm Monday to Friday, 9am to 1pm Saturday. The Mexpost express mail office is next door on Correo. There's a DHL office opposite, plus FedEx and UPS nearby.

Pay phones are plentiful in the center, and there's a caseta in the bus station. Telecomm, at Correo 16, two doors from the post office, has fax service.

La Conexión (☎ 152-16-87), Aldama 1, is one of several places offering mailboxes, express mail service to the US and 24-hour fax, Internet access and phone message services.

Internet 2000, Juárez 7, opposite Jardín San Francisco, has pretty fast connections for about US$2.25 per hour; it's open about 9am to 9pm daily. Plenty of other places offer Internet access at similar rates.

Travel Agencies Viajes Vertiz (☎ 152-18-56), Hidalgo 1A, sells domestic and international air tickets.

Library & Bookstores The public library, Insurgentes 25, also functions as an educational and cultural center with an emphasis on children's activities. It has an excellent collection of books in English and Spanish on Mexican art, crafts, architecture, history, literature and more. There are English and Spanish sections for general reference books, novels and magazines. Hours are 10am to 2pm and 4pm to 7pm Monday to Friday, 10am to 2pm Saturday. The library has a good little restaurant and a small souvenir shop.

El Colibrí bookstore (☎ 152-07-51), Diez de Sollano 30, has paperbacks, art books and magazines in English and Spanish, plus a few in French and German. El Tecolote (☎ 152-73-95), Jesús 11, is another good bookshop, with many titles in English and Spanish (closed Monday).

Media The expatriate community puts out a weekly English-language newspaper, *Atención San Miguel* (US$0.80); its office is in the public library. It's full of local news and events, plus ads for rooms, apartments or houses to sell, rent or exchange, and information about classes in yoga, Spanish, art or dance. You can buy it at the public library and elsewhere. The same sorts of things are advertised on notice boards in the public library and the language schools. The Escuela de Bellas Artes has a notice board that features local cultural events and activities.

A San Miguel home page can be found at ⓦ www.portalsanmiguel.com.

Laundry Laundromats charge around US$3.25 to wash and dry a 3kg load. Two good ones are Arco Iris, in an arcade off Mesones, and Lavandería El Reloj, Reloj 34A, both open Monday to Saturday.

Parroquia de San Miguel Arcángel

The pink 'wedding cake' towers of the parish church dominate the Jardín. These strange pinnacles were designed by indigenous stonemason Zeferino Gutiérrez in the late 19th century. He reputedly based the design on a postcard of a Belgian church and instructed builders by scratching plans in the sand with a stick. Most of the rest of the church dates from the late 17th century. The crypt contains the remains of a 19th-century Mexican president, Anastasio Bustamante. In the chapel to the left of the main altar is the much-revered image of the Cristo de la Conquista (Christ of the Conquest), made in Pátzcuaro from cornstalks and orchid bulbs, probably in the 16th century. Irish visitors will be pleased to find a statue of St Patrick.

Iglesia San Rafael, the church to the east of here, was founded in 1742 and has undergone Gothic-type alterations.

Museo Histórico de San Miguel de Allende

Near the parroquia stands the house where Ignacio Allende was born, now a museum *(☎ 152-24-99, cnr Cuna de Allende & Umarán; admission US$3.25; open 10am-4pm Tues-Sun)*. Exhibits relate the interesting history of the San Miguel area, with special displays on Allende and the independence movement. An inscription in Latin on the façade says '*Hic natus ubique notus*,' which means 'Here born, everywhere known.' Another plaque points out that the more famous independence hero, Miguel Hidalgo, only joined the movement after being invited by Allende.

Casa del Mayorazgo de Canal

This house of the Canal family, one of the most imposing of San Miguel's old residences, now houses offices of the Banamex bank, on the west side of the Jardín. It's a handsome neoclassical structure with some late baroque touches. The original entrance is at Canal 4 and retains beautiful carved wooden doors.

Templo de San Francisco

This church on the north side of the small Jardín de San Francisco, at San Francisco and Juárez, has an elaborate late-18th-century Churrigueresque façade. An image of St Francis of Assisi is at the top. A museum (☎ 152-09-47) of religious painting is due to open in the old convent beside the church; ask at the tourist office for details.

Capilla de la Tercera Orden

This chapel on the west side of the Jardín de San Francisco was built in the early 18th century and, like the San Francisco church, was part of a Franciscan monastery complex. The main façade shows St Francis and symbols of the Franciscan order.

Oratorio de San Felipe Neri

This multitowered and domed church, built in the early 18th century, stands near the east end of Insurgentes, on the Plaza Cívica. The pale pink main façade is baroque with an indigenous influence. A passage to the right of this façade leads to the east wall, where a doorway holds the image of Nuestra Señora de la Soledad (Our Lady of Solitude). You can see into the cloister from this side of the church.

Inside the church are 33 oil paintings showing scenes from the life of San Felipe Neri, the 16th-century Florentine who founded the Oratorio Catholic order. In the east transept is a painting of the Virgin of Guadalupe by Miguel Cabrera. In the west transept is a lavishly decorated chapel, the

Santa Casa de Loreto, built in 1735. It's a replica of a chapel in Loreto, Italy, legendary home of the Virgin Mary. If the chapel doors are open you can see tiles from Puebla, Valencia and China on the floor and walls, gilded cloth hangings and the tombs of chapel founder Conde Manuel de la Canal and his wife María de Hervas de Flores. Behind the altar, the *camarín* has six elaborately gilded baroque altars. In one is a reclining wax figure of San Columbano; it contains the saint's bones.

Templo de La Salud

This church, with a blue and yellow tiled dome and a big shell carved above its entrance, is just east of San Felipe Neri. The façade is early Churrigueresque. The church's paintings include one of San Javier by leading colonial painter Miguel Cabrera. San Javier (St Francis Xavier in English; 1506-52) was a founding member of the Jesuits.

Colegio de Sales

This was once a college, founded in the mid-18th century by the San Felipe Neri order. It's next door to the Templo de La Salud, which was once part of the same college. Many of the 1810 revolutionaries were educated here. The local Spaniards were locked up here when the rebels took San Miguel.

Templo de La Concepción

A couple of blocks west of the Jardín down Canal is the splendid church of La Concepción, with a fine altar and several magnificent old oil paintings. Painted on the interior doorway are a number of wise sayings to give pause to those entering the sanctuary. The church was begun in the mid-18th century; its dome, added in the late 19th century by the versatile Zeferino Gutiérrez, was possibly inspired by pictures of Les Invalides in Paris.

Escuela de Bellas Artes

The **Centro Cultural Nigromante** (☎ 152-02-89, *Hernández Macías 75; open 9am-8pm*) is housed in the beautiful former monastery of La Concepción church. It was converted into the Escuela de Bellas Artes (School of Fine Arts) in 1938. It's officially named the Centro Cultural Ignacio Ramírez, after a leading 19th-century liberal thinker who lived in San Miguel. His nickname was El

Nigromante (The Sorcerer), and the center is also commonly called by this name.

One room in the cloister is devoted to an unfinished mural by Siqueiros, done in 1948 as part of a course in mural painting for US war veterans. Its subject – though you wouldn't guess it – is the life and work of Ignacio Allende. (There is a light switch to the right of the door just before you enter.)

Instituto Allende
This large building with several patios and an old chapel at Ancha de San Antonio 4 was built in 1736 as the home of the Conde Manuel de la Canal. Later it was used as a Carmelite convent, eventually becoming an art and language school in 1951 (see Courses, later). Above the entrance is a carving of the Virgin of Loreto, patroness of the Canal family.

Mirador & Parque Juárez
One of the best views over the town and surrounding country is from the *mirador* (overlook), on Vargas (also known as the Salida a Querétaro) in the southeast of town. If you take Callejón del Chorro, the track leading directly downhill from here, and turn left at the bottom, you reach El Chorro, the spring where the town was founded. Today it gushes out of a fountain built in 1960, and there are still public washing tubs here. A path called Paseo del Chorro zigzags down the hill to the shady Parque Benito Juárez.

Botanical Gardens
The large **Jardín Botánico El Charco del Ingenio** *(off Antiguo Camino Real a Querétaro; admission US$1.25; open sunrise-sunset),* devoted mainly to cacti and other native plants of this semiarid area, is on the hilltop about 1.5km northeast of the town center. It's a lovely place for a walk, particularly in the early morning or late afternoon, though women alone should steer clear of its more secluded parts. Pathways range along the slope above a reservoir and a deep canyon. The garden is managed by CANTE, a nonprofit organization that promotes conservation.

The direct approach to the garden is to walk uphill from the Mercado El Nigromante along Homobono and Cuesta de San José, then fork left up Montitlan past the Balcones housing development. Keep walking another few minutes along the track at the top and about 100m after the track levels out, look for a small street sign on the left saying 'Paloma.' If the gate here is shut, follow the fence east to the other entrance.

Alternatively, a 2km vehicle track leads north from the Gigante shopping center, which is 2.5km east of the center on the Querétaro road. Gigante can be reached on 'Gigante' buses from the bus stop on the east side of Jardín de San Francisco. A taxi to the gardens from the center costs about US$1.75.

CANTE also administers **Los Pocitos** *(Santo Domingo 38),* an orchid garden with 2000 plants covering 230 species. It's at its best in February, March and April.

Galleries
Galería San Miguel *(☎ 152-04-54, Plaza Principal 14; open 9am-2pm & 4pm-7pm Mon-Sat, 11am-2pm Sun),* on the north side of the Jardín, and **Galería Atenea** *(☎ 152-07-85, Jesús 2; open 10am-2pm & 4pm-8pm daily)* are two of the best and most established commercial art galleries. The Escuela de Bellas Artes and Instituto Allende (see Courses) stage art exhibitions year-round. Many other galleries are advertised in *Atención San Miguel.*

Activities
Rancho La Loma *(☎ 152-21-21, Carretera Dolores Hidalgo s/n, ✆ rancholaloma@ hotmail.com; horses US$30 per hour)* rents horses and can arrange instruction and guides.

Posada de la Aldea *(☎ 152-10-22, Ancha de San Antonio 15; admission US$2.75)* opens its pool to nonguests most days, but it's more enjoyable to visit the *balnearios* (bathing spots) in the surrounding countryside (see the Around San Miguel section).

Courses
Several institutions offer Spanish courses, with group or private lessons, and optional classes in Mexican culture and history. There are also many courses in painting, sculpture, ceramics, music, dance and so on, at levels from enthusiastic dabbler to experienced professional. Most courses are available year-round, except for a three-week break in December. For classes in

meditation, yoga, tai chi and the like, look for notices in *Atención San Miguel.*

Instituto Allende *(☎ 152-01-90, fax 152-45-38,* **W** *www.instituto-allende.edu.mx, Ancha de San Antonio 20; postal address Instituto Allende, Box 85, San Miguel de Allende 37700, Gto, Mexico)* Monthly fees for Spanish classes 50 minutes a day US$120, 6 hours a day US$465, art & craft classes US$210, registration US$20, insurance US$15. The venerable Instituto Allende offers courses in fine arts, crafts and Spanish. Art and craft courses can be joined at any time and usually entail nine hours of attendance a week. Spanish courses begin about every four weeks and range from conversational to total impact (maximum six students per class).

Academia Hispano Americana *(☎ 152-03-49, fax 152-23-33, Mesones 4)* 2/4/8-week classes US$300/450/800, private classes US$12 per hour. This place runs courses in the Spanish language and Latin American culture. The cultural courses are taught in elementary Spanish. One-on-one language classes, for any period you like, are also available. The school can arrange accommodations with a Mexican family with a private room and three meals per day for about US$20 per day.

Escuela de Bellas Artes *(☎ 152-02-89, Hernández Macías 75 at Canal)* Monthly fees for 9 hours a week US$95. This school offers courses in art, dance, crafts and music. Most are given in Spanish and cost around US$95 a month, plus materials costs. Registration is at the beginning of each month. Some classes are not held in July, and there are none in August.

Other organizations offering Spanish courses include ***Centro Bilingüe*** *(☎ 154-79-60,* **W** *www.geocities.com/centrobilingue, Potrero 1, Colonia San Antonio)* and ***Warren Hardy Spanish*** *(☎ 154-40-17, 152-47-28, San Rafael 6,* **W** *www.warrenhardy.com).*

Organized Tours

Promotion of Mexican Culture *(PMC, ☎ 152-16-30, fax 152-01-21,* **W** *www.pmexc.com, Cuna de Allende 11)* Walking tours US$10-15, bus tours US$55. This company conducts two-hour historical walking tours of central San Miguel, plus a variety of day tours by bus. Stop by their office in Hotel Vista Hermosa Taboada for a brochure.

Asociación de Guías de Turistas *(☎ 154-51-31, booth on the north side of the Jardín)* Walking tours from US$8. This tour company also offers a variety of walking and bus tours in town and the surrounding area at similar prices.

A tour of the lovely private houses and gardens in San Miguel sets off at noon every Sunday from the public library. Tickets are on sale from 11am. Cost is around US$16 for the two-hour tour, with three different houses visited each week. Saturday tours of nearby ranches, haciendas and ruins are also offered for around US$16, in aid of the disabled children's school; call El Centro de Crecimiento Zamora *(☎ 152-03-18)* for the current program.

Aventuras San Miguel *(☎ 152-64-06, Recreo 10,* **e** *aventurasma@yahoo.com)* Tours US$30 per day for groups of 3 or more. Open 9am-2pm Mon-Sat. This company conducts hiking, biking, camping and horseback riding trips, as well as small group trips to many destinations in central Mexico.

Bici-Burro *(☎ 152-15-26, Hospicio No 1; trips US$38-70)* conducts mountain bike tours for groups of two or more, including guide, bike, helmet, gloves and vehicular transport if required. Popular trips include five- or six-hour excursions to Atotonilco or Pozos. They also rent bikes for the day (US$22).

Special Events

Being so well endowed with churches and patron saints (it has six), San Miguel has a multitude of festivals every month. You'll probably learn of some by word of mouth – or the sound of fireworks – while you're there.

Blessing of the Animals – This happens in several churches, including the parroquia, on January 17.

Allende's Birthday – On January 21 various official events celebrate this occasion.

Cristo de la Conquista – This image in the parroquia is feted on the first Friday in March, with scores of dancers in elaborate pre-Hispanic costumes and plumed headdresses in front of the parroquia.

San Patricio – March 17 sees a parade, but celebrations are more saintly than in cities with an Irish tradition.

Semana Santa – Two weekends before Easter pilgrims carry an image of the Señor de la

Columna (Lord of the Column) from Ato-tonilco, 19km north, to the church of San Juan de Dios in San Miguel on Saturday night or Sunday morning. During Semana Santa itself, the many activities include the lavish Procesión del Santo Entierro on Good Friday and the burning or exploding of images of Judas on Easter Day.

Fiesta de la Santa Cruz – This unusual, rather solemn festival has its roots in the 16th century. Try to be as unobtrusive as possible and not intrude on the events. It happens on the last weekend in May at Valle del Maíz, 2km from the center of town. Oxen are dressed in lime necklaces and painted tortillas, and their yokes festooned with flowers and fruit. One beast carries two boxes of 'treasure' (bread and sugar) and is surrounded by characters in bizarre costumes on horses or donkeys. A mock battle between 'Indians' and 'Federales' follows, with a wizard appearing to heal the 'wounded' and raise the 'dead.'

Corpus Christi – This movable feast in June features dances by children in front of the parroquia.

Chamber Music Festival – The Escuela de Bellas Artes sponsors an annual festival of chamber music *(música de cámara)* in the first two weeks of August.

San Miguel Arcángel – Celebrations honoring the town's chief patron saint are held on the third Saturday of September. There are cockfights, bullfights and *pamplonadas* (bull-running) in the streets, but the hub of a general town party is provided by traditional dancers from several states who meet at Cruz del Cuarto, on the road to the train station. Wearing bells, feather headdresses, scarlet cloaks and masks, groups walk in procession to the parroquia carrying flower offerings called *xuchiles*, some playing armadillo-shell lutes. The roots of these events probably go back to pre-Hispanic times. Dances continue over a few days and include the Danza Guerrero in front of the parroquia, which represents the Spanish conquest of the Chichimecs.

San Miguel Music Festival – This largely classical music festival presents an almost daily program with Mexican and international performers throughout the second half of December. Most concerts are at the fine Teatro Ángela Peralta, built in 1910, on the corner of Mesones and Hernández Macías.

Places to Stay

Some of the better-value places are often full; book ahead if you can, especially during the high seasons.

Many hotels give discounts for long-term guests. If you're planning to stay a while in San Miguel, there are houses, apartments and rooms to rent. Check the newspapers, notice boards and real-estate agents. Expect to pay from US$400 a month for a decent two-bedroom house. House-sitting is another possibility.

Budget *Lago Dorado KDA Trailer Park* (☎ 152-23-01) Sites US$10. Situated near the reservoir a few km south of town, this park has a lounge, Laundromat and 80 shady spaces with full hookups. It's cheaper for longer stays. From town, take the Celaya road, then after 3km turn right at the Hotel Misión de los Ángeles and continue another 2km toward the lake, crossing the train tracks.

Trailer Park La Siesta (☎ 152-02-07, Carretera Celaya 2km) Sites US$12. La Siesta is on the grounds of the Motel La Siesta, 2km south of town. It has 60 spaces with full hookups.

Hostal Internacional (☎ 152-31-75, ✉ hostma@unisono.net.mx, Jaime Nunó 28) Dorm beds US$6.50, with student or hostel card US$5.50, private rooms US$13. The friendly Internacional is about seven blocks northwest of the center. The building is nothing special, but it has a good kitchen/dining area and seats outside in the courtyard. The price includes coffee, tea and continental breakfast. The hostel may have to move when the lease expires on the current building.

Hostal Alcatraz (☎ 152-85-43, ✉ alcatraz hostel@yahoo.com, ⩊ http://mexlinks.com/hostel.htm, Reloj 54) Dorm beds US$11, with hostel card US$10. This HI-affiliated hostel is centrally located and appealing, with TV room and kitchen available to guests.

Casa de Huéspedes (☎ 152-13-78, Mesones 27) Singles/doubles with bath US$16.50/22. This clean, pleasant upstairs hostelry has a rooftop terrace with a good view. You pay slightly more with a kitchenette, but you can probably get a discount for a longer stay or at off-peak times.

Hotel Vianey (☎ 152-45-59, Aparicio 18) Singles & doubles US$16.50. A couple blocks up the hill from Casa de Huéspedes, the Vianey has small, plain, comfortable rooms surrounding a plant-filled courtyard. It's a good budget option.

Posada Cholita (☎ 152-28-98, Hernández Macías 114) Singles/doubles from US$17/27. Another budget possibility is the Posada Cholita, a few blocks southwest of the center on a pretty street. Smallish, dark rooms vary in quality; the cheapest ones have a shared bathroom.

Posada El Mayorazgo (☎ 152-13-09, Hidalgo 8) Singles/doubles US$21/23. Also close to the center, this place has comfortable, modern rooms around a sunny courtyard and also an apartment suitable for four adults.

Hotel Sautto (☎ 152-00-51, Hernández Macías 59) Singles/doubles US$22/27, large rooms for 3/4 people US$33/38. The Sautto is an interesting old building around a big, quiet courtyard, just north of the Escuela de Bellas Artes. Rooms have high ceilings and bright tiled bathrooms.

Mid-Range Mid-range options in San Miguel run from adequate but uninspiring accommodations for around US$30, to very attractive places that are quite good values at around US$40.

Hotel Vista Hermosa Taboada (☎ 152-00-78, fax 152-26-33, Cuna de Allende 11) Singles & doubles from US$33. South of the Jardín, the Vista Hermosa Taboada is in the former category, with 17 rooms with fireplace, carpet and double bed.

Parador de San Sebastián (☎ 152-70-84, Mesones 7) Singles/doubles from US$24/27. This place is quiet, clean and very attractive. The newer rooms are smallish, but very clean and mostly OK. The nicest rooms, with fireplaces, are the older ones around the courtyard, and they cost considerably more – generally over US$33.

Posada de las Monjas (☎ 152-01-71, fax 152-62-27, e bigboy@prodigy.net.mx, Canal 37) Singles/doubles from US$33/40. The welcoming Posada de las Monjas is a monastery turned motel, and one of the better values in San Miguel. The 65 rooms are comfortable and nicely decorated, and the bathrooms all have slate floors and hand-painted tiles. Rooms in the new section out back are in better condition than those in the old section and just as charming. Numerous terraces give lovely views over the valley. Restaurant, bar, laundry and parking are available. Prices are more for larger rooms and those with fireplaces.

Hotel Quinta Loreto (☎ 152-00-42, fax 152-36-16, e hqloreto@terra.com.mx, Loreto 15) Singles/doubles US$35/43. This motel-style place is a longtime favorite with visitors from the US. The 38 pleasant rooms,

some with small private patio, are set around large grounds with trees, tennis courts and plenty of parking space. The restaurant is good. Discounts are available for a stay of a week or longer. Reservations are recommended.

Posada Carmina (☎ 152-04-58, fax 152-01-35, Cuna de Allende 7) Singles/doubles from US$44/60, suites from US$109. Close to the Jardín, the Carmina is a former colonial mansion with large, attractive rooms, tiled bathrooms and amenities like phones and color TV. In the leafy courtyard there's a pleasant restaurant-bar.

Hotel Mansión Virreyes (☎ 152-08-51, fax 152-38-65, e mansionvirreyes@prodigy .net.mx, Canal 19) Singles/doubles US$38/60. This is another colonial place with 22 rooms around two courtyards and a restaurant-bar in the rear patio. It is just half a block from the Jardín.

Hotel Mesón de San Antonio (☎ 152-05-80, fax 152-28-97, Mesones 80) Standard rooms with breakfast US$54. Centrally located, this hotel has rooms set around an attractive courtyard with a lawn and a small swimming pool.

Top End **Posada San Francisco** (☎ 152-00-72, 800-714-68-70, e hposadasanfrancisco@ prodigy.net.mx, w www.naftaconnect.com/ hsanfrancisco, Plaza Principal 2) Singles & doubles US$72. The San Francisco is a great value for its perfect location on the Jardín and for its classic colonial courtyard, though the spacious, comfortable rooms are modern and not especially charming.

Posada de la Aldea (☎ 152-10-22, w www.naftaconnect.com/hotellaaldea, Ancha de San Antonio 15) Singles & doubles US$74. Opposite the Instituto Allende, this modern hotel has wide lawns, a pool, and 66 large, well-equipped rooms.

Hotel Aristos (☎ 152-03-92, fax 152-16-31, e arissma@prodigy.net, Calzada del Cardo 2) Singles & doubles US$83. In the spacious grounds behind the Instituto Allende, the Aristos has tennis courts, a big pool and modern rooms with terraces and parking.

Casa de Sierra Nevada (☎ 152-70-40, fax 152-14-36, e sierranevada@prodigy.net.mx, Hospicio 35) Singles & doubles US$228, suites US$322-491. The most luxurious, elegant and expensive place in town is the

Casa de Sierra Nevada, which was converted from four colonial mansions. It has a swimming pool, fine restaurant, views over the town, and superbly appointed rooms.

B&Bs San Miguel now has a slew of B&Bs offering comfortable accommodations at quite high prices.

Casa Murphy (☎/fax 152-37-76, e *reservations@smahotels.com, San Antonio Abad 22)* Singles & doubles US$80-90. Off Canal, about 400m northwest of the Jardín, Casa Murphy offers luxurious rooms in an old colonial house, and two larger *casitas* with kitchen, spa bath and private patio.

Pensión Casa Carmen (☎ *152-08-44,* e *ccarmen@unisono.net.mx,* w *www.com/casacarmen, Correo 31)* Singles/doubles US$55/75. Centrally located in an old colonial home, Casa Carmen has 12 rooms with high-beamed ceilings, set around a pleasant courtyard with a fountain, orange trees and flowers. The price includes a delicious breakfast and lunch in the elegant dining room.

La Mansión del Bosque (☎ *152-02-77,* e *manruth@unisono.net.mx,* w *www.infosma.com/mansion, Aldama 65)* Singles US$33-42, doubles US$69-88 with breakfast & dinner. This popular place, opposite Parque Benito Juárez, has 23 different rooms, all comfortable with good furniture and original art. Winter and July/August rates are higher. Reserve well in advance. Mailing address is Apartado Postal 206, San Miguel de Allende, Gto 37700.

Long-Term Accommodations If you want to stay in San Miguel for more than a few weeks, as many people do, consider renting a house or apartment. Many lovely, fully furnished homes are only used for a few weeks a year, usually in winter, and are otherwise available for rental for periods as short as a month. Contact one of the local real estate offices like Casas de San Miguel (☎ 152-44-16), Remax (☎ 152-79-52, w www.realestate-sma.com), Century 21 (☎ 152-18-42, w www.century21mexico.com) and Abrahám Cadena Hernández (☎ 152-16-38, e ach@unisono.net.mx).

Places to Eat

San Miguel restaurants serve a wide variety of quality international cuisine, but for cash-strapped budget travelers there are a few economical options aimed more at local families than trendy expatriates.

Budget For quick cheap eats, there are some excellent *bakeries* around town, while food *stands* on the east side of the Jardín offer cheap, tasty Mexican fare like *elotes* (steamed ears of corn), hamburgers, hot dogs or tamales for around US$2. The *taquería* on Mesones, just uphill from El Infierno, stays open late. *Mercado El Nigromante*, with all the usual Mexican market eateries, is on Colegio about four blocks from the Jardín, but light years away from the San Miguel gringo scene. For self-catering, try Espino's supermarket, at Codo 36, which has a large range of necessities for US and Canadian expatriates, and fresh fruit and vegetables are sold just outside.

Restaurant Flamingo's (no ☎, Juárez 15) Prices US$5-6. Open 9am-10pm daily. Northeast of the Jardín, Flamingo's serves a good-value comida corrida (US$5) from 1pm to 4pm, but its main line is take-out chicken, which you'll see turning on the spit out front.

El Infierno (☎ *152-23-55, Mesones 25)* Prices US$5-6. El Infierno will do a full meal of soup, chicken, french fries and vegetables, but like Flamingo's, it also sells a lot of take-out chicken.

Café Colón (no ☎, Insurgentes 2) Prices US$3. Open 8am-5pm. Around the corner from El Infierno, this cafe is popular with locals for its inexpensive set breakfasts and lunches.

Villa de Pancho (☎ *152-12-47, Quebrada 12)* Prices US$4. Open 9am-9pm. A few blocks northwest of the Jardín, Pancho's is a cheap and cheerful little place offering breakfasts, a tasty set lunch (US$4) and inexpensive beers.

South of the Jardín, several inexpensive places cater mostly to visitors.

La Piñata (☎ *152-20-60, cnr Jesús & Umarán)* Prices US$3-5. Open 9am-8pm Wed-Mon. Just one block west of the Jardín, the convivial La Piñata is popular for juices, breakfasts, salads, sandwiches and quesadillas.

El Buen Café (☎ *152-58-07, Jesús 23)* Prices US$5-7. Open 9am-8pm Mon-Sat. Apart from the good coffee, this place does healthy, economical breakfasts, Mexican dishes, and home-style southern-US specialties.

El Ten Ten Pie (☎ 152-71-89, *Cuna de Allende 21*) Prices US$2-4. Open 9am-midnight. This little family-run restaurant serves up home-style Mexican cooking with excellent chili sauces. Try the inexpensive comida corrida, or antojitos like the tasty cheese and mushroom tacos.

Downhill toward Instituto Allende, on the corner of Ancha San Antonio and tree-shaded Calle Nueva, two or three food *stands* assemble in the evenings, selling ice cream, tacos and other snacks. They're very clean, the cost is minimal, the tastes are a treat, and the experience is delightful.

El Tomato (☎ 154-61-50, *Mesones 62*) Prices US$4. Open 9am-9pm daily. For *cocina naturista*, try El Tomato, where light meals include pasta, whole wheat sandwiches and salads, and feature fantastically fresh and tasty ingredients like lettuce you can really taste. There are also freshly squeezed fruit and vegetable juices, and the comida corrida is a great value at US$5.75.

Mid-Range & Top End There are several lively places around the Jardín, open from around 9am to 10pm, but you pay a premium for the position.

Rincón de Don Tomás (☎ 152-37-80, *Portal de Guadalupe 2*) Prices US$7. On the northeast corner of the Jardín, this good mid-range restaurant has a solid menu of classic Mexican dishes like *chiles en nogada* and *gorditas* using handmade tortillas.

Café del Jardín (☎ 152-50-06, *Portal Allende 2*) Prices US$6-8. Open 7am-midnight. On the southwest corner of the Jardín, this café is OK for ice cream, coffee, cakes and late-night snacks, but not a great value for a full meal.

La Terrazza (☎ 152-01-51, *Correo s/n*) Prices US$6-10. Under the arches next to the tourist office, La Terrazza and some other eateries have tables on a balcony at the corner of the Jardín. It's often crowded with people who come to see people, and it's a great spot, though the food is ordinary and the prices quite high.

If you want to blow your budget on some fine food, San Miguel is one of the best places in Mexico to do it.

El Pegaso (☎ 152-13-51, *Corregidora 6*) Prices US$5-9. Open 8.30am-10pm Mon-Sat. You could start spending madly here with an excellent breakfast of fruit, eggs

Benedict, fresh bread and coffee. For a light lunch, try their fancy sandwiches such as smoked turkey or smoked salmon with cream cheese. For dinner, there's an intriguing choice of Mexican, Italian and Asian-inspired dishes.

Rincón Español (☎ 152-29-84, *Correo 29*) Prices US$6-10. Open noon-10pm or 11pm daily. The long-standing Rincón Español has traditional Mexican and Spanish dishes, which are a little on the pricey side but worth it if you come in the evening when flamenco dancers perform. The comida corrida is more affordable at about US$5. And Rincón Español has recently opened a sushi bar, just beside its front door.

Mama Mía (☎ 152-20-63, *Umarán 8*) Prices US$5-10. Open 8am-after midnight. Just west of the Jardín, this San Miguel institution has a restaurant, several bars, a disco and a live music venue. The restaurant, in a cool and pleasant courtyard, features a wide range of dishes, with pastas, well-prepared steak and seafood. Breakfasts are a much better deal, but Mama Mía is most popular at night (see Entertainment).

La Fragua (☎ 152-11-44, *Cuna de Allende 3*) Prices from US$9. Open 6pm-2am daily. This is a long popular courtyard restaurant-bar, with live music every night and a happy hour from 6pm to 8pm. It's becoming more popular as a bar than a restaurant, but it's still an enjoyable place to eat.

La Capilla (☎ 152-06-98, *Cuna de Allende 10*) Prices US$9-14. Open noon-midnight Wed-Mon. The location is central but strange – almost underneath the parroquia – but the atmosphere is magic and the food superb at this most recommendable of restaurants, offering 'tastes from Mexico and around the world.'

La Grotta (☎ 152-37-90, *Cuadrante 5*) Prices from US$7.50. Around the corner from Cuna de Allende, this Italian restaurant is said to serve the best pizza in Mexico – a number of places make this claim – but La Grotta supports it with a truly excellent product. The pasta here is also good, and the homemade desserts are delicious.

Tío Lucas (☎ 152-49-96, *Mesones 103*) Prices US$7-11. Open noon-midnight daily. This US-style place is well known for its beef and also serves a good range of soups and salads; the Caesar salad is especially recommended. It often has live blues or jazz at night.

Café Olé Olé (☎ 152-08-96, *Loreto 66*) Prices US$7. Open 1pm-9pm daily. A fun place near the market, this friendly family-run cafe is brightly decorated with bullfighting memorabilia. It's been popular for years for its grilled chicken and beef, and its special chicken fajitas.

La Trattoria (☎ 152-38-90, *cnr Zacateros & Codo*) Prices US$8-14. La Trattoria does a good range of Italian and vegetarian dishes, and is one of the best places southwest of the center.

Entertainment

Every evening at sunset, the Jardín hosts a free concert of birdsong as the trees fill with twittering, whistling and preening birds, while the paths below fill with people doing much the same. These days, gray-haired gringos can outnumber flirting teenagers, but it's a delight to be there, as the air cools and the fragrance of flowers and food stalls floats across the plaza.

For more formal entertainment, check *Atención San Miguel* for news about what's on in town. The *Escuela de Bellas Artes* hosts a variety of events including art exhibitions, concerts, readings and theater; check its notice board for the current schedule. Some events are held in English.

Villa Jacaranda (☎ 152-10-15, *Aldama 53*) Admission US$5.50. Villa Jacaranda shows recent releases of US movies on a big screen at 7.30pm daily. Entry includes a drink and popcorn. The library shows quality movies at 4pm, 5.30pm and 7.30pm Tuesday to Saturday.

Several restaurants double as drinking, dancing and entertainment venues. Most of the action is on Thursday, Friday and Saturday nights, but at holiday times some places will have live music and more any night of the week.

Mama Mía (☎ 152-20-63, *Umarán 8*) Open 8pm-2am or 3am daily. The perennially popular Mama Mía has a main bar featuring live rock (Friday to Saturday) or South American music (Thursday), sometimes with a US$3 to US$5 cover. At night the restaurant features more live music and an older crowd. A bar at the front shows big-screen sports and music videos, and another

bar upstairs offers a fine view of the town. Serious nightlife gets going around 11pm.

El Grito (☎ 152-00-48, *Umarán 15*) Open 10pm-2am Thur-Sat. An oversized face shouts above the doorway of this upscale disco, just across the street from Mama Mía.

Char Rock Bar/Café (☎ 152-73-73, *upstairs at Correo & Diez de Sollano*) This café has live bands doing classic rock covers and occasional cheap drink specials to get the students in early, but later on it's mostly an older crowd.

Antika (☎ 152-19-58, *Mesones 99*) Admission US$3-5. Open 10.30pm-3am Wed, Fri & Sat. This disco, spinning techno and dance music, is popular with a young, affluent crowd.

100 Ángeles (☎ 512-59-37, *Mesones 97*) Admission US$3-5. Open 10pm-4am Fri-Sat. Cien Ángeles disco/dance club is San Miguel's premier gay venue, with a '70s ambiance from the music to the glitter ball. Just to the right of the front door, *El Caporal* bar has a small stage for acoustic music and comedy acts.

El Ring (☎ 152-19-98, *Hidalgo 25*) Admission US$4-6. Open 10pm-3am Thur-Sat. This flashy place is the most popular club in town, blasting a mix of Latin, US, and European dance music. From midnight it's usually full (sometimes packed) with young Mexicans and foreigners.

La Cucaracha (☎ 152-01-96, *Zacateros 22*) Open 9pm-3am daily. You won't have to dress up for this skanky watering hole, where Mexican students and assorted gringos come for the large pool tables and cheap beers.

Agave Azul (☎ 152-51-51, *Mesones 80*) Open 1pm-1am or later. The restaurant at Hotel Mesón de San Antonio morphs into a bar after 9pm, when live music kicks in and the long tequila list looks tempting.

Shopping

San Miguel has one of the biggest and best concentrations of craft shops in Mexico, selling folk art and handicrafts from all over the country. Local crafts include tinware, wrought iron, silver, brass, leather, glassware, pottery and textiles. Most of these crafts are traditions going back to the 18th century. Prices are not low, but quality is high and the range of goods is mind-boggling.

Casa Maxwell (☎ 152-02-47, Canal 14) A block west from the Jardín, this rambling store offers a tremendous array of decorative and household goods. There are many, many more within a few blocks, especially on Canal, San Francisco and Zacateros.

Mercado de Artesanías is a collection of handicraft stalls in the alleyway between Colegio and Loreto; prices are lower than in San Miguel's smarter shops, but the quality is very variable. The daily **Mercado El Nigromante**, on Colegio, sells fruit, vegetables and assorted goods for the local community.

The biggest *market* takes place on Tuesday out of town beside the Gigante shopping center, 2.5km east of the center on the Querétaro road. Take a 'Gigante' or 'Placita' bus (10 minutes) from the east side of the Jardín de San Francisco.

Getting There & Away

Air The nearest airport is Bajío international (BJX), between León and Silao (see the León section for flight information). Mexico City airport is served by many more direct flights than BJX, and they may be slightly cheaper, but BJX is more convenient for San Miguel.

Bus The small Central de Autobuses has a telephone caseta, snack bar and not much else. It's on Canal, about 1km west of the center. ETN, Primera Plus and Pegasso Plus tickets can be bought at PMC Tours (☎ 152-16-30), Cuna de Allende 11. Daily departures include:

Celaya – 52km, 1¼ hours; frequent 2nd-class Flecha Amarilla (US$3)

Dolores Hidalgo – 43km, 1 hour; frequent 2nd-class Flecha Amarilla and Herradura de Plata (US$2)

Guadalajara – 380km, 6 hours; 2 deluxe ETN (US$35), 3 1st-class Primera Plus (US$29)

Guanajuato – 94km, 1-1½ hours; 2 deluxe ETN (US$9), 4 1st-class Primera Plus (US$6.50), 2 1st-class Ómnibus de México and Servicios Coordinados (US$5.50), 10 2nd-class Flecha Amarilla (US$5)

León – 138km, 2¼ hours; 2 deluxe ETN (US$15), 3 1st-class Primera Plus and Servicios Coordinados (US$11), 2 2nd-class Flecha Amarilla (US$9)

Mexico City (Terminal Norte) – 280km, 3½-4 hours; 4 deluxe ETN (US$23), 2 1st-class Primera Plus, 2 1st-class Herradura de Plata

(US$17), frequent 2nd-class Flecha Amarilla semidirect (US$14)

Querétaro – 60km, 1 hour; 3 deluxe ETN (US$5.50), frequent 2nd-class Flecha Amarilla (US$3.50)

Other 1st-class services go to San Luis Potosí, Aguascalientes, and Monterrey while Americanos buses go at 5pm daily to San Antonio, Houston, Dallas and Chicago.

Car If you need a car for more than a few days, it may be worth going to Querétaro, or at least calling the agencies there. The only car rental place based in San Miguel is Hola (☎ 152-01-98), in the Posada San Francisco. Prices start around US$60 per day for a VW Beetle. You should book at least a week ahead, especially in the winter and summer holiday periods.

Getting Around

A few operators will provide transport to Bajío international airport, if there are enough paying passengers to fill the vehicle. Try PMC Tours (☎ 152-16-30), Asociación de Guías de Turistas (☎ 154-51-31), Aventuras San Miguel (☎ 152-64-06) and Viajes Vertiz (☎ 152-18-56). Alternatively, take a bus to Silao and get a taxi from there to the airport. For Mexico City airport, get a bus to Querétaro, and a bus direct to the airport from there.

Local buses run 7am to 9pm daily and cost US$0.30. 'Central' buses go every few minutes between the bus station and the town center. Coming into town these go up Insurgentes, wind through the town a bit and terminate on the corner of Mesones and Colegio. Heading out from the center, you can pick one up on Canal.

A taxi between the center and the bus station costs US$2.25, as do most taxi trips around town.

AROUND SAN MIGUEL DE ALLENDE
Hot Springs

Natural hot springs *(admission from US$5 per day)* near San Miguel have been developed as balnearios, with swimming pools where you can soak in mineral waters amid pleasant surroundings; the soaking is supposedly good for the skin, and definitely good for relaxation. The balnearios are accessed via the highway north of San Miguel – take a Dolores Hidalgo bus from the San Miguel bus station, or a 'Santuario' minibus (half-hourly) from the bus stop on Puente de Umarán, off Colegio and opposite the Mercado El Nigromante. This will stop out front, or within walking distance, of all the main balnearios. Returning to town, hail one of the buses that speed along the highway. Taxis are a good option if you can get a few people together. They cost around US$8 each way, and you can ask the driver to return for you at an appointed time.

The most popular balneario is **Taboada** (☎ 415-152-08-50; open 9am-6pm Wed-Mon), 8km north of San Miguel and then 3km west along a signposted side road. It has a large lawn area and three swimming pools: one Olympic-size with warm water, a smaller pool for children, and a thermal spa that can get quite hot. A small kiosk and a bar provide snacks and drinks. Minibuses to 'Xote,' hourly from the Puente de Umarán bus stop, will get you most of the way to Taboada. Get off where the bus turns off the Taboada side road and walk the remaining 1km to the hot springs.

Other balnearios include **Santa Verónica**, right beside the highway to Dolores Hidalgo, at the Taboada turnoff. Nine kilometers from San Miguel, **Parador del Cortijo** (☎ 415-152-17-00) is a hotel-restaurant with a thermal pool, sauna, whirlpool bath and massages. Nearby **Balneario Xote** (☎ 415-614-58-89) is an inexpensive spa and pool.

Only 100m or so beyond the Parador del Cortijo, on the same side of the highway, **La Gruta** (☎ 415-152-25-30) has three small pools into which the waters of a thermal spring have been channeled. The hottest is in a cave entered through a tunnel, with hot water gushing from the roof, lit by a single shaft of sunlight.

The favorite **Escondido Place** balneario has two warm outdoor pools and three connected indoor pools, each progressively hotter. The picturesque grounds have plenty of space for picnicking, and there's a small kiosk for drinks and snacks. It's 8km from San Miguel, on the road to Dolores Hidalgo.

Santuario de Atotonilco

Turning west off the Dolores Hidalgo highway about 15km north of San Miguel and going about 3km will bring you to the hamlet of Atotonilco, dominated by its sanctuary founded in 1740 as a spiritual retreat. Here Ignacio Allende was married in 1802. Eight years later he returned with Miguel Hidalgo and the band of independence rebels en route from Dolores to San Miguel to take the shrine's banner of the Virgin of Guadalupe as their flag.

Today a journey to Atotonilco is a goal of pilgrims and penitents from all over Mexico, and the starting point of an important and solemn procession two weekends before Easter, in which the image of the Señor de la Columna is carried to the church of San Juan de Dios in San Miguel. Inside, the sanctuary has six chapels and is vibrant with statues, folk murals and other paintings. Extensive restoration has been underway for some time. Traditional dances are held here on the third Sunday in July.

Pozos

• pop 130 • elev 2305m ☎ 412

Less than a hundred years ago, Mineral de Pozos was a flourishing silver- and copper-mining center of about 50,000 people, but as the minerals played out the population dwindled and abandoned houses, mine workings and a large but unfinished church. Now visitors enjoy exploring the well-worn buildings, old mines and abandoned mine structure, and touring the surrounding area by horseback or mountain bike. Replicas of pre-Hispanic musical instruments, including deerskin drums and rainmakers, are still produced here, providing a livelihood for some of the residents. The instruments are used to accompany the pre-Hispanic dances that feature in local fiestas.

Casa Mexicana Hotel (☎ 293-00-14, e pozosmex@yahoo.com, Jardín Principal 2) Doubles with breakfast US$70-83. This 100-year-old hacienda was the first place to be converted to tourist lodging, and it has been very well done. The rooms are spacious and elegant with great views.

Casa Montana (☎ 293-00-32, Jardín Principal 4) Prices US$93-120. A total renovation has turned this antique building into a comfortable B&B, restaurant and art gallery.

Pozos is 14km south of San Luis de la Paz, a detour east of highway 57. To get there by bus from San Miguel, go first to Dolores Hidalgo, then to San Luis de la Paz, and then take a third bus from there to

Pozos. By car it's about 35 minutes from San Miguel. *Aventuras San Miguel* (☎ 152-64-06) runs trips to Pozos from San Miguel, and *Bici-Burro* (☎ 152-15-26) does it as a bike tour.

CELAYA
• pop 263,900 • elev 1760m ☎ 461

Founded in 1570, Celaya grew as the center of a rich agricultural region supplying the mining towns farther north and also as a transit point on the trade routes between Mexico City and the mines. Industries grew rapidly in the mid-19th century, producing thread, cloth and the delicious caramel sweets called *cajetas*, which are still a local specialty. Today, Celaya has a key position in the rapidly developing industrial region from Querétaro to Guadalajara, with important food-processing, chemical and engineering plants, though it may be better known as home to one of Mexico's major football teams.

The tourist office (☎ 612-74-76), Juárez 204, in the 17th century Casa del Diezmo, opens 9am to 4pm Monday to Friday.

The main attraction for visitors is the legacy of neoclassical architect Eduoardo Tresguerras, born here in 1759. The 1802 **Templo del Carmen**, at the corner of Madero and Obregón, is his masterpiece, noted for its domed ceiling and one of Tresguerras' own paintings inside. Other Tresguerras works (all in the historic center of town) include the façade and altars of **Templo San Francisco** (1683-1820), the 1820 **Templo de Tercera Orden** and the **Columna de la Independencia** monument. Also worth seeing in the city center are **Torre Hidraulica**, a 1910 water tower with a strange sci-fi look, and Octavio Ocampo's optical illusionary murals in the Presidencia Municipal.

Places to Stay
Hotel Guadalupe (☎ 612-18-39, Portale Guadalupe 18B) Singles & doubles US$8, US$10 with bath. This basic budget hotel is very central, and was reputedly used by revolutionary leader Miguel Hidalgo in 1810.

Hotel Gómez (☎ 612-00-01, Morelos 101A) Singles/doubles US$22/25. Some rooms in this comfortable hotel have views over the city.

Plaza Bajío Inn (☎ 613-86-00, Libertad 133) Singles/doubles US$38/41. The business traveler's choice is this modern multistory hotel a few blocks from the city center.

Getting There & Away
The bus station, about 1km southeast of the city center, has frequent services along the main highways east (to Querétaro and Mexico City) and west (to Irapuato, León and Guadalajara). Regular 2nd-class services go north to San Miguel de Allende.

Querétaro State

Querétaro is primarily an agricultural and livestock-raising state. Industry has developed around Querétaro city and certain other places, notably San Juan del Río. The state also turns out opals, mercury, zinc and lead. Apart from Querétaro city, with its fine colonial architecture, there are other areas worth visiting, like pretty Tequisquiapan with its thermal springs. In the northeast of the state, the rugged fringe of the Sierra Madre has little-visited archaeological sites, and a dramatic road descending to old mission towns on the fringe of the Huasteca.

QUERÉTARO
• pop 523,800 • elev 1762m ☎ 442

Querétaro's museums, monuments and colonial architecture are less spectacular than those of Guanajuato or Zacatecas, but it's a lively city. It's prettiest at night when many of its handsome buildings are floodlit, and wandering the streets and plazas is a real pleasure. It especially warrants a visit if you're interested in Mexico's history, in which it has played an important role. In 1996 the city officially took back its old name, Santiago de Querétaro, but it's generally known as just Querétaro.

History
The Otomí founded a settlement here in the 15th century that was later absorbed into the Aztec empire, then by Spaniards in 1531. Franciscan monks used it as a base for missions not only to Mexico but also to what is now the southwestern USA. In the early 19th century, Querétaro became a center of intrigue among disaffected criollos plotting to free Mexico from Spanish rule. Conspirators, including Miguel Hidalgo, met secretly at the house of Doña Josefa Ortiz (La Corregidora),

QUERÉTARO

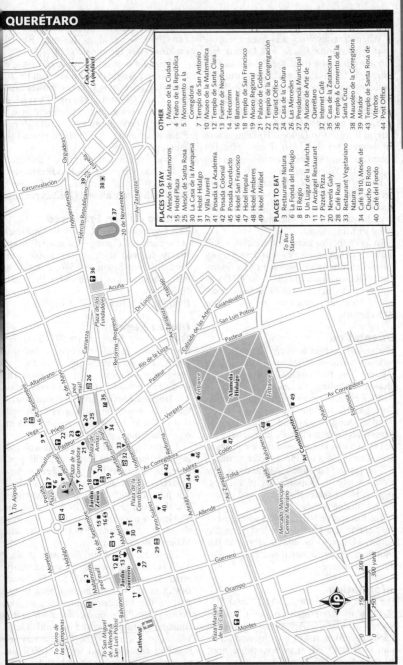

PLACES TO STAY
2 Mesón de Matamoros
15 Hotel Plaza
25 Mesón de Santa Rosa
30 La Casa de la Marquesa
31 Hotel Hidalgo
37 Villa Juvenil
41 Posada La Academia
42 Posada Colonial
45 Posada Acueducto
46 Hotel San Francisco
47 Hotel Impala
48 Hotel Amberes
49 Hotel Mirabel

PLACES TO EAT
3 Restaurante Natura
6 La Fonda del Refugio
8 El Regio
9 Un Lugar de la Mancha
11 El Arcángel Restaurant
17 Pizzeta Pizza
20 Nevería Galy
28 Café Real
33 Restaurant Vegetariano
   Natura
34 Café 1810, Mesón de
   Chucho El Roto
40 Café del Fondo

OTHER
1 Museo de la Ciudad
4 Teatro de la República
5 Monumento a la
   Corregidora
7 Templo de San Antonio
10 Museo de la Matemática
12 Templo de Santa Clara
13 Fuente de Neptuno
14 Telecomm
16 Bancomer
18 Templo de San Francisco
19 Museo Regional
21 Palacio de Gobierno
22 Templo de la Congregación
23 Tourist Office
24 Casa de la Cultura
26 Las Mercedes
27 Presidencia Municipal
29 Museo de Arte de
   Querétaro
32 Internet Café
35 Casa de la Zacatecana
36 Templo & Convento de la
   Santa Cruz
38 Mausoleo de la Corregidora
39 Mirador
43 Templo de Santa Rosa de
   Viterbos
44 Post Office

who was the wife of a former *corregidor* (district administrator) of Querétaro.

When the conspiracy was discovered, the story goes, Doña Josefa was locked in a room in her house (now the Palacio de Gobierno) but managed to whisper through a keyhole to a coconspirator, Ignacio Pérez, that their colleagues were in jeopardy. Pérez galloped off to inform another conspirator in San Miguel de Allende, who in turn carried the news to Dolores Hidalgo, where on September 16, 1810, Padre Hidalgo issued his famous Grito, the call to arms that initiated the War of Independence.

In 1867 Emperor Maximilian surrendered to Benito Juárez's general Escobedo at Querétaro, after a siege lasting nearly 100 days. It was here that Maximilian was executed by firing squad.

In 1917 the Mexican constitution – still the basis of Mexican law – was drawn up by the Constitutionalist faction in Querétaro. The PNR (which later became the PRI) was organized in Querétaro in 1929, and it dominated Mexican politics for the rest of the 20th century.

Orientation
The historic center is fairly compact, with pedestrian streets called *andadores* linking a number of lively plazas – it makes for pleasant strolling. The heart of things is Jardín Zenea, the main plaza, with Avenida Corregidora, the main downtown street, running along its east side. The Plaza de Armas (also called Plaza de la Independencia) is two blocks east, and the small Plaza de la Corregidora is a block to the north.

The large and shady Alameda, a few blocks south, is popular for picnicking, jogging, roller-skating, strolling and generally just taking it easy.

The bus station is about 5km southeast of the center, and local buses link it to the center. Madero-5 de Mayo serves as the boundary between north-south and east-west street addresses.

Information
The tourist office (☎ 212-14-12, 800-715-17-42, Ⓦ www.queretaro.com.mx), Pasteur Norte 4 off Plaza de Armas, has reasonable maps and brochures of the city, and information about tourist attractions throughout the state. Hours are 8am to 8pm daily.

There are several banks on and near the Jardín Zenea, most with ATMs. The American Express agent is Turismo Beverly (☎ 216-15-00), Tecnológico 118.

The main post office, Arteaga 7, is oper 8am to 7pm Monday to Friday, 9am to 1pm Saturday. Telecomm, with fax, money order *(giro)* and Western Union 'Dinero er Minutos' services, is at Allende Norte 4 There are card phones on Jardín Zenea Plaza de Armas and elsewhere around the center.

Handy Internet places are at Libertad 32 and in Las Mercedes, the handicrafts store on the corner of Carranza and Río de la Loza; both charge around US$2.25 per hour

Templo de San Francisco
This impressive church is on Jardín Zenea, at the corner of Corregidora and 5 de Mayo. Pretty colored tiles on the dome were brought from Spain in 1540, around the time construction of the church began. Inside are some fine religious paintings from the 17th, 18th and 19th centuries.

Museo Regional
The Regional Museum (☎ 212-20-31, cnr *Corregidora & Jardín Zenea; admission US$3.50; open 10am-7pm Tues-Sun)* is beside the Templo de San Francisco. The ground floor holds artifacts and exhibits on pre-Hispanic Mexico, archaeological sites in Querétaro state, the early Spanish occupation of the area and the state's various indigenous groups.

Upstairs are exhibits on Querétaro's role in the independence movement, the post-independence history of Mexico and Querétaro, and many religious paintings. The table at which the Treaty of Guadalupe Hidalgo was signed in 1848, ending the Mexican-American War, is on display, as is the desk of the tribunal that sentenced Maximilian to death.

The museum is housed in part of what was once a huge monastery and seminary, attached to the Templo de San Francisco. Begun in 1540, the seminary became the seat of the Franciscan province of San Pedro y San Pablo de Michoacán by 1567. Building continued on and off until at least 1727. The tower was the highest vantage point in the city, and in the 1860s the monastery was used as a fort both by imperialists supporting Maximilian and by the forces who finally defeated him in 1867.

Museo de Arte de Querétaro

Querétaro's Art Museum (☎ 212-23-57, Allende Sur 14; admission US$1.50, free Tues; open 11am-7pm Tues-Sun) is in a former monastery, adjacent to the Templo de San Agustín. The monastery was built between 1731 and 1748 and is a splendid example of baroque architecture. There are angels, gargoyles, statues and other ornamental details all over the building, particularly around the courtyard.

The ground-floor display of 16th- and 17th-century European painting traces interesting influences, from Flemish to Spanish to Mexican art. On the same floor you'll find 19th- and 20th-century Mexican painting, a collection of 20th-century Querétaro artists, and a hall for temporary exhibitions. The top floor has a photographic display on the history of the monastery and rooms with more art, from 16th-century mannerism to 18th-century baroque.

Museo de la Ciudad

The 11-room City Museum (☎ 212-47-02, Guerrero Norte 29; admission US$0.60; open 11am-5pm Tues-Sun) has some quite good contemporary art, and not terribly interesting displays on the city's recent history.

Teatro de la República

One block north of the Jardín Zenea, this lovely old theater (☎ 212-03-39, cnr Juárez & Peralta; admission free; open 10am-3pm & 5pm-8pm Tues-Sun) was where a tribunal met in 1867 to decide the fate of Emperor Maximilian. Mexico's constitution was signed here on January 31, 1917. The stage backdrop lists the names of its signatories and the states they represented. In 1929, politicians met in the theater to organize Mexico's ruling party, the PNR (now the PRI).

Palacio de Gobierno (Casa de la Corregidora)

The Casa de la Corregidora, Doña Josefa Ortiz's home, where she informed Ignacio Pérez of the plans to arrest the independence conspirators, stands on the north side of Plaza de Armas. Today the building is the Palacio de Gobierno, the state government building. The room where Doña Josefa was locked up

is upstairs, over the entrance – it's now the governor's conference room. On one side of the landing as you go up the stairs a plaque records Doña Josefa's place in history. The building can be visited during normal office hours, but there's not much to see.

Convento de la Santa Cruz

About 10 minutes' walk east of the center is one of the city's most interesting sights, the Convento de la Santa Cruz (☎ 212-03-35, cnr Acuña & Independencia; donation requested; open 9am-2pm Tues-Fri, 9am-4.30pm Sat). This monastery was built between 1654 and about 1815 on the site of a battle in which a miraculous appearance of Santiago (St James) had led the Otomí to surrender to the conquistadors and Christianity. Emperor Maximilian had his headquarters here while under siege in Querétaro from March to May 1867. After his surrender and subsequent death sentence, he was jailed here while awaiting the firing squad. Today the monastery is used as a religious school.

A guide will provide insight into the Convento's history and artifacts, which include an ingenious water system and unique colonial ways of cooking and refrigeration. The guide will also relate several of the site's miracles, including the legendary growth of a tree from a walking stick stuck in the earth by a pious friar in 1697. The thorns of the tree form a cross.

Entry to the building is free, but your guide will request a donation to the convent at the end of your tour. Tours are given in English or Spanish.

Acueducto & Mirador

Walk east along Independencia past the Convento de la Santa Cruz then fork right along Ejército Republicano, and you come to a **mirador** with a view of 'Los Arcos,' Querétaro's emblematic 1.28km aqueduct, with 74 towering arches built between 1726 and 1735. The **aqueduct** runs along the center of Avenida Zaragoza and still brings water to the city from about 12km away.

Across the street from the mirador is the **Mausoleo de la Corregidora**, the resting place of Doña Josefa Ortiz (La Corregidora) and her husband, Miguel Domínguez de Alemán. Behind the tomb is a shrine with pictures and documents relating to Doña Josefa's life.

Other Central Sights

Plaza de la Corregidora is dominated by the **Monumento a la Corregidora**, a 1910 statue of doña Josefa Ortiz bearing the flame of freedom.

One block west of the Jardín Zenea is the **Fuente de Neptuno** (Neptune Fountain), designed by the noted Mexican neoclassical architect Eduardo Tresguerras in 1797. The 17th-century **Templo de Santa Clara**, adjacent, has an ornate baroque interior. On Madero at Ocampo is the rather plain 18th-century **cathedral**. Hidalgo, which runs parallel to Madero two blocks north, is lined with many fine mansions.

At the intersection of Arteaga and Montes stands the 18th-century **Templo de Santa Rosa de Viterbos**, Querétaro's most splendid baroque church, with its pagoda-like bell tower, unusual exterior paintwork and curling buttresses and lavishly gilded and marbled interior. The church also boasts what some say is the earliest four-sided clock in the New World.

Other notable colonial churches include the **Templo de San Antonio** on Peralta at Corregidora Norte, with two large pipe organs, elaborate crystal chandeliers, red wallpaper and several oil paintings; and the **Templo de la Congregación** on Pasteur Norte at 16 de Septiembre, with beautiful stained-glass windows and a splendid pipe organ.

The newly opened **Casa de la Zacatecana** (☎ 224-07-58, Independencia 59; admission US$2.25; open 11am-7pm daily) is a finely restored 17th century house with its own murder mystery – look for the skeletons in the basement. The main attraction is the collection of 18th- and 19th-century furniture and decorations.

The one-room **Museo de la Matemática** (no ☎, 16 de Septiembre 57 Ote; admission US$0.60; open erratically 10am-2pm & 4pm-6pm Mon-Fri), in the university building, has a fun collection of science models, optical illusions, math puzzles and other educational stuff. It's all in Spanish, but easy enough to enjoy.

Cerro de las Campanas

In the west of the city, a good 35-minute walk from the center, is the Cerro de las Campanas (Hill of the Bells), the site of Maximilian's execution. The emperor's family constructed a chapel on the spot.

Today the area is a park, with a statue of Benito Juárez, a café and the **Museo del Sitio (Siege)** de Querétaro (☎ 215-20-75, near Hidalgo; admission US$0.10; open 10am-6pm daily). You can get there on a 'Tecnológica' bus going west on Zaragoza at the Alameda Hidalgo. Get off at the Ciudad Universitaria.

Courses

Olé Spanish Language School (☎ 214-40-23, fax 224-16-28, ⓦ www.ole.edu.mx, Universidad Pte 1D) offers a range of courses at all levels, with homestay options and extracurricular programs.

Organized Tours

Guided walking tours of the city center, in English or Spanish, leave the **tourist office** up to six times daily, depending on demand. They cost US$1.75 per person and last around two hours. **Queretour** (☎ 223-08-33, Velázquez 5, Colonia Pathé) does city tours (US$15) and longer trips to other attractions in the surrounding region.

Special Events

Querétaro's Feria Internacional in the first two weeks of December is one of Mexico's biggest state fairs. While it focuses on livestock, it also covers industry, commerce and artisanry and is the excuse for varied entertainment and fun.

Places to Stay

Budget Villa Juvenil (☎ 223-31-42, Ejército Republicano s/n) Dorm beds US$3.50, discount for HI members. The youth hostel is in the back of a sports complex, a pleasant 1km walk east of the center. Dorms and bathrooms are clean, and guests can use a kitchen, swimming pool and gym.

Hotel San Francisco (☎ 212-08-58, Corregidora Sur 144) Singles/doubles with bath US$14/17.50. This is a three-story place with lots of smallish but decent rooms, all with TV.

Posada Colonial (☎ 212-02-39, Juárez Sur 19) Singles & doubles with bath US$18.50; without bath US$6.50/10. Some of the rooms here are very basic while others have extras like TV and a private bathroom.

Posada La Academia (☎ 224-27-29, Pino Suárez 52) Singles & doubles with shared bath from US$6.50. This place has dark, cell-like rooms, some with black-and-white TV.

Hotel Hidalgo (☎ 212-00-81, Madero Pte 11) Singles/doubles US$14/17. Just a few doors off the Jardín Zenea, the Hidalgo is an old-style building where the rooms vary greatly in size and appeal. The cheapest rooms are pokey; larger rooms with two beds cost more, and the largest rooms can hold up to seven people. They all have private bathrooms, and some upper-floor rooms have small balconies. There's parking in the courtyard.

Posada Acueducto (☎ 224-12-89, Juárez Sur 64) Singles/doubles with bath US$23/26, US$31 with 2 beds. The attractive lodgings here feature well-kept rooms, color TV and colorful paintwork.

Mesón de Matamoros (☎ 214-03-75, e posadamatamoros@hotmail.com.mx, Matamoros 8) Singles/doubles US$22/24. In a quiet position on a pedestrian street, this new and comfortable *posada* is a pleasant place to stay.

Mid-Range **Hotel Plaza** (☎ 212-11-38, Juárez Nte 23) Singles/doubles from US$22/28. A respectable place beside Jardín Zenea, the Plaza has 29 tidy, comfortable, charm-free rooms. Some have French doors and small balconies facing the Jardín, offering plenty of light, air and noise.

Hotel Impala (☎ 212-25-70, fax 212-45-15, Colón 1) Singles/doubles US$27/38. This modern four-story hotel is on the corner of Corregidora Sur and Zaragoza, opposite the Alameda Hidalgo. It has underground parking and 114 rooms with TV, carpet and phone. Some rooms have a view of the park; interior rooms are quieter and bright enough. Rooms vary, so check first.

Hotel Amberes (☎ 212-86-04, fax 212-41-51, e hamberes@qro.1.telmex.net.mx, Corregidora Sur 188) Singles US$38, doubles US$49, triples US$60. Hotel Amberes, also facing the Alameda, is similar but a bit smarter.

Top End **Hotel Mirabel** (☎ 214-39-29, fax 214-35-85, w www.hotelmirabel.com.mx, Avenida Constituyentes Ote 2) Singles/doubles from US$53/73. Business travelers go for the modern Mirabel, facing the south side of the Alameda. The comfortable carpeted rooms have color TV, air-

conditioning and phone, and some have a view over the park.

La Casa de la Marquesa (☎ 212-00-92, fax 212-00-98, e marquesa@albec.net.mx, Madero 41) Singles & doubles and suites from US$230. For something superb, La Casa de la Marquesa is a magnificent 18th-century baroque/Mudéjar mansion transformed into a hotel and filled with lavish period furnishings, carved stone, tiles and frescoes (some original). The 25 suites have names such as Alhambra and Maximiliano y Carlota, with style to match, and all rooms have cable TV and air-con. The price includes continental breakfast and welcome cocktail. Slightly less expensive rooms are in a separate building, Casa Azul, a couple of doors west on the corner of Madero and Allende. Children under 12 are not admitted.

Mesón de Santa Rosa (☎ 224-26-23, fax 212-55-22, e starosa@sparc.ciateq.mx, Pasteur Sur 17) Singles & doubles from US$98, suites US$152. On the east side of the Plaza de Armas, Mesón de Santa Rosa is another finely restored colonial building. It's built around three patios: one with a heated swimming pool, one with a fountain, and one with restaurant tables. The elegant and comfortable rooms each come with a safe and satellite TV.

Places to Eat
Plaza de la Corregidora is bounded on two sides by restaurants with outdoor tables and a vibrant atmosphere in the evening. Most of them will have a menu posted out front, so you can stroll around and take your pick.

La Fonda del Refugio (☎ 212-07-55, Plaza de la Corregidora 26) Prices US$6-8. This restaurant has a pretty standard menu, with chicken dishes and steaks, and special nights for *parrillada* (barbecue) and *pozole*. It's not cheap, but it's an enjoyable place to eat, especially after 8pm Thursday to Saturday when live music plays.

El Regio (☎ 214-12-75, Plaza de la Corregidora & 16 de Septiembre) Prices around US$10. El Regio has a similar setup, serving well-prepared Mexican standards at breezy outdoor tables.

Pizzeta Pizza (☎ 212-40-33, 16 de Septiembre 14) Prices US$4-8. On the south side of the plaza, Pizzeta is an economical option, with a good range of pizzas.

The surrounding pedestrian streets have plenty of mid-range restaurants and cafés catering to shoppers, workers and snackers.

Un Lugar de la Mancha (☎ 212-33-33, *Vega 1*) Prices US$3-7. University staff congregate at this café-cum-bookshop, enjoying light meals and excellent coffee.

Nevería Galy (no ☎, *5 de Mayo 20*) Prices US$1.50. This Querétaro institution is known for its homemade ice cream. Specialties include *nieve de limón* (lemon sorbet) with mineral water, or cola or red wine.

Plaza de Armas has a handful of more expensive restaurants with indoor and outdoor tables.

Mesón de Chucho El Roto (☎ 212-42-95, *Andador Libertad 60*) Prices US$9. This place boasts *alta cocina mexicana* and offers many interesting variants on the classic Mexican dishes.

Café 1810 (☎ 214-33-24, *Andador Libertad 62*) Prices US$7. Café 1810 is a little less expensive than its next-door neighbor Mesón de Chucho El Roto. It has a more standard menu of international and Mexican dishes; try the local specialty *enchiladas queretanas* (fried enchiladas with chili sauce, cheese and onions).

Café del Fondo (☎ 212-09-05, *Pino Suárez 9*) Prices from US$2.50. Open 7.30am-10pm daily. Café del Fondo is a relaxed, rambling place with soothing background music from a creaky old sound system. You can get a set breakfast with eggs, *frijoles*, bread roll, juice and coffee, or a four-course comida corrida with plenty of choices. At other times, just linger over a snack and a coffee.

Café Real (☎ 212-00-92, *cnr Madero & Allende*) Prices around US$8. Open 7am-5pm daily. Part of the hotel La Casa de la Marquesa, this attractive courtyard restaurant has a gurgling fountain, fine food and a good value comida corrida.

El Arcángel Restaurant (☎ 212-65-42, *southwest cnr of Jardín Guerrero*) Prices US$3-6. For a quiet breakfast or a relaxing lunch, it's hard to go past this pleasant, old-fashioned place.

Restaurante Natura (☎ 244-22-12, *Juárez 47 Nte*) Prices US$2.50. Open 8am-9.30pm daily. Vegetarians and natural-food fans will find the comida corrida is an excellent value, as are the soyburgers with mushrooms and cheese.

Restaurante Vegetariano Natura (☎ 214-10-88, *Vergara 7*) Prices US$2.50-3. Open 8am-9pm Mon-Sat. This inexpensive little vegetarian restaurant on a quiet pedestrian street serves set breakfasts, salads and a good value comida corrida.

Entertainment

Querétaro has cultural activities befitting a state capital and university city. You can pick up a calendar of events from the tourist office. Sit in the Plaza Principal any Sunday evening with local families enjoying concerts; the state band performs from around 7pm to 9pm, sometimes with dancers. A callejoneada kicks off from the Plaza de Armas at 8pm Saturday in summer.

Casa de la Cultura (*5 de Mayo 40*) sponsors concerts, dance, theater, art exhibitions and other events; stop by during office hours to pick up their monthly schedule.

Most of the fashionable bars and nightclubs are outside the historic center, some right out in the suburbs. Check the entertainment section of Friday's *Diario de Querétaro*, or ask the tourist office to suggest some happening nightspots. There's a slew of bars, clubs and discos along Avenida Constituyentes, southeast of the historic center (get a taxi). *QIU* (☎ 213-72-39, *Avenida Constituyentes 1192*) is a currently popular disco. Two reliable standbys are *JBJ Bar* (☎ 213-43-07, *Boulevard Bernardo Quintana 109*), which has live music on weekends, and the local branch of *Carlos 'n Charlies* (☎ 213-90-36, *Boulevard Bernardo Quintana 160*). They're on the city's eastern ring road, south of the aqueduct.

Getting There & Away

Air Aeroméxico (☎ 215-64-74) has regular flights to/from Mexico City and Monterrey, while Aerolitoral (☎ 224-27-88) has one or two flights daily to/from Guadalajara with connections to Pacific coast resorts. Aeromar (☎ 220-69-35) also has some services. Turismo Beverly (☎ 216-15-00), Tecnológico 118, can book flights.

Bus Querétaro is a hub for buses in many directions; the big, modern Central Camionera is 5km southeast of the center on the south side of the Mexico City-León highway. There's one building for deluxe and 1st class, another for 2nd class. Both buildings have cafeterías, telephone casetas, coin-operated pay phones, shops and luggage storage. Daily departures include:

Guadalajara – 377km, 4½-5½ hours; 7 deluxe ETN (US$32), frequent 1st-class Primera Plus and Ómnibus de México (US$23), frequent 2nd-class Flecha Amarilla and Oriente (US$22)

Guanajuato – 154km, 2½-3 hours; 2 1st-class Ómnibus de México (US$9), 5 2nd-class Flecha Amarilla (US$8), or take one of the frequent buses to Irapuato, from where buses frequently leave for Guanajuato

Mexico City (Terminal Norte) – 215km, 2½-3 hours; 39 deluxe ETN (US$19), frequent 1st-class Primera Plus (US$15), 14 1st-class Ómnibus de México (US$14), frequent 2nd-class Flecha Amarilla (many direct), frequent 2nd-class Herradura de Plata (US$11)

Mexico City (Terminal Poniente) – 215km, 3 hours; frequent 2nd-class Herradura de Plata (US$10)

Mexico City Airport – 230km, 3 hours; 18 1st-class Aeroplus (US$18)

Morelia – 195km, 3-4 hours; 22 1st-class Primera Plus and Servicios Coordinados (US$10-11), 12 2nd-class Flecha Amarilla (US$9.50)

San Luis Potosí – 202km, 2½ hours; 3 deluxe ETN (US$16), frequent 1st-class Servicios Coordinados and Primera Plus (US$14), hourly 2nd-class Flecha Amarilla (US$11)

San Miguel de Allende – 60km, 1 hour; 3 deluxe ETN (US$5.50), frequent 2nd-class Herradura de Plata and Flecha Amarilla (US$3.50)

Tequisquiapan – 70km, 1 hour; half-hourly 2nd-class Flecha Azul (US$2.25)

Car If you want a car to explore the Sierra Gorda, Express Rent-a-Car (☎ 216-04-44) has competitive rates. Golf's (☎ 212-11-47) and Auto Rentals del Bajío (☎ 214-23-39) are also worth checking.

Getting Around
Once you have reached the city center, you can easily get to most sights on foot. The airport is an 8km taxi ride northeast of the center (US$3.50).

City buses run from 6am until 9pm or 10pm and cost US$0.40. They can be infuriatingly slow. They leave from an open lot a few hundred meters from the bus terminal; turn right from the 2nd-class terminal, left from the 1st-class side. Several routes go to the center including Nos 8 and 19, which both go to the Alameda Hidalgo then up

Ocampo. For a taxi, get a ticket first from the bus station booth (US$2.50).

To get out to the bus station from the center, take city bus No 19, No 25 Zaragoza, or No 36 or any other saying 'Terminal de Autobuses' heading south on the east side of the Alameda Hidalgo.

TEQUISQUIAPAN
● pop 24,000 ● elev 1880m ☎ 414

This small town ('teh-kees-kee-AP-an'), 70km southeast of Querétaro, is a quaint, pleasant retreat from Mexico City or Querétaro, popular with city-dwellers on weekends. It used to be known for its thermal spring waters – Mexican presidents came here to ease their aches and tensions. Some local industries now use most of the hot water, but there are still some delightful cool-water pools, some set in pretty gardens at attractive hotels and posadas. It's a pleasure to simply stroll the streets, lined with brilliant purple bougainvillea and colorful colonial buildings. Tequisquiapan's name is sometimes playfully abbreviated to just TX, pronounced 'TEH-kees.'

Orientation & Information
The bus station is a vacant lot on the southwest outskirts of town, a 10-minute walk along Niños Héroes from the center. A local bus (US$0.30) to the Mercado will let you off on Carrizal, a two-minute walk northeast of the central Plaza Principal.

The tourist office (☎ 273-02-95) is on the northeast side of the Plaza Principal, normally open Wednesday to Sunday, with maps, brochures and information on Tequisquiapan and the state of Querétaro. There's a Bancomer branch nearby, with an ATM.

Things to See & Do
The wide and traffic-free **Plaza Principal** is surrounded by *portales* (arcades) glowing in rich orange-pink hues, overlooked by the 19th-century Templo de Santa María de la Asunción on the north side.

The main market, on Ezequiel Montes, and the **Mercado de Artesanías** (Crafts Market) on Carrizal, are just a couple of blocks away through little lanes. The large, verdant **Parque La Pila** is a short distance past the Mercado de Artesanías along Ezequiel Montes.

Most hotel swimming pools are for guests only, but the large, cool **pool** *(admission US$3.25; open 8am-6pm daily Apr-Oct, Sat & Sun only Nov-Mar)* at the Hotel Neptuno (see Places to Stay) is open to the public. Other balnearios are just north of town along highway 120.

Look for migratory birds at the **Santuario de Aves Migratorios La Palapa** by the dam at the north end of the lake just south of town; you'll see it on the right if you approach Tequis from San Juan del Río. Other things you can do include horseback riding, tennis and golf (ask at the tourist office or your hotel).

Special Events
The Feria Internacional del Queso y del Vino (International Wine and Cheese Fair), from late May to early June, attracts people from far and wide for tastings, music, charreadas and other events.

Places to Stay
Most places are pretty pricey; the best budget options are the posadas along Moctezuma. Demand is low from Monday to Thursday, so you may be able to negotiate a discount.

Posada Tequisquiapan (☎ 273-00-10, *Moctezuma 6)* Singles/doubles US$22/38. This hotel has pretty gardens and a splendid grottolike swimming pool. Rooms are spacious, with cable TV.

Posada San Francisco (☎ 273-02-31, *Moctezuma 2)* Singles/doubles US$23/37. The Posada San Francisco also has a large garden and a swimming pool (overlooked by a statue of a ruminating nymph), and rooms at similar prices to the Tequisquiapan.

Hotel/Balneario Neptuno (☎ 273-02-24, *Juárez Oriente 5)* Singles/doubles US$33/54. Two blocks east of the Plaza Principal, the Balneario Neptuno has a big pool and lots of rooms, including larger family rooms.

Hotel La Plaza (☎ 273-00-56, fax 273-02-89, *Juárez 10)* Singles & doubles US$35-65. Located on the Plaza Principal, Hotel La Plaza has a pool, restaurant, bar, parking and a choice of 17 various rooms and suites.

Hotel El Relox (☎ 273-00-66, fax 273-00-66, *Morelos Pte 8)* Singles & doubles US$81. Hotel El Relox, 1½ blocks north of the Plaza Principal, is set in extensive gardens with a restaurant, several swim-

ming pools, gym, tennis courts and private thermal pools.

Places to Eat
The cheapest place for a meal or snack is the rear of the main market, where many clean little *fondas* (food stalls) have tables under awnings in the patio. They're open daily from around 8am to 8pm.

Restaurants on the plaza specialize in long lunches for large family groups and tend to be expensive.

K'puchinos (☎ 273-10-46, *Morelos 4)* Prices US$4-8. With indoor and outdoor tables, this place is a good choice for lunch or dinner. The menu is standard Mexican fare, with well-prepared main courses, pastas, antojitos, and a big choice of coffees.

Getting There & Away
Tequisquiapan is about 20km northeast on highway 120 from the larger town of San Juan del Río, which is on highway 57. Buses to/from Tequis are all 2nd class. Flecha Azul runs every 30 minutes, 5.30am to 7pm, to Querétaro (70km, 1 hour, US$2.25); Flecha Amarilla has regular connections to/from Mexico City's Terminal Norte (184km, 2¾ hours, US$9).

NORTHEAST QUERÉTARO STATE
Bernal
• **pop 5200** ☎ 441

North of Tequisquiapan, a 10km detour west of highway 120, Bernal is a quaint, cute little town with a thriving weekend tourist trade. The attraction is the rocky peak called Peña de Bernal (2370m), a natural pyramid believed (by some at least) to impart a cosmic energy. It's said that Bernal's residents enjoy extraordinary longevity. Bernal's visitors enjoy lengthy lunches at the various restaurants around town, and lengthy browsing through numerous craft and souvenir shops.

Posada Peña (☎ 277-12-77, *Turbidé 3)* Singles & doubles US$9. This is a plain hotel, but clean and central. Some rooms have rock views.

Regular 2nd-class buses from Querétaro go past Bernal, and will drop you off on the highway; the last back will be at about 5pm.

Highway 120
Those heading to/from northeast Mexico, or with a hankering to get off the beaten

track, might consider following highway 120 northeast from Tequisquiapan over the scenic Sierra Gorda to the lush Huasteca area (covered in the Central Gulf Coast chapter). It's possible to get to most places on the way by bus, but it's much better with your own transport.

Heading north from Tequisquiapan, you pass Ezequiel Montes (the turnoff for Bernal) and then the **Freixenet Winery** (☎ 441-277-01-47; open 11am-3pm daily), where you can see wine being made by *método champenoise.*

The next big town is Cadereyta, 38km from Tequis. On the eastern edge of town, signs point to the **Quinta Fernando Schmoll**, a botanical garden with over 4400 varieties of cactus.

After another 38km there's a turnoff going east to San Joaquín. Follow the good but very winding road for about 32km through the rugged mountains; stay on that road straight through San Joaquín, and continue a few steeply climbing kilometers to the little-visited **Ranas** *(admission US$2.75; open 9am-4pm daily)*. This is an archaeological site, with well-built walls and circular steps incorporated into a steep hillside. There are ball courts and a small hilltop pyramid. Dating from as early as the 8th century, the site is appealing for its rugged forest setting. San Joaquín has very basic lodgings and some places to eat.

Continuing north on highway 120, the road twists and turns up to 2300m at Pinal de Amoles and makes several dramatic descents and climbs before reaching **Jalpan** at 760m. This attractive town centers on the old mission church, constructed by Franciscan monks and their indigenous converts in

the 1750s. **Museo de la Sierra Gorda** *(☎ 441-296-01-65, Fray Junípero Serra No 1; admission US$0.60; open 10am-4pm daily)* outlines the pre-Hispanic cultures here, and the mission-building period.

Hotel María del Carmen *(☎ 441-296-03-28, Independencia 8)* Singles/doubles US$15/20. This hotel is on the plaza opposite the church, and has clean, comfortable rooms.

Hotel Misión Jalpan *(☎ 441-296-01-64, Fray Junípero Serra s/n)* Singles & doubles US$60. The Misión Jalpan is on the west side of the plaza. It's especially attractive, with a good restaurant, big swimming pool, cable TV, carpets, phones and all the comforts of home.

Inexpensive restaurants on Jalpan's plaza serve up solid Mexican fare.

In the mid-18th century, Franciscans established four other beautiful missions in this remote region. Their leader was Fray Junípero Serra, who later went on to found another chain of missions in California. The churches have all been restored and are notable for their colorful façades carved with symbolic figures. Going east from Jalpan on highway 120, there are missions at **Landa de Matamoros** (1760-68); **Tilaco** (1754-62), about 10km south of the highway; and **Tancoyol** (1753-60), about 20km north of the highway. There's another mission located north of Jalpan on highway 69, at **Concá** (1754-58).

Northwest of Jalpan, **Reserva de la Biosfera Sierra Gorda** *(☎ 441-296-02-42 in Jalpan, ℮ sierrago@ciateq.mx)* covers a range of altitudes and is notable for the diversity of its ecological systems, from subtropical valleys to high deserts to coniferous forests.

Central Gulf Coast

Long neglected as merely a travel corridor, the coastal plain between the Gulf of Mexico and the Sierra Madre Oriental is gradually being rediscovered by foreign visitors. It was here that Cortés landed, marking the start of his bloody march through the mountains to Tenochtitlán. Later, the port of Veracruz flowered as the terminus of colonial trade routes. Jalapa, now the capital of Veracruz state, also blossomed as an inland transportation hub.

Today, while most foreigners continue to blow through the coastal area, some adventurers stop to enjoy the region's offshore diving, wild rivers and spectacular Pico de Orizaba, Mexico's tallest mountain. Mexican families have long made the central Gulf Coast a popular vacation destination, resulting in a proliferation of enjoyable and inexpensive accommodations and food options. The city of Veracruz is famous for its tropical-port ambience, festive atmosphere and riotous Carnaval. Cooler and more relaxed, Jalapa offers many cultural and colonial attractions and is surrounded by pretty towns dotting the foothills. Other attractive spots include Córdoba, another colonial center, and Tlacotalpan, a once-important river port.

Pre-Totonac El Tajín heads the list of important archaeological sites; ruins buffs may also want to visit smaller spots such as Zempoala. Although southern Veracruz state was the Olmec heartland, little evidence remains of their existence, even at San Lorenzo, the Olmec center. However, several Olmec artifacts are superbly preserved at Jalapa's Museo de Antropología.

This chapter covers the coast and hinterland from Ciudad Madero in the north to Acayucan in the south – about 600km as the crow flies but more than 800km by highway 180, which follows the coastal curve.

History

Though the central Gulf Coast lacks spectacular Maya or Aztec sites, it served as a cradle of Mesoamerican culture.

Olmec The Olmecs, Mesoamerica's earliest known civilization, built their first great center around 1200 BC at San Lorenzo, in

Highlights

- Plazas – in the region, by far the best spots to mingle, dance, smooch and ogle
- Las Pozas – Xilitla's surreal world of convoluted concrete buildings and sculptures, set amid swimming holes and waterfalls
- El Tajín – mystical jungle-ringed ruins, constituting an extensively reconstructed city of the Classic Veracruz culture
- Voladores – an ancient Totonac ceremony involving costumed men whirling upside down around a 30m-high pole
- Museum of Anthropology, Jalapa – a regional gem, featuring seven huge Olmec heads and hundreds of ancient artifacts, superbly exhibited
- Veracruz – Mexico's historic, heroic port, also a steamy nightlife capital and tropical holiday hot spot
- Gulf Coast beaches – a 500km coastline featuring everything from secluded coves to Mexican holiday madness
- Laguna Catemaco – a crystalline lake surrounded by verdant terrain, abounding in hiking and wildlife-watching possibilities
- Wild water – rivers from the sierra, offering exciting rafting and wonderful waterfalls in the lush rain forests of the Huasteca
- Pico de Orizaba – Mexico's tallest peak, a perfect volcanic cone that throws down the gauntlet for visiting climbers

Tampico & the Huasteca page 690
Tampico page 691
Tuxpan page 699
El Tajín page 704
Zempoala page 709
Jalapa page 711
Central Jalapa page 712
Veracruz page 717
Central Veracruz page 719
Orizaba page 732
Córdoba page 728
Los Tuxtlas page 736
Catemaco page 739

Gulf of Mexico

OTHER MAPS
Central Gulf Coast page 687

CENTRAL GULF COAST

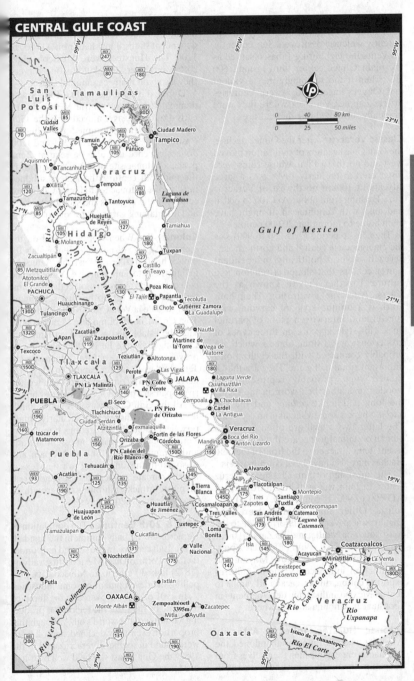

southern Veracruz. There they prospered until about 900 BC, when their city was apparently violently destroyed. Subsequently, La Venta in neighboring Tabasco served as the main Olmec center until around 600 BC, when it too seemingly met a violent end. Olmecs lingered for several centuries at Tres Zapotes, Veracruz, where they were gradually subsumed by other cultures.

Classic Veracruz After the Olmec decline, the Gulf Coast centers of civilization moved west and north. El Pital, whose ruins were discovered in the early 1990s, was a large city about 100km northwest of Veracruz port. Existing from about AD 100 to 600, it had links with Teotihuacán. It might have been home to more than 20,000 people.

The Classic period (AD 250 to 900) saw the emergence in central and northern Veracruz of several politically independent power centers that shared a religion and culture. Together they're known as the 'Classic Veracruz' civilization. Their hallmark is a unique style of carving, with curving and interwoven pairs of parallel lines. This style appears on three types of mysterious carved stone objects, which are probably connected with the civilization's important ritual ball game. They are the U-shaped *yugo*, probably representing a wooden or leather belt worn in the game; the long paddlelike *palma;* and the flat *hacha*, shaped somewhat like an ax head. The latter two, which are often carved in human or animal forms, are thought to represent items attached to the front of the belt. Hachas may also have been court markers.

The most important Classic Veracruz center, El Tajín, was at its height from about AD 600 to 900. It contains at least 11 ball courts. Other main centers were Las Higueras, near Vega de Alatorre, close to the coast south of Nautla; and El Zapotal, near Ignacio de la Llave, south of Veracruz port. Classic Veracruz sites show Mayan and Teotihuacán influences. Veracruz cultures exported cotton, rubber, cacao and vanilla to central Mexico, influencing developments in Teotihuacán, Cholula and elsewhere.

Totonac, Huastec, Toltec & Aztec By AD 1200, when El Tajín was abandoned, the Totonacs were establishing themselves from Tuxpan in the north to beyond Veracruz in the south. North of Tuxpan, the Huastec civilization, another web of small, probably independent states, flourished from AD 800 to 1200. The Huastecs were Mexico's chief cotton producers. As skilled stone carvers, they also built many ceremonial sites.

During this time, the warlike Toltecs, who dominated much of central Mexico in the early Postclassic age, moved into the Gulf Coast area. They occupied the Huastec Castillo de Teayo between AD 900 and 1200. Toltec influence can also be seen at Zempoala, a Totonac site near Veracruz port. In the mid-15th century, the Aztecs subdued most of the Totonac and Huastec areas, exacting tributes of goods and sacrificial victims and maintaining garrisons to control revolts.

Colonial Era When Cortés arrived on the scene in April 1519, he made Zempoala's Totonacs his first allies against the Aztecs by telling them to imprison five Aztec tribute collectors and vowing to protect them against reprisals. Cortés set up his first settlement, Villa Rica de la Vera Cruz (Rich Town of the True Cross), north of modern Veracruz port. Then he established a second settlement at La Antigua, where he scuttled his ships to prevent desertion before advancing to Tenochtitlán, the Aztec capital. In May 1520 he returned to Zempoala and defeated the rival Spanish expedition sent to arrest him.

All the Gulf Coast was in Spanish hands by 1523. New diseases, particularly smallpox, decimated the indigenous population. Veracruz harbor became an essential trade and communications link with Spain and was vital for anyone trying to rule Mexico, but the climate, tropical diseases and threat of pirate attacks inhibited the growth of coastal Spanish settlements.

19th & 20th Centuries The population of Veracruz city actually shrank in the first half of the 19th century. In the second half, under dictator Porfirio Díaz, Mexico's first railway (1872) linked Veracruz to Mexico City, propelling the development of some industries.

In 1901 oil was discovered in the Tampico area, and by the 1920s the region was producing a quarter of the world's oil. Although that proportion eventually declined, new oil fields were found in southern Veracruz, and in the 1980s the Gulf Coast still held well over half of Mexico's reserves and refining capacity.

Geography & Climate

More than 40 rivers run from the inland mountains to the central Gulf Coast, most passing through a well-watered, hilly landscape. Some offer ideal white-water rafting or dramatic waterfalls. The north is primarily an undulating coastal plain, while the flood-prone southeast is low-lying, with marshes and jungles that extend into Tabasco.

The region is generally warm and humid, hotter along the coast, wetter in the foothills, hottest and wettest of all in the southeast. Two-thirds or more of the rain falls between June and September. Veracruz city receives about 1650mm of rain annually. From April to October it features temperatures well over 30°C, falling into the teens at night only from December to February. Tuxpan and Tampico, on the north coast, are a bit drier, a little hotter in summer and a fraction cooler in winter. Coatzacoalcos, in the southeast, gets 3000mm (more than 10 feet!) of rain a year.

Population & People

With about seven million people, Veracruz is Mexico's third-most-populous state. The descendants of Africans shipped over as slaves, along with later (and contemporary) immigrants from Cuba, contribute a visible African element to the population and culture. Of the region's nearly 500,000 indigenous people, the most numerous are the 150,000 Totonacs and 150,000 Huastecs.

Tampico & the Huasteca

Industrial, developed Tampico contrasts sharply with the verdant Huasteca, inland where the coastal plain meets the fringes of the Sierra Madre Oriental. Spread over southern Tamaulipas, eastern San Luis Potosí, northern Veracruz and small corners of Querétaro and Hidalgo, the Huasteca is named after the Huastec people, who have lived here for about 3000 years.

Heading inland from the Huasteca to the Bajío region and Mexico City, four steep, winding routes cross the *sierra*: highway 70, from Ciudad Valles to San Luis Potosí; highway 120, from Xilitla toward Querétaro; highway 85, from Tamazunchale to Ixmiquilpan (near which you can turn off toward

Querétaro), Pachuca and Mexico City; and highway 105, from Huejutla to Pachuca and on to Mexico City via highway 85.

TAMPICO & CIUDAD MADERO

Wedged between seafront sleaze and unattractive urban sprawl, downtown Tampico is a surprisingly lively, refreshing area. At the southern tip of Tamaulipas state, just a few kilometers upstream from the Río Pánuco's mouth, this oil town (pop 313,400, ☎ 833) remains Mexico's busiest port – a tropical place where bars stay open late and the market area is sweaty, smelly, seedy, but always jolly. Mexican families flock to the wide beaches of Ciudad Madero (pop 192,200, ☎ 833), to the north, but foreign visitors may be more interested in Tampico's artfully redeveloped Plaza de la Libertad, surrounded by 19th-century French-style buildings. And although prices are inflated by the oil business, you don't have to hunt too hard for bargain accommodations and seafood.

History

Upon defeating the native Huastecs in 1523, Cortés founded the colony of San Estéban, now Pánuco, 30km upriver from Tampico. In the next few years he prevailed over both rebellious Huastecs and Spanish rivals. Nuño de Guzmán was named royal governor of the Pánuco area in 1527, but was pressured by Cortés to move to western and northern regions, where he concentrated on pillage, slaughter and slave raids until being recalled to Spain.

In the 1530s a mission was established in Tampico to convert the Huastecs to Christianity. The town was destroyed by pirates in 1684 but was refounded in 1823 by families from Altamira, to the north. After the 1901 discovery of oil in the area, Tampico suddenly became the world's biggest oil port – rough, tough and booming. Although the city experienced its heyday in the 1920s, the oil and its profits were under foreign control until 1938, when the industry was nationalized by President Lázaro Cárdenas following a strike by Tampico oil workers.

Mexico's 1970s and '80s oil boom took place farther down the coast, but the Tampico-Ciudad Madero area remains important. Pipelines and barge fleets bring oil from fields north and south, on- and offshore,

TAMPICO & THE HUASTECA

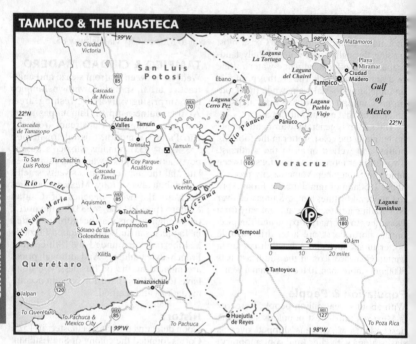

to the area's refineries and harbor. Ciudad Madero remains the headquarters of the powerful oil workers' union, the STPRM.

Orientation

Set in a marshy region near the mouth of the Río Pánuco, Tampico is ringed by several lakes, including Laguna del Chairel, which is used for recreation, and unattractive Laguna del Carpintero, which isn't. You'll cross numerous small estuaries as you approach the city from the north or west. Going south, the spectacular Puente Tampico (Tampico Bridge) crosses the Río Pánuco to Veracruz state.

Downtown Tampico centers on two plazas. The *zócalo,* or Plaza de Armas, features a grand rotunda and a 20th-century cathedral on its north side. One block south and one block east is the elegant Plaza de la Libertad, with balconied buildings on three sides. Hotels and restaurants of all grades are within a few blocks of these two plazas. The bus station is north of the downtown area.

Down a gentle hill south of either plaza you come to a sketchy area containing the

market, train station and riverside docks. East and south of Plaza de la Libertad are several blocks frequented by prostitutes and clients. Those who wish to avoid unsavory attention should stay clear after dark. It would be especially unwise to walk in the unlit streets around the market and down toward the waterfront.

Addresses on east-west streets usually have the suffix 'Ote' (Oriente; east) or 'Pte' (Poniente; west), while those on north-south streets are 'Nte' (Norte; north) or 'Sur' (south). The dividing point is the junction of Colón and Carranza, at the zócalo's northwest corner.

Ciudad Madero's center is about 8km northeast of central Tampico. Industrial zones extend east from there to Playa Miramar, on the Gulf of Mexico.

Information

The new, minuscule tourist office is in the Palacio Municipal, off the zócalo. It offers a range of brochures and maps, and it's open 8am to 3pm Monday to Thursday. Check the tourist office or telephone directory for a list of local consulates.

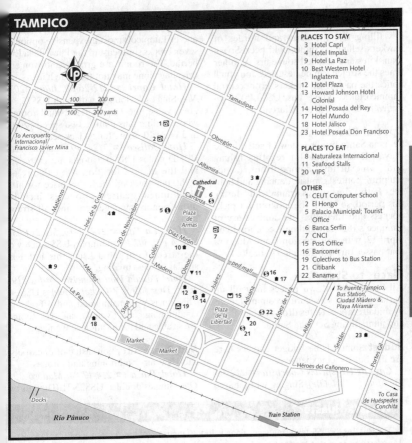

TAMPICO

PLACES TO STAY
3 Hotel Capri
4 Hotel Impala
9 Hotel La Paz
10 Best Western Hotel Inglaterra
12 Hotel Plaza
13 Howard Johnson Hotel Colonial
14 Hotel Posada del Rey
17 Hotel Mundo
18 Hotel Jalisco
23 Hotel Posada Don Francisco

PLACES TO EAT
8 Naturaleza Internacional
11 Seafood Stalls
20 VIPS

OTHER
1 CEUT Computer School
2 El Hongo
5 Palacio Municipal; Tourist Office
6 Banca Serfin
7 CNCI
15 Post Office
16 Bancomer
19 Colectivos to Bus Station
21 Citibank
22 Banamex

Banca Serfin, Bancomer, Banamex and Citibank are on or around the central plazas. They change traveler's checks and have ATMs.

The main post office is at Madero 309, on the north side of Plaza de la Libertad. CEUT computer school, on 20 de Noviembre, offers Internet access for US$1 per hour, seven days a week. Next door, El Hongo offers the same services without the air-conditioning or crowds of students. CNCI, off the zócalo, is often full but is a great value at US$0.50 per hour of Internet access.

Museo de la Cultura Huasteca

The modest Museum of Huastec Culture (☎ 210-22-17, 10 de Mayo and Sor Juana Inés de la Cruz; admission free; open 10am-5pm Mon-Fri, 10am-3pm Sat), in Ciudad Madero's Instituto Tecnológico, features archaeological displays and artifacts from pre-Hispanic Huastec culture, as well as a worthwhile bookstore. From central Tampico take a 'Boulevard' bus (US$0.45) north on Alfaro and ask for 'Tecnológico de Madero.'

Playa Miramar

The 10km-long Playa Miramar is about 15km from downtown Tampico; to get there you pass central Ciudad Madero and several kilometers of petrochemical installations. The beach is wide and reasonably clean, and the lukewarm water is clear, if not crystalline. A long line of simple restaurants features *mariscos* and margaritas, and each joint rents out the shady *palapas* and plastic chairs on its stretch of sand. On holidays and weekends the beach is crowded, with families filling every palapa and hordes of hawkers selling coconuts, cold beer, Styrofoam kites and seashell souvenirs. At other times the stretch can be deserted, and you'll notice the passing oil tankers. From central Tampico, take a 'Playa' bus (US$0.45) or *colectivo* (US$2) north on Alfaro.

Special Events

Semana Santa brings a slew of activities to Playa Miramar; look for regattas, fishing and windsurfing competitions, sand-sculpture contests, music, dancing and bonfires. Petty crime spikes dramatically during this period, so be on the lookout for pickpockets and their ilk. The anniversary of Tampico's 1823 refounding is celebrated on April 12, with a procession from Altamira that passes through Tampico's zócalo.

Places to Stay

All decent downtown places may fill up during holidays, so secure accommodations by midafternoon. Rates drop at quiet times and jump during Semana Santa.

Budget Some of the budget choices here are iffy, but very inexpensive.

Casa de Huéspedes Conchita (☎ 212-38-41, Madero 814 Ote) Singles with shared bath US$4, doubles with private bath US$9. Putting the 'dirt' back in 'dirt cheap,' this is one of Tampico's most inexpensive options, seven blocks southeast of the Plaza de la Libertad. The rooms are grungy, and women traveling alone may not feel safe here.

Hotel Capri (☎ 212-26-80, Juárez 202 Nte) Singles & doubles with bath US$15. A great value, the Capri offers small rooms whose ceiling fans feature two speeds: zero and Warp 10. Some toilets lack seats.

Hotel Jalisco (☎ 212-27-92, La Paz 120 Pte) Doubles US$20. Rooms are cramped and the market location a bit dodgy at night, but you can't beat this price for air-conditioned quarters. Bonuses include ultra-friendly management and off-street parking.

Hotel La Paz (☎ 214-11-19, fax 214-03-82, La Paz 307 Pte) Doubles US$22. Down the street from the Jalisco, this hotel is similar but less inviting.

Hotel Posada Don Francisco (☎/fax 219-28-35, Díaz Mirón 710 Ote) Doubles US$29. This inn is well maintained and offers air-conditioning, color TV and a café-bar. Rooms are sizable and the location convenient.

Mid-Range All options listed offer carpets, cable TV, air-conditioning and phones.

Hotel Plaza (☎ 214-17-84, Madero 204 Ote) Singles/doubles US$25/31. Though by

---

Whassa Huastec?

The Huastec ('WASS-tek') language, along with the languages of the Yucatán and Chiapas Maya, is classified as one of the Mayance family – possibly stemming from a single tongue once spoken all down the Gulf Coast. The language may have split from the rest of the family around 900 BC, when the Olmec culture arose in the intervening area. The central-Mexican feathered-serpent god Quetzalcóatl was probably of Huastec origin.

The Huastecs' greatest period was roughly AD 800 to 1200. Under a number of independent rulers, they built many ceremonial centers, practiced sometimes excruciating phallic fertility rites and expanded as far west as northeast Querétaro and Hidalgo. They developed great skill in making pottery and carving stone and shells. The two most interesting Huastec sites nowadays are Tamuín (see Ciudad Valles & Around) and Castillo de Teayo (see Around Tuxpan), though neither is spectacular.

After the Spanish conquest, during the second half of the 16th century, slavery and imported diseases cut the Huastec population from an estimated one million to fewer than 100,000. Rebellions began and continued into the 19th century. Today, about 150,000 Huastecs live in the Huasteca, mostly between Ciudad Valles and Tamazunchale, and east of Tantoyuca. Many of the women still wear *quechquémitls*, colorfully embroidered with traditional trees of life, animals, flowers and two-armed crosses. Huastecs still practice land-fertility ceremonies, particularly dances.

no means gargantuan, the Plaza's rooms are immaculately kept and comfy.

Hotel Posada del Rey (☎ 214-10-24, e posadadelrey@yahoo.com.mx, Madero 218 Ote) Singles/doubles US$31/37. With a prime location (some rooms overlook the Plaza de la Libertad), this hotel features handsome rooms and warm, sociable common areas.

Hotel Mundo (☎ 212-03-60, fax 212-65-53, Díaz Mirón 413 Ote) Singles/doubles US$42/45. The Mundo's rooms are slightly worn and the place carries an air of mustiness. OK, so the beds are king-size, the rooms are large and the TVs get CNN in English. It's still not the most spectacular value in town.

Hotel Impala (☎ 212-09-90, fax 212-06-84, e hotelimpala@prodigy.net.mx, Díaz Mirón 220 Pte) Singles/doubles US$42/53. The gleaming Impala offers friendly management and nicely decorated rooms, rendering it a solid mid-range choice.

Top End A quartet of good hotels represents Tampico's top end.

Best Western Hotel Inglaterra (☎ 219-28-57, 800-715-71-23, e beweingl@tamnet .com.mx, Díaz Mirón Ote 116) Doubles US$90. As the top downtown place, this Best Western hotel offers 120 huge air-conditioned rooms with all the modern conveniences. The restaurant is fancy but reasonably priced, the swimming pool is inviting, and shuttle service to and from the airport is complimentary.

Howard Johnson Hotel Colonial (☎ 212-76-76, fax 212-06-53, e tampico@hj.com.mx, Madero 210 Ote) Singles/doubles US$85/101. Rooms at this central hotel are spic 'n' span and delightfully decorated.

Hotel Camino Real (☎ 213-88-11, Avenida Hidalgo 2000) Doubles from US$197. Out toward the airport along the suburban strip mall of Avenida Hidalgo, the Camino Real is Tampico's most luxurious hotel, with spacious rooms and bungalows facing a tropical garden-courtyard and a large pool.

Club Maeva Miramar (☎ 230-02-02, 800-849-19-87, fax 211-50-48, in the USA ☎ 888-739-0113, w www.maevamiramar.com.mx, Blvd Costero s/n) Singles/doubles from US$134/222. Out by the beach, the Maeva Miramar is a large, imposing resort hotel.

The price includes all meals, live entertainment and access to a private strip of beach. The enormous rooms come with all the comforts.

Places to Eat

No one will mistake Tampico for a gourmet paradise, but the seafood is good. A local specialty is *carne asada tampiqueña* – steak marinated in garlic, oil and oregano and usually served with guacamole, strips of chili and corn chips. The smart restaurant at **Best Western Hotel Inglaterra** does a good version for US$10. Inexpensive *comedores* and restaurants stay open late around the zócalo and to the east; the farther east you go, they cheaper and seedier they get. A row of **seafood stalls** on Olmos south of the plaza offers great *cocteles* and other treats for around US$4.

Naturaleza Internacional (*Aduana 107 Nte*) Meals US$4 and up. Vegetarians (and others) should try Naturaleza, which has a good whole-meal bakery, as well as an excellent vegetarian *comida corrida*.

VIPS (*Madero 410 Ote*) Prices US$4-7. Right on the Plaza de la Libertad, this branch of VIPS is popular with prosperous *tampiqueños*. It offers a large (if slightly bland) selection of salads and American and Mexican dishes, with speedy service and a bright and cheery atmosphere. It's also open late every day, providing a refreshing alternative to grimy comedores for night owls.

Getting There & Away

Passenger trains no longer serve Tampico.

Air Mexicana (☎ 228-36-62), whose city office is at Universidad 700-1, flies daily to Mexico City. Aerolitoral (☎ 228-08-57) flies to Monterrey and Veracruz, with connections to Villahermosa.

Bus Tampico's bus station is seven annoying kilometers from downtown, on Rosalio Bustamente. It has a left-luggage room and a few pay phones, but it lacks a restaurant and has no place to sit down until you've bought a ticket and are admitted to the departure lounges.

Most of the bus companies don't display their timetables, so you have to ask at each desk for departure times.

Buses are available to most major towns north of Mexico City and down the Gulf Coast. The following daily departure information is for 1st-class and deluxe services; 2nd-class buses also run to most of these destinations.

Matamoros – 570km, 7 hours; 3 Futura, 7 ADO (US$27)

Mexico City (Terminal Norte) – 515km, 10 hours; 1 UNO (US$45), 10 ADO, 9 Ómnibus de México (US$29)

Monterrey – 530km, 7½ hours; 10 Futura, 1 Ómnibus de México (US$33)

Nuevo Laredo – 755km, 11 hours; 4 Futura (US$45)

Poza Rica – 250km, 5 hours; 1 UNO (US$25), hourly ADO, 1 Ómnibus de México (US$15)

San Luis Potosí – 410km, 8 hours; 2 Ómnibus de México, 4 Futura (US$27)

Tuxpan – 190km, 3½ hours; hourly ADO (US$12)

Veracruz – 490km, 10 hours; 1 UNO (US$45), 20 ADO (US$27)

Long-distance 1st-class buses also go to Reynosa, Soto la Marina, Villahermosa and Jalapa. Towns in the Huasteca are mostly reached by 2nd-class local buses. The quickest options are probably Vencadora for Ciudad Valles and Tamazunchale, and Autobuses Blancos for Huejutla.

Car & Motorcycle Highway 180 north of Tampico is a good four-lane divided highway for about 80km, then it's two-lane northeast to Aldama or northwest on highway 81 to Ciudad Victoria. Heading south from Tampico, highway 180 soars across the Puente Tampico and continues down to Tuxpan. It's an adequate two-lane road, but avoid driving it at night.

If you want a car to explore the Huasteca, contact one of several rental agencies in Tampico, including Dollar (☎ 227-25-75), Avis (☎ 228-05-85) and Budget (☎ 227-18-80).

Getting Around

Tampico's colectivo taxis are large, old US cars with destinations painted on the doors. They are inexpensive but slower than a regular taxi because they stop frequently.

Aeropuerto Internacional Francisco Javier Mina is 15km north of downtown. Transporte Terrestre (☎ 228-45-88) runs colectivo combis from the airport to anywhere

in Tampico-Ciudad Madero for about US$3.50, depending on distance.

Taxi tickets from the bus station to the city center cost US$3. Colectivos wait outside the station and are a little cheaper. From the city center to the bus station, take a 'Perimetral' or 'Perimetral-CC' colectivo from Olmos, a block south of the zócalo (US$0.45).

CIUDAD VALLES & AROUND
• pop 108,700 • elev 80m ☎ 481

Ciudad Valles is a simple town at the intersection of highways 85 (the Pan-American) and 70 (which runs east-west from Tampico to San Luis Potosí). The city lies just south of the halfway point between Monterrey and Mexico City. It's a convenient motorist stop and a good base for trips into the Huasteca. Cattle and coffee are among its most important commercial products.

The town is pleasant enough, but the real attractions are in the surrounding countryside. They're most conveniently seen by car, but local buses can also get you there…eventually.

Orientation & Information

Highway 85, called Boulevard México-Laredo in town, curves north-south through the city. To reach the main plaza, head six blocks west on Avenida Juárez or Avenida Hidalgo. Highway 70 bypasses town on the south side. The main bus station is at the southern edge. A small, helpful tourist booth is on the west side of highway 85, north of the bus station (open 8am-2pm Mon-Fri, 8am-1.30pm Sat) – ask here about transportation to nearby attractions.

Archaeological Sites

The important Huastec ceremonial center of **Tamuín** *(admission free; open 7am-6pm daily)* flourished from AD 700 to 1200. Today it's one of the few Huastec sites worth visiting, though don't expect anything spectacular. The only cleared part of the 170,000-sq-m site is a plaza with platforms made of river stones on all four sides. Look for a low bench with two conical altars, extending from a small platform in the middle of the plaza. The bench has the faded remains of some 1000-year-old frescoes that may represent priests of Quetzalcóatl.

Southwest of that site are two unrestored pyramids (on private property), and farther southwest is Puente de Dios (God's Bridge), a notch in a ridgeline on the horizon. At the winter solstice, around December 22, you can stand on the main Tamuín platform and watch the sun set into the Puente de Dios, with the pair of pyramids exactly between them, all aligned with the Río Tampaón.

To get to the Tamuín site, go first to the modern town of Tamuín, 30km east of Ciudad Valles on highway 70. A kilometer or so east, turn south from the highway down a road marked 'Zona Arqueológica' and 'San Vicente.' Follow it roughly south for 5km to another 'Zona Arqueológica' sign, then head west 800m.

Frequent buses between Tampico and Ciudad Valles go through Tamuín. The rest of the way you must walk or take a taxi (US$4.50).

Waterfalls & Swimming Spots

Many rivers flow east from the well-watered slopes of the sierra, forming cascades, waterfalls and shady spots for cool swims. One of the nicest areas is around Tamasopo, 5km north of highway 70, about 55km west of Ciudad Valles. **Cascadas de Tamasopo** has good swimming and a beautiful natural arch.

The **Cascadas de Micos** are north of highway 70, just a few kilometers west of Ciudad Valles. They're not so good for swimming, but rental canoes are available on weekends.

Another fun place to get wet is **Coy Parque Acuático** (☎ 382-41-59; admission US$5.50). From April to August it's open daily; at other times, you'll have to visit on a weekend. On highway 85 south of town, the park features water slides and a swimming pool. For detailed information about these and other watery attractions, ask at the Ciudad Valles tourist information booth.

Taninul

To reach this small village, head south off highway 70 between Ciudad Valles and Tamuín. The turnoff is marked by a sign for Hotel Taninul. Here, the **Museo Lariab** (admission free; open 9am-3pm Tue-Sun) has exhibits on the Huasteca, ancient and contemporary.

Places to Stay & Eat

Several budget hotels lie near the bus station in Ciudad Valles.

Hotel San Carlos (☎ 381-21-42) Doubles US$19. Right across the street from the bus station, this ordinary-looking hotel offers well-kept, cozy rooms with air-conditioning and TV.

Hotel Piña (☎/fax 382-01-83, e hotel_pina @yahoo.com.mx, Juárez 210) Singles/doubles with fan US$18/22, with air-conditioning and TV US$25/33. A block east of the plaza, this good budget hotel features a choice of cute, spotless rooms and ample parking.

Hotel Rex (☎ 381-04-11, fax 382-33-35, Hidalgo 418) Singles/doubles US$22/28. The Rex is 3½ blocks east of the plaza. With moderately sized rooms and parking, it's merely OK and not as good a value as the Piña.

Hotel San Fernando (☎ 382-22-80, fax 382-01-84, Blvd Mexico-Laredo 17 Nte) Singles/doubles US$32/38. Stepping up in price, the San Fernando is a well-run place offering comfortable but characterless rooms with air-conditioning, TV, phone and parking.

Hotel Valles (☎ 382-00-50, fax 382-00-22, e hotelvalles@prodigy.net.mx, Boulevard México-Laredo 36 Nte) Trailer sites US$10 per person, singles/doubles US$54/64 and up. A few blocks north of the town center on the east side of the street is this very stylish motel with a delightful tropical garden and a big swimming pool. Rooms are large and air-conditioned. A campground/trailer park offers sites with full hookups.

Hotel Taninul (☎/fax 388-01-43, Carretera Valles-Tampico Km 15) Singles/ doubles US$38/48. The Taninul offers hot mineral springs and moderately luxurious accommodations.

The best places to eat are the hotel restaurants. **La Troje**, in Hotel Piña, does US and Mexican standards for around US$3. **Hotel Valles** has two restaurants, including a good steak house (dishes US$4-11), as well as an open-air bar. **Hotel San Fernando**'s restaurant is open 24 hours.

Getting There & Away

Bus East of highway 85 on the way to Tamazunchale and Mexico City, the user-friendly bus terminal offers pay phones and a left-luggage room. A booth sells taxi tickets to the center of town for US$1.75.

The principal 1st-class lines are TransPaís, Ómnibus de Oriente, Línea Azul and Transportes Frontera. Flecha Roja and other companies offer 2nd-class service. Many buses are *de paso*. The following daily schedule is for 1st-class buses; 2nd-class buses run more frequently and cost about 10% less:

Matamoros – 544km, 10 hours; 15 buses (US$32)

Mexico City (Terminal Norte) – 495km, 10 hours; 12 buses (US$22)

Monterrey – 514km, 8 hours; 18 buses (US$33)

San Luis Potosí – 262km, 4½-5 hours; dozens of buses (US$18)

Tampico – 138km, 2½ hours; frequent buses (US$9.50)

Regular buses also go to Pachuca, Ciudad Victoria, Tamazunchale and Xilitla.

Car & Motorcycle West to San Luis Potosí (262km), highway 70 is spectacular as it rises across the Sierra Madre to the Altiplano Central. It's a twisting road, and you can get stuck behind slow trucks and buses, so don't count on doing it in a hurry. East to Tampico, highway 70 is in worse condition but is straighter and faster. Going south, highway 85 heads to Tamazunchale and then southwest toward Mexico City. You can also continue east from Tamazunchale to Huejutla, circling the Huasteca back to Tampico.

AQUISMÓN & AROUND
● pop 1700 ☎ 482

The poor and mildly depressing Huastec village of Aquismón, 5km up a side road west of highway 85, holds its market on Saturday. An area specialty is the Zacamsón dance, which in its full version has more than 75 parts, danced at different times of the day and night. At festivals much drinking of sugarcane alcohol accompanies the performances. Traditional dances are also performed for festivals of San Miguel Arcángel and the Virgen de Guadalupe (see Tancanhuitz later).

About 30km north of Aquismón by rough roads and a walk (allow 1½ hours from Aquismón), the **Cascada de Tamul** plunges 105m into the pristine Río Santa María. Alternatively, you can reach the falls from Tanchachin, south of highway 70, by a 2½-hour river trip (this option is unavailable during flooding, at which time the falls can be up to 300m wide).

About 1½ hours southwest of Aquismón on a rough and roundabout road, the **Sótano de las Golondrinas** (Pit of the Swallows) is a 300m-deep hole, home to tens of thousands of swallows and parakeets and a draw for serious spelunkers. The birds fly out en masse just after sunrise and return in the afternoon around 5pm to 5.30pm.

TANCANHUITZ
● pop 3000 ☎ 482

The bustling town of Tancanhuitz, called 'Ciudad Santos' on highway signs, is in the heart of the area inhabited by modern-day Huastecs. It's in a narrow, tree-covered valley 52km south of Ciudad Valles, 3km east of highway 85. A lively market takes place on Sunday, and pre-Hispanic Huastec remains can be seen near **Tampamolón**, a few kilometers east.

Tancanhuitz and Aquismón are centers for the festivals of San Miguel Arcángel on September 28 and 29 and the Virgen de Guadalupe on December 12. Huastec dances performed include Las Varitas (Little Twigs) and Zacamsón (Small Music), which both imitate the movements of wild creatures.

XILITLA
● pop 5300 ☎ 489

On the slopes of the sierra at about 1000m, diminutive Xilitla boasts a 16th-century church and mission, a temperate climate and a rain-forest with abundant bird life, wild orchids, stunning waterfalls, caves and walking trails. The most bizarre attraction, however, is **Las Pozas** *(the Pools; admission US$2; open 9am-sunset daily)* – a truly bizarre concatenation of concrete buildings, bridges, pavilions, sculptures and spiral stairways leading nowhere, the surreal fantasy of Sir Edward James (see 'An English Eccentric'). It can be a magical place – a child's dream, but a parent's nightmare: guardrails are nonexistent, and one false step can lead to a nasty end.

Skillfully cast by local workers in the 1960s and '70s, the concrete and reinforcing rod is already deteriorating in the jungle environment. Swimming holes and waterfalls make this a popular weekend picnic spot, but it can be deserted during the week. The site is on a dirt road a few kilometers east of

An English Eccentric

Edward James, born in 1907, was descended from the not uncommon union of an American multimillionaire and the lesser English aristocracy. Educated at Eton and Oxford, James was well endowed with money, charm and social connections, and he soon became part of London's lavish social and artistic set. He bankrolled the publication of poems by John Betjeman, supported Dylan Thomas for a short time and sponsored a ballet so his own wife could play the lead.

Haunted by women who tormented him (his mother considered him a social nuisance, while his wife wanted everything to do with his money and nothing to do with him), James entered a period of depression after the breakup of his marriage in the early 1930s. He moved to Europe and became absorbed in modern art, especially surrealism. He collected Picassos, was a patron of Magritte and commissioned work by Dalí (he acquired the original Dalí-designed sofa in the shape of Mae West's lips).

As WWII threatened, James moved to the USA – mixing with film people in Hollywood and writers and artists in Taos, New Mexico – and visited Mexico for the first time. Among other projects, he donated money to save the bizarre Watts Towers, a creatively unaesthetic monument in southern Los Angeles that was slated for destruction.

In 1945 James discovered Xilitla and was besotted by the exotic plants and birds of the rain forest. Initially he devoted himself to cultivating local orchids, but when a cold snap destroyed his collection in 1962, James turned to a more enduring medium. With the help of his Mexican friend Plutarco Gastelum (who was quite an eccentric in his own right), he hired local workers to craft giant, colored, concrete flowers beside his idyllic jungle stream.

For the next 17 years, James and Gastelum created ever larger and stranger structures, many of which were never finished and all of which were totally impractical. James died in 1984, making no provision to maintain his creation, which is already decomposing into yet another Mexican ruin. As Salvador Dalí reputedly said: 'Edward James is crazier than all the surrealists put together. They pretend, but he is the real thing.'

Xilitla – turn left after the bridge about 2km from town.

El Castillo (☎ 365-00-38, fax 365-00-55, Ⓦ *www.junglegossip.com, Ocampo 105*) Doubles US$40-80. Built by Edward James' friend and foreman, Plutarco Gastelum, this wonderfully winding mansion is now a guest house providing comfortable, unconventional accommodations (advance bookings recommended). The genial management is a superb source of area information, and the atmosphere is heartily convivial.

Hotel San Ignacio (☎ 365-00-94) Singles/doubles US$14/17. If you insist on banging the budget drum, try this place. Down the street from El Castillo, it's cramped, dark and not terribly friendly, but it keeps the rain off your head.

La Casa Vieja Café Mains US$4-9. On the plaza, this place serves excellent, inexpensive Italian food and American snacks.

Xilitla can be reached by bus from Ciudad Valles, Tampico or Querétaro.

Highway 120, west to Jalpan then southwest toward Querétaro, is an exciting route through the Sierra Gorda (see the Northeast Querétaro State section in the Northern Central Highlands chapter).

TAMAZUNCHALE
• pop 21,000 • elev 20m ☎ 483

Bustling, noisy Tamazunchale, 95km south of Ciudad Valles on highway 85, is in a low-lying area of tropical vegetation with exuberant bird life and an attractive river. Unfortunately, the colorful Sunday market offers few Huastec handicrafts. For the Day of the Dead (November 2), denizens spread carpets of confetti and marigold petals on the streets. There's no single bus station: buses pull in at various company offices on Avenida 20 de Noviembre (the commercial stretch of highway 85 through town).

Hotel González (☎ 362-15-44, fax 362-01-36, 20 de Noviembre 301) Singles/doubles US$18/20. The cheapest decent place in town, the González offers basic rooms with fan and TV.

Hotel Mirador (☎ 362-01-90, fax 362-00-04, 20 de Noviembre 61) Singles/doubles US$18/21. A little airier than the González, the Mirador offers similar rooms.

Hotel Tropical (☎ 362-00-41, fax 362-08-09, 20 de Noviembre 404) Singles/doubles US$22/28. With a delightful entrance and air-conditioned rooms, the Tropical is a smooth mid-range choice.

Hotel Tamazunchale (☎/fax 362-04-96, 20 de Noviembre 122) Singles/doubles US$37/59. Glittery and genial, this place pounds your wallet but pampers you with attentive service and gorgeous rooms.

Southwest of Tamazunchale, highway 85 climbs steeply to Ixmiquilpan, then continues to Pachuca. This is the most direct route from the Huasteca to Mexico City. It's a steep but scenic route over the Sierra Madre. Start early to avoid mist and fog.

HUEJUTLA DE REYES
• pop 32,600 • elev 30m ☎ 789

On the northern edge of Hidalgo state, but still in the semitropical lowlands, Huejutla is a cheery town with a wacky, huge central plaza. It boasts a 16th-century fortress-monastery, built when this area was frontier territory and foreign newcomers were subject to attack by indignant indigenous folks. The big Sunday market attracts many Nahua people from outlying villages.

Hotel Oviedo (☎ 896-05-59, Morelos 12) Singles/doubles US$13/17. A smashing deal, the Oviedo features bright, clean rooms with air-conditioning and TV.

Hotel Fayad (☎ 896-00-40, cnr Hidalgo & Morelos) Singles/doubles US$15/20. Come here only if the Oviedo's full: the rooms aren't quite as nice, and they're more expensive.

SOUTH OF HUEJUTLA
Highway 105 rolls through lush, hilly farmland near Tampico, but south of Huejutla it climbs into the lovely Sierra Madre Oriental. It's a tortuous, foggy road to Pachuca. On the way you'll pass old monasteries at **Molango** and **Zacualtipán**.

The highway then leaves the Sierra Madre and drops several hundred meters to scenic **Metzquititlán**, in the fertile Río Tulancingo Valley. The village of **Metztitlán**,

23km northwest up the valley, sports a fairly well preserved monastery. It was the center of an Otomí state that the Aztecs couldn't conquer.

Back on highway 105, an 800m climb up from the Tulancingo Valley, about 100km by road, brings you to **Atotonilco El Grande**, 34km from Pachuca (see Around Pachuca in the Around Mexico City chapter).

Northern Veracruz

South of Tampico lies the relatively poor state of Veracruz, whose northern half is mostly rolling plains between the coast and the southern end of the Sierra Madre Oriental. The Laguna de Tamiahua stretches 90km along the coast, separated from the Gulf of Mexico by a series of sandbars and islands. It shelters isolated though sometimes polluted beaches, as well as opportunities for fishing and birding. The major archaeological attraction is El Tajín, usually reached from Papantla. Although your vehicle may be stopped and searched at army checkpoints along this coast, the soldiers are usually courteous to tourists.

TUXPAN
• pop 74,700 ☎ 783

Tuxpan (sometimes spelled 'Túxpam') is a fishing town and minor oil port near the mouth of the Río Tuxpan, 300km north of Veracruz and 190km south of Tampico. With a wide river, shaded parks and nothing much to do, the town is a tranquil and inexpensive place to break a journey. A nearby beach, 12km away, is popular with vacationing Mexicans, though it's no idyllic seaside resort.

Orientation & Information
The downtown area, on the Río Tuxpan's north bank, spreads six blocks upstream from the high bridge spanning the river. The riverfront road, Boulevard Heroles, passes under the bridge and runs east to Playa Norte. A block inland from Heroles is hotel-heavy Avenida Juárez. Parque Reforma, at Juárez's west end, serves as the heart of downtown and is popular in the evening.

The tourist office (☎ 834-01-77), in the Palacio Municipal, is open 9am to 8pm Monday to Saturday. It offers to the public

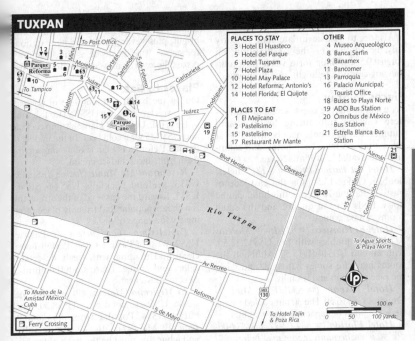

TUXPAN

PLACES TO STAY
- 3 Hotel El Huasteco
- 5 Hotel del Parque
- 6 Hotel Tuxpam
- 7 Hotel Plaza
- 10 Hotel May Palace
- 12 Hotel Reforma; Antonio's
- 14 Hotel Florida; El Quijote

PLACES TO EAT
- 1 El Mejicano
- 2 Pastelísimo
- 15 Pastelísimo
- 17 Restaurant Mr Mante

OTHER
- 4 Museo Arqueológico
- 8 Banca Serfin
- 9 Banamex
- 11 Bancomer
- 13 Parroquia
- 16 Palacio Municipal; Tourist Office
- 18 Buses to Playa Norte
- 19 ADO Bus Station
- 20 Ómnibus de México Bus Station
- 21 Estrella Blanca Bus Station

Río Tuxpan

To Post Office
To Tampico
To Museo de la Amistad México-Cuba
To Agua Sports & Playa Norte
To Hotel Tajín & Poza Rica

Ferry Crossing

CENTRAL GULF COAST

some brochures and telephone numbers, but not much more. There are pay phones in Parque Reforma, and an ATM-endowed Banamex is nearby. Banca Serfin and Bancomer, on Juárez, also have ATMs. The post office is on Mina, a few blocks north of Juárez.

Museums

On the west side of Parque Reforma, a humble **Museo Arqueológico** (*admission free; open 9am-1pm & 4pm-8pm Mon-Fri*) exhibits Totonac and Huastec artifacts. On the river's south side, the **Museo Histórico de la Amistad México-Cuba** (*Mexican-Cuban Friendship Museum; Obregón s/n; donation requested; open 8am-7pm daily*) commemorates Fidel Castro's 1956 stay in Tuxpan. After planning the Cuban revolution here, he sailed for Cuba with 82 comrades in a converted private yacht. The museum has a tepid collection of maps, B&W photos and a model of Cuba depicting Castro's campaign. More worthwhile are displays on José Martí and Ché Guevara.

To reach the museum, take one of the small boats across the river (US$0.15), walk several blocks south to Obregón, then turn

right. The museum is at the end of Obregón, just before you reach the river again. The walk takes about 10 minutes.

Playa Norte

Tuxpan's beach is a wide strip stretching 20km north from the Río Tuxpan's mouth, 12km east of town. Its beauty is diminished by a power station 2km north of the river mouth, but the water and sand are fairly clean and, apart from holidays and weekends, it's almost empty. Palapas serve seafood and sell souvenirs. Local buses marked 'Playa' leave every 20 minutes from the south side of Boulevard Heroles and drop you at the south end of the beach (25 minutes; US$0.75).

Diving

Aqua Sports (☎ 837-02-59, *Carretera a la Playa Km 7; trips start around US$175 per person*), a few kilometers from downtown on the Playa Norte road, is an established scuba-diving operation. They offer trips to the nearby reefs comprising four dives with a group of six or seven, or six-dive trips to Isla de Lobos. Aqua Sports can also arrange fishing trips, water-skiing and windsurfing.

Special Events

A big fishing tournament brings hundreds of visitors to Tuxpan in late June or early July. Festivities for the Assumption, on August 15, continue for a week with folk-dancing contests, bullfights and fireworks.

Places to Stay

As usual along the coast, accommodations here can be full during holidays and summer, but discounts may be available at other times. A few cheap hotels and camp-sites are available at Playa Norte.

Hotel del Parque (☎ 834-08-12) Singles/doubles US$11/13.50. On the east side of bustling Parque Reforma, this hotel can be noisy. Beds vary in quality, and the small rooms can be grungy.

Hotel El Huasteco (☎ 834-18-59, *Morelos 41*) Singles/doubles with fan US$12/13.50, with air-con US$14.50/15.50. Although the rooms here are somewhat small and dark, the place is clean and friendly.

Hotel Tuxpam (☎ 834-41-10, *Mina 2*) Doubles US$16.50. The 30 fan-cooled rooms here are plain but spacious and well lit.

Hotel Florida (☎ 834-02-22, *fax 834-06-50*, ⓦ *www.tuxpamver.com.mx, Juárez 23*) Singles/doubles US$37/46. At Hotel Florida, you pay for quality. The medium-size rooms boast good beds, air-conditioning and cable. Try for a river view.

Hotel Plaza (☎ 834-07-38, *Juárez 39*) Singles/doubles US$35/41. Rooms here are larger than at the Florida, but the lack of river views is disappointing. Nonetheless, it's a workable mid-range option.

Hotel May Palace (☎ 834-88-81, *fax 834-88-82, Juárez 44*) Singles/doubles US$57/67. With a central location, well decked out rooms and a cute swimming pool, the May Palace is a solid place to splurge. River views cost extra.

Hotel Reforma (☎ 834-02-10, *fax 834-06-26*, ⓦ *www.tuxpan.com.mx, Juárez 25*) Singles/doubles US$50/59. If you want luxury but the May Palace is full, try the Reforma. Rooms are smallish, but wooden furnishings add ambience. Bonuses include a relaxing courtyard, a happy fountain and a sparkly at-mosphere throughout the establishment.

Hotel Tajín (☎ 834-22-60, *fax 834-54-29*, ⓔ *misiontajin@prodigy.net.mx, Carretera a Cobos Km 2.5*) Doubles US$71. So what if the yellow-and-blue paint scheme is remi-niscent of your elementary school? The Tajín offers the best rooms in town, large and bright, plus several entertainment options for guests. The downside is the location – across the river, removed from downtown.

Places to Eat

Out at the beach is a long line of palapas, where you typically pay US$4.50 for fish soup or fresh fish, US$6 for a large shrimp cocktail and US$1.25 for a cold beer. In the middle of Parque Reforma is a circle of *tiendas* serving fresh fruit, juices and ice cream.

Restaurant Mr Mante (*Juárez 8*) Snacks US$3, seafood cocktails US$4-6, steaks US$7. Toward the east end of the street, this is a cheap, popular and friendly place offer-ing a wide range of dishes.

Pastelísimo (*Garizurieta 2*) Pastries US$2. West of Parque Cano, Pastelísimo is clean and inviting, with fresh, delectable cakes and coffee. There's another branch next to El Mejicano.

El Mejicano (*Morelos 49*) Snacks US$2, steaks US$6, seafood soup US$8.50, lunch buffet US$4. Popular from *desayuno* to *cena*, El Mejicano offers fantastic values and a bar that must be the bane of the local AA chapter. Don't miss the midday bargain buffet.

Antonio's (*Juárez 25*) Snacks US$4, steaks US$10. In Hotel Reforma, this is the fanciest, chilliest place in town.

El Quijote (*Juárez 23*) Snacks US$4, seafood US$8. Hotel Florida's answer to Antonio's, El Quijote is always bustling and efficient.

Getting There & Away

Book 1st-class buses out of Tuxpan as far ahead as possible, as all are *de paso* and only a limited number of seats are reserved for passengers boarding here. You might have to take a 2nd-class bus to Poza Rica and a 1st-class one from there. The modern ADO (1st-class) station, on Rodríguez half a block north of the river, is also used by UNO deluxe buses. Ómnibus de México (ODM) is under the bridge on the north side of the river. Es-trella Blanca (EB), on the corner of Constitu-ción and Alemán, two blocks east of the bridge, offers regular 2nd-class service; Turis-tar, Futura, ABC Blanco, and Coordinados offer a few 1st-class buses from this station. Daily departures include the following:

Jalapa – 350km, 5½ hours; 2 ADO GL (US$19), 5 ADO (US$16)

Matamoros – 760km, 11 hours; ADO at 12.10am and 6pm (US$39), several 2nd-class

Mexico City (Terminal Norte) – 355km, 4 hours; 1 UNO (US$26.50), 3 ADO GL (US$19), 13 ADO (US$17), 7 ODM (US$17)

Papantla – 90km, 1¼ hours; 7 ADO (US$3.50)

Poza Rica – 60km, 45 minutes; 3 ADO GL (US$3.50), 53 ADO (US$3), 1 ODM (US$3), 2nd-class every 20 minutes

Tampico – 190km, 3½ hours; 26 ADO, 1 ODM (US$12.50), 2nd-class every 30 minutes

Veracruz – 300km, 5½ hours; 15 ADO (US$15.50)

Villahermosa – 780km, 12 hours; 4 ADO (US$44)

AROUND TUXPAN

Tamiahua (pop 5500 ☎ 768), 43km north from Tuxpan by paved road, is at the southern end of Laguna de Tamiahua. It has a few seafood-shack restaurants, and you can rent boats for fishing or trips to the lagoon's barrier island. From Tuxpan take a 1st-class ODM bus (US$1.50) or a more frequent 2nd-class bus.

Castillo de Teayo (pop 4300 ☎ 746), 23km up a bumpy road west off highway 180 (the turnoff is 18km from Poza Rica), was from about AD 800 one of the southernmost points of the Huastec civilization. Beside its main plaza is a steep, 13m-high restored pyramid topped by a small temple. It's in Toltec style and was probably built during that civilization's rule of the area, sometime between AD 900 and 1200.

Around the base of the pyramid are some stone sculptures that have been found in the surrounding area. Some of these are in Huastec style, while others are thought to be the work of Aztecs who controlled the area briefly before the Spanish conquest.

POZA RICA

• **pop 161,600** • **elev 28m** ☎ **782**

Congested and polluted, the oil city of Poza Rica is at the junction of highways 180 and 130. You might have to change buses here, but it's really not worth staying the night.

Hotel Farolino (☎ 824-34-66) Singles/doubles US$10/13.50. Although its rooms are grimy and tiny, this is the least sketchy of the sleazy spots near the bus station. Turn left out of the station and walk a block.

Best Western Hotel Poza Rica (☎ 822-01-12, fax 823-20-32, cnr Avenida Kehoe and 10

Ote) Singles/doubles US$60/67. If, for some strange reason, you have to come to downtown Poza Rica, this is the best choice. Rooms are as pleasant and predictable as vanilla ice cream.

The main Poza Rica bus station, on Calle Puebla east off Boulevard Lázaro Cárdenas, has 2nd-class and some 1st-class departures. Most 1st-class buses go from the adjoining ADO building. Daily services include the following:

Mexico City (Terminal Norte) – 260km, 5 hours; UNO deluxe at 1am (US$23), 31 ADO (US$14), regular 2nd-class

Pachuca – 209km, 4 hours; ADO at 1.40am, 1.40pm and 3.30pm (US$9.50)

Papantla – 25km, 30 minutes; 27 ADO (US$1), frequent 2nd-class

Tampico – 250km, 4 to 5 hours; 3 UNO deluxe (US$23), 40 ADO (US$15)

Tuxpan – 60km, 45 minutes; 50 ADO (US$3), 2nd-class every 20 minutes

Veracruz – 250km, 5 hours; 3 UNO deluxe (US$22.50), 21 ADO (US$12.50)

For El Tajín, take one of Transportes Papantla's frequent buses to Coyutla (US$0.75) and ask to get off at the 'Desviación El Tajín,' about 30 minutes from Poza Rica. Autotransportes Coatzintla and other 2nd-class buses to El Chote, Agua Dulce or San Andrés will also go past the El Tajín turnoff.

POZA RICA TO PACHUCA

The 200km Poza Rica-Pachuca road, highway 130, is the direct approach to Mexico City from the northern part of Veracruz state. This scenic, misty route climbs up to the Sierra Madre, across the semitropical north of Puebla state and into Hidalgo. The area's population has a high proportion of Nahua and Totonac indigenous people.

Huauchinango, roughly halfway between Poza Rica and Pachuca, is the center of a flower-growing area. You'll also find embroidered textiles in the busy Saturday market. A weeklong flower festival, known as the *feria*, includes traditional dances and reaches its peak on the third Friday in Lent. Readers have recommended this as a fascinating time to visit the town. **Acaxochitlán**, 25km west of Huauchinango, has a Sunday market; specialties include fruit wine and preserved fruit.

The traditional Nahua village of **Pahuatlán** is the source of many of the cloths woven with multicolored designs of animals and plants. Reach it by turning north off highway 130, about 10km past Acaxochitlán. A spectacular 27km dirt road winds several hundred meters down to the village, which holds a sizable Sunday market. About half an hour's drive beyond Pahuatlán is **San Pablito**, an Otomí village where colorfully embroidered blouses abound.

Highway 130 climbs steeply to Tulancingo, in the state of Hidalgo. See the Around Pachuca section in the Around Mexico City chapter for details on the rest of this route to Pachuca.

PAPANTLA
• pop 49,900 • elev 198m ☎ 784

Set on a hillside, Papantla dangles on the edge of the southern Sierra Madre Oriental. It's a convenient base for visiting El Tajín as well as a laid-back, *alegre* destination in its own right. The central zócalo is delightful on Sunday evenings, when half the town is out dancing and smooching. Some Totonacs still wear traditional costume here – men in baggy white shirts and trousers, women in embroidered blouses and *quechquémitls*. Because the town is in the center of a vanilla-growing region, a fresh, sweet aroma pervades the area.

Orientation & Information
Papantla lies just off highway 180, which runs southeast from Poza Rica. The center of town is uphill from the main road. From the zócalo, uphill (facing the cathedral) is south, downhill is north. Now you know.

To get to the town center from the ADO bus station, turn left as you go out, then follow Avenida Carranza a couple of hundred meters west to Calle 20 de Noviembre. Turn left and climb 20 de Noviembre past the Transportes Papantla bus terminal and market to the zócalo. The tourist office (theoretically open 9am-3pm and 6pm-9pm Monday to Friday) is hidden away on the ground floor of a government building opposite the cathedral on 16 de Septiembre, a block uphill from the zócalo.

Zócalo
Officially called 'Parque Téllez,' the main plaza is terraced into the hillside, below the Iglesia de la Asunción. Beneath the cathedral, a 50m-long mural facing the square depicts Totonac and Veracruz history. A serpent stretches along most of the mural linking a pre-Hispanic stone carver, E. Tajín's Pirámide de los Nichos, *voladores* and an oil rig.

Volador Monument
At the top of the hill, above the cathedral, towers a 1988 statue of a volador musician playing his pipe as preparation for the four fliers to launch themselves into space. A red light adorns one of his fingers to warn off passing aircraft. Take the street heading uphill from the southwest corner of the cathedral yard to reach the statue. Inscriptions around its base give an explanation of the ritual. The spot serves as Lovers' Point on weekend nights.

Museo de Cultura Totonaca
On the edge of town, this humble museum *(admission US$1.50; open 9am-6pm Mon-Sat)* on the road to El Chote and El Tajín has exhibits on Totonac culture from pre-Hispanic times to the present. Spanish-speaking Totonac guides give detailed explanations and can answer questions. White micros from 16 de Septiembre can get you here for a couple of pesos.

Facts about the Totonacs

Approximately 260,000 Totonacs survive in modern Mexico, mostly living between Tecolutla on the Veracruz coast and the southern Sierra Madre Oriental in northern Puebla. Roman Catholicism has been superimposed on their ancient beliefs, with traditional customs stronger in the mountain areas. The chief Totonac deities are ancestors, the sun (which is also the maize god) and St John (also the lord of water and thunder). Venus and the moon are identified with Qotiti, the devil, who rules the kingdom of the dead beneath the earth. Some Totonacs believe that the world is flat, the sky is a dome and the sun travels beneath the earth at night. The Feast of the Holy Cross (May 3) coincides with ceremonies for fertility of the earth and the creation of new seeds.

Special Events

The Corpus Christi festival, in late May and early June, is the big annual event. In Papantla it's a celebration of Totonac culture, and the town is thronged for the parades, dances and other cultural events. The main procession is on the first Sunday, voladores fly two or three times a day, and costumed performers do traditional dances.

Places to Stay

Hotel Pulido (☎ 842-10-79, Enríquez 205) Doubles US$14.50. The Pulido is 250m east from the downhill side of the zócalo. Rooms are small and sometimes grimy.

Hotel Totonacapán (☎ 842-12-16, cnr 20 de Noviembre & Olivo) Singles/doubles US$25/28.50. Downhill (north) of the zócalo, this place offers sparse but large and comfy air-conditioned rooms.

Hotel Tajín (☎/fax 842-06-44, Núñez 104) Singles/doubles US$29/41, with air-con US$40/53. This hotel is in a blue building a few meters east of the zócalo mural's left end. It sports homey, sizable, well-kept rooms; those in front have balconies overlooking the town.

Hotel Provincia Express (☎ 842-16-45, Enríquez 101) Doubles US$42. Formerly the Hotel Premier, this place offers sterile, spacious air-conditioned rooms. For peaceful sleepin', stay away from the plaza-fronting quarters.

Places to Eat

Papantla's cuisine is strictly Mexican, with an emphasis on meat – try the beef fillets starting at around US$7 at the **Hotel Tajín's** restaurant.

Restaurant Sorrento (Enríquez 105) Dishes US$2-3, comida corrida US$3. On the downhill side of the zócalo, this spot offers adequate, inexpensive breakfasts and a typical comida corrida.

Plaza Pardo (Enríquez 103) Dishes US$3-5. Upstairs on the same street as the Sorrento, this is the most pleasant place in town. Balcony tables overlook the zócalo. Main courses are filling, desserts scrumptious, and the cocktails kickin'.

Shopping

As Mexico's leading vanilla-growing center, Papantla offers good vanilla extract, vanilla pods and vanilla figuras (pods woven into the shapes of flowers, insects, human figures or crucifixes). Also try the regional vanilla liquor. **Mercado Hidalgo**, at the northwest corner of the zócalo, has some pretty Totonac costumes, good baskets and vanilla souvenirs. **Mercado Juárez**, at the southwest corner opposite the cathedral, sells mainly food.

Getting There & Away

Few long-distance buses stop here. Most are de paso, so book your bus out of town as soon as possible. If desperate, go to Poza Rica and get one of the much more frequent buses from there. ADO is the only 1st-class line serving Papantla. The main 2nd-class alternative is Transportes Papantla (TP), with slow, old vehicles.

Jalapa – 260km, 4 hours; 10 ADO (US$12.50), several TP

Mexico City (Terminal Norte) – 290km, 5 hours; 6 ADO (US$15)

Poza Rica – 25km, 30 minutes; 15 ADO (US$1), TP every 15 minutes

Tampico – 275km, 5-6 hours; 5 ADO (US$16)

Tuxpan – 90km, 1 hour; 4 ADO (US$3.50)

Veracruz – 230km, 4 hours; 6 ADO (US$10), 8 TP (US$8)

White microbuses go on the hour to El Tajín from 16 de Septiembre, the street on the uphill side of the cathedral (about 30 minutes; US$0.80). Alternatively, you can do the trip in two stages by getting a bus from the same stop to El Chote, then any of the frequent buses going west (to the right) from El Chote to the El Tajín turnoff ('Desviación El Tajín'). Other buses from Papantla to El Chote leave from the TP terminal.

EL TAJÍN

Among verdant hills a few kilometers from Papantla lies the site of El Tajín – Totonac for 'thunder,' 'lightning' or 'hurricane,' all of which can happen here in summer. The ancient Totonacs may have occupied El Tajín in its later stages, but most of it was built before that civilization became important. It is the highest achievement of Classic Veracruz civilization, about which little is known.

El Tajín was first occupied about AD 100, but most of what's visible was built around AD 600 or 700. The years AD 600 to 900 saw its zenith as a town and ceremonial

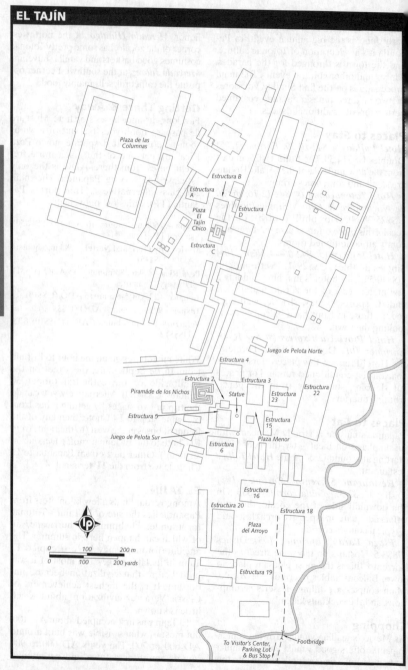

EL TAJÍN

Plaza de las Columnas

Estructura B

Estructura A

Plaza El Tajín Chico

Estructura D

Estructura C

Juego de Pelota Norte

Estructura 4

Estructura 2

Estructura 3

Pirámade de los Nichos

Statue

Estructura 23

Estructura 22

Estructura 5

Estructura 15

Juego de Pelota Sur

Plaza Menor

Estructura 6

Estructura 16

Estructura 20

Estructura 18

Plaza del Arroyo

Estructura 19

0   100   200 m
0   100   200 yards

To Visitor's Center,
Parking Lot
& Bus Stop

Footbridge

enter. Around AD 1200 the site was abandoned, possibly after attacks by Chichimecs, and lay unknown to the Spaniards until about 1785, when an official found it while looking for illegal tobacco plantings.

Among El Tajín's special features are rows of square niches on the sides of buildings, numerous ball courts, and sculptures depicting human sacrifice connected with the ball game. The archaeologist who did much of the excavation here, José García Payón, believed that El Tajín's niches and stone mosaics symbolized day and night, light and dark, and life and death in a universe composed of pairs of opposites, though many are skeptical of this interpretation. Despite extensive reconstruction in 1991, El Tajín retains an aura of mystery and a peaceful 'lost in the jungle' feel.

Information

The whole site *(admission US$4, free Sun; open 8am-7pm daily)* covers about 10 sq km, and you need to walk a few kilometers to see it all. There's little shade and it can get very hot, especially in the middle of the day – a water bottle and hat are highly recommended.

Outside are a parking lot and stalls selling food and handicrafts. The visitor's center has a restaurant, souvenir shops, a left-luggage room, an information desk and an excellent museum with a model of the whole site. Exhibits are labeled in English and Spanish (there are no interpretive signs on the site itself). Those who want more information should look for the booklet *Tajín: Mystery and Beauty,* by Leonardo Zaleta, which may be available (in English, French, German and Spanish) at some of the souvenir shops.

Totonac Voladores

Totonacs carry out the exciting voladores rite most days from a 30m-high steel pole beside the visitor's center. Performances are usually around 2pm and 4pm; before they start, a Totonac in traditional dress requests donations from the audience (US$2).

Around the Site

Two main parts of the site have been cleared and restored: the lower area, containing the Pirámide de los Nichos (Pyramid of the Niches), and, uphill, a group of buildings known as 'El Tajín Chico' (Little Tajín). Most features of the site are known by the labels used in a 1966 INAH survey, with many called simply 'Estructura' (Structure) followed by a number or letter.

Plaza Menor Beyond the unremarkable Plaza del Arroyo, you reach the Plaza Menor (Lesser Plaza), part of El Tajín's main ceremonial center, with a low platform in the middle. A statue on the first level of Estructura 5, a pyramid on the plaza's west side, represents either a thunder-and-rain god who was especially important at El Tajín, or Mictlantecuhtli, a death god. All of the structures around this plaza were probably topped by small temples, and some were decorated with red or blue paint.

Juego de Pelota Sur Some 17 ball courts have been found at El Tajín. The Juego de Pelota Sur (Southern Ball Court), between Estructuras 5 and 6, dates from about 1150 and is the most famous of the courts owing to the six relief carvings on its walls depicting various aspects of the ball-game ritual.

The panel on the northeast corner (on the right as you enter the court from the Plaza Menor) is the easiest to make out. At its center, three ballplayers wearing knee pads are depicted carrying out a ritual postgame sacrifice: One player is about to plunge a knife into the chest of another, whose arms are held by the third. A skeletal death god on the left and a presiding figure on the right look on. Another death god hovers over the victim.

The central north wall panel depicts the ceremonial drinking of *pulque* – a figure holding a drinking vessel signals to another leaning on a pulque container. Quetzalcóatl sits cross-legged beside Tláloc, the fanged god of water and lightning. The panel at the northwest corner of the same wall is thought to represent a ceremony that preceded the ball game. Two players face each other, one with crossed arms, the other holding a dagger. Speech symbols emerge from their mouths. To their right is a figure with the mask of a coyote, the animal that conducted sacrificial victims to the next world. The death god is on the right.

The southwest corner panel seems to show the initiation of a young man into a

Outdoing the Dervishes

The voladores rite – a sort of slow-motion quadruple bungee jump – starts with five men in colorful costumes climbing to the top of a very tall pole. Four of them sit on the edges of a small, square, wooden frame atop the pole, arrange their ropes and then rotate the square to twist the ropes around the pole. The fifth man dances, bangs a drum and plays a whistle while standing on a tiny platform above them. Suddenly he stops and the others launch themselves backward into thin air. Upside down, arms outstretched, they revolve gracefully around the pole and descend slowly to the ground as their ropes unwind.

This ancient ceremony is packed with symbolic meanings. One interpretation is that it's a fertility rite and the fliers are macaw-men who make invocations to the four corners of the universe before falling to the ground, bringing with them the sun and rain. It is also noted that each flier circles the pole 13 times, giving a total of 52 revolutions. The number 52 not only is the number of weeks in the modern year but also was an important number in pre-Hispanic Mexico, which had two calendars – one corresponding to the 365-day solar year, the other to a ritual year of 260 days. A day in one calendar coincided with a day in the other calendar every 52 solar years.

While it's sad in a way to see a sacred rite turned into a show for tourists (the people who do it say they need the money), the dangerous feat is a spectacular sight.

A Totonac Indian flies through the voladores rite.

band of warriors associated with the eagle. A central figure lies on a table; to the left, another holds a bell. Above is an eagle-masked figure, possibly a priest. The central south wall panel, another pulque-drinking scene, shows Tláloc squatting as he passes a gourd to someone in a fish mask who appears to be in a pulque vat. On the left is the maguey plant, from which pulque is made. Maguey is not native to this part of Mexico, which points to influences from central Mexico (possibly Toltec) at this late stage of El Tajín. On the **southeast corner** panel, a man offers spears or arrows to

another, perhaps also in the eagle-warrior initiation ceremony.

Pirámide de los Nichos The Pyramid of the Niches, 35m square, is just off the Plaza Menor by the northwest corner of Estructura 5. The six lower levels, each surrounded by rows of small square niches, climb to a height of 18m. The wide staircase on the east side was a late addition, built over some of the niches. Archaeologists believe that there were originally 365 niches, suggesting that the building may have been used as a kind of calendar. The insides of the niches were painted red, and their frames blue. The only similar known building, probably an earlier site, is a seven-level niched pyramid at Yohualichán near Cuetzalán, 50km southwest of El Tajín.

El Tajín Chico The path north toward El Tajín Chico passes the Juego de Pelota Norte (Northern Ball Court), which is smaller and older than the southern court but also bears carvings on its sides.

Many of the buildings of El Tajín Chico have geometric stone mosaic patterns known as 'Greco' (Greek); similar patterns are found in decorations of Mitla (Oaxaca), a later site. The main buildings, probably 9th century, are on the east and north sides of Plaza El Tajín Chico. Estructura C, on the east side, with three levels and a staircase facing the plaza, was initially painted blue. Estructura B, next to it, was probably home to priests or officials. Estructura D, behind Estructura B and off the plaza, has a large lozenge-design mosaic and a passage underneath.

Estructura A, on the plaza's north side, has a façade like a Mayan roof comb, with a stairway leading up through an arch in the middle. This corbeled arch – its two sides jutting closer to each other until they are joined at the top by a single slab – is typical of Mayan architecture, and its presence here is yet another oddity in the confusing jigsaw puzzle of pre-Hispanic cultures.

Uphill to the northwest of Plaza El Tajín Chico is the as-yet-unreconstructed Plaza de las Columnas (Plaza of the Columns), one of the site's most important structures. It originally housed an open patio inside, with adjoining buildings stretching over the hillside to cover an area of nearly 200m by 100m. Most of this area is heavily overgrown and fenced off with 'no access' signs. Some reassembled columns are displayed in the museum at the visitor's center.

Getting There & Away

Frequent buses journey here from Papantla and Poza Rica – see the sections on those towns, earlier in this chapter, for details. To return, catch a local bus from the area next to the parking lot or on the main Poza Rica-El Chote road.

SOUTH OF PAPANTLA

Highway 180 runs near the coast for most of the 230km from Papantla to Veracruz.

> ## The Legend of El Tajín
>
> On the walls of the museum at El Tajín is inscribed a poem that curators insist was a myth told by the ancient city's inhabitants. The legend tells of 12 thunder gods who took a boy as their protégé. In a plot twist suspiciously reminiscent of Disney's *Sorcerer's Apprentice*, the boy steals the gods' robes and proceeds to unleash the elements on earth. To prevent Armageddon, the gods bind the boy with a rainbow and a lock of virgin's hair, then banish him to the ocean floor.
>
> How such a story might have survived, and the source of the text, remain unclear.
>
>

Strong currents can make for risky swimming here.

Tecolutla
• pop 3600 ☎ 766

This minor seaside resort has a relaxed, enjoyable atmosphere on holidays, when it's crowded with families and students. A wide, sandy, palm-fringed beach lines one side of town, and the mouth of Río Tecolutla is on the other. Launches make trips into the mangroves for fishing and wildlife watching. Prices for accommodations skyrocket during high season, quadrupling during Semana Santa.

Hotel Álbatros (☎ 846-00-02, cnr Hidalgo & Prieto) Singles/doubles US$16.50/28, with air-con US$28/38. A block off the central plaza, this hotel offers bright, comfortable rooms and plenty of plants.

Hotel Oasis (☎/fax 846-02-75, Agostín Lara 8) Doubles US$14. Right on the beach, a 10-minute walk from the plaza, the Oasis features basic but large rooms with the tiniest TVs you've ever seen. The friendly managers can pick you up from the town center if you call ahead.

Tecolutla abounds in cheap, good restaurants. You can reach this town by a side road that branches off highway 180 at Gutiérrez Zamora. ADO and Transportes Papantla buses go to and from Papantla.

Costa Esmeralda

The 20km 'Emerald Coast' sports a scattering of hotels, holiday homes and trailer parks along a strip between highway 180 and the dark, sandy, sometimes deserted beach. It's a popular summer and holiday spot but very quiet most of the year. At the north end of the coast, **La Guadalupe** is an OK stop. One solid option here is *Hotel Catán*, right on the highway. The comfortable, fan-cooled cabin rooms (US$16.50 in low season) sleep one to four people. As you continue south, hotels get more upscale and expensive, culminating in *Hotel El Doral (☎/fax 232-321-00-04, Carretera 180 Km 81)*, 12km away, near the village of Casitas. Large, well-equipped doubles run US$40 in low season.

At the mouth of the Río Bobos, the small fishing town of **Nautla** dozes on the south side of a toll bridge. Seafood is sold at a couple of simple places near the brown beach.

Laguna Verde & Villa Rica

Mexico's controversial first nuclear power station is at Laguna Verde, about 80km north of Veracruz port, on the coastal side of highway 180. The first unit came into operation in 1989, the second in 1996, but government plans for more reactors have been abandoned in the face of public protest. Concerns about the safety of this reactor have led to suggestions that it be replaced with natural-gas-powered generators.

Now just a fishing village, 69km north of Veracruz, Villa Rica is the probable site of the first Spanish settlement in Mexico. Here you can explore traces of a fort and a church on the Cerro de la Cantera or bask on a very nice beach. The nearby Totonac tombs of **Quiahuiztlán** are superbly situated on a hill overlooking the coast.

Central Veracruz

Highway 180 follows the coast past the ruins of Zempoala to Cardel, where a side road leads to the beach at Chachalacas and highway 140 branches west to Jalapa, the state capital. The countryside around Jalapa shelters appealing villages, striking landscapes and dramatic river gorges that are increasingly popular for rafting trips. The very early colonial ruins at La Antigua are worth a stop on the way to the bustling port of Veracruz, 35km south of Cardel. From Veracruz, highway 150D heads southwest to

Córdoba, Fortín de las Flores and Orizaba, on the edge of the Sierra Madre. Southeast of Veracruz is a flat, hot, wet coastal plain crossed by many rivers and sheltering the serene port town of Tlacotalpan.

COASTAL COMMUNITIES
☎ 296

North of the city of Veracruz lies the central coastal area, a popular vacation spot for Mexican holidaymakers and home to the Totonac ruins of Zempoala. Cardel, the area's transportation hub, provides a good base for exploring the central coast's historical sites, and decent beaches for those who don't want to make the trip up from Veracruz.

Zempoala

The pre-Hispanic Totonac town of Zempoala holds a key place in the story of the Spanish conquest. Its ruins stand 42km north of Veracruz and 4km west of highway 180 in modern Zempoala. The turnoff is by a Pemex station, 7km north of Cardel. Voladores regularly perform at the ruins, especially on holidays and on weekends, around 10am, noon and 2pm. Zempoala is most easily reached through Cardel – take a bus marked 'Zempoala' (US$1) from the Cardel bus station, or a taxi (US$6).

History Zempoala became a major Totonac center after about AD 1200 and may have been the leader of a federation of southern Totonac states. It fell subject to the Aztecs in the mid-15th century; thus, many of the buildings are in Aztec style. The town boasted defensive walls, underground water and drainage pipes and, in May 1519 when the Spanish came, about 30,000 people. As Cortés approached the town, one of his scouts reported back that the buildings were made of silver – but it was only white plaster or paint shining in the sun.

Zempoala's portly chief, Chicomacatl, known to history as 'the fat cacique' from a description by Bernal Díaz del Castillo, struck an alliance with Cortés for protection against the Aztecs. But his hospitality didn't stop the Spanish from smashing his gods' statues and lecturing the Zempoalans on the virtues of Christianity. Zempoalan carriers went with the Spaniards when they set off for Tenochtitlán in 1519. The following year, it was at Zempoala that Cortés defeated

he Pánfilo de Narváez expedition, which
had been sent out by orders from the governor of Cuba to arrest Cortés.

By the 17th century Zempoala had virtually ceased to exist. Its population, devastated by diseases, was down to eight
families. Eventually the town was abandoned. The present town dates from 1832.

Zempoala Ruins After you enter Zempoala, take a right where a sign says 'Bien-
venidos a Zempoala.' You'll find the main
archaeological site *(admission US$5, free
Sun; open 9am-6pm daily)* at the end of this
short road.

The site is green and lovely, with palm
trees and a mountain backdrop. Most of the
buildings are faced with smooth, rounded
riverbed stones, but many were originally
plastered and painted. A typical feature is
battlement-like 'teeth' called *almenas*.

The **Templo Mayor** (Main Temple) is an
11m-high, 13-platform pyramid, originally
plastered and painted. A wide staircase
ascends to the remains of a three-room
shrine on top (you're not allowed to climb
it). In 1520 this was probably Pánfilo de
Narváez's headquarters, which Cortés' men
captured by setting fire to its thatched roof.

On their first visit to Zempoala, the conquistador and his men lodged in **Las Chimeneas**. The hollow columns in front of the
main structure were thought to be chim-
neys – hence the name. A temple probably
topped the seven platforms here.

There are two main structures on the west
side. One is known as the Gran Pirámide or
Templo del Sol, with two stairways climbing
its front side to three platforms on top, in
typical Toltec-Aztec style. It faces east and
was probably devoted to the sun god. To its
north, the **Templo de la Luna** has a rectangular platform and ramps in front, and a round
structure behind, similar to Aztec temples to
the wind god Ehecatl.

East of Las Chimeneas, beyond the irrigation channel, you'll see a building called
Las Caritas (Little Heads) on your right. Its
niches once held several small pottery
heads. Three other structures formerly
stood east of Las Caritas, in line with the
rising sun. Another large wind-god temple,
known as **Templo Dios del Aire**, is in the
town itself – just go back south on the site
entrance road, cross the main road in town

and then go around the corner to the right.
The ancient temple, with its characteristic
circular shape, is beside an intersection.

Chachalacas

A few kilometers northeast of Cardel, this
unpretentious seaside 'resort' has miles of uncrowded beaches and some wild sand dunes
north of town. Most of the accommodations
are geared to family groups, and at holiday
times they ask about US$40 for a large room.

*La Pingüi (☎/fax 962-50-01, e lapingui@
prodigy.net.mx, López Aries 2)* Doubles
US$29, with air-con US$35. Though a far
cry from budget, this is the best value
around – it'll be on your right on the way
downtown. It has a small pool, and the
helpful owners can arrange snorkeling on
the reefs and trips to the dunes.

*Chachalacas Hotel-Club (☎ 962-52-36,
800-900-38-00, fax 962-52-42, e chachalacas@
prodigy.com)* Singles US$76, singles/doubles
with meals and entertainment US$108/162.
Another resort in the Maeva chain, this hotel
boasts large pools, bright tropical decor and
spacious quarters, but it doesn't have the
gleam you'd expect from a five-star spot.

CENTRAL GULF COAST

Games, music and other forms of recreation are available.

Several restaurants line up along the beach, generally charging around US$6 for fresh fish.

Cardel

The area's main town, Cardel (or José Cardel) is a stop on the way to the ruins and the beach. It has banks and restaurants, as well as adequate accommodations at *Hotel Cardel* (☎ 962-00-14, cnr Zapata & Martínez), where singles/doubles go for US$15.50/22, US$20/26 with air-conditioning. It's a block off the main plaza.

From the Veracruz bus station, regular 1st-class ADO buses to Cardel cost US$3; frequent 2nd-class AU buses cost US$2.

La Antigua

Intriguing La Antigua (population 1000) is 2km east of the coastal highway 150, 23km north of Veracruz. A Spanish settlement was established here near the mouth of Río Huitzilapan in 1525, after Villa Rica was abandoned and before Veracruz was founded. The picturesque ruined building, its walls overgrown with tree roots, was the 16th-century customhouse (though it's commonly called the 'Casa de Cortés'). The Ermita del Rosario church, probably dating from 1523, is one of the oldest in the Americas. Kids will guide you around the sites for a small tip. Slightly buggy riverside accommodations are available at *Hotel La Malinche*, where singles/doubles go for US$16.50/28. Nearby, small seafood restaurants are popular with day-trippers from Veracruz.

JALAPA

- pop 341,100 • elev 1427m ☎ 228

Cool, cultured Jalapa is truly a capital city. Sometimes spelled 'Xalapa' (but always pronounced 'ha-LA-pa'), this urban delight houses not only the government of Veracruz state but also the Universidad Veracruzana, a lively artistic and entertainment scene, a convivial café life and a sophisticated, stylish population.

Visitors can enjoy Jalapa's rolling hills and terraced parks (which offer satisfying vistas), revel in the cool mountain climate and fuel their explorations with some of the Gulf Coast's finest cuisine. The city's high-light, the superb anthropological museum, i a particularly enjoyable retreat on one o Jalapa's many misty, drizzly days, when the traffic noise and fumes grow too vile to bear. Allow a couple of days to get to know this town.

A pre-Hispanic town on this site became part of the Aztec empire around 1460, and Cortés and his men passed through in 1519 The Spanish town didn't take off until the annual trade fair of Spanish goods was firs held here in 1720 (it ran until 1777). Today Jalapa is a commercial hub for the coffee and tobacco grown on the slopes, and the city is also well known for its flowers. The surrounding area shelters attractive towns and offers dramatic landscapes with rivers gorges and waterfalls.

Orientation

The city center is on a hillside, with the plaza Parque Juárez, more or less in the middle of things. Uphill is north. Jalapa's cathedral is on Enríquez, just east of the plaza. Many of the mid-range hotels and restaurants are a little to the east, on Enríquez and Zaragoza. CAXA, the bus station, is 2km east of the city center, and the unmissable anthropology museum is a few kilometers north.

Information

Tourist Offices Don't count on the tourist information desk at the bus station (theoretically open 8am-9pm Mon-Sat, 8am-noon Sun) to be open when you need it. The very helpful municipal tourist information booth (☎ 842-12-00 ext 3025) is under the arches of the Palacio Municipal, facing Parque Juárez (open 9am-4pm Mon-Fri).

Another good tourist resource is the information desk (☎ 815-07-08) on the right as you enter the Museo de Antropología. The state tourist office (☎ 812-85-00, Colón 5) is inconveniently located in the Torre Ánimas skyscraper, 3km east of the center on the highway into town.

Money Banca Serfin, Bancomer and Banamex on Enríquez/Gutiérrez Zamora have ATMs. Casa de Cambio Jalapa (Gutiérrez Zamora 36) offers quicker exchange services and has slightly longer hours (9am-2pm and 4pm-6pm Mon-Fri, 10am-2pm Sat).

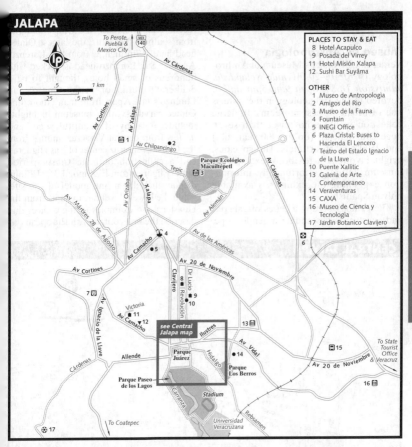

JALAPA

To Perote,
Puebla &
Mexico City

Av Cárdenas

0   5   1 km

0   .25   .5 mile

PLACES TO STAY & EAT
8   Hotel Acapulco
9   Posada del Virrey
11 Hotel Misión Xalapa
12 Sushi Bar Suyåma

OTHER
1   Museo de Antropología
2   Amigos del Rio
3   Museo de la Fauna
4   Fountain
5   INEGI Office
6   Plaza Cristal; Buses to
    Hacienda El Lencero
7   Teatro del Estado Ignacio
    de la Llave
10 Puente Xallitic
13 Galeria de Arte
    Contemporaneo
14 Veraventuras
15 CAXA
16 Museo de Ciencia y
    Tecnologia
17 Jardin Botanico Clavijero

CENTRAL GULF COAST

Post & Communications The post office is a few blocks east of the city center, at the corner of Gutiérrez Zamora and Diego Leño. The Telecomm office, with fax, telex and telegram services, is next door. You can access the Internet for US$1.25 an hour at Compupapel, on Primo Verdad south of Enríquez (open 9am-8.30pm daily).

City Center

The central **Parque Juárez** is like a terrace, with its elevated south side overlooking the valley below and (when the weather is clear) snowcapped mountains in the distance. Tucked *beneath* the plaza is the **Pinacoteca Diego Rivera** (☎ 818-18-19; admission free; open 10am-8pm Tue-Sat). It's a nifty little art museum with a permanent exhibit of

works from throughout Rivera's life. Rotating exhibits feature prints and paintings by other Mexican artists. You can reach the museum via the steps leading down from the west side of the plaza.

On the plaza's north side are the arcades of the **Palacio Municipal**. On the east side is the **Palacio de Gobierno**, the seat of the Veracruz state government. The Palacio de Gobierno sports a fine **mural** by Mario Orozco Rivera depicting the history of justice; it's above the stairway you'll reach from the eastern entrance on Camacho. Facing the Palacio de Gobierno across Enríquez is the unfinished **cathedral** (started in 1772), from where Revolución and Dr Lucio both lead up to the bustling area above the market. Farther north, Dr Lucio crosses a deep valley via **Puente Xallitic**, a high, arched bridge.

Museo de Antropología

Veracruz University's Museum of Anthropology (☎ 815-09-20, Avenida Xalapa s/n; admission US$3; open 9am-5pm daily), devoted to the archaeology in the state, is one of Mexico's best museums. Its large collection includes no fewer than seven huge Olmec heads (up to 3000 years old) and 2500 superb artifacts. The spacious, bright layout is a textbook example of museum design. Unfortunately, information explaining the exhibits is available only in Spanish.

The exhibits occupy a series of galleries and courtyards descending a gentle slope,

and they're arranged from oldest to most recent. First you reach the Olmec material from southern Veracruz; the largest Olmec head here, 2.7m high, is from San Lorenzo. Another San Lorenzo head is pocked with hundreds of small holes, thought to be a deliberate mutilation at the time of San Lorenzo's fall. Apart from many more fine Olmec carvings, other museum highlights include an array of beautiful *yugos* and *hachas* from central Veracruz, murals from the Classic Veracruz center of Las Higueras, and a collection of huge Classic-period pottery figures from El Zapotal. The El Tajín display includes a fine model of the site, while the lowest level has exhibits from the Huasteca and examples of the codices that describe the first contact with Europeans.

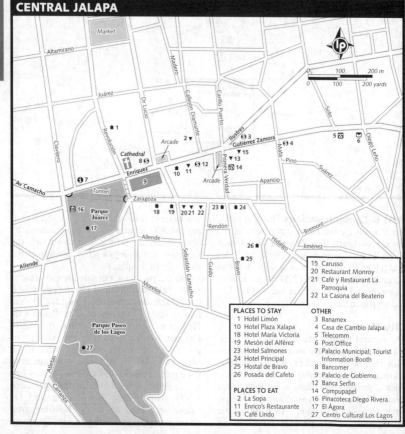

CENTRAL JALAPA

PLACES TO STAY
1 Hotel Limón
10 Hotel Plaza Xalapa
18 Hotel María Victoria
19 Mesón del Alférez
23 Hotel Salmones
24 Hotel Principal
25 Hostal de Bravo
26 Posada del Cafeto

PLACES TO EAT
2 La Sopa
11 Enrico's Restaurante
13 Café Lindo
15 Carusso
20 Restaurant Monroy
21 Café y Restaurant La Parroquia
22 La Casona del Beaterio

OTHER
3 Banamex
4 Casa de Cambio Jalapa
5 Telecomm
6 Post Office
7 Palacio Municipal; Tourist Information Booth
8 Bancomer
9 Palacio de Gobierno
12 Banca Serfin
14 Compupapel
16 Pinacoteca Diego Rivera
17 El Ágora
27 Centro Cultural Los Lagos

The museum is on the west side of Avenida Xalapa, 4km northwest of the city center – look for the spacious gardens and the building with a fountain outside. Take a 'Tesorería-Centro-SEP' or 'Museo' bus (US$0.50) west from in front of the Palacio Municipal on Enríquez. To return, take a bus marked 'Centro.' Buses can be infrequent or full, so a taxi may be worth the US$1.50 fare. It costs US$1.50 extra to bring in a camera, but you can't use a flash.

Galería de Arte Contemporáneo

This state-run art gallery (☎ 818-04-12, *Xalapeños Ilustres 135; admission free; open 10am-8pm Tue-Sun*) is in a fine renovated colonial building 1km east of the city center, just past Arteaga. It houses worthwhile temporary exhibitions; contact the gallery to find out what's on.

Museo de Ciencia y Tecnología

The eclectic collection here includes old trains, assorted cars, airplanes, ecology displays and hands-on scientific exhibits. Thematic galleries cover the human body, earth sciences, water, transportation and space exploration. Exhibits are high-quality and particularly excellent for children who can read Spanish. The museum (☎ 812-51-10, *Avenida Vidal s/n; admission US$5 with IMAX theater; open 9am-6pm Tue-Fri, 10am-7pm Sat & Sun*) is on the southeast side of town – take a Murillo Vidal bus (US$0.40) or a taxi (US$2).

Parks

Just south of Parque Juárez is **Parque Paseo de los Lagos**, winding for 1km along either side of a lake. At its northern end is the **Centro Cultural Los Lagos**, a lovely, sophisticated escape that hosts courses, concerts and temporary cultural exhibits. If you're lucky, you'll hear the strains of orchestras practicing as you stroll through the grounds.

On a hill in the north of the city, **Parque Ecológico Macuiltépetl** is the thickly wooded cap of an old volcano; the turnoff is about 200m south of the anthropology museum. Paths spiral to the top, which offers good views. At the summit, the small **Museo de la Fauna** (*admission US$0.90; open 11am-5pm Tue-Sun*) has

some tethered eagles, regionally endemic reptiles and a taxidermist's dream array of displays.

Southwest of the town center the attractive **Jardín Botánico Clavijero** has a fine collection of subtropical plants.

White-Water Rafting

Jalapa is the base for a number of 'adventure tourism' operators, several offering rafting trips on nearby rivers. **Veraventuras** (☎ 818-95-79, 800-712-65-72, fax 818-96-80, W *www.dpc.com.mx/veraventuras, Santos Degollado 81-8*) does trips ranging from a half-day outing on the Río Filo-Bobos (US$53 per person) to a three-day expedition on the class IV rapids of the Barranca Grande, on the upper reaches of Río Pescados (US$210). To find the company's office, go up the driveway and look for the building behind the parking lot.

Another established rafting operator is **Amigos del Río** (☎/fax 815-88-17, W *www .amigosdelrio.com.mx, Chilpancingo 205*). Rafting trips usually require a minimum of four to eight participants, so it's a good idea to contact the operator ahead of time. Weekend trips offer the best chance of joining up with other people.

Organized Tours

BTT Xalapa (☎ 812-00-81, fax 828-96-02, e *victoursxalapa_btt@hotmail.com; prices from US$20 to US$60 per person*) offers daily tours of the city as well as excursions to nearby towns and to archaeological and historical sites. Some guides speak English. **EcoTours** (*contact Laura Elida Amador Zaragoza* ☎ 842-18-00 ext 3504, e *elida@ecologia.edu.mx*) offers bird watching, boat trips to Laguna Mancha and wildlife-observing expeditions.

Places to Stay

Despite the big-city location, decent accommodations don't break the bank in Jalapa.

Budget Several good low-cost options can be found in Jalapa.

Hotel Limón (☎ 817-22-04, fax 817-93-16, *Revolución 8*) Singles/doubles US$10/10.50. The yellow-tiled rooms here are mini-everything, with tiny beds, televisions, bathrooms and floor space. However, they are clean and the price is right.

CENTRAL GULF COAST

Hotel Plaza Xalapa (☎ *817-33-10, fax 818-27-14, Enríquez 4*) Singles/doubles US$12/14.50, US$16.50 with two beds. The adequate rooms here are spacious but can be dark and noisy. Get a room facing away from the street, or risk bed rage at 3am from the noise.

Hotel Principal (☎ *817-64-00, Zaragoza 28*) Singles/doubles US$16.50/19. Rooms here boast cable TV but can be dim and musty. Again, beware of streetside quarters.

Hostal de Bravo (☎ *818-90-38, Bravo 11*) Singles/doubles US$18.50/21. Popular with backpackers, this place offers comfortable, well-equipped rooms that sparkle in a way the previous three options just don't.

Hotel Salmones (☎/fax *817-54-31, Zaragoza 24*) Singles/doubles US$21/23.50, newer ones US$23.50/28. With a small garden, big lobby, nice restaurant and old-fashioned style, this is a decent mid-range choice. Though slightly worn, rooms come with carpet, phone and TV (renovated rooms are much more shipshape).

Hotel Acapulco (☎ *815-16-41, Julián Carrillo 6*) Singles/doubles US$12/15.50. Though a little out of the way (a kilometer north of the plaza), this is a good stop for clean, serviceable rooms. Don't expect any frills other than friendly management.

Mid-Range & Top End About 300m uphill from the town center, you'll find *Posada del Virrey* (☎ *818-61-00, fax 818-68-80,* e *posadadelvirrey@infosel.net.mx, Dr Lucio 142*) Singles/doubles US$28/32. This is a comfortable, modern hotel with TV, phones, a bar and a restaurant. The management can be a bit snobby.

Hotel María Victoria (☎ *818-60-11, 800-260-08-00, fax 818-05-21, Zaragoza 6*) Singles/doubles US$47/56. Close to the town center, this hotel sports 114 ultraclean, large, well-maintained rooms with phones, cable, air-conditioning and heating. Amenities include a restaurant and a bar with occasional live entertainment.

Mesón del Alférez (☎/fax *818-01-13,* e *mesonalferez@hotmail.com.mx, Sebastián Camacho 4-6*) Singles/doubles US$41/48. An interesting place with character in a central location, this hotel is in a renovated old building. Rooms have magnificent wooden furniture and are arranged around a plant-filled inner courtyard.

Posada del Cafeto (☎/fax *817-00-23* e *p_cafeto@xal.megared.net.mx, Canovas 8*) Singles/doubles US$26/31. Tucked away in a quiet neighborhood, this reader-recommended *posada* offers airy, fan-cooled rooms with separate (private) toilets and showers.

Hotel Misión Xalapa (☎ *818-22-22, cnr Victoria & Bustamante*) Doubles US$81. The top place in town is this modern 200-room hotel, 1km west of the city center, 1½ blocks uphill from Avenida Camacho. The central part is built around a swimming pool, and the complex holds bars, a restaurant and a good cafeteria. The majority of the clientele are suit-clad businesspeople.

Places to Eat

Jalapa has plenty of excellent, inexpensive eateries, with one local specialty being *chiles rellenos* (stuffed peppers). And where do you think the *jalapeño* got its name?

La Sopa (*Callejón Diamante 2*) Meals US$2.50. Very popular La Sopa offers a fine lunchtime comida corrida and main courses in the evening. There's live music Friday and Saturday nights and a convivial atmosphere anytime.

Enrico's Restaurante (*Enríquez 6*) Dishes US$1-6. Next to Hotel Plaza Xalapa, Enrico's is a good place to rest your feet and enjoy a cappuccino or a glass of juice. There is a good-value set lunch and à la carte main courses.

Carusso (*Gutiérrez Zamora 12*) Unlimited buffet US$4. East of Enrico's, Carusso serves very tasty pizza and pasta – a small, thin-crust pizza fills one person.

Café Lindo (*Primera Verdad 21*) Dishes US$1-6. Just south of Enríquez/Zamora, Café Lindo is one of Jalapa's trendiest places, with a bright, cheerful atmosphere, cozy chairs, live music and an indoor fountain. You can have cappuccino or espresso, sandwiches and snacks, and beef or chicken main courses.

Café y Restaurant La Parroquia (*Zaragoza 18*) Dishes US$5-8. Another local institution is this café, where the efficient staff serves up good, solid fare. Treat yourself to a set dinner of soup, chicken and fries, or a variety of set breakfasts and other snacks and meals.

Restaurant Monroy (*Zaragoza 16*) Dishes US$5-8. Open 24 hours. This restaurant serves up a wide assortment of *antojitos* around the clock and a hearty four-course comida corrida at lunchtime.

La Casona del Beaterio (Zaragoza 20) Prices US$4-9. Next to La Parroquia, this place has an even more inviting ambience in its pretty courtyard or in colorful rooms with photos of old Jalapa. The long menu of reliable choices includes fruit, granola, and yogurt with honey for breakfast, as well as spaghetti, crêpes, enchiladas and meat dishes. The five-course comida corrida is a bargain.

Sushi Bar Suyâma (Camacho 54A) Gyoza US$2, *teppanyaki* US$10. With loud music and an upscalish atmosphere, this new joint brings quality Japanese fare to Jalapa. It's a good place for groups.

Entertainment

El Ágora (☎ 818-57-30) Open 10am-10pm Tue-Sun, 9am-6pm Mon. This is an arts center under the Parque Juárez containing a cinema, theater and gallery; it's the focus of Jalapa's busy arts scene. It also shelters a bookstore and café. For news of what's happening around town, look here or on the notice board in the Café La Parroquia (see Places to Eat).

The *Teatro del Estado Ignacio de la Llave* (☎ 818-08-34), the state theater, on the corner of Avenidas Camacho and Ignacio de la Llave, offers performances by the Orquesta Sinfónica de Jalapa and the Ballet Folklórico of the Universidad Veracruzana.

Jalapa has a notoriously evolving nightlife scene. Check the tourist information booth in the Palacio Municipal for suggestions.

Getting There & Away

As an inland transportation hub, Jalapa offers excellent connections throughout the state.

Bus Jalapa's gleaming, modern, well-organized bus station, 2km east of the city center, is known as the Central de Autobuses de Xalapa (CAXA). Deluxe service is offered by UNO and ADO GL, 1st-class service by ADO, and 2nd-class service by AU (many 2nd-class services are direct, and not much slower, or cheaper, than 1st class).

Cardel – 72km, 1½ hours; 23 ADO (US$3), AU every 20 minutes 5.15am-7.15pm (US$3)

Mexico City (TAPO) – 315km, 5 hours; 5 UNO (US$27.50), 8 ADO GL (US$19), 16 ADO (US$16.50), 17 AU (US$14.50)

Papantla – 260km, 5 hours; 8 ADO (US$12.50)

Puebla – 185km, 3 hours; 9 ADO (US$9.50), 14 AU (US$8.50)

Tampico – 525km, 11 hours; 1 ADO at 10.30pm (US$28)

Veracruz – 100km, 2 hours; ADO every 20 to 30 minutes 5am-11pm (US$5.50), 24 AU (US$5)

Villahermosa – 575km, 8 hours; UNO at 11.30pm (US$46), ADO GL at 1.45am (US$33), 4 ADO (US$30)

Other places served by ADO include Acayucan, Campeche, Catemaco, Córdoba, Fortín de las Flores, Mérida, Orizaba, Poza Rica, San Andrés Tuxtla and Santiago Tuxtla. AU also goes to Salina Cruz.

Car & Motorcycle For cheap car rentals, try Kanguro (☎ 817-78-78) or Alsad (☎ 817-70-46). Highway 140 to Puebla is narrow and winding until Perote; Jalapa-Veracruz road is very good. Going to the northern Gulf Coast, it's quickest to go to Cardel, then turn north on highway 180; the inland road via Tlapacoyan is scenic but slow.

Getting Around

For buses from CAXA to the city center, follow the signs to the taxi stand, then continue downhill to the big road, Avenida 20 de Noviembre. Turn right to the bus stop, from where any microbus or bus marked 'Centro' will take you within a short walk of Parque Juárez (US$0.50). For a taxi to the city center, buy a ticket in the bus station (US$2), then walk down the ramp and through the tunnel to the taxi stand. To return to the bus station, take a 'CAXA' bus east along Zaragoza.

AROUND JALAPA

The countryside around Jalapa is very scenic, and some appealing old towns lie nearby.

Hacienda El Lencero

About 12km from Jalapa on the Veracruz highway, a signposted road branches right for a few kilometers to the Museo Ex-Hacienda El Lencero *(admission US$1.50; open 10am-6pm Tue-Sun)*. The former estate rests on land once granted to a soldier from the army of Cortés. One of the first inns between Mexico City and Veracruz was established here, and the extensive ranch was developed to provide horses and cattle for travelers. Onetime dictator General Antonio López de Santa Anna owned the property from 1842 to the mid-1850s; the hacienda, chapel and other buildings date mostly from this period. The grand, superbly restored house is beautifully furnished with fine period pieces, and the gardens and lake are delightful (the vast fig tree is said to be 500 years old). The building and grounds are well worth a visit.

From Jalapa, catch one of the regular 'Banderia' buses from outside the Plaza Cristal shopping center (US$2).

El Carrizal
South of the Veracruz road, 44km from Jalapa, El Carrizal hot springs feed several sulfurous pools. The site also houses a restaurant and a spa-hotel. For information in Jalapa, contact ☎ 818-97-74, fax 818-96-80.

Coatepec & Xico
Coatepec (population 44,700), a charming colonial town 15km south of Jalapa, is known for its coffee and orchids. The María Cristina orchid garden, on the main square, is open daily. Xico (population 15,000) is a pretty colonial village, 8km south of Coatepec. From Xico it's a pleasant 2km walk to the photogenic 40m **Texolo waterfall**.

Buses go about every 15 minutes to Coatepec or Xico from Avenida Allende, about 1km west of central Jalapa (US$3).

Parque Nacional Cofre de Perote
The 4274m-high Cofre de Perote volcano is southwest of Jalapa but often obscured by mist. From the town of Perote, 50km west of Jalapa on highway 140, Calle Allende continues southwest to become a dirt road that climbs 1900m in 24km, finishing just below the summit. There's no public transportation here.

Valle Alegre
To reach this 'happy valley' take the highway toward Puebla and turn south after 15km, just west of Las Vigas. Follow the side road through El Llanillo to Tembladeras, where you'll find **Valle Alegre Hostel** (☎ 282-818-34-84, e valle_alegre@ correoweb.com), surrounded by an ecological reserve, which offers myriad hiking and wildlife-watching possibilities. On Sunday at 10am, an AU bus leaves Jalapa's CAXA for an overnight trip to the valley and back (US$6 including accommodations).

VERACRUZ
• pop 401,200 ☎ 229

O heroic town! Festive, frenetic Veracruz revels in peripatetic mariachis, pleasingly aesthetic colonial buildings and a kinetic fervor that starts in its zócalo and pervades its denizens (jarochos). Bands flock to town during Carnaval, which stands as Mexico's biggest and wildest. Land and seashore offer you chances to cruise past historical attractions, to booze and party with locals or merely to snooze in a shaded plaza: in Veracruz, tropical hedonism is the norm.

Though tourists may take the city by storm, it retains an almost small-town charm – warm, vivacious and vibrant. Whatever form your visit takes, beware. You'd best believe that when time comes to go, you may not want to leave.

History
The coast here was occupied by Totonacs, with influences from Toltec and Aztec civilizations. This mix of pre-Hispanic cultures can be seen at Zempoala, 42km to the north (see Zempoala, earlier in this chapter). After the Spanish conquest, Veracruz provided Mexico's main gateway to the outside world for 400 years. Invaders and pirates, incoming and exiled rulers, settlers, silver and slaves – all came and went to make the city a linchpin in Mexico's history.

Spanish Conquest & Pirate Raids Cortés made his first landing here at an island 2km offshore, which he named 'Isla Sacrificios' because of the remains of human sacrifices he found there. He anchored off another island, San Juan de Ulúa, on Good Friday (April 21), 1519, where he made his first contact with Moctezuma's envoys. Cortés founded the first Spanish settlement at Villa Rica, 69km north, but this was later moved to La Antigua, and finally to the present site of Veracruz in 1598.

Veracruz became the Spaniards' most important anchorage, and until 1760 it was the only port allowed to handle trade with Spain. Tent cities blossomed for trade fairs when the fleet from Spain made its annual arrival, but because of seaborne raids and tropical diseases (malaria and yellow fever were rampant) Veracruz never became one of Mexico's biggest cities.

In 1567 nine English ships under John Hawkins sailed into Veracruz harbor, with the intention of selling slaves in defiance of the Spanish trade monopoly. They were trapped by a Spanish fleet, and only two ships escaped. One of them, however, carried Francis Drake, who went on to harry the Spanish in a long career as a sort of licensed pirate. The most vicious pirate attack of all came in 1683, when the Frenchman Laurent de Gaff, with 600 men, held the 5000 inhabitants of Veracruz captive in the church with little food or water. They killed any who tried to escape, piled the Plaza de Armas with loot, got drunk, raped many of the women and threatened to blow up the church unless the people revealed their secret stashes. They left a few days later, much richer.

19th & 20th Centuries In 1838 General Antonio López de Santa Anna, who had been routed in Texas two years earlier, fled Veracruz in his underwear under bombardment from a French fleet in the 'Pastry War' (the French were pressing various claims against Mexico, including that of a French pastry cook whose restaurant had been wrecked by unruly Mexican officers). But the general responded heroically, expelling the invaders and losing his left leg in the process.

When the 10,000-strong army of Winfield Scott attacked Veracruz in 1847 during the Mexican-American War, over 1000 Mexicans were killed in a weeklong bombardment before the city surrendered.

In 1859, during Mexico's internal Reform War, Benito Juárez's Veracruz-based liberal government promulgated the reform laws that nationalized church property and put education into secular hands. In 1861 when Juárez, having won the war, announced that Mexico couldn't pay its foreign debts, a joint French-Spanish-British force occupied Veracruz. The British and Spanish planned only to

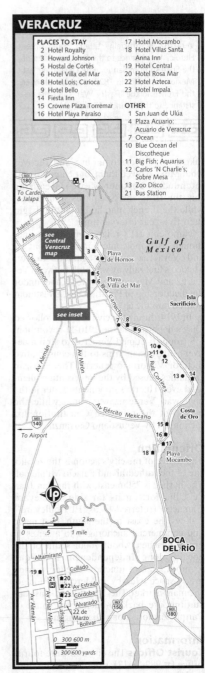

VERACRUZ

PLACES TO STAY
2 Hotel Royalty
3 Howard Johnson
5 Hostal de Cortés
6 Hotel Villa del Mar
8 Hotel Lois; Carioca
9 Hotel Bello
14 Fiesta Inn
15 Crowne Plaza Torremar
16 Hotel Playa Paraíso
17 Hotel Mocambo
18 Hotel Villas Santa Anna Inn
19 Hotel Central
20 Hotel Rosa Mar
22 Hotel Azteca
23 Hotel Impala

OTHER
1 San Juan de Ulúa
4 Plaza Acuario; Acuario de Veracruz
7 Ocean
10 Blue Ocean del Discotheque
11 Big Fish; Aquarius
12 Carlos 'N Charlie's; Sobre Mesa
13 Zoo Disco
21 Bus Station

The Heroic City

Veracruz is officially titled 'Four Times Heroic,' in reference to the final expulsion of the Spanish from San Juan de Ulúa (their last Mexican toehold) in 1825; the triumph over the French in the 'Pastry War'; and the resistance to the US in 1847 and 1914.

take over the customhouse and recover what Mexico owed them, but Napoleon III intended to conquer Mexico. Realizing this, the Brits and Spaniards went home, while the French marched inland to begin their five-year intervention.

Napoleon III's reign came to an end, though, as Napoleonic reigns are wont to, and Veracruz again began to flower. Mexico's first railway was built between Veracruz and Mexico City in 1872, and, under the dictatorship of Porfirio Díaz, investment poured into the city.

In 1914, during the civil war that followed Díaz's departure in the 1910-11 revolution, US troops occupied Veracruz to stop a delivery of German arms to the conservative dictator Victoriano Huerta. The Mexican casualties caused by the intervention alienated even Huerta's opponents. Later in the civil war, Veracruz was for a while the capital of the reformist Constitutionalist faction led by Venustiano Carranza.

Orientation

The center of the city's action is the zócalo, site of the cathedral and Palacio Municipal. The harbor is 250m east, with the San Juan de Ulúa fort on its far side. Boulevard Camacho (referred to as 'El Boulevard') follows the coast to the south, past naval and commercial anchorages, to a series of grimy beaches. About 700m south of the zócalo along Independencia is Parque Zamora, a road junction circling a wide green space. Nearby is Mercado Hidalgo, the main market. The 1st- and 2nd-class bus stations are back-to-back, 2km south of Parque Zamora along Díaz Mirón.

Information

Tourist Offices The city and state tourist office (☎ 989-88-17) is on the ground floor of the Palacio Municipal (open 9am to 8pm Monday to Saturday, 10am to 6pm Sunday). The staffers are super-sweet and eager to please. Some speak English. They offer maps, discount-coupon books and cheesy brochures.

Money Banamex and Bancomer are both on Independencia in the block north of the zócalo – they have ATMs and change traveler's checks. Banorte is nearby. Casa de Cambio Puebla (Juárez 112) gives good rates (open 9am to 6pm Monday to Friday, 9am to 2pm Saturday).

Post & Communications The main post office (Plaza de la República 213) is a five-minute walk north of the zócalo (open 8am to 4pm Monday to Friday, 9am to 1pm Saturday). Next door, the Telecomm office offers public fax, telegram and telex services (open 8am to 7pm Monday to Friday, 9am to 5pm Saturday, 9am to noon Sunday). There are pay phones on the zócalo.

Netchatboys (Lerdo 369) offers lightning-speed Internet access for US$1.60 per hour (open 9am to 8.30pm Monday to Friday, noon to 7pm Saturday, noon to 5pm Sunday).

Zócalo

Veracruz's zócalo, also called the 'Plaza de Armas,' 'Plaza Lerdo' and 'Plaza de la Constitución,' is the hub of the city for jarochos and visitors alike. It's a fine-looking place with *portales* (arched arcades), palm trees, a fountain, the 17th-century Palacio Municipal on one side and an 18th-century cathedral on another. The level of activity accelerates as the day progresses, from breakfast and coffee under the arches, through a leisurely lunch, to afternoon entertainment on an outdoor stage. In the evening, as the sweat cools off Veracruz bodies, the zócalo becomes a swirling, multifaceted party, with cool drinks and competing street musicians (see Entertainment, later).

Harbor & Malecón

Veracruz's harbor is still busy, though oil ports such as Tampico and Coatzacoalcos now handle greater tonnages. The Paseo del Malecón (also called Insurgentes) is a pleasant waterfront walk; starting with the Plaza de las Artesanías, colorful souvenir stalls opposite the plaza sell a mind-boggling

CENTRAL VERACRUZ

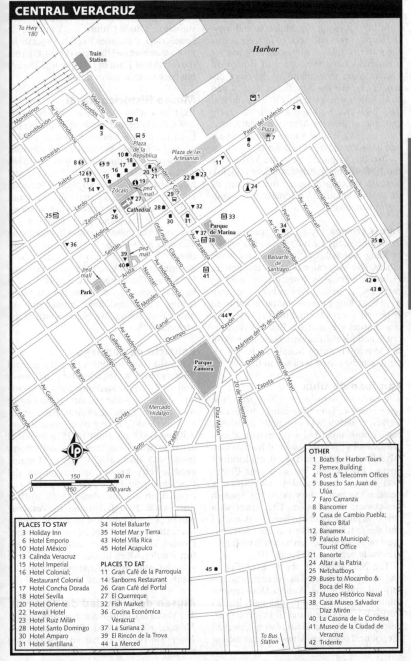

To Hwy 180

Harbor

Train Station

CENTRAL GULF COAST

To Bus Station

PLACES TO STAY
3   Holiday Inn
6   Hotel Emporio
10 Hotel México
13 Calinda Veracruz
15 Hotel Imperial
16 Hotel Colonial;
    Restaurant Colonial
17 Hotel Concha Dorada
18 Hotel Sevilla
20 Hotel Oriente
22 Hawaii Hotel
23 Hotel Ruiz Milán
28 Hotel Santo Domingo
30 Hotel Amparo
31 Hotel Santillana

34 Hotel Baluarte
35 Hotel Mar y Tierra
43 Hotel Villa Rica
45 Hotel Acapulco

PLACES TO EAT
11 Gran Café de la Parroquia
14 Sanborns Restaurant
26 Gran Café del Portal
27 El Querreque
32 Fish Market
36 Cocina Económica
    Veracruz
37 La Suriana 2
39 El Rincón de la Trova
44 La Merced

OTHER
1   Boats for Harbor Tours
2   Pemex Building
4   Post & Telecomm Offices
5   Buses to San Juan de
    Ulúa
7   Faro Carranza
8   Bancomer
9   Casa de Cambio Puebla;
    Banco Bital
12 Banamex
19 Palacio Municipal;
    Tourist Office
21 Banorte
24 Altar a la Patria
25 Netchatboys
29 Buses to Mocambo &
    Boca del Río
33 Museo Histórico Naval
34 Casa Museo Salvador
    Díaz Mirón
40 La Casona de la Condesa
41 Museo de la Ciudad de
    Veracruz
42 Tridente

0   150   300 m
0   150   300 yards

selection of seashell knickknacks and tacky T-shirts.

Stroll out along the Malecón and view the ships, cranes and ancient fortress across the water, or take a sightseeing boat trip for a closer look. At the corner of Boulevard Camacho are monuments to the city's defenders against the Americans in 1914 and to all sailors who gave their lives to the sea. The high-rise building here is an early example of modern Mexican architecture; built in 1940, it now houses Pemex offices and has some interesting murals.

Two blocks inland from the Malecón is the 1998 **Altar a la Patria**, a solemn obelisk beneath which are buried the remains of those who defended Veracruz during its numerous conflicts.

Faro Carranza Facing the waterfront on the Malecón, the Faro Carranza is a yellow building that holds a lighthouse and navy offices. The Mexican navy goes through an elaborate parade in front of the building early each morning. Venustiano Carranza lived here during the revolution, in 1914 and 1915, and it was here that the 1917 Mexican constitution was drafted. Exhibits on Carranza and his political struggles are now in the Museo Histórico Naval; the Faro Carranza building itself is closed to the public.

San Juan de Ulúa

This fortress (admission US$3, free Sun; open 9am-4.30pm Tue-Sun) protecting Veracruz harbor was originally an island, but it's now connected to the mainland by a causeway. In 1518 the Spaniard Juan de Grijalva landed here during an exploratory voyage from Cuba. The next year Cortés also landed here, and it subsequently became the main entry point for Spanish newcomers to Mexico. The Franciscan chapel is thought to have been built in 1524 and the first fortifications in the 1530s, but most of what can be seen now was built progressively between 1552 and 1779.

The central part of the fortress, Fuerte San José, has also acted as a prison, most notoriously during the Porfirio Díaz regime. Under Díaz, three damp, stinking cells – El Purgatorio, La Gloria and El Infierno (Purgatory, Heaven and Hell) – were reserved for political prisoners. Many inmates died of yellow fever or tuberculosis.

Today San Juan de Ulúa is an empty ruin of passageways, battlements, bridges and stairways. Guided tours are available in Spanish and, sometimes, English. To get there, take a 'San Juan de Ulúa' bus (US$0.45) from the east side of Plaza de la República. The last bus back to town leaves at 6pm.

Museo Histórico Naval

Built as a school for naval officers in the 1890s, this large and handsome building has been beautifully restored, and in 1997 it opened as a museum (cnr Arista & Morelos; admission free; open 9am-5pm Tue-Sun) covering Mexico's maritime heritage and naval history, with an inexplicable focus on knot-tying. As well as rooms full of weapons and model ships, the museum holds beautifully presented (and guilt-inspiring, for Americans) exhibits on the US attacks on Veracruz in 1847 and 1914, and on revolutionary hero Venustiano Carranza, whose government-in-exile was based in Veracruz for a time. The displays are well laid out in large, air-conditioned rooms, but the information is in Spanish only. The museum entrance is on Arista, two blocks south of the Malecón.

Baluarte de Santiago

From the 16th to 19th centuries, central Veracruz was surrounded by a defensive wall that incorporated nine forts. The only one remaining is the Baluarte (Bastion) de Santiago (cnr Canal & 16 de Septiembre; admission US$3.30, free Sun; open 10am-4.30pm Tue-Sun), built in 1526 beside a canal at what was then the waterfront. Inside is a small exhibit of pre-Hispanic gold jewelry known as 'Las Joyas del Pescador' (the Fisherman's Jewels). The name refers to some fabulous gold artifacts discovered by a fisherman in Veracruz harbor in 1976, but most pieces on display here, though gorgeous, come from other sources. The price covers admission to the fort interior, which houses the gold exhibit; you can walk around the outside battlements anytime at no cost.

Museo de la Ciudad de Veracruz

The Veracruz City Museum (cnr Zaragoza & Morales; admission US$2.75, free Sun; open 10am-6pm Wed-Mon) has fine displays and presentations ranging from the city's early history (particularly slavery) to the present. Temporary exhibits tend not to be as good.

Casa Museo Salvador Díaz Mirón

Once the home of celebrated poet Salvador Díaz Mirón (1853-1928), this house (☎ 989-88-00 ext 146, Zaragoza 322; admission free; open 10am-7pm Mon-Sat) is now a center for literary and theatrical workshops. Some rooms upstairs are restored and decorated in late-19th-century style. There's not a whole lot to see, but with some imagination, you can feel as though you're in the presence of greatness. Furthermore, the genial curators will be delighted that you're interested in Mirón's work and life.

Acuario de Veracruz

Veracruz's aquarium (admission child/adult US$1.50/3.30; open 10am-7pm daily) is inside the Plaza Acuario shopping mall at Playa de Hornos, about 2km south of the city center. The most impressive exhibit is the huge, donut-shaped tank in which sharks, rays and giant turtles swim right around and over viewers. Numerous smaller tanks and ponds show lots of fish (both freshwater and saltwater species), turtles, coral and so on.

Beaches & Lagoons

In general, the farther south you go, the cleaner the beaches get. Hence, few people venture into the water at Playa de Hornos, just south of the city center, or at Playa Villa del Mar, a little farther south. The beaches are more acceptable 5km south of the city at **Costa de Oro** and 7km south at **Playa Mocambo**.

Still farther south, the road goes to **Boca del Río**, with popular seafood restaurants. Over the bridge, the coastal road continues to **Mandinga**, where you can hire a boat to explore the lagoons, and **Antón Lizardo**.

Diving & Snorkeling

The beaches near Veracruz may not be inviting, but there is good diving (including at least one accessible wreck) on the reefs near the offshore islands. Part of the area has been designated an underwater natural park. **Tridente** (☎/fax 931-79-24, Boulevard Camacho 165A; diving trips US$65 per person) is a PADI dive school that arranges dive and snorkel trips from Veracruz and Antón

Lizardo (45 minutes down the coast). With a group of four people, you can do a day trip with two dives, a guide and equipment. Other diving operations are a few blocks south of Tridente on the boulevard; still more are based in Boca del Río and Antón Lizardo.

Organized Tours

Boats from the Malecón offer hourlong harbor tours for US$5 per person – they leave when they're full (about every 30 minutes 7am-7pm). Also leaving from the Malecón, imitation tramcars make a 40-minute circuit of the city's attractions (US$2).

Special Events

Carnaval – Veracruz busts out into a nine-day party before Ash Wednesday (February or March; 46 days before Easter Sunday) each year. Starting the previous Tuesday, colorful parades wind through the city daily, beginning with one devoted to the 'burning of bad humor' and ending with the 'funeral of Juan Carnaval.' Other events include fireworks, dances, salsa and samba music, handicrafts, folklore shows and children's parades. See the tourist office for a program of events.

Festival del Caribe – High point of the summer holiday season is the festival of Afro-Caribbean culture in the last two weeks of August. Various Caribbean nations participate in academic forums, trade shows and business conferences, but the main attractions are the dance and music performances (many of them free), film screenings and art expositions.

Places to Stay

The busiest time in Veracruz is Carnaval, when the town is packed, hotels are booked weeks or months ahead, and prices soar. Other busy periods, when reservations are recommended, are Semana Santa, the summer from mid-July to mid-September (especially weekends) and the period from mid-November to mid-January. At other times, plenty of rooms are available, and you should be able to get a discount off the prices listed here.

It's convenient, fun and not too expensive to stay on or just off the zócalo. Some of the seafront hotels can offer good value too. The cheaper places are around the zócalo and near the bus stations, while the most expensive are the resort hotels in the beach suburb of Mocambo, 7km south of the city center.

Budget Even the cheapest hotels should have hot water, but check for adequate ventilation and a working fan.

Zócalo Area Just around the corner from the zócalo is *Hotel México* (☎ *932-43-60, Morelos 343*) Singles/doubles US$19/28. This basic hotel has lots of brown tiles and quiet rooms with TV and fan. Housekeeping could be more assiduous about cleaning out dust and cobwebs, though.

Hotel Sevilla (☎ *932-42-46, Morelos 359*) Singles/doubles US$14.50/15.50. Just east of the zócalo, the Sevilla has big, spare rooms with ceiling fan, TV and private bath. The place is dimly lit and can feel creepy at night.

Hotel Santo Domingo (☎ *931-63-26, Serdán 451*) Singles/doubles US$15/17. With cell-block concrete rooms and minuscule private bathrooms, the Santo Domingo is best for those who don't plan to spend a ton of time in the room.

Hotel Amparo (☎ *932-27-38, Serdán 482*) Singles/doubles US$10.50/13.50, US$3 more for TV. Across from the Santo Domingo, the older Amparo is a simple but clean place with fluorescent lighting, tiled floors and a slightly dingy feel. Rooms are well sized and come with small desks and bathrooms.

Hotel Santillana (☎ *932-31-16, Landero y Cos 209*) Doubles US$16.50. The cute rooms here are endowed with TVs, fine bathrooms and happy wallpaper. The purple-and-green courtyard adds to the festive atmosphere.

City Seafront Budget travelers who want to be by the ocean might choose *Hotel Villa Rica* (☎ *932-48-54, Boulevard Camacho 7*) Singles/doubles US$18/22. The Villa Rica's small rooms are not a fantastic value, but they're tidy and well ventilated.

Bus Station Area Right opposite the 2nd-class bus station is *Hotel Rosa Mar* (☎ *937-07-47, Lafragua 1100*) Singles/doubles US$19/21.50, US$3 more for air-con. The Rosa Mar may be a bit noisy (get a room in the back), but it's clean, friendly and respectable.

Hotel Azteca (☎/fax *937-42-41, 22 de Marzo 218*) Doubles US$22. A block east from the 2nd-class bus station, at Orizaba, this jolly green place offers clean rooms with air-conditioning, phone and TV, as well as garrulous management and a small courtyard.

Hotel Acapulco (☎ *932-34-92, fax 931-87-27, Uribe 1327*) Singles/doubles US$19/23. Though not in the world's most convenient location, the Acapulco is a great value. The immaculate, bright, spacious rooms are worth the nine-block walk from the bus station or city center.

Mid-Range Mid-range options in Veracruz range from elegant to characterless, but almost all offer good values. Air-conditioning, cable TV and good water pressure are standard in this category.

Zócalo Area Just off the zócalo is *Hotel Concha Dorada* (☎/fax *931-29-96*, ☎ *800-712-53-42*, e *conchadorada@yahoo.com.mx, Lerdo 77*) Singles/doubles US$28/34. The rooms are dark and the bathrooms are tiny, but the place is immaculately kept, and the air-conditioning is mighty but quiet.

Hotel Colonial (☎/fax *932-01-93*, e *hcolonial@ifosel.net.mx, Lerdo 117*) Singles/doubles US$37/47, with balcony US$54/68. Despite its perfect location and elegant furnishings, the 180-room Colonial suffers from rushed management and a weirdly institutional feeling, as well as a pervasive musty odor. Rooms are luxurious but vary, so check one out before you check in.

Hotel Imperial (☎ *932-12-04, fax 931-45-08*, w *www.hotelimperial-veracruz.com, Lerdo 153*) Singles/doubles US$61/67. The Imperial has an elegant lobby, old-fashioned elevator, towering columns and a stained-glass ceiling. The spacious rooms come with a marble-floored bathroom. It's a good spot to treat yourself.

Hotel Oriente (☎/fax *931-24-90, Lerdo 20*) Singles/doubles US$32/39. Hotel Oriente is centrally located and comes with clean, mid-size rooms featuring TV and phone. Outside rooms have balconies but also more noise. Air-conditioners in some rooms have been known to fall apart at 1am.

Hotel Baluarte (☎ *932-52-22/fax 932-54-42, Canal 265*) Singles/doubles US$40/50. Southeast from the zócalo, the Hotel Baluarte boasts quiet, enormous, immaculately kept rooms. Bonuses include a sparkling lobby area and a nice elevator; the management's indifference is a minus.

Harbor & City Seafront 'Big and busy' describes *Hotel Mar y Tierra* (☎ *931-38-66, fax*

932-6096, **e** *hotelmarytierra@terra.com.mx, cnr Boulevard Camacho & Figueroa)* Singles/doubles US$29/37. Mar y Tierra has rooms in an older front section or in a preferable rear extension. All rooms have air-conditioning, satellite TV and carpet, but some are a bit claustrophobia-inducing, so look first.

Hotel Royalty (☎ 932-39-88, fax 932-70-96, Abasolo 34) Doubles US$22, US$32 with air-con. A little farther from the city center, the Hotel Royalty has clean, no-frills rooms with balconies; the upper floors have good views. The place won't blow you away, but it offers good value for the area.

*Hostal de Cortés (☎ 932-12-00, 800-112-98-00, fax 932-12-09, **w** www.hostaldecortes .com.mx, cnr Boulevard Camacho & Las Casas)* Doubles with breakfast from US$59. This friendly spot, opposite Playa Villa del Mar (2.5km south of the zócalo), offers 98 motel-style rooms, some with sea-view balconies, as well as a pool, great views and the world's slowest elevators.

Hotel Bello (☎ 922-48-28, fax 922-48-35, Ruiz Cortines s/n) Doubles US$63. Also near the nightlife, the Bello has some comfortable if unspectacular rooms with sea views and others facing the Carnaval parade route; all have air-conditioning. Rates plummet during low season. The restaurant is decent and reasonably priced.

Bus Station Area Your peso packs a lot of punch at the *Hotel Impala (☎ 937-01-69, Orizaba 650)* Doubles US$28. Though a teensy bit cramped, rooms here smell fresh and come with air-conditioning, TV and phones.

Hotel Central (☎ 937-22-22, fax 937-98-09, Díaz Mirón 1612) Doubles US$30. Half a block north of the bus station, this busy hotel offers mid-size, dark and noisy rooms. You do, however, get air-conditioning and comfortable beds – but the Impala is a better value for such luxuries.

Mocambo A short walk from Playa Mocambo is *Hotel Villas Santa Anna Inn (☎ 922-47-57, Suárez 1314)* Doubles from US$44, bungalows US$89. The Villas Santa Anna Inn is good for families, with a garden, pool, and pleasant, spacious, air-conditioned rooms. The hotel faces the inland side of the Carretera Veracruz-Boca

del Río; enter from the first street on the right a couple of hundred meters south of the traffic circle by the Hotel Mocambo. An unbelievably unhelpful sign for the hotel appears several meters *beyond* the turnoff.

Top End Beyond the eroding charm of Veracruz's venerable elder institutions, most hotels at the top end have little to offer in terms of personality. Efficient service and plenty of gleam are the hallmarks of this price range.

Zócalo Area The rooftop pool has a superb view at *Calinda Veracruz (☎ 931-22-33, **w** www.hotelescalinda.com, cnr Independencia & Lerdo)* Doubles from US$104. The most central top-end place here, the fully modernized Calinda Veracruz overlooks the zócalo. Beautiful corridors resemble those in Mughal palaces; the rooms, although well decorated and air-conditioned, are surprisingly small. More expensive rooms have balconies.

*Holiday Inn (☎ 932-45-50, fax 932-42-55, **e** hichvera@prodigy.net.mx, Morelos 225)* Singles/doubles US$73/84. Around the corner and two blocks from the zócalo, this modern hotel is housed in a stylishly renovated old building. It has a lovely courtyard swimming pool and comfortable rooms with all the modern conveniences.

Harbor & City Seafront The harbor view is the only selling point at *Hotel Ruiz Milán (☎/fax 932-27-72, ☎ 800-221-42-60, **e** ruiz milan@ver.megared.net.mx, cnr Paseo del Malecón & Farías)* Old doubles US$72, remodeled doubles US$86. On the Malecón, but a handy six blocks from the city center, the Ruiz Milán has some 'economical' fan-cooled rooms and better rooms with air-conditioning and harbor vistas.

*Hawaii Hotel (☎ 938-00-88, fax 932-55-24, **e** Hawaii@infosel.net.mx, Paseo del Malecón 458)* Singles/doubles US$72/83. A better value than the Ruiz Milán, this place offers white, cool, cheery rooms and a lobby reminiscent of a garden party.

*Howard Johnson (☎ 931-00-11, fax 931-08-67, **e** hojover@ver.megared.net.mx, Boulevard Camacho 1263)* Doubles US$55-102. Rooms here vary in proportion to their quality and views. All are relatively luxurious, however, and the festive atmosphere makes you feel better about dishing out the cash.

Hotel Emporio (☎ 932-00-20, 800-295-20-00, **e** emporio@ver.megared.net.mx, Paseo del Malecón 244) Singles/doubles US$122/133. Towering over the harbor, the Emporio features an outside elevator that soars above three swimming pools to a rooftop garden. The myriad luxuries that come with a large 'standard' room include a bathtub, hair dryer and separate faucet for drinking water.

Hotel Villa del Mar (☎ 931-33-66, fax 932-71-35, **e** hvilladelmar@ver.megared .net.mx, Boulevard Camacho s/n) Doubles US$109. Farther south from the Hostal de Cortés, this spot isn't a great value unless you bargain down the price or can get a discount. Also, get a room away from the noisy road. The air-conditioned rooms and garden bungalows, nicely decorated with pastel paintings, abut a pleasantly breezy courtyard and an outdoor pool.

Hotel Lois (☎ 937-82-90, 800-712-91-36, fax 937-80-89, **e** htlois@net.iaiver.com.mx, Avenida Ruiz Cortines 10) Doubles US$144, US$80 in low season. At the center of the nightlife action, the Hotel Lois is near the seafront Boulevard Camacho. It's very new and smart, with modern air-conditioned rooms resembling those of the Crowne Plaza Torremar (see below). Those on the north side have a good view of the Carnaval parade. The lobby could well have been designed by sir Edmund James, creator of Las Pozas (see 'An Eccentric Englishman' in the Xilitla section, earlier).

Mocambo Luxury places here include pools, gardens and private beaches.

Hotel Mocambo (☎ 922-02-05, 800-290-01-00, fax 922-02-12, **e** hmocambo@ ifosel.net.mx, Ruiz Cortines 4000) Doubles US$93. The original luxury resort hotel in this area is the venerable Hotel Mocambo, 7km south of the city center. Once the best in Veracruz, it's now ever-so-slightly faded but still offers more character and style than most of the more modern places. It has terraced gardens, three sizable pools (two indoors) and more than 100 enormous rooms with air-conditioning, TV and a variety of views. Playa Mocambo is just a minute's walk from the foot of the terraced gardens.

Crowne Plaza Torremar (☎ 989-21-00, fax 989-21-21, Ruiz Cortines 4300) Rooms from US$109. This eight-story hotel has scores of excellent, large rooms. It's just been purchased by the Holiday Inn corporation, so expect imminent renovations and possible price hikes.

Hotel Playa Paraíso (☎ 923-07-00, **w** www.playaparaiso.com.mx, Ruiz Cortines 3500) Doubles from US$91, bungalows US$124. Smaller than its neighbors, the Playa Paraíso has rooms and suites that all sport lime green walls, smallish baths and breezy balconies.

Fiesta Inn (☎/fax 923-10-10, Boulevard Camacho s/n) Doubles from US$160. With an enormous pool, a bright lobby and simply gorgeous rooms, the Fiesta Inn is a very solid top-end choice.

Places to Eat

Food in Veracruz is nothing short of wonderful. Veracruzana sauce, found on fish all over Mexico, is made from onions, garlic, tomatoes, olives, green peppers and spices. A wide array of international cuisine is available – but with so much great, cheap Mexican fare around, why bother?

Zócalo Area The cafés under the portales are as much for drinks and atmosphere as for food. Stroll along the line and find one that appeals to you, or stop at any one with a free table. Typically, fish dishes run US$6, seafood cocktails US$4 and beer around US$1.50.

Restaurant Colonial Snacks US$2, steak US$9. At the Hotel Colonial, this bright, air-conditioned spot has pretty good food, but expect to burn a bit of cash.

Sanborns Restaurant Dishes US$2-13. On the west corner of the zócalo, Sanborns sits under its own set of portales. It's a tame, upscale and somewhat insipid alternative to the main square, but it offers the usual good-quality Sanborns snacks and meals in a squeaky-clean setting at reasonable prices.

El Querreque Dishes US$3-5. On the quieter southeast side of the zócalo, this restaurant offers good value and atmosphere. Main courses include a range of well-prepared seafood dishes.

Gran Café del Portal (Independencia 105) Coffee US$1.50, meals US$3-9. Open 6am-midnight daily. Years ago this spot was the site of a Veracruz institution known as the Gran Café de la Parroquia. After a change in ownership and moniker, it remains a cavernous, convivial café, and customers still request a refill of *café con leche* by clinking spoons on glasses, but so much of the atmosphere is gone. No more are the conspicuous coffee-making contraptions and colorful decorations, and the large-screen television detracts from the ambience. On the other hand, the food is better than ever, with typical dishes like fish veracruzano or steak tampiqueño. Particularly good are the pasta dishes and the famous milk coffee. If you wish for peace and quiet, avoid this place: it's a magnet for marimbas and mariachis, especially in the evening.

Cocina Económica Veracruz (cnr Zamora & Madero) Comida corrida US$2. Two blocks southwest of the zócalo, this place is aimed at locals, not tourists. It serves cheap, basic, wholesome Mexican food at unbeatable prices.

El Rincón de la Trova (Callejón Héroes de Nacozari s/n) Prices US$2-5. Two blocks south of the zócalo, look for the quaint Callejón Héroes de Nacozari, between Serdán and Arista. During the day here, popular places serve lunches at outdoor tables. In the evenings, the alley becomes more lively. El Rincón de la Trova turns on a large selection of alcoholic drinks and live music Friday and Saturday nights. The menu is limited to simple items such as tostadas, empanadas and tamales.

Harbor Inheriting the name, if not the ambience, of the original institution near the zócalo is *Gran Café de la Parroquia (Paseo del Malecón s/n)* Coffee US$1.50, meals US$3-9. Open 6am-midnight daily. Inheriting the name, if not the ambience, of the original institution near the zócalo is this vast restaurant-coffeehouse faces the harbor. The menu is the same as the Gran Café del Portal's, and it gets just as crowded. It's especially popular for breakfast, when the café con leche is in high demand.

The top floor of the municipal *fish market*, on Landero y Cos, is packed until early evening with *comedores* doing bargain fish filets and shrimp *al mojo de ajo*. Not for the faint of stomach, the market is heavy on atmosphere and fishy aromas.

La Suriana 2 (Zaragoza 286) Dishes US$2-8. La Suriana has a friendly family feel and excellent seafood at budget prices – come here for *cocteles*, soup and the freshest of fish.

Parque Zamora Area Between Zaragoza and Clavijero is *La Merced (Rayón s/n)* Prices US$3-8. This is Parque Zamora's jolly answer to the Gran Cafés. The filling comida corrida includes chicken soup, rice, chicken, sweets and a drink; also available are meat and fish dishes and antojitos.

Down the Coast Restaurants at Playa Mocambo tend to be pricey and boring. However, enjoying a seafood meal in the river-mouth village of Boca del Río, 10km south of Veracruz's center, is an indispensable part of a visit to Veracruz for many Mexicans – a long Sunday lunch is the favorite way to do it. *Pardiño's (Zamora 40)*, in the village center, is the best-known restaurant, but there are several more equally worthwhile ones along the riverside.

Mandinga, about 8km farther down the coast from Boca del Río, is also known for its seafood (especially prawns) and has a clutch of small restaurants.

Entertainment
A café seat under the zócalo portales is a ringside ticket to some of the best entertainment in town. There you might witness, in two blinks, crazily dancing couples, families with out-of-control kids, cruising transvestites and vendors hawking foam-rubber lizards – all to the accompaniment of wandering mariachis, marimba bands and guitarists vying to be heard above each other. Some evenings there's scheduled entertainment too, in the form of visiting musicians or dancers on a temporary stage. The level of excitement depends on the crowd – sometimes there are whole groups of revelers going wild; other times it's all staid tourists sitting at their tables waiting for something to happen.

You can watch the show for nothing from the paths and benches around the zócalo, but it's not too expensive to enjoy a drink in the portales. A beer is only US$1.50; mixed drinks run to US$4, and they're generous with the booze. Places at the east end of the portales, east of the plaza proper, are cheapest.

Rivaling the portales, especially for the under-thirty set, is the happening nightclub,

CENTRAL GULF COAST

The Crafty Countess

Local myth has it that during the colonial era, a countess who made her home in Veracruz didn't take too well to her husband's protracted absences. To while away the time, she took lovers from among the city's lesser nobility – and, to preserve her reputation, had a set of tunnels built between the buildings she visited most often.

Fanciful as such proceedings may seem, they are probably more accurate than further tales that have the countess murdering the lovers with whom she got bored. According to these stories, the tunnels served as escape routes from the crime scenes.

Rumor has it that tunnels still exist between the Palacio Municipal site and the cathedral, extending as far as the building presently housing the establishment known as 'La Casona de la Condesa.'

bar and disco scene along the waterfront Boulevard Camacho near the junction with Avenida Ruiz Cortines. The purple neon tower of **Hotel Lois** is the most conspicuous focus, and its lobby bar attracts a well-dressed crowd.

Most of the discos in this area charge a cover of US$3 to US$10. Women often get in cheaper, and Friday and Saturday nights are more expensive. Particularly popular discos for the beautiful set include **Ocean**, across from Hotel Lois; **Blue Ocean**, farther south; **Aquarius** and **Big Fish**, adjacent to each other; and **Zoo Disco**, about 2km beyond Blue Ocean. If you're serious about salsa dancing, try **Carioca**, in the Hotel Lois' building – but know your *pasos* beforehand to avoid embarrassment.

A bustling stop for mixed drinks, cheap beer and (appropriately enough) dancing on the tables is **Sobre Mesa**, adjacent to the chain behemoth **Carlos 'N' Charlie's**, which is home to an older (twenty- to thirty-something) crowd. Neither of these spots charges cover.

During holiday times, the entire boulevard area becomes an outdoor party, with bars and snack stalls along Boulevard Camacho, live, loud music, and dancing in the streets. It's quite the scene.

Those looking for a more relaxing, less teenybopper-oriented evening might try **La Casona de la Condesa**, which offers great mixed drinks and solid live music Thursday to Sunday nights. It's near the zócalo, adjacent to El Rincón de la Trova (see Places to Eat).

If you hanker for something more sedate, ask the tourist office for information on concerts and cultural events. A slew of cinemas show recent-release movies.

Getting There & Away

Passenger train service to Veracruz is, sadly, no more.

Air Frequent flights between Veracruz and Mexico City are offered by Mexicana (☎ 921-75-08) and Aeroméxico (☎ 800-021-40-00); the latter also flies to and from Tampico and Villahermosa, and Mexicana flies to Tampico and to Cancún via Mérida. Aerocaribe (☎ 922-52-05) has direct flights to Minatitlán, with onward connections to Cancún and other destinations.

Bus Veracruz is a major hub, with good services up and down the coast and inland along the Córdoba-Puebla-Mexico City corridor. Buses to and from Mexico City can be heavily booked at holiday times.

The renovated bus station is about 3km south of the zócalo. The 1st-class/deluxe area fronts Díaz Mirón on the corner with Xalapa and has mostly ADO (Autobuses de Oriente) 1st-class services, as well as some deluxe UNO and ADO GL buses. It's very modern, but quite inconvenient for users. The waiting area has phones and a snack bar, but you might not be allowed in if you don't have a ticket. The left-luggage room closes at night, and the only alternative is to buy a token for an over-priced locker. Behind the ADO station, the 2nd-class side is entered from Avenida Lafragua and has mostly AU and TRV services. There's a 24-hour luggage room here. Note that AU bus prices are 10% lower than 1st-class fares.

Acayucan – 250km, 3½ hours; 15 ADO (US$13), frequent AU

Catemaco – 165km, 3 hours; 7 ADO (US$8), 10 AU *directos*

Córdoba – 125km, 1½ hours; 27 ADO (US$6.50), hourly AU directos

Jalapa – 100km, 2 hours; ADO every 20 to 30 minutes 2.45am to 11.30pm (US$5.50), 25 AU

Mexico City (TAPO) – 430km, 5 hours; 7 UNO (US$37), 15 ADO GL (US$27), 15 ADO (US$23.50), 15 AU

Oaxaca – 460km, 6½ hours; ADO at 8.40am, 3.20pm and 10.30pm (US$27), 1 AU directo

Orizaba – 150km, 2 hours; frequent ADO (US$7.50) and AU directos

Papantla – 230km, 4 hours; 6 ADO (US$11.50), hourly AU

Poza Rica – 250km, 5 hours; 3 UNO (US$22.50), 22 ADO (US$11.50)

Puebla – 300km, 4 hours; 7 ADO (US$16.50), some AU directos

San Andrés Tuxtla – 155km, 2¾ hours; 22 ADO (US$7.50), frequent AU

Santiago Tuxtla – 140km, 2½ hours; 15 ADO (US$6.50), frequent AU

Tampico – 490km, 10 hours; 3 UNO (US$46), 17 ADO (US$27)

Tuxpan – 300km, 5½ hours; 8 ADO (US$15.50)

Villahermosa – 480km, 8 hours; 2 UNO (US$39), 13 ADO (US$23)

Buses leaving Veracruz also go to Campeche, Cancún, Chetumal, Matamoros, Mérida and Salina Cruz.

Car Many car rental agencies have desks at Veracruz's airport. The larger agencies scattered around town include National (☎ 931-17-56), Hertz (☎ 937-47-76), Budget (☎ 937-57-06) and Powerfull (☎ 932-85-73). Smaller agencies are worth calling if you're shopping around – try Today's (☎ 935-70-15) or Kanguro (☎ 937-95-77).

Getting Around
To/From the Airport Veracruz's airport is 11km southwest of town near highway 140. There is no bus service to or from town; taxis cost around US$12.

To/From the Bus Stations For the city center, take a bus marked 'Díaz Mirón y Madero' (US$0.45) from in front of the 1st-class bus station. It will head to Parque Zamora then up Madero. For the zócalo, get off on the corner of Madero and Lerdo and turn right. Returning to the depots, pick up the same bus going south on 5 de Mayo. At the booth outside the 1st-class depot you can buy a taxi ticket to the zócalo for US$2.30.

Down the Coast A bus marked 'Mocambo-Boca del Río' (US$0.45 in town, US$1 to Boca del Río) leaves every few minutes from the corner of Zaragoza and Serdán near the zócalo; it goes to Parque Zamora then down Boulevard Camacho to Mocambo (20 minutes; get off at Expover exhibition hall on Calzada Mocambo and walk down the street left of the Hotel Mocambo to the beach) and Boca del Río (30 minutes).

AU buses to Antón Lizardo stop at Boca del Río and Mandinga. They leave from the 2nd-class bus station every 20 minutes until 8.45pm; the last one back to town leaves around 8pm.

CÓRDOBA & FORTÍN DE LAS FLORES
Although Córdoba (pop 139,000, elev 924m, ☎ 271) lacks big-ticket natural or cultural attractions, this proud colonial town is worth a stop for its atmosphere alone. About 125km from Veracruz, the city lies in the foothills of Mexico's central mountains, surrounded by enticing, fecund countryside. Its inhabitants enjoy a cool, temperate climate, a laid-back lifestyle and some first-class cuisine.

In 1618, 30 Spanish families founded Córdoba to stop escaped black slaves from attacking travelers between Mexico City and the coast; consequently, the town is known as 'La Ciudad de los Treinta Caballeros' (City of the 30 Knights). Today it's a commercial and processing center for sugarcane, tobacco and coffee from the nearby hillsides and fruit from the lowlands.

Just west of Córdoba, Fortín de las Flores (pop 20,000, elev 970m, ☎ 271) is a center for commercial flower production, though most of the color is confined to the nurseries and to private gardens. Peaceful Fortín is popular as a weekend retreat for the Mexico City middle class, but there's very little for most travelers here.

Orientation
Córdoba's central Plaza de Armas sports fine 18th-century portales on three sides, with a row of busy cafés under the arches on the northeast. The city streets have numbers, not names. Avenidas 2, 4, 6 etc are northeast of the plaza; Avenidas 3, 5, 7 etc are southwest of the plaza. The *calles* are at

right angles to the Avenidas, with Calles 2, 4, 6 etc northwest of the plaza and the odd-numbered calles to the southeast.

Fortín's big, open plaza, the Parque Principal, shelters the Palacio Municipal in the middle and a cathedral on the south side. It's 7km from central Córdoba, but the towns have grown into each other along highway 150.

Information

Córdoba's tourist office (☎ 712-25-31) is in the Palacio Municipal, on the northwest side of the plaza (open 8.30am to 8pm Monday to Friday, 8.30am to 1pm Saturday). Its friendly staff offers some handy maps, brochures and a monthly schedule of activities, all in Spanish.

Córdoba's post office is on Avenida 3, just west of the Plaza de Armas. Banks around the plaza have ATMs and change traveler's checks, and a couple of casas de cambio on Avenida 3, southeast of the plaza, also change traveler's checks.

Internet access costs US$1.60 per hour at CETEC, a computer school on the west corner of Córdoba's plaza (open 7am to 9pm Monday to Friday, 8am to 6pm Saturday and Sunday). However, connections can be slow, and sometimes all the machines are being used for computer classes. Similar hours are kept by Cybermania, just off the plaza, which charges US$1.10 and boasts better connection speeds.

Things to See & Do

The **Ex-Hotel Zevallos**, built in 1687, is not a hotel but the former home of the *condes* (counts) of Zevallos. It's on the northeast side of Córdoba's Plaza de Armas, behind the portales. Plaques in the courtyard record that Juan O'Donojú and Agustín de Iturbide met here after mass on August 24, 1821, and agreed on terms for Mexico's independence. O'Donojú, the new viceroy, had concluded it was useless for Spain to try to cling to its colony; Iturbide, leader of the anti-imperial forces, was a former royalist general who had changed sides. Contrary to the Plan de Iguala, in which Iturbide and Vicente Guerrero had proposed a European monarch as Mexican head of state, O'Donojú and Iturbide agreed that a Mexican could hold that office. Iturbide went on to a brief reign as Emperor Agustín I. The building is now notable mainly for its excellent restaurants (see Places to Eat).

At the southeast end of Plaza de Armas, the sprawling late-18th-century church is **La Parroquia de la Inmaculada Concepción**, famous for its loud bells.

Just off the plaza, the **Museo de Antropología** *(Calle 3 s/n; admission free;*

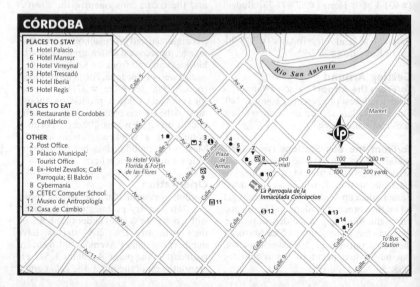

CÓRDOBA

PLACES TO STAY
1 Hotel Palacio
6 Hotel Mansur
10 Hotel Virreynal
13 Hotel Trescadó
14 Hotel Iberia
15 Hotel Regis

PLACES TO EAT
5 Restaurante El Cordobés
7 Cantábrico

OTHER
2 Post Office
3 Palacio Municipal; Tourist Office
4 Ex-Hotel Zevallos; Café Parroquia; El Balcón
8 Cybermania
9 CETEC Computer School
11 Museo de Antropología
12 Casa de Cambio

open 9am-2pm & 4pm-8pm daily) has a modest but well-presented collection of originals and replicas of indigenous artifacts from around the area. Displays include a Classic Veracruz *palma* and some beautifully crafted personal ornaments.

In Fortín, the most fulfilling activity is to pick out a choice spot in the central plaza as the shadows lengthen, kick back with a cool drink and revel in the fresh-smelling tranquility of the town.

Activities

Faraventuras (W *http://communities.msn .com.mx/faraventuras*) runs trips to waterfalls, caves, underground rivers and other natural attractions in the area. Climbs on Pico de Orizaba, for a group of six, cost around US$60 per person per day with guide, equipment and food. A three-day expedition to the summit, with all equipment, accommodations and food, runs US$250 per person in a group of six. You can contact the company at its head office in the Xochítl travel agency (☎ 713-16-95, Avenida 3 Pte), at Calle 2, in Fortín de las Flores – it's just a couple of blocks from the plaza.

Special Events

On the evening of Good Friday, Córdoba marks Jesus' crucifixion with a procession of silence, in which thousands of residents walk through the streets behind an altar of the Virgin. Everyone holds a lit candle, no one utters a word, and the church bells are eerily quiet.

April, May and June are the best months to see flowers blooming; Fortín's annual flower festival runs for a week in late April or early May.

Places to Stay

Inexpensive but acceptable accommodations huddle together on Avenida 2 in Córdoba, only three blocks downhill from the plaza.

Hotel Trescadó (☎ 712-23-74, Avenida 2 No 909) Singles/doubles US$6/7, US$1 extra for cruddy TV. The Trescadó is very bare and basic. Rooms lack fans, and only a low wall separates them from grimy private bathrooms, but they sure are cheap. Parking is an extra US$1.

Hotel Iberia (☎ 712-13-01, Avenida 2 No 919) Singles/doubles US$12/14.50. The Iberia has small, modern rooms with TV and fan, set around a courtyard. Pretty paintings and amiable management lend the establishment a cozy atmosphere.

Hotel Regis (☎ 712-12-10, Avenida 2 No 929) Doubles US$9.50, US$14 with two beds. Rooms here are cramped and musty, but they're still a better value than the holes at the Trescadó.

Hotel Virreynal (☎ 712-23-77, fax 712-03-95, Avenida 1 No 309) Singles/doubles US$24.50/26.50. Housed in a colonial building, this hotel provides sumptuous, immaculate fan-cooled rooms. Viceroy-worthy decor and services render it a fantastic value.

Hotel Mansur (☎ 712-60-00, 712-69-89, Avenida 1 No 301) Singles/doubles US$34/38. If you're looking for historical character, it doesn't get much better than the Mansur. The lobby is elegant and the rooms well decked out, with cable TV, phone and air-conditioning. It's not a great value unless you manage to wrangle an upstairs room overlooking the plaza.

Hotel Palacio (☎ 712-21-88, fax 712-60-78, Avenida 3 No 200) Singles/doubles US$22/28. The modern Palacio is lacking in style, but the rooms are spacious and clean, and the air-conditioning is whisper-quiet. Many of the upper rooms have wonderful views of Pico de Orizaba, while others have windows facing the corridor.

Hotel Villa Florida (☎ 716-33-33, fax 716-33-36, e *vflorida@ver1.telmex.net.mx, Avenida 1 No 3002)* Singles/doubles US$83/110. Cocky in its self-awareness as Córdoba's most upmarket option, the Villa Florida will reach deep into your pocket. The location, 1.5km northwest of the center, is not the most convenient, but facilities are wonderful (including a big pool, lovely gardens with a fountain, a restaurant and 82 tasteful, fresh-smelling, air-conditioned rooms).

Hotel Posada Loma (☎ 713-06-58, fax 712-1454, e *posada66@prodigy.net.mx, Km 33 Boulevard Córdoba-Fortín)* Large rooms (up to four guests) US$56. If you're vacillating on splurging in the area, stay here. The rooms are well equipped and a good value in themselves, but what really makes this place is the environs: acres of gardens and terraces offering countless opportunities for bird watching and plant identifying (don't miss the orchid collection). Breakfast in the

CENTRAL GULF COAST

restaurant, which offers a spectacular view of the Pico de Orizaba, is unbeatable. An inviting pool and friendly management sweeten the deal. This attractive hotel is off the south side of highway 150, about 2km from Fortín de las Flores.

Hotel El Pueblito (☎ 713-00-33, fax 713-10-88, Avenida 2 Ote 503) Singles/doubles US$26.50/33.50. This 'little village' is a slightly humbler option than the Villa Florida, but it's quite charming in its own right. The spacious, comfortable rooms are named, not numbered, and laid out to resemble a small town. A gem of a swimming pool, tennis courts and bulk bougainvillea combine to create a delightful atmosphere. Look for the entrance between Calles 9 and 11 Nte.

Places to Eat

Food in Córdoba is far superior to the offerings in Fortín. For fine seafood, try the restaurants on Calle 15 between Avenidas 5 and 7. Ultrafresh fish dishes and seafood cocktails are yours for around US$6, and chefs are happy to be creative if requested. At the time of research, local favorite *Restaurant-Bar Díaz* was closed, but it may open up again by the time you arrive.

The Plaza de Armas' portales, also in Córdoba, are lined with high-quality cafés and restaurants where you can eat well at any hour or just enjoy the local coffee.

Café Parroquia Prices US$3-8. Egg dishes, antojitos, and fish and meat dishes are all splendid here, and the coffee caps off a meal nicely.

Restaurante El Cordobés Comida corrida US$4.50. Popular and pricey, El Cordobés isn't a great bargain unless you come in time for the four-course set lunch.

El Balcón Dishes US$6-10. Upstairs in the Ex-Hotel Zevallos building, overlooking the plaza, this spot enjoys one of the town's best locations. The steaks are solid and the desserts delectable.

Cantábrico (Calle 3 No 9) Dishes US$8-10. Slightly upscalish in ambience, the Cantábrico charges a little extra for its well-prepared main courses. If you're looking for quality cuisine, this is an excellent choice.

Crepas Y Carnes Los 30's (Avenida 9 s/n) Crêpes US$8-10. A lively spot for a late lunch or early dinner, this place is tucked

between Calles 20 and 22. It's a good trek from the zócalo but worth it for the colorful decor, party atmosphere and big selection of mouthwatering sweet and savory crêpes.

Colorines (Calle 1 Nte s/n) Dishes US$4-6. Fortín doesn't offer too many exciting eating options. This steak house, just north of the plaza, will get you the beef, but it ain't nothing to write home to the ranch about.

Lolo (Calle 1 Nte s/n) Prices US$5-10. A block north of Colorines, Lolo is to seafood as Colorines is to steak. You'll leave feeling satisfied but not thrilled.

Getting There & Away

Bus Córdoba's bus station, with deluxe (UNO and ADO GL), 1st-class (ADO and Cristóbal Colón) and 2nd-class (AU) services, is at Avenida Privada 4, 3km southeast of the plaza. To get to the town center from the station, take a local bus marked 'Centro' or buy a taxi ticket (US$1.50). To Fortín de las Flores and Orizaba, it's more convenient to take a local bus (US$1.10) from Avenida 11 than to go out to the Córdoba bus station. As always, 2nd-class buses run more often to mid-range destinations, take longer and cost 10% less than the corresponding 1st-class service. Long-distance deluxe and 1st-class buses from Córdoba include the following:

Jalapa – 260km, 3½ hours; 17 ADO (US$9)

Mexico City (TAPO) – 305km, 4½ hours; 2 UNO (US$28.50), 6 ADO GL (US$21), 23 ADO (US$18)

Oaxaca – 317km, 6 hours; ADO at 12.10am and 10am (US$20.50)

Puebla – 175km, 3 hours; 14 ADO (US$11)

Veracruz – 125km, 2 hours; 27 ADO (US$6.50)

In Fortín, local buses arrive and depart from Calle 1 Sur, on the west side of the plaza. A small ADO depot on the corner of Avenida 2 and Calle 6 has mainly de paso services to Mexico City, Veracruz, Puebla and Jalapa. UNO has two daily deluxe buses to Mexico City; ADO GL has one. Prices are more or less the same as those from Córdoba.

Car & Motorcycle Córdoba, Fortín de las Flores and Orizaba are linked by the toll road (highway 150D), which buses take, and the much slower highway 150. A scenic back road goes through the hills from Fortín, via Huatusco, to Jalapa.

ORIZABA
• pop 120,300 • elev 1219m ☎ 272

Orizaba, 16km west of Córdoba, was founded by the Spanish to guard the Veracruz-Mexico City road. It retains a few colonial buildings and church domes, though much was lost in the 1973 earthquake. An industrial center in the late 19th century, its factories were early centers of the unrest that led to the unseating of dictator Porfirio Díaz. Today it has a big brewery and cement, textile and chemical industries.

Though a major economic hub, the city isn't particularly compelling, and most foreign visitors use it only as a base for climbing Pico de Orizaba, one of Mexico's most spectacular volcanoes and its highest peak. One jewel in the Orizaba rough, though, is the excellent art museum.

Orientation & Information
Orizaba's central plaza is the Parque del Castillo, with the irregularly shaped Parroquia de San Miguel on its north side. Madero, a busy street bordering the plaza's west side, divides *avenidas* into Oriente (Ote; east) and Poniente (Pte; west). Avenida Colón, on the south side, is the boundary between the Norte and Sur streets. All other streets have numbers rather than names – check out the map to learn the strange logic of the system. Avenida Pte 7/Avenida Ote 6, three blocks south of the plaza, is the main east-west artery.

The tourist office (☎ 726-58-71) is back in its old digs at the Ex-Palacio Municipal, just off the main plaza (open 8am to 9pm Monday to Friday, 8am to 3pm Saturday). Avenida Ote 2, a block south of the plaza, houses a couple of banks with ATMs. Access the Internet in the next block at Cybercity for US$1.10 per hour (open 8.30am to 10pm Monday to Saturday). The post office is on the corner a block farther east.

Parque del Castillo
Although Orizaba's central plaza isn't as attractive or festive as one might wish, it does abut some noteworthy attractions. The **Parroquia de San Miguel**, the big parish church on the park's north side, is mainly

17th century in style, with several towers and some Puebla-type tiles.

The **Ex-Palacio Municipal**, off the northwest corner of the plaza, was the Belgian pavilion at the Paris International Exhibition in the late 19th century. Orizaba bought the prefabricated cast-iron and steel building for US$13,800 and had it dismantled, shipped to Mexico and reassembled as a town hall. Many municipal offices have been moved to the new Palacio Municipal, and the renovated old building now holds only the tourist office, some other government chambers and a café.

Museo de Arte del Estado
The highlight of Orizaba is the State Art Museum (☎ 724-32-00, Avenida Ote 4; admission US$1.10, free Sun; open 10am-5pm Tue-Sun), between Calles 25 and 27. This masterpiece is housed in a splendidly restored colonial building dating from 1776 that has been at times a church, a hospital and a military base. The museum itself consists of many rooms, each of which adheres to a different theme. In one room, exquisite paintings depict key moments in the history of Veracruz state. Another has contemporary works by regional artists; still another depicts Veracruz through the eyes of travelers. Although some of the works by Diego Rivera have been moved to Jalapa, there's still a respectable collection of 20th-century Mexican paintings and drawings.

Activities
The canyon beside the Hotel Fiesta Cascada (see Places to Stay) features a beautiful waterfall emerging from dense forest, offering spectacular hiking possibilities. A forest-flanked trail begins a few meters west of the hotel and descends to the canyon floor, where it forks. To the left, the trail follows the river for several kilometers. To the right, it crosses a footbridge beside the waterfall and a small power station, then reaches a rough road that winds northwest into the mountains, through forest and farmland.

Looming over the Alameda park west of town, the Cerro del Barrego offers brilliant views if you get to the top very early, before the mist rolls in.

Turismo Aventura Desafío (☎ 725-06-96, Pte 3 No 586) arranges various adventure

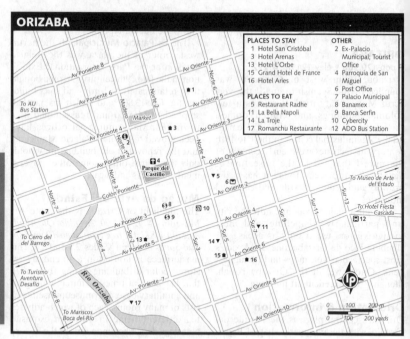

ORIZABA

PLACES TO STAY
1 Hotel San Cristóbal
3 Hotel Arenas
13 Hotel L'Orbe
15 Grand Hotel de France
16 Hotel Aries

PLACES TO EAT
5 Restaurant Radhe
11 La Bella Napoli
14 La Troje
17 Romanchu Restaurante

OTHER
2 Ex-Palacio
  Municipal; Tourist
  Office
4 Parroquia de San
  Miguel
6 Post Office
7 Palacio Municipal
8 Banamex
9 Banca Serfin
10 Cybercity
12 ADO Bus Station

activities in nearby hills, mountains and canyons, including climbs of the Pico de Orizaba (see Around Orizaba). A one-day climb costs about US$170 per person.

Places to Stay

Hotel Arenas (☎ 725-23-61, e abelac@ prodigy.net.mx, Nte 2 No 169) Singles/ doubles with bath US$12/17. Orizaba's best budget value is this friendly, family-run hotel, which boasts a central location and a quiet courtyard garden. The helpful management has good information about the area. Clean rooms come with cable TV, but the bathrooms can be odoriferous.

Hotel San Cristóbal (☎ 725-11-40, Nte 4 No 243) Singles/doubles US$9/13. Cheaper than the Arenas but less charming is the San Cristóbal. Its smallish, tiled rooms are modern and clean, but those facing the street can be noisy.

Grand Hotel de France (☎ 725-23-11, fax 725-44-44, Ote 6 No 186) Old singles/doubles US$20/21, remodeled ones US$26/30. With cheerfully decorated rooms surrounding an old-fashioned courtyard, this hotel empow-

ers your peso. Renovated rooms aren't that much better than the old ones.

Hotel Aries (☎ 725-35-20, Ote 6 No 263) Singles/doubles US$22/27. For more modern amenities, try this reasonably priced hotel. Bright, comfortable rooms come with cable TV, phone, air-conditioning and cute paintings.

Hotel L'Orbe (☎ 725-50-33, fax 725-53-44, Pte 5 No 33) Singles/doubles US$33/39. Enormous, squeaky-clean rooms render this hotel an even better mid-range value than the Aries. The remodeled quarters feature air-conditioning, cable TV and phones.

Hotel Fiesta Cascada (☎ 724-15-96, fax 724-55-99, Carretera Puebla-Córdoba Km 275) Singles/doubles US$39/44. If you don't mind the long hike or taxi ride (head down highway 150D and look for two Pemex stations opposite each other, about 2km east of the center), you should consider staying here. The Cascada sits above a gorgeous canyon and has a pool, gardens and a private patch of rain forest. Charming, spacious rooms with minibar, TV and phone come at an unbeatable price.

Places to Eat
Some decent taco joints lie around the plaza, and the market, as always, offers cheap eats. Most of the moderately priced restaurants close early – Orizaba is far from a party town.

Restaurant Radhe (Sur 5) Dishes US$5. This place offers respectable, if not completely authentic, Indian vegetarian food. It's a nice break from tacos and carne asada.

La Troje (Sur 5) Comida corrida US$4. Farther south, La Troje offers an upscale atmosphere and an excellent five-course comida corrida. Mexican specialties are the order of the day.

La Bella Napoli (Sur 7) Dishes US$5-11. Come here for the best pizza in town.

Romanchu Restaurante (Pte 7) Dishes US$5-9. A nonvegetarian paradise, the large and colorful Romanchu is popular for its exquisite beef dishes.

Mariscos Boca del Río (Pte 7) Seafood US$5-7. Don't be deterred by its humble appearance: this is the best seafood restaurant in town. A few blocks west of the Romanchu, it offers large and reasonably priced shrimp, fish and squid dishes. An imposter restaurant of the same name lies north of the plaza.

Getting There & Away
Bus Local buses from Fortín or Córdoba stop four blocks north and six blocks east of the town center, around Ote 9 and Nte 14. The AU (2nd-class) bus station is at Zaragoza Pte 425, northwest of the center. To reach the city center from here, turn left outside the depot, cross the bridge, take the first fork right and head for the church domes.

The 1st-class bus station, on Ote 6 at Sur 13, has been fully modernized and handles all ADO, ADO GL and deluxe UNO services (one day it may even replace the inconveniently located 2nd-class station).

Jalapa – 240km, 4 hours; 10 ADO (US$10)

Mexico City (TAPO) – 285km, 4 hours; 2 UNO (US$27), 3 ADO GL (US$19.50), 13 ADO (US$17), frequent AU

Puebla – 160km, 2½ hours; 14 ADO (US$10), frequent AU

Veracruz – 150km, 2¼ hours; 25 ADO (US$7.50), frequent AU directo

There is also 1st-class service to Oaxaca, Tehuacán, Tampico and Villahermosa.

Car & Motorcycle Toll highway 150D, which bypasses central Orizaba, goes east to Córdoba and west, via a spectacular ascent, to Puebla (160km). Toll-free highway 150 runs east to Córdoba and Veracruz (150km) and southwest to Tehuacán, 65km away over the hair-raising Cumbres de Acultzingo.

AROUND ORIZABA
Pico de Orizaba
Mexico's tallest mountain (5611m), called 'Citlaltépetl' (Star Mountain) in the Náhuatl language, is 25km northwest of Orizaba. The dormant volcano has a small crater and a three-month snowcap. From the summit, in good weather, one can see Popocatépetl, Iztaccíhuatl and La Malinche to the west and the Gulf of Mexico 96km to the east. The only higher peaks in North America are Mt McKinley in Alaska and Mt Logan in Canada.

The most common route up Orizaba is from the north, using the small town of **Tlachichuca** as a base. Tlachichuca can be reached by white microbuses departing the bus terminal in Ciudad Serdán (1 hour, US$0.90). Serdán, in turn, can be reached from Puebla (2 hours, US$3) or Orizaba (2 hours, US$3.30). Infrequent AU buses also run directly between Tlachichuca and Puebla (4 hours, US$4).

Unless you have navigation skills and a good map, and your group has some experience of snow- and ice-climbing techniques, you should not attempt this climb without a guide. Remember to allow several days for acclimatization beforehand. From Tlachichuca, take a taxi to Villa Hidalgo at 3400m (15km, US$15), then walk 10km farther to the mountain hut (*refugio* or *albergue*) called 'Piedra Grande,' at 4200m. This walk will help with acclimatization, though it's also possible to charter a 4WD all the way to Piedra Grande. The refugio is big but basic, and you'll need to bring a sleeping mat, sleeping bag, stove and cooking gear. Most climbers start at about 2am for the final climb and try to reach the summit around sunrise or shortly after, before mist and cloud envelop the mountain. The climb is moderately steep over snow that is usually hard – it's not technically difficult (though classified as 'extreme' by international standards), but crampons are essential (especially for the descent), as are ropes and ice axes for safety. Allow five to 10 hours for the ascent (depending on the conditions and your abilities) and another three hours to return to the refugio. You can arrange to be picked up by 4WD at Piedra Grande after returning from the climb.

An alternative and less-used route is from the south, via the villages of Atzitzintla and Texmalaquilla and a refugio at 4750m. A guide is recommended for this route.

Experienced climbers doing the northern route can make all the necessary arrangements in Tlachichuca, but get maps well in advance. The 1:50,000 INEGI map is supposed to be the best, but it can be hard to obtain. Some specialist books on climbing in Mexico have adequate maps, including *Mexico's Volcanoes*, by RJ Secor. The best climbing period is October to March, with the most popular (and crowded) time being December and January.

In Tlachichuca, the Reyes family runs *Servimont* (☎ 245-451-50-09, fax 245-451-50-19, [e] info@servimont.com.mx, [w] www .servimont.com.mx, Ortega 1A), a climber-owned and -operated outfit that offers a wide range of trips up the mountain. Basic accommodations and good meals are available in a charming former soap factory that also serves as the company office. Servimont also acts as a Red Cross rescue facility and has an excellent reputation for safety. It's the longest-running operation in the area by far. Make reservations two to three months in advance. A three-day trip, including guide and rentals, costs about US$500 per person.

Other guides also operate in Tlachichuca and you can book them in Orizaba and elsewhere. They may offer lower rates than Servimont, but a few have been known to cut corners when it comes to safety. A reader-recommended guide in Tlachichuca is Joaquín Canchola Limón (☎/fax 245-451-40-82, Avenida 3 Pte No 3). It's even possible to make Pico de Orizaba trips from as far away as Oaxaca, where the adventure tourism firm Tierra Dentro (see 'Turismo Alternativo' in the Oaxaca State chapter) offers a range of trips lasting between three and six days for US$200 to US$650 per person. Some start with an acclimatization night at an atmospheric abandoned hacienda in Tlaxcala.

If you're not staying with Servimont, you can hole up in Tlachichuca at *Hotel Las 3 Garcías* (☎ 245-451-50-35, Juárez 52) or the more friendly and commodious *Hotel Gerar* (☎ 245-451-50-75, Avenida 20 de Noviembre 200). Both offer basic rooms for US$13; the latter can help with arranging guides and providing information. On the plaza, *La Casa Blanca* serves up a righteous steak for US$4.50.

Zongolica

A road leads 38km south from Orizaba to this mountain village, where isolated indigenous groups have unique styles of weaving. Buses leave from Ote 3 between Nte 12 and Nte 14 every half-hour.

TLACOTALPAN

• pop 9000 • elev 155m ☎ 288

A very quiet old town beside the wide Río Papaloapan, Tlacotalpan was a major port in the 19th century and has preserved its broad plazas, colorful houses and pretty streets.

The best entertainment in town consists of sitting by the riverbank and watching the water go by. If that's a little too *tranquilo*, head for the **Museo Salvador Ferrando** (*Alegre 6; admission US$0.90; open 10.30am-5pm Tue-Sun*), facing Plaza Hidalgo, which displays an eclectic, confusing slew of assorted furniture and artifacts recalling Tlacotalpan's glory days. The pink **Casa de la Cultura**, six blocks east on Carranza off Plaza Zaragoza, features memorabilia from Agustín Lara (1900-70), a local musician, composer and pioneering radio personality.

Tlacotalpan's lively Candelaria festival, in late January and early February, features bull-running in the streets and an image of the Virgin floating down the river followed by a flotilla of small boats.

Hotel Reforma (☎ 884-20-22, Carranza 2) Singles/doubles US$16.50/22, US$25/31 with air-con. Right off Plaza Zaragoza, this hotel is clean, cool, sunny and friendly.

Posada Doña Lala (☎ 884-25-80, fax 884-24-55, Carranza 11) Singles/doubles US$20/25, US$26/30 with air-con. Doña Lala is near the river, a block from the Reforma, and boasts a bit o' character. Rooms are spotless and spacious.

For good eats, try the Doña Lala's restaurant or one of the breezy eateries along the riverfront (fish and meat dishes US$4-5).

Highway 175 runs from Tlacotalpan up the Papaloapan valley to Tuxtepec, then twists and turns over the mountains to Oaxaca (320km from Tlacotalpan). ADO offers service to Mexico City, Puebla, Jalapa and Veracruz, while Cuenca and TLT buses run along local routes.

Los Tuxtlas & Southeast Veracruz

South and southeast of Tlacotalpan, around the towns of Santiago Tuxtla and San Andrés Tuxtla, is a hilly, green and fertile region known as Los Tuxtlas ('TOOKS-lahs'), home to myriad lakes and waterfalls, as well as an agreeable climate. Mexican vacationers are attracted to Catemaco, a small lakeside resort, while the undeveloped coastline is increasingly popular with foreign visitors.

Los Tuxtlas is the western fringe of the ancient Olmec heartland, and Olmec artifacts can be observed at Santiago Tuxtla, Tres Zapotes and San Lorenzo. The basalt for the huge Olmec heads was quarried from Cerro Cintepec in the east of the Sierra de los Tuxtlas and then moved, probably by roller and raft, to San Lorenzo, 60km to the south.

The southeastern end of Veracruz state, bordering Tabasco and Chiapas, is home to oil metropolises such as Minatitlán and Coatzacoalcos, neither of which holds any attractions for visitors other than the fun of pronouncing their names.

SANTIAGO TUXTLA
• pop 16,000 • elev 285m ☎ 294

Santiago, founded in 1525, is a quiet valley town in the rolling green foothills of the volcanic Sierra de los Tuxtlas. Though a soothing stopover in its own right, it's worth visiting mainly for the Olmec artifacts around town and at Tres Zapotes, 23km away.

Orientation & Information

ADO and AU buses arriving in Santiago drop you where Calle Morelos runs off the highway. Go south (downhill) down

Morelos a little and the Transportes Los Tuxtlas office will be on your left; turn right (west) here onto Ayuntamiento to reach the museum, on the south side of the zócalo. The post office is also on the zócalo, as are banks that change traveler's checks.

Things to See & Do

The **Olmec head** in the zócalo is known as the 'Cobata head,' after the estate west of Santiago where it was found. Thought to be a very late or even post-Olmec production, it's the biggest known Olmec head and unique in that its eyes are closed.

The **Museo Regional Tuxteco** (☎ 947-10-76; admission US$3, free Sun; open 9am-6pm Mon-Sun), on the plaza, exhibits Olmec stone carvings, including another colossal head (this one from Nestepec west of Santiago), a rabbit head from Cerro de Vigía and a copy of Monument F, or 'El Negro,' from Tres Zapotes, which is an altar or throne with a human form carved into it. Countless small tools and other artifacts are also on display here.

Special Events

Santiago celebrates the festivals of San Juan (June 24) and Santiago Apóstol (St James; July 25) with processions and dances including the Liseres, in which the participants wear jaguar costumes. The dance costumes also come out the week before Christmas.

Places to Stay & Eat

Hotel Morelos (☎ 947-04-74, Obregón 12) Singles/doubles US$13.50/18, twins US$22. This family-run hotel has its entrance on Obregón, which runs off Morelos almost opposite the Transportes Los Tuxtlas bus station, a block south of Ayuntamiento. The rooms are small, cozy and neat; some are brighter than others. All have cable TV, fans and private bath with hot water.

Hotel Castellanos (☎ 947-02-00, fax 947-04-00, cnr 5 de Mayo & Comonfort) Singles/doubles US$26/28.50. The modern Castellanos, in a circular building on the north side of the zócalo, is an unbelievable value. It's a beautiful establishment with all the modern facilities – surprising for a town of this size. The charming, round rooms are complemented by a refreshing swimming pool and incredible views. The restaurant serves

LOS TUXTLAS

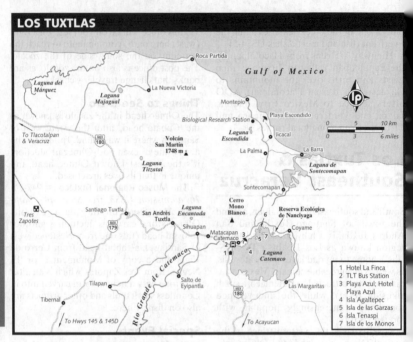

1 Hotel La Finca
2 TLT Bus Station
3 Playa Azul; Hotel Playa Azul
4 Isla Agaltepec
5 Isla de las Garzas
6 Isla Tenaspi
7 Isla de los Monos

decent main courses for around US$3.50. Cheaper eateries line up on the south side of the zócalo.

Getting There & Away

If no convenient services are available out of Santiago Tuxtla, go first to San Andrés Tuxtla by the frequent but suspension-free buses of Transportes Los Tuxtlas (30 minutes, US$0.60) or less frequent Cuenca vehicles (20 minutes, US$0.70).

ADO and AU both use the same office beside the main road, where buses stop on the way through. Cuenca is a local company using the same office. From Santiago, ADO has eight de paso buses a day going west to Veracruz (2½ hours, US$6.50) via Alvarado, five a day going east to Coatzacoalcos (2 hours, US$8) via Catemaco (1 hour, US$1.75), and four a day to Acayucan (2 hours, US$5). Cuenca has three buses a day to Tlacotalpan (US$4). Cheaper but less comfortable Transportes Los Tuxtlas buses depart every 10 minutes for San Andrés Tuxtla, Catemaco and Veracruz, and hourly for Acayucan. Colectivo taxis frequently leave Ayuntamiento for San Andrés Tuxtla (US$2.50).

TRES ZAPOTES
• pop 3500 ☎ 294

The important late-Olmec center of Tres Zapotes is now just a series of mounds in maize fields, but many interesting finds are displayed at the museum in the village of Tres Zapotes, 23km west of Santiago Tuxtla.

History

Tres Zapotes was occupied for over 2000 years, from around 1200 BC to AD 1000. It was probably first inhabited while the great Olmec center of La Venta (Tabasco) still flourished. After the destruction of La Venta (about 600 BC), the city carried on in what archaeologists regard as an 'epi-Olmec' phase – a period when the spark had gone out of Olmec culture, and other civilizations, notably Izapa, were adding their marks. Most of the finds are from this later period.

At Tres Zapotes in 1939, Matthew Stirling, the first great Olmec excavator, unearthed part of an interesting chunk of basalt. One side was carved with an epi-Olmec 'were-jaguar,' the other with a series of bars and dots, apparently part of a date in the Mayan

celebrating Día de Todos los Santos, Morelia

Friendly neighbors, Michoacán

Planting blue agave for future tequila shots

Guadalajara food market

Mariachi, Guadalajara

GREG ELMS

Habanero chiles for everyone, Veracruz

GREG ELMS

Fish seller, Veracruz

GREG ELMS

A peck of papayas, Veracruz

GREG ELMS

A spoonful of shrimp cocktail, Veracruz

JOHN NEUBAUER

Museo de Antropología, Jalapa

Long Count system. Stirling decoded the date as September 3, 32 BC, which meant that the Olmecs preceded the Maya; until then, the Maya were believed to have been Mexico's earliest civilization. Much debate followed, but later finds supported Stirling's discovery. In 1969 a farmer came across the rest of the stone, now called Stela C, which bore the missing part of Stirling's date.

Museo Arqueológico

At the Tres Zapotes museum (admission US$2.50, free Sun; open 8am-6pm daily), the objects are arranged on a disappointingly small cross-shaped platform. On the far side is the Tres Zapotes head, dating from about 100 BC, which was the first Olmec head to be discovered in modern times; it was found by a hacienda worker in 1858. Opposite the head is Stela A, the biggest piece, with three human figures in the mouth of a jaguar. This originally stood on its end. To the right of Stela A are two pieces. One is a sculpture of what may have been a captive with hands tied behind his or her back. The other piece has a toad carved on one side and a skull on the other.

Beyond Stela A is an altar or throne carved with the upturned face of a woman, and beyond that, in the corner, is the less interesting part of the famous Stela C. (The part with the date is in the Museo Nacional de Antropología, but a photo of it is on the wall here.) The museum attendant is happy to answer questions (in Spanish) or give a tour (be nice and tip him US$0.50 or so).

Getting There & Away

The road to Tres Zapotes goes southwest from Santiago Tuxtla (a 'Zona Arqueológica' sign points the way from highway 180). Eight kilometers down this road, you fork right onto a newly paved stretch for the last 15km to Tres Zapotes village. It comes out at a T-junction next to the Sitio Olmeca taxi stand. From here you walk to the left, then turn left again to reach the museum.

To get to Tres Zapotes, take a green-and-white taxi from Santiago Tuxtla (US$1.75 if it's going colectivo, US$10 if you have it all to yourself). They leave from the Sitio Puente Real, on the far side of the pedestrian bridge at the foot of Zaragoza, the street going downhill beside the Santiago

Tuxtla museum. Infrequent TLT buses also make the trip (US$1.10).

SAN ANDRÉS TUXTLA
• pop 56,900 • elev 365m ☎ 294

San Andrés is in the center of Los Tuxtlas, surrounded by countryside producing maize, bananas, beans, sugarcane, cattle and tobacco (the town is Mexico's cigar capital). San Andrés itself is bustling but not particularly interesting; however, several scenic attractions are nearby, including the dormant Volcán San Martín (1748m).

Orientation & Information

The main bus station is on Juárez, a full annoying kilometer northwest of the plaza. The cathedral is on the plaza's north side, the Palacio Municipal on the west side and a Banamex on the south side. The market is three blocks west.

The post office is on Lafragua; head down 20 de Noviembre directly across the plaza from the Palacio Municipal and follow it around to the left. From the post office, turn left on Suárez and head a block uphill to find Internépolis, which offers lickety-split Internet access for US$1.10 per hour (open 8am-11pm daily).

Things to See & Do

You can see and smell the *puros* being rolled by hand at the **Santa Clara cigar factory** (*admission free; open 8am-5pm Mon-Fri, 8am-11am Sat*), on the highway a block or so from the bus station. Cigars in assorted shapes and sizes are available for purchase at factory prices.

Twelve kilometers from San Andrés, a 242-step staircase leads down to the **Salto de Eyipantla**, a 50m-high, 40m-wide waterfall. Follow highway 180 east for 4km to Sihuapan, then turn right down a dirt road to Eyipantla; frequent Transportes Los Tuxtlas buses make the trip (US$1).

The **Laguna Encantada** (Enchanted Lagoon), a lake that rises in dry weather and falls when it rains, occupies a small volcanic crater 3km northeast of San Andrés. A dirt road goes there but no buses; some travelers have reported muggings in the area.

At Cerro del Gallo near **Matacapan**, just east of Sihuapan, is a pyramid in Teotihuacán style, dating from AD 300 to 600. It may

CENTRAL GULF COAST

have been on the route to Kaminaljuyú in Guatemala, the farthest Teotihuacán outpost.

Places to Stay

For the cheapest hotels, turn left when you hit the plaza from Juárez, then take the second right, where the road ends; this is Pino Suárez. For mid-range places to stay and eat, turn right down Madero when approaching the plaza from Juárez.

Hotel Figueroa *(☎ 942-02-57, Pino Suárez 10)* Singles/doubles US$11/13.50, US$3 more with TV. The Figueroa offers clean, dim and cramped rooms for a decent price. All rooms have hot water and fan; rooms 34 to 42 have views.

Hotel Colonial *(☎ 942-05-52, cnr Pino Suárez & Domínguez)* Singles US$5.50, larger singles/doubles US$7.50/9. A nicely cheap choice, this place provides tiny but well-maintained rooms with decent beds and hot water.

Hotel Catedral *(☎ 942-02-37, cnr Pino Suárez & Bocanegra)* Singles/doubles US$6.50/8.50. Rooms here are small and unsparkly, but the glittery price allows you to overlook any small defects.

Hotel Posada San José *(☎ 942-10-10, Domínguez 10)* Singles/doubles US$13.50/ 16.50, US$21/28 with air-con. A few doors up Domínguez from the Figueroa is the Posada San José, which offers 30 tidy, pleasantly decorated rooms around a peaceful closed courtyard. Some toilets lack seats.

Hotel del Parque *(☎ 942-01-98, fax 942-30-50, Madero 5)* Singles/doubles US$26/32.50. Right on the zócalo, this hotel offers bright and clean but insipid rooms with fan and air-conditioning in the same room!

Hotel de los Pérez *(☎ 942-07-77, 800-290-3900, fax 942-36-46, Rascón 2)* Singles/ doubles US$24.50/33.50. The Hotel de los Pérez is just down the street beside the Hotel del Parque and offers similar amenities without the big lobby. Rooms are well kept and sizable.

Places to Eat

Cafe Winni's (Madero s/n) Dishes US$3-4.50. An excellent dining choice is Winni's, just down from the plaza. Options include soup, egg dishes and antojitos, as well as substantial main courses. Try 'Sabana Winni's,' a toothsome steak smothered with ham and melted cheese.

Hotel del Parque *(Dishes US$5-8)* The restaurant here has outdoor tables facing the plaza, where regular customers have enjoyed their evening coffee for years. The food is a touch overpriced.

Restaurant & Cafetería del Centro Dishes US$4-5. Open 7am-midnight. Beneath the Hotel de los Pérez, this restaurant is good for American-style breakfasts, snacks and set meals; they whip up a mean burger.

Getting There & Away

San Andrés is the transport center for Los Tuxtlas, with fairly good bus services in every direction – 1st-class with ADO and good 2nd-class with AU. Transportes Los Tuxtlas (TLT) buses are old and bouncy, but because of their frequent departures they're often the quickest way of getting to local destinations. TLT buses leave from the corner of Cabada and Solana Nte, a block north of the market; they skirt the north side of town on 5 de Febrero (highway 180), and you can get on or off at most intersections. They charge 10% less than ADO buses.

Acayucan – 95km, 1½ hours; 15 ADO (US$4.20), TLT every 10 minutes

Campeche – 785km, 12½ hours; ADO at 9.15pm and 10.45pm (US$36.50)

Catemaco – 12km, 20 minutes; 16 ADO (US$0.60), TLT every 10 minutes

Mérida – 965km, 15 hours; ADO at 9.15pm and 10.35pm (US$45)

Mexico City (TAPO) – 550km, 9 hours; ADO at 9.45pm, 10.30pm and 11.10pm (US$31), AU at 12.05pm, 9.40pm and 10.05pm (US$27.50)

Puebla – 420km, 5 hours; ADO at 9.45pm and 10.30pm (US$23.50), AU at 9.50pm (US$22.50)

Santiago Tuxtla – 14km, 20 minutes; 12 Cuenca (US$0.65), TLT every 10 minutes

Veracruz – 155km, 2 hours; 22 ADO (US$7.50), AU at 12.05pm and 9.50pm (US$6.50), TLT every 10 minutes

Villahermosa – 320km, 4 hours; 11 ADO (US$17)

CATEMACO

● pop 25,000 ● elev 370m ☎ 294

This town on the western shore of beautiful Laguna Catemaco makes most of its living from fishing and from Mexican families who flood in during July and August and for Christmas, New Year and Semana Santa. It's one of the state's few real tourist towns, with hawkers and pushers bugging travelers right and left. The annual convention of *brujos* (witch doctors), held on Cerro Mono Blanco (White Monkey Hill), north of Catemaco, on the first Friday in March, has become more a tourist event than a supernatural one.

Orientation & Information

Catemaco slopes gently down to the lake. A tourist information office in the *municipalidad,* on the north side of the zócalo, offers limited information (open 9am to 3pm Monday to Friday). The post office has moved from near the bus station to a few blocks west of the central plaza.

Bancomer, on Aldama, changes cash but not traveler's checks, usually in the mornings only. In a pinch, try the Hotel Los Arcos, which sometimes changes American Express traveler's checks at not very good rates. There's an ATM at the Catemaco Hotel.

Laguna Catemaco

The lake, ringed by volcanic hills, is roughly oval and 16km long. Streams flowing into it are the source of Catemaco and Coyame mineral water. East of town are a few gray-sand beaches where you can swim in murky water.

The lake contains several islands; on the largest, Isla Tenaspi, Olmec sculptures have been discovered. **Isla de los Monos** (Monkey Island), also called Isla de los Changos, holds about 60 red-cheeked *Macaca arctoides* monkeys, originally from Thailand. They belong to the University of Veracruz, which acquired them for research. Despite pleas from the university for the animals to be left alone, boat operators bring food so tourists can get close-up photos.

Boats moored along the lakeside offer trips around the islands and across to the ecological reserve at Nanciyaga (see below) – the posted price for up to six people is US$40, or US$5.50 per person if you go as an individual.

On the north shore of the lake lies the **Reserva Ecológica de Nanciyaga** *(☎/fax 943-01-99, Carretera Catemaco-Coyame Km 7; admission US$2.80; open 9am-6pm daily).* Dedicated to promoting 'responsible tourism,' it preserves a small piece of rain forest. A guided walk (in Spanish) includes the chance to sample mineral water and to test the cosmetic benefits of smearing black mud on your face. The not-so-wild wildlife includes toucans, monkeys, tortoises, peccaries, raccoons and crocodiles, all in enclosures. Replicas of Olmec ruins are scattered about the site. It's quite interesting but a bit contrived – indeed, *Medicine Man,* a Sean Connery film, was shot here. The reserve can be reached by *pirata* (pickup truck, US$0.75) or by boat.

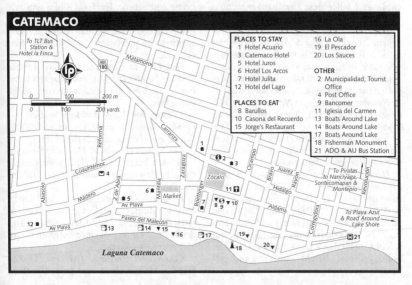

CATEMACO

PLACES TO STAY
1 Hotel Acuario
3 Catemaco Hotel
5 Hotel Juros
6 Hotel Los Arcos
7 Hotel Julita
12 Hotel del Lago

PLACES TO EAT
8 Barullos
10 Casona del Recuerdo
15 Jorge's Restaurant

16 La Ola
19 El Pescador
20 Los Sauces

OTHER
2 Municipalidad; Tourist Office
4 Post Office
9 Bancomer
11 Iglesia del Carmen
13 Boats Around Lake
14 Boats Around Lake
17 Boats Around Lake
18 Fisherman Monument
21 ADO & AU Bus Station

To TLT Bus Station & Hotel la Finca

Matamoros

MEX 180

0   100   200 m
0   100   200 yards

Reforma
Carranza
Cuauhtémoc
Abasolo
Madero
2 de Abril
Mantilla
Boettinger
Zaragoza
Ocampo
Bravo
Juárez
Rayón
Hidalgo
Aldama
Corregidora
Revolución

Zócalo
Market
Av Playa
Paseo del Malecón
Av Playa

To Piratas, to Nanciyaga, Sontecomapan & Montepío

To Playa Azul & Road Around Lake Shore

Laguna Catemaco

Places to Stay

Catemaco has lodging in all price ranges, all over the place. Air-conditioning is standard in mid-range places.

Hotel Julita (☎ 943-00-08, Avenida Playa 10) Singles/doubles US$11/20. Near the waterfront just down from the zócalo, the Julita is a decent budget bargain, with large rooms including fan, hot water and private bath, as well as friendly critters such as lizards and flies.

Hotel Acuario (☎ 943-04-18, Carranza 10) Doubles/quads US$11/19. Right by the zócalo, the Acuario sports small, plain quarters with the bathroom right there in the middle of the room! Watch out for uneven steps in the stairwell.

Hotel Los Arcos (☎ 943-00-03, e arcos@catemaco.net, Madero 7) Doubles US$40. On the corner of Mantilla, Los Arcos has helpful staff, a swimming pool and clean and bright (though smallish) rooms with balconies.

Hotel Juros (☎ 943-00-84, Avenida Playa 14) Doubles US$25.50, US$46 with air-con. Rooms at the Juros are large and pretty, and the renovated air-conditioned ones are far superior to the musty older set.

Catemaco Hotel (☎ 943-02-03, fax 942-00-45, e hotel@catemaco.net, Carranza 8) Singles/doubles from US$35/49. On the north side of the zócalo, the Catemaco features a huge pool and unhuge rooms with cable and balconies. The management is affable, but it's not a super value.

Hotel del Lago (☎ 943-01-60, fax 943-04-31, cnr Avenida Playa & Abasolo) Doubles US$42. Rooms at this lakefront hotel are adequate but not really worth the inflated price. A decent restaurant and a small pool soften the blow to your wallet somewhat.

Reserva Ecológica de Nanciyaga (☎ 943-01-99) Tent sites US$3.30 per person, cabañas US$45 for two. The ecological reserve (see Laguna Catemaco earlier) offers basic tent sites in La Jungla, a nearby stretch of forest, and a few simple cabins on site.

Hotel Playa Azul (☎ 943-00-01, e set@axtel.net) Trailer sites US$11, doubles US$82, bungalows for six US$111. Situated 2.5km east of town by the lake, the Playa Azul adjoins a patch of rain forest and promotes itself as an 'ecoadventure' destination, but it looks much like a mass-market American holiday motel. Bright, coral-colored air-conditioned rooms are surrounded by a garden and parking lot. Facilities include satellite TV, a swimming pool, restaurant and (in high season) a discotheque.

Hotel La Finca (☎ 943-03-22, 800-523-46-22, e lafinca@catemaco.net, Carretera 180 Km 47) Doubles US$89. The lakeside, four-star La Finca is 2km west of town on the Acayucan road. It's a stylish modern building with 36 comfortable rooms, most with large balconies and lake views. Discounts off the rack rate are often available.

Places to Eat

The lake provides the specialties here, among them the *tegogolo*, a snail reputed to be an aphrodisiac and best eaten in a sauce of chili, tomato, onion and lime; *chipalchole*, a soup with shrimp or crab claws; *mojarra*, a type of perch; and *anguilas* (eels). *Tachogobi* is a hot sauce sometimes served on mojarra; eels may come with raisins and hot chilies. Many eating spots can be depressingly empty out of season and tend to close early.

Jorge's Restaurant (Paseo del Malecón) Dishes US$3-7. Offering decent breakfasts and local fish dishes, Jorge's is one of two of the most popular and pleasant of Catemaco's many restaurants. It's right beside the lake, with a breezy garden eating area.

La Ola (Paseo del Malecón) Dishes US$3-6. Next door to Jorge's, La Ola is its prime competitor. The food is of a similarly high standard, and prices are virtually identical. The only difference is that La Ola seems to be patronized by a slightly older clientele.

Hotel Julita (see Places to Stay) Dishes US$4-6. Not far from the lakeside, this hotel has a good budget restaurant with basic, filling fare.

El Pescador (Paseo del Malecón) Seafood US$4-8. This is a popular spot for eating, drinking and socializing in the evening.

Los Sauces (Paseo del Malecón) Seafood US$3-8, lobster US$12. This joint closely rivals El Pescador for sunset entertainment and fare.

Barullos (Aldama) Dishes US$5-7. Open only for dinner, Barullos offers excellent vittles, such as a juicy filet mignon. The decor strikes a nice balance between classy and warmly welcoming.

Casona del Recuerdo (Aldama) Dishes US$4-7. Half a block east from Barullos, this place features delightful balcony tables, friendly service and budget prices, all in a very pretty gardenlike setting. It specializes in seafood dishes.

Getting There & Away

Few long-distance buses reach Catemaco, so you may have to travel via San Andrés Tuxtla (12km west on highway 180) or Acayucan (80km south), taking the more frequent but less comfortable local buses to or from Catemaco.

ADO and AU buses operate from a small terminal by the lakeside at the corner of Avenida Playa and Revolución. The local Transportes Los Tuxtlas buses pull up at the main road junction on the west side of town. ADO and AU mid- to long-distance services include the following:

Acayucan – 8 ADO (US$3.60), AU at 2.45am (US$3.20)

Córdoba – AU at 9pm (US$11.50)

Jalapa – 4 ADO (US$13.50), AU at 9.15pm (US$11.80)

Mexico City (TAPO) – ADO at 10pm (US$31), AU at 11.30am, 9pm and 9.30pm (US$28)

Puebla – ADO at 10pm (US$23), AU at 9.15pm (US$21.50)

Santiago Tuxtla – AU at 11.30am, 9pm and 9.40pm (US$1.10)

Veracruz – 6 ADO (US$7.50), AU at 11.30am and 9.15pm (US$7)

Getting Around

To explore the villages and country east of the lake, where the mountain Santa Marta stands out, take a *pirata* (pickup truck) going to Las Margaritas (around US$2). They leave every hour or two from a corner five blocks north of the ADO station.

AROUND CATEMACO

About 4km northeast of Catemaco, the road forks. The section to the right follows the east side of the lake past the Reserva Ecológica Nanciyaga to Coyame and Las Margaritas; the road to the left is sealed and scenic as it goes over the hills toward the coast. At Sontecomapan, 15km from Catemaco, you can turn right (east) off the main road and go down to the lagoon side, where there are a few restaurants; stroll to the left for 100m to find the idyllic Pozo de los Enanos (Well of the Dwarves) swimming hole. From this

backwater you can rent boats for excursions into the mangroves around Laguna de Sontecomapan. It's 20 minutes by boat to the mouth of the lagoon, where you may be able to camp on the beach near the fishing village of **La Barra** – but ask first and bring everything you'll need. La Barra can also be reached by a side road from La Palma, 8km north of Sontecomapan.

The road is rough after Sontecomapan, but the countryside is lovely – mainly cattle ranches and rain forest, with green hills rolling down to the shore. About 5km past La Palma, a sign points down another rough side road to Playa Escondida. This takes you past **Jicacal**, a small, poor fishing village with a long gray-sand beach, one restaurant and some basic bungalows. **Playa Escondida** itself is about 4km from the main road. Accommodations in this area were in flux at the time of writing, but there should be lodging and dining opportunities at the site.

Back on the 'road' you pass a biological research station next to one of the few tracts of unspoiled rain forest on the Gulf Coast. A turnoff here leads to pretty Laguna Escondida, hidden in the mountains. The end of the road is at **Montepío**, where you'll find a nice beach at the river mouth, with two places to eat. *Posada San José* (☎ 294-942-10-10) offers reasonably comfortable singles/doubles for US$13.50/15.50, US$21/26.50 with air-conditioning.

Getting There & Away

Public transportation to Sontecomapan and beyond is by *camionetas* (pickup trucks with benches in the back), also called 'piratas.' They leave Catemaco every half hour or so (when they're full) 6am to 3pm, from the corner of Revolución and the Playa Azul road (from the northeast corner of the plaza, walk five blocks east and six blocks north, and look for vehicles congregating). The full 39km trip to Montepío, with numerous stops, takes about 2 hours and costs US$3.

ACAYUCAN

● pop 51,800 ● elev 150m ☎ 924

Lively Acayucan lies where highway 180 (between Veracruz and Villahermosa) meets highway 185 (which goes south across the Isthmus of Tehuantepec to the Pacific coast).

The new east-west *autopista* (toll road), highway 145D, also passes nearby. You may have to change buses here, but try to avoid it – most buses are de paso, the 1st-class bus station is not a great setup (no left-luggage storage), and the 2nd-class buses go from offices scattered in surrounding streets. If you do get stuck in Acayucan, don't fret: it's a cheerily busy junction town with plenty of opportunities to mingle with locals, who don't often see travelers. If you have your own vehicle and are a true archaeology buff, you might want to seek out the Olmec site of San Lorenzo, 35km to the southeast.

Orientation & Information
The bus stations are on the east side of town. To reach the central plaza, walk uphill through (or past) the market to Avenida Hidalgo, turn left and walk six blocks. The plaza has a modern church on the east side and the town hall on the west. Bancomer and Banamex, both near the plaza, have ATMs and change traveler's checks. A generic Internet café provides access on the south side of the plaza for US$1.10 per hour.

Plaza Central
In the evening, especially on weekends, Acayucan's central plaza fills with happily chattering schoolkids, romantically entwined couples, wizened town elders and solo pedestrians out for a stroll. It's the best place to strike up a conversation while sipping a cool drink.

Places to Stay & Eat
Hotel Ancira (☎ 245-00-48, *Bravo 2*) Singles/doubles US$8/8.50. Half a block southwest of the plaza, the Ancira offers rooms with fan, phone, private bathroom and hot water. Some are a little sketchy, so ask to see yours before checking in.

Hotel Joalicia (☎/fax 245-08-77, *Zaragoza 4*) Singles/doubles US$10.50/14.50, US$18/24.50 with air-con. On the plaza's south side, the Joalicia is a better value than the Ancira. Rooms are decently sized and well maintained.

Hotel Arcos del Parque (☎ 245-65-06, fax 245-00-18, *Hidalgo 14*) Singles/doubles US$31/33, US$39 with balcony. Fronting the plaza's north side, this place features sterile but large and comfortable rooms. The staff's towel-folding skills are remarkable.

Hotel Kinaku (☎/fax 245-04-10, *Ocampo Sur 7*) Singles/doubles US$44/51. You might have to pay through the nose at the Kinaku, but the enormous, sparkling rooms with air-conditioning and cable are worth it. The Kinaku's restaurant, open 24 hours, is the smartest place in town but is somewhat pricey, with US$5 chicken dishes and US$8 beef and pork dishes.

La Parrilla Beef dishes US$6-7. Housed in the Hotel Arcos' building, this restaurant does satisfyingly beefy main meals.

Los Tucanes Cafetería Snacks US$3, meat dishes US$5-6. Open 24 hrs. On the pedestrian street a block west of the plaza, this popular and pleasant spot attracts a diverse clientele.

Getting There & Around
Bus Most 1st-class buses (ADO and Cristóbal Colón) are de paso, but the computerized reservation systems indicate if seats are available. UNO and ADO GL run a few deluxe services, while AU and Sur provide quite good 2nd-class service. All these companies operate from the same terminal at the lower side of the market. Transportes Los Tuxtlas (TLT) provides very rough services to the Tuxtlas area from a terminal on the edge of the market, for 15% less than the 1st-class price. Travel times given below are by autopista where available, on a directo bus.

Catemaco – 80km, 1½ hours; 8 ADO (US$3), frequent TLT

Juchitán – 195km, 3 hours; 9 ADO, Sur every 30 minutes (US$5.75)

Mexico City (TAPO) – 650km, 7 hours; UNO at 10pm (US$62), ADO GL at 10.45pm and 11pm (US$42), 7 ADO (US$36), 5 AU (US$32)

San Andrés Tuxtla – 95km, 2 hours; 5 ADO (US$4.25), AU at 7.30pm (US$3.75), frequent TLT

Santiago Tuxtla – 110km, 2¼ hours; hourly TLT (US$3)

Tapachula – 580km, 10 hours; Colón at 11.20pm and 11.25pm (US$28), Sur at 11.40am and 10.40pm (US$23.50)

Tuxtla Gutiérrez – 440km, 8 hours; ADO at 1.10am, 5.25am and 10.10pm (US$19), 3 Colón (US$19.50)

Veracruz – 250km, 3½ hours; UNO at 3am (US$26), 18 ADO (US$13)

Villahermosa – 225km, 3½ hours; 14 ADO (US$11.50)

Car & Motorcycle The new toll highway, 145D, passes south of town. Heading east, it's signposted to Minatitlán (which is clear enough); heading west, toward Córdoba or Veracruz, it's marked to 'Isla' (referring to the inland town of Isla, not to any island). The tolls are expensive – it costs over US$30 to get to Córdoba.

Local Transportation You can generally hoof it wherever you need to be. For those carrying tons of luggage, local buses run between the terminal and city center (US$0.30); a taxi costs US$1.

SAN LORENZO

Near the small town of Tenochtitlán, 35km southeast of Acayucan, San Lorenzo was the first of the two great Olmec ceremonial centers. It saw its heyday from about 1200 to 900 BC.

Ten Olmec heads and numerous smaller artifacts have been found here, but most of the finds are in museums elsewhere. Some heavy stone thrones, with figures of rulers carved in the side, were also found. Tools made from the black volcanic glass obsidian were imported from Guatemala or the Mexican highlands, and basalt for the heads and thrones was transported from the Sierra de los Tuxtlas. Such wide contacts, and the organization involved in building the site, demonstrate how powerful the rulers of San Lorenzo were. Other features include an elaborate stone-pipe drainage system and evidence of cannibalism. During San Lorenzo's dramatic destruction, which occurred around 900 BC, most of the big carvings were mutilated, dragged onto the ridges and covered with earth.

The main structure was a platform about 50m high, 1.25km long and 700m wide, with ridges jutting from its sides, but now the San Lorenzo site is nothing more than a low hill. The 'museum' *(admission free; open 8am-5pm daily)* here is just two disappointingly tiny rooms of stone artifacts and a single large head.

Another site, **El Azazul**, is in the countryside about 7km farther south. The hill here seems to have been a large pyramid but is completely overgrown. Halfway up it, under a shelter, are some remarkably well carved kneeling stone figures. They are said to be over 1000 years old, but they're in such good condition that it's hard to believe. Often there are people in the hut who will show you around in return for a tip of a couple of pesos.

Getting There & Away

Unless you're rabid about archaeology, it's really not worth visiting these sites by public transportation. From Acayucan take a bus to Texistepec (south of the Minatitlán road), then another to the town of Tenochtitlán (also called San Lorenzo-Tenochtitlán). Then take a local bus or taxi to the 'zona arqueológica' south of town, and look for the cream-colored buildings behind a chain-link fence on the left side of the road. The entire trip costs about US$7 and takes about three centuries (fine, 2½ hours, but who's counting by now?). The El Azazul site is virtually inaccessible by public transportation, but a taxi driver might consent to take you for about US$2. If you're driving, head 7km past the San Lorenzo museum and look for a road branching left and a hut on the right. Exploring these sites is much less traumatic with your own wheels.

Oaxaca State

The rugged southern state of Oaxaca ('wah-HAH-kah') reaches to within 250km of Mexico City, but in atmosphere it's a world away from central Mexico. Barriers of sparsely populated mountains – today traversed by the spectacular highway 135D from the north – have always permitted Oaxaca to pursue its own destiny.

Oaxaca enjoys a slower, sunnier existence and a magical quality that has something to do with its dry, rocky landscape, its bright southern light and its large indigenous population. Indigenous people are the driving force behind the state's fine handicrafts and booming art scene.

The beautiful, colonial state capital, Oaxaca city, is one of Mexico's major handicrafts and arts centers. Around the city, in the Valles Centrales (Central Valleys), are thriving village markets and spectacular ruins of pre-Hispanic towns such as Monte Albán, Mitla and Yagul. On the spectacular Oaxaca coast, Mexico's latest tourist resort is growing up on the lovely Bahías (Bays) de Huatulco, but travelers continue to enjoy a very relaxed beach scene at other spots such as Puerto Escondido, Puerto Ángel and Zipolite, just as they have for decades.

The fascinating backcountry of the region is as far from Oaxaca city in culture and traveling time as Oaxaca is from Mexico City – but becoming more accessible thanks to an exciting new wave of 'alternative tourism' ventures based in Oaxaca city.

Occupying a region where temperate and tropical climatic zones and several mountain ranges meet, Oaxaca has spectacularly varied landscapes and a biodiversity greater than any other Mexican state. Cloud forests and big stands of oak and pine grow in the highlands, while lower-lying areas and Pacific-facing slopes support deciduous tropical forest.

History

Zapotecs & Mixtecs The Valles Centrales have always been the hub of Oaxacan life, and the pre-Hispanic cultures reached heights rivaling those of central Mexico. The hilltop city of Monte Albán here became the center of the Zapotec

Highlights

- Oaxaca city – beautiful colonial city with great arts, shopping and entertainment
- Monte Albán – ruins of the ancient Zapotec capital on a superb hilltop site
- Pueblos Mancomunados – walks and bike rides through cool highland forests
- Puerto Ángel, Zipolite, Mazunte – great tropical beaches, cool travelers' scene, boat trips, snorkeling, sea turtles, crocodiles
- Puerto Escondido – tropical resort-cum-fishing town with superb surfing
- Laguna Manialtepec & Lagunas de Chacahua – mangrove-fringed lagoons teeming with bird life, pristine ocean beaches
- Bahías de Huatulco – low-key modern resort on a set of exquisite bays

OTHER MAPS
Oaxaca State page 746

Gulf of Mexico

Oaxaca City page 749
Central Oaxaca City pages 752-753

Yagul page 776

Monte Albán page 773

Mitla page 777

Valles Centrales page 771

Puerto Escondido page 785

Bahías de Huatulco page 807

Puerto Ángel page 796

Santa Cruz Huatulco page 812
La Crucecita page 810

PACIFIC OCEAN

OAXACA STATE

culture, which extended its control over much of Oaxaca by conquest, peaking between AD 300 and 700. Monte Albán declined suddenly; by about AD 750 it was deserted, as were many other Zapotec sites in the Valles Centrales. From about 1200, the surviving Zapotecs came under growing dominance by the Mixtecs from Oaxaca's northwest uplands, renowned

OAXACA STATE

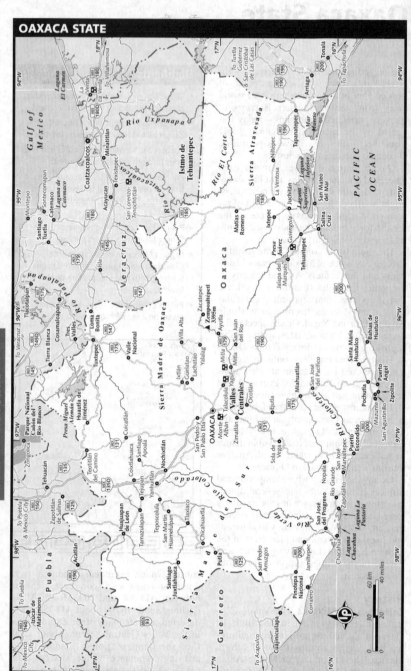

potters and metalsmiths. Mixtec and Zapotec cultures became entangled in the Valles Centrales before the Aztecs conquered them in the 15th and early 16th centuries.

Colonial Era The Spaniards had to send at least four expeditions before they felt safe enough to found the city of Oaxaca in 1529. Cortés donated large parts of the Valles Centrales to himself and was officially named Marqués del Valle de Oaxaca. In colonial times, the indigenous population dropped disastrously. The population of the Mixteca region in the west is thought to have fallen from 700,000 at the Spanish arrival to about 25,000 in 1700. Rebellions continued into the 20th century, but the indigenous peoples rarely formed a serious threat.

Juárez & Díaz Benito Juárez, the great reforming leader of mid-19th-century Mexico, was a Zapotec. He served two terms as Oaxaca state governor before being elected Mexico's president in 1861. (See 'Benito Juárez' in this chapter.)

Juárez appointed Porfirio Díaz, son of a Oaxaca horse trainer, as state governor in 1862, but Díaz rebelled against Juárez's presidency in 1871. He went on to control Mexico with an iron fist from 1877 to 1910. While his rule brought the country into the industrial age, it also fostered corruption, repression and, eventually, the revolution. In Valle Nacional in northern Oaxaca, tobacco planters set up virtual slave plantations, most of whose 15,000 workers had to be replaced annually after dying from disease, beating or starvation. Indigenous lands were commandeered by foreign and mestizo coffee planters.

Oaxaca Today After the revolution about 300 *ejidos* (peasant land-holding cooperatives) were set up, but land ownership remains a source of conflict today. With little industry, Oaxaca is one of Mexico's poorest states, and many of its residents leave home to work in the cities or the USA. The situation is made worse in some areas, notably the Mixteca, by deforestation and erosion. Tourism thrives in Oaxaca city and nearby villages and in a few places on the coast, but underdevelopment still prevails in the backcountry.

Geography & Climate

The western two-thirds of the state are rugged and mountainous; the eastern third lies on the hot, low-lying Isthmus of Tehuantepec (Istmo de Tehuantepec). Oaxaca also has a thin plain along the Pacific coast and a low-lying north-central region bordering Veracruz state.

The Sierra Madre del Sur (average height 2000m), running parallel to the Pacific coast, meets the Sierra Madre de Oaxaca (average height 2500m), which runs down from Mexico's central volcanic belt, roughly in the center of the state. Between them, converging at the city of Oaxaca, lie the three Valles Centrales.

The Valles Centrales are warm and dry, with most rain falling between June and September. On the coast and in low-lying areas it's hotter and a bit wetter.

Population & People

Oaxaca's population of 3.4 million includes 15 indigenous groups, numbering somewhere between 1 million and 2 million people in total. Each group has its own language, but most also speak Spanish. Colorful traditional costumes are seen less than they used to be, but you'll still notice a strong indigenous presence in the villages and markets and strong indigenous influence on markets and festivals. Indigenous land and housing are, however, usually the poorest in the state.

The approximately 400,000 Zapotecs live mainly in and around the Valles Centrales and on the Isthmus of Tehuantepec. You're sure to come into contact with them, though few obvious signs identify them. Most are farmers, but they also make and trade handicrafts, mezcal and other products. Many emigrate temporarily for work.

About 300,000 Mixtecs are spread around the mountainous borders of Oaxaca, Guerrero and Puebla states, with more than two-thirds of them in Oaxaca. The state's other large indigenous groups include 160,000 or so Mazatecs in the far north, 100,000 Mixes in the highlands northeast of the Valles Centrales and 100,000 Chinantecs around Valle Nacional, in the north.

In Oaxaca city you may well see Triquis, from western Oaxaca; the women wear bright red *huipiles* and populate craft markets. The Triquis are only about 15,000 strong and have

Oaxaca Bus Companies

The following abbreviations for 2nd-class bus companies are used in this chapter:

AU	Autobuses Unidos
AVN	Autotransportes Valle del Norte
EB	Estrella Blanca
ERS	Estrella Roja del Sureste
EV/OP	Estrella del Valle/Oaxaca Pacífico
FYPSA	Fletes y Pasajes
TOI	Transportes Oaxaca-Istmo

a long history of violent conflict with mestizos and Mixtecs over land rights.

Internet Resources

Oaxaca's Tourist Guide (**W** http://oaxaca-travel.com) is an excellent photo-filled Web site with everything from information on beaches and hotels to regional recipes and biographies of famous Oaxacans. Oaxaca's Forum (**W** http://bbs.oaxaca.com) is a bulletin board where you can look for rented accommodations or shared transport or just ask any old question. Oaxaca's Index (**W** http://index.oaxaca.com) has language schools and lodgings listings. The Oaxaca state tourism department's site (**W** http://oaxaca.oaxaca.gob.mx/sedetur) has lots of interesting material, but at the time of writing most of it was in Spanish only.

Dangers & Annoyances

Buses and other vehicles traveling isolated stretches of highway, including the coastal highway 200 and highway 175 from Oaxaca city to Pochutla, have occasionally been stopped and robbed. The best way to avoid this risk is not to travel at night.

Oaxaca City

- **pop 255,000** - **elev 1550m** ☎ **951**

The state's capital and only sizable city has a colonial heart of narrow, straight streets, liberally sprinkled with lovely stone buildings. Oaxaca is relaxed but stimulating, remote but cosmopolitan. Its dry mountain heat, manageable scale, old buildings, broad shady plazas and leisurely cafés help slow the pace of life. At the same time, diverse Oaxacan, Mexican and international currents create a spark of excitement. The city has some first-class museums and galleries, arguably the best handicrafts shopping in Mexico, and a bright cultural, restaurant, bar and music scene. It's a capital of the modern Mexican art world and an ever more popular location for learning Spanish, venturing outside the city on 'alternative tourism' activities, or simply hanging out.

Head first for the *zócalo* to get a taste of the atmosphere. Then ramble and see what markets, crafts, galleries, cafés, bars and festivities you run across. Allow time, if you can, for more than one trip out to the many fascinating places in the Valles Centrales.

History

The Aztec settlement here was called Huaxyacac (meaning 'In the Nose of the Squash'), from which 'Oaxaca' is derived. The Spanish laid out a new town around the existing zócalo in 1529. It quickly became the most important place in southern Mexico.

Eighteenth-century Oaxaca grew rich on exports of cochineal, a red dye made from tiny insects living on the prickly pear cactus, and on the weaving of textiles. By 1796 it was probably the third-biggest city in Nueva España, with about 20,000 people (including 600 clergy) and 800 cotton looms.

In 1854 an earthquake destroyed much of the city. Only decades later, under the presidency of Porfirio Díaz, did Oaxaca began to grow again; in the 1890s its population exceeded 30,000. In 1931 another earthquake left 70% of the city uninhabitable.

Oaxaca's major expansion has come in the past two decades, with tourism, new industries and rural poverty all encouraging migration from the countryside. The city's population has roughly doubled in 20 years, and today Oaxaca sprawls well past its old limits, especially to the northwest.

Orientation

Oaxaca centers on the zócalo and the adjoining Alameda plaza in front of the cathedral. Calle Alcalá, running north from the cathedral to the Iglesia de Santo Domingo (a famous Oaxaca landmark), is mostly pedestrian-only.

The road from Mexico City and Puebla traverses east across the northern part of

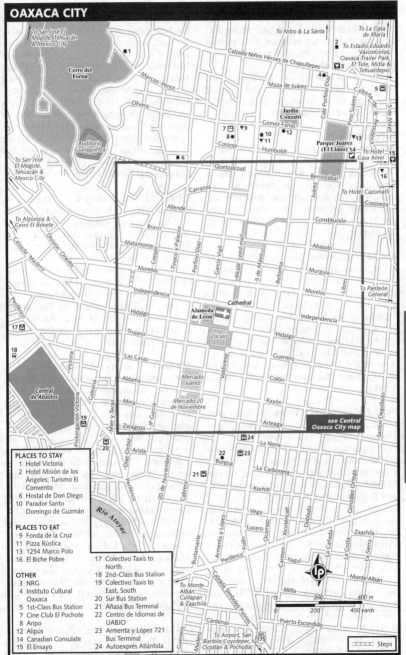

OAXACA CITY

To San José El Mogote, Tehuacán & Mexico City

Cerro del Fortín

Auditorio Guelaguetza

To San José El Mogote, Tehuacán & Mexico City

To Atzompa & Cerro El Bonete

Calzada Niños Héroes de Chapultepec

To Nitro & La Santa

To La Casa de María

To Estadio Eduardo Vasconcelos, Oaxaca Trailer Park, El Tule, Mitla & Tehuantepec

Marcos-Pérez

Olivera

Maza de Juárez

Jardín Conzatti

Gómez Farías

Cosijopi

Humboldt

Parque Juárez (El Llano)

To Hotel Casa Amel

Quetzalcóatl

Berriozábal

To Hotel Cazomalli

Carranza

Allende

Cosijoeza

Bravo

Constitución

Matamoros

Abasolo

Morelos

Murguia

Independencia

Morelos

To Panteón General

Hidalgo

Cathedral

Independencia

Trujano

Alameda de León

Zócalo

Hidalgo

Las Casas

Guerrero

Aldama

Mercado Juárez

Colón

Mina

Mercado 20 de Noviembre

Rayón

Zaragoza

Arteaga

see Central Oaxaca City map

Central de Abastos

La Noria

La Carbonera

Xochitl

Vega

Lucero

Río Atoyac

To Monte Albán, Cuilapan & Zaachila

Puerto Escondido

Monte Albán

Mitla

To Airport, San Bartolo Coyotepec, Ocotlán & Pochutla

PLACES TO STAY
1 Hotel Victoria
2 Hotel Misión de los Ángeles; Turismo El Convento
6 Hostal de Don Diego
10 Parador Santo Domingo de Guzmán

PLACES TO EAT
9 Fonda de la Cruz
11 Pizza Rústica
13 1254 Marco Polo
16 El Biche Pobre

OTHER
3 NRG
4 Instituto Cultural Oaxaca
5 1st-Class Bus Station
7 Cine Club El Pochote
8 Aripo
12 Alipús
14 Canadian Consulate
15 El Ensayo

17 Colectivo Taxis to North
18 2nd-Class Bus Station
19 Colectivo Taxis to East, South
20 Sur Bus Station
21 Añasa Bus Terminal
22 Centro de Idiomas de UABJO
23 Armenta y López 721 Bus Terminal
24 Autoexprés Atlántida

OAXACA STATE

0   200   400 m
0   200   400 yards

Steps

Oaxaca as Calzada Niños Héroes de Chapultepec. The 1st-class bus station is on this road, 1.75km northeast of the zócalo. The 2nd-class bus station is almost 1km west of the center, near the main market, the Central de Abastos.

The blocks north of the zócalo are smarter, cleaner and less traffic-infested than those to the south and, especially, the southwest, which is the commercial area.

Information

Tourist Offices The Oaxaca state tourist office (☎ 516-01-23) is at Independencia 607, facing the Alameda. It's open 8am to 8pm daily. Someone in attendance can usually speak English, and staff will dig out almost any answer they don't already know. A branch office (☎ 511-50-40) is at the airport.

Money There are plenty of banks and ATMs around the center. The best exchange rates for US dollars (cash or traveler's checks) are often found at Casa de Cambio Puebla, García Vigil 106L, open 9am to 6pm Monday to Friday, 9am to 2pm Saturday. Banks with reasonable exchange rates include Banamex on Valdivieso, open 11am to 7pm Monday to Friday, and Bital, on Armenta y López one block east of the zócalo, open 8am to 7pm daily except Sunday.

Post & Communications The main post office, on the Alameda, is open 8am to 6pm Monday to Friday, 9am to 1pm Saturday.

Pay phones are available on the zócalo and elsewhere, and many telephone *casetas* are scattered about. Those marked on the Central Oaxaca City map on Independencia and Trujano offer fax service too.

C@fe Internet, handily placed upstairs at the corner of Valdivieso and Independencia, one block from the zócalo, is open 8am to 11pm Monday to Saturday and 10am to 10pm Sunday, with Internet charges graduated from US$0.60 for 15 minutes up to US$1.50 for an hour. Mega Plaza, Guerrero 104 just off the zócalo, charges US$1.25 an hour and is open 7.30am to 9pm daily. For low hourly rates, try @.web, Abasolo 213 (US$0.90 an hour, open 9.30am to 9.30pm daily), or Virtuali@, Pino Suárez 501 (US$0.70 an hour).

Bookstores & Map Shops Amate, at Alcalá 307-2 (in Plaza Alcalá), is probably the best English-language bookstore in all Mexico, stocking almost every Mexico-related title in print in English. Librería Universitaria, Guerrero 108 just off the zócalo, also sells books in English about Oaxaca and Mexico. Proveedora Escolar, Independencia 1001 (at Reforma), has a good upstairs section on local history, archaeology and anthropology (mostly in Spanish). Oaxaca's INEGI map sales center at Independencia 805 sells a great range of topographical maps covering Oaxaca, Chiapas and Tabasco states.

Libraries The Biblioteca Circulante de Oaxaca (Oaxaca Lending Library), Alcalá 305, has a sizable collection of books and magazines on Oaxaca and Mexico, in English and Spanish. It's open 10am to 1pm and 4pm to 7pm Monday to Friday, 10am to 1pm Saturday. A two-month visitor membership (US$23 plus US$67 refundable deposit) allows you to borrow books.

The excellent library of the Instituto de Artes Gráficas de Oaxaca, Alcalá 507, covers art, architecture, literature, botany, ecology and history.

Media Two free monthly English-language papers aimed at tourists, *Oaxaca Times* and *Oaxaca,* are available around town. They contain some useful practical information and small ads. These and the Spanish-language *Noticias* have rental ads for apartments and houses.

Notice boards at Plaza Gonzalo Lucero, 5 de Mayo 412, and the Biblioteca Circulante, Alcalá 305 (see Libraries), are covered in ads for accommodations, classes (in everything from Spanish to yoga) and other interesting stuff.

Well worth dipping into is **w** www.realoaxaca.com, the site of Stan Gotlieb and Diana Ricci, a US writer-photographer couple resident in Oaxaca – it's full of Oaxaca news, anecdotes and gossip. The *Oaxaca Times* newspaper's Web site (**w** www.oaxacatimes.com) includes classified ads where you can look for an apartment.

Cultural Centers The Alianza Francesa (☎ 516-39-34), Morelos 306, maintains a small *mediateca* with French books as well as periodicals. The institute presents exhibitions and French films. It closes all August.

Laundry Same-day wash-and-dry laundry service is available at several laundries. Lavandería Azteca, at Hidalgo 404 and Superlavandería Hidalgo, at the corner of Hidalgo and JP García, charge US$5 for up to 3.5kg, and open 8am to 8pm Monday to Saturday (plus 10am to 2pm Sunday at the Azteca). Lavandería Antequera, Murguía 408, washes 3kg for US$4.50 and is open 8am to 2pm and 4pm to 8pm Monday to Saturday.

Medical Services Clínica Hospital Carmen (☎ 516-26-12), Abasolo 215, is open 24 hours daily and has several English-speaking doctors.

Emergency For any emergency service, you can call ☎ 066. The Centro de Protección al Turista (Ceprotur, ☎ 516-01-23), in the tourist office at Independencia 607, helps tourists with legal problems; if you have a complaint, or if you've lost documents or had things stolen, you can report it here.

Zócalo & Alameda
Shady, traffic-free and surrounded by *portales* (arcades) sheltering numerous cafés and restaurants, the zócalo is the perfect place to sit back and watch the city go by. The adjacent Alameda, also traffic-free but without the cafés, is another popular local gathering place.

On the south side of the zócalo stands the **Palacio de Gobierno**, whose stairway mural by Arturo García Bustos depicts famous Oaxacans and Oaxacan history. At the top of the mural are revolutionary Ricardo Flores Magón (left); Benito Juárez and his wife, Margarita Maza (center); and José María Morelos (right). Porfirio Díaz appears below Juárez, in blue, with a sword. At the bottom, toward the right, Vicente Guerrero's execution at Cuilapan is shown. The left wall shows ancient Mitla. At the center of the right wall is Juana Inés de La Cruz, the 17th-century nun and love poet.

Oaxaca's **cathedral**, begun in 1553 and finished (after several earthquakes) in the 18th century, stands just north of the zócalo. Its main façade, facing the Alameda, features some fine baroque carving.

Buildings near the Zócalo
Fine carved façades adorn two colonial churches: **La Compañía**, just off the southwest corner of the zócalo; and the popular **San Juan de Dios**, on Aldama at 20 de Noviembre, which dates from 1526 and is the oldest church in Oaxaca. The 17th-century baroque **Templo de San Felipe Neri**, on Independencia at JP García, is where Benito Juárez and Margarita Maza were married in 1843; Maza was the daughter of Don Antonio Maza, who had employed Juárez's sister as a family cook and had taken in young Benito on his arrival in Oaxaca.

The 1903 **Teatro Macedonio Alcalá**, on 5 de Mayo at Independencia, is in the French style that was fashionable under Porfirio Díaz. It has a marble stairway and a five-tier auditorium that holds 1300 people.

Calle Alcalá
Closed to traffic and with its colonial-era stone buildings cleaned up and restored, Alcalá makes a fine pedestrian route from the city center to the Iglesia de Santo Domingo, dotted with attractive shops, cafés and restaurants.

The **Museo de Arte Contemporáneo de Oaxaca** *(MACO,* ☎ *514-22-28, Alcalá 202; admission US$1.25, free Sun; open 10.30am-8pm Wed-Mon)* occupies a lovely colonial house built around 1700. It exhibits recent art from around the world and work by leading modern Oaxacan artists such as Rufino Tamayo, Francisco Toledo, Rodolfo Morales, Rodolfo Nieto and Francisco Gutiérrez. Toledo, one of the museum's founders, is a leading campaigner for the cultural life of the city.

Iglesia de Santo Domingo
Santo Domingo *(cnr Alcalá & Gurrión; open 7am-1pm & 5pm-8pm daily),* four blocks north of the cathedral, is the most splendid of Oaxaca's churches. It was built mainly between 1570 and 1608, for the city's Dominican monastery. The finest artisans from Puebla and elsewhere helped with its construction. Like other large buildings in this earthquake-prone region, it has immensely thick stone walls. During the 19th-century wars and anticlerical movements it was used as a stable and warehouse.

Amid the fine carving on the baroque façade, the figure holding a church is Santo

CENTRAL OAXACA CITY

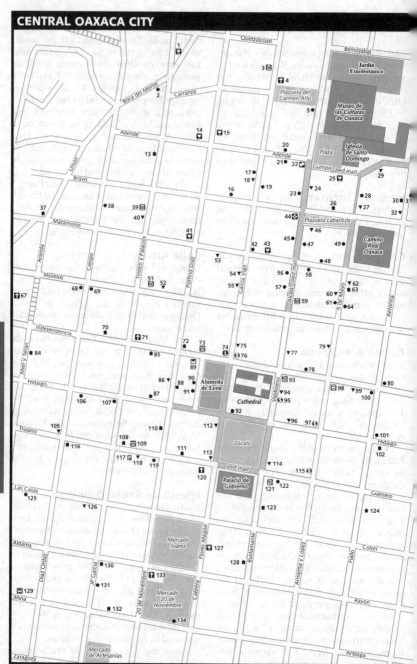

OAXACA STATE

CENTRAL OAXACA CITY

70 Hotel Posada del Centro
72 Hotel Antonio's
81 Hotel Santa Clara
82 Hostel Luz de Luna Nuyoo
84 Hostal Santa Isabel
85 Youth Hostel
   Plata/Gelatina
92 Hotel Marqués Del Valle;
   Turismo Marqués Del Valle
102 Casa de Sierra Azul
108 Hotel Mesón del Rey
110 Hotel Francia
111 Hotel Las Rosas
116 Casa Paulina
123 Hotel Gala
124 Magic Hostel
128 Hotel Aurora
130 Hotel Posada Catarina
132 Hotel Pasaje

PLACES TO EAT
18 La Brew
24 Pizzeria Alfredo da Roma
27 Coffee Beans
29 Los Pacos; Galería
   Quetzalli
32 Café La Antigua
40 Restaurant Manantial
   Vegetariano
46 El Topil
52 Restaurant Flor de Loto
53 Panini
54 Cafetería Bamby
55 Bamby Bakery
60 Coffee Beans
62 Decano
75 Tito's
77 Quickly Restaurant
79 1254 Marco Polo
86 Restaurant Colonial
94 El Sagrario
96 El Mesón
99 Pastelería Quemen
103 El Buen Gourmet
105 Café Alex
112 La Primavera
113 Café Del Jardín; El Asador
   Vasco
114 Terranova Café
118 Restaurante El Naranjo
126 Rosticería El Chinito

BARS
1 La Caracola
7 El Sol y La Luna
14 La Resistencia
15 Club 502
25 La Divina
41 La Cucaracha
43 La Tentación
50 Candela
127 La Casa del Mezcal

OTHER
2 Tierraventura
3 Museo Casa de Juárez
4 Templo & Ex-Convento
   del Carmen Alto
5 Instituto de Artes Gráficas
   de Oaxaca
6 Tierra Dentro
9 Aviacsa
11 Virtuali@
16 Becari Language School
17 Bicicletas Bravo
19 Expediciones Sierra Norte
20 Galería Índigo
21 Galería Punto y Línea
22 US Consulate
23 El Cactus
28 Plaza Gonzalo Lucero
   (Cantera Tours; Café
   Gecko)
33 Vinigúlaza
34 @.web
35 Clínica Hospital Carmen
38 Centro de Esperanza
   Infantil
39 Museos Comunitarios del
   Estado de Oaxaca
42 Casa de las Artesanías de
   Oaxaca
44 Plaza Alcalá (Instituto de
   Comunicación y Cultura;
   Corazón El Pueblo; Amate;
   La Crêpe; Hostería de
   Alcalá)
45 Biblioteca Circulante de
   Oaxaca
47 Centro Cultural Ricardo
   Flores Magón
48 Arte de Oaxaca
49 Budget
51 Museo Rufino Tamayo
56 La Mano Mágica
57 Aerotucán
58 Casa Cantera
59 Museo de Arte
   Contemporáneo de
   Oaxaca
61 Alamo
64 MARO
65 Centro Fotográfico
   Álvarez Bravo
66 Lavandería Antequera
67 Basílica de la Soledad
68 Alianza Francesa
69 Fonart
71 Templo de San Felipe Neri
73 Telephone Caseta
74 Tourist Office
76 Casa de Cambio Puebla
78 INEGI
80 Proveedora Escolar
83 Amigos del Sol
87 Aeroméxico
88 Ticket Bus
89 Post Office
90 Transportes Aeropuerto
91 Hotel Monte Albán;
   Aerovega
93 C@fe Internet
95 Banamex
97 Banamex
98 Teatro Macedonio Alcalá
100 Mexicana
101 Aerocaribe
104 Iglesia de La Merced
106 Lavandería Azteca
107 Superlavandería Hidalgo
109 Telephone Caseta
115 Bital
117 Estacionamiento Trujano
119 Viajes Turísticos Mitla;
   Hostal Santa Rosa
120 Iglesia de La Compañía
121 Mega Plaza
122 Librería Universitaria
125 El Rey de los Mezcales
129 Autobuses Turísticos (to
   Monte Albán); Viajes
   Turísticos Mitla; Hotel
   Rivera del Ángel
131 Bicicletas Pedro Martínez
133 Iglesia de San Juan de Dios
134 Posada Chocolate

PLACES TO STAY
8 Las Mariposas
10 La Casa de mis
   Recuerdos
12 Parador del Dominico
13 Hotel Las Golondrinas
26 Posada Margarita;
   Hertz
30 Hotel Villa de León
31 Las Bugambilias; Café
   La Olla
36 Hostal Guadalupe
37 Hotel Azucenas
63 Hotel Principal

Parque Juárez
(El Llano)

Juárez
Cosijoeza
Pino Suárez
Constitución
Abasolo
Murguía
Morelos
Libres
Independencia

0   50   100 m
0   50   100 yards

⊥⊥⊥⊥ Steps

OAXACA STATE

Domingo de Guzmán (1172-1221), the Spanish monk who founded the Dominican order. The Dominicans observed strict vows of poverty, chastity and obedience, and in Mexico they protected the indigenous people from other colonists' excesses.

The interior, lavish with gilded and colored stucco, has a magically warm glow during candlelit evening masses. Just inside the main door, on the ceiling, is an elaborate family tree of Santo Domingo de Guzmán. The 18th-century Capilla de la Virgen del Rosario (Rosary Chapel), on the south side, is a profusion of yet more gilt.

Museo de las Culturas de Oaxaca

The beautifully restored Ex-Convento de Santo Domingo houses the large, excellent and modern Museum of Oaxacan Cultures (☎ 516-29-91, adjoining Iglesia de Santo Domingo; admission US$4, free Sun; open 10am-8pm Tues-Sun). These old monastery buildings were used as military barracks for over 100 years until 1994. The museum, opened in 1998, takes you right through the history and cultures of Oaxaca state up to the present day. Explanatory material is in Spanish, but you can rent good audio guides in other languages for US$4.50.

A beautiful stone cloister serves as an antechamber to the museum proper. The museum emphasizes the direct lineage between Oaxaca's pre-Hispanic and contemporary indigenous cultures, illustrating continuity in such areas as crafts, medicine, food, drink and music. A video in one room shows members of each of the state's 15 indigenous peoples speaking their own languages. Other exhibits feature plenty of archaeological relics and colonial art. The greatest highlight is the Mixtec treasure from Tumba 7 at Monte Albán, in Sala 3. This treasure dates from the 14th century, when Mixtecs reused an old Zapotec tomb to bury one of their kings and his sacrificed servants. With the bodies they placed a hoard of beautifully worked silver, turquoise, coral, jade, amber, jet, pearls, finely carved jaguar and eagle bone and, above all, gold. The treasure was discovered in 1932 by Alfonso Caso.

Jardín Etnobotánico

This garden of Oaxaca state plants, in the former monastic grounds behind the Museo

de las Culturas, has only been growing since the mid-1990s but is already a fascinating demonstration of the state's biodiversity. Visits are by free guided tour only. These are given in English at noon on Tuesday, Thursday and Saturday (maximum 15 people; put your name down at the museum's ticket desk earlier the same morning), and in Spanish at 1pm and 6pm (5pm November to March) Tuesday to Saturday (get tickets at the museum's ticket desk).

Instituto de Artes Gráficas de Oaxaca

The Graphic Arts Institute (☎ 516-69-80, Alcalá 507; admission free; open 9.30am-8pm daily), almost opposite Santo Domingo, is in a beautiful colonial house donated by artist Francisco Toledo. It offers changing exhibitions of graphic art as well as a superb arts-focused library.

Museo Casa de Juárez

The Juárez House Museum (☎ 516-18-60, García Vigil 609; admission US$3, free Sun & holidays; open 10am-7pm Tues-Sun), opposite the Templo del Carmen Alto, is where Benito Juárez found work as a boy with bookbinder Antonio Salanueva (see 'Benito Juárez' in this chapter). The renovated house shows how the early-19th-century Oaxacan middle class lived. The binding workshop is preserved, along with pictures and a death mask and other memorabilia of Juárez.

Museo Rufino Tamayo

This excellent museum of pre-Hispanic art (☎ 516-47-50, Morelos 503; admission US$2.25; open 10am-2pm & 4pm-7pm Mon & Wed-Sat, 10am-3pm Sun), in a fine 17th-century house, was donated to Oaxaca by its most famous artist, the Zapotec Rufino Tamayo (1899-1991). The collection focuses on the aesthetic qualities of pre-Hispanic artifacts and is arranged to trace artistic developments in preconquest times. It has some beautiful pieces and is strong on the Preclassic era and lesser-known civilizations such as those of Veracruz and western Mexico.

Basílica de la Soledad

The image of Oaxaca's patron saint, the Virgen de la Soledad (Virgin of Solitude), resides in this 17th-century church, about

Benito Juárez

Benito Juárez (1806-72) was born in the mountain village of Guelatao, 60km northeast of Oaxaca. His Zapotec parents died when he was three. At the age of 12, knowing only a few words of Spanish, he walked to Oaxaca and found work at the house of Antonio Salanueva, a bookbinder. Salanueva saw the boy's potential and decided to help pay for an education Juárez otherwise might not have received.

Juárez trained for the priesthood but abandoned it to work as a lawyer for poor villagers. He became a member of the Oaxaca city council and then of the Oaxaca state government. As state governor from 1848 to 1852, he opened schools and cut bureaucracy. The conservative national government exiled him in 1853, but he returned to Mexico in the 1855 Revolution of Ayutla that ousted General Santa Anna. Juárez became justice minister in Mexico's new liberal government. His Ley Juárez (Juárez Law), which transferred the trials of soldiers and priests charged with civil crimes to ordinary civil courts, was the first of the Reform laws, which sought to break the power of the Catholic Church. These laws provoked the War of the Reform of 1858 to 1861, in which the liberals eventually defeated the conservatives.

Juárez was elected Mexico's president in 1861 but had only been in office a few months when France, supported by conservatives and clergy, invaded Mexico and forced him into exile again. In 1866-67, with US support, Juárez ousted the French and their puppet emperor, Maximilian.

One of Juárez's main political achievements was to make primary education free and compulsory. He died in 1872, a year after being elected to his fourth presidential term. Today he is one of the few Mexican national heroes with an unambiguous reputation. Countless statues, streets, schools and plazas preserve his name and memory, and his sage maxim *'El respeto al derecho ajeno es la paz'* ('Respect for the rights of others is peace') is widely quoted.

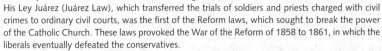

3½ blocks west of the Alameda along Independencia. The church, with a richly carved baroque façade, stands where the image is said to have miraculously appeared in a donkey's pack a few centuries ago. In the mid-1990s, the virgin's 2kg gold crown was stolen, along with the huge pearl and many of the 600 diamonds with which she was adorned. The adjoining convent buildings contain a religious museum.

Galleries

As capital of a state that has produced many top-notch Mexican artists, Oaxaca attracts artists and dealers from far and wide. Several of the city's commercial galleries display some of the best in contemporary Mexican art (admission is free to all of them). One, **Arte de Oaxaca** (☎ 514-09-10, **w** www.artedeoaxaca.com.mx, Murguía 105; open 10am-2pm & 5pm-8pm Mon-Fri,

10am-2pm Sat), is part of the Fundación Cultural Rodolfo Morales, set up in 1990 by Morales, a native of Ocotlán and one of Mexico's leading 20th-century artists, to promote the arts, education, heritage and social welfare of Oaxaca's Valles Centrales. The gallery includes a room devoted to the work of Morales himself.

Galería Quetzalli (☎ 514-26-06, **w** http://quetzalli.com, Constitución 104) has a reputation as Oaxaca's leading serious gallery, free of 'folklorism.' It handles some of the biggest names in Oaxacan art such as Francisco Toledo, Luis Zárate and Sergio Hernández. **Galería Punto y Línea** (Allende 107) and **Galería Índigo** (Allende 104) are two further classy galleries well worth a look. The **Centro Fotográfico Álvarez Bravo** (☎ 516-45-23, Murguía 302; open 9.30am-8pm Wed-Mon) puts on good photo exhibitions and has a library of photography books.

Centro de Esperanza Infantil

This center (☎ 516-21-04, *Crespo 308*) sponsors and cares for Oaxaca's street children, many of whom are homeless after fleeing political violence elsewhere in the state. Despite Oaxaca's apparent wealth, poverty is rife. The center has a kitchen, library, classrooms and kindergarten. The staff here are doing a terrific job and welcome donations and volunteers.

Courses

Language Oaxaca is naturally a popular place to study Spanish. Most students at the city's language schools seem pleased with their experiences. All schools offer group instruction at a variety of levels, Monday to Friday, and most emphasize the spoken language. Most offer private classes too, and they can also arrange accommodations for students, either in hotels or self-catering or with families. Staying with a family costs US$15 to US$20 a day including two meals.

Amigos del Sol (☎ 514-34-84, W *www .oaxacanews.com/amigosdelsol.htm, Libres 109*) US$75 a week for 3 hours daily. This is a small school with maximum class size of five; students may start any Monday or other weekday (go to the school at 8.45am). There's no minimum duration and no charge for registration or textbooks.

Becari Language School (☎ 514-60-76, W *www.becari.com.mx, Plaza San Cristóbal, Bravo 210*) US$75/100/150 a week for 15/20/30 hours. Becari is a medium-size school with a maximum class size of five. Class hours are divided between two or three teachers. You can start any Monday morning. A US$50 registration fee is charged.

Centro de Idiomas, Universidad Autónoma Benito Juárez de Oaxaca (*UABJO,* ☎/fax *516-59-22,* e *cedio@ hotmail.com, Burgoa s/n*) Group classes US$4 per hour. UABJO is part of the city's university. Courses of four hours daily classes for one, two, three or four weeks are offered, with an average eight students per class. Students can start at the beginning of any month. You can also study literature, culture and the Zapotec and Mixtec languages here.

Instituto de Comunicación y Cultura (☎/fax *516-34-43,* W *www.iccoax.com, Plaza Alcalá, Alcalá 307*) US$100/145 a week for

3/4 hours daily. Classes are in groups of three to five, starting any Monday, with a nonrefundable deposit of US$50. The school emphasizes its teachers' qualifications and experience. Special courses are offered in business and medical Spanish, translation, Mexican literature and Spanish for children.

Instituto Cultural Oaxaca (☎ *515-34-04,* W *www.instculturaloax.com.mx, Juárez 909*) 'Total-immersion' 4-week courses US$400. The Instituto Cultural has experienced, qualified teachers, and its courses include workshops and lectures in arts, crafts and culture; many classes are held in the school's spacious gardens and terraces. It's possible to enroll for less than the full four weeks. There's a US$50 registration fee.

Vinigúlaza (☎ *514-64-26,* W *www.mex online.com/vinigulaza.htm, Abasolo 209*) US$45/67.50/90 a week for 2/3/4 hours daily. Maximum class size at this competitively priced school is five. Start any Monday.

Private tutors are not hard to find; check notice boards (see Media, earlier in this chapter) or ask at the schools. One-on-one instruction costs around US$10 an hour.

Cooking *Seasons of My Heart* (☎ *518-77-26,* W *www.seasonsofmyheart.com*) 1-day class US$75 per person; 1-week course US$1595. This cooking school at a ranch in the Valle de Etla is run by American chef and Oaxacan food expert Susana Trilling. It offers English-language classes in Mexican and Oaxacan cooking, from one-day group lessons (usually on Wednesday) to long-weekend and weeklong courses. Classes incorporate market trips to buy ingredients, and we've heard glowing reports from participants.

Organized Tours

Several agencies offer city tours and trips out to places in the Valles Centrales. A typical three- or four-hour group trip to Monte Albán, or to El Tule, Teotitlán del Valle and Mitla, costs around US$17 per person plus any admission fees to museums, archaeological sites, etc. Agencies with a wide choice of itineraries include the following:

Cantera Tours (☎ *516-05-12, Plaza Gonzalo Lucero, 5 de Mayo 412*)

Turismo El Convento (☎ *513-40-97, Hotel Misión de los Ángeles, Calzada Porfirio Díaz 102-1*)

Turismo Marqués Del Valle (☎ 514-69-62, *Hotel Marqués Del Valle, on the zócalo at Portal de Clavería s/n)*

Viajes Turísticos Mitla (☎ 514-31-52, *Hotel Rivera del Ángel, Mina 518; and* (☎ 514-78-00) *Hostal Santa Rosa, Trujano 201)*

Special Events

All major national festivals are celebrated here, and Oaxaca has some unique fiestas of its

own. The most spectacular is the Guelaguetza (see '¡Guelaguetza!'), but others include:

Virgen del Carmen – The streets around the Templo del Carmen Alto on García Vigil become a fairground for a week or more before the day of the Virgen del Carmen, July 16. The nights are lit by processions and fireworks.

Blessing of Animals – Pets are dressed up and taken to Iglesia de La Merced, on Independencia, about 5pm on August 31.

Turismo Alternativo

'Alternative tourism' is a loose term gaining currency in Mexico to refer to a broad span of activities from hiking, biking and climbing to spotting birds or chatting with *curanderos* (traditional medical practitioners) in remote villages. All foster close contact with Mexican nature or Mexican communities and most reach destinations that few other visitors get to. The state of Oaxaca is an alternative tourism hub, and the state government even has a Web site devoted to it (W www.activemexico.com). Several organizations in the city offer exciting ventures:

Bicicletas Bravo (☎ 516-09-53, e roger@spersaoaxaca.com.mx, *García Vigil 409)* Bicicletas Bravo does easy-to-challenging mountain bike trips of four or five hours in the Valles Centrales for around US$33 per person (minimum two), and a two-day trip in the Santiago Apoala area in the Mixteca. They rent bikes too (see Getting Around).

Bicicletas Pedro Martínez (☎ 514-31-44, W www.bicicletaspedromartinez.com, *JP García 509)* The amiable Pedro Martínez, a champion mountain biker himself, offers day rides for a minimum of two people in the Valles Centrales, Sierra Norte and Mixteca (from US$34/65 per person without/with support vehicle), and four-day Oaxaca-Puerto Escondido expeditions (minimum three people) for around US$650. Keen bikers of all levels enjoy Pedro's trips. He rents bikes too (see Getting Around).

Expediciones Sierra Norte (☎ 514-82-71, W www.sierranorte.org.mx, *García Vigil 406)* This well-run rural community organization offers walking, mountain biking and accommodations in the beautiful Sierra Norte, northeast of the city; see the Pueblos Mancomunados section, later.

Museos Comunitarios del Estado de Oaxaca (☎/fax 516-57-86, W www.umco.org, *Tinoco y Palacios 311, Depto No 12)* Open 10am-6pm Mon-Fri. About 15 Oaxacan villages have set up community museums to foster their unique cultures and keep their archaeological and cultural treasures 'at home.' Organized in conjunction with the museums is a program of day tours with villager guides, including lunch with a family, activities such as horse or bicycle rides or walks to little-known archaeological sites, and craft, cooking or agricultural demonstrations. Groups of three to five can usually arrange a tour at one day's notice (US$21 to US$32 per person). For an English-speaking guide, you may need to ask a few days ahead. Usually no one at the office speaks English.

Tierra Dentro (☎ 514-92-84, W www.tierradentro.com, *Reforma 528B)* Tierra Dentro offers climbing for beginners near Oaxaca and Yagul (US$34 to US$45 per half-day), birding (around US$70 for a seven-hour trip), mountain bike trips including a four-day expedition to Puerto Escondido (around US$550), and ascents of Mexico's highest mountain, Pico de Orizaba (see Around Orizaba in the Central Gulf Coast chapter), practicable even for those without high-altitude climbing experience (three to six days, US$200 to US$650).

Tierraventura (☎ 514-38-43, W www.tierraventura.com, *Boca del Monte 110)* Run by a multilingual Swiss and German couple, Tierraventura takes groups of up to six on trips in the Valles Centrales, Sierra Norte, Mixteca or along the Pacific coast. They include some fairly remote destinations and focus on hiking, nature, crafts, meeting locals, and traditional medicine, working with local communities and using local guides where possible. Prices range between US$45 and US$65 per person per day.

Oaxaca's beautiful Pacific coast presents many further energetic ways of spending your time; see the Oaxaca Coast section, later.

OAXACA STATE

Día de Muertos – Day of the Dead is a big happening here, with a festive atmosphere building beforehand, and a program of music and dance events at the main cemetery, the Panteón General, on Calzada del Panteón about 1.25km east of the zócalo. A local specialty is colored sand sculptures – look for them in front of the cathedral and at the cemetery. Some guesthouses and agencies put on excursions to village celebrations.

Christmas Events – December 16 is the first of nine nights of *posadas*, neighborhood processions of children and adults symbolizing Mary and Joseph's journey to Bethlehem. December 18, the Día de la Virgen de la Soledad, sees processions and traditional dances, including the Danza de las Plumas, at the Basílica de la Soledad. On the Noche de los Rábanos (Night of the Radishes), December 23, amazing figures carved from radishes are displayed in the zócalo. On December 24, processions called *calendas* leave from churches and converge on the zócalo about 10pm, bringing music, floats and fireworks.

Places to Stay

The tourist high seasons in Oaxaca are from about mid-December to mid-January, a week each side of Easter, mid-July to mid-August, and a week each side of Día de Muertos. Many establishments, except in the real budget bracket, raise their prices by somewhere between 15% and 30% during these periods.

¡Guelaguetza!

The Guelaguetza, a brilliant feast of Oaxacan folk dance, takes place in the big open-air Auditorio Guelaguetza on Cerro del Fortín, the hill in the north of the city, on the first two Mondays after July 16. (The only time the dates vary is when July 18, the anniversary of Benito Juárez's death, falls on a Monday. Guelaguetza then happens on July 25 and August 1.) Thousands of people flock into the city for these and a slew of associated events, turning Oaxaca into a feast of celebration and regional culture.

On the appointed Mondays, known as Los Lunes del Cerro (Mondays on the Hill), Cerro del Fortín comes alive with hawkers and picnickers. From about 10am to 1pm, magnificently costumed dancers from the seven regions of Oaxaca state perform a succession of dignified, lively or comical traditional dances, tossing offerings of produce to the crowd as they finish. Excitement climaxes with the incredibly colorful pineapple dance by women of the Papaloapan region, and the stately, prancing Zapotec Danza de las Plumas (Feather Dance), which reenacts, symbolically, the Spanish conquest.

Seats in the amphitheater (which holds perhaps 10,000) are divided into four *palcos* (areas). For the two palcos nearest the stage, tickets (around US$40 and US$33) go on sale months beforehand from the tourist office on Independencia. Nearer festival time they're also available at other outlets in the city. Tickets guarantee a seat, but you should still arrive before 8am if you want one of the better ones. The two much bigger rear palcos are free and fill up early – if you get in by 8am you'll get a seat, but by 10am you'll be lucky to get even standing room. For all areas take a hat and something to drink, as you'll be sitting under the naked sun for hours.

In recent years a number of other events have grown up around the Guelaguetza. Highlights include the processions of the regional delegations, in the city center on the two Saturday afternoons before the Guelaguetza Mondays; the Bani Stui Gulal, a vibrant show of music, fireworks and dance telling the history of the Guelaguetza, on the two Sunday evenings in the Plaza de la Danza by the Basílica de la Soledad; a weeklong mezcal fair; and lots of concerts and craft and food stalls. Programs of events are widely available.

The origins of the Guelaguetza lay in pre-Hispanic rites in honor of maize and wind gods, held about the same time of year on Cerro del Fortín. After the Spanish conquest the indigenous festivities became fused with Christian celebrations for the Virgen del Carmen (July 16). In the 18th century a new tradition emerged of giants and grotesquely big-headed figures dancing on the hill.

Celebrations in something like their present form began in 1932, and the purpose-built amphitheater was opened in 1974. Guelaguetza is a Zapotec word meaning mutual help, cooperation or exchange of gifts, referring to the tradition of people helping each other out at such times as weddings, births and deaths.

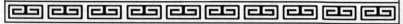

Budget For camping, there's the moderately shabby *Oaxaca Trailer Park* (☎ 515-27-96, *Violetas 900*), which is 3.5km northeast of the center. Turn north off Calzada Niños Héroes de Chapultepec, half a kilometer east of the 1st-class bus station, and go seven blocks up Avenida Manuel Ruiz (which becomes Calle Violetas). For a car or van, the rate is US$10 for two people; for a trailer with hookups, it's US$11.50/17 for one/two people.

Hostels Oaxaca has more backpacker-oriented hostels than any other city in Mexico. All have guest kitchens and shared bathrooms unless stated.

Hostel Luz de Luna Nuyoo (☎ 516-95-76, e *mayoraljc@hotmail.com*, *Juárez 101*) Dorm beds US$7.25 including breakfast. This is a friendly small hostel run by two young Oaxacan musician brothers. Separate bunk rooms for women, men and couples open to a patio, and at the front is an inexpensive café run by the brothers' mom. Internet use costs US$0.90 an hour.

Hostal Santa Isabel (☎ 514-28-65, *Mier y Terán 103*) Dorm beds US$4.50, doubles/triples US$13.50/17. Tranquil, friendly Santa Isabel has room for about 40 in bunk dormitories (one for women only) and varied bedrooms, around two patios with plants. Internet is US$1.25 an hour, and there are bicycles to rent.

Hostal Guadalupe (☎ 516-63-65, *Juárez 409*) Dorm beds US$5/5.75 with/without hostel card. This small, clean, calm hostel, north of the zócalo, offers separate-sex bunk rooms.

Youth Hostel Plata/Gelatina (☎ 514-93-91, *Independencia 504*) Dorm bunks US$5.75, singles/doubles US$11.50/13.50. Plata/Gelatina is a rambling, friendly, small hostel-cum-gallery-cum-artists' storehouse, close to the zócalo. It has separate-sex bunk dorms and a couple of small rooms – plus Ping-Pong.

Magic Hostel (☎ 516-76-67, *Fiallo 305*) Dorm bunks & beds US$6.75, rooms US$8 per person. The Magic is an untidy, social backpackers' hostel with plentiful sitting areas but little care wasted on the dorms or bathrooms. It has about 45 places in women-only and mixed dorms, 11 rooms holding from two to five people, and a beer bar next to the kitchen and roof lounge. Guests get 15 minutes' free Internet daily.

Casa Paulina (☎ 516-20-05, e *hpaulina@prodigy.net.mx*, *Trujano 321*) Dorms US$7.25 per person, doubles/triples/quads US$9/18/27. Casa Paulina, with an unmissable bright yellow exterior, is almost brand new and impeccably clean, with eight-bunk dorms and rooms holding one double bed and one pair of bunks. Lockers are provided. The hostel has a pretty little interior garden, and a cafeteria under construction on our visit, but no guest kitchen.

Hostal de Don Diego (☎ 516-92-60, *Callejón del Carmen 102*) Dorm bunks US$5.75, doubles US$13.50. Don Diego is another friendly hostel with eight dorm rooms, two private rooms and a shared courtyard. Bike rental is also available for US$5.75 a day.

Hotels Though hostel dorms provide the cheapest accommodations, several budget hotels offer good value if you want your own room.

Hotel Aurora (☎ 516-41-45, e *ernestor@prodigy.net.mx*, *Bustamante 212*) Singles/doubles/triples/quads with bath US$17/25/30/34. Close to the zócalo, the Aurora has 30 decent, if in some cases rather airless, rooms, with hot water. A restaurant is under construction. Staff are amiable.

Hotel Pasaje (☎ 516-42-13, *Mina 302*) Singles US$14.50, doubles US$18-23. The Pasaje has small, clean rooms with small bathrooms, on two floors around a patio with plenty of plants. A long-time travelers' favorite, it has suffered like other cheap hotels from the hostels boom but remains a fair value if you want a room. Sadly, Lorenzo the parrot has passed away.

Posada Margarita (☎ 516-28-02, *Plaza de la Virgen, Plazuela Labastida 115*) Singles/doubles with shared bath US$11.50/16, with private bath US$19/23. The Margarita has 12 simple, plain, clean rooms. Its location, a stone's throw from Alcalá and Santo Domingo, is its main plus.

Hotel Santa Clara (☎ 516-11-38, *Morelos 1004*) Singles/doubles with bath US$14.50/23. This little hotel is not a bad value. It's friendly, with fair-sized, clean rooms.

Hotel Villa de León (☎ 516-19-77, *Reforma 405*) Singles/doubles US$19/26. The Villa de León offers adequate rooms with fan, TV and carpets.

Hotel Casa Arnel (☎ 515-28-56, ⓦ *http://oaxaca.com.mx/arnel, Callejón Aldama 404)* Singles/doubles with shared bath US$12.50/25, singles & doubles with private bath from US$28, triples with private bath from US$31; suites US$56-84. Family-run Casa Arnel is in quiet, cobbled Colonia Jalatlaco, five minutes' walk south from the 1st-class bus station and 20 minutes northeast from the city center. It's a long-running travelers' hangout with clean but still mostly basic rooms around a big, leafy courtyard, plus a few suites for up to four people. Casa Arnel also offers a travel agency (village tours available), economical car rental, breakfast, a clothes-washing sink and a fabulous roof terrace.

Mid-Range Rooms in this range nearly all have private bathrooms with hot water.

Hotels The first five hotels here are all within 1½ blocks of the zócalo.

Hotel Las Rosas (☎ 514-22-17, *Trujano 112)* Singles/doubles US$32/40, triples/quads US$48/60. The dependable Las Rosas offers clean, fan-cooled rooms with TV, on two levels around a pleasant courtyard. It also provides free drinking water, tea and coffee. The entrance is up a flight of stairs from the street.

Hotel Mesón del Rey (☎ 516-00-33, ⓔ *mesonrey@oax1.telmex.net.mx, Trujano 212)* Singles/doubles US$32/41. The 27-room Mesón del Rey is another clean, comfy abode. Rooms are carpeted and have TV and fan.

Hotel Francia (☎ 516-48-11, fax 516-42-51, ⓦ *www.mexonline.com/francia.htm, 20 de Noviembre 212)* Singles/doubles/triples US$38/45/56. The venerable, 65-room Francia was recently brightened up and its rooms are now quite pleasant though still moderate-sized. They have fan, phone and TV. This is a clean, amiable place (and DH Lawrence stayed here!).

Hotel Antonio's (☎ 516-72-27, fax 516-36-72, *Independencia 601)* Singles or doubles (one bed) US$28, triples or quads (two double beds) US$39. Antonio's has 15 nice, bright, sizable rooms. The best are those above the courtyard restaurant.

Hotel Gala (☎ 514-22-51, fax 516-36-60, *Bustamante 103)* Singles/doubles/triples US$52/58/67. The Gala, just off the zócalo,

has a highly impressive lobby decked with art and elegant furnishings. The rooms are less imposing but good enough, all possessing TV, phone and fan. Those on the street side are biggest.

Hotel Posada Catarina (☎ 516-42-70, ⓔ *aesperon@oax1.telmex.net.mx, Aldama 325)* Singles & doubles US$34-44, triples & quads US$50. The Posada Catarina is on a busy street in a grungy part of town, southwest of the zócalo, but it's large and rambling, with two patios (one with a garden) and really nice rooms, traditional in style but with modern comforts including TV and fan. Contemporary art decks the walls.

Hotel Posada del Centro (☎/fax 516-18-74, ⓦ *www.mexonline.com/posada.htm, Independencia 403)* Singles/doubles/triples/quads with shared bath US$17/20/26/28, with private bath & TV US$35/39/53/55. Posada del Centro, with two large patios, was converted only a few years ago to an attractive hotel. The 22 rooms have fans and pleasing Oaxacan artisanry. It's just three blocks west of the cathedral.

The following are all in the attractive northern part of the city center.

Hotel Las Golondrinas (☎ 514-32-98, ⓔ *lasgolon@prodigy.net.mx, Tinoco y Palacios 411)* Singles US$32-40, doubles US$40-50, triples US$48. This excellent small hotel, lovingly tended by friendly owners and staff, has about 18 rooms opening onto three leafy little patios. It's often full, so try to book ahead. None of the rooms is huge but all are tastefully decorated and immaculately clean. Good breakfasts (not included in room rates) are available.

Hotel Principal (☎ 516-25-35, ⓔ *jdbrena@prodigy.net.mx, 5 de Mayo 208)* Singles/doubles/twins/triples US$22/33/43/52. The Principal is a long-running travelers' haunt providing about 16 rooms at reasonable prices. Most are large and surround a sunny, peaceful courtyard. The few rear rooms are smaller and less attractive.

Hotel Cazomalli (☎ 513-86-05, ⓦ *www.mexonline.com/cazomalli.htm, El Salto 104)* Singles & doubles US$45, triples/quads US$53/64. The comfortable, 18-room Cazomalli is 1.5km northeast of the zócalo and five minutes' walk from the 1st-class bus station, in quiet Colonia Jalatlaco. The hotel has a covered patio and is decorated with tasteful *artesanías*. Breakfast and Internet access (US$1.25 an hour) are available, and the roof terrace has lovely views.

Hotel Azucenas (☎ 514-79-18, fax 514-93-80, **W** www.hotelazucenas.com, Aranda 203) Singles/doubles/triples US$39/45/50. The Azucenas is a small hotel in a tastefully restored colonial house. Its top feature is an inviting roof terrace with good vistas, where a delicious buffet breakfast (US$3) is served.

Parador del Domínico (☎ 513-18-12, **e** dominico@infosel.net.mx, Pino Suárez 410) Singles/doubles US$68/73 including breakfast. This hotel is almost new but in an attractive traditional style, with a lovely stone-columned patio bar. The 30 or so rooms have air-con, cable TV, computer hookups and safe. There's a restaurant too.

B&Bs Most 'B&Bs' in Oaxaca are actually attractive guesthouses.

Las Bugambilias (☎/fax 516-11-65, **W** www.mexonline.com/bugambil.htm, Reforma 402) Singles US$37-61, doubles US$49-74, double/triple/quad suites US$97/107/122. This delightful B&B, entered through Café La Olla, is a colonial house with a pretty garden, library, TV/sitting room and eight individually decorated rooms with tiled bathrooms. Some have terraces. Prices include a healthy, traditional breakfast.

La Casa de mis Recuerdos (☎ 515-56-45, ☎ 515-84-83, **W** www.misrecuerdos.net, Pino Suárez 508) Singles US$33-43, doubles US$59-71 (prices fall a few dollars from August to late October and from March to May, except around Semana Santa). A big Oaxacan breakfast, served in the family dining room, is a feature of this charming guesthouse. Five of the nine rooms have private bath, and the best overlook a central garden.

Las Mariposas (☎/fax 515-58-54, **W** www.mexonline.com/mariposas.htm, Pino Suárez 517) Singles/doubles US$28/39, studio apartments US$39/50. Las Mariposas offers six studio apartments (with small kitchen) and four rooms along a pretty patio. There's an open-air guest kitchen too. All rooms are simply but prettily decorated, and it's a tranquil, friendly place.

La Casa de María (☎ 515-12-02, **W** http://oaxacalive.com/maria.htm, Belisario Domínguez 205, Colonia Reforma) Singles/doubles from US$36/46 including continental breakfast. Tucked behind a high wall in the north of town, this attractive guesthouse is an oasis of calm run by the lively and friendly María. The 16 comfortable rooms and two self-catering bungalows are set around two lovely garden areas. There's a roof terrace and a TV/sitting room too. From the 1st-class bus station, it's four blocks north along Emiliano Carranza, then 1½ blocks west along Belisario Domínguez.

You'll find more B&Bs advertised in the *Oaxaca Times* and *Oaxaca* newspapers and on the Internet.

Apartments & Houses Check notice boards and the press (see Media, earlier) for apartments and houses to let.

Parador Santo Domingo de Guzmán (☎ 514-10-19, **e** suitesparador@prodigy .net.mx, Alcalá 804) Singles/doubles/triples US$62/69/74, per week US$374/410/432. These comfortable apartments are 8½ blocks north of the zócalo. Each has two double beds, a sitting room, bathroom, cable TV and well-equipped kitchen. Other amenities include a pool and hotel-style room service with clean sheets daily.

La Casa de mis Recuerdos (see B&Bs) has three nearby apartments for rent at US$500 a month.

Top End Top-end accommodations range from a converted colonial convent to modern resort-type hotels.

Camino Real Oaxaca (☎ 516-06-11, fax 516-07-32, **W** www.caminoreal.com, 5 de Mayo 300) Singles/doubles from US$228/254. Four blocks northeast of the zócalo, the Camino Real was created in the 1970s in the 16th-century former Santa Catalina convent. The old chapel is a banquet hall, one patio contains an enticing swimming pool, and the bar is lined with books on otherworldly devotion. Thick stone walls keep the place cool. There are 91 varied rooms, well decorated in colonial styles and some reserved for non-smokers. If you can, choose one upstairs and away from kitchen noise.

Casa de Sierra Azul (☎/fax 514-84-12, **W** www.mexonline.com/sierrazul.htm, Hidalgo 1002) Singles/doubles US$78/96. The Sierra Azul is a 200-year-old house recently converted to a fine small hotel, centered on a broad courtyard with a fountain and stone pillars. The 13 good-sized, tasteful rooms have high ceilings, old-fashioned-style furnishings and good tiled bathrooms.

Hotel Marqués Del Valle (☎ *516-36-77, fax 516-99-61,* e *hmarques@prodigy.net.mx, Portal de Clavería s/n)* Singles/doubles/triples US$74/90/106, doubles/triples with balcony US$96/116. You're paying for an incomparable location on the north side of the zócalo. The 100-room Marqués Del Valle has spacious, comfortable rooms, some with great views.

Hotel Misión de los Ángeles (☎ *515-15-00,* w *www.misiondelosangeles.com, Calzada Porfirio Díaz 102)* Singles & doubles US$117, triples US$139, suites for 4 US$152. North of the center, the Misión de los Ángeles has 145 large rooms in extensive tropical gardens, plus tennis courts and a large pool. Standard rooms all have two double beds. Choose one well away from the road. Promotional offers sometimes include free accommodations for children under 12.

Hotel Victoria (☎ *515-26-33, fax 515-24-11,* w *www.hotelvictoriaoax.com.mx, Lomas del Fortín 1)* Singles & doubles US$170, villas for up to 4 US$208, suites for up to 5 from US$247. The Victoria stands on the lower slopes of Cerro del Fortín. Many of the 150 large rooms and suites overlook the city, and the hotel has an Olympic-size pool in big gardens. The restaurant gets good reports. The hotel runs a free shuttle to/from the city center.

Places to Eat

Many places offer Oaxacan specialties, but four spots that really feature them are Restaurante El Naranjo, Fonda de la Cruz, El Biche Pobre and El Topil (see the following sections). For places where you can enjoy music with a meal, see the Entertainment section. If you're a vegetarian or a caffeine addict, your best bet is the area north of the zócalo.

Markets Cheap *oaxaqueño* meals can be had in the *Mercado 20 de Noviembre*, south of the zócalo. Most of the many small *comedores* here serve up local specialties such as chicken in *mole negro*. Few post prices, but a typical main dish is about US$1.75 to US$3. Pick a comedor that's busy – those are the best. Many stay open until early evening,

but their food is freshest earlier in the day. More comedores can be found in the big *Central de Abastos* (see Shopping, later).

On & Near the Zócalo All the cafés and restaurants beneath the zócalo arches are great spots for watching Oaxaca life, but quality and service vary.

Café Del Jardín (*Portal de Flores 10)* The Jardín has a peerless position at the southwest corner of the zócalo. Its food is ordinary but the cappuccino is nice.

La Primavera (☎ *516-25-95, Portal de Flores 1C)* Mains US$2.75-4.50. This is a fairly good restaurant with some vegetarian options. Three quesadillas with mushrooms, guacamole, the herb *epazote* and pumpkin flower cost US$3.75.

El Asador Vasco (☎ *514-47-55, Portal de Flores 11)* Mains US$8-13.50. Open noon-11.30pm Mon-Sat. Upstairs at the southwest corner of the square, the Asador Vasco serves good Mexican, Spanish and international food. It's strong on meat and seafood. For a table overlooking the zócalo on a warm evening, book earlier in the day.

Terranova Café (☎ *514-05-33, Portal Juárez 116)* Mains & *comida corrida* US$5-7.50. This cafe, on the east side of the zócalo, is one of the best places on the square, serving good breakfasts till 1pm (with a US$7.50 unlimited buffet on Sunday), and a big range of *antojitos*, baguettes and other light eats as well as lunches and dinners.

El Mesón (☎ *516-27-29, Hidalgo 805)* Buffet meals US$5. Open 8am-midnight daily. El Mesón, just off the zócalo, prepares tasty, mainly charcoal-grilled Mexican food. You tick off your order on a printed list. Tacos and quesadillas are the specialties, mostly at US$2 to US$3 for a serving of two or three. There are also reasonable self-serve buffets available for all three meals.

El Sagrario (☎ *514-03-43, Valdivieso 120)* Mains US$4.50-9. This popular and reliable spot half a block north of the zócalo serves Mexican, Italian and international food on three floors. They do a US$7.25 all-you-can-eat buffet from 1pm to 5pm.

West of the Zócalo *Café Alex* (☎ *514-07-15, Díaz Ordaz 218)* Breakfasts US$3.25-4.50. Open 7am-9pm Mon-Sat, 7am-noon Sun. The clean, busy Alex is well worth hunting out for great-value breakfasts, served till noon. Nineteen deals are on offer: US$3.75 will buy you scrambled eggs with potatoes, ham and onion, plus beans, tortillas or bread, juice or fruit, and coffee or tea, and servings are generous. There's usually a mixed Mexican and foreign crowd here, and service is quick.

Restaurant Colonial *(20 de Noviembre 112)* Comida corrida US$3. Open 1pm-4pm Mon-Sat. The Colonial's 10 or so tables fill up for the good-value comida, which includes soup, rice, a main course such as

pollo a la naranja (chicken à l'orange), dessert and *agua de fruta*.

Restaurante El Naranjo *(☎ 514-18-78, Trujano 203)* Mains US$6.50-8. Open 1pm-10pm Mon-Sat. This excellent courtyard restaurant features oaxaqueño food with a modern touch. It's not cheap and the clientele is nearly all foreign, but the owner/chef is a local woman who picked up some imaginative ideas during a spell in Mexico City, and she can cook. Each of the seven Oaxacan moles is served one day of the

Cocina Oaxaqueña

Good oaxaqueño regional cooking is spicily delicious, and the seven traditional Oaxacan *moles* (sauces) are renowned. Specialties include:

amarillo (con pollo) – a yellow-orange cumin and chili mole (with chicken)

chapulines – grasshoppers! They come fried, often with chili powder, onion and garlic; high in protein and good with a squeeze of lime – vendors sell them from baskets in the zócalo and you can find them in food markets too

chíchilo – a dark, rich mole made with varied chilies

coloradito – a brick-red chili-and-tomato mole, usually served over pork or chicken

colorado – a dark red mole

manchamanteles – 'tablecloth-stainer': a mole made with pineapple and bananas

memelitas – small tortillas with varied toppings

mole negro – the monarch of Oaxacan moles, sometimes called just *mole oaxaqueño:* a dark, spicy, slightly sweet sauce made with many ingredients including chilies, bananas, chocolate, pepper and cinnamon; usually served with chicken

picadillo – spicy minced or shredded pork, often used for the stuffing in *chiles rellenos*

quesillo – Oaxacan stringy cheese

verde (con espinazo) – a green mole (with pork back) made from beans, chilies, parsley and *epazote* (goosefoot or wild spinach)

tamal oaxaqueño – a tamal with a mole and (usually) chicken filling

tasajo – a slice of pounded beef

tlayuda or *tlalluda* – a big crisp tortilla, traditionally served with salsa and chili but now topped with almost anything, making it into a kind of pizza

GREG ELMS

Chapulinas (grasshoppers) for sale

week, with chicken breast or pork fillet. The *chiles rellenos*, with innovative fillings, are another good choice.

Rostería El Chinito (*Las Casas 405*) Quarter/half chicken US$2/3. Your roast bird comes with rice, salad and tortillas at cheap, cheerful Chinito.

East of the Zócalo *El Buen Gourmet* (*Independencia 1104*) Mains US$1.50-2.25. The straightforward Buen Gourmet turns out good, straightforward Mexican dishes like chiles rellenos and chicken in *mole poblano* at straightforward prices. Soups and salads are only US$0.60 to US$1.25.

North of the Zócalo These listings are in approximate south-to-north order.

Tito's (☎ 516-19-71, *García Vigil 116*) Prices US$2-5. Tito's prepares quite a range of mainly Mexican food, from *tortas* and salads to meat main courses. Tito's snack bar next door is good for a quick taco, torta or baguette.

Quickly Restaurant (☎ 514-23-11, *Alcalá 100B*) Mains around US$4.50. Quickly is reliable for an inexpensive if bland feed. *Parrilladas* – grilled vegetable and rice platters topped with melted cheese and served with tortillas and guacamole – will fill you up. Some have meat too.

1254 Marco Polo (☎ 514-43-60, *5 de Mayo 103*) Mains US$6-11. Open 8am-10.30pm Mon-Sat. Marco Polo is Oaxaca's best downtown fish and seafood restaurant. Soups and seafood cocktails for starters cost US$4 to US$5.

Decano (*5 de Mayo 210*) Prices US$3-4.50. Open 8am-midnight daily. Decano satisfies a range of food needs from breakfast to a good *menú del día* or tasty light eats (*'el super munchies'*). In the evening it's a popular spot for young oaxaqueños to down a beer or two. Host Carlos has our favorite Oaxaca restaurant music collection!

Cafetería Bamby (☎ 516-25-10, *García Vigil 205*) Breakfasts US$2.50-4.50, mains US$3.50-5. Open 8am-10pm Mon-Sat. This bright, clean café serves sizable portions of plain but good Mexican and gringo food – salads, spaghetti, chicken and meats. The three-course comida is US$4.

Panini (*Matamoros 200A*) Prices US$1.50-3. This is a great little place to drop into for a fine ciabatta torta (with

vegetarian varieties available), salad or sweet crêpe.

Hostería de Alcalá (☎ 516-20-93, *Plaza Alcalá, Alcalá 307*) Mains US$5-10, wines from US$20. Open 8am-11pm daily. This courtyard restaurant is one of Oaxaca's classiest eateries. The steaks, at the top end of the price range, are a specialty. For something more economical, try pasta or a salad.

La Crêpe (☎ 516-22-00, *Plaza Alcalá, Alcalá 307*) Crêpes US$1.50-4. Enjoy a sweet or savory crêpe with wine, beer or coffee here, upstairs in Plaza Alcalá.

El Topil (☎ 514-16-17, *Plazuela Labastida 104*) Prices US$3.50-6. Open 7.30am-11.30pm daily. El Topil serves individualistic dishes with the touch of home cooking; *tasajo* with guacamole and frijoles is one specialty. The menu also offers soups, *tlayudas*, chiles rellenos, and some good antojitos.

Pizzeria Alfredo da Roma (☎ 516-50-58, *Alcalá 400*) 2-person pizzas US$6.75-8.50. Alfredo's, just below the Iglesia de Santo Domingo, has reasonable, well-priced Italian food. Pizzas come in more than 20 combinations and five sizes. Rinse them down with sangria or wine.

Los Pacos (☎ 516-17-04, *Constitución 104*) Mains US$5-10. Los Pacos, set in a pleasant patio, offers tasty Oaxacan and international food and good service. Servings are generous.

La Brew (☎ 514-96-73, *García Vigil 409B*) Prices US$1-4. Open 8am-8pm Mon-Sat, 8am-2pm Sun. Come to American-owned La Brew for waffles, BLT sandwiches, yogurt and granola, homemade brownies and chocolate chip cookies.

Fonda de la Cruz (☎ 513-91-60, *García Vigil 716*) Mains from US$3.50. This atmospheric spot specializes in yummie Oaxacan and Yucatán dishes. You can eat at the table in the kitchen and watch the intricate preparations of your meal. Try the *pan de cazón*, a thick pancake with fish and a piquant tomato sauce, or *panuchos*, corn pizzas with pork and onion in a spicy sauce. The *botana oaxaqueña*, an assortment of Oaxacan dishes, is recommended too.

Pizza Rústica (☎ 516-75-00, *Alcalá 804*) Pizzas US$6-10. Open 1pm-11pm or midnight daily. Rústica's pizzas are big and tasty – a *grande* should satisfy three. Salads are good too, and there's wine aplenty.

1254 Marco Polo (☎ 513-43-08, *Pino Suárez 806*) Breakfasts US$2.50-3, antojitos

US$3.50, fish & seafood more. Open 8am-6.30pm Wed-Mon. This popular breakfast spot has a large garden dining area, attentive waiters and good food. From noon till closing, antojitos and oven-baked seafood are the main draws.

El Biche Pobre (☎ 513-46-36, Calzada de la República 600) Mains around US$3.50-6. Open 1pm-9pm daily. El Biche Pobre, 1.5km northeast of the zócalo, is an informal place with about a dozen tables, some long enough to stage lunch for a whole extended Mexican family. A big variety of Oaxacan food is available at reasonable prices. For an introduction to the local cuisine, you can't beat the US$5 *botana surtida*, a dozen assorted little items that add up to a tasty meal.

Vegetarian Many restaurants have vegetarian options, but the following have more than most.

Café La Olla (☎ 516-66-68, Reforma 402) Prices US$2.50-9. Open 8am-10pm Mon-Sat. This excellent café serves good whole-grain tortas, juices, salads, meat dishes and regional specialties. It's a fine place for breakfast (US$3-4).

Restaurant Flor de Loto (Morelos 509) Dishes from US$3. Flor de Loto makes a reasonable stab at pleasing a range of palates from vegan to carnivore. The *crepas de espinacas* (spinach pancakes) and *verduras al gratin* (vegetables with melted cheese) are both good. The US$3.75 comida corrida, with a veggie version available, is a real meal.

Restaurant Manantial Vegetariano (☎ 514-56-02, Tinoco y Palacios 303) Breakfasts US$1.75-3.50, menú del día US$3, 25-plate lunch buffet (2pm-4pm daily) US$5.75. Open 9am-9pm Mon-Sat, 9am-6pm Sun. This veggie restaurant has a pleasant atmosphere with tables in an open-air courtyard.

Cafés & Bakeries A handy everyday bakery for cakes, *bolillos* and large *pan integral* loaves is *Bamby (García Vigil at Morelos)*.

Coffee Beans (5 de Mayo 205; 5 de Mayo 400C) Coffees US$1.50-3. The two branches of Coffee Beans offer a vast range of real caffeine fixes, which you can accompany with crêpes, cakes or pastries.

Café Gecko (☎ 514-80-24, Plaza Gonzalo Lucero, 5 de Mayo 412) Prices US$1-2.50.

This peaceful café in a leafy courtyard is a good spot for coffee and a sandwich or quesadillas.

Café La Antigua (☎ 516-57-61, Reforma 401) Coffees US$1.50-3. The popular Antigua has a long list of gourmet coffees.

Pastelería Quemen (Independencia 902) Cakes & pastries US$1-1.50. Sweet tooths should head directly for the divine fruit tarts at this bakery 2½ blocks northeast of the zócalo.

Entertainment

Oaxaca has an ever livelier entertainment and cultural scene, thanks to its student and tourist populations. Some kind of what's-on publication is usually available.

Live Music Venues Free *concerts* in the zócalo are given several evenings each week at 7pm, and around noon on Sunday, by the state marimba ensemble or state band.

Candela (☎ 514-20-10, Murguía 413) Admission US$3-4. Open 1pm-1.30am Tues-Sat. Candela's writhing salsa band and beautiful colonial-house setting have kept it at the top of the Oaxaca nightlife lists for several years. Arrive fairly early (9.30pm to 10.30pm) to get a good table, and either learn to dance or learn to watch. Candela is a restaurant too, with a good lunchtime menú (US$4) prepared by a Paris-trained chef. Drinks start around US$1.75.

El Sol y La Luna (☎ 514-80-69, Reforma 502) Admission US$3.50. Open 6pm-1am Mon-Sat. El Sol y La Luna offers smooth Latin music, or sometimes jazz, starting around 9.30pm several nights a week. The setting is another colonial-style house and the crowd tends to be a refined one of dining couples and art lovers. Pasta, salads, crêpes, chicken and meat dishes cost between US$4.50 and US$8.

La Caracola (☎ 516-38-16, Tinoco y Palacios 604) Admission around US$5. Open from 6pm Mon-Sat. La Caracola is an atmospheric café/bar/restaurant with frequent live music, often jazz, and an indoor/outdoor layout that makes the most of a pedestrian area with a fountain.

La Tentación (Matamoros 101) Admission US$3. Open 9pm-2am Tues-Sat. A casual but erratic alternative to Candela, La Tentación puts on live salsa Thursday to Saturday, and some DJ nights midweek. It's close to the zócalo and has a relaxed door policy.

Other places with regular live music are *El Ensayo*, *La Cucaracha* and *La Resistencia (see Bars)*.

Bars *La Cucaracha* (☎ 514-20-42, *Porfirio Díaz 301A)* Open 7pm-2am Mon-Sat. If you wish to make close acquaintance with some classic Mexican beverages, a good place to start is La Cucaracha. This specialist bar stocks 40 varieties of mezcal and 100 of tequila, costing around US$1.75 to US$5 a shot. Everyone's welcome (it's not a cantina), food is available, and there's live Latin music and a lively atmosphere on weekends.

La Resistencia (*Porfirio Díaz 503)* Open 8.30pm-1am Tues-Sun. This revolution-theme bar, popular with a mainly Mexican 20s and 30s crowd, has good draft beers and good service. Some nights you might catch some offbeat live music.

La Divina (☎ 582-05-08, *Gurrión 104)* Open approx 12.30pm-1am Tues-Sun. Loud, busy La Divina, across the street from the Iglesia de Santo Domingo, has a disco-esque interior and music from Spanish-language rock to house to English pop. A mixed-nationality crowd generates a warm atmosphere that spills out on to the street if you're lucky. Drinks start around US$1.75.

La Casa del Mezcal (*Flores Magón 209)* Open 9am-9pm daily. Open since 1935, this is one of Oaxaca's oldest bars, 1½ blocks south of the zócalo. It's a cantina, but a safe one. One room has a large stand-up bar and shelves full of mezcal (US$1 to US$2.50 a shot); the other room has tables where *botanas* are served. Most patrons are men, but there are often a few women in there too.

Club 502 (☎ 516-60-20, *Porfirio Díaz 502)* Admission US$4.50 (including a drink) Fri & Sat. Open 11pm-dawn Thur-Sat. Club 502 is Oaxaca's only non-underground gay nightclub and offers the best house music in town. It's the only club downtown with a late-opening license. Ring the bell to enter, and be prepared for a strict door policy.

El Ensayo (☎ 513-87-42, *cnr 5 de Mayo & Alianza, Colonia Jalatlaco)* Open 2pm-11pm Tues-Sat. This art-focused hangout in Oaxaca's cobblestoned oldest quarter, northeast of the center, incorporates a bar, restaurant, bookstore and study center. You

can enjoy excellent food (around US$15 for lunch, more for dinner) while listening to live music including Spanish guitar and occasionally even flamenco.

Discos & Clubs Colonia Reforma, the middle-class suburb north of the center, is home to Oaxaca's best discos. They're generally open Wednesday to Saturday, with cover charges around US$5. Closest to downtown is *NRG (cnr Calzada Niños Héroes de Chapultepec & Calzada Porfirio Díaz)*, which has a regular following and innovative management who offer numerous events and promotions to lure their crowd. About four blocks north on Calzada Porfirio Díaz, *Nitro* pulls a younger crowd with the aid of beer promotions and themed events such as foam parties. A third place, good on Friday and Saturday, is *La Santa*, a further couple of blocks north on Calzada Porfirio Díaz.

Guelaguetza Shows If you're not lucky enough to be in Oaxaca for the Guelaguetza (see '¡Guelaguetza!'), there are worthwhile imitations.

Casa Cantera (☎ 514-75-85, *Murguía 102)* Admission US$11. A lively mini-Guelaguetza is staged here at 8.30pm nightly, in colorful costume with live music. To book, phone or stop by during the afternoon. Food and drinks are available.

Hotel Monte Albán (☎ 516-27-77, *Alameda de León 1)* Admission US$6.75. This hotel presents a 1½-hour version at 8.30pm nightly.

Camino Real Oaxaca (☎ 516-06-11, *5 de Mayo 300)* Admission US$32 including dinner. The classy Camino Real stages a highly colorful Guelaguetza show at 7pm Friday.

Other Entertainment *Cine Club El Pochote* (☎ 514-11-94, *García Vigil 817)* Admission free (donations accepted). Screenings usually 6pm & 8pm Tues-Sun. El Pochote shows international movies in their original language, usually with a different theme each month.

Centro Cultural Ricardo Flores Magón (☎ 514-03-95, *Alcalá 302)* This center puts on varied musical, dance and theater shows most nights. Many are free; drop by to see the program.

Spectator Sports

Oaxaca's **Guerreros** (W *http://guerreros deoaxaca.com*) play Liga Mexicana baseball from March to August at the Estadio Eduardo Vasconcelos, on Calzada Niños Héroes de Chapultepec, 400m east of the 1st-class bus station. Games are usually at 6pm Saturday or Sunday and 7.30pm other days. Admission ranges from US$0.60 to US$6.

Shopping

The state of Oaxaca has probably the richest, most inventive folk art scene in Mexico, and the city is its chief clearing-house. The classiest work is generally in shops, but prices are lower in the markets. You may not pay more for crafts in the city than in the villages where most of them are made, but in the city a lot of your money may be going to intermediaries. Some artisans have grouped together to market their own products directly: MARO (see Craft Shops, below) is one such enterprise.

Though artisans' techniques remain pretty traditional – back-strap and pedal looms, hand-turning of pottery – new products frequently appear in response to the big international demand for Oaxaca crafts. The wooden fantasy animals known as *alebrijes* were developed only a few years ago from toys that Oaxacans had been carving for their children for centuries.

Special crafts to look out for include the distinctive black pottery from San Bartolo Coyotepec; blankets, rugs and tapestries from Teotitlán del Valle; huipiles and other indigenous clothing from anywhere; the creative pottery figures made by the Aguilar sisters of Ocotlán; and stamped and colored tin from Oaxaca itself.

Rugs or blankets with muted colors are less likely to have been made with synthetic dyes than some of the more garish offerings. To assess the quality of a woven rug you can:

- gently tug at the fibers to see how tightly it's woven;
- rub your fingers or palm on it for about 15 seconds – if balls appear, the quality is poor;
- crumple it up a bit, then spread it on the floor – the creases will disappear from good rugs.

Jewelry is also sold here, and you'll find pieces using gold, silver or precious stones,

Chocolate

Oaxacans love their chocolate. A bowl of steaming hot chocolate with sweet bread to dunk is the perfect warmer when winter sets in 1500m above sea level. The mix to which hot milk or water is added typically contains cinnamon, almonds and lots of sugar as well as ground-up cocoa beans.

The area around the south end of Oaxaca's Mercado 20 de Noviembre is filling up with shops specializing in this time-honored Mexican treat – and not just chocolate for drinking but also chocolate for *moles,* hard chocolate for eating, and more. You can sample chocolate with or without cinnamon, light or dark chocolate with varying quantities of sugar, and many other varieties at any of these places. Most of them have vats where you can watch the mixing. We like the **Posada Chocolate,** which has a café (and even lodging rooms) as well as a shop. Or try a cup of steaming hot chocolate, with a sweet bun for dipping, in the market itself for around US$1.50.

but prices are a bit higher than in Mexico City or Taxco.

Just as fascinating in its way as the fancy craft stores is Oaxaca's commercial area stretching over several blocks southwest of the zócalo. Oaxacans flock here, and to the big Central de Abastos market, for all their everyday needs.

Markets The vast main market, the **Central de Abastos** (Supplies Center), is on the Periférico in the western part of town. Saturday is the big day, but the place is a hive of activity daily. If you look long enough, you can find almost anything here. Each type of product has a section to itself, so you'll find 20 or so woven-basket sellers here, a couple dozen pottery stalls there, and so on. The care that goes into the displays of food, particularly vegetables, is amazing.

The indoor **Mercado Juárez**, a block southwest of the zócalo, concentrates on food (more expensive than the Central de Abastos) but also has flowers and some crafts. The **Mercado 20 de Noviembre**, a block farther south, is mainly occupied by comedores, but you'll find a few inexpensive craft stalls on its west side. The **Mercado de Artesanías** (Handicrafts Market), a block southwest of Mercado 20 de Noviembre, gets fewer customers because it's slightly off the beaten track – so you may pick up some bargains. It's strong on pottery, rugs and textiles.

Two smaller craft markets function daily on plazas off Alcalá. On Plazuela Labastida you'll find jewelry, alebrijes, leather belts and artists at work, while Plazuela del Carmen Alto has weavings, embroideries, rugs and other textiles, mainly made and sold by the indigenous Triqui people.

Craft Shops MARO (☎ 516-06-70, 5 de Mayo 204) Open 9am-8pm daily. This is a sprawling store with a very wide range of good crafts at good prices, all made by the 300 members of the MARO women artisans' cooperative around Oaxaca state. Whether you buy a stamped tin mirror or a wooden skeleton on springs, you know your money is going direct to the people who made it.

The highest-quality crafts are mostly found in the smart stores on and near Alcalá, 5 de Mayo and García Vigil.

La Mano Mágica (☎ 516-42-75, Alcalá 203) This place sells particularly classy and expensive stuff, including weavings by one of its owners, the Teotitlán del Valle master weaver Arnulfo Mendoza. Some Mendoza

pieces go for thousands of dollars. The store is also a gallery of contemporary art.

Fonart (☎ 516-57-64, Crespo 114) This is a good government-run shop strong on ceramics and textiles.

El Cactus (☎ 514-03-05, Alcalá 401) El Cactus is good for blankets and rugs.

Aripo (☎ 514-40-30, García Vigil 809) Open 9am-8pm Mon-Fri, 10am-6pm Sat, 11am-4pm Sun. Aripo, run by the Oaxaca state government, stocks beautiful textiles and a range of other local crafts.

Casa de las Artesanías de Oaxaca (Matamoros 405) This shop has a patio surrounded by several rooms full of varied crafts.

Corazón El Pueblo (Alcalá 307) Upstairs in Plaza Alcalá, Corazón El Pueblo is yet another outlet for beautiful crafts.

Many shops can mail things home for you. Typical shop hours are 10am to 2pm and 4pm to 8pm Monday to Saturday.

Getting There & Away

Air Direct flights to and from Mexico City (1 hour) are operated by Mexicana four times daily and Aeroméxico three times (both costing around US$150) and Aviacsa once (US$120).

Aerocaribe has a daily multistop flight to/from Tuxtla Gutiérrez (around US$250 one-way), Villahermosa (US$280) and Mérida (US$350).

Over the years a variety of airlines have offered flights over the Sierra Madre del Sur to Puerto Escondido and Bahías de Huatulco on the Oaxaca coast – a spectacular half-hour hop. Currently Aerocaribe and Aerotucán (with 14-seat Cessnas) fly daily to/from both destinations, with fares to either starting around US$100 one-way. Aerovega flies a five-seater to/from Puerto Escondido daily (US$100).

Airline offices include: Aerocaribe (☎ 516-02-66), Fiallo 117; Aeroméxico (☎ 516-32-29), Hidalgo 513; Aerotucán (☎ 501-05-30), Alcalá 201, Interior 204 Altos; Aerovega (☎ 516-49-82), Hotel Monte Albán, Alameda de León 1; Aviacsa (☎ 518-45-55), Pino Suárez 604; and Mexicana (☎ 516-84-14), Fiallo 102.

Bus The 1st-class bus station, used by UNO (deluxe service), ADO and Cristóbal Colón (deluxe or 1st-class), is at Calzada Niños Héroes de Chapultepec 1036, 1.5km northeast of the zócalo. The 2nd-class bus station

---

Mezcal

Central Oaxaca state – especially around Santiago Matatlán and the Albarradas group of villages, south and east of Mitla – produces probably the best mezcal in Mexico (and therefore the world). Just like its cousin tequila, mezcal is made from the maguey plant and is usually better when *reposado* or *añejo* (aged). There are also some delicious *crema* varieties with fruit or other flavors.

Several Oaxaca shops southwest of the zócalo specialize in mezcal. Try **El Rey de los Mezcales** (Las Casas 509). US$10 will buy you a decent bottle but some US$3 mezcals are also fine. For fancy export mezcals (up to US$45 a bottle), head for **Alipús** (☎ 515-23-35, Gómez Farías 212B), north of the center.

ncient Zapotec capital of Monte Albán, Oaxaca

Vatermelons, Oaxaca

Café, Oaxaca City

Oaxacan dancer

uerto Escondido's harbor

RICHARD NEBESKY

Oaxacan history mural by Arturo García Bustos, Palacio de Gobierno, Oaxaca City

DAN HERRICK

Checking out the headlines, Oaxaca City

is 1km west of the zócalo along Trujano or Las Casas; the main long-distance companies using it are EV/OP, FYPSA and TOI. Unless otherwise noted, buses mentioned below use one of these two main stations.

It's advisable to book a day or two in advance for some of the less frequent services, including buses to San Cristóbal de Las Casas and the better buses to the coast. Ticket Bus, at 20 de Noviembre 103D in the city center, sells tickets for UNO, ADO and Colón buses throughout Mexico.

Mexbus The backpackers' van service Mexbus began in 2001 with daily service between Mexico City and Oaxaca for US$28, stopping at hostels and budget hotels in both cities. The service was planned to extend to Chiapas and the Yucatán Peninsula in 2002 (see the Bus section in the Getting Around chapter for more information).

Oaxaca Coast Some buses to the coast head down highway 175 through Miahuatlán and Pochutla; some go by Salina Cruz then west along the coast, a longer way around though the roads are in better condition; and a few 2nd-class buses take highway 131 (paved but in bad condition) direct to Puerto Escondido. To Pochutla (the jumping-off point for Puerto Ángel, Zipolite and other nearby beaches), it's 245km and about 6½ hours by highway 175 (a spectacular, winding, downhill ride), or 450km and 8½ hours via Salina Cruz. Puerto Escondido is 65km (1½ hours) west of Pochutla, by the coastal highway 200, or 200km from Oaxaca (8-9 hours) by highway 131.

All in all, highway 175 is the happy medium in terms of distance and road condition. At the time of writing the best service on highway 175 was EV/OP's *directo* 2nd-class service (at 10am, 2.30pm, 10.45pm) to Pochutla (US$10) and Puerto Escondido (US$11) from a terminal at Armenta y López 721, 500m south of the zócalo. The 10am bus is best of all because it's safest to travel in daylight. EV/OP also runs 10 *ordinarios* to Pochutla (US$8) and Puerto Escondido (US$9) and a 10pm *directo* to Santa Cruz Huatulco (7½ hours, US$12), all by highway 175.

An alternative to buses to Pochutla is the air-conditioned Chevrolet Suburban vans of Autoexprés Atlántida from La Noria 101, four times daily by highway 175 for US$13.50.

Cristóbal Colón (1st-class) was using only the Salina Cruz route at the time of writing, with four buses daily to Bahías de Huatulco (7½ hours, US$18), Pochutla (8½ hours, US$18) and Puerto Escondido (10 hours, US$19).

Services by highway 131 to Puerto Escondido are from the 2nd-class bus station by ERS (US$9-10, four daily) and Transol (US$9-13, seven daily).

Other Destinations Other daily buses from Oaxaca include:

Mexico City (most to TAPO, a few to Terminal Sur) – 440km, 6½ hours; 5 UNO (US$44), 8 Colón (US$28-32), 24 ADO (US$28), 8 FYPSA (US$23); see also Mexbus, above

Puebla – 340km, 4½ hours; 9 ADO, 8 Colón (both US$21-24), 9 FYPSA (US$16)

San Cristóbal de Las Casas – 625km, 12 hours; 3 Colón (US$28-35)

Tehuantepec – 245km, 4½ hours; 12 Colón (US$11.50-13.50), many FYPSA, TOI (US$8.75)

Tuxtla Gutiérrez – 540km, 10 hours; 4 Colón (US$25-30), several FYPSA, TOI (US$20)

Veracruz – 460km, 7 hours; 1 Colón (US$32), 3 ADO (US$27)

Villahermosa – 700km, 12 hours; 5 ADO (US$35)

Car & Motorcycle Car tolls from Mexico City to Oaxaca on highways 150D and 135D total US$28 (from Puebla, US$19); the trip takes about six hours. For some reason, the 135D is also numbered 131D for some stretches. The main toll-free alternative, via Huajuapan de León on highway 190, takes several hours longer.

The best rental deals we found were at Budget (VW sedans for US$67 a day with unlimited kilometers). The airport desks may come up with offers. Rental agencies include:

Alamo (☎ 514-85-34) 5 de Mayo 203; (☎ 511-62-20) Airport
Avis (☎ 511-57-36) Airport
Budget (☎ 516-44-45) 5 de Mayo 315A
Hertz (☎ 516-24-34) Local 4, Plaza de la Virgen, Plazuela Labastida 115; (☎ 511-54-78) Airport

Getting Around
To/From the Airport Oaxaca airport is 6km south of the city, 500m off highway 175.

Transporte Terrestre *combis* from the airport will take you to anywhere in the city center for US$2.25. A taxi costs about US$8.

You can book a combi seat from the city to the airport, a day or more ahead, at Transportes Aeropuerto (☎ 514-43-50), Alameda de León 1G, facing the cathedral (closed Sunday).

Bus Most points of importance in the city are within walking distance of each other, but you might want to use city buses (US$0.30) to and from the bus stations.

From the 1st-class bus station, a west-bound 'Juárez' or 'Av Juárez' bus will take you down Juárez and Ocampo, three blocks east of the zócalo; a 'Tinoco y Palacios' bus will take you down Tinoco y Palacios, two blocks west of the zócalo. To return to the bus station from downtown, take an 'ADO' or 'Gigante' bus north up Xicoténcatl or Pino Suárez, four blocks east of the zócalo, or up Díaz Ordaz or Crespo, three blocks west of the zócalo.

Buses between the 2nd-class bus station and the center pass slowly along congested streets, and it's almost as quick to walk. 'Centro' buses head toward the center along Trujano, then turn north up Díaz Ordaz. Going out to the 2nd-class bus station, 'Central' buses head south on Tinoco y Palacios, then west on Las Casas.

Car & Motorcycle There are several guarded parking lots in the city center. Estacionamiento Trujano, at Trujano 219, 1½ blocks west of the zócalo, is open 6am to 11pm daily. An overnight stay (8pm to 8am) is US$3.50.

Taxi A taxi anywhere within the central area, including the bus stations, costs US$2.25.

Bicycle You can rent mountain bikes for US$11.50 a day at Bicicletas Pedro Martínez (☎ 514-31-44), JP García 509, or Bicicletas Bravo (☎ 516-09-53), García Vigil 409. Both outfits offer bike tours too (see 'Turismo Alternativo,' earlier).

Valles Centrales

Three valleys radiate from the city of Oaxaca: the Valle de Tlacolula, stretching

50km east; the Valle de Etla, reaching about 40km north; and the Valle de Zimatlán, stretching about 100km south.

In these Valles Centrales (Central Valleys), all within day-trip distance of Oaxaca city, you'll find much to fascinate – pre-Hispanic ruins, craft-making villages and thronged country markets. The people are mostly Zapotec.

Market Days

The markets are at their busiest in the morning, and most start to wind down in early afternoon. Here are the main ones:

Sunday – Tlacolula
Tuesday – Atzompa
Wednesday – San Pedro y San Pablo Etla
Thursday – Zaachila and Ejutla
Friday – Ocotlán, Santo Tomás Jalieza and San Bartolo Coyotepec

Places to Stay

The Oaxaca state tourism department, Sedetur, runs six small self-catering units called *tourist yú'ùs* in the Valles Centrales. ('Yú'ù,' pronounced 'you,' means 'house' in the Zapotec language.) Most sleep about six people in bunks and a few have a separate room with a couple of beds. They're generally well kept, with equipped kitchens and bedding, towels and showers provided. Cost is between US$5.75 and US$10 per person. It's best to book ahead at the main tourist office in Oaxaca, though you can also call a few yú'ùs direct.

Getting There & Away

Most of the places in the Valle de Tlacolula, east of Oaxaca, are on or within walking distance of the Oaxaca-Mitla road, highway 190. TOI's buses to Mitla, every few minutes from Gate 9 of Oaxaca's 2nd-class bus station, will drop you anywhere along this road. South from Oaxaca, highway 175 goes through San Bartolo Coyotepec, Ocotlán, Ejutla and Miahuatlán. Separate roads go to Monte Albán and to Cuilapan and Zaachila. Further details on bus services are given under the individual sites and villages.

An alternative to traveling by bus, costing twice as much (still cheap!), is to take a *colectivo* taxi. These run to places north of Oaxaca (such as Atzompa and San José el

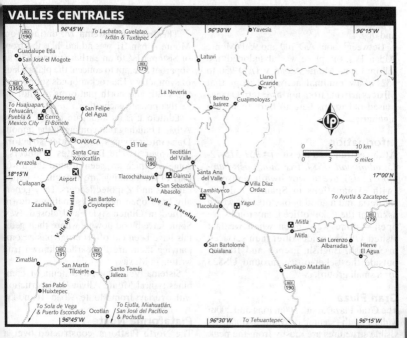

VALLES CENTRALES

Mogote) from Trujano on the north side of the 2nd-class bus station; and to places east, south and southwest (including El Tule, Teotitlán del Valle, San Bartolo Coyotepec, Ocotlán, Arrazola, Cuilapan and Zaachila) from Prolongación Victoria just east of the Central de Abastos market. They leave when they're full (five or six people).

MONTE ALBÁN

The ancient Zapotec capital Monte Albán ('MONH-teh ahl-BAHN,' meaning White Mountain) stands on a flattened hilltop, 400m above the valley floor, just a few kilometers west of Oaxaca. The views from here are spectacular.

History

The site was first occupied around 500 BC, probably by Zapotecs from the outset. It probably had early cultural connections with the Olmecs to the northeast.

Archaeologists divide Monte Albán's history into five phases. The years up to about 200 BC (Monte Albán I) saw the leveling of the hilltop, the building of temples and probably palaces, and the growth of a town of 10,000 or more people on the hillsides. Carvings of hieroglyphs and dates in a dot-and-bar system from this era may well mean that the elite of Monte Albán were the first to use writing and the written calendar in Mexico. Between 200 BC and about AD 300 (Monte Albán II) the city came to dominate more and more of Oaxaca. Buildings were typically made of huge stone blocks and had steep walls.

The city was at its peak from about AD 300 to 700 (Monte Albán III), when the main and surrounding hills were terraced for dwellings, and the population reached about 25,000. Most of what we see now dates from this time. Monte Albán was the center of a highly organized, priest-dominated society, controlling the extensively irrigated Valles Centrales, which held at least 200 other settlements and ceremonial centers. Many Monte Albán buildings were plastered and painted red, and *talud-tablero* architecture indicates influence from Teotihuacán. Nearly 170 underground tombs from this period have been found, some of them elaborate and decorated with frescoes. Monte Albán's people ate tortillas, beans, squashes, chilies, avocados and other vegetarian fare, plus sometimes deer, rabbit and dog.

Between about AD 700 and 950 (Monte Albán IV), the place was abandoned and fell into ruin. Monte Albán V (AD 950 to 1521) saw minimal activity, except that Mixtecs arriving from northwestern Oaxaca reused old tombs here to bury their own dignitaries.

Information

At the entrance to the site (☎ 951-516-12-15; admission US$4, free Sun; open 8am-6pm daily) are a worthwhile museum (with explanations in Spanish only), a cafeteria and a good bookstore. It's worth asking at the ticket office if any tombs are open – none were open when we last visited. Official guides offer their services, in Spanish, English, French and Italian, outside the ticket office (around US$23 for a small group).

Gran Plaza

The Gran Plaza, about 300m long and 200m wide, was the center of Monte Albán. Its visible structures are mostly from the peak Monte Albán III period. Some were temples, others residential. The following description takes you clockwise around the plaza. On our last visit, most of the structures in and around the plaza were cordoned off to prevent public access.

The stone terraces of the deep, I-shaped Juego de Pelota (Ball Court) were probably part of the playing area, not stands for spectators. The Pirámide (Edificio P) was topped by a small pillared temple. From the altar in front of it came a well-known jade bat-god mask, now in the Museo Nacional de Antropología. The Palacio (Palace) has a broad stairway and, on top, a patio surrounded by the remains of typical Monte Albán III residential rooms. Under the patio is a cross-shaped tomb.

The big Plataforma Sur (South Platform), with its wide staircase, is still good for a panorama of the plaza. Edificio J, an arrowhead-shaped Monte Albán II building riddled with tunnels and staircases (unfortunately you can't go in), stands at an angle of 45 degrees to the other Gran Plaza structures and is believed to have been an observatory. Figures and hiero-glyphs carved on its walls probably record military conquests.

The front of Sistema M, dating from Monte Albán III, was added, like the front of Sistema IV, to an earlier structure in an apparent attempt to conceal the plaza's lack of symmetry. (The rock mounds supporting the south and north platforms are not directly opposite each other.)

Edificio L is an amalgam of the Monte Albán I building that contained the famous Danzante carvings and a later structure built over it. The Danzantes (Dancers), some of which are seen around the lower part of the building, are thought to depict captives and Zapotec leaders. They generally have open mouths (sometimes downturned in Olmec style) and closed eyes. Some have blood flowing where their genitals have been cut off. Hieroglyphs accompanying them are the earliest known true writing in Mexico.

Sistema IV, the twin to Sistema M, combines typical Monte Albán II construction with overlays from Monte Albán III and IV.

Plataforma Norte

The North Platform, constructed over a rock outcrop, is almost as big as the Gran Plaza. It was rebuilt several times over the centuries. Chambers on either side of the main staircase contained tombs, and columns at the top of the stairs supported the roof of a hall. On top of the platform is a ceremonial complex built between AD 500 and 800; it's composed of Edificios D, VG and E (which were topped with adobe temples) and the Templo de Dos Columnas. Also atop the platform is the Patio Hundido (Sunken Patio), with an altar at its center.

Tombs

Tumba 104 Dating from AD 500 to 700, this is the tomb that you have most chance of finding open. Above its underground entrance stands an urn in the form of Pitao Cozobi, the Zapotec maize god, wearing a mask of Cocijo, the rain god whose forked tongue represents lightning. The tomb walls are covered with colorful frescoes in a style similar to Teotihuacán. The figure on the left wall is probably Xipe Tótec, the Zapotec flayed god and god of spring; on the right wall, wearing a big snake-and-feather headdress, is Pitao Cozobi again.

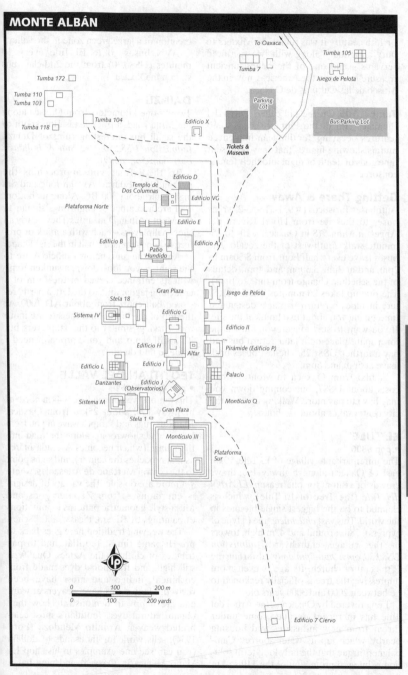

MONTE ALBÁN

To Oaxaca

Tumba 7

Tumba 105

Juego de Pelota

Parking Lot

Tickets & Museum

Bus Parking Lot

Tumba 172

Tumba 110
Tumba 103

Tumba 118

Tumba 104

Edificio X

Edificio D

Templo de Dos Columnas

Edificio VG

Plataforma Norte

Edificio E

Edificio B

Patio Hundido

Edificio A

Gran Plaza

Juego de Pelota

Stela 18

Sistema IV

Edificio G

Edificio II

Edificio H

Altar

Pirámide (Edificio P)

Edificio L

Edificio I

Palacio

Danzantes

Edificio J (Observatorios)

Sistema M

Monticulo Q

Stela 1

Gran Plaza

Monticulo III

Plataforma Sur

0   100   200 m
0   100   200 yards

Edificio 7 Ciervo

OAXACA STATE

Tumba 7 This tomb, just off the parking lot, dates from Monte Albán III, but in the 14th or 15th century it was reused by Mixtecs to bury a dignitary along with two sacrificed servants – and one of the richest ancient treasure hoards in the Americas, now in the Museo de las Culturas de Oaxaca.

Tumba 105 On the hill called Cerro del Plumaje (Hill of the Plumage), this tomb features decaying Teotihuacán-influenced murals showing figures that may represent nine gods of death or night and their female consorts.

Getting There & Away

Autobuses Turísticos (☎ 951-516-53-27) runs buses to the site from Hotel Rivera del Ángel, at Mina 518 in Oaxaca, a 10- to 15-minute walk southwest of the zócalo. The buses leave every half hour from 8.30am to 2pm, and at 3pm, 3.30pm and 4pm (details of the schedule change from time to time). The ride up takes 20 minutes. The US$2.50 fare includes a return trip at a designated time, giving you about two hours at the site. If you want to stay longer, you must hope for a spare place on a later return bus and pay a further US$1.25. The last buses back leave at 5pm and 6pm.

A taxi from Oaxaca to Monte Albán costs about US$7, but coming down you may have to pay more. Walking up from the city center takes about 1½ hours.

EL TULE
• pop 6800

The unremarkable village of El Tule, 10km east of Oaxaca along highway 190, draws crowds of visitors for one reason: *El Árbol del Tule* (the Tree of El Tule), which is claimed to be the biggest single biomass in the world. This vast *ahuehuete* tree (a type of cypress), 58m around and 42m high, towers in the village churchyard *(admission US$0.30; open 9am-5pm daily)*, dwarfing the 17th-century church. Its age is even more impressive; the tree is officially reckoned to be between 2000 and 3000 years old.

Long revered by Oaxacans, the Árbol del Tule has in recent decades come under threat from new industries and housing nearby, which tap its water sources. Campaigners argue that the only long-term solution is integral protection of the 110-sq-km

basin that supplies the tree's water, including reforestation in the mountains above and creation of a large green zone in the valley.

AVN buses go to El Tule every 10 minutes (US$0.30) from the 2nd-class bus station in Oaxaca.

DAINZÚ

Twenty-one kilometers from Oaxaca along the Mitla road, a track leads 1km south to the small but interesting ruins of Dainzú *(admission US$2.50, free Sun & holidays; open 8am-5pm daily)*.

To the left as you approach is the pyramid-like Edificio A, 50m long and 8m high, built about 300 BC. Along its bottom wall are a number of engravings similar to the Monte Albán Danzantes. They nearly all show ballplayers – each with a mask or protective headgear and a ball in the right hand.

Among the ruins below Edificio A are, to the right as you look down, a sunken tomb with its entrance carved in the form of a crouching jaguar and, to the left, a partly restored ball court from about AD 1000. At the top of the hill behind the site are more rock carvings similar to the ballplayers, but it's a stiff climb, and you'd probably need a guide to find them.

TEOTITLÁN DEL VALLE
• pop 4600 ☎ 951

This famous weaving village is 4km north of highway 190, about 25km from Oaxaca. Blankets, rugs and sarapes wave at you from houses and showrooms along the road into the village (which becomes Avenida Juárez as it approaches the center), and signs point to the central **Mercado de Artesanías**, where yet more are on sale. The variety of designs is enormous – from Zapotec gods and Mitla-style geometric patterns to imitations of paintings by Rivera, Picasso and Escher.

The weaving tradition here goes back to pre-Hispanic times: Teotitlán had to pay tributes of cloth to the Aztecs. Quality is still high, and traditional dyes made from cochineal, indigo and moss have been revived. Many shops have weavers at work and are happy to demonstrate how they obtain natural dyes. Teotitlán's most celebrated weaver, Arnulfo Mendoza (born 1954), sells work for thousands of dollars (you can see fine examples in his shop La Mano Mágica in Oaxaca) and now has a large house overlooking the north end of the village.

Facing the Mercado de Artesanías on the central plaza is the **Museo Comunitario Balaa Xtee Guech Gulal** *(admission US$0.60; open 10am-6pm daily)*, with local archaeological finds and material on local crafts and traditions. From the plaza, steps rise to a fine broad churchyard with the handsome 17th-century **Templo de la Preciosa Sangre de Cristo** in one corner. The village's regular daily market is behind the top of the churchyard.

Turismo de Aventura Teotitlán *(☎ 524-41-03, Avenida Juárez 59)* offers mountain biking, horseback riding, hiking and birding in the vicinity, mostly with English-speaking guides, for US$15 to US$35 depending on the activity.

Places to Stay & Eat

Tourist yú'ù (500m from highway 190 on approach road to village) US$8 per person. The yú'ù is not very convenient to the village, which is 3km farther up the road.

Calle 2 de Abril No 12 (☎ 524-41-64, 2 de Abril 12) US$20 per person including dinner & breakfast. This house belonging to friendly, English-speaking Elena González has three nice, almost new upstairs rooms with private bath and hot water.

Restaurante Tlamanalli (Avenida Juárez 39) Mains US$6-9. Open 1pm-4pm Tues-Sun. This restaurant serves excellent Oaxacan lunches; exhibits on weaving add to the interest.

Getting There & Away

AVN buses run hourly from 7am to 9pm daily except Sunday to Teotitlán (50 minutes, US$0.60) from Gate 29 at Oaxaca's 2nd-class bus station; the last bus back from the village leaves about 7pm. Or get any Mitla- or Tlacolula-bound bus to the signposted Teotitlán turnoff (US$0.50) on highway 190, then a local bus or a colectivo taxi (US$0.40) to the village.

LAMBITYECO

This small archaeological site *(admission US$2.50, free Sun & holidays; open 8am-5pm daily)* is on the south side of the Mitla road, 29km from Oaxaca. Between AD 600 and 800, Lambityeco seems to have become a sizable Zapotec center of about 3000

people. The interest lies in two patios. In the first are two carved stone friezes, each showing a bearded man holding a bone (a symbol of hereditary rights) and a woman with Zapotec hairstyle. Both these couples, plus a third in stucco on a tomb in the patio, are thought to have occupied the building around the patio and to have ruled Lambityeco in the 7th century.

The second patio has two heads of the rain god Cocijo. On one, a big headdress spreading above Cocijo's stern face forms the face of a jaguar.

TLACOLULA
• pop 11,000

This town 31km from Oaxaca holds one of the Valles Centrales' major markets every Sunday, when the area around the church becomes a packed throng. Some crafts, an array of foods and plenty of everyday goods are on sale. It's a treat for lovers of market atmosphere.

The church was one of several founded in Oaxaca by Dominican monks. Inside, the domed 16th-century Capilla del Santo Cristo is a riot of golden, indigenous-influenced decoration comparable with the Capilla del Rosario in Santo Domingo, Oaxaca. Martyrs can be seen carrying their heads under their arms.

Frequent TOI and FYPSA buses run to Tlacolula from Oaxaca's 2nd-class bus station (1 hour, US$1).

SANTA ANA DEL VALLE
• pop 2250 ☎ 951

Santa Ana, 4km north of Tlacolula, is another village with a time-honored textile tradition. Today it produces woolen blankets, sarapes and bags. Natural dyes have been revived, and traditional designs – flowers, birds, geometric patterns – are still in use. Prices in the cooperatively run **Mercado de Artesanías**, on the main plaza, are considerably lower than in Teotitlán del Valle or Oaxaca shops. Also on the plaza are the richly decorated 17th-century **Templo de Santa Ana** and the **Museo Comunitario Shan-Dany** *(admission US$0.60; open 10am-2pm & 3pm-6pm Mon-Sat)*, which has exhibits on local textiles, archaeology and history and the Zapotec Danza de las Plumas. The village also has a few textile shops and workshops open to visitors.

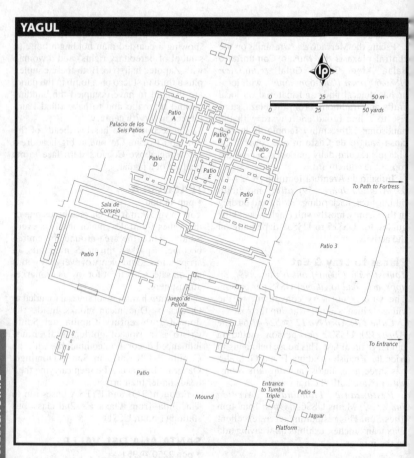

YAGUL

A *tourist yú'ù* (☎ 562-03-43), charging US$8.50 per person, is on the approach road from Tlacolula, about 500m from the village center. You can arrange guided horseback or bicycle rides there. Buses and minibuses run frequently from Tlacolula until about 6pm.

YAGUL

The ruins of Yagul *(admission US$3, free Sun & holidays; open 8am-5pm daily)* are finely sited on a cactus-covered hill, 1.5km off the Oaxaca-Mitla road. The signposted turnoff is 34km from Oaxaca.

Yagul was a leading Valles Centrales settlement after the decline of Monte Albán. Most of what's visible was built after AD 750.

Patio 4 was surrounded by four temples. On the east side is a carved-stone animal, probably a jaguar. Next to the central platform is the entrance to one of several underground **Tumbas Triples** (Triple Tombs).

The beautiful **Juego de Pelota** (Ball Court) is the second biggest in Mesoamerica (after one at Chichén Itzá). To its west, on the edge of the hill, is **Patio 1**, with the narrow **Sala de Consejo** (Council Hall) along its north side.

The labyrinthine **Palacio de los Seis Patios** (Palace of the Six Patios) was probably the leader's residence. Its walls were plastered and painted red.

It's well worth climbing the **Fortress**, the huge rock that towers above the ruins. The path passes **Tumba 28**, made of cut stone.

OAXACA STATE

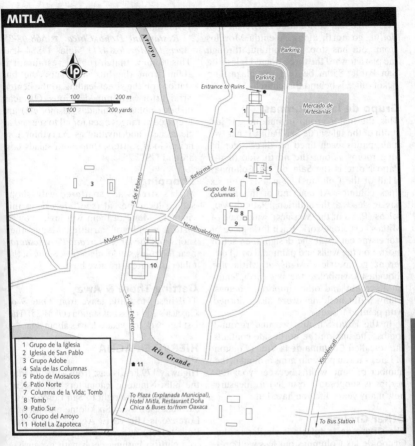

MITLA

1 Grupo de la Iglesia
2 Iglesia de San Pablo
3 Grupo Adobe
4 Sala de las Columnas
5 Patio de Mosaicos
6 Patio Norte
7 Columna de la Vida; Tomb
8 Tomb
9 Patio Sur
10 Grupo del Arroyo
11 Hotel La Zapoteca

Parking

Parking

Entrance to Ruins

Mercado de Artesanías

Grupo de las Columnas

Arroyo

Reforma

5 de Febrero

Nezahualcóyotl

Madero

5 de Febrero

Río Grande

Xicoténcatl

To Plaza (Explanada Municipal), Hotel Mitla, Restaurant Doña Chica & Buses to/from Oaxaca

To Bus Station

0   100   200 m
0   100   200 yards

Several overgrown ruins perch atop the Fortress – and the views are marvelous.

MITLA
• pop 7500 ☎ 951

The pre-Hispanic stone 'mosaics' of Mitla, 46km southeast of Oaxaca, are unique in Mexico. Today they are surrounded by a dusty modern Zapotec town.

History

The ruins date almost entirely from the last two or three centuries before the Spanish conquest, when Mitla was probably the most important Zapotec religious center, dominated by high priests who performed literally heart-wrenching human sacrifices. Evidence points to a short period of Mixtec domination here in the 14th century, followed by a Zapotec reassertion before the Aztecs arrived in 1494. Somewhere beneath the town may be a great undiscovered tomb of Zapotec kings; the 17th-century monk Francisco de Burgoa wrote that Spanish priests found it but sealed it up.

It's thought that each group of buildings we see at Mitla was reserved for specific occupants – one for the high priest, one for lesser priests, one for the king and so forth.

Orientation & Information

If you tell the bus conductor from Oaxaca that you're heading for *las ruinas*, you should be dropped at a junction signed 'Zona Arqueológica' soon after you enter Mitla (the bus station is 600m farther east from this stop). For the ruins *(admission US$3, free Sun & holidays; open 8am-5pm daily)*, go north along Avenida Morelos from your bus stop, and continue through the plaza toward the three-domed Iglesia de San Pablo, 850m beyond the plaza. The ticket office is behind this church.

Grupo de las Columnas

This, the major group of buildings, is just south of the Iglesia de San Pablo. It has two main patios, each lined on three sides by long rooms. Along the north side of the Patio Norte is the **Sala de las Columnas** (Hall of the Columns), 38m long with six thick columns. At one end of this hall, a passage leads to the additional **Patio de Mosaicos** (Patio of the Mosaics), with some of Mitla's best stonework. Each little piece of stone was cut to fit the design, then set in mortar on the walls and painted. The 14 different geometric designs at Mitla are thought to symbolize the sky, earth, feathered serpent and other important beings. Many Mitla buildings were also adorned with painted friezes.

In the Patio Sur are two underground tombs. The one on the north side contains the so-called **Columna de la Vida** (Column of Life) – if you put your arms around it, the number of hand widths between your fingertips is supposed (absurdly) to measure how many years' life you have left.

Other Groups

The **Grupo de la Iglesia** is similar to the Grupo de las Columnas but less well preserved. The church was built over one of the group's patios in 1590. The **Grupo del Arroyo** is the most substantial of the other groups. Remains of forts, tombs and other structures are scattered for many kilometers around.

Places to Stay & Eat

Hotel Mitla (☎ 568-01-12, Juárez 9) Singles/doubles US$17/23. This basic and over-priced but friendly hotel, just off the town's central plaza, has fanless rooms with lumpy beds and private bath. It serves straightforward food at reasonable prices.

Hotel La Zapoteca (☎ 568-00-26, 5 de Febrero 8) Singles or doubles US$14 (double bed), US$19 (twin beds). Located between the plaza and the ruins, La Za-

poteca has bare, fanless rooms and another restaurant.

Restaurant Doña Chica (☎ 568-02-25, Avenida Morelos 411) Mains US$4-4.50. This homey, thatch-roofed restaurant is 100m from the bus stop (not the bus station) on the street leading to the center. Straightforward but delicious Oaxacan dishes (moles, enchiladas, tasajo, etc) are prepared at ranges open for all to see and as clean, neat and inviting as everything else here. Good starters, soups and salads cost around US$2.25.

Shopping

Mitla's streets are spattered with shops selling local mezcal (see 'Mezcal' in this chapter). Many of them will invite you to taste a couple of varieties. Many other shops, and the large *Mercado de Artesanías* near the ruins, sell local textiles. Some of the tablecloths are attractive buys.

Getting There & Away

TOI buses to Mitla leave from Gate 9 of Oaxaca's 2nd-class bus station (US$1.25). The last bus back to Oaxaca leaves about 8pm.

HIERVE EL AGUA
☎ 951

Highway 179 heads east from Mitla up into the hills. Nineteen kilometers out, a signpost points to the right to San Lorenzo Albarradas, 3km away. Six kilometers past San Lorenzo is Hierve El Agua ('The Water Boils'). Here mineral springs run into icy-cold clifftop bathing pools with expansive panoramas. This cliff and another nearby are encrusted with petrified minerals, giving them the appearance of huge frozen waterfalls. Altogether it's one of the more unusual bathing experiences you'll ever have. The waters here were used for irrigation as long ago as 1300 BC.

Hierve El Agua is a popular oaxaqueño weekend excursion. Above the pools and cliffs are a number of comedores, a good *tourist yú'ù (☎ 562-09-22)* costing US$6.75 per person and six similar *cottages* (some without kitchens) at the same price. You can also camp here for US$5.75 per tent.

The area is dotted with maguey fields: San Lorenzo Albarradas, nearby San Juan del Río and the other 'Albarradas' villages produce some of Oaxaca's finest mezcal.

Viajes Turísticos Mitla, at the Hotel Rivera del Ángel, Mina 518 in Oaxaca, runs two daily trips to Hierve El Agua, giving you three hours there (US$13.50 return). Several Oaxaca tour agencies offer day trips combining Hierve El Agua with Mitla, Teotitlán del Valle and El Tule for US$25 to US$30 per person.

A FYPSA bus runs from Oaxaca's 2nd-class bus station to Hierve El Agua (US$3) at 8am daily, passing through Mitla about 9.15am. From Hierve El Agua it returns to Mitla, then leaves Mitla again at noon for Hierve El Agua (US$1.75), finally returning from Hierve El Agua at 2pm to Mitla and Oaxaca.

SAN BARTOLO COYOTEPEC
• pop 2800 ☎ 951

All the polished, black, surprisingly light pottery you find around Oaxaca comes from San Bartolo Coyotepec, a small village about 12km south of the city. Look for the signs to the **Alfarería Doña Rosa** (☎ 551-00-11, Juárez 24; open 9am-6.30pm daily), a short walk east off the highway. Several village families make and sell the barro negro (black ware), but it was Rosa Real Mateo (1900-80) who invented the method of burnishing it with quartz stones for the distinctive shine. Her family pottery workshop (alfarería) is the biggest in the village, and demonstrations of the process are given whenever a tour bus rolls in (several times a day). The pieces are hand-molded by an age-old technique using two saucers functioning as a rudimentary potter's wheel. Then they are fired in pit kilns; they turn black because of the iron oxide in the local clay and because smoke is trapped in the kiln.

Buses run to San Bartolo (20 minutes, US$0.50) every few minutes from the terminal at Armenta y López 721, 500m south of the Oaxaca zócalo.

SAN MARTÍN TILCAJETE & SANTO TOMÁS JALIEZA

The village of San Martín Tilcajete, just west of highway 175 about 27km south of Oaxaca, is the source of many of the bright copal alebrijes (animal figures) seen in Oaxaca. You can see and buy them in makers' houses.

Santo Tomás Jalieza, just east of highway 175 a couple of kilometers farther south, holds a textiles market on Friday to coincide with the Ocotlán market. Women weave high-quality textiles on back-strap looms here; their cotton waist sashes have pretty animal or plant designs. Colectivo taxis run from Ocotlán.

OCOTLÁN
• pop 11,500

The bustling Friday market at Ocotlán, 32km south of Oaxaca, dates back to pre-Hispanic times and is one of the biggest in the Valles Centrales. Ocotlán's most renowned artisans are the four Aguilar sisters and their families, who create whimsical, colorful pottery figures of women with all sorts of unusual motifs. The Aguilars' houses are together by the highway before you get into the town center – spot them by the pottery women on the wall. Most renowned are Guillermina Aguilar and her family, at Prolongación de Morelos 430, who turn out, among other things, miniature Frida Kahlos.

Ocotlán was also the hometown of artist Rodolfo Morales (1925-2001), who turned his international success to Ocotlán's benefit by setting up the Fundación Cultural Rodolfo Morales. Aside from providing the town with its first ambulance, establishing a computer center and planting 3500 jacaranda trees, the Morales foundation has renovated Ocotlán's handsome 16th-century church, the Templo de Santo Domingo, and turned the neighboring ex-convent, formerly a dilapidated jail, into a museum of popular and religious art (including some of his own works).

Buses to Ocotlán (45 minutes, US$1) leave every few minutes from the terminal at Armenta y López 721 in Oaxaca.

SAN JOSÉ DEL PACÍFICO
☎ 951

The small village of San José del Pacífico, about an hour south of Miahuatlán on highway 175 to Pochutla, is just outside the Valles Centrales but en route to the coast. It's famed for its magic mushrooms but is also a good base for walks through the cool mountain pine forests.

You can get basic singles/doubles with shared bath at **Cabañas Rayito del Sol**, in the village, for US$6.75/13.50, and better rooms and cabañas with bath for US$23 a double or US$45 for up to four people at

Cabañas y Restaurante Puesta del Sol, on highway 175, 500m north of the village. You can book both places by calling the village telephone caseta (☎ 572-01-11).

All highway 175 buses between Oaxaca and Pochutla stop at San José.

ARRAZOLA
• pop 1000

Below the west side of Monte Albán and about 4km off the Cuilapan road, Arrazola produces many of the colorful copal alebrijes that are sold in Oaxaca. You can see and buy them in artisans' homes.

CUILAPAN
• pop 11,200

Cuilapan, 12km southwest of Oaxaca, is one of the few Mixtec enclaves in the Valles Centrales. It's the site of a beautiful, historic Dominican monastery, the **Ex-Convento de Santiago Apóstol** *(admission US$2.50; open 9am-5pm daily)*, whose pale stone seems almost to grow out of the land.

In 1831 the Mexican independence hero Vicente Guerrero was executed at the monastery by soldiers supporting the rebel conservative Anastasio Bustamante, who had just deposed the liberal Guerrero from the Mexican presidency. Guerrero had fled by ship from Acapulco, but the ship's captain put in at Huatulco and betrayed him to the rebels. Guerrero was transported to Cuilapan to die.

From the monastery entrance you reach a long, low, unfinished church that has stood roofless since work on it stopped in 1560. Beyond is the church that succeeded it. Around its right-hand end is a two-story Renaissance-style cloister, whose rear rooms have 16th- and 17th-century murals. A painting of Guerrero hangs in the room where he was held, and outside is a monument where he was shot. The main church is usually closed, but is said to contain the tomb of Juana Donají (daughter of Cocijo-eza, the last Zapotec king of Zaachila).

The Añasa line runs buses to Cuilapan (US$0.40) about every 15 minutes from its terminal at Bustamante 604, five blocks south of Oaxaca's zócalo.

ZAACHILA
• pop 12,000

This part-Mixtec, part-Zapotec village, 6km beyond Cuilapan, has a busy Thursday market. Zaachila was a Zapotec capital from about 1400 until the Spanish conquest. Its last Zapotec king, Cocijo-eza, became a Christian with the name Juan Cortés and died in 1523. Six pre-Hispanic monoliths and the village church stand on the main plaza.

Up the road behind the church, then along a path to the right marked 'Zona Arqueológica,' are mounds containing at least two **tombs** *(admission US$2.50, free Sun & holidays; open 8am-5pm daily)* used by the ancient Mixtecs. In one of them, Tumba 2, was found a Mixtec treasure hoard comparable with that of Tumba 7 at Monte Albán. It's now in the Museo Nacional de Antropología in Mexico City. The famous Mexican archaeologists Alfonso Caso and Ignacio Bernal were forced to flee by irate Zaachilans when they tried to excavate the tombs in the 1940s and 1950s. Roberto Gallegos excavated them under armed guard in 1962.

Zaachila is served by the same buses as for Cuilapan (see the previous section).

ATZOMPA
• pop 9180

Atzompa, 6km northwest of Oaxaca, is a village with many potters. A lot of their very attractive, colorful work is sold at excellent prices in the **Mercado de Artesanías** *(Avenida Libertad 303)*, on the main road entering the village from Oaxaca. This market is open daily and has a restaurant.

From the church up in the village center, a 2.5km road (mostly dirt) leads south up **Cerro El Bonete**. The road ends a few minutes' walk from the top of the hill, which is dotted with unrestored pre-Hispanic ruins.

Choferes del Sur, at Gate 39 of Oaxaca's 2nd-class bus station, runs buses every few minutes to Atzompa (US$0.30). If driving yourself, follow Calzada Madero northwest out of downtown Oaxaca, turn left along Masseu (signposted 'Monte Albán') at a big intersection on the fringe of town, then go right at traffic signals after 1.5km.

SAN JOSÉ EL MOGOTE

Fourteen kilometers northwest of central Oaxaca on highway 190, a westward turnoff signposted to Guadalupe Etla leads about 2km to San José el Mogote, a tiny village indicated by a 'Museo Comunitario Ex-Hacienda El Cacique' sign. Long ago, before Monte Albán became important, Mogote was the major settlement in Oaxaca. It was at its peak between 650 and 500 BC, and flourished again between 100 BC and AD 150. Its main plaza was almost as big as Monte Albán's. The major surviving structures (partly restored) are a ball court and a sizable pyramid-mound on the village periphery. The interesting **community museum** *(in village center; admission US$1; open 9am-6pm daily)* is in the former landowner's hacienda. If you find it closed, just ask around for someone to find the keeper. A highlight of the museum is 'El Diablo Enchilado' (the Chilied Devil), a pre-Hispanic brazier in the form of a bright red grimacing face. The museum also has interesting material on the villagers' 20th-century struggle for land ownership.

Colectivo taxi is a fairly easy way to get to Mogote; see the Valles Centrales introductory Getting There & Away section.

Mixteca

The rugged, mountainous west of Oaxaca state is known as the Mixteca, for its Mixtec indigenous inhabitants. It was from here in about the 12th century that Mixtec dominance began to spread to the Valles Centrales. The Mixtecs were famed workers of gold and precious stones, and it's said the Aztec emperor Moctezuma would eat only off their fine Mixteca-Puebla ceramics.

Today much of the Mixteca is over-farmed, eroded and deforested, and politics and business are dominated by mestizos. Many Mixtecs have to emigrate for work. Foreign visitors are uncommon here, though a few guided trips are now available from Oaxaca (see 'Turismo Alternativo,' earlier).

Things to See & Do

The small village of **Santiago Apoala**, in a beautiful green valley 40km north of Nochixtlán by unpaved road, is an increasingly popular center for hiking, mountain biking and climbing. The scenery around here is spectacular, with the 60m waterfall Cascada Cola de la Serpiente and the 400m-deep Cañón Morelos ranking among the highlights. Several Oaxaca alternative-tourism agencies run trips here, and the village tourism committee (☎ 55-5151-9154) offers accommodations, meals and excur-

sion packages costing from about US$20 per person with one night camping to US$45 per person with two nights in Apoala's good little tourist yú'ù.

The beautiful 16th-century **Dominican monasteries** *(admission US$2.50 each; open 10am-5pm daily)* in the Mixteca villages of Yanhuitlán, Coixtlahuaca and Teposcolula are among colonial Mexico's finest architecture. Their restrained stonework fuses medieval, plateresque, Renaissance and indigenous styles. The one at Coixtlahuaca is perhaps the most beautiful of the group. Its church has a lovely rib-vaulted ceiling and pure Renaissance façade, beside which stands a graceful, ruined *capilla abierta* (open chapel), used for preaching to crowds of indigenous people. The weightier monastery at Yanhuitlán, designed to withstand earthquakes and serve as a defensive refuge, towers over highway 190, 120km from Oaxaca. The cloister has an interesting little museum. The church contains valuable works of art, and a fine Mudéjar timber roof supports the choir. Teposcolula's monastery features a stately capilla abierta of three open bays, outside the monastery church.

About 25km south of Teposcolula, just off highway 125, is San Martín Huamelulpan, where the **Museo Comunitario Hitalulu** *(Plaza Cívica; officially open 9am-6pm daily)* focuses on traditional medicine (the practitioners here are renowned for their powers) and archaeology. Also well worth a visit is the Mixtec archaeological site 500m from the village.

Tlaxiaco, 43km south of Teposcolula on highway 125, was known before the Mexican Revolution as París Chiquita (Little Paris), for the quantities of French luxuries such as clothes and wine imported for its few rich families. Today the only signs of that elegance are the arcades around the main plaza and a few large houses with courtyards. The market area is off the southeast corner of the plaza – Saturday is the main day.

South of Tlaxiaco, highway 125, all paved, winds through the remote Sierra Madre del Sur to Pinotepa Nacional, on coastal highway 200. The major town is **Putla**, 95km from Tlaxiaco. Just before Putla is **San Andrés Chicahuaxtla**, in the small territory of the indigenous Triquis. The Amuzgo people of **San Pedro Amuzgos**, 73km south of Putla, are known for their fine huipiles.

Places to Stay

You could visit the Mixteca in a long day trip from Oaxaca, but basic hotels or *casas de huéspedes* are available in Nochixtlán, Coixtlahuaca, Tamazulapan, Teposcolula and Putla, and better ones in Tlaxiaco and Huajuapan de León. Santiago Apoala and San Martín Huamelulpan have *tourist yú'ùs* (see the Valles Centrales introductory Places to Stay section, earlier), costing US$8 per person at Apoala and US$5.75 at Huamelulpan.

Accommodations in Tlaxiaco include *Hotel Del Portal (☎ 953-552-01-54, Plaza de la Constitución 2)*, on the main plaza, where big, clean doubles with bath and TV, around a pleasant courtyard, cost US$22 to US$27; and *Hotel México (☎ 953-552-00-86, Hidalgo 13)*, which has singles/doubles with shared bath for US$9/10, or with private bath for US$20/22.

Getting There & Away

Yanhuitlán, on highway 190, is served by several 1st- and 2nd-class buses daily from Oaxaca (2½ hours, US$6 1st-class). For Coixtlahuaca, FYPSA runs from Oaxaca's 2nd-class bus station (US$7), or you can take a Huajuapan-bound bus to Tejupan, where colectivo taxis run to Coixtlahuaca. Santiago Apoala has a bus service three days a week to/from Nochixtlán, which is served by the same buses as Yanhuitlán. You could also reach Apoala by taxi from Nochixtlán.

Teposcolula (3 hours, US$5-7.25), Tlaxiaco (3½ hours, US$6.50-9.25) and other places on highway 125 are served from Oaxaca daily by a couple of 1st-class Cristóbal Colón buses, 11 Sur 2nd-class buses from the Sur terminal on the Periférico, and a dozen or so 2nd-class FYPSA and TOI buses from the 2nd-class bus station. Many of these continue south to Pinotepa Nacional (US$14-19).

Buses run from Mexico City's Terminal Oriente (TAPO) to several Mixteca towns.

Northern Oaxaca

Highway 175, scenic but rough in parts, crosses Oaxaca's northern sierras to Tuxtepec, the main town in a low-lying region of far northern Oaxaca that in culture and geog-raphy is akin to neighboring Veracruz. In the Sierra Mazateca west of Tuxtepec is **Huautla de Jiménez**, where according to legend the likes of Bob Dylan, the Beatles, Timothy Leary and Albert Hoffman (the inventor of LSD) used to go to trip on the local *hongos* (hallucinogenic mushrooms) under the guidance of María Sabina, Huautla's famed *curandera*. María Sabina died in 1985, but others carry on her work and a trickle of foreigners still make their way to Huautla. Fresh mushrooms appear in the rainy season, June to August. Locals disapprove of mushroom-taking just for thrills.

GUELATAO & IXTLÁN
☎ 951

On highway 175, 60km from Oaxaca, Guelatao village was the birthplace of Benito Juárez (see 'Benito Juárez' in this chapter). By the pretty lake at the center of the village is a statue of the boy Benito as a shepherd. Among the adjacent municipal buildings are two statues of Juárez and a small exposition, the **Sala Homenaje a Juárez** *(admission free; open 9am-4pm Wed-Sun)*.

In the small town of Ixtlán, 3km beyond Guelatao on highway 175, is the baroque **Templo de Santo Tomás**, where baby Benito was baptized. Note the finely carved west façade. On Ixtlán's plaza is a **Museo de la Biodiversidad** (Museum of Biodiversity), where you'll also find a community ecotourism venture, **Schiaa-Rua-Via** *(☎/fax 553-60-75, ℮ eco_ixt@hotmail.com)*. Ixtlán has a couple of basic *hotels*.

The Benito Juárez and Flecha del Zempoaltépetl bus lines serve Guelatao (1½ hours, US$2.75) and Ixtlán 10 times daily from Oaxaca's 2nd-class bus station.

PUEBLOS MANCOMUNADOS

The Pueblos Mancomunados (Commonwealth of Villages) are eight remote Zapotec villages in Oaxaca's Sierra Norte, the beautiful, damp highlands north of Teotitlán del Valle. For centuries, in a unique form of cooperation, the villages have pooled the natural resources of their 290-sq-km territory, which include extensive pine and oak forests. The profits from forestry and other enterprises are shared among all the families of the Pueblos Mancomunados. Nevertheless several villages have suffered a severe population drain as people have moved to Mexican cities and the USA in search of higher income.

Now, in an effort to stanch the emigration and maintain sustainable uses of their forests, the villages have set up an excellent ecotourism program, **Expediciones Sierra Norte** (☎ *951-514-82-71*, e *sierranorte@ oaxaca.com*, w *www.sierranorte.org.mx, García Vigil 406, Oaxaca*). Expediciones Sierra Norte offers simple but decent lodgings, and walking and mountain-biking along more than 100km of scenic tracks and trails. It's a great way for travelers to experience this unique region of Oaxaca, completely different from the dry Valles Centrales or the tropical Pacific coast. Elevations here range between 2200m and over 3200m, and there's great natural diversity: over 400 bird species, 350 butterflies, all six Mexican wild cats (including the jaguar) and nearly 4000 plants have been recorded in the Sierra Norte. One highlight walk is the beautiful Latuvi-Lachatao canyon trail, which follows a pre-Hispanic track that connected Oaxaca's Valles Centrales with the Gulf of Mexico and passes through cloud forests festooned with bromeliads and hanging mosses.

You can go on your own, or with trained local guides, who almost certainly will only speak Zapotec and Spanish but who will be knowledgeable about the plants, wildlife and ecology of these sierras. For accommodations, you can stay in simple but comfortable *cabañas* with dormitory beds (in each village), or use a few designated *camping grounds*. In every village are *comedores* where you can eat cheap local meals.

The best first step is to contact Expediciones Sierra Norte's office at García Vigil 406, Oaxaca. The friendly, English-speaking people here have full information on trails, tracks, accommodations and how to prepare, and you can book both guided and independent trips. They also sell a very useful guide/map for US$4. Be ready for much cooler temperatures: in the Sierra Norte's higher, southern villages, it can freeze in winter. The rainiest season is from late May to September, but there's little rain from January to April.

Prices for visiting the Pueblos Mancomunados are: guide for up to five people US$11.50/17 per half/full day; cabaña accommodations US$8 per person; camping US$5.75; bike rental US$9.50/13.50 per half/full day; *huentzee* (contribution to maintenance costs) US$5.75 per visit. Expediciones Sierra Norte also offers fully organized trips of up to three days including meals, accommodations and transportation.

The most common starting villages are Cuajimoloyas (elevation 3180m) and Benito Juárez (2750m), which are at the higher southern end of the Sierra Norte, so that northbound walks or rides starting here will be more downhill than up. Both villages possess more than the average amount of accommodations, all costing US$8 per person. In Benito Juárez there's a 14-person *tourist yú'ù* with double rooms as well as bunks, as well as cozy *cabañas* for up to four people with bathroom and kitchen. In the village center are a good comedor, a helpful information office (☎ 954-545-99-94), where you can organize guides, and a 17th-century church, beside which a Sunday market is held. Cuajimoloyas has a similar information office, at Avenida Oaxaca 15.

A good place to end up is Lachatao in the north, today almost a ghost village but with a large 17th-century church, the fruit of nearby colonial gold mines.

It's also possible simply to base yourself in one village and take local walks or rides from there, with or without guides. Some superb lookout points are accessible from the southern villages, such as the 3000m El Mirador, a 2.5km walk from Benito Juárez, or the 3280m Yaa-Cuetzi lookout, 1km from Cuajimoloyas. From Yaa-Cuetzi in clear weather you can see such distant mountains as Pico de Orizaba and Zempoaltépetl.

Getting There & Away

Cuajimoloyas has the best bus links with Oaxaca: five daily buses from the 2nd-class bus station by the Flecha del Zempoaltépetl company (2 hours, US$2.75). For Benito Juárez, Transportes Ya'a-Yana buses (2 hours, US$2) leave from Calle Niño Perdido 306, Colonia Ixcotel in Oaxaca, at 4pm Tuesday, Friday and Saturday (5pm during the daylight saving period). The stop is next to a Pemex gas station on the Mitla road (highway 190), a couple of kilometers east of the 1st-class bus station; taxi is the easiest way there from the city center. These buses leave Benito Juárez for Oaxaca at 5am on the same days. Another way to reach Benito

Juárez is to take a Cuajimoloyas-bound bus to the Benito Juárez turnoff (desviación de Benito Juárez), 1¾ hours from Oaxaca, and walk 3.5km west along the unpaved road to the village.

Transportes Ya'a-Yana also runs buses from Lachatao to Oaxaca (3 hours, US$3.50) and back. Departures from Lachatao are at 6am daily plus 4pm Sunday.

Oaxaca Coast

A laid-back spell on the beautiful Oaxaca coast is the perfect complement to the inland attractions of Oaxaca city and the Valles Centrales. The trip down highway 175 from Oaxaca is spectacular: south of Miahuatlán you climb into pine forests, then you descend into ever lusher and hotter tropical forest.

The once remote fishing villages and former coffee ports of Puerto Escondido and Puerto Ángel are now also informal tourist resorts. But the operative word is informal. Puerto Escondido has famous surf and a lively travelers' scene, while Puerto Ángel is the hub for a series of wonderful beaches with limitless low-cost accommodations – among them the fabled Zipolite and its increasingly popular neighbor Mazunte. To the east, a bigger new tourist resort has been developed on the lovely Bahías de Huatulco.

West of Puerto Escondido, nature lovers can visit the lagoons of Manialtepec and Chacahua, teeming with bird life, and hang out in dirt-cheap beach cabañas at Chacahua village.

The coast of Oaxaca is hotter and much more humid than the state's highlands. Most of the year's rain falls between June and September, turning everything green. From October the landscape starts to dry out, and by March many of the trees are leafless. May is the hottest month.

The peak tourism seasons on this coast are from mid-December to mid-January and the months of July and August. At other times hotel prices may come down anywhere between 10% and 40% from the prices we list.

The Web site Pacific Coast of Oaxaca (**w** www.tomzap.com) is a mine of information about the coast, with a useful message board headed 'Visitors' Comments.'

The Oaxaca coast is a rather impoverished region apart from its few tourism honey pots. Be on your guard against theft in Puerto Escondido and the Puerto Ángel-Zipolite area.

PUERTO ESCONDIDO
• pop 40,000 ☎ 954

Known to surfers since before paved roads reached this part of Oaxaca, Puerto Escondido (Hidden Port) remains relatively relaxed and inexpensive but has developed a lively travelers' scene. It has several beaches, a steadily improving range of accommodations, some excellent restaurants, plenty of cafés and a spot of active nightlife. Several interesting ecotourist destinations are close by.

Any breath of breeze is a blessing in Puerto, and you're more likely to get one up the hill a little bit than down at sea level.

Orientation
The town rises above the small, south-facing Bahía Principal. Highway 200, here called the Carretera Costera, runs across the hill halfway up, dividing the upper town – where buses arrive and most of the locals live and work – from the lower, tourism-dominated part. The heart of the lower town is El Adoquín, the pedestrianized section of Avenida Pérez Gasga (adoquín is Spanish for paving stone). The west end of Pérez Gasga winds up the slope to meet highway 200 at an intersection with traffic signals, known as El Crucero.

Bahía Principal curves around at its east end to the long Playa Zicatela, the hub of the surf scene, with loads more places to stay and eat.

Information
Tourist Offices The very helpful tourist information office (**e** ginainpuerto@yahoo .com) at the west end of El Adoquín is open 9am to 2pm and 4pm to 6pm Monday to Friday, 10am to 2pm Saturday. Gina Machorro, the energetic, multilingual information officer usually found there, can answer almost any question you could throw at her. The head tourist office (☎ 582-01-75) is about 2.5km west of the center on the road to the airport, at the corner of Boulevard Juárez.

Money There's a handy Bital ATM on El Adoquín. Banamex, on the corner of Pérez

PUERTO ESCONDIDO

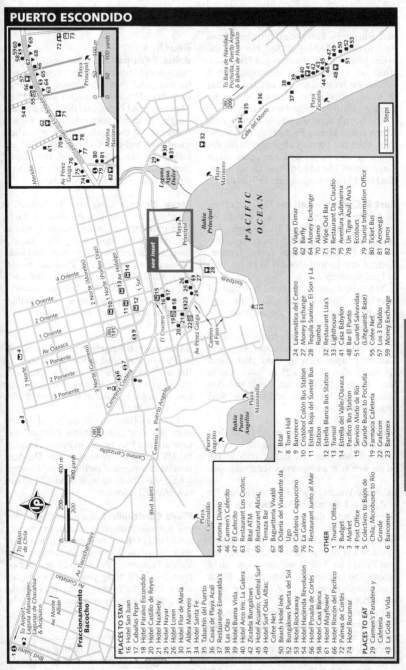

PLACES TO STAY
16 Hotel San Juan
17 Cabañas Pepe
18 Hotel Paraíso Escondido
20 Hotel Castillo de Reyes
21 Hotel Naxhiely
25 Hotel Nayar
26 Hotel Loren
30 Hotel Flor de María
31 Aldea Marinero
34 Hotel Santa Fe
35 Tabachín del Puerto
36 Casas de Playa Acali
37 Restaurante Esmeralda's
38 Las Olas
39 Hotel Buena Vista
40 Hotel Arco Iris; La Galera
42 Zicatela Bungalows
45 Hotel Acuario; Central Surf
49 Hotel Surf Olas Altas;
   Cofee Net
50 Beach Hotel Inés
52 Bungalows Puerta del Sol
53 Hotel Rockaway
54 Hotel Hacienda Revolución
56 Hotel Posada de Cortés
58 Hotel Casa Blanca
61 Hotel Mayflower
66 Hotel Rincón del Pacifico
72 Palmas de Cortés
74 Hotel Rocamar

PLACES TO EAT
29 Carmen's Panadería y
   Cafetería
43 La Gota de Vida
44 Aroma Divino
46 Carmen's Cafecito
47 El Cafecito
63 Restaurant Los Crotos;
   Bital ATM
65 Restaurant Alicia;
   Terraza Bar
67 Baguettería Vivaldi
68 Osteria del Viandante da
   Ugo
69 Cafetería Cappuccino
76 La Galería
77 Restaurant Junto al Mar

OTHER
1 Tourist Office
2 Budget
3 Market
4 Post Office
5 Colectivos to Bajos de
   Chila; Microbuses to Río
   Grande
6 Bancomer

7 Bital
8 Town Hall
10 Cristobal Colón Bus Station
11 Estrella Roja del Sureste Bus
   Station
13 Estrella Blanca Bus Station
13 Transol
14 Estrella del Valle/Oaxaca
   Pacifico Bus Station
15 Servicio Mixto de Río
   Grande Buses to Pochutla
19 Farmacia Cafetería
22 Graficom
23 Banamex

24 Lavamática del Centro
27 Money Exchange
28 Tequila Sunrise; El Son y La
   Rumba
32 Restaurant Liza's
33 Lighthouse
41 Casa Babylon
48 Bar El Punto
51 Cuartel Salvavidas
   (Lifeguards' Base)
55 Cofee Net
57 Los 3 Diablos
59 Money Exchange

60 Viajes Dimar
62 Barfly
64 Money Exchange
70 Alamo
71 Wipe Out Bar
73 Restaurant Da Claudio
75 Aventura Submarina
78 Un Tigre Azul; Ana's
   Ecotours
79 Tourist Information Office
80 Ticket Bus
81 Aerovega
82 Tarros

OAXACA STATE

Gasga and Unión, changes US dollars traveler's checks, cash US and Canadian dollars and European currencies; it's open from 9am to 2pm Monday to Saturday. In the upper part of town Bancrecer at Hidalgo 4, Bital on 1 Norte and Bancomer on 3 Poniente offer similar exchange service 9am to noon Monday to Friday, and can be quicker. All these banks have ATMs.

The town's several casas de cambio – all simply called Money Exchange – give worse rates than the banks but change a similar range of currencies and are open much longer hours. The one on Pérez Gasga opposite Hotel Loren is open 8am to 9pm daily.

Post & Communications The post office, on Avenida Oaxaca at 7 Norte, is a 20- to 30-minute uphill walk from El Adoquín, but you can take a 'Mercado' bus or colectivo taxi up Avenida Oaxaca. Postal services operate 9am to 4pm Monday to Friday, 9am to 1pm Saturday.

You'll find pay phones and a couple of telephone casetas on the Adoquín, and more pay phones along Calle del Morro on Zicatela.

Puerto has heaps of cybercafés. On Pérez Gasga uphill from the Adoquín, Farmacia Cafetería (open 8am to 11pm daily) and Graficom charge US$1.25 an hour. Cofee Net charges US$1.75 an hour and has branches on El Adoquín and in Hotel Surf Olas Altas on Zicatela.

Media The free bimonthly paper *El Sol de la Costa*, in Spanish and English, is full of information about what's on and what to do. It's on the web at **W** www.puertoconnection.com.

Laundry You can wash 3.5kg of clothes for US$1.75 at Lavamática del Centro on Pérez Gasga. It's open daily.

Dangers & Annoyances We haven't heard of any dire incidents lately, but in the past Puerto has had an up-and-down safety record. The murder of an American artist in broad daylight on Playa Zicatela in 1998 was widely publicized.

To minimize any risks, avoid isolated or empty places, and stick to well-lit areas at night (or use taxis). Take special care on the beach at Playa Zicatela and in the rocks area between Zicatela and Playa Marinero,

and it's probably best to avoid the coastal walkway passing the lighthouse.

Beaches

Bahía Principal The main town beach is long enough to accommodate restaurants at its west end, sun worshipers and young body-boarders at its east end (called Playa Marinero) and occasional flocks of pelicans winging in inches above the waves. Fishing boats bob on the swell, and a few hawkers wander up and down. The smelly water entering the bay at times from the inaptly named Laguna Agua Dulce will put you off dipping away from Playa Marinero.

Playa Zicatela Long, straight Zicatela is Puerto's hip beach, with enticing cafés, restaurants and accommodations as well as the waves of the 'Mexican Pipeline,' just offshore, which draw surfers from far and wide. Nonsurfers beware: the Zicatela waters have a lethal undertow and are definitely not safe for the boardless. Lifeguards rescue several careless people most months (their base, the Cuartel Salvavidas, is in front of Hotel Surf Olas Altas).

Bahía Puerto Angelito The sheltered bay of Puerto Angelito, about 1km west of Bahía Principal, has two small beaches separated by a few rocks. Playa Manzanilla, the eastern one, is quieter because vehicles can't reach it.

Lanchas (fast, open, outboard boats) from the west end of Bahía Principal will take three or four people to Puerto Angelito for US$2.25 per person each way. The boat returns at an agreed pick-up time. By land, it's a 20- to 30-minute walk or a US$1.75 taxi ride from El Adoquín.

Playa Carrizalillo Just west of Puerto Angelito, small Carrizalillo beach is in a rockier cove but is OK for swimming. It has a bar with a few *palapas* for shade. Lanchas from Bahía Principal (about US$6 per person roundtrip) will bring you here too. A path down from the former trailer park on the cliff top immediately north of the beach also reaches the cove.

Activities

You can rent boards for **surfing** and **bodyboarding** in a few places on Playa Zicatela.

One is **Central Surf** (☎ 582-22-85, Ⓦ www.centralsurfshop.com, Morro s/n; US$4.50/11.50 per hour/day for surfboard or body board & fins), in the Hotel Acuario building. Central Surf also offers surfing lessons. Local kids sometimes rent body boards on Playa Marinero for around US$1.25 an hour.

Lanchas from the west end of Bahía Principal will take groups of four or five out for about an hour's **turtle-spotting** (and, in winter, sometimes dolphin-spotting) for around US$33, with a dropoff at Puerto Angelito or Playa Carrizalillo, if you like, afterwards.

Local marlin fishers and sailfishers will take two to four people **fishing** with them for three hours for US$100. Ask at the lancha kiosk at the west end of Bahía Principal. The price includes cooking some of the catch for you at one of the town's seafood restaurants.

Diving is another possibility. Apparently the San Andreas Fault begins not far out to sea from Zicatela. **Aventura Submarina** (☎ 582-23-53, Pérez Gasga 601A; one/two-tank dive trips US$39/62 per person) teaches diving courses and leads dive trips.

Special Events

Semana Santa is a big week for local partying; a local surf carnival is held at this time. At least two international surf contests are held on Zicatela each year, usually in August or September, and the national surfing championships happen on the last weekend of November.

November is a big month in other ways too: the Festival Costeña de la Danza, a fiesta of Oaxaca coastal dance, and a sailfish-fishing contest and art exhibitions all take place over the second and/or third weekends of the month.

Places to Stay

The two main accommodation zones are the central Avenida Pérez Gasga area and the surf beach Playa Zicatela. In the peak seasons the most popular places will probably be full. Your best chance of getting into a place you like, if you haven't booked ahead, is to ask early in the day, about 9am or 10am.

Many accommodations lack heated water, but the tap water is usually fairly warm anyway.

Several apartments and houses are available for short and long stays. Apartments start around US$400/800 a month in low/ high season; houses overlooking the beach are around US$675/1350. Ask at the tourist information office on Pérez Gasga.

Budget For campers, the small tree-shaded site **Palmas de Cortés** (Bahía Principal) has showers, electrical hookups, fireplaces and 24-hour supervision. Rates are US$3.50 per person, plus US$3.50 per vehicle.

Playa Marinero & Playa Zicatela Budget options near the beaches are limited, but there are a couple of good-value places along Zicatela.

Aldea Marinero (1ª Entrada a Playa Marinero) Singles/doubles US$5/8. These cabañas, on a small lane going back from Playa Marinero, have mosquito nets, hammocks out front and clean shared bathrooms. They're better and more secure than the other cabaña places on this street.

Restaurante Esmeralda's (Playa Zicatela) Singles or doubles US$11.50. Esmeralda's, right on the Zicatela sands, has a few small rooms with bath. The price is good but the location is not very private: lock up well.

Las Olas (☎ 582-09-19, Ⓔ zazielucassen@ hotmail.com, Morro 15) Singles & doubles US$23, triples US$34. Las Olas has 12 good cabañas and rooms, each with attached bath, fan, screens and fridge; some have cookers and most have TV.

Hotel Buena Vista (☎ 582-14-74, Morro s/n) Singles & doubles US$16-23 (US$50-56 in Semana Santa). The plain, well-kept Buena Vista stands on the hillside, reached by a flight of steps from Calle del Morro. The 16 reasonably sized rooms all have mosquito screens or nets. The most expensive have kitchens, and many have breezy balconies with splendid views.

Hotel Rockaway (☎ 582-06-68, fax 582-24-20, Morro s/n) Singles/doubles/triples/ quads US$11.50/17/23/28. The popular Rockaway has good, solid cabañas with showers, nets and fans, around a pool, plus a bar and handy little grocery store.

Avenida Pérez Gasga & Around There are just a handful of budget spots in this area.

Hotel Mayflower (☎ 582-03-67, fax 582-04-22, Ⓔ minnemay7@hotmail.com, Andador

Libertad s/n) Dorm beds US$6, singles/ doubles US$18/22. The Mayflower, beside the steps leading down to El Adoquín from the east end of Merklin, has three fan-cooled dormitories with 15 places in all. Rates include fridge, microwave and filtered water. The pleasing single and double rooms have fan and bath. There's a bar open in the evenings.

Hotel Naxhiely (☎ *582-30-75, Pérez Gasga 301)* Singles/doubles/triples/quads US$17/20/24/27. This small hotel has 11 plain, smallish but good clean rooms with fan, TV and bathroom. Security is good and there's a small cafeteria.

Cabañas Pepe (☎ *582-20-37, Merklin 201)* Rooms for up to 4 people US$17. Not far below El Crucero, friendly, family-run Pepe's is geared to backpackers and offers rooms with two double beds, fan, nets and bathroom. Most are in good shape and some have superb views.

Mid-Range Attached baths are standard in this range.

Playa Marinero & Playa Zicatela There's plenty of choice near the beaches in this price range.

Hotel Flor de María (☎ *582-05-36, fax 582-26-17,* W *www.mexonline.com/florde maria.htm, 1ª Entrada a Playa Marinero)* Singles or doubles US$30-50. A friendly Canadian couple run this good hotel on a lane behind Playa Marinero. The 24 ample rooms, around a columned patio, all have two double beds and safes and are really pretty, with individually painted murals and door panels. Extras include a rooftop pool and bar and a good international restaurant. Many North American 'snowbirds' migrate here every spring.

Tabachín del Puerto (☎ *582-11-79,* W *www.tabachin.com.mx, at the end of a short lane behind Hotel Santa Fe)* Singles or doubles US$45-65 including breakfast. The American-owned Tabachín offers six studio-rooms of various sizes, all with kitchen, air-con, TV and phone, and some with computer hookups. Most have balcony access; decor and furniture range from folksy Mexican to classical fine-art. The vegetarian breakfast, which includes organically grown coffee and fruits from the owners' farm in the sierra town of Nopala, is a feature here.

Casas de Playa Acali (☎ *582-07-54, Morro s/n)* Single & double cabañas US$28, triple cabañas US$34, single & double bungalows US$62, triple/quad bungalows US$73/84. Acali provides eight wooden cabañas, each with one double and one single bed, and 16 bungalows with two double beds, air-con and a kitchen. All have mosquito nets. A pool and bar add to its attraction.

Hotel Arco Iris (☎/fax *582-04-32,* e *arco iris@ptoescondido.com.mx, Morro s/n)* Singles & doubles US$40-48, triples US$45-54, quads US$50-59. The Arco Iris has 32 big, clean rooms with balconies or terraces, most looking straight out to the surf, plus a large pool and a good upstairs restaurant/ bar open to the breeze. It all adds up to one of Zicatela's most attractive hotels. All rooms have two double beds and ceiling fans, and some have a kitchen.

Zicatela Bungalows (☎ *582-07-98, Morro s/n)* Doubles/triples/quads US$39/45/50, with kitchen US$50/56/62, with kitchen & air-con US$67/78/89. Next door to the Arco Iris, the Zicatela has a sociable pool and restaurant. All 40-odd accommodations have mosquito-netted windows and are solidly built, even if they're squeezed a little tightly together.

Hotel Acuario (☎ *582-10-27, fax 582-06-31,* e *bunacuario@hotmail.com, Morro s/n)* Doubles US$28-45; US$5.75 per extra person. The 30 or so accommodations here range from wooden cabañas to spacious upstairs rooms with terrace and beach view. All have mosquito nets and there's a nice pool.

Hotel Surf Olas Altas (☎ *582-23-15, ☎/fax 582-00-94,* W *www.surfolasaltas.com.mx, Morro 310)* Singles/doubles/triples/quads with fan (ground floor) US$50/56/64/73, with air-con US$62/67/75/84, suites US$84/89/100/112. Zicatela's biggest hotel is a modern place with 57 rooms. It has less character than some of the smaller places but the rooms are fine; most have two double beds and all have satellite TV. The hotel has a pool and a restaurant out front.

Beach Hotel Inés (☎/fax *582-07-92,* W *www.hotel-ines.com, Morro s/n)* Singles or doubles US$11.50-37. German-run Inés has a range of cabañas, rooms, bungalows and suites; some will take four or more people for US$40 and up. At the center of things is a pleasant pool area with a café serving good food.

Bungalows Puerta del Sol (☎ 582-29-22, Morro s/n) Singles & doubles US$33, triples/quads US$39/44. Just east of Hotel Inés, this place has a good pool and 10 spacious, solidly built rooms, each with two double beds, hammock and fan.

Avenida Pérez Gasga & Around There's a good range of places here too.

Hotel Rincón del Pacífico (☎ 582-00-56, fax 582-01-01, e rconpaci@prodigy.net.mx, Pérez Gasga 900) Singles/doubles/triples/quads with fan US$25/30/35/41, with air-con US$38/47/57/66. This hotel on El Adoquín has 20-odd big-windowed rooms with TV around a palmy courtyard. Staff are helpful and the hotel has a beachside café/restaurant.

Hotel Casa Blanca (☎ 582-01-68, Pérez Gasga 905) Singles/doubles/triples/quads US$25/34/38/43. The friendly Casa Blanca is right at the heart of things on the inland side of El Adoquín, and it fills up with guests quickly. It has 21 large rooms; the streetside ones have balconies.

Hotel Posada de Cortés (☎ 582-07-74, fax 582-02-09, e cortes@ptoescondido.com.mx, Pérez Gasga 218) Singles & doubles US$28, triples/quads US$34/39. Posada de Cortés is set around a pleasant patio/garden, just above El Adoquín. The standard rooms ('bungalows') include kitchen. There are also more expensive 'suites.' For air-con, you pay US$8 extra.

Hotel Hacienda Revolución (☎/fax 582-18-18, w www.haciendarevolucion.com, Andador Revolución 21) Singles/doubles/triples/quads US$17/28/34/39. This place, on a flight of steps leading up from El Adoquín, has 11 nice, spacious rooms around a garden-courtyard. They have attractively tiled bathrooms and colorful paintwork, and most have a patio and hammock.

Hotel Rocamar (☎ 582-03-39, Pérez Gasga s/n) Singles & doubles US$34, triples US$39. The Rocamar, at the west end of El Adoquín, is not a bad value. The rooms, of varied size, have no frills but are clean, and some have balconies overlooking the street.

Hotel Loren (☎ 582-00-57, fax 582-05-91, Pérez Gasga 507) Singles & doubles with fan US$39, triples with fan US$45, singles & doubles with air-con US$50, triples with air-con US$56. A minute uphill from El Adoquín, this friendly, sky-blue-and-lobster-colored hotel has bare but spacious rooms. All have two double beds, cable TV and balconies, but not all catch a sea view. There's a pool.

Hotel Nayar (☎ 582-01-13, fax 582-03-19, Pérez Gasga 407) Singles or doubles US$33 with fan, US$42 with air-con. The predominant color here is apricot. The Nayar gets a good breeze in its wide sitting areas/walkways, and the 40 rooms have hot water, TV and small balconies. Some have sea views. Like the Loren, the Nayar has a pool.

Hotel Paraíso Escondido (☎ 582-04-44, Unión 10) Singles & doubles US$55, triples US$66. Owned by a group of architects and designers, the Paraíso Escondido is a rambling whitewash-and-blue place decorated with tiles, pottery, stained glass and stone sculpture by well-known Mexican sculptors. It has an attractive restaurant/bar/pool area, and the 20 clean though moderately sized rooms have air-con.

Hotel Castillo de Reyes (☎/fax 582-04-42, Pérez Gasga 210) Singles/doubles/triples/quads US$23/29/32/34. The 18 sizable and clean rooms here all have two double beds and fan.

Hotel San Juan (☎ 582-05-18, fax 582-06-12, e sanjuanhotel@prodigy.net.mx, Merklin 503) Singles/doubles/triples/quads US$23/27/37/43. The friendly San Juan, just below El Crucero, has 31 good, straightforward rooms. All have hot water, mosquito screens and cable TV; some have terraces and excellent views. The hotel also boasts a pool and a rooftop sitting area for catching sun, view or breeze.

Top End Hotel Santa Fe (☎ 582-01-70, e info@hotelsantafe.com.mx, Morro s/n) Singles/doubles US$84/100, single/double bungalows US$95/111. The Santa Fe, behind the rocky outcrop dividing Playa Marinero from Playa Zicatela, has 51 rooms attractively set around small terraces and a palm-fringed pool. Rooms vary in size and view, but good design, with tiles cleverly used, makes most of them agreeable. Many have air-con. Also available are eight appealing bungalows with kitchens.

Places to Eat

Puerto has some excellent eateries, a large proportion of them Italian thanks to the tide of Italian travelers drawn here by the movie *Puerto Escondido*. Many are at least partly open-air.

Playa Zicatela These listings are in north-to-south order.

Hotel Santa Fe (see Places to Stay) Mains US$6-14. The airy restaurant here, looking down Zicatela, has some tasty seafood and vegetarian fare, but be ready for your choice to be unavailable. It's medium to expensive in price, with fish and seafood among the costlier offerings.

La Galera (in Hotel Arco Iris; see Places to Stay) Mains US$6-10. This restaurant has a good, open-air, upstairs setting, and a limited but tasty mix of Mexican and international fare. Main dishes focus on fish and meat; salads and antojitos cost US$3.50 to US$7.25.

Zicatela Bungalows (see Places to Stay) The restaurant here is a good value – try the burgers (meat, soy or fish) at US$2 including salad and fries.

La Gota de Vida (Morro s/n) Dishes US$2.25-5.75. This is an excellent vegetarian restaurant, with salads, crêpes, good pasta, and tempeh, tofu and stir-fries. Many ingredients are homemade. Sate your thirst from a huge range of juices or *licuados* made from all sorts of bases including yogurt and almond milk.

Aroma Divino (☎ 582-34-27, Playa Zicatela) Food US$2-4.50. Open 7am-8pm Mon-Sat. The Aroma Divino has a prime site on the sands looking straight out to the surf break. Run by a Christian surfers' group, it serves a good array of burritos, tortas, tacos, egg dishes, salads and chicken and prawn dishes. Devise your own juice combination for US$1.50 to US$2.

Carmen's Cafecito (☎ 582-05-16, Morro s/n) Prices US$0.75-7. Open 6am-10pm daily. Carmen's, run by an inspired Mexican/Canadian couple, does a roaring trade morning, noon and night. Great pastries, croissants and cakes cost just US$0.75, coffee refills are free, and whole-meal tortas (including the superb scrambled egg, ham, cheese and tomato creation) go for around US$2. A vast helping of French toast and fruit for breakfast is US$2 too. Homemade lunch and dinner dishes, including Mexican options, cost from US$2.25 to US$7. *El Cafecito*, next door, has the same owners and menu, plus a breezy upstairs area.

Zicatela has two or three small *grocery stores*, including a 24-hour one at Hotel Rockaway.

Playa Marinero *Carmen's Panadería y Cafetería (1ª Entrada a Playa Marinero)* Breakfasts around US$2. Open 7am-3pm Mon-Sat, 7am-noon Sun. This is a brilliant café for breakfast or lunchtime snacks, run by the same people as Carmen's Cafecito on Zicatela, and with an outdoor terrace overlooking tropical greenery. Breakfasts include big servings of fruit salad, yogurt and granola, or whole wheat French toast with honey and lots of fruit. A bakery section sells great bread and baked goods.

Avenida Pérez Gasga *La Galería (☎ 582-20-39, Pérez Gasga s/n)* Mains US$4.50-5.75. At the west end of El Adoquín, La Galería is one of Puerto's best Italian spots, with art on the walls and good fare on the tables. The pasta dishes are original and tasty, and the mixed green salad (US$3.50) is a real treat.

Restaurant Junto al Mar (☎ 582-12-72, Pérez Gasga 600) Mains US$6.25-10. On the bay side of El Adoquín (as its name implies), the Junto al Mar has a terrace overlooking the beach and serves up excellent fresh seafood. Try a whole juicy snapper with rice or fries and salad.

Restaurant Los Crotos (☎ 582-00-25, Pérez Gasga s/n) Mains US$5.75-9. Los Crotos serves similar fare to the Junto al Mar in a similar attractive setting between El Adoquín and the beach.

Restaurant Alicia (Pérez Gasga s/n) Dishes US$1.75-5. The little Alicia, around the middle of El Adoquín, is a good value, with multiple spaghetti variations, seafood cocktails and good fish dishes. It does cheap breakfasts too.

Baguettería Vivaldi (Pérez Gasga s/n) Breakfasts & baguettes US$2-3.50. Vivaldi serves good breakfasts (named for German cities) and baguettes on white or whole wheat bread.

Ostería del Viandante da Ugo (Pérez Gasga s/n) Dishes US$3-5.75. Italian-run Ugo's makes a range of pastas and one-person pizzas, and good salads.

Cafetería Cappuccino (☎ 582-03-34, Pérez Gasga s/n) Breakfasts & mains US$2.50-8. The Cappuccino serves good coffee and other fare ranging from breakfasts and salads to steaks and seafood.

Altro Mondo (Pérez Gasga 609B) Mains US$5-13. The Altro Mondo is one of the better and more upmarket Italian joints, with offerings ranging from salads and pizza to seafood with fettuccine and salad.

Entertainment

The two-story music bar *Barfly* on El Adoquín was the epicenter of the travelers' social scene at the time of writing, pulling in a hip crowd nightly. Rival establishments on this street are *Un Tigre Azul*, *Wipe Out Bar*, *Terraza Bar*, *Los 3 Diablos* and, around the corner on Marina Nacional, *Tarros*. Some of these places hold happy hours, with two-for-the-price-of-one on some drinks, from around 9pm to 11pm to get people in early. *El Son y La Rumba (Marina Nacional 15)* has a good salsa/Latin band playing several nights a week. If you fancy a further change of mood try *Tequila Sunrise* disco next door, open from 10pm Tuesday to Sunday (admission US$1.75).

A few bars overlooking the sea, such as *Restaurant Liza's* on Playa Marinero or the *Hotel Arco Iris* on Zicatela, have happy hours from about 5pm to 7pm to help you enjoy Puerto's spectacular sunsets.

Also on Zicatela, *Casa Babylon (Morro s/n)* is a hip travelers' bar, open in the evenings, with board games and a big selection of secondhand books to sell or exchange. *El Punto* bar, on the Zicatela sands, plays cool music and has a bit of space to dance. It sort of warms up around 2am.

The 1992 Italian travel-and-crime movie *Puerto Escondido* is shown at 8pm nightly at *Restaurant Da Claudio*, just off El Adoquín. This film has attracted thousands of Italians and others to Puerto and is well worth seeing, even if it makes the place seem more remote than it really is.

Shopping

The Adoquín is great for a browse – shops and stalls sell fashions from surf designers and from Bali, new-age and silver jewelry, tacky cheap souvenirs and classy crafts that are real works of art.

Getting There & Away

Air See the Oaxaca City section for details on flights to/from Oaxaca. Aerocaribe

(☎ 582-20-24 at Puerto Escondido airport) flies nonstop to/from Mexico City daily (1 hour, from US$175 one-way). You can buy air tickets at agencies such as Viajes Dimar (☎ 582-15-51), Pérez Gasga 905B. The Aerovega office (☎ 582-01-51) is on Marina Nacional, just off El Adoquín.

Bus The bus terminals are all in the upper part of town, a couple of blocks above El Crucero. The EB yard is entered from 1 Oriente; EV/OP, Transol and ERS are on Avenida Hidalgo; and Cristóbal Colón is on 1 Norte. The only true 1st-class services are Colón's and a couple of the EB Mexico City runs.

It's advisable to book ahead for Colón buses and the better services to Oaxaca. Ticket Bus, a national reservations service for Cristóbal Colón, has an office on Marina Nacional just off El Adoquín.

Oaxaca Important: See Getting There & Away in the Oaxaca city section, earlier, for an explanation of the three possible routes between Oaxaca and Puerto Escondido. Daily departures from Puerto to Oaxaca are:

Via highways 200 & 175 – 8 hours; 10 EV/OP (US$9/11 ordinario/directo)

Via highway 131 – 8-10 hours; 6 ERS (US$9-10, most overnight), 8 Transol (US$9-13)

Via highways 200 & 190 – 10-11 hours; 1 Colón (US$19)

Other Destinations Keep a particularly close eye on your baggage when going to or from Acapulco and be sure to get a ticket for any bags placed in the baggage hold. We've heard tales of stolen luggage on this route.

Daily departures include:

Acapulco – 400km, 7 hours; 15 EB (US$14/19 ordinario/semi-directo)

Bahías de Huatulco – 115km, 2½ hours; 5 Colón (US$5.25), 8 EB (US$4/6 ordinario/semi-directo)

Pochutla – 65km, 1½ hours; 7 Colón (US$3.25), 8 EB (US$2.50/4 ordinario/semi-directo), Servicio Mixto de Río Grande buses from El Crucero every 20 minutes, 5am to 7pm (US$2)

Colón also runs two daily buses each to Tuxtla Gutiérrez (US$26), San Cristóbal de Las Casas (US$30) and Mexico City via highway 175 (US$43). EB (US$40-43) goes

OAXACA STATE

to Mexico City too. Colón and EB go to Salina Cruz (5 hours, US$11-12), and Colón runs to Juchitán (6 hours, US$14).

Car Alamo (☎/fax 582-30-03), on El Adoquín, rents VW sedans for US$77 a day with unlimited kilometers; per-km offers might be more economical. Budget (☎ 582-03-12) has a rental office opposite the tourist office on Boulevard Juárez in Fraccionamiento Bacocho.

Getting Around

The airport (☎ 582-04-92) is 4km west of the center on the north side of highway 200. A taxi costs around US$2.50, if you can find one (look on the main road outside the airport). Otherwise, colectivo combis (US$4 per person) will drop you anywhere in town. You should have no problem finding a taxi from town to the airport for about US$2.50.

Taxis and lanchas (see Beaches, earlier in this section) are the only transportation between the central Pérez Gasga/Bahía Principal area and the outlying beaches if you don't want – or think it's unsafe – to walk. Taxis wait at each end of El Adoquín. The standard fare to Playa Zicatela or Puerto Angelito is US$1.75.

AROUND PUERTO ESCONDIDO
Laguna Manialtepec

This lake, 6km long, begins 14km west of Puerto Escondido along highway 200. It's home to ibis, roseate spoonbills, parrots, pelicans and several species of hawk, falcon, osprey, egret, heron, kingfisher and iguana. The best months for observing birds are December to March, and they're best seen in the early morning. The lagoon is mainly surrounded by mangroves, but tropical flowers and palms accent the ocean side.

Several restaurants along the lake's north shore (just off highway 200) run boat trips on the lake. To reach these places from Puerto Escondido, take a Río Grande-bound microbus from 2 Norte just east of the Carretera Costera, in the upper part of town, leaving about every half hour.

Restaurant Isla del Gallo (halfway along the lake) 2-hour trip including ocean-beach stop US$40 for up to 10 people; colectivo service US$8 per person in peak tourism periods. 8am-5pm daily. The boats are shaded and the boatmen know their

birds. Good grilled fish is available at the restaurant for around US$6.

Puesta del Sol (towards west end of lake) This restaurant is another recommended embarkation point, with the same prices as the Isla del Gallo.

A good guide speaking your language can greatly enhance your experience. Several four-to-five-hour options are available from Puerto Escondido.

Hidden Voyages Ecotours (W www.wincom.net/~pelewing) Morning & sunset tours (Dec 1 to about Apr 1) US$32 per person. These excellent trips are run by knowledgeable Canadian ornithologist Michael Malone. Book at Viajes Dimar (☎ 954-582-15-51), Pérez Gasga 905B.

Ana's Ecotours (☎ 954-582-29-54, W www.anasecotours.com, Un Tigre Azul, Pérez Gasga) US$34 per person (minimum 4). Ana's, run by Ana Márquez, an excellent, English-speaking local guide, provides good Manialtepec tours year-round.

Bajos de Chila

The Mixtec ball game *(pelota mixteca)*, a five-a-side team sport descended from the pre-Hispanic ritual ball game, is played at 3pm every Saturday in the village of Bajos de Chila, 10km west of Puerto Escondido along highway 200. If this living relic of Mexico's ancient culture sparks your curiosity, wander along and have a look. The playing field, called the *patio* or *pasador*, is easy to find in the village. Colectivos to Bajos de Chila (15 minutes, US$0.60) leave about every 30 minutes from 2 Norte just east of the Carretera Costera, in the upper part of Puerto Escondido.

Barra de Navidad

The Los Naranjos and Palmazola coastal lagoons, near this village 6km southeast of Puerto Escondido along highway 200, offer another chance to get close to the abundant bird life of the Oaxaca coast – and to the local crocodile population. Villagers have formed a society to protect the lagoons and offer **guided visits** *(US$11.50)* lasting about 1¼ hours, including a half-hour boat ride. It's best to go in the early morning or late afternoon. Unaccompanied visits are not permitted. Barra de Navidad is a short walk south from highway 200 on the east side of the Río Colotepec bridge; take a 'La Barra' colectivo from the highway at the east end of Pérez Gasga in Puerto.

Other Destinations

The mainly Mixtec town of **Jamiltepec**, 105km west of Puerto Escondido on highway 200, holds a colorful Sunday market with many people in traditional clothing.

The town of **Nopala**, about 35km northwest of Puerto Escondido off highway 131, is set in the foothills of the Sierra Madre del Sur in the indigenous Chatino region. You can visit organic coffee plantations and see ancient steles, and a regional museum focusing on local archaeology and Chatino and Afro-Mexican cultures was due to open in 2002. The Tabachín del Puerto (see Places to Stay in the Puerto Escondido section) has a pleasant winter posada, the *Posada Nopala*, there.

Agencies such as *Ana's Ecotours* and *Viajes Dimar* (see the Laguna Manialtepec section, earlier) offer day trips to these destinations for around US$34 per person, usually with a minimum of four people.

LAGUNAS DE CHACAHUA

Highway 200, heading west from Puerto Escondido toward Acapulco, runs along behind a coast studded with lagoons, pristine beaches and prolific bird and plant life. The population in this region includes many descendants of African slaves who escaped from the Spanish.

The area around the coastal lagoons of Chacahua and La Pastoría forms the beautiful **Parque Nacional Lagunas de Chacahua**. Birds from Alaska and Canada migrate here in winter. Mangrove-fringed islands harbor roseate spoonbills, ibis, cormorants, wood storks, herons and egrets, as well as mahogany trees, crocodiles and turtles. El Corral, a mangrove-lined waterway filled with countless birds in winter, connects the two lagoons.

Zapotalito

Sixty kilometers from Puerto Escondido, a 5km road leads south from highway 200 to Zapotalito, a small fishing village at the eastern end of La Pastoría lagoon. A few simple restaurants flank the lagoon. A cooperative here runs four-to-six-hour *lancha tours* of the lagoons (*US$78 for up to 10 people*). The trips visit islands, channels to

the ocean and the fishing village of Chacahua, at the western end of the park.

You can travel straight to Chacahua village on colectivo boats (US$3.50 per person), which you'll find about 300m further around the shore beyond the lancha tours departure point. These leave when they have seven or eight passengers. The 25km journey takes about 45 minutes. The colectivo boats also run from Chacahua back to Zapotalito.

Chacahua

Chacahua village straddles the channel that connects the west end of Chacahua lagoon to the ocean. The ocean side of the village, fronting a wonderful beach, is a perfect place to bliss out – for the day, or longer. The waves here can be good for surfers, but there are some strong currents; check where it's safe to swim. The inland half of the village contains a crocodile-breeding center with a sad-looking collection of creatures kept for protection and reproduction. Chacahua's croc population (not human-eating) has been decimated by hunters.

Organized Tours

It's fun to get to Chacahua on your own, and an independent day trip from Puerto Escondido is quite feasible, but several Puerto Escondido agencies offer good day trips (see the earlier Laguna Manialtepec section for details of the following operators).

Hidden Voyages Ecotours US$35 per person, Thur only, Dec 1 to about Apr 1.

Ana's Ecotours US$39 per person (minimum 6), daily.

Places to Stay & Eat

Several places along the beach at Chacahua village offer basic cabañas, hammocks or tent space.

Restaurante Siete Mares Camping or hammock US$2.25 per person, cabañas US$11.50/13.50 for 2/4 people; main dishes US$6.75. The Siete Mares, at the west end of the beach, has the best food, with fish and seafood prepared in a variety of ways, and is also in charge of some of Chacahua's better cabañas, 300m along the beach, with two beds, fan, nets and clean bathrooms.

Palapa de Chano Double cabañas US$6.75. Chano's, a little east of the Siete

Mares, has very basic cabañas with nets and vile shared toilets.

Palapa de Bertha Bertha lets you pitch a tent or sleep in a hammock for free as long as you eat here too; a fish meal is US$4.50.

Getting There & Away

From Puerto Escondido, you first have to get to the town of Rio Grande, 50km west on highway 200. Río Grande-bound microbuses (1 hour, US$1.50) leave 2 Norte just east of the Carretera Costera, in the upper part of Puerto Escondido, about every half hour. All EB buses between Puerto Escondido and Acapulco stop at Río Grande too. From the microbus stop in Río Grande, cross the road and get a colectivo taxi (US$0.70) to Zapotalito, 14km southwest. For information on getting from Zapotalito to Chacahua, see Zapotalito, above.

Chacahua village is linked to San José del Progreso, 29km north on highway 200, by a sandy track that is impassable in the wet season.

PINOTEPA NACIONAL
• pop 23,500 ☎ 954

This is the biggest town between Puerto Escondido (140km east) and Acapulco (260km west). To the southwest there's a fine beach, **Playa Corralero**, near the mouth of Laguna Corralero (from 'Pino' go about 25km west on highway 200, then some 15km southeast). You can stay in palapas at Corralero village; two *camionetas* (pickups) run there daily from Pinotepa.

Hotel Marissa (☎ 543-21-01, *Avenida Juárez 134)* Singles or doubles US$12-16.50. The Marissa, conveniently located half a block east of Pino's central plaza, has clean rooms with bath and fan, and parking.

Hotel Carmona (☎ 543-23-22, *Porfirio Díaz 401)* Singles or doubles with fan US$24, with air-con US$34. This hotel, on the main road about 500m west of the main plaza, is one of the best in Pino. Rooms have bath and TV and there's a pool.

All EB buses between Puerto Escondido and Acapulco stop at Pinotepa (from Puerto Escondido: 3 hours, US$5/6.75 ordinario/semi-directo). First-class Cristóbal Colón buses and 2nd-class FYPSA and TOI buses travel north on highway 125 through the Mixteca, some reaching Oaxaca that way.

POCHUTLA
• pop 10,300 ☎ 958

This bustling, sweaty market town is the starting point for transportation to the nearby beach spots Puerto Ángel, Zipolite, San Agustinillo and Mazunte. It also has the nearest banks to those places.

Orientation

Highway 175 from Oaxaca runs through Pochutla as Cárdenas, the narrow north-south main street, and meets the coastal highway 200 about 1.5km south of town. Hotel Izala marks the approximate midpoint of Cárdenas. Long-distance bus stations cluster on Cárdenas 300 to 400m south of the Izala. The main square, Plaza de la Constitución, is a block east of the Izala along Juárez.

Information

At least four banks – Scotiabank Inverlat, Bital and Bancomer, in south-north order on Cárdenas, and Banamex on Plaza de la Constitución – have ATMs, though it's quite possible to find none of the machines providing money at any given moment. Bital changes traveler's checks and US dollars 8am to 5.30pm Monday to Friday, 8am to 3pm Saturday. Bital and Scotiabank provide over-the-counter Visa-card cash advances (take your passport).

The post office, open 8am to 3pm Monday to Friday, is on Avenida Progreso behind Plaza de la Constitución. Caseta Cybeltel, Cárdenas 62 almost opposite the Hotel Izala, open 7am to 10pm daily, offers 15/30/60 minutes' Internet access for US$1.25/1.75/3.50, plus long-distance telephone service.

Places to Stay

Hotel Santa Cruz (☎/fax 584-01-16, *Cárdenas s/n)* Singles/doubles US$10/13.50. The Santa Cruz has simple, just-about-adequate rooms with bathroom and fan. It's about 150m north of the main cluster of bus stations.

Hotel Izala (☎ 584-01-19, *Cárdenas 59)* Singles/doubles with fan US$14.50/23, with air-con US$28/34. The Izala has plain, clean rooms with bathroom and TV, around a courtyard.

Hotel Costa del Sol (☎ 584-03-18, fax 584-00-49, *Cárdenas 47)* Singles or doubles with fan US$28, with air-con US$34. Pochutla's best hotel, 1½ blocks north of the Izala, has hot water and cable TV in all rooms.

Getting There & Away

The three main bus stations, in north-south order near the south end of Cárdenas, are EB (2nd-class) on the west side of the street, EV/OP (2nd-class) on the east side, and Cristóbal Colón (1st-class) on the west side.

Oaxaca Oaxaca is 245km away by highway 175 (six to eight hours) or 450km by the better highways 200 and 190 (via Salina Cruz, nine to 10 hours). At the time of research Colón had one daily bus by each route, both costing US$18.50 – but schedules and routings are changeable. The 13 daily EV/OP buses take highway 175 (US$8/10 ordinario/directo). Autoexprés Atlántida at Hotel Santa Cruz runs four daily air-conditioned Chevrolet Suburban vans by highway 175 for US$13.50.

Puerto Ángel & Nearby Coast Transportation services to the nearby coast change frequently. When things are going well, frequent buses, microbuses and colectivo taxis run along the paved road from Pochutla to Puerto Ángel, Zipolite, San Agustinillo and Mazunte, usually starting at the EV/OP station or nearby on Cárdenas. But at the time of writing these services had been suspended for several months because of a turf battle among the area's drivers. From about 7am to 7pm daily, frequent colectivo taxis to Puerto Ángel (US$0.60, 20 minutes, 13km) were still leaving from a stand on Cárdenas 200m north of the EB bus station. But vehicles from Pochutla could not carry passengers beyond Puerto Ángel to Zipolite, San Agustinillo or Mazunte. For these destinations, you either had to change to another vehicle at Puerto Ángel or – longer but easier – take one of the camionetas leaving frequently between about 7am and 7pm daily from beside Ferretería RoGa, on Cárdenas 300m north of the Hotel Izala. These headed to Mazunte (20km, 30 minutes, US$0.80), San Agustinillo (21km, 35 minutes, US$0.80) and Zipolite (25km, 45 minutes, US$0.80), via San Antonio on highway 200 northwest of Mazunte (not via Puerto Ángel).

Other Destinations Daily bus departures include:

Acapulco – 465km, 8 hours; 6 EB (US$16.50/23 ordinario/semi-directo)

Bahías de Huatulco – 50km, 1 hour; 4 Colón (US$2.25), 5 EB (US$2.25), Transportes Rápidos de Pochutla buses every 15 minutes, 5.30am to 8pm, from yard opposite EB (US$1.50)

Puerto Escondido – 65km, 1½ hours; 6 Colón (US$3.25), 6 EB (US$2.50/4 ordinario/semi-directo), Servicio Mixto de Río Grande buses every 20 minutes, 5am to 7pm, from Allende, one block south and half a block east of Hotel Izala (US$2)

San Cristóbal de Las Casas – 590km, 11 hours; 2 Colón (US$27)

Tuxtla Gutiérrez – 505km, 10 hours; 2 Colón (US$23)

Colón runs to Salina Cruz, Tehuantepec and Juchitán. EB also serves Salina Cruz. Both these companies go to Mexico City.

PUERTO ÁNGEL
● pop 2500 ☎ 958

The small fishing town, naval base and travelers' hangout of Puerto Ángel ('PWAIR-toh AHN-hel') straggles around a picturesque bay between two rocky headlands, 13km south of Pochutla. Many travelers prefer to stay out on the beaches a few kilometers west at Zipolite, San Agustinillo or Mazunte, but the marginally more urban Puerto Ángel can be a good base too. It offers its own little beaches, some excellent places to stay and eat, and easy transportation to/from Zipolite.

Orientation

The road from Pochutla emerges at the east end of the small Bahía de Puerto Ángel. The road winds around the back of the bay, over an often-dry *arroyo* (creek) and up a hill. It then forks – right to Zipolite and Mazunte, left down to Playa del Panteón.

Information

The nearest banks are in Pochutla, but several accommodations and restaurants will change cash or traveler's checks at their own rates. The post office is on Avenida Principal at the east end of town and is open 8.30am to 3pm Monday to Friday. Gel@net, Vasconcelos 3, has telephone, fax and

PUERTO ÁNGEL

PLACES TO STAY
1 La Buena Vista
2 Casa Arnel
4 Hotel Puesta del Sol
5 Casa de Huéspedes Anati; G@l@p@gos
7 Casa de Huéspedes Gundi y Tomás
8 Penelope's
9 Casa de Huéspedes El Capy

12 Villa Florencia
13 El Almendro
14 Posada Rincón Sabroso
15 Posada Cañon Devata
16 Hotel La Cabaña

PLACES TO EAT
10 Rincón del Mar
17 Restaurante Susy; Other Beach Restaurants
19 Restaurant Marisol

OTHER
3 Caseta Telefónica Lila's
6 Market
11 Naval Base
18 Azul Profundo
20 Taxi Stand
21 Farmacia El Ángel
22 Gel@net
24 Post Office

Internet (US$3.50 an hour), plus a travel agency that can make flight reservations from Puerto Escondido and Bahías de Huatulco. Gel@net is open 8am to 10pm daily. Caseta Telefónica Lila's, on Boulevard Uribe, has phone and fax service too. Other places offering Internet access (also US$3.50 an hour) are G@l@p@gos in Casa de Huéspedes Anati, Casa Arnel and Hotel Puesta del Sol.

The *simpático* Dr Constancio Aparicio (☎ 584-30-58) is a doctor recommended by foreign residents. He's based at Farmacia El Ángel on Vasconcelos.

Theft and robbery can be a problem, especially on the Zipolite road.

Beaches

Playa del Panteón The beach on the west side of Bahía de Puerto Ángel is shallow and calm, and its waters are cleaner than those near the fishers' pier across the bay.

Playa Estacahuite Half a kilometre up the road toward Pochutla, a sign points right along a path to this beach 700m away. The three tiny, sandy bays here are all good for

snorkeling, but watch out for jellyfish. A couple of shack restaurants serve good, reasonably priced seafood or spaghetti, and they may have snorkels to rent.

Playa La Boquilla The coast northeast of Estacahuite is dotted with more good beaches, none of them very busy. A good one is Playa La Boquilla, on a small bay about 5km out, site of the Bahía de la Luna accommodations and restaurant (see Places to Stay). You can get there by a 3.5km road from a turnoff 4km out of Puerto Ángel on the road toward Pochutla. A taxi from Puerto Ángel costs around US$5 each way, but more fun is to go by boat – you can get a fisher to take a few people from Playa Panteón or from the pier across the bay for around US$11 per person, including a return trip at an agreed time.

Activities

Snorkeling and **fishing** are popular and you can go **diving** too. The drops and canyons out to sea from Puerto Ángel are suitable for very deep dives; another dive is to a ship wrecked in 1870.

OAXACA STATE

Some of the café-restaurants on Playa del Panteón rent snorkel gear (US$2.75/6.75 per hour/day). **Byron Luna** (☎ 584-31-15; 2-3-hour trips US$11 per person) offers snorkeling and fishing trips to four beaches. He provides the equipment and transport from your hotel. Byron is great fun and enjoys spotting dolphins, orcas and turtles. Look for him at his home across the street from Hotel La Cabaña. **Azul Profundo** (☎ 584-31-09, Playa del Panteón) is a dive shop offering more or less the same deal on snorkeling and fishing trips, plus dives at all levels. One-tank dives cost US$44.50, four-tank dives US$123. A first-timer session costs US$50 and a seven-day PADI course US$389.

Places to Stay

Places with an elevated location are more likely to catch any breeze. Mosquito screens are a big plus too. Some places have a water shortage; there's not always enough water to wash clothes. The following accommodations in town are listed in east-to-west order.

Hotel Soraya (☎ 584-30-09, Vasconcelos s/n) Singles & doubles US$34, with air-con US$50. Overlooking the pier, the Soraya's 32 rooms with fan, bath and TV are clean though a bit rundown. All have a balcony and many have good views.

Posada Rincón Sabroso (☎ 584-30-95, Boulevard Uribe s/n) Singles/doubles US$23/30. This greenery-shaded hotel is up a flight of stairs from the street. It has 10 fan-cooled rooms, each with bathroom, terrace and hammock.

El Almendro (☎ 584-30-68, off Boulevard Uribe) Singles/doubles US$11.50/17. Set in a shady garden up a little lane a few meters past the Rincón Sabroso steps, El Almendro has similarly clean rooms, plus a bungalow for up to six people.

Villa Florencia (☎/fax 584-30-44, Boulevard Uribe s/n) Singles/doubles/triples US$28/39/45, air-con US$3.50 extra. The Villa Florencia has 13 pleasant but smallish rooms with private bath, fan and screens. There's a cool sitting area. There are also two apartments for up to five people at US$278 a month.

Casa de Huéspedes Gundi y Tomás (☎ 584-30-68, ⓦ www.reisen-mexiko.de, off Boulevard Uribe) Singles US$11.50, doubles US$16-20. Owned by the same friendly German woman as El Almendro,

this guesthouse has a tranquil atmosphere and a variety of rooms, all with fans and mosquito nets and/or screens. The more expensive ones have private bathrooms. In an emergency you can hang or rent a hammock for US$4.50. Good food is available, including homemade bread and vegetable juices. Decent breakfasts and dinners (7pm to 9pm) cost US$4 and US$5. Other amenities include pleasant sitting areas, a safe for valuables and exchange service for cash or traveler's checks.

Casa Arnel (☎/fax 584-30-51, ⓦ www.oaxaca.com.mx/arnel, Azueta 666) Singles/doubles/triples US$17/22.50/26; discounts for stays longer than a week. Casa Arnel is along the lane past the market. Owned by members of the same welcoming family as Hotel Casa Arnel in Oaxaca, it has five clean rooms with fan and bath. *Refrescos,* coffee and tea are available, and there's a breezy hammock area.

La Buena Vista (☎/fax 584-31-04, ⓦ www.labuenavista.com, La Buena Compañía s/n) Doubles US$35-46. The 16 or so big rooms and couple of excellent mud-brick bungalows here are kept scrupulously clean. All have private bathrooms with pretty tiles, fans, mosquito screens and breezy balconies with hammocks. There's a good restaurant too.

Casa de Huéspedes Anati (Boulevard Uribe s/n) Doubles US$9, quads US$17. This guesthouse on the main drag has a few small, basic but clean rooms, with fan and bath.

Hotel Puesta del Sol (☎/fax 584-30-96, ⓦ www.puertoangel.net, Boulevard Uribe s/n) Singles US$11.50, doubles US$15-18.50, triples US$22; with private bath doubles US$30-34, triples US$34-37, quads US$40. The German/Mexican-owned Puesta del Sol offers sizable, clean rooms, with fan and screens. Some sleep up to six people. The more expensive ones have their own terraces. There's a small library, and satellite TV and videos are available in the sitting room. Hammocks out on the breezy terrace invite relaxation, and breakfast is available.

Casa de Huéspedes El Capy (☎/fax 584-30-02, Carretera Playa del Panteón) Singles/doubles/triples from US$12.25/20/23. This establishment on the road descending to Playa del Panteón has 20 cool but smallish rooms with fan, bath and (mostly) good views.

Hotel La Cabaña (☎ *584-31-05, Saenz de Barandas s/n)* Doubles/triples US$31/34. This bigger hotel is behind Playa del Panteón. Its 23 comfortable rooms have bath, fan and screens.

Posada Cañon Devata (☎ *584-31-37, off Saenz de Barandas; postal address: Apartado Postal 1, Puerto Ángel 70902, Oaxaca)* Singles/doubles with fan & bath US$23/28; 2-room units US$39-50 for 2, plus US$6 per extra adult (maximum 6). Along the road from La Cabaña and up some steps to the right, the friendly Cañon Devata has a variety of attractive accommodations scattered among hillside foliage. It's a good place for those seeking a quiet retreat and is still run by the ecologically-minded López family. Fine Mexican and vegetarian food is available. The posada is closed in May and June.

Penelope's (☎ *584-30-73, 3″ Curva Camino a Zipolite)* Singles/doubles/triples US$17/28/34. Penelope's, with just four rooms, is set in a quiet, leafy neighborhood high above Playa del Panteón. It's just off the Zipolite road, clearly signposted a couple of hundred meters beyond the fork to Playa del Panteón. The clean, spacious rooms have private bath with hot water, fan and mosquito screens. There's an attractive terrace restaurant with economical meals prepared by the attentive Penelope, as well as a small library.

Bahía de la Luna (☎ *584-61-86, fax 584-30-74, e bahia-de-la-luna@usa.net, w www .totalmedia.qc.ca/bahiadelaluna, Playa La Boquilla)* Singles/doubles/triples with bath US$46/53/69, 5-person bungalow US$55, house for 8 US$208. This Canadian-owned spot, out at Playa La Boquilla (see Beaches, earlier), has nice adobe bungalows. It also has a good beachside restaurant-café with moderate prices – a whole fish with rice and vegetables is around US$8, and good salads start at US$3. Inner development workshops in yoga, astrology, stress control and dream interpretation are offered here; check the Web site.

Places to Eat

La Buena Vista (*see Places to Stay)* Breakfast US$3-4, dinner US$5-6. Open for breakfast & dinner Mon-Sat. On an airy terrace overlooking the bay, La Buena Vista's restaurant offers Mexican and American fare, from hotcakes to *chiles*

rellenos with a *quesillo* (Oaxacan cheese) filling. The food is well prepared, even if the Mexican dishes are a little bland.

Posada Cañon Devata (*see Places to Stay)* Dinner US$9.50. Open for breakfast 8.30am-noon daily, dinner from 7.30pm daily; closed May & June. This is another guesthouse restaurant where all are welcome. A good three-course dinner is served at long tables in a lovely palm-roofed, open-sided dining room. Fare is Mexican and whole-food vegetarian. It's best to book early in the day.

Rincón del Mar (*above walkway to Playa del Panteón)* Dishes US$2.25-6. This place has great views from its cliffside location, reached by steps up from the walkway. The food's good too. The fish specialty, *filete a la cazuela,* is prepared with olives, peas, onions and tomatoes. Or you could pick octopus, prawns or *verduras al vapor* (steamed vegetables). Out of high season, it's only open from 4pm to 11pm daily.

Villa Florencia (*see Places to Stay)* Dishes US$2.25-7.25. This Italian restaurant usually manages good pasta. It also serves good cappuccino, salads, Mexican fare, inexpensive breakfasts, and pizzas. Drinks are costly, though.

Casa de Huéspedes El Capy (*see Places to Stay)* Dishes US$2-5. This terrace restaurant is best in the cool of the evening. The long menu includes fish, shrimp, chicken, meat and salads.

The restaurants on Playa del Panteón offer fish and seafood for US$8 to US$11, plus cheaper fare such as *entomatadas* and eggs. Be careful about the freshness of seafood in the low season. The setting is very pretty after dark. ***Restaurante Susy*** (☎ *584-30-19)* is one of the better beachside establishments.

You'll also find several places to eat on the main town beach. They're economical but none is very well frequented. ***Restaurant Marisol***, close to the pier, has good-value food and cheap drinks (beer US$0.80, margarita US$1.50).

Getting There & Away

See the Pochutla section for details of transportation from there. A taxi to or from Zipolite costs US$0.60 colectivo, or US$3 for the whole cab (US$4.50 after dark and even more after 10pm or 11pm). You can ind cabs on Boulevard Uribe; there's a stand at the corner of Vasconcelos.

A taxi to Huatulco airport costs US$34; to Puerto Escondido airport, US$45.

ZIPOLITE
• pop 800 ☎ 958

The beautiful 1.5km stretch of pale sand called Zipolite, beginning about 2.5km west of Puerto Ángel, is fabled as southern Mexico's perfect place to lie back and do as little as you like, *in* as little as you like, *for* as little as you like (well, almost).

Once just a small fishing settlement with a few comedores, Zipolite has grown a lot in recent years. Budget places to stay and eat now line nearly the whole beach, but most are still reassuringly ramshackle and wooden.

Zipolite is as great a place as ever to take it easy, with a magical combination of pounding sea and sun, open-air sleeping, eating and drinking, unique scenery and the travelers' scene. It's the kind of place where you may find yourself postponing departure over and over again. The cluster of larger establishments toward the beach's west end is the hub of Zipolite for many, but there's plenty of room elsewhere if you're looking to really chill out.

Beware: The Zipolite surf is deadly, literally. It's fraught with riptides, changing currents and a strong undertow. Locals don't swim here, and going in deeper than your knees can be risking your life. Most years several people drown here. Local voluntary lifeguards *(salvavidas)* have rescued many, but they don't maintain a permanent watch. If you do get swept out to sea, your best hope is to try to swim calmly parallel to the shore to get clear of the current pulling you outward.

Theft can be a problem at Zipolite, and it's inadvisable to walk along the Puerto Ángel-Zipolite road after dark. And if you buy any drugs, be very careful who you buy them from.

Total nudity is more common at the west end of the beach.

Orientation & Information
The eastern end of Zipolite (nearest Puerto Ángel) is called Colonia Playa del Amor, the middle part is Centro, and toward the western end (divided from Centro by a narrow lagoon-cum-creek) is Colonia Roca Blanca. The few streets behind the beach are mostly nameless.

The nearest banks are in Pochutla, but some accommodations may change cash US dollars. Internet access is available in Colonia Roca Blanca at Caseta Oceana on Avenida Roca Blanca, a block back from the beach (open 8am to 10pm daily), and Zipolnet round the corner (open 9am to 9pm daily). Both charge US$1.50 an hour and also provide long-distance phone service. Lola's, at the east end of the beach, has another telephone caseta.

Places to Stay
Most Zipolite accommodations are right on the beach, where nearly every building rents small rooms, cabañas or hammocks. Wander along and pick one that suits you – it makes sense to choose one where your belongings can be locked up. Few rooms or cabañas cost less for one person than for two.

The following selection starts at the low-key east end of Zipolite (nearest Puerto Ángel) and moves west.

Trailer Park Las Palmeras *(Fernando's Camp Ground, Carretera Puerto Ángel-Zipolite)* US$1.75-2.25 per tent or vehicle, US$1.25 per person. This small park, beside the road from Puerto Ángel as you enter Zipolite, has a grassy plot edged with trees. Rates include electrical hookups, fairly clean showers and toilets, water for washing and 24-hour caretaking.

Chololo's (☎ 584-31-59) Singles or doubles with shared bath US$8, with private bath US$17. Chololo's, with just a few simple rooms, is the easternmost place on the beach. The friendly Mexican and Italian hosts, Guille and Genaro, prepare good food too.

Lola's (☎ 584-32-01) Singles/doubles/triples/quads US$13.50/17/23/28. Lola's is a larger place and has better rooms, with private bath, fan and mosquito screens. Prices rise about US$4 at peak times. It has a popular restaurant.

Casa de Huéspedes Lyoban (☎ 584-31-77, **W** www.lyoban.com.mx) Hammocks US$4, singles/doubles/triples with shared bath US$8/13.50/17. Lyoban, very popular with gay travelers, has basic, clean accommodations and a spacious, sociable bar/restaurant area, plus pool table and library. The hammock price includes a locker and shower usage.

Posada María Hammocks US$3, singles/doubles US$8/9. Run by a friendly older *señora,* Posada María offers box-sized but breezy wooden rooms and has a lockup baggage store. Inexpensive food is available: US$4 for fish fillet, rice, salad and tortillas.

Palapa Katy (☎ 584-31-79 *for messages*) Hammocks US$3, cabañas US$5.75-11.50. Katy's cabañas have mosquito nets. Well-priced Italian food is available, with spaghetti, pizza and salad all between US$2.25 and US$3.50.

Posada Itzama (*Calle El Palmar*) Single/double cabañas US$5.75/6.75. The Itzama's good prices reflect its non-beachfront location, but it's only a few meters from the beach, on the inland side of a lane. The half-dozen solidly built wooden cabañas have double bed, mosquito net and window.

Cabañas Zipolite (*formerly Cabañas Monte Bello*) Single/double cabañas US$4.75/8 facing the beach, US$3.50/6.75 behind. These are ramshackle basic wooden accommodations with mosquito net and shared bath.

La Choza (☎ 584-31-90) Singles or doubles US$11.50. La Choza, Cabañas Zipolite's larger, more solid neighbor, has decent if bare rooms with fan and bath. It offers 24-hour security and will lock away valuables for you. At the front is one of the beach's most popular restaurants.

La Jaula Hammocks US$1.75. Like La Choza, La Jaula had to be rebuilt after a fire in 2001 that destroyed several places. While building new cabañas, its friendly family owners offered hammocks, plus simple fish meals for the same price.

The next two places westward, *El Eclipse* and *Tao*, were also burnt down, but both had been among Zipolite's more popular accommodations, and they should be back.

Posada San Cristóbal (☎ 584-31-91) Single/double cabañas US$8/11.50. The San Cristóbal provides bare accommodations with double bed, net, fan and shared bath, alongside a leafy garden.

Hotel Posada San Cristóbal (☎ 584-31-91, *Avenida Roca Blanca*) Singles/doubles US$11.50/17. This annex of Posada San Cristóbal, on the street behind it, has rooms with two beds, bath, fan and nets.

Posada Esmeralda (*Avenida Roca Blanca*) Singles or doubles with shared bath US$9, with private bath US$17. One block back from the beach, behind Posada San Cristóbal, the Esmeralda has 10 simple rooms of reasonable size and cleanliness with fan, in a solid two-story building.

Lo Cósmico Double cabañas US$11.50-20, plus US$3.50 per extra person. The varied cabañas of Mexican/Swiss-owned Lo Cósmico are built around a tall rock outcrop near the west end of the beach. Each has a double bed, hammock, fan and net. A few are available for single occupancy at US$9 to US$10. There's a good restaurant.

Shambhala Posada Hammocks US$2, singles/doubles US$7/8, single & double cabañas US$12, triple cabañas US$18. Known as Casa Gloria, after its owner, a long-time American Zipolite resident, the popular, long-established Shambhala climbs the hill at the west end of the beach, with great views back along it. The above prices for its varied, basic accommodations are estimates because Shambhala was temporarily closed at the time of research. Rooms have mosquito nets and Shambhala has a restaurant and a luggage room to keep your stuff safe. The shared bathrooms are OK.

Places to Eat

Eating and drinking in the open air a few steps from the surf is an inimitable Zipolite experience. Most accommodations have a restaurant of some kind, and there are also some good stand-alone restaurants. Most of the best eateries are towards the west end of the beach and in the streets behind there.

La Choza (☎ 584-31-90, *Colonia Roca Blanca*) Mains US$3.50-8. The beachside restaurant here has a wide-ranging menu and does most of it well, with generous servings. A big fruit salad with yogurt and granola is US$2.25.

El Eclipse (*Colonia Roca Blanca*) Mains US$4-9. El Eclipse, just west of La Choza, does very good Italian fare, with pasta and pizza costing US$4 to US$5.75, and seafood and meat a bit more. There's even wine (US$3/12 a glass/bottle).

Restaurant Posada San Cristóbal (☎ 584-31-91, *Colonia Roca Blanca*) Dishes US$2.50-9. This popular place does a wide variety of food pretty well, from *pan francés* (French toast), antojitos or salads to whole fish, prawns, octopus or chicken.

Lo Cósmico (*see Places to Stay*) Dishes US$2.75-3.50. Lo Cósmico, on the rocks near the end of the beach, has an open-air restaurant with good food from an impeccably clean kitchen. Especially tasty are the crêpes (sweet and savory) and salads.

El Alquimista (west end Playa Zipolite) Mains US$4-8.50. Popular El Alquimista is one of Zipolite's best, with a great site in the cove between Lo Cósmico and Shambhala. The very wide-ranging fare runs from the likes of falafel tortas (US$2.25) to good meat and chicken dishes (US$4.25 to US$8.50). There's excellent espresso coffee too.

The following places are all a block or two behind the western part of the beach.

Peter's Pan (on the street linking Colonia Roca Blanca to the main road) Breakfasts US$1.75-4. Open 7am-noon Mon-Sat (8am-1pm in summer). The breakfasts here, with fresh whole-grain or white bread from the bakery inside, go well with a visit to Zipolnet next door.

El Chupón (just north of Peter's Pan) Most dishes US$3-6. Open 6pm-2am daily. Probably the best of Zipolite's many Italian eateries, El Chupón serves a big range of pasta with some tasty sauces, and also fish and meat.

Piedra de Fuego (along the lane between Peter's Pan & El Chupón) Dinners US$3.50. At this simple but excellent family-run place, you'll get a generous serving of whatever they're offering on the night (fish, prawns, chicken, etc), with rice, salad and tortillas. Big jugs of *agua de fruta* are US$1.50.

Pizzeria 3 de Diciembre (along the street opposite El Chupón) Prices US$1.25-5. Open 7pm-2am Wed-Sun. The 3 de Diciembre serves not only excellent pizzas (US$4 to US$5) but also good pastry pies (US$1.25 to US$4) with fillings like cauliflower-and-parmesan or baked spinach. Great for late-night munchies!

Entertainment

Zipolite's beachfront restaurant-bars have unbeatable locations for drinks around sunset and after dark. Those towards the west end of the beach are generally the most popular – especially *El Alquimista* (see Places to Eat), which plays cool music and serves cocktails for US$2.25 to US$3 as well as the usual beer, mezcal, etc.

For slightly more active nightlife Zipolite has two open-air *discotecas,* where nothing much happens before midnight (nothing

much may happen after midnight either, but you might as well have a look). *La Puesta* is next door to Zipolnet in Colonia Roca Blanca; *Zipolipa's* opens onto the beach next to Casa de Huéspedes Lyoban.

Getting There & Away

See the Pochutla and Puerto Ángel sections for details on transportation from those places. The camionetas between Pochutla, Mazunte, San Agustinillo and Zipolite terminate on the main road at the far west end of Zipolite (about 2km from the east end of the beach). Colectivo taxis from Puerto Ángel will go to the same spot too, but pass along the length of Zipolite en route, so are probably a better bet if you're heading for the east end of the beach.

After dark, a non-colectivo taxi is your only option for getting to Puerto Ángel or San Agustinillo. They cost around US$4.50 till about 10pm, but more after that.

SAN AGUSTINILLO
☎ 958

West from Zipolite, other glorious beaches stretch almost unbroken all the way to Puerto Escondido. Long, straight Playa Aragón – in the Zipolite mold, but almost empty – stretches west from the headland at the west end of Zipolite to the tiny village of San Agustinillo. Footpaths behind Shambhala Posada cross the headland from Zipolite, or you can take the road, which loops inland then comes back down to San Agustinillo (4km from Zipolite).

San Agustinillo is set on a small curved bay, with waves that are perfect for **body-boarding** and often good for **body-surfing**. There are several relaxed little places to stay and a line of open-air beach comedores serving mainly seafood. You can rent body boards at **México Lindo y qué Rico!** for US$3.50 an hour. **Palapa Olas Altas** offers lancha trips at US$39 an hour for **turtle-viewing** (and occasionally dolphin-viewing) or **fishing.** (See Places to Stay & Eat, below, for details on these places.)

The coast between Zipolite and Puerto Escondido is a major sea turtle nesting ground. Until hunting and killing sea turtles was banned in Mexico in 1990, San Agustinillo was the site of a gruesome slaughterhouse (now demolished) where some 50,000 turtles were killed per year for their meat and shells.

OAXACA STATE

Places to Stay & Eat

Palapa de Evelia (west end Playa San Agustinillo) Singles & doubles US$17, main dishes around US$5.50. This place, the third along from the west end of the beach, has a few bare and basic but clean rooms with bath, fan and mosquito net. The food is the best on the beach, with straightforward but well-prepared fish and seafood, and great guacamole for US$2.25.

México Lindo y qué Rico! (e *fafin yleila@latinmail.com, west end Playa San Agustinillo)* Singles & doubles US$23, main dishes around US$5.50. Next door to Evelia's, México Lindo's handful of rooms are San Agustinillo's best – especially the breezy upstairs pair under the tall palapa roof. They're large, with bath, fan, double bed and net. The owners, Fausto and Leila, are young, friendly and serve good food.

Palapa Olas Altas (☎ 583-97-60, east end Playa San Agustinillo) Singles & doubles US$9-13.50, main dishes US$5-8. Olas Altas has 13 upstairs rooms – only one with sea view but all with mosquito nets. The restaurant serves decent food.

Cabañas Sol y Mar (☎ 584-07-56, west end Playa Aragón) Hammocks US$3, singles & doubles US$6.75-13.50. The Sol y Mar has rooms on both sides of the road, plus breezy upstairs hammocks on the beach side. Cookers are available if you want to cut your eating costs.

Cabañas María (west end Playa Aragón) Singles & doubles without/with view US$11/17. This unusually tall building wasn't finished when we checked it out but it was up and running. The owner is friendly and the rooms are good-sized, with showers. Cookers, pots and pans are available if you ask.

Two places have stunning positions atop the steep slope backing Playa Aragón. Both are reachable by drivable tracks from the road or by paths up from the beach.

Rancho Hamacas (☎ 584-05-49, e b_Silva_Mendez@hotmail.com, Playa Aragón) Hammocks US$3.50, cabañas US$28. Rancho Hamacas has a couple of adobe cabañas with double bed, mosquito net, fridge and cooker. There's a separate patio for hammock-hanging. The owners make beautiful, strong hammocks (around US$100).

Rancho Cerro Largo (fax 584-30-63, e ranchocerrolargomx@yahoo.com, Playa Aragón) Single/double cabañas US$56/67. Farther east on the hilltop from Rancho Hamacas, this place has just a handful of superior, fan-cooled cabañas, and the price includes an excellent breakfast and dinner.

Getting There & Away

See the Pochutla section for information on transportation from there. Camionetas to or from Zipolite or Mazunte cost US$0.40.

MAZUNTE
• pop 450 ☎ 958

Like San Agustinillo, Mazunte, 1km farther west, grew up around the turtle industry. When this was banned in 1990, many villagers turned to slash-and-burn cultivation, threatening nearby forests. Encouraged by a Mexico City-based environmental group, Ecosolar, in 1991 Mazunte declared itself an ecological reserve, attempting to preserve the environment while creating a sustainable economy. Projects included printing and natural cosmetics workshops, construction of ecological toilets and garbage separation. A key element was tourism, which the government-funded Centro Mexicano de la Tortuga, opened in 1994, was also intended to encourage. After Hurricane Pauline in 1997, which caused great damage at Mazunte, Ecosolar's influence waned, but by then the village was well established on the tourism map, and today it's a travelers' hangout almost as popular and hip as Zipolite. The waters of the fine, curving, sandy beach are generally safe, though the waves can be quite big.

Orientation

The paved road running west from Zipolite to highway 200 passes through the middle of Mazunte. The Centro Mexicano de la Tortuga is beside this main road towards the east end of the village. Three sandy lanes run from the road to the beach (about 500m). The western one is sometimes called Camino al Rinconcito, as the west end of the beach is known as El Rinconcito.

Things to See & Do

The **Centro Mexicano de la Tortuga** *(Mexican Turtle Center, ☎ 584-30-55; admission US$2.25; open 10am-4.30pm Tues-Sat)* is a turtle aquarium and research center containing specimens of all seven of

Mexico's marine turtle species, on view in fairly large tanks. It's enthralling to get a close-up view of these creatures, some of which are *big*. Visits are guided (in Spanish) and start every 10 to 15 minutes.

Mazunte's natural cosmetics workshop and store **Cosméticos Naturales** *(open 9am-4pm daily)* is by the roadside toward the west end of the village. This small cooperative makes shampoo and cosmetics from natural sources such as maize, coconut, avocado and sesame seeds. It also sells organic coffee, peanut butter, natural mosquito repellents and handicrafts made elsewhere.

Temazcal and **massage** are available at **Cabañas Balamjuyuc** *(see Places to Stay; temazcal US$11.50 per person including dinner, massage US$17 for 1½ hours)*. A temazcal is a traditional herbal steam bath – a kind of pre-Hispanic sauna!

Cabañas Balamjuyuc will take small groups out on *boat trips* to see turtles and dolphins at US$5.75 per person for around 2½ hours.

Punta Cometa This rocky cape, jutting out from the west end of Mazunte beach, is the southernmost point in the state of Oaxaca and a fabulous place to be at sunset, with great long-distance views in both directions along the coast. You can walk there in 20 to 30 minutes over the rocks from the end of Mazunte beach, or take the Camino a Punta Cometa, a path that starts through the woods almost opposite the entrance to Cabañas Balamjuyuc (see Places to Stay).

Playa Ventanilla Some 2.5km along the road west from Mazunte, a sign points left to Playa Ventanilla, 1.2km down a dirt track. The settlement here includes a handful of simple homes, a couple of comedores and the palapa of **Servicios Ecoturísticos La Ventanilla** *(1½-hour lagoon tours US$4/1.75 adult/child; 6am-6pm daily)*. Servicios Ecoturísticos is a local cooperative providing interesting canoe trips on a mangrove-fringed lagoon, the Estero de la Ventanilla, a few hundred meters along the beach. You'll see river crocodiles (there are about 200 in the lagoon), lots of water birds (most prolific during July and August) and, in an enclosure on an island in the lagoon, a few white-tailed deer. Servicios Ecoturísticos also offers horseback rides *(US$17)* to

another lagoon farther west, where more boat trips *(US$5.75)* are available – about three hours in total.

Frequent camionetas run from Mazunte to the Playa Ventanilla turnoff for US$0.40.

Places to Stay

Most places along the beach (including restaurants) have basic rooms or cabañas, hammocks to rent and often tent space. Prices often rise or fall according to season and demand. December is the busiest time; May and June are quiet. The following beachfront places are listed in east-to-west order.

Cabañas Ziga Singles/doubles with shared bath US$11.50/16, doubles/triples/quads with private bath US$18/24/32. On a breezy beachside elevation a little west of the turtle center, Ziga has decent little rooms with fan and mosquito net, plus a restaurant.

Restaurant Yuri Singles & doubles US$11.50. Yuri's rooms for rent are plain but adequate.

Restaurant Omar Camping US$3 per person, hammocks US$3.50, singles & doubles US$11.50, triples US$17. Omar is beside the end of the middle lane to the beach. The rooms have mosquito nets and two double beds.

Restaurante El Arbolito Camping or hammocks US$2.25 per person. Just west of Omar, El Arbolito is one of the cheaper beachside places.

Palapa El Mazunte Camping or hammocks US$3.50 per person, single or double cabañas US$11.50. This is one of the most popular spots along this part of the beach.

Palapa El Pescador Camping or hammocks US$3 per person. This popular restaurant has a small tent/hammock area on the sand.

Backpackers Youth Hostel Carlos Einstein *(just off Camino al Rinconcito)* Hammocks US$4, dorm beds US$5.75, including continental breakfast. Squeezed between a sluggish creek and a large rock west of Palapa El Pescador, Einstein's is run by an effervescent, eccentric ex-photojournalist named Carlos Aguilera. The accommodations have fresh air but are pretty tightly packed: the beds are small and hard but have mosquito nets. You can use the kitchen for US$0.60 a day (free if you're sleeping in a bed).

OAXACA STATE

Posada del Arquitecto (**e** *laposadade larquitecto@yahoo.com, El Rinconcito*) Cabañas with shared bath US$9 per person, with bath US$11.50-13.50 per person, hammocks US$4.50 (dry season only). On a rocky outcrop near the west end of the beach, the friendly Posada del Arquitecto belongs to an Italian/Mexican couple who have constructed their seven cabañas cleverly around the natural features of the land, using predominantly natural materials.

El Agujón (**e** *elagujonmazunte@yahoo .com.mx, El Rinconcito*) Single/double cabañas US$6.75/13.50. El Agujón, across the street from the Posada del Arquitecto, has 10 small but clean cabañas on the hill-

side just above its restaurant. Bathrooms are shared.

Cabañas Balamjuyuc (**e** *balamjuyuc@ hotmail.com, Camino a Punta Cometa*) Hammocks US$4, double cabañas US$11.50-34. Balamjuyuc is perched on a hilltop above the west end of the beach, with superb views. It's run by a friendly, alternative-minded Mexican/Argentine couple, using solar electricity. The half-dozen cabañas are large, airy and mosquito-netted, and breakfast and dinner are available. You can take a temazcal, massage or boat trip too (see the earlier sections on these). In low season cabañas rent for as little as US$170 a month including use of

Mexico's Turtles

Of the world's eight sea turtle species, seven are found in Mexican waters. Their nesting sites are scattered all along Mexico's coasts.

Female turtles usually lay their eggs on the beaches where they were born, some swimming huge distances to do so. They come ashore at night, scoop a trough in the sand and lay 50 to 200 eggs in it. Then they cover the eggs and go back to the sea. Six to 10 weeks later, the baby turtles hatch, dig their way out and crawl to the sea at night. Only two or three of every 100 make it to adulthood.

Playa Escobilla, just east of Puerto Escondido, is one of the world's main nesting grounds for the small **olive ridley turtle** (*Lepidochelys olivacea,* or *tortuga golfina* to Mexicans), the only unendangered sea turtle species. Between May and January, about 700,000 olive ridleys come ashore here in about a dozen waves – known as *arribadas* – each lasting two or three nights, often during the waning of the moon. Playa Escobilla's turtles are guarded by armed soldiers, and there is no tourist access to the beach.

The rare **leatherback** (*Dermochelys coriacea,* or *tortuga Laúd* or *tortuga de altura*) is the largest sea turtle. It grows up to 3m long and can weigh one ton and live 80 years. One leatherback nesting beach is Playa Mermejita, between Punta Cometa and Playa Ventanilla, near Mazunte. Another is Barra de la Cruz, east of Bahías de Huatulco.

The smallest and most endangered sea turtle, the **Kemp's ridley**, or parrot turtle (*Lepidochelys kempii,* or *tortuga lora*), lives only in the Gulf of Mexico. Its nesting beaches are nearly all in the Mexican state of Tamaulipas. In recent years a joint Mexican-US program has had some success in reversing the decline of the Kemp's ridley, giving hope that the species may be brought back from the brink of extinction (see the South of Matamoros section in the Northeast Mexico chapter).

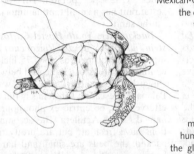

The **green turtle** (*Chelonia mydas,* or *tortuga verde*) is a vegetarian that grazes on marine grasses. Most adults are about 1m long. For millennia, the green turtle's meat and eggs have provided protein to humans in the tropics. European exploration of the globe marked the beginning of the turtle's the kitchen. Balamjuyuc is 400m up from Camino al Rinconcito (signposted). You can also get there by steps up from El Rinconcito beach.

Alta Mira *(☎/fax 584-31-04,* **w** *www .labuenavista.com/alta_mira/, Camino a Punta Cometa)* Doubles US$37-43. The Alta Mira is next door to Cabañas Balamjuyuc, with the same approach routes. It's run by the people from La Buena Vista at Puerto Ángel, and its 10 or so rooms, all with nice tiled bathrooms, mosquito nets, and terrace with hammock, are Mazunte's classiest and comfiest. They're strung beside steps leading down the hillside, and most catch some breeze and excellent views. There's a restau-

rant serving breakfast and dinner, with a similar menu to La Buena Vista's.

Posada Lalo Doubles US$8. One of a few places along the street heading inland from the main road in the middle of Mazunte (and thus about 750m from the beach), Lalo's is a shady spot with friendly young owners. Its few simple rooms have mosquito nets and the price includes kitchen usage.

Places to Eat

Most places to stay are also places to eat. On the beach, most have similar prices. ***Palapa El Pescador*** is one of the best and most popular, with fish and seafood for

---

Mexico's Turtles

decline. In the 1960s, the Empacadora Baja California in Ensenada, Baja California, was canning as many as 100 tons of turtle soup a season.

The **loggerhead turtle** *(Caretta caretta,* or *tortuga caguama),* weighing up to 100kg, is famous for the vast distances it crosses between its feeding grounds and nesting sites. Loggerheads born in Japan and even, it's thought, Australia, cross the Pacific to feed off Baja California. Females later return to their birthplaces – a yearlong journey – to lay their eggs.

The **hawksbill turtle** *(Eretmochelys imbricata,* or *tortuga de carey)* nests along both of Mexico's coasts and can live 50 years. Mexico's seventh species, the **black turtle** *(Chelonia agassizi,* or *tortuga negra* or *tortuga prieta),* sticks to the Pacific.

Turtle nesting seasons vary, but July to September are peak months in many places.

Despite international conservation efforts, turtle flesh and eggs continue to be eaten, and some people still believe the eggs to be aphrodisiac. Turtle skin and shell are used to make clothing and adornments. The world's fishing boats kill many turtles by trapping and drowning them in nets.

In Mexico, hunting and killing sea turtles was officially banned in 1990, but illicit killing and egg-raiding still goes on – one clutch of eggs can be sold for more than a typical worker makes in a week. Environmentalists gained an important victory in 2001, however, when a project for a new hotel at the Caribbean beach of Xcacel was annulled by the Mexican government. Xcacel is an important nesting beach for loggerhead and green turtles, and environmentalists had waged a three-year campaign against the project.

See the Turtle Trax Internet site at **w** www.turtles.org for more fascinating turtle facts.

To help the turtles that use Mexican beaches – and most people who have seen these graceful creatures swimming at sea will want to do that – follow these tips if you find yourself at a nesting beach:

- Try to avoid nesting beaches altogether between sunset and sunrise.
- Don't approach turtles emerging from the sea, or disturb nesting turtles or hatchlings with noise or lights (lights on or even near the beach can cause hatchlings to lose their sense of direction on their journey to the water).
- Keep vehicles, even bicycles, off nesting beaches.
- Don't build sand castles or stick umbrellas into the sand.
- Never handle baby turtles or carry them to the sea – their arduous scramble is vital to their development.
- Boycott shops or stalls selling products made from sea turtles or any other endangered species.

US$5 to US$6.75; lighter eats such as quesadillas, tacos, fruit salad and eggs for US$2.25 to US$3; and tortas around US$1.50. *El Agujón* has another good restaurant, with a very wide range from large and excellent French-bread tortas (US$2 to US$2.25) to crêpes (US$1.50 to US$3.25), fish (US$5 to US$6) and, in the evening, pizzas (US$4.50 to US$6.75).

Aldea Cocos (Main road, west of turtle center) Breakfasts US$1.75-3, comida corrida US$2.25-4, meat/fish mains US$3-5. Aldea Cocos serves some of Mazunte's most economical meals. A lunch of soup, rice, a main dish with beans and tortillas, coffee and dessert is just US$3.25.

La Dulce Vita (Main road, east of Cosméticos Naturales) Mains US$4-8. This Italian restaurant is one of Mazunte's best eateries.

Entertainment

La Barra de Mazunte (Off Camino al Rinconcito) La Barra, nestled deep among the trees on a minor track east of Camino al Rinconcito, is the place to check out if you're after late-night music and a spot of dancing. It's more mellow than the equivalent places at Zipolite.

Getting There & Away

See the Pochutla section for information on transportation from Pochutla. Camionetas between Mazunte and San Agustinillo or Zipolite cost US$0.40.

BAHÍAS DE HUATULCO

• pop 18,000 ☎ 958

Mexico's newest big coastal resort is arising along a series of beautiful sandy bays, the Bahías de Huatulco ('wah-TOOL-koh'), 50km east of Pochutla. Until the 1980s this stretch of coast had just one small fishing village and was known to just a few lucky people as a great place for a quiet swim in translucent waters. Huatulco's developers appear to have learned some lessons from other modern Mexican resorts. Pockets of development are separated by tracts of unspoiled shoreline. The maximum building height is six stories, and no sewage goes into the sea. For now, Huatulco is still an enjoyable, relatively uncrowded resort with a succession of lovely beaches lapped by beautiful water and backed by forest. You can have a pretty active time here – agencies offer all sorts of energetic pursuits from rafting and horseback riding to diving and kayaking. Huatulco is not a place to stay long on a tight budget, however.

The Parque Nacional Huatulco, declared in 1998, protects 119 sq km of land, sea and shoreline west of Santa Cruz Huatulco but is under pressure as developers seek to open up new areas.

Orientation

A divided road leads about 5km down from highway 200 to La Crucecita, the service town for the resort. La Crucecita has the bus stations, market, most of the shops and the only cheap accommodations. One kilometer south, on Bahía de Santa Cruz, is Santa Cruz Huatulco, site of the original village (no trace remains), with some hotels and a harbor. The other main developments so far are at Bahía Chahué, 1km east of Santa Cruz; Tangolunda, 4km farther east; and El Faro, near Playa La Entrega, 2.5km west of Santa Cruz.

The Huatulco bays are strung along the coast about 10km in each direction from Santa Cruz. From west to east, the main ones are San Agustín, Chachacual, Cacaluta, Maguey, El Órgano, Santa Cruz, Chahué, Tangolunda and Conejos.

Bahías de Huatulco airport is 400m north of highway 200, 12km west of the turnoff to La Crucecita.

Information

Tourist Offices There's an information kiosk on La Crucecita's Plaza Principal, open 9am to 2pm and 4pm to 7pm Monday to Saturday. The Sedetur Oaxaca state tourist office (☎ 581-01-76, e sedetur@oaxaca.gob.mx), Boulevard Benito Juárez s/n, is in Tangolunda, on the left as you arrive from the west. It's open 9am to 5pm Monday to Friday, 9am to 1.30pm Saturday. The Asociación de Hoteles de Huatulco (☎ 587-08-48), on Boulevard Santa Cruz in Santa Cruz, also provides tourist information and has similar hours.

Money In La Crucecita, there's a Bancrecer ATM on the south side of Plaza Principal. Bancrecer, Bugambilias 1104, and Bital, Bugambilias 1504, change cash and traveler's checks. Bital has longer hours (8am to

BAHÍAS DE HUATULCO

6pm Monday to Saturday). Banamex and Bancomer on Boulevard Santa Cruz in Santa Cruz also change cash and traveler's checks and have ATMs.

Post & Communications La Crucecita's post office, on Boulevard Chahué, 400m east of the Plaza Principal, is open 8am to 3pm Monday to Friday and 9am to 1pm Saturday.

You can use the Internet at Mare 2000, Guanacastle 203 in La Crucecita, for US$2 an hour. It's open 10am to 9pm Monday to Friday, 10am to 4pm Saturday. Porticos Internet Cafe, Gardenia at Tamarindo, has much better computers with faster access, but it's more expensive at US$3.50 an hour. However, it has the best coffee in town!

Laundry Lavandería Estrella, on Flamboyan at Carrizal in La Crucecita, will wash 3kg of laundry for US$3.50 with same-day pick-up, less for the following day. Open hours are 8am to 9pm Monday to Saturday. Lavandería Abril, Gardenia 1403, charges the same.

Medical Services Some doctors speak English at the Hospital IMSS (☎ 587-11-84), on Boulevard Chahué, halfway between La Crucecita and Bahía Chahué. The big hotels have English-speaking doctors on call.

Parque Ecológico Rufino Tamayo
This park on the edge of La Crucecita is composed mainly of natural vegetation, with some paved paths and tile-roofed shelters with benches.

Beaches
Huatulco's beaches are sandy with clear waters (though boats and Jet Skis leave an oily film here and there). As throughout Mexico, all beaches are under federal control, and anyone can use them even when hotels appear to treat them as private property. Some have coral offshore and excellent snorkeling, though visibility can be poor in the rainy season.

Lanchas will whisk you out to most of the beaches from Santa Cruz Huatulco's harbor anytime between 8am and 4pm or 5pm, and they'll return to collect you by dusk. Taxis can get you to most beaches for less money, but a boat ride is more fun. Lancha tickets are sold at a hut beside the harbor. Roundtrip rates for up to 10 people include: Playa La Entrega, US$17; Bahía Maguey, US$38; Bahía El Órgano, US$44. Another possibility for a fun day is a 6½-hour, *seven-bay boat cruise* (US$17 per person; 11am daily) with an open bar.

Bahía de Santa Cruz At Santa Cruz Huatulco, the small **Playa Santa Cruz** is kept pretty clean but is inferior to most Huatulco beaches.

Playa La Entrega lies toward the outer edge of Bahía de Santa Cruz, a five-minute lancha trip or 2.5km by paved road from Santa Cruz. This 300m-long beach, backed by a line of seafood palapas, can get crowded, but it has calm water and good snorkeling in a large area from which boats are cordoned off. 'La Entrega' means 'The Delivery': here in 1831, Mexican independence hero Vicente Guerrero was betrayed to his enemies by an Italian sea captain for 50,000 pieces of gold. Guerrero was taken to Cuilapan, near Oaxaca, and shot.

West of Bahía de Santa Cruz Some of the western bays are accessible by road. A 1.5km paved road diverges to **Bahía Maguey** from the road to La Entrega, about half a kilometer out of Santa Cruz. Maguey's fine, 400m beach curves around a calm bay between forested headlands. It has a line of seafood palapas but is less busy than La Entrega. There's good snorkeling around the rocks at the left (east) side of the bay. **Bahía El Órgano**, just east of Maguey, has a 250m beach. You can reach it by a narrow 10-minute footpath that heads into the trees halfway along the Santa Cruz-Maguey road. El Órgano has calm waters good for snorkeling, but it lacks comedores.

The beach at **Bahía Cacaluta** is about 1km long and protected by an island, though there can be undertow. Snorkeling is best around the island. Behind the beach is a lagoon with bird life. The road from Maguey to Cacaluta is paved except for the last section to the beach. There is a research station here investigating turtles and purple sea snails (a traditional source of purple and mauve dyes).

Bahía Chachacual, inaccessible by land, has a headland at each end and two beaches. The easterly Playa La India is one of Huatulco's most beautiful and is the best place for snorkeling.

Thirteen kilometers down a dirt road from a crossroads on highway 200, 1.7km west of the airport, is **Bahía San Agustín**. After 9km the road fords a river. The beach is long and sandy, with a long line of palapa comedores, some with hammocks to rent for overnight. It's popular with Mexicans on weekends and holidays, but quiet at other times. Usually the waters are calm and the snorkeling is good (some of the comedores rent equipment).

East of Bahía de Santa Cruz A paved road runs to the eastern bays from La Crucecita and Santa Cruz, continuing eventually to highway 200. **Bahía Chahué** has a beach at its west end and a small harbor at its east end. Farther east, **Bahía Tangolunda** is the site of the major top-end hotel developments to date. The sea is sometimes rough here, and you should beware of currents and heed the colored-flag safety system. Tangolunda has an 18-hole golf course too. Three kilometers farther east is the long sweep of **Playa Punta Arena**, on Bahía Conejos. Around a headland at the east end of Bahía Conejos is the more sheltered **Playa Conejos**, unreachable by road.

About 2 to 3km beyond Bahía Conejos, the road runs down to the coast again at **La Bocana**, at the mouth of the Río Copalita, where you'll find a handful of seafood comedores and a hotel. Another long beach stretches to the east.

The small fishing village of **Barra de la Cruz**, at the mouth of the Río Zimatán, has good surf. Access is by a 1½km dirt road from highway 200 around 20km east of Santa Cruz.

Activities
You can sail, snorkel, dive, kayak, fish, raft, canoe, walk in the jungle, bird-watch, ride horses, rappel, canyon, cycle, visit a coffee plantation and more. Half-day outings generally cost US$17 to US$19.

Snorkeling & Diving You can rent snorkeling gear beside the lancha kiosk at Santa Cruz harbor for US$5.75 a day. At Playa Maguey you can rent a snorkel, mask and fins for US$4.50 a day. These prices may rise in high season. A tour guide will take you snorkeling for US$17 to US$25.

These companies will take you diving and offer instruction from beginner's sessions through to full certification courses:

Buceo Sotavento – Leeward Dive Center, ☎ 587-21-66, Local 18, Interior, Plaza Oaxaca, La Crucecita; four-hour introduction US$72

Hurricane Divers – ☎ 587-11-07, Hotel Fiesta Mexicana, Boulevard Juárez, Chahué; single dive US$39, PADI programs US$95 to US$375

Triton Dive Center – ☎ 587-08-44, harborside, Santa Cruz

Rafting The Copalita and Zimatán Rivers near Huatulco have waters ranging from class 1 to class 4/5 in rafting terms. They're at their biggest in the rainy season, between July and November. Rafting and kayaking trips are operated out of La Crucecita by **Copalita River Tours** (☎ 587-05-35, *Posada Michelle, Gardenia 8; 4-hr beginner or family outing US$33 per person; longer, more challenging trip US$66),* **Aventuras Piraguas** (☎ 587-13-33, **W** *www.piraguas.com, Local 19, Plaza Oaxaca, 4-hr trip US$50, full day US$89)* and **Turismo Conejo** (☎ 587-00-09, *Plaza Conejo, Guamuchil 208; various levels, 3-8 hrs).*

Places to Stay

Budget All these hotels are in La Crucecita.

Hotel Arrecife (☎ 587-17-07, fax 587-14-12, Colorín 510) Singles with fan US$23, doubles & triples with fan US$28-39, with air-con US$45. The Arrecife has a small pool and a good little restaurant and is in a quiet, leafy neighborhood. The best rooms are sizable, with two double beds, air-con, balcony and TV; others are small and open straight onto the street. All have private bath, but in some cases it's outside the room.

Hotel Benimar (☎ 587-04-47, *Bugambilias 1404)* Singles & doubles with fan & bath US$23, triples with fan & bath US$28. This family-run hotel has 12 clean and adequate rooms.

Hotel Busanvi I (☎ 587-00-56, *Carrizal 601)* Singles & doubles with fan/air-con US$17/27, larger triples with air-con US$34. The Busanvi I has plain rooms with bath and TV (not cable).

Mid-Range There are mid-range hotels in La Crucecita, Santa Cruz Huatulco and Tangolunda.

The cheaper places in this category are in La Crucecita.

Hotel Posada Del Parque (☎ 587-02-19, **e** *hdelparque@huatulco.net.mx, Flamboyan 306, Plaza Principal)* Singles & doubles with fan US$39, with air-con US$54, including breakfast. This hotel has fairly comfortable and sizable rooms. The pricier ones have hot water and TV.

Posada Michelle (☎ 587-05-35, *Gardenia 8)* Singles/doubles/triples US$34/56/89. The Michelle is next to the EB bus station and can be noisy. But it's a friendly place, and the dozen or so rooms are brightly decorated and have fan, air-con, bath and cable TV.

Hotel Plaza Conejo (☎ 587-00-09, **e** *turismoconejo@hotmail.com, Guamuchil 208)* Singles/doubles US$39/45. This friendly hotel, in Plaza Conejo, half a block from the Plaza Principal, has five tidy, bright rooms with bath and hot water, fan, telephone and TV. Energetic guides lead tours from here. Plaza Conejo has an Internet café and a good, almost-vegetarian restaurant.

Hotel Suites Begonias (☎ 587-03-91, fax 587-13-90, Bugambilias 503) Suites US$55. The small Suites Begonias has comfortable two-room suites with two double beds, TV, fan and pretty tiled bathrooms, opening on upstairs walkways.

Hotel Flamboyant (☎ 587-01-13, **e** *flamboyant@huatulco.net.mx, Plaza Principal)* Singles & doubles US$58 including breakfast. This pink hotel has a pleasant courtyard, helpful staff, a nice pool, its own restaurant and air-conditioned rooms. Decor is Oaxacan folksy. There's free transportation to Playa La Entrega.

Misión de los Arcos (☎ 587-01-65, **W** *www.misiondelosarcos.com, Gardenia 902)* Singles & doubles with fan/air-con US$34/39, suites US$45. This is a fairly new 13-room hotel embellished by a touch of interior greenery. It has nice, big, bright rooms.

Santa Cruz's mid-range options are more luxurious than those in La Crucecita.

Hotel Marlin (☎ 587-00-55, **e** *hmarlin@huatulco.net.mx, Mitla 28)* Singles & doubles US$78. The Marlin offers nicely decorated, colorful rooms with TV and air-con. It has a good restaurant and small pool too.

Hotel Meigas Binniguenda (☎ 587-00-77, **e** *binniguenda@huatulco.net.mx, Boulevard Santa Cruz 201)* Singles & doubles US$78. This is Huatulco's oldest hotel, dating from all of 1987. It has a garden, pool, restaurant and 195 spacious, air-conditioned rooms with TV.

These mid-range hotels are of a similar standard to those in Santa Cruz Huatulco.

Posada Chahué (☎ 587-09-45, **W** *www.huatulco.com.mx/posadachahue, Mixe 75)* Singles/doubles US$61/78. Family-owned Posada Chahué, affiliated with the Best Western group, is about 1km east of La Crucecita and 500m from Playa Chahué.

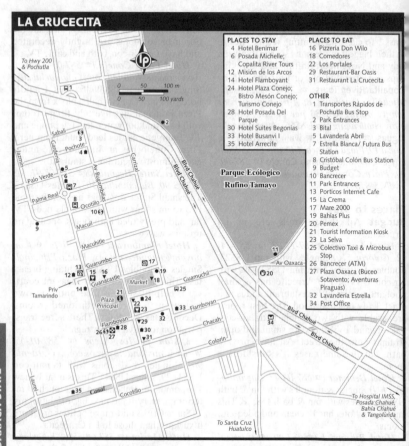

LA CRUCECITA

PLACES TO STAY
4 Hotel Benimar
6 Posada Michelle;
  Copalita River Tours
12 Misión de los Arcos
14 Hotel Flamboyant
24 Hotel Plaza Conejo;
  Bistro Mesón Conejo;
  Turismo Conejo
28 Hotel Posada Del
  Parque
30 Hotel Suites Begonias
33 Hotel Busanvi I
35 Hotel Arrecife

PLACES TO EAT
16 Pizzería Don Wilo
18 Comedores
22 Los Portales
29 Restaurant-Bar Oasis
31 Restaurant La Crucecita

OTHER
1 Transportes Rápidos de
  Pochutla Bus Stop
2 Park Entrances
3 Bital
5 Lavandería Abril
7 Estrella Blanca/ Futura Bus
  Station
8 Cristóbal Colón Bus Station
9 Budget
10 Bancrecer
11 Park Entrances
13 Porticos Internet Cafe
15 La Crema
17 Mare 2000
19 Bahías Plus
20 Pemex
21 Tourist Information Kiosk
23 La Selva
25 Colectivo Taxi & Microbus
  Stop
26 Bancrecer (ATM)
27 Plaza Oaxaca (Buceo
  Sotavento; Aventuras
  Piraguas)
32 Lavandería Estrella
34 Post Office

Parque Ecólogico
Rufino Tamayo

Going down Boulevard Chahué toward Bahía Chahué, take the second turn to the left (east) after the Pemex station. There are 12 attractive rooms, most with two king-size beds, all with air-con, fans and color TV, plus a moderately priced restaurant and small pool.

Hotel Plaza Huatulco (☎ 581-00-35, e plazahuatulco@hotmail.com, Boulevard Juárez 23) Singles/doubles US$50/56, suites US$100-150. The small Plaza Huatulco is across the street from the Barceló Resort in Tangolunda. All units have air-con and cable TV; the suites also have terraces and kitchenettes.

Top End If what you want is a holiday in a top-end Huatulco hotel, a package is your best bet. If you're already in Mexico, ask a travel agent. Around US$700 could buy two people return flights from Mexico City and three nights in a top hotel.

Santa Cruz's top-end choices are at the moderate end of the price spectrum.

Hotel Castillo Huatulco (☎ 587-01-44, w www.hotelcastillohuatulco.com, Boulevard Santa Cruz 303) Doubles US$89-100. The colonial-style Castillo Huatulco has a decent pool, a restaurant and 112 good-sized, air-conditioned rooms, with TV. Transportation to the Castillo's beach club on Bahía Chahué is free.

Hotel Marina Resort (☎ 587-09-63, w http://hotelmarinaresort.com, Tehuantepec 112) Singles/doubles US$97/114 including breakfast. The 50-room Marina Resort, on the east side of the harbor, has three pools, a temazcal and youthful managers.

Chahue's top-end hotel is another with moderate prices.

Hotel Villablanca (☎ 587-06-06, w *www .villablancahotels.com.mx, Boulevard Juárez s/n at Zapoteco)* Singles & doubles US$89, suites from US$123, including breakfast. This hotel, located about 250m back from Playa Chahué, has a large, clean pool and offers pleasant air-conditioned rooms with cable TV. Packages offer a third night for free. Main dishes in its restaurant are inexpensive.

Tangolunda is real top-end territory.

Quinta Real (☎ 581-04-28, w *www .quintareal.com, Paseo Juárez 2)* Suites from US$280. The gorgeous Quinta Real has a hilltop position at the west end of Tangolunda. Its 27 suites have Jacuzzi and ocean view; some have private pools. The grounds extend down to the beach, with a pool area near the beach.

Barceló Resort (☎ 581-00-55, e *barcelo@ huatulco.net.mx, Boulevard Juárez s/n)* Singles & doubles from US$223. East of the Quinta Real, the Barceló has more than 300 rooms, all with ocean view. Its big pool sits in a beachside garden, and you'll find all the amenities you'd expect: restaurants, bars, tennis courts, gymnasium, water sports, shops and nightly mariachi entertainment. Packages for two people including meals for US$165 are sometimes available.

Hotel Gala (☎ 581-00-00, w *www.gala resorts.com.mx, Boulevard Juárez s/n)* Singles/doubles US$180/300 including all meals & drinks, land & water sports & entertainment. Next door to the Barceló, and strangely similar in color and architecture, the Gala has four pools, a disco and 300 air-conditioned rooms. Low-season packages can bring the price down to US$180 for two people.

Camino Real Zaashila (☎ 581-04-60, w *www.caminoreal.com/zaashila, Boulevard Juárez 5)* Singles & doubles US$200-250. A little farther around the bay from the Gala, and more tranquil, this hotel is very attractive with a big pool in lovely gardens. The more expensive rooms have their own small pool too. Promotional rates cut room prices by almost half at times.

Casa del Mar (☎ 581-02-03, w *http:// hotels.baysofhuatulco.com.mx/casadelmar, Balcones de Tangolunda 13)* Suites US$166.

One kilometer beyond the Zaashila is the elegant Casa del Mar, with 25 air-conditioned suites and a beautifully sited pool.

Places to Eat

La Crucecita The very clean *mercado* (market) has several comedores serving up fish or shrimp platters for US$4 to US$5 and *enfrijoladas* or *entomatadas* for US$2.75.

Restaurant-Bar Oasis (☎ 587-00-45, *Flamboyan 211, Plaza Principal)* Prices US$1.20-10. The Oasis has good, moderately priced fare, from tortas to *filete de pescado* (fish fillet) or steaks. It does Oaxacan specialties and takes a stab at Japanese food too.

Los Portales (☎ 587-00-70, *Bugambilias 603, Plaza Principal)* Dishes US$4-8. Los Portales is also good, with offerings such as an *alambre de pechuga de pollo* (chicken breast kebab) with bell peppers and onions, or a *farolado de pollo* (two flour tortillas with chicken, bacon and cheese). There are vegetarian choices too.

Pizzería Don Wilo (☎ 587-06-23, *Plaza Principal)* Mains US$4.50-14. You could try a pizza with prawns, but the Oaxacan dishes, including tamales and tlayudas, are very popular.

Bistro Mesón Conejo (*Plaza Conejo, Guamuchil)* Prices US$2.75-5. Open from 7am daily. This restaurant has a spotless kitchen and offers several vegetarian choices.

Restaurant La Crucecita (*Bugambilias at Chacah)* Prices US$2.50-6. Open 7am-10pm daily. This inexpensive spot is a block from the plaza. Its *sincronizadas a la mexicana* make a good antojito. Tangy licuados with yogurt or milk are a specialty (US$2.25).

Santa Cruz Huatulco Food at the eateries on Playa Santa Cruz is mostly average.

Restaurant Ve El Mar (☎ 587-03-64, *Playa Santa Cruz)* Mains US$6-9.50. This place at the east end is an exception to the rule. The seafood is fine, the salsas picante and the margaritas potent. Try a whole fish, an octopus or shrimp dish or, if you have US$17 to spare, lobster.

Café Huatulco (☎ 587-12-28, *Kiosko de Santa Cruz, Plaza Santa Cruz)* Prices US$2-2.50. This café in the plaza near the harbor serves good local Pluma coffee in many

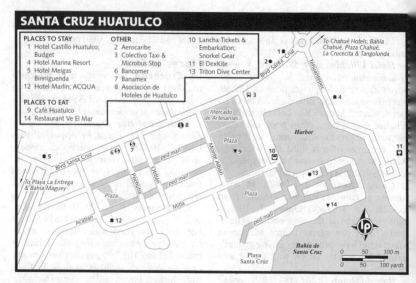

SANTA CRUZ HUATULCO

PLACES TO STAY
1 Hotel Castillo Huatulco; Budget
4 Hotel Marina Resort
5 Hotel Meigas Binniguenda
12 Hotel Marlin; ACQUA

PLACES TO EAT
9 Café Huatulco
14 Restaurant Ve El Mar

OTHER
2 Aerocaribe
3 Colectivo Taxi & Microbus Stop
6 Bancomer
7 Banamex
8 Asociación de Hoteles de Huatulco

10 Lancha Tickets & Embarkation; Snorkel Gear
11 El DexKite
13 Triton Dive Center

different ways – the *capuchino frío* (cold cappuccino with a dollop of ice cream) is well worth a splash.

Tangolunda The big hotels offer a choice of expensive bars, coffee shops and restaurants. The *Casa del Mar* (*see Places to Stay*) has one of the best restaurants, with a great view. You'll spend US$30 to US$50 for a full dinner with wine.

There are also a few medium to expensive restaurants along Tangolunda's two streets. *La Casa de la Nona* (☎ 581-00-35, *Boulevard Juárez s/n*) Prices US$3.50-15. This Italian/Argentine restaurant opposite the Barceló Resort offers well-priced pastas, steaks, pizzas and salads.

Restaurant La Pampa Argentina (☎ 581-01-75, *Boulevard Juárez s/n*) Prices US$11-27. Open 1pm-1am daily. La Pampa is a good place for a steak-out.

Beaches The seafood palapas at La Entrega are ordinary, but we had a fine meal at Maguey – US$9 for a whole *huachinango* (snapper). The comedores at La Bocana will cook you up a tasty grilled fish with fries or salad for less.

Entertainment
La Crema (☎ 587-07-02, *Plaza Principal, La Crucecita*) Admission free. Open 7pm-3am

daily. This upstairs bar, entered from Gardenia, pulls a cool crowd. A shot of tequila starts at US$2. Pizzas are available too.

La Selva (☎ 587-10-63, *Bugambilias 601, La Crucecita*) La Selva is a laid-back, open-air bar overlooking the Plaza Principal.

Santa Cruz has a couple of nightspots, open from around 10pm Thursday to Sunday. Cover charges are typically US$7 per person, but different nights have different deals.

ACQUA (☎ 587-00-55, *Mitla, beside Hotel Marlin*) The building is blue and distinctively Arabic.

El DexKite (☎ 587-09-71, *harborside*) This is *the* hottest place in Huatulco. The fun goes on all night, assisted by drinks measured by the liter.

Noches Oaxaqueñas (☎ 581-00-01, *Boulevard Juárez s/n, Tangolunda*) Admission US$17. Noches Oaxaqueñas, beside the Tangolunda traffic circle, presents a Guelaguetza regional dance show Friday, Saturday and Sunday evening (drinks and/or dinner cost extra).

Getting There & Away
Air Mexicana offers two to four flights daily to/from Mexico City (from US$153). For flights to/from Oaxaca, see the Oaxaca City Getting There & Away section. Cheap charters from Canada and the US are occasionally available.

Mexicana (☎ 587-02-23, airport ☎ 581-90-08) has an office at Local 3, Plaza Chahué, Boulevard Juárez. Aerocaribe (☎ 587-12-20, airport ☎ 581-90-30) has an office next to the Hotel Castillo Huatulco in Santa Cruz. The travel agency Bahías Plus (☎ 587-09-32), at Carrizal 704 in La Crucecita, can help with air tickets.

Bus The main bus stations are on Gardenia in La Crucecita. Some buses coming to Huatulco are marked 'Santa Cruz Huatulco,' but they still terminate in La Crucecita. Make sure your bus is *not* headed to Santa María Huatulco, which is a long way inland.

Cristóbal Colón (1st-class; ☎ 587-02-61) is on Gardenia at Ocotillo, four blocks from the plaza. Most of its buses are *de paso*. EB & Futura (☎ 587-01-03), Gardenia at Palma Real, have *'primera'* services that are quick and fairly comfortable, and *ordinario* buses which are typical ordinario. Daily departures include:

Oaxaca – 405km, 7½ hours, via Salina Cruz; 2 Colón overnight (US$19)

Pochutla – 50km, 1 hour; 7 Colón (US$2.25), 7 EB (US$1.75-2.25); Transportes Rápidos de Pochutla every 15 minutes to about 8.30pm, from the main road opposite Bugambilias (US$1.50)

Puerto Escondido – 115km, 2½ hours; 7 Colón (US$5.25), 7 EB (US$4.25-5.50)

Salina Cruz – 145km, 2½ hours; 5 Colón (US$8.75), 3 EB (US$6.50)

Colón also runs a few buses to Tehuantepec, Juchitán, Tuxtla Gutiérrez, San Cristóbal de Las Casas (US$24) and Tapachula. EB goes to Acapulco (US$24). Colón and EB go to Mexico City.

Car Auto-rental agencies include:

Budget (☎ 587-00-10) Ocotillo at Jazmín, La Crucecita; (☎ 587-01-35) Hotel Castillo Huatulco, Santa Cruz Huatulco; (☎ 581-90-00) Airport

Dollar (☎ 581-00-55 ext 787) Barceló Resort, Tangolunda; (☎ 581-00-00 ext 18) Hotel Gala, Tangolunda; (☎ 581-90-16) Airport

Budget and Dollar rent VW beetles for around US$60 a day with unlimited kilometers, taxes and insurance, as well as other cars starting at around US$85.

Getting Around

To/From the Airport Transportación Terrestre (☎ 581-90-14, 581-90-24) provides colectivo combis for US$7.50 per person from the airport to La Crucecita, Santa Cruz or Bahía Chahué and for US$8.75 to Tangolunda. Get tickets at the company's airport kiosk. For a whole cab at a reasonable price, walk just outside the airport gate, where you can pick one up for about US$10 to La Crucecita, Santa Cruz or Tangolunda, or US$13.50 to Pochutla. Even cheaper, walk 400m down to highway 200 and catch a microbus for US$0.60 to La Crucecita or US$1.25 to Pochutla. Those heading to La Crucecita may be marked 'Santa Cruz' or 'Bahías Huatulco' or something similar.

Bus & Colectivo Colectivo taxis and a few microbuses provide transportation between La Crucecita, Santa Cruz Huatulco and Tangolunda. In La Crucecita catch them on Guamuchil at Carrizal, one block from the Plaza Principal. In Santa Cruz they stop by the harbor, and in Tangolunda at the traffic circle outside the Hotel Gala. Fares are the same in either type of vehicle: from La Crucecita to Santa Cruz US$0.40, to Tangolunda US$0.60.

Bicycle Arasto Rojas (☎ 587-16-95) rents mountain bikes and takes groups cycling along the bays. You can also arrange bicycles through Eco Discover Tours, Plaza Las Conchas, Tangolunda, opposite the Barceló Resort.

Taxi Taxis are plentiful. From La Crucecita you pay around US$1.50 to Santa Cruz, US$2.25 to Tangolunda and US$6.25 to Bahía Maguey.

Isthmus of Tehuantepec

Eastern Oaxaca is the southern half of the 200km-wide Isthmus of Tehuantepec ('teh-wahn-teh-PECK'), Mexico's narrowest point. This is sweaty, flat country, but Zapotec culture is strong here. If you spend a night or two here, you'll probably be agreeably surprised by the people's liveliness and friendliness. Government proposals for a new fast road and/or rail transit corridor across the isthmus, as a 21st-century rival to the Panama Canal, along with associated petrochemical and industrial development projects, provoke mixed reactions from *istmeños* wary that the beneficiaries will be outsiders.

Fifteen kilometers northeast of Juchitán, around La Ventosa (where highway 185 to Acayucan diverges from highway 190 to Chiapas), strong winds sweep down from the north and sometimes blow high vehicles off the road.

History & People

In 1496 the isthmus Zapotecs repulsed the Aztecs from the fortress of Guiengola, near Tehuantepec, and the isthmus never became part of the Aztec empire. Later there was strong resistance to the Spanish here.

Isthmus women are noticeably open and confident and take a leading role in business and government. Many older women still wear embroidered huipiles and voluminous printed skirts. For the numerous *velas* (fiestas), Tehuantepec and Juchitán women turn out in velvet or sateen huipiles, gold and silver jewelry (a sign of wealth), skirts embroidered with fantastically colorful silk flowers and a variety of odd headgear. Many isthmus fiestas feature the *tirada de frutas,* in which women climb on roofs and throw fruit on the men below!

TEHUANTEPEC

• pop 39,000 ☎ 971

Tehuantepec is a friendly town, often with a fiesta going on in one of its *barrios.*

Orientation & Information

The Oaxaca-Tuxtla Gutiérrez highway (190) meets highway 185 from Salina Cruz about 1km west of Tehuantepec. Highway 190 then skirts the north edge of town. All Tehuantepec's bus stations, collectively known as El Terminal, cluster just off highway 190, 1.5km northeast of the town center. Local buses to/from Salina Cruz also stop, more conveniently, where highway 190 passes the end of 5 de Mayo, a minute's walk from the central plaza. To reach the plaza from El Terminal on foot, follow Avenida Héroes until it ends at a T-junction, then turn right along Guerrero for four blocks to another T-junction, then go one block left along Hidalgo.

Some tourist information may be available at the Ex-Convento Rey Cosijopí (when it's open). A couple of banks around the central plaza have ATMs. The dark, almost medieval market is on the west side of the plaza. There's an Internet café next door to the Hotel Oasis on Cruz.

Ex-Convento Rey Cosijopí

This former Dominican monastery *(Callejón Rey Cosijopí),* on a short street off Guerrero, is Tehuantepec's Casa de la Cultura, holding classes and occasional exhibitions. Built in the 16th century, the monastery is named for the local Zapotec leader of the day (who paid for it) and features stout two-story construction around a central courtyard. It served as a prison before being restored in the 1970s. It was closed for further work in 2001.

Guiengola

The hillside Zapotec stronghold of Guiengola, where king Cosijoeza rebuffed the Aztecs, is north of highway 190 from a turnoff about 11km out of Tehuantepec. A sign points to 'Ruinas Guiengola 7' just past the Km 240 marker. You can see the remains of two pyramids, a ball court, a 64-room complex known as El Palacio and a thick defensive wall. There are fine views over the isthmus.

To get there take a bus bound for Jalapa del Marqués from El Terminal. Get off at Puente Las Tejas, from which it's a walk of about 2½ hours. Start early, 6am or before, to take advantage of the morning cool. You may be able to find a guide by asking in the Ex-Convento Rey Cosijopí (if it's open).

Places to Stay

Hotel Donají (☎ 715-00-64, Juárez 10) Singles/doubles with fan US$11/16, with air-con US$16/21. The recently revamped Donají is two blocks south of the east side of the central plaza, and has clean rooms with private bath on two upper floors with open-air walkways.

Hotel Oasis (☎ 715-00-08, Ocampo 8) Singles/doubles with fan US$11/14.50, with air-con US$18/22. The Oasis, a block south of the west side of the plaza, is basic but has warm showers. Parking is available in the courtyard, and it has a restaurant and an art gallery containing paintings by the owner.

Places to Eat

Cafe Colonial (☎ 715-01-15, Romero 66) Dishes US$3.50-6.25. This café 1½ blocks south of the plaza serves generous chicken and meat dishes and antojitos.

Restaurante Scarú (Leona Vicario 4) Dishes US$4.50-9. Open 7am-11pm daily. Up a side street a block east of the Hotel Donají, the Scarú occupies an 18th-century house with a courtyard and colorful modern murals of Tehuantepec life. The menu offers varied fish, seafood, meat and chicken dishes. On weekends old-timers play a marimba.

Getting There & Away

The 245km trip from Oaxaca takes 4½ hours in a 1st-class bus. The road winds downhill for the middle 160km.

Cristóbal Colón and ADO (1st-class) and Sur and AU (2nd-class) share one building. Most 1st-class buses are de paso, often in the wee hours. Colón runs 10 daily buses to Oaxaca (US$11.50 to US$13.50) and a few each to Tuxtla Gutiérrez, San Cristóbal de Las Casas, Bahías de Huatulco, Pochutla, Puerto Escondido, Mexico City and Tapachula. ADO runs three buses to Villahermosa and a night bus to Palenque. AU has a few buses to Veracruz. Sur runs frequent buses to Arriaga.

TOI (2nd-class), just east of Colón, has hourly buses to Oaxaca (US$9) around the clock, plus four to Tuxtla Gutiérrez (US$10.25).

Across the street from Colón are local buses to Juchitán (25km, 45 minutes, US$1.25) and Salina Cruz (15km, 30 minutes, US$0.80). They go at least every half hour during daylight hours.

Getting Around

A curious form of local transportation is the *motocarro* – a kind of three-wheel buggy in which the driver sits on a front seat while passengers stand behind on a platform. They congregate by the railway track behind the market.

SALINA CRUZ
• pop 75,000 ☎ 971

Once an important railway terminus and port, then undermined by the cutting of the Panama Canal, Salina Cruz has revived as an oil pipeline terminal with a refinery. It's a windy city with a rough-and-ready feel.

Orientation & Information

Highway 200 from Puerto Escondido and Pochutla meets the Salina Cruz-Tehuantepec road, highway 185, on the northern edge of Salina Cruz. Avenida Tampico runs 2km south from this junction to the center, with the combined bus station of Cristóbal Colón, ADO, Sur and AU just off Avenida Tampico on Laborista, seven blocks north of the center. EB is on Avenida Tampico at Frontera, four blocks north of the center.

Reaching the center, Avenida Tampico passes one block west of the wide, windy plaza. Banks with ATMs and an Internet café are on the plaza.

Places to Stay & Eat

Hotel Posada del Jardín (☎ 714-01-62, Camacho 108) Singles/doubles/triples with fan US$13.50/17.50/20.50, with air-con US$19/23/28.50. Posada del Jardín, 1½ blocks north of the main plaza, has clean little rooms with shower, around a leafy courtyard.

Hotel Costa Real (☎ 714-02-93, fax 714-51-11, Progreso 22) Singles/doubles/triples US$22/25/43. The modern Costa Real, two blocks north of the plaza, is a reasonable choice. Carpeted, air-conditioned rooms have color TV. It also has a decent restaurant (closed on Sunday) and parking too.

Viña del Mar (Camacho 110) Prices US$2-7. This bright, fan-cooled little café, a few doors north of the Posada del Jardín, does an excellent lime juice and has lots of fish and seafood dishes.

Getting There & Away

Frequent buses to Tehuantepec (30 minutes, US$0.80) and Juchitán (1½ hours, US$2) leave from the corner of Avenida Tampico and Progreso, one block west and two north from the plaza.

Cristóbal Colón and ADO run 1st-class buses; the other lines are 2nd-class. Five or more Colón and four EB buses run daily to Bahías de Huatulco (2½ hours, US$6.75), Pochutla (US$9, 3½ hours) and Puerto Escondido (5 hours, US$11). Colón also runs five buses to Oaxaca (5 hours, US$12.50), three to Tuxtla Gutiérrez and two to San Cristóbal de Las Casas (8 hours, US$18). There's 1st-class service to Tapachula, Veracruz, Villahermosa and Mexico City.

OAXACA STATE

Getting Around

Local buses run along Avenida Tampico between the bus stations and town center. Going out to the bus stations, they're marked 'Refinería' or 'Refi.'

JUCHITÁN

- pop 65,000 ☎ 971

Istmeño culture is strong in this friendly town, which is visited by few gringos.

Orientation & Information

Prolongación 16 de Septiembre leads into Juchitán from a busy intersection with traffic signals on highway 190, on the north edge of town. The main bus terminal is about 100m toward town from the intersection. The street curves left, then right, then divides into 5 de Septiembre (the right fork) and 16 de Septiembre (left). These emerge as opposite sides of the central plaza, Jardín Juárez, after seven blocks.

There are two banks with ATMs on the Jardín. Compubyte on 16 de Septiembre, three blocks north of the Jardín, has Internet access.

Things to See & Do

Jardín Juárez is a lively central square. A busy market on its east side spills into the surrounding streets. Comedores here may have iguana on the menu.

Juchitán's Lidxi Guendabiaani (Casa de la Cultura, José F Gómez; admission free; open 10am-3pm & 5pm-8pm Mon-Fri, 10am-2pm Sat), a block south of Jardín Juárez, has an interesting archaeological collection and an art collection with works by leading 20th-century Mexican artists, including Rufino Tamayo and juchiteco Francisco Toledo. It's housed around a big patio beside the Iglesia de San Vicente Ferrer.

Places to Stay & Eat

Casa de Huéspedes Echazarreta (Juárez 23) Singles & doubles with bath & fan US$9. This hotel on the south side of Jardín Juárez has small, clean rooms.

Both these hotels have medium-priced restaurants.

Hotel Santo Domingo del Sur (☎ 711-10-50, e stodgo@istmored.com.mx, Carretera Juchitán-Tehuantepec) Singles/doubles with air-con US$28/37. Located by the highway 190 crossroads, the popular Santo Domingo has decent rooms, a swimming pool and plenty of parking space.

Hotel López Lena Palace (☎ 711-13-88, fax 711-13-89, 16 de Septiembre 70) Singles/doubles with air-con US$28/37. The López Lena Palace, about halfway between the bus station and town center, has reasonable rooms with multichannel TV and bath. They're not as fancy as the hotel's exterior suggests.

Casagrande Restaurant (☎ 711-34-60, Juárez 12) Prices US$3.50-16. Open 7am-10pm daily. This is the best eatery in town, in a pleasant covered courtyard with ceiling fans on the south side of Jardín Juárez. It offers all sorts of goodies, from regional dishes or pasta to seafood.

Café Santa Fé (☎ 711-15-46, Cruce de Carretera Transístmica) Prices US$3-8. Open 24 hours. For cool air and good food, try this restaurant handily wedged between the main bus station and the highway. It does an excellent breakfast buffet.

Getting There & Away

Cristóbal Colón and ADO (1st-class) and Sur and AU (2nd-class) use the main bus terminal on Prolongación 16 de Septiembre. Frequent 2nd-class Autotransportes Istmeños buses to Tehuantepec (45 minutes, US$1.25) and Salina Cruz (1½ hours, US$2) stop at the next corner south on Prolongación 16 de Septiembre during daylight hours. FYPSA (2nd-class) has its own terminal, separated from the main one by a Pemex station.

Many buses are de paso and leave in the middle of the night. To Oaxaca (285km, 5 hours, US$12.50-14.50) there are nine Colón and four ADO buses daily, as well as FYPSA departures about hourly around the clock. Colón runs five daily buses to Bahías de Huatulco (US$8.75) and at least three each to Pochutla, Puerto Escondido, San Cristóbal de Las Casas and Tapachula. Colón and FYPSA go several times daily to Tuxtla Gutiérrez. Sur has frequent service to Acayucan. ADO runs four buses to Villahermosa and one at 2am to Palenque. Colón and AU go to Mexico City, Veracruz and Puebla.

Getting Around

'Terminal-Centro' buses run between the bus station and Jardín Juárez. A taxi costs US$1.50.

Tabasco & Chiapas

Just east of the Isthmus of Tehuantepec, Mexico's narrow 'waist,' lie the states of Tabasco and Chiapas. Their differences define them: Chiapas is wealthy in natural resources but most of its people are poor, whereas Tabasco is oil-rich. Tabasco, with a long coastline on the Gulf of Mexico, is mostly well-watered lowland, hot and humid, but in its south start to rise the hills that become the cool, pine-clad Altos (Highlands) of Chiapas. Chiapas' indigenous history is Mayan, Tabasco's is chiefly Olmec.

There are river routes into neighboring Guatemala from both states.

Tabasco

Tabasco is kept fertile by huge rivers that meander across it en route to the Gulf of Mexico. It was here, between about 1200 and 600 BC, that the Olmecs developed Mesoamerica's first great civilization. In recent decades Tabasco's mineral riches, particularly petroleum, have brought great prosperity.

History

La Venta, the second great Olmec center (after San Lorenzo, Veracruz) was in western Tabasco. Olmec religion, art, astronomy and architecture deeply influenced all Mexico's later pre-Hispanic civilizations.

Cortés, who disembarked on the Tabasco coast in 1519, initially defeated the Maya and founded a settlement called Santa María de la Victoria. The Maya regrouped and offered stern resistance until they were defeated by Francisco de Montejo, around 1540. Later, pirate attacks forced the original settlement to be moved inland from the coast and it was renamed Villahermosa de San Juan Bautista.

After Mexico won independence from Spain, various local land barons tried to assert their power over the area, causing considerable strife. The economy languished until after the Mexican Revolution, when exports of cacao, bananas and coconuts started to increase.

Highlights

- Jungle-enshrouded Palenque, most romantic of Mayan cities
- The colonial highland town of San Cristóbal de Las Casas and nearby Mayan villages
- The Mayan ruins of Bonampak and Yaxchilán, deep in the Lacandón Jungle
- Villahermosa's Parque-Museo La Venta, a fascinating zoo and outdoor Olmec archaeological museum
- Remote, serene Laguna Miramar, the largest lake in the Lacandón Jungle

Gulf of Mexico

Villahermosa page 819
Central Villahermosa page 823
Parque-Museo La Venta page 821
Palenque pages 862-863
Palenque Ruins page 865
Cañón del Sumidero page 838
Yaxchilán page 876
Tuxtla Gutiérrez page 832
San Cristóbal de Las Casas pages 840-841
Bonampak page 872
Comitán page 879
Around San Cristóbal de Las Casas page 852
Lagos de Montebello page 881
PACIFIC OCEAN
Guatemala
Tapachula page 886
OTHER MAPS
Tabasco & Chiapas page 818

In the 20th century, US and British petroleum companies discovered oil, and Tabasco's economy began to revolve around this resource. During the 1970s, Villahermosa became an oil boomtown. This prosperity yielded a sophistication that cuts right through the tropical heat, stamping Tabasco as different from neighboring Chiapas and Campeche.

Geography & Climate

Tabasco's topography changes from flatland near the coast to undulating hills as you

TABASCO & CHIAPAS

TABASCO & CHIAPAS

near Chiapas. Due to heavy rainfall (about 1500mm annually, mostly between May and October), there is much swampland, lush tropical foliage and sticky humidity. Outside Villahermosa, Tabasco can be quite bug-infested (particularly near the rivers), so bring repellent. The state is rather sparsely populated, with 1.9 million people inhabiting 24,475 sq km.

VILLAHERMOSA
● pop 331,000 ☎ 993

Hot, crowded and untidy, downtown Villahermosa is anything but the 'beautiful city' that its name implies, despite its situation on the banks of the Río Grijalva. Courtesy of the Tabasco oil boom, however, outer areas of the city enjoy some tree-shaded boulevards, spacious parks, fancy hotels and excellent cultural institutions.

To see everything here, you'll have to stay at least one night. The chief attractions are the Parque-Museo La Venta, an excellent open-air combination of Olmec archaeological museum and the Tabasco zoo; the Museo Regional de Antropología; and Yumká, a kind of safari park outside the city.

Orientation

In this sprawling city you'll find yourself walking some distances in the sticky heat, and occasionally hopping on a minibus (*combi*) or taking a taxi.

The older commercial center of the city, known as the Zona Luz, extends from the Plaza de Armas in the south to Parque

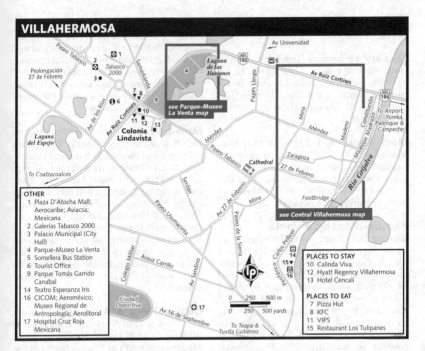

VILLAHERMOSA

OTHER
1 Plaza D'Atocha Mall;
  Aerocaribe; Aviacsa;
  Mexicana
2 Galerías Tabasco 2000
3 Palacio Municipal (City
  Hall)
4 Parque-Museo La Venta
5 Somellera Bus Station
6 Tourist Office
9 Parque Tomás Garrido
  Canabal
14 Teatro Esperanza Iris
16 CICOM; Aeroméxico;
   Museo Regional de
   Antropología; Aerolitoral
17 Hospital Cruz Roja
   Mexicana

PLACES TO STAY
10 Calinda Viva
12 Hyatt Regency Villahermosa
13 Hotel Cencali

PLACES TO EAT
7 Pizza Hut
8 KFC
11 VIPS
15 Restaurant Los Tulipanes

Juárez in the north, and is roughly bounded by Calles Zaragoza, Madero and Juárez. It's a lively area, busy with shoppers.

The main visitor attraction in Villahermosa, the Parque-Museo La Venta, lies 2km northwest of the Zona Luz, beside Avenida Ruiz Cortines, the main east-west highway crossing the city. About 1km west of Parque-Museo La Venta is the Tabasco 2000 district, where you'll find modern commercial and government buildings.

Information

Tourist Offices The main tourist office (☎ 316-36-33) is inconveniently situated at the corner of Avenida de los Ríos and Calle 13 in the Tabasco 2000 district, in the northwest of the city. It's open 9am to 3pm and 7pm to 9pm Monday to Friday, 9am to 1pm Saturday. Staff are helpful and have a lot of printed information on Tabasco state. To get there from the Zona Luz, take a 'Fracc Carrizal' combi from Madero just north of Parque Juárez, get off at the big traffic circle surrounded by banks after you cross Avenida Ruiz Cortines, and walk one block to the left along Avenida de los Ríos.

There is a small tourist office at the entrance to Parque-Museo La Venta.

Money There are many banks in the Zona Luz, most with ATMs (see the Central Villahermosa map). Bital on Juárez has particularly long hours (8am to 7pm Monday to Saturday).

Post & Communications The main post office, at Sáenz 131 on the corner of Lerdo de Tejada, is open 8am to 3pm Monday to Friday, 8am to noon Saturday and holidays.

C@fé Internet Zona Luz, in the Howard Johnson Hotel, Aldama 404, charges US$1.75 a half hour for Internet access. It's open 8am to 10pm Monday to Friday, 8am to 8pm Saturday, and noon to 8pm Sunday. La Net, Saenz 130, is cheaper at US$1.25 an hour and open 7am to midnight daily.

Travel Agencies Viajes Villahermosa (☎ 312-54-56), at Méndez 724, sells international and domestic tickets; staff speak English and can arrange excursions. Hours are 9am to 8pm Monday to Friday, 9am to 4pm Saturday. Closer to the center,

Turismo Nieves (☎ 314-18-88), Sarlat 202, can do the same.

Laundry Lavandería Top Klen next to Hotel Madero charges US$1.75 per kg for next-day service. Super Lavandería La Burbuja, north of the Zona Luz at Hermanos Bastar Zozaya 621, is cheaper but less convenient.

Medical Services The Hospital Cruz Roja Mexicana (☎ 315-55-55) is at Avenida Sandino 716, a short ride southwest of the Zona Luz. Unidad Médica Guerrero Urgencias (☎ 314-56-97/98), at 5 de Mayo 444 in the center, is open 24 hours.

Parque-Museo La Venta

History The Olmec city of La Venta, built on an island near where the Río Tonalá runs into the Gulf some 130km west of Villahermosa, flourished in the centuries before 600 BC. Danish archaeologist Frans Blom did the initial excavations in 1925, and work was continued by archaeologists from Tulane University and the University of California. Matthew Stirling is credited with having discovered, in the early 1940s, five colossal Olmec heads sculpted from basalt. The largest weighs over 24 tons and stands more than 2m tall. It is a mystery how the Olmecs managed to move these massive basalt heads and other weighty religious statues some 100km to La Venta without the use of the wheel.

When petroleum excavation threatened the La Venta site, the most significant finds, including three of the Olmec heads, were moved to Villahermosa to found the Parque-Museo La Venta, which is now a fascinating combined outdoor museum and tropical zoo.

Admission Plan at least two hours, preferably three, for your visit to the Parque-Museo La Venta (☎ 314-16-52, Avenida Ruiz Cortines; admission US$1.75; open 8am-4pm daily). Independent guides charge US$17 to take one to four people around the Parque. Snack stands and a little cafetería provide sustenance. Be warned: you really do need to slap on the mosquito repellent.

Zoo Once inside, this is the section you come to first. It's devoted to animals from Tabasco and nearby regions: colorful macaws and toucans, pumas, jaguars, lynxes, ocelots, white-tailed deer, spider monkeys, crocodiles, boa constrictors, peccaries and plenty more. Stop at the informative display with text in English and Spanish on Olmec history and archaeology as you go through. The zoo is closed Monday.

Museum A giant ceiba (the sacred tree of the Olmecs and Mayas) marks the starting point of a trail through lush tropical verdure past the 34 Olmec stone sculpture exhibits ranging from the famous heads and other human figures to deities, dolphins and even a stone mosaic mask laid out on the ground. The trail is 1km long and takes at least an hour to walk if you spend a few minutes at each exhibit. Along the way, many trees bear signs giving their names and species. There are also more animal enclosures. Some animals that pose no danger, such as coatis, roam freely.

Getting There & Away Parque-Museo La Venta is 3km from the Zona Luz. A 'Fracc Carrizal' combi (US$0.50) from Madero just north of Parque Juárez in the Zona Luz will drop you at the corner of Paseo Tabasco and Avenida Ruiz Cortines. Then walk 1km northeast across Parque Tomás Garrido Canabal and along the Malecón de las Ilusiones, a pleasant lakeside path, to the entrance. A taxi from the Zona Luz costs US$1.75.

CICOM & Museo Regional de Antropología

The Centro de Investigación de las Culturas Olmeca y Maya (CICOM) is a complex of buildings on the bank of the Río Grijalva, 1km south of the Zona Luz. Its centerpiece is the Museo Regional de Antropología Carlos Pellicer Cámara (☎ 312-63-44, Periférico Carlos Pellicer, admission US$1.25; open 9am-7pm Tues-Sun) named for the scholar and poet responsible for the preservation of the Olmec artifacts in the Parque-Museo La Venta. Besides the museum, the complex holds a theater, research center, arts center and other buildings. Just inside the front door of the museum is a massive Olmec head, one of those wonders from La Venta.

The best way to tour the museum is to take the elevator to the top floor and work

PARQUE-MUSEO LA VENTA

Museo de Historia Natural

To Central Villahermosa

0   50   100 m
0   50   100 yards

Aviary

Zoológico

Small Felines

Turtles, Crocodiles

Big Felines

Parque Museo-La Venta

Av Ruiz Cortines

Malecón de las Ilusiones

Laguna de las Ilusiones

Plaza de Artesanías

Crafts Shop

Jaguar Compound

Parque Tomás Garrido Canabal

Malecón de las Ilusiones

Footbridge

To Paseo Tabasco

25   Altar Cuadrangular (Quadrangular Altar)
26   Personaje con Estandarte (Figure with Standard)
27   Cabeza Hendida (Cloven Head)
28   La Silueta (Silhouette)
29   Lápida con Incisiones (Stone with Incisions)
30   Altar del Diálogo (Dialogue Altar)
31   Altar Erosionado (Eroded Altar)
32   Altar de los Tecolotes (Altar of the Owls)
33   Altar Felino (Feline Altar)
34   El Gobernante (Governor)
35   Cabeza Tatuada (Tattooed Head)
36   Fragmentos (Fragments)
37   Estela del Rey (Royal Stele)
38   Mosaico-Mascarón (Mosaic Mask)
39   Cabeza del Guerrero (Warrior's Head)
40   Altar del Jaguar (Jaguar Altar)
41   Basalt Column (Columna de Basalto)
42   El Contorsionista (Contortionist)
43   Jaguar Niño (Jaguar Child)
44   El Delfín (Dolphin)
45   Mono Mirando el Cielo (Monkey Looking at the Sky)
46   Pond with Crocodiles
47   Mirador de las Águilas

○ Toilets
◪ Shelters

15   Tumba (Tomb)
16   Mosaico-Mascarón (Mask Mosaic)
17   El Hombre Barbado (Bearded Man)
18   La Abuela (Grandmother)
19   El Trono (Throne)
20   El Caminante (Walker)
21   Diosa Joven (Young Goddess)
22   Cabeza Inconclusa (Unfinished Head)
23   Altar de los Niños (Altar of the Children)
24   Altar de los Niños (Altar of the Children)

ZOOLÓGICO
1   Peccaries
2   Crocodiles; Turtles
3   Snakes
4   Toucans; Parrots
5   Nocturnal Animals
6   Entrance; Tourist Office
7   Deer
8   Spider Monkeys
9   Los Olmecas de La Venta Display
10   Spider Monkeys
11   Cafeteria
20   Giant Ceiba Tree

MUSEUM/NATURE TRAIL
12   El Viejo Guerrero (Old Warrior)
13   El Joven Guerrero (Young Warrior)
14   Estacada de Columnas Naturales (Palisade of Natural Basalt Columns)

your way down. Although the museum's explanations are all in Spanish, they are accompanied by photos, maps and diagrams.

On the top floor, exhibits outline Mesoamerica's many civilizations, from the oldest Stone Age inhabitants to the relatively recent Aztecs. After you've brushed up on the broad picture, descend to the middle floor, which concentrates on the Olmec and Mayan cultures. Especially intriguing are the displays concerning Comalcalco, the ruined Mayan city not far from Villahermosa.

Finally, the ground floor holds a room of particularly big Olmec and Mayan sculptures, plus temporary exhibits.

CICOM is 1km south of the Zona Luz. You can walk there in about 15 minutes, or catch any 'CICOM' combi or microbus heading south on Madero or the malecón south of Madero.

Museo de Historia

The History Museum (*Juárez 402; admission US$0.60; open 10am-8pm Tues-Sat, 10am-5pm Sun*), in a blue-tiled building, deals with Tabasco history.

Torre del Caballero

This lookout tower rising from the footbridge over the Río Grijalva near the city center affords medium-distance panoramas of the area, as well as potentially embarrassing encounters with young couples who come here for semisecluded smooching.

Tabasco 2000

The Tabasco 2000 complex, with its modern government buildings, chic boutiques in the Galerías Tabasco 2000 mall, convention center and pretty fountains, is a testimony to the prosperity oil brought to Villahermosa. From the Zona Luz, take a 'Fracc Carrizal' combi from Madero just north of Parque Juárez.

Places to Stay

Budget The Zona Luz has plenty of cheap hotels, but few are very inviting. Keep street noise in mind when choosing one, and consider splurging on a pleasant, air-conditioned room.

Hotel del Centro (☎ *312-59-61, Pino Suárez 209*) Singles/doubles with fan US$12.50/16, with air-con US$23/36. The Hotel del Centro is better kept than most cheapies. The 20 bright, clean rooms come with TV and bathroom.

Hotel San Miguel (☎ *312-15-00, Lerdo de Tejada 315*) Singles/doubles/triples US$11/14/17.50, singles/doubles with air-con & TV US$23/27. This hotel is small and cheap, with plain rooms.

Hotel Oriente (☎ *312-01-21, Madero 425*) Singles/doubles US$13.50/20, with TV & air-con US$23/29. Just around the corner from the Hotel San Miguel, the Oriente is better, though the front rooms are noisier.

Hotel San Francisco (☎ *312-31-98, Madero 604*) Singles/doubles US$18/22. This hotel is better than most budget places. An elevator does away with the sweaty hike upstairs, where you'll find 28 rooms with air-con and TV. Some have balconies, but this street can be *very* noisy.

Hotel Palma de Mallorca (☎ *312-01-44, Madero 516*) Singles/doubles with fan US$11.50/15 with double bed, US$15/17 with twin beds, singles/doubles with air-con US$17/20.50. This is another acceptable option if price is crucial.

Mid-Range Most middle-range hotels are in the Zona Luz.

Hotel Miraflores (☎ *312-00-22,* e *miraflores@miraflores.com.mx, Reforma 304*) Singles/doubles US$56/61. The very popular 74-room Miraflores, on a pedestrian street just off Madero, offers large, clean air-conditioned rooms with good bathrooms and numerous TV channels. The hotel has a

restaurant, a coffee shop serving meals and a rather dire music bar.

Hotel Madan (☎/*fax 314-33-73,* e *madan@intrasur.net.mx, Madero 408*) Doubles with bath US$41-44. The lollypop-pink Madan has 40 comfortable air-conditioned rooms with bath and TV and an intimate little restaurant serving up economical breakfasts.

Hotel Pakaal (☎ *314-46-48, Lerdo de Tejada 106*) Singles/doubles/triples US$39/45/56. The Pakaal's fair-size air-conditioned rooms have cable TV. It has a distinctive, partly plant-covered façade.

Hotel Provincia Express (☎ *314-53-76,* e *villaop@prodigy.net.mx, Lerdo de Tejada 303*) Singles/doubles US$42/45. This hotel has 50 bright, newly refurbished but not enormous air-conditioned rooms with bath and cable TV.

Hotel Plaza Independencia (☎ *312-12-99,* w *www.hotelesplaza.com.mx, Independencia 123*) Singles/doubles/triples US$56/64/78. This hotel with comfortable rooms is tucked a little away from the thick of things, yet close to the center. Its other draw card is a swimming pool.

Top End As an oil town, Villahermosa has no shortage of luxury hotels.

Howard Johnson Hotel (☎/*fax 314-46-45,* ☎ *800-201-09-09,* w *www.hojo.com.mx, Aldama 404*) Singles/doubles US$64/74, twins US$84. The 100-room Howard Johnson has small but comfortable rooms in the Zona Luz's pedestrian zone. Its restaurant makes a good breakfast choice.

Casa Inn (☎ *358-01-02, 800-201-09-09,* w *www.casainn.zl.com.mx, Madero 418*) Singles & doubles US$84 including breakfast (US$62 Fri & Sat). This downtown hotel, the former Don Carlos, has had a substantial makeover. Its 100 comfy but moderate-size rooms have modem connections. There's a restaurant, bar and parking.

Many top-end hotels are close to the main east-west highway, which crosses northern Villahermosa as Avenida Ruiz Cortines.

Hotel Best Western Maya Tabasco (☎ *314-44-66, 800-237-77-00,* w *www.best western.com/thisco/bw/70071/70071, Avenida Ruiz Cortines 907*) Singles & doubles US$120, suites US$175. The Maya Tabasco is 1km north of the Zona Luz. It has good,

CENTRAL VILLAHERMOSA

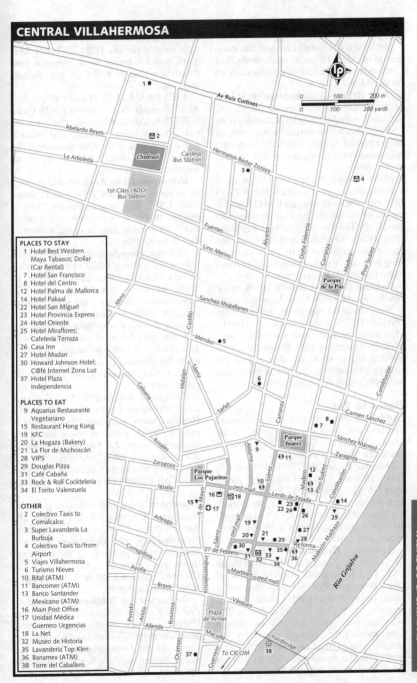

PLACES TO STAY
1 Hotel Best Western
   Maya Tabasco; Dollar
   (Car Rental)
7 Hotel San Francisco
8 Hotel del Centro
12 Hotel Palma de Mallorca
14 Hotel Pakaal
22 Hotel San Miguel
23 Hotel Provincia Express
24 Hotel Oriente
25 Hotel Miraflores;
   Cafetería Terraza
26 Casa Inn
27 Hotel Madan
30 Howard Johnson Hotel;
   C@fé Internet Zona Luz
37 Hotel Plaza
   Independencia

PLACES TO EAT
9 Aquarius Restaurante
   Vegetariano
15 Restaurant Hong Kong
19 KFC
20 La Hogaza (Bakery)
21 La Flor de Michoacán
28 VIPS
29 Douglas Pizza
31 Café Cabaña
33 Rock & Roll Cocktelería
34 El Torito Valenzuela

OTHER
2 Colectivo Taxis to
   Comalcalco
3 Super Lavandería La
   Burbuja
4 Colectivo Taxis to/from
   Airport
5 Viajes Villahermosa
6 Turismo Nieves
10 Bital (ATM)
11 Bancomer (ATM)
13 Banco Santander
   Mexicano (ATM)
16 Main Post Office
17 Unidad Médica
   Guerrero Urgencias
18 La Net
32 Museo de Historia
35 Lavandería Top Klen
36 Banamex (ATM)
38 Torre del Caballero

Av Ruíz Cortines

Abelardo Reyes

La Arboleda

Chedraui

Cardesa
Bus Station

1st-Class (ADO)
Bus Station

Hermanos Bastar Zozaya

Fuentes

Lino Merino

Sanchez-Magallanes

Méndez

Mina

Castillo

Sáenz

Hidalgo

Galeana

Rosales

Zaragoza

Iguala

Aldama

5 de Mayo

Arteaga

Corregidora

Ayutla

Peredo

Arista

Rovirosa

Bravo

Vásquez

Macuilz

Guerrero

Ocampo

Allende

Martínez

27 de Febrero

Reforma

Zaragoza

Sánchez Mármol

Carmen Sánchez

Constitución

Malecón Madrazo

Río Grijalva

Doña Fidencia

Carranza

Madero

Pino Suárez

Alvarez

Sarlat

Parque
de la Paz

Parque
Juárez

Parque
Los Pajaritos

Parque
de Armas

Plaza
de Armas

Lerdo de Tejada

Independencia

Footbridge

To CICOM

TABASCO & CHIAPAS

modern rooms and attractive gardens with a large pool.

The next three hotels are near the intersection of Paseo Tabasco and Avenida Ruiz Cortines, a pleasant few minutes' walk from Parque-Museo La Venta.

Hyatt Regency Villahermosa (☎ 315-12-34, 🌐 www.hyatt.com, Avenida Juárez 106, Colonia Lindavista) Singles & doubles from US$181. This is the poshest hotel, with all the expected luxury services, including swimming pool, tennis courts and modem connections.

Hotel Cencali (☎/fax 315-19-99, 🌐 www .cencali.com.mx, cnr Avenida Juárez & Paseo Tabasco) Singles & doubles US$117 including buffet breakfast. The Cencali neighbors the Hyatt. The hotel's setting, away from noisy streets, is excellent, and the rooms are air-conditioned and modern. There's a swimming pool in tropical gardens running down to the Laguna de las Ilusiones.

Calinda Viva (☎ 315-00-00, 🌐 www .hotelescalinda.com.mx, cnr Avenidas Juárez & Ruiz Cortines) Singles & doubles from US$119. This is a three-story, motel-style, white stucco building built around a beautiful, large swimming pool. Rooms are comfortable, and promotions often reduce the rates by 10% or 15%. The hotel boasts a spa with gym, sauna and massage services.

Places to Eat

Zona Luz Madero and the pedestrian streets of the Zona Luz (Lerdo de Tejada, Juárez, Reforma, Aldama) have lots of snack and fast-food shops.

Douglas Pizza (☎ 312-76-76, Lerdo de Tejada 105) Small pizzas US$5, large pizzas from US$12. Open 4pm-11.30pm Mon-Sat, 2pm-9.30pm Sun. Opposite Hotel Pakal, this place offers pizzas with a wide assortment of toppings. There's a pleasant ambiance, and pasta and salads too.

Aquarius Restaurante Vegetariano (☎ 312-05-79, Zaragoza 513) Breakfasts US$2.75-3.50, comida corrida US$4.75. Open 8am-6pm Mon-Sat. Aquarius has a small, open-air courtyard with a touch of greenery and is close to Parque Juárez. The offerings are largely vegetarian, though some menu items contain meat. Try the granola, yogurt, fruit and honey, the soyburgers, or the mushroom cocktail. There's a well-stocked lunch buffet too.

Cafetería Terraza (☎ 312-00-22, Hotel Miraflores, Reforma 304) Mains US$7.50-9.50, comida corrida US$5.75. This café is good, with fair prices. Try antojitos or one-fourth of a chicken with fries and salad, or meats and fish.

VIPS (☎ 314-39-71, Madero 402; ☎ 315-44-55, Avenida Ruiz Cortines 1503) Mains US$5.75-9. This countrywide chain restaurant offers reliable Mexican and international food in very clean surroundings. The Ruiz Cortines branch is near the Hyatt Regency Villahermosa.

Restaurant Hong Kong (☎ 312-59-96, 5 de Mayo 433) Set meal US$10, main dishes from US$7. This is an upstairs Chinese restaurant with a six-page menu. Set meals run from wonton soup through a chicken dish to fortune cookies.

El Torito Valenzuela (☎ 314-11-89, 27 de Febrero 202) Tacos US$0.70 each, comida corrida US$4.50. Open 8am-midnight. El Torito Valenzuela is a popular taquería. It serves varied tacos and the daily comida corrida has four courses.

Rock & Roll Cocktelería (☎ 312-05-93, Reforma 307) Seafood cocktails US$4-9. This place is always busy in the late afternoon. Try a cocktel (fish or seafood, tomato sauce, lettuce, onions and a lemon squeeze) with crackers.

Eating or drinking on the run? There are a few options on Juarez near Reforma. **La Hogaza** bakery has croissants, doughnuts, Danish pastries, yogurt or boxed juices. Just across the street, **La Flor de Michoacán** offers thirst-quenching fresh juices, licuados, frozen yogurt and fruit cocktails. The sidewalk **Café Cabaña** brews excellent coffee.

Elsewhere The luxury hotels near the intersection of Avenida Ruiz Cortines and Paseo Tabasco all have good restaurants; the **Hyatt Regency Villahermosa** has a particularly high reputation. In Tabasco 2000, there are plenty of restaurants in the **Galerías Tabasco 2000** mall, including an economical food court.

Restaurant Los Tulipanes (☎ 312-92-17, Periférico Carlos Pellicer 511) Fish dishes US$6.50, steaks US$8.50. Open 8am-10pm Mon-Sat, noon-6pm Sunday. Los Tulipanes overlooks the river near the Museo Regional de Antropología. Seafood and steaks are the specialties here. On Sunday, the buffet with Tabascan specialties is definitely worth its US$13.50 price tag.

Entertainment

Teatro Esperanza Iris (☎ 314-42-10, Periférico Carlos Pellicer) This theater, just north of CICOM, often stages folkloric dance, theater, cinema and music performances.

Live music, usually with dancing, is featured at the bars of several hotel including the *Calinda Viva*, *Hyatt Regency*, *Cencali*, *Best Western Maya Tabasco* and *Miraflores*.

Getting There & Away

Air Nonstop or one- or two-stop direct flights to/from Villahermosa include the following:

Cancún – Aerocaribe daily
Guadalajara – Aeroméxico daily
Havana, Cuba – Aerocaribe daily
Houston, Texas – Aeroméxico twice weekly
Mérida – Aerocaribe twice daily, Aviacsa daily
Mexico City – 8-9 flights daily between Aeroméxico, Mexicana, Aviacsa and Aerocaribe
Monterrey – Aeroméxico and Mexicana daily
Oaxaca – Aerocaribe daily
San Antonio, Texas – Mexicana 5 days weekly
Tuxtla Gutiérrez – Aerocaribe daily
Veracruz – Aerolitoral daily

Mexicana (☎ 316-31-32) is at Locales 5 and 6, Plaza D'Atocha Mall, Tabasco 2000. Aerocaribe (☎ 316-50-46) and Aviacsa (☎ 316-57-00) are in the same mall at Locales 9 and 10, respectively. Aeroméxico and Aerolitoral (both ☎ 800-021-40-00) are in the CICOM complex at Periférico Carlos Pellicer 511-2. The airport is at ☎ 356-01-57.

Bus The 1st-class (ADO) bus station, Mina 297 (☎ 312-76-92) is three blocks south of Avenida Ruiz Cortines and about 12 blocks north of the city center. It has a luggage room (US$0.40 per hour) and a selection of little eating places. Deluxe and 1st-class buses of UNO, ADO and Cristóbal Colón run from here, as well as a few AU 2nd-class buses.

Though Villahermosa is an important transportation point, many buses serving it are *de paso*, so buy your onward ticket as early as possible. Daily departures (most in the evening) include these:

Campeche – 380km, 6 hours; 15 buses (US$21-26)
Cancún – 875km, 12 hours; 10 buses (US$43-67)
Chetumal – 580km, 8 hours; 6 buses (US$26)
Mérida – 560km, 9 hours; 12 buses (US$30-35)
Mexico City (TAPO) – 780km, 11 hours; 22 buses (US$47-75)
Oaxaca – 700km, 12 hours; 3 buses (US$35)
Palenque – 140km, 2½ hours; 12 buses (US$7)
Playa del Carmen – 850km, 12 hours; 6 buses (US$40)
San Cristóbal de Las Casas – 305km, 7 hours; 2 buses (US$14.50); or go via Tuxtla Gutiérrez
Tuxtla Gutiérrez – 285km, 6 hours; 6 buses (US$14)
Veracruz – 590km, 8 hours; 16 buses (US$18-23)

Only a few destinations within Tabasco, including Comalcalco and Tenosique, are served by this bus station. More buses to these and other Tabasco destinations are run by smaller companies from other terminals in Villahermosa.

Car Most rental companies have desks at the airport. Offices in the city include Advantage (☎ 315-58-48), Paseo Tabasco 1203; Budget (☎ 314-37-90), Malecón Madrazo 761; and Dollar (☎ 315-48-30), Paseo Tabasco 600, next to the cathedral. Dollar has another office (☎ 314-44-66) at the Hotel Best Western Maya Tabasco, Avenida Ruiz Cortines 907.

Getting Around

Villahermosa's Aeropuerto Rovirosa is 13km east of the center on highway 186. A taxi from city to airport costs US$11-13 (from airport to city US$16) and takes about 20 minutes. Alternatively, go to the road outside the airport parking lot and pick up a colectivo taxi into the city for US$0.90 per person. These terminate on Carranza half a block south of Ruiz Cortines, about 1km north of the Zona Luz. Take a 'Dos Montes' vehicle from there to return to the airport.

To get from the ADO bus station to the Zona Luz, take a 'Centro' combi (US$0.50) or a taxi (US$1.50), or walk 15 to 20 minutes. To walk, go out of the bus station's side (south) door, turn left onto Lino Merino and walk five blocks to Parque de la Paz, then turn right on Carranza.

From the Zona Luz to the ADO bus station, take a 'Chedraui' bus or combi north on Malecón Madrazo. Chedraui is a big store just north of the bus station.

Any taxi ride within the area between Avenida Ruiz Cortines, the Río Grijalva and Paseo Usumacinta costs US$1.50. Combi rides within the same area are US$0.50.

YUMKÁ

Yumká (☎ 993-356-01-07, Camino de Yumka s/n, Dos Montes; admission US$3.50, lake US$1.25 extra; open 9am-5pm daily), 18km east of Villahermosa (4km past the airport), is the city's version of a safari park. It's divided into jungle, savanna and lake areas – representing Tabasco's three main ecosystems. Visits take the form of guided tours of the three areas (30 minutes each). In the jungle, on foot, you come across Tabascan species such as howler monkeys, jaguars, macaws, deer and peccaries (the big cats are enclosed). The savanna is viewed from a tractor-pulled trolley. There is an African section with elephants, giraffes and hippos and an Asian section with axis deer, antelope, nilgai and gaur, the largest ox in the world. You tour the lake by boat and should see plenty of birds. Yumká is named for the legendary jungle-protecting spirit of the local indigenous Chontal people.

It's hardly a Kenya game drive, but if you fancy a dose of space, greenery and animals, go. Drinks and snacks are available. A taxi from the Zona Luz costs US$17.

COMALCALCO

The Chontal Mayan city of Comalcalco (3km northeast of Comalcalco town; admission US$3.50, free Sun & holidays; open 10am-5pm daily) flourished during the late Classic period, between AD 500 and 900, when the region's agricultural productivity allowed population expansion. Comalcalcans traded the cacao bean with other Mayan settlements, and it is still the chief local cash crop.

Resembling Palenque in architecture and sculpture, Comalcalco is unique because it is built of bricks made from clay, sand and, ingeniously, oyster shells. Mortar was made with lime from the oyster shells.

As you enter the ruins, the substantial structure to your left may surprise you, as the pyramid's bricks look remarkably like the bricks used in construction today. Look on the right-hand side for remains of the stucco sculptures that once covered the pyramid. In the northern section of the acrópolis are remains of fine stucco carvings.

Although the west side of the acrópolis once held a crypt comparable to that of Palenque's Pakal, the tomb was vandalized centuries ago and the sarcophagus stolen. Continue up the hill to the Palacio, and from this elevation enjoy the breeze while you gaze down on unexcavated mounds.

Getting There & Away

The 55km journey from Villahermosa to Comalcalco town takes about 1¼ hours. Colectivo taxis leave Abelardo Reyes, one street north of the north side of the ADO bus station in Villahermosa, charging US$3 per person. Frequent 2nd-class buses go from the Cardesa bus station on Hermanos Bastar Zozaya and from the Somellera bus station, northwest of the center on Avenida Ruiz Cortines.

The ruins are about 3km from Comalcalco town. You can cover the distance by taxi or by a Paraíso-bound combi. Combis may go right to the ruins or they may drop you at the entrance, from which it's about a 1km walk. Excursions to Comalcalco offered by Villahermosa travel agents cost from US$73 to US$95. The US$95 tour run by Turismo Nieves (see Travel Agencies in the Villahermosa section) also visits La Hacienda de la Luz, a nearby cacao plantation, and concludes with lunch and a lagoon trip at Paraíso, on the coast.

TO/FROM GUATEMALA VIA TENOSIQUE

The river route from Tabasco into Guatemala is along the Río San Pedro from La Palma in southeast Tabasco. Compared to the more commonly taken route via Frontera Corozal in Chiapas, the San Pedro gives you a longer river ride, but the connecting transportation is less convenient.

First you have to get to the town of Tenosique, served by 10 buses a day (US$9.75, 3½ hours) from Villahermosa's ADO bus station. From Palenque, there's an ADO bus to Tenosique at 6am (US$5.50, 2 hours) and 10 daily Transportes Palenque combis (US$5), the first at 5.15am. A taxi is about US$55. The last combi back from Tenosique to Palenque leaves at 5.30pm.

From Tenosique, colectivo taxis (US$2.25) and combis (US$2) to La Palma

(45 minutes) leave from 5am to 5pm from Abarrotes La Fortuna, Calle 28 No 602. A whole taxi costs US$10.

A daily boat leaves La Palma at 8am for the four-hour trip (100km, US$23) through jungle and cut-down jungle to the village of El Naranjo, Guatemala. El Naranjo has a few basic lodging places including *Posada San Pedro*, by the river, which has good singles/doubles with fan and cold water for US$6.75/9 and a restaurant.

About five buses daily go from El Naranjo to Flores, Guatemala (about US$4, 4-5 hours). The buses on this route are 2nd-class, with the better ones being *directo* (no stops).

Coming from Guatemala, the scheduled boat leaves El Naranjo about 1pm. If you miss the last bus out of La Palma, there should be trucks.

There are economical hotels in Tenosique and Emiliano Zapata.

Viajes Na Chan Kan and *Viajes Yax-Há* (see Organized Tours in the Palenque section) are among the Palenque travel agencies offering packages along this route. The full trip from Palenque to Flores is roughly 13 hours, with arrival in Flores between 7 and 8pm. Viajes Yax-Há charges US$85 per person (minimum four people) including the bus trip from El Naranjo to Flores. Viajes Na Chan Kan charges US$39 to take you in their own van to La Palma, from where you make your own way by boat to El Naranjo and bus to Flores.

Chiapas

Mexico's southernmost state has enormous variety, fascinating to anyone with a curiosity about natural wonders, ancient civilizations or modern indigenous peoples. At the center of Chiapas is San Cristóbal de Las Casas, a cool, tranquil hill-country colonial town surrounded by mysterious indigenous Maya villages. Two hours' drive west, and nearly 1600m lower, the surprisingly modern state capital, Tuxtla Gutiérrez, has probably the best zoo in Mexico, devoted entirely to the varied fauna of Chiapas. Only a few kilometers from Tuxtla is the 800m-deep Cañón del Sumidero (Sumidero Canyon), through which you can take an awesome boat ride.

North of San Cristóbal are the Agua Azul waterfalls, which are among Mexico's most spectacular, and the Mayan ruins of Toniná and Palenque – the latter perhaps the most beautiful of all ancient Mayan sites. In the east of Chiapas is the Selva Lacandona (Lacandón Jungle), one of the largest areas of tropical rain forest in Mexico. Within the jungle you can visit further Mayan sites such as Yaxchilán and Bonampak, look for toucans, monkeys and macaws, or hang out at Laguna Miramar, a pristine lake. You can cross the jungle-flanked Río Usumacinta into Guatemala, en route to Flores and Tikal.

Chiapas also has a steamy Pacific coastal region, largely ignored by the tourism promoters but with plenty of attractions for those in the know, such as the beaches of laid-back Puerto Arista, the lagoons, wildlife (and more beaches) of La Encrucijada Biosphere Reserve, and the 4110m volcano Tacaná on the Guatemalan border, near Tapachula.

Dangers & Annoyances

Since the 1994 Zapatista uprising, the security situation in Chiapas has been volatile. Keep your ear to the ground about where it is and is not advisable to go, especially if you are thinking of leaving the main highways. The situation in 2001, the first year of the Fox presidency in Mexico, was more relaxed than a couple of years previously, with the Mexican military adopting a much lower profile. The army was still there in big numbers, though, even if less visible. If traveling off the main tourist routes, be prepared for military checkpoints and make sure your tourist card and passport are in order. If the purpose of your visit is anything other than plain tourism (human rights observation, for instance), you can ask in advance at a Mexican consulate or embassy about visa requirements.

In some little-visited areas outside San Cristóbal de Las Casas, unknown outsiders could be at risk because of local politico-religious conflicts. Take local advice about where not to go. The far east of Chiapas is an area where many illegal drugs are smuggled into Mexico, and the area has a dangerous reputation for that reason.

When traveling by bus, take care of your belongings and don't accept food or drink from other passengers. At the time of writing we had not heard of any highway holdups for a couple of years, but those who are driving themselves should always take soundings: the Ocosingo-Agua Azul-Palenque road, in particular, still has a dodgy reputation.

History

Chiapas state has always been intimately connected with Guatemala. Major pre-Hispanic civilizations straddled what's now

the Chiapas-Guatemala border, and for most of the Spanish colonial era Chiapas was governed from Guatemala.

Pre-Hispanic Chiapas may have been the site of Mexico's first permanent human settlements. The little-known Mokaya culture, which didn't even receive a name from archaeologists until the 1990s, established year-round villages along the coast some time around 1500 BC. Later, Chiapas came

The Zapatistas

Subcomandante Marcos

On January 1, 1994, an armed left-wing peasant group calling itself the Ejército Zapatista de Liberación Nacional (EZLN; Zapatista National Liberation Army) sacked and occupied government offices in the Chiapas towns of San Cristóbal de Las Casas, Ocosingo, Las Margaritas and Altamirano. The Mexican army evicted the Zapatistas within a few days, with about 150 people (the majority of them Zapatistas) killed in the fighting. The rebels retreated to forest hideouts on the fringes of the Lacandón Jungle, having drawn the world's attention to Chiapas. Their goal was to overturn a corrupt, wealthy minority's centuries-old hold on land, resources and power in the state, where many indigenous peasants were impoverished, marginalized and lacking in education, health care and fundamental civil rights. The Mexican Revolution of 1910-20 had had little impact here.

Though the Zapatistas were militarily far outnumbered and outgunned, they attracted broad support and sympathy, and their leader, a masked figure who is known as Subcomandante Marcos, became a cult figure for many in Mexico and beyond.

During 1994, while Marcos waged a propaganda war from his jungle hideout, demanding justice and reform in Mexican politics, peasants took over hundreds of farms and ranches in Chiapas, especially in Las Cañadas (the area between Ocosingo, Comitán and the Montes Azules Biosphere Reserve). Ultimately the government bought some of these properties from their previous owners and handed them over to the peasants. Las Cañadas, settled since the 1960s by thousands of dispossessed and land-hungry campesinos from highland Chiapas, has always been the main hotbed of Zapatista support.

Eventually an agreement on indigenous rights was reached between EZLN and government negotiators at San Andrés Larráinzar, a center of Zapatista support in the Chiapas highlands, in 1996. The deal gave a degree of autonomy to Mexico's indigenous peoples, but it soon became clear that the government did not intend to turn the San Andrés accords into law.

The rebels, encircled by government troops in a remote pocket of jungle territory near the Guatemalan border, continued to wage a propaganda war, using the Internet and staging a series of high-profile conventions, including an 'intercontinental encounter against neoliberalism' at their headquarters, the village of La Realidad, 85km southeast of Ocosingo.

In 1997 and 1998, tension and killings escalated in Chiapas. The Zapatistas set up some 'autonomous municipalities,' ousting officials of the ruling PRI party. The Zapatistas' enemies

under Olmec influence, and Izapa, near Tapachula, which peaked between 200 BC and AD 200, is thought to be a link between the Olmecs and the Maya.

During the Classic era (approximately AD 250-900), coastal and central Chiapas were relative backwaters, but low-lying, jungle-covered eastern Chiapas gave rise to splendid Mayan city-states such as Palenque, Yaxchilán, Bonampak and Toniná, which flourished in the 7th and 8th centuries.

After the Classic Mayan collapse, highland Chiapas and Guatemala came to be divided among a number of often-warring kingdoms, many with cultures descended from the Maya but some also claiming central Mexican Toltec ancestry. Coastal Chiapas, a rich source of cacao, was conquered by the Aztecs at the end of the 15th century and became their most distant province, under the name Xoconochco (from which its present name, Soconusco, is derived).

The Zapatistas

formed paramilitary organizations to drive Zapatista supporters from their villages and oppose the autonomous municipalities. Some of these paramilitaries were led by prominent local members of the PRI. Violence reached its worst point with the Acteal massacre in December 1997 (see 'Indigenous Peoples of Chiapas,' later in this chapter) and continued in 1998.

In 1999 the EZLN organized a nationwide 'consultation' about indigenous rights. The 2.85 million respondents, it said, overwhelmingly favored enactment of the San Andrés accords and special constitutional rights for indigenous people.

The Mexican army had approximately 60,000 troops in Chiapas by 1999, along with lots of imposing new bases and roadblocks. That year troops, police and paramilitaries launched a campaign of intimidation against dozens of pro-Zapatista villages in Las Cañadas and the Lacandón Jungle. Thousands fled their villages, and the number of Chiapas indigenous people displaced from their homes grew to an estimated 21,000.

Hopes of a fresh start in tackling Chiapas' problems rose in 2000 when Vicente Fox was elected as Mexico's new president and Pablo Salazar as the Chiapas state governor. Both were the first non-PRI incumbents of these positions in a long time, with Salazar representing a multiparty anti-PRI coalition at state level.

Early in 2001, the Zapatistas staged a much-publicized two-week journey from Chiapas to Mexico City, the 'Zapatour.' President Fox presented Mexico's Congress with a bill for constitutional changes granting special rights to Mexico's indigenous peoples, closely based on the San Andrés accords. Congress, however, watered down the provisions, and the Zapatistas rejected the resulting law as a basis for peace talks. The Mexican army adopted a lower profile in Chiapas and tension ebbed, but few troops were actually pulled out. Some refugees started to return home, but by early 2002 there were still an estimated 10,000 or more people in camps, and the right-wing paramilitary organizations were far from vanquished. They and their allies even won local political power in municipal elections in places like Chenalhó, north of San Cristóbal, and Tila, in the north of the state.

A fresh attempt to resolve the conflict was made in February 2002 when, in response to heavy criticisms of the watered-down indigenous rights law of 2001, the original national legislation based directly on the 1996 San Andrés accords was reintroduced into Congress. The legislation was known as the Cocopa law, after a congressional committee involved in the mid-1990s negotiations with the Zapatistas.

Underlying – literally – the whole complex conflict may be oil, large quantities of which are rumored to be sitting beneath several areas of eastern Chiapas.

To get the Zapatista point of view firsthand, visit the EZLN's Web site (w www.ezln.org). Further background on this complicated situation is available from organizations such as Global Exchange (w www.globalexchange.org), SIPAZ (w www.nonviolence.org/sipaz) and the Centro de Derechos Humanos Fray Bartolomé de Las Casas (w www.laneta.apc.org/cdhbcasas).

Spanish Era Central Chiapas was brought under Spanish control by the 1528 expedition of Diego de Mazariegos, who defeated the dominant, warlike Chiapa people, many of whom jumped to their death in the Cañón del Sumidero rather than be captured. Outlying areas were subdued in the 1530s and 1540s, though Spain never gained full control over the scattered inhabitants of the Lacandón Jungle. New diseases arrived with the Spaniards, and an epidemic in 1544 killed about half the indigenous people of Chiapas.

Administration from Guatemala for most of the Spanish era meant that Chiapas lacked supervision for long periods, and there was little check on the excesses of the colonists against the indigenous people.

The only real light in the darkness was the work of some Spanish church figures. Preeminent was Bartolomé de Las Casas (1474-1566), appointed the first bishop of Chiapas in 1545. Las Casas had come to the Caribbean as a colonist, but he entered the Dominican order in 1510 and spent the rest of his life fighting for indigenous rights in the new colonies. His achievements, including the passing of laws reducing compulsory labor (1542) and banning indigenous (though not black) slavery (1550), earned him the hostility of the colonists but the affection of the native people. (See 'A Different Sort of Liberator,' in the History section of the Facts about Mexico chapter).

19th & 20th Centuries In 1822 newly independent Mexico annexed Spain's former Central American provinces (including Chiapas), but when Mexican emperor Agustín de Iturbide was overthrown in 1823, the United Provinces of Central America declared their independence. A small military force under General Vicente Filísola, which Iturbide had sent to the Guatemala/Chiapas region, managed to persuade Chiapas to join the Mexican union, and this was approved by a referendum in Chiapas in 1824.

From then on, a succession of governors appointed in Chiapas by Mexico City, along with local landowners, maintained an almost feudal control over the state. Periodic uprisings and protests bore witness to bad government, but the world took little notice until January 1, 1994, when a group calling itself the Ejército Zapatista de Lib-

eración Nacional (EZLN, Zapatista National Liberation Army) briefly occupied San Cristóbal de Las Casas and nearby towns by military force. The Zapatistas, fighting for a fairer deal for indigenous peoples, won widespread support around and beyond Mexico, but no real concessions. From remote jungle bases they continued to maintain a chiefly political and propaganda campaign for democratic change and better treatment for indigenous peoples. After the advent of the non-PRI Fox government in 2000, hopes for a final settlement of the conflict were dashed when conservatives in Mexico's national Congress watered down new legislation on indigenous rights (see 'The Zapatistas,' earlier in this chapter, and History in the Facts about Mexico chapter).

Geography & Climate

Chiapas' 74,000 sq km fall into five distinct bands, all roughly parallel to the Pacific coast. The heaviest rain in all of them falls from May to October.

The hot, fertile coastal plain, 15km to 35km wide, is called El Soconusco. Rising inland of the Soconusco is the Sierra Madre de Chiapas mountain range, mostly between 1000m and 2500m in height, though Tacaná volcano on the Guatemalan border reaches 4110m. The Sierra Madre continues into Guatemala, pimpled by several more volcanoes.

Inland from the Sierra Madre is the wide, warm, fairly dry Río Grijalva Valley, also called the Central Depression of Chiapas, 500m to 1000m high.

Next come the Chiapas highlands, Los Altos, mostly 2000m to 3000m high and also extending southeast into Guatemala. San Cristóbal de Las Casas, in the Valle de Jovel in the middle of these uplands, has a very temperate climate.

To the north and east of the highlands, the land slopes down to almost sea level on the southern fringes of Mexico's Gulf coast plain (in northern Chiapas) and in the Usumacinta valley (eastern Chiapas). These areas contain some of Mexico's few remaining areas of tropical rain forest. The eastern rain forests, known as the Selva Lacandona (Lacandón Jungle), have shrunk from around 15,000 sq km in 1940 to perhaps 5000 sq km now, as a result of timber-cutting.

colonization by landless peasants from elsewhere and clearing by cattle ranchers (see 'The Lacandón Jungle & the Lacandones,' later in this chapter).

Economy

Chiapas has little industry but is agriculturally rich. The fertile Soconusco and adjacent slopes are major banana- and coffee-growing regions. Tapachula is the commercial hub of the Soconusco.

Chiapas also contributes natural gas and oil to the Mexican economy, and the Río Grijalva, flowing across the center of the state, generates more electricity at several big dams than any other river in Mexico. But in this resource-rich state, one-third of the homes do not have running water, and rates of illiteracy and child mortality are among the highest in Mexico. Most *chiapanecos* are very poor, and wealth is concentrated in a small oligarchy.

TUXTLA GUTIÉRREZ

• pop 425,000 • elev 532m ☎ 961

Chiapas' lively state capital has several things worth stopping for, among them one of Mexico's best zoos (devoted to the fauna of Chiapas) and easy access to exhilarating boat trips through the 800m-deep Cañón del Sumidero, though both of these trips could also be made in a long day from San Cristóbal de Las Casas.

Tuxtla Gutiérrez lies toward the west end of Chiapas' hot, humid central valley. Its name comes from the Náhuatl word *tuchtlan* (meaning 'where rabbits abound'), and from Joaquín Miguel Gutiérrez, a leading light in Chiapas' early-19th-century campaign to not be part of Guatemala. Tuxla Gutiérrez was not an important city until it became the state capital in 1892.

Orientation

The city center is Plaza Cívica, with the cathedral on its south side. The main east-west street, here called Avenida Central, runs past the north side of the cathedral. As it enters the city from the west, this same street is Boulevard Dr Belisario Domínguez; to the east it becomes Boulevard Ángel Albino Corzo.

East-west streets are called Avenidas and are named Norte or Sur depending whether they're north or south of Avenida Central. North-south streets are Calles and are called Poniente (Pte) or Oriente (Ote) depending whether they're west or east of Calle Central. Each street name also has a suffix indicating whether it is east (Oriente, Ote), west (Poniente, Pte), north (Norte) or south (Sur) of the intersection of Avenida Central and Calle Central. So the address 2ª Avenida Norte Pte 425 refers to No 425 on the western (Pte) half of 2ª Avenida Norte.

The best source for maps is INEGI, southwest of the center on 6ª Avenida Sur Pte between Calles 5ª and 6ª Poniente Sur, which sells 1:25,000 and 1:50,000 maps of many parts of Chiapas and other Mexican states. It's open 8.30am to 4.30pm Monday to Friday.

Information

Immigration The Instituto Nacional de Migración (☎ 614-32-88, 613-32-91) is well out of the center, on Libramiento Norte Ote. If you need to go there, a taxi is the best option (15 minutes, US$1.75). It's open 9am to 5pm Monday to Friday.

Tourist Offices The Oficina Municipal de Turismo (City Tourism Office, ☎ 612-55-11 ext 214) is at Calle Central Norte and 2ª Norte Ote, in the underpass at the northern end of Plaza Cívica. It's open 9am to 9pm Monday to Saturday, 9am to 2pm Sunday. A free left luggage service is offered, and in the afternoons there's a team of cheerful, youthful volunteers to supplement the regulars.

Chiapas' state tourism ministry, Sedetur, has a tourist information office (☎ 800-280-35-00) at Boulevard Domínguez 950, 1.6km west of Plaza Cívica, in the Secretaría de Desarrollo Económico building, which has a big Mayan-head statue outside. It's open 8am to 4pm Monday to Friday. Also out front is a tourist kiosk with friendly staff who can answer most questions. It's open 9am to 9pm Monday to Friday, 9am to 8pm Saturday, 9am to 3pm Sunday.

Money Bancomer, at the corner of Avenida Central Pte and 2ª Avenida Norte Pte, and Bital, on the west side of Plaza C\'ivica, do foreign exchange 9am to 3pm Monday to Friday. These and many other city-center banks have ATMs. Elektra, a shop on Calle Central Norte facing Plaza Cívica, does Western Union money transfers.

TUXTLA GUTIÉRREZ

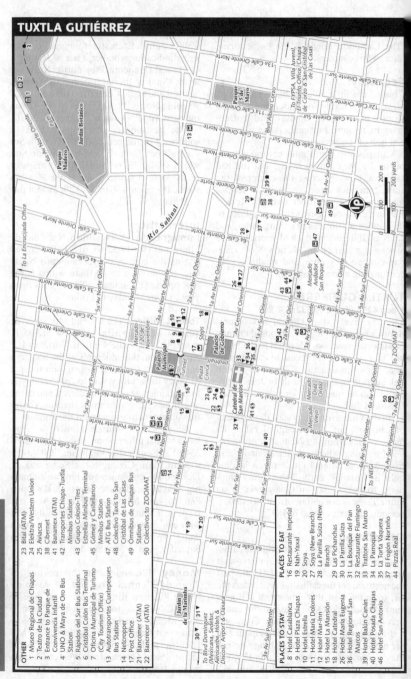

OTHER
1 Museo Regional de Chiapas
2 Teatro de la Ciudad
3 Entrance to Parque de Convivencia Infantil
4 UNO & Maya de Oro Bus Station
5 Rápidos del Sur Bus Station
6 Cristóbal Colón Bus Terminal
7 Oficina Municipal de Turismo (City Tourism Office)
13 Autotransportes Cuxtepeques Bus Station
14 Netcropper
17 Post Office
21 Bancomer (ATM)
22 Bancrecer (ATM)
23 Bital (ATM)
24 Elektra/Western Union
25 Aviacsa
38 Cibernet
41 Banamex (ATM)
42 Transportes Chiapa-Tuxtla Minibus Station
43 Grupo Colosio-Tres
45 Estrellas Minibus Terminal
    Gómez y Castellanos Minibus Station
47 ATG Bus Station
48 Colectivo Taxis to San Cristóbal de Las Casas
49 Omnibus de Chiapas Bus Station
50 Colectivos to ZOOMAT

PLACES TO STAY
8 Hotel Casablanca
9 Hotel Plaza Chiapas
10 Hotel Estrella
11 Hotel María Dolores
12 Hotel Mar-Inn
15 Hotel La Mansión
18 Hotel Catedral
26 Hotel María Eugenia
36 Hotel Regional San Marcos
39 Hotel Balún Canán
40 Hotel Posada Chiapas
46 Hotel San Antonio

PLACES TO EAT
16 Restaurante Imperial
19 Nah-Yaxal
20 Soya
27 Soya (New Branch)
28 La Parrilla Suiza (New Branch)
29 Las Pichanchas
30 La Parrilla Suiza
31 La Boutique del Pan
32 Restaurante Flamingo
33 Trattoria San Marco
34 La Parroquía
35 La Torta Vaquera
37 El Fogón Norteño
44 Pizzas Real

Post & Communications The post office, on a pedestrian-only block of 1ᵃ Avenida Norte Ote just off Plaza Cívica, is open 9am to 5pm Monday to Friday, 9am to 1pm Saturday. There are plenty of pay phones around the plaza.

Netcropper, 2ᵃ Avenida Norte Pte 427, is open 9am to 9pm daily and charges US$1.25 an hour for Internet access. Cibernet, Avenida Central Ote 768, charges the same and is open 10am to midnight Monday to Saturday and 4pm to midnight Sunday.

Plaza Cívica & Cathedral

Tuxtla's broad, lively main plaza occupies two blocks, with the modern Catedral de San Marcos facing it across Avenida Central at the south end. On the hour the cathedral's clock tower tinkles out a tune to accompany a revolving parade of apostles' images on one of its upper levels.

Zoológico Miguel Álvarez del Toro

Chiapas, with its huge range of natural environments, claims the highest concentration of animal species in North America – among them several varieties of big cat, 1200 types of butterfly and over 600 kinds of birds. About 180 of these species, many of them in danger of extinction, are on view in relatively spacious enclosures at Tuxtla's zoo (☎ 612-37-54, El Zapotal; admission free; open 8.30am-5pm Tues-Sun).

The Zoológico Miguel Álvarez del Toro (ZOOMAT), on a forested hillside just south of the city, was closed for improvement works at the time of research. It was due to reopen in late 2002, but ask in the city before you make the trip.

Among the creatures here are ocelots, jaguars, pumas, tapirs, red macaws, toucans, a rattlesnake, a boa constrictor, spider monkeys, a monkey-eating harpy eagle (águila arpia) and a pair of quetzal birds. The zoo has a clear conservation message and is named after Miguel Álvarez del Toro, the eminent Chiapas conservationist who founded it.

To get there take a 'Cerro Hueco, Zoológico' colectivo (US$0.40) from the corner of 1ᵃ Calle Ote Sur and 7ᵃ Avenida Sur Ote. They leave about every 20 minutes and take 20 minutes. A taxi is US$3.

Parque Madero

This museum-theater-park area is 1.25km northeast of the city center. If you don't want to walk, take a colectivo along Avenida Central to Parque 5 de Mayo at the corner of 11ᵃ Calle Ote, then another colectivo north along 11ᵃ Calle Ote.

The modern Museo Regional de Chiapas (☎ 612-04-59, Calzada de los Hombres Ilustres s/n; admission US$3.50, free Sun & holidays; open 9am-4pm Tues-Sun) has archaeological and colonial history exhibits and costume and craft collections, all from Chiapas, plus temporary exhibitions. Next door is the 1200-seat Teatro de la Ciudad. Nearby is a shady Jardín Botánico (Botanical Garden; Calzada de los Hombres Ilustres s/n; admission free; open 9am-6pm Tues-Sun).

Also in Parque Madero is a children's park, the Parque de Convivencia Infantil (Parque Madero; admission free; open 9am-8.30pm Tues-Fri, 9am-9.30pm Sat & Sun), with a minitrain, mechanical rides, swings, climbing equipment and minigolf. You pay for the individual rides and activities.

Places to Stay

Budget *La Hacienda Hotel & Trailer Park* (☎ 602-90-26, Boulevard Domínguez 1197) Trailer sites US$12.50-17 per double. This park is 3km west of Plaza Cívica, beside a traffic circle with a large 'cow horn' sculpture. It has all hookups, a coffee shop and a tiny pool. The park area is very small and close to the busy highway.

Villa Juvenil Chiapas (☎ 613-54-78, Boulevard Albino Corzo 1800) Dorm beds US$5.75, buffet meals US$1.75-2.75. Tuxtla's youth hostel is part of a sports center nearly 2km east of Plaza Cívica. Beds are in small, clean, separate-sex dormitories. You don't need a hostel card. From the city center take a 'Ruta 1' colectivo east along Avenida Central to the yellow footbridge just before a statue of Albino Corzo.

There are many hotels on and near 2ᵃ Avenida Norte Ote, off the northeast corner of Plaza Cívica.

Hotel Casablanca (☎ 611-03-05, ℮ amhm _chis@chiapas.net, 2ᵃ Avenida Norte Ote 251) Singles/doubles with fan & shower US$10/15, with TV US$15/18, air-con doubles with TV US$28. The Casablanca has plain, small rooms, but they're very clean and the whole place is brightened by leafy indoor plants. The hotel has parking.

Hotel Plaza Chiapas (☎ *613-83-65, 2ª Avenida Norte Ote 229*) Singles/doubles with fan & bath US$11/13.50. The Plaza Chiapas has a shiny lobby but the bare, clean rooms are nothing fancy. There is hot water, however.

Hotel María Dolores (☎ *612-36-83, 2ª Calle Ote Norte 304*) Singles/doubles with bath US$7.75/10. Across the side street from the Plaza Chiapas, the María Dolores has very plain rooms, with hot water from 6am to 10am only.

Hotel Estrella (☎ *612-38-27, 2ª Calle Ote Norte 322*) Singles/doubles with shared bath US$6.75/9, with private bath and hot water US$7.75/10. This is another basic place a couple of doors from the María Dolores.

Hotel Mar-Inn (☎ *612-57-83, 2ª Avenida Norte Ote 347*) Singles/doubles with fan, bath & hot water US$14.50/18.50. Half a block east of the Plaza Chiapas, the Mar-Inn has 60 decent rooms and wide, plant-lined walkways, but its roof traps humidity.

Hotel Catedral (☎ *613-08-24, 1ª Avenida Norte Ote 367*) Singles/doubles/triples/quads US$17/20/24/27. In the next block south from the above hotels, the Catedral has decent, clean rooms with bath, fans, hot water and cable TV.

Hotel San Antonio (☎ *612-27-13, 2ª Avenida Sur Ote 540*) Singles/doubles with bath & fan US$10/13.50. This is an amicable, modern place southeast of Plaza Cívica, with a small courtyard and clean rooms for good prices.

Hotel La Mansión (☎ *612-21-51, 1ª Calle Pte Norte 221*) Singles/doubles/triples with bath and fan US$13.50/16/18, with air-con US$18/20/23. This is a good-value hotel west of Plaza Cívica, with decent-size rooms. French travelers seem to congregate here.

Hotel Posada Chiapas (☎ *612-33-54, 2ª Calle Pte Sur 243*) Singles/doubles US$9/16. Posada Chiapas has clean but smallish rooms with fan, TV and bath.

Mid-Range *Hotel Regional San Marcos* (☎ *613-19-40,* e *sanmarcos@chiapas.net, 2ª Calle Ote Sur 176*) Singles/doubles US$25/28, with air-con US$30/35. A minute's walk from Plaza Cívica, this hotel has medium-size rooms with TV and bath. Bright, flower-patterned furniture lends a little sparkle.

Hotel Balún Canán (☎ *612-30-48, fax 612-31-02, Avenida Central Ote 944*) Singles/doubles/triples/quads US$32/34/37/39. East of the center, the Balún Canán has adequate but slightly shabby rooms with air-con, bath and TV.

La Hacienda Hotel (☎ *602-90-26, Boulevard Domínguez 1197*) Singles/doubles with fan US$39/47, with air-con US$46/52. La Hacienda is 3km west of Plaza Cívica and has clean, spacious rooms and friendly management.

Top End *Hotel María Eugenia* (☎ *613-37-67, fax 613-28-60,* e *heugenia@ prodigy.net.mx, Avenida Central Ote 507*) Singles/doubles US$63/71. This is the most comfortable downtown hotel. It has an excellent restaurant, parking, and attractive air-conditioned rooms, all with two double beds and cable TV. There's even a swimming pool. Prices can be knocked down a bit when business is slow.

Hotel Bonampak (☎ *613-20-50, fax 612-77-37, Boulevard Domínguez 180*) Singles/doubles/triples with air-con US$/64/72/79. Almost opposite the state tourist office, 1.6km west of Plaza Cívica, the Bonampak has comfortable rooms with cable TV. It boasts a pool, travel agency, parking and a copy of one of the famous murals at Bonampak ruins.

Hotel Camino Real (☎ *617-77-77,* w *www.caminoreal.com/tuxtla, Boulevard Domínguez 1195*) Singles & doubles US$195. Tuxtla's most luxurious hostelry, the modern, 210-room Camino Real rises like some huge, colored-concrete castle of the hospitality industry, 1.5km west of Hotel Bonampak. The interior is spectacular, with a pool and waterfall in a large, verdant inner courtyard. It has very comfortable air-conditioned rooms, wheelchair access and plenty of top-end facilities. Promotional packages sometimes offer doubles with breakfast for US$125.

Hotel Flamboyant (☎ *615-09-99,* e *flamboyant@correo.chiapas.com, Boulevard Domínguez 1081*) Singles & doubles US$111. This hotel is 1km west of the Camino Real and is in handsome modern Arabic style, with a big pool set in lovely gardens.

Places to Eat
Restaurante Imperial (*Calle Central Norte*) Egg dishes & antojitos US$1-2.75, comida

corrida US$3. This good, clean, busy place faces the west side of Plaza Cívica, convenient to the 1st-class bus station. The three-course comida corrida offers lots of main-course choice. Breakfast items include cornflakes, eggs and hotcakes, and there's good chocolate to drink.

The next three places are in a row of popular restaurants with outdoor tables, behind the cathedral on Callejón Ote Sur. Most are open from around 7am to midnight.

Trattoria San Marco (☎ 612-69-74, *Plaza San Marcos Local 5)* Prices US$2.50-6. You can enjoy 23 varieties and six sizes of pizza here, as well as subs, baguettes, salads, *papas al horno* (potatoes with filling) or savory *crepas*.

La Parroquia *(Callejón Ote Sur)* Grills US$5-9. Next door to Trattoria San Marco, the Parroquia specializes in *a la parrilla* grills, from bacon to T-bone.

La Torta Vaquera (☎ 613-20-94, *Callejón Ote Sur)* Snacks from US$0.50. This place is popular for coffee, tacos and *quesadillas*.

Restaurante Flamingo (☎ 612-09-20, *1ª Calle Pte Sur 17)* Prices US$3-11. Open 7am-10pm daily. Along a passage off a downtown street, this quiet, efficient, air-conditioned restaurant will do you a full hotcakes breakfast, an order of luncheon tacos or enchiladas, or bigger meat and fish dishes.

Pizzas Real *(2ª Avenida Sur Ote 557)* Comida corrida US$1.50. For a decent-size meal at a small price, try Pizzas Real, opposite Hotel San Antonio. The comida corrida includes rice and two other dishes. No pizzas, though!

Hotel María Eugenia (☎ 613-37-67, *Avenida Central Ote 507)* Comida corrida US$4. This hotel restaurant is great for all meals. The comida corrida is one of the best values in town – or join the local bureaucrats for the breakfast buffet.

Soya (☎ 613-36-16, *Avenida Central Pte)* Ice cream US$1.50-2. A few blocks west of the center, this branch of Soya sells whole-wheat breads, fresh yogurt and yogurt ice cream, for which you can select a range of toppings and fruits to be crushed into it.

Nah-Yaxal (☎ 613-96-48, *6ª Calle Pte Norte 124)* Breakfasts & antojitos US$2.50-3.50, lunch US$4.75. Open 7am-9pm Mon-Sat, 7am-4pm Sun. Clean, bright, vegetarian Nah-Yaxal is around the corner from Soya. Come here for whole wheat *tortas, antojitos,*

an *energética* breakfast salad of fruit, granola, yogurt and honey, or an economical three-course lunch.

Soya (☎ 611-12-47, *Avenida Central Ote 525)* Prices US$1.50-4.75. This newer branch of Soya has a Nah-Yaxal restaurant in the back, and combines the offerings of both the preceding listings.

La Boutique del Pan (☎ 613-35-17, *Avenida Central Pte 961)* Snacks US$1-4. This good bakery, facing the Jardín de la Marimba, has a nice, bright, air-conditioned café section where you can sit down for a pastry, sandwich or coffee.

La Parrilla Suiza (☎ 614-44-74, *Avenida Central Pte 1013;* ☎ 612-20-41, *Central Oriente 731)* Tacos al pastor US$0.50, two-person grills US$7.25. Open 4pm-4am. The Parrilla Suiza's two branches are popular for economical meat fixes large and small.

Cafetería Bonampak (☎ 613-20-50, *Hotel Bonampak, Boulevard Domínguez 108)* Mains US$5.50-8. This hotel restaurant is extremely popular, attractively decked out and reasonably priced.

Las Pichanchas (☎ 612-53-51, *Avenida Central Ote 837)* Mains US$3-8. Open noon-midnight daily. Six blocks east of Plaza Cívica, Las Pichanchas is a courtyard restaurant with a long menu of local specialties and chiapaneco entertainment. Marimbas play in the afternoon and evening, and there's Chiapas folkloric dance in the evening too. Try *chipilín*, a cheese-and-cream soup with a maize base; and for dessert *chimbos,* made from egg yolks and cinnamon. In between, have tamales, vegetarian salads (beets and carrots) or *carne asada*.

El Fogón Norteño (☎ 611-38-61, *Avenida Central Ote 784)* Grills for two US$7.25, salads US$1.75-2.50. This very popular restaurant offers a similar meaty menu to the fairly new branch of Parrilla Suiza across the street.

Entertainment
Popular, free marimba concerts are held from 7pm to 10pm Saturday and Sunday in the Jardín de la Marimba, a pleasant park beside Avenida Central Pte, eight blocks west of Plaza Cívica.

Tuxtla's most popular discos, both attracting a mixed-ages crowd, are **Baby Rock** (☎ 615-14-28, *Calzada Emiliano Zapata 207),* off Boulevard Domínguez opposite the Camino Real hotel, and *La Uno (☎ 615-29-57, Boulevard Las Fuentes 101)*, just outside the Camino Real's main door.

Shopping

Casa de las Artesanías de Chiapas (☎ 612-22-75, Boulevard Domínguez 2035) Open 10am-8pm Mon-Sat, 10am-3pm Sun. This place, though an unhandy 2km west of Plaza Cívica, sells a good range of Chiapas crafts. There's also a very pretty Museo Etnográfico here, smelling sweetly of the countryside, with exhibits on seven Chiapas indigenous groups.

Getting There & Away

Air Aerocaribe flies to/from Mexico City, Oaxaca, Villahermosa, Veracruz, Tapachula, Palenque, Mérida, Cancún and Havana (Cuba), all at least once daily. Aviacsa flies several times daily to/from Mexico City (US$192).

The Aerocaribe office (☎ 602-56-49, airport ☎ 671-55-51) is at Avenida Central Pte 1748, out west beyond the Hotel Bonampak and beside a Pizza Hut. Aviacsa (☎ 611-08-90, airport ☎ 671-52-46), is at Avenida Central Pte 160, just west of Plaza Cívica.

Bus A new bus station is projected for a site several kilometers east of the center near the Central de Abastos Libramiento Sur (Libramiento Sur Market). Meanwhile, there are numerous bus stations. The main one is the Cristóbal Colón terminal (☎ 612-51-22) at 2ª Avenida Norte Pte 268, two blocks west of the main plaza. Colón's 1st-class and 1st-cum-2nd-class (Altos) services, and ADO's 1st-class buses operate from here. The 2nd-class line RS (Rápidos del Sur) is next door, and UNO and Maya de Oro deluxe services are across the street. There's no baggage checkroom, but there are private ones outside on 2ª Norte Pte: look for 'Se guardan maletas' or 'Se guardan equipaje' signs.

Most 2nd-class companies' terminals are east of the center:

Autotransportes Cuxtepeques – 10ª Calle Ote Norte at 3ª Norte Ote

Autotransportes Tuxtla Gutiérrez (ATG) – 3ª Avenida Sur Ote 712

Fletes y Pasajes (FYPSA) – 9ª Avenida Sur Ote 1882

Grupo Colosio-Tres Estrellas – 2ª Avenida Sur Ote 521

Ómnibus de Chiapas (OC) – 3ª Avenida Sur Ote 884

Daily departures from Tuxtla include:

Comitán – 175km, 3½ hours; 1 Maya de Oro (US$9.25), 12 Colón (US$7-7.75), 17 Cuxtepeques (US$5.50)

Mérida – 820km, 13 hours; 1 Maya de Oro (US$45), 2 ATG (US$29)

Mexico City (most to TAPO, a few to Norte) – 980km, 17 hours; 1 UNO (US$91), 4 Maya de Oro (US$66), 8 Colón/ADO (US$49-55)

Oaxaca – 540km, 10 hours; 1 Maya de Oro (US$30), 3 Colón (US$25), 8 FYPSA (US$20)

Palenque – 275km, 6 hours; 3 Maya de Oro (US$16), 8 Colón (US$12.50-14.50), 3 ATG (US$9.50-10.50)

Puerto Escondido – 560km, 11½ hours; 2 Colón (US$26)

San Cristóbal de Las Casas – 85km, 2 hours; 5 Maya de Oro (US$4.75), 18 Colón (US$3.75), 8 ATG (US$3.25), frequent Colosio-Tres Estrellas minibuses (US$4), every 45 minutes 6am to 6pm (US$2.25), frequent colectivo taxis (US$4.50) from 3ª Avenida Sur Ote 847

Tapachula – 390km, 8 hours; 1 UNO (US$30), 6 Maya de Oro (US$22), 13 Colón (US$18), 29 RS (US$16)

Villahermosa – 285km, 7 hours; 3 Maya de Oro (US$17), 7 Colón (US$12.50-14), 3 ATG (US$10-13)

Car Rental companies, most also with desks at the airport, include:

Arrendadora Express (☎ 612-26-66) Avenida Central Ote 725

Autos Gabriel (☎ 612-07-57) Boulevard Domínguez 780

Budget (☎ 615-06-83) Boulevard Domínguez 2510

Hertz (☎ 615-53-48) Hotel Camino Real, Boulevard Domínguez 1195

Getting Around

Tuxtla's Aeropuerto Francisco Sarabia (☎ 612-29-20), also called Aeropuerto Terán, is 3km south of highway 190 from a signposted turnoff 5km west of Plaza Cívica. A taxi from the center to the airport costs US$5.50.

All colectivos (US$0.40) on Boulevard Domínguez-Avenida Central-Boulevard Albino Corzo run at least as far as the Hotel

Bonampak and state tourist office in the west, and 11ª Calle Ote in the east. Official stops are marked by *'parada'* signs but they'll sometimes stop for you elsewhere. Taxi rides within the city cost US$1.75 to US$2.25.

CHIAPA DE CORZO
• pop 29,400 • elev 450m ☎ 961

This pleasant colonial town on the Río Grijalva, 12km east of Tuxtla Gutiérrez, is the main starting point for trips into the Cañón del Sumidero.

History

Chiapa de Corzo has been occupied almost continuously since about 1500 BC. Its sequence of pre-Hispanic cultures makes it invaluable to archaeologists, but there's little to see in the way of remains.

In the couple of centuries before the Spaniards arrived, the warlike Chiapa – the dominant people in western Chiapas at the time – had their capital, Nandalumí, a couple of kilometers downstream from present-day Chiapa de Corzo, on the opposite bank of the Grijalva near the canyon mouth. When the Spaniards under Diego de Mazariegos invaded the area in 1528, the Chiapa, realizing defeat was inevitable, apparently hurled themselves by the hundreds, men, women and children, to death in the canyon rather than surrender.

Mazariegos founded a settlement that he called Chiapa de los Indios here, but quickly shifted his base to another new settlement, Villa Real de Chiapa (now San Cristóbal de Las Casas), where he found the climate and natives were more agreeable.

At Chiapa in 1863, liberal forces, organized by Chiapas state governor Ángel Albino Corzo, defeated conservatives supporting the French invasion of Mexico. The name of Corzo, who was also born in the town and died here, was added to the name Chiapa in 1888.

Orientation & Information

Buses and minibuses from and to Tuxtla stop on the north side of Chiapa's spacious plaza, named for Albino Corzo. The Chiapa *embarcadero* for Cañón del Sumidero boat trips is two blocks south of the plaza along 5 de Febrero, the street on the plaza's west side.

There's a tourist information office just off the southwest corner of the plaza on Calle 5 de Febrero. Hours are 9am to 7pm Monday to Friday and 9am to 3pm Saturday. Banamex, with an ATM, is on the west side of the plaza. Port@net, on the south side of the plaza, offers Internet access.

Things to See & Do

Impressive **arcades** frame three sides of the plaza, a statue of General Corzo rises on the west side, and **La Pila**, an elaborate castle-like colonial brick fountain in Mudéjar-Gothic style, said to resemble the Spanish crown, stands toward the southeast corner.

The large **Templo de Santo Domingo de Guzmán**, one block south of the plaza, was built in the late 16th century by the Dominican order. Its adjoining convent is now the Centro Cultural, holding an exposition

---

Cross-Dressing & Blond Conquistadors

Some of Mexico's most colorful and curious fiestas, together known as the Fiesta de Enero, happen in Chiapa de Corzo every January.

Starting January 9, young men, known as Las Chuntá, dress as women and dance through the streets nightly – a custom said to derive from a distribution of food to the poor by the maids of a rich woman of colonial times, Doña María de Angulo.

Processions and dances of the bizarre Parachicos, men representing Spanish conquistadors and wearing bright striped sarapes, staring wooden masks and bushes of blond 'hair,' take place in daytime on January 15, 17 and 20.

There's a musical parade on January 19; then on the night of January 21 comes the Combate Naval, an hour-long mock canoe battle on the river, which features spectacular fireworks.

The flower-patterned dresses worn by Chiapa's women during these festivities are among the most vividly colorful you'll ever see.

TABASCO & CHIAPAS

of Mexican prints and the absorbing **Museo de la Laca** (☎ 616-00-55, Avenida Mexicanidad Chiapaneca 10; admission US$2.25; open 10am-6pm), which features the local craft specialty, lacquered gourds. There are pieces dating back to 1606 and even some from Asia, where lacquerwork also evolved.

Places to Stay
Casa de Huéspedes Los Ángeles (☎ 616-00-48, Plaza Albino Corzo) Singles/doubles with bath US$14.50/17. This hotel, at the southeast corner of the plaza, has basic rooms with hot water and TV.

Hotel La Ceiba (☎ 616-07-73, e laceiba chiapadecorzo@hotmail.com, Domingo Ruiz 300) Singles/doubles with air-con US$39/45. La Ceiba, with an inviting pool, is two blocks west of the plaza, and has attractive rooms with fans and folksy decor.

Places to Eat
By the embarcadero are eight *restaurants* with almost identical menus and loud music. All are equally overpriced, though the view of the river is nice. Near the market, across from the Museo de la Laca, are the standard ultracheap market *comedores*.

Restaurant Los Corredores (☎ 616-07-60, 5 de Febrero at Madero) Fish mains US$6.75. This restaurant, facing the southwest corner of the plaza, has good cheap breakfasts, reasonably priced fish plates and lots of local specialties.

Restaurant Jardines de Chiapa (☎ 616-01-98, Madero 395) Mains US$4.50-6.50. One block along Madero from Los Corredores, and popular with tour groups, this place is set around a garden patio. The food is fine and the coffee acceptable.

Restaurant El Campanario (☎ 616-03-90, Urbina 5) Mains US$5-8. Stroll half a block east of the plaza to this good-value restaurant with folksy decor and a plant-filled patio. The ambiance is relaxed, the food list extensive, with plenty of fish, seafood and regional specialties, and the prices are good.

Getting There & Away
Minibuses from Tuxtla Gutiérrez to Chiapa de Corzo are run by Gómez y Castellanos, at 3ª Avenida Sur Ote 380, and Transportes Chiapa-Tuxtla, on 2ª Avenida Sur Ote at 2ª Ote Sur. Both depart every few minutes

from 5.30am to 10.30pm for the 20-minute US$0.70 trip, and will also stop at Embarcadero Cahuaré if you wish (see the next section).

Buses to/from San Cristóbal de Las Casas don't pass through central Chiapa de Corzo but most will stop at a gas station on highway 190 on the northeast edge of town. Microbuses (US$0.50) run between the *gasolinera* and the top end of Chiapa's plaza.

CAÑÓN DEL SUMIDERO
The Cañón del Sumidero (Sumidero Canyon) is a daunting fissure in the earth a few kilometers east of Tuxtla Gutiérrez, with the Río Grijalva flowing northward through it. In 1981 the Chicoasén hydroelectric dam was completed at its northern end, and the canyon became a narrow 25km-long reservoir.

The canyon can be viewed from above from at a couple of *miradores* (lookout points) reached by road from Tuxtla, but more exciting is to take a trip through it by boat. Fast motorboats carry visitors through the canyon between towering sheer rock walls. The fare per person for a round trip of

CAÑÓN DEL SUMIDERO

about 2¼ hours, in a boat holding around 10 people, is US$9.50.

Highway 190 crosses the canyon mouth at Cahuaré, between Tuxtla and Chiapa de Corzo. Just east of the bridge is the Embarcadero Cahuaré. You can board one of the open, fiberglass motorboats *(lanchas)* here, or at the embarcadero in Chiapa de Corzo a couple of kilometers farther upstream, between roughly 8am and 4pm. You'll rarely have to wait more than half an hour for a boat to fill up. Bring something to drink, something to shield you from the sun and, if the weather is not hot, a layer or two of warm clothing.

It's about 35km from Chiapa de Corzo to the dam. Soon after you pass under highway 190, the sides of the canyon tower an amazing 800m above you. Along the way you'll see a variety of birds – herons, egrets, cormorants, vultures, kingfishers – plus probably a crocodile or two. The boat operators will point out a couple of caves and a few odd formations of rock and vegetation, including one cliff face covered in thick, hanging moss resembling a giant Christmas tree, where in rainy periods water cascades down the 'branches.' Some boat operators are in a real hurry to get the trip over, so you may want to spell it out to them if you particularly want to take your time and study the bird life closely.

At the end of the canyon, the fast, brown river opens out behind the dam. The water beneath you is 260m deep.

SAN CRISTÓBAL DE LAS CASAS
• pop 113,000 • elev 2100m ☎ 967

Highway 190 from Tuxtla Gutiérrez seems to climb endlessly into the clouds before descending into the temperate, pine-clad Valle de Jovel, where lies the beautiful colonial town of San Cristóbal ('cris-TOH-bal').

San Cristóbal has been a favorite travelers' haunt for decades: its rewards come from rambling its streets, discovering the many intriguing nooks and corners, visiting nearby indigenous villages and absorbing the unique atmosphere. San Cristóbal has a bohemian, artsy, floating community of Mexicans and foreigners, a lively bar and music scene and wonderfully clear highland light – and accommodations and meals are inexpensive.

History
The ancestors of the indigenous Maya people of the San Cristóbal area, the Tzotziles and Tzeltales, are thought to have moved to these highlands after the collapse of lowland Maya civilization, more than 1000 years ago. Diego de Mazariegos founded San Cristóbal as the Spanish regional base in 1528. For most of the colonial era San Cristóbal was a neglected outpost governed ineffectively from Guatemala. Its Spanish citizens made fortunes from wheat; the indigenous people lost their lands and suffered diseases, taxes and forced labor.

The church afforded some protection against colonist excesses. Dominican monks reached Chiapas in 1545 and made San Cristóbal their main base. The town is now named after one of them, Bartolomé de Las Casas, who was appointed bishop of Chiapas that year and became the most prominent Spanish defender of indigenous people in colonial times. In modern times Bishop Samuel Ruiz, who retired in 1999 after a long tenure, followed very much in Las Casas' footsteps. He supported the oppressed indigenous people of Chiapa and earned the violent hostility of the Chiapas establishment for his pains (see 'A Different Kind of Liberator' in the Facts about Mexico chapter).

San Cristóbal was the Chiapas state capital from 1824 to 1892 but remained relatively isolated until the 1970s, when tourism began to influence its economy. Another change since the 1970s has been an influx of around 20,000 people who were expelled by village authorities from Chamula and other indigenous villages for turning Protestant under the influence of foreign missionaries. These people live in what locals call the Cinturón de Miseria (Belt of Misery), a series of squalid, violence-ridden, makeshift colonies around San Cristóbal's Periférico (ring road). Lacking work, schools and many basic amenities, these people represent a social time bomb for the beautiful colonial town they encircle. Most of the craft sellers around Santo Domingo church and the underage chewing-gum hawkers around town are drawn from their numbers.

San Cristóbal was catapulted into the limelight on January 1, 1994, when the Zapatista rebels selected it as one of four places in which to launch their revolution, seizing and sacking government offices in the town

SAN CRISTÓBAL DE LAS CASAS

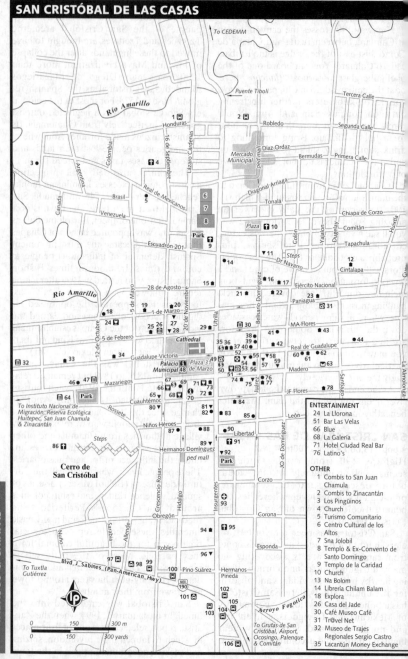

ENTERTAINMENT
24 La Llorona
51 Bar Las Velas
66 Blue
68 La Galería
71 Hotel Ciudad Real Bar
76 Latino's

OTHER
1 Combis to San Juan
   Chamula
2 Combis to Zinacantán
3 Los Pingüinos
4 Church
5 Turismo Comunitario
6 Centro Cultural de los
   Altos
7 Sna Jolobil
8 Templo & Ex-Convento de
   Santo Domingo
9 Templo de la Caridad
10 Church
13 Na Bolom
14 Librería Chilam Balam
18 Explora
26 Casa del Jade
30 Café Museo Café
31 Tr@vel Net
32 Museo de Trajes
   Regionales Sergio Castro
35 Lacantún Money Exchange

before being driven out within a few days by the Mexican army.

Orientation

San Cristóbal is easy to walk around, with straight streets rambling up and down several gentle hills. The Pan-American Highway (190) passes through the southern part of town. Officially named Boulevard Juan Sabines, it's more commonly called 'El Bulevar.'

Nearly all transportation terminals are on or just off the Pan-American. From the Cristóbal Colón bus terminal, it's six blocks north up Insurgentes to the central square, Plaza 31 de Marzo, which has the cathedral on its north side.

Information

Immigration The Instituto Nacional de Migración (☎ 678-02-92), Diagonal El Centenario 30 (at the corner of the Pan-American Highway, 1.2km west of the Cristóbal Colón bus station), is open 9am to 2pm Monday to Friday.

Tourist Offices The municipal tourist office (☎ 678-06-65) is in the north end of the Palacio Municipal, on the west side of Plaza 31 de Marzo. It's open 8am to 8pm, Monday to Saturday, and has helpful staff and plenty of printed information.

The Sedetur (Chiapas state) tourist office (☎ 678-65-70) is just off Plaza 31 de Marzo at Hidalgo 1B – open 8am to 8pm Monday to Saturday, 9am to 2pm Sunday. Usually at least one staff member on duty speaks English.

Money For those who can't use ATMs, Banamex on Plaza 31 de Marzo is efficient at currency exchange, and Bital bank, half a block west of the plaza on Mazariegos, is open long hours: 8am to 7pm Monday to Saturday, 10am to 2pm Sunday. For speedier service or exchange outside bank hours (but at worse rates) you can use Viajes Chincultik at the Casa Margarita, Real de Guadalupe 34, or Lacantún Money Exchange, Real de Guadalupe 12A.

Post & Communications The post office, at Madero 52, is open 9am to 3pm Monday to Friday, 9am to 1pm Saturday. You'll find pay phones at both ends of Plaza 31 de

Marzo and in the Cristóbal Colón bus station. La Pared bookstore, Hidalgo 2, offers bargain international calls: at the time of research, US$0.90 a minute to the USA, Canada, Europe and Australia.

San Cristóbal has many cybercafés, some very cheap and most open long hours (9am to 10pm daily is typical). Restaurant Chamula's, Real de Guadalupe 1C, charges just US$0.60 an hour. The Central pool hall, Madero 14, and Tr@vel Net, Paniagua 29A, charge US$0.50/0.80 per 30/60 minutes. The Youth Hostel at Juárez 2 offers fast connections for US$1.50 an hour.

Bookstores & Libraries La Pared (e lapared9@hotmail.com), Hidalgo 2, has an excellent selection of new and used books in English. Run by a friendly American, Dana Burton, it also buys and trades used books.

Librería Chilam Balam, in a courtyard at Utrilla 33, has a few guidebooks in English and French, and lots of history, anthropology and literature in Spanish. Libros Soluna, Real de Guadalupe 13B, has some books on Chiapas and Mexico in English, and many more in Spanish.

The more than 11,000 books and documents at Na Bolom (Guerrero 33, see Na Bolom, later in this section) make up one of the world's biggest collections on the Maya and their lands. This library is open from 10am to 4pm Monday to Friday.

Laundry Lavomart, Real de Guadalupe 70A, open 8.15am to 8pm daily, will wash, dry and fold 3/5/8kg for US$4.50/5.75/9. Lavasor, Belisario Domínguez 8D, and Lavandería La Rapidita, Insurgentes 9, have the same price for 3kg but are costlier for larger loads. But La Rapidita lives up to its name, with a full wash, dry and fold service within 2½ hours. It also lets you do your own washing for a lower cost if you wish.

Medical Services San Cristóbal doctors generally charge foreigners US$50 per consultation. Foreign residents have recommended Dr Roberto Lobato (☎ 678-77-77), Belisario Domínguez 17. There's a general hospital (☎ 678-07-70) on Insurgentes.

Plaza 31 de Marzo
The main plaza, sometimes called the zócalo, was used for markets until the early 20th century. Today it's a fine place to sit and watch life happen around you.

The cathedral, on the north side of the plaza, was begun in 1528 but completely rebuilt in 1693. Its gold-leaf interior has a baroque pulpit and altarpiece, and the detailed stonework on the west façade has been attractively picked out in yellow, red and white paint.

The Hotel Santa Clara, on the plaza's southeast corner, was the house of Diego de Mazariegos, the Spanish conqueror of Chiapas. It's one of the few secular examples of plateresque style in Mexico.

Templo & Ex-Convento de Santo Domingo
North of the center on 20 de Noviembre, the Templo de Santo Domingo is the most beautiful of San Cristóbal's many churches, especially when its pink façade is floodlit at night. The church and adjoining monastery were built between 1547 and 1560. The church's baroque façade – on which can be seen the double-headed Hapsburg eagle, symbol of the Spanish monarchy in those days – was added in the 17th century. There's plenty of gold inside, especially on the ornate pulpit.

Chamulan women and bohemian types from elsewhere conduct a super-colorful daily crafts market around Santo Domingo and the neighboring Templo de La Caridad (built in 1712). You'll find local and Guatemalan textiles, leather bags and belts, homemade toys and dolls, hippie jewelry, *animalitos* from Amatenango del Valle and more.

The Ex-Convento (Ex-Monastery) attached to Santo Domingo contains two interesting exhibits. One is the showroom of **Sna Jolobil** *(20 de Noviembre s/n; open 9am-2pm & 4pm-6pm Mon-Sat)*, a cooperative of 800 indigenous women weavers from the Chiapas highlands. Here you can see very fine huipiles, hats, blouses, skirts, rugs and other woven items. Prices range from a few dollars for smaller items to over US$1000 for the best huipiles and ceremonial garments. The weavers of Sna Jolobil, which was founded in the 1970s to foster the important indigenous art of backstrap-loom weaving, have revived forgotten techniques and designs, and developed dyes from plants, soil, bark and other natural sources.

Traditional Highland Dress

Each indigenous village in the Chiapas highlands has its own unique costume. The men of Zinacantán have distinctive pink tunics embroidered with flower motifs and may sport flat, round, ribboned palm hats. Zinacantán women wear pink or purple shawls over white embroidered blouses.

In San Juan Chamula, most men wear loose homespun tunics of white wool (sometimes, in cool weather, thicker black wool), but *cargo*-holders – those with important religious and ceremonial duties – wear a sleeveless black tunic and a white scarf on the head. Chamula women wear fairly plain white or blue blouses and/or shawls.

Many of the seemingly abstract designs on these costumes are in fact stylized snakes, frogs, butterflies, pawprints, birds, saints and other beings. Some motifs have religious-magical functions: scorpions, for example, can be a symbolic request for rain, since they are believed to attract lightning. The rhombus shape on some huipiles from San Andrés Larraínzar is also found on garments shown on Lintel 24 at the ancient Maya city of Yaxchilán. The shape represents an old Mayan conception of the universe, according to which the sky had four corners.

The sacredness of traditional costume is shown by the dressing of saints' images in old and revered garments at festival times.

The **Centro Cultural de los Altos** (*20 de Noviembre s/n; admission US$3, free Sun & holidays; open 10am-5pm Tues-Sun*), also in the Ex-Convento buildings, is a museum dealing mainly with the history of San Cristóbal, though it has a rundown of Mayan history on the lower floor. Explanatory material is in Spanish. The museum is set around a large courtyard and has wide, dramatic balconies. It brims with atmosphere, a result of its simple architecture and slightly unkempt state.

Mercado Municipal

The flavor of outlying indigenous villages can be sampled at San Cristóbal's busy municipal market, eight blocks north of the main plaza between Utrilla and Belisario Domínguez, from early morning to late afternoon, Monday through Saturday. Many of the traders are villagers for whom buying and selling is the main reason to come to town.

Centro de Desarrollo de la Medicina Maya (CEDEMM)

Anyone who's curious about the beliefs and lives of Chiapas' indigenous people will be interested to visit the Maya Medicine Development Center (☎ 678-54-38, Ⓦ *www.laneta .apc.org/omiech, Avenida Salomón Gonzá- lez Blanco 10; museum admission US$1.75; open 9am-2pm & 3pm-6pm Tues-Fri, 10am-* 4pm Sat & Sun). It's on the northward continuation of Utrilla, in the north of town. Traditional Maya medicine is a matter not of pills and chemical formulae but of prayers, candles, incense, bones and herbs. The center contains an award-winning museum showing how pulse readers, midwives, herbalists, prayer specialists and other traditional practitioners work, a medicinal plant garden and a *casa de curación*, where treatments are carried out. Herbal medicines are on sale too. CEDEMM was founded by OMIECH, the Organization of Indigenous Doctors of Chiapas, which was set up in the 1980s to develop traditional medicine.

Casa del Jade

The House of Jade (☎ *678-11-21, 16 de Septiembre No 16; guided visits free; open noon to 9pm daily*) is a classy jeweler's shop with a two-room museum. One room contains jade reproductions of ancient Olmec carvings; the other has a full-size replica of the tomb of king Pakal at Palenque, depicted at the moment of Pakal's interment.

Museo del Ámbar de Chiapas

The Chiapas Amber Museum (*Diego de Mazariegos s/n; admission US$1.25; open 10am-2pm & 4pm-7pm Tues-Sun*) is housed in the Ex-Convento de la Merced. Opened in 2000, the museum has some excellent exhibits, including pieces with embedded insects. All is explained in several languages, and there are guided tours. Apparently Chiapas amber is known for its clarity and diverse colors.

Museo de las Culturas Populares de Chiapas

The recently opened Popular Cultures Museum *(Diego de Mazariegos 37; admission by donation; open 10am-2pm & 4pm-6pm Tues-Sun)* is across the road from the Amber Museum. Initially it was housing only temporary exhibits: we saw an excellent display of photographs of Lacandones from Najá.

Museo de Trajes Regionales Sergio Castro

The Museum of Regional Costumes *(☎ 678-42-89, Guadalupe Victoria 61; admission by donation)* can only be visited by appointment, best made between 5pm and 7pm daily. This is a private collection of indigenous costumes belonging to Sergio Castro, a Mother Teresa-type figure (but male and Mexican) who works with the indigenous peoples around San Cristóbal. (One of the main things he does is treat burns suffered by people sleeping too close to open fires.) The impressive collection occupies three rooms, through which you are attentively guided by the man himself, who speaks English, French and Italian plus three indigenous languages.

Cerro de San Cristóbal & Cerro de Guadalupe

The most prominent of the small hills over which San Cristóbal undulates are the tree-covered Cerro de San Cristóbal southwest of the center, reached by steps up from Allende, and the Cerro de Guadalupe, seven blocks east of the main plaza. Both are crowned by churches and afford good views, but it's not advisable to go up after dark.

Café Museo Café

This combined café and coffee museum *(☎ 678-78-76, w http://members.es.tripod.de/cafemuseocafe, MA Flores 10; admission free; open 9am-9pm daily)* is a venture of Coopcafé, a group of 15,000 small-scale, mainly indigenous, Chiapas coffee growers. The three-room museum covers the history

of coffee and its cultivation in Chiapas, indigenous coffee growing and organic coffee. In the café you can taste some of that good organic coffee. Snacks and breakfasts (US$2.50-3.50) are served too.

Na Bolom

A visit to this lovely 19th-century house *(☎ 678-14-18, w www.ecosur.mx/nabolom, Guerrero 33; admission US$3 for 1½-hour tours in English and Spanish at 11.30am and 4.30pm daily)* is an intriguing experience. For many years Na Bolom was the home of Swiss anthropologist and photographer Gertrude (Trudy) Duby-Blom (1901-93), who with her Danish archaeologist husband Frans Blom (1893-1963) bought the house in 1950.

The couple shared a fascination for Chiapas. While Frans explored, surveyed and dug at ancient Mayan sites including Palenque, Toniná and Chinkultic, Trudy devoted much of her life to studying, photographing and trying to protect the scattered, isolated Lacandón people of eastern Chiapas and the jungle they inhabited (see 'The Lacandón Jungle & the Lacandones,' later in this chapter). Since her death Na Bolom has continued as a museum, guest house and institute for the study and preservation of Chiapas' indigenous cultures, under a board of trustees. The thrust of the Bloms' work is maintained through community and environmental programs in indigenous areas.

The name Na Bolom means 'Jaguar House' in the Tzotzil language, as well as being a play on its former owners' name. The house, visited by around 25,000 people a year, is full of photographs, archaeological and anthropological relics and books (see Bookstores & Libraries, earlier in this chapter). Behind the house is an organic garden and tree nursery.

Na Bolom also offers guest rooms and meals (see Places to Stay and Places to Eat), and takes volunteers for work on some of its programs.

Language Courses

Instituto Jovel (☎/fax 678-40-69, w www.mexonline.com/jovel.htm, MA Flores 21) 5 days tuition and 7 days family accommodation US$185 individual, US$145 group; hourly individual/group classes US$9/6 per hour. Instituto Jovel receives excellent reports from students. Most tuition here is one-to-one, with three hours' teaching a day. Group classes are only possible if other students at your level are also wanting to take a group class.

Centro Bilingüe El Puente (☎ *678-37-23, Real de Guadalupe 55)* Individual/group classes US$133/100 per week. El Puente has an attached café, Internet access and cinema, and is aimed at travelers. The weekly rates are for 15 hours of group instruction, or 12 hours one-to-one, including several hours of chat sessions. Accommodations are extra.

Organized Tours

For tours of indigenous villages, see the Around San Cristóbal section. Agencies in San Cristóbal also offer tours farther afield, often with guides who speak English, French or Italian. All the destinations can be reached independently, but some people may prefer a tour. Here are some typical prices per person (usually with a minimum of four people): Chiapa de Corzo and Cañón del Sumidero, 7 to 8 hours, US$24; Lagos de Montebello, Chinkultic ruins, Amatenango del Valle, Grutas de San Cristóbal, 9 hours, US$27; Palenque ruins, Agua Azul, Misol-Ha, 14 hours, US$38; Toniná, Grutas de San Cristóbal, 12 hours, US$27.

Viajes Chincultik (☎ *678-09-57, Real de Guadalupe 34)*. This agency at the Casa Margarita knows what people want and generally provides a good value.

Other agencies worth checking out include the following:

Astur (☎ *678-39-17, Portal Oriente B, Zócalo)*
Kanan-Ku Viajes (☎ *678-61-01, Niños Héroes 2C)*
Turística Chan-Balum (☎ *678-76-56, Real de Guadalupe 26G)*
Zapata Tours (☎ *674-51-52, Restaurant Madre Tierra, Insurgentes 19)*

Turismo Comunitario (☎ *678-96-01, ℯ turismocomunitario@yahoo.com.mx, Real de Mexicanos 16)* 3-hr tours in town US$7-9.50 per person. This grouping of community tourism and crafts organizations offers guided tours of indigenous sites and craft workshops within San Cristóbal and to places of interest farther afield. It's committed to the environment and collective principles and to spreading the benefits of tourism more widely.

Explora (☎ *678-42-95,* ₩ *www.prodigy web.net.mx/explora, 1 de Marzo 45)* 4-6 day raft & canoe trips US$395-520 per person. Explora offers adventure trips in remote areas of Chiapas for groups of three to 12 people. The rafting and canoeing happens along the Lacanjá and Lacantún rivers in the Lacandón Jungle of eastern Chiapas and the canyons of the Río La Venta in the west of the state. Explora also offers caving in the western part of the state.

Another option from San Cristóbal is a four-day trip to Laguna Miramar (see that section, later in this chapter, for details).

Special Events

Semana Santa sees the crucifixion acted out on Good Friday in the Barrio de Mexicanos in the northwest part of town. The Saturday afternoon is the start of the annual town fair, the Feria de la Primavera y de la Paz (Spring and Peace Fair), with parades, bullfights and so on. Sometimes the celebrations of the anniversary of the town's founding (March 31) fall in the midst of it all too!

Also look out for events marking the feast of San Cristóbal (July 17 to 25), as well as other fiestas celebrated nationwide.

Places to Stay

Budget *Rancho San Nicolás* (☎ *678-00-57)* US$3.50 per person. This camping and trailer park, nearly 2km east of the center on an eastward extension of León, is a friendly place with grassy lawns, tall trees, clean bathrooms and a central fireplace.

There are a couple of reasonably priced hostels in town.

Albergue Juvenil/Youth Hostel (☎ *678-76-55,* ℯ *yout@sancris.com.mx, Juárez 2)* Dorm bunks with shared/private bath US$3.50/4.50. This hostel offers bunks in very clean four- to six-person rooms; there's also one single and one double room. The door is locked at 11pm.

Magic Hostel (☎ *678-05-61, Guadalupe Victoria 47)* Dorms US$4.50 per person. This hostel was opened by the people from the Magic Hostel in Oaxaca shortly before we went to press. It's in a courtyarded colonial building, with kitchen, TV (free movies nightly), Internet and safe. As well as dorms, there are double rooms, some with private bath.

There is no shortage of hotels and posadas that provide suitable accommodations without overtaxing a limited budget. The following can be found on or near Real de Guadalupe and Madero.

Hotel Real del Valle (☎ 678-06-80, fax 678-39-55, e hrvalle@mundomaya.com.mx, Real de Guadalupe 14) Singles/doubles/triples/quads US$23/28/34/39. The Real del Valle has a nice courtyard and 36 clean rooms with bath.

Hotel San Martín (☎/fax 678-05-33, e rmleon1@prodigy.net.mx, Real de Guadalupe 16) Singles/doubles/triples/quads US$23/23/28/34. This hotel offers reasonable, clean rooms with small bathrooms.

Hotel Posada del Barón (☎/fax 678-08-81, e hotelbarondelascasas@yahoo.com.mx, Belisario Domínguez 2) Singles/doubles/triples with bath US$14.50/19/28. The Posada del Barón has 12 simple, clean rooms along a wood-pillared patio.

Casa Margarita (☎ 678-09-57, e agchin cultik@hotmail.com, Real de Guadalupe 34) Singles/doubles/triples US$9/13.50/18.50, quads/quintuples US$23/27. The Margarita, a long-popular travelers' halt run by a friendly family, has decent, clean rooms. The shared bathrooms, with hot water, are kept very clean and there are plenty of them. There's a wide courtyard, a handy in-house travel agency and a good restaurant under the same ownership next door.

Posada Casa Real (☎ 678-13-03, Real de Guadalupe 51) Singles/doubles US$5.75/11.50. This friendly, quiet place, popular with women travelers, has just eight nice, clean rooms. There's a pleasant upstairs sitting area. The door is locked at 11pm.

Posada Las Casas (☎ 678-28-82, Madero 81) Dorm beds US$3.50, singles/doubles/triples with shared bathrooms US$4.50/8/11.50, with private bath US$5.75/10/13.50. Posada Las Casas offers straightforward, clean rooms with hot water, at very good prices. The rooms are on two floors along an open-air courtyard. A restaurant should be open on the premises by the time you get there.

There are two places worth checking out on or near Insurgentes:

Logis La Media Luna (☎ 678-88-14, e paint@hotmail.com, JF Flores s/n) Singles/doubles US$11/13.50, with bath & TV US$17/19. The friendly Media Luna, off

Insurgentes two blocks south of the main plaza, has just a handful of rooms around a nice yard.

Hotel Lucella (☎ 678-09-56, Insurgentes 55) Singles/doubles/triples with bath US$6.75/14/20. The Lucella, opposite Santa Lucía church, is run by a friendly family and has simple, clean rooms around a patio.

There are also a number of acceptable lodgings both north and west of the center.

Posada Jovel (☎ 678-17-34, e posada_jovel@latinmail.com, Paniagua 28) Singles/doubles with shared bath US$9/11.50, with private bath US$11.50/15.50, superior singles/doubles/triples/quads with bath and TV US$17/23/28/34. Posada Jovel is tidy, friendly, well kept and popular. The 10 superior rooms, added in the past few years, are in a separate house across the street. Both sections have terraces with great views across San Cristóbal's tiled rooftops. There's a breakfast restaurant too. Rates come down 10% to 15% in low season.

Posada San Agustín (☎ 678-18-16, Ejército Nacional 7) Singles/doubles/triples with shared bath US$8/11.50/14.50, with private bath US$10/17/20. Family-run San Agustín has 14 good, clean rooms, plenty of hot water and good views from the roof.

Posada Doña Rosita (☎ 678-09-23, e 393@correoweb.com, Ejército Nacional 13) Dorm beds US$4-5, singles/doubles/triples/quads US$8/9/13.50/18, all including continental breakfast. This is a hostel-type place run by a friendly señora who also practices natural medicine. The rooms, most with shared bathrooms, are plain but clean, and there's a kitchen available from noon to 8.30pm.

Posada 5 (e posada5@yahoo.com, Ejército Nacional 14) Dorm beds US$4, singles/doubles/triples with shared bath US$8/9/13.50. Relaxed Posada 5 is run by Roberto, the son of Doña Rosita from across the street. It's popular with young travelers and has a sociable little 24-hour kitchen area.

Hotel El Cerrillo (☎/fax 678-12-83, Belisario Domínguez 27) Singles/doubles/triples/quads US$20/20/32/32. Friendly El Cerrillo has a flowery courtyard and good-size, prettily painted rooms with bathroom and cable TV. Some larger rooms (US$39-50) hold up to seven people. There are a roof terrace, restaurant and bar, too.

La Casa di Gladys (☎ 678-57-75, e casagladys@hotmail.com, Cintalapa 6) Dorm beds US$4.50, doubles/triples/quads with shared bath US$12.50/14.50/16.50. The 28-room Casa di Gladys has a very friendly travelers' atmosphere. Amenities include a TV area, Internet (US$1.25 an hour), a sink for washing clothes, breakfast (US$2) and evening kitchen use (US$1.25).

Hotel Adriana (☎/fax 678-81-39, 1 de Marzo 29) Singles & doubles with shared bath US$11-13.50, doubles with private bath & TV US$22-31, 4- & 5-bed rooms US$34-50. This hotel has rooms set around a prettily lit courtyard.

Mid-Range The following is just a selection from the many choices. New hotels are opening all the time, often in attractive colonial buildings.

Look for the following near the city center.

Posada San Cristóbal (☎ 678-68-81, Insurgentes 3) Singles/doubles/triples/quads US$32/36/43/49. The San Cristóbal, a block south of the main plaza, has about ten good, large, airy rooms around a pleasant, old-fashioned courtyard, and smaller, newer rooms in the rear.

Hotel La Noria (☎ 678-68-78, Insurgentes 18A) Singles/doubles/triples US$28/38/48. This fairly new hotel has bright decor and dry, comfortable rooms along covered passageways on two levels, with attractive tiles. All rooms have cable TV.

Hotel Santa Clara (☎ 678-11-40, fax 678-10-41, e hotelstaclara@correoweb.com, Insurgentes 1) Singles/doubles/triples/quads US$42/44/55/67. The historic Santa Clara, on the main plaza, has sizable, comfortable rooms, a courtyard with caged red macaws, a restaurant, a bar/lounge and a pool. Watch out for off-season deals that include breakfast.

Hotel Mansión de los Ángeles (☎ 678-11-73, fax 678-25-81, Madero 17) Singles/doubles/triples/quads with TV & bath US$45/52/58/65. This is a colonial-style, three-story building with 19 pleasant rooms around two patios. Indigenous costume prints add an attractive touch, and one patio contains a wood-and-glass-roofed restaurant.

There are also the following suitable lodgings west of the center.

Hotel Español Flamboyant (☎ 678-00-45, fax 678-05-14, e correo@flamboyant .com.mx, 1 de Marzo 15) Singles/doubles US$50/61 (doubles US$74 at Semana Santa and Christmas). This is an old hotel recently upgraded. It has a pretty garden with lots of trees, flowers and birds. Graham Greene stayed here in the 1930s.

El Paraíso (☎ 678-00-85, fax 678-51-68, w www.geocities.com/hparaisosc, 5 de Febrero 19) Singles/doubles/triples/quads US$38/51/63/75. El Paraíso has a cheery, flower-filled courtyard, an amiable atmosphere and comfortable rooms. The excellent restaurant serves Swiss and Mexican dishes and whips up a good margarita.

Hotel Catedral (☎ 678-53-56, Guadalupe Victoria 21) Singles/doubles/triples/quads US$53/59/72/83. This classy, colonial-style hotel has 65 attractive rooms on four levels around a covered courtyard. There are also suites with Jacuzzi. Rooms cater for most needs with satellite TV and even telephones in the bathroom. A good-size pool occupies an additional courtyard.

These mid-range lodging options are east of the center.

Hotel Casavieja (☎/fax 678-68-68, w www.casavieja.com.mx, MA Flores 27) Singles/doubles/triples US$50/61/67. The Casavieja is an almost-new hotel in an 18th-century house, very attractive and comfortable. Rooms are arranged around grassy, flowered courtyards, and there's a neat restaurant.

Na Bolom (☎ 678-14-18, fax 678-55-86, e nabolom@sclc.ecosur.mx, Guerrero 33) Singles/doubles with bath US$40/54. This museum/research institute (see the Na Bolom section, earlier in this chapter) has 14 good guest rooms, with meals available.

Top End *Hotel Casa Mexicana* (☎ 678-06-98, fax 678-26-27, w www.hotelcasamexicana .com, 28 de Agosto 1) Singles/doubles/triples US$60/78/92. With its sky-lighted garden, fountains, plants, art and sculpture, the Casa Mexicana exudes colonial charm.

Hotel Diego de Mazariegos (☎ 678-08-33, fax 678-08-27, e reserva@diegode mazariegos.com.mx, 5 de Febrero 1) Singles/doubles/triples/suites US$67/77/84/111. This hotel occupies two fine buildings either side of Utrilla one block north of the main plaza. The 77 rooms are tastefully furnished and

50 have fireplaces. The hotel has a very pleasant sitting room with fireplace, a reasonable restaurant and a nightclub.

Casa Dr Felipe Flores (☎ 678-39-96, W *www.felipeflores.com, JF Flores 36)* Doubles US$75-90 including full breakfast. Casa Flores is a charming colonial house with five attractive guest rooms around two flowery courtyards. The welcoming American owners, Nancy and David Orr, have decorated the house with local art and artisanry, and furnishings from Mexico and Guatemala. Each room has a fireplace, as do the shared living room, dining room and den.

Places to Eat

San Cristóbal offers a variety of cuisines and plenty of choice for vegetarians. Some eateries try to please everyone with long lists of multinational imitations; those with more focused efforts tend to be better.

Real de Guadalupe This is a good street for economical breakfasts. Eggs, toast, butter, jam, juice and coffee will cost you US$2 at *Hamburguesas Juanito (Real de Guadalupe 9)* and US$2.75 at the two branches of *Cafetería del Centro (Real de Guadalupe 15 and Pasaje Mazariegos mall, Real de Guadalupe 7)*.

Restaurante Margarita (☎ 678-09-57, *Real de Guadalupe 34)* Mains US$4-8. This restaurant adjoining Casa Margarita offers a broad choice of dependably good food. The family here has been in the business of pleasing travelers' palates for at least two decades.

Todo Natural (Belisario Domínguez south of Real de Guadalupe) Big plates of fruit, yogurt and granola US$2. Todo Natural is good for juice combos, too.

Insurgentes *Restaurant Kukulkan (in Posada San Cristóbal – see Places to Stay, above)* Mains US$4-5. This hotel restaurant does a wide range of adequate if uninspired Mexican and international fare. Breakfasts (US$2.50-3.50) are a decent value.

Restaurante Tuluc (☎ 678-20-90, *Insurgentes 5)* Breakfasts US$2.25-3.25, mains US$3-4. Open 6.30am-10pm daily. Tuluc, 1½ blocks south of the main plaza, scores with efficient service, good food and reasonable prices.

Madre Tierra (☎ 678-42-97, *Insurgentes 19)* Prices US$2.25-4.50. Open 8am-10pm daily. Long-running Madre Tierra has an eclectic and appetizing vegetarian menu, with filling soups, whole-grain sandwiches, salads and spinach cannelloni. There are big breakfasts and a US$6 daily set lunch. Excellent whole-grain bread is served with all meals.

Los Merenderos (Insurgentes s/n) Mains & egg dishes US$1.75-2.25. These food stalls around the Mercado de Dulces y Artesanías serve up some of the cheapest meals in town.

Restaurante El Sol (Insurgentes 71) Breakfasts & comida corrida US$2-3. El Sol is a small restaurant serving economical breakfasts and a good-value comida corrida of four courses and coffee.

Madero *Restaurante Maya Pakal* (☎ 678-59-11, *Madero 21A)* Mains US$2.75-4. Open 7.30am-11pm daily. There are about eight restaurants on Madero within a block of Plaza 31 de Marzo. Few stand out, but the Maya Pakal's good prices and generous portions make it constantly busy. The Mexican dishes are best, and the three-course vegetarian comida and cheap breakfasts are popular too.

El Gato Gordo (☎ 678-04-99, *Madero 28)* Breakfasts & veg comida US$2-2.50. Open 9am-10.30pm Wed-Mon. The friendly, economical Gato Gordo attracts budget travelers. Apart from the set menus, you can go for crêpes, pasta, chicken or meat.

Hidalgo & Rosas *Emiliano's Moustache* (☎ 678-72-46, *Rosas 7)* Prices US$2.25-6.75. Open 9am-1am daily. Carnivores flock here for the meat *filetes*, though vegetarian possibilities exist too (including veggie tacos). A specialty is the filling order of five tacos with combinations of meat, vegetable or cheese.

Café La Selva (☎ 678-72-43, *Rosas 9)* Baguettes, sandwiches & croissants US$2.50-4. Sit in the courtyard or in either of two clean, bright rooms to enjoy your baguette with any of 39 types of organic, indigenous-grown Chiapas coffee.

North of the Center *Restaurant El Teatro* (☎ 678-31-49, *1 de Marzo 8)* Dinner US$10-12. Open 1pm-10pm Tues-Sun. This is one of the more upscale restaurants in town. The European-based menu includes chateaubriand, crêpes, fresh pasta, pizzas and desserts.

El Fogón de Jovel (☎ 678-11-53, 16 de Septiembre No 11) Mains US$5-8. Open noon-10.30pm daily. The Fogón serves up good chiapaneco food in a bright courtyard setting with live marimba music – it's fun!

Restaurant Los Magueyes (☎ 678-06-98, 28 de Agosto 1) Prices US$3.25-8.50. The Hotel Casa Mexicana's restaurant has something to please everyone.

La Casa del Pan (☎ 678-58-95, Dr Navarro 10) Prices US$2.50-4.25. Open 8am-10pm Tues-Sun. This is an excellent bakery-restaurant with lots of vegetarian fare: whole-wheat sandwiches, vegan salads, *hojaldres* (vegetable strudels) and vegetarian antojitos. Try a 'high-energy breakfast' of orange juice, fruit, yogurt, granola, organic Chiapas coffee and croissant or whole-grain bread.

Na Bolom (see the Na Bolom section, earlier in this chapter) Dinner US$8.75. For unique ambiance, eat at Na Bolom. Guests sit at one long wooden table in the Bloms' old dining room. Dinner is at 7pm; book an hour or two ahead. You can also go for lunch.

Entertainment

You can choose from half a dozen live music spots almost any night; the musicians are enthusiastic, though not always the most professional! At the time of research, reggae was very much the vogue, but you can also hear *trova*, Cuban son, salsa, rock, pop, blues or jazz.

Latino's (☎ 678-99-27, Madero 23) Admission free. This is the funkiest place for Latin music, with a good band from 10pm to 2am Monday to Saturday, space to dance, and reasonably priced food.

Blue (☎ 678-65-99, Rosas 2) Admission free. Open 9pm-3am daily. Blue is one of the hippest locales in town. It has a courtyard area with space for live bands and dancing, plus a bar with a pool table. Live music starts nightly about 11pm. Reggae was in high favor here when we were last in town.

La Galería (☎ 678-15-47, Hidalgo 3) Admission free. Open daily. This gallery-bar, in a 16th-century house where San Cristóbal's founder, Diego de Mazariegos, once lived, has assorted live music starting at 8.30pm nightly. It's popular with a young Mexican and traveler crowd and has a good atmosphere.

Bar Las Velas (Madero 14) Admission US$1.25. Open from about 9pm daily. One of the hippest places, attracting young locals and travelers alike, at the time of research Las Velas had a live reggae band about midnight. They search you at the door.

La Llorona (1 de Marzo 14B) Open from 5pm, Wed-Mon. This cafe/pub has cushions and hammocks so that you can really lie back and relax. Films are shown nightly at 7pm. There are also books, newspapers, board games and vegetarian food.

La Casa del Pan (see Places to Eat, above) Admission free-US$2. This vegetarian restaurant has varied and sometimes quite original live music most nights, from around 8.30pm to 10.30pm.

The bars of the ***Hotel Santa Clara*** and ***Hotel Ciudad Real*** on Plaza 31 de Marzo are two more busy spots with nightly music. There's no cover at either.

Cinema El Puente (☎ 678-37-23, Real de Guadalupe 55) Admission US$1.25. This mini-cinema in the Centro Bilingüe El Puente shows a well-publicized program of good films. Usually there are three different films a day, Monday to Saturday, ranging from documentaries on Chiapas to Hollywood 'A' releases.

Shopping

Most San Cristóbal shops open from 9am to 2pm and 4pm to 8pm, Monday to Saturday. Hosts of them sell Chiapas indigenous crafts. Artistically speaking, the outstanding local *artesanías* are textiles such as huipiles, blouses and blankets: Tzotzil weavers are some of the most skilled and inventive in Mexico (see the boxed text 'Traditional Highland Dress,' earlier in this chapter). Another Chiapas specialty is amber jewelry, sold in numerous San Cristóbal shops: ***La Pared*** (Hidalgo 2) has good-quality stock. Amber, which is fossilized pine resin, is mined near Simojovel, north of San Cristóbal, but beware of plastic imitations: real amber is never cold and never heavy.

The heaviest concentration of **craft shops** is along Real de Guadalupe (prices go down as you move away from Plaza 31 de Marzo), but there's also a huge range of wares at good prices at the busy daily **crafts market** around Santo Domingo and La Caridad churches. At the market you're expected to bargain: the first price quoted is traditionally significantly more than the going rate for the item. Also next to Santo Domingo is the showroom/shop of *Sna Jolobil*, with some of the finest textiles in Mexico (see Templo & Ex-Convento de Santo Domingo, earlier in this section). The *Casa de las Artesanías de Chiapas* (cnr Niños Héroes & Hidalgo) sells a good range of Chiapas crafts at good prices (it also has a small exhibition area on the costumes and crafts of various villages). *La Galería* (Hidalgo 3) has a really great selection of jewelry in turquoise, amber, silver, gold and more.

If you like your shopping to have a political dimension, *Nemizapata (Real de Guadalupe 45)* sells Zapatista-made and pro-Zapatista crafts, and Subcomandante Marcos dolls in little black balaclavas are commonplace. Several shops sell Zapatista videos, including *El Mono de Papel (Libertad)*.

Getting There & Away

Air San Cristóbal airport is about 15km out of town on the Palenque road. At the time of writing the only passenger flights were to/from Mexico City daily by Aeromar (☎ 674-30-03 at the airport). One-way fares start around US$200; Kanan-Ku Viajes (see Organized Tours) is one agency selling tickets. There are many more flights from Tuxtla Gutiérrez. A taxi to Tuxtla airport costs about US$40.

Bus, Suburban & Taxi Each company has its own terminal. All of them are on or just off the Pan-American Highway, except for a few serving nearby villages (see Around San Cristóbal).

The deluxe and 1st-class companies, Cristóbal Colón, ADO and UNO, share a terminal at the corner of Insurgentes and the Pan-American Highway. You can buy tickets for buses on all these lines at Ticket Bus, Belisario Domínguez 8C, in the center.

Transportes Lacandonia (TL), 2nd-class, is 150m west of Colón along the highway, and Autotransportes Tuxtla Gutiérrez (ATG), also 2nd-class, is just north of the highway on Allende.

The basic 1st-class bus line TRF (Transportes Dr Rodulfo Figueroa) and 2nd-class Ómnibus de Chiapas (OC) have a joint terminal on the south side of the highway, and various Suburban-type vans and colectivo taxi services have their depots on the highway

in the same area. The Suburbans and colectivos run all day from 6am or earlier and leave when the vehicle is full. See the San Cristóbal de las Casas map for locations.

Daily departures from San Cristóbal include the following:

Cancún – 990km, 16 hours; 5 from Colón terminal (US$45-56), 2 ATG (US$35)

Chiapa de Corzo – 70km, 1¼ hours; take a 2nd-class bus, van, or colectivo heading for Tuxtla Gutiérrez, but check first that it will let you off in Chiapa de Corzo

Ciudad Cuauhtémoc (Guatemalan border) – 170km, 2½ hours; 6 Altos (US$7), leave early if you want to get any distance into Guatemala the same day

Comitán – 90km, 1½ hours; 10 from Colón terminal (US$3.75-4.50), other buses and Suburbans (US$3) and colectivo taxis (US$3.50) from south side of Pan-American Highway

Mérida – 735km, 11 hours via Campeche; 2 from Colón terminal (US$33-40), 1 ATG (US$29)

Mexico City (TAPO) – 1065km, 19 hours; 6 from Colón terminal (US$53-92), 1 ATG (US$47)

Oaxaca – 625km, 12 hours; 3 from Colón terminal (US$28-35)

Ocosingo – 88km, 1½ hours; 8 from Colón terminal (US$3.75-4.75), 3 Figueroa (US$3.50), 6 ATG (US$3.25), 11 TL (US$2.25), Suburbans (US$3.50) from north side of Pan-American Highway

Palenque – 190km, 4 hours; 10 from Colón terminal (US$9-11.50), 6 ATG (US$8), 3 Figueroa (US$8), 10 TL (US$6.75)

Puerto Escondido – 645km, 13 hours; 2 Colón (US$30)

Tuxtla Gutiérrez – 85km, 1½ hours; 11 from Colón terminal (US$4-6.50), 8 ATG (US$3.25), 3 Figueroa (US$3.25), OC every 40 minutes during daytime (US$2.25), colectivo taxis (US$3.50) by Taxis Jovel, Suburbans (US$3.50) by Corazón de María

Villahermosa – 305km, 7 hours; 2 from Colón terminal (US$13.50-14.50), 3 ATG (US$13)

Buses of various classes from the Colón terminal also run to Tapachula, Bahías de Huatulco, Campeche, Chetumal, Playa del Carmen, Pochutla, Tulum and Veracruz.

To take the pain out of getting to Guatemala, Viajes Chincultik (see Organized Tours, earlier in this section) runs a shuttle service (on Tuesday and Friday) to La Mesilla (2½ hours, US$20), Quetzaltenango (5½ hours, US$40), Panajachel (7½ hours, US$50) and Antigua (9½ hours, US$60).

Car Budget (☎ 678-31-00), at Mazariegos 39 in the lobby of the Hotel Mansíon del Valle, has VW sedans for US$57 a day including unlimited kilometers, insurance and taxes. Its Nissan Tsurus are US$78 on the same basis. Excellent Rent a Car (☎ 678-76-56), Real de Guadalupe 26G, has VW sedans for a few dollars more.

Getting Around

Combis go up Rosas from the Pan-American Highway to the town center. A typical taxi trip within the town costs US$1.50.

Los Pingüinos (☎ 678-02-02), Ecuador 4B, rent mountain bikes with lock and maps at US$6/8/9 for three/four/five hours, US$10 for a day (daylight hours) or US$12.50 for 24 hours. You need to deposit some security such as your passport with them. Staff there can advise on good and safe routes; they also conduct guided bicycle tours (see the Around San Cristóbal section, below). They're closed Sunday.

AROUND SAN CRISTÓBAL

The indigenous villagers of the beautiful Chiapas highlands are descended from the ancient Maya and maintain some unique customs, costumes and beliefs.

Dangers & Annoyances

Security in the Chiapas highlands has been shaky ever since the Zapatista uprising in 1994, because of a combination of political, religious and social conflicts. Villages north of San Cristóbal such as San Andrés Larraínzar, a center of strong Zapatista support, and San Pedro Chenalhó, head of the municipality where the 1997 Acteal massacre took place, remained tense at the time of writing.

San Juan Chamula, Zinacantán and Amatenango del Valle were considered safe to visit at that time. In all cases, if you're going independently, make prior inquiries about security, and make sure you get back to San Cristóbal well before dark. Walking or riding by horse or bicycle by day along the main roads to Chamula and Zinacantán should not be risky, but wandering into unfrequented areas or down isolated tracks could still be dangerous.

In some villages cameras are at best tolerated – and sometimes not even that. Photography is banned completely in the church and during rituals at San Juan Chamula, and in the church and churchyard at Zinacantán. You may put yourself in physical danger if you take photos without permission. If in any doubt at all, ask before taking a picture.

Organized Tours

A good guide can give you a feel for indigenous village life that you could never know alone. The following all offer well-received daily trips to local villages, usually San Juan Chamula and Zinacantán.

Alex and Raúl (☎ 678-37-41) 4½-hour tours, US$10 per person. We have enjoyed this English-language minibus trip. You can find Alex and/or Raúl beside San Cristóbal cathedral at 9.30am daily.

Viajes Chincultik (☎ 678-09-57, Casa Margarita, Real de Guadalupe 34) 4½-hour trip to CEDEMM, Chamula and Zinacantán, US$12.50; with extension to San Andrés Larraínzar, US$17. These trips are led by a sociologist member of the family that runs the Casa Margarita.

Mercedes Hernández Gómez 5-6-hour trips around US$10. Mercedes waits just before 9am daily near the kiosk in San Cristóbal's main plaza, twirling a colorful umbrella. Her tours, traveling by minibus and on foot, have been popular for years. A fluent English-speaker who grew up in Zinacantán, she's a strong character who has on occasions reportedly ejected participants in mid-tour if she didn't like their vibe.

Further village tours are offered by agencies such as Astur, Kanan-Ku Viajes and Zapata Tours (see Organized Tours in the San Cristóbal section).

Bicycle Tours *Los Pingüinos (☎ 967-678-02-02, Ecuador 4B, San Cristóbal)* 3-6½-hour trips US$18-25 per person (2-8 people). The friendly English-, German- and Spanish-speaking folk at Los Pingüinos lead mountain-bike tours of 20 to 42km. Most go to little-visited, scenic country areas east of San Cristóbal, but Chamula and Zinacantán are also options. The routes are predominantly off-road but without long, hard gradients. Book one day or more ahead.

Horseback Riding Almost any travel agency or place to stay in San Cristóbal can arrange a three- or four-hour guided ride to

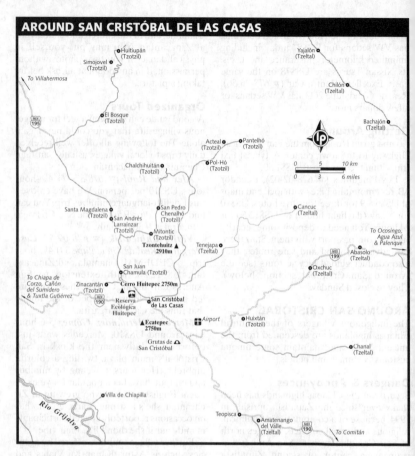

AROUND SAN CRISTÓBAL DE LAS CASAS

San Juan Chamula for around US$10. You might want to ask about the animals: are they horses or just ponies, fiery or docile, fast or slow? Rides with Viajes Chincultik at Casa Margarita have received good reports of late.

Markets & Special Events

Weekly markets at the villages are nearly always on Sunday. Proceedings start very early, with people arriving from outlying settlements as early as dawn, and wind down by lunchtime.

Festivals often give the most interesting insight into indigenous life, and there are plenty of them. Occasions like Carnaval (for which Chamula is famous), Semana Santa, el Día de Muertos (November 2) and el Día de la Virgen de Guadalupe (December 12) are celebrated almost everywhere. At some of these fiestas much *posh,* an alcoholic drink made from sugarcane, is drunk. At Carnaval, groups of minstrels stroll the roads in tall, pointed hats with long, colored tassels, strumming guitars and chanting.

Getting There & Away

Transportation to most villages leaves from points around the Mercado Municipal in San Cristóbal. Check latest return times before you set out: some services wind down by lunchtime. Combis to San Juan Chamula (US$0.70) leave from Calle Honduras fairly frequently from 5am up to about 6pm; for Zinacantán, combis (US$0.90) and colectivo taxis (US$1.25) go at least hourly, 6am to 5pm, from a yard off Robledo.

Indigenous Peoples of Chiapas

Of the 3.9 million people of Chiapas, about 1 million are indigenous (mostly Mayan groups). At least nine languages are spoken in the state. Spanish is the idiom of commerce, most education and government in the cities. In the countryside in various parts of the state, indigenous peoples speak the Chol, Chuj, Lacandón, Mam, Tojolabal, Tzeltal, Tzotzil and Zoque languages. Although all derived from ancient Mayan, most of these tongues are now mutually unintelligible, so local inhabitants use a second language such as Spanish or the fairly widely understood Tzeltal to communicate with other groups. The indigenous languages also define ethnic groups that have common beliefs, traditions and dress customs.

The indigenous people who travelers are most likely to come into contact with are the 330,000 or so Tzotziles, who mainly live in a highland area centered on San Cristóbal de Las Casas and stretching about 50km from east to west and 100km from north to south. Tzotzil clothing is among the most varied, colorful and elaborately worked in Mexico. It not only identifies wearers' villages but also marks them as inheritors of ancient Mayan traditions (see 'Traditional Highland Dress,' earlier in this chapter).

You may also encounter the Tzeltales, numbering about 350,000, who inhabit the region between San Cristóbal and the Lacandón Jungle. Both groups are among Mexico's most traditional indigenous peoples. Their nominally Catholic religious life involves some distinctly pre-Hispanic elements and goes hand in hand with some unusual forms of social organization (see 'Burdens of Honor,' later in this chapter). Most of the people live in the hills outside the villages, which are primarily market and ceremonial centers.

Other Chiapas indigenous peoples include about 180,000 Choles, mainly in the north of the state, and some 40,000 Zoques in the northwest.

Chiapas' indigenous peoples are 2nd-class citizens in economic and political terms, living, on the whole, on the least productive land in the state. Some have emigrated to the Lacandón Jungle to clear new land, or to the cities in search of work. Their plight was the major reason for the 1994 Zapatista uprising.

But not everyone supports the Zapatistas, and violence between opposing indigenous factions has been an ugly side of the Zapatista upheaval. One series of revenge killings between pro-PRI and pro-Zapatista Tzotziles culminated in a 1997 massacre at the village of Acteal, in the municipality of Chenalhó, north of San Cristóbal. Some 45 people, mostly women and children, from Las Abejas (the Bees), a Catholic pacifist group sympathetic to the Zapatistas, were gunned down in a chapel by pro-PRI paramilitaries. As a result of this and other incidents, somewhere between 10,000 and 20,000 people fled their homes for refugee camps, chiefly in northern areas of Chiapas. By 2001, some were finally returning home, but the release from jail at the same time of some of the 34 men convicted of the Acteal massacre raised tensions again in the Chenalhó area.

Despite their problems, indigenous peoples' identities and self-respect survive. Traditional festivals, costumes, crafts and often ancient religious practices assist in this. These people generally remain suspicious of outsiders, and may resent interference, especially in their religious observances. But they also will be friendly and polite if treated with due respect.

Reserva Ecológica Huitepec

The entrance to Huitepec Ecological Reserve *(self-guided visits US$1.75; open 9am-4pm Tues-Sun)* is about 3.5km from San Cristóbal, on the road to San Juan Chamula. The reserve is set on the slopes of 2700m Cerro Huitepec, rising from evergreen oak woods to rare cloud forest, and has some 60 resident bird species and over 40 winter visitors. The self-guided trail is 2km long. If you're interested in plants, it's well worth taking a three-hour guided tour with the Tzotzil guide, Javier, who speaks some English and focuses on the medical and spiritual properties of plants. This tour costs US$23 per group (up to eight people), and you need to book one day before at Pronatura (☎ 967-678-50-00), Juárez 11B in

San Cristóbal. Javier also gives four-hour early-morning bird tours.

San Juan Chamula
• pop 2900 • elev 2200m

The Chamulans put up strong resistance to the Spaniards in 1524 and launched a famous rebellion in 1869, attacking San Cristóbal. Today they are one of the largest subgroups of the Tzotzil people, about 80,000 strong. Their main village, San Juan Chamula, 10km northwest of San Cristóbal, is the center for some unique religious practices. A big sign at the entrance to the village strictly forbids photography in the village church or anywhere rituals are being performed. Nearby, around the shell of an older church, is the village graveyard, with black crosses for people who died old, white for the young, and blue for others. Near the old church is the small village museum, **Ora Ton** (*admission US$0.60; open 9am-6pm daily*).

Starting at dawn on Sunday, people from the hills stream into San Juan Chamula for the weekly market and to visit the church. Busloads of tourists also stream in, so you might prefer to come another day. Artesanías (mainly textiles) are sold every day for the passing tourist trade.

The **Templo de San Juan**, Chamula's main church, white with a colorfully painted door arch, stands beside the main plaza. A sign tells visitors to obtain tickets (US$0.60) at the tourist office (open 9am-6pm daily), at the side of the plaza, before entering the church. Do not wear a hat inside. The candles, incense and the worshipers kneeling with their faces to the pine needle-carpeted floor make a powerful impression. Chanting *curanderos* may be rubbing patients' bodies with eggs or bones. Images of saints are surrounded with mirrors and dressed in holy garments. Chamulans revere San Juan Bautista (St John the Baptist) above Christ, and his image occupies a more important place in the church. Coca-Cola also occupies an important place in the Chamulan cosmography – it facilitates burping in the church, which is believed to expel evil spirits. The family with the Coca-Cola franchise here has a large house in the middle of the village, in marked contrast to the humble homes of most of its clients. An aggressive marketing campaign to flood large parts of the Chiapas highlands with

the brown liquid was under way as we researched this edition.

Christian festivals are interwoven with older ones here: the important Carnaval celebrations also mark the five 'lost' days of the ancient Mayan Long Count calendar, which divided time into 20-day periods (18 of these make 360 days, leaving five to complete a year). Other festivals include ceremonies for San Juan Bautista (June 22-25, with up to 20,000 people gathering to dance and drink on the 24th) and the annual change of *cargos* (December 30 to January 1; see 'Burdens of Honor,' later in this chapter). Conflicts between adherents of traditional Chamulan 'Catholicism' and converts to Protestantism in the past couple of decades have resulted in the expulsion of many thousands of Chamulans from their villages, and they now inhabit the shantytowns around San Cristóbal.

San Lorenzo Zinacantán
• pop 3500

The road to the orderly village of San Lorenzo Zinacantán, about 11km northwest of San Cristóbal, forks left off the Chamula road before descending into a valley. This is the main village of the Zinacantán municipality (population 45,000). Zinacantán people are Tzotzil, and the predominantly pink and purple colors of their costume are very distinctive.

A market is usually held only at fiesta times. The most important celebrations are for the festival of la Virgen de la Candelaria, around August 10.

Zinacantecos are great flower growers and have a particular love for the geranium, which along with pine branches is offered in rituals performed to bring a wide range of benefits.

The village has two churches. The central **Iglesia de San Lorenzo** has been rebuilt following a 1975 fire. Photography is banned in the church and churchyard. There are also two **museums**, one devoted to local textiles and the other focusing on Zinacantán culture.

Grutas de San Cristóbal

The *grutas (admission US$1.25; open 8am-5pm daily)* are in fact a single long cavern 9km southeast of San Cristóbal. The entrance is among pine woods, a five-minute

Burdens of Honor

Traditional community leadership positions in Chiapas highland villages are known as *cargos* (charges or duties) and are held by men. Women focus on domestic work, including weaving, though they also take a leading role in market trading.

Men take turns as cargo-holders. The duties normally last for one year, and include caring for the images of saints in churches and for the masks and costumes used in religious ceremonies. Other cargos entail organizing and paying for the ceremonies and celebrations that mark saints' days.

Taking on a cargo is both an honor and a burden. Only fairly prosperous villagers can afford the considerable expense involved: their wealth is thus turned to the benefit of all.

Among the Tzotziles, senior cargo-holders, called *mayordomos,* are responsible for the care of the saints' images. A mayordomo's expenses in San Juan Chamula can amount to US$5000 a year (and the village's patron saint San Juan Bautista has eight mayordomos). Other cargo-holders, *alféreces,* organize and pay for fiestas, while *capitanes* dance and ride horses at the fiestas. After successfully carrying out several cargos, men enter the ranks of the *principales,* or village elders.

walk south of the Pan-American Highway. The first 350m or so of the cave have a wooden walkway and are lit.

To get there take a Teopisca-bound combi from the Pan-American Highway, about 150m southeast of the Cristóbal Colón bus station, and ask for 'Las Grutas.'

Amatenango del Valle
• pop 3350

The women of this Tzeltal village, by the Pan-American Highway 37km southeast of San Cristóbal, are renowned potters. Amatenango pottery is still fired by a pre-Hispanic method, building a wood fire around the pieces rather than putting them in a kiln. In addition to everyday pots and jugs that the village has turned out for generations, young girls now find a ready tourist market with animalitos – little animal figures that are in-

expensive but fragile. If you visit the village, expect to be surrounded within minutes by girls selling these.

Amatenango women wear white huipiles with red and yellow embroidery, wide red belts and blue skirts.

From San Cristóbal, take a Comitán-bound bus or combi.

OCOSINGO
• pop 26,500 • elev 900m ☎ 919

Around the halfway mark of the 180km journey from San Cristóbal to Palenque, a trip that takes you down from cool, misty highlands to steaming, lowland jungle, is the town of Ocosingo, a busy market hub for a large area.

Ocosingo is only a few kilometers from the impressive Mayan ruins of Toniná, near which is a lovely guest ranch, Rancho Esmeralda, that is one of the most enjoyable places to stay in Chiapas. Ocosingo is also a jumping-off point for beautiful Laguna Miramar.

The market area, three blocks east downhill from the main plaza, is the liveliest part of town. Its Tianguis Campesino (Peasants' Market) section is for peasant producers to sell their goods direct: they sit on the bare ground to do so.

Although today there's no overt evidence, Ocosingo saw the bloodiest fighting in the 1994 Zapatista rebellion, with about 50 rebels killed here by the Mexican army.

Orientation & Information
Ocosingo spreads east (downhill) from highway 199, the San Cristóbal-Palenque road. Avenida Central runs down from the main road to the central plaza.

Serfin bank, on Calle Central Norte, which runs off the plaza beside Hotel Central, changes cash US dollars and US-dollar traveler's checks and has an ATM. Banamex on the plaza has another ATM. Red Toniná and Tu Espacio, both on Avenida 1 Norte almost opposite Serfin, provide Internet access for US$1.75 an hour.

Places to Stay
Hotel Central (☎ 673-00-24, Avenida Central 5) Singles/doubles/triples US$16/20/23. This hotel has a prime location on the north side of the main plaza, and simple, clean rooms with fan, bath and TV.

Hotel Nakum (☎ 673-02-80, *Calle Central Norte 19*) Singles/doubles/triples US$23/27/30. The Nakum, half a block north of Hotel Central, has the town's best rooms – recently upgraded and, again, with fan, bath and TV.

Hospedaje Las Palmas (*Avenida 1 Norte*) Singles/doubles with shared bath US$5.75/8. This adequately clean, family-run place is one block west and one north from the plaza.

Places to Eat

Ocosingo is known for its *queso amarillo* (yellow cheese), which comes in three-layered 1kg balls. The two outside layers are chewy, the middle is creamy.

You can get a comida for US$1.50 at comedores in the *mercado* on Avenida Sur Ote.

Restaurant La Montura (☎ 673-00-24, *Avenida Central 5*) Mains US$4.50-6.75. Set on the Hotel Central's veranda overlooking the plaza, this is a reliable restaurant, where a big breakfast of fruit, eggs, bread and coffee will cost you US$3.75.

Restaurant Los Portales (*Avenida Central 19*) Mains US$3-3.50. Los Portales, a few doors east of La Montura, is a straightforward place offering home-style cooking at good prices.

Pizzas El Desván (☎ 673-01-17, *Avenida 1 Sur Ote*) Pizzas US$4.50-13. Across the plaza from Los Portales, El Desván has bright orange and blue paintwork and a good upstairs location. Apart from pizzas there are other possibilities, including breakfasts.

Getting There & Away

The company Servicios Aéreos San Cristóbal (☎ 673-01-88) does small-plane charters from Ocosingo's airstrip, about 4km out of town along the Toniná road. Possible destinations include Bonampak and Yaxchilán (around US$150 a person for four or five people) or San Quintín (near Laguna Miramar; see that section, later in this chapter).

The main transportation terminals are on highway 199, in the three blocks north (downhill) from the intersection of Avenida Central. First, on the east side of the road after 1½ blocks, is the stop for the 2nd-class buses of Transportes Lacandonia (TL) and Autotransportes Yaxnichil (AY). *Camione-*

tas (pickups) to Palenque go from the side street opposite here. Autotransportes Tuxtla Gutiérrez (ATG, 2nd-class buses) and Cristóbal Colón (1st-class buses) are on the left (west), 1½ blocks on down the highway, with Transportes Dr Rodulfo Figueroa (TRF, 1st-class) opposite them.

Most buses are *de paso*. Departures include the following:

Palenque – 103km, 2½ hours; 12 Colón (US$5.50-7), 4 TRF (US$5), 6 ATG (US$5), TL/AY every 30 minutes 5am-5pm (US$4.50), irregular camionetas (US$4.50)

San Cristóbal de Las Casas – 88km, 1¾ hours; 10 Colón (US$3.75-4.75), 4 TRF (US$3.50), 6 ATG (US$3.25), TL/AY every 30 minutes 5am-5pm (US$2.25)

Tuxtla Gutiérrez – 170km, 3½ hours; 10 Colón (US$7-9.25), 4 TRF (US$6), 6 ATG (US$5.75)

Colón and/or ATG also run buses to Campeche, Cancún, Chetumal, Mérida, Mexico City and Villahermosa.

TONINÁ
● elev 900m ☎ 919

The Mayan ruins of Toniná, 14km east of Ocosingo, don't match Palenque, 95km north, for beauty or extent, but they form an expansive and intriguing site overlooking a lovely pastoral valley, and they have a very interesting history. Also, an excellent site museum has recently opened here. It's worth taking a flashlight to help you explore some of the passages.

Toniná was not excavated until 1979. Since then archaeologists have concluded that it was Toniná that brought about the downfall of Palenque. The prelude to Toniná's heyday was the inauguration of the Snake Skull-Jaguar Claw dynasty in the late 7th century. The new rulers, who seem to have had an extraordinarily bleak and harsh view of the world, demolished their predecessors' palaces and temples, erected new ones, and declared war on Palenque about AD 690. At least three Palenque leaders were held prisoner at Toniná. One, Kan-Xul II, probably had his head lopped off here around AD 720.

Toniná was at its most powerful in the decade following its devastation of Palenque in 730. It became known as the Place of the Celestial Captives, for in some of its chambers were held the captured rulers of Palenque and other Maya cities, destined either to be ransomed for large sums or to be decapitated. A recurring image in Toniná sculpture is that of captives before decapitation, thrown to the ground with their hands tied.

Around AD 900 Toniná was rebuilt again, in a simpler, austere style. But Jaguar Serpent, in 903, was the last Toniná ruler of whom any record has been found. Classic Mayan civilization was ending here, as elsewhere.

The Site

There are few explanatory signs at the ruins (admission US$3.50, free Sun; open 9am–4pm daily), but the new **museum** near the site entrance explains Toniná's history and background, in Spanish.

Many of the site's stone facings and interior walls were originally covered in paint or frescoes. The path from the entrance and museum crosses a stream and climbs to the broad, flat **Gran Plaza**. At the south end of the Gran Plaza is the **Templo de la Guerra Cósmica** (Temple of Cosmic War), with five altars in front of it. Off a side of the plaza is a **juego de pelota** (ball court), which was inaugurated around 780 under the rule of the female regent Smoking Mirror. A decapitation altar stands beside it.

To the north rises the great pyramid of Toniná, a semi-natural hillside terraced into a number of platforms. At the right-hand end of the steps rising from the first to the second platform is the entry to a **ritual labyrinth** of passages.

Higher up on the right-hand side is the **Palacio de las Grecas y de la Guerra** (Palace of the Grecas and War), a greca being a band of geometrical decoration, in this case a zigzag X-shape in the stone facing of one of the walls. The zigzag may represent Quetzalcóatl and is also a flight of steps (and you're not allowed to step on it!). To the right of the X is a rambling series of chambers, passages and stairways, believed to have been Toniná's administrative headquarters.

Higher again, still toward the right-hand side of the stepped-and-terraced hillside, is the most remarkable sculpture of Toniná, the **Mural de las Cuatro Eras** (Mural of the Four Eras). Created sometime between AD 790 and 840, this stucco relief of four panels (the first, from the left end, has been lost) represents the four suns, or four eras of

human history, in Maya belief. At the center of each panel is the upside-down head of a decapitated prisoner. Blood spurting from the prisoner's neck forms a ring of feathers and, at the same time, a sun. In one panel, a dancing skeleton holds a decapitated head with its tongue out. To the left of the head is a lord of the underworld, who resembles an enormous rodent. This mural was created at a time when a wave of destruction was running through the Maya world. The people of Toniná believed themselves to be living in the fourth sun, that of winter, mirrors, the direction north and the end of human life.

Near the middle of the same level you'll find a tomb with a stone sarcophagus. Up the next steps is the seventh level, with remains of four temples. Behind the second temple from the left, steps descend into the very narrow **Tumba de Treinta Metros** (Thirty-Meter Tomb), which is definitely not for the claustrophobic or obese!

Above here is the acropolis, the abode of the rulers of Toniná and site of its eight most important temples – four on each of two levels. The right-hand temple on the lower level, the **Templo del Monstruo de la Tierra** (Temple of the Earth Monster), has Toniná's best-preserved roof comb, built around AD 713.

The topmost level has two tall temples behind and two smaller ones in front. The top of the tallest, the **Templo del Espejo Humeante** (Temple of the Smoking Mirror), is 80m above the Gran Plaza. This temple was built by Zots-Choj, who took the throne in AD 842. In that era of the fourth and final sun and the direction north, Zots-Choj needed to raise this, Toniná's northernmost temple, higher than all the others, which necessitated a large, artificial northeast extension of the hill.

Places to Stay

Rancho Esmeralda (fax 673-07-11, **W** www.ranchoesmeralda.net) Singles & doubles US$28-33, 4- or 5-person cabañas US$48, camping US$5.75 per person. The relaxing, immaculate Rancho Esmeralda is set amid rolling, green countryside just a 15-minute walk from Toniná ruins (but a loop of about 6km by road). Its welcoming American owners, Ellen Jones and Glen Wersch, settled here in 1994 because the altitude is just right for the macadamia grove they have planted. Their comfortable guest cabañas are set on grassy lawns. A separate camping and RV area lies beyond a small stream. Excellent meals are served (breakfast US$4.50, dinner US$8). Horse rides on the ranch's well-kept animals are popular, and they can also arrange day trips by plane to Yaxchilán and Bonampak.

Getting There & Away
Combis to Toniná (US$1.25) leave from a stop opposite the Tianguis Campesino in Ocosingo, every half-hour from early morning to 5pm or 6pm.

A taxi from Ocosingo to Rancho Esmeralda is around US$5. Alternatively, take a Toniná-bound combi from Ocosingo and get off after about 8km at a signed turnoff opposite a military base, from which it's 1.5km along a dirt road to the *rancho*.

LAGUNA MIRAMAR
• elev 400m
Beautiful, pristine Laguna Miramar, 100km southeast of Ocosingo, is the largest lake in the Lacandón Jungle. It's accessible to visitors thanks to a successful community ecotourism project by the village near its western shore, Ejido Emiliano Zapata.

Surrounded by hills covered in rain forest and echoing with the roars of howler monkeys, the 16-sq-km lake has a beautiful temperature all year and is virtually unpolluted, one of the last expanses of water in Mexico of which that can be said. The lake is within the Montes Azules biosphere reserve and the four *ejidos* (communal landholdings) surrounding it have agreed to use no motorboats on the lake and to keep a 1km band around it free of settlement, farming and extractive activities.

A visit to Miramar is a unique close encounter with nature. Ejido life in Emiliano Zapata – a poor but well-ordered community of 800 people, founded in 1968 by Chol and Tzotzil settlers from northern Chiapas – is fascinating too. It is forbidden to bring alcohol or drugs into the community.

You can visit Miramar in an organized group or on your own. Prices for independent visitors are reasonable. In either case it's a good idea to contact in advance the architect of the ecotourism project, Fernando Ochoa, in San Cristóbal (see Organized

Tours, below, for contact details). Fernando, who speaks excellent English, takes groups to the lake and will provide other visitors with important information and advice.

Ideally, try to visit outside the rainy period from late August to the end of October, when land access can be more difficult and foot trails muddy.

When you reach Emiliano Zapata, ask for the Presidente de la Laguna (the villager in charge of lake matters) and/or the Comisariado (equivalent to the mayor). Fernando Ochoa can tell you the names of the people currently occupying these posts. Through them you must arrange details of your visit and pay for the services you need – US$11 a day for a guide (US$22 with an overnight stay at the lake), US$3.50 per person for a night's stay, US$5.50 for a porter to or from the lake (optional), US$11 a day for use of a *cayuco* (canoe; optional). The village is a spread-out place of huts and a few concrete communal buildings, on a gentle slope running down to the Río Perlas, which is the village's beautiful bathing place.

The 7km walk from village to lake, through milpas and forest, takes about 1½ hours. Guides will point out trees like the *caoba* (mahogany) and what they call the *matapalo*, which strangles other trees. Around the lake you hear the incessant growls of howler monkeys (*saraguatos*) and may see these and spider monkeys (*monos arañas*). You may hear jaguars at night. Birdlife includes macaws, toucans and prolific butterflies. Locals fish for perch (*mojarra*) in the lake, and will assure you that its few crocodiles are not dangerous.

It takes about 45 minutes to canoe across to Isla Lacan-Tun, an island covered in overgrown remains from the pre-Hispanic Chol-Lacantún people, who survived here unconquered by the Spanish until the 1580s.

Organized Tours
Fernando Ochoa (☎ 967-678-04-68, ⓔ don fer8a@prodigy.net.mx, Calle Dr Navarro 10, Barrio del Cerrillo, San Cristóbal de Las Casas) Trips for groups of three to eight last four days (and three nights) from San Cristóbal, and cost US$350 a person including transportation from San Cristóbal to Ocosingo and back, flights from Ocosingo to San Quintín and back,

equipment, good food, porters and all other fees at the ejido and lake.

Turismo Comunitario (see Organized Tours in the San Cristóbal section, earlier in this chapter) also offers Miramar trips.

Places to Stay & Eat

At the lakeshore you can camp or sling a hammock under a *palapa* shelter. A small guest house next to the Río Perlas in Ejido Emiliano Zapata, *Posada Zapata*, with five rooms, a hammock area, showers and lockers, was due to open in 2002. Costs for lodging (in addition to the regular US$3.50 per person overnight fee) were to be US$3.50 per person in a hammock and US$13.50/17 for single/double rooms, with breakfast and dinner available in villagers' homes.

Food supplies in Emiliano Zapata's couple of stores are very basic. You may be able to obtain tortillas in the mornings. There are a few slightly better stocked stores and a couple of simple comedores in neighboring San Quintín.

Getting There & Away

To reach Emiliano Zapata you must first get to the neighboring ejido, San Quintín, which has an airstrip and a large Mexican army base. From the bus stop in San Quintín, walk five minutes along the airstrip and turn down a dirt road to the right, opposite a complex of military buildings. From here it's a 15- or 20-minute walk to the middle of Ejido Emiliano Zapata.

Air Small planes of Servicios Aéreos San Cristóbal (see Getting There & Away in the Ocosingo section) leave Ocosingo most mornings for San Quintín. If you're at the airstrip by 9.30am you should get a place. The one-way fare is US$39. Return flight times are less reliable, but there's one most days.

Bus & Truck You can get to San Quintín from Ocosingo and from Las Margaritas, 17km east of Comitán. The latter is quicker if you're starting from San Cristóbal de Las Casas.

From Ocosingo, four or five buses, microbuses or passenger-carrying trucks (*'tres toneladas'*) run daily to San Quintín from a stop a few meters south of the town's Tianguis Campesino. There's nearly always something leaving at 9am or 9.30am, and

often 10am or 11am too. The 130km trip costs US$7 and takes up to eight hours, nearly all along a dirt road following some of the river valleys east of Ocosingo known as Las Cañadas de Ocosingo. Inhabited mainly by Tzeltal indigenous people, this is one of the main areas of support for the Zapatistas. Your documents may be checked at Mexican army checkpoints as you travel through; keep your passport and tourist card handy.

Vehicles head back from San Quintín to Ocosingo at 8am, 2pm and midnight.

To go from Las Margaritas, first take a combi or colectivo taxi (both US$1, 20-30 minutes) to Las Margaritas from 6ª Calle Sur Ote 51 in Comitán. (Comitán is served by frequent transportation from San Cristóbal – see the San Cristóbal de Las Casas section, earlier.) Microbuses or trucks to San Quintín (US$8, about six hours) normally leave Las Margaritas plaza at 10am and 1pm daily. The Las Margaritas-San Quintín road is also unpaved, but it's a shorter trip than from Ocosingo. On the way you pass the village of La Realidad, the main Zapatista base.

AGUA AZUL, AGUA CLARA & MISOL-HA

Three short detours off the Ocosingo-Palenque road lead to beautiful water attractions: the thundering cascades of Agua Azul, the turquoise Río Shumulha at Agua Clara and the spectacular waterfall of Misol-Ha.

All three can be visited in an organized day tour from Palenque – perhaps best if time is precious – but it's quite possible to go independently, and there are accommodations at Misol-Ha.

The road between Ocosingo and Palenque has at times been the scene of highway robberies. It's not advisable to be waiting around for transportation on highway 199 after about 5pm.

Agua Azul

The turnoff for the superb waterfalls of Agua Azul is about halfway between Ocosingo and Palenque. Scores of dazzling white waterfalls thunder into turquoise pools surrounded by jungle.

On holidays and weekends the place is thronged; at other times you'll have few companions. Note that the beautiful blue water color that gives the place its name may be evident only in April and May. Silt can cloud the waters in other months.

The temptation to swim is great but take extreme care. The current is deceptively fast, and there are many submerged hazards like rocks and dead trees. Use your judgment to identify slower, safer areas. People do drown here.

The falls are in the territory of an **ejido** *(admission US$1.75 per person on foot, US$2.25 per car)*. A paved road leads 4.5km down from highway 199 to a parking lot and the cluster of *comedores* near the main falls. Most of the comedores have similar menus, charging around US$3.50 for fish/meat/chicken dishes.

It's worth walking 1km or so up the riverside path to get away from the crowds: you pass the main falls but the tropical river is just as beautiful, and in places safer for swimming. People walking alone have occasionally been robbed in isolated spots up here, so exercise caution.

About 2km downstream is another set of falls, Cascadas Bolón-Ahau, just before the river from Agua Azul flows into the Río Shumulhá.

Agua Clara

About 8km after the Agua Azul turnoff, heading toward Palenque, another signed detour leads 2km by paved road to Agua Clara. Here the Río Shumulhá (or Tulijá) is a beautiful, broad, shallow expanse of turquoise water that's a delight to swim in (but test the current before choosing your spot). You can also take a stroll across a hanging footbridge or, in winter, rent a kayak (US$3.50 an hour).

Misol-Ha

About 20km south of Palenque, the Río Misol-Ha drops 35m into a wide pool surrounded by lush tropical vegetation. A path behind the main fall leads into a cave with some smaller trickles of water. The waterfall is 1.5km off highway 199 and the turn is signposted. Admission is US$1.75 per person.

Centro Turístico Ejidal Cascada Misol-Ha (☎/fax 916-345-12-10) Single or double cabins US$17, family cabin with kitchen US$32. These good wooden cabins near the falls have bathrooms and mosquito netting. There's a restaurant nearby, open till 6pm.

Getting There & Away

Many Palenque travel agencies offer daily trips to Misol-Ha and Agua Azul, with Agua Clara as a possible extra. See the list of agencies under Organized Tours in the Palenque section, then check out a few current deals. Most trips last around seven hours, spending half an hour at Misol-Ha and three hours at Agua Azul. The basic price is about US$9 including admission fees but not food. Add a couple of dollars each for extras such as breakfast or air-conditioned transportation. You may also have to pay more if you wish to visit Agua Clara.

To do it independently, take a *camioneta* (pickup) from Cárdenas, off Juárez a block west of the Colón/ADO bus station in Palenque, or any 2nd-class bus along highway 199; they will drop you at any of the three intersections. The fare from Palenque to the Agua Azul junction *(crucero)* is US$2.25. From San Cristóbal, a Figueroa bus will take you to the Agua Azul junction for US$5.75.

The distances from the highway to Misol-Ha and Agua Clara are manageable on foot. For the 4.5km between the Agua Azul crucero and Agua Azul itself, there are camionetas for US$1. Check out times of camionetas going back to the crucero, as it's uphill in that direction.

A taxi from Palenque to Misol-Ha with a one-hour wait costs around US$28; to Agua Azul with a two-hour wait should be US$55.

PALENQUE
• pop 30,000 • elev 80m ☎ 916

The ancient Mayan city of Palenque, with its superb jungle setting and exquisite architecture and decoration, is one of the marvels of Mexico. Modern Palenque town, a few kilometers to the east, is a sweaty, humdrum place with little attraction except as a base for visiting the ruins.

History

The name Palenque (Palisade) is Spanish and has no relation to the city's ancient name, which according to current theories was probably Baak. Palenque was first occupied around 100 BC. It flourished from about AD 600 to 700, and what a glorious century that was! The city rose to prominence under K'inich Hanab Pakal (generally known just as Pakal), a club-footed king who reigned from AD 615 to 683. Archaeologists have determined that Pakal is represented by hieroglyphics of sun and shield, and he is also referred to as Sun Shield (in Spanish, Escudo Solar) or White Macaw (Guacamaya Blanca). He lived to the age of 80.

During Pakal's reign, many plazas and buildings, including the superlative Templo de las Inscripciones (Pakal's own mausoleum), were constructed in Palenque. The structures were characterized by mansard roofs and very fine stucco bas-reliefs.

Pakal was succeeded by his son K'inich Kan Balam II, who is symbolized in hieroglyphics by the jaguar and the serpent (and also called Jaguar Serpent II). Kan Balam continued Palenque's political and economic expansion and artistic development. He completed his father's crypt in the Templo de las Inscripciones and presided over the construction of the Grupo de las Cruces temples, placing sizable narrative stone steles within each.

During Kan Balam II's reign, the rival Maya city of Toniná, 65km to the south, declared war on Palenque. Toniná's hostility was probably the major factor in Palenque's precipitous decline after Kan Balam's death in 702. Kan Balam's brother and successor, K'an Hoy Chitam II, was captured by forces from Toniná and probably executed there. Palenque may have enjoyed a brief final resurgence under K'inich Ahkal Mo' Nahb' III, who took the throne in 722 and added many substantial buildings during a rule of perhaps 15 years.

After AD 900 Palenque was largely abandoned. In an area that receives the heaviest rainfall in Mexico, the ruins were soon overgrown.

Orientation

Highway 199 meets Palenque town's main street, Juárez, at the Glorieta de la Cabeza Maya, an intersection with a large statue of a Maya chieftain's head, at the west end of the town. From here Juárez heads 1km east to the central square, El Parque. The main bus stations are on Juárez just east of the Maya head statue.

A few hundred meters south of the Maya head, the 7.5km road to the Palenque ruins diverges west off highway 199. This road passes the site museum after 6km, then winds on 1.5km to the main entrance to the ruins.

Information

The helpful tourist office (no ☎), on Juárez at Abasolo, has reliable town and transportation information and a few maps. It's open 9am to 9pm Monday to Saturday, 9am to 1pm Sunday.

The Instituto Nacional de Migración (☎ 345-07-95) is about 6km north of town on highway 199. It's normally open 8am to 2pm and 5pm to 8pm daily. You can get there by Transportes Otolum or Transportes Palenque combis from their terminals on Allende.

Bancomer, on Juárez 1½ blocks west of El Parque, changes US dollars cash and US-dollar traveler's checks from 9am to noon Monday to Friday. Outside those hours, try travel agents if you don't have a card for the ATMs at Bancomer or at Banamex, a block farther west on Juárez.

The post office, at Independencia and Bravo one block from El Parque, is open 7am to 4pm Monday to Friday and 8am to noon Saturday. You'll find pay phones around El Parque, along Juárez and elsewhere, and a few telephone casetas on Juárez. TNet, on Independencia just south of El Parque, is open 8am to 11pm daily, with Internet access for US$1.25 an hour. Red M@ya, Juárez 133, offers air-conditioned Internet access for US$1.25/1.75 per half-hour/hour, 8.30am to midnight daily.

The *lavandería* on 5 de Mayo opposite Hotel Kashlan will wash and dry 3kg for US$4.50 (same-day service if you drop off in the morning). It's open Monday to Saturday.

A recommended English-speaking doctor is Dr Alfonso Martínez at Clínica Palenque (☎ 345-15-13), Velasco Suárez 33.

Palenque Ruins

Ancient Palenque *(site & museum admission US$4, free Sun & holidays; site open 8am-5pm daily, museum 9am-4pm daily)* stands at the precise point where the first hills rise out of the Gulf Coast plain, and the dense green jungle covering these hills forms a superb backdrop to Palenque's outstanding Maya architecture. The ruins are

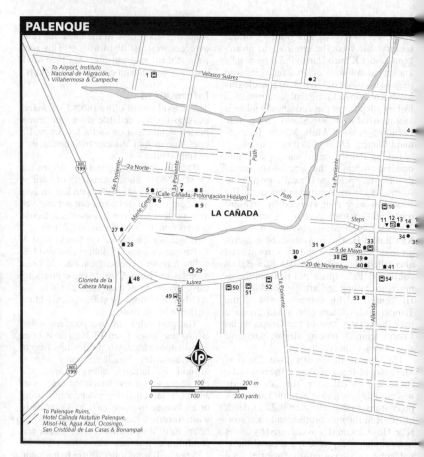

PALENQUE

To Airport, Instituto
Nacional de Migración,
Villahermosa & Campeche

Velasco Suárez

2a Norte

(Calle Cañada, Prolongación Hidalgo)

LA CAÑADA

Path

Steps

5 de Mayo

20 de Noviembre

Glorieta de la
Cabeza Maya

Juárez

0   100   200 m
0   100   200 yards

To Palenque Ruins,
Hotel Calinda Nututun Palenque,
Misol-Ha, Agua Azul, Ocosingo,
San Cristóbal de Las Casas & Bonampak

made up of some 500 buildings spread over
15 sq km, but only relatively few, in a fairly
compact central area, have been excavated.
Everything you see here was built without
metal tools, pack animals or the wheel. As
you explore the ruins, try to picture the gray
stone edifices as they would have been at
the peak of Palenque's power: painted
bright red. The forest around them is home
to toucans, ocelots and monkeys; you may
hear the howler monkeys, especially if you
stay near the ruins.

The best way to visit is to take a combi or
taxi to the main (upper) entrance, see the
major ruins (the Templo de las Inscripciones
group, El Palacio and the Grupo de las
Cruces), exploring nearby lesser ones as you
please, then walk downhill to the museum,

visiting minor ruins along the way (with a
dip in the pools along Arroyo Otolum if the
fancy takes you). From the museum you can
catch a combi back to town.

A good time to visit is at opening time,
when it's cooler and not too crowded and
morning mist may still be wrapping the
temples in a picturesque haze.

Bring sunscreen. Refreshments, hats and
souvenirs (including quivers of arrows sold
by Lacandones) are available from the
hawker circus outside the entrance, and
there are cafés here and at the museum.
Guides are available from a kiosk by the entrance (a two-hour tour for up to seven
people costs US$38).

An excellent place to read up on
Palenque is the official Web site of some

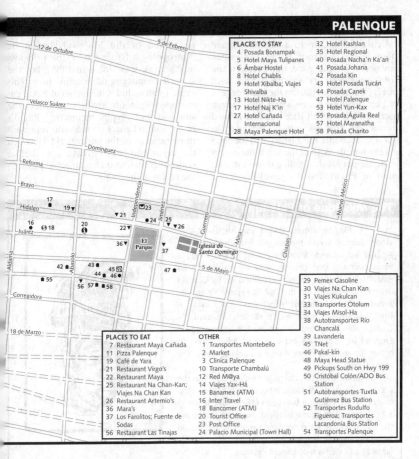

PALENQUE

PLACES TO STAY
4 Posada Bonampak
5 Hotel Maya Tulipanes
6 Ámbar Hostel
8 Hotel Chablis
9 Hotel Xibalba; Viajes Shivalba
13 Hotel Nikte-Ha
17 Hotel Naj K'in
27 Hotel Cañada Internacional
28 Maya Palenque Hotel
32 Hotel Kashlan
35 Hotel Regional
40 Posada Nacha'n Ka'an
41 Posada Johana
42 Posada Kin
43 Hotel Posada Tucán
44 Posada Canek
47 Hotel Palenque
53 Hotel Yun-Kax
55 Posada Águila Real
57 Hotel Maranatha
58 Posada Charito

PLACES TO EAT
7 Restaurant Maya Cañada
11 Pizza Palenque
19 Café de Yara
21 Restaurant Virgo's
22 Restaurant Maya
25 Restaurant Na Chan-Kan; Viajes Na Chan Kan
26 Restaurant Artemio's
36 Mara's
37 Los Farolitos; Fuente de Sodas
56 Restaurant Las Tinajas

OTHER
1 Transportes Montebello
2 Market
3 Clínica Palenque
10 Transporte Chambalú
12 Red M@ya
14 Viajes Yax-Há
15 Banamex (ATM)
16 Inter Travel
18 Bancomer (ATM)
20 Tourist Office
23 Post Office
24 Palacio Municipal (Town Hall)
29 Pemex Gasoline
30 Viajes Na Chan Kan
31 Viajes Kukulcan
33 Transportes Otolum
34 Viajes Misol-Ha
38 Autotransportes Río Chancalá
39 Lavandería
45 TNet
46 Pakal-kin
48 Maya Head Statue
49 Pickups South on Hwy 199
50 Cristóbal Colón/ADO Bus Station
51 Autotransportes Tuxtla Gutiérrez Bus Station
52 Transportes Rodulfo Figueroa; Transportes Lacandonia Bus Station
54 Transportes Palenque

of the archaeologists who are working here, **w** www.mesoweb.com/palenque.

Templo de las Inscripciones Group As you emerge through the trees from the entrance, a line of temples rising in front of the jungle on your right comes into view. Below them is the tomb of archaeologist Alberto Ruz Lhuillier.

First (at the western end of the group) is Templo XII, called the **Templo de la Calavera** (Temple of the Skull) for the relief sculpture of a rabbit or deer skull at the foot of one its pillars. The second temple has little interest. Third is **Templo XIII**, containing a tomb where in 1994 was found a female skeleton, colored red as a result of treatment with cinnabar. You can enter this

'Tumba de la Reina Roja' (Tomb of the Red Queen) to see her sarcophagus. With the skeleton were found a malachite mask and about 1000 pieces of jade, but no inscriptions to tell who the 'queen' was. Some speculate, from resemblances to Pakal's tomb next door, that she was his wife.

The line of temples culminates in the **Templo de las Inscripciones** (Temple of the Inscriptions), the tallest and most stately of Palenque's buildings. Owing to inevitable damage to its murals from the humidity exuded by hordes of visitors, in 2001 this temple was closed for restoration work: it was expected to reopen on a very restricted basis, with a maximum of 20 visitors per day, possibly only between 4 and 5pm.

TABASCO & CHIAPAS

Constructed on eight levels, the Templo de las Inscripciones has a central front staircase rising 25m to a series of small rooms. The tall roof comb that once crowned it is long gone, but between the front doorways are stucco panels with reliefs of noble figures. On the interior rear wall are the three panels with a long Mayan inscription, for which Ruz Lhuillier named the temple. The inscription, dedicated in AD 692, recounts the history of Palenque and the temple. Also at the top is the access to the slippery stairs leading down into the tomb of Pakal. Pakal's jewel-bedecked skeleton and jade mosaic death mask were removed to Mexico City, and the tomb was re-created in the Museo Nacional de Antropología (from where the priceless death mask was stolen in 1985), but the stone sarcophagus lid remains here. This carved slab includes the image of Pakal encircled by serpents, mythical monsters, the sun god and glyphs recounting Pakal's reign. Stucco figures on the walls represent the nine lords of the underworld. Between the crypt and the staircase, a snakelike hollow ventilation tube connected Pakal to the realm of the living.

The Mystique of Palenque

In 1773, Mayan hunters told a Spanish priest that stone palaces lay in the jungle. Father Ordóñez y Aguilar led an expedition to Palenque and wrote a book claiming that the city was the capital of an Atlantis-like civilization. An expedition led by Captain Antonio del Río set out in 1787 to explore Palenque. Although his subsequent report was locked away in the Guatemalan archives, a British resident of Guatemala translated it and had it published in England in 1822. This led a host of adventurers to brave malaria and other dangers tracking down the hidden city.

Among the most colorful of these characters was the eccentric Count de Waldeck, who, in his 60s, lived atop one of the pyramids for two years (1831-33). He wrote a book, complete with fraudulent drawings that made the city resemble great Mediterranean civilizations. In Europe, Palenque became mythologized as a lost Atlantis or an extension of ancient Egypt.

In 1837, John L Stephens, an amateur archaeology enthusiast from New York, reached Palenque with artist Frederick Catherwood. Stephens wrote insightfully about the six pyramids he started to excavate and the city's aqueduct system. His was the first scientific investigation, paving the way for research by other serious scholars, over some of whom Palenque has exerted a lifetime's enchantment. Among these would definitely be counted Alberto Ruz Lhuillier, the tireless Mexican archaeologist who revealed many of Palenque's mysteries – including King Pakal's secret crypt in 1952 – and American Merle Green Robertson, who has compiled a unique record of Palenque's art in the form of drawings, tracings or rubbings of practically every stone in the place.

In 1973 Dr Robertson organized the first Palenque Round Table, an innovative, interdisciplinary get-together of experts, which gave Maya studies a big impetus. Dr Robertson has a street named for her in Palenque and in 1994 received the highest Mexican honor bestowable on foreigners, the Aztec Eagle.

Frans Blom, a mid-20th-century investigator, remarked: 'The first visit to Palenque is immensely impressive. When one has lived there for some time this ruined city becomes an obsession.' It's not hard to understand why.

alla lilies going to market, Chiapas

)awn in San Cristóbal de Las Casas

Villahermosa's pedestrian mall

Ancient Mayan city of Palenque, Chiapas

RICHARD I'ANSON

Atop El Castillo, Chichén Itzá, Yucatán

JOHN ELK III

Museo Regional de Antropología, Mérida

DALE BUCKTON

Blanket for sale, Isla Mujeres, Quintana Roo

ERIC L WHEATER

Mayan girls sharing a joke, Yucatán

SCOTT DOGGETT

Cancún's party scene

SCOTT DOGGETT

Sunbathers, Cancún

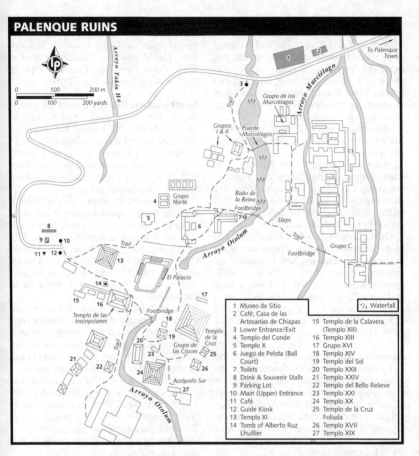

PALENQUE RUINS

```
0    100    200 m
0    100    200 yards
```

To Palenque Town

Arroyo Tukin Ha

Arroyo Murciélago

3 — Trail

Grupo de los Murciélagos

Grupos I & II — Puente Murciélagos

Grupo Norte — 4

5 — 6

Baño de la Reina Footbridge — 7

Steps

Arroyo Otolum

Trail — Grupo C

Footbridge

8 — 9 — 10 — 11 — 12 — Trail

13 — El Palacio

14 — 17

15 — 16 — Footbridge — 18

Templo de las Inscripciones — 19 — Templo de la Cruz

20 — 23 — 25

21 — 22 — 24 — 26

Grupo de las Cruces — Acrópolis Sur — 27

Arroyo Otolum

Waterfall

1	Museo de Sitio
2	Café; Casa de las Artesanías de Chiapas
3	Lower Entrance/Exit
4	Templo del Conde
5	Templo X
6	Juego de Pelota (Ball Court)
7	Toilets
8	Drink & Souvenir Stalls
9	Parking Lot
10	Main (Upper) Entrance
11	Café
12	Guide Kiosk
13	Templo XI
14	Tomb of Alberto Ruz Lhuillier
15	Templo de la Calavera (Templo XII)
16	Templo XIII
17	Grupo XVI
18	Templo XIV
19	Templo del Sol
20	Templo XXII
21	Templo XXIV
22	Templo del Bello Relieve
23	Templo XXI
24	Templo XX
25	Templo de la Cruz Foliada
26	Templo XVII
27	Templo XIX

El Palacio Diagonally opposite the Templo de las Inscripciones is the Palace, a large, complex structure divided into four main courtyards, with a maze of corridors and rooms. Its tower, restored in 1955, has fine stucco reliefs on the walls, but is not open to visitors. Archaeologists believe the tower was constructed so that Mayan royalty and priests could observe the sun falling directly into the Templo de las Inscripciones during the winter solstice.

The northeastern courtyard, the Patio de los Cautivos (Patio of the Captives), contains a collection of relief sculptures that seem disproportionately large for their setting: it's conjectured that they are representations of conquered rulers and were brought from elsewhere.

Grupo de las Cruces Although Pakal had only one building dedicated to him during his 68-year reign (the Templo de las Inscripciones), his son Kan Balam II had four. Known today as the Grupo de las Cruces (Group of the Crosses), these are arranged in beautiful formation around a plaza southeast of the Templo de las Inscripciones. The 'cross' carvings figuring in some buildings here symbolize the ceiba tree which in Maya belief held up the universe.

The **Templo del Sol** (Temple of the Sun) on the west side of the plaza has the best-preserved roof comb at Palenque. Carvings inside, commemorating Kan Balam's birth in AD 635 and accession in 684, show him facing his father. At least one guide at Palenque will have you believe that some of the carvings on the roof represent a Chinese dragon and the Buddha, and that all this stuff about Pakal, Kan Balam and company is so much hocus-pocus. Others view this beautiful building as sure proof that Palenque's ancient architects were inspired by the same magic mushrooms as some modern-day travelers enjoy around here. Make up your own mind!

The smaller, less well preserved **Templo XIV** has tablets showing Kan Balam doing a ritual dance.

Steep steps climb to the **Templo de la Cruz** (Temple of the Cross), the largest in this group. Carvings in the central sanctuary show the God L smoking tobacco, and Kan Balam. Behind is a reproduction of a panel depicting Kan Balam's accession.

On the **Templo de la Cruz Foliada** (Temple of the Foliated Cross), the corbel arches are fully exposed, revealing how Palenque's architects designed these buildings. A well-preserved inscribed tablet shows a king (probably Pakal) with a sun shield emblazoned on his chest, corn growing from his shoulder blades and the sacred quetzal bird on his head.

Acrópolis Sur In the jungle south of the Grupo de las Cruces is the Southern Acropolis, where archaeologists have focused their most recent excavations. You may find part of the area roped off. The Acrópolis Sur appears to have been constructed as an extension of the Grupo de las Cruces, with both groups set around what was probably a single long open space.

Templo XVII, between the Cruces group and the Southern Acropolis, contains a reproduction carved panel depicting a standing figure with a bound captive kneeling before him.

In **Templo XIX**, in 1999 diggers made the most important Palenque find for decades, an 8th-century limestone platform with beautiful carvings of seated figures and hieroglyphic texts. A reproduction is in its place now. The central of the seven figures on the long south side of the platform is the ruler in whose reign this temple was dedicated, K'inich Ahkal Mo' Nahb' III. Also on view is a reproduction of a colorful tall stucco relief.

In **Templo XX**, a tomb of an unknown personage, with many murals, was found in 1999.

Grupo Norte North of El Palacio are a **ball court** and the handsome buildings of the Northern Group. Crazy Count de Waldeck (see 'The Mystique of Palenque') lived in the so-called Templo del Conde (Temple of the Count), constructed in AD 647.

Northeastern Groups East of the Grupo Norte, the main path crosses Arroyo Otolum. Some 70m beyond the stream, a right fork will take you to **Grupo C**, a set of buildings and plazas on different levels, thought to have been lived in from about AD 750 to 800. Large trees now grow from some of these buildings.

If you stay on the main path, you'll find it descends steep steps to a group of low, elongated buildings, thought to have been occupied residentially around AD 770 to 850. The path goes alongside the Arroyo Otolum, which here tumbles down a series of small falls forming delicious natural bathing pools known as the **Baño de la Reina** (Queen's Bath).

The path continues to another residential quarter, the **Grupo de los Murciélagos** (Bat Group), then crosses the **Puente Murciélagos** (Bat Bridge), a suspension footbridge across Arroyo Otolum. The stream here has another series of inviting falls and pools.

Across the bridge and a bit farther downstream, a path goes west to **Grupos 1 and 2**, a short walk uphill. These ruins, only partly uncovered, are in a beautiful jungle setting. The main path continues downriver to the road, where the museum is along to the right a short distance.

Museo de Sitio Palenque's Site Museum does a fine job of displaying finds from the site and interpreting Palenque's history. It includes a copy of the lid of Pakal's sarcophagus. Next door are a pleasant café and a shop selling some of Chiapas' best handicrafts.

Getting There & Away A paved roadside footpath, some parts shaded, runs from the Maya head statue all the way to the museum, about 6km.

Transporte Chambalú, on Allende at Hidalgo, and Transportes Palenque, Allende at 20 de Noviembre, operate combis to the ruins about every 15 minutes from around 6am to 6pm daily (US$0.80 one way). The vehicles will pick you up anywhere along the town-to-ruins road. A taxi from town to ruins costs US$4.50.

Organized Tours

Several agencies in Palenque offer transportation packages to Agua Azul, Agua Clara and Misol-Ha, to Bonampak and Yaxchilán, and to Flores (Guatemala). See the sections To/From Guatemala via Tenosique and Agua Azul, Agua Clara & Misol-Ha, earlier, and Bonampak, Yaxchilán & the Carretera Fronteriza later in this chapter for more information. Agencies include the following:

Inter Travel (☎ 345-15-66, Juárez 48)

Pakal-kin (☎ 345-11-97, Independencia s/n)

Transporte Chambalú (☎ 345-08-67, Hidalgo at Allende)

Transportes Palenque (Allende at 20 de Noviembre)

Viajes Kukulcan (☎ 345-15-06, Juárez s/n)

Viajes Misol-Ha (☎ 345-08-16, Juárez 27)

Viajes Na Chan Kan (☎ 345-02-63, Hidalgo at Jiménez, and Juárez s/n)

Viajes Shivalba (☎ 345-04-11, Merle Green 9, La Cañada)

Viajes Yax-Há (☎ 345-07-98, Juárez 123)

Places to Stay

Many places to stay are in Palenque town but there are others (including campgrounds) along the road to the ruins. Combis from town will stop anywhere on the ruins road.

Prices given here are for the high season, which at most establishments is from mid-July to mid-August, mid-December to early January, and Semana Santa. Rates at some places fall by up to 35% at other times.

Budget You have plenty of options both in the town and along the 7.5km road to Palenque ruins.

Several of the places strung along the road to the ruins have camping space. They include **La Aldea del Halach-Uinic**, with tent sites for US$3; **Beto's** at El Panchán, with hammock space or camping for US$2.25 per person; and **Elementos Naturales**, with hammock space or camping at US$3.50 per person, and hammocks to rent for a further US$1.75, including breakfast – see later in this section for more on all these.

Mayabell Hotel Trailer Park (☎ 345-01-25, e mayabell82@hotmail.com, Carretera Palenque-Ruinas Km 6) Hammock space or camping US$3 per person, hammocks to rent US$1.25, small vehicle without hookups US$1.25, vehicle sites with full hookups for one/two people US$11.50/13.50, single/double/triple/quad rooms with fan US$18/22/25/28, air-con singles/doubles/triples US$34/39/45; deposit of US$17 or passport per room or rented hammock. The Mayabell is the most convenient place to stay for the ruins – just 400m from the site museum. Campers and hammock-dwellers share clean toilet and shower blocks. There's plenty of space, with some shade, and palapas for slinging hammocks. All 15 rooms have private bath: rooms with air-con are comfortable, those with fan are basic. In the pleasant restaurant few items cost more than US$3.50. Lockers are US$1.25 a day. A taxi from town is US$3.50 by day and US$4.50 by night.

There are a number of suitable budget hostels, hotels and posadas in town.

Ámbar Hostel (☎ 345-10-08, e ambar hostel@hotmail.com, Merle Green s/n) Dorm places US$5.75, singles & doubles US$23. This hostel, in the quiet, leafy La Cañada area, has a couple of dorms with bunks and double beds, and rooms with fan and bath. There's a kitchen, a sink for washing clothes and table tennis. It's kept pretty clean and the atmosphere is friendly.

Posada Bonampak (☎ 345-09-25, Domínguez 33) Singles & doubles US$6.25-6.75. The Bonampak, four blocks north of Juárez, is the best of the rock-bottom cheapies. Definitely no frills here, but the rooms are well kept and of reasonable size, with fan and attached tiled bathrooms.

Posada Johana (20 de Noviembre s/n) Singles/doubles/triples US$6.75/11.50/13.50. The Johana, run by a friendly young couple, offers bare, basic rooms with double bed and bath.

Posada Canek (☎ 345-01-50, 20 de Noviembre 43) Dorm beds US$5.75, singles/doubles/triples/quads US$11.50/13.50/17/23. Posada Canek, southwest of El Parque, has largish rooms with bathroom and fan. The dorms have private toilets and shared showers. Reception provides safe boxes for valuables.

Posada Charito (☎ 345-01-21, 20 de Noviembre 15) Singles/doubles/triples/quads

US$6.75/11.50/13.50/23. The Charito's rooms are dark and short on fresh air, but they're cheap, they have fan and shower and they've had a fairly recent coat of paint.

You can get a much better room for a few dollars more at the following places.

Hotel Yun-Kax (☎ 345-07-25, *Corregidora 87)* Singles/doubles/triples/quads with fan US$20/23/28/34, with air-con US$25/28/34/43. The Yun-Kax, handily placed between the bus stations and town center, has clean rooms with shower, arranged around a little patio.

Posada Nacha'n Ka'an (e *pnachankaan@ hotmail.com, 20 de Noviembre 25)* Dorm beds US$5.50, singles/doubles/triples/quads US$13.50/15/22/27. The friendly Nacha'n Ka'an, a block north of the Yun-Kax, offers a rooftop dorm with fresh air, clean, good-size rooms with ample bathrooms and hot water, and a café for breakfast. Reception staff speak some English.

Hotel Kashlan (☎ 345-02-97, *fax 345-03-09, 5 de Mayo 117)* Singles/doubles with fan & bath US$17/23, with air-con US$45/57. This plain hotel has received a lick of paint, which makes the rooms more agreeable. All have bathroom with hot water. The air-con rooms are not worth the money, however.

Hotel Regional (☎ 345-01-83, e *regional@ tnet.net.mx, Juárez 119)* Singles/doubles/triples/quads US$20/20/28/40. The Regional has adequate rooms with shower and fan, around a small, plant-filled courtyard.

Posada Kin (☎ 345-17-14, *Abasolo 1)* Singles/doubles/triples/quads with breakfast (except Sun) US$13.50/17/20/23. Posada Kin has clean, decent-size rooms with bathroom and ceiling fan, on four floors around a small patio.

Hotel Posada Tucán (☎ 345-18-59, *5 de Mayo 5)* Singles/doubles/triples/quads US$13.50/17/23/28. Posada Tucán is a welcome, fairly recent newcomer, with a breezy upstairs location. The rooms are clean and reasonably-sized, with fan and bathroom, and the friendly family here plan to add a restaurant and splash-pool.

Posada Águila Real (☎/fax 345-00-04, *20 de Noviembre s/n)* Singles & doubles with fan/air-con US$23/28, air-con triples & quads US$34. This small, newish posada offers spick-and-span rooms with tile floors, TV and bathroom.

Hotel Maranatha (☎ 345-10-07, *20 de Noviembre 19)* Singles US$11.50, doubles US$13.50-17, quads US$23. The Maranatha is another small, fairly new place, offering good, clean, tile-floored rooms with fan and bath.

There are also suitable hostels, hotels and posadas on the road to the ruins:

La Aldea del Halach-Uinic (☎ 345-16-93, *Carretera Palenque-Ruinas Km 2.7)* Singles/doubles US$9/16. Some 4km from town, the Halach-Uinic has simple palapa-roofed cabañas amid green gardens. Each room has two beds and two hammocks on a little porch. There's a small pool, clean shared toilets and showers and a restaurant.

If you go 1.7km farther toward the ruins, you will come to **El Panchán** (*Carretera Palenque-Ruinas Km 4.4),* a group of simple places to stay in a beautiful patch of forest. Some places here serve excellent food, and El Panchán has something of a travelers' scene. Once ranchland, the area has been re-forested by the remarkable Morales family, one of whom headed the team of archaeologists recently working at Palenque ruins.

Rakshita's (e *rakshita@yahoo.com, El Panchán)* Cabañas with shared bath US$4.50 per person, double cabaña with private bath US$13.50. Rakshita's also has an exotically painted meditation center with a good and inexpensive vegetarian restaurant. The cabañas have mosquito-netted windows.

Margarita & Ed Cabañas (e *edcabanas @yahoo.com, El Panchán)* Singles US$11.50-12.50, doubles US$13.50-14.50. Margarita and Ed, a friendly Mexican/US couple, have clean rooms with bath and hot water on the ground floor of their house, and eight more rooms being built in a separate two-story block behind, plus a few more rustic cabañas. Some rooms have kitchens available for an extra US$1.25.

Beto's (*El Panchán)* Singles & doubles US$8.

Elementos Naturales (*Carretera Palenque-Ruinas Km 5)* Dorm bunks US$5.75, double cabañas US$13.50, including breakfast. It's 700m farther from El Panchán to this calm spot with cabañas and palapa shelters scattered around grassy grounds. The breakfast is generous, the dorms and cabañas have fan and electric light, the bathrooms are clean. They'll look after your valuables at the desk.

Mid-Range *Hotel Nikte-Ha* (☎ 345-13-80, *Juárez 133)* Singles/doubles/triples

US$28/34/39. This place offers small, clean, modern rooms with bath, air-con and TV.

Hotel Naj K'in (☎ 345-11-26, Hidalgo 72) Doubles/triples/quads with fan US$28/38/45, with air-con US$33/45/50. This is a pleasant place with average rooms and good bathrooms with hot water.

Hotel Palenque (☎/fax 345-01-88, e htlpque@tnet.net.mx, 5 de Mayo 15) Rooms with fan US$50, air-con US$62. Just east of El Parque, this is the town's oldest hotel, recently spruced up. Rooms are set around a garden courtyard, and all hold up to four people, with TV, phone and free bottled water.

Several mid-range and top-end hotels cluster in the leafy La Cañada area west of the center.

Hotel Chablis (☎ 345-08-70, fax 345-03-65, e hotelchablis@hotmail.com, Merle Green 7) Singles & doubles/triples/quads US$39/45/50. The Chablis is a smallish hotel whose good-size rooms have two double beds, air-con, fan and TV.

Hotel Xibalba (☎ 345-04-11, fax 345-03-92, e shivalva@tnet.net.mx, Merle Green 9) Singles & doubles with fan US$28, air-con US$39. Opposite the Chablis is the 14-room Xibalba, with reasonably attractive rooms in two buildings. Some have TV.

Hotel Cañada Internacional (☎/fax 345-20-93, Juárez 1) Singles & doubles US$25-36, triples & quads US$30-47. The Cañada Internacional has comfortable rooms all with two beds (at least one double) and TV. The more expensive ones are bigger, newer and air-conditioned.

Hotel Villas Kin-Ha (☎ 345-05-33, fax 345-05-44, e kin_ha@hotmail.com, Carretera Palenque-Ruinas Km 2.7) Singles/doubles/triples US$56/56/62. On the road to the ruins, 4km from town, the Kin-Ha offers palapa-roofed duplex concrete cabañas. The rooms, with fan, aren't big, but the gardens hold a good-size pool and open-sided palapa restaurant.

Top End *Hotel Maya Tulipanes* (☎ 345-02-01, e reservas@mayatulipanes.com .mx, Cañada 6) Singles/doubles/triples US$76/76/83. The Maya Tulipanes, in the La Cañada area at the west end of town, has large, comfortable rooms with good bathrooms, cable TV, air-con and fan. There's a small pool and a restaurant.

Maya Palenque Hotel (☎ 345-07-80, fax 345-09-07, e hmayapal@tnet.net.mx, cnr Merle Green & Juárez) Singles/doubles/triples/quads US$88/88/96/104. The Maya Palenque, at the west end of town, has good air-conditioned rooms with two double beds and cable TV, plus a large pool.

Hotel Calinda Nututun Palenque (☎ 345-01-00, fax 345-06-20, e cnututun@ tnet.net.mx, Carretera Palenque-Ocosingo Km 3.5) Singles/doubles/triples US$100/100/156. The Calinda, 3.5km south of town on the road to San Cristóbal, has motel-style buildings with large, comfortable, air-con rooms in spacious tropical gardens. A big attraction is the beautiful bathing spot in the Río Chacamax, which flows through the hotel property, but the hotel restaurant is ordinary. A taxi from Palenque center costs US$3.

Chan-Kah Resort Village (☎ 345-11-00, fax 345-08-20, Carretera Palenque-Ruinas Km 3.2) Singles/doubles/quads US$99/99/114. This resort on the road to the ruins, 4.5km from town, has handsome wood-and-stone cottages with generous bathrooms, ceiling fans and air-conditioning. An enormous stone-bound swimming pool and lush jungle gardens add to the appeal.

Places to Eat

Palenque is definitely not the gastronomic capital of Mexico, but there are enough places to satisfy your hunger at a fair price. The cheapest are the taquerías along the eastern side of El Parque. Try *Los Farolitos* or neighboring *Fuente de Sodas* for a plate of tacos at around US$3.

Restaurant Las Tinajas (20 de Noviembre 41) Mains US$4-6.75. For a huge feed of excellent home-style cooking, head straight to Las Tinajas, where the portions really are plenty for two. An excellent choice is *pollo a la mexicana,* a chicken-with-lots-of-vegetables dish. If you seriously like hot chilies, go for *filete a la cazuela.*

Mara's (☎ 345-15-76, Juárez 1) Mains US$5-8.50, breakfasts US$3.50-5. Mara's has a prime location facing El Parque, with a handful of sidewalk tables and an abundance of whirring fans inside. With varied, reliable and unexciting food, it's always busy.

Restaurant Maya (☎ 345-02-16, cnr Independencia & Hidalgo) Mains US$4.50-8. This busy place, facing the northwest corner of El

TABASCO & CHIAPAS

Parque, offers similar value to Mara's, but we didn't like the waiter who went round the tables suggesting how much people should tip.

Restaurant Na Chan-Kan (☎ 345-02-63, *cnr Hidalgo & Jiménez*) Set meals US$2.50-5. Na Chan-Kan, facing the northeast corner of El Parque, does reasonable-value two-course meals with a drink.

Restaurant Artemio's (☎ 345-02-63, *Hidalgo 14*) Prices US$3-7. Family-run Artemio's serves pizzas, set menus from US$3.25 to US$5, breakfasts and a big range of antojitos.

Restaurant Virgo's (☎ 345-20-57, *Hidalgo 5*) Antojitos & mains US$3.50-8. This upstairs restaurant offers good open-air dining half a block west of El Parque. Try the burritos with guacamole, one of the pasta plates or a meat dish. There's wine, too.

Café de Yara (*cnr Hidalgo & Abasolo*) Prices US$2-4. The bustling, modern Yara is good for breakfast, snacks, salads and organic Chiapas coffee.

Pizza Palenque (☎ 345-03-32, *Juárez 168*) Pizzas US$5.75-9. The pizzas here won't win prizes, but they fill your stomach.

Restaurant Maya Cañada (☎ 345-00-42, *Merle Green s/n*) Mains US$5-10. This is the best place to eat in the La Cañada area, with friendly service and a range of well-prepared food including good steaks with baked potatoes. It's open to the air and has a cool upstairs terrace.

El Panchán, amid the forest 4.5km along the road to the ruins (see Places to Stay, earlier), contains several excellent places to eat.

Don Mucho's (*El Panchán*) Set menus US$3-4, snacks US$1.75-3. Don Mucho's serves good food at good prices and often parties on late.

Rakshita's (*El Panchán*) Menú del día US$3, snacks US$1-1.75. Vegetarian Rakshita's has veggie burgers, great cakes and licuados, and a different set meal (for example, curry, rice, chapati and chutney) every day.

Getting There & Away

Flight schedules from Palenque's small airport are very variable. At the time of research, Aerocaribe (☎ 345-06-18) flew to/from Mérida and Tuxtla Gutiérrez daily. Sometimes there are flights to/from Cancún or Flores, Guatemala.

Buses serving Palenque, especially night buses to/from Mérida, have had a bad record for theft. Take special care of your possessions, don't accept drinks from strangers and don't leave anything of value in the overhead rack or under the seats.

Westernmost of the main bus terminals on Juárez is the joint deluxe and 1st-class terminal of Cristóbal Colón and ADO. A block east is Autotransportes Tuxtla Gutiérrez (ATG, 2nd-class), and together half a block farther east, at Juárez 159, are Transportes Rodulfo Figueroa (TRF; basic 1st-class) and Transportes Lacandonia (TL, 2nd-class).

It's a good idea to buy your outward ticket a day in advance. Daily departures include the following:

Campeche – 365km, 5 hours; 4 Colón/ADO (US$16-20), 2 ATG (US$15)

Cancún – 870km, 13 hours; 5 Colón/ADO (US$36-46), 2 ATG (US$33)

Mérida – 545km, 8 hours; 4 Colón/ADO (US$24-31), 2 ATG (US$19)

Mexico City (TAPO) – 1010km, 16 hours; 2 ADO (US$54)

Oaxaca – 815km, 15 hours; 1 ADO (US$40)

Ocosingo – 103km, 2½ hours; 11 Colón/ADO (US$4.50-6.25), 7 TRF (US$5), 6 ATG (US$5), 9 TL (US$4.50)

Playa del Carmen – 805km, 12 hours; 4 Colón/ADO (US$34-40), 1 ATG (US$29)

San Cristóbal de Las Casas – 190km, 4½ hours; 10 Colón/ADO (US$8.50-11.50), 7 TRF (US$8), 6 ATG (US$8), 9 TL (US$6.75)

Tulum – 745km, 11 hours; 3 Colón/ADO (US$31-34)

Tuxtla Gutiérrez – 275km, 6½ hours; 8 Colón/ADO (US$12.50-16), 6 ATG (US$11), 7 TRF (US$11.50)

Villahermosa – 140km, 2½ hours; 11 ADO (US$6), 3 ATG (US$5.75)

For travel to or from Guatemala, see the sections To/From Guatemala via Tenosique (in the Tabasco section of this chapter) and Bonampak, Yaxchilán & the Carretera Fronteriza (later in this chapter).

Getting Around

The airport is a couple of kilometers north of the Maya head statue along highway 199. Yellow Transportación Terrestre cabs from airport to town cost US$0.40. In town, taxis wait at the northeast corner of El Parque and at the Colón/ADO bus station. They charge US$2 to the airport.

BONAMPAK, YAXCHILÁN & THE CARRETERA FRONTERIZA

The ancient Maya cities of Bonampak and Yaxchilán, southeast of Palenque, have become much more accessible in recent years because of the Carretera Fronteriza, a paved road completed in 2000 which runs parallel to the Mexico-Guatemala border all the way round from Palenque to the Lagos de Montebello. Bonampak is 148km by road from Palenque; Yaxchilán is 173km by road then about 22km by boat down the Río Usumacinta.

Visiting this area independently doesn't necessarily work out cheaper than taking a tour from Palenque, but it allows you time to explore an intriguing region at leisure. You can cross into Guatemala at Frontera Corozal or Benemérito de las Américas.

This part of Mexico does not observe daylight saving time, so you should triple-check all transportation schedules! And don't forget insect repellent.

Organized Tours

See Organized Tours in the Palenque and San Cristóbal de Las Casas sections for details about agencies.

Bonampak & Yaxchilán Several Palenque travel agencies offer 13- to 14-hour day tours to Bonampak and Yaxchilán for around US$55-60 per person, usually including entry fees, two meals and transportation in an air-conditioned van. There's also a two-day version, with the night spent camping at or near Lacanjá Chansayab, and the possibility of river or walking excursions from there: this costs around US$90-100 depending exactly how many meals and so on are included (ask carefully about these details). There are also tours from San Cristóbal de Las Casas.

Guatemala Palenque agencies also offer transportation packages to Flores (near Tikal) for around US$33. Check carefully the details of what the agencies are offering: the deal usually includes an air-conditioned van to Frontera Corozal, river launch from there to Bethel, Guatemala, and public 2nd-class bus from Bethel to Flores – 10 or 11

hours altogether. Some agencies include a visit to Bonampak for a few dollars more.

Rafting & Kayaking Explora, based in San Cristóbal de Las Casas but also with a camp at Lacanjá Chansayab (see those sections, earlier in this chapter), offers trips along the rivers of the Lacandón Jungle.

Getting There & Away

Autotransportes Río Chancalá at 5 de Mayo 120 in Palenque runs combis to Frontera Corozal (3 hours, US$5) four times daily between 6am and 2.30pm, and to Benemérito (3 hours, US$5.75) 13 times between 4.30am and 4.15pm. Transportes Montebello, on Velasco Suárez two blocks west of Palenque market, runs buses to Frontera Corozal (4 hours, US$5) at noon, to Benemérito (4 hours, US$5) nine times daily, and all the way along the Carretera Fronteriza to Comitán (11 hours, US$17) three times. Both these companies, like the region they travel to but unlike the rest of Palenque, tend to ignore daylight saving time in summer – meaning that by Palenque time, departures during that period are one hour after posted times.

All the above-mentioned services stop at San Javier (US$4.25, 2¼ hours), 140km from Palenque, where a side road branches to Bonampak and Lacanjá Chansayab. They also stop at Crucero Corozal, the intersection for Frontera Corozal. There are *comedores* at Crucero Corozal.

Several military checkpoints are dotted along the Carretera Fronteriza.

Bonampak

Bonampak's setting in dense jungle hid it from the outside world until 1946. Stories of how it was revealed are full of mystery and innuendo, but it seems that Charles Frey, apparently a young WWII conscientious objector from the US, and John Bourne, heir to the Singer sewing machine fortune, were the first outsiders to visit the site when Chan Bor, a Lacandón, took them there in February 1946. Later in 1946 an American photographer, Giles Healey – who had apparently fallen out with Frey and Bourne during an earlier expedition to film the Lacandones – was also led to the site by Chan Bor and found the Templo de las Pinturas with its famous murals. Frey drowned in

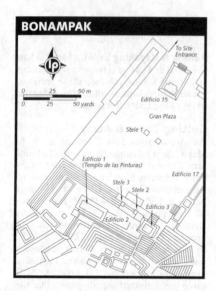

BONAMPAK

To Site Entrance

Edificio 15

Gran Plaza

Stele 1

Edificio 1
(Templo de las Pinturas)

Edificio 17

Stele 3

Stele 2

Edificio 3

Edificio 2

0   25   50 m
0   25   50 yards

1949, when his canoe capsized on another expedition to Bonampak.

The Bonampak site *(admission US$3.50, free Sun & holidays; open 8am-4pm daily)* spreads over 2.4 sq km, but all the main ruins stand around the rectangular Gran Plaza. At different periods Bonampak was an enemy and an ally of more powerful Yax-chilán. The major surviving monuments were built under Bonampak's Chaan Muan II, who took the throne in AD 776 at a time of alliance with Yaxchilán. He was a nephew of the Yaxchilán ruler Escudo Jaguar II and was married to Yaxchilán royalty. The 6m-high Stele 1 in the Gran Plaza represents Chaan Muan at the height of his reign. He also features in Steles 2 and 3 on the Acrópolis, which rises from the south end of the plaza.

The masterly frescoes painted for Chaan Muan inside the Templo de las Pinturas (Edificio 1) on the Acrópolis steps are what give Bonampak its fame (and its name: Bonampak means 'Painted Walls' in Yu-catecan Maya and was coined by the 20th-century Mayanist Sylvanus Morley).

Diagrams outside the temple help interpret these murals, which have weathered badly since their discovery and would otherwise be very hard to understand, despite restoration in the 1990s. Room 1, on the left as you face the temple, shows the consecration of an infant heir – probably Chaan Muan II's son – who is seen held in arms toward the top of the right end of the room's south wall, which faces you as you enter. The central Room 2 on the south wall shows a battle, and, on the north wall, the torture (by fingernail removal) and sacrifice of prisoners, a scene presided over by Chaan-Muan II in jaguar-skin battle dress. A severed head lies below him, beside the foot of a sprawling captive. Room 3 shows a celebratory dance on the Acrópolis steps by lords wearing huge headdresses, and on its east wall three white-robed women puncture their tongues in a ritual bloodletting. By one interpretation, the prisoner sacrifices, the bloodletting and the dance may all have been part of the ceremonies surrounding the new heir.

The infant prince probably never got to rule Bonampak; the place was abandoned before the murals were finished, as Classic Maya civilization imploded.

Refrescos and snacks are sold at a café at the Monumento Nacional Bonampak entrance, 9km before the ruins, and at a house by the archaeological site entrance.

Places to Stay *Camping Margarito (at Lacanjá Chansayab turnoff)* Camping per person US$1.25, hammock sites US$2.25, rented tents/hammocks per person US$2.25/3.50. This Lacandón-run camping ground 9km from Bonampak, with a grassy camping area and a palapa for hammocks, is the closest you can stay to the ruins. Meals are available and there are showers and toilets.

Getting There & Away Bonampak is 12km from San Javier, a small junction settlement on the Carretera Fronteriza. The first 3km, to the Lacanjá Chansayab turnoff, is paved; the rest is good gravel/dirt road through the forest. Just past the start of the gravel/dirt section is the entrance to the Monumento Nacional Bonampak protected zone: here you can rent bicycles for US$1 an hour or take an irregular bus to the ruins for US$8 roundtrip.

A taxi from San Javier to Bonampak ruins and back, with time to visit the ruins, costs US$5.75 per person. You may have to wait a while at San Javier before one turns up, however. Hitching is possible.

Lacanjá Chansayab
• pop 500 • elev 320m

Just 12km from Bonampak is the largest village of the indigenous Lacandón people, Lacanjá Chansayab. This spread-out settlement, where there is an inviting river pool you can bathe in, was founded around 1980. The villagers here are now predominantly Presbyterian.

Villagers can guide you to Bonampak (around US$10) and to other places of interest in the nearby forests such as the little-explored Maya ruins of Lacanjá, the 2.5km-long Laguna Lacanjá or the Cascadas Lacanjá. Wildlife you can hope to see includes toucans and macaws in addition to coatis.

Some villagers make and sell attractive pottery, wood carvings, seed necklaces, arrows and drums.

Places to Stay & Eat Several villagers have set up simple *campamentos* where you can pitch a tent and/or rent a hammock – look for their signs or ask for Carlos Cham Bor Kin, Kin Bor, Vicente or Manuel Chan Bor. You pay around US$1.25 per person to pitch a tent and US$2.25 to rent a hammock under a shelter. These campings should be able to provide a meal or two for a small number of visitors, but bring food supplies if you plan to stay more than a night. Camping Margarito (see Bonampak, earlier) is also nearby.

Campamento Río Lacanjá (2km south of village entrance) Cabins US$6.75 per person in bunks, US$20 with double bed; meals US$3-4. These accommodations, a grade better than the others, were created by a villager in collaboration with the Explora adventure travel firm (see Organized Tours in the San Cristóbal de Las Casas section, earlier in this chapter). Wooden cabins stand near the jungle-shrouded Río Lacanjá, most with two bunks and all with mosquito nets, terrace and hammock. There's a clean, separate bathroom block. All meals are available, and you can also take interesting rafting or combined rafting and walking outings. To reach Campamento Río Lacanjá head south along the airstrip from the village and keep going along the track.

Getting There & Away Lacanjá Chansayab is 6.5km by paved road from San Javier on the Carretera Fronteriza. A taxi is US$6 (US$1.50 *colectivo*) but you might have to walk or hitch.

Frontera Corozal
• pop 5000 • elev 200m

This frontier town (formerly called Frontera Echeverría) spreads back from the bank of the Río Usumacinta, 16km by paved road from Crucero Corozal junction on the Carretera Fronteriza. The broad Usumacinta, flowing swiftly between jungle-covered banks, forms the Mexico-Guatemala border here. Frontera Corozal is an essential stepping-stone both to the ruins of Yaxchilán and for onward travel into Guatemala.

Long, outboard-powered launches come and go from the river embarcadero, below a cluster of wooden buildings that includes a few inexpensive *comedores*. Almost everything you'll need is on the paved main street leading inland from here – including the immigration office, where you should hand in/obtain a tourist card if you're leaving for/arriving from Guatemala.

To make a phone call to Frontera Corozal, use ☎ Miditel (dial the Mexico City number 55-5350-9624 preceded by any necessary codes, then await new tone, then dial local number). There's a telephone caseta at Escudo Jaguar (see Places to Stay & Eat, below).

Places to Stay & Eat *Escudo Jaguar* (☎ 5201-6441) Small singles & doubles/triples with shared bath US$12.50/19, large singles & doubles/triples & quads with private bath US$28/42. A short distance along the road back from the embarcadero, Escudo Jaguar is easily the most comfortable accommodations. The spotless rooms, in pink palapa-roofed huts, come with fans and mosquito screens, and there's a good if slightly pricey restaurant (main dishes US$5-6.75), officially open from 7am to 8pm.

The alternative to Escudo Jaguar is a bare, basic room in one of the town's rock-bottom posadas. Best of this bad lot is the *Hospedaje*, two blocks off the main street a few hundred meters back from Escudo Jaguar (signposted). Rooms for up to four, with common bathrooms, cost US$5.75.

Getting There & Away If you can't get a bus or combi direct to Frontera Corozal, get one to Crucero Corozal, 20 minutes southeast of San Javier on the highway, where you can get a taxi (US$2.25 per person *colectivo*, US$5.75 otherwise) to Frontera Corozal.

At the time of writing, combis left Frontera Corozal for Palenque at about 5am, 10am, noon and 3pm, and a Transportes Montebello bus left at 3am. The last Palenque-bound combi passes Crucero Corozal about 5pm.

If you want to go to Guatemala, fast river launches *(lanchas)* go from Frontera Corozal to the village of Bethel, on the Guatemalan bank of the Usumacinta 40 minutes upstream. Ask at the Contratación de Lanchas office in Escudo Jaguar, or the Sociedad Cooperativa Tikal Chilam, just above the embarcadero. A boat for up to six people costs around US$30; for seven to 10 people it's about US$40. The launches can carry bicycles and even motorcycles. Another option is to take a boat from Frontera Corozal to the small Guatemalan village of La Técnica, directly across the Usumacinta (US$0.60 per person). From La Técnica there's a bus at 11am along the dirt road to Bethel (two hours, US$2.50).

At the time of writing 2nd-class buses were leaving Bethel for Santa Elena near Flores (US$4, four hours) at 3am, noon and 2pm. Bethel's *Posada Maya (☎ 502-801-1799)* has camping, hammock space and cabañas on the banks of the Usumacinta.

Yaxchilán

Yaxchilán *(admission US$3.50, free Sun & holidays; open 8am-4.45pm daily)* has a marvelous jungle setting above a loop of the Usumacinta. Archaeologically, it's famed for its ornamented building façades and roof combs, and stone lintels carved

The Lacandón Jungle & the Lacandones

Mexico harbors 10% of the earth's living species, on 1.4% of the earth's land. The Selva Lacandona (Lacandón Jungle) in eastern Chiapas occupies just one quarter of 1% of Mexico. Yet it contains more than 4300 plant species, about 17% of the Mexican total; 450 types of butterfly, 42% of the national total; at least 340 birds, 32% of the total; and 163 mammals, 30% of the Mexican total. Among these are such emblematic creatures as the jaguar, red macaw, toucan, howler monkey, spider monkey, ocelot, tapir and harpy eagle.

This great fund of natural resources, genetic diversity and protection against global warming is the southwest end of a 30,000-sq-km corridor of tropical rain forest stretching into northern Guatemala, Belize and the south of the Yucatán Peninsula. But the Selva Lacandona is going, fast. In the 1950s it covered 15,000 sq km between the Chiapas highlands and the Río Usumacinta. Today perhaps 5000 sq km remain (some estimates are as low as 3000 sq km). Most of that is in the eastern half of the Reserva de la Biósfera Montes Azules.

Those 10,000 vanished square kilometers of jungle have mostly been turned into *milpas* (cornfields) and cattle pasture by some 150,000 land-hungry settlers from other parts of Mexico.

The ancient Maya developed major cities such as Yaxchilán and Bonampak in the Selva Lacandona. When the Spanish came, the jungle was probably inhabited by Chol people, some of whom managed to survive unconquered in forest hideaways until the late 17th century. Then conquest and new diseases removed the Lacandón Choles from history. (The modern-day Choles, around 180,000 strong, live mainly in northern Chiapas.)

In the late 19th century, loggers moving up the Río Usumacinta in search of mahogany and cedar reported encounters with small, scattered groups of jungle dwellers. These were the people known today as the Lacandones. They are thought to have reached the Selva Lacandona in the 18th century, fleeing either from the Spanish in the Yucatán or Guatemala or from the British in Belize. They avoided permanent contact with the outside world until the 1950s. Their language is related to Yucatecan Maya, and they call themselves Hach Winik, the True People.

You will almost certainly have seen Lacandones if you have visited the ruins at Palenque, where they sell quivers of arrows and are readily recognizable in their long white tunics with their long black hair cut in a fringe.

(often on their undersides) with conquest and ceremonial scenes. A flashlight (torch) is a help in exploring some parts of the site.

Another feature of these ruins is the howler monkeys that come to feed in some of the tall trees here. You'll almost certainly hear their roars, and you stand a good chance of seeing some.

Conquests and alliances made Yaxchilán one of the most important pre-Hispanic cities in the Usumacinta region. It peaked in power and splendor between AD 681 and 800 under the rulers Escudo Jaguar I (Shield Jaguar I, 681-742), Pájaro Jaguar IV (Bird Jaguar IV, 752-768) and Escudo Jaguar II (772-800). It was abandoned around AD 810.

Yaxchilán's inscriptions tell more about its 'Jaguar' dynasty than is known of almost any other Mayan ruling clan. The names by which the rulers are known come from the hieroglyphs representing them: the shield-and-jaguar symbol appears on many Yaxchilán buildings and steles. Pájaro Jaguar IV's hieroglyph is a small jungle cat with feathers on its back and a bird superimposed on its head.

At the site, refrescos are sold at a shack near the river landing. Signs in three languages including English explain what most of Yaxchilán's buildings were.

As you walk toward the ruins, a signed path to the right leads up to the Pequeña Acrópolis, a group of ruins on a small hilltop. You can visit this later, at the end of a circuit of the site. Staying on the main path, you soon reach the labyrinthine passages of El Laberinto (Edificio 19), built between AD 742 and 752, during the interregnum between Escudo Jaguar I and Pájaro Jaguar IV. From this complicated two-level building you emerge at the northwest end of the Gran Plaza.

The Lacandón Jungle & the Lacandones

There are about 800 Lacandones today. Most live in the village of Lacanjá Chansayab near Bonampak, just outside the Montes Azules Biosphere Reserve. They congregated here in 1979 after the reserve was declared. As a result of Christian missionary efforts, the predominant religion in Lacanjá Chansayab today is Presbyterianism. Najá, another Lacandón village, about 50km farther northwest, remains truer to Lacandón traditions.

At the same time as Lacandones gathered in Lacanjá Chansayab, many of the Chol and Tzeltal people who had settled in the Lacandón Jungle in the previous couple of decades gathered in two other new towns near the reserve's eastern fringe, the Choles in Frontera Corozal and the Tzeltales in Nueva Palestina. These three groups today jointly administer an area of over 6000 sq km called the Comunidad Lacandona, which includes much of the Montes Azules and Lacantún biosphere reserves.

The first waves of settlers deforested the northern third of the Selva Lacandona by about 1960. Also badly deforested are the far eastern area called Marqués de Comillas, settled since the 1970s, and Las Cañadas, the area between the Montes Azules reserve and Ocosingo, which received many chiapaneco settlers in the 1950s, '60s and '70s.

Many settlers in Las Cañadas, as elsewhere in the Lacandón, found that their new land deteriorated fast. Cleared jungle makes a fertile milpa for a couple of years, but then yields rapidly drop. It will subsequently support grass and cattle for a few years before the grass turns to weeds, leaving the settlers little better off than before. Struggling Las Cañadas settlers have always had some of the Zapatistas' strongest support.

Traditional Lacandón agriculture, by contrast, makes it possible to live almost indefinitely off small areas of land. Leaving some plots fallow allows land to regenerate, and many varied crops are planted under a canopy of big trees that are not felled. But like other traditional Lacandón ways, these methods are now threatened by the onslaught of the outside world. Few Lacandones now maintain the Mayan religion or social customs that were common until recently. Selling crafts to tourists has become the major source of income for many Lacandones.

Little can stop the Selva Lacandona from continuing to be cut down. From time to time logging is banned, or attempts are made to slow immigration to the area. But steady erosion of the jungle continues.

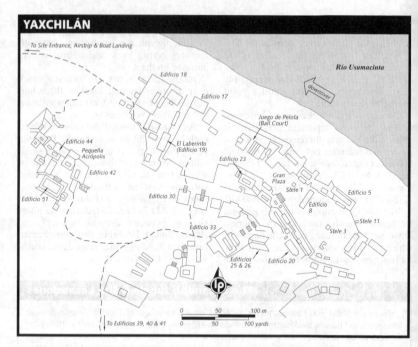

YAXCHILÁN

To Site Entrance, Airstrip & Boat Landing

Río Usumacinta

downriver

Edificio 18

Edificio 17

Juego de Pelota
(Ball Court)

Edificio 44

Pequeña
Acrópolis

El Laberinto
(Edificio 19)

Edificio 23

Edificio 42

Gran
Plaza

Stele 1

Edificio 5

Edificio
8

Edificio 51

Edificio 30

Stele 11

Stele 3

Edificio 33

Edificios
25 & 26

Edificio 20

0   50   100 m
0   50   100 yards

To Edificios 39, 40 & 41

Though it's hard to imagine anyone here ever wanting to be hotter than they already were, Edificio 17 was apparently a sweathouse. About halfway along the plaza, Stele 1, flanked by weathered sculptures of a crocodile and a jaguar, shows Pájaro Jaguar IV in a ceremony that took place in 761. Edificio 20, from the time of Escudo Jaguar II, was the last significant structure built at Yaxchilán. Stele 11, now at the northeast corner of the Gran Plaza, was originally found in front of Edificio 40. The bigger of the two figures visible on it is Pájaro Jaguar IV.

A grand stairway climbs from Stele 1 to Edificio 33, the best-preserved building at Yaxchilán, with about half its roof comb remaining. The final step in front of the building is carved with many ball-game scenes. There are fine relief carvings on the undersides of the lintels. Inside is a decapitated statue of Pájaro Jaguar IV; he lost his head to treasure-seeking 19th-century timber cutters.

From the clearing behind Edificio 33, a path leads into the trees. About 20m along this, fork left uphill. Go left at another fork after about 80m, and in 10 minutes – mostly uphill – you reach three buildings on a hilltop, Edificios 39, 40 and 41. You can climb to the top of Edificio 41 for great views across the top of the jungle to the distant mountains of Guatemala.

Getting There & Away You can reach Yaxchilán by chartered plane from places such as Palenque and Ocosingo, or by boat from Frontera Corozal.

River launches take 40 minutes running downstream from Frontera Corozal, and one hour returning upstream. You can arrange for a boat at two places in Frontera Corozal: the Contratación de Lanchas office at Escudo Jaguar, and Sociedad Cooperativa Tikal Chilam, just above the embarcadero. For a round trip to Yaxchilán, including about three hours at the ruins, Escudo Jaguar charges US$50 for up to six people and US$67 for seven or more. Tikal Chilam's prices are similar, but staff there also quoted us US$45 for two people.

Obviously, you can save money by finding other travelers to share a boat. Failing that, one or two people might be able to join with a tour group. These come most days, especially during the peak tourist seasons, arriving at Escudo Jaguar as early as 8.30am. You could pay US$10 to US$15 per person this way, but you'll need the group guide's agreement first.

Benemérito de las Américas
• pop 6150 • elev 200m

South of Frontera Corozal you soon enter the area of far eastern Chiapas known as Marqués de Comillas (for its Spanish former landowner). After oil explorers opened tracks into this jungle region in the 1970s, land-hungry settlers poured in from all over Mexico. Now it's one of the most deforested parts of the Lacandón Jungle. Cattle and logging have made many settlers richer than they could have hoped to be where they came from. Marqués de Comillas is also a route for drugs entering Mexico. You may receive warnings about violence associated with this.

The main town is Benemérito de las Américas, on the bank of the Río Salinas, an Usumacinta tributary that forms the Mexico-Guatemala border here. It has traces of 'Wild West' atmosphere but no attractions except as a staging post.

The main street is a 1.5km-long stretch of the highway. A side street beside the Farmacia Arco Iris, toward the north end of town, leads 1.25km east to the river. Benemérito has no immigration post; you must pick up or hand in Mexican tourist cards at Frontera Corozal.

For making phone calls, you need to use ☎ Miditel (dial the Mexico City number ☎ 55-5350-9624, then await new tone, then dial local number).

Places to Stay *Hotel de Las Américas* (☎ 029-40-60, beside highway at south end of town) Singles/doubles US$11.50/13.50. This hotel already looks dilapidated although at the time of writing they hadn't finished building it. The rooms, with bathroom and fan, are all right, but for security check that the windows close properly.

Hospedaje Siempre Viva (beside Autotransportes Río Chancalá terminal) Singles & doubles US$6.75, with private bath US$13.50. This is the second choice. Rooms have fans.

Getting There & Away Autotransportes Río Chancalá has its combi terminal on the highway, toward the north end of town. Combis run to Palenque (US$5.75, 3 hours) 12 times daily, the last at 4pm. There's a taxi stand across the road. From the Transportes Montebello bus stop, about 350m south, buses leave for Palenque (US$5, 4 hours) nine times between 4am and 2pm, and for Comitán (US$12, 7 hours) via the southern stretch of the Carretera Fronteriza four times between 5am and 12.45pm, with a couple of others going just to Ixcán.

For travel between Chiapas and Guatemala, you can hire a lancha for around US$150 to take you up the Río Salinas and its tributary the Río de la Pasión to Sayaxché (Guatemala) in three to four hours. Sayaxché is a base for visiting several Mayan ruins and has lodgings and buses to Flores, near Tikal. On the way, there may be Guatemalan immigration checks at Pipiles, and you have the opportunity to stop to see more ruins at Pipiles and Altar de Sacrificios. Cargo boats are cheaper (around US$8 per person) but are infrequent and take all day.

An alternative is to take a lancha a short distance downriver to Laureles on the Guatemalan side (US$1.25 *colectivo*, US$9 *especial*). From Laureles buses leave at 3am and 5am (Guatemalan time) for El Subín (2½ hours, US$2.50), where you could change for Sayaxché, and Santa Elena (4 hours, US$3) near Flores.

Benemérito de las Américas to Lagos de Montebello

South of Benemérito, the Carretera Fronteriza heads 60km south before turning due west for the 150km stretch to Tziscao in the Lagos de Montebello. East of Ixcán you're passing through jungle or semicleared jungle, crossing several tropical rivers. West of Ixcán you climb more than 1000m up to the cooler, pine-clad highlands around the Lagos de Montebello. There are numerous villages along the way, nearly all founded since the 1960s.

For information on transportation along the highway, see Getting There & Away in the introduction to this Bonampak, Yaxchilán & the Carretera Fronteriza section and under Benemérito de las Américas (above), and in the Comitán section, later in this chapter.

Ecolodges

Two projects at remote ejidos in the southern Selva Lacandona aim to preserve the environment by providing local people with an income from non-destructive tourism.

Las Guacamayas Las Guacamayas, also called Ara Macao, is on the edge of Reforma Agraria ejido, about 40km southwest of Benemérito de las Américas by unpaved road. Because of its remote location and lack of publicity it receives few visitors, but if you're dying to see red macaws, try it, for one of the center's goals is the protection of these beautiful birds. You may see howler monkeys, toucans and white-tailed deer in the 12-sq-km forest reserve here. Accommodations are in good-quality cabins, costing around US$30 for up to four people. For further information try a Chiapas state tourist office in Tuxtla Gutiérrez or elsewhere, or Escudo Jaguar in Frontera Corozal.

To get here, take a combi from Palenque or Benemérito to Pico de Oro (four daily; from Palenque, 4 hours, US$6.75; from Benemérito, one hour, US$1.25), then a taxi to Reforma Agraria (about 20 minutes, US$5). In Reforma Agraria, ask for Don Germán Hernández.

Estación Ixcán This is a solar-powered ecolodge beside the Río Lacantún, at the southern tip of the Montes Azules Biosphere Reserve. Boat trips and guided jungle walks (by night as well as day), plus swimming, a library and videos are available. You stand a good chance of seeing howler monkeys (among other wildlife), and there are Mayan ruins in the vicinity too. Unless you camp (US$11.50 per site), it's not cheap: singles/doubles/triples/quads cost US$34/55/88/99, meals are US$9-10 each, and guided excursions cost between US$17 and US$55 for up to seven people.

Estación Ixcán (☎ 55-5151-3030, **w** www .ixcan.com.mx) is on the territory of Ejido Ixcán, which is just off the Carretera Fronteriza at Km 340, approximately 100km east of Tziscao. You can reach Ejido Ixcán by bus along the Carretera Fronteriza (see Getting There & Away in the Benemérito de las Américas section, earlier in this chapter, and Getting There & Around in the Comitán section, below). Then it's a half-hour boat ride (US$44 for up to seven people) to the Estación. You can book up to 15 days ahead through Conservation International,

(☎/fax 961-602-90-32, **e** mmorales@ ci-mexico.org.mx), Boulevard Comitán 191, Colonia Moctezuma, Tuxtla Gutiérrez.

COMITÁN
• pop 70,000 • elev 1635m ☎ 963

Comitán, a pleasant, orderly town with what must be the cleanest streets in Mexico, is the last place of any size on highway 190 before the Guatemalan border. With a few minor but interesting museums and archaeological sites in and around the town, and the Lagos de Montebello an hour away, you could easily spend an enjoyable couple of days based here.

The first Spanish settlement here, San Cristóbal de los Llanos, was founded in 1527. Today the town is officially called Comitán de Domínguez, after Belisario Domínguez, a local doctor who was a national senator during the presidency of Victoriano Huerta. Domínguez spoke out in 1913 against Huerta's record of political murders and was accordingly murdered himself.

Orientation & Information
Comitán is set on hilly terrain, with a wide, attractive main plaza. North-south streets are Avenidas and east-west ones are Calles.

The Chiapas state tourist office (☎ 632-40-47), on the north side of the main plaza, has fairly well informed staff. It's open 9am to 4pm, Monday to Friday. The municipal tourist office (☎ 632-19-31), upstairs in the Palacio Municipal a couple of doors farther west, is open 9am to 2pm and 5pm to 7pm, Monday to Friday.

Bancomer, at the southeast corner of the main plaza, does currency exchange from 9am to 5pm Monday to Friday and has an ATM.

The post office is at Avenida Central Sur 45. Pay phones and telephone casetas are dotted around the central area.

Café Inter Net, at Local 12, Pasaje Morales, offers email and Internet access for US$0.90/1.75 per half-hour/hour, from 9am to 8pm daily. Cyber Centro, 1ª Calle Norte Pte 12A, has similar prices and stays open till 1am Monday to Saturday nights.

Museums
The **Casa de la Cultura**, on the southeast corner of the plaza, includes an exhibition

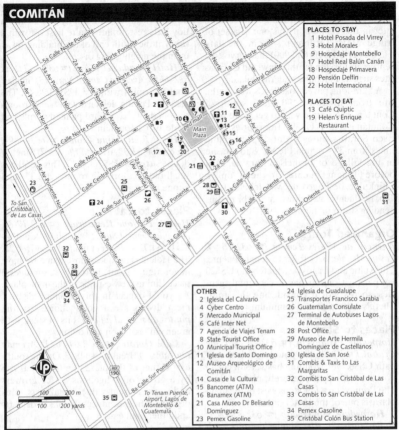

COMITÁN

PLACES TO STAY
1 Hotel Posada del Virrey
3 Hotel Morales
9 Hospedaje Montebello
17 Hotel Real Balún Canán
18 Hospedaje Primavera
20 Pensión Delfin
22 Hotel Internacional

PLACES TO EAT
13 Café Quiptic
19 Helen's Enrique
   Restaurant

OTHER
2 Iglesia del Calvario
4 Cyber Centro
5 Mercado Municipal
6 Café Inter Net
7 Agencia de Viajes Tenam
8 State Tourist Office
10 Municipal Tourist Office
11 Iglesia de Santo Domingo
12 Museo Arqueológico de
   Comitán
14 Casa de la Cultura
15 Bancomer (ATM)
16 Banamex (ATM)
21 Casa Museo Dr Belisario
   Domínguez
23 Pemex Gasoline
24 Iglesia de Guadalupe
25 Transportes Francisco Sarabia
26 Guatemalan Consulate
27 Terminal de Autobuses Lagos
   de Montebello
28 Post Office
29 Museo de Arte Hermila
   Domínguez de Castellanos
30 Iglesia de San José
31 Combis & Taxis to Las
   Margaritas
32 Combis to San Cristóbal de Las
   Casas
33 Combis to San Cristóbal de Las
   Casas
34 Pemex Gasoline
35 Cristóbal Colón Bus Station

gallery as well as an auditorium. You can walk through it to the small **Museo Arqueológico de Comitán** (☎ 632-06-24, 1ª Calle Sur Oriente; admission free; open 10am-5pm Tues-Sun), with artifacts from the area's archaeological sites. The misshapen pre-Hispanic skulls on display – deliberately 'beautified' by squeezing infants' heads between boards – make you wonder what kind of thoughts would have taken shape inside such distorted brains.

The **Casa Museo Dr Belisario Domínguez** (Avenida Central Sur 35; admission US$0.60; open 10am-6.45pm Tues-Sat, 9am-12.45pm Sun), the martyr-hero's family home, provides fascinating insights into medical practices and the life of the professional classes in early-20th-century Comitán. It's half a

block from the main plaza. One block farther down this street is a neat little art museum, the **Museo de Arte Hermila Domínguez de Castellanos** (☎ 632-20-82, Avenida Central Sur 53; admission US$0.60; open 10am-2pm & 4pm-6pm Mon-Fri, 10am-4pm Sat, 10am-1pm Sun), with paintings by many leading 20th-century Mexican artists, including Rufino Tamayo, Francisco Toledo and José Guadalupe Posada.

Tenam Puente

This Maya archaeological site (open 9am-4pm daily; admission free), 14km south of town, features three ball courts and several pyramids and other structures rising from a terraced, wooded hillside. It has a pleasant rural setting and good long-distance views

TABASCO & CHIAPAS

from the topmost structures. Like Chinkultic (see the Lagos de Montebello section, later in this chapter) it was one of a set of fringe Maya settlements from the late Classic period (AD 600-900) that survived a century or two longer than lowland Chiapas sites such as Palenque and Yaxchilán.

A 5km-long paved road leads west to the site from highway 190, 9km south of Comitán. The simple way to get there from Comitán is a taxi (US$9). Transportes Francisco Sarabia buses go at unpredictable times from 3ª Avenida Pte Sur 8 to the site or the village of Francisco Sarabia, 2km before Tenam Puente. To head on to Chinkultic or Lagos de Montebello from Tenam Puente, flag down a combi or bus heading south on highway 190.

Organized Tours

Agencia de Viajes Tenam (☎ 632-16-54, *Pasaje Morales 8A)* Tours to Tenam Puente, Chinkultic and Lagos de Montebello US$20 per person. Comitán has no car-rental agencies, so it's worth considering this tour. There's a three-person minimum.

Places to Stay

Hospedaje Primavera (☎ 632-20-41, *Calle Central Pte 4)* Singles/doubles with shared bath US$6.75/9. Comitán has several cheap posadas with small, severely plain rooms. The Primavera, a few steps west of the main plaza, is one of the better ones.

Hospedaje Montebello (☎ 632-35-72, *1ª Calle Norte Pte 10)* Singles/doubles with shared bath US$5.75/11.50, with private bath US$8/13.50. This cheapie has clean rooms around a courtyard.

Hotel Morales (☎ 632-04-36, *Avenida Central Norte 8)* Singles & doubles with bath US$17, with phone & cable TV US$23. The Morales has no sign outside, and the inside resembles an aircraft hangar, with small rooms perched around an upstairs walkway, but it's clean.

Pensión Delfín (☎ 632-00-13, *Avenida Central Sur 11)* Singles/doubles with bath & TV US$21/25. The Delfín, on the west side of the main plaza, has a pleasant rear patio and decent-size rooms, but they're not as clean as you'd hope.

Hotel Internacional (☎ 632-01-10, *fax 632-01-12, Avenida Central Sur 16)* Singles & doubles US$33, triples/quads US$40/45.

A block from the plaza, this is the best downtown hotel, with comfy rooms and a tidy little restaurant. You're best off with a room at the south end of the building, away from the neighboring disco.

Hotel Posada del Virrey (☎ 632-18-11, *fax 632-44-83, Avenida Central Norte 13)* Singles/doubles/triples with TV US$23/28/40. The pleasant Posada del Virrey has small rooms surrounding a courtyard painted purple and white, with a fountain.

Hotel Real Balún Canán (☎ 632-10-94, *fax 632-00-31, 1ª Avenida Pte Sur 7)* Singles/doubles/triples US$26/30/35. This hotel has small but comfortable rooms with TV and phone.

Places to Eat

Helen's Enrique Restaurant (☎ 632-17-30, *Avenida Central Sur 9)* Breakfasts & antojitos US$1.75-4.50, meat mains US$3.75-6.25. The Helen's Enrique, whose name we have never figured out, is the best of several places lining the west side of the main plaza. As you'd expect in this ranching district, meat dishes are a good choice: try the *puntos de filete al albañil*, bits of steak with green chilies, bacon and onion.

Café Quiptic (☎ 632-04-00, *1ª Avenida Ote Sur s/n)* Breakfasts US$3. On the southeast corner of the plaza, the Quiptic is run by a group of indigenous coffee growers and serves great-value breakfasts, plus organic coffee, sandwiches, salads, desserts and other light eats.

Getting There & Around

Comitán is 90km southeast down the Pan-American Highway from San Cristóbal, and 83km from the Guatemalan border. The Cristóbal Colón bus station (deluxe, 1st class and 2nd class) is on the Pan-American Highway, which passes through the western part of town, about a 20-minute walk from the main plaza. The highway here is named Boulevard Dr Belisario Domínguez and called simply 'El Bulevar.' Daily departures include:

Ciudad Cuauhtémoc – 83km, 1¼ hours; 7 buses (US$3.75)

Mexico City (TAPO) – 1155km, 20 hours; 5 buses (US$56-73)

San Cristóbal de Las Casas – 90km, 1½ hours; 16 buses (US$3-4), also Suburban vans (US$3) from Boulevard Dr Belisario Domínguez between 1ª and 2ª Calle Sur Pte

Tapachula – 245km, 5½ hours (via Motozintla); 7 buses (US$10.50)

Tuxtla Gutiérrez – 175km, 3½ hours; 17 buses (US$6.75-8.50)

Colón also serves Oaxaca, Palenque, Villahermosa, Playa del Carmen and Cancún.

Buses and combis to the Lagos de Montebello and along the Carretera Fronteriza go from the Terminal de Autobuses Lagos de Montebello at 2ª Avenida Pte Sur 23. Combis to Laguna Bosque Azul (US$2, 1 hour) run about every 30 minutes from 5.30am to 5.30pm. Other combis and buses head to Tziscao (US$2, 1¼ hours, 20 or more daily), Ixcán (US$5.50, 3 hours, about 12 daily), Benemérito de las Américas (US$12, 7 hours, four daily) and even Palenque (US$17, 11 hours, two daily).

'Centro' microbuses, across the road from the Colón bus station, will take you to the main plaza for US$0.40. A taxi is US$1.75.

LAGOS DE MONTEBELLO

The temperate forest along the Guatemalan border southeast of Comitán is dotted with 59 small lakes of varied colors, the Lagos (or Lagunas) de Montebello. The area is refreshing and quiet, and if you want to stretch your legs you can follow some of the little-used vehicle tracks through the forest. At the western edge of the lake district are the Mayan ruins of Chinkultic.

Orientation

The paved road to Montebello turns east off highway 190 just before the town of La Trinitaria, 16km south of Comitán. It passes Chinkultic after 30km, and enters the forest and the Parque Nacional Lagunas de Montebello 5km beyond. At the park entrance (no fee) the road splits. One road continues 3km north to end at Laguna Bosque Azul. The other heads east to the village of Tziscao (9km), beyond which it becomes the Carretera Fronteriza, continuing east to Ixcán and ultimately Palenque (see the Ixcán and Benemérito de las Américas to Lagos de Montebello sections, earlier in this chapter).

Chinkultic

These dramatically sited ruins *(admission US$3; open 10am-5pm daily)* lie 2km north of La Trinitaria-Montebello road. The access road is paved.

Chinkultic was on the far western edge of the ancient Mayan area. Dates carved here extend from AD 591 to 897. Of the 200 mounds scattered over a wide area here, only a few have been cleared, but they're worth the effort.

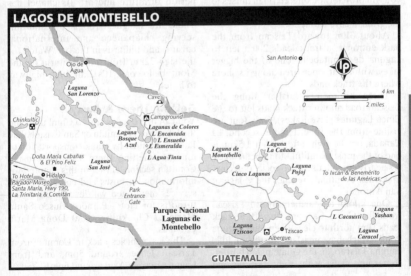

LAGOS DE MONTEBELLO

From the entrance, take the path to the left, which curves around to the right. On the hill to the right of this path stands one of Chinkultic's biggest structures, E23, still covered in thick vegetation. The path reaches an open area with several steles, some carved with human figures, and a long ball court on the right.

The other path from the entrance passes a couple of mounds on the right, then the Plaza Hundida (Sunken Plaza), then crosses a stream. It then climbs steeply up to the Acrópolis, a partly restored temple atop a rocky eminence. From the Acrópolis you have fine views over the surrounding lakes and forests and down into a *cenote* 50m below – into which the Maya used to toss offerings of pottery, beads, bones and obsidian knives.

The Lakes
The road straight on from the park entrance leads through the **Lagunas de Colores**, a group of five lakes whose hues range from turquoise to deep green. The first, on the right after about 2km, is **Laguna Agua Tinta**. Then on the left come **Laguna Esmeralda** and **Laguna Encantada**, with **Laguna Ensueño** on the right opposite Encantada. The fifth and biggest is **Laguna Bosque Azul**, on the left where the paved road ends. There are a couple of comedores here, and you will probably be offered small horses to rent: 800m along the path straight ahead is the *gruta*, a cave shrine.

About 3km toward Tziscao from the park entrance, a track leads 200m left to **Laguna de Montebello**, one of the bigger lakes, with a flat, open area along its shore where the track ends.

Three kilometers farther along the Tziscao road another track leads left to the **Cinco Lagunas** (Five Lakes). Only four are visible from the road, but the second, **La Cañada**, on the right after about 1.5km, is one of the most beautiful Montebello lakes; it's nearly cut in half by two rocky outcrops. The track eventually reaches the village of San Antonio.

One kilometer farther toward Tziscao from the Cinco Lagunas turnoff, a track leads 1km north to clear, deep blue **Laguna Pojoj**, which has an island in the middle. **Laguna Tziscao**, on the Guatemalan border, comes into view on the right, 1km beyond

the Laguna Pojoj turnoff. The junction for Tziscao village, a pleasant, spread-out place, is a little farther, again on the right.

Places to Stay
Doña María Cabañas *(La Orquidea; Carretera La Trinitaria-Lagos de Montebello Km 31.5)* Cabins US$2.25 per person. You can rent a rustic cabin and eat inexpensive food here, a few hundred meters east of the Chinkultic turnoff. The elderly owner, Señora María Domínguez Figueroa, has been looking after travelers since the 1930s. The cabins have electric light; showers and toilets are shared.

El Pino Feliz *(Carretera La Trinitaria-Lagos de Montebello Km 31.5)* Cabins US$3 per person. Right next door to Doña María's, the 'Happy Pine' has newer cabins and also provides meals.

In Tziscao village a formerly unkempt youth hostel by the lakeside has been upgraded into the ***Albergue Turístico*** with reasonable rooms for around US$11 single or double, camping space, cabins and a restaurant.

Hotel Parador-Museo Santa María *(☎/fax 963-632-51-16, Carretera La Trinitaria-Lagos de Montebello Km 22)* Singles & doubles US$68. By far the best hostelry in the region, the Santa María is a restored 19th-century hacienda, decorated with period furniture and art. Its chapel has been turned into a religious art museum. There are six guest rooms, a restaurant serving chiapaneco and international cuisine, and billiards in the bar. Watch for the sign 22km from La Trinitaria on the Montebello road. It's 2km from highway to hotel.

Getting There & Away
You can make a day trip to Chinkultic and the lakes from Comitán or San Cristóbal de Las Casas, either by public transportation or tour. See Getting There & Around in the Comitán section, earlier in this chapter, for information on buses and combis. All the services mentioned will let you off at the turnoffs for Hotel Parador-Museo Santa María or Chinkultic, or at Doña María Cabañas.

The last vehicles back to Comitán from Tziscao leave around 5pm, and from Laguna Bosque Azul around 6pm.

CIUDAD CUAUHTÉMOC
• pop 2000

This 'city' amounts to little more than a few houses and a comedor or two, but it's the last/first place in Mexico on the Pan-American Highway (190). Comitán is 83km north. Ciudad Cuauhtémoc is the Mexican border post; the Guatemalan one is 4km south at La Mesilla. Colectivo taxis (US$1.50) ferry people between the two sides. There's a bank on the Guatemalan side of the border, and money changers on both sides. Expect to be charged small fees of a couple of dollars by Guatemalan officials as you enter or leave their country.

If you get stuck at this border, the best place to stay is *Hotel Mily's*, at La Mesilla, which has doubles with fan, cable TV and bath for around US$15.

Getting There & Away
Fairly frequent buses and combis run to and from Comitán and San Cristóbal. See sections on those two cities, earlier in this chapter, for bus details.

Guatemalan buses depart La Mesilla about every half hour from 8am to about 4pm for main points inside Guatemala, such as Huehuetenango (US$1.25, 1½-2 hours) and Quetzaltenango (US$4, 3½ hours). If there's no bus to your destination, take one to Huehuetenango, where you may be able to get an onward bus.

RESERVA DE LA BIÓSFERA EL TRIUNFO
The luxuriant cloud forests high in the remote El Triunfo Biosphere Reserve in the Sierra Madre de Chiapas are a bird-lovers' paradise and a bizarre world of trees and shrubs festooned with epiphytes, ferns, bromeliads, mosses and vines. The cool cloud forest is formed by moist air rising from the hot, humid lowlands to form clouds and rain on the uplands.

The Sierra Madre de Chiapas is home to more than 30 bird species that are nonexistent or rare elsewhere in Mexico. El Triunfo is the one place in the country where it's fairly easy to see the resplendent quetzal. Other birds here include the extremely rare horned guan (big as a turkey, but dwelling high in the trees), the azure-rumped tanager, the black guan, the blue-tailed and wine-throated hummingbirds and the blue-throated motmot.

Visits are controlled fairly strictly. Avoid the May-to-October wet season. For a permit and arrangements, contact – at least one month in advance – Sonja Bartelt, Coordinadora del Programa de Visitas Guiadas, Ecoturismo, Reserva de la Biósfera El Triunfo, Calle Argentina 389, Colonia El Retiro, 29040 Tuxtla Gutiérrez, Chiapas (☎ 961-614-07-79, e ecotriunfo@hotmail.com). There's a minimum group size of four, and a minimum cost of about US$190 per person. For that you get four nights at the basic Campamento El Triunfo, 1850m high in the heart of the reserve, guides who are expert bird-spotters and some help with transportation from/to the nearest town, Jaltenango. Campamento El Triunfo is a three- to four-hour uphill hike (mules will take the baggage) from Finca Prusia, a coffee plantation near Jaltenango. Jaltenango is served by Autotranportes Cuxtepeques buses from Tuxtla Gutiérrez.

EL SOCONUSCO
The Soconusco is Chiapas' hot, fertile coastal plain, 15 to 35km wide. It's hot and sweaty year-round, and plenty of rain falls from mid-May to mid-October. The steep, lushly vegetated Sierra Madre de Chiapas, sweeping up from the plain, provides an excellent environment for coffee, bananas and other crops.

Tonalá
• pop 31,000 • elev 45m ☎ 966

Tonalá, on highway 200, is the jumping-off point for Puerto Arista. You can find a tourist office (☎ 663-27-87, cnr Hidalgo & 5 de Mayo) on the main street (Hidalgo), two blocks east of the main plaza, Parque Esperanza.

Hotel Tonalá (☎ 663-04-80, Hidalgo 172) Singles/doubles with fan & TV US$18/23. The Tonalá, between Parque Esperanza and the Colón bus station, is a reasonable moderate-price choice if you're stuck here.

Getting There & Away Cristóbal Colón (deluxe and 1st-class) and Rápidos del Sur (RS, 2nd-class) share a bus station toward the west end of town on Hidalgo, six blocks from Parque Esperanza. Frequent buses go to Tuxtla Gutiérrez (US$8-9.50, 3½ hours), Escuintla (US$7-9, 2½ hours) and Tapachula (US$10-13.50, 4 hours) from

TABASCO & CHIAPAS

early morning until evening. Colón also runs buses to Mexico City, Oaxaca and Puerto Escondido.

For Puerto Arista, combis and micro-buses (US$0.90) leave from Juárez and 5 de Mayo, one block east of the market, until 6pm. Colectivo taxis (US$1.25) run as late as 8pm from Matamoros and 5 de Mayo, one block uphill from the combi stop. A taxi is around US$7.

Puerto Arista
• pop 850 ☎ 994

Puerto Arista, 18km southwest of Tonalá, stretches lazily for about 2km along part of a 30km-long gray beach. Though the past few years have seen several substantial concrete buildings added to its collection of palm shacks, it remains a sleepy place – most of the time. On weekends a few hundred chiapanecos cruise in from the towns, and at Semana Santa and Christmas they come by the thousands, and the few permanent residents make most of their money for the year. The rest of the time, the most action you'll see is when a piglet breaks into a trot because a dog has gathered the energy to bark at it. You get through a lot of *refrescos* while you listen to the crashing of the Pacific waves.

The ocean is clean here but take care where you go in: riptides, known as *canales,* can sweep you a long way out in a short time.

Puerto Arista's only real street, interchangeably called Matamoros or Zapotal, runs along the back of the beach. The road from Tonalá hits it at a T-junction by a lighthouse, the midpoint of town.

A nice outing is to **Boca del Cielo**, a lagoonside village 15km southeast, where you can take a *lancha* across to a sandbar, with a few seafood comedores, between lagoon and ocean – almost suspended between water and sky. The road to Boca del Cielo turns southeast off the Puerto Arista-Tonalá road around 1km inland: combis from Tonalá run along it fairly frequently.

Places to Stay & Eat There are plenty of places in both directions from the lighthouse. The following is just a selection, starting at the southeast end of town and moving northwest.

José's Camping Cabañas (☎ 600-90-48) Camping US$2.25 per person, singles/ doubles/triples US$6.75/11.50/16. Head about 800m southeast from the lighthouse, then turn left (inland) by Hotel Lucero to reach this excellent place, run by a hospitable Canadian. Eleven cute cabañas, with mosquito screens, fan and electric light, are dotted about a coconut and citrus grove. The shared showers and toilets are immaculate. Good food (including vegetarian) is available at about US$6 for a typical fish meal, US$2.25 for beans and rice. Lots of birds inhabit a channel at the back.

Cabañas Maya Bell (☎ 600-90-50) Camping US$2.25 per person, singles/ doubles/triples US$8/10/13.50. Mexican-run Maya Bell, just along the street from José's, has cabañas with small built-in bathrooms. Boat rides along the channel behind cost US$6.75.

Hotel Lucerito (☎ 600-90-41, *Matamoros 800*) Singles & doubles/quads US$ 34/50. This is the best hotel at the east end of town, with air-conditioned rooms, pool and restaurant. It doesn't front the beach, though. Prices sometimes rise on the weekend.

Restaurant Playa Escondido (☎ 600-90-52) Singles & doubles US$5.75, quads US$11.50. Just 150m southeast of the lighthouse, this is typical of several beachfront comedores, with a few basic, bare little rooms. They come with fan and bathroom.

Hotel Lizeth (☎ 600-90-38) Rooms with one double bed US$15/27 with fan/air-con, with two double beds US$23/34. Three-story Lizeth is almost opposite the lighthouse. The rooms are OK and have private bath, but are a bit dark and stuffy. Add US$5 on the weekend.

Restaurant Hospedaje Brisas del Mar (☎ 600-90-47) Rooms with two double beds, fan & bath US$23/34 with fan/air-con. Fronting the beach one block northwest of the Lizeth, this place has bare, medium-size rooms at the back of its restaurant area.

Hotel Arista Bugambilias (☎ 600-90-44) doubles US$62, suites for four US$94. Almost 1km northwest of the lighthouse, this is the top hotel, with a pool, restaurant and bar in beachfront gardens. Rooms are not enormous but pleasant enough, with air-con and TV. Add 25% in high season.

Getting There & Away See the Tonalá section, above.

Reserva de la Biósfera La Encrucijada

This large biosphere reserve protects a 1448-sq-km strip of coastal lagoons, sandbars, wetlands, forest and Mexico's tallest mangroves (some above 30m). It's a vital wintering and breeding ground for migratory birds, and a well-preserved, important ecosystem. Inhabitants include one of Mexico's biggest populations of jaguars, plus ocelots, spider monkeys, white-tailed deer, eight turtle species, river crocodiles, caimans, boa constrictors, fishing bats, anteaters, fishing eagles and lots of waterfowl. Many of these species are in danger of extinction. There are also about 27,000 people in scattered settlements.

A ride in a lancha through the reserve will take you between towering mangroves and past palm-thatched lagoonside villages. You'll see plenty of birds any time of year but best is the November-to-March nesting season.

The biosphere reserve has offices at Avenida Central 4, Acapetahua (6km southwest of Escuintla; ☎ 918-647-00-84), and 3ª Calle Ote Norte 162, Barrio La Pimienta, Tuxtla Gutiérrez (☎ 961-618-21-05, e laencrucijada@infosel.net.mx). Contact either office, at least a week beforehand, about visits to the reserve's study and vigilance center, Campamento La Concepción, which has guides available (for costs, see Places to Stay & Eat, below). La Concepción is a 25km lancha ride southeast from Embarcadero Las Garzas, which is 16km southwest of Acapetahua.

Nearer to Embarcadero Las Garzas is Barra de Zacapulco, a small settlement on a sandbar between ocean and lagoon, with a handful of palapa comedores and a sea turtle breeding center nearby.

Places to Stay & Eat
At the *Barra de Zacapulco comedores* you can camp or sling a hammock for a minimal fee. A big plate of fresh prawns with salad and tortillas costs around US$5.

Campamento La Concepción (see above) Visits of two days and two nights for one/two/three/four people US$205/295/387/478. The price includes food, guided excursions and transportation. There's accommodation for up to 20 people.

Hotel El Carmen (☎ 918-647-00-62, Avenida Central, Acapetahua) Singles & doubles US$11.50. This hotel on Acapetahua's main street has air-con rooms with bath and TV.

Getting There & Away
Take a bus along highway 200 to Escuintla, then get a colectivo taxi to Acapetahua (US$0.60, 6km). Beside the railway in Acapetahua, get a combi or bus to Embarcadero Las Garzas (US$1.50, 16km). These run about every 30 minutes.

From Embarcadero Las Garzas, a colectivo lancha to Barra de Zacapulco takes 25 minutes for US$3. The last lancha back to Embarcadero Las Garzas may leave Barra de Zacapulco as early as 3.30pm, and the last combi from Embarcadero Las Garzas to Acapetahua about 4.30pm.

A three-hour private lancha tour from Embarcadero Las Garzas costs around US$55.

TAPACHULA
* pop 180,000 ☎ 962

Mexico's southernmost city is a gateway to Guatemala and a busy commercial center. It has few redeeming features, but the surrounding area, dominated by 4110m-high Tacaná, the first of a chain of volcanoes stretching southeast into Guatemala, has its attractions.

Orientation & Information
The central Parque Hidalgo is the site of the tourist office, banks, cathedral and museum. Bus stations and places to stay are scattered around the central area.

The municipal tourist office (no ☎), on 8ª Norte facing Parque Hidalgo, is open 9am to 9pm Monday to Friday and 9am to 1pm Saturday.

The Instituto Nacional de Migración (☎ 626-91-02) is at Carretera del Antiguo Aeropuerto Km 1.5, about 2.5km south of the center.

There are banks with ATMs around Parque Hidalgo (see the Tapachula map). You can also change cash at Centro Cambiario Casa Santa, 2ª Norte 6, open 8.30am to 5.30pm Monday to Friday, 8.30am to 2.30pm Saturday.

The post office, east of the center on 1ª Oriente, opens 9am to 3pm Monday to Saturday. @cuan@utas, 5ª Pte 17, and Ciber Pacheco, just along the street, charge

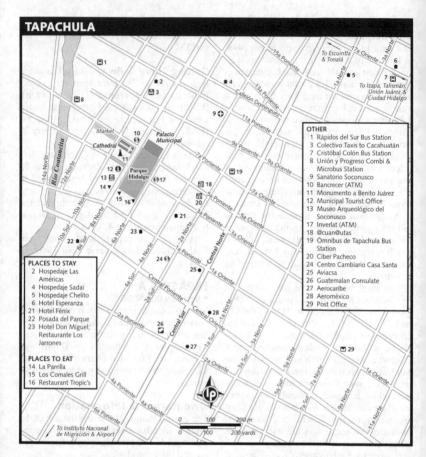

TAPACHULA

OTHER
1 Rápidos del Sur Bus Station
3 Colectivo Taxis to Cacahuatán
7 Cristóbal Colón Bus Station
8 Unión y Progreso Combi &
   Microbus Station
9 Sanatorio Soconusco
10 Bancrecer (ATM)
11 Monumento a Benito Juárez
12 Municipal Tourist Office
13 Museo Arqueológico del
   Soconusco
17 Inverlat (ATM)
18 @cuan@utas
19 Ómnibus de Tapachula Bus
   Station
20 Ciber Pacheco
24 Centro Cambiario Casa Santa
25 Aviacsa
26 Guatemalan Consulate
27 Aerocaribe
28 Aeroméxico
29 Post Office

PLACES TO STAY
2 Hospedaje Las
   Américas
4 Hospedaje Sadai
5 Hospedaje Chelito
6 Hotel Esperanza
21 Hotel Fénix
22 Posada del Parque
23 Hotel Don Miguel;
   Restaurante Los
   Jarrones

PLACES TO EAT
14 La Parrilla
15 Los Comales Grill
16 Restaurant Tropic's

US$1.25 an hour for Internet access. Both are open from 8am to 10pm daily.

For medical services, Sanatorio Soconusco (☎ 626-50-74, 4ª Norte 68) handles *urgencias* (emergencies).

Museo Arqueológico del Soconusco

The Soconusco Archaeological Museum (☎ 625-54-09, 8ª Norte; admission free; open 10am-5pm Tues-Sun), facing Parque Hidalgo, displays some of the best finds from the nearby Izapa ruins, including stone sculptures and a gold-and-turquoise-encrusted skull.

Places to Stay

Budget All rooms in these places have attached bathrooms.

Hospedaje Las Américas (☎ 626-27-57, 10a Nte 47) Singles US$6.75, doubles US$9-11.50, triples US$13.50-16. Four blocks from Parque Hidalgo, this cheapie has a leafy patio and clean rooms with fan.

Posada del Parque (☎ 626-51-18, 8ª Sur 3) Singles US$10, doubles US$11.50-15, air-con singles & doubles US$17.50. The rooms are muggy, despite fans, but they're clean, with small curtained-off bathrooms.

Hospedaje Chelito (☎ 626-24-28, 1ª Norte 107) Singles/doubles/triples with fan and cable TV US$17/19.50/22, with air-con US$23/23/27. A short walk from the Cristóbal Colón bus station, Chelito has clean, good-size rooms.

Hospedaje Sadai (☎ 626-38-20, Callejón Domínguez 17) Singles/doubles/triples

TABASCO & CHIAPAS

US$8/9/13.50. The Sadai has rooms on two floors, arranged around a patio where cars park. Rooms are adequately clean but drab and dark.

Mid-Range *Hotel Esperanza (☎/fax 625-91-35, 17ª Oriente 8)* Singles/doubles/triples with fan US$23/27/32, with air-con US$32/35/42. Across the street from the Colón bus station, the Esperanza offers nice, clean, new rooms with cable TV.

Hotel Fénix (☎ 625-07-55, fax 626-47-47, ☒ www.fenix.com.mx, 4ª Norte 19) Singles/doubles with fan US$19/24, with air-con US$32/39, with air-con & cable TV US$40/50. The Fénix's most expensive rooms, which have been remodeled, are good; some of the others are small and dark.

Hotel Don Miguel (☎ 626-11-43, fax 626-10-59, 1ª Pte 18) Singles/doubles US$47/58, suites from US$69. The Don Miguel is the best city-center hotel. Rooms are clean and bright, with air-con and TV. But beware attempts to short-change you at reception.

Places to Eat
Los Comales Grill (☎ 626-24-05, Portal Pérez) Antojitos & egg dishes US$1.75-4, meat dishes US$4.50-9. Open 24 hours daily. Los Comales, the best of several restaurants lined up along the south side of Parque Hidalgo, serves a bit of everything: the *filetes* and steaks are good.

Restaurant Tropic's (Portal Pérez) Antojitos & egg dishes US$1.75-3.50, meat dishes US$3.50-6.75. Tropic's is a cheaper option, a few doors from Los Comales.

La Parrilla (☎ 626-40-62, 8ª Norte 28) Antojitos US$1.75-3.50, meat dishes US$4.50-8. Open 7am-12.30am daily. Across the street from Los Comales, La Parrilla has another wide-ranging menu. Tasty *tortas a la plancha* cost under US$3; good, big plates of fruit salad are US$3.50. Try a thirst-quenching *agua de maracuyá* (passion fruit juice).

Restaurante Los Jarrones (Hotel Don Miguel, ☎ 626-11-43, 1ª Pte 18) Breakfasts US$3.50-6.75, mains US$5.75-11.50. This air-conditioned hotel restaurant is one of the best and most popular places in town, with a big choice of Mexican and international fare.

Getting There & Around
Air Aviacsa (☎ 626-14-39), Central Norte 18, and Aeroméxico (☎ 800-021-40-10),

Central Oriente 4, both fly at least twice daily to/from Mexico City, with connections there for other destinations.

Aerocaribe (☎ 626-98-72), 2ª Oriente 4, flies daily to/from Mérida via Tuxtla Gutiérrez and Palenque, and to/from Veracruz Monday to Friday.

Tapachula's airport is 20km southwest of the city off the Puerto Madero road. Transporte Terrestre (☎ 625-12-87), 2ª Sur 68, charges around US$5 per person from the airport to any hotel in the city, or vice-versa.

Bus Cristóbal Colón (☎ 626-28-81), on 17ª Oriente 1km northeast of Parque Hidalgo, operates deluxe and 1st-class buses. The main 2nd-class bus stations are Rápidos del Sur (RS) at 9a Pte 62, and Ómnibus de Tapachula (OT) at 7ª Pte 5.

Departures include:

Comitán – 245km, 6 hours (via Motozintla); 6 Colón (US$10.50)

Escuintla – 85km, 1 hour; 9 Colón (US$4), 31 RS (US$2.25), 53 OT (US$1.75)

Mexico City (TAPO or Norte) – 1110km, 18 hours; 7 Colón (US$62)

Oaxaca – 670km, 12 hours; 3 Colón (US$32-37)

San Cristóbal de Las Casas – 335km, 7½ hours; 6 Colón (US$14)

Tonalá – 220km, 4 hours; 12 Colón (US$10-13.50), 31 RS (US$8.50)

Tuxtla Gutiérrez – 390km, 7 hours; 18 Colón (US$18-22), 31 RS (US$16)

Colón also goes daily to Palenque, Bahías de Huatulco, Pochutla, Puerto Escondido, Cancún, Villahermosa and Veracruz.

To travel to and from Guatemala, there are a few companies that run buses from the Colón station to Guatemala City and also other main Central American cities. Transportes Galgos runs to/from Guatemala City (US$22, 6 hours) twice daily. Its Guatemala City terminal (☎ 230-5058) is at 7ª Avenida 19-144, Zona 1. Tica Bus leaves at 7am for Guatemala City (US$17, 6 hours) and San Salvador (US$26, 10 hours). You can buy tickets through to Chuluteca, Honduras (US$43), Managua (US$54) and San José, Costa Rica (US$65), involving overnight stops at San Salvador and Managua. Tica's Guatemala City terminal (☎ 331-4279) is at 11a Calle 2-72, Zona 9.

For destinations this side of Guatemala City you need to get a bus from the border (see the Guatemalan Border Towns section, later in this chapter).

AROUND TAPACHULA
Izapa

The Pre-Hispanic ruins at Izapa are important to archaeologists but of limited interest to the nonenthusiast. Izapa flourished from approximately 200 BC to AD 200, and the Izapa carving style (typically seen on tall slabs known as steles, fronted by round altars) shows descendants of Olmec deities, with their upper lips unnaturally lengthened. Early Mayan monuments in northern Guatemala are similar, and Izapa is thus considered an important 'bridge' between the Olmecs and the Maya.

Izapa is around 11km east of Tapachula on the Talismán road. There are three groups of ruins, at each of which the caretaking family will ask you for US$0.50 or so.

The northern part of the site is on the left of the road if you're coming from Tapachula: watch for the small pyramids. As well as a few low pyramids, you'll see here a ball court and several carved steles and altars. The warden, whose home, piglets and chicks are all part of the site, has a basic information sheet in Spanish.

From the northern area, go 700m back toward Tapachula and take a signposted dirt road to the left. You'll pass houses with 2000-year-old sculptures lying in their gardens. After 800m you reach a fork with signs to Izapa Grupo A and Izapa Grupo B, each about 250m farther. Grupo A is a set of weathered stele-and-altar pairings around a field. Grupo B is a couple of grass-covered mounds and more stone sculpture, including three curious ball-on-pillar affairs.

Getting There & Away Take a Unión y Progreso combi or microbus (US$0.70) from 5ª Pte 53 in Tapachula.

Santo Domingo, Unión Juárez & Volcán Tacaná
☎ 962

Dormant Tacaná towers on the Guatemalan border northeast of Tapachula. Even if you're not interested in climbing to the summit, two villages on its gorgeously verdant lower slopes make an attractive side trip and are

several agreeable degrees cooler than Tapachula.

Santo Domingo (population: 3500) lies 34km northeast of Tapachula amid coffee plantations. The splendid three-story wooden 1920s *casa grande* of the German immigrants who formerly owned the coffee plantation here has been restored as the **Centro Turístico Santo Domingo** (☎ 629-12-75, admission free), with a restaurant, video bar, small coffee museum and well-tended tropical garden.

Nine kilometers up the paved road beyond Santo Domingo, Unión Juárez (population 2500, elevation 1300m) is the starting point for ascents of Tacaná. Tapachula folk like to come up here on weekends and holidays to cool off and tuck into a *parrillada*, a big plate of grilled meat and a few vegetables. The best month to climb the mountain is December, which is cold but dry. Guatemalans even hold a small food and drink market at the summit (which is on the Mexico-Guatemala border) over the Christmas holiday period. Climbing conditions are worse during the wet months, April to October.

There are two routes up the mountain from Unión Juárez. Neither requires any technical climbing, but you need to allow two or three days for either, plus time to acclimatize. Be prepared for extreme cold at the top. If you have a vehicle (preferably 4WD) the better option is first to drive 12km up to Chiquihuite. From there it's a three-hour walk to Papales, where you can sleep in huts for US$0.90. From Papales to the summit is about a five-hour ascent. If you're without a vehicle, the preferable route is via Talquián (about two hours' walk from Unión Juárez) and Trigales (five hours from Talquián). It's about a six-hour climb from Trigales to the summit.

It's a good idea to get a guide in Unión Juárez, especially for the Chiquihuite-Papeles route, which is harder to follow. Brothers Fernando and Diego Valera (ⓔ dievaletacana@hotmail.com) charge between US$30 and US$50 for most ascents: ask for them at the Hotel Colonial Campestre. Diego speaks passable English.

Another place to head for in the area is **Pico del Loro**, a parrot's-beak-shaped overhanging rock that offers fine panoramas. The rock is 5km up a driveable track that leaves the Santo Domingo-Unión Juárez road about halfway between the two villages.

La Ventana (the Window) is a lookout point over Guatemala and the valley of the Río Suchiate (which forms the border): it's about a 20-minute from the road 2km below Unión Juárez. The turnoff is about 300m above the Km 27 marker. Or ask directions to the **Cascadas Muxbal** waterfalls, about one hour's walk from Unión Juárez.

Places to Stay & Eat *Hotel Santo Domingo* (☎ *629-90-73*) Singles/doubles/triples & quads US$17/23/34. A short walk from the Centro Turístico, Santo Domingo's old Casa del Pueblo has been converted into a hotel with reasonable fan-cooled rooms with bath.

Hotel Colonial Campestre (☎ *647-20-00, fax 647-20-15, 1½ blocks below Unión Juárez plaza*) Singles/doubles/triples US$27/23/34. Restaurant main dishes US$4.50-6.50. Rooms are sizeable, with bath, and most have TV and good views. In the restaurant a big meaty parrillada for two is US$13.50.

Hotel Aljoad (☎ *647-21-06, half a block from top of Unión Juárez plaza*) Singles/doubles US$11.50/23. The rooms here are more economical than the above hotels, but still have hot-water bathrooms. Food is commensurately cheaper too.

Centro Turístico Santo Domingo (☎ *629-12-75*) Salads & antojitos US$3, chicken/meat US$4-6. The restaurant here has some tables outside on the attractive multiple verandahs.

There are more *restaurants* around Unión Juárez plaza.

Getting There & Away From Tapachula you must first get to the small town of Cacahuatán, 20km north. Unión y Progreso microbuses (US$0.80, 1 hour) go every few minutes from 5ª Pte 53, as do colectivo taxis (US$1.25, 30 minutes) from 10a Norte between 9a and 11a Pte. From where these services terminate in Cacahuatán, Transportes Tacaná combis head on to Santo Domingo (US$0.70, 30 minutes) and Unión Juárez (US$0.80, 45 minutes).

Guatemalan Border Towns

The road from Tapachula to Izapa heads a further 9km northeast to the international border at Talismán bridge, opposite El Carmen, Guatemala. A branch south off the Talismán road leads to another cross-border bridge at Ciudad Hidalgo (37km from Tapachula), opposite Ciudad Tecún Umán, Guatemala. Both crossings are open 24 hours and have money-changing facilities. The Guatemalan border posts may make various small charges as you go through, and they may insist on being paid in either dollars or quetzals, so get some before you leave Tapachula.

Getting There & Away Microbuses of Unión y Progreso leave for Talismán from 5ª Pte 53 in Tapachula every few minutes, 5.30am to 10.30pm (US$0.80). You can also catch them on the street outside the Cristóbal Colón bus station as they leave town. A taxi from Tapachula to Talismán takes 20 minutes and costs around US$7.

Rápidos del Sur buses from 9a Pte 62 in Tapachula make the 45-minute journey to Ciudad Hidalgo every 20 minutes from 6am to 6.30pm (US$1.25). In the opposite direction, the buses run from 7am to 7.30pm.

Frequent buses leave Ciudad Tecún Umán for Guatemala City (about five hours away) by the coastal slope route through Retalhuleu and Escuintla. From El Carmen there's colectivo taxi service to Malacatán, on the road to Quetzaltenango. If you're heading for Lake Atitlán or Chichicastenango, you need to get to Quetzaltenango (Xela) first, for which you can get buses at Retalhuleu or Malacatán.

The Yucatán Peninsula

The Yucatán Peninsula is the realm of the Maya. Inheritors of a glorious and often violent history, they live today where their ancestors lived a millennium ago. They are proud to be Mexican, but even prouder to be Maya, and it is the Mayab – the lands of the Maya, which also include Guatemala, parts of Belize and Honduras and much of Chiapas – that they consider their true country.

When the Spanish conquered the Mayan city of T'hó in 1542, they founded Mérida, now the capital of Yucatán state, in its place. For centuries, Mérida answered directly to Spain, rather than Mexico City. Conse-

quently, the peninsula has always looked upon itself as distinct from the rest of Mexico.

The flat and hot Yucatán Peninsula has surprising diversity. Comprising three Mexican states – Quintana Roo, Yucatán and Campeche – the peninsula is home to numerous archaeological sites, several handsome colonial cities, Mexico's most popular seaside resort and plenty of quiet coastlines. The rainy season is mid-August to mid-October, when you'll get afternoon showers most days. A good time to visit is in November or early December, when it's less crowded and less expensive.

Highlights

- Chichén Itzá – an extensive Maya-Toltec ceremonial center with unique and exceptionally fine architecture
- Cenotes – limestone sinkholes filled with water, holding fantastic formations for great swimming, snorkeling and diving
- Campeche – colonial walls, bastions, forts and houses, and a small museum brimming with archaeological treasures
- Caribbean beaches – crystalline water, a vast barrier reef and world-class diving

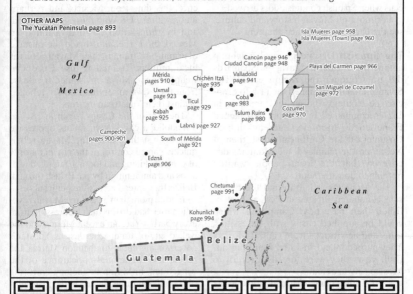

OTHER MAPS
The Yucatán Peninsula page 893

Gulf of Mexico

Isla Mujeres page 958
Isla Mujeres (Town) page 960

Cancún page 946
Ciudad Cancún page 948

Playa del Carmen page 966

Mérida pages 910
Chichén Itzá page 935
Valladolid page 941

San Miguel de Cozumel page 972

Uxmal page 923
Ticul page 929
Cobá page 983

Kabah page 925
Tulum Ruins page 980
Cozumel page 970

Labná page 927

Campeche pages 900-901
South of Mérida page 921

Edzná page 906

Chetumal page 991
Caribbean Sea

Kohunlich page 994

Belize

Guatemala

History

The Maya At the height of the Mayan culture, during the late Classic period (AD 600-900), the Mayan lands were ruled not as an empire but as a collection of independent but also interdependent city-states. Each city-state had its noble house, headed by a king who was the social, political and religious focus of the city's life.

By the end of the period, the focus of Mayan civilization had shifted from Guatemala and Belize to the Yucatán Peninsula, where a new civilization developed at Chichén Itzá, Uxmal, Labná, Kabah, Edzná, Sayil and elsewhere.

Prevailing expert opinion has it that classic Mayan civilization collapsed in the 9th and 10th centuries. One story has it that a Toltec king named Topiltzin led an invasion of the Yucatán Peninsula in 987 and easily conquered the Maya. Through battles previously won, Topiltzin had taken on legendary status, and his name became virtually inseparable from that of the great god Quetzalcóatl or, in Maya, Kukulcán. He established himself on the Yucatán Peninsula at Uucil-abnal (Chichén Itzá), and upon his death, it was said he would one day return from the direction of the rising sun and initiate a new era. This legend haunted many Mesoamericans when Spanish conquistadors arrived.

For more on Mayan history and culture, see the Facts about Mexico chapter.

The Spanish Despite political infighting among the Yucatecan Maya, the Spaniards did not conquer the region easily. The Spanish monarch assigned the task to Francisco de Montejo, who set out from Spain in 1527 accompanied by his son, also named Francisco de Montejo. Landing first at Cozumel off the Caribbean coast, then at Xel-ha on the mainland, the Montejos discovered that the local people wanted nothing to do with them.

The Montejos sailed around the peninsula, conquered Tabasco in 1530, and established their base near Campeche, which could be supplied easily with necessities, arms and new troops from central Mexico. They pushed inland, but after four long, difficult years they were forced to return to Mexico City in defeat.

In 1540, the younger Montejo took up the cause again, with his father's support. He returned to Campeche with a cousin named – you got it – Francisco de Montejo, and the two pressed inland with speed and success. Allying themselves with the Xiú Maya against the Cocom Maya, they defeated the Cocoms and gained the Xiús as converts to Christianity.

The Montejos founded Mérida in 1542 and within four years had brought almost all of the Yucatán Peninsula under Spanish rule. The once proud and independent Maya became peons working for Spanish masters.

Independence Period When Mexico won its independence from Spain in 1821, the new Mexican government urged the peoples of the Yucatán Peninsula, Chiapas and Central America to join it in the formation of one large new state. Yucatán and Chiapas accepted the offer. Mayan claims to ancestral lands were largely ignored, and huge plantations were created for the cultivation of tobacco, sugarcane and henequen (agave rope fiber). The Maya, though legally free, were enslaved in debt peonage to the great landowners.

War of the Castes Not long after ties with Spain were broken, the Yucatecan ruling classes were again dreaming of independence, this time from Mexico, and perhaps union with the US. With these goals in mind, and in anticipation of an invasion from Mexico, the *hacendados* made the mistake of arming and training their Mayan peons as local militias. Trained to use European weaponry, the Maya envisioned a release from their own misery and boldly rebelled against their Yucatecan masters.

The War of the Castes began in 1847 in Valladolid, a city known for its oppressive laws against the Maya. The Mayan rebels quickly gained control of the city in an orgy of vengeful killing and looting. Supplied with arms and ammunition by the British through Belize, they spread across the peninsula.

In little more than a year, the Mayan revolutionaries had driven their oppressors from every part of Yucatán except Mérida and the walled city of Campeche. Just as Yucatán's governor was about to abandon Mérida, the rebels saw the annual appearance of the winged ant. In Mayan mythology, corn (the staff of life) must be planted at the first sighting of the winged ant. If the sowing is delayed,

THE YUCATÁN PENINSULA

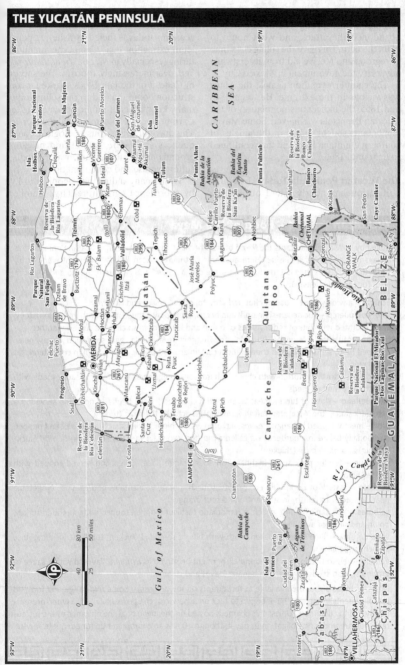

Chac, the rain god, will be affronted and respond with a drought. Thus, the rebels abandoned the attack and went home to plant the corn. This gave the ruling class time to regroup and receive aid from its erstwhile adversary, the government in Mexico City.

The counterrevolution against the Maya was vicious in the extreme. Between 1848 and 1855, the indigenous population of the Yucatán Peninsula was halved. Some Mayan combatants sought refuge in the jungles of southern Quintana Roo, and they continued to fight until 1866.

The Yucatán Peninsula Today Henequen cultivation has nearly faded out on the peninsula, though the fiber is still imported from Brazil and made into rope. The economy today is fueled by fisheries, petroleum extraction near Campeche, manufacturing (especially in Mérida's *maquiladoras)* and, ever increasingly, tourism. The success of Cancún in the late 1960s sparked a construction boom that led to the selling off of many kilometers of public beach along the Caribbean coast to commercial developers. This has had disastrous ecological consequences as wildlife habitat and breeding grounds are destroyed and water supplies suffer overuse and contamination.

While many indigenous people still live by subsistence agriculture, large numbers

Yucatecan Cuisine – Food of the Maya

Called by its Maya inhabitants the 'Land of the Pheasant and the Deer,' the Yucatán Peninsula has always had a distinctive cuisine. Here are some of the Yucatecan dishes you might want to try (note that squash is the US term for what some call 'marrow,' and cilantro is the US and Mexican term for coriander leaves):

achiote – a widely used sauce of chopped tomato, onion, chilies and cilantro

frijol con puerco – Yucatecan-style pork and beans, topped by a sauce made with grilled tomatoes, and decorated with bits of radish, slices of onion and leaves of fresh cilantro; served with rice

huevos motuleños – 'eggs Motul style'; fried eggs atop a tortilla, garnished with beans, peas, chopped ham, sausage, grated cheese and a certain amount of spicy chili – high in cholesterol, fat and flavor

papadzules – tortillas stuffed with chopped hard-boiled eggs and topped with a sauce made with squash or cucumber seeds

pavo relleno – slabs of turkey meat layered with chopped, spiced beef and pork and served in a rich, dark sauce; the Yucatecan *faisán* (pheasant) is actually the *pavo* (turkey)

pibil – meat wrapped in banana leaves, flavored with achiote, garlic, sour orange, salt and pepper, traditionally baked in a barbecue pit called a *pib*; the two main varieties are *cochinita pibil* (suckling pig) and *pollo pibil* (chicken)

poc-chuc – tender pork strips marinated in sour orange juice, grilled and served topped with pickled onions

puchero – a stew of pork, chicken, carrots, squash, potatoes, plantains and *chayote* (vegetable pear), spiced with radish, fresh cilantro and sour orange

salbutes – Yucatán's favorite snack: a handmade tortilla fried then topped with shredded turkey, onion and slices of avocado

sopa de lima – 'lime soup'; chicken broth with bits of shredded chicken, tortilla strips, lime juice and chopped lime

venado – venison, a popular traditional dish, might be served as a *pipián*, flavored with a sauce of ground squash seeds, wrapped in banana leaves and steamed

Many of these dishes are available at restaurants on the peninsula. Some mid-range and top-end establishments in the area have begun to tack on a *'servicio'* charge (usually 10%) when presenting the bill to customers. Unless this charge is posted on the menu or at the entrance of the restaurant, you are under no obligation to pay it, though 10% is an appropriate tip for adequate service.

work in the service industries and construction. Some individuals and communities, often with outside encouragement, are having a go at ecotourism, opening their lands to tourists and/or serving as guides.

The Yucatán Peninsula is widely regarded as one of the safest areas in Mexico today, and large numbers of people from other parts of the country continue to settle here, attracted by the security, tourist dollars and high employment rate.

Geography & Geology

The Yucatán Peninsula is one vast, flat limestone shelf rising only a dozen meters above sea level. The shelf extends outward below sea level from the shoreline for several kilometers. If you approach the peninsula by air, you should have no trouble seeing the barrier reef that marks the limit of the shelf. It's the longest in the Northern Hemisphere, extending from southern Belize to Isla Mujeres off the northern coast of Quintana Roo. On the landward side of the reef, the water is usually no more than 5m to 10m deep. On the seaward side of the reef, the water plunges to a depth of several thousand meters only 10km out.

The underwater shelf makes Yucatán's coastline wonderful for aquatic sports, keeping the waters warm and the marine life (fish, crabs, lobsters, tourists) abundant, but it makes life difficult for traders, who cannot bring their oceangoing vessels near shore to dock.

Anomalies on the otherwise flat peninsula include rolling hills rising to several hundred meters in the Puuc region of Yucatán state, near Uxmal, and the hills in the heavily forested southern section of the peninsula along the Mexico-Guatemala border.

The peninsula has few lakes and exposed rivers, but thanks to the porous limestone it does have underground rivers and pools. Yucatecans have traditionally drawn their freshwater from *cenotes* (limestone caverns with collapsed roofs), which serve as natural cisterns. And south of the Puuc region, in the Chenes region, the inhabitants get water from the *chenes* (limestone pools) that gave the region its name; the pools are more than a hundred meters below ground.

Campeche State

Campeche is the first of the Yucatán Peninsula's three states that travelers coming overland from other parts of Mexico hit, but it is the least visited. Campeche is proudly preparing to take its place among Mexico's top tourist destinations, however, as rapid excavation, restoration and reconstruction work continue at many locations throughout the state. Visitors can enjoy the uncrowded Mayan archaeological sites of Edzná, Calakmul and Chicanná; the impressive walled city of Campeche, with its colonial fortifications and architecture; and the Reserva de la Biósfera Calakmul, Mexico's largest biosphere reserve.

The 56,000-sq-km state is largely flat, like other parts of the peninsula, but instead of light forest and brush, 30% of Campeche is covered with jungle. Marshlands, ponds and inlets are common along the state's coastline, which faces the dark and generally uninviting waters of the Gulf of Mexico.

ESCÁRCEGA TO XPUJIL

Highway 186 heads nearly due east across southern-central Campeche state, from grubby Escárcega through jungle to Chetumal, in Quintana Roo, a 261km, three-hour ride. It passes near several fascinating Mayan sites and through the ecologically diverse and archaeologically rich Calakmul Biosphere Reserve. The largest settlement between Escárcega and Chetumal – and the only one with accommodations – is Xpujil, on highway 186 about 20km west of the Campeche-Quintana Roo border. The only gasoline station in the same stretch is about 5km east of Xpujil.

Many of the numerous archaeological sites between Escárcega and Xpujil are being restored. The most significant historically is Calakmul, which is also one of the most difficult to reach (no buses). It and most of the other sites in this section can be visited by taxis hired in Xpujil or tours booked either through hotels in Xpujil or through Corazón Maya in Campeche (see Organized Tours in the Campeche section).

The predominant architectural styles of the region's archaeological sites are Río Bec and Chenes. The former is characterized by long, low buildings that look as though they're divided into sections, each with a huge serpent or 'monster' mouth for a door. The façades are decorated with smaller masks, geometric designs (with many X forms) and columns. At the corners of the buildings are tall, solid towers with extremely small, steep, nonfunctional steps and topped by small false temples. Many of these towers have roofcombs. The Chenes style shares most of these characteristics except for the towers.

Escárcega
• pop 25,000 ☎ 982

These days many buses between Villahermosa, in Tabasco, and the Yucatán Peninsula bypass Escárcega, taking coastal highway 180 through Ciudad del Carmen. But some still stop here, as do many coming from Palenque. Unless you must break your journey to rest, there is no reason to stay in this town at the junction of highways 186 and 261, 150km south of Campeche and 301km from Villahermosa. Indeed, as most buses arrive in town full and depart in the same condition, you may find it difficult to get out of Escárcega if you break your trip here.

The town is spread out along 2km of highway 186 toward Chetumal. The ADO station is at the junction of the highways; the 2nd-class Sur bus terminal is 1.7km east on highway 186. Most hotels are nearer to the Sur terminal than to the ADO; most of the better restaurants are nearer the ADO terminal.

Balamkú

Balamkú *(Chunhabil; admission US$3.50, free Sun & holidays; open 8am-5pm daily)* is 60km west of Xpujil (less than 3km west of Conhuas), then just under 3km north of the highway along a rough unpaved road. Discovered only in 1990, the site boasts recently uncovered frescoes with still-visible red paint, and an exquisite, ornate stucco frieze showing a jaguar flanked by two large mask designs and topped with images of a king in various forms. Another section has figures as well (look for the toad). The unusual design bears little resemblance to any of the known decorative elements in the Chenes and Río Bec styles and has mystified archaeologists.

The frieze is well preserved; a structure has been built over it, with skylights, but a flashlight can come in handy. Exploration and restoration continue.

A roundtrip taxi ride from Xpujil with a one-hour visit costs US$44.

Calakmul

Most Mayanists agree that Calakmul *(Adjacent Mounds; admission US$3.50, free Sun & holidays; open 8am-5pm daily)* is an important site. Discovered in 1931 by American botanist Cyrus Lundell, it's larger than Tikal, in Guatemala. But so far only a fraction of its 100-sq-km expanse has been cleared, and few of its 6500 buildings have been consolidated, let alone restored. Exploration and restoration are ongoing, however. The turnoff to Calakmul is 59km west of Xpujil, and the site is 59km farther south on a paved road.

Lying at the heart of the vast, untrammeled Calakmul Biosphere Reserve – one of the two Unesco-designated biosphere regions on the Yucatán Peninsula (Sian Ka'an is the other) – the ruins are surrounded by rain forest, which is best viewed from the top of one of the several pyramids. Visiting the site is a good opportunity to explore the area without risk of getting lost in the jungle. Visitors are likely to see wild turkeys, parrots, toucans and other of the huge number of species living within the reserve.

From about AD 250 to 695, Calakmul was the leading city in a vast region known as the Kingdom of the Serpent's Head. Its perpetual rival was Tikal, and its decline began with the power struggles and internal conflicts that followed the defeat by Tikal of Calakmul's king Garra de Jaguar (Jaguar Paw).

As at Tikal, there are indications that construction occurred over a period of more than a millennium. Beneath Edificio VII, archaeologists discovered a burial crypt with some 2000 pieces of jade, and tombs continue to yield spectacular jade burial masks; many of these objects are on display in Campeche city's Museo Arqueológico. Calakmul holds at least 120 carved stelae, though many are eroded.

At the Semarnat post 20km from the highway, rangers allow camping; they appreciate a donation if you use the shower and toilets. They've built a small, screened palapa that can sometimes be rented.

Santuario de la Virgen de Izamal, Yucatán

JOHN ELK III

Carrying rope materials, Yucatán

ERIC L WHEATER

Fantasy or reality? A limestone sinkhole, Yucatán

STUART WASSERMAN

Chichén Itzá, Yucatán

ERIC L WHEATER

DALE BUCKTON

A hatchling turtle, Quintana Roo

TOM BOYDEN

Señor *Crocodylus moreletii*

DAVID M WATSON

Single male lizard hoping to meet warm sunny rock.

TOM BOYDEN

Boat-billed heron shuns the press.

SCOTT DOGGETT

Flamingoes in flight

GREG ELMS

Wild nopal cactus breaking into bloom

A toll of US$4.50 per car (more for heavier vehicles) and US$2.25 per person is levied at the turnoff from highway 186, to fund the constant road maintenance. From the parking lot to the ruins is a 500m walk. A full-day roundtrip excursion by taxi from Xpujil costs about US$66.

Chicanná

Almost 12km west of Xpujil and 500m south of the highway, Chicanná *(House of the Snake's Jaws; admission US$3, free Sun; open 8am-5pm daily)* is a mixture of Chenes and Río Bec architectural styles buried in the jungle. The city was occupied from about AD 300 to 1100.

Enter through the modern palapa admission building, then follow the rock paths through the jungle to Grupo D and Estructura XX (AD 830), which boasts not one but two monster-mouth doorways, one above the other, the pair topped by a roofcomb.

A five-minute walk along the jungle path brings you to Grupo C, with two low buildings (Estructuras X and XI) on a raised platform; the temples bear a few fragments of decoration.

The buildings in Grupo B (turn right when leaving Grupo C) have some intact decoration as well, and there's a good roofcomb on Estructura VI.

Shortly beyond is Chicanná's most famous building, Estructura II (AD 750 to 770) in Grupo A, with its gigantic Chenes-style monster-mouth doorway, believed to depict the jaws of the god Itzamná, lord of the heavens, creator of all things. If you photograph nothing else here, you'll want a picture of this, best taken in the afternoon.

Take the path leading from the right corner of Estructura II to reach nearby Estructura VI.

Chicanná Ecovillage Resort *(☎/fax 983-871-60-74, **e** chicanna@campeche.sureste .com)* Singles/doubles/triple US$97/108/113. The former Ramada is 500m north of the highway and directly across it from the road to the ruins. Large, airy rooms with ceiling fans are grouped mostly four to a bungalow and set amid well-tended grass lawns. There's a pool, and the small dining room/ bar serves decent but expensive meals.

Roundtrip taxi fare from Xpujil to Chicanná is US$5.50 plus US$5.50 per hour of wait.

Becán

Becán *(admission US$3.50, free Sun & holidays; open 8am-5pm daily)*, 8km west of Xpujil, sits atop a rock outcrop; a 2km moat snakes its way around the entire city to protect it from attack. (Becán – literally 'path of the snake' – is Mayan for 'canyon' or 'moat.') Seven causeways crossed the moat, providing access to the city. Becán was occupied from 550 BC until AD 1000.

This is among the largest and most elaborate sites in the area. The first thing you'll come to is a plaza. Walk keeping it to your left to pass through a rock-walled passageway and beneath a corbeled arch. You will reach a huge twin-towered temple with cylindrical columns at the top of a flight of stairs. This is Estructura VIII, dating from about AD 600 to 730. The view from the top of this temple has become partially obscured by the trees, but on a clear day you should still be able to see structures at the Xpujil ruins to the east.

Northwest of Estructura VIII is Plaza Central, ringed by 30m-high Estructura IX (the tallest building at the site) and the more interesting Estructura X. At X's far south side, in early 2001, a stucco mask still bearing some red paint was uncovered. It is enclosed in a wooden shelter with window.

In the jungle to the west are more ruins, including the Plaza Oeste, which is surrounded by low buildings and a ball court. Much of this area is still being excavated and restored, so it's open to the public only intermittently.

Loop back east, through the passageway again, to the plaza; cross it diagonally to the right, climbing a stone staircase to the Plaza Sureste. Around this are Estructuras I through IV; a circular altar (Estructura III-a) lies on the east side. Estructura I has the two towers typical of the Río Bec style. You can go around the plaza counterclockwise and descend the stone staircase on the southeast side or go down the southwest side and head left. Both routes lead to the exit.

A taxi visit from Xpujil will run about US$3.50 plus US$5.50 per hour of waiting time.

XPUJIL
Orientation & Information

The hamlet of Xpujil ('shpu-HEEL') lies at the junction of east-west highway 186 and

Campeche highway 261 (not to be confused with Mexico highway 261), which leads north to Hopelchén and eventually Mérida. A good base from which to explore the area's sites, Xpujil is growing rapidly in anticipation of a tourist boom. But it still has no bank or laundry, and the nearest gasoline station is 5km east of town. Several restaurants, a couple of hotels and a taxi stand are near the bus depot.

From the junction, the Xpuhil ruins are less than 1km west, Becán is 8km west, Chicanná is 11.5km west, and Balamkú is 60km west.

Ruins

Xpuhil *(admission US$3, free Sun & holidays; open 8am-5pm daily),* 'Place of the Cattails' in Mayan, flourished during the late Classic period from AD 400 to 900, though there was a settlement here much earlier. The site's entrance is on the west edge of town on the north side of highway 186, at the turnoff for the airport, less than 1km west of the junction.

One large building and three small ones have been restored. Estructura I in Grupo I, built about AD 760, is a fine example of the Río Bec architectural style, with its lofty towers. The three towers (rather than the usual two) have traces of the impractically steep ornamental stairways reaching nearly to their tops, and several fierce jaguar masks (go around to the back of the tower to see the best one). About 60m to the east is Estructura II, an elite residence.

Xpuhil is a far larger site than may be imagined from these buildings. Three other structure groups have been identified, but it may be decades before they are restored.

Places to Stay & Eat

Restaurant-Hotel Calakmul (☎ 983-871-60-29) Cabins with shared bath US$22, doubles with fan & private bath US$39. The Calakmul is about 350m west of the junction. Rooms at the back are large, modern and clean, with lots of tile, if rather overpriced.

El Mirador Maya (☎/fax 983-871-60-05) Bungalows US$28, rooms US$39. About 1km west of the junction, this hotel has eight bungalows and two rooms. Each bungalow has a fan and two beds. The rooms are new and have air-con but are very small, and the air-con is poorly placed. There is a restaurant here as well.

Getting There & Around

Xpujil is 220km south of Hopelchén, 153km east of Escárcega and 120km west of Chetumal. Stopping in Xpujil are six buses daily to Escárcega (US$6.75), four to Campeche (US$14) and five to Chetumal (US$5.75). No buses originate in Xpujil, so you must hope to luck into a vacant seat on one passing through. The bus terminal is just east of the Xpujil junction, on the north side of the highway.

The Xpuhil ruins are within walking distance of Xpujil junction. You may be able to hitch a ride to the access roads for Becán, Chicanná and Balamkú, but for other sites you will need to book a tour or hire a cab.

HORMIGUERO & RÍO BEC

Hormiguero

This site *(admission US$2.50, free Sun & holidays; open 8am-5pm daily)* is reached by heading 14km south from Xpujil junction, then turning right and heading another 8km west (the roads are paved). Hormiguero (Spanish for 'anthill') is an old site, with some buildings dating as far back as AD 50. The city flourished during the late Classic period, however. Hormiguero has one of the most impressive buildings in the region. Entering the site you will see the 50m-long **Estructura II**, which has a giant Chenes-style monster-mouth doorway with much of its decoration in good condition. You'll also want to see **Estructura V**, 60m to the north; Estructura E-1, in the East Group, should be a sight once it is excavated.

A roundtrip taxi ride will run US$8, plus waiting time.

Río Bec

The entrance to the collective farm Ejido 20 de Noviembre is 10km east of the Xpujil junction and signed 'Río Bec.' The unpaved ejido road leads 5km to the collective itself and its U'lu'um Chac Yuk Nature Reserve. Look for the small store on the left side of the road, and ask there for guides to show you the various sites about 13km farther down the very rough road. 'Río Bec' is the designation for an agglomeration of small sites, 17 at last count, in a 50-sq-km area southeast of Xpujil. It gave its name to the prevalent architecture style in the region. Of these many sites, the most interesting is certainly Grupo B, followed by

Grupos I and N. The best example is Estructura I at Grupo B, a late Classic building dating from around AD 700. Though not restored, Estructura I has been consolidated and is in a condition certainly good enough to allow appreciation of its former glory. At Grupo I look for Estructuras XVII and XI. At Grupo N, Estructura I is quite similar to the grand one at Grupo B.

The road is passable only when dry, and even then you need a high-clearance vehicle. The way is unsigned as well; you're best off hiring a guide with or without a 4WD truck. A taxi to the ejido will charge around US$4 for drop-off service; negotiate waiting time. Though it looks closer on the map, access to Río Bec from the road to Hormiguero is all but impossible.

CAMPECHE
• pop 205,000 ☎ 981

In 1999 Unesco added the city of Campeche to its list of World Heritage Sites. *Campechanos* are rightly proud of this and are doing an excellent job of improving the colonial heart of the city while retaining the best of the old. Many structures have been restored, repainted or, in some cases, reconstructed from scratch.

During Campeche's heyday, wealthy Spanish families built mansions, many of which still stand. Two segments of the city's famous wall have survived the times as well, as have no fewer than seven of the *baluartes* (bastions or bulwarks) that were built into it, and two perfectly preserved colonial forts guard the city's outskirts. One of them contains a small archaeological museum with world-class pieces.

Adding to Campeche's charm is its location on the Gulf of Mexico. A broad waterfront boulevard provides the perfect place for cloud- and sunset-watching; add a thunderstorm rolling in off the Gulf and you have a sound-and-light show nonpareil.

History
Once a Mayan trading village called Ah Kim Pech (Lord Sun Sheep-Tick), Campeche was first entered by the Spaniards in 1517. The Maya resisted, and for nearly a quarter century the Spaniards were unable to conquer the region. Colonial Campeche was founded in 1531 but later abandoned owing to Mayan hostility. By 1540 the conquistadors, led by Francisco de Montejo the Younger, had gained enough control to establish a settlement that survived. They named it Villa de San Francisco de Campeche.

The settlement soon flourished as the major port of the Yucatán Peninsula. Locally grown timber, chicle and dyewoods were major exports to Europe, as were gold and silver mined from other regions and shipped from Campeche.

Such wealth did not escape the notice of pirates, who arrived only six years after the town was founded. For two centuries, they terrorized Campeche. Not only were ships attacked, but the port itself was invaded, its citizens robbed, its women raped and its buildings burned. In the most gruesome assault, in early 1663, various pirate hordes set aside their rivalries to converge as a single flotilla upon the city, where they massacred many of Campeche's citizens.

This tragedy finally spurred the Spanish monarchy to take preventive action, but it was not until five years later, in 1668, that work on the 3.5m-thick ramparts began. After 18 years of building, a 2.5km hexagon incorporating eight strategically placed *baluartes*, or bastions, surrounded the city. A segment of the ramparts extended out to sea so that ships literally had to sail into a fortress, easily defended, to gain access to the city.

Today the local economy is largely driven by shrimping and offshore petroleum extraction, and the prosperity brought by these activities has helped fund the downtown area's renovation.

Orientation
Though the bastions still stand, the city walls themselves have been mostly razed and replaced by Avenida Circuito Baluartes, which rings the city center just the way the walls once did. Many of the streets making up the circuit are paved with stone taken from the demolished wall.

According to the compass, Campeche is oriented with its waterfront to the northwest, but be aware that locals giving directions usually follow tradition and convenience, which dictate that the water is to the west, inland is east.

A multilane boulevard with bicycle and pedestrian paths on its seaward side extends

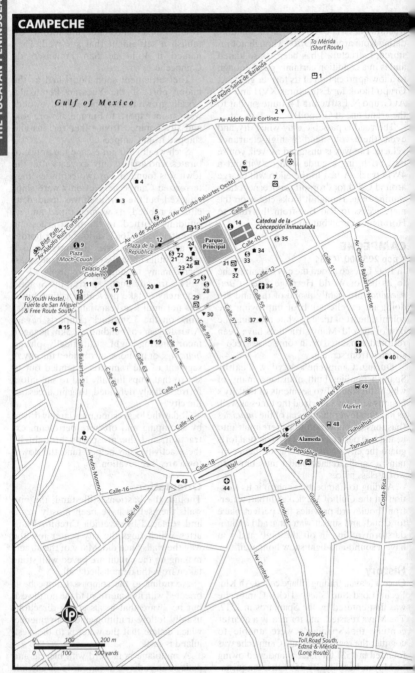

CAMPECHE

Gulf of Mexico

To Mérida
(Short Route)

Av Pedro Sáinz de Barandá

2 ▼

Av Aldofo Ruiz Cortinez

🚲 Bike Path

Av Aldofo Ruiz Cortinez

1

8

6

7

4

3

5

Calle 8

Wall

13

14

Catedral de la
Concepción Inmaculada

35

Calle 51

Av Circuito Baluartes Norte

Av 16 de Septiembre (Av Circuito Baluartes Oeste)

12

Plaza de la
República

Parque
Principal

Calle 10

34

9

Plaza
Moch-Couoh

Palacio de
Gobierno

24

22

21

25

26

23

33

31

32

Calle 53

Calle 51

11

17

18

20

27

28

36

To Youth Hostel,
Fuerte de San Miguel
& Free Route South

10

29

30

37

Calle 55

15

16

19

38

Calle 59

Calle 57

39

40

Av Circuito Baluartes Sur

Calle 61

Calle 63

Calle 65

Calle 14

Calle 16

49

Market

42

Calle 16

Av Circuito Baluartes Este

48

Chihuahua

46

Alameda

Tamaulipas

45

Pedro Moreno

Calle 18

Wall

Av República

47

43

44

Calle 16

Calle 18

Av Central

Honduras

Guatemala

Costa Rica

0   100   200 m
0   100   200 yards

To Airport,
Toll Road South,
Edzná & Mérida
(Long Route)

several kilometers in either direction along Campeche's shore, changing names a few times. The stretch closest to the city center is named Avenida Adolfo Ruiz Cortínez and is commonly referred to as *el malecón* (the seafront drive).

Information

Tourist Offices The state-run Secretaría de Turismo (☎ 816-67-67), in Plaza Moch-Couoh just off Avenida Ruiz Cortínez, has good maps of the city and literature about what's on. It's open 8am to 9pm Monday to Friday, 9am to 2pm and 4pm to 8pm Saturday and Sunday. The Secretaría also has a module in the Centro Cultural Casa Número 6, on the southeast side of the Parque Principal; it's staffed from 9am to 9pm daily.

The city tourist office is on Calle 55 at Calle 8, northwest of the cathedral. It's open 9am to 3.30pm and 6pm to 9pm Monday to Friday. A desk in the main bus terminal is open ostensibly from 9am to 1pm and 5pm to 8pm daily.

Money Campeche has numerous banks with ATMs, open 9am to 4pm Monday to Friday, 9am to 1pm Saturday. See the map for some locations.

Post & Communications The central post office is at the corner of Avenida 16 de Septiembre and Calle 53, in the Edificio Federal (Federal Building). There are plenty of card phones around town. The Telmex office is on Calle 8 near Calle 51.

Diversiones del Centro, a pool hall at Calle 55 between Calles 10 and 12, has Internet access for US$0.90 a half hour. Ciber & Chat, at the corner of Calles 12 and 59, charges US$0.70 a half hour. A few blocks north of town center, the long-running Cibernet (☎ 816-67-02), Calle 12 No 48 at Calle 45, charges US$1.75 an hour for decent connections; you may get to hear Louis Armstrong and Limp Bizkit at the same time, both at high volume.

Laundry Lavandería Campeche is on Calle 55 between Calles 12 and 14. You can drop off clothing here in the morning and usually get it back cleaned, dried and folded in the afternoon. Cost is about US$4.75 for a large load. It's open 8am to 4pm Monday to Saturday.

Medical Services The IMSS Hospital is at the corner of Avenida Circuito Baluartes Este and Avenida Central. In an emergency, call the Red Cross at ☎ 815-24-11.

Walking Tour

Seven of the eight bulwarks still stand, and all can be visited on a 2km walk around Avenida Circuito Baluartes, taking in other sights on the way. Because of traffic, some of the walk is not very pleasant; you might want to limit your excursion to the first three or four baluartes described, which house museums and gardens.

First stop, at the corner of Calles 10 and 63, the **ex-Templo de San José** is a visual delight. Its façade is covered in striking blue and yellow tiles, and one spire is topped by a lighthouse complete with weather vane.

A block northwest is the bizarre, ultra-modern **Palacio Legislativo** (Congress Building). Undoubtedly meant to evoke a baluarte with slitted windows, it looks more like the Mothership landing. Just southwest along Calle 8 is its colonial inspiration, the **Baluarte de San Carlos** (admission free; open 9am-2pm Mon, 8am-8pm Tues-Sat, 8am-2pm Sun), which contains the modest Museo de la Ciudad. There's a good scale model of the old city, historical photos, specimens of dyewood and the like. You can visit the dungeon and look out over the sea from the roof.

Head northeast back along Calle 8 to its intersection with Calle 59 to see the **Puerta del Mar** (Sea Gate), which provided access to the city from the sea before the surrounding area was filled in. The gate was demolished in 1893 but rebuilt in 1957 when its historical value was realized. A short section of re-erected wall connects the gate to the **Baluarte de Nuestra Señora de la Soledad**, which holds the **Museo de Estelas Maya** (admission US$2.50, free Sun; open 8am-2pm Mon, 8am-7.30pm Tues-Sat, 8am-1pm Sun). Many of the Mayan artifacts here are badly weathered, but the precise line drawing next to each stone shows you what the designs once looked like. You can visit the roof here as well.

Just northeast of the Baluarte de Nuestra Señora is a newly built replica of the original Palacio Municipal, housing a public library. Across Calle 8 from the library is the **Parque Principal**, Campeche's main plaza. It's a pleasant place where locals go to sit and

think, chat, smooch, plot, snooze, have their shoes shined or stroll and cool off after the heat of the day. Come for the concerts on Sunday evenings.

On the park's southwest side is **Centro Cultural Casa Número 6** (admission free; open 9am-9pm daily), an 18th-century building furnished with pieces from the 18th and 19th centuries; it gives a good idea of how the city's high society lived back then. The center also contains several computer-interactive exhibits providing information about the main tourist attractions in the city and state of Campeche. There is a free guided tour of the building (in Spanish only).

Construction was begun on the **Catedral de la Concepción Inmaculada**, on the northeast side of the plaza, in the mid-16th century shortly after the conquistadors established the town, but it wasn't finished until 1705.

Back on Calle 8 head northeast again for two blocks beyond the park to **Baluarte de Santiago**. It houses a minuscule yet lovely tropical garden, the **Jardín Botánico Xmuch Haltún** (admission free; open 9am-4pm daily), with 250 species of tropical plants set around a lovely courtyard of fountains.

Walk back on Calle 8 a few steps and turn left (inland) onto Calle 51. Follow it to Calle 18, passing the **Iglesia de San Juan de Dios** (1652) on the way. The **Baluarte de San Pedro** (admission free; open 9am-1pm & 5pm-8pm Mon-Fri) is in the middle of a complex traffic intersection at the beginning of Avenida Gobernadores. Within the bulwark is the Exposición Permanente de Artesanías, a regional crafts sales center, and an agency that will book tours of the city and region.

If you're still game, head southwest from the Baluarte de San Pedro along Avenida Circuito Baluartes to the **Baluarte de San Francisco**, on Calle 57, and, a block farther, the **Puerta de Tierra** (Land Gate) on Calle 59. Linked to the gate by Campeche's other stretch of wall is **Baluarte de San Juan**, at the intersection of Calles 18 and 65. From here you bear right along Calle 67 (Avenida Circuito Baluartes) to the **Baluarte de Santa Rosa**, at the corner of Calles 14 and 67. Admission is free to all four of these.

Evening Stroll

To see some beautiful houses, many painted in cheerful pastels with white trim, walk through Campeche's streets – especially

Calles 55, 57 and 59 – in the evening, when the sun is not blazing, and interior lighting illuminates courtyards, salons and alleys.

Museo Arqueológico & Fuerte de San Miguel

Four kilometers southwest of Plaza Moch-Couoh a road turns left off the malecón and climbs for about 600m to the Fuerte de San Miguel, a colonial fortress now home to the excellent archaeological museum (☎ 816-24-60; admission US$2.50, free Sun; open 8.30am-7.30pm Tues-Sun). Here you can see objects found at the ancient Mayan sites of Calakmul, Edzná and Jaina, an island north of the city once used as a burial site for Mayan aristocracy.

Among the objects on display are stunning pieces of jade jewelry and exquisite vases, masks and plates. The star attractions are the jade burial masks from Calakmul. Also displayed are stelae, arrowheads, weapons, seashell necklaces and clay figurines.

The fort is itself a thing of beauty. In mint condition, it's compact and equipped with a dry moat and working drawbridge, and it's topped with several cannons. The views are great too.

For US$0.30, 'Lerma' or 'Playa Bonita' buses depart from the market (at the northeast edge of the center) and travel counterclockwise most of the way around the circuito before heading down the malecón. Tell the driver you're going to the Fuerte de San Miguel. The turnoff for the fort, Avenida Escénica, is across from the old San Luis artillery battery. To avoid the strenuous walk from the coastal road up the hill (about 700m), you can take a taxi or the tranvía (see Organized Tours, below).

Organized Tours

Two different tours by motorized tranvía (trolley) depart from the Parque Principal daily; both cost US$2.25. At 9.30am, 6pm and 8pm, the 'Tranvía de la Ciudad' heads off on a tour of the principal neighborhoods of the historic town center. At 9am and 5pm, 'El Guapo' goes to the Fuerte de San Miguel and its twin on the north side of the city, the Fuerte de San José, which contains a modest maritime museum. You don't get enough time to take in the archaeological museum; if it's your goal, just use the tram to get there, then walk down the hill.

Corazón Maya (☎/fax 811-37-88, e tour corazonmaya@hotmail.com, Baluarte de San Pedro) This company offers archaeological tours to Edzná, Calakmul, and the various sites around Xpujil in eastern Campeche, among other places. You can get contact information at the baluarte for other tour outfits as well.

Places to Stay

Budget Of the cheapest hotels, only a few are worth trying, and they're fairly dumpy.

Villa Deportiva Universitaria (☎ 816-18-02) Dorm beds US$2.75. Campeche's youth hostel is in a university sports complex on Avenida Agustín Melgar, which comes off the malecón 3.5km southwest of Plaza Moch-Couoh. The hostel has an 11pm curfew; doors unlock at 7am. Buses marked 'Avenida Universidad' will take you there. Ask the driver to let you off at the albergue de juventud or Villa Deportiva. Avenida Melgar heads inland between a Volkswagen dealership and a Pemex fuel station. The hostel is 150m up on the right. Enter the signed gate and keep turning right.

Hotel Roma (☎ 816-38-97, Calle 10 between Calles 59 & 61) Rooms without/with bath US$5/9. The Roma's rooms have fans.

Hotel Castelmar (☎ 816-28-86, Calle 61 No 2, at Calle 8) Rooms US$10. In spite of the potted plants around its courtyard, the Castelmar feels like the kind of seedy place the protagonist in a noir novel might hole up in.

Hotel Campeche (☎ 816-51-83, Calle 57 No 2) Rooms with 1 bed US$12, 2 beds US$15.50, 3 beds US$18. It's very basic, with sagging beds and dark rooms around two courtyards, but it's centrally located, facing the Parque Principal.

Hotel Colonial (☎ 816-22-22, Calle 14 No 122) Singles/1-bed doubles/2-bed doubles/triples US$13.50/17/18/22. Hotel Colonial is popular with budget travelers. Some readers have complained of noise, but others recommend it highly. Housed in what was once the mansion of Doña Gertrudis Eulalia Torostieta y Zagasti, former Spanish governor of Tabasco and Yucatán, the rooms have good showers with hot water and a fan. Add US$7.25 for air-con.

Posada del Ángel (☎ 816-77-18, Calle 10 No 307) Singles/doubles/triples with fan

US$19.50/24/27, with air-con US$29/33/36. This hotel is a good value with 14 spartan, modern, clean rooms.

Mid-Range & Top End *Hotel López* (☎/fax 816-33-44, e *lopezh@elsitio.com, Calle 12 No 189)* Rooms with fan/air-con US$36/47. The López has clean, agreeable rooms and multiple courtyards.

Hotel del Paseo (☎ *811-01-00, 811-00-77, fax 811-00-97,* e *cslavall@etzna.uacam.mx, Calle 8 No 215)* Singles/doubles/suites US$44/49/70. The 48 like-new rooms here are very reasonably priced. All have air-con, cable TV and phone. There's a restaurant and bar as well.

Both of the places listed below have pools and restaurants.

Hotel Baluartes (☎ *816-39-11, fax 816-24-10,* e *baluarte@campeche.sureste.com, Avenida 16 de Septiembre 128, enter from Calle 61)* Singles/doubles/triples US$50/54/62. Though showing its age a bit, this hotel offers a good value. The trick is to get a room on one of the upper floors, the higher the better, with a good view of the sea or the city. Rooms are perfectly serviceable and have good air-con.

Hotel Del Mar (☎ *811-91-91, fax 811-16-18,* e *delmarcp@camp1.telmex.net.mx, Avenida Ruiz Cortínez 51)* Rooms with city view/sea view US$88/104. This 119-room hotel was formerly a Ramada hotel.

Places to Eat

While in town, be sure to try the regional specialty *pan de cazón,* which is dogfish – a small shark – cooked between layers of tortillas in a dark sauce. If it smells like ammonia, though, send it back; the shark has gone bad. Another regional specialty is *camarones al coco,* consisting of shrimp rolled in ground coconut and fried. It's often served with marmalade and when done right tastes much better than it sounds.

San Francisco de Asís This supermarket is across Avenida Ruiz and north of the Baluarte de Santiago; the selection is broad and prices low.

Restaurant Marganzo (Calle 8 between Calles 57 & 59) Breakfast US$2.75-5, lunch & dinner mains US$3.25-10. This popular upscale, air-conditioned restaurant faces the Baluarte de Nuestra Señora. It serves good

breakfasts and juices (carrot and beet among them) and has an extensive seafood menu. Alas, the camarones al coco are not up to par.

Restaurant Campeche (Calle 57) Mains US$4-7.25. Opposite the Parque Principal, this place is in the building that saw the birth of Justo Sierra, founder of Mexico's national university. It's popular and offers a wide selection of dishes.

Panificadora Nueva España (cnr Calle 10 & Calle 59) This place has a large assortment of fresh baked goods at very low prices.

Nutri Vida (Calle 12 No 167) Open 8am-2pm & 5.30pm-8.30pm Mon-Fri, 8am-2pm Sat. Nutri Vida is a health food store serving up soy burgers and the like.

Restaurant-Bar Familiar La Parroquia (Calle 55 No 8) Breakfast US$2.50-3.50, lunch & dinner under US$10. La Parroquia is the complete family restaurant-café-hangout, open 24 hours. Breakfast is served from 7am to 10am. Substantial lunches and dinners of traditional and regional dishes are mostly *well* under US$10.

Entertainment

From September to May, the state tourism authorities sponsor free performances of folk music and dancing. The performances take place on Saturday at 7pm (weather permitting) in the Plaza de la República and on Thursday at 8.30pm in the Centro Cultural Casa No 6. Every Sunday at 7pm in the Parque Principal you can hear popular campechana music performed by the Banda del Estado (State Band). There's no cost to attend and it's a pleasant way to pass time. Arrive early for a good seat.

Getting There & Away

Air The airport is at the end of Avenida López Portillo (Avenida Central), which is 3.5km southeast from Plaza Moch-Couoh. Aeroméxico (☎ 800-021-40-00) flies to Mexico City at least once daily for US$183. Aerocaribe (☎ 8-6-90-74) flies four times a week to Cancún.

Bus Campeche's main bus terminal (sometimes called the ADO terminal) is on Avenida Gobernadores, 1.7km from Plaza Moch-Cuouh, or about 1.5km from most hotels. The terminal has a restaurant and a tourist information counter. The 2nd-class area is farther off the street in the same building.

Though most of its buses leave from the main terminal, Sur has a terminal for buses to Champotón on Avenida República across from the Alameda (which is south of the market). Rural buses for Edzná and other parts depart from here as well.

There have been reports of theft on night buses, especially to Chiapas; keep a close eye on your bags.

Daily buses from Campeche include:

Bolonchén de Rejón – 116km, 3-4 hours; 4 2nd-class (US$4.50)

Cancún – 512km, 6-7 hours; 1st-class ADO direct (US$26) at 10pm & 11.30pm, 1 2nd-class TRP, via Mérida (US$23)

Chetumal – 422km, 6¼-9 hours; 1st-class ADO (US$19.50) at noon, 2nd-class buses (US$15.50) at 8.15am & 10pm

Edzná – 55km, 1½ hours; buses leave at 6am and 10am, then roughly hourly until 5pm, from the Sur Champotón terminal (US$1.50); see the Edzná section for further information

Escárcega – 150km, 2½ hours; 5 1st-class ADO (US$7.25), many 2nd-class buses (US$5.50)

Hopelchén – 86km, 2 hours; several 2nd-class (US$3.25)

Mérida – 195km, 2½-3 hours (short route via Bécal); 12 1st-class ADO (US$8.75), ATS (US$7.25) every 30 minutes

Mérida – 250km, 4 hours (long route via Uxmal); 4 2nd-class Sur (US$7.25) at 6am, noon, 2.30pm and 5pm

Mexico City (TAPO) – 1360km, 18 hours; 4 1st-class ADO (US$68)

Palenque – 362km, 5 hours; 1 deluxe Maya de Oro (US$23) at midnight, 3 1st-class ADO (US$17), 1 1st-class Altos (US$16) at 9.45pm; some Villahermosa-bound buses can drop you at Catazajá (the Palenque turnoff), 27km north of Palenque town

San Cristóbal de Las Casas – 820km, 14 hours; 1 deluxe Maya de Oro (US$33) at midnight, 1 1st-class Altos (US$25) at 9.45pm

Villahermosa – 450km, 6 hours; 15 buses (US$18.50-25)

Xpujil – 306km, 6-8 hours; 1 1st-class ADO (US$14) at noon, 4 2nd-class Sur (US$11)

Car & Motorcycle If you're heading for Edzná, the long route to Mérida or the fast toll road going south, take Avenida Central and follow signs for the airport and Edzná.

For the free route south you can just head down the malecón.

For the short route to Mérida head north on the malecón; it curves right eventually and hits the highway at a Pemex station.

Getting Around

Local buses all originate at the market. Most charge US$0.30 and go at least partway around the Avenida Circuito Baluartes counterclockwise before heading to their final destinations. Ask a local where along the circuito you can catch the bus you want.

Taxis have set prices for destinations on a sign posted in the back seat, but agree on a price with the driver before you go. By the hour they are US$7.50. The fare between the bus terminal and the center is around US$2.25. Between the airport and the center should be US$4.50 (but it's hard to get this price). *Colectivo* taxis from the airport charge US$3 per person.

CAMPECHE TO MÉRIDA – SHORT ROUTE (HIGHWAY 180)

The *ruta corta* is the fastest way to get between the two cities, and it's the road more traveled by buses. If you'd prefer to go the long way via Kabah and Uxmal, ask for a seat on one of the less-frequent long-route buses. If you'd like to stop at one of the towns along the short route, catch a 2nd-class bus.

From Campeche it's 109km to **Bécal**, a center of the Yucatán Peninsula's panama hat trade just inside the border of Campeche state. The soft, pliable hats, called *jipijapas* by the locals, have been woven by townsfolk from the fibers of the huano palm tree in humid limestone caves since the mid-19th century. The caves – there's at least one on every block, generally reached by a hole in the ground in someone's backyard – provide just the right atmosphere for shaping the fibers, keeping them pliable and minimizing breakage. Each cave is typically no larger than a bedroom. About 1000 of the town's 3000 adult residents make their living weaving hats. The hats cost from under US$10 to well over US$50, depending on quality. If you're shopping for one, be sure to visit the cooperative on the main street, a stone's throw from Bécal's dominating church. From Bécal it's 85km to Mérida.

CAMPECHE TO MÉRIDA – LONG ROUTE (HIGHWAY 261)

Most travelers take the long route from Campeche to Mérida in order to visit the various ruin sites on the way. It's often referred to as 'la Ruta Chenes,' for the *chenes* (wells) that give the region its name.

Edzná

The closest major ruins to Campeche are about 53km to the southeast. Edzná *(admission US$3.50, free Sun & holidays; open 8am-5pm daily)* covered more than 17 sq km and was inhabited from approximately 600 BC to the 15th century AD. Most of the visible carvings date from AD 550 to 810. Though it's a long way from such Puuc Hills sites as Uxmal and Kabah, some of the architecture here has elements of the Puuc style. What led to Edzná's decline and gradual abandonment remains a mystery.

Beyond the ticket office is a palapa sheltering carvings and stelae from the elements. A path from here leads about 400m through vegetation to the zone's big draw, the Plaza Principal (follow the signs for the Gran Acrópolis), which is 160m long, 100m wide and surrounded by temples. On your right as you enter from the north is the **Nohochná** (Big House), a massive, elongated structure that was topped by four long halls likely used for administrative tasks, such as the collection of tributes and the dispensation of justice. The built-in benches facing the main plaza clearly were designed to serve spectators of special events in the plaza.

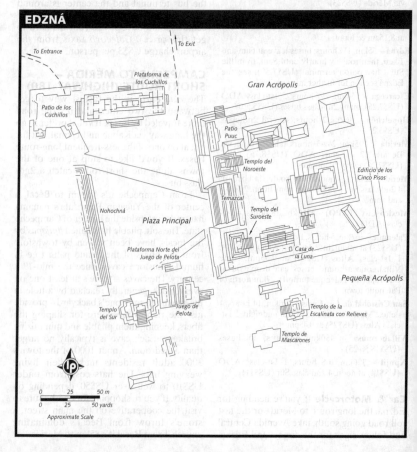

EDZNÁ

Across the plaza is the Gran Acrópolis, a raised platform holding several structures, including Edzná's major temple, the 31m-high **Edificio de los Cinco Pisos** (Five-Story Building). It rises five levels from its vast base to the roofcomb and contains many vaulted rooms. A great central staircase of 65 steps goes right to the top. Some of the weathered carvings of masks, serpents and jaguars' heads that formerly adorned each level are now in the palapa near the ticket office.

The current structure is the last of four remodels and was done primarily in the Puuc architectural style. Scholars generally agree that this temple is a hybrid of a pyramid and a palace. The impressive roofcomb is a clear reference to the sacred buildings at Tikal in Guatemala.

In the Pequeña Acrópolis to the south of the main plaza is the palapa-protected **Templo de Mascarones** (Temple of Masks), which features carved portrayals of the sun god. The central motif is the anthropomorphic head of a Maya man whose face has been modified to give him the appearance of a jaguar.

Getting There & Away From Campeche, dilapidated rural buses leave from outside the Sur Champotón terminal at 6am and 10am, then roughly hourly until 6pm (55km, 1½ hours, US$1.50); it's a good idea to check the day before. Most drop you about 200m from the site entrance; ask before boarding. The last bus returning to Campeche passes near the site at 2pm, so if you're coming here on a day trip from the city you'll want to catch one of the two early buses leaving Campeche.

Coming from the north and east, get off at San Antonio Cayal and hitch or catch a bus 20km south to Edzná. If you're headed north on leaving Edzná, you'll have to depend on hitching or the occasional bus to get you to San Antonio Cayal, where you can catch a Chenes Route bus north to Hopelchén, Bolonchén de Rejón and ultimately Uxmal.

Coming by car from Campeche, take Avenida Central out of town and follow the signs to the airport and Edzná. If you drove to Edzná from the north and are headed to Campeche city, don't retrace your route to San Antonio; just bear left shortly after leaving the parking lot and follow the signs westward.

Tours of Edzná from Campeche start at about US$20 per person. Corazón Maya is among the companies offering them; see Organized Tours in the Campeche city section.

Bolonchén de Rejón & Xtacumbilxunaan

Forty kilometers east of San Antonio Cayal is Hopelchén, where highway 261 turns north; there's a Pemex station on the west side of town. The next town to appear out of the flat, dry jungle is Bolonchén de Rejón, after 34km. Its local festival of Santa Cruz is held each year on May 3.

Bolonchén is near the **Grutas de Xtacumbilxunaan** (*'SHTAA-koom-beel-shoo-NAHN'; admission US$2.25; open 8am-6pm daily*), about 3km south of town. Lighted steps lead down to a barely visible cenote, beyond which a passage leads 100m farther. There are few stalactites or stalagmites, but the climb back up to the green forest surrounding the cave is dramatic, and with future improvements the cenote may be visible.

Highway 261 continues into Yucatán state to Uxmal, with a side road leading to the ruins along the Ruta Puuc. See the Uxmal and La Ruta Puuc sections later in this chapter for more information.

Yucatán State

The state of Yucatán is a pie slice at the top of the Yucatán Peninsula. Until the development of Cancún in neighboring Quintana Roo, it was the peninsula's economic engine. While Quintana Roo's tourist-driven economy has surpassed Yucatán's in recent years, historically and culturally Yucatán remains paramount. Here you'll find the peninsula's most impressive Mayan ruins (Chichén Itzá, Uxmal), its finest colonial cities (Mérida and Valladolid) and two coastal communities nationally famous for their wild red flamingoes.

As a tourist destination, traditional Yucatán complements commercial Quintana Roo extremely well, and travel between the two states is convenient and affordable. A high-speed highway served by numerous 1st-class buses links Cancún and Mérida, and the trip to one of Mexico's oldest cities following a visit to one of its most modern resorts is highly recommended.

MÉRIDA
• pop 685,000 ☎ 999

Mérida has been a center of Mayan culture in the Yucatán region since before the conquistadors arrived. Today the capital of the state of Yucatán is a prosperous city of narrow streets, colonial buildings and shady parks. Every night of the week something's on: folkloric dance or music, theatrical performances, film showings.

There are hotels and restaurants of every class and price range and good transportation services to any part of the peninsula and the country, and the city makes a good base for numerous excursions around the region.

Mérida's drawbacks are traffic, pollution and heat. Noisy buses pump clouds of noxious fumes into the air, and the region's high temperatures seem even higher here, where buildings catch and hold the heat. The buses and the crowded, narrow sidewalks have led for calls to ban vehicular traffic from the colonial center, a move that would enhance the city's already considerable charm.

History
Francisco de Montejo the Younger founded a Spanish colony at Campeche, about 160km to the south, in 1540. From this base he was able to take advantage of political dissension among the Maya, conquering T'hó (now Mérida) in 1542. By the end of the decade, Yucatán was mostly under Spanish colonial rule.

When Montejo's conquistadors entered defeated T'hó, they found a major Mayan settlement of lime-mortared stone that reminded them of Roman architectural legacies in Mérida, Spain. They promptly renamed the city and proceeded to build it into the regional colonial capital, dismantling the Mayan structures and using the materials to construct a cathedral and other stately buildings. Mérida took its colonial orders directly from Spain, not from Mexico City, and Yucatán has had a distinct cultural and political identity ever since.

During the War of the Castes, only Mérida and Campeche were able to hold out against the rebel forces. On the brink of surrender, the ruling class in Mérida was saved by reinforcements sent from central Mexico in exchange for Mérida's agreement to take orders from Mexico City. Although Yucatán is certainly part of Mexico, there is still a strong feeling in Mérida and other parts of the state that the local people stand a breed apart.

Mérida today is the peninsula's center of commerce, a bustling city that has benefited greatly from the *maquiladoras* that opened in the 1980s and '90s and the tourism that picked up during those decades.

Orientation
The Plaza Grande, as *meridanos* call the main square, has been the city's center since Mayan times. Most of the services visitors want are within five blocks of the square. Odd-numbered streets run east-west, and their numbers increase by twos going from north to south (for example, Calle 61 is a block north of Calle 63); even-numbered streets run north-south, and increase by twos from east to west.

House numbers may increase very slowly, and addresses are usually given in this form: 'Calle 57 No 481 x 56 y 58' (between Calles 56 and 58).

Information
Tourist Offices The tourist information booths at the airport and the main bus terminal, Terminal CAME, are not of much use, but there are three helpful tourist offices downtown (two run by the state, one by the city) that provide brochures, maps and current information. The first of the state-run offices is in the entrance to the Palacio de Gobierno, on the Plaza Grande, open 8am to 10pm daily; a second office (☎ 924-92-90) is less than two blocks north, at the corner of Calles 60 and 57A off the northeast edge of Parque de la Madre, open 8am to 9pm daily. An English-speaker is usually on hand.

The city tourist office (☎ 923-08-83), at the corner of Calles 59 and 62, is staffed with helpful English-speakers and open 8am to 8pm daily.

Money *Casas de cambio* offer faster, better service than banks, though they often have poorer rates. Try Money Marketing, in the Gran Hotel on Parque Hidalgo; Finex, just south of the cathedral;

or Cambistas Peninsulares, on the east side of Calle 60 between Calles 55 and 57.

Banks and ATMs are scattered throughout the city. There is a cluster of both along Calle 65 between Calles 60 and 62, one block south of the Plaza Grande. Most are open 9am to 5pm Monday to Friday, and some are also open 9am to 1pm or 2pm Saturday. See the Mérida map for other locations.

Post & Communications The main post office (☎ 921-25-61) is just north of the market, on Calle 65 between Calles 56 and 56A. It's open 8am to 3pm Monday to Friday and, for stamps only, 9am to 1pm Saturday. Postal service booths at the airport and bus terminal are open Monday through Friday.

Card phones can be found throughout the city. Among the many Internet places around town, those with decent connections and air-con include the following. Cybernet, on Calle 57A between Calles 58 and 60, charges US$0.10 per minute with a 15-minute (US$1.50) minimum (closed Sunday). Ciber-café Santa Lucí@, on Calle 62 at Calle 55, is open daily and charges US$1.65 per hour, US$0.85 per half hour and US$0.05 per minute, with free coffee. La Net@, at Calles 58 and 57 (upstairs), has similar prices and is closed Sunday. Near the bus terminals is CenterNet, on Calle 64 between Calles 69 and 71, south of Parque de San Juan. It's small but no-nonsense, with fax and scanning services. Net access is US$1.75 an hour, US$0.95 per half hour; it's closed Sunday.

Travel Agencies Asatej, the Argentine youth organization, has an agency (☎ 944-33-76, e merida@asatej.com.mx) in the north of town at Calle 54 No 370, Colonia Benito Juárez, Plaza Villas La Hacienda. The office will book flights, make low-cost changes and so forth.

Laundry Lavandería La Fe, Calle 64 between Calles 55 and 57, charges US$4.50 per 3kg load to wash and dry. It's open 8am to 6pm Monday to Friday, 8am to 2pm Saturday. You also can drop off your clothing at Lavandería Flamingo, on Calle 57 between Calles 56 and 58, and pick it up in the late afternoon. It charges per item (for example, US$0.35 per shirt, US$0.10 for each under-garment...yes, it's US$0.20 for a pair of socks). It's open 9am to 6pm Monday to Friday, 9am to 3pm Saturday.

Most hotels in the mid-range category and above, including the Gran Hotel, offer overnight laundry service.

Medical Services Hospital O'Horán (☎ 924-48-00), the largest hospital in Mérida, is near the Parque Zoológico Centenario on Avenida de los Itzáes. For most treatment (prescriptions, consultations) you're best off going to a private clinic. Ask at your consulate or hotel for a recommendation. In an emergency, call the Cruz Roja (Red Cross, ☎ 924-98-13).

Dangers & Annoyances Guard against pickpockets, bag-snatchers and bag-slashers in the market district and in any crowd, such as at a performance. Buses drive fast along the narrow streets and don't slow down for anything; sidewalks are often narrow and crowded.

Plaza Grande

This large but at times surprisingly intimate square is the most logical place to start a tour of Mérida. Also known as 'El Centro' (as in the center of town) or the Plaza Principal, the Plaza Grande was the religious and social center of ancient T'hó; under the Spanish it was the Plaza de Armas (parade ground), laid out by Francisco de Montejo the Younger. The plaza is surrounded by some of the city's most impressive and harmonious colonial buildings, and its carefully tended laurel trees provide welcome shade. On Sunday hundreds of meridanos take their *paseo* (stroll) here. Various events take place around the plaza on weekly schedules.

Cathedral On the plaza's east side, on the former site of a Mayan temple, is Mérida's hulking, severe cathedral *(open 6am-noon & 4pm-7pm)*, begun in 1561 and completed in 1598. Some of the stone from the Mayan temple was used in its construction. The massive crucifix behind the altar is **Cristo de la Unidad** (Christ of Unity), a symbol of reconciliation between those of Spanish and Maya stock. To the right over the south door is a painting of Tutul Xiú, cacique of the town of Maní, paying his respects to his ally Francisco de Montejo at T'hó (de Montejo and Xiú jointly defeated the

THE YUCATÁN PENINSULA

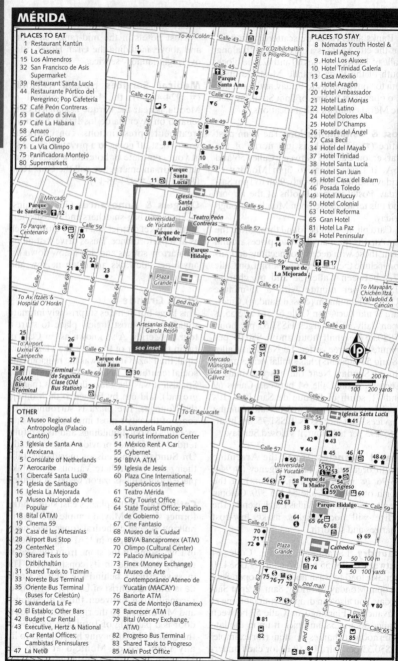

MÉRIDA

PLACES TO EAT
1 Restaurant Kantún
6 La Casona
15 Los Almendros
32 San Francisco de Asís Supermarket
39 Restaurant Santa Lucía
44 Restaurante Pórtico del Peregrino; Pop Cafetería
52 Café Peón Contreras
53 Il Gelato di Silvia
57 Café La Habana
58 Amaro
66 Café Giorgio
71 La Vía Olimpo
75 Panificadora Montejo
80 Supermarkets

PLACES TO STAY
8 Nómadas Youth Hostel & Travel Agency
9 Hotel Los Aluxes
10 Hotel Trinidad Galería
13 Casa Mexilio
14 Hotel Aragón
20 Hotel Ambassador
21 Hotel Las Monjas
22 Hotel Latino
24 Hotel Dolores Alba
25 Hotel D'Champs
26 Posada del Ángel
27 Casa Becil
34 Hotel del Mayab
37 Hotel Trinidad
38 Hotel Santa Lucía
41 Hotel San Juan
45 Hotel Casa del Balam
46 Posada Toledo
49 Hotel Mucuy
50 Hotel Colonial
63 Hotel Reforma
65 Gran Hotel
81 Hotel La Paz
84 Hotel Peninsular

OTHER
2 Museo Regional de Antropología (Palacio Cantón)
3 Iglesia de Santa Ana
4 Mexicana
5 Consulate of Netherlands
7 Aerocaribe
11 Cibercafé Santa Lucí@
16 Iglesia de Santiago
16 Iglesia La Mejorada
17 Museo Nacional de Arte Popular
18 Bital (ATM)
19 Cinema 59
23 Casa de las Artesanías
28 Airport Bus Stop
29 CenterNet
30 Shared Taxis to Dzibilchaltún
31 Shared Taxis to Tizimín
33 Noreste Bus Terminal
35 Oriente Bus Terminal (Buses for Celestún)
36 Lavandería La Fe
40 El Establo; Other Bars
42 Budget Car Rental
43 Executive, Hertz & National Car Rental Offices; Cambistas Peninsulares
47 La Net@

48 Lavandería Flamingo
51 Tourist Information Center
54 México Rent A Car
55 Cybernet
56 BBVA ATM
59 Iglesia de Jesús
60 Plaza Cine International; Supersónicos Internet
61 Teatro Mérida
62 City Tourist Office
64 State Tourist Office; Palacio de Gobierno
67 Cine Fantasio
68 Museo de la Ciudad
69 BBVA Bancapromex (ATM)
70 Olimpo (Cultural Center)
72 Palacio Municipal
73 Finex (Money Exchange)
74 Museo de Arte Contemporáneo Ateneo de Yucatán (MACAY)
76 Banorte ATM
77 Casa de Montejo (Banamex)
78 Bancrecer ATM
79 Bital (Money Exchange, ATM)
82 Progreso Bus Terminal
83 Shared Taxis to Progreso
85 Main Post Office

Cocomes; Xiú converted to Christianity, and his descendants still live in Mérida).

In the small chapel to the left of the altar is Mérida's most famous religious artifact, a statue called **Cristo de las Ampollas** (Christ of the Blisters). Local legend says the statue was carved from a tree that was hit by lightning and burned for an entire night without charring. It is also said to be the only object to have survived the fiery destruction of the church in the town of Ichmul (though it was blackened and blistered from the heat). The statue was moved to the Mérida cathedral in 1645.

Other than these, the cathedral's interior is largely plain, its rich decoration having been stripped away by angry peasants at the height of anticlerical feeling during the Mexican Revolution.

Around the Cathedral South of the cathedral, housed in the former archbishop's palace, is the **Museo de Arte Contemporáneo Ateneo de Yucatán** (Macay, ☎ 928-31-91; admission US$2.25, free Sun; open 10am-6pm Wed-Mon). This attractive museum holds permanent exhibits of Yucatán's most famous painters and sculptors, changing exhibits of local arts and crafts, and a cafeteria.

The **Casa de Montejo** (Palacio de Montejo; open 9am-5pm Mon-Fri, 9am-2pm Sat) is on the south side of the Plaza Grande and dates from 1549. It originally housed soldiers but soon was converted into a mansion that served members of the Montejo family until 1970. These days it shelters a bank, and you can enter and look around during bank hours. At other times, content yourself with a close look at the façade, where triumphant conquistadors with halberds hold their feet on the necks of generic barbarians (who are not Maya, but the association is inescapable). Also gazing across the plaza from the façade are busts of Montejo the Elder, his wife and his daughter.

Across the square from the cathedral is Mérida's **Palacio Municipal** (City Hall). Originally built in 1542, it was twice refurbished, in the 1730s and the 1850s. Adjoining it to the north is the **Olimpo**, Mérida's municipal cultural center. Attempts to create a modern exterior for the building were halted by government order, to preserve the colonial character of the plaza.

The ultramodern interior serves as a venue for music and dance performances as well as other exhibitions. Schedules for these and frequent film showings are posted outside.

On the north side of the plaza, the **Palacio de Gobierno** (admission free; open 8am-9pm daily) houses the state of Yucatán's executive government offices (and one of its tourist information offices). It was built in 1892 on the site of the palace of the colonial governors. Inside are murals painted by local artist Fernando Castro Pacheco; completed in 1978, they were 25 years in the making and portray a symbolic history of the Maya and their interaction with the Spaniards.

Museo de la Ciudad

The City Museum (no ☎, Calle 61 between 58 & 60; admission free; open 10am-2pm & 4pm-8pm Tues-Fri, 10am-2pm Sat-Sun) is small but worthwhile, with artifacts, exhibits and good photos of the city and region. Signs in English explain such subjects as Mayan traditions, history and the process of henequen production.

Walking up Calle 60

A block north of the Plaza Grande, just beyond shady Parque Hidalgo, rises the 17th-century **Iglesia de Jesús**, also called Iglesia de la Tercera Orden. Built by the Jesuits in 1618, it is the sole surviving edifice from a complex of buildings that once filled the entire city block. Always interested in education, the Jesuits founded schools that later gave birth to the nearby Universidad de Yucatán.

North of the church is the enormous bulk of the **Teatro Peón Contreras**, built between 1900 and 1908, during Mérida's henequen heyday. It boasts a main staircase of Carrara marble and a dome with faded frescoes by Italian artists. The main entrance to the theater is at the corner of Calles 60 and 57. Outside of performance hours, the guard may allow you in to see the theater.

Across Calle 60 from the theater is the main building of the **Universidad de Yucatán**. Though the Jesuits provided education to Yucatán's youth for centuries, the modern university was established in the 19th century by Governor Felipe Carrillo Puerto and General Manuel Cepeda Peraza.

A block north of the university, at the intersection of Calles 60 and 55, is pretty little **Parque Santa Lucía**, with arcades on the north and west sides. When Mérida was a lot smaller, this was where travelers would get on or off the stagecoaches that linked towns and villages with the provincial capital. The **Bazar de Artesanías**, the local handicrafts market, is held here at 11am Sunday.

To reach the Paseo de Montejo, discussed below, walk four blocks north and two east.

Paseo de Montejo

The Paseo de Montejo was an attempt by Mérida's 19th-century city planners to create a wide boulevard similar to the Paseo de la Reforma in Mexico City or the Champs Élysées in Paris. Though more modest than its predecessors, the Paseo de Montejo is still a beautiful swath of green, relatively open space in an urban conglomeration of stone and concrete.

Europe's architectural and social influence can be seen along the paseo in the fine mansions built by wealthy families around the end of the 19th century. The greatest concentrations of surviving mansions are north of Calle 37 – which is three blocks north of the Museo Regional de Antropología – and on the first block of Avenida Colón west of Paseo de Montejo.

Museo Regional de Antropología

The great white Palacio Cantón houses the Regional Anthropology Museum of the Yucatán *(cnr Paseo de Montejo & Calle 43; admission US$3.25, free Sun; open 8am-8pm Tues-Sat, 8am-2pm Sun)*. Construction of the mansion lasted from 1909 to 1911. Its owner, General Francisco Cantón Rosado (1833-1917), lived here for only six years before his death. Its splendor and pretension make it a fitting symbol of the grand aspirations of Mérida's elite during the last years of the Porfiriato, the period from 1876 to 1911 when Porfirio Díaz held despotic sway over Mexico.

The museum covers the peninsula's history since the age of mastodons. Exhibits on Mayan culture include explanations (many in Spanish only) of forehead-flattening, which was done to beautify babies, and other cosmetic practices such as sharpening teeth and implanting them with tiny jewels. If you plan to visit archaeological sites near Mérida, you can study the exhibits here – some with plans and photographs – covering the great Mayan cities of Mayapán, Uxmal and Chichén Itzá, as well as lesser-known sites such as Ek' Balam. There's also a good bookstore with many archaeological titles.

Parque Centenario

About 12 blocks west of the Plaza Grande lies the large, verdant Parque Centenario *(admission free; open 6am-6pm Tues-Sun)*, bordered by Avenida de los Itzáes, which leads to the airport and becomes the highway to Campeche. The park's **zoo** *(admission free; open 8am-5pm Tues-Sun)* features the fauna of Yucatán, as well as some exotic species. To get there, take a bus west along Calle 61 or 65.

Museo Nacional de Arte Popular

The National Museum of Popular Art *(Calle 59 between Calles 48 and 50; admission US$1.25; open 8am-6pm Tues-Sat)* is six blocks northeast of the Plaza Grande and holds displays of the best of local arts and crafts. It will satisfy your curiosity about the embroidering of colorful *huipiles*, carving of ceremonial masks, weaving of hammocks and hats, turning of pottery and construction of musical instruments.

Organized Tours

Transportadora Turística Carnaval (☎ 927-61-19) Bus tour of Mérida US$8.25. Carnaval conducts two-hour guided tours in English on its Paseo Turístico bus, departing from Parque Santa Lucía, Calle 55 at Calle 60, at 10am, 1pm, 4pm and 7pm Monday to Saturday, and 10am and 1pm Sunday. Seating capacity is 30 people. You can buy your tickets ahead of time at the nearby Hotel Santa Lucía, among other places.

You can choose from many group tours to sites around Mérida. Ask at your hotel reception desk for brochures, or consult any of the various travel agencies along Calle 60. Some common prices are: Celestún (US$40), Chichén Itzá (US$27; with drop-off in Cancún US$47), Uxmal and Kabah (US$27), Uxmal light-and-sound show (US$27), Ruta Puuc (Puuc Route, US$51) and Izamal (US$24). All prices are per person and most include transportation, guide and lunch.

Nómadas Youth Hostel and Travel Agency (☎/fax 924-52-23, e nomadas1@ prodigy.net.mx, Calle 62 No 433) Nómadas offers better prices on most of the tours listed above, and arranges a variety of others, from do-it-yourself trips in your rented car or on public transportation (with written instructions), to nearly all-inclusive (some meals) trips in private buses. Many include lodging at other hostels as well as insurance. Nómadas will also help to match up travelers into groups for sharing cars and such.

Special Events

For most of the month of February the Universidad de Yucatán celebrates its anniversary with free performances by the Ballet Folklórico, concerts of Afro-Cuban and *son* music and other manifestations of Yucatán's cultural roots.

Prior to Lent, in February or March, Carnaval features colorful costumes and nonstop festivities. It is celebrated with greater vigor in Mérida than anywhere else in Yucatán state. Also during the last days of February or the beginning of March (the dates vary) is Kihuic, a market that fills the Plaza Grande with handicrafts artisans from all over Mexico.

Between September 22 and October 14, *gremios* (guilds or unions) venerate the Cristo de las Ampollas (Christ of the Blisters) statue in the cathedral with processions.

Another big religious tradition is the Exposición de Altares, held the night of November 1, when the Maya welcome the spirits of their ancestors with elaborate dinners outside their homes. Although this custom is more apparent in the countryside, Mérida observes it with elaborate festivities in the center of town from 11am November 1 until 11am the next day.

Places to Stay

Many hotels' rates have been approaching unreasonable levels for what is offered, though the downturn in tourism following the 2001 terrorist attacks may reverse this trend. A lot of mid-range and top-end hotels raise prices 10% to 15% in December and during Semana Santa. These times and July and August (which see price increases as well at some places) tend to be the busiest; it's wise to book ahead. When business is slow many places will discount, some without

being asked (it never hurts to ask for a *promoción* if they don't). If you're arriving at the CAME bus terminal, check at the tourism desk for flyers offering hotel discounts. Rooms have private baths unless noted.

Wherever possible, high-season rates have been given here.

Budget Almost all hotels in this range provide purified drinking water at no extra charge. Sometimes the water bottles are not readily evident, so ask for *agua purificada*. Spending the extra money for air-con is worth it in the hotter months.

Nómadas Youth Hostel (☎/fax 924-52-23, ☎ 800-800-26-25, e nomadas1@prodigy .net.mx, W www.hostels.com.mx, Calle 62 No 433 at Calle 51) Hammock with mosquito net or tent with air mattress US$4.50/5 with/ without HI card, dorm beds with/without card US$6.50/7 with continental breakfast. Nómadas has a total of 28 beds in one coed and two women's dorms and a couple of other rooms. Guests have use of a full kitchen with fridge and purified water, 24-hour hot showers and hand-laundry facilities. Basic foods are provided on an honor system, as is good Internet access. Luggage lockers are free while you stay, US$1 a day while you travel. Between the two of them, the owners speak Spanish, good French and English and some Italian. Bring mosquito repellent and earplugs, and be warned: it gets hot.

Hotel La Paz (☎ 923-94-46, Calle 62 between Calles 65 & 67) Singles/doubles US$11/13.50. It ain't the Ritz, but the dark rooms are fairly quiet and have semiprivate bathrooms (they're in-room but with half-height walls).

Hotel Las Monjas (☎/fax 928-66-32, Calle 66A No 509) Singles/doubles US$11/12-14. This cozy hotel is just off Calle 63. All 31 rooms have ceiling fans and sinks or good private bathrooms with hot and cold water. Most rooms are tiny and dark, but they're clean.

Hotel Latino (☎ 923-50-87, Calle 66 No 505 between Calles 61 & 63) Singles/doubles with fan US$8.75/10, rooms with air-con US$16.50. This hotel offers 29 rather spartan rooms with good mattresses. It can get noisy.

Hotel Mucuy (☎ 928-51-93, fax 923-78-01, Calle 57 No 481 between Calles 56 & 58) Singles/doubles/triples with fan US$18/22/27.

This recommended hotel has 24 tidy rooms on two floors facing a long, narrow garden courtyard. The señora and her daughter speak English and French as well as Spanish.

Casa Becil (☎ 924-67-64, fax 924-24-24 during office hours, Calle 67 No 550C between Calles 66 & 68) 1-bed/2-bed doubles US$13.50/19. Near the main bus terminals, this is a friendly 13-room house with a high-ceilinged sitting-room/lobby and small, sometimes hot, but clean rooms with fans and good mattresses.

Hotel del Mayab (☎ 928-51-74, fax 928-60-47, Calle 50 No 536A between Calles 65 & 67) Doubles with fan/air-con US$16.50/26. The Mayab is clean and low-key. Streetside rooms can be noisy, but interior rooms are quiet, and there's a swimming pool.

Hotel Peninsular (☎ 923-69-96, fax 923-69-02, Calle 58 No 519 between Calles 65 & 67) Doubles with fan/air-con US$17/22. This 45-room hotel is in the heart of the market district, three blocks from the Plaza Grande. You pass through a long corridor to find a neat restaurant and a maze of rooms; most are spacious and have windows opening onto the interior, though some of those with fan are quite hot. Throw in a small swimming pool and you have a pretty good deal.

Posada del Ángel (☎ 923-27-54, fax 926-07-58, Calle 67 No 535 between Calles 66 & 68) Singles/doubles/triples with fan US$18/26/33, with air-con US$25/33/42. This neocolonial 30-room hotel is three blocks northeast of Terminal CAME and is quieter than most other hotels in this neighborhood.

Hotel Aragón (☎ 924-02-42, fax 924-11-22, W www.hotelaragon.com, Calle 57 No 474 between Calles 52 & 54) Rooms US$25. Hotel Aragón offers 18 very clean air-conditioned rooms on three floors overlooking a charming little courtyard. Purified water, tea and coffee are available free 24 hours.

Hotel Reforma (☎ 924-79-22, fax 928-32-78, e hreforma@yuc1.telmex.net.mx, Calle 59 No 508 between Calles 60 & 62) Singles/doubles with fan US$27/31, with air-con US$30/33; all include breakfast. The Reforma has 50 rooms ringing a courtyard with a swimming pool. Each room contains a TV, telephone and ceiling fan. The facilities are deteriorating slightly, but the air-con is good.

Hotel Dolores Alba (☎ 928-56-50, 800-849-50-60, fax 928-31-63, W www.doloresalba .com, Calle 63 between Calles 52 & 54)

Doubles US$27 with fan, US$30-42 with air-con (no credit cards). The Dolores Alba is a Mérida institution and an excellent value. Rooms are around two large courtyards; all those in the new, modern wing are quite large and face the lovely, chlorine-free pool. The hotel has secure parking and is quiet, well managed and friendly.

Hotel Trinidad (☎ 924-98-06, fax 924-11-22, e info@hoteltrinidad.com, Calle 62 No 464 between Calles 55 & 57) Doubles with shared/private bath US$22/28 with continental breakfast. This colonial hotel is run by artists; it's quirky and a tiny bit run-down, but in a good way. It has a lovely, quiet courtyard, and each of the 19 fan-cooled rooms has its own unique decor and charm. There's 24-hour tea and a small café, and guests can use the pool at the Trinidad's sister hotel, the Hotel Trinidad Galería.

Hotel Trinidad Galería (☎ 923-24-63, fax 924-23-19, Calle 60 No 456 near Calle 51) Singles/doubles/triples US$31/37/44. The Galería is a former appliance showroom, and farther-out in appearance than its sister hotel. It has a bar, art gallery and an impressively shady courtyard. Both the public areas and presentable, fan-cooled rooms offer up a multitude of visual delights.

Hotel Santa Lucía (☎ 928-26-62, ☎/fax 928-26-72, Calle 55 No 508 between Calles 60 & 62) Singles/doubles/triples US$34/37/43. Clean, secure and very popular, this hotel has a pool and 51 rooms with air-con, TV and telephone. It's pretty nice, all in all.

Hotel San Juan (☎/fax 924-17-42, Calle 55 No 497A near Calle 58) Singles/doubles US$35/39. This hotel offers a pool, parking and 63 clean, roomy units with phone, TV and aging air-con.

Posada Toledo (☎ 923-16-90, ☎/fax 923-22-56, e hptoledo@pibil.finred.com.mx, Calle 58 No 487 at Calle 57) Doubles with air-con US$36. This is a colonial mansion with small, somewhat modernized rooms arranged on two floors around the classic courtyard, and a dining room (breakfast only) straight out of the 19th century. The newer, upstairs rooms are larger than the ground-floor rooms.

Mid-Range Mérida's mid-range places provide surprising levels of comfort for what you pay. Most charge between US$60 and US$80 for a double with air-con, ceiling fan and private shower (and often TV and phone). Most have restaurants, bars and small swimming pools as well.

Hotel D'Champs (☎ 924-86-55, 800-849-09-34, fax 923-60-24, Calle 70 No 543 at Calle 67) Singles/doubles US$55/61. Just a block from the two main bus terminals, this hotel is in a classy old building with modernized interior. It has a massive open courtyard with pool and trees, a restaurant and 90 decent-sized rooms with TV, air-con and phones.

Gran Hotel (☎ 924-77-30, fax 924-76-22, e granh@sureste.com, Calle 60 No 496 between Calles 59 & 61) Singles/doubles US$51/57. This grand hotel was built in 1901 and retains many delightful decorative flourishes. The 28 air-conditioned rooms have period furnishings, and some overlook Parque Hidalgo.

Casa Mexilio (☎/fax 928-25-05, ☎ 800-538-6802 in the USA, e casamexilio@prodigy.net.mx, Calle 68 No 495 between Calles 57 & 59) Rooms with fan US$55, with air-con US$78. This charming pensión is in a well-preserved historical house with a maze of quiet, beautifully appointed rooms. All room rates include a good breakfast in the period dining room. There's a small pool with Jacuzzi.

Hotel Ambassador (☎ 924-21-00, fax 924-27-01, w www.ambassadormerida.com, Calle 59 No 546 near Calle 68) Doubles/triples/suites US$66/76/82. The Ambassador offers 100 comfortable, modern rooms with satellite TV and minibars, a pool, a pleasant courtyard and a travel agency and car-rental outfit. Try asking for a discount.

Hotel Colonial (☎ 923-64-44, 888-886-2982 in the USA, fax 928-39-61, e reservas@hotelcolonial.com.mx, Calle 62 No 476 cnr Calle 57) Doubles/triples US$78/92. This hotel features 73 comfortable air-conditioned rooms in a fairly modern building with a small pool.

Top End Top-end hotels charge between about US$80 and US$230 for a double with air-con in high season. Most have restaurants, bars, nightclubs and swimming pools, and many will offer other services such as a newsstand, hairdresser or travel agency.

If you reserve your top-end room through your travel agent at home, you're likely to pay international-class rates. But if you walk in and ask about *promociones* (promotional rates) or – even better – look through local newspapers and handouts for special rates aimed at a local clientele, you can lower your lodging bill substantially.

Hotel Los Aluxes (☎ 924-21-99, fax 923-38-58, 800-782-8395 in the USA, e aluxes@finred.com.mx, w www.aluxes.com.mx, cnr Calle 60 & Calle 49) Doubles US$83. This very modern and comfortable hotel has 109 rooms; it's popular with tour groups.

Hotel Casa del Balam (☎ 924-21-50, 800-624-8451 in the USA, fax 924-50-11, w www.yucatanadventure.com.mx, Calle 60 No 488 near Calle 57) Doubles US$107. The Balam is wearing at the edges a bit, but it's centrally located and has a great pool and large, quiet rooms with powerful central air-con. Hefty discounts are available when things aren't busy.

Fiesta Americana Mérida (☎ 942-11-11, 800-343-7821 in the USA, fax 942-11-12, e ventasmd@fiestaamericana.com.mx, w www.fiestaamericana.com, Calle 56A No 451) Rooms & junior suites US$191-228. This enormous, modern neocolonial luxury hotel is part of a complex housing shops, travel agencies, airline offices and restaurants. Though the official address doesn't indicate it, the hotel occupies a large stretch of Avenida Colón, on the northern edge of the colonial center.

Hyatt Regency Mérida (☎ 942-02-02, fax 925-70-02, e hyatt@sureste.com, w www.hyatt.com, Avenida Colón 344) Rooms from US$232. Not far from the Fiesta Americana, the 17-story Hyatt is Mérida's most expensive hotel. It has 300 rooms, tennis courts, a gym and steam bath, and a great pool with swim-up bar.

Places to Eat

As in other touristed areas of the Yucatán Peninsula, many restaurants in Mérida have begun adding a service charge (usually 10%) to the bill. Check the menu carefully before you order to see if this is official policy; if there's no mention, use your own judgment when it comes time to pay.

Budget Mérida's least-expensive eateries are in the Mercado Municipal Lucas de Gálvez on Calle 56A; most are open from early morning until early evening. Upstairs joints have tables and chairs and more varied menus; main-course platters of beef, fish or chicken go for as little as US$1.25. Downstairs at the north end are some cheap taquerías where you sit on a stool at a narrow counter, while near the south end are *coctelerías* serving shrimp, octopus and conch cocktails starting at around US$2.

For good, cheap breakfasts, try a selection of *panes dulces* (sweet rolls and breads) from one of Mérida's several *panificadoras*, such as **Panificadora Montejo** on the southwest corner of the main plaza. A full bag of breads usually costs US$2.50.

A few blocks east of the Plaza Grande are side-by-side **supermarkets** *(Calle 56 between Calles 63 & 65)*, as well as a branch of **San Francisco de Asís** *(cnr Calles 67 & 54A)*, a market/department-store chain.

Il Gelato di Silvia *(Calle 57A near Calle 58)* Ice cream! In a variety of good flavors.

Mid-Range *Café La Habana (cnr Calles 59 & 62)* Breakfast & soups US$1.50-4, sandwiches US$3.25-5, mains US$4-10, set meals US$4.75. Open 24 hrs. This air-conditioned restaurant is one of the most popular in town. It serves decent food at decent prices. Meaty *menúes* are a good deal.

La Vía Olimpo *(Calle 62 between Calles 61 & 63)* Mains US$3-6. Open 24 hrs. Olimpo is an upscale and trendy restaurant-café on the west side of the Plaza Grande, closed only between 11pm Monday and 7am Tuesday. Try the *baguette de pavo lomo ahumado* (smoked turkey sandwich, US$5.50). Internet access is also available, though it's fairly slow.

Cafe Peón Contreras *(Calle 60)* Breakfast US$4.75-5.75, pizzas US$5.75-10. A few steps north of Parque Hidalgo, this café has espresso drinks and a long, varied menu, including a combination plate of Yucatecan specialties for around US$10.

Pop Cafetería *(Calle 57 between Calles 60 & 62)* Breakfasts US$2.50-3.75, mains US$3.75-5.50. The Pop is plain, modern and well cooled. It has tasty, cheap breakfast combinations and a good variety of Mexican dishes; try the chicken in *mole* (US$3.25) or the delicious guacamole (US$2.25).

Café Giorgio *(Calle 60 No 496 between Calles 59 & 61)* Breakfasts US$3.50-5.50, mains US$4.50-6. On the Parque Hidalgo, this place serves generous, reasonably priced breakfasts, as well as ample portions of pasta

and other dishes and mediocre pizza. The outdoor tables offer prime people-watching opportunities.

Restaurant Santa Lucía *(Calle 60 near Calle 55)* The Santa Lucía serves good lunches and dinners at good prices and has a pleasing ambiance.

Amaro *(Calle 59 between Calles 60 & 62)* Dishes US$4.75-6.50. Open noon-1am daily. Amaro is a romantic dining spot, especially at night. It's set in the courtyard of the house in which Andrés Quintana Roo – poet, statesman and drafter of Mexico's Declaration of Independence – was born in 1787. The restaurant has Yucatecan food and a good variety of vegetarian plates, as well as some continental dishes and pizzas. There's a full bar. Service and food are good.

Restaurant Kantún *(Calle 45 between Calles 64 & 66)* Mains US$6-8. Open 11am-6pm Thur-Sun. This family-run, neighborhood place serves some of the best seafood in town. Entrées are all prepared to order and superbly seasoned or sauced; try the *filete Normanda*, a fillet stuffed with smoked oysters and topped with anchovies (US$7.50). There are a few meat dishes for nonfishy types, and you can eat well for under US$10.

Top End *Restaurante Pórtico del Peregrino (☎ 928-61-63, Calle 57 between Calles 60 & 62)* Meals US$12-20. Several pleasant, traditional-style dining rooms (some air-conditioned) surround a small courtyard here. Yucatecan dishes are the forte, but you'll find many continental dishes and a broad range of seafood as well. Readers recommend it highly.

La Casona *(Calle 60 between Calles 47 & 49)* Dishes US$12-25. Open for dinner only. La Casona is a fine old city house, with tables set out on a portico next to a small but lush garden; dim lighting lends an air of romance (but bring repellent if you're eating outside). Excellent Italian dishes and a few Yucatecan choices are served.

Los Almendros *(Calle 50A between Calles 57 & 59)* Meals US$13-20. Los Almendros serves a wide variety of authentic Yucatecan country cuisine and is famous for its zingy *poc-chuc*, an onion-and-tomato pork dish. This is hearty, stick-to-your-ribs food. The maître d' might try to dictate the amount of tip you pay.

Entertainment

Mérida offers almost nightly folkloric and musical events in parks and historic buildings, put on by local performers of considerable skill. Admission is free to many of these; check with one of the tourist information offices for information and to learn of special events.

Among the most popular events are the Monday night *vaquerías* (traditional Yucatecan dances), which are performed to live music in front of the Palacio Municipal (on the west side of Plaza Grande) from 9pm to 10pm. The dance and music reflect a mixture of Spanish and Mayan cultures and date from the earliest days of the Vaquería Regional, a local festival that celebrated the branding of cattle on neighboring haciendas. You should arrive early in order to get a good seat.

Mérida has several cinemas, most of which show some first-run Hollywood fare in English, with subtitles (ask *'¿en inglés?'* if you need to be sure). *Teatro Mérida (Calle 62 between Calles 59 & 61)* often shows classic Hollywood and international flicks.

El Establo (Calle 60 between Calles 57 & 55) Open 9pm-3am Thur-Sun. This is one of a cluster of bars on this block of Calle 60 that have live music and dancing on Friday and Saturday night.

Shopping

Mérida is a fine place for buying Yucatecan handicrafts. Purchases to consider include traditional Mayan clothing such as the colorful embroidered *huipiles* (women's tunics), panama hats woven from palm fibers and of course the wonderfully comfortable Yucatecan hammocks.

Yucatecan Hammocks: The Only Way to Sleep

The fine strings of Yucatecan hammocks make them supremely comfortable. In the sticky heat of a Yucatán summer, most locals prefer sleeping in a hammock, where the air can circulate around them, rather than in a bed. Many inexpensive hotels used to have hammock hooks in the walls of all guestrooms, though the hooks are not so much in evidence today.

Yucatecan hammocks are normally woven from strong nylon or cotton string and dyed in various colors. There are also natural, undyed cotton versions. Some sellers will try to fob these off as henequen, telling you it's much more durable (and valuable) than cotton. Don't be taken in; real henequen hammocks are very rough and not something you'd want near your skin. In the old days, the finest, strongest, most expensive hammocks were woven from silk, but these are no longer seen (don't pay silk prices for nylon!).

Hammocks come in several widths. The *sencillo* (for one person) has about 50 pairs of end strings (each pair consisting of at least four strands) and should run from about US$12 to US$16. The *doble* (also called *número 4*) is made with 100 to 120 pairs and costs roughly US$17 to US$22. Next comes the *matrimonial/número 5* (150 pairs, US$20 to US$23), and finally the *matrimonial especial/número 8* (175 or more pairs, US$26 to US$32). De croché (very tightly woven) hammocks can take several weeks to produce and cost double or triple the prices given here.

When selecting a hammock, you must check to be sure that you're really getting the width you're paying for. Because hammocks fold up small and the larger hammocks are more comfortable (though more expensive), consider the bigger sizes.

During your first few hours in Mérida you will be approached on the street by hammock peddlers. They may quote very low prices, but a low price is only good if the quality is high, and street-sold hammocks are mediocre at best. Check the hammock very carefully.

You can save yourself a lot of trouble by shopping at a hammock store with a good reputation. Getting away from the heavily touristed areas helps. Hamacas El Aguacate (☎ 928-64-69), at the corner of Calles 58 and 73, has quality hammocks and decent prices, and there's no hard sell.

It's interesting to venture out to the nearby village of Tixcocob to watch the hammocks being woven. A bus runs regularly from the Progreso bus station, Calle 62 No 524, between Calles 65 and 67 south of the main plaza.

Mercado Municipal Lucas de Gálvez Mérida's main market is bounded by Calles 56 and 56A at Calle 67, southeast of the Plaza Grande. The surrounding streets are all part of the large market district, lined with shops selling everything one might need. Guard your valuables extra carefully in the market area. Watch for pickpockets, purse-snatchers and bag-slashers.

Handicrafts *Casa de las Artesanías (Calle 63 between Calles 64 & 66)* Open 9am-8pm Mon-Sat, 10am-2pm Sun. This is a government-supported market for local artisans selling just about everything: earthenware, textiles, wicker baskets, sandals, wind chimes, ceramic dolls, vases, purses and pouches, figurines of Mayan deities and bottles of locally made liqueurs. Prices are fixed and reasonable; you can have a look at the stuff here, then try to bargain down independent sellers elsewhere, but it's often not worth the amount you save.

Panama Hats Locally made panama hats are woven from jipijapa palm leaves in caves, where humid conditions keep the fibers pliable when the hat is being made. Once exposed to the relatively dry air outside, the panama hat is surprisingly resilient and resistant to crushing. The Campeche town of Bécal is the center of the hat-weaving trade, but you can buy good examples of the hatmaker's art in Mérida.

The best quality hats have a fine, close weave of slender fibers. The coarser the weave, the lower the price should be. Prices range from a few dollars for a hat of basic quality to US$50 or more for top quality. They can be found at the Casa de las Artesanías and elsewhere.

Getting There & Away

Air Mérida's modern airport is a 10km, 20-minute ride southwest of the Plaza Grande off highway 180 (Avenida de los Itzáes). It has car rental desks, an ATM and currency exchange booth and a tourist office that can help with hotel reservations.

Most international flights to Mérida are connections through Mexico City or Cancún. Nonstop international services are provided by Aeroméxico (daily from Miami), Continental (Houston) and Aviateca (Guatemala City). Scheduled domes-

tic flights are operated mostly by smaller regional airlines, with a few flights by Aeroméxico and Mexicana.

Aerocaribe (☎ 928-67-90), Paseo de Montejo 500B, flies between Mérida and Cancún, Chetumal, Veracruz and Villahermosa, with connections to Tuxtla Gutiérrez, Havana (Cuba) and other destinations.

Aerolíneas Bonanza (☎ 928-06-09, fax 927-79-99), Calle 56A No 579, between Calles 67 and 69, flies roundtrips daily from Mérida to Cancún, Chetumal and Palenque.

Aeroméxico (☎ 920-12-60, 920-12-93), Hotel Fiesta Americana, Avenida Colón at Paseo Montejo, flies to Mexico City and Miami.

Aviacsa (☎ 925-68-90 at Hotel Fiesta Americana, ☎ 946-18-50 at airport) flies to Cancún and Mexico City.

Continental Airlines (☎ 800-900-50-00), at the airport, flies nonstop between Houston and Mérida.

Mexicana (☎ 924-69-10), Paseo de Montejo 493, has nonstop flights to Mexico City.

Bus Mérida is the bus transportation hub of the Yucatán Peninsula. Take care with your gear on night buses and those serving popular tourist destinations (especially 2nd-class buses); Lonely Planet has received many reports of theft on the night runs to Chiapas and of a few daylight thefts on the Chichén Itzá route and other lines.

Bus & Combi Terminals Mérida has a variety of bus terminals, and some lines operate out of (and stop at) more than one terminal. Tickets for departure from one terminal can often be bought at another, and destinations overlap greatly among lines. Following are some of the stations, bus lines operating out of them and areas served.

Terminal CAME – Pronounced 'KAH-meh,' and sometimes referred to as the 'Terminal de Primera Clase,' Mérida's main terminal (reservations ☎ 924-83-91) is seven blocks southwest of the Plaza Grande, on Calle 70 between Calles 69 and 71. Come here for (mostly 1st-class) buses to points around the Yucatán Peninsula and well beyond, for example, Campeche, Cancún, Mexico City, Palenque, San Cristóbal de Las Casas and Villahermosa. Lines include ADO, Altos (providing 'directo económico' service, with air-con and few stops, but no bathroom), Maya de Oro, Super Expresso and UNO.

CAME has card phones and an ATM and runs counters for tourist, bus and hotel information.

Terminal de Segunda Clase – Also known as Terminal 69 ('Sesenta y Nueve') or simply Terminal de Autobuses, this is on Calle 69, just around the corner from CAME. ATS, Mayab, Omnitur del Caribe, Oriente, Sur, TRP and TRT run mostly 2nd-class buses to points in the state and around the peninsula. The terminal has an ATM and a luggage checkroom (US$0.30 an hour, open 7am to 11pm).

Terminal Noreste – The Noreste bus line's terminal is on Calle 67 between Calles 50 and 52; LUS uses it as well. Service here is to many small towns in the northeast part of the peninsula, including Tizimín and Río Lagartos, as well as frequent service to Cancún and points along the way, and small towns south and west of Mérida, including Ticul and Oxkutzcab.

Terminal Celestún – This is a small open-air terminal on Calle 50, around the corner from Terminal Noreste. Occidente buses for Celestún depart from here, as do some Oriente buses (for Izamal and Tizimín, for example). Other Oriente buses depart from Terminal 69.

Parque de San Juan – On Calle 69 between Calles 62 and 64, this is the terminus for vans and Volkswagen *combis* going to Dzibilchaltún Ruinas, Muna, Oxkutzcab, Peto, Sacalum, Tekax and Ticul.

Progreso – The separate bus terminal for Progreso is at Calle 62 No 524 between Calles 65 and 67.

Hotel Fiesta Americana – This small 1st-class terminal on the west side of the hotel complex on Avenida Colón near Calle 56A is aimed at guests of the luxury hotels on Avenida Colón, far from the center. Don't catch a bus to here unless you'll be staying at the Fiesta or Hyatt. ADO GL and Super Expreso have service between here and Cancún, Campeche, Chetumal and Playa del Carmen.

Bus Routes Destinations served from Mérida include the following:

Campeche – 195km (short route via Bécal), 2½-3 hours; 250km (long route via Uxmal), 4 hours; 29 2nd-class ATS (US$7.25), 27 1st-class ADO (US$8.75)

Cancún – 320km, 4-6 hours; 15 2nd-class Oriente (US$12), 7 deluxe Super Expreso (US$16.50), many other buses

Celestún – 95km, 2 hours; 17 2nd-class Occidente from Celestún terminal (US$3.50)

Chetumal – 456km, 6-8 hours; 8 deluxe Omnitur del Caribe and Super Expreso (US$18.50), 3 2nd-class Mayab (US$15.50)

Chichén Itzá – 116km, 2½ hours; 2nd-class Oriente Cancún-bound buses stop at Chichén Itzá during open hours, otherwise at nearby Pisté (US$4.75)

Cobá – 270km, 3½ hours; deluxe Super Expreso at 6.30am and 1pm (US$11)

Escárcega – 345km, 5-5½ hours; 1 1st-class Altos (US$14), 5 1st-class ADO (US$16), 1 2nd-class Sur (US$13)

Felipe Carrillo Puerto – 310km, 5½ hours; 9 2nd-class Mayab (US$11.50), 3 2nd-class TRP (US$12)

Izamal – 72km, 1½ hours; frequent 2nd-class Oriente (from Terminal Celestún; US$2.75)

Mayapán Ruinas – 48km, 2 hours; 2nd-class LUS at 8.30am daily and 2pm Saturday only (from Noreste terminal; US$3.50 one-way)

Mexico City (Norte) – 1514km, 19 hours; 1st-class ADO at 12.05pm and 2.45pm (US$76)

Mexico City (TAPO) – 1504km, 20 hours; 4 1st-class ADO between 10am and 9.15pm (US$76)

Palenque – 556km, 8-9 hours; 1 deluxe Maya de Oro (US$29), 3 1st-class ADO (US$26), 1 Altos (US$24)

Playa del Carmen – 385km, 4½-8 hours; 10 deluxe Super Expreso (US$20), 6 2nd-class Mayab (US$17.50), several others

Progreso – 33km, 1 hour; buses leave every 20 minutes, 8am-9pm, from the Progreso bus terminal (US$1.25); for the same ticket price, shared vans (some with air-con) take off from a parking lot located on Calle 60 between Calles 63 and 65

Río Lagartos – 261km, 3-4 hours; 1st-class Noreste at 5.30pm (US$10), 2nd-class Noreste at 9am and 4pm (US$8)

Ticul – 85km, 1¾ hours; frequent 2nd-class Mayab (US$3.25), 2nd-class LUS (US$3.50) at 6.15am, 10.15am and 4.30pm; frequent minibuses (combis and vans) from Parque de San Juan (US$2.75)

Tizimín – 210km, 2½-4 hours; several 1st-class Noreste (US$7.50), several 2nd-class Noreste (US$6.50), 3 2nd-class Oriente (US$7)

Tulum – 320km (via Cobá), 4 hours; deluxe Super Expreso at 6.30am and 1pm (US$11); there is 2nd-class service to Tulum, but it costs more and takes much longer.

Tuxtla Gutiérrez – 820km, 13-16 hours; 1 deluxe Maya de Oro at 9.30pm (US$44), 1 Altos at 7.15pm (US$36); or change at Palenque or Villahermosa

Valladolid – 160km, 2½-3½ hours; many buses, including deluxe Super Expreso (US$8.25), 2nd-class Oriente (US$6.25) and ATS

Villahermosa – 560km, 9 hours; 10 1st-class ADO (US$30), superdeluxe UNO at 9.30pm and 11pm (US$49), air-conditioned 2nd-class TRP at 11am and 9pm (US$26)

Car Rental car is the optimal way to tour the many archaeological sites south of Mérida, especially if you have two or more people to share costs. Assume you will pay a total of US$40 to US$60 per day (tax, insurance and gas included) for short-term rental of the cheapest car offered, usually a bottom-of-the-line Volkswagen or Nissan. Getting around town is better done on foot or with public transportation, so hold off renting your car until you've seen most of Mérida, or at least gotten well oriented.

México Rent A Car (☎ 923-36-37, fax 927-49-16, e mexicorentacar@hotmail.com), Calle 57-A between Calles 58 and 60, offers rates the big-name agencies often can't touch, especially if you're paying cash. It's sometimes possible to get a VW Beetle for as little as US$25 a day, and long-term rentals can bring prices lower than that, even on higher-quality cars. Cars are in very good condition, and the friendly managers speak good English.

Several other agencies have branches at the airport as well as on Calle 60 between 55 and 57, including Budget (☎ 928-66-59), Executive (☎ 923-37-32) and Hertz (☎ 924-28-34).

See Cancún's Getting There & Away section for a warning about the overpriced toll highway between Mérida and Cancún.

Getting Around

To/From the Airport Bus 79 ('Aviación') travels between the airport and the city center every 15 to 30 minutes until 9pm, with occasional service until 11pm. The half-hour trip (US$0.40) is via a very roundabout route; the best place to catch the bus is on Calle 70 just south of Calle 69, near the corner of the CAME terminal.

Transporte Terrestre (☎ 946-15-29) provides speedy service between the airport and the center, charging US$10.50 per carload (same price for hotel pick-up). A taxi from the center to the airport should run about US$8.25 (but it's hard to get this price *from* the airport).

Bus Most parts of Mérida that you'll want to visit are within five or six blocks of the Plaza Grande and are thus accessible on foot. Given the slow speed of city traffic, particularly in the market areas, travel on foot is also the fastest way to get around.

City buses are cheap at US$0.40, but routes are confusing. Most start in suburban

neighborhoods, meander through the city center and terminate in another distant suburban neighborhood. To travel between the Plaza Grande and the upscale neighborhoods to the north along Paseo de Montejo, catch the Ruta 10 at the corner of Calles 58 and 59, half a block east of the Parque Hidalgo, or catch a 'Tecnológico' bus on Calle 60 and get out at Avenida Colón. To return to the city center, catch any bus heading south on Paseo de Montejo that is displaying the destination 'Centro.'

Taxi Taxis in Mérida are not metered. Rates are fixed, with an outrageous US$3.50 minimum fare, which will get you from the bus terminals to all downtown hotels. Most rides within city limits do not exceed US$5.50. Taxi stands can be found at most of the barrio parks, or dial ☎ 928-53-22 or 923-12-21; service is available 24 hours (dispatch fees are an extra US$1 to US$2).

SOUTH OF MÉRIDA
Hacienda Yaxcopoil

Hacienda Yaxcopoil *(☎ 999-927-26-06; admission US$4; open 8am-6pm Mon-Sat, 9am-1pm Sun)* is on the west side of highway 261, 33km southwest of central Mérida. A vast estate that grew and processed henequen, its numerous French Renaissance-style buildings have been restored and turned collectively into a museum of the 17th century. Frequent buses pass Yaxcopoil running between Mérida and Ticul.

Mayapán

These ruins *(admission US$2.50, free Sun & holidays; open 8am-5pm daily)* are some 50km southeast of Mérida, on Yucatán state highway 18. Though far less impressive than many Mayan sites, Mayapán is historically significant, its main attractions are clustered in a compact core, and visitors usually have the place to themselves.

Don't confuse the ruins of Mayapán with the Mayan village of the same name, some 40km southeast of the ruins, past the town of Teabo.

History Mayapán was supposedly founded by Kukulcán (Quetzalcóatl) in AD 1007, shortly after the former ruler of Tula arrived in Yucatán. His dynasty, the Cocom, organized a confederation of city-states

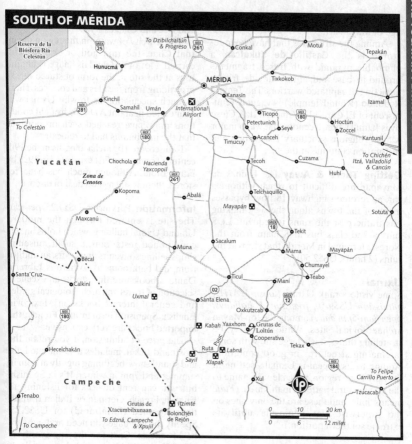

SOUTH OF MÉRIDA

that included Uxmal, Chichén Itzá and many other notable cities. Despite their alliance, animosity arose between the Cocomes of Mayapán and the Itzáes of Chichén Itzá during the late 12th century, and the Cocomes stormed Chichén Itzá, forcing the Itzá rulers into exile. The Cocom dynasty emerged supreme in all of northern Yucatán.

Cocom supremacy lasted for almost 2½ centuries, until the ruler of Uxmal, Ah Xupán Xiú, led a rebellion of the oppressed city-states and overthrew Cocom hegemony. The great capital of Mayapán was utterly destroyed and remained uninhabited ever after.

But struggles for power continued in the region until 1542, when Francisco de Montejo the Younger conquered T'hó and

established Mérida. At that point the current lord of Maní and ruler of the Xiú people, Ah Kukum Xiú, proposed to Montejo a military alliance against the Cocomes, his ancient rivals. Montejo accepted, and Xiú was baptized as a Christian, taking the name Francisco de Montejo Xiú. The Cocomes were defeated and – too late – the Xiú rulers realized that they had signed the death warrant of Mayan independence.

The Site The city of Mayapán was large, with a population estimated to be around 12,000; it covered 4 sq km, all surrounded by a great defensive wall. Over 3500 buildings, 20 cenotes and traces of the city wall were mapped by archaeologists working in the 1950s and in 1962. The Late Postclassic workmanship is inferior to that of the great age of Mayan art.

Among the structures that have been restored is the **Castillo de Kukulcán**, a climbable pyramid with fresco fragments around its base and, at its rear side, friezes depicting decapitated warriors. The **Templo Redondo** (Round Temple) is vaguely reminiscent of El Caracol at Chichén Itzá. Close by is Itzmal Chen, a cenote that was a major Mayan religious sanctuary. Excavation and restoration continue at the site.

Getting There & Away The Ruinas de Mayapán are difficult to reach without a car, as rerouted highway 18 now bypasses many of the towns along the way, making bus traffic past the ruins infrequent. LUS runs a 2nd-class bus at 8.30am from the Noreste terminal in Mérida that stops at the ruins (2 hours, US$2.50).

Uxmal

Some visitors rank Uxmal *('oosh-MAHL'; admission US$9.50, free Sun & holidays; open 8am-5pm daily)* among the top Mayan archaeological sites. While this may be stretching things, it is a large site with some fascinating structures in good condition. Adding to its appeal is Uxmal's setting in the hilly Puuc region, which lent its name to the architectural patterns in this area. *(Puuc* means 'hills,' and these are the only ones on the otherwise flat peninsula until its extreme southern portion.)

History Uxmal was an important city in a region that encompassed the satellite towns of Sayil, Kabah, Xlapak and Labná. Although Uxmal means 'Thrice Built' in Mayan, it was actually constructed five times.

That a sizable population flourished in this dry area is yet more testimony to the engineering skills of the Maya, who built a series of reservoirs and *chultunes* (cisterns) lined with lime mortar to catch and hold water during the dry season. First settled about AD 600, Uxmal was influenced by highland Mexico in its architecture, most likely through contact fostered by trade. This influence is reflected in the town's serpent imagery, phallic symbols and columns. The well-proportioned Puuc architecture, with its intricate, geometric mosaics sweeping across the upper parts of elongated façades, was strongly influenced by the slightly earlier Río Bec and Chenes styles.

The scarcity of water in the region meant that Chac, the rain god or sky serpent, carried a lot of weight. His image is ubiquitous at the site in the form of stucco masks protruding from façades and cornices. There is much speculation as to why Uxmal was abandoned in about AD 900; drought conditions may have reached such proportions that the inhabitants had to relocate.

Rediscovered by archaeologists in the 19th century, Uxmal was first excavated in 1929 by Frans Blom. Although much has been restored, there is still a good deal to discover.

Information Parking is US$1.25 per car. The site is entered through the modern Unidad Uxmal building, which holds an air-conditioned restaurant, a small museum, shops selling souvenirs and crafts, an auditorium and bathrooms. Also here is Librería Dante, a bookstore that stocks an excellent selection of travel and archaeological guides and general-interest books on Mexico in English, Spanish, German and French; the imported books are very expensive.

The price of admission, if you retain the wristband-ticket, includes a 45-minute light and sound show, beginning nightly at 8pm in summer and 7pm in winter. It's in Spanish, but you can rent devices for listening to English, French, German or Italian translations (beamed via infrared) for US$2.75. Specify the language you need or it may not be broadcast. Cost for the show only is US$3.50, applicable toward the next day's site admission.

As you pass through the turnstile and climb the slope to the ruins, the rear of the Casa del Adivino comes into view.

Casa del Adivino This tall temple (the Magician's House), 39m high, was built on an oval base. The smoothly sloping sides have been restored; they date from the temple's fifth incarnation. The four earlier temples were covered in the rebuilding, except for the high doorway on the west side, which remains from the fourth temple. Decorated in elaborate Chenes style (which originated farther south), the doorway proper forms the mouth of a gigantic Chac mask.

At the time of research climbing the temple was not allowed.

UXMAL

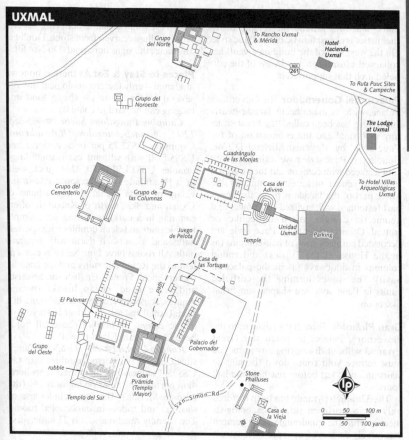

To Rancho Uxmal
& Mérida

Hotel
Hacienda
Uxmal

MEX
261

To Ruta Puuc Sites
& Campeche

The Lodge
at Uxmal

Grupo
del Norte

Grupo del
Noroeste

Cuadrángulo
de las Monjas

Casa del
Adivino

To Hotel Villas
Arqueológicas
Uxmal

Grupo del
Cementerio

Grupo de
las Columnas

Juego
de Pelota

Temple

Unidad
Uxmal

Parking

Casa de
las Tortugas

El Palomar

path

Grupo
del Oeste

rubble

Palacio del
Gobernador

Gran
Pirámide
(Templo
Mayor)

Templo del Sur

Stone
Phalluses

San-Simón-Rd

Casa de
la Vieja

0   50   100 m
0   50   100 yards

Cuadrángulo de las Monjas The 74-room, sprawling Nuns' Quadrangle is directly west of the Casa del Adivino. Archaeologists guess variously that it was a military academy, royal school or palace complex. The long-nosed face of Chac appears everywhere on the façades of the four separate temples that form the quadrangle. The northern temple, grandest of the four, was built first, followed by the southern, then the eastern and then the western.

Several decorative elements on the façades show signs of Mexica, perhaps Totonac, influence. The feathered-serpent (Quetzalcóatl, or in Mayan, Kukulcán) motif along the top of the west temple's façade is one of these. Note also the stylized depic-

tions of the *na* (Mayan thatched hut) over some of the doorways in the northern and southern buildings.

Passing through the corbeled arch in the middle of the south building of the quadrangle and continuing down the slope takes you through the **Juego de Pelota** (ball court). Turn left and head up the steep slope and stairs to the large terrace.

Casa de las Tortugas To the right at the top of the stairs is the House of the Turtles, which takes its name from the turtles carved on the cornice. The Maya associated turtles with the rain god, Chac. According to Mayan myth, when the people suffered from drought so did the turtles, and both prayed to Chac to send rain.

The frieze of short columns, or 'rolled mats,' that runs around the temple below the turtles is characteristic of the Puuc style. On the west side of the building a vault has collapsed, affording a good view of the corbeled arch that supported it.

Palacio del Gobernador The Governor's Palace, with its magnificent façade nearly 100m long, has been called 'the finest structure at Uxmal and the culmination of the Puuc style' by Mayanist Michael D Coe. Buildings in Puuc style have walls filled with rubble, faced with cement and then covered in a thin veneer of limestone squares; the lower part of the façade is plain, the upper part festooned with stylized Chac faces and geometric designs, often latticelike or fretted. Other elements of Puuc style are decorated cornices, rows of half-columns (as in the House of the Turtles) and round columns in doorways (as in the palace at Sayil). The stones forming the corbeled vaults in Puuc style are shaped somewhat like boots.

Gran Pirámide Though it's adjacent to the Governor's Palace, to reach the Great Pyramid without disobeying any signs you must retrace your route down the hillside stairs and turn left before reaching the ball court.

The 32m-high pyramid has been restored only on its northern side. Archaeologists theorize that the quadrangle at its summit was largely destroyed in order to construct another pyramid above it. That work, for reasons unknown, was never completed. At the top are some stucco carvings of Chac, birds and flowers.

El Palomar West of the Great Pyramid sits a structure whose roofcomb is latticed with a pattern reminiscent of the Moorish pigeon houses built into walls in Spain and northern Africa – hence the building's name (the Dovecote, or Pigeon House). The nine honeycombed triangular 'belfries' sit on top of a building that was once part of a quadrangle. The base is so eroded that it is hard for archaeologists to guess its function.

Casa de la Vieja Off the southeast corner of the Palacio del Gobernador is a small complex, largely rubble, known as the Casa de la Vieja (Old Woman's House). In front of it is a small palapa sheltering several large phalluses carved from stone. Don't get any ideas; the signs here read 'Do Not Sit.'

Places to Stay & Eat As there is no town at Uxmal – only the archaeological site and several top-end hotels – cheap food and lodging can be hard to come by.

Camping Bungalows Sacbé (☎ 985-858-12-81, e sacbebungalow@hotmail.com) Campsites US$2.75 per person, dorm bed US$5/5.50 with/without card, small/large doubles US$13.50/15.50. This quiet, well-kept HI affiliate is on the south side of the village of Santa Elena, 16km southeast of Uxmal and 8km north of Kabah. It offers camping in a parklike setting, four simple but pleasant and clean doubles with spotless baths and a four-bed dorm with separate bath. All rooms have fans. Sacbé is convenient to the Ruta Puuc ruins, and the friendly owners speak French, English and Spanish, and serve good, cheap breakfasts and dinners. To get here, catch a southbound bus from Uxmal and ask the driver to let you off at the *campo de béisbol* (baseball field) beyond the Santa Elena turnoff.

Rancho Uxmal (☎ 997-972-62-54) Campsites US$2.75 per person, doubles with fan US$25. Campers can pitch their tents here, 4km north of the ruins on highway 261 (the road to Mérida). The fee includes use of showers and toilets in unoccupied rooms. The friendly rancho also has 23 basic, serviceable guestrooms with good ventilation, and a shaded, welcoming restaurant serving three meals.

More budget lodgings are 30km east of Uxmal in Ticul (see that section).

Hotel Villas Arqueológicas Uxmal (☎/fax 997-976-20-20, ☎ 800-258-2633 in the USA, ☎ 801 80 28 03 in France, e villauxm@sureste.com) Singles/doubles/triples US$66/75/86. This is an attractive Club Med-run hotel with a swimming pool, tennis courts, a restaurant and air-conditioned guestrooms, not far from the ruins entrance.

The Lodge at Uxmal (☎ 997-976-21-02, 800-235-4079 in the USA, fax 997-976-20-11, e uxmal1@sureste.com, w www.mayaland.com) Doubles with fan/air-con US$78/90. Mayaland Resorts' lodge, just opposite the entrance to the archaeological site, is Uxmal's newest, most luxurious hotel.

There are two pools and a restaurant-bar with OK food.

Hotel Hacienda Uxmal (☎ 997-976-20-12, 800-235-4079 in the USA, fax 997-976-20-11, e uxmal1@sureste.com, w www.maya land.com) Doubles with fan/air-con US$78/134. This is another Mayaland Resort, 500m from the ruins and across the highway. It originally housed the archaeologists who explored and restored Uxmal. Wide, tiled verandas, high ceilings and a beautiful swimming pool make this an exceptionally comfortable place to stay. The fan-cooled rooms are in a more modest annex.

Salón Nicté-Ha Open 1pm-8pm daily. Just across the highway from the road to the ruins, on the grounds of the Hotel Hacienda Uxmal, this is an informal air-conditioned restaurant offering sandwiches, fruit salads and similar fare at prices slightly higher than those at the Yax-Beh at Unidad Uxmal. There's a swimming pool for restaurant patrons.

Getting There & Away Uxmal is 80km (1½ hours) from Mérida. The inland route between Mérida and Campeche passes Uxmal, and most buses coming from either city will drop you there, or at Kabah or the Ruta Puuc turnoff. But when you want to leave, passing buses may be full (especially Saturday and Monday).

ATS buses depart Mérida's Terminal de Segunda Clase at 8am daily on a whirlwind excursion (US$6) to the Ruta Puuc sites, Kabah and Uxmal, heading back from Uxmal's parking lot at 2.30pm. This 'tour' is transportation only; you pay all other costs. The time spent at each site is enough to get only a nodding acquaintance, though some say the two hours at Uxmal is sufficient, if barely.

Organized tours of Uxmal and other sites can be booked in Mérida (see Organized Tours in the Mérida section).

If you're going from Uxmal to Ticul, first take a northbound bus to Muna (20 minutes, US$0.50) then catch one of the frequent buses from there to Ticul (30 minutes, US$0.80).

Kabah

The ruins of Kabah (admission US$3, free Sun & holidays; open 8am-5pm daily), just over 23km southeast of Uxmal, are right astride highway 261. The guard shack/souvenir shop (selling snacks and cold drinks) and the bulk of the restored ruins are on the east side of the highway.

On entering, head to your right to climb the stairs of the structure closest to the highway, **El Palacio de los Mascarones** (Palace of Masks). The façade is an amazing sight, covered in nearly 300 masks of Chac, the rain god or sky serpent. Most of their huge curling noses are broken off; the best intact beak is at the building's south end. These noses may have given the palace its modern Mayan name, Codz Pop (Rolled Mat).

When you've had your fill of noses, head around back to check out the two restored **atlantes** (an atlas – plural 'atlantes' – is a male figure used as a supporting column). These are especially interesting, as they're among the very few three-dimensional human figures you'll see at a Mayan site. One is headless and the other wears a jaguar mask atop his head. A third statue stands by the office near the entrance; the two others that were discovered here are in museums.

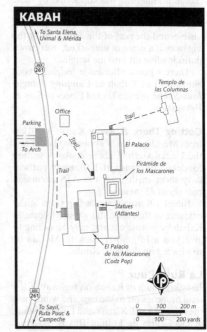

KABAH

To Santa Elena,
Uxmal & Mérida

MEX 261

Templo de
las Columnas

Office

Parking

Trail

Trail

To Arch

El Palacio

Trail

Pirámide de
los Mascarones

Statues
(Atlantes)

El Palacio
de los Mascarones
(Codz Pop)

MEX 261

To Sayil,
Ruta Puuc &
Campeche

0   100   200 m
0   100   200 yards

Descend the steps near the atlantes and turn left, passing the small **Pirámide de los Mascarones**, to reach the plaza containing **El Palacio**. The Palace's broad façade has several doorways, two of which have a column in the center. These columned doorways and the groups of decorative *columnillas* (little columns) on the upper part of the façade are characteristics of the Puuc architectural style.

Steps on the north side of El Palacio's plaza put you on a path leading a couple of hundred meters through the jungle to the **Templo de las Columnas**. This building has more rows of decorative columns on the upper part of its façade.

West of El Palacio, across the highway, a path leads up the slope and passes to the south of a high mound of stones that was once the **Gran Pirámide** (Great Pyramid). The path curves to the right and comes to a large restored **monumental arch**. It's said that the *sacbé*, or cobbled and elevated ceremonial road, leading from here goes through the jungle all the way to Uxmal, terminating at a smaller arch; in the other direction it goes to Labná. Once, all of the Yucatán Peninsula was connected by these marvelous 'white roads' of rough limestone.

At present, nothing of the sacbés is visible, and the rest of the area west of the highway is a maze of unmarked, overgrown paths leading off into the jungle.

There's good, affordable lodging about 8km north of Kabah at *Camping Bungalows Sacbé*; see the Uxmal Places to Stay & Eat section.

Getting There & Away Kabah is 101km from Mérida, a ride of about two hours. See the Uxmal Getting There & Away section for details on transport. Kabah gets particularly short shrift from the ATS excursion bus; about 25 minutes.

Buses will usually make flag stops at the entrance to the ruins. Many visitors come to Kabah by private car and may be willing to give you a lift, either back to Mérida or southward on the Puuc Route.

La Ruta Puuc

Just 5km south of Kabah on highway 261, a road branches off to the east and winds past the ruins of Sayil, Xlapak and Labná, ending at the Grutas de Loltún. This is the Puuc Route, and its sites offer some marvelous architectural detail and a deeper acquaintance with the Puuc Mayan civilization.

See the Uxmal Getting There & Away section for details on the ATS excursion bus, the only regularly scheduled public transport on the route. Though during the busy winter season it's usually possible to hitch rides from one site to the next, the best way year-round to appreciate the sites is by rented car.

Sayil The ruins of Sayil *(admission US$3, free Sun & holidays; open 8am-5pm daily)* are 4.5km from the junction of the Puuc Route with highway 261.

Sayil is best known for **El Palacio**, the huge three-tiered building with a façade some 85m long reminiscent of the Minoan palace on Crete. The distinctive columns of Puuc architecture are used here over and over, as supports for the lintels, as decoration between doorways and as a frieze above them, alternating with huge stylized Chac masks and 'descending gods.'

Ascending the Palacio beyond its first level is not allowed.

Taking the path south from the palace for about 400m and bearing left, you come to the temple named **El Mirador**, whose roosterlike roofcomb was once painted a bright red. About 100m beyond El Mirador, beneath a protective palapa, is a stela bearing the relief of a fertility god with an enormous phallus, now badly weathered.

Xlapak From the entrance gate at Sayil, it's 6km east to the entrance gate at Xlapak *('shla-PAK'; admission US$2.50, free Sun & holidays; open 8am-5pm daily)*. The name means 'Old Walls' in Mayan and was a general term among local people for ancient ruins.

If you're going to skip any of the Ruta Puuc sites, Xlapak should be it. The ornate **palace** at Xlapak is smaller than those at Kabah and Sayil, measuring only about 20m in length. It's decorated with the inevitable Chac masks, columns and colonnettes and fretted geometric latticework of the Puuc style. The building is slightly askew, looking as though it doesn't know which way to fall. There's not much else here.

Labná If Xlapak is the skippable Puuc site, Labná *(admission US$3, free Sun & holidays;*

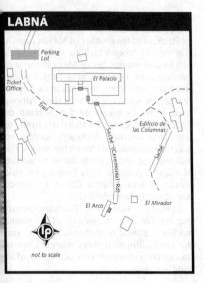

LABNÁ

Parking Lot

Ticket Office

El Palacio

Trail

Sacbé (Ceremonial Rd)

Edificio de las Columnas

Sacbé

El Arco

El Mirador

not to scale

open 8am-5pm daily) is the one not to miss. Its setting on a flat, open area is unique in the region, and if no one has been through before you for a while, at each doorway you approach you're likely to startle groups of long-tailed mot-mots (clock birds) into flight. Between the birds and the vegetation growing atop the Palacio, you can almost imagine yourself one of the first people to see the site in centuries.

Archaeologists believe that at one point in the 9th century, some 3000 Maya lived at Labná. To support such numbers in these arid hills, water was collected in *chultunes*. At Labná's peak there were some 60 chultunes in and around the city; several are still visible. From the entrance gate at Xlapak, it's 3.5km east to the gate at Labná.

El Palacio The first building you come to at Labná is one of the longest in the Puuc region, and much of its interesting decorative carving is in good shape. On the west corner of the main structure's façade, straight in from the big tree near the center of the complex, is a serpent's head with a human face peering out from between its jaws, the symbol of the planet Venus. Toward the hill from this is an impressive Chac mask, and nearby is the lower half of a human figure (possibly a ballplayer) in loincloth and leggings.

The lower level has several more well-preserved Chac masks, and the upper level contains a large chultún that still holds water. The view of the site and the hills beyond from there is impressive.

From the Palace a limestone-paved sacbé leads to El Arco.

El Arco Labná is best known for its magnificent arch, once part of a building that separated two quadrangular courtyards. It now appears to be a gate joining two small plazas. The corbeled structure, 3m wide and 6m high, is well preserved, and the reliefs decorating its upper façade are exuberantly Puuc in style.

Flanking the west side of the arch are carved *na* (thatched structures) with multi-tiered roofs. Also on these walls, the remains of the building that adjoined the arch, are lattice patterns atop a serpentine design. Archaeologists believe a high roofcomb once sat over the fine arch and its flanking rooms.

El Mirador Standing on the opposite side of the arch and separated from it by the sacbé is a pyramid known as El Mirador, topped by a temple. The pyramid itself is largely stone rubble. The temple, with its 5m-high roofcomb, is well positioned to be a lookout, thus its name.

Grutas de Loltún
North and east of Labná 15km, an over-grown sign points out the left turn to the Grutas de Loltún, 5km farther northeast. The road passes through lush orchards and some banana and palm groves, an agreeable sight in this dry region.

The Loltún Caverns *(admission US$5.25; open 9am-5pm daily),* one of the largest and most interesting cave systems on the Yucatán Peninsula, provided a treasure trove of data for archaeologists studying the Maya. Carbon dating of artifacts found here reveals that the caves were used by humans 2500 years ago. Chest-high murals of hands, faces, animals and geometric motifs were apparent as recently as 20 years ago, but so many people have touched them that scarcely a trace remains. Today, visitors to the illuminated caves see mostly natural limestone formations, some of which are quite lovely.

To explore the labyrinth, you must take a scheduled guided tour at 9.30am, 11am, 12.30pm, 2pm, 3pm or 4pm, but they may depart early if enough people are waiting, or switch languages if the group warrants it. The services of the English-speaking guides are included in the admission price.

Restaurant El Guerrero Dishes US$3.50-5. If you drove from Labná, you passed this restaurant on your left just before the junction where the caves lie. If you're on foot, it's a walk of eight to 10 minutes (600m) along a marked path from the far side of the parking lot near the cave entrance. Dishes are tasty and are accompanied by enough sides to fill you up. Ask the price before ordering drinks.

Food is also available at a ***parador turístico*** across the highway from the caves' parking lot.

Getting There & Away At the time of research, LUS had just begun service from the Noreste terminal in Mérida to the Grutas (2½ hours, US$4), with departures at 7.30am, 11am and 2.45pm, returning at 11.30am, 2.20pm and 6.05pm. Other buses run frequently between Mérida and Oxkutzcab ('osh-kootz-KAHB') via Ticul. Loltún is 7km southwest of Oxkutzcab, and there is usually some transportation along the road. *Camionetas* (pickups) and *camiones* (trucks) charge US$1 for a ride (the locals' price of US$0.60 may be hard to get). A taxi from Oxkutzcab may charge US$6 or so, one-way.

If you're driving from Loltún to Labná, turn right out of the Loltún parking lot and take the next road on the right, which passes Restaurant El Guerrero's driveway. Do not take the road marked for Xul. After 5km turn right at the T intersection to join the Puuc Route west.

Ticul

• pop 27,000 ☎ 997

Ticul, 30km east of Uxmal and 14km northwest of Oxkutzcab, is the largest town in this ruin-rich region. It has decent hotels and restaurants and good transportation. Although there is no public transportation to the Puuc Route from Ticul, it is possible to stay the night here and take an early morning bus to Muna, arriving there in time to catch a tour bus to the Puuc Route ruins; see Getting There & Away. Ticul is also a center for fine huipil weaving, and ceramics made here from

the local red clay are renowned throughout the Yucatán Peninsula.

Because of the number of Mayan ruins in the vicinity from which to steal building blocks and the number of Maya in the area needing conversion to Christianity, Franciscan friars built many churches in the region that is now southern Yucatán state. Among them is Ticul's **Iglesia de San Antonio de Padua**, construction of which dates from the late 16th century. Although looted on several occasions, the church has some original touches, among them the stone statues of friars in primitive style flanking the side entrances and a Black Christ altarpiece ringed by crude medallions.

Saturday mornings in Ticul are picturesque: Calle 23 in the vicinity of the public market is closed to motorized traffic, and the street fills with three-wheeled cycles transporting shoppers between the market and their homes.

Orientation & Information Ticul's main street is Calle 23, sometimes called the Calle Principal, going from the highway northeast past the market and the town's best restaurants to the main plaza, or Plaza Mayor. A post office faces the plaza, as does a bank, and the bus terminal is less than 100m away. Catercorner to the Plaza Mayor is the recently built Plaza de la Cultura, which is all cement and stone but nevertheless an agreeable place to take the evening breeze, enjoy the view of the church and greet passing townspeople.

Places to Stay *Hotel San Miguel* (☎ 972-03-82, Calle 28 No 215D) Singles/1-bed doubles/2-bed doubles US$6.50/8.50/10. This place is near Calle 23 and the market. The friendly management offers worn rooms with fan and bath.

Hotel Sierra Sosa (☎/fax 972-00-08, Calle 26 No 199A) Singles/doubles with fan US$10.50/14, with air-con US$15/18.50. This hotel is just northwest of the plaza. A few rooms at the back have windows, but most are dark.

Hotel Plaza (☎ 972-04-84, fax 972-00-26, cnr Calles 23 & 26) Rooms with fan/air-con US$29/33. This is the best hotel in town, though some rooms get very hot and lack cold water. Air-conditioned rooms have telephone and cable TV.

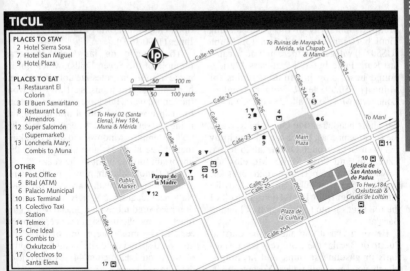

TICUL

PLACES TO STAY
2 Hotel Sierra Sosa
7 Hotel San Miguel
9 Hotel Plaza

PLACES TO EAT
1 Restaurant El Colorín
3 El Buen Samaritano
8 Restaurant Los Almendros
12 Super Salomón (Supermarket)
13 Lonchería Mary; Combis to Muna

OTHER
4 Post Office
5 Bital (ATM)
6 Palacio Municipal
10 Bus Terminal
11 Colectivo Taxi Station
14 Telmex
15 Cine Ideal
16 Combis to Oxkutzcab
17 Colectivos to Santa Elena

Places to Eat *Public Market (Calle 28A between Calles 21 & 23)* Ticul's lively market provides all the ingredients for picnics and snacks. It also has lots of those wonderful eateries where the food is good, the portions generous and the prices low.

Super Salomón Across Calle 23 from the public market is this small supermarket with a big variety of groceries and household items.

El Buen Samaritano (Calle 23) The Samaritano is west of Calle 26 and bakes bread and sweet rolls.

Restaurant El Colorín (Calle 26 No 199B) Set meals US$3.25. For a homemade meal, try this cheap restaurant, half a block northwest of the plaza.

Lonchería Mary (Calle 23 east of Calle 28) This is a clean, family-run place.

Restaurant Los Almendros (Calle 23 No 207 between 26A & 28) Mains US$4.50-5.50. The original Almendros (now with fancier branches in Mérida and Cancún) specializes in hearty Yucatecan food. The menu has photos and descriptions of the food. The restaurant's renowned *poc-chuc* (pork with tomatoes, onions and a sour-orange sauce) runs US$4.75.

Getting There & Away
Bus Ticul's bus terminal is on Calle 24 behind the massive church. Mayab runs frequent

2nd-class buses between Mérida and Ticul (85km, 1½ hours, US$3.25) from 4.30am to 9.45pm. There are 11 buses to Felipe Carrillo Puerto (4 hours, US$8.25), frequent ones to Oxkutzcab (US$0.70) in addition to five a day to Chetumal (6½ hours, US$12.50). There are also six Mayab buses to Cancún each day (US$16.50), three of which also serve Tulum (US$12.50) and Playa del Carmen (US$15). Super Expresso has less frequent 1st-class service to some of these destinations.

Colectivo vans direct to Mérida's Parque de San Juan (1½ hours, US$2.75) depart from the intersection of Calles 24 and 25 as soon as they're full between 5am and 7pm. Combis for Oxkutzcab (16km, 30 minutes, US$0.80) leave from Calle 25A on the south side of the church between 7am and 8.30pm.

Colectivos going to Santa Elena (15km, US$0.80), the village between Uxmal and Kabah, depart from Calle 30 just south of Calle 25 between 6.15am and 7.45pm. They take highway 02 and drop you to catch another bus northwest to Uxmal (15km) or south to Kabah (3.5km). You can also take a combi or bus to Muna (see below) on highway 261 and another south to Uxmal (16km).

Ruta Puuc-bound travelers can catch one of the early-morning buses from Ticul to Muna and pick up the ATS tour bus (US$5) for Labná, Sayil, Xlapak, Kabah and Uxmal at 9am on its way from Mérida. It returns to Muna at 3pm. Any of the buses leaving Ticul between 6am and 8am for Muna (US$0.60) will get you there in time to catch the Ruta Puuc bus (all 2nd-class Mérida-bound buses stop in Muna). Combis for Muna (US$0.90) leave from in front of Lonchería Mary on Calle 23 near Calle 28.

Car Those headed east to Quintana Roo and the Caribbean coast by car can take highway 184 from Ticul through Oxkutzcab to Tekax, Tzucacab and José María Morelos. At Polyuc, 130km from Ticul, a road turns left (east), ending after 80km in Felipe Carrillo Puerto, 210km from Ticul. The right fork of the road goes south to the region of Laguna Bacalar.

Between Oxkutzcab and Felipe Carrillo Puerto or Bacalar there are very few restaurants or gasoline stations, and no hotels. Mostly you see small, typical Yucatecan villages, with their traditional Mayan thatched houses, *topes* (speed bumps) and agricultural activity.

Getting Around The local method of getting around is to hire a *triciclo,* Mexico's version of the ricksha. You'll see them on Calle 23 just up from the market; the fare is about US$0.50 for a short trip.

DZIBILCHALTÚN

Lying about 17km due north of downtown Mérida, Dzibilchaltún *(Place of Inscribed Flat Stones; admission US$5.50, free Sun & holidays; open 8am-5pm daily)* was the longest continuously utilized Mayan administrative and ceremonial city, serving the Maya from 1500 BC or earlier until the European conquest in the 1540s. At the height of its greatness, Dzibilchaltún covered 15 sq km. Some 8500 structures were mapped by archaeologists in the 1960s; few of these have been excavated and restored.

Enter the site along a nature trail that terminates at the modern, air-conditioned **Museo del Pueblo Maya** *(open 8am-4pm Tues-Sun),* featuring artifacts from throughout the Mayan regions of Mexico, including some superb colonial-era religious carvings and other pieces. Exhibits explaining Mayan daily life and beliefs from ancient times until the present are labeled in Spanish and English. Beyond the museum, a path leads

to the central plaza, where you will find an open chapel that dates from early Spanish times (1590-1600).

The **Templo de las Siete Muñecas** (Temple of the Seven Dolls), which got its name from seven grotesque dolls discovered here during excavations, is a 1km walk from the central plaza. It is most unimpressive but for its precise astronomical orientation: the rising and setting sun of the equinoxes 'lights up' the temple's windows and doors, making them blaze like beacons and signaling this important turning point in the year.

The **Cenote Xlacah**, now a public swimming pool, is more than 40m deep. In 1958 a National Geographic Society diving expedition recovered more than 30,000 Mayan artifacts, many of ritual significance, from the cenote. The most interesting of these are now on display in the site's museum. South of the cenote is **Estructura 44**, at 130m one of the longest Mayan structures in existence.

Parking costs US$1.25. Minibuses and colectivo taxis depart frequently from Mérida's Parque de San Juan, on Calle 69 between Calles 62 and 64, for the village of Dzibilchaltún Ruinas (15km, 30 minutes, US$0.80), only a little over 1km from the museum.

PROGRESO

● pop 40,000 ☎ 969

If Mérida's heat has you dying for a quick beach fix, or you want to see the longest wharf (7km) in Mexico, head to Progreso (also known as Puerto Progreso). Otherwise there's little reason to visit this dual-purpose port-resort town. The beach is fine, well groomed and long, but it's nearly shadeless and is dominated by the view of the wharf, giving it a rather industrial feel. Winds hit here full force off the Gulf in the afternoon and can blow well into the night. As with other Gulf beaches, the water is murky; visibility even on calm days rarely exceeds 5m. None of this stops meridanos from coming in droves on weekends, especially in the summer months. Even on spring weekdays it can be difficult to find a room with a view.

Progreso's street grid confusingly employs two different numbering systems 50 numbers apart. The city center's streets are numbered in the 60s (10s), 70s (20s) and 80s (30s). This text uses the high numbers.

Even-numbered streets run east-west and decrease by twos eastward; odd ones decrease by twos northward. The bus terminal is on Calle 79 west of Calle 82, a block north (toward the water) from the main plaza. It's six short blocks from the plaza on Calle 80 to the waterfront Malecón (Calle 69) and *muelle* (wharf); along the way are two Banamexes, one with an ATM.

Places to Stay & Eat

All hotels and restaurants listed are no more than a total of 11 blocks north and east of the station. Room rates are high season.

Hotel Miralmar (☎ 935-05-52, Calle 77 No 124 at Calle 76) Doubles US$14.50-20; with air-con US$30. This hotel offers rooms with private shower and fan. Rooms on the upper floor are not as dungeonlike as the ground-floor rooms. The three bubble-shaped rooms look a tad bizarre but offer the best ventilation.

Tropical Suites (☎ 935-12-63, fax 935-30-93, cnr Malecón & Calle 70) Singles US$22/28/31 without fan/with fan/with air-con, doubles US$33-39 with air-con. This seaside hotel has 21 tidy rooms, some with sea views.

Hotel Real del Mar (☎ 935-07-98) Doubles US$20-39. Across the street from Tropical Suites, this place features 15 air-conditioned rooms with various configurations of beds and views.

Restaurant Los Pelícanos (cnr Malecón & Calle 70) Mains US$4.50-14.50. By the Hotel Real del Mar, this restaurant has a shady terrace, sea views, a good menu and moderate prices, considering its location.

Restaurant Mary Doly (Calle 75 between Calles 74 & 76) Breakfasts US$1.75-2.75, lunch & dinner mains US$3.50-6. Near the Hotel Miralmar, this is a homey place with good, cheap seafood, meat and breakfasts.

Restaurant El Cordobes Also near Hotel Miralmar, this restaurant is on the north side of the plaza in a 100-year-old building with character. Its menu and prices are similar to those at Restaurant Mary Doly.

Getting There & Away

Progreso is 33km due north of Mérida along a fast four-lane highway that's basically a continuation of the Paseo de Montejo. If you're driving, head north on the Paseo and follow signs for Progreso. For bus information see the Mérida Getting There & Away section.

CELESTÚN
• pop 5200 ☎ 988

Celestún is in the middle of a wildlife sanctuary abounding in resident and migratory waterfowl, with flamingoes as the star attraction. It makes a good beach-and-bird day trip from Mérida, and it's also a great place to kick back and do nothing for a few days, especially if you've become road-weary. Fishing boats dot the appealing white-sand beach that stretches to the north for kilometers, and afternoon breezes cool the town on most days.

Though the winds can kick up sand and roil the sea, making the already none-too-clear water unpleasant for swimming, they are less intense than in Progreso. Celestún is sheltered by the peninsula's southward curve, resulting in an abundance of marine life. It's a fine place to watch the sun set into the sea, and if you are from a west coast anywhere you'll feel perfectly oriented. If you're not from a west coast, all you need to know is that Calle 11 is the road into town (due west from Mérida), ending at Calle 12, the dirt road paralleling the beach along which lie most of the restaurants and hotels.

Flamingo Tours

The Ría Celestún Biosphere Reserve's 591 sq km are home to a huge variety of animal life, including a large flamingo colony.

Given the winds, the best time to see birds is in the morning, though from 4pm onward they tend to concentrate in one area after the day's feeding, which can make for good viewing. There are two places to hire a boat for bird-watching: from the bridge on the highway into town (about 1.5km from the beach), and from the beach itself.

Tours from the beach last 2½ to three hours and begin with a ride south along the coast for several kilometers, during which you can expect to see egrets, herons, cormorants, sandpipers and many other species of bird. The boat then turns into the mouth of the *ría* (estuary) and passes through a 'petrified forest,' where tall coastal trees once belonging to a freshwater ecosystem were killed by saltwater intrusion long ago and remain standing, hard as rock.

Continuing up the ría takes you under the highway bridge where the other tours begin and beyond which lie the flamingos. Depending on the tide, the hour and the season, you may see hundreds or thousands of the colorful birds. Don't encourage your captain to approach them too closely; a startled flock taking wing can result in injuries and deaths (for the birds). In addition to taking you to the flamingoes, the captain will wend through a 200m mangrove tunnel and go to one or both (as time and inclination allow) of the freshwater cenote/springs welling into the saltwater of the estuary, where you can take a refreshing dip.

Asking price for this tour is US$100 per boatload (up to six passengers). Boats depart from several beachside spots, including from outside Restaurant Celestún, at the foot of Calle 11. The restaurant's beachfront palapa is a pleasant place to wait for a group to accumulate.

Tours from the bridge, where there is a parking lot, ticket booth and a place to wait for fellow passengers, are cheaper. For US$40 per boat (again up to six passengers) plus US$2.25 per passenger, you get the latter part of the tour described earlier: flamingoes, mangrove tunnel and spring. It's also possible to tour from the bridge south to the 'petrified forest' and back (also US$40), or combine the two (each lasts about 1¼ hours).

With either operation, bridge or beach, your captain may or may not speak English. English-speaking guides can be hired at the bridge; this reduces the maximum possible number of passengers, of course. Bring snacks, water and sunscreen for the longer tours, and cash for any of them. There is no bank in town, and neither credit cards nor traveler's checks are accepted by the tour operators.

Places to Stay

Celestún's hotels are all on Calle 12, within a short walk of one another. The following list runs from north to south. Try to book ahead if you want a sea view, especially on weekends.

Eco Hotel Flamingos Playa (☎ 999-929-57-08 in Mérida) Doubles US$28. About three blocks north of Calle 11, the recently built Flamingos has decent rooms with air-con, fan, TV and purified water. There's a small beachside pool, a restaurant and bar, and the hotel was in the process of installing Internet facilities.

Hotel San Julio (☎ 916-20-62, 923-63-09 in Mérida, Calle 12) Singles/doubles/triples US$11/13.50/16.50. Also north of Calle 11, the San Julio is old and a little beat-up but has its own charm. It's right on the beach, and the eight fan-cooled rooms are clean, with new mattresses. Try for the front room.

Hospedaje Sofía (no ☎, Calle 12) Singles/doubles with fan US$11/22. Across the street and south a bit, this whitewashed *hospedaje* has eight spotless rooms (four with TV), updated with new tile, fresh paint and other nice touches. It also has secure parking.

Hotel María del Carmen (☎/fax 916-21-70, Calle 12) Doubles with fan/air-con US$22/31. South of Calle 11, this hotel has 14 clean and pleasant beachfront rooms. Those on the upper floors have balconies facing the sea. Prices drop when things are slow.

Places to Eat

Celestún's specialties are crab, octopus and, of course, fresh fish. Service and decor vary from restaurant to restaurant in Celestún, but the menu for the most part does not, and most restaurants have outdoor areas on the beach. Eat early on weeknights or you may find every place closed.

Prices vary, but expect to pay about US$5.50 for either the catch of the day, delicious ceviche, or crab prepared in a variety of ways, and US$3 for a conch, shrimp, crab or octopus cocktail.

La Playita, a few doors north of the foot of Calle 11, offers large portions of good food. Other places include ***Restaurant Celestún***, ***La Boya*** and ***Ávila***.

Getting There & Away

Buses from Mérida head for Celestún (95km, 2 hours, US$3.50) 17 times daily between 5am and 8pm from the terminal on Calle 50 between Calles 67 and 65. The route terminates at Celestún's plaza, a block inland from Calle 12. Returning to Mérida, buses run from 5am to 8pm.

Nómadas Youth Hostel and Travel Agency (see the Mérida Organized Tours section) books day trips to see the flamingoes for around US$40, leaving Mérida at

9am and returning at 5pm. They include transportation, guide, a boat tour and lunch.

IZAMAL

• pop 14,900 ☎ 988

In ancient times, Izamal was a center for the worship of the supreme Mayan god, Itzamná, and the sun god, Kinich-Kakmó. A dozen temple pyramids were devoted to these or other gods. Perhaps these bold expressions of Mayan religiosity are why the Spanish colonists chose Izamal as the site for an enormous and impressive Franciscan monastery, which today stands at the heart of this town just under 70km east of Mérida.

The Izamal of today is a quiet, colonial gem of a provincial town, nicknamed La Ciudad Amarilla (the Yellow City) for the traditional yellow that most buildings are painted. It is easily explored on foot and makes a great day trip from Mérida.

Things to See & Do

When the Spaniards conquered Izamal, they destroyed the major Mayan temple, the Ppapp-Hol-Chac pyramid, and in 1533 began to build from its stones one of the first monasteries in the Western Hemisphere. Work on **Convento de San Antonio de Padua** *(admission free; open 6am-8pm daily)* was finished in 1561. Under the monastery's arcades, look for building stones with an unmistakable mazelike design; these were clearly taken from the earlier Mayan temple.

The monastery's principal church is the **Santuario de la Virgen de Izamal**, approached by a ramp from the main square. The ramp leads into the **Atrium**, a huge arcaded courtyard in which the fiesta of the Virgin of Izamal takes place each August 15.

At some point, the 16th-century **frescoes** beside the entrance of the sanctuary were completely painted over. For years they lay concealed under a thin layer of whitewash until a maintenance worker who was cleaning the walls discovered them a few years ago. The church's original altarpiece was destroyed by a fire believed to have been started by a fallen candle. Its replacement, impressively gilded, was built in the 1940s. In the niches at the stations of the cross are some superb small figures.

In the small courtyard to the left of the church, look up and toward the Atrium to see the original sundial projecting from the roof's edge.

The best time to visit is in the morning, as the church is occasionally closed during the afternoon siesta.

Three of the town's original 12 Mayan **pyramids** have been partially restored so far. The largest is the enormous Kinich-Kakmó, three blocks north of the monastery. You can climb it for free.

Places to Stay & Eat

In front of the monastery are two very modest budget hotels and several inexpensive eateries.

Hotel Canto Singles/doubles US$7/10. The Canto is the more attractive of the two hotels, with tiny skylights and colorful murals brightening the worn but clean rooms.

Hotel Kabul 1-bed/2-bed doubles US$11/13.50. Though no Taliban are in evidence here, it's not the friendliest place, and rooms are rather shabby.

Macan-Che B&B (☎/fax 954-02-87, e macanche@umanet.com.mx, Calle 22 No 305) Doubles US$28-55 with breakfast. About three long blocks east of the monastery, this charming B&B has a cluster of cottages in a jungle setting, with 12 pretty rooms in all. The most expensive has air-con and a kitchenette.

Restaurant Kinich-Kakmó (☎ 954-08-89, Calle 27 between Calles 28 & 30) This restaurant is casual and extremely friendly, offering fan-cooled patio dining beside a garden. It specializes in traditional Yucatecan food, and you can have an absolute feast for less than US$10.

Getting There & Away

Oriente operates frequent buses between Mérida and Izamal (1½ hours, US$2.75) from the 2nd-class terminal. There are buses from Valladolid (2 hours, US$3.50) as well. Coming from Chichén Itzá you must change buses at Hóctun. Izamal's bus terminal is just one block west of the monastery.

Other services from Izamal include buses to Tizimín (US$5.25) and Cancún (6 hours, US$9, 5 buses). Driving from the west, turn north at Hóctun to reach Izamal; from the east, turn north at Kantunil.

CHICHÉN ITZÁ

The most famous and best restored of the Yucatán Peninsula's Mayan sites, Chichén Itzá *(Mouth of the Well of the Itzáes; admission US$9.50, free Sun & holidays; open 8am-6pm daily)* will awe even the most jaded visitor. Many mysteries of the Mayan astronomical calendar are made clear when one understands the design of the 'time temples' here. Other than a few minor passageways, El Castillo is now the only structure at the site you're allowed to climb or enter.

At the vernal and autumnal equinoxes (March 20 to 21 and September 21 to 22), the morning and afternoon sun produces a light-and-shadow illusion of the serpent ascending or descending the side of El Castillo's staircase. Chichén is mobbed on these dates, however, making it difficult to get close enough to see, and after the spectacle, parts of the site are sometimes closed to the public. The illusion is almost as good in the week preceding and following each equinox, and is re-created nightly in the light-and-sound show year-round.

Heat, humidity and crowds can be fierce; try to spend the night nearby and do your exploration of the site (especially climbing El Castillo) either early in the morning or late in the afternoon.

History

Most archaeologists agree that the first major settlement at Chichén Itzá, during the late Classic period, was pure Mayan. In about the 9th century, the city was largely abandoned for reasons unknown. It was resettled around the late 10th century, and shortly thereafter it is believed to have been invaded by the Toltecs, who had migrated from their central highlands capital of Tula, north of Mexico City. Toltec culture was fused with that of the Maya, incorporating the cult of Quetzalcóatl (Kukulcán, in Mayan). You will see images of both Chac, the Mayan rain god, and Quetzalcóatl, the plumed serpent, throughout the city.

The substantial fusion of highland central Mexican and Puuc architectural styles makes Chichén unique among the Yucatán Peninsula's ruins. The fabulous El Castillo and the Plataforma de Venus are outstanding architectural works built during the height of Toltec cultural input.

The warlike Toltecs contributed more than their architectural skills to the Maya. They elevated human sacrifice to a near obsession, and there are numerous carvings of the bloody ritual in Chichén demonstrating this. After a Maya leader moved his political capital to Mayapán while keeping Chichén as his religious capital, Chichén Itzá fell into decline. Why it was subsequently abandoned in the 14th century is a mystery, but the once-great city remained the site of Mayan pilgrimages for many years.

Orientation

Most of Chichén's lodgings, restaurants and services are ranged along 1km of highway in the village of Pisté, to the western (Mérida) side of the ruins. It's 1.5km from the ruins' main (west) entrance to the first hotel (Pirámide Inn) in Pisté, or 2.5km from the ruins to Pisté village plaza, which is shaded by a huge tree. Buses generally stop at the plaza; you can make the hot walk to and from the ruins in 20 to 30 minutes.

On the eastern (Cancún) side, it's 1.5km from the highway along the access road to the eastern entrance to the ruins.

Information

Filming with a video camera costs US$3.25 extra; tripods are forbidden. Hold onto your wristband ticket; it gives you in-and-out privileges and admission to that evening's light-and-sound show. Parking costs US$1.25. Explanatory plaques are displayed in Spanish and English.

The main entrance is the western one, with a large parking lot and a big, modern entrance building, the Unidad de Servicios, open 8am to 10pm. The Unidad has a small but worthwhile **museum** *(open 8am-5pm)* with sculptures, reliefs, artifacts and explanations of these in Spanish, English and French.

The Chilam Balam Auditorio, next to the museum, sometimes has video shows about Chichén and other Mexican sites. The picture quality can be truly abominable, but the air-con is great. In the central space of the Unidad stands a scale model of the archaeological site, and off toward the toilets is an exhibit on Edward Thompson's excavations of the Sacred Cenote. Facilities include two bookstores with a good assortment of guides and maps; a currency-exchange desk (open 9.30am to 3pm Monday to Friday);

CHICHÉN ITZÁ

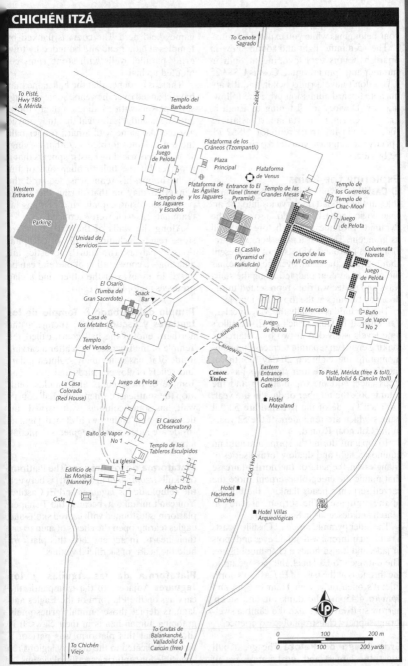

To Cenote Sagrado

To Pisté, Hwy 180 & Mérida

Templo del Barbado

Sacbé

Gran Juego de Pelota

Plataforma de los Cráneos (Tzompantli)

Plaza Principal

Plataforma de Venus

Templo de los Guerreros, Templo de Chac-Mool

Western Entrance

Parking

Plataforma de las Águilas y los Jaguares

Templo de los Jaguares y Escudos

Entrance to El Túnel (Inner Pyramid)

Templo de las Grandes Mesas

Juego de Pelota

Unidad de Servicios

El Castillo (Pyramid of Kukulcán)

Grupo de las Mil Columnas

Columnata Noreste

Juego de Pelota

El Osario (Tumba del Gran Sacerdote)

Snack Bar

El Mercado

Baño de Vapor No 2

Casa de los Metates

Templo del Venado

Juego de Pelota

Causeway

Causeway

La Casa Colorada (Red House)

Juego de Pelota

Cenote Xtoloc

Eastern Entrance Admissions Gate

To Pisté, Mérida (free & toll), Valladolid & Cancún (toll)

Trail

Hotel Mayaland

El Caracol (Observatory)

Baño de Vapor No 1

Templo de los Tableros Esculpidos

La Iglesia

Edificio de las Monjas (Nunnery)

Gate

Akab-Dzib

Old Hwy

Hotel Hacienda Chichén

MEX 180

Hotel Villas Arqueológicas

To Chichén Viejo

To Grutas de Balankanché, Valladolid & Cancún (free)

0   100   200 m
0   100   200 yards

and, around the corner from the ticket desk, a free *guardaequipaje* where you can leave your belongings while you explore the site.

The 45-minute light-and-sound show in Spanish begins each evening at 8pm in summer and 7pm in winter. Cost is US$3.25 if you don't have a ruins ticket, and it's applicable toward admission price the following day. Devices for listening to English, French, German or Italian translations (beamed via infrared) rent for US$2.75. Specify the language you need or it may not be broadcast.

Exploring the Ruins

El Castillo As you approach from the turnstiles at the Unidad de Servicios into the archaeological zone, El Castillo (also called the Pyramid of Kukulcán) rises before you in all its grandeur. The first temple here was pre-Toltec, built around AD 800, but the present 25m-high structure, built over the old one, has the plumed serpent sculpted along the stairways and Toltec warriors represented in the doorway carvings at the top of the temple.

The pyramid is actually the Mayan calendar formed in stone. Each of El Castillo's nine levels is divided in two by a staircase, making eighteen separate terraces that commemorate the eighteen 20-day months of the Vague Year. The four stairways have 91 steps each; add the top platform and the total is 365, the number of days in the year. On each façade of the pyramid are 52 flat panels, which are reminders of the 52 years in the Calendar Round.

To top it off, during the spring and autumn equinoxes, light and shadow form a series of triangles on the side of the north staircase that mimic the creep of a serpent (note the carved serpent's heads flanking the bottom of the staircase). The serpent ascends in March and descends in September.

The older pyramid *inside* El Castillo boasts a red jaguar throne with inlaid eyes and spots of jade, and it also holds a chac-mool figure. The entrance to El Túnel, the passage up to the throne, is at the base of El Castillo's north side; it's open only from 11am to 3pm and 4pm to 4.45pm. The dank air and steep, narrow stairway can make the climb a sweltering, slippery, claustrophobic experience.

Gran Juego de Pelota The great ball court, the largest and most impressive in Mexico, is only one of the city's eight courts, indicative of the importance the games held here. The court is flanked by temples at either end and bounded by towering parallel walls with stone rings cemented up high.

There is evidence that the ball game may have changed over the years. Some carvings show players with padding on their elbows and knees, and it is thought that they played a soccerlike game with a hard rubber ball, the use of hands forbidden. Other carvings show players wielding bats; it appears that if a player hit the ball through one of the stone hoops, his team was declared the winner. It may be that during the Toltec period the losing captain, and perhaps his teammates as well, were sacrificed.

Along the walls of the ball court are stone reliefs, including scenes of decapitations of players. The court's acoustics are amazing – a conversation at one end can be heard 135m away at the other, and a clap produces multiple loud echoes.

Templo del Barbado & Templo de los Jaguares y Escudos The structure at the northern end of the ball court, called the Temple of the Bearded Man after a carving inside of it, has some finely sculpted pillars and reliefs of flowers, birds and trees. The Temple of the Jaguars and Shields, built atop the southeast corner of the ball court's wall, has some columns with carved rattlesnakes and tablets with etched jaguars. Inside are faded mural fragments depicting a battle.

Plataforma de los Cráneos The Platform of Skulls (*tzompantli* in Náhuatl) is between the Templo de los Jaguares and El Castillo. You can't mistake it, because the T-shaped platform is festooned with carved skulls and eagles tearing open the chests of men to eat their hearts. In ancient days this platform held the heads of sacrificial victims.

Plataforma de las Águilas y los Jaguares Adjacent to the tzompantli, the carvings on the Platform of the Eagles and Jaguars depict those animals gruesomely grabbing human hearts in their claws. It is thought that this platform was part of a temple dedicated to the military legions responsible for capturing sacrificial victims.

Cenote Sagrado A 300m rough stone road runs north (a five-minute walk) to the huge sunken well that gave this city its name. The Sacred Cenote is an awesome natural well, some 60m in diameter and 35m deep. The walls between the summit and the water's surface are ensnared in tangled vines and other vegetation. There are ruins of a small steam bath next to the cenote, as well as a modern drinks stand with toilets. See 'Dredging Chichén's Sacred Cenote' for the historical details.

Grupo de las Mil Columnas Comprising the **Templo de los Guerreros** (Temple of the Warriors), **Templo de Chac-Mool** (Temple of Chac-Mool) and **Baño de Vapor** (Sweat House or Steam Bath), this group behind El Castillo takes its name (Group of the Thousand Columns) from the forest of pillars stretching south and east.

Structures are adorned with stucco and stone-carved animal deities. Archaeological work in 1926 revealed the Temple of Chac-Mool beneath the Temple of the Warriors. You can walk through the columns on its south side to reach the Columnata Noreste, notable for the 'big-nosed god' masks in its façade. Some have been reassembled on the ground around the statue. Just to the south are the remains of a Mayan sweat house, with an underground oven and drains for the water. The sweat houses were regularly used for ritual purification.

El Osario The Ossuary, otherwise known as the Bonehouse or the Tumba del Gran Sacerdote (High Priest's Grave), is a ruined pyramid southwest of El Castillo. As with most of the buildings in this southern section, the architecture is more Puuc than Toltec. It's notable for the serpent heads at the base of its staircases. There's a snack bar with phone and toilets nearby.

El Caracol Called El Caracol (the Snail) by the Spaniards for its interior spiral staircase, this observatory is one of the most fascinating and important of all the Chichén Itzá buildings. Its circular design resembles some central highlands structures, although, surprisingly, not those of Toltec Tula. In a fusion of architectural styles and religious imagery, there are Mayan Chac rain-god masks over four external doors facing the cardinal directions. The windows in the observatory's dome are aligned with the appearance of certain stars at specific dates. From the dome the priests decreed the times for rituals, celebrations, corn-planting and harvests.

Edificio de las Monjas & La Iglesia
Thought by archaeologists to have been a palace for Mayan royalty, the so-called Edificio de las Monjas (Nunnery), with its myriad rooms, resembled a European convent to the conquistadors, hence their name for the building. The building's dimensions are imposing: its base is 60m long, 30m wide and 20m high. The construction is Mayan rather than Toltec, although a Toltec sacrificial stone stands in front of the building. A smaller adjoining building to the east,

---

Dredging Chichén's Sacred Cenote

Around 1900 Edward Thompson, a Harvard professor and US consul to Yucatán, bought the hacienda that included Chichén Itzá for US$75. No doubt intrigued by local stories of female virgins being sacrificed to the Mayan deities by being thrown into the cenote, Thompson resolved to have the cenote dredged.

He imported dredging equipment and set to work. Gold and jade jewelry from all parts of Mexico and as far away as Colombia was recovered, along with other artifacts and a variety of human bones. Many of the artifacts were shipped to Harvard's Peabody Museum, but some have since been returned to Mexico.

Subsequent diving expeditions in the 1920s and '60s turned up hundreds of other valuable artifacts. It appears that all sorts of people, including children and old people, the diseased and the injured, and the young and the vigorous, were forcibly obliged to take an eternal swim in Chichén's Sacred Cenote.

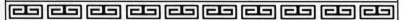

known as La Iglesia (the Church), is covered almost entirely with carvings.

Akab-Dzib On the path east of the Nunnery, the Puuc-style Akab-Dzib is thought by some archaeologists to be the most ancient structure excavated here. The central chambers date from the 2nd century. The name means 'Obscure Writing' in Maya and refers to the south-side Annex door, whose lintel depicts a priest with a vase etched with hieroglyphics that have never been translated.

Grutas de Balankanché

In 1959 a guide to the Chichén ruins was exploring a cave on his day off when he came upon a narrow passageway. He followed the passageway for 300m, meandering through a series of caverns. In each, perched on mounds amid scores of glistening stalactites, were hundreds of ceremonial treasures the Maya had placed there 800 years earlier: ritual *metates* and *manos* (grinding stones), incense burners and pots. In the years following the discovery, the ancient ceremonial objects were removed and studied. Eventually most of them were returned to the caves, placed exactly where they were found.

The caverns *(admission US$5.25, ticket booth open 9am-5pm daily)* are 6km east of the ruins of Chichén Itzá and 2km east of the Hotel Dolores Alba on the highway to Cancún. Second-class buses heading east from Pisté toward Valladolid and Cancún will drop you at the Balankanché road. The entrance to the caves is 350m north of the highway.

Outside the caves you'll find a botanical garden (displaying native Yucatecan flora), a small museum, a shop selling cold drinks and souvenirs, and a ticket booth. The museum features large photographs taken during the exploration of the caves, and descriptions (in English, Spanish and French) of the Mayan religion and the offerings found in the caves. Also on display are photographs of modern-day Mayan ceremonies called Ch'a Chaac, which continue to be held in all the villages on the Yucatán Peninsula during times of drought and consist mostly of praying and making numerous offerings of food to Chac.

Compulsory 40-minute tours (minimum six people, maximum 30) have recorded narration (difficult to hear and losing its at-

tempted dramatic effect): English is at 11am, 1pm and 3pm; Spanish is at 9am noon, 2pm and 4pm; and French is at 10am

Be warned that the cave is unusually hot and ventilation is poor in its farther reaches. The lack of oxygen makes it difficult to draw a full breath until you're outside again.

Cenote Ik Kil

A little more than 3km east of the eastern entrance to the ruins is *Ik Kil Parque Ecoarqueológico* (☎ 985-851-00-00; admission adult/child US$4.50/2.25; open 9am-5pm daily), whose cenote has been developed into a divine swimming spot. Small cascades of water plunge from the high limestone roof, which is ringed by greenery. A good buffet lunch runs an extra US$4.50. Get your swim in by no later than 1pm to beat the tour groups.

Places to Stay

No matter what you plan to spend on a bed, don't hesitate to haggle in the off-season (May, June, September and October), when prices should be lower.

Budget There's *camping* at the agreeable Pirámide Inn, in Pisté (see Mid-Range). For US$4.50 per person you can pitch a tent or hang a hammock under a palapa, enjoy the Pirámide Inn's pool and watch satellite TV in the lobby. Campers have use of tepid showers, clean shared toilet facilities and a safe place to stow gear.

Hotel Posada Maya (☎ 985-851-02-11) Hammock sites US$4.50, singles/doubles US$16.50/22. Just north of the highway (look for the sign), around the corner from the Oriente ticket office, this hotel has clean rooms with showers, fans and good beds.

Posada Olalde (☎ 985-851-00-86, Calle 6 between Calles 15 & 17) Singles/doubles US$15/20. Two blocks south of the highway by Artesanías Guayacán, this is the best of Pisté's several small pensiones, offering seven clean, quiet and attractive rooms. There are four rustic bungalows (US$18) on the premises as well, and the friendly manager speaks good English.

Posada Poxil (☎ 985-851-01-16) Doubles/triples US$20/25. This hotel at the western end of Pisté has relatively clean, quiet rooms and an inexpensive restaurant serving big breakfasts (US$2.75) and Yucatecan dishes.

Posada Chac-Mool Singles/doubles US$18/20 with fan, US$33/37 with air-con. Just east of the Hotel Chichén Itzá on the opposite (south) side of the highway in Pisté, the Chac-Mool has basic doubles. Good air-con is available in all rooms.

Mid-Range *Hotel Chichén Itzá* (☎ 985-851-00-22, fax 985-851-00-23, e *chichen@ valladolid.com.mx*) Doubles with air-con and TV US$44-88. On the west side of Pisté, this place has 42 pleasant rooms with tile floors and old-style brick-tile ceilings. Rooms in the upper range face the pool and nicely landscaped grounds, and they come with breakfast.

Pirámide Inn (☎ 985-851-01-15, fax 985-851-01-14, w *www.piramideinn.com*) Doubles/triples US$44/49. On the main street in Pisté, next to the eastern bus stop, this hotel was entirely renovated in 1999. All 42 rooms have air-con, and there's a book exchange and deep swimming pool. The restaurant serves international and vegetarian cuisine. Here you're as close as you can stay to the archaeological zone's western entrance.

Hotel Dolores Alba (☎ 985-858-15-55, 999-928-56-50 in Mérida, fax 999-928-31-63, w *www.doloresalba.com, highway 180 Km 122*) Doubles US$42. This hotel is across the highway from Cenote Ik Kil, just over 3km east of the eastern entrance to the ruins and 2km west of the Grutas de Balankanché. Its 40 air-conditioned rooms are simply but pleasingly decorated and face two inviting swimming pools. There's a restaurant, and staff will transport you to and from the Chichén ruins.

Top End All of these hotels have air-con, swimming pools, restaurants, bars, well-kept tropical gardens, comfortable guestrooms and tour groups coming and going. They're very close to the eastern entrance to the archaeological zone.

Hotel Mayaland (☎ 998-887-24-50, 800-235-4079 in the USA, fax 998-884-45-10, w *www.mayaland.com*) Doubles US$159, bungalows from US$214. Less than 100m from the ruins' entrance, this hotel was built around 1923 and is the most gracious in Chichén's vicinity, with multiple pools and restaurants and vast, beautifully green grounds. Rooms and garden bungalows are very nicely appointed.

Hotel Hacienda Chichén (☎ 999-924-21-50 in Mérida, ☎ 800-624-8451 in the USA, fax 999-924-50-11, e *balamhtl@finred.com .mx*, w *www.yucatanadventure.com.mx*) Doubles US$100-117. About 200m farther from the entrance, this is an elegant converted colonial estate that dates from the 16th century. It was here that the archaeologists who excavated Chichén during the 1920s lived. Their bungalows have been refurbished, new ones have been built, and a swimming pool has been added. Guests give it high marks.

Hotel Villas Arqueológicas (☎ 985-851-00-34, 800-258-2633 in the USA, ☎ 801 802 803 in France, fax 985-851-00-18, e *chic chef01@clubmed.com*) Singles/doubles/ triples US$72/83/95. This Club Med hotel is 300m from the east entrance. It is an exact clone of the villas at Cobá and Uxmal except the beds are larger and it somehow lacks their charm. The 40 air-conditioned rooms are smallish but comfortable.

Places to Eat

The *restaurant* in the Unidad de Servicios, at the western entrance to the archaeological zone, serves decent food at decent prices.

The highway through Pisté is lined with more than 20 small restaurants. The cheapest are the market eateries on the main plaza opposite the huge tree. The others are ranged along the highway from the town square to the Pirámide Inn. *Los Pájaros* and *Restaurant y Cocina Económica Chichén Itzá* are among the cheapest ones, serving sandwiches, omelets, enchiladas and quesadillas for around US$3.25.

Lonchería Sayil Facing the Hotel Chichén Itzá, this restaurant offers good values; *bistec, cochinita* or *pollo pibil* are US$2.25.

Hotel Dolores Alba Good set lunches US$6.25, dinners US$9. The restaurant at this hotel (see Places to Stay), 4km east of Pisté, specializes in Yucatecan food.

Restaurant Hacienda Xaybe'h Buffet lunch & dinner US$9. Set back from the highway opposite the Hotel Chichén Itzá (see Places to Stay), this big restaurant has decent food. Diners can use its swimming pool free; others pay about US$2.

Getting There & Away

A modern airport lies about 14km east of Pisté. At the time of research it had yet to receive other than local charter flights.

When all goes well, Oriente's 2nd-class buses pass through Pisté bound for Mérida (2½ hours, US$4.50) hourly between 7.30am and 9.30pm. Hourly Oriente buses to Valladolid (50 minutes, US$1.75) and Cancún (4½ hours, US$7.50) pass between 7.30am and 8.30pm. One bus for Chiquilá (to reach Isla Holbox; 4 hours, US$7) passes at 1.30am.

First-class buses serve Mérida (1¾ hours, US$6.25) at 3pm and 5pm, Cancún (2½ hours, US$12) at 4.30pm, Cobá (1½ hours, US$5.50) and Tulum (2½ hours, US$7.25) at 8am, 2.25pm and 4.30pm. The last two continue to Playa del Carmen (3½ hours, US$15.50).

Shared vans to Valladolid (40 minutes, US$1.75) pass through town regularly.

Getting Around

Buses passing through Pisté stop near the east and west sides of town; during Chichén Itzá's opening hours they also stop at the ruins (check with the driver), and they will take passengers from town for about US$0.60 when there's room. For a bit more, 2nd-class buses will also take you to the Hotel Dolores Alba/Cenote Ik Kil and the Grutas de Balankanché (be sure to specify your destination when buying your ticket).

There is a taxi stand near the west end of town; the asking price to the ruins is US$2.75. There are sometimes cabs at Chichén's parking lot, but make advance arrangements if you want to be sure of a ride.

VALLADOLID

• pop 53,000 ☎ 985

Valladolid is relatively small, manageable and affordable, with an easy pace of life, many handsome colonial buildings and several good hotels and restaurants. It's a fine place to stop and spend a day or three getting to know the real Yucatán, and it makes a good base from which to visit the surrounding area, including Chichén Itzá.

History

Valladolid was once the Mayan ceremonial center of Zací ('sah-KEE'). The initial attempt at conquest in 1543 by Francisco de Montejo, nephew of Montejo the Elder, was thwarted by fierce Mayan resistance, but the Elder's son Montejo the Younger ultimately took the town. The Spanish laid out a new city on the classic colonial plan.

During much of the colonial era, Valladolid's physical isolation from Mérida kept it relatively autonomous from royal rule. The Maya of the area suffered brutal exploitation, which continued after Mexican independence. Barred from entering many areas of the city, the Maya made Valladolid their first point of attack in 1847 when the War of the Castes began. After a two-month siege, the city's defenders were finally overcome. Many fled to the safety of Mérida; the rest were slaughtered.

Today Valladolid is a prosperous seat of agricultural commerce, with some light industry thrown in. Many *vallisetanos* still speak Spanish with the soft and clear Mayan accent.

Orientation & Information

The old highway passes through the center of town, though all signs urge motorists toward the toll road north of town. To follow the old highway eastbound, take Calle 41; westbound, take Calle 39.

Most hotels are on the main plaza, called Parque Francisco Cantón Rosado, or within a block or two of it. The tourist office (☎ 856-20-63 ext 15) is on the east side of the plaza. It has maps and somewhat accurate information and is open 9am to 8pm daily (except during siesta).

A few doors north is the main post office. Various banks, most with ATMs, are near the center of town and are generally open 9am to 5pm Monday to Friday, 9am to 1pm Saturday.

Most Internet places in town charge about US$0.05 per minute and have annoying 'reminder' software of one form or another. A happy exception is @lbert's PC, on Calle 43 near Calle 40, which charges US$1.75 an hour.

Templo de San Bernardino & Convento de Sisal

The Church of San Bernardino de Siena and the Convent of Sisal, just under a kilometer southwest of the plaza, are said to be the oldest Christian structures in Yucatán. They were constructed in 1552 to serve the dual functions of fortress and church.

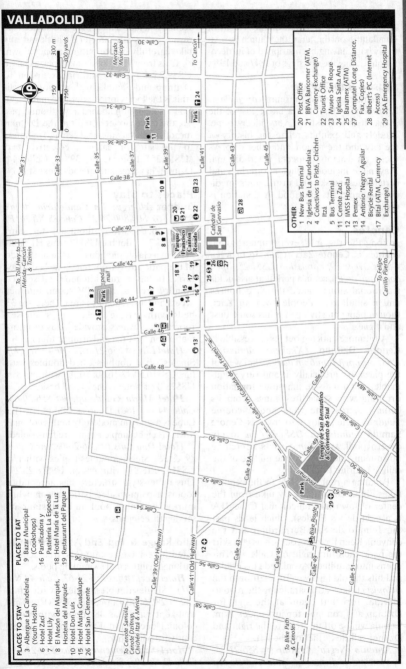

VALLADOLID

If the convent is open, you can go inside. Apart from the likeness of the Virgin of Guadalupe on the altar, the church is relatively bare, having been stripped of its decorations during the uprisings of 1847 and 1910.

Museo San Roque

This church turned museum *(open 9am-9pm daily)* is less than a block east of the plaza. It is modest but very nicely done. Models and exhibits relate the history of the city and the region, and other displays focus on various aspects of traditional Mayan life, including religious offerings and ceremonies, masks and instruments, medicines, handicrafts and food. A donation is requested.

Cenotes

Among the region's several underground cenotes is **Cenote Zací** *(Calle 36 between Calles 37 & 39; admission US$1.25; open 8am-5pm daily)*, set in a park that also holds traditional stone-walled thatched houses and a small zoo. People swim in Zací, though being mostly open it has some dust and algae.

A bit more enticing but less accessible is **Cenote Dzitnup** *(Xkekén; admission US$1.50; open 7am-6pm daily)*, 7km west of the plaza. It's artificially lit and very swimmable, and a massive limestone formation dripping with stalactites hangs from its ceiling. Across the road and a couple hundred meters closer to town is **Cenote Samulá** *(admission US$1.25)*, a lovely cavern pool with *álamo* roots stretching down many meters from the middle of the ceiling to drink from it.

Pedaling a rented bicycle to the cenotes takes about 20 minutes. By bike from the center of town take all-colonial Calle 41A (Calzada de los Frailes), which leads past the Templo de San Bernardino and the convent. Keep them to your left as you skirt the park, then turn right on Calle 49. This opens into tree-lined Avenida de los Frailes and hits the old highway. Turn left onto the *ciclopista* (bike path) paralleling the road to Mérida. Turn left again at the sign for Dzitnup and continue for just under 2km; Samulá will be off this road to the right and Dzitnup a little farther on the left.

Antonio 'Negro' Aguilar (☎ 856-21-25, ⓔ *vinicio@chichen.com, Calle 44 between*

Calles 39 & 41) Bike rental US$0.55 per hr. Rentals include a lock, map and advice (the owner is a real character). Check out any bike carefully before putting money down.

Taxis from Valladolid's main plaza charge US$9.25 for the roundtrip excursion to Dzitnup and Samulá, with an hour's wait (this is the locals' price; your rate may vary). You also can hop aboard a westbound bus, ask the driver to let you off at the Dzitnup turnoff, then walk the final 2km (20 minutes) to the site; or catch a colectivo taxi (US$1.25) from Calle 39 at Calle 44. Dzitnup has a restaurant and drinks stand.

Places to Stay

Budget *Albergue La Candelaria* (☎/*fax 856-22-67, 800-800-26-25, Calle 35 No 201F)* Dorm beds with/without hostel card US$6.75/7.25, double US$17. This HI affiliate is in a classic old house on the north side of the park across from Iglesia de la Candelaria. It has a full kitchen, self-service laundry area, a cable TV room, Internet access and a serene back area. There are 33 beds with private lockers in single-sex rooms. The owners provide loads of information on the area and arrange tours.

Hotel Lily (☎ *856-21-63, Calle 44 No 190)* Singles/1-bed doubles/2-bed doubles with fan US$10.50/13/16.50, triple with air-con US$28. This hotel is cheap and basic.

Hotel María Guadalupe (☎ *856-20-68, Calle 44 No 188)* Doubles US$14.50. The Lupe is a study in modernity in this colonial town. Its eight simple rooms are fan-cooled.

Hotel Don Luis (☎ *856-20-08, cnr Calles 39 & 38)* Singles/doubles/triples with fan US$14.50/18/21, with air-con US$18/23/29. This motel-style structure has acceptable rooms, a palm-shaded patio, a somewhat murky swimming pool and a restaurant serving three meals.

Mid-Range & Top End All of the hotels listed here have restaurants, free secure parking facilities and swimming pools.

Hotel Zací (☎/*fax 856-21-67, Calle 44 No 191)* Singles/doubles/triples with fan US$21/28/36, with air-con US$29/34/39. This well-kept place has 48 rooms with mock colonial decor and TVs around a quiet courtyard with a bar.

Hotel San Clemente (☎/*fax 856-22-08, Calle 42 No 206)* Singles/doubles US$25/30.

An excellent value, the San Clemente has a pool and 64 rooms with air-con, cable TV and decor nearly identical to the Zací's. It's on the corner of the plaza, across from the cathedral.

El Mesón del Marqués (☎ *856-20-73, fax 856-22-80,* e *h_marques@chichen.com.mx, Calle 39 No 203*) Standard/deluxe doubles US$40/51. The best hotel in town is on the north side of the plaza. It has two colonial courtyards, a pool, a good restaurant and guestrooms with air-con and ceiling fans.

Places to Eat
Valladolid has several good bakeries, including *Panificadora y Pastelería La Especial* (*Calle 41*) less than a block west of the plaza, open afternoons only.

Bazar Municipal (*cnr Calles 39 & 40*) Set meals US$2.25. This is a collection of market-style cookshops at the plaza's northeast corner, popular for their big, cheap breakfasts. At lunch and dinner there are *comidas corridas* (set meals) – check the price before you order.

Restaurant del Parque (*cnr Calles 41 & 42*) Set meals US$2.25. The old-fashioned, high-ceilinged Parque offers good Yucatecan standards and amiable, if sometimes bumbling, service.

Hotel María de la Luz (*Calle 42 No 193*) Breakfast buffet & set meals US$4.50. This hotel has breezy tables overlooking the plaza and serves a tasty and bountiful breakfast.

Hostería del Marqués (*Calle 39 No 203*) Mains US$4-6.25. The best restaurant in town is in the Hotel El Mesón del Marqués. It serves delicious food in the beautiful and tranquil outer courtyard. Try the superb *pan de cazón* (dogfish – a small shark – in layers of tortillas, US$5), a specialty of Campeche.

Getting There & Away
Bus Valladolid has two bus terminals: the convenient old one on Calle 39 at Calle 46, two blocks from the plaza, and a newer terminal five blocks farther northwest, on Calle 37 at Calle 54. All buses going through town stop at both. Many 1st-class buses running between Cancún and Mérida don't go into town at all but drop passengers near the toll road's off-ramp. Free shuttles then take them into town.

The principal services are Oriente and Expresso (2nd-class) and Super Expresso (1st-class). Travel times given are for 1st-class unless there is only 2nd-class service; in most cases 2nd-class costs about 30% less and takes at least one-third longer.

Cancún – 165km, 2-3 hours; 9 1st-class (US$8.25), 13 2nd-class (US$6) 8.30am to 9.30pm

Chetumal – 357km, 6 hours; 2 2nd-class (US$11.50)

Chiquilá (for Isla Holbox) – 155km, 2½ hours; 2nd-class (US$6) at 2.30am

Cobá – 60km, 1-1½ hours; 3 1st-class (US$3), 3 2nd-class (US$2.25)

Izamal – 115km, 2 hours; 3 2nd-class (US$3.25)

Mérida – 165km, 2-3 hours; 9 1st-class (US$8.25), 17 2nd-class

Pisté/Chichén Itzá – 40km, 45 minutes; 17 2nd-class (US$1.75) Mérida-bound buses 7.30am to 6pm; buses stop near ruins during opening hours

Playa del Carmen – 169km, 3-3½ hours; 2 1st-class (US$10.50), 3 2nd-class (US$6.25)

Tizimín – 51km, 1 hour; 8 2nd-class (US$2)

Tulum – 106km, 2 hours; 3 1st-class (US$4.75), 3 2nd-class (US$4.25)

Colectivos Often faster, more reliable and more comfortable than buses are the shared vans that leave for various points as soon as their seats are filled. Direct services to Mérida (from in front of the old terminal, US$5.50) and Cancún (from west side of the plaza, US$6.50) take two hours – confirm it's nonstop. Passengers for Pisté and Chichén Itzá (40 minutes, US$1.75) use a waiting room across Calle 46 from the old bus terminal.

EK' BALAM
The turnoff for this fascinating archaeological site *(admission US$2.50, free Sun & holidays; open 8am-5pm daily)* is due north of Valladolid, 17km along the road to Tizimín. Ek' Balam is another 10.5km east. There is usually someone at the site willing to act as a guide; tips are appreciated.

Vegetation still covers much of the area, but excavations and restoration continue to add to the sights, including an interesting ziggurat-like structure near the entrance, as well as a fine arch and a ball court.

Most impressive is the main pyramid – a massive, towering structure sporting a huge jaguar mouth with 360-degree dentition. At its base are stucco skulls, and to its right side are unusual winged human figures (some call them Mayan angels). From the top of the pyramid you can see pyramids at Chichén Itzá and Cobá.

It's possible to catch a colectivo from Calle 44 between Calles 35 and 47 in Valladolid for the village of Santa Rita (US$1.75), a 2km walk from Ek' Balam. A roundtrip taxi ride from Valladolid with an hour's wait at the ruins will cost around US$20. Hostel La Candelaria in Valladolid can arrange tours.

TIZIMÍN
• pop 38,000 ☎ 986

Travelers bound for Río Lagartos change buses in Tizimín, a ranching center. There is little to warrant an overnight stay, but the tree-filled Parque Principal is pleasant, particularly at sundown.

Two great colonial structures – Parroquia Los Santos Reyes de Tizimín (Church of the Three Wise Kings) and its former Franciscan monastery (the ex-convento) – are worth a look.

Both Bital, on the southwest side of Parque Principal, and Bancomer, at Calles 48 and 51, have ATMs.

Places to Stay & Eat
Posada María Antonia (☎ 863-23-84, fax 863-28-57, Calle 50 No 408) Rooms with air-con US$18 for up to four people. Just north of the church, this place has 12 fairly basic rooms. You can place international calls at the reception desk.

Panificadora La Especial (Calle 55) This bakery lies down a pedestrian lane from the Parque Principal.

Pizzería César's This popular joint near the Posada María Antonia serves pizza, pasta, sandwiches and burgers. Few items are over US$5.

The *market*, two blocks north of the church, has the usual cheap eateries.

Getting There & Away
Oriente (shared with Mayab, both 2nd-class only) and Noreste (1st- and 2nd-class) have terminals around the corner from one another, just east of the market.

Cancún – 194km, 3-3½ hours; 5 Mayab (US$7.25) between 3.30am and 5.15pm, 7 1st-class Noreste (US$7.75) and 2nd-class Noreste, 3am to 6pm

Izamal – 109km, 2½ hours; Oriente (US$5.25) at 5.15am, 11.20am and 6pm

Mérida – 180km, 2¼ hours; 10 1st-class Noreste (US$7.50) between 4.30am and 6.30pm

Playa del Carmen – 270km, 5 hours; 1 Oriente (US$10) at 8.30am

Río Lagartos – 50km, 1 hour; 10 Noreste (US$2.25) between 5am and 7.45pm; some buses continue another 12km west to San Felipe

Valladolid – 51km, 1 hour; 7 Oriente (US$2) between 5.30am and 6pm

Taxis to Río Lagartos or San Felipe charge US$23.

RÍO LAGARTOS
• pop 2100 ☎ 986

The most spectacular flamingo colony in Mexico warrants a trip to this fishing village, 103km north of Valladolid, 52km north of Tizimín and lying within the Ría Lagartos Biosphere Reserve. The mangrove-lined estuary is also home to snowy egrets, red egrets, tiger herons, snowy white ibis, hundreds of other bird species and a small number of the crocodiles that gave the town its name (Alligator River).

The Maya knew the place as Holkobén and used it as a rest stop on their way to the nearby lagoons (Las Coloradas) from which they extracted salt. (Salt continues to be extracted, on a much vaster scale now.) Spanish explorers mistook the inlet for a river and the crocs for alligators, and the rest is history.

Flamingo Tours
The brilliant orange-red birds can turn the horizon fiery when they take wing. For their well-being, however, please ask your boat captain not to frighten the birds into flight. You can generally get to within 100m of flamingoes before they walk or fly away. Depending on your luck, you'll see either hundreds or thousands of them.

The four primary haunts, in increasing distance from town, are Punta Garza, Yoluk, Necopal and Nahochín (all flamingo feeding spots named for nearby mangrove patches). Prices vary with boat, group size (maximum five) and destination. The lowest you can expect to pay is around US$39; a full boat to Nahochín runs as much as US$66.

Ismael Navarro and Diego Núñez Martínez are licensed guides with formal training both as guides and naturalists. They speak English and Italian and are up on the area's fauna and flora, including the staggering number of bird species. They also offer night rides looking for crocodiles and, from May through September, sea turtles. Follow the signs for Restaurante-Bar Isla Contoy (turn left when you reach the water), visit **w** www.ismaelnavarro.gobot.com, or call Holkobén Expeditions (☎ *986-862-00-00*, **e** *nunez@chichen.com*).

Alternatively, you can negotiate with one of the eager men in the waterfront kiosks near the entrance to town. They speak English and will connect you with a captain (who usually doesn't).

Places to Stay & Eat
Most residents aren't sure of the town's street names, and signs are few. The road into town is north-south Calle 10, which ends at the waterfront Calle 13.

Posada Leyli (no ☎, cnr Calles 14 & 11) Singles with shared/private bath US$13/15, doubles with bath US$20. Two blocks south of Calle 10, this place has six pleasant, fan-cooled rooms.

Hotel Villas de Pescadores (☎ *862-00-20, Calle 14 s/n*) Doubles US$33. This hotel is two blocks north of the Leyli, near the water's edge, and offers 12 very clean rooms, each with good cross-ventilation (all face the estuary), two beds and a fan. The owner rents bicycles and canoes as well; if he's not around, ask for his neighbor Benigno.

Cabañas Escondidas (Calle 19 at waterfront) Cabañas US$17. There are five simple cabañas with fans at this friendly place next door to the Isla Contoy.

Restaurante-Bar Isla Contoy (Calle 19 at waterfront) Seafood US$4.25-7. This popular spot is a good place to meet other travelers and form groups for the boat tours.

Getting There & Away
Several buses run between Tizimín (50km, US$2.25, Noreste), Mérida (2½-4 hours, US$6.50 2nd-class, US$7.50 1st-class, Noreste) and Cancún (3-4 hours, US$7.25-7.75, Noreste and Mayab). Noreste also serves San Felipe (20 minutes, US$1) several times a day.

SAN FELIPE
This seldom-visited fishing village 12km west of Río Lagartos makes a nice day trip or overnight. Birding and beach are the main attractions, just across the estuary at Punta Holohit.

Hotel San Felipe de Jesús (☎ *986-862-20-27*, **e** *sanfelip@prodigy.net.mx*) Rooms US$27-39. To get to this friendly, clean and cleverly constructed hotel, turn left at the water and proceed 100m. Six of the 18 rooms are large and have private balconies and water views. All rooms have good cross-ventilation and are super bargains. The restaurant offers tasty seafood at low prices.

By public transportation you pretty much have to come through Río Lagartos (20 minutes, US$1). Six buses a day go from San Felipe to Tizimín (US$2.25), continuing to Valladolid (US$3).

Quintana Roo

The state of Quintana Roo, Mexico's only Caribbean real estate, stretches north from the border with Belize to the extreme northeastern tip of the Yucatán Peninsula. Its barrier reef runs almost this entire distance, stopping at Isla Mujeres. This and the other reefs along the coast, all bathed in crystal-clear Caribbean waters teeming with tropical fish, provide a profusion of excellent diving and snorkeling sites ranked among the world's best. Quintana Roo is also home to several impressive Mayan ruins and to resorts of every size and flavor.

Owing in part to its geographic isolation and the effects of the War of the Castes, the region did not have an official name until 1902, when it was given the status of territory and named after Andrés Quintana Roo, the poet-warrior-statesman who presided over the drafting of Mexico's constitution. In 1974, largely as a result of the development of Cancún, the territory achieved statehood.

CANCÚN
• pop 385,000 ☎ 998
In the 1970s Mexico's ambitious tourism planners decided to outdo Acapulco with a brand-new, world-class resort located on the Yucatán Peninsula. The place they chose was a deserted sand spit offshore from the little fishing village of Puerto Juárez, on the peninsula's eastern shore. The name of the place was Cancún. Vast sums were sunk

CANCÚN

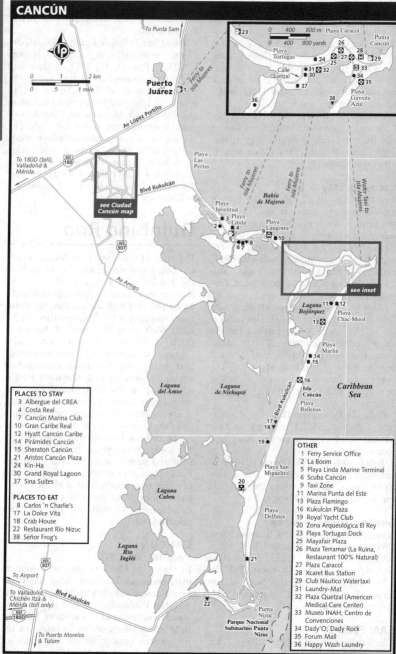

PLACES TO STAY
3 Albergue del CREA
4 Costa Real
7 Cancún Marina Club
10 Gran Caribe Real
12 Hyatt Cancún Caribe
14 Pirámides Cancún
15 Sheraton Cancún
21 Aristos Cancún Plaza
24 Kin-Ha
30 Grand Royal Lagoon
37 Sina Suites

PLACES TO EAT
8 Carlos 'n Charlie's
17 La Dolce Vita
18 Crab House
22 Restaurant Río Nizuc
38 Señor Frog's

OTHER
1 Ferry Service Office
2 La Boom
5 Playa Linda Marine Terminal
6 Scuba Cancún
9 Taxi Zone
11 Marina Punta del Este
13 Plaza Flamingo
16 Kukulcán Plaza
19 Royal Yacht Club
20 Zona Arqueológica El Rey
23 Playa Tortugas Dock
25 Mayafair Plaza
26 Plaza Terramar (La Ruina,
     Restaurant 100% Natural)
27 Plaza Caracol
28 Xcaret Bus Station
29 Club Náutico Watertaxi
31 Laundry-Mat
32 Plaza Quetzal (American
     Medical Care Center)
33 Museo INAH; Centro de
     Convenciones
34 Dady'O; Dady Rock
35 Forum Mall
36 Happy Wash Laundry

into landscaping and infrastructure, yielding straight, well-paved roads, potable tap water and great swaths of sandy beach. Cancún's raison d'être is to shelter planeloads of tourists who fly in to spend one or two weeks in a resort hotel before flying home again. More than 2 million visitors descend on Cancún each year.

During their stay they can get by with speaking only English, spending only US dollars and eating only familiar food. In the daytime, tourists enjoy the beaches, rent a car or board a bus for an excursion to Chichén Itzá, Xcaret or Tulum, or browse in air-conditioned shopping malls straight out of Dallas. At night they dance and drink in clubs and discos to music that's the same all over the world. They have a good time. This is the business of tourism.

Hordes of US university students descend on Cancún during Spring Break (usually in March), driving up lodging prices and the blood pressure of locals, many of whom are scandalized by the public displays of drunkenness and other debauchery that ensue. Not surprisingly, accident and crime rates (including sexual assaults) tend to go up at this time also.

Orientation

Cancún is actually two places in one: Ciudad Cancún and the Zona Hotelera.

Ciudad Cancún On the mainland lies Ciudad Cancún, a planned city founded as the service center of the resort. The area of interest to tourists is referred to as *'el centro'* ('downtown'). The main north-south thoroughfare is Avenida Tulum, a 1km-long tree-shaded boulevard lined with banks, shopping centers and restaurants.

Those who are content to trundle out to the beach by bus or taxi can save pots of money by staying downtown in one of the smaller, low- to medium-priced hotels, many of which have swimming pools. Restaurants in the city center range from ultra-Mexican taco joints to fairly smooth and expensive salons.

Zona Hotelera The sandy spit of an island, Isla Cancún, is usually referred to as the Zona Hotelera ('SO-na oh-te-LE-ra'). Boulevard Kukulcán, a four-lane divided avenue, leaves Ciudad Cancún and goes eastward out on the island several kilometers, passing condominium developments, a youth hostel, several moderately priced hotels, some expensive larger ones and several shopping complexes, to Punta Cancún (Cancún Point) and the Centro de Convenciones (Convention Center).

From Punta Cancún, the boulevard heads south for 13km, flanked on both sides for much of the way by mammoth hotels, shopping centers, dance clubs and many restaurants and bars, to Punta Nizuc (Nizuc Point), where it turns westward and rejoins the mainland. From there, the boulevard cuts through light tropical forest for a few more kilometers to its southern terminus at Cancún's international airport.

Few of the buildings in the Zona Hotelera have numbered addresses. Instead, because the vast majority of them are on Boulevard Kukulcán, their location is described in relation to their distance from Km 0, the boulevard's northern terminus in Ciudad Cancún, identified with a roadside 'Km 0' marker. Each kilometer is similarly marked

The airport is about 8km south of the city center. Puerto Juárez, the port for passenger ferries to Isla Mujeres, is about 3km north of the center. Punta Sam, the dock for the slower car ferries to Isla Mujeres, is about 7km north of the center.

Information

Tourist Offices There is a sporadically staffed tourist information booth in the international arrivals section of the airport. Downtown, the state tourism office (☎ 884-80-73) is in the Edificio Fonatur, Avenida Náder at Avenida Cobá; it's open 9am to 9pm daily and usually has English-speakers on staff.

Immigration For visa and tourist-card extensions, visit the Instituto Nacional de Migración (☎ 884-14-04), Avenida Náder 1 at Avenida Uxmal downtown. The office handles extension requests from 9am to 1pm Monday to Friday.

Money There are at least three banks in the Zona Hotelera: Banco Bilbao Vizcaya in Mayafair Plaza, across from the Fiesta América Cancún hotel; a Banamex with currency exchange and ATM next door in

THE YUCATÁN PENINSULA

CIUDAD CANCÚN

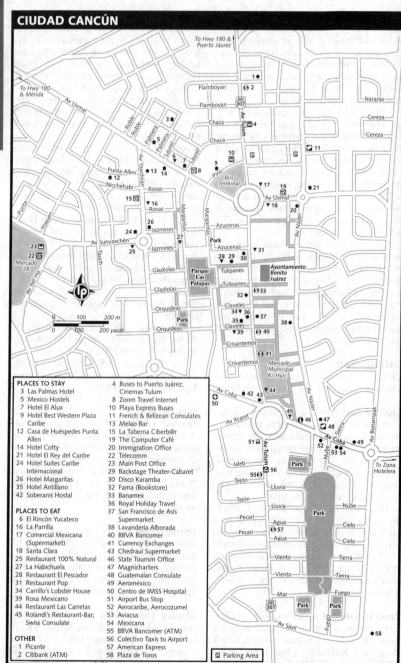

PLACES TO STAY
3 Las Palmas Hotel
5 Mexico Hostels
7 Hotel El Alux
9 Hotel Best Western Plaza Caribe
12 Casa de Huéspedes Punta Allen
14 Hotel Cotty
21 Hotel El Rey del Caribe
24 Hotel Suites Caribe Internacional
26 Hotel Margaritas
35 Hotel Antillano
42 Soberanis Hostal

PLACES TO EAT
6 El Rincón Yucateco
16 La Parrilla
17 Comercial Mexicana (Supermarket)
18 Santa Clara
25 Restaurant 100% Natural
27 La Habichuela
28 Restaurant El Pescador
31 Restaurant Pop
34 Carrillo's Lobster House
39 Rosa Mexicano
44 Restaurant Las Carretas
45 Rolandi's Restaurant-Bar; Swiss Consulate

OTHER
1 Picante
2 Citibank (ATM)

4 Buses to Puerto Juárez; Cinemas Tulum
8 Zoom Travel Internet
10 Playa Express Buses
11 French & Belizean Consulates
13 Melao Bar
15 La Taberna Ciberb@r
19 The Computer Café
20 Immigration Office
22 Telecomm
23 Main Post Office
29 Backstage Theater-Cabaret
30 Disco Karamba
32 Fama (Bookstore)
33 Banamex
36 Royal Holiday Travel
37 San Francisco de Asís Supermarket
38 Lavandería Alborada
40 BBVA Bancomer
41 Currency Exchanges
43 Chedraui Supermarket
46 State Tourism Office
47 Magnicharters
48 Guatemalan Consulate
49 Aeroméxico
50 Centro de IMSS Hospital
51 Airport Bus Stop
52 Aerocaribe, Aerocozumel
53 Aviacsa
54 Mexicana
55 BBVA Bancomer (ATM)
56 Colectivo Taxis to Airport
57 American Express
58 Plaza de Toros

P Parking Area

Plaza Terramar; and Bital, at the Centro de Convenciones, a full-service bank open 8am to 7pm Monday to Saturday. There are ATMs and casas de cambio (open long hours) inside practically all the malls and at Punta Cancún. Most of the resorts on the island will change money, but they offer poor exchange rates and sometimes limit transactions to guests only. Exchange rates on the island are generally less favorable than those downtown, but not enough to warrant a special trip.

ATMs are common downtown, and there are several banks on Avenida Tulum between Avenidas Cobá and Uxmal, including a Bancomer and a Banamex. Most banks are open 9am to 5.30pm Monday to Friday, but they sometimes limit foreign-exchange transactions to between 10am and noon. More convenient are the many currency-exchange booths on the east side of Avenida Tulum halfway between Avenida Cobá and Avenida Uxmal (and scattered elsewhere throughout the city); most are open 8am to 8pm daily.

Post & Communications There is no post office in the Zona Hotelera, but most hotels' reception desks sell stamps and will mail letters. The main post office is downtown at the west end of Avenida Sunyaxchén. It's open 8am to 6pm Monday to Friday, and, for buying stamps only, 9am to 1pm Saturday.

There are numerous Telmex pay phones throughout Cancún that accept prepaid phone cards. Beware of phones accepting credit cards; charges can be very high. The call center at Soberanis Hostal (see Places to Stay) offers good rates on international calls.

At the time of research, Internet access in the Zona Hotelera was scarce, expensive and sketchy. An unnamed place south of the Museo INAH (on the south side of the Centro de Convenciones) charges US$2.75 for 15 minutes. A single terminal in the Holanda ice-creamery in Plaza Caracol charges US$0.10 per minute.

Public Internet facilities in downtown Cancún sprout and die off like mushrooms. One of the longest standing is La Taberna Ciberb@r, Avenida Yaxchilán 23, an adjunct to a popular neighborhood bar managed by friendly English-speaking people. They charge US$1.75 an hour and are open 10am to 4am daily. There are several places across Pino from the bus terminal and along Avenida Tulum north of it. The Computer Café, on Avenida Uxmal between Avenidas Tulum and Náder, has good connections and charges US$1.75 an hour.

Many of these facilities can send faxes; most hotels will oblige if you insist that you have a document that must be faxed right away, and other businesses in town offer fax services as well.

Travel Agencies In the Zona Hotelera, most big hotels have travel agencies. A reputable independent agency is Thomas Moore (☎ 885-02-66), in the Royal Yacht Club complex at Boulevard Kukulcán Km 16.

Downtown there's the centrally located Royal Holiday Travel (☎ 887-34-00, fax 884-58-92, e royalh@telmex.com.mx), Avenida Tulum 33, which has a professional, English-speaking staff.

Bookstores The main bookstore in the Zona Hotelera is Librería Dalí in Kukulcán Plaza on the 2nd floor; it has thousands of books in Spanish and English and an impressive selection of books on the Yucatán Peninsula.

Fama, a bookstore downtown at Avenida Tulum 105, near the southern end of Tulipanes, has a large variety of domestic and international magazines, and a fair selection of Mexican road atlases and books in various languages. Most of the books are about Cancún, the Yucatán Peninsula and the ancient Mayan civilization.

Laundry All the resorts in the Zona offer laundry service, but if you want to save some money try Happy Wash Laundry, on Paseo Pok-Ta-Pok near the Hotel Suites Laguna Verde. Laundry Mat, on Boulevard Kukulcán at Km 7.5, charges US$2.75 per kilogram for wash and dry service, or US$2.25 per washer and US$2.75 per drier for self-service.

Lavandería Alborada at Avenida Náder 5, downtown, charges US$1.25 per washer.

Medical Services The American Medical Care Center (☎ 883-10-01), in Plaza Quetzal, Boulevard Kukulcán Km 8, provides good medical attention and accepts insurance plans from around the world. As its name suggests, it is American owned and operated. From downtown Cancún it's a 15-minute bus ride to the hospital.

The Centro de IMSS (Social Security Center, ☎ 884-19-63) is downtown, on Avenida Cobá at Avenida Tulum.

Dangers & Annoyances Cancún has a reputation for being safe, but as is the case everywhere, don't leave valuables unattended in your hotel room or beside your beach towel.

Vehicular traffic on Boulevard Kukulcán, particularly as it passes between the malls, bars and discotheques at Punta Cancún, is a serious concern. Pedestrians (many of them drunk) are regularly hit by cars. Traffic cops watching for speeders station themselves throughout the Zona Hotelera, but buses routinely speed and tailgate nonetheless.

Mayan Ruins

There are two sets of Mayan ruins in the Zona Hotelera, and though neither is particularly impressive, both are worth a look if time permits. In the **Zona Arqueológica El Rey** *(admission US$3, free Sun; open 8am-5pm daily)*, on the west side of Boulevard Kukulcán between Km 17 and Km 18, are a small temple and several ceremonial platforms. Visitors are occasionally 'required' to be accompanied by a guide. The other, much smaller, site is **Yamil Lu'um** *(admission free)*, atop a beachside knoll on the parklike grounds separating the Sheraton Cancún and Pirámides Cancún towers. Only the outward-sloping remains of the weathered temple's walls still stand, but the ruin makes for a pleasant venture, as much for its lovely setting as anything else. To reach the site visitors must pass through either of the hotels flanking it or approach it from the beach – there is no direct access from the boulevard.

The tiny Mayan structure and chac-mool statue on the beautifully kept grounds of the Sheraton Hotel are authentic and were found on the spot.

Museo INAH

The archaeological museum *(☎ 883-03-05; admission US$3.25, free Sun & holidays; open 9am-8pm Tues-Fri, 10am-7pm Sat-Sun),* operated by the National Institute of Anthropology and History (INAH), is on the south side of the Centro de Conven-

ciones in the Zona Hotelera. Most of the items – including jewelry, masks and intentionally deformed skulls – are from the Postclassic period (AD 1200-1500). Also here are part of a Classic-period hieroglyphic staircase (inscribed with dates from the 6th century) and the stucco head that gave the local archaeological zone its name of El Rey (the King).

Most of the informative signs are in Spanish only, but at the ticket counter you can get a fractured-English information sheet detailing the contents of the museum's 47 showcases.

Beaches

Under Mexican law you have the right to walk and swim on every beach in the country except those within military compounds. In practice, it is difficult to approach many stretches of beach without walking through the lobby of a hotel, particularly in the Zona Hotelera. However, unless you look suspicious or unless you look like a local (the hotels tend to discriminate against locals, particularly the Maya), you'll usually be permitted to cross the lobby and proceed to the beach.

Starting from Ciudad Cancún in the northwest, all of Isla Cancún's beaches are on the left-hand side of the road (the lagoon is on your right). The first beaches are Playa Las Perlas, Playa Linda, Playa Langosta, Playa Tortugas and Playa Caracol; after rounding Punta Cancún, the beaches to the south are Playa Gaviota Azul, Playa Chac-Mool, Playa Marlin, the long stretch of Playa Ballenas and finally, at Km 17, Playa Delfines.

Delfines is about the only beach with a public parking lot; unfortunately, its sand is coarser and darker than the exquisite fine sand of the more northerly beaches.

Beach Safety Cancún's ambulance crews respond to as many as a dozen near-drownings per week. The most dangerous beaches seem to be Playa Delfines and Playa Chac-Mool.

As experienced swimmers know, a beach fronting on open sea can be deadly dangerous, and Cancún's eastern beaches are no exception. Though the surf is usually gentle, undertow is a possibility, and sudden storms (called *nortes*) can blacken the sky and sweep in at any time without warning. The local authorities have devised a system of colored pennants to warn beachgoers of potential dangers. Look for the pennants on the beaches where you swim:

Blue	normal, safe conditions
Yellow	use caution, changeable conditions
Red	unsafe conditions; use a swimming pool instead

Water Sports

For decent **snorkeling**, you need to travel to one of the nearby reefs. Resort hotels, travel agencies and various tour operators in the area can book you on day-cruise boats that take snorkelers to the barrier reef, as well as to other good sites within 100km of Cancún. To see the sparse aquatic life off Cancún's beaches, you can rent snorkeling equipment for about US$10 a day from most luxury hotels.

For diving, try **Scuba Cancún** (☎ 849-75-08, e scuba@cancun.com.mx, Boulevard Kukulcán Km 5), a family-owned, PADI-certified operation with many years of experience. The bilingual staff are safety oriented and environmentally aware, and they offer a variety of dive options (including cenote dives), as well as snorkeling and fishing trips, at reasonable prices.

Deep-sea fishing excursions can also be booked through a travel agent or one of the large hotels. Most of the major resorts rent **kayaks** and the usual water toys; a few make them available to guests free.

AquaWorld is an enormous, impersonal operation with a very poor environmental record. The company offers everything from diving and snorkeling tours to 'submarine' rides and equipment rental.

Organized Tours

Most hotels and travel agencies work with companies that offer tours to surrounding attractions. Some of the places visited, and approximate prices, are: Chichén Itzá (US$48, including buffet lunch and admission), Tulum and Xel-Há (US$58, including admission), and Xcaret (US$70, including admission).

Places to Stay

As happens in other popular Yucatán Peninsula destinations, the rates at some of Cancún's hotels change with the tourist seasons, and every hotelier's idea of when these seasons are is slightly different. Rate changes occur more at mid-range and top-end establishments, though during Semana Santa (Easter Week) rates can rise at budget hotels as well. Broadly, Cancún's high season is from mid-December through March. All prices quoted here are for that high season unless otherwise specified; off-season rates can be significantly lower.

When business is slow, getting a significant discount can be as easy as showing hesitation about a place. It's always worth asking for a *promoción* (discount), regardless of season.

Budget Except for the first hostel described below, all budget accommodations are downtown. 'Budget' is a relative term; prices in Cancún are higher for what you get than anywhere else in Mexico.

Albergue del CREA (☎ 849-43-61, fax 849-43-60, Boulevard Kukulcán Km 3.2) Camping US$5.50 per person, dorm beds US$11. Near the northern edge of the Zona Hotelera, the dilapidated hostel is 4km from the bus terminal, on the left-hand side of the road as you come from downtown. There are better dorm facilities downtown; camping near the water's edge is the

Cancún's spring break hysteria

main reason to stay here. Campers get a locker and use of the hostel's shower and bathroom facilities. There is no age limit and space is usually available. The beach here is silty and shallow.

Much of Cancún's cheap lodging is within a few blocks of the bus terminal. Go northwest on Avenida Uxmal to reach the first four places described here.

Mexico Hostels (☎ 887-01-91, 800-800-26-25, e *frontdesk@mexicohostels.com*, w *www.mexicohostels.com, Palmera 30)* US$10/11 per dorm bed with/without card; includes continental breakfast. This hostel has 50 beds, lockers, Internet access and a full rooftop kitchen. Rooms are clean, with good ventilation, though things can get a bit cramped when they're full.

Hotel El Alux (☎ 884-66-13, fax 884-30-65, Avenida Uxmal 21) Singles/1-bed doubles/2-bed doubles US$28/32/38. The reader-recommended Alux has 35 air-conditioned rooms, each with hot shower, phone and TV.

Hotel Cotty (☎ 884-05-50, fax 884-13-19, *Avenida Uxmal 44)* Singles/doubles/triples US$33/37/39. Each of the 38 rooms here has a shower, air-con, cable TV, phone and two comfortable double beds. There is off-street parking. The 2nd-floor rooms in the rear get club noise from Avenida Yaxchilán.

Las Palmas Hotel (☎ 884-25-13, Palmera 43) Doubles US$25/28 with fan/air-con. Las Palmas has clean, cool rooms with comfy beds and TV. Good, cheap meals are also available.

Casa de Huéspedes Punta Allen (☎ 884-02-25, e *puntaallen@yahoo.com, Punta Allen 8)* Doubles US$31-35. From Avenida Uxmal, walk south along Avenida Yaxchilán and take the first right, Punta Allen, to find this family-run guesthouse. Rooms have bath and air-con, and a light breakfast is included.

Soberanis Hostal (☎ 884-45-64, 800-101-01-01, fax 887-51-38, e *soberani@cancun .com.mx, Avenida Cobá 5)* Bed in 4-bed room US$10/12 with/without card, doubles with continental breakfast US$39. This recently refurbished place is a very good value. All rooms have strong air-con, comfortable beds, tile floors, cable TV and nicely appointed bathrooms. It is primarily a hotel. Only one hostel room was ready at the time of research, but more are in the works, as

are Internet service, an activity center, Asatej travel agency, cafetería and other niceties.

Mid-Range 'Mid-range' in Cancún is a two-tiered category; the downtown area is much cheaper than the Zona Hotelera and only a short bus ride away from the Zona's beaches.

Downtown *Hotel El Rey del Caribe* (☎ 884-20-28, fax 884-98-57, e *reycarib@ cancun.com.mx, w www.reycaribe.com, cnr Avenidas Uxmal & Náder)* Double suites US$60 (US$10 per extra person). The 24 air-conditioned suites have fully equipped kitchenettes, supercomfy beds and safes (you can use your own lock). There's a lush courtyard, a lovely small pool, a Jacuzzi and off-street parking. There is no extra charge for up to two children under 11. The rooms at the back are very nice lodgings indeed. El Rey is a true eco-tel that composts, uses solar collectors and cisterns, gardens with gray water and even has a few composting toilets. Its owners are also educating other hotels and businesses in the area about such methods.

Hotel Antillano (☎ 884-15-32, fax 884-18-78, e *antillano@infosel.net.mx, Claveles 1)* Singles/doubles US$55/62. Just off Avenida Tulum, this pleasant hotel has a pool and 48 guestrooms with air-con and cable TV.

Hotel Margaritas (☎ 884-93-33, fax 884-13-24, e *ventashic@sybcom.com, Avenida Yaxchilán 41)* Doubles US$86. This cheerful hotel has 100 guestrooms with air-con, TV and bath. There's a pool, a restaurant, a bar and attentive service.

Hotel Suites Caribe Internacional (☎ 884-39-99, fax 884-19-93, Avenida Sunyaxchén 36)* Doubles/suites US$62/74. This place has 80 standard rooms with air-con and cable TV, as well as numerous junior suites with two beds, sofa and kitchenette. Amenities include secure parking and a small pool in a pleasant courtyard. The rates are negotiable depending on occupancy; ask for a discount.

Hotel Best Western Plaza Caribe (☎ 884-13-77, 800-528-1234 in the USA, fax 884-63-52, e *plazacbe@cancun.com.mx, w www .hotelplazacaribe.com)* Doubles US$99. Directly across Pino from the bus terminal, between Avenidas Tulum and Uxmal, this franchise hotel offers 140 comfortable air-conditioned rooms with all the amenities. A pool and restaurant are on the premises.

Zona Hotelera In choosing a moderately priced hotel in the Zona Hotelera (that is, one that's under US$135 for two people), bear in mind that those close to Boulevard Kukulcán are close to cheap, convenient transportation.

Grand Royal Lagoon (☎ 883-28-99, fax 883-00-03, Quetzal 8) Rooms US$98. This hotel, 100m off Boulevard Kukulcán Km 7.7, has 36 air-conditioned rooms with cable TV; most have two double beds (some have kings). There's also a pool on the premises.

Sina Suites (☎ 883-10-17, fax 883-24-59, e suitessina@cancun.novenet.com.mx, Quetzal 33) Suites US$106-143. Each of the 33 spacious suites here has a kitchen, 1½ baths, two double beds, a separate living room (with a sofa bed) and satellite TV. Other amenities include a pool, bar and restaurant.

Aristos Cancún Plaza (☎ 885-33-33, 800-527-4786 in the USA, fax 885-02-36, e intl.sales@aristoshotels.com, Boulevard Kukulcán 20.5) Rooms US$101. Considering its beachfront location and amenities, this place offers one of the best values of the Zona's moderately priced digs. All rooms have marble floors, cable TV and balconies with sea or lagoon views. The hotel also has a restaurant and two pools.

Cancún Marina Club (☎ 849-49-99, 800-719-55-23, fax 849-49-70, Boulevard Kukulcán 5.5) Standard rooms US$130. This popular hotel has a water-sports center, a very inviting pool and a pleasant restaurant-bar overlooking the lagoon. Among the 75 rooms are 10 penthouses, two with Jacuzzis.

Top End Rates in this category start at US$160 double. All of these resorts are in the Zona Hotelera and border the Caribbean. All guestrooms in this price category have air-con and satellite TV, and many have balconies with sea views. Often the best room rates available are contained in hotel-and-airfare packages; shop around. Because the rates offered by each resort vary greatly depending on when and where guests book reservations, and because all of the resorts are conveniently located along Boulevard

Kukulcán, these listings are arranged by location along the boulevard rather than by cost.

Costa Real (☎ 881-13-00, 800-543-7556 in the USA, e costa@bestday.com, w www.realresorts.com.mx, Blvd Kukulcán Km 4) Doubles US$200. This large resort has attractive grounds, both all-inclusive and room-only rate plans and a shared-facilities agreement with the much more spectacular Gran Caribe Real to the east.

Gran Caribe Real (☎ 881-73-00, 800-543-7556 in the USA, fax 881-73-99, e pleon@real.com.mx, Blvd Kukulcán Km 5.7) Rooms from US$320. There are 504 deluxe rooms (all with ocean views), 52 junior suites and two three-story, three-bedroom penthouse suites here. All come with private terraces that overlook a dazzling swimming pool and 200m of beach. An all-inclusive plan runs US$210 per person, double occupancy.

Kin-Ha (☎ 883-23-77, fax 883-21-47, kinha3@mail.caribe.net.mx, Blvd Kukulcán Km 8) Rooms/suites US$200/250. This self-contained hotel has 162 rooms and suites in four buildings. All rooms feature a balcony and two double beds or one king-size bed. A travel agency, car rental, mini-market, bars and a gym are on the premises.

Hyatt Cancún Caribe (☎ 848-78-00, 800-633-7313 in the USA, fax 883-15-14, w www.hyatt.com, Blvd Kukulcán Km 10.3) Rooms from US$340. The luxurious Hyatt has a range of accommodations among its 226 lovely guestrooms and suites. Multiple pools, restaurants and tennis courts are among the amenities here, and the location is prime beachfront.

Pirámides Cancún (☎ 885-13-33, fax 885-01-13, e reservascancun@parkroyal.com.mx, w www.parkroyal.com.mx, Blvd Kukulcán Km 11.75) Rooms from US$219. This place has 289 charming rooms and suites. The grounds are idyllic and the beach particularly deep. The resort 'shares' a real Mayan ruin with its neighbor to the south, the Sheraton Cancún.

Sheraton Cancún (☎ 883-19-88, 800-325-3535 in the USA, fax 885-09-74, e sheratoncancun.reservations@sheraton.com, w www.sheraton.com/cancun, Blvd Kukulcán Km 12.5) Singles/doubles US$158/169. The Sheraton has tremendous appeal, from the elegant lobby to the immaculate gardens to the gorgeous tiled art in the restaurant.

Places to Eat

Budget Though you can find a meal in any price range in the Zona Hotelera, the best selection of budget eats is available downtown, away from the big resorts.

Downtown The main market is set back from the street, west of the post office. Its official name is long; locals simply call it Mercado Veintiocho (Market 28). The eateries are mostly in the inner courtyard. The likes of *Restaurant Margely* and *Cocina La Chaya* offer set meals for as little as US$3 and sandwiches for less.

El Rincón Yucateco (Avenida Uxmal 24) Set meals US$3.25. Across from the Hotel Cotty, this place serves excellent yet inexpensive Yucatecan food, with good comidas corridas.

Restaurant Pop (Avenida Tulum) Dishes US$6. This air-conditioned restaurant is about a block south of Avenida Uxmal and serves tasty salads, soups, pastas, fish and meat dishes.

Santa Clara (Avenida Uxmal) Santa Clara specializes in ice cream.

Restaurant Las Carretas (Avenida Tulum 16) Meals US$4-9. This open-air restaurant serves up decent Mexican and American food.

Comercial Mexicana (cnr Avenida Tulum & Avenida Uxmal) This centrally located supermarket has a good selection of produce, meats, cheeses and cookies.

Zona Hotelera For budget eats in the Zona Hotelera, try the food courts, which can be found in every large mall.

La Ruina (Plaza Terramar) Mains US$6.25. This place faces Boulevard Kukulcán near Km 8.5. The highlights here are the delicious Mexican traditionals.

Restaurant Río Nizuc Under US$7.75. Open 11am-7pm daily. At the end of a short, nameless road near Boulevard Kukulcán Km 22, this outdoor restaurant, which is flanked by mangroves, is a nice place to settle in a chair under a palapa and watch convoys of snorkelers in sporty little boats pass by. Octopus, conch and fish are served in various ways.

Mid-Range As with budget restaurants, the downtown area has a wider variety of middle-priced places than the Zona Hotelera.

Downtown Restaurant El Pescador (Tulipanes 28) Meals from US$14. This restaurant has been serving dependably good seafood meals for many years.

Rolandi's Restaurant-Bar (☎ 883-25-27, Avenida Cobá 12) 1-person pizzas US$5.50-8, mains US$7-10. This attractive Italian eatery, between Avenidas Tulum and Náder just off the southern roundabout, serves elaborate pizzas, spaghetti plates and more substantial dishes of veal and chicken.

Restaurant 100% Natural (Cien por Ciento Natural, ☎ 884-36-17, Avenida Sunyaxchén) Mains US$4-9. Near Avenida Yaxchilán, this is one of a chain of restaurants serving juice blends, a wide selection of yogurt-fruit-vegetable combinations and pasta, fish and chicken dishes. There's a bakery on the premises, and the place is very nicely decorated and landscaped.

Rosa Mexicano (☎ 884-63-13, Claveles 4) Mains US$10-18.50. A long-standing favorite, this is the place to go for unusual Mexican dishes in a pleasant hacienda atmosphere. Try the squid sautéed with three chilies or the shrimp in a *pipián* sauce (made of ground pumpkin seeds and spices).

La Parrilla (☎ 887-61-41, Avenida Yaxchilán 51) Mains US$9.50-16. This traditional Mexican restaurant is popular with locals and tourists alike. Mains include tasty *calamares al mojo de ajo* (squid in garlic sauce), steaks and sautéed grouper. *Mole* enchiladas and superb piña coladas both run US$6.50.

Zona Hotelera The Zona Hotelera's mid-range choices are mostly franchise places serving upscale American fast food with some Mexican options. Some are of the kind where waiters pour liquor down patrons' throats straight out of the bottle, to chanting crowds.

Señor Frog's (Boulevard Kukulcán Km 9.8) Dishes US$10-17.

Carlos 'n Charlie's (Boulevard Kukulcán Km 5.5) Dishes US$10-17.

Restaurant 100% Natural (Plaza Terramar, Boulevard Kukulcán Km 8.65) This is a smaller and less aesthetically pleasing branch of the downtown restaurant (see Downtown, just above), charging slightly higher prices.

Plaza Flamingo and the Forum mall hold other options.

Top End Though there are many establishments in this category in the Zona Hotelera, their prices sometimes reflect their location more than the quality of food.

Downtown La Habichuela (☎ 884-31-58, *Margaritas 25*) Mains US$10-17. The specialty at this elegant restaurant just off Parque Las Palapas is shrimp and lobster in curry sauce served inside a coconut with tropical fruit (US$26).

Carrillo's Lobster House (*no ☎, Claveles 35*) Shrimp & fish dishes US$10-16.50, lobster dishes around US$33. This somewhat formal restaurant is the place to head for lobster.

Zona Hotelera The Crab House (☎ 885-39-36, *Boulevard Kukulcán Km 14.8*) Dishes US$12-35. A lovely view of the lagoon complements the seafood here. The long menu includes many shrimp and fillet-of-fish dishes. Crab and lobster are priced by the pound (US$10 to US$50).

La Dolce Vita (☎ 885-01-61, *Boulevard Kukulcán Km 14.8*) Mains US$12-22. Overlooking the lagoon, this is one of Cancún's fanciest Italian restaurants.

Ruth's Chris Steak House (☎ 883-33-01, *Kukulcán Plaza*) Steaks US$22-33. The Ruth's Chris chain is known internationally for its aged, corn-fed, USDA prime beef.

Entertainment

Much of the Zona Hotelera's nightlife is aimed toward a young crowd and is loud and booze-oriented (often with an MC urging women to display body parts). Most of the dance clubs charge around US$12 admission (some have open bar nights for about US$24); some don't open their doors before 10pm, and none are hopping much before midnight.

Dady'O (*Boulevard Kukulcán Km 9*) Opposite the Forum mall, this is one of Cancún's hottest dance clubs. The setting is a five-level black-walled faux cave with a two-level dance floor and zillions of laser beams and strobes, and the beat is pure disco.

Dady Rock This steamy rock 'n' roll club with live music is next door to Dady'O.

La Boom (*Boulevard Kukulcán Km 3.8*) Top 40 tunes are featured here, played at many decibels.

Downtown clubs are mellower. In the lower level of the Plaza de Toros (*cnr Avenidas Bonampak & Sayil*) there are several bars, some with music, that draw a largely local crowd.

Melao Bar (*Avenida Yaxchilán opposite Punta Allen*) For live Cuban music, visit this intimate upstairs club. There's no cover, but the performances often don't begin until after 11pm.

Gay & Lesbian Venues There's a significant gay scene downtown, but it's not apparent until well after sunset.

Backstage Theater-Cabaret (☎ 887-91-06, *Tulipanes 30*) Admission US$3.50. This place has terrific ambiance and a joyful crowd. It features drag shows, strippers (male and female), fashion shows and musicals.

Disco Karamba (*cnr Azucenas & Avenida Tulum*) Open Tues-Sun. Above the Ristorante Casa Italiana, this disco is famous for its frequent drink specials.

Picante Set back from Avenida Tulum a few blocks north of Avenida Uxmal, Picante is mainly for talkers, not dancers.

Shopping

For last-minute purchases before flying out of Cancún, try the **Mercado Municipal Ki-Huic** (*Avenida Tulum north of Avenida Cobá*), a warren of stalls and shops carrying a wide variety of souvenirs and handicrafts. It's 100% tourist trap, so even hard bargaining may not avail.

Getting There & Away

Air Cancún's international airport (☎ 886-00-49) is the busiest in southeastern Mexico. The best place to change money is the Bital bank just outside the domestic arrivals and departures area; it has an ATM and there are other machines nearby. There are baggage lockers just outside customs at the international arrival area; they cost US$5.50 for 24 hours.

Cancún is served by many direct international flights (see the Getting There & Away chapter).

Between Mexicana and its subsidiaries Aerocaribe and Aerocozumel there is at least one flight daily to each of the following: Mexico City (US$130), Oaxaca (US$166), Tuxtla Gutiérrez (US$226), Villahermosa (US$200) and Veracruz (US$217).

The airlines have a total of two flights daily to Chetumal (US$145) and to Mérida (US$95), and they offer five flights daily to Cozumel (US$50). They also fly twice daily to Havana, Cuba (US$310), but you can get better package deals through local travel agents.

Aviacsa, a regional carrier based in Tuxtla Gutiérrez, has flights from Cancún to Mérida, Mexico City, Oaxaca, Tapachula, Tuxtla Gutiérrez, Villahermosa and Chetumal, as well as points in central and northern Mexico. Magnicharters flies to Monterrey, León, Guadalajara and Mexico City.

Aviateca runs flights from Cancún to Flores, Guatemala (US$164), and on to Guatemala City (US$329) several times a week.

If you intend to fly from Cancún to other parts of Mexico, reserve your airline seat ahead of time to avoid any unpleasant surprises. Airline contact information is:

Aerocaribe & Aerocozumel (☎ 884-20-00), Avenida Cobá 5, Plaza América (downtown)

Aeroméxico (☎ 884-10-97), Avenida Cobá 80, just west of Avenida Bonampak (downtown)

American Airlines (☎ 886-01-63, 800-904-60-00), airport counter

Aviacsa (☎ 887-42-11, fax 884-65-99), Avenida Cobá 37 (downtown)

Aviateca (☎ 884-39-28), airport counter

Continental (☎ 886-00-40, 800-900-50-00, fax 886-00-07), airport counter

Magnicharters (☎ 884-06-00), Avenida Náder 93 (downtown)

Mexicana (☎ 881-90-90 downtown, 24-hr toll-free ☎ 800-502-20-00), Avenida Cobá 39 (downtown)

Northwest (☎ 886-00-46, 800-225-25-25), airport counter

Bus Cancún's bus terminal occupies the wedge formed where Avenidas Uxmal and Tulum meet. Services are 2nd-class, 1st-class and any of several luxury flavors. Across Pino from the bus terminal, a few doors from Avenida Tulum, is the ticket office and miniterminal of Playa Express, which runs shuttle buses down the Caribbean coast to Tulum and Felipe Carrillo Puerto at least every 30 minutes until early evening, stopping at major towns and points of interest along the way; Riviera has instituted frequent, more comfortable 1st-class service.

The staff at the ADO/Riviera information counter in the bus terminal are in touch with their routes and can tell you all about it.

Following are some of the major routes serviced daily:

Chetumal – 382km, 5½-6½ hours; many 1st-class (US$17) and 2nd-class (US$14.50)

Chichén Itzá – 205km, 3-4 hours; 1 1st-class Riviera (US$13) at 9am, hourly 2nd-class Oriente (US$7.50) 5am to 5pm

Felipe Carrillo Puerto – 230km, 3½-4 hours; 8 1st-class Riviera (US$10.50), hourly 2nd-class Mayab (US$9)

Mérida – 320km, 4-6 hours; 15 deluxe and 1st-class UNO, ADO GL and Super Expresso (US$20-25), hourly 2nd-class Oriente (US$12) 5am to 5pm

Mexico City – 1821km, 22-24 hours; 2 deluxe ADO GL to TAPO (US$107); 2 1st-class ADO to Terminal Norte, 3 to TAPO (US$81)

Playa del Carmen – 68km, 45 minutes to 1¼ hours; 1st-class Riviera (US$3.50) every 15 minutes 5am to midnight, 2nd-class Playa Express (US$3) every half hour until 4.30pm

Puerto Morelos – 36km, 40 minutes; Playa Express every 30 minutes until 4.30pm, numerous others (US$1.25-1.75)

Ticul – 395km, 6 hours; 6 2nd-class Mayab (US$16.50)

Tizimín – 212km, 3-4 hours; 9 2nd-class by Noreste and Mayab (US$7.25-7.75)

Tulum – 134km, 2-2½ hours; 7 1st-class Riviera (US$6), 2nd-class Playa Express (US$5) every 30 minutes, numerous others

Valladolid – 160km, 2-3 hours; 12 1st-class ADO (US$8.25), 18 2nd-class Oriente (US$6)

Villahermosa – 947km, 12 hours; 11 1st-class (US$43)

Car Alamo (☎ 886-01-33), Avis (☎ 886-02-21), Europcar (☎ 887-32-72), Hertz (☎ 886-01-50) and Thrifty (☎ 886-03-93), among others, have counters at the airport. You can often receive better rates if you reserve ahead of time, but it doesn't hurt to do some comparison shopping after arriving.

Be warned that highway 180D, the 238km toll road running part of the way between Cancún and Mérida, costs almost US$26 for the distance and has only two exits, at Valladolid (US$16.50) and Pisté (for Chichén Itzá, US$22).

Getting Around

To/From the Airport If you don't want to pay US$38 for a taxi ride into town, there are a few options. Comfortable shared vans charging US$9.25 leave from the curb in front of the international terminal about every 15 minutes, heading for the Zona Hotelera via Punta Nizuc. They head into town after the island, but it can take up to 45 minutes from the airport. If volume allows, however, they will separate passengers into downtown and Zona groups. To get downtown more directly and cheaply, exit the terminal and pass the parking lot to a smaller dirt lot between the Budget and Executive car rental agencies. There is a ticket booth there for buses (US$4.50 in pesos, US$5 in dollars) that leave the lot every 20 minutes or so between 5.30am and midnight. They travel up Avenida Tulum, one of their most central stops being across from the Chedraui supermarket on Avenida Cobá (confirm your stop with the driver as there are two Chedrauis in town).

If you follow the access road out of the airport and past the traffic-monitoring booth (a total of about 300m), you can often flag down a taxi leaving the airport empty that will take you for much less than US$38 (try for US$4) because the driver is no longer subject to the expensive regulated airport fares.

To get to the airport you can catch the airport bus on Avenida Tulum just south of Avenida Cobá, outside the Es 3 Café, or a colectivo taxi from the stand in the parking area a few doors south. These operate between 6am and 9pm, charge US$3.25 per person and leave when full. The official rate for private taxis from town is US$14.50.

Riviera runs 11 express 1st-class buses from the airport to Playa del Carmen between 7am and 7.30pm (45 minutes to 1 hour, US$7.25). Tickets are sold at a counter in the international section of the airport.

Bus To reach the Zona Hotelera from downtown, catch any bus with 'R1,' 'Hoteles' or 'Zona Hotelera' displayed on the windshield as it travels south along Avenida Tulum or east along Avenida Cobá. The fare each way is US$0.60.

To reach Puerto Juárez and the Isla Mujeres ferries, catch a Ruta 13 ('Pto Juárez' or 'Punta Sam', US$0.40) bus at the stop in front of Cinemas Tulum (next to McDonald's), on Avenida Tulum north of Avenida Uxmal.

Taxi Cancún's taxis do not have meters. There is a sign listing official fares on the northeast outside wall of the bus terminal; if you can't refer to it you'll probably have to haggle. From downtown to Punta Cancún is US$7.75, to Puerto Juárez US$2.75.

ISLA MUJERES
• pop 8500 ☎ 998
Isla Mujeres (Island of Women) has a reputation as a backpackers' Cancún – a quieter island where many of the same amenities and attractions cost a lot less. That's not as true today – Cancún makes itself felt each morning as boatloads of package tourists arrive for a day's excursion. But Isla Mujeres continues to offer good values, a popular sunbathing beach and plenty of dive and snorkel sites. Though its character has changed, the island's chief attributes are still a relaxed tropical social life and waters that are turquoise blue and bathtub warm.

History
Although many locals believe Isla Mujeres got its name because Spanish buccaneers kept their lovers there while they plundered galleons and pillaged ports, a less romantic but still intriguing explanation is probably more accurate. In 1517 Francisco Hernández de Córdoba sailed from Cuba to procure slaves for the mines there. His expedition came upon Isla Mujeres, and in the course of searching it the conquistadors located a stone temple containing clay figurines of Mayan goddesses. Córdoba named the island after the icons.

Today some archaeologists believe that the island was a stopover for the Maya en route to worship their goddess of fertility, Ixchel, on the island of Cozumel. The clay idols are thought to represent the goddess.

Orientation
The island is 8km long, 300m to 800m wide and 11km off the coast. The town of Isla Mujeres is at the island's northern tip, and the ruins of the Mayan temple are at the southern tip. The two are linked by Avenida Rueda Medina, a loop road that hugs the coast. Between them are a handful of small fishing villages, several saltwater lakes, a string of westward-facing beaches, a large lagoon and a small airport.

THE YUCATÁN PENINSULA

ISLA MUJERES

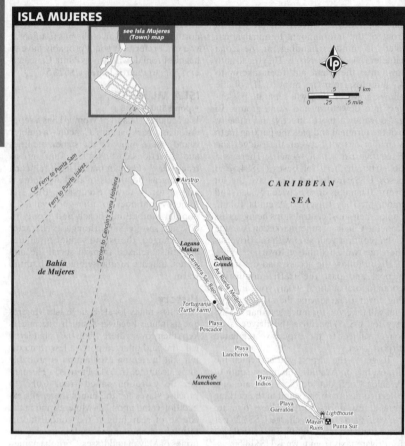

The best snorkeling sites and some of the best swimming beaches are on the island's southwest shore; the eastern shore is washed by the open sea, and the surf there is dangerous. The ferry docks, the town and the most popular sand beach (Playa Norte) are at the northern tip of the island.

Information

Tourist & Immigration Offices The tourist information office (☎ 877-07-67) is on Avenida Rueda Medina between Madero and Morelos. One member of its friendly staff speaks English; the rest speak Spanish only. It's usually open 8am to 8pm Monday to Friday, 9am to 2pm Saturday and Sunday. The immigration office is next door and usually open 8am to 5pm Monday to Friday, 8am to noon Saturday and Sunday.

Money Within a couple of blocks of the ferry docks lie several banks, including a Bital on Avenida Rueda Medina directly across from the Zona Hotelera ferry dock. Most exchange currency, have ATMs and are open 8.30am to 5pm Monday to Friday, 9am to 2pm Saturday.

Post & Communications The post office, on Guerrero at López Mateos, is open 9am to 4pm Monday to Friday. Telmex card phones are abundant. CompuIsla, on Abasolo just south of Juárez, provides Internet and email services from 8am to 10pm daily for US$0.55 for up to 10 minutes, and

US$1.50 an hour. Cosmic Cosas (see Bookstores) has five terminals and charges US$2.25 to US$3.25 (depending on time of day) for good Internet access. They also rent out a digital camera and allow you to email your photos or upload them straight to the Internet.

Bookstores Cosmic Cosas, at Matamoros 82, just north of Hidalgo, is a nifty store that buys, sells and trades mostly English-language books (largely novels, but also some travel guides, history and books on the Maya). The store has a comfortable living room where visitors are welcome to relax and play board games. The friendly owners enjoy offering tourist information as well. It's open 10.30am to 10.30pm daily.

Laundry Laundries in town will wash, dry and fold 4kg of clothes for US$3.50 to US$4.50. Among them are Lavandería Automática Tim Phó, on Juárez at Abasolo, and Lavandería JR, on Abasolo between Avenida Rueda Medina and Juárez. Lavandería Ángel, just off Hidalgo in Plaza Isla Mujeres, is the cheapest of the three unless you want colors washed separately. Most are open 7am to 9pm Monday to Saturday, 9am to 1pm Sunday.

Tortugranja (Turtle Farm)

Three species of sea turtle lay eggs in the sand along the island's calm western shore. Although they are endangered, sea turtles are still killed throughout Latin America for their eggs and meat, considered a delicacy. In the 1980s efforts by a local fisherman led to the founding of the **Isla Mujeres Turtle Farm** (☎ 877-05-95, Carretera Sac Bajo Km 5; admission US$2.25; open 9am-5pm daily), which protects the turtles' breeding grounds and places wire cages around their eggs to protect against predators. Hatchlings live in three large pools for up to a year, at which time they are tagged for monitoring and released. Because most turtles in the wild die within their first few months, the practice of guarding them until they are a year old greatly increases their chances of survival. Moreover, the turtles that leave this protected beach return each year, which means their offspring receive the same protection. The main draw here is several hundred sea turtles, ranging in weight from 150g to more

than 300kg. The farm also has a small but good quality aquarium, displays on marine life and a gift shop. Tours are available in Spanish and English. The facility is best reached by taxi (about US$2.50). If you're driving, bear right at the unsigned 'Y' south of town.

Mayan Ruins

At the south end of the island lie the severely worn remains of a temple dedicated chiefly to Ixchel, Mayan goddess of the moon and fertility. (The conquistadors found various clay female figures here; whether they were all likenesses of Ixchel or instead represented several goddesses is unclear.) In 1988 Hurricane Gilbert nearly finished the ruins off. Except for a still-distinguishable stairway and scattered remnants of stone buildings, there's little left to see other than the sea (a fine view) and, in the distance, Cancún. The ruins are beyond the lighthouse, just past Playa Garrafón (see Beaches). From downtown, a taxi costs about US$4.

Beaches

Walk west along Calle Hidalgo or Guerrero to reach the town's principal beach, **Playa Norte**, sometimes called Playa Los Cocos or Cocoteros. The slope of the beach is gradual, and the transparent and calm waters are only chest-high even far from shore. Playa Norte is well supplied with bar/restaurants and can get crowded at times.

South of town 5km is **Playa Lancheros**, the southernmost point served by local buses. The beach is less attractive than Playa Norte, but it sometimes has free musical festivities on Sunday. A taxi ride to Lancheros is US$1.85.

Another 1.5km south of Lancheros is **Playa Garrafón**, with translucent waters and colorful fish. Unfortunately the reef here has been heavily damaged by hurricanes and careless visitors. The water can be very choppy, sweeping you into jagged areas, so it's best to stay near shore. Avoid the over-hyped Parque Natural and visit instead the **Garrafón de Castilla Club** (☎ 877-01-07, Carretera Punta Sur Km 6; admission US$2.25; open 9am-5pm daily), which offers chairs, umbrellas, showers and baths with the entrance fee. Snorkeling gear is US$6.75 extra. It has an enclosed swimming area

ISLA MUJERES (TOWN)

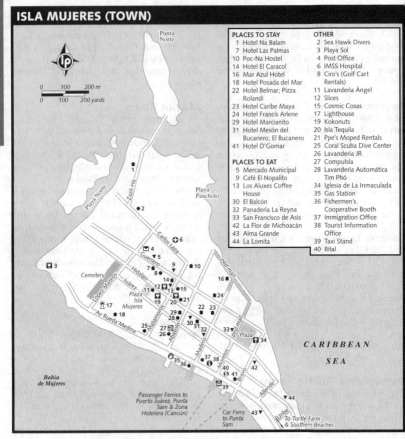

PLACES TO STAY
1 Hotel Na Balam
7 Hotel Las Palmas
10 Poc-Na Hostel
14 Hotel El Caracol
16 Mar Azul Hotel
18 Hotel Posada del Mar
22 Hotel Belmar; Pizza Rolandi
23 Hotel Caribe Maya
24 Hotel Francis Arlene
29 Hotel Marcianito
31 Hotel Mesón del Bucanero; El Bucanero
41 Hotel D'Gomar

PLACES TO EAT
5 Mercado Municipal
9 Café El Nopalito
13 Los Aluxes Coffee House
30 El Balcón
32 Panadería La Reyna
33 San Francisco de Asis
42 La Flor de Michoacán
43 Alma Grande
44 La Lomita

OTHER
2 Sea Hawk Divers
3 Playa Sol
4 Post Office
6 IMSS Hospital
8 Ciro's (Golf Cart Rentals)
11 Lavandería Ángel
12 Slices
15 Cosmic Cosas
17 Lighthouse
19 Kokonuts
20 Isla Tequila
21 Ppe's Moped Rentals
25 Coral Scuba Dive Center
26 Lavandería JR
27 CompuIsla
28 Lavandería Automática Tim Phó
34 Iglesia de La Inmaculada
35 Gas Station
36 Fishermen's Cooperative Booth
37 Immigration Office
38 Tourist Information Office
39 Taxi Stand
40 Bital

and a resident nurse shark, as well as a restaurant and snack bar, and rents lockers and towels. Taxis from town cost about US$3.75.

Diving & Snorkeling

Within a short boat ride of the island are a handful of lovely reef dives, such as Barracuda, La Bandera, El Jigueo and Manchones. A popular nonreef dive is the one to a cargo ship resting in 30m of water 90 minutes by boat northeast of Isla Mujeres. Known as **El Frío** (the Deep Freeze) because of the unusually cool water found there, the site contains the intact hull of a 60m-long cargo ship thought to have been deliberately sunk.

At all the reputable dive centers you need to show your certification card, and

you will be expected to have your own gear, though any piece of scuba equipment is usually available for rent. One relable shop is **Coral Scuba Dive Center** (☎ 877-07-63, fax 877-03-71, e coral@coralscubadivecenter.com, w www.coralscubadivecenter.com), at Matamoros & Avenida Rueda Medina. They offer dives for US$29 to US$98 and snorkel trips for US$14. Another reliable place is friendly **Sea Hawk Divers** (☎ 877-12-33, fax 877-02-96, e seahawkdivers@hotmail.com), on Carlos Lazo. They speak good English and offer dives for US$45 to US$55, as well as snorkeling tours from US$20.

The fisherfolk of Isla Mujeres have formed a cooperative that offers snorkeling tours of various sites from US$13.50, including the reef off Playa Garrafón (see Beaches, earlier), as well as day trips to Isla Contoy. You can book through their office at the foot of Madero, in a palapa steps away from the dock.

Places to Stay

Each hotel seems to have a different 'high season'; prices here are for mid-December through March, when you can expect many places to be booked solid by midday (earlier during Easter week). Some places offer substantially lower rates in off-season periods.

Budget *Poc-Na Hostel (☎/fax 877-00-90, 800-800-26-25,* e *pocna@soberanis.com.mx, cnr Matamoros & Carlos Lazo)* Campsites US$2.75 per person, dorm beds US$5.50, doubles US$11-22. The fan-cooled eight- and 14-bed dormitories accommodate men and women together; lockers are free (bring your own lock). Not the cleanest place in the past, the Poc-Na recently changed ownership and is undergoing renovations that should greatly improve the atmosphere and facilities.

Hotel Las Palmas (☎ 877-09-65, Guerrero 20) Doubles US$19. Across from the Mercado Municipal, this hotel offers basic but clean rooms with fan.

Hotel Caribe Maya (☎ 877-06-84, Madero 9) Doubles US$22/28 with fan/air-con. Rooms here, though a bit musty and with small baths, are a solid value.

Hotel El Caracol (☎ 877-01-50, fax 877-05-47, Matamoros between Hidalgo & Guerrero) Doubles US$28/37 with fan/air-con. This place offers 18 clean, well-furnished rooms with insect screens and tiled bathrooms; many have two double beds.

Hotel Marcianito (☎ 877-01-11, Abasolo 10) Rooms US$33-39. The 'Little Martian' is a neat, tidy hotel offering eight acceptable, fan-cooled rooms, each containing one double bed.

Mid-Range *Hotel D'Gomar (☎ 877-05-41, Avenida Rueda Medina between Morelos & Bravo)* Singles/doubles US$44/50, a view adds US$5.50. A friendly place facing the ferry dock, the D'Gomar has four floors of attractive, amply sized rooms with double beds, air-con and large baths.

Hotel Francis Arlene (☎/fax 877-03-10, e *hfrancis@prodigynet.mx, Guerrero 7)* Rooms US$50. This hotel offers good-sized, comfortable rooms with fan and fridge. Most have a king bed or two doubles, and many have balconies and sea views.

Mar Azul Hotel (☎ 877-01-20, Madero) Singles/doubles US$56/58. A block north of Guerrero right on the eastern beach, this hotel has a pool, restaurant and 91 nice, sizable rooms on three floors. All have balconies and most have wonderful sea views.

Hotel Belmar (☎ 877-04-30, fax 877-04-29, Hidalgo between Abasolo & Madero) Doubles with air-con US$56, suite with Jacuzzi US$95. Hotel Belmar is above the Pizza Rolandi restaurant and is run by the same friendly family. All rooms are comfy and well kept.

Hotel Mesón del Bucanero (☎ 877-01-26, 800-712-35-10, fax 877-02-10, e *bucaneros@ bucaneros.com,* w *www.bucaneros.com, Hidalgo between Abasolo & Madero)* Doubles US$32-67. Above El Bucanero restaurant, the charming rooms (most with air-con) all have TV and come with various combinations of beds, balcony, tub and fridge.

Top End All rooms in this category have air-con.

Hotel Posada del Mar (☎ 877-00-44, fax 877-02-66, e *hotelposada@posadadelmar .com,* w *www.posadadelmar.com, Avenida Rueda Medina between López Mateos & Matamoros)* Bungalow doubles US$80, rooms US$90. This is an agreeable newer place with 30 rooms (most with sea views) in a three-story building and 12 bungalows ringing a swimming pool.

Hotel Na Balam (☎ 877-02-79, fax 877-04-46, e *nabalam@cancun.rce.com.mx,* w *www.nabalam.com, Calle Zazil-Ha)* Rooms US$150. This place faces Playa Norte on the northern tip of the island. Most of the 31 spacious rooms (including beachfront bungalows) have fabulous sea views and numerous nice touches, and there's a pool.

Places to Eat

The remodeled *mercado municipal* (town market) has four open-air restaurants serving simple but tasty and filling meals at the best prices on the island.

San Francisco de Asís This supermarket, on the plaza, has a solid selection of groceries and snacks.

Panadería La Reyna (*cnr Madero & Juárez*) Closed Sun. This is the place for breakfast buns and snacks.

Los Aluxes Coffee House (*Matamoros between Guerrero & Hidalgo*) The friendly Aluxes serves bagels with cream cheese, croissants, muffins and espresso drinks, including excellent iced mocha.

Café El Nopalito (*Guerrero near Matamoros*) Breakfast US$2.75-4.50. Open 8am-1pm. This is an intimate cafe with beautifully painted tables and chairs. It specializes in healthful but fancy food and serves delicious breakfasts, as well as espresso, crêpes, sandwiches and ice cream.

La Lomita (*Juárez between Allende & Uribe*) Mains US$4-5.50. 'The Little Hill' serves good, inexpensive Mexican food. Seafood and chicken dishes predominate.

Alma Grande (*Avenida Rueda Medina between Allende & Uribe*) Mains US$5.50-7.75. The Alma is a tiny, colorfully painted shack dishing up cocktails of shrimp, conch and octopus, heaping plates of delicious ceviche, and seafood soups.

El Balcón (*Hidalgo just east of Abasolo*) Mains US$4.50-8. This is an airy, casual 2nd-floor eatery popular with tourists. El Balcón serves good fruit drinks, some veggie dishes and a large selection of seafood. Try the rich *camarones a la Reina* if you have friend who can help out.

El Bucanero (*Hidalgo between Abasolo & Madero*) Mains US$5.50-11. Below the Hotel Mesón del Bucanero, this fan-cooled, mostly outdoor restaurant has a pleasing ambiance and a variety of alcoholic and nonalcoholic tropical shakes and drinks. The best deal is the *menú ejecutivo*: for about US$7 you can choose either a fish, meat or veggie dish, accompanied by soup, beans, rice and coffee.

Pizza Rolandi (*Hidalgo between Abasolo & Madero*) Mains US$6-8, pizzas US$5.50-11. Below the Hotel Belmar, Rolandi bakes very good thin-crust pizzas and calzones in a wood-fired oven. The menu also includes pasta, fresh salads, fish, good coffee and some Italian specialties.

La Flor de Michoacán (*cnr Hidalgo & Bravo*) Head to this spot near the plaza for excellent milk shakes, fruit drinks and shaved ices.

Entertainment

Isla Mujeres is fairly sedate Sunday through Thursday. The current focal point for nightlife is Hidalgo. Two loud disco/bar/restaurants – *Slices* and *Kokonuts* – lie on opposite sides of the street, near the corner with Matamoros.

Isla Tequila (*cnr Hidalgo & Matamoros*) This is quieter than its neighbors. Some Tex-Mex food and snacks are available, but the emphasis is on reasonably priced beer and mixed drinks.

Playa Sol (*Playa Norte*) The Sol is a happening spot day and night, with volleyball, a soccer area and good food and drinks at decent prices. It's a great spot for watching the sunset, and in high season bands play reggae, salsa, merengue or other danceable music.

Hotel Na-Balam (*Calle Zazil-Ha*) The beach bar at the Na-Balam is a popular spot on weekend afternoons (every other week in off-season), with live music, dancing and a three-hour-long happy hour.

Getting There & Away

There are five main points of embarkation to reach Isla Mujeres. The following description starts from the northernmost port and progresses southeast. (See the Cancún map.) To reach Puerto Juárez or Punta Sam from downtown Cancún, catch a bus (US$0.40) displaying those destinations from in front of the Cinemas Tulum, on Avenida Tulum north of Avenida Uxmal.

Punta Sam Car ferries, which also take passengers, depart from Punta Sam, about 8km north of Cancún center, and take about an hour to reach the island. Departure times are 8am, 11am, 2.45pm, 5.30pm and 8.15pm from Punta Sam; from Isla Mujeres they are 6.30am, 9.30am, 12.45pm, 4.15pm and 7.15pm. Walk-ons and vehicle passengers pay US$1.75; cars cost US$19.50, vans US$24, motorcycles US$7.50 and bicycles US$6 (operator included in each fare). If you're taking a car in high season, it's good to get in line an hour or so before departure time. Tickets go on sale just before the ferry begins loading.

Puerto Juárez About 4km north of the Cancún city center is Puerto Juárez, from which express boats head to Isla Mujeres every 30 minutes from 6am to 8pm (25 minutes, US$4 one-way), with a final departure at 9pm. Slower boats (45 minutes, US$2 one-way) run roughly every hour from 5am to 5.30pm.

Playa Linda Terminal *The Shuttle* departs from Playa Linda in the Zona Hotelera approximately seven times between 9.30am and 4.15pm, returning from Isla Mujeres at 12.30pm, 3.30pm and 5.15pm. The roundtrip fare is US$15 and includes soft drinks on board. Show up at the terminal at least 20 minutes before departure so you'll have time to buy your ticket and get a good seat on the boat. It's the beige building between the Costa Real Hotel and the channel, on the mainland side of the bridge (Boulevard Kukulcán Km 4).

Playa Tortugas The *Náutica Shuttle* departs the Zona Hotelera from the dock near Fat Tuesday's on Playa Tortugas beach (Km 6.35) at 9.15am, 11.30am, 1.45pm and 3.45pm, returning from Isla Mujeres at 10.15am, 12.30pm, 3.30pm and 6.30pm. Fare is US$9 one-way.

Club Náutico Dock This dock shares a parking lot with the Xcaret bus terminal and is next to the Fiesta Americana Coral Beach. From here the *Watertaxi* leaves to Isla Mujeres at 9am, 11am and 1pm. Boats return to the Zona Hotelera at 10am, noon and 5pm. Fare for the 40-minute trip is US$9 one-way, US$15 roundtrip.

Getting Around

With all rented transportation it's best to deal directly with the shop supplying it. They're happier if they don't have to pay commissions to touts, and the chances for misunderstandings are fewer.

Bus & Taxi By local (and infrequent) bus from the market or dock, you can get within 1.5km of Playa Garrafón; the terminus is Playa Lancheros. The owners of Cosmic Cosas bookstore can give you an idea of the bus's erratic schedule. Unless you're pinching pennies, you'd be better off taking a taxi anyway – the most expensive one-way trip on the island is under US$4. Taxi rates are set by the municipal government and are posted at the ferry dock, though the sign is sometimes defaced.

Motorcycle If you rent a scooter or 50cc Honda 'moped,' shop around, compare prices and look for new or newer machines in good condition, with full gas tanks and reasonable deposits. Cost per hour is usually US$6 or US$7 with a two-hour minimum, US$28 all day. Shops away from the busiest streets tend to have better prices, but not necessarily better equipment. Ciro's, on Guerrero north of Matamoros, has fairly new scooters.

Bicycle Bicycles can be rented from a number of shops on the island for about US$2/6.50 an hour/day. Before you rent, compare prices and the condition of the bikes in a few shops, then arrive early in the day to get one of the better bikes. Most places ask for a deposit of about US$10.

Golf Cart Many people find golf carts a good way to get around the island, and caravans of them can be seen tooling down the roads. Ciro's, on Guerrero north of Matamoros, has a huge inventory of carts for US$14 an hour, US$44 for a 9am-to-5pm day. Ppe's Moped Rentals, on Hidalgo between Matamoros and Abasolo, also has carts, but no mopeds.

PARQUE NACIONAL ISLA CONTOY

From Isla Mujeres it's possible to take an excursion by boat to tiny, uninhabited Isla Contoy, a national park and bird sanctuary 25km north. Its dense foliage is home to more than 100 species, including brown pelicans, olive cormorants, turkey birds, brown boobies and red-pouched frigates, and it's subject to frequent visits by red flamingoes, snowy egrets and white herons.

There is good snorkeling both en route to and just off Contoy, which sees about 1500 visitors a month. Bring mosquito repellent.

Getting There & Away

At least two outfits on Isla Mujeres offer trips to Isla Contoy. Coral Scuba Dive Center (☎ 998-877-07-63, fax 877-03-71), on the corner of Matamoros and Avenida Rueda Medina, charges US$37 for a day trip that includes lunch and opportunities to snorkel and bird-watch. The fishermen's cooperative (☎ 998-877-05-00; see Diving & Snorkeling in the Isla Mujeres section) does daily trips for US$42 per person. The tours include a light breakfast, a lunch (including fish caught en route), stops for snorkeling (gear provided), scientific information on the island and your choice of purified water or soft drinks. Try to book on one of the faster boats; this will give more time for activities and less time on the hard seats. You can also book at your hotel.

ISLA HOLBOX
• pop 1600 ☎ 984

With its friendly fishing families and hammock-weaving cottage industry, Isla Holbox ('hol-BOSH') is a beach site not yet overwhelmed by gringos, though many foreigners (particularly Italians) are settling in and building guesthouses. The island is 25km long and 3km wide, with seemingly endless beaches, tranquil waters and a galaxy of shells in various shapes and colors. There are also red flamingoes and the occasional roseate spoonbill. The water is not the translucent turquoise common to Quintana Roo beach sites, because here the Caribbean waters mingle with those of the darker Gulf. During the rainy season there are clouds of mosquitoes; bring repellent and be prepared to stay inside for a couple of hours each evening.

The town of Holbox has sand streets and few vehicles. Everything is within walking distance of the central plaza ('el Parque'), and locals are happy to direct visitors.

Places to Stay & Eat
Development has arrived on Holbox, and cabañas are sprouting everywhere. The rates given here are for the high season.

Don Wach (☎ 875-20-88) Doubles US$5.50. This modest place is on the Parque (the sign outside reads 'Abarrotes Addy'). Rooms are rather dark and musty, but they have fans, private baths and a price that can't be beat.

A few other places in town charge around US$17, including *Pensión Ingrid*, *Posada Los Arcos* and *Posada La Raza*.

Posada Mawimbi (☎/fax 875-20-03) Doubles US$40/46 without/with kitchenette. The pleasant, two-story Mawimbi is one of several places just off the beach. Most rooms have a fan, balcony, comfortable beds and a hammock.

Villas Delfines (☎ 884-86-06, e uni terra@prodigy.net.mx, w www.holbox.com)

Doubles US$100. This charming place is an eco-tel that composts waste, catches rainwater and uses solar power. Its large beach bungalows are built on stilts, fully screened and fan-cooled. Very reasonable meal plans are also available.

Restaurant El Parque Mains US$4.50-7.25. This local restaurant has excellent fresh seafood, especially its delicious ceviches.

Getting There & Away
A launch ferries passengers (25 minutes, US$3.50) to Holbox from the port village of Chiquilá eight times a day from 5am to 6pm in winter, 6am to 7pm in summer. It is usually timed to meet arriving and departing buses. Two Mayab buses leave Cancún daily for Chiquilá (3½ hours, US$6) at 8am and 12.45pm. There are also Oriente buses from Valladolid (2½ hours, US$6). Another way to go is to take a 2nd-class bus traveling between Mérida and Cancún to El Ideal, on Highway 180 about 73km south of Chiquilá. From there you can take a cab (about US$23) or catch one of the Chiquilá-bound buses coming from Cancún, which pass through El Ideal around 10.30am and 3.30pm. All schedules are subject to change, so try to verify ahead of time.

If you're driving, you can either park your car in Chiquilá (US$2.25 a day) or try to catch the infrequent car ferry to Holbox. It doesn't run on a daily schedule, and you won't have much use for a car once you arrive.

PUERTO MORELOS
• pop 830 ☎ 998

Puerto Morelos, 33km south of Cancún, is a quiet fishing village known principally for its car ferry to Cozumel. It has some good hotels, and travelers who spend the night here find it refreshingly free of tourists. A handful of scuba divers come to explore the splendid stretch of barrier reef 600m offshore, reachable by boat.

Two kilometers south of the turnoff for Puerto Morelos is the **Jardín Botánico Dr Alfredo Barrera** *(admission US$3; open 9am-5pm Mon-Sat)*, with 3km of trails through several native habitats. The orchids, bromeliads and other flora are identified in English, Spanish and Latin. Buses may be hailed directly in front of the garden.

Places to Stay & Eat

Posada Amor (☎ 871-00-33, fax 871-01-78, e *pos_amor@hotmail.com*) Singles US$18.50/31 with shared/private bath, doubles US$37/43. The Amor is 100m southwest of the plaza and has been in operation for many years. It has plenty of plants, rooms are fan-cooled, and meals are available.

Hotel Hacienda Morelos (☎/fax 871-00-15) Doubles US$62/74 low/high season. On the waterfront, about 150m south of the plaza, the Morelos has appealing, breezy rooms with sea views, kitchenettes and fans (some rooms have air-con for the same price). There's also a pool and a good restaurant.

Rancho Libertad (☎/fax 871-01-81, e *rancholibertad@puertomorelos.com .mx*, w *www.rancholibertad.com*) Doubles downstairs/upstairs US$49/59 Apr-Dec, US$69/79 Jan-Mar; singles US$10 less, triples US$10 more. This mellow B&B, beyond the ferry terminal, is the best place in town and has 15 charming guestrooms in one- and two-story thatched bungalows. All rooms have private bath and good ventilation; some have air-con. There's a pleasing beach, and room rates include breakfast for two and use of bikes and snorkel gear (as available). The hotel is managed by a friendly multinational team; massage (and other bodywork) is available.

Caffè del Puerto, on the plaza, has baguettes, bagels, pasta, deli food and ice cream.

Lonchería Petita is north of the plaza, opposite the lighthouse. It's a very local place serving delicious whole fried fish for about US$4. Cheap lobster is sometimes available.

Johnny Cairo's Mains US$5-10. At Hotel Hacienda Morelos, this place serves very well prepared American and Mexican dishes.

Getting There & Away

Playa Express and Riviera buses traveling between Cancún and Playa del Carmen drop you on the highway. Some Mayab buses enter town.

The plaza is 2km from the highway. Taxis are usually waiting by the turnoff to shuttle people into town, and there's usually a taxi or two near the square to shuttle them back over to the highway. The official local rate is US$1.25 each way, for as many people as you can stuff in.

The *transbordador* (vehicle ferry, ☎ 871-06-14, 987-872-09-50 in Cozumel) to Cozumel leaves Puerto Morelos at 5am daily, with an additional departure Sunday and Monday at 2pm. Other days a second departure occurs sometime between 10am and 4pm. All times are subject to change according to season or the weather; during high seas, the ferry won't leave at all. Unless you plan to stay awhile on Cozumel, it's really not worth shipping your vehicle. You must get in line at least two hours before departure and hope there's enough space. The voyage takes anywhere from 2½ to four hours and costs US$81 per car (driver included), US$6.25 per person. Departure from Cozumel is from the dock in front of the Hotel Sol Caribe, south of town along the shore road.

PLAYA DEL CARMEN
• pop 18,000 ☎ 984

For decades Playa was a simple fishing village that foreigners passed through on their way to a ferry that would take them to Cozumel. But with the construction of Cancún, the number of travelers roaming this part of the Yucatán Peninsula increased dramatically, as did the number of hotels and restaurants serving them. Playa has overtaken Cozumel as the preferred resort town in the area; its beaches are better and nightlife groovier, and the reef diving is just as good. Many of the town's accommodations are owned and managed by Europeans, and several of its restaurants serve delicious European and Asian cuisine.

What's to do in Playa? Hang out. Swim. Dive. Shop. Eat. Drink. Walk the beach. Get some sun. Listen to beach bands. Dance in clubs. In the evening, Playa's pedestrian mall, Quinta Avenida (5th Avenue), is a popular place to stroll and dine, or drink and people-watch, or any combination of the above, though the number of restaurant and time-share touts can be dismaying at times.

Nudity is tolerated on at least three beaches north of the town center. Never leave valuables unattended, especially on isolated stretches of beach. Run-and-grab thefts while victims are swimming or sleeping is common.

THE YUCATÁN PENINSULA

PLAYA DEL CARMEN

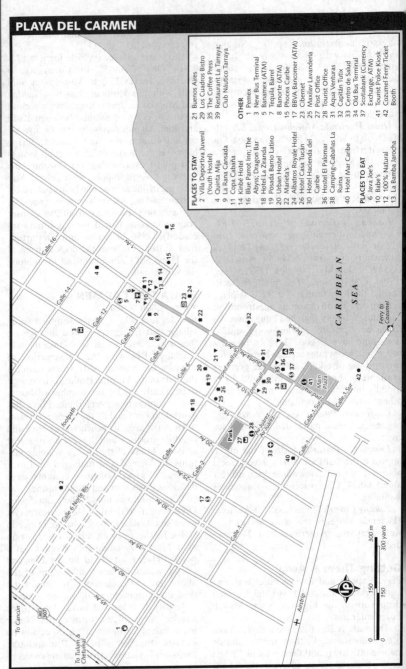

PLACES TO STAY
2 Villa Deportiva Juvenil (Youth Hostel)
4 Quinta Mija
9 La Rana Cansada
11 Copa Cabaña
14 Kinbé Hotel
16 Blue Parrot Inn; The Abyss; Dragon Bar
18 Hotel La Ziranda
19 Posada Barrio Latino
20 Urban Hostel
22 Marieta's
24 Albatros Royale Hotel
26 Hotel Casa Tucán
30 Hotel Hacienda del Caribe
36 Hostel El Palomar
38 Camping-Cabañas La Ruina
40 Hotel Mar Caribe

PLACES TO EAT
6 Java Joe's
10 Babe's
12 100% Natural
13 La Bamba Jarocha
21 Buenos Aires
29 Los Cuadros Bistro
35 The Coffee Press
39 Restaurant La Tarraya; Club Náutico Tarraya

OTHER
1 Pemex
3 New Bus Terminal
5 Banamex (ATM)
7 Tequila Barrel
8 Banorte (ATM)
15 Phocea Caribe
17 BBVA Bancomer (ATM)
23 Cibernet
25 Maxilav Lavandería
27 Post Office
28 Tourist Office
31 Aqua Venturas
32 Capitán Tutix
33 Centro de Salud
34 Old Bus Terminal
37 Scotiabank (Currency Exchange, ATM)
41 Tourist Police Kiosk
42 Cozumel Ferry Ticket Booth

CARIBBEAN SEA

Ferry to Cozumel

Main Plaza

To Cancún
MEX 307

To Tulum & Chetumal

Airstrip

300 m
300 yards

Orientation & Information

Playa is laid out on an easy grid. The pedestrian stretch of Quinta Avenida is the most happening street in town; the old bus terminal (serving most destinations on the Yucatán Peninsula) and main plaza are at the intersection of Quinta Avenida and Avenida Juárez. The tourist information office (☎ 873-28-04), Avenida Juárez at 15 Avenida, is open 9am to 9pm Monday to Saturday, 9am to 5pm Sunday. A tourist police kiosk (☎ 873-02-91) is in the plaza.

There's a Scotiabank with ATM and a currency-exchange counter across Quinta Avenida from the old bus terminal. Bancomer has a branch with ATM four blocks west on Avenida Juárez, and Banamex has one at the corner of Calle 12 and 10 Avenida.

For medical treatment, try the Centro de Salud on 15 Avenida near Avenida Juárez.

The post office is at the corner of 15 Avenida and Avenida Juárez, a couple blocks inland from the main plaza. Internet places bloom and wilt rapidly in Playa; you needn't walk far to find one. Air-conditioned Cibernet, on Calle 8 just east of Quinta Avenida, charges US$1.75 per hour for generally good connections.

The Coffee Press on Calle 2 at Quinta Avenida has a two-for-one book exchange.

Water Sports

Club Náutico Tarraya (☎ 873-20-40, fax 873-20-60, e gmillet@yuc1.telmex.net.mx, Avenida Juárez), at Restaurant La Tarraya, rents **kayaks** and offers several options for **diving**, **snorkeling** and **fishing**.

Other dive centers are:

The Abyss (☎ 873-21-64, e abyss@playadel carmen.com), foot of Calle 12, at the Blue Parrot Inn

Aqua Venturas (☎/fax 873-09-69, e aquaven@ prodigy.net.mx), Quinta Avenida between Calles 2 and 4

Phocea Caribe (☎ 873-12-10, fax 873-10-24, e phocea@prodigy.net.mx), 1 Avenida between Calles 10 & 12

Places to Stay

Playa del Carmen has been developing and changing rapidly for several years. You can expect new hotels by the time you arrive, as well as a number of changes in the existing ones. The room prices given below are for the busy winter tourist season (roughly January to March). Prices at many places can be up to 30% lower at most other times. Note that what many places call 'cabañas' are merely rooms in a thatched-roof building.

Budget *Villa Deportiva Juvenil* (☎/fax 873-15-08, Calle 8 at end of 35 Avenida) Bunk beds US$4.50, cabañas US$22. This hostel offers cheap clean lodging in single-sex, somewhat worn dorms with lockers. It's a trek to the beach, but there's table tennis, TV area and skateboard park.

Camping-Cabañas La Ruina (☎/fax 873-04-05, Calle 2) Tents & hammocks US$5.50 per person, doubles US$18-25 with shared bath, US$31-40 with private bath. You can pitch your tent or hang your hammock (they're available for rent) in a large lot near the beach. Some rooms have ceiling fans, some have air-con. The cheapest are bare, with no view.

Urban Hostel (☎ 879-93-42, e urban hostel@yahoo.com, 10 Avenida between Calles 4 & 6) Dorm beds US$10 with breakfast. No smoking. Guests have use of kitchen facilities, lockers, a lounge (with TV) and a safe-deposit box. The nearly new hostel is centrally located, quiet and a good place to meet other travelers, though the single-sex dorms are rather cramped.

Hostel El Palomar (☎ 878-03-16, e elpalomarhostel@myrealbox.com, Quinta Avenida between Avenida Juárez & Calle 2) Dorm beds US$11, doubles US$33, both with breakfast. No smoking. This recently opened hostel has 18-bed, single-sex dorms facing the sea. Modest doubles have balconies with hammock and sea view, and shared baths. A rooftop terrace has great views of the Caribbean.

Hotel Mar Caribe (☎ 873-02-07, cnr 15 Avenida at Calle 1) 1-bed/2-bed rooms US$28/39. This nine-room place is simple, secure and very clean. Rooms have fans, and the owners speak French, Spanish and some English.

Hotel Casa Tucán (☎/fax 873-02-83, e casatucan@playadelcarmen.com, Calle 4 between 10 & 15 Avenidas) Rooms US$31, 2-room apartment US$50. This German/ Texan-run hotel features 16 rooms (a couple with kitchenettes), four cabañas, an apartment and a swimming pool. Its restaurant, in a pleasant tropical garden, serves excellent, affordable breakfasts.

Hotel La Ziranda (☎ 876-24-76, e infoa@ hotelziranda.com, Calle 4 between 15 & 20 Avenidas) Rooms US$33-39. Constructed in late 2000, the Ziranda's two buildings have 15 nice rooms, all with balconies or terraces and two double beds or one king. The grounds are agreeably landscaped and the staff is friendly.

Posada Barrio Latino (☎/fax 873-23-84, e posadabarriolatino@yahoo.com, Calle 4 between 10 & 15 Avenidas) Rooms with fan/ air-con US$33/42. This hotel offers 16 clean, pleasant rooms with good ventilation, tiled floors, ceiling fans and hammocks (in addition to beds). The friendly Italian owners speak English and Spanish and maintain strict security. Other amenities include off-street parking, bicycles for rent and a free safe for valuables.

Marieta's (☎ 873-02-24, e marieta@ playa.com.mx, Quinta Avenida between Calles 6 & 8) Rooms US$33-65. Centrally located Marieta's has a variety of rooms, some with kitchenettes or balconies, all centered around a relaxing, leafy courtyard.

Copa Cabaña (☎ 873-0218, Quinta Avenida between Calles 10 & 12) Singles/ doubles with fan US$33/44, with air-con US$44/55. Copa Cabaña boasts 30 comfortable rooms and a lush courtyard with Jacuzzi.

Mid-Range *La Rana Cansada* (☎ 873-03-89, e ranacansada@playadelcarmen.com, Calle 10 between Quinta & 10 Avenidas) Doubles US$44-50. Recently built, tidy and peaceful, the Tired Frog's rooms, each with a hammock out front, are grouped around a great central garden and bar area. They have fans, while cheaper 'cabaña' rooms (US$33) don't.

Kinbé Hotel (☎ 873-04-41, fax 873-22-15, e hotelkinbe@prodigy.net.mx, Calle 10 near 1 Avenida) Rooms US$45-75. This Italian-owned and -operated hotel has 19 clean, modern rooms, all with air-con and fan.

Quinta Mija (☎/fax 873-01-11, e info@ quintamija.com, w www.quintamija.com, Quinta Avenida at Calle 14) Twins US$58, apartments with kitchenettes US$82. The Mija offers Internet access as well as a peaceful tropical courtyard with a pool and bar.

Top End *Hotel Hacienda del Caribe* (☎ 873-31-32, fax 873-11-49, w www.hacienda delcaribe.com, Calle 2 between Quinta &

10 Avenidas) Doubles US$77, suites US$95. The large, quiet, comfortable rooms here have lovely decor, air-con and cable TV. There's a small pool in the courtyard, and parking in a nearby lot is free while you stay.

Albatros Royale Hotel (☎ 873-00-01, 800-538-6802 in the USA, fax 873-00-02, Calle 8) Doubles with fan/air-con US$81/94. This hotel next to the beach has 37 lovely rooms, all with fridge and hammock.

Blue Parrot Inn (☎ 873-00-83, 888-854-4498 in the USA, fax 873-00-49, w www .blueparrot.com, Calle 12) Rooms/bungalows/villas US$73/135/157. This is the place most people wish they were staying when they wander up the beach and discover it. Many of its charming rooms have terraces or sea views, and there are also a number of beachside bungalows and villas. The inn's beachfront bar has swing chairs and the occasional live band.

Places to Eat
As in other tourist-oriented places on the Yucatán Peninsula, many Playa restaurants add a service charge to the bill.

Java Joe's (Quinta Avenida between Calles 10 & 12) Head here to feed the caffeine monkey some great coffee drinks.

The Coffee Press (Calle 2) Breakfast US$2.50-3.75, lunch mains US$3. This is another place for a caffeine fix, with a selection of gourmet coffees and teas. The breakfasts are excellent, and there's café food in the afternoon as well as a book exchange.

Restaurant La Tarraya (Calle 2) This eatery at the beach is one of the few in town that dates from the 1960s. It continues to offer good food (including breakfast) at decent prices, including guacamole for US$2.25, fried fish for US$9.50 per kg and *pulpo* (octopus) for US$3.50.

100% Natural (cnr Quinta Avenida & Calle 10) Mains US$3.50-9. Yes, it's a franchise, but the trademark fruit and vegetable juice blends, salads, chicken dishes and other healthy foods are delicious and filling, the green courtyard is inviting, and service is excellent.

Babe's (Calle 10 between Quinta & 10 Avenidas) Mains US$4.75-8.75. Babe's serves fabulous Thai food, including a perfectly spiced, home-style *tom ka gai* (chicken and coconut-milk soup) brimming with veggies.

Also recommended are the Vietnamese salad (with shrimp and mango), and smoked salmon wasabi noodles (both US$4.75).

Buenos Aires *(Quinta Avenida between Calles 4 & 6)* Mains US$6-12. This grill is tucked away down an alley behind two mediocre restaurants. It's famous for its steaks, ribs, burgers and other meaty items, made only with Angus beef.

La Bamba Jarocha *(Calle 10 between Quinta & 1 Avenidas)* Mains US$6.75-10. La Bamba is a good choice for seafood and Mexican dishes, and the menu (if they haven't retranslated it yet) makes for fun reading.

Los Cuadros Bistro *(Calle 2 between Quinta & 10 Avenidas)* Mains US$7-10. Good French and Mexican dishes are on offer here, with daily specials.

Entertainment

Tequila Barrel *(Quinta Avenida between Calles 10 & 12)* This sparkling clean bar pours a huge selection of…tequilas.

Dragon Bar *(Calle 12 at the beach)* Admission free. The party's hearty at the Blue Parrot Inn's open-sided palapa bar, where bands often play.

Capitán Tutix *(Calle 4)* Admission free. A band playing reggae, rock, calypso or salsa starts up most nights at this restaurant near the beach.

Other music and party scenes can be found along Quinta Avenida most nights.

Getting There & Away

Bus Playa has two bus terminals. The new one, at 15 Avenida just east of Calle 12, is mainly for 1st-class buses serving destinations outside the Yucatán Peninsula, but it does have departures for Mérida and Valladolid. A taxi to the main plaza will run about US$1.25.

The old terminal, at the corner of Avenida Juárez and Quinta Avenida, has frequent peninsular service, both 1st- and 2nd-class. Buses to Cancún and its airport have a separate ticket counter, on the Avenida Juárez side of the terminal.

Cancún – 68km, 1 hour; 1st-class Riviera (US$3.50) every 10 minutes

Cancún International Airport – 64km, 45 minutes to 1 hour; 11 direct 1st-class Riviera (US$7.25) between 7am and 7.30pm

Chetumal – 315km, 5-5½ hours; 12 1st-class Riviera (US$14), 11 2nd-class Mayab (US$12)

Chichén Itzá – 272km, 3½ hours; 1 1st-class Riviera (US$15.50) at 7.30am

Cobá – 113km, 1½ hours; 1 1st-class Riviera (US$4.50) at 7.30am

Mérida – 385km, 5-8 hours; 10 1st-class Super Expresso (new terminal, US$20), 9 2nd-class Mayab (old terminal, US$17.50)

Palenque – 800km, 10 hours; 1 deluxe Maya de Oro (US$42), 1 1st-class Altos (US$33)

San Cristóbal de Las Casas – 990km, 16 hours; 1 deluxe Maya de Oro (US$53), 1 1st-class Occidental (US$45), 1 1st-class Altos (US$42), all from new terminal

Tulum – 63km, 1 hour; 11 1st-class Riviera (US$3.25), 11 2nd-class Mayab (US$3), Playa Express (US$2.75) every 15 minutes

Valladolid – 169km, 2½-3½ hours; 1 1st-class Riviera (US$10.50), 2 1st-class Super Expresso (from new terminal, US$10.50), 3 2nd-class Mayab (US$6.25)

Boat Ferries to Cozumel run nearly every hour on the hour from 6am to 11pm (US$8 one-way). The open-air boat takes 45 minutes to an hour, while the air-conditioned catamaran leaving from the opposite side of the pier takes closer to half an hour (same ticket, same price, though it doesn't always stick to schedule).

COZUMEL

• pop 70,000 ☎ 987

Cozumel, 71km south of Cancún, is a teardrop-shaped coral island ringed by crystalline waters. It is Mexico's only Caribbean island and, measuring 53km by 14km, it is also the country's largest. Called Ah-Cuzamil-Peten (Island of Swallows) by its earliest inhabitants, Cozumel has been a favorite destination for divers since 1961, when a Jacques Cousteau documentary on its glorious reefs appeared on TV. Today, no fewer than 100 world-class dive sites have been identified within 5km of Cozumel, and no less than a dozen of them are shallow enough for snorkeling. But except for the diving and snorkeling, there's little reason to visit Cozumel.

History

Mayan settlement here dates from AD 300. During the Postclassic period, Cozumel flourished as a trade center and, more importantly, a ceremonial site. Every Maya woman on the Yucatán Peninsula and beyond was expected to make at least one pilgrimage here to pay tribute to Ixchel, the goddess of fertility and the moon, at a temple erected in her honor at San Gervasio, near the center of the island.

At the time of the first Spanish contact with Cozumel (in 1518, by Juan de Grijalva and his men), there were at least 32 Mayan building groups on the island. According to Spanish chronicler Diego de Landa, Cortés a year later sacked one of the Mayan centers but left the others intact, apparently satisfied with converting the island's population to Christianity. Smallpox introduced by the Spanish wiped out half the 8000 Maya, and of the survivors, only about 200 escaped genocidal attacks by conquistadors in the late 1540s.

The island remained virtually deserted into the late 17th century, its coves providing sanctuary for several notorious pirates, including Jean Lafitte and Henry Morgan. In 1848 Indians fleeing the War of the Castes began to resettle Cozumel. At the beginning of the 20th century the island's now mostly mestizo population grew, thanks to the craze for chewing gum. Cozumel was a port of call on the chicle export route, and locals harvested chicle on the island. After the demise of chicle Cozumel's economy remained strong owing to the construction of a US air base here during WWII.

When the US military departed, the island fell into an economic slump, and many of its people moved away. Those who stayed fished for a living until 1961, when Cousteau's

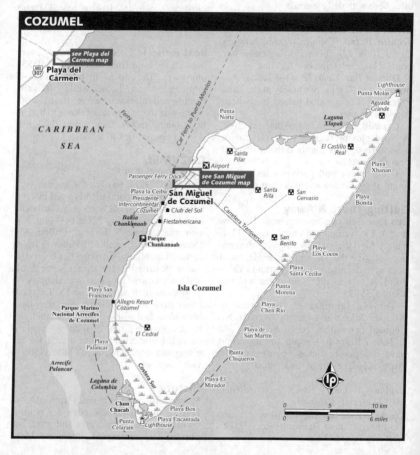

documentary broadcast Cozumel's glorious sea life to the world. The tourists began arriving almost overnight.

Orientation

It's easy to make your way on foot around the island's only town, **San Miguel de Cozumel**. The waterfront boulevard is Avenida Rafael Melgar; along Melgar south of the main ferry dock (the 'Muelle Fiscal') is a narrow sand beach. The main plaza is just opposite the ferry dock. Lockers are available for rent at the landward end of the Muelle Fiscal for US$2.25 per day, but they're not big enough for a full backpack. The airport is 2km north of town.

Information

Cozumel's tourist information office (☎ 872-75-63), open 9am to 3pm Monday to Friday, is hidden upstairs in the Plaza del Sol, a shopping area on the southeast side of the main plaza. It operates a branch at the foot of the ferry dock, open 8am to 4pm Monday to Saturday. The helpful tourist police patrol the island and staff a kiosk at the northeast edge of the plaza from 9am to 11.30pm daily.

Money For currency exchange, try any of the banks near the main plaza shown on the map. Many have ATMs and all are open 8am or 9am to 4.30pm Monday to Friday and on Saturday morning; Banca Serfin keeps longer hours.

The many casas de cambio around town may charge as much as 3.5% commission (versus the bank rate of 1%) to cash a traveler's check, but they keep longer hours. Most of the major hotels, restaurants and stores will also change money. Many establishments charge a percentage when accepting credit cards; always ask beforehand.

Post & Communications The post office is on Calle 7 Sur at Avenida Melgar. The Telecomm office next door handles faxes, money orders and such. Telmex card phones are abundant.

Most Internet places in town offer painfully slow access. Coffee Net's lightning-fast connections are worth the extra expense. Its air-conditioned facilities include a small branch at the foot of the ferry pier, where access costs US$0.10 per minute, and a large 2nd-floor branch in a courtyard off the north side of the main plaza, where access costs US$9 per hour with a US$3 (15-minute) minimum.

Bookstores The Gracia Agencia de Publicaciones, on the southeast corner of the plaza, sells English, French, German and Spanish books, and English and Spanish periodicals. Fama, a bookstore one block north along Avenida 5 Norte, carries books and periodicals in English and Spanish.

Laundry The large washers at Margarita Laundromat, on Avenida 20 Sur near Calle 3 Sur, cost US$1.75 per load (soap is US$0.50 extra); 10 minutes of dryer time is US$1.25. It's open daily.

Museo de la Isla de Cozumel

Exhibits at this fine museum *(Avenida Melgar between Calles 4 & 6 Nte; admission US$3; open 9am-6pm daily)* present a clear and detailed picture of the island's flora, fauna, geography, geology and ancient Mayan history. Thoughtful and detailed signs in English and Spanish accompany the exhibits. It's a good place to learn about coral before hitting the water, and it's one not to miss before you leave the island. Hours may vary seasonally.

Diving & Snorkeling

Cozumel is one of the most popular diving destinations in the world. Its diving conditions are unsurpassed for many reasons, chief among them the fantastic year-round visibility (50m and greater) and jaw-droppingly awesome variety of marine life.

There are scores of dive centers on Cozumel and dozens more in Playa del Carmen. Prices vary, but in general, expect to pay about US$70 for a two-tank dive (less if you bring your own BCD and regulator), US$60 for an introductory 'resort' course and US$350 for PADI open-water-diver certification. Multiple-dive packages and discounts for groups or those paying in cash can bring these rates down significantly. For more information, pick up a copy of Lonely Planet's Pisces *Diving & Snorkeling Cozumel*, with detailed descriptions of local dive sites and operators.

There are dozens of dive shops on Cozumel. Listed below are some reputable

SAN MIGUEL DE COZUMEL

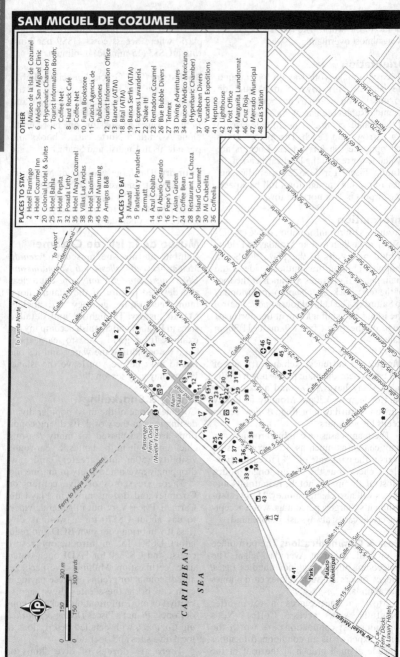

OTHER
1 Museo de la Isla de Cozumel
6 Medica San Miguel Clinic
  (Hyperbaric Chamber)
7 Tourist Information Booth;
  Coffee Net
8 Hard Rock Café
9 Coffee Net
10 Fama Bookstore
11 Gracia Agencia de
   Publicaciones
12 Tourist Information Office
13 Banorte (ATM)
18 Bital (ATM)
19 Banca Serfín (ATM)
21 Express Lavandería
22 Shake It!
23 Rentadora Cozumel
26 Blue Bubble Divers
27 Telmex
33 Diving Adventures
34 Buceo Médico Mexicano
   (Hyperbaric Chamber)
37 Caribbean Divers
40 Yucatech Expeditions
41 Neptuno
42 Lighthouse
43 Post Office
44 Margarita Laundromat
46 Cruz Roja
47 Mercado Municipal
48 Gas Station

PLACES TO STAY
2 Hotel Flamingo
4 Hotel Cozumel Inn
20 Colonial Hotel & Suites
25 Hotel Bahia
31 Hotel Pepita
32 Posada Letty
35 Hotel Maya Cozumel
38 Villas Las Anclas
39 Hotel Saolima
45 Hotel Marruang
49 Amigos B&B

PLACES TO EAT
3 Manati
5 Pastelería y Panadería
  Zermatt
14 Azul Cobalto
15 El Abuelo Gerardo
16 Pepe's Grill
17 Asian Garden
24 Coffee Bean
28 Restaurant La Choza
29 Island Gourmet
30 Mi Chabelita
36 Coffeelia

ones, all of which are in downtown San Miguel. Most of those listed also have facilities at hotels outside of town, and some offer snorkeling and deep-sea fishing trips as well as dives and diving instruction.

Blue Bubble Divers (☎/fax 872-18-65, ☎ 800-878-8853 in the USA), Calle 3 Sur 33; gear storage, rinse and delivery service as well as a variety of dive packages

Caribbean Divers (☎ 872-10-80, fax 872-14-26, e caridive@cozumel.com.mx, w www.cozumel-diving.net/caribbean_divers), Calle 3 Sur at Avenida 5 Sur

Diving Adventures (☎/fax 872-30-09, ☎ 888-338-0388 in the USA, e dive@divingadventures.net, w www.divingadventures.net), Calle 5 Sur between Avenidas Melgar and 5 Sur

Yucatech Expeditions (☎ 872-56-59, fax 872-14-17, e yucatech@prodigy.net.mx, w www.cozumel-diving.net/yucatech), Avenida 15 Sur between Rosado Salas and Calle 1 Sur; specializes in diving the region's caves and caverns

There are two hyperbaric chambers in San Miguel: Buceo Médico Mexicano (☎ 872-23-87, 872-14-30, fax 872-18-48), Calle 5 Sur between Avenidas Melgar and 5 Sur; and Cozumel Hyperbaric Research (☎ 872-01-030), Calle 6 Nte between Avenidas 5 and 10 Nte, in the Médica San Miguel clinic.

Snorkelers: All of the best sites are reached by boat. A half-day tour will cost US$30 to US$50, but you'll do some world-class snorkeling. If you want to be penny-wise and fish-foolish, you can save on the boat fare and walk into the gentle surf at Playa La Ceiba, Bahía Chankanaab, Playa San Francisco and elsewhere.

Touring the Island

In order to see most of the island you will have to rent a bicycle, moped or car, or take a taxi. The following route will take you south from San Miguel, then counterclockwise around the island. There are some places along the way to stop for food and drink, but all the same it's good to bring water.

Several signs along the west coast of the island offer horseback riding. The asking price is US$16.50 an hour; bargain hard.

Parque Chankanaab This park (*admission US$10; open 6am-6pm daily*) on the bay of

the same name is a very popular snorkeling spot, though there's not a lot to see in the water beyond brightly colored fish and some deliberately sunken artificial objects. The beach is a beauty, though, and 50m inland is a limestone lagoon surrounded by iguanas and inhabited by turtles. You're not allowed to swim or snorkel there, but it's picturesque nevertheless. The beach is lined with palapas and fiberglass lounge chairs, and you can rent snorkel and dive equipment or try out 'snuba' (diving with a helmet that requires no special training).

Dolphin and sea lion shows are included in the admission price. The grounds also hold a small archaeological park containing replica Olmec heads and Mayan artifacts, a small museum holding objects imported from Chichén Itzá, and a botanical garden with 400 species of tropical plants. Other facilities include a restaurant, bar and snack shops, as well as dressing rooms, lockers and showers (included in the admission fee). A taxi from town costs US$9 one-way.

Playa Palancar Palancar, about 17km south of town, is one of the island's nicest publicly accessible beaches. There's a *restaurant* at the beach. To scuba dive or snorkel at nearby Arrecife Palancar (Palancar Reef), you will have to sign on for a day cruise or charter a boat.

Punta Celarain The southern tip of the island has a picturesque lighthouse, accessible via a dirt track, 4km from the highway. To enjoy truly isolated beaches en route, climb over the sand dunes. There's a fine view of the island from the top of the lighthouse.

The East Coast The eastern shoreline is the wildest part of the island and highly recommended for beautiful seascapes. Unfortunately, except at Punta Chiqueros, Playa Chen Río and Punta Morena, swimming is dangerous on Cozumel's east coast because of riptides and undertows. There are a few small restaurants along the road serving seafood; most are expensive, but have great views of the sea.

Punta Molas Beyond where the east coast highway meets the Carretera Transversal, intrepid travelers may take a

THE YUCATÁN PENINSULA

poorly maintained, infrequently traveled road toward Punta Molas, the island's northeast point, accessible only by 4WD or on foot. About 17km down the road are the Mayan ruins known as El Castillo Real, and a few kilometers farther is Aguada Grande. Both sites are quite far gone, their significance lost to time. In the vicinity of Punta Molas are some fairly good beaches and a few more minor ruins. If you head down this road be aware of the risk: if your vehicle breaks down, you can't count on flagging down another motorist for help.

The best camping spot along the road is Playa Bonita. Playa Xhanan isn't nearly as pretty, and there are no sandy beaches north of it.

Places to Stay

All hotel rooms come with private bath and fan, unless otherwise noted. Prices in all categories are winter rates and may be much lower at other times of year. Whatever the season, if business is slow, most places are open to negotiation.

Budget Camping is prohibited along the coast within the Parque Marino Nacional Arrecifes de Cozumel. For camping north of the park, permits are available at the Oficina de Urbanismo y Ecología (☎ 872-51-95), downstairs in the Palacio Municipal on Calle 13 Sur just off Avenida Melgar; it's open 8am to 3pm Monday to Friday. You'll also need to go next door to the Seguridad Pública office to inform them of where you'll be camping (this is for your safety). The best spots are along the relatively un-populated eastern shore.

Hotel Saolima (☎ 872-08-86, *Rosado Salas 33*) Rooms US$22. The Saolima has simple, musty rooms opening onto a plant-filled patio strip. Upstairs room get more light.

Posada Letty (☎ 872-02-57, *cnr Avenida 15 Sur & Calle 1 Sur*) Singles/doubles US$25-28. Rooms here are no-frills.

Hotel Pepita (☎/fax 872-00-98, *Avenida 15 Sur between Calle 1 Sur & Rosado Salas*) Doubles/triples US$31/36. The friendly Pepita's rooms are well maintained and grouped around a garden. All have two double beds, insect screens, refrigerators and air-con, and there's free

morning coffee. This is one of the best deals in town.

Hotel Cozumel Inn (☎ 872-03-14, *fax 872-31-56, Calle 4 Nte between Avenidas Melgar & 5 Nte*) Doubles with fan/air-con US$31/37. This hotel has 30 decent rooms and a small, murky swimming pool.

Hotel Marruang (☎ 872-16-78, *Rosado Salas 440*) Rooms US$33. This hotel, entered from a passageway across from the municipal market, is simple and clean, if a bit overpriced in high season.

Mid-Range *Hotel Maya Cozumel* (☎/fax 872-00-11, *Calle 5 Sur between Avenidas Melgar & 5 Sur*) Singles/doubles/triples US$40/45/50. This hotel has rooms with air-con, fridge and TV. There's also an inviting pool surrounded by lawn and bougainvillea. It's a good value, though some of the downstairs rooms are musty.

Hotel Flamingo (☎ 872-12-64, e *flamingo@cozumel.com.mx, Calle 6 Nte between Avenidas 5 Nte & Melgar*) Doubles with fan/air-con US$55/83. The 22 rooms here are nothing out of the ordinary, but there's a leafy courtyard and a rooftop sundeck with good views.

Colonial Hotel & Suites (☎ 872-90-80, *800-227-2639, fax 872-90-73, e colonial@cozumel-hotels.net, w www.cozumel-hotels.net/colonial*) Studios/suites US$62/73, including breakfast. The Colonial is down a passageway off Avenida 5 Sur near Rosado Salas. It has studios and nice, spacious, one-bedroom suites (some sleep four people) with kitchenettes. All rooms have cable TV, fridge and air-con.

Hotel Bahía (☎ 872-90-80, *800-227-2639, fax 872-90-73, e bacocame@dicoz.com, cnr Avenida Melgar & Calle 3 Sur*) Rooms US$57/78. Some rooms have sea views at this hotel, and all have the same amenities as the Colonial (they're under the same management). Some suites are also available. The unmarked entrance is on Calle 3 Sur, just past the Pizza Hut.

Club del Sol (☎/fax 872-37-77, *fax 872-58-77, e clubdelsol@cozunet.finred.com.mx, Carretera a Chankanaab Km 6.8*) Doubles US$55-70. South of town and across the street from the water, this hotel has two restaurants and 28 spacious rooms with air-con and good beds; some have kitchenettes. Reserve directly for a 20% discount.

Amigo's B&B (☎ 872-38-68, fax 872-35-28, W www.bacalar.net, Calle 7 Sur between Avenidas 25 & 30 Sur) Doubles/triples US$65/70 with breakfast. It's worth the hike from the center to enjoy one of the three well-appointed, cottage-style rooms here. All have air-con and full kitchenettes, and there's a huge garden with fruit trees and an inviting pool. Book ahead.

Villas Las Anclas (☎ 872-61-03, fax 872-54-76, W www.lasanclas.com, Avenida 5 Sur between Calles 3 & 5 Sur) Suites US$95 with breakfast. Lovely, roomy two-story suites with air-con and kitchenettes are clustered around a leafy garden. The excellent breakfasts are served in your suite.

Top End Beginning several kilometers south of town are the big luxury resort hotels. See the Cozumel map for locations.

Presidente Intercontinental Cozumel (☎ 872-95-00, fax 872-13-61, e cozumel@interconti.com, W www.cozumel.interconti.com, Carretera a Chankanaab Km 6.5) Rooms US$350-420. There are 253 guestrooms here, many with sea views, set amid tropical gardens and swimming pools. Wild iguanas roam the grounds.

Fiesta Americana (☎ 872-26-22, 800-343-7821 in the USA, fax 872-26-66, W www.fiestamericana.com, Carretera a Chankanaab Km 7.5) Singles/doubles US$250/300. This dive resort has plenty of gardens, a spectacular swimming pool, 172 mostly ocean-view rooms (with balconies, safes and full minibars) and 56 'Tropical Casitas' behind the main building.

Allegro Resort Cozumel (☎ 872-34-43, 800-858-2258 in the USA, fax 872-45-08, W www.allegroresorts.com, Carretera a Chankanaab Km 16.5) Singles/doubles around US$215/320 all-inclusive. The Allegro has 300 rooms in two-story, Polynesian-style thatched-roof villas. There are three swimming pools, one with a swim-up bar, and hammocks all over. Rooms are smallish, but bathrooms are large and sparkling clean. There's a great private beach on the premises and a playground for kids with its own pool. Rates include three meals a day plus snacks, drinks (except imported alcohol) and activities (including attending shows, dancing, snorkeling and renting equipment).

Places to Eat

Budget Cheapest of all eating places, with tasty food, are the little market *loncherías* next to the Mercado Municipal on Rosado Salas between Avenidas 20 and 25 Sur. All offer soup and a main course for around US$3, with a large selection of dishes available; ask about cheap comidas corridas not listed on the menu.

Pastelería y Panadería Zermatt (cnr Avenida 5 Nte & Calle 4 Nte) Try this place for delicious baked goods.

Coffee Bean (Calle 3 Sur, just off Avenida Melgar) This joint serves the latest trendy java recipes.

Coffeelia (Calle 5 Sur between Avenidas Melgar & 5 Sur) Breakfasts US$3.25-5.50. Enjoy your breakfast or coffee in a relaxed atmosphere among fellow travelers.

Mi Chabelita (Avenida 10 Sur between Calle 1 Sur & Rosado Salas) Mains US$4-4.50. This is an inexpensive eatery serving up decent portions of decent food.

Mid-Range *Island Gourmet* (cnr Avenida 10 Sur & Rosado Salas) Mains US$4-11. This is a casual corner joint that whips up some excellent seafood. The coconut shrimp and delicious handmade pasta are the biggest sellers, but there are great deli sandwiches and other goodies as well.

El Abuelo Gerardo (Avenida 10 Nte between Avenida Juárez & Calle 2 Nte) Mains US$6-12. The menu here is extensive (mostly Mexican) and includes seafood. Guacamole and chips are on the house.

Restaurant La Choza (cnr Rosado Salas & Avenida 10 Sur) Entrées US$7.50-10. This is an excellent and popular restaurant specializing in authentic regional cuisine. All entrées include soup.

Manatí (☎ 872-51-69, cnr Calle 8 Nte & Avenida 10 Nte) Mains US$7.25-12.50. Manatí serves inventive cuisine in a good ambiance. There's usually a veggie dish on the menu, as well as pastas, chicken, meat and fish, plus espresso drinks. Phone ahead, as it's often closed.

Azul Cobalto (Avenida Juárez between Avenidas 5 & 10 Nte) Mains US$7.75-15.50. Good pizzas from a wood-fired oven and pleasing decor are the draws at this spot on pedestrian Avenida Juárez.

Asian Garden (Avenida 5 Sur between Calle 1 Sur & Rosado Salas) Mains around

US$7.75-19, lunch specials US$5.50. The Garden serves good rice plates and a wide variety of authentic Chinese seafood, veggie and meat dishes.

Top End *Pepe's Grill (Avenida Melgar, just south of Rosado Salas)* Mains US$20-25. This is Cozumel's traditional place to dine well and richly. It's mostly meat (steaks and prime rib), but there's also charcoal-broiled lobster (available at market price, typically around US$35).

Entertainment

Most of the year, Cozumel can't keep up with Playa del Carmen as a nightlife destination. But if you're here a couple of hours after sunset and looking for a happening scene, there are a few places to go.

Hard Rock Café (Avenida Melgar) Near the main ferry dock, the Hard Rock has live music most nights of the week. Go on, add another T-shirt to your collection!

Shake It! (cnr Avenida 10 Sur & Rosado Salas) Open Thur-Sun 10pm-4am. The band (reggae, rock or other dance music) starts around 11pm at this small, air-conditioned nightspot.

Neptuno (cnr Avenida Melgar & Calle 11 Sur) Open Thur-Sat nights. The only disco in town worth the title; it's huge.

Getting There & Away

Air There are some direct flights from the US, but European flights are usually routed via the US or Mexico City. Continental (☎ 872-04-87, 800-900-50-00, 800-523-3273 in the USA, ⓦ www.continental.com) has direct flights from Dallas and Houston, while Aeroméxico (☎ 800-021-40-10) flies to Atlanta Friday through Sunday. Mexicana (☎ 872-02-63) flies to Mexico City Thursday, Saturday, Sunday and Monday.

Aerocozumel (☎ 872-09-28), with offices at the airport, flies between Cancún and Cozumel (US$50).

Ferry Passenger ferries run from Playa del Carmen, and vehicle ferries run from Puerto Morelos. See those sections for details.

Getting Around

To/From the Airport The airport is about 2km north of town. You can take a minibus from the airport into town for about US$2 (slightly more to the hotels south of town), but you'll have to take a taxi (US$4.50 from town, US$9 from southern hotels) to return to the airport.

Taxi Fares in and around town are US$2 per ride; luggage may cost extra. There is no bus service.

Car Rates for rental cars usually run US$35 (for a beat-up VW Beetle) to US$55 per day, all inclusive though you'll pay more during late December and January. There are plenty of agencies around the main plaza. Rentadora Cozumel (☎ 872-11-20), on Avenida 10 Sur between Rosado Salas and Calle 1 Sur, rents cars, bicycles and scooters. If you rent, observe the law on vehicle occupancy. Usually only five people are allowed in a vehicle. If you carry more, the police will fine you.

Note that some agencies will deduct tire damage from your deposit, even if tires are old and worn. Be particularly careful about this if you're renting a 4WD for use on unpaved roads; straighten out the details before you sign.

There's a gas station on Avenida Juárez five blocks east of the main square.

Motorcycle Motorbikes are one way to tour the island on your own, and rental opportunities abound. The standard price is US$28 a day (US$20 in the off-season), but you may be able to haggle down to as little as US$15 per day, gas, insurance and tax included.

To rent, you must have a valid driver's license, and you must leave a credit card slip or put down a deposit (usually US$100). There is a helmet law and it is enforced (the fine for not wearing one is US$25), although most moped-rental people won't mention it. Before you sign a rental agreement, be sure to request a helmet.

The best time to rent is first thing in the morning, when all the machines are there. Choose one with a working horn, brakes, lights, starter, rearview mirrors and a full tank of fuel; remember that the price asked will be the same whether you rent the newest machine or the oldest rattletrap.

Bring a towel to toss on the bike's seat when parked – the black plastic can get blisteringly hot in the sun. Keep in mind that you're not the only one unfamiliar with the road here, and some of your fellow travelers may be hitting the bottle. Drive carefully.

Bicycle Bicycles typically rent for US$5.50 for 24 hours and can be a great way to get to Bahía Chankanaab and other spots on this flat island.

XCARET

Once a precious spot open to all, Xcaret (*'shkar-ET,'* ☎ 984-871-40-00; admission adult/child US$45/22; open 8.30am-10pm daily), about 10km south of Playa del Carmen, is now a heavily Disneyfied 'ecopark.' There are still Mayan ruins and a beautiful inlet on the site, but much of the rest has been created or altered using dynamite, jackhammers and other terraforming techniques. The park offers a cenote and 'underground river' for swimming, a restaurant, an evening show of 'ancient Mayan ceremonies' worthy of Las Vegas, a butterfly pavilion, a botanical garden and nursery, orchid and mushroom farms and a wild-bird breeding area.

Package tourists from Cancún fill the place every day, happily paying the admission fee (children under five get in free), plus additional fees for many of the attractions and activities, such as swimming with captive dolphins.

PAAMUL

Paamul, 87km south of Cancún, is a de facto private beach on a sheltered bay. Like many other spots along the Caribbean coast, it has signs prohibiting entry to nonguests, and parking is limited.

The attractions here are the beach and the great diving. The sandy beach is fringed with palms, but it holds many small rocks, shells and spiked sea urchins in the shallows offshore, so take appropriate measures. The large RV park here is a favorite with snowbirds; the 'BC' license plates you see here are from British Columbia, not Baja California. There is also an attractive alabaster sand beach about 2km north.

Scuba-Mex (☎/fax 984-873-06-67, **w** www .scubamex.com) offers diving trips to any of 30 superb sites for a reasonable price and has dive packages and certification courses.

Paamul Hotel (☎/fax 984-875-10-51, **e** paamulmx@yahoo.com) Campsites US$8 per double, recreational vehicle sites US$18, cabaña doubles US$70. This place has beachfront cabañas consisting of spacious, if worn, duplexes. Each cabaña has two beds, a ceiling fan and a private bathroom with hot water. Numerous spaces for recreational vehicles have full hookups.

Giant sea turtles come ashore here at night in July and August to lay their eggs. If you run across one during an evening stroll along the beach, keep a good distance away and don't shine a flashlight at it, as that will scare it off. Do your part to contribute to the survival of the turtles, which are endangered; let them lay their eggs in peace.

To reach Paamul by bus requires a 600m walk from the highway to the hotel and beach.

XPU-HÁ

'Shpoo-HA' is a beach area, about 95km south of Cancún, that extends for several kilometers. It's reached by numbered access roads (most of them private).

Hotel Villas del Caribe (☎/fax 984-873-21-94, cellular ☎ 984-876-99-45, **w** www .cafedelmarxpuha.com) Cabañas US$22, rooms US$45-53. At the end of X-4 (Xpu-Há access road 4), this laid-back place sits on a lovely stretch of beach whose northern reaches are nearly empty. All rooms have a terrace or balcony and are very clean and quiet, with fans and good beds. The owners between them speak Spanish, English, French, Italian, Hebrew, German and Dutch, and they do massage and physiotherapy and run an excellent restaurant on the premises.

AKUMAL

Famous for its beautiful beach, Akumal (Place of the Turtles) does indeed see some sea turtles come ashore to lay their eggs in the summer, although fewer and fewer arrive each year thanks to resort development. Akumal is one of the Yucatán Peninsula's oldest resort areas and consists primarily of pricey hotels and condominiums on nearly 5km of wide beach bordering four consecutive bays.

Activities

Although increasing population is taking a heavy toll on the reefs that parallel Akumal, diving remains the area's primary attraction. Dive trips and deep-sea fishing excursions are available from two shops: **Akumal Dive Shop** (☎ 984-875-90-32, fax 984-875-90-33, W www.akumal.com); and **Akumal Dive Center** (☎/fax 984-875-90-25, W www .akumaldivecenter.com).

Places to Stay & Eat

For the lowdown on most of the lodgings available in Akumal or to make a reservation, call ☎ 800-448-7137 in the USA. There are few rooms in Akumal under US$100 per day.

Villa Las Brisas (☎/fax 984-876-21-10, fax 984-875-90-31, ℮ villaslasbrisas@ hotmail.com) 1- & 2-bedroom condos US$73-185. On the beach in Aventuras Akumal (whose turnoff is 2.5km south of Playa Akumal's), this attractive, modern place has condos and a studio apartment – all under one roof. The owners speak English, Spanish, German, Italian and some Portuguese.

Hotel Club Akumal Caribe/Hotel Villas Maya (☎ 984-875-90-12, 800-351-1622 in the USA or Mexico, fax 915-581-6709 in the USA, ℮ clubakumal@aol.com, W www.hotelakumalcaribe.com) Bungalows from US$129. All rooms have air-con, and there's a pool. Meal plans start at US$28 per person per day.

Just outside the entrance of Akumal is a *grocery store* that stocks a good selection of inexpensive food. *Lol Ha* and *El Café del Pescador* are two restaurants within the complex.

CENOTE TOURS

On the west side of the highway south of Paamul are several cenotes (limestone sinkholes/caverns filled with water) you can visit (and usually swim in) for a price. A few kilometers south of Akumal is the turnoff for Cenote Dos Ojos, which provides access to the Nohoch Nah Chich cave system, the largest underwater cave system in the world. You can take guided snorkel and dive tours of some amazing underwater caverns, floating past illuminated stalactites and stalagmites in an eerie wonderland.

Hidden Worlds (☎ 984-877-85-35, ℮ info@hiddenworlds.com.mx, W www .hiddenworlds.com.mx) is an American-run outfit offering two- to three-hour snorkeling tours for US$25 to US$40, and one- and two-tank dive tours for US$50 and US$80, respectively. The snorkeling price includes flashlights, wet suit, equipment and transportation to the cenotes on a unique 'jungle mobile.' The drive through the jungle is a unique experience in itself, and the guides are very knowledgeable and informative. The diving tours are at 9am, 11am and 1pm daily; equipment rental costs extra. You don't need to make a reservation, but it never hurts to call.

These are cavern (as opposed to cave) dives and require only standard open-water certification. Don't try doing it on your own, however. Cavern diving without an experienced guide (preferably one with cave certification) can be just as deadly as cave diving.

TULUM
• pop 3800 ☎ 984

Tulum lies some 130km south of Cancún. Its main attractions are at water's edge: Mayan ruins, beautiful beaches and a profusion of cabañas for rent. The area's foreign population has been steadily increasing as new hotels and restaurants (many Italian-owned) open in town and at the beach.

Orientation & Information

Approaching from the north the first thing you reach is Tulum Crucero, the junction of highway 307 and the old access road to the ruins. The new access road is 400m farther south and leads another 600m to the ruins themselves. Another 1.5km south on the highway brings you to the Cobá junction; turning right (west) takes you to Cobá. The road to the left leads about 3km to the north-south road servicing the Zona Hotelera, the string of waterfront lodgings extending 10km south from the ruins. This road eventually enters the Reserva de la Biósfera Sian Ka'an, continuing some 50km past Boca Paila to Punta Allen.

The town, Tulum Pueblo, flanks the highway (called Avenida Tulum through town) south of the Cobá junction. It has Telmex pay phones, numerous currency-exchange booths and at least one bank with ATM. The Weary Traveler hostel (see Places to Stay & Eat) has several terminals with fast Internet access (US$0.07 per minute). John, the friendly operator, also offers travelers' information, free valuables storage (recommended if you're staying out at the beach cabañas), free incoming phone calls and faxes (up to two pages), a big two-for-one book exchange and coffee and juice drinks for sale. The hostel is open 24 hours.

Savana's also offers Internet access (at a similar price), along with copier, fax and telephone services and a book exchange. It's about four blocks north of the Weary Traveler, across the street.

Tulum Ruins

The ruins of Tulum *(admission US$4, free Sun; open 8am-5pm daily)*, though well preserved, would hardly merit rave reviews if it weren't for their setting. The grayish-tan buildings dominate a palm-fringed beach lapped by turquoise waters. Even on dark, stormy days, the majestic cliff-top ruins overlooking vast stretches of pristine beach look fit for the cover of a magazine. But don't come to Tulum expecting anything comparable to Chichén Itzá or Uxmal. The buildings here, decidedly Toltec in influence, were the product of a Mayan civilization in decline.

Tulum is a prime destination for tour buses. To best enjoy the ruins, visit them either early in the morning or late in the afternoon, when the tour groups aren't there. Parking costs US$2.75, and the optional shuttle to the site (about a seven-minute walk) is US$2.25 roundtrip.

History Most archaeologists believe that Tulum was occupied during the Late Postclassic period (AD 1200-1521) and that it was an important port town during its heyday. When Juan de Grijalva sailed past in 1518, he was amazed by the sight of this walled city, its buildings painted a gleaming red, blue and yellow and a ceremonial fire flaming atop its seaside watchtower.

The ramparts that surround three sides of Tulum (the fourth side being the sea) leave little question as to its strategic function as a fortress. Several meters thick and standing 3m to 5m high, the walls protected the city during a period of considerable strife between Mayan city-states. Not all of Tulum was situated within the walls. The vast majority of the city's residents lived outside

them; the civic-ceremonial buildings and palaces likely housed Tulum's ruling class.

The city was abandoned about 75 years after the Spanish conquest. It was one of the last ancient cities to be abandoned; most others had been given back to nature long before the arrival of the Spanish. Maya pilgrims continued to visit over the years, and Indian refugees from the War of the Castes took shelter here from time to time.

The name 'Tulum' is Mayan for 'wall,' though that was not how its residents knew it. They called it Zama, or 'Dawn.' 'Tulum' was apparently applied by explorers during the early 20th century.

The Site The two-story **Templo de Las Pinturas** was constructed in several stages around AD 1400-1450. Its decoration was among the most elaborate at Tulum and included relief masks and colored murals on an inner wall. The murals have been partially restored but are nearly impossible to make out. This monument might have been the last built by the Maya before the Spanish conquest, and with its columns, carvings, two-story construction and the stela out front, it's probably the most interesting structure at the site.

Overlooking the Caribbean is Tulum's tallest building, a watchtower appropriately named **El Castillo** (the Castle) by the Spaniards. Note the Toltec-style serpent columns at the temple's entrance, echoing those at Chichén Itzá.

The **Templo del Dios Descendente** (Temple of the Descending God) is named for the relief figure above the door – a diving figure, partly human, that may be related to the Maya's reverence for bees. This figure appears at several other east coast sites and at Cobá.

The restored **Templo de la Estela** (Temple of the Stela) is also known as the Temple of the Initial Series. Stela 1, now in the British Museum, was found here. The stela was inscribed with the Mayan date corresponding to AD 564 (the 'initial series' of Mayan hieroglyphs in an inscription gives its date). At first this confused archaeologists, who believed Tulum had been settled several hundred years later than this date. It's now believed that Stela 1 was brought to Tulum from Tankah, 4km to the north, a settlement dating from the Classic period.

TULUM RUINS

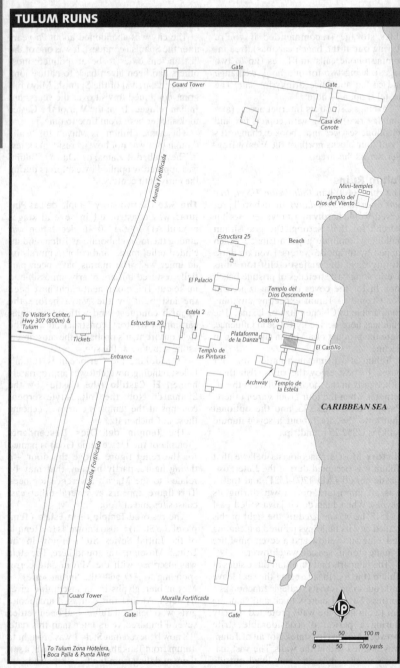

Gate

Guard Tower

Gate

Casa del
Cenote

Mini-temples

Templo del
Dios del Viento

Muralla fortificada

Estructura 25

Beach

El Palacio

Templo del
Dios Descendente

Oratorio

Estela 2

Estructura 20

Plataforma
de la Danza

El Castillo

To Visitor's Center,
Hwy 307 (800m) &
Tulum

Tickets

Templo de
las Pinturas

Archway

Templo de
la Estela

Entrance

CARIBBEAN SEA

Muralla Fortificada

Guard Tower

Muralla Fortificada

Gate

Gate

To Tulum Zona Hotelera,
Boca Paila & Punta Allen

0   50   100 m
0   50   100 yards

If you're anxious for a look at the sea, go through the corbeled arch to the right of the temple and turn left.

El Palacio (the Palace) features a beautiful stucco carving of a diving god over its main doorway.

The **Templo del Dios del Viento** (Temple of the Wind God) provides the best views of El Castillo juxtaposed with the sea below. It's a great place for snapping photos, though it can get pretty crowded.

Places to Stay & Eat

The following listings give high-season lodging rates. Off-season rates can be as much as 50% lower.

Tulum Pueblo Several hotels and restaurants have sprung up in town in recent years. They offer better accessibility and security than the seaside lodgings and are the logical place to stay if you're just passing through or only want to visit the ruins.

The Weary Traveler (☎ 871-24-61, ⓔ hostel@tulum.com, Avenida Tulum s/n) Bed in 4-bed room US$5.50 with breakfast and dinner. The Traveler is across the main street from the bus terminal and one block south. Each room has two bunk beds, one with single mattresses and one with double, and a fan, toilet, shower and sink. Guests can use the kitchen facilities to elaborate on the pancake breakfasts and rice-and-bean dinners. Other pluses are nightly video viewings, ready Internet access and a large hammock area. It's a great place to meet fellow travelers.

Kin-Ha Suites (☎/fax 871-23-21, ⓔ hotel kinha@tulum.cc, Orión between Sol & Venus) Doubles US$39/44 with fan/air-con. The Kin-Ha is about seven blocks northeast of the bus terminal. Pleasant rooms, each with a hammock out front, surround a small courtyard garden.

Don Cafeto (Avenida Tulum s/n) Breakfasts US$3.25-5.50, lunch & dinner mains US$7.25-11. Good breakfasts and Mexican food (including seafood dishes) make this a popular choice with diners.

L'Hotelito (Avenida Tulum s/n) The restaurant at this hotel, on the west side of the highway three blocks north of the bus terminal, serves good breakfasts, espresso drinks and great Italian food at reasonable prices.

Zona Hotelera Along the coastal road leading to Punta Allen (Carretera Tulum Ruinas – Boca Paila), which begins less than 1km south of the ruins, is a string of cabaña hotels. Many cater primarily to backpackers, and most have simple restaurants but no telephones. Of those places that have electricity, many shut it off at 9pm or 10pm.

The cheapest way to sleep here is to have your own hammock and mosquito net; if you don't, several of the inexpensive places rent them for about US$3.50 a night. In the cheapest places you'll have to supply your own towel and soap. Most places (even the expensive ones, though they have nets over beds) aren't well screened against bugs; bring repellent. See the boxed text for more tips on Tulum cabañas.

These places appear in the order you'd find them if you were to travel south from the ruins; not all establishments are listed. The first three are north of the intersection with the road to town, the rest are south of it.

Cabañas El Mirador (☎ 879-60-19) Tent & hammock sites, dorm cabañas all US$5.50, doubles with bed US$20. This place is closest to the ruins. It has 28 cabins (half with sand floors), most with beds (some with hammocks), but no fans or anything else. There's a beach out front and a decent restaurant (mains US$4.50 to US$7, more for seafood) above it. They'll store valuables.

Cabañas Magsal Cabañas US$11-31. This popular place (the late Don Armando's) is only a 10-minute walk from the ruins. It has a dive center, a restaurant/bar and a nice stretch of beach. Its driveway is marked mainly by a Corona beer sign. The cabaña's poles have been filled in with concrete, which makes them more secure but prevents ventilation. Rates vary depending on room features, such as lockable doors, hammocks and number of beds. Room lighting is by candles.

Cabañas Playa Condesa Cabañas US$17-44. Located 500m south of Magsal, Cabañas Playa Condesa has 18 comfortable cabañas (eight with private bath), each with a bed suspended by rope from the ceiling, mosquito netting, a concrete floor and slat-pole siding with good ventilation. There's a restaurant, and power runs till midnight. Cabañas have light (from solar power) all night.

Tips for Tulum's Cabañas

The waterfront cabañas south of the Tulum ruins are world famous among backpackers. The first four sit side by side within 1km of the ruins. Thereafter, they are mixed in with more expensive places and spread out over the next 9km. Here are a few tips to keep in mind if you intend to stay at one of them:

- Cabañas closest to the ruins are usually fully occupied by 10am or 11am every day from mid-December through March and in July and August. Arrive early, or make a reservation the night before.
- Taxis are recommended to cover the distance between the cabañas and the bus terminal or the bus stops at Tulum Crucero and the Zona Arqueológica.
- The cheapest cabañas are made of sticks and built on sand (some have concrete floors). Bring a mosquito net to hang over yourself at night.
- Few of the flimsy, primitive cabañas can be reliably secured. Thieves lift the poles in the walls to gain entrance, or burrow beneath through the sand, or jimmy the locks. At least one theft a month is reported. Never leave valuables unattended in a cabaña.
- Bring a pair of sandals or flip-flops. Most of the cabañas, even at the pricier places, have shared bathrooms. Shoes help you keep sand out of your bed and reduce the chance of catching athlete's foot.

Hotel Diamante K (☎ 871-23-76, W www .diamantek.com) Dorm beds US$11, rooms with/without bath from US$65/22. Lovely cabañas have suspended beds and a table for candles (the electricity goes off at 11.30pm). The Diamante K has a small beach and a fine restaurant/bar, and it often fills up even in the low season.

Papaya Playa (☎ 871-20-91, fax 871-20-92, e sertrapote@hotmail.com) Teepees & hammocks US$5.50, cabañas US$14.50/20 with sand/cement floor, rooms US$50. This popular place is just south of the road that links the coastal road and Tulum town, and its stretch of beach is fairly secluded. There are 13 small, bare cabañas and four big rooms with private bath, furniture and beds. All lodgings have ocean views, and electricity runs until 11pm. Food is available and there's a cozy bar, plus a free safe-deposit box. Reservations are recommended.

Cabañas Copal (☎ 871-24-81, ☎/fax 871-24-82, e info@cabanascopal.com, W www .cabanascopal.com) Bunk in 4-bed cabaña US$8/9 with/without hostel card; doubles US$30 with shared bath, US$40-50 with private bath; quads with private bath US$60. All cabañas here have mosquito nets, firm mattresses and good ventilation; price depends on location, beds and flooring.

Cabañas La Conchita (fax only 871-20-92, include 'attn La Conchita') Rooms US$105 with breakfast. About 5km south of the ruins, this family-run place has eight rooms. These are a major step up from those described thus far. Most have cool, concrete walls, standard windows with some degree of sea view and lockable doors (good security). The beach and landscaping here are lovely.

Restaurant y Cabañas Nohoch Tunich (☎ 871-22-71, fax 871-20-92) Cabañas US$44, rooms US$77. This place offers both tidy, appealing hotel rooms with porches and electricity (until 11pm), and handsome thatch-and-board cabañas with wooden floors, very near the beach.

Hotel Cabañas La Perla (☎/fax 871-23-82, e laperlatulum@hotmail.com) Cabañas US$22, 1-bed/2-bed rooms US$44/55. Friendly La Perla offers six rooms with private bath and two rustic cabañas. It has a restaurant/bar and shares a small beach with the neighboring hotels.

Zamas (☎ 415-387-9806 in the USA, fax 871-20-67, W www.zamas.com) Cabañas US$80/95 with garden/sea view. Just south of La Perla, Zamas' romantic cabañas all have terraces with two hammocks, 24-hour light, purified drinking water, big, private baths and two comfy beds with mosquito nets (you'll need 'em, as screens don't extend to the roof). The lovely restaurant overlooks the rocks, sea and beach (small at high tide) and serves good food (mains US$6.75 to US$11).

Maya Tulum (☎ *888-515-4580 in the USA,* ⓦ *www.mayatulum.com*) Cabañas with shared bath US$85, with private bath US$85-195. The focus is on meditation and spiritual growth at this place approximately 500m south of Zamas. There are five grades of cabañas, a gorgeous beach nearby, a yoga room (massages available also) and a vegetarian restaurant.

Getting There & Around
You can walk from Tulum Crucero to the ruins (800m). The cabañas begin about 600m south of the ruins and can be reached by taxi from Tulum Pueblo; fares are fixed and cheap. At the center of town you'll see the large sign of the Sindicato de Taxistas, on which the rates are posted. To the ruins it's US$2.75, to most of the cabañas US$5.

The bus terminal is toward the southern end of town (look for the two-story building with 'ADO' painted on it in huge letters). When leaving Tulum, you can also wait at Tulum Crucero for a Playa Express or regular intercity bus. Here are some distances, travel times and prices for buses leaving Tulum:

Cancún – 132km, 2 hours, US$5.25-6.25
Chetumal – 251km, 3½-4 hours, US$9.50-11.50
Chichén Itzá – 190km, 3 hours, US$7.25
Cobá – 45km, 45 minutes, US$2.25
Felipe Carrillo Puerto – 98km, 1¼ hours, US$4-4.75
Mérida – 320km, 7 hours, US$15
Playa del Carmen – 63km, 1 hour, US$3.25
Valladolid – 106km, 2 hours, US$4.25-4.75

If you're headed for Valladolid, be sure your bus is traveling the short route through Chemax, not via Cancún.

GRAND CENOTE
A little over 3km from Tulum on the road to Cobá is Grand Cenote, a worthwhile stop on your way between Tulum and the Cobá ruins, especially if it's a hot day. You can snorkel (US$4.50) among small fish in the caverns here if you bring your own gear.

COBÁ
Among the largest of Mayan cities, Cobá, 50km northwest of Tulum, offers the chance to explore mostly unrestored antiquities set deep in tropical jungle.

History
Cobá was settled earlier than Chichén Itzá or Tulum, and construction reached its peak between AD 800 and 1100. Archaeologists believe that this city once covered 50 sq km and held 40,000 Maya.

Cobá's architecture is a mystery; its towering pyramids and stelae resemble the architecture of Tikal, which is several hundred kilometers away, rather than the much nearer sites of Chichén Itzá and the northern Yucatán Peninsula.

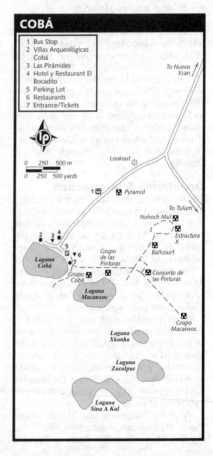

COBÁ

1 Bus Stop
2 Villas Arqueológicas Cobá
3 Las Pirámides
4 Hotel y Restaurant El Bocadito
5 Parking Lot
6 Restaurants
7 Entrance/Tickets

0   250   500 m
0   250   500 yards

To Nuevo Xcan
Lookout
1 🅿 Pyramid
To Tulum
Nohoch Mul
Estructura X
2 3 4
5
🅿 ▼6
●7
Grupo de las Pinturas
Ballcourt
Laguna Cobá
Grupo Cobá
Conjunto de las Pinturas
Laguna Macanxoc
Grupo Macanxoc
Laguna Xkanha
Laguna Zacalpuc
Laguna Sina A Kal

Some archaeologists theorize that an alliance with Tikal was made through marriage to facilitate trade between the Guatemalan and Yucatecan Maya. Stelae appear to depict female rulers from Tikal holding ceremonial bars and flaunting their power by standing on captives. These Tikal royal females, when married to Cobá's royalty, may have brought architects and artisans with them.

Archaeologists are also baffled by the extensive network of *sacbés* (stone-paved avenues) in this region, with Cobá as the hub. The longest runs nearly 100km from the base of Cobá's great pyramid Nohoch Mul to the Mayan settlement of Yaxuna. In all, some 40 sacbés passed through Cobá, parts of the huge astronomical 'time machine' that was evident in every Mayan city.

The first excavation was by the Austrian archaeologist Teobert Maler in 1891. There was little subsequent investigation until 1926, when the Carnegie Institute financed the first of two expeditions led by Sir J Eric S Thompson and Harry Pollock. After their 1930 expedition, not much happened until 1973, when the Mexican government began to finance excavation. Archaeologists now estimate that Cobá contains some 6500 structures, of which just a few have been excavated and restored, though work is ongoing.

Orientation & Information

The small village of Cobá, 2.5km west of the Tulum-Nuevo Xcan road, has a small cheap hotel and several small, simple and low-cost restaurants. At the lake, turn left for the ruins, right for the upscale Villas Arqueológicas Cobá hotel.

The **archaeological site** (*admission US$4 Mon-Sat, free Sun & holidays; open 7am-6pm daily*) has a parking lot charging US$1.25 per passenger car.

Be prepared to walk several kilometers on paths, depending on how much you want to see. Bring insect repellent and water; the shop next to the ticket booth sells both at reasonable prices, but there are no drinks stands within the site. Avoid the midday heat if possible. Most people spend around two hours at the site.

A short distance inside, at the Grupo Cobá, are bicycles renting at US$2.75 for the day. These are useful if you really want to get around the farther reaches, and the breeze they create is cooling. If the site is crowded it's probably best to walk.

You may want to buy a book on Cobá before coming. On-site signage and maps are minimal and cryptic. Guides near the entrance size you up and ask whatever they think you're worth, anywhere from US$8 to over US$66, depending on the length of the tour. They can be worth it, as they are up on the latest restoration work. At the time of research, the Nohoch Mul pyramid was the only structure the public was allowed to climb.

Grupo Cobá

Walking just under 100m along the main path from the entrance and turning right brings you to the **Templo de las Iglesias** (Temple of the Churches), the most prominent structure in the Cobá Group. It's an enormous pyramid, with views from the top of the Nohoch Mul pyramid and surrounding lakes (but climbing it is forbidden).

Back on the main path, you pass through the *juego de pelota* (ball court), 30m farther along. It's been restored quite well.

Grupo Macanxoc

About 500m beyond the juego de pelota, the path forks. Going straight gets you to the Grupo Macanxoc, a group of stelae that bore reliefs of royal women who are thought to have come from Tikal. They are badly eroded, and it's a 1km walk; the flora along the way is interesting, however.

Conjunto de las Pinturas

Though it's signed to the left at the fork, if you're on foot you can reach the Conjunto de las Pinturas (Group of Paintings) by heading toward the Grupo Macanxoc a very short distance and turning left. The temple here bears traces of glyphs and frescoes above its door and remnants of richly colored plaster inside.

You approach the temple from the southeast. Leave by the trail at the northwest (opposite the temple steps) to see several stelae. The first of these is 20m along beneath a palapa. Here, a regal figure stands over two others, one of them kneeling with his hands bound behind him.

Sacrificial captives lie beneath the feet of a ruler at the base. Continue along the path past another badly weathered stela and a small temple to rejoin the Nohoch Mul path and turn right.

Nohoch Mul

A walk of 800m more brings you to Nohoch Mul (Big Mound), also known as the Great Pyramid, built on a natural hill. Along the way is another ball court, at whose north end lie weathered stelae; the track then bends between piles of stones – a ruined temple – before passing Templo 10 and Stela 20. The exquisitely carved stela bears a picture of a ruler standing imperiously over two captives. Eighty meters beyond stands the Great Pyramid.

At 42m high, the Great Pyramid is the tallest Mayan structure on the Yucatán Peninsula. There are two diving gods carved over the doorway of the temple at the top (built in the Postclassic period, AD 1100-1450), similar to the sculptures at Tulum. The view is spectacular.

From Nohoch Mul, it's a 1.4km, half-hour walk back to the site entrance.

Places to Stay & Eat

There's no organized campsite, but you can try finding a place along the shore of the lake, which is inhabited by crocodiles (local children can show you a safe swimming spot).

Hotel y Restaurant El Bocadito (no ☎) Singles/doubles US$6.75/9. Meals US$7.25. The hotel has very simple, fan-cooled rooms with private bath. The restaurant is very well run and serves a great *menú* (set meal). They'll store luggage while you visit the ruins. El Bocadito also serves as Cobá's bus terminal and colectivo taxi terminus.

Villas Arqueológicas Cobá (☎/fax 998-874-20-87, ☎ 800-258-2633 in the USA) Singles/doubles/triples US$66/75/86. This Club Med hotel next to the lake has a swimming pool and mediocre restaurant to complement the air-conditioned rooms. It's a nice place to relax and the best value among the Villas Arqueológicas on the Yucatán Peninsula.

Restaurant Las Pirámides Mains US$5.50. A few doors down from the Club Med, this restaurant has good lake views and friendly service.

Pyramid Scheme

Every year people lose their footing on the steps of ancient pyramids in Mexico and tumble to their deaths. You should always wear snug footwear with good traction (or go barefoot) when you climb.

Give this sure-fire technique a try: zigzag up the steps, making diagonal passes to either side of the stairway. This is an especially useful method if your feet are too large for the shallow steps. It works well on the descent, also, as it prevents you from looking straight down (a view that can be quite vertiginous and unnerving). Use the entire width of the stairway, and to keep your stride smooth, try to ascend or descend a stair with each step you take if you feel comfortable doing so.

Once you master this style, you'll never descend again using the embarrassing sit-and-bump-down-on-your-butt method.

There are several small restaurants by the site parking lot, including **Restaurant El Faisán** and **Restaurant El Caracol**, both of which serve inexpensive meals.

Getting There & Away

There are four buses daily between Tulum and Cobá (US$2.25 to US$2.50); one of them serves Playa del Carmen as well (1½ hours, US$4.50). Combis between Cobá and Tulum charge US$4.75 per person. There is also bus service to Valladolid (1½ hours, US$2.25), Chichén Itzá (2 hours, US$5.25) and Mérida (3½ hours, US$11).

A more comfortable but expensive way to reach Cobá is by taxi from Tulum Crucero. Find some other travelers interested in the trip and split the cost, about US$50 roundtrip, including two hours at the site.

The 31km road from Cobá to Chemax is arrow-straight and in good shape. If you're driving to Valladolid or Chichén Itzá this is the way to go.

TULUM TO PUNTA ALLEN

Punta Allen is at the end of a narrow spit of land that stretches south nearly 40km from its start below Tulum. There are some charming beaches along the way, with plenty of privacy, and most of the spit is within the protected, wildlife-rich Reserva de la Biósfera Sian Ka'an.

A van makes the trip from the taxi cooperative in the middle of Tulum Pueblo to Punta Allen once a day, around 11.30am, taking 1½ to 2½ hours and charging tourists US$11. Motorists: no fuel is available on the route, and the road can be a real muffler-buster between gradings, especially when holes are filled with water from recent rains, making it impossible to gauge their depth. The southern half, south of the bridge, is the worst stretch.

Reserva de la Biósfera Sian Ka'an

Over 5000 sq km of tropical jungle, marsh, mangroves and islands on Quintana Roo's coast have been set aside by the Mexican government as a large biosphere reserve. In 1987 the United Nations appointed it a World Heritage Site – an irreplaceable natural treasure.

Sian Ka'an (Where the Sky Begins) is home to howler monkeys, anteaters, foxes, ocelots, pumas, crocodiles, eagles, raccoons, tapirs, peccaries, giant land crabs, jaguars and hundreds of bird species, including *chocolateras* (roseate spoonbills) and some flamingoes. There are no hiking trails through the reserve; it's best explored with a professional guide.

Three Punta Allen locals with training in English, natural history, interpretation and birding conduct bird-watching, snorkeling and nature tours, mostly by boat, for about US$110 for five to six people: Baltazar Madera (☎ 984-879-82-34 in Tulum), Marcos Nery (reachable through the local telephone office, ☎ 984-871-24-24) and Chary Salazar (inquire in town). The latter two are experts on endemic and migratory bird species, and Chary also does walking tours when she's around.

Punta Allen

Although it suffered considerable damage from the ferocious winds of Hurricane Gilbert in 1988, Punta Allen still sports a laid-back ambiance reminiscent of the Belizean cayes. There's also a healthy reef 400m from shore that offers snorkelers and divers wonderful sights. Between the reef and the beach there's lots of sea grass; that's a turnoff to a lot of people, but it provides food and shelter for numerous critters and is one of the reasons the snorkeling and diving are so good.

The area is known primarily for its bone-fishing, and for that many people come a long way. The guides listed above, as well as cooperatives in town, do fishing trips for about US$200, including lunch.

Places to Stay & Eat *Tres Marías* (no ☎) Doubles US$25. This is a set of simple cabañas in the middle of town, locally run.

Posada Sirena (☎ 984-878-77-95, fax 984-871-20-92, e savanna_tulum@hotmail.com, w www.casasirena.com) Doubles US$30-40. Fully furnished cabañas here have kitchens and hot-water showers.

Sol Caribe (☎ 984-874-18-58, e welcome@cancun.com) Doubles US$95 Dec-June, US$65 July-Nov. At Km 48 on the road from Tulum, this place has three lovely rooms (more in the works) with fans, lights, comfy beds, hammocks and big baths. It's on a long stretch of beautiful beach, very secluded and swimmable. The owners have a restaurant with bar and offer massage therapy. They'll do their best to stock your advance food requests. Breakfasts run up to US$7, lunches to US$11, and dinners are US$12-15.

Muelle Viejo Mains US$6.75-9. The Old Wharf is just off Punta Allen's sandy main square, near the old wharf. Its specialty is tasty fried fish (US$6.75); lobster goes for US$14.50.

FELIPE CARRILLO PUERTO
• pop 17,000 ☎ 983

Now named for a progressive governor of Yucatán, this crossroads town 95km south of Tulum was once known as Chan Santa Cruz, the rebel headquarters during the War of the Castes.

Carrillo Puerto offers the visitor little in the way of attractions, but it's a transit hub and the first town of consequence if you're arriving from the Mérida/Ticul/Uxmal area. There's a gas station on the highway and inexpensive air-conditioned accommodations. At the time of research no bank in town would change money or cash traveler's checks.

History

In 1849, when the War of the Castes turned against them, the Maya of the northern Yucatán Peninsula made their way to this town seeking refuge. Regrouping, they were ready to sally forth again in 1850 when a 'miracle' occurred. A wooden cross erected at a cenote on the western edge of the town began to 'talk,' telling the Maya they were the chosen people, exhorting them to continue the struggle against the whites, and promising victory. The talking was actually done by a ventriloquist who used sound chambers, but the people looked upon it as the authentic voice of their aspirations.

The oracular cross guided the Maya in battle for more than eight years, until their great victory conquering the fortress at Bacalar. For the latter part of the 19th century, the Maya in and around Chan Santa Cruz were virtually independent of governments in Mexico City and Mérida. In the 1920s a boom in the chicle market brought prosperity to the region, and the Maya decided to come to terms with Mexico City, which they did in 1929.

Some of the Maya, unwilling to give up the cult of the talking cross, left Chan Santa Cruz to take up residence at small villages

Time among the Maya

The history of the Talking Cross is not over. Every year on May 3, the Feast of the Holy Cross, Mayas gather in Felipe Carrillo Puerto – known to them as Noh Cah Santa Cruz Balam Na – to celebrate ancient Mayan traditions and specifically the Talking Cross, the last great symbol of Mayan independence.

Just a short drive inland from this city, Mayan villagers observe many aspects of traditional life, including use of the ancient Mayan calendar.

In the mid-1980s, English writer Ronald Wright came here in search of Mayas who still understood the Long Count and lived by the dictates of the *tzolkin*, the ancient Mayan almanac. Wright wrote about his experiences in a fascinating book, *Time among the Maya*, in 1989.

Wright found what he was seeking in X-Cacal Guardia and nearby villages, where descendants of the survivors of the 19th-century War of the Castes settled. Enveloped in the Yucatecan jungle, away from the centers of wealth and power, they guard their ancient crosses and religious beliefs while accepting innovations such as electric light, automobiles and Coca-Cola.

The 25m-long church at X-Cacal Guardia is guarded by men with rifles, its inner sanctum to be entered only by the Nohoch Tata (Great Father of the Holy Cross) himself. It may be that Chan Santa Cruz's famous Talking Cross, spirited away from the doomed city by the Mayas retreating from the last battle of the War of the Castes, has come to rest here. That is Ronald Wright's guess.

deep in the jungle, where they still revere the talking cross to this day. You may see some of them visiting the site where the cross spoke, especially on May 3, the day of the Holy Cross.

The **Santuario de la Cruz Parlante** (Sanctuary of the Talking Cross) is five blocks west of the gas station on highway 307. There isn't much to see there, and the town's residents do not like strangers in the sanctuary; they will try to take your camera if they see you using it there. More interesting and accessible is the **Casa de Cultura** on

THE YUCATÁN PENINSULA

the plaza, which has art exhibitions, work-shops, and the occasional exhibit on the War of the Castes. Be sure to check the mural outside.

Places to Stay & Eat

Hotel Esquivel (☎ 834-03-44, fax 834-03-13, ℮ hotelesquivelfcp@todito.com, Calle 65 No 746) Doubles US$13.50/16.50/22 bare/with fan & TV/with air-con & TV. The Esquivel is around the corner from the plaza and bus terminal.

El Faisán y El Venado (☎ 834-07-02, Avenida Juárez 7812) Doubles US$22. The 30 air-conditioned rooms of this hotel feature private bath, firm mattresses, TV and ceiling fans; there's also a good, inexpensive restaurant.

Restaurant 24 Horas This friendly restaurant is a few dozen meters south with food a bit cheaper than El Faisán's.

Getting There & Away

Most buses serving Carrillo Puerto are *de paso* (they don't originate there).

Cancún – 230km, 3½-4 hours; 8 1st-class (US$10.50), hourly 2nd-class (US$9)

Chetumal – 155km, 2-3 hours; 8 1st-class (US$7.25), 11 2nd-class (US$5.75)

Mérida – 310km, 5½ hours; 3 2nd-class (US$12)

Playa del Carmen – 159km, 2½ hours; 8 1st-class (US$7.50), 15 2nd-class (US$6.25)

Ticul – 200km, 4½ hours; 3 2nd-class (US$8.75); change there or at Muna for Uxmal

Tulum – 96km, 1¾ hours; 16 1st-class (US$4.75), 15 2nd-class (US$3.75)

Note that there are very few services such as hotels, restaurants or gas stations between Carrillo Puerto and Ticul, and there's no gas station between Carrillo Puerto and Chetumal.

XCALAK & COSTA MAYA

The coast south of the Reserva de la Biósfera Sian Ka'an to the small fishing village of Xcalak ('shka-LAK') is often referred to as the Costa Maya. Development of the area has been in fits and starts: Xcalak is now linked to highway 307 by a paved road, and the town of Mahahual to the north has a cruise-ship pier and airport, though ships have had much difficulty docking, and the airport sees little traffic. Realtors' advertise-ments and 'Land for Sale' signs are abundant on the coastal road, but Xcalak remains for the moment a relatively primitive part of Mexico. There are very few services, and most residents have electricity only six hours a day.

Xcalak's appeal lies in its quiet atmo-sphere, decaying Caribbean-style wooden homes, swaying palms and pretty beaches. Another draw is the little-explored **Reserva de la Biósfera Banco Chinchorro**, the largest coral atoll in the Northern Hemisphere, 40km northeast. In addition to its many natural beauties, the atoll is a wreck diver's paradise. So many vessels have collided with the ring of islands that parts of it re-semble a ship graveyard; many are easily snorkeled. The barrier reef is much closer and provides some very interesting diving and snorkeling opportunities.

Aventuras Xcalak to Chinchorro Dive Center (☎ 983-831-04-61, ℮ divextc@pocket mail.com, ⓦ www.xcalak.com.mx), south of the Hotel Tierra Maya, offers dive and snorkel trips to Banco Chinchorro and other dive spots, and rents equipment.

Places to Stay & Eat

Hotel Caracol (no ☎) Rooms US$11. This six-room hotel is the town's only cheap place to stay, offering decent rooms with fan and cold-water private bath. Electricity is available from 6pm to 10pm. Look for the owner, Sra Mauricia Garidio, next door to the hotel.

The following places are among a handful on the old coastal road leading north from town (most run by Americans or Canadians); rates given are the higher winter prices. All listed have purified drink-ing water, ceiling fans, 24-hour electricity (from solar or wind with generator backup), bikes and/or sea kayaks for guests' use, and private hot-water bathrooms. The snorkel-ing is good, and the first two have docks to swim off.

Hotel Tierra Maya (☎ 983-831-04-04, ☎ 800-480-4505 in the USA, ℮ fantasea@ xcalak.com, ⓦ www.tierramaya.net) Small/ large doubles US$73/84 with light buffet breakfast. This is a modern beachfront hotel 2km north of town. It features six lovely rooms (three quite large), each tastefully appointed and with many architectural details. Each of the rooms has mahogany furniture and a balcony facing the sea – the bigger rooms even have small refrigerators. Air-con is US$8 extra per night (available in some rooms). Mains at the pleasant restaurant (dinner only) are around US$10.50.

Casa Carolina (☎ 983-831-04-44, W www.casacarolina.net) Doubles US$84 with continental breakfast. Carolina is just up the road from the previous listing. Its four guestrooms have large balconies facing the sea, with hammocks. Each room has a kitchen with fridge, and the bathrooms try to outdo one another with their beautiful Talavera tile. All levels of scuba instruction (NAUI) are offered here, as well as recreational dives at the barrier reef.

Villas La Guacamaya (☎/fax 983-831-03-34, e villaslaguacamaya@yahoo.com) Doubles US$87. This place is 10km north of Xcalak. It has two rooms that face the sea and share use of a fully equipped gourmet kitchen. Each room has a double and a single bed. There's also a separate apartment with kitchen set back from the beach. One of the friendly owners is a family nurse practitioner and certified diving medical technician; she speaks English, Spanish and Portuguese.

Grocery trucks service the coast road, and there are a very few small restaurants near the center of Xcalak keeping sporadic hours. **Lonchería Silvia** is the most likely to be open, and it's good, they say. If you're lucky enough to catch the **Restaurant Bar Xcalak Caribe** open (it's about one block south of the wharf and just across the street from the beach), enjoy. Delicious fried fish is US$5, ceviche runs US$9, and a huge serving of lobster will set you back US$16.50.

Getting There & Around
From highway 307, take the signed turnoff for Mahahual. The turnoff is 68km south of Felipe Carrillo Puerto (1km south of Limones) and 46km north of Bacalar. About 55km east, a few kilometers before Mahahual, turn right (south) and follow the signs to Xcalak (another 60km).

Expect to be stopped at least once at a military checkpoint; they're only searching for contraband. The road passes through young mangroves and is frequented by diverse wildlife. Watch out for the usual herons and egrets, as well as jabirus, iguanas, javelinas (peccaries) and other critters.

Rickety Sociedad Cooperativa del Caribe buses depart Chetumal's main bus terminal for Xcalak (200km, 5 hours, US$5.50) daily at 5am and 3pm. From Felipe Carrillo Puerto catch a bus to Limones; from there buses to Xcalak (US$4.25) depart at around 6.30am and 4.30pm.

A taxi now works the town, serving the northern hotels for US$11 and hiring out for excursions to farther destinations.

LAGUNA BACALAR
A large, clear, turquoise freshwater lake with a bottom of gleaming white sand, Laguna Bacalar comes as a surprise in this region of tortured limestone and scrubby jungle.

The small, sleepy town of Bacalar, just east of the highway, 125km south of Felipe Carrillo Puerto, is the only settlement of any size on the lake. It's noted mostly for its old Spanish fortress and its popular *balneario* (swimming facility).

The fortress was built above the lagoon to protect citizens from raids by pirates and Indians. It served as an important outpost for the whites in the War of the Castes. In 1859 it was seized by Maya rebels, who held the fort until Quintana Roo was finally conquered by Mexican troops in 1901. Today, with formidable cannons still on its ramparts, the fortress remains an imposing sight. It houses a **museum** (admission US$0.60; open 10am-6pm Tues-Sun) exhibiting colonial armaments and uniforms from the 17th and 18th centuries.

A divided avenue runs between the fortress and the lakeshore north a few hundred meters to the balneario. There are some small restaurants along the avenue and near the balneario, which is very busy on weekends.

Costera Bacalar & Cenote Azul
The road that winds south along the lakeshore from Bacalar town to highway 307 at Cenote Azul is called the Costera Bacalar. It passes a few lodging and camping places along the way. Cenote Azul is a 90m-deep natural pool on the southwest shore of Laguna Bacalar, 200m east of highway 307. (If you're approaching from the north by bus, get the driver to let you off here.) There's a *restaurant* (meals US$6-9) overlooking the cenote.

Hotel Laguna (☎ *983-834-22-06, fax 983-834-22-05*) Doubles US$39. This place is 2km south of Bacalar town along the Costera, only 150m east of highway 307. Clean, cool and hospitable, it boasts a small swimming pool, a restaurant, bar and great views of the lake, directly below the hotel.

Los Coquitos Camping US$4.50 per person. Only 700m south of the Hotel Laguna along the Costera is this very nice camping area on the lakeshore. Water and soft drinks are sometimes for sale, but it's best to bring your own food and water; the nearest meals are at the Hotel Laguna's restaurant.

Getting There & Away

Coming from the north, have the bus drop you in Bacalar town, at the Hotel Laguna or at Cenote Azul, as you wish; check before you buy your ticket to see if the driver will stop.

Departures from Chetumal's minibus terminal on Primo de Verdad at Hidalgo to the town of Bacalar are about once an hour from 5am to 7pm (39km, 40 minutes, US$1.25); some northbound buses departing from the bus terminal will also drop you near the town of Bacalar (US$1.50).

Heading west out of Chetumal, take highway 307 north 25km to the turn on the right marked for the Cenote Azul and Costera Bacalar.

CHETUMAL

● pop 149,000 ☎ 983

Before the Spanish conquest, Chetumal was a Mayan port for shipping gold, feathers, cacao and copper to the northern Yucatán Peninsula. After the conquest, the town was not actually settled until 1898, when it was founded to put a stop to the illegal trade in arms and lumber carried on by the descendants of the War of the Castes rebels. Dubbed Payo Obispo, the town changed its name to Chetumal in 1936. In 1955, Hurricane Janet virtually obliterated it.

The rebuilt city is laid out on a grand plan with a grid of wide boulevards along which traffic speeds (be careful at stop signs).

Chetumal is the gateway to Belize. With the peso so low against the neighboring currency, Belizean shoppers come to Chetumal frequently.

Orientation & Information

Despite Chetumal's sprawling layout, the city center is easily manageable on foot, and it contains several hotels and restaurants.

A tourist information kiosk (☎ 832-36-63), on Avenida de los Héroes right in the center of town, is open 9am to 2pm and 6pm to 9pm Monday through Saturday.

The post office (☎ 832-00-57) is at the corner of Plutarco Elías Calles and 5 de Mayo. The immigration office (☎ 832-63-53) is on Avenida de los Héroes on the left about four blocks north of Avenida Insurgentes (and the bus terminal); it's open 9am to 11pm Monday to Friday for tourist-card extensions and such. There are several banks and ATMs around town, including a Bital ATM in the bus terminal. Cambalache, on Avenida de los Héroes between Elías Calles and Zaragoza, is a currency exchange.

Abra Internet, at the east end of Efraín Aguilar, provides decent Internet access for US$1.75 per hour. Universonet, at Lázaro Cárdenas 186, has good air-con and OK Internet connections for US$1.25 an hour.

Museo de la Cultura Maya

This museum (*Avenida de los Héroes between Colón & Avenida Gandhi; admission US$5.50, free Sun; open 9am-7pm Tues-Thur & Sun, 9am-8pm Fri-Sat*) is the city's claim to cultural fame – a bold showpiece designed to draw visitors from as far away as Cancún.

The museum is organized into three levels, mirroring Mayan cosmology. The main floor represents this world, the upper floor the heavens, and the lower floor the underworld. Though the museum is short on artifacts, the various exhibits (labeled in Spanish and English) cover all of the lands of the Maya and seek to explain their way of life, thought and belief. There are beautiful scale models of the great Mayan buildings as they may have appeared, replicas of stelae from Copán, Honduras, reproductions of the murals found in Room 1 at Bonampak and artifacts from sites around Quintana Roo. Among the most impressive exhibits: an ingenious device with crank and wheels that graphically illustrates the complex Mayan calendar, and an abacus-like counting machine that does the same for the Mayan numerical system.

CHETUMAL

PLACES TO STAY
1 Hotel Cristal
9 Hotel Ucum
12 Holiday Inn Chetumal Puerta Maya
19 Hotel Los Cocos
33 Hotel Mariá Dolores; Restaurant Sosilmar
35 Hotel Caribe Princess
36 Instituto Quintanaroense de la Juventud (Youth Hostel)

PLACES TO EAT
10 Restaurant Pantoja
21 Restaurant Vegetariano La Fuente
26 El Taquito de Don Julio
28 Café-Restaurant Los Milagros
32 Pollo Brujo
34 Sergio's Pizzas
39 Panadería y Pastelería La Invencible
42 Café Espresso

OTHER
2 Minibus Terminal
3 Public Library
4 ADO Bus Ticket Office
5 Combi Stand
6 Colectivos to Bus Terminal
7 Taxi Stand
8 Museo de la Cultura Maya
11 Clinica de Chetumal
13 Cruz Roja
14 Hospital Morelos
15 Abra Internet
16 Tourist Information Kiosk
17 Telmex

18 Banco Santander Mexicano
20 BBV Bancomer (ATM)
22 Banorte; BanCrecer (ATM)
23 Universo.net
24 Aviacsa
25 Post Office
27 Cambalache (Casa de Cambio)
29 BBV Bancomer (ATM)
30 Banamex
31 Banca Serfin (ATM)
37 Teatro Constituyentes
38 Pemex Station
40 Bital
41 Palacio de Gobierno

To Guatemalan Consulate

To Bus Terminal & Immigration Office

To Nuevo Mercado Lázaro Cárdenas (Buses to Belize)

Av Primo de Verdad

Cristóbal Colón

Av José María Morelos
Av Francisco I Madero
Av Independencia
Av Benito Juárez
Av Belice
Av de los Héroes

Av Mahatma Gandhi

To Belizean Consulate

Efraín Aguilar

Héroes de Chapultepec

Lázaro Cárdenas

Plutarco Elías Calles

To Airport, Hwy 186, Hwy 307, Belize, Escárcega & Cancún

Ignacio Zaragoza

Av Álvaro Obregón

Othón P Blanco

Carmen Ochoa de Merino

22 de Enero

Blvd Bahía

General Heriberto Lara
Felipe Carrillo Puerto
José María Luis Moya
Francisco Márquez
Eberto Frías

Calzada Veracruz

Juan Escuita

Juan de la Barrera

Augustin Melgar

Francisco Márquez

Fernando Montes

Calzada Tampico

Héroes de Chapultepec

Av 16 de Septiembre
Av Miguel Hidalgo

Mercado Ignacio Manuel Altamirano ped mall

Av de los Héroes
Av 5 de Mayo
Av 16 de Septiembre
Av Miguel Hidalgo
Av Reforma
Calzada Veracruz
Av Cozumel

Heroica Escuela Naval

Park

ped mall

Clock Tower

Blvd Bahía

Bahía Chetumal

ped mall

Park

LP

0   100   200 m
0   100   200 yards

P Parking Area

Unfortunately, displays are beginning to suffer from lack of maintenance.

The museum's courtyard (admission free) has salons for temporary exhibits of modern artists (such as Rufino Tamayo) and paintings reproducing Mayan frescoes. Just walk past the ticket window.

Places to Stay

Instituto Quintanarroense de la Juventud (☎ 832-05-25, fax 832-00-19, Heroica Escuela Naval) Dorm beds US$3.50. Off Calzada Veracruz just past the eastern end of Avenida Obregón, this hostel is the cheapest place in town. It has single-sex dorms (four bunks to a room) and serves three meals a day, each for under US$2.25. The doors lock at 11pm but you can arrange to be let in later.

Hotel María Dolores (☎ 832-05-08, Avenida Obregón 206) Singles/doubles US$13.50/15-16.50. This hotel, west of Avenida de los Héroes, is the best for the price. Beds are a bit saggy, but some of the fan-cooled rooms are good sized, and there's off-street parking.

Hotel Ucum (☎ 832-07-11, 832-61-86, Avenida Gandhi 167) Doubles with fan US$16.50-19, with air-con US$25. Hotel Ucum has lots of plain rooms around a bare central courtyard/parking lot; cheaper rooms have no TV. The hotel restaurant is inexpensive and good.

Hotel Cristal (☎ 832-38-78, Colón 207) Singles/doubles/triples with fan US$12.50/18/21, doubles/triples with air-con US$23/27. The interior of this hotel bears a striking resemblance to a prison cell block, but the rooms are clean and the air-con good.

Hotel Caribe Princess (☎/fax 832-09-00, Avenida Obregón 168) Singles/doubles/triples US$31/37/42. This quiet hotel is well run and nicely appointed. All rooms have air-con, phone and TV, and there's off-street parking.

Hotel Los Cocos (☎ 832-05-44, fax 832-09-20, e hotelcocos@correoweb.com, cnr Avenida de los Héroes & Calle Héroes de Chapultepec) Doubles with air-con & TV US$66. This hotel has a nice swimming pool, a guarded parking lot and a popular sidewalk restaurant. Rooms are good and have fridges.

Holiday Inn Chetumal Puerta Maya (☎ 835-04-00, fax 832-16-76, e hotel@

holidayinnmaya.com.mx, Avenida de los Héroes 171) Doubles US$104. This place is two blocks north of Los Cocos along Avenida de los Héroes, near the tourist information kiosk. Its comfortable rooms overlook a small courtyard with a swimming pool set amid tropical gardens; there's a restaurant and bar. This is the best in town.

Places to Eat

Across from the Holiday Inn and the tourist information kiosk is the *Mercado Ignacio Manuel Altamirano* and its row of small, simple eateries serving meals for US$2.25 to US$3.25. Similar is the upstairs area in the *Nuevo Mercado Lázaro Cárdenas*, on Calzada Veracruz.

Restaurant Sosilmar (Álvaro Obregón 206) Open Mon-Sat. Mains US$4.25-6.25. Beneath the Hotel María Dolores, this bright and simple restaurant serves filling platters of fish or meat.

Panadería y Pastelería La Invencible (Calle Carmen Ochoa de Merino) West of Avenida de los Héroes, this is a good pastry shop.

Pollo Brujo (Álvaro Obregón between Avenidas de los Héroes & Juárez) This restaurant is west of the Sosilmar. A roasted half chicken costs US$3.50; take it with you or dine in the air-conditioned salon.

Restaurant Vegetariano La Fuente (Lázaro Cárdenas 222) Meals US$4. Open Mon-Sat. La Fuente is a tidy meatless restaurant next to a homeopathic pharmacy.

Café-Restaurant Los Milagros (Calle Ignacio Zaragoza between Avenidas 5 de Mayo & de los Héroes) Breakfast US$2.75-4, mains US$3.50-5. This place serves espresso and meals indoors and outdoors. It's a favorite with Chetumal's student and intellectual set.

Restaurant Pantoja (cnr Avenida Gandhi & 16 de Septiembre) Mains US$2.75-5. The Pantoja is a family-run restaurant that opens early for breakfast and later provides enchiladas and other entrées.

Café Espresso (cnr 22 de Enero & Avenida Miguel Hidalgo) Breakfast US$2.50-4, mains US$6-9. Open for breakfast and dinner. Try this café facing the bay for your coffee fix. It has an upscale ambiance and a good selection of omelets and other breakfasts; the *huevos chetumaleños* (eggs, cheese, chaya – a spinach-like green – tomato and onion, US$2.75) are excellent. Dinner adds various cuts of meat to the menu.

El Taquito de Don Julio (Plutarco Elías Calles 220) In the airy, simple dining room, small tacos cost US$0.80 each, slightly more with cheese, and the daily comida corrida is US$4. The jukebox occasionally duels with the radio.

Sergio's Pizzas (Avenida Obregón 182) Pizza US$4.50-18, mains US$5.50-14.50. Air-conditioned Sergio's has pizzas and cold beer in frosted mugs, plus Mexican and continental dishes and an extensive wine list.

If you're busing into town, stock up at the **Supermercado San Francisco de Asís** just west of the bus terminal.

Getting There & Away
Air Chetumal's small airport is less than 2km northwest of the city center along Avenida Obregón. Mexicana's regional carrier Aerocaribe (☎/fax 832-63-36) flies direct from Chetumal to Cancún and Mérida with onward connections.

Aviacsa (☎ 832-77-65, 832-77-87 at the airport, fax 832-76-54, 832-76-98 at the airport) flies to Mexico City. Its in-town office is on Avenida Cárdenas at 5 de Mayo.

For flights to Belize City (and on to Tikal) or to Belize's cayes, cross the border into Belize and fly from Corozal.

Bus The bus terminal is about 2km north of the center near the intersection of Avenidas Insurgentes and Belice. ADO, Sur, Cristóbal Colón, Omnitur del Caribe, Maya de Oro, Mayab and Novelo's, among others, provide service. The terminal has lockers, a bus information kiosk, ATM, post office, international phone and fax services, an exchange counter, cafetería and shops. East of the terminal is a huge San Francisco de Asís department store.

You can also buy ADO tickets and get information about most bus services at the ADO office on Avenida Belice, just west of the Museo de la Cultura Maya.

Many local buses, and those bound for Belize, begin their runs from the Nuevo Mercado Lázaro Cárdenas, on Calzada Veracruz at Confederación Nacional Campesina (also called Segundo Circuito), about 10 blocks north of Avenida Primo de Verdad. From this market, some Belize-bound buses continue to the long-distance terminal and depart from there 15 minutes later. Tickets can be purchased at the market, on board the buses or at the main terminal.

The minibus terminal, at the corner of Avenidas Primo de Verdad and Hidalgo, has services to Bacalar and other nearby destinations. Departures listed below are from the main terminal unless otherwise noted.

Bacalar – 39km, 45 minutes; hourly minibuses (US$1.25) from the minibus terminal; many Mayab buses (US$1.75) departing from the main terminal

Belize City, Belize – 160km, 3-4 hours; 20 1st-class (US$6.75) and 2nd-class (US$5) Novelo's and Northern buses, departing from Nuevo Mercado between 4.30am and 6pm, some departing main terminal 15 minutes later

Campeche – 422km, 6½-9 hours; 1 1st-class ADO (US$19.50) at noon, 2 2nd-class (US$15.50)

Cancún – 382km, 5½-6½ hours; many 1st-class (US$17) and 2nd-class (US$14.50)

Corozal, Belize – 30km, 1 hour with border formalities; 2nd-class (US$2.25); see Belize City schedule

Escárcega – 273km, 4-6 hours; 11 buses between 7am and 9pm (US$10.50-12.50)

Felipe Carrillo Puerto – 155km, 2-3 hours; 8 1st-class (US$7.25), 11 2nd-class (US$5.75)

Flores, Guatemala (for Tikal) – 350km, 8 hours; 1st-class Servicio San Juan and Mundo Maya buses (US$36) at 7am, 8am, 3pm and 4pm

Mérida – 456km, 6-8 hours; 8 deluxe Omnitur del Caribe and Super Expresso (US$18.50), 3 2nd-class Mayab (US$15.50)

Orange Walk, Belize – 91km, 2¼ hours; 1st-class (US$3.50), 2nd-class (US$2.75); see Belize City listing, above

Playa del Carmen – 315km, 4½-6 hours; many buses (US$12-14.50)

Ticul – 352km, 6 hours; 6 buses (US$12.50)

Tulum – 251km, 3½-4 hours; many buses (US$9.25-11.50)

Valladolid – 357km, 6 hours; 2 2nd-class (US$11.50)

Veracruz – 1037km, 16 hours; 2 1st-class (US$49)

Villahermosa – 565km, 7-9 hours; 7 buses (US$22-26)

Xcalak – 200km, 5 hours; 2nd-class Sociedad Cooperativa del Caribe (US$5.50) at 6am and 3.15pm

Xpujil – 120km, 2-3 hours; 10 buses (US$4.75-5.75)

Getting Around
Taxis from the stand at the bus terminal charge US$1.25 to the center (agree on the

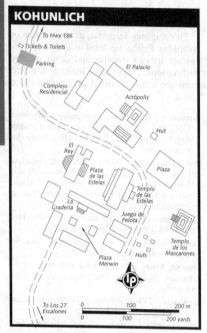

price before getting in; some will try to charge per person). You can try to avoid haggles by walking out of the terminal to the main road (Avenida Insurgentes), turning left (east), and walking a little over a block to the traffic circle at Avenida de los Héroes to hail a taxi. From here you can also catch the cheapest ride to the center (US$0.30), in an eastbound ('Santa María' or 'Calderitas') combi. The route will be circuitous. To reach the terminal from the center, head for the combi and taxi stands on Avenida Belice behind the Museo de la Cultura Maya. By combi, ask to be dropped off at the *glorieta* (traffic circle) at Avenida Insurgentes. Head left (west) to reach the terminal.

KOHUNLICH

The archaeological site of Kohunlich (*admission US$2.75 Mon-Sat, free Sun & holidays; open 8am-5pm daily*) is being aggressively excavated, though most of its nearly 200 mounds are still covered in vegetation. The surrounding jungle is thick, but the archaeological site itself has been cleared selectively and is now a delightful forest park. Drinks

are sometimes sold at the site. The toilets are usually locked and 'under repair.'

These ruins, dating from the Late Preclassic (AD 100-200) and the Early Classic (AD 250-600) periods, are famous for the great **Templo de los Mascarones** (Temple of the Masks), a pyramid-like structure with a central stairway flanked by huge, 3m-high stucco masks of the sun god. The thick lips and prominent features are reminiscent of Olmec sculpture. Of the eight original masks, only two are relatively intact following the ravages of archaeology looters.

The masks themselves are impressive, but the large thatch coverings that have been erected to protect them from further weathering obscure the view; you can see the masks only from close up. Try to imagine what the pyramid and its masks must have looked like in the old days as the Maya approached it across the sunken courtyard at the front.

A few hundred meters southwest of Plaza Merwin are the **27 Escalones** (27 Steps), the remains of an extensive residential area, with photogenic trees growing out of the steps themselves.

The hydraulic engineering used at the site was a great achievement; 90,000 of the site's 210,000 sq meters were cut to channel rainwater into Kohunlich's once enormous reservoir.

Getting There & Away

At the time of writing, there was no public transportation running directly to Kohunlich. To visit the ruins without your own vehicle, you need to start early, taking a bus to the village of Francisco Villa near the turnoff to the ruins, then either hitching or walking the 8.5km to the site.

Better still, take a taxi from Chetumal to the ruins, have the driver wait for you, and then return. Roundtrip taxi fare, with the wait, will cost about US$60 per party. Another means is to travel to Xpujil and book a tour from there. For US$30 per person you can visit Kohunlich and Dzibanché (see Xpujil in the Campeche State section, earlier).

To return by bus to Chetumal or head west to Xpujil or Escárcega you must hope to flag down a bus on the highway; not all buses will stop.

SOUTH TO BELIZE & GUATEMALA

Corozal, 18km south of the Mexico-Belize border, is a pleasant, sleepy, laid-back farming and fishing town and an appropriate introduction to Belize. It has several hotels and restaurants catering to a full range of budgets.

Buses run directly from Chetumal's market to Belize City via Corozal and Orange Walk; all connect with buses to Melchor de Mencos in Guatemala. From there continue onward to Flores, Tikal and points in Guatemala. There are also buses from Chetumal to Flores (Tikal is an hour beyond Flores). See the Chetumal Getting There & Away section for details.

Language

Pronunciation

Pronunciation of Spanish is not difficult, given that many Spanish sounds are similar to their English counterparts, and there is a clear and consistent relationship between pronunciation and spelling. Unless otherwise indicated, the English words used below to approximate Spanish sounds take standard American pronunciation.

Vowels Spanish has five vowels: a, e, i, o and u. They are pronounced something like the highlighted letters of the following English words:

a as in 'father'
e as in 'met'
i as in 'feet'
o as in the British 'hot'
u as in 'put'

Diphthongs A diphthong is one syllable made up of two vowels, each of which conserves its own sound. Here are some diphthongs in Spanish, and their approximate pronunciations:

ai as in 'hide'
au as in 'how'
ei as in 'hay'
ia as in 'yard'
ie as in 'yes'
oi as in 'boy'
ua as in 'wash'
ue as in 'well'

Consonants Many consonants are pronounced in much the same way as in English, but there are some exceptions:

c is pronounced like 's' in 'sit' when before 'e' or 'i'; elsewhere it is like 'k'
ch as in 'choose'
g as the 'g' in 'gate' before 'a,' 'o' and 'u'; before 'e' or 'i' it is a harsh, breathy sound like the 'h' in 'hit.' Note that when 'g' is followed by 'ue' or 'ui' the 'u' is silent, unless it has a dieresis (ü), in which case it functions much like the English 'w':
    guerra 'GEH-rra'
    güero 'GWEH-ro'
h always silent
j a harsh, guttural sound similar to the 'ch' in the Scottish 'loch'

ll as the 'y' in 'yard'
ñ nasal sound like the 'ny' in 'canyon'
q as the 'k' in 'kick'; always followed by a silent 'u'
r a very short rolled 'r'
rr a longer rolled 'r'
x like the English 'h' when it comes after 'e' or 'i,' otherwise it is like English 'x' as in 'taxi'; in many Indian words (particularly Mayan ones) 'x' is pronounced like English 'sh'
z the same as the English 's'; under no circumstances should 's' or 'z' be pronounced like English 'z' – that sound does not exist in Spanish

There are a few other minor pronunciation differences, but the longer you stay in Mexico, the easier they will become. The letter ñ is considered a separate letter of the alphabet and follows 'n' in alphabetically organized lists and books, such as dictionaries and phone books.

Stress There are three general rules regarding stress:

• For words ending in a vowel, 'n' or 's,' the stress goes on the penultimate (next-to-the-last) syllable:
    naranja na-RAHN-ha   *joven* HO-ven   *zapatos* sa-PA-tos

- For words ending in a consonant other than 'n' or 's,' the stress is on the final syllable:

  estoy   es-TOY   *ciudad*   syoo-DAHD   *catedral*   ka-teh-DRAL

- Any deviation from these rules is indicated by an accent:

  México   MEH-hee-ko   *mudéjar*   moo-DEH-har   *Cortés*   cor-TESS

Gender

Nouns in Spanish are either masculine or feminine. Nouns ending in 'o,' 'e' or 'ma' are usually masculine. Nouns ending in 'a,' 'ión' or 'dad' are usually feminine. Some nouns take either a masculine or feminine form, depending on the ending; for example, *viajero* is a male traveler, *viajera* is a female traveler. An adjective usually comes after the noun it describes and must take the same gender as the noun.

Greetings & Civilities

Hello/Hi.	*Hola.*
Good morning/Good day.	*Buenos días.*
Good afternoon.	*Buenas tardes.*
Good evening/Good night.	*Buenas noches.*
See you.	*Hasta luego.*
Good-bye.	*Adiós.*
Pleased to meet you.	*Mucho gusto.*
How are you? (to one person)	*¿Como está?*
How are you? (to more than one person)	*¿Como están?*
I am fine.	*Estoy bien.*
Please.	*Por favor.*
Thank you.	*Gracias.*
You're welcome.	*De nada.*
Excuse me.	*Perdóneme.*

People

I	*yo*	they (f)	*ellas*
you (familiar)	*tú*	my wife	*mi esposa*
you (formal)	*usted*	my husband	*mi esposo, mi marido*
you (pl, formal)	*ustedes*	my sister	*mi hermana*
he/it	*el*	my brother	*mi hermano*
she/it	*ella*	Sir/Mr	*Señor*
we	*nosotros*	Madam/Mrs	*Señora*
they (m)	*ellos*	Miss	*Señorita*

Useful Words & Phrases

Yes.	*Sí.*	I am ...	*Estoy ...*
No.	*No.*	(location or temporary condition)	
What did you say?	*¿Mande?* (colloq)	here	*aquí*
	¿Cómo?	tired (m/f)	*cansado/a*
good/OK	*bueno*	sick/ill (m/f)	*enfermo/a*
bad	*malo*	happy (m/f)	*contento/a*
better	*mejor*		
best	*lo mejor*	I am ...	*Soy ...*
more	*más*	(permanent state)	
less	*menos*	a worker	*trabajador*
very little	*poco* or *poquito*	a woman	*(una) mujer*

LANGUAGE

Buying

How much?	¿Cuánto?
How much does it cost?	¿Cuánto cuesta? or ¿Cuánto se cobra?
How much is it worth?	¿Cuánto vale?
I want ...	Quiero ...
I do not want ...	No quiero ...
I would like ...	Quisiera ...
Give me ...	Déme ...
What do you want?	¿Qué quiere?
Do you have ...?	¿Tiene ...?
Is/are there ...?	¿Hay ...?

Nationalities

American (m/f)	(norte)americano/a
Australian (m/f)	australiano/a
British (m/f)	británico/a
Canadian (m & f)	canadiense
English (m/f)	inglés/inglesa
French (m/f)	francés/francesa
German (m/f)	alemán/alemana

Languages

I speak ...	Yo hablo ...
I do not speak ...	No hablo ...
Do you speak ...?	¿Habla usted ...?
Spanish	español
English	inglés
German	alemán
French	francés

I understand.	Entiendo.
I do not understand.	No entiendo.
Do you understand?	¿Entiende usted?
Please speak slowly.	Por favor hable despacio.

Crossing the Border

birth certificate	certificado de nacimiento
border (frontier)	la frontera
car-owner's title	título de propiedad
car registration	registración
customs	aduana
driver's license	licencia de manejar
identification	identificación

immigration	inmigración
insurance	seguro
passport	pasaporte
temporary vehicle import permit	permiso de importación temporal de vehículo
tourist card	tarjeta de turista
visa	visado

Getting Around

street	calle
boulevard	bulevar, boulevard
avenue	avenida
road	camino
highway	carretera
corner (of)	esquina (de)
corner/bend	vuelta
block	cuadra
to the left	a la izquierda
to the right	a la derecha

forward, ahead	adelante
straight ahead	todo recto or derecho
this way	por aquí
that way	por allí
north	norte (Nte)
south	sur
east	este
east (in an address)	oriente (Ote)
west	oeste
west (in an address)	poniente (Pte)

Where is ...?	¿Dónde está ...?
the bus station	el terminal de autobuses/ central camionera
the train station	la estación del ferrocarril
the airport	el aeropuerto
the post office	el correo

a telephone	*un teléfono*
bus	*camión* or *autobús*
minibus	*colectivo, combi* or (in Mexico City) *pesero*
train	*tren*
taxi	*taxi*
ticket sales counter	*taquilla*
waiting room	*sala de espera*
baggage check-in	*(recibo de) equipaje*
toilet	*sanitario*
departure	*salida*
arrival	*llegada*
platform	*andén*
left-luggage room/checkroom	*guardería* (or *guarda*) *de equipaje*

How far is . . . ?	*¿A qué distancia está . . . ?*
How long? (How much time?)	*¿Cuánto tiempo?*
short route (usually a toll highway)	*vía corta*

Driving

gasoline	*gasolina*	full	*lleno* or *ful*
fuel station	*gasolinera*	oil	*aceite*
unleaded	*sin plomo*	tire	*llanta*
fill the tank	*llene el tanque; llenarlo*	puncture	*agujero*

How much is a liter of gasoline?	*¿Cuánto cuesta el litro de gasolina?*
My car has broken down.	*Se me ha descompuesto el carro.*
I need a tow truck.	*Necesito un remolque.*
Is there a garage near here?	*¿Hay un garaje cerca de aquí?*

Highway Signs

Though Mexico mostly uses the familiar international road signs, you should be prepared to encounter these other signs as well:

road repairs	*camino en reparación*
keep to the right	*conserve su derecha*
do not overtake	*no rebase*
dangerous curve	*curva peligrosa*
landslides or subsidence	*derrumbes*
slow	*despacio*
detour	*desviación*
slow down	*disminuya su velocidad*
school (zone)	*escuela (zona escolar)*
men working	*hombres trabajando*
road closed	*no hay paso*
danger	*peligro*
continuous white line	*raya continua*
speed bumps	*topes* or *vibradores*
road under repair	*tramo en reparación*
narrow bridge	*puente angosto*
toll highway	*vía cuota*
short route (often a toll road)	*vía corta*
have toll ready	*prepare su cuota*
one-lane road 100 meters ahead	*un solo carril a 100m*

Accommodations

hotel	*hotel*	shower	*ducha* or *regadera*
guesthouse	*casa de huéspedes*	hot water	*agua caliente*
inn	*posada*	air-conditioning	*aire acondicionado*
room	*cuarto, habitación*	blanket	*manta, cobija*
room with one bed	*cuarto sencillo*	towel	*toalla*
room with two beds	*cuarto doble*	soap	*jabón*
room for one person	*cuarto para una*	toilet paper	*papel higiénico*
	persona	the check (bill)	*la cuenta*
room for two people	*cuarto para dos*	What is the price?	*¿Cuál es el precio?*
	personas	Does that include taxes?	
double bed	*cama matrimonial*	¿Están incluidos los impuestos?	
twin beds	*camas gemelas*	Does that include service?	
with bath	*con baño*	*¿Está incluido el servicio?*	

At the Table

Note that *el menú* can mean either the menu or the special fixed-price meal of the day. If you want the menu, ask for *la carta*. Please see the Food & Drink Glossary for more vocabulary.

fork	*tenedor*	wineglass	*copa*
knife	*cuchillo*	napkin	*servilleta*
spoon	*cuchara*	waiter	*mesero/a*
plate	*plato*	check (bill)	*cuenta*
cup	*taza*	tip	*propina*
glass	*vaso*		

Money

money	*dinero*
traveler's checks	*cheques de viajero*
bank	*banco*
exchange bureau	*casa de cambio*
credit card	*tarjeta de crédito*
exchange rate	*tipo de cambio*
ATM	*caja permanente* or *cajero automático*
I want/would like to change some money.	*Quiero/quisiera cambiar dinero.*
What is the exchange rate?	*¿Cuál es el tipo de cambio?*
Is there a commission?	*¿Hay comisión?*

Telephones

telephone	*teléfono*
telephone call	*llamada*
telephone number	*número telefónico*
telephone card	*tarjeta telefónica*
area or city code	*clave*
prefix for long-distance call	*prefijo*
local call	*llamada local*
long-distance call	*llamada de larga distancia*
long-distance telephone	*teléfono de larga distancia*
card-operated telephone	*teléfono de tarjetas telefónicas*
long-distance telephone office	*caseta de larga distancia*
tone	*tono*
operator	*operador(a)*
person to person	*persona a persona*
collect (reverse charges)	*por cobrar*
dial the number	*marque el número*

Please wait.	*Favor de esperar.*
busy	*ocupado*
toll/cost (of call)	*cuota/costo*
time and charges	*tiempo y costo*
Don't hang up.	*No cuelgue.*

Times & Dates

Monday	*lunes*	Friday	*viernes*
Tuesday	*martes*	Saturday	*sábado*
Wednesday	*miércoles*	Sunday	*domingo*
Thursday	*jueves*		

yesterday	*ayer*
today	*hoy*
tomorrow (also at some point, or maybe)	*mañana*
right now (meaning in a few minutes)	*horita, ahorita*
already	*ya*
morning	*mañana*
tomorrow morning	*mañana por la mañana*
afternoon	*tarde*
night	*noche*
What time is it?	*¿Qué hora es?*

Numbers

0	*cero*	14	*catorce*	60	*sesenta*
1	*un, uno* (m), *una* (f)	15	*quince*	70	*setenta*
2	*dos*	16	*dieciséis*	80	*ochenta*
3	*tres*	17	*diecisiete*	90	*noventa*
4	*cuatro*	18	*dieciocho*	100	*cien*
5	*cinco*	19	*diecinueve*	101	*ciento uno*
6	*seis*	20	*veinte*	143	*ciento cuarenta*
7	*siete*	21	*veintiuno*		*y tres*
8	*ocho*	22	*veintidós*	200	*doscientos*
9	*nueve*	30	*treinta*	500	*quinientos*
10	*diez*	31	*treinta y uno*	700	*setecientos*
11	*once*	32	*treinta y dos*	900	*novecientos*
12	*doce*	40	*cuarenta*	1000	*mil*
13	*trece*	50	*cincuenta*	2000	*dos mil*
				1,000,000	*millón*

Mexican Slang

Pepper your conversations with a few slang expressions! You'll hear many of these slang words and phrases all around Mexico, but others are particular to Mexico City.

¿Qué onda?	What's up?, What's happening?
¿Qué pex?	What's up?
¿Qué pasión? (Mexico City only)	What's up?, What's going on?
¡Qué padre!	How cool!
fregón	really good at something, way cool, awesome
Este club está fregón.	This club is way cool.
El cantante es un fregón.	The singer is really awesome.
ser muy buena onda	to be really cool, nice

Mi novio es muy buena onda.	My boyfriend is really cool.
Eres muy buena onda.	You are really cool (nice).
estar de pelos	to be super, awesome
La música está de pelos.	The music is awesome.
pisto (in the north)	booze
alipús	booze
echarse un alipús, echarse un trago	to go get a drink
Echamos un alipús/trago.	Let's go have a drink.
tirar la onda	try to pick someone up, flirt
ligar	to flirt
irse de reventón	go partying
¡Vámonos de reventón!	Let's go party!
reven	a 'rave' – huge party, lots of loud music and wild atmosphere
un desmadre	a mess
Simón.	Yes.
Nel.	No.
No hay tos.	No problem. (literally 'There's no cough.')
¡Órale! – positive	Sounds great! (responding to an invitation)
¡Órale! – negative	What the *#*!? (taunting exclamation)
¡Caray!	Shit!
¿Te cae?	Are you serious?
Me late.	Sounds really good to me.
Me vale.	I don't care. Whatever.
Sale y vale.	I agree. Sounds good.
¡Paso sin ver!	I can't stand it! No thank you!
¡Guácatelas! ¡Guácala!	How gross! That's disgusting!
¡Bájale!	Don't exaggerate! Come on!
¡¿Chale?! (Mexico City only)	Really?! No way!
¡Te sales! ¡Te pasas!	That's it! You've gone too far!
¿Le agarraste?	Did you understand? Do you get it?
un resto	a lot
lana	money, dough
carnal	brother
cuate, cuaderno	buddy
chavo	guy, dude
chava	girl, gal
jefe	father
jefa	mother
la tira, la julia	the police
chapusero	a cheater (at cards, for example)

Glossary

For food and drink terms, see the Food and Drink Glossary; for transportation terms, see the Getting Around chapter; for general terms, see the Language chapter.

AC – *antes de Cristo* (before Christ); equivalent to BC

adobe – sun-dried mud brick used for building

aduana – customs

agave – family of plants including the *maguey*

Alameda – name of formal parks in several Mexican cities

albergue de juventud – youth hostel

alfarería – potter's workshop

alfiz – rectangular frame around a curved arch; an Arabic influence on Spanish and Mexican buildings

Altiplano Central – dry plateau stretching across north central Mexico between the two Sierra Madre ranges

amate – paper made from tree bark

Ángeles Verdes – Green Angels; government-funded mechanics who patrol Mexico's major highways in green vehicles; they help stranded motorists with fuel and spare parts

antro – bar with (often loud) recorded music and usually some space to dance

Apdo – abbreviation for Apartado (Box) in addresses; hence Apdo Postal means Post Office Box

arroyo – brook, stream

artesanías – handicrafts, folk arts

atlas (s), **atlantes** (pl) – sculpted male figure(s) used instead of a pillar to support a roof or frieze; a *telamon*

atrium – churchyard, usually a big one

autopista – expressway, dual carriageway

azulejo – painted ceramic tile

bahía – bay

balneario – bathing-place, often a natural hot spring

baluarte – bulwark, defensive wall

barrio – neighborhood of a town or city, often a poor neighborhood

billete – bank note

boleto – ticket

brujo, -a – witch doctor, shaman; similar to *curandero, -a*

burro – donkey

caballeros – literally 'horsemen,' but corresponds to 'gentlemen' in English; look for it on toilet doors

cabaña – cabin, simple shelter

cabina – Baja Californian term for a telephone *caseta*

cacique – regional warlord or political strongman

calle – street

callejón – alley

callejoneada – originally an Spanish tradition, still enjoyed in cities such as Guanajuato and Zacatecas, in which musicians lead a crowd of revelers through the streets, singing and telling stories as they go

calzada – grand boulevard or avenue

calzones – long baggy shorts worn by indigenous men

camarín – chapel beside the main altar in a church; contains ceremonial clothing for images of saints or the Virgin

camión – truck or bus

camioneta – pickup truck

campesino, -a – country person, peasant

capilla abierta – open chapel; used in early Mexican monasteries for preaching to large crowds of indigenous people

casa de cambio – exchange house; place where currency is exchanged, faster to use than a bank

caseta de larga distancia, caseta de teléfono, caseta telefónica – public telephone call station

cazuela – clay cooking pot; usually sold in a nested set

cenote – a limestone sinkhole filled with rainwater, used in Yucatán as a reservoir

central camionera – bus terminal

cerro – hill

Chac – Mayan rain god

chac-mool – pre-Hispanic stone sculpture of a hunched, belly-up figure; the stomach may have been used as a sacrificial altar

charreada – Mexican rodeo

charro – Mexican cowboy

chilango, -a – citizen of Mexico City

chinampas – Aztec gardens built from lake mud and vegetation; versions still exist at Xochimilco, Mexico City

chingar – literally 'to fuck'; it has a wide range of colloquial usages in Mexican Spanish equivalent to those in English

chultún – cement-lined brick cistern found in the *chenes* (wells) region in the Puuc hills south of Mérida

Churrigueresque – Spanish late-baroque architectural style; found on many Mexican churches

cigarro – cigarette

clavadistas – the cliff divers of Acapulco and Mazatlán

Coatlicue – mother of the Aztec gods

colectivo – minibus or car that picks up and drops off passengers along a predetermined route; can also refer to other types of transport, such as boats, where passengers share the total fare

coleto, -a – citizen of San Cristóbal de Las Casas

colonia – neighborhood of a city, often a wealthy residential area

completo – no vacancy, literally 'full up'; a sign you may see at hotel desks

conde – count (nobleman)

conquistador – early Spanish explorer-conqueror

cordillera – mountain range

correos – post office

coyote – person who smuggles Mexican immigrants into the USA

criollo – Mexican-born person of Spanish parentage; in colonial times considered inferior by peninsular Spaniards (see *gachupines, peninsulares*)

Cristeros – Roman Catholic rebels of the late 1920s

cuota – toll; a *vía cuota* is a toll road

curandero, -a – literally 'curer'; a medicine man or woman who uses herbal and/or magical methods and often emphasizes spiritual aspects of disease

damas – ladies; the sign on toilet doors

danzantes – literally 'dancers'; stone carvings at Monte Albán

DC – *después de Cristo* (after Christ); equivalent to AD

de lujo – deluxe; often used with some license

de paso – a bus that began its route somewhere else, but stops to let passengers on or off at various points – often arriving late; a *local* bus is preferable

delegación – a large urban governmental subdivision in Mexico City comprising numerous *colonias*

descompuesto – broken, out of order

DF – Distrito Federal (Federal District); about half of Mexico City lies in the DF

edificio – building

ejido – communal landholding

embarcadero – jetty, boat landing

encomienda – a grant made to a *conquistador* of labor by or tribute from a group of indigenous people; the conquistador was supposed to protect and convert them, but usually treated them as little more than slaves

enramada – literally a bower or shelter, but it often refers to a thatch-covered, open-air restaurant

enredo – wraparound skirt

entremeses – hors d'oeuvres; also theatrical sketches, such as those performed during the Cervantino festival in Guanajuato

escuela – school

esq – abbreviation of *esquina* (corner) in addresses

estación de ferrocarril – train station

estípite – long, narrow, pyramid-shaped, upside-down pilaster; the hallmark of Churrigueresque architecture

ex-convento – former convent or monastery

excusado – toilet

faja – waist sash used in traditional indigenous costume

feria – fair or carnival, typically occurring during a religious holiday

ferrocarril – railway

ficha – a locker token available at bus terminals

fraccionamiento – subdivision, housing development; similar to a *colonia,* often modern

frontera – a border between political entities

gachupines – derogatory term for the colonial *peninsulares*

giro – money order

gringo, -a – US or Canadian (and sometimes European, Australasian, etc) visitor to Latin America; can be used derogatorily

grito – literally 'shout'; the Grito de Dolores was the 1810 call to independence by parish priest Miguel Hidalgo, which sparked the struggle for independence from Spain

gruta – cave, grotto

guarache – also *huarache;* woven leather sandal, often with tire tread as the sole

guardería de equipaje – room for storing luggage, eg, in a bus station

guayabera – also *guayabarra;* man's shirt with pockets and appliquéd designs up the front, over the shoulders and down the back; worn in place of a jacket and tie in hot regions

güero, -a – fair-haired, fair-complexioned person; a more polite alternative to *gringo*

hacendado – *hacienda* owner

hacha – flat carved-stone object from the Classic Veracruz civilization; connected with the ritual ball game

hacienda – estate; Hacienda (capitalized) is the Treasury Department

hay – there is, there are; you're equally likely to hear *no hay* (there isn't, there aren't)

henequén – agave fiber used to make sisal rope; grown particularly around Mérida

hombres – men; sign on toilet doors

huarache – see *guarache*

huevos – eggs; also slang for testicles

huipil, -es – indigenous woman's sleeveless tunic, usually highly decorated; can be thigh-length or reach the ankles

Huizilopochtli – Aztec tribal god

iglesia – church

INAH – Instituto Nacional de Antropología e Historia; the body in charge of most ancient sites and some museums

indígena – indigenous, pertaining to the original inhabitants of Latin America; can also refer to the people themselves

INI – Instituto Nacional Indígenista; set up in 1948 to improve the lot of indigenous Mexicans and to integrate them into society; sometimes accused of paternalism and trying to stifle protest

ISH – *impuesto sobre hospedaje;* lodging tax on the price of hotel rooms

isla – island

IVA – *impuesto de valor agregado,* or 'ee-bah'; a 15% sales tax added to the price of many items

ixtle – *maguey* fiber

jaguar – jaguar, a panther native to southern Mexico and Central America; principal symbol of the Olmec civilization

jai alai – the Basque game *pelota,* brought to Mexico by the Spanish; a bit like squash, played on a long court with curved baskets attached to the arm

jarocho, -a – citizen of Veracruz

jefe – boss or leader, especially a political one

jipijapa – Yucatán name for a Panama hat

jorongo – small poncho worn by men

Kukulcán – Mayan name for the plumed serpent god Quetzalcóatl

lada – short for *larga distancia*

ladino – more or less the same as *mestizo*

lancha – fast, open, outboard boat

larga distancia – long-distance; usually refers to telephones

latifundio – large landholding; these sprang up after Mexico's independence from Spain

latifundista – powerful landowner who usurped communally owned land to form a *latifundio*

libramiento – road, highway

licenciado – university graduate, abbreviated as Lic and used as an honorific before a person's name; a status claimed by many who don't actually possess a degree

lista de correos – literally 'mail list,' a list displayed at a post office of people for whom letters are waiting; similar to General Delivery or Poste Restante

lleno – full, as with a car's fuel tank

local – can mean premises, such as a numbered shop or office in a mall or block, or can mean local; a *local* bus is one whose route starts at the bus station you are in

machismo – Mexican masculine bravura

madre – literally 'mother,' but the term can be used colloquially with an astonishing array of meanings

maguey – a type of agave, with thick pointed leaves growing straight out of the ground; *tequila* and *mezcal* are made from its sap

malecón – waterfront street, boulevard or promenade

mañana – literally 'tomorrow' or 'morning'; in some contexts it may just mean 'some time in the future'

maquiladora – assembly-plant operation, importing equipment, raw materials and parts for assembly or processing in Mexico, then exporting the products

mariachi – small ensemble of street musicians playing traditional ballads on guitars and trumpets

marimba – wooden xylophone-type instrument, popular in Veracruz and the south

Mayab – the lands of the Maya

mercado – market; often a building near the center of a town, with shops and open-air stalls in the surrounding streets

Mesoamerica – the region inhabited by the ancient Mexican and Mayan cultures

mestizaje – 'mixedness,' Mexico's mixed-blood heritage; officially an object of pride

mestizo – person of mixed (usually indigenous and Spanish) ancestry, ie, most Mexicans

metate – shallow stone bowl with legs, for grinding maize and other foods

Mexican Hat Dance – a courtship dance in which a girl and boy dance around the boy's hat

milpa – peasant's small cornfield, often cultivated by the slash-and-burn method

mirador, -es – lookout point(s)

Montezuma's revenge – Mexican version of Delhi-belly or travelers' diarrhea

mordida – literally 'little bite,' a small bribe to keep the wheels of bureaucracy turning

mota – marijuana

Mudéjar – Moorish architectural style, imported to Mexico by the Spanish

mujeres – women; seen on toilet doors

municipio – small local-government area; Mexico is divided into 2394 of them

na – Mayan thatched hut

NAFTA – North American Free Trade Agreement – see *TLC*

Náhuatl – language of the Nahua people, descendants of the Aztecs

naos – Spanish trading galleons

norteamericanos – North Americans, people from north of the US-Mexican border

Nte – abbreviation for *norte* (north), used in street names

Ote – abbreviation for *oriente* (east), used in street names

paceño, -a – person from La Paz, Baja California Sur

palacio de gobierno – state capitol, state government headquarters

palacio municipal – town or city hall, headquarters of the municipal corporation

palapa – thatched-roof shelter, usually on a beach

palma – long, paddle-like, carved-stone object from the Classic Veracruz civilization; connected with the ritual ball game

panga – fiberglass skiff for fishing or whale-watching in Baja California

parada – bus stop, usually for city buses

parado – stationary, or standing up, as you often are on 2nd-class buses

parque nacional – national park; an environmentally protected area in which human exploitation is supposedly banned or restricted

parroquia – parish church

paseo – boulevard, walkway or pedestrian street; also the tradition of strolling in a circle around the plaza in the evening, men and women moving in opposite directions

Pemex – government-owned petroleum extraction, refining and retailing monopoly

peña – evening of Latin American folk songs, often with a political protest theme

peninsulares – those born in Spain and sent by the Spanish government to rule the colony in Mexico (see *criollo, gachupines*)

periférico – ring road

pesero – Mexico City's word for *colectivo*

petate – mat, usually made of palm or reed

peyote – a hallucinogenic cactus

pinacoteca – art gallery

piñata – clay pot or papier-mâché mold decorated to resemble an animal, pineapple, star, etc; filled with sweets and gifts and smashed open at fiestas

playa – beach

plaza de toros – bullring

plazuela – small plaza

poblano, -a – person from Puebla, or something in the style of Puebla

pollero – same as a *coyote*

Porfiriato – Porfirio Díaz's reign as president-dictator of Mexico for 30 years, until the 1910 revolution

portales – arcades

potosino – from the city or state of San Luis Potosí

presidio – fort or fort's garrison

PRI – Partido Revolucionario Institucional (Institutional Revolutionary Party); the political party that ruled Mexico for most of the 20th century

propina – tip; different from a *mordida,* which is closer to a bribe

Pte – abbreviation for *poniente* (west), used in street names

puerto – port

quechquémitl – indigenous woman's shoulder cape with an opening for the head; usually colorfully embroidered, often diamond-shaped

quetzal – crested bird with brilliant green, red and white plumage, native to southern Mexico, Central America and northern South America; quetzal feathers were highly prized in pre-Hispanic Mexico

Quetzalcóatl – plumed serpent god of pre-Hispanic Mexico

rebozo – long woolen or linen shawl covering the head or shoulders

refugio – a very basic cabin for shelter in the mountains

regiomontano, -a – person from Monterrey

reja – wrought-iron window grille

reserva de la biósfera – biosphere reserve; an environmentally protected area where human exploitation is steered towards ecologically unharmful activities

retablo – altarpiece; or small painting on wood, tin, cardboard, glass, etc, placed in a church to give thanks for miracles, answered prayers, etc

río – river

s/n – *sin número* (without number); used in street addresses

sacbe (s), **sacbeob** (pl) – ceremonial avenue(s) between great Mayan cities

sanatorio – hospital, particularly a small private one

sanitario(s) – toilet(s), literally 'sanitary place'

sarape – blanket with opening for the head, worn as a cloak

Semana Santa – Holy Week, the week from Palm Sunday to Easter Sunday; Mexico's major holiday period, when accommodations and transport get very busy

servicios – toilets

sierra – mountain range

sitio – taxi stand

stele (s), **-es** or **stelae** (pl) – standing stone monument(s), usually carved

supermercado – supermarket; anything from a small corner store to a large, US-style supermarket

Sur – south; often seen in street names

taller – shop or workshop; a *taller mecánico* is a mechanic's shop, usually for cars; a *taller de llantas* is a tire-repair shop

talud-tablero – stepped building style typical of Teotihuacán, with alternating vertical *(tablero)* and sloping *(talud)* sections

tapatío, -a – person born in the state of Jalisco

taquilla – ticket window

telamon – statue of a male figure, used instead of a pillar to hold up the roof of a temple; see also *atlas*

telar de cintura – backstrap loom; the warp (lengthwise) threads are stretched between two horizontal bars, one of which is attached to a post or tree and the other to a strap around the weaver's lower back, and the weft (crosswise) threads are then woven in

teleférico – cable car

templo – church; anything from a wayside chapel to a cathedral

teocalli – Aztec sacred precinct

Tezcatlipoca – multifaceted pre-Hispanic god, lord of life and death and protector of warriors; as a smoking mirror he could see into hearts, as the sun god he needed the blood of sacrificed warriors to ensure he would rise again

tezontle – light-red, porous volcanic rock used for buildings by the Aztecs and *conquistadores*

tianguis – indigenous people's market

tienda – store

típico, -a – characteristic of a region; particularly used to describe food

Tláloc – pre-Hispanic rain and water god

TLC – Tratado de Libre Comercio, the North American Free Trade Agreement (NAFTA)

topes – speed bumps; found on the outskirts of many towns and villages, they are only sometimes marked by signs

trapiche – mill; in Baja California usually a sugar mill

tzompantli – rack for the skulls of Aztec sacrificial victims

UNAM – Universidad Nacional Autónoma de México (National Autonomous University of Mexico)
universidad – university

viajero, -a – traveler
villa juvenil – youth sports center, often the location of an *albergue de juventud*
voladores – literally 'fliers,' the Totonac ritual in which men, suspended by their ankles, whirl around a tall pole

War of the Castes – bloody 19th-century Mayan uprising in the Yucatán Peninsula
were-jaguar – half-human, half-jaguar being, portrayed in Olmec art

yácata – ceremonial stone structure of the Tarascan civilization
yugo – U-shaped carved-stone object from the Classic Veracruz civilization; connected with the ritual ball game

zaguán – vestibule or foyer, sometimes a porch
zócalo – main plaza or square; a term used in some (but by no means all) Mexican towns
Zona Rosa – literally 'Pink Zone'; an area of expensive shops, hotels and restaurants in Mexico City frequented by the wealthy and tourists; by extension, a similar area in another city

Food & Drink Glossary

a la parrilla – grilled, perhaps over charcoal
a la plancha – 'planked': grilled on a hot-plate
a la tampiqueña – 'Tampico style': sautéed, thinly sliced meat, officially also marinated in garlic, oil and oregano
a la veracruzana – 'Veracruz style': topped with tomato, olive and onion sauce
abarrotes – groceries
abulón – abalone
aceite – oil
aceitunas – olives
adobado – marinated, seasoned and dried
agua – water
agua de fruta – drink made by adding sugar and water to fruit juice or a syrup made from mashed grains or seeds (also called *agua fresca* or *agua preparada*)
agua mineral – mineral water
aguacate – avocado
aguardiente – literally 'burning water'; strong liquor usually made from sugarcane
ahumado – smoked
al carbón – charcoal-grilled
al horno – baked
al mojo de ajo – in garlic sauce
al pastor – 'shepherd-style': roasted on a stake or spit
alambre – shish kebab, 'en brochette'
almejas – clams
antojitos – literally 'little whims,' traditional Mexican snacks or light dishes
arrachera – skirt steak
arroz – rice
arroz con leche – rice pudding
asada – grilled
atole – sweet, hot drink thickened with *masa* (corn dough) and flavored with chocolate, cinnamon or various fruits
atún – tuna
avena – porridge
aves – poultry
azúcar – sugar

barbacoa – literally 'barbecued,' but meat is usually covered and placed under hot coals
betabel – beet
bien cocido – well-done

birria – stew-cum-broth of kid or mutton and chopped onion
bistec, bisteck, bistec/bisteck de res – beefsteak
bocadillo – sandwich, often in a long roll (see *sandwich*)
bolillo – bread roll
burrita – flour tortilla folded over a filling of ham and cheese, heated a little to make the cheese melt
burrito – any combination of beans, cheese, meat, chicken or seafood seasoned with salsa or chili and wrapped in a wheat-flour tortilla – especially popular in northern Mexico

cabeza – head
cabra – goat
cabrito – kid (young goat)
café – coffee
café americano – black coffee
café con crema – coffee with cream, served separately
café con leche – coffee with hot milk, half-and-half
café negro – black coffee
cafetería – a snack bar or coffeehouse
calabaza – squash or pumpkin
calamar – squid
caldo – broth (*caldo tlalpeño* is a hearty chicken, vegetables and chili variety)
camarones – shrimp
camarones gigantes – prawns
cangrejo – large crab
caracol – snail
carne – meat, usually beef if not otherwise specified
carnero – mutton
carnitas – deep-fried pork
catsup – ketchup; US-style spiced tomato sauce
cebolla – onion
cecina – thin-sliced beef, soaked in lemon or orange and salt, then grilled
cerdo – pork
cerveza – beer
ceviche – cocktail of raw seafood marinated in lime and mixed with onions, chilies, garlic and tomatoes
chabacano – apricot

champiñones – mushrooms
chícharos – peas
chicharrón – deep-fried pork rind; pigskin cracklings
chilaquiles – fried tortilla chips with sauce or scrambled eggs, often with grated cheese on top
chile – chili pepper
chiles rellenos – chilies stuffed with cheese, meat or other foods, deep fried and baked in sauce
chipotle – chilies dried, then fermented in vinegar; many Mexicans feel a meal is not complete without it
chorizo – spicy pork sausage
chuleta – chop (such as a lamb chop)
cilantro – fresh coriander leaf
cochinita – suckling pig
cocido – boiled
coco – coconut
coctel – appetizer (seafood, fruit, etc) in sauce
col – cabbage
coliflor – cauliflower
comedor – literally 'eating place,' usually a sit-down stall in a market or a small, cheap restaurant
comida corrida – set lunch or dinner special
conejo – rabbit
cordero – lamb
corvina – bass
costillas – ribs
crema – cream
crepa – crêpe; thin pancake

durazno – peach

ejotes – green beans
elote – corn on the cob; commonly served from steaming bins on street carts
empanada – small pastry with savory or sweet filling
empanizado – breaded
enchilada – ingredients similar to those used in burritos and tacos rolled up in a tortilla, dipped in sauce and then baked or partly fried; *enchiladas suizas* (Swiss enchiladas) come smothered in a blanket of thick cream
enfrijolada – soft tortilla in a frijole sauce with cheese and onion on top
ensalada de frutas – plain mixed seasonal fruits
ensalada (verde) – (green) salad

entomatada – soft tortilla in a tomato sauce with cheese and onion on top
entremeses – hors d'oeuvres
epazote – a common Mexican herb, sometimes translated as goosefoot or wild spinach
espárragos – asparagus
espinaca – spinach
espresso – espresso, brewed using steam pressure

faisán – pheasant; turkey
fajitas – short beef strips, good fried with the likes of onion, peppers and tomato
filete – fillet (as of fish or meat)
filete de pescado – fish fillet
flan – custard; crème caramel
flor de calabaza – pumpkin flower
fonda – eating stall in market; small restaurant
fresa – strawberry or other berry
frijoles – beans, usually black
frito – fried
fruta – fruit

galletas – cookies/biscuits
gazpacho – chilled vegetable soup spiced with hot chilies
gelatina – Jell-O (jelly)
gordita – fried maize dough filled with refried beans, topped with cream, cheese and lettuce
guacamole – mashed avocados mixed with onion, chili, lemon, tomato and other ingredients
guajolote – turkey
guanábana – green pearlike fruit
guayaba – guava (better yellow than pink)

hamburguesa – hamburger
helado – ice cream
hígado – liver
higo – fig
hongos – mushrooms
huachinango – red snapper
huevos – eggs
huevos cocidos – harder-boiled eggs (specify the number of minutes if you're in doubt)
huevos estrellados – fried eggs
huevos fritos (con jamón/tocino) – fried eggs (with ham/bacon)
huevos mexicanos – eggs scrambled with tomatoes, chilies and onions (representing the red, green and white of the Mexican flag)

huevos motuleños – tortilla topped with slices of ham, fried eggs, cheese, peas and tomato sauce
huevos pasados por agua – lightly boiled eggs (too lightly for many visitors' tastes)
huevos poches – poached eggs
huevos rancheros – fried eggs on tortillas, covered in salsa
huevos revueltos – scrambled eggs
huitlacoche – corn fungus, considered a delicacy since Aztec times; grows on some maize ears in the rainy season – often prepared with garlic and onions, it's used as a filling for quesadillas, or to make soup, or in an increasing number of other ways

jaiba – small crab
jamón – ham
jitomate – tomato (not to be confused with *tomate*)
jugo – juice

langosta – lobster
leche – milk
lechuga – lettuce
legumbres – legumes
lengua – tongue
lentejas – lentils
licuado – drink made from fruit juice, water or milk, and sugar
limón – lime or lemon
lomo – loin

mamey – sweet, orange tropical fruit
mango – mango
mantequilla – butter
manzana – apple
margarina – margarine
mariscos – shellfish
melón – melon
menudo – tripe soup made with the spiced entrails of various four-legged beasts
mezcal – strong alcoholic drink produced from sap of the maguey plant
milanesa – breaded Italian-style
mixiotes – stew of sliced lamb
mojarra – perch
mole – spicy sauce made with chilies and other ingredients (sometimes including chocolate), often served over poultry
mole poblano – delicious Puebla-style mole, with many ingredients, including hot chilies and bitter chocolate
molleja – gizzard

naranja – orange
Nescafé – any instant coffee (*agua para Nescafé* is a cup of boiled water presented with a jar of instant coffee)
nieve – sorbet
nopales – green prickly-pear cactus ears

ostiones – oysters

paleta – flavored ice on a stick
pan (integral) – (whole-grain) bread
panadería – bakery, pastry shop
papas – potatoes
papas fritas – french fries (chips)
papaya – papaya
pastel – pastry or cake
patas – trotters (feet)
pato – duck
pavo – turkey
pay – fruit pie
pechuga – chicken breast
pepino – cucumber
pera – pear
pescado – fish after it has been caught
pez – fish that's still alive in the water
pez espada – swordfish
pibil – meat (usually suckling pig or chicken) flavored with ingredients such as garlic, pepper, chili, oregano and orange juice, then baked (best the traditional way – in a pit called a *pib*)
pierna – leg
pimienta – pepper
piña – pineapple
plátano – banana
poco cocido – rare
pollo – chicken
postre – dessert
pozole – rich, spicy stew of hominy (large maize kernels) with meat and vegetables
puerco – pork
pulpo – octopus
pulque – thick, milky, alcoholic drink of fermented maguey juice

quesadilla – flour tortilla topped or filled with cheese and occasionally other ingredients and then heated
queso – cheese
queso fundido – melted cheese served with tortillas

rábano – radish
refrescos – bottled or canned soft drinks

res – beef
robalo – sea bass

sal – salt
salchicha – spicy pork sausage
salmón (ahumada) – (smoked) salmon
salsa roja/verde – red/green sauce made with chilies, onions, tomato, lemon or lime juice and spices
sandwich – toasted sandwich
sincronizada – a lightly grilled or fried flour-tortilla 'sandwich,' usually with a ham and cheese filling
sopa – soup
sopa de arroz – rice pilaf
sope – thick patty of corn dough lightly grilled then served with *salsa verde* or *salsa roja* and frijoles, onion and cheese

taco – the Número Uno Mexican snack: soft corn tortilla wrapped or folded around the same fillings as a burrito
tamal – corn dough stuffed with meat, beans, chilies or nothing at all, wrapped in corn husks or banana leaves and then steamed
taquería – place where you buy tacos
té – tea
té de manzanilla – chamomile tea
té negro – black tea, to which you can add *leche* (milk) if you wish

tequila – liquor produced, like *pulque* and *mezcal,* from the maguey plant
ternera – veal
Tex-Mex – Americanized version of Mexican food
tiburón – shark
tocino – bacon
tomate or **tomatillo** – green tomato-like fruit used to make salsa verde
toronja – grapefruit
torta – Mexican-style sandwich in a roll
tortilla – the essence of Mexican eating: a thin round pancake of pressed corn *(maíz)* dough or wheat-flour *(harina)* dough
tostada – crisp-fried, thin tortilla that may be eaten as a nibble while you're waiting for the rest of a meal or can be topped with meat or cheese, tomatoes, beans and lettuce
trucha – trout
tuna – nopal (prickly pear) cactus fruit

uva – grape

venado – deer (venison)
verduras – vegetables
vino – wine

zanahoria – carrot
zapote – sweet fruit of the chicle tree, best liquidized with, for example, orange juice or Kahlua

Thanks

Many readers wrote with helpful information and suggestions, including the following (please note that an X was used for readers who did not give their surnames):

Edward Abse, Campamento Adame, Mike Agnew, Erik Agterhuis, Luis Enrique Lopez Aguilar, Carlos Aguilera, Roberto Alcalar, JM Aldrich, Curtis Allan, Wim Allegaert, Anne Allen, Danny Allen, Emily Allen, Kurt Allen, Christine Alles, William Allsup, Graeme Alston, Javier Amaro, Kaia Ambrose, Jeff Ames, Roger Amiot, Francesca Ancona, Mikael Andersen, Sheila Anderson, Sid Anderson, Veronica Anderson, Lotta Andersson, Rachel Andrews, Kinal Antzetik, William Apt, Deborah Arambula, Jan E Arctander, Ronald Ariesen, David Arlt, Gloria Asbel, Nicholas Aster, Marvin & Judith Atchley, Suzanne Aubry, Jorg Ausfelt, Judy Avisar, John Ayre, Aspy & Homai Ayrton, Stefan Bachschmid, Mike Bada, Rebecca Bader, Christina Baez, Elaine Bainard, Lisa Baird, Danielle Baker, Grace Ann Baker, John Baker, Deborah Bakker, Ingeborg Baltussen, André & Katia Balty, Michele Bandini, Kevin Banker, Abi Bankole, Sola Bankole, Grahame Bann, Bass Bannick, Paul Barber, Zoe Barker, Samantha Barletta, Deborah Barlow, Jo & Liz Barlow, Carlos Barragan, Nallely Barragan, Gavin Barratt, Sue Barreau, John Barreiro, Aharon Barth, Kati Bassler, Lynne Bateman, Dorothy Batz, Lee Bayer-Shapiro, Sarah Bayly, Jack Beard, P Beauchamp, Sallie G Beck, Petra Beckmann, Eric Beecroft, Graham Beedie, Theo Beekman, Georgina Behrens, Natasha Belenkin, Beverly Bell, Jack Bell, Stacy Bell, Alessia Bello, Nicki Beltchev, Gary Benedyk, Assaf Ben-Yishai, Brian & Caryl Bergeron, Mauricio Bergstein, Manuel Bernal Guerra, Ventura Bernat, Adam Bernd, Claudia Bernrieder-Kulla, Melanie Best, John Beston, Alejandra Betancourt, Jan Betts, Steve Bey, Martha Bibbins, Joanna Biggs, Luke Biggs, Sarah Billyack, Trista Bilmer, Roderick Binns, Scott Bishopp, Helle Bjerre, Clara Bjorkelund, John Black, Theresa Black, J David Blagg, Rachel Blair, Gon Bloemendal, Dick Blom, Dan Bloomingdale, Janina Blume, Steve Boanas, Olivier Bonin, Andre Bookelmann, K Boom!, Tjeerd Boonman, Kim Borchard, Art Borkent, Christina Boses, Erik Boshuizen, Erik Botsford, Phillip Boulton, David Bowen, Kathy Bowman, Patrick Boylan, Charlotte Brauer, Agnes Bray, Michael Bray, Sharon Bray, Lorraine Brecht, Regina Brecht, Connie Breedlove, Dirk Bremecke, Raffaella & Filippo Brigante, Elizabeth Briggs, Tracey Brignole, Ricardo Briseo Milln, Wade Brittingham, George Broché, Mary Ann Broder, Hugh R Brodie, Barry Brolley, Tom Brosnahan, Joanna Brown, Nigel Brown, Joe Bruckner, Louise Brule, Christopher Bruno, Jake Bryant, Dan Brylde, Simon Bucknall, Anita Bueno, Yvonne Buijink, Jan Bulman, April Burge, Anke Burger, Mark Burgess, Jeannine Burk, Craig Burton, Ian Burton, Delores Bushong, Jose Cabrara Priego, Rebecca Cague, Eric Calder, Robey Callahan, Murray Cambie, Bubu Camdiani, Claude Camirand, Frank Campbell, KW Campbell, Keith Campbell, Ben Capell, Judith & Kirby Capen, Javier Carbajal, Robert Card, Peggy Carlson, Ingeman Carlsson, Kristen Carney, C Carol, Geoff Carr, Marco Carricato, Eleanor Carrington-Finch, Sandy Cartwright, Carla M & Scott Healey Carvalho, Chuck Cassity, June Challoner, E & J Chanecka, Bob Chase, Pablo Chemor, Sally Childs, Joannie Chiung-Yueh Chang, Dianne Christy, John Ciampi, Adam Clark, Gordon Clark, Kitty Clark, Michael Clark, Wayne Clarke, Janet Clements, Jen Clent, Stacey Clinesmith, Joann Clirftn, Lida Clouser, Amy Coates, Ray Coe, Chris Cogburn, Seth Cohen, Valerie P Cohen, Jeff Collard, Margaret Collins, Pere Colls, Laura Coloma, Jaume Rovira Colomer, Tania Columba, Glen Coming, Kevin Connor, William Constandse, Geoff Cook, Thomas Cook, Pamela Cooper, Dan Coplan, Maria Cordes, Joan Corman, William Corrin, Seymour Cottage, Nicholas Couis, Marie-Lou Coulombe, Grere Coutie, Rob & Lorri Cracknell, Christopher Craig, Rob Craig, David Croome, George N Cull, A Currier, Lucy Curry, Irene Czurda, M Dahl, Rosario & Patty D'Alessandro, Lee Daneker, Chantel Daniel, Christopher & Victoria Darke, Graham Darling, Pamela Darling, Maria Darlington, Amanda Dates, Justin Davenport, Georgie & Rob Davidson, Jimmy Davies, Brenda Davis, Lisa Davis, Simon Davis, Susann Davis, Sandra Day, Guido de Bie, Koen De Boeck, Irene de Bruijn, Rosita De Decker, Anka de Dood, Thibaut de Groen, Simone de Haan, Ilsa de Jager, Jeroen de Leeuw den Bouter, Jeroen de Leeuw den Bouter, Henry de Marigny, Sven De Potter, Frank de Roeck, Hans de Roo Sr, Alex de Vet, A de Vries, Paul De Zardain, Morgan Dean, Anne-Laure Degove, Maria del Pilar Costa, Jose Enrique del Valle, Pablo Del Valle, David Delaney, Dimitri Deloste, Bill Denny, Yann Deredec, Vincent Desloges, Kate Deters, Barry & Kathy Devine, Samuel Eitan Diamond, Michael Dickson, Paic Diego Quiroz, Cisco Craig Dietz, Kai Artur Diers, Martin Dillig, Carsten Dittmann, Anna Doddridge, Martin & Michaela Dohnalkova, Debbi Dolan, Claudio Carrasco Dominguez, Scott Donahue, Anouk Donker, Annick Donkers, Julia Dotson, Julia K Dotson, Norma Douglas, Silvie Dresselhaus, Marcel Driessen, Erika Drucker, Eddie Dry, Jean-Marc Dumont, K Dunk, Sarah Dunn, Alex Dunne,

Jim Dutkiewycz, Mr & Mrs J Dutton, Zsolt Edelenyi, Anna Eder, Joyce Edling, Bindi Edmonds, Alberta R Edwards, Libby Edwards, Eve Eidelson, Naomi Eisenstein, Werner Eitel, Anna Elfors, Carole Elicker, Mei-Ling Ellerman, Jocelyn Elliot, Sue Elliott, David Ellis, Bijan Elmdust, Kari Eloranta, Peter Epanchin, Louisa Ersanilli, Andres Escalante, Carlos Escudero Albarran, Emily Espinosa, Margaret Stewart Evans, Craig Faanes, Florence Fabre, Austen Fairbairn, Annabel Falk, Manuel Falkenberg, Thomas Farrell, Megan Faunce, Roi Faust, Renée Feather, Brian Fenn, Keith Ferguson, Enrique Fernandez, Joachim Ferneding, Carmen Ferrant, Maurice Ficheroux, Arnold Fieldman, Eva Filius, Brian Fillmore, Daniel Finke, Nick Fischer, Joel Fisler, Sean Fitzgerald, Andrea Fitzsimmons, Judy Johnson Flaherty, Isac Flaishman, Anne Fleming, Rachael Flowerday, Tom Fogarty, Cristina Folgueras, M Fonteyn, Jan Ford, Lisa Foresee, Michael Forrest, Mark Forster, Stephane Fortin, John Foster, Amy Fox, Julie Francesio, Caroll & Bill Fraser, Robert C Freese, Dana A Freiburger, Astrid Frey, Beth Fridinger, Aviv Fried, Mirit Friedland, David Frier, Flair Friesen, Thomas Fritzsche, Graham Frogley, Franco Fubini, Geraldine Fuller, Gerry Fuller, Erik Futtrup, Tom Fyfe, Dick Gabriel, Casarotti Gabriele, Rikke Gade-gaard, Paulo Gaeta, Kate Gale, Lucy Garbutt, Del-phine Garcia, Ken Gardner, Mathilde Garnier, Michele Garrett, Micheline Garrity, Alma & Joe Gaskill, RWJ Gates, Pat Gaudry, Damon Gautama, Dana Gay Burton, Tobias Gayer, Mike Gaze, Ellen Geertsema, Katrin Gehrich-Schroter, Mneesha Gellman, Adam Gerle, Gregoire Gerlier, Raad German, Dominique Geurden, Rita Geysens, Massimo Giannini, Iain Gibbs, Carmelia Giger, Eric W Gilliam, David W Gillio, Pamela Ginder, Paolo Giubellino, Sue Glenn, Jackie & Steven Gloor, Julie Gloss, Warren Glover, Robert Goad, Stefan Goed-dertz, Charles P Goff, Peter Gohler, Jonathan Gold-berg, Adam Goldstein, Peter Goltermann, Antonio J Gonzalez, Gerardo Gonzalez, Nicolas Gonze, Saul Goodwin, Ernie Gorrie, Donna Gottardi, Kevin Gottesman, Richard Grabman, Denis Grady, Albert Graf, Brian Graham, Ted Graham, Catherine Grange, Rachel Grant, Carrol Greenbaum, Mark Gregory, Caroline Greig, Martí Gríera, Ben Griffin, Sherry Griffiths, Christel Grosse Bockhorn, Yosi & Ayala Grosskop, Sarah Groves, Sasha Gubser, Ale-jandro Guerra, Olivier Guidet, Jenny Gunter, Alex Gunz, Shamir Gurfinkel, Camilla Gustafsson, Arturo Gutierrez, Simone de Haan, Magda Haas, Gad Hachlili, Malreen Haentjens, Helen Hagan, Oliver Hagemann, Jessie Hahn, Michael Hahne, Em & Steve Hahoney, Stefan & Katarzyna Haider, Mirén Haines, Marc Hale, Olivia Hall, Ian Halling, Sven Hamann, Emily Hamilton, Laura Beth Hamilton, Jon Hampson, Neil Hancock, Ladislav R Hanka, Carla Hanson, Angie Harding, James Hardy, Megan Harker, Dylan Harris, Fred Hart, Paul Hartvigson, Faye Haskins, Earl Hastings, Mary Hatch, Lewis Haupt, Steve Hauser, Shirley Hawatt, Michelle Hawk, Gay Haworth, Josephine Haynes, Julie Haynes, C Heard, Ian-Michael Hebert, Tina Hebert, Jeff A Heermann, Jacob Hegner, Robert Heil, Pavel Heimlich, Mike Hellemn, Rasmus Hemph, Bas Hen-driks, David Henry, Miguel Hernandez, Robert Ian Herre, Miguel Herrera-Martinez, Barbara & Art Hess, Bob & Art Hess, Steen & Helene Hest, NG Hetterley, Marcel Heutmekers, Dawn Hewett, Dr Thomas Hewitt, Jeff Hicks, Patricia Hicks, Andresch Hiepel, Anneloes & Tim Hilbers, Michael Hill, Graeme Hind, Howard Hjelm, Winston & Esther Ho, David Hobson, Richard Hoch, Frits Hoefman, Frank Hoffman, John Hoffman, Jorg Hoffmann, Katrina Hoffman, Diane Hofstetter, Bruce Hogg, David C Holcomb, Ralf Hollmann, Victoria Holtelies, David Holyrod, Tanya Bianca Hoppe, Marco Hop-staken, Edward Horne, Rachel Horsley, Antonio & Hostel Soberanis Laviada, Leland Housman, Karin Van Hout, Alistair How, Julian & Lydia Howarth, Sherry Howell, Tony Hoyt, Ron Hruby, Teri Hruska, Wayne Hsu, Johannes Huber, Grace Hucul, Marian Hudson, Sarah Hughlock, Stephan & Humboldt-Universitaet zu Berlin Roch, Errol Hunt, Tasneem Hussain, Karen Inkster, Martin & Elizabeth Inwood, Jim Isaacs, Philip M Isaacson, Marko Istenic, David Ito, Christian Iyer, David Iza, Kimi Jackson, Erik Ja-cobsen, Vibeke Jansteen, Alex Jantzen, Andrew Jeffery, Tony Jenkins, Marla Jensen, Thomas Jensen, Chris Johansson, Berit Johns, Kay Johnson, Julie Johnston, Ryan Johnston, Cheryl Hayden, Don, Lynne & Doug Jones, Fred Jones, Ken Jones, Natalie Jones, Werner Joos, Mark Jordan, Wiley Jordan, Xavi Juanico, Zianny Juarez, Faisal Juma, Nancy Jusari, Rachel Kahn, Vladimir Kalista, Andy Kaltenbach, B Kane, Ofir Kanter, Stephan Karkowsky, Nik Katsourides, Volker Katz, John Kay, Ufuk Kayserilioglu, Juan Kdiaz-Roche, George Kechagiouglou, Steve Kelleher, Pascal Kellenberg, Geoff Kelley, Cyndi Kelly, John Kelly, Susan Kelly, Wendy Kennan, Denise Kennedy, Jim Kentch, Dietmar Kenzle, Bas Kerkhoff, Joachim Kernstock, Tracy Keshek, Monique Kettelarij, Herb Kieklak, Tuomas Kiiski, Mark Kiker, Russell Kilday-Hicks, Eliz-abeth Killeen, Jeff King, Kimberly King, Matt King, Rache Kirk, Michele Kitagawa, Jeanine Kitchel, Joanne Kitson, Russel Kivell, Leslie Klein, Raymond Klomp, Andrea Knaf, Susanne Knauer Lucile, Sandra Knenzi, Linda Knight, David Knox, Lindsay S Koehler, Mike Koehler, Steven Koenig, Ulli Koester, Simone Koliwyzer, Naama Kostiner, George Kouseras, Robert Kramps, Robert Krauser, Susan Kroll, Ulrike Kuhnert, Agniesia Kulik, Christine Labri-ola, Paul Lack, Eric Lacy, Bernard Lamarche, Miguel Angel Hernandez Lamas, Matt Lamon, Kerry Lamont, Rachele Lamontagne, Alison Land, Louise

Lander, Leslie Lane, Kevin Lang, R Langello, Callie Langlois, Christy Lanzl, Noga Laor, Leah Larkin, Anne Larsen, Carol Larson, Lynn Larson, Robert M Larson, Sunny Larson, Sallie Latch, Wendy Lawton, Andrew Lay, Cristina Laz, Denis Le Cam, Brian Leach, Daniel Lebidois, Bill Lee, Jonathan Lee, Debbie Lee Keltz, Stephan Leinert, Rolf Lenherr, AH Lenz, Scott Leonard, Thibaut Lespagnol, Milton Lever, Shira R Levine, Irving Levinson, Yoram Levy, Robin LeWinter, Danny Lewis, Marina Lewis, Jeremy Lian, Guy F Liardet, Gabriela Licini, Steve Lidgey, HME Lier, Frederico Lifsichtz, T Liljeberg, Nino Lind, Matthew Linnell, Esmé-Jane Lippiatt, Amanda Lireg, Dana Lissy, Vicki Littlefield, Elisa Llamas, David Lloyd, Joann Lo, Ingrid Lobet, Bill Locascio, Ellen & Jos Lommerse, Mirco Lomuth, Giovanna Longhi, Giovanni Longo, Christy Loop, Gustavo Lopez, Joanne Dinsmore de López, Andreas Lots, Anthony Lott, Gary Love, Markus Low, Gareth Lowndes, Ernesto Lozano, Francisco Lozano, Coby Lubliner, Carey Luff, Jane Luis, Francisco Luis Avina Cervantes, Jorge Luna, Daniel Lund, Birgit Lutz, Peter & Lene Lykke-Olesen, Freya Maberly, Adriana Madrazo, Jim Madsen, Fernando Ochoa Magana, Liz Maher, Matt Mahlau, Olivier de la Maisonneuve, Mary Makena, Erika Malitzky, Thyra Mangan, Alessandro Marcolin, Boris Marie, Marcia Marini, Birgit Maris, Seija Marjamaa, Bob van der Mark, Mateja Markovic, Ole Markussen, Roger Marsden, Alison Marsh, Gregory Martin, Jacques Martin, Neil Martin, Paolo Marzitta, Julian Mason, Larry Matheson, Stefano Mattana, Mia Matusow, Evelyn Mau, Eduardo Maubert, Gordon Maul, Chris S Maun, Cheryl Maxwell-Buckeridge, Mary Lou & Ted Mayer, Leonard G Mazzone, Beth McCall, Chris McCauley, Keely McCauley, Mike McConnell, Brian McCumber, Gaelynn McDermott, Dan McDougall, Sarah McGowan, Bruce McGrew, MA McIntosh, Chris McKenna, Edith McLaren, Martha McLean, Grant McMillan, Cameron McPherson, Ramon Medina, Kathleen Meehan, Hanneke Meerpoel, Andreas Meier, Annalise Mellor, Lilia Mendoza, Aditya Menon, David Mercer, Roberta Merighi Perosa, David Merrill, David Mestres Ridge, Mervyn Metcalf, Susanne Metzger, Famille Meunier, Helene Meunier, Stuart Michael, M Michael Menzel, Sophie Michard, Ty Milford, Geovanni Millan, Angela Millar, Phyllis & Larry Miller, Jason Milligan, Lisa Mills, Stéphanie Mills, Ute Minckert, Yaniv Minkov, Carolina A Miranda, Max Miranda, Jordan Mitchell, Vicki Moellgaard, Lester H Moffatt, Dennis Mogerman, Rubina Mohamed, Rachel Moilliet, Peter Moller, Rich Molter, Andrew G Moncrieff, Rosalia Mondragon Sosa, Patrick Monney, A Montondo, Paul Montore, Frank Moore, Alexis Morgan, Dan Morris, John Morrison, Lenie Mosaic, Alex Moss, Tania Moy, Maira Muchnik, W Mueller, Jobst Muhlbach,

Ashish Mukharji, Shayo Mukhopadhyay, Barbara Müller, Maren Müller, Steph Munro, Todd Munro, Jack Munsee, Jean Munsee, Paolo A Muraro, Christy Murphy, Geoff & Jean Murphy, Roberta Murray, Andreas Musolff, Mark Myska, Eli Nadel, Leila Nafissi, Nancy Nancarrow, Miguel Naranjo, Daniel Nardin, Jeanne Nash, Norris Nash, Barbara Naylor, Linda Neal, Nicoletta Negri, Jan Nesnidal, Jorongo Net, Adam Nevin, Susan & Kirk Nevin, Mark Nicklas, Gitte Nielsen, Maggie Niemkiewicz, B Norman, Larry Norris, Daniel Novak, Ippolita Novali, Joan & Peter O'Brien, Andrew O'Connor, Betty Odell, Josefin Ohlsson, Karyn Okazaki, Marian Oker, Paula Oliveira, Nick Oliver, John S Oliverio, David Olson, Eleni Isis & Brian O'Neill, Peter Ormand, Carlos Ortega, Chris Osterbauer, Lawrence Oswald, Valentina Otaoio, Mike Otoole, Thomas Ottillinger, Alisa Ouellette, Roy & Velia Ovenden, Patty Owen, Aydin Ozkaya, Axel B Pajunk, Jos ven der Palen, Esa Palmborg, Paul Palmera, Luigi Palmieri, Carine Paques, Alicia Park, Lucie Parker, Sujata Patil, Darren Patterson, Steve Patti, John Payne, Brendan Peace, Nigel Peacock, Kristi Peargin, Stefan Pedall, Bjarke Busk Pedersen, Loretta Pedersen, Jerry Peek, Sibyl Peic, Jorge Penagos Cruz, Laurie & Chuck Pence, Deborah Pencharz, Angélica Pérez, Javier Perez Vicente, Geri & Len Perkins, Roberta Perosa, Charles Perreault, Nisse Perry, Iris Persak, Oliver Peter, Ooi Lin Pheh, Esther Phillips, Stefano Piazzardi, Lisa Pidruchney, Wenceslao Pigretti, Melissa Pike, Anna Judith Piller, Darlene S Pinch, Julie Pingue, Paul Pinn, Natasa Platise, Edna Platzer, Leonard Plompen, Flor Podesta, Bartek Pogoda, Daniel Pöhlke, Frantoise Pohm, Judith Polak, Gunnar Polner, Lynne Pope, Scott Pope, Simon & Alison Porges, Hans Possin, Jim Power, Ellen Powers, Toni Pozo, Harald Praschinger, Jacqueline Pratt, Philip Preston, Neil Pyatt, Boyd Pyper, Brooke Quarnstrom, Hugh E Quetton, Kenyatta Quinones-Street, Anne Quinton, Ann Rabin, Nigel Rains, Glenn Rajaram, Rafael Ramirez, Mandy Rampling, Rosemary Ranck, Grethe Rand, Billy Rangetree, Kris B Prasada Rao, Dr Rapp, Helle Rasmussen, Henrik Rasmussen, Fabrizio Rasore, Maria Rausse, Cristiano Ravalli, Dev Ray, Brian Rayner, George & Concern Worldwide Redman, Sri Redy, Jay Collier Reed, Willow Regnery, Keith Reher, Daniel Reigada, Signe Reimer-Sorensen, Hans Reip, Holly Reiter, Julian Remnant, Morgane Remter, R Rensing, Pamela Rey, Allan Rhodes, Lawrence Rich, Tom Richards, Rolf Richardson, Ryc & Penny Rienks, Virginia Rincon, Jose Luis Rivera Escudero, Nicola Rizzi, Wayne Roberts, Paul Robinson, Ricardo Robledo Carmona, Elizabeth Roche, Pinhas Rodan, Alan Rodgers, Eduardo Rodriguez, Valerie Roedenbeck-Galli, Andrea Rogge, Steve Rogowski, Pilar Rojas-Wong, Patrick Römer, Ana Roque, Lia Rosa, Eric

Rose, Mark Rosenfeld, Pierre Ross, Mary & Mike Rossignoli, Bridgit Roth, Paul Rotheroe, Kevin Rouse, John Rowe, Linnéa Rowlatt, Michael Rubin, Deborah Rubio, Julian Rubio, Anne-Marie Runfola, Frances Runnalls, Bob Russel, Kerry Russell, Stefan Ruthner, Amber Ruyter, Fleming Rysholm, Ed Sacchette, Alessandro Sacerdoti, Pekka Salo, Lysa Salsbury, Kevin Samarasingha, Michael Samuel, Salvador Sanchez, Marietta Sander, Pablo Santaella, Rebecca Sarah, Kirsti Sarheim, Manuela Sartory, Nathan Sato, Diana Sayers, Daniela Schempp, Florentine Schepers, Louse Schlein, Christopher Schlichting, Stefan Schmeja, Emery Schmel, Ralph Schmens, Richard Schmitt, Laura Schmulewitz, Cindy Schneider, David Schnur, Markus Schocker, Martina Schoefberger, Marius Schoenberg, Markus Schrader, Wim Schramms, Bob & Karen Schrey, Teresa L Schriever, Wolfgang Schuler, Corinna Schüller, John Schultz, Brenda & Lee Schussman, Gunter Schwarz, Thomas Schwarz, Robert Schweiger, Sandra Scofield, Claire Scott, Stephen Scott, Vicky Scrivens, Russell Seager, Thijs Vancay Seele, Kim Segal, William Seibert, Rossana Seitter, Erin Sellers, Inge Sels, Scott Semyan, Gus Sevier, Brigid Seymour-East, Katie Shannon, Joli Sharp, Tanya Sharp, Craig Shaw, Ken Shaw, Peter & Florence Shaw, P Shenkin, Tersina Shieh, Roland & Bettina Shulze, Luc Sicard, Laura Siklossy, Mark Simkin, Chris Simon, Christopher Simons, Richard Simpkins, Alan Simpson, Deborah Simpson, Marco Sims, David Sindall, Thomas Singh Suzuki, Marit Sivertsen, Agnete Skaarup, Hana Skockova, Dan Skog, Mitsy Sleurs, William Sleurs, Stacey Sloan, Mary Slusser, David Smallwood, Dan Smith, Ellen Smith, Gary Smith, Gemma Smith, Gordon Smith, Iain Smith, Tom Smoyer, Ben Snyder, Jason Snyder, Laura Sobel, Georg Sollfrank, Kjell Solli, Kurt Sollinger, Janne Solpark, Alfredo Sosa, Leopold Soucy, Regina Soucy, Patrick Spanjaard, Tina Sparks, Kathrin Speidel, Erin Spiess, John Spiess, Detlef Spötter, Imelda Stack, Christian Staeubli, Marco Stambul, Jochen Stange, Robert W Stanton, Susi Stead, Susan Steed, John Steedman, Hugo Steeds, Fiona Steggles, Daniel Stein, Jack Stein, David Steinberg, Megan Stelmach, Daniel & Anja Stenberg, David Stephens, Edel Stephenson, Louisa Stevens, Patrick Stoddard, Stefan Stoffels, Auke van Stralen, Bruce Stroud, Dagmar Sturm, Koen Stuyck, Jean Su, JW Suddart, Meike Suesse, Murray Sugden, Miha Svalj, Christian Svane, Karen Svanholm, Josip Svoboda, Rajat Swani, Sam Symonds, Els 't Hooft, Else Tamayo, John Tanner, Amadeo Tatje, Arthur Tauck, Kevin Taylor, Krysta Taylor, Linnet Taylor, Neil & Anne Taylor, WJ Taylor, Ellen Anne Teigen, Kasper Tesser, Ge Teunissens, Dan Thatcher, Frédéric Thébaud, Jeroen Thijs, Raphaël Thiry, Christobel Thomas, Ross Thomasson, Jackie Thompson, Rod Thompson, Trish Thompson, Nick Thorpe, Alessandro Tieghi, Vanessa Tierney, Mary Tiesen, Paul Tilley, Tina Tin, Mark Tipping, R Tokgoz, Maarten Tol, Sara Tolbert, Jackie & Bob Tomlinson, Cesar Torres, Rachel Toyen, Minh-Try Tran, Catherine Trencher, Darren Trentepohl, Clare & Chris Trimbur, Sissy Trinh, Susan Tripp, John Trotter, Heidi Tschanz, E Tsitrone, John Tuffrey, Paolo & Annalis Turetta, Eric Turlot, Anne-Marie Turner, Ben Turner, Salome Twinberger, Hester van Hees & Sandra Ubbink, Evelyne Udry, J Ulmanis, Joerg Umpfenbach, BL Underwood, Dan Unger, Anna Utech, Alegra Vaca, Sarah Valinsky, Cor & Jenny Valk, Jerry Van Belle, Jessica van Dam, Sebastian van de Beek, Annet Van de Kreke, Maurits van den Boorn, Noor van der Beek, Hans Van der Linden, Thomas van der Ljke, Andre van der Plas, Dreas van Donselaar, Klaartje van Engelen, Berit Van Laneshem, Marc & Mirjan van Maastricht, Marieke van Putten, Peter Paul van Reenen, Michael Van Wyk, Thijs Vancay Seele, Krista Vanggaard, Merry Varney, Mike L Vasey, Mary Jo Vath, Torben Vejloe, Martin Velazquez, Willem Veldhuizen, David M Vella, Carol Ventura, Steven Verdekel, Bart Verlinden, R Vermaire, Vikki Vermod, Heidi Verstraate, Matt Vesce, Heather & Tony Vilardi, Erica Visser, Eirik Krogh Visted, Daniel Von Kritter, Johan & Marie Von Matern, Peter von Zezschwitz, Peter Vreeswijk, F Wagner, Aron Wahl, Shahar Waks, Michael Walensky, Clive Walker, Jamie Walker, Richard Walker, M Wallenburg, Sigrit Walloe, Dyimpna Walsh, Kevin Walters, Kylie Walzak, Margaret Ward, Daniel Ware, Tom & Martha Waring, Ingrid Warren, Kim Watkins, Thomas Watrous, Paul Watson, Cheryl Watts, Bonita Wauls, Emma Weatherup, David Webb, Guido Weber, Gabriel Wechter, Bart Weekers, Susan Weeks, Robert & Owen Weinstein, Ramona Weiss, Susan van der Welt, MW Wenner, Sandi Wermes, Dorothy C Wertz, Annemieke Wevers, Fiona Whiddon, Chandra White, Michael White, Paul White, Karen Whitlow, Beth Whitman, Robert Wickham, Borre Wickstrom, Sharen Wiggins, John Wight, Eleanore Wilde, John D Wildi, Scott Wilhelm, Patrick William-Powlett, Ann & Dave Williams, Martin Williams, Michael Williams, Stuart Williams, Tia & Spencer Williams, Tim Williams, John & Rosa Wilson, Nick Wilson, Robert Wilson, Pip Witheridge, William Wolf, Jung Won Kim, Jung Won King, Julia Wood, Karen Wood, Sara Wood, Chris & Judy Woods, Ken Woods, Tim Woods, Christopher Wortley, Holly Worton, Barrie Wraith, CA Wright, Jeffrey Wright, Pat Wright, Patrick Wullaert, Anita X, Ian X, Lalita X, Liliane X, Massimo X, Sharon Yarwood, Be Yeo, Donald Yeo, Basil Yokarinis, Aiko Yokozuka, Anna Young, Rebecca Young, Sally Young, Steve Zabinsky, Dave Zapanta, Salome Zapf, Judy Zavos, Carmen Zeisler, Eric Ziegler, Lars Zimmermann, Sabine Zimmermann, Dario Zito, Felipe Zuniga, Magda Zupancic, Wanda Zyla.

LONELY PLANET

You already know that Lonely Planet produces more than this one guidebook, but you might not be aware of the other products we have on this region. Here is a selection of titles which you may want to check out as well:

World Food Mexico
ISBN 1 86450 023 9
US$11.95 • UK£6.99

Central America on a shoestring
ISBN 1 86450 186 3
US$21.99 • UK£13.99

Latin American Spanish phrasebook
ISBN 0 86442 558 9
US$6.95 • UK£4.50

Diving & Snorkeling Cozumel
ISBN 0 86442 574 0
US$14.95 • UK£8.99

Healthy Travel Central & South America
ISBN 1 86450 053 0
US$5.95 • UK£3.99

Belize, Guatemala & Yucatán
ISBN 1 86450 140 5
US$19.99 • UK£13.99

Available wherever books are sold.

Lonely Planet Guides by Region

L onely Planet is known worldwide for publishing practical, reliable and no-nonsense travel information in our guides and on our Web site. The Lonely Planet list covers just about every accessible part of the world. Currently there are 16 series: Travel guides, Shoestring guides, Condensed guides, Phrasebooks, Read This First, Healthy Travel, Walking guides, Cycling guides, Watching Wildlife guides, Pisces Diving & Snorkeling guides, City Maps, Road Atlases, Out to Eat, World Food, Journeys travel literature and Pictorials.

AFRICA Africa on a shoestring • Botswana • Cairo • Cairo City Map • Cape Town • Cape Town City Map • East Africa • Egypt • Egyptian Arabic phrasebook • Ethiopia, Eritrea & Djibouti • Ethiopian Amharic phrasebook • The Gambia & Senegal • Healthy Travel Africa • Kenya • Malawi • Morocco • Moroccan Arabic phrasebook • Mozambique • Namibia • Read This First: Africa • South Africa, Lesotho & Swaziland • Southern Africa • Southern Africa Road Atlas • Swahili phrasebook • Tanzania, Zanzibar & Pemba • Trekking in East Africa • Tunisia • Watching Wildlife East Africa • Watching Wildlife Southern Africa • West Africa • World Food Morocco • Zambia • Zimbabwe, Botswana & Namibia
Travel Literature: Mali Blues: Traveling to an African Beat • The Rainbird: A Central African Journey • Songs to an African Sunset: A Zimbabwean Story

AUSTRALIA & THE PACIFIC Aboriginal Australia & the Torres Strait Islands • Auckland • Australia • Australian phrasebook • Australia Road Atlas • Cycling Australia • Cycling New Zealand • Fiji • Fijian phrasebook • Healthy Travel Australia, NZ and the Pacific • Islands of Australia's Great Barrier Reef • Melbourne • Melbourne City Map • Micronesia • New Caledonia • New South Wales • New Zealand • Northern Territory • Outback Australia • Out to Eat – Melbourne • Out to Eat – Sydney • Papua New Guinea • Pidgin phrasebook • Queensland • Rarotonga & the Cook Islands • Samoa • Solomon Islands • South Australia • South Pacific • South Pacific phrasebook • Sydney • Sydney City Map • Sydney Condensed • Tahiti & French Polynesia • Tasmania • Tonga • Tramping in New Zealand • Vanuatu • Victoria • Walking in Australia • Watching Wildlife Australia • Western Australia
Travel Literature: Islands in the Clouds: Travel in the Highlands of New Guinea • Kiwi Tracks: A New Zealand Journey • Sean & David's Long Drive

CENTRAL AMERICA & THE CARIBBEAN Bahamas, Turks & Caicos • Baja California • Belize, Guatemala & Yucatán • Bermuda • Central America on a shoestring • Costa Rica • Costa Rica Spanish phrasebook • Cuba • Cycling Cuba • Dominican Republic & Haiti • Eastern Caribbean • Guatemala • Havana • Healthy Travel Central & South America • Jamaica • Mexico • Mexico City • Panama • Puerto Rico • Read This First: Central & South America • Virgin Islands • World Food Caribbean • World Food Mexico • Yucatán
Travel Literature: Green Dreams: Travels in Central America

EUROPE Amsterdam • Amsterdam City Map • Amsterdam Condensed • Andalucía • Athens • Austria • Baltic States phrasebook • Barcelona • Barcelona City Map • Belgium & Luxembourg • Berlin • Berlin City Map • Britain • British phrasebook • Brussels, Bruges & Antwerp • Brussels City Map • Budapest • Budapest City Map • Canary Islands • Catalunya & the Costa Brava • Central Europe • Central Europe phrasebook • Copenhagen • Corfu & the Ionians • Corsica • Crete • Crete Condensed • Croatia • Cycling Britain • Cycling France • Cyprus • Czech & Slovak Republics • Czech phrasebook • Denmark • Dublin • Dublin City Map • Dublin Condensed • Eastern Europe • Eastern Europe phrasebook • Edinburgh • Edinburgh City Map • England • Estonia, Latvia & Lithuania • Europe on a shoestring • Europe phrasebook • Finland • Florence • Florence City Map • France • Frankfurt City Map • Frankfurt Condensed • French phrasebook • Georgia, Armenia & Azerbaijan • Germany • German phrasebook • Greece • Greek Islands • Greek phrasebook • Hungary • Iceland, Greenland & the Faroe Islands • Ireland • Italian phrasebook • Italy • Kraków • Lisbon • The Loire • London • London City Map • London Condensed • Madrid • Madrid City Map • Malta • Mediterranean Europe • Milan, Turin & Genoa • Moscow • Munich • Netherlands • Normandy • Norway • Out to Eat – London • Out to Eat – Paris • Paris • Paris City Map • Paris Condensed • Poland • Polish phrasebook • Portugal • Portuguese phrasebook • Prague • Prague City Map • Provence & the Côte d'Azur • Read This First: Europe • Rhodes & the Dodecanese • Romania & Moldova • Rome • Rome City Map • Rome Condensed • Russia, Ukraine & Belarus • Russian phrasebook • Scandinavian & Baltic Europe • Scandinavian phrasebook • Scotland • Sicily • Slovenia • South-West France • Spain • Spanish phrasebook • Stockholm • St Petersburg • St Petersburg City Map • Sweden • Switzerland • Tuscany • Ukrainian phrasebook • Venice • Vienna • Wales • Walking in Britain • Walking in France • Walking in Ireland • Walking in Italy • Walking in Scotland • Walking in Spain • Walking in Switzerland • Western Europe • World Food France • World Food Greece • World Food Ireland • World Food Italy • World Food Spain **Travel Literature:** After Yugoslavia • Love and War in the Apennines • The Olive Grove: Travels in Greece • On the Shores of the Mediterranean • Round Ireland in Low Gear • A Small Place in Italy

Lonely Planet Mail Order

onely Planet products are distributed worldwide. They are also available by mail order from Lonely Planet, so if you have difficulty finding a title, please write to us. North and South American residents should write to 150 Linden St, Oakland, CA 94607, USA; European and African residents should write to 10a Spring Place, London NW5 3BH, UK; and residents of other countries to Locked Bag 1, Footscray, Victoria 3011, Australia.

INDIAN SUBCONTINENT & THE INDIAN OCEAN Bangladesh • Bengali phrasebook • Bhutan • Delhi • Goa • Healthy Travel Asia & India • Hindi & Urdu phrasebook • India • India & Bangladesh City Map • Indian Himalaya • Karakoram Highway • Kathmandu City Map • Kerala • Madagascar • Maldives • Mauritius, Réunion & Seychelles • Mumbai (Bombay) • Nepal • Nepali phrasebook • North India • Pakistan • Rajasthan • Read This First: Asia & India • South India • Sri Lanka • Sri Lanka phrasebook • Tibet • Tibetan phrasebook • Trekking in the Indian Himalaya • Trekking in the Karakoram & Hindukush • Trekking in the Nepal Himalaya • World Food India **Travel Literature:** The Age of Kali: Indian Travels and Encounters • Hello Goodnight: A Life of Goa • In Rajasthan • Maverick in Madagascar • A Season in Heaven: True Tales from the Road to Kathmandu • Shopping for Buddhas • A Short Walk in the Hindu Kush • Slowly Down the Ganges

MIDDLE EAST & CENTRAL ASIA Bahrain, Kuwait & Qatar • Central Asia • Central Asia phrasebook • Dubai • Farsi (Persian) phrasebook • Hebrew phrasebook • Iran • Israel & the Palestinian Territories • Istanbul • Istanbul City Map • Istanbul to Cairo • Istanbul to Kathmandu • Jerusalem • Jerusalem City Map • Jordan • Lebanon • Middle East • Oman & the United Arab Emirates • Syria • Turkey • Turkish phrasebook • World Food Turkey • Yemen **Travel Literature**: Black on Black: Iran Revisited • Breaking Ranks: Turbulent Travels in the Promised Land • The Gates of Damascus • Kingdom of the Film Stars: Journey into Jordan

NORTH AMERICA Alaska • Boston • Boston City Map • Boston Condensed • British Columbia • California & Nevada • California Condensed • Canada • Chicago • Chicago City Map • Chicago Condensed • Florida • Georgia & the Carolinas • Great Lakes • Hawaii • Hiking in Alaska • Hiking in the USA • Honolulu & Oahu City Map • Las Vegas • Los Angeles • Los Angeles City Map • Louisiana & the Deep South • Miami • Miami City Map • Montréal • New England • New Orleans • New Orleans City Map • New York City • New York City City Map • New York City Condensed • New York, New Jersey & Pennsylvania • Oahu • Out to Eat – San Francisco • Pacific Northwest • Rocky Mountains • San Diego & Tijuana • San Francisco • San Francisco City Map • Seattle • Seattle City Map • Southwest • Texas • Toronto • USA • USA phrasebook • Vancouver • Vancouver City Map • Virginia & the Capital Region • Washington, DC • Washington, DC City Map • World Food New Orleans **Travel Literature**: Caught Inside: A Surfer's Year on the California Coast • Drive Thru America

NORTH-EAST ASIA Beijing • Beijing City Map • Cantonese phrasebook • China • Hiking in Japan • Hong Kong & Macau • Hong Kong City Map • Hong Kong Condensed • Japan • Japanese phrasebook • Korea • Korean phrasebook • Kyoto • Mandarin phrasebook • Mongolia • Mongolian phrasebook • Seoul • Shanghai • South-West China • Taiwan • Tokyo • World Food Hong Kong • World Food Japan **Travel Literature:** In Xanadu: A Quest • Lost Japan

SOUTH AMERICA Argentina, Uruguay & Paraguay • Bolivia • Brazil • Brazilian phrasebook • Buenos Aires • Buenos Aires City Map • Chile & Easter Island • Colombia • Ecuador & the Galápagos Islands • Healthy Travel Central & South America • Latin American Spanish phrasebook • Peru • Quechua phrasebook • Read This First: Central & South America • Rio de Janeiro • Rio de Janeiro City Map • Santiago de Chile • South America on a shoestring • Trekking in the Patagonian Andes • Venezuela **Travel Literature:** Full Circle: A South American Journey

SOUTH-EAST ASIA Bali & Lombok • Bangkok • Bangkok City Map • Burmese phrasebook • Cambodia • Cycling Vietnam, Laos & Cambodia • East Timor phrasebook • Hanoi • Healthy Travel Asia & India • Hill Tribes phrasebook • Ho Chi Minh City (Saigon) • Indonesia • Indonesian phrasebook • Indonesia's Eastern Islands • Java • Lao phrasebook • Laos • Malay phrasebook • Malaysia, Singapore & Brunei • Myanmar (Burma) • Philippines • Pilipino (Tagalog) phrasebook • Read This First: Asia & India • Singapore • Singapore City Map • South-East Asia on a shoestring • South-East Asia phrasebook • Thailand • Thailand's Islands & Beaches • Thailand, Vietnam, Laos & Cambodia Road Atlas • Thai phrasebook • Vietnam • Vietnamese phrasebook • World Food Indonesia • World Food Thailand • World Food Vietnam

ALSO AVAILABLE: Antarctica • The Arctic • The Blue Man: Tales of Travel, Love and Coffee • Brief Encounters: Stories of Love, Sex & Travel • Buddhist Stupas in Asia: The Shape of Perfection • Chasing Rickshaws • The Last Grain Race • Lonely Planet...On the Edge: Adventurous Escapades from Around the World • Lonely Planet Unpacked • Lonely Planet Unpacked Again • Not the Only Planet: Science Fiction Travel Stories • Ports of Call: A Journey by Sea • Sacred India • Travel Photography: A Guide to Taking Better Pictures • Travel with Children • Tuvalu: Portrait of an Island Nation

LONELY PLANET

ON THE ROAD

Travel Guides explore cities, regions and countries and supply information on transport, restaurants and accommodation, covering all budgets. They come with reliable, easy-to-use maps, practical advice, cultural and historical facts and a rundown on attractions both on and off the beaten track. There are more than 200 titles in this classic series, covering nearly every country in the world.

Lonely Planet Upgrades extend the shelf life of existing travel guides by detailing any changes that may affect travel in a region since a book has been published. Upgrades can be downloaded for free from **www.lonelyplanet.com/upgrades.**

For travelers with more time than money, **Shoestring** guides offer dependable, first-hand information with hundreds of detailed maps, plus insider tips for stretching money as far as possible. Covering entire continents in most cases, the six-volume shoestring guides are known around the world as 'backpackers bibles.'

For the discerning short-term visitor, **Condensed** guides highlight the best a destination has to offer in a full-color, pocket-sized format designed for quick access. They include everything from top sights and walking tours to opinionated reviews of where to eat, stay, shop and have fun.

CitySync lets travelers use their Palm™ or Visor™ hand-held computers to guide them through a city with handy tips on transport, history, cultural life, major sights, and shopping and entertainment options. It can also quickly search and sort hundreds of reviews of hotels, restaurants and attractions and pinpoint their locations on scrollable street maps. CitySync can be downloaded from **www.citysync.com.**

MAPS & ATLASES

Lonely Planet's **City Maps** feature downtown and metropolitan maps, as well as transit routes and walking tours. The maps come complete with an index of streets, a listing of sights and a plastic coat for extra durability.

Road Atlases are an essential navigation tool for serious travelers. Cross-referenced with the guidebooks, they also feature distance and climate charts and a complete site index.

LONELY PLANET

ESSENTIALS

Read This First books help new travelers to hit the road with confidence. These invaluable predeparture guides give step-by-step advice on preparing for a trip, budgeting, arranging a visa, planning an itinerary and staying safe while still getting off the beaten track.

Healthy Travel pocket guides offer a regional rundown on disease hot spots and practical advice on predeparture health measures, staying well on the road and what to do in emergencies. The guides come with a user-friendly design and helpful diagrams and tables.

Lonely Planet's **Phrasebooks** cover the essential words and phrases travelers need when they're strangers in a strange land. They come in a pocket-sized format with color tabs for quick reference, extensive vocabulary lists, easy-to-follow pronunciation keys and two-way dictionaries.

Miffed by blurry photos of the Taj Mahal? Tired of the classic 'top of the head cut off' shot? *Travel Photography: A Guide to Taking Better Pictures* will help you turn ordinary holiday snaps into striking images and give you the know-how to capture every scene, from frenetic festivals to peaceful beach sunrises.

Lonely Planet's **Travel Journal** is a lightweight but sturdy travel diary for jotting down all those on-the-road observations and significant travel moments. It comes with a handy time-zone wheel, a world map and useful travel information.

Lonely Planet's eKno is an all-in-one communication service developed especially for travelers. It offers low-cost international calls and free email and voicemail so that you can keep in touch while on the road. Check it out at **www.ekno.lonelyplanet.com**.

FOOD GUIDES

For people who live to eat, drink and travel, **World Food** guides explore the culinary culture of each country. Entertaining and adventurous, each guide is packed with details on staples and specialties, regional cuisine and local markets, as well as sumptuous recipes, comprehensive culinary dictionaries and lavish photos good enough to eat.

LONELY PLANET

OUTDOOR GUIDES

For those who believe the best way to see the world is on foot, Lonely Planet's **Walking Guides** detail everything from family strolls to difficult treks, with 'when to go and how to do it' advice supplemented by reliable maps and essential travel information.

Cycling Guides map a destination's best bike tours, long and short, in day-by-day detail. They contain all the information a cyclist needs, including advice on bike maintenance, places to eat and stay, innovative maps with detailed cues to the rides, and elevation charts.

The **Watching Wildlife** series is perfect for travelers who want authoritative information but don't want to tote a heavy field guide. Packed with advice on where, when and how to view a region's wildlife, each title features photos of more than 300 species and contains engaging comments on the local flora and fauna.

With underwater color photos throughout, **Pisces Books** explore the world's best diving and snorkeling areas. Each book contains listings of diving services and dive resorts, detailed information on depth, visibility and difficulty of dives, and a roundup of the marine life you're likely to see through your mask.

LONELY PLANET

OFF THE ROAD

Journeys books, travel literature written by renowned travel authors, capture the spirit of a place or illuminate a culture with a journalist's attention to detail and a novelist's flair for words. These are tales to soak up while you're actually on the road or dip into as an at-home armchair indulgence.

The new range of lavishly illustrated **Pictorial** books is just the ticket for both travelers and dreamers. Off-beat tales and vivid photographs bring the adventure of travel to your doorstep long before the journey begins and long after it is over.

Lonely Planet **Videos** encourage the same independent, tough-minded approach as the guidebooks. Currently airing throughout the world, this award-winning series features innovative footage and an original soundtrack.

Yes, we know, work is tough, so do a little deskside dreaming with the spiral-bound Lonely Planet **Diary** or a Lonely Planet **Wall Calendar**, filled with great photos from around the world.

TRAVELERS NETWORK

Lonely Planet Online, Lonely Planet's award-winning Web site, has insider information on hundreds of destinations, from Amsterdam to Zimbabwe, complete with interactive maps and relevant links. The site also offers the latest travel news, recent reports from travelers on the road, guidebook upgrades, a travel-links site, an online book-buying option and a lively traveler's bulletin board. It can be viewed at **www.lonelyplanet.com** or AOL keyword: lp.

Comet, our free monthly email newsletter, is loaded with travel news, advice, dispatches from authors, raging debates, travel competitions and letters from readers. To subscribe, click on the newsletters link on the front page of our Web site or go to **www.lonelyplanet.com/comet/**.

Planet Talk is a free quarterly print newsletter full of travel advice, tips from fellow travelers, author articles, news about forthcoming Lonely Planet events and a complete list of Lonely Planet books and other products. It provides an antidote to the being-at-home blues and helps you dream about and plan your next trip. To join our mailing list, contact any Lonely Planet office or email us at talk2us@lonelyplanet.com.au.

OFF THE ROAD

TRAVELLERS NETWORK

Index

Bold indicates maps.

Boxed Text

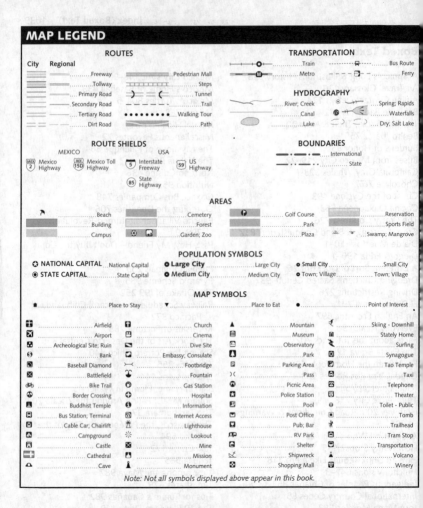

MAP LEGEND

ROUTES

City **Regional**

Freeway
Tollway
Primary Road
Secondary Road
Tertiary Road
Dirt Road

Pedestrian Mall
Steps
Tunnel
Trail
Walking Tour
Path

ROUTE SHIELDS

MEXICO

(MEX 2) Mexico Highway
(MEX 15D) Mexico Toll Highway

USA

(5) Interstate Freeway
(59) US Highway
(85) State Highway

TRANSPORTATION

Train
Metro
Bus Route
Ferry

HYDROGRAPHY

River; Creek
Canal
Lake
Spring; Rapids
Waterfalls
Dry; Salt Lake

BOUNDARIES

International
State

AREAS

Beach
Building
Campus
Cemetery
Forest
Garden; Zoo
Golf Course
Park
Plaza
Reservation
Sports Field
Swamp; Mangrove

POPULATION SYMBOLS

⊘ NATIONAL CAPITAL ... National Capital
◉ STATE CAPITAL ... State Capital
● **Large City** ... Large City
● **Medium City** ... Medium City
● Small City ... Small City
● Town; Village ... Town; Village

MAP SYMBOLS

■ ... Place to Stay
▼ ... Place to Eat
● ... Point of Interest

Airfield	Church	Mountain	Skiing - Downhill
Airport	Cinema	Museum	Stately Home
Archeological Site; Ruin	Dive Site	Observatory	Surfing
Bank	Embassy; Consulate	Park	Synagogue
Baseball Diamond	Footbridge	Parking Area	Tao Temple
Battlefield	Fountain	Pass	Taxi
Bike Trail	Gas Station	Picnic Area	Telephone
Border Crossing	Hospital	Police Station	Theater
Buddhist Temple	Information	Pool	Toilet - Public
Bus Station; Terminal	Internet Access	Post Office	Tomb
Cable Car; Chairlift	Lighthouse	Pub; Bar	Trailhead
Campground	Lookout	RV Park	Tram Stop
Castle	Mine	Shelter	Transportation
Cathedral	Mission	Shipwreck	Volcano
Cave	Monument	Shopping Mall	Winery

Note: Not all symbols displayed above appear in this book.

LONELY PLANET OFFICES

Australia
Locked Bag 1, Footscray, Victoria 3011
☎ 03 8379 8000 fax 03 8379 8111
email talk2us@lonelyplanet.com.au

USA
150 Linden Street, Oakland, California 94607
☎ 510 893 8555, TOLL FREE 800 275 8555
fax 510 893 8572
email info@lonelyplanet.com

UK
10a Spring Place, London NW5 3BH
☎ 020 7428 4800 fax 020 7428 4828
email go@lonelyplanet.co.uk

France
1 rue du Dahomey, 75011 Paris
☎ 01 55 25 33 00 fax 01 55 25 33 01
email bip@lonelyplanet.fr
www.lonelyplanet.fr

World Wide Web: www.lonelyplanet.com *or* AOL keyword: lp
Lonely Planet Images: lpi@lonelyplanet.com.au